A Hebrew And English Lexicon To The Old Testament

A

HEBREW AND ENGLISH LEXICON

TO

THE OLD TESTAMENT;

INCLUDING THE

BIBLICAL CHALDEE.

EDITED, WITH IMPROVEMENTS, FROM THE GERMAN WORKS

OF

GESENIUS,

BY

JOSIAH W. GIBBS, A.M.

OF THE THEOLOGICAL SEMINARY, ANDOVER, U. S.

LONDON:

PRINTED FOR

HOWELL AND STEWART,

SUCCESSORS TO

OGLE, DUNCAN & C°.

295, HOLBORN.

MDCCCXXVII.

PREFACE.

The increasing attention to the study of the Hebrew language in this country, the dissatisfaction and discouragement which many experience from the imperfect helps that they possess, and the great improvements lately made by Gesenius in Hebrew philology, seem to demand that his works should be made accessible to all that pursue this important branch of sacred learning.

The results of Gesenius's laborious and successful investigations, so far as the grammar of the Hebrew language is concerned, have already been given to the public by Prof. Stuart in his invaluable work on that subject, and have been received with general approbation. This has opened the way for publishing in this country the results of Gesenius's original investigations in Hebrew lexicography, in which he has adopted the same style of criticism and the same principles of philology as are found in his grammatical works. The Lexicons here referred to, are, *Hebräisch-Deutsches Handwörterbuch über die Schriften des Alten Testaments mit Einschluss der Geographischen Nahmen und der Chaldaïschen Wörter beym Daniel und Esra. Ausgearbeitet von D. Wilhelm Gesenius, ausserordentlicher Professor der Theologie zu Halle.* 2 Theile, pp. 1344. 8vo. Leips. 1810-12.—And *Neues Hebraïsch-Deutsches Handwörterbuch über das Alte Testament mit Einschluss des Biblischen Chaldaismus. Ein Auszug aus dem grössern Werke in vielen Artikeln desselben umgearbeitet vornehmlich für Schulen. Von W. Gesenius, u. s. w.* pp. 920. 8vo. Leips. 1815.

It may be proper here to state the grounds of the preference which is due to the lexicons of Gesenius.

The intrinsic value of a critical lexicon consists chiefly in the views of lexicography held by the author. The leading trait of Gesenius, in this respect, is judgment. He makes a sober and temperate use of the various means for determining the signification of a Hebrew word. His reasoning from grammatical analogy, from the usage of the Hebrew language, from the context, from the kindred dialects, and from the ancient versions, spontaneously commends itself to the understanding. It is not sufficient to say that he rejects all mystical derivations. He has also avoided the error, nearly as dangerous, into which some modern lexicographers have run—I mean, their extravagant use of Arabic derivations, in disregard of the fact that the Hebrew is a distinct dialect, and as such has its peculiarities. But although Gesenius has restricted himself in this particular, yet his accurate knowledge of the Oriental languages, especially of their constructions and inflexions, sheds a constant and powerful light on Hebrew criticism.

Much too depends on the arrangement of the various significations. Here Gesenius has been very successful in seizing hold of the primary physical acceptation of a word. This he has placed first, and the other significations in the order in which they might be supposed to be derived from the primary. Each signification and each construction is supported by pertinent citations, which, when attended with any peculiar difficulty, are written out and accompanied with a literal translation. Such a view of the different meanings of a word is the best commentary on all the passages cited. Where the different significations of a root appear to have no logical connexion, they are distinguished by Roman numerals; in other cases, only by Arabic numerals.

Gesenius has introduced into his lexicons many things, which other lexicographers either wholly or partially omit; as (1.) A full account of the construction of verbs with different prepositions and particles. This is the more necessary, as the Hebrews have no composite verbs, but vary the signification of the verb, by means of the preposition following, as in other languages by the preposition in composition. (2.) A full explanation of phrases and idioms; a very important part of a good lexicon. (3.) A notice of poetical words and inflexions, with the corresponding prosaic expression. (4.) A notice of the peculiarities of the more modern Hebrew, in distinction from the more ancient. (5.) An account of those words which are defective in some of their forms; which are therefore borrowed from some other word, like the anomalous verbs in Greek. Gesenius first attended to this class of words in the Hebrew.

The alphabetical arrangement in Gesenius would alone give that lexicon a superiority over every other. The etymological arrangement, or the arrangement of words under their roots, was universally practised, till Gesenius, in 1810, opened the new path. The etymological order is not found expedient in the western languages; but has been adopted and retained in the Hebrew, on the false principle that all the words in that language are reducible to triliteral roots. This principle has been supported by the adoption of many hypothetical, refined, and far-fetched derivations. These fanciful derivations being given up, the number of verbal derivatives of all kinds is probably not greater in Hebrew than in many of the occidental languages. Why then should we follow this order in Hebrew more than in the languages with which we are familiar? Why should we, to support this arrangement, derive אָב *father* from

אָבָה *to acquiesce;* אָח *brother,* from אָחָה in the kindred dialects *to join together;* אֵם *mother,* from אָמַם Arab. أَمَّ *to go before;* derivations which we should reject with contempt, if proposed in any other language? But these derivations are plausible, compared with many others which might be given.—Some may not acquiesce in our view of this subject; but every one can see, that the etymological order supposes the *student* to be already a *proficient* in the language; and of course, however true in principle, it is not suited to a beginner. After all, every advantage of the ancient arrangement is secured in this edition, by mentioning under each derivative the root from which it springs, and under each root all the derivatives which do not immediately follow in the order of the lexicon.

The preceding remarks apply to both lexicons of Gesenius. The smaller work contains only the more important proper names of persons and places, has fewer references under the more common words, has fewer passages written out, and omits some extended critical discussions.

The basis of the present work is the abridgment or smaller lexicon. But his Thesaurus or larger work has been constantly consulted, and additions made from it. Also some corrections have been made from his later philological works, particularly his "Ausführliches grammatisch-kritisches Lehrgebäude der Hebraïschen Sprache mit Vergleichung der verwandten Dialecte," published in 1817, and his Commentary on Isaiah published in 1820-1. It is but rarely that the translator has had occasion to differ from his author. In these cases he has sometimes made an alteration conformably to his own views.

The present editor has, as he hopes, improved the work, (1.) By mentioning under each noun which is found inflected in the O.T. the declension to which it belongs.* (2.) By breaking the articles into paragraphs, and making each signification of a word to commence a new paragraph. A similar improvement has been made in the British editions of Schleusner's Greek Lexicons. (3.) By correcting many errors and oversights which have necessarily crept into a work of this kind.

J. W. G.

ANDOVER, (MASS.), JAN. 1824.

* The declensions of feminines are, for the convenience of reference, numbered X. XI. XII. XIII. instead of I. II. III. IV.

SYRIAC AND ARABIC ALPHABETS

COMPARED WITH THE HEBREW.

	Arabic Alphabet.				Syriac Alphabet.					
	Final.	Medial.	Initial.	Arabic Names.	Final.	Medial.	Initial.	Syriac Names.	Corresp. Hebrew.	
1.	ا ـا	ـا	ا	*Elif*	ܐ ܐ	ܐ	ܐ	*Olaph*	א	1.
2.	ب ـب	ـبـ	بـ	*Be*	ܒ ܒ	ܒ	ܒ	*Beth*	ב	2.
3.	ج ـج	ـجـ	جـ	*Jim*	ܓ	ܓ	ܓ	*Gomal*	ג	3.
4.	د ـد	ـد	د	*Dal*	ܕ ܕ	ܕ	ܕ	*Dolath*	ד	4.
	ذ ـذ	ـذ	ذ	*Dhal*						
5.	ه ـه	ـهـ	هـ	*He*	ܗ ܗ	ܗ	ܗ	*He*	ה	5.
6.	و ـو	ـو	و	*Vau*	ܘ ܘ	ܘ	ܘ	*Vau*	ו	6.
7.	ز ـز	ـز	ز	*Ze*	ܙ ܙ	ܙ	ܙ	*Zain*	ז	7.
8.	ح ـح	ـحـ	حـ	*Ha*	ܚ	ܚ	ܚ	*Heth*	ח	8.
	خ ـخ	ـخـ	خـ	*Kha*						
9.	ط ـط	ـطـ	طـ	*Ta*	ܛ	ܛ	ܛ	*Teth*	ט	9.
	ظ ـظ	ـظـ	ظـ	*Tha*						
10.	ي ـي	ـيـ	يـ	*Ye*	ܝ	ܝ	ܝ	*Yud*	י	10.
20.	ك ـك	ـكـ	كـ	*Kef*	ܟ	ܟ	ܟ	*Coph*	כ ך	20.
30.	ل ـل	ـلـ	لـ	*Lam*	ܠ ܠ	ܠ	ܠ	*Lomad*	ל	30.
40.	م ـم	ـمـ	مـ	*Mim*	ܡ ܡ	ܡ	ܡ	*Mim*	מ ם	40.
50.	ن ـن	ـنـ	نـ	*Nun*	ܢ ܢ	ܢ	ܢ	*Nun*	נ ן	50.
*	——	—	—	wanting	ܣ	ܣ	ܣ	*Semcath*	ס	60.
70.	ع ـع	ـعـ	عـ	*Ain*	ܥ ܥ	ܥ	ܥ	*Ee*	ע	70.
	غ ـغ	ـغـ	غـ	*Gain*						
80.	ف ـف	ـفـ	فـ	*Fe*	ܦ	ܦ	ܦ	*Pe*	פ ף	80.
90.	ص ـص	ـصـ	صـ	*Tsad*	ܨ ܨ	ܨ	ܨ	*Tsode*	צ ץ	90.
	ض ـض	ـضـ	ضـ	*Dhad*						
100.	ق ـق	ـقـ	قـ	*Kaf*	ܩ	ܩ	ܩ	*Kuph*	ק	100.
200.	ر ـر	ـر	ر	*Re*	ܪ ܪ	ܪ	ܪ	*Rish*	ר	200.
*60.	س ـس	ـسـ	سـ	*Sin*	—	—	—	wanting	ש	
300.	ش ـش	ـشـ	شـ	*Shin*	ܫ	ܫ	ܫ	*Shin*	ש	300.
400.	ت ـت	ـتـ	تـ	*Te*	ܬ ܬ	ܬ	ܬ	*Tau*	ת	400.
	ث ـث	ـثـ	ثـ	*The*						

BRIEF REMARKS ON THE ORIENTAL LANGUAGES.

1. The Chaldaic Dialect has a very close resemblance to the Syriac; hence they are both frequently referred to under the common name of Aramean. Its alphabetical character and mode of writing are the same with the Hebrew. Its conjugations are, I. Peal (i. q. Heb. Kal), pass. Ithpeel; II. Pael (i. q. Heb. Piel), pass. Ithpaal; III. Aphel (i. q. Heb. Hiphil).

2. The Syriac Vowels are *five;* viz.

Pethoho	ـܰ	ـܲ	or	ـܱ	a.
Rebotso	ـܶ	ـܳ	or	ـܴ	e.
Hebotso	ـܺ			ـܻ	i.
Zekopho	ـܳ			ـܴ	o.
Etsotso	ـܽ	ܘـܽ	or	ܘ ـ	u.

The three first characters in the left-hand column are written either above or below the line. The Syriac has no sign for Dagesh nor for Sheva. The linea occultans ـ̱ is placed under a letter to shew that it is mute; thus ܒܪ̱ܬ *bath* (not *barth*) *a daughter.* The other diacritical signs are of minor importance. The conjugations are, I. Peal, pass. Ethpeel; II. Pael, pass. Ethpaal; III. Aphel.

3. The Arabic Letters are arranged in the Table according to the order of the Hebrew and Syriac Alphabets. The usual arrangement in Arabic Grammars and Lexicons is different. It will be seen by the Table that several of the letters in Hebrew (as ד, ח, etc.) have two corresponding letters in Arabic. The Arabic Vowels are only *three;* viz.

Fatha	ـَ	a, e.
Kesra	ـِ	e, i.
Dhamma	ـُ	o, u.

These vowels become long when followed by a homogeneous quiescent. When followed by any other quiescent, they form diphthongs; as لَوْ *lau.*

The Diacritical Signs are,

Jesm ـْ or quiescent Sheva.

Teshdid ـّ or Dagesh forte.

Hamza ـٔ placed over Elif when *radical.*

Wesla ـٱ placed over initial Elif, shewing that the word is joined in pronunciation with the preceding.

Medda ـٓ placed over Elif, as a sign of prolongation.

Nunnation, or double final vowels, ـً ـٍ ـٌ, shewing that they are to be pronounced *an, en* or *in, on* or *un.* It occurs only in the Kôran and in poetry.

The Conjugations in Arabic are very numerous, and numbered I. II. III. etc.

4. The Ethiopic is a branch of the Arabic, has a distinct character, but is quoted in this work in Hebrew letters.

5. The Samaritan is intermediate between Hebrew and Aramean. It has a peculiar character, but is here represented in Hebrew letters.

6. The Persian has many Arabic words intermingled, but is not itself a kindred dialect with the Hebrew. Yet many Persian words are found in the Hebrew written after the captivity, and some, as it is now admitted by the learned, even in ancient Hebrew. The Persians use the Arabic alphabet with the addition of پ for *p;* چ for *ch,* as in *church;* گ or ݣ for *g* hard; and ژ for *zh.*

7. Words relating to Egypt, or denoting usages or natural productions brought from Egypt, are sometimes illustrated from the Coptic language, which is here expressed in Greek characters.

TABLE OF ABBREVIATIONS

MADE USE OF IN THIS WORK.

I. In English.

Absol.	absolutely, *i.e.* not followed by an object.
accus.	accusative.
adv.	adverb.
Aph.	Aphel.
Aqu.	Aquila, the author of a Greek version.
Aram.	Aramean, *i.e.* Syriac and Chaldaic.
art.	article, or articles.
caus.	causative.
collect.	collectively.
com. gen.	common gender.
comp.	compare.
conj.	conjugation, also for conjunction.
const.	construct state.
C. V.	common English version.
dec.	declension.
denom.	denominative.
deriv.	derivative.
e. g.	for example.
emph.	emphatic state.
Ethiop.	Ethiopic.
Ethpa.	Ethpaal.
Ethpe.	Ethpeel.
f. fem.	feminine.
fut.	future.
Gr. Venet.	A Greek version discovered at Venice.
Gr. anon.	The unknown author of a Greek version.
Heb.	Hebrew.
Hiph.	Hiphil.
Hithpa.	Hithpael.
Hithpo.	Hithpoel.
Hithpol.	Hithpolel.
Hithpal.	Hithpalel.
Hithpalp.	Hithpalpal.
Hoph.	Hophal.
Hothpa.	Hothpaal.
ibid.	in the same place.
i.e.	that is.
i.q.	the same as.
imper.	imperative.
infin.	infinitive.
intrans.	intransitive.
Ithpe.	Ithpeel.
Ithpa.	Ithpaal.
liter.	literally.
med. Vav.	having the middle radical Vav.
m. masc.	masculine.
N. T.	New Testament.
Niph.	Niphal.
obsol.	obsolete.
O. T.	Old Testament.
Onk.	Onkelos, the author of a Targum on the Pentateuch.
Pa.	Pael.
Pi.	Piel.
Po.	Poel.
Pu.	Pual.
pass.	passive.
parag.	paragogic.
prim.	primitive.
prob.	probably.
q. v.	which see.
recipr.	reciprocal.
reflex.	reflexive.
Samar.	Samaritan.
Sept.	Septuagint.
spec.	specifically.
suff.	suffix or suffixes.
Symm.	Symmachus, the author of a Greek version.
Syr.	Syriac.
synon.	synonymous.
subst.	substantive.
Targ.	Targum, that is, the Chaldaic version of the O.T.
Theod.	Theodotion, the author of a Greek version.
trans.	transitive.
trop.	tropically or figuratively.
Vulg.	the Latin vulgate.
=	(sign of equality), *the same as.*
[ ]	The figures in brackets shew the chapter and verse in our common version, when they differ from the number in the Hebrew Bible. When the difference is only one verse, as in many of the Psalms, no notice is taken of it.

II. In Hebrew.

פּ׳	פְּלוֹנִי (*aliquis*) *any one*, in the account of general phrases.
וגו׳	וְגוֹמַר (*et completio*) *and so forth*, an abbreviation common in Rabbinical writings.

HEBREW LEXICON.

א, the first letter of the alphabet, called in Hebrew אָלֶף *Aleph*.

The name אָלֶף is a Segolate noun, synonymous with אֶלֶף *ox, bull.* (Comp. שֶׁל=עָל.) So Plutarch, speaking of τὸ ἄλφα, says: διὰ τὸ Φοίνικας οὕτω καλεῖν τὸν βοῦν. Quæst. Sympos. ix. 2. The letter is so called probably with reference to its original form. Several forms of this letter are found on Hebrew coins. One of these (<), particularly when inverted (v), is a rude representation of a *bull's* head with horns; and from it were evidently derived the Greek and Latin A. If the Chaldee or common square form of this letter were the more ancient, then we might, as Simonis and others have done, compare א with ♉ the character which stands for *taurus* in the zodiac.

The force of א as a *consonant*, probably consisted, like the spiritus lenis (ʼ) of the Greeks, in a gentle emission of the breath from the throat, or rather lungs, and differed from ה, or the spiritus asper (ʽ), in being more smooth. But its sound is generally neglected by us in reading, and no more heard than the French *h* in *habit, homme*. In the middle of a word, however, it has a sensible effect in dividing syllables; e. g. יִשְׁאַל *yish-al*, not *yi-shal*.

In Hebrew, it is more commonly a consonant, and quiesces more rarely than ו or י.

Where א has neither the force of a consonant, nor of a vowel, it is said to be *in otio*, and is then absolutely destitute of sound; e. g. in חֵטְא.

The interchange of א with the kindred sound ה occurs, sometimes in Hebrew itself, but much more frequently in a comparison of cognate dialects; e. g. אֵיךְ and הֵיךְ *how?* אָמוֹן Jer. 52:15 for הָמוֹן *multitude;* הַל (whence .הַ) Arab. אַל the article; etc. Also, as the second radical, in כָּאָה and כָּהָה *to be fainthearted, desponding;* לָאָה and לָהָה *to be wearied, exhausted.*

א is commuted for the guttural ע. This is seen particularly in a comparison of Hebrew words with Aramean. E.g. אָגַם and עָגַם *to be sad;* אוד and עוד (both are found also in Ethiop.) *to turn back, to go round;* עֲנַק Chald. אֲנַק *to fit;* אָמִיר Syr. ܥܡܝܪܐ *verdure, foliage.* As the second rad. in גָּאַל Chald. גְּעַל *to pollute;* תָּאַב and תָּעַב *to abhor.* As the third rad. in גָּמָא Chald. גְּמַע *to drink, to swallow;* פִּתְאֹם *in a moment, suddenly,* from פֶּתַע; etc.

As a middle radical, א is exchanged with ו and י, especially in relation to the Aramean; e. g. רְאֵם and רִים *buffalo;* רָאַם Zech. 14:10 i. q. רום *to be high;* לָאַט i. q. לוט *to cover.* Its commutation with י, as the first rad., takes place more rarely, as אָשַׁם and יָשַׁם *to be desolated.*

The Hebrews sometimes omit א in the beginning of words; e. g. אֲנַחְנוּ, נַחְנוּ *we;* אֲשֶׁר in later Heb. שֶׁ *who;* אֶחָד and חַד (Ezek. 33:30) *one;* הָסוּרִים Ecc. 4:14 for הָאֲסוּרִים.

They also frequently employ a prosthetic אֶ. See the articles אֲבַטִּיחִים, אֶנְפִּים, אֲבַעְבֻּעוֹת, אַדְרִפּוֹן. Particularly does this happen, when two consonants, without an intervening vowel, commence a word, (in which case אֶ becomes אָ or אֲ,) as זְרוֹעַ, אֶזְרוֹעַ *arm*; תְּמוֹל, אֶתְמוֹל *yesterday*; אֶשְׁכֹּל *cluster of grapes*, Aram. סְגוֹל; in which cases both forms now exist. Here belong also אֶפְרֹחַ (for פְּרוֹחַ) *young birds*; אֶגְרֹף (for גְּרוֹף) *fist*; אֶתְנַן (for תְּנַן) *gift*; אַכְזָב (for כְּזָב) *deceitful*. Comp. in Greek χθὲς and ἐχθὲς *yesterday*; and in the transition of Latin words into French, *spiritus, esprit*; *status, état*. In imitation of the Syriac, א is put before י in אִישַׁי 1 Chr. 2: 13 for יִשַׁי *Jesse*. This perhaps made no difference in the pronunciation, for it is not improbable that the Hebrews, in some cases, pronounced יִ and אִי alike. See C. B. Michaëlis' Lum. Syr. § 8. Verbals derived from Hiphil, (or Chald. Aphel,) which sometimes begin with א, as e.g. אַזְכָּרָה, ought carefully to be distinguished from examples like those given above, where the א is merely prosthetic.

I. **אָב** m. prim. irreg. const. and before grave suff. אֲבִי, with light suff. אָבִי, אָבִיךָ, אָבִיךְ, אָבִיו and אָבִיהוּ, אָבִיהָ, אָבִינוּ; Plur. אָבוֹת, const. and before suff. אֲבוֹת.

1. *father*, properly so called; freq.

2. *grandfather, forefather, ancestor*. Gen. 28 : 13. 1 K. 15 : 11 *and Asa did that which pleased Jehovah, like David his father*. 1 Chr. 2 : 45. Fig. Gen. 4 : 20, 21 אֲבִי כָּל־תֹּפֵשׂ כִּנּוֹר וְעוּגָב *the father of all that play on the harp and cornet*, i. e. the inventor of these instruments. Plur. אָבוֹת *forefathers*; freq.

3. *maker, creator*. Job 38 : 28 הֲיֵשׁ לַמָּטָר אָב *has the rain a father* other than me? (Parall. *Who* but Jehovah *begets the drops of the dew?*) In this sense, rather perhaps than in that of *benefactor* of men, it is applied to Jehovah, Is. 63 : 16. 64 : 7 *Jehovah, thou art our father; we are the clay, and thou our potter*. Deut. 32 : 6. (Concerning Job 34 : 36, see אָב No. II.)

4. *benefactor, guardian*. Job 29 : 16 *I was a father to the poor*. Ps. 68 : 6. Among the epithets applied to the expected Messiah is אֲבִי עַד *the eternal father* of his people, Is. 9 : 5. Eliakim, a principal officer at Jerusalem, is called *a father to the inhabitants of Jerusalem*, Is. 22 : 21. David, in addressing Saul, says, *my father!* 1 Sam. 24 : 12. The expression, however, may be taken literally, as Saul was his *father-in-law*.

5. a title of respect for prophets and priests, even from kings. 2 K. 6 : 21. 13 : 14. (Hence in chap. 8 : 9, the king calls himself a *son* of the prophet.) Judg. 17 : 10 הֱיֵה־לִי לְאָב וּלְכֹהֵן *be to me a father and priest*. 18 : 19. The leading idea, in these instances, is that of *teacher*, particularly of one invested with divine authority; whence the frequent use of the expression, *my son! my daughter!* in the poetical books, Prov. 4 : 10, 20. 5 : 1, 20. 6 : 1, 3. 7 : 1, 24. Ps. 45 : 11. Christian teachers and priests have also borne similar titles; e. g. *abbot* (Syr. אבא), *pope* (Greek πάππας), *father*, etc.

6. *father of the king* is an oriental expression to designate *a vizier* or *prime-minister*. Thus Gen. 45 : 8 וַיְשִׂימֵנִי לְאָב לְפַרְעֹה *and he has made me a father to Pharaoh*, i.e. his prime-minister. So Haman is called δεύτερος πατὴρ of Artaxerxes, Est. 13 : 6. Comp. 16 : 11. 1 Mac. 11 : 32. 2 Chr. 2 : 13. 4 : 16. The viziers among the Arabians have a similar title, viz. *Atabeg*; see Jablonskii Opusc. ed. Te Water, T. 1. p. 206. This is also the meaning of אַבְרֵךְ *father of the king*, or *of the land*, Gen. 41 : 43; if the ancient versions and Luther are correct. The prominent idea in this phrase is *counsellor*, which is allied to that of *teacher*.

7. It is used in a figurative sense, Job 17:14 לַשַּׁחַת קָרָאתִי אָבִי אָתָּה *I say to the grave, Thou art my father*, parall. *to corruption, My mother, and my sister;* i. e. they are, as it were, my nearest relatives. Comp. Ps. 88 : 19.

Note 1. In compound proper names the construct state is sometimes אַב, as in אַבְשָׁלוֹם, אַבְרָהָם; (once אֲבִי after the Chaldee form, as in אֲבִיגַל 1 Sam. 25: 18 Keth.) but most frequently אֲבִי, as in אֲבִימֶלֶךְ, אֲבִישַׁי. Out of composition the const. state is אֲבִי as given above, except in Gen. 17 : 4, 5, where אַב is used in order to illustrate the etymology of אַבְרָהָם. Among these proper names are also some names of *women;* e. g. אֲבִיגַל 2 Sam. 3: 4. אֲבִיחַיִל 2 Chron. 11 : 18.

Note 2. The feminine termination of the plural does not affect the gender, which is the same in both numbers. Such anomalies are frequent in the kindred dialects, e.g. رَاعٍ *a shepherd*, plur. رُعَاةٌ, and appear to refer back to an early stage of these languages, when the gender was not distinguished so exactly by the termination, as it was afterwards.

II. **אָב** prob. verbal from אָבָה, dec. II. a. *wish, desire.* Job 34 : 36 אָבִי יִבָּחֵן אִיּוֹב *my wish is that Job may be tried.* So the Chaldee and many translators. Others, *I will cause that*, etc. making אָבִי equivalent to אָבִיא. Others, e. g. Vulg. Luther, with less propriety, *my father!* (addressed to God.)

אַב, suff. אֲבִי, אֲבוּךְ, אֲבוּהִי; Plur. אֲבָהָן (with epenthetic ה, comp. אַמְהָה.) Chald. *father*, as in Heb. Dan. 2 : 23. 5:13.

אֵב m. verbal from obs. אָבַב, dec. VIII. b. *greenness, verdure.* Job 8 : 12 עֹדֶנּוּ בְאִבּוֹ *whilst it is yet green.* Cant. 6 : 11 אִבֵּי הַנָּחַל *the verdure of the valley.* Vulg. *poma*, according to the Chaldee usage.

אֵב, suff. אִנְבֵּהּ. Chald. *fruit.* Dan. 4 : 9, 11, 18. [4 : 12, 14, 21.] The Targums use it for the Heb. פְּרִי.

אָבַב a root not found in the original scriptures. In Chaldee, Pa. אַבֵּב *to bring forth fruit.* In Syriac, the kindred הַבַּב *to blossom.* In Hebrew, as in Arabic, it appears also to have signified, *to be green, to produce* generally. Deriv. אֵב, אָבִיב.

אֲבַגְתָא m. proper name of an eunuch or chamberlain of Ahasuerus. Est. 1 : 10. The name is probably of Persian origin. Comp. בִּגְתָן, בִּגְתָא, 1:10. 2 : 21.

אָבַד, fut. יֹאבַד and יֹאבֵד. 1. *to be lost, to fail;* with לְ of the person, 1 Sam. 9 : 3, 20. with מִן, Deut. 22 : 3. Job 11 : 20 מָנוֹס אָבַד מִנְהֶם *refuge has failed them.* Jer. 25 : 35. Ps. 142 : 5. Job 30 : 2. Ezek. 7 : 26 תֹּאבַד תּוֹרָה מִכֹּהֵן וְעֵצָה מִזְּקֵנִים *the law shall fail the priest, and wisdom the aged*, comp. Jer. 18:18. 49 : 7. Hence Deut. 32 : 28 גּוֹי אֹבַד עֵצוֹת *a people void of counsel* or *wisdom*, (אֹבַד is participle in const. state,) Jer. 4 : 9 יֹאבַד לֵב הַמֶּלֶךְ *the heart*, i.e. the understanding, *of the king shall fail* through fear, consternation. Job 8 : 13 וְתִקְוַת חָנֵף תֹּאבֵד *and the hope of the profligate man fails*, i.e. is frustrated. Ps. 9 : 19. 112 : 10. Prov. 10 : 28. Ps. 1 : 6 דֶּרֶךְ רְשָׁעִים תֹּאבֵד *the designs of the ungodly shall come to nought.* Ezek. 12 : 22 אָבַד כָּל־חָזוֹן *every prophecy faileth.*

2. *to wander, go astray*, spoken of cattle. Ps. 119 : 176 שֶׂה אֹבֵד *a stray sheep.* Comp. Jer. 50 : 6. Ezek. 34 : 4, 16. Hence also of persons, Is. 27 : 13 הָאֹבְדִים בְּאֶרֶץ אַשּׁוּר *the exiles in the land of Assyria.* (Parall. נִדָּח.) Deut. 26 : 5 אֲרַמִּי אֹבֵד *a wandering Syrian.*

3. *to perish;* spoken of a harvest, Joel 1 : 11. of a country, Ex. 10 : 7. Jer. 9 : 11. of houses, Am. 3 : 15. of men and animals, Job 4 : 11. Judges 5 : 31. Num. 17 : 27 [12] אָבַדְנוּ כֻּלָּנוּ אָבָדְנוּ *we perish, we all perish.* Hence it signifies *to be destroyed, rooted out*, Deut.

7:20. 8:19. often with the addition מֵעַל הָאָרֶץ Deut. 4:26. 11:17. Josh. 23: 13, 16.

4. Also simply *to be unfortunate, unhappy*, spoken of men; as Part. אֹבֵד *the unfortunate, forsaken*, Job 29:13. 31:19. Prov. 31:6.

Note 1. The future with Tseri יֹאבֵד is used at the end of a clause, the future with Pattah יֹאבַד in the beginning or middle; comp. Job 8:13, with Ps. 9:19.

Pi. אִבֵּד, fut. יְאַבֵּד. 1. caus. of Kal no. 1. *to lose, to cause to fail.* Ecc. 3:6. 7:7 יְאַבֵּד אֶת־לֵב מַתָּנָה *a bribe perverts the understanding*, comp. Jer. 4:9. Construed with מִן, Jer. 51:55.

2. caus. of Kal no. 2. *to lead* flocks *astray*. Jer. 23:1.

3. caus. of Kal no. 3. *to ruin, destroy, kill.* Est. 3:9, 13. 2 K. 11:1. 13:7. 19:18. Num. 33:52. Deut. 12:2. יְאַבֵּד הוֹן *to destroy*, or *waste one's substance*, Prov. 29:3.

Note 2. אַבֶּדְךָ Syr. for אֲאַבֶּדְךָ, Ez. 28:16.

Hiph. הֶאֱבִיד i. q. Pi. but especially 1. caus. of Kal no. 1. Job 14:19. Jer. 25:10.

2. caus. of Kal no. 3. *to destroy* men, nations. Deut. 7:10. 8:20. 9:3. Often followed by מִקֶּרֶב הָעָם *from amidst the people*, Lev. 23:30. or by מִתַּחַת הַשָּׁמָיִם *from under heaven*, Deut. 7:24.

Note 3. אֹבִידָה Chald. for אַאֲבִידָה 1 per. sing. fut. Jer. 46:8.

אֲבַד, fut. יֵאבַד. Chald. *to perish*, as in Heb. Jer. 10:11 *they shall perish*.

Aph. הוֹבֵד, fut. יְהוֹבֵד, *to destroy*, Dan. 2:12, 24. perhaps also *to perish*, 2:18.
Hoph. הוּבַד *to be destroyed*. Dan. 7:11.

אֹבֵד m. verbal from אָבַד, *ruin, destruction*. Num. 24:20, 24.

Note. The form of this noun is that of the common participle, but the signification is abstract, comp. גֹּלָה, יֹתֵר.

אֲבֵדָה f. verbal from אָבַד, dec. x. 1. *something lost*. Ex. 22:8. Lev. 5:22, 23.

2. i.q. אֲבַדּוֹן *the region of the dead.* Prov. 27:20 Keth.

אֲבַדּוֹן m. verbal from אָבַד.

1. *destruction.* Job 31:12.

2. *place of destruction*, hence i. q. שְׁאוֹל ᾅδης, *the subterranean world, the region of the dead.* Job 26:6. 28:22. Prov. 15:11.

אַבְדַן m. verbal from אָבַד, *destruction*. Est. 9:5.

אָבְדָן m. verbal from אָבַד, dec. II. b. *id.* Est. 8:6.

אָבָה, fut. יֹאבֶה, preceded by a negative in every instance, except Is. 1:19. Job 39:9.

1. i.q. Lat. *volo*; followed by an infinitive with and without לְ. Ex. 10:27 לֹא אָבָה לְשַׁלְּחָם *he would not let them go.* Job 39:9 הֲיֹאבֶה רֵים עָבְדֶךָ *will the buffalo serve thee?* Gen. 24:5, 8. Lev. 26:21. Deut. 2:30. 10:10.

2. *to consent, obey*; used absolutely, Is. 1:19 אִם תֹּאבוּ וּשְׁמַעְתֶּם *if ye consent and obey.* Prov. 1:10. with a dative of the person, Ps. 81:12. (Parall. שָׁמַע לְ.) Deut. 13:9. Prov. 1:30. with an accusative of the thing, Prov. 1:25.

3. In the derivatives appear the kindred ideas, *to wish*, (see אֵב no. II.) *to desire, long for*, (see אֲבִיּוֹנָה); *to want, need*, (see אֶבְיוֹן).

Note. תֵּבֵא Chald. for תֹּאבֶה, Prov. 1:10. אבוא Arab. for אָבוּ, Is. 28:12.

אֵבֶה m. found only Job 9:26 אֳנִיּוֹת אֵבֶה *swift ships*, or *boats.* The connexion makes this rendering necessary, but the rationale of it is attended with some difficulty. The usual solution is, *naves desiderii* (from אָבָה) i. e. cum desiderio ad portum properantes. Symm. ναυσὶ σπευδούσαις. But this is too far-fetched. A better explanation is derived from the Arab. אבא *reeds, papyrus*; namely, *boats made of papyrus*, which were celebrated in antiquity for their fast sailing, (see Is. 18:2. Plin. N. H. vii. 57. xiii. 22. Lucani Phars. iv. 136.) or from the Ethiop. אַבִּי *a* *rapid stream,* the poet having, perhaps, before his eyes the swift boats in the Tigris. The reading איבה found in more than 40 MSS. ought probably to be pointed אֵיבָה *hostility,* and the phrase might then be rendered *naves prædatoriæ,* which agrees with the Syriac version, and is not unsuitable to the context. The common text also, if pointed thus אֵבֶה, may have the same signification, and the other reading איבה deserves attention as a good gloss or scholium on the text.

אֲבוֹי interj. formed by an onomatopœia. *wo! alas!* found only Prov. 23:29, where it is used substantively, like אוֹי in the same verse.

אֵבוּס m. (Syr. for אֲבוּס) verbal from אָבַס, dec. III. g. *barn, stall, stable.* Is. 1:3. Job 39:9. The ancient versions generally render it *crib;* but the sense given above is supported by the connexion Prov. 14:4 *where no oxen are, the barn is empty; but much produce is through the strength of the ox;* also by the root אָבַס q. v. and the other derivative מַאֲבוּס.

אִבְחָה or אֲבָחָה f. found only Ezek. 21:20 [15] אִבְחַת־חֶרֶב probably *the threatening of the sword,* i.e. the threatening sword. The root אָבַח then is i.q. Arab. وبخ or أبخ *to threaten, censure, punish,* whence it may also be rendered *sword of punishment.* According to others, *the destruction of the sword,* i.e. the destroying sword, making אבח = Arab. باح (עו) which in Conj. x. signifies *to destroy.*

אֲבַטִּיחִים m. plur. (with prosth. א, see p. 2.) *melons.* Once Num. 11:5. In Arab. بطيخ or طبيخ *melon,* from طبخ *to ripen;* as in Greek πέπων, from πέπτω *to ripen.* The water-melon particularly (*Cucurbita Citrullus,* Linn.) is at this day cultivated on the banks of the Nile, and serves the Egyptians for food, drink, and medicine. See Hasselquist's Voyages, p. 255.

אֲבִי עַלְבוֹן m. *(father of strength,* i.e. strong,) proper name of one of David's heroes, 2 Sam. 23:31; which is written אֲבִיאֵל *(idem)* 1 Chr. 11:32. Comp. Arab. غلب *prævaluit.*

אָבִיב m. verbal from obs. אָבַב.

1. *ear of corn.* Lev. 2:14. Ex. 9:31 הַשְּׂעֹרָה (בְּ) אָבִיב *hordeum fuit in arista, the barley was in the ear.*

2. חֹדֶשׁ הָאָבִיב *the month of green corn,* in later Heb. called נִיסָן, answering to part of March and part of April in our calendar. Ex. 13:4. 23:15. Deut. 16:1.

אֲבִיָּהוּ m. (*will of Jehovah*) proper name of a king of Judah, son and successor to Rehoboam. 2 Chr. 13:20, 21. He is called also אֲבִיָּה 2 Chr. 11:22. 13:1. and אֲבִיָּם 1 K. 14:31. 15:1, 7, 8. In 1 K. 14:31, some MSS. and editions have אֲבִיָּה.

אֶבְיוֹן verbal adj. from אָבָה, (see אָבָה no. 3.) dec. I. b.

1. *poor, needy.* Deut. 15:4, 7, 11. Ps. 72:4 *sons of the poor,* i.e. the poor, see בֵּן.

2. *unhappy, afflicted, distressed.* Frequently connected with עָנִי, Ps. 40:18 וַאֲנִי עָנִי וְאֶבְיוֹן *and I am afflicted and distressed.* 70:6. 86:1. 109:22. Like עָנִי, it often includes the idea of innocency, or of suffering unjustly, Am. 2:6. (Parall. צַדִּיק *righteous.*) It also relates, like עָנִי, rather to public than to personal affliction.

אֲבִיּוֹנָה f. found only Ecc. 12:5. According to the Sept. Syr. Arab. and Vulg. *the caper,* which, considered as a stimulant to appetite and lust, suits the connexion. We are not, however, to understand by this word the *buds* of the plant, which are sometimes pickled, but the *berries,* which contain a sharp stimulating seed, like pepper. Plin. N. H. xiii. 44. In Rabbinic, אֲבִיּוֹנוֹת

denotes *small berries* whether of the *caper*, or of the myrtle, olive, etc. It is prob. derived from אָבָה no. 3. *to desire*, having reference to the stimulating properties of the caper.

אֲבִימָאֵל m. proper name of a descendant of Joktan. Gen. 10:28. 1 Chr. 1:22. He and his brethren probably represent in these passages different Arabian tribes; but no name has yet been discovered in the Arabian writers, which clearly corresponds to *Abimael*.

אֲבִימֶלֶךְ m. (*father of the king*, or perhaps *royal father*.)

1. common title of the Philistine kings, as פַּרְעֹה of the Egyptian. Gen. 20:2 ff. 21:22 ff. 26:1 ff. Ps. 34:1. So at the present day among the Ethiopians the king is called אב נגש *pater rex*. Comp. אָב nos. 5. and 6.

2. proper name of a son of Gideon. Judg. 8:31. 9:1.

3. also of a chief priest, in the time of David. 1 Chron. 18:16.

אֲבִינֵר m. (*father of light*) proper name of the general of Saul's armies. 1 Sam. 14:50. More usually called אַבְנֵר.

אֲבִיעֶזֶר m. (*father of help*, comp. Germ. Adolf *Adolphus*, from atta *father*, and holf *help*,) proper name.

1. son of Gilead. Josh. 17:2. By a metonymy, *his posterity*, Judg. 6:34. 8:2. The patronymic noun is אֲבִי הָעֶזְרִי *the Abiezrite*, Judg. 6:11, 24. 8:32. From these are formed, by contraction, אִיעֶזֶר and הָאִיעֶזְרִי Num. 26:30.

2. one of David's heroes. 2 Sam. 23:27. 1 Chr. 11:28. 27:12.

אֲבִיר m. verbal adj. from obs. אָבַר no. I. dec. III. a. *strong*, *mighty*; but only in the connexion אֲבִיר יִשְׂרָאֵל, יַעֲקֹב *the mighty one of Israel*, *of Jacob*, i. e. Jehovah. Gen. 49:24. Is. 49:26. 1:24.

אַבִּיר verbal adj. from obs. אָבַר, no. 1. dec. I. b.

1. *strong*, *stout*, *robust*. Hence applied to men, *valiant*, and used as a subst. *a valiant man*, *a hero*, Judg. 5:22. Lam. 1:15. Jer. 46:15. Is. 10:13. Ps. 76:6 אַבִּירֵי לֵב *the stout-hearted*. But as an epitheton ornans, it is also used by the poets without a substantive following, to denote (1.) *the bull*, Ps. 22:13 אַבִּירֵי בָשָׁן *the strong ones*, i.e. the bulls, *of Bashan*. 50:13. 68:31. Is. 34:7. (2.) *the horse*, only in Jer. 8:16. 47:3. 50:11.

2. *illustrious*, *chief*, *noble*. Job 24:22. 34:20. Ps. 78:25 לֶחֶם אַבִּירִים *princely food*, i.e. delicate, savoury food, (comp. Judg. 5:25.) 1 Sam. 21:8 אַבִּיר הָרֹעִים *the chief of the shepherds*.

3. with לֵב, *stiffnecked*. Is. 46:12. Comp. חֲזַק לֵב.

אָבַךְ prob. i. q. Arab. بَاكَ (عو) *to entangle*, *involve*. Hence Hithpa. *to involve* or *roll one's self*, applied to rising smoke, found only Is. 9:17 יִתְאַבְּכוּ גֵּאוּת עָשָׁן *they mount up in columns of smoke*.

אָבַל, fut. יֶאֱבַל. 1. *to mourn*, *be in mourning*. Hos. 10:5. Am. 8:8, etc. It denotes the external marks of sorrow, including also lamentation, see אֵבֶל.

2. *to be* or *appear gloomy*, *desolate*, applied to inanimate nature. Am. 1:2 אָבְלוּ נְאוֹת הָרֹעִים *the pastures of the shepherds are desolate*. Is. 24:4. 33:9. 24:7 אָבַל תִּירוֹשׁ אֻמְלְלָה־גָפֶן *the new wine is wasted*, *the winestock is withered*.

Hiph. הֶאֱבַלְתִּי 1. caus. of Kal no. 1. Ezek. 31:15.

2. caus. of Kal no. 2. Lam. 2:8.

Hithpa. 1. i.q. Kal, with this difference, that Kal occurs in poetry, but this conj. in prose. It is construed with אֶל and עַל of the person or thing lamented. 1 Sam. 15:35. 2 Sam. 13:37. Ezek. 7:12, 27.

2. *to feign one's self a mourner*. 2 Sam. 14:2.

אָבֵל verbal adj. from אָבַל, (with Tseri impure,) dec. V. f. *mourning*, *gloomy, desolate.* Gen. 37:35. Lam. 1:4 דַּרְכֵי צִיּוֹן אֲבֵלוֹת *the ways to Zion are desolate.* Ps. 35:14 אֲבֵל־אֵם *one mourning for his mother.* Is. 61:3 אֲבֵלֵי צִיּוֹן *the mourners of Zion.* The last syllable is written fully in Arabic אביל; and also in Samar. text Gen. 37:35.

אָבֵל f. with Tseri impure, dec. V. f. Comp. Arab. ابل *fresh grass;* ابيلة *a bundle of grass;* ابل the name of certain villages; Syr. ܐܒܠܐ *fresh grass.*

1. as an appellative, prob. *a grassy plain.* 1 Sam. 6:18.

2. proper name of a city in the north of Palestine, 2 Sam. 20:18, of considerable size, as it is called in the next verse *a mother in Israel.* To distinguish it from other cities of the same name, it is called אָבֵל בֵּית־מַעֲכָה 2 Sam. 20:14, (ו here is exegetical,) 15. 1 K. 15:20. 2 K. 15:29. and אָבֵל מַיִם 2 Chr. 16:4. comp. 1 K. 15:20. The addition *Beth Maachah* appears to place it in the country east of Jordan and below Mt. Libanus. See מַעֲכָה. Eusebius also speaks of an Ἀβιλὰ in Phenicia, between Paneas and Damascus. See Reland's Palæst. p. 524 ff. Josephus (Antiq. vii. 11. 7.) calls this place Ἀβελμαχέα. Comp. Luke 3:1. —Βελμὲν, Judith 4:4, is perhaps a corruption of *Abelmaim.*

3. אָבֵל הַשִּׁטִּים (*place of acacia*) a place in the plains of Moab. Numb. 33:49. It appears to be the same which is called barely שִׁטִּים, 25:1. Mic. 6:5. According to Josephus (Antiq. v. 1. 1.) it was 60 stadia distant from the Jordan.

4. אָבֵל כְּרָמִים (*place of vineyards*) a village of the Ammonites. Judg. 11:33. According to Eusebius it abounded in his time with vineyards, and was six Roman miles from Rabbath-Ammon.

5. אָבֵל מְחוֹלָה (*place of the dance*) the birth-place of Elisha, in the tribe of Issachar, between Scythopolis and Neapolis. Judg. 7:22. 1 Kings 4:12. 19:16.

6. אָבֵל מִצְרַיִם name of a threshing-floor not far from the Jordan, i. q. אֵבֶל מִצְרַיִם *the mourning of the Egyptians,* as explained Gen. 50:11.

Note. אָבֵל in these compositions may be considered as in apposition, see Gesen. Lehrgeb. p. 566.

אֵבֶל m. verbal from אָבַל, dec. VI. j. *mourning, lamentation.* Est. 4:3. 9:22. Especially for a person deceased, Gen. 27:41. אֵבֶל יָחִיד *the mourning for an only son,* Am. 8:10. Jer. 6:26. עָשָׂה אֵבֶל לְ *to institute mourning for one deceased,* Gen. 50:10. — Mic. 1:8 וְאֵבֶל כִּבְנוֹת יַעֲנָה *and I make a mourning like the ostriches,* which are noted for their doleful cry.

אֲבָל conj. prim. i. q. Arab. بل. 1. advers. *but, yet, nevertheless.* Ezra 10:13. Dan. 10:7, 21. 2 Chr. 33:17. Also as Lat. *imo, nay rather,* Gen. 17:19.

2. explet. *indeed, truly.* Gen. 42:21. 2 Sam. 14:5.

אֶבֶן f. (m. only 1 Sam. 17:40.) prim. dec. VI. b.

1. *stone.* Gen. 31:46. Job 28:2 *one melts the stone,* or *ore, into copper.* Is. 30:30 אֶבֶן בָּרָד *hailstones;* hence Josh. 10:11 אֲבָנִים גְּדֹלוֹת *great hailstones,* i. q. אַבְנֵי הַבָּרָד in the succeeding verse. Comp. Ezek. 13:11, 13.

2. by way of eminence, *a precious stone;* often with an addition אֶבֶן יְקָרָה, 1 K. 10:2, 11. but also by itself, Pr. 26:8. Ex. 35:33.

3. *rock, fortress,* in a metaphorical sense. Gen. 49:24 אֶבֶן יִשְׂרָאֵל i. q. צוּר יִשְׂרָאֵל *the rock of Israel,* that is, Jehovah.

4. *a weight,* which no doubt was frequently, as with us, of stone. Zech. 5:8 אֶבֶן הָעֹפֶרֶת *the weight* or *mass of lead.* 4:10 אֶבֶן הַבְּדִיל *the plummet.* Is. 34:11 אַבְנֵי־בֹהוּ *the plummet of destruction.* (Comp. as a parallel in sense, Am. 7:8.)—אֶבֶן וָאָבֶן *two kinds of weights,* Deut. 25:13. Prov. 20:10, 23.

5. אֶבֶן הָעֵזֶר (*stone of help*) proper name of a stone placed by Samuel between Mizpeh and Shen. 1 Sa. 4:1. 5:1. 7:12.

6. אֶבֶן הָאָזֶל (*stone of departure*) proper name. 1 Sam. 20:19.

אֶבֶן, emph. אַבְנָא. Chald. *stone*, as in Heb. Dan. 2:34, 35.

אַבְנָה 2 K. 5:12 Keth. for אֲמָנָה q.v. See also the letter ב.

אָבְנַיִם dual. 1. *a potter's wheel*, once Jer. 18:3 *the potter* עֹשֶׂה מְלָאכָה עַל הָאָבְנָיִם *was executing a work on the wheel.* So the Chald. Syr. Vulg. and Jerome in his Comment. To render it *the seat* of the potter seems less suitable.

2. perhaps *a stone bathing-trough* for newly-delivered women and their infants, once Ex. 1:16 *When ye deliver the Hebrew women,* וּרְאִיתֶן עַל הָאָבְנָיִם *and see by the bathing-vessel, whether it is a son, then kill it; but if it is a daughter, then it may live,* or, *then watch over the bathing-vessel, if it is a son,* etc.—According to these explanations, אָבְנַיִם may in both passages be the dual of אֹבֶן=אֶבֶן *stone.*—Others understand in the former passage *the seat* of the potter, and in the latter *sellam mulieris parturientis.* So Kimchi, the Chaldee and both the Arabic versions. In this case אָבְנַיִם is perhaps from a sing. אָבְנָה (root בָּנָה) *building, frame, seat.* No form, however, analogous to this, is known. A greater knowledge of ancient manners and customs is necessary to determine the meaning of this word.

אַבְנֵט m. with prosth. א, and Tseri impure, (in Samar. text אבניט,) dec. I. b. *girdle* of the priests, Ex. 28:4. 39:40. or of the magistrates, Is. 22:21. In Arabic بنيقة signifies *a weaver;* and in Chald. בֵּנֶד, פּוּנְדָּא, אֲפוּנְדָּא *a girdle.*

אַבְנֵר m. (*father of light*) prop. name of the general of Saul's armies. 1 Sam. 14:51. 17:55, 57. 20:25. Sometimes אֲבִינֵר. Sept. 'Αβεννήρ.

אָבַס 1. i. q. Arab. أبش, *to heap up.* In Hebrew, only in the derivatives אֵבוּס, מַאֲבוּס.

2. as in Chald. *to fatten.* Part. pass. 1 K. 5:3. [4:23.] Prov. 15:17.

אֲבַעְבֻּעֹת fem. plur. (with prosth. א.) *blains, blisters, pustules.* Ex. 9:9, 10. Comp. Chald. בַּעְבַּע *to bubble, boil;* Syr. ܒܥܒܘܥܐ *swellings, tumours;* and the kindred roots בָּעָה no. II. and נָבַע.

אָבַק only in Niph. נֶאֱבַק *to wrestle,* construed with עִם. Gen. 32:25, 26. It is a denom. from אָבָק *dust,* because in wrestling the dust is put in motion. So in Greek, παλαίω from πάλη, συγκονίομαι from κόνις; and in Chald. אִתְעַפַּר from עפר *dust.*

אָבָק m. prim. dec. IV. c. *fine dust,* such as is easily blown about, different from עָפָר. Is. 5:24. Ez. 26:10. Ex. 9:9.

אֲבָקָה fem. of אָבָק, dec. XI. d. *idem.* Cant. 3:6 אַבְקַת רוֹכֵל *aromatic dust,* or *powder of the merchant.*

I. **אָבַר** *to be strong, stout,* only in deriv. אָבִיר, אַבִּיר.

II. **אָבַר**, Hiph. *to fly,* being a denom. from אֵבֶר *a wing.* Job 39:26.

אֵבֶר m. prob. prim. dec. VI. j. and אֶבְרָה fem. of אֵבֶר, dec. X. (In Aram. אֶבְרָא *idem.*)

1. *quill* or *hard feather of the wing.* Ezek. 17:3. Job 39:13. (Is. 40:31.?)

2. *wing, pinion.* Ps. 55:7. 91:4. Deut. 32:11. Is. 40:31.

אַבְרָהָם m. *Abraham,* the well-known progenitor of the Jews. In the book of Genesis to chap. 17:4, 5, he is uniformly called אַבְרָם (*father of elevation,* or *high father*) Sept. Ἄβραμ; but in this passage he receives the promise of a numerous posterity, and also the name אַבְרָהָם Sept. Ἀβραάμ, which he bears through the remainder of the sacred volume. This name signifies *father of a multitude;* comp. Arab. رهام *numerus copiosus;*) and the sacred writer himself explains it by אַב הֲמוֹן גּוֹיִם father of a multitude of nations.—אֱלֹהֵי אַבְרָהָם God of Abraham, i.e. Jehovah, 2 Chr. 30:6. Ps. 47:10. זֶרַע אַבְרָהָם seed of Abraham, i.e. the Israelites, Ps. 105:6. Is. 41:8.

אַבְרֵךְ Gen. 41:43. If the word be Hebrew, then it is 1 pers. fut. Hiph. for אַבְרִיךְ *I will bow the knee*, or *have men bow it;* or imper. (with Chald. form, comp. Jer. 25:3) for הַבְרֵךְ *bow the knee;* or, which is preferable, infin. abs. (with Chald. form) used instead of the imper. Vulg. *clamante præcone, ut omnes coram eo genu flecterent.* But the word is probably of Egyptian origin, and perhaps so altered by the Hebrew writer as to have an apparent significancy in his own language. (Comp. מֹשֶׁה.) If such is the fact, it will be difficult to determine the Egyptian word, since it may have a different meaning from that which the word presents in Hebrew. The most plausible conjectures, however, are that of Pfeiffer, Copt. *αυ ρεκ inclinet se quisque*, and that of De Rossi, Copt. *απι ρεκ inclinare caput.* Luther renders it: *this is the father of the country*, namely אַב *father* and רֵךְ i. q. Chald. רֵךְ *rex, regnum.* See אָב no. 6.

אַבְרָם see **אַבְרָהָם**.

אַבְשָׁלוֹם m. *(father of peace)* proper name of the third son of David, famous for his insurrection against his father. 2 Sam. xiii—xviii. Sept. Ἀβεσσαλώμ. Syr. ܐܒܫܠܘܡ. Arab. إِبِيشَالُوم.

אֲגַג m. name of two kings of the Amalekites, perhaps a common name of all their kings. Comp. פַּרְעֹה, אֲבִימֶלֶךְ. Num. 24:7. 1 Sam. 15:8, 9, 20, 32.

אֲגֻדָּה f. dec. X. The root אָגַד signifies in Chald. *to bind together;* and its derivatives, in Arabic, *a solid arch* or *edifice*, from the binding together of its parts. See אָחַז.

1. *band, tie, knot.* Is. 58:6 אֲגֻדּוֹת מוֹטָה *the bands of the yoke.*

2. *bunch, bundle.* Ex. 12:22.

3. *band* or *body of men.* 2 Sam. 2:25. Comp. חֶבֶל.

4. *arch* or *vault of heaven.* Am. 9:6.

אֱגוֹז m. prim. (In Syr. and Arab. גוז.) *nut.* Once Cant. 6:11.

אָגוּר m. Prov. 30:1. proper name of a wise man, to whom the thirtieth chapter of Proverbs is ascribed, otherwise unknown. As an appellative, אגורא in Syr. signifies *qui studio sapientiæ se applicat;* whence it is possible that the name may be significant and allegorical. Comp. אִיתִיאֵל.

אֲגוֹרָה f. dec. X. name of a small coin. Once 1 Sam. 2:36. Sept. ὀβολός, Vulg. *nummus.* According to the Jewish commentators, i.q. גֵּרָה, see גֵּרָה no. II.

אֶגֶל m. dec. VI. j. found only Job 38:28 אֶגְלֵי־טָל *the drops of the dew.* Vulg. *stillæ roris.* So most of the ancient translators. The root אָגַל in Arab. conj. II. signifies *to collect water*, whence others render this phrase, *the magazines* or *reservoirs of the dew;* comp. verse 22.

אֶגְלַיִם proper name of a village in the country of Moab, in Eusebius Ἀγαλλείμ, 8 miles S. of Areopolis. Probably the place which Josephus (Antiq. xiv, 1. 4.) calls Ἄγαλλα. Once Is. 15:8.

אָגַם a root not found in the Heb. SS. but which probably signified

1. as in Arab. *to burn, be hot.* Deriv. אַגְמוֹן no. 1.

2. as in Arab. *to become tepid* or *corrupted*, as stagnant water. Der. אֲגַם *pool.*

3. as in Chald. i. q. עָגַם *to suffer pain, to be sad.* Deriv. אָגֵם *sad.*

I. **אָגֵם** verbal adj. from obs. אָגַם no. 3, dec. IV. c. *mournful, sad.* Is. 19:10 אַגְמֵי נָפֶשׁ *sad of spirit.*

II. **אֲגַם** m. verbal from obs. אָגַם no. 2. const. אֲגַם; Plur. אֲגַמִּים, const. אַגְמֵי. *pond, pool, marsh.* Is. 35:7. 42:15. Ex. 7:19. 8:1. [5.] Ps. 107:35.

I. **אַגְמוֹן** m. verbal from obs. אָגַם no. 1. *boiling caldron.* Job 41:12. [20.]

II. **אַגְמוֹן** m. denom. from אֲגַם *marsh*,

by adding the adjective termination וֹן; literally *growing in marshes.*

1. *reed, rush.* Is. 58:5. Concerning Is. 9:13. 19:15, see כִּפָּה.

2. *cord* or *rope,* made of twisted reeds. Job 40:26. [41:2.] Comp. Greek σχοῖνος.

אַגָּן m. const. אַגַּן; Plur. אַגָּנוֹת. *bowl, goblet.* Cant. 7:3. Ex. 24:6. Is. 22:24. (In Arab. إِجَّانَةٌ *idem.*)

אֲגַפִּים m. plur. (with prosth. א, see p. 2) dec. VIII. a. *warlike hosts* or *bands.* Only Ezek. 12:14. 17:21. 38:6, 9, 22. 39:4. It corresponds to Chald. גַּף, אֲגַף, *wing;* hence literally *wings of an army, alæ exercitus;* comp. כְּנָפַיִם Is. 8:8.

אָגַר, fut. יֶאֱגֹר. *to gather, collect* a harvest. Deut. 28:39. Prov. 6:8. 10:5.

אִגְּרָא f. emph. אִגַּרְתָּא. Chald. i. q. Heb. אִגֶּרֶת *letter, epistle.* Ezra 4:8, 11. 5:6.

אִגֶּרֶת f. dec. XIII. h. *letter, epistle.* Only in later Hebrew; e. g. 2 Chr. 30:1, 6. Est. 9:26, 29. Neh. 2:7, 8, 9. 6:5, 17, 19. The word is most probably of Persian origin, and kindred to the modern Pers. انگاریدن *to paint, write;* whence انگاره *a writing.* From it is derived the Greek ἄγγαρος *a Persian post* or *courier,* who transmitted the royal edicts and letters; comp. Pers. سخرك *angariatio, the forcible requisition of public service by a courier;* and see commentators on Mat. 5:41.

אֶגְרֹף m. (with prosth. א, see p. 2.) dec. I. b. *fist.* Ex. 21:18. Is. 58:4. So Sept. and Vulg. in both passages, and the Rabbins use the word in this sense.

אֲגַרְטָל m. dec. II. b. found only Ezra 1:9 אֲגַרְטְלֵי זָהָב, כֶסֶף *golden, silver basins.* The derivation of the word is doubtful. The Jewish interpreters derive it from the Greek κάρταλλος; which word has been adopted into Arabic, Syriac, and Rabbinic, but signifies a *basket, fruit-basket,* and not a *basin.* There is, however, in the Shemitish languages no etymology which is more plausible.

אֵד m. dec. I. a. *vapour, mist, cloud.* Gen. 2:6. Job 36:27. (In Chald. איד *idem.*)

אֹדוֹת see **אוּדוֹת.**

אָדַב by metath. for דָּאַב *to faint, fail,* found only in Hiph. infin. לַאֲדִיב for לְהַאֲדִיב, 1 Sam. 2:33. Comp. especially Deut. 28:65.

אָדוֹן m. dec. III. a. (with suff. and in plur. written defectively אֲדֹנִי ,אֲדֹנִים) *master, lord, owner.* Gen. 24:9, 12, 14 ff. 45:8 אָדוֹן לְכָל־בֵּיתוֹ *lord over his whole house.* 1 K. 16:24 אֲדֹנֵי הָהָר שֹׁמְרוֹן *owner of the hill Samaria.* (Concerning the plural, see below.) Josh. 3:11, 13 אֲדוֹן כָּל־הָאָרֶץ *lord of the whole earth.* Also without addition used of Jehovah by way of eminence, Ps. 114:7.—אֲדֹנִי *my lord,* a polite and respectful address employed by the Hebrews in conversing with a superior; also with a father, Gen. 31:35. a brother, Num. 12:11. a royal consort, 1 K. 1:17, 18. *my lord* is then substituted for the pronoun of the second person, *thou;* as *thy servant, thy handmaid,* for the first person, *I;* Gen. 33:8, 13, 14, 15. 44:7, 9, 19 אֲדֹנִי שָׁאַל אֶת־עֲבָדָיו *my lord asked his servants,* i. e, thou askedst us. Yet more servile is the application of *my lord* to an absent person; Gen. 32:4. The wife calls the husband *her lord,* Gen. 18:12. Comp. Judg. 19:26, 27. and art. בַּעַל.

Plur. אֲדֹנִים *lords,* Is. 26:13, (with a plural verb.) In the same sense with the suff. ־ַי אֲדֹנַי *my lords,* Gen. 19:2, 18. Elsewhere is אֲדֹנִים אֲדֹנֵי (and with the other suff. ־ֶיךָ, ־ָיו, ־ֵיכֶם, etc.) uniformly pluralis excellentiæ, and synonymous with the singular, Gen. 39:2 ff. (sometimes with a singular adjective, Is. 19:4 אֲדֹנִים קָשֶׁה *a hard master.*) Gen. 42:30, 33 אֲדֹנֵי הָאָרֶץ *the lord of the land.* Deut. 10:17 אֲדֹנֵי הָאֲדֹנִים *the Lord of lords,* i. e. God. The root is probably דּוּן *to judge,* which idea is in the eastern languages closely connected with that of *ruling.* This word does not occur in the kindred dialects, except that in the Phenician a vestige of it remains in Ἄδωνις; and perhaps in Auodoni (*hail, my lord!*) Plaut. Pœn. v. 2.

אֲדֹנָי *the Lord*, used exclusively of God. ־ָי is an ancient plur. termination for ־ִים (see שַׁדַּי) and plur. excellentiæ; but the form ־ָי was chosen instead of ־ַי to distinguish it from אֲדֹנַי *my lords*. Gen. 18:3. Ex. 4:10, 13. Some consider the termination ־ָי as used for the suffix ־ַי; but (1.) the form with ־ָי has always the plural signification; and (2.) Jehovah calls himself אֲדֹנָי, Is. 8:7. Job 28:28.

אֱדַיִן adv. Chald. i. q. Heb. אָז or אֲזַי *then*. Dan. 2:15, 17, 19. בֵּאדַיִן *idem*, Dan. 3:3. מִן־אֱדַיִן *from that time on*, Ezra 5:16.

אַדִּיר verbal adj. from אָדַר, dec. I. b.

1. *great, mighty, powerful;* applied to the waves of the sea, Ps. 93:4. to kings, Ps. 136:18. to nations, Ezek. 32:18.

2. *distinguished, chief;* hence Plur. *nobles, princes, rulers*, 2 Chr. 23:20. Neh. 10:30. Judg. 5:25 סֵפֶל אַדִּירִים *bowl of princes*, i. e. a princely bowl. Jer. 25:34, 35, 36 אַדִּירֵי הַצֹּאן *rulers of the flocks*, i. q. parall. רֹעִים *shepherds*.

3. *splendid, glorious, majestic.* Ps. 8:2. *how glorious is thy name in all the earth!* Is. 33:21.

אָדַם *to be red.* Lam. 4:7. Some translators, (e. g. Bochart, Hieroz. II. lib. v. c. 6, 7.) understand here simply *brilliancy, lustre*, without the idea of *redness*, (comp. *purpureus color*, Hor. Od. iv. 1. 10.) but without sufficient proof from the analogy of the *oriental* languages.

Pu. אָדַם *to be red coloured.* Nah. 2:4. Ex. 25:5. 35:7, 23.

Hiph. i. q. Kal. Is. 1:18. Several verbs denoting colour preserve the intransitive signification in Hiphil; comp. הִלְבִּין.

Hithpa. *to shew itself red, to sparkle*, applied to wine. Prov. 23:31.

אָדָם m. prim. 1. *man*, i. q. Lat. *homo*, and collectively *men*. The two following are subordinate meanings under this head; (1.) *other men*, in opposition to those already named, Jer. 32:20 בְּיִשְׂרָאֵל וּבָאָדָם *both on Israel and on other men*, i. e. the Egyptians. Judg. 18:7, 28. Ps. 73:5. Judg. 16:7 כְּאַחַד הָאָדָם *as one of other men*, in opposition to Samson. Somewhat analogous to this is the idea, *common men*, in opposition to better men, Job 31:33 כְּאָדָם *as common men*, i. e. after the usual human manner. Hos. 6:7. Ps. 82:7. also *wicked men*, Ps. 124:2. (2.) *men of inferior rank*, when opposed to אִישׁ *men of higher rank*, Is. 2:9. 5:15. The plurals of these nouns are בְּנֵי אָדָם and בְּנֵי אִישׁ (rarely אִישִׁים, see אִישׁ), Ps. 49:3. 62:10. Prov. 8:4.—אֶבְיוֹנֵי אָדָם *the poor among men*, a Hebraism for simply *the poor*, Is. 29:19. So זֹבְחֵי אָדָם *sacrificers*, Hos. 13:2; comp. בֹּגְדִים בְּאָדָם Prov. 23:28.

2. *man*, i. q. אִישׁ=Lat. *vir*, very rarely. Ecc. 7:28 *one man* (אָדָם,) *have I found among a thousand, but a woman* etc.

3. *any one.* Lev. 1:2.

4. proper name of the first man, although it preserves here its force as an appellative, and has the article almost without exception. The woman (אִשָּׁה) has an appropriate name *Eve* (חַוָּה); but the man (אָדָם) has none. On the contrary in Gen. 5:2, they are both named אָדָם. In a translation it would be better to render it as an appellative *the man*; though the old versions have treated it as a proper name.

5. proper name of a city on the Jordan. Once Josh. 3:16.

6. בֶּן אָדָם *son of man*, i. q. אָדָם. Used especially in poetry, Num. 23:19. Job 25:6. very frequently in Ezekiel, where God addresses the prophet, בֶּן־אָדָם *man! mortal!* 2:1, 3. 3:1, 3, 4, 10, 25, intimating thereby the unworthiness of a weak mortal to receive so exalted revelations. In Syriac, ܒܰܪ ܢܳܫܳܐ *son of man* is the usual expression for *man*. The plural בְּנֵי אָדָם *men* is used as the plural of אָדָם which has no grammatical plural, 2 Sam. 7:14. especially in poetry, Deut. 32:8. Ps. 11:4. 12:2, 9. 14:2. 21:11. Comp. Chald. בַּר אֱנָשׁ under art. אֱנָשׁ.

אֹדֶם f. verbal from אָדַם, *carnelian*, a gem of a red colour. Ex. 28:17. 39:10. Ezek. 28:13. Sept. σάρδιον, Vulg. *sardius*.

אָדֹם, fem. **אֲדֻמָּה** verbal adj. from אָדַם. dec. VIII. d. *red*. Cant. 5:10. spoken also of a *reddish-brown* heifer, Num. 19:2. and of a *fox-coloured* horse, Zech. 1:8. 6:2.

אֱדוֹם (*red*, comp. the etymology Gen. 25:30) proper name.

1. son of Isaac, elder twin-brother of Jacob, more commonly called *Esau*. But on the contrary, *Edom* is the usual word to designate

2. his posterity, *the Edomites, Idumeans*, and their country, *Idumea*, on the south of Palestine. As the name of the people, it is of the masc. gender, Num. 20:20; as the name of the country, of the fem. gender, Jer. 49:17. Comp. the names יַעֲקֹב and יִשְׂרָאֵל. The gentile noun is אֱדוֹמִי *an Edomite*, Deut. 23:8.

אֲדַמְדָּם fem. **אֲדַמְדֶּמֶת** verbal adj. from אָדַם. Plur. אֲדַמְדַּמּוֹת. *reddish*. Lev. 13:19 ff. 14:37.

אֲדָמָה f. prim. dec. XI. d.

1. *earth*, the element. Gen. 2:19 *out of earth Jehovah formed every beast*. Ex. 20:24 *an altar of earth*. 1 Sam. 4:12, etc.

2. *earth, ground*, which we cultivate. Gen. 4:2. 2 Chr. 26:10 אֹהֵב אֲדָמָה *a lover of husbandry*.

3. *land, country*. Gen. 28:15. Is. 14:2 אַדְמַת יְהוָֹה *the land of Jehovah*, i.e. Canaan; comp. Hos. 9:3.

4. *the globe, whole earth*. Gen. 4:11. 6:1. 7:4.

Plur. found only Ps. 49:12 עֲלֵי אֲדָמוֹת *super terris*.

אַדְמָה one of the five cities, which were destroyed with the valley of Siddim, and sunk in the Dead Sea. Gen. 10:19. 14:2. Hos. 11:8.

אַדְמוֹנִי verbal adj. from אָדַם, *red-haired*; spoken of Esau, Gen. 25:25. of David, 1 Sam. 16:12. 17:42. So the ancient versions with one consent, and not as some render it *of a ruddy countenance*.

אֲדָמִי a city in the tribe of Naphtali. Josh. 19:33. It ought perhaps to be joined with the succeeding word אֲדָמִי־הַנֶּקֶב.

אֶדֶן m. perhaps prim. dec. VI. a.

1. *base, pedestal*, under the boards and pillars of the tabernacle, in order to support them. Ex. 26:19 ff. 27:10 ff. 36:38. According to the description, they were metal plates of a rectangular form with a mortise or socket in the middle. Two of these plates were put under each board, and each board had two tenons (יָדוֹת) which entered into their sockets, and supported the boards. The pillars had only one such plate or pedestal.—In Cant. 5:15, a more elegant pedestal appears to be intended.

2. *foundation of a building*; applied figuratively to the earth, Job 38:6.

אָדַר not found in Kal, but its primary signification appears to have been, *to be wide, broad*, see deriv. אֶדֶר, אַדֶּרֶת; hence 2. *to be great, illustrious, noble*, see deriv. אַדִּיר. Comp. הָדַר.

Niph. *to make oneself glorious*. Ex. 15:6, 11.

Hiph. fut. יַאְדִּיר. *to make glorious*. Is. 42:21.

אֶדֶר m. verbal from אָדַר, dec. VI.

1. *broad mantle*, i.q. אַדֶּרֶת. Mic. 2:8.

2. *splendour, magnificence*. Zech. 11:13. אֶדֶר הַיְקָר *splendour of price*, i.e. splendid price; ironically.

אִדַּר Chald. *threshing-floor*. Da. 2:35.

אֲדָר m. *Adar*, the sixth month of the civil year, corresponding to part of February and part of March. It first occurs, like most of the names of the months, in the later books. Est. 3:7, 13. 8:12.

אֲדַרְגָּזְרִין m. pl. Chald. *chief judges*. Dan. 3:2, 3. Compounded of אֲדַר=אֶדֶר *honour, dignity*, and גְּזַר *to decide, judge*.

אַדְרַזְדָּא Chald. Ezra 7:23. *quickly*, or *carefully, exactly*. Sept. ἑτοίμως. Most probably, according to Moser, the

Greek ἀδειάστα=ἀδειάστως *not transiently, carefully.* The ד is changed after ו into ר, as in הִדְוֵשׁ.

אֲדַרְכֹּן 1 Chr. 29:7. Ezra 8:27. i.q. דַּרְכְּמוֹן *the Persian daric,* a gold coin, which was in circulation among the Jews during their subjection to the Persians. The אֲ is prosthetic, and דַּרְכּוֹן occurs in the Rabbins. The word is of Persian origin, from دارا (dara) *king,* or from درگاه (dargah) *royal court.* Its value was an Attic χρυσοῦς, which the moderns estimate at 1½ ducats. The distinguishing mark of this coin was an archer, hence it is called in numismatics *Sagittarius.* See Ekhel's Doct. Numm. P. I. Vol. III. p. 551.

אַדְרַמֶּלֶךְ (*mighty king*) found only 2 K. 17:31. an idol of the Sippharenes, to which they offered human sacrifices, otherwise wholly unknown.

אֶדְרָע Chald. with א prosthetic, i. q. דְּרָע *arm.* Ezra 4:23.

אַדֶּרֶת f. verbal from אָדַר, dec. XIII. a.

1. *wide mantle, mantle* generally. 1 K. 19:13, 19. אַדֶּרֶת שִׁנְעָר *a Babylonish mantle,* i. e. one curiously worked in Babylonish manner, Josh. 7:21. See Plin. VIII. 48. אַדֶּרֶת שֵׂעָר *a hairy mantle,* perhaps *a fur cloak,* Zech. 13:4. Gen. 25:25.

2. *glory, splendour.* Ezek. 17:8. Zech. 11:3.

אָדַשׁ i. q. דּוּשׁ *to thresh.* Once Is. 28:28 אָדוֹשׁ יְדוּשֶׁנּוּ *he threshes it constantly.* Comp. Jer. 8:13.

אָהַב and **אָהֵב**, fut. יֶאֱהַב (in 1 pers. אֹהַב and אֹהֵב,) inf. אֱהֹב, more frequently אַהֲבָה.

1. *to love.* Construed with an accusative, more rarely with לְ, Lev. 19:18, 34. with בְּ, Ecc. 5:9. Part. אֹהֵב *intimate friend, confidant,* (more than רֵעַ *acquaintance.*) Prov. 18:24. Est. 5:10, 14. See שָׂנֵא.

2. *to desire, rejoice in.* Ps. 40:17 אֹהֲבֵי תְשׁוּעָתֶךָ *those who desire thy help.* 70:5. Comp. 2 Tim. 4:8 τοῖς ἠγαπηκόσι τὴν ἐπιφάνειαν αὐτοῦ *who desire his appearing.* Ps. 116:1 אָהַבְתִּי כִּי יִשְׁמַע יְהוָה *I rejoice because Jehovah has heard.* When construed with לְ before an infin. i. q. French *aimer à faire quelque chose, to like to do a thing,* Hos. 12:8. Is. 56:10. Jer. 14:10.

Niph. part. *lovely.* 2 Sam. 1:23.

Pi. part. מְאַהֵב *lover, paramour.* Ezek. 16:33, 36, 37. 23:5.

אַהֲבָה f. dec. X. 1. infin. of the preceding. Is. 56:6 לְאַהֲבָה אֶת־שֵׁם יְהוָה *to love the name of Jehovah.* Deut. 7:8 מֵאַהֲבַת יְהוָה אֶתְכֶם *since Jehovah loves you.* 1 K. 10:9. 2 Chr. 2:10. 9:8.

2. *love.* Prov. 10:12. 2 Sam. 1:26. Cant. 8:6, 7.

3. *object of love, mistress.* Cant. 2:7. 3:5. 8:4.

4. adv. *charmingly, elegantly.* Cant. 3:10.

אֲהָבִים m. plur. verbal from אָהַב.

1. *fornication,* figuratively for *foreign alliances.* Hos. 8:9. Comp. זָנָה, Is. 23:17.

2. *loveliness.* Prov. 5:19 אַיֶּלֶת אֲהָבִים *the lovely hind,* among the Orientals, a word of amorous endearment.

אֳהָבִים m. pl. verbal from אָהַב. *love, sexual enjoyment.* Prov. 7:18.

אֲהָהּ interj. expressive of grief, formed by an onomatopœia. *Ah! wo! alas!* most generally in the connexion אֲהָהּ אֲדֹנָי יְהוָה *Ah, Lord God!* Judg. 6:22. Jer. 1:6. 4:10. also Judg. 11:35. and with a dative, Joel 1:15 אֲהָהּ לַיּוֹם *alas the day!*

אֱהִי i. q. אֵי or אַיֵּה *where?* Hos. 13:10 אֱהִי אֵפוֹא as in other places frequently אֵי אֵפוֹא *where then?* So the Sept. Vulg. Chald. agreeably to the context.

אָהַל, fut. **יֶאֱהַל**, i. q. נָסַע, perhaps denom. from אֹהֶל. *to take up one's tent and move about as a Nomade,* Gen. 13:12, 18. In the last passage the Sam. text has adopted a correct gloss וַיֵּלֶךְ into the text.

Hiph. *idem.* Fut. יַאֲהִל by contr. יַהֵל Is. 13:20 *the Arabian shall not pitch tent there.* But יַאֲהִיל is prob. Syr. for יָהֵל=יַהֲלִיל the Hiph. of הָלַל *to shine,*

Job 25:5 הֵן עַד יָרֵחַ וְלֹא יַאֲהִיל *behold even the moon, it shineth not clear*, or, *is not pure*. Comp. צַאֲלִים Syr. for צְלָלִים. Others render Job 25:5 *he abides not there*, which is not suited to the context. The various reading יָהֵל in one of Kennicott's MSS. is to be regarded as a correct gloss or explanation.

אֹהֶל m. prob. prim. const. אֹהֶל, with ה local אֹהֱלָה, with suff. אָהֳלִי, אָהָלְךָ [oholcha]; Plur. אֹהָלִים with light suff. אֹהָלֶיךָ, אֹהָלָיו, const. and before grave suff. אָהֳלֵי.

1. *tent*. אֹהֶל מוֹעֵד, הָעֵדוּת, *the tent* or *tabernacle of meeting*, (see מוֹעֵד, עֵדוּת,) for which also stands אֹהֶל simply, 1 K. 1:39. In larger tents אֹהֶל denotes, in a restricted sense, *the external covering*, consisting for the most part of skins, and is opposed to מִשְׁכָּן *the inward lining*, Ex. 26:1, 7. 36:8, 14, 19.

2. *the temple*, because it took the place of the tabernacle just mentioned. Ezek. 41:1.

3. *habitation* generally. Prov. 14:11. Ps. 52:7. 91:10. Is. 16:5 אֹהֶל דָּוִד *house*, i. e. citadel, *of David*.

אֲהָלִים m. plur. Num. 24:6. Prov. 7:16. and אֲהָלוֹת Ps. 45:9. Cant. 4:14. *lign aloes* or *aloes wood*, the ξυλαλόη, or ἀγάλλοχον of the Greeks, the fragrant and very costly wood of a tree growing in the East Indies, with red fruit resembling pepper-corns, *Excæcaria Agallocha*, Linn. In Num. 24:6, the *tree* itself is intended, which, though foreign, the Hebrew poet might speak of, as our poets would of the *palm:* in the other passages the *wood*, as a perfume, is intended. See especially Celsii Hierob. T. I. p. 135—170.

אָהֳלָה f. name of a lewd woman, allegorically representing Samaria. Ezek. 23:4 ff. Most probable derivation is אָהֳלָהּ (she has *her own tent*, i. e. temple.)

אָהֳלִיבָה f. name of a lewd woman, allegorically representing idolatrous Jerusalem. Ezek. 23:4 ff. It is explained by אָהֳלִי בָהּ (*my tent*, i. e. temple, *is with her*) in opposition to אָהֳלָה q. v.

אָהֳלִיבָמָה f. (*tent of exaltation*) proper name of a wife of Esau. Gen. 36:2, 14. The same name is afterwards employed to denote an Edomitish tribe, ver. 41. just as תִּמְנַע the concubine of Eliphaz (v. 12.) gave name to another tribe, v. 40.

אַהֲרֹן m. proper name of the brother of Moses, and first high-priest of the Hebrews. Ex. 4:14. 6:20. בְּנֵי אַהֲרֹן *the children of Aaron*, Josh. 21:4, 10, 13. and בֵּית אַהֲרֹן *the house of Aaron*, Ps. 115:10, 12. 118:3. i. e. the priests. Also *the high-priest* generally, Ps. 133:2. The root אהר is not found in Hebrew, but from it is derived Syr. ܐܗܪܢܐ *lewd, wanton*.

אוֹ conj. prim. 1. *if, if perhaps*. 1 Sa. 20:10 *who will tell me*, אוֹ מַה־יַּעַנְךָ אָבִיךָ קָשָׁה *if thy father answer thee somewhat roughly*. Sept. ἐάν, Vulg. si forte. Gen. 24:55 יָמִים אוֹ עָשׂוֹר *some days, if* it were *perhaps ten*, i. e. about ten days. Sept. ἡμέρας ὡσεὶ δέκα, Vulg. *saltem decem dies*. Lev. 26:11.

2. *but if*. Ex. 21:36. 2 Sam. 18:13. Is. 27:5. (i. q. אוֹ כִּי Lev. 13:16, 24.)

3. *and if*. Lev. 4:23.

4. most frequently, *or*. When repeated, *either, or*. Lev. 25:19.

אוֹ Prov. 31:4 Keth. probably to be pointed אֵו i. q. אַוָּה *desire, inclination*, verbal from אָוָה no. I.

I. **אוֹב** m. dec. I. a.

1. *necromancer, a conjurer who calls up the dead to learn from them the future*. (See particularly 1 Sa. 28:7–19.) Deut. 18:11. 2 K. 21:6. 1 Chr. 33:6.

2. *the spirit of divination in such a conjurer*. Lev. 20:27 *a man, or woman, in whom is* אוֹב *a spirit of necromancy*. 1 Sam. 28:8. Hence בַּעֲלַת־אוֹב *a woman that hath such a spirit, sorceress*, 1 Sam. 28:7.

3. *the ghost itself which is raised*. Is. 29:4 וְהָיָה כְּאוֹב מֵאֶרֶץ קוֹלֵךְ *and thy voice shall be as that of a ghost from the earth*.

Plur. fem. אֹבוֹת *women exercising ne-*

cromancy, sorceresses, Lev. 19:31. 20:6. 1 Sam. 28:3, 9. Is. 8:19. 19:3.

II. אוֹבוֹת f. plur. *skin bottles.* Job 32:19.

Also proper name of an encampment of the Israelites in the wilderness. Num. 21:10. 33:43.

אוּבָל and אֻבָל dec. II. b. *river, lake, marsh.* Dan. 8:2, 3, 6. Comp. Arab. وبل *imbrem effudit.*

אוּד m. dec. I. *firebrand.* Is. 7:4. Am. 4:11. Zech. 3:2.

אוֹדוֹת fem. plur. dec. X. *causes;* only in the connexion עַל אוֹדוֹת *because of, on account of,* Gen. 21:11, 25. Ex. 18:8. עַל־כָּל־אוֹדוֹת אֲשֶׁר *because that,* Jer. 3:8.—In 2 Sam. 13:16, instead of אַל אוֹדוֹת read אֶל א׳.

I. אָוָה only in Pi. אִוָּה *to wish, desire,* generally spoken of נֶפֶשׁ *the soul.* 2 Sam. 3:21. 1 K. 11:37. Deut. 12:20. 14:26.

Hithpa. הִתְאַוָּה, fut. apoc. יִתְאָו *idem;* without נֶפֶשׁ. Construed with an acc. Am. 5:18. with a dative, Prov. 23:3, 6. 24:1. הִתְאַוָּה תַאֲוָה *cupidinem cupere, to desire ardently, to long* or *lust after, to covet,* Num. 11:4. Ps. 106:14. Prov. 21:26.

Deriv. out of course אַו, תַּאֲוָה, מַאֲוַיִּים.

II. אָוָה as in Arab. *to lodge, dwell.* Whence Hithpa. according to the present punctuation, Num. 34:10 הִתְאַוִּיתֶם לָכֶם *take to yourselves for a dwelling;* but according to the versions, *measure off for yourselves,* as if i. q. תְּתָאוּ לָכֶם (verses 7, 8.) from תָּאָה *to measure.* This renders it probable that the first form is derived from תָּאָה, which may be, if we point it as the Hiphil from a quadriliteral תָּאָה=הִתְאָה *to measure,* after the analogy of נָאָה=נָאוָה. In that case the root אָוָה no. II. is to be rejected.

אַוָּה f. verbal from אָוָה no. I. dec. X. *desire.* Deut. 12:15, 20. 18:6. Jer. 2:24. Constantly joined with נֶפֶשׁ, except Hos. 10:10.

אוּזָל found only Gen. 10:27, proper name of a descendant of Joktan, probably the head of some Arabian tribe. According to many testimonies from very different sources, this was the ancient name of the city Sana, the capital of Arabia Felix. See Bochart; and, for further confirmation, J. D. Michaelis Spicil. Geogr. Hebræorum Exter. T. II. p. 164 ff.

אוֹי interj. formed by an onomatopœia, expressive of grief, *wo! alas!* generally with a dat. 1 Sam. 4:8 אוֹי לָנוּ *wo unto us!* or of threatening, Num. 21:29.

אוֹיָה interj. *idem.* Ps. 120:5.

אֱוִיל verbal from obs. אָוַל, dec. I. adj. *foolish* and subst. *a fool,* sometimes connected with the idea of *impiety,* which is more frequent in its synonymes, especially נָבָל. Most common in Proverbs; chap. 1:7. 10:14, 21. 12:15, 16.

אֱוִילִי denom. from אֱוִיל by adding the adjective termination ִי *idem.* Zech. 11:15.

אֱוִיל מְרֹדַךְ m. proper name of a king of Babylon and successor of Nebuchadnezzar. 2 K. 25:27. Jer. 52:51. The latter part of this compound name is the name of a Babylonish idol (see מְרֹדַךְ): the former signifies in Hebrew *foolish,* but is without doubt an entirely different Assyrian or Persian word, which has been somewhat altered, so as to sound like Hebrew. Syncellus writes the name *Evidan-merodach.*

אוּל and איל an obsolete root, which probably signified *to be strong, mighty.* Deriv. אֵילִים, אֵלִים *the mighty;* אֵל *might, God;* perhaps also אַיִל *ram,* אֵלָה *turpentine-tree,* both so named from their *strength;* and with a moveable ,י אֱיָל, אֱיָלוּת *strength.* An entirely different word from this is

אָוַל a root also obsolete, *to be foolish.* Deriv. אֱוִיל *foolish,* אִוֶּלֶת *foolishness.* By metath. this verb becomes יָאַל=אָוַל Niph. *to be foolish,* q. v.

אוּל m. dec. I. a.

1. *mighty.* (See root אול.) 2 K. 24:15 Keth. אֻלֵי הָאָרֶץ *the mighty* or *the nobles of the land,* instead of which the Keri substitutes the more usual form אֵלֵי.

2. *body.* Ps. 73:4 *their body is fat.* (In Arab. اِلّ, آل *corpus.*)

I. אוּלַי *perhaps,* Gen. 16:2. 24:5. *if perhaps,* Hos. 8:7.

II. אוּלַי *Eulæus,* a river flowing by Susa in Persia. Dan. 8:2.

I. אוּלָם, also אֻלָם, m. (with Kamets impure,) Pl. אֻלַמִּים more commonly אֵילַמִּים, אֵלַמִּים, אֵלַמּוֹת, (from אֵלָם.) *a covered walk with pillars, a portico, piazza, porch.* 1 K. 7:6 ff. Ezek. 40:7 ff. Particularly the porch in front of Solomon's temple, πρόναος, 1 K. 6:3. Joel 2:17. In the passage in Kings, this porch is described only as to its length and breadth, whence it would be most natural to suppose its height to be that of the temple itself; but the parallel passage in 2 Chr. 3:4, gives it the towering height of 120 cubits, which would not conform to our ideas of architecture, and leads us to suspect some error. Hirt (Tempel Salomo's, p. 24.) makes it probable that its height was short of 20 cubits, and therefore less than that of the temple. The word has no root in Hebrew; but in Egyptian, ιλαμ signifies *a portico.* See Jablonskii Opusc. ed. Te Water. T. I p. 85. But Gesenius (Lehrgeb. p. 495, 844.) gives a different origin to this word.

II. אוּלָם (once אֻלָם Job 17:10.) Comp. Arab. أَوَّل *præcessit,* and see Gesen. Lehrgeb. p. 624, 844.

1. conj. advers. *but, nevertheless,* Sept. οὐ μὴν ἀλλά. Job 2:5. 5:8. 13:3. More frequent is וְאוּלָם *idem.* Job 1:11. 12:7. 33:2.

2. more rarely, conj. causal, i. q. כִּי in the beginning of a proposition, *for, for indeed, enimvero.* Job 13:4 *for ye invent false words.* 14:18.

אִוֶּלֶת f. verbal from obs. אָוַל, dec. XIII. a.

1. *folly.* Prov. 12:23. 13:16. Hence

2. *sin, transgression.* Ps. 38:6. Comp. נְבָלָה.

3. perhaps *might, high rank,* borrowing its signification from אול. Prov. 14:24 אִוֶּלֶת כְּסִילִים אִוֶּלֶת *the elevation of fools is still folly.* There would then be an antanaclasis, or a play upon the double signification of the word אִוֶּלֶת; but perhaps it ought the first time to be differently pointed. Others: *the foolishness of fools continues foolishness,* which does not accord with the parallel clause.

אָוֶן m. dec. VI. e. (Kindred to אַיִן *nothingness, defect,* and as an adv. *not.*)

1. *nothingness, vanity, falsehood.* Is. 41:29. (Parall. אֶפֶס.) Zech. 10:2. It is applied particularly to idolatry, (comp. הֶבֶל,) 1 Sam. 15:23. and to every thing pertaining to it; e. g. to the idol itself, Is. 66:3. Hence Hosea names the idolatrous city בֵּית־אֵל *(house of God)* in derision בֵּית אָוֶן *(house of an idol)* Hos. 4:15. 5:8. 10:5. and simply אָוֶן 10:8.

2. *wickedness, sin, transgression.* Job 36:21. Is. 1:13. מְתֵי־אָוֶן, אַנְשֵׁי *wicked men,* Job 22:15. 34:36. פֹּעֲלֵי אָוֶן *evil-doers,* Job 31:3. 34:8, 22. Used prob. as a concrete Prov. 11:7 אוֹנִים for אַנְשֵׁי אָוֶן (so the Sept. Syr. Arab. Chald.)

3. *evil, trouble, sorrow, affliction,* i. q. עָמָל no. 3. Ps. 55:4 *they bring trouble upon me.* Prov. 22:8 *he who sows iniquity, reaps affliction.* Ps. 90:10, Job 15:35. Gen 35:18 בֶּן־אוֹנִי *son of my sorrow.*—לֶחֶם אוֹנִים *bread of sorrow, funeral meal,* Hos. 9:4. comp. Deut. 26:14.—Hab. 3:7 תַּחַת אָוֶן *in affliction.*—As this word, when joined with suffixes, is exactly like און below, whose signification is essentially and radically different, care should be taken not to confound them.

אָוֶן prop. name. 1. a pleasant valley in Syria of Damascus, now called *Un,* and used proverbially for a pleasant vale. Am. 1:5.

2. i. q. אוֹן *Heliopolis.* Ezek. 30:17.

אוֹן m. dec. 1. a.

1. *strength.* Job 18:7, 12. 40:16.

Hos. 12:4. Particularly *the power of generation,* רֵאשִׁית אוֹן *firstling of one's strength, first-begotten,* Gen. 49:3. Deut. 21:17. Ps. 105:36. Plur. אוֹנִים, Is. 40:26, 29. Ps. 78:51.

2. *wealth, riches,* Hos. 12:9. Job 20:10. Comp. חַיִל. According to others, i. q. הוֹן, by interchanging א and ה.

אוּפָז Jer. 10:9. Dan. 10:5. *Uphaz,* a country rich in gold, the situation of which is nowhere pointed out.

אוֹפִיר, also **אוֹפִר**, *Ophir,* a celebrated country, famous for its gold, which Solomon's ships visited in company with the Phenician. They brought back from thence gold, precious stones, and sandal-wood, (1 K. 9:28. 10:11. 2 Chr. 8:18. 9:10. also (according to 1 K. 10:22, where Ophir indeed is not mentioned, but is intended) silver, ivory, apes, and peacocks, (קֹפִים according to others *pheasants.*) The Bible speaks frequently of the gold *of Ophir,* Job 28:16. Ps. 45:10. 1 Chr. 29:4. In Job 22:24, אוֹפִיר stands alone for *Ophiritic gold.* Were we obliged to suppose all these articles the actual productions of Ophir, then this country must, as Bochart, Reland and others have thought, be looked for only in India; and the LXX appear to have had this opinion, in rendering it Σωφίρ, Σουφίρ, Σωφιρά, which is the Egyptian name for India. (Josephi Antiq. Jud. viii. 6. 4. comp. Jablonskii Opusc. ed. Te Water. T. I. p. 337.) But in Gen. 10:29, Ophir stands in the midst of other Arabian countries, and the arguments preponderate for placing it in Arabia; yet possibly it is mentioned in that connexion only on account of its being an Arabian colony planted abroad. If it was in Arabia, the articles mentioned above, except apes, precious stones, and perhaps pheasants, must have come to Ophir in the way of commerce, and it is probable that they were brought from the East coast of Africa. (אוֹפִיר is thought to mean *Africa* itself by the Chaldee interpreter and by some others in Origen on Job 22:24.) Antiquity has constantly ascribed a great abundance of gold to the nations of Arabia, (comp. art. שְׁבָא; concerning the Midianites, Num. 21:22, 50. Judges 8:24, 26; and concerning the passages in the classics, Bochart;) although it is probable that gold was never produced there. See Mannert's Geographie der Griechen und Römer. Th. vi. H. 1. p. 8. The very name *El Ophir* has lately been pointed out as a city in Oman, in former times the centre of a very active Arabian commerce. Comp. Bochart's Phaleg. ii. c. 27. Reland's Dissert. Miscell. i. 4. J. D. Michaëlis Spicileg. T. II. p. 184 ff. Bredow's histor. Untersuchungen. Th. ii. p. 253 ff. Seetzen in Zach's monatl. Correspondenz. B. XIX. p. 331 ff.

אוֹפַן m. dec. VIII. a. *wheel.* Ex. 14:25. Prov. 20:26 וַיָּשֶׁב עֲלֵיהֶם אוֹפָן *and brings over them the wheel* of the threshing waggon or sledge. Comp. דּוּשׁ.

אוּץ 1. *to be narrow.* Josh. 17:15.

2. trans. *to press.* Ex. 5:13.

3. *to press oneself, to hasten.* Josh. 10:13. Prov. 19:2. 28:20. When construed with מִן, *to take one's self away, to withdraw,* Jer. 17:16 לֹא־אַצְתִּי מֵרֹעֶה אַחֲרֶיךָ for מִהְיוֹת רֹעֶה *I have not withdrawn myself from following thee as a shepherd,* i. e. as a prophet.

Hiph. *to press on* any one, construed with בְּ, Gen. 19:15. Is. 22:4.

אוֹצָר m. verbal from אָצַר, dec. II. Plur. אוֹצָרוֹת.

1. *store, stores;* e. g. of provisions, 2 Chr. 11:11. 1 Chr. 27:27. Job 38:22 *stores of the snow, of the hail.* Especially of costly articles; hence *a treasure,* Prov. 21:20. often *the treasure* of the temple, 1 K. 7:51. of the royal house, 14:26. בֵּית הָאוֹצָר *treasure-house,* Neh. 10:39.

2. i. q. בֵּית הָאוֹצָר *storehouse,* Joel 1:17. *treasure-house,* 2 Chr. 32:27.

אוֹר 1. *to be* or *become light;* applied to the morning, Gen. 44:3. to the sun, Prov. 4:18. to the eyes, 1 Sa. 14:27, 29.

Used impers. אוֹר *it is light, it is day,* 1 Sam. 29:10.

2. used figuratively. Is. 60:1 *up, to the light, for thy light is come.*

Niph. נָאוֹר, fut. יֵאוֹר. *to become light,* 2 Sam. 2:32. *to be enlightened,* Job 33:30. Part. נָאוֹר *shining, illustrious, glorious,* Ps. 76:5.

Hiph. הֵאִיר 1. *to illumine, enlighten.* Ps. 77:19. 97:4. 105:39. Particularly (1.) with עֵינַיִם, *to enlighten the eyes* of any one, Ps. 13:4 *enlighten mine eyes,* (antith. *sleeping the sleep of death;*) elsewhere *to gladden, make joyful,* Prov. 29:13. Ps. 19:9. (Parall. *rejoicing the heart.*) Ezra 9:8. (2.) with פָּנִים, *to enlighten the countenance* of any one, *to make it serene,* Ecc. 8:1. *a man's wisdom shall make his face serene, but his haughty countenance shall be disfigured.* Ps. 80:4, 8. When construed with אֶל, בְּ, עַל, *to make one's face to shine on* any one, *to be propitious to* him, Ps. 31:17. 119:135. Dan. 9:17. Also without פָּנִים in the same sense, Ps. 118:27. (3.) *to instruct.* Ps. 119:130.

2. *to shine,* strictly *to make it light.* Gen. 1:15. Ex. 13:21.

3. *to kindle, set on fire.* Mal. 1:10. Is. 27:11. Comp. אוּר *fire.*

Deriv. out of course, מָאוֹר.

אוֹר m. (fem. perhaps Job 36:32.) verbal from אוֹר, dec. I. a. *light.* Gen. 1:3—5. Particularly (1.) *daylight, daybreak.* 1 Sam. 14:36. Neh. 8:3 מִן־הָאוֹר עַד־מַחֲצִית הַיּוֹם *from daybreak to mid-day.* Job 24:14. (2.) *the sun.* Job 31:26. 37:21. Hab. 3:4. (3.) *light of life, life.* Job 3:16, 20. in full, אוֹר הַחַיִּים Ps. 56:14. (4.) *light,* as an emblem of *happiness;* the figure sometimes being preserved, Job 22:28. Is. 9:1. 30:26. and sometimes not, Ps. 97:11. Parall. שִׂמְחָה. (5.) *light* as an emblem of *instruction.* Is. 49:6 אוֹר גּוֹיִם *light of the gentiles,* i. e. their teacher. 51:4. 2:5 *let us walk in the light of Jehovah,* see verse 3. Comp. Prov. 6:23 *the commandment is a lamp, and the law is light.* Probably also in this sense Jehovah is called *the light of Israel,* Is. 10:17. (60:3.?) (6.) אוֹר פָּנִים *light* or *serenity of countenance.* Job 29:24. When applied to God, to a king, *a propitious countenance,* Prov. 16:15 *in the serene,* i. e. propitious, *countenance of the king.* Ps. 4:7. 44:4.

I. **אוּר** m. verbal from אוֹר, dec. I. a. *fire.* Ezek. 5:2. Is. 44:16. 47:14. 50:11. See verb אוֹר Hiph. no. 3.

Plur. אוּרִים or אֻרִים, sometimes alone Num. 27:21. but generally with וְתֻמִּים. Luth. *Licht und Recht;* Sept. more correctly δήλωσις καὶ ἀλήθεια; perhaps plurales excellentiæ, *light,* i. e. revelation, *and truth,* the sacred lot of the Hebrews which the high-priest bore in or on his breast-plate (חֹשֶׁן) and consulted in difficult cases. Ex. 28:30. Lev. 8:8. Ezra 2:63. Neh. 7:65. Of what it consisted is a matter of dispute. Josephus (Antiq. iii. 8. 9.) and the Rabbins say, that it consisted of the gems in the breast-plate; but a more probable opinion is derived from Ex. 28:30, (comp. Philo de vita Mosis, Opp. T. II. p. 152. ed. Mangey.) that the Urim and Thummim were two small oracular images, similar to the Teraphim, and personifying *Revelation* and *Truth,* which were placed in the cavity of the breast-plate. There appears to have been a very similar custom among the Egyptians, see Diod. Sic. i. 48, 75. Æliani Var. Hist. xiv. 34.

II. **אוּר** Gen. 11:28. Neh. 9:7. proper name of a city in Mesopotamia, which is also mentioned by the same name in Ammian. Marc. xxv. 8.

אוּרִים or **אֻרִים** found only Is. 24:15. probably *the north country.* Comp. نور *septentrio.* This explanation does not form an exact antithesis to אִיֵּי הַיָּם *the islands of the western sea* in the parallel clause; but such exactness ought not to be required, see Am. 8:12. Ps. 107:3. Deut. 33:23.

אוֹרָה fem. of אוֹר, dec. X. *light.* Ps. 139:12. Fig. *happiness,* Est. 8:16.

Plur. אוֹרֹת *herbs, vegetables.* 2 K. 4:39. (In the Shemitish languages, the ideas of *sprouting, being green, flourishing,* are connected in many words with that of *shining.* See נָצַץ. In the Samar. version יאר is used for דֶּשֶׁא *an herb,* Gen. 1:11, 12.) So perhaps Isaiah 26:19 כִּי טַל אוֹרֹת טַלֶּךָ *for a dew of plants is thy dew,* i. e. refreshing, healing, as the dew of plants. Others: *morning dew.* Others: *the dew of life.*

אֻרָוֺת by metath. for אֻרָוֺת *stalls* or *cribs.* 2 Chr. 32:28.

אוּרִיָּה (*light of Jehovah*) proper name. 1. a Hittite, husband of Bathsheba, caused to be murdered by David. 2 Sam. 11:3.

2. a high-priest under Ahaz, contemporary with Isaiah. Is. 8:2. 2 K. 16:10.

אוֹת com. dec. I. Plur. אֹתוֹת. *sign.* Particularly (1.) *sign, flag, standard.* Num. 2:2 ff. namely, such as each tribe carried, and different from דֶּגֶל a common standard for three tribes. (2.) *sign, memorial, pledge,* e. g. of a covenant. Thus circumcision, Gen. 17:11, and the sabbath, Ex. 31:13, 17. Ezek. 20:12, 20, are called *signs of the covenant* between Jehovah and the Jews. Hence, in a more general sense, *sacred rites, religious institutions, offerings and the like,* Ps. 74:9 אוֹתֹתֵינוּ לֹא־רָאִינוּ *our sacred rites we see not.* So verse 4. (3.) *sign, memorial, remembrance,* e. g. of something to be done, Ex. 13:9, 16. Deut. 6:8. or avoided. Ezek. 14:8. Num. 17:25. [10.] Deut. 28:46. (4.) *sign, token, pledge, omen,* of a promise to be performed, or of a prediction to be fulfilled. The deity, or the prophet as his interpreter, predicts a special event, the fulfilment of which is a pledge for the accomplishment of the whole prophecy. Ex. 3:12. 1 Sam. 2:34. 10:7, 9. 2 K. 19:29. 20:8, 9. Is. 7:11, 14. 38:7, 22. Jer. 44:29. Comp. מוֹפֵת no. 1. with which it is sometimes joined, Deut. 13:2. In a more general sense, *sign* or *proof* of a divine mission, Judg. 6:17. (5.) *emblem, type, symbol,* of a future event, synonymous with מוֹפֵת no. 2. Ezek. 4:3 אוֹת הִיא לְבֵית יִשׂ׳ *let this be a type to the house of Israel.* Is. 8:18. 20:3. (6.) *sign in heaven, a prodigy.* Jer. 10:2. Particularly *a miracle* wrought by God or by his messengers, and then synonymous with מוֹפֵת no. 1. with which it is very frequently connected. Deut. 4:34. 6:22. 7:19. Ex. 4:8, 9, 17 ff. Also in classical Greek and Latin authors, the same words which denote *a mark, sign,* likewise denote *a miracle.* Comp. σῆμα, σημεῖον, τέρας, monstrum, portentum, ostentum, prodigium.

אוּת or **אוֹת** only in Niph. נֵאוֹת, 1 pers. pl. fut. נֵאוֹת, 3 pers. יֵאוֹתוּ *to consent.* 2 K. 12:9. Construed with a dative of the person, Gen. 34:15, 22, 23.

אוֹת or **אֹת,** with suffixes a sign of the accusative case. See אֵת no. II.

אָז adv. prim. 1. *then, at that time,* Germ. *damals.* Gen. 12:6. Josh. 14:11. In this sense it refers back to past time, but has a verb after it in the future tense, which must be rendered as if in the preterite, Josh. 10:12. Ex. 15:1. Deut. 4:41.

2. *then, at some future time,* Germ. *dann.* Ps. 96:12 אָז יְרַנְּנוּ *then shall they rejoice.* Zeph. 3:9. Job 3:13. Often at the beginning of the latter member of a sentence, Job 13:20. Prov. 2:5.

3. *therefore, on that account.* Jer. 22:15. Ps. 40:8 *therefore I said, Behold, I come.*

4. מֵאָז and מִן־אָז formed like the French *depuis, dès lors.* (1.) *from that time on, after, since;* construed with a verb finite and infin. Ex. 5:23 מֵאָז בָּאתִי אֶל פַּרְעֹה *since I came to Pharaoh.* Gen. 39:5. Ex. 4:10 מֵאָז דַּבֶּרְךָ *since thou hast spoken.* Josh. 14:10. also with substantives, Ruth 2:7 מֵאָז הַבֹּקֶר *from the morning on.* Ps. 76:8 מֵאָז אַפֶּךָ *from the time of thine anger onward,* i. e. when thine anger has once broken out. (2.) used absolutely, *formerly, in times past, long ago,* 2 Sam. 15:34. Is. 44:8. 45:21. 48:3, 5, 7. also *from ancient times,* Prov. 8:22.

אֲזָא and **אֲזָה** Chald. *to kindle, heat.* Part. pass. אֵזֵה, Dan. 3:22. infin. מֵזֵא, with suff. מֵזְיֵהּ, 3:19.

אֲזַד Chald. found only Dan. 2:5, 8 מִלְּתָא מִנִּי אַזְדָּא *the word from me is fixed,* i. e. my command is unchangeable. So Aben Ezra compares the Talmudic אַזְדָּא *robur, firmitas.* Perhaps *the command has gone forth from me,* making אֲזַד=אֲזַל *to depart, go out;* comp. Dan. 9:23. Is. 45:23.

אֵזוֹב m. (Syr. for אֵיזוֹב) *hyssop,* a bunch of which was used in the sacred sprinklings. Ex. 12:22. Lev. 14:4, 6, 49, 51. This word, like the names of many other oriental plants, passed from the eastern nations to the Greeks. Comp. Greek ὕσσωπος.

אֵזוֹר m. (Syr. for אֵיזוֹר) verbal from אָזַר, dec. III. g.

1. *girdle.* Ps. 5:27. Jer. 13:1 ff.

2. *fetter.* Job 12:18. Vulg. *funis.*

אֲזַי adv. i. q. אָז then. Ps. 124:3—5. The Chald. אֱדַיִן is nearly related to this word.

אַזְכָּרָה f. verbal from Hiph. of זָכַר, dec. X. *praise-offering* or *remembrance-offering,* i. e. in the ritual language, that part of the meat-offering which was burnt. Sept. μνημόσυνον. Vulg. *memoriale.* Lev. 2:2, 9, 16. 5:12. 6:8 [15.] Num. 5:26. The priest took from the meat-offering a handful of the flour, some of the oil, and the whole incense, and burnt them on the altar to Jehovah. The rest fell to the priest; see Lev. 2:2, 3, 9, 10.—In Lev. 24:7, the incense scattered on the shew-bread is also called אַזְכָּרָה. This word is a verbal, (or strictly speaking, Chald. infin. Aphel,) from הִזְכִּיר. Comp. הִזְכִּיר לְבֹנָה *to burn incense,* Is. 66:3. a technical expression of the ritual service.

I. אָזַל fut. תֵּזְלִי for תֵּאזְלִי, Jer. 2:36. also אֹזֵל לוֹ Prov. 20:14.

1. *To go away.* Prov. 20:14 אֹזֵל לוֹ אָז יִתְהַלָּל *going his way, then he boasteth.* Jer. 2:36 *why goest thou away so much?*

2. *to go away, disappear;* applied to the drying up of water, Job 14:11. to the consumption of the articles of living, 1 Sam. 9:7. to the disappearing of succour, Deut. 32:36.

אֲזַל Chal. 1. *to go.* Ezra 4:23. 5:8, 15.

2. *to go away.* Dan. 2:17. 6:19.

II. אָזַל *to spin, weave.* (Comp. Talmud. אַזְלָא *a weaver;* and Syr. and Arab. غزل *to spin;* and see letter א, p. 1.) Part. Pu. מְאוּזָּל *something spun or woven.* Ezek. 27:19.

אָזַן i. q. Arab وَزَنَ *to weigh,* whence מֹאזְנַיִם *scales.* In Heb. found only in Pi. אִזֵּן *to weigh, examine.* Ecc. 12:9. In Rabbin. אִזֵּן *to be weighed, proved.*

אָזֵן m. dec. V. b. found only Deut. 23:14. *implement, utensil.* In Chald. זֵינִין denotes *arms, weapons,* a very kindred idea, from Aram. זַיֵּן, زين *to arm.*

אֹזֶן f. dec. VI. p. Dual אָזְנַיִם. *ear;* freq.—דִּבֶּר בְּאָזְנֵי פ׳ *to speak in the ears,* i.e. in the presence, *of any one.* Gen. 20:8. 23:16. 44:18. Ex. 10:2. Hence

Hiph. הֶאֱזִין denom. from אֹזֶן *to hear, give ear, to perceive by the ear;* construed with an acc. Gen. 4:23. Job 33:1. with לְ, Job 34:2. with אֶל, Ps. 77:2. with עַל, Prov. 17:4. with עַד, Num. 23:18. of the person or thing heard.

2. applied to God anthropopathically, *to hear.* Ps. 5:2. 17:1. 39:13. 54:4, In both these significations it is used almost solely in the more elevated poetic style.

3. *to hearken to, obey.* Neh. 9:30. Ex. 15:26.

Note. The א quiesces and falls away in אֹזִין for אַאֲזִין, Job 32:11. מֵזִין part. for מַאֲזִין, Prov. 17:4.

אֲזִקִּים with prosth. א, i. q. זִקִּים *chains, fetters.* Jer. 40:1, 4. In verse 1, the א is wanting in several MSS.

אָזַר, fut. יֶאְזֹר.

1. *to gird, to gird up* or *about;* spoken of a garment, with an accusative of the person, Job 30:18. with an acc. of the part girded, Job 38:3 אֱזָר־נָא חֲלָצֶיךָ *gird up thy loins,* i. e. make thyself ready. 40:7. Jer. 1:17.

2. *to gird on, to gird one's self,* construed with an acc. of the thing, 1 Sam. 2:4 אָזְרוּ חָיִל *they gird themselves with*

strength. 2 K. 1:8 אֵזוֹר אָזוּר *girded with a girdle.*

Niph. *to be girded about.* Ps. 65:7.

Pi. *to gird,* construed with a double accusative of the person and thing. Ps. 18:33, 40 תְּאַזְּרֵנִי חַיִל *thou hast girded me with strength.* Comp. 30:12. Is. 50:11 מְאַזְּרֵי זִיקוֹת *girded,* i. e. armed, *with fiery darts.* Comp. other verbs of clothing; e. g. לָבַשׁ.

Hithpa. *to gird, arm one's self.* Is. 8:9. with an acc. Ps. 93:1.

אֶזְרוֹעַ i. q. זְרוֹעַ *the arm* (with prosth. א, see letter א, p. 2.) Jer. 32:21. Job 31:22.

אֶזְרָח m. verbal from זָרַח *to rise, sprout up.*

1. *a tree still standing in its original soil, and not transplanted.* Ps. 37:35.

2. *a native, one born in a place, not a foreigner, indigena.* Lev. 16:19. 18:26.

אֶזְרָחִי a patronymic noun (from אֶזְרָח), *an Ezrahite, descendant of Ezrah;* applied to Ethan, 1 K. 5:11. [4. 31.] Ps. 89:1. and to Heman, Ps. 88:1. Both of these persons were descendants of Zerah (זֶרַח) the son of Judah, 1 Chr. 2:6; whence אֶזְרָח, is probably only another form of the name זֶרַח, which became the usual one in the patronymic.

I. **אָח** m. prim. irreg. const. and before grave suff. אֲחִי, with light suff. אָחִי, אָחִיו, אָחִינוּ, אָחִיךָ; Plur. אַחִים, (for אָחִים) const. and before grave suff. אֲחֵי, with light suff. אַחַי, אַחֶיךָ, אַחֶיךָ, אֶחָיו (for אַחָיו), אַחֵינוּ, אַחֵיהֶ.

1. *brother;* freq. When it is not important to fix the exact degree of kindred, it denotes also *a half brother,* Gen. 42:15. 43:3. but the more accurate expression for the latter is בֶּן אָב, בֶּן אֵם.—Sometimes, with emphasis, *an own brother,* Gen. 44:20.

2. *cousin, kinsman* of any degree. Gen. 14:16 *Lot, his brother,* i. e. his nephew. 13:8. 29:12, 15.

3. *one belonging to the same tribe, contribulis.* 2 Sam. 19:13. The Levites are so called in respect to each other, Num. 8:26. 16:10. Neh. 3:1.

4. *fellow countryman.* Judg. 14:3. Ex. 2:11. 4:18. Also kindred nations are called אַחִים; e. g. Edomites and Hebrews, Gen. 9:25. 16:12. 25:18. Num. 20:14.

5. *confederated, bound together by a league;* e. g. Tyrians and Hebrews, Am. 1:9.

6. *friend, companion.* Job's friends are so called, Job 6:15. (19:13.?) Hiram gives this name to Solomon, 1 K. 9:13. Comp. Neh. 5:10, 14.

7. *neighbour, fellowman,* i. q. רֵעַ. Lev. 19:17. Hence following after אִישׁ, *one, another; alter, alter.* Gen. 13:11 אִישׁ מֵעַל אָחִיו *the one from the other, from one another.* 26:31. Ex. 16:15. This mode of expression is applied also to inanimate objects of the masc. gender, Ex. 25:20 *and the faces of the cherubim were* אִישׁ אֶל אָחִיו *towards one another.* 37:9.

8. It is applied metaphorically to persons and things which have resemblance. Job. 30:29 *I am a brother of the jackal,* i. e. I moan like him. Prov. 18:9. Ezek. 18:10.

II. **אָח** interj. of lament. *Ah! alas!* construed with the dative, Ezek. 6:11. 21:20. [15.]

III. **אָח** f. (comp. Arab. أَجَّ *ardeo*) *a fire-pan,* such as is employed in the east for warming chambers. This pan, called in Pers. and Turk. *tennor,* or *tendur,* is placed in a small cavity in the midst of a winter apartment: when the fire is burnt down, a cover, like a dish, is placed upon it, and round the whole a carpet is spread to retain the heat. Jer. 36:22, 23.

אַח Chald. *brother,* as in Heb. Plur. with suff. אַחָךְ, Ezra 7:18.

אַחְאָב m. (*father's brother*) proper name of a king of Israel about the year 900 before Christ, characterized as a weak prince and an idolater. 1 K. 16:28. 22:40. He was followed on the throne by his two sons Ahaziah and Jehoram in succession, but his family was afterwards utterly rooted out by Jehu.

אֹחִים plur. found only Is. 13:21. a species of howling animals, perhaps *owls*, or *uhus*, comp. אָח interj. of lament. According to others: *howlings, lamentations.* So the Sept.

אָחַד not found in Kal, but instead of it יָחַד *to unite.*

Hithpa. Ezek. 21:21 [16] הִתְאַחֲדִי *unite thyself,* i. e. rage with united strength, (addressed to the triple sword.)

אֶחָד m. const. אַחַד; and **אַחַת** (for אַחֶדֶת) f. in pause אֶחָת.

1. *one;* freq.

2. *first.* Only in numbering the days of the month, (the use of the cardinals for the ordinals is generally limited to notices of time;) e. g. Ezra 10:16, 17 יוֹם אֶחָד לַחֹדֶשׁ *the first day of the month,* i. q. בְּאֶחָד לַחֹדֶשׁ *on the first* day *of the month,* Gen. 8:5, 13. In other passages, e. g. Gen. 1:5. 2:11, the usual signification is retained, as in Lat. *unus, alter, tertius,* e. g. Suet. Oct. 101.

3. *any one, some one.* אַחַד הָעָם *one of the people.* אֵין אֶחָד, לֹא אֶחָד *no one.* Hence

4. it is used in later Hebrew for the indefinite article *a, an.* 1 K. 20:13 נָבִיא אֶחָד *a prophet,* προφήτης τις. Dan. 8:3 אַיִל אֶחָד *a ram.* 1 K. 19:4.

5. When doubled, *one, the other.* Ex. 17:12. 18:3, 4. sometimes repeated thrice, 1 Sam. 10:3. Also when repeated, used distributively, *one apiece, one by one, one each,* Num. 13:2. אִישׁ אֶחָד אִישׁ אֶחָד לַמַּטֶּה *one man from each tribe.* 34:18.

6. כְּאֶחָד *as one, together, in company.* Ezra 2:64. כָּל־הַקָּהָל כְּאֶחָד *the whole congregation together.* 3:9. 6:20. Ecc. 11:6 שְׁנֵיהֶם כְּאֶחָד *both alike.* Is. 65:25. The same signification has כְּאִישׁ אֶחָד Judg. 20:8. 1 Sam. 11:7. In Chald. כַּחֲדָא *idem.*

7. אַחַת (פַּעַם being omitted) *once.* 2 K. 6:10. Ps. 62:12.—בְּאַחַת *idem,* also i. q. כְּאֶחָד *together,* Jer. 10:8. also *at once, suddenly,* Prov. 28:18.

Plur. אֲחָדִים 1. *the same.* Gen. 11:1.

2. *joined in one.* Ezek. 37:17 *the two sticks* הָיוּ לַאֲחָדִים *shall become one.*

3. *some, several;* hence *a few,* Gen. 27:44. 29:20.

אָחוּ m. Gen. 41:2, 18. Job 8. 11. *Grass, reeds,* growing in marshy grounds, and forming pasture for cattle. The word is of Egyptian origin, and is also preserved in the Greek of the Sept. (Is. 19:7.) and of Sirach (Ecclus. 40:16.) in the form Ἄχει, Ἄχι. Jerome on Is. 19:7, says: Quum ab eruditis quærerem, quid Ἄχει significaret, audivi, ab Ægyptiis hoc nomine lingua eorum *omne quod in palude virens nascitur* significari. See Jablonskii Opusc. ed. Te Water. T. I. p. 45. T. II. p. 160.

אַחֲוָה f. dec. X. *information, argument, defence.* Job 13:17. It is a verbal from the Hiph. of חָוָה *to inform,* of which in Heb. only the Piel, but in Chald. the Hiph. or Aphel occurs.

אַחֲוָה f. denom. from אָח no. I. *brotherhood.* Zech. 11:14.

אַחֲוָיָה Chald. *explanation.* Dan. 5:12. Strictly infin. Aph. from חֲוָה *to shew, explain.*

אָחוֹר dec. III. 1. *hinder side, back part.* Only in plur. אֲחוֹרִים Ezek. 8:16. 1 K. 7:25. In the singular it is used adverbially, and signifies (1.) *behind.* Ezek. 2:10. 1 Chr. 19:10. Antith. פָּנִים *before.* (2.) *back, backwards.* Gen. 49:17. Hence אָחוֹר, נָסוֹג, הָלַךְ, *to decline, fall away,* particularly from the service of God. So לְאָחוֹר, Jer. 7:24. Hence

2. *the west side,* antith. קֶדֶם. Is. 9:11. Also adverbially, *westward,* Job 23:8.

Note. The Shemite, in speaking of the quarters of the heavens, supposes his face turned toward the east; so that the east is before him, the west behind, the south on the right hand, etc. Comp. שְׂמֹאל, יָמִין, קֶדֶם, תֵּימָן.

3. *the future, time to come:* hence לְאָחוֹר *for the future,* Is. 41:23. 42:23.

אָחוֹת f. (for אַחֲוָת from masc. אָחוּ Chald. and Arab. for אָח) irreg. const.

and before suff. אֲחוֹת (once אֲחוֹתוֹ Num. 6:7); Plur. with suffixes, אַחְיֹתֵיכֶם, אֲחוֹתַיִךְ, etc. (as from a sing. אָחָה); also אַחְיוֹתַיִךְ, אַחְיוֹתֵיהֶם, אַחְיוֹתַי, etc. (as from a sing. אַחְוָה fem. of אַחְוָ.)

1. *sister;* freq.

2. *one more distantly related, a kinswoman.* Job 42:11. In Gen. 24:60, the mother and brother of Rebekah say to her, אֲחֹתֵנוּ אַתְּ *thou art our sister.*

3. It is applied figuratively to kindred states, Ezek. 16:46. 23:31. and kingdoms, Jer. 3:7, 8.

4. It is used as a word of endearment to an object beloved. Cant. 4:9 ff.

5. *female companion*, i. q. רְעוּת; freq. Hence

6. with אִשָּׁה preceding, *one, another; altera, altera.* Applied also to inanimate objects of the fem. gender, Ex. 26:3 *five curtains shall be joined* אִשָּׁה אֶל־אֲחֹתָהּ *one to another.* verses 5, 6, 17. Ezek. 1:9. 3:13.

7. It is used figuratively in such phrases as Prov. 7:4 *say to wisdom, thou art my sister.* Job 17:14. Comp. the other names of kindred, especially אָב no. 7. אָח no. 8.

אָחַז, fut. יֹאחֵז (rarely יֶאֱחֹז 1 K. 6:10. Ecc. 7:18.)

1. *to seize, lay hold of;* construed with an accusative, Judg. 12:6. with בְּ, Ex. 4:4. 15:14 חִיל אָחַז יֹשְׁבֵי פְּלָשֶׁת *terror seizes the inhabitants of Philistia.* v. 15. Ps. 48:7. Also inverted, Job 18:20 קַדְמֹנִים אָחֲזוּ שָׂעַר *the forefathers lay hold of fear*, i.e. fear lays hold of them. 21:6. So the Arabians say: *cepit metum alicujus rei.*

2. *to take, catch,* in hunting, fishing. Cant. 2:15. Ecc. 9:12.

3. *to hold;* construed with an acc. 1 Chr. 13:9. 2 Chr. 25:5. with בְּ, Gen. 25:26. אָחַז דֶּרֶךְ *to pursue one's course,* Job 17:9. — Part. pass. with act. signification, Cant. 3:8 אֲחֻזֵי חֶרֶב *holding the sword.*

4. *to bind, join, fasten.* (The ideas, *to take, to hold on, to adhere,* are combined in many verbs; comp. לָכַד and לָקַח in Hithpa. and in Greek, ἔχομαι τινὸς *to adhere to any thing,* ἐχόμενος *connected.*) Ezek. 41:6 וְלֹא־יִהְיוּ אֲחוּזִים בְּקִיר הַבַּיִת *but so that they were not fastened in the wall of the temple.* 1 K. 6:6. Hence

5. *to close, fasten, bar,* as in Syriac. Neh. 7:3.

6. i. q. Lat. *contigno, to bind beams together, to cover* a house. 1 K. 6:10 *he covered the house with cedar-wood.* Comp. תָּפַשׂ Hab. 2:19.

7. *to take out,* (from a great number,) particularly passively *to be drawn out by lot.* (The same signification has the synon. לָכַד in Niph. and also אחז in Ethiop.) Num. 31:30 *of the children of Israel's half* תִּקַּח אֶחָד אָחֻז מִן־הַחֲמִשִּׁים *take one out of fifty.* verse 46. 1 Chr. 24:6 בֵּית־אָב אֶחָד אָחֻז לְאֶלְעָזָר *one family was drawn from Eleazar.*

Niph. 1. pass. of Kal no. 2. Ecc. 9:12.

2. pass. of Kal no. 3. Gen. 22:13.

3. *to take possession.* Gen. 34:10. 47:27. Josh. 22:9, 19. Comp. deriv. אֲחֻזָּה, and also Syr. אחד *to possess.*

Pi. i. q. Kal no. 5. *to close.* Job 26:9 *he closes,* i. e. covers, *the face of his throne.*

Hoph. pass. of Kal no. 4. *to be fastened.* 2 Chr. 9:18.

אָחָז m. proper name of a king of Judah, contemporary with Isaiah, Hosea, and Micah, a weak prince and an idolater. 2 K. 16:1 ff. 2 Chr. 28:16 ff. Is. 7:1 ff. 38:8. Sept. Ἄχαζ.

אֲחֻזָּה f. verbal from אָחַז, dec. X. *possession.* Gen. 17:8. 23:4. See אָחַז Niph. no. 3.

אֲחַזְיָה and **אֲחַזְיָהוּ** (*Jehovah has seized*) prop. name. 1. son of Ahab, king of Israel. 1 K. 22:40. 2 K. 1:2. 2 Chr. 20:35. Sept. Ὀχοζίας.

2. son of Jehoram, king of Judah. 2 K. 8:24. 9:16. 2 Chr. 22:1. He is called in 2 Chr. 22:6, עֲזַרְיָהוּ an evident corruption; for 12 MSS. Sept. Syr. Vulg. and Arab. retain the usual name. The same person is also called יְהוֹאָחָז i. q. אֲחַזְיָהוּ by metathesis, 2 Chr. 21:17. Here too the Sept. Syr. Chald.

Arab. and cod. Kennicott. 332 are in favour of אֲחִיָּה, but the common Heb. text may be retained, as the two names are synonymous.

אֲחִידָה Chald. with prosth. א, i. q. Heb. חִידָה *riddle*. Dan. 5:12.

אֲחִימֶלֶךְ m. (*brother of the king*) prop. name. 1. a priest at Nob and friend of David, 1 Sam. 21:2. 22:9. Ps. 52:2. and afterwards a chief-priest under him, 2 Sam. 8:17. He is probably the same person with אֲחִיָּה, as each of them is called a son of Ahitub. Comp. 1 Sam. 14:3, with 22:9.

2. a Hittite, companion of David. 1 Sam. 26:6.

אַחֲלַי Ps. 119:5. and **אַחֲלֵי** 2 K. 5:3. adv. of wishing. *O that! would God!* Probably derived from חָלָה no. II.

אַחְלָמָה f. Ex. 28:18. 39:12. name of a precious stone, which the Sept. Vulg. have translated ἀμέθυστος, *amethystus*. In its form, it is a verbal, from the Hiph. of חָלַם *to dream;* hence the story of the Rabbins, that this gem has the property of causing dreams.

אַחְמְתָא Ezra 6:2. *Ecbatana*, capital of Media, and summer residence of the Persian monarchs, probably near the modern *Hamadan*.

אָחַר *to stay, tarry*. Hence 1 pers. fut. אֵחַר, Gen. 32:5.

Pi. אִחַר, fut. יְאַחֵר *to tarry, delay*, as in Kal. Judg. 5:28. Ps. 40:18. construed with לְ before the infin. Deut. 23:22. with an acc. Ex. 22:28 *the abundance of thy grain thou shalt not delay*, i.e. hold back.

2. *to abide long, tarry late*. Prov. 23:30 מְאַחֲרִים עַל־הַיָּיִן *who tarry late at the wine*. Is. 5:11. Comp. Ps. 127:2.

3. caus. *to retard, hinder*. Gen. 24:56.

אַחֵר, fem. **אַחֶרֶת** (with Dagesh forte implied;) Plur. אֲחֵרִים, אֲחֵרוֹת, (as if from אָחַר) *other*. אֵל אַחֵר *another* or *strange God*, i. e. an idol. Is. 42:8. Deut. 6:14. 7:4. 8:19. — Ps. 16:4 אַחֵר מָהָרוּ *they hasten to another*, i.e. they decline from Jehovah to idols.

אַחַר 1. originally a subst. *the hinder part*. Plur. 2 Sam. 2:23 בְּאַחֲרֵי הַחֲנִית *with the hinder end of the spear*.

2. adv. (1.) *behind*. Once Gen. 22:13, (where, however, the Samar. text, 42 Heb. MSS. Sept. and Syr. favour the easier reading אֶחָד,) Vulg. *post tergum*. (2.) more frequently, *afterwards*. Gen. 18:5. Ex. 5:1. Num. 19:7. Also adverbially in this sense אַחֲרֵי, Pr. 28:23.

3. prep. Plur. אַחֲרֵי, with suff. אַחֲרַי, אַחֲרָיו, etc. (1.) *after, behind*. Thus הָלַךְ אַחֲרֵי *to go after, to follow*. Hence, in a geographical sense, *to the west of*, (comp. אָחוֹר no. 2.) Ex. 3:1 *west of the desert*. (2.) *after, since*, construed with an infin. Gen. 5:4. with אֲשֶׁר and a finite verb, Josh. 9:16. Judg. 11:36. (3.) אַחֲרֵי כֵן (literally *after it was so*,) *upon that, afterwards*. 2 Sam. 2:1. Hence אַחֲרֵי כֵן אֲשֶׁר (liter. *after it was so that*,) *after*, as in Lat. *posteaquam* for *postquam*, Gen. 6:4. Also אֲשֶׁר being omitted, 2 Sam. 24:10. comp. עַל־כֵּן for עַל־כֵּן אֲשֶׁר under art. כֵּן.

Combined with other prepositions (1.) מֵאַחֲרֵי *from after, away from*. 2 Sam. 20:2. 2 K. 17:21. Also, the force of מִן being lost, simply *behind, after*, Ex. 14:19. Josh. 8:2. Ecc. 10:14. Jer. 9:21. hence מֵאַחֲרֵי כֵן *afterwards*, 2 Sam. 3:28. (2.) אֶל אַחֲרֵי *behind*, construed with an acc. 2 K. 9:18. (3.) עַל אַחֲרֵי *behind*, construed with a dative, Ezek. 41:15.

אַחֲרוֹן, fem. ־ָה, denom. from אַחַר, with adj. termination וֹן, dec. I. b.

1. *hinder*. Gen. 33:2. Hence *western*, (see אָחוֹר no. 2.)—הַיָּם הָאַחֲרוֹן *the western sea*, i. e. the Mediterranean, in opposition to the eastern or Dead sea, Deut. 11:24. 34:2. Joel 2:20.

2. *following, future*. Ps. 48:14. 78:4, 8 דּוֹר אַחֲרוֹן *the future generation*.—יוֹם אַחֲרוֹן *the following day*, or *time to come*, Prov. 31:25. Is. 30:8. — Plur. אַחֲרֹנִים *posterity*, Job 18:20. Ecc. 4:16.

3. *last*. Is. 44:6 *I am the first, and I am the last*. 2 Sam. 19:12, 13.

The fem. stands adverbially for *a second time*, Dan. 11:29. with prefix לְ and בְּ, *afterwards*, Deut. 13:10. Ec. 1:11.

אַחֲרֵי prep. Chald. *after*, as in Heb. Dan. 2:29.

אָחֳרִי adj. Chald. *another*. Dan. 2: 39. 7:5, 6.

אַחֲרֵין adv. Chald. Dan. 4:5 [8] עַד אָחֳרֵין *at the last, finally*.

אַחֲרִית f. denom. from אַחַר, dec. I. b. 1. *last, hindermost*, or *remotest part*. Ps. 139:9.

2. more frequently of time, *end, latter end*. Deut. 11:12. Job 8:7. 42:12. Prov. 5:11. (Antith. רֵאשִׁית.) Prov. 5:4 אַחֲרִיתָהּ מָרָה *her end*, i. e. the end which the adulteress leads to, *is bitter*; comp. 23:21. Especially *a happy end* or *conclusion*, 23:18. 24:14.

3. *futurity*. Frequently in the phrase בְּאַחֲרִית הַיָּמִים *in process of time*, Is. 2:2. Gen. 49:1. Mic. 4:1.

4. as a concrete, *posterity, remains*. Dan. 11:4. Ps. 109:13. Am. 4:2. 9:1. Ezek. 23:25.

אַחֲרִית Chald. *end*, as in Heb. Dan. 2:28.

אָחֳרָן Chald. *another*. Dan. 2:11.

אֲחֹרַנִּית adv. from אָחוֹר. *backwards*. Gen. 9:23. 1 Sam. 4:18.

אֲחַשְׁדַּרְפְּנִים masc. plur. Est. 3:12. 8:9. 9:3, etc. *high satraps, chief governors*, Persian officers nearly analogous to the present Turkish pachas. These satraps or high satraps had the civil and military jurisdiction over several smaller provinces, each of which had its own פֶּחָה *governor*. The word is of Persian origin, and probably compounded. The first part אֲחַשׁ is the Pers. اخش *excellence, worth*. (See the following articles.) But the latter part is perhaps more uncertain. The letters agree very well with דרבאן *a door-keeper, porter*, or *a courtier* generally; but the explanation is to be preferred, which makes שתרף=שתרפן or Pers. ستَرب *a satrap*, with the termination ַן as in אֲחַשְׁתְּרָנִים.

אֲחַשְׁדַּרְפְּנִין masc. plur. Chald. i. q. Heb. Dan. 3:2, 3, 27. 6:2, 3.

אֲחַשְׁוֵרוֹשׁ a name or title which is given to several different Persian kings. Dan. 9:1. Ezra 4:6. Est. 1:1. The signification of the first part of this name has just been given in the preceding article. The latter part is either ורוש, Pers. بروش or بروشان *prince*, (ב and ו being commuted, see letter ב,) or Pehlvi, *Zwaresch (a hero)*.

אֲחַשְׁתְּרָנִים plur. masc. *mules of a superior breed*. A Persian word compounded of اخش *excellence, price*, and استار *mule*. Est. 8:10. It appears from what follows that they were bred between an ass and a mare.

אַחַת see אֶחָד.

אַט subst. from obs. אָטַט. *a going softly* or *slowly*. Hence אַט, לְאַט, לְאִט, for the most part used adverbially, (1.) *slowly, softly*, applied to walking, 1 K. 21:27. to the running of water, Is. 8:6. Gen. 33:14 לְאִטִּי *in my slow pace*, i. e. gradually as I am accustomed to go. (2.) *mildly, gently*. 2 Sam. 18:5 לְאַט־לִי לַנַּעַר deal *gently for my sake with the lad*. Job 15:11 וְדָבָר לָאַט עִמָּךְ *and our language so full of mildness to you*.

אִטִּים masc. plur. *conjurers, magicians*. Once Is. 19:3. The root אָטַט signifies in Arab. *to make a gentle noise, to mutter*, and in this derivative has reference to the muttering over of magical spells. Comp. לַחַשׁ.

אָטָד m. name of a prickly shrub, *the southern buckthorn, Christ's thorn, rhamnus, (rhamnus paliurus*, Linn.) Judg. 9:14, 15. Psalm 58:10. In the Arab. أطد but more frequently عوسج).

אֵטוּן m. (Syr. for אֵטוּן) dec. III. g. found only Prov. 7:16 אֵטוּן מִצְרָיִם *Egyptian tapestry*. In Chald. אֵטוּן signifies *a cord, rope, instita*, somewhat kindred to the sense given above. Sept. ἀμφίταπα τὰ ἀπ' Αἰγύπτου. Others think it an Egyptian word: *athi-ouniau*, (*stamen lini;*) whence also the Greek ὀθόνη, ὀθόνιον, *linen*, is said to be derived.

אָטַם *to shut, close, stop*, e. g. the mouth, ears. Prov. 17:28. 21:13. חַלּוֹנִים אֲטֻמוֹת *closed windows*, i. e. prob. lattices inserted into the wall in such a manner, as not to be raised or opened, Ezek. 40:16. 41:16, 26. The same is somewhat differently expressed 1 K. 6:4.

Hiph. *idem*. Ps. 58:5.

אָטַר, fut. יֶאְטַר *to shut, close*. Once Ps. 69:16. In Arabic this verb has the kindred signif. *to surround, to enclose*.

אִטֵּר verbal adj. from אָטַר *bound, impeded*, followed by יַד יְמִינוֹ *bound in his right hand*, i. e. only left-handed. Judg. 3:15. 20:16. The verb in Arabic, Conj. v. signifies *to be bound, hindered*.

אֵי 1. adv. of interr. prim. *where?* with suff. אַיֶּכָּה *where* art *thou?* Gen. 3:9. אַיּוֹ *where* is *he?* אַיָּם *where* are *they?* אֵיפֹה is synonymous with אֵי.

2. Connected with other adverbs or with pronouns, it simply gives them an interrogative signification, just as אֲשֶׁר gives them the force of relatives. Comp. in English, *wherein* for *in which*. Hence (1.) אֵי זֶה *who? what?* Job 38:19, 24. 2 K. 3:8. also *where?* (from זֶה *here*.) Est. 7:5. 1 Sam. 9:18. 1 K. 22:24. In the indirect inquiry, Ecc. 11:6. Also as one word אֵיזֶה, see below. (2.) אֵי־מִזֶּה *whence? from what?* Gen. 16:8. Job 2:2. Jon. 1:8 אֵי־מִזֶּה עַם *from what people?* 2 Sam. 15:2 אֵי מִזֶּה עִיר *from what city?* (3.) אֵי לָזֹאת *on what account?* (from לָזֹאת *on this account*.) Jer. 5:7.—Several other adverbs are joined with אֵי; but always in one word. See אֵיכָה ,אֵיכָה ,אֵיפֹה. (3.) In Prov. 31:4, the Keri אֵי is usually explained as i. q. אַיִן *not*. But we may retain the usual sense of this word, and translate the clause thus: *and it is not becoming for princes* to say, *Where is strong drink?*

I. **אִי**, more frequently in plur. אִיִּים, (once אִיִּן Ezek. 26:18.) m. (fem. perhaps Is. 23:2. unless we consider it as an instance of the constructio ad sensum, as is the case with עִיר in the preceding verse,) by contr. for אֱוִי verbal from אָוָה = Arab. أوى *to take for an habitation, to inhabit*, (comp. כִּי for כְּוִי, ... ,...)

1. *habitable, dry land*, in opposition to water. Is. 42:15 שַׂמְתִּי נְהָרוֹת לָאִיִּים *I will make the rivers dry land;* comp. 43:19, 20. 47:2. 50:2.

2. *coast, shore, sea-coast;* of Ashdod, Is. 20:6. of Tyre, 23:2, 6. of Chittim and Elishah, Ezek. 27:6, 7.

3. *island*. Jer. 47:4 אִי כַפְתּוֹר *isle of Caphtor*, i. e. prob. Cyprus. אִיֵּי הַיָּם *the islands of the sea*, Est. 10:1. Antith. אֶרֶץ *main land;* comp. Ps. 97:1. Particularly did the Hebrews employ אִיִּים, also אִיֵּי הַגּוֹיִם (Gen. 10:5.) and אִיֵּי הַיָּם to denote *the islands and remote coasts of the west*, of which they had acquired an obscure knowledge through the navigation of the Phenicians. Gen. 10:5. Ps. 72:10 (in connexion with Tarshish.) Is. 11:11. 24:15. 66:19. Ezek. 26:15, 18. 27:3, 15. Dan. 11:18. The idea is made clear by a paraphrase, Jer. 25:22 הָאִי אֲשֶׁר בְּעֵבֶר הַיָּם. Often perhaps in a more general sense, *remote coasts, distant lands, lands beyond sea;* the Hebrews having in mind the vast extent of country to the west. Is. 40:15. 41:5. 42:15. 49:1, etc.

II. **אִי** (for אֱוִי verbal from אָוָה = Arab. أوى i. q. عوى *to howl*.) 1. subst. *howling*. Hence as a concrete, *the howler*, or a *jackal*, so called from his doleful howling, especially at night. Found only in the plur. אִיִּים Is. 13:22. 34:14. Jer. 50:39. In Arab. he is called ابن اوى *son of howling*, i. e. the howler.

2. adv. or interj. *alas!* Ecc. 4:10. 10:16.

III. **אִי** adv. *not*. found only Job 22:30, and in the proper name אִי־כָבוֹד (*inglorious*) 1 Sam. 4:21. In Ethiop. and Rabbin. *idem*.

אָיַב *to hate, be an enemy to*. found only Ex. 23:22.—Part. אֹיֵב *enemy, adversary*, Gen. 22:17. 49:8. sometimes as a participle governing the case of its verb, 1 Sam. 18:29 אֹיֵב אֶת־דָּוִד *an enemy of David.* Fem. אֹיֶבֶת *female adversary,* Mic. 7:8, 10.

אֵיבָה f. verbal from אָיַב, dec. X. *enmity, hostility.* Gen. 3:15. Num. 35:21. Contracted from אֲיֶבָה, as אֵימָה from אֲיֻמָּה.

אֵיד m. dec. I. a, *distress, ruin, destruction.* Job 18:12. 21:17. 30:12. Prov. 1:26, 27. 6:15. The root אוד in Arab. signifies *to press, bend down;* and its derivatives, *oppression, misfortune.*

אַיֵּה i. q. אַי *where?* (with ה־ paragogic, comp. הֵן=הִנֵּה *behold.*) Gen. 3:9. 18:9. Used indefinitely, Nah. 3:17. Job 15:23 *he wanders about for bread* אַיֵּה *where* it may be found.

אַיָּה fem. name of some bird of prey, perhaps *a falcon, hawk,* or *vulture.* Lev. 11:14. Job 28:7. Sept. ἰκτίν, and γύψ. Vulg. *vultur.*

אִיּוֹב m. *Job.* the hero of the book which bears his name, occurring also Ezek. 14:14, 20. The name is most probably fictitious, having reference to the description which is given of his life and fortune, and signifying *persecuted,* (namely, by adverse fortune,) from אָיַב. Comp. יִלּוֹד *born* from יָלַד *to bear.* Another explanation, viz. *serio resipiscens* is given by the Koran, (Sur. 38:40, 44.) The eastern people, at the present day, consider him as a real person, and a descendant of Esau; but their opinion is not conclusive evidence.

אִיזֶבֶל f. proper name of the wife of Ahab, king of Israel, notorious for her cruelty, her persecution of the prophets, and her introduction of the worship of the Phenician Baal. 1 K. 16:31. 18:4, 13. 21:5 ff. 2 K. 9:7 ff. Hence the name *Isabella.* Several plausible derivations of this word have been proposed, but none of them is certain.

אֵיזֶה *where?* Job 38:19, 24. Compounded of the interrogative particle אֵי (see אִי no. 2.) and זֶה *here.*

אֵיךְ *how?* by contr. for אֵיכָה. Gen. 26:9. Sometimes as an interj. of lament. *Ah how,* Ps. 73:19. Is. 14:4. So Ecc. 2:16 *Ah how dies the wise man with the fool!* Used indefinitely, Ruth 3:18. 2 K. 17:28.

אֵיכָה compounded of אֵי no. 2. and כָּה i. q. כֹּה *here, thus.* 1. *where?*

2. *how?* Deut. 1:12, often as an interj. *Ah how,* Is. 1:21. Lam. 1:1. Used indefinitely, Deut. 12:30.

אֵיכֹה 2 K. 6:13 Keth. or אֵיפֹה Keri. *idem.*

אֵיכָכָה *how?* Cant. 5:3. Est. 8:16. from אֵי and כָּה=כָּכָה or כֹּה *thus.*

אַיִל m. dec. VI. f.

1. *ram.* Gen. 15:9. Plur. אֵילִים Ex. 25:5. See root אוּל.

2. a technical expression in architecture, the exact meaning of which has not yet been discovered. 1 K. 6:31. Ezek. 40:9 ff. 41:3 ff. Comp. in Chald. אִלַּת סִפַּיָּא for אַמּוֹת הַסִּפִּים Is. 6:4. These passages will have the clearest sense, if we render this word *pillars* or *pilasters,* with which the doors and walls of the temple were ornamented. The name אַיִל (*ram*) may refer perhaps to the twisted form of the capital, as e. g. in Corinthian pillars. Vulg. *frontes,* Luth. *Erker;* neither of which suits the connection. More plausible is the explanation of Cocceius, *projectura parietis in imo prominentis.*

אֱיָל m. verbal from obs. אוּל. *strength.* Once Ps. 88:5.

אַיִל m. verbal from אוּל, dec. I. plur. אֵילִם. 1. *the mighty, noble.* Ex. 15:15. Ezek. 17:13. 2 K. 24:15 Keri.

2. *turpentine-tree, terebinthus,* for which the fem. אֵלָה is more common. So in the prop. name אֵיל פָּארָן, Sept. τερέβινθος τῆς Φαράν. Gen. 14:6. Plur. אֵילִים Is. 61:3.

אֵילִם (*turpentine-trees*) proper name of the second encampment of the Israelites after they left Egypt, with 12 wells of water, and 70 palm-trees. Ex. 15:27. 16:1. Num. 33:9. Now called *Girondel,* a valley well watered, and abounding in palm-trees.

אַיָּל com. (fem. e. g. Ps. 42:2.) prim. *stag, hart.* Deut. 12:15. 14:5. Is. 35:6. Plur. ־ִים Cant. 2:9, 17.

אַיָּלָה fem. of אַיָּל. *hind.* Gen. 49:21. (here as an epicene joined with a masc. participle.) Plur. אַיָּלוֹת, const. אַיְלוֹת. 2 Sa. 22:34. Cant. 2:7.

אֵילוֹן (*turpentine-tree,* see אֵלוֹן) prop. name of a city in the tribe of Dan. Josh. 19:43. 1 K. 4:49.

אַיָּלוֹן (from אַיָּל, as if *deer pasture*) proper name. 1. a Levitical city in the tribe of Dan. Josh. 10:12. 19:42. 21:24. Judg. 1:35.

2. a city in the tribe of Zebulun. Judg. 12:12.

אֵילוֹת see **אֵילַת**.

אֱיָלוּת f. dec. I. a. i. q. אֱיָל *force, strength.* Once Ps. 22:20. See אול.

אֵילָם and **אֵלָם** m. Plur. אֵילַמִּים and אֵילַמּוֹת; i. q. אוּלָם *hall, porch, portico.* Ezek. xl.

אִילָן *m.* Chald. *tree.* Dan. 4:7, 8 ff. It corresponds to the Heb. אֵלוֹן *turpentine-tree,* but has this wider signification.

אֵילַת Deut. 2:8. also אֵילוֹת, אֵלוֹת 1 K. 9:26. 2 K. 16:6. *Elath,* a well-known port in Idumea, in Greek Αἴλανα, now *Ailah.* It lies on a bay of the Arabian gulf, to which it gives name.

אַיֶּלֶת fem. of אַיָּל. *female deer, hind.* Among the Orientals it is used as a word of endearment to a wife. So Prov. 5:19. The title of Ps. xxii. עַל אַיֶּלֶת הַשַּׁחַר is of difficult interpretation. Perhaps *after the hind of the dawn,* i.e. to be sung after a song or tune called *the hind of the morn.* Comp. קֶשֶׁת. By *hind of the dawn,* perhaps the sun is meant, which the Arabian poets sometimes call *gazelle.*—Were it a note of time, then the best explanation consists in the Rabbin. אַיַּלְתָּא וְשַׁחְרָא *break of day.*

אָיֹם, fem. **אֲיֻמָּה,** adj. *terrible, dreadful.* Hab. 1:7. Cant. 6:4, 10. In Chald. Pa. אַיֵּם *to terrify.*

אֵימָה (for אֵמָה) f. verbal from obs. אִים, dec. X.

1. *terror.* Deut. 32:25. The genitive following is often to be understood passively, Prov. 20:2 אֵימַת מֶלֶךְ *the terror which a king causes.* Job 33:7 אֵימָתִי *fear of me.* With ה parag. אֵימָתָה Ex. 15:16. Plur. ־וֹת Ps. 55:5. and ־ִים Ps. 88:16.

2. Plur. אֵימִים *idols.* Jer. 50:38. Literally *objects of fear* or *terror;* comp. e. g. מִפְלֶצֶת.

אֵימִים and **אֵמִים** plur. masc. *Emims,* an ancient people, the original inhabitants of Moab. Gen. 14:5. Deut. 2:11. As an appell. *the terrible ones, the strong ones.* Chald. *fortes.*

I. **אַיִן,** const. **אֵין,** properly a subst. *nothingness, defect, non-existence,* (comp. אָוֶן.) but more frequently used as an adv. of negation.

1. *not,* but constantly including the subst. verb *to be* in its various persons and tenses; of course i. q. לֹא יֵשׁ. Gen. 37:29 אֵין־יוֹסֵף בַּבּוֹר *Joseph was not in the pit.* Num. 14:42. It deserves particular remark (1.) that if a personal pronoun is the subject of the proposition, it is suffixed to this word; whence the following forms arise אֵינֶנִּי *I am* or *was not,* אֵינְךָ, אֵינֵךְ, אֵינֶנּוּ, אֵינֶנָּה, אֵינְכֶם, אֵינָם, אֵינָמוֹ. These suffixes here express the subject or nominative. (2.) Since אֵין includes the subst. verb, it is very often joined with the participle. Ex. 5:16 תֶּבֶן אֵין נִתָּן *straw is not given.* Josh. 6:1 אֵין יוֹצֵא וְאֵין בָּא *there was not any one going out and coming in,* i.e. no one went out or came in. Lev. 26:6. *No one* is often expressed in this manner; see Gen. 41:8, 15, 24, 39. Deut. 22:27. (3.) אֵין לִי *mihi non est* is the usual expression for *I have not.* Construed with לְ and an infin. it often signifies *it is not permitted;* e.g. Est. 4:2 אֵין לָבוֹא *it is not permitted to enter.* Ruth 4:4. Ecc. 3:14. (4.) אֵין אִישׁ *no man,* אֵין דָּבָר, אֵין מְאוּמָה *nothing,* אֵין כֹּל *nothing at all.* Num. 11:6. Ecc. 1:9.

2. If there is no other predicate of the proposition, אֵין includes the predicate itself, and signifies *not to be, not to exist,*

not to be extant. 1 Sam. 9:4 *and they passed through the land of Shalim* וָאַיִן *and they were not there.* 10:14. 1 K. 18:10. Frequently with suff. which express the subject; e. g. אֵינֶנּוּ *he was no more,* for *he lived no longer,* Gen. 5:24. 42:13, 32, 36.

3. *nothing,* often, as above, including the verb. 1 K. 8:9. Ps. 19:7. לְאַיִן *to nothing,* Is. 40:23.

4. *without,* for the more full בְּאֵין, Ex. 21:11. Joel 1:6 אֵין מִסְפָּר *without number.*

5. Combined with prepositions are (1.) בְּאֵין literally *in the non-existence of,* hence *before that, without.* Prov. 8:24 בְּאֵין־תְּהֹמוֹת *before the floods were.* Ezek. 38:11 בְּאֵין חוֹמָה *without walls.* Prov. 11:14. 15:22. 26:20. (2.) כְּאַיִן liter. *about nothing,* hence *nothing was wanting, almost.* Ps. 73:2. Parall. כִּמְעַט *about a little, little was wanting, almost.* (3.) לְאֵין *to him who.... not* for לַאֲשֶׁר אֵין, Is. 40:29. Neh. 8:10. 2 Chr. 14:10. *so that.... not.* Ezra 9:14. 2 Chr. 20:25. (4.) מֵאֵין *because.... not,* Is. 50:2. *so that.... not,* Is. 5:9. barely *not,* Jer. 10:6, 7. 30:7. (Concerning the double negation, see מִן.)

Note. If we consider אַיִן as a subst. in the absolute state, and אֵין as a subst. in the const. state, the reason will be seen why the former stands only at the close of a proposition, but the latter only in connexion with something following; e. g. Num. 20:5 מַיִם אַיִן, *water was not there,* which inverted would become אֵין מַיִם, as in Ex. 17:1.

II. **אַיִן** adv. of interr. *where?* i. q. אֵי, אַי, with paragogic ן, (comp. אָזַי, אָזְנַיִן) found only with prefix מ, מֵאַיִן *whence?* Gen. 29:4, etc.

אִין found only 1 Sam. 21:9. i. q. אֵין *not,* but here used interrogatively for הַאֵין *is there not?*

אֵיפָה more rarely **אֵפָה,** dec. X. f. a corn measure, containing 3 seahs or 10 omers. Ex. 16:36. Its definite capacity is not known. Josephus (Antiq. xv. 12.) compares it with the *Attic medimnus,* which is about a Berlin bushel. That it was a considerable measure appears from Zech. 5:6 ff.—אֵיפָה וְאֵיפָה *two kinds of measure,* Prov. 20:10.

אֵיפֹה (compounded of אֵי and פֹּה *here, thus,*) *where?* Ruth 2:19. *how?* Judg. 8:18. used indefinitely, *where,* Jer. 36:19.

אֵיפוֹא i. q. **אֵפוֹא** *now, then.* Judg. 9:38.

אִישׁ m. prim. irreg. Plur. very rarely אִישִׁים (Ps. 141:4. Prov. 8:4.) but instead of it is commonly used אֲנָשִׁים const. אַנְשֵׁי (from an obs. sing. אֱנוֹשׁ=אֱנָשׁ *man.*)

1. *man,* i. q. Lat. *vir.* Sometimes used collectively, and construed for the most part with the plural; e. g. Judg. 8:22 וַיֹּאמְרוּ אִישׁ יִשׂ׳ *then spake the Israelites.* Often in apposition before other substantives, as אִישׁ סָרִיס *an eunuch,* Jer. 38:7. Used as an appropriate designation of sex, even in animals, Gen. 7:2. hence *a husband,* Gen, 3:16. Hos. 2:18. [16.]

2. joined with many substantives, especially those which designate quality, it denotes a possessor of that quality, or some connexion with the thing expressed by the noun; as אִישׁ אָוֶן *a wicked wretch,* אִישׁ מְדָנִים *a contentious man,* אִישׁ מִלְחָמָה *a warrior.*

3. followed by אָחִיו or רֵעֵהוּ, *the one.... the other.* See אָח and רֵעַ. So אִישׁ repeated, Is. 3:5.

4. *any one, some one.* Ex. 16:29. Cant. 8:7.

5. *every one.* Ex. 16:29. Gen. 40:5. In this signification the signs of cases are often omitted, Num. 26:54 אִישׁ יֻתַּן *to every one shall be given.* Instead of this stands also אִישׁ אִישׁ, Ex. 36:4. אִישׁ וָאִישׁ, Est. 1:8. The repetition of אִישׁ also expresses distribution, Num. 1:4.

6. used impersonally like the French *on* or Germ. *man,* 1 Sam. 9:9 *formerly in Israel* כֹּה־אָמַר הָאִישׁ *man said thus,* i. e. it was thus said.

7. בְּנֵי אִישׁ in oppos. to בְּנֵי אָדָם, see אָדָם no. 1. (2.)

אִישׁוֹן m. (according to others, com. comp. Ps. 17:8.) dimin. from אִישׁ, dec. I. b.

1. *homulus, mannikin, little man;*

joined with עַיִן, Deut. 32:10. Prov. 7:2 *the little man in the eye,* i. e. the apple of the eye, so called from the little image of himself, which the beholder sees therein. This beautiful figure is found in many languages of the ancient world. Arab. إِنْسَانُ الْعَيْنِ (*man of the eye.*) Greek κόρη, κοράσιον; Lat. pupa, pupilla, pupula; (*little damsel, puppet.*) The more full expresion is אִישׁוֹן בַּת־עַיִן *the little man, daughter of the eye,* Ps. 17:8. see בַּת.

2. figuratively *middle.* (So in Arabic, يُؤْيُؤ *apple of the eye,* stands for *middle, head, summit.*) Thus Prov. 7:9 *middle of the night.* 20:20 *midst of darkness.* In the last passage the Keri reads אֱשׁוּן *time,* a gloss which gives a very unsatisfactory explanation.

אִיתוֹן m. found only Ezek. 40:15 Keri. *entrance,* verbal from אָתָה i. q. בּוֹא *to come, to enter.* In the Kethib יאתון Yod is transposed.

אִיתַי Chald. i. q. Heb. יֵשׁ; from which it is formed by changing שׁ into ת, prefixing prosthetic א, and annexing the termination ־ַי, (comp. אַשׁ, אֲנִי.)

1. It has the force of the subst. verb *to be,* in all its persons, particularly the third. Dan. 5:11 אִיתַי גְּבַר בְּמַלְכוּתָךְ *there is a man in thy kingdom.* 3:12, 25. With the participle it forms a periphrasis for the finite verb, Dan. 3:17. If the subject of the proposition is a pronoun, it is suffixed to אִיתַי in the following manner; אִיתָךְ *thou art,* אִיתוֹהִי *he is,* אִיתַנָא *we are,* אִיתֵיכוֹן *ye are,* Dan. 2:26. 3:14, 15, 18. The suffix pronoun of the third person is often pleonastic, Dan. 2:11.

2. *there exists, is found, is extant.* Dan. 2:10, 11. 3:29. 4:32 [35.]

3. with לִי, *I have, mihi est.* Ezra 4:16.

אִיתִיאֵל m. (for אִתִּי אֵל *God is with me,* or for אִיתַי אֵל *there is a God,*) prop. name, found only Prov. 30:1. Ithiel and Ucal were probably Agur's scholars or children, to whom he directed his instructions.

אִיתָמָר m. (*island of the palm-tree*) proper name of a son of Aaron. Ex. 6:23. 28:1.

אֵיתָן adj. and subst. dec. I. prob. verbal from obs. יָתַן=Arab. وَتَنَ *perennis et indesinens fuit* aqua.

1. *constant, lasting, never-failing, perennis,* applied especially to water. Deut. 21:4. Am. 5:2 נַחַל אֵיתָן *a never-failing brook.* Also without נַחַל *idem,* 1 K. 8:2 יֶרַח הָאֵתָנִים *the month of flowing brooks,* (otherwise called *Tisri,*) which corresponds to part of Sept. and part of October. In a neuter or abstract sense, it is used substantively, and placed after another noun as a genitive, Ps. 74:15 נַהֲרוֹת אֵיתָן *the never-failing streams.* Hence *the stream, channel itself,* Ex. 14:27.

2. *firm, strong, mighty.* This signification is kindred to the preceding.) Jer. 5:15 גּוֹי אֵיתָן *a strong nation.* Job 12:19 אֵיתָנִים *the mighty.* Vulg. *optimates.* (33:19?) As a subst. *firmness, strength,* Gen. 49:24 תֵּשֶׁב בְּאֵיתָן קַשְׁתּוֹ *his bow abides strong.*

3. prob. *hard, inflexible;* hence, (by a common association of ideas in the Shemitish languages,) *harsh, severe, pernicious.* Prov. 13:15 *the way of transgressors is pernicious.* So Luther: *bringt wehe.* Job 33:19 רִיב עֲצָמָיו אֵיתָן *the contest in his bones is severe.*

4. *rock,* (perhaps only poetically,) literally *something fast, firm, solid.* Mic. 6:2 הָאֵתָנִים מוֹסְדֵי אָרֶץ *ye rocks, foundations of the earth.* Jer. 49:19. 50:44 נְוֵה אֵיתָן *dwelling of the rocks,* (comp. 49:16 חַגְוֵי הַסֶּלַע.)

5. proper name of an Ezrahite, (see אֶזְרָחִי,) celebrated for his wisdom, 1 K. 5:11, [4:31,] and supposed author of Ps. lxxxix.

אַךְ conj. prim. 1. *only.* Gen. 7:23. Ex. 10:17 אַךְ הַפַּעַם *only this once.* Deut. 16:15 אַךְ שָׂמֵחַ *only joyful,* i. e. entirely joyful.

2. *but, yet, nevertheless.* Gen. 20:12. 26:9. Lev. 11:4. Often in strong antitheses, *but on the contrary, nay rather, imo vero, quin,* Is. 14:15. 43:24.

3. *scarcely, only just now.* Gen. 27:30. Judg. 7:19.

4. *also.* Gen. 9:4.

5. *indeed, certainly, surely.* in the begining of a proposition, i.q. כִּי. Is. 19:11. Job 16:7. 19:13. Ps. 139:11.

אַכַּד name of a city built by Nimrod. Once Gen. 10:10. Sept. Ἀχάδ. According to the Targums, Jerome, and Ephrem Syrus, *Nisibis* in Mesopotamia. Ephrem Syrus, however, reads אכר.

אַכְזָב verbal adj. from כָּזַב. *deceitful;* hence particularly *a deceitful brook,* (opposite of אֵיתָן,) which, drying up suddenly, disappoints the traveller who visits it. Jer. 15:18. Mic. 1:14. We may suppose נַחַל *brook* to be understood.

אַכְזִיב (*deceived, deception,*) prop. name.

1. a maritime city in the tribe of Asher, between Acco and Tyre, *Ecdippa,* now *Zib.* Josh. 19:29. Judg. 1:31.

2. a city in the tribe of Judah. Josh. 15:44. Mic. 1:14. Comp. כְּזִיב, and כֹּזֵבָה.

אַכְזָר m. adj. Comp. Syr. ܟܢܙܪ *vir strenuus.*

1. *daring, bold.* Job 41:2.

2. *hostile;* substantively, *an enemy.* Job 30:21.

3. *cruel, unmerciful.* Lam. 4:3.

4. *destructive, pernicious,* applied to poison. Deut. 32:33.

אַכְזָרִי denom. from אַכְזָר, with adj. termination ־ִי.

1. *cruel, unmerciful.* Prov. 5:9. 11:17. Jer. 6:23.

2. *destructive, pernicious.* Prov. 17:11 *a messenger of destruction,* i.e. one who brings awful tidings, e.g. the sentence of death, or the like. Is. 13:9. Jer. 30:14.

אַכְזְרִיּוּת f. denom. from אַכְזָרִי, *cruelty, fierceness,* applied to anger. Prov. 27:4.

אֲכִילָה f. verbal from אָכַל. *food, what is eaten.* 1 K. 19:3.

אָכִישׁ m. proper name of a king of the Philistine city Gath. 1 Sam. 21:11. 27:2, 1 K. 2:39.

אָכַל, fut. יֹאכַל and יֹאכֵל; see art. אָבַד note 1.

1. *to eat;* applied to men and animals, and construed with an accusative. When construed with בְּ, it signifies *to eat of, partake of,* Ex. 12:43—45. 48. Judg. 13:16. Zech. 11:1. Applied figuratively to the sword, (comp. פֶּה,) 2 Sam. 2:26. to fire, Num. 16:35. 26:10. to hunger, pestilence, and sicknesses, Job 18:13. Ezek. 7:15. The following phrases ought also to be noticed (1.) אָכַל לֶחֶם *to eat bread,* i.e. to take a meal, Gen. 43:16, 25, 32. Jer. 41:1. 52:33. Comp. Mat. 15:2. (2.) אָכַל בָּשָׂר *to eat the flesh* of any one, i.e. to seek for one's life, spoken of bloodthirsty enemies, Ps. 27:2. comp. Job 19:22. (3.) *to eat one's own flesh,* i.e. to waste away, Ecc. 4:5. (4.) Jer. 15:16 *thy words came to me, and I did eat* or *devour them,* i.e. I received them eagerly. Hence the figure of eating a book, Ezek. 3:1 ff.

2. *to consume, destroy;* e.g. a people, spoken of an enemy, Deut. 7:16 וְאָכַלְתָּ אֶת־כָּל־הָעַמִּים *and thou shalt destroy all the nations.* Jer. 10:25. 30:16. 50:7, 17. 51:34. Hos. 7:7 אָכְלוּ אֶת־שֹׁפְטֵיהֶם *they have destroyed* or *killed their magistrates.* Hence also אָכַל עֲנִיִּים *to consume the poor* or *unfortunate, to prey upon their property,* or, as we by a similar figure say, *to drain their blood,* Prov. 30:14. Hab. 3:14.

3. *to enjoy;* e.g. sexual pleasure, Prov. 30:20. Construed with בְּ, Job 21:25 וְלֹא אָכַל בַּטּוֹבָה *and does not enjoy good.*

Niph. נֶאֱכַל passive of Kal; also *to be permitted to be eaten,* Lev. 11:47.

Pu. pass. of Kal. Neh. 2:3.

Hiph. הֶאֱכִיל, fut. יַאֲכִיל, once 1 pers. sing. אוֹכִיל (Hos. 11:4.) infin. הַאֲכִיל once הָכִיל (Ezek. 21:33. [28.]).

1. caus. of Kal, *to give* to any one *to eat, to feed,* construed with two accusa-

tives, Ex. 16:32. Num. 11:18. Prov. 25:21. *to give to enjoy*, Is. 58:14.

2. i. q. Kal, *to consume;* spoken of the sword, Ezek. 21:33. [28.] of fire, Job 20:26.

Hoph. found only Ezek. 42:5 יוּכְלוּ for אֻכְּלוּ *they were made shorter, they came short*, literally, *they were cut off*. Comp. יָצַר *to cut off, to eat*, and intransitively, *to come short, to fail*.

Deriv. out of course מַאֲכָל, מַאֲכֶלֶת, מַאֲכֹלֶת, מַכֹּלֶת.

אֲכַל, fut. יֵאכֻל. Chald. *to eat*, as in Heb. Concerning the phrase אֲכַל קַרְצִין *to accuse, calumniate*, see קְרַץ.

אֹכֶל m. verbal from אָכַל, dec. VI. m. *food*, particularly *grain, produce of the field*, Gen. 41:35. 42:7, 10.

אֻכָל proper name, see אִיתִיאֵל.

אָכְלָה fem. of אֹכֶל. *food*. Gen. 1:29,30.

אָכֵן i. q. כֵּן *thus*, with א prosth.

1. *truly, certainly*. Gen. 28:16. Ex. 2:14. Jer. 8:8.

2. *but, yet*. Ps. 31:23. Is. 53:4.

אָכַף (comp. Syr. ܐܟܦ *solicitavit*.) *to urge on to labour*. Once Prov. 16:26. Vulg. *compulit*.

אֶכֶף or **אַכַּף**, with suff. אַכְפִּי, prob. i. q. כַּף *hand*. Once Job 33:7 *my hand cannot lie heavy upon thee*. Sept. ἡ χείρ μου. Comp. 13:21. In the form אַכְפִּי, the א would be prosthetic, as in Chald. גַּן=אִגַּן *garden*. The form אַכְפִּי, may be illustrated by comparing דּוּשׁ=אֶדְרֹשׁ. Others: *my burden, the weight of my character;* comparing Chald. אוּכָף *ephippium, sella equi;* and Arab. أكف *clitellas imposuit*.

אִכָּר m. dec. I. *ploughman, farmer, husbandman*. Is. 61:5. Jer. 14:4. 31:24. The root אָכַר signifies in Arabic, conj. V. *foveam fodit*, and is cognate with כָּרָה.

אַכְשָׁף a city in the tribe of Asher. Josh. 12:20. 19:25.

אַל from obs. אָלַל, strictly a subst. *nothingness*, but by usage only a particle of negation.

1. *lest, that .... not*, especially before a future, to express a prohibition, dehortation. Gen. 43:23 אַל־תִּירָאוּ *fear ye not*. 15:1. Ps. 40:18 אַל־תְּאַחַר *delay not*. Gen. 19:7, 8.

2. i. q. לֹא *not*, but more rarely. Am. 5:14.

3. *nay, no*. Ruth 1:13 אַל בְּנֹתַי *no, my daughters*.

4. *nothing*. Job 24:25.

5. interrogatively for הֲלֹא. 1 Sa. 27:10.

אַל Chald. *idem*. Dan. 2:24.

I. **אֵל** m. verbal (with participial form) from obs. אוּל, and synonymous with אַיִל, dec. I. a.

1. *strong, mighty*. Ezek. 31:11 אֵל גּוֹיִם *the mighty one*, i. e. the prince, *of the nations*. Plur. אֵלִים, Job 41:17. [25.] Ez. 32:21 אֵלֵי גִבּוֹרִים *the strongest of the heroes*. The reading אֵיל is also found in all these passages. (Is. 9:5 אֵל גִּבּוֹר *the mighty hero;* see Gesenius' Jesaia, p. 25.?)

2. as an abstract noun, *strength, power*. Only in the phrase יֶשׁ־לְאֵל יָדִי *it is in the power of my hand*, or *in my power*, Gen. 31:29. Prov. 3:27. Mic. 2:1. and negatively אֵין לְאֵל יָדֶךָ *it is not in thy power, thou canst not help thyself*, Deut. 28:32. Neh. 5:5.

3. most frequently *God*. The name is general, and applied both to Jehovah and to the heathen gods. Is. 44:10, 15. 45:20. Frequently with epithets subjoined; as אֵל עֶלְיוֹן *the most high God*, אֵל שַׁדַּי *almighty God*, אֵל חַי *the living God*, אֵל זָר, אֵל אַחֵר *a strange god*, אֵל גִּבּוֹר *the mighty God*, Is. 10:21. So Is. 9:5, see Rosenmüller in loc.—בְּנֵי אֵלִים Ps. 89:7. 29:1 *sons of the gods*, i. e. angels, subordinate gods, who are also called בְּנֵי אֱלֹהִים, Job 1:6.—Whatever was great, excellent, or sacred, the Hebrews were accustomed to call *divine* or *from God*. Thus *cedars of God*, Ps. 80:11. *mountains of God*, Ps. 36:7. Comp. in Homer, δῖος Ὀδυσσεύς, Ἀχιλλεύς.

Note. Together with the usual form

אֵל (from אול,) the Hebrews had also another, after the analogy of verbs לה, which is seen in the proper names, אֱלִימֶלֶךְ, אֶלְיָשִׁיב, אֶלְיָקִים, אֱלִיעֶזֶר. Concerning such double forms, see Gesen. Lehrgeb. p. 481.

II. **אֵל, הָאֵל** pron. plur. i. q. אֵלֶּה *these.* Only in the Pentateuch and 1 Chr. 20 : 8.

אֵל Chald. *idem.* Ezra 5 : 15 Keri.

III. **אֵלִים** *turpentine-trees,* see **אֵלָה**.

IV. **אֶל** prep. prim. with Makkeph אֶל־; Plur. אֱלֵי (only poet.) with suff. אֵלַי, אֵלֶיךָ, אֲלֵיהֶם, etc.

1. *to,* a sign of the dative case from which is formed, by contraction, the prefix לְ.

2. *towards, even to, up to;* e. g. אֶל־הַמִּדְבָּר *towards the desert,* Num. 24 : 1. אֶל הַשָּׁמַיִם *up to heaven.*

3. *at, on, near;* e. g. אֶל מָקוֹם *at a place.* אֶל שֻׁלְחָן *at the table,* 1 K. 13 : 20. הִנְנִי אֲלֵיכֶם *behold, I am upon you,* to wit, for punishment, Ezek. 13 : 8. 21 : 8. 34 : 10. Jer. 50 : 31. 51 : 25. also in a good sense, Ezek. 36 : 9.

4. *about, concerning, de.* Gen. 20 : 2. Ps. 2 : 7. 69 : 27. Hence שָׁמַע אֶל, דִּבֶּר *to say, hear concerning* any one.

5. *in, into;* e. g. אֶל־הַתֵּבָה *into the ark,* Gen. 8 : 9. אֶל־לִבּוֹ *in his heart,* 6 : 6.

6. *among.* 1 Sam. 10 : 22. Ezek. 2 : 6.

7. *through.* Ezek. 44 : 7 *through all your abominations.*

8. *for, on account of.* 1 K. 14 : 5. (Gen. 37 : 35.?)

9. In combination with other prepositions it implies direction *to* or *towards* a place; e. g. אַחֲרַי simply *behind me,* אֶל אַחֲרַי *away behind me;* אֶל בֵּינִי *to between me;* מִחוּץ לְ *without, on the outside of,* with אֶל *to the outside of.* The exceptions are rare; as 1 Sam. 21 : 5 אֶל־תַּחַת־יָדִי *in my hand,* where אֶל is redundant. So Job 5 : 5 אֶל מִן *out of;* unless perhaps it signifies *even out of.*

Note. What verbs are construed with this preposition, is mentioned under the several articles. In these constructions, the preposition may require very diverse interpretations in our modern languages, although the real force of the original word continues the same.

אֶלְגָּבִישׁ m. *hail.* Ezek. 13 : 11, 13. 38 : 22. Comp. Arab. جَمَسَ *concrevit, congelavit,* and Heb. גָּבִישׁ prob. *ice, crystal* Job 28 : 19. אֶל is prob. the Arabic article, which appears to have been retained in several words derived from the Arabic; e. g. אַלְקוּם. The same is the case with many words in Syriac. This is better than to derive אֶל from אֵל no. 1. 2. *strength, power,* rendering אֶלְגָּבִישׁ *power of hail,* i. e. powerful hail.

אַלְגּוּמִּים see **אַלְמֻגִּים**.

I. **אָלָה** 1. *to swear.* 1 K. 8 : 31. Hos. 4 : 2.

2. *to curse.* Judg. 17 : 2.

Hiph. *to cause to swear, to require an oath of* any one. 1 K. 8 : 31. 2 Chr. 6 : 22. 1 Sam. 14 : 24 וַיֹּאֶל fut. apoc. from יַאֲלֶה for יֹאלֶה.

Deriv. out of course תַּאֲלָה.

II. **אָלָה** as in Syriac, *to lament.* Once Joel 1 : 8 אֱלִי *lament.*

אָלָה f. verbal from אָלָה no. 1. dec. X.

1. *oath.*—בּוֹא בְאָלָה *to enter into an oath, to swear,* Neh. 10 : 29. Hence הֵבִיא בְאָלָה *to administer an oath, to take an oath* of any one, Ezek. 17 : 13. Comp. Virg. Æn. iv. 339. *hæc in fœdera veni.* אָלָתִי *the oath made to me,* Gen. 24 : 41.

2. particularly *a covenant confirmed by an oath.* Gen. 26 : 28. Deut. 29 : 12, 14. Ezek. 16 : 59.

3. *imprecation, curse.* Num. 5 : 21. Is. 24 : 6. שְׁבֻעַת הָאָלָה *oath of imprecation,* Num. 5. 21. הָיָה לְאָלָה *to become a curse,* Num. 5 : 27. Jer. 44 : 12.

אֵלָה, Plur. אֵלִים, f. verbal from obs. אול, dec. X. *turpentine-tree, pistacia terebinthus,* Linn. a common tree in Palestine, which grows to a considerable height, and has evergreen leaves with clustering fruit. It attains to a very great age; and the earliest history, on that account, often employed single trees of this kind, under special names, to designate particular places. Gen. 35 : 4. Judg. 6 : 11;19. 1 Sam. 17 : 2,19. 2 Sam. 18 : 9, 14. Ezek. 31 : 14. It is synonymous with אַלּוֹן.

אֵלֶּה pron. plur. com. gen. *these*, employed as the plural of זֶה and זֹאת.

אֵלֶּה Chald. *idem.* Jer. 10 : 11.

אֵלָה f. *oak.* Once Josh. 24 : 26. More frequent is אַלּוֹן.

אֱלָהּ m. emph. אֱלָהָא. Chald. i. q. Heb. אֱלוֹהַּ *God.* Plur. אֱלָהִין *the gods,* Dan. 2 : 11. 5 : 4, 11, 14, 23. בַּר אֱלָהִין *son of the gods,* 3 : 25.

אֲלוּ Chald. i. q. אֲרוּ (ל and ר being interchanged, see letter ל.) *see, behold.* Dan. 2 : 31.

אִלּוּ (prob. compounded of אִם and לוּ, comp. Syr. ܐܶܠܽܘ.) *if,* only in later Hebrew, Ecc. 6 : 6. Est. 7 : 4.

אֱלוֹהַּ m. prim. dec. I. (Comp. Arab. اله (אָלַהּ) *to fear, reverence;* which is probably derived from the noun.) *God,* spoken by way of eminence of Jehovah, but also of other gods. Dan. 11 : 37—39. In the singular, only in the later books and in poetry, Neh. 9 : 17. 2 Chr. 32 : 15. Deut. 32 : 15, 17. very frequently in Job, chap. 3 : 4. 4 : 9. 5 : 17, etc. The later Hebrew in this respect agrees with the Chaldaic and Syriac usage.—Job 12 : 6 אֲשֶׁר הֵבִיא אֱלוֹהַּ בְּיָדוֹ *who bears the divinity in his hand,* i. e. whose fist is his God. Comp. Hab. 1 : 11.

Plur. אֱלֹהִים. 1. *gods,* in the plural number. Ex. 20 : 3, 20. Deut. 4 : 28. Hence *godlike forms* or *appearances,* 1 Sam. 28 : 13 אֱלֹהִים רָאִיתִי עֹלִים מִן־הָאָרֶץ *I see gods ascending from the earth,* i. e. godlike or spirit-like forms. Also i. q. בְּנֵי אֱלֹהִים *sons of God,* or *kings,* Ps. 82 : 1, 6. (It has been supposed to designate also *magistrates* and *judges;* e. g. Ex. 21 : 6. 22 : 7, 8. But Deut. 19 : 17 shows that אֱלֹהִים in these passages is *God himself,* whom the priests in their judicial capacity represented.)

2. as a pluralis excellentiæ *God* in the singular, (comp. אֲדֹנִים, בְּעָלִים.) Spoken of a false god, 2 K. 1 : 2, 3. 1 K. 11 : 33. Ex. 32 : 4, 23. Judg. 16 : 23. but preeminently of Jehovah. It is sometimes construed, (contrary to the general rule concerning the pluralis excellentiæ,) with plural adjectives; e. g. 1 Sam. 4 : 8. 17 : 26. but the verb is almost constantly in the singular, as in Gen. 1 : 1. The exceptions are Gen. 20 : 13. 31 : 53. 2 Sam. 7 : 23. Ps. 58 : 12. The following phrases, formed with אֱלֹהִים, are yet to be noticed.

3. בֶּן־אֱלֹהִים *son of God;* (1.) applied to kings, Ps. 2 : 7. 82 : 6. comp. 2 Sam. 7 : 14. also Ps. 89 : 27, where David is called *the first-born,* i. e. the most beloved, *son of Jehovah.* The ancient nations generally supposed the kingly power to be derived from God; hence the frequent expression in Homer, διογενὴς βασιλεύς; comp. Il. I. 279. II. 196, 197. To this it may be added that almost divine reverence was paid to eastern monarchs, which led to their being called *Gods* (comp. Ps. 82 : 6. 45 : 7, 8.) (2.) In the plural בְּנֵי אֱלֹהִים, applied to subordinate gods, angels, Gen. 6 : 2. (so Gesenius, but see below.) Job 1 : 6. 2 : 1. 38 : 7. (3.) applied to servants or worshippers of God, Deut. 14 : 1. Ps. 73 : 15. Prov. 14 : 26. Gen. 6 : 2, (comp. 4 : 26.)

4. אִישׁ אֱלֹהִים *man of God;* applied to angels, Judg. 13 : 6, 8. to prophets, 1 Sam. 2 : 27. 9 : 6. 1 K. 13 : 1. and to other servants of God, as to Moses, Deut. 33 : 1. to David, Neh. 12 : 24, 36.—So נְשִׂיא אֱלֹהִים *prince of God,* spoken of Abraham with reference to his princely dignity, Gen. 23 : 6.

5. *great before God,* i. e. great in the judgment of God, for *very great.* Jon. 3 : 3 *a city great before God,* i. e. a very great city. Comp. Acts 7 : 20. Gen. 10 : 9.

אֱלוּל m. the sixth month of the Hebrew ecclesiastical year, corresponding to part of August, and part of September. Neh. 6 : 15. The etymology is obscure.

אֵלוֹן m. dec. I. i. q. אֵלָה *turpentine-tree.* Gen. 12:6. Judg. 9:6, 37. Plur. אֵלוֹנִים, Gen. 13:18. 14:13.

אַלּוֹן m. dec. I. i. q. אַלָּה *oak.* Gen. 35:8. Ezek. 27:6.

I. **אַלּוּף** verbal from אָלַף, dec. I. b.

1. as an adj. *tame, brought up to hand.* Jer. 11:19 כֶּבֶשׂ אַלּוּף *a lamb brought up to hand.*

2. as a subst. *friend, confidant.* Ps. 55.14. Prov. 16:28. 17:9. Mic. 7:5. Comp. אָלַף no.1.

3. i. q. אֶלֶף no.I. *ox.* Ps. 144:14. It is an epicene noun of the masc. gender, even when applied to female animals.

II. **אַלּוּף** (denom. from אֶלֶף no. II. 2. *family.*) dec. I. b. *head of a family* or *tribe,* φύλαρχος, χιλίαρχος, Zech. 9:7. 12:5, 6. Applied particularly to the heads of the Edomitish tribes, Gen. 36:15 ff. Ex. 15:15. 1 Chr. 1:51 ff.

אָלוּשׁ (in Talmudic, *turma hominum*) proper name of an encampment of the Israelites, Num. 33:13.

אָלַח found only in Niph. *to be corrupted,* in a moral sense. Ps. 14:3. 53:4. Job 15:16. This verb in Arabic, conj. VIII. signifies *to become sour,* spoken of milk.

אַלְיָה f. *the fat tail* of a certain species of eastern sheep, (ovis laticaudia, Linn.) which is said to weigh from 12 to 20 pounds. It is placed on a two-wheeled truckle-cart, which the sheep draws after him. Lev. 3:9. 7:3. 8:25. 9:19. See Herod. III. 113. Comp. Arab. أَلْيَةٌ *cauda ovis adiposa,* أَلِيَ *carnosos clunes habuit vir.*

אֵלִיָּה m. (*Jehovah is my God*) *Elijah,* a celebrated prophet, in the time of Ahab king of Judah. 1 K. xvii.—2 K. ii. Equally common is אֵלִיָּהוּ. Concerning his re-appearance as the forerunner of the Messiah, see Mal. 3:23, 24. Besides the prophet, there are in the Scriptures several other persons of the same name.

אֱלִיהוּא, אֱלִיהוּ proper name of a friend and disputant of Job. Only Job xxxii.—xxxv.

אֱלִיל verbal from obs. אָלַל, dec. I.

1. as an adj. *vain, null, nothing-worth.* 1 Chr. 16:26. Ps. 96:5. Lev. 19:4 *the nothing-worth,* i. e. idols. 26:1. Comp. הֶבֶל.

2. as a subst. *nothingness, vanity, weakness.* Job 13:4 רֹפְאֵי אֱלִל *vain comforters;* comp. Zech. 11:17.

אִלֵּין and **אִלֵּן** Chald. pron. plur. com. gen. i. q. Heb. אֵלֶּה *these, those.* Dan. 2:44. 6:7.

אֶלְיָקִים (*God raises up*) prop. name.

1. a præfectus palatii under Hezekiah. 2 K. 18:18. 19:2. Is. 22:20. 36:3.

2. a king of Judah, son of Josiah, whose name was afterwards changed by Nechoh king of Egypt into יְהוֹיָקִים (*Jehovah raises up.*) 2 K. 23:34. 24:1. Jer. 1:3. 1 Chr. 3:15.

אֱלִישָׁה a Grecian province from which purple was brought to Tyre. This circumstance suits the Peloponnessus, and the name most probably is kindred to *Elis,* (the Samar. text has אליש,) which in a wider sense is used for the whole Peloponnessus. Gen. 10:4. Ezek. 27:7. According to others: *Hellas.* See Bocharti Phaleg. iii. 4. Michaëlis Spicileg. Geogr. Hebr. T. I. p. 80.

אֱלִישָׁע m. (perhaps for אֱלִישָׁעָה *God sees*) *Elisha,* a prophet who wrought miracles in the kingdom of Israel, successor of Elijah. 2 K. ii.—xiii. Sept. Ἐλίσα, Ἐλισσαιὲ, Ἐλισσαῖος. In Luke 4:27, Ἐλισσαῖος.

אִלֵּךְ Chald. pron. plur. masc. gen. i. q. Heb. אֵלֶּה *these, those.* Dan. 3:12, 13.

I. **אָלַל** an obsolete root, *to be nothing,* or *of no worth.* Deriv. אֱלִיל *of no worth,* and אַל *not, nothing.*

II. **אָלַל** *to lament,* see the following article.

אַלְלַי interj. joined with לִי, *wo to me!* Job 10:15. Mic. 7:1. The root אָלַל, (comp. Arab. آلَ,) is synonymous with the more frequent forms אָלָה, יָלַל *to lament.*

אָלַם not found in Kal, but its significations appear to have been

1. *to bind;* see Piel.—Deriv. אֲלֻמָּה.

2. passively *to be bound, silent, dumb;* see Niphil.—Deriv. אִלֵּם, אֵלֶם.

3. *to be solitary, forsaken, widowed,* (a meaning which is often connected with the preceding; e.g. in the Arab. بَكِمَ *to be dumb, unmarried.*) Deriv. אַלְמָן, אַלְמֹן.

Niph. *to be,* or *become dumb,* Ps. 31:19. 39:3,10. Is. 53:7. *to be silent,* Ezek. 33:22.

Pi. *to bind.* Gen. 37:7.

אֵלֶם m. prob. verbal from אָלַם no. 2. *dumbness.* Ps. 58:2 הַאֻמְנָם אֵלֶם צֶדֶק *is justice indeed silent?* Ps. 56:1 יוֹנַת אֵלֶם רְחֹקִים *the dumb dove among strangers.* This appears to be the name of a song or tune, after which Ps. lvi. was to be sung. Comp. אַיֶּלֶת. Others: *upon the oppression of distant princes,* reading אֵלִם with other points.

אִלֵּם m. verbal adj. from אָלַם no. 2. dec. VII. c. *dumb.* Ex. 4:11.

אֻלָם see **אוּלָם**.

אַלְמֻגִּים 1 K. 10:11, 12. and by metath. אַלְגּוּמִּים 2 Chr. 2:7. 9:10,11. a costly wood, which Solomon obtained, by the way of Ophir, from the East Indies. Most probably, as many Rabbins explain it, *red sandal-wood,* which in India and Persia is wrought into various costly vessels. Others render it *corals,* and in Rabbinic the word has this signification; but this is to be regarded as a more extended use of the word, than that which it originally possessed. Comp. Celsii Hierob. P. i. p. 171 ff.

אַלְמוֹדָד Gen. 10:26. a people or tribe in Yemen, sprung from Joktan. Arabian authors speak of a *Modar* (מצ׳ר), who was descended from Kachtan or Joktan. If this name be the same, then אַל may be regarded as the Arabic article, and the change of ר into ד as an ancient error of the copyist.

אֲלֻמָּה f. verbal. from אָלַם no. 1. dec. X. Plur. ־ִים and ־וֹת. *sheaf* or *bundle of corn.* Gen. 37:7. Ps. 126:6.

אַלְמָן m. verbal from אָלַם no. 3. *deserted, forsaken, widowed.* Jer. 51:5.

אַלְמֹן m. verbal from אָלַם no. 3. *widowhood.* Once Is. 47:9.

I. **אַלְמָנָה** fem. of אַלְמָן, dec. XI. a. *widowed, a widow.* Gen. 38:11. Ex. 22:21. Lev. 21:14.

II. **אַלְמָנוֹת** fem. plur. Is. 13:22. *palaces,* i.q. אַרְמְנוֹת, as some MSS. read (ר and ל being interchanged.) See אַרְמוֹן.—Perhaps also Ezek. 19:7.

אַלְמָנוּת f. denom. from אַלְמָן, dec. III. c. Plur. אַלְמְנוּתִים, *widowhood.* Gen. 38:14, 19. Is. 54:4.

אַלְמֹנִי m. *some one, a certain one.* Always joined with פְּלֹנִי q.v. It is probably a verbal from אָלַם no. 2. signifying, literally, *not named,* or *passed over in silence.*

אֵלֶן see **אִלֵּין** *these, those.*

אֶלָּסָר found only Gen. 14:1. proper name of an unknown country. Vulg. *Pontus.* A more plausible conjecture is *Assyria,* although the name אַשּׁוּר occurs in Genesis.

אֶלְעָזָר m. (*God helps*) proper name of a son of Aaron and head of a Levitical family. Ex. 6:23 ff.

אֶלְעָלֵה and **אֶלְעָלֵא** a village in the tribe of Reuben, one mile from Heshbon. Num. 32:3, 37. Is. 15:4. 16:9. Jer. 48:34.

אָלַף, fut. **יֶאֱלַף**. 1. probably as in Arabic, *to accustom one's self, to become familiar with* any thing; also spoken of animals, *to become tame.* Deriv. אַלּוּף no. I. אֶלֶף no. I.

2. *to learn.* Prov. 22:25. Comp. לָמַד.

Pi. *to teach.* Construed with one

accusative, Job. 15 : 5. 35 : 11. with a double acc. of the person and thing, Job 33 : 33.—מַלְּפֵנוּ Aram. for מְאַלְּפֵנוּ part. Job 35 : 11.

Hiph. see אֶלֶף no. II.

I. **אֶלֶף** masc. epicene, dec. VI. b. *ox, animal of the ox kind.* Deut. 7 : 13. 28 : 4. Ps. 8 : 8. Comp. אַלּוּף no I. 3.—Perhaps prim. but more probably verbal from אָלַף no. I. denoting, literally, *tame cattle.*

II. **אֶלֶף** m. prim. dec. VI. b.

1. *thousand.* Dual אַלְפַּיִם *two thousand.* Plur. אֲלָפִים *thousands,* שֵׁשֶׁת אֲלָפִים 6000; but מֵאָה אֶלֶף 100,000. אַלְפֵי אֵילִים *thousands of rams,* Mic. 6 : 7. אַלְפֵי רְבָבָה *a thousand times ten thousand,* Gen. 24 : 60.

2. *family, subdivision of a tribe,* consisting originally of *a thousand,* but afterwards without any reference to that number, i. q. מִשְׁפָּחָה. Judg. 6 : 15. 1 Sam. 10 : 19. 23 : 23. Num. 1 : 16. 10 : 4. Jos. 22 : 21, 30. In the division of Palestine, there appears to have been assigned to each family (אֶלֶף) a portion of the territory belonging to the tribe (מַטֶּה); and each of these districts, like the whole tribe, had its capital village, or place of concourse for the family. Hence Micah says of Bethlehem, chap. 5 : 1 צָעִיר לִהְיוֹת בְּאַלְפֵי יְהוּדָה אַתָּה *thou art too small to be ranked among the chief princes in Judah.* Comp. אַלּוּף no. II.

Hiph. הֶאֱלִיף denom. from אֶלֶף no. II. *to produce thousands.* Ps. 144 : 13.

אֲלַף, אֶלֶף Chald. *thousand.* Dan. 5 : 1. 7 : 10.

אָלַץ, Pi. **אִלֵּץ** *to press, urge* any one. Once Judg. 16 : 16. (In Syr. ܐܠܨ *idem.*)

אַלְקוּם found only Prov. 30 : 31. perhaps i. q. Arab. القوم *the people,* which is here retained with the article. (See אַלְגָּבִישׁ.) מֶלֶךְ אַלְקוּם עִמּוֹ *the king whose people are with him.* Sept. δημηγορῶν ἐν ἔθνει. According to others it is compounded of אַל *not* and קוּם *to rise up;* (comp. אַל־מָוֶת Prov. 12 : 28;) namely *the king, against whom no one rises up* or *resists,* i. e. the victorious king.

אֶלְקֹשִׁי a gentile noun, *an Elkoshite.* Spoken only of Nahum, chap. 1 : 1. The cities which may have given birth to this prophet are chiefly (1.) *Alkush* (القوش) in Assyria, not far from Mosul, where Nahum may have been born of Israelitish colonists; and (2.) *Elcese,* according to Jerom, a small village in Galilee.

אֵם f. prim. dec. VIII. b. Plur. אִמּוֹת.

1. *mother.* Gen. 2 : 24. Also *grandmother,* 1 K. 15 : 10.—בְּנֵי אִמֶּךָ *thy mother's sons,* poetically for *thy brethren,* Gen. 27 : 29.—Figuratively Job 17 : 14.

2. *protectress, instructress.* Judg. 5 : 7. Comp. אָב nos. 4. 5.

3. *mother city, chief city, metropolis.* 2 Sam. 20 : 19. See אַמָּה no. 2.

4. with דֶּרֶךְ, *mother of the way,* for *a cross road.* Ezek. 21 : 26. [21.]

אִם a primitive particle.

1. adv. of time, *when;* referring either to time past, like the Germ. *da, als,* Am. 7 : 2 *when they had entirely eaten off,* or to time present or future, like the Germ. *wenn,* Is. 24 : 13. אִם־כָּלָה בָצִיר *when the vintage is over.* Gen. 38 : 9. Ps. 63 : 7. So in the phrases עַד אִם, עַד אֲשֶׁר אִם *till that,* Gen. 24 : 19. 28 : 15.

2. conj. condit. *if, supposing that;* very frequently.

3. conj. concess. *although.* Judg. 13 : 16. Am. 5 : 22. Job 9 : 20.

4. adv. of wishing, *O that! utinam!* Gen. 30 : 27. Ps. 81 : 9. 139 : 19. Joined with לוּ pleonastically, Gen. 23 : 13.

5. אִם—אִם *whether.... or.* Ex. 19 : 13 אִם־בְּהֵמָה אִם־אִישׁ לֹא יִחְיֶה *whether it be beast or man, it shall not live.*

6. in swearing, the form of imprecation being omitted by an ellipsis, *not, that not.* 2 Sam. 11 : 11 *as sure as thy soul liveth,* אִם־אֶעֱשֶׂה אֶת־הַדָּבָר הַזֶּה *I will not*

do this. 1 Sam. 14 : 45. 2 Sam. 20 : 20. 2 K. 3 : 14. Cant. 2 : 7. Ps. 95 : 11. The literal meaning in these cases is *if*, (as in no. 2.) which is evident when the ellipsis is supplied, as in 2 Sam. 3 : 35 *let God deal with me thus and thus, if* etc. 1 Sam. 24 : 7 *Jehovah forbid it, if* etc. (Comp. אִם לֹא.) The signification *not* occurs also, though more rarely, where there is no oath, Is. 22:14. Judg. 5 : 8. Prov. 27 : 24.

7. perhaps *that, quod.* Gen. 31 : 52. Ex. 1 : 16.

8. adv. interrog. i.q. הֲ, Lat. *an*. Jer. 3 : 5. Hence in a double question, הֲ—אִם, *an?....utrum?* In Job 21 : 4. אִם merely strengthens the interrogative force of מַדּוּעַ which follows.

9. in the indirect inquiry, *whether*. Cant. 7 : 13. When preceded by הֲ, *whether....or*. Num. 13 : 20.

10. *nonne?* (הֲ sometimes has this meaning.) Hos. 12 : 12 אִם־גִּלְעָד אָוֶן *is not Gilead mere iniquity?* Job 39 : 13 *has not the stork wings and feathers?* 17 : 13, 16. 19 : 5. Jer. 31 : 30. Prov. 3 : 34. The ancient translators have often in these instances omitted the interrogation, and correctly rendered the word, *behold, yea, surely*. Comp. הֲלֹא and הַאִם.

11. *whether....not.* Est. 4 : 14.

12. הַאִם i.q. הֲלֹא *nonne? ecce!* Num. 17 : 28. Job 6 : 13.

13. אִם־לֹא (1.) *if not.* (2.) *but.* Gen. 24 : 38. (3.) in swearing, the form of imprecation being omitted, (comp. אִם no. 6.) *yea, surely.* Job 1 : 11. Is. 5 : 9. When the ellipsis is supplied, *if not*, 2 Sam. 19 : 14. (4.) *nonne?* Job 22 : 20. 30 : 25: Several examples usually placed under no. (3.) may, with as much propriety, be placed here.

אָמָה f. prim. irreg. with suff. אֲמָתִי, אֲמָתוֹ; Plur. אֲמָהוֹת (with epenthetic ה, as in Chald. אֲבָהָן *fathers*,) const. and before suff. אַמְהוֹת. *handmaid, maidservant, female slave.* אֲמָתְךָ *thy handmaid* is frequently used for the pronoun *I*, in addressing a superior, 1 Sam. 1 : 11, 16. 25 : 24 ff. 2 Sam. 14 : 15. (comp. אָדוֹן.)

בֶּן־אָמָה *son of a handmaid, a slave,* Exod. 23 : 12. Ps. 116 : 16.

אַמָּה f. dec. X.

1. *lower part of the arm from the elbow to the wrist, cubitus.* Deut. 3 : 11 בְּאַמַּת־אִישׁ *after the cubit of a man.*

2. *cubit*, a measure. Dual אַמָּתַיִם *two cubits.* With larger numbers it is often joined thus; מֵאָה בָּאַמָּה *an hundred on the cubit*, or *a hundred cubits.* Ex. 26 : 8, 16. 36 : 15. Jer. 15 : 13 בָּא קִצֵּךְ אַמַּת בִּצְעֵךְ *thine end is come, the measure of thine extortion (is full).* A kind of zeugma.

3 fem. of אֵם, *mother city, metropolis.* 2 Sam. 8 : 1. *David took* אֶת־מֶתֶג הָאַמָּה מִיַּד פְּלִשְׁתִּים *the bridle of the chief city out of the hand of the Philistines*, i. e. he brought it into subjection. The Arabians have very similar phrases; e. g. *I do not deliver up my bridle*, i. e. I do not subject myself.

4. Is. 6 : 4 אַמּוֹת הַסִּפִּים probably *the mothers*, i. e. the foundations, *of the thresholds.* The Arab. أُمّ *mother* and the Talmud. אַמָּה are used in a similar manner. According to others: *posts*, the angle which they make with the threshold being like an *elbow.*

5. proper name of a hill on the way of the desert of Gibeon. Once 2 Sam. 2 : 24.

אַמָּה f. Plur. אַמִּין. Chald. *cubit*, as in Heb. Dan. 3 : 1. Ezra 6 : 3.

אֻמָּה f. *family, tribe, people.* (In Arab. أُمَّة, Syr. ܐܽܘܡܬܳܐ *idem.*) In Hebrew found only in the plural אֻמּוֹת, Num. 25 : 15. and אֻמִּים, Ps. 117 : 1.

אֻמָּה, Plur. אֻמַּיָּא, Chald. *people*, as in Heb. Dan. 3 : 4, 29.

I. אָמוֹן com. gen. verbal from אָמַן no. 3. *child, foster-child*, spoken of wisdom, Prov. 8 : 30. Others: *artist, artificer*, i. q. אָמָּן. But the want of a feminine termination is a greater difficulty in the way of the latter than of the former explanation: and the rest of the verse agrees best with the idea of child.

II. אָמוֹן i. q. הָמוֹן *multitude of people* (א and ה being interchanged,) Jer. 52:15.

III. אָמוֹן *Amon*, an Egyptian idol, worshipped with peculiar honour at Thebes, which hence received the name נֹא־אָמוֹן; see נֹא. Jer. 46:25. (but comp. Ezek. 30:15.)

אֵמוּן m. (Syr. for אֱמֻן) verbal from אָמַן, dec. III. g. *truth, faithfulness.* Deut. 32:20. אִישׁ אֱמוּנִים *a faithful man*, Prov. 20:6. comp. 13:17. 14:5.

אֱמוּנָה fem. of אֵמוּן, dec. X.

1. *steadiness.* Ex. 17:12 (בְּ) אֱמוּנָה *with steadiness*, i. e. steady.

2. *truth, faithfulness, honesty, uprightness.* Deut. 32:4. Ps. 89:25. Ps. 40:11. Prov. 12:22. Ps. 37:3 *seek to be faithful.*

אַמִּיץ m. verbal adj. from אָמַץ, dec. I. b. *strong, powerful.* Job 9:4, 19. As a subst. *strength*, Is. 40:26.

אָמִיר m. *foliage* of a tree. Is. 17:6. בְּרֹאשׁ אָמִיר *at top in the foliage.* ver. 9. The root אָמַר in Hithpa. signifies *to boast one's self*, comp. Arab. أمير *a prince, emir;* hence, as some suppose, in our derivative, *height, summit, top.* This derivation, however, is unsatisfactory. It is better to compare the Syr. and Arab. עָמִיר (א and ע being commuted, see א) *grass, hay*, (perhaps literally *what is woolly*, see צַמֶּרֶת;) which is at least a kindred signification.

אָמַל *to wither, languish.* In Kal, only in the participle, Ezek. 16:30 מָה אֲמֻלָה לִבָּתֵךְ *how did thine heart languish through lust!*

Pual. אֻמְלַל. 1. *to wither, be withered, to languish;* spoken of plants, Is. 24:7. Joel 1:12. of fields, Is. 16:8. Nah. 1:4. of a sick person, Ps. 6:3, where אֻמְלַל is a participle for מְאֻמְלַל.

2. *to mourn, lament.* Is. 19:8. 33:9. Jer. 14:2. Lam. 2:8.

אֲמֵלָל m. verbal adj. from אֻמְלַל, dec. I. b. *weak, feeble.* Neh. 3:34. [4:2.]

אָמַן 1. *to be firm, secure.* In Kal, not used in this sense.

2. in a moral sense, *to be true, faithful.* Part. pass. אָמוּן, plur. אֱמוּנִים *the faithful*, Ps. 12:2. 31:24.

3. *to nurse, take care of, bring up* a child. (So in Arabic, the kindred form مان *idem.*) Hence אֹמֵן *a nursing father, one who brings up* or *educates children*, Num. 11:12. Est. 2:7. 2 K. 10:1, 5. Fem. אֹמֶנֶת *a nurse*, Ruth 4:16. 2 Sam. 4:4. The idea of *bearing* is often conveyed by this word, Lam. 4:5 הָאֱמֻנִים עֲלֵי תוֹלָע *those who are borne on crimson.* Comp. Num. 11:12. Is. 60:4.

Niph. 1. *to be firm, secure.* מָקוֹם נֶאֱמָן *a firm place*, Is. 22:23, 25.

2 *to be durable, lasting, of long continuance;* e. g. בַּיִת נֶאֱמָן *a durable house*, i. e. a lasting posterity, 1 Sam. 2:35. 25:28. 2 Sam. 7:16. 1 K. 11:38. Applied to lingering sicknesses, Deut. 28:59. to constantly-flowing water, Is. 33:16. Jer. 15:18. Comp. אֵיתָן.

3. in a moral sense, *to be true, faithful.* Jer. 42:5. Is. 1:21. Applied to God and his law, Deut. 7:9. Ps. 19:8. 93:5. to a servant, 1 Sam. 3:20. 22:14. Ps. 78:8 וְלֹא־נֶאֶמְנָה אֶת־אֵל רוּחוֹ *and whose spirit was not faithfully devoted to God.* (Comp. שָׁלֵם, תָּמִים עִם אֵל.) Neh. 9:8. Also, *to be tried, proved, found skilful*, in an art or science, Job 12:20. *he takes away speech from the most skilful* in their art, i.e. from the eloquent.

4. *to be true, prove true, be verified*, Gen. 42:20. Hence *to be fulfilled*, 1 K. 8:26. 1 Chr. 17:23.

5. pass. of Kal no. 3. *to be borne*, spoken of a child. Is. 60:4.

Hiph. הֶאֱמִין. 1. *to lean or rest* on any thing. Is. 28:16.

2. *to trust, to confide in;* construed with an acc. Judg. 11:20. with בְּ, Job 4:18. 15:15. 1 Sam. 27:12. especially הֶאֱמִין בַּיהוָה *to confide in God*, Gen. 15:6. Ex. 14:31. הֶאֱמִין בְּחַיָּיו *to confide in one's life*, or *feel secure of life*, Deut. 28:66. Job 24:22.

3. *to believe, regard as true.* Ex. 4:5. Construed with an infin. Job 15:22. with לְ of the person, Gen. 45:26. Ex. 4:1, 8, 9.

4. intrans. i. q. Niph. no. 1. *to stand firm, to stand still.* Job 39:24 *he* (the horse) *stands not still, when the trumpet hath sounded;* comp. Virg. Georg. III. 84. *stare loco nescit.*

Deriv. out of course אֵמוּן no. I. אָמוֹן, אֻמָּה.

II. **אָמַן**, Hiph. הֶאֱמִין for הֵימִין *to go to the right.* Is. 30:21.

אֲמַן Chald. only in Aph. הֵימִן (formed with ה, as in Hebrew,) *to confide in,* construed with בְּ. Dan. 6:24. Part. pass. מְהֵימַן *certain, true, faithful,* Dan. 2:45. 6:5.

אָמָּן m. verbal from אָמַן *workman,* literally *one approved* or *found skilful* in his art, (see אָמַן Niph. no. 3. especially Job 12:20.) Cant. 7:2. (In Chal. אוּמָן, in the Mishnah also אָמָּן *idem.*)

אָמֵן verbal from **אָמַן**.

1. subst. *truth, faithfulness.* אֱלֹהֵי אָמֵן *the true God,* Is. 65:16.

2. adv. *truly, certainly, so be it, fiat.* Jer. 11:5. 28:6. It was used especially, (1.) when an individual person, or the whole congregation, confirmed the oath, or covenant, which had been recited before them. Num. 5:22. Deut. 27:15 ff. Neh. 5:13. 8:6. (2.) at the close of a doxology in a song or prayer, being sometimes repeated. Ps. 41:14. 72:19. 89:53. comp. Matth. 6:13.

אֹמֶן m. verbal from **אָמַן**. *truth, faithfulness.* Is. 25:1.

אֲמָנָה f. verbal from **אָמַן**.

1. *firm covenant,* (In Arab. أَمَانَةٌ.) Neh. 10:1.

2. *fixed task* or *stated allowance.* Neh. 11:23.

3. proper name of a part of Mount Libanus. Cant. 4:8. From it flows a river of the same name, 2 K. 5:12 Keri, called in Greek *Chrysorrhoas,* now *Barrady.*

אֹמְנָה 2 K. 18:16. *a pillar, doorpost,* probably verbal from אָמַן *to be firm,* of course *to be supported,* here trans. *to support.* In the Chald. סִקְפָּא *a beam, threshold, lintel.*

אָמְנָה f. verbal from **אָמַן**.

1. *truth.* Only as an adv. *in truth,* Gen. 20:12. Josh. 7:20.

2. *education, bringing up.* Est. 2:20. Comp. אָמַן no. 3.

אָמְנָם and **אֻמְנָם** adv. (from אֹמֶן with the adverbial termination ־ָם) *certainly, truly, indeed.* Job 9:2. 12:2. 1 K. 8:27. Ps. 58:2.

אָמֵץ fut. יֶאֱמַץ. 1. *to be strong.* Gen. 25:23.

2. *to be firm, courageous.* Generally in this connexion, חֲזַק וֶאֱמָץ *be strong and courageous,* Josh. 1:6, 7, 9, 18, etc.

Pi. 1. *to strengthen.* Job 4:4.

2. *to strengthen* or *repair* a house, i. q. חִזַּק no. 2. 2 Chr. 24:13. *to establish,* Prov. 8:28 בְּאַמְּצוֹ שְׁחָקִים מִמָּעַל *when he established the clouds above.*

3. *to inspire courage.* Deut. 3:28. Job 16:5.

4. with לֵב, *to harden the heart.* Deut. 2:30. 15:7. 2 Chr. 36:13.

5. *to establish* or *confirm;* e. g. as king, 2 Chr. 11:17. Ps. 80:18 בֶּן־אָדָם אִמַּצְתָּ לָּךְ *the son of man, whom thou hast established for thyself.* So verse 16.

6. with בְּ, *to lay hold of, to take.* Is. 44:14 וַיְאַמֶּץ־לוֹ בַּעֲצֵי־יָעַר *and he took,* i. e. chose for himself, *among the trees of the wood.*

Hiph. intrans. *to be strong, courageous.* i. q. Kal no. 2. Ps. 27:14 וְיַאֲמֵץ לִבֶּךָ *let thine heart be courageous.* 31:25.

Hithpa. 1. *to strengthen one's self, to collect one's strength.* 2 Chr. 13:7. 1 K. 12:18 הִתְאַמֵּץ לַעֲלוֹת *he hastened with all his might to ascend.*

2. *to firmly resolve.* Ruth 1:18.

Deriv. out of course אַמִּיץ, מַאֲמָץ.

אֹמֶץ m. verbal from אָמֵץ. *strength.* Once Job 17:9.

אָמֹץ, plur. אֲמֻצִּים Zech. 6:3, as an attribute of horses, *strong, stout.* Sept.

Chald. *ash-coloured, gray;* but without support from etymology.

אַמְצָה f. verbal from אָמֵץ. *strength, power.* Zech. 12:5.

אֲמַצְיָה m. (*strength of Jehovah*) proper name of a son of Joash, king of Judah. 2 K. 12:22. 13:12. Equally common is אֲמַצְיָהוּ, 14:1, 9, 11. Sept. Ἀμεσσίας. Vulg. *Amasias.*

אָמַר, fut. יֹאמַר and יֹאמֵר, (see art. אָבַד note 1.) with ו conversive וַיֹּאמֶר; infin. לֵאמֹר, אֱמֹר.

1. *to say, dico.* It differs from דִּבֶּר *to speak, loquor,* especially in this, that אָמַר is almost uniformly followed, directly or indirectly, by the words spoken; while דִּבֶּר is not: hence the two verbs are often connected thus, דַּבֵּר אֶל־בְּנֵי יִשְׂרָאֵל וְאָמַרְתָּ אֲלֵיהֶם *speak to the children of Israel, and say to them,* Lev. 1:2. More frequently, however, the latter verb stands in the infinitive, thus, לֵאמֹר *saying,* after which the direct words follow. The accusative of the thing said is more rare; e.g. וְאָמַרְתָּ אֲלֵיהֶם אֶת־הַדָּבָר הַזֶּה *and say to them this,* Jer. 14:17. מַה־נֹּאמַר *what shall we say?* Gen. 44:16. כַּאֲשֶׁר אָמַר י׳ *as Joseph had said,* 41:54. Rarely also is this verb followed by כִּי *that,* Job 36:10. It is used absolutely, like דִּבֶּר, only in a few cases, principally in the later writers, who also use דִּבֶּר for אָמַר, 2 Chr. 2:10 וַיֹּאמֶר חוּרָם בִּכְתָב *and Huram spake,* i.e. gave an answer, *by writing.* 32:24 וַיֹּאמֶר לוֹ *and God spake to him.* Ps. 139:20 יֹמְרוּךָ *they speak concerning thee.* (Comp. Dan. 7:16.) Also Gen. 4:8. belongs here, if there is no omission in the text.—The person *to* whom any one speaks, is preceded by אֶל and לְ. The person *concerning* whom any thing is said, by לְ, Gen. 20:13 אִמְרִי־לִי *say concerning me.* Ps. 3:3. 71:10. Judg. 9:54. or is put in the accusative, Gen. 43:27 *your old father* אֲשֶׁר אֲמַרְתֶּם *of whom ye said, quem dixistis.* ver. 29. Num. 14:31. Ps. 139:20. Lam. 4:20.

2. *to think.* (*Speaking* and *thinking,* to a man of lively imagination, especially when he is alone, are the same thing, and they are therefore frequently expressed by one word. Comp. φημί in Homer. Forster informs us of savages in the South Sea, who use the phrase *to speak in the belly* for *to think.* In Heb. see שִׂיחַ.) 2 Sam. 21:16 וַיֹּאמֶר לְהַכּוֹת *he thought to slay.* Ex. 2:14 הַלְהָרְגֵנִי אַתָּה אֹמֵר *thinkest thou to kill me?* Gen. 44:28 וָאֹמַר אַךְ טָרֹף טֹרָף *and I think, he is surely torn in pieces.* 1 Sam. 20:4 מַה־תֹּאמַר נַפְשְׁךָ *what does thy soul think or desire?* Used absolutely, Ps. 4:5 *think,* i.e. meditate, *in your hearts upon your bed.*

3. *to command.* (This is the prevailing signification in Arabic, but in Hebrew it is found chiefly in the later books.) Construed frequently with an infin. Est. 1:17 אָמַר לְהָבִיא *he commanded to bring.* 4:13. 9:14. 1 Chr. 21:17. or with וְ following, Neh. 13:9 וָאֹמְרָה וַיְטַהֲרוּ *and I commanded, and they cleansed.* 2 Chr. 24:8 וַיֹּאמֶר הַמֶּלֶךְ וַיַּעֲשׂוּ *the king commanded, and they made.* Ps. 105:31, 34. (In Chaldaic, as examples of the former construction, comp. Dan. 2:46. 3:13, 19, 20. as an example of the latter, 5:29.) 2 Chr. 29:24 כִּי לְכָל־יִשְׂרָאֵל אָמַר הַמֶּלֶךְ הָעוֹלָה *because for all Israel had the king commanded this burnt-offering.* 1 K. 11:18 לֶחֶם אָמַר לוֹ *he commanded food for him,* i.e. assigned to him a supply of food.

4. *to praise.* Ps. 40:11. 145:6, 11. Is. 3:10.

Niph. *to be said,* construed with לְ. Is. 4:3 קָדוֹשׁ יֵאָמֶר לוֹ *holy shall be said to him,* or *he shall be called holy,* i.e. in the language of Isaiah, he shall be holy. 61:6. 62:4.

Hiph. i. q. Kal, but intensitively, *to declare solemnly, to promise,* construed with an accus. of the person. Deut. 26:17, 18.

Hithpa. *to boast one's self.* Ps. 94:4. Or, *to exercise dominion,* (as in Arab. Conj. I. V.)

Deriv. out of course, מַאֲמָר.

אֲמַר Chald. *idem.* especially no. 3. *to command.* Pret. fem. אֲמָרַת for אַמְרַת, Dan. 5:10. fut. יֵאמַר, infin. מֵאמַר also מֵמַר, Ezra 5:11.

אֹמֶר verbal from אָמַר.

1. *word, speech,* (only in poetry.) Ps. 19:3.

2. *a matter, thing,* i.q. דָּבָר. Job 22:28. (In Arabic, more frequent.)

3. *triumphal song.* Ps. 68:12. So prob. also Hab. 3:9.

אֵמֶר m. verbal from אָמַר, dec. VI. g.

1. *word, speech,* (only poet.) i.q. דָּבָר. Prov. 22:21.—אִמְרֵי־אֵל *oracles of God,* Num. 24:16; comp. Job 6:10. Ps. 107:11.

2. *promise.* Job 20:29 נַחֲלַת אִמְרוֹ מֵאֵל *the inheritance of his promise,* i.e. his promised inheritance, *from God.*

3. Gen. 49:21 *Naphtali is a slender hind* הַנֹּתֵן אִמְרֵי־שָׁפֶר perhaps *which brings forth beautiful young,* אִמְרֵי here denoting perhaps *the young stag,* as in Chaldaic, אִמַּר *a young sheep.* Bochart, (Hieroz. I. p. 895.) and most critics since his day read this verse with a change of the vowel-points אֵילָה and אֲמִירֵי; and render it thus: *Naphtali is a tall turpentine-tree, which puts forth goodly branches.*

אִמַּר. plur. אִמְּרִין. Chald. *lamb.* Ezra 6:9, 17. 7:17.

אִמְרָה fem. of אֵמֶר, dec. XII. b. *word, speech,* (only poet.) Deut. 32:2. Gen. 4:23. Ps. 12:7, etc.

אֶמְרָה fem. of אֵמֶר, dec. XII. b. *idem.* Lam. 2:17.

אֱמֹרִי m. a gentile noun, *Amorite,* or collect. *Amorites,* a Canaanitish people, inhabiting at first the mountainous parts of Judea, Gen. 14:7, 13. 48:22. 2 Sam. 21:2. but, when the country was invaded by the Israelites, found principally beyond Jordan between the rivers Jabbok and Arnon, Num. 21:13, 24—26, 32. Used by way of eminence for *a Canaanite* generally, Gen. 15:16. Am. 2:9, 10. Deut. 1:20. Comp. Relandi Palæstina, p. 138.

אַמְרָפֶל m. proper name of a king of Shinar, (Babylonia,) contemporary with Abraham. Gen. 14:1, 9. The probable Assyrian etymology of this word is obscure.

אֶמֶשׁ subst. and adv. *the preceding night, the last night,* Gen. 19:34. 31:29, 42. *yesterday,* 2 K. 9:26. Probably used for *night* generally, Job 30:3 אֶמֶשׁ שׁוֹאָה וּמְשׁוֹאָה *the night of wasting and desolation.* Comp. Jer. 2:6, 31. So the Chald. Drusius, and others. אֶמֶשׁ signifies *yesternight, evening and night* generally, as בֹּקֶר *tomorrow morning,* and *early morn* generally. Comp. Arab. أمس *heri.*

אֱמֶת f. for אֱמֶנֶת fem. of אָמֵן, with suff. אֲמִתּוֹ.

1. *duration, continuance.* Is. 39:8 שָׁלוֹם וֶאֱמֶת *prosperity and continuance,* i.e. lasting prosperity. Jer. 33:6. comp. שְׁלוֹם אֱמֶת Jer. 14:13.

2. *certainty.* Josh. 2:12 אוֹת אֱמֶת *a certain sign.*

3. *truth, faithfulness;* applied to Jehovah, Ps. 54:7. 57:11. 108:5. to men, denoting *uprightness* generally, Ex. 18:21. *faithful attachment to religion,* 1 Sam. 12:24. 1 K. 2:4. 2 Chr. 31:20. 32:1.—חֶסֶד וֶאֱמֶת *grace and truth,* (often thus connected,) spoken of God, Ps. 25:10. 40:11. Gen. 32:10. of a king, Prov. 20:28. of men, signifying *kindness and truth,* or *true kindness,* Gen. 24:49. 47:29.—דִּבְרֵי שָׁלוֹם וֶאֱמֶת *words of peace and truth,* Est. 9:30.

4. *truth, something true.* Gen. 42:16. 24:48. especially *religious truth, true religion,* Dan. 8:12. 9:13. comp. Ps. 25:5. 26:3.

אַמְתַּחַת f. (verbal from מָתַח *to stretch out,*) dec. XIII. a. *sack.* Gen. 42:27 ff.

אֲמִתַּי m. (from אֱמֶת with the adjective termination ־ַי, *true,*) proper name of the father of the prophet Jonah. 2 K. 14:25. Jon. 1:1. Others without sufficient reason regard it as the name of his mother.

אֵימְתָנִי f. (for ־ִית) Chald. *strong, powerful.* Dan. 7:7. The root מְתַן signifies in Arabic, *to be firm, stable, strong.*

אָן adv. interrog. contraction of אַיִן no. II. *where?* also *whither?* 1 Sam. 10:14. Hence מֵאָן *whence?* 2 K. 5:25 Keth. עַד־אָן *how far? how long?* Job 8:2. With ה local, אָנָה *whither?* also without interrogation, Josh. 2:5. Neh. 2:16. *where?* Ruth 2:19. עַד־אָנָה *till when? how long?* Ex. 16:28. Ps. 13:2. אָנָה וָאָנָה *hither and thither,* 1 K. 2:36, 42.

אֲנָא and **אֲנָה** Chald. *I,* also *I am.*

אָנָּא [*anna*] interj. of entreating, (compounded of אָהּ or אָהָהּ and נָא.) *Ah, I pray you! ah, quæso.* Gen. 50:17. Dan. 9:4. Sometimes written אָנָּה, Jon. 1:14. 4:2.

I. **אָנָה** i. q. אָנַן *to mourn, lament.* Is. 3:26. 19:8.

Deriv. out of course, תַּאֲנִיָּה, אֲנִיָּה.

II. **אָנָה** i. q. Arab. أَنَى *to be* or *happen at a proper time.*

Pi. *to bring* or *cause to come at a proper time.* Ex. 21:13.

Pu. *to happen to* or *befall* any one; spoken of a misfortune. Prov. 12:21. Ps. 91:10.

Hithpa. construed with לְ, *to seek occasion against* any one. 2 K. 5:7. See תֹּאֲנָה.

אָנָה see **אָן**.

אֲנָה see **אֲנָא**.

אָנָּה see **אָנָּא**.

אֲנוּ pron. com. gen. *we.* Once Jer. 42:6 Keth. which is the true reading, for the Keri אֲנַחְנוּ is only a gloss which has substituted the usual for the unusual form. An abbreviation of this pronoun is seen in קְטַלְנוּ and in the suffixes נוּ, ־ֵנוּ, ־ָנוּ.

אִנּוּן m. **אִנִּין** f. Chald. pron. plur. *these.* (In Syr. ܗܢܘܢ *idem.*)

אֱנוֹשׁ m. prim. *man,* also collect. *men.* In the singular, except 2 Chr. 14:11. it is found only poetically, in Job, Isaiah, and the Psalms. The prose expression is אָדָם. Sometimes it denotes (1.) *common men, ordinary men;* hence Is. 8:1 בְּחֶרֶט אֱנוֹשׁ *with the pen of the common man,* i. e. in the common legible character; comp. Rev. 13:18. 21:17. (2.) *wicked men.* Ps. 56:2. Comp. אָדָם no. 1.

Plur. אֲנָשִׁים, const. אַנְשֵׁי, (formed from an obs. sing. אֱנָשׁ) employed as the plur. of אִישׁ *man,* (q. v.) denoting *men* generally. Gen. 32:29.

אָנַח found only in Niph. *to sigh, groan.* Ex. 2:23. Joel 1:18, etc. (In Aram. Ethpa. *idem.*) Construed with עַל, Ezek. 21:12. [7.] or מִן Ex. 2:23. The following verbs appear to be kindred to each other, נָאַק, אָנַן, אָנַק, אָנַח, אָנָה.

אֲנָחָה f. verbal from אָנַח, dec. XI. d. *a sigh, sighing.* Ps. 31:11. Lam. 1:22.

אֲנַחְנָא and **אֲנַחְנָה** Chald. i. q. Heb. אֲנַחְנוּ.

אֲנַחְנוּ pron. plur. com. gen. *we.* Comp. נַחְנוּ. (In Arab. نَحْنُ *idem.*)

אֲנִי in pause אָנִי pron. prim. com. gen. *I.* Also written אָנֹכִי. The form אָנִי also occurs in the phrase חַי אָנִי, (see חַי.) Hence, by abbreviation, the suffixes ־ִי, ־ַי, ־נִי.

אֳנִי m. *ship,* and collect. *ships, a fleet.* 1 K. 9:26, 27. 10:11. (The parallel passage in Chronicles has the plural.) Also used collectively in the fem. gen. 1 K. 10:22. Is. 33:21.

אֳנִיָּה fem. of אֳנִי, dec. X. *idem.* Gen. 49:13. Judg. 5:17. 2 Chr. 8:18 Keri. The Kethib in the last passage is אוניות, which is to be attributed to the later incorrect mode of writing the vowels fully.

אֲנִיָּה f. verbal from אָנָה. *mourning, sorrow.* Is. 29:2.

אֲנָךְ m. prim. *lead;* hence *a plumb, plummet, perpendicle,* Am. 7:7 חוֹמַת אֲנָךְ *a perpendicular wall, murus perpendiculi.* verse 8. (In Arabic, *lead* and *tin.*)

אָנֹכִי in pause אָנֹכִי (penacute,) pron. com. gen. *I.* Otherwise אֲנִי.

אָנַן *to groan, murmur, complain,* found only in Hithpoel, הִתְאוֹנֵן *idem,* Num. 11:1. Lam. 3:39.

אָנַס (more frequent in Aram. אֲנַס, انس) *to press, constrain, compel* any one. Once Est. 1:8.

אֲנַס Chald. *idem.* Once Dan. 4:6. [9] *no secret presses you,* i. e. gives you trouble.

אָנַף, fut. יֶאֱנַף, *to breathe, to snort,* especially from anger; hence *to be angry,* construed with בְּ of the person, 1 K. 8:46. Ps. 2:12. 60:3. 79:5.

Hithpa. *idem;* also construed with בְּ, Deut. 1:37. 4:21.

Deriv. out of course אַף.

אַנְפִּין Chald. *face, countenance.* Only Dan. 2:46. 3:19. See Heb. אַפַּיִם.

אֲנָפָה f. Lev. 11:19. Deut. 14:18. an unclean bird of several species. (לְמִינָהּ.) Sept. χαραδριός. C. V. *heron.* Comp. Bocharti Hieroz. II. p. 335 ff.

אָנַק, fut. יֶאֱנַק, *to groan, cry out from pain,* spoken of a wounded person. Once Ezek. 26:15.

Niph. pass. Only Ezek. 9:4. 24:17.

אֲנָקָה f. verbal from אָנַק, const. אֶנְקַת.

1. *groaning, cry of anguish.* Ps. 12:6. 79:11.

2. a species of lizard. Once Lev. 11:30.

אָנַשׁ *to be sick,* especially *to be dangerously sick.* (In Syr. ܢܫ which form is also found in Hebrew, Ps. 69:21.) Part. pass. אָנוּשׁ, אֲנוּשָׁה (1.) *malignant, dangerous, incurable;* spoken of a wound, Jer. 15:18. Mic. 1:9. Job 34:6. of pain. Is. 17:11 (i. q. נַחֲלָה, חוֹלָה.) (2.) figuratively, יוֹם אָנוּשׁ *a sorrowful day,* Jer. 17:16; comp. יוֹם נַחֲלָה Jer. 17:11.

3. *wicked,* spoken of the heart. Jer. 17:9.

Niph. *to be very sick.* 2 Sam. 12:15.

אֲנָשִׁים *men,* see אִישׁ.

אֱנָשׁ Chald. i. q. Heb. אֱנוֹשׁ *man.* Dan. 2:10. 3:10. 5:5, 7, etc.—בַּר אֱנָשׁ *son of man, a man,* (see בֶּן אָדָם.) Dan. 7:13 *behold, in the clouds of heaven came one* כְּבַר אֱנָשׁ *like a son of man,* i. e. in a human form.

Plur. אֲנָשִׁים Dan. 4:14.

אַנְתָּה Chald. pron. masc. gen. *thou.* Found only in biblical Chaldee. The author undoubtedly intended that it should be pronounced after the Hebrew manner אַנְתָּה, but the Masoretes sought to amend it in conformity with the Chaldee אַנְתְּ (com. gen.) by placing under it the vowel-points which belong to this form.

אַנְתּוּן Chald. pron. plur. *ye.* Once Dan. 2:8.

אָסָא m. *(curing, physician)* proper name of a king of Judah, the third after Solomon. 1 K. 15:8 ff.

אָסוּךְ m. verbal from סוּךְ. *ointment-bottle, oil-cup.* 2 K. 4:2.

אָסוֹן m. *hurt, injury, mischief,* which befalls any one. Gen. 42:4, 38. Ex. 21:22, 23. Probably a verbal from obs. אָסָה i. q. אָוָה = Arab. أَذِيَ *læsus fuit, noxam percepit.* See the letters ו and ס.

אֵסוּר (Syr. for אֱסוּר) m. verbal from אָסַר, dec. III. g. *band, fetter.* Ecc. 7:26.—בֵּית הָאֵסוּר Jer. 37:15, בֵּית הָאֲסוּרִים and by contract. הָסוּרִים. Ecc. 4:14. *prison-house.*

אֱסוּר Chald. *idem.* Dan. 4:12. [15.] Ezra 7:26.

אָסִיף m. verbal from אָסַף. *harvest-time.* Ex. 23:16. 34:22.

אָסִיר m. verbal from אָסַר, dec. III. a. *prisoner, captive.* It differs from the part. pass. אָסוּר in being used substantively; comp. Gen. 39:20.

אַסִּיר m. verbal from אָסַר. *idem.* Is. 10:4. 24:22. 42:7.

אָסָם m. dec. IV. c. *storehouse, granary,* perhaps *a subterranean one,* (comp. Mat. 6:19.) Deut. 28:8. Prov. 3:10. The root is either שׂוּם=סוּם signifying *to heap up, to lay up,* like the Syr. ܣܳܡ and Arab. شَامَ or אָסַם = Chald. אֲסַן and Syr. ܐܣܡ having the same signification. Comp. the letter ם.

אָסְנַפַּר m. Chald. proper name of an Assyrian king, or general. Ezra 4:10. He is thought to be the same person with *Esar-haddon;* see verse 2.

אָסְנַת f. proper name of the wife of Joseph in Egypt, daughter of the priest Poti-pherah. Gen. 41:45. 46:20. The etymology is undoubtedly Egyptian, but obscure.

אָסַף, fut. יֶאֱסֹף, plur. יַאַסְפוּ; also יֹאסֵף, but always written defectively יֹסֵף (1 Sam. 15:6. 2 Sam. 6:1. Ps. 104:29.)

1. *to gather, collect, assemble;* e.g. fruits, Ex. 23:10. the people, Num. 21:16. gold, 2 K. 22:4. Construed with אֶל, *to gather into* any place, Gen. 42:17 וַיֶּאֱסֹף אֹתָם אֶל־מִשְׁמָר *he brought them together into ward.* Ezek. 24:4. Gen. 6:21. Jos. 2:18. From this it signifies

2. *to take to one's self, to receive* even an individual person or thing. Deut. 22:2. Jos. 20:4 וְאָסְפוּ אֹתוֹ הָעִירָה אֲלֵיהֶם *they shall take him to themselves into the city.* 2 Sam. 12:28. Ps. 27:10.— אָסַף מִצָּרַעְתּוֹ 2 K. 5:3, 6, 7, 11. *to receive* one *again from his leprosy,* i.e. to cure him, and thereby restore him to society.

3. *to withdraw, draw back, take back.* Gen. 49:33 וַיֶּאֱסֹף רַגְלָיו אֶל הַמִּטָּה *and he drew back his feet upon the bed.* 1 Sam. 14:20 אֱסֹף יָדֶךָ *draw back thine hand.* Ps. 104:29 תֹּסֵף רוּחָם יִגְוָעוּן *thou takest back* or *away their life, they die.* 26:9. Job 34:14. Joel 2:10 *the stars* אָסְפוּ נָגְהָם *take back* or *withdraw their shining.* Gen. 30:23 אָסַף אֱלֹהִים אֶת חֶרְפָּתִי *God has taken away my reproach.* Is. 4:1. Ps. 85:4.— אָסַף נַפְשׁוֹ *to take away one's own life,* i.e. to be the occasion of one's own death, Judg. 18:25.

4. *to take out of the way, to kill, destroy.* 1 Sam. 15:6 פֶּן אֹסִפְךָ עִמּוֹ *lest I kill thee with him.* Ezek. 34:29.

5. *to bring up the rear, be a rereward, agmen claudere.* Is. 58:8; since the rear *completes* the whole army. Comp. Pi. no. 2.

Niph. 1. pass. and reflex. of Kal no. 1.

2. pass. of Kal no. 2. *to be received,* spoken of a leper, Num. 12:14. reflex. of the same, *to withdraw itself, spoken* of the sword, Jer. 47:6.

3. *to be taken away, disappear, cease.* Is. 16:10. 57:1. Jer. 48:33. Spoken of the moon, *to withdraw itself,* or *become dark,* Is. 60:20.

4. *to perish.* Hos. 4:30.

5. נֶאֱסַף אֶל־עַמָּיו Gen. 25:8. 49:29, 33. and אֶל־אֲבוֹתָיו Judg. 2:10. also without addition Num. 20:26. (Is. 57:1.?) *to be gathered to one's people, to one's fathers,* i.e. *to die, to go to the regions of the dead, where the fathers are;* something more, as the connexion of these passages clearly shews, than *being buried in a tomb with one's forefathers;* although Gen. 15:15. 2 K. 22:20, appear to favour the latter supposition.

Pi. 1. i.q. Kal nos. 1, 2. *to gather, receive.* Judg. 19:18.

2. *to bring up the rear* of an army. Num. 10:25. Jos. 6:9, 13. Is. 52:12. See Kal no. 5.

Pu. pass. of Kal no. 1. Is. 24:22. 33:4.

Hithpa. reflex. Deut. 33:5.

Deriv. out of course אֹסֶף.

אָסָף m. (*collector*) proper name of a Levite, who was one of David's chief musicians, and a poet, and had the title of חֹזֶה (*a seer.*) 1 Chr. 6:24. [39.] 15:17. 16:5. 2 Chr. 29:30. To him are ascribed many of the Psalms; e.g. L. LXXIII.—LXXXIII.

אֹסֶף m. verbal from אָסַף, dec. VI. m.

1. *a gathering in, a harvest.* Is. 32:10. Mic. 7:1.

2. *an eating up, consuming.* Is. 33:4.

אֲסֵפָה f. verbal from אָסַף. *a gathering together.* Once Is. 24:22. where it gives intensity to the finite verb.

אֲסֻפָּה f. verbal from אָסַף, dec. X. *an assembly,* especially of wise men. Ecc. 12:11 בַּעֲלֵי אֲסֻפּוֹת *masters,* i.e. members, *of the assemblies of wise men.* i.q. parall. חֲכָמִים. The Rabbins use this word with the same signification.

אֲסֻפִּים masc. plur. verbal from אָסַף, dec. I. b. *stores.* 1 Chr. 26 : 15 בֵּית הָאֲסֻפִּים, and verse 17, without בֵּית, *storehouse,* an apartment of the outer temple towards the south.—Neh. 12 : 25 אֲסֻפֵּי הַשְּׁעָרִים *the store-rooms of the gates.*

אֲסַפְסֻף m. verbal from אָסַף. *collection of people, a rabble.* With the article, הָאסַפְסֻף (Syr. for הָאֲסַפְסֻף). Once Num. 11 : 4.

אָסְפַּרְנָא (penacute) Chald. adv. *carefully, diligently, speedily.* Ezra 5 : 8. 6 : 8, 12, 13. 7 : 17, 21, 26. The word is most probably not of Shemitish, but of Assyrian or Persian origin, (comp. the proper name אַסְפְּנַז.) Its meaning is evident, from the connexion in which it is used.

אָסַר, fut. יֶאְסֹר, and יַאְסֹר, part. act. אֹסְרִי poet. for אֹסֵר (Gen. 49 : 11.)

1. *to bind.* Gen. 49 : 11. Ps. 118 : 27.

2. *to bind with fetters.* Gen. 42 : 24. Judg. 16 : 5 ff. Hence

3. *to imprison,* even without binding. 2 K. 17 : 4. 23 : 33. (comp. Gen. 42 : 16.) אָסוּר *imprisoned,* Gen. 40 : 3, 5. (In Arab. أسر *idem.*)

4. *to yoke.* 1 Sam. 6 : 7, 10. 1 K. 18 : 44.—אָסַר מֶרְכָּבָה *to harness a chariot,* Gen. 46 : 29. Ex. 14 : 6.

5. with מִלְחָמָה, *to join battle,* for *to make an attack.* 1 K. 20 : 14. 2 Chr. 13 : 3.

6. אָסַר אִסָּר עַל נַפְשׁוֹ *to take on one's self a vow of abstinence,* different from נָדַר *to vow that one will do something.* Num. 30 : 3 ff. e. g. verse 10 כֹּל אֲשֶׁר אָסְרָה עַל נַפְשָׁהּ *every thing whereto she has bound herself,* i. e. to restrain herself from the same. In Chaldaic, אֲסַר signifies *to bind* and *to forbid;* in Arabic, חרם has the same significations, חלל signifies *to loose* and *to permit.*

Niph. pass. of Kal nos. 1, 2. Gen. 42 : 16.

Pu. *to be taken prisoner.* Is. 22 : 3.

Deriv. out of course אֵסוּר, אָסִיר, אַסִּיר, מוֹסֵרִים, מַסֹּרֶת.

אֱסָר and **אִסָּר** m. verbal from אָסַר, dec. I. *vow of abstinence.* Num. 30 : 3 ff. See אָסַר no. 6.

אֱסָר m. Chald. *prohibition.* Dan. 6 : 8 ff.

אֵסַר־חַדּוֹן m. *Esar-haddon,* son of Sennacherib, king of Assyria. 2 K. 19 : 37. Is. 37 : 38. Ezra 4 : 2. In Tob. 1 : 21, this name is written Σαχερδονός; in Ptolemy, *Asaradin.*

אָע Chald. *wood,* Ezra 5 : 8, etc. i. q. Heb. עֵץ; ע being changed into א, and צ into ע; see the letters א, ע, and צ.

אֶסְתֵּר f. proper name of a Jewess, the heroine of the book which bears her name, who, according to chap. 2 : 7, was at first called הֲדַסָּה *Hadassah.* If, with Hiller, we regard the name אֶסְתֵּר as a Persian translation of the Hebrew הֲדַסָּה (*myrtle,*) then the former may be explained by comparing the Pers. اس تر *green myrtle.* The Jewish commentators, however, derive the name from the Pers. استاره *a star.*

I. **אַף** conj. prim. 1. *also.*

2. *and.* Cant. 1 : 16. Job 14 : 3 *and upon such an one directest thou thine eyes?*

3. *yea rather, imò,* i. q. גַּם no. 2. Prov. 22 : 19 הוֹדַעְתִּיךָ אַף אָתָּה *I teach thee, yea thee.*

4. *but, yet.* Ps. 44 : 10. 58 : 3. Ecc. 2 : 9.

5. i. q. אַף כִּי *how much less.* Job 4 : 19.

6. אַף כִּי literally *also when.* It also signifies (1.) *how much more,* after an affirmation, 1 Sam. 14 : 30. 2 Sam. 4 : 11. *how much less,* after a negation, 1 K. 8 : 27. (2.) i. q. כִּי *yea.* Hab. 2 : 5. (3.) Gen. 3 : 1, for הַאַף כִּי *is it indeed so that?* Luther correctly: *yea, should God have said?*

אַף Chald. *idem.* Dan. 6 : 23.

II. **אַף** m. contraction of אַנְף verbal from אָנַף *to breathe,* (In Arabic أنف), dec. VIII. h.

1. *nose.*—גֹּבַהּ אַף *pride of nose,* i. e. of countenance, Ps. 10 : 4. רוּחַ אַף *the breathing of the nose,* i. e. anger, Job 4 : 9. Hence

2. *anger.*—בַּעַל אַף *an angry man*, Prov. 22:24. Of very frequent occurrence is the phrase, חָרָה אַף *anger is enkindled*. See this and other phrases under the particular verbs.

Dual אַפַּיִם. 1. *nostrils, nose*. Gen. 2:7. Ex. 15:8.

2. *anger*; especially in the phrases, קְצַר אַפַּיִם *passionate, irascible*; אֶרֶךְ אַפַּיִם *long-suffering*. See these words.

3. *face, countenance*. (Syr. ܐܦܐ) Gen. 3:19. Frequently occurs the expression, *he fell down* אַפַּיִם אַרְצָה *with his face towards the ground*, Gen. 19:1. 42:6, etc. לְאַפֵּי דָוִד *before the face of David*, 1 Sam. 25:23, for the usual לִפְנֵי.

4. *two persons*. (So Syr. ܐܦ̈ܐ signifies *face*, and *person*, like πρόσωπον, פָּנִים.) 1 Sam. 1:5 מָנָה אַחַת אַפָּיִם *a portion for two persons*, i. e. a double portion.

אָפַד *to put on, to clothe, gird*. Only Ex. 29:4. Lev. 8:7. where it is applied to the girding on of the ephod.

אֲפֻדָּה f. verbal from אָפַד, dec. X.

1. i. q. infin. of אָפַד; *the girding on* of the ephod. Only Ex. 28:8 חֵשֶׁב אֲפֻדָּתוֹ אֲשֶׁר עָלָיו *the girdle for girding it on*, i. e. the girdle with which one girds on the ephod, *which is upon it*, etc. 39:5.

2. *the overlaying* or *plating* of a statue with gold or silver. Once Is. 30:22. Parall. צִפּוּי. Comp. Bar. 6:8, 57.

אַפֶּדֶן, dec. VI. a. i. q. Syr. ܐܦܕܢܐ *palace*. Once Dan. 11:45 אָהֳלֵי אַפַּדְנוֹ *his palace tents* or *royal pavilions*. (Comp. Jer. 43:10 Targ.)

אָפָה, fut. יֹאפֶה. *to bake*. Gen. 19:3. Part. masc. אֹפֶה, fem. אֹפָה *a baker*, Gen. 40:1. 1 Sam. 8:13. A peculiar construction occurs Lev. 24:5, *thou shalt take meal*, וְאָפִיתָ אֹתָהּ שְׁתֵּים עֶשְׂרֵה חַלּוֹת *and bake thereof twelve cakes*.

Niph. pass. Lev. 6:10. [17.]

Deriv. out of course מַאֲפֶה.

אֵפוֹ and **אֵפוֹא** (to be carefully distinguished from אֵיפֹה *where?*) a primitive particle, *now, then*, used as an expletive and intensitive; (1.) after an interrogative word, אַיֵּה אֵפוֹא *where now? where then?* Job 17:5. Judg. 9:38. Is. 19:12. Hos. 13:10. מִי אֵפוֹא *who then?* מָה אֵפוֹא *what then?* Gen. 27:37. Ex. 33:16. (2.) דְּעוּ אֵפוֹא *know then, know now*, 2 K. 10:10. Job 19:6. לְכָה אֵפוֹא *come on then!* Gen. 27:37. עֲשֵׂה זֹאת אֵפוֹא בְּנִי *do this then, my son*, Prov. 6:3.—Gen. 43:11 אִם כֵּן אֵפוֹא *if it is so then*. Job 19:23 מִי יִתֵּן אֵפוֹ *O that now*.

אֵפוֹד m. (Syr. for אֵפֹד) ver. from אָפַד.

1. *the ephod*, a covering for the breast or shoulders, in the dress of the high-priest. It was a short coat, one cubit long, consisting of two parts, one of which went before and the other behind. These were connected over the shoulders by buckles. Ex. 28:6—12. The garment under it is called מְעִיל הָאֵפוֹד, 28:31. 29:5. Besides the high-priest, it was also worn by David, while engaged in a religious service, 2 Sam. 6:14; by Samuel, while a youth ministering before the Lord, 1 Sam. 2:18; and by many priests of the lower order.

2. *idol*, (comp. אֲפֻדָּה no. 2.) Judg. 8:27. probably Judg. 17:5. 18:17—20. perhaps also Hos. 3:4.

אָפִיל verbal adj. from obs. אָפַל, dec. III. a. literally *dark*, (see אֹפֶל, אָפֵל;) hence *late, backward as to growth*, from want of the fertilizing influence of the sun. (Comp. Jer. 2:6, 31.) Once Ex. 9:32.

I. **אָפִיק** m. verbal adj. from אָפַק dec. III. a. *strong*. Job 12:21. (parall. נְדִיב.) 41:7 אֲפִיקֵי מָגִנִּים *the strong of his shields*, for *his strong shields*, spoken of the scales of the crocodile.

II. **אָפִיק** perhaps prim. dec. III. a.

1. *valley, dale*, (parall. גַּיְא.) Ezek. 6:3. 34:13. 35:8. 36:4, 6. especially one wherein brooks collect, i. q. נַחַל.

2. *brook*. Ps. 126. 4.—אֲפִיקֵי מַיִם *water-brooks*, 42:2. Joel 1:20. Cant. 5:12. אֲפִיק נְחָלִים *brook of the valleys*, Job 6:15.

3. *bed* or *channel* of a river. Is. 8:7. Ezek. 32:6.—אֲפִיקֵי יָם *bottom of the sea*, 2 Sam. 22:16.

4. perhaps *canal, pipe.* Job 40:18 אֲפִיקֵי נְחוּשָׁה *brazen pipes.* Others, according to no. I. *robora æris, strong (bars) of brass.*

אָפִיק see אָפַק.

אָפַל an obs. root, i.q. Arab. أفل *to set,* spoken of the sun; *to become dark.* Deriv. out of course מַאְפֵּלְיָה, מַאֲפֵל, אָפֵל.

אָפֵל verbal adj. from obs. אָפַל. *dark.* Am. 5:20.

אֹפֶל m. and אֲפֵלָה, plur. אֲפֵלוֹת, f. verbal from obs. אָפַל.

1. *darkness.* Ps. 11:2. Ex. 10:22.

2. figuratively *misfortune.* Job 23:17. comp. חֹשֶׁךְ no. 2. (1.)

אֹפֶן see אוֹפָן.

אָפְנַיִם or אָפְנָיִם m. with suff. אָפְנָיו *suitable time, convenient time.* Once Prov. 25:11. (In Arab. إفّان *idem.*)

אָפֵס *to cease, fail, have an end.* Gen. 47:15, 16. Ps. 77:9. Is. 16:4.

אֶפֶס m. verbal from אָפֵס, dec. VI. a.

1. *end, extreme boundary.* אַפְסֵי אָרֶץ *the ends of the earth,* hyperbolically, for *very remote countries,* Ps. 2:8. 22:28, etc. Dual אָפְסַיִם Ezek. 47:3. according to the Chald. Syr. Vulg. *ankles.* Others: *soles of the feet.* (Comp. Chald. פַּס i.q. כַּף *vola, planta;* so אֶפֶס=כַּף.)

2. adv. *not.*—הַאֶפֶס *is there not?* 2 Sam. 9:3. בְּאֶפֶס i.q. בְּלֹא *without,* Job 7:6. Prov. 14:28. 26:20. Dan. 8:25. Also i.q. אַיִן *there is not, non est,* Deut. 32:36. Is. 5:8.

3. *nothing,* Is. 34:12. *no one,* 46:9.

4. *only.* Num. 22:35. 23:13. Is. 47. 8, 10 אֲנִי וְאַפְסִי עוֹד *I and only I further,* i.e. no one besides me. Zeph. 2:15.

5. אֶפֶס כִּי *only that, but, yet, nevertheless.* Num. 13:28. Deut. 15:4. Am. 9:8.

אֶפֶס דַּמִּים proper name of a place in the tribe of Judah. Once 1 Sam. 17:1. In 1 Chr. 11:13, פַּס דַּמִּים.

אֶפַע found only Is. 41:24 פָּעָלְכֶם מֵאָפַע according to some, *your work (is worse) than (that of) the adder,* making אֶפַע= אֶפְעֶה. But the close resemblance of this passage with verses 12, 29, renders it highly probable that the true reading is אֶפֶס. It is so rendered by the Chald. Vulg. Saad.

אֶפְעֶה m. *adder, viper, poisonous serpent.* (In Arab. أفعى *idem,* from the root فعى *tumido ore flavit,* also perhaps *sibilavit.*) Job 20:16. Is. 30:6. 59:5.

אָפַף *to compass, surround;* construed with an acc. 2 Sam. 22:5. Ps. 18:5. 116:3. Jon. 2:6. with עַל, Ps. 40:13. It retains in its inflection the double פ; thus אֲפָפוּנִי, אָפְפוּ.

אָפַק, in Kal unused, but probably signifying *to be strong.* See deriv. אָפִיק no. I. (In Arab. أفق *to excel, be distinguished,* kindred with فاق *to be superior.*)

Hithpa. literally *to make one's self strong, to take to one's self strength.* 1 Sam. 13:12 וָאֶתְאַפַּק *then I strengthened myself,* i.e. I took courage to transgress the command. Especially *to restrain one's self, to refrain, not to give vent to one's feelings,* Gen. 45:1 *Joseph could not restrain himself.* 43:31. Is. 42:14. Est. 5:10. Is. 63:15 רַחֲמֶיךָ אֵלַי הִתְאַפָּקוּ *thy love towards me restrains itself,* or *is become inactive.* 64:12.

אֲפֵק proper name.

1. a city in the tribe of Asher. Jos. 13:4. 19:30. also called אֲפִיק Judg. 1:31. The same city is probably intended 1 K. 20:26—34.

2. another city, probably in the tribe of Issachar. 1 Sam. 4:1. 29:1. comp. 28:4. Which of the two places is meant Jos. 12:18, is uncertain. Different from these is

אֲפֵקָה a city in the mountainous district of Judah. Once Jos. 15:53.

אֵפֶר m. *ashes.* Gen. 18:27. etc.

אֲפֵר m. found only 1 K. 20:38, 42. *head-band, turban, a covering for the head.* By metath. for פְּאֵר (q. v.) or else i.q. עֲטַר (א being put for ע; see א.) from עטר in Syr. Ettaph. *indutus est cum cidari.*

אֶפְרֹחַ m. (with prosth. א) dec. I. b. *a young bird.* (Comp. פִּרְחָה, and Arab. فرخ *pullus avis.*) Deut. 22:6. Ps. 84:4. It is a verbal from פָּרַח, in Hebrew signifying *to sprout,* spoken of plants; but in Arabic also *to have young,* spoken of animals.

אַפִּרְיוֹן found only Cant. 3:9. *sedan, litter, portable couch.* Sept. φορεῖον. Vulg. *ferculum.* In Syr. ܦܘܪܝܐ signifies *solium, sella, lectulus.* Concerning the א, see p. 2. In Talmudic, this word signifies *a nuptial bed.*

אֶפְרַיִם proper name.

1. Joseph's second son, who inherited equally with the sons of Jacob; hence *the tribe descended from him,* or *their territory,* the limits of which are given, Jos. 16:5—10.

2. also, the tribe of Ephraim, being the most powerful of the ten tribes, *the whole kingdom of Israel.* Hos. 12:1, etc.

Note. As the name of a country, it is of the fem. gen. Hos. 5:9.

אֲפָרְסָיֵא Chald. masc. plur. name of a people out of which a colony was brought to Samaria. Ezra 4:9. Some make them *the Parrhasii,* in the east of Media; others, *the Persians.*

אֲפַרְסְכָיֵא Ez.5:6. and **אֲפַרְסַתְכָיֵא** Ezra 4:9. Chald. masc. plur. the names, in like manner, of two nations which were in subjection to the Assyrians. The latter name has been compared with *Parasitaceni, Parætaceni,* a people of Media.

אֶפְרָת Gen. 48:7. and **אֶפְרָתָה** (penacute) Gen. 35:16, 19. Ruth 4:11.

1. proper name of a city; also called *Beth-lehem of Judah,* and *Beth-lehem Ephratah.* Mic. 5:1.

2. probably i. q. אֶפְרַיִם, Ps. 132:6.

אֶפְרָתִי a gentile noun, from אֶפְרָת.

1. *an Ephrathite.* Ruth 1:2. 1 Sam. 17:12.

2. *an Ephraimite.* 1 K. 11:26. 1 Sa. 1:1.

אַפְּתֹם Chald. found only Ezra 4:13 וְאַפְּתֹם מַלְכִים תְּהַנְזִק usually rendered, *and it shall endamage the royal treasury;* comp. verses 15, 22, in which אפתם is omitted. This explanation is destitute of etymological proof. The ancient translators only give the sense.

אֶצְבַּע f. (with prosth. א) perhaps prim. dec. II. c. (In Chald. אֶצְבַּע. Arab. اصبع, but in modern Arabic without the prosth. א.)

1. *finger.* Ex. 31:18. especially *fore-finger,* Lev. 4:6 ff. 14:16. Ex. 8. 15 אֶצְבַּע אֱלֹהִים הִוא *this is the finger of God,* i. e. God's power is here displayed. In plur. אֶצְבְּעוֹת *fingers, hand.* Ps. 8:4. 144:1.

2. with רַגְלַיִם, *toes.* 2 Sam. 21:20.

אָצִיל dec. III. a. 1. *noble, chief.* Ex. 24:11. (In Arab. أَصِيل *sprung from an ancient and noble stock;* أَصْل *root, stock, nobility.*)

2. אֲצִילֵי הָאָרֶץ Is. 41:9, *distant countries of the earth,* joined with קְצוֹת הָאָרֶץ *ends of the earth.* Probably i. q. אַצִּיל *shoulder,* applied figuratively to the earth, like יַרְכְּתַיִם, כְּנָפוֹת. Others explain this passage from no. 1.

אַצִּיל (verbal from אָצַל i. q. יָצַל= Arab. وَصَلَ *to join,*) dec. I. b. *a joining, juncture.* Hence אַצִּיל יָדַיִם *juncture of the hands,* or *of the arms,* for *the arm-pit,* or *shoulder,* Jer. 38:12. Ezek. 13:18. 41:8. The passage in Jer. particularly favours this interpretation. The other passages seem to require *wrist,* or, according to some, *the juncture of the fingers with the hand.* It is difficult to decide.

I. **אָצַל** 1. *to take back,* construed with מִן of the thing. Num. 11:17 *I will take back of the spirit.*

2. *to refuse, keep back,* construed with מִן. Ecc. 2:10 *I refused it not to them.*

3. *to reserve,* construed with לְ of the person. Gen. 27:36. (Comp. הִבְדִּיל and גָּרַע with לְ.)

Niph. *to be drawn back, to be contracted.* Ezek. 42:6.

Hiph. fut. וַיָּאצֶל, i. q. Kal. Num. 11:25.

II. **אָצַל** (acute) found only Zech. 14:5 in pause, (probably for אָצֵל,) appears to be the proper name of a place. As the proper name of a person, it stands also in pause 1 Chr. 8:33. 9:44, for אָצֵל 8:37. 9:43. If it denoted *foot of a mountain,* i. q. Arab. أصل, it would be pointed אֵצֶל, in pause אָצֶל.

אֵצֶל adv. *by the side of, by, near.* (Derived from אָצַל i. q. יָצַל=Arab. وَصَلَ *to join, unite.* Comp. אָצִיל.) With suff. אֶצְלִי etc.—מֵאֵצֶל i.q. מֵעִם *from beside, de chez,* 1 K. 3:20. 1 Sam. 20:41 מֵאֵצֶל הַנֶּגֶב *from the south.* also, the force of מִן being lost, i.q. אֵצֶל, Ezek. 40:7.

אֶצְעָדָה f. (strictly i. q. צְעָדָה, with א prosth.) *clasp, bracelet.* 2 Sam. 1:10. Num. 31:50.

אָצַר *to heap up, lay up.* 2 K. 20:17. Am. 3:10. Deriv. אוֹצָר.

Niph. pass. of Kal. Is. 23:18.

Hiph. denom. from אוֹצָר, 1 pers. fut. אוֹצְרָה Chald. for אַאֲצִירָה. *to appoint for a treasurer,* construed with עַל. Neh. 13:13.

אֶקְדָּח m. verbal from קָדַח. name of a precious stone, perhaps a *carbuncle.* Once Is. 54:12. The derivation shows it to be of a *fiery sparkling* nature.

אַקּוֹ m. prob. *wild-goat.* Once Deut. 14:5. So the Targums, 2 Arab. Syr. and many Rabbins. We may compare this name with the Arab. عَنَاق *a goat* (a Samar. MS. has עַקוֹ) and with אַקָּא *a he-goat* in the Talmud.

אֹר see **אוֹר** *light,* and **יְאֹר** *river.*

אֶרְאֶלָּם found only Is. 33:7. prob. *the heroes,* formed from אֲרִאֵל i.q. אֲרִיאֵל *a hero,* by adding the termination ־ָם, which gives the noun the force of a collective, as in קָם. Others: *their heroes,* making ־ָם a suffix, and אראל a collective.

אָרַב, fut. יֶאֱרֹב.

1. strictly *to tie, nectere,* as in Arabic. Only in deriv. אֹרְבָה, אֲרֻבָּה.

2. figuratively *to lay snares, suere dolos, κακὰ ῥάπτειν*; and particularly, *to lay wait, to lie in ambush* for any one, construed with לְ, Deut. 19:11. Prov. 1:11, 18. 24:15. with עַל, Judg. 9:34. Part. אֹרֵב *one laying wait,* collect. *a party lying in ambush, an ambush,* Jos. 8:14, 19, 21. Judg. 20:33, 36, 37, 38. sometimes with a plur. verb, verse 37 וְהָאֹרֵב הֵחִישׁוּ *the ambush hastened.* Comp. Jos. 8:12.

Pi. *idem.* Judg. 9:25.

Hiph. fut. וַיָּרֶב for וַיַּאֲרֵב, 1 Sam. 15:5. *to place an ambush.*

Deriv. out of course מַאֲרָב.

אֲרָב proper name of a city in the hilly country of Judah. Josh. 15:52. Hence the gentile noun אַרְבִּי, 2 Sa. 23:35.

אֶרֶב m. verbal from אָרַב.

1. *a laying wait.* Job 38:40.

2. *dens* or *lurking-places,* for wild beasts. Job 37:8.

אֹרֶב verbal from אָרַב, dec. VI. m. *ambush, snares, fraud.* Jer. 9:7.

אַרְבֵּאל Hos. 10:14. see בֵּית אַרְבֵּאל.

אַרְבֶּה m. (verbal from רָבָה *to multiply,*) *the locust.* Ex. 10. 4 ff. Lev. 11:22. Joel 1:4. Ps. 78:46. It is often mentioned in connexion with the various species of locusts, in which the east is so abundant, (Bocharti Hieroz. T. II. p. 447.) and then denotes a particular species, perhaps *the common migratory locust, (gryllus gregarius,* Linn.) Some suppose that the different names in Lev. xi. and Joel i. do not denote different species of locusts, but different states or conditions of the same species. But this idea is incorrect, for in Lev. 11:22 it is added, after each of these names, לְמִינוֹ *after his kind.*

אֲרֻבָּה, plur. אֲרֻבּוֹת, const. אָרְבּוֹת. Is. 25:11 *he (Jehovah) humbles his pride* עִם אָרְבּוֹת יָדָיו *and* punishes *the craft of* *his hands*, (by a natural zeugma.) Others explain אֻרְבַּת יָדַיִם *the tying, closing*, or *clinching of the hand*, i. e. the fist, as an emblem of violence.

אֲרֻבָּה f. verbal from אָרַב no. 1. dec. X. strictly a *grate, lattice.* Hence

1. *window.* Ecc. 12:3.

2. with הַשָּׁמַיִם, *windows* or *sluices of heaven*, by the opening of which showers of rain descend. Gen. 7:11. 8:2. 2 K. 7:19. Is. 24:18. Mal. 3:10.

3. *dove-hole. dove-window.* Is. 60:8.

4. *chimney, opening through which the smoke rises.* Hos. 13:3.

אֲרֻבּוֹת proper name of a place, probably in the tribe of Judah. Once 1 K. 4:10.

אַרְבַּע f. and **אַרְבָּעָה**, const. אַרְבַּעַת m. a prim. numeral. *four.* It stands for רֶבַע, the א being prosthetic, and wanting in all the derivatives; e. g. רֶבַע, רְבִיעִי, רָבַע, etc. With suff. אַרְבַּעְתָּם *they four*, Ezek. 1:8, 10. Dual אַרְבַּעְתַּיִם *fourfold*, 2 Sam. 12:6.

Plur. אַרְבָּעִים *forty.* Gen. 8:6. Like *seven* and *seventy*, it is also used by the Shemite for a round number. Comp. Gen. 7:17. Jon. 3:4. Ezek. 4:6. Matt. 4:2. So in Persian; e. g. *Chil minar*, (*forty pillars*,) a long colonnade, applied to the ruins of Persepolis.

אַרְבַּע and **עַרְבְּעָה** Chald. *idem.*

אַרְבַּע (*four*) proper name of one of the Enakite giants. Josh. 14:15. 15:13. 21:11. See קִרְיַת־אַרְבַּע.

אָרַג, fut. יֶאֱרֹג 1. *to twist.* Judg. 16:13.

2. *to weave.* Is. 59:5. Part. masc. אֹרֵג, fem. אֹרְגָה *a weaver*, Ex. 28:32. 2 K. 23:7.

אֶרֶג m. verbal from אָרַג.

1. *web.* Judg. 16:14.

2. *weaver's shuttle, radius.* Job 7:6.

אַרְגֹּב proper name of a country held by Og king of Bashan, having sixty cities. Deut. 3:4, 13. 1 K. 4:13.

אַרְגְּוָן Chald. i. q. Heb. אַרְגָּמָן *purple.* Dan. 5:7, 16, 29. (In Arab. أرجوان, Syr. ܐܪܓܘܢܐ *idem.*) Also in Hebrew. 2 Chr. 2:6.

אַרְגַּז m. *box, chest, coffer*, fixed to the side of a waggon. 1 Sam. 6:8, 11, 15. Probably from רָגַז *to shake, tremble*; whence in Arab. رجازة *a bag of stones*, which was wont to be placed on the camel's side to preserve the balance. The א is prosthetic.

אַרְגָּמָן m. *reddish purple* or *any thing coloured therewith.* Ex. xxv.—xxvii. It was obtained from a shell-fish, common on the Syrian coast, called in Greek πορφύρα, *purpura*; and is to be distinguished from the *violet* or *bluish purple*, תְּכֵלֶת (q. v.) The etymology is uncertain. Bochart (Hieroz. II. p. 740 ff.) and others consider אַרְגָּן as the original word, and as equivalent to אֲרַמְגָּן *Syrian colour*, from אֲרָם *Syria*, and ܓܘܢܐ *colour.*

אָרָה *to gather.* Cant. 5:1. With an accus. of the plant, *to strip*; e. g. the vine. Ps. 80:13. (In Ethiopic אר and ארר *idem.*)

אֲרוּ Chald. *see! behold!* Dan. 7:5,6. It is like the Arabic imper. أرو *see.* Comp. אֲלוּ.

אַרְוַד proper name. *Aradus*, a Phenician city, situated on a small island near the main land. Ezek. 27:8, 11. The gentile noun is אַרְוָדִי, Gen. 10:18. The island is now called *Ruad.*

אָרוּז adj. denom. from אֶרֶז, dec. III. c. *made of cedar.* Ezek. 27:24. According to others, i. q. Arab. أرز *firm, stable.*

אֲרוּכָה and **אֲרֻכָה** f. dec. X. (Probably a verbal from obsolete אָרַךְ = Arab. أرك *to be healed*; which has a deriv. أريكة *a binding up, a healing.*)

1. *bandage of a wound.*—הֶעֱלָה אֲרֻכָה לְ *to put a plaster* or *bandage on* any one,

Jer. 30:17. 33:6. (for the most part figuratively.) Hence passively, Jer. 8:22. עָלְתָה אֲרֻכָה *the bandage is laid on.*

2. figuratively *healing, cure, health;* the figure being generally preserved, Neh. 4:1 [7] עָלְתָה אֲרוּכָה לְחוֹמוֹת *the walls were made whole* or *repaired.* 2 Chr. 24:13. but sometimes not, Is. 58:8 אֲרֻכָתְךָ מְהֵרָה תִצְמָח *thy health shall spring forth speedily.*

אֲרוּמָה proper name of a city not far from Shechem. Once Judg. 9:41. Some compare רוּמָה 2 K. 23:36.

אֲרוֹמִים 2 K. 16:6 Kethib, for אֲרַמִּים *Syrians.* But the reading of the Keri אֲדוֹמִים *Edomites,* is to be preferred.

אָרוֹן com. (m. 1 Sam. 6:8. f. 2 Chr. 8:11.) dec. III. a. Whether the ן is radical or servile, is uncertain. If it is servile, this noun may be derived from אָרָה *to gather.*

1. *chest, box.* 2 K. 12:10, 11.—אֲרוֹן אֱלֹהִים *chest of God,* 1 Sam. 3:3. אֲרוֹן הַבְּרִית *chest of the covenant,* Josh. 3:6. and א׳ הָעֵדוּת *chest of the law,* Ex. 25:22. which are different names for *the holy chest* or *ark,* containing the tables of the law, and placed in the tabernacle, and afterwards in the temple.

2. *coffin, mummy-chest.* Gen. 50:26.

אֻרָוֹת plur. fem. const. אֻרְוֹת, 2 Chr. 32:28. 1 K. 5:6. [4:26.] and אֻרְיוֹת, const. אֻרְיוֹת, 2 Chr. 9:25. *separate stalls in a stable for large cattle,* or *the stable itself.* (Arab. إِرِيٌّ and آرِيٌّ, Aram. אוּרְיָא, אוּרְוָה and ܐܘܪܝܐ *stall, crib.*) To such a stall always belonged a certain number of horses or oxen, so that this word was also used for *the animals* themselves. (Comp. the word *team* in English.) See 1 K. 5:6. also 2 Chr. 9:25. Comp. 1 K. 10:26.

אֶרֶז m. dec. VI. a. *cedar-tree.* Lev. 14:4, 6, 49. In Chaldaic and Syriac, occurs the same word; and the inhabitants of Lebanon at the present day call this tree *ars.* In Aram. this name is applied to several similar trees; e.g. to *the pine-tree;* on which account the ancient versions differ in rendering this word. Hence *cedar wainscoting,* 1 K. 6:18. Deriv. אַרְזָה.

אַרְזָה fem. of אֶרֶז, used collectively. *cedar-work, cedar wainscoting.* Zeph. 2:14. Comp. עֵצָה fem. collect. from עֵץ.

אָרַח *to go, to travel.* Job 34:8. Part. אֹרֵחַ *travelling, a traveller.* Judg. 19:17. 2 Sam. 12:4. Jer. 9:1.

אֹרַח, plur. אֳרָחוֹת, com. gen. verbal from אָרַח, dec. VI. n.

1. *way, path,* i. q. דֶּרֶךְ. (In Hebrew it is used only in poetry. In Aram. it is the usual word.) Gen. 49:17. Judg. 5:6. and often in Job, Isaiah, Psalms, and Proverbs.

2. *traveller,* i. q. אִישׁ אֹרַח. Job 31:32. Also collectively, *a caravan,* i. q. אֹרְחָה, Job 6:19 אָרְחוֹת תֵּימָא *the caravans of Tema.*

3. figuratively *manner of conducting, conduct,* comp. דֶּרֶךְ no. 2. Ps. 17:4. 25:10.

4. *lot, fate, destiny.* Job 8:13 *such is the fate of all who forget God.* Pr. 1:19.

5. *way, manner.* Job 22:15. Also in prose, Gen. 18:11 חָדַל לִהְיוֹת לְשָׂרָה אֹרַח כַּנָּשִׁים *it had ceased to be with Sarah after the manner of women.* Comp. 31:35 דֶּרֶךְ נָשִׁים לִי *it is with me after the manner of women.*

אֹרַח, plur. אֹרְחָן, Chald. *idem.* Dan. 4:34. [37.] 5:23.

אֹרְחָה f. verbal from אָרַח, dec. X. *step, course, going.* Is. 3:12. דֶּרֶךְ אֹרְחֹתֶיךָ *the way in which thou goest.* Prov. 3:6. 9:15.

2. *company of travellers, a caravan.* Gen. 37:25. Is. 21:13.

אֲרֻחָה f. dec. X. *stated portion,* especially of food which is regularly furnished to any one, 2 K. 25:30. Jer. 52:34. *a portion* generally, Prov. 15:17 אֲרֻחַת יָרָק *a portion of herbs.* Jer. 40:5. Derived from obs. אָרַח = Arab. ارخ *to fix* the time, *to date.*

אֲרִי and אַרְיֵה (with ה ֵ parag. comp. אִשֶּׁה, הִנֵּה) m. *lion.* Is. 21:8 וַיִּקְרָא אַרְיֵה *then he cried as a lion.* Comp. Rev. 10:3. Plur. אֲרָיִים 1 K. 10:20. and

אֲרָיוֹת Judg. 14:5. The latter is also of the masc. gen. 1 K. 7:36. 10:19.

אַרְיֵה Chald. plur. אַרְיָן, m. *idem.* Dan. 6:8. 7:4.

אֲרִיאֵל m. (compounded of אֲרִי and אֵל.)

1. *lion of God,* a name which the Arabians also give to *a bold hero.* Bocharti Hieroz. I. p. 716, 757. 2 Sam. 23:20.

2. *altar of God,* (compounded of אֲרִי i. q. إِرَةٌ for إِرْيَةٌ *fire-hearth,* from أري *to burn,* and אֵל.) So the *altar of burnt-offering* is called, Ezek. 43:15, 16. and *Jerusalem,* Is. 29:1, 2, because the altar of God was there.

אַרְיוֹךְ an Assyrio-chaldean proper name.

1. a king of Ellasar. Gen. 14:1, 9.

2. a captain of the body-guard in the Chaldean court. Dan. 2:14.

אֲרָיוֹת see **אֻרְווֹת**.

אָרַךְ *to be* or *grow long.* Ezek. 31:5. Gen. 26:8 וַיְהִי כִּי אָרְכוּ־לוֹ שָׁם הַיָּמִים *when he had been there a long time.* Comp. Ezek. 12:22.

Hiph. 1. trans. *to make long, lengthen, prolong.* Here pertain the phrases: (1.) הֶאֱרִיךְ נַפְשׁוֹ Job 6:11. and אַפּוֹ Is. 48:9. Prov. 19:11. *to be patient, long-suffering.* (2.) הֶאֱרִיךְ יָמָיו *to prolong his days, to live long.* Deut. 4:26, 40. 5:30. [33.] 17:20, etc. Also without יָמִים, Prov. 28:2. Ecc. 7:15 רָשָׁע מַאֲרִיךְ בְּרָעָתוֹ *a wicked man living long in his wickedness.* 8:12. (3.) with לָשׁוֹן, *to stick out the tongue* in derision. Is. 57:4.

2. intrans. *to be long.* 1 K. 8:8. Applied to time, *to be prolonged,* הֶאֱרִיכוּ יָמָיו *his days are prolonged, he lives long,* Ex. 20:12. Deut. 5:16. 6:2. 25:15.

3. *to tarry, delay;* strictly, *to make it long.* Num. 9:19, 22.

אֲרַךְ Chald. *idem.* But part. אָרִיךְ *meet, suitable.* (So in Talmud אָרַךְ i. q. עָרַךְ *to fit, adjust.*) Ezra 4:14.

אָרֵךְ verbal adj. from אָרַךְ, dec. V. c. found only in the const. state אֶרֶךְ. *long.* Ezek. 17:3 אֶרֶךְ הָאֵבֶר *with long feathers.* Ecc. 7:8 אֶרֶךְ רוּחַ *long-suffering.* Besides these, only in the common phrase אֶרֶךְ אַפַּיִם *long-suffering,* Ex. 34:6, etc. Jer. 15:15 אַל לְאֶרֶךְ אַפְּךָ תִּקָּחֵנִי *take me not away by being long-suffering,* i. e. through thy long-suffering (towards my enemies). לְאֶרֶךְ stands here for לִהְיוֹת אֶרֶךְ.

אֶרֶךְ proper name. Found only Gen. 10:10. According to the Targums, Jerome, and Ephrem Syrus, *Edessa,* in Mesopotamia, now called *Ourfa.* See Michaëlis Spicileg. Geogr. T. I. p. 220 ff. The gentile noun אַרְכִּי 2 Sam. 15:32. 16:16. may refer to this place; as also, with more certainty, the Chald. אַרְכְּוָיֵא Ezra 4:9.

אֹרֶךְ m. verbal from אָרַךְ, dec. VI. m. *length.* Gen. 6:15. with יָמִים, *length of life,* Ps. 21:5. לְאֹרֶךְ יָמִים *one's life long,* 23:6.

אָרֹךְ, fem. אֲרֻכָּה verbal adj. from אָרַךְ. *long, lasting.* 2 Sam. 3:1. Job 11:9.

אַרְכָּה f. Chald. *lengthening, prolongation.* Dan. 4:24. [27.] 7:12.

אֲרֻכָה see **אֲרוּכָה**.

אַרְכֻּבָה f. Chald. *knee.* Dan. 5:6. In the Targums, without prosthetic א, רְכוּבָא, רְכוּב by metath. i. q. Heb. בֶּרֶךְ.

אֲרָם f. *Aramea, Syria,* and (as masc.) *the Syrians,* 1 K. 20:26. This name, which in its widest sense includes Mesopotamia, was known also to the Greeks, at least as the name of a people, Ἄριμοι, Ἀραμαῖοι. See Strabo, XIII. p. 627. XVI. p. 785.—According to Gen. 10:22, Aram was a son of Shem; and in chap. 22:21, the same name is given to one of his remote descendants, the son of Nahor. The different parts of Aramea are distinguished thus, (1.) אֲרַם נַהֲרַיִם *Syria of the two rivers, the land between the Tigris and Euphrates, Mesopotamia,* Gen. 24:10. also called פַּדַּן אֲרָם *the plain of Syria,* Gen. 25:20. 28:2, 5, 6, 7. 31:18. (2.) אֲרַם צוֹבָה *Syria of Zobah,* a kingdom, north-east of Damascus, frequently engaged in war with Israel. See צוֹבָה.

(3.) אֲרַם דַּמֶּשֶׂק *Syria of Damascus.* (4.) אֲרַם בֵּית־רְחוֹב *Syria of Beth-rehob,* 2 Sam. 10:6, its capital רְחֹבוֹת הַנָּהָר on an arm of the Euphrates.

אֲרַמִּי, fem. ־ִית a gentile noun, from אֲרָם, *an Aramean, Syrian.* Plur. אֲרַמִּים 2 K. 8:29.

אֲרָמִי *idem;* but found only in the fem. אֲרָמִית an adv. *in Aramean, in the Aramean,* i.e. the Syrian or Chaldaic, *language.* Dan. 2:4. Ezra 4:7.

אַרְמוֹן m. Plur. אַרְמְנוֹת, const. אַרְמְנוֹת (from an obs. sing. form אַרְמֶן.) Probably derived from אָרַם i.q. Arab. وَرِمَ and Heb. רוּם *to be high.*

1. *palace.* Is. 25:2. Jer. 30:18. Am. 1:4, 7, 10, 12, etc.

2. In 1 K. 16:18. 2 K. 15:25, it must be *a part* of the royal citadel or palace; hence אַרְמוֹן בֵּית הַמֶּלֶךְ perhaps *the harem of the royal palace.* (So we use *seraglio* sometimes for the whole royal residence, and sometimes for the harem.)

אֹרֶן m. name of a tree. Once Is. 44:14. Usually rendered (on account of the similarity of the names, which in plants is of considerable weight,) *ornus, an ash.* But according to Celsius (Hierobot. P. I. p. 192.) i. q. Arab. أُرَانٌ a prickly tree of Arabia Petrea, producing berries in clusters, which at first are green and bitter, but afterwards of a dark red colour, and which are used as a medicine. The same names, however, have sometimes different significations in the different dialects.

אַרְנֶבֶת (in Arab. أَرْنَبٌ) f. epicene. prim. *hare.* Only Lev. 11:6. Deut. 14:7.

אַרְנוֹן a brook and valley of the same name, forming the northern boundary of the country of Moab. Num. 21:13. Deut. 3:8, 12, 16. 4:48. According to Seetzen, its present name is *Mujeb.*

אַרְעָא, אֲרַע, Chald.

1. *the earth,* i. q. Heb. אֶרֶץ. Dan. 2:35. Jer. 10:11. Concerning the interchange of ע and צ, see the letter ע.

2. adv. *below;* with מִן, *lower than, inferior to.* Dan. 2:39. Hence the grammatical expression מִלְּרַע for מִלְּאַרַע (*accented*) *below,* i. e. on the last syllable, ὀξύτονον. Hence

אַרְעִי Chald. adj. from אֲרַע *low.* Fem. ־ִית *what is low, the bottom.* Dan. 6:25.

אַרְפָּד a city and country in Syria, near Hamath, with which it is often joined, and which for a time had its own kings. 2 K. 18:34. 19:13. Is. 10:9. Jer. 49:23. Some confound it with אַרְוַד (q. v.)

אַרְפַּכְשַׁד Gen. 10:22, 24. 11:12, 13. name of a son of Shem. The names of his brethren are most of them also names of countries. If this is the case with Arphaxad, the most probable supposition is that of Josephus, that it denotes *Chaldea.* It may be compounded of ארף, Arab. أَرْفٌ *limits, territory,* and כֶּשֶׂד the root from which comes כַּשְׂדִּי *Chaldean.* The name of Chesed was preserved in the family of Arphaxad, see Gen. 22:22.

אֶרֶץ com. gen. (masc. rarely, Gen. 13:6. Is. 9:18.) prim. dec. VI. b.

1. *earth;* also *inhabitants of the earth,* Gen. 6:11. 11:1.

2. *land;* e. g. אֶרֶץ מִצְרַיִם *the land of Egypt.*—Sometimes, by way of eminence, *Palestine,* Joel 1:2.—אַרְצִי *my land,* says the Hebrew, for *my native country,* Jon. 1:8. Gen. 30:25.

3. *jurisdiction of a city.* Josh. 8:1.

Plur. אֲרָצוֹת *lands.* Gen. 10:5, 20, 31. In the later Hebrew style, אֲרָצוֹת denotes *other lands, heathen lands,* in opposition to Palestine, (as גּוֹיִם *other nations, gentile nations;*) e. g. עַמֵּי הָאֲרָצוֹת *the people of* (*other*) *lands,* 2 Chr. 13:9. 32:13, 17. 2 K. 18:35. Ezra 9:1, 2, 11. Neh. 9:30. 10:29. מַמְלְכוֹת הָאֲרָצוֹת *the kingdoms of* (*other*) *lands,* 1 Chr. 29:30. 2 Chr. 12:8. 17:10. comp.

Ezra 9 : 7. In Ezekiel and several passages of Jeremiah we see this usage in its origin, comp. Ezek. 5 : 6. 11 : 17. 12 : 15. 20 : 23. 22 : 15. especially 20 : 32. 22 : 4.—With ה local, אַרְצָה *to the earth*, freq. In some places the He is only paragogic, and אַרְצָה i. q. אֶרֶץ, Job 31 : 13. 37 : 12. Is. 8 : 23. The accent on the penult shows that it is not a feminine form.

אֲרַק Chald. i. q. אֲרַע, (the ע, which the ancients sometimes pronounced like *g* hard, being commuted into ק.) *earth*. Once Jer. 10 : 11. In the Targums frequent.

אָרַר *to curse, execrate*, construed with an acc. Gen. 12 : 3. 27 : 29. Job 3 : 8 אֹרְרֵי יוֹם *those who curse the day*, i. e. magicians, to whose execrations a certain efficacy was attributed. Imper. אָרָה Num. 22 : 6. 23 : 7.

Niph. part. נֵאָר Mal. 3 : 9, after the form נָחַל.

Pi. אֵרַר 1. i. q. Kal. Gen. 5 : 29.

2. *to bring a curse*. Num. 5 : 22 ff. הַמַּיִם הַמְאָרְרִים *the waters bringing a curse.*

Hoph. pass. Num. 22 : 6.

Deriv. מְאֵרָה.

אֲרָרַט a province of Armenia, (between the Araxes and the lakes Van and Ormias,) still having this name among the Armenians. Is. 37 : 38. Jer. 51 : 27.—הָרֵי אֲרָרָט *mountains of Ararat* or *Armenia*, Gen. 8 : 4.

אָרַשׂ found only in Pi. אֵרַשׂ, in full אֵרַשׂ לוֹ אִשָּׁה *to purchase for one's self*, or *betroth a wife*. Deut. 20 : 7. 28 : 30. Hos. 2 : 21, 22. [2 : 19, 20.] The price of purchase is preceded by בְּ, 2 Sam. 3 : 14. (In Chald. אֲרַס *idem.*)

Pu. אֹרַשׂ *to be betrothed*, spoken of a maiden. Ex. 22 : 15.

אֲרֶשֶׁת f. found only Ps. 21 : 3. *request, desire*. Sept. δέησις. Vulg. *voluntas*. Derived from אָרַשׁ i. q. Arab. وَرِشَ *to desire.*

אַרְתַּחְשַׁשְׂתָּא Ezra 4 : 8, 11, 23, אַרְתַּחְשַׁסְתְּא 7 : 7, and אַרְתַּחְשַׁשְׂתָּא 4 : 7, *Artaxerxes*, a king of the Persians. This name is derived from the ancient Persian *Artahshetr* (ארתחשתר,) which is found upon the inscriptions of Nakschi-Roustam. The latter part of this word is the Zendish *khshethro*, also *sherao*, (*king.*) But the syllable *art*, (which is found in several Persian names, e. g. *Artabanus, Artaphernes, Artabazus,*) appears to have signified *to be great*, or *mighty :* at least the Greeks gave it this interpretation. Thus Hesychius: Ἀρταῖοι, οἱ ἥρωες, παρὰ Πέρσαις. Comp. Alberti on this passage: P. I. p. 552. Steph. Byzant. de Urbib. p. 173. Reland de Veteri Lingua Pers. § 23. In accordance with this, Herodotus (VI. 98.) explains, Ἀρταξέρξης by μέγας ἀρήιος. This signification is now lost in the Persian. —Out of that original *Artashetr*, the modern Persians formed *Ardeshir*, اردهشير, also اردشير, (a name borne by three kings of the dynasty of the Sassanides;) the Armenians, *Artashir;* the Greeks, *Artaxerxes;* the Hebrews, *Artachshashta*. See Silv. de Sacy Mémoires sur diverses Antiquités de la Perse. (Paris, 1793.) p. 32, 100, 111.

אֵשׁ com. gen. (masc. rarely, e. g. Job 20 : 26. Ps. 104 : 4.) prim. with suff. אֶשְׁכֶם, אִשִּׁי.

1. *fire*—אֵשׁ הָאֱלֹהִים *fire of God, lightning*, Job 1 : 16. Figuratively *the scorching heat of the sun*, Joel 1 : 19, 20.

2. *shining, glittering;* e. g. of steel, Nah. 2 : 4.

אֶשָּׁא, emph. אֶשָּׁא, Chald. *idem*. Dan. 7 : 11.

אִשׁ 2 Sam. 14 : 19. Mic. 6 : 10. for אִישׁ (with prosth. א) i. q. יֵשׁ *there is*. Concerning the prosth. א, comp. Chald. אִיתַי, and see p. 2.

אֹשׁ, plur. אֻשַּׁיָּא, Chald. *foundation*. Only Ezra 4 : 12. 5 : 16. 6 : 3.

אֶשֶׁד m. *the pouring out, running down*. (Comp. Aram. ܐܫܕ *fudit, effudit.*) Num. 21 : 15 אֶשֶׁד הַנְּחָלִים *the running down of the brooks*, perhaps *the lower* *countries amidst brooks.* See the following article.

אֲשֵׁדָה, plur. אַשְׁדוֹת, *the foot of a mountain.* Josh. 10:40. 12:8.—אַשְׁדוֹת הַפִּסְגָּה *the foot of Pisgah,* Deut. 3:17. 4:49. Strictly, *the place where torrents run down and collect.* See אָשַׁד.

אַשְׁדּוֹד *Ashdod,* one of the five principal cities of the Philistines, in Greek Ἄζωτος. Josh. 11:22. 15:46. 1 Sam. 5:1. There is now at this place a village called *Esdud* or *Atzud.* The gentile noun is אַשְׁדּוֹדִי, fem. ־ִית; the latter being also used adverbially, *in Ashdoditish, in the dialect of Ashdod,* Neh. 13:24.

אִשֶּׁה m. const. אִשֵּׁה; Plur. const. אִשֵּׁי. (strictly i.q. אֵשׁ *fire,* with parag. ־ֶה, comp. אֲרִי, אַרְיֵה, עֶשְׂרֵה,) a word peculiar to the ritual service, *firing, something on fire, an offering.* It is a generic word, and includes every species of offering. In Lev. 24:7, it is applied to the incense scattered on the shew-bread, though not burnt; and in verse 9, the shew-bread itself is reckoned among the אִשֵּׁי יְהוָה. It occurs most frequently at the close of a ritual precept in this phrase רֵיחַ נִיחוֹחַ אִשֶּׁה לַיהוָה הוּא *a sweet savour, an offering (acceptable) to Jehovah is this,* Ex. 29:18, 25, 41. or אִשֵּׁה רֵיחַ נִיחוֹחַ לַיהוָה *an offering of a sweet savour unto Jehovah,* Lev. 1:9, 13, 17. 2:2. 3:5. Num. 15:10, 13, 14, etc. Besides very frequently in the plural אִשֵּׁי יְהוָה Lev. 2:3, 10. 6:10, 11. [6:17, 18.]

אִשָּׁה (for אִנְשָׁה fem. of אֱנוֹשׁ) irreg. const. אֵשֶׁת (for אִישֶׁת fem. of אִישׁ) with suff. אִשְׁתִּי. אִשְׁתְּךָ; Plur. once אִשּׁוֹת (Ezek. 23:44.) usually נָשִׁים by aphaer. for אֲנָשִׁים.)

1. *woman.*—Applied as a designation of sex, even in animals, Gen. 7:2. Frequently for *wife,* hence אֵשֶׁת אָב *father's wife,* i.e. a stepmother, Lev. 18:8. comp. 1 Cor. 5:1.

2. It often stands with genitives denoting quality, as אֵשֶׁת חֵן *a lovely woman,* Prov. 11:16. אֵשֶׁת חַיִל *a woman of firmness* or *integrity,* Ruth 3:11. אֵשֶׁת מִדְיָנִים *a contentious woman, Zankerin,* Prov. 27:15. Also in apposition, as אִשָּׁה זוֹנָה *a harlot,* Josh. 2:1. אִשָּׁה נְבִיאָה *a prophetess,* Judg. 4:4. אִשָּׁה אַלְמָנָה *a widow,* 1 K. 7:14.

3. with אֲחוֹת (*sister,*) and רְעוּת *female companion*) for *the one.... the other.* See these articles.

4. *some one.*

5. *every one.* Ex. 3:22.

Note. The form אֵשֶׁת occurs sometimes for the absolute state, Ps. 58:9. Deut. 21:11. 1 Sam. 28:7.

אֶשָּׁה f. i.q. אֵשׁ *fire.* This is the best explanation of the Kethib in Jer. 6:29 מֵאֶשְׁתָּם עֹפָרֶת *by their fire the lead (is consumed).* The Keri has the more easy reading מֵאֵשׁ תַּם ע' *by the fire is consumed the lead.*

אֲשׁוּיָה see **אֲשִׁיָּה.**

אֱשׁוּן m. Prov. 20:20 Keri, according to Chaldee usage, *time,* or perhaps *obscurity.* It is an explanation of the more difficult, but more poetical reading אִישׁוֹן (q. v.)

אֲשֻׁר f. verbal from אָשַׁר, dec. I.

1. *step, walk, course.* Prov. 14:15. Job 23:11. See אָשַׁר no. 1.

2. Ezek. 27:6, according to the explanation most generally adopted, i.q. תְּאַשּׁוּר which is usually interpreted *box-tree;* hence in our passage שֵׁן בַּת־אֲשֻׁרִים *ivory, daughter of the box-wood,* i.e. ivory set in box-wood. So in Virgil, *ebur inclusum buxo.* Æn. x. 137. Simonis, in his Lexicon, compares the Arab. أَشَرَ *incidit striatim.* أُشُورٌ *striæ;* and translates thus, *ebur, filia striarum,* i.e. ivory in stripes or streaks.

אַשּׁוּר 1. f. verbal from אָשַׁר dec. I. b. *step, walk, course.* Job 31:7. See אָשַׁר, no. 1.

2. proper name. *Assyria* and *Assyrians,* (in the former sense, fem. in the latter, masc. e.g. Is. 19:23.) Gen. 10:10, 22. 2 K. xv—xx. etc. In a wider sense, the name *Assyria* embraces *Babylonia,* (comp. Herod. I. 106.) on account of the close connexion which often existed between these two countries.

The kingdom of Persia is also so called; comp. Ezra 6 : 22, where Darius is called King of Assyria. Comp. also Num. 24 : 22, 24. That the classics often confound the names *Syria* and *Assyria*, does not apply here, since the eastern nations kept these names distinct. See Bocharti Phaleg. lib. II. cap. 3.

3. אַשּׁוּרִם plur. name of an Arabian tribe. Once Gen. 25 : 3.

אָשְׁיָה f. dec. X. *support*. Once Jer. 50:15 Keri. (Comp. Arab. أسية *pillar, support*.) In the Chald. Syr. Vulg. *foundations*. In Kethib אָשְׁוִיָּה, a form similar to that of many Arabic words.

אֲשִׁימָא 2 K. 17 : 30, an idol of the people of Hamath. According to an uncertain tradition of the Jews, it was in the form of a bald he-goat.

אֲשֵׁרָה see **אֲשֵׁירָה**.

אֲשִׁישׁ m. found only Is. 16 : 7 אֲשִׁישֵׁי קִיר־חֲרֶשֶׂת in C. V. *the foundations of Kir-hareseth*. Comp. Chald. אֹשׁ, אֻשִּׁין, and Arab. أسيس *foundation* from أسس *to found*. But in the parallel passage of a subsequent writer, Jer. 48 : 31, instead of this word stands אַנְשֵׁי. This may be regarded as an explanation of the original word in Isaiah, as is often the case in such changes, then is אִישֵׁי=אֲשִׁישֵׁי or אַנְשֵׁי. Comp. הִתְאֹשָׁשׁוּ *show yourselves men*, Is. 46 : 8. under art. אִשׁ.

אֲשִׁישָׁה f. Plur. ־ִים and ־וֹת. *a cake, libum;* in full Hos. 3 : 1 אֲשִׁישֵׁי עֲנָבִים *a cake* or *hardened sirup made of grapes*, here in reference to the worship of idols, but in other places as a refreshment, Cant. 2 : 5, particularly on a journey, 2 Sam. 6 : 19. 1 Chr. 16 : 3. (according to the Sept. in Samuel, *a pan-cake*, and in 1 Chr. *a honey-cake*.) In the Chaldee version by Pseudo-Jonathan, אֶשְׁיָתָא is used Ex. 16 : 31, for the Hebrew צַפִּיחִת *cakes;* and in the Mishnah (apud Surenhus. T. III. p. 125.) the same word denotes a kind of lentile-cake.—Some derive אֲשִׁישָׁה from אֵשׁ *fire*, namely, a *fire-cake;* but the signification is more certain, than the etymology.

אֶשֶׁךְ m. *testicle*. Lev. 21 : 20. (In Syr. ܐܫܟܐ *idem*.)

אֶשְׁכֹּל (with prosth. א). Plur. אֶשְׁכְּלוֹת and אַשְׁכְּלוֹת (as if from an obs. sing. אַשְׁכָּל, comp. אַרְמוֹן.)

1. strictly *the stem* or *stalk on which berries or flowers grow in clusters, racemus*, spoken of the vine and other similar plants; e. g. of the plant called by Arabians *alhenna*, Cant. 1 : 14 אֶשְׁכֹּל הַכֹּפֶר *a cluster of alhenna*. of the palm, or date-tree, 7 : 8 *clusters* (*of dates*). of a vine-stem with flowers and unripe grapes, Gen. 40 : 10 הִבְשִׁילוּ אַשְׁכְּלֹתֶיהָ עֲנָבִים literally *the unripe clusters ripened into ripe grapes*. So the Latin *racemus* stands for *unripe grapes*. Virg. Georg. lib. II. l. 60. On account of this extended use of the word, in order to restrict its meaning to *clusters of the vine*, it is followed sometimes by הַגֶּפֶן, Cant. 7 : 9. or עֲנָבִים, Num. 13 : 23.

2. without addition, *grapes*, Is. 65 : 8. Mic. 7 : 1.

3. proper name of a valley in the land of Canaan. Num. 13 : 23, 24. 32 : 9. Deut. 1 : 24.

אַשְׁכְּנַז Gen. 10 : 3. Jer. 51 : 27. a people of northern Asia, as appears from their being joined with Gomer (the Cimmerians) in the first passage, and with Ararat a province of Armenia in the second; otherwise unknown. The modern Jews understand *Germany* (!) and use the word with this signification.

אֶשְׁכָּר m. (with prosth. א) *gift, present*. Only Ezek. 27 : 15. Ps. 72 : 10. Derived from שָׁכַר=Arab. شكر *to give thanks, to reward, to make a present* to any one.

אֵשֶׁל i. q. Arab. أثل a species of tamarisk, which grows to the height of a middling-sized tree, is prickly, and on the knots of the branches bears small yellowish brown berries of the size of a pea, *tamarix orientalis*, Linn. Only Gen. 21:33. 1 Sam. 22:6. 31:13. In the parallel passage 1 Chr. 10:12, instead of אֵשֶׁל stands אֵלָה *a turpentine-tree.* How the two passages are to be reconciled does not appear.

I. **אָשַׁם** and **אָשֵׁם**, fut. יֶאְשַׁם. (In Arab. أثم.)

1. *to be in fault, to be guilty.* Lev. 4:13, 22, 27. 5:2, 3. Construed with לְ of the person, whom one has injured, Num. 5:7 לַאֲשֶׁר אָשַׁם לוֹ *to him whom he has injured.* So with לַיהוָה, Lev. 5:19. 2 Chr. 19:10. The thing wherein one has sinned is preceded by לְ, Lev. 5:5. by בְּ, Hos. 13:1. Ezek. 25:12.

2. *to feel one's self guilty.* Hos. 5:15. Zech. 11:5.

3. *to suffer* or *be punished for sin.* (In Arab. أثم.) Ps. 34:22, 23. Is. 24:6. Prov. 30:10. Hos. 14:1.

Niph. i. q. Kal no. 3. Joel 1:18.

Hiph. *to cause to suffer, to punish.* Ps. 5:11.

II. **אָשַׁם** i. q. שָׁמֵם and שָׁמַם *to be laid waste* or *destroyed.* Ezek. 6:6.

אָשֵׁם verbal adj. from אָשַׁם, dec. V. b.

1. *guilty.* Gen. 42:21. 2 Sam. 14:13.

2. *one who presents a trespass-offering.* Ezra 10:19. (Comp. חַטָּא.)

אָשָׁם m. verbal from אָשַׁם, dec. IV. c.

1. *guilt, guiltiness.* Gen. 26:10. Jer. 51:5. Ps. 68:22.

2. *damage* or *injury done to another.* Num. 5:7, 8.

3. *trespass-offering.* Lev. 5:6, 7, 15, 25. [6:6.] 1 Sam. 6:3. 2 K. 12:17. Is. 53:10. The Hebrew ritual made a distinction between חַטָּאת *a sin-offering,* and אָשָׁם a *trespass-offering.* The ceremonies accompanying them were somewhat different. See concerning the former, Lev. 6:18—23. [25—30.] concerning the latter, 7:1—10. The law specified the particular cases in which a trespass-offering should be brought; though no generic distinction has yet been discovered between the two classes of sins. In one case a lamb of a year old was brought for a trespass-offering, and another lamb for a sin-offering at the same time, Lev. 14:10—19. The opinion, that the trespass-offering was for sins of omission, and the sin-offering for sins of commission, cannot be supported; comp. Lev. 5:17—19. Other distinctions, which have been thought of, are not more satisfactory. Comp. Warnekros hebr. Alterthümer, p. 151—155. Bauer's gottesdienstliche Verfassung der Hebräer. Th. I. p. 146.

אַשְׁמָה f. verbal from אָשַׁם, dec. XII. a.

1. i. q. infin. of אָשַׁם, (comp. יִרְאָה, אַהֲבָה.) Lev. 5:26 [6:7] לְאַשְׁמָה בָהּ *to be guilty therein.* Comp. 4:3 לְאַשְׁמַת הָעָם *so that the people is guilty.*

2. *guilt, guiltiness.* 1 Chr. 21:3. 2 Chr. 24:18. 28:10. Ezra 9:7. 10:10. Am. 8:14 אַשְׁמַת שֹׁמְרוֹן *the sin of Samaria,* i. e. his idols. 2 Chr. 28:13 לְאַשְׁמַת יְהוָה עָלֵינוּ *to bring upon us guilt against Jehovah.*

3. *trespass-offering,* or rather *the presenting of a trespass-offering,* (also i. q. infin.) Lev. 6:5 בְּיוֹם אַשְׁמָתוֹ *on the day in which he brings a trespass-offering.* Comp. adj. אָשֵׁם no. 2. also אֲפֻדָּה no. 1.

אַשְׁמַנִּים plur. masc. *deep night, darkness.* Once Is. 59:10. (In Syr. ܐܘܛܡܢܐ *idem.*) So Gesenius in his Lexicon; but in his Commentary on Isaiah (Leip. 1820) he has adopted a different interpretation, namely *fat fields, fertile fields,* from comparing שְׁמָנִים and מִשְׁמַנִּים (q. v.)

אַשְׁמֻרָה f. (verbal from שָׁמַר *to watch*) const. אַשְׁמֹרֶת; Plur. אַשְׁמֻרוֹת. *a watch of the night, vigilia,* φυλακή. It appears from Judg. 7:19, where the *middle* watch is spoken of, that the Hebrews, in more ancient times, counted only 3 watches. The first is רֹאשׁ אַשְׁמֻרוֹת Lam. 2:19. the last, אַשְׁמֹרֶת הַבֹּקֶר Ex. 14:24. Sam. 11:11. In the N. T. four night-watches are mentioned, which may have been a Roman custom.

אֶשְׁנָב m. with prosth. א, (verbal

from obs. שָׁנַב = Arab. شَنِبَ *to be cool*, spoken of the air.) dec. VIII. *lattice-window*, for the admission of cool air. Judg. 5:28. Prov. 7:6.

אַשָּׁף m. dec. I. b. *magician, astrologer*. Dan. 1:20. 2:2. In Syr. ܐܫܘܦܐ *idem*.

אָשַׁף m. Chald. Plur. אָשְׁפִין, emph. אָשְׁפַיָּא. *idem*. Dan. 2:10, 27. 4:4. [7.] 5:7.

I. אַשְׁפָּה f. dec. X. *quiver*. Job 39:23. Is. 22:6. 49:2.—בְּנֵי אַשְׁפָּתוֹ *sons of the quiver, arrows*, Lam. 3:13.

II. אַשְׁפָּה found only in the plur. אַשְׁפּוֹת *dung, dunghill*. Ps. 113:7. 1 Sam. 2:8. Hence שַׁעַר הָאַשְׁפּוֹת Neh. 2:13. 3:14. 12:31. and (the א being suppressed, comp. Ecc. 4:13.) שַׁעַר הַשְּׁפוֹת Neh. 3:13. *the dung-gate*. The singular occurs in the Mishnah, (T. III. p. 80. IV. p. 133, 178. ed. Surenhus.) and from T. IV. p. 133. it appears that its proper signification was *fimetum*. Comp. אַשְׁפֹּת.

אֶשְׁפָּר found only 2 Sam. 6:19. 1 Chr. 16:3. From the connexion, probably a certain kind of food. Vulg. *a roasting of beef*, deriving it perhaps from אֵשׁ *fire*, and פַּר *bull*. Syr. and Chald. *a piece of flesh*. The etymology is very obscure. From the root שָׁפַר *to be beautiful*, it could denote *a small ornament*, or the like.

אַשְׁפֹּת f. i. q. אַשְׁפָּה no. II. found only in the plur. אַשְׁפַּתּוֹת *dung, mire*. Lam. 4:5 *they embrace dunghills*, i.e. they lie in the dust. Comp. Job 24:8. The plural is formed without losing the ת, as in דֶּלֶת *door*, plur. דְּלָתוֹת; comp. שְׁנָת.

אַשְׁקְלוֹן *Askelon*, one of the five princely cities of the Philistines, situated on the Mediterranean Sea. 1 Sam. 6:17. The gentile noun is אֶשְׁקְלוֹנִי, Josh. 13:3. There is now in its place a village called *Ascalan*.

אָשַׁר strictly i. q. יָשַׁר *to be straight*. Hence

1. *to go straight*, (comp. Pi.) *to go, to proceed*. Prov. 9:6. Comp. the deriv. אַשּׁוּר and אֲשׁוּר.

2. *to be right, suitable*; hence *to be successful, prosperous*. Comp. יָשַׁר Hab. 2:4. and כָּשֵׁר.

Pi. 1. *to lead* or *guide straight*, Prov. 23:19. Is. 1:17. *to guide* generally, Is. 3:12 מְאַשְּׁרֶיךָ מַתְעִים *thy guides are seducers*. 9:15.

2. intrans. i. q. Kal, *to go*. Prov. 4:14.

3. *to pronounce happy, to bless*. Gen. 30:13. Job 29:11. Mal. 3:12, 15.

Pu. אֻשַּׁר and אֻשָּׁר.

1. *to be guided*. Is. 9:15.

2. *to be pronounced happy*, hence *to be happy*. Ps. 41:3. Prov. 3:18.

אָשֵׁר m. proper name.

1. a son of Jacob, progenitor of one of the tribes of Israel. The territory of this tribe lies along the sea-coast in the north of Palestine. See Josh. 19:24—31. The gentile noun is אָשֵׁרִי, Judg. 1:32.

2. a city not far from Shechem. Josh. 17:7.

אֶשֶׁר *happiness, prosperity*; found only in the plur. const. אַשְׁרֵי *the happiness of*, i.e. prosperity to (any one), Ps. 1:1. 2:12. 32:1, 2. 33:12. Prov. 3:13. 8:34. With suff. אַשְׁרֶיךָ *prosperity to thee*, Deut. 33:29. אַשְׁרֵךְ for אַשְׁרַיִךְ, Ecc. 10:17. אַשְׁרָיו *prosperity to him*, Prov. 14:21. The punctuation of אַשְׁרֶיךָ, אַשְׁרָיו is irregular, for אֲשָׁרֶיךָ, אֲשָׁרָיו, like פִּלַגְשִׁים from פִּילֶגֶשׁ.

אֲשֶׁר 1 pron. relat. indecl. of both genders and numbers, *who, qui, quæ, quod; qui, quæ, quæ*.—When preceded by prepositions, it includes its antecedent; as לַאֲשֶׁר *to him, her*, or *them who*; מֵאֲשֶׁר *from him*, etc. *who*. The idea of *place* or *time* is also sometimes involved in this antecedent; as אֶל אֲשֶׁר *to the place where*.

2. this pronoun is often merely a sign of relation, which gives to other pronouns and to adverbs the force of relatives, (as אֵי no. 2. gives them the force of interrogatives.) Thus אֲשֶׁר־שָׁם *where*,

(from שָׁם *there;*) אֲשֶׁר־מִשָּׁם *whence,* (from מִשָּׁם *thence;*) אֲשֶׁר־שָׁמָּה *whither,* (from שָׁמָּה *thither.*) Most generally these words are separated by the intervention of one or more words, as in Gen. 13:3 *to the place* אֲשֶׁר־הָיָה שָׁם אָהֳלֹה *where his tent had been.* Gen. 20:13. but sometimes immediately connected, as in 2 Chr. 6:11. When joined with the oblique cases of the pronouns, it forms oblique cases of the relative, as אֲשֶׁר־לוֹ *to whom,* (from לוֹ *to him;*) אֲשֶׁר אוֹתָם *whom, quos;* אֲשֶׁר בּוֹ *wherein;* אֲשֶׁר מִמֶּנּוּ *from whom, whence;* אֲשֶׁר בְּאַרְצָם *in quorum terrâ;* אֲשֶׁר־תַּחַת־כְּנָפָיו *under whose wings,* Ruth 2:12. The Swiss dialect has something similar, using the particle *wo* (*where*) as a sign of relation; e.g. *the stranger where thou hast eaten with him,* for *the stranger with whom thou hast eaten.* Comp. *whence* and *thence* in English.

3. אֲשֶׁר לְ (*which belongs to*) sometimes serves for a periphrasis of the sign of the genitive case, especially where two genitives follow in succession, the latter of which is then expressed by אֲשֶׁר לְ; as 1 Sa. 21:8 אַבִּיר הָרֹעִים אֲשֶׁר לְשָׁאוּל *the overseer of the shepherds of Saul.* 2 Sam. 2:8 שַׂר־צָבָא אֲשֶׁר לְשָׁאוּל *the general of Saul's armies.* Cant. 1:1 שִׁיר הַשִּׁירִים אֲשֶׁר לִשְׁלֹמֹה *a song of the songs of Solomon.* Comp. 1 Sam. 17:40 כְּלִי הָרֹעִים אֲשֶׁר לוֹ *his shepherd's pouch.* 1 K. 15:20 שָׂרֵי הַחֲיָלִים אֲשֶׁר־לוֹ *the captains of his forces.* In these last cases suffixes might otherwise stand. In the later writings, in which שֶׁ (q.v.) took the place of אֲשֶׁר, שֶׁל became the usual sign of the genitive case, as in Aram. דִּי, דְּ, דִּ and before suff. דִּיל, ܕܝܠ.

4. אֲשֶׁר is also used as an adv. or conjunction, like the Greek ὅτι and Lat. *quod;* and signifies (1.) *that, to the end that, ut;* construed with a future. Gen. 11:7. Deut. 4:40. (2.) *that, how that, quod.* Ex. 11:7. Comp. the more full expressions, such as שָׁמַעְנוּ אֵת אֲשֶׁר־הוֹבִישׁ יְהוָה *we have heard how that Jehovah has dried up,* Jos. 2:10. 1 Sam. 24:19. 2 Sam. 11:20. 2 K. 8:12. Deut. 29:15. (3.) *because.* Gen. 34:27. 1 K. 8:33. especially when compounded thus, עַל אֲשֶׁר, יַעַן אֲשֶׁר. (4.) *if.* Lev. 4:22. Deut. 11:27. (5.) *for.* Deut. 3:24. Gen. 31:49. Zech. 1:15. (6.) *when.* 2 Chr. 35:20. (7.) *as.* 1 K. 8:39. Jer. 33:22. (8.) *where.* Num. 20:13.

5. בַּאֲשֶׁר (1.) *in the place where, where,* (see above no. 1.) Ruth 1:17. *whither,* 1 Sam. 23:13. (2.) *because.* Gen. 39:9, 23.

6. כַּאֲשֶׁר (1.) *according to what, as.* Gen. 7:9. 34:12. (2.) *as if.* Job 10:19. (3.) *because.* Num. 27:14. Mic. 3:4. (4.) *when,* (after וַיְהִי.) Ex. 32:19. Deut. 2:16. Gen. 12:11. 27:40. Ex. 17:11. Josh. 4:1.

אֲשֵׁרָה f. rarely אֲשִׁירָה (Mic. 5:13. Deut. 7:5.) Plur. אֲשֵׁרִים and אֲשֵׁרוֹת. name of a Syrian goddess often worshipped by the Hebrews, and of her images, probably i.q. עַשְׁתֹּרֶת *Astarte.* See especially 1 K. 15:13. 2 K. 21:17. 23:7, 15. Judg. 6:25, 28, 30. Like עַשְׁתֹּרֶת it stands as a female divinity, joined with the male one Baal, 1 K. 18:19. 2 K. 23:4. Judg. 3:7. (Comp. 2:13.) The plural denotes *statues* or *images of Astarte,* i.q. עַשְׁתָּרוֹת. The usual explanation of this word is, that it denotes (1.) as rendered in the Sept. ἄλσος, *a grove;* and (2.) by a metonymy, *an idol worshipped in a grove, a sylvan goddess;* but the incorrectness of this interpretation has been shown very satisfactorily by Gesenius, in his larger lexicon under this article. Comp. Castelli Lex. Heptaglott. col. 2937. Some make אֲשֵׁרָה to be *the goddess of fortune,* from אָשַׁר no. 2.

אֹשֶׁר m. verbal from אָשַׁר, dec. VI. m. *prosperity.* Gen. 30:13.

אֻשַּׁרְנָא m. Chald. *wall.* Ezra 5:3. Vulg. *muri.* Comp. in Talmud. אַשֵּׁר *to make strong.*

אשש found only in Hithpo. *to show one's self firm,* or *strong,* i.q. Talmud. הִתְאֹשָׁשׁוּ. Is. 46:8. Comp. Arab. أسس

to found, establish; Chald. אֻשַּׁיָּא; and Heb. אֻשִּׁים. Another opinion adopted by Gesenius in his commentary on Isaiah, makes הִתְאֹשָׁשׁוּ a denom. from איש in conj. Hithpalel, *to show one's self a man.*

אֵשֶׁת see **אִשָּׁה**.

אֶשְׁתָּאֹל proper name of a city of the Danites, situated in the low country of the tribe of Judah. Jos. 15:33. 19:41. Judg. 13:25. 16:31. This word resembles, as to its form, the Arab. infin. conj. VIII. of שׁאל. The gentile noun occurs 1 Chr. 2:53.

אֶשְׁתַּדּוּר Chald. *insurrection, sedition.* Ezra 4:15, 19. It is verbal from the Ithpa. of שְׁדַר for שְׁדַל Ithpa. *moliri, conari.*

אֶשְׁתְּמֹה Jos. 15:50. and **אֶשְׁתְּמוֹעַ** Josh. 21:14. 1 Sam. 30:28. 1 Chr. 6:42. [57.] a Levitical city in the mountainous country of the tribe of Judah. According to Eusebius, it was a great village in the southern part of Judea. The form of this noun is like the Arab. infin. Conj. VIII. of שמה and שמע.

אָת com. gen. Chald. i. q. Heb. אוֹת *sign, miracle,* synonymous with תְּמַהּ. Dan. 3:32, 33. 6:28.

אַתְּ i. q. אַתָּה *thou* (masc.) q. v.

אַתְּ, in pause אָתְּ, more rarely אַתִּי Judg. 17:2. 1 K. 14:2. *thou* (fem.) The Yod in אַתִּי stands in otio, as in the Syr. ܐܢ݁ܬܝ; but becomes vocal, when another syllable is annexed; e. g. in the verb with suffix קְטַלְתִּיהוּ *thou* (fem.) *hast killed him.* Others regard the punctuation as incorrect, and read אַתְּ. It stands sometimes as a *masc.* Num. 11:15. Ezek. 28:14. a mere incorrectness introduced from the language of common life. See אַתָּה.

I. **אֵת** m. subst. *ploughshare.* It is inflected in two ways; אֵתוֹ, אִתִּים 1 Sam. 13:20, 21. and אִתִּים Is. 2:4. Joel 4:10. [3:10.] The first mode is favoured by several MSS. which read אִיתוֹ, אִיתִים. The signification above is supported by the authority of most of the old versions, (see the different interpretations collected in Michaëlis' Supplem.) but in 1 Sam. 13:20, 21, the word is used in conjunction with מַחֲרֵשָׁה, which from its etymology undoubtedly has that meaning, and cannot be supposed synonymous with אֵת. This difficulty may be removed by rendering it, with the Jewish commentators, *hoe, mattock.* So the Vulg. *ligo,* and Luther in Samuel, *haue.* Or, by rendering it *coulter,* as in C. V. Nothing can be determined from etymology or the kindred dialects.

I. **אֵת**, with Makk. אֶת־; with suff. אֹתִי; אֹתְךָ, in pause and fem. אֹתָךְ; אֹתוֹ, אֹתָהּ; אֹתָנוּ; אֶתְכֶם, also אֹתְכֶם; אֹתָם, also אֶתְהֶם, אֹתָן, rarely אֹתְהֶן (the forms with Holem are also written in full;) a primitive particle.

1. a sign of the accusative case, (in Aram. ܝܳܬ, יָת.) But this accusative case of the Hebrews, which is denoted by אֵת, is often used in circumstances in which other languages employ the nominative; namely, (1.) with a passive verb, Gen. 17:5. לֹא־יִקָּרֵא עוֹד אֶת־שִׁמְךָ אַבְרָם *no more shall thy name be called Abram.* Josh. 7:15 *he who is taken with the accursed thing, shall be burned with fire,* אֹתוֹ וְאֶת־כָּל־אֲשֶׁר־לוֹ *he and all that he hath.* Ex. 10:8. Lev. 10:18. Num. 26:55. Jer. 35:14. 36:22. 38:4. (2) with a neuter verb, 2 Sam. 11:25. אַל יֵרַע בְּעֵינֶיךָ אֶת־הַדָּבָר הַזֶּה *let not this thing displease thee.* (3.) with the subst. verb *to be,* even when only implied, Ezek. 35:10. Jos. 22:17 הַמְעַט־לָנוּ אֶת־עֲוֹן פְּעוֹר *is the iniquity of Peor not sufficient for us?* (4.) sometimes before a nominative of the subject; e. g. 1 Sam. 17:34 *there came a lion* וְאֶת־הַדּוֹב *and a bear.* 2 K. 6:5. Neh. 9:19. This singular use of the Hebrew accusative might be explained by supposing אֵת to be a kind of article which is placed usually before the accusative, but also more rarely before the nominative. The Arabians, however, actually employ the accusative in most of the cases

mentioned; e.g. *exibit album, evasit facies ejus nigram*, (comp. C. B. Michaëlis de Solœcismo Casuum, § 6. 20.) and we may infer that the Hebrew idiom here agrees with the Arabic, especially as the Shemitish languages generally are somewhat irregular in the use of cases.

III. **אֵת**, with Makk. ־אֶת; with suff. אִתִּי, אִתְּךָ, אִתּוֹ, אִתְּכֶם; also with suff. like no. II. (though more rarely,) especially in Kings and in the prophets; prep. prim.

1. *with, together with*. Gen. 4:1 אֶת־יְהוָה *with God*, i.e. with his aid, *Deo juvante*. 1 Chr. 20:5 *there was war with* (אֶת) *the Philistines*.—הִתְהַלֵּךְ אֶת־הָאֱלֹהִים *to walk with God*, i.e. in a manner well pleasing to him, Gen. 5:22.

2. *with, near by*. Here belongs Gen. 39:6 לֹא־יָדַע אִתּוֹ מְאוּמָה *he took no concern about any thing with him, (Joseph,)* i.e. under Joseph's care. So verse 8. and 30:29 *thou knowest how thy cattle has been with me*, i.e. under my care. Like the Lat. *penes* and the synon. עִם (see עִם no. 2.) it signifies *with* in a figurative or intellectual sense, Job 12:3 אֶת־מִי־אֵין כְּמוֹ אֵלֶּה *with whom were not such things as these?* i.e. who knew not such things? Is. 59:12. Job 14:4 *if the number of his months is with thee*, i.e. is determined by thee.

3. *in* or *on* a place. 1 Sam. 7:16 *he judged Israel* אֵת כָּל־הַמְּקוֹמוֹת הָאֵלֶּה *in all these places*. 1 K. 9:25 וְהַקְטֵיר אִתּוֹ אֲשֶׁר לִפְנֵי יְהוָה *and burnt incense on this (altar,) which was before Jehovah*.

4. *besides*, (a modification of *with, together with*.) 1 K. 11:25.

5. *towards, erga*. Ruth 2:20. 2 Sam. 16:17.

אָתָה *to come*; in Arab. and Aram. the usual word to express this idea; in Hebrew more rare and only in poetry, Deut. 33:2. The forms which occur are almost all inflected after the Aramean analogy, or otherwise irregularly. Pret. אָתָא Is. 21:12. but in some copies אָתָה, plur. אָתָנוּ Jer. 3:22. Fut. יֶאֱתֶה and וַיֵּתֵא, תֵּאתֶה Deut. 33:21. and apoc. יֵאת Is. 41:25. plur. יֶאֱתָיוּ Ps. 69:32. Imp. אֵתָיוּ Is. 21:12. Syr. for אֱתָיוּ. Part. plur. אֹתִיּוֹת *future things*. Is. 41:23. 44:7.

Hiph. הֵתָיוּ contraction of הַאֲתָה, plur. imper. הֵתָיוּ *bring!* Is. 21:14. Jer. 12:9.

Deriv. אֵיתָן.

אֲתָה Chald. *to come*. Dan. 7:22. Infin. מֵיתֵא Dan. 3:2.

Aph. הַיְתִי, infin. הַיְתָיָה, *to bring*. Dan. 3:13. 5:2, 13. Pass. הֵיתָיוּ *to be brought*. 3 pers. sing. fem. הֵיתָיִת Dan. 8:18. plur. הֵיתָיוּ Dan. 3:13. (In the Targums, Ithpe. is used instead of this passive.)

אַתָּה pron. pers. *thou* (masc.) The Dagesh forte stands for an assimilated Nun, which in Aram. and Arab. is written out אַנְתְּ, ܐܢ̱ܬ, اَنْتَ, although in Syr. it is omitted in the pronunciation. In pause it becomes penacute, and is sounded אָתָּה. It occurs without ה, (אַתְּ,) five times, Ecc. 7:22. Job 1:10. Neh. 9:6 Keth. 1 Sam. 24:19. Ps. 6:4. Comp. fem. אַתְּ, and plur. אַתֶּם, אַתֵּן.

אָתוֹן f. *she-ass*. Num. 22:23, 33. 2 K. 4:24. (In Syr. and Arab. *idem*.)

אַתּוּן com. gen. Chald. *oven, furnace*, i. q. Syr. ܐܬܘܢܐ. Dan. 3:6, 11, 15 ff.

אַתּוּק Ezek. 41:15 Keth. for the following אַתִּיק.

אַתִּי *thou* (fem.) i. q. אַתְּ (q. v.)

אַתִּיק dec. I. b. an obscure expression in architecture, found only Ezek. 41:15, 16. 42:5. Probably *pillars*, or *some decorations of the same*. The Targums, Ezek. 41:16, have עַתִּיק; which may denote *an ornament, decoration*; comp. עָתִיק, עָתַק *beautiful, shining*.

אַתֶּם pron. pers. *ye* (masc.) It is used for the fem. Ezek. 13:20. probably an incorrectness of the language of common life here admitted into that of writing.

אֵתָם a place on the border of the desert of Shur in Arabia. Ex. 13:20. Num. 33:6. From it the adjoining part of the desert is named, Num. 33:8. Sept. 'Οθώμ. It is thought to be the Egyptian word *atiom* (*border of the sea*).

אֶתְמוֹל and **אֶתְמוּל** adv. with prosth. א, i.q. תְּמוֹל *yesterday*. 1 Sam. 4:7. 14:21. 19:7. Ps. 90:4.

אֶתֵּן in some editions and MSS. for אֵיתָן (q.v.) especially Mic. 6:2. Job 33:19.

אַתֵּן pron. pers. *ye* (fem.) Ezek. 34:31. where, however, some copies have אַתֶּן, like אַתֶּם. Also אַתֵּנָה Gen. 31:6. Ezek. 13:11, 20. 34:17. In Ezek. 13:20, it is written in some editions אַתֵּנָה (after the analogy of הֵנָּה, הֵמָּה.)

אֶתְנָה f. verbal from תָּנָה. *gift, reward;* especially of an harlot. Hos. 2:14. [12.]

אֶתְנַן m. (with א prosth.) verbal from תָּנָה, dec VIII. a.

1. *wages* or *hire of an harlot.* Ezek. 16:31, 34. hence with תָּנָה, Deut. 23:19.

2. applied figuratively to riches, fruits of the earth, etc. which were regarded by idolaters as presents from their gods, (paramours,) Hos. 9:1. to the riches of Samaria, considered as a present from their idols, Mic. 1:7. comp. Is. 23:17, 18. also Hos. 2:7, 14. [2:5, 12.]

אָתָר m. dec. IV. c. probably, as in Aramean, *place, region, country.* Num. 21:1 דֶּרֶךְ הָאֲתָרִים *the way to (his) regions.* Others: *the way to* or *the way from Atharim.*

אֲתַר Chald. *place.* Ezra 5:15. 6:5, 7.—6:3 אֲתַר דִּי *the place where, where.* So in Syr. ܐܬܪ ܕ, in later Heb. מְקוֹם אֲשֶׁר.

ב

The name בֵּית i.q. בַּיִת signifies *a house*, and refers probably to the common square form of this letter.

Beth is sometimes interchanged with the harder sound ף; e.g. בַּרְזֶל Aram. פַּרְזֶל *iron;* בָּזַר and פָּזַר *to scatter;* (more frequently in the kindred dialects.)

Also with מ; (these two sounds are more nearly alike in the lips of an Orientalist than with us, so that *Mecca* sounds almost as *Becca.*) E.g. דִּיבוֹן and דִּימוֹן the name of a city; בָּרִיא and מְרִיא *fat;* זְמַן Syr. ܙܒܢܐ *time.* So in Greek βλίττω *to cut the honey-comb*, for μελίττω, from μέλι *honey;* and in modern languages, French *marbre* from Latin *marmor;* *cable* from Greek κάμιλος.

בְּ a prefix preposition, occurring in various connexions and significations, which in other languages must be expressed by many different particles. The principal of these are

1. *in* or *into* a place or subject. Also of time, as בְּיָמִים אֲחָדִים *in some days;* בַּשָּׁנָה הַשֵּׁנִית *in the second year.*

2. *with*, noting an instrument, concomitance, or aid; as בַּחֶרֶב *with the sword.* בְּעַם כָּבֵד *with much people*, Num. 20:20. בְּמַקְלִי *with my staff*, Gen. 32:11. Ps. 18:30 *with thee* (בְּךָ) *I assailed troops.* Hence verbs of *coming*, construed with בְּ, denote *bringing;* see בּוֹא, יָרַד, פָּקַד.

3. *on, at, near;* as בָּעַיִן *at the fountain.* בַּקִּיר *on the wall.* הֶחֱזִיק בְּ, אָחַז, *to lay hold of* or *on.* קָרָא בְ *to call on.*

4. *by.* Also in swearing, Gen. 22:16. Cant. 2:7.

5. *through.* Num. 12:2.

6. *upon;* as בָּאֹהֶל *upon the tabernacle*, Num. 14:10.

7. *to* a place or thing; as בְּאָשֵׁר *to Asher*, Judg. 6:35. שׁוּב בְּ *to return to*, Hos. 12:7. Gen. 9:10. בָּעוֹף בַּבְּהֵמָה וגו' *to fowl, to cattle*, etc.

8. *against;* as יָדוֹ בַכֹּל *his hand against every one*, Gen. 16:12. 2 Sam. 24:17. נִלְחַם בְּ *to contend against.* מָעַל, בָּגַד, מָרָה בְּ *to deal treacherously against* any one. עָנָה בְ *to testify against* any one.

9. *concerning, de;* as דִּבֶּר בְּ *to speak concerning* any thing.

10. *out of, from;* as בְּצֶמֶר *from the wool;* בִּשְׁגָגָה *from negligence;* בְּשִׂנְאָה *from hatred;* מָרַד, פָּשַׁע בְּ *to revolt from* any one. שָׁתָה בְּ *to drink out of* a vessel, Gen. 44:5; comp. the French *boire dans la tasse.*

11. *among;* as בַּגּוֹיִם *among the nations.* יָפָה בַּנָּשִׁים *the fair,* i.e. the fairest, *among women,* a periphrasis for the superlative degree, Cant. 1:8.

12. *before,* as בְּעֵינֵי פ' *before the eyes of any one.*—Gen. 23:18 *before* (בְּ) *all who entered through the gate of his city.*

13. *for;* as נֶפֶשׁ בְּנֶפֶשׁ *life for life,* Deut. 19:21. בְּנַפְשׁוֹתָם *with danger of their lives,* 2 Sam. 23:17. בְּבִתְּךָ *for thy daughter,* Gen. 29:18.

14. *on account of.* Gen. 18:28 בַּחֲמִשָּׁה *on account of the five.* 2 K. 14:6. Jon. 1:14.

15. *after, according to.* Gen. 1:26 בְּצַלְמֵנוּ *after our likeness.* Lev. 5:15. בִּדְבַר־ *according to the word* or *command* of any one. Hence

16. *as.* Job 34:36. Hos. 10:15.

17. Verbs of sense and some others, construed with בְּ, imply that the action is performed with pleasure, more rarely that it is connected with pain. Comp. אָכַל, שָׁמַע, רָאָה.

18. The following construction is common in Arabic, in Hebrew more rare. Ps. 118:7 יְהוָה בְּעֹזְרָי *Jehovah is among my helpers,* i.e. is my helper. Ps. 54:6. Judg. 11:35. Ps. 99:6. Also in the sing. Ex. 32:22 *thou knowest the people,* כִּי בְרָע הוּא *that they are wicked.* Hos. 13:9 כִּי בִי בְעֶזְרֶךָ *for with me is thy help.* This בְּ is called *Beth essentiæ.*

19. before an infin. *when, while,* Gen. 2:4. *after,* Gen. 33:18. *since, because,* Ex. 16:7.

With suff. בִּי; בְּךָ, in pause and fem. בָּךְ; בּוֹ, בָּהּ; בָּנוּ; בָּכֶם; בָּהֶם and בָּם, בָּהֶן. In poetry for בְּ occurs בְּמוֹ, בְּמוֹ; see כְּמוֹ, לְמוֹ.

בְּאוּשׁ Chald. adj. *bad, wicked.* Once Ezra 4:12.

בָּאַר in Kal not used, *to dig.* Comp. deriv. בְּאֵר, בּאֹר.

Pi. בֵּאֵר 1. *to engrave* on stones or tablets. Deut. 27:8. Hab. 2:2.

2. *to explain, eruere sensum.* Deut. 1:5.

בְּאֵר f. verbal from בָּאַר; Plur. בְּאֵרוֹת, const. בְּאֵרֹת.

1. *a well.* Gen. 21:25, 30. 26:15, 20, 21.

2. *pit* generally. Ps. 55:24. 69:16.

3. proper name of an encampment of the Israelites in the wilderness. Num. 21:16—18.

4. also of a place in the tribe of Judah, on the way from Jerusalem to Shechem. Judg. 9:21.

בְּאֵר אֵלִים (*well of the turpentine-trees*) a place in Moab. Once Is. 15:8.

בְּאֵר לַחַי רֹאִי (*well of life, of vision,* i.e. where one sees God and yet lives,) name of a well in the desert between Palestine and Egypt. Gen. 24:62. 25:11. The etymological signification is given by Moses, Gen. 16:14.

בְּאֵרוֹת (*wells*) proper name of a city in the tribe of Benjamin, between Jerusalem and Shechem. 2 Sam. 4:2. The gentile noun is בְּאֵרֹתִי, 2 Sam. 4:2, 3, 23, 37.

בְּאֵרוֹת בְּנֵי יַעֲקָן (*wells of the sons of Jaakan*) an encampment of the Israelites in the wilderness; also written without בְּאֵרוֹת. Deut. 10:6. Num. 33:31.

בֹּאר (Syr. for בּוֹר verbal from בָּאַר) i.q. the more common בּוֹר *cistern.* Only once Jer. 2:13; for in the Kethib of 2 Sam. 23:15, 16, 20, בְּאֵר (*well*) is probably the true punctuation. The Keri and the parallel passage in Chronicles have בּוֹר.

בְּאֵר שֶׁבַע (i.q. בְּאֵר שְׁבוּעָה *well of the oath,* as explained Gen. 21:31. 26:33.) a place on the southern boundary of Palestine; hence the phrase, *all Israel* מִדָּן וְעַד־בְּאֵר שָׁבַע *from Dan to Beersheba,* 2 Sam. 17:11. Now called, according to Seetzen, *Bîr-Szábéa.*

I. **בָּאַשׁ,** fut. יִבְאַשׁ. *to have an offensive smell, to stink.* Ex. 7:18, 21. 16:20.

Niph. reflex. of Hiph. *to make one's self loathsome* or *odious* to any one, construed with בְּ and אֶת of the person. 1 Sam. 13:4. 2 Sam. 10:6. 16:21. Comp. the French *être en bonne, en mauvaise odeur*.

Hiph. 1. *to cause to stink, to corrupt*. Ecc. 10:1. Figuratively, *to render odious* to any one, construed with בְּ of the person, Gen. 34:30. also, the figure being drawn out, Ex. 5:21 הִבְאַשְׁתֶּם אֶת רֵיחֵנוּ *ye have made our savour to stink*, i.e. ye have made us odious.

2. i. q. Kal, *to stink*, Ex. 16:24. figuratively, *to be loathsome* or *odious*, 1 Sam. 27:12.

Hithpa. *to make one's self odious*, construed with עִם. 1 Chr. 19:6.

II. בָּאַשׁ i. q. בּוֹשׁ *to be ashamed*.

Hiph. *to act shamefully* or *basely*. Prov. 13:5 רָשָׁע יַבְאִישׁ וְיַחְפִּיר *the wicked man acts basely and shamefully*. Comp. חָפֵר no. 3.

בְּאֵשׁ Chald. *to be evil, wicked; construed with* עַל, *to be displeasing;* i. q. Heb. רַע, רָעַע. Dan. 6:14. In the eastern languages a pleasant savour is often attributed to pleasant objects generally, and an unpleasant savour to objects which are not pleasant.

בְּאשׁ m. *stink, stench*. Am. 4:10. with suff. בָּאְשׁוֹ Joel 2:20. בָּאְשָׁם Is. 34:3.

בָּאְשָׁה f. Job 31:40. and בְּאֻשִׁים Is. 5:2, 4. *monk's-hood*, a well-known poisonous herb, which produces berries like grapes, *aconitum napellus*, Linn.

בָּאתַר Chald. prep. i. q. בָּתַר *after*. Dan. 7:6.

בָּבָה f. dec. X. in the phrase בָּבַת עַיִן *apple of the eye*. Once Zech. 2:12. [8.] In Syr. ܒܒܘܬܐ *pupil;* in Chald. בְּבוּאָה *image, shadow*. It appears from this that בָּבַת עַיִן properly denotes *the image* or *little man in the eye*, like אִישׁוֹן (q. v.)

בָּבֶל f. *Babel, Babylon*, on the Euphrates, the celebrated metropolis of Babylonia; freq. With ה local, בָּבֶלָה *to Babylon*.—According to Gen. 11:9, it signifies *confusion* (*of languages*); comp. Syr. ܒܠܒܠܐ *hesitancy of speech, stammering, stuttering*. It stands by syncope for בַּלְבֵּל from בָּלַל; comp. גֻּלְגֹּלֶת Chald. גּוּלְגַּלְתָּא *scull*.

בַּג found only Ezek. 25:7. Keth. If this reading is correct, i. q. Arab. בג *food*. (comp. פַּתְבַּג,) but all the ancient versions favour the reading of the Keri בַּז *spoil*.

בָּגַד, fut. יִבְגֹּד 1. *to act faithlessly, perfidiously*. 1 Sam. 14:33. Job 6:15. Construed with בְּ, *to deal treacherously against* any one, Judg. 9:23. with בַּיהוָה, *faithlessly to forsake Jehovah*, Jer. 5:11. Hos. 5:7. 6:7. with בְּאִשָּׁה, *to forsake one's wife*, Mal. 2:14, 15, 16. Ex. 21:8. Construed more rarely with מִן, Jer. 3:20 בָּגְדָה אִשָּׁה מֵרֵעָהּ *a wife forsakes her husband*. But מֵרֵעַ may be considered as a noun, for this verb sometimes governs the accus. directly, as Ps. 73:15 הִנֵּה דוֹר בָּנֶיךָ בָגָדְתִּי *behold, I should deal faithlessly against the generation of thy children*.

2. *to be arrogant, wicked*. Hab. 2:5. הַיַּיִן בּוֹגֵד *the wine*, i. e. the drunken man, *is wicked*. Plur. בֹּגְדִים *the arrogant, wicked*. Prov. 2:22. 11:3, 6. 13:2. 22:12.

3. *to rob, destroy*. Is. 21:2. 24:16. 33:1. According to some, *to strip of one's garment*, as if a denom. (with a privative sense) from בֶּגֶד. Others place these examples under no. 2.

I. בֶּגֶד m. verbal from בָּגַד. *faithlessness, perfidy*. Jer. 12:1. Is. 24:16.

II. בֶּגֶד com. (generally masc.)

1. *cloth, covering*. Num. 4:6—13. especially of a bed, 1 Sam. 19:13. 1 K. 1:1.

2. *garment*, especially *the outer garment* of the Orientalist. Gen. 24:53.

With suff. בִּגְדִי; Plur. בְּגָדִים, const. בִּגְדֵי; with the termination ־וֹת only Ps. 45:9.

בֹּגְדוֹת plur. fem. verbal from בָּגַד. *treachery*. Zeph. 3:4. Concerning the form, see art. אֵגֹד, note.

בָּגוֹד verbal adj. from בָּגַד, found only in the fem. בָּגוֹדָה *faithless, perfidious.* Jer. 3 : 7, 10.

בִּגְלַל *on account of*, see גָּלַל.

I. **בַּד** dec. VIII. h.

1. *vain speaking, boasting, lying.* Job 11 : 3. Is. 16 : 6. Jer. 48 : 30.

2. *liar, boaster.* Is. 44 : 25. Jer. 50 : 36.

Root בָּדַד i. q. בְּדָה in Syr. and Arab. *to lie, boast;* kindred with בָּרָא *to imagine, invent.*

II. **בַּד** strictly a verbal from בָּדַד, denoting *the being single* or *separate, separation.* Hence לְבַד adv. (1.) *in separation, separately, apart, seorsim.* Ex. 26 : 9 *five curtains by themselves* (לְבָד) *and six curtains by themselves* (לְבָד.) 36 : 16. Judg. 7 : 5. (2.) *only, alone.* Ecc. 7 : 29. Is. 26 : 13. (3.) לְבַד מִן and מִלְּבַד *besides, except,* Ex. 12 : 37 לְבַד מִטָּף *besides children.* Gen. 26 : 1 מִלְּבַד הָרָעָב הָרִאשׁוֹן *besides the first famine.*—לְבַד עַל־ *besides that which;* once Ezra 1 : 6. (4.) Very frequently joined with suffixes in the following manner, אֲנִי לְבַדִּי *I alone* or *by myself,* (also without the first pronoun, if it is implied in the verb,) Num. 11 : 14. אַתָּה לְבַדְּךָ *thou alone,* Ex. 18 : 14. יַעֲקֹב, מֹשֶׁה לְבַדּוֹ *Jacob, Moses alone.* לוֹ לְבַדּוֹ *for him alone.* Gen. 43 : 32. Ps. 71 : 16 צִדְקָתְךָ לְבַדֶּךָ *thy righteousness, even thine only,* (strictly *justitia tui, tui solius.*) — בַּד בְּבַד *in equal parts,* Ex. 30 : 34.

Plur. בַּדִּים strictly *separations, things which are separate;* hence (1.) *boughs, branches.* Ezek. 17 : 6. 19 : 14. (2.) *poles, staves.* Ex. 25 : 13 ff. Num. 4 : 6 ff. (3.) *bars.* Job 17 : 16. Figuratively perhaps, *princes, leaders,* (as if *the bars, shields* of the people,) Hos. 11 : 6. Others take it literally. (4.) בַּדֵּי עוֹר and simply בַּדִּים Job 18 : 13. 41, 4. [12] poetically *members* or *limbs of the body.*

III. **בַּד** m. *white, fine linen,* i. q. שֵׁשׁ. Ex. 28 : 42. 39 : 28. Lev. 6 : 10. Plur. בַּדִּים *linen garments.* Ezek. 9 : 2, 3. Dan. 10 : 5.

בָּדָא *to imagine, invent, devise.* 1 K. 12 : 33. Neh. 6 : 8 בּוֹדָאם Syr. for בּוֹרְאָם. Comp. בַּד no. 1.

בָּדַד *to separate one's self.* (In Arab. *idem.*) Part. בּוֹדֵד *solitary, separate, alone.* Ps. 102 : 8. Hos. 8 : 9. Deriv. בַּד no. II. and בָּדָד.

בָּדָד verbal from בָּדַד. *the being separate* or *alone.* Hence לְבָדָד and בָּדָד adv. *alone.* Jer. 49 : 31 בָּדָד יִשְׁכֹּנוּ *they dwell alone.* Is. 27 : 10 עִיר בְּצוּרָה בָּדָד *the defenced city (stands) alone.* Lam. 1 : 1. The idea of *desolation* is also implied in the two last passages.

בְּדִי i. q. בְּ; see דַּי.

בְּדִיל m. verbal from בָּדַל, dec. I. a.

1. the *stannum* of the ancients, i. e. lead intermixed with the silver ore, and *separated* from it by fusion. Comp. בָּדַל *to separate.* See Plin. H. N. xxxiv. 16. and Schneider's griech. Wörterbuch, art. *κασσίτερος.* Is. 1 : 25 אָסִירָה כָּל־בְּדִילָיִךְ *I will take away all thy tin,* i. e. the impure metal mixed with thee.

2. *tin, plumbum album* of the ancients. Num. 31 : 22.

בָּדַל in Kal not used.

Hiph. 1. *to divide, separate.* It is construed with בֵּין....וּבֵין, Ex. 26 : 33. with בֵּין....לְ, Gen. 1 : 6. with בֵּין....לְבֵין, Is. 59 : 2. with מִן, Lev. 20 : 24. It is also used absolutely, Lev. 1 : 17 *he shall tear the bird on its wings,* וְלֹא יַבְדִּיל *but not make a separation.*

2. *to separate, single out,* or *appoint* to any thing; construed with לְ, Deut. 29 : 20. Num. 16 : 9. also without this dat. Deut. 4 : 41 אָז יַבְדִּיל מֹשֶׁה שָׁלֹשׁ עָרִים *then Moses appointed three cities.* 10 : 8. 19 : 7. Ezek. 39 : 14.

Niph. 1. *to be separated,* 1 Chr. 23 : 13. Ezra 10 : 8. *to separate one's self,* construed with מִן, Num. 16 : 21. Ezra 9 : 1. 10 : 11. *to separate one's self (and go)* to any one, construed with אֶל, 1 Chr. 12 : 8.

2. *to be appointed.* Ezra 10 : 16.

Deriv. בְּדִיל, מִבְדָּלוֹת.

בָּדָל m. verbal from בָּדַל, dec. IV. a.

piece, part; with אֹזֶן, *piece* or *tip of an ear.* Once Am. 3:12.

בְּדֹלַח m. Gen. 2:12. Num. 11:7. according to Aquila, Symm. Theod. in Num., the Vulg. in both passages and Josephus, *bdellium*, βδέλλιον, a transparent gum, of a sweet scent and resembling wax, obtained from a tree which grows in Arabia, India and Media, perhaps the wine-palm (borassus flabelliformis, Linn.). According to the Sept. ἄνθραξ. Others: *beryl.* The Arab. *pearls.*

בָּדַק 1. *to tear in pieces.* (In Arab. בזק *idem.*) Deriv. בֶּדֶק.

2. denom. from בֶּדֶק *to repair* a breach, or a decayed building. 2 Chr. 34:10.

בֶּדֶק m. verbal from בָּדַק, dec. VI. h. *breach, chink.* 2 K. 12:5—12. Ezek. 27:9.

בְּדַר Chald. i.q. Heb. בָּזַר *to scatter.* Pa. imper. Dan. 4:11. [14.]

בֹּהוּ m. subst. *emptiness, desolation, a waste,* for בֹּהוּ (after the form קֹדֶשׁ) from the root בָּהָה in Arabic *to be empty, waste,* spoken of a house. Always joined with תֹּהוּ, Gen. 1:2. Jer. 4:23. Is. 34:11 אַבְנֵי בֹהוּ; see אֶבֶן.

בַּהַט m. Est. 1:6. probably a species of marble. Sept. σμαραγδίτης, by which is perhaps meant *the green antique porphyritic marble* of Egypt.

בְּהִילוּ f. Chald. *haste.* Once Ezra 4:23.

בָּהִיר adj. *bright, shining.* Once Job 37:21. (The root בהר in Chald. and Arab. signifies *to be bright, shining.*)

בָּהַל in Kal not used.

Niph. 1. *to be violently moved* or *shaken* (by fear or anxiety), *to be alarmed* or *confounded.* Ex. 15:15. 1 Sam. 28:21. 2 Sam. 4:1. Ps. 6:3 נִבְהֲלוּ עֲצָמָי *my bones tremble.*

2. *to flee in amazement.* Judg. 20:41.

3. *to be disordered, destroyed.* Ps. 104:29 *thou hidest thy face* יִבָּהֵלוּן *they* (creatures) *are destroyed.* Hence Part. fem. used substantively, *destruction.* Zeph. 1:18.

4. *to hasten* after any thing, construed with לְ. Prov. 28:22.

Pi. בִּהַל, fut. יְבַהֵל.

1. *to terrify, perplex, confound.* Ezra 4:4. 1 Chr. 32:18. Job 22:10.

2. *to be in haste,* Ecc. 5:1. 7:9.

3. *to hasten,* Est. 2:9.

Pu. *to hurry, be in haste.* Est. 8:14. Prov. 20:21 Keri נַחֲלָה מְבֹהֶלֶת *hastened substance,* i.e. substance too hastily and avariciously acquired.

Hiph. 1. i.q. Pi. no. 1. Job 23:16.

2. i.q. Pi. no. 2. Est. 6:14.

3. *to drive out in haste.* 2 Chr. 26:20.

בְּהַל Chald. Pa. *to terrify, trouble.* Dan. 4:2, 16. [4:5, 19.] 7:15.

Ithpa. pass. 5:9.

Ithpe. infin. הִתְבְּהָלָה, substantively, *haste.* Dan. 2:25. 3:24. 6:20.

בֶּהָלָה f. verbal from בָּהַל, dec. X.

1. *terror, consternation.* Lev. 26:16.

2. *destruction.* Is. 65:23.

בְּהֵמָה f. prim. irreg. const. בֶּהֱמַת with suff. בְּהֶמְתְּךָ; Plur. בְּהֵמוֹת, const. בַּהֲמוֹת.

1. *beast, quadruped.* Ecc. 3:19, 21. Lev. 11:2.

2. *tame cattle,* in opposition to חַיָּה *wild beast.* Gen. 1:24—26. 3:14. 7:21. Lev. 25:7. In Lev. 1:2, it includes צֹאן and בָּקָר *small* and *large cattle.*

3. *large cattle,* in opposition to מִקְנֶה *small cattle.* Gen. 34:23.

4. *wild beast of the field.* Deut. 32:24. Hab. 2:17. generally with the addition of הָאָרֶץ, Deut. 28:26. Is. 18:6. of הַשָּׂדֶה, שָׂדַי 1 Sam. 17:44. Joel 1:20. 2:22. or of יַעַר Mich. 5:7. The discourse is here, for the most part, of ravenous animals.

Plur. בְּהֵמוֹת *animals.* Also as a pluralis excellentiæ denoting only one, Ps. 73:22. So *the Behemoth,* Job 40:15. From the description, especially verse 18, it is pretty evident that *the hippopotamus* was intended by the poet, (comp. Bocharti Hieroz. II. p. 753. Ludolfi Hist. Æth. I. c. 11;) and not the elephant, as Grotius, Schultens, and Michaëlis have supposed. Although a

Hebrew would regard this word as an example of the pluralis excellentiæ, yet it may have originated from the Egyptian word *Pehemout*, (river ox.) Comp. אַבְנָךְ.

בֹּהֶן f. with יָד, *the thumb;* with רֶגֶל, *the great toe.* Lev. 8 : 23, 24. 14 : 17, 18. Plur. בְּהֹנוֹת Judg. 1 : 6, 7. from a sing. בְּהוֹן, which the Samar. text always substitutes for בֹּהֶן.

בֹּהַק m. found only Lev. 13 : 39. name of a harmless eruption on the skin, of a dull whitish colour, still called *bohak* by the Arabians. The root בָּהַק in Syr. conj. Aphel signifies *to be white,* spoken of the leprosy.

בַּהֶרֶת f. *the white scab* of a person affected with the leprosy, λεύκη of Hippocrates, *morphea* or *vitiligo alba* of the Latins. Lev. 13 : 2—39. Plur. בֶּהָרוֹת verses 38, 39. Comp. בָּהִיר.

בּוֹא 1. *to go* or *come in, to enter.* Gen. 6 : 18. 7 : 9, 13. 39 : 14, 17. Frequently opposed to יָצָא; see under no. (4.) It is construed with בְּ, אֶל, or an accus. (like *ingredi urbem.*) Ps. 100 : 4 בֹּאוּ שְׁעָרָיו *enter into his gates.* Ps. 105 : 18. Hence with a genitive בָּאֵי שַׁעַר *those who enter at the gate,* Gen. 23 : 10, 18. Particularly (1.) spoken of the sun, *to go in* (below the horizon,) *to set, go down.* Gen. 15 : 17. 28 ; 11. (Antith. יָצָא *to rise.*) (2.) בּוֹא אֶל אִשָּׁה *to lie with a woman, inire feminam.* Gen. 16 : 2. 30 : 3. 38 ; 8. Deut. 22 : 13. 2 Sam. 16 : 21. also with עַל, Gen. 19 : 31. Deut. 25 : 5. (3.) spoken of a maiden, *to enter the house of her husband.* Josh. 15 : 18. Judg. 1 : 14. (4.) בָּא וְיָצָא *to go in and out,* a common periphrasis for *to conduct, act,* (like הָלַךְ.) 1 K. 3 ; 7 לֹא אֵדַע צֵאת וָבֹא *I know not how to go in and out,* i. e. how to live, or to act. 1 Sam. 29 : 6. 2 K. 19 ; 27 (with the addition יָשַׁב *to sit.*) Comp. Deut. 28 : 6. Ps. 121 ; 8. With the addition לִפְנֵי הָעָם *before the people,* i. q. to lead or direct the people. Num. 27 : 16. 1 Sam. 18 ; 16. 2 Chr. 1 : 10. also Deut. 31 : 2. Jos. 14 : 11. without that addition. (5.) *to come in,* as profit or revenue. 1 K. 10 : 14. 2 Chr. 9 : 13. (Antith. יָצָא *to be expended.*) (6.) בּוֹא בִּבְרִית *to enter into a covenant.* See בְּרִית.

2. *to come,* construed with עַד, עַל, אֶל, or an accus. Lam. 1 : 10. Jer. 32 : 24 סוֹלְלוֹת בָּאוּ הָעִיר *the mounds reach to the city.* Lam. 1 : 4 בָּאֵי מוֹעֵד *those who come to the feast.* Particularly (1.) *to come upon* any one, *to happen to* or *befall* him; construed with an acc. Ezek. 32 : 11 *the sword*....תְּבוֹאֶךָּ *shall come upon thee.* Job 22 : 21 תְּבוֹאַתְךָ טוֹבָה *good shall befall thee.* Ps. 35 : 8. 44 : 18 כָּל־זֹאת בָּאַתְנוּ *all this has befallen us.* 109 : 17. 119 : 41, 77. Prov. 10 : 24. Also with עַל, Job 2 : 11. 3 : 25. 4 : 25. and לְ, Is. 47 : 9. (2.) *to come to pass, to be fulfilled;* spoken of a wish, Prov. 13 : 12. of a request, Job 6 : 8. of a predicted sign, 1 Sam. 10 : 7. especially of a prophecy, 1 Sam. 9 : 6. Deut. 13 : 2. 18 : 22. (3.) with בְּ, *to come with* any thing, *to bring* it. Ps. 66 : 13. See בְּ no. 2. (4.) *to come at* any thing, *to obtain* it; construed with בְּ. Ps. 69 : 28. (5.) *to fall to* any one, construed with אֶל. Num. 32 : 19.

לָבֹא and עַד לָבֹא *till one come,* i. e. unto. Num. 34 : 8 לְבֹא חֲמָת *even to Hamath.* Num. 13 : 21 עַד רְחֹב לְבֹא חֲמָת *to Rehob and Hamath.* Instead of this occurs also עַד בֹּאֲךָ *till thou comest,* i. e. till one comes, Gen. 19 : 22. Judg. 6 : 4. 11 : 33. and simply בֹּאֲךָ, Gen. 20 : 19, 30. 13 : 10.—מִלְּבֹא....עַד *from.... to,* 1 K. 8 : 65. 2 K. 14 : 25. Am. 7 : 14.

3. more rarely *to go.* (So ἔρχομαι, *to come* and *to go.*) Jon. 1 : 3 *he found a ship* בָּאָה תַרְשִׁישׁ *which went to Tarshish.* Hence with עִם and אֵת, *to be concerned with* any one, (like הָלַךְ עִם.) Ps. 26 : 4. Prov. 22 : 24.

Hiph. הֵבִיא 1. caus. of Kal no. 1. *to bring in, to carry in;* e. g. the produce from the field, 2 Sam. 9 : 10. Hag. 1 : 6. —*to lead Israel in and out,* i. e. to direct or govern them, Num. 27 : 16. 1 Chr. 11 : 2. (Comp. Kal. no. 1. (4.)

2. *to cause to come, to lead, to bring.* Gen. 4 : 4, etc. Figuratively, *to let happen,* Is. 37 : 26. 46 : 11. Ps. 78 : 29.

Hoph. pass. Lev. 10:18.
Deriv. תְּבוּאָה, מָבוֹא, בִּיאָה.

בּוּב in Kal not used, *to be hollow and empty.*

Niph. part. נָבוּב *hollow.* Ex. 27:8. 38:7. Jer. 52:11. Figuratively, *empty-headed, stupid,* Job 11:12.

בּוּז, fut. יָבוּז, *to despise*, construed with an accus. Prov. 1:7. more frequently with לְ, Prov. 11:12. 13:13. 14:21. Cant. 8:7. Prov. 6:30 לֹא־יָבוּזוּ לַגַּנָּב *they do not overlook a thief,* i.e. they do not let him go unpunished. (In Zech. 4:10, בַּז stands for בָּז, as if from בָּזַז.)

I. **בּוּז** m. verbal from בּוּז. *contempt.* Ps. 123:4. Job 31:34.

II. **בּוּז** proper name of the second son of Nahor the brother of Abraham. Gen. 22:21. Hence a people and country in the desert of Arabia, Jer. 25:23, 24. The gentile noun is בּוּזִי, Job 32:2.

בּוּזָה fem. of בּוּז. *contempt, object of contempt.* Once Neh. 3:36. [4:4.]

בּוּזִי see **בּוּז** no. II.

בּוּךְ found only in Niph. נָבוֹךְ *to be entangled, confounded,* or *in consternation.* Est. 3:15 וְהָעִיר שׁוּשָׁן נָבוֹכָה *and the city Shushan was in consternation.* Ex. 14:3 נְבֻכִים הֵם בָּאָרֶץ *they are entangled in the land,* i.e. they wander about in confusion. Joel 1:18 (spoken of herds of cattle.) In Arab. *idem.* Deriv. מְבוּכָה.

I. **בּוּל** (for יְבוּל verbal from יָבַל no. I, i.q. בּוֹא.) dec. I. a.

1. *produce, proventus.* Once Job 40:15.

2. בּוּל עֵץ after the Chaldaic usage, *stick* or *log of wood.* Once Is. 44:19.

II. **בּוּל** (for יְבוּל verbal from יָבַל no. II. *to rain violently.*) *the rain month,* the eighth month of the Hebrews, answering to part of October and part of November. Once 1 K. 6:38.

בּוּם see **בָּמָה**.

בּוּן see **בִּין** *to perceive, understand.*

בּוּס, fut. יָבוּס, part. בּוֹסִים. *to tread* or *trample upon.* Prov. 27:7. For the most part figuratively, *to tread down* or *to the ground,* namely, the enemy. Ps. 44:6. 60:14. Is. 63:6.

Pil. בּוֹסֵס *to tread* a place *under foot.* Jer. 12:10. Is. 63:18. Here, of the *treading* of the sanctuary by profane persons, or of its *being profaned* by them; comp. *καταπατεῖσθαι τὰ ἅγια, τὸ ἁγίασμα,* 1 Mac. 3:45, 51. and מִרְמָס, Dan. 8:13.

Hoph. *to be trodden under foot.* Is. 14:19.

Hithpal. הִתְבּוֹסֵס Ezek. 16:6, 22. *to be exposed to be trodden under foot, conculcandum se præbere.*

Deriv. תְּבוּסָה, מְבוּסָה.

בּוּץ m. *byssus, the finest white cotton* of the Egyptians, obtained from several species of the gossypium, also from the more costly bombax gossypinum in Egypt. Also *cloth made of this cotton.* It is synonymous with שֵׁשׁ, but בּוּץ occurs only in the later books. 1 Chr. 15:27. 2 Chr. 2:12, 13. 3:14. 5:12. Est. 1:6. 8:15. Ezek. 27:16. Root בּוּץ or בִּיץ = Arab. بَاضَ *to be white* or *shining,* (comp. Rev. 19:8, 14.) From the same root is בֵּיץ *an egg.* Comp. J. R. Forster de bysso antiquorum liber singularis. Lond. 1776. 8vo. Celsii Hierobotan. II. p. 167 ff.

בּוּקָה f. *emptiness, desolation.* Once Nah. 2:11. Root בּוּק = בָּקַק *to be empty.*

בּוֹקֵר m. (denom. from בָּקָר *herd of oxen,* but in Syriac a *herd* simply.) *herdsman.* Am. 7:14. That the word is not restricted to a feeder of oxen is evident from chap. 1:1.

I. **בּוֹר**, plur. בֹּרוֹת, m. dec. I. a. (strictly for בְּאֵר, בְּאֵר verbal from בָּאַר *to dig.*)

1. *pit.* 1 Sam. 13:6. 1 Chr. 11:22.

2. especially *a cistern.* Gen. 37:20 ff. בֹּרוֹת חֲצֻבִים *hewn-out cisterns.* Deut. 6:11. Since the empty cisterns were used as places of confinement, (see Zech. 9:11. Jer. 38:6 ff.) hence

3. *a prison.* Is. 24:22. particularly בֵּית הַבּוֹר, Jer. 37:16. Ex. 12:29.

4. *grave*. Of frequent occurrence in the phrase יוֹרְדֵי־בוֹר *who go down to the grave, the dying*, Ps. 28:1. 143:7. Prov. 1:12. Is. 14:19 יוֹרְדֵי אֶל־אַבְנֵי־בוֹר *those who are* or *should be laid in tombs built of stone*. עַד בּוֹר *to the grave*, Prov. 28:17. Hence

5. *the regions of the dead*. Is. 14:15 יַרְכְּתֵי בוֹר *the depths of the lower regions*.

II. בּוֹר i. q. בֹּר (q. v.)

בּוּר i. q. בָּרַר no. 3. *to examine*. Once Ecc. 9:1.

I. בּוֹשׁ, pret. בּוֹשׁ, בֹּשְׁתִּי; fut. יֵבוֹשׁ. *to be ashamed*. Job 6:20. 19:3. Ezra 8:22. 9:6. construed with מִן of the thing, Ezek. 36:32. (comp. 43:10, 11.)

2. *to be made ashamed*, especially *to be deceived* in one's expectation, or in the issue of one's undertaking, with which shame is usually connected. Ps. 22:6 בְּךָ בָטְחוּ וְלֹא בוֹשׁוּ *they trusted in thee, and were not made ashamed*. 25:2, 3, 20. 31:2, 18. 71:13 יֵבֹשׁוּ שֹׂטְנֵי נַפְשִׁי *may they who lie in wait for my life be brought to shame!* The object of disappointed hope is preceded by מִן, Jer. 2:36 גַּם מִמִּצְרַיִם תֵּבוֹשִׁי כַּאֲשֶׁר בֹּשְׁתְּ מֵאַשּׁוּר *thou shalt also be disappointed in Egypt, as thou wast disappointed in Assyria*. 12:13. 48:13. Hos. 4:19. 10:6. Ps. 69:7 אַל יֵבֹשׁוּ בִי קֹוֶיךָ *let not those who wait on thee be disappointed in* or *through me*. Here belongs the phrase עַד־בּוֹשׁ, e. g. Judg. 3:25 *they waited* עַד בּוֹשׁ *till they were ashamed*, i. e. very long. 2 K. 2:17. 8:11. In the last passage, perhaps, *till he was embarrassed*.

3. figuratively of inanimate nature, Hos. 13:15 יֵבוֹשׁ מְקוֹרוֹ *his spring shall be ashamed*, i. e. dried up. Comp. בּוֹשׁ no. II. According to others, בּוֹשׁ here is i. q. יָבֵשׁ *to dry up*.

Hiph. הֵבִישׁ. 1. caus. of Kal nos. 1. 2. *to shame, make ashamed, disappoint* any one. Ps. 14:6. 44:8. 119:31, 116 אַל תְּבִישֵׁנִי מִשִּׂבְרִי *let me not be disappointed in my hope*.

2. *to bring disgrace* on any one. Prov. 29:15.

3. intrans. *to act basely, shamefully*. (Prov. 13:5.) Hence part. מֵבִישׁ *base, contemptible, foolish;* often in opposition to מַשְׂכִּיל *wise*. Prov. 10:5. 12:5. 14:35. 17:2. 19:26.

Another Hiph. see under יָבֵשׁ no. II.

Hithpal. הִתְבֹּשֵׁשׁ *to be ashamed*. Gen. 2:25.

Deriv. out of course, בָּשְׁנָה, בֹּשֶׁת and מְבוּשִׁים.

II. בּוֹשׁ found only in Pil. בֹּשֵׁשׁ *to delay*. Ex. 32:1. Judg. 5:28. It may also be formed from בָּשַׁשׁ.

בּוּשָׁה f. verbal from בּוֹשׁ. *shame, disgrace*. Ps. 89:46. Mic. 7:10.

בּוּת Chald. *to pass the night*. Dan. 6:19. Hence the Heb. בַּיִת, plur. בָּתִּים, *house*.

בַּז m. verbal from בָּזַז, dec. VIII. f. *booty*, whether of men, (i. q. שְׁבִי,) of animals, (i. q. מַלְקוֹחַ,) or of other possessions. Num. 14:3 נָשֵׁינוּ וְטַפֵּנוּ יִהְיוּ לָבַז *that our wives and our children should become a prey*. Jer. 15:13 חֵילְךָ וְאוֹצְרוֹתֶיךָ לָבַז אֶתֵּן *thy substance and thy treasures will I give for a prey*. Very frequent is the phrase הָיָה לָבַז *to become a prey*, Num. 14:31. Deut. 1:39. Is. 42:22. Jer. 2:14. and נָתַן לָבַז *to give for a prey*. Ezek. 25:7.

בָּזָא Arab. بزا *to subject to one's self*. Only Is. 18:2, 7 *whose land the rivers overflow*. According to the Chald. Vulg. and some Rabbins, i. q. בָּזַז *to lay waste*. So also the reading בזו in 4 MSS.

בִּזָּה fem. of בַּז *booty, prey*. 2 Chr. 14:14. Est. 9:10, 15, 16. Often joined with שְׁבִי and שָׁלָל, 2 Chr. 28:14. Ezra 9:7. Dan. 11:24, 33.

בָּזָה i. q. בּוּז *to despise, esteem lightly;* construed with an accus. Num. 15:21. more frequently with לְ, 2 Sam. 6:16: 2 K. 19:21. once with עַל, Neh. 2:19.—Est. 3:6 וַיִּבֶז בְּעֵינָיו לִשְׁלֹחַ *it appeared to him contemptible to lay hands*, etc. Prov. 19:16 בּוֹזֵה דְרָכָיו *he who despises his ways*, i. e. is indifferent about them. Is. 49:7 לִבְזֹה נֶפֶשׁ *to the despising of men*, i. e. to him whom men despise.

Niph. Part. נִבְזֶה *despised.* Ps. 15 : 4. Is. 53 : 3.

Hiph. i. q. Kal. Est. 1 : 17.

Deriv. out of course prob. נִבְזֶה.

בִּזָּיוֹן m. verbal from בָּזָה. *contempt.* Once Est. 1 : 18.

בָּזַז, plur. בָּזְזוּ, בָּזַזְנוּ, also בָּזוּנוּ; fut. יָבֹז.

1. *to spoil, plunder;* (1.) used absolutely, Num. 31 : 53. 1 Sam. 14 : 36 נָבֹזָּה בָהֶם *let us make spoil among them.* (2.) construed with an accus. *to take as booty, to make spoil of* any thing, Gen. 34 : 29. Deut. 2 : 35 רַק הַבְּהֵמָה בָּזַזְנוּ לָנוּ *only the cattle we took as a prey to ourselves.* 3 : 7. 20 : 14. Josh. 8 : 17. Ps. 109 : 11. Ezek. 26 : 12. (3.) construed with an accus. of the place, Gen. 34 : 27 וַיָּבֹזּוּ הָעִיר *and they plundered the city.* 2 K. 7 : 16. Ezek. 39 : 10. 2 Chr. 14 : 14.

Niph. נָבֹז, plur. נָבֹזּוּ; infin. הִבּוֹז; fut. יִבּוֹז. *to be made a prey of, to be plundered.* Am. 3 : 11. Is. 24 : 3.

Pu. *idem.* Jer. 50 : 37.

Deriv. בַּז, בִּזָּה.

בָּזָק m. found only Ezek. 1 : 14. According to the versions, *lightning.* Root בָּזַק, in Syr. and Arab. *to scatter, to break in pieces;* in Arab. also *to beam, to emit rays.*

בֶּזֶק proper name of a city lying south of Bethshan or Scythopolis. Only Judg. 1 : 4. 1 Sam. 11 : 8.

בָּזַר, fut. יִבְזֹר, i. q. פָּזַר *to scatter.* Once Dan. 11 : 24.

Pi. *idem.* Once Ps. 68 : 31. In Arab. *idem.* In Aram. בְּדַר (q. v.)

בָּחוֹן m. verbal from בָּחַן. *one who examines metals, a metallurgist.* Once Jer. 6 : 27. This form often has an active signification; comp. עָשׁוֹק=עֹשֵׁק *oppressor.*

בַּחוּן m. dec. I. found only Is. 23 : 13 Keri, prob. *a tower,* raised by a besieging enemy; comp. בֹּחַן. Chald. *specula.* The root is either בחן = Arab. بحن conj. IX. XI. *to be raised up;* or the Heb. בָּחַן in the sense of *exploring, spying,* as if i. q. בָּחַן.

בָּחוּר, plur. בַּחוּרִים בַּחוּרֵי (with Dagesh forte implied, to distinguish it from בְּחִירִים.) m. *a youth, young man.* Deut. 32 : 25. Prob. verbal from בָּחַר *to choose,* and literally signifying *chosen,* particularly as a young man for military service. Otherwise (ח and כ being interchanged) it may be compared with בֶּכֶר=Arab. بكر *a young man.*

בְּחוּרִים masc. plur. Num. 11 : 28. and **בְּחוּרוֹת** fem. plur. denom. from בָּחוּר. *youth, period of youth.* Ecc. 11 : 9. 12 : 1.

בַּחִין Is. 23 : 13 Keth. see בַּחוּן.

בָּחִיר verbal adj. and subst. from בָּחַר, dec. III. a. *one chosen* or *elected* of God. Is. 42 : 1. 43 : 20. 45 : 4. Ps. 106 : 23.

בָּחַל 1. *to loathe, abhor,* construed with בְּ. Zech. 11 : 8. So in Aram.

2. as in Arab. *to be covetous.* part. Pu. fem. Prov. 20 : 21 Kethib מְבֻחֶלֶת *penuriously acquired.*

בָּחַן fut. יִבְחַן, *to examine, try, prove,* spoken properly of a metallurgist, who examines and purifies his metals in the fire. Jer. 9 : 6. Zech. 13 : 9. Ps. 66 : 10. hence metaphorically Job 23 : 10 *he tries me, I come forth as gold.* Also without this figure, Ps. 7 : 10 *thou triest the hearts and reins.* 17 : 3. Jer. 11 : 20. 17 : 10. Spoken of men who try or tempt God, Mal. 3 : 10, 15.

Deriv. out of course בָּחוֹן.

בַּחַן m. prob. *tower.* Once Is. 32 : 14. Comp. בַּחוּן.

בֹּחַן m. verbal from בָּחַן. *examination, trial.* Is. 28 : 16.

בָּחַר fut. יִבְחַר, *to choose, select, elect;* construed with an acc. Josh. 24 : 15. 2 Sam. 24 : 12. 1 K. 18 : 25. more frequently with בְּ, Num. 16 : 5. 17 : 20. [5.] Deut. 7 : 6. with לְ, only 1 Sam. 20 : 30 (where many MSS. have בְּ.) with עַל, Job 36 : 21. When followed by מִן, *to choose, to prefer rather,* Ps. 84 : 11.

2. *to take pleasure* in any thing or

any body, *to like, be pleased,* (comp. *diligere* and *delectari,*) construed with an acc. or with בְּ. Gen. 6:2 מִכֹּל אֲשֶׁר בָּחָרוּ *of all whom they liked.* Is. 1:29. 2 Sam. 15:15 כְּכֹל אֲשֶׁר־יִבְחַר אֲדֹנִי *according to all which my lord shall please.* 2 Sam. 19:38 כֹּל אֲשֶׁר תִּבְחַר עָלַי *all which thou desirest of me.* Prov. 1:29. 3:31. Is. 14:1. Zech. 1:17. 2:12. 3:2.

3. as in Aram. *to prove, examine.* Is. 48:10. בְּחַרְתִּיךָ בְּכוּר עֹנִי *I have tried thee in the furnace of affliction.* 1 MS. has in this place בְּחַנְתִּיךָ an explanatory gloss. Comp. Job 34:4.

Part. בָּחוּר, plur. const. בְּחוּרֵי (whereby it is distinguished from בַּחוּרִים *young men.*) *chosen, selected.* Judg. 20:15. שְׁבַע מֵאוֹת אִישׁ בָּחוּר *seven hundred chosen men.* 16:34. 1 Sam. 24:3. 2 Sam. 6:1 אֶת־כָּל־בָּחוּר בְּיִשְׂרָאֵל *all the chosen men in Israel.*

Niph. part. נִבְחָר.

1. *worthy to be chosen, choice, excellent, eligendus.* Prov. 16:16 קְנוֹת בִּינָה נִבְחָר מִכָּסֶף *to possess wisdom is more excellent than silver.* 22:1. Jer. 8:3. Prov. 10:20. 8:10, 19.

2. *pleasant, acceptable.* Prov. 21:3 נִבְחָר לַיהוָה מִזָּבַח *more acceptable to Jehovah than sacrifice.*

Deriv. מִבְחוֹר, מִבְחָר, בָּחִיר.

בָּטָא and **בָּטָה** *to speak inconsiderately* or *rashly.* Part. בּוֹטֶה, Prov. 12:18.

Pi. בִּטֵּא, Lev. 5:4 נֶפֶשׁ כִּי תִשָּׁבַע לְבַטֵּא בִשְׂפָתַיִם *if any one swears, so as to speak inconsiderately with his lips.* The addition of the word שְׂפָתַיִם, which occurs also Ps. 106:34. Num. 30:7, 9. gives intensity to the idea of *rash talking.* Comp. אִישׁ שְׂפָתַיִם. Deriv. מִבְטָא.

בָּטַח 1. *to trust* or *confide in;* construed most commonly with בְּ, Ps. 13:6. 28:7. also with עַל, 2 K. 18:20, 21, 24. and אֶל, Ps. 4:6. 31:7. Judg. 20:36. A dative of personal advantage is sometimes added, Jer. 7:4 אַל תִּבְטְחוּ לָכֶם אֶל דִּבְרֵי הַשֶּׁקֶר *trust ye not in lying words.* ver. 8. 2 K. 18:21. (comp. Is. 36:6, where לְךָ is omitted.) Is. 36:9.

2. used absolutely, *to be quiet, secure, without fear.* Is. 12:2 *behold, God is my help,* אֶבְטַח וְלֹא אֶפְחָד *therefore am I secure and fear nothing.* Prov. 11:15 שֹׂנֵא תֹקְעִים בּוֹטֵחַ *he who hateth suretiship is sure* or *secure.* (Antith. רַע יֵרוֹעַ.) Sometimes, in a bad sense, *to be careless, thoughtless,* especially in the part. בּוֹטֵחַ *careless, thoughtless.* Judg. 18:7 שֹׁקֵט וּבֹטֵחַ *secure and thoughtless.* verses 10, 27. Is. 32:9 בָּנוֹת בֹּטְחוֹת *ye careless daughters.* ver. 10, 11. Jer. 12:5. Prov. 14:16. (Comp. the articles שַׁאֲנָן, שָׁלָה, שַׁלְוָה.)

Part. pass. בָּטוּחַ *confident, trusting,* with an active signification, (comp. Lat. *confisus.*) Is. 26:3. Ps. 112:7.

Hiph. *to cause to trust, to inspire confidence.* Jer. 28:15. 29:31. 2 K. 18:30. Ps. 22:10.

Deriv. out of course מִבְטָח.

בֶּטַח m. verbal from בָּטַח. *confidence, security.* Is. 32:17. Hence לָבֶטַח and בֶּטַח used adverbially, *confidently, securely, without fear and without danger, securè et tutò.* Gen. 34:25. hence frequently, יָשַׁב, שָׁכַן בֶּטַח, *to dwell quietly, securely,* 1 Sam. 12:11. 1 K. 4:25. Jer. 23:6. also *carelessly, thoughtlessly,* Jer. 49:31. Judg. 8:11.

בֶּטַח proper name of a city in the country of Aram Zobah, 2 Sam. 8:8. which in the parallel passage 1 Chr. 18:8. is called טִבְחַת.

בִּטְחָה f. Is. 30:15. and

בִּטָּחוֹן m. Is. 36:4. Ecc. 9:4. verbals from בָּטַח. *confidence.*

בַּטֻּחוֹת fem. plur. verbal from בָּטַח. *idem.* Job 12:6.

בָּטַל *to cease* or *leave off* from labour. Once Ecc. 12:3. In Arab. and Syr. *idem.*

בְּטֵל Chald. *idem.* Ezra 4:24.

Pa. בַּטֵּל, plur. בַּטִּלוּ, infin. בַּטָּלָא. *to cause to cease, to hinder.* Ezra 4:21, 23. 5:5. 6:8.

בֶּטֶן f. prim. dec. VI. g. 1. *body, belly.* Judg. 3:21. particularly *womb,* Gen. 25:23, 24. Job 3:10 כִּי לֹא סָגַר

דַּלְתֵי בִטְנִי *because it shut not up the doors of my mother's womb.*—מִבֶּטֶן אִמִּי *from the womb of my mother*, Judg. 16:17. Ps. 22:10, 11. פְּרִי בֶטֶן *fruit of the body* or *womb, children;* used also in reference to the male, Deut. 7:13. 28:4, 11. 30:9. Mich. 6:7. Job 19:17 בְּנֵי בִטְנִי *my children*, (spoken by Job.)

2. metaphorically, as the seat of thought and feeling, i. q. the breast, heart. Job 15:2, 35. 32:18.—חַדְרֵי בֶטֶן *the inmost part of the breast*, Prov. 18:8. 20:27. 26:22.

3. used in architecture, for a belly-like protuberance in pillars. 1 K. 7:10.

בָּטְנִים masc. plur. found only Gen. 43:11. *pistich nuts*, the fruit of the Pistacia vera, Linn. a species of oblong nuts, like hazel nuts, but with a double shell, and flat on one side. They are native in Palestine. Comp. Celsii Hierob. T. I. p. 24—27.

בִּי particle of entreaty, found only in the phrase בִּי אֲדֹנִי or בִּי אֲדֹנָי *pray* or *hear, my lord*, or *Lord!* Gen. 43:20. 44:18. Ex. 4:10, 13. Num. 12:11. Sept. δέομαι, δεόμεθα. Vulg. *obsecro.* This, like many similar particles, is perhaps primitive and underived. The most probable derivations, however, which have been proposed, are (1.) בִּי *per me* (scil. *obsecro.*) The Arabians use oaths in this way; and the expressions for swearing and for supplication often coincide. Others compare the expression used by the Germans on the Rhine, *mein!* (2.) בִּי for בְּעִי *entreaty* (q. v.) by contraction; comp. בַּל=בְּעַל. A noun in the accusative is often used as a particle. The Aramean translators render it by this word, בְּבָעוּ *cum obsecratione, quæso.*

בִּיאָה f. verbal from בּוֹא. *entrance.* Once Ezek. 8:5.

בִּין, pret. בִּן, בִּנֹתָה and בִּינוֹתִי, fut. יָבִין, strictly, as in Arab. *to be separated*, (hence בֵּין *between*,) *to be distinct, clear.*

1. *to see, perceive, observe.* (Comp. Germ. merken *to observe* with Marke *boundary;* Lat. vidēre *to see*, with vidĕre (whence dividere, vidua) *to divide;* intelligere, literally *to discern;* cernere, decernere, *to divide* and *to see.*) Construed with an accusative, Prov. 7:7. Dan. 10:1. with בְּ, Neh. 13:7. Ezra 8:15. and לְ, Job 23:8.

2. *to see into, to understand.* Is. 6:9. Dan. 12:8.

3. *to know.* Ps. 139:2 בַּנְתָּה לְרֵעִי מֵרָחוֹק *thou knowest my thoughts afar off.* 19:13. Here belongs בִּין דַּעַת *to know* or *possess knowledge*, Prov. 29:7. and בִּין מִשְׁפָּט *to know what is right*, Job 32:9. Prov. 28:5.

4. used absolutely, *to have understanding, to be wise* or *intelligent.* Ps. 49:21. Part. בָּנִים *the intelligent, prudent.*

Niph. נָבוֹן i. q. Kal no. 4. Is. 10:13. Part. נָבוֹן *intelligent.* Gen. 41:33, 39. Deut. 1:13.—נְבוֹן דָּבָר *intelligent of speech, eloquent*, 1 Sam. 16:18. comp. Is. 3:3.

Pil. בּוֹנֵן found only Deut. 32:10. *to observe, take care of.*

Hiph. הֵבִין. 1. caus. of Kal, *to make to understand, to explain.* Dan. 8:16.

2. *to teach, instruct*, Neh. 8:9 מְבִינִים אֶת הָעָם *who taught the people.* Ps. 119:34, 73, 130. Construed with two accusatives, Ps. 119:27 דֶּרֶךְ פִּקּוּדֶיךָ הֲבִינֵנִי *the way of thy commandments teach thou me.* More rarely with לְ of the person, Job 6:24 *wherein I have erred*, הָבִינוּ לִי *teach ye me.* Dan. 11:33. or of the thing, Neh. 8:7.

3. *to make wise.* Job 32:8.

4. intrans. as in Kal, *to observe, perceive, attend.* Dan. 8:5, 17 הָבֵן בֶּן־אָדָם *attend mortal!* 9:23. 10:11, 12.

5. *to know.* Job 28:23 אֱלֹהִים הֵבִין דַּרְכָּהּ *God knows the way thereto.* Construed with אֶל, Ps. 33:15. with בְּ, Dan. 1:17. Part. מֵבִין *skilled*, especially in writing, *learned*, 1 Chr. 27:32. Ezra 8:16.

6. *to be wise, intelligent.* Part. מֵבִין Prov. 8:9. 17:10, 24.

Hithpal. הִתְבּוֹנֵן.

1. *to observe, attend, regard.* Used absolutely, Jer. 2:10. with an acc. Job 37:14. Ps. 119:95. with אֶל, 1 K.

3:21. Is. 14:16. with עַל, Job 31:1. Ps. 37:10. with עַד, Job 32:12. 38:18. with בְּ, Job 30:20.

2. *to understand.* Job 26:14 *the thunder of his power,* מִי יִתְבּוֹנָן *who hath understood it.*

3. *to be skilful, intelligent.* Ps. 119:100.

Deriv. out of course תְּבוּנָה, תָּבוּן.

בַּיִן, const. בֵּין, strictly a subst. *intermediate space, interval, midst;* hence dual בֵּנַיִם, 1 Sam. 17:4, 23 אִישׁ הַבֵּנַיִם *a middle-man, umpire, champion.* Hence בְּבֵין Is. 44:4. and בֵּין (with suff. בֵּינִי, בֵּינְךָ, also בֵּינֶךָ, בֵּינֵיכֶם, and בֵּינוֹתֵינוּ, בֵּינוֹתָם,) used as a preposition *between.* For *between this and that,* stands בֵּין....וּבֵין Ex. 11:7. בֵּין....לְבֵין Gen. 26:28. בֵּין....לְ Is. 59:2.—בֵּין עֲשֶׂרֶת יָמִים *within ten days,* Neh. 5:18.—Prov. 26:13. בֵּין הָרְחֹבוֹת *in the streets.* Many verbs of *seeing, knowing,* and *teaching,* are construed with בֵּין, and signify *to see, know,* or *teach a difference between,* etc. Thus Mal. 3:18 וּרְאִיתֶם בֵּין צַדִּיק לְרָשָׁע *ye shall see the difference between the righteous and the wicked.* So with יָדַע 2 Sam. 19:36. Jon. 4:11. with הֵבִין 1 K. 3:9. with הוֹרָה *to teach,* Ezek. 44:23. comp. Lev. 27:12.

In combination with other prepositions, (1.) אֶל בֵּין *between, ad medium,* governing an acc. Ezek. 10:2. 31:10. (2.) מִבֵּין *from between, out of, e medio.* Ps. 104:12 *from between the branches.* Num. 17:2. [16:37.] Deut. 28:57 *the after-birth* הַיּוֹצֵאת מִבֵּין רַגְלֶיהָ *which cometh out from between her feet.* (Comp. Il. xix. 110.) Gen. 49:10 *there shall not depart* מְחֹקֵק מִבֵּין רַגְלָיו *the sceptre from his feet,* i.e. from its proper place between the feet of the king. More rarely מִבֵּין is merely i.q. בֵּין, 2 K. 16:14. (3.) מִבֵּינוֹת לְ *between, intra,* (comp. מִן לְ, מִתַּחַת לְ.) Ezek. 10:2.

בֵּין prep. Chald. *between,* as in Hebrew.

בִּינָה f. verbal from בִּין, dec. X.

1. *the act of understanding* Is. 33:19.

2. *understanding, wisdom, knowledge.* Prov. 2:3. Job 28:12, 20. Is. 11:2.—יָדַע בִּינָה *to have* or *acquire knowledge,* Job 38:4. Prov. 4:1. Is. 29:24. יֹדֵעַ בִּינָה *intelligent, prudent,* 2 Chr. 2:12.—1 Chr. 12:32 יֹדְעֵי בִינָה לָעִתִּים *understanding the times,* i.q. יֹדְעֵי הָעִתִּים Est. 1:10.

3. *explanation, interpretation,* of a vision. Dan. 8:15. comp. 9:22.

בֵּיצָה f. dec. I. a. *egg.* Deut. 22:6. Root בּוּץ or בִּיץ, signifying in Arab. *to be white.* Comp. בּוּץ.

בִּיר i.q. בְּאֵר *a spring* or *well.* Found only Jer. 6:7 Keri. comp. Arab. بِئْر.

בִּירָה f. dec. X. 1. *castle, fortress, citadel, palace.*—שׁוּשַׁן הַבִּירָה *the fortress Susa,* Neh. 1:1. Est. 1:2. 2:3, 8. 3:15. Dan. 8:2. All these passages can be understood of a proper citadel. Mention is also made, in the same connexion, of הָעִיר שׁוּשָׁן *the city of Susa,* Est. 3:15. 8:15. In other places it is used for the *whole city,* Est. 9:6, 11, 12. Compare the notice of Herodotus, that Susa at first was the name only of a citadel, and afterwards was transferred to the whole city. In speaking of Jerusalem, it is applied to the *fortress* of the temple, Neh. 2:8. 7:2, which in Josephus (J. A. xv. 14. xviii. 6. B. J. i. 16. vi. 15.) is called βάρις.

2. *temple,* as if *palace of God.* 1 Chr. 29:1, 19. (In Syr. ܒܝܪܬܐ *palatium, arx.*)

בִּירָה Chald. *idem.* Ezra 6:2.

בִּירָנִית f. denom. from בִּירָה, found only in the plur. בִּירָנִיּוֹת, *castle, citadel.* 2 Chr. 17:12. 27:4.

בַּיִת m. (concerning Prov. 2:18, see שׁוּחַ,) verbal from בּוּת; const. בֵּית, plur. בָּתִּים (*bottim*) for בַּתִּים or בָּתְּתִים from an obs. sing. בַּתָּה, (comp. in Syr. ܒܝܬܐ, plur. ܒܬܐ.)

1. *house, dwelling.*—בֶּן הַבַּיִת *son of the house, a slave born in the house, verna.* Gen. 15:3. Ecc. 2:7. בֵּית עוֹלָם *the eternal house, the grave,* Ecc. 12:5. אֲשֶׁר

אֲשֶׁר עַל הַבַּיִת *one who is placed over the house, a steward*, Gen. 44:1.—The accusative בַּיִת frequently stands for בְּבַיִת *in the house*, Gen. 24:23. Num. 30:11. With He local, בַּיְתָה *into the house*, Gen. 19:10. const. בֵּיתָה, e.g. בֵּיתָה יוֹסֵף *into the house of Joseph*, 43:17.

2. *tent*. Gen. 33:17. 2 K. 23:7. Ps. 5:8. (In Arab. بيت *idem*.)

3. *palace, temple*.—בֵּית פַּרְעֹה *palace of Pharaoh*. Gen. 12:15. בֵּית הַמֶּלֶךְ *royal palace*. אֲשֶׁר עַל הַבַּיִת *overseer of the palace, præfectus palatii*, one of the great officers of the crown, 1 K. 4:6. 2 K. 15:5. 19:2. Is. 36:3. comp. Dan. 2:49. בֵּית דָּגוֹן *temple of Dagon*, 1 Sam. 5:2. בֵּית יְהֹוָה *temple of Jehovah*, applied also to the tabernacle of the congregation, Ex. 23:19.—Spoken of a magnificent sepulchre, or mausoleum, Is. 14:18.

4. applied to *part* of a house or palace; e.g. בֵּית מִשְׁתֵּה הַיַּיִן *banqueting-hall*, Est. 7:8. (comp. Dan. 5:10.) בֵּית הַנָּשִׁים *harem*, Est. 2:3.

5. in an extended sense, *a repository, place*, or *container of any thing*. בָּתֵּי הַנֶּפֶשׁ *smelling bottles*, Is. 3:20. בָּתִּים לְבְרִיחִים לַבַּדִּים, *the places for the staves*, Ex. 26:29. 36:34. 37:14. 38:5. בֵּית עַכָּבִישׁ *the spider's web*, Job 8:14.—1 K. 18:32 *a trench* כְּבֵית סָאתַיִם *about the capacity of two seahs*.—בֵּית אֲבָנִים *a vein of stones*, (in the earth,) Job 8:17.—Neh. 2:3 הָעִיר בֵּית קִבְרוֹת אֲבוֹתַי *the city where my fathers are buried*. Ezek. 41:9 בֵּית צְלָעוֹת אֲשֶׁר לַבָּיִת *the place for the side-chambers of the house*. Prov. 8:2 בֵּית נְתִיבוֹת *the place where several roads meet*.

6. *the inner part, within*, (antith. חוּץ *without*.) בַּיְתָה *within, ad intus*, Ex. 28:26. 39:19. מִבַּיִת *from within, ab intus*, Gen. 6:14. בֵּית לְ Ezek. 1:27. מִבַּיִת לְ 1 K. 6:16. and לְמִבַּיִת לְ Num. 18:6. *within*. אֶל מִבַּיִת לְ *within, ad intus*, 2 K. 11:15.

7. figuratively, *family, kindred, tribe, people*. (Comp. in Arab. أهل *tent, family, tribe, people*.) Ex. 12:4. Gen. 7:1. 50:4. בֵּית פַּרְעֹה *the people*, i.e. the servants, *of Pharaoh*. Ex. 2:1. בֵּית לֵוִי *the tribe of Levi*. בֵּית יְהוּדָה . יִשְׂרָאֵל *the people of Judah, of Israel*.—בֵּית יְהוָֹה *the family* or *people of Jehovah*, i.e. Israel, Hos. 8:1. 9:8, 15. Jer. 12:7. comp. 1 Tim. 3:15. Heb. 3:6.

8. particularly *posterity*. Gen. 18:19. Hence Ruth 4:11 בָּנוּ בֵּית יִשְׂרָאֵל *they have built the house of Israel*, i.e. have given posterity to Israel. בָּנָה בַּיִת לְ *to raise up posterity to any one*, i. q. הֵקִים שֵׁם לְ *to raise up a name to any one*, spoken of him who marries a brother's widow, Deut. 25:9. When spoken of God, *to give posterity*, 2 Sam. 7:27. 1 K. 11:38. In the same sense occurs עָשָׂה בַּיִת לְ 2 Sam. 7:11. 1 K. 2:24.

9. בֵּית אָב strictly *one's father's house*. Gen. 24:23. hence *one's father's family, kindred*, Gen. 46:31 *Joseph spake to his brethren, and to his father's house*. 47:13. and *family*, a subdivision of a tribe, smaller than מִשְׁפָּחָה (q. v.) Num. 1:2 *number the children of Israel* לְמִשְׁפְּחֹתָם לְבֵית אֲבוֹתָם *according to their generations and families*. ver. 18 ff. רָאשֵׁי בֵּית אֲבוֹתָם *heads of their families*, Ex. 6:14. or רָאשִׁים לְבֵית אֲבוֹתָם 1 Chr. 5:24. also elliptically רָאשֵׁי אָבוֹת 1 Chr. 8:6. 26:32. Num. 31:26. Josh. 14:1. likewise שָׂרֵי אָבוֹת 1 Chr. 29:6. נְשִׂיאֵי הָאָבוֹת 2 Chr. 5:2. (Syr. [Syriac] *patriarch*.)

בֵּית is used before many proper names of places. The most remarkable of these combinations are the following:

1. בַּיִת a city of Moab, Is. 15:2. elsewhere written more in full בֵּית בַּעַל מְעוֹן.

2. בֵּית אָוֶן (*house of idols*) a city in the tribe of Benjamin. Josh. 7:2. 18:12. 1 Sam. 13:5. 14:23. This name, by way of reproach, is also given by the prophets to בֵּית־אֵל the city which follows. See אָוֶן no. 1.

3. בֵּית אֵל (*house of God*) a city between Shechem and Jerusalem, at first called לוּז, after the time of Jeroboam the seat of the worship of the golden calf, hence called by the prophets בֵּית אָוֶן (*house of idols*). Concerning the origin of the name, see Gen. 28:19. 35:1—

15. The gentile noun is בֵּית הָאֱלִי 1 K. 16:34.

4. בֵּית הָאֵצֶל a place not far from Samaria, Mic. 1:11.

5. בֵּית בַּעַל מְעוֹן Josh. 13:17, a place in the tribe of Reuben, afterwards taken possession of by the Moabites, called also simply בַּעַל מְעוֹן.

6. בֵּית בָּרָה found only Judg. 7:24, a place on the Jordan, prob. for בֵּית־עֲבָרָה (*domus transitûs,*) perhaps Βηθαβαρά, John 1:28.

7. בֵּית גָּדֵר (*house of inclosure*) a place in the tribe of Judah, 1 Chr. 2:51, otherwise called גְּדֵרָה Josh. 15:36, and גֶּדֶר 12:13.

8. בֵּית דָּגוֹן (*temple of Dagon*) a city in the tribe of Judah, Josh. 15:41. Also another of the same name in the tribe of Asher, 19:27. Comp. 1 Mac. 10:83.

9 בֵּית חוֹרֹן a Levitical city in the tribe of Ephraim, 2 Chr. 25:13. Josh. 21:22. otherwise called *the upper Bethhoron*, to distinguish it from *the lower*, on the borders of the tribes Ephraim and Benjamin, Josh. 16:3, 5. 18:13.

10. בֵּית לֶחֶם (*house of bread*) a village in the tribe of Judah, the birth-place of David, and of our blessed Saviour. Mic. 5:1. Ruth 1:2. Comp. אֶפְרָתָה. Also a city in the tribe of Zebulun, Josh. 19:15. The gentile noun is בֵּית הַלַּחְמִי 1 Sam. 16:1, 18.

11. בֵּית מִלּוֹא a citadel not far from Shechem, Judg. 9:6, 20. probably also 2 K. 12:20. where, however, some understand מִלּוֹא on mount Zion.

12. בֵּית נִמְרָה Num. 32:36. Josh. 13:27. also simply נִמְרָה Num. 32:3. a city in the tribe of Gad, in Eusebius called Βηθναβρίς.

13. בֵּית עֶדֶן Am. 1:5. a village on the west of Damascus, with a valley of the same name, which is also retained at the present day.

14. בֵּית פְּעוֹר a city of Moab, not far from Jordan, celebrated for the worship of Baal-Peor. Deut. 3:29. 34:6.

15. בֵּית צוּר (*house of the rock*) a strong city in the mountainous country of the tribe of Judah, between Jerusalem and Hebron. Josh. 15:58. Neh. 3:16. 1 Chr. 2:45. 2 Chr. 11:7. comp. Joseph. A. J. VIII. 3. XII. 1. 14. XIII. 9. 1 Mac. 4:29. 6:7, 26.

16. בֵּית רְחוֹב a city or province in Syria, once at war with David. Judg. 18:28. 2 Sam. 10:6.

17. בֵּית שְׁאָן (*house of rest*) Josh. 17:11, 16. also בֵּית שַׁן 1 Sam. 31:10, 12. and בֵּית שָׁן 2 Sam. 21:12. a city in the tribe of Manasseh, on the west of Jordan, afterwards called Σκυθόπολις, and in the Talmud *Baisan*.

18. בֵּית שֶׁמֶשׁ (*house of the sun*). (1.) a Levitical city in the tribe of Judah, near the bounds of the Philistines. Josh. 21:16. 1 Sam. 6:12. 1 K. 4:9. 2 K. 14:11. 1 Chr. 6:59. 2 Chr. 28:18. The gentile noun is בֵּית־הַשִּׁמְשִׁי 1 Sam. 6:14, 18. (2.) a place in the tribe of Naphtali. Josh. 19:38. Judg. 1:33. (3.) a place in the tribe of Issachar or Zebulun. Josh. 19:22. (4.) i. q. *On*, or *Heliopolis*, in Egypt. Jer. 43:13.

19. בֵּית אַרְבֵאל a village in the neighbourhood of Sephoris, afterwards fortified by Josephus, called in 1 Mac. 9:2. Ἄρβηλα. Hos. 10:14.

בַּיִת Chald. emph. בַּיְתָא, בַּיְתָה. i. q. Heb. בַּיִת.

1. *house, temple, palace.* Ezra 5:3 ff.

2. *a place in which any thing is contained.*—בֵּית גִּנְזַיָּא דִּי מַלְכָּא *royal treasure chamber*, Ezra 5:17. 7:20. בֵּית סִפְרַיָּא *archives*, Ezra 6:1.

בִּיתָן m. const. בִּיתַן, denom. from בַּיִת, dec. II. b. *palace*. Est. 1:5. 7:7, 8.

I. **בָּכָא** m. dec. IV. a. prob. *the baca plant* or *tree*, (Arab. بكا,) which grows in Arabia about Mecca, and resembles the balsam plant. 2 Sam. 5:23, 24. 1 Chr. 14:15. According to the Rabbins, *mulberry-tree*.

II. **בָּכָא** i. q. בְּכִי, בָּכָה, *a weeping*. Ps. 84:7 עֵמֶק הַבָּכָא *valley of weeping*, i.e. vale of tears. Others: *valley of the* *plant baca*, i. e. a dry valley. Others render it as a proper name.

בָּכָה, fut. יִבְכֶּה, apoc. יֵבְךְּ. *to weep, to weep for, to bewail;* construed with an acc. Gen. 23:2. 37:35. 50:3. Lev. 10:6. with עַל, Judg. 11:37, 38. Lam. 1:16. also with אֶל, 2 Sam. 1:24. with לְ, Jer. 22:10. Job 30:25. The construction with עַל has also other significations; e. g. Num. 11:13 יִבְכּוּ עָלַי לֵאמֹר *they wept unto me*, i. e. they implored me, *and said*. Gen. 45:15 *he kissed all his brethren*, וַיֵּבְךְּ עֲלֵיהֶם *and wept over them*, i. e. in their embraces. Gen. 45:15. 50:1. Judg. 14:16.

Pi. *to bewail;* construed with an acc. Ezek. 8:14. with עַל, Jer. 31:15.

Deriv. out of course, בְּכִית, בְּכִי, בָּכוּת, perhaps בָּכָא.

בֶּכֶה m. verbal from בָּכָה. *a weeping.* Once Ezra 10:1.

בְּכוֹר m. verbal from בָּכַר, dec. I.

1. *first-born*, spoken of men and cattle. Ex. 11:5. 12:29, etc. Plur. fem. בְּכוֹרוֹת used as a neuter, *firstlings, primogenita*, Gen. 4:4. Deut. 12:17.

2. figuratively, Is. 14:30 בְּכוֹרֵי דַלִּים *the first-born of the poor*, i. e. the very poor, the poorest of all. Job 18:13 בְּכוֹר מָוֶת *death's first-born*, i. e. a most awful death, a most terrible sickness. For the feminine occurs the form בְּכִירָה (from an obs. masc. בָּכִיר.)

בְּכוֹרָה, fem. of בְּכוֹר, dec. X.

1. *earlier birth, seniority, primogeniture.* Gen. 43:33.—מִשְׁפַּט הַבְּכֹרָה *the right of primogeniture*, Deut. 21:17.

2. *the right of primogeniture, birthright.* Gen. 25:31, 34. 27:32, 36. (Comp. בְּאֻלָּה.)

בִּכּוּרִים and **בִּכֻּרִים** plur. masc. verbal from בָּכַר. *first-fruits*, spoken of fruit and grain. Lev. 2:14. 23:17.—לֶחֶם הַבִּכּוּרִים *the bread of the first-fruits*, i. e. the first bread from the new corn, Lev. 23:20. 2 K. 4:42. יוֹם הַבִּכּוּרִים *festival of first-fruits*, otherwise called *the feast of weeks*, or *pentecost*.

בִּכּוּרָה, f. plur. בִּכּוּרִים. *early fig*, (in Arab. *Bokkore*, in Span. *Albacora*,) which ripens in June, the common fig not being eatable till August. Hos. 9:10. Mic. 7:1. Is. 28:4. In the same sense occurs תְּאֵנֵי הַבַּכֻּרוֹת Jer. 24:2.

בָּכוּת f. verbal from בָּכָה. *a weeping.* Gen. 35:8.

בְּכִי, in pause בֶּכִי, with suff. בִּכְיִי, verbal from בָּכָה, dec. VI. 1.

1. *a weeping.* בָּכָה בְּכִי גָדוֹל *to weep bitterly*, 2 Sam. 13:36. Is. 38:3. Comp. Jer. 31:15 בְּכִי תַמְרוּרִים רָחֵל מְבַכָּה *with bitter weeping Rachel wept*, etc.

2. *oozing* or *trickling down* of water in mines. Job 28:11. So in Greek and Lat. *δάκρυον, lacryma.*

בְּכִירָה adj. (from an obs. masc. בָּכִיר,) used as the fem. of בְּכוֹר, *oldest, first-born.* Gen. 19:31 ff.

בְּכִית f. verbal from בָּכָה, dec. I. *a weeping, mourning.* Once Gen. 50:4.

בָּכַר in Kal not used in Hebrew, but in Arab. signifying, *to precede, be forward, to hasten*, (kindred with בָּקַר.) Hence in Hebrew,

Pi. 1. *to bear early* or *new fruit.* Ezek. 47:12.

2. denom. of בְּכוֹר, *to constitute one first-born, to give him the rights of primogeniture.* Deut. 21:16.

Pu. *to be a first-born* or *firstling.* Lev. 27:26.

Hiph. *to bear for the first time.* Jer. 4:31.

Deriv. בְּכוֹר, בְּכִירָה, בִּכּוּרִים.

בֵּכֶר m. and **בִּכְרָה** f. *young camel.* (Arab. بَكْر and بَكْرَة.) Is. 60:6. Jer. 2:23. Others: *swift camel, dromedary.*

בַּל properly a subst. i. q. בְּלִי (from בָּלָה) *consumption, destruction;* hence, only in poetical usage,

1. adv. *not, non.* Is. 26:10, 14. Prov. 10:30. 24:23.

2. conj. *lest, that not, ne.* Is. 14:21.

בָּל Chald. m. *heart.* Once Dan. 6:15. (In Syr. and Arab. *idem.*)

בֵּל contraction of בְּעֵל i. q. בַּעַל *Bel*,

Belus, the god of the Babylonians. Only Is. 46:1. Jer. 50:2. 51:44. See the History of Bel and the Dragon; and comp. Cicero de nat. deorum, III. 16.

בְּלָא Chald. i.q. Heb. בָּלָה.

Pa. *to wear out, afflict, oppress.* Once Dan. 7:25. See בָּלָה Pi. no. 3.

בַּלְאֲדָן m. *Baladan*, the father of king Merodach-Baladan. 2 K. 20:12. Is. 39:1. Probably compounded of בֵּל *Baal*, and אֲדָן i.q. אָדוֹן *lord.*

בָּלַג in Kal not used in Hebrew, but signifying in Arabic, *to shine, to shine forth*, as the dawn. Conj. II. *to rejoice*, or *have a shining countenance;* see (אוֹר.) Conj. V. *to smile, be serene.* So in Hebrew,

Hiph. 1. *to cause to rise*, in a figurative sense, Am. 5:9 הַמַּבְלִיג שֹׁד עַל עָז *he causes destruction to rise*, i.e. to come, *on the mighty.* Comp. the very similar metaphors, Is. 42:9. 47:11. 58:8.

2. intrans. *to be serene, joyful.* Ps. 39:14 הָשַׁע מִמֶּנִּי וְאַבְלִיגָה *look away from me, and I shall again rejoice.* Job 9:27. 10:20.

Deriv. מַבְלִיגִית.

בָּלָה, fut. יִבְלֶה. 1. *to be old, worn, to wear out*, spoken of garments. Josh. 9:13. Neh. 9:21. hence the constructio prægnans, בָּלָה מֵעַל *to wear out and fall off from* any one, Deut. 8:4. 29:5. Applied figuratively to the heavens and earth, Is. 50:9. 51:6. Ps. 102:27.

2. *to be old, faded*, spoken of persons. Gen. 18:12.

3. *to be consumed.* (In Arab. applied e.g. to the consuming of bones by rottenness, or by worms.) Ps. 32:3 בָּלוּ עֲצָמָי *my bones are consumed.* Job 13:28 וְהוּא כְּרָקָב יִבְלֶה *and he is consumed, as a rotten thing.*

Pi. 1. *to cause to grow old* or *waste away.* Lam. 3:4.

2. *to consume, spend, enjoy.* Job 21:13 יְבַלּוּ בַטּוֹב יְמֵיהֶם *they spend their days in happiness.* Is. 65:22 *they shall enjoy the work of their own hands.* Ps. 49:15.

3. *to wear out, afflict, oppress, attero.* 1 Chr. 17:9. Comp. Chald. בְּלָא.

Deriv. out of course בְּלוֹאִים, בְּלִי, בַּל, תַּבְלִית.

בָּלֶה, fem. בָּלָה, dec. IX. b. *old, worn out;* spoken of garments, Josh. 9:4, 5. of persons, Ezek. 23:43 בָּלָה נִאוּפִים *adulteriis effœta.*

בָּלַהּ found only in Pi. בִּלֵּהּ i.q. בִּהֵל *to terrify.* Once Ezra 4:4 Kethib. Comp. בָּהַל and בָּלָה. (In Syr. ܒܠܗܒ a quadriliteral, *to terrify.*

בַּלָּהָה verbal from בָּלַהּ dec. XI. a. generally in the plural, 1. *terror.* Job 18:11. 24:17. 27:20. 30:15. 18:14 מֶלֶךְ בַּלָּהוֹת *the king of terrors*, i.e. of hades.

2. *sudden destruction.* Ps. 73:19. תַּמּוּ מִן־בַּלָּהוֹת *they perish by sudden destruction.* Is. 17:14. Used as a concrete, Ezek. 26:21 בַּלָּהוֹת אֶתְּנֵךְ וְאֵינֵךְ *I will make thee destruction*, i.e. a thing to be destroyed, *and thou shalt be no longer.* 27:36. 28:19.

בְּלוֹ Chald. *a tax on consumable articles, an excise;* or rather *an oppressive tax* (comp. בָּלָה no. 3.) *a tribute* generally. Comp. the etymology of מִכְסָה. Ezra 4:13, 20. 7:24.

בְּלוֹאִים masc. plur. Jer. 38:12, and **בְּלוֹיִים** verse 11, *old garments, rags.* (In Syr. ܒܠܘܐ *idem.*)

בֵּלְטְשַׁאצַּר m. a Chaldean name, which was given to Daniel in the Babylonian court, Dan. 1:7. 2:26. 4:5. It differs but little, perhaps, in its signification from בֵּלְשַׁאצַּר (see below); and probably signifies *Bel* (*est*) *rex princeps*, from בֵּל *Bel*, شاه *king*, and سر *chief* or *Belis princeps*, the syllable *tsha*, in *Belteshazzar*, being the suffix in the Zendish language, to denote the genitive case. Concerning the termination אצַּר, see article נְבוּכַדְנֶאצַּר.

בְּלִי verbal from בָּלָה. 1. as a subst. *destruction.* Is. 38:17. Hence

2. as an adv. *not.* 2 Sam. 1:21. Job 41:18. [26.] Whence (1.) בִּבְלִי *without;* e.g. בִּבְלִי־דַעַת *without knowing it, unawares,*

Deut. 4:42. 19:4. also simply בְּלִי in the same sense, Job 8:11. 24:10. 31:39. 33:9. Sometimes closely connected with a following noun, Job 30:8 בְּנֵי בְלִי שֵׁם *ignominious brood.* (2.) לִבְלִי *idem.* Josh. 5:14. Job 41:25. (3.) מִבְּלִי *because....not, so that....not,* i.q. מֵאֵין. Jer. 2:15 מִבְּלִי יֹשֵׁב *so that there is no inhabitant.* Zeph. 3:6. Job 4:20. Lam. 1:4 מִבְּלִי בָּאֵי מוֹעֵד *because none come to the feast.* It is usually followed (like מֵאֵין) by the participle, once Deut. 28:55 by the finite verb, and 9:28 מִבְּלִי יְכֹלֶת יְהוָֹה *because Jehovah could not,* by the infin. The negative is sometimes repeated, הֲמִבְּלִי אֵין *is it because....not,* 2 K. 1:16. Ex. 14:11. The word מִבְּלִי also signifies *without,* Is. 5:13. Job 6:6.—מִבְּלִי אֲשֶׁר לֹא *except that....not,* Ecc. 3:11. (4.) עַל בְּלִי *because....not.* Gen. 31:20. (5.) עַד בְּלִי *till....not.* Ps. 72:7.

בְּלִיל m. verbal from בָּלַל, dec. I. *mixt provender, meslin, farrago.* Job 6:5. 24:6. Is. 30:24. The two latter passages are rendered perfectly clear, by adopting the meaning of the Latin *farrago,* which consisted of barley or oats, mixed with vetches and beans, which were both sown and reapt together. See Plin. H. N. xviii. 15. 41.

בְּלִימָה *nothing.* Job 26:7. Compounded of בְּלִי *not* and מָה *any thing.*

בְּלִיַּעַל compounded of בְּלִי *not* and יַעַל prob. *use, profit;* comp. יָעַל Hiph. *to be useful.*

1. *perniciousness, worthlessness, wickedness.* אִישׁ בְּלִיַּעַל *a wicked man,* 1 Sam. 25:25. 30:22. Frequently in the plur. אֲנָשִׁים ,אַנְשֵׁי ,בְּנֵי בְלִיַּעַל *wicked people,* Deut. 13:13. Judg. 20:43. 2 Sam. 2:12. 1 K. 21:10. בַּת בְּלִיַּעַל *a wicked woman,* 1 Sam. 1:16. עֵד ב׳ *an ungodly witness,* Prov. 19:18. דְּבַר בְּלִיַּעַל *a wicked* or *base action,* Ps. 41:9. 101. 3. comp. Deut. 15:9 *lest there be a wicked thought in thine heart.*

2. *something pernicious, destruction.* Nah. 1:11. יֹעֵץ בְּלִיַּעַל *one who plans destruction.* Ps. 18:5 נַחֲלֵי בְלִיַּעַל *streams of destruction,* as an emblem of misfortune, or great dangers. Others incorrectly: *streams of hades,* (a signification, which does not belong to בְּלִיַּעַל.) Equally incorrect is the rendering, *king of hades.*

3. as a concrete, i. q. אִישׁ ב׳ *a wicked man,* Job 34:18. 2 Sam. 23:6. *a destroyer, waster,* Nah. 2:1.

I. **בָּלַל**, fut. יָבֹל, *to moisten, wet, anoint.* (In Arab. *idem.*) Hence part. בָּלוּל בַּשֶּׁמֶן *anointed over with oil.* Num. 2:4, 5. 7:10, 12. 14:21, etc. Intransitively, Ps. 92:11 בַּלֹּתִי בְּשֶׁמֶן רַעֲנָן *I am anointed with fresh oil.*

II. **בָּלַל** 1. *to mingle, confuse, confound.* (In Syr. ܒܠܒܠ *to mix, confuse.* Arab. بَلْبَلَ *idem.* II. *to stammer.*) Gen. 11:9 כִּי שָׁם בָּלַל יְהוָֹה שְׂפַת *for there Jehovah confounded the language of the whole earth.*

2. denom. from בְּלִיל, *to give fodder.* Judg. 19:21 וַיָּבָל לַחֲמוֹרִים *he gave to the asses fodder.*

Hithpo. *to mix one's self, to be mixed.* Hos. 7:8 *Ephraim is mixed with the nations,* i. e. he is familiar with them.

Deriv. תֶּבֶל, תְּבַלֻּל, בְּלִיל.

III. **בָּלַל** i. q. נָבַל *to wither, fade.* Hence fut. Hiph. וַנָּבֶל *we fade,* Is. 64:5.

בָּלַם *to bind, confine, restrain,* as a horse or mule with a bridle. Once Ps. 32:9. (In Syr. ܒܠܡ *to bind, confine,* the mouth. ܒܠܡܐ *a muzzle.*)

בָּלַס (denom. from Arab. and Ethiop. בָּלָס *figs,* also *sycamore fruit.*) *to gather, cultivate,* or *live on figs,* συκάζω. Once Am. 7:14 בּוֹלֵס שִׁקְמִים *one who scrapes* or *rubs sycamore fruit,* i. e. one who ripens or cultivates it by this necessary management. Sept. κνίζων συκάμινα. Comp. שִׁקְמִים and Bocharti Hieroz. 1. p. 384.

בָּלַע (In Arab. بَلَعَ.) 1. *to swallow, swallow up, devour.* Gen. 41:7, 24. Ex. 7:12. Jon. 2:1. Num. 16:30 *the* *earth opens her mouth and swallows them up.* ver. 32. 26:10. Ps. 106:17. Used proverbially, Job 7:19 עַד בִּלְעִי רֻקִּי *till I can swallow my spittle.* i.e. only a moment. The Arabs use a very similar expression: *let me swallow my spittle,* i.e. give me a moment's time. Perhaps it was used in this sense elliptically, without רֹק; hence Num. 4:20 וְלֹא־יָבֹאוּ לִרְאוֹת כְּבַלַּע אֶת־הַקֹּדֶשׁ *and they shall not for a moment see the sanctuary.* Sept. ἐξάπινα. Others: *when it is covered.* Others: *to their destruction.*

2. figuratively *to destroy,* (see Piel,) but without giving up the figure. Prov. 1:12 *let us swallow them up, as the grave the living.* Jer. 51:34 *he swallows me up, like a sea monster.*

Pi. בִּלַּע *to swallow up.* Figuratively בִּלַּע אָוֶן *to swallow up iniquity,* i.e. to commit it abundantly, Prov. 19:23. comp. Job 15:16.

2. *to destroy,* but without giving up the figure, (see Ps. 124:3.) Comp. אָכַל no.2. Job 2:3 *thou hast excited me against him, to destroy him without cause.* 10:8. 37:20. Ps. 21:10 בְּאַפּוֹ יְבַלְּעֵם *in his anger he destroys them.* Is. 3:12 וְדֶרֶךְ אֹרְחֹתֶיךָ בִּלֵּעוּ *they destroy thy path.* 19:3 וַעֲצָתוֹ אֲבַלֵּעַ *and I will destroy,* i.e. frustrate, *his purpose.* 25:7 וּבִלַּע בָּהָר הַזֶּה פְּנֵי הַלּוֹט *and he will destroy,* i.e. remove, *in that mountain the veil,* etc. verse 8 בִּלַּע הַמָּוֶת לָנֶצַח *he will destroy death for ever.* Applied to the *laying waste* of a country, 2 Sam. 20:19, 20. Lam. 2:2, 5, 8. The same metaphorical application is found in the Chald. בְּלַע *to swallow* and *to destroy;* and also in καταπίνω of the N. T. 2 Cor. 2:7. 5:4. 1 Pet. 5:8.

Pu. pass. of Pi. no. 2. Is. 9:15. Job 37:20. 2 Sam. 17:16 פֶּן יְבֻלַּע לַמֶּלֶךְ *so that the king be not destroyed.*

Niph. 1. pass. of Pi. no. 2. Hos. 8:8. Is. 28:7 נִבְלְעוּ מִן־הַיַּיִן *they are disordered by wine.* (comp. 28:1 הֲלוּמֵי יָיִן *smitten by wine.*) Others find in this passage a distinct root, namely, the Arab. بَلَغَ *to conquer,* which in Arabic is applied also to wine, which overcomes a man, and, as it were, smites him to the ground. Comp. שֵׁכָר no. 5. and רוּן.

Hithpa. Once Ps. 107:27 כָּל־חָכְמָתָם תִּתְבַּלָּע *all their wisdom is destroyed.*

בֶּלַע, with suff. בִּלְעוֹ, verbal from בָּלַע.

1. *something swallowed.* Jer. 51:44.

2. *destruction.* Ps. 52:6. [4.]

3. proper name of a small city on the southern extremity of the Dead Sea, afterwards called צֹעַר. With the four cities which were destroyed, it formed the Pentapolis, or district of five cities. Gen. 14:2, 8. 19:20—22.

בִּלְעֲדֵי and **בַּלְעֲדֵי,** with suff. בִּלְעָדַי, בִּלְעָדֶיךָ. Compounded of בַּל *not,* and עַד, עֲדֵי *to.*

1. properly *non ad, nihil ad.* Gen. 41:16 בִּלְעָדָי אֱלֹהִים יַעֲנֶה וגו' *it is not in me, God may answer Pharaoh peaceably.* 14:24 בִּלְעָדַי *nothing for me.*

2. *besides.* Job 34:32 בִּלְעֲדֵי אֶחֱזֶה *besides that which I see.* Is. 45:6.

3. *without.* Gen. 41:44. But more frequently

מִבַּלְעֲדֵי (1.) *besides* Ps. 18:32 מִי אֵל מִבַּלְעֲדֵי יְהוָה *who is God, besides Jehovah?* Num. 5:20. Josh. 22:19. (2.) *without.* Is. 36:10. (In Syr. occurs the singular form, ܒܠܥܕ, which is construed with ܡܢ.)

בִּלְעָם m. (prob. for בְּלַע עָם *absorptio populi,* i.q. Greek Νικόλαος.) proper name of a prophet hired by the Moabites against Israel. Num. 22:5 ff. In Greek Βαλαάμ.

בָּלַק *to pour out, to make empty* or *desolate.* (In Arab. is بلق *to open,* but بَلُوقَة *a waste, desert.*) Is. 24:1. Parall. בָּקַק.

Pu. pass. Nah. 2:11.

בָּלָק m. (*a waste, emptiness*) proper name of a king of the Moabites. Num. 22:2. Josh. 24:9. Judg. 11:25. Mic. 6:5.

בֵּלְשַׁאצַּר Dan. 5:1, 2. and בֵּלְאשַׁצַּר 7:1. proper name of the last king of the Chaldeans. From a comparison of Dan. v. with Herod. I. 191. and Xenoph. Cyrop. VII. 5:15 ff. it appears that he was the same who is called by the Greeks *Nabonned* and *Labynetus*. Comp. בֵּלְשַׁאצַּר.

בִּלְתִּי perhaps properly a subst. *separation*, from בָּלַת i. q. Arab. بلت *to separate*, intrans. *to be separated;* whence בֶּלֶת, with Yod paragogic, בִּלְתִּי.

1. adv. *not.* 1 Sam. 20:26.

2. prep. *without, besides, except.* Gen. 21:26. Ex. 22:19.—בִּלְתִּי אֶל־ *even to, except*, Num. 11:6. With suff. בִּלְתֶּךָ 1 Sam. 2:2.

3. בִּלְתִּי אִם *except, unless*, after a preceding negation, Gen. 47:18 *there is nothing left* בִּלְתִּי אִם גְּוִיָּתֵנוּ *except our body.* Judg. 7:14. Am. 3:3,4.

4. conj. *unless, besides that.* Gen. 43:3 בִּלְתִּי אֲחִיכֶם אִתְּכֶם *unless your brother is with you.* Dan. 11:18.

The following combinations also occur;

1. לְבִלְתִּי (1.) before an infin. *not to*, (the negative before an infinitive with לְ, is always expressed in this manner.) Gen. 3:11 לְבִלְתִּי אֲכָל *not to eat.* Ruth 2:9 לְבִלְתִּי נָגְעֵךְ *not to touch thee.* Gen. 38:9. Ex. 8:18, 25. *so that.....not, lest*, Gen. 4:15. *since....not*, Jer. 42:13.—לְבִלְתִּי לְ־ *so that not*, 2 K. 23:10. (2.) before a finite verb, *that not, lest.* Jer. 23:14 לְבִלְתִּי שָׁבוּ *that they do not return.* 27:18. but in Ezek. 13:3 לְבִלְתִּי רָאוּ *without that they see*, i. e. without having visions.

2. מִבִּלְתִּי *since not*, (the mode of expressing the negation before the infin. with מִן.) Num. 14:16. Ezek. 16:28 מִבִּלְתִּי שָׂבְעָתֵךְ *since thou art not satisfied.*

3. עַד־בִּלְתִּי *till not*, construed with the pret. Num. 21:35. Deut. 3:3. Josh. 8:22. Job 14:12 עַד בִּלְתִּי שָׁמַיִם *till the heavens are no more.*

בָּמָה f. with Kamets impure, as if from a root בּוּם, (comp. Pers. بام *above, a roof, arch,*) dec. X.

1. *height, high place.* 1 Sam. 9:12, 13, 14 ff. 10:5, 13. 1 Chr. 16:39. 21:29. Ezek. 36:2 בָּמוֹת עוֹלָם *the ancient high places.* Ps. 18:34 עַל בָּמוֹתַי יַעֲמִידֵנִי *he sets me upon my high places*, i.e. in secure places. On high places, the Hebrews frequently sacrificed to idols, and, also, before the idea arose or became prevalent that unity of place was necessary in religious worship, to Jehovah. Such worship is usually stigmatized by the Jewish historians as illegal. Hence כֹּהֲנֵי הַבָּמוֹת *priests of the high places*, 1 K. 12:32. 2 K. 17:32. 23:9.—בָּתֵּי הַבָּמוֹת, *houses* or *temples of the high places*, prob. *small chapels, sacella,* (in honour of Jehovah or of false gods,) 1 K. 13:32. 2 K. 17:29,32. 23:19. Hence

2. i.q. בֵּית הַבָּמָה *a chapel* or *sanctuary*, devoted to this illegal worship. 1 K. 11:7. 14:23. 2 K. 21:3. 23:8. These chapels were found, e.g. in the cities of Judah, 2 K. 17:9. on the mountains of Judah, 2 Chr. 21:11. in the valley of Hinnom, Jer. 7:31. This word is distinguished from מִזְבֵּחַ *altar*, 2 K. 23:15. 2 Chr. 14:2. 32:12. From Ezek. 16:16, according to which בָּמוֹת טְלֻאוֹת were made of garments, we may infer that these chapels were tents, or moveable temples, like the tabernacle of testimony, (comp. 2 K. 23:7. and Am. 5:26.)

Plur. בָּמוֹת (with *singular* meaning,) (1.) *high place.* Jer. 26:18. Mic. 3:12.

2. *grave, monument, mausoleum.* Is. 53:9. With suff. בְּמֹתָיו (the Kamets in this case being pure and mutable.)

Plur. const. (with double plural termination, comp. מְרַאֲשֹׁתֵי 1 Sam. 26:12.) בָּמוֹתֵי, or according to the Keri בָּמֳתֵי (read *bāmŏthe,*) *high places.* According to the reading בָּמֳתֵי, the וֹ is shortened as in עֲשָׂרִים ,עֶשֶׂר. Thus in the phrase דָּרַךְ עַל בָּמֳתֵי אֶרֶץ *to march upon the heights of the earth*, or *of the land*, a poetical description of a triumphant conqueror, or of the advancing Deity, Deut. 33:29. Mic. 1:3. Am. 4:13. also with רָכַב, Deut. 32:13. Is. 58:14. In the same connexion occurs בָּמֳתֵי־יָם *the high waves of the sea*, Job 9:8. בָּמֳתֵי עָב *the heights of the clouds*, Is. 14:14.

בְּמוֹ i. q. בְּ; see מוֹ.

בֵּן (for בְּנֶה) m. prim. (compare, however, the verb בָּנָה *to build*, in Arab. conj. I. II. VIII. *to beget, bear, have children;* and see, concerning this trope, under art. בַּיִת no. 8.) irreg. const. בֶּן, more rarely בִּן (Prov. 30:1, and before the proper name נוּן,) once בְּנִי (like אֲבִי) Gen. 49:11, and בְּנוֹ Num. 24:3, 15. with suff. בְּנִי, בִּנְךָ, בְּנוֹ; Plur. בָּנִים, בְּנֵי (as if from בְּנֶה, בֵּן.)

1. *son*, in the plural *sons* or *children.* Gen. 4:25. 43:29. 3:16. Deut. 4:10. This word is used in Hebrew in a very extended sense, and employed in many phrases unknown to our western languages, but parallel for the most part with those found under the articles אָב, אַח, etc. namely;

2. *grandson, descendant.* Gen. 29:5. 32:1. The more exact expression, however, for grandchildren is בְּנֵי בָנִים *children's children.* Hence (1.) בְּנֵי יִשְׂרָאֵל *the children of Israel, Israelites;* בְּנֵי עַמּוֹן *Ammonites;* בְּנֵי לֵוִי *Levites;* instead of which occur also the patronymics, יִשְׂרְאֵלִים, לְוִיִּם, etc. Nearly allied to these phrases is (2.) the joining of בֵּן with the names of nations and countries, to denote the members and inhabitants of the same. בְּנֵי צִיּוֹן *inhabitants of Zion*, Ps. 149:2. *the sons of the Greeks* for *the Greeks*, Joel 4:6. [3:6.] *the sons of the Ethiopians* for *the Ethiopians*, Am. 9:7. comp. υἷες Ἀχαιῶν in Homer. To this is also allied (3.) the periphrastic expression, such as *sons of strangers* for *strangers*, Ps. 18:45. *sons of the poor* for *the poor*, Ps. 72:4. *sons of nobles*, Ecc. 10:17. comp. δυστήνων παῖδες, Iliad, φ. 151. See also בֶּן־אָדָם under the art. אָדָם.

3. *pupil, disciple, follower, worshipper* of any one, (comp. אָב no. 5.) Thus בְּנֵי נְבִיאִים *sons of the prophets*, i. e. disciples of the prophets, (as in Persian, *filii magorum.*) 1 K. 20:35. 2 K. 2:3, 5, 7, 15, etc. (comp. Am. 7:14. Is. 19:11. and in Greek, παῖδες μουσικῶν, φιλοσοφῶν, for μουσικοί, φιλοσοφοί.)—בְּנֵי אֱלֹהִים *worshippers of God;* see art. אֱלֹהִים no. 3. The didactic poet addresses the reader thus, *my son!* Prov. 2:1. 3:1, 21. 4:10, 20. 5:1. 6:1. 7:1. Comp. בַּת Ps. 45:11. So in Prov. 10:5 בֵּן מַשְׂכִּיל, מֵבִישׁ *a wise son, a foolish son,* (so called in reference to the poet,) for *a wise person, a foolish person* generally.

4. *a client, favourite.* Thus the Israelitish nation is called *Jehovah's son,* Ps. 80:16. Hos. 11:1. Ex. 4:22. Perhaps the phrase *son of God*, when applied to kings, is to be understood in this way. See אֱלֹהִים no. 3. (1.)

5. In combination with substantives which express age, quality, or something similar, it denotes one who has this age or this quality. Gen. 5:32 *a son of* 500 *years*, i. e. 500 years old. Lev. 12:6 *a son of years*, i. e. aged. Jon. 4:10 שֶׁבִּן לַיְלָה הָיָה וּבִן לַיְלָה אָבָד *which as a son of a night*, i. e. during a night, *arose, and during a night perished.* (In Syr. ܒܪ ܝܘܡܗ *eodem die.*)—בֶּן חַיִל *a man of courage*, Deut. 3:18. בֶּן בְּלִיַּעַל *a wicked man, a worthless fellow,* (see בְּלִיַּעַל.)—*sons of surety*, i. e. hostages, 2 K. 14:14.—Is. 5:1 קֶרֶן בֶּן שָׁמֶן *a hill, son of fatness*, i. e. a fruitful hill. (Comp. אִישׁ, בַּעַל.)

6. used figuratively in other phrases; e. g. *son of death*, i. e. one deserving of death, 1 Sam. 20:31. So *son of stripes,* Deut. 25:2. *sons of the quiver*, i. e. arrows, Lam. 3:13. *sons of the bow,* i. e. arrows, Job 41:19. *son of the dawn,* i. e. morning-star, Is. 14:12. *sons of the bear* (a constellation in the heavens,) i. e. the three stars in his tail, Job 38:32.

7. applied to animals of every kind, *young.* בֶּן יוֹנָה *a young dove*, Ex. 12:6. בְּנֵי עֹרֵב *young ravens*, Ps. 147:2. בֶּן בָּקָר *a calf*, (see בָּקָר.) Applied also to eggs, (comp. in Syr. ܒܪܬܐ *daughter*, and *egg*,) Job 39:16. *she cruelly entreats her young ones as if they were not hers*, speaking of the ostrich's treatment of her eggs.

8. applied to plants, *a sprout, shoot, sucker*, as if *son of the tree.* (Comp. יוֹנֵק and יוֹנֶקֶת; and in Lat. *pullus* and *pullulare.*) Then, because it denotes an

inanimate substance, joined with a feminine adj. (as a substitute for the neuter,) Gen. 49:22 בֵּן פֹּרָת prob. *a fruitful sprout* or *branch*. (But see Lehrgeb. p. 474.) According to some, also Ps. 80:16.

בֵּן Chald. *idem*. Found only in the plural בְּנִין, בְּנֵי (בַּר being used in the sing.) —בְּנֵי גָלוּתָא *the exiles*, Dan. 2:25. בְּנֵי תוֹרִין *bullocks*, Ezra 6:9. (So in Syr. ܒܪ Plur. ܒܢܝ̈ܐ.)

בֶּן־הֲדַד m. common name of several kings of Syria of Damascus. 1 K. 15:18. 20:1. 2 K. 6:24. 8:7. 13:3. Jer. 49:27. Am. 1:4. Comp. הֲדַד and הֲדַדְעֶזֶר.

בֵּנַיִם, see בַּיִן.

בִּנְיָמִין m. (*son of prosperity;* see Gen. 35:18. and comp. יָמִין no. 4.) *Benjamin*, the youngest son of Jacob; also the tribe which was named from him, the boundaries of which are given Josh. 18:11 ff. The gentile noun is בֶּן־הַיְמִינִי, see יְמִינִי,

בָּנוֹת *daughters*, see בַּת.

בָּנָה, fut. יִבְנֶה, יִבֶן. 1. *to build, erect, make*, construed with an acc. Gen. 8:20. 10:11. 12:7, 8. rarely in an improper sense, as Gen. 2:22 וַיִּבֶן יְהוָה אֱלֹהִים אֶת־הַצֵּלָע לְאִשָּׁה *and the Lord God made the rib into a woman*, i. e. made a woman out of it. The material, out of which any thing is made, stands regularly in the accusative, 1 K. 18:32 וַיִּבְנֶה אֶת־הָאֲבָנִים מִזְבֵּחַ *and he built the stones into an altar*, i.e. built an altar out of the stones. 1 K. 15:22. Ex. 20:25. Deut. 27:6. Is. 9:9. Ezek. 27:5. comp. Niph. 1 K. 6:7. Rarely with בְּ prefixed to the material of which any thing is made, as 1 K. 15:22 at the close. The following constructions are worthy of notice, 1 K. 16:24 וַיִּבֶן אֶת־הָהָר *he built the mountain*, i. e. built upon it. 6:15 וַיִּבֶן אֶת־קִירוֹת הַבַּיִת מִבַּיְתָה בְּצַלְעוֹת אֲרָזִים *he built*, i. e. overlaid, *the walls of the temple inwardly with cedar boards*. Construed with בְּ, *to work on any thing, to labour on a building*, Zech. 6:15. Neh. 4:4, 11.

2. *to rebuild, build up* what has been destroyed. Am. 9:14 בָּנוּ עָרִים נְשַׁמּוֹת *they shall rebuild the desolate cities*. Ps. 122:3. 147:2. Josh. 6:26.—בָּנָה חֳרָבוֹת *to cultivate desert places anew;* see חָרְבָּה.

3. used figuratively of persons and nations, *to build them up, to give them a permanent habitation, to make them prosperous*. Jer. 24:6 וּבְנִיתִים וְלֹא אֶהֱרֹס וּנְטַעְתִּים וְלֹא אֶתּוֹשׁ *I will build them up and not pull them down, I will plant them and not pluck them up*. 31:4. 33:7. 42:10. Ps. 28:5. Comp. the other verbs of the quoted passages. So Ex. 1:22 *he* (*God*) *built for them houses*. (In Arab. also metaphorically, *to confer favours* or *blessings* on any one.)

4. בָּנָה בַיִת לְ *to raise up*, or *give posterity* to any one. See בַּיִת no. 8. comp. Niph. no. 3.

Niph. 1. *to be built, rebuilt*. Deut. 13:17. Job 12:14.

2. figuratively, *to be built up, to be made prosperous, to prosper again*. Jer. 12:16 וְנִבְנוּ בְּתוֹךְ עַמִּי *then shall they prosper among my people*. Mal. 3:15. Job 22:23.

3. pass. of Kal no. 4. Gen. 16:2 אוּלַי אִבָּנֶה מִמֶּנָּה *perhaps I shall acquire posterity through her*. 30:3. (Arab. بنا conj. I. II. and VIII. *to beget, bear, have children*.)

Deriv. מִבְנֶה, תַּבְנִית, בִּנְיָן, בִּנְיָה; and, according to some, בֵּן and בַּת.

בְּנָא, בְּנָה Chald. *to build*. Ezra 4:12. 5:2. Part. pass. בְּנֵה, 5:11. Infin. מִבְנֵא and מִבְנְיָה, 5:9.

Ithpe. pass. construed with an acc. of the material. Ezra 5:8 וְהוּא מִתְבְּנֵא אֶבֶן גְּלָל *and it is builded out of hewn stones*.

בִּנְיָה f. Ezek. 41:13. and

בִּנְיָן m. Ezek. 40:5. verbals from בָּנָה, *a building, structure*. According to Ezek. 41:12, 15. a special building within the circuit of the temple, appears to be intended. In Chald. Ezra 5:4. (Syr. ܒܶܢܝܳܢܳܐ, Arab. بُنْيَان *idem*.)

בְּנַס Chald. *to be angry*. Dan. 2:12. In the Targums more frequent.

בָּסַס see בּוּס Hithpa.

בֹּסֶר m. dec. VI. g. Job 15:33. and בֹּסֶר Is. 18:5. Jer. 31:29. *unripe grape.* (Syr. ܒܣܪܐ *idem*, ܒܣܪܐ *vinegar*.

בְּעַד and בַּעַד, with suff. בַּעֲדוֹ, בַּעֲדִי, בַּעַדְכֶם; prep.

1. *behind, after*, (Arab. بعد *after*.) Gen. 7:16. Judg. 3:22. 9:51. Am. 9:10 לֹא־תַגִּישׁ וְתַקְדִּים בַּעֲדֵינוּ הָרָעָה *the evil shall not overtake us, nor come up with us.* 2 Sam. 20:21 בְּעַד הַחוֹמָה *over the wall*, perhaps for מִבַּעַד *from behind the wall.*

2. *for.* 1 Sam. 7:9. 2 Sam. 10:12. Jer. 21:2.—הָיָה בְעַד i. q. הָיָה לְ, *to be for*, i. e. to become, Is. 32:14.—Job 2:4 עוֹר בְּעַד עוֹר *skin for skin.* (Ethiop. בער *to exchange, barter.*) Hence frequently, הִתְפַּלֵּל, כִּפֶּר בְּעַד *to pray for* any one, *to make atonement for* any person or thing.

3. *through.* Joel 2:8, 9 בְּעַד הַחַלּוֹנִים *through the lattices.* Gen. 26:8. Josh. 2:15. Judg. 5:28. Joined with מִן, מִבַּעַד (the only case in which the form בַּעַד is used before nouns,) *from through* or *between*, Cant. 4:1, 3. 6:7.

4. *about, round about.* Ps. 139:11 *then is the night light about me.* Job 3:23. Lam. 3:7 גָּדַר בַּעֲדִי *he has hedged round about me.* In this signification it follows many verbs of closing, (i. e. closing about,) and may be omitted in translating; e. g. after סָגַר 1 Sam. 1:6. after עָצַר Gen. 20:18. after חָתַם *to seal*, Job 9:7. Comp. הֵגֵן בְּעַד *to protect, defend*, Ps. 3:4. Zech. 12:8.

5. *by.* 1 Sam. 4:18 בְּעַד יַד הַשַּׁעַר *by the side of the gate.*

I. בָּעָה *to search, inquire*, (as in Arab. and Aram.) Is. 21:12.

Niph. pass. Obad. 6 *how are his secret places searched!*

Deriv. בְּעִי.

II. בָּעָה *to swell;* applied to water, *to boil, to boil up.* (Comp. Arab. بغي *to swell;* Chald בַּעְבַּע *to bubble, to boil;* and the Heb. אֲבַעְבֻּעֹת *blains, blisters.*) Is. 64:1 מַיִם תִּבְעֶה אֵשׁ *the fire makes the water to boil.*

Niph. Is. 30:13 *as a breach ready to fall*, נִבְעֶה בְּחוֹמָה *swelling out in the wall.*

בְּעָה and בְּעָא Chald. 1. *to seek.* Dan. 2:13. 6:5.

2. *to request, pray;* construed with מִן and מִן קֳדָם. Dan. 2:16, 18, 23. Hence

בָּעוּ f. Chald. *request, prayer.* Dan. 6:8, 14.

בְּעוֹר m. proper name of the father of Balaam. Num. 22:5. 24:3. Josh. 24:9. Mic. 6:5. In the N. T. 2 Pet. 2:15, this name is written Βοσόρ, perhaps by a commutation of the sounds of ע and צ. See the letter ע.

בֹּעַז proper name. 1. a kinsman of Ruth, to whom she was afterwards married. Ruth 2:1.

2. a pillar in front of Solomon's temple, so called after the architect, or the benefactor at whose expense it was built. 1 K. 7:21. 2 Chr. 3:17.

בְּעִי m. verbal from בָּעָה no. I. *request, prayer.* Once Job 30:24 לֹא בְעִי *prayer* avails *nothing.* Others regard it as a compound of בְּ, and עִי *hill, grave.*

בְּעִיר m. verbal from בָּעַר, (see בָּעַר no. I. 1.) dec. 1. *cattle.* In Syr. and Arab. *idem.*) Gen. 45:17. Ex. 22:5. Num. 20:4, 8, 11.

בָּעַט *to kick behind.* Deut. 32:15. hence, figuratively, *to spurn at, despise, be unmindful of benefits*, construed with בְּ, 1 Sam. 2:29 *wherefore despise ye my offering, and my oblation, which I have appointed?* Vulg. *Quare calce rejecistis—?* (Syr. ܒܥܛ *calcavit, recalcitravit.*)

בָּעַל, fut. יִבְעַל. 1. *to possess, command, rule over.* Is. 26:13 בְּעָלוּנוּ אֲדֹנִים זוּלָתֶךָ (*other*) *lords besides thee have ruled over us.* Construed with לְ, 1 Chr. 4:22.

2. *to take for a wife, to marry*, (the husband being considered the lord of the wife.) Deut. 21:13. 24:1. Is. 62:5. Part. בֹּעֲלַיִךְ (as a pluralis excellentiæ,)

thy husband, Is. 54:5. Part. pass. בְּעוּלָה and בְּעֻלַת־בַּעַל *a married woman*, Gen. 20:3. Deut. 22:22. (In Syr. and Arab. *idem.*)

3. construed with בְּ, *to despise, loathe.* (In Arab. بعل بـ *idem.* comp. Pococke ad Port. Mosis, p. 2.) Jer. 3:14 *return, rebellious children; though I have loathed you, yet will I* etc. 31:32.

Niph. *to be taken again for a wife.* Prov. 30:23. Figuratively, Is. 62:4.

בַּעַל verbal from בָּעַל, with suff. בַּעְלוֹ, בְּעָלֶיהָ (as a pluralis excellentiæ with singular meaning) Ex. 21:29, 34, 36. Is. 1:3. but בַּעְלֵיהֶן Est. 1:17, 20 (with plural meaning.)

1. *lord, owner.* בַּעַל הַבַּיִת, הַשּׁוֹר *the owner of the house, of the ox.* Ex. 21:28. Judg. 19:22. Also in the following phrases, Prov. 3:27 *withhold not a favour* מִבְּעָלָיו *from its lord*, i. e. from the poor man, to whom it is due. 17:8. 16:22 מְקוֹר חַיִּים שֵׂכֶל בְּעָלָיו *a well-spring of happiness is wisdom to its possessor.* 1:19. Ecc. 8:8 *wickedness delivers not* אֶת־בְּעָלָיו *him who practises it.* comp. 7:12.

2. *husband*, (as the lord of the wife.) 2 Sam. 11:20. Ex. 21:22 בַּעַל הָאִשָּׁה *the woman's husband;* but in verse 3 בַּעַל אִשָּׁה *a married man.* Joel 1:8 בַּעַל נְעוּרִים *the husband of one's youth.*

3. Joined with many substantives of different significations, it denotes one who possesses or is otherwise connected with the thing denoted by the noun, (comp. אִישׁ no. 2. בֵּן no. 5.) e. g. בַּעַל דְּבָרִים *one who has a lawsuit*, Ex. 24:14. בַּעַל קְרָנַיִם, כָּנָף *horned, winged*, Prov. 1:17. Dan. 8:6, 20. So *master of points* or *teeth*, i. e. having teeth, Is. 41:15. *master of dreams*, i. e. a dreamer, Gen. 37:19. *masters of arrows*, i. e. archers, Gen. 49:23. *masters of an oath, a covenant*, i. e. confederate, Gen. 14:13. Neh. 6:18. etc. Joined with the name of a city, it denotes, *an inhabitant, a citizen*, Josh. 24:11. Judg. 9:2 ff. 1 Sam. 23:11, 12. Here בַּעֲלֵי is synonymous with אַנְשֵׁי, בְּנֵי, (comp. 2 Sam. 21:12. with 2:4, 5.) and it is so regarded by all ancient versions. Others incorrectly; *rulers, proceres*, relying perhaps on Judg. 9:51 כָּל־הָאֲנָשִׁים וְהַנָּשִׁים וְכֹל בַּעֲלֵי הָעִיר, which ought to be rendered: *all the men and women, all the inhabitants of the city*, וְ being explanatory or exegetical, as in Josh. 6:23.

4. name of the tutelary god of the Phenicians and Syrians, to whose worship the Hebrews also were frequently inclined; constantly with the article, הַבַּעַל, לַבַּעַל, בַּבַּעַל, as Judg. 6:25 ff. 1 K. 18:18 ff. 2 K. 10:18 ff. He appears under the same name on Phenician monuments and medals, and in many Punic prop. names, as Hannibal i. e. חַנִּיבַעַל *grace of Baal;* Hasdrubal; Adherbal, etc.) Upon some of those inscriptions, which have a Greek translation accompanying them, this name is rendered Ἡρακλῆς; and this is the usual name, which the Greeks, led by the similarity of character between Baal and Hercules, have given to the national God of the Tyrians. Herod. II. 44. Arrian. Exped. Alex. XI. 16. On 1 K. 19:18, comp. Cic. in Verrem, IV. 43. Plur. הַבְּעָלִים *the Baals* or *Baalim*, (like עַשְׁתָּרוֹת *the Astartes*,) either meaning *statues of Baal*, or else referring to the different epithets, under which he was worshipped; as (1.) בַּעַל בְּרִית *Baal of the covenant*, Judg. 8:33. 9:4, 46. comp. Ζεὺς ὅρκιος. (2.) בַּעַל זְבוּב *the fly Baal;* comp. Ζεὺς ἀπόμυιος. See זְבוּב. (3.) בַּעַל פְּעוֹר see פְּעוֹר.

Connected with no. 3. is the use of this word before geographical names, denoting *the place where any thing is found*, i. q. בֵּית. The principal proper names of this kind are,

1. בַּעַל גָּד a city in the valley of Lebanon, on the border of Palestine. Josh. 11:17. 12:7. 13:5.

2. בַּעַל הָמוֹן Cant. 8:11. otherwise unknown. One of these two cities may, perhaps, be the celebrated *Balbec* or *Heliopolis of Syria*, the ruins of which are still admired by travellers.

3. בַּעַל חֶרְמוֹן a part of mount Antilibanus. Judg. 3:3. 1 Chr. 5:23.

4. בַּעַל מְעוֹן Ezek. 25:9. Josh. 13:17.

also בֵּית מְעוֹן Jer. 48:23. a place in the tribe of Reuben, afterwards taken possession of by the Moabites, according to Eusebius, near Baaru in Arabia.

5. בַּעַל פְּרָצִים (*place of discomfiture*) a place where David smote the Philistines. 2 Sam. 5:20.

6. בַּעַל צְפוֹן a city in Egypt, Ex. 14:2. Num. 33:7. usually called *Heroopolis*, from the worship of Typhon.

7. בַּעַל תָּמָר (*place of palms*) Judg. 20:33.

בְּעֵל Chald. *idem.* Ezra 4:8. See טְעֵם.

בַּעֲלָה fem. of בַּעַל, dec. X.

1. *female owner* or *possessor.* 1 K. 17:17.—בַּעֲלַת אוֹב, כְּשָׁפִים *sorceress.* See these words.

2. a city in the tribe of Judah, otherwise called *Kirjath Jearim.* Josh. 15:9. 1 Chr. 13:6.

בְּעָלוֹת a city in the southern part of the tribe of Judah. Josh. 15:24. 1 K. 4:16.

בַּעֲלִיס m. proper name of a king of the Ammonites. Jer. 40:14.—16 MSS. and Josephus (A. J. IX. 3.) read בַּעֲלִים.

בַּעֲלָת f. 1. a city in mt. Lebanon, 1 K. 9:18. 2 Chr. 8:6.

2. i. q. בַּעֲלָה no. 2. Josh. 19:44.

בָּעַר, fut. יִבְעַר. 1. prob. *to feed, graze, consume by grazing.* Not used in Kal in this sense, but see Pi. no. 1. Hiph. no. 1. Hence בְּעִיר *cattle*, so called from their *grazing.*

2. *to burn up, consume.* (Comp. אָכַל spoken of fire.) Ps. 83:15 כְּאֵשׁ תִּבְעַר יָעַר *as the fire consumes the forest.* More frequently construed with בְּ, Job 1:16 *the fire of God is fallen from heaven,* וַתִּבְעַר בַּצֹּאן וּבַנְּעָרִים *and has consumed the sheep and the young men.* Num. 11:3. Ps. 106:18. Is. 42:25. Also intrans. *to burn up, to be consumed by fire,* Ex. 3:3. Is. 1:31. Judg. 15:14. and inchoat. *to take fire, to kindle, to burn;* spoken of fire, Jer. 20:9. Is. 62:1. of the burning material, Ex. 3:2. Deut. 4:11: or figuratively of anger, Ps. 2:12 כִּי יִבְעַר כִּמְעַט אַפּוֹ *for his anger shall be suddenly kindled.* Ps. 79:6. 89:46. Est. 1:12. Ps. 18:9 גֶּחָלִים בָּעֲרוּ מִמֶּנּוּ *coals took fire from him,* i. e. glowing coals proceeded from him.

3. *to be dumb, brutish*, denom. from בְּעִיר *cattle.* Jer. 10:8. Part. בּוֹעֵר, Ps. 94:8. Ezek. 21:36. [31.]

Niph. נִבְעַר *to be dumb, brutish,* (see Kal no. 3.) Jer. 10:14, 21. 51:17. Is. 19:11. (Syr. ܐܬܒܥܪ *ferus factus est, ferociit, stulte fecit.*)

Pi. בִּעֵר, infin. בַּעֵר, fut. יְבַעֵר.

1. *to let* cattle *feed,* Ex. 22:4. Construed with an accusative, *to feed upon,* Is. 3:14. 5:5.

2. *to kindle, set on fire, burn.* Ex. 35:3. Lev. 6:5. [12.] Is. 44:15 וְהָיָה לְאָדָם לְבָעֵר *and it shall serve for a man to burn.* Is. 40:16 *Lebanon would not suffice* לְבָעֵר *to burn* for him a sacrifice. Neh. 10:35. 2 Chr. 4:20. 13:11.

3. *to remove, put away, take away.* Deut. 26:13, 14. 2 Sam. 4:11. 1 K. 22:46 *and the other sodomites* בִּעֵר מִן הָאָרֶץ *he removed out of the land.* Here belongs the expression in Deuteronomy, respecting the infliction of capital punishment, בִּעַרְתָּ הָרָע מִקִּרְבֶּךָ *thou shalt remove the evil from the midst of thee,* Deut. 13:6. 17:7. 19:19. 21:21. 22:21, 24. 24:7. also with מִיִּשְׂרָאֵל 17:12. 22:22. (In the earlier laws the correspondent expression is נִכְרְתָה נֶפֶשׁ מֵעַמָּם, or some similar phrase. But that הָרָע is here to be taken abstractly, is evident from 22:21, 24. where it otherwise would be in the feminine or in the plural.) Also construed with אַחֲרֵי, 1 K. 14:10 בִּעַרְתִּי אַחֲרֵי בֵית יָרָבְעָם *I will remove away the house of Jeroboam, as a man removes dung.* 21:21.

Pu. *to burn.* Jer. 36:22.

Hiph. 1. *to feed upon.* Ex. 22:4.

2. *to kindle, set on fire,* Ex. 22:5. *to burn* any thing, Nah. 2:14. 2 Chr. 28:3.

3. *to remove, put away;* construed with אַחֲרֵי. 1 K. 16:3.

Deriv. out of course תַּבְעֵרָה.

בָּעֵר verbal adj. from בָּעַר, *burning.* Is. 4:4.

בַּעַר m. denom. from בְּעִיר, *brutish, stupid,* like cattle. (See בָּעַר no. 3.) Ps. 49:11. 73:22. 92:7.

בְּעֵרָה fem. of בָּעֵר, *a fire, burning.* Ex. 22:5.

בַּעְשָׁא proper name of a king of Israel, son of Ahijah. 1 K. 15:16. 2 Chr. 16:1. Sept. Βαασά. Vulg. *Baasa.* (Root בעש in Chald. i.q. בָּאַשׁ *to be wicked.*)

בָּעַת in Kal not used. (In Syr. *to fear, to be afraid.*)

Pi. בִּעֵת, fut. יְבַעֵת. 1. *to frighten, terrify.* Ps. 18:5. Job 9:34. 13:11. 15:24.

2. *to come upon suddenly.* 1 Sam. 16:14 וּבִעֲתַתּוּ רוּחַ רָעָה *an evil spirit came upon him suddenly.* ver. 15. (Arab. بغت *to happen suddenly;* conj. III. *to come upon suddenly.*)

Niph. *to fear, be afraid.* Dan. 8:17. construed with מִפְּנֵי, מִלִּפְנֵי, 1 Chr. 21:30. Est. 7:6.

בְּעָתָה f. verbal from בִּעֵת. *terror.* Jer. 8:15. 14:19.

בִּעוּתִים masc. plur. verbal from בִּעֵת, dec. 1. *idem.* Job 6:4. Ps. 88:17.

בֹּץ m. Jer. 38:22. and בִּצָּה f. Job 8:11. 40:21. *marsh, mire.* (In Chald. *idem.*) Plur. with suff. בִּצֹּאתָיו Ezek. 47:11, an incorrect orthography for בִּצּוֹתָיו (Root בצץ i.q. Arab. بضّ *to be moist, to moisten;* بضّ *moisture, scanty water.*)

בָּצִיר m. verbal from בָּצַר, dec. III. a.
1. subst. *vintage.* Lev. 26:5. Judg. 8:2. See בָּצַר no. 1.
2. adj. i.q. בָּצוּר *fortified, strong.* Zech. 11:2. Keri.

בָּצָל m. *onion.* Plur. בְּצָלִים, Num. 11:5. In Syr. and Arab. *idem.* Root בצל i.q. Arab. بصل *to peel off;* comp. Heb. פָּצַל.

I. בָּצַע (Arab. بضع *to cut off, to cut in pieces,*) *to break off, to break down.* Am. 9:1 וּבְצַעַם בְּרֹאשׁ כֻּלָּם *and break them down on the head of all,* i.e. so that the pieces fall on the head of all. The form בְּצַעַם is put for בַּצְּעֵם. Joel 2:8 *they rush through drawn swords,* לֹא יִבְצָעוּ *and break not their course.*

Pi. 1. *to cut off,* Is. 38:12.

2. *to finish, make an end.* Is. 10:12. Zech. 4:9. Job 6:9 *may he loose his hand* וִיבַצְּעֵנִי *and make an end of me.* 27:8 *when (God) maketh an end (of him,)* i.e. taketh away his life. Lam. 2:17 בִּצַּע אֶמְרָתוֹ *he has finished,* i.e. fulfilled, *his word.*

II. בָּצַע (Arab. بضع) *to heap up, collect;* particularly ill-gotten wealth. Part. בּוֹצֵעַ בֶּצַע *one who seeks unrighteous gain,* Prov. 1:19. 15:27. Jer. 6:13. 8:10. Infin. Ezek. 22:27.

Pi. *to take advantage of* any one construed with an accus. Ezek. 22:12.

בֶּצַע m. with suff. בִּצְעוֹ, verbal from בָּצַע, dec. VI.

1. *gain.* Gen. 37:26 מַה־בֶּצַע *what is the gain?* Ps. 30:10. Job 22:3. Especially *unrighteous gain,* 1 Sam. 8:3. Ex. 18:21 שֹׂנְאֵי בָצַע *hating unrighteous gain, enemies of extortion.* Prov. 28:16. Jer. 51:13. Hence

2. *ill-gotten wealth.* Ezek. 22:13. בִּצְעֵךְ אֲשֶׁר עָשִׂית *thy ill-gotten wealth which thou hast procured.* Mic. 4:13. See בָּצַע בֶּצַע, under art. בָּצַע no. II.

3. *covetousness.* Is. 57:17.

בָּצֵק *to swell.* Only Deut. 8:4. Neh. 9:21. (In Samar. אבזק *idem.*)

בָּצֵק m. verbal from בָּצֵק, dec. V. a. *dough,* (so called from its *swelling.*) Ex. 12:34, 39. 2 Sam. 13:8.

בָּצְקַת (*vicus elatior,* according to the Arab. بصقة) a place in the plain of the tribe of Judah. Josh. 15:39. 2 K. 22:1. In Josephus (J. A. x. 5.) Βόσκεθ.

בָּצַר, fut. יִבְצֹר 1. *to cut off, to gather.* (Comp. in Syr. ܒܨܪ Pa. *to shorten, to lessen.*) Used almost exclusively of the *gathering* of grapes in vintage. Lev. 25: 5, 11. Construed with an accusative of the vineyard, Deut. 24:21. Judg. 9:27. Part. בּוֹצֵר *a vintager*, Jer. 6:9. and this as an image of a formidable enemy, Jer. 49:9. Obad. 5. (comp. Rev. 14:18, 19.) Metaphorically, Ps. 76:13 יִבְצֹר רוּחַ נְגִידִים *he cuts off the spirit of princes.*

2. *to make inaccessible*, and hence to *fortify*. Part. בָּצוּר (1.) *inaccessible, high.* חוֹמָה בְצוּרָה *an inaccessible wall*, Deut. 28: 52. Is. 2:15. Metaphorically גְּדֹלוֹת וּבְצֻרוֹת *magna et ardua* (*intellectu*,) Jer. 33:3. (2.) applied to cities, *fortified.* Deut. 1: 28. 3:5. 2 Sam. 20:6.

Niph. *to be cut off, forbidden, restrained*, construed with מִן. Gen. 11: 6. Job 42:2 וְלֹא יִבָּצֵר מִמְּךָ מְזִמָּה *no undertaking is forbidden*, or *too difficult for thee.*

Pi. *to fortify* cities. Is. 22:10. Jer. 51:53. See מִבְצָר.

I. בֶּצֶר Job 22:24. and Plur. בְּצָרִים verse 25. a precious metal or something costly, which can be determined with certainty, neither from etymology, nor from the ancient versions, nor from Jewish tradition. According to David Kimchi: *gold;* according to Aben Ezra and others: *silver.* The parallel clause ver. 24, has *gold of Ophir;* verse 25, *treasures of silver.*

II. בֶּצֶר proper name of a Levitical city and city of refuge, in the tribe of Reuben. Deut. 4:43. Josh. 20:8. 21: 36. Vulg. *Bosor.*

בְּצַר i. q. בֶּצֶר no. I. Job 36:19.

בָּצְרָה f. 1. *a fold, pen.* Mic. 2:12. (from בָּצַר no. 2. comp. מִכְלָא from כָּלָא.) In Chald. בְּצוּרְתָּא *septum, conclave.*

2. a city in Idumea, Gen. 36:33. Is. 34:6. 63:1. Jer. 49:13, 22. Am. 1:12. another in Moab, Jer. 48:24.

בִּצָּרוֹן m. verbal from בָּצַר, *a fortified place, a strong hold.* Zech. 9:12.

בַּצֹּרֶת f. Jer. 17:8. and Plur. בַּצָּרוֹת 14:1. *the holding back of rain, drought.* (comp. בָּצַר.) In Chald. more frequent. Root בְּצַר *to cut off, eheck, restrain.*

בַּקְבּוּק m. dec. 1. *flask, bottle, flagon.* 1 K. 14:3. Jer. 19:1, 10. Formed from the sound which a bottle makes when emptied. (Comp. Arab. بقبق *sonum edidit* amphora *inter evacuandum;* Syr. ܩܘܩܒܐ *laguncula;* and Greek βομβύλιον.)

בְּקִיעַ m. verbal from בָּקַע dec. I. *a cleft, breach, fissure.* Am. 6:11. especially *a breach in a wall*, Is. 22:9.

בָּקַע, fut. יִבְקַע (In Syr. ܒܩܥ.)

1. *to divide, cleave;* e. g. the sea, Ex. 14:16. Neh. 9:11. *to cleave out*, Ps. 74:15.

2. *to cleave and enter, to break in.* 2 Sam. 23:16 *then the three mighty men broke into the camp.* Hence *to make an irruption into*, or *to take* a hostile city. 2 Chr. 32:1. 21:17.

3. *to break open* or *hatch* eggs. Is. 34:15 וַתְּמַלֵּט וּבָקְעָה וְדָגְרָה *she* (*the serpent*) *lays her eggs, and hatches them, and broods* (*over her young.*)

4. *to rip up* a woman with child. Am. 1:13.

5. *to tear in pieces*, spoken of wild animals. Hos. 13:8.

Niph. 1. *to divide itself, to open*, spoken of the earth. Num. 16:31. Zech. 14:4. Hence *to be rent with noise, to shake*, spoken of the earth, 1 K. 1:40. also *to burst*, spoken of skin-bottles, Job 32:19.

2. *to be broken up, to be taken*, spoken of a city. 2 K. 25:4. Jer. 52:7. Ezek. 30:17.

3. *to break out*, (see Pi. no. 2.) spoken of water, Is. 35:6. Prov. 3:20. of light, Is. 58:8.

4. *to be hatched, to come out of the egg.* Is. 59:5.

5. *to be rent.* Job 26:8.

6. *to be dashed in pieces*, 2 Chr. 25:12.

Pi. בִּקַּע 1. i. q. Kal no. 1. *to cleave, split;* e. g. wood, Gen. 22:3. the rocks, Ps. 78:15.

2. *to cause to break out.* Job 28:12. Hab. 3:9.

3. i. q. Kal no. 3. *to hatch eggs.* Is. 59:5.

4. i. q. Kal no. 4. 2 K. 8:12. 15:16.

5. i. q. Kal no. 5. 2 K. 2:24.

Pu. 1. *to be rent.* Josh. 9:4.

2. pass. of Kal no. 2. Ezek. 26:10.

3. pass. of Kal and Pi. no. 4. Hos. 14:1. [13:16.]

Hiph. i. q. Kal no. 2. 2 K. 3:26. Is. 7:6.

Hoph. pass. Jer. 39:2.

Hithpa. *to divide itself, to be cleft.* Mic. 1:4. Is. 9:13.

בֶּקַע m. verbal from בָּקַע, *a half,* especially *a half shekel.* Gen. 24:22. Ex. 38:26.

בִּקְעָה f. verbal from בָּקַע, dec. XII. b. *valley, low plain.* (Syr. ܦܩܥܬܐ, Arab. بقعة بقيع *a plain.*) Gen. 11:2. Ezek. 37:1, 2.—בִּקְעַת הַלְּבָנוֹן *valley of Lebanon,* i. e. *the valley of Bukka* between Libanus and Antilibanus, Josh. 11:17. 12:7.

בִּקְעָה f. Chald. *valley,* as in Heb. Dan. 3:1.

בָּקַק properly *to pour out, to empty out.* (Arab. بقبق, see בַּקְבּוּק.) Hence

1. *to make empty, to depopulate* a country. Is. 24:1. Nah. 2:3.—Jer. 19:7 בַּקֹּתִי אֶת עֲצַת יְהוּדָה *I empty the counsel of Judah,* i. e. I deprive him of counsel or wisdom.

2. intrans. *to pour itself out, to spread out wide.* Hos. 10:1 גֶּפֶן בּוֹקֵק *a wide-spread* or *luxuriant vine.* (Arab. بق *to have many children.*)

Niph. נָבַק, infin. הִבּוֹק, fut. יִבּוֹק, pass. of Kal no. 1. Is. 24:3. 19:3 נָבְקָה רוּחַ מִצְרַיִם *the spirit of the Egyptians shall fail,* (נָבְקָה for נָבַקָּה).

Poel i. q. Kal no. 1. Jer. 51:2.

בָּקַר found only in Pi. בִּקֵּר.

1. *to see, behold, look;* when construed with בְּ, *to behold with pleasure, to rejoice in the sight of,* Ps. 27:4 לְבַקֵּר בְּהֵיכָלוֹ *to rejoice in his sanctuary.*

2. *to look after, to search for* any thing; construed with לְ, Gen. 13:36. with בֵּין, Lev. 27:33.

3. *to think on, to reflect, meditate.* Prov. 20:25. 2 K. 16:15.

4. *to look after, to take care of* any thing, *prospicere* alicui rei, i. q. פָּקַד Ezek. 34:11, 12.

בְּקַר Chald. found only in Pa. בַּקַּר *to seek, search.* Ezra 4:15, 19. 5:17. and Ithpa. אִתְבַּקַּר *idem.* Ezra 5:17.

בָּקָר com. gen. dec. IV. a. collect. *oxen, neat cattle, a herd of oxen,* without distinction of age or sex. Gen. 12:16. 13:5. 18:7. 20:14. 21:27. The nomen unitatis is שׁוֹר; hence Ex. 21:37 [22:1] *if a man shall steal an ox* (שׁוֹר) *then he shall restore* חֲמִשָּׁה בָקָר *five oxen.* (In Arab. بقرة *an ox,* بقر *oxen.* In Heb. comp. שֶׂה and צֹאן.) בָּקָר עָלוֹת *milch kine, cows,* Gen. 33:13. בֶּן בָּקָר *a son of the herd, a calf,* Gen. 18:7, 8. פַּר בֶּן בָּקָר *a young bullock,* Num. 29:2, 8. or עֵגֶל בֶּן בָּקָר *a young calf,* Lev. 9:2.—Jer. 31:12 בְּנֵי צֹאן וּבָקָר *young oxen and sheep.* More rarely the plur. בְּקָרִים, Am. 6:12. Neh. 10:37. 2 Chr. 4:3.

בֹּקֶר, plur. בְּקָרִים, m. dec. VI. p.

1. *the dawn, the morning.* Gen. 1:5 ff.—בַּבֹּקֶר בַּבֹּקֶר *every morning,* Ex. 30:7. 34:2. לַבֹּקֶר *idem,* Am. 4:4. 1 Chr. 16:40. לַבְּקָרִים *idem,* Ps. 73:14. 10:8. Is. 33:2.

2. i. q. מָחָר *to-morrow, the morrow, cras.* Ex. 16:7. Num. 16:5. hence לַבֹּקֶר *on the morrow,* i. e. *soon, suddenly.* Ps. 49:15. 90:14. 143:8. The ground of this signification is this, that when we think of the morrow, the morning presents itself to the mind, (comp. αὔριον;) but when we think of yesterday, the evening, (see אֶמֶשׁ.)

בַּקָּרָה f. (with Kamets impure) dec. X. *the looking after,* or *taking care of* flocks. Ezek. 34:12. Properly Aram. infin. Pael.

בִּקֹּרֶת f. *chastisement, punishment.* Lev. 19:20. Root בקר in Chald. *to punish*, i. q. Heb. פָּקַד.

בָּקַשׁ found only in Pi. בִּקֵּשׁ.

1. *to seek, quæro.* Gen. 37:15, 16. 1 Sam. 10:14. When construed with לְ, *to seek after, inquire into,* Job 10:6. Construed with an infin. with and without לְ, Ex. 2:15. 4:24. 1 Sam. 19:2. Jer. 26:21. The following phrases are worthy of notice, (1.) בִּקֵּשׁ רָעָה לְ *to seek the harm of* any one. Num. 35:23. 1 Sam. 24:10. 25:26. The contrary phrase is בִּקֵּשׁ טוֹבָה לְ *to seek the welfare of* any one, Neh. 2:10. (2.) בִּקֵּשׁ יְהוָה *to seek Jehovah,* i. e. to turn one's self to him, to supplicate him. Deut. 4:29. 2 Chr. 20:4. מְבַקְשֵׁי יְהוָה *those who seek Jehovah,* Ps. 40:17. 69:7. 105:3. (3.) *to seek the face of the king,* for *to desire to see him,* 1 K. 10:24. or *to solicit his favour,* Prov. 29:26. Hence (4.) *to seek the face of Jehovah,* for *to worship him in his temple,* Ps. 24:6. 27:8. 105:4. *to inquire of him,* 2 Sam. 21:1. or *to supplicate him* generally, 2 Sam. 12:16.

2. *to strive after any thing, peto.* Num. 16:10.—בִּקֵּשׁ נֶפֶשׁ פ׳ *to seek the life of any one,* Ex. 4:19. 1 Sam. 19:16. also in a good sense, *to be zealous for another's life,* Pro. 29:10.

3. *to require, demand.* Neh. 5:18. Construed with מִן, Neh. 5:12. Ps. 104:21. or with מִיַּד, Gen. 31:39. 43:8. Is. 1:12 מִי בִקֵּשׁ זֹאת מִיֶּדְכֶם *who hath required this from you?* Especially בִּקֵּשׁ דָּם מִיַּד פ׳ *to require a man's blood from the hand of any one,* i. e. to take revenge from him for bloodshed, 2 Sam. 4:11. Ezek. 3:18, 20. also in the same sense without דָּם, 1 Sam. 20:16. Comp. Josh. 22:23. יְהוָה הוּא יְבַקֵּשׁ *then let Jehovah himself revenge it.*

4. *to beg, entreat, pray,* construed with מִן. Ezra 8:21. Dan. 1:8. Est. 7:7 'וְהָמָן עָמַד לְבַקֵּשׁ עַל נַפְשׁוֹ מִ *and Haman stood up to entreat Esther for his life.* So Ezra 8:23. and Est. 4:8, (with לְפָנָי.)

בַּקָּשָׁה f. (with Kamets impure) verbal from בִּקֵּשׁ, dec. I. *request, petition, prayer.* Est. 5:7, 8. 7:3.

I. **בַּר** m. with suff. בְּרִי, *son,* as in Chald. but in Hebrew used only poetically. Prov. 31:2. Ps. 2:12 *kiss the son,* to wit, *Jehovah's son,* i. e. the king mentioned in verse 6. Others derive בַּר in this passage from בָּרַר no. 2. as if it signified, *the appointed, the chosen one;* but even the more ancient poetical language of the Hebrews frequently approximates to the Chaldaic.

II. **בַּר**, fem. **בָּרָה** verbal adj. from בָּרַר, dec. VIII. k. (Arab. بَرّ.)

1. *pure, clear, unspotted.* Cant. 6:8, 9. especially in a moral sense, Job 11:4.—בַּר לֵבָב *pure of heart,* Ps. 24:4. 73:1.

2. *empty.* Prov. 14:4.

III. **בַּר** and **בָּר** m. *corn, grain.* Gen. 41:35, 49. 42:3, 25. rarely spoken of standing corn, Ps. 65:14. (Arab. بُرّ *wheat.*)

בַּר m. Chald. with suff. בְּרֵהּ, plur. בְּנִין, (see בֵּן,) verbal from בְּרָא no. I. (see Niph.) *son.* Dan. 6:1.—בַּר אֱלָהִין *son of the gods, an angel,* Dan. 3:25.

2. *grandson.* Ezra 5:1.

בַּר m. *field.* Job 39:4. See the following article.

בַּר Chald. emph. בָּרָא. Dan. 2:38. 4:18, 20, 22, 29. [4:21, 23, 25, 32.] *field, open country.* (In Arab. بَرّ, بَرِّيَّة, Syr. ܒܪܐ *idem,* properly *what is without;* comp. بَرًّا *without, abroad,* and the Heb. חוּצוֹת.)

בֹּר m. verbal from בָּרַר, dec. I.

1. *purity;* joined with יָדַיִם and כַּפַּיִם, *purity of hands,* as indicative of innocence, Ps. 18:21, 25. Job 22:30.

2. a cleansing or purifying substance, i. q. בֹּרִית *alkali, lye;* perhaps also *borax,* which was formerly used in the fusing of metallic ores. (The two things are denoted by one word in Arabic.) Is. 1:

25 כְּבֹר *as with alkali*, or rather *borax*. Job 9:30 וַהֲזִכּוֹתִי בְּבֹר כַּפָּי *and I washed my hands with lye.*

I. בָּרָא 1. strictly, *to hew, to hew out.* (See Piel; and comp. Arab. برا and بري *to cut, to cut out, to plane.*)

2. *to form, make, produce.* (Arab. برا. The order of the significations is, as in the Arab. خلق, (1.) *to be smooth.* (2.) *to make smooth, to plane.* (3.) *to form, to make.*) Gen. 1:1, 21, 27. 2:3, 4. Is. 43:1, 7. Am. 4:13. (Syn. עָשָׂה, יָצַר) Ps. 51:12. Is. 45:7. Jer. 31:22 בָּרָא אֱלֹהִים חֲדָשָׁה *God will create something new.* Is. 65:18 הִנְנִי בוֹרֵא אֶת יְרוּשָׁלַיִם גִּילָה *behold, I will make Jerusalem a rejoicing.*

Niph. 1. pass. of Kal no. 2. Gen. 2:4. 5:2.

2. *to be born.* Ezek. 21:35 [30] בִּמְקוֹם אֲשֶׁר־נִבְרֵאת *in the place where thou wast born.* Ps. 102:19 עַם נִבְרָא יְהַלֶּל יָהּ *let the people, who are born, praise Jehovah.* (In Chald. בְּרָא *genuit;* hence בַּר *son.*)

Pi. בֵּרֵא 1. *to hew, cut down;* e.g. a wood, Josh. 17:15, 18.

2. *to cut down* (with the sword,) *to kill.* Ezek. 23:47.

3. *to form, engrave, mark out.* (Parall. שִׂים יָד.) Ezek. 21:24. [19.]

Deriv. בְּרִיאָה.

II. בָּרָא denom. from בָּרִיא, *to make fat, to fatten.* 1 Sam. 2:29.

בְּרֹאדַךְ בַּלְאֲדָן *Berodach Baladan,* king of Babylon. 2 K. 20:12. instead of which *Merodach Baladan* occurs Is. 39:1. See art. מְרֹדַךְ.

בַּרְבֻּרִים m. found only 1 K. 5:3. [4:23.] According to the Sept. (in some MSS. (Syr. Chald. Vulg. *birds, fowls.* (In Samar. ברברי is the name of a particular bird, by which the Heb. יַנְשׁוּף is rendered Lev. 11:17. Comp. Syr. ܒܪܒܘܪܐ *avis diversicolor,* according to others, *cygnus.*) Others: *game, venison,* from בַּר *field.*

בָּרַד 1. as in Aram. *to scatter, sprinkle.* See בָּרֹד.

2. *to hail.* Is. 32:19. In Arab. *idem.*

בָּרָד m. verbal from בָּרַד, *hail.* Ex. 9:18 ff.

בֶּרֶד proper name of a place in the desert of Shur. Gen. 16:14.

בָּרֹד, plur. בְּרֻדִּים, verbal adj. from בָּרַד, *spotted, speckled, party-coloured.* Gen. 31:10, 12. Zech. 6:3, 6. (In Syr. ܒܪܘܕܐ *idem;* especially *spotted with red.*)

I. בָּרָה *to eat.* 2 Sam. 12:17. 13:6, 10. In Chald. בְּרָה *idem.* It is kindred with Arab. وري *to be fat, full of marrow;* مرا *to fatten, become fat;* and Chald. מְרָא *to feed, fatten;* whence מְרִיא and בָּרִיא *fat.*

Pi. *idem.* Lam. 4:10.

Hiph. *to cause to eat, to give to eat;* construed with a double accus. 2 Sam. 3:35. 13:5.

Deriv. בִּרְיָה, בָּרוּת.

II. בָּרָה i. q. בָּרַר *to choose.* 1 Sam. 17:8 ברו *choose.* (In Arab. برا for برو *distinxit, separavit,* i. q. ברר.)

בָּרוּךְ (*blessed*) proper name, particularly of the friend of Jeremiah, to whom he dictated his prophecies, and from whom the apocryphal book of Baruch derives its name. Jer. 32:16. 36:4.

בְּרֹמִים masc. plur. Ezek. 27:24. *damask, cloth interwoven with various colours,* i. q. Greek *πολύμιτα.* (In Arab. برم conj. II. IV. *to turn the spindle, to twist threads;* hence بريم *a twisted, two-coloured thread,* and مبرم *cloth made out of such threads.*)

בְּרוֹשׁ m. dec. I.

1. *a fir* or *pine tree.* 1 K. 5:22. [8.] 6:15, 34. 9:11. So the Vulg. uniformly. (In Arab. بروث, Syr. ܒܪܘܬܐ *idem.*) Others: *cypress.* Perhaps it included several kindred species of trees, which the ancients did not minutely

distinguish. See Celsii Hierobot. I. p. 74 ss.

2. hence *a pine lance* or *spear*. Nah. 2:4.

3. *a musical instrument made of this wood.* 2 Sam. 6:5.

בְּרוֹת m. with Syriac orthography, i. q. בְּרוֹשׁ *fir*, found only in plur. Cant. 1:17.

בֵּרוֹתָה Ezek. 47:16. and **בֵּרוֹתַי** 2 Sam. 8:8. *Berytus*, a maritime city in Phenicia, with a harbour, celebrated in the middle ages, now called *Barut* or *Bairut*.

בָּרוּת f. verbal from בָּרָה no. I. *meat, food.* Ps. 69:22.

בַּרְזֶל m. prim. with suff. בַּרְזִלּוֹ, dec. VIII. g. (Aram. פַּרְזֶל, ܦܪܙܠܐ.)

1. *iron.* Num. 35:16.

2. *an iron tool.* 2 K. 6:5. Ecc. 10:10.

3. *iron fetters.* Ps. 105:18. 107:10.

בָּרַח 1. *to flee.* Gen. 31:22, 27. Construed with מִפְּנֵי, Gen. 35:7. 1 K. 2:7. with מִלִּפְנֵי, Jon. 1:3. and with מִן, Is. 48:20. *to flee before* any one. In the imperative it is usually joined with a dative of the pronoun, as בְּרַח לְךָ *flee thou*, Gen. 27:43. Num. 24:11. Am. 7:12. (comp. French *s'enfuir.*) When construed with אַחֲרֵי, *to flee after* any one, 1 Sam. 22:20.

2. *to pass through, to stretch across.* Ex. 36:33 *he made the middle bar* לִבְרֹחַ בְּתוֹךְ הַקְּרָשִׁים *to pass through the midst of the boards.* Hence בְּרִיחַ *a bar.*

Hiph. הִבְרִיחַ 1. *to put to flight, to chase away.* 1 Chr. 8:13.

2. i. q. Kal no. 2. Ex. 16:28.

Deriv. מִבְרָח, בָּרִיחַ, בְּרִיחַ.

בָּרִיחַ see **בָּרַח**.

I. **בְּרִי** adj. i. q. בָּרִיא *fat.* Whence the feminine בְּרֻיָּה (which ought perhaps to be pointed בְּרִיָּה,) Ezek. 34:20. Several MSS. have בריאה.

II. **בְּרִי** m. *clear weather, serene sky.* Job 37:11. Root בָּרַר=בָּרָה *to be pure;* comp. Chald. בְּרִירוּתָא *serenitas.* Others consider בְּ as a preposition. See art. רִי.

בָּרִיא m. dec. III. a. *fat, fatted, plump;* spoken of animals, Gen. 41:2 ff. of men, Judg. 3:17. Ps. 73:4. Dan. 1:15. *of food,* Hab. 1:16. Root בָּרָא = בָּרָה no. I. (q. v.)

בְּרִיאָה f. verbal from בָּרָא, *something effected by God,* especially *something wonderful* or *extraordinary.* Nu. 16:30.

בִּרְיָה f. verbal from בָּרָה no. I. *meat, food.* 2 Sam. 13:5, 7, 10.

בָּרִיחַ m. verbal adj. from בָּרַח. (Put for בָּרִחַ; hence with Kamets impure, see Is. 43:14. but also with Kamets pure, see Is. 15:5.)

1. *flying, fugitive, runaway.* Is. 15:5. 43:14.

2. as an epithet of the serpent, Is. 27:1. also of the serpent as a constellation, Job 26:13. *Flying* or *swift serpent* would not suit the latter passage, at least it would be very bold; perhaps better: *extended serpent.* comp. בָּרַח no. 2.

בְּרִיחַ m. verbal from בָּרַח no. 2. dec. I. *bar;* and particularly (1.) *cross-bar* for the fastening of gates. Deut. 3:5. Neh. 3:3. used poetically of the bars of the earth, Jon. 2:7. (2.) *cross-piece* for the binding together of the boards, in the tabernacle of the congregation. Ex. 26:26 ff. 36:31 ff.

בְּרִיעָה proper name of a son of Ephraim, according to the etymology 1 Chr. 7:23. i. q. בְּרָעָה *in misfortune.*

בְּרִית f. dec. I. 1. *covenant, league, compact.* (Root ברה i. q. Arab. بَرَى *præcidit, præsecuit,* from the custom of cutting in pieces the victims sacrificed on such occasions, and of passing through them; see כָּרַת.) The verbs employed to denote a making or entering into a covenant are כָּרַת, הֵקִים, עָבַר בְּ, בּוֹא בְּ; those to denote its violation are הֵפֵר, חִלֵּל. The genitive often denotes the person with whom the covenant is made, Lev. 26:45 בְּרִית רִאשֹׁנִים *the covenant with their ancestors.* Deut. 4:31 בְּרִית אֲבֹתֶיךָ *the covenant with thy fathers;* hence with a double genitive, Lev. 26:42 בְּרִיתִי יַעֲקוֹב *my covenant with Jacob.*

2. Often the terms of the covenant on one side only are intended; hence, in speaking of the covenant of God with the Israelites, it is sometimes equivalent to *law;* as אֲרוֹן הַבְּרִית *the law chest* or *ark of the covenant*, Josh. 3:6. לֻחוֹת הַבְּרִית *tables of the law*, Deut. 9:9. סֵפֶר הַבְּרִית *book of the law*, a statute book out of which Moses read to the people, Ex. 24:7. and the institution of the passover is cited, 2 K. 23:21.—דִּבְרֵי הַבְּרִית עֲשֶׂרֶת הַדְּבָרִים *the words of the covenant, the ten words*, i.e. the ten commandments, Ex. 34:28.

3. used as a concrete, i.q. אִישׁ בְּרִית *one who makes a covenant.* Is. 42:6 בְּרִית עָם *one who establishes a covenant with the nations.* Is. 49:8.

בֹּרִית f. Jer. 2:22. Mal. 3:2. *alkali, lye, lixivium*, especially the vegetable alkali, (the mineral was called נֶתֶר,) which was procured from the ashes of several alkaline plants, (e.g. salsola kali, soda fruticosa, anabasis, Linn.) The ancients made use of this alkali, or of a solution of it, in connexion with oil, for cleansing and washing clothes, Jer. 2:22. hence Mal. 3:2 בֹּרִית מְכַבְּסִים *the alkali of the fullers.* As to its form, it is probably a denom. from בֹּר *purification, cleansing;* hence with the adjective termination, בֹּרִי, בֹּרִית *what serves for cleansing* or *purifying.* Comp. Bocharti Hieroz. II. p. 45. Celsii Hierob. I. 449. J. Th. Hartmann's Hebräerin. Th. 1. p. 163 ff. See art. בֹּר.

בָּרַךְ, fut. יִבְרַךְ. 1. *to bend the knee, to kneel.* 2 Chr. 6:13 וַיִּבְרַךְ עַל בִּרְכָּיו *he kneeled upon his knees.* Ps. 95:6. (In Syr. and Arab. *idem.*) Probably a denom. from בֶּרֶךְ *a knee.*

2. *to bless*, as in Piel. In Kal found only in the infin. absol. Josh. 24:10. and part. pass. בָּרוּךְ, Gen. 9:26. hence בָּרוּךְ יְהוָֹה Gen. 24:31. 26:29. and בָּרוּךְ לַיהוָֹה Judg. 17:2. *blessed of Jehovah.*

Niph. pass. of Pi. *to be blessed, prospered.* Only Gen. 12:3. 18:18. 28:14.

Pi. 1. בֵּרַךְ *to bless, pronounce a blessing.* (Whether this signification is connected with that of *kneeling* is doubtful. According to some, strictly *to cause* one *to kneel down*, as the posture for receiving a blessing. According to others; *to kneel down one's self*, as the posture of salutation, or religious worship. But most probably the two senses are independent of each other.) Applied e.g. to aged parents blessing their children, Gen. 27:4, 7, 10, 19 ff. 48:9. to a priest's benediction on the people, Lev. 9:22, 23. Num. 6:23. 2 Chr. 30:27. to a prophet, Num. 23:11. Deut. 33:1. to God, Gen. 1:22, 28. 9:1. In the latter case, (by a metonymy of the cause for the effect,) it signifies *to make happy, to prosper*, Gen. 12:3. 24:1, 35. When construed with a double accus. *to bless any one with any thing*, Deut. 12:7. 15:14.

2. *to greet, to salute* any one, which was connected with a blessing, 2 K. 4:29. and this either at first meeting, Gen. 47:7. 2 Sam. 6:20. or on taking leave, Gen. 47:10.

3. *to bless God*, i.e. to praise, laud, or thank him; (very frequent in the Psalms.) Ps. 16:7. 26:12. 34:2. 63:5. 66:8. Deut. 8:10. also בֵּרַךְ בְּשֵׁם יְהוָֹה, Deut. 10:8. 21:5. 1 Chr. 23:13. *to call on* or *invoke God*, spoken of the priests, in imitation of the phrase קָרָא בְשֵׁם יְהוָֹה.—Is. 66:3 מְבָרֵךְ אָוֶן *one who worships an idol.*

4. Closely connected with no. 2. where it is spoken of one's taking leave, is perhaps the signification, *to leave, to renounce* any one. Hence בֵּרַךְ אֶת יְהוָֹה *to renounce God*, Job 1:5. 2:5. also associated with the idea of calumny and blasphemy, 1 K. 21:10 בֵּרַכְתָּ אֱלֹהִים וָמֶלֶךְ *thou hast reviled God and the king.* Ps. 10:3. (But perhaps this word was originally taken in a neutral signification, being applied equally in a good and bad sense, to *wishing good*, and *wishing evil;* like the Lat. *sacer.* Comp. under the art. נָקַב.)

Pu. בֹּרַךְ pass. of Pi. Ps. 37:22. 113:2.

Hiph. caus. of Kal, *to make to kneel*, or *couch*, as camels to rest. Gen. 24:11. Comp. אַבְרֵךְ.

Hithpa. i. q. Niph. Gen. 22:18. 26:4. Ps. 72:17. reflex. *to bless one's self*, Deut. 29:18.

בְּרַךְ Chald. *to kneel*. Dan. 6:10, with the addition עַל בִּרְכוֹהִי *upon his knees*.

Pa. *to bless, praise*. Dan. 2:19, 20. 3:28.

בֶּרֶךְ f. dec. VI. h. *knee*. Is. 45:23. Dual בִּרְכַּיִם *knees*, used also of more than two, e. g. כָּל־בִּרְכַּיִם *all knees*, Ezek. 7:17. 21:12. [7.] Often, like the Greek τὰ γόνατα in phrases in which we use *lap*, *bosom*. Gen. 30:3. 50:23. comp. Job 3:12. Is. 66:12.

בְּרַךְ or **בֶּרֶךְ** Chald. *idem*. Dan. 6:11.

בְּרָכָה f. (once בְּרָכָה Gen. 27:38.) verbal from בֵּרֵךְ, dec. XI. c.

1. *a blessing, benediction*. Gen. 27:12, 41.—נָתַן בְּרָכָה עַל־ *to bestow a blessing on* any one, Ex. 32:29. Also *a blessing* from God, Gen. 49:25 בִּרְכֹת שָׁמַיִם *blessings of the heavens*.

2. *an object of blessing, one blessed*. Ps. 21:7 תְּשִׁיתֵהוּ בְרָכוֹת לָעַד *thou makest him blessings for ever*, i. e. thou blessest him for ever. Zech. 8:13. Gen. 12:2.

3. *a gift, present*, primarily one which is given on occasion of saluting, welcoming, or bidding farewell to another, (see בֵּרֵךְ no. 2.) Gen. 33:11. 1 Sam. 25:27. and then used also in a more general sense, 1 Sam. 30:26. 2 K. 5:15. Josh. 15:19. נֶפֶשׁ בְּרָכָה *the beneficent* or *liberal soul*, Prov. 11:25. (In Syr. ܒܘܪܟܬܐ *idem*. See Michaelis' edition of Castell's Lex. Syr. and also Michaelis' Supplem.)

4. probably *peace*. (The ideas, *blessing, prosperity, peace*, are closely related to each other.) 2 K. 18:31 עֲשׂוּ אִתִּי בְרָכָה *make peace with me*. Is. 36:16.

בְּרֵכָה f. (with Tseri impure) dec. X. *pond, pool*. 2 Sam. 2:13. Ecc. 2:6. Cant. 7:4. Arab. بِرْكَةٌ *idem*, properly *a reservoir of water at which the camels kneel to drink*. See הִבְרִיךְ.

בְּרַם Chald. conj. *but, yet*. Dan. 4:12. [15.] 5:17. In Syr. *idem*.

בָּרַק *to lighten, send forth lightning*. Ps. 144:6. (Also in Syr. and Arab.)

בָּרָק m. verbal from בָּרַק, dec. IV. a.

1. *lightning, a flash of lightning*. Ex. 19:16. Spoken figuratively of the sword, בְּרַק חַרְבִּי *the glittering of my sword*, i. e. my glittering sword, Deut. 32:41; comp. Nah. 3:3. Hence without addition *a glittering sword*, Job 20:25. Ezek. 21:15, 20. [21:10, 15.] (Comp. Arab. بَرَقَ *to shine, glitter*, spoken of the sword.) Plur. בְּרָקִים *lightnings*, Job 38:35.

2. proper name of a patriot, who, with the aid of Deborah, smote the Canaanites. Judg. 4:6, 8. 5:1. Comp. the Punic *Barcas*.

בָּרֶקֶת f. Ex. 28:17. and **בָּרְקַת** Ezek. 28:13. a precious stone, probably so called from its *glittering brightness*, (see בָּרַק,) according to Braun (De Vestitu Sacerdotum Hebr. p. 518 ff.) *the emerald*. Some fancy a connexion in its sound with μάραγδος, (Arab. *Sbaragd*,) *an emerald*.

בַּרְקָנִים masc. plur. Judg. 8:7, 16. *threshing wagon* or *sledge*. Sept. in some MSS. and Symm. τρίβολοι literally *briers*. But the Sept. also uses τρίβολοις for τρίβολα, *tribula* or *tribulum*, a threshing machine, a board, armed beneath with pointed stones, which was drawn over the grain. Comp. חָרוּץ. (In Arab. بُرْقَةٌ *stony ground*.

בָּרַר 1. *to separate*. Ezek. 20:38 וּבָרוֹתִי מִכֶּם הַמֹּרְדִים *I will separate the rebellious from you*. (Arab. بَرَّ conj. VIII. *to be separated*. Comp. בָּרָה no. II.)

2. hence *to select* for any object, *to appoint*. Part. *appointed, chosen*. 1 Chr. 9:22 כֻּלָּם הַבְּרוּרִים לְשֹׁעֲרִים *all these, who were chosen to be porters*. 16:41. (Comp.

(.הִבְדִּיל.) Neh. 5:18 צֹאן בְּרֻרוֹת *choice sheep.*

3. *to separate what is unclean, to cleanse, purify.* Part. בָּרוּר *pure,* in a moral sense, Zeph. 3:9 שָׂפָה בְרוּרָה *a pure lip.* Used adverbially, *purely, sincerely,* Job 33:3. See Niph. Hiph.

4. *to burnish* or *sharpen* an arrow. Part. pass. *sharpened,* Is. 49:2. See Hiph.

5. *to search out, examine, prove.* (In Arab. بر conj. X. and بار.) Ecc. 3:18 לְבָרָם *for to prove them.* This form of the infin. is like סֹךְ. In Ecc. 9:1. the infin. בּוּר occurs in the same sense; see בּוּר.

Niph. נָבַר *to purify one's self.* Is. 52:11. Part. נָבָר *morally pure,* Ps. 18:27.

Pi. *to purify, refine,* as metals. Dan. 11:35.

Hiph. 1. *to clear, cleanse,* as corn from the chaff. Jer. 4:11.

2. *to burnish* or *sharpen* an arrow. Jer. 51:11.

Hithpa. 1. *to purify one's self.* Dan. 12:10.

2. *to conduct one's self as pure, to show one's self pure.* Ps. 18:27. In the parallel passage 2 Sam. 22:27 occurs הִתַּבָּר Chald. for הִתְבָּרֵר.

Deriv. בַּר, בֹּר, בְּרִית; comp. also בְּרִי no. II.

בְּשׂוֹר a brook, which flows into the sea, on the north of Gaza. 1 Sam. 30:9, 10, 21.

בָּשָׂם m. dec. IV. a. *an aromatic plant;* here perhaps specially *the balsam-bush.* Cant. 5:1. (Arab. بَشَام.)

בֶּשֶׂם Ex. 30:33. and **בֹּשֶׂם**, plur. בְּשָׂמִים.

1. *sweet odour, spicy fragrance, perfume.* קִנְּמָן־בֶּשֶׂם *sweet cinnamon,* Ex. 30:23. קְנֵה־בֹשֶׂם *sweet cane, sweet calamus,* ibid. Plur. Cant. 4:16 יִזְּלוּ בְשָׂמָיו *that its spicy odours may flow out,* i. e. be scattered.

2. *spice, spicery.* Ex. 30:23. 35:28. 1 K. 10:10. Ezek. 27:32. בְּרֹאשׁ כָּל־בֹּשֶׂם *with the most costly spices.* Plur. 1 K. 10:2. Cant. 4:10, 14.

3. perhaps *the balsam-bush.* Cant. 5:13. עֲרוּגַת הַבֹּשֶׂם *an espalier,* (according to others *a bed,*) *of balsam-bushes.* 6:1. (Syr. ܒܣܡ *to be sweet;* Aph. *to smell sweet, to be fragrant;* ܒܣܡܐ *sweet odour, spice.*)

בָּשְׂמַת proper name. 1. the wife of Esau, and daughter of Elon the Hittite, Gen. 26:34. also called *Adah,* 36:2.

2. the wife of Esau, and daughter of Ishmael. Gen. 36:3 ff.

3. the daughter of Solomon. 1 K. 4:15.

בָּשַׂר found only in Pi. 1. *to bring joyful news;* construed with an accusative of the person, 2 Sam. 18:19 אֲבַשְּׂרָה אֶת הַמֶּלֶךְ *I will bear the king the joyful news.* 1 Sam. 31:9. 1 Chr. 10:9. Used absolutely, 2 Sam. 4:10 הָיָה כִמְבַשֵּׂר בְּעֵינָיו *he thought to bring joyful news.* Also with an accusative of the news announced, 1 Chr. 16:23 בַּשְּׂרוּ מִיּוֹם אֶל יוֹם יְשׁוּעָתוֹ *declare from day to day his salvation.* Is. 60:6 תְּהִלֹּת יְהוָֹה יְבַשֵּׂרוּ *they shall declare the praises of Jehovah.* Ps. 40:10.

2. more rarely *to bring news* generally, 2 Sam. 18:20, 26. sometimes even of an unpleasant nature, 1 Sam. 4:17. Hence with an addition, בִּשֵּׂר טוֹב *to bring good tidings,* 1 K. 1:42. Is. 52:7. (In Arab. بشر I. II. *to bring joyful news,* also *to bring news of a contrary nature,* when specially noticed. In Syr. by transposition ܣܒܪ *idem.*)

Hithpa. *to receive joyful news.* 2 Sam. 18:31. (In Arab. med. Kesr. and conj. IV. X.)

בְּשׂרָה f. verbal from בִּשֵּׂר. 1. *joyful tidings.* 2 Sam. 18:22. also with the epithet טוֹבָה, verse 27.

2. *reward for bringing news.* 2 Sam. 4:10.

בָּשָׂר m. dec. IV. a. 1. *flesh.* Ps. 102:6 דָּבְקָה עַצְמִי לִבְשָׂרִי *my bones cleave to my flesh,* a description of great leanness; comp. Ps. 22:16. (Others take בָּשָׂר here, like the Arab. بَشَرَة, for *skin.*)

2. *body.* Num. 8:7. Prov. 14:30 חַיֵּי בְשָׂרִים *health of the body.* Ps. 16:9. 84: 3 לִבִּי וּבְשָׂרִי *my soul and my body.* Ecc. 12:12 יְגִעַת בָּשָׂר *weariness of the body.* Hence, like σάρξ in the N. T. *the fleshly appetites and passions,* Ecc. 2:3. 5:5.

3. כָּל בָּשָׂר *all flesh,* for *all living creatures,* Gen. 6:13, 17. 7:15. Ps. 136: 25. and, in a more restricted sense, *all men,* Gen. 6:12. Joel 3:1. [2:28.] (So in Arab. بَشَر frequently, e. g. in opposition to angels.) Hence בָּשָׂר often denotes *what is human, frail, mortal,* in opposition to *God,* or *what is divine,* Gen. 6:3. Ps. 56:5. 78:39. Job 10:4. Is. 31:3.—זְרוֹעַ בָּשָׂר *a fleshly arm,* i. e. human power, 2 Chr. 32:8.

4. עַצְמִי וּבְשָׂרִי *my bone and my flesh,* i. e. my relative. Gen. 29:14. Judg. 9: 2. 2 Sam. 5:1. 19:12, 13. Also בָּשָׂר alone in the same sense, Gen. 37:27 כִּי אָחִינוּ בְשָׂרֵנוּ הוּא *for he is our brother, our flesh.* Is. 58:7 בְּשָׂרְךָ *thy fellow man.* (Arab. لَحِيم *one kindred by blood,* لُحْمَة *blood relationship;* from لَحْم *flesh.*) In Heb. see שְׁאֵר.

5. by a euphemism, *pudenda viri.* Lev. 15:2, 3, 7, 19. Ezek. 16:26.

בְּשַׂר m. Chald. *flesh,* as in Heb. Dan. 2:11. 4:9. [12.]

בָּשַׁל 1. *to boil, to be a boiling.* Ezek. 24:5.

2. *to be ripe, ripen.* Joel 4:13. [3: 13.] So in Aram. בְּשַׁל, ܒܫܠ; comp. πέπτω, Lat. *coquitur vindemia, messis,* also Chald. שְׁלַק.

Pi. *to boil* flesh. Ex. 23:19. 16:23.

Pu. pass. of Piel. Ex. 12:9.

Hiph. *to ripen,* as in Kal. Gen. 40: 26. 10.

בָּשֵׁל, fem. **בְּשֵׁלָה**, verbal adj. from בָּשַׁל. *boiled, sodden.* Ex. 12:9. Num. 6: 19.

בָּשָׁן proper name of a country beyond Jordan, between the rivers Jabbok and Arnon, celebrated for its pastures, whence the mention made of the bulls and rams of Bashan. Num. 21:33. 32: 33. Deut. 3:1. Ps. 22:13. Am. 4:1. In Greek Βαταναία, now *El Bottin.*

בָּשְׁנָה f. verbal from בּוֹשׁ. *shame.* Hos. 10:6. The termination נָה, as the afformative of a verbal noun, is otherwise unknown; but is analogous with ־ָן.

בָּשַׁס found only in Po. בּוֹשֵׁס *to tread down, to trample upon.* Once Am. 5: 11, construed with עַל, like its synonyme בּוֹסֵס. Ought it not perhaps to be read בּוֹשֵׁס?

בֹּשֶׁשׁ see בּוֹשׁ no. II.

בֹּשֶׁת f. verbal from בּוֹשׁ, dec. XIII. e.

1. *shame;* for the most part joined with פָּנִים, *shame* or *confusion of face,* Ps. 44:16. Dan. 9:7, 8. 2 Chr. 32:21. —לָבַשׁ בֹּשֶׁת figuratively *to be clothed with shame,* Job 8:22. Ps. 35:26.—עָטָה בֹשֶׁת *idem,* Ps. 109. 29.

2. *the secret parts.* Mic. 1:11 עֶרְיָה־בֹשֶׁת *nuda pudendis.*

3. *idol,* Hos. 9:10. Jer. 3. 24. 11:13.

בַּת f. (contraction of בֶּנֶת fem. of בֵּן,) with suff. בִּתִּי; plur. בָּנוֹת, const. בְּנוֹת (analogous with בָּנִים.)

1. *daughter;* freq. Its other significations are parallel for the most part with those under בֵּן.

2. *grand-daughter, female descendant.* בְּנוֹת כְּנַעַן *the daughters of Canaan,* Gen. 36:2. also joined with names of cities, to denote *female inhabitants;* as בְּנוֹת צִיּוֹן *daughters,* i. e. female inhabitants, *of Zion,* Is. 3:17.

3. In apposition with names of cities and countries, it forms a poetical personification, known also to other eastern writers, whereby those cities or countries are regarded as young women or mothers; e. g. applied to cities, בַּת צֹר *the daughter of Tyre,* i. e. Tyre herself, Ps. 45:13. בַּת בָּבֶל *daughter of Babylon,* Ps. 137:8. בַּת יְרוּשָׁלַיִם, Is. 37:22. בַּת צִיּוֹן, Is. 10:32. applied to countries, בַּת כַּשְׂדִּים, Is. 47:1, 5. בַּת מִצְרַיִם, Jer. 46:11. בַּת עַמִּי *the daughter of my people,* i. e. my people, my native country, Is. 22:4. Jer. 4:11. 8:22. etc. Sometimes the ex-

pression is more full, בְּתוּלַת בַּת צִידוֹן *virgin daughter of Zidon*, Is. 23:12. בְּתוּלַת בַּת עַמִּי, Jer. 14:17. comp. Jer. 46:11. Lam. 1:15. 2:13.

4. בְּנוֹת הָעִיר *daughters of a city*, i. e. small villages under its jurisdiction. Num. 21:25, 32. Judg. 11:26. Josh. 15:45.

5. also other phrases; as Gen. 17:17 *a daughter of ninety years*, i. e. ninety years old. בַּת בְּלִיַּעַל *a wicked* or *vile woman*, 1 Sam. 1:16. בְּנוֹת הַשִּׁיר *daughters of song*, i. e. singing birds, Ecc. 12:4. בַּת עַיִן *daughter of the eye*, i. e. the apple of the eye, Lam. 2:18, (a similar phrase is formed with אִישׁוֹן q. v.) בַּת נְשִׂים *a princess*, Dan. 11:17.

בַּת m. dec. VIII. h. *a bath*, a measure for liquids, containing the tenth part of a homer. 1 K. 7:26, 38. Ezek. 45:10.

בַּת Chald. i. q. Heb. בַּת *a bath*. Ezra 7:22.

בָּתִּים *houses*, see בַּיִת.

בָּתָה f. Is. 5:6. and plur. בַּתּוֹת 7:19. according to the connexion and the ancient versions, *desolation*. (Root בתת = Arab. بتّ *to cut off, to break off, to finish entirely*; بَتَات *a finished business*; and بَتَّةً *completely, entirely*. Comp. כָּלָה *destruction* from כָּלָה *to finish*. This derivation would lead us to prefer the punctuation בַּתָּה.)

בְּתוּלָה f. prim. dec. X. *maid, virgin*. Gen. 24:15 וְהַנַּעֲרָ בְּתוּלָה וְאִישׁ לֹא יְדָעָהּ *and the damsel was a virgin, and no man had known her*. 2 Sam. 13:2.— נַעֲרָה בְתוּלָה *a damsel who is a virgin*, Deut. 22:23, 28. Judg. 21:12. Applied also to a new-married wife, Joel 1:8. So *puella*, in Virg. Æn. IV. 458. and *virgo*, Idyll. VI. 47. Hor. Od. II. 8. 23. Often applied to cities and countries, by means of a personification, (see בַּת no. 3.) also without בַּת, as בְּתוּלַת יִשְׂרָאֵל Jer. 18:13. 31:4, 21. Am. 5:2.

בְּתוּלִים m. denom. from בְּתוּלָה, dec. I.

1. *the state* or *condition of a virgin, virginity*. Lev. 21:13 וְהוּא אִשָּׁה בִבְתוּלֶיהָ יִקָּח *and he shall take a wife as a virgin*. Judg. 11:37. Applied figuratively to the people of Israel, *freedom from idolatry*, Ezek. 23:3, 8.

2. *sign* or *token of virginity, the bridal sheet kept by the friends of the bride*. Comp. Deut. 22:14 ff. with Niebuhr's Description de l'Arabie, p. 31 ff.

בָּתַק Pi. *to cut in pieces, thrust through*. Ezek. 16:40. (Arab. بتك *to cut in pieces*, כ and ק being interchanged.)

בָּתַר and **בִּתֵּר** *to cut in pieces*. Gen. 15:10. In Arabic, *to cut off*; comp. بطر *to divide*.

בָּתַר Chald. *after*. Dan. 2:39. 7:7. In verse 6, it is written fully בָּאתַר. Syr. ܒܳܬܰܪ.

בֶּתֶר verbal from בָּתַר, dec. VI. h. *part cut off, piece*; spoken of the parts of the sacrificial victim. Gen. 15:10. Jer. 34:18, 19.

2. *separation*. Cant. 2:17 *mountains of separation*, i. e. the solitary mountains.

ג

THE name of this letter, *Gimel*, (גִּמֶל or גִּימֶל i. q. גָּמָל or גְּמַל *camel*,) is most easily illustrated by its form in the Phenician alphabet ٦, ᛧ, in which we find a rude delineation of a *camel's* neck. It is most frequently interchanged with the kindred palatals; (1.) with כ, as גָּפְרִית Syr. ܟܒܪܝܬܐ Ar. كبريت *brimstone*; Heb. and Syr. גּוּמָץ Chald. כּוּמְצָא and קוּמְצָא *a pit*; זְכוּכִית Syr. ܙܓܘܓܝܬܐ *crystal*; סָגַר and סָכַר *to close*; רָגַל and רָכַל *to run about, to travel*. (2.) with ק, as גָּבִיעַ *a cup*, Arab. قبيعة *the cup of a flower*, comp. מִצְנֶפֶת ;צְנֵפָה *a priest's cap, a turban*, כּוֹבַע and קוֹבַע *a helmet*, Syr. ܩܘܦܥܐ *a hat*, Arab. قبع *to cover the head.* Comp. Bocharti Hieroz. T. II. p. 888. J. D. Michaelis Arab. Grammatik. p. 91.

גֵּא i. q. גֵּאֶה verbal from גָּאָה. *proud, arrogant, puffed up.* Is. 16:6.

גָּאָה, fut. יִגְאֶה. 1. *to be lifted up, to rise.* Job 10:16 וְיִגְאֶה *and should it* (my head) *be lifted up.* Others: *and it* (my affliction) *increases.* Spoken of water, Ezek. 47:5.

2. spoken of plants, *to grow up.* Job 8:11.

3. *to be exalted, majestic, excellent.* Ex. 15:1, 21. In Syr. applied to beauty, pomp, splendour. In Hebrew used only in the poetical portions of the Bible.

Deriv. out of course גֵּא, גֵּאָה, גָּאוֹן, גֵּאוּת, גֵּוָה, גַּאֲיוֹן.

גֵּאֶה, plur. גֵּאִים, verbal adj. from גָּאָה.

1. *elated, proud.* Job 40:11, 12 רְאֵה כָל־גֵּאֶה *behold every thing proud.* Is. 2:12.

2. *arrogant, bold, violent, wicked.* (So זֵד, and many words denoting *pride*, include the idea of *violence and wickedness;* as, on the contrary, *humility* often denotes *virtue and piety.* Comp. in Greek, ἀγήνωρ, ὑπερήνωρ.) Plur. גֵּאִים, Ps. 94:2. 140:6. Prov. 15:25. 16:19.

גֵּאָה f. verbal from גָּאָה. *pride, arrogancy.* Prov. 8:13.

גַּאֲוָה f. verbal from גָּאָה, dec. X.

1. *exaltation, majesty, greatness;* spoken of God. Deut. 33:26, 29. Ps. 68:35.

2. *pride, arrogance, violence.* Ps. 10:2. 31:19, 24. 36:12. 46:4 יִרְעֲשׁוּ הָרִים בְּגַאֲוָתוֹ *the mountains shake through its violence*, i. e. through the raging of the sea. Job 41:6 גַּאֲוָה אֲפִיקֵי מָגִנִּים *his strong shields are his pride.* (Others make it in this passage i. q. גֵּוָה *back, body.*)

גָּאוֹן m. verbal from גָּאָה, dec. III.

1. *exaltation, greatness, majesty*, especially of God. Ex. 15:7. Mic. 5:3. Job 37:4 קוֹל גְּאוֹנוֹ *his* (God's) *majestic voice*, i. e. the thunder. Job 40:10 עֲדֵה נָא גָאוֹן וָגֹבַהּ *deck thyself with majesty and excellency.* Is. 60:15.

2. *pride, haughtiness, arrogance.* Job 38:11 גְּאוֹן גַּלֶּיךָ *pride of the waves*, i. e. proud waves. Ezek. 7:24. 16:49, 56. Prov. 16:18. Is. 14:18. Am. 6:8.

3. *that whereof any one is proud.* Ps. 47:5 גְּאוֹן יַעֲקֹב *the pride of Jacob*, i.e. the Promised Land. Am. 6:8.

4. גְּאוֹן הַיַּרְדֵּן *the pride* or *glory of Jordan*, Jer. 12:5. 49:19. 50:44. Zech. 11:3. i. e. the banks and shores of Jordan, which were overgrown with reeds, willows, and thickets, and formed a residence for wild beasts. Comp. Jerome on Zech. 11:3. Relandi Palæstina, p. 274. That the above is a correct explanation of the phrase, is evident from the parall. אַדֶּרֶת Zech. 11:3. Others, thinking a poetical expression here unsuitable, regard this word as a contraction of גָּאוֹן=גַּאֲוָה, גַּיְא *a valley;* but in this case the Tseri would be impure.

גֵּאוּת f. verbal from גָּאָה.

1. *rising up*, as of smoke. Is. 9:17.

2. *exaltation, majesty, excellency.* Ps. 93:1. Is. 12:5 כִּי גֵאוּת עָשָׂה *for he has done excellently.*

3. *pride, arrogance, raging.* Ps. 17:10. 89:10 אַתָּה מוֹשֵׁל בְּגֵאוּת הַיָּם *thou rulest the raging of the sea.*

גַּאֲיוֹן verbal adj. from גָּאָה, *proud.* Ps. 123:4 Kethib גַּאֲיוֹנִים *the proud.* The Keri has גְּאֵי יוֹנִים *the proud of the oppressors*, i. e. the proud oppressors.

גֵּאָיוֹת plur. fem. *valleys.* Ezek. 7:16. 31:12. 32:5. It forms the plural of גַּיְא ,גַּי *a valley;* and appears to be transposed for גֵּיאוֹת, which would be the regular plural.

I. גָּאַל, fut. יִגְאַל. 1. *to demand back* one's property; hence (1.) *to repurchase, buy again* an estate which has been sold. Lev. 25:25. comp. Ruth 4:4, 6. (2.) *to redeem* what has been vowed or is otherwise due to the priests. Lev. 27:13, 15, 19, 20. (3.) *to require satisfaction for bloodshed, to avenge the blood of one slain, sanguinem repetere.* Found only in part. גֹּאֵל הַדָּם *an avenger of blood,*

Num. 35:19 ff. Deut. 19:6, 12. 20: 5, 9. without הַדָּם, Num. 35:12.

2. *to redeem, ransom.* Lev. 25:49. hence in general *to deliver, set free,* Gen. 48:16. Ex. 6:6. Frequently spoken of God in the Psalms and Prophets, Ps. 19:15. 103:4. 106:10. Is. 44:22. 48:20. 52:9.

3. because the right of repurchase and of redemption, as well as of the avenging of blood, pertained, by the Jewish law, only to the nearest of kin; the part. גֹּאֵל comes to signify *one nearest of kin.* Lev. 25:25 גֹּאֲלוֹ הַקָּרֹב אֵלָיו *his nearest kinsman.* Ruth 3:12 גֹּאֵל קָרוֹב מִמֶּנִּי *a nearer kinsman than I.* 1K.16:11.—מִגֹּאֵל *the nearest of kin but one,* Ruth 2:20. (So שְׁאֵר *one nearest of kin,* and ثَائِر *an avenger of blood,* in which example the order of significations is inverted.)

4. because the nearest of kin was under obligation to marry the widow of his deceased relative, hence the verb גָּאַל is used to express this idea. Ruth 3: 13 אִם יִגְאָלֵךְ טוֹב יִגְאָל וְאִם לֹא יַחְפֹּץ לְגָאֳלֵךְ וּגְאַלְתִּיךְ אָנֹכִי *if he will take thee to wife, well, let him do so; but if he will not take thee to wife, then I will take thee.* Comp. Tob. 3:17.

Niph. *to be redeemed.* Lev. 25:30. 27:20 ff. reflex. *to redeem one's self.* 25:49.

II. גָּאַל *to defile, pollute, disgrace,* like the Chald. גְּאַל (comp. under the letter א.) Job 3:5 יִגְאָלֻהוּ חֹשֶׁךְ וְצַלְמָוֶת *let darkness and death-shade disgrace it.*

Pi. גֵּאַל *idem.* Mal. 1:7.

Pu. part. מְגֹאָל *polluted, ceremonially unclean.* Mal. 1:7, 12.

Niph. pass. נִגְאָל Zeph. 3:1. Instead of this we find Is. 59:3. Lam. 4:14 נְגֹאֲלוּ, a peculiar grammatical form. Is it not perhaps a trace of the passive of Niphal, like the Arab. اُنقتِل ?

Hiph. with Syr. form, אֶגְאָלְתִּי *I have polluted* or *stained,* Is. 63:3.

Hithpa. *to defile* or *pollute one's self.* Dan. 1:8.

III. גָּאַל *to reject, exclude.* (In Syr. Aph. *to reject,* Ethp. *to be rejected.* Verbs א״ע and ע״ע are often commuted, especially in Syriac.)

Pu. pass. Ezra 2:62. Neh. 7:64 וַיְגֹאֲלוּ *they were rejected,* i. e. removed from the priesthood.

גֹּאַל m. plur. const. גָּאֳלֵי, verbal from גָּאַל, *pollution, defilement.* Neh. 13:29.

גְּאֻלָּה f. verbal from גָּאַל, dec. X.

1. *repurchase, redemption.* Ruth 4: 7. verse 6 גְּאַל אַתָּה אֶת גְּאֻלָּתִי *redeem thou instead of me.*—מִשְׁפַּט הַגְּאֻלָּה *the right of redemption,* Jer. 32:7. comp. verse 8.

2. *the right of repurchase* or *redemption.* Lev. 25:24, 29 יָמִים תִּהְיֶה גְאֻלָּתוֹ *his right of redemption shall last a year,* verses 31, 48. Jer. 32:8.

3. *price of redemption, ransom.* Lev. 25:51, 52.

4. *relationship, kindred.* (Comp. גָּאַל no. 1. 3.) Ezek. 11:15 אַנְשֵׁי גְאֻלָּתֶךָ *thy relatives* or *kindred.*

גַּב m. with suff. גַּבִּי, plur. גַּבִּים and גַּבּוֹת, dec. VIII. h. *something curved, arched,* or *vaulted.* (Chald. גִּבְּבָא *a bunch, hill.*) Particularly

1. *the back* of men and animals. (Comp. Germ. *Buckel.*) Ezek. 10:12. Ps. 129:3 עַל־גַּבִּי חָרְשׁוּ חֹרְשִׁים *they furrowed my back.*

2. *boss of a shield* or *buckler, umbo.* Job 15:26 *he ran against him* בַּעֲבִי גַּבֵּי מָגִנָּיו *with the thick bosses of his bucklers.* In Arabic the expression is almost proverbial, *he turned against him the boss of his buckler,* i. e. he became his unrelenting adversary. Further the Arab. جَوْب denotes *the shield* itself; comp. the French *bouclier* from *boucle.*

3. *citadel, intrenchment;* applied figuratively to conclusions, or arguments, behind which men, as it were, intrench themselves. Job 13:12. (So in Arab. ظهر *a back* and also *a citadel.*)

4. *arch, arched building, vault;* probably, like the Lat. *fornix* for a *brothel.*

(Sept. and Vulg. *a brothel;* Syr. *an arched house.*) Ezek. 16:24, 31, 39. As no traces of arches are found in the Egyptian and Persepolitan ruins, it has been denied that the Hebrews were acquainted with them. (Goguet's Origin of Laws, etc. Part III. Jahn's Archäol. I. 1. p. 208.) But the Babylonians were acquainted with the building of arches, according to Strabo (XVI. p. 738, 739.) and the etymology of גַּב and אֲגֻדָּה prove the same as to the Hebrews. Applied to an arched part of the altar, Ezek. 43:13.

5. *the circumference of a wheel, felloe, apsis.* 1 K. 7:33. Ezek. 1:18.

6. *bow of the eye, eye-brow.* Lev. 14:9. (Arab. جَبَّة *the bone just below the eye-brow.*)

גַּב Chald. *side.* (Syr. ܓܒܐ Arab. جَنْب.) Hence עַל גַּב and עַל גַּבֵּי *on the side of, by, upon.* Syr. ܠܘܬ ܓܒ *idem.*) Dan. 7:6 Kethib עַל גביה, (read גַּבַּהּ) Keri עַל גַּבַּהּ *on him.* Sept. ὑπεράνω αὐτῆς. Vulg. *super se.* Others, after the Hebrew usage, *on his back.*

גֵּב m. dec. I. a.

1. *board, plank.* 1 K. 6:9. (Root גּוּב i. q. Arab. جَابَ *to cut, cleave;* hence in Syr. ܓܘܒܐ *a board.*)

2. *cistern, reservoir of water.* Jer. 14:3. 2 K. 3:16. (Chald. גּוּב, גֻּבָּא, גּוּבָא, Syr. ܓܘܒܐ, Arab. جُبّ *idem.*)

3. plur. גֵּבִים *locusts.* Is. 33:4. Comp. גּוֹב, with which it is synonymous.

4. plur. גֵּבִים proper name of an unknown place. Is. 10:31. Sept. Γιββείρ.

גֹּב m. emph. גֻּבָּא, Chald. *pit, cavern, den.* Dan. 6:7 ff.

גבים 2 K. 25:12 Kethib, probably to be pointed גֹּבִים *ploughmen,* i. q. יֹגְבִים in Keri. Root גּוּב, i. q. יָגַב *to plough, to till;* comp. the Arab. جَابَ *to cut, to cleave;* conj. VIII. *to dig* a well. The Keri is a correct gloss.

גֶּבֶא m. dec. VI. a. 1. *cistern.* Is. 30:14.

2. *pool, swamp, marsh.* Ezek. 47:11. Root גָּבָא i. q. جبا and جبى (with which also جبا conj. IV. agrees,) *to collect water;* hence جَابِيَة *a great reservoir of water;* جبا *collected water.*

גָּבַהּ, fut. יִגְבַּהּ, infin. גָּבְהָה (Zeph. 3:11.)

1. *to be high;* spoken of a tree, Ezek. 31:5, 10. of stature, 1 Sam. 10:23 וַיִּגְבַּהּ מִכָּל־הָעָם *and he was higher than any of the people.*

2. *to be lifted up, to be exalted.* Job 36:7. Is. 5:16. 52:13.

3. גָּבַהּ לִבִּי *my heart is elated,* i. e. proud, arrogant, haughty. Ps. 131:1 לֹא־גָבַהּ לִבִּי *my heart is not haughty.* Prov. 18:12. 2 Chr. 26:16. 32:25. Ezek. 28:2, 16. In a good sense 2 Chr. 17:6 וַיִּגְבַּהּ לִבּוֹ בְּדַרְכֵי יְהוָה *his heart was elated,* i. e. courageous, *in the ways of Jehovah.* Hence

4. by itself, *to be proud, arrogant, haughty.* (Comp. גַּבָּה.) Is. 3:16 כִּי גָבְהוּ בְּנוֹת צִיּוֹן *because the daughters of Zion are haughty.* Jer. 13:15. Ezek. 16:50. Zeph. 3:11.

Hiph. הִגְבִּיהַּ 1. *to make high, exalt.* 2 Chr. 33:14. Ezek. 17:24. Prov. 17:19 מַגְבִּיהַּ פִּתְחוֹ, *who exalteth his gate,* i. e. buildeth it too high. Jer. 49:16. כִּי תַגְבִּיהַּ כַּנֶּשֶׁר קִנֶּךָ *though, like the eagle, thou buildest thy nest on high.* So Obad. 4. with the omission of קִנֶּךָ which may be supplied from the following clause.

2. when joined with the infinitive of another verb, it may be rendered as an adverb, and the infinitive as a finite verb. (See הִשְׁפִּיל, הֶעֱמִיק.) Ps. 113:5 הַמַּגְבִּיהִי לָשָׁבֶת *who sitteth* or *dwelleth on high.* Job 5:7 יַגְבִּיהוּ עוּף *they fly high.* Hence without עוּף, probably in the same signification, 39:27 אִם עַל פִּיךָ יַגְבִּיהַּ נָשֶׁר *doth the eagle mount up at thy command?*

גָּבֹהַּ verbal from גָּבַהּ, const. גְּבַהּ and גְּבֹהַּ, fem גְּבֹהָה, plur. גְּבֹהִים.

1. *high;* spoken of trees, mountains, towers. Is. 2:15. 30:25. 40:9. 57:7. 1 Sam. 9:2.

2. *haughty, proud.* Is. 5:15 עֵינֵי גְבֹהִים *the eyes of the proud.* 1 Sam. 2:3 אַל־תַּרְבּוּ תְדַבְּרוּ גְּבֹהָה גְבֹהָה *talk no more exceeding proudly.* Further in the phrases גְּבַהּ־עֵינַיִם *with haughty eyes,* Pr. 101:5. גְּבַהּ לֵב *of a proud heart,* Prov. 16:5 ג׳ רוּחַ *of a proud spirit,* Ecc. 7:8.

3. as a subst. גֹּבַהּ קוֹמָתוֹ *the height of his stature,* 1 Sam. 16:7. comp. Ex. 15:16.

גֹּבַהּ m. verbal from גָּבַהּ, dec. VI. n.

1. *height.* Job 22:12.

2. *exaltation, majesty.* Job 40:10.

3. *arrogance.* Jer. 48:29. also with the addition of אַף, Ps. 10:4. of לֵב, 2 Chr. 32:26. of רוּחַ, Prov. 16:18.

גַּבְהוּת m. verbal from גָּבַהּ. *pride, arrogance.* Is. 2:11, 17.

גְּבוּל and **גְּבֻל** verbal from גָּבַל, dec. I.

1. *bound, limit, border.* Num. 34:3 ff. Deut. 3:16, 17. Josh. 13:23, 27. 15:47.

2. *territory.* Ex. 10:14 כָּל גְּבוּל מִצְרַיִם *the whole territory of Egypt.*

3. *edge, border, margin.* Ezek. 43:13, 17, 20.

Plur. גְּבוּלִים *territory,* like the Lat. *fines.* 1 Sam. 5:6. 2 K. 15:16. 18:8.

גְּבוּלָה fem. of גְּבוּל, dec. X. *territory, place.* Is. 28:25. frequently in the plural גְּבוּלוֹת *idem.* Deut. 32:8.

גִּבּוֹר and **גִּבֹּר** verbal from גָּבַר, dec. I.

1. *strong, mighty.* Gen. 10:8 וְהוּא הֵחֵל לִהְיוֹת גִּבֹּר בָּאָרֶץ *and he began to be mighty on the earth.* 1 Chr. 1:10. Ps. 112:2. Hence spoken of God, Deut. 10:17 הָאֵל הַגָּדֹל הַגִּבֹּר וְהַנּוֹרָא *a great God, mighty and terrible.*

2. *brave, valiant,* and substantively *a hero.* 2 Sam. 17:8. Gen. 10:9 גִּבֹּר צַיִד *a brave hunter.* Used ironically, Is. 5:22 גִּבּוֹרִים לִשְׁתּוֹת יָיִן *heroes to drink wine.* Frequently in the phrase גִּבּוֹר חַיִל *brave hero, mighty man of valour,* Judg. 6:12. 11:1. 1 Sam. 16:18. 2 K. 5:1. and sometimes merely *warrior,* Josh. 1:14. 8:3. 10:7. Cant. 3:7. 4:4. In a different sense,

3. גִּבּוֹר חַיִל *one great in substance, a man of wealth.* 1 Sam. 9:1. Ruth 2:1. 2 K. 15:20. also *an active, enterprising man.* 1 K. 11:28. Neh. 11:14. (Comp. גִּבּוֹר תָּמִים *a righteous man,* 2 Sam. 22:26.)

4. particularly, *leader of an army.* 2 Sam. 23:8. 1 K. 1:8. 1 Chr. 29:24. 2 Chr. 32:3. also generally, *a leader, chief,* 1 Chr. 9:26 גִּבֹּרֵי הַשֹּׁעֲרִים *the chief porters.* So גִּבּוֹר חַיִל *the leader* or *general of an army,* 1 Chr. 11:26. 2 Chr. 32:21.

5. in a bad sense, *violent, tyrannical,* i. q. Arab. جَبَّار. Ps. 52:3. 126:4.

גְּבוּרָה f. verbal from גָּבַר, dec. X.

1. *strength, might, power.* Ecc. 9:16. Plur. Job 41:4. [12.] Ps. 147:10.

2. *valour, courage, spirit, fortitude.* 2 K. 18:20. Judg. 8:21. Job 39:19 הֲתִתֵּן לַסּוּס גְּבוּרָה *canst thou give to the horse spirit?* Mic. 3:8. Used as a concrete in the phrase גְּבוּרָתוֹ אֲשֶׁר עָשָׂה *his valiant deeds which he did,* 1 K. 16:27. 22:46. comp. 16:7. 2 K. 13:12. etc.

3. *power, omnipotence* of God, Ps. 54:3. 66:7. 99:14. etc. Plur. גְּבוּרוֹת יְהוָֹה *God's mighty deeds* or *wonders,* Deut. 3:24. Ps. 106:2. 150:2. In Syr. ܓܒܘܪܬܐ *idem.*

4. *victory.* Ex. 32:18. comp. the verb, chap. 17:11.

גְּבוּרָה Chald. emph. גְּבוּרְתָא, *idem.* Dan. 2:20.

גִּבֵּחַ m. Lev. 13:41. *having too high a forehead, bald before, forehead bald, recalvaster,* different from קֵרֵחַ. (Root גבח in Samar. i. q. גָּבַהּ *to be high.* The Arabians use this word specifically of *the high forehead;* hence جَبْهَة *high forehead,* and أَجْبَه *having a high forehead.*)

גַּבַּחַת f. with suff. גַּבַּחְתּוֹ, denom. from גִּבֵּחַ.

1. *bald forehead.* Lev. 13:42, 43.

2. metaphorically, *baldness,* or *bare-*

ness of hair, on the outer, front, or *right side of cloth.* Lev. 13:55.

גְּבִינָה *curdled milk, cheese.* Job 10: 10. (Syr. ܓܒܝܢ with omission of Nun, and Arab. جبن *idem.* The root in Syr. Ethpe. and in Arab. conj. V. signifies *to curdle* as milk, *to form cheese.*)

גָּבִיעַ m. dec. III. a. 1. *cup.* Gen. 44:2 ff. Jer. 35:5. In the latter passage, גָּבִיעַ appears to denote a larger drinking vessel, *a goblet, crater;* and כּוֹס, a smaller one, *wine glass, cyathus,* into which they drew from the other.

2. *the cup* or *calix* of a flower. Ex. 25:33. (So the Arab. قبعة. Comp. קֻבַּעַת.)

גְּבִיר m. verbal from גָּבַר. *master, ruler, lord.* Found only Gen. 27:29, 37.

גְּבִירָה fem. of גְּבִיר, *mistress, female ruler, reigning queen.* 1 K. 11:19. 15: 13 וַיְסִרֶהָ מִגְּבִירָה *he removed her from being queen.* 2 Chr. 15:16.

גָּבִישׁ m. found only Job 28:18. The connexion shows that it is something costly, a precious stone or a precious metal. Most probably *crystal;* comp. אֶלְגָּבִישׁ Ezek. 13:11 *hail.* So in Greek κρύσταλλος denotes *ice* and *crystal.* Some of the Rabbins render it *pearls;* others of them, *a green precious stone.*

גָּבַל, fut. יִגְבֹּל *to bound, to set up a boundary;* spoken (1.) of the boundary itself, Josh. 18:20 *the Jordan* יִגְבֹּל אֹתוֹ *shall bound it.* (2.) of one who fixes the boundaries, Deut. 19:14 *thou shalt not remove thy neighbour's land-mark,* אֲשֶׁר גָּבְלוּ רִאשֹׁנִים *which the forefathers have fixed.*

Hiph. *to set bounds* to a person, or about a thing. Ex. 19:12 *set bounds to the people.* verse 23 *set bounds about the mount.*

Deriv. out of course גְּבָל, מִגְבָּלָה.

גְּבַל proper name of a Phenician city, called by the Greeks *Byblus* and by the modern Arabians *Geble, Gebail,* and *Esbele.* Ezek. 27:9. comp. Josh. 13:5. 1 K. 5:32. The gentile noun is גִּבְלִי; 1 K. 5:32. Josh. 13:5.

גְּבָל Ps. 83:8. probably the Arab. جبال *Gebalene,* a mountainous country beyond Jordan. Reland's Palæstina, p. 82—85.

גְּבֻל see גְּבוּל.

גַּבְלֻת f. verbal from גָּבַל, prob. *bordering, bounding.* Ex. 28:22 and 39: 15 שַׁרְשְׁרֹת גַּבְלֻת *bordering chains,* or *cords,* to separate the different rows of precious stones on the breast-plate. Comp. מִגְבָּלֹת 28:14. Others: *catenæ æqualiter terminatæ, chains of equal length;* but the idea of equality is arbitrarily introduced. Others: *elegantly-formed chains,* from גבל in Syr. and Arab. *to form.*

גִּבֵּן m. *hump-backed, hunch-backed.* Lev. 21:20. So Sept. Vulg. Syr. Arab. See the following article.

גַּבְנֻנִּים masc. plur. *protuberances, knobs, hills.* Ps. 68:16 הַר גַּבְנֻנִּים *a mountain having many summits,* ὄρος πολυκόρυφος. verse 17 הָרִים גַּבְנֻנִּים *idem,* where the latter word is used adjectively, or they both stand in apposition. Comp. the Syr. ܓܒܢܘܢܐ *summit, eyebrow;* Talmud. גַּבְנוּנִית *summit, crown of the head;* גַּבְנוּן *puffed up, proud.*

גֶּבַע (*height, hill*) proper name of a Levitical city in the tribe of Benjamin, the northernmost boundary of Judea, Josh. 18:24. 2 Sam. 5:25. also called *Geba of Benjamin,* Judg. 20:10. 1 K. 15:22.

גִּבְעָה f. plur. גְּבָעוֹת, dec. XII. b.

1. *hill.* Ex. 17:9. 2 Sam. 2:25. etc.

2. proper name of a city in the tribe of Benjamin, also called גִּבְעַת שָׁאוּל *Gibeath-Saul,* because Saul was born there, and made it his royal residence. 1 Sam. 11.4. 26:1. 2 Sam. 21:1—9. The gentile noun is גִּבְעָתִי.—Gibeath-Phinehas, Josh. 24:33. is a different place.

גִּבְעוֹן (*hill*) proper name of a city in the tribe of Benjamin, somewhat more to the north than Gibea, anciently inhabited by the Hivites, (Josh. 9:1. 11:19.) and famous for the deception which the inhabitants played on the Israelites.

גִּבְעֹל found only Ex. 9:31 וְהַפִּשְׁתָּה גִּבְעֹל Vulg. *cum linum jam folliculos germinaret.* Luther: *the flax had knotted.* C.V. *the flax was bolled.* Sept. Arab. and Samar. render it: *had seeds, or was impregnated.* Perhaps: *was in blossom,* so that this quadriliteral were compounded of גָּבִיעַ *calix of a flower,* and גֹּל i. q. Syr. ܡܘܦܠ *bud, flower.* In the Talmud, גבעול occurs for *stem, stalk,* Mishnah, P. VI. p. 307. ed. Surenhus.

גָּבַר and גָּבֵר (2 Sam. 1:23.) fut. יִגְבַּר, perhaps a denom. from גֶּבֶר.

1. *to be strong, powerful.* Lam. 1:16. Construed with מִן, *to be stronger than, to prevail over,* 2 Sam. 1:23. Ps. 65:4. Construed with עַל, in the same sense, 2 Sam. 11:23. Gen. 49:26.

2. *to increase;* e.g. as water, Gen. 7:18, 24.—גָּבַר חַיִל *to increase in substance,* Job 21:7.

3. *to conquer, get the upper hand.* Ex. 17:11. 1 Sam. 2:9. (Arab. جبر *to bind fast, to fortify;* conj. V. *to become strong, to acquire strength.*)

Pi. *to make strong, to establish.* Ecc. 10:10. Zech. 10:6, 12.

Hiph. 1. *to make strong, to confirm.* Dan. 9:27 הִגְבִּיר בְּרִית לָרַבִּים *he makes a firm covenant with many.*

2. intrans. i. q. Kal. Ps. 12:5 לִלְשֹׁנֵנוּ נַגְבִּיר *through our tongue we are strong.*

Hithpa. 1. *to prevail, be superior;* construed with עַל. Is. 42:13.

2. *to conduct one's self proudly* or *arrogantly.* Job 15:25. 36:9. (Arab. conj. V. *to exalt one's self against God.*)

Deriv. גִּבּוֹר, גְּבוּרָה, גְּבִיר.

גֶּבֶר m. prob. prim. dec. VI.

1. *man, vir,* i. q. אִישׁ, almost exclusively in poetry. לַגְּבָרִים *man by man,* Josh. 7:14, 17, 18.—Ps. 34:9 אַשְׁרֵי הַגֶּבֶר *happy is the man.* 40:5. 52:9. 94:12.

2. as a distinguishing name of sex, *male, mas,* i. q. זָכָר. Deut. 22:5. spoken even of new-born babes, Job 3:3 וְהַלַּיְלָה אָמַר הֹרָה גָבֶר *the night which said: a man,* i. e. a man-child, *is conceived.*

3. in a general sense, for *man, homo;* especially in opposition to God. Prov. 20:24 מֵיהוָה מִצְעֲדֵי גָבֶר *a man's goings are of the Lord.* Job 4:17. 10:5. 14:10, 14. Lam. 3:35.

4. *every one,* like אִישׁ. Joel 2:8 גֶּבֶר בִּמְסִלָּתוֹ יֵלֵכוּן *every one marches in his path.* Lam. 3:39.

גְּבַר m. (with Chaldaic form,) *idem.* Ps. 18:26.

גְּבַר m. plur. גֻּבְרִין (as if from גֻּבַר,) Chald. *idem.* Dan. 2:25. 5:11. 3:8, 12.

גִּבָּר Chald. i. q. Heb. גִּבּוֹר *hero.* Dan. 3:20.

גְּבֶרֶת f. with suff. גְּבִרְתִּי, fem of גְּבִיר, dec. XIII. b. *mistress,* in opposition to handmaid. Gen. 16:4, 8. Prov. 30:23. 2 K. 5:3.—*mistress of kingdoms,* Is. 47:5, 7.

גַּבְרִיאֵל m. (*man of God*) proper name of one of the seven archangels in the writings of the later Jews. Dan. 8:16. 9:21. Comp. Luc. 1:19, 26.

גִּבְּתוֹן proper name of a Philistine city in the limits of the tribe of Dan. Josh. 19:44. 21:23. 1 K. 15:27. Eusebius calls it Γαβαθὼν τῶν ἀλλοφύλων; Josephus, Γαβαθώ.

גָּג m. prim. with suff. גַּגּוֹ. plur. גַּגּוֹת.

1. *flat roof* or *top* of an oriental house. Josh. 2:6, 8. Prov. 21:9. 1 Sam. 9:25.

2. *surface* or *top* of an altar. Ex. 30:3. 37:26.

I. גַּד Is. 65:11. name of a divinity, which was worshipped by the idolatrous Hebrews, perhaps *the god* or *goddess of fortune.* Comp. גַּד. Sept. Τύχη. Vulg. *Fortuna.* According to some Jewish commentators, this word denotes in

Arabic *the star Jupiter*. Hence perhaps בַּעַל גָּד *Baal Gad*, the name of a place.

II. גַּד m. according to Sept. Vulg. Chald. Syr. Arab. and the Jewish commentators, *coriander*, a highly aromatic plant. The seeds are round, and of the size of pepper-corns. In Ex. 16:31. Num. 11:7, the appearance of manna is compared to these seeds.

I. גָּד m. 1. *fortune, prosperity*. Found only Gen. 30:11 Kethib בְּגָד *fortunately, happily.* Sept. ἐν τύχῃ. Vulg. *feliciter.* Keri בָּא גָד *good fortune comes*. Others make it i. q. גְּדוּד *a crowd, troop, turma,* but unsuitably to the context.

2. proper name of a son of Jacob and of the tribe named from him, whose possessions lay beyond Jordan between Reuben and Manasseh. The limits are given more minutely, Josh. 13:24—28. The gentile noun is גָּדִי, Deut. 3:12. Josh. 1:12.

II. גָּד or גָּדָה found only in the plur. const. גְּדוֹת *banks*. Josh. 3:15. 4:18. 12:15. Is. 8:8.

גְּדָבְרִין Chald. Dan. 3:2, 3. i. q. גִּזְבְּרִין *treasurers* (q. v.)

גֻּדְגֹּדָה found only Deut. 10:7. proper name of a place in the Arabian desert. In the parallel passage Num. 33:32, חֹר הַגִּדְגָּד.

I. גָּדַד *to cut in, to cut off*, (as in Syr. and Arab.) Found only in Hithpo. הִתְגּוֹדֵד *to cut one's self* in the body; as a superstitious and idolatrous rite, Deut. 14:1. 1 K. 18:28. and as a sign of mourning, Jer. 16:6. 41:5. 47:5. See גְּדוּד.

II. גָּדַד i. q. גּוּד *to press*, (found only in Hebrew,) construed with עַל, Ps. 94:21 יָגוֹדּוּ עַל־נֶפֶשׁ צַדִּיק *they press upon the life of the righteous*. (53 MSS. of Kennicott have יָגֹדּוּ,)

Hithpo. *to collect into one place*, from fear or terror, Mic. 4:14. [5:1.] *to assemble* any where, Jer. 5:7.

גְּדַד Chald. *to cut down, to hew down* a tree. Dan. 4:11, 20. [4:14, 23.]

I. גְּדוּד m. plur. גְּדוּדוֹת, verbal from גָּדַד no. I.

1. *an incision in the skin.* Jer. 48:37.

2. *an incision in the ground, a furrow.* Ps. 65:11.

II. גְּדוּד m. plur. גְּדוּדִים, *crowd, band of warriors*, particularly of light-armed troops for predatory excursions. Gen. 49:19. 1 Sam. 30:8, 23. 2 Sam. 3:22. 2 K. 6:23. 13:20, 21. 24:2. 2 K. 5:2. See especially 2 K. 5:2 אֲרָם יָצְאוּ גְדוּדִים *the Syrians had gone out in plundering parties*. Also *a band of robbers*, Hos. 7:1.—בְּנֵי הַגְּדוּד *men of the plundering party, predatory soldiers*, 2 Chr. 25:12. בַּת גְּדוּד *daughter of plundering parties*, Mic. 4:14.

גָּדֹל, גָּדוֹל, const. גְּדוֹל, גְּדֹל, (גְּדָל־ Ps. 145:8. Nah. 1:3. Keri,) verbal adj. from גָּדַל, dec. III. a. and h.

1. *great.*—מֶלֶךְ הַגָּדוֹל *the great king*, a title of the Assyrian monarch, equivalent to *king of kings*, 2 K. 18:19, 28. הַכֹּהֵן הַגָּדוֹל *the high-priest*, Hag. 1:1, 12, 14. Zech. 3:1, 8. גְּדוֹל חֶסֶד ,כֹּחַ *of great kindness, of great power*, Ps. 145:8. Nah. 1:3. Keth.—Gen. 29:7 עוֹד הַיּוֹם גָּדוֹל *it is yet high day;* comp. the French *grand jour.*—As a subst. Ex. 15:16 גְּדֹל זְרוֹעֲךָ *the greatness of thine arm*, i. e. thy great arm. Plur. גְּדֹלוֹת *wonderful works;* of a prophet, 2 K. 8:4. and especially of God, Job 5:9. 9:10. Ps. 106:21. — Ps. 12:4 *the tongue, which speaketh great things*, i. e. which is arrogant and boasting.

2. *elder in age, major natu.* Gen. 27:1. 1 Sam. 17:13. 1 K. 2:22. 29:16.

3. *respectable, rich, mighty, distinguished.* Ex. 11:3 הָאִישׁ משֶׁה גָּדוֹל מְאֹד בְּאֶרֶץ מִצְרַיִם *the man Moses was much distinguished in the land of Egypt.* Lev. 19:15. 2 Sam. 19:32. 2 K. 4:8 אִשָּׁה גְדוֹלָה *a distinguished woman.* 5:1 אִישׁ גָּדוֹל לִפְנֵי אֲדֹנָיו *a great man with his master.* Job 1:3.—Plur. גְּדֹלִים *the great, mighty, noble*, Prov. 18:16. 25:6.—גְּדֹלֵי הַמֶּלֶךְ

the nobles of the king, Jon. 3:7. גְּדֹלֵי הָעִיר *the nobles of the city*, 2 K. 10:6, 11.

4. *weighty, important, gravis.* Ecc. 9:13.

גְּדֻלָּה, גְּדוּלָּה and **גְּדֻלָּה** f. verbal from גָּדַל, dec. X.

1. *greatness, majesty;* e. g. of God, Ps. 145:3. of a king, Est. 1:4. of a noble in a court, Est. 10:2. 6:3.

2. as a concrete, *mighty deeds* of God. 2 Sam. 7:21. 1 Chr. 17:19. Ps. 145:6.

גִּדּוּף verbal from גָּדַף, found only in plur. גִּדּוּפִים and גִּדּוּפֹת *reproaches, revilings, scoffs.* Is. 43:28. 51:7.

גִּדּוּפָה f. verbal from גָּדַף, *idem.* Ezek. 5:15.

גְּדִי m. dec. VI. 1. *kid, hœdus.* Ex. 23:19. generally with the addition עִזִּים, *a kid of the goats,* Gen. 38:17, 20. etc. plur. גְּדָיִים, גְּדָיִם, 1 Sam. 10:3. Gen. 27:9, 16.

I. **גְּדִיָּה** fem. of גְּדִי. *a female kid, capella.* Found only in the plur. גְּדִיֹּת, Cant. 1:8. (The singular occurs in the Mishnah, P. III. p. 111. ed. Surenhus.)

II. **גְּדִיּוֹת** i. q. **גְּדוֹת** *banks.* 1 Chr. 12:15 Kethib.

גְּדִלִים masc. plur. *plaited work, twisted threads,* from the root גָּדַל, which in Syr. and Arab. signifies *to twist, to weave.* Spoken (1.) of the sacred tufts or tassels on the four corners of the upper garment, Deut. 22:12. (2.) of ornaments on the chapiter of a pillar, 1 K. 7:17.

גָּדִישׁ m. 1. *pile of sheaves in the field, a stack, shock* of corn. Ex. 22:5. Judg. 15:5. Job 5:26. (Syr. and Arab. *idem.*)

2. *grave, tomb.* Job 21:32.

גָּדֵל and **גָּדַל**, fut. יִגְדַּל.

1. *to be great,* Gen. 38:14. Job 2:13. etc. *to become great, to wax great,* Gen. 21:8. 25:27. 1 K. 12:8, 10. Job 31:18 גְּדֵלַנִי כְאָב for גָּדַל עִמָּדִי *he has grown up with me as with a father.* Before the suffix ־ַנִי, the preposition עִם or לְ is to be supplied. Jerome: *crevit mecum.*

2. metaphorically *to be* or *become great, rich, distinguished.* Gen. 16:13 עַד כִּי גָדַל מְאֹד *till he became very great,* i. e. very rich. 24:35. 41:40 רַק הַכִּסֵּא אֶגְדַּל מִמֶּךָּ *only as to the throne will I be greater than thou.* 2 Sam. 5:10. 1 K. 10:23. Jer. 5:27.

3. *to be exalted, magnified, praised,* Ps. 35:27 יִגְדַּל יְהוָה *praised be Jehovah.* 40:17. 2 Sam. 7:26.

4. *to be highly valued, precious, dear.* 1 Sam. 26:24 *as thy life was precious in my eyes this day,* i. e. as I spared thy life; comp. verse 21, where יָקַר stands in the same connexion.

Pi. גִּדֵּל, גַּדֵּל. 1. *to make great, cause to grow;* e. g. the hair, Num. 6:5. plants, Is. 44:14. Ezek. 31:4.

2. *to bring up, to educate* children. Is. 1:2. 49:21. 51:18. 2 K. 10:6. *to nourish,* or *support,* in general, Dan. 1:5. Pu. pass. Ps. 144:12.

3. *to make great, mighty,* or *distinguished.* Est. 3:1. 5:11. 10:2. Josh. 3:6. 4:14.

4. *to exalt, to praise* God. Ps. 69:31. construed with לְ, Ps. 34:4.

Note. The form גַּדֵּל occurs at the end of a clause, Is. 49:21.; the form גִּדֵּל in the beginning or middle, Josh. 4:14. Est. 3:1.

Hiph. הִגְדִּיל. 1. *to make great.* Gen. 19:19 וַתַּגְדֵּל חַסְדְּךָ עִמָּדִי *thou hast made great thy kindness towards me,* i. e. thou hast shown me great favour. comp. Is. 9:2. 28:29. Ps. 18:29. Ecc. 1:9.

2. הִגְדִּיל אֶת פִּיו *to make great one's mouth, to make arrogant speeches, to act proudly* or *insolently.* Obad. 12. comp. Ezek. 35:13 וַתַּגְדִּילוּ עָלַי בְּפִיכֶם *ye have boasted against me with your mouth.* also, with the omission of פֶּה or בְּפֶה, in the same sense, Dan. 8:5, 8. 11:25. and with עַל of the person, Ps. 35:26. 38:17. 55:13. Job 19:5. Jer. 48:26, 42.

3. with the infinitives of other verbs, used adverbially; thus הִגְדִּיל לַעֲשׂוֹת *to do*

great things, Ps. 126:2, 3. Joel 2:21. also *to act proudly, insolently*, Joel 2:20. It has the former signification sometimes, when this infinitive is omitted, 1 Sam. 12:24 אֵת אֲשֶׁר־הִגְדִּיל עִמָּכֶם *what great things he has done for you.* 1 Sam. 20:41 *they both wept* עַד דָּוִד הִגְדִּיל *till David exceeded*, or *wept very loud.*

4. *to make high, to lift up.* Ps. 41:10.

Hithpa. 1. *to magnify one's self.* Ezek. 38:23.

2. *to conduct proudly* or *insolently.* Is. 10:15. Dan. 11:36, 37.

גָּדֵל m. verbal from גָּדַל, dec. V. a. *great.* Ezek. 16:26.

גֹּדֶל m. with suff. גָּדְלוֹ, once גֻּדְלוֹ (Ps. 150:2.) verbal from גָּדַל, dec. VI. m. and o.

1. *greatness;* e.g. of a tree, Ezek. 31:7.—גֹּדֶל זְרוֹעֲךָ *the greatness of thy might*, Ps. 79:11.

2. *greatness, honour, majesty;* of a king, i. q. כָּבוֹד, Ezek. 31:2, 18. of God, (frequent in Deut.) Deut. 3:24. 5:21. 9:26. 11:2. 32:3 הָבוּ גֹדֶל לֵאלֹהֵינוּ *give honour to our God.* Ps. 150:2.

3. with לֵבָב, *arrogance.* Is. 9:8. 10:12.

גָּדֹל see גָּדוֹל.

גְּדֻלָּה see גְּדוּלָּה.

גָּדַע 1. *to break in pieces;* e.g. a staff, Zech. 11:10.—1 Sam. 2:31 *I break in pieces thine arm, and the arm of thy father's house.* i. e. I destroy your strength. The same sense is attached to the phrase, *to break in pieces the horn*, Lam. 2:3. comp. in Pi. Ps. 75:11.

2. *to root out;* e.g. trees, (see Pual.) men, Judg. 21:6 נִגְדַּע הַיּוֹם שֵׁבֶט אֶחָד *we have this day rooted out a tribe.*

Pi. i. q. Kal, *to break in pieces;* e.g. a bar, Is. 45:2. Ps. 107:16. a horn, Ps. 75:11. especially *to break down* images of the gods, Deut. 12:3. 2 Chr. 34:4, 7.

Pu. pass. *to be rooted out.* Is. 9:9.

Niph. *to be broken in pieces, to be broken down.* Jer. 48:25. Is. 14:12 נִגְדַּעְתָּ לָאָרֶץ *thou art broken down (and thrown) to the ground.*

גִּדְעוֹן proper name of a judge in Israel. Judg. 6:11. 7:1 ff. Sept. Γεδεών.

גָּדַף found only in Pi. גִּדֵּף.

1. *to reproach, revile.* See the deriv. גִּדּוּף, גְּדוּפָה.

2. especially *to blaspheme* or *reproach* God. 2 K. 19:6, 22. This may be done by actions as well as words, Num. 15:30 *but he who does it presumptuously, blasphemes Jehovah*, i. e. expresses contempt to his positive command. Ezek. 20:27. (In Syr. Pa. and Arab. conj. II. *idem.*)

גָּדַר *to build a wall, to wall up.* (Arab. جَدَرَ I. II. *idem.*) Part. גֹּדֵר *a mason*, 2 K. 12:13. Often figuratively, Ezek. 13:5 *ye have not built a wall (for protection) about Israel.* (comp. 22:30.) More frequently in the following figure. Job 19:8 אָרְחִי גָדַר *he has walled up my path.* Lam. 3:7 גָּדַר בַּעֲדִי *he has walled about me.* verse 9. Hos. 2:8. [6.]

גָּדֵר com. gen. (comp. Ps. 62:4. Ezek. 42:7.) const. גְּדֵר, verbal from גָּדַר, dec. V. c.

1. *wall.* Mic. 7:11. Ezek. 13:5. especially about a vineyard, Num. 22:24. Ecc. 10:8. Is. 5:5.

2. *place walled in, place of protection.* Ezra 9:9. (Arab. جَدْرٌ *wall*, جَدِيرٌ *place walled in.*)

גְּדֵרָה fem. of גָּדֵר, dec. XI. b. *wall* of a city. Ps. 89:41. More frequently *a place surrounded with a wall*, into which the shepherds drove their flocks by night for security against wild animals. Hence גִּדְרוֹת הַצֹּאן *sheep-folds*, Num. 32:16, 24, 36. 1 Sam. 24:4. Zeph. 2:6. Comp. Odyss. IX. 185. But Nah. 3:17, appears to require *a quick-hedge*, yet we may understand here the thorn-bushes growing on a garden-wall, (Greek αἱμασιά.)

גְּדֶרֶת fem. of גָּדֵר. *idem.* Ezek. 42:12.

גֵּה Ezek. 47:13, undoubtedly a corrupt reading for זֶה *this*, as in verse 15. It is so read by the Sept. Vulg. Chald. and in 14 MSS. The two letters are very easily confounded.

גָּהָה according to the Jewish commentators, *to heal, cure.* Once Hos. 5:13 לֹא יִגְהֶה מִכֶּם מָזוֹר *he will not heal your wounds.* The moderns, on account of the Syr. ܓܗܐ *to escape*, render this passage, *the wound will not depart from you,* which does not suit the parallel clause. Hence

גֵּהָה f. verbal from גָּהָה. *healing, cure.* Prov. 17:22 *a joyful heart* יֵיטִב גֵּהָה *favours healing* or *health*, i. e. is salutary to the body. Sept. εὐεκτεῖν ποιεῖ. Comp. 16:24. The moderns, on account of the Arab. جِهَة i. q. وَجْه *face, countenance,* render the passage, *makes the countenance serene*, but not in accordance with the parallel clause, *dries up the bones.*

גָּהַר *to bend one's self down.* 2 K. 4:34, 35 וַיִּגְהַר עָלָיו *and he bent himself over him* to the ground. 1 K. 18:42 וַיִּגְהַר אַרְצָה *he bent himself to the ground.* So according to the context and the ancient versions. In Arabic, according to Schindler and Calasio, اجهر *incubuit, incurvatus fuit,* مجهور *incurvatus.*

גֵּו m. with suff. גֵּוִי, גֵּוָם, dec. VIII. h. i. q. גַּו, גַּב *the back.*—הִשְׁלִיךְ אַחֲרֵי גֵווֹ *to cast behind himself, to despise.* (See הִשְׁלִיךְ.)

גַּו, const. גּוֹ, with suff. גַּוַּהּ, גַּוֵּהּ, Chald. *the middle, midst.* (In Syr. ܓܘ.)—With בְּ simply *in*, like בְּתוֹךְ, Ezra 5:7 כְּדְנָה כְּתִיב בְּגַוֵּהּ *thus was written therein.* 4:15 בְּגַוַּהּ *in the same.* 6:2 כֵּן כְּתִיב בְּגַוַּהּ דִּכְרוֹנָה *thus was written in this record.* (The pronoun הּ is here, as frequently in Aramean, suffixed to the preposition, and signifies *this, the same*; e. g. בַּהּ שַׁעֲתָא *in the same hour*, Dan. 3:6, 15. 4:30. 5:5.) Dan. 3:25 בְּגוֹ נוּרָא *in the fire.* 7:15. Comp. גּוֹא.

גֵּו m. with suff. גֵּוִי, גֵּוְךָ, dec. VII. f.

1. *the back.* Prov. 10:13. 19:29. 26:3. Is. 38:17 כִּי הִשְׁלַכְתָּ אַחֲרֵי גֵוְךָ כָּל־חֲטָאָי *for thou castest all my sins behind thy back,* i. e. thou disregardest them, forgivest them.

2. *the middle,* i. q. Chald. גַּו. Job 30:5 מִן גֵּו יְגֹרָשׁוּ *from the midst* (*of men*) *they are driven.*

גּוֹא Chald. i. q. גַּו, גֵּו *the middle, midst.* Dan. 3:26. 4:7. [10.]

גּוֹב, *the locust*, plur. גֹּבַי, Am. 7:1. Nah. 3:17 גּוֹב גֹּבָי *locusta locustarum*, a construction like קֹדֶשׁ קֳדָשִׁים, used here to express the vast multitude. (Chald. גּוֹבָא, גּוֹבָא, plur. emph. גּוֹבַאי Ps. 105:34 Targ. as if from a sing. גּוֹבַי,) Bochart (Hieroz. II. p. 443.) compares in Arab. جَابٌ for جَابِي *locuts,* from جبا *to creep out from the ground,* as the young locusts do in the spring; comp. in Ethiop. אנבב *locusts* from נבב *to creep out from the ground.*

גּוֹג proper name. Ezek. 38:3, 14 ff. 39:11. prince of the people of Magog, which, according to Ezek. XXXVIII. XXXIX. was to invade Israel from the north, and there suffer a defeat. See מָגוֹג. The eastern writers have much to say concerning Gog, which with them is the name of *a country* or *nation*, as it appears to be in Rev. 20:8.

גּוּד *to press*, i. q. גָּדַד no. II. Gen. 49:19. Hab. 3:16.

I. גֵּוָה f. *body.* Job 20:25. Kindred with גֵּו and גַּו, and synonymous with גְּוִיָּה.

II. גֵּוָה contraction of גַּאֲוָה verbal from גָּאָה.

1. *exaltation.* Job 22:29 וַתֹּאמֶר גֵּוָה *then thou sayest, an exaltation.*

2. *pride, arrogance.* Job 33:17. Jer. 13:17.

גֵּוָה Chald. *pride.* Dan. 4:34. [37.]

גּוּז i. q. Arab. جَازَ = עָבַר *to pass over, to pass beyond.* Ps. 90:10 כִּי גָז חִישׁ *for it passes away suddenly.* Also caus. like Hiph. Num. 11:31 וַיָּגָז שַׂלְוִים מִן הַיָּם

and brought quails over from the sea. Sept. ἐξεπέρασεν. Usually derived from גָּזַז, *it* (the wind) *cuts* or *hurries them away from the sea.*

גּוֹזָל m. dec. II. b. *a young bird.* Deut. 32:11. especially *a young pigeon,* Gen. 15:9. (Arab. جوزل Syr. by metath. ܝܘܙܠܐ *a young pigeon.*)

גּוֹזָן a city or country in northern Mesopotamia, 2 K. 17:6. 18:11. 19:12. Is. 37:12. where it is joined with Haran and the river Habor; in Ptolemy *Gauzanitis,* now *Kauschan.*

גּוֹחַ see גִּיחַ *to break forth.*

גּוֹי m. with suff. גּוֹי (Zeph. 2:9.) Plur. גּוֹיִם, const. גּוֹיֵי.

1. *people, nation,* in the widest sense, and of general application. Spoken of the Israelites, Deut. 32:43. Poetically of troops or swarms of certain animals; e.g. of locusts, Joel 1:6. comp. עַם Prov. 30:25, 26. and Hom. Iliad, II. 87.

2. especially *foreign nations, nations not Hebrew,* i.q. τὰ ἔθνη, *gentes,* in ecclesiastical usage. Gen. 10:5, 32. Neh. 5:8. often in the sense of *enemies, barbarians,* Ps. 9:6, 16, 20, 21. 10:16. 59:6, 9.—גְּלִיל הַגּוֹיִם *Galilee of the gentiles,* Is. 9:1. (In Rabbin. גּוֹי, גּוֹיָה denotes *one not a Jew, a heathen* or *Christian.*)

3. Gen. 14:1. Josh. 12:23, the proper name of a people, of whose residence nothing further is known.

גְּוִיָּה f. dec. X.

1. *body.* Dan. 10:6. Gen. 47:18 *there is nothing left,* בִּלְתִּי אִם גְּוִיָּתֵנוּ וְאַדְמָתֵנוּ *except our body,* i.e. our person, *and our land.* Neh. 9:37 עַל גְּוִיֹּתֵינוּ מֹשְׁלִים וּבִבְהֶמְתֵּנוּ *they have dominion over our bodies and over our cattle.*

2. *dead body, carcass, corpse,* of men or animals. Judg. 14:8, 9. 1 Sam. 31:10, 12. Nah. 3:3. (Syr. ܓܘܝܐ *venter.*)

גּוּל see גִּיל *to rejoice.*

גּוֹלָה, rarely גֹּלָה, strictly part. Kal fem. from גָּלָה *to emigrate.*

1. *emigration, removal, captivity.*—עַד הַגּוֹלָה *till the captivity,* 1 Chr. 5:22. כְּלֵי הַגּוֹלָה *furniture for travelling,* Ezek. 12:7. הָלַךְ, יָצָא בַּגּוֹלָה *to go into exile* or *captivity,* Jer. 29:16. 48:7, 11. 49:3. בְּנֵי הַגּוֹלָה *exiles,* also *those returned from exile,* Ezra 4:1. 6:19, 20. 10:7.

2. *the emigrants themselves, captives.* Est. 2:6. Jer. 28:6. Ezek. 1:1. 3:11, 15. 11:24, 25. also *those who have returned from captivity,* Ezra 10:8 קְהַל הַגּוֹלָה *the congregation of those that had been carried away.*

גּוֹלָן a city in Bashan or Batanea, afterwards belonging to the tribe of Manasseh. Deut. 4:43. Josh. 20:8. 21:27, (where the Kethib has גָּלוֹן.) 1 Chr. 6:56. Eusebius writes it (according to the Syriac pronunciation,) Γαυλων, and calls it a great place in Batanea. It gave name to the province of Gaulonitis, which, however, Josephus distinguishes from Batanea, and places to the west of the same, immediately on the Jordan. Its capital he calls Γαυλάνη, J. A. VIII. 2. J. B. I. 4. II. 25. III. 2. See Reland's Palæstina, p. 199, 318.

גּוּמָּץ m. *pit.* Once Ecc. 10:8. (In Syr. *idem.* In Chald. also written with כ and ק.)

גָּוַע, fut. יִגְוַע. *to breathe out one's life, to expire, die,* i.q. מוּת. Gen. 6:17. 7:21. Num. 17:27. 20:3. Sometimes joined with מוּת, Gen. 25:8 וַיִּגְוַע וַיָּמָת אַבְרָהָם *and Abraham expired and died.* verse 17. 35:29.

גּוּף found only in Hiph. *to close.* Neh. 7:3. (Arab. conj. IV. *idem.* and in Syr. Ethpa. pass.)

גּוּפָה f. dec. X. *body, corpse.* 1 Chr. 10:12. (Arab. جوف *belly,* جيفة *corpse.*)

גּוּר 1. *to sojourn, to dwell any where for a time, to live as not at home.* Gen. 12:10. 19:9. 20:1. Judg. 17:7. 19:1. Ruth 1:1. Is. 11:6. The person with whom one resides is preceded by עִם, Gen. 32:5. by אֵת, Ex. 12:19. or stands in the accus. Ps. 120:5 כִּי גַרְתִּי מֶשֶׁךְ *that I dwell with Mesech*, i. e. with the Moschians. Job 19:15 גָּרֵי בֵיתִי *those who dwell in my house, the inmates of my family, inquilini mei.* Ex. 3:22 גָּרַת בֵּיתָהּ *the lodger in her house.* The accusative also denotes the place, Is. 33:14 מִי יָגוּר לָנוּ אֵשׁ אוֹכֵלָה *who can dwell with the devouring fire?*—גּוּר בְּאֹהֶל יְהוָה *to dwell in the tabernacle of Jehovah*, i. e. to visit it uninterruptedly, to be, as it were, an inmate of God, and enjoy his protection. Ps. 15:1: (39. 13?) 61:5. The name of God is also put in the accus. 5:5 לֹא יְגֻרְךָ רָע *the wicked shall not dwell with thee.* (In Arab. جار conj. III. *to live any where as a guest;* with an accus. *to be on hospitable terms with any one.* Hence جاور الله *to be on intimate terms with God, to be ardently devoted to him.*)

Deriv. out of course מָגוּר, גֵּרוּת, גֵּיר, גֵּר.

2. *to gather together, to assemble.* (So the Jewish commentators and the Chaldaic version. The synonymous word in Arabic أوى signifies in conj. I. *to reside, to dwell,* in conj. V. *to assemble in one place.*) Ps. 56:7 יָגוּרוּ יִצְפּוֹנוּ הֵמָּה *they assemble and lie in wait.* 59:4. יָגוּרוּ עָלַי עַזִּים *the mighty gather themselves together against me.* Perhaps transitively Ps. 140:3 יָגוּרוּ מִלְחָמוֹת *they gather up contentions.* Or גּוּר in this last passage is i. q. גָּרָה; hence *they excite contentions.* Is. 54:15.

Deriv. מְגוּרָה.

Hithpo. הִתְגּוֹרֵר 1. *to reside*, i. q. Kal. no. 2.

II. גּוּר also גּוּר לוֹ (Job 19:29.)

1. *to be afraid*, i. q. יָגֹר and Arab. وجر. It is construed with מִן, Job 41:17. with מִפְּנֵי, Num. 22:3. Deut. 1:17. 9:19. 18:22. with an acc. Deut. 32:27. Judg. 5:17 וְדָן לָמָּה יָגוּר אֳנִיּוֹת *and Dan, wherefore fears he the (hostile) ships?* (Sept. Vulg. Luth. according to no. I. *wherefore dwells Dan (quietly) in his ships?* unaptly, as this tribe is not situated on the sea-coast.

2. *to fear, reverence, worship.* Ps. 22:24. 33:8.

Deriv. מָגוֹר, מְגוּרָה.

גּוּר m. plur. גּוּרִים and גֻּרוֹת. *a young animal, a whelp, cub, catulus.* Usually in the connexion, גּוּר אַרְיֵה *a young lion*, Gen. 49:9. Ezek. 19:3 ff. but in Lam. 4:3, spoken of the young of a jackal. (Syr. ܓܘܪܝܐ, ܓܘܪܝܬܐ, ܓܘܪܐ, Arab. جرو *a young lion, or dog*, applied also to other animals, especially to beasts of prey. Bocharti Hieroz. I. p. 714.)

גּוֹרָל m. plur. גּוֹרָלוֹת, prim. dec. II. b.

1. *lot.* (The primary signification *a small stone*, as is used for casting lots, is found in the Arab. جرل *a stone.*) The phrases formed with this word are יָדָה, יָרָה הַגּוֹרָל *to cast lots*, Josh. 18:6. Joel 4:3. So with הִשְׁלִיךְ, Josh. 18:8 ff. with הִפִּיל, Neh. 10:34. with הֵטִיל, Prov. 16:33. with נָתַן, Lev. 16:8. On the contrary עָלָה גוֹרָל עַל, Lev. 6:9. or יָצָא לְ, Josh. 19:1 ff. *the lot falls to any one*, i. e. the lot of any one comes out (of the shaken urn.) The thing, about which lots are cast, is preceded by עַל, Ps. 22:19. Joel 3:8. Obad. 11.

2. *that which falls to any one by lot;* e. g. his inheritance, Judg. 1:3 *come up with me into my lot.* Ps. 16:5. 125:3. Is. 57:6.

3. *lot, destiny*, in general. Jer. 13:25. Is. 17:14. Dan. 12:13 וְתַעֲמֹד לְגֹרָלְךָ *and thou shalt stand up to receive thy lot*, namely, in the Messiah's kingdom. Comp. Acts 26:18. Col. 1:12. Rev. 20:6.

גּוּשׁ found only Job 7:5. *a clod of earth*, i. q. Chald. גּוּשְׁא. In Kethib גִּישׁ. —לָבַשׁ בְּשָׂרִי רִמָּה וְגוּשׁ עָפָר *worms and clods of dust clothe my body.* The latter is here applied figuratively to the dirty colour and scabby appearance of the sick person.

גֵּז m. with suff. גִּזִּי, plur. גִּזִּים, verbal from גָּזַז, dec. VIII. b.

1. *the shearing, wool shorn off, fleece,*

vellus. Deut. 18:4 גֵּז צֹאנְךָ *the shearing of thy sheep.* Job 31:20. See גִּזָּה.

2. *the mowing of meadows.* Ps. 72:6. Am. 7:1 גִּזֵּי הַמֶּלֶךְ *the king's mowings.*

גִּזְבָּר Heb. and Chald. *treasurer.* Ezra 1:8. Plur. גִּזְבְּרִין, Ezra 7:21. and with the flat pronunciation, גְּדָבְרַיָּא, Dan. 3:2, 3. (In Syr. ܓܙܒܪܐ and ܓܝܙܒܪܐ also ܓܙܘܒܪܐ. In Pers. گنجور ganjwar *idem.*) It is compounded of גִּז contraction of גְּנַז *treasure, royal income,* and the Pers. termination בר or ור; comp. חִדְבָר. The first word is properly Shemitish, but was adopted very early by the Persians; hence the ancient writers quote it as Persian. See for example Quint. Curt. III. 13. 5.

I. **גָּזָה** prob. i. q. جزا *to recompense,* and also (like the synonymes גָּמַל, ولى) *to bestow benefits.* Ps. 71:6 מִמְּעֵי אִמִּי אַתָּה גוֹזִי *from the womb of my mother thou hast been my benefactor.* Sept. σκεπαστής. Syr. *fiducia mea.* It is usually derived from גוז *transiit,* here taken transitively, (as in Num. 11:31.) *from my mother's womb thou hast taken me.* So the Chald.

II. **גָּזָה** *to work on stone, wood,* as in Aram. See גָּזִית.

גִּזָּה fem. of גֵּז, dec. X. *the shearing, wool shorn off, fleece, vellus,* i. q. גֵּז. Judg. 6:37 ff.

גָּזַז, fut. יָגֹז, infin. גֹּז.

1. *to shear* sheep. Gen. 31:19. 38:12, 13. 1 Sam. 25:4, 7.

2. *to shear* or *poll* the hair of the head, as a sign of mourning. Job 1:20. Mic. 1:16.

3. *to mow* corn, as in Arabic. See גֵּז no. 2.

Niph. *to be cut off,* or *destroyed,* by enemies, (comp. the figure Is. 7:20.) Nah. 1:12 נָגֹזּוּ *they are cut off.* The Chald. and some MSS. read נָגוֹזוּ from גוז (as in Ps. 90:19.) which is not unsuited to the context.

גָּזִית f. verbal from obs. גָּזָה, no. II.

1. *the hewing of stones;* hence אַבְנֵי גָזִית *hewn stones, square stones.* 1 K. 5:17.

2. without אַבְנֵי, *hewn stones.* Ex. 20:25. Am. 5:11. 1 K. 6:36. 7:9, 11, 12.

גָּזַל, fut. יִגְזֹל. (In Syr. by metath. ܓܠܙ.)

1. *to tear away* any thing, *to take away by violence.* 2 Sam. 23:21 *he plucked the spear out of the hand of the Egyptian.* Gen. 31:31 *for I feared thou mightest take away thy daughters from me.* Deut. 28:31. Job 20:19. 24:19 צִיָּה גַם חֹם יִגְזְלוּ מֵימֵי שֶׁלֶג *drought and heat carry off the snow water.* Mic. 2:2.

2. *to pull off, to strip off, to flay.* Mic. 3:2 גֹּזְלֵי עוֹרָם מֵעֲלֵיהֶם *who strip off their skin from them,* i. e. oppress them.

3. *to rob, take away, carry off.* Lev. 5:23. [6:4.] Judg. 21:23. Job 24:2. —גָּזַל מִשְׁפַּט פ׳ *to take away one's right,* Is. 10:2. comp. Ecc. 5:7.

4. with an accus. of the person, *to rob* or *plunder* any one. Judg. 9:25. 21:23. Ps. 35:10.

5. *to oppress, take advantage of,* i. q. עָשַׁק. Lev. 19:13. Prov. 22:22.

גָּזֵל m. const. גְּזֶל, verbal from גָּזַל, dec. V. c. *robbery, plunder, spoil.* Lev. 5:21. [6:2.] Ezek. 18:18. 22:29. Ecc. 5:7.

גְּזֵלָה fem. of גָּזֵל, dec. X. *idem.* Lev. 5:23. [6:4.] Is. 3:14 גְּזֵלַת הֶעָנִי *the spoil of the poor.*

גָּזָם a species of locust, Joel 1:4. 2:25. Am. 4:9. The Chald. and Syr. render it זַחְלָא, ܡܟܣܡܐ *the young unfledged locust, bruchus,* which is very suitable to the passage in Joel, where the גָּזָם begins its ravages before the locust. Sept. κάμπη. Vulg. *eruca.* The root גָּזַם, in Arab. and in the Talmud, *to cut off,* is kindred with כָּסַם.

גֶּזַע m. with suff. גִּזְעוֹ, *stock,* or *stump* of a tree that hath been cut down. Is. 11:1. 40:24. Job 14:8. (In Syr. ܓܘܙܥܐ

idem; Arab. جزع VIII. *to cut wood from a tree.*)

גָּזַר fut. A. and O. properly *to cut, divide.* Particularly

1. *to cut asunder, to divide.* 1 K. 3: 25, 26. Ps. 136:13 גֹּזֵר יַם סוּף *who divided the sea of reeds.*

2. *to fell* trees. 2 K. 6:4. Hence מַגְזֵרָה *an axe.*

3. *to eat, devour, vorare.* Is. 9:19. with a fut. יִגְזֹר. In Arab. by metath. جزر.

4. figuratively, *to decide, resolve,* (the prevailing signification in Aramean.) Job 22:28. with a fut. יִגְזַר.

5. intrans. *to decrease, to fail, deficere.* Hab. 3:17 גָּזַר מִמִּכְלָה צֹאן *the cattle fails in the folds.*

Niph. 1. *to be separated, excluded.* 2 Chr. 26:21 כִּי נִגְזַר מִבֵּית יְהוָה *he was excluded from the house of Jehovah.* Ps. 88:6. וְהֵמָּה מִיָּדְךָ נִגְזָרוּ *and they* (the dead) *are removed from thy hand,* i. e. from thy protection. Is. 53:8 *taken away from the land of the living.*

2. *to be cut off, destroyed, to perish.* Lam. 3:54 נִגְזָרְתִּי *I am undone.* Ezek. 37:11 נִגְזַרְנוּ לָנוּ *we are destroyed,* (לָנוּ is here a pleonastic dative of the pronoun.)

3. pass. of Kal no. 4. Est. 2:1.

גְּזַר Chald. as in Heb. 1. *to cut, divide, separate.* See Ithpe.

2. *to decide, appoint, fix.* Comp. גְּזֵרָא *fate,* also *the influence of the stars upon it;* גְּזֵרִין *art of divination, astrology,* (*numeri Babylonii,* Hor. Od. I. 11, 2.) Part. plur. גָּזְרִין Dan. 2:27. 5:11. *diviners, astrologers.*

Ithpe. *to be detached, separated.* Dan. 2:34, 35.

גֶּזֶר a Levitical city, on the western border of the tribe of Ephraim, not far from Bethhoron, anciently the residence of a Canaanitish king. Josh. 10:33. 12:12. 16:3, 10. 21:21. Judg. 1:29. 1 Chr. 14:16. Solomon rebuilt it after it was destroyed by the Egyptians, 1 K. 9:16, 17. In 1 Mac. 8:45, it is called Γάζηρα.

גְּזָרִים plur. *divided parts, pieces, halves.* Gen. 15:17. Ps. 136:13 *who divided the sea of reeds into* (*two*) *parts.*

גְּזֵרָה f. (26 MSS. גזירה) Lev. 16:22. אֶל אֶרֶץ גְּזֵרָה *into a desert land,* i. q. מִדְבָּר, by which word it appears to be afterwards explained. Sept. γῆ ἄβατος. Vulg. *terra solitaria.* (Syr. ܓܙܝܪܐ *sterilis;* Arab. by metath. جرز *unfruitful land.* Others compare the Arab. جزيرة *an island,* also *an island, as it were, in a sea of sand, an oasis.*)

גְּזֵרָה f. Chald. (with Tseri impure.) 1. *decree.* Dan. 4:14. [17.] (Syr. ܓܙܝܪܬܐ.) Comp. גְּזַר no. 4.

2. *the thing decreed* or *appointed.* Dan. 4:21. [24.]

גִּזְרָה f. dec. X. 1. *body, breast.* Lam. 4:7. (In Arab. by metath. جرز.) Others: *appearance.* If so, we may compare קֶצֶב *appearance, form,* from קָצַב *to cut;* and French *taille.*

2. an expression in architecture, the exact meaning of which is not known. Ezek. 41:12—15. 42:1, 10, 13.

גִּזְרִי m. proper name of a people upon whom David made war, between Shur and Egypt. 1 Sam. 27:8.

גָּחוֹן m. dec. III. a. *belly,* or *under part of the body,* of reptiles. Gen. 3:14. Lev. 11:42. In Chald. גְּחַן *to stoop to bow.* So in German, bauch (*belly*) and sich bücken (*to stoop*) are etymologically connected.

גַּחֶלֶת f. Plur. גֶּחָלִים, const. גַּחֲלֵי; *burning coals.* Ps. 18:9. Prov. 25:22 כִּי גֶחָלִים אַתָּה חֹתֶה עַל רֹאשׁוֹ *for thou shalt heap coals of fire upon his head,* i. e. shame and repentance shall burn him, like coals on his head. (comp. Rom. 12:20.)

גַּי const. גֵּי, and **גַּיְא** const. גֵּיא; Plur. גיאות (read גֵּאָיוֹת) 2 K. 2:16 Kethib, but in Keri, and in other places by metath. גֵּאָיוֹת (q. v.) before suff. גֵּיאוֹתֶיךָ; com. gen. (generally masc.) *valley.* The Hebrews appear to have discriminated between this and several other words usually rendered *valley;* for to the same place they uniformly apply the same name. The distinction may have been this; גַּי *a valley without a brook;* נַחַל *a valley with a brook;* עֵמֶק and בִּקְעָה *a low plain.* The following places bear the name גַּי or גֵּיא; (1.) גֵּיא הִנֹּם, בֶּן־הִנֹּם *valley of Hinnom, of the son of Hinnom,* on the south-eastern side of Jerusalem, consecrated to Moloch. Josh. 15:8. 18:16. 2 Chr. 28:3. 33:6. Jer. 7:32. (2.) גֵּי מֶלַח *the valley of salt,* in the neighbourhood of the Dead Sea. 2 Sam. 8:13. 2 K. 14:7. 1 Chr. 19:12. (3.) גֵּי הַצְּבֹעִים (*valley of beasts of prey*) once 1 Sam. 13:18. (Arab. جية and جيئة *low ground where water collects,* جواء *broad valley, plain.*)

Note. גֵּיא occurs once in the absolute state, Zech. 14:4. and גַּיא Is. 40:4.

גִּיד m. dec. I. *nerve, tendon.* Gen. 32.33. Job 10:11. 40:17. (In Syr. and Chald. *idem.*)

גִּיחַ and גּוּחַ, fut. יָגִיחַ.

1. *to break* or *burst forth;* e. g. as a stream, Job 40:23. In Syr. ܓܳܚ *idem.* In Chald. גִּיחַ signifies especially *to rush forth to battle.* So Ezek. 32:2 וַתָּגַח בְּנַהֲרוֹתֶיךָ *thou rushest forth* (*to battle*) *down thy streams, per flumina cum impetu ferebaris.* Applied also to a child's breaking forth from the womb, Job 38:8.

2. transit. *to draw forth* from the womb, and, spoken of the mother, *to bring forth, to be in labour,* Ps. 22:10. אַתָּה גֹחִי מִבָּטֶן אִמִּי *thou drewest me from my mother's womb.* Mic. 4:10. חוּלִי וָגֹחִי בַּת צִיּוֹן *tremble, be in labour, O daughter of Zion.*

Hiph. intrans. *to arise,* or *rush forth,* from an ambush, Judg. 20:33.

גִּיחַ or גּוּחַ Chald. Aph. *to break forth,* spoken of the winds. Dan. 7:2.

גִּיחוֹן proper name; (literally *a stream* from גִּיחַ no. 1. comp. جيحان or جيحون, a term applied to several Asiatic rivers, as the Ganges, Araxes; and used by way of eminence for the latter. See Michaelis Suppll. ad Lexx. Heb. p. 297.)

1. a water-course near Jerusalem, otherwise called שִׁלֹחַ. 1 K. 1:33. 2 Chr. 32:30. 33:14.

2. one of the four rivers of paradise. Gen. 2:13. From what is said above, it is usually supposed to be the *Oxus* or *Araxes;* but in that case כּוּשׁ must be taken in an unusual acceptation. Josephus considers it *the Nile,* (J. A. I. 1. 3.) and this river is said to be called *Guyon* by the Abyssinians. The writer of Gen. II. would appear then to have selected four large streams, (the Nile, Tigris, Euphrates, and probably the Ganges,) as specimens of the mighty rivers which God originally formed.

I. גִּיל and גּוּל (Prov. 23:24 Keth.) *to rejoice, exult,* with a more intense signification than שָׂמַח. Job 3:22 הַשְּׂמֵחִים אֱלֵי גִיל *who rejoice even to exultation.* The object of joy stands with בְּ, Ps. 9:15. 13:6. 21:2. 149:2. with עַל, Zeph. 3:17. Hos. 10:5.—גִּיל בְּיהוָה *to rejoice in God,* Ps. 89:17. Is. 29:19. 41:16. 61:10. Spoken also of inanimate nature, 1 Chr. 16:31. Ps. 96:11. (The original idea probably was, *to jump round, to leap for joy,* comp. Arab. جَالَ *to move in a circle.*)

II. גִּיל *to fear, to reverence,* (like the Arab. وَجِلَ *to tremble, to fear.*) Ps. 2:11 גִּילוּ בִּרְעָדָה *fear with trembling.* Hos. 10:5. So the Heb. גּוּר, יָגֹר, corresponds to the Arab. وجر.

גִּיל m. verbal from גִּיל, dec. I. a.

1. *joy, exultation.* Ps. 45:16. 65:13.

2. *age, generation.* Dan. 1:10 הַיְלָדִים אֲשֶׁר כְּגִילְכֶם *young people of your age.* In Arab. جِيل *generatio,* in Samar. גיל, *generatio, ætas.* (This meaning is connected with that of the Arab. جَالَ *to*

move in a circle; comp. דּוֹר *generation,* which has a similar origin.)

גִּילָה fem. of גִּיל, dec. X. *exultation.* Is. 35:2.

גִּילֹנִי see גָּלָה.

גִּיר m. Is. 27:9. *chalk, lime.* Arab. جير.

גִּיר Chald. *idem.* Dan. 5:5.

גִּיר i. q. גֵּר *a stranger.* 2 Chr. 2:16.

גִּישׁ see גּוּשׁ *a clod of earth.*

גַּל m. plur. גַּלִּים, verbal from גָּלַל *to roll,* dec. VIII. h.

1. *a heap,* especially *a heap of stones,* with and without אֲבָנִים. Gen. 31:46 ff. Josh. 7:26. Is. 25:2. In the plur. *heaps of stones, ruins,* Jer. 9:10 וְנָתַתִּי אֶת יְרוּשָׁלִַם לְגַלִּים *I will make Jerusalem ruins.* 51:37.

2. *running spring.* Ecc. 4:12. Job 8:17. In the plur. *waves of the sea,* Ps. 42:8. 89:10. 107:25, 29. (Syr. ܓܠܠܐ *fluctus, unda.*)

גֹּל m. dec. VIII. d. *oil-cruise, oil-vessel,* i. q. גֻּלָּה no. 2. Zech. 4:2.

גִּלָּא see גָּלָה.

גַּלָּב m. dec. I. b. *barber.* Ezek. 5:1. (Syr. ܓܠܒܐ *a razor;* Chald. גַּלָּב *idem.*)

גִּלְבֹּעַ proper name of a chain of mountains in the tribe of Issachar, upon which king Saul was slain by the Philistines. 1 Sam. 28:4. 31:1. 2 Sam. 1:6, 21. At its foot rises the fountain Tubania. In Josephus, Γιλβουὲ, Γιλβοέ.

גַּלְגַּל, plur. גַּלְגַּלִּים, verbal from גָּלַל, dec. VIII. f.

1. *wheel.* Is. 5:28. Ezek. 10:2, 6. 23:24. 26:10. *a wheel to draw water with,* Ecc. 12:6.

2. *whirlwind.* Ps. 77:19. Ezek. 10:13. (Syr. ܓܠܓܠܐ.) Hence

3. *things driven about by a whirlwind, chaff, stubble.* Ps. 83:14 אֱלֹהַי שִׁיתֵמוֹ כַגַּלְגַּל *my God, make them as the whirlwind;* parall. *as stubble before the wind.* Is. 17:18 כְּגַלְגַּל לִפְנֵי סוּפָה *as dust before the whirlwind.* Parall. מֹץ. (Aram. ܓܠܐ, גִּלָּא *dust, stubble driven about by the wind;* Arab. جل *idem.*)

גַּלְגַּל Chald. *wheel.* Dan. 7:9.

גִּלְגָּל m. verbal from גָּלַל, dec. II. b.

1. *wheel.* Is. 28:28.

2. proper name of a place on the east of Jericho and on this side of Jordan. Josh. 4:19, 20. 9:6. 10:6. 14:6. Its etymology from גָּלַל, is given Josh. 5:9. In subsequent times it was the seat of idolatry, Hos. 4:15. Am. 5:5. It is called בֵּית הַגִּלְגָּל, Neh. 12:29. and Γάλγαλα, 1 Mac. 9:2.

גֻּלְגֹּלֶת f. verbal from גָּלַל, dec. XIII. e. *the human scull,* from its *spherical* shape. 2 K. 9:35. It is used to denote *an individual,* (as we use the term *poll, head,*) Ex. 16:16 עֹמֶר לַגֻּלְגֹּלֶת *an omer a head,* or *for an individual.* Num. 1:2. כָּל־זָכָר לְגֻלְגְּלֹתָם *every male according to their polls.* verses 18, 20, 22. 3:47. In Rabbin. כֶּסֶף הַגֻּלְגֹּלֶת *poll-tax.* In Syr. ܓܓܘܠܬܐ (ל being omitted) *a scull.* In Arab. still more contracted جلجة *idem.* In the name Γολγοθᾶ, Matt. 27:33, there is a similar omission of the second ל.

גֶּלֶד, with suff. גִּלְדִּי, dec. VI. h. *hide, skin.* (In Arab. and Aram. *idem.*) Job 16:15.

I. גָּלָה, fut. יִגְלֶה, apoc. יִגֶל. *to uncover, open, disclose, reveal.* (Arab. جلا *idem.*) In Kal, for the most part in a figurative sense, particularly, (1.) גָּלָה אֹזֶן פ׳ *to uncover* or *open the ear of any one,* i. e. to reveal something to him. 1 Sam. 9:15. 20:2 *my father does nothing great or small,* וְלֹא יִגְלֶה אֶת אָזְנִי *which he has not revealed to me.* verses 12, 13. 22:8, 17. 2 Sam. 7:26. Ruth 4:4. Also spoken of God in a somewhat different sense, Job 36:10 וַיִּגֶל אָזְנָם לַמּוּסָר *he openeth their ear to correction.* verse 15. 33:16. (2.) גָּלָה סוֹד *to reveal a secret.* Am.

3:7. Prov. 20:19. Part. גָּלוּי *open*, spoken of a book. Jer. 32:11, 14.

Pi. גִּלָּה, fut. יְגַלֶּה, apoc. יְגַל.

1. *to uncover, make bare.* Ruth 3:4, 7 וַתְּגַל מַרְגְּלֹתָיו *she uncovered a place at his feet.*—גִּלָּה עֶרְוַת אִשָּׁה *to uncover the nakedness of a woman,* applied to sexual intercourse, particularly that which is incestuous, Lev. 18:6 ff. 20:11 ff.—Hos. 2:12. [10.] Mic. 1:6 וִיסֹדֶיהָ אֲגַלֶּה *and her foundations I will make bare,* (through her destruction.)

2. when construed with an accusative of the garment or covering, *to uncover, remove, take off.* Deut. 22:30 וְלֹא יְגַלֶּה כְּנַף אָבִיו *and he shall not remove the covering,* i. e. the bed covering, *of his father.* 27:20. (both in the sense explained under no. 1.) Is. 22:8. 47:2 גַּלִּי צַמָּתֵךְ *uncover* or *remove thy veil.* Nah. 3:5. Job 41:5.

3. גִּלָּה אֶת עֵינֵי פ׳ *to open the eyes of any one,* (spoken of God,) i. e. to let one see what he otherwise would not have seen, particularly what is concealed from mortal eyes. Num. 22:31 *then opened Jehovah the eyes of Balaam, and he saw the angel of Jehovah stand in the way.* 24:4, 16. Ps. 119:18. See a similar phrase under פָּקַח.

4. figuratively *to discover, disclose, reveal.* Job 20:27. Ps. 98:2 *before the eyes of the nations he reveals his righteousness.* Is. 16:3 נֹדֵד לֹא תְּגַלִּי *the fugitive thou shalt not discover,* i. e. betray. 26:21. Prov. 11:13. 25:9. Construed with עַל, Lam. 2:14.

5. *to cause to appear, to bring upon* any one. Jer. 33:6 וְגִלֵּיתִי לָהֶם עֲתֶרֶת שָׁלוֹם *I bring upon them abundance of prosperity.*

Pu. pass. Nah. 2:8.

Niph. נִגְלָה, infin. absol. נִגְלֹה.

1. *to be uncovered, made bare.* Ex. 20:26. Ezek. 13:14. Job 38:17. Reflex. *to make one's self bare.* 2 Sam. 6:20.

2. *to be removed, taken off.* Jer. 13:21 נִגְלוּ שׁוּלַיִךְ *thy trains* or *trails are removed.*

3. *to reveal* or *shew one's self, to appear.* 1 Sam. 14:8 *behold, we will pass over to the men* וְנִגְלִינוּ אֲלֵיהֶם *and shew ourselves to them.* verse 11. Gen. 35:7 *for there had God appeared to him.* 1 Sam. 2:27. 3:21. Ezek. 16:57.

4. *to be revealed,* 1 Sam. 3:7. Dan. 10:1. Is. 53:1. *to be manifest* or *known,* Ezek. 21:29. [24.] Is. 22:14.

Hithpa. 1. *to uncover one's self.* Gen. 9:21.

2. *to reveal one's self.* Prov. 18:2.

II. גָּלָה (in Arab. جلا and جلي) fut. יִגְלֶה, apoc. יִגֶל.

1. *to remove, emigrate, go into exile* or *captivity.* Ezek. 12:3. for the most part spoken of whole nations, 2 K. 17:23 *and Israel was carried away out of his land into Assyria.* 24:14. 25:21. Is. 5:13.

2. figuratively, *to disappear, vanish, cease.* 1 Sam. 4:21, 22 *glory is departed* or *ceased from Israel.* Is. 24:11 גָּלָה מְשׂוֹשׂ הָאָרֶץ *the mirth of the land has ceased.* 38:12.

Niph. pass. of Hiph. of course i. q. Kal. Is. 38:12.

Hiph. הִגְלָה and הֶגְלָה, fut. apoc. וַיֶּגֶל *to carry* a people *into captivity.* 2 K. 15:29. 17:6, 11, 27. 18:11.

Hoph. i. q. Kal. Est. 2:6. etc.

Deriv. גּוֹלָה, גָּלוּת.

גְּלָה and **גְּלָא** Chald. *to reveal.* Dan. 2:22, 28, 29. Part. Pehil גְּלֵי and גֲּלִי, verses 19, 30.

Aph. הַגְלִי *to carry into captivity.* Ezra 4:10. 5:12.

גִּלֹה proper name of a city in the hilly country of the tribe of Judah. Josh. 15:51. 2 Sam. 15:12. The gentile noun is גִּילֹנִי.

גֹּלָה see **גּוֹלָה** *captivity.*

גֻּלָּה f. verbal from גָּלַל, dec. X.

1. i. q. גַּל *a spring.* Josh. 15:19. Judg. 1:15.

2. i. q. גֹּל *oil-cup* or *oil-vessel,* (in the sacred chandelier.) Zech. 4:3. Ecc. 12:6 *before the silver chain is severed,* וְתָרֻץ גֻּלַּת הַזָּהָב *and the golden oil-cup is broken in pieces.* The Greeks and Ro-

mans also were wont to suspend their lamps by a chain.

3. in architecture, the name of some part of the chapiter of a pillar, *the bowl.* 1K. 7:41, 42. 2 Chr. 4:12, 13.

גִּלּוּלִים plur. masc. a nick-name or word of derision for idols, perhaps *logs, blocks,* (from גָּלַל *to roll.*) Lev. 26:30. Deut. 29:17. Of frequent occurrence, especially in Ezekiel, chap. 6:4, 5, 9, 13. 14:3. 20:17. 23:7. According to the Jewish commentators: *sordidi, stercorei* (from גֵּל *stercus.*) According to others: *the great, mighty,* (from גלל, which in Arab. signifies *to be great, mighty.*)

גְּלוֹם m. verbal from גָּלַם, dec. I. *mantle, robe, covering.* Ezek. 27:24. (Chald. גּוּלְמָא, גְּלִימָא, גְּלֵם *idem.*)

גָּלוּת and **גָּלֻת** (with Kamets impure) verbal from גָּלָה no. II. dec. I. i. q. גּוֹלָה.

1. *captivity, exile.* Ezek. 33:21.

2. *exiles,* or *those who have been exiles.* Jer. 24:5. 28:4. 29:22.

גָּלוּת Chald. *idem.* Dan. 2:25. 5:13. בְּנֵי גָלוּתָא *the exiles,* Ezra 6:16.

גִּלַּח found only in Pi. גִּלַּח *to shave;* e.g. the beard, 2 Sam. 10:4. the hair of the head, 2 Sam. 14:26. The following accusative is either the head, Num. 6:9. Deut. 21:12. or the hair, Lev. 14:8.—Once reflex. *to shave one's self,* Gen. 41:14. and once caus. *to cause to shave,* Judg. 16:19. Figuratively, Is. 7:20, *on that day the Lord will shave, with a hired razor, the head and the hair of the feet,* i. e. he will cut off or lay waste the whole land.

Pu. *to be shaven.* Judg. 16:17.

Hithpa. *to shave one's self.* Lev. 13:33.

גִּלָּיוֹן verbal from גָּלָה no. I. (comp. פִּדְיוֹן, נִקָּיוֹן from נָקָה, כָּלָה,) dec. III. d. *tablet* of wood, metal, or stone, for writing on. Is. 8:1. (comp. לוּחַ, Is. 30:8. Hab. 2:2.) In Chald. גִּלָּיוֹן signifies *the vacant margin of a writing.*

Plur. גִּלְיֹנִים Is. 3:23. probably *mirrors,* (here as a female ornament, comp. Ex. 38:8.) literally *metallic plates.* So the Vulg. and Chald. According to the Sept. *thin transparent garments;* comp. Arab. جلوة *vestis splendida;* Syr. ܓܠܝܐ *indumentum.*

גָּלִיל verbal from גָּלַל, dec. III. a.

1. as an adj. *turning, that is easily turned, versatilis.* 1 K. 6:34. comp. Ezek. 41:24.

2. as a subst. *a ring.* Est. 1:6. Cant. 5:14 *his arms as gold rings, set with Tarshish stones.* In these similitudes, the ground of comparison is not to be sought for in the form or colour.

3. *circuit, border, district, country;* hence as a proper name, *Galilee,* the northernmost district of Palestine, between Sidon and Samaria, with undefined bounds towards the south. 1 K. 9:11. Josh. 20:7. 21:32. With He paragogic, 2 K. 15:29. More full גְּלִיל הַגּוֹיִם *(country of the* heathen *nations) Galilee of the Gentiles,* Is. 8:23. [9:1.]

גְּלִילָה fem. of גָּלִיל, dec. X. *circuit, country,* i. q. גָּלִיל no. 3. Ezek. 47:8.—גְּלִילוֹת הַפְּלִשְׁתִּים Josh. 13:2. and גְּלִילוֹת פְּלָשֶׁת Joel 4:4. [3:4.] *the borders of the Philistines.*—ג׳ הַיַּרְדֵּן Josh. 22:10, 11. *the regions of the Jordan.*

גָּלְיָת proper name of a Philistine giant, well known for his combat with David. 1 Sam. 17:4. 21:10. 22:10. —It would appear from 2 Sam. 21:19, as the text now stands, that Goliath was slain by Elhanan the Bethlehemite; but the reading in 1 Chr. 20:5, removes this apparent contradiction.

גָּלַל plur. גָּלֲלוּ, but in the sing. גַּלּוֹתִי; infin. and imper. גֹּל, also גַּל (Ps. 119:22.)

1. *to roll;* e.g, a stone, Gen. 29:3, 8. Josh. 10:18.

2. figuratively, *to roll away* reproach. Josh. 5:9. Ps. 37:5 גּוֹל עַל יְהוָה דַּרְכֶּךָ *roll* or *devolve on Jehovah thy way,* i. e. commit or commend thy concerns to

him. A similar phrase occurs with מַעֲשֶׂיךָ, Prov. 16:3. Also elliptically, Ps. 22:9 גֹּל אֶל יְהוָה *he commends to Jehovah (his ways.)* גֹּל stands here for גֹּל עַל, the infinitive for the finite verb. Others regard it as the preterite of גּוּל, גִּיל, *he rejoices in Jehovah.*

Niph. נָגֹל, fut. יִגַּל, *to be rolled together*, as a book, Is. 34:4. *to roll on*, as a stream, Am. 5:24. Comp. גַּלִּים.

Poal *to be rolled about.* Is. 9:4.

Hithpo. *to wallow, welter.* 2 Sam. 20:12. Gen. 43:18 לְהִתְגֹּלֵל עָלֵינוּ *that he roll himself*, i. e. rush, *upon us.*

Pilpel גִּלְגֵּל i. q. Kal. Is. 51:25.

Hithpalp. *to rush upon*, spoken of an invading enemy. Job 30:14.

Hiph. הֵגַל *to roll.* Gen. 29:10.

Deriv. out of course גַּל, גֹּל, גֻּלָּה, גִּלְגַּל, גָּלִיל, מְגִלָּה, גֻּלְגֹּלֶת, גִּלְגָּל, and perhaps גִּלּוּלִים.

גָּלָל (Arab. جَلَّة) m. *dung, ordure.* 1 K. 14:10. Literally, *roundish dung*, as of camels, horses, etc. from the root גָּלַל.

גָּלָל literally, *thing, business*, (Arab. جَلَل,) but in use only as an adv. בִּגְלַל, with suff. בִּגְלָלְךָ, בִּגְלַלְכֶם, *on account of.* Gen. 12:13. 30:27. 39:5. Deut. 15:10. (Arab. مِن اجلك *on thy account.*)

גְּלָל m. Chald. Ezra 5:8. 6:4 אֶבֶן גְּלָל *hewn stones.* Sept. λίθοι ἐκλεκτοί. 1 Esd. 6:9 λίθοι ξυστοὶ πολυτελεῖς. It derives its signification perhaps from גָּלָה i. q. Arab. جلي *detersit, polivit*, ξέειν. Comp. גִּלָּיוֹן. In the Talmud גללא by itself signifies *a stone*, as כלי גללין *vessels of stone.*

גֵּלֶל m. plur. גְּלָלִים, const. גֶּלְלֵי, verbal from גָּלַל, dec. VI. j. *dung.* Zeph. 1:17. Ezek. 4:12, 17. Job 20:7 כְּגֶלְלוֹ לָנֶצַח יֹאבֵד *like his dung he perishes for ever.* Comp. the similar figure 1 K. 14:10.

גָּלַם, fut. יִגְלֹם, *to wrap together, fold up.* Once 2 K. 2:8. Deriv. out of course גֹּלֶם.

גֹּלֶם m. verbal from גָּלַם, dec. VI. p. literally, *something wrapt* or *folded together, a mass* or *lump;* hence applied to *the unformed fœtus* or *embryo in the womb*, Ps. 139:16. (In the Talmud גולם *any unformed mass, a fœtus*, also *an uncultivated man.*)

גַּלְמוּד a quadrilateral adj. *barren, unfruitful.* Is. 49:21. Job 3:7. 15:34. 30:3. (In Arab. جُلْمُود *a rough unfruitful rock.* The kindred simple roots, of which this word appears to be compounded, are גמד = Arab. جمد *to be hard, hard-hearted*, and גלמא = Syr. ܓܠܡܐ *a stony soil where nothing grows.* In Rabbin. גַּלְמוּד *a woman who keeps by herself on account of some levitical uncleanness.*

גָּלַע in Kal not used. In Arab. conj. III. *to contend with* any one, especially in drinking and gaming. So in Hebrew, Hithpa. *to grow angry, to be irritated*, in a contention. Prov. 20:3 *it is an honour for a man to cease from contention*, וְכָל־אֱוִיל יִתְגַּלָּע *but every fool becomes angry.* 18:1 בְּכָל־תּוּשִׁיָּה יִתְגַּלָּע *he is angry against every thing rational.* Also, spoken of a contention, *to grow warm*, Prov. 17:14.

גִּלְעָד proper name.

1. a son of Machir and grandson of Manasseh. Num. 26:29.

2. a mountain (Gen. 31:23. Cant. 4:1.) and province beyond Jordan; in a more restricted sense, *the country south of Bashan and Argob*, Deut. 3:13. Josh. 17:1. 13:25, 31. 2 Sam. 24:6. Num. 32:39. in a wider sense, *the whole country east of Jordan*, afterwards called *Perea.* Num. 32:26, 29. Josh. 22:9. Jer. 8:22. Zech. 10:10. For the etymology of the word, namely גַּלְעֵד *heap of witness*, see Gen. 31:47.

3. a city in the abovementioned province. Hos. 6:8.

גָּלַשׁ prob. i. q. Arab. جلس *to sit, to lie down;* conj. II. *to move*, especially up hill. Cant. 4:1 *as a flock of goats* שֶׁגָּלְשׁוּ מֵהַר גִּלְעָד *which lie down on* *mount Gilead.* 6:5. מִן here signifies *on,* or *towards;* comp. Cant. 2:9. 5:4.

גַּם a primitive particle.

1. conj. cop. *also.*—In the poetical style, i. q. וְ *and,* Joel 1:12 רִמּוֹן גַּם תָּמָר וְתַפּוּחַ *the pomegranate-tree, the palm-tree also, and the apple-tree.*

2. at the beginning of a sentence, i. q. כִּי *yea!* Job 18:5 גַּם אוֹר רְשָׁעִים יִדְעָךְ *yea, the light of the wicked is put out.* Prov. 14:20. 17:26. 18:9. 19:2. 20:11. Used also in the emphatic repetition of the same word, 1 Sam. 24:12 רְאֵה גַּם רְאֵה *see, yea, see.* Gen. 20:5 הִיא־גַם־הִיא *she, yea, she.* Gen. 27:34. 4:26. 10:21. Ecc. 2:15. Ps. 9:7. 1 K. 21:19 אֶת־דָּמְךָ גַּם אָתָּה *thy blood, yea, thine, sanguinem tui, imò tui.* Prov. 23:15. Sometimes the word is nearly pleonastic, Prov. 17:15 תּוֹעֲבַת יְהוָה גַּם־שְׁנֵיהֶם *they both are an abomination to Jehovah.* 20:10, 12.

3. conj. concess. *although.* Ps. 95:9. Neh. 6:1. Jer. 36:25. גַּם כִּי *idem,* Is. 1:15.

4. conj. advers. *yet.* Ps. 129:2. Ezek. 16:25. Ecc. 4:16. 8:12.

5. גַּם־גַּם (1.) *both....and, as well...as, et....et, tàm....quàm.* Gen. 24:25. Ex. 12:31. (2.) *as....so.* Jer. 51:12.

גָּמָא in Kal not used, *to swallow, sip, drink.*

Pi. *idem.* Job 39:24 יְגַמֶּא אֶרֶץ *he (the horse) swallows the ground,* i. e. sweeps it away with him in his rapid course. (The Arabians also say: *the horse swallows the ground,* i. e. runs swiftly over it. See Bocharti Hieroz. I. p.142—148.)

Hiph. *to let drink.* Gen. 24:17.

גֹּמֶא m. verbal from גָּמָא, *the Egyptian papyrus plant,* so called from its *imbibing* water. (Comp. the phrase *bibula papyrus,* Lucan. IV. 136.) Job 8:11. Is. 35:7. Out of the skin or fibres of this plant the ancients made mats, cords, boats, (Plin. XIII. 21—26.) Hence Ex. 2:3 תֵּבַת גֹּמֶא *a small boat made of papyrus.* Is. 18:2.

גֹּמֶד m. *cubit.* Once Judg. 3:16. (In Syr. ܓܘܪܡܕܐ, *elbow, cubit;* ܓܘܪܕܡܐ ܓܘܪܡܕܐ *idem.*)

גַּמָּדִים masc. plur. Ezek. 27:11. proper name of a people, probably of Phenicia, of whom nothing farther is known. Others: *bold* or *stout people,* from Arab. جَمَدَ *to be hard, unmerciful.*

גְּמוּל m. verbal from גָּמַל, dec. I. also גְּמוּל יָדַיִם (Judg. 9:16. Prov. 12:14. Is. 3:11.)

1. *one's actions* or *conduct in relation to another, one's treatment of another, merit, desert.* Judg. 9:16. Is. 3:11.—הֵשִׁיב גְּמוּלוֹ לְ *to render to* any one *his desert,* or *to recompense one's actions upon* him, Ps. 28:4 הָשֵׁב גְּמוּלָם לָהֶם *render to them their desert.* Prov. 12:14. also with עַל, Ps. 94:2.—שִׁלֵּם גְּמוּל לְ *idem,* Ps. 137:8. Prov. 19:17. Is. 59:18. also with עַל Joel 4:4. [3:4.]

2. *recompense.* Is. 35:4.

3. *benefit.* Ps. 103:2.

גְּמוּלָה fem. of גְּמוּל, dec. X. *idem.* 2 Sam. 19:37. Is. 59:18. Jer. 51:56.

I. גָּמַל fut. יִגְמֹל.

1. *to shew* or *bring upon* any one (good or evil,) with a double accusative of the person and thing, (comp. in Greek εὖ or κακῶς πράττειν τινά.) 1 Sam. 24:18 אַתָּה גְּמַלְתַּנִי הַטּוֹבָה *thou hast shewn me good.* Gen. 50:15 *all the evil* אֲשֶׁר גָּמַלְנוּ אֹתוֹ *which we have shewn him.* verse 17. Prov. 3:30. 31:12. Is. 63:7. Also with לְ of the person, Is. 3:9 גָּמְלוּ לָהֶם רָעָה *they shew to themselves evil,* i. e. they bring evil on themselves. Ps. 137:8 גְּמוּלֵךְ שֶׁגָּמַלְתְּ לָנוּ *that which thou hast brought upon us.*

2. especially *to shew good, to treat kindly, to favour.* Prov. 11:17 גֹּמֵל נַפְשׁוֹ *that does good to his own soul* or *to himself.* More frequently with עַל, Ps. 13:6. 116:7. 119:17. 142:8.

3. *to recompense, requite,* (good or evil.) Construed with an acc. Ps. 18:21 יִגְמְלֵנִי יְהוָה כְּצִדְקִי *Jehovah recompenses me according to my righteousness.* with

עַל, 2 Chr. 20:11. Ps. 103:10. with לְ Deut. 32:6, (according to another division of the words, the noun is here in the accusative.)

Deriv. out of course גְּמוּל, תַּגְמוּל.

II. גָּמַל, fut. יִגְמֹל. 1. *to wean* a child from the breast of its mother. (In Is. 28:9, מֵחָלָב is subjoined.) 1 Sam. 1: 23, 24. 1 K. 11:20.

2. spoken of fruit, *to ripen, to bring to maturity*, Num. 17:23. [8.] *to grow ripe*, Is. 18:5.

Niph. *to be weaned.* Gen. 21:8. 1 Sam. 1:22.

גָּמָל com. gen. prim. plur. גְּמַלִּים, dec. VIII. a. *a camel*, male or female. Where the discrimination of sex is unimportant, the gender is usually masc. as 1 K. 10:2. When used to denote a female camel, it is fem. as Gen. 32:15.—This word has passed with a slight change from the eastern into our western languages.

גָּמַר, fut. יִגְמֹר. 1. *to finish, accomplish, execute.* Ps. 57:3 אֵל גֹּמֵר עָלָי *God who executes for me*, i.e. who manages my affairs for me. So with בְּעַד, Ps. 138:8.

2. *to come to an end, to cease, fail.* Ps. 7:10. 12:2. 77:9. (In Aram. *idem.*)

גְּמַר Chald. *idem.* Part. pass. גְּמִיר *finished, skilful, learned*, Ezra 7:12.

גֹּמֶר *Cimmerians, Cimbri*, common name of a little-known and barbarous northern nation. Only Gen. 10:2, 3. Ezek. 38:6. If this name was known to the people themselves, and was derived from them to the southern nations, then we may compare it with *Kymr*, the ancient name of the Welsh.

גַּן, with suff. גַּנִּי, com. gen. verbal from גָּנַן, dec. VIII. h. *garden*, (literally *a place hedged in.*) Gen. 2:8 ff.—גַּן יָרָק *a garden of herbs*, Deut. 11:10. 1 K. 21:2. גַּן יְהוָה *garden of Jehovah*, as if planted by him, (comp. Gen. 2:8. Ps. 104:16.) Gen. 13:10. Is. 51:3. Ezek. 31:8, 9. Plur. גַּנִּים, Cant. 4:15. 6:2.

גָּנַב, fut. יִגְנֹב. 1. *to steal;* construed with an acc. of the thing, Gen. 31:19. 30:32. or of the person, 2 Sam. 19: 42. Deut. 24:7. Job 21:18 וּכְמֹץ גְּנָבַתּוּ סוּפָה *and as chaff which the whirlwind carries away.* 27:20.

2. *to deceive*, like the Greek κλέπτειν. Gen. 31:27 וַתִּגְנֹב אֹתִי *thou hast deceived me.* verse 20 וַיִּגְנֹב יַעֲקֹב אֶת לֵב לָבָן *and Jacob deceived Laban.* verse 26. Part. pass. with paragogic Yod, גְּנֻבְתִי, Gen. 31:39.

Niph. pass. Ex. 22:11.

Pi. i.q. Kal. 1. *to steal.* Jer. 23:30.

2. *to deceive, seduce.* 2 Sam. 15:6.

Pu. pass. Job 4:12 אֵלַי דָּבָר יְגֻנָּב *an oracle was secretly brought to me.* Infin. absol. גֻּנֹּב, Gen. 40:15.

Hithpa. 2 Sam. 19:4 וַיִּתְגַּנֵּב הָעָם בַּיּוֹם הַהוּא לָבוֹא הָעִיר *and the people stole themselves that day into the city.* (Syr. ܓܢܒ ܢܦܫܗ *to steal one's self away.*)

גַּנָּב m. verbal from גָּנַב, dec. I. *thief.* Ex. 22:1, 6, 7.

גְּנֵבָה f. verbal from גָּנַב, dec. X. *something stolen.* Ex. 22:3.

גַּנָּה fem. of גַּן dec. X. *garden.* Is. 1: 30. Job 8:16. Plur. גַּנּוֹת, Am. 4:9. 9:14.

גִּנָּה fem. of גַּן, dec. X. *idem.* More frequent, as it appears, in the later books. Est. 1:5. 7:7, 8. Cant. 6:11.

גְּנָזִים, const. גִּנְזֵי, dec. VI. g.

1. *treasures.* Est. 3:9. 4:7.

2. *chests*, in which to pack up and preserve valuable articles, as the Greek θησαυροί. Ezek. 27:24. (Chald. גְּנַז *to hide, lay up, preserve;* Arab. جنز *to cover, collect.* Kindred with כָּנַס.)

גִּנְזִין Chald. masc. plur. *treasures.* Ezra 6:1.—בֵּית גִּנְזַיָּא *treasure-house*, Ezra 5:17. 7:20.

גַּנְזַךְ m. dec. VIII. h. *treasure-chambers* in the temple. 1 Chr. 28:11. The ךְ is afformative as in אַלְךְ, דִּךְ, and other Chaldaic words.

גָּנַן *to protect, defend*, (strictly *to cover*, like the Arab. جَنَّ, which, construed with عَلَى, signifies *to protect;* and on this account גָּנַן like verbs of covering, is construed with עַל.) 2 K. 20 : 6 וְגַנּוֹתִי עַל הָעִיר הַזֹּאת *I will defend this city.* (In chap. 19 : 34, with אֶל.) Is. 37 : 35. 38: 6. Pret. גַּנּוֹתִי. Infin. absol. גָּנוֹן, Is. 31 : 5.

Hiph. fut. יָגֵן, *idem.* Is. 31 : 5. construed with עַל, Zech. 9 : 15. with בְּעַד, (see בְּעַד no. 4.) 12 : 8.

Deriv. גַּן, גַּנָּה, גִּנָּה, מָגֵן.

גָּעָה *to low, bellow,* as kine. 1 Sam. 6 : 12. Job 6 : 5. (In Aram. more frequent, and in a general sense *to cry.*)

גָּעַל *to reject, throw away* (from disgust and aversion,) *to abhor;* construed with an acc. Lev. 26 : 30 וְגָעֲלָה נַפְשִׁי אֶתְכֶם *my soul shall abhor you.* verses 11, 44. So of the Israelites, verse 15 מִשְׁפָּטַי תִּגְעַל נַפְשְׁכֶם *your soul shall abhor my laws.* verse 43. Ezek. 16 : 45 גֹּעֶלֶת אִישָׁהּ וּבָנֶיהָ *who rejecteth her husband and her children.* Construed with בְּ, Jer. 14 : 19.

Niph. *to be thrown away.* 2 Sam. 1: 21 כִּי שָׁם נִגְעַל מָגֵן גִּבּוֹרִים *for there the shield of the mighty was thrown away.* Vulg. *abjectus est clypeus.*

Hiph. i. q. Kal. Job 21 : 10 שׁוֹרוֹ עִבַּר וְלֹא יַגְעִל *his cow becomes pregnant, and casts not* (her calf,) i. e. suffers no abortion.

גֹּעַל m. verbal from גָּעַל, *abhorrence, loathing.* Ezek. 16 : 5.

גָּעַר *to assail with harsh words, to chide, reprove, rebuke;* construed with an accus. or with בְּ. (In Syr. *idem.*) Gen. 37 : 10. Ruth. 2 : 16. Jer. 29 : 27. Frequently spoken of God, who rebukes men in order to restrain them, Is. 17 : 13. Zech. 3 : 2 יִגְעַר יְהוָה בְּךָ הַשָּׂטָן *the Lord rebuke thee, Satan,* i. e. the Lord check thee. Mal. 3 : 11 וְגָעַרְתִּי לָכֶם בָּאֹכֵל *I will rebuke the devourer for your sakes,* i. e. I will drive away destructive insects from you. 2 : 3 הִנְנִי גֹעֵר לָכֶם אֶת הַזֶּרַע *behold, I rebuke the seed for your sakes,* i. e. I deny to you the seed. Applied to Jehovah's rebuking his enemies, Ps. 9 : 6. 68 : 31. 119 : 21. to his rebuking or controlling the elements, Ps. 106 : 9 וַיִּגְעַר בְּיַם־סוּף וַיֶּחֱרָב *he rebuked the sea of reeds, and it dried up.* Nah. 1 : 4.

Deriv. out of course מִגְעֶרֶת.

גְּעָרָה f. verbal from גָּעַר, dec. XI.

1. *rebuke, reproof;* e. g. from one's parents. Prov. 13 : 1 וְלֵץ לֹא שָׁמַע גְּעָרָה *and the scorner hearkens not to reproof.* 17 : 10. Ecc. 7 : 5 טוֹב לִשְׁמֹעַ גַּעֲרַת חָכָם *it is better to hear the reproof of a wise man, than* etc.

2. *threatening, menace.* Is. 30 : 17. Especially applied to God's threatening the elements, Ps. 104 : 7. Is. 50 : 2 בְּגַעֲרָתִי אַחֲרִיב יָם *through my threatening I dry up the sea.* to God's pronouncing destruction, Ps. 76 : 7. 80 : 17.

גָּעַשׁ *to be moved violently, to shake, to tremble;* spoken of the earth. Ps. 18 : 8.

Pu. גֹּעַשׁ *idem.* Job 34 : 20 יְגֹעֲשׁוּ עָם *the people shall be moved* or *troubled.*

Hithpa. *to be moved, to roll,* spoken of the earth, the floods. Ps. 18 : 8. Jer. 5 : 22. 46 : 7, 8.

Hithpo. *to stagger,* spoken of a drunken man. Jer. 25 : 16.

גַּעַשׁ proper name of a mountain, which forms a part of mount Ephraim. Josh. 24 : 30. Judg. 2 : 9.

גַּף m. (kindred with גַּב,) dec. VIII. h.

1. *the body.* Ex. 21 : 3 בְּגַפּוֹ *with his body* (*only,*) i. e. without wife or family. verse 4.

2. *back, height.* Prov. 9 : 3 עַל גַּפֵּי מְרֹמֵי קָרֶת literally, *on the back of the heights of the city.*

גַּף Chald. plur. גַּפִּין, *wing.* Dan. 7 : 4, 6. Comp. אֲגַף.

גֶּפֶן, with suff. גַּפְנִי, com. gen. (masc. rarely, Hos. 10 : 1. 2 K. 4 : 39.) dec. VI. a.

1. *vine, grape-vine*—More definitely גֶּפֶן הַיַּיִן Num. 6 : 4. But the word is extended to other similar plants, thus גֶּפֶן שָׂדֶה *the wild cucumber-vine,* 2 K. 4 : 39. (see פַּקֻּעוֹת.)—גֶּפֶן סְדֹם *the vine of Sodom,* probably no particular plant, Deut. 32: 32.

2. *the fruit of the vine.* 2 K. 18 : 31. Is. 36 : 16.

גֹּפֶר m. found only Gen. 6 : 14 עֲצֵי גֹפֶר

fir or pine wood. According to the Chald. and the Jewish commentators, *cedar.* It is without doubt a species of resinous tree; hence גָּפְרִית *brimstone,* perhaps also *pitch.*

גָּפְרִית f. denom. from גֹּפֶר, *brimstone.* (Syr. ܟܒܪܝܬܐ, Arab. كبريت, Chald. גּוּפְרִית.) Is. 30:33. Gen. 19:24.

גֵּר, fem. גָּרָה, participial noun from גּוּר, dec. I. a. *inmate, lodger, sojourner.* Job 19:15. Ex. 3:22.

גָּר perhaps *the foot of a mountain,* (like the Arab. جر.) Job 28:4 פָּרַץ נַחַל מֵעִם־גָּר *one opens a passage from the foot of the mountain.* But it may be rendered, *one opens a passage from his dwelling,* as if by ellipsis for מֵעִם אֲשֶׁר גָּר שָׁם *from the place where he dwells.*

גָּר m. participial noun from גּוּר (q. v.) *a stranger.*

גֹּר i. q. גּוּר *catulus.* Plur. גּוֹרִים, Jer. 51:38. and גֹּרוֹת, Nah. 2:13.

גָּרָב m. *scurvy,* perhaps of a malignant kind. Sept. ψώρα ἀγρία. Vulg. *scabies jugis.* Lev. 21:20. 22:22. (In Syr. and Arab. *leprosy, itch.*)

גַּרְגַּר m. dec. VII. i. *berry,* e. g. of the olive. Is. 17:6. (So in Chald. and Arab.)

גַּרְגְּרוֹת plur. fem. *neck.* Prov. 1:9. 3:3, 22. 6:21. (In Arab. جرجر a denom. *to gargle,* جرية *craw, crop.*)

גִּרְגָּשִׁי proper name of a Canaanitish people. Gen. 10:16. 15:21. Josh. 24:11. The name Γεργεσηνοί occurs Mat. 8:28. but the reading is supposed to be a mere conjecture of Origen.

גָּרַד *to scratch, scrape, rub.*

Hithpa. *to scrape one's self.* Job 2:8. (So in Arab. and Aram.)

גָּרָה in Kal not used.

Pi. גֵּרָה *to excite, stir up* contention. Prov. 15:18 אִישׁ חֵמָה יְגָרֶה מָדוֹן *the passionate man stirs up contention.* 28:25. 29:22. (In Arab. غرا conj. II. IV. *to excite hostility.* In Aram. גְּרֵי, ܓܪܐ *idem.*)

Hithpa. 1. *to be excited, to be angry* with any one, construed with בְּ. Prov. 28:4 שֹׁמְרֵי תוֹרָה יִתְגָּרוּ בָם *the observers of the law are angry with them.* Dan. 11:10 at the beginning.

2. *to contend, to engage in war with* any one, construed with בְּ. Deut. 2:5, 19 אַל תִּתְגָּר בָּם *contend not with them.* With the addition מִלְחָמָה, *to excite* or *wage war,* verses 9, 24. With בַּיהוָה *to contend against Jehovah,* Jer. 50:24.—2 K. 14:10 לָמָּה תִתְגָּרֶה בְּרָעָה *wherefore wilt thou contend with evil?* Dan. 11:10 יִתְגָּרֶה עַד מָעֻזֹּה *he shall be excited anew, (and march) even to his fortress.* verse 25. יִתְגָּרֶה לַמִּלְחָמָה *he shall be stirred up to battle.* (Syr. and Chald. Ethpa. *to be irritated,* also *to wage war.*) Deriv. תִּגְרָה.)

I. גֵּרָה f. verbal from גָּרַר no. 2. dec. X. *the cud, the food which the animal brings up and chews again.* Found only in the phrases, הֶעֱלָה גֵרָה *to ruminate,* or *chew the cud,* Lev. 11:3 ff. Deut. 14:6, 7. and גָּרַר גֵּרָה *idem,* once Lev. 11:7.

II. גֵּרָה f. *a gerah,* the smallest weight of the Hebrews, being the twentieth part of the shekel, used also as a coin; literally, *a bean, grain,* (comp. גַּרְגַּר *a berry,* in Chald. *a grain, kernel;* also Arab. خرخر *a bean.*) The Hebrews without doubt made use of a kernel or grain for a weight, as the Greeks and Romans did of the κεράτιον, and the moderns of barley and pepper-corns.

גָּרוֹן m. const. גְּרוֹן, dec. III. a. The form of this word is from גָּרָה, but the signification from גָּרַר no. 3. See גַּרְגְּרוֹת.

1. *neck.* Is. 3:16 נְטוּוֹת גָּרוֹן *with stretched-out necks.* Ezek. 16:11.

2. *throat, swallow.* Ps. 149:6 רוֹמְמוֹת אֵל בִּגְרוֹנָם liter. *exaltations of God are in their throat.* Is. 58:1 קְרָא בְגָרוֹן *call from a (full) throat,* i. e. cry aloud. Ps. 69:

4. 115:7. Ps. 5:10 קֶבֶר פָּתוּחַ גְּרוֹנָם *their throat is an open sepulchre.* Jer. 2:24.

גֵּרוּת f. denom. from גֵּר, *habitation.* Jer. 41:17.

גָּרַז i. q. גָּזַר, by a metathesis which prevails in this word also in Arabic. Found only in Niph. *to be cut off* or *taken away.* Ps. 31:23 נִגְרַזְתִּי מִנֶּגֶד עֵינֶיךָ *I am taken away from thine eyes.* (comp. Ps. 88:6.) But 8 MSS. read נגזרתי.

גִּרְזִי name of a Canaanitish people, found only 1 Sam. 27:8 Kethib, (Vulg. *Gerzi,*) the Keri being גִּזְרִי. Perhaps synonymous with גִּרְגָּשִׁי Gen. 10:16.

גְּרִזִּים proper name, *Gerizim,* a peak of mt. Ephraim, over against mt. Ebal. Between the two the city Shechem was situated. Deut. 11:29. 27:12. This mountain became in subsequent times the seat of the religious worship of the Samaritans. The Samar. text, and the Samaritans join in one word הרגריזים *mount Gerizim,* as it is written in Eupolemus Αργαριζιν. See Reland de monte Garizim, in his Dissert. Miscellan. P. I, no. 3.

גַּרְזֶן m. *axe, hatchet.* Deut. 19:5. 20:19. 1 K. 6:7. This quadriliteral appears to be derived from גָּזַר = גָּרַז *to cut, to hew.*

גְּרָל or גְּרָל־ Prov. 19:19 Kethib, prob. a corrupt reading instead of גְּדָל־. Theodot. μεγαλόθυμος.

גֹּרָל see גּוֹרָל *lot.*

I. גָּרַם properly, *to cut off,* as in Syr. and Arab. Hence, construed with לְ, *to reserve,* Zeph. 3:3 לֹא גָרְמוּ לַבֹּקֶר *they reserve nothing till the morning.* (Comp. הִבְדִּיל לְ, אָצַל לְ.)

II. גֵּרֵם Pi. denom. from גֶּרֶם, *to gnaw* or *break in pieces* a bone. Num. 24:8 עַצְמֹתֵיהֶם יְגָרֵם *he shall break their bones.* Hence metaphorically, Ezek. 23:34 *thou shalt drink it (the cup,) and suck it out,* וְאֶת חֲרָשֶׂיהָ תְּגָרֵמִי *and its sherds thou shalt gnaw,* i. e. thou shalt completely exhaust it. (In Arab. جرم is i. q. جلم *to pick* or *gnaw flesh from a bone,* a denom. from جلم *flesh.* In Chald. also it signifies *to pick a bone,* Ps. 27:2 Targ.)

גֶּרֶם m. prim. dec. VI. a.

1. *bone.* Prov. 17:22. 25:15.—חֲמוֹר גֶּרֶם *an ass of bone,* i. e. a strong-built ass, Gen. 49:14. The Arabs say in like manner, حمار جرم فرس, *a strong horse, ass,* and جريم *strong-boned.*)

2. *self,* (like עֶצֶם *bone* and *self,*) as is common in Chald. and Samaritan. 2 K. 9:13 עַל גֶּרֶם הַמַּעֲלוֹת *on the stairs themselves.* Others: *on one of the stairs,* (comp. Arab. جرم *part,* and the expression بعضهم *one of them,* literally, *a part of them.*)

גְּרַם m. Chald. *bone,* as in Hebrew. Dan. 6:25.

גֹּרֶן f. plur. גְּרָנוֹת, const. גָּרְנוֹת; prim. dec. VI. p.

1. *an open level place, area;* e. g. before the gate, 1 K. 22:10. 2 Chr. 18:9.

2. especially *a threshing-floor, a circular level plat of ground in the open air,* where corn was trodden by oxen. Ruth. 3:2 ff.—תְּבוּאַת גֹּרֶן *the produce of the threshing-floor.* Num. 18:30.—Is. 21:10 בֶּן גָּרְנִי *son of my threshing-floor,* i. e. (if spoken of the Israelites,) *my bruised broken people,* or (if spoken of the Babylonians,) *thou who shalt soon be broken on my threshing-floor.* Comp. דוש.

3. *the grain itself.* Job 39:12.

גָּרַס *to be bruised, crushed,* or *broken in pieces.* (Syr. ܓܪܣ *to break in pieces;* Arab. جرش *to break into large pieces.*) Ps. 119:20 גָּרְסָה נַפְשִׁי לְתַאֲבָה *my soul is broken,* or languisheth, *from desire.*

Hiph. Lam. 3:16 וַיַּגְרֵס בֶּחָצָץ שִׁנָּי *he causes my teeth to bite gravel stones.*

גָּרַע 1. *to take off* (the beard,) *to shave.* Is. 15:2. Jer. 48:37. (In Syriac, *idem.*)

R

2. *to take* or *draw off* or *away*, *to withdraw* from a person or thing. Job 36:7 לֹא יִגְרַע מִצַּדִּיק עֵינָיו *he withdraws not his eyes from the righteous.* In this way the ellipsis is to be supplied in Ezek. 5:11 וְגַם אֲנִי אֶגְרַע *I also will withdraw* (mine eye;) especially as עֵינִי follows soon after. Jer. 26:2 אַל תִּגְרַע דָּבָר *take nothing away.* Often absolutely, *to take away*, without specifying what is taken away, (comp. יָסַף no. 1.) Deut. 4:2 *and ye shall not take away from it.* 13:1. [12:32.] Ex. 5:8, 19. Ecc. 3:14 עָלָיו אֵין לְהוֹסִיף וּמִמֶּנּוּ אֵין לִגְרֹעַ *there is nothing to be added to it, and nothing to be taken from it.* Hence

3. construed with an accus. of the thing, *to diminish, lessen, shorten.* Ex. 21:10. Ezek. 16:27. Job 15:4 וְתִגְרַע שִׂיחָה לִפְנֵי אֵל *thou lessenest prayer before God.*

4. as in Arabic, *to suck up* or *draw in* (water), *to imbibe.* Job 15:8 וְתִגְרַע אֵלֶיךָ חָכְמָה *hast thou imbibed wisdom to thyself?*

Pi. i. q. Kal no. 4. Job 36:27 כִּי יְגָרַע נִטְפֵי מָיִם *has he drawn up* (*to himself*) *the drops of water?*

Niph. *to be taken away.* Num. 36: 3, 4. 27:4. Often used in a somewhat impersonal manner, without specifying the object taken away, נִגְרַע מִן *something is taken away* or *is wanting*, Num. 36: 3 at the end. Ex. 5:11. Lev. 27:18. Hence *to be diminished, lessened, restrained*, Num. 9:7 לָמָּה נִגָּרַע לְבִלְתִּי *wherefore should we be restrained, so as not*, etc.

Deriv. מִגְרָעוֹת.

גָּרַף *to carry* or *wash away.* (In Arab. and Syr. *idem.*) Once Judg. 5: 21 נַחַל קִישׁוֹן גְּרָפָם *the brook Kishon carries them away.* Deriv. מֶגְרָפָה.

גָּרַר, fut. יָגֹר, יָגֹר. 1. *to draw*, especially *to carry off, to sweep away.* (In Syr. and Arab. *idem.*) Hab. 1:15 יְגֹרֵהוּ בְחֶרְמוֹ *one draws them in his net.* Prov. 21:7.

2. *to draw* (with the saw,) *to saw, saw in pieces.* (The kindred form נגר has this signification in Syr. and Arab.) Deriv. מְגֵרָה *a saw.* See Poal.

Niph. *to bring up again* (the food,) *to ruminate.* (In Arab. conj. IV. VIII. Syr. Ethpe. *idem.*) Fut. יִגָּר Lev. 11:7.

Poal, *to be sawn.* 1 K. 7:9. See Kal no. 2.

Hithpo. i. q. Kal no. 1. Jer. 30:23.

גְּרָר proper name of a city of the Philistines, and residence of a king. Gen. 20:1. 26:1.—נַחַל גְּרָר *the valley of Gerar*, Gen. 26:17.

גֶּרֶשׂ, with suff. גִּרְשָׂהּ, verbal from גָּרַשׂ =גָּרַס, dec. VI. h. *something pounded* or *beaten fine.* Lev. 2:14, 16.

גָּרַשׁ 1. *to drive out.* Ex. 34:11. Lev. 21:7. More frequent in Piel.

2. *to drive*, or *carry along with itself, to wash away.* Is. 57:20 וַיִּגְרְשׁוּ מֵימָיו רֶפֶשׁ וָטִיט *and his waters carry along mire and dirt.*

3. *to empty, strip, pillage.* Ezek. 36: 5 לְמַעַן מִגְרָשָׁהּ לָבַז *to pillage it* (*the uninhabited land*) *for booty.* מִגְרַשׁ is the Aramean infinitive.

Pi. גֵּרֵשׁ *to drive away, to drive out.* Gen. 3:24. 4:14. 21:10. etc.

Pu. גֹּרַשׁ pass. Ex. 12:39.

Niph. 1. *to be driven out.* Jon. 2:5.

2. *to be carried* or *swept along.* Am. 8:8 וְנִגְרְשָׁה וְנִשְׁקְעָה כִּיאוֹר מִצְרָיִם *it shall be carried along and overflowed as* (*by*) *the river Egypt.*

3. *to be agitated.* Is. 57:20 יָם נִגְרָשׁ *the agitated* or *troubled sea, mare impulsum.*

Deriv. out of course מִגְרָשׁ.

גֶּרֶשׁ m. verbal from גָּרַשׁ, *produce, proventus.* Deut. 33:14. (The root which usually signifies *to drive out*, has here the kindred meaning *to produce.*)

גְּרֻשָׁה f. verbal from גָּרַשׁ, dec. X. *expulsion* (from one's possessions,) *exactions.* Ezek. 45:9.

גֵּרְשֹׁם (*expulsion*, from גָּרַשׁ) proper name of a son of Moses. Ex. 2:22. 18:3. The patronymic noun גֵּרְשֻׁנִּי Num. 3:21. 26:57. is made from the form גֵּרְשׁוֹן.

גְּשׁוּר literally, *a bridge*, (comp. Arab. جِسْر, Syr. ܓܶܫܪܳܐ *idem.*) But in Hebrew used only as a proper name.

1. a country on the east of Jordan, inhabited by Canaanites. Deut. 3:14. Josh. 12:5. 13:13.

2. a country in the south of Palestine, in the neighbourhood of the Philistines. Josh. 13:2. 1 Sam. 27:8.

3. a place in Syria, subject to a king, whose daughter David married. 2 Sam. 3:3. 13:37. 15:8.

גָּשַׁם in Kal not used.

Hiph. *to cause to rain.* Jer. 14:22.

גֶּשֶׁם m. plur. גְּשָׁמִים, const. גִּשְׁמֵי, verbal from גָּשַׁם, dec. VI. h. *a heavy rain, shower,* differing from מָטָר *a light rain.* Comp. 1 K. 18:45. Prov. 25:23. Ezek. 13:11. 38:22. The combination of the two synonymes, as in Job 37:6 גֶּשֶׁם, מָטָר and Zech. 10:1 מְטַר גֶּשֶׁם, gives intensity to the signification.

גֹּשֶׁם, with suff. גָּשְׁמָהּ verbal from גָּשַׁם, dec. VI. o. *idem.* Ezek. 22:24.

גְּשֵׁם, with suff. גִּשְׁמֵהּ, גִּשְׁמְהוֹן, Chald. *body.* Dan. 4:30. [33.] 5:21. (Syr. ܓܘܫܡܐ and ܓܫܡܐ, Arab. جسم also جثمان *idem.*)

גֹּשֶׁן 1. *Goshen,* proper name of a country in Egypt, in which the Israelites dwelt from the time of Jacob to that of Moses. Gen. 45:10. 46:28, 34. 47:27. 50:8. Ex. 8:22. 9:26. The Greek geographers, living at a later period, have made no mention of Goshen. Its situation can only be limited in general to the eastern side of lower and middle Egypt, towards Palestine and Arabia. The most important data for its situation are found in Gen. 46:29. Ex. 13:17. 1 Chr. 7:21. To this may be added the rendering of the Sept. by Γεσὲμ Ἀραβίας Gen. 45:10. and Ἡρώων πόλις ἐν γῇ Ῥαμεσσῆ 46:28. The different opinions may be found stated and examined in Bellermann's Hanbuch der bibl. Literatur, Th. IV. p. 191—220. comp. Jablonski's 8 dissertations De Terra Gosen, reprinted also in his Opuscula T. II. p. 77—224. ed. Te Water. and, as advocating a different opinion, J. D. Michaëlis' Supplem. p. 371—381. The pronunciation of the Sept. Γεσέμ corresponds to the Coptic form of the word ΓΕϹΕΜ, ΝΓΕϹΕΜ, ΝΟΥΕϹΕΜ.

2. also of a city and country in the mountain of Judah. Josh. 10:41. 11:16. 15:51.

גָּשַׁשׁ found only in Pi. *to grope after* any thing, construed with an accus. Is. 59:10. (In Arab. and Aram. *idem.*)

גַּת, plur. גִּתּוֹת, f. (prob. for גֶּנֶת or יְגֶנֶת verbal from גָּן = Arab. وجن *pressit.*) dec. VIII. f.

1. *wine-press,* or rather *the trough in which the grapes were trodden,* and out of which the juice ran into the tub (יֶקֶב) placed at the side. Joel 4:13. [3:13.] —דָּרַךְ גַּת *to tread the wine-press,* Neh. 13:15. Lam. 1:15,

2. proper name of one of the five princely cities of the Philistines, the birth-place of Goliath. Josh. 13:3. 1 Sam. 6:17. 21:10. 1 K. 2:39, 40.

3. גַּת חֵפֶר (*dug wine-press*) a place in the tribe of Zebulun, (with He local גִּתָּה חֵפֶר.) Josh. 19:13.

4. גַּת רִמּוֹן (*pomegranate-press*) a place in the tribe of Dan. Josh. 19:45.

גִּתִּי a gentile noun from גַּת, *a Gittite.* 2 Sam. 6:10, 11. 15:18. The fem. גִּתִּית appears in Ps. 8:1. 81:1. 84:1. to be the name of a musical instrument, perhaps invented at Gath, or so called from גַּת *a wine-press,* because used at the joyful season of vintage.

גִּתַּיִם (*two wine-presses*) proper name of a city in the tribe of Benjamin. Neh. 11:33.

גֶּתֶר found only Gen. 10:23. a son of Aram, perhaps representing a people of Syria.

ד

THE name דָּלֶת i. q. דֶּלֶת *a door*, refers probably to the common square form of this letter.

Daleth is most nearly related to ז, (especially where this letter corresponds with the Arab. ذ, sounded like *ds*, but in some Arabic dialects like *d* simply.) Comp. דָּעַךְ and זָעַךְ *to be extinguished;* גֶּדַע *truncus* and גָּזַע *to cut down;* נָדַר Arab. نذر *to vow;* and on the other hand נֵזֶר *a crown*, as if from Arab. نذر *to be distinguished;* etc. It corresponds very rarely with the Arab. ز; e. g. קַרְדֹּם Arab. كرزم *an axe.*

It is sometimes commuted with the harder consonants of the same organ; e. g. דִּבָּה Aram. טִבָּא *slander;* بدن and بطن *body, belly;* בָּדַל Arab. بتل *to divide.*

דָּא Chald. pron. denom. fem. i.q. Heb. זֹה and זֹאת *this*, (otherwise דְּנָה, דֵּךְ.) Dan. 4:27. [30.] 5:6 דָּא לְדָא *one another.*

דָּאַב i. q. דּוּב (q.v.) *to languish, faint, waste away.* Jer. 31:12 וְלֹא יוֹסִיפוּ לְדַאֲבָה עוֹד *and they shall not languish any more.* Spoken of the eye, Ps. 88:10 *mine eye languisheth from affliction.* (Comp. עָשֵׁשׁ.) Spoken of the soul, Jer. 31:25.

דְּאָבָה f. verbal from דָּאַב, literally, a *wasting away*, from anxiety, consternation; hence, *anxiety, sorrow.* Job 41: 14. [22.] Comp. כַּעַס.

דְּאָבוֹן m. const. דַּאֲבוֹן, verbal from דָּאַב, dec. III. *a languishing, faintness.* joined with נֶפֶשׁ. Deut. 28:65.

דָּאג i. q. דָּג *fish.* Neh. 13:16.

דָּאַג 1. *to be afflicted* or *troubled about* any thing; construed with לְ, 1 Sam. 9:5 וְדָאַג לָנוּ *and be troubled about us.* 10:2. with מִן, Ps. 38:19 אֶדְאַג מֵחַטָּאתִי *I am afflicted on account of my sin.*

2. *to fear.* Jer. 17:8. construed with an acc. Jer. 38:19. Is. 57:11. with מִן, Jer. 42:16.

דֹּאֵג (*afflicted*) proper name of an Idumean, in the retinue of Saul, and hostile to David. 1 Sam. 21:8. 22:9. Ps. 52:2. The Kethib 1 Sam. 22:18, 22, has דּוֹיֵג, after the Syriac pronunciation.

דְּאָגָה f. verbal from דָּאַג, *affliction, sorrow.* Prov. 12:25.

2. *fear, apprehension, anxiety.* Ezek. 4:16. 12:18, 19. Jer. 49:23.

דָּאָה, fut. יִדְאֶה, apoc. יֵדֶא (Ps. 18:11.) *to fly;* spoken of the swift eagle, Deut. 28:49. Jer. 48:40. 49:22. of the Deity, Ps. 18:11 וַיֵּדֶא עַל כַּנְפֵי רוּחַ *and he flew on the wings of the wind.* For 2 K. 17:21, see נָדָא.

דָּאָה found only Lev. 11:14. (רָאָה being in the parallel passage Deut. 14: 13, though perhaps merely a corruption;) name of a swift bird of prey. So much is evident from the etymology and the context. Its specific meaning cannot be determined. Sept. γύψ, *vulture.* Vulg. *milvus.* Comp. Bocharti Hieroz. T. II. p. 191.

דָּאר see **דּוֹר**.

דֹּב and **דּוֹב** prim. masc. epicene, dec. VIII. d. *bear.* 1 Sam. 17; 34, 36, 37. 2 Sam. 17:8. Prov. 17:12. Hos. 13:8 דֹּב שַׁכּוּל *a she-bear robbed of her whelps.* Plur. דֻּבִּים f. *she-bears,* 2 K. 2: 24. (Arab. دُبّ, دُبَّة *a he-bear, a she-bear.*)

דֹּב Chald. *idem.* Dan. 7:5.

דֹּבֶא m. dec. VI. p. found only Deut. 33:25 כְּיָמֶיךָ דָּבְאֶךָ *as thy days,* i. e. the days of thy life, *so thine old age,* or *thine end, death.* Vulg. *senectus tua.* (Others: *strength;* not suiting the context.) The primary idea is either *rest* (comp. دبا *to rest,*) or *wasting away,*

(as if from דָּבָא i. q. דָּאַב, דוב *to languish.*)

דָּבַב according to the Jewish commentators, strictly, *to speak,* (whence דִּבָּה,) hence causatively, spoken of wine, Cant. 7:10 דּוֹבֵב שִׂפְתֵי יְשֵׁנִים *which makes the lips of the sleeping to speak,* (as in dreaming.) But the root of דִּבָּה is more probably the Arab. دَبَّ *to creep,* also *to flow gently,* whence our passage may be rendered, *which flows gently over the lips of the carousers.*

דִּבָּה m. *slander, ill report.*— הוֹצִיא דִבָּה *to spread an ill report,* Num. 14:36. Prov. 10:18. The following genitive may be taken actively, as Ps. 31:14 כִּי שָׁמַעְתִּי דִּבַּת רַבִּים *for I hear the slanders of many.* Jer. 20:10. or passively, as Num. 13:32. 14:37. Gen. 37:2. Prov. 25:10 וְדִבָּתְךָ לֹא תָשׁוּב *and thine ill report turn not away.* (In Arab. دَبُوب and دَبِيب *a secret slanderer.* In Syr. ܕܒܬܐ *reputation, report;* and ܐܕܒ *to spread a report, to slander.* In Chald. מִבָּה *ill report, infamy.* Concerning the root, see דָּבַב.)

דְּבוֹרָה f. prim. dec. X.

1. *bee,* Is. 7:18. Plur. דְּבֹרִים, Judg. 14:8. Ps. 118:12. Deut. 1:44. (Syr. ܕܒܘܪܬܐ *bee, wasp;* Arab. دَبْر, collect. *bees, wasps.*)

2. proper name of a celebrated judge and prophetess in Israel. Judg. 4:4. 5:1.

דְּבַח Chald. i. q. Heb. זָבַח *to offer* a sacrifice. Ezra 6:3. Deriv. out of course מַדְבַּח *altar.*

דְּבַח, plur. דִּבְחִין, Chald. *sacrifice.* Ezra 6:3.

דִּבְיוֹנִים masc. plur. 2 K. 6:25 Keri. *doves' dung.* The Masoretes have substituted this word, as appearing to them less offensive, for the reading of the Kethib חֲרֵי יוֹנִים. The first part of this compound, the syllable דִּב, appears to be derived from דבה = Chald. דוב and Syr. ܕܒ *fluxit,* and is probably an euphemism for חֶרֶא, (comp. ῥεῦμα γαστρός, διάῤῥοια, *alvi profluvium.*)

דְּבִיר m. 1. a portion of the temple, (otherwise called קֹדֶשׁ הַקֳּדָשִׁים *the holy of holies,*) embracing a third part of its area towards the west, and 20 cubits square, *adytum.* 1 K. 6:5, 19—22. 8:6, 8. 2 Chr. 3:16. 4:20. 5:7, 9. Jerome renders the word *oraculum, oraculi sedes,* (from דִּבֶּר *to speak,*) because the Deity reveals his oracles there; but the more probable root is דבר i. q. Arab. دَبَرَ *to be behind;* hence, *the hinder,* i. e. the western, *part of the temple,* (comp. אָחוֹר.)

2. proper name of a city in the tribe of Judah, otherwise called *Kirjath-sepher.* Judg. 1:11.

דְּבֵלָה f. const. דְּבֶלֶת, Plur. דְּבֵלִים, dec. XI. f. *a round cake of dried figs pressed together,* i. q. Greek παλάθη. 1 Sam. 25:18. 1 Chr. 12:40. With the addition תְּאֵנִים (*figs,*) 2 K. 20:7. (In Syr. *idem.* Root דבל, which in Arabic signifies *to press together, to make round.*) See Celsii Hierobot. T. II. p. 377—379.

דִּבְלָה Ezek. 6:14. **דִּבְלָתַיִם** Num. 33:46. and **בֵּית דִּבְלָתָיִם** Jer. 48:22. proper name of a city of Moab. Jerome (Onomast. s. v. Jaffa,) says; et usque hodie ostenditur inter Medabam et Deblatai.

דָּבַק and **דָּבֵק**, fut. יִדְבַּק, infin. דָּבְקָה. (In Syr. ܕܒܩ *adhæsit;* Arab. دَبِقَ *firmiter adhæsit.*)

1. *to cleave* or *stick to, to adhere;* construed with בְּ, לְ, or אֶל. Ps. 102:6. Lam. 4:4 דָּבַק לְשׁוֹן יוֹנֵק אֶל חִכּוֹ *the tongue of the suckling cleaves to his palate,* (from thirst, dryness.) Ps. 22:16. The same phrase is also used in another sense, Job 29:10 וּלְשׁוֹנָם לְחִכָּם דָּבֵקָה *their tongue clave to their palate,* i. e. they were silent, (from veneration, respect.) Ps. 137:6. (comp. Hiph. Ezek. 3:26.) Deut. 13:18 *let nothing cleave to thine hand,* i. e. purloin nothing. Job 31:7.

2. *to attach one's self to* a person, *to keep by* him. Ruth 2:8, 21. construed with בְּ, verse 23. Hence, *to stick close to*, or *to love*, e.g. the king, God, one's wife, construed with בְּ, or לְ, Deut. 10:20. 11:22. 2 Sam. 20:2. 1 K. 11:2. Josh. 23:12. Gen. 2:24. 34:3. with אַחֲרֵי, Ps. 63:9 דָּבְקָה נַפְשִׁי אַחֲרֶיךָ *my soul cleaveth to thee.*

3. *to overtake* any one, construed with an acc. with בְּ, or with אַחֲרֵי. Gen. 19:19. Deut. 28:60. Jer. 42:16 שָׁם יִדְבַּק אַחֲרֵיכֶם *it (hunger) shall overtake you there.* Synonymous with הִשִּׂיג. See Hiph. no. 3.

Pu. pass. *to cleave together*. Job 38:38. 41:9. [17.]

Hiph. 1. caus. of Kal no. 1. *to cause to cleave* or *stick*. Ezek. 3:26. 29:4. Jer. 13:11.

2. *to pursue;* construed with an acc. Judg. 18:22. 2 Sam. 1:6. and with אַחֲרֵי, Judg. 20:45 וַיַּדְבִּקוּ אַחֲרָיו *and they pursued him.* 1 Sam. 14:22. 31:2.

3. *to overtake*, i.q. Kal no. 3. Gen. 31:23. Judg. 20:42. also causat. *to make to overtake*, Deut. 28:21.

Hoph. *to cleave* or *adhere*. Ps. 22:16.

דְּבַק Chald. *idem*. Dan. 2:43.

דָּבֵק verbal from דָּבַק, dec. V. a. *cleaving, adhering*. 2 K. 3:3. Prov. 18:24.

דֶּבֶק m. verbal from דָּבַק, dec. VI. h

1. *the soldering* or *welding* of metals. Is. 41:7.

2. plur. דְּבָקִים 1 K. 22:34. 2 Chr. 18:33. probably *the joints* of the coat of mail. So the Chald.—Others: *shoulders;* comp. Chald. מִדְבְּקֵי יְדָךְ Jer. 28:12 Targ.

דָּבַר 1. prob. as its primary signification, *to lead, to drive*, (as in the Syr. ܕܒܰܪ, and in Arab. conj. II.) Comp. Hiph. Hence the deriv. דֹּבֶר, מִדְבָּר, דֹּבְרָה.

2. *to put in order, to arrange, connect*, (as in Arabic;) and hence *to connect words, to speak, serere verba*, (whence *sermo*.) In Kal found only in the part. דֹּבֵר and דָּבֻר Prov. 25:11. and in the infin. דָּבְרֶךָ Ps. 51:6. But much more common in

Pi. דִּבֶּר, דִּבֵּר, fut. יְדַבֵּר.

1. *to speak, loquor*, (different from אָמַר *to say, dico*, which is followed by the words spoken; see אָמַר no. 1.) (1.) used absolutely. Job 11:5 מִי יִתֵּן אֱלוֹהַּ דַּבֵּר *O that God would speak.* Is. 1:2 כִּי יְהוָה דִּבֵּר *for Jehovah speaketh.* (2.) construed with an acc. (in cases where אָמַר is likewise used.) Ex. 6:29 דַּבֵּר אֶל פַּרְעֹה אֵת כָּל־ אֲשֶׁר אֲנִי דֹּבֵר אֵלֶיךָ *speak thou to Pharaoh all which I say to thee.* 24:7 כֹּל אֲשֶׁר דִּבֶּר יְהוָה נַעֲשֶׂה *all which Jehovah says, we will do.* Jer. 1:17. Dan. 10:11. Jon. 3:2. Frequently in such phrases as the following, דִּבֶּר שֶׁקֶר, שָׁוְא, כָּזָב, צֶדֶק *to speak deceit, falsehood, lying, righteousness*, Ps. 101:7. Is. 45:19. 59:3. Dan. 11:27. Hos. 10:4 דִּבְּרוּ דְבָרִים *they speak (vain) words*, i. e. give words for deeds, *verba dant*. (3.) very rarely, followed by the words spoken; like אָמַר, or perhaps לֵאמֹר being understood. Gen. 41:17. Ex. 32:7 וַיְדַבֵּר יְהוָה אֶל מֹשֶׁה לֶךְ־ *and Jehovah said unto Moses, go*, etc. 1 K. 21:5. 2 K. 1:7, 9. Ezek. 40:4. Dan. 2:4.

The person spoken *to* or addressed, is most commonly preceded by לְ or אֶל, also by עִם, Gen. 31:29. Deut. 5:4. by אֵת (אֶת,) Gen. 23:8. 42:30. and by בְּ, especially in the sense of a revelation from a higher being, Zech. 1:9 הַמַּלְאָךְ הַדֹּבֵר בִּי *the angel who spake with me.* verse 14. 2:7. [3.] 4:1, 4 ff. Hab. 2:1. Jer. 31:20. Num. 12:6, 8. In one instance the person spoken *to* is put in the acc. Gen. 37:4. (Comp. λέγειν τινά *to say to any one*, and *of any one*.)

The person or thing spoken *of*, is put in the accus. Ruth 4:1 הַגֹּאֵל עֹבֵר אֲשֶׁר דִּבֶּר בֹּעַז *the kinsman passed by, of whom Boaz had spoken, quem dixerat Boaz.* Gen. 19:21. 23:16. or is preceded by בְּ, 1 Sam. 19:3 וַאֲנִי אֲדַבֵּר בְּךָ אֶל אָבִי *and I will speak to my father concerning thee.* or by עַל, 1 K. 2:19. especially where the promises or oracles of God are spoken of, 1 K. 2:4. Dan. 9:12. Jer. 25:13. 42:19.

The person spoken *against* is preceded by עַל, Ps. 109:20. Jer. 6:10. 29:32. Deut. 13:6. or by בְּ, Num. 21:

7 דִּבַּרְנוּ בַיהוָה וָבָךְ *we have spoken against Jehovah, and against thee.* Job 19:18. Ps. 50:20. 78:19.—דִּבֶּר בְּ also signifies *to speak by* or *through* any one, (i. q. דִּבֶּר בְּיַד,) Num. 12:2. 2 Sam. 23:2. 1 K. 22:28.

The following applications and combinations of this word ought to be noticed; (1.) *to promise.* Deut. 19:8. Jon. 3:10. Construed with an acc. Deut. 6:3. (2.) דִּבֶּר עַל לֵב פ׳ *to speak to any one in a friendly manner,* especially, *to comfort him.* (Comp. παραμυθέομαι, *to address,* and also *to comfort;* so the Lat. *alloquor.*) Gen. 34:3. 50:21. Ruth 2:13. 2 Sam. 19:8. 2 Chr. 30:22. 32:6. (3.) דִּבֶּר אֶל, עַל לִבּוֹ *to speak with one's self,* or *in one's heart, to meditate.* Gen. 24:45. 1 Sam. 1:13 מְדַבֶּרֶת עַל לִבָּהּ *she spake in her heart.* Also with עִם, בְּלִבּוֹ, Ecc. 1:16. 2:15. Ps. 15:2. (4.) דִּבֶּר טוֹב, טוֹבָה עַל *to speak* or *promise good concerning* any one, spoken of God. Num. 10:29. 1 Sam. 25:30. Jer. 18:20. דִּבֶּר רָעָה עַל פ׳ *to pronounce evil concerning any one,* 1 K. 22:23. Jer. 11:17. 19:15. 26:19. 35:14. 36:31. This phrase is used somewhat differently Est. 7:9 מָרְדֳּכַי אֲשֶׁר דִּבֶּר טוֹב עַל הַמֶּלֶךְ *Mordechai, who had spoken to the safety of the king,* (comp. 6:2.) (5.) דִּבֶּר טוֹבוֹת אֶת אֶל, *to speak kindly with* any one. 2 K. 25:28. Jer. 12:6. (6.) דִּבֶּר שָׁלוֹם *to speak kindly* or *peaceably;* construed with עִם, Ps. 28:3. with אֶת, Jer. 9:7. *to wish peace,* or *prosperity,* construed with אֶל, Ps. 85:9. with בְּ, Ps. 122:8 אֲדַבְּרָה־נָּא שָׁלוֹם בָּךְ *I wish thee prosperity.* with לְ, Est. 10:3 דֹּבֵר שָׁלוֹם לְכָל־זַרְעוֹ *wishing peace to all his seed.* Used absolutely, Ps. 35:20. לֹא שָׁלוֹם יְדַבֵּרוּ *they do not speak peace.* (7.) דִּבֶּר מִשְׁפָּט אֶת *to pass sentence against,* also *to contend in law with* any one. See מִשְׁפָּט.

2. *to destroy.* 2 Chr. 22:10. (comp. אִבֵּד in the parallel passage 2 K. 11:1.) Derived from the primary signification, in this manner; first, *to drive away,* then *to persecute, to destroy.* Hence דֶּבֶר *pestilence.* (In Arab. conj. II. *to prepare for death;* III. *to be hostile.*)

Pu. pass. Ps. 87:3 נִכְבָּדוֹת מְדֻבָּר בָּךְ *glorious things are spoken,* i. e. designed by God, *concerning thee.* Cant. 8:8 בַּיּוֹם שֶׁיְּדֻבַּר בָּהּ *when one shall speak for her,* i. e. to have her to wife. (Comp. דִּבֶּר בְּ used in a similar connexion 1 Sam. 25:39.)

Niph. recip. of Pi. *to speak together* or *among themselves,* Mal. 3:16. construed with בְּ, Ezek. 33:30. Ps. 119:23. with עַל, Mal. 3:13.

Hiph. prob. i. q. Kal no. 1. *to drive together, to subject, to subdue.* Ps. 18:48 וַיַּדְבֵּר עַמִּים תַּחְתָּי *and he subdued nations under me.* 47:4.

Hithpa. i. q. Pi. no. 1. Found only in the part. מִדַּבֵּר, 2 Sam. 14:13. Ezek. 2:2.

דָּבָר m. verbal from דִּבֶּר, dec. IV. a.

1. *word, speech.*—דָּבָר לִי אֵלֶיךָ *I have a word to say to thee.* אִישׁ דְּבָרִים *an eloquent man,* Ex. 4:10. נְבוֹן דָּבָר *skilful of speech, eloquent.* 1 Sam. 16:18. Used particularly to denote, (1.) *command;* as דְּבַר־מַלְכוּת *a royal command,* Est. 1:19.—Josh. 1:13. 1 Sam. 17:29 הֲלֹא דָּבָר הוּא *was it not a command?* (2.) *promise.* 1 K. 2:4. 8:20. 12:16. Ps. 33:4. 56:5. (3.) *sentiment, doctrine, instruction.* Ecc. 1:1 דִּבְרֵי קֹהֶלֶת *the words,* or *sentiments of Koheleth.* Prov. 4:4, 20. 30:1. 31:1. especially *an oracle, revelation,* וַיְהִי דְבַר יְהוָה *an oracle from God was made known,* construed with אֶל, Jer. 1:4, 11. 2:1. 13:8. Ezek. 3:16. 6:1. 7:1. 11:14. with עַל, 1 Chr. 22:8. Job 4:12 וְאֵלַי דָּבָר יְגֻנָּב *a divine oracle was secretly revealed to me.* (4.) Plur. דְּבָרִים *words,* for *narration, history.* דִּבְרֵי שְׁלֹמֹה *the history of Solomon,* 1 K. 11:41. דִּבְרֵי הַיָּמִים *the history of days, journal, chronicle,* 1 Chr. 27:24. Est. 6:1.

2. *matter, thing.* (The same change of signification is also found in the Aram. מִלָּה, ܡܶܠܬܳܐ; also in פִּתְגָם; in the Arab. أمر and خطب; in the Greek ἔπος, ῥῆμα.) Ecc. 7:8.—הַדָּבָר הַזֶּה *this thing, this,* Gen. 20:10. 21:11, 26. כָּל־הַדְּבָרִים הָאֵלֶּה *all these things, all this,* Gen. 20:8. כַּדָּבָר הַזֶּה Gen. 18:25. 32:19. 44:7.

and כַּדְּבָרִים הָאֵלֶּה 24:28. 39:17, 19. *as this, thus.*—אַחַר הַדְּבָרִים הָאֵלֶּה *upon this, after this,* 15:1. 22:1. 39:7.—דְּבַר יוֹם *a daily rate* or *task;* hence דְּבַר יוֹם בְּיוֹמוֹ *the daily task in its day,* i. e. day by day, Ex. 5:13, 19. 16:4. Lev. 23:37. 1 K. 8:59. So דְּבַר יוֹם בְּיוֹם 2 Chr. 8:13. and לִדְבַר יוֹם בְּיוֹמוֹ verse 14. 31:16. in the same sense.—Often redundant, like the Greek χρῆμα, 1 Sam. 10:2 נָטַשׁ אָבִיךָ אֶת דִּבְרֵי הָאֲתֹנוֹת *thy father has given up the asses.* Ps. 65:4 דִּבְרֵי עֲוֹנֹת גָּבְרוּ מֶנִּי *iniquities prevail against me.* Ps. 105:27. 145:5.

3. *something.* Gen. 18:14.—לֹא, אֵין דָּבָר *nothing.* כָּל־דָּבָר *every thing,* Num. 31:23. Deut. 17:1. דָּבָר טָמֵא *something unclean,* Lev. 5:2. עֶרְוַת דָּבָר *something shameful* or *unbecoming,* Deut. 23:15. 24:1. comp. 2 K. 4:41. 1 Sam. 20:2. Also in plur. דְּבָרִים טוֹבִים *something good,* 2 Chr. 12:12.

4. *manner, state, condition.* 1 K. 9:15 זֶה דְּבַר הַמַּס *this is the manner of the levy.* Deut. 15:1. 19:4. (Comp. דִּבְרָה.)

5. *cause.* Josh. 5:4. Hence עַל דְּבַר *on account of, by reason of,* Gen. 12:17. 20:11. 43:18. עַל דִּבְרֵי *idem,* Deut. 4:21. Jer. 7:22. 14:1. עַל דְּבַר אֲשֶׁר before verbs, *because,* Deut. 22:24. 23:5. 2 Sam. 13:22. (Comp. דִּבְרָה.)

6. *a suit at law, causa.* Ex. 18:16 כִּי יִהְיֶה לָהֶם דָּבָר *if they have a suit at law.* verse 22. 22:8. עַל כָּל־דְּבַר פֶּשַׁע *in every suit concerning a breach of trust.*—24:14 בַּעַל דְּבָרִים *one who has a law-suit.*

דֶּבֶר m. plur. דְּבָרִים, verbal from דָּבַר, dec. VI. a. *pestilence.* Ex. 9:3. Lev. 26:25. Deut. 28:21. Hos. 13:14. (In Arab. دبر *death;* in Heb. comp. דִּבֵּר no. 2. The ideas *death* and *pestilence* are often expressed by the same word, see מָוֶת no. 4.)

דֹּבֶר i. q. מִדְבָּר verbal from דָּבַר no. 1. dec. VI. p. *a fold, pasture.* Mic. 2:12. Is. 5:17. (Comp. Syr. ܕܒܪܐ and ܕܒܪܐ *a field;* Arab. دبر *idem.*)

דֹּבְרוֹת plur. fem. verbal from דָּבַר, *floats* or *rafts,* from their being impelled or *driven* along. 1 K. 5:23. [9.]

דִּבְרָה f. verbal from דָּבַר, 1. i. q. דָּבָר no. 4. *state, condition, manner.* Ps. 110:4 *thou art a priest for ever* עַל דִּבְרָתִי מַלְכִּי־צֶדֶק *after the manner of Melchisedek.* (The ִי is paragogic, see Gesenius' Lehrgeb. p. 547.)

2. i. q. דָּבָר no. 5. *cause.* Hence עַל דִּבְרַת *on account of,* Ecc. 3:18. 8:2. עַל דִּבְרַת שֶׁ *so that,* Ecc. 7:14.

3. i. q. דָּבָר no. 6. *suit at law, matter in controversy.* Job 5:8.

דִּבְרָה f. Chald. *cause.* Dan. 2:30 עַל דִּבְרַת דִּי *so that, to the end that.*

דַּבְּרָה f. verbal from דִּבֵּר, plur. דַּבְּרוֹת *words, oracles.* Found only Deut. 33:3 יִשָּׂא מִדַּבְּרֹתֶיךָ *he (Israel) receives of thy oracles* or *commands.* So Sept. Vulg. Others read, with a change of the vowel-points, יִשָּׂא מִדַּבְּרוֹתֶךָ *he (Jehovah) undertakes the guidance of thee,* as if מִדְבָּרָה were a verbal from דָּבַר no. 1.

דְּבַשׁ m. prim. with suff. דִּבְשִׁי, dec. VI. r. (Arab. دبس.)

1. *honey.* Lev. 2:11. 1 Sam. 14:26, 27, 30, 45. Prov. 16:24. 24:13.

2. *wine sirup, new wine boiled down to the consistency of sirup,* (Greek ἕψημα; Lat. *sapa, defrutum;* Ital. *mósto cótto;*) an article, which at the present day is exported from Palestine, especially from the country about Hebron, to Egypt. Gen. 43:11. Ezek. 27:17. See E. F. C. Rosenmüller on Gen. 43:11.

דַּבֶּשֶׁת f. dec. XIII.

1. according to the connexion, the Vulg. Chald. Syr. *a bunch* or *protuberance* on the back of a camel. Once Is. 30:6. (The etymology is unknown.)

2. name of a place. Once Josh. 19:11.

דָּג m. prim. dec. II. a. once דָּאג q. v. Plur. דָּגִים, דְּגֵי; *a fish.* Jon. 2:1, 11. Gen. 9:2. Num. 11:22. 1 K. 4:33. Hence the verbs דָּגָה *to increase* like fishes; and דּוּג *to fish.*

דָּגָה fem. of דָּג, dec. XI. a. *idem.*

Deut. 4:18. Jon. 2:2. in other places used collectively, like סִקָה, Ex. 7:18, 21. Num. 11:5.

דָּגָה denom. from דָּג, *to increase, multiply*, like fishes. Once Gen. 48:16. Comp. נגן.

דָּגוֹן m. (denom. from דָּג *a fish*,) *Dagon*, an idol of the Philistines at Ashdod. From 1 Sam. 5:4, it seems to have resembled a fish in the lower part, with a human head and hands. Such deities are very common on that coast, as the idols Derceto and Atergatis prove. Comp. De Wette's Hebr. jüd. Archäologie, p. 282.

דֶּגֶל m. with suff. דִּגְלוֹ, Plur. דְּגָלִים, const. דִּגְלֵי; dec. VI. h. *standard, flag, banner*. In the march of the Israelites through the wilderness, each of the twelve tribes had its אוֹת or *lesser standard;* and every three tribes, its דֶּגֶל or *greater standard*. Num. 1:52. 2:2, 3, 10, 18, 25. 10:14 ff. Cant. 2:4 וְדִגְלוֹ עָלַי אַהֲבָה *and his banner over me is love*. (The versions render it, on account of the context, *band*, a meaning kindred to that already given; comp. the old German Fähnlein, *a flag*, also *a band of soldiers*.)

דָּגַל denom. from דֶּגֶל, *to carry* or *raise up standards*. Ps. 20:6 וּבְשֵׁם אֱלֹהֵינוּ נִדְגֹּל *to the honour of our God we will raise up banners* (*of victory*.) (Sept. μεγαλυνθησόμεθα, probably because they read נִגְדַּל.) Part. pass. דָּגוּל probably, *distinguished, chief*, (like *insignis* from *signum*,) Cant. 5:11 *my beloved is fair and ruddy*, דָּגוּל מֵרְבָבָה *distinguished before ten thousand*.

Niph. *to be provided with flags* or *banners*. Cant. 6:4, 10 אֲיֻמָּה כַּנִּדְגָּלוֹת *terrible as those provided with banners*, probably a poetical phrase for *armies*, or *warlike camps*. Symm. ὡς τάγματα παρεμβολῶν.

דָּגָן m. dec. IV. a. *corn, grain*. Gen. 27:28, 37. Num. 18:26. (In Arab. دَاجِن *idem*.)

דָּגַר 1. *to gather, heap up*, applied particularly to a female bird's gathering her eggs or young ones, and brooding over them. (In Chald. *idem*.) Jer. 17:11 קֹרֵא דָגַר וְלֹא יָלָד *as the partridge broods over eggs, which she has not laid, so he that acquires riches, but not by right*, etc. Sept. πέρδιξ συνήγαγεν, ἃ οὐκ ἔτεκεν. Is. 34:15 *she lays her eggs, and hatches them, and gathers* (*her young*) *under her shadow*. Vulg. in both passages correctly: *fovere*.

דַּד, whence dual דַּדַּיִם, dec. VIII. h. *breasts*, i. q. שָׁדַיִם. Ezek. 23:3, 8, 21. Prov. 5:19.

דָּדָה *to move slowly* or *solemnly*, particularly in a festival procession. (In Chald. and Talmud. דַּדָּה *to lead slowly*, e. g. a child.) Found only in Hithpa. Ps. 42:5 אֶדַּדֵּם עַד־בֵּית אֱלֹהִים *as I moved in procession with them to the house of God*. The suffix pronoun ־ָם is used here for עִמָּם, unless we prefer to point the verb, as if in Piel אֲדַדֵּם *as I led them*. Is. 38:15 אֶדַּדֶּה כָל־שְׁנוֹתַי עַל מַר נַפְשִׁי *I will go in solemn procession* (*to the temple*) *all my years, on account of the sufferings of my soul*, namely, those out of which God had delivered him.

דְּדָן, plur. דְּדָנִים, proper name of a people and country in Arabia, frequently mentioned in connexion with places in Idumea. Jer. 25:23. 49:8. Ezek. 25:13. 27:15, 20. Is. 21:13. There was a Dedan, the grandson of Cush, Gen. 10:7. and another, the grandson of Abraham by Keturah, Gen. 25:3. Hence it is not impossible that there were different tribes known by this name.

דֹּדָנִים masc. plur. Gen. 10:4. proper name of a people, situated to the west of the Hebrews, perhaps of Grecian origin. The proper name of a people or place is frequently so altered and corrupted in a foreign language, as greatly to obscure the original appellation. This appears to be the case here. Dodanim is usually thought to have some connexion with *Dodona* in Epirus. But the Samar. text, and Sept. in Gen. and the Heb. in 1 Chr. 1:7. read רֹדָנִים, which the Sept. renders 'Ῥόδιοι, and Bochart refers to the river *Rhodanus* or *Rhone*.

דְּהַב m. Chald. emph. דַּהֲבָא, *gold*, i. q. Heb. זָהָב. Dan. 2:32. 3:1, 5, 7.

דֶּהָיֵא (in Kethib דהוא) masc. plur. Chald. proper name of a people, from which a colony was carried by the Assyrians to Samaria. Ezra 4:9. Comp. the *Daæ* or *Dahæ*, above mt. Imaus and the Caspian Sea, in Quint. Curt. (IV. 12.) joined with the Susiani, as is the case in our passage.

דָּהַם found only in part. Niph. Jer. 14:9 כְּאִישׁ נִדְהָם *as one taken by surprise, perplexed*, or *astonied*. (In Arab. دهم *to fall upon suddenly*, e.g. as misfortune, the night; دهيم *fatuus*.) Others: *as one accidentally passing by*, since دهم also signifies *supervenit, accidit*.

דָּהַר *to pursue, chase, move quickly*, spoken of a horse or rider. Nah. 3:2 סוּס דֹּהֵר *the prancing horse*. Hence,

דַּהֲרָה f. verbal from דָּהַר, dec. X. *pursuit, rapid movement, haste*. Judg. 5:22 *then the hoofs of the horses struck the earth*, מִדַּהֲרוֹת דַּהֲרוֹת אַבִּירָיו *from the haste, the haste of their heroes*, i.e. their riders, (See Bocharti Hieroz. P. I. p. 97. Michaëlis Supplem. p. 401.)

דּוֹב i. q. דֹּב *a bear*, (q. v.)

דּוּב i. q. דָּאַב *to languish, faint*. (Arab. ذاب *idem*; Syr. ܕܳܒ *to melt, dissolve*.) Hiph. caus. Lev. 26:16.

דּוּג and **דִּיג** denom. from דָּג; *to fish*. Jer. 16:16 וְדִיגוּם *and they shall fish them*. Deriv. דַּיָּג and דּוּגָה *fisher*.

דַּוָּג m. verbal from דּוּג, dec. I. b. *fisher*. Ezek. 47:10. and Jer. 16:16 Kethib.

דּוּגָה f. verbal from דּוּג, *fishery*. Amos 4:2 סִירוֹת דּוּגָה *fish-hooks*.

דּוֹד m. with suff. also defectively דֹּדוֹ, דֹּדָהּ, dec. I. a.

1. *one beloved, a friend, lover*. Cant. 1:13, 14, 16. 2:3, 8, 9, 10, 16, 17 ff. Plur. דּוֹדִים, 5:1. (Root דוד i. q. יָדַד = Arab. وَدَّ *to love*.)

2. *father's brother, uncle by the father's side*. (Syr. ܕܳܕܳܐ.) Lev. 10:4. 18:14. 20:20. 1 Sam. 10:14. 16:15. Est. 2:15. Jer. 32:7, 8, 9. In verse 12, it appears to stand for בֶּן דּוֹד. (Comp. in Chald. חֲבִיב *one beloved*; חֲבִיבָא *an uncle*; and חֲבִיבְתָּא *a mother-in-law*.)

3. plur. דּוֹדִים *love, amores*. Cant. 1:2, 4. 4:10. Ezek. 16:8 עֵת דֹּדִים *season of love, mature age*. 23:17 מִשְׁכַּב דֹּדִים *bed of love*. Prov. 7:18 לְכָה נִרְוֶה דֹדִים *come on, let us drink deeply of love*.

דּוֹדָה fem. of דּוֹד, dec. X. *father's brother's wife, father's sister*. Ex. 6:20. Lev. 18:14. 20:20.

דּוּד 1. dec. VI. a. *pot, kettle*. Job 41:12. [20.] 1 Sam. 2:14. Plur. דּוּדִים, 2 Chr. 35:13. (Syr. ܕܘܕܐ *a great pot*; ܕܘܕܐ *a kettle*; Samar. דודיה *pots*.)

2. dec. I. *basket*. Jer. 24:2. *a labourer's basket*, Ps. 81:7. Plur. דּוּדִים, 2 K. 10:7.

דָּוִד m. (prob. *beloved*, from דוד = יָדַד *to love*,) *David*, son of Jesse, king of Israel. 1 Sam. XVI. ff. 2 Sam. 1 Chr. XII.—XXX.— עִיר דָּוִד *the city of David*, *Zion*, 1 K. 3:1. 8:1. 9:24. בֵּית דָּוִד *the posterity of David, the royal family of the kingdom of Judah*, Is. 7:2, 13. Jer. 21:12.—In the later books, such as Chronicles, Ezra, Nehemiah, Zechariah, it is written דָּוִיד, in the earlier books more rarely.

I. **דּוּדָאִים** masc. plur. a plant having a (pleasant) smell, Cant. 7:14. and supposed to render barren women fruitful, Gen. 30:14, 15, 16. According to the ancient versions, *the mandrake*, (*atropa mandragora*, Linn.) an herb with a turnip-shaped root, white and reddish flowers, and reddish fruit, of the size of small apples. The fruit ripens from May to July, and is thought, in the east, at the present day, to help conception. See Schulze's Leitungen des Höchsten, Th. v. p. 197. Herbelot's Bibliotheque Orientale, p. 17. Also Celsii Hierobot. T. I. p. 1 ff. Michaëlis Supplem. p. 410 ff. Oedmann's verm. Sammlungen aus der Naturkunde no. 5. p. 94 ff.— The form of the singular was probably דודי *amatorius*, from דוד = דוד *amator*, by adding the Aramean adjective termination י; hence the plural דודאים, as צְבִי, plur. צְבָאִים. Comp. לוּלָאוֹת.

II. דּוּדָאִים plur. *baskets.* Jer. 24:1. see דוד no. 2.

דָּוָה 1. *to be sick, out of health, infirm.* (In Arab. دوي *idem.*) Hence the derivatives דְּוַי, דַּוָּי and מַדְוֶה. Particularly *to be sick,* as females during their monthly courses. Lev. 12:2 נִדַּת דְּוֹתָהּ *separation for uncleanness on account of her courses.* (This phrase is nearly inverted 15: 35.) Comp. דָּוָה.

2. *to be sad.* See דָּוֶה.

דָּוֶה verbal adj. from דָּוָה. 1. *sick,* as females with their monthly courses. Lev. 15:33 הַדָּוָה בְּנִדָּתָהּ *one who is sick with her monthly courses.* also without addition, 20:18. — Is. 30:22 תִּזְרֵם כְּמוֹ דָוָה *thou shalt cast them away as an unclean garment,* i. e. as a garment soiled by this disease.

2. *faint, sad,* spoken of the heart. Lam. 5:17.

3. *unhappy.* Lam. 1:13. (In Syr. ܕܘܐ *to be sad, to be unhappy;* Aph. *to afflict, make unhappy;* ܕܘܝܐ *unhappy;* ܕܘܝܘܬܐ *affliction, unhappiness.*)

דּוּחַ found only in Hiph. הֵדִיחַ.

1. *to drive away, cast out.* Jer. 51: 34. Comp. the kindred forms נָדַח and דָּחָה. (In Arab. داخ *to be vile and abject;* conj. VI. *to cast away.*)

2. *to wash, to purify;* e. g. a burnt offering, 2 Chr. 4:6. Ezek. 40:38. *to wash away* blood-guiltiness, Is. 4:4.

דְּוַי m. verbal from דָּוָה 1. *sickness.* Ps. 41:4 עֶרֶשׂ דְּוָי *the sick-bed.*

2. *impurity, loathsomeness.* Job 6:6, 7 *can that which is unsavoury be eaten without salt? is there taste in the white of an egg? I cannot touch it,* הֵמָּה כִּדְוֵי לַחְמִי *and this is as the loathsomeness of my food,* i. e. as my loathsome food. Others, less correctly, make כִּדְוֵי i. q. כְּדֵי *as.*

דַּוָּי m. verbal from דָּוָה, *sick, faint,* spoken of the heart. Is. 1:5. Jer. 8:18. Lam. 1:22.

דּוּךְ i. q. דָּכָה *to pound* or *bruise in pieces.* Num. 11:8. (Arab. داك *idem.*) Hence מְדֹכָה *a mortar.*

דּוּכִיפַת f. Lev. 11:19. Deut. 14: 18. name of an unclean bird; according to the Sept. Vulg. and Arab. *the hoopoe.* The etymology presents nothing definite; although we may compare the Arab. ديك *the cock.* Simonis derives the last syllable פת from the Arab. فتّ *excrevit stercus;* and adopts the interpretation, *dung-cock,* i. e. the hoopoe. The Chaldaic translator renders it *mountain cock,* probably deriving it from דוך כיפא *gallus rupis.* Comp. Bocharti Hieroz. T. II. p. 346.

דּוּם an obsolete root, i. q. דָּמַם no. I. *to be silent.* Hence the three following derivatives.

דּוּמָה f. verbal from obs. דום.

1. *the land of silence, the regions of the dead.* Ps. 94:17. 115:17.

2. proper name of an Ishmaelitish tribe in Arabia. Gen. 25:14. Is. 21: 11. Modern geographers make mention of a place called *Dumah* and *Dumath-algandel* (*the rocky Dumah,*) in a rocky valley on the borders of Syria and Arabia. See Michaëlis Supplem. p. 419. Niebuhr's Arabien, p. 344.

דּוּמִיָּה f. verbal from obs. דום.

1. *silence.* Ps. 39:3 נֶאֱלַמְתִּי דוּמִיָּה *I was dumb (in) silence,* i. e. I was dumb and silent.

2. *silent submission* to God. Ps. 62: 2 אַךְ אֶל־אֱלֹהִים דּוּמִיָּה נַפְשִׁי *my soul is (entire) submission to God.* 65:2 לְךָ דֻמִיָּה תְהִלָּה

to thee (is due) submission (and) praise.

3. *quietness, peace.* Ps. 22:3.

דּוּמָם adv. from obs. דום *to be silent.*

1. *in silence.* Is. 47:5 שְׁבִי דוּמָם *sit thou in silence.* Hab. 2:19 אֶבֶן דּוּמָם *the silent motionless stone;* (the adverb is here used as a noun in the genitive; comp. חִנָּם.)

2. *submissively, with confidence in God.* Lam. 3:26.

דּוּמֶּשֶׂק a proper name, 2 K. 16:10. i. q. דַּמֶּשֶׂק or דַּרְמֶשֶׂק *Damascus;* but occuring more rarely. The same form is found in Syriac.

דּוּן or **דִּין** prob. i. q. דִּין *to judge,* also *to rule, direct, govern.* (Hence אָדוֹן *lord.*) Gen. 6:3 לֹא־יָדוֹן רוּחִי בָאָדָם לְעֹלָם *my spirit shall not always rule* or *act in man.* The spirit of God appears here, as in Ps. 104:30, to be the animating principle in creatures; hence this meaning: *I will take away from man the breath of life, they shall live no longer.* The Sept. renders יָדוֹן by καταμείνῃ; Vulg. *permanebit;* Syr. Arab. *habitabit;* (perhaps because they read ידום, from דום, which in Arab. signifies, *to continue.*) Others make דון i. q. Arab. دان (*med. Vau*) *to be vile, to be contemned;* hence they render the passage: *my spirit shall not always be debased in man.* See on this text Michaëlis Supplem. p. 423. Vater's Comment. in locum. Rosenmüller de Vers. Pentat. Persicâ, p. 19.

דּוֹנַג and **דֹּנַג** m. prim. *wax.* Ps. 68:3. 97:5. Mic. 1:4.

דּוּץ i. q. Syr. ܕܘܨ *to dance, leap, exult.* Job 41:14 [22] וּלְפָנָיו תָּדוּץ דְּאָבָה *and sorrow exults before him.*

דּוּק Chald. i. q. דָּקַק intrans. *to be broken in pieces.* Plur. דָּקוּ, Dan. 2:35.

דּוֹר and **דֹּר** m. 1. *age, generation.* (Root דור i. q. Arab. دار *to go about, to move in a circle;* comp. Lat. *periodus.* The Arabic word corresponding to the Heb. דור is دهر *time, age, century, eternity;* comp. similar commutations under the letter ה. Yet we also find داران *the two ages, the present and future life.*) Deut. 23:2, 3, 9 דּוֹר שְׁלִישִׁי, עֲשִׂירִי *the third, the tenth generation.* Job 42:16. Judg. 2:10 דּוֹר אַחֵר *another generation.* Num. 32:13 עַד־תֹּם כָּל־הַדּוֹר *till the whole generation was consumed.*—דֹּר וָדֹר *from generation to generation, for ever and ever,* a phrase employed to denote a long time, Ps. 61:7. Joel 2:2 עַד שְׁנֵי דּוֹר וָדוֹר *to the years of the remotest generations.* Ps. 45:18 בְּכָל־דֹּר וָדֹר *in all future generations.* 145:13. Applied also to time past, Deut. 32:7 שְׁנוֹת דּוֹר וָדוֹר *the years of past generations.* Is. 58:12. 60:15. *For ever* is also expressed by לְדֹר דֹּר, Ex. 3:15. לְדֹר וָדֹר, Ps. 10:6. 33:11. 49:14. Joel 4:20. [3:20.] עַד דּוֹר וָדוֹר, Ps. 100:5. Is. 13:20. מִדֹּר דֹּר, Ex. 17:16. In the time of the patriarchs, an age appears to have been reckoned at 100 years; (so originally among the Romans, as is shown by the word *seculum;* see Censorin. de die natali, cap. 17.) Hence Gen. 15:16 *in the fourth generation they shall return hither.* This is explained in verse 13, and in Ex. 12:40, to be 400 years.

2. *a race* or *class of men;* sometimes in a good sense, Ps. 14:5. 24:6. 73:15. 112:2. and sometimes in a bad sense, Deut. 32:5 דּוֹר עִקֵּשׁ וּפְתַלְתֹּל *a perverse and crooked generation.* verse 20. Jer. 7:29 דּוֹר עֶבְרָתוֹ *the generation with which he is angry.*

3. *dwelling,* i. q. Arab. دار. Is. 38:12. Ps. 49:20 דּוֹר אֲבוֹתָיו *the dwelling of his fathers,* i. e. the grave. (See the verb דּוּר.)

Plur. דּוֹרִים and דֹּרוֹת, (both masc.) but used in different connexions. The former occurs only in the phrase דּוֹר דּוֹרִים *generations of generations, secula seculorum,* i. e. eternity, Ps. 72:5. 102:25. Is. 51:8. Elsewhere the plural with termination וֹת uniformly occurs. This plural denotes also *future generations, posterity.* Lev. 23:43 לְמַעַן יֵדְעוּ דֹרֹתֵיכֶם

so that your posterity may know. 22:3. Num. 9:10 לָכֶם אוֹ לְדֹרֹתֵיכֶם *to you or to your posterity.* 15:14. Often in the legal phrase חֻקַּת עוֹלָם לְדֹרֹתֵיכֶם *an eternal statue for your future generations,* Lev. 3:17. 16:9. 23:14, 31, 41. and in a similar manner, Gen. 17:7, 9, 12. Ex. 12:14, 17. 16:32, 33.

דּוֹר or **דֹּאר** Josh. 17:11. and נָפַת דּוֹר, נָפוֹת דּוֹר Josh. 11:2. 12:23. 1 K. 4:11. proper name of a city with a harbour, not far from mount Carmel. It occurs 1 Mac. 15:11 ff. under the name Δωρᾶ.

דּוּר 1. as in Arabic, *to move in a circle.* Deriv. דּוֹר no. 1. and דּוּר.

2. as in Chaldaic, *to dwell.* Ps. 84:11. Deriv. דּוֹר no. 2.

דּוּר Chald. *to dwell.* Dan. 4:9, 18. [4:12, 21.] Part. דָּאְרִין, in Keri דָּיְרִין, Dan. 2:38. 3:31. 6:26. Deriv. מְדָר, מְדוּרָה, מָדוֹר.

דּוּר m. verbal from דּוּר.

1. *circle.* (Arab. دَوْر.) Is. 29:3 כַּדּוּר *as in a circle, round about.*

2. *ball.* Is. 22:18.

3. *round pile* of wood or bones for a fire. Ezek. 24:5. (comp. מְדוּרָה verse 9.)

דּוּרָא Chald. proper name of a plain in Babylonia. Dan. 3:1. According to Polybius, (v. 48. comp. Isidor. Characensis, p. 4.) it is in Mesopotamia, at the mouth of the Chaboras. See Miscellan. Lips. nova, T. V. p. 274.

דּוּשׁ and **דִּישׁ** (Deut. 25:4.) (In Arab. دَاسَ, in Syr. ܕܳܫ.)

1. *to tread down* or *under foot.* Job 39:15. Hab. 3:12.

2. *to tread out* corn, spoken of the ox; hence *to thresh.* (Comp. the art. מוֹרַג, חָרוּץ.) Jer. 50:11 עֶגְלָה דָשָׁה *a threshing heifer.* Hos. 10:11. Deut. 25:4. Spoken also of the person leading the ox or heifer, 1 Chr. 21:20 וְאָרְנָן דָּשׁ חִטִּים *and Ornan was threshing wheat.*

3. spoken of a cruel mode of capital punishment, sometimes inflicted by the Hebrews on their prisoners, which consisted in drawing over them a threshing wagon armed with iron teeth. Am. 1:3.

Niph. pass. of Kal no. 1. Is. 25:10.

Hoph. pass. Is. 28:27.

Deriv. מְדוּשָׁה, דַּיִשׁ.

דּוּשׁ Chald. *to tread under foot.* Dan. 7:23.

דָּחָה *to push down, to thrust away, overthrow.* Ps. 35:5. 118:13 דָּחֹה דְחִיתַנִי לִנְפֹּל *thou pushedst me down so that I fell.* 140:5. Ps. 62:4 גָּדֵר הַדְּחוּיָה *a wall thrown down.*

Niph. 1. pass. of Kal. Prov. 14:32. comp. Jer. 23:12, where יִדַּחוּ borrows its form from דָּחַח.

2. *to be cast out* or *driven away.*— נִדְחֵי יִשְׂרָאֵל *the outcasts of Israel,* Ps. 147:2. Is. 11:12. 56:8.

Pu. pass. of Kal. Ps. 36:13.

Deriv. מִדְחֶה, דְּחִי.

Note. The same signification is likewise found in Arab. Syr. and Chald. The leading idea, *to push, to push on, to drive on, to press,* is found in many forms which appear to be closely related. Comp. דָּחַף, דָּחַק, דָּחָה, דָּחַח, דּוּחַ, and נָדַח; (in the dialects also دحب, دحم, دحر, and דְּחַם, ܕܚܫ.) With these the following roots may be compared, both as to sound and signification, דּוּךְ, דָּכָא, דָּכָה, דָּכַךְ, and דּוּק, דָּקַק *to beat* or *bruise in pieces.*

דַּחֲוָה f. plur. דַּחֲוָן, Chald. *concubine.* (Root דחה i. q. Arab. دَحَا and دَحَا *subegit fœminam.*) Dan. 6:19 וְדַחֲוָן לָא־הַנְעֵל קָדָמוֹהִי *and his concubines he did not call in,* Theodot. and the Syr. *food.*

דָּחַח i. q. דָּחָה. The form יִדַּחוּ Jer. 23:12, is properly derived from this root.

דְּחִי, in pause דֶּחִי, m. *a falling, stumbling.* Ps. 56:14. 116:8.

דְּחַל Chald. *to be afraid,* construed with מִן קֳדָם of the person. Dan. 5:19. Part. pass. דְּחִיל *terrible,* Dan. 2:31. 7:7. Comp. Heb. זָחַל no. 2.

Pa. דַּחֵל *to terrify.* Dan. 4:2. [5.]

דֹּחַן m. (Arab. دُخْن.) Ezek. 4:9. (*holcus dochna*, Linn.) a kind of grain, of which several species were cultivated in Italy, Syria, and Egypt. While green it served for fodder, and the ripe grain was used for making bread and starch. Comp. Oedmann's verm. Sammlungen aus der Naturkunde, Th. v. p. 92 of the German translation.

דָּחַף *to press on, to hasten.* Part. דָּחוּף *hastened, concitatus,* Est. 3:15. 8: 14.

Niph. נִדְחַף *to urge one's self on, to make haste.* 2 Chr. 26:20. Est. 6:12. Deriv. מַדְחֵפֹת.

דָּחַק *to push, press, oppress.* Joel 2: 8. Part. דֹּחֵק *an oppressor* (of a people,) Judg. 2:18. (In Aram. more frequent. In Arab. دحق *to drive back* or *away.*)

דַּי const. דֵּי, with suff. דַּיִּי, dec. VIII. j.

1. *sufficient, enough.* Mal. 3:10. Est. 1:18 וּכְדַי בִּזָּיוֹן וָקָצֶף *and* (*there will be*) *contempt and altercation enough.* The noun or pronoun, which follows in the genitive, denotes regularly the person or thing, *to* or *for* which there is a sufficiency, Prov. 25:16 דַּיֶּךָּ *what is sufficient for thee.* Ex. 36:7 דַּיָּם *sufficient for them.* Obad. 5. Jer. 49:9. Lev. 5:7 דֵּי שֶׂה *so much as is sufficient for a sheep.* 12:8. 25:26 כְּדֵי גְאֻלָּתוֹ *sufficient for its redemption.* Neh. 5:8 כְּדֵי בָנוּ *according to the sufficiency in us,* i. e. after our ability. The genitive following denotes more rarely that *of* which there is a sufficiency, Prov. 27:27 דֵּי חֲלֵב עִזִּים *enough of goat's milk.*

2. The status constructus דֵּי is sometimes suffixed to the prepositions בְּ, כְּ, מִן, without affecting their signification; as is likewise the case with the syllable מוֹ. Hence (1.) בְּדֵי i. q. בְּ. Job 39:25 בְּדֵי שׁוֹפָר for בְּשׁוֹפָר *among the trumpets.* Jer. 51: 58. Hab. 2:13. (2.) כְּדֵי i. q. כְּ. Deut. 25:2 כְּדֵי רִשְׁעָתוֹ *according to his fault.* Judg. 6:5 כְּדֵי־אַרְבֶּה *as the locusts.* (3.) מִדֵּי i. q. מִן 1 Sam. 7:16 מִדֵּי שָׁנָה בְּשָׁנָה *from year to year.* Zech. 14:16. Is. 66:23 מִדֵּי חֹדֶשׁ בְּחָדְשׁוֹ *from month to month.* When used before an infinitive, *so often as,* 1 Sam. 18:30 וַיְהִי מִדֵּי צֵאתָם *and it came to pass so often as they went forth.* Comp. 1:7. 1 K. 14:28 וַיְהִי מִדֵּי בֹא הַמֶּלֶךְ *and it happened, so often as the king came,* etc. Is. 28:19.—Jer. 20:8 מִדֵּי אֲדַבֵּר *since I spake.*

דִּי Chald. i. q. Heb. אֲשֶׁר. Syr. ܕ.) Etymologically related to the Hebrew demonst. זֶה.

1. pron. relative, indec. *who, which,* of both genders and numbers.—The Aramean often inserts דִּי in phrases, where the relative is usually omitted in Hebrew; as before the prepositions בְּ, מִן; e. g. הֵיכְלָא דִּי בִירוּשְׁלֶם *the temple which is in Jerusalem,* Dan 5:2. בְּבִירְתָא דִּי בְמָדַי *the citadel which is in Media,* Ezra 6:2. Dan. 6:14. especially 2:34. comp. Est. 1:12, with verse 15. This pronoun was used especially before the genitive, hence it became

2. a sign of the genitive case, (comp. אֲשֶׁר לְ.)—The preceding substantive stands then either in the absolute state; as נְהַר דִּי נוּר *a stream of fire,* Dan. 7:10. or in the emphatic state; as in Dan. 2: 15. or finally with a pleonastic suffix pronoun; as שְׁמֵהּ דִּי אֱלָהָא *God his name,* or *God's name,* Dan. 2:20. קַרְצֵיהוֹן דִּי יְהוּדָיֵא *accusations of the Jews,* 3:8. comp. 4:23. [26.] 6:25. The prefix לְ is placed before pronouns; as Dan. 2:20. דִּי חָכְמְתָא וּגְבוּרְתָא דִּי לֵהּ הִיא *for wisdom and might is his.* The following genitive sometimes denotes the material, out of which a thing is made; as Dan. 2:32 רֵאשֵׁהּ דִּי דְהַב טָב *his head of fine gold.* Ezra 6:4.

4. often (like אֲשֶׁר) merely a sign of relation.—דִּי תַמָּה *where,* Ezra 6:1. דִּי מְדָרְהוֹן *whose dwelling,* Dan. 2:11. דִּי אִנּוּן *who,* Dan. 7:17.

4. conj. *that, to the end that, ut.* Dan. 2:16, 18.

5. *that, quod.* Dan. 2:47.

6. *for, since.* Dan. 4:15. [18.]

7. redundant, like כִּי or ὅτι, in the beginning of a speech, Dan. 2:25 *and he said thus unto him:* דִּי הַשְׁכַּחַת גְּבַר *a man*

has been found, etc. verse 37. 5:7. 6: 6, 14.

8. compositions, as (1.) כְּדִי i. q. כַּאֲשֶׁר *when.* Dan. 3:7. 5:20. 6:11, 15. (2.) מִן־דִּי *from the time that, ex quo.* Dan. 4:23. [26.] Ezra 5:2. (3.) כָּל־, קֳבֵל־דִּי see קֳבֵל.

דִּי זָהָב (*possessor of gold,* i. e. a place rich in gold; comp. Arab. ذو and ذي *lord,* and בַּעַל no. 5.) proper name of a place in the desert, not far from mt. Sinai, probably so called from its abounding in gold. Deut. 1:1.

דִּיבוֹן name of a city in the country of Moab, afterwards in the tribe of Gad, but finally possessed again by the Moabites. Num. 32:3, 34. Josh. 13:9, 17. Is. 15:2. Jer. 48:18, 22. In Is. 15: 9, it is written דִּימוֹן, by a commutation of ם and ב.

דִּיג *to fish,* see דּוּג.

דַּיָּג m. verbal from דִּיג, dec. I. *fisher.* Is. 19:8. and Jer. 16:16 Keri.

דַּיָּה f. dec. I. Deut. 14:13. Is. 34: 15. name of some bird of prey which inhabits ruins. Sept. ἴκτινος. Vulg. *milvus.* C. V. *vulture.*

דְּיוֹ m. (analogous in form to פְּרִי, צְבִי,) *ink.* Once Jer. 36:18. (Aram. דְּיוֹתָא, ܕܝܘܬܐ *ink;* Arab. دواة, and Pers. دويت *inkstand.*) The Hebrews made use of various colours for writing, (Josephus J. A. XII. 2. 11.) but black (μέλαν) is expressly mentioned in the N. T. and has the analogy of other ancient nations in its favour. Comp. Lat. *atramentum.*

דִּימוֹן Is. 15:9. i. q. דִּיבוֹן proper name of a city of Moab, (q. v.)

דִּימוֹנָה Jos. 15:22. i. q. דִּיבוֹן Neh. 11:25. proper name of a city in the tribe of Judah.

דִּין, rarely דּוּן (q. v.) fut. יָדִין, pret. דָּן; for the most part in poetry, i. q. שָׁפַט. (Chald. דִּין, דּוּן, Syr. ܕܶܢ *to judge;* Arab. دان (med. Je) *to requite,* also *to judge.*)

1. *to judge.* Gen. 49:16 דָּן יָדִין עַמּוֹ *Dan judges his people.* Often spoken of God, as judge of nations, Ps. 7:9. 9:9. 50: 4. 72:2. 96:10. Is. 3:13.

2. *to manage, plead, or defend the cause of* any one, as an advocate; *to give* one *his right, to do* him *justice,* as a judge. Prov. 31:9 דִּין עָנִי וְאֶבְיוֹן *plead the cause of the afflicted and distressed.* Gen. 30:6 דָּנַנִּי אֱלֹהִים *God has done me justice.* Ps. 54:3 בִּגְבוּרָתְךָ תְדִינֵנִי *through thy power do me justice,* i. e. avenge me. Sometimes the expression is more full, Jer. 5:28. 22:16 דָּן דִּין עָנִי וְאֶבְיוֹן *he pleaded the cause of the afflicted and distressed.* 30:13. (Comp. שָׁפַט no. 2. and רִיב no. 2.)

3. *to pass sentence against* any one, *to punish.* Gen. 15:14 *the people whom they shall serve,* דָּן אָנֹכִי *I will punish.* Job 36:31. Construed with בְּ, Ps. 110:6.

4. construed with עִם, *to contend together,* i. q. Niphal. Ecc. 6:10.

5. *to rule, govern.* 1 Sam. 2:10. Zech. 3:7. Comp. דּוּן, and the deriv. אָדוֹן. *Judging* and *ruling* are closely connected in the languages, as well as in the political constitutions of the eastern nations. Comp. שָׁפַט; also Arab. حكم and دان *to rule,* also *to judge.*

Niph. נָדוֹן recip. *to contend together.* Once 2 Sam. 19:10. Comp. the synon. נִשְׁפַּט. (In Arab. حكم *to judge;* conj. III. VI. *to contend in law.*)

Deriv. מָדוֹן, מְדִינָה, מִדְיָן, מְדָנִים.

דִּין and **דּוּן** Chald. *idem.* Part. Ezra 7:25.

דִּין m. verbal from דִּין, dec. I. a.

1. *judgment, act of judging.* Ps. 79: 9.—כִּסֵּא דִין *throne of judgment,* Prov. 20:8.

2. *cause, right, matter in controversy.* Deut. 17:8 בֵּין דִּין לְדִין *between the right of one and of the other.* Prov. 29:7.—עָשָׂה דִין, i. q. דָּן דִּין *to defend the cause of* any one, Ps. 140:13. Est. 1:13 כָּל יֹדְעֵי דָּת וָדִין *all who know law and right.* In

Job 36: 17, דִּין is opposed to מִשְׁפָּט, as guilt to punishment.

3. *contention, quarrel.* Prov. 22:10.

דִּין Chald. 1. *judgment.* As a concrete, *those sitting at judgment, judges,* (i. q. Arab. دِيوَان *a divan* or *senate.*) Dan. 7:10 דִּינָא יְתִב *the judges were seated.* verse 26.

2. *righteousness, justice,* Dan. 4:34 [37] אֹרְחָתֵהּ דִּין *his ways are righteousness,* 7:22 וְדִינָא יְהִב לְקַדִּישֵׁי עֶלְיוֹנִין *and (till) justice was done to the saints of the Most High.*

3. *punishment.* Ezra 7:26 דִּינָה לֶהֱוֵא מִתְעֲבֵד מִנֵּהּ *let punishment be inflicted on him.*

דִּינָיֵא masc. plur. Chald. name of a people removed to Samaria by the Assyrians. Ezra 4:9.

דַּיָּן m. verbal from דִּין, dec. II. b.

1. *judge.* 1 Sam. 24:16.

2. *defender, advocate.* Ps. 68:6.

דַּיָּן Chald. *idem.* Ezra 7:25.

דִּיפַת 1 Chr. 1:6. instead of which רִיפַת stands in the parallel passage Gen. 10:3. Also, in the passage in Chronicles, several MSS. and the Sept. and Vulg. read רִיפַת (q. v.)

דָּיֵק m. prob. *a line of circumvallation, a wall thrown up round about a place besieged.* 2 K. 25:1. Jer. 52:4. Ezek. 4:2. 17:17. 21:27. [22.] 26:8. It is therefore always joined with בָּנָה *to build,* while סֹלְלָה *a mound,* which often occurs in the same connexion, is joined with שָׁפַךְ *to cast up.* (Root דּוּק i. q. Arab. دَاقَ (*med. Vau*) conj. IV. *to surround.*)

דִּישׁ i. q. דּוּשׁ *to thresh.* Deut. 25:4.

דַּיִשׁ m. verbal from דּוּשׁ, *threshing-time.* Lev. 26:5.

דִּישׁוֹן m. 1. a. species of gazel or antelope. Deut. 14:5. Sept. πύγαργος; C. V. *pygarg;* i. e. white buttocks, deriving the word perhaps from דֶּשֶׁן *ashes.* The Syr. and Chald. רִים, in like manner a species of gazel. The two Arabic translators الاروي a species of wild goat. The word is perhaps kindred with the Aram. דִּיצָא, ܪܝܡܐ, also denoting a species of gazel, from דּוּץ *to spring, to leap.* Comp. Bocharti Hieroz. edid. Rosenmüller. T. II. p. 270.

2. proper name of a son of Seir, and of a place in Idumea named from him. Gen. 36:21, 30. 1 Chr. 1:38.

3. also of a grandson of Seir. Gen. 36:25. 1 Chr. 1:41.

דַּךְ m. verbal adj. from דָּכָא=דָּכַךְ or דָּכָה, dec. VIII. h. *oppressed, afflicted, cast down, attritus.* Ps. 9:10. 10:18. 74:21. Prov. 26:28 לְשׁוֹן שֶׁקֶר יִשְׂנָא דַכָּיו *a false tongue hates those whom it will injure.* The word דַּךְ here signifies *atterendus,* and not *attritus,* which is its usual signification; the participles *amatus* and *amandus,* being expressed in Hebrew by the same form. Others make דַּכָּיו i. q. דַּכָּיו or דַּכָּא *the oppressed,* (comp. עָנָו, עָנָיו.) Others in an inverted order, *those who are injured by it, hate the false tongue;* which does not accord with the parallel clause.

דִּךְ m. Chald. pron. demon. *this.* Ezra 5:16, 17. 6:7, 8. Fem. דָּךְ, Ezra 4:15, 16, 18. 5:8. (In the Targums, דֵּךְ, דִּיכִי, דֵּיכִי, דֵּיךְ is used for the Heb. הוּא. It corresponds to the Arab. ذَاكَ, and is formed from the demonst. זֶה, by adding the suffix of second person; as in Arabic, ذا *this* gives rise not only to ذاك, but also to ذَلِكَ, and if several persons are addressed, ذَالكم.)

דָּכָא i. q. דָּכָה, דּוּךְ, and Arab. دَكَّ, *to be bruised.* In Kal not used.

Pi. דִּכָּא 1. *to bruise, break in pieces.* Ps. 72:4 וִידַכֵּא עוֹשֵׁק *and he (God) breaks in pieces the oppressor.* 89:11. 143:3. Job 6:9 וְיֹאֵל אֱלוֹהַּ וִידַכְּאֵנִי *and that God would please to break me in pieces.* Figuratively, Job 19:2 וּתְדַכְּאוּנַנִי בְמִלִּים *and* (*how long*) *will ye break me in pieces with words?*

2. *to tread down, to trample under foot.* Lam. 3:34. Hence, *to oppress,* Is. 3:15. Ps. 94:5. especially before a court, Prov. 22:22.

Niph. part. *depressed, humble, contrite.* Is. 57:15.

Pu. 1. *to be broken in pieces.* Job 22:9.

2. *to be bruised, smitten.* Is. 53:5.

3. *to be afflicted, humbled, sorrowful.* Jer. 44:10. Is. 19:10.

Hithpa. הִדַּכָּא pass. of Kal no. 2. Job 5:4. 34:25.

דַּכָּא verbal adj. from דָּכָא, dec. II. b.

1. *broken in pieces.* Ps. 90:3 תָּשֵׁב אֱנוֹשׁ עַד־דַּכָּא *thou lettest man return, till* (*he is*) *broken in pieces,* namely, as the dust.

2. *broken, contrite, humble.* Is. 57:15. Ps. 34:19 דַּכְּאֵי־רוּחַ *those of a contrite spirit.*

דָּכָה i. q. דָּכָא *to be bruised* or *crushed.* In Kal found only Ps. 10:10 Kethib וְדָכָה יָשֹׁחַ *and crushed he sinks to the ground.* (Others read וְדָכָה, which gives the same sense.) In the Keri, יִדְכֶּה in the future tense.

Pi. *to bruise, to break.* Ps. 44:20. 51:10 תָּגֵלְנָה עֲצָמוֹת דִּכִּיתָ *that* (*my*) *bones may rejoice,* (*which*) *thou hast broken,* namely, through a consciousness of guilt.

Niph. pass. Ps. 38:9 נְפוּגוֹתִי וְנִדְכֵּיתִי *I am feeble and broken.* 51:19 לֵב נִשְׁבָּר וְנִדְכֶּה *a broken and contrite heart.*

Deriv. out of course דֳּכִי.

דַּכָּה f. verbal from obs. דָּכַךְ, *bruising.* Deut. 23:2 פְּצוּעַ דַּכָּה *mutilated by bruising,* namely, of his testicles, which was one of the modes of castration. Vulg. *eunuchus attritis testiculis.* The Greeks called one castrated in this way θλαδίας, from θλάω, *to crush, bruise.*

דֳּכִי m. verbal from דָּכָה, dec. VI. q. *the dashing,* or *striking together* of waves. Hence, *raging, roaring,* Ps. 93:3 יִשְׂאוּ נְהָרוֹת דָּכְיָם *the floods increase their raging.* (In Arab. دكّا *to strike, to smite;* conj. VI. *to smite together;* and دَاكَ conj. VI. *to urge each other in the tumult of battle;* دَوْكَةٌ *contention, tumult.*)

דִּכֵּן Chald. i. q. דֵּךְ *this.* Dan. 2:31. 7:20.

דְּכַר, plur. דִּכְרִין, Chald. *ram.* Ezra 6:9, 17. 7:17. (Comp. Heb. זָכָר *male,* which in Chaldaic denotes, by way of eminence, *a ram;* also Greek ἄῤῥην *male,* which is etymologically connected with αἰγὴν, ἄρς, *aries,* all signifying *a ram.*)

דִּכְרוֹנָה f. Chald. *record, memoir,* ὑπόμνημα. Ezra 6:2. Root דְּכַר i. q. Heb. זָכַר *to remember.*

דָּכְרָן m. Chald. *idem.* Ezra 4:15 סְפַר דָּכְרָנַיָּא *the book of records,* i.e. annals or chronicles of the empire, composed by the historiographer (Heb. מַזְכִּיר).

I. **דַּל** m. prim. i. q. fem. דֶּלֶת *a door.* Ps. 141:3 נִצְּרָה עַל־דַּל שְׂפָתָי *watch over the door of my lips.* (comp. Mic. 7:5.) Sept. θύρα. Vulg. *ostium.*

II. **דַּל**, plur. דַּלִּים, verbal adj. from דָּלַל, dec. VIII. h.

1. *lean, meagre.* Gen. 41:19. 2 Sam. 13:4 מַדּוּעַ אַתָּה כָּכָה דַּל *why art thou so lean?*

2. *weak, without strength.* 2 Sam. 3:1. *David waxed stronger and stronger,* וּבֵית שָׁאוּל הֹלְכִים וְדַלִּים *and the house of Saul waxed weaker and weaker.* Judg. 6:15 אַלְפִּי הַדַּל בִּמְנַשֶּׁה *my family is the weakest in Manasseh.*

3. *low, poor, tenuis.* Ex. 23:3. Lev. 14:21. 19:15. 1 Sam. 2:8. Ruth 3:10. Ps. 41:2. 72:13. Prov. 10:15. 14:31. 19:4.

דָּלַג *to leap, spring.* In Kal once, Zeph. 1:9.

Pi. *idem.* Is. 35:6 אָז יְדַלֵּג כָּאַיָּל פִּסֵּחַ *then shall the lame man leap as an hart.* Construed with עַל, Cant. 2:8. with an accus. Ps. 18:30 בֵּאלֹהַי אֲדַלֶּג שׁוּר *with* (*the aid of*) *my God I leaped over walls.* (In Chald. *idem.*)

דָּלָה *to draw water.* (Arab. دَلَا and

دَلَى, Syr. ܕܠܳܐ idem.) Ex. 2:16, 19. Figuratively, Prov. 20:5 *counsel in the heart of a man is (as) deep water,* וְאִישׁ תְּבוּנָה יִדְלֶנָּה *yet a wise man will draw it out.*

Pi. 1. *to draw up* (out of a well), hence, figuratively, *to deliver, set free,* Ps. 30:2 אֲרוֹמִמְךָ כִּי דִלִּיתָנִי *I will exalt thee, for thou hast delivered me.*

2. prob. *to take away, tollere, auferre.* (Comp. in Lat. *haurire pectus, latus, ventrem,* in Virg. and Ov.) Prov. 26:7 דַּלְיוּ שֹׁקַיִם מִפִּסֵּחַ וּמָשָׁל בְּפִי כְסִילִים *take away legs from the lame man, and a proverb which is in the mouth of fools;* implying that both are equally useless to their possessors. דַּלְיוּ here stands for דַּלּוּ imper. Piel, the radical Yod being retained, as in תְּדַמְּיוּנִי Is. 40:25. (comp. Ps. 36:9. Is. 21:12, 14.) Sept. ἀφελοῦ πορείαν σκελῶν.

Deriv. out of course דְּלִי, דֳּלִי.

דְּלָת dec. XI. a. i. q. דֶּלֶת *a door.* Is. 26:20 Keri.

דַּלָּה f. verbal from דָּלַל, dec. X.

1. *fine threads,* particularly *the thrums which unite the web to the beam,* Is. 38:12 מִדַּלָּה יְבַצְּעֵנִי *from the thrums of the web he has cut me off.* (Chald. דְּלִיל *a thread, something made of threads.*)

2. *head of hair.* Cant. 7:6. Vulg. *coma capitis.* (Comp. דָּלַל no. 4.)

3. *lowness, poverty.* As a concrete, *low* or *poor people,* 2 K. 24:14 דַּלַּת עַם־הָאָרֶץ *the poorer people of the land.* 25:12. In the plur. דַּלּוֹת הָעָם Jer. 52:15. and דַּלּוֹת הָאָרֶץ verse 16. *idem.*

דָּלַח *to trouble* or *disturb water with the feet,* Ezek. 32:2, 13. (Syr. ܕܠܰܚ *idem.*)

דְּלִי m. verbal from דָּלָה, *a vessel* or *bag to draw water with, a water-bucket.* Is. 40:15. (Arab. دَلْو.)

דֳּלִי m. verbal from דָּלָה, dec. VI. q. *idem.* Num. 24:7 יִזַּל מַיִם מִדָּלְיָו *water flows from his buckets.* דָּלְיָו is either from a dual דָּלְיַיִם, or from a plural formed like עֳפָרִים.

דָּלִיּוֹת plur. fem. (with Kamets impure) *boughs, branches.* Jer. 11:16. Ezek. 17:6, 23. 31:7, 9, 12. (Syr. ܕܳܠܺܝܬܳܐ *idem.* Arab. דלה conj. V. تَدَلَّى *to hang down,* spoken of the branches of a tree.)

דְּלִילָה f. (*weak, languishing*) proper name of a Philistine woman, beloved of Samson. Judg. 16:4—18.

דָּלַל pret. דַּל, דַּלּוֹתִי, and דָּלְלוּ.

1. *to be exhausted, emptied.* Is. 19:6 דָּלְלוּ וְחָרְבוּ יְאֹרֵי מָצוֹר *the streams of Egypt shall be exhausted and dried up.*

2. *to be brought low, to be afflicted, distressed.* Ps. 79:8. 116:6. 142:7.

3. spoken of the eyes, *to long* or *languish after* any thing. Is. 38:14 דַּלּוּ עֵינַי לַמָּרוֹם *mine eyes languished for heaven.* Comp. דָּלָה.

4. connected with signif. no. 1. *to hang down.* (Chald. דקן מדולדל *a beard hanging down;* Arab. دَلِّى conj. V. *deorsum pependit.* In Hebrew, compare דָּלָה and דָּלִיּוֹת.) Hence spoken of miners who let themselves down into the shaft of a mine, Job 28:4 דַּלּוּ מֵאֱנוֹשׁ נָעוּ *they descend, they remove from men.*

Niph. pass. of Kal no. 1. Judg. 6:6 וַיִּדַּל יִשְׂרָאֵל מְאֹד מִפְּנֵי מִדְיָן *and Israel was exceedingly impoverished before the Midianites.* (comp. 2 Sam. 3:1.) Is. 17:4.

Deriv. דַּל, דַּלָּה.

דָּלַף, fut. יִדְלֹף. 1. *to drip, to have drops falling from it,* spoken of a house. Ecc. 10:18 יִדְלֹף הַבָּיִת *the house drips,* i. e. it lets in the rain through the leaky roof. See דֶּלֶף.

2. *to flow in tears, to weep,* spoken of the eye. Job 16:20 אֶל אֱלוֹהַּ דָּלְפָה עֵינִי *mine eye weeps unto God.* Ps. 119:28 דָּלְפָה נַפְשִׁי *my soul weeps.*

In Aram. *idem;* in Arab. دَلَفَ *to move slowly, to creep;* conj. VII. *to be poured out, to flow.* Comp. רבב.

דֶּלֶף m. verbal from דָּלַף, *the dropping of rain from a roof.* Prov. 19:13. 27:15.

דָּלַק, fut. יִדְלֹק. 1. *to burn.* (In Aram.

idem.) Obad. 18. Ps. 7:14 חִצָּיו לְדֹלְקִים יִפְעָל *he makes his arrows burning*, i.e. he shoots burning arrows. Prov. 26:23 שְׂפָתַיִם דֹּלְקִים *burning lips*, i.e. lips making warm professions.

2. construed with אַחֲרֵי, *to burn after, to pursue ardently* or *hotly*. Gen. 31:36 כִּי דָלַקְתָּ אַחֲרָי *that thou pursuest hotly after me.* 1 Sam. 17:53. Construed with an accusative in the same sense, Lam. 4:19 עַל הֶהָרִים דְּלָקֻנוּ *they pursued us upon the mountains.*

3. figuratively, *to be filled with anguish*, inasmuch as violent anguish is compared with heat, (comp. Is. 13:8. Ps. 39:4.) Ps. 10:2 בְּגַאֲוַת רָשָׁע יִדְלַק עָנִי *through the arrogance of the wicked, the afflicted man is filled with anguish.*

Hiph. 1. *to kindle.* Ezek. 24:10.

2. *to heat, inflame.* Is. 5:11.

דְּלַק Chald. *to burn.* Dan. 7:9.

דַּלֶּקֶת f. verbal from דָּלַק, *burning fever.* Deut. 28:22.

דֶּלֶת fem. of דַּל (q. v.) with suff. דַּלְתִּי, *a door, gate.* Cant. 8:9 אִם דֶּלֶת הִיא *if she be a door*, i. e. if she be open to honourable proposals.

Dual דְּלָתַיִם, const. דַּלְתֵי, (as if from the form דְּלָה;) *double doors, folding doors, fores*, also *doors* generally. Deut. 3:5. Figuratively, Job 3:10 דַּלְתֵי בִטְנִי *the doors of my mother's womb.* 41:5 [13] דַּלְתֵי פָנָיו *the doors of his* (*the crocodile's*) *face*, i. e. his ravenous jaws. 38:8 *he shut up the sea with doors*; comp. verse 10.

Plur. דְּלָתוֹת (the ת being treated as if radical,) fem. (masc. Neh. 13:19.) const. דַּלְתוֹת.

1. *doors, gates.* Judg. 3:23—25. 19:27. Ezek. 26:2 נִשְׁבְּרָה דַּלְתוֹת הָעַמִּים *she is broken, the gates of the nations*, i. e. Jerusalem, where the nations assembled.

2. *leaves* or *folds of a door.* 1 K. 6:31 וְאֵת פֶּתַח הַדְּבִיר עָשָׂה דַּלְתוֹת עֲצֵי־שָׁמֶן *and for the door of the most holy place he made leaves of olive wood.* Ezek. 41:24 וּשְׁתַּיִם דְּלָתוֹת לַדְּלָתוֹת *and two leaves to the doors*, i. e. to each door.

3. *lid* of a chest. 2 K. 12:10.

4. *leaf* or *column of a roll* or *book.* Jer. 36:23.

I. דָּם m. prim. const. דַּם, with suff. דָּמוֹ, דִּמְכֶם (Gen. 9:5.) dec. II. a.

1. *blood.*—אָכַל עַל הַדָּם *to eat* (*flesh*) *with the blood*, 1 Sam. 14:32 ff. Ezek. 33:25. (a violation of the Mosaic law, Lev. 17:11. Deut. 12:23.) דָּם נָקִי *innocent blood*, 2 K. 21:16. Ps. 106:38. also *the innocent person himself*, Ps. 94:21 וְדָם נָקִי יַרְשִׁיעוּ *they condemn innocent blood.* Instead of this phrase we find frequently דַּם נָקִי *blood of the innocent*, Deut. 19:10, 13. 27:25. Jer. 19:4. 22:17.—דַּם עֵנָב, עֲנָבִים *blood of grapes*, poetically for (*red*) *wine*, Gen. 49:11. Deut. 32:14. Plur. *idem.*—אִישׁ דָּמִים *a blood-thirsty man*, Ps. 5:7. 26:9.

2. *bloodshed, murder, bloodguiltiness.* Gen. 37:26. Lev. 17:4 דָּם יֵחָשֵׁב לָאִישׁ הַהוּא *as bloodguiltiness it shall be imputed to that man.* 19:16 לֹא תַעֲמֹד עַל דַּם רֵעֶךָ *thou shalt not stand up against the blood*, i. e. the life, *of thy neighbour.* Deut. 17:8 בֵּין דָּם לְדָם *between bloodguiltiness and bloodguiltiness.* Numb. 35:27 אֵין לוֹ דָּם *he has no bloodguiltiness.* Plur. *idem.*—בַּיִת, עִיר דָּמִים, *house, city, on which rests the guilt of bloodshed*, 2 Sam. 21:1. Ezek. 22:2. 24:6, 9. דָּמָיו בּוֹ *his bloodguiltiness is upon him*, Lev. 20:9. Ezek. 18:13. דְּמֵיהֶם בָּם *their bloodguiltiness is upon them*, Lev. 20:11 ff.

II. דָּם or דַּם verbal from דָּמָה no. I. *similarity, likeness.* Ezek. 19:10 בְּדָמְךָ *after thy likeness.* So among the older translators the Chald. and Jarchi.

I. דָּמָה (Aram. דְּמָא, ܕܡܐ,) *to be like, to resemble*; construed with לְ or אֶל. Ps. 102:7. 144:4. Ezek. 31:2, 8, 18. Cant. 2:9. 7:8. To the imperative a pleonastic dative of the pronoun is sometimes joined, Cant. 2:17 דְּמֵה לְךָ דוֹדִי לִצְבִי *be thou like, my beloved, to the gazelle.* 8:14.

Niph. *to be made like*; construed with בְּ, Ps. 49:13, 21. with an acc. Ezek. 32:2.

Pi. דִּמָּה 1. *to liken, compare.* Cant.

1:9. Is. 40:18, 25. 46:5. Lam. 2:13 מָה אֲדַמֶּה לָּךְ *what shall I liken to thee?*

2. *to imagine, conceive, think.* Ps. 50:21 דִּמִּיתָ הֱיוֹת־אֶהְיֶה כָמוֹךָ *thou thoughtest, I was altogether as thyself.* Est. 4:13. Is. 10:7.

3. *to think, intend, purpose.* Num. 33:56. Judg. 20:5 אֹתִי דִּמּוּ לַהֲרֹג *they intended to kill me.* Is. 14:24.

4. *to think of, to make mention of.* Ps. 48:10 דִּמִּינוּ אֱלֹהִים חַסְדֶּךָ *we make mention, O God, of thy grace.*

Hithpa. 1. pers. sing. fut. אֶדַּמֶּה Is. 14:14. *to liken one's self.*

Deriv. דָּם no. II. דְּמוּת, דִּמְיוֹן.

II. **דָּמָה** i. q. דָּמַם no. II. *to destroy.* Hos. 4:5 דָּמִיתִי אִמֶּךָ *I will destroy thy mother,* i. e. thy metropolis. Jer. 6:2 *O fair and delicate (damsel,)* דָּמִיתִי בַּת צִיּוֹן *I destroy the daughter of Zion,* i. e. I announce to thee destruction. (The noun itself is here repeated instead of the pronoun; comp. Is. 5:1. Ps. 45:6.)

Niph. *to be destroyed, to perish;* spoken of persons, Hos. 10:15 בַּשַּׁחַר נִדְמֹה נִדְמָה מֶלֶךְ יִשְׂרָאֵל *in the morning the king of Israel shall utterly be destroyed.* Is. 6:5. אוֹי לִי כִּי נִדְמֵיתִי *wo is me, for I perish.* of a people, Zeph. 1:11. Hos. 4:6. of cities, countries, Is. 15:1. Jer. 47:5. Hos. 10:7. (All these examples are in the preterite, the fut. יִדַּמּוּ, תִּדַּמּוּ is formed in Niphal from דָּמַם no. II.)

Pi. דִּמָּה *to destroy.* Hos. 12:11 בְּיַד הַנְּבִיאִים אֲדַמֶּה *by the hand of the prophets I destroy,* i. e. announce destruction. Construed with לְ, 2 Sam. 21:5.

III. **דָּמָה** i. q. דָּמַם no. I. *to be quiet or still, to rest, cease.* Jer. 14:17 *mine eyes shall run down with tears night and day,* וְאַל תִּדְמֶינָה *and shall not cease.* Lam. 3:49 עֵינִי נִגְּרָה וְלֹא תִדְמֶה *mine eye flows in tears and ceases not.* Deriv. דֳּמִי *rest.* דְּמִי *the standing still (of the sun,) midday.* (דּוּמִיָּה *rest?*)

דְּמָה Chald. *to be like.* Dan. 3:25. 7:5.

דֻּמָּה f. verbal from דָּמַם, found only Ezek. 27:32. prob. *destruction,* but in this passage *the destroyed (city.)*

דְּמוּת f. (Syr. ܕܡܘܬܐ) verbal from דָּמָה no. I. dec. I.

1. *image, likeness.* Gen. 1:26 כִּדְמוּתֵנוּ *after our likeness.* 5:1, 3 *he begat a son* בִּדְמוּתוֹ כְּצַלְמוֹ *after his image and likeness.* 2 Chr. 4:3 דְּמוּת בְּקָרִים *images of oxen,* i. e. carved, molten oxen. Is. 40:18 מַה־דְּמוּת תַּעַרְכוּ לוֹ *what likeness will ye compare to him?*

2. *model, pattern, copy.* 2 K. 16:10.

3. *form.* Ezek. 1:16 דְּמוּת אֶחָד לְאַרְבַּעְתָּן *all four had one form.* In Ezekiel the indefinite language of vision is often denoted by this word in different combinations, 1:5 וּמִתּוֹכָהּ דְּמוּת אַרְבַּע חַיּוֹת *and therein was the form of four animals,* i. e. something like four animals. verse 26 דְּמוּת כִּסֵּא *something like a throne.* verse 28. 8:2. 10:1, 21. Dan. 10:16. Sometimes מַרְאֶה is added besides.

4. as an adv. *as, like as.* Is. 13:4.—כִּדְמוּת *idem,* Ps. 58:5.

דְּמִי m. *rest* or *standing still* of the sun, (verbal from דָּמָה no. III. i. q. דָּמַם no. I. 4. דּוּם and Arab. دوم spoken of the apparent rest of the sun at noon;) hence *noon* or *mid-day.* Is. 38:10 בִּדְמִי יָמַי *the mid-day of my life.* Sept. ἐν τῷ ὕψει τῶν ἡμερῶν μου. Vulg. *in dimidio dierum meorum.*

דֳּמִי m. verbal from דָּמָה no. III. *rest, quietness, inactivity, silence.* Ps. 83:2 אֱלֹהִים אַל דֳּמִי לָךְ *O God, be not quiet,* i. e. behold not our sufferings quietly or without relieving them; (comp. חָרַשׁ, חָשָׁה.) Is. 62:6, 7.

דִּמְיוֹן m. i. q. דְּמוּת verbal from דָּמָה no. I. dec. I. *likeness, resemblance.* Ps. 17:12.

I. **דָּמַם**, pret. דַּמּוּ, imper. and infin. דֹּם, fut. יִדֹּם, plur. יִדְּמוּ (with Chaldaic inflection,) i. q. דָּמָה no. III.

1. *to be silent, to hold one's peace.* Lev. 10:3. Lam. 3:28. Ezek. 24:17 הֵאָנֵק דֹּם *sigh in silence;* Vulg. *ingemisce tacens.* Job 29:21 וְיִדְּמוּ לְמוֹ עֲצָתִי *they were silent to my counsel,* i. e. they listened to it in silence.

2. *to be struck dumb*, from amazement or pain. Ex. 15:16 בִּגְדֹל זְרוֹעֲךָ יִדְּמוּ כָּאָבֶן *through the greatness of thy might they shall be struck dumb as a stone.* (comp. Hab. 2:19 אֶבֶן דּוּמָם *a motionless stone.*) Is. 23:2 דֹּמּוּ יֹשְׁבֵי אִי *be dumb,* (from terror or amazement,) *ye inhabitants of the isle.* Lam. 2:10 יֵשְׁבוּ לָאָרֶץ יִדְּמוּ זִקְנֵי בַת־צִיּוֹן *the elders of Zion sit upon the ground in silent pain.*

3. *to rest, to be quiet, to keep still.* Ps. 4:5. 1 Sam. 14:9. Job 31:34. Lam. 2:18 אַל תִּדֹּם בַּת עֵינֵךְ *let not the apple of thine eye rest,* i. e. let it not cease to weep. Job 30:27 מֵעַי רֻתְּחוּ וְלֹא דָמּוּ *my bowels were in commotion and rested not.*

4. *to stand still.* Josh. 10:12 שֶׁמֶשׁ בְּגִבְעוֹן דּוֹם *O sun, stand still in Gibeon.* verse 13 וַיִּדֹּם הַשֶּׁמֶשׁ *and the sun stood still.*

5. דָּמַם לַיהוָֹה *to submit quietly to Jehovah, to hope patiently in him.* Ps. 37:7. 62:6. (comp. דּוּמִיָּה.)

Po. דּוֹמֵם *to command silence, to quiet, compose.* Ps. 131:2.

Deriv. דְּמָמָה, and (as if formed from דּוּם,) דּוּמָה, דּוּמָם.

II. דָּמַם i. q. דָּמָה no. II. *to destroy, lay waste.* In Kal not used.

Niph. נָדַם, plur. נָדַמּוּ (Jer. 25:37.) fut. יִדַּם also תִּדֹּמִּי (Jer. 48:2.) *to be destroyed, to perish,* spoken of persons, 1 Sam. 2:9 רְשָׁעִים בַּחֹשֶׁךְ יִדָּמּוּ *the wicked perish in darkness.* Jer. 49:26. 50:30. 51:6. *to be laid waste,* spoken of countries, Jer. 25:37. 48:2. Here we may place also Jer. 8:14 *let us enter into the defenced cities,* וְנִדְּמָה שָׁם *and there perish,* i. e. wait for destruction. (נִדְּמָה stands here for נִדַּמָּה.)

Hiph. הֵדַם *to destroy.* Jer. 8:14.

Note. The signification of דָּמַם no. II. may, perhaps, be derived from that of דָּמַם no. I. For the idea of *resting, being still,* naturally leads to that of *being uncultivated, desolate, waste.* Compare the articles שָׁמֵם, שָׁבַת, and שָׁאָה. In the same way דָּמָה nos. II. and III. may be connected. See Gesen. Auszug, Vorrede, s. VII.

דְּמָמָה f. verbal from דָּמַם no. I. *a silent* or *gentle breeze.* 1 K. 19:12. Ps. 107:29. Job 4:16 דְּמָמָה וָקוֹל אֶשְׁמָע *a gentle breeze and a voice I heard.*

דֹּמֶן m. *dung.* (Arab. دمن and دمان.) 2 K. 9:37. Jer. 8:2. 16:4. 25:33.

דָּמַע *to weep, shed tears.* Jer. 13:17. (In Aram. and Arab. *idem.*) Hence,

דֶּמַע m. verbal from דָּמַע, dec. VI. i. *a tear;* hence figuratively, *the juice of pressed grapes and olives, wine and oil.* Ex. 22:28.

דִּמְעָה fem. of דֶּמַע, dec. XII. b. *a tear,* and collect. *tears.* Ps. 6:7. 39:13. 56:9. 80:6. The phrase frequent in Jeremiah, תֵּרֵד עֵינִי דִּמְעָה *mine eye flows down in tears,* will be found explained under the art. יָרַד.

דַּמֶּשֶׂק, Arab. دمشق, Syr. ܕܪܡܣܘܩ, (comp. דַּרְמֶשֶׂק, 1 Chr. 18:5,6.) a proper name.

1. *Damascus,* one of the principal cities in Syria, situated on the river Chrysorrhoas, in an extensive and pleasant plain below mt. Antilibanus; hence called by the Orientalists the earthly paradise. It is mentioned in the history of Abraham, Gen. 14:15. 15:2; was conquered by David, 2 Sam. 8:6, but made itself independent again under king Solomon, 1 K. 11:24, 25.

2. *an inhabitant of Damascus, a Damascene.* Gen. 15:2. Here is an ellipsis of אִישׁ; comp. כְּנַעַן *a Canaanite,* Hos. 12:7.

דְּמֶשֶׁק (in other MSS. דְּמֶשֶׂק and דַּמֶּשֶׂק) Am. 3:12. a kind of cloth, *silk tapestry;* either derived, with some alteration, from the proper name דַּמֶּשֶׂק *Damascus,* where the cloth was perhaps first manufactured, as is the English word, *damask,* Ital. *damasco;* or from the Arab. دمسق, دمشق, and دمقس *silk, silk cloth.* The last word, however, appears to be of Persian origin, from دم

a thread, and قز or قَزّ *silk;* and such words are rare in the Hebrew writers before the exile.

דָּן (*judge*) a proper name.

1. a son of Jacob; also the tribe named from him, the boundaries of which are given Josh. 19:40—48.

2. a city on the northern boundary of Palestine, at first called לַיִשׁ. Gen. 14: 14. Josh. 19:47. Judg. 18:29.

דֵּן com. gen. emph. דְּנָה, Chald. pron. demon. i. q. זֶה, זאת *this.* Dan. 2:18, 28, 30, 36, 43, 47.—כִּדְנָה *as this, thus, such,* Ezra 5:7 כִּדְנָה כְתִיב *it was written thus.* Jer. 10:11. Dan. 2:10 מִלָּה כִדְנָה *such a thing.*—עַל דְּנָה *on this account,* Dan. 3: 16. Ezra 4:14, 15. בָּאתַר, אַחֲרֵי דְנָה *upon this, after this,* Dan. 2:29. 7:6, 7. (In the Targums, we find the more usual דֵּין, הָדֵין, הָדֵין for זֶה *this;* and כְּדֵין *thus.*)

דִּנְהָבָה proper name of an Idumean city. Gen. 36:32. 1 Chr. 1:43.

דָּנִיֵּאל m. (*judge of God*) proper name of a Hebrew prophet and wise man, who lived in the Chaldean court at Babylon. Dan. 1:6. Also written דָּנִאֵל Ezek. 14:14, 20. 28:38.

דֵּעַ m. dec. VII. f. strictly infin. of יָדַע but in use only as a subst. *opinion.* Job 32:10 אֲחַוֶּה דֵעִי אַף אָנִי *I also will show my opinion.* verses 6, 17. 36:3. Plur. תְּמִים דֵּעִים *perfect in wisdom,* Job 37:16.

דֵּעָה fem. of דֵּעַ, dec. X. *knowledge;* governing an acc. Is. 11:9 דֵּעָה אֶת־יְהוָה *knowledge of Jehovah.* It also occurs 28:9. Ps. 73:11. Job 36:4.

דְּעָה Prov. 24:14. imper. from יָדַע, with paragogic ה. Hence כֵּן דְּעֶה חָכְמָה לְנַפְשֶׁךָ *so* (*as honey*) *know,* i. e. mayest thou experience, *wisdom to thy soul.*

דָּעַךְ (Syr. ܕܥܟ) 1. *to be extinguished, to go out.* Is. 43:17. נֵר רְשָׁעִים יִדְעָךְ *the lamp of the wicked goeth out,* Prov. 13:9. 24:20. Job 21:17. comp. 18:5, 6. Prov. 20:20. (Similar to this, the Arabians have a proverb: *adverse fortune has extinguished my light,* i. e. it has destroyed my happiness and my hopes.)

2. *to dry up,* spoken of water; as in Latin, *exstinguere aquam,* Liv. v. 16. comp. Curt. vi. 4.

Niph. pass. Job 6:17 בְּחֻמּוֹ נִדְעֲכוּ מִמְּקוֹמָם *through the heat they dry up from their place.*

Pu. *to be put out, extinguished,* spoken of enemies. Ps. 118:12.

דַּעַת f. infin. of יָדַע, (like דֵּעַ and דֵּעָה.)

1. *knowledge, act of knowing;* sometimes governing an accus. Jer. 22:16 הַדַּעַת אֹתִי *the knowledge of me,* or *to know me.*— דַּעַת אֱלֹהִים *knowledge* or *reverence of God,* Hos. 4:1. 6:6. בִּבְלִי דַעַת *without knowing it, unawares,* Deut. 4:42. 19: 4. Josh. 20:5.

2. *understanding, intelligence, wisdom,* i. q. תְּבוּנָה, חָכְמָה. Prov. 1:4. 2:6. 24:5. etc.—בִּבְלִי דַעַת *without knowledge, foolishly,* Job 34:35. 35:12, 16. 38:2. 42:3. יָדַע דַּעַת *to possess wisdom,* Prov. 17:27.

דָּפִי, in pause דֹּפִי, m. found only Ps. 50:20. i. q. דִּבָּה רָעָה *slander,* according to the Jewish commentators, but perhaps merely as a conjecture from the parallel clause. The root דָּפָה i. q. Arab. دفا, دفي, signifies *to push, thrust, wound,* also *to kill;* whence the sense *destruction* may be derived.

דָּפַק 1. *to drive,* here *to drive too hard, to urge on too violently,* as cattle. Gen. 33:13.

2. *to knock* (at a door.) Cant. 5:2.

Hithpa. i. q. Kal no. 2. Judg. 19:22.

דָּפְקָה proper name of a station of the Israelites in the desert. Num. 33: 12. Seetzen found there a place called *El Tobbacha.*

דַּק, fem. דַּקָּה, verbal adj. from דָּקַק.

1. *small, fine,* spoken of dust. Is. 29: 5 אָבָק דַּק *fine dust.* Lev. 16:12. Hence, *something small* or *like dust, dust itself,* Ex. 16:14. Is. 40:15.

2. *fine, thin, lean.* Lev. 13:30 שֵׂעָר דַּק *thin hair.* Gen. 41:3 *kine lean in flesh.* verses 4, 6 *thin ears.* verse 7.—

Lev. 21:20 *thin, consumptive*, or perhaps *having a withered limb.*

3. *light, gentle.* 1 K. 19:12 דְּמָמָה דַקָּה *a gentle breeze.*

דֹּק m. verbal from דָּקַק *thinness, something thin;* hence, *a fine thin garment*, Is. 40:22.

דִּקְלָה f. found only Gen. 10:27. proper name of a country in Joktanitish Arabia, of which nothing farther is known. Bochart compares the Arab. دَقَل, Syr. ܕܩܠܐ *a palm-tree*, and supposes it to denote *a country rich in palms*, of which there are many in Arabia. Equally uncertain is the comparison of the Syr. ܕܩܠܬ, *the Tigris*, as if it meant a country on the Tigris.

דָּקַק, pret. דַּק, fut. יָדֹק. (In Arab. دَقّ.)

1. *to be broken in pieces, to be small, fine.* Ex. 32:20 וַיִּטְחַן עַד אֲשֶׁר דָּק *and he ground (it) till it was fine* (as dust). Deut. 9:21.

2. trans. *to bruise in pieces, to beat small.* Is. 41:15 תָּדוּשׁ הָרִים וְתָדֹק *thou threshest the mountains and beatest them small.* 28:28.

Hiph. הֵדַק *to stamp* or *beat small.* 2 K. 23:15 *the altar* הֵדַק לְעָפָר *he stamped to dust.* verse 6. 2 Chr. 15:16. 34:4, 6. Infin. הָדֵק used adverbially, *fine* (as dust), Ex. 30:36. Figuratively, Mic. 4:13 *thou beatest in pieces many nations.* Infin. הָדֵק, 2 Chr. 34:7. Fut. with suff. אֲדִקֵּם, 2 Sam. 22:43.

Hoph. pass. Is. 28:28.

Deriv. דַּק, דֹּק.

דְּקַק Chald. *to be broken in pieces.* In Peal only דָּקוּ Dan. 2:35, which borrows its form from דּוּק.

Aph. הַדֵּק *to break in pieces.* 3 pers. pret. fem. הַדֶּקֶת Dan. 2:34, 45. fut. תַּדִּק, יַדִּק; part. מְהַדֵּק, fem. מַדְּקָה, Dan. 7:7, 19.

דָּקַר *to thrust through, to pierce, stab*, as with a sword or spear. (In Aram. *idem.*) Num. 25:8. Judg. 9:54. 1 Sam. 31:4.

Niph. pass. Is. 13:15.

Pu. *idem.* Jer. 37:10. 51:4. Lam. 4:9 *the slain with the sword are better than the slain with hunger,* שֶׁהֵם יָזוּבוּ מְדֻקָּרִים מִתְּנוּבֹת שָׂדָי *who pined away, being slain, because the fruits of the field failed.* מְדֻקָּרִים *pierced through* is here applied by a bold metaphor to those who are killed by hunger, as in the first member of the verse חַלְלֵי רָעָב is put in opposition to חַלְלֵי־חֶרֶב. מִ denotes defect. Vulg. *contabuerunt consumpti a sterilitate terræ.* Others apply here the signification of the Arab. دقر *to be nourished, pampered;* and render the passage thus, *for those* (*the slain by the sword*) *bled, being nourished by the fruits of the earth;* but in accordance neither with the parallel phrase חַלְלֵי רָעָב, nor with the Hebrew use of this participle.

דַּר m. found only Est. 1:6. i.q. Arab. دُرّ, دُرَّة *a pearl*, especially *one of a large size.* Bochart, (Hieroz. II. 708 ff.) from the accounts of Asiatic luxury, brings examples to show that pearls, as here דַּר, were actually inlaid in pavements. But on account of its connexion in this place with other stones, it means perhaps only *a pearl-like stone,* (Sept. πίννινος λίθος *pearl stone,*) as also in German a species of alabaster goes by the name of *Perlenmutterstein*, perhaps of *Perlenmutter.*

דָּר Chald. i.q. דּוֹר *age, generation.* Dan. 3:33. [4:3.] 4:31. [4:34.]

דֹּר see דּוֹר.

דֵּרָאוֹן m. dec. III. d. *detestation, disgrace, contempt.* Dan. 12:2 *these to shame,* לְדִרְאוֹן עוֹלָם *to everlasting disgrace.* (Root. דרא i.q. Arab. درأ *to repel, drive away,* especially an evil.) Theod. αἰσχύνη. Syr. ܚܣܕܐ.

דֵּרָאוֹן m. Is. 66:24. *idem*, or rather *the object of abhorrence* or *detestation.* From the same root.

דָּרְבוֹנָה f. dec. X. Ecc. 12:11. *goad, sting.* Root. דָּרַב i.q. Arab. ذَرِب *to be sharp, pointed.*

דָּרְבָן *an ox goad, stimulus,* βούκεντρον. 1 Sam. 13:21.

דַּרְדַּע proper name of a wise man contemporary with Solomon, 1 K. 5:11. [4:31.] called דָּרַע in the parallel passage 1 Chr. 2:6.

דַּרְדַּר m. *thorn, thistle, tribulus;* perhaps a particular species of the same. Gen. 3:18. Hos. 10:8. (Syr. ܕܪܕܪܐ used for the Greek τρίβολος in N. T. Arab. دردر *idem.* Root perhaps در *to flow abundantly,* also, *to grow exuberantly,* spoken of herbs.

דָּרוֹם m. of uncertain derivation.

1. *the south,* or *south country.* Ezek. 40:24 ff. 42:12 ff. Ecc. 1:6.

2. *the south wind.* Job 37:17.

דְּרוֹר 1. *freedom, deliverance,* (found only in Hebrew.)—קָרָא דְרוֹר לְ *to announce freedom* or *deliverance to* any one, Is. 61:1. Jer. 34:8, 15, 17. Lev. 25:10. —שְׁנַת הַדְּרוֹר *the year of deliverance* (to slaves,) i. e. the year of jubilee, Ezek. 46:17.—מָר־דְּרוֹר *myrrh flowing spontaneously,* Ex. 30:23.

2. Ps. 84:4. Prov. 26:2. name of a bird, (צִפּוֹר *the sparrow* stands in the parallel clause of both passages,) probably according to the Jewish commentators, *the swallow,* (perhaps so called from its flying freely.) According to the versions, *turtle dove,* (probably from its similarity with תֹּר,) but less suitably.

דָּרְיָוֶשׁ *Darius,* the common name of several Persian kings. In Persian we find دارا and داراب (dara, darab,) *a king;* (see the art. אֲדַרְכֹּן.) The ground of the Hebrew name probably lies in the Pers. داريش daraweseh (with a suffix שׁ,) which appears to have been known to Strabo, (L. XVI. p. 785. or § 27. fin.) who mentions as the original form Δαριαυης, or, as Salmasius conjectures it should be written, Δαριαυης, B and K being easily mistaken in writing. The O. T. mentions three kings of this name, (1.) *Darius, the Mede,* or *Cyaxares* II. Dan. 6:1. 9:1. (2.) *Darius, the son of Hystaspes.* Ezra 4: 5. 5:5. Hagg. 1:1. Zech. 1:1. (3.) *Darius Nothus.* Neh. 12:22.

דַּרְיוֹשׁ probably a corrupt reading for דְּרוֹשׁ *to search, examine,* Ezra 10: 16.

דָּרַךְ, fut. יִדְרֹךְ, *to tread, to tread on;* construed with an accus. Job 22:15. Judg. 5:21 תִּדְרְכִי נַפְשִׁי עֹז *O my soul, thou hast trodden on the mighty.* with עַל, Ps. 91:13. 1 Sam. 5:5. with בְּ, Mic. 5:4 כִּי יִדְרֹךְ בְּאַרְמְנֹתֵינוּ *when he shall tread our palaces.* Is. 59:8. Deut. 11:24, 25. Josh. 1:3. 14:9. When construed with מִן, *to step forth, to arise,* Num. 24: 17. Especially (1.) דָּרַךְ יֶקֶב Job 24:11. or גַּת, גִּתָּה Lam. 1:15. Is. 63:2. *to tread the wine-press;* also דָּרַךְ יַיִן בַּיְקָבִים Is. 16: 10 and simply דָּרַךְ Judg. 9:27. Jer. 25: 30. *idem.*—דָּרַךְ זַיִת *to tread olives,* Mic. 6:15. Metaphorically, *to tread down* or *destroy* one's enemies, Is. 63:3. (2.) דָּרַךְ קֶשֶׁת *to bend* or *stretch the bow,* namely, by resting it on the ground, and treading on it. Ps. 7:13. 11:3. 37:14. 1 Chr. 5:18. 8:40. 2 Chr. 14:8. Is. 5:28. Also, in an improper sense, דָּרַךְ חִצִּים Ps. 58:8. 64:4. *to stretch the arrows.*

Hiph. 1. *to cause to tread* or *walk.* Is. 11:15. construed with בְּ, Ps. 107: 7 וַיַּדְרִיכֵם בְּדֶרֶךְ יְשָׁרָה *and he caused them to walk,* i. e. he led them, *the right way.* 119:35. Is. 42:16. 48:17. Prov. 4:11. Ps. 25:5 הַדְרִיכֵנִי בַאֲמִתֶּךָ *cause me to walk in thy truth.* verse 9.

2. intrans. as in Kal, construed with an acc. Job 28:8 לֹא הִדְרִיכֻהוּ בְנֵי שָׁחַץ *wild beasts have not trodden it.* Also, *to bend* (the bow,) in a figurative sense, Jer. 9:2 וַיַּדְרְכוּ אֶת לְשׁוֹנָם קַשְׁתָּם שֶׁקֶר וְלֹא לֶאֱמוּנָה *they bend their tongues, (as) their bows, for lying, and not for truth.*

3. as in Arab. ادرك and in Syr. Aph. *to overtake.* Judg. 20:43.

דֶּרֶךְ com. gen. (m. 1 Sam. 21:6. f. Ezra 8:21.) dual דְּרָכַיִם (as if from דֶּרֶךְ,) plur. דְּרָכִים, const. דַּרְכֵי, verbal from דָּרַךְ, dec. VI. a.

1. *way.* The place to which the way

leads is put in the genitive; as, דֶּרֶךְ עֵץ *the way to the tree*, Gen. 3:24. comp. 16:7. 35:19. 38:14. Ex. 13:17. הָלַךְ לְדַרְכּוֹ *to go on one's way*, Gen. 19:2. 32:2. Num. 24:25. Josh. 2:16. דֶּרֶךְ הַמֶּלֶךְ *the king's way*, i. e. the high-way, Num. 20:17. 21:22.—1 K. 2:1 אָנֹכִי הֹלֵךְ בְּדֶרֶךְ כָּל־הָאָרֶץ *I go the way of all things earthly*, i. e. I die. Josh. 23:14.—As an adv. *on the way to* any place, *towards*, as, דֶּרֶךְ הַדָּרוֹם *towards the south*, Ezek. 8:5. comp. 1 K. 8:48.

2. *walk, manner of life, conduct*. (So in Arabic almost all words which denote *way*.) Prov. 12:15 דֶּרֶךְ אֱוִיל יָשָׁר בְּעֵינָיו *the conduct of the fool is right in his own eyes*. 1:31 פְּרִי דַרְכָּם *the fruit*, i. e. the consequences, *of their own conduct*. 1 Sam. 18:14. *and David behaved himself wisely* לְכָל־דְּרָכָיו *in his whole conduct*. —הָלַךְ בְּדֶרֶךְ, בְּדַרְכֵי פְּלוֹנִי *to walk in the ways of any one, to follow him, to imitate him*, 1 K. 16:26. 22:43. 2 K. 22:2. 2 Chr. 17:3. 21:12. 22:3.—*The ways of God* denote, (1.) *his conduct towards men*, Ps. 18:31. (2.) *his will* or *law*, Ps. 27:11. 25:4.

3. especially *religious walk, devotion to God, religion*. Am. 8:14 דֶּרֶךְ בְּאֵר־שָׁבַע *the religion* or *worship at Beersheba*, *cultus Beersebæ*. Ps. 139:24 דֶּרֶךְ עֹצֶב *the way*, i. e. the worship, *of idols*. in the same verse דֶּרֶךְ עוֹלָם *the way of antiquity*, i. e. the religion of our fathers, as, שְׁבִילֵי עוֹלָם Jer. 18:15. (Comp. ὁδὸς *the Christian religion*, Acts 19:9, 23. 9:2.)

4. *way, manner, method*. Gen. 31:35 דֶּרֶךְ נָשִׁים לִי *it happens to be with me after the manner of women*. 19:31 כְּדֶרֶךְ כָּל־הָאָרֶץ *after the manner of all the world*. Is. 10:24, 26 בְּדֶרֶךְ מִצְרָיִם *after the manner of the Egyptians*. comp. Am. 4:10.

5. *work*. Job 40:19 הוּא רֵאשִׁית דַּרְכֵי־אֵל *he is the chief of the works of God*. Job 26:14. Prov. 8:22 יְהוָה קָנָנִי רֵאשִׁית דַּרְכּוֹ *Jehovah created me the first of his works*.

דַּרְכְּמוֹן Ezra 2:69. Neh. 7:70, 71, 72. i. q. אֲדַרְכֹּן *the Persian daric*. (Also two MSS. in Ezra 8:27, read אֲדַרְכְּמֹנִים.)

דַּרְמֶשֶׂק 1 Chr. 18:5, 6. the Syriac orthography for דַּמֶּשֶׂק *Damascus*, Syr. ܕܪܡܣܘܩ. In the usual orthography, the ר is assimilated, as in כִּסֵּא, כֻּרְסֵא *throne*.

דְּרָע Chald. i. q. Heb. זְרוֹעַ *the arm*. Dan. 2:32.

דָּרַשׁ, fut. יִדְרֹשׁ.

1. *to seek, look for, search for*. Lev. 10:16. Prov. 31:13. Construed with לְ, Job 10:6 וּלְחַטָּאתִי תִדְרוֹשׁ *and (that) thou searchest after my sin*. with אַחַר, Job 39:8. Also in the following phrases, (1.) דָּרַשׁ שְׁלוֹם וְטוֹבַת פ׳ *to seek the peace and prosperity of any one*, Deut. 23:7. Ezra 9:12. also דָּרַשׁ לְשָׁלוֹם לְ in the same sense, Jer. 38:4.—דָּרַשׁ רָעָה *to seek* one's *hurt*, Ps. 38:13. (2.) *to seek God*, i. e. to turn to him, to supplicate him; usually construed with an accus. in the later books with לְ, 2 Chr. 15:13. 17:4. 31:21. with אֶל, Job 5:8.

2. *to seek unto, to visit* or *frequent* a place, especially for religious worship. 2 Chr. 1:5 וַיִּדְרְשֵׁהוּ שְׁלֹמֹה וְהַקָּהָל *and Solomon and the congregation frequented it* (*the altar*.) Am. 5:5. Deut. 12:5 (with אֶל.) Is. 62:12 דְּרוּשָׁה עִיר *a frequented city*.

3. *to require, demand*. Deut. 22:2. 23:22. Mic. 6:8. Ps. 109:10 וְדָרְשׁוּ מֵחָרְבוֹתֵיהֶם *they demand* (*bread*,) i. e. beg, *far from their desolate houses*.—Especially, דָּרַשׁ דָּם מִיַּד, מֵעִם *to require blood of any one*, i. e. to punish him for bloodshed, Gen. 9:5. 42:22. Ezek. 33:6. Also without דָּם, Deut. 18:19 *and whosoever hearkeneth not unto my words* אֶדְרֹשׁ מֵעִמּוֹ *I will require it of him*, i. e. I will punish him for it. Ps. 10:4.

4. *to ask about, to inquire into, to examine*. Deut. 13:15. 17:4, 9. The subject inquired about or examined, is put in the acc. 2 Chr. 32:31 לִדְרֹשׁ הַמּוֹפֵת *to inquire into the miracle*. 1 Chr. 28:9 כָּל־לְבָבוֹת דּוֹרֵשׁ יְהוָה *Jehovah examineth all hearts*. or construed with לְ, 2 Sam. 11:3. Construed with עַל of the person *of* whom, and of the thing *about* which inquiry is made, 2 Chr. 31:9. Especially *to inquire of* or *consult* (an oracle, Jehovah, an idol, a magician;) construed with an acc. of the person, Gen. 25 : 22. Ex. 18 : 15. 2 K. 22 : 13 (here with עַל of the thing.) with בְּ, 1 Sam. 28 : 7. 2 K. 1 : 2 ff. 1 Chr. 10 : 14. 2 Chr. 16 : 12. with אֶל, Is. 8 : 19. 19 : 3. Deut. 18 : 11. with לְ, Ezek. 14 : 7. The person *through* whom God is consulted stands with מִן, 2 K. 8 : 8. with לְ, Ezek. 14 : 7.

5. *to regard, care for, observe.* Deut. 11 : 12 אֶרֶץ אֲשֶׁר יְהוָה דֹּרֵשׁ אֹתָהּ *a land which Jehovah careth for.* Job 3 : 4. Ps. 9 : 13. Ps. 142 : 5 דּוֹרֵשׁ לְנַפְשִׁי *caring for my life,* or *for me.*—דָּרַשׁ מִצְוֹת, חֻקֵּי, פִּקּוּדֵי יְהוָה *to observe God's commands,* Ps. 119 : 45, 156. 1 Chr. 28 : 8. דָּרַשׁ מִשְׁפָּט *to observe righteousness,* Is. 1 : 17. 16 : 5.

Niph. 1. *to be sought for.* 1 Chr. 26 : 31.

2. pass. of Kal no. 4. *to be inquired of;* hence, *to answer, to hear,* spoken of God, construed with a dative, otherwise synonymous with עָנָה. Ezek. 14 : 3 הַאִדָּרֹשׁ אִדָּרֵשׁ לָהֶם *should I hear them?* 20 : 3, 31. 36 : 37 עוֹד זֹאת אִדָּרֵשׁ לְבֵית יִשׂ' לַעֲשׂוֹת לָהֶם *also in this I will hearken to the house of Israel to do it for them.* Is. 65 : 1 נִדְרַשְׁתִּי לְלוֹא שָׁאָלוּ *I hearken to those who supplicate me not.* The form אִדָּרֹשׁ is the infin. pleonastic.

דָּשָׁא *to wax green, to flourish.* Joel 2 : 22.

Hiph. *to cause to flourish, to bring forth.* Gen. 1 : 11. Hence,

דֶּשֶׁא m. verbal from דָּשָׁא, *young tender herb,* different from עֵשֶׂב *a plant already in the seed.* Gen. 1 : 11, 12. Deut. 32 : 2. Prov. 27 : 25.

דָּשֵׁן *to wax fat.* Deut. 31 : 20. (Arab. دسم *idem,* ם and ן being often commuted.)

P. 1. *to make fat,* or *full of marrow.* Prov. 15 : 30 שְׁמוּעָה טוֹבָה תְּדַשֶּׁן עָצֶם *a good report maketh the bones fat.* Hence, *to anoint,* Ps. 23 : 5.

2. *to regard* or *pronounce fat.* Ps. 20 : 4 עוֹלָתְךָ יְדַשְּׁנֶה *thine offering he regardeth as fat,* i. e. he accepts of it. (ה ֶ is paragogic, as in 1 Sam. 28 : 15.)

3. denom. from דֶּשֶׁן, *to purify from ashes, to remove ashes.* Ex. 27 : 3. Num. 4 : 13.

Pu. figuratively, *to be abundantly satisfied.* Prov. 11 : 25. 13 : 4 וְנֶפֶשׁ חָרֻצִים תְּדֻשָּׁן *the desire of the diligent shall be satisfied.* 28 : 25.

Hothpa. *to be soiled with fat,* spoken of the sword. Is. 34 : 6.

דָּשֵׁן verbal adj. from דָּשֵׁן, dec. V. a.

1. *fat, fruitful,* spoken of the earth. Is. 30 : 23.

2. *full of sap,* spoken of trees. Ps. 92 : 15.

3. *rich, opulent,* spoken of men. Ps. 22 : 30.

דֶּשֶׁן m. with suff. דִּשְׁנִי, verbal from דָּשֵׁן, dec. VI. h.

1. *fatness,* Judg. 9 : 9. *rich food, delicacy,* Job 36 : 16. Is. 55 : 2. Jer. 31 : 14. *fruitfulness, blessing,* Ps. 65 : 12.

2. *ashes,* (perhaps because the ancients made use of them for manure, comp. Plin. XVII. 9.) Lev. 1 : 16.

דָּת f. plur. דָּתִים, dec. I. a. found only in later Hebrew.

1. *law, a law.* Est. 1 : 13, 15, 19. 2 : 12. כְּדָת הַיּוֹם *according to the edict this day, as this day,* 9 : 13.

2. *an order made public, an edict.* Est. 3 : 14. 8 : 13. 9 : 14. (The word appears to be of Persian origin. For from دادن *to give, command, appoint,* is derived داد *justice, equity, law;* in Pehlvi *dadha, dadestan;* in Zend, *daetie,* in Armen. *dat, judicium.*)

3. Deut. 33 : 2. according to the usual reading אֵשׁ דָּת *fire of the law,* i. e. fiery law. (Vulg. *lex ignea,* so the Syr. Chald. Arab.) But 50 MSS. read אשדת, also 2 Samar. MSS. אשדות,) i. e. either אֲשֵׁדוֹת *streams of water,* (see אֶשֶׁד;) or rather *the strong,* (comp. اسد *the lion.*) The form then were feminine, as in פְּרָעוֹת Judg 5 : 2. and it would correspond to the parallel clause רִבְבֹת קֹדֶשׁ *holy myriads.*

דָּת f. Chald. 1. *law.* Dan. 6:9, 13, 16. דָּתָא דִי אֱלָהּ *the law of God,* Ezra 7: 12, 21.

2. *religion, religious rites.* Dan. 6:6. בְּדָת אֱלָהֵהּ *in his religion;* comp. 7:25. (The Rabbins call the Christian and Mahommedan religion דָּת.)

3. *edict, decree.* Dan. 2:13, 15.

4. *meaning, purpose.* Dan. 2:9. חֲדָה הִיא דָתְכוֹן *this only is your purpose.*

דִּתְאָ, emph. דִּתְאָה, Chald. i. q. Heb. דֶּשֶׁא *young tender herb.* Dan. 4:12, 20. [4:15, 23.]

דְּתָבַר m. Chald. (strictly Persian,) Dan. 3:2, 3. *one skilled in the law, a judge;* compounded of דָּת *law,* and the termination בַר, وار (comp. גִּזְבָּר.) In Pehlvi, we find datouber, *one who directs, commands, a judge;* in Pers. داذواران *lawyers.*

דֹּתָיִן (*two wells,* dual of דּוֹת in Chald. *a well;*) Gen. 37:17. also דֹּתָן 2 K. 6: 13. proper name of a place situated to the north of Samaria, in Greek Δωθαϊμ Judith 4:6. 7:3. Δωταϊα 3:9.

דָּתָן proper name of an associate with Korah, in the conspiracy against Moses. Num. 16:1. 26:9. Deut. 11:9. Ps. 106:7.

ה

ה, the fifth letter of the alphabet, called in Hebrew הֵא *He.* The signification of the name is unknown.

As a guttural it is intermediate between the gentler breathing א and the stronger ח. Examples of its commutation with א may be found on page 1. In the kindred dialects, though not in the Hebrew itself, it is sometimes interchanged with ח; e.g. Syr. ܓܗܢ Chald. גְּחַן *to stoop;* Chald. זְהוֹרִי, Syr. ܙܚܘܪܐ *crimson,* kindred with זָהַר *to shine;* גָּבַהּ Samar. גבח *to be high;* גִּבֵּחַ *having a high forehead,* comp. جبهة *a high forehead;* etc.

More frequently the ה, as a middle radical, is interchanged with Vav quiescent (as in the case also with א, see page 1, 2.) e. g. בּוֹשׁ Aram. בְּהַת, ܒܗܬ *to be ashamed;* דּוֹר Arab. دهر *generation;* לְהָטִים *magic arts,* comp. לָאט and לוּט; מוּל Chald. מְהַל *to circumcise,* comp. Is. 1:22; נוּר Aram. נְהַר, ܢܗܪ *to shine;* רוּץ Aram. ܪܗܛ *to run.*

הַ a prefix, (before the gutturals and ר pointed with Kamets, but before ח generally, and before ה often, with Pattah, and before gutturals having Kamets, regularly pointed הֶ;) the Hebrew article, a contraction of the ancient complete form הַל i. q. ال (אַל.) The Lamed assimilates itself in Arabic to the succeeding consonant in sound, at least before what are called the solar letters, but is constantly retained in the writing, as الشمس (ashshams.) The Hebrews, however, both speak and write הַשֶּׁמֶשׁ, instead of the original הַלְשֶׁמֶשׁ. (Another example of the assimilated Lamed is in יִקַּח for יִלְקַח.) The plural pronoun אֵל, אֵלֶּה, *these,* was probably originally related to the article הַל. This article is used,

1. for the definite article, *the.*

2. for the denom. pron. *this;* as, הַיּוֹם *this day,* Ex. 2:18. 1 K. 20:13. הַפַּעַם *this time,* Ex. 9:27.

3. for the indef. art. *a;* as, הָעַלְמָה *a virgin,* Is. 7:14. הַיּוֹם *on a day, once, formerly,* 1 Sam. 1:4. 2 K. 4:18. Job 1:6.

4. before the vocative; as, הַמֶּלֶךְ *O king,* Est. 7:3. הַבַּעַל *O Baal,* 1 K. 18: 26.—Cant. 6:1.

5. for the relative, *who, which;* as the Germ. *der die das* for *welcher welche welches;* and as ὁ in Homer for *this*

and *who;* (comp. הַ.) Josh. 10:24 *he spake to the captains of the soldiers* הֶהָלְכוּא אִתּוֹ *who went with him.* Judg. 13:8 *what we shall do to the child* הַיּוּלָּד *which shall be born.* Ezra 8:25. Dan. 8:1. Ps. 34:13. So Gen. 27:33 מִי אֵפוֹא הוּא הַצָּד צַיִד וַיָּבֵא לִי *who then is he that hunted venison and brought it to me?* In this instance, therefore, there is no change in the construction from the participle to the finite verb.

Note. It is to be observed, that in the construction of a noun with a following genitive, the article, if used, is placed before the genitive; as, גִּבּוֹר חַיִל *a hero,* Judg. 11:1. גִּבּוֹרֵי הַחַיִל *the heroes,* Josh. 1:14. גִּבּוֹר הֶחָיִל *O hero,* Judg. 6:12. אִישׁ הַדָּמִים *thou bloodhound,* 2 Sam. 16:7. comp. verse 8.

הֲ a prefix, (before gutturals pointed with Pattah, but before gutturals having Kamets, with Segol; sometimes, like the article, followed by Dagesh forte, especially before letters with Sheva, as Gen. 17:17. 18:21. 37:32.) i. q. Arab. أَ.

1. a sign of the direct inquiry, i. q. Lat. *an? num?* Gen. 4:9 הֲשֹׁמֵר אָחִי אָנֹכִי *am I my brother's keeper?* In such an inquiry a negation is sometimes implied, (comp. הֲלֹא *nonne?* for *ecce!*) 2 Sam. 7:5 הַאַתָּה תִּבְנֶה לִּי בַיִת *wilt thou build for me a house?* i. e. thou shalt not build me a house; hence, in the parallel passage, 1 Chr. 17:4 לֹא אַתָּה תִּבְנֶה *thou shalt not build,* etc. So Am. 5:25.

2. in the indirect inquiry, *whether.* Gen. 8:8 *to see* הֲקַלּוּ הַמַּיִם *whether the waters were abated.* 24:23. Cant. 6:11. Also where there is no inquiry; as, Gen. 43:1 *to tell the man* הַעוֹד לָכֶם אָח *that ye had yet a brother.* It is sometimes followed by אִם *or,* Gen. 18:21. 27:21. (In Arab. أَ...أَمْ.)

3. *nonne?* Gen. 30:2 הֲתַחַת אֱלֹהִים אָנֹכִי *stand I not under God?* 50:19. Job 20:4 הֲזֹאת יָדַעְתָּ *knowest thou not this?* 40:33. 1 Sam. 2:27. 2 Sam. 23:17. Jer. 31:20. Ezek. 20:4.

4. sometimes i. q. אִם *if.* Ex. 33:16 *whereby shall it be known*—הֲלוֹא בְּלֶכְתְּךָ עִמָּנוּ *if not in this that thou goest with us.*

הָא Chald. *see! behold!* Dan. 3:25. (Syr. ܗܳܐ *idem.*)

הֵא *lo! behold!* Gen. 47:23. Ezek. 16:43.

הָא Chald. *idem.* Dan. 2:43 הָא כְדִי *behold, as,* for *as* simply. So in Syr. ܗܳܐ is often redundant.

הֶאָח interj. formed by an onomatopœia, *aha!* expressive of exultation, Is. 44:16. Job 39:25. Ps. 35:21, 25. *of scorn,* Ps. 40:16. Ezek. 25:3.

הַב imper. of יָהַב.

הַבְהָבִים masc. plur. verbal from יָהַב *to give; presents, offerings.* Hos. 8:13.

הָבַל, fut. יֶהְבַּל, *to be vain, to cherish vain thoughts.* Job 27:12 לָמָּה זֶּה הֶבֶל תֶּהְבָּלוּ *why do you cherish so vain a thought?* Ps. 62:11 וּבְגָזֵל אַל תֶּהְבָּלוּ *be not vain in robbery,* i. e. indulge not vain hopes from it. 2 K. 17:15 וַיֵּלְכוּ אַחֲרֵי הַהֶבֶל וַיֶּהְבָּלוּ *they went after vain idols, and became vain,* i. e. practised idolatry. Jer. 2:5.

Hiph. *to make vain, to seduce to idolatry.* Jer. 23:16.

הֶבֶל, m. with suff. הֶבְלִי; Plur. הֲבָלִים, const. הַבְלֵי; verbal from הָבַל, dec. VI. a. and k.

1. *breath, vapour,* (Aqu. ἀτμίς, Symm. ἀτμὸς, so Kimchi;) for the most part, as an image of transientness. Job 7:16 כִּי הֶבֶל יָמָי *for my days are a breath.* Prov. 13:11 הוֹן מֵהֶבֶל יִמְעָט *riches pass away more rapidly than a vapour.* 21:6. 31:30. Ps. 39:6. Ecc. 1:2, 14. 2:11, 17, 23. 4:4, 8. 5:9. 6:9. Applied in a peculiar manner to an untimely birth, Ecc. 6:4 כִּי בַהֶבֶל בָּא וּבַחֹשֶׁךְ יֵלֵךְ *for it came in a breath, and departed in darkness.*

2. figuratively, *something vain, foolish,* or *of no value.* Lam. 4:17 עֶזְרָתֵנוּ הָבֶל *our vain help.* Jer. 10:3, 8.

3. especially *idols, idolatry.* In the

singular, 2 K. 17:15. Jer. 2:5. in the plural, Jer. 8:19. 14:22. Deut. 32: 21. Ps. 31:7 הַבְלֵי שָׁוְא *vain idols.* Jon. 2:9.

4. adv. *in vain, to no purpose.* Job 9:29. 21:34. 35:16. Is. 30:7. Ps. 39:7.

5. a proper name, *Abel,* (Sept. Ἄβελ,) Adam's second son. The meaning of the name (*transientness* or *short continuance*) has probably a designed reference to his early death. Gen. 4:2.

הֲבֵל *idem,* (with Chaldaic form.)— הֲבֵל הֲבָלִים *vanity of vanities,* Ecc. 1:2. 12:8.

הָבְנִים masc. plur. found only Ezek. 27:15. *ebony, ebenum,* ἔβενος. So among the ancients Symmachus and Jerome, comp. Bocharti Hieroz. T. II. p. 141. The similarity of the names is also of great weight in a production of the east, the name of which usually passed, with the article itself, into Greece. The names of several other kinds of costly wood, (as שִׁטִּים, אַלְגֻּמִּים,) are used only in the plural; probably because the wood was brought from abroad divided into planks, (φάλαγγες.)

הָבַר found only Is. 47:13 הֹבְרֵי שָׁמַיִם, Sept. ἀστρολόγοι τοῦ οὐρανοῦ. Vulg. *augures cœli.* Probably *those who cut up the heavens,* or *divide them into fields* or *houses,* (as they are called,) for the purpose of taking auguries, i.e. astrologers; from the root هبر *to cut off.* Others make הָבַר i.q. Arab. خبر *to know.*

I. **הָגָה,** fut. יֶהְגֶּה. (In Syr. ܗܓܐ *to meditate, to read by syllables; Pa. to meditate, consider;* Ethpa. *to read.*)

1. *to meditate on* any thing; construed with בְּ, for the most part applied to religious reflection, Josh. 1:8 וְהָגִיתָ בּוֹ יוֹמָם וָלַיְלָה *thou shalt meditate thereon* (*on the law*) *day and night.* Ps. 1:2. 63:7. 77:13 וְהָגִיתִי בְכָל־פָּעֳלֶךָ *I will meditate on all thy works.* 143:5. (parall. שִׂיחַ.) Used absolutely, Prov. 15:28 לֵב צַדִּיק יֶהְגֶּה לַעֲנוֹת *the heart of the righteous meditates in order to answer.* Construed with an accus. *to think on* any thing, *to remember.* Is. 33:18 לִבְּךָ יֶהְגֶּה אֵימָה *thy heart shall remember the time of terror.* also in an evil sense, *to imagine, invent, devise,* Ps. 2:1. וּלְאֻמִּים יֶהְגּוּ רִיק (*wherefore*) *do the nations imagine a vain thing?* i.e. vain sedition. Prov. 24:2. Is. 59:13.

2. *to speak, utter.* Job 27:4. Ps. 35: 28 וּלְשׁוֹנִי תֶּהְגֶּה צִדְקֶךָ *my tongue shall speak,* i.e. celebrate, *thy righteousness.* 37:30. 71:24. 115:7. Is. 59:3. Prov. 8:7.

3. *to sigh, mourn, lament.* Jer. 48: 31. Is. 16:7.

4. *to mourn* or *coo,* spoken of doves. Is. 38:14 אֶהְגֶּה כַּיּוֹנָה *I mourned as a dove.* 59:11.

5. *to roar,* spoken of lions. Is. 31:4.

Po. infin. הֹגוֹ i.q. Kal no. 2. Is. 59: 13.

Hiph. part. plur. מַהְגִּים, *to mutter,* (as sorcerers do their incantations,) or *to coo* or *sigh* (as necromancers, in imitating the voice of the manes.) Is. 8:19.

II. **הָגָה** i.q. יָגָה no. II. *to be separated,* (comp. הָלַךְ and יָלַךְ,) and trans. *to separate.* Prov. 25:4 הָגוֹ סִיגִים מִכָּסֶף *separate the dross from the silver.* The infin is here used for the imper. Symm. καθαίρε. Vulg. *aufer.* verse 5. (Others read הֹגוֹ, as if Hiph. from יָגָה.) Probably also Is. 27:8 הָגָה בְּרוּחוֹ הַקָּשָׁה בְּיוֹם קָדִים *he sweeps them away with a violent wind, in the day of the east wind.*

הֶגֶה m. verbal from הָגָה.

1. *a thought.* Ps. 90:9.

2. *sighing, mourning.* Ezek. 2:10.

3. *roaring* (of thunder.) Job 37:2.

הָגוּת f. (with Kamets impure) verbal from הָגָה dec. I. *thought, meditation.* Ps. 49:4.

הָגִיג m. verbal from obs. הָגַג prob. i.q. הָגָה, (comp. דָּמָה and דָּמַם, חָקַק and חָקָה, רָנַן and רָנָה,) dec. III. a. *mourning, sighing.* Ps. 5:2 יְהוָה בִּינָה הֲגִיגִי *Jehovah, hear my mourning.* 39:4 בַּהֲגִיגִי תִבְעַר אֵשׁ literally, *in my mourning a fire was kindled,* i.e. I became impatient. According to the first signification of הָגָה, it may be translated in the latter passage, *musing, meditation;* and in the former, *meditation, prayer.* So De Wette.

הִגָּיוֹן m. prob. *a poem, song.* (The Syriac translator gives this meaning to the root הָגָה Is. 8:19. and it is easily derived from the signification *meditari*, scil. (*carmen.*) Ps. 92:4 עֲלֵי הִגָּיוֹן בְּכִנּוֹר, Sept. μετ' ᾠδῆς ἐν κιθάρᾳ, *with a song on the harp.* So Vulg. Jerome. Ps. 9:17 הִגָּיוֹן סֶלָה (a musical expression,) Sept. ᾠδὴ διαψάλματος, *an interlude, chorus.* So Symm. Aqu. Vulg. According to others, הִגָּיוֹן in both cases denotes a musical instrument.

הֶגְיוֹן m. verbal from הָגָה, dec. I.

1. *meditation.* Ps. 19:15.

2. *intention, purpose,* (comp. הָגָה Ps. 2:1.) Lam. 3:62.

הָגִין m. adj. dec. III. a. found only Ezek. 42:12. *convenient, fit, suitable.* (In the Talmud. הגון *becoming, fit, suitable.*)

הָגָר a proper name, *Hagar*, an Egyptian, hand-maid to Sarah, and mother of Ishmael. Gen. 16:1. 25:12. The root of this word signifies in Arabic, *to flee, to leave one's country,* (whence Hegira, *the flight* of Mahommed;) hence הָגָר signifies *fugitive*, a name which agrees with her history. See הָבַל.

הַגְרִים masc. plur. Ps. 83:7. and **הַגְרִיאִים** 1 Chr. 5:10, 19, 20. 11:38. 27:31. proper name of a people, in the east of Gilead, with which the tribes beyond Jordan were frequently at war. Steph. Byzant. speaks of a people in that country called Ἀγραῖοι; Dionys. Perieget. (v. 956.) of the Ἀγρέες, in the neighbourhood of the Nabatheans. The moderns compare هَجَر i. e. the province *Baharein;* or حِجْر, a city in Arabia Petrea. The Jewish commentators make them the posterity of Hagar.

הֵד i. q. הֵידָד *shout of joy, rejoicing,* Ezek. 7:7 הֵד הָרִים *the rejoicing upon the mountains.* (comp. Is. 16:9, 10.)

הַדָּבְרִין plur. masc. Chald. *state counsellors, ministers, viziers.* Dan. 3:24. 4:33. [36.] 6:8. also הַדָּבְרֵי מַלְכָּא 3:27, *royal counsellors.* The Ottoman Porte, for example, has six counsellors, besides the grand vizier. The termination בַר, (see גְּזָבָר, דְּתָבָר) shews that the word is of Persian origin, but the meaning of the first syllable הד is not easily defined.

הֲדַד proper name of a king of the Idumeans. Gen. 36:35. 1 Chr. 1:46. comp. verse 50.

הֲדַדְעֶזֶר a proper name, *Hadadezer*, king of Syria of Zobah. 2 Sam. 8:3 ff. Other passages read הֲדַרְעֶזֶר, as 2 Sam. 10:16, 19. 1 Chr. 19:16, 19. but here also individual MSS. have the first reading.

הֲדַדְרִמּוֹן proper name of a place in the plain of Megiddo. Zech. 12:11. According to Jerome afterwards called *Maximianopolis.*

הָדָה *to stretch out* (the hand.) Once Is. 11:8. In Arab. and Syr. هدي and ܗܕܳܐ *to lead, direct.*

הֹדּוּ (for הֹנְדּוּ) Syr. ܗܶܢܕܽܘ, Arab. هند, *India.* Est. 1:1. 8:9.

הֲדוֹרָם Gen. 10:27. name of an Arabian tribe of the race of Joktan. The Arabic genealogists also mention a הדראם, هدرام. See Bocharti Phaleg, Lib. II. p. 128. Michaëlis Spicil. Geogr. P. II. p. 162.

הָדַךְ *to overthrow, to tread to the ground.* Job 40:12. In Arab. هدك *to throw to the ground,* as a house.

הַדָּם Chald. *a piece.*—עֲבַד הַדָּמִין Dan. 2:5. 3:29. (μέλη ποιεῖν 2 Mac. 1:16.) *to make one into pieces, to hew in pieces,* a mode of capital punishment, in use among several ancient nations, otherwise in Syr. ܗܰܕܡܳܐ (Chald. הַדֵּם *to cut in pieces;* Syr. ܗܰܕܳܡܳܐ *a member.* Ethpa. ܐܶܬܗܰܕܰܡ *to be dismembered.*)

הֲדֹם m. joined with רַגְלַיִם, *a footstool.* (Root הדם, in Arabic, *to spread upon the ground, to make level with the ground.*) Is. 66:1 *the earth is the footstool of my feet.* Ps. 110:1 *till I make thine enemies thy footstool.* Especially is the ark of the covenant called the footstool of God, because Jehovah was considered as seated upon it, 1 Chr. 28:2. Ps. 99:5. 132:7. Lam. 2:1.

הֲדַס m. plur. הֲדַסִּים dec. VIII. h. *myrtle.* Neh. 8:15. Is. 41:19. 55:13. Zech. 1:8, 10, 11. See Celsii Hierobotanicon, P. II. p. 17 ff. (Arab. هدس in the dialect of Yemen, i. q. آس *a myrtle*).

הֲדַסָּה (*myrtle*) the earlier name of the Jewish maiden Esther. Est. 2:7.

הָדַף, fut. יֶהְדֹּף. 1. *to thrust, strike, ferire.* Num. 35:20, 22. Ezek. 34:21. Job 18:18 מֵאוֹר יֶהְדְּפֻהוּ אֶל חֹשֶׁךְ *they shall thrust him out of light into darkness.*

2. *to thrust down, to overthrow.* Jer. 46:15.

3. *to thrust away, to keep back, withhold.* 2 K. 4:27. Prov. 10:3.

4. *to drive away.* Deut. 6:19. 9:4. Josh. 23:5.

הָדַר, fut. יֶהְדַּר. 1. prob. *to be wide, broad,* (like the kindred אָדַר,) also *to be extended in height, tumidum esse.* (Arab. اهدر *tumidus,* comp. حدر *intumuit.*) Is. 45:2 וַהֲדוּרִים אֲיַשֵּׁר *I will level the high places, loca tumida complanabo.* Sept. ὄρη ὁμαλιῶ.

2. *to adorn, decorate.* Is. 63:1 *adorned in his apparel.*

3. *to honour, respect, reverence;* construed with an accus. or with פְּנֵי פ׳, Lev. 19:32. also, *to have respect of persons, to be partial in judging,* i. q. נָשָׂא פָנִים, Ex. 23:3. Lev. 19:15.

Niph. pass. of Kal no. 3. Lam. 5:12.

Hithpa. *to make one's self broad, to make a display.* Prov. 25:6.

הֲדַר Chald. Pa. הַדַּר *to honour, to respect.* Dan. 4:31, 34. [4:34, 37.]

הָדָר m. verbal from הָדַר, dec. IV. c.

1. *ornament.* Ezek. 16:14. Ps. 110. 3 הַדְרֵי קֹדֶשׁ *sacred ornaments* or *attire.*—Prov. 20:29 הֲדַר זְקֵנִים שֵׂיבָה *gray hairs are the ornament of old men.* Lev. 23:40 עֵץ הָדָר *beautiful trees.*

2. *pomp, splendour, majesty.* Ps. 104:1 הוֹד וְהָדָר לָבָשְׁתָּ *thou puttest on glory and majesty.* Job 40:5. Ps. 29:4 קוֹל יְהוָה בֶּהָדָר *the voice of Jehovah is full of majesty.*

3. *honour.* Ps. 149:9.

הֲדַר m. verbal from הָדַר, *ornament, honor, glory.* Dan. 11:20 מַעֲבִיר נוֹגֵשׂ הֶדֶר מַלְכוּת *one who shall send an officer through the glory of his kingdom,* i. e. through Palestine. The expression is parallel with צְבִי verse 16. comp. Zech. 9:8 As a parallel in sense, see 2 Mac. 3:1 ff.

הֲדָרָה f. const. הַדְרַת, fem. of הָדָר, dec. XI. d. *ornament, honor.* Prov. 14:28.—הַדְרַת־קֹדֶשׁ *sacred ornaments* or *attire,* Ps. 29:2. 96:9.

הָהּ interj. of lament. formed by an onomatopœia i. q. אֲהָהּ *wo! alas!* Ezek. 30:2.

הוֹ i. q. הוֹי interj. *alas!* Am. 5:16.

הוּא 1. pron. prim. of the third person sing. masc. *he,* and as a neuter *it.* (Syr. ܗܘ, Arab. هو.) In the Pentateuch this form is of the common gender, and stands for the fem. הִיא, which occurs only 11 times in the writings of Moses, (comp. the Masora on Gen. 38:25.) The authors of the vowel-points, to whom this use of the word appeared strange, sought to remedy it, at least so far as the vowel-points are concerned, by writing it הִוא, where we must of course suppose a Keri הִיא. The same punctuation occurs also 1 K. 17:15. Job 31:11. Is. 30:33. where הִוא is without doubt the correct reading.

2. *self, same, selfsame.* Is. 7:14 יִתֵּן אֲדֹנָי הוּא לָכֶם אוֹת *the Lord himself will give you a sign.* Ps. 44:5. 1 Chr. 17:26. especially with the article בַּמָּקוֹם הַהוּא *in the same place.*

3. It serves to express the substantive verb *to be*, i. e. the copula in the logical sense. Is. 43:25 אָנֹכִי הוּא מֹחֶה *I am he that blotteth out, ego sum abstergens.*

Note. Under one of the three preceding numbers, all those cases probably belong, in which הוּא has been supposed to designate *Jehovah.* (See Simonis Onomast. V. T. p. 549.) E. g. under no. 1. Deut. 32:39 רְאוּ כִּי אֲנִי אֲנִי הוּא וְאֵין אֱלֹהִים עִמָּדִי *see that I, even I, am he, and besides me there is no God.* Is. 43:10, 13, 25. 48:12. Jer. 14:22. under no. 2. Ps. 102:28 אַתָּה הוּא *thou (art) the same.* under no. 3. 2 Sam. 7:28 אַתָּה הוּא הָאֱלֹהִים *thou art God.*

הוּא Chald. *idem.* Dan. 2:21.

הֲוָא Chald. see **הֲוָה**.

הוֹד dec. I. a.

1. *ornament, decoration.* Zech. 10:3. 6:13.

2. *splendour, glory, majesty;* (1.) spoken of God, and joined with הָדָר, Ps. 21:6. 96:6. 104:1. 111:3. Job 40:10. (2.) of a king, 1 Chr. 29:25. Dan. 11:21. (3.) of the voice, Is. 30:30 הוֹד קוֹלוֹ *his majestic voice.* Job 39:20 הוֹד נַחְרוֹ אֵימָה *his mighty snorting is terrible.*

3. *bloom of youth, blooming countenance, comeliness.* Dan. 10:8 הוֹדִי נֶהְפַּךְ עָלַי *my comeliness was changed upon me.* Hos. 14:7 כַּזַּיִת הוֹדוֹ *as the olive-tree is his comeliness.* (Comp. זִיו.)

הָוָה i. q. הָיָה *to be,* (the current word in Aramean, but in Hebrew confined to the poets and later writers.) Part. הֹוֶה, Neh. 6:6. Ecc. 2:22. Imper. הֱוֵה, הֱוִי, Gen. 27:29. Is. 16:4. Job 37:6 כִּי לַשֶּׁלֶג יֹאמַר הֱוֵא אָרֶץ *for he saith to the snow, be thou on the earth.* Sept. γίνου ἐπὶ γῆς. Others: *fall upon the earth;* comparing the Arab. هوي *to fall.* Vulg. *ut descendat in terram.* Fut. יְהוּא Ecc. 11:3, for the apoc. יְהִי from יִהְיֶה.

הֲוָה and **הֲוָא** Chald. *to be,* i. q. Heb. הָיָה. Fut. יֶהֱוֵה, sometimes joined with the prefix לְ, signifying *that,* the preformative of the future being omitted; e. g. לֶהֱוֵן *that they may* or *might be,* Dan. 2:43. 6:2, 3. לֶהֱוֵא 5:17. The Chaldeans use this word very frequently with the participles of other verbs to express the tense of narration; e. g. חָזֵה הֲוֵית *I saw,* Dan. 4:7, 10. [4:10, 13.] 7:2, 4.

הַוָּה f. (also הַיָּה in the Kethib of Job 6:2. 30:13.) dec. X.

1. *desire.* Prov. 10:3 הַוַּת רְשָׁעִים יֶהְדֹּף *he withholds the desire of the wicked.* Parall. נֶפֶשׁ צַדִּיק. (In Arab. هوى *idem,* from هوي *to desire, will, love.*)

2. *mischief, evil, wickedness.* 5:10 קִרְבָּם הַוּוֹת *their inward part is very wickedness.* 38:13 דִּבְּרוּ הַוּוֹת *they speak evil.* 52:4, 9. 55:12. Prov. 11:6. 17:4 מֵזִין עַל לְשׁוֹן הַוֹּת *listening to a wicked tongue.* Job 6:30.

3. *ruin, destruction, calamity.* Ps. 57:2 עַד יַעֲבֹר הַוּוֹת *till the calamities are past.* 91:3 דֶּבֶר הַוּוֹת *the destructive pestilence.* 94:20. Prov. 19:13. Job 6:2 Keri 30:13 Keri (Comp. هَوِيّ *fall, ruin,* from هوي *to fall.*)

הֹוָה i. q. הַוָּה no. 3. *destruction, calamity.* Is. 47:11. Ezek. 7:26.

הוֹי 1. interj. of threatening, *wo! alas!* construed with an acc. Is. 1:4 הוֹי גּוֹי חֹטֵא *alas! sinful nation.* 5:8, 11, 18, 20, 21. with אֶל, Jer. 48:1. with עַל, 50:27. Ezek. 13:3. with לְ, 13:18.

2. of grief, *ah! alas!* 1 K. 13:30 הוֹי אָחִי *alas! my brother.*

3. of exhorting, *come on! ho!* Lat. *heus!* Zech. 2:10. [6.] Is. 55:1.

הוּךְ Chald. *to go.* Fut. יְהָךְ, Ezra 5:5. 6:5. 7:13. Infin. מְהָךְ, 7:13.

הוֹלֵלָה f. plur. הוֹלֵלוֹת, verbal from Poel of הָלַל, dec. X. *foolishness, madness.* Ecc. 1:17. 2:12.

הוֹלֵלוּת f. verbal from Poel of הָלַל, *idem.* Ecc. 10:13.

הוֹלֶם m. (Milêl) verbal from הָלַם, *a stroke* (with the hammer.) Is. 41:7. The part. הוֹלֵם (Milra) would appear to suit the connexion better. But הֹלֶם

(Milêl) may itself be regarded as this participle, the accent being drawn back, and the last syllable shortened, on account of the following penacuted dissyllable, as Gesenius has shewn in his Lehrgeb. p. 308. and in his Isaiah, note on chap. 41:7.

הוּם *to confound, throw into consternation.* Deut. 7:23 וְהָמָם מְהוּמָה גְדוֹלָה *he shall throw them into great consternation.*

Niph. fut. יֵהוֹם *to be thrown into commotion,* (by an unexpected occurrence,) spoken of a city or country. Ruth 1:19. 1 Sam. 4:5. 1 K. 1:45. For the forms תְּהִימֶנָה, אֲהִימָה, see under הִים.

Deriv. מְהוּמָה.

הוּן i. q. Arab. هَانَ *to be light, small;* conj. II. IV. X. *to regard as a light thing, to lightly esteem, to despise.* So Hiph. Deut. 1:41 וַתָּהִינוּ לַעֲלוֹת *and ye regarded it as a light thing to go up,* i. e. ye were going up in a thoughtless manner. Others: *and ye despised (the divine command) and went up;* comp. Num. 14:44.

הוֹן m. dec. I. a. 1. *riches, wealth, substance.* Prov. 1:13. 6:31. 8:18. Ps. 44:13 בְּלֹא הוֹן *for that which is not wealth,* i. e. for nought. Plur. הוֹנִים, Ezek. 27:33.

2. adv. *enough, sufficient.* Prov. 30:15, 16. Sept. ἀρκεῖ. So also the Chald. Syr. Arab. (Arab. هَوْن *ease, convenience;* comp. أَانَ *to live quietly, pleasantly;* أَوْن *quiet, convenience.*)

הוֹר and **הֹר** 1. i. q. הַר *a mountain,* being the more ancient and unusual form. Gen. 49:26 הוֹרֵי עַד *the eternal mountains.* Parall. גִּבְעֹת עוֹלָם *the everlasting hills.* The Masoretic punctuation of this phrase is הוֹרַי עַד, according to which הוֹרַי signifies *parentes mei,* (part. from הָרָה,) as rendered by the Vulg. and Chald. and עַד is to be joined to the following clause. But the parallel passages Deut. 33:15. Hab. 3:6. as well as the parallel clause גִּבְעֹת עוֹלָם, decide against this punctuation. The true punctuation is probably הוֹרֵי עַד.

2. proper name of a mountain on the borders of Edom. Num. 20:22. 33:32.

3. of another in Lebanon. Num. 34:7, 8.

הוֹשֵׁעַ (*save*) a proper name.

1. the earlier name of Joshua, servant and successor to Moses. Num. 13:8, 16.

2. a king of Israel. 2 K. 15:30. 17:1 ff. 18:1 ff.

3. a prophet. Hos. 1:1, 2.

הוּת or **הָתַת** found only in Pilel or Poel, Ps. 62:4 עַד אָנָה תְּהוֹתְתוּ עַל אִישׁ *how long will ye rage against a man?* Sept. ἐπιτίθεσθε. Vulg. *irruitis.* Comp. هَاتَ *intulit malum, grassatus est.* Aquila and Jerome less suitably, ἐπιβουλεύετε, *insidiamini;* comp. حَاتَ conj. III. So R. Jona.

הָזָה *to dream, to speak in one's sleep.* Is. 56:10. Sept. ἐνυπνιαζόμενοι. Aqu. φανταζόμενοι. Symm. ὁραματισταί. (In Arab. هَذَى and هَذَا *to be delirious,* especially from sickness; so הָזָה in the Talmud.)

הִי for נְהִי, (as בַּל for יְבַל,) verbal from נָהָה, *lamentation.* Ezek. 2:10.

הִיא f. 1. pron. of the third person sing. *she,* and as a neuter *it.* Syr. ܗܝ Arab. هِيَ. Comp. the masc. הוּא.

2. with the article, הַהִיא *this, the same.*

3. used for the subst. verb. Lev. 11:39.

הִיא Chald. *idem.* Dan. 2:9.

הֻיְּדוֹת plur. fem. Neh. 12:8. *songs of praise, psalms;* comp. 11:17. It is without doubt a verbal from the Hiphil of יָדָה *to praise, celebrate;* and is synonymous with תּוֹדוֹת; but no analogous form is known.

הֵידָד m. prim. formed by an onomatopœia, *joyful acclamation, shout of* *joy, rejoicing;* spoken (1.) of the vintager, and presser of grapes, Jer. 25: 30. 48:33. (2.) of the warrior, Jer. 51:14. In Is. 16:9, 10. the two significations are put in antithesis to each other.

הָיָה, fut. יִהְיֶה, apoc. יְהִי, וַיְהִי, infin. הֱיוֹת, הֱיֹה, once הָיֵה Ezek. 21:15. [10.]

1. *to be.*—הָיָה לִי *I have, mihi est,* Ex. 20:3. Otherwise construed with a dative of the person and thing, *to serve for* any thing, Ex. 4:16. Num. 10:31. or *to be* any thing, 1 Sam. 4:9 הֱיוּ לַאֲנָשִׁים *be men,* (or *become men.*) Construed with לְ before an infinitive, it forms in many phrases a periphrasis for the future, Gen. 15:12 וַיְהִי הַשֶּׁמֶשׁ לָבוֹא *and the sun was about to set.* 2 Chr. 26:5 וַיְהִי לִדְרֹשׁ אֱלֹהִים *and he sought God.* The verb in the infinitive must often be translated passively, Deut. 31:17 הָיָה לֶאֱכֹל *he shall be to consume,* i. e. he shall be consumed. Josh. 2:5 וַיְהִי הַשַּׁעַר לִסְגּוֹר *and the gate was to be shut.* Is. 6:13.—הָיָה עִם אִשָּׁה *rem habere cum fœmina,* Gen. 39: 10. 2 Sam. 13:20.

2. *to become.*—הָיָה לְ *to become* any thing, Ex. 4:4, 9. הָיָה לְאִישׁ *to be enjoyed by a man, rem habere cum viro,* Hos. 3:3. Jer. 3:1. Deut. 24:2.

3. *to happen.*—וַיְהִי כִּ *it happened that.*—Sometimes, *to succeed, to prosper,* Is. 19:15 לֹא יִהְיֶה לְמִצְרַיִם מַעֲשֶׂה *no work shall succeed to the Egyptians.*

Niph. נִהְיָה i. q. Kal, but occurring more rarely.

1. *to be,* (strictly pass. of an obsolete Hiphil, *to be brought about.*) 1 K. 1:27. 12:24.

2. *to become,* (literally, *to be made.*) Construed with לְ, *to become* any thing, Deut. 27:9. *to be made* or *received by* any one, Zech. 8:10.

3. *to be done* or *brought to pass.* Neh. 6:8. Deut. 4:32. Judg. 19:30. 20 3, 12.

4. *to be done, finished, wearied out,* like Lat. *confici.* Dan. 8:27 נִהְיֵיתִי וְנֶחֱלֵיתִי *I was wearied out and sick.* Vulg. *langui et ægrotavi.* Dan. 2:1 וּשְׁנָתוֹ נִהְיְתָה עָלָיו *and his sleep went from him;* (עָלָיו for מֵעָלָיו.) Theod. ἐγένετο ἀπ' αὐτοῦ. Vulg. *fugit ab illo.*

הַיָּה f. in the Kethib of Job 6:2. 30:13. i. q. Keri הַוָּה *suffering, calamity.*

הֵיךְ Chaldaic form for אֵיךְ *how?* 1 Chr. 13:12. Dan. 10:17. (In Chald. more frequent.)

הֵיכָל m. plur. ־ִים, once וֹת (Hos 8: 14.) dec. II. b.

1. *a great* or *magnificent building, a palace.* Prov. 30:28. Is. 39:7. Dan. 1:4.

2. *a temple;* generally, הֵיכַל יְהוָה 2 K. 24:13. 2 Chr. 3:17. Also applied, before the building of the temple, to the tabernacle of the congregation, 1 Sam. 1:9. 3:3.

3. in a more restricted sense, *the sanctuary,* part of the temple, in opposition to *the holy of holies,* (דְּבִיר.) 1 K. 6:5, 17. 7:50.

הֵיכַל m. Chald. *idem.* Dan. 4:26. [29.]

הֵילֵל m. prob. *the morning star,* and so בֶּן שָׁחַר may be regarded as an epithet. Is. 14:12. Sept. ἑωσφόρος. Vulg. *Lucifer.* Root הָלַל *to shine.* For the form, comp. הֵיכָל. But Gesenius in his Isaiah, (Leips. 1820.) makes it a verb in the imperative mode from יָלַל *to lament.*

הֵילְכָה Prov. 31:27 Keth. i. q. the Keri הֲלִיכָה. The form is that of a verbal from the Hiph. הֵילִיךְ (Ex. 2:9.)

הִים i. q. הוּם and הָמָה.

1. *to make a great noise.* Mic. 2:12 תְּהִימֶנָה מֵאָדָם *they shall make a great noise from the multitude of men.*

2. *to rage, to be disquieted* or *uneasy.* Ps. 55:3 אָהִימָה *I am disquieted.* Others make it the Hiphil of הוּם, but it has not the transitive signification.

הֵימָן a proper name, (perhaps i. q. מְהֵימַן in Chald. and Syr. *true, faithful.*)

1. a Levitical chorister in the time of David. 1 Chr. 6:18. [33.] 15:17.

2. an Ezrahite, 1 Chr. 2:6. celebrated for his wisdom, 1 K. 5:11. [4: 31.] and called the author of Ps. LXXXVIII. See אֶזְרָחִי.

הִין m. a measure for liquids, containing 12 logs (לֻגִּים,) or according to Josephus (A. J. III. 9.) 2 χόας of the Athenians. Num. 15:4 ff. 28:5, 7, 14. Ezek. 4:11. Sept. εἵν, ἵν, ὕν.

הָכַר i. q. Arab. هكر *to be astonished, motionless, obstupere.* Hence, in Hiph. *to amaze, stun, stupefacere, obtundere.* Job 19:3 תַּהְכְּרוּ לִי *ye amaze me,* i. e. ye strike me dumb. (תַּהְכְּרוּ prob. for תְּהַכְּרוּ; comp. Jer. 9:2.) Sept. ἐπίκεισθέ μοι. Vulg. *opprimentes me.* (The signification, *to be hard, insensible,* which Schultens gives to the Arabic root, is not sufficiently confirmed.)

הַכָּרָה f. verbal from Hiph. of נָכַר, (comp. הַצָּלָה) dec. X. *respect, regard.* Hence Is. 3:9 הַכָּרַת פְּנֵיהֶם *their respect to persons,* i. e. their partiality or corruption in judgment. Vulg. *agnitio vultus ipsorum.*

הַל Deut. 32:6, (according to the MSS. of the Nehardensians which write separately הַל יְהוָה,) an adverb of interrogation, *an? num?* (Arab. هَلْ.) The verb גָּמַל is then construed with an accus.

הָלָא *to remove, put at a distance,* in Kal not used. Found only in Niph. part. fem. הַנַּהֲלָאָה *the far removed,* used collectively, Mic. 4:7. (In Syriac we find the kindred form הלהל, ܗܠܗܠ *elongavit, rejecit, removit.* It can also be regarded as a denom. from the following noun.

הָלְאָ (a segolate form like אֶרֶץ, מָוֶת,) subst. *remoteness, distance,* but found only with He parag. הָלְאָה (Milêl, but without Metheg,) as an adv. *to a distance, farther, beyond, onward;* (1.) spoken of space, Gen. 19:9 גֶּשׁ־הָלְאָה *approach farther this way.* 1 Sam. 10:3 מִשָּׁם וָהָלְאָה *from thence and farther.* 20:22 מִמְּךָ וָהָלְאָה *from thee and beyond,* i. e. beyond thee. verse 37. Num. 32:19.—מֵהָלְאָה לְ *beyond,* Am. 5:27 מֵהָלְאָה לְדַמֶּשֶׂק *beyond Damascus.* (2.) spoken of time, 1 Sam. 18:9 מֵהַיּוֹם הַהוּא וָהָלְאָה *from that day and forward.* Lev. 22:26. (In Syr. ܠܗܠ ܡܢ ܠܗܠ, from a verb ܗܠ, *idem;* construed with ܡܢ *beyond.* In Chald. לְהָלְאָה, לְהַלָּא and לְהַלָּה.)

הִלּוּלִים plur. masc. *a joyful feast, festival,* (at the gathering in of the fruits of the year.) Judg. 9:27. Lev. 19:24.

הֲלוֹם see הֲלֹם.

הַלָּז com. gen. *this.* Used as a masc. Judg. 6:20. Zech. 2:8. Dan. 8:16. as a fem. 2 K. 4:25. The more common form is

הַלָּזֶה m. *this.* Gen. 24:65. 37:19. It corresponds to the Arab. اَلَّذِي, which, however, in that dialect is a relative. See the article הַ no. 5.

הַלֵּזוּ i. q. הַלָּזֶה *this,* once Ezek. 36:35, but prob. *fem.* being construed with אֶרֶץ.

הֲלִיךְ m. verbal from הָלַךְ, dec. I. Job 29:6 הֲלִיכַי *my steps,* poetically for *my feet.*

הֲלִיכָה f. verbal from הָלַךְ, dec. X. found only in the plural.

1. *ways, goings.* Nah. 2:6. Especially *ways* or *goings of God,* Ps. 68:25. Hab. 3:6. Figuratively, Prov. 31:27 הֲלִיכוֹת בֵּיתָהּ *the ways of her house,* i. e. how things go in her house.

2. *companies of travellers, caravans.* Job 6:19. Parall. אֹרְחוֹת.

הָלַךְ, fut. יֵלֵךְ, יֵלֶךְ, (from יָלַךְ,) but poetically יַהֲלֹךְ, imper. לֵךְ, infin. absol. הָלוֹךְ, infin. const. לֶכֶת, with suff. לֶכְתִּי, part. הֹלֵךְ.

1. *to go,* in whatever manner, applied to things both animate and inanimate; e. g. to the ark floating, Gen. 7:18. to a boundary extending itself, Josh. 16:8. to a report circulating, 2 Chr. 26:8.—2 Sam. 15:20 אֲנִי הוֹלֵךְ עַל אֲשֶׁר־אֲנִי הוֹלֵךְ *I go whither I am going,* i. e. whither my lot leads me; comp. 1 Sam. 23:13. —The place *whither* is most frequently preceded by לְ or אֶל, but sometimes stands in the accus. e. g. Judg. 19:18. 2 Chr. 9:21 אֳנִיּוֹת הֹלְכוֹת תַּרְשִׁישׁ *the ships*

went to Tarshish.—The most remarkable constructions of this word are the following, (1.) with an accusative, *to go through* a place. Deut. 1:19 וַנֵּלֶךְ אֵת כָּל־הַמִּדְבָּר *then we went through the whole wilderness.* 2:7. Job 29:3. (2.) with בְּ, *to go with* any thing. Ex. 10:9. Hence, *to bring* or *carry*, Hos. 5:6. (Comp. בְּ no. 2.) (3.) with עִם or אֵת (אֶת,) *to be conversant with, to associate with.* Job 34:8. Prov. 13:20. Comp. Job 31:5. (4.) with אַחֲרֵי, *to go after, to follow.* Gen. 24:5, 8. 37:17.—הָלַךְ אַחֲרֵי אֱלֹהִים, בְּעָלִים, *to go after God, Baalim,* i. e. to serve or be devoted to them, Deut. 4:3. 1 K. 14:8. Jer. 2:8. Also, *to pursue, persecute,* Jer. 48:2 אַחֲרַיִךְ תֵּלֶךְ חָרֶב *the sword shall pursue thee.* (5.) with a pleonastic dative, הָלַךְ לוֹ, like the French *s'en aller;* Ital. *andarséne, to be gone.* Cant. 4:6 אֵלֶךְ לִי *I will go,* or *get me.* Especially in the imper. לֶךְ לְךָ *go,* or *get thee,* Gen. 12:1. 22:2.

2. *to walk,* figuratively for *to live,* (comp. דֶּרֶךְ no. 2.) Ps. 15:2 הוֹלֵךְ תָּמִים *walking uprightly.* 1:1. Construed more rarely with an accus. (like הָלַךְ דֶּרֶךְ,) Is. 33:15 הֹלֵךְ צְדָקוֹת *walking in righteousness.* Mic. 2:11 הֹלֵךְ רוּחַ וָשֶׁקֶר *walking in wind and falsehood.* Prov. 6:12 הוֹלֵךְ עִקְּשׁוּת פֶּה *walking in perverseness of mouth.*

3. *to depart, to die.* Gen. 15:2. Ps. 39:14.

4. *to pass away, to perish.* Ps. 78:39 רוּחַ הוֹלֵךְ *a breath which passes away.* Job 19:10. 14:20. (Arab. هلك *idem.*)

5. *to run, flow,* spoken of water. Is. 8:8. It is common with the Hebrews to say, *the hills run down with milk, water,* for *milk* or *water runs down the hills,* Joel 4:18. [3:18.] So also Ezek. 7:17. 21:12 כָּל־בִּרְכַּיִם תֵּלַכְנָה מַּיִם, Vulg. *omnia genua fluent aquis,* (a low representation of strong fear.) Comp. the Latin phrase, *auro plurima fluxit,* Virg. Georg. II. 166.

6. *to go on, continue, last.* The Hebrews express the continuation or continued increase of an action, by means of this verb in various constructions; (1.) with the pleonastic infin. הָלוֹךְ, and a participle or adjective of the action continued or continually increasing. Gen. 26:13 וַיֵּלֶךְ הָלוֹךְ וְגָדֵל *and he waxed greater and greater,* Judg. 4:24. וַתֵּלֶךְ יַד בְּנֵי־יִשְׂרָאֵל הָלוֹךְ וְקָשָׁה *and the hand of the children of Israel prevailed more and more.* 1 Sam. 14:19. 2 Sam. 5:10. 18:25. (2.) instead of the first הָלַךְ we sometimes find a finite verb of the continued action. Gen. 8:3 וַיָּשֻׁבוּ הַמַּיִם מֵעַל הָאָרֶץ הָלוֹךְ וָשׁוֹב *and the waters ran off continually from the surface of the earth.* 12:9. comp. Gen. 8:5. (3.) with the participle הוֹלֵךְ, and a participle or adjective of the continued action. 1 Sam. 17:41 וַיֵּלֶךְ הַפְּלִשְׁתִּי הֹלֵךְ וְקָרֵב *and the Philistines drew nearer and nearer.* Also, the finite verb being omitted, 1 Sam. 2:26 וְהַנַּעַר שְׁמוּאֵל הֹלֵךְ וְגָדֵל וָטוֹב *and the child Samuel waxed greater and better.* 2 Sam. 3:1. Est. 9:4. Jon. 1:11. Prov. 4:18. 2 Chr. 17:12. Comp. in French, *la maladie va toujours en augmentant et en empirant, the disease constantly increased and waxed worse.*

Niph. נֶהֱלַךְ pass. of Hiph. of course i. q. Kal, *to pass away, disappear.* Ps. 109:23.

Pi. הִלֵּךְ 1. i. q. Kal, *to go, walk,* only poetically, (except 1 K. 21:27.) Job 24:10. 30:28. Ps. 38:7. (In Chald. and Syr. this conjugation is commonly used instead of Kal.)

2. perhaps *grassari* (an intensitive from *gradior,*) hence מְהַלֵּךְ *a highwayman, robber, grassator,* Prov. 6:11. (Parall. אִישׁ מָגֵן.) Others: *a stroller, vagabond.* Comp. Hithpa. no. 3.

Hiph. הוֹלִיךְ (from יָלַךְ,) also הֵילִיךְ Ex. 2:9, and part. מַהְלְכִים Zech. 3:7, (from הָלַךְ,) the latter with Chaldaic inflection.

1. *to make* or *cause to go, to lead.* Deut. 8:2. 2 K. 24:15. Is. 42:16. Zech. 3:7.—2 Sam. 13:13 אָנָה אוֹלִיךְ אֶת־חֶרְפָּתִי *whither shall I go with my shame?* Also, *to bear* or *carry* things, Zech. 5:10. Ecc. 10:20.

3. causat. of Kal no. 4. *to cause to perish, to destroy.* Ps. 125:5.

3. causat. of Kal no. 5. *to cause to*

flow. Ezek. 32:14. Also, *to cause to run off,* Ex. 14:21.

Hithpa. הִתְהַלֵּךְ 1. as in Kal, but implying a dative of personal advantage, *for one's self.* Hence, *to walk,* Ps. 35:14. Ezek. 28:14. *to walk abroad,* Ex. 21:19. *to take a walk,* Gen. 3:8. 2 Sam. 11:2. *to march up and down,* Job 1:7. Zech. 1:10, 11. 6:7. Construed (like Kal) with an accus. Job 22:14 וְחוּג שָׁמַיִם יִתְהַלָּךְ *he walks upon the arch of heaven.*

2. figuratively, like Kal no. 2., *to live.* הִתְהַלֵּךְ בֶּאֱמֶת, בְּתֹם *to walk* or *live in truth, innocence,* Ps. 26:3. 101:2. Prov. 20:7. 23:31.—הָלַךְ לִפְנֵי יְהוָה *to walk before God,* i.e. to live in a manner well-pleasing to him, Gen. 17:1. 24:40. 48:15. also construed with אֵת, 5:22, 24. 6:9.

3. Part. מִתְהַלֵּךְ Prov. 24:34. *a robber* or *vagrant;* comp. Pi. no. 2.

Deriv. out of course מַהֲלָךְ, הֲלִיכָה, הֵלֶךְ, תַּהֲלוּכָה.

הֲלַךְ Chald. Pa. *to go, walk.* 4:26. [29.]

Aph. *idem.* Part. מַהְלְכִין *walking,* Dan. 3:25. 4:34. [37.]

הֵלֶךְ m. verbal from הָלַךְ, dec. VI.

1. *course, journey;* hence i.q. אִישׁ הֵלֶךְ *a traveller, stranger.* 2 Sam. 12:4.

2. *a stream.* 1 Sam. 14:26 הֵלֶךְ דְּבַשׁ *a stream of honey.*

הֲלָךְ m. Chald. *toll.* Ezra 4:13, 20. 7:24.

הָלַל 1. *to shine, give light,* i.q. Arab. هلّ. Job 29:3 בְּהִלּוֹ נֵרוֹ *when it shines, (namely,) his light.* (הִלּוֹ is an infin. of the form שֹׁךְ, or חֹן, צֵל, with a pleonastic pronoun, as in Ezek. 10:3. Job 33:20.) Comp. Hiph.

2. *to shine, to glitter.* Comp. Pi.

3. *to be haughty, arrogant.* Ps. 75:5. Part. הוֹלְלִים *the arrogant,* connected with the idea of wickedness, Ps. 5:6. 73:3. 75:5. Hence,

4. *to be mad, foolish.* (In the idiom of the Hebrews, a wicked or irreligious man is called *a fool,* and a good man is termed *wise;* comp. נָבָל.) See Poel.

Pi. הִלֵּל *to make to shine, to give lustre;* hence, *to praise, commend, celebrate.* (In Syr. and Arab. *idem.*) Gen. 12:15 וַיְהַלְלוּ אֹתָהּ אֶל־פַּרְעֹה *and they commended her to Pharaoh.* Prov. 27:2. 28:4. Most frequently, *to praise* (God,) construed with an accus. as הַלְלוּ־יָהּ *praise Jehovah,* Ps. 116:19. 146:1. in later Hebrew with לְ, 1 Chr. 16:36. 25:3. 2 Chr. 20:21. 30:21. Ezra 3:11. with בְּ, Ps. 44:9. Intrans. *to glory, boast,* Ps. 56:5 בֵּאלֹהִים אֲהַלֵּל *I will glory in God.* Comp. 10:3.

Pu. הֻלַּל *to be praised* or *celebrated.* Ezek. 26:17. Part. מְהֻלָּל *worthy of praise,* spoken of God, Ps. 48:2. 96:4. 145:3.—Ps. 78:63 וּבְתוּלֹתָיו לֹא הוּלָּלוּ, according to the present punctuation, *and their maidens are not praised,* namely, in nuptial songs; comp. Chald. הִלּוּלָא *a nuptial song.* But this rendering does not suit the parallel clause in verse 64, which seems to require that הוּלָּלוּ should be pointed הֵילִילוּ=הוֹלִלוּ *they lamented.*

Hithpa. 1. *to be praised, to deserve praise.* Prov. 31:30.

2. *to glory, boast.* 1 K. 20:11. Prov. 20:14 אֹזֵל לוֹ אָז יִתְהַלָּל *going his way, then he boasteth,* namely of his bargain. Construed with בְּ, Prov. 25:14. 27:1. especially *to glory* (in God,) Ps. 34:3. 64:11. 105:3. Once with עִם, Ps. 106:5.

Po. הוֹלֵל, fut. יְהוֹלֵל, causat. of Kal no. 4. *to make foolish, to deprive of reason.* Ecc. 7:7. Hence, *to shew to be foolish, to shame, disgrace,* Job 12:17. Is. 44:25 קֹסְמִים יְהוֹלֵל *he shews the diviners to be fools.* Poal part. מְהוֹלָל *made foolish, mad, raving.* Ps. 102:9 מְהוֹלָלַי *those who rave against me;* (like קָמַי.) Ecc. 2:2.

Hithpo. 1. *to be* or *become mad, foolish.* Jer. 25:16. 51:7. Nah. 2:5 יִתְהוֹלְלוּ הָרֶכֶב *the chariots are tumultuous.* Jer. 50:38 בָּאֵימִים יִתְהֹלָלוּ *they madly trust in idols,* (constructio prægnans.)

2. *to feign one's self mad.* 1 Sam. 21:13.

Hiph. causat. of Kal no. 1. *to cause to shine.* Job 41:10. [18.] Is. 13:10. also i. q. Kal, *to shine,* Job 31:26. On Job 25:5, see אָהַל.

Deriv. הִלּוּל, מַהֲלָל, תְּהִלָּה; הוֹלֵלָה, הוֹלֵלוֹת.

הָלַם 1. *to strike, smite.* Judg. 5:26 הָלְמָה סִיסְרָא *she smote Sisera.* Is. 41:7. Ps. 141:5.

2. *to beat down, to break in pieces.* Ps. 74:6. Is. 16:8.

3. *to be scattered, dispersed,* spoken of an army. 1 Sam. 14:16 וַיֵּלֶךְ וַהֲלֹם *and they were more and more dispersed.*

4. *to stamp* or *strike* the ground; spoken of the hoofs of horses. Judg. 5:22.

5. הֲלוּמֵי יָיִן Is. 28:1. *smitten by wine, drunken,* Greek οἰνοπλήξ, Lat. *vino saucius.* Comp. בָּלַע in Niph.

Deriv. out of course מַהֲלֻמוֹת.

הֲלֹם adv. of place. 1. *here.* Gen. 16:13.

2. *hither.* Ex. 3:5. Judg. 18:5. 1 Sam. 10:22.—עַד־הֲלֹם *hither,* 2 Sam. 7:18. (In Arab. هَلُمَّ *come hither,* which is inflected like a verb in the imper. mode; as fem. هَلُمِّي.)

הַלְמוּת f. verbal from הָלַם, *hammer.* Judg. 5:26.

הָם or **הַם** proper name of a place, inhabited by the Zuzims, otherwise unknown. Gen. 14:5.

הֵם or **הָם** prob. i. q. הָמוֹן *multitude.* Plur. const. Ezek. 7:11 מֶהֱמֵהֶם prob. for מֵהֲמֵיהֶם *from their multitude,* or *from their riches.* It is here connected, by way of paronomasia, with מֵהֶם, מֵהֲמוֹנָם; which accounts in some measure for the use of a rare or obsolete form.

הֵם and **הֵמָּה** 1 pron. of the third pers. plur. masc. *they.*—Sometimes, (probably an incorrectness drawn from the language of common life,) used in reference to women, Zech. 5:10. Cant. 6:8. Ruth 1:22.

2. הֵמָּה, הָהֵם *these, the same.*

3. It is used for the subst. verb in the third pers. plur. 1 K. 8:40. 9:20. Gen. 25:16. Also for the subst. verb in the second person, Zeph. 2:12 *also ye Cushites* חַלְלֵי חַרְבִּי הֵמָּה *shall be slain by my sword.*

הָמָה, fut. יֶהֱמֶה. 1. *to make a noise, to bluster, to rage, to roar, to be in commotion;* spoken particularly of waves, Ps. 46:4. Is. 51:15. Jer. 5:22. 31:35. 51:55. of a great multitude of people, 1 K. 1:41. Ps. 46:7 הָמוּ גוֹיִם *the heathen raged.* 59:7. 83:3. Is. 17:12. Prov. 1:21 הֹמִיּוֹת *the noisy* or *bustling,* poetically for *the bustling streets* or *the bustling crowds.* Prov. 20:1 לֵץ הַיַּיִן הֹמֶה שֵׁכָר *wine is a mocker, and strong drink is raging.* Comp. Zech. 9:15.

2. applied figuratively to emotions in the soul, such as anguish, sorrow, compassion. Ps. 42:6, 12 מַה־תֶּהֱמִי עָלָי (*O my soul,*) *why art thou disquieted in me?* Jer. 4:19 *my heart is disquieted in me,* i. e. I have no rest through anguish. 31:20 *therefore are my bowels moved for him* (*Ephraim,*) *I will have compassion on him, saith Jehovah;* comp. Cant. 5:4.—As הָמָה denotes the various tones of musical instruments, (comp. Is. 14:11.) so this commotion of the inward parts is sometimes compared to musical sounds. (So Forster says of the savages, that they call compassion, *a barking of the bowels.*) Is. 16:11 מֵעַי לְמוֹאָב כַּכִּנּוֹר יֶהֱמוּ *my bowels sound for Moab, like an harp.* Jer. 48:36 לִבִּי לְמוֹאָב כַּחֲלִלִים יֶהֱמֶה *my heart sounds for Moab, like pipes.*

3. *to sigh, mourn, lament.* Ps. 55:18. 77:4. Also where this mourning is compared with the *moaning* of doves, Ezek. 7:16. with the *growling* of bears, Is. 59:11. *we growl* (נֶהֱמֶה) *all like bears, and moan* (נֶהְגֶּה) *sore like doves.* Applied to the *howling* of dogs, Ps. 59:7, 15.

4. *to be noisy, clamorous.* Prov. 7:11. 9:13. Comp. the somewhat synonymous הָגָה.

Deriv. הָמוֹן, הֶמְיָה.

הָמוֹ see **הָמוֹן**.

הָמוֹן masc. (fem. only Job 31:34.) verbal from הָמָה, dec. III. a.

1. *sound, noise;* e. g. of rain, 1 K. 18:41. of music, Ezek. 26:13. Am. 5:23. especially *the bustle* or *tumult* of a crowd of people, 1 Sam. 4:14. 14:19. Job 39:7. Hence,

2. *a multitude* or *crowd of people.* קוֹל הָמוֹן *noise of a multitude*, Is. 13:4. 33:3. Dan. 10:6.—הֲמוֹן גּוֹיִם *multitude of nations*, Gen. 17:4, 5. הֲמוֹן עַמִּים *idem*, Is. 17:12. הֲמוֹן נָשִׁים *multitude of wives*, 2 Chr. 11:23. especially *a warlike host* or *army*, Judg. 4:7. Dan. 11:11, 12, 13.

3. *a multitude* generally; e. g. of waters, Jer. 10:13. 51:15. and without addition, *multitude of possessions, abundance, riches*, Ps. 37:16. Ecc. 5:9. Is. 60:5.

4. *inward commotion.* Is. 63:15 הֲמוֹן מֵעֶיךָ *the moving of thy bowels*, i. e. thy compassion; comp. הָמָה no. 2.

הִמּוֹ and **הִמּוֹן** Chald. pron. of the third pers. plur. masc. i. q. Heb. הֵם *they*. Dan. 2:34. Ezra 4:10, 23.

הֶמְיָה f. verbal from הָמָה, dec. X. *sound, noise*, (of musical instruments.) Is. 14:11. See הָמָה no. 2.

הֲמֻלָּה and **הֲמוּלָּה** f. probably *noise, bustle, tumult*, i. q. הָמוֹן. Ezek. 1:24 בְּלֶכְתָּם קוֹל הֲמֻלָּה כְּקוֹל מַחֲנֶה *when they went, there was a noise, as the noise of a camp.* (Comp. קוֹל הָמוֹן Is. 13:4. 33:3. 1 K. 20:13, 28. especially Dan. 10:6.) Jer. 11:16. The root הָמַל, which in Arabic signifies, *to flow, to rain*, in Hebrew was probably synonymous with הָמָה.

הָמַם, fut. יָהֹם i. q. the less frequent הוּם.

1. *to terrify, confound, discomfit.* Spoken especially of God, Ex. 14:24. 23:27. Josh. 10:10. Ps. 144:6 שְׁלַח חִצֶּיךָ וּתְהֻמֵּם *send forth thine arrows and confound them* (*the enemy.*) Ps. 18:15. 2 Chr. 15:6 אֱלֹהִים הֲמָמָם בְּכָל־צָרָה *God terrified them with every distress.* Hence,

2. *to consume entirely, to destroy.* Deut. 2:15. Est. 9:24 (synon. אִבֵּד.) Jer. 51:34 (synon. אָכַל.)

3. *to drive on.* Is. 28:27 וְהָמַם גַּלְגַּל עֶגְלָתוֹ *he drives on the wheel of his cart.*

הָמַן. To this root is usually assigned Ezek. 5:7 יַעַן הֲמָנְכֶם מִן הַגּוֹיִם; as if הֲמָנְכֶם were an infin. with suff. But the explanation of R. Menahem, (in Rashi,) is comparatively the easiest; *because ye rage*, i. e. rebel against God, *more than the heathen.* הֲמָנְכֶם is then i. q. הֲמוֹנְכֶם (from הָמוֹן,) a verbal noun construed as an infinitive. Compare הָגָה Ps. 2:1. הָמָה Ps. 46:7. and other passages in which *noise* and *blustering* occur as an expression of *arrogance*. The form הֲמָנְכֶם is like שְׁלֹשׁ־ Ex. 21:11. מְחָר־ for מְחֹר, etc.

הָמָן proper name of a Persian nobleman, famous as a persecutor of the Jews. Est. 3:1 ff. (In Persian همان signifies *only, solely.*)

הַמְנִיךְ, or according to the Kethib, הַמּוֹנִיךְ, Chald. Dan. 5:7, 16, 29. *a chain* for the neck or arm. (In Syr. ܗܡܝܢܟܐ, ܗܡܢܝܟܐ. It is the Greek *μανιάκης*, otherwise *μάνος, μάννος*; comp. Polyb. II. 31. The ה is prosthetic; hence we also find מְנִיכָא.)

הֲמָסִים masc. plur. found only Is. 64:1. According to several Jewish commentators, *brushwood, small sticks.* Comp. Arab. هشم (with letters transposed) *to break* (something dry;) whence هشيم *dry brushwood, chips for burning, stubble.*

1. **הֵן** pron. of the third pers. plur. fem. *they.*—Used incorrectly in reference to men, Ruth 1:13. Comp. הֵנָּה.

II. **הֵן**, with Makkeph הֶן־.

1. *see! behold!* but more frequently הִנֵּה.

2. *if.* Lev. 25:20 *what shall we eat in the seventh year*, הֵן לֹא נִזְרָע *if we shall not sow.* Jer. 3:1. Job 40:23. Especially 2 Chr. 7:13, where it is interchanged with אִם.

3. *whether, num*, in the indirect inquiry; or i. q. Lat. *an?* in the direct inquiry. Jer. 2:10. (In Chald. *idem.*

The Arabians use إِنَّ see! behold! in a similar manner; and the Syr. ܗܳܐ behold! is often synonymous with אִם and with the interrogative הֲ; as ܗܳܐ ܠܳܐ nonne?)

הֵן Chald. 1. *if.* Dan. 2:5, 6. 3:15, 18.

2. *whether.* Ezra 5:17.

3. הֵן—הֵן *whether....or, sive....sive.* Ezra 7:26.

4. for הֲלָא *nonne?* as a strong affirmation. Dan. 3:17.

הֵנָּה 1. i. q. הֵן pron of the third pers. plur. fem. *they, eæ,* and as a neuter *ea.* Hence,

2. as an adv. of place, (1.) *hither, in hæc* scil. *loca.* Gen. 45:8. Josh. 3:9. Also of time, Gen. 15:16.—הֵנָּה וָהֵנָּה *hither and thither,* Josh. 8:20.—1 Sam. 20:21 מִמְּךָ וָהֵנָּה *from thee and hither,* i. e. on this side of thee. (2.) *here, in his* scil. *locis.* Gen. 21:29. הֵנָּה—הֵנָּה *here....there,* Dan. 12:5. הֵנָּה וָהֵנָּה *here and there,* 1 K. 20:40.

הִנֵּה, rarely הִנָּה (Gen. 19:2.) interj. *see! behold!* Very frequent. With suff. (which here are nominatives,) הִנְנִי *behold me,* or *see,* (*here am*) *I,* more rarely הִנֵּנִי ; הִנֶּךָ ; הִנּוֹ ; הִנֵּנוּ ; הִנְּנוּ ; הִנְּכֶם ; הִנָּם. הִנְנִי—*here am I,* is often used as the answer to a call.

הֲנָחָה f. verbal from Hiph. of נוּחַ, *a permission to rest, rest.* Esth. 2:18. The Sept. and Chald. make it *a release from tribute.* Josephus, (J. A. xi. 6.) *a general festival* throughout the empire.

הֵנַע proper name of a city in Mesopotamia. Is 37:13. 2 K. 18:34.

הָסָה in Kal not used.

Pi. *to be silent.* Found only in the imper. הַס *be silent, be still,* Hab. 2:20. Zeph. 1:7. Zech. 2:17. [13.] and as an exclamation, *hush! be still!* Judg. 3:19. Am. 6:10. As an adv. *silently,* Am. 8:3. Sept. σιωπήν. Plur. הַסּוּ, Neh. 8:11.

Hiph. *to make silent, to quiet, still.* Num. 13:30.

הֲפוּגָה f. verbal from Hiph. of פּוּג, dec. X. *intermission, cessation.* Lam. 3:49.

הָפַךְ, fut. יַהֲפֹךְ. 1. trans. *to turn, to turn about.* 2 K. 21:13. Hos. 7:8.—הֲפֹךְ יָדְךָ *turn thy hand,* i. e. turn about, 1 K. 22:34, 2 Chr. 18:33. comp. 2 K. 9:23.—הָפַךְ דְּבָרִים *to pervert words,* Jer. 23:36.—הָפַךְ עֹרֶף לִפְנֵי *to fly before* any one, *terga vertere,* Josh. 7:8.

2. intrans. *to turn one's self, to turn.* 2 K. 5:26. 2 Chr. 9:12 וַתַּהֲפֹךְ וַתֵּלֶךְ *she turned herself and went.* Hence, *to turn about, to flee* (in battle,) *to retreat.* Judg. 20:39, 41. Ps. 78:9.

3. *to overturn* or *destroy* (a city,) *evertere.* Gen. 19:21, 25. Deut. 29:22. Construed with בְּ, Am. 4:11.

4. *to change.* Ps. 105:25. Lev. 13:55. Construed with לְ, *to change into* any thing, Ps. 66:6. 105:29. 114:8. Jer. 31:13. also with an accus. Lev. 13:3 שֵׂעָר בַּנֶּגַע הָפַךְ לָבָן *the hair in the plague has become white.* verses 4, 10, 13, 20.

Niph. נֶהְפַּךְ 1. *to turn one's self, to turn about.* Josh. 8:20 (spoken of an army.) Job 19:19 נֶהְפְּכוּ בִי *they have turned themselves against me.* 1 Sam. 4:19 נֶהֶפְכוּ עָלֶיהָ צִירֶיהָ *her pains came upon her;* comp. Dan. 10:16.—Prov. 17:20 נֶהְפָּךְ בִּלְשׁוֹנוֹ *he is perverse with his tongue.*—*To be turned to,* construed with לְ, Lam. 5:2. with עַל, Is. 60:5.

2. *to be destroyed.* Jon. 3:4.

3. *to be changed.* Ex. 7:15. Lev. 13:16, 17. 1 Sam. 10:6 (with לְ.) Construed with an accus. Lev. 13:25. Especially, *to be changed for the worse, to degenerate, in pejus mutari,* Jer. 2:21; comp. Ps. 32:4. Dan. 10:8.

Hoph. *to be rolled.* Job 30:15.

Hithpa. 1. *to turn one's self, to turn.* Gen. 3:24 חֶרֶב מִתְהַפֶּכֶת *a sword constantly turning itself,* i. e. a glittering brandished sword. Job 37:12.

2. *to change itself.* Job 38:14.

3. *to roll down.* Judg. 7:13. comp. Hoph.

Deriv. out of course מַהְפֵּכָה, מַהְפֶּכֶת, תַּהְפֻּכוֹת,

הֲפֶךְ and הֵפֶךְ m. verbal from הָפַךְ, *the contrary, the opposite*. Ezek. 16: 34.

הֲפֵכָה f. verbal from הָפַךְ, *destruction, overthrow*. Gen. 19:29. See הָפַךְ no. 3.

הֲפַכְפַּךְ m. verbal from הָפַךְ *crooked, perverse*. Prov. 21:8.

הַצָּלָה f. verbal from Hiph. of נָצַל, *deliverance*. Est. 4:14.

הֹצֶן found only Ezek. 23:24, (many MSS. read חֹצֶן,) according to the Targ. and Kimchi, *weapons*; comp. Arab. حصن *to be firm, fortified*; حصنة *weapon, dart*; Ethiop. חצין *iron, iron work*. Perhaps also i. q. חֹסֶן *strength, force*; here, *a warlike force, army*; (ה being often interchanged with ח, see under the letter ה).

הַר m. with the article הָהָר, with ה local, once הָרָה (Gen. 14:10.) in other places הָהָרָה; Plur. הָרִים, with the article הֶהָרִים; prim. dec. VIII. k. *a mountain*, often *a chain of mountains, mountainous country*. Gen. 14:10.—הַר יְהוּדָה *the mountain of Judah*, a chain of mountains, in the south of Palestine, in the tribes of Judah, and Simeon, Josh 21: 11. also called, by way of eminence, הָהָר, Josh. 10:40. 11:16.—הַר אֶפְרַיִם *the mountain of Ephraim*, in the tribes of Ephraim and Benjamin, Josh. 17:15, 16, 18.—הַר הָאֱלֹהִים *the mount of God*, i. e. Sinai, (comp. Olympus in the mythology of the Greeks,) Ex. 3:1. 4:27. 18:5. הַר הַקֹּדֶשׁ *the holy mount*, namely, that on which the temple was built, Ps. 2:6. 48:3. Comp. הָרָר and הוֹר.

הֹר see הוֹר.

הַר חֶרֶס (*mount of the sun*) a city in the tribe of Dan. Judg. 1:35.

הַר יְעָרִים see יַעַר.

הָרָא 1 Chr. 5:26. proper name of a country to which the Israelites were carried away by the Assyrians. Bochart (Phaleg, Lib. III. p. 225 ff.) compares it with Aria, the northern part of Media.

הַרְאֵל (*mount of God*) name of the altar of burnt offerings. Ezek. 43:15. instead of which אֲרִיאֵל occurs in the context. See אֲרִיאֵל.

הָרַג, fut. יַהֲרֹג. *to kill, slay*; construed with an accus. of the person, rarely with לְ, 2 Sam. 3:30. Job 5:2. with בְּ, 2 Chr. 28:9 *ye have slain them*. Ps. 78:31. Figuratively, Ps. 78:47 יַהֲרֹג בַּבָּרָד גַּפְנָם *he killed their vines with hail*. Comp. *interfice messes*, Virg. Georg. IV. 330.

Niph. pass. Ezek. 26:6, 15.

Pu. הֹרַג *idem*. Is. 27:7.

הֶרֶג m. verbal from הָרַג, *slaughter*. Est. 9:5. Prov. 24:11.

הֲרֵגָה f. verbal from הָרַג, *slaughter*. צֹאן הַהֲרֵגָה *sheep for slaughter*. Zech. 11:4, 7. גֵּיא הַהֲרֵגָה *the valley of slaughter*, Jer. 7:32. 19:6.

הָרָה 1. *to conceive, to be* or *become pregnant*. Gen. 4:1, 17. 16:4. 21:2. 25:21. 29:32. Construed with לְ, *to become pregnant by* any one, Gen. 38: 18. Part. הוֹרָה *one that bears, a mother*, Cant. 3:4. Hos. 2:7. [5.]

2. figuratively, Ps. 7:15 הָרָה עָמָל וְיָלַד שָׁקֶר *he hath conceived mischief, and brought forth falsehood*. Job 15:35. Is. 53:11. 59:4.

Pu. pass. Job 3:3.

Po. הֹרָה, infin. הֹרוֹ, i. q. Kal no. 2. Is. 59:13.

Deriv. out of course הֵרָיוֹן, הֵרוֹן.

הָרָה, fem. הָרָה, verbal adj. from הָרָה, dec. X. *pregnant*. Gen. 16:11.—הָרָה לָלֶדֶת *pregnant to bring forth*, i. e. in the last stages of pregnancy, 1 Sam. 4:19. —הֲרַת עוֹלָם *eternally pregnant*, Jer. 20: 17. Once in the plural הָרִיּוֹתָיו *their women with child*, Hos. 14:1. [13:16.]

הַרְהֹר Chald. (from הַרְהֵר *to think*,) *thoughts*. Like the synonymous רַעְיוֹן (Dan. 2:29, 30. 4:16. [19.]) it is applied to *thoughts in sleep*, or *nocturnal spectres*. Dan. 4:2. [5.]

הֵרֹן m. (with Tseri impure) verbal from הָרָה, dec. I. *pregnancy*. Gen. 3:16.

הֵרָיוֹן m. verbal from הָרָה, *conception*. Ruth. 4:13. Hos. 9:11.

הֲרִיסָה f. verbal from הָרַס, dec. X. *something torn down, a ruin.* Am. 9:11.

הֲרִיסוּת f. verbal from הָרַס, dec. I. *destruction.* Is. 49:19.

הַרְמוֹן m. found only Am. 4:3. most prob. i. q. אַרְמוֹן no. 2. *a seraglio, harem.* So Kimchi. Others make it i. q. חֶרְמוֹן name of a mountain. Others, the name of an (unknown) distant place.

הָרַס, fut. יַהֲרֹס and יֶהֱרֹס.

1. *to tear down, to destroy* (houses, walls, cities,) Ezek. 16:39. 26:4, 12. Lam. 2:2, 17. *to beat in* (the teeth,) Ps. 58:7 אֱלֹהִים הֲרָס־שִׁנֵּימוֹ בְּפִימוֹ *O God, beat their teeth into their mouth.*—Is. 22:19 *from thy station he shall tear thee down.* Comp. בָּנָה no. 3.

2. intrans. *to break through.* Ex. 19:21 פֶּן יֶהֶרְסוּ אֶל אֵל *lest they break through unto God.* verse 24.

3. *to lay waste* (a country), Prov. 29:4. *to destroy* (a people), Ex. 15:7.

Niph. *to be thrown down;* spoken also of mountains. Ezek. 38:20.

Pi. i. q. Kal no. 1. Ex: 23:24.

Deriv. out of course הֲרִיסָה, הֲרִיסוּת.

הֶרֶס m. *destruction,* or what is preferable, according to the Syriac usage (ܗܘܪܣܐ *liberatio,*) *deliverance.* Is. 19:18 עִיר הַהֶרֶס יֵאָמֵר לְאֶחָת *one* (*of these cities*) *shall be called a city of deliverance;* i.e. (in the style of Isaiah,) it shall be a delivered city. Comp. 47:1, 4, 5. 56:7. 60:14. Others make it the proper name of an Egyptian city. See חֶרֶס.

הָרָר found only with suff. הֲרָרִי Jer. 17:3. and **הָרָר**, with suff. הַרְרִי Ps. 30:8. Plur. const. הַרְרֵי, with suff. הֲרָרֶיהָ; i. q. הַר *mountain,* but only in poetry.

הֲרָרִי 2 Sam. 23:33. and **הָרָרִי** verse 11. *a mountaineer* of mount Ephraim or Judah.

הַשְׁמָעוּת f. verbal from Hiph. of שָׁמַע, *a causing to hear, a making known.* Ezek. 24:26.

הִתּוּךְ m. verbal from Hiph. of נָתַךְ, *a melting.* Ezek. 22:22.

הָתַל found only in Pi. הֵתֵל (for הִתֵּל, the long vowel making compensation for the Dagesh omitted,) infin. הָתֵל, fut. יְהָתֵל and יְהַתֵּל.

1. *to mock, deride.* 1 K. 18:27.

2. *to deceive.* Gen. 31:7. Judg. 16:10, 13, 16. Job 13:9. Jer. 9:4. These two significations are also united in the Latin *ludere,* and Greek παίζειν. For the form תְּהַתֵּלּוּ Job 13:9, comp. יַחֵל for יְיַחֵלוּ Job 29:21 (The Dagesh is euphonic.)

Pu. הוּתַל pass. Is. 44:20.

In Arab. compare ختل *to deceive,* (ה and ח being commuted.)

Deriv. מַהֲתַלּוֹת, הֲתֻלִּים.

הֲתֻלִּים masc. plur. verbal from הָתַל, *mockings;* and as a concrete *mockers.* Job 17:2.

ו

The name *Vav* וָו, (according to others וָיו,) signifies *a nail, peg, hook.* Its form in the original alphabet must therefore have resembled its present form.

As a consonant, it answers to the Latin *v,* or Germ. *w;* perhaps in the beginning of words to the English *w* in *ware.* As a vowel it was pronounced like *o* or *u,* according as it was written וֹ or וּ.

As the first radical, it appears very rarely in Hebrew, since in this dialect all verbs פו exchange it for י, in all the forms which should regularly begin with ו. Verbs strictly פו stand, therefore, under י; only a few derivatives occur here.

וְ a prefix, (before a simple Sheva or the letters ב, מ, ף, written וּ; before a composite Sheva with the corresponding short vowel; before the tone-syllable וָ;) conj. *and;* (hence usually called *Vav copulativum.*) Used much more extensively than the conjunction *and* in

English. It was a part of the simplicity of ancient language to mark merely the connexion of ideas, without expressing those nice distinctions of thought, which are designated by the use of causal, adversative, disjunctive, and other conjunctions. The prefix וְ retains this variety of signification, though other more definite conjunctions are also in use. It may be observed likewise, that plain men incline to the use of some one particular connective, and that there is nothing in which those who are unaccustomed to writing oftener fail, than in the use of the conjunctions. The principal uses of וְ are,

1. as merely connective, *and, also;* freq.

2. as adversative, *but, yet.* Gen. 17:21 *but with Isaac will I establish my covenant.*

3. as illative, *since, quandoquidem.* Gen. 26:27 *wherefore have ye come to me,* וְאַתֶּם שְׂנֵאתֶם אֹתִי *since ye hate me?* 15:2. Ruth. 1:21.

4. as causal, *for.* Gen. 20:3 *for she is married.* Is. 39:1.

5. to express a result, consequence, *that, quod;* as וַיְהִי וְ *it happened that.*—Num. 23:19 *God is not a man* וִיכַזֵּב *that he should lie.*

6. as final or perfective, *that, to the end that, ut.* Judg. 6:30. Ex. 8:8.

7. as concessive, *though.* Mal. 2:14.

8. before the closing member of a sentence, where in English no particle is used, like the Germ. *so.* Gen. 3:5. 44:9. Frequently after the nominative absolute, Ex. 12:15 כָּל־אֹכֵל חָמֵץ וְנִכְרְתָה הַנֶּפֶשׁ *every one who eateth leaven, that soul shall be cut off.* 1 Sam. 25:27. Prov. 23:24. Job 23:12. Obad. 8. Prov. 24:27.

9. to express a comparison, *so, as,* Job 5:7. 12:11. 14:18, 19. Prov. 25:25. 1 Sam. 12:15.

10. *otherwise.* Job 6:14. Ps. 51:18: 143:7.

11. as explanatory, *namely,* or where apposition is employed in other languages. 1 Sam. 28:3 בָרָמָה וְעִירוֹ *in Ramah his city.* 17:40. Ps. 68:10. Gen. 30:32 *to day I will go through thy flocks, to separate all the speckled and spotted small cattle, namely,* (וְ) *all the black among the sheep, and all the speckled and spotted among the goats.* Num. 34:6 וְהָיָה לָכֶם הַיָּם הַגָּדוֹל וּגְבוּל *and the great sea shall be to you as a border.* 2 Sam. 15:34. Ps. 55:20. Job 4:6. Gen. 49:25 *from the God of thy father* וְיַעְזְרֶךָּ *he helped thee, and from the Almighty* וִיבָרְכֶךָּ *he blessed thee.* In this and similar connexions it may be translated *who;* though this word is not to be regarded as the signification of וְ. The same is the case with the 73 significations, which Noldius has enumerated under this particle, all of which may be referred to the above and a few kindred meanings.

12. וְ—וְ *both....and, et....et.* Num. 9:14. also, *whether....or, sive....sive,* Ex. 21:16. Lev. 5:3.

וַ a prefix, as in וַיִּקְטֹל *he killed.* Usually called *Vav conversivum futuri.* It is most probably a contraction of the old form הָוָה or הֲוֵי i.q. הָיָה *it happened,* which is placed before the future, like the Arabic كَانَ and جَعَلَ, in order thereby to express the tense of narration. The initial ה, which in Syriac is often dropped in pronunciation, falls away entirely, (the Hebrews usually omitting to write letters that are not pronounced,) and וַי יִקְטֹל is contracted into וַיִּקְטֹל. The only objection to this comparison is, that the Arabic كَانَ and جَعَلَ when thus used, are inflected, which could not have been the case in Hebrew.

וְדָן proper name of a place in Arabia. Ezek. 27:19. That the וְ belongs to the word itself and is not a prefix, has been rightly observed by Michaëlis (Spicileg. Geogr. Heb. p. 274.) yet it is not necessary to read דָּן.

וָהֵב a doubtful reading, Num. 21:14. It is generally regarded as the proper name of an (unknown) place. But Kimchi found some MSS. which read אתהבב in one word. It would then be the Aram. Hithp. from יהב=وهب to give; namely, *Jehovah dedit se in turbine.* The passage, however, appears to be corrupted.

וָו, plur. וָוִים m. *a nail, hook;* found only Ex. XXVI. XXVII. XXXVI. XXXVIII. where it is applied to the hooks on which the curtains of the tabernacle were suspended.

וָזָר m. Prov. 21:8. *guilty, laden with transgression.* Comp. the Arab. وزر *to bear;* in the passive *to be laden with a crime.*

וָלָד m. verbal from יָלַד, (Arab. ولد.) *son, child.* Gen. 11:30.

וָלֶד m. *idem.* 2 Sam. 6:23. The Keri and the western MSS. read יֶלֶד.

ז

The name זַיִן *Zain* probably signifies i. q. Syr. ܙܝܢܐ *a weapon, sword.* To this name the form of the letter answers in all the more ancient alphabets.

In the Arabic alphabet we find two letters which correspond to the Hebrew Zain, namely ذ sounded like *ds,* and ز sounded like *z;* e. g. זָבַח Arab. ذبح *to sacrifice;* but זָרַע Arab. زرع *seed.* In the first case, it is changed in the Aramean into ד, in the latter it remains unchanged; thus, Aram. ܕܒܚ, דְּבַח *to sacrifice;* Aram. ܙܪܥ, זְרַע *to sow.* Comp. the letter ד. There are some roots, whose orthography is the same in Hebrew, but whose signification varies according to the two Arabic roots with ذ and ز, to which they correspond; e. g. זָלַל *to be despised,* and *to shake;* זָרַע *to sow,* and זְרוֹעַ *the arm;* q. v.

Sometimes, however, ذ and ز are interchanged; e. g. עָזַר Arab. عزر and Syr. ܥܕܪ *to help;* גֶּזַע *a stock,* Arab. جذع and جزع.

Zain is commuted with צ (*ts;*) e. g. זָעַק and צָעַק *to cry;* עָלַז and עָלַץ *to rejoice;* זָהָב *gold* and צָהֹב *yellow like gold,*

Also with ס, שׂ; e. g. זוּר and סוּר *to go back;* עָלַז, עָלַס *to rejoice;* זָמַם Syr. ܣܡܡ *to despise;* אָסוֹן *injury,* probably from اذي *to injure,*

זְאֵב m. prim. (with Tseri impure) dec. I.

1. *wolf.* Gen. 49:27. Is. 11:6. 65:25. Jer. 5:6. זְאֵבֵי עֲרָב *wolves which prowl at night,* Hab. 1:8. Zeph. 3:3.

2. proper name of a Midianitish prince. Judg. 7:25. 8:3. Ps. 83:12.

זֹאת *this,* fem. of זֶה (q. v.)

זָבַד *to present* (with a gift.) Found only Gen. 30:20. So Sept. Chald. Vulg. Saad. (In Arab. زبد according to Geuhari, *donum dedit de opibus suis;* زبد *donum, munus.*)

זֶבֶד m. verbal from זָבַד, *gift, present.* Gen. 30:20. From the same root come many proper names, as, זָבָד, זַבְדִּי, זְבַדְיָה (Ζεβεδαῖος.)

זְבוּב m. prim. dec. I. *fly, gadfly.* Is. 7:18. Ecc. 10:1 זְבוּבֵי מָוֶת *poisonous flies.* —בַּעַל זְבוּב *Fly-Baal,* i. e. the god Baal, as *deus averruncus muscarum,* 2 K. 1:2, 3, 16. an oracular deity of the Ekronites, similar to the Ζεὺς ἀπόμυιος of the Greeks, (Pausan. Eliac. c. 14.) or to the Deus Myiagros, (Solin. c. 1.) Comp. further the epithets of Hercules, ἰπόκτονος, κορνοπίων, etc. It has been incorrectly regarded as a name of reproach; see Carpzov Apparat. Antiquit. Heb. p. 497.

זְבוּל and **זְבֻל** m. verbal from זָבַל

dec. I. ***dwelling, habitation***, especially of God. 1 K. 8:13. 2 Chr. 6:2. Ps. 49:15. Is. 63:15. Also Hab. 3:11 שֶׁמֶשׁ יָרֵחַ עָמַד זְבֻלָה ***the sun and the moon stood still in their habitation***, i. e. in their place in the heavens. The ה־ָ is paragogic; hence the word is Milêl.

זְבוּלֻן, זְבוּלֹן, זְבוּלוּן, and **זְבֻלוּן**, (*dwelling*, see Gen. 30:20.) a proper name.

1. the tenth son of Jacob by Leah. Hence,

2. the tribe of Zebulun, the boundaries of which are given Josh. 19:10—16. The gentile noun is זְבוּלֹנִי from the form זְבוּלֹן, Num. 26:27.

זָבַח (kindred with טָבַח.)

1. *to slay, kill.* 1 Sam. 28:24. 1 K. 19:21. Ezek. 39:17.

2. especially *to slay for sacrifice, to sacrifice;* construed with לְ, 1 K. 8:63. and לִפְנֵי, 1 K. 8:62. 2 Chr. 7:4. of the person to whom the sacrifice is offered.

Pi. זִבַּח, fut. יְזַבֵּחַ, *idem.* 1 K. 3:2. 8:5. 22:44.

Deriv. out of course מִזְבֵּחַ.

זֶבַח m. with suff. זִבְחִי, Plur. זְבָחִים, const. זִבְחֵי, once זְבָחוֹת (Hos. 4:19.) verbal from זָבַח dec. VI. i.

1. ***an animal killed, a repast on animals killed.*** Gen. 31:54. Ezek. 39:17. Prov. 17:1 זִבְחֵי־רִיב ***feastings with strife.***

2. ***a sacrifice***, partly in opposition to ***the unbloody offering*** (מִנְחָה,) 1 Sam. 2:29. Ps. 40:7. partly in opposition to ***the burnt-offering***, (עֹלָה,) and embracing those offerings which were not entirely consumed, such as the sin-offering, trespass-offering, and thank-offering, Ex. 10:25. Lev. 17:8. Num. 15:5. זֶבַח שְׁלָמִים ***thank-offering***, Lev. 3:1. 4:10. Hence applied to great anniversary sacrifices and feasts generally, as זֶבַח הַיָּמִים ***the yearly sacrifice***, 1 Sam. 1:21. 20:6. זֶבַח הַמִּשְׁפָּחָה ***the family sacrifice***, 20:29. comp. 9:12, 13. 16:3.

זָבַל ***to dwell, cohabit.*** Found only Gen. 30:20 יִזְבְּלֵנִי ***he shall dwell with me.*** Verbs of dwelling are usually construed with an acc.

Deriv. זְבוּל.

זְבַן (Syr. ܙܒܢ) *to buy, to gain.* Dan. 2:8 *that ye would gain time.*

זָג m. Num. 6:4. *the external transparent skin of the grape.* Root זָגַג or זוּג *to be clear, transparent;* comp. the Samar. זגג and Chald. זגג.

זֵד m. verbal adj. from זוּד or זִיד, dec. I. *arrogant, proud;* hence, by a common transition, (comp. הָלַל nos. 3, 4.) *bold, wicked, profane.* Is. 13:11. Jer. 43:2. Ps. 19:14. 119:21, 51, 69, 78, 85, 122.

זָדוֹן m. const. זְדוֹן (as if from זָדָה i. q. זִיד,) dec. III. a.

1. *arrogance, pride.* Prov. 11:2. 21:24.—זְדוֹן לִבְּךָ *the pride of thine heart*, Jer. 49:16. Obad. 3.

2. *wickedness, impiety.* Deut. 17:12:

3. as a concrete, *proud.* Jer. 50:31.

זֶה, fem. **זֹאת** (prob. for זָאת fem. of זא, Arab. ذا.)

1. pron. denom. *this.*—When doubled, *one....the other,* 1 K. 22:20. Is. 6:3. Job 1:16. Sometimes it implies contempt, like the Greek οὗτος, or Lat. *ille,* Ex. 32:1 כִּי זֶה מֹשֶׁה *for as to this Moses.* verse 23. 10:7. 1 Sam. 10:27. Ezra 3:12. Comp. however Ps. 48:15. Used as a plural, Job 19:19. 1 Sam. 29:3.

2. more rarely in poetry as a relative, *who,* like the Germ. *der.* (Comp. the art. הַ.) Ps. 104:8 אֶל־מְקוֹם זֶה יָסַדְתָּ לָהֶם *to the place which thou hast prepared for them.* Prov. 23:22. Also merely as a sign of relation, (comp. אֲשֶׁר no. 2.) Ps. 78:54. 74:2 הַר צִיּוֹן זֶה שָׁכַנְתָּ בּוֹ *mount Zion which thou inhabitest.*

3. *here,* for בָּזֶה *in hoc* scil. *loco.* Gen. 28:17.—מִזֶּה *hence,* 37:17. (Comp. אֵי־זֶה and אֵי־מִזֶּה.)—Dan. 10:17 אֲדֹנִי זֶה *my lord here.*

4. before numbers and dates, *now, already,* to give emphasis. Gen. 27:36. זֶה פַעֲמַיִם *these two times,* i. e. now twice. 31:38 זֶה עֶשְׂרִים שָׁנָה *now twenty years.* verse 41. 43:10. 45:6. Zech. 7:3 זֶה כַּמֶּה שָׁנִים *now so many years.*

5. after many particles, especially of

interrogation and exclamation, it is used as an intensitive, like the English *now, then.* Gen. 27:21 הַאַתָּה זֶה בְּנִי עֵשָׂו אִם־לֹא *whether thou then art my son Esau, or not.*—מַה־זֶּה *how then?* Gen. 27:20. *why then?* Judg. 18:24. 1 K. 21:5. לָמָּה־זֶּה *why then?* Gen. 18:13. 25:22. הִנֵּה־זֶה *behold now!* Cant. 2:9. עַתָּה־זֶה *this very time, now then,* Ruth 2:7 מֵאָז הַבֹּקֶר וְעַד עַתָּה זֶה *from the morning until this very time.* 1 K. 17:24.

6. Compounded with prepositions, (1.) בָּזֶה *here,* Gen. 38:21. Ex. 24:14. *when,* Est. 2:13. (2.) כָּזֶה וְכָזֶה *so and so, thus and thus,* Judg. 18:4. 1 K. 14:5. also, *this as well as that,* 2 Sam. 11:25.

זֹה f. *this,* i. q. זֹאת. Found only Ecc. 2:2. 5:15, 18. 7:23. 9:13. Comp. זוֹ and זוּ.

זָהָב m. prim. const. זְהַב, once זֲהַב (Gen. 2:12.) dec. IV. a.

1. *gold.* Gen. 24:22, 53. 36:39. Ex. 3:22. When used after numerals, *shekel* (שֶׁקֶל) is to be supplied, as Gen. 24:22 עֲשָׂרָה זָהָב *ten (shekels of) gold.*

2. figuratively, *the golden splendour* (of the firmament,) Job 37:22. *gold-coloured oil,* Zech. 4:12.

זָהַם in Kal not used in Hebrew; but in Arabic signifying *to be fœtid, rancid,* spoken of corrupted oil; and in Chaldaic, *to be dirty, loathsome.* Hence in Pi. *to loathe, abhor,* Job 33:20 וְזִהֲמַתּוּ חַיָּתוֹ לָחֶם *his life abhorreth it, (namely) bread.*

זָהַר in Kal not used, *to shine,* (as in Syr. and Arab.) comp. צֹהַר *light.*

Hiph. הִזְהִיר. 1. intrans. *to be bright, to shine.* Dan. 12:3. (In Chald. אַזְהִיר *idem.*)

2. *to enlighten;* but only figuratively, (1.) *to teach,* construed with two accusatives, Ex. 18:20. With an accusative of the person only, 2 Chr. 19:10. (2.) *to warn against* any thing. 2 K. 6:10. Construed with מִן of the thing, Ezek. 3:18 לְהַזְהִיר רָשָׁע מִדַּרְכּוֹ הָרְשָׁעָה *to warn the wicked from his wicked way.* Also construed with מִן in a somewhat different sense, Ezek. 3:17. 33:7 וְהִזְהַרְתָּ אֹתָם מִמֶּנִּי *thou shalt warn them from me,* i.e. on my account. (In Syr. Pa. and Aph. in Chald. Aph. *idem.*)

Niph. 1. *to be instructed,* Ps. 19:12. *to receive instruction* or *counsel,* Ecc. 4:13.

2. *to take warning.* Ezek. 33:4, 5, 6. Construed with מִן, Ecc. 12:12.

זְהַר Chald. *idem.* Part. pass. זְהִיר *admonished, cautious, prudent.* Ezra 4:22. (In Syr. Ethpe. *to take heed, attend, watch.*)

זֹהַר m. verbal from זָהַר, dec. VI. *brightness* (of the firmament.) Ezek. 8:2. Dan. 12:3.

זוֹ f. i. q. זֹה and זֹאת *this.* Hos. 7:16. Used as a relative, Ps. 132:12.

זוּ com. gen. for זֶה and זֹאת.

1. as a pron. denom. *this.* Ps. 12:8.

2. more frequently as a relative, *who, which.* Ex. 15:13. Ps. 9:16. 142:4. Is. 43:21. Hab. 1:11 זוּ כֹחוֹ לֵאלֹהוֹ *his strength is his god.*

זִו m. 1 K. 6:1, 37. (in many MSS. זִיו,) the second month of the Hebrew year, answering to part of April and part of May. This word signifies in Chaldaic, *splendour, brightness,* (see זִיו;) an idea which in the eastern languages is closely connected with that of *flourishing, blossoming;* hence perhaps *the month of flowers,* as in the Chaldee version יְרַח זִיו נִצָּנַיָּא *month of the flourishing of flowers.* (In Arab. زها *to be bright, to flower;* زهو *a flower;* comp. زهر *to shine,* whence زهر *a flower*).

זוּב 1. *to flow.* Ps. 78:20. 105:41. Is. 48:21. Also spoken of the person or place, *in, on,* or *from* which any thing flows. (Comp. הָלַךְ no. 5.) Jer. 49:4 זָב עִמְקֵךְ *thy valley flows (with blood.)* So אֶרֶץ זָבַת חָלָב וּדְבַשׁ *a land flowing (with) milk and honey,* Ex. 3:8, 17. 13:5. 33:3. Lev. 20:24. Num. 13:27. 14:8. 16:14.

2. applied especially to the catame-

nia or monthly courses of women, Lev. 15:25. and in the latter part of the verse to the women themselves, תָּזוּב *she has her courses.* Part. זָבָה *having her courses,* verse 19.

3. also to the gonorrhœa in men, Lev. 15:2. Hence זָב *a man having a gonorrhœa,* Lev. 15:4 ff. 22:4. Num. 5:2. 2 Sam. 3:29.

4. *to pine away, to die.* Lam. 4:9.

In Aram. ܕܘܒ, דּוּב *to flow,* especially in the significations nos. 2, 3. also *to melt down, to dissolve.* In Arab. ذَابَ *to pine away,* from hunger, sickness.

זוֹב m. verbal from זוּב, dec. I. a.

1. *gonorrhœa, fluxus seminis virilis.* Lev. 15:1—15.

2. *the monthly courses of females, fluxus sanguinis muliebris.* Lev. 15:16 ff.

זוד see זִיד.

זוּזִים masc. plur. found only Gen. 14:5. a people on the borders of Palestine, otherwise entirely unknown. Sept. ἔθνη ἰσχυρὰ, which is also expressed by several ancient translators. (Comp. Arab. زَوَازِيَةٌ *stout* or *thickset people.*)

זָוִיָּה (with Kamets impure) f. dec. X. *a corner.* Zech. 9:15 כְּזָוִיּוֹת מִזְבֵּחַ *as the corners of the altar.* Ps. 144:12 בְּנוֹתֵינוּ כְזָוִיֹּת מְחֻטָּבוֹת literally, *our daughters as corner pillars elegantly hewn.* Aqu. ὡς ἐπιγώνια. Vulg. *quasi anguli.*

זוּל found only Is. 46:6 הַזָּלִים זָהָב מִכִּיס *who pour out gold from the purse.* Comp. the Arab. زَالَ (med. Vav and Je) i. q. אָזַל *to go away,* intrans. *to remove;* or זָלַל no. 2. *to squander, to spend.*

זוּלָה f. verbal from זוּל, dec. X. *removal, separation, defect,* (comp. زَالَ *to be removed, to fail;*) but found only in the construct state זוּלַת, and with suff. זוּלָתִי, זוּלָתְךָ, as a preposition, *besides, except, only,* 2 K. 24:14. Is. 45:5, 21. Sometimes with Yod paragogic זוּלָתִי, Deut. 1:36. 4:12.

זוּן *to nourish.* Deriv. מָזוֹן.

Hoph. Jer. 5:8 Kethib סוּסִים מְיֻזָּנִים *well-fed horses.* The Keri reads מְיֻזָּנִים, which Schultens derives from יָזַן = Arab. وزن *to weigh;* namely, *ponderibus instructi* (*pondera* i. q. *testes,* as in Catull. 62. 5. Stat. Sylv. III. 4. 77.) *bene vasati.* Sept. ἵπποι θηλυμανεῖς.

זוּן Chald. *idem.*

Ithpe. pass. Dan. 4:9. [12.]

זוֹנָה f. *a harlot,* part. fem. from זָנָה, q. v.

זוּעַ (in Aram. frequent.) 1. *to move one's self.* Est. 5:9.

2. *to tremble, to be moved with alarm.* Ecc. 12:3.

Pilp. part. מְזַעְזְעַ, *to trouble, vex, agitare, divexare.* Hab. 2:7. (In Aram. and Arab. *idem.*)

זוּעַ Chald. *to tremble, to be afraid;* construed with מִן. Part. זָאֲעִין, or as in the Keri זָיְעִין, Dan. 5:19. 6:27.

זְוָעָה f. verbal from זוּעַ, with Vav moveable.

1. *object of oppression* or *ill-treatment, objectum agitationis, divexationis.* Jer. 15:4 נְתַתִּים לְזַוָעָה לְכֹל מַמְלְכוֹת הָאָרֶץ *I will give them to be ill-treated by all the kingdoms of the earth.* 24:9. 29:18. 34:17. 2 Chr. 29:8. In the Keri of all these passages, we find זַעֲוָה, (q. v.) a form of more easy pronunciation.

2. *terror.* Is. 28:19.

I. **זוּר** or **זוֹר** 1. *to press* or *squeeze together, to crush* (Syr. ܙܪ, ܙܘܪ *to take into the hand* or *fist;* Arab. زَرَّ *to press, to pinch.*) Judg. 6:38 וַיָּזַר אֶת־הַגִּזָּה *and he pressed together the fleece.* Job 39:15 וַתִּשְׁכַּח כִּי־רֶגֶל תְּזוּרֶהָ *she* (*the ostrich*) *forgetteth that the foot may crush them* (*the eggs.*) Is. 59:5 הַזּוּרֶה *that which is crushed,* part. pass. fem. with ־ֶה instead of ־ָה

2. *to be pressed together,* as the lips of a wound. Is. 1:6 לֹא זֹרוּ *they are not pressed together,* namely, so as to cleanse them from blood. The form זֹרוּ (not זָרוּ)

is chosen on account of the intransitive signification.

Deriv. מָזוֹר no. 1.

II. זוּר *to be estranged, alienated.* Job 19:13. Ps. 78:30. Especially *to be alienated from God, to sin,* Ps. 58:4. (In Arab. زور conj. VI. VIII. IX. XI. *declinavit.* Comp. in Heb. סוּר.)

2. *to be strange* or *a stranger.* Job. 19:17 רוּחִי זָרָה לְאִשְׁתִּי *my spirit,* i. e. I, *am become a stranger to my wife.* (Comp. verses 13, 15. Ps. 69:9.) Part זָר *a stranger, another,* variously modified, (1.) *a foreigner, one who is not an Israelite.* Ex. 30:33. often in the sense of *an enemy, barbarian,* (like ξεῖνος, *hostis,*) Ps. 109:11 *let enemies plunder his substance.* Is. 1:7. Ezek. 11:9. 28:10. 30:12. Hos. 7:9. 8:7. Obad. 11. Here also we may place אֵל זָר *a strange god,* Ps. 44:21. 81:10. and זָרִים *strange gods,* Deut. 32:16. Jer. 3:13. 5:19. (2.) *another,* in opposition to *one's self.* Prov. 11:15. 14:10. 20:16. 27:2, 13. 1 K. 3:18.—אֵשׁ זָרָה *other,* i. e. unconsecrated, *fire,* Lev. 10:1. comp. Ex. 30:9. (3.) זָרָה *the wife of another,* comp. אֵשֶׁת רֵעַ Prov. 6:24, 29.) in opposition to one's own wife, especially in reference to criminal intercourse with her; hence, *an adulteress.* Prov. 2:16. 5:3, 20. 7:5. 22:14. 23:33. So זָרִים *other men,* i. e. adulterers, Jer. 2:25. Ezek. 16:32.—בָּנִים זָרִים *strange children,* i. e. children born out of wedlock, Hos. 5:7.

Niph. i. q. Kal no. 1. Is. 1:4.

Hoph. part. מוּזָר *estranged.* Ps. 69:9.

Deriv. מָזוֹר no. II.

זוּרֶה Is. 59:5 וְהַזּוּרֶה תִּבָּקַע אֶפְעֶה *and as to that which is crushed, a viper cometh out.* See זוּר no. I. 1. It ought perhaps to be pointed וְהַזּוּרָה.

זָחַח found only in Niph. *to move one's self, to move from one's place.* Ex. 28:28. 39:21. (In Arab. زحّ and زحزح, in Aram. ܙܚ, זָחַח *idem.*)

זָחַל 1. *to creep.* Part. זֹחֲלֵי עָפָר *creepers in the dust, serpents,* Deut. 32:24. Mic. 7.17.

2. *to fear, to be afraid,* (like the Aram. דְּחַל, ܕܚܠ) Job 32:6 עַל־כֵּן זָחַלְתִּי וָאִירָא *wherefore I feared and was afraid.*

I. **זִיד** in Kal and Hiph.

1. *to act proudly, rashly;* of course, *to be disobedient towards God.* Deut. 17:13. Neh. 9:16, 29. Deut. 1:43 וַתָּזִדוּ וַתַּעֲלוּ הָהָרָה *ye acted rashly and went up into the mountain,* namely, against the divine command.

2. construed with עַל, *to deal wickedly with* any one. Neh. 9:10 כִּי יָדַעְתָּ כִּי הֵזִידוּ עֲלֵיהֶם *for thou knewest that they* (*the Egyptians*) *dealt wickedly against them* (*the Hebrews.*) Ex. 18:11. 21:14 כִּי יָזִד אִישׁ עַל רֵעֵהוּ לְהָרְגוֹ בְעָרְמָה *if any one deals wickedly with his neighbour, to slay him with guile.* (In this passage its signification approaches to that of צָדָה, צוּד *to lie in wait.*)

Deriv. זָדוֹן, זֵידוֹן, זֵד.

II. **זִיד** *to prepare pottage.* Gen. 25:29 וַיָּזֶד יַעֲקֹב נָזִיד *and Jacob prepared pottage.* Sept. ἥψησε δὲ Ἰακὼβ ἕψημα (φακοῦ). Vulg. *coxit autem Jacob pulmentum.* Chald. בַּשֵּׁל תַּבְשִׁילָא. Deriv. נָזִיד *pottage,* from the synonymous root נזד. (Comp. Arab. زاد *food,* especially *food for a journey;* and Heb. צֵדָה, צָדָה.)

זִיד or **זוּד** Chald. i. q. Heb. זִיד no. I. Aph. infin. Dan. 5:20.

זֵידוֹן verbal adj. from זִיד no. I. dec. I. *proud, swelling,* spoken of the waves. Ps. 124:5.

זִיו m. Chald. *brightness, splendour.* Dan. 2:31. 4:33. [36.] hence, in the plural, *a bright, healthy countenance,* Dan. 5:6, 9 זִיוֹהִי שָׁנַיִן עֲלוֹהִי *his countenance was changed upon him,* i. e. it became pale. verse 10. 7:28. Comp. in Heb. chap. 10:8. (Syr. ܙܝܘܐ *brightness;* Arab. زيّ and زيّ *ornament, dress.* Comp. זִו.)

זִיז literally, *motion, life, activity.*

(In Chald. זוּז to move, whence also מְזוּזָה.) Hence,

1. זִיז שָׂדַי poetically for *wild beasts of the field*, Ps. 50:11. 80:14.

2. perhaps *abundance* generally. Is. 66:11 זִיז כְּבוֹדָהּ *the abundance of her glory*. Others make it i. q. Syr. ܙܝܘܢ *pride*.

זִיף proper name of a city in the tribe of Judah. Josh. 15:55. 2 Chr. 11:8. In its neighbourhood was a desert of the same name, 1 Sam. 23:14, 15. The gentile noun is זִיפִי, 1 Sam. 23:19. 26:1.

זִיקוֹת fem. plur. *burning arrows, fiery darts, burning torches*. Is. 50:11. i. q. זִקִּים Prov. 26:18. (where also many MSS. read זִיקִים.) In Syr. ܙܝܩܐ *telum, fulmen*.

זַיִת m. dec. VI. f. 1. *olive-tree*. Judg. 9:9. also זֵית שֶׁמֶן *idem*, Deut. 8:8.—שֶׁמֶן זַיִת *olive oil*, Ex. 27:20. 30:24. Lev. 24:2. הַר הַזֵּיתִים *the Mt. of Olives*, near Jerusalem, Zech. 14:4.

2. *the olive*.—עֵץ הַזַּיִת *the olive-tree*, Hag. 2:19.—דָּרַךְ זַיִת *to press olives*, Mic. 6:15.

3. *an olive branch*. Zech. 4:11; comp. verse 12.

זַךְ and **זָךְ**, fem. זַכָּה, verbal adj. from זָכַךְ, dec. VIII. *pure*, (1.) in a physical sense; spoken of oil, Ex. 27:20. of incense, 30:34. (2.) in a moral sense, Job 8:6. 11:4. 33:9. Prov. 16:2. 20:11. 21:8.

זָכָה *to be pure*, only in a moral sense. Job 15:14. 25:4. Ps. 51:6. Mic. 6:11.

Pi. *to purify, cleanse*. Ps. 73:13 זִכִּיתִי לְבָבִי *I have cleansed my heart*. Prov. 20:9. Ps. 119:9 בַּמֶּה יְזַכֶּה נַּעַר אֶת־אָרְחוֹ *how can a young man keep his conduct pure?*

Hithpa. See זָכַךְ Niph.

In Aram. ܙܟܐ, דְּכָא *to be pure*; also ܙܟܐ, זְכָא; the latter more in a moral sense.

זָכוּ f. Chald. *purity, innocence*. Dan. 6:22.

זְכוּכִית f. verbal from זָכַךְ, found only Job 28:17. *glass* or *crystal*. (Arab. زجاج, Syr. ܙܓܘܓܝܬܐ *idem*.)

זָכוּר m. i. q. זָכָר *male*, spoken of men and animals. Ex. 23:17. 34:23.

זָכַךְ i. q. זָכָה *to be pure*; in a physical sense, Lam. 4:7. in a moral sense, Job 15:15. 25:5.

Hiph. *to make clean, to wash*. Job 9:30.

Niph. *to make one's self clean*. Is. 1:16. But this form may better be regarded as the Hithpael from זָכָה.

Deriv. זַךְ, זְכוּכִית.

זָכַר, fut. יִזְכֹּר, *to remember, to think of*. Deut. 5:15. 15:15. 16:12. Construed with an accus. of the person or thing, Gen. 8:1. 19:29.—זָכַר אֶת־יְהוָה *to remember Jehovah*, Deut. 8:18.—Ps. 98:3 זָכַר חַסְדּוֹ וֶאֱמוּנָתוֹ *he remembered his grace and truth*.—Also with לְ of the person, *to remember* any thing *for* any one, Neh. 5:19 זָכְרָה לִּי אֱלֹהַי לְטוֹבָה כֹּל אֲשֶׁר *remember for me, O my God, for good, all that* etc. 13:22. Jer. 2:2. Ps. 79:8. More rarely with לְ of the person or thing, Ex. 32:13. Deut. 9:27. Ps. 25:7. 136:23. with בְּ, Jer. 3:16.

Niph. נִזְכַּר *to be remembered, to be thought of*. Job 24:20 עוֹד לֹא יִזָּכֵר *he shall no more be remembered*. Jer. 11:19. Is. 23:16. Zech. 13:2. Est. 9:28 הַיָּמִים אֵלֶּה נִזְכָּרִים וְנַעֲשִׂים *these days should be remembered and kept*. Construed with לְ of the person, (see Kal,) *to be remembered concerning* or *for* any one, Ezek. 18:22. 33:16.—Construed with אֶל, *to be remembered by* any one, Ps. 109:14 יִזָּכֵר עֲוֹן אֲבֹתָיו אֶל יְהוָה *let the iniquity of his fathers be remembered by Jehovah*. Also with לִפְנֵי in the same sense, Num. 10:9.

Hiph. הִזְכִּיר *to bring to remembrance*. Gen. 40:14 הִזְכַּרְתַּנִי אֶל פַּרְעֹה *bring me into remembrance with Pharaoh*. 1 K. 17:18. Ezek. 21:29. [24.] 29:16. Jer. 4:16 הַזְכִּירוּ לַגּוֹיִם *announce (it) to the nations*. Also in the superscriptions of Psalms XXXVIII. LXX. לְהַזְכִּיר *to bring (one's self) into remembrance (with God,)* a meaning, which suits the contents of those Psalms.

2. *to make mention of.* (Arab. conj. IV. *to mention, to praise.*) 1 Sam. 4: 18. Ps. 87:4. Especially, *to mention with commendation, to praise,* Is. 63:7. 1 Chr. 16:4. Cant. 1:4 נַזְכִּירָה דֹדֶיךָ מִיַּיִן *we praise thy love more than wine.* Ps. 45: 18. 71:16. 77:12. also with שֵׁם יְהוָה, Is. 26:13. and בְּשֵׁם, Josh. 23:7. Ps. 20:8. Am. 6:10. (comp. קָרָא בְּשֵׁם.) Is. 48:1. Once causat. *to cause to mention* or *praise,* Ex. 20:24.

3. as in Kal, *to remember.* Gen. 41: 9. Is. 19:17. 49:1.

4. in the ritual language, מַזְכִּיר לְבֹנָה *one who burns incense,* i. e. one who brings a remembrance-offering, or praise-offering, of incense. Is. 66:3. See אַזְכָּרָה.

5. *to write down, memoriæ prodere.* Part. מַזְכִּיר as a subst. 1 K. 4:3. 2 K. 18:18, 37. 2 Chr. 34:8. Is. 36:3, 22. *the recorder* or *historiographer,* a great officer of the crown among the Hebrews, whose business was to record the events of the nation, especially what related to the king. Among the Persians this officer is called *Vakia-Nuwis,* and under the later Roman emperors *magister memoriæ.*

זָכָר m. *male, of the male kind, mas,* the appropriate word for the distinction of sex in men and animals. Its opposite is נְקֵבָה Gen. 1:27. 5:2. 6:19. Hence as a denominative, in

Niph. נִזְכַּר *to be born a male.* Ex. 34: 19. (In Arab. ذكر conj. IV. *to bear a male child.*)

זֵכֶר and **זֶכֶר** m. with suff. זִכְרִי, verbal from זָכַר, dec. VI. g. and h.

1. *memory, remembrance.* Ex. 17:14 *I will destroy the remembrance of Amalek.* Deut. 25:19. 32:26.

2. *name, appellation,* i. q. שֵׁם. Ex. 3: 15 זֶה שְּׁמִי לְעֹלָם וְזֶה זִכְרִי לְדֹר דֹּר *this is my name for ever, and this is my appellation unto all generations.* Ps. 30:5 הוֹדוּ לְזֵכֶר קָדְשׁוֹ *praise his holy name.* Hos. 14:8 זִכְרוֹ כְּיֵין לְבָנוֹן *his name is as the wine of Lebanon.* comp. Cant. 1:3 שֶׁמֶן תּוּרַק שְׁמֶךָ *as ointment poured out is thy name.*

3. *praise, celebration.* Ps. 6:6. 102: 13. (Arab. ذكر *praise.*)

זִכָּרוֹן m. const זִכְרוֹן, plur. ־ִים and וֹת, verbal from זָכַר, dec. III. d.

1. *memory, remembrance.* Josh. 4.7. Ex. 12:14. Ecc. 1:11. 2:16.—אַבְנֵי זִכָּרוֹן *stones of remembrance,* spoken of the two precious stones on the shoulder-pieces of the high-priest's ephod, Ex. 28:12. 39:7.

2. *memorial,* Ex. 13:9.

3. *an event committed to writing, a memoir.* Ex. 17:14 כְּתֹב זֹאת זִכָּרוֹן בַּסֵּפֶר *write this as a memoir in a book.*—סֵפֶר זִכָּרוֹן *a book of remembrance,* Mal. 3:16.—סֵפֶר הַזִּכְרֹנוֹת *the book of memoirs,* i. e. the chronicles of the kingdom, Est. 6:1

4. *a sacred day, festival.* (Comp. the verb, Est. 9:28. Ex. 20:8.) Lev. 23:24.

5. *a memorable speech, maxim, proverb,* i. q. מָשָׁל. Job 13:12.

זְכַרְיָה and **זְכַרְיָהוּ** (*Jehovah remembers*) a proper name, (in Greek Ζαχαρίας).

1. a king of Israel, son of Jeroboam II. 2 K. 14:29.—15:11.

2. a prophet. Zech. 1:1, 7. Ezra 5: 1. 6:14.

זֻלּוּת f. usually rendered *vileness, baseness,* as if from זָלַל no. 1. Ps. 12:9. Better: *terror,* from זָלַל no. II.

זַלְזַל dec. VIII. h. found only in the plur. זַלְזַלִּים *twigs, branches of the vine,* so called from their *tremulous* motion. Is. 18:5. Root. זלל *to shake;* see זָלַל no. II.

I. **זָלַל** 1. *to be low, vile, contemptible.* (Arab. ذل, Syr. ܙܠ *idem.*) Part. Lam. 1:11. Jer. 15:19.

2. causat. *to regard as vile, to lightly esteem, to squander, spend.* Part. זוֹלֵל *a spendthrift, glutton,* Prov. 23:21. 28: 7. Deut. 21:20. Prov. 23:20 זֹלְלֵי בָשָׂר *wasters of their own body,* namely, through debauchery.

Hiph. הֵזִיל (with Chaldaic inflection) *to lightly esteem, to despise.* Lam. 1:8.

II. זָלַל found only in Niph. *to be shaken, to quake.* Is. 63:19 [64:1] מִפָּנֶיךָ הָרִים נָזֹלּוּ *at thy presence the mountains quake.* Judg. 5:5. (Arab. زلزل *to shake the earth;* زلزال *an earthquake.*) Comp. זֻלּוּת, זַלְזַלִּים.

זַלְעָפָה, זִלְעָפָה f. dec. XI. *heat, glow.* (In Arab. زلعب conj. IV. *ambusta et ustulata fuit cutis.* The quadriliteral is formed from זָעַף by the insertion of ל.) Ps. 11:6 רוּחַ זִלְעָפוֹת *a hot wind,* like the simoom. Lam. 5:10 זַלְעֲפוֹת רָעָב *the heats of hunger;* comp. λιμὸς αἴθων in Hesiod, and *ignea fames* in Quintilian. Applied to hot anger, Ps. 119:53.

זִמָּה f. verbal from זָמַם dec. X.

1. *plan, purpose;* in a good sense, Job 17:11. in a bad sense, Prov. 24:9. 21:27.

2. *wickedness, mischief, crime.* Ps. 26:10. 119:150. Especially, *unchastity,* Lev. 18:17 זִמָּה הִיא *it is wickedness.* Job 31:11. Ezek. 16:27. 22:9, 11.

זְמוֹרָה f. plur. זְמֹרִים, verbal from זָמַר no. I. dec. X.

1. *a branch of the vine.* Num. 13:23.

2. *a branch* generally. Is. 17:10. Ezek. 15:2. 8:17 *and behold, they hold the branch before their nose;* an allusion to the religious custom of the Parsees, who while praying to the rising sun hold a bundle of brush-wood (called *bersam*) in their hands.

זַמְזֻמִּים masc. plur. proper name of a race of giants in Palestine, extinct before the time of Moses. Deut. 2:20.

זָמִיר m. verbal from זָמַר no. I. (after the form קָצִיר, חָרִישׁ.) *time of pruning the vine.* Cant. 2:12. According to others, *the time of the singing of birds;* but against the usage of זָמַר no. II.

זָמִיר, plur. זְמִירוֹת, verbal from זָמַר no. II. *a song.* Is. 25:5. Ps. 119:54. 2 Sam. 23:1. Especially, *a song of praise,* Job. 35:10 *who giveth songs of praise,* i. e. prosperity, *in the night* (*of adversity.*)

זָמַם, pret. זָמַמְתִּי and זַמֹּתִי, fut. יָזֹם, plur. יָזְמוּ for יָזֹמּוּ.

1. *to purpose, resolve.* Jer. 51:12. Lam. 2:17. Gen. 11:6. comp. Job 42:2. Construed with an accus. Prov. 31:16 זָמְמָה שָׂדֶה *she thinks on a field.*

2. especially *to purpose evil.* Prov. 30:32 וְאִם זַמּוֹתָ *and if thou purposest (evil.)* comp. Deut. 19:19. Zech. 8:14. and the noun זִמָּה.

3. construed with a dative, *to plot, to lie in wait.* Ps. 37:12.

Deriv. out of course מְזִמָּה, זִמָּה.

זָמָם m. verbal from זָמַם, dec. IV. a. *plan, purpose.* Ps. 140:9.

זָמַן, Pi. זִמֵּן *to appoint,* as in Chaldaic. Found only in Pu. part. עִתִּים מְזֻמָּנִים Ezra 10:14. Neh. 10:35. and עִ׳ מְזֻמָּנוֹת 13:31 *the appointed times.*

זְמָן m. plur. זְמַנִּים, dec. VIII. a. *time,* especially *an appointed time.* (Arab. زمن, زمان *time;* Syr. ܙܒܢ *idem.*) Ecc. 3:1 לַכֹּל זְמָן *every thing has its time.* Neh. 2:6. Est. 9:27, 31.

זְמַן Chald. found only in Pa. *to appoint, prepare.*

Ithpa. הִזְדַּמַּן *to meet, to agree, to concert, inter se convenire.* Dan. 2:9 Keri הִזְדְּמִנְתּוּן *ye have agreed.* Comp. Am. 3:3 Targum. The Kethib is to be read הַזְמִנְתּוּן in Aphel, in which conjugation this verb is found in Chaldaic and Samaritan.

זְמָן and זְמַן m. emph. זִמְנָא, plur. זִמְנִין, Chald.

1. *time, appointed time.* Dan. 2:16. בֵּהּ זִמְנָא— *at the same time.* 3:7, 8. 4:33. [36.] עַד זְמַן וְעִדָּן *for a time and season,* 7:12. Also, *a sacred time,* or *festival,* Dan. 7:25. Comp. מוֹעֵד no. 1. (2.)

2. Plur. *times, repetitions of any thing,* i. q. Lat. *vices.* Dan. 6:11 זִמְנִין תְּלָתָה *three times.* (So the Syr. ܙܒܢ, and in Arab. وقت, *tempus,* plur. *vices.*)

I. זָמַר *to prune* (the vine.) Lev. 25:3, 4.

(Arab. زبر, the letters מ and ב being commuted.)

Niph. pass. Is. 5:6.

Deriv. מַזְמֵרָה, זְמוֹרָה, זָמִיר, מְזַמְּרוֹת.

II. זָמַר found only in Pi. זִמֵּר.

1. *to sing, to sing praises, to celebrate.* (In Syr. and Arab. *idem.* Some derive this signification from the former, *to prune*, on account of the *cæsura* or break in singing, but erroneously.) Construed with a dative of the person sung or celebrated, Judg. 5:3. Ps. 9:12. 30:5. 47:7. or with an accus. Ps. 47:7. 66:2. 68:5, 33.

2. *to play* on an instrument, ψάλλειν. Ps. 33:2. 71:22.

Deriv. out of course זָמִיר, מִזְמוֹר.

זְמָר m. Chald. *music, instrumental music.* Dan. 3:5, 7, 10, 15.

זַמָּר m. Chald. *a singer.* Ezra 7:24.

זֶמֶר m. found only Deut. 14:5. an (unknown) animal of the stag or gazel kind. (In Arab. زمر *saliit caprea.*)

זִמְרָה f. verbal from זָמַר no. I. dec. X.

1. *song.* Ps. 81:3. 98:5.

2. *sound* of musical instruments. Am. 5:23.

3. figuratively, זִמְרַת הָאָרֶץ *the song of the land,* i. e. its most celebrated and valued productions. Gen. 43:11.

זִמְרִי m. (*my song*) proper name of a king of Israel, the murderer and successor of Elah. 1 K. 16:9, 10. 2 K. 9:31. In Sept. Ζαμβρί.

זִמְרָת f. i. q. זִמְרָה Ex. 15:2 עָזִּי וְזִמְרָת יָהּ *Jehovah is my glory and song.* Ps. 118:14. Is. 12:2.

זַן m. plur. זְנִים, dec. VII. i. *manner, sort.* Ps. 144:13. מִזַּן אֶל זַן *of every sort.* 2 Chr. 16:14.

זַן m. Chald. *idem.* Dan. 3:5, 7, 10.

זָנָב m. prim. plur. זְנָבוֹת, const. זַנְבוֹת, dec. IV. f. *tail* (of an animal.) Judg. 15:4. Job 40:17. Figuratively, שְׁנֵי זַנְבוֹת הָאוּדִים *the two ends of the fire-brands,* Is. 7:4. Used proverbially for *something small* or *contemptible,* Deut. 28:13 *Jehovah shall make thee the head and not the tail.* verse 44. Is. 9:13. 19:15. Hence,

Pi. זִנֵּב denom. from זָנָב, *to smite in the rear, to smite the rear-guard* (of an army). Deut. 25:18. Josh. 10:19. Literally, *to wound the tail.* Comp. the Greek οὐρά, οὐραγία *the rear of an army.*

זָנָה (Syr. ܙܢܳܐ, Arab. زنى,) *to commit fornication, to whore;* and figuratively, *to practise idolatry,* since the Hebrews regarded Jehovah as the husband of his people, to whom they were under bonds of conjugal fidelity; idolatry, therefore, was *unfaithfulness* to him. (See for example Ezek. 16:8, 22. Hos. 1:2.) The person *with* whom fornication is committed, either literally or figuratively, is put in the accus. Jer. 3:1. Ezek. 16:28 וַתִּזְנִים *and thou committest fornication with them;* or is preceded by אֶל, Num. 25:1. Ezek. 16:26, 28. by בְּ, Ezek. 16:17. but most frequently by אַחֲרֵי *to go a whoring after* any one, i. e. to run after him for the purposes of whoredom, Judg. 2:17 זָנוּ אַחֲרֵי אֱלֹהִים אֲחֵרִים *they went a whoring after strange gods.* So Lev. 17:7. 20:5, 6. Deut. 31:16. —זָנָה אַחֲרֵי הָאוֹבוֹת *to go a whoring after necromancers,* Lev. 20:6.—The person sinned *against* is preceded by מִן, Ps. 73:27. by מֵאַחֲרֵי, Hos. 1:2. by מִתַּחַת, Hos. 4:12. by תַּחַת, Ezek. 23:5. (comp. Num. 5:19, 29.) or by מֵעַל, Hos. 9:1. —More rarely, *to have intercourse with foreign nations,* Is. 23:17 וְזָנְתָה אֶת־כָּל־מַמְלְכוֹת הָאָרֶץ *thou* (*Tyre*) *hast committed fornication with all the kingdoms of the earth.* (Comp. Nah. 3:4.)

Part. fem. זוֹנָה, more frequently אִשָּׁה זוֹנָה, *a harlot,* Lev. 21:7, 14. Deut. 23:19. Josh. 2:1.

Pu. זוּנָה Ezek. 16:34.

Hiph. הִזְנָה, fut. apoc. יֶזֶן.

1. *to seduce to fornication,* Ex. 34:16. *to cause to commit fornication,* Lev. 19:29.

2. i. q. Kal. Hos. 4:10, 18.

Deriv. out of course זְנוּנִים, זְנוּת, תַּזְנוּת.

זָנוֹחַ name of two places in the tribe

of Judah. Josh. 15:34, 56. Neh. 3: 13. 11:30. 1 Chr. 4:18.

זְנוּנִים masc. plur. verbal from זָנָה, dec. I.

1. *whoredom.* Gen. 38:24. Hos. 1: 2 אֵשֶׁת זְנוּנִים וְיַלְדֵי זְנוּנִים *a woman of whoredom, and children of whoredom.* 2:6. [4.] 4:12. 5:4. 2:4 [2] וְתָסֵר זְנוּנֶיהָ מִפָּנֶיהָ *that she may remove her whoredom,* i.e. her whorish looks, *from her face;* (comp. Ezek. 6:9.)

2. *idolatry.* 2 K. 9:22.

3. *intercourse with foreign nations,* (like the verb, Is. 23:17.) Nah. 3:4.

זְנוּת f. plur זְנוּתִים, dec. I.

1. *whoredom, idolatry.* Jer. 3:2, 9. Ezek. 23:27. 43:7, 9. Hos. 4:11.

2. *disobedience to God* generally, *transgression of his commands;* applied to murmuring against him, Num. 14:33 וְנָשְׂאוּ אֶת־זְנוּתֵיכֶם *they shall bear your transgressions,* i.e. the punishment for them.

זָנַח 1. perhaps i. q. Arab. زنخ *to have an offensive smell, to be rancid.* (See Hiph. no. 1.)

2. trans. *to regard as offensive,* hence, *to reject, cast off.* (Comp. זָהַם. The signification, however, is more certain than this connexion.) Hos. 8:3 זָנַח יִשְׂרָאֵל טוֹב *Israel rejects what is good.* Most frequently applied to Jehovah, Ps. 43:2 לָמָה זְנַחְתָּנִי *wherefore dost thou reject me?* 44: 10, 24. 60:3, 12. 74:1. 77:8. 89:39. Construed with מִן, Lam. 3:17 וַתִּזְנַח מִשָּׁלוֹם נַפְשִׁי *thou rejectest me from prosperity,* i.e. thou robbest me of prosperity.

Hiph. 1. i. q. Kal no. 1. Here we may place Is. 19:6 הֶאֶזְנִיחוּ נְהָרוֹת *the rivers begin to stink,* i.e. they become shallow, stagnant. Sept. Vulg. *deficient flumina.* (The form has either arisen from compounding two different readings הִזְנִיחוּ and the Chald. אַזְנִיחוּ, and is of course corrupted; or else it is a denom. from an adjective אֶזְנָח.) The signification is more certain than the etymological derivation.

2. causat. of Kal no. 2. *to make contemptible, to profane.* 2 Chr. 29:19.

3. *to reject, cast off.* 1 Chr. 28:9. Construed with מִן, 2 Chr. 11:14.

זָנַק in Kal not used.

Pi. *to rush out, to leap forth,* as a beast of prey. Deut. 33:22. In Syr. *to shoot* an arrow.

זֵעָה f. dec. X. i. q. זֵעַ *sweat.* Gen. 3: 19. (In Talmud. זִיעָא *sweat,* הֵזִיעַ *to sweat;* Syr. ܕܘܥܬܐ *sweat.*)

זַעֲוָה f. by transposition for זְוָעָה, (as עֲלָה for עַוְלָה,) *object of oppression* or *ill-treatment.* Deut. 28:25. Ezek. 23: 46. Also in the Keri of Jer. 15:4. 24:9. 29:18. 34:17.

זְעֵיר m. *a little,* μικρόν, (a Chaldaic form.) Job 36:2. Comp. מִזְעָר.

זְעֵיר Chald. *small,* i.q. Heb. צָעִיר. Dan. 7:8. (Aram. זְעַר, زغر *to be small.*)

זָעַךְ i. q. דָּעַךְ *to be extinguished, to be cut short.* Found only in Niphal, Job 17:1. (3 MSS. read this word with ד, which gives a correct gloss.)

זָעַם 1. *to be angry with, to have indignation against,* hence, *to punish with indignation.* Construed with an accus. Mal. 1:4. Zech. 1:12 עָרֵי יְהוּדָה אֲשֶׁר זָעַמְתָּה *the cities of Judah against which thou hast had indignation.* Is. 66:14. with עַל, Dan. 11:30.—Part. זְעוּם יְהוָה *he with whom Jehovah is angry,* Prov. 22:14.

2. *to curse, to execrate.* Num. 23:7, 8. Prov. 24:24. Mic. 6:10.

Niph. (as if pass. of Hiph.) *to be angry.* Prov. 25:23 פָּנִים נִזְעָמִים *an angry* or *sullen countenance.* Vulg. *facies tristis.* (Comp. זָעַף.)

זַעַם m. verbal from זָעַם, dec. VI. c. *anger,* especially *the punitive anger* of God. Is. 10:5, 25. 26:20.—בְּיוֹם זַעַם *in the day of (God's) anger,* Ezek. 22:24.—Dan. 11:36 עַד כָּלָה זַעַם *till (God's) anger is over;* comp. chap. 8:19.—Hos. 7:16 מִזַּעַם לְשׁוֹנָם *through the pride of their (the princes') tongue.*

זָעַף i. q. זָעַם, (comp. the letter ב).

1. *to be angry;* construed with עַל, Prov. 19:3. with עִם, 2 Chr. 26:19. (In Syr. *to be hot,* comp. זַלְעָפָה; in Samar.

to breathe, (comp. Germ. *schnauben*;) both of which may lead us to the primary physical signification of the word.)

2. *to be* or *look sullen, sad*, or *peevish*. (For this connexion of ideas, see e. g. עָצַב.) Part. זֹעֲפִים *sad, sorrowful*, Gen. 40 : 6. (comp. רָעִים verse 7.) Dan. 1 : 10 פְּנֵיכֶם זֹעֲפִים *a sad* or *sunken countenance*, namely, from the want of nourishment. Theod. correctly σκυθρωπὰ ; comp. Mat. 6 : 16.

זָעֵף m. verbal adj. from זָעַף, *angry, displeased*. 1 K. 20 : 43. 21 : 4.

זַעַף m. verbal from זָעַף, dec. VI. c. *anger, rage*, 2 Chr. 16 : 10. 28 : 9. *agitation*, as of the sea, Jon. 1 : 15.

זָעַק fut. יִזְעַק, imper. זְעַק, infin. זְעֹק; i. q. צָעַק *to cry out, to call*, especially from pain, sorrow. The person *to* whom one cries is preceded most commonly by אֶל, Ps. 142 : 6. 22 : 6. Hos. 7 : 14. sometimes by לְ, 1 Chr. 5 : 20. or put in the accus. Judg. 12 : 2. Neh. 9 : 28. Also construed with an accus. of the thing, besides a dative of the person, Hab. 1 : 2 אֶזְעַק אֵלֶיךָ חָמָס *(how long) shall I cry to thee because of violence?* comp. Job 19 : 7. In other passages, the thing *concerning* which one cries out is preceded by עַל, Jer. 30 : 15, or by לְ, Is. 15 : 5. Jer. 48 : 31.

Niph. (pass. of Hiph. no. 1.)

1. *to be called together*. Judg. 18 : 22, 23. Hence,

2. *to gather together, to assemble one's self*. 1 Sam. 14 : 20. Judg. 6 : 34, 35.

Hiph. 1. *to call together, to assemble*. 2 Sam. 20 : 4, 5.

2. as in Kal, *to call*. Jon. 3 : 7. Job 35 : 9. Construed with an accus. Zech. 6 : 8.

זְעַק Chald. *to cry*. Dan. 6 : 21.

זַעַק m. verbal from זָעַק, dec. VI. c. *a cry*. Is. 30 : 19.

זְעָקָה f. verbal from זָעַק, dec. XI. d. *a cry*. Jer. 18 : 22. 20 : 16. 50 : 46. The following genitive is also used passively, Gen. 18 : 20 זַעֲקַת סְדֹם *the cry concerning Sodom*.

זִפְרֹנָה a city in the north of Palestine. Once Num. 34 : 9.

זֶפֶת f. *pitch*. Ex. 2 : 3. Is. 34 : 9. (Arab. زِفْت, Syr. ܙܶܦܬܳܐ *idem*.)

זִקִּים masc. plur. 1. i. q. זִיקוֹת *burning arrows, fiery darts*. Prov. 26 : 18. The forms with ִי and those with ִ followed by Dagesh, are often commuted with each other; e. g. פִּלֶּגֶשׁ and פִּילֶגֶשׁ, קִמּוֹשׂ and קִימוֹשׂ, מוֹרִגִּים and מוֹרִיגִים.

2. *fetter, chain*. Ps. 149 : 8. Is. 45 : 14. Nah. 3 : 10. Job 36 : 8. (In Chald. זִיקִין *idem*, in Talmud. also זִיקִים; from the root זָקַק *to bind*.)

זָקָן com. gen. dec. IV. a. *the bearded chin* of a man; hence, *beard*, and *chin*. 2 Sam. 20 : 9. Lev. 13 : 29, 30. 19 : 27. (Arab. ذَقَن *chin;* Syr. ܕܩܢܐ *beard, chin*.)

זָקֵן, fut. יִזְקַן, *to be old*. Gen. 18 : 12, 13.

Hiph. intrans. *to wax old*. Prov. 22 : 6. Spoken also of inanimate nature, Job 14 : 8.

זָקֵן, m. const. זְקַן; Plur. זְקֵנִים, const. זִקְנֵי; verbal from זָקֵן, dec. V. a. *an old man*. Gen. 24 : 2.—זִקְנֵי יִשְׂרָאֵל, מִצְרַיִם, הָעִיר *the elders of Israel, of Egypt, of the city*, often for *the chief men, the magistrates, proceres*, without reference to their age, Ex. 3 : 16. 4 : 29. Deut. 19 : 12. 21 : 3, 4, 6. 22 : 7, 15, 17, 18. The same is true of the Arab. شَيْخ and the modern words *Signore, Seigneur, Señor*, (formed from the Lat. *senior*.) Plur. fem. זְקֵנוֹת Zech. 8 : 4.

זֹקֶן m. verbal from זָקֵן, *old age*. Once Gen. 48 : 10.

זִקְנָה f. verbal from זָקֵן, dec. X. *idem*. Ps. 71 : 9, 18. Is. 46 : 4.

זְקֻנִים masc. plur. denom. from זָקֵן, dec. I. *idem*. Gen. 21 : 2, 7. 37 : 3. 44 : 20.

זָקַף *to raise up* (one who is bowed down.) Ps. 145 : 14. 146 : 8. In Syr. ܙܩܦ *idem*.)

זְקַף Chald. *to raise up, to suspend;* applied to the suspending of a malefactor on an upright stake. (Syr. ܙܩܦ *to crucify.*) Ezra 6:11.

זָקַק 1. *to pour out.* Job 36:27.

2. *to filter,* hence *to refine* wine. Comp. Pual.

3. *to refine* metals. Job 28:1.

Pi. זִקֵּק *to purify* or *refine* gold. Mal. 3:3.

Pu. *to be refined,* spoken of wine, Is. 25:6. spoken of metals, 1 Chr. 28:18. 29:4. Ps. 12:7.

זֵר m. dec. I. *crown, wreath, border;* e.g. of a table, chest. Ex. 25:11, 24, 25. 37:2, 11, 26. (Syr. ܙܪܐ *a necklace;* Arab. زِرّ *border, stripe.*)

זָרָא found only Num. 11:20. *loathsomeness.* Vulg. *nausea.* (This signification belongs in Arabic to the root זור, ذار (med. Je;) which shews the ־ָא to be a feminine termination for ־ָה.)

זָרַב i. q. Syr. ܙܪܒ *to be straitened.* Hence in Pual, *to be straitened,* spoken of rivers. Once Job 6:17 בְּעֵת יְזֹרְבוּ *at the time when they are straitened.*

זֶרֶד m. proper name of a valley or brook (נַחַל.) Num. 21:12. Deut. 2:13, 14.

זָרָה 1. *to scatter, disperse, cast away.* Num. 17:2. [16:37.] Is. 30:22.

2. especially *to winnow,* i. e. to throw grain against the wind for the purpose of cleansing it. Jer. 4:11. Ruth 3:2 הִנֵּה הוּא זֹרֶה אֶת־גֹּרֶן *behold, he winnoweth upon the threshing-floor.* Figuratively, *to winnow* or *scatter* vanquished enemies, Jer. 15:7. Is. 41:16. Ezek. 5:2.

Pi. זֵרָה 1. *to scatter,* frequently *to scatter* or *disperse* a people. Lev. 26:33. Ezek. 5:10. 6:3. 12:15. 30:26. Prov. 20:8 *the king....by his look scatters every thing evil.*—Prov. 15:7 *the lips of the wise spread abroad knowledge.*

2. *to fan* or *winnow.* Prov. 20:26. Hence,

3. *to sift* or *search, eventilare;* and, of consequence, *to know, to understand.* Ps. 139:3 אָרְחִי וְרִבְעִי זֵרִיתָ *thou knowest my path and my lying down.* Jerôme, *eventilasti.* Others compare the Arab. دري *to know.*

Pu. 1. *to be scattered,* Job 18:15. *to be spread,* Prov. 1:17.

2. *to be winnowed.* Is. 30:24.

Niph. *to be scattered.* Ezek. 6:8. 36:18.

Deriv. מִזְרֶה.

זְרֻבָּבֶל a proper name, *Zerubbabel,* a descendant of David, and leader of the first Jewish colony which returned from the Babylonish captivity. Ezra 2:2. 3:2. Hag. 1:1. In Greek Ζοροβάβελ.

זְרוֹעַ com. gen. but more frequently fem. Plur. ־ִים m. and ־וֹת f. also m. (Dan. 11:15, 22.) dec. I.

1. *the arm,* in animals *the shoulder* or *fore-leg,* βραχίων. Num. 6:19, 20. Deut. 18:3. (So the Latin *armus* denotes *arm* or *shoulder* of men and animals. Compare our English word *arm.*) By way of eminence, *the forepart of the arm,* (see Job 31:22.) hence also in Arabic, *cubitus.*—גָּדַע, שָׁבַר, דִּכָּא זְרוֹעַ פְּלֹנִי, *to break the arm of any one,* i. e. to take away his strength, 1 Sam. 2:31. Job 22:9. 38:15. Ps. 10:5. 37:17.

2. figuratively, *strength, force.* 2 Chr. 32:8 זְרוֹעַ בָּשָׂר *human strength.* Is. 17:5. —אִישׁ זְרוֹעַ *a mighty man,* Job 22:8. זְרֹעֵי יָדָיו *the strength of his hands,* Gen. 49:24.—Especially *a military force, host,* Dan. 11:15, 22, 31.

3. *help, assistance.* Ps. 83:9. Is. 33:2.

זֵרוּעַ m. verbal from Piel of זָרַע, (comp. the form תַּפּוּחַ) dec. I. *a sowing, what is sown.* Lev. 11:37. Plur. זֵרוּעִים *seed sown,* Is. 61:11.

זַרְזִיף m. found only Ps. 72:6. *a violent shower.* (Root זרף i. q. Arab. ذرف *to flow;* Syr. ܙܪܝܦܬܐ *rain, shower;* Talmud. זרזיפי דמיא *adspersiones aquæ, guttæ.*)

זַרְזִיר m. found only Prov. 30:31 זַרְזִיר מָתְנַיִם *the girded on the loins,* an epithet of the war-horse; comp. Bocharti

Hieroz. T. 1. p. 102. and Schultens in locum. (Root זור i. q. زار to surround, to bind; or زرّ to buckle, to clasp. Comp. also the Chald. זְרַז to gird. According to others, the zebra, as if the ringstreaked on the loins. According to some Jewish commentators, the greyhound.

זָרַח 1. to rise; spoken of the sun, Gen. 32:31. Ps. 104:22. of the light, Ps. 112:4. of the majesty of Jehovah, Is. 60:1, 2.

2. to break out; spoken of the leprosy, 2 Chr. 26:19. of a child coming from its mother's womb, i. q. יָצָא, compare the etymology of זֶרַח Gen. 38:30.

Deriv. out of course אֶזְרָח, מִזְרָח.

זֶרַח m. verbal from זָרַח, dec. VI. d.

1. a rising. Is. 60:3.

2. proper name of a son of Judah by his daughter-in-law, Tamar. Num. 26:20. The derivation of the name is found in Gen. 38:30. In Greek, Ζαρά.

זָרַם to flow, to pour out. Construed with an accus. to overflow, to carry away, Ps. 90:5. (Syr. زرف, Chald. זְרַב to flow; by commutation with ב and ף; see ב.)

Po. to pour out. Ps. 77:18.

זֶרֶם m. verbal from זָרַם, a violent rain, a sudden shower. Is. 4:6. 25:2. 28:4. זֶרֶם בָּרָד a shower of hail, Is. 28:2.

זִרְמָה f. verbal from זָרַם, dec. X. the emission of seed. Ezek. 23:20.

זָרַע, fut. יִזְרַע.

1. to sow. Judg. 6:3. Construed with an accus. of the place sown, Gen. 47:23. Ex. 23:10. with two accusatives, Judg. 9:45 וַיִּזְרָעֶהָ מֶלַח and he sowed it with salt. Lev. 19:19. Also figuratively, Jer. 31:27.—Gen. 1:29 עֵשֶׂב זֹרֵעַ זֶרַע herb yielding seed. Figuratively, to sow good, evil, for to do good or evil, Job 4:8. Prov. 22:8. comp. Ps. 97:11.

2. to scatter, disperse. Zech. 10:9.

3. to set out or plant a branch or slip, like the Lat. serere; construed with two accusatives, Is. 17:10. Hence, to plant a nation, to fix it firmly, Hos. 2:25. [23.]

Niph. 1. to be sown. Lev. 11:37. Figuratively, Nah. 1:14 of thy name, i. e. thy reputation, shall nothing more be sown, i. e. spread abroad.

2. to be made fruitful, to conceive, spoken of a woman. Num. 5:28.

Pu. to be sown. Is. 40:24.

Hiph. 1. i. q. Kal. Gen. 1:11.

2. i. q. Niphal no. 2. to conceive. Lev. 12:2.

Deriv. out of course זֵרוּעַ, מִזְרָע.

זֶרַע m. verbal from זָרַע, dec. VI. d.

1. seed (of plants.) Gen. 1:11, 12, 29. corn, grain in general, Job 39:12. hence, seed-time, winter, Gen. 8:22. Lev. 26:5. fields of corn, 1 Sam. 8:15.

2. semen virile. Lev. 15:16, 18, 32. 19:20.

3. Hence, children, posterity; even in the singular, Gen. 4:25—זֶרַע אֲנָשִׁים male offspring, 1 Sam. 1:11.

4. race, tribe, people. זֶרַע הַמֶּלֶךְ, הַמַּמְלָכָה, the royal family, 2 K. 11:1, 14. זֶרַע מְרֵעִים a race of evil doers, Is. 1:4.

זְרַע Chald. idem. Dan. 2:43. In Hebrew, Num. 11:7.

זֵרֹעִים and **זֵרְעֹנִים** food from the vegetable kingdom, vegetables. Dan. 1:12, 16. (In Chald. and Talmud. more frequent. Syr. ܙܪܥܘܢܐ idem.)

זָרַק fut. יִזְרֹק. 1. to scatter, as solids. Ex. 9:8. Job 2:12.

2. to sprinkle, as water, blood. Ex. 24:6. 29:16, 20. Figuratively, Hos. 7:9. גַּם־שֵׂיבָה זָרְקָה בּוֹ etiam canities ei sparsa est; זָרְקָה must here be taken intransitively. So Propertius, III. 4. 24.

Pu. זֹרַק pass. Num. 19:13, 20.

זָרַר found only in Po. זוֹרֵר to sneeze. 2 K. 4:35. So the Rabbins explain it. In Chaldaic we find זְרִיר a sneezing. Vulg. oscitavit.

זֶרֶת a span. Ex. 28:16. 39:9. 1 Sam. 17:4. (Aram. ܙܪܬܐ, ܙܪܬ, זרתא idem.) Prob. from זָרָה, which signifies, to spread out, hence זַר (for זָרָה,) fem. זֶרֶת.

ח

The name *Heth* חֵית probably signifies *a hedge, wall,* (from the Arab. حَاطَ, Syr. ܚܳܛ *to surround, to hedge in;*) and refers to its figure in the Phenician alphabet *H*, which is in some measure retained in the Greek H.

In Arabic we find two letters corresponding to the Hebrew *Heth;* namely, ح *Hha,* a strong aspirate or double *h,* and خ *Kha,* sounded like the Swiss *ch* or Span. *j.* This diversity of sound probably existed in the Hebrew, when it was a living language; at least, several roots have different significations, according as their ח corresponds to an Arab. ح or خ; comp. the articles חָבַל nos. I. and III. חָפַר nos. I. and II. But these two sounds ح and خ, on account of their general resemblance, are sometimes commuted for each other; e. g. רָצַח *to kill;* comp. رضح and رضخ, *to break* or *bruise in pieces.*

חֹב m. with suff. חֻבִּי, dec. VIII. d. *bosom.* Job 31: 33. (In Chald. חוּבָּא, חֻבָּא, חֻבָּא, *idem.*)

חָבָא in Kal not used. (Arab. خَبَأَ *to hide, conceal;* also خبأ conj. X. *to hide one's self.*)

Niph. *to be concealed, to conceal one's self;* construed with בְּ and אֶל of the place. Josh. 10: 16. 1 Sam. 10: 22. Job 29: 8 רָאוּנִי נְעָרִים וְנֶחְבָּאוּ *the young men saw me and hid themselves,* i. e. retired. verse 10 קוֹל־נְגִידִים נֶחְבָּאוּ *the voice of nobles hid itself,* i. e. it was restrained. Gen. 31: 27 לָמָּה נַחְבֵּאתָ לִבְרֹחַ *wherefore didst thou flee away secretly?* (comp. λανθάνω construed with a participle.)

Pu. *to creep away.* Job 24: 4.

Hiph. הֶחְבִּיא *to hide, conceal.* Josh. 6: 17, 25.

Hoph. pass. Is. 42: 22.

Hithpa. *to hide one's self.* 1 Sam. 14: 11.

Deriv. מַחֲבֹא, מַחֲבֵא.

חָבַב *to love.* Once Deut. 33: 3. (In Arab. حَبَّ, Aram. ܚܰܒ, ܚܰܒܶܒ, and חָבַב *idem.*)

חָבָה i. q. חָבָא *to hide one's self.* Imper. חֲבִי, Is. 26: 20. Infin. Niph. הֵחָבֵה, 1 K. 22: 25. 2 K. 7: 12.

Deriv. חֶבְיוֹן.

חֲבוּלָה f. Chald. *fault, crime.* Dan. 6: 23. comp. the root חבל Neh. 1: 7.

חָבוֹר *Chaboras,* the proper name of a river in Mesopotamia, which rises in mount Masius and empties into the Euphrates at Circesium. 2 K. 17: 6. 18: 11. 1 Chr. 5: 26. Arab. خابور. Otherwise written כְּבָר (q. v.)

חַבּוּרָה and חֲבֻרָה (Is. 53: 5.) f. dec. X. *wound, bruise, scar.* Gen. 4: 23. Is. 1: 6. 53: 5. Especially *a running sore,* Ps. 38: 6.

חָבַט, fut. יַחְבֹּט.

1. *to beat off with a stick,* as fruit from a tree. Deut. 24: 20. Is. 27: 12.

2. *to beat out* grain *with a stick.* Judg. 6: 11. Ruth. 2: 17.

Niph. pass. Is. 28: 27.

חֶבְיוֹן m. verbal from חָבָה, dec. I. *covering.* Hab. 3: 4.

I. חָבַל 1. i. q. Arab. خبل *to corrupt, injure, destroy.* See Piel.

2. *to be mad, foolish.* Hence, in Hebrew, *to act foolishly* or *wickedly,* Job 34: 31 לֹא אֶחְבֹּל *I will no more act wickedly.* Construed with לְ, Neh. 1: 7. (with עַל, Job 24: 9?)

Niph. *to be destroyed, to perish.* Prov. 13: 13.

Pi. *to destroy.* Ecc. 5: 5. Used in reference to persons, Is. 32: 7. or to countries, namely, *to lay* them *waste,* Is. 13: 5. 54: 16. Mic. 2: 10.

Pu. pass. Job 17:1 רוּחִי חֻבָּלָה *my breath*, i. e. my life, *is destroyed*. Is. 10:27.

II. **חָבַל**, fut. יַחְבֹּל, often יַחְבֹּל, תַּחְבֹּל. (Arab. خبل conj. IV. *to lend*; حبل *interest, usury*; Syr. ܚܘܒܠܐ, Chald. חֲבוּלָא *usury*.)

1. *to take a pledge of* any one, *to bind* him *by a pledge*; construed with an accusative of the person. Job 22:6. Prov. 20:16. 27:13.

2. *to take* any thing *as a pledge*, construed with an accus. of the thing. Deut. 24:6, 17. Ex. 22:24. Job 24:3. Perhaps construed with עַל, Job 24:9. But others render חָבַל in this passage, *to chain*, (after no. III.) Also see above, no. I. Part. חָבוּל *taken as a pledge*, Am. 2:8.

Deriv. חֲבֹל.

III. **חָבַל** i. q. Arab. حبل.

1. *to tie with a cord, to twist, to bind*. Deriv. חֶבֶל.

2. *to experience pain, torture*, (comp. the Lat. *tormentum, tortor*, from *torquere*.) Zech. 11:7, 14. Deriv. חֵבֶל.

Pi. *to bring forth with pain, to be in labour*. Cant. 8:5. Ps. 7:15.

חַבֵּל Chald. Pa. 1. *to injure, hurt*. Dan. 6:23.

2. *to destroy, to overturn*. Dan. 4:20. [23.] Ezra 6:12.

Ithpa. *to be destroyed, to perish*; spoken of a kingdom. Dan. 2:44. 6:27. 7:14.

Deriv. חֲבוּלָה.

חֵבֶל (Is. 66:7.) usually in the plur. חֲבָלִים, const. חֶבְלֵי, verbal from חָבַל no. III. 2. dec. VI. j. *pains* or *throes* of a woman in childbirth, ὠδῖνες. Is. 13:8. Jer. 13:21. 22:23 בְּבֹא־לָךְ חֲבָלִים *when pangs come upon thee*. Is. 66:7. Hos. 13:13.—Job 39:3 חֶבְלֵיהֶם תְּשַׁלַּחְנָה (*when*) *they are delivered of their pains*, i. e. of their young.—Spoken of pain generally, once Job 21:16.

חֶבֶל m. (once fem. Zeph. 2:6.) with suff. חֶבְלִי, Plur. חֲבָלִים, const. חַבְלֵי and חֶבְלֵי, verbal from חָבַל no. III. 1. dec. VI. a. and k.

1. *line, rope, cord*. Josh. 2:15. Ecc. 12:6 חֶבֶל הַכֶּסֶף *the silver cord*.

2. especially *a measuring-line*. Am. 7:17. 2 Sam. 8:2. Hence,

3. *a portion of land measured out, and assigned to any one by lot*. Josh. 17:14. 19:9. Hence, *an inheritance, possession*, Ps. 16:6. חֲבָלִים נָפְלוּ לִי בַּנְּעִמִים *my inheritance has fallen to me in a pleasant country*. Deut. 32:9 יַעֲקֹב חֶבֶל נַחֲלָתוֹ *Jacob is his possession*.

4. *a district of country, a region*. Deut. 3:4. 13:14.

5. *a snare, net*. Ps. 140:6. Job 18:10.—חֶבְלֵי מָוֶת, שְׁאוֹל *the snares of death, of hades*, Ps. 18:5, 6. 116:3.

6. *a band* or *company* of men. 1 Sam. 10:5, 10.

חֲבֹל m. verbal from חָבַל no. II. *a pawn, pledge*. Ezek. 18:12, 16. 33:15.

חֲבֹלָה fem. of חֲבֹל, *idem*. Ezek. 18:7.

חֲבָל m. Chald. *hurt, injury*. Dan. 3:25.

חֲבָל m. Chald. *injury*. Ezra 4:22.

חִבֵּל m. found only Prov. 23:34. a part of a ship, probably *the mast*, so called from the ropes (חֶבֶל,) by which it is made fast. Others: *the rudder*.

חֹבֵל m. denom. from חֶבֶל *a rope*;) *a shipman, seaman*. Jon. 1:6. Ezek. 27:8, 27—29. Comp. תַּחְבֻּלוֹת.

חֲבַצֶּלֶת f. Cant. 2:1. Is. 35:1. name of a flower, according to the ancient versions, *a lily*, or *a narcissus*. See Celsii Hierobotan. T. I. p. 488. The corresponding Syr. ܚܒܨܠܝܬܐ signifies i. q. the Greek ἐφήμερον, *meadow-saffron*, (*colchicum autumnale*, Linn.)

חָבַק, more frequently in Pi. חִבֵּק.

1. *to embrace, twine round*, Construed with an accus. Ecc. 3:5. 2 K. 4:16. with לְ, Gen. 29:13. 48:10.—חִבְּקוּ צוּר אַשְׁפַּתּוֹת, *they embrace the rock, the dunghill*, a proverbial phrase for *they lie on the rock*, or *on the dunghill*, Job 24:8. Lam. 4:5.

2. חֹבֵק יָדַיִם *to fold the hands*, spoken of the idler. Ecc. 4:5.

חִבֻּק m. verbal from Piel of חָבַק, dec. I. *the folding* of the hands, spoken of the sluggard. Prov. 6:10. 24:33.

חֲבַקּוּק m. (*embracing*, after the form שַׁעֲרוּר,) *Habakkuk*, proper name of a prophet. In the Sept. Ἀμβακούμ, as if derived from the punctuation חַמְבַּקּוּק and a corruption of κ into μ.

חָבַר 1. *to be joined* or *bound together*. Ex. 26:3. Also, *to be confederated*, spoken of nations, Gen. 14:3 כָּל־אֵלֶּה חָבְרוּ אֶל עֵמֶק הַשִּׂדִּים *all these were confederated (and came) to the valley of Siddim*. comp. Hos. 4:17 חֲבוּר עֲצַבִּים *confederated with idols*.

2. חָבַר חֶבֶר *to exercise magic*, namely, by means of certain magical knots *to bind* some (distant) object. Perhaps more particularly *the charming* of poisonous serpents. Deut. 18:11. Ps. 58:6. (The ideas of *binding* and *magic* are united in several languages: comp. the Greek καταδεσμός; Lat. *fascinare, ligare ligulam;* and Germ. *Nesteln knüpfen*. Others derive the idea, *to exercise magic*, from the Arab. خبر *to be wise;* but it appears from Deut. 18:11. that a particular species of magic is intended.)

Pi. חִבֵּר *to bind, join*. Ex. 26:6 ff. 2 Chr. 20:36.

Pu. חֻבַּר pass. Ex. 28:7. Ps. 94:20 הַיְחָבְרְךָ כִּסֵּא הַוּוֹת *shall the throne of wickedness be joined with thee?* i. e. shall it have fellowship with thee?

Hithpa. *to join one's self*. 2 Chr. 20:35, 37. Dan. 11:6.—In verse 23, the Syriac infinitive form הִתְחַבְּרוּת occurs as a noun.

Hiph. *to bind, join*, perhaps in an artificial manner. Job. 16:4 אַחְבִּירָה עֲלֵיכֶם בְּמִלִּים *I could join together words against you*, i. e. compose artificial speeches against you. (The prefix בְּ appears superfluous.)

Deriv. out of course מַחְבָּרָה, מְחַבְּרוֹת.

חַבָּר m. Job. 40:30. [41:6.] verbal from חָבַר dec. I. usually rendered, *a companion;* perhaps *a sorcerer, magician*. Syr. ܚܒܳܪܳܐ Comp. חֶבֶר no. III.

חָבֵר m. verbal from חָבַר, dec. V. b. *associate, companion*. Cant. 1:7. 8:13. —Judg. 20:11 כְּאִישׁ אֶחָד חֲבֵרִים *all associated together*. Ps. 149:63.

חַבַר m. Chald. *idem*. Dan. 2:13, 17, 18.

חֶבֶר m. verbal from חָבַר dec. VI. k.

1. *company, society*. Hos. 6:9. Prov. 21:9 בֵּית חָבֶר *a house of company*, i. e. a common house. 25:24.

2. *magic, enchantment*. Is. 47:9, 12.

חֲבַרְבֻּרוֹת fem. plur. dec. I. *the variegated spots* (of the leopard). Jer. 13:23. (Arab. حبر *mark, spot, colour.*)

חַבְרָה fem. of חָבֵר, Chald. *a female companion*, hence, (like רְעוּת,) *the other*. Dan. 7:20.

חֶבְרָה fem. of חֶבֶר, *company, society*. Job 34:8.

חֶבְרוֹן proper name of an ancient city in the tribe of Judah, also called קִרְיַת־אַרְבַּע Gen. 13:18. 14:13. 23:2. afterwards the royal residence of David for seven years, 2 Sam. 2:1. 5:5.

חֲבֶרֶת fem. of חָבֵר dec. XIII. c. *female companion, wife*. Mal. 2:14.

חֹבֶרֶת f. verbal from חָבַר, *joining, place of joining*. Ex. 26:4, 10.

חָבַשׁ, fut. יַחְבֹּשׁ, once יַחֲבוּשׁ (Job 5:18.)

1. *to bind, to bind on, to bind about*. Ezek. 27:24. particularly, *to bind on* a turban, Ex. 29:9. Lev. 8:13. Jon. 2:6 סוּף חָבוּשׁ לְרֹאשִׁי *the sea-reed is bound about my head*, i. e. it composes my turban. Ezek. 16:10 וָאֶחְבָּשֵׁךְ בַּשֵּׁשׁ *I bound thee (thy head) about with fine cotton*.

2. *to bind up* (a wound.) Job 5:18. Is. 3:7. 30:26. Construed with לְ, (comp. נָשָׂא לְ,) Ezek. 34:4, 16. Is. 61:1.

3. *to saddle*, construed with an accus. Gen. 22:3. Num. 22:21. Judg. 19:11. 2 Sam. 17:23.

4. *to bind up, to close, cover*. Job 40:13 פְּנֵיהֶם חֲבֹשׁ בַּטָּמוּן *cover their face in darkness*. See Pi. no. 2.

5. *to exercise power, to rule, imperio coercere*. Job 34:17 הַאַף שׂוֹנֵא מִשְׁפָּט יַחֲבוֹשׁ

can also he that hateth righteousness exercise power? (Comp. עָצַר *to rule*, 1 Sam. 9:17.)

Pi. 1. *to bind up*, construed with לְ. Ps. 147:3.

2. *to bind, to stop, restrain;* spoken of the miner who stops the oozing of water in the shaft. Job 28:11 מִבְּכִי נְהָרוֹת חִבֵּשׁ *he stops the streams from trickling down.*

Pu. *to be bound up*. Is. 1:6. Ezek. 30:21.

חֲבִתִּים masc. plur. *pans*. 1 Chr. 9:31. Comp. מַחֲבַת. Root perhaps خبت *to be low*, spoken of a field; hence, *shallow pans*. According to others, *pastry*.

חַג, const. חַג with suff. חַגִּי, dec. VIII. a.

1. *a feast, festival*. Ex. 10:9. 12:14. —עָשָׂה חַג, חַג חָג *to celebrate a festival*, Lev. 23:39. Deut. 16:10.—In the Talmudical writers it denotes, by way of eminence, *the feast of tabernacles;* so 2 Chr. 5:3. comp. 1 K. 8:2.

2. by a metonymy, *the festival sacrifice, victim*. Ps. 118:27 אִסְרוּ־חַג בַּעֲבֹתִים *bind the victim with cords*. Ex. 23:18 חֵלֶב חַגִּי *the fat of my sacrifice*. Mal. 2:3. comp. מוֹעֵד 2 Chr. 30:22.

חָגָּא i. q. חָגָה (which is also found in several MSS.) *fear, trembling*. Is. 19:17. Root חָגַג, perhaps *to be giddy* or *to tremble* (through fear,) *to be afraid;* comp. חוּל.

חָגָב m. dec. IV. c. *the locust*. According to Lev. 11:22. a winged and eatable species of this insect. Num. 13:33. Is. 40:22.

חָגַג (kindred with חוּג) *to move round in a circle*. Hence,

1. *to dance*. 1 Sam. 30:16.

2. *to keep* or *celebrate* a feast, namely, by dancing. Ex. 5:1. Lev. 23:41. Num. 29:12. Ps. 42:5 הָמוֹן חוֹגֵג *the multitude keeping a holiday*. (Syr. ܚܓܐ, ܚܓܓ *idem;* Arab. حجّ *to make a pilgrimage* or *to march in procession on a festival*.)

3. *to be giddy, to stagger*, spoken of a drunkard. Ps. 107:27.

חֲגָוִים masc. plur.—חַגְוֵי הַסֶּלַע *the heights, cliffs of the rocks*, or *the refuges among the rocks*. Cant. 2:14. Obad. 3. Jer. 49:16. (In Arab. حجا *confugit, refugit;* and مَحْجَأ *refugii locus, asylum;* but on the contrary Syr. ܚܓܘܐ, ܚܓܘ *a precipice, steep cliff*.)

חֲגוֹר m. verbal from חָגַר, dec. III. a.

1. *a girdle*. 1 Sam. 18:4.

2. as an adj. i. q. חֹגֵר *girded, clothed*. חֲגוֹרֵי אֵזוֹר *girded with a girdle*. comp. 2 K. 3:21.

חֲגוֹרָה fem. of חֲגוֹר, dec. X.

1. *a girdle*. 2 Sam. 18:11.

2. *an apron*. Gen. 3:7.

חַגַּי (*festive*, from חַג and the termination ־ַי i. q. ־ִי) *Haggai*, the proper name of a prophet. Sept. Ἀγγαῖος. Hag. 1:1.

חָגַר, fut. יַחְגֹּר. 1. *to gird, to gird up, to gird on*. It is construed, (1.) with an accus. of the part girded, Prov. 31:17 חָגְרָה בְעוֹז מָתְנֶיהָ *she girded her loins with strength*. 2 K. 4:29. 9:1. (2.) with an accus. of the garment or girdle, (comp. לָבַשׁ,) as חָגַר אֶת־הַחֶרֶב *to gird on the sword*, 1 Sam. 17:39. 25:13. Ps. 45:4. חָגַר שַׂק *to gird on sackcloth*, Is. 15:3. Jer. 49:3. Part. act. 2 K. 3:21 מִכֹּל חֹגֵר חֲגֹרָה *from all who girded on the girdle*, i. e. who were capable of bearing arms. Part. pass. חָגוּר אֵפוֹד *girded* or *clothed with an ephod*, 1 Sam. 2:18. Also put in the const. state, Joel 1:8 חֲגֻרַת־שַׂק *girded with sackcloth*. Elliptically, Joel 1:13 חִגְרוּ *gird yourselves*, i. e. gird on sackcloth. 2 Sam. 21:16 וְהוּא חָגוּר חֲדָשָׁה *and he was girded with a new* (*sword*.)—Metaphorically, Ps. 65:13 גִּיל גְּבָעוֹת תַּחְגֹּרְנָה *the hills gird on joy*. (comp. Ps. 65:14.) Ps. 76:11. (3.) with a double accus. of the person and girdle, Ex. 29:9. Lev. 8:13. Also with בְּ of the girdle, Lev. 8:7. 16:4.

2. *to gird one's self*. Ezek. 44:18. 1 K. 20:11. Here likewise we may place, (if the reading is correct,) 2 Sam. 22:46 וְיַחְגְּרוּ מִמִּסְגְּרוֹתָם *and they gird themselves*

(and go) out of their citadels; or, according to Syriac usage, *they hobble forth,* comp. Mic. 7:17. Hos. 11:11.

Deriv. מַחֲגֹרֶת, חֲגוֹר.

חַד fem. חֲדָא and חֲדָה, Chald.

1. *one,* i. q. Heb. אֶחָד. (See א.)—Sometimes used for the indefinite article, *a, an,* Dan. 2:31 צְלֵם חַד *an image.* 6:18. Ezra 4:8.

2. *the first.* Dan. 7:1.

3. when used before numerals, *times,* Lat. *vices.* Dan. 3:19 חַד־שִׁבְעָה עַל דִּי *seven times more than.* (So the Syr. ܚܕ)—כַּחֲדָה *at the same time, together,* i. q. Heb. כְּאֶחָד, Dan. 2:35.—חַד *one* occurs once also in Hebrew, Ezek. 33:30.

חַד, fem. חַדָּה, verbal adj. from חָדַד, dec. VIII. h. *sharp,* spoken of the sword. Ezek. 5:1. Ps. 57:5. Prov. 5:4.

חָדַד 1. *to be sharp,* i. q. Arab. حَدَّ (fut. 1.)

2. *to be swift, nimble.* Hab. 1:8. (Several words denoting *sharpness* have this signification; comp. in Greek, ὀξύς, θοός; in Lat. *acer;* in Syr. ܚܪܝܦ.) Others: *to be sharp-sighted.* Comp. חָרַץ.

Hoph. pass. Ezek. 21:14, 15, 16. [21:9, 10, 11.]

Deriv. חַד.

I. **חָדָה,** fut. apoc. יִחַדְּ, *to rejoice.* Ex. 18:9. Job 3:6 אַל יִחַדְּ בִּימֵי שָׁנָה *let it not rejoice among the days of the year.*

Pi. *to make serene* or *joyful.* Ps. 21:7.

Deriv. חֶדְוָה.

II. **חָדָה** i. q. חדד *to be* or *become sharp.*

Hiph. *to sharpen.* Prov. 27:17 בַּרְזֶל בְּבַרְזֶל יָחַד וְאִישׁ יַחַד פְּנֵי־רֵעֵהוּ *iron becomes sharp on iron, so one man sharpens the countenance of another.* יָחַד in the former part of the verse is the fut. apoc. of Kal; in the latter part, the fut. apoc. of Hiphil.

חַדּוּדִים masc. plur. dec. I. Job 41:22. [30.] *points;* חַדּוּדֵי חָרֶשׂ *sharp potsherds,* spoken of the scales of the crocodile; comp. Ælian. Hist. Anim. x. 24.

חֶדְוָה f. verbal from חָדָה no. I. dec. X. *joy, gladness.* 1 Chr. 16:27. Neh. 8:10.

חֶדְוָה f. Chald. *idem.* Ezra 6:16.

חָדִיד proper name of a city of the Benjamites, situated on a mountain. Ezra 2:33. Neh. 7:37. 11:34. In 1 Mac. 12:38, it is called Ἀδιδά. Comp. Josephus J. A. III. 11.

חֲדִין plur. Chald. *breast,* i. q. Heb. חָזֶה. Dan. 2:32. (In the Targums we find the singular חֲדִי.)

חָדַל and **חָדֵל** fut. יֶחְדַּל. 1. *to cease, desist, leave off,* (from doing any thing.) Am. 7:5. Construed with an infin. Is. 1:16. especially with לְ and an infin. Gen. 11:8. 41:49. 1 Sam. 12:23. With an accus. of the noun, Job 3:17. Spoken also of the thing desisted from, Ex. 9:34 חָדַל הַמָּטָר *the rain ceased.* verses 29, 33. Is. 24:8.

2. *to omit, to forbear, not to do.* 1 K. 22:6, 15 הֲנֵלֵךְ—אִם נֶחְדָּל *shall we go, ... or shall we omit it?* Ezek. 2:5. Jer. 40:4. Construed with לְ and an infinitive, Num. 9:13. Deut. 23:23.

3. *to quit, let alone, desert, give up, leave off;* (1.) construed with מִן of the person, Ex. 14:2 חֲדַל מִמֶּנּוּ *let us alone.* Job 7:16. 19:14 חָדְלוּ קְרוֹבָי *my kinsfolk desert me.*—In a different sense 2 Chr. 35:21 חֲדַל לְךָ מֵאֱלֹהִים אֲשֶׁר עִמִּי *desist from God, who is with me,* i. e. be afraid of him. Is. 2:22. (2.) with מִן of the thing, 1 Sam. 9:5. Prov. 23:4. Ps. 49:9 *he gives it up for ever.* With an accus. of the thing, Judg. 9:9 ff. (3.) with מִן and an infin. of the action, 1 K. 15:21 *he left off building.* Hence, *to avoid* doing any thing, Ex. 23:5.

4. *to be idle, to rest, to keep holiday.* 1 Sam. 2:5. Job 14:6. Judg. 5:6 חָדְלוּ אֳרָחוֹת *the highways were idle,* i. e. deserted; (comp. Is. 33:8.)

5. *to cease to be, to fail, to be wanting.* Deut. 15:11 לֹא יֶחְדַּל אֶבְיוֹן *the poor shall not fail.* Judg. 5:7. Job 14:7.

Note. The imperative חֲדַל is construed with a dative of the pronoun לְךָ, לָכֶם, 2 Chr. 25:16. 35:21. Is. 2:22.

חָדֵל verbal adj. from חָדַל, dec. V. b. 1. *one who forbears.* Ezek. 3:27.

2. *frail, transitory*. Ps. 39:5.

3. חֲדַל־אִישִׁים *forsaken by men*. Is. 53:3. comp. Job 19:14.

חֶדֶל m. verbal from חָדַל, *place of rest, regions of the dead, hades*. Is. 38:11. See חדל no. 4. and comp. דּוּמָה.

חֵדֶק Mic. 7:4. and **חֶדֶק** Prov. 15:19. a species of thorn or thorn-bush. Arab. حدق a thorn-bush of Phenicia, perhaps *solanum insanum*, Linn.

חִדֶּקֶל *the river Tigris*. Gen. 2:14. Dan. 10:4. Aram. דִּיגְלַת, ܕܩܠܬ; Arab. دجلة.

חָדַר found only Ezek. 21:19 חֶרֶב הַחֹדֶרֶת לָהֶם usually rendered (as if a denom. from חֶדֶר,) *which penetrates into their inward parts*. Better according to the ancient versions, *which terrifies them*, i. q. חָרַד by transposition. According to the Syriac usage, *to surround in a hostile manner*.

חֶדֶר m. const. חֲדַר, with suff. חֶדְרוֹ; Plur. חֲדָרִים, const. חַדְרֵי; dec. VI. a. and k. (In Arab. خدر *a curtain which separates the inner part of a tent from the outer*.)

1. *the inner apartment* or *chamber of a tent* or *house*. Gen. 34:30. Judg. 16:9, 12. whether *a bed-chamber*, 2 Sam. 4:7. 13:10. *woman's chamber*, Cant. 3:4. *bride-chamber*, Judg. 15:1. Joel 2:16. or *store-chamber*, Prov. 24:4.

2. figuratively, חַדְרֵי־תֵימָן Job 9:9. *the remotest south, penetralia austri*; (comp. יַרְכְּתֵי צָפוֹן;) also without תֵּימָן in the same sense, 37:9. But perhaps in these two passages it means *the chambers* or *store-houses of the south wind*.—חַדְרֵי־בֶטֶן *the innermost parts of the belly*, Prov. 18:8. 26:22.—חַדְרֵי־מָוֶת *the chambers of hades*, Prov. 7:27.

חַדְרָךְ Zech. 9:1. anciently a great city, east of Damascus, giving name to the surrounding country. See Michaëlis Supplem. p. 676. and Ugolini Thes. T. VII. no. 20.

חָדַשׁ *to be new*. In Kal not used.

Pi. *to renew, make new*. Job 10:17. Ps. 51:12. especially, *to rebuild* or *repair* cities, buildings. Is. 61:4. 2 Chr. 24:4.

Hithpa. *to renew one's self*. Ps. 103:5.

חָדָשׁ verbal adj. from חָדַשׁ dec. IV. c. *new*, in all its various significations.—*Fresh, recens*, (antith. יָשָׁן,) Lev. 26:10. —*new, unheard of*, Ecc. 1:9, 10.— חֲדָשָׁה *something new*. Is. 43:19. Plur. חֲדָשׁוֹת *new things*, Is. 42:9.

חֹדֶשׁ m. verbal from חָדַשׁ, dec. VI. m.

1. *the new-moon, the first day on which the moon is visible*, kept by the Israelites as a festival. Num. 29:6. 1 Sam. 20:5, 18, 24.—Ex. 19:1 בַּחֹדֶשׁ הַשְּׁלִישִׁי *on the first day of the third month, tertiis calendis*. Hos. 5:7 עַתָּה יֹאכְלֵם חֹדֶשׁ *now shall the new-moon consume you*, i. e. ye shall be consumed on the new moon.

2. *a month*, which the Hebrews began with the new moon. Gen. 7:11, etc.— חֹדֶשׁ יָמִים *a month long, a whole month*, (see יָמִים,) Gen. 29:14. Num. 11:20, 21.

חֲדַת adj. Chald. *new*. Ezra 6:4.

חַוָּא see **חַוָּה**.

חוּב *to be guilty, to owe, to transgress*, as in Aram. and Arab.

Pi. חִיֵּב *to make guilty, to cause to owe*. Dan. 1:10.

חוֹב m. verbal from חוּב, *debt*. Ezek. 18:7.

חוֹבָה proper name of a place north of Damascus. Once Gen. 14:15. comp. Χωβὰ Judith 4:4. 15:4.

חוּג *to draw a circle, to measure with a compass*. Job 26:10. Deriv. out of course מְחוּגָה.

חוּג m. verbal from חוּג, *circle, arch*; spoken of the arch of heaven, Prov. 8:27. Job 22:14. of the circle of the earth, Is. 40:22.

חוּד denom. from חִידָה, (like מָשַׁל from מָשָׁל,) always joined with חִידָה.

1. *to propose a riddle*. Judg. 14:12 ff.

2. *to propose an allegory.* Ezek. 17:2.

חָוָה found only in Piel חִוָּה, in poetry, i. q. הִגִּיד, *to shew, declare.* Job 32:10, 17. Construed with an accus. of the person, Job 32:6. with suff. 15:17. 36:2. but likewise with a dative, Ps. 19:3.

חֲוָה or חֲוָא, Pa. חַוֵּא Chald. *idem.* Dan. 2:11. Construed with לְ of the person, 2:24. with an accus. 5:7.

Aph. *idem.* Construed with לְ, Dan. 2:16, 24, 27. with an accus. 2:6, 9. (In Syr. *idem.* In Arab. by transposition وحي.)

חַוָּה f. proper name of the first woman. Gen. 3:20. 4:1. In the first passage it is explained as if synonymous with חַיָּה *life.* Sept. Εὔα, (comp. חַוִּי Εὐαῖος.) Vulg. *Eva.*

חַוּוֹת plur. fem. dec. X. *villages of moveable tents, encampments of wandering shepherds.* Num. 32:41. Deut. 3:14. Josh. 13:30. Comp. חַיָּה no. 4. (Root Arab. حوي *to collect, assemble.*)

חוֹחַ m. dec. I. a. and VI. *a.*

1. *a thorn, thorn-bush.* Job 31:40. Prov. 26:9. 2 K. 14:9. Plur. חוֹחִים Cant. 2:2. and חֲוָחִים 1 Sam. 13:6. *thorn-bushes.*

2. i. q. חַח *a hook,* or perhaps *ring,* such as was put through the nose of great fishes, to let them down again into the water. Job 40:26. [41:2.] Comp. Œdmann's verm. Sammlungen aus der Naturkunde, Th. v. p. 5.

3. a similar instrument used for the confining of prisoners. 2 Chr. 33:11. comp. Am. 4:2.

חוּט Chald. *to sew together.* Aph. *to repair* (a wall.) Ezra 4:12.

חוּט m. (comp. Chald. חוּט *to sew together.*)

1. *a thread.* Ecc. 4:12. Used proverbially, Gen. 14:23 מִחוּט וְעַד שְׂרוֹךְ נַעַל *from a thread even to a shoe-latchet,* i. e. not the least thing. So the Latins, *ne hilum* (i. q. filum) *quidem, not even a thread;* whence *nihil.*

2. *a line, cord.* Josh. 2:18.

3. *a band, fillet.* Cant. 4:3.

חִוִּי a gentile noun, *the Hivites,* a Canaanitish tribe at the foot of Mount Hermon, Josh. 11:3. also in Mount Lebanon, Judg. 3:3.

חֲוִילָה a proper name. 1. two districts in Yemen, the one inhabited by Hamites, Gen. 10:7. and the other by Shemites, verse 29. comp. 25:18. 1 Sam. 15:7. (Probably the districts now called خَوْلَان, see Niebuhr's Description de l'Arabie.)

2. Gen. 2:11. *Havilah,* a gold country, perhaps a general name for Arabia (and India,) which accords best with the supposition that *the Pison* is *the Ganges.* See art. פִּישׁוֹן. Others, with less probability, *Chwala* on the Caspian Sea; whence the Caspian Sea is called in Russian *Chwalinskoje More.*

I. חוּל and חִיל literally, *to turn, to twist.* (Arab. حال, whence حَوْلَ *round about.*)

1. *to be pained,* (as if *torqueri,* comp. חָבַל no. III.) Jer. 5:3. especially *to be in labour, to travail,* Is. 13:8. 23:4. 26:18. 66:7, 8. Mic. 4:18. Figuratively, Mic. 1:12 *for she is pained for the good* (*which she has lost.*) Hence,

2. *to tremble,* (as a woman in labour.) Deut. 2:25. Joel 2:6. Construed with מִן 1 Sam. 31:3. 1 Chr. 10:3.

3. *to dance.* Judg. 21:21.

4. *to bring forth.* Is. 54:1.

5. *to rush, fall upon.* Jer. 30:23 *a sweeping whirlwind* עַל רֹאשׁ רְשָׁעִים יָחוּל *shall fall on the head of the ungodly.* So 23:19. 2 Sam. 3:29 *let it* (*the blood of Abner*) *fall upon the head of Joab.* Hos. 11:6 חָלָה חֶרֶב בְּעָרָיו *the sword shall fall on his cities.* Lam. 4:6 לֹא חָלוּ בָהּ יָדַיִם *no hands fell on her.* (This signification of חוּל is found in the Targums.)

6. *to be strong, lasting, permanent.* (On the connexion of this with the primary signification, see חָזַק, קָשַׁר. In Arab. حال (med. Vav) *idem.* In Aram.

Pa. חַיֵּל *to strengthen.* Deriv. חַיִל *strength.*) Ps. 10:5 יָחִילוּ דְרָכָו *his ways are strong,* i.e. his actions prosper. Job 20:21 לֹא יָחִיל טוּבוֹ *his prosperity shall not be lasting.* (Others connect this signification with that of *waiting;* see חול no. II.)

Hiph. causat. of Kal no. 2. *to shake.* Ps. 29:8.

Hoph. *to be made to bring forth.* Is. 66:8.

Pilel חוֹלֵל 1. *to dance in a circle.* Judg. 21:23.

2. i.q. Kal no. 2. *to tremble.* Job 26:5.

3. i.q. Kal no. 4. *to bring forth.* Job 39:1. Prov. 25:23. *to form, to make* generally, Deut. 32:18. Ps. 90:2. Causat. Ps. 29:9.

Pulal חוֹלַל pass. *to be born.* Job 15:7. Prov. 8:24, 25. Ps. 51:7.

Hithpalel הִתְחוֹלֵל.

1. *to be pained* or *tormented.* Job 15:20.

2. *to rush.* Jer. 23:19.

Hithpalp. הִתְחַלְחֵל *to be pained* or *grieved.* Est. 4:4.

Deriv. out of course חִיל, מְחוֹלָה, חַלְחָלָה.

II. חוּל and חִיל i.q. יָחַל *to wait, tarry.* Gen. 8:10. Judg. 3:25.

Pilel חוֹלֵל *idem.* Job 35:14.

Hithpal. *idem.* Ps. 37:7.

חוֹל m. 1. *sand.* Ex. 2:12. generally in the phrase חוֹל יַמִּים, חוֹל הַיָּם *sand of the sea,* as indicative of multitude, Gen. 32:13. 41:49. and of weight, Job 6:3. Prov. 27:3.

2. Job 29:18. according to the Jewish commentators, *the bird phœnix,* but perhaps a mere conjecture from the context. The Babylonian MSS read חוּל.

חוּל proper name of an Aramean country. Once Gen. 10:23. It is supposed by some to be *Cœlesyria,* from the Chald. חֵיל *a valley;* but the etymological grounds are insufficient.

חוּם m. adj. *black.* Gen. 30:32 ff. The root חוּם is kindred with חָמַם *to be hot,* which in Arabic signifies also *to be burnt by the sun, to be black.*

חוֹמָה f. dec. X. *a wall.* Ex. 14:22, 29. Deut. 3:5. 28:52. Root prob. חָמָה i.q. Arab. حمى *to surround, protect.*

Plur. חוֹמוֹת (with *singular* meaning, like בָּמוֹת,) *a wall.* Jer. 1:18. comp. 15:20. Hence,

Dual בֵּין הַחֹמֹתַיִם *between the two walls (of Jerusalem),* 2 K. 25:4. Is. 22:11. Jer. 39:4.

חוּס, fut. יָחוּס, יָחֹס, also יָחֹס.

1. *to have compassion, to pity;* construed with עַל of the person. Ps. 72:13. Also *to be grieved* or *troubled,* construed with עַל of the thing, Jon. 4:10 אַתָּה חַסְתָּ עַל הַקִּיקָיוֹן *thou art grieved on account of the ricinus.* (comp. Gen. 45:20.)

2. *to spare,* construed with עַל. Neh. 13:22. Jer. 13:14. Ezek. 24:14. Joel 2:17. (In Aram. ܚܣ construed with ܥܠ.)

3. Instead of the simple construction given above, we find more commonly in the significations nos. 1. and 2. the following phraseology, תָּחוֹס עֵינִי עַל *mine eye looks with pity* or *indulgence on* any one. Gen. 45:20 וְעֵינְכֶם אַל־תָּחֹס עַל־כְּלֵיכֶם *and be not troubled about your utensils.* Deut. 7:16 לֹא תָחוֹס עֵינְךָ עֲלֵיהֶם *thou shalt not spare them.* 13:9. 19:13, 21. 25:12. Is. 13:18. Ezek. 5:11. 7:4, 9. Once with the omission of עַיִן, 1 Sam. 24:11 וַתָּחָס עָלֶיךָ *and (mine eye) looked with compassion on thee,* i.e. I spared thee from compassion. Similar examples in which actions are attributed to particular members of the body, are very common; (comp. קָשָׁה joined with יָד, חָזַק with the same, Judg. 7:11. 2 Sam. 16:21. מָלֵא with עַיִן; etc.)

חוֹף, חֹף m. dec. I. *coast, shore.* Gen. 49:13. Deut. 1:7. Josh. 9:1. (Arab. حافة *margin, bank, shore.*)

חוּץ 1. as an adv. *without, abroad;* denoting the place where, as מוֹלֶדֶת חוּץ *one born out of the house,* Lev. 18:9. also the place whither, Deut. 23:13. With ה parag. חוּצָה in the same senses, 1 K. 6:6. Ex. 12:46. Joined with prepositions, (1.) בַּחוּץ *without, in the street.* Gen. 9 : 22. (2.) לַחוּץ *idem,* Ps. 41 : 7. and לַחוּצָה *idem,* 2 Chr. 32 : 5. (3.) מִחוּץ *from without, outwardly,* the opposite of מִבַּיִת. Gen. 6 : 14. מֵהַחוּץ *idem,* Ezek. 41 : 25. מִן הַחוּץ *idem,* 2 K. 4 : 3. (4.) מִחוּץ לְ as a prep. *without.*—מִחוּץ לָעִיר *without the city,* Gen. 19 : 16. 24 : 11 מִחוּצָה לְ *idem,* Ezek. 40 : 40, 44. (5.) אֶל מִחוּץ לְ as a prep. *to the outside of.* Num. 5 : 3, 4 אֶל מִחוּץ לַמַּחֲנֶה *to the outside of the camp.* Deut. 23 : 11. Lev. 4 : 12. (6.) חוּץ מִן as a prep. figuratively, *besides.* Ecc. 2 : 25. (So in Chald. בַּר מִן.)

2. as a subst. dec. I. (1.) *what is without the house, the street.* Jer. 37 : 21. Job 18 : 17. Plur. חוּצוֹת, Is. 5 : 25. 10 : 6. (2.) *what is without the city, fields, pastures, deserts.* Job 5 : 10. (Aram. בַּר *idem.*) Hence put in opposition to אֶרֶץ, Prov. 8 : 26 אֶרֶץ וְחוּצוֹת *(cultivated) land and deserts.* Comp. Mark 1 : 45.

Deriv. חִיצוֹן.

חוק (ו or י) i. q. חֵיק *the bosom.* Ps. 74 : 11 Keth.

חָוַר, fut. יֶחֱוַר *to become white, to grow pale,* spoken of the face. Is. 29 : 22. (Aram. ܚܘܰܪ, חֲוַר *idem.*)

I. חוּר m. *fine white linen* or *cotton.* Est. 1 : 6. 8 : 15. Sept. *βύσσος.* Arab. حرير *white silk;* which may be the meaning of the Hebrew word, for Median garments were made of silk. Ethiop. ሐሪር (hhărîr) *white silk.*

II. חוֹר and חֹר, dec. I. i. q. חוֹר no. II. *hole, cavity.* Is. 11 : 8. 42 : 22. (In Arab. with خ.)

I. חוֹר i. q. חוּר no. I. *white linen,* (or *silk.*) With an uncommon plural termination חוֹרָי, Is. 19 : 9.

II. חוֹר m. dec. I. 1. *a hole.* 2 K. 12 : 10. Applied to the opening for a window, Cant. 5 : 4. to the cavity for the eye, Zech. 14 : 12.

2. *a cave, cavern.* Job 30 : 6. 1 Sam. 14 : 11.

חִוָּר m. Chald. *white.* Dan. 7 : 9.

חוּרָם *Huram,* 1. proper name of a king of Tyre, contemporary with Solomon. 2 Chr. 2 : 2. Otherwise called חִירָם, 2 Sam. 5 : 11. 1 K. 5 : 15. [5 : 1.]

2. of a Tyrian artist, 2 Chr. 4 : 11. also called חִירוֹם 1 K. 7 : 40.

חַוְרָן proper name of a district beyond Jordan. Ezek. 47 : 16, 18. In Greek, Αὐρανῖτις, Ἀὐρανῖτις.

I. חוּשׁ 1. *to make haste, to hasten.* Is. 8 : 1, 3. 1 Sam. 20 : 38. Deut. 32 : 35. Ps. 70 : 6 אֱלֹהִים חוּשָׁה לִּי *O God, hasten to me.* 141 : 1. Part. pass. חֻשִׁים *hastening* or *in haste,* with an active signification, (comp. אָחוּז,) Num. 32 : 17.

2. *to move violently, to rage, to be ardent.* Job 20 : 2 בַּעֲבוּר חוּשִׁי בִי *on account of my ardour within me.*

Hiph. 1. *to urge on, to hasten.* Is. 5 : 19. 60 : 22. Ps. 55 : 9.

2. intrans. as in Kal, *to make haste.* Judg. 20 : 37.

3. *to be afraid, to flee.* Is. 28 : 16. (These significations are also united in בהל, חוּשׁ. In Arab. حاش (med. Je) *to be afraid* and *to hasten.*)

II. חוּשׁ as in Chaldaic, *to perceive by the senses, to feel,* for example, pain, joy, pleasure. Ecc. 2 : 25 מִי יָחוּשׁ *who has enjoyed pleasure?*

חוּת. For Hab. 2 : 17, see חָתַת.

חוֹתָם m. verbal from חָתַם, dec. I. *a seal, a seal-ring.* The inhabitants of the east often carried a seal suspended by a string, round the neck, between their outer and inner garments, as the Persians do at this day. Gen. 38 : 18. Cant. 8 : 6.

חֲזָאֵל m. *Hazael,* proper name of a king of Syria. 1 K. 19 : 15, 17. 2 K. 8 : 9, 12.—בֵּית ח' *the house of Hazael,* i. e. Damascus, Am. 1 : 4.

חָזָה 1. in poetry, i. q. רָאָה *to see, behold.* Job 24 : 1. Ps. 46 : 9. 58 : 9. Construed with בְּ, *to see* or *regard with satisfaction,* Ps. 27 : 4. 63 : 3. Cant. 7 : 1. [6 : 13]. Job 36 : 25. In a different sense, Is. 47:13 הֹזִים בַּכּוֹכָבִים *the gazers on the stars.*

2. used especially in a religious sense; e. g. חָזָה אֶת הָאֱלֹהִים *to see God,* Ex. 24:11. Job 19:26. and applied particularly to the supernatural visions and internal revelations given to the prophets, Num. 24:4. Hab. 1:1 הַמַּשָּׂא אֲשֶׁר חָזָה חֲבַקּוּק *the oracle which Habakkuk saw,* i. e. which was revealed to him. Ezek. 13:6 חָזוּ שָׁוְא *they see lies,* i. e. they have false revelations. Zech. 10:2.

3. *to look out, choose, select.* Gen. 18:21. comp. רָאָה לוֹ Gen. 22:8.

4. figuratively, *to see into, to understand.* Job 15:17. 27:12.

Deriv. out of course חָזוֹן, חָזוּת, חָזוֹת, מַחֲזֶה, מֶחֱזָה, חִזָּיוֹן.

חֲזָה and **חֲזָא** Chald. *to see.* Dan. 5:5, 23. 3:19 שִׁבְעָה עַל דִּי חֲזֵה לְמֵזְיֵהּ *seven times more than it had ever been seen,* i. e. known, *to be heated.* Infin. מֶחֱזָא, Ezra 4:14. (In Syr. *idem.*)

חָזֶה m. dec. IX. b. *the breast,* spoken only of animals. Ex. 29:26, 27. Lev. 7:30, 31. Plur. חָזוֹת, Lev. 9:20, 21.

חֹזֶה m. verbal from חָזָה, dec. IX. a.

1. *a seer, prophet,* in later Hebrew, i. q. רֹאֶה, נָבִיא. 1 Chr. 21:9. 25:5. 29:29.

2. i. q. חָזוּת no. 3. (q. v.) *a covenant, agreement.*

חֵזוּ m. Chald. 1. *vision.* Dan. 2:28. 4:2, 7. [4:5, 10.] 7:7, 13.

2. *form, appearance.* 7:20. (Syr. ܚܶܙܘܳܐ.)

חָזוֹן m. verbal from חָזָה dec. III. a.

1. *sight, vision.* Dan. 1:17. 8:1. 9:24.

2. *a divine revelation.* 1 Sam. 3:1. 1 Chron. 17:15. Prov. 29:18.

3. especially *an oracle,* often collectively. (Comp. ὅραμα, Acts 11:5. 16:9.) Is. 1:1. Obad. 1. Nah. 1:1.

חָזוֹת f. verbal from חָזָה, dec. III. a. *vision, revelation.* 2 Chr. 9:29.

חֲזוֹת Chald. *sight.* Dan. 4:8, 17. [4:11, 20.]

חָזוּת f. (with Kamets impure) verbal from חָזָה, dec. I.

1. *form,* especially *a great* or *beautiful form,* (comp. מַרְאֶה.) Dan. 8:5 קֶרֶן חָזוּת *a great horn, cornu conspicuum.* verse 8 וַתַּעֲלֶנָה חָזוּת אַרְבַּע *and there rose up four great (horns.)* The latter verse might be rendered, *something like four (horns),* comp. דְּמוּת no. 3. but the meaning given above appears preferable on account of verse 5.

2. *a prophetic vision.* Is. 21:2. 29:11.

3. *a revelation, law;* hence, *a covenant, agreement.* The Hebrews connected these two ideas, inasmuch as they regarded their religion as a covenant with God. Is. 28:18. comp. חֹזֶה verse 14.

חִזָּיוֹן m. const. חֶזְיוֹן, plur. חֶזְיוֹנוֹת, verbal from חָזָה, dec. III. e.

1. *sight, vision.* Job 4:13. 7:14. 20:8.

2. *a revelation.* 2 Sam. 7:17.—גֵּיא חִזָּיוֹן Is. 22:5. (whence the superscription in verse 1.) *valley of vision* or *revelation,* i. e. Jerusalem, or some part of it, allegorically represented. According to some, it is, in this passage, a translation of the name מוֹרִיָּה supposed to signify *vision.*

חֲזִיז m. dec. I. *lightning.* Job 28:26. 38:25. Kindred with חֵץ. (Arab. حز *transfixit telum fulminis.*)

חֲזִיר m. prim. *a swine.* Lev. 11:7. (Syr. and Arab. *idem.*)

חָזַק, fut. יֶחֱזַק. 1. *to bind fast, to tie strait.* (Arab. حزق and حزك *idem;* Syr. ܚܙܩ *to gird,* comp. Piel.) Intrans. *to be bound fast,* Is. 28:22.

2. *to adhere* or *stick fast,* 2 Sam. 18:9 וַיֶּחֱזַק רֹאשׁוֹ בָאֵלָה *and his head stuck fast to the turpentine-tree.* Hence, ח׳ בְּתוֹרָה *to adhere to the law,* 2 Chr. 31:4. Construed with לְ and an infin. *to adhere to doing any thing.* Deut. 12:23. Josh. 23:6.

3. *to strengthen.* (Strength is acquired from bracing the muscles and

from girding one's self; hence this transfer of signification is found in several words. Comp. אזר no. 6. קָשַׁר; and for examples in Arabic, see Bocharti Hieroz. I. p. 514 ff.) Ezek. 30:21. More frequently intrans. *to be* or *become strong*, Josh. 17:13. Judg. 1:28. Gen. 41:56, 57. Construed with מִן *to be stronger than, to conquer*, 1 Sam. 17:50. Construed with עַל, *idem*, 2 Chr. 8:3. 27:5. Also with an accus. in the same sense, 1 K. 16:22. 2 Chr. 28:20. Spoken of a command, *to prevail, to get the upper hand*, 2 Sam. 24:4. 1 Chr. 21:4.

4. *to urge on*, construed with עַל. Ex. 12:33. Ezek. 3:14. with an accus. Jer. 20:7.

5. *to be recovered* from a sickness. Is. 39:1.

6. figuratively, *to be firm, strong, undaunted*.—חֲזַק וֶאֱמָץ *be strong and courageous*, Deut. 31:7, 23. comp. Dan. 10:19.—חָזְקוּ יְדֵי פ׳ *the hands of any one are strong*, i. e. he himself is strong, undaunted, Judg. 7:11. 2 Sam. 16:21. (comp. חוש joined with יָדַיִן.)

7. *to be hard, obstinate, inflexible*, i. q. קָשָׁה, Mal. 3:13. Hence, spoken of the heart, *to be hardened* or *rendered obdurate*, Ex. 7:13, 22.

8. *to be confirmed, established*. 2 K. 14:5. 2 Chr. 25:3 (with עַל.)

Pi. חִזֵּק 1. *to gird*, construed with two accusatives. Is. 22:21. Nah. 2:2.

2. *to fortify* or *intrench*, 2 Chr. 11:11, 12. 26:9. *to repair* what is decayed, 2 K. 12:8, 9, 13, 15. construed with לְ, 1 Chr. 26:27. *to build anew*, Neh. 3:19.

3. *to strengthen*. Judg. 16:28.

4. *to heal*. Ezek. 34:4, 16.

5. figuratively, *to strengthen the hands of any one*, i. e. to urge him on, to inspire him with courage. Judg. 9:24. Jer. 23:14. Job 4:3. 1 Sam. 23:16 וַיְחַזֵּק אֶת־יָדוֹ בֵּאלֹהִים *he gave him courage with God*.—חִזֵּק יָדַיִם *to strengthen one's own hands, to take courage*, Neh. 2:18.

6. *to support, help, assist*. 2 Chr. 29:34. Ezra 6:22. 1:6 *and all their neighbours* חִזְּקוּ בִידֵיהֶם בִּכְלֵי־כֶסֶף *assisted*, i. e. presented *them with silver vessels*, etc.

7. construed with לֵב, *to harden the heart*. Ex. 4:21.—חִזֵּק לִבּוֹ, עֹרֶף *to shew one's self stiff-necked*, Josh. 11:20. Jer. 5:3. Ps. 64:6 יְחַזְּקוּ לָמוֹ דָּבָר רָע *they are resolute in a wicked deed*.

Hiph. הֶחֱזִיק 1. *to bind fast*, especially *to fasten the hand on* any thing; hence, *to seize* or *take hold of*, in Greek ἐμφῦναι τινί. The original construction is found Gen. 21:18 הַחֲזִיקִי אֶת יָדֵךְ בּוֹ *fasten thine hand on him*, i. e. hold him in thine hand. Hence the verb is construed with בְּ, Ex. 4:4. Deut. 22:25. 25:11. more rarely with an accus. Is. 41:9, 13. Jer. 6:23, 24. 8:21. 50:43. Mic. 4:9 הֶחֱזִיקֵךְ חִיל *pangs take hold of thee*. Also with an inverted construction, Jer. 49:24 רֶטֶט הֶחֱזִיקָה *she seizes hold of terror;* comp. אָחַז Job 18:20. 21:6. Construed with לְ, 2 Sam. 15:5. with עַל, Job 18:9. This verb often signifies (1.) *to hold back*, Ex. 9:2. or *to oblige to stay*, Judg. 19:4. (2.) *to contain, to hold*, 2 Chr. 4:5. (3.) *to get possession of*, Dan. 11:21.

2. *to hold fast, to adhere closely;* e. g. to one's integrity, Job 2:3, 9. 27:6. Construed with עַל of the person, Neh. 10:30.

3. *to strengthen, fortify;* hence, *to build up again*. Neh. 5:16. Ezek. 27:9, 27.

4. *to make strong*, Ezek. 30:23. and intrans. *to become strong, to conquer*, 2 Chr. 26:8. Dan. 11:32.

5. *to help, assist;* construed with בְּ Lev. 25:35. Comp. מַחֲזִיק *an helper*, Dan. 11:1. construed with an accus. verse 6.

Hithpa. *to be strengthened, established*, or *confirmed;* spoken of a new king, 2 Chr. 1:1. 12:13. 13:21. *to gather one's strength*, Gen. 48:2.

2. *to feel one's self strengthened*, 1 Sam. 30:6. Ezra 7:28. *to take courage*, 2 Chr. 15:8. 23:1. 25:11.

3. *to act courageously*. 2 Sam. 10:12. Construed with לִפְנֵי *to oppose*, 2 Chr. 13:7, 8.

4. *to assist* any one, construed with בְּ and עִם. 2 Sam. 3:6. 1 Chr. 11:10. Dan. 10:21.

חָזָק m. verbal adj. from חָזַק, dec. IV. e.

1. *strong, mighty, vehement.* Ex. 3:19. 10:19.

2. *firm, hard.* Ezek. 3:9.—חִזְקֵי־לֵב ,מֵצַח *stiff-necked, obdurate,* Ezek. 2:4. 3:7. comp. verse 8.

חָזֵק m. verbal adj. from חָזַק, *idem.* Ex. 19:19. 2 Sam. 3:1.

חֵזֶק with suff. חִזְקִי, verbal from חָזַק, dec. VI, g. *strength, help.* Ps. 18:2.

חֹזֶק m. verbal from חָזַק, dec. VI. m. *idem.* Ex. 13:3, 14, 16.

חֶזְקָה f. dec. X. strictly an infin. from חָזַק.

1. כְּחֶזְקָתוֹ 2 Chr. 12:1. 26:16. *when he had gained strength.*

2. כְּחֶזְקַת־הַיָּד Is. 8:11. *when the hand (of God) urged me.* Comp. the verb Ezek. 3:14. Jer. 20:7.

3. Dan. 11:2 כְּחֶזְקָתוֹ בְעָשְׁרוֹ *as he supports himself on his riches.*

חִזְקִיָּה and **חִזְקִיָּהוּ** m. (*the strength of Jehovah*) *Hezekiah,* the proper name of a king of Judah. 2 K. 18:1, 10. Also called יְחִזְקִיָּה, Hos. 1:1. Is. 1:1.

חָזְקָה fem. of חֹזֶק. 1. *force, violence.* בְּחָזְקָה *by force* or *violence,* 1 Sam. 2:16. Ezek. 34:4. *vehemently, mightily, vehementer,* Judg. 4:3. 8:1.

2. *the repairing* (of a building). 2 K. 12:13. comp. the verb Pi. no. 2.

חָח m. with suff. חַחִי, plur. חַחִים, (with Dagesh forte implied, as in אָח, plur. אַחִים); i.q. חוֹחַ, literally, *a thorn;* hence,

1. *a ring,* such as was put through the nose of wild animals, and to which the bridle was fastened. 2 K. 19:28. Is. 37:29. Also such an one as was passed through the jaws of sea-monsters, Ezek. 29:4. comp. Job 40:26, [41:2,] under חוֹחַ no. 2.

2. Ex. 35:22. *nose-ring,* a female ornament; or according to Kimchi *a buckle* or *clasp,* to fasten together one's garment; (comp. French épingle, *a pin,* from Lat. spinula, *a small thorn,* and Tac. Germ. 17.)

חָטָא 1. *to slip, to fall.* Prov. 19:2.

2. *to err, go astray, to miss the goal.* (Comp. Hiph. Judg. 20:16.) Prov. 8:36 וְחֹטְאִי חֹמֵס נַפְשׁוֹ *he who misseth me wrongeth his own soul.* Antith. מֹצְאִי verse 35. Job 5:24 *thou visitest thy dwelling* וְלֹא תֶחֱטָא *and missest nothing,* i.e. thy hope is not frustrated, nothing is wanting. (In Ethiop. חטא *frustrari spe potiundi, carere.*)

3. *to sin,* since virtue is regarded as a path from which the sinner *strays,* or on which he *slips.* (Comp. the Greek *ἁμαρτάνω,* and Eng. *to err.*) The person *against* whom one sins, is preceded by לְ, as, חָטָא לַיהוָה *to sin against Jehovah,* Gen. 20:6, 9. 1 Sam. 2:25. 7:6. The person or thing *in respect to* which, or the action *by* which one sins, is preceded by בְּ, Gen. 42:22. Lev. 4:23 חָטָא בָהּ *in which he hath sinned.* Neh. 9:29. by עַל, Lev. 5:5. Num. 6:11. Neh. 13:26. or put in the accus. Lev. 5:16 אֵת אֲשֶׁר חָטָא מִן הַקֹּדֶשׁ *what he hath sinfully taken from the sanctuary.*

4. *to owe, to forfeit;* construed with an accus. Lev. 5:7. comp. verse 11. Prov. 20:2 חוֹטֵא נַפְשׁוֹ *he forfeits his own life,* or *brings it into danger;* comp. Hab. 2:10.

Pi. חִטֵּא 1. *to be punished,* or *to suffer for anything;* construed with an accus. Gen. 31:39.

2. *to offer as a sin-offering.* Lev. 6:19 [26] הַמְחַטֵּא אֹתָהּ *he that offers it as a sin-offering.* 9:15 וַיְחַטְּאֵהוּ *and he offered it as a sin-offering.*

3. *to purify, to cleanse,* i.q. כִּפֶּר; as persons, Num. 19:19. Ps. 51:9. as sacred utensils, the temple, etc. Ex. 29:36. (construed with עַל.)

Hiph. הֶחֱטִיא 1. i.q. Kal no. 2. *to miss the mark,* spoken of archers. Judg. 20:16. (In Arab. conj. IV.)

2. causat. of Kal no. 3. *to cause to sin, to seduce.* Ex. 23:33. 1 K. 15:26 וּבְחַטָּאתוֹ אֲשֶׁר הֶחֱטִיא אֶת־יִשְׂרָאֵל *and in his sin, wherewith he made Israel to sin.* 16:26. 2 K. 3:3. 10:29.

Hithpa. 1. *to purify one's self.* Num. 19:12 ff. 31:20.

2. *to be beside one's self,* (from anguish, terror.) Job 41:17. [25.] Many

verbs of erring (comp. Kal no. 2. Hiph. no. 1.) have this change of signification; e.g. חָטָא Is. 21:4. also the Arab. ضَلَّ, زَلَّ.

חֵטְא m. with suff. חֶטְאִי, plur. חֲטָאִים, const. חֶטְאֵי, verbal from חָטָא, *sin, transgression.* Lev. 19:17. 22:9. הָיָה בְךָ חֵטְא *a sin rests upon thee,* Deut. 15:9.

חַטָּא m. (with Kamets impure) verbal from חָטָא, dec. I.

1. *a sinner.* Gen. 13:13.

2. *one liable to punishment, an offender.* 1 K. 1:21.

חֲטָאָה f. verbal from חָטָא, *a sin.* Gen. 20:9.

חַטָּאָה fem. of חַטָּא.

1. *a sin.* Ex. 34:7.

2. *a sinful woman, peccatrix.* Am. 9:8.

חַטָּאָה f. Chald. *a sin-offering.* Ezra 6:17 Keri.

חַטָּאת f. const. חַטַּאת, plur. חַטָּאוֹת, fem. of חַטָּא, dec. XIII. o.

1. *a fall, stumbling, misfortune.* Prov. 10:16. (antith. חַיִּים.) perhaps also 21:4.

2. *a sin.*—Also *that wherein one sins,* Deut. 9:21.

3. *expiation, purification.* Num. 8:7 מֵי חַטָּאת *water of purification,* i.q. מֵי נִדָּה.

4. *a sin-offering.* Lev. 6:25, 30. (For its distinction from אָשָׁם, see that article.)

5. *punishment.* Zech. 14:19.

חָטַב *to hew* wood, *to form by hewing.* Deut. 29:11. Josh. 9:21, 23. (Comp. חָצַב *to hew* stones.)

Pu. *to be hewn out.* Ps. 144:12.

חֲטֻבוֹת fem. plur. Prov. 7:16. *variegated coverings.* (Arab. خَطَبَ *to be particoloured;* Syr. ܡܚܛܒܐ *a particoloured garment.*)

חִטָּה f. *wheat.* Ex. 9:32. Plur. ־ִים Gen. 30:14. and ־ִין Ezek. 4:9. The singular denotes *the plant,* the plural *the grain.*

חָטַם *to make an animal tractable,* by putting a muzzle on his mouth, or a ring through his nose. (Arab. خطم.) Metaphorically, Is. 48:9 אֶחֱטָם־לָךְ *I tame (my anger)* or *I restrain (myself) towards you.* For the ellipsis, see נָטַר, שָׁמַר.

חָטַף i.q. חָתַף *to seize, take.* Judg. 21:21. Ps. 10:9. (In Aram. frequent. In Arab. خطف.)

חֹטֶר m. 1. *a branch, twig.* Is. 11:1.

2. *a rod.* Prov. 14:3 *in the mouth of a fool arrogance is a rod.* (Syr. ܚܘܛܪܐ *staff, rod.*)

חַי, const. חֵי, fem. חַיָּה, plur. חַיִּים, const. חַיֵּי, verbal from חָיָה, dec. VIII. j.

1. as an adj. *living, lively.* Josh. 8:23.—כָּל־חַי *every living person,* Gen. 3:20.—נֶפֶשׁ חַיָּה *a living creature,* Gen. 1:20. חֵי־עוֹלָם *he that liveth forever, the Eternal,* Dan. 12:7.—חַי־יְהוָה *as true as God lives, vivus (est) Jehova,* Ruth 3:13. a form of swearing; also חַי אָנִי, *vivus ego,* when Jehovah himself swears, Num. 14:21, 28. Deut. 32:40.

2. *fresh, flowing,* spoken of water. Gen. 26:19. Lev. 14:5, 50.

3. *raw, fresh,* spoken of flesh. 1 Sam. 2:15. Lev. 13:13 ff.

4. *reviving, living again;* in the phrase כָּעֵת חַיָּה Gen. 18:10, 14. 2 K. 4:16, 17. *when the season revives,* i.e. in the coming year, περιπλομένου ἐνιαυτοῦ. (Hom. Od. XI. 247.)

5. as a subst. *life.* In the singular only Lev. 25:36. 1 Sam. 25:6. and in the formulas of swearing, חֵי פַרְעֹה *(by) the life of Pharaoh,* Gen. 42:15, 16. חֵי נַפְשְׁךָ *(by) the life of thy soul,* 1 Sam. 1:26. 17:55. Before the name of Jehovah, חַי is used; hence, חַי־יְהוָה וְחֵי נַפְשְׁךָ *as Jehovah liveth, and as thy soul liveth,* 1 Sam. 20:3. 25:26.—But this signification we find more commonly in the Plur. חַיִּים, חַיִּין (Job 24:22.)

1. *life.*—רוּחַ חַיִּים *breath of life,* Gen. 6:17. עֵץ הַחַיִּים *tree of (immortal) life,* Gen. 2:9. comp. 3:22, 24.

2. *means of living, sustenance.* Prov. 27:27.

3. *refreshment.* Prov. 3:22. Job 3:20.

4. *happiness, prosperity.* Ps. 34:13.

Prov. 4:22, 23. 12:28. 13:14. 14:27. —אֹרַח חַיִּים *the way to happiness*, 2:19. 5:6.

חִידָה f. dec. X. literally, *something intricate* or *complicated*, (from חוּד i. q. Arab. حاد *to bend off;* conj. II. *to tie knots.*) Hence,

1. *cunning, artifice.* Dan. 8:23.

2. *a riddle,* i. e. an intricate speech; comp. חוּד חִידָה—מְלִיצָה *to give out a riddle,* הִגִּיד הַחִידָה *to solve a riddle,* Judg. 14:12—19.

3. i. q. מָשָׁל, only implying greater intricacy; hence, *a proverb*, Prov. 1:6. *a parable*, Ezek. 17:2. *a song*, Ps. 49:5. 78:2. comp. Hab. 2:6. *an oracle, vision*, Num. 12:8.

חָיָה, fut. יִחְיֶה, apoc. יְחִי.

1. *to live*, often, *to be in good health.* Deut. 8:1. 30:16. Neh. 9:29.—יְחִי לְבַבְכֶם *let your heart live*, i. e. be joyful, Ps. 22:27. 69:33.

2. *to continue alive.* Num. 14:38. —וְחָיְתָה נַפְשִׁי *my soul shall live*, i. e. I shall be preserved alive, Gen. 12:13. 19:20.

3. *to come to life again*, Ezek. 37:5 ff. 1 K. 17:22. *to revive*, Judg. 15:19. Gen. 45:27.

4. *to be restored to health.* Gen. 20:7. Josh. 5:8. Construed with מִן, 2 K. 1:2. 8:8.

Pi. חִיָּה 1. *to make alive, to restore to life.* Ps. 30:4. 1 Sam. 2:7.

2. *to permit to live, to preserve alive.* Gen. 12:12. Ex. 1:17. Construed with נֶפֶשׁ, 1 K. 20:31.—חִיָּה זֶרַע *to preserve seed*, Gen. 7:3. in a different sense, 19:32, 34.—חִיָּה בָּקָר *to raise cattle*, Is. 7:21. Hos. 14:8 יְחַיּוּ דָגָן *they raise corn*, namely, in a desolate land.

3. metaphorically, *to rebuild* (a city.) 1 Chr. 11:8. comp. Neh. 3:34 [4:2] הַיְחַיּוּ אֶת־הָאֲבָנִים *will they revive the stones again?* i. e. form them again into a building?

Hiph. 1. *to restore to life.* 2 K. 8:1, 5.

2. *to save alive*, Gen. 6:19, 20. Construed with נֶפֶשׁ, Gen. 19:19. Also, *to save life*, Gen. 47:25. 50:20. Once construed with לְ, Gen. 45:7.

Deriv. out of course מִחְיָה, חַיּוּת, חַי.

חֲיָה and **חֲיָא** Chald. *idem.* Dan. 2:4 מַלְכָּא לְעָלְמִין חֱיִי *O king, live forever,* the usual salutation to a king. 3:9. 5:10. 6:6. 7:22. Comp. Neh. 2:3 הַמֶּלֶךְ לְעוֹלָם יִחְיֶה *let the king live forever.* 1 K. 1:31.

Aph. part. מַחֵא *preserving alive*, (Syr. ܡܚܐ.) Dan. 5:19.

חָיֶה verbal adj. from חָיָה, dec. IX. a. Plur. fem. חָיוֹת. *lively, strong, vigorous,* Ex. 1:19.

חַיָּה f. const. חַיַּת, also poetically חַיְתוֹ, (See Gesenius' Lehrgeb. § 127. 3.) fem. of חַי, dec. X.

1. *living;* hence, *a living soul, an animal.* Gen. 37:20, 33.—Often collectively, as כָּל־הַחַיָּה *every animal*, Gen. 7:14. 8:1, 17, 19. חַיַּת הָאָרֶץ, הַשָּׂדֶה, *the beasts of the field*, often opposed to tame animals (בְּהֵמָה,) Gen. 1:24, 25. but sometimes including them, Lev. 11:2, 47.

2. as an abstract noun, *life;* but only in poetry, (otherwise חַיִּים,) Job 33:18, 22, 38. Ps. 143:3.

3. i. q. נֶפֶשׁ *desire, hunger, appetitus.* Job 33:20. 38:19. comp. Is. 57:10.

4. i. q. חַיָּה *a band* or *company of men.* 2 Sam. 23:11, 13.

חֵיוָא f. emph. חֵיוְתָא, Chald. *an animal.* Dan. 4:13 ff. [4:16 ff.]

חַיּוּת f. verbal from חָיָה, *life.* 2 Sam. 20:3.

חָיַי i. q. חָיָה *to live*, but inflected as a verb Ain doubled, like the Arab. حيّ. Hence the pret. חַי *he lived*, Gen. 5:5 כָּל־יְמֵי אָדָם אֲשֶׁר־חַי *all the days of Adam which he lived.* 3:22 וְאָכַל וָחַי לְעֹלָם *and he shall eat and live forever.* Num. 21:8 וְרָאָה אֹתוֹ וָחָי *and he shall see it and be cured.* These examples ought not to be confounded with those in which חַי is an adj.; as Gen. 43:7 הַעוֹד אֲבִיכֶם חַי *is your father yet alive? an pater vester adhuc vivus* scil. *est?*

חִיל see **חוּל**.

חַיִל m. const. חֵיל, plur. חֲיָלִים, dec. VI. β. (see חיל no. 6.)

1. *power, strength, courage.* Ps. 18: 33, 40. 33:16. עָשָׂה חַיִל *to shew courage, to do valiantly,* Num. 24:18. Deut. 8: 18. Ps. 60:12. 108:14.

2. *a military force, a host.* Ex. 14: 28. שַׂר הַחַיִל *a captain of the host,* 2 Sam. 24:2. בְּנֵי חַיִל, אַנְשֵׁי חַיִל *men of war, soldiers,* Deut. 3:18. 1 Sam. 14:52. Ps. 110:3 בְּיוֹם חֵילֶךָ *in the day of thy power,* i. e. at the time of drawing out thy forces.

3. *substance, riches, wealth.* Gen. 34: 29. Job 20:15. עָשָׂה חַיִל *to acquire wealth,* Deut. 8:17, 18. Ruth 4:11.

4. figuratively, *integrity, virtue,* i. q. Lat. *virtus.* אַנְשֵׁי חַיִל *men of activity* or *integrity,* Gen. 47:6. Ex. 18:21, 25. אֵשֶׁת חַיִל *a virtuous woman,* Ruth 3:11. Prov. 12:4. 31:10. בֶּן־חַיִל *honest, virtuous,* 1 K. 1:52. עָשָׂה חַיִל *to act virtuously,* Prov. 31:29.

5. *the strength of a tree,* poetically for *its fruit.* Joel 2:22. comp. כֹּחַ Job 31:39.

חֵיל m. Chald. 1. *strength.* Dan. 3:4.
2. *a host.* Dan. 3:20. 4:32. [35.]

חֵיל and **חֵל** m. dec. I. a.

1. *a host.* 2 K. 18:17. Once חֵל Obad. 20. also in the Keri of Ps. 10:10 חֵל־כָּאִים *the multitude of the desponding;* but the Kethib is preferable. See חֵלְכָה.

2. i. q. Lat. *pomœrium, a space without the wall of a city,* but considered as a part of its defence, perhaps somewhat raised, like a small wall. 2 Sam. 20:15. Is. 26:1. Nah. 3:8. Lam. 2:8. comp. 1 K. 21:23. Ps. 48:14. 122:7. Perhaps figuratively, Hab. 3:19. Sept. προτείχισμα, περίτειχος. Vulg. *antemurale.* (In the Talmudical writers, חֵיל denotes *a space,* 10 cubits broad, *round the wall of the temple;* see Lightfooti Opp. T. II. p. 193.)

חִיל m. and **חִילָה** f. (Job 6:10.) See חול nos. 1, 2.

1. *pain,* especially of childbirth. Ps. 48:7. Jer. 6:24. 22:23. Mic. 4:9.

2. *trembling, fear.* Ex. 15:14.

חֵילָה Ps. 48:14. according to the usual punctuation, i. q. חֵיל no. 2. But the Sept. Vulg. Syr. Chald. Jerome and 18 MSS. read with Mappik חֵילָהּ from חֵיל.

חֵילָם 2 Sam. 10:16. and **חֵלָאם** verse 17. a city not far from the Euphrates, where David smote Hadadezer.

חִילֵן a sacerdotal city in the tribe of Judah. Once 1 Chr. 6:43. [58.]

חִין m. Job 41:4. [12.] a Chaldaic form for חֵן *grace, beauty, gratia.* (In Chald. חִין, also חִינָא, חִנָּא i. q. Heb. חֵן.)

חַיִץ m. *a wall.* Ezek. 13:10. (In Chald. and Arab. *idem.*)

חִיצוֹן, fem. חִיצוֹנָה, denom. adj. from חוּץ, *outer, external,* Ezek. 10:5. 40: 17, 31. *civil,* in opposition to *sacred,* 1 Chr. 26:29. in a somewhat different sense, Neh. 11:16. לַחִיצוֹן *without,* 1 K. 6:29, 30.

חֵיק, rarely חֵק, m. dec. I. a.

1. *the bosom.* 1 K. 3:20. Ex. 4:6, 7. שָׁכַב בְּחֵיק *to lie on the bosom,* i. e. to have conjugal intercourse, 1 K. 1:2. Mic. 7:5. אֵשֶׁת חֵיקֶךָ *the wife that rests on thy bosom,* Deut. 13:7. 28:54. comp. verse 56. שֹׁחַד בַּחֵק *a present in the bosom,* i. e. a secret present, Prov. 21:14. comp. 17:23. הֵשִׁיב אֶל חֵיק *to render into the bosom* of any one, i. e. to recompense him, Ps. 79:12. Is. 65:6, 7.

2. *the bosom* or *lap of a garment.* Prov. 16:33.

3. figuratively, *sinus currûs, the hollow cavity of a chariot* or *wagon,* 1 K. 22:35. *the cavity* of an altar where the fire burns, Ezek. 43:13.

4. *the inward part* generally. Job 19: 27.

חִישׁ i. q. חוּשׁ *to be in haste.* Hence, חִישָׁה Ps. 71:12 Kethib; and

חִישׁ adv. *in haste, soon.* Ps. 90:10.

חֵךְ m. with suff. חִכִּי, dec. VIII. b. (Arab. حَنَكٌ, Aram. ܚܢܟܐ,) *the palate;* (1.) as the organ of taste, Job 12: 11. comp. 6:30. Ps. 119:103. (2.) as the organ of speech, Prov. 8:7 כִּי אֱמֶת

חִכִּי יֶהְגֶּה אֱמֶת *for my palate speaks truth.* Job 31:30 *I suffered not my palate to sin;* comp. 33:2. Hos. 8:1 *the trumpet to thy palate!* i. e. to thy mouth!

חָכָה *to wait.* Once Is. 30:18.

Pi. חִכָּה *idem.* 2 K. 7:9. Construed with an accus. or with לְ, *to wait for,* Job 3:21. 32:4. especially חִכָּה לַיהוָה *to wait (with confidence) on Jehovah,* Ps. 33:20. Is. 8:17. Infin. with Chaldaic form חַכֵּי, Hos. 6:9.

חַכָּה f. *an angle, hook.* Job 40:25. [41:1.] Is. 19:8. Hab. 1:15. Probably fem. of חֵךְ *the palate,* as the hook catches in *the palate* or *throat* of the fish. (Also in Chald.)

חֲכִילָה proper name of a hill in the desert of Ziph. 1 Sam. 23:19. 26:1, 3.

חַכִּים Chald. *wise.* Dan. 2:21. especially *a wise man, a Magian,* Dan. 2:27. 5:15.

חַכְלִילִי m. *red,* spoken of the eyes inflamed with wine. (Root חכל i. q. Arab. حكل *oculus rubedine suffusus est.*) Gen. 49:12. Hence,

חַכְלִלוּת f. denom. from חַכְלִילִי, *redness,* as of the eyes from drinking wine. Prov. 23:29.

חָכַם, fut. יֶחְכַּם, *to be* or *become wise, to act wisely.* Prov. 6:6. 23:19. Construed with an accus. Ecc. 2:19 עֲמָלִי שֶׁעָמַלְתִּי וְשֶׁחָכַמְתִּי *my substance, which I have earned by my wisdom.*

Pi. *to make wise.* Job 35:11.

Hiph. *idem.* Ps. 19:8.

Hithpa. 1. *to think one's self wise.* Ecc. 7:16.

2. *to act wisely,* construed with לְ Ex. 1:10.

חָכָם verbal adj. from חָכַם, dec. IV. c.

1. *skilful, dexterous.* Is. 3:3. (Sept. σοφός.) Ex. 28:3. כָּל־חַכְמֵי־לֵב *all who are skilful workmen.* 31:6. 35:10. 36:1, 2, 8. Jer. 10:9 מַעֲשֵׂה חֲכָמִים *a work of skilful men.* Comp. the Homeric expression εἰδυῖαι πραπίδεσ.

2. *wise, intelligent, prudent.*—Also *artful, cunning,* 2 Sam. 14:2. Job 5:13. *learned, abounding in knowledge;* compare what is said of Solomon 1 K. 5:9—14. [4:29—34.] *to be virtuous;* freq. For the connexion between *wisdom* and *virtue* in the view of the ancient Hebrews, see the maxim, Job 28:28.

3. plur. חֲכָמִים *the wise men in a royal court, statesmen, philosophers, Magians.* Gen. 41:8. Ex. 7:11. Fem. חֲכָמוֹת Jer. 9:16. *women skilled (in lamentation).* Parall. *mourning women.*

חָכְמָה f. verbal from חָכַם, dec. X.

1. *skill, dexterity.* Ex. 28:3. 31:6. Also joined with לֵב, 35:26, 35.

2. *wisdom, intelligence.* Prov. 1:2. 7:4.

חָכְמָה Chald. *wisdom.* Dan. 2:30.

חָכְמוֹת f. verbal from חָכַם, *wisdom.* Construed as a singular, (like שִׂמְלוֹת,) Prov. 9:1. (comp. 14:1.) as a plural, 24:7. In other passages doubtful, 1:20 (where תָּרֹנָּה may also be plural). Ps. 49:4.

חַכְמוֹת f. *wisdom;* construed as a singular, Prov. 14:1.

חֵל see חֵיל

חֹל m. verbal from חָלַל Pi. no. 4. dec. I. *profane, common,* in opposition to *holy* or *consecrated.* Lev. 10:10. 1 Sam. 21:5, 6.

חָלָא 2 Chr. 16:12. i. q. חָלָה *to be sick, diseased.* Deriv. תַּחֲלוּא.

חֲלָאִים plural of חֳלִי.

חֶלְאָה f. dec. X. *rust,* for example, of brazen pots. Ezek. 24:6 ff. (Root perhaps חלא i. q. Arab. حلأ *to rub, to scrape off.*)

חָלָב m. const. חֲלֵב (as if from חָלָב), with suff. חֲלָבִי, dec. IV. c. *milk, sweet milk,* different from חֶמְאָה. Gen. 18:8. 49:12. Prov. 27:27. Is. 60:16.

חֵלֶב and חֵלֶב m. with suff. חֶלְבּוֹ, plur. חֲלָבִים, const. חֶלְבֵי, dec. VI. j and k.

1. *fat.* Gen. 4:4. Lev. 3:3. figuratively, *the best* or *most eminent of its kind,* Num. 18:12.—חֵלֶב הָאָרֶץ *the fat of*

the land, i. e. its best productions, Gen. 45:14. חֵלֶב חִטִּים Ps. 81:17. 147:14. and חֵלֶב כִּלְיוֹת חִטָּה Deut. 32:14. (comp. Is. 34:6.) *the fat, the kidney fat of wheat*, i. e. the finest wheat. comp. Num. 18:12.

2. figuratively, *a fat*, i. e. an unfeeling, *heart*. Ps. 17:10. comp. 73:7. (Others comp. the Arab. خِلْب *pericardium.*)

חֶלְבָּה Judg. 1:31. proper name of a city in the tribe of Asher.

חֶלְבּוֹן Ezek. 27:18. in Greek Χαλυβών, now *Aleppo*, a city of Syria, celebrated for its wine, the common drink of the Persian kings.

חֶלְבְּנָה f. *galbanum*, a powerful and very fragrant gum procured from a Syrian plant. Ex. 30:34. Comp. Celsii Hierobot. T. I. p. 267.

חֶלֶד m. dec. VI. k. 1. *length of life*. Ps. 39:6. 89:48. (Root Arab. خَلَدَ *to last, endure.*)

2. *life*. Job 11:17.

3. *world*. (Comp. עוֹלָם.) Ps. 49:2. 17:14 מְתִים מֵחֶלֶד *men of the world*, i. q. κόσμος, John 15:18, 19.

חֹלֶד m. *a mole*. Lev. 11:29. (Syr. and Arab. *idem*. Root ܚܠܕ *to dig.*)

I. חָלָה 1. *to be weak, feeble*. Judg. 16:7 ff.

2. *to be pained*. Prov. 23:35.

3. *to be sick*. Gen. 48:1. 2 K. 13:14. —חָלָה אֶת רַגְלָיו *he was diseased in his feet*, 1 K. 15:23. *to suffer from a wound*, 2 K. 1:2. 1 Sam. 31:3. רָעָה חוֹלָה *a sore evil*, Ecc. 5:12, 15.

4. *to be concerned about* any one, construed with עַל. 1 Sam. 22:8.

Niph. נֶחֱלָה 1. *to be exhausted, wearied*, Jer. 12:13. *to be weak, sick*, Dan. 8:27. Part. fem. נַחְלָה, as מַכָּה נַחְלָה *a sore wound*, Jer. 14:17. 30:12. comp. 10:19. Nah. 3:19.

2. *to be troubled about* any thing, construed with עַל. Am. 6:6. Hence, יוֹם נַחֲלָה *a grievous* or *sorrowful day*, Is. 17:11. (comp. Jer. 17:16.)

Pi. חִלָּה *to afflict with sickness*, Deut. 29:21. Passively, Ps. 77:11 חַלּוֹתִי הִיא *this is my infirmity*.

Pu. pass. *to become weak*. Is. 14:10.

Hiph. pret. הֶחֱלִי Is. 53:10. Mic. 6:13.

1. *to cause* a wound *to be malignant*; hence, metaphorically, *to afflict, to grieve*. Prov. 13:12.

2. intrans. Hos. 7:5 *on the (festival) day of our king* הֶחֱלוּ שָׂרִים חֲמַת מִיָּיִן *the princes fell ill from the heat of wine*.

Hoph. *to be wounded*. 1 K. 22:34.

Hithpa. 1. *to become sick*, from grief. 2 Sam. 13:2.

2. *to feign one's self sick*. 2 Sam. 13:5, 6.

Deriv. חֳלִי, מַחֲלָה, מַחֲלֶה.

II. חָלָה found only in Piel, and in the phrase חִלָּה פְּנֵי פ׳ which signifies (1.) *to flatter* or *caress*, namely, a prince, in order to obtain some favour. Job 11:19. Prov. 19:6. Ps. 45:13 *the rich among the people shall flatter thee*. (2.) *to supplicate* any one, *to ask his favour*. Ex. 32:11. 1 Sam. 13:12. 1 K. 13:9. 2 K. 13:14. Dan. 9:13. (In Kal probably i. q. Arab. حَلَا, Syr. ܚܠܐ *to be sweet, pleasant, acceptable*; hence literally, in Piel, *to make the face of any one serene, to make him friendly*.)

חַלָּה f. dec. X. *a cake*. 2 Sam. 6:19. especially one presented as an offering, Lev. 8:26. 24:5. Root חלל, *to bore through*; probably because the cakes were *perforated*, as among the Arabians and modern Jews.

חֲלוֹם m. plur. חֲלוֹמוֹת, verbal from חָלַם, dec. I. *a dream*. Gen. 20:3, 6. 31:10, 11, 24.

חַלּוֹן com. gen. (m. Josh. 2:18. f. Ezek. 41:16.) Plur. ־ִים Joel 2:9. and וֹת Ezek. 40:16. *a window*.—בְּעַד הַחַלּוֹן *through the window*, Gen. 26:8. Josh. 2:15. Judg. 5:28.

חֹלוֹן Josh. 15:51. 21:15. Jer. 48:21. a sacerdotal city in the tribe of Judah; perhaps the same with חִילֵז 1 Chr. 6:43. [6:58.]

חֲלוֹף m. *act of leaving behind.* Prov. 31 : 8 בְּנֵי חֲלוֹף *children left behind, orphans.* (Arab. خلف conj. II. *to leave children behind.*)

חֲלוּשָׁה f. verbal from חָלַשׁ, *overthrow, defeat.* Ex. 32 : 18.

חֲלַח *Calachene,* proper name of a province in the northern part of Assyria. 2 K. 17 : 6. 18 : 11.

חַלְחָלָה f. verbal from Pilpel of חול.

1. *pain,* as of a woman in travail. Is. 21 : 3.

2. *pain, distress, terror.* Nah. 2 : 11. Ezek. 30 : 4, 9.

חָלַט found only 1 K. 20 : 33 וַיְמַהֲרוּ וַיַּחְלְטוּ הֲמִמֶּנּוּ prob. *they hastened and sought confirmation whether it were from him.* In the Mishnah (T. V. p. 216. T. IV. p. 42. 142. ed. Surenhus.) חָלַט signifies *to confirm ;* hence perhaps in our passage causatively, *to seek confirmation.* The form may be regarded as the fut. Hiph. (see הָכַר ;) or perhaps it should be pointed יַחְלְטוּ.

חֲלִי m. plur. חֲלָאִים, dec. VI. *an ornament for the neck, a necklace.* Prov. 25 : 12. Cant. 7 : 2. (Arab. حلي *idem.*)

חֳלִי in pause חֹלִי, plur. חֳלָיִים, verbal from חָלָה no. I. dec. VI. q.

1. *sickness.* Deut. 7 : 15. 28 : 61. Is. 1 : 5 כָּל־רֹאשׁ לָחֳלִי *the whole head is become sickness,* i. e. is very sick.

2. *a moral evil,* (in the constitution of the world). Ecc. 6 : 2.

3. *grief, affliction.* Ecc. 5 : 16.

חֶלְיָה fem. of חֲלִי, dec. X. *a necklace.* Hos. 2 : 15. [13.]

חָלִיל m. verbal from חָלַל, dec. III. a. *a flute, pipe.* Is. 5 : 12. 30 : 29. 1 K. 1 : 40.

חָלִילָה and חָלִלָה adv. *far be it, God forbid.* (Liter. *base, profane,* see חָלַל Pi. and Hiph.) 1 Sam. 20 : 2 חָלִילָה לֹא תָמוּת *God forbid; thou shalt not die;* comp. 2 : 30.—חָלִילָה לִּי construed with מִן and an infinitive, *far be it from me so to act,* Gen. 18 : 25. 44 : 7, 17. Josh. 24 : 16. comp. Job 34 : 10. or with אִם and a finite verb, in the same sense, Job 27 : 5. 1 Sam. 14 : 45 (without לְ) 2 Sam. 20 : 20. In each of the above constructions we sometimes find מֵיְהוָה *before Jehovah* inserted, 1 Sam. 24 : 7. 26 : 11. 1 K. 21 : 3. Hence, Josh. 22 : 29 חָלִילָה לָּנוּ מִמֶּנּוּ לִמְרֹד בַּיהוָה *God forbid that we should rebel against him.* We find a different phraseology 1 Sam. 20 : 9, *far be it from thee* (instead of *me*) *that I should know .... and not tell thee.*

חֲלִיפָה f. verbal from חָלַף, dec. X. *change, alternation.* 2 K. 5 : 5 עֶשֶׂר חֲלִיפוֹת בְּגָדִים *ten changes of raiment,* i. e. ten complete suits. verses 22, 23. Judg. 14 : 12, 13. Gen. 45 : 22. also without בְּגָדִים, Judg. 14 : 19.—Job 10 : 17 חֲלִיפוֹת וְצָבָא *changes and armies,* i. e. armies constantly recruiting.—Job 14 : 14 חֲלִיפָתִי *my change,* i. e. the happy change of my destiny. Plur. חֲלִיפוֹת as an adv. *by courses, alternately,* 1 K. 5 : 28. [14.]

חֲלִיצָה f. verbal from חָלַץ, dec. X. *spoils stripped from an enemy, booty, exuviæ.* 2 Sam. 2 : 21. Judg. 14 : 19.

חֶלְכָה (for חֶלְכָא) adj. masc. Ps. 10 : 8. in pause חֵלְכָה verse 14. Plur. חֵלְכָאִים verse 10. *poor, unfortunate.* Root, Arab. حلك *to be dark, to be unfortunate.* The word is quadriliteral, and the ָה or ָא (like ָה in אַרְיֵה), originally a He paragogic, but afterwards regarded and treated as a radical. It is, however, doubtful whether the vowel-points are correct; for the present points belong to the Keri חֵלְכָה *thy host,* and plur. חֵל כָּאִים *the company of the desponding.* A short vowel in the first syllable would be more conformable to analogy.

חָלַל 1. *to bore* or *pierce through,* (Arab. خل ;) and intrans. *to be pierced through* or *wounded.* Ps. 109 : 22. Deriv. חָלִיל, חַלָּה, חַלּוֹן, חָלָל. Comp. Pi. and Pu.

2. *to loose, to open, to break.* (In Arab. حل, but probably kindred with خل.) See Pi. and Hiph.

Pi. 1. *to wound, smite.* Ezek. 28 : 9.

2. *to break, violate* (a covenant). Ps. 55 : 20. 89 : 35. Mal. 2 : 10.

3. *to open, make common.*—חִלֵּל בַּת *to prostitute one's daughter*, Lev. 19 : 29. comp. 21. 7, 14. Hence, because what is *permitted* or *common* is opposed to what is *sacred*,

4. *to profane, pollute, defile;* e. g. the priest, the sanctuary, Lev. 19 : 8. 21 : 9 ff. Mal. 2 : 11. the sabbath, Ex. 31 : 14. the name of God, Lev. 18 : 21. 19 : 12. the bed of one's father, (by incest,) Gen. 49 : 4.—Ps. 89 : 40 חִלַּלְתָּ לָאָרֶץ נִזְרוֹ *thou profanest (and castest) to the ground his diadem.* Comp. 74 : 7. Ezek. 28 : 16.—חִלֵּל הַכֶּרֶם *to profane a vineyard*, namely, by gathering its fruits, after it had been consecrated, (see Lev. 19 : 23.); hence, in general, *to use* or *improve it*, Deut. 20 : 6. 28 : 30. Jer. 31 : 5.

5. denom. from חָלִיל, *to blow the flute* or *pipe.* 1 K. 1 : 40.

Pu. pass. of Piel no. 1. Ezek. 32 : 26. pass. of Piel no. 4. Ezek. 36 : 23. Deriv. חֹל *profane.*

Niph. נִחַל (for נִחַל). infin. הֵחַל (like הִסֵּם), fut. יֵחַל, יֵחֵל; pass. of Pi. no 4. Ezek. 7 : 24. 20 : 9, 14, 22. Lev. 21 : 4.

Hiph. הֵחֵל 1. *to loose, set free.* Hos. 8 : 10 (with מִן).

2. *to break* or *violate* (a promise). Num. 30 : 3.

3. i. q. Pi. no. 4. *to profane.* Ezek. 39 : 7.

4. *to open, to begin;* construed for the most part with an infin. either with or without לְ, Gen. 10 : 8. Deut. 2 : 25, 31. rarely with a finite verb, Deut. 2 : 24, 31. 1 Sam. 3 : 12 הָחֵל וְכַלֵּה *beginning and ending*, i. e. from beginning to end. Gen. 9 : 20 וַיָּחֶל נֹחַ אִישׁ הָאֲדָמָה *and Noah began to be an husbandman.*

Hoph. pass. *to be begun.* Gen. 4 : 26. Deriv. תְּחִלָּה.

חָלָל m. verbal adj. from חָלַל, dec. IV. c.

1. *pierced through;* hence, *mortally wounded*, Job 24 : 12. Ps. 69 : 27. Jer. 51 : 22. and more frequently, *slain* (in battle), Deut. 21 : 1, 2, 3, 6.—חַלְלֵי חֶרֶב *slain with the sword*, Num. 19 : 16. also, as an antithesis to this phrase, חַלְלֵי רָעָב *the slain with hunger*, Lam. 4 : 9. comp. Is. 22 : 2.

2. *profane, unholy.* (See the verb in Pi. no. 4.) Ezek. 21 : 30. [25.] Fem. חֲלָלָה (joined with זוֹנָה), *a defiled*, i. e. defloured, *virgin*, Lev. 21 : 7, 14.

I. חָלַם, fut. יַחֲלֹם, *to dream.* Gen. 37 : 5 ff. Divine revelations were often communicated through dreams; hence, חֹלֵם חֲלוֹם *a dreamer of dreams*, i. q. נָבִיא *a prophet*, Deut. 13 : 2. comp. Joel 3 : 1. [2 : 28.] Num. 12 : 6.

Hiph. causat. of Kal, *to cause to dream.* Jer. 29 : 8.

II. חָלַם as in Syriac, *to be strong, healthy.* Job 39 : 4.

Hiph. causat. of Kal, *to restore to health, to recover.* Is. 38 : 16.

חֵלֶם m. emph. חֶלְמָא, Chald. *a dream.* Dan. 2 : 4 ff. 4 : 2 ff. [4 : 5 ff.]

חַלָּמוּת f. found only Job 6 : 6. prob. according to the Targums and the Jewish commentators, i. q. חֶלְמוֹן and חַלְבּוֹן *the yelk of an egg;* hence, רִיר חַלָּמוּת *the saliva of the yelk, the white of an egg.*

חַלָּמִישׁ m. a quadriliteral, *a hard stone, flint.* Job 28 : 9. Ps. 114 : 8. Joined with צוּר, Deut. 8 : 15. 32 : 13.

חָלַף, fut. יַחֲלֹף, poetically for עָבַר.

1. *to pass, to go by, to go away.* Job 4 : 15. 9 : 26. Cant. 2 : 11.

2. *to go on.* 1 Sam. 10 : 3.

3. *to perish, disappear.* Is. 2 : 18.

4. *to transgress* (the law). Is. 24 : 5.

5. *to go through;* but only causatively *to pierce through.* Judg. 5 : 26. Job 20 : 24.

6. *to attack, to press in a hostile manner.* Job 9 : 11. 11 : 10. Spoken of the wind, Is. 21 : 1. of a stream, 8 : 8.

7. *to put forth new shoots, to become verdant, to renew its youth.* Ps. 90 : 5, 6. Hab. 1 : 11 אָז חָלַף רוּחַ *then his courage shall renew itself.* (Syr. in Aph. Arab. conj. IV. *idem.*)

Pi. *to change* (one's garments). Gen. 41 : 14. 2 Sam. 12 : 20. (Syr. Pa. *idem.*)

Hiph. 1. *to change, exchange.* Gen. 35:2. Lev. 27:10. Ps. 102:27.

2. *to alter.* Gen. 31:7, 41.

3. causat. of Kal no. 7. *to cause to grow,* Is. 9:9. and intrans. *to sprout* or *grow,* Job 14:7. Hence, with כֹּחַ, *to renew one's strength,* Is. 40:31. 41:1. also without כֹּחַ, in the same sense, Job 29:20.

Deriv. out of course חֲלִיפָה, חֲלוֹף.

חֲלַף Chald. *to pass,* spoken of time. Dan. 4:13, 20, 29. [4:16, 23, 32.]

חֵלֶף strictly a subst. *exchange,* (from חָלַף); hence, as a prep. *for, in exchange for.* Num. 18:21, 31.

חָלַץ 1. *to loose* or *pull off* (the shoe). Deut. 25:9, 10. Is. 20:2.

2. *to draw out* (the breast). Lam. 4:3.

3. *to withdraw one's self,* construed with מִן. Hos. 5:6.

Pi. 1. *to pull out;* e. g. stones from a wall, Lev. 14:40, 43.

2. *to deliver.* 2 Sam. 22:20. Ps. 6:5. 50:15. 81:8.

3. as in Syriac, *to rob, plunder.* Ps. 7:5 וָאֲחַלְּצָה צוֹרְרִי רֵיקָם *and have robbed him who was my enemy without cause.* Comp. חֲלִיצָה. It is better, however, with the Chaldaic version, to make חִלֵּץ i. q. לָחַץ *to oppress;* namely, *I oppressed my enemy without cause.*

Niph. *to be delivered.* Prov. 11:8. Ps. 60:7. 108:7.

Deriv. מַחֲלָצוֹת.

II. **חָלַץ** in Kal not used.

Niph. *to prepare for action, to arm for battle.* (Comp. Syr. ܡܚܠܨ *accinctus ad opus.*) Prob. a denom. from חָלָץ *the loins,* namely, *to gird up one's loins.* Num. 32:17, 20. 31:3. Part. חָלוּץ and חֲלוּץ צָבָא *prepared for battle, in battle-array,* Num. 32:21, 27, 29 ff. Deut. 3:18. Josh. 6:7 ff. Is. 15:4 חֲלֻצֵי־מוֹאָב *the warriors of Moab;* (in the parallel passage Jer. 48:41 גִּבּוֹרֵי־מוֹאָב).

Hiph. *to strengthen, alacrem, expeditum reddere.* Is. 58:11.

חֲלָצַיִם dual, dec. IV. c. *loins.* Job 38:3 *gird up now thy loins like a man,* i. e. prepare for contest. 40:7. Gen. 35:11 *kings shall come out of thy loins,* i. e. shall be begotten of thee.

חָלַק, fut. יַחֲלֹק. 1. *to be smooth.* (Arab. خلق *idem.*) Hos. 10:2. Metaphorically, *to be flattering,* Ps. 55:22.

2. *to divide.* (Arab. حلق *idem.*) Josh. 14:5. 18:2. 22:8. most frequently, *to divide among themselves, to share,* 2 Sam. 19:29. 1 Sam. 30:24 יַחְדָּו יַחֲלֹקוּ *they shall share alike.* Prov. 17:2 *and shall share* or *partake of the inheritance among the brethren.* (Num. 18:20.) comp. Job 27:17. Construed with עִם, *to share with* any one, Prov. 29:24. with לְ, *to divide to* any one, Deut. 4:19. 29:25. Neh. 13:13. with לְ of the person and בְּ of the thing, *to give one a part in* any thing, Job 39:17 וְלֹא־חָלַק לָהּ בַּבִּינָה *and hath not given her* (*the ostrich*) *understanding.* 2 Chr. 28:21 *Ahaz divided the house of God and the house of the king and of the princes,* i. e. he plundered them of their treasures. Sept. ἔλαβεν τὰ ἐν τῷ οἴκῳ. Comp. חֵלֶק *booty.* Job 17:5.

Niph. 1. *to divide one's self.* Gen. 14:15 וַיֵּחָלֵק עֲלֵיהֶם *he divided himself* (*and came*) *upon them.* Job 38:24.

2. *to be divided out.* Num. 26:53, 55.

Pi. 1. as in Kal, *to divide,* e. g. the booty. Gen. 49:27. Ps. 68:13. Construed with לְ, *to distribute among,* 2 Sam. 6:19. Is. 34:17. 53:12 אֲחַלֶּק לוֹ בָרַבִּים *I will assign to him* (*his lot*) *among the mighty.*

2. *to scatter.* Gen. 49:7. Lam. 4:16.

Pu. pass. Is. 33:23.

Hithpa. *to divide for themselves.* Josh. 18:5.

Hiph. 1. *to smooth, labour,* spoken of an artificer. Is. 41:7.

2. joined with לָשׁוֹן Ps. 5:10. Prov. 28:23. or with אֲמָרִים Prov. 2:16. 7:5. *to make smooth one's tongue, one's words,* i. e. to flatter; also without these additions in the same sense, Prov. 29:5 גֶּבֶר מַחֲלִיק עַל רֵעֵהוּ *a man who flatters* or *dissembles to his neighbour.* Ps. 36:3.

3. causat. of Kal no. 2. Jer. 37:12 לַחֲלֹק מִשָּׁם *to fetch his inheritance from thence.* Others: *to escape from thence.* (On the order of the significations, see מָלַט.)

Deriv. out of course מַחֲלְקָה, מַחֲלֹקֶת.

חָלָק m. verbal adj. from חָלַק.

1. *smooth, without hair.* Gen. 27:11. Spoken of a mountain, *uncovered,* Josh. 11:17. 12:7. Figuratively, Prov. 5:3.

2. *flattering.* Prov. 26:28.

3. *false, deceitful.* Ezek. 12:24. comp. 13:7.

חֲלָק Chald. *part, lot, portion.* Ezra 4:16. Dan. 4:12, 20. [4:15, 23.] Comp. חֵלֶק.

חֲלַקּוֹת plur. fem. verbal from חָלַק, *flatteries.* Dan. 11:32.

חֵלֶק m. with suff. חֶלְקִי, verbal from חָלַק, dec. VI. j.

1. *smoothness.* Is. 57:6 בְּחַלְּקֵי נַחַל *the smooth,* i. e. unwooded, *parts of the valley.* (comp. חָלָק no. 1. The Dagesh in ל is euphonic.) Hence, figuratively, *flattery.* Prov. 7:21.

2. *part, portion.* Josh. 14:4. חֵלֶק כְּחֵלֶק *in equal portions,* Deut. 18:8. Especially (1.) *a portion of the booty.* Gen. 14:24. hence, *the booty itself,* Job 17:5 לְחֵלֶק יַגִּיד רֵעִים (*who*) *betrays his friends for booty.* (2.) יֵשׁ ,אֵין לִי חֵלֶק וְנַחֲלָה עִם ,אֶת פְּלוֹנִי *I have* or *have not a portion with any one,* Deut. 10:9. 12:12. 14:27, 29. or with בְּ of the thing, Ecc. 9:6. Also figuratively, *to have* or *not have some concern* or *something to do with* any one, 2 Sam. 20:1. 1 K. 12:16. Ps. 50:18. (3.) חֵלֶק יַעֲקֹב *the portion of Jacob,* i. e. Jehovah, the object of his worship. Jer. 10:16. 51:19. comp. Deut. 4:19. Ps. 16:5. 142:6.

2. *a portion of land, a field.* 2 K. 9:10, 36, 37. Hence, *land,* in opposition to *sea,* Am. 7:4.

3. *lot,* μοῖρα. Ecc. 2:10. 3:22. 5:17. Job 20:29. 31:2 חֵלֶק אֱלוֹהַּ *lot ordained of God.*

חַלֻּק verbal adj. from חָלַק, dec. I. *smooth.* 1 Sam. 17:40 חֲמִשָּׁה חַלֻּקֵי אֲבָנִים *five smooth among the stones,* i. e. five smooth stones. Comp. similar phrases Is. 29:19. Hos. 13:2.

חֶלְקָה f. verbal from חָלַק, dec. XII. c.

1. *smoothness.* Gen. 27:16. Plur. *smooth* or *slippery places,* Ps. 73:18.

2. *flattery.* Prov. 6:24. Plur. חֲלָקוֹת *idem,* Is. 30:10. שְׂפַת חֲלָקוֹת *a flattering lip,* Ps. 12:3, 4.

3. *a part,* or *portion;* hence, with שָׂדֶה *a piece of land,* Gen. 33:19. Ruth 2:3. also without addition in the same sense, 2 Sam. 14:30, 31. 23:12.

חֲלֻקָּה f. verbal from חָלַק, dec. X. *division.* 2 Chr. 35:5.

חִלְקִיָּה and **חִלְקִיָּהוּ** m. (*portion of Jehovah*) *Hilkiah,*

1. a high-priest under king Josiah. 2 K. 22:8, 12.

2. the father of Jeremiah. Jer. 1:1.

חֲלַקְלַקּוֹת plur. fem. verbal from חָלַק.

1. *slippery places.* Ps. 35:6. Jer. 23:12.

2. *flatteries, arts of dissimulation.* Dan. 11:21, 34.

חָלַשׁ 1. fut. יַחֲלֹשׁ, *to discomfit, defeat.* Ex. 17:13. Construed with עַל, Is. 14:12. Deriv. חֲלוּשָׁה.

2. fut. יֶחֱלַשׁ, *to be weak, frail, to pass away.* Job 14:10. (Syr. Ethpe. *debilitatus est;* ܡܚܠܫܐ *debilis.*) Deriv. חַלָּשׁ.

חַלָּשׁ m. verbal from חָלַשׁ, *weak, feeble.* Joel 4:10. [3:10.]

I. **חָם** m. with suff. חָמִיךְ ,חָמִיהָ, prim. irreg. *a father-in-law.* Gen. 38:13, 25. (Comp. חָמוֹת.)

II. **חָם** a proper name.

1. *Ham,* son of Noah, from whom, according to Gen. 10:6—20, most of the southern nations were descended. The name literally denotes perhaps *warm* or *southern.* See חָמַם, and comp. תֵּימָן.

2. a poetical name for *Egypt,* probably of Egyptian derivation, but to the Hebrew presenting the same literal signification as above. (In Egypt. χημι,

χημι, i. e. *black.* Ps. 78:51. 105:23, 27. 106:22.

III. חָם verbal adj. from חָמַם, dec. VIII. a. *hot, warm.* Josh. 9:12. Plur. חַמִּים, Job 37:17.

חֹם m. verbal from חָמַם, *heat, warmth.* Gen. 8:22.

חֵמָא see חֵמָה.

חֵמָא, חֲמָא f. Chald. *heat, anger,* i. q. Heb. חֵמָה. Dan. 3:13, 19.

חֶמְאָה f. 1. *thick* or *curdled milk.* (In Arab. خما *spissum et velut durum fuit lac.*) Gen. 18:8. Is. 7:15, 22. 2 Sam. 17:29. In the poetic parallelism, it acquires perhaps the same meaning as חָלָב, Job 20:17. Judg. 5:25. Deut. 32:14.

2. *cheese.* Prov. 30:33. (This word is often rendered *butter,* which, however, is hardly known to the orientalists, except as a medicine.)

חָמַד fut. יַחְמֹד. 1. *to desire, covet, lust after, strive for.* Gen. 20:17. 34:24. Mic. 2:2.

2. *to take pleasure in, to delight in.* Ps. 68:17. Is. 1:29. Prov. 12:12. With a pleonastic dative לוֹ, Prov. 1:22. Part. חָמוּד *what is most pleasant* or *beautiful,* Job 20:20. Ps. 39:12. Is. 44:9 חֲמוּדֵיהֶם *their pleasant things,* i. e. their idols; (comp. Dan. 11:37.)

Niph. part. נֶחְמָד 1. *lovely, pleasant, desirable.* Gen. 2:9. 3:6.

2. *costly, precious.* Ps. 19:11. Prov. 21. 20.

Pi. *to take delight in,* construed with בְּ. Cant. 2:3.

Deriv. out of course מַחְמָד.

חֶמֶד m. verbal from חָמַד, *pleasantness, beauty.* Ezek. 23:6.—שְׂדֵי־חֶמֶד *pleasant fields,* Is. 32:12. comp. Am. 5:11.

חֶמְדָּה fem. of חֶמֶד, dec. III. c.

1. *a wishing, desiring, longing.* 2 Chr. 21:20 בְּלֹא חֶמְדָּה *without being lamented, nemini desideratus.*

2. *object of desire.* 1 Sam. 9:20. Dan. 11:37 חֶמְדַּת נָשִׁים *the desire of women,* perhaps the goddess of the Syrians.

3. *pleasantness, preciousness.* אֶרֶץ חֶמְדָּה *a pleasant land,* Jer. 3:19. Ezek. 26:12. כְּלֵי חֶמְדָּה, *costly vessels,* 2 Chr. 32:27. 36:10.

חֲמֻדוֹת and חֲמוּדוֹת fem. plur. verbal from חָמַד *preciousness, precious things.* Dan. 11:38, 43.—בִּגְדֵי, כְּלֵי חֲמֻדוֹת *beautiful garments, costly vessels,* Gen. 27:15. 2 Chr. 20:25. לֶחֶם חֲמֻדוֹת *rich food,* (which those who fast must abstain from,) Dan. 10:3. אִישׁ חֲמֻדוֹת Dan. 10:11, 19. and without אִישׁ 9:23. *a man greatly beloved, a favourite* (*of heaven*).

חַמָּה fem. of חַם, dec. X.

1. strictly a fem. adj. *the hot, glowing;* but used poetically for *the sun.* Job 30:28. Cant. 6:10. Is. 30:26. (In the Mishnah often in this sense.)

2. *warmth, heat.* Ps. 19:7.

I. חֵמָה f. (for יֶחְמָה) const. חֲמַת, verbal from יָחַם, dec. XI. b. *heat, anger,* Gen. 27:44. Jer. 6:11.—כּוֹס הַיַּיִן הַחֵמָה Jer. 25:15. and כּוֹס חֲמָתוֹ Is. 51:17. *the wine cup of his wrath,* which Jehovah causes the nations to drink. Comp. Apoc. 16:19. and Job 21:20 *of the wrath of the Almighty he shall drink.*

2. *poison,* from its *hot* burning nature. Deut. 32:24. Ps. 58:5.

II. חֵמָה i. q. חֶמְאָה *milk.* Job 29:6.

חָמוֹץ m. verbal from חָמֵץ, no. II. *an evildoer,* i. q. חוֹמֵץ. Is. 1:17.

חַמּוּק m. verbal from חָמַק, dec. I. *circuit, compass.* Cant. 7:2 חַמּוּקֵי יְרֵכַיִךְ *the circuits of thy thighs.*

I. חֲמוֹר, חֲמֹר m. dec. I. *a he-ass.* Gen. 49:14. Ex. 13:13. So called perhaps from his *reddish* colour, whence the ass is also called in Span. *burro, burrico.*

II. חֲמוֹר, חֲמֹר m. dec. I. i. q. חֹמֶר no. III. *a heap.* So on account of the paronomasia, Judg. 15:16 בִּלְחִי הַחֲמוֹר חֲמוֹר חֲמֹרָתָיִם *with an ass' jawbone,* (*I smote*) *one heap, two heaps.*

חָמוֹת f. (for חֲמוֹת fem. of חָמוֹ i. q. חָמִי or חָם; comp. the form אָחוֹת;) dec.

III. a. *a mother-in-law.* Ruth 1:14. 2:11.

חֹמֶט m. found only Lev. 11:30. prob. a species of lizard. Sept. σαῦρα. Vulg. *lacerta.*

חָמִיץ m. adj. *salted.* Is. 30:24 בְּלִיל חָמִיץ *salted fodder*, i. e. fodder sprinkled with salt, or mixed with salt hay. Comp. Bocharti Hieroz. T. I. p. 113. Faber zu Harmer's Beobachtungen über d. Orient, Th. I. p. 409.

חֲמִישִׁי and חֲמִשִׁי, fem. ־ִית, *fifth.* —חֲמִישִׁית *the fifth part*, (חֵלֶק being omitted,) Gen. 47:24. Plur. חֲמִישִׁתָיו *its fifth parts*, Lev. 5:24. [6:5.]

חָמַל, fut. יַחְמֹל, infin. חֶמְלָה (Ezek. 16:5).

1. *to have compassion, to pity;* construed with עַל of the person, Ex. 2:6. 1 Sam. 23:21.

2. *to spare, to save.* 1 Sam. 15:3, 15. 2 Chr. 36:15, 17. Construed with אֶל, Is. 9:18.

3. in reference to things, *to spare, withhold.* Jer. 50:14. 2 Sam. 12:4.

חֶמְלָה f. verbal from חָמַל, dec. X. *pity, mercy, kindness.* Gen. 19:16. Is. 63:9.

חָמַם, fut. יֵחַם, *to be* or *become warm.* Ex. 16:21.—כְּחֹם הַיּוֹם *at mid-day*, Gen. 18:1. 1 Sam. 11:9.—Impers. חַם לוֹ *he had heat*, 1 K. 1:2. Ecc. 4:11.

Niph. fut. יֵחַמּוּ Hos. 7:7. part. נֵחָמִים Is. 57:5. *to be hot* with zeal or passion.

Pi. *to warm.* Job 39:14.

Hithpa. *to warm one's self.* Job 31:20.

חַמָּנִים masc. plur. dec. I. *idols, images.* Lev. 26:30. Is. 17:8. 27:9. Ezek. 6:4, 6. comp. 2 Chr. 34:4. Usually interpreted more definitely, *pillars consecrated to the sun*, as if from חַמָּה *the sun*, but that word in this signification occurs only in later poetic usage. Others, *tutelary deity*, as if from חמה i. q. Arab. حمى *to protect.*

חָמַס, fut. יַחְמֹס, *to tear off, to pluck;* e. g. fruit, Job 15:33. foliage, Lam. 2:6.

2. *to treat with violence, to oppress, to injure.* Jer. 22:3. Prov. 8:36 חֹמֵס נַפְשׁוֹ *injuring himself.* Job 21:27 *I know* מְזִמּוֹת עָלַי תַּחְמֹסוּ *the opinions whereby ye injure me,* i. e. which ye injuriously attribute to me. חָמַס תּוֹרָה *to violate* or *transgress the law,* Ezek. 22:26. Zeph. 3:4.

Niph. *to be treated with violence;* hence, in Jer. 13:22, *to be made bare by force.* (These two significations are also united in עָוַל and עָשַׁק.)

חָמָס m. verbal from חָמַס, dec. IV. c.

1. *violence, wrong.* Gen. 6:11, 13. 49:5.—אִישׁ חָמָס *a violent man,* Ps. 18:49. Prov. 3:31. עֵד חָמָס *a false witness,* Ex. 23:1.—The following genitive is often used passively, חֲמָסִי *the wrong done to me,* Gen. 16:5. comp. Joel 4:19. [3:19.] Obad. 10. also actively, Ps. 7:17.

2. *ill-gotten wealth.* Am. 3:10. Plur. חֲמָסִים Prov. 4:17.

I. חָמֵץ, fut. יֶחְמַץ, infin. חֻמְצָה, *to be sour* or *bitter;* hence, spoken of bread, *to be leavened,* Ex. 12:39.

Hiph. part. intrans. מַחְמֶצֶת *something leavened.* Ex. 12:19, 20.

Hithpa. *to be embittered, pained,* or *grieved.* Ps. 73:21. (Chald. Pa. *to occasion sorrow* or *pain.*)

II. חָמֵץ i. q. חָמַס *to do wrong, to commit an unlawful action.*—חוֹמֵץ *an evildoer,* Ps. 71:4. (Rabbin. חַמְצָן *raptor,* from חָמֵץ=חָמַס.) This signification may, however, be connected with no. I. comp. حامض *vir corruptus;* literally, *vappa,* ὀξίνης.—Comp. חָמוּץ and חָמֵץ.

III. חָמֵץ, part. Paul חָמוּץ Is. 63:1. *red.* So the Sept. and Syr. comp. verse 2. (Syr. Ethpa. *to blush, to be ashamed.*)

חָמֵץ m. verbal from חָמֵץ no. I.

1. *something leavened.* Ex. 12:15. 13:3, 7.

2. perhaps *ill-gotten wealth.* Am. 4:5. (See חָמֵץ no. II.) But the usual signification may be retained in this passage, *burn leavened bread for a thank-offering.*

חֹמֶץ m. verbal from חָמֵץ no. I. *vinegar.* Num. 6:3. Ruth 2:14. Ps. 69:22. Prov. 10:26.

חָמַק 1. *to go away, to depart.* Cant. 5:6.

2. *to go about, to wander.* So in Hithpa. Jer. 31:22.

Deriv. חַמּוּק.

I. **חָמַר** (Arab. حمر) 1. *to be red,* spoken of wine. Ps. 75:9.

2. denom. from חֵמָר, *to cover with pitch.* Ex. 2:3.

Pualal חֳמַרְמַר *to be made red,* as the countenance by weeping. Job 16:16.

II. **חָמַר** Arab. خمر) *to be agitated, to be in a ferment.* Ps, 46:4.

Pualal, *to be in commotion,* spoken of the bowels, indicating violent pain. Lam. 1:20. 2:11.

חֵמָר m. *asphaltos, Jew's pitch,* a combustible bitumen found in and near the Dead Sea, and in the neighbourhood of Babylon, which the ancient Babylonians used for mortar. Gen. 11:3. 14:10. Ex. 2:2. (Arab. حمر and حمر, prob. so called from its reddish colour.)

חֶמֶר m. verbal from חָמַר no. II. *wine,* so called from its *fermenting.* Deut. 32:14. Is. 27:2.

חֲמַר m. Chald. emph. חַמְרָא *idem.* Ezra 6:9. 7:22. Dan. 5:1, 2, 4, 23.

I. **חֹמֶר** m. 1. *clay, loam,* as a cement in building, Gen. 11:3. *potter's clay,* Job 10:9. Is. 45:9. *clay for receiving impressions,* Job 38:14.

2. *mud, mire.* Is. 10:6. Job 30:19.

Comp. חֵמָר.

II. **חֹמֶר** m. verbal from חָמַר no. II. *roaring, raging.* Hab. 3:15.

III. **חֹמֶר** m. dec. VI. m. 1. *a heap.* Ex. 8:10. [14.] (Root חמר i. q. Arab. حمر conj. IV. *to collect.*)

2. *a homer,* a larger measure, containing ten baths in liquid, or ten ephahs in dry measure. Lev. 27:16. Num. 11:32. Ezek. 45:11, 13, 14.

חָמֵשׁ, const. חֲמֵשׁ, f. and חֲמִשָּׁה, const. חֲמֵשֶׁת, m. *five.*

Plur. חֲמִשִּׁים *fifty.*—שַׂר חֲמִשִּׁים *a captain of fifty,* πεντηκόνταρχος, a military officer, 2 K. 1:9—14. Is. 3:3. Hence,

חִמֵּשׁ Pi. denom. from חָמֵשׁ, *to cause to pay one fifth part as a tithe* or *tax.* Gen. 41:34.

חֲמֻשִׁים adj. plur. Ex. 13:18. Josh. 1:14. 4:12. Judg. 7:11. *armed, in battle-array,* spoken of an army, (i. q. חֲלוּצִים Josh. 4:12. comp. verse 13). Aqu. ἐνοπλιζόμενοι. Vulg. *armati.* So Symm. Onk. Syr. Arab. (In the kindred dialects we find the Arab. حمش *to assemble,* also, *to excite to battle,* conj. VIII. X. *to rush to battle;* and حمس *strong, courageous;* but perhaps it is a denom. from חֹמֶשׁ no. II. like חָלוּץ from חֲלָצַיִם.) Others: *divided into companies of fifty.*

I. **חֹמֶשׁ** m. denom. from חָמֵשׁ, *the fifth part,* paid by the Egyptians as a tribute. Gen. 47:26.

II. **חֹמֶשׁ** m. *belly, abdomen.* 2 Sam. 2:23. 3:27. (Syr. *idem.*)

חֲמִשִׁי see **חֲמִישִׁי**,

חֵמֶת Gen. 21:15, 19. const. חֵמַת verse 14. *a leather bag* or *bottle.*

חֲמָת *Hamath,* on the northern boundary of Canaan, a colony of the Phenicians, and residence of a king in friendship with David, by the Greeks called Ἐπιφάνεια. Num. 13:21. 34:8. Judg. 3:3. 2 Sam. 8:9. (Arab. حماة.) Called in Am. 6:2, חֲמַת רַבָּה *Hamath the great;* and in 2 Chr. 8:3, חֲמַת צוֹבָה *Hamath Zobah.* The inhabitants are called חֲמָתִי Gen. 10:18.

חֵן m. with suff. חִנִּי, verbal from חָנַן, dec. VIII. b.

1. *grace, favour, kindness.*—מָצָא חֵן בְּעֵינֵי פְלֹנִי *to find favour in the eyes of any one,* i. e. to obtain his favour. Gen. 6:8. 19:19. 32:5. 33:10 אִם־נָא מָצָאתִי חֵן בְּעֵינֶיךָ *if I have obtained thy favour.* 18:3. 30:27. 47:29. 50:4. With נָשָׂא in

the same sense, only Est. 2:15, 17.— Ex. 3:21 וְנָתַתִּי אֶת־חֵן הָעָם הַזֶּה בְּעֵינֵי מִצְרָיִם *and I will give to this people favour with the Egyptians*, i. e. will make the Egyptians favourable to them. 11:3. 12: 39. Gen. 39:21.

2. *grace, beauty, loveliness*. Prov. 31: 30. 5:19 יַעֲלַת חֵן *the lovely roe*.

3. *an ornament*. Prov. 3:22.—אֶבֶן חֵן *a precious stone*, 17:8.

4. *supplication*. Zech. 12:10. See the verb in Hithpa.

חָנָה, fut. apoc. יִחַן. 1. *to decline*. Judg. 19:9 חֲנוֹת הַיּוֹם *the declining* or *closing of the day*.

2. *to station one's self, to pitch one's tent*, Gen. 26:17. *to encamp*, Ex. 13: 20. 17:1. 19:2.—Num. 1:51 בַּחֲנֹת הַמִּשְׁכָּן *when the tabernacle is pitched*. (1.) Construed with עַל, *to encamp against* any one, Ps. 27:3. 2 Sam. 12:28. Is. 29:3. So חֹנָךְ for חֹנֶה עָלֶיךָ Ps. 53:6. (2.) Construed with לְ, *to encamp about* any one, for his protection, Zech. 9:8. Ps. 34:8.

3. *to dwell*. Is. 29:1.

Deriv. מַחֲנֶה, חָנוּת.

חַנָּה f. plur. חַנּוֹת verbal from חָנַן, dec. X.

1. *grace, compassion*. Ps. 77:10.

2. *Hannah*, the mother of Samuel. 1 Sam. 1:2 ff. In Greek Ἄννα.

חֲנוֹךְ m. (*initiated* or *initiating*,) a proper name.

1. the son of Cain; also a city named from him. Gen. 4:17, 18.

2. the father of Methuselah, taken away on account of his piety, Gen. 5: 18—24. According to the more modern Jews, and the Arabians, (who call him *Idris the learned*,) he was the inventor of letters, arithmetic and astronomy; probably an inference from the etymology of the name.

חַנּוּן m. verbal adj. from חָנַן, *merciful, gracious;* spoken of God. Ps. 111: 4. 112:4.

חָנוּת f. plur. חֲנֻיּוֹת, Jer. 37:16. according to the Syr. ܚܢܘܬܐ *a shop, cell, dwelling;* in the Rabbins also the proper name of a building or place on Mount Moriah, where in later times the Jewish Sanhedrim was held. So prob. in our passage. According to others, i. q. מַהְפֶּכֶת *a pillory, the stocks;* from حنا *to bend, incline*, like κύφων from κύπτω.

חָנַט *to season, to spice;* hence,

1. *to embalm, condire cadaver*. Gen. 50:2, 3, 26. (In Arab. حَنَّطَ conj. II. *idem*.)

2. *to give a flavour;* hence, *to ripen* fruit. Cant. 2:13.

חִנְטִין masc. plur. Chald. i. q. Heb. חִטִּים *wheat*. Ezra 6:9. 7:22.

חָנִיךְ m. verbal from חָנַךְ, dec. III. a. literally, *initiated;* hence, *experienced, proved*. Gen. 14:14.

חֲנִית f. plur. חֲנִיתִים and וֹת—, dec. I. *a dart, javelin, spear, lance*. 1 Sam. 18:11. 19:10. 20:33.

חָנַךְ, fut. plur. יַחְנְכוּ, i. q. Arab. حنك.

1. *to consecrate*, e. g. a house, Deut. 20:5. *a temple*, 1 K. 8:63. 2 Chr. 7:6.

2. hence, *to instruct, to initiate*. (So also in the Mishnah.) Prov. 22:6 חֲנֹךְ לַנַּעַר עַל פִּי דַרְכּוֹ *instruct a young man concerning his conduct*.

Deriv. out of course חָנִיךְ.

חֲנֻכָּה f. verbal from חָנַךְ, dec. X. *a consecration*. Ps. 30:1. Num. 7:11. Also, *a consecration-offering*, verse 10.

חֲנֻכָּה f. Chald. *idem*. Dan. 3:2, 3 Ezra 6:16, 17.

חִנָּם adv. (from חֵן, by adding the termination ָם.)

1. literally, *for mere favour, for thanks' sake*, like Lat. *gratis*, contraction of *gratiis;* hence, *without recompense* or *reward, for nothing*, Gen. 29:15. Job 1:9. *without cost*, 2 Sam. 24:24.

2. *without cause* or *occasion, undeservedly*. Job 2:3. 9:17.—1 K. 2:31 דְּמֵי חִנָּם *innocent blood*. Prov. 26:2.

3. *in vain, to no purpose, frustra*.

Prov. 1:17.—אֶל חִנָּם, Ezek. 6:10. (So the Greek δωρεάν in the N.T. the old Lat. *frustra*, and the Germ. *umsonst*, signify *for nothing*, and also in *vain.*)

חֲנָמַל a quadriliteral, *hail.* Once Ps. 78:47.

חָנַן, fut. יָחֹן and יֶחֱנַן (Am. 5:15). with suff. יְחָנְךָ for יָחָנְךָ, infin. חֲנַנְכֶם (Is. 30:18). and חֶנְנָהּ (Ps. 102:14).

1. *to be favourable* or *gracious to* any one, *to have compassion on him;* construed with an accus. Ex. 33:19. Lam. 4:16. Prov. 14:31.—חָנֵּנִי, חָנֵּנוּ, (once חָנְנֵנִי Ps. 9:14.) *have compassion on me, on us*, Ps. 4:2. 6:3. 31:10.

2. *to give graciously*, construed with two accus. Gen. 33:5. Ps. 119:29. Judg. 21:22. with one accus. Prov. 19:17. without cases, Ps. 37:21, 26.

3. perhaps as in Hithpael, *to supplicate, weep.* (Comp. Arab. حن *to sigh, lament.*) Job 19:17 חַנֹּתִי לִבְנֵי בִטְנִי *my sighing* (*is strange*) *to my own children.* Others: *I am loathsome* etc. (comp. خن conj. X. *fœtorem emisit.*)

Niph. נֵחַן (after the form נֵחַל, נֵחַת,) pass. of Po. no. 2. *to be pitied, to be deserving of pity.* Jer. 22:22.

Pi. *to make friendly.* Prov. 26:25.

Po. 1. i. q. Kal no. 1. Prov. 14:21.

2. *to compassionate, lament.* Ps. 102:15.

Hoph. *to be pitied, to receive pity.* Prov. 21:10.

Hithpa. *to supplicate for pity, to entreat;* construed with לְ, Est. 4:8. Job 19:16. with אֶל, 1 K. 8:33, 47. or with לִפְנֵי, 2 Chr. 6:24.

Deriv. חֵן, חַנָּה, חַנּוּן, תְּחִנָּה, תַּחֲנוּנִים.

חֲנַן Chald. *to have compassion*, construed with an accus. Infin. מִחַן Dan. 4:24. [27.]

Ithpa. *to make supplication.* Dan. 6:12.

חֲנַנְאֵל proper name of a tower in Jerusalem. Jer. 31:38. comp. Zech. 14:10. Neh. 3:1. 12:39.

חָנֵס found only Is. 30:4. proper name of a city in Egypt, perhaps Ἄνυσις mentioned Herod. II. 137.

חָנֵף fut. יֶחֱנַף. 1. *to be* or *become profaned*, or *polluted.* Ps. 106:38. Is. 24:5.

2. *to be profane, ungodly.* Jer. 23:11.

3. causat. as in Hiph. *to profane, defile.* Jer. 3:9.

Hiph. 1. *to profane* or *pollute* (a land). Num. 35:33. Jer. 3:2.

2. *to make profane* or *heathenish, to lead to apostacy.* Dan. 11:32. (Syr. ܚܢܦܐ *a heathen, a profane man;* ܐܚܢܦ *to apostatize* from a religious sect.)

חָנֵף m. verbal from חָנֵף, dec. V. b. *profane, ungodly, profligate.* Job 8:13. 13:16. 15:34. 17:8.

חֹנֶף m. verbal from חָנֵף, *profligacy, contempt of God.* Is. 32:6.

חֲנֻפָּה f. verbal from חָנֵף, *idem.* Jer. 23:15.

חָנַק found only in Pi. *to strangle*, spoken of lions. Nah. 2:13.

Niph. *to strangle one's self.* 2 Sam. 17:23. (Arab. and Syr. *idem.*)

Deriv. מַחֲנָק.

חָסַד *to be good, kind, benevolent.* See חֶסֶד. and Hithpa.

Pi. as in Aramean, *to reproach, to put to shame.* Prov. 25:10.

Hithpa. *to shew one's self kind.* Ps. 18:26.

Deriv. out of course חָסִיד, חֲסִידָה.

חֶסֶד m. verbal from חָסַד, dec. VI. a.

1. *love, kindness;* and, spoken of God, *grace, mercy.*—עָשָׂה חֶסֶד עִם *to shew kindness to* any one, Gen. 21:23. 2 Sam. 3:8. 9:1, 7. 2 Sam. 9:3 אֶעֱשֶׂה עִמּוֹ חֶסֶד אֱלֹהִים *I will exercise towards him the kindness of God.* More rarely with אֵת, Zech. 7:9. (comp. Ruth 2:20. 2 Sam. 16:17.) with עַל, 1 Sam. 20:8. and with לְ, which latter is used more especially where God is spoken of, *to shew mercy* or *grace to* any one, Ex. 20:6. Deut. 5:10. also with עִם, Gen. 24:12, 14.—Gen. 39:21 וַיֵּט אֵלָיו חֶסֶד *he*

inclined favour to him, i.e. let him gain favour.—By a metonymy, *object of love or piety,* spoken of God, Ps. 144 : 2. Jon. 2 : 9.

2. *beneficence, liberality.* Prov. 19 : 22. 20 : 6. Plur. חֲסָדִים, Ps. 89 : 2. 107 : 43.

3. as in Aramean, *a reproach.* Prov. 14 : 34. Spoken of incest, Lev. 20 : 17. See the verb in Piel.

חָסָה *to seek protection, to trust;* construed with בְּ of the place. Is. 30 : 2. Ps. 57 : 2. 61 : 5. Especially with בַּיהוָֹה *to seek protection in Jehovah, to confide firmly in him,* Ps. 2 : 12. 5 : 12. 7 : 2. 25 : 20. 31 : 2. 37 : 40. Without cases, Ps. 17 : 7. Prov. 14 : 32 *the righteous man hath confidence even in his death.* Deriv. חָסוּת, מַחְסֶה.

חָסֹן m. verbal adj. from חָסַן, *strong.* Am. 2 : 9. Also collectively, *the strong, the mighty,* Is. 1 : 31.

חָסוּת f. verbal from חָסָה, *trust, confidence.* Is. 30 : 3.

חָסִיד verbal adj. from חָסַד, dec. III. a.

1. *kind, benevolent, humane.* Ps. 12 : 2. 18 : 26. 43 : 1. Spoken of God, *gracious, merciful,* Jer. 3 : 12. Ps. 145 : 17.

2. *pious, virtuous.*—חֲסִידֵי יְהוָֹה *the pious ones of Jehovah, his pious worshippers,* Ps. 30 : 5. 31 : 24. 37 : 28. also חָסִיד לוֹ Ps. 4 : 4.

חֲסִידָה f. strictly *(avis) pia,* (as if fem. of חָסִיד,) hence, *the stork,* a bird celebrated by the ancients for its affection towards its parents. Lev. 11 : 19. Deut. 14 : 18. Job 39 : 13. Ps. 104 : 17. Jer. 8 : 7. Zech. 5 : 9. See Bocharti Hieroz. ed. Rosenmüller. T. III. p. 85 ff. Others: *the heron.*

חָסִיל m. strictly, *the waster, devourer,* (see חָסַל,) hence the name of a species of locust. 1 K. 8 : 37. Ps. 78 : 46. Is. 33 : 4. Joel 1 : 4. Sept. βροῦχος, i. e. the unfledged locust.

חָסִין m. verbal adj. from חָסַן, *strong, mighty.* Ps. 89 : 9.

חַסִּיר adj. Chald. *defective,* i. q. חָסֵר. Dan. 5 : 27.

חָסַל *to eat off, consume;* spoken of the locust. Deut. 28 : 38. (In Chald. *idem.*) Deriv. חָסִיל.

חָסַם *to stop, obstruct.* Deut. 25 : 4 *thou shalt not stop* or *muzzle the ox.* Ezek. 39 : 11 וְחֹסֶמֶת הִיא אֶת־הָעֹבְרִים usually rendered, *and it (the valley) shall stop (the nose of) the passengers,* namely, through the strong stench. Better perhaps after the Syriac translation, *it shall obstruct the passengers,* namely, through the multitude of corpses.

חָסַן 1. as in Syr. and Chald. *to be strong.* Deriv. חָסֹן, חָסִין, חֹסֶן.

2. *to keep, preserve, lay up.* (Arab. خزن, whence مخزن *a magazine.*)

Niph. *to be laid up.* Is. 23 : 18. (See חֹסֶן no. 2.)

חֲסַן Chald. Aph. *to possess, to have in possession.* Dan. 7 : 18, 22.

חֱסֵן m. Chald. emph. חִסְנָא, *might, power.* Dan. 2 : 37. 4 : 27. [30.]

חֹסֶן m. verbal from חָסַן.

1. *strength, might.* Is. 33 : 6.

2. *riches, property.* Prov. 15 : 6. 27 : 24. Jer. 20 : 5. Ezek. 22 : 25. (Chald. אַחְסֵן *to possess.*)

חֲסַף m. Chald. *potters' work, burnt clay.* Dan. 2 : 33 ff.

חַסְפַּס a quadriliteral, part. pass. מְחֻסְפָּס Ex. 16 : 14. *something scaled off, something like scales.* (Comp. חָשַׂף *to peel off;* and the Arab. خزف in the plur. *sherds, scales.*)

חָסֵר, fut. יֶחְסַר, plur. יַחְסְרוּ.

1. *to want, lack,* or *be without* any thing, construed with an accus. Deut. 2 : 7. 8 : 9. Ps. 34 : 11. Prov. 31 : 11. Gen. 18 : 28 אוּלַי יַחְסְרוּן חֲמִשִּׁים הַצַּדִּיקִם חֲמִשָּׁה *perhaps the fifty righteous shall lack five,* i. e. five of the fifty righteous shall be lacking.

2. used absolutely, *to suffer want.* Ps. 23 : 1. Prov. 13 : 25.

3. *to fail, be wanting.* Ecc. 9:8. Deut. 15:8.

4. *to decrease.* Gen. 8:3, 5.

Pi. *to cause to want, to make inferior.* Ps. 8:6. Construed with מִן of the thing, *to deprive,* Ecc. 4:8.

Hiph. 1. used absolutely, *to suffer want.* Ex. 16:18.

2. causat. *to cause to fail, to take away.* Is. 32:6. (In Syr. *idem.*)

Deriv. out of course מַחְסוֹר.

חָסֵר verbal adj. from חָסֵר, dec. V. b. *wanting, lacking;* construed with an accus. 1 K. 11:22. with מִן, Ecc. 6:2. —חֲסַר לֶחֶם *lacking bread,* 2 Sam. 3:29. —חֲסַר־לֵב *lacking understanding,* Prov. 6:32. 7:7. 9:4. also as a subst. *want of understanding,* Prov. 10:21.

חֶסֶר m. verbal from חָסֵר, *want, poverty.* Prov. 28:22. Job 30:3.

חֹסֶר m. verbal from חָסֵר, dec. VI. *idem.* Am. 4:6.

חֶסְרוֹן m. verbal from חָסֵר, *idem.* Ecc. 1:15.

חַף m. verbal adj. from obsolete חָפַף no. II. *pure,* in a moral sense. Job 33:9.

חָפָא perhaps i. q. חָפָה *to cover.* Hence, Pi. *to do in secret.* 2 K. 17:9. Others, by conjecture, *to devise.*

חָפָה *to cover,* the head, face. 2 Sam. 15:30. Est. 6:12. 7:8. (Syr. and Arab. *idem.*)

Pi. *to overlay* with gold, silver, or wood; construed with two accus. 2 Chr. 3:5, 7, 8, 9.

Niph. pass. of Pi. Ps. 68:14.

חֻפָּה f. verbal from חָפַף no. I. dec. X.

1. *a covering, protection.* Is. 4:5.

2. *a bride-bed, bride-chamber;* perhaps, strictly, *the canopy* or *curtain* of a bed, and so *the chamber itself.* Ps. 19:6. Joel 2:16.

חָפַז, fut. יַחְפֹּז. 1. *to be alarmed, disturbed, perplexed.* Ps. 31:23. 116:11.

2. *to flee in perturbation.* 2 K. 7:15 Keri. Job 40:23.

3. *to make haste.* 2 Sam. 4:4.

Niph. 1. *to flee.* Ps. 48:6. 104:7.

2. *to make haste* generally. 1 Sam. 23:26. The Latin *trepidus, fugere,* and many similar words often denote only *haste.*

חִפָּזוֹן m. verbal from חָפַז, *hasty flight.* Ex. 12:11. Deut. 16:3.

חָפְנַיִם dual, dec. I. *the hollow hands.* Ezek. 10:2, 7. Ex. 9:8. (In Aram. and Arab.)

I. **חָפַף** i. q. חָפָה *to cover,* construed with עַל, (comp. קָשָׁה;) hence, *to protect, defend.* Deut. 33:12. (comp. גָּנַן.) Deriv. חֻפָּה.

II. **חָפַף** like the Aram. חֲפַף and Arab. حف *to rub, wash, scrape off.* Deriv. חַף.

חָפֵץ fut. יַחְפֹּץ and יַחְפֵּץ.

1. i. q. Arab. حفض *to bend, incline,* in a physical sense. Job 40:17 יַחְפֹּץ זְנָבוֹ *he bends his tail.*

2. intrans. and figuratively, *to be favourably inclined towards* any one, *to take delight in* him, *to love* him; construed with בְּ, Gen. 34:19. 2 Sam. 20:11. also, in reference to things, 24:3.—Spoken of God, Num. 14:8. 2 Sam. 22:20.—Construed with an accus. Ps. 40:7. Mic. 7:18. Job 33:32 כִּי חָפַצְתִּי צַדְּקֶךָּ *for I desire thy justification.*

3. *to have a desire, be willing,* or *be pleased to do any thing;* construed with לְ and an infin. Deut. 25:8. Ps. 40:19. 1 Sam. 2:25. without לְ, Is. 53:10. Job 13:3. 9:3. Used absolutely, Cant. 2:7. 3:5.

חָפֵץ m. (with Tseri impure) verbal adj. from חָפֵץ, dec. V. f. *willing, desiring, delighting.*—נֶפֶשׁ חֲפֵצָה *a willing mind,* 1 Chr. 28:9.—Joined with the personal pronouns it forms a periphrasis for the verb; e. g. 1 K. 21:6 אִם חָפֵץ אַתָּה *if thou wilt.* Mal. 3:1.

חֵפֶץ m. with suff. חֶפְצִי, verbal from חָפֵץ dec. VI. j.

1. *pleasure, delight* taken in any thing. 1 Sam. 15:22. Ps. 1:2. 16:3. 1 K. 10:13 כָּל־חֶפְצָהּ *all wherein she took delight.*

2. *wish, desire.* Job 31:16.

3. *preciousness, costliness.* (Comp. יָקָר and חֶמֶד.)—אַבְנֵי־חֵפֶץ *precious stones,* Is. 54:12. Plur. חֲפָצִים *costly things,* Prov. 3:15. 8:11.

4. *business, concern, affair.* (So the Lat. *studium* is sometimes nearly equivalent to *negotium, occupatio.*) Ecc. 3:1 וְעֵת לְכָל־חֵפֶץ *and every business has its proper time.* verse 17. 5:7, 8. 8:6. (So in Syr. ܨܒܘ *matter, business,* from ܨܒܐ i.q. חָפֵץ.) The transition to this signification is found in such passages as Is. 53:10 חֵפֶץ יְהוָה בְּיָדוֹ יִצְלָח *the business of Jehovah prospers in his hand.* Job 21:21. 22:3.

I. חָפַר fut. יַחְפֹּר, Arab. حَفَرَ.

1. *to dig,* e.g. a well, a pit. Gen. 21:30. 26:15 ff. Ecc. 10:8. Spoken of spirited horses, Job 39:21 יַחְפְּרוּ בָעֵמֶק *they paw in the valley.*

2. *to lay snares, to dig a pit* for any one. Ps. 35:7.

3. *to espy, discover.* Job 39:29 *from thence he espies the prey.* Construed with an accus. *to spy out, explore* (a country). Deut. 1:22. Josh. 2:2, 3.

II. חָפֵר, fut. יֶחְפַּר and יַחְפֹּר, Arab. خَفِرَ, *to blush, to be ashamed,* i.q. בּוֹשׁ; generally denoting, *to be made ashamed, to be frustrated in one's expectation.* Ps. 35:4, 26. 40:15. 70:3. 83:18. Applied to פָּנִים, Ps. 34:6.—Job 11:18 וְחָפַרְתָּ לָבֶטַח תִּשְׁכָּב *(though now) thou art disappointed, (yet then) thou shalt rest in safety.* The object *wherein* one's expectation is disappointed, is preceded by מִן, Is. 1:29. (comp. בּוֹשׁ.)

Hiph. 1. *to cause shame, to act shamefully.* Prov. 13:5. 19:26.

2. intrans. as in Kal. Is. 54:4. Spoken of inanimate nature, Is. 33:9.

חֵפֶר (*a grave, pit,*) proper name of a Canaanitish royal city. Josh. 12:17. (comp. 1 K. 4:10.)

חֲפַרְפָּרוֹת fem. plur. probably the correct reading in Is. 2:20. and signifying, according to Jerome, *mice, moles,* so called from חָפַר *to dig.* The context certainly requires that it should denote some animal, which can stand in the parallelism with *the bat.* Others: *pits, holes.*

חָפַשׂ *to seek;* in Kal only in a figurative sense, *to search after* (wisdom), Prov. 2:4. *to search into* (the heart), 20:27.—Ps. 64:7 יַחְפְּשׂוּ עוֹלֹת *they search out or devise evil deeds.*

Niph. pass. *to be searched through.* Obad. 6.

Pi. *to seek, to search.* Gen. 31:35. 44:12. Construed with an accus. *to search for,* 1 Sam. 23:23. *to search through,* 1 K. 20:6. Zeph. 1:12. Metaphorically once Ps. 77:7 וַיְחַפֵּשׂ רוּחִי *my spirit makes search.*

Pu. 1. *to be devised.* Ps. 64:7.

2. *to be sought for,* hence, *to be concealed.* Prov. 28:12. comp. verse 28. and Hithpa.

Hithpa. literally, *to conceal one's self,* (see Pu.). Hence, *to disguise one's self,* 1 Sam. 28:8. 1 K. 20:38 וַיִּתְחַפֵּשׂ בָּאֲפֵר עַל עֵינָיו *and he disguised himself by a turban over his eyes.* 22:30. Job 30:18 בְּרָב־כֹּחַ יִתְחַפֵּשׂ לְבוּשִׁי literally, *through the violence (of the disease) my garment,* i.e. my skin, *is changed.* Others, in accordance with the parallel clause, *it (pain) has become my garment,* i.e. it encompasses me as a garment.

חֵפֶשׂ m. verbal from חָפַשׂ, *a device, purpose.* Ps. 64:7. See Pu. no. 1.

חָפַשׁ 1. *to be prostrate, weak,* i.q. Arab. خَفَشَ, (comp. חָפְשִׁי no. 1. and חָפְשׁוּת.)

2. in Pu. *to be set free.* Lev. 19:20. (Perhaps strictly, in Pual, *to be regarded as weak, infirm;* hence, spoken of a slave, *to be set free.* The signification, however, is clear, though this derivation of it is doubtful.)

חֹפֶשׁ m. verbal from חָפַשׁ, *a spreading, stratio.* Once Ezek. 27:20 בִּגְדֵי חֹפֶשׁ לְרִכְבָּה *tapestry for riding, tapetes stratæ ad vehendum.*

חָפְשָׁה fem. of חֹפֶשׁ, *liberty, freedom.* Lev. 19:20. See the verb in Pual.

חָפְשִׁי adj. (formed from חֹפֶשׁ i. q. חֻפְשָׁה *freedom*, and the adjective termination ִי,) plur. חָפְשִׁים.

1. *prostrate, weak.* Ps. 88:6.

2. *free*, not a slave nor a prisoner. Job 3:19.—שִׁלַּח חָפְשִׁי *to set free*, Deut. 15:12, 13, 18. also with לַחָפְשִׁי, Ex. 21:26, 27.—יָצָא חָפְשִׁי לַחָפְשִׁי, *to become free*, (see יָצָא;) also, *to be freed from the taxes and burdens of a subject*, 1 Sam. 17:25.

חָפְשׁוּת and **חָפְשִׁית** f. denom. from חָפְשִׁי no. 1. *sickness*; hence, בֵּית הַחָפְשִׁית *a house for the sick*, 2 K. 15:5. 2 Chr. 26:21. (Arab. حفشا *a house of mourning whither widows were wont to retreat.* See Judah Ben Karish in Eichh. Biblioth. III. p. 970.)

חֵץ m. with suff. חִצִּי, plur. חִצִּים, verbal from חָצַץ, dec. VIII. b.

1. *an arrow.*—בַּעֲלֵי חִצִּים *the archers*, Gen. 49:23.—*the arrows of God*, i. e. the lightning, Hab. 3:11. לְאוֹר חִצֶּיךָ יְהַלֵּכוּ *at the shining of thine arrows they pass away.*

2. *an arrow-wound, a wound* generally. Job 34:6.

3. חֵץ הַחֲנִית 1 Sam. 17:7 Keth. *the staff of the spear*, like the Lat. *hasta, hastile.* The parallel passages 2 Sam. 21:19. 1 Chr. 20:5. and the Keri in 1 Sam. 17:7. have the simpler reading עֵץ.

חָצַב and **חָצֵב**, fut. יַחְצֹב.

1. *to hew, to hew out*, especially stones, (comp. חָטַב.) Deut. 6:11. Is. 5:2. Prov. 9:1. Part. חֹצֵב *a stonecutter*, 2 K. 12:13. sometimes, *a hewer both of wood and stone*, 1 K. 5:29. [15.] *a hewer of wood*, Is. 10:15.

2. figuratively, *to destroy, to kill.* Hos. 6:5 חָצַבְתִּי בַנְּבִיאִים *I destroy them through the prophets*, i. e. I announce their destruction.

3. Ps. 29:7 *the voice of Jehovah divides flames of fire*, i. e. throws out divided flames of fire.

Niph. *to be engraven.* Job 19:24.

Pu. *to be hewn out*, or *formed.* Is. 51:1.

Hiph. i. q. Kal no. 2. Is. 51:9.

Deriv. מַחְצֵב.

חָצָה 1. *to divide into two parts, to halve.* Gen. 32:8. Num. 31:27, 42. Ps. 55:24 לֹא יֶחֱצוּ יְמֵיהֶם *they shall not halve their days*, i. e. they shall not live out half of them.

2. *to divide* generally. Judg. 9:43. Job 40:30. [41:6.]

Niph. *to divide itself*, or *be divided.* 2 K. 2:8, 14. Dan. 11:4.

Deriv. מֶחֱצָה, חֲצוֹת, חֵצִי, מַחֲצִית.

חָצוֹר (*a court*) proper name of several places.

1. a city in the tribe of Naphtali, which Solomon caused to be fortified. Josh. 11:1. 12:19. 19:36. Judg. 4:2. 1 K. 9:15. 2 K. 15:29.

2. another in the tribe of Benjamin. Neh. 11:33.

3. a country in Arabia, mentioned in connexion with Kedar. Jer. 49:28.

חֲצוֹצְרָה see **חֲצֹצְרָה** *a trumpet.*

חֲצוֹת f. verbal from חָצָה, *middle, midst.* Job 34:20. Ps. 119:62. Ex. 11:4.

חֲצִי and **חֶצְיִ** m. const. חֲצִי, with suff. חֶצְיוֹ, verbal from חָצָה, dec. VI.

1. *middle, midst.* Judg. 16:3.

2. *half.* (Comp. *medium, dimidium.*) Ex. 24:6.—חֶצְיֵנוּ *the half of us*, 2 Sam. 18:3.

3. i. q. חֵץ *an arrow.* 1 Sam. 20:36, 37, 38. 2 K. 9:24.

I. **חָצִיר** m. verbal from obs. חָצַר no. II. dec. III. a.

1. *grass.* Job 8:12. 40:15. Ps. 104:14.

2. *garlick.* Num. 11:5.

II. **חָצִיר** i. q. חָצֵר *a dwelling.* Is. 34:13.

חֹצֶן dec. VI. m. Is. 49:22. Neh. 5:13. and חֵצֶן dec. VI. g. Ps. 129:7. masc. *the bosom, the folds of the dress covering the breast, sinus.*

חֲצַף Chald. *to be hard, strict, severe;*

and (especially in Pa. and Aph.) *to press, to hasten.*

Aph. part. *strict, urgent, hasty,* Dan. 2:15. 3:22.

חָצַץ i. q. חָצָה *to divide;* and intrans. *to be divided.* (Comp. חֵץ *an arrow,* so called from its *dividing* or *cleaving.*) Prov. 30:27 *the locusts have no king,* וַיֵּצֵא חֹצֵץ כֻּלּוֹ *yet they all march out divided (into bands).* Comp. Gen. 14:15.

Pi. part. מְחַצְצִים usually rendered, *the archers,* (as if a denom. from חֵץ;) perhaps *those who divide the prey.* Judg. 5:11.

Pu. *to be allotted* or *assigned.* Job 21:21.

חָצָץ m. dec. IV. c. 1. *small stones, gravel stones.* Prov. 20:17. Lam. 3:16. (Syr. ܚܨܨܐ, Arab. حصى.) Strictly, *small parts* or *pieces,* from חָצַץ.

2. i. q. חֵץ *an arrow;* hence, *lightning,* Ps. 77:18.

חַצְצוֹן־תָּמָר, חַצֲצוֹן־תָּמָר (*pruning of the palm*) Gen. 14:7. 2 Chr. 20:2. proper name of a city in the desert of the tribe of Judah, celebrated for its forests of palms, afterwards called עֵין גֶּדִי (q. v.)

חֲצֹצְרָה and חֲצוֹצְרָה f. dec. X. *a trumpet.* Num. 10:2 ff. 31:6. Hos. 5:8. 2 K. 12:14. See חָצַר no. III.

I. חָצַר i. q. Arab. حصر *to shut in, to surround;* whence, حصار *a court, villa.* See חָצֵר and חָצִיר no. II.

II. חָצַר i. q. Arab. خضر *to be green.* See חָצִיר no. I.

III. חָצַר i. q. حضر literally, *to be present.* Hence in Hebrew, in Poel, חוֹצֵר literally, *to call together,* (Arab. conj. X.) which was done by means of a trumpet; hence, *to blow the trumpet.* Part. מחצרים, (read מַחְצְצְרִים,) in the Kethib of 1 Chr. 15:24. 2 Chr. 5:13. 7:6. 13:14. 29:28. The Keri rejects one צ, forming the participle in Piel or Hiphil; but against the analogy of the verbal noun חֲצֹצְרָה. In 2 Chr. 5:12, we find מחצררים, after the form of the conj. Pilel, unless the reading is corrupt.

חָצֵר com. gen. plur. ־ִים and ־וֹת, verbal from obs. חָצַר no. I. dec. V. b.

1. *court before a building.* Neh. 8:16. Est. 5:2. especially of the tabernacle and temple, Ex. 27:9 ff.—הֶחָצֵר הַפְּנִימִית *the inner* or *priests' court* (of the temple), 1 K. 6:36. הֶחָצֵר הַחִיצוֹנָה *the outer court,* or *court of the people,* Ezek. 46:21.

2. *a small place, village,* such as were attached to larger towns, (otherwise called בְּנוֹת הָעִיר.) Josh. 13:23, 28. 15:32 ff. Lev. 25:31. Spoken also of the moveable villages of the Nomades, Gen. 25:16. Is. 42:11. comp. Cant. 1:5.)

This word also forms a part of many names of places; as,

1. חֲצַר אַדָּר (*court of Addar*) a place on the borders of the tribe of Judah, Num. 34:4. which in Josh. 15:3. is called simply אַדָּר.

2. חֲצַר סוּסָה Josh. 19:5. and חֲצַר סוּסִים 1 Chr. 4:31. (*court of horses*) in the tribe of Simeon.

3. חֲצַר עֵינוֹן Ezek. 47:17. and חֲצַר עֵינָן 48:1. Num. 34:9, 10. (*court of wells*) on the northern boundary of Palestine.

4. חֲצַר שׁוּעָל (*court of foxes*) Josh. 15:28. 19:3. 1 Chr. 4:28. Neh. 11:27. in the tribe of Simeon.

5. חָצֵר הַתִּיכוֹן (*the middle court*) Ezek. 47:16. on the borders of Hauran or Auranitis.

6. Plur. חֲצֵרוֹת a station of the Israelites in Arabia. Num. 11:35. 12:16. 33:17. Deut. 1:1.

חֲצַרְמָוֶת proper name of a district of Arabia, on the east of Yemen, now retaining the same name حضرموت *Hadramaut.* Gen. 10:26. See Niebuhr's Description de l'Arabie, Tom. II. p. 126 ff. It is the same name with *Hadrumetum* on the African coast.

חֵק see חֵיק.

חֹק m. before Makkeph חָק, with suff. חֻקִּי, חֻקְּךָ, Plur. חֻקִּים, const. חֻקֵּי (Ezek. 20:18.) verbal from חָקַק, dec. VIII. d.

literally, *something fixed* or *appointed*, as לֶחֶם חֻקִּי *food appointed* or *suitable for me*, Prov. 30:8. comp. Ezek. 16:27. 45:14. Job 23:14 חֻקִּי *what is appointed for me*. Especially,

1. *an appointed labour, a task, pensum*. Ex. 5:14. Prov. 31:15.

2. *a bound, goal*. Job 26:10. Prov. 8:29. לִבְלִי־חֹק *without bounds, boundless*, Is. 5:14.—עָשָׂה חֹק *to set a bound*, Job 28:26.

3. *a definite time*. Job 14:13. Mic. 7:11.

4. *law*, also *custom, usage*. Judg. 11:39. Applied to the laws of nature, Job 28:26. Plur. חֻקִּים, most frequently, *the laws* (of God), Deut. 4:5, 8, 14. 6:24. 11:32. 12:1. Hence, *a declaration of Jehovah, an oracle*, Ps. 2:7 אֲסַפְּרָה אֶל חֹק *I will declare concerning the oracle*; (comp. Is. 8:16.) Comp. חֻקָּה.

חָקָה i. q. חָקַק *to engrave*, and so i. q. Greek *γράφειν, to mark out, portray, paint*. (So the French *dessiner* from the Lat. *designare*.)

Pu. part. מְחֻקֶּה *something portrayed* or *painted*, Ezek. 8:10. comp. 23:14. *something engraven*, 1 K. 6:35.

Hithpa. Job 13:27 *about my feet thou drawest a mark*, i. e. thou markest out for my feet how far they should go.

חֻקָּה fem. of חֹק, dec. X. *a law* of heaven or of nature, Job 38:33. Jer. 31:35. 33:25. of God, as חֻקַּת עוֹלָם לְדֹרֹתָם *an eternal law for their generations*, Ex. 27:21. Lev. 3:17. הָלַךְ בְּחֻקּוֹת הַגּוֹיִם *to walk in*, i. e. to live after, *the laws of the heathen*, 2 K. 17:8. Lev. 20:23.

חָקַק 1. *to engrave* (a writing or picture). Is. 30:8. Ezek. 4:1. Also *to dig out*, Is. 22:16. (comp. the parallel verb חָצַב.)

2. i. q. *γράφειν, to paint*. Ezek. 23:14.

3. *to establish, institute*. Prov. 8:27 בְּחֻקוֹ חוּג עַל פְּנֵי תְהוֹם *when he established an arch over the face of the deep*. verse 29 בְּחוּקוֹ מוֹסְדֵי אָרֶץ *when he established the pillars of the earth*; (בְּחוּקוֹ for בְּחֻקּוֹ).

4. *to resolve, decree*. Is. 10:1. Part. חֹקֵק *a ruler, leader, prince*, Judg. 5:9.

Pu. part. מְחֻקָּק *law, right*. Prov. 31:5.

Hoph. *to be engraven, to be written down*. Job 19:23.

Po. i. q. Kal no. 4. Prov. 5:15. Part. מְחֹקֵק (1.) *a lawgiver*, Deut. 33:21. Is. 33:22. *a leader*, Judg. 5:14. (2.) *a sceptre*. Num. 21:18. Ps. 60:9. Gen. 49:10.

Deriv. out of course חֹק.

חֵקֶק m. verbal from חָקַק, dec. VI. g. found only in the plur. const. חִקְקֵי, *deliberations, decrees*. Judg. 5:15. Is. 10:1.

חָקַר, fut. יַחְקֹר, *to make search, to search*. Deut. 13:15. Ezek. 39:14. Construed with an accus. of the person or thing, 1 Sam. 20:12. Judg. 18:2. Ps. 139:1. Job 5:27. 13:9. Prov. 28:11 *the rich man is wise in his own eyes*, וְדַל מֵבִין יַחְקְרֶנּוּ *yet the poor man that hath understanding searcheth him out*. Sept. καταγνώσεται. Aqu. and Theod. ἐξιχνιάσει.

Pi. i. q. Kal. Ecc. 12:9.

Niph. pass. of Kal. Jer. 31:37. 1 K. 7:47 לֹא נֶחְקַר מִשְׁקַל הַנְּחֹשֶׁת *for the weight of the brass was not to be estimated*. Comp. אֵין חֵקֶר.

חֵקֶר verbal from חָקַר, dec. VI. g.

1. *examination*. Job 34:24. Judg. 5:16 גְּדֹלִים חִקְרֵי־לֵב *great deliberations of heart*.—אֵין חֵקֶר *unsearchable*, Prov. 25:3. hence, *innumerable*, Job 5:9. 9:10. 36:26.

2. *what is examined, a secret, the inner part*. Job 11:7. 38:16 חֵקֶר תְּהוֹם *the innermost depths of the sea*.

חֹר m. found only in the plur. חֹרִים, חוֹרִים *the noble, free born*. 1 K. 21:8, 11. Neh. 2:16. 4:14. (Comp. the Arab. حُرّ for حرر *to be free, free born, of noble descent*; حُرّ *noble, free born*.)

חֹר *a hole*. See חוּר no. II.

חֲרָאִים masc. plur. Is. 36:12. *dung*. (Arab. خَرِئَ *to ease nature*.) The Masoretes, regarding it as a low word, have placed under it the vowel-points of צֹאָה. (See חָרֵי יוֹנִים.)

חָרֵב, fut. יֶחֱרַב and יֶחֱרָב.

1. *to be dry, to be dried up.* Gen. 8: 13. Job 14:11.

2. *to be desolated,* or *laid waste,* spoken of a country or city. (The transition to this signification from no. 1. may be seen in Is. 42:15. 48:21.) Is. 34:10. Jer. 26:9. Spoken of sanctuaries, Am. 7:9. of nations, *to be destroyed,* Is. 60: 12.

3. actively, *to destroy.* Jer. 50:21, 27.

4. *to be astonished, confounded.* Jer. 2:12. Synonymous with שָׁמֵם and שָׂעַר. Comp. particularly שָׁמֵם.

Niph. 1. *to be laid waste.* Ezek. 26: 19. 30:7.

2. recipr. *to seek each other's destruction;* hence, *to contend, fight.* 2 K. 3:23.

Pu. *to be dried.* Judg. 16:7, 8.

Hiph. 1. *to dry up.* Is. 50:2.

2. *to lay waste,* e. g. cities, countries, Ezek. 19:7. Judg. 16:24. *to destroy,* e. g. nations, 2 K. 19:17.

Hoph. pass. of no. 2. Ezek. 26:2. 29:12.

חָרֵב verbal adj. from חָרַב dec. V. b.

1. *dry.* Lev. 7:10. Prov. 17:1.

2. *desolate, waste.* Jer. 33:10, 12. Neh. 2:3, 17. Plur. חֳרָבוֹת, Ezek. 36: 35.

חֶרֶב f. verbal from חָרַב dec. VI. a.

1. *a sword.*—הִכָּה לְפִי חֶרֶב *to smite with the edge of the sword, to put to death,* Deut. 13:16. 20:13. Josh. 6:21. 8: 24. 10:28.

2. also other instruments for cutting; as *a knife for circumcising,* Josh. 5:2, 3. *a razor,* Ezek. 5:1. *a pickaxe,* Ex. 20:25. *a battering ram,* Ezek. 26:9.

3. *dryness, drought.* Deut. 28:22.

חֹרֵב and **חוֹרֵב** the western summit of mount Sinai, now generally called *Sinai.* Ex. 3:1. 17:6. Deut. 1:2. Mal. 3:22.

חֹרֶב m. verbal from חָרֵב.

1. *dryness.* Judg. 6:37, 39. Hence, *heat,* Gen. 31:40. Job 30:30.

2. *desolation.*—עָרֵי חֹרֶב *desolate cities,* Is. 61:4. Ezek. 29:10.

חָרְבָּה fem. of חֹרֶב, plur. חֳרָבוֹת, with the article הֶחֳרָבוֹת, *a desolation, waste.* Lev. 26:31 וְנָתַתִּי אֶת־עָרֵיכֶם חָרְבָּה *I will make your cities a waste.*—בָּנָה חֳרָבוֹת *to build up waste places,* Ezek. 36:10, 33. 38; 12. comp. Job 3:14.

חָרָבָה f. (for חֲרֵבָה,) verbal from חָרֵב *dry,* especially *the dry land.* Gen. 7:22. Ex. 14:21.

חֲרָבוֹן m. verbal from חָרֵב, dec. I. *drought, heat.* Ps. 32:4.

חָרַג found only Ps. 18:46. prob. *to fear, tremble.* (Chald. חַרְגָּא *horror, timor, trepidatio.*) Hence, וְיַחְרְגוּ מִמִּסְגְּרוֹתֵיהֶם *they tremble out of their strong holds,* i. e. they leave them trembling. Comp. Mic. 7:17. Hos. 11:11.) According to others, i. q. Arab. خرج *to go out;* which gives a sense, nearly the same, but not so forcibly expressed as the parallel clause would lead us to expect.

חַרְגֹּל found only Lev. 11:22. a species of locust, eatable and winged. (In Arab. حَرْجَل *a troop of horses, a swarm of locusts.*)

חָרַד, fut. יֶחֱרַד. 1. *to tremble, to quake, to be terrified.* Ex. 19:16. 1 Sam. 28: 5. Is. 10:29. Construed with לְ, *to tremble because of* any thing, Job 37:1. Often in the constructio prægnans, as Gen. 42:28 וַיֶּחֶרְדוּ אִישׁ אֶל אָחִיו לֵאמֹר *and they addressed one another in terror, saying.* Comp. 1 Sam. 13:7.

2. *to have care* or *concern for* any one, construed with אֶל. 2 K. 4:13.

3. *to hasten,* like the Lat. *trepidare, trepidè accurrere.* (Comp. חוּשׁ Niph.) Hos. 11:10, 11. 1 Sam. 16:4. 21:2.

Hiph. *to put in consternation, to make afraid.* Judg. 8:12. 2 Sam. 17:2. Lev. 26:6 אֵין מַחֲרִיד *no one makes you afraid.* Job 11:19. Is. 17:2.

חָרֵד verbal adj. from חָרַד, dec. V. b.

1. *timid, timorous.* Judg. 7:3. Construed with עַל, 1 Sam. 4:13.

2. *fearing, reverencing,* in a religious sense. Ezra 10:3 הַחֲרֵדִים בְּמִצְוַת אֱלֹהֵינוּ *who fear the commandment of our God;* comp. 9:4. Is. 66:2 וְחָרֵד עַל דְּבָרִי *he that fears my words.* In verse 5, construed with אֶל.

חֲרָדָה f. const. חֶרְדַּת, verbal from חָרֵד, dec. XI. e.

1. *fear, terror, trembling.* Gen. 27:33 וַיֶּחֱרַד יִצְחָק חֲרָדָה גְּדֹלָה *and Isaac trembled exceedingly.* Prov. 29:25 חֶרְדַּת אָדָם *fear of men.* 1 Sam. 14:15 חֶרְדַּת אֱלֹהִים *fear of God,* i. e. a panic terror sent from God. Plur. Ezek. 26:16.

2. *care, concern.* 2 K. 4:13. See the verb, signif. no. 2.

3. proper name of a station of the Israelites. Num. 33:24.

חָרָה, fut. יֶחֱרֶה, apoc. יִחַר; (kindred with חָרַר).

1. *to burn, to be kindled;* spoken only of anger. It is found in the following connexions; (1.) חָרָה אַפּוֹ *his anger burns,* Ex. 22:23. Construed with בְּ of the person offending, Gen. 30:2 וַיִּחַר אַף יַעֲקֹב בְּרָחֵל *and the anger of Jacob was kindled against Rachel.* 44:18. Job 32:2, 3. 42:7. rarely with אֶל, Num. 24:10. or with עַל, Zech. 10:3. (2.) used impersonally, אַף being omitted, חָרָה לוֹ *(his anger) was kindled,* i. e. he was angry, Gen. 31:36 וַיִּחַר לְיַעֲקֹב *and Jacob was angry.* 34:7. 1 Sam. 15:11. 2 Sam. 19:43. (3) construed in the same way with בְּעֵינֵי, Gen. 31:35 אַל יִחַר בְּעֵינֵי אֲדֹנִי *let not my lord be angry.* 45:5. In several passages, these phrases express rather *grief* than *anger;* hence it is often rendered in the Sept. by λυπεῖσθαι; comp. 2 Sam. 6:8. Gen. 4:5. Jon. 4:5, 10. For this connexion of ideas, comp. נָחַם Niph. עָצַב Hithpa.

2. *to be angry,* used personally. Hab. 3:7 הֲבִנְהָרִים חָרָה יְהוָה *is Jehovah angry with the rivers?*

Niph. *to be angry,* construed with בְּ. Cant. 1:6 בְּנֵי אִמִּי נִחֲרוּ בִי *my mother's children were angry with me;* (the form is analogous to the fut. Kal יִחַר). Is. 41:11. 45:25.

Hiph. 1. *to be hot, ardent, zealous.* Neh. 3:20 אַחֲרָיו הֶחֱרָה הֶחֱזִיק בָּרוּךְ *after him Baruch zealously repaired.*

2. *to cause to burn, to kindle;* e. g. anger. Job 19:11.

Hithpa. *to be angry.* Ps. 37:1, 7, 8. Prov. 24:19.

Deriv. חָרִי, חָרוֹן. Comp. תַּחֲרָה.

חֲרוּזִים masc. plur. *chains* of pearls, corals, or the like. Cant. 1:10. (Syr. ܚܪܙܐ; comp. the Arab. خرز *to bore through,* especially for the purpose of stringing; خرز *a necklace* of precious stones, berries, or the like.)

חָרוּל dec. VIII. Job 30:7. Zeph. 2:9. Plur. חֲרֻלִּים, Prov. 24:31. *a thorn, a thorn-bush.* Comp. Celsii Hierobot. T. II. p. 166.

חָרוֹן m. verbal from חָרָה, dec. III. a.

1. *a burning.* Ps. 58:10.

2. חֲרוֹן אַף *glow of anger,* i. e. anger itself. Num. 25:4. 32:14. 1 Sam. 28:18 וְלֹא עָשִׂיתָ חֲרוֹן אַפּוֹ בַּעֲמָלֵק *and thou hast not executed his anger against Amalek;* comp. Hos. 11:9. More rarely חָרוֹן alone, used especially of *divine anger.* Neh. 13:18. Ps. 2:5. Plur. Ps. 88:17.

חָרוּץ m. (with Kamets impure, but examples of the plural occur only under no 2.)

1. strictly an adj. *pointed, sharp,* (see חָרַץ;) hence as a poetical epithet of מוֹרַג, Is. 41:15 מוֹרַג חָרוּץ *the sharp threshing sledge* or *wagon,* and also without מוֹרַג in the same sense, Is. 28:27. Am. 1:3. Job 41:22. For a description of this instrument, see מוֹרַג.

2. *a trench,* perhaps including also the mound. Dan. 9:25. (Chald. חֲרִיץ. Comp. the root no. 2. in this case signifying *to dig.*) The verb נִבְנְתָה *it is built* is spoken of חָרוּץ by the figure called zeugma.

3. *industrious, diligent.* (See the verb no. 3.) Prov. 10:4. 12:24, 13:4. 21:5.

4. *judgment, sentence.* (See the verb no. 4.) Joel 4:14 [3:14] בְּעֵמֶק הֶחָרוּץ *in the valley of judgment,* i. e. of punishment. Sept. ἐν κοιλάδι τῆς δίκης.

5. a poetical word for *gold.* Ps. 68:14. Prov. 3:14. 8:10. 12:27. 16:16. Zech. 9:3. perhaps, literally, *desired, coveted,* (as if from the Arab. حرص *avide cupiit, quæsivit.*) A. Schultens supposes it a peculiar species of massy gold, *aurum sponte effissum ex terræ gremio,* but the expression appears rather general and poetic, than special and technical.

חַרְחֻר m. verbal from חָרַר, *inflammation, fever.* Deut. 28:22. Sept. ἐρεθισμός. Vulg. *ardor.*

חֶרֶט m. Ex. 32:4. Is. 8:1. *a pen* or *style,* for writing on a tablet. Comp. עֵט. (Syr. ܚܪܛ *to cut in, to engrave.*)

חַרְטֻמִּים masc. plur. *diviners, soothsayers, persons skilled in hieroglyphics;* in the Egyptian court, Gen. 41:8, 24. Ex. 7:11, 22. 8:3, 14, 15. 9:11. perhaps the kind of Egyptian priests called by the Greeks ἱερογραμματεῖς; in the Chaldean court, Dan. 1:20. 2:2. a kind of Magians. (If the word is Shemitish, it may be compounded of חֶרֶט *a style* or *pen,* and חרם *to be sacred;* hence i. q. ἱερογραμματεῖς. Others derive it from the Copt. Ἐρταμ or Ἐρσαμ, *a worker of miracles.* Others, with more probability, from the Pers. خردمند *a wise man,* from خرد *knowledge,* and مند *endowed.* See Michaëlis Supplem. p. 920. Rosenmülleri not. in Bocharti Hieroz. T. II. p. 468. Jablonskii Opusc. ed. te Water. T. I. p. 401.

חַרְטֻמִּין Chald. plur. *idem.* Dan. 2:10, 27. 4:4, 6. [4:7, 9:] 5:11.

חֳרִי m. verbal from חָרָה, *heat, burning,* i. q. חָרוֹן. Ex. 11:8. Is. 7:4.

I. חֹרִי *bread, white* or *wheaten bread,* (comp. חוּר no. I.) Gen. 40:16 סַלֵּי חֹרִי *baskets of white bread;* Vulg. *canistra farinæ;* Sept. κανᾶ χονδριτῶν. (In Arab. حُوَّارَى *white bread;* and in the Mishnah (Edajoth c. 3, 10.) חרי a kind of pastry.)

II. חֹרִי (perhaps, *dwelling in caverns,* from חוֹר no. II. and the adjective termination ־ִי,) proper name of a people dwelling in Mount Seir, Gen. 14:6. afterwards driven out by the Edomites, Deut. 2:12, 22. Their chiefs, however, are mentioned in connexion with those of the Edomites, Gen. 36:20—30.

חֲרֵי יוֹנִים masc. plur. 2 K. 6:25 Kethib. *doves' dung,* comp. חֲרָאִים. It can be taken literally, (comp. Celsii Hierobot. P. II. p. 30. Rosenmülleri not. in Bocharti Hieroz. T. II. p. 582.) but it may also stand for any other despicable food. That the name *doves' dung* is applied in the Shemitish languages to certain vegetable substances is shewn in Bocharti Hieroz. T. II. p. 44 ff.

חָרִיט m. dec. III. a. *a money-bag, a purse.* 2 K. 5:23. Spoken of as a female ornament, Is. 3:22. (Arab. خريطة *a leathern purse.*)

I. חָרִיץ dec. III. a. i. q. חָרוּץ no. 1. *a threshing wagon, threshing machine.* 2 Sam. 12:31. 1 Chr. 20:3.

II. חֲרִיצֵי הֶחָלָב 1 Sam. 17:18. *cheeses.* So the Sept. τρυφαλίς. Vulg. *formella casei.* Chald. and Syr. *idem.* (In Arab. كريض *caseus molliusculus,* by a commutation of ח and כ.)

חָרִישׁ m. verbal from חָרַשׁ, dec. III. a. *a ploughing, time of ploughing:* 1 Sam. 8:12. Gen. 45:6. Ex. 34:21.

חֲרִישִׁי adj. strictly, *still, quiet.* Jon. 4:8 רוּחַ קָדִים חֲרִישִׁית prob. *a still* or *sultry east wind.* Chald. *quietus.*

חָרַךְ *to catch, seize.* Once Prov. 12:27 לֹא יַחֲרֹךְ רְמִיָּה צֵידוֹ, according to the ancient versions, *laziness seizes not its prey.* Comp. the following article.

חֲרַכִּים masc. plur. Cant. 2:9. strictly, *a net;* here, *a lattice window.* Sept. δίκτυα.

חֲרַךְ Chald. *to singe, to burn.*
Ithpa. pass. Dan. 3 : 27. (In Syr. *idem.* Arab. حَرَقَ.)

I. חָרַם in Kal not used. (Arab. حَرَمَ *to prohibit;* in several derivatives also *to consecrate.*)

Hiph. הֶחֱרִים 1. *to devote to Jehovah,* and in such a way as not to be redeemed. Lev. 27 : 28. Mic. 4 : 13.

2. This was done frequently to hostile cities, after the taking of which, the men and animals were put to the sword, the city was burnt, and a curse imposed on those who should rebuild it. The *devotion* and *destruction* are both expressed by this word. Deut. 2 : 34. 3 : 6. 7 : 2. 20 : 17. Josh. 8 : 26. 10 : 28, 37. 11 : 21. 1 Sam. 15 : 3 ff. Sometimes with the addition לְפִי חֶרֶב *with the edge of the sword,* Josh. 11 : 12. 1 Sam. 15 : 8. Construed with אַחֲרֵי, Jer. 50 : 21. (comp. 1 K. 14 : 10. 21 : 21.)—Is. 11 : 15 וְהֶחֱרִים יְהוָה אֵת לְשׁוֹן יָם־מִצְרַיִם *and Jehovah devotes to destruction the tongue of the Egyptian sea.* The effect of this curse we may conceive to be the drying up of the gulf spoken of.

Hoph. הָחֳרַם pass. spoken of persons, *to be destroyed* or *killed,* (as if devoted to God,) Ex. 22 : 19. Lev. 27 : 29. of things, *to be devoted to God,* Ezra 10 : 8.

II. חָרַם i. q. Arab. خَرَمَ *to tear off, to cut off,* intrans. *to have one's nose broken;* conj. II. *to break one's nose.* Part. חָרֻם Lev. 21 : 18. *flat nosed, mutilated in the nose.*

I. חֵרֶם m. with suff. חֶרְמִי, verbal from חָרַם no. I. dec. VI. j.

1. *something devoted to Jehovah without the possibility of redemption,* differing in that respect from other consecrated things. See Lev. 27 : 21. 28 : 29. Num. 18 : 14. Deut. 7 : 26. 13 : 18. Josh. 6 : 17, 18. 7 : 1 ff. 1 Sam. 15 : 21. Ezek. 44 : 29.

2. *anathema, curse.* 1 K. 20 : 42 אִישׁ חֶרְמִי *the man whom I anathematize;* comp. Is. 34 : 5. Mal. 3 : 24. Zech. 14 : 11.

II. חֵרֶם m. dec. VI. j. *net* (of a fisher or fowler). Hab. 1 : 16, 17. Ezek. 26 : 5, 14. In Chald. *idem.*

חָרְמָה (*curse*) proper name of a Canaanitish royal city, which was afterwards allotted to the tribe of Simeon. Num. 14 : 45. 21 : 3. Deut. 1 : 44. Josh. 12 : 14. 19 : 4. According to Judg. 1 : 14, originally called צְפַת.

חֶרְמוֹן proper name of a mountainous ridge of Antilibanus, which according to Deut. 3 : 9. was called by the Amorites שְׂנִיר, by the Sidonians שִׂרְיֹן. In 1 Chr. 5 : 22, however, *Hermon* is distinguished from *Senir.* According to Deut. 4 : 48, it is the same as שִׂיאֹן. See also Josh. 11 : 3, 17. Ps. 29 : 6. 89 : 13. 133 : 3. Plur. חֶרְמוֹנִים Ps. 42 : 7. Now *Jebel es Shech.* (For its appellative signification, comp. خُرْم *a high mountain.*)

חֶרְמֵשׁ m. *a sickle.* Deut. 16 : 9. 23 : 26. (This word appears to be compounded of חרם no. II. and חרש.)

חָרָן proper name of a city in Mesopotamia, in Greek Κάῤῥαι. Gen. 11 : 31. 12 : 5. 27 : 43. 2 K. 19 : 12. In later times famous for the overthrow of Crassus. The same city is perhaps intended Ezek. 27 : 23. comp. 2 K. 19 : 12.

חֹרֹנַיִם proper name of a Moabitish city. Is. 15 : 5. Jer. 48 : 3, 5, 34. The gentile noun is חֹרֹנִי, Neh. 2 : 10, 19. A different place is intended by בֵּית חוֹרֹן.

I. חֶרֶס m. *the sun.* Job 9 : 7. Judg. 8 : 13. Also חַרְסָה with ה paragogic 14 : 18. (comp. לַיִל and לַיְלָה.)

II. חֶרֶס *the itch.* Deut. 28 : 27. (Root Arab. حَرِشَ *to scratch, to be rough, scabby.*)

III. חֶרֶס Is. 19 : 18. in the majority of MSS. editions, and versions, עִיר הַחֶרֶס (in the common text עִיר הַהֶרֶס,) according to Symm. Vulg. Saad. *the city of the sun,* i. e. Heliopolis; but perhaps both readings have the same sense, and חֶרֶס denotes i. q. חֶרֶס *deliverance*, comp. the Arab. حرس *to preserve, guard.*

חַרְסוּת f. Jer. 19:2 Keth. (in the Keri חַרְסִית,) proper name of a gate, in the city of Jerusalem, which led to the valley of Hinnom. Vulg. and Luther, *potsherd gate,* (from חֶרֶשׂ.) Others, *sun* or *east gate,* (from חֶרֶס;) comp. שַׁעַר הַמִּזְרָח Neh. 3:29.

I. **חָרַף** fut. יֶחֱרַף *to mock, reproach, revile,* construed with an accus. Ps. 119:42. Prov. 27:11. Job 27:6 לֹא יֶחֱרַף לְבָבִי מִיָּמָי *my heart reproaches none of my days.* More frequently in

Pi. חֵרֵף *idem.* 1 Sam. 17:26, 36. Construed with לְ, 2 Chr. 32:17. with בְּ, 2 Sam. 23:9.—Judg. 5:18 זְבֻלוּן עַם חֵרֵף נַפְשׁוֹ לָמוּת *Zebulun is a people that lightly esteemed their life, even unto death,* i. e. they exposed themselves to the greatest dangers; (comp. Schnurrer on this passage).

II. **חָרַף** found only in Niph. Lev. 19:20 שִׁפְחָה נֶחֱרֶפֶת לְאִישׁ *a bondmaid betrothed to a man.* (In Talmud. חֲרוּפָה *a woman betrothed,* i. q. אֲרוּסָא strictly, *a woman purchased.* Comp. the Arab. حرف *to exchange, bargain;* since a wife was obtained by *purchase.* See אָרַשׂ and מֹהַר.)

III. **חָרַף** denom. from חֹרֶף, *to winter, to pass the winter.* Once Is. 18:6 וְכָל־בֶּהֱמַת הָאָרֶץ עָלָיו תֶּחֱרָף *and all the beasts of the field shall winter upon them.* Antith. קִיץ *to pass the summer,* denom. from קַיִץ *summer.* So the Chald. Jerome, and Luther; and the context greatly confirms it. Also in Arabic the significations of the verb خرف are for the most part derived from a noun denoting *autumn* or *winter.* Others, after no. 1., *the beasts of the field shall insult them.*

חֹרֶף m. dec. VI. m. *autumn,* or rather, since the Hebrews distinguished only two seasons of the year, *autumn and winter* together. Hence the antithesis, קַיִץ וָחֹרֶף *summer and winter,* Gen. 8:22. Ps. 74:17. Zech. 14:8.—בֵּית הַחֹרֶף *the winter palace,* Am. 3:15.—Job 29:4 בִּימֵי חָרְפִּי *in my autumnal days,* or, as we should say, *in my vernal days,* since the Hebrews and other eastern nations began the year with autumn. Jerome: *diebus adolescentiæ meæ.* (Hence, יוֹרֶה *the rain which falls in our autumn* is called by the Hebrews the *early* rain; and מַלְקוֹשׁ *that which falls in spring,* the *latter* rain. So חַרְפָן in Chaldaic denotes *early fruit,* in opposition to אֲפִילֵי *late fruit.*)

חֶרְפָּה f. plur. חֲרָפוֹת, verbal from חָרַף no. I. dec. XII. c.

1. *scorn, reproach, contumely.* Job 16:10. Ps. 39:9. 79:12. Mic. 6:16 חֶרְפַּת עַמִּי *the reproach which my people cast on me.*

2. *reproach, shame, disgrace.* Is. 25:8. 54:4 *the reproach of widowhood.* Josh. 5:9 *the reproach of Egypt,* i. e. that which cleaves to you from Egypt to this place.

3. *object of scorn, derision.* Neh. 2:17. Ps. 22:7. Joel 2:17, 19.

חָרַץ, fut. יֶחֱרַץ.

1. *to sharpen to a point, to sharpen.* Found only in the proverbial phrase Ex. 11:7 וּלְכֹל בְּנֵי יִשְׂרָאֵל לֹא יֶחֱרַץ־כֶּלֶב לְשֹׁנוֹ *against all the children of Israel shall no dog point or draw out his tongue,* i. e. no one shall injure them. Josh. 10:21. Comp. Judith 11:19. Deriv. חָרוּץ no. I.

2. *to rend, tear, lacerate.* Part. Paul חָרוּץ Lev. 22:22. *lacerated, having a small wound.*

3. *to be quick, active, diligent, acrem esse.* (In Arab. حرص conj. I. VIII. *idem.* Comp. חוּשׁ.) 2 Sam. 5:24 אָז תֶּחֱרָץ *then be quick* or *hasten.* See חָרוּץ no. 3.

4. *to determine, decide, decree.* 1 K. 20:40. Job 14:5 אִם חֲרוּצִים יָמָיו *if his days are determined.* Is. 10:22 כִּלָּיוֹן חָרוּץ *the destruction is decreed.*

Niph. Part. נֶחֱרָצָה and נֶחֱרֶצֶת as a subst. *something decreed, sentence of punishment.* Is. 10:23 כָּלָה וְנֶחֱרָצָה *destruction and the decree,* a hendiadys for *the de-*

creed destruction. 28:22. Dan. 9:27. 11:36. Dan. 9:26 נֶחֱרֶצֶת שֹׁמֵמוֹת *the decreed desolations.*

חֲרַץ Chald. *loins,* i.q. Heb. חֲלָצַיִם. Syr. ܚܰܨܳܐ. Dan. 5:6 קִטְרֵי חַרְצֵהּ מִשְׁתָּרַיִן *the joints of his loins were loosed,* i.e. he could not stand up.

חַרְצֻבּוֹת plur. 1. *tight cords* or *bands.* Is. 58:6. (In Arab. by transposition حضرب *to bind a cord tight.*)

2. *pains, torments.* Ps. 73:4. comp. חֶבֶל no. III. and חיל no. I.

חַרְצַנִּים masc. plur. found only Num. 6:4. *unripe grapes,* out of which a kind of food was prepared. (Arab. حصرم *unripe grapes;* by a transposition of צ and ר; and a commutation of ם and נ.)

חָרַק, fut. יַחֲרֹק, i.q. Arab. حرق *to gnash.* Job 16:9 חָרַק עָלַי בְּשִׁנָּיו *he gnashes upon me with his teeth.* In other places construed with an accus. Ps. 35:16. 37:12. 112:10. Lam. 2:16.

חָרַר, Arab. حر, *to be hot, burnt, dried.* Job 30:30 וְעַצְמִי חָרָה מִנִּי חֹרֶב *my bones are dried with heat.* Ezek. 24:11. Is. 24:6 חָרוּ יֹשְׁבֵי אֶרֶץ *the inhabitants of the land shall be consumed as it were with fire, quasi igne absumentur incolæ terræ.* (Comp. Joel 1:18—20.)

Niph. נִחַר *to be burnt, dried.* Jer. 6:29. Ezek. 15:4. Fut. יֵחַר, Ezek. 15:5. 24:10. There is another form of the pret. נִחַר (like נִחַל from חָלַל, נִחַת from חָתַת,) Ps. 69:4 נִחַר גְּרוֹנִי *my throat is dried.* 102:4.

Pilp. infin. חַרְחַר *to kindle* (contention). Prov. 26:21.

חֲרֵרִים plur. verbal from חָרַר, *dry* or *parched places.* Jer. 17:6.

חֶרֶשׂ m. *a sherd, potsherd,* Job 2:8. 41:22. [41:30.] Ps. 22:16. *an earthen vessel,* Prov. 26:23. for which last we more frequently find כְּלִי חֶרֶשׂ Lev. 6:21. [28.] 11:33. 14:5, 50. 15:12. (Arab. حرش *to have a rough skin;* and خرش *to scrape.* Comp. חֶרֶס *the itch.*)

חָרַשׁ, 1. fut. יַחֲרֹשׁ, *to cut, to cut in, engrave.* Jer. 17:1. Deriv. חָרָשׁ no. 1.

2. *to work, labour,* especially metals. Gen. 4:22. 1 K. 7:14. Used metaphorically like the Lat. *fabricari, machinari,* Prov. 3:29. 6:14. 14:22.

3. *to plough, till.* (Arab. حرث.) Deut. 22:10. Job 1:14. 4:8. Ps. 129:3 עַל גַּבִּי חָרְשׁוּ חֹרְשִׁים *they ploughed upon my back.* Metaphorically, Hos. 10:13 *ye have ploughed in wickedness, and ye have reaped iniquity.* Deriv. חָרִישׁ, מַחֲרֵשָׁה.

4. fut. יֶחֱרַשׁ, *to be dumb, silent.* (It appears to be an intrans. from the preceding; as the Lat. *tusus, obtusus.* (*blunted,*) from *tundere;* Greek κωφός, (*dumb, deaf,*) from κόπτω; German *stumm* kindred with *stumpf.* The Arabs, however, have here a different orthography, namely خرش.) Used especially of God, *to be quiet, inactive,* (in regard to the prayers of men,) Ps. 35:22 רָאִיתָה יְהוָה אַל תֶּחֱרַשׁ *thou seest it, Jehovah, be not inactive.* 39:13. 83:2. 109:1. Construed with מִן, Ps. 28:1 צוּרִי אַל תֶּחֱרַשׁ מִמֶּנִּי *my rock, turn not silently away from me,* i.e. be not inactive to help me. (Comp. דָּמִי and חָשָׁה.)

5. *to be deaf.* Mic. 7:16. Deriv. חֵרֵשׁ, חֶרֶשׁ.

Hiph. 1. i.q. Kal no. 2. 1 Sam. 23:9.

2. i.q. Kal no. 4. *to be silent, to keep silence.* Gen. 34:5. Ps. 32:3. 50:21. Construed with לְ, *to be silent about* any thing, Num. 30:5, 8, 12, 15. with מִן, *to be silent before* any one, Job 13:13. with אֶל, in the same sense, Is. 41:1. Construed with an accus. *to conceal,* Job 41:4. [12.] *to be silent about* any thing, Job 11:3.—Especially, as is common in Kal, *to keep still, to be inactive,* 2 Sam. 19:11. Jer. 38:27 וַיַּחֲרִשׁוּ מִמֶּנּוּ *they went quietly away from him,* i.e. they let him alone. Also spoken of God, Hab. 1:13. Also spoken of God in the difficult passage Zeph. 3:17 יַחֲרִישׁ בְּאַהֲבָתוֹ usually, *he is quiet or appeased in his love,* as the context seems to require; but the usage of the verb in other places does not support this interpretation.

We should rather expect a negation, *he is not inactive in his love.*

3. i. q. Kal no. 5. *to be deaf.* 1 Sam. 10:27.

Hithpa. *to keep still.* Judg. 16:2.

חָרָשׁ m. const. חָרַשׁ, plur. חָרָשִׁים, const. חָרָשֵׁי, verbal from חָרַשׁ.

1. *a stonecutter.* Ex. 28:11.

2. *a workman* in stone, wood, or metal, i. q. Lat. *faber.* Ex. 35:35. Deut. 27:15. Sometimes more accurately defined by what follows, חָרַשׁ בַּרְזֶל *a workman in iron, a smith,* Is. 44:12. חָרַשׁ אֶבֶן, עֵצִים *a workman in stone, a workman in wood,* Is. 44:13. 2 Sam. 5:11. Metaphorically, Ezek. 21:36 [31] חָרָשֵׁי מַשְׁחִית *workmen of destruction.*

חֵרֵשׁ m. plur. חֵרְשִׁים, verbal adj. from חָרַשׁ, dec. VII. a. *deaf.* Ex. 4:11. Lev. 19:14. Ps. 38:14. See the root no. 5.

חֶרֶשׁ m. verbal from חָרַשׁ, dec. VI. k.

1. *mechanic work, business of a* חָרָשׁ. Is. 3:3 חֲכַם חֲרָשִׁים *the cunning artificer, peritus fabricationum.* Hence, גֵּיא חֲרָשִׁים 1 Chr. 4:14. Neh. 11:35. *the carpenters' valley,* near Jerusalem.

2. *silence,* and as an adv. *silently, secretly.* Jos. 2:1.

חוֹרֵשׁ m. verbal from חָרַשׁ, (with the form of the common participle, compare יוֹצֵר, אֹמֵר;) dec. VII. a. literally, *the cutter, worker;* hence, *an instrument.* Gen. 4:22 כָּל־חֹרֵשׁ נְחֹשֶׁת *every instrument of brass.*

חֹרֶשׁ m. dec. VI. m. *a thick wood, an intricate thicket.* (In Chald. חֲרַשׁ *to be entangled,* חוּרְשָׁא *a thicket,* חוּרְשָׁא *a wood.*) Is. 17:9. Ezek. 31:3. With ה paragogic חֹרְשָׁה *into the wood,* 1 Sam. 23:16. Also with prepositions, בַּחֹרְשָׁה *in the wood,* verses 15, 18. Plur. חֳרָשִׁים 2 Chr. 27:4.

חֲרֹשֶׁת f. verbal from חָרַשׁ.

1. *a labouring* or *working* in wood, stone. Ex. 31:5. 35:33.

2. חֲרֹשֶׁת הַגּוֹיִם Judg. 4:2, 13, 16. a place on the river Kishon, in the north of the country east of Jordan.

חָרַת found only Ex. 32:16. i. q. חָרַשׁ no. 1. *to engrave.* (Aram. חֲרַת *idem.*)

חָשִׂיף m. found only 1 K. 20:27 שְׁנֵי חֲשִׂפֵי עִזִּים *two small flocks of goats.* Sept. δύο ποίμνια αἰγῶν. Vulg. *duo parvi greges caprarum.* So also the Chaldaic interpreter, Kimchi, and other Jewish commentators. Others: *a couple of kids* or *young roes;* comp. the Arab. خِشْفٌ *a young roe,* perhaps *the young of the goat and stag* generally.

חָשַׂךְ fut. יַחְשֹׂךְ, (Aram. חֲשַׂךְ, ܚܣܟ.)

1. *to hold back, to restrain.* Prov. 10:19. Job 7:11. 16:5. Is. 58:1. *cry aloud,* אַל תַּחְשֹׂךְ *hold not back* (*the voice*). Construed with מִן of the thing, Gen. 20:6. 1 Sam. 25:39. 2 Sam. 18:16.

2. hence, *to deliver,* construed with מִן of the thing. Prov. 24:11. Ps. 78:50. Job 33:18.

3. *to deny* any thing *to* any one, construed with an accus. of the thing and מִן of the person. Gen. 39:9. 22:12. Without מִן, verse 16.

4. *to spare, withhold.* Prov. 11:24. 13:24 *he who spareth the rod hateth his son.* 21:26. Construed with לְ of the object *for* which, Job 38:23.

5. *to spare,* in reference to persons. Is. 14:6. 2 K. 5:20.

Niph. 1. *to be assuaged,* spoken of pain. Job 16:6.

2. *to be spared, saved.* Job 21:30.

חָשַׂף fut. יֶחֱשֹׂף 1. *to strip, make bare,* as trees of their bark or leaves. Joel 1:7. Ps. 29:9.

2. *to make bare, to uncover.* Is. 52:10 *Jehovah hath made bare his holy arm.* Is. 20:4 חֲשׂוּפַי שֵׁת *with naked buttocks, nudati nates,* (־ַי is the construct state after the Syriac form, or the state absolute followed by an accus. or else it ought to be pointed ־ֵי) Construed with an accus. of the person, Jer. 49:10. with an accus. of the garment, Is. 47:2 חֶשְׂפִּי שֹׁבֶל *remove the trail.* Jer. 13:26.

3. *to draw, to draw off.* Is. 30:14. Hag. 2:16.

Deriv. מַחְשׂף.

חָשַׁב, fut. יַחְשֹׁב. 1. *to think, intend,*

purpose; construed with לְ and an infinitive. Ps. 140:5 אֲשֶׁר חָשְׁבוּ לִדְחוֹת פְּעָמָי *who thought to overthrow my steps.* 1 Sam. 18:25.

2. *to imagine, invent, devise.* Generally in a bad sense, as חָשַׁב מַחֲשָׁבוֹת עַל *to devise plans against* any one, Jer. 11:19. 18:11, 18. with אֶל, Jer. 49:20. 50:45.—חָשַׁב רָעָה עַל *to imagine evil against* any one, Gen. 50:20.

3. *to think, reckon,* or *account to be* any thing; construed usually with לְ, Gen. 38:15. 1 Sam. 1:13. Job 13:24. sometimes with כְּ, Job 19:11.

4. used absolutely, *to esteem, to regard highly.* Is. 13:17. 33:8. 53:3. Construed with לְ, Ps. 40:18.

5. *to impute,* construed with לְ of the person and an accus. of the thing. 2 Sam. 19:20. Ps. 32:2. Gen. 15:6.

6. *to invent, devise,* as a mechanic. Am. 6:5. Ex. 31:3, 4. (Comp. חִשְּׁבֹנוֹת). Part. חֹשֵׁב *an artificer,* 2 Chr. 26:15. especially, *a weaver, a worker in damask,* different, however, from רֹקֵם, Ex. 26:1, 31. 28:6. 35:35. 36:8. 39:8.

Niph. 1. pass. of Pi. no. 4. *to be reckoned, counted.* 2 K. 22:7.

2. *to be counted to* any thing; construed with לְ, Josh. 13:3. with עַל, 2 Sam. 4:2. comp. Lev. 25:31.

3. *to be regarded* or *esteemed as* any thing. Construed with a nomin. Prov. 17:28 חָכָם יֵחָשֵׁב *he is esteemed wise.* Gen. 31:15. Neh. 13:13. with כְּ, Job 18:3 מַדּוּעַ נֶחְשַׁבְנוּ כַבְּהֵמָה *wherefore are we accounted as beasts?* 41:21. with לְ, 1 K. 10:21. Is. 29:17. 32:15. with בְּ, Is. 2:22. with עִם, Ps. 88:5.

4. *to be imputed to* any one. Lev. 7:18. 17:4.

Pi. חִשֵּׁב 1. i. q. Kal no. 1. Prov. 24:8. Jon. 1:4 *the ship thought to be broken,* i. e. it was near being wrecked.

2. i. q. Kal no. 2. Prov. 16:9. in a bad sense, Dan. 11:24, 25. Construed with אֶל, Nah, 1:9. Hos. 7:15.

3. i. q. Kal no. 4. *to esteem.* Ps. 144:3.

4. *to reckon, to count.* Lev. 25:27, 50, 52. 27:18, 23. 2 K. 12:16.

5. *to consider, reflect on.* Ps. 77:6 חִשַּׁבְתִּי יָמִים מִקֶּדֶם *I consider the years of former times.* 119:59. comp. 73:16.

Hithpa. *to reckon one's self,* construed with בְּ. Num. 23:9.

חֲשַׁב Chald. *to reckon, esteem.* Dan. 4:32. [35.]

חֵשֶׁב m. verbal from חָשַׁב, *the girdle of the high priest's ephod,* so called from *the damask work* of which it was made. (See חָשַׁב no. 6.) Ex. 28:8, 27, 28. 29:5. 39:5, 20, 21.

חֶשְׁבּוֹן m. verbal from חָשַׁב.

1. *wisdom, understanding.* Ecc. 7:25, 27. 9:10. Vulg. *ratio.* (In Chald. חוּשְׁבָּן *reckoning, account, amount;* which would suit Ecc. 7:25, 27.)

2. proper name of a city of the Amorites, which, after the settlement of the Israelites in Palestine, lay on the borders of the tribes of Gad and Reuben, and was reckoned sometimes to one and sometimes to the other of these tribes. It also belonged for some time to Moab. Now called *Husban.* Num. 21:25. 32:3. Josh. 13:26. 21:37. Cant. 7:5. Is. 15:4.

חִשְּׁבֹנוֹת plur. fem. verbal from חָשַׁב.

engines, especially *engines of war,* to cast stones or darts, *tormenta.* (Comp. חָשַׁב no. 6. So the modern Lat. *ingenia,* whence *ingenieur.*) 2 Chr. 26:15.

2. *artifices, devices, artes.* Ecc. 7:29.

I. חָשָׁה 1. *to be silent.* Ecc. 3:7. Ps. 107:29.

2. *to keep still, not to act,* spoken of God. Is. 62:1, 6. 64:11. 65:6. Construed with מִן, Ps. 28:1 פֶּן תֶּחֱשֶׁה מִמֶּנִּי *lest thou turn away silently from me.* (Comp. חָרַשׁ no. 4.)

Hiph. הֶחֱשָׁה, part. מַחְשֶׁה.

1. i. q. Kal no. 1. *to be silent.* 2 K. 2:3, 5. 7:9. Ps. 39:3 הֶחֱשֵׁיתִי מִטּוֹב *I was silent concerning (their) prosperity*

2. i. q. Kal no. 2. Is. 57:11. 1 K. 22:3. Comp. הֶחֱרִישׁ.

3. trans. *to quiet, appease.* Neh. 8:11.

II. חָשָׁה i. q. חוּשׁ *to be in haste.* Here belongs, according to the present punctuation, the fut. apoc. יָחֵשׁ Job 31:5. Perhaps also Judg. 18:9 וְאַתֶּם מַחְשִׁים אַל תֵּעָצְלוּ *and do ye hasten and delay not.*

חֲשׁוֹךְ Chald. *darkness.* Dan. 2:22.

חֲשׁוּקִים see חֲשֻׁקִים.

חֲשַׁח Chald. 1. *to think necessary,* construed with לְ and an infin. Dan. 3:16.

2. *to be necessary.* Ezra 6:9 וּמָה חַשְׁחָן *et quæ opus sunt.* (Syr. ܚܫܚ *to be useful, suitable.*)

חַשְׁחוּת f. *need.* Ezra 7:20.

חָשַׁךְ fut. יֶחְשַׁךְ, *to be darkened, obscured, dim;* spoken of the light or of the sun, Job 18:6. Is. 5:30. 13:10. of the earth, Ex. 10:15. of the eyes, Lam. 5:17. Ps. 69:24.—Ecc. 12:3 חָשְׁכוּ הָרֹאוֹת בָּאֲרֻבּוֹת *they are dark that look through the windows.* Part. pass. חֲשֻׁכִּים *mean men, homines obscuri,* Prov. 22:29. (Chald. חֲשׁוֹכָא, חֲשִׁיכָא *low, mean, obscure.*)

Hiph. 1. *to make dark.* Am. 5:8. Construed with לְ, 8:9 Metaphorically, Job 38:2 מִי זֶה מַחְשִׁיךְ עֵצָה *who is it that darkeneth,* i. e. censureth, *(my) counsel;* comp. חֹשֶׁךְ 37:19.

2. intrans. *to be dark.* Ps. 139:12. Jer. 13:16.

Deriv. out of course מַחְשָׁךְ.

חֹשֶׁךְ m. verbal from חָשַׁךְ, dec. VI. m.

1. *darkness.* Gen. 1:2 ff. Ex. 10:21, 22. hence, *hades, the regions of the dead,* Ps. 88:13. comp. Job 10:21.

2. used metaphorically for (1.) *misfortune, destruction.* (In opposition to אוֹר *light, prosperity.*) Is. 9:1. Job 15:22 לֹא־יַאֲמִין שׁוּב מִנִּי־חֹשֶׁךְ *he expects not to escape destruction.* verses 23, 30. 20:26 *every misfortune is reserved for him.* 23:17. Am. 5:18, 20. Ps. 18:29. (2.) *sadness.* Ecc. 5:16. (3.) *ignorance.* Job 37:19. comp. 12:25, with verse 24.

חֲשֵׁכָה f. verbal from חָשַׁךְ, dec. X. *darkness.* Gen. 15:12. Is. 8:23. Ps. 82:5. Also חֲשֵׁיכָה, Ps. 139:12. Plur. חֲשֵׁכִים, Is. 50:10.

חֶשְׁכָּה f. verbal from חָשַׁךְ, dec. X. *idem.* Ps. 18:12.

חֶשְׁכָה fem. of חֹשֶׁךְ, *idem.* Mic. 3:6.

חָשַׁל i. q. חָלַשׁ no. 2. *to be weak.*

Niph. נֶחֱשָׁלִים *the feeble, exhausted.* Deut. 25:18.

חֲשַׁל Chald. *to be thin.*

Pa. *to make thin* or *small, to bruise in pieces,* i. q. הֵדַק. Dan. 2:40.

חַשְׁמַל m. Ezek. 1:4, 27. 8:2. Sept. ἤλεκτρον, Vulg. *electrum;* meaning prob. thereby *a bright metal compounded of gold and silver,* much esteemed in ancient times, (see Plin. XXXIII. 4. 23.) To a similar idea we are led by the common derivation from נְחָשׁ or נְחֹשֶׁת *brass,* (dropping the initial נ, comp. חַי for חַיִּי,) and מַלְלָא *virgin gold;* namely, *golden brass, aurichalcum,* which by some writers is said to have been dearer than gold. The ancients were acquainted with several species of copper, which, by a natural or artificial mixture of gold, acquired a remarkably brilliant lustre. In Rev. 1:15, we find in a similar connexion the Greek word χαλκολίβανον, which is of equally difficult explanation. Others explain the syllable מַל by *lustre,* as if from מָלַל *to rub, polish,* hence, *polished brass,* i. q. נְחֹשֶׁת קָלָל verse 7. See Bocharti Hieroz. T. II. p. 870—878.

חַשְׁמַנִּים masc. plur. found only Ps. 68:32. probably, according to the Rabbins, *princes, viri magni et principes.* (In Arab. حشيم *magnus magnique famulitii vir.*) Others render it as a gentile noun, *Chasmoneans, inhabitants of the Egyptian province Ashmunein,* اشمونين.

חֹשֶׁן m. in full חֹשֶׁן הַמִּשְׁפָּט Ex. 28:15, 30. *the breast-plate of the high-priest,* a kind of gorget, on the outside set with 12 precious stones, and in the inside hollow to receive the Urim and Thummim. See Ex. 28:22 ff. 39:8 ff. and comp. אוּרִים. Perhaps, literally, *ornament,* as if from the Arab. حسن *to be beautiful,* conj. II. V. *to adorn.*

חָשַׁק 1. *to cleave* or *be attached to*

any one, (from affection). Construed with בְּ, Deut. 7:7. 10:15. 21:11. Gen. 34:8. Employed in an elliptical construction, Is. 38:17 חָשַׁקְתָּ נַפְשִׁי מִשַּׁחַת בְּלִי *thou lovedst (and deliveredst me) from the pit of destruction.*

2. *to have a desire to* do any thing, construed with לְ and an infin. 1 K 9:19. 2 Chron. 8:6.

Pi. חִשֵּׁק *to bind, join, connect.* Ex. 38:28.

Pu. pass. Ex. 27:17.

חֵשֶׁק m. verbal from חָשַׁק, dec. VI. g. *desire, pleasure.* 1 K. 9:1, 19. Is. 21:4 נֶשֶׁף חִשְׁקִי *the night of my desire.*

חֲשֻׁקִים and **חֲשׁוּקִים** masc. plur. dec. I. *poles* or *rods*, by means of which the upright pillars or lathes of the court were *joined together* at the top, and on which the curtains were hung. Ex. 27:10, 11. 38:10 ff.

חִשֻּׁקִים m. verbal from חָשַׁק, dec. I. *spokes* of a wheel, *radii*, which *connected* the nave and felloe. 1 K. 7. 33.

חַשְׁרָה or **חֲשָׁרָה** f. *a collection.* (Comp. the Arab. حشر *to collect.*) Once 2 Sam. 22:12. In the parallel passage Ps. 18:12, חֶשְׁכַת.

חִשֻּׁרִים masc. plur. dec. I. *naves* of a wheel, *modioli*, where the spokes *unite.* 1 K. 7:33.

חֲשַׁשׁ m. *hay, dried grass.* Is. 5:24 חֲשַׁשׁ לֶהָבָה *fœnum flammæ, hay set on fire.* 33:11. (Arab. حشيش *idem.*)

חַת m. with suff. חִתְּכֶם, plur. חַתִּים, verbal from חָתַת.

1. adj. *broken*, spoken of the bow. 1 Sam. 2:4.

2. *terrified, dismayed.* Jer. 46:5.

3. subst. *fear, dread.* Gen. 9:2.

4. as a proper name, בְּנֵי חֵת *children of Heth*, and חִתִּי, plur. חִתִּים, *a Hittite* or *Hittites*, a Canaanitish tribe, dwelling in the neighbourhood of Hebron. Gen. 23:7. 15:20. Deut. 7:1. Josh. 1:4.—מַלְכֵי הַחִתִּים 2 K. 7:6. for *Canaanitish kings* gen. ally.

חָתָה 1. *to take* (fire or coals from an hearth). Is. 30:14 לַחְתּוֹת אֵשׁ מִיָּקוּד *to take fire from the hearth.* Prov. 6:27. 25:22 כִּי גֶחָלִים אַתָּה חֹתֶה עַל רֹאשׁוֹ *for thou takest (and layest) coals upon his head.*

2. *to seize, lay hold of.* Ps. 52:7 יַחְתְּךָ וְיִסָּחֲךָ מֵאֹהֶל *he shall seize thee and pluck thee from thy tent.*

Deriv. מַחְתָּה.

חִתָּה f. verbal from חָתַת, dec. X. *terror.* Once Gen. 35:5.

חִתּוּל m. verbal from חָתַל, *bandage of a wound.* Ezek. 30:21.

חַתְחַתִּים masc. plur. verbal from חָתַת, *terrors*, Ecc. 12:5.

חִתִּית f. verbal from חָתַת, dec. I. *terror, fear.* Ezek. 32:23. חִתִּיתָם *the fear of them*, 32:24—26.

חָתַךְ *to determine, destine.* Niph. pass. Dan. 9:24 *seventy weeks* נֶחְתַּךְ עַל עַמְּךָ *are determined concerning thy people.* (In Chald. *to cut, decide.*)

חָתַל *to wrap in swaddling-clothes.*

Hoph. pass. Ezek. 16:4.

Pu. pass. Ezek. 16:4.

חֲתֻלָּה f. verbal from חָתַל dec. X. *swaddling-band.* Job 38:9. Comp. חִתּוּל.

חֶתְלֹן proper name of a city in Syria of Damascus. Ezek. 47:15. 48:1.

I. **חָתַם**, fut. יַחְתֹּם.

1. *to seal, to seal up;* construed with an accus. Also with בְּעַד, Job 9:7. (see בַּעַד no. 4.) and with בְּ, Job 37:7 בְּיַד כָּל־אָדָם יַחְתּוֹם *he sealeth up every man's hand*, i. e. hinders him from using it. (Comp. אָטַר.)

2. as the roll or letter, when completed, was sealed up, hence, *to complete, finish, fulfil.* (In Arab. *idem.*) Dan. 9:24 לַחְתֹּם חָזוֹן וְנָבִיא *till the vision and the prophets*, i. e. their oracles, *are fulfilled.* Vulg. *et impleatur visio et prophetia.* Ezek. 28:12 חוֹתֵם תָּכְנִית *complete in beauty*, i. e. a model of beauty, i. q. כְּלִיל יֹפִי.

Niph. *to be sealed.* Est. 3:12. 8:8.

Pi. *to shut up.* Job 24:16 יוֹמָם חִתְּמוּ לָמוֹ *in the day-time they shut themselves up*, literally, *obsignant sibi.* (The ancients often sealed up what we are wont only to close, Dan. 6:18. Mat. 27:66. Lipsius in Tac. Annal. II. 2.)

Hiph. *idem.* intrans. *to be closed* or *stopped up.* Lev. 15:3.

Deriv. out of course חוֹתָם.

II. חָתַם prob. i. q. Arab. ختم *to reveal* or *suggest to* any one, construed with בְּ. Job 33:16 בְּמֹסָרָם יַחְתֹּם *he revealed their admonition,* i. e. revealed to them admonition. Others, after the usual signification, *he impresses* or *inculcates on them admonition.*

חֲתַם Chald. *to seal.* Dan. 6:18.

חֹתָם *a seal,* see חוֹתָם.

חֹתֶמֶת fem. of חוֹתָם, *idem.* Gen. 38:25.

חָתַן found only in the part. חֹתֵן *a father-in-law,* namely, *a wife's father,* (*a husband's father* in Hebrew is חָם). Ex. 18:1 חֹתֵן מֹשֶׁה *the father-in-law of Moses.* Judg. 19:4 ff. Fem. חֹתֶנֶת *a wife's mother, a mother-in-law,* Deut. 27:23.

Hithpa. *to contract affinity by marriage,* namely, by marrying the daughter of any one, or by giving him his own daughter in marriage. Construed with אֶת, Gen. 34:9. 1 K. 3:1. with בְּ, Deut. 7:3. Josh. 23:12. 1 Sam. 18:22, 23, 26, 27. Ezra 9:14. with לְ, 2 Chron. 18:1. (Arab. ختن conj. III. *to contract affinity by marriage;* خَتَن *a son-in-law, a wife's relation.*)

חָתָן m. verbal from חָתַן, dec. IV. c.

1. *a son-in-law.* Gen. 19:12. Judg. 15:5, 6.

2. *a bridegroom.* Ps. 19:6. Is. 62:5. Ex. 4:25 חֲתַן דָּמִים *a bloody bridegroom,* on account of the child just circumcised. Perhaps expressive of a symbolical union with Jehovah, (comp. כַּלָּה;) and perhaps also containing an allusion to the signification of חתן i. q. Arab. ختن *to circumcise.*

3. *a kinsman by marriage,* in reference to the husband. 2 K. 8:27.

חֲתֻנָּה f. verbal from חָתַן, dec. X. *a marriage, wedding.* Cant. 3:11.

חָתַף i. q. חָטַף *to lay hold of, to seize, rapere* (*more leonis*). Job 9:12.

חֶתֶף verbal from חָתַף, *prey, spoil,* probably for אִישׁ חֶתֶף *a robber,* (comp. הֵלֶךְ for אִישׁ הֵלֶךְ 2 Sam. 12:4.) Prov. 23:28.

חָתַר 1. *to break through,* e. g. a wall; construed with בְּ. Ezek. 8:8. 12:5, 7, 12. Am. 9:2 אִם יַחְתְּרוּ בִשְׁאוֹל *if they break through* or *into hades.* Construed with an accus. Job 24:16.

2. *to row,* i. e. to break through the waves. (Only in Heb.) Jon. 1:13.

Deriv. מַחְתֶּרֶת.

חָתַת 1. *to break* or *be broken in pieces.* comp. Niph. Pi. Hiph.

2. *to be terrified, confounded.* (Several verbs of breaking have this change of signification; comp. שְׁבָרִים.) Especially, *to be thrown into consternation, to be made ashamed,* kindred with בּוֹשׁ, Job 32:15 חַתּוּ לֹא עָנוּ עוֹד *they were thrown into consternation, they answered no more.* Jer. 8:9. 14:4. 48:1, 20, 39. 50:2.

Niph. נִחַת (not to be confounded with נִחַת from נָחַת,) fut. יֵחַת, plur. יֵחַתּוּ.

1. *to be broken* or *shattered in pieces.* Is. 7:8. 51:6 וְצִדְקָתִי לֹא תֵחָת *my goodness shall not be broken,* i. e. it shall not cease.

2. *to be terrified, to despond.* Frequently joined with יָרֵא, Deut. 1:21. 31:8. Josh. 1:9. 8:1. 10:25. Construed with מִפְּנֵי, *to be afraid of* any one, Jer. 1:17. Ezek. 2:6. 3:9. with מִן, in the same sense, Is. 30:31. 31:4. Jer. 10:2.—Mal. 2:5 מִפְּנֵי שְׁמִי נִחַת הוּא *and he feared my name.*—Also, *to be confounded,* Jer. 17:18.

Pi. 1. intrans. *to be broken in pieces.* Jer. 51:56.

2. trans. *to terrify.* Job 7:14.

Hiph. הֵחַת, הַחִתֹּתִי (Jer. 49:37).

1. *to break in pieces.* Is. 9:3.

2. *to terrify, to make afraid,* Jer. 49:37. *to make ashamed,* Job 31:34. So

in Hab. 2:17 יְחִיתַן, for יְחִיתֵּן. ־ִי stands for Hirik with Dagesh forte following, (comp. קִים;) and ־ַן stands in pause for ־ֵן. Vulg. *deterrebit eos.*

Deriv. out of course חַת, חִתָּה, חִתִּית, מְחִתָּה, חַתְחַתִּים.

חֲתַת m. verbal from חָתַת, *terror.* Job 6:21.

ט

THIS letter is called in Hebrew טֵית, and as a numerical sign denotes 9. In composition טו denotes 15, (9 + 6.) In Arabic there are two corresponding letters, namely ط and ظ. The former is more common, as the latter approaches to the צ. It is often commuted with ת; as חָתַף and חָטַף *to seize;* קָטַל Arab. قتل *to kill;* תָּעָה and טָעָה, Syr. ܛܥܳܐ *to err;* comp. קָטַל no. II. etc. For its interchange with ד, see page 124.

טְאֵב Chald. *to be joyful, glad.* Dan. 6:24. Syr. ܛܐܶܒ *to be glad.* See טוֹב no. 3.

טֵאטֵא *to sweep out* or *away.* (In Talmud. טַאטֵא, also טַיְאֵט *idem,* טֵיאוּט *a sweeping out,* kindred with טִיט *mud, mire.*) Is. 14:23 וְטֵאטֵאתִיהָ בְּמַטְאֲטֵא הַשְׁמֵד *and I will sweep her (Babylon) away with the besom of destruction;* (so the Vulg. Chald.) indicative of entire destruction; comp. 1 K. 14:10. 21:21. A similar figure is found under מָחָה. Others compare the Arab. طأطأ *profundam effecit fossam;* hence, in our passage, *I will sink them into the pit of destruction;* which, however, is not sufficiently confirmed. In a similar manner, the Sept. θήσω αὐτὴν πηλοῦ βάραθρον εἰς ἀπώλειαν, evidently deriving it from טִיט *mire,* πηλός.

טָב Chald. *good.* Dan. 2:32. Ezra 5:17 הֵן עַל מַלְכָּא טָב *if (it seem) good unto the king.* Comp. טוֹב Est. 1:19. 3:9.

טְבוּלִים masc. plur. *bandages, headbands, turbans.* Ezek. 23:15. (Usually derived from טָבַל *to colour;* but more probably from the Ethiop. טבלל *to wind round, to swathe with bandages.*)

טַבּוּר m. *a height, hill, mountain.* Judg. 9:37 יֹרְדִים מֵעִם טַבּוּר הָאָרֶץ *descending from the height of the land;* (comp. רָאשֵׁי הֶהָרִים verse 36.) Ezek. 38:12 יֹשְׁבֵי עַל טַבּוּר הָאָרֶץ *dwelling upon the height of the land.* (Comp. הָרֵי יִשְׂרָאֵל *mountains of Israel* for *the country* generally, 6:2. 33:28. 35:12. 38:8.) In Samar. טבור *a mountain;* in Talmud. טִיבּוּר *the navel;* thus, too, the Sept. and Vulg. translate טַבּוּר in both places. Most translators have followed them, though the figure appears very unnatural.

טָבַח kindred with זָבַח.

1. *to slaughter, kill,* as animals. Ex. 21:37. [22:1.] Especially to dress them for the table, 1 Sam. 25:11. Prov. 9:2. (In Arabic we find only the latter idea, طبخ *to cook, to roast.*)

2. *to cut down, destroy.* Ps. 37:14. Lam. 2:21.

טַבָּח m. verbal from טָבַח, dec. I. literally, *a slaughterer;* hence,

1. *a cook.* 1 Sam. 9:23, 24.

2. *an executioner, one who inflicts capital punishment.* This task in the east belonged to the body guards of the king. רַב טַבָּחִים 2 K. 25:8 ff. Jer. 39:9 ff. and שַׂר הַטַּבָּחִים Gen. 37:36. 39:1. 40:3, 4. 41:10, 12. *the captain of the body guard,* who was also the king's chief executioner, like the Captain Pacha of the Ottoman Porte.

טַבָּח Chald. *an executioner, member of the body guard.* Dan. 2:14.

טֶבַח m. verbal from טָבַח, dec. VI. i.

1. *cattle for slaughter;* also, *a feast on them.* Prov. 9:2 טָבְחָה טִבְחָהּ *she killeth her beasts,* or *prepares her feast.* Gen. 43:15. comp. זֶבַח no. 1.

2. *the slaughtering-bench, the slaughter.* Prov. 7:22. Is. 53:7.

3. *a slaughter* or *destruction of men.* Is. 34:2, 6.

טִבְחָה fem. of טֶבַח, dec. X.

1. *beasts slain, a feast on them.* 1 Sam. 25:11.

2. *the slaughter.* Ps. 44:23.

טַבָּחָה fem. of טַבָּח, dec. X. *a female cook.* 1 Sam. 8:13.

טִבְחַת 1 Chr. 18:8. proper name of a city in Syria of Zobah, which in the parallel passage 2 Sam. 8:8, is called בֶּטַח.

טָבַל, fut. יִטְבֹּל, *to dip in*, construed with בְּ. Gen. 37:31. Deut. 33:24. Ruth 2:14. Also without an accus. Ex. 12:22. 2 K. 5:14 *he went down* וַיִּטְבֹּל בַּיַּרְדֵּן שֶׁבַע פְּעָמִים *and dipped in the Jordan seven times.* 8:15.

Niph. pass. Josh. 3:15.

טָבַע 1. *to sink*, e.g. into the mud, into a pit. Ps. 9:16. 69:3, 15. Lam. 2:9 טָבְעוּ בָאָרֶץ שְׁעָרֶיהָ *her gates are sunk to the ground.*

2. *to penetrate, infigi.* 1 Sam. 17:49 וַתִּטְבַּע הָאֶבֶן בְּמִצְחוֹ *and the stone penetrated into his forehead.*

3. as in Arabic, *to seal;* literally, trans. of the preceding signification, *to make an impression on a soft substance.* Deriv. טַבַּעַת.

Pu. i. q. Kal no. 1. Ex. 15:4.

Hoph. *idem.* Jer. 38:22. *to settle down* or *subside*, spoken of the foundations of the earth, Job 38:6. of the mountains, Prov. 8:25.

טַבַּעַת f. plur. טַבָּעוֹת, const. טַבְּעוֹת, verbal from טָבַע, dec. XIII. m.

1. *a seal-ring, a signet.* Gen. 41:42. Est. 3:10. See טָבַע no. 3.

2. *a ring* generally, even without a seal, or not intended for the finger. Ex. 35:22 ff. 37:3 ff.

טַבָּת Judg. 7:22. a place not far from Abel-meholah in the tribe of Ephraim.

טֵבֵת name of the tenth month, corresponding partly to December and partly to January of our calendar. Est. 2:16. "Decimus mensis, qui Hebræis appellatur Tebeth, et apud Ægyptios Τωβι (in *La Croze* Τωβι, in a Vienna MS. Τωβι, Arab. طوبة), apud Romanos Januarius." Jerome on Ezek. 39:1.

טָהוֹר, const. טְהוֹר, sometimes טְהָר (Job 17:9.) verbal adj. from טָהֵר, dec. III. a. and h. *pure;* particularly, (1.) *unmixed*, as gold. Ex. 25:11. (2.) *clean, not dirty.* Zech. 3:5. (3.) *clean*, in a ceremonial sense, Lev. 13:17. hence, spoken of animals permitted to be eaten, Gen. 7:2. 8:8, 20. (4.) *pure*, in a moral sense. Ps. 12:7. 19:10. 51:12 לֵב טָהוֹר *a pure heart.* Job 14:4. Used abstractly as a subst. *purity*, Prov. 22:11.

טָהֵר *to be* or *become pure;* in a physical sense, 2 K. 5:12, 13. especially in a ceremonial sense, opposite of טָמֵא, Lev. 7:19. 10:10. 11:36. also in a moral sense, Job 4:17. Prov. 20:9.

Pi. טִהַר, fut. יְטַהֵר.

1. *to purify;* e. g. a people, country. Ezek. 24:13. 36:33. 39:12, 14.

2. *to pronounce clean* or *pure*, spoken of the priest. Lev. 13:13, 17 ff.

Pu. pass. Ezek. 22:24.

Hithpa. הִטַּהֵר and הִטַּהַר *to purify* or *cleanse one's self.* Gen. 35:2. Lev. 14:4 ff.

טֹהַר m. verbal from טָהֵר, dec. VI. n.

1. *purity, brightness, clearness*, spoken of the firmament. Ex. 24:10.

2. *purification.* Lev. 12:4, 6.

טְהָר m. verbal from טָהֵר, dec. I. *lustre, majesty, glory.* Ps. 89:45 הִשְׁבַּתָּ מִטְּהָרוֹ *thou makest his glory to cease.* For the construction with מִן, comp. 1 K. 18:5. Mich. 4:2.

טָהֳרָה fem. of טֹהַר, dec. X.

1. *purity.* 2 Chr. 30:19.

2. *purification.* Lev. 13:35. 14:2. —דְּמֵי טָהֳרָה, *blood of purification*, from which the lying-in-woman is cleansed, Lev. 12:4, 5.

טוֹב, pret. טוֹב, טֹבוּ, (instead of the future, יִיטַב is in use from יָטַב).

1. *to be good;* but only used impersonally, (1.) טוֹב לִי *it goes well with me.* Deut. 5:30. 15:16. 19:13. Job 13:9 הֲטוֹב כִּי *will it go well* (*with you*) *that*

etc.—Also, *it helps one*, Job 10 : 3. *to be well* (*in mind*), 1 Sam. 16 : 16. (2.) טוֹב בְּעֵינַי *it pleases me.* Num. 24 : 1. In the later books we find עַל instead of בְּעֵינֵי, 1 Chr. 13 : 2. Est. 1 : 19 אִם עַל הַמֶּלֶךְ טוֹב *if it please the king.* 3 : 9. 5 : 4, 8. 7 : 3. Neh. 2 : 5. comp. Ezra 5 : 17.

2. *to be fair, lovely.* Num. 24 : 5. Cant. 4 : 10.

3. *to be serene, joyful,* (the prevalent meaning in Syriac,) spoken of the heart. 1 Sam. 25 : 36. 2 Sam. 13 : 28. Est. 1 : 10.

Hiph. הֵטִיב, (הֵיטִיב from יָטַב occurs more frequently).

1. *to do well.* 1 K. 8 : 18. 2 K. 10 : 30.

2. *to do good.* Ezek. 36 : 11.

3. *to make fair* or *beautiful.* Hos. 10 : 1.

טוֹב, fem. **טוֹבָה**, verbal adj. from טוֹב, dec. I.

1. *good.*—הָיָה טוֹב לִי *it goes well with me,* Ecc. 8 : 12, 13. לְטוֹב לָנוּ, לָהֶם *that it might be well with us, with them,* Deut. 6 : 24. 10 : 13. Jer. 32 : 39. (strictly for לִהְיוֹת טוֹב לְ, comp. לְרַע לָהֶם, בְּצַר לִי.)—טוֹב לִי *happy am I,* Ps. 119 : 71. Lam. 3 : 27. —טוֹב בְּעֵינַי *that which pleases me,* (Num. 24 : 1.?) Deut. 6 : 18. Gen. 16 : 6 עֲשִׂי לָהּ הַטּוֹב בְּעֵינָיִךְ *do to her what pleases thee.* 19 : 8. Judg. 10 : 15. 19 : 24. Also, in the same sense, with לְפָנַי, Ecc. 2 : 26. and לְ, (Job 10 : 3.?) Deut. 23 : 17.—לֹא טוֹב sometimes for *evil, wicked,* Prov. 18 : 5. 20 : 23.—Also as an adv. *well! come on!* 2 Sam. 3 : 13. Ruth 3 : 13. and as a subst. *something good, a good,* Job 7 : 7. Ps. 16 : 2. and placed as a genitive after another noun, e. g. בִּרְכַּת טוֹב *benedictio boni,* i. e. bona.—לְטוֹב *for good,* for the most part in phrases otherwise ambiguous, (see טוֹבָה,) Ps. 119 : 122. Deut. 30 : 9.

2. *fair, beautiful,* spoken of persons and things. Ex. 2 : 2. Gen. 6 : 2. Often with the addition מַרְאֶה, Gen. 24 : 16. Est. 1 : 11. 2 : 3, 7.

3. *pleasant, lovely.* Cant. 1 : 2. 4 : 10. Especially, *of a pleasant smell, fragrant,* שֶׁמֶן הַטּוֹב *the fragrant ointment,* Ps. 133 : 2. Is. 39 : 2.

4. *happy, prosperous.* Jer. 44 : 17. Ps. 112 : 5 טוֹב־אִישׁ *happy is the man.* Ecc. 5 : 4, 17. 7 : 18. comp. Lam. 3 : 36. Amos 6 : 2.

5. *great.* Ps. 69 : 17 כִּי טוֹב חַסְדֶּךָ *for thy goodness is great.* 109 : 21. (Comp. Ruth 3 : 10.) Syr. ܛܒ adv. *valde.*

6. *joyful.* Est. 8 : 8. 1 K. 8 : 66.—טוֹב לֵב *with a joyful heart,* Ecc. 9 : 7.

7. טוֹב עַיִן *having a compassionate eye, merciful.* (So the Sept. Vulg.) Opposite of רַע עַיִן. Prov. 22 : 9.

טוֹב proper name of a country beyond Jordan. Jud. 11 : 3. 2 Sam. 10 : 6. Probably the same with Τωβίος 1 Mac. 5 : 13.

טוּב m. verbal from טוֹב, dec. I.

1. *goodness, good condition.* Ps. 119 : 66 טוּב טַעַם *goodness of judgment,* i. e. good judgment. Often spoken of God, Ps. 25 : 7. 27 : 13. 31 : 20. 145 : 7. Jer. 31 : 14.

2. *what is good* or *best, the best part.* Gen. 45 : 18, 20. Especially, *the best productions* (of a country), Gen. 45 : 23. Is. 1 : 19. Ezra 9 : 12.

3. *goods, riches.* Gen. 24 : 10. Deut. 6 : 11.

4. *joyfulness,* spoken of the heart. Deut. 28 : 47. Is. 65 : 14.

5. *prosperity, happiness.* Job 20 : 21. 21 : 16. Prov. 11 : 10.

6. *beauty, glory.* Hos. 10 : 11. Zech. 9 : 17. Ex. 33 : 19 אֲנִי אַעֲבִיר כָּל־טוּבִי *I will make all my glory to pass before thee.*

טוֹבָה fem. of טוֹב, dec. X.

1. *what is good, goodness.*—לְטוֹבָה *for good,* Neh. 5 : 19 *remember it, O God, to me for good.* 13 : 31. Also in phrases otherwise ambiguous, Ps. 86 : 17. Jer. 14 : 11. 24 : 6. Ezra 8 : 22.

2. *goodness, blessing,* (of God.) Ps. 65 : 12.

3. *happiness, prosperity.* Ps. 16 : 2. 106 : 5.

טָוָה *to spin.* Ex. 35 : 25, 26. (Arab. طوي *to fold up, to wind about.*)

Deriv. מַטְוֶה.

טוּחַ (comp. Arab. طاخ med. Je) *to cover, overlay;* hence, *to close* (the eyes), Is. 44:18. *to plaster over* (a wall), Lev. 14:42. 1 Chron. 29:4. Construed with two accusatives, Ezek. 13:10—15. 22:28.—In Is. 44:18, the pret. is טַח, as if from טָחַח.

Niph. pass. Lev. 14:43, 48.

Deriv. טִיחַ, טֻחוֹת.

טוֹטָפוֹת plur. fem. *bracelets, frontlets;* especially, *scrolls of parchment, with passages of the Mosaic law* (such as Ex. 13:1—10. 11—16. Deut. 6:4—9. 11:13—21.) *written upon them,* commanded to be worn on the forehead and left wrist, Ex. 13:16. Deut. 6:8. 11:18. These were afterwards regarded as amulets. They are called by the modern Jews תְּפִלִּין, and in the N. Test. φυλακτήρια, *phylacteries.* (Chald. טוֹטֶפְתָּא, טוֹטְפָא, *a bracelet, turban.*)

טוּל in Kal not used. In Arab. طَالَ *to be long.*

Hiph. הֵטִיל *to extend along, to throw, to cast,* 1 Sam. 18:11. 20:33. Jon. 1:5, 12, 16. *to cast out* (of a country), Jer. 16:13. 22:26. Applied to the *sending* of a wind, Jon. 1:4.

Hoph. *to be cast,* spoken of a lot, Prov. 16:33. *to be cast down,* Ps. 37:24. Job 41:1. [41:9.] *to be cast out,* Jer. 22:28.

Pilp. טִלְטֵל *to throw* or *cast away.* Is. 22:17. Deriv. טַלְטֵלָה.

טוּר m. dec. I.

1. *a row.* Ex. 28:17 ff. 39:10 ff.

2. *a wall, border, boundary.* Ezek. 46:23. (Arab. طَوْر *a boundary wall;* طِوَار *septum.*)

טוּר Chald. *a mountain, rock.* Dan. 2:35, 45.

טוּשׂ *to fly.* Job 9:26. (Syr. ܛܳܫ.)

טְוָת Chald. *a fasting;* as an adv. *with fasting.* Dan. 6:19. (After the form קְנָת, from טְוָה i. q. Arab. طَوِيَ *to fast.*)

טֻחוֹת plur. fem. according to the Jewish commentators, *the reins,* (from טוּחַ *to cover,* because the reins are *covered* with fat; comp. חֵלֶב.) Ps. 51:8 *behold thou lovest truth in the reins* or *inward parts.* Job 38:36 *who puts wisdom in the inward parts?* So the Chald. Vulg. *in visceribus hominis.* (Parall. שֶׂכְוִי *heart.*) The explanation of the latter passage has this difficulty, that it does not suit the context, verses 34, 35, 37, 38, which all speak of appearances in the atmosphere. Some, therefore, have attempted to accommodate verse 36 to the rest, by rendering טֻחוֹת *clouds,* and שֶׂכְוִי *a meteor;* but it would be better to suppose an abruptness in the course of thought, or verse 36 to be transposed out of its place, than to reject what appears the obvious meaning of the verse.

טָחָה hence, Pilel part. מְטַחֲוֵי־קֶשֶׁת *the archers,* Gen. 21:16. (Comp. طحا *expandit.*) The form is like נָאוָה, שָׁאָה; and הִשְׁתַּחֲוָה, שָׁחָה.

טָחַח see **טוּחַ**.

טְחוֹן m. verbal from טָחַן, *a mill, handmill.* Lam. 5:13.

טְחֹרִים masc. plur. dec. I. *a difficulty in going to stool, tumours on the fundament, hemorrhoids, piles;* or *the fundament itself,* as the seat of disease; for the most part only in the Keri for עֳפָלִים, Deut. 28:27. 1 Sam. 5:6, 9. but sometimes in the text itself, 6:11, 17. The Keri probably contains the less offensive expression. (Syr. ܛܚܰܪ *to strain hard in discharging the fæces;* ܛܚܘܿܪܳܐ *difficulty in discharging the fæces, the fundament.* The Aramean translators use this word for the Heb. עֳפָלִים.)

טָחַן *to grind, to bruise in pieces.* Ex. 32:20. Num. 11:8.—טָחַן פְּנֵי עֲנִיִּים *to grind the face of the poor,* i. e. to oppress him greatly, Is. 3:15.—Job 31:10 תִּטְחַן לְאַחֵר אִשְׁתִּי *my wife may grind for a stranger,* i. e. become his mill-maid, or most abject slave; (comp. Ex. 11. 5. Is. 47:2.). The Sept. Vulg. Chald. on account of the antithesis in verse 9, and the parallel clause in verse 10, render it, *she may have criminal intercourse* *with another;* comp. the Greek *μύλλειν* and Latin *molere*, both used in this sense. But in this case we should expect the verb to have been in the passive voice.

Deriv. out of course טְחוֹן.

טְחֹנָה f. verbal from טָחַן, *the plaster* of a wall. Ezek. 13:12.

טִיט m. 1. *clay, potters' clay.* Is. 41:25. Nah. 3:14.

2. *mud, mire.* Ps. 18:43. 69:15.

טִין m. Chald. *clay.* Dan. 2:41, 43. (In Syr. and Arab. *idem.*)

טִירָה f. dec. X.

1. *a fold*, or *enclosure for cattle,* such as the Nomades used; also, *a cottage with conveniences for cattle,* and perhaps *a village of moveable tents.* Gen. 25:16. Num. 31:10. 1 Chr. 6:39. [54.] Ps. 69:26.

2. i. q. טוּר no. 2. *a walk.* Ezek. 46:23.

3. *a tower, palace.* Cant. 8:9.

טַל m. in pause טָל, with suff. טַלִּי, dec. VIII. h. *a dew,* which in the east sometimes resembles a gentle rain. Gen. 27:28, 39. (Arab. طَلّ *a gentle rain.*)

טַל Chald. *idem.* Dan. 4:12. [15.]

טָלָא *to patch, to mend.* (Chald. טְלָא *idem.*) Josh. 9:5 נְעָלוֹת מְטֻלָּאוֹת *mended shoes.* Part. טָלוּא *spotted, party-coloured,* Gen. 30:32 ff. Ezek. 16:16. (So the Germ. *flecken* signifies both *to patch* and *to spot.*)

טְלָאִים see טְלִי and טָלֶה.

טָלֶה m. dec. IX. b. *a tender lamb.* 1 Sam. 7:9. Is. 65:25. (Arab. طَلًا *the young of any animal,* especially *of the gazelle;* Syr. ܛܠܝܐ *a youth.*)

טַלְטֵלָה f. verbal from טוּל, *a throw, cast, projectio.* Is. 22:17. See the verb in Pilp.

טְלִי plur. טְלָאִים, dec. VI. *a tender lamb.* Is. 40:11.

טָלַל found only in Pi. טִלֵּל *to cover, to cover with a roof,* i. q. קָרָה. Neh. 3:15.—For טַלְטֵל, see טוּל.—(Arab. ظَلَّ conj. II. IV. *to overshadow,* kindred with צָלַל no. III.)

טְלַל Chald. Aph. אַטְלֵל *to lie in the shade, to rest.* Dan. 4:9. [12.] Comp. the Heb. צָלַל.

טֶלֶם Josh. 15:24. proper name of a city in the tribe of Judah, according to Kimchi and others the same with טְלָאִים 1 Sam. 15:4.

טָמֵא, infin. טָמְאָה. 1. *to be* or *become unclean* or *impure,* especially in a ceremonial sense, spoken of persons and things. Lev. 11:24 ff. Construed with בְּ, *to be rendered unclean by* any thing, Lev. 15:32. 18:20, 23.

Pi. טִמֵּא *to render unclean, to pollute, defile.* Lev. 15:31. Ps. 79:1. comp. 2 K. 23:8, 10, 13.

2. *to pronounce unclean,* spoken of the priest. Lev. 13:3, 8, 11 ff.

3. *to permit to be polluted.* Ezek. 20:26.

4. *to deflour, defile,* (a woman.) Gen. 34:5, 13, 27. Ezek. 18:6, 15.

Pu. pass. Ezek. 4:14.

Niph. נִטְמָא and Hithpa. הִטַּמֵּא *to defile* or *pollute one's self,* construed with לְ (Num. 5:2. 6:7. 9:6.) and בְּ (Ezek. 20:7.) of the thing *whereby* one is polluted; also, *to defile one's self by adultery,* spoken of a woman, Num. 5:27, 29.

Hothpa. הֻטַּמָּא *idem.* Deut. 24:4.

טָמֵא fem. טְמֵאָה, verbal adj. from טָמֵא, dec. V. e. and dec. X. *unclean, impure;* (1.) in a ceremonial sense, spoken of men, animals, and things, Lev. 5:2. Deut. 14:19. (2.) in a moral sense, Job 14:4. טְמֵאַת הַשֵּׁם *infamous of character,* Ezek. 22:5.

טֻמְאָה f. verbal from טָמֵא, dec. X. *impurity, uncleanness, pollution.* Lev. 5:3. 7:21. also, *something unclean,* Judg. 13:7, 14.

טָמָה i. q. טָמֵא, found only in Niph. Lev. 11:43. Job 18:3 נִטְמִינוּ *we are un-*

clean, i. e. reputed vile, *in your sight*. Vulg. *sorduimus*. Others without sufficient ground make טמה i. q. טמם, אטם *to be stopped, closed;* hence, *to be dumb*.

טָמַן 1. *to hide, conceal*, as in the ground, *to bury*. Gen. 35 : 4. Ex. 2 : 12. Josh. 7 : 21, 22.—טָמַן פַּח לְ *to lay a snare privily*, or, *to spread a net for* any one, Ps. 140 : 6. 142 : 4. with רֶשֶׁת in the same sense, Ps. 9 : 16. 31 : 5. comp. 64 : 6.

2. *to hide* generally. Josh. 2 : 6. Job 31 : 33. 3 : 16 נֵפֶל טָמוּן *an unnoticed abortion*. 20 : 26 כָּל־חֹשֶׁךְ טָמוּן לִצְפוּנָיו *every trouble is reserved in his treasures*.

2. *to put in, to dip in*. Prov. 19 : 24 *the slothful man puts his hand into the dish*. This word depicts the inactivity of the slothful man.

Niph. pass. Is. 2 : 10.

Hiph. i. q. Kal, 2 K. 7 : 8.

Deriv. מַטְמוֹן.

טֶנֶא m. dec. VI. a. *a basket*. Deut. 26 : 2, 4. (Chald. טַנְיָא *idem*.)

טָנַף found only in Pi. *to pollute, make dirty*. Cant. 5 : 3. (Aram. ܛܢܦ *to be polluted*.)

טָעָה i. q. תָּעָה *to err, deviate from a way*. Comp. the Aram. טְעָא ܛܥܐ.

Hiph. *to cause to err, to seduce*. Ezek. 13 : 10.

טָעַם (also in Arab. and Aram.)

1. *to taste, to try the taste of* any thing. Job 12 : 11.

2. *to taste, to eat a little of* any thing. 1 Sam. 14 : 24, 29, 43.

3. *to taste, to enjoy the taste of* any thing. 2 Sam. 19 : 36.

4. metaphorically, *to perceive, enjoy, experience*. Prov. 31 : 18. Ps. 34 : 9 טַעֲמוּ וּרְאוּ כִּי טוֹב יְהוָה *experience and see that Jehovah is good*.

Deriv. out of course מַטְעַמִּים.

טְעֵם Chald. *idem*.

Pa. *to cause to eat, to feed*. Dan. 4 : 22. [25.] 5 : 21.

טַעַם m. verbal from טָעַם, dec. VI. c.

1. *taste*, as of food. Num. 11 : 8. Jer. 48 : 11. Especially, *pleasant taste, savouriness*, Job 6 : 6.

2. metaphorically, *intellectual taste, discernment, wisdom*. Comp. Lat. *sapere*, (*to be wise;*) *insipiens*, (*unwise*.) 1 Sam. 25 : 33. Ps. 119 : 66. Job 12 : 20.—אִשָּׁה סָרַת טָעַם *a woman without understanding*, Prov. 11 : 22.—מְשִׁיבֵי טָעַם *those who answer wisely*, Prov. 26 : 16.

3. after the Chaldaic usage, *a royal decree* or *edict*. Jon. 3 : 7.

טַעַם m. Chald. *will, command*. Ezra 6 : 14. 7 : 13. More frequently טְעֵם, which see, especially signif. no. 3.

טְעֵם m. Chald. 1. *taste*, particularly *a pleasant taste*. Dan. 5 : 2 בִּטְעֵם חַמְרָא *when he had tasted* or *felt the effects of the wine*.

2. *wisdom, understanding*. Dan. 2 : 14.

3. *will, command, royal edict*. Dan. 3 : 10, 29.—שִׂים טְעֵם *to publish an edict*, Ezra 4 : 19, 21. 5 : 3, 9, 13. 6 : 1.—Also, *a matter for royal decision, causa*, Ezra 5 : 5.—בְּעֵל טְעֵם *a deputy*, literally, *a master of the rolls, dominus edictorum* seu *causarum*, an officer under the Persian government, at Samaria, Ezra 4 : 8, 9, 17.

4. *reckoning, account, ratio*. Dan. 6 : 3.

5. *regard, respect*. שִׂים טְעֵם עַל *to have regard to* any one, Dan. 3 : 12.

I. טָעַן *to load*, especially beasts for a journey. Gen. 45 : 17. (Aram. טְעַן, ܛܥܢ *to be loaded*.)

II. טָעַן *to thrust through*. Pu. pass. Is. 14 : 19. (Arab. طعن *idem*.)

טַף m. with suff. טַפְּכֶם, dec. VIII. h. a collective noun, *little ones, children*. Gen. 34 : 29. 43 : 8. 45 : 19. 46 : 5. comp. Ezek. 9 : 6, where it is used in opposition to *young men and young women;* and Ex. 12 : 37, where it is opposed to *men capable of bearing arms*. Often in a wider sense, *one's whole family*, Ex. 10 : 10. Num. 32 : 16, 24, 26. Comp. 2 Chr. 20 : 13 גַּם טַפָּם נְשֵׁיהֶם וּבְנֵיהֶם *their family*, (*namely*,) *their wives and children.* 2 Chr. 31:18. Gen. 47:12 לְפִי הַטָּף *after the number of the family.*—Derived from טָפַף, unless this verb is rather a denom. from טַף.

טָפַח literally, *to be broad, extended, spreading.* (Syr. ܛܦܚ *to spread out.* Kindred with מתח, whence טְפִיחוֹת.) Deriv. out of course מִטְפַּחַת.

Pi. טִפַּח 1. *to spread out, to extend.* Is. 48:13.

2. *to bear upon the arms,* as small children, a denom. from טֶפַח, here in the sense of *palma.* Lam. 2:22.

טֶפַח m. plur. טְפָחוֹת, verbal from טָפַח dec. VI.

1. *a palm, hand-breadth,* a measure of length. 1 K. 7:26. 2 Chr. 4:5. (comp. Jer. 52:21.) Ps. 39:6 הִנֵּה טְפָחוֹת נָתַתָּה יָמַי *behold! thou makest my days as an hand-breadth.*

2. in architecture, prob. *the coping, corbil, projecting stone on which a timber is laid, mutulus.* 1 K. 7:9. Sept. γεῖσος, i. e. *epistylium.*

טֹפַח m. verbal from טָפַח, *a hand-breadth.* Ex. 25:25. 37:12. Ezek. 40: 5, 43.

טִפֻּחִים masc. plur. verbal from טָפַח no. 2. *the bearing* or *nursing of children.* Lam. 2:20.

טָפַל *to invent, contrive;* joined with שֶׁקֶר, Ps. 119:69. Job 13:4. Used elliptically, Job 14:17 וַתִּטְפֹּל עַל־עֲוֹנִי *thou inventest (falsehood) to my transgression,* i. e. thou chargest me with evil falsely. (In Arab. طفل *to labour one's discourse;* in Talmud. *to join on, to sew on.*)

טִפְסַר m. Jer. 51:27. Plur. טַפְסְרִים Nah. 3:17. name of a military officer among the Assyrians and Medes. In the Targum of Jonathan Deut. 28:12, it occurs as the name of a chief angel. The word is perhaps of Assyrian origin. The second syllable is most probably i.q. שַׂר Pers. سر *princeps;* and the first syllable טַף may be compared with the Pers. تاب (*tab*) *altitudo, potentia.*

טָפַף, Arab. طفّ and دفّ, *to take many and short steps, to trip, to mince,* spoken of affected coquettes. Is. 3:16 הָלוֹךְ וְטָפֹף תֵּלַכְנָה *they mince as they walk.* Luth. *sie treten einher und schwänzen.* Deriv. טַף *children,* (q.v.) perhaps so called from their manner of walking.

טְפַר, plur. טִפְרִין, Chald. i.q. Heb. צִפֹּרֶן.

1. *nail* (of a human finger or toe.) Dan. 4:30. [33.]

1. *claw* (of an animal.) Dan. 7:19.

טָפַשׁ *to be fat;* hence, metaphorically, *to be stupid, insensible;* comp. παχύς, *pinguis.* Ps. 119:70.

טָרַד, in Arab. and Syr. *to thrust away;* conj. IV. *to follow one another continually,* namely, by pushing one another forward. So applied to flowing water, Prov. 19:13. 27:15 דֶּלֶף טֹרֵד *a continual dropping from a roof.*

טְרַד Chald. *to thrust forth, to drive out.* Dan. 4:22, 29, 30. [4:25, 32, 33.]

טרום (read **טְרוֹם**) i. q. טֶרֶם *yet not.* Ruth 3:14 Keth.

טָרַח, in Arab. طرح conj. I. IV. *to cast forth* or *away.* Hence, Hiph. Job 37:11 אַף בְּרִי יַטְרִיחַ עָב *also the clear sky drives away the clouds.* Others: *with showers he loads the clouds,* comp. טֹרַח; but not so accordant with the parallel clause.

טֹרַח m. dec. VI. p. *burden, trouble.* Deut. 1:12. Is. 1:14. (In Chald. טְרַח *to fatigue one's self by labour, to weary one's self.*)

טָרִי adj. found only in the fem. טְרִיָּה *fresh, recens.* (Arab. طري and طرق *to be fresh.*) Spoken of a wound, Is. 1:6. of a jaw-bone, Judg. 15:15.

טֶרֶם conj. *yet not;* construed with a future, Gen. 2:5. Ex. 10:7. Josh. 2: 8. with a preterite, 1 Sam. 3:7.—בְּטֶרֶם *when not yet, before,* Jer. 1:5 בְּטֶרֶם תֵּצֵא *before thou camest out.* Ruth 3:14 Keri. 2 K. 2:9. Also without בְּ in the same sense, Josh. 3:1. Ps. 119:67.—In Zeph.

2:2, לֹא is also added, of course there is a double negation.—בְּטֶרֶם *when not yet,* Hag. 2:15.

טָרַף, fut. יִטְרֹף, once יִטְרָף (Gen 49:27.) *to tear in pieces, to raven,* spoken properly of wild animals. Deut. 33:20. Ps. 22:14. Nah. 2:13. Used metaphorically of God, Ps. 50:22 פֶּן אֶטְרֹף וְאֵין מַצִּיל *lest I tear you in pieces and there be none to deliver.* Hos. 6:1.

Niph. pass. Ex. 22:12. Jer. 5:6.

Pu. *idem.* Gen. 37:33. 44:28.

Hiph. *to cause to eat, to feed,* as men. Prov. 30:8.

טָרָף adj. *fresh, recens,* spoken of a leaf. Gen. 8:11. (Arab. طَرُفَ *to be new.*)

טֶרֶף m. verbal from טָרַף, dec. VI. a

1. *prey,* (of a wild animal.) Job 4:11. 29:17. 38:39.

2. *food.* Prov. 31:15. Mal. 3:10. Ps. 111:5. Comp. the verb in Hiph.

3. *a leaf.* Ezek. 17:9. (Aram. טַרְפָא, ܛܪܦܐ *idem,* perhaps so called from its *freshness;* comp. טָרָף.)

טְרֵפָה f. verbal from טָרַף, *something torn in pieces by wild animals.* Gen. 31:39. Ex. 22:12, 30. Lev. 7:24.

טַרְפְּלָיֵא Chald. Ezra 4:9. name of a people, which were brought into Palestine by the Assyrian kings. Sept. Ταρφαλαῖοι.

THE name *Yod* יוֹד probably signifies i.q. יָד *a hand,* (comp. יוֹם plur. יָמִים,) and has reference to its figure in the Phenician alphabet 𐤉, which represents three fingers stretched out, or a rude drawing of *a hand.*)

יָאַב *to desire earnestly, to long for* any thing, construed with לְ. Ps. 119:131. In Syr. ܝܐܒ a quadriliteral, Pa. and Ethpa. *idem.* Kindred with אָבָה and אָוָה no. I.

יָאָה *to be fair, becoming, suitable, due,* i.q. נָאָה (Ps. 33:1. Prov. 17:7.) Jer. 10:7 כִּי לְךָ יָאָתָה *for it is due to thee.* Sept. σοὶ γὰρ πρέπει. (Syr. ܝܐܐ *fair,* most frequently with ܠ, *becoming, due,* i.q. πρέπον.)

יְאוֹר see **יְאֹר** *a river.*

יָאִיר (*he shines*) a proper name, *Jair,* the son of Manasseh. Num. 32:41. In Greek Ἰάειρος Mark 5:22.

I. **יָאַל** for אָוַל, *to be foolish,* i.q. אָוַל (whence אֱוִיל,) by transposition.

Niph. נוֹאַל *to be foolish, to act foolishly,* Num. 12:11. Jer. 5:4. Hence, *to appear as fools, to be made ashamed,* Is. 19:13. Jer. 50:36 חֶרֶב אֶל הַבַּדִּים וְנֹאָלוּ *a sword is upon the lying prophets, and they appear as fools.* Comp. הוֹלֵל Job 12:17. Is. 44:25.)

II. **יָאַל**, Hiph. הוֹאִיל. 1. *to begin.* Deut. 1:5. Josh. 17:12 וַיּוֹאֶל הַכְּנַעֲנִי לָשֶׁבֶת בָּאָרֶץ *and the Canaanites began to dwell,* i.e. to fix themselves, *in that land.* Judg. 1:27, 35. Hence, *to undertake, to venture,* Gen. 18:27, 31.

2. *to will* or *please* to do a thing. Hos. 5:11. Judg. 17:11. Ex. 2:21. Judg. 19:6 הוֹאֶל־נָא וְלִין *be pleased, I pray thee, and tarry all night;* comp. 2 Sam. 7:29. 2 K. 5:23.

Note. This verb is construed with לְ before an infinitive; and with a finite verb with (Judg. 19:6.) or without Deut. 5:1. Hos. 5:11.) a copula.

יְאֹר and **יְאוֹר** once **אוֹר** (Am. 8:8.) m. dec. I. *a river,* a word of Egyptian origin, namely, *Jaro* and *Jero.* Hence used almost exclusively of the Nile, Gen. 41:1 ff. Ex. 1:22. 2:3. 7:15 ff. and only rarely of any other stream, Dan. 12:5, 6, 7.

Plur. יְאֹרִים *brooks, streams, canals.* Job 28:10. Is. 33:21. Applied especially to the canals and arms of the Nile, Ezek. 29:3 ff. 30:12. Ps. 78:44. Is. 7:18. 19:6. 37:25.

יָאַשׁ, Arab. يأس *to despair* or *be out of hope* concerning any thing. In Kal not used.

Niph. *idem*, construed with מִן. 1 Sam. 27:1. Part. נוֹאָשׁ *one in despair*, Job 6:26. Also used impersonally, *it is in vain, there is no hope, desperatum est*, Is. 57:10. Jer. 2:25. 18:12.

Pi. infin. יַאֵשׁ *to cause to despair*. Ecc. 2:20.

יֹאשִׁיָּהוּ m. (*Jehovah heals*, from יֹאשֶׁה fut. of אָשָׁה = أسا *to heal*, and יָהּ;) proper name of a king of Judah, in whose reign the book of the law, which had been lost, was found. 2 K. 23:23. 2 Chr. 34:33. In Greek Ἰωσίας.

יָבַב found only in Pi. יִבֵּב *to call, to cry aloud*. Judg. 5:28. (In Aram. *to cry aloud, to shout.*)

יְבוּל m. verbal from יָבַל no. 1. (comp. תְּבוּאָה *proventus*, from בּוֹא,) dec. I. *produce of the earth*. Lev. 26:4, 20. Deut. 11:17. Ps. 67:7. 85:13. Job 20:28 יִגֶל יְבוּל בֵּיתוֹ *the produce*, i. e. the substance, *of his house shall disappear*.

יְבוּס the ancient name of Jerusalem. Judg. 19:10, 11. 1 Chr. 11:4, 5. The gentile noun is יְבוּסִי Gen. 10:16. 15:21. Josh. 15:63. 2 Sam. 5:6. But this form appears also to denote the city, Josh. 18:28. Zech. 9:7.

יָבֵישׁ see **יָבֵשׁ**.

יָבַל I. *to go*. See Hiph. Deriv. יבל no. I. יְבוּל, and perhaps תֵּבֵל.

2. *to flow, run;* (comp. הָלַךְ no. 5.) Arab. وبل *vehementer pluit*. Deriv. יבל no. II. יָבָל, יוּבַל, אוּבָל, מַבּוּל.

Hiph. הוֹבִיל (Syr. ܐܘܒܠ i. q. הֵבִיא, used only in poetry.

1. *to bring, lead*, as persons. Ps. 60:11. 108:11.

2. *to bring, present*, as gifts, offerings. Ps. 68:30. 76:12. Zeph. 3:10.

Hoph. הוּבַל 1. *to be brought, led*, spoken of persons. Ps. 45:15, 16.

2. *to be brought*, spoken of things. Is. 18:7. Hos. 10:6. 12:2.—Also *to be carried* (to the grave), Job 10:19. 21:30—32.

יְבַל Chald. found only in Aph. הֵיבֵל *to bring*. Ezra 5:14. 6:5.

יָבָל m. verbal from יָבַל no. 2. dec. IV. a.

1. *a stream*.—יִבְלֵי־מַיִם *streams of water*, Is. 30:25. 44:4.

2. *Jabal*, proper name of a son of Lamech, the first who led a Nomadic life. Gen. 4:20.

יִבְלְעָם (from יִבְלֶה and עָם, *the people wastes away*,) a city in the tribe of Manasseh. Josh. 17:11. Judg. 1:27. 2 K. 9:27.

יַבָּל, found only in the fem. יַבֶּלֶת *having excrescences, blains*, or *warts;* spoken of cattle. Lev. 22:22. Vulg. *papulas habens*. (So in Chald. and Rabbin. The Mishnah (Erubhin 10. § 11.) treats of the cutting off of such warts. In Arab. وَابِلَة *defluxus pilorum*, but the former explanation is preferable.)

יָבָם m. dec. IV. a. *a brother-in-law*, or *husband's brother*, Lat. *levir*, who, by the Mosaic law, was bound to marry the widow of his brother deceased without issue. Deut. 25:5—9. Hence,

יִבֵּם Pi. denom. from יָבָם, *to perform the duty of a husband's brother* or *of a levir*. Deut. 25:5—9. Gen. 38:8.

יְבֵמֶת fem. of יָבָם, with suff. יְבִמְתֵּךְ, יְבִמְתּוֹ, dec. XIII. b. *a sister-in-law* or *brother's wife*. Deut. 25:7, 9. Also, *a brother-in-law's wife*, Ruth 1:15.

יַבְנְאֵל (*God builds.*)

1. proper name of a city in the tribe of Judah. Josh. 15:11.

2. also of a city in the tribe of Naphtali. Josh. 19:33.

יַבְנֶה a place in Philistia, on the Mediterranean sea, in later times the seat of a celebrated Jewish school

2Chr. 26:6. In Greek. Ἰαμνία, 1 Mac. 4:15. and Ἰάμνεια 5:58. 2 Mac. 12:8.

יַבֹּק proper name of a stream or small river (נַחַל) which flows into the Jordan below the sea of Galilee; Arab. *Yarmuc*, also *Jiryat Musa*, Lat. *Hieromiax*. According to others, *the Jiryat Manadra*. Seetzen in Zach's Monatl. Correspondenz, XVIII. p. 381. Gen. 32:23. Deut. 2:37. Josh. 12:2. Judg. 11:13.

I. יָבֵשׁ, fut. יִיבַשׁ, plur. יָבְשׁוּ, infin. יְבוֹשׁ, const. יְבֹשׁ, יְבֹשֶׁת, *to be* or *become dry;* Josh. 9:5, 12. spoken of rivers or of the sea, Job 14:11. of the earth, Gen. 8:14. of plants, *to wither* or *dry up*, Is. 15:6. 19:7. 40:7, 9. Ps. 22:16 יָבֵשׁ כַּחֶרֶשׂ כֹּחִי *my strength is dried up as a potsherd.* Applied particularly to a paralysis or withering of the hand, 1 K. 13:4. Zech. 11:17. comp. in the New Testament, Mark 3:1. etc.

Pi. יִבֵּשׁ *to make dry, to dry up.* Job 15:30. Prov. 17:22. In Nah. 1:4, we find וַיַּבְּשֵׁהוּ for וַיְיַבְּשֵׁהוּ.

Hiph. הוֹבִישׁ *to dry up, to make dry.* Josh. 2:10. 4:23.

I. יָבֵשׁ, Hiph. הוֹבִישׁ i. q. הֵבִישׁ from בּוּשׁ.

1. *to make ashamed, to shame.* 2 Sam. 19:5.

2. intrans. like בּוֹשׁ in Kal, *to be brought to shame, to be disappointed in one's hope*, Joel 1:11. Jer. 10:14. Zech. 9:5. *to be disgraced*, Jer. 2:26. 6:15. 8:12.

3. *to become a disgrace, to perish;* spoken of the harvest, Joel 1:10, 12, 17. of cities, Jer 48:1, 20. 50:2. Joel 1:12 הוֹבִישׁ שָׂשׂוֹן מִן בְּנֵי אָדָם *the joy of the children of men has perished.*

4. *to conduct shamefully.* Hos. 2:7. [2:5.]

יָבֵשׁ, fem. יְבֵשָׁה, verbal adj. from יָבֵשׁ no. I. dec. V. f. and X.

1. *dry.* Job 13:25. Ezek. 17:24. 20:47.

2. proper name of a city in Gilead, also called יָבֵישׁ 1 Sam. 11:1, 3.

יַבָּשָׁה f. verbal from יָבֵשׁ no. I. *the dry, the dry land.* Gen. 1:9. Ex. 4:9. Jon. 1:9, 13. 2:11. — בַּיַּבָּשָׁה *on dry ground, with dry feet,* Ex. 14:16, 22, 29. Josh. 4:22.

יַבֶּשֶׁת f. *idem.* Ex. 4:9. Ps. 95:5.

יַבֶּשֶׁת f. Chald. emph. יַבֶּשְׁתָּא, *idem.* Dan. 2:10.

יָגַב *to plough, till.* Part. יֹגְבִים *ploughmen, husbandmen,* 2 K. 25:12 Keri. Jer. 52:16. This root is kindred with גוב, see the art. גֵּבִים.

יָגֵב m. verbal from יָגַב, dec. V. a. *a field.* Jer. 39:10.

יָגְבְּהָה, with ה paragogic יָגְבְּהָה (*he is lifted up*, Hoph. of גָּבַהּ,) a place in the tribe of Gad. Num. 32:35. Judg. 8:11.

I. יָגָה *to be afflicted, grieved.* In Kal not used.

Pi. יִגָּה *to afflict, grieve.* Fut. יַגֶּה for יְיַגֶּה Lam. 3:33.

Hiph. הוֹגָה *to afflict, grieve, vex.* Job 19:2. Lam. 1:5, 12. 3:32. Is. 51:23.

Niph. נוּגָה (for נוֹגָה.) Part. נוּגֶה (for נוֹגֶה) *afflicted, grieved,* Zeph. 3:18 נוּגֵי מִמּוֹעֵד *the disconsolate for*, i. e. for want of, *the solemn assembly.* Lam. 1:4 בְּתוּלֹתֶיהָ נּוּגוֹת *her virgins are afflicted.*

Deriv. יָגוֹן, תּוּגָה.

II. יָגָה *to be separated.*

Hiph. הוֹגָה *to separate, to remove.* 2 Sam. 20:13. (Arab. وجي conj. IV. *to remove;* comp. in Heb. הָגָה no. II.)

יָגוֹן m. verbal from יָגָה no. I. dec. III. a. *affliction, sorrow.* Gen. 42:38. 44:31. Ps. 13:3.

יָגִיעַ m. verbal from יָגַע, dec. III. a.

1. adj. *wearied.* Job 3:17.

2. subst. *labour*, particularly, *fatiguing labour, strenuous exertion.* Gen. 31:42 יְגִיעַ כַּפַּי *the labour of my hands.* Job 10:3 יְגִיעַ כַּפֶּיךָ *the labour of thine hands*, i. e. thy work.

3. *what is produced* or *earned by labour, possession, substance, wealth.* Is. 45:14. 55:2. Jer. 3:24. 20:5. Ezek. 23:29. Ps. 109:11. Neh. 5:13. So יְגִיעַ כַּפַּיִם, in the same sense Hag. 1:11. That this word denotes especially the

labour and produce of the field is evident from Ps. 78:46. 128:2.

יְגִיעָה, fem. of יְגִיעַ, dec. X. *fatiguing labour, weariness.* Ecc. 12:12.

יָגַע, fut. יִיגַע. 1. *to labour, to exert one's self.* Job 9:29. Prov. 23:4. Is. 49:4. 65:23. The thing *about* which a man labours, is preceded by בְּ, Josh. 24:13. Is. 62:8. 47:12. or put in the accus. verse 15.

2. *to be wearied.* 2 Sam. 23:10. Is. 40:31. Ps. 6:7 יָגַעְתִּי בְאַנְחָתִי *I am wearied with my groaning.* 69:4. Jer. 45:3. In a somewhat different sense Is. 43:22 כִּי יָגַעְתָּ בִּי יִשְׂרָאֵל *for thou hast been weary of me, O Israel.*

Pi. *to fatigue, make weary.* Josh. 7:3. Ecc. 10:15.

Hiph. הוֹגִיעַ. 1. *to load, burden.* Is. 43:23 לֹא הוֹגַעְתִּיךָ בִּלְבוֹנָה *I have not burdened thee with incense,* i. e. in requiring incense.

2. *to weary, be troublesome.* Is. 43:24. Mal. 2:17.

Deriv. out of course יְגִיעַ.

יְגָע m. verbal from יָגַע, *what is produced* or *earned by labour.* Job 20:18.

יָגֵעַ verbal adj. from יָגַע, dec. V. a. *wearisome, tiresome,* Ecc. 1:8 כָּל־הַדְּבָרִים יְגֵעִים *all words would be tiresome.* Also *weary, fatigued,* Deut. 25:18. 2 Sam. 17:2.

יְגַר m. Chald. *a hill, a heap of stones.* Gen. 31:47. (Syr. ܝܓܪܐ *idem.*)

יָגֹר, 2 pers. יָגֹרְתָּ, i. q. גּוּר no. II. *to fear, to be afraid of,* construed with an accus. Job 3:25. 9:28. Ps. 119:39. or with מִפְּנֵי, Deut. 9:19. 28:60.

יָגֹר verbal adj. or part. from יָגֹר, *fearing,* used with the pronouns to form a periphrasis for the finite verb. Jer. 22:25. 39:17.

יָד com. gen. (more frequently fem.) const. יַד, with suff. יָדִי, יֶדְכֶם, prim. dec. II. a.

1. *the hand.* The following phrases are worthy of notice; (1.) יָדִי עִם, אֶת פְּלֹנִי *my hand (is) with any one,* i. e. I assist him. 1 Sam. 22:17. 2 Sam. 3:12. 2 K. 15:19. (2.) יָדִי הָיְתָה בְּ *my hand is against* any one, (Gen. 16:12.) *I bring evil upon* him. Gen. 37:27. 1 Sam. 18:17, 21. 24:13, 14. 2 Sam. 24:17. Josh. 2:19.—יַד יְהוָה בְּ *the hand of Jehovah is against* or *brings destruction on* any thing, Ex. 9:3. Deut. 2:15. Judg. 2:15. Job 23:2 יָדִי כָּבְדָה *the hand (of God) upon me is heavy.* Also construed with אֶל in the same sense, Ezek. 13:9. This phrase is sometimes, though very rarely, taken in a good sense, *to be for* any one, *to be favourable to* him, 2 Chr. 30:12. Ezra 9:2. Hence in Judg. 2:15, the meaning is made more definite by adding לְרָעָה. (3.) הָיְתָה יַד יְהוָה עַל־ *the hand of Jehovah came upon* any one, i. e. the Deity began to inspire him, (as a prophet). Ezek. 1:3. 3:14, 22. 37:1. 2 K. 3:15. Construed with אֶל in the same sense, 1 K. 18:46. Ezek. 8:1 וַתִּפֹּל עָלַי שָׁם יַד אֲדֹנָי *and there the hand of the Lord fell upon me,* (הָיָה is used in the same sense, Ezek. 11:5.) Jer. 15:17 מִפְּנֵי יָדְךָ *because of thy hand which has inspired me.* (4.) יַד יְהוָה עַל פְּלֹנִי *the hand of Jehovah rests (graciously) upon any one.* Ezra 7:6, 28. 8:18, 31. The more full expression is יַד אֱלֹהִים הַטּוֹבָה *the good hand of God,* Ezra 7:9. Neh. 2:8. comp. Ezra 8:22. Is. 1:25. It is used in a bad sense only Am. 1:8. (5.) נָתַן יָד *to give the hand to* any one, i. e. to promise or make sure by striking hands. Ezra 10:19. 2 K. 10:15. Used particularly of the party which in making a covenant *submits* or *devotes itself* to the other, Ezek. 17:18. Lam. 5:6. Jer. 50:15 נָתְנָה יָדָהּ *she (Babel) hath submitted.* 2 Chr. 30:8. So נָתַן יָד תַּחַת *to submit one's self,* 1 Chr. 29:24. (6.) לֹא בְיָד Job 34:20. and בְּאֶפֶס יָד Dan. 8:25. *without the hand (of man),* i. e. without human aid; comp. Dan. 2:34, 45. Lam. 4:6. (7.) יָד לְיָד *from hand to hand,* i. e. from generation to generation; and joined with a negative participle, *never.* Prov. 11:21. 16:5.

In the following combinations with a preposition, the force of יָד is often lost, and the signification of the preposition only remains. (1.) בְּיַד (a.) *in the hand of*, also simply, *with, by*. 1 Sam. 14: 34 אִישׁ שׁוֹרוֹ בְּיָדוֹ *each one his ox with him.* 16:2. 1 K. 10:29. Jer. 38:10 קַח בְּיָדְךָ מִזֶּה שְׁלֹשִׁים אֲנָשִׁים *take hence thirty men with thee.* Deut. 33:3. Comp. in Chald. Ezra 7:25. (b.) *through the hand of*, also simply *through*. Num. 15:23 *all which Jehovah has commanded* בְּיַד מֹשֶׁה *through Moses.* 2 Chr. 29:25. Is. 20: 2. 1 K. 12:15. Jer. 37:2. (c.) *into the hand, under the power* or *charge of* any one; after verbs of delivering up. Gen. 9:2. 14:20. Ex. 4:21. Hence, צֹאן יָדוֹ *the flock under his charge*, Ps. 95: 7. Comp. also 2 Sam. 18:2. Num. 31: 49. (d.) *before, in conspectu*, i. q. לִפְנֵי, ἐν χερσί. 1 Sam. 21:14 *he feigned himself mad* בְּיָדָם *before them.* Job 15:23 יָדַע כִּי נָכוֹן בְּיָדוֹ יוֹם־חֹשֶׁךְ *he knows that a day of darkness is prepared for*, i. e. threatens, *him.* (e.) *because of*. Job 8: 4. Is. 64:6. (2.) מִיַּד, מִידֵי *from* or *out of the hand* or *hands of*, also simply *from, out of*; after verbs of requiring, freeing, receiving. Gen. 9:5. 32:12. 33:19. Num. 5:25. 24:24. 35:25. Job 5:20. 1 Sam. 17:37. (3.) עַל־יַד, עַל־יְדֵי (a) *into the hand* or *hands of* any one, after verbs of delivering up, committing. 1 K. 14:27. 2 K. 10:24. 12:12. 22:5, 9. Ezra 1:8. Hence, *under the oversight* or *direction*, 1 Chr. 25:2, 3, 6 עַל יְדֵי אֲבִיהֶם *under the direction of their father.* (b.) *through*. Jer. 18:21. Ps. 63:11.

Dual. יָדַיִם *hands* (of the human body).

Plur. יָדוֹת *artificial hands, something resembling hands*; as, (1.) *a tenon* (in timber). Ex. 26:17, 19. 36:22, 24. (2.) *the axle-tree* (of a wheel). 1 K. 7: 32, 33.

2. prob. *the arm*, (as يد also in Arab.) See אַצִּיל יָדַיִם *the shoulder*; literally, *the juncture of the arms.*

3. metaphorically, *might, power, aid, succour*. Ex. 14:30. Deut. 32:36 כִּי אָזְלַת יָד *that succour disappears.*—בְּיָד *with might* or *power*, Is. 28:2. Ezek. 13:7.— Ps. 76:6 *and none of the men of might found their hands*, i. e. their strength was gone.

4. *manner*.—כְּיַד הַמֶּלֶךְ *after the manner of a king, as it becomes a king*, Est. 1: 7. 2:18. 1 K. 10:13. עַל יְדֵי דָוִיד *ex more a Davide instituto*, Ezra 3:10. 2 Chr. 29:27.

5. *side*; hence, לְיַד *at the side, near*, 1 Sam. 19:3. Also, בְּעַד יַד 1 Sam. 4:18. אֶל יַד 2 Sam. 18:4. עַל יַד, עַל יְדֵי Job 1:14. Neh. 3:2 ff. in the same sense. Dual יָדַיִם *sides*; often in the phrase רְחַב יָדַיִם *wide on all sides* or *hands, spacious*, Gen. 34:21. Ps. 104:25. Is. 33:21. Plur. יָדוֹת *ledges* or *borders*, 1 K. 7:35, 36. *the side railings* (of a throne), 1 K. 10:19.

6. *place*. Deut. 23:13. Num. 2:17 אִישׁ עַל־יָדוֹ *each one in his place.* Dual *idem.* Josh. 8:20.

7. *part*. Dan. 12:7. Plur. יָדוֹת 1 K. 11:7 וּשְׁתֵּי הַיָּדוֹת בָּכֶם *and the two (third) parts among you.* Gen. 47:24 אַרְבַּע הַיָּדוֹת *the four (fifth) parts.* Neh. 11:1. The same sense is also expressed in other places by פֶּה.—יָדוֹת *parts* for *times*, Latin *vices*, Dan. 1:20. Gen. 43:33. 2 Sam. 19:44.

8. *a monument, trophy*, i. q. שֵׁם. 1 Sam. 15:12. 2 Sam. 18:18.

יַד Chald. emph. יְדָא, with suff. יְדָךְ, יְדוֹהִי, dual יְדַיִן, i. q. Heb. יָד.

יְדָא Chald. found only in Aph. part. מְהוֹדֵא Dan. 2:23. and מוֹדֵא 6:11. *praising, giving thanks.*

יָדַד i. q. יָדָה *to cast* or *throw*, as lots. Pret. plur. יַדּוּ, Joel 4:3. [3:3.] Nah. 3:10. Obad. 11.

I. **יָדָה** *to throw, cast*, i. q. יָדַד. Imper. יְדוּ Jer. 50:14.

Pi. fut. וַיַּדּוּ for וַיְיַדּוּ Lam. 3:53. Infin. יַדּוֹת Zech. 2:4 [1:21] *to cast down the horns of the Gentiles.*

II. **יָדָה** found only in Hiph. הוֹדָה.

1. *to own, acknowledge, confess.* (Arab. ودي conj. X. Syr. Aph. *idem.*) Prov. 28:13. Construed with עַל, Ps. 32:5 *I will make confession concerning my sins.*

2. *to praise.* Gen. 49 : 8. Especially *to praise* Jehovah, construed with an accus. or with לְ, also with שֵׁם or לְשֵׁם, 1 K. 8 : 33. Ps. 54 : 8. 106 : 46. 122 : 4.

Hithpa. הִתְוַדָּה. 1. *to confess, to make confession.* Lev. 5 : 5. Construed most frequently with an accus. Lev. 16 : 21. 26 : 40. sometimes with עַל, Neh. 1 : 6. 9 : 2.

2. *to praise,* construed with לְ. 2 Chr. 30 : 22.

Deriv. הֻיְּדוֹת, תּוֹדָה, also the proper name יְהוּדָה.

יְדוּתוּן and יְדִיתוּן proper name of a Levite, one of David's choristers. 1 Chr. 9 : 16. 16 : 38, 41, 42. 25 : 1. Also his descendants, *the Jeduthunites,* likewise musicians, 2 Chr. 35 : 15. Neh. 11 : 17. In the latter signification it occurs also in the superscriptions of Psalms XXXIX. LXII. LXXVII. But Aben Ezra supposes it here to be the beginning of a song; and Jarchi, the name of a musical instrument.

יָדִיד m. dec. III. a. (Syr. ܝܰܕܺܝܕܳܐ *one beloved;* Arab. وَدّ *to love.* Kindred with דּוֹד).

1. subst. *one beloved, a friend.* Is. 5 : 1.—יְדִיד יְהוָה *the friend* or *favourite of Jehovah,* Ps. 127 : 2. Deut. 33 : 12. Spoken of the Israelites, Ps. 60 : 7. 108 : 7.

2. adj. *lovely, pleasant.* Ps. 84 : 2.

3. subst. Plur. יְדִידוֹת *loveliness.* Ps. 45 : 1 שִׁיר יְדִידֹת *a lovely song;* a commendatory title, probably of later date. Others: *a song of love.*

יְדִידוּת f. denom. from יָדִיד, *love,* also *the object of love.* Jer. 12 : 7.

יְדִידְיָה m. (*favourite of Jehovah*) a name given to Solomon at his birth by the prophet Nathan. 2 Sam. 12 : 25.

יָדַע, fut. יֵדַע, (once יִדַּע,) infin. absol. יָדֹעַ, const. דַּעַת.

1. *to know, to understand, to know how,* Lat. *scire.* Usually construed with an accus. or with an infin. with (Ecc. 4 : 13. 10 : 15.) and without (Jer. 1 : 6. 1 Sam. 16 : 18.) the preposition לְ; sometimes with a finite verb, Job 32 : 22. לֹא יָדַעְתִּי אֲכַנֶּה *I know not how to flatter.* 23 : 3. 1 Sam. 16 : 16. Neh. 10 : 29.—לֹא יָדַע טוֹב וָרָע *not to discern between good and evil,* as descriptive of childhood, Deut. 1 : 39. (comp. Is. 7 : 15. Gen. 2 : 17.) or of childish old age, 2 Sam. 19 : 36.—מִי יוֹדֵעַ *who knoweth?* construed with a future, a mode of expressing a weak or doubtful hope, 2 Sam. 12 : 22. Joel 2 : 14. Jon. 3 : 9.—Also, *to know about* any thing, construed with בְּ, 1 Sam. 22 : 15. with עַל, Job 37 : 16.—Sometimes it is construed with a pleonastic pronoun or dative of personal advantage, Cant. 1 : 8 תֵּדְעִי לָךְ *thou knowest.*—Part. יוֹדְעִים i. q. חֲכָמִים *the wise, skilful,* Job 34 : 2. Ecc. 9 : 11.

2. *to know, to be acquainted with,* Lat. *noscere.* Gen. 29 : 5.—יָדַע בְּשֵׁם *to know by name,* i. e. intimately, minutely, Ex. 33 : 12, 17. (comp. קָרָא בְשֵׁם.)—Also, inchoatively, *to learn to know, to become acquainted with,* Num. 14 : 31. Deut. 9 : 24.—Part. יֹדְעִים *acquaintances, friends,* Job 19 : 13. Part. pass. יָדוּעַ *known, respected, esteemed,* Deut. 1 : 13, 15. Is. 53 : 3 יְדוּעַ חֹלִי *distinguished through grief.*

3. *to perceive, observe, discern.* Gen. 19 : 33, 35. Judg. 13 : 21. Also with the addition עִם לֵבָב, Deut. 8 : 5.—Construed with בְּ, Gen. 15 : 8. 24 : 14. Ex. 7 : 17. Job 35 : 15.

4. *to learn, to be informed, to learn by experience.* Gen. 9 : 24. Lev. 5 : 3. Neh. 13 : 10. Especially in promises and threatenings, Ex. 6 : 7 *ye shall know that I am Jehovah your God.* Ezek. 6 : 7, 13. 7 : 4, 9. 11 : 10. Job 21 : 19 יְשַׁלֵּם אֵלָיו וְיֵדָע *he (God) should recompense him, so that he may know or feel it.* Hos. 9 : 7 יֵדְעוּ יִשְׂרָאֵל *Israel shall experience it.* Is. 9 : 8. Ps. 14 : 4. Ecc. 8 : 7. See Niph. no. 3.

5. *to imagine, expect.* Ps. 35 : 8 *let destruction come upon him,* לֹא יֵדָע *before he expects it,* i. e. unawares, suddenly. Job 9 : 5 *he removes the mountains* לֹא יָדָעוּ *suddenly.* Prov. 5 : 6.

6. *to concern one's self about, to take care of* any thing. Gen. 39 : 6. Prov. 27 : 23 יָדֹעַ תֵּדַע פְּנֵי צֹאנֶךָ *take diligent care of thy flock.* Hence, spoken of God, *to take an interest in* any one, *to love* him, Ps. 144 : 3. Amos 3 : 2. Nah. 1 : 7. spoken of men, *to know* (God), *to esteem or reverence* him, Hos. 8 : 2. Ps. 36 : 11. 9 : 11 יֹדְעֵי שְׁמֶךָ *those who reverence thy name.* Job 18 : 21 זֶה מְקוֹם לֹא יָדַע אֵל *this is the place of him who knows not God.*

7. as an euphemistic expression, (comp. signif. no. 4.) *to lie with* one of the other sex; spoken of the man, Gen. 4 : 17, 25. 1 Sam. 1 : 19. of the woman, Gen. 19 : 8. Judg. 11 : 39. expressed more fully, Num. 31 : 17. Used also of unnatural lust, Gen. 19 : 5. (Many verbs of *knowing* in different languages suffer this change of signification; as in Syr. ܝܕܥ *to know;* In Arab. عرف *idem;* in Greek γινώσκω, in Lat. *cognosco.* See Pfochenius de Purit. Styli N. T. p. 10.)

Niph. נוֹדַע 1. *to be known.* Ex. 2 : 14. 21 : 36. Lev. 4 : 14. Construed with לְ of the person, 1 Sam. 6 : 3. Ruth 3 : 3. Est. 2 : 22.—Gen. 41 : 21 וְלֹא נוֹדַע כִּי בָאוּ אֶל קִרְבֶּנָה *and it was not known that they* (*the fat kine*) *had passed into their belly.*

2. *to be known,* pass. of Kal no. 2. Ps. 9 : 17. 76 : 2. Prov. 31 : 23.

3. i. q. Kal no. 4. (strictly pass. of Hiph. no. 3.) Prov. 10 : 9 מְעַקֵּשׁ דְּרָכָיו יִוָּדֵעַ *he who perverteth his ways shall be made to feel,* i. e. shall be punished. Jer. 31 : 19 אַחֲרֵי הִוָּדְעִי *after I was made to feel.* C. V. *after I was instructed.*

Pi. *to make to know.* Once Job 38 : 12.

Pu. part. מְיֻדָּע *an acquaintance.* Ps. 31 : 12. 55 : 14. 88 : 9, 19.

Po. יוֹדַע *to appoint, direct,* (to a place), elsewhere הוֹעִיד. 1 Sam. 21 : 3.

Hiph. הוֹדִיעַ, imper. הוֹדַע.

1. *to cause to know, to inform, shew* any one; construed (1.) with two accusatives, Gen. 41 : 39. Ex. 33 : 12, 13. Ezek. 20 : 11. 22 : 2. 1 Sam. 14 : 12 נוֹדִיעָה אֶתְכֶם דָּבָר *we will shew you something.* (2.) with an accus. of the thing and dative of the person, Ex. 18 : 20. Deut. 4 : 9. Ps. 145 : 12. Neh. 9 : 14. (3.) with only an accus. of the person, Josh. 4 : 22. 1 K. 1 : 27. (4.) with an accus. of the thing, Ps. 77 : 15. 98 : 2. Job 26 : 3.

2. *to instruct* any one; construed with an accus. of the person, Job 38 : 3. 40 : 7. 42 : 4. with a dative, Prov. 9 : 9.

3. *to cause to feel, to punish,* causat. of Kal no. 4. Judg. 8 : 16 (*he took*) *thorns of the wilderness and threshing wagons,* וַיֹּדַע בָּהֶם אֵת אַנְשֵׁי סֻכּוֹת *and punished with them the men of Succoth.* This explanation, however, is not perfectly satisfactory. Perhaps the author wrote וירע *contrivit,* which is the sense given by the ancient versions.

Hoph. הוּדַע *to be known.* Lev. 4 : 23, 28.

Hithpa. הִתְוַדַּע *to make one's self known,* Gen. 45 : 1. *to reveal one's self,* Num. 12 : 6. Construed with אֶל.

Deriv. out of course דֵּעַ, דַּעַת, מַדָּע, מוֹדָע.

יְדַע Chald. fut. יִנְדַּע.

1. *to know.*

2. *to be informed.* Dan. 6 : 11.

3. *to understand.* Dan. 4 : 14, 22. [4 : 17, 25.] Part. pass. יְדִיעַ לֶהֱוֵא לְמַלְכָּא *be it known unto the king.* Ezra 4 : 12, 13.

Aph. הוֹדַע, fut. יְהוֹדַע, *to shew, make known.* Construed with a dative of the person, Dan. 2 : 15, 17, 28. with suffix pronouns, Dan. 2 : 23, 29. 4 : 15. [4 : 18.] 5 : 15, 16, 17. 7 : 16.

Deriv. מַנְדַּע.

יִדְּעֹנִי m. plur. יִדְּעֹנִים, verbal from יָדַע.

1. *a wise man, a soothsayer.* Lev. 19 : 31. 20 : 6. Deut. 18 : 11. 1 Sam. 28 : 3, 9. (Comp. the Arab. عَالِم *knowing,* hence, *a wise man, Magian;* and also חבר no. 2.)

2. *a spirit of divination.* Lev. 20 : 27. Comp. אוֹב.

יָהּ an abbreviation of יְהוָֹה or rather יַהְוָה (as it was anciently pronounced) יַהְוָה. It was first abridged by apocope into יָהוּ, (like וַיִּשְׁתַּחוּ for וַיִּשְׁתַּחֲוֶה,) and this again into יָה. These two contracted forms, (the latter without Mappik,) are used indiscriminately in many proper names; as אֵלִיָּהוּ and אֵלִיָּה, יִרְמְיָהוּ and יִרְמְיָה. The name יָהּ is frequently used, for the sake of conciseness, in the burden or repeated verses of the psalms; as, הַלְלוּ־יָהּ *praise Jehovah*, Ps. 104 : 36. 105 : 45. 106 : 1, 48. 111 : 1. 112 : 1. 113 : 1. Sometimes in other places, as Ps. 89 : 9. 94 : 7, 12. Is. 38 : 11. Ex. 15 : 2 עָזִּי וְזִמְרָת יָהּ *Jehovah is my glory and my song*. Ps. 118 : 14. Is. 12 : 2. Ps. 68 : 5 בְּיָהּ שְׁמוֹ *Jehovah is his name*, בְּ being here the Beth essentiae; (comp. Is. 47 : 4. 48 : 2. 54 : 5.) Is. 26 : 4 בְּיָהּ יְהוָה *Jehovah is Jehovah*, i. e. an unchangeable, eternal God.

יָהַב *to give, put, place*, i. q. נָתַן. In the preterite found only Ps. 55 : 23 הַשְׁלֵךְ עַל יְהוָה יְהָבְךָ *cast upon Jehovah what he allots you*, i. e. commit to Jehovah your destiny; (אֲשֶׁר is to be supplied before יְהָבְךָ.) Others make יְהָב a substantive, signifying *burden*. Elsewhere only in the imper. הַב (Prov. 30 : 15.) הָבָה, fem. הָבִי (Ruth 3 : 15.) plur. הָבוּ. (1.) *give, give here*. Gen. 29 : 21. Job 6 : 22. 2 Sam. 16 : 20 הָבוּ לָכֶם עֵצָה *give counsel*, (לָכֶם is pleonastic.) (2.) *place, appoint*. 2 Sam. 11 : 15. Deut. 1 : 13 הָבוּ לָכֶם אֲנָשִׁים *appoint for yourselves men*. Josh. 18 : 4. (3.) *come on*. Gen. 11 : 3, 4, 7. 38 : 16. Ex. 1 : 9.—הֵבוּ, if the reading is correct, probably for הָבוּ, Hos. 4 : 18 אָהֲבוּ הֵבוּ *amant dant*, for *amant dare*.

יְהַב Chald. 1. *to give*, Dan. 2 : 37, 38, 48. *to give up*, Dan. 3 : 28.

2. *to lay, place*, as a foundation. Ezra 5 : 16. Only the preterite יְהַב, the imper. הַב, and the participles יָהֵב and יְהִיב occur; the future and infinitive are supplied from the verb נְתַן, which again is defective in the tenses first mentioned. (The same is also the case in Syriac.)

Ithpe. אִתְיְהֵב *to be given* or *given up*. Dan. 4 : 13. [16.] 7 : 25.

יָהַד, Hithpa. הִתְיַהֵד, denom. from יְהוּדִי *to profess Judaism*. Esth. 8 : 17.

יֵהוּא m. (perhaps i. q. יְהִיא, Ecc. 11 : 3. *he shall be*.)

1. proper name of a king of Israel, who destroyed the family of Ahab. 2 K. 9 : 11.

2. also of an Israelitish prophet in the time of king Baasha. 1 K. 16 : 1. 2 Chr. 19 : 2. 20 : 34.

יְהוֹאָחָז m. (*Jehovah holds*.)

1. proper name of a son of Jehu, king of Israel. 2 K. 13 : 1—9.

2. also of a son of Josiah, king of Judah. 2 K. 23 : 30. 2 Chr. 36 : 1. Also written יוֹאָחָז 2 Chr. 36 : 2. Sept. Ἰωάχαζ.

יְהוֹאָשׁ m. 1. proper name of a son of Ahaziah, king of Judah. 2 K. 12 : 1. 14 : 13. Also written יוֹאָשׁ 11 : 2. 12 : 20.

2. also of a son of Jehoahaz, king of Israel. 2 K. 13 : 10—25. In like manner written יוֹאָשׁ verse 9. Sept. Ἰωάς. Its appellative signification is probably *Jehovah gives*, from אוּשׁ i. q. Arab. أس *donavit*.

יְהוּד Chald. a collective noun, *the Jews*. (Arab. هُودٌ, يَهُودُ *idem*.) Dan. 2 : 25 מִן בְּנֵי גָלוּתָא דִּי יְהוּד *of the captives from the Jews*. 5 : 13. 6 : 14. Ezra 5 : 1, 8. 6 : 14.

יְהוּדָה a proper name.

1. the fourth son of Jacob; also *the tribe descended from him*, the boundaries of whose territory are given Josh. xv.—הַר יְהוּדָה *the hill-country in the tribe of Judah*, Josh. 15 : 48 ff.

2. after the division of the kingdom in the time of Rehoboam, *the kingdom and people of Judah*, (of the fem. gen. when denoting the kingdom, and of the masc. gen. when denoting the people, Is. 3 : 8.) consisting of the tribes of Judah and Benjamin, and also of a part of the tribes of Dan and Simeon. Comp. De Wette hebr. jüdische Archäologie, p. 173.—אַדְמַת יְהוּדָה *the country* or *kingdom of Judah*, Is. 19 : 17. עִיר יְהוּדָה *the (chief) city of Judah*, i. e. Jerusalem, 2 Chron. 25 : 28. It is worthy of remark, that this division of the kingdom is alluded to in the time of David and even earlier; as in Josh. 11 : 16, 21.

2 Sam. 2:10. 5:5. 19:40. 20:2. 24:9. 1 Chr. 21:5. Either, therefore, there is an anachronism in these writers, or the division took place earlier in common speech.

3. after the captivity, *the whole country of Israel.* Hag. 1:1, 14. 2:3.

יְהוּדִי, plur. יְהוּדִים, also יְהוּדִיִּים, fem. יְהוּדִית and ־ִית. (see no. 4.) a gentile noun from יְהוּדָה.

1. *a Jew* or *Jewess, one belonging to the tribe of Judah.*

2. *a citizen of the kingdom of Judah.* 2 K. 16:6. 25:25.

3. after the captivity of the ten tribes, *an Israelite* or *Hebrew* generally. Jer. 32:12. 38:19. 40:11. 43:9. especially 34:9, where it is synonymous with עִבְרִי. Neh. 1:2. 3:33. 4:6. Est. 2:8. 3:4. 5:13.

4. fem. יְהוּדִית used adverbially, *in Jewish* or *Hebrew,* i. e. in the Hebrew language, (comp. signif. no. 3.) 2 K. 18:26. Neh. 13:24.

יְהוּדִי Chald. *a Jew.* Found only in the plur. יְהוּדָיִן, emph. יְהוּדָיֵא, Dan. 3:8, 12. Ezra 4:12, 23. 5:1, 5.

יְהֹוָה the proper name of the Deity among the ancient Hebrews.

It is worthy of remark, that this word has not its own original punctuation, but derives its vowels from the word אֲדֹנָי, (except that simple Sheva is used under י instead of ־ֲ.) This name *Adonai* the Jews, in conformity with an ancient superstition, are accustomed to read instead of the ineffable name יהוה, just as the Septuagint has used Κύριος for the same word. Hence, with the prefixes, it is written מֵיְהֹוָה, בַּיהֹוָה, לַיהֹוָה, (the vowels being conformed to the word אֲדֹנָי,) and where אדני יהוה stands in the text, it is pointed אֲדֹנָי יֱהֹוִה, and read אֲדֹנָי אֱלֹהִים.

The inquiry then arises, What is the correct pronunciation of יהוה? Many critics make it יַהֹוָה, relying on the testimony of several ancient writers that the Hebrews called their God ΙΑΩ. See Diod. Sic. I. Macrob. Saturn. I. 18. Iren. adv. hær, II. cap. ult. and others, particularly Theodoret. Quæst. ad Exod. XV. καλουσι δε αυτο Σαμαρειται ΙΑΒΕ, Ιουδαιοι δε ΙΑΩ. The objection to this is, that יָהוֹ has not the form of a Hebrew noun. The same objection lies against יַהְוֹה, a pronunciation which some derive from the ΙΕΥΩ of Philo Byblius, (Euseb. de Præp. Evang. I. 9.) Its true pronunciation, therefore, was probably יַהְוֶה (comp. the passage quoted above from Theodoret,) like the future of הָיָה. From this the abbreviations יְהוֹ and יָהּ (q. v.) are most easily formed. Comp. Relandi Decas Dissert. de vera Pronuntiatione Nominis Jehovæ. Traj. 1707. 8vo. The pronunciation of the Masoretic points is defended by Reland, Simonis, J. D. Michaëlis (Suppl. ad Lex. Hebr. p. 554.)

The pronunciation יַהְוֶה *he shall be* is supported also by the etymological explanation given by Moses, Ex. 3:14. 6:3. comp. Rev. 1:4, 8. namely, *he who is as he shall be,* i. e. the eternal, unchangeable, true. To this interpretation, an allusion is also made Hos. 12:6 יְהֹוָה זִכְרוֹ *he is called* or *is Jehovah,* i. e. the unchangeable.—When used in the beginning of proper names it is written יְהוֹ and by contraction יוֹ; when used in the end יָהוּ, יָה.

יְהוֹחָנָן m. (*Jehovah is gracious*) proper name of a general under Jehoshaphat. Hence the Greek names 'Ιωαννᾶς and 'Ιωάννης are formed.

יְהוֹיָדָע m. (*Jehovah knows*) proper name of a distinguished priest in the court of the kings of Israel, who destroyed the queen Athaliah, and raised Jehoash to the government. 2 K. 11:4 ff. Also the name of several other persons.

יְהוֹיָכִין m. (*Jehovah founds*) proper name of a son of Jehoiakim, king of Judah, 2 K. 24:8—17. under whom the first transportation to Babylon took place. He is also called יוֹיָכִין Ezek. 1:2. יְכָנְיָה Est. 2:6. Jer. 27:20. 28:4. יְכָנְיָהוּ Jer. 24:1 Keth. and כָּנְיָהוּ Jer. 22:24, 28. 37:1. The latter names stand for יָכִין יָהּ (*Jehovah stands up.*)

יְהוֹיָקִים m. (*Jehovah raises up*) proper name of a son of Josiah, king of Judah, at first called אֶלְיָקִים, (q. v.) 2 K. 23:34, 24:1. Jer. 1:3.

יְהוֹיָרִיב and יוֹיָרִיב m. (*Jehovah contends*) proper name of a distinguished priest in Jerusalem. 1 Chr. 9:10. 24: 7. Ezra 8:16. Neh. 11:10. 12:6, 19. Hence the Greek name Ἰωαρίβ 1 Mac. 2:1.

יְהוֹנָדָב and יוֹנָדָב m. (*Jehovah urges on*, or *is willing, liberal*,) proper name of a Rechabite, from whom the vow of the Rechabites was derived. 2 K. 10:15. Jer. 35:6. See רֵכָב.

יְהוֹנָתָן and יוֹנָתָן m. (*Jehovah gives*) *Jonathan*, the son of Saul, celebrated for his heroic friendship towards David, 1 Sam. XIII.—XXXI. Also the name of several other persons.

יְהוֹסֵף a Chaldaic form for יוֹסֵף, Ps. 81:6. here denoting *Israel*. See יוֹסֵף.

יְהוֹרָם and יוֹרָם m. (*Jehovah is exalted*.)

1. proper name of a king of Judah, son of Jehoshaphat. 2 K. 8:16—24.

2. also of a son of Ahab, king of Israel. 2 K. III.

יְהוֹשֶׁבַע f. (*the oath of Jehovah*) proper name of a daughter of king Joram, wife of the priest Jehoiada. 2 K. 11:2. Also written יְהוֹשַׁבְעַת 2 Chr. 22: 11.

יְהוֹשׁוּעַ and יְהוֹשֻׁעַ m. (*the help of Jehovah*; comp. אֱלִישׁוּעַ, אֲבִישׁוּעַ.)

1. proper name of a son of Nun, servant and armourbearer of Moses, and afterwards his successor, and leader of the Israelites. Ex. 17:9. 24:13. He was called at first הוֹשֵׁעַ, Num. 13:16. See also יֵשׁוּעַ.

2. also of a high-priest after the exile. Zech. 3:1. Hag. 1:1, 12. See in like manner יֵשׁוּעַ. Sept. Ἰησοῦς. Vulg. *Josua*.

יְהוֹשָׁפָט m. (*Jehovah judges*) proper name of a son of Asa, king of Judah. 2 K. 22:41—51. Also of a valley between Jerusalem and mount Olivet, named after this king, Joel 4:2, 12. [3:2, 12.]

יָהִיר adj. *proud, arrogant*. Prov. 21:24. Hab. 2:5. (In Chald. and Talmud. אִתְיְהַר *superbire*; יְהִיר *superbus*; יְהִירוּת, יְהִירָא *superbia*.)

יַהֲלֹם m. Ex. 28:18. 39:11. Ezek. 28:13. name of a precious stone, which cannot be defined with certainty. Comp. Braun de Vestitu Sacerdotum. p. 542 ff.

יַהַץ and יַהְצָה proper name of a Moabitish city, which was afterwards reckoned to the tribe of Reuben, but allotted to the priests. Num. 21:23. Deut. 2:32. Josh. 13:18. Is. 15:4. Jer. 48:21, 34. (As an appellative, perhaps i. q. Arab. وَهْصَةٌ *terra depressa et rotunda*.)

יוֹאֵל m. (*Jehovah is God*) proper name of a prophet. Joel 1:1.

יוֹאָשׁ i. q. יְהוֹאָשׁ q. v.

יוֹב proper name of a son of Issachar, Gen. 46:13. instead of which we find יָשׁוּב Num. 26:24. 1 Chr. 7:1 Keri. Hence the first name may be merely a corruption. Some have identified this name with אִיּוֹב the hero of the book of Job, but without reason.

יוֹבָב proper name of an Arabian tribe, of the family of Joktan. Gen. 10: 29. Bochart supposes it the same with the Ἰωβαρίταις on the Salachian gulf; the true spelling, in his opinion, being Ἰωβαβίταις, since P is very easily corrupted into B. Bocharti Geogr. T. I. p. 190.

יוֹבֵל com. gen. 1. name of a wind instrument. Ex. 19:13. The full name is קֶרֶן הַיּוֹבֵל Josh. 6:5. and in the plural שׁוֹפְרוֹת יוֹבְלִים Josh. 6:6. שׁוֹפְרוֹת הַיּוֹבְלִים Josh. 6:4, 8, 13. *Jubel horns* or *trumpets*. Hence the phrase, מָשַׁךְ בְּקֶרֶן הַיּוֹבֵל Josh. 6: 5. Ex. 19:13. *to blow with this instrument*; comp. מָשַׁךְ. The literal signification is doubtful. The Chaldaic version and the Jewish commentators render יָבַל *a ram;* hence, *rams' horns, trumpets made of rams' horns.* It is said by Rabbi Levi and Akiba to have this signification in Arabic, but it is not found in our present Arabic Lexicons. See Bocharti Hieroz. P. I. lib. II. cap. 43. Others make it *sonus tractus* (as if from יָבַל,) which, however, does not suit the context.

2. שְׁנַת הַיּוֹבֵל Lev. 25:13, 15, 18, 40. and simply יֹבֵל verse 28: 30:33. *the year of jubilee,* every 50th (others erroneously every 49th) year, which, according to the Mosaic law, was a year of general release, 25:10 ff. Sept. ἔτος τῆς ἀφέσεως, ἄφεσις. Vulg. *annus jubilei, annus jubileus.* The etymology is uncertain, but it is most probably derived from signif. no. 1. this year being perhaps announced with Jubel horns, as the new year was with trumpets. Comp. further Carpzov. Apparat. ad Antiquit. Sac. Cod. p. 447 ff.

יוּבַל m. verbal from יָבַל no. 2.

1. *a river* or *wet ground.* Jer. 17:8.

2. proper name of a son of Lamech, the inventor of the harp and cornet. Gen. 4:21.

יוֹם m. prim. dec. I.

1. *day.*—Hence, (1.) הַיּוֹם *this day;* hence, *to-day,* also *now,* 1 Sam. 12:17. *immediately,* 14:33. and *once, formerly,* i. e. on a certain day; (see p. 147.) (2.) בְּיוֹם with an infinitive following, *on the day when* any thing happens or happened; also simply, *as soon as, when,* Gen. 2:17 בְּיוֹם אֲכָלְךָ מִמֶּנּוּ *as soon as thou eatest thereof.* 3:5. Ex. 10:28. Ruth 4:5. Construed with a finite verb, Lev. 7: 35. (3.) בַּיּוֹם *on the day;* also *immediately, yet on the same day,* Prov. 12: 16. Neh. 3:34. [4:2.] (4.) כַּיּוֹם *now.* Gen. 25:31, 33. Hence, in reference to an action which is to take place soon, *immediately, presently, first,* 1 Sam. 2: 16. 1 K. 22:5. (5.) יוֹם בְּיוֹם, יוֹם יוֹם Neh. 8:18. (comp. Ezra 3:4 עֹלַת יוֹם בְּיוֹם *the daily burnt-offering.*) כְּיוֹם בְּיוֹם 1 Sam. 18:10. *daily.* (6.) מִיּוֹם *from the day on, since.* Ex. 10:6. Deut. 9:24.

The following special uses of the word are worthy of notice; (1.) *a day of misfortune,* or *calamity.* Obad. 12 יוֹם אָחִיךָ *the calamitous day of thy brother.* Job 18:20 *at his day,* i. e. at his destruction, (יוֹמוֹ,) *posterity are astonished.* Ps. 37: 13. 137:7. 1 Sam. 26:10. Ezek. 21: 29. (2.) more rarely, *a day of prosperity* or *rejoicing, a festival day.* Hos. 7:5 יוֹם מַלְכֵּנוּ *the festival day of our king,* perhaps *his birth* or *coronation day.* 2: 15 [2:13] יְמֵי הַבְּעָלִים *the festivals of Baalim.* 1:11. [2:2.] *one's birth day,* Job 3:1. (3.) *day of Jehovah,* for *his day of judgment* or *punishment.* Joel 1:15. Ezek. 13:5. Is. 2:12.

2. *time* generally, (like the Greek ἡμέρα, and the Lat. *dies.*)—כְּהַיּוֹם הַזֶּה *about this time,* Gen. 39:11. בְּלֹא יוֹמוֹ *before its time,* Job 15:32. כָּל־הַיּוֹם *constantly,* Gen. 6:5.

Dual יוֹמַיִם *two days.* Hos. 6:2 מִיֹּמָיִם בַּיּוֹם הַשְּׁלִישִׁי *after two days, on the third day;* comp. Luc. 13:32, 33.

Plur. יָמִים (from an obsolete sing. יָם,) also יָמִין after the Chaldaic form (Dan. 12:13.) const. יְמֵי rarely יְמוֹת (Deut. 32: 7. Ps. 90:15.)

1. *days,* especially *days of one's life.* Gen. 6:3.—כָּל־הַיָּמִים *all one's days, all one's life long,* Gen. 43:9. 44:32.—מִיָּמֶיךָ *since thou livest,* 1 Sam. 25:28.—Gen. 8:22 כָּל־יְמֵי הָאָרֶץ *so long as the earth stands.*—בָּא בַּיָּמִים *advanced in age, ætate provectus,* Gen. 24:1. Josh. 13:1.—הֶאֱרִיךְ יָמִים *to prolong one's days, to live long;* see אָרַךְ.

2. *time* generally. Gen. 47:8 יְמֵי שְׁנֵי חַיֶּיךָ *the time of the years of thy life.*—בִּימֵי אַבְרָהָם, דָּוִד *in the time of Abraham, of David,* Gen. 26:1. 2 Sam. 21:1. 1 K. 10:21. וַיְהִי בַּיָּמִים הָהֵם *and it came to pass in these days,* Ex. 2:11. Judg. 18: 1. 19:1. 1 Sam. 28:1. כָּל־הַיָּמִים *constantly, for ever,* like the Homeric phrase, ἤματα πάντα, Deut. 4:40. 5:29. 6: 24. 1 Sam. 2:32, 35. 22:14. Job 1: 5. It is sometimes added after the time how long; as, שְׁלשָׁה שָׁבֻעִים יָמִים *three weeks as to time,* i. e. three weeks long, (others, incorrectly, *three whole weeks,*) Dan 10:

2, 3. חֹדֶשׁ יָמִים *a month long*, Gen. 29:14. יֶרַח יָמִים *idem*, Deut. 21:13. 2 K. 15:13. שְׁנָתַיִם יָמִים *two years long*, Gen. 41:1. Jer. 28:3, 11.

3. *some* or *several days*. Neh. 1:4. Dan. 8:27. (like שָׁנִים *some years*, Dan. 11:6, 8.) Hence, *some* or *a considerable time*, Gen. 40:4 וַיִּהְיוּ יָמִים בְּמִשְׁמָר *and they were some time in custody*. Num. 9:22 יֹמַיִם אוֹ חֹדֶשׁ אוֹ יָמִים *two days or a month or a longer time*. 1 Sam. 29:3 *who has been with me* זֶה יָמִים אוֹ זֶה שָׁנִים *some time or perhaps some years*. שָׁנִים here denotes more than יָמִים. מִיָּמִים *after some time*, Judg. 11:4. 14:8. 15:1. מִקֵּץ יָמִים *idem*, Gen. 4:3. 1 K. 17:7.

4. *a year*. (This definite signification is found also in the Aram. יְמָן, ܙܒܢ, *time*. Some make it elliptical for תְּקוּפַת יָמִים but this phrase never denotes *a year*.) Lev. 25:29. Judg. 17:10. זֶבַח הַיָּמִים *the yearly sacrifice*, 1 Sam. 2:19. מִיָּמִים יָמִימָה *from year to year*, Ex. 13:10. Judg. 11:40. 21:19. 1 Sam. 1:3. 2:19. Also with numerals, 2 Chr. 21:19 כְּעֵת צֵאת הַקֵּץ לְיָמִים שְׁנַיִם *about the time of the expiration of the second year*. Less certain is Am. 4:4 לִשְׁלֹשֶׁת יָמִים *every three years*, but perhaps *every three days*, in irony. (פָּנִים in like manner has both a plural and singular signification.)

יוֹם m. Chald. *day*, as in Heb. plur. יוֹמִין, emph. יוֹמַיָּא, const. fem. יוֹמָת (Ezra 4:15, 19.) const. masc. after the Hebrew form יְמֵי (Ezra 4:7.)

יוֹמָם adv. (from יוֹם with the adverbial termination ־ָם,) *by day*. יוֹמָם וָלַיְלָה *by day and by night*, Lev. 8:35. Num. 9:21. בְּיוֹמָם *by day*, Neh. 9:19. (comp. the Syr. ܝܘܡܐ *day*, ܝܘܡܐܝܬ *daily*.)

יָוָן proper name. 1. Gen. 10:2. Dan. 8:21. Is. 66:19. Ezek. 27:13. *the people and country of the Ionians*, the tribe of the Greeks which lay the nearest to the Shemitish nations, and had the greatest intercourse with them; and by which the Hebrews, like the Syrians and Arabians, appear to have understood *the Greeks* generally. Syr. ܝܘܢ, ܝܘܢ, ܝܘܢ *Greece*; Arab. يونانيّ *a Greek*.) בְּנֵי הַיְּוָנִים *the sons of the Greeks*, i. e. the Greeks themselves, Joel 4:6. [3:6.]

2. Ezek. 27:19. perhaps a city in Arabia Felix. (Arab. يون, يوان *oppidum Jemen*.)

יָוֵן m. const. יְוַן, *mire*. Ps. 69:3. 40:3 טִיט הַיָּוֵן *the miry clay*, two synonymes being used to express intensity; comp. Dan. 2:41.

יוֹנָה f. plur. יוֹנִים, dec. X.

1. *a dove*. Gen. 8:8 ff. Used as a word of endearment, יוֹנָתִי *my dove*, Cant. 2:14. 5:2. 6:9. עֵינַיִךְ יוֹנִים *thine eyes are doves* (*eyes*). Cant. 1:15. 4:1 בְּנֵי יוֹנָה *young doves*, Lev. 5:7.

2. proper name of a celebrated prophet. Jon. 1:1. 2 K. 14:25.

Note. Another יוֹנָה may be found under יָנָה.

יוֹנֵק m. Is. 53:2. and **יוֹנֶקֶת** f. dec. XIII. a. verbals from יָנַק, *a sprout* or *shoot from the stock* or *root*, as it were, *a sucker*. Job 8:16. 14:7. 15:30. Ezek. 17:22. Hos. 14:7. For similar metaphors, comp. the Greek μόσχος; the Lat. *pullus*, *pullulus*, whence *pullulare*; and the Eng. *sucker*.

יוֹסֵף m. proper name of the youngest son (except Benjamin) of Jacob, who became prime minister to Pharaoh king of Egypt. Each of his two sons Ephraim and Manasseh inherited a portion with the sons of Jacob. Hence יוֹסֵף and בֵּית יוֹסֵף denote (1.) *the two tribes of Ephraim and Manasseh*. Josh. 17:17. 18:5. Judg. 1:23, 35. So בְּנֵי יוֹסֵף in the same sense, Josh. 14:4. (2.) after the division of the kingdom under Rehoboam, *the kingdom of the ten tribes*, *the kingdom of Israel*, in opposition to *the kingdom of Judah*; (the tribe of Ephraim being the most powerful of the ten tribes.) Ps. 78:67. Ezek. 37:16—19. Zech. 10:6. (3.) *the Israelites* generally. Ps. 80:2. 81:6. Am. 5:6, 15. 6:6.

Note. In Gen. xxx. there appear to be two derivations of this name given; namely, one from יֹאסֵף he takes away, (comp. אָסַף=יָסַף 2 Sam. 6:1.) in verse 23; and the other from יֹסֵף he adds, in verse 24. The form יְהוֹסֵף Ps. 81:6. favours the latter.

יוֹצֵר 1. *a potter.* See יָצַר.

2. Zech. 11:13. i. q. אוֹצָר *a treasure, the treasury of the temple;* the change in the orthography being probably derived from the Aramean pronunciation; (comp. אִיתַי, אִישׁ, יֵשׁ.) This explanation is supported by the various readings בית יצר, אל בית יצר, and אל אוצר, the authors of which must certainly have given it this signification. The true punctuation is probably יֹצֵר. The Syriac version renders it *treasury.*

יוֹרֶה m. verbal from יָרָה no. 1. *the early rain,* which in Palestine falls from the latter part of October to the first part of December. Deut. 11:14. Jer. 5:24. See the root no. 3. *to sprinkle,* Hos. 6:3.

יוֹתָם proper name of a son of Azariah, king of Judah. 2 K. 15:32—38.

יוֹתֵר m. verbal from יָתַר, (with the form of the participle).

1. *advantage, pre-eminence;* literally, *something remaining over* or *exceeding.* Ecc. 6:8.

2. *more, further.* Ecc. 2:15. 7:11. (Chald. and Rabbin. יוֹתֵר, with מִן, *more than.*)

3. *too much, over much.* Ecc. 7:16.

4. *besides,* like יֶתֶר. Est. 6:6 יוֹתֵר מִמֶּנִּי *besides myself.* Ecc. 12:9 וְיֹתֵר שֶׁהָיָה קֹהֶלֶת חָכָם *besides, because Koheleth was wise.* 12:12.

יוֹתֶרֶת fem. of יוֹתֵר; literally, *something superfluous, projecting over, redundans;* used particularly in the phrase הַיֹּתֶרֶת עַל הַכָּבֵד Ex. 29:13. Lev. 3:4. or יֹתֶרֶת הַכָּבֵד Ex. 29:22. and יֹתֶרֶת מִן הַכָּבֵד Lev. 9:10. *the great liver lobe, major lobus hepatis.* Sept. λοβὸς τοῦ ἥπατος. Saad. زِيَادَة *idem,* and with the same etymology, for زَادَ denotes i. q. יָתַר. See Bocharti Hieroz. T. I. p. 498 ff. Although this lobe makes a part of the liver itself, yet we may say, *the lobe over the liver.* This is better than to understand it of *the caul over the liver, omentum minus hepaticogastricum,* (Vulg. *reticulum hepatis,*) which is inconsiderable in size, and has but little fat.

יָזֹם Gen. 11:6. see זָמַם.

יָזַן see זוּן.

יֶזַע m. *sweat.* Once Ezek. 44:18. (Comp. זֵעָה *sweat;* and the verb وَذَعَ in Arabic, *to flow,* and in Ethiop. *to sweat.*)

יִזְרְעֶאל and **יִזְרְעֵאל** (*God sows;* comp. Hos. 1:4. 2:25.)

1. proper name of a city in the tribe of Manasseh, at times the residence of the kings of Israel. 1 K. 18:46. 2 K. 9:15. In its neighbourhood was עֵמֶק יִזְרְעֶאל *the valley of Jezreel,* Josh. 17:16. Judg. 6:33. In later times called *Esdrelom, Esdrelon, Stradela.* The gentile noun is יִזְרְעֵאלִי 1 K. 21:1. fem. יִזְרְעֵאלִית, יִזְרְעֵלִית 1 Sam. 27:3. 30:5.

2. also of a town in the hill-country of the tribe of Judah. Josh. 15:56. 1 Sam. 29:1.

יָחַד, fut. יֵחַד, (kindred with אָחַד, אָחַד,) *to be united, joined.* Construed with בְּ, Gen. 49:6. with אֵת (אֶת,) Is. 14:20.

Pi. יִחֵד *to unite.* Ps. 86:11.

Deriv. out of course יָחִיד.

יַחַד m. verbal from יָחַד, dec. VI. c. *union.* 1 Chr. 12:17. Hence, as an adv. 1. *together, with one another, in the same place,* 1 Sam. 11:11. 17:10. *at the same time,* 2 Sam. 21:9.

2. with and without כֹּל, *all together.* Job 34:15 כָּל־בָּשָׂר יַחַד *all flesh together.* Job 3:18. 24:4. 38:7 בְּרָן־יַחַד כּוֹכְבֵי בֹקֶר *when all the morning stars rejoiced.* Deut. 33:5.—Without a substantive, Job 16:10. 17:16. 19:12. With a negation, *no one at all,* Hos. 11:7.

3. *entirely.* Job 10:8 יַחַד סָבִיב *all about.* Ps. 141:10.

With a suffix, יַחְדָּיו and יַחְדָּו literally *they together,* like כֻּלּוֹ; hence, 1. *together, in the same place.* Gen. 13:6. 36:7. Deut. 25:5. Gen. 22:6, 8 וַיֵּלְכוּ שְׁנֵיהֶם יַחְדָּו *and they went both of them together.*

2. *mutually;* as, נִצָּה יַחְדָּו *to contend together,* Deut. 25:11. comp. 1 Sam. 17:10.

3. *at the same time.* Ps. 4:9.

4. with and without כֹּל, *all together.* Ps. 14:3. 1 Chr. 10:6. Job 24:17.

יְחֶזְקֵאל m. (for יְחַזֵּק אֵל *God strengthens,* like אֲכַלְךָ Ex. 33:3. for אֲכַלֶּךָ,) proper name of a well-known prophet, the son of Buzi. Ezek. 1:3. 24:24. Sept. Ἰεζεκιήλ, so Ecclus. 49:8. Vulg. *Ezechiel;* comp. יְחִזְקִיָּה, חִזְקִיָּה, Vulg. *Ezechias.*

יְחִזְקִיָּה m. (*Jehovah strengthens*) i. q. חִזְקִיָּה *Hezekiah,* king of Judah, q. v.

יָחִיד, fem. יְחִידָה, verbal from יָחַד, dec. III. a. and X.

1. *alone, only;* used particularly of an only child. Gen. 22:2, 12, 16. also without בֵּן or בַּת, in the masc. Jer. 6:26. Zech. 13:10. Prov. 4:3. in the fem. Judg. 11:34.

2. *solitary, forsaken, desolate.* Ps. 25:16. 68:7.

3. fem. יְחִידָה *the only, the most beloved, the darling;* a poetical expression for *one's life.* Ps. 22:21. 35:17. comp. כָּבוֹד. Others: *the forsaken (soul).*

יָחִיל m. verbal adj. from יָחַל, *waiting* or *hoping for.* Lam. 3:26.

יָחַל in Kal not used.

Pi. יִחֵל 1. *to wait.* Job 6:11. The person or thing waited *for* is preceded by לְ, Job 29:23. 30:26. by אֶל, Is. 51:5. Ps. 130:6. 131:3. Frequently in the phrase יִחֵל לַיהוָה *to wait with confidence on Jehovah, to hope in him,* Ps. 31:25. 33:22.

2. trans. *to cause to hope, to inspire hope.* Ezek. 13:6. Ps. 119:49.

Hiph. הוֹחִיל *to wait,* as in Pi. 1 Sam. 10:8. 13:8. Construed with לְ, Job 32:11. Ps. 42:6.

Niph. נוֹחַל, fut. יִיָּחֵל (with לְ, *to wait,* as in Piel and Hiph. Gen. 8:12. Ezek. 19:5.

Deriv. יָחִיל, תּוֹחֶלֶת.

יָחַם found only in the fut. יֵחַם and יֵחַם (1 K. 1:1) i. q. חָמַם which is used only in the preterite.

1. *to be* or *become warm.* Ezek. 24:11. Impers. יֵחַם, יֵחַם לוֹ *he is warm.* 1 K. 1:1. Ecc. 4:11. (The preterite חַם from חָמַם is also used impersonally.)

2. *to glow with anger.* Deut. 19:6.

3. *to rut* or *copulate,* as animals. Gen. 30:38, 39.

Note. The future יֵחַם is formed differently in Gesenius' Lehrgeb. p. 366.

Pi. 1. i. q. Kal no. 3. *to copulate,* spoken of animals. Gen. 30:41. 31:10.

2. *to conceive,* spoken of a woman. Ps. 51:7 וּבְחֵטְא יֶחֱמַתְנִי אִמִּי *and in sin my mother conceived me.* (The form יֶחֱמַתְנִי is used for יְחֵמַתְנִי, as אַחֲרוּ for אֵחֲרוּ or אֵחֲרוּ Judg. 5:28.)

Deriv. חֵמָה.

יַחְמוּר Deut. 14:5. 1 K. 5:3. [4:23.] Arab. يحمور, an animal of the deer kind, of a reddish colour, with horns indented like a saw, which it sheds every year; prob. *the fallow deer.* See Bochart's Hieroz. P. I. p. 913. (T. II. p. 284 of the new edition.)

יָחֵף m. *barefoot.* 2 Sam. 15:30. Is. 20:2, 3, 4. Jer. 2:25.

יָחַר i. q. אָחַר *to delay.* Found only 2 Sam. 20:5 Kethib ויחר (read וַיִּיחַר) *and he delayed.* The Keri וַיּוֹחֶר is the Hiph. (with Chaldaic form) from אָחַר.

יַחַשׂ m. in later Hebrew, *a generation, family, tribe.* Once Neh. 7:5 סֵפֶר הַיַּחַשׂ *a family register.* (Chald. יַחַס used for the Hebrew מִשְׁפָּחָה and in the plur. for תּוֹלְדוֹת.) Hence,

Hithpa. הִתְיַחֵשׂ *to be entered* or *enrolled in a family register,* ἀπογράφεσθαι, *censeri.* 1 Chr. 5:1, 7, 17. 9:1. Neh. 7:5. The infin. הִתְיַחֵשׂ is used as a noun, *a register, catalogue,* 1 Chr. 7:5, 7, 9, 40. 2 Chr. 31:16, 17. 12:15 *the deeds of Rehoboam are written in the book of*

Shemaiah, לְהִתְיַחֵשׂ *in the family register.*

יָטַב used only in the fut. יִיטַב, יֵיטַב, (once תֵּיטְבִי Nah. 3:8.) i. q. טוֹב.

1. *to be good.* Nah. 3:8. Ecc. 7:3. Elsewhere used impersonally, (1.) יִיטַב לִי *it shall be well with me.* Gen. 12:13. 40:14. Deut. 4:40. (2.) וַיִּיטַב בְּעֵינַי *and it pleased me.* Gen. 41:37. 45:16. Lev. 10:19, 20. more rarely with לִפְנֵי, Est. 5:14. Neh. 2:5, 6. with לְ, Ps. 69:32.

2. *to be joyful,* spoken of the heart. Judg. 19:6. Ruth 3:7.

Hiph. הֵיטִיב, fut. יֵיטִיב, more rarely יֵטִיב, (once יֵיטִב.)

1. *to make good, to do well.* Deut. 5:25 [28] הֵיטִיבוּ כָּל־ אֲשֶׁר דִּבֵּרוּ *they have done well all that they have spoken,* i. e. they have spoken well. 18:17. Construed with an infin. Jer. 1:12 הֵיטַבְתָּ לִרְאוֹת *thou hast rightly seen.* 1 Sam. 16:17 מֵיטִיב לְנַגֵּן *one who can play well.* Comp. Ezek. 33:32. The infin. absol. הֵיטֵב *doing well,* is used adverbially for *well, exactly, carefully, diligently.* Deut. 9:21. 13:15. 17:4. 19:18. 27:8.

2. הֵיטִיב דְּרָכָיו *to make good one's ways,* i.e. to conduct well. Jer. 2:33. 7:3, 5. with מַעֲלָלִים, 35:15. Hence, elliptically, Jeremiah 4:22 וּלְהֵיטִיב לֹא יָדָעוּ *but to do good, they have no knowledge.* 13:23. The infin. used as an adv. *acting well, rightly,* Jon. 4:4, 9.

3. *to do good to* or *benefit* any one; construed with לְ, Gen. 12:16. Ex. 1:20. with an accus. Deut. 8:16. 30:5. with עִם, Gen. 32:10, 13. Num. 10:32.

4. *to make joyful.* Judg. 19:22.

5. *to adjust, prepare.* (Syr. ܛܝܒ.) Ex. 30:7. 2 K. 9:30. וַתֵּיטֶב אֶת־רֹאשָׁהּ *she adjusted her head (dress), composuit capillos.*

6. intrans. *to be good.* Mic. 2:7. Hence, construed with אֶל, *to please,* as in Kal, 1 Sam. 20:13.

Deriv. מֵיטָב.

יְטַב, fut. יִיטַב, Chald. *to be good.* Construed with עַל, *to be pleasing.* Ezra 7:18.

יָטְבָתָה Num. 33:33. Deut. 10:7. proper name of a station of the Israelites in the desert, abounding in brooks. Probably different from יָטְבָה 2 K. 21:19.

יְטוּר m. proper name of a son of Ishmael. Gen. 25:15. 1 Chron. 1:31. Hence, *his posterity, the Itureans,* who were engaged in war with the tribes beyond Jordan, 1 Chron. 5:19, 20. This agrees with the situation of Iturea, (Luke 3:1.) a mountainous district between Syria and the desert of Arabia. See Reland's Palæstina, p. 106.

יַיִן m. prim. dec. VI. f.

1. *wine.*

2. *intoxication.* Gen. 9:24. 1 Sam. 1:14. 25:37.

יַךְ 1 Sam. 4:13 Kethib, an evident corruption for יַד *on the side,* which stands in the Keri.

יָכַח in Kal not used, prob. i. q. Arab. وجه, وجح, *to be clear, evident,* (כ and ג being interchanged.)

Hiph. הוֹכִיחַ.

1. *to shew, prove.* Job 13:15 אַךְ־דְּרָכַי אֶל־פָּנָיו אוֹכִיחַ *surely I will prove my ways (righteous) before him,* i.e. I will justify my ways before him, 19:5.

2. *to correct, reprove, convince, refute.* Job 32:12. Construed with לְ, Prov. 9:7, 8. 15:12. 19:25. Used absolutely, Ezek. 3:26. comp. Prov. 25:12. Amos 5:10. Is. 29:21. Particularly with reproach or censure, hence,

3. *to rebuke, reproach, censure.* Job 6:25 מַה־יּוֹכִיחַ הוֹכֵחַ מִכֶּם *what does your reproaching prove?* 13:10. 40:2 מוֹכִיחַ אֱלוֹהַּ *he that reproacheth God.* Gen. 21:25 וְהוֹכִחַ אַבְרָהָם אֶת אֲבִימֶלֶךְ *and Abraham reproached Abimelech.* Also, *to revile,* 2 K. 19:4. Is. 37:4.

4. *to punish,* spoken particularly of God. Job 5:17. Prov. 3:12. Ps. 6:2. 38:2. 94:10. 105:14. 141:5. (Often parall. with יִסַּר.)

5. *to judge, decide,* spoken of a judge, i. q. שָׁפַט. Is. 11:3. Hence, construed with לְ, *to do justice* to any one, (like

(שָׁפַט ,דִּין,) 11:4. construed with בֵּין, *to decide between* parties, Gen. 31:37. Job 9:33.

6. construed with לְ, *to appoint* or *destine for* any one. Gen. 24:14, 44.

7. *to contend with* any one, (comp. נָדוֹן ,נִשְׁפַּט and Niph.) construed with אֶל, Job 13:3. with לְ, 16:21. with an accus. 22:4. Literally, *to seek to confute* any one.

Hoph. pass. of no. 4. Job 33:19.

Niph. נוֹכַח 1. *to be confuted*. Gen. 20:16 וְנֹכָחַת *and she (Sarah) was confuted*, i. e. she could say nothing in her defence.

2. recipr. *to contend with* any one. Job 23:7. Is. 1:18.

Hithpa. הִתְוַכַּח i. q. Niph. no. 2. Mic. 6:2.

Deriv. תּוֹכֵחָה ,תּוֹכַחַת.

יָכֹל rarely יָכוֹל 2 Chr. 7:7. 32:14. fut. יוּכַל (strictly fut. Hoph. but in use the same as fut. Kal,) inf. absol. יָכוֹל, const. יְכֹלֶת.

1. *to be able.* Construed generally with לְ and an infin. Gen. 13:6, 16. 45:1, 3. Ex. 7:21, 24. sometimes without לְ, Ex. 2:3. 18:23. Num. 22:6. also with a finite verb, Est. 8:6 אֵיכָכָה אוּכַל וְרָאִיתִי *how can I see* etc.? with an accus. Job 42:2. Also in a moral sense, Gen. 37:4 *they could not speak peaceably unto him.* Job 4:2. Hos. 8:5 עַד־מָתַי לֹא יוּכְלוּ נִקָּיֹן *how long shall they be unable*, i. e. indisposed, (*to do*) *what is innocent*, supply לַעֲשׂוֹת.

2. *to be permitted* (by law). Gen. 43:32. Num. 9:6. Deut. 12:17.

3. *to be able to endure, to suffer.* (We may supply לָשֵׂאת from Jer. 44:22. Prov. 30:21. or הָכִיל from Amos 7:10.) Ps. 101:5. Is. 1:13.

4. *to prevail*, or *obtain the mastery over* any one; construed with לְ of the person, Gen. 32:26. with a suffix, Jer. 20:10. Ps. 13:5. Applied to the mind, Ps. 139:6. Used absolutely, *to conquer, to get the upper hand*, Gen. 30:8. 32:28. Hos. 12:4. Also, in general, *to go through* or *execute* any thing, Jer. 3:5. 20:7. 1 K. 22:22.

יְכִל ,יְכֵל Chald. fut יִכֻּל Dan. 3:29. 5:16. and with the Hebrew form יוּכַל 2:10.

1. *to be able*, construed with לְ and an infin. Dan. 2:47. 3:17. 4:34. [4:37.]

2. *to prevail over*, construed with לְ. Dan. 7:21.

יָלַד and **יָלֵד** (Arab. وَلَدَ,) fut. יֵלֵד, infin. absol. יָלוֹד and לֶדֶת ,יָלֹד, const. לֶדֶת, once לֵת (1 Sam. 4:19.) with suff. לִדְתָּהּ.

1. *to bring forth*, as a mother. Gen. 4:1, 22. 16:1, 15. Part. fem. יוֹלֵדָה *one that brings forth*, used poetically for *a mother*, Prov. 17:25. 23:25. Cant. 6:8. Sometimes elliptically, Gen. 6:4. וְיָלְדוּ לָהֶם *and they bare to them (children).* 16:1. וְשָׂרַי אֵשֶׁת אַבְרָם לֹא יָלְדָה לוֹ *and Sarai, Abram's wife, did not bear to him (children).* 30:1. (comp. Niph. and Pual.) Frequently used metaphorically, as in Job 15:35 *they conceive mischief and bring forth wickedness.* Ps. 7:15. comp. Is. 33:11.

2. *to beget*, as a father. Gen. 4:18. 10:8, 13. So metaphorically Jehovah, addressing the Messiah or king of Israel, says, Ps. 2:7 *thou art my son, this day have I begotten thee;* without a figure, *thou art a king, to day do I appoint thee.* Hence, metaphorically, *to make, produce, form, create*, Deut. 32:18. Jer. 2:27. (Comp. אָב no. 3.)

3. *to lay (eggs), parere (ova).* Jer. 17:11.

Niph. נוֹלַד *to be born;* often with אֵת before the nominative of the subject, Gen. 4:18 וַיִּוָּלֵד לַחֲנוֹךְ אֶת־עִירָד *and unto Enoch was born Irad.* 21:15. 46:20. Num. 26:60. Also used elliptically, like Kal no. 1. Gen. 17:17 הַלְּבֶן מֵאָה־שָׁנָה יִוָּלֵד *shall (a son) be born to one an hundred years old?*

Note. The form נוּלְּדוּ 1 Chr. 3:5. 20:8. is the pret. Niph. with Dagesh euphonic, for נוֹלְדוּ.

Pi. יִלֵּד *to help to bring forth, to deliver*, as a midwife. Ex. 1:16. Part. fem. מְיַלֶּדֶת *a midwife*, Ex. 1:17 ff.

Pu. יֻלַּד and יוּלַּד *to be born*, as in Niph. Gen. 4:26. also elliptically, as in Kal and Niph. Gen. 10:21 וּלְשֵׁם יֻלַּד גַּם הוּא *and to Shem, also to him were (sons) born.* Used metaphorically of inanimate nature, Ps. 90:2.

Hiph. הוֹלִיד 1. *to cause to bring forth* (children). Is. 66:9. Used metaphorically of the earth, *to cause to bring forth* (fruit). Is. 55:10.

2. *to beget*, as a father. Gen. 5:4, 7, 10, 13 ff. 11:11 ff. Figuratively Job 38:28 מִי־הוֹלִיד אֶגְלֵי־טָל *who begat the drops of the dew?*

Hoph. only in the infin. הֻלֶּדֶת Gen. 40:20 and הוּלֶּדֶת Ezek. 16:4, 5. *a being born*, as Gen. 40:20 יוֹם הֻלֶּדֶת אֶת־פַּרְעֹה *the birthday of Pharaoh.*

Hithpa. הִתְיַלֵּד *to be enrolled in the family registers*, (סֵפֶר תּוֹלְדוֹת.) Num. 1:18. see הִתְיַחֵשׂ.

Deriv. out of course מוֹלֶדֶת, תּוֹלְדוֹת, וָלָד, וָלָד, יִלּוֹד, יָלִיד.

יֶלֶד m. verbal from יָלַד, dec. VI. a. and h.

1. *a child, boy, youth.* Gen. 21:8 ff. Ex. 2:3 ff.—Is. 2:6 יַלְדֵי נָכְרִים *sons of strangers*, i. e. simply strangers, like the Greek υἷες Ἀχαιῶν. Is. 57:4 יַלְדֵי פֶשַׁע *children of transgression*, i. e. transgressors. The plur. יְלָדִים is sometimes used of both sexes, like בָּנִים, 1 Sam. 1:2. Ezra 10:1.

2. *the young* of animals. Is. 11:7.

יַלְדָּה fem. of יֶלֶד, dec. XII. a. *a girl, a young woman.* Gen. 34:4. Joel 4:3. [3:3.]

יַלְדוּת f. denom. from יֶלֶד, dec. X.

1. *boyhood, youth.* Ecc. 11:9, 10.

2. *young men.* Ps. 110:3.

יִלּוֹד m. verbal from יָלַד, dec. I. a. *born.* Ex. 1:22. Josh. 5:5.

יָלוּן see **לוּן**.

יָלִיד m. verbal from יָלַד, dec. III. a. *born, a son, natus.* Num. 13:22 יְלִידֵי הָעֲנָק *the sons of Anak.* 2 Sam. 21:16 יְלִידֵי הָרָפָה *the sons of Raphah*, i. q. רְפָאִים. More frequently יְלִיד בַּיִת *a slave born in one's house, verna*, Gen. 14:14. 17:12, 13.

יָלַךְ i. q. הָלַךְ *to go*, which forms some of its tenses from this verb. See הָלַךְ.

יָלַל found only in Hiph. הֵילִיל, fut. יְיֵלִיל *to lament, to wail.* Is. 13:6. 15:4. 23:1, 14. Jer. 25:34. Am. 8:3 הֵילִילוּ שִׁירוֹת הֵיכָל *the songs of the palace shall wail*, i. e. be turned into wailings. Is. 52:5 מֹשְׁלָיו יְהֵילִילוּ *their princes lament.* For הוּלָלוּ Ps. 78:63, see under הָלַל.

יְלֵל m. verbal from יָלַל, *lamentation, wailing*, or perhaps *howling* of wild animals. Once Deut. 32:10.

יְלָלָה f. const. יִלְלַת, verbal from יָלַל, dec. XI. c. *lamentation.* Is. 15:8. Jer. 25:36. Zech. 11:3.

יָלַע probably i. q. לָעָה *to speak inconsiderately* or *rashly*, (synon. בָּטָא.) Prov. 20:25. (Arab. لغي *idem;* see Cor. Sur. II. 225.)

יַלֶּפֶת f. Lev. 21:20. 25:22. a kind of itching scab or tetter. Sept. λειχήν. Vulg. *impetigo.* Root perhaps ילף=Arab. ولف *to adhere, stick.*

יֶלֶק m. a species of locust, Ps. 105:34. Joel 1:4. 2:25. Nah. 3:15. It was winged, Nah. 3:16. and bristly or hairy, Jer. 51:27. Root ילק according to some i. q. Arab. يلق *to be white;* but more prob. i. q. לקק *to lick, to eat off*, comp. לחך Num. 22:4. See Bocharti Hieroz. P. II. p. 443.

יַלְקוּט m. verbal from לָקַט, *a sack, pouch, bag.* 1 Sam. 17:40.

יָם m. prim. (with Kamets impure, even before Makkeph, except in the phrase יַם־סוּף.) plur. יַמִּים, dec. VIII. a.

1. *a sea, an inland sea* or *lake.*—יָם־כִּנֶּרֶת *the Sea of Chinnereth*, Num. 34:11. afterwards called *the Lake of Gennesaret, or Sea of Galilee.* יָם־הַמֶּלַח *the salt Sea*, Gen. 14:3. also called יָם הָעֲרָבָה *the sea of the desert*, Deut. 3:17. i. q. the Dead Sea. יַם־סוּף *the Sea of Reeds, the Red Sea*, Ex. 15:4—The Mediterranean Sea is called הַיָּם by way of emi-

nence, הַיָּם הַגָּדוֹל *the Great Sea*, Num. 34 : 6, 7. or הַיָּם הָאַחֲרוֹן *the Western Sea*, Deut. 11 : 24. The Galilean Sea is also called הַיָּם Is. 8 : 23. [9 : 1.]

2. *a large river;* spoken of the Nile, Is. 19 : 5. Nah. 3 : 8. of the Euphrates, Jer. 51 : 36. Plur. יַמִּים spoken of the streams of the Nile, Ezek. 32 : 2. (So the Arab. يَمّ is sometimes used.)

3. *the west*, since the Mediterranean Sea lay to the *west* of Palestine.—Hence, רוּחַ יָם *a west wind*, Ex. 10 : 19. פְּאַת־יָם *the west side*, Ex. 27 : 12. 38 : 12. יָמָּה *towards the west*, Gen. 28 : 14. Ex. 26 : 22. (also, *towards the sea*, Ex. 10 : 19. but in this sense more frequently הַיָּמָּה.) מִיָּם *on the west*, 12 : 8. מִיָּם לְ *on the west of*, Josh. 8 : 9, 12, 13.—In two passages, Ps. 107 : 3. Is. 49 : 12. יָם stands opposed to מִצָּפוֹן, but ought still to be rendered *the west;* comp. Am. 8 : 12. Deut. 33 : 23.

4. יָם הַנְּחֹשֶׁת 2 K. 25 : 13. 1 Chr. 18 : 8. *the brazen sea*, a great basin in the priests' court of the temple.

יָמִים plur. of יוֹם, q. v.

יָמוֹת *idem.*

יֵמִים masc. plur. found only Gen. 36 : 24. most prob. *hot springs*, (perhaps those of Calirrhoë, which are found in the country spoken of.) So Vulg. *aquæ calidæ:* and according to Jerome, the word continued to have this signification in Punic. Syr. *aquæ*. The Samar. text has הָאֵימִים *Emims, giants;* so Onkelos and Pseudo-Jonathan. In the Arabic and Veneto-Greek versions, *mules*.

יָמִין subst. dec. III. a.

1. masc. gen. *the right side.*—עַל יָמִין *to the right*, Gen. 24 : 49. 30 : 12. Also simply יָמִין (as an accus. used adverbially,) *to the right, towards the right.* Num. 20 : 17. 22 : 26. Deut. 2 : 26. 5 : 32. Hence used as a genitive after other substantives, שׁוֹק הַיָּמִין *the right shoulder*, literally, *the shoulder of the right side*, Ex. 29 : 22. עֵין יָמִין *the right eye*, 1 Sam. 11 : 2. יַד יְמִינִי *my right hand*, Ps. 73 : 23. Jer. 22 : 24.

2. without יָד, *the right hand.* In this sense it is both masc. and fem. (as if the name of a double member,) e. g. masc. Lam. 2 : 4. Prov. 27 : 16. elsewhere fem.—Ps. 80 : 18 אִישׁ יְמִינֶךָ *the man of thy right hand*, i. e. the man whom thy right hand guideth. Ps. 16 : 8 *he is at my right hand*, i. e. he assists me. Ps. 119 : 31. 121 : 5.

3. *the south side, the south.* (See אָחוֹר Note.) 1 Sam. 23 : 19 מִימִין הַיְשִׁימוֹן *on the south of the desert.* verse 24. 2 Sam. 24 : 5. Also, *in the south*, Job 23 : 9.

4. *prosperity*. (Arab. يُمْن.) So in the proper name בִּנְיָמִין. Gen. 35 : 18. Hence,

Hiph. הֵימִין and הֵמִין (2 Sam. 14 : 19.) denom. from יָמִין.

1. *to turn to the right.* Gen. 13 : 9. Ezek. 21 : 21. In this signification we likewise find תַּאֲמִינוּ Is. 30 : 21.

2. *to use the right hand, to be right-handed.* 1 Chr. 12 : 2 מַיְמִינִים *using the right hand.*

יְמִינִי 1. i. q. יְמָנִי *dexter*, but found only in the Kethib of 2 Chr. 3 : 17. Ezek. 4 : 6.

2. בֶּן־יְמִינִי *a Benjamite*, a gentile noun from בִּנְיָמִין *Benjamin*. 1 Sam. 9 : 21. Ps. 7 : 1. With the article, בֶּן־הַיְמִינִי *the Benjamite*, Judg. 3 : 18. 2 Sam. 16 : 11. Plur. בְּנֵי יְמִינִי *Benjamites*, Judg. 19 : 16. 1 Sam. 22 : 7. So in the same sense אִישׁ יְמִינִי, 1 Sam. 9 : 1. 2 Sam. 20 : 1. Est. 2 : 5.—אֶרֶץ יְמִינִי *the country of Benjamin*, 1 Sam. 9 : 4.

יְמָנִי fem. יְמָנִית, denom. adj. from יָמִין, *dexter, dextra, dextrum.* Ex. 29 : 20. Lev. 8 : 23, 24.

יָמַר Hithpa. הִתְיַמֵּר *to boast one's self*, or *to exercise dominion*. Is. 61 : 6. comp. הֶאֱמִיר Ps. 94 : 4. (Also in Arabic the verbs אמר, ימר, ومر, interchange their signification in several conjugations.)

יָמַשׁ i. q. מָשַׁשׁ, but doubtful. Once Judg. 16 . 26 Kethib הימשני (read הֲמִישֵׁנִי) *let me touch.* The Yod, however, may be merely a mater lectionis.

יָנָה, fut. יִינֶה. 1. *to exercise violence.* Part. Zeph. 3:1 הָעִיר הַיּוֹנָה *the oppressive city.*—חֶרֶב הַיּוֹנָה *the oppressive sword,* Jer. 46:16. 50:16. without חֶרֶב 25:38 חֲרוֹן הַיּוֹנָה prob. *the anger of the oppressive sword.*

2. *to annihilate, destroy.* Ps. 74:8. נִינָם יָחַד *let us destroy them all.*

Hiph. הוֹנָה, fut. יוֹנֶה, *to oppress* any one, in civil matters, (synon. עָשַׁק,) Ex. 22:20. Lev. 19:33. Ezek. 18:7 ff. *to overreach,* in buying and selling, Lev. 25:14, 17. *to oppress* a people, Is. 49:26. *to dispossess,* construed with מִן, Ezek. 46:18. (Chald. Aph. אוֹנִי *idem.*)

יָנוֹחַ (*he rests*) proper name of a place on the borders of the tribes Ephraim and Manasseh. 2 K. 15:29. with ה local יָנוֹחָה, Josh. 16:6, 7.

ינח found only in Hiph. הִנִּיחַ (with assimilated Yod,) kindred with נוּחַ *to rest.*

1. *to lay* or *put down.* 1 K. 13:29, 30. especially, *to deposit* before Jehovah, Ex. 16:33, 34. Num. 17:4.—Ezek. 22:20 וְהִנַּחְתִּי וְהִתַּכְתִּי אֶתְכֶם *so will I put you (in the furnace) and melt you.*

2. *to erect* or *set up* an idol. 2 K. 17:29.

3. *to remove* or *transfer* (to another place). Ezek. 37:14. Is. 14:1. 2 Chr. 1:14. הִנִּיחַ בְּמִשְׁמָר *to imprison, to put under arrest,* Lev. 24:12. Num. 15:34.

4. *to throw out* or *away,* as ashes. Num. 19:9. Figuratively, Am. 5:7 וּצְדָקָה לָאָרֶץ הִנִּיחוּ *and they throw righteousness to the ground.* Intrans. *to cast itself down,* spoken of a storm of hail. Is. 28:2.

5. *to let, leave,* (kindred in sense with עָזַב, נָטַשׁ,) in many constructions; as (1.) *to leave behind.* Gen. 42:33. Judg. 2:23. 3:1. (2.) *to leave undisturbed, to let alone, to suffer.* Est. 3:8. Hence, הַנִּיחָה לִּי *let me alone,* Ex. 32:10. Hos. 4:17. 2 Sam. 16:11 הַנִּחוּ לוֹ וִיקַלֵּל *let him curse me.* Also, Judg. 16:26 הַנִּיחָה אוֹתִי *suffer me.* (3.) הִנִּיחַ יָד מִן *to withdraw* or *withhold the hand from* any thing. Ecc. 7:18. 11:6. (4.) *to forsake,* Jer. 14:9, *to give over to* any one, construed with לְ. Ps. 119:121. (5.) *to leave remaining,* Ex. 16:23, 24. Lev. 7:15. Construed with a dative of the person *for* whom, Ps. 17:14. Ecc. 2:18. (6.) *to suffer to do* any thing, construed with an accusative of the person, and לְ of the action, (comp. the construction with נָטַשׁ Gen. 31:28, and with נָתַן.) Ps. 105:14 לֹא הִנִּיחַ אָדָם לְעָשְׁקָם *he suffered no one to oppress them.* In the parallel passage 1 Chr. 16:21, we find לְאִישׁ.

6. i. q. הֵנִיחַ *to pacify, prevent.* Ecc. 10:4.

Hoph. הֻנַּח *to be put down.* Zech. 5:11. (comp. Dan. 7:4.) Part. מֻנָּח *left remaining,* spoken of the space between two walls, Ezek. 41:9, 11.

יְנִיקָה f. verbal from יָנַק, dec. X. i. q. יוֹנֶקֶת, *a sprout, shoot, sucker.* Ezek. 17:4. It is a passive form with an active signification. (Aram. יְנִיק, יְנוּק, ܝܢܘܩܐ *a suckling.*)

יָנַק, fut. יִינַק, *to suck,* (at the mother's breast.) Job 3:12. Construed with an accus. Cant. 8:1. Joel 2:16. comp. Job 20:16. Metaphorically, *to enjoy,* Deut. 33:19 כִּי שֶׁפַע יַמִּים יִינָקוּ *for they shall enjoy the abundance of the seas.* Is. 60:16. 66:11, 12. Part. יוֹנֵק *a suckling* or *suckling child,* Deut. 32:25. Ps. 8:3. (For the signification, *a sucker,* see יוֹנֵק.)

Hiph. הֵינִיק 1. *to give suck, to suckle* (a child). Gen. 21:7. Ex. 2:7, 9. 1 Sam. 1:23. Spoken also of animals, Gen. 32:15. Part. מֵינֶקֶת *one who suckles, a nurse;* with suff. מֵינִקְתּוֹ 2 K. 11. 12. plur. מֵינִיקוֹת Is. 49:23.

2. metaphorically, *to cause to enjoy.* Deut. 32:13.

Deriv. יוֹנֵק, יְנִיקָה.

יַנְשׁוּף m. and יַנְשׁוֹף (Is. 34:11.) a species of bird, which is mentioned Lev. 11:17. Deut. 14:16. in connexion with several waterfowls, and in Is. 34:11, is said to inhabit the desert with the raven. Sept. and Vulg. *Ibis.* According to Bochart (Hieroz. P. II. p. 231 ff.) *owl* from נֶשֶׁף *twilight.*

יָסַד *to found* or *lay the foundation* (of a building). Ezra 3:12. Is. 54:11. This primary signification is more frequent in Piel, for in Kal the verb is used commonly in a metaphorical sense, as of the founding of the earth, Ps. 24:2. 78:69. Job 38:4. of the heavens, Am. 9:6.

2. metaphorically, *to establish, appoint, ordain.* Hab. 1:12 וְצוּר לְהוֹכִיחַ יְסַדְתּוֹ *O rock, for correction hast thou appointed it (the people of the Chaldees);* compare the exactly parallel member יְהוָה לְמִשְׁפָּט שַׂמְתּוֹ *O Jehovah, for judgment thou hast ordained it.* Comp. Pi. no. 2. Ps. 104:8 *to the place which thou hast appointed for them.*

3. *to throw up in a heap, to heap up.* 2 Chr. 31:7. (So יָדָה and רָמָא *to throw, to throw up, to found.*) Comp. עֲרֵמָה.

Niph. נוֹסַד 1. *to be founded,* spoken of a kingdom. Ex. 9:18. Is. 44:28.

2. denom. from סוֹד (for יְסוֹד) *a circle* or *body of counsellors;* hence, *to sit together and take counsel, to consult.* Ps. 2:2. 31:14. See סוֹד.

Pi. יִסַּד 1. *to found* (a building). Josh. 6:26. 1 K. 16:34. With an accus. of the material, 1 K. 5:31 [17] לְיַסֵּד הַבָּיִת אַבְנֵי גָזִית *to found the house with hewed stones.* For a similar construction, comp. בָּנָה.

2. metaphorically, *to appoint, ordain.* Ps. 8:3.

3. *to prepare, establish.* Est. 1:8. 1 Chr. 9:22 הֵמָּה יִסַּד דָּוִיד *them David had established.*

Pu. יֻסַּד *to be founded.* 1 K. 6:37. Construed with an accus. of the material. 1 K. 7:10.

Hoph. *idem.* Ezra 3:11. Infin. הוּסַד *the foundation,* 2 Chr. 3:3.

Deriv. out of course מוּסָד, מוֹסָד, מְיֻסָּד, סוֹד, יְסוּדָה, יְסוֹד.

יְסֹד m. verbal from יָסַד, *a foundation,* and metaphorically, *a beginning.* Ezra 7:9.

יְסוֹד m. verbal from יָסַד, dec. I. *basis, foundation;* e. g. of an altar, Ex. 29:12. Lev. 4:7 ff. Plur. יְסוֹדִים Mic. 1:6. and יְסוֹדוֹת Lam. 4:11. Ezek. 30:4.

יְסוּדָה f. verbal from יָסַד, dec. X. *a foundation.* Ps. 87:1.

יִסּוֹר m. verbal from יָסַר, (after the form גִּבּוֹר,) *a censurer, reproacher.* Job 40:2 הֲרֹב עִם שַׁדַּי יִסּוֹר *shall the reproacher (of God) contend with the Almighty.* (רֹב is the infin. absol. from רִיב, and is used for the finite verb; comp. Judg. 11:25.)

יָסוּר m. verbal from סוּר, (like יָרִיב from רִיב,) *one who departs.* Jer. 17:13 Kethib יְסוּרַי *they who depart from me,* for יְסוּרִים, like קָמַי for קָמִים עָלַי, שֹׂטְנַי. In the Keri סוּרַי.

יָסַךְ found only Ex. 30:32 לֹא יִיסָךְ *it shall not be poured.* It has the passive signification from סוּךְ, נָסַךְ, (like יָשַׂם from שׂוּם.) Perhaps it should be written יִסַּךְ.

יָסַף (in Kal and Hiphil,) fut. יֹסִיף, יֹסֵף, וַיֹּסֶף, infin. הוֹסִיף, part. יוֹסֵף (Is. 29:14. 38:5.) and מוֹסִיף (Neh. 13:18.)

1. *to add,* construed with an accus. and עַל, Lev. 5:16. 22:14. 27:13 ff. Deut. 19:9. or אֶל, 2 Sam. 24:3. Often used absolutely, *to add,* without specifying what is added, Deut. 12:32 לֹא תֹסֵף עָלָיו וְלֹא תִגְרַע מִמֶּנּוּ *thou shalt add nothing, and take nothing away;* comp. 4:2. Prov. 30:6. Ecc. 3:14. Hence,

2. *to increase, enlarge, addere (aliquid) ad—.* Ps. 71:14 וְהוֹסַפְתִּי עַל כָּל־תְּהִלָּתֶךָ *I will increase all thy praise.* 115:14. Ezra 10:10. Also construed with אֶל, Ezek. 23:14. with לְ, Is. 26:15. with an accus. Lev. 19:25. Job 42:10 וַיֹּסֶף יְהוָה אֶת־כָּל־אֲשֶׁר לְאִיּוֹב לְמִשְׁנֶה *and Jehovah increased all that Job had twofold.* Ecc. 1:18. *To increase* any thing to a person, is sometimes i. q. *to give* or *bestow in abundance,* Ps. 120:3 מַה־יִּתֵּן לְךָ וּמַה־יֹּסִיף לָךְ לָשׁוֹן רְמִיָּה *what does a false tongue give or bestow upon thee?* comp. Lev. 26:21. Ezek. 5:16.—*To enlarge* any thing is sometimes i. q. *to exceed,* 2 Chr. 9:6. comp. 1 K. 10:7.

3. Construed with an infin. of another verb, or with a finite verb, with and

without a copula, (e.g. Prov. 23:35. Is. 52:1. Hos. 1:6.) it expresses *the repetition* or *continuance* of an action, and may be rendered in English by various adverbs; as (1.) *again, once more, a second time.* Gen. 4:2 וַתֹּסֶף לָלֶדֶת *and she brought forth again.* 8:10, 12. 18:29 וַיֹּסֶף עוֹד לְדַבֵּר *he spake yet again.* 25:1. (2.) *further, longer.* Gen. 4:12 לֹא־תֹסֵף תֵּת־כֹּחָהּ לָךְ *it (the ground) shall no longer yield to thee its fruit.* Num. 32:15. Josh. 7:12. 1 Sam. 19:8. 27:4. Is. 47:1, 5. (3.) *more.* Gen. 37:5. וַיּוֹסִפוּ עוֹד שְׂנֹא אֹתוֹ *and they hated him yet more.* ver. 8. 1 Sam. 18:29. 2 Sam. 3:34. The action itself, the repetition or continuance of which is intended, is often omitted, and must be supplied from the context, Job 20:9. 34:32. 38:11. 40:5, 32. Ex. 11:6 *there has been none like this,* וְכָמֹהוּ לֹא תֹסִף, namely לִהְיוֹת, *and there shall be none again like it.* Num. 11:25 *and when the spirit rested upon them they prophesied,* וְלֹא יָסָפוּ, namely לְהִתְנַבֵּא, *and (afterwards) never again.*

Note. The future of this verb is sometimes written יֹאסֵף, Ex. 5:7. 1 Sam. 28:29. On the other hand יוֹסֵף Ps. 104:29. 2 Sam. 6:1. has the signification of אָסַף, being used for יֶאֱסֹף.—For the imper. Kal we twice find סְפוּ, which, however, with the infin. סְפוֹת, may be derived from a form סָפָה.

Niph. נוֹסַף 1. *to be added, to add* or *join one's self.* Ex. 1:10. Num. 36:3, 4.

2. *to be increased, to increase, augeri divitiis.* Prov. 11:24.

יְסַף Chald. *idem.*

Hoph. הוּסַף *to be added.* Dan. 4:33. [4:36.]

יָסַר in Kal only fut. אֶסֳּרֵם Hos. 10:10. Is. 8:11. and part. יֹסֵר Prov. 9:7. Ps. 94:10. elsewhere in

Pi. יִסַּר, fut. יְיַסֵּר, infin. also יַסְּרָה Lev. 26:18. and יַסֵּר Ps. 118:18.

1. *to instruct, admonish.* Prov. 9:7. Job 4:3. (comp. Hos. 7:15.) Ps. 16:7 אַף־לֵילוֹת יִסְּרוּנִי כִלְיוֹתָי *also by night my reins admonish me,* namely, to thankfulness. Used particularly of the admonitions of parents to children, Deut. 21:18. and of God to men, Deut. 4:36. 8:5. Ps. 94:12. Construed with two accusatives, Prov. 31:1. As this admonition is often connected with, or contained in, *correction, punishment;* hence

2. *to correct, chastise.* 1 K. 12:11, 14. Used of the chastisement of children, Prov. 19:18. 29:17. and of men by the Almighty, Lev. 26:18, 28. Ps. 6:2. (The ideas *to instruct* and *to chastise* are, as in Hebrew, also united in the words παιδεύειν, *castigare.*)

Hiph. i. q. Pi. אַיְסִירֵם Hos. 7:12.

Niph. נוֹסַר *to be warned, to receive warning.* Lev. 26:18. Ps. 2:10. Jer. 6:8. Prov. 29:19. The form נִוַּסְּרוּ Ezek. 23:48, is, according to the present punctuation, an example of the (Rabbinical) conjugation. Nithpa. for נִתְיַסְּרוּ. Perhaps it should be pointed נוֹסְרוּ.

Deriv. מוּסָר, יִסּוֹר.

יָע m. (for יָעֶה) verbal from יָעָה, dec. I. usually rendered, *shovel.* Vulg. *forceps.* (In Arabic some derivatives from وعى signify a *vessel.*) Ex. 27:3. 38:3. Num. 4:14. 1 K. 7:40, 45.

יָעַד, fut. יִעַד.

1. *to fix, appoint,* (a time, or place.) Jer. 47:7. 2 Sam. 20:5.

2. *to appoint* (a punishment), *to threaten.* Mic. 6:9.

3. *to appoint for a wife* or *concubine, to betroth, desponsare.* Ex. 21:8, 9.

Niph. נוֹעַד 1. reflex. *to come to the place agreed upon with* any one, *to meet with* any one; construed with לְ, Ex. 25:22. 29:42, 43. 30:6, 36. with אֶל, Num. 10:4.

2. recipr. *to agree upon a place of meeting, to meet by appointment.* Neh. 6:2, 10. Job 2:11. Amos 3:3. Hence

3. *to come together* generally. Josh. 11:5. 1 K. 3:5. Construed with עַל *against* any one, spoken of conspirators, Num. 14:35. 16:11. 27:3.

Hiph. הוֹעִיד *to appoint for* any one, especially a day for trial. Job 9:19. מִי יוֹעִידֵנִי *quis diem mihi dicet?* Jer. 49:19. 50:44.

Hoph. 1. *to be placed.*

2. *to be directed,* spoken of the face. Ezek. 21: 21. [16.]

Deriv. עֵדָה, מוֹעֵד, מוֹעָד, מוֹעָדָה, מוּעָדָה.

יָעָה found only Is. 28:17. *to clear away, to sweep away.* (Arab. وعي i. q. אָסַף *to collect, to sweep away;* Ethiop. ותי *totum absumsit.*) See יָע.

יָעַז prob. i. q. עָזַז, found only in Niph. Is. 33:19 עַם נוֹעָז *a strong* or *wicked people.*

יְעוֹרִים masc. plur. *woods,* i. q. יְעָרִים. Ezek. 34:25 Kethib.

יַעְזֵר and יַעְזֵיר a city in the tribe of Gad, on the east of Jordan, on the borders of Ammon. Num. 21:32. 32:1. Is. 16:8. In Greek Ἰαζὴρ 1 Mac. 5:8.

יָעַט i. q. עָטָה *to clothe.* Once Is. 61:10 יְעָטָנִי.

יְעַט Chald. i. q. Heb. יָעַץ *to counsel, advise.* Part. יָעֵט *a counseller* or *minister of the king,* Ezra 7:14, 15.

Ithpa. *to consult together.* Dan. 6:8.

Deriv. עֵטָא.

יָעַל in Kal not used. Probably *to be useful;* comp. יַעַל in the compound בְּלִיַּעַל.

Hiph. הוֹעִיל, 1. *to profit, to help.* Used absolutely, Prov. 10:2. 11:4. Jer. 2:8 אַחֲרֵי לֹא יוֹעִלוּ הָלָכוּ *they follow after those who profit nothing,* i. e. after idols. Construed with a dative of the person, Is. 30:5. Jer. 23:32. or of the thing, Job 30:13 לְהַוָּתִי יֹעִילוּ *they help my fall.* With suff. יוֹעִילוּךְ Is. 57:12.

2. intrans. *to receive profit,* or *to gain,* from any thing, *proficere.* Job 21:15 מַה־נּוֹעִיל *what shall we gain?* 35:3. Is. 47:12.

יָעֵל m. plur. יְעֵלִים, const. יַעֲלֵי, dec. V. b. *a wild he-goat,* Arab. وَعِل, comp. Bocharti Hieroz. P. I. p. 915 ff. 1 Sam. 24:3 צוּרֵי הַיְּעֵלִים (*the rocks of the wild goats*) proper name of certain rocks in the desert of Engedi. In the Arabic and Hebrew, the word probably denoted also *the chamois-goat.*

יַעֲלָה fem. of יָעֵל, dec. X. *a wild she-goat,* or *chamois;* but used as a word of endearment to a lovely female, as the word gazelle is used in Arabic. Prov. 5:19. The Arabians have the phrase, *more beautiful than a wild goat,* (الوعل.) Bochart I. 899.

יַעַן (for יַעֲנֶה) subst. *purpose, aim,* from the verb עָנָה i. q. Arab. عني *to intend, mean, have in view.* Hence

1. as a prep. *on account of.* Ezek. 5:9. Hag. 1:9. Is. 37:29.

2. as a conj. *because.* Num. 20:12. 2 K. 22:19. often joined with אֲשֶׁר *because that,* (construed with a pret.) Judg. 2:20. *so that,* (construed with a fut.) Ezek. 20:16. or with כִּי. Num. 11:20.

3. יַעַן וּבְיַעַן Lev. 26:43. Ezek. 13:10. and without ו, 36:3. *because, even because,* as an intensitive.

יְעֵנִים masc. epicene. Lam. 4:3 Keri *the ostriches,* i. q. בְּנוֹת יַעֲנָה, here spoken of the female. Sept. ὡς στρουθίον. Vulg. *sicut struthio.* (For a parallel in sense, comp. Job 39:17.)

יַעֲנָה fem. of the preceeding, but found only in the phrase בַּת הַיַּעֲנָה, plur. בְּנוֹת יַעֲנָה, *the ostrich.* Comp. יָעֵל, fem. יַעֲלָה. (In like manner the ostrich is called in Arab. نعام, نعامة and بنت نعامة, and the latter expression sometimes includes the male.) See Bocharti Hieroz. P. II. p. 230. Lev. 11:16. Deut. 14:15. This bird inhabits the waste places, Is. 13:21. 34:13. and is noted for its doleful cry, Mic. 1:8. Job 30:29. comp. Shaw's Travels, p. 449, 455. According to others, *the owl,* but in opposition to the ancient versions, and by a false derivation from ענה. The word is probably primitive.

יָעַף, fut. יִיעַף, Arab. وغف.

1. *to run swiftly.* See Hoph. and Deriv. יְעָף and תּוֹעָפוֹת.

2. *to be weary, fatigued,* e. g. by running, Jer. 2:24 מְבַקְשֶׁיהָ לֹא יִיעָפוּ Luth.

they who seek her need not run far. Is. 40:30, 31. by hard labour, Is. 40:28. 44:12. Hab. 2:13. comp. Jer. 51:58.

Hoph. Dan. 9:21 מֻעָף בִּיעָף *being caused to run quickly.* Sept. ταχυ φερομενος.

יָעֵף m. verbal from יָעַף, *wearied, fatigued.* Is. 40:29. 30:4.

יְעָף m. verbal from יָעַף, *rapid course.* Dan. 9:21.

יָעַץ, fut. יִיעַץ, imper. twice עֻצוּ (from עוּץ) Judg. 19:30. Is. 8:10.

1. *to advise, to give advice.* 2 Sam. 17:11, 15. also יָעַץ עֵצָה in the same sense, 16:23. 17:7. Construed with a dative of the person, Job 26:3. with a suff. Ex. 18:19. 1 K. 1:12. 12:8, 13.

2. *to take counsel, to purpose, resolve.* Ps. 62:5. 2 Chr. 25:16. Construed with עַל, *against* any one. Is. 7:5. 19:17. and with אֶל, Jer. 49:20.—יָעַץ זִמּוֹת *to form evil purposes,* Is. 32:7.

3. *to consult* or *provide for* any one, *consulere alicui.* With a suff. Ps. 16:7. 32:8 אִיעֲצָה עָלֶיךָ עֵינִי an elliptical construction for אִיעָצְךָ וְאָשִׂימָה עָלֶיךָ עֵינִי *I will consult for thee and direct mine eye to thee,* i. e. I will be gracious to thee. (In Old German and Swiss *Rath* (*counsel*) signifies also *care, support.*)

4. *to predict, foretel.* Num. 24:14. (In Arab. وعظ *to admonish, to instruct concerning the future.*)

Part. יוֹעֵץ *an adviser,* Prov. 11:14. 24:6. hence *a counsellor* or *minister of the king,* 1 Chr. 27:32, 33. Ezra 7:28. 8:25. (comp. 7:24, 25.) spoken of the seven principal Persian ministers. Hence יוֹעֲצִים often parallel with kings, princes, Job 3:14. 12:17. Is. 1:26.

Niph. נוֹעַץ. 1. reflex. *to receive advice* or *counsel.* Prov. 13:10.

2. recipr. *to consult together, to advise mutually.* Ps. 71:10. 83:6. Construed with עִם, 1 Chr. 13:1. with אֶת, Is. 40:14. 1 K. 12:6, 8. with אֶל, 2 K. 6:8. 2 Chr. 20:21.

3. *to advise, give counsel.* 1 K. 12:6. 9. Spoken also of individuals, *to take counsel,* 1 K. 12:28. 2 Chr. 30:23.

Hithpa. i. q. Niph. no. 2. Ps. 83:4.

Deriv. עֵצָה, מוֹעֵצָה.

יַעֲקֹב m. (*holding the heel, supplanting;* comp. Gen. 25:26. 27:36. Hos. 12:4.) proper name of the second son of Isaac, and progenitor of the Israelites. Gen. xxv.—l.—אֱלֹהֵי יַעֲקֹב *the God of Jacob, Jehovah,* Is. 2:3. Ps. 20:2.—בֵּית יַעֲקֹב and simply יַעֲקֹב *the Israelitish people, the Israelites,* i. q. יִשְׂרָאֵל; but used only in the poetical books and in the prophets, where it is often parallel with יִשְׂרָאֵל; comp. יְשֻׁרוּן. But in the historical books we always find יִשְׂרָאֵל used. Sometimes the people are considered as a single person; e. g. Is. xli. xliii. etc. It is comparatively seldom, that it is used for *the kingdom of Israel,* in opposition to that of Judah, as Hos. 12:3. or like Israel in the later books for *the kingdom of Judah,* as Obad. 18.

I. **יַעַר** m. plur. ־ִים and ־וֹת, dec. VI. c.

1. *a wood, forest.* Deut. 19:5. Josh. 17:15, 18. (Syr. ܥܵܒܵܐ *a thicket.*)—בֵּית הַיַּעַר *the house of the forest,* Is. 22:8. and more fully בֵּית יַעַר הַלְּבָנוֹן *the house of the forest of Lebanon,* 1 K. 7:2. 10:17. namely, *the arsenal of king Solomon,* otherwise called נֶשֶׁק Neh. 3:19.

2. proper name, prob. i. q. קִרְיַת יְעָרִים Ps. 132:6.

II. **יַעַר** m. dec. VI. c. Cant. 5:1. and יַעְרַת הַדְּבַשׁ f. 1 Sam. 14:27. *a honeycomb, favus mellis.*

יָפָה, fut. יִיפֶה, יִיף, *to be fair, beautiful.* Cant. 4:10. 7:1, 6.

Pi. *to make beautiful, to adorn.* Jer. 10:4.

Pu. a rare conjugation, formed by the reduplication of the two first radicals, יָפְיָפִיתָ *to be very beautiful.* Ps. 45:3.

Hithpa. *to adorn one's self.* Jer. 4:30.

Deriv. out of course יְפִי, יֳפִי.

יָפֶה m. const. יְפֵה, dec. IX. b. fem. יָפָה, const. יְפַת, with suff. יָפָתִי, dec. XI. a. verbal adj. from יָפָה.

1. *fair,* spoken of persons. 2 Sam. 13:1. 14:25. often with the addition מַרְאֶה,

1 Sam. 17 : 42. or יְפֵה מַרְאֶה, Gen. 29 : 17. Also spoken of animals, Gen. 41 : 2 ff. of countries, Ps. 48 : 3.

2. *proper, suitable, becoming.* Ecc. 3 : 11.

יְפֵה־פִיָּה f. Jer. 46 : 20. *beautiful*, after the form פְּקַחְקֹחַ, only ה quiescing in the middle of a word should be changed into י. This circumstance probably has occasioned its being divided into two words.

יָפוֹ Jon. 1 : 3. also יָפוֹא Ezra 3 : 7. in Greek Ἰόππη, a city, on the Mediterranean, with a celebrated harbour, in the limits of the tribe of Dan; now called *Jaffa*. Relandi Palæstina, p. 864.

יְפִי m. Ezek. 28 : 7. and יֳפִי, in pause יֹפִי, with suff. יָפְיוֹ, verbal from יָפָה, *beauty*. Ps. 50 : 2. Ezek. 27 : 3.

יָפַח i. q. פּוּחַ, נָפַח, *to blow, to breathe.* Found only in Hithpa. *to breathe with difficulty, to sigh.* Jer. 4 : 31.

יָפֵחַ verbal adj. from יָפַח, *efflans.* Ps. 27 : 12 וִיפֵחַ חָמָס *efflans scelus.* Comp. הֵפִיחַ no. 3.

יָפַע found only in Hiph. הוֹפִיעַ.

1. *to shine, to give light.* Job 3 : 4. 10 : 3. Used particularly of Jehovah, *to appear in a bright light, to shine forth,* Deut. 33 : 2. Ps. 50 : 2. 80 : 2. 94 : 1.

2. *to cause to shine.* Job 37 : 15.

יִפְעָה f. verbal from יָפַע, dec. X. *brightness, beauty,* (of a city). Ezek. 28 : 7, 17.

יֶפֶת (for יַפְתְּ fut. Hiph. from פָּתָה *to be wide, extended,*) proper name of a son of Noah, Gen. 5 : 32. 7 : 13. 9 : 18 ff. who in Gen. 10 : 2—5, is represented as the progenitor of the nations scattered on the North and West of Palestine. Comp. חָם, and De Wette Kritik der Israëlitischen Geschichte. Th. I. p. 72. Sept. Ἰάφεθ. Vulg. *Japhet.*

יִפְתָּח (*he opens*) proper name of an Israelitish judge, who, in accordance with his vow, sacrificed his daughter to Jehovah. Judg. 11 : 12. 1 Sam. 12 : 11. In Greek Ἰεφθάε, Ἰεφθάες. Vulg. *Jephtha.*

יָצָא, fut. יֵצֵא, imper. צֵא, infin. absol. יָצֹא, const. צֵאת, *to go out, to go forth.* Construed with מִן of the place left; also with an accus. like the Lat. *egredi urbem*, Gen. 44 : 4 הֵם יָצְאוּ אֶת־הָעִיר *they went out of the city.* Amos 4 : 3 פְּרָצִים תֵּצֶאנָה *they go out through the breaches.* Part. יֹצְאֵי הָעִיר *they who go out of the city,* Gen. 34 : 24. comp. 9 : 10.—In Amos 5 : 3, it is spoken of the object, out of which something proceeds, (comp. הָלַךְ no. 5.) thus הָעִיר הַיֹּצֵאת אֶלֶף *a city which goes out by thousands.* The following special significations are worthy of notice; (1.) *to arise,* spoken of the sun and stars. Gen. 19 : 23. Ps. 19 : 6. Neh. 4 : 15. (Antith. בּוֹא.) (2.) *to spring up,* spoken of plants. Job 5 : 6. Deriv. צֶאֱצָאִים. (3.) *to spring from* any one, *to be begotten* or *descended from* him, Gen. 17 : 6. More frequently with the addition מִמְּעֵי, מִבֶּטֶן, Job 1 : 21. Gen. 46 : 26. (4.) *to expire, to be finished,* spoken of time. Ex. 23 : 16 בְּצֵאת הַשָּׁנָה *at the close of the year.* Spoken also of a boundary, *to run out, to extend itself,* Josh. 15 : 3, 4, 9, 11. (5.) יָצָא חָפְשִׁי Ex. 21 : 5. and יֵצֵא לַחָפְשִׁי verse 2. *to become free.* Also simply יָצָא Ex. 21 : 3, 4, 11. Likewise used of inanimate things, which in the year of jubilee were restored without compensation to their original owners, Lev. 25 : 28, 30. (6.) *to be laid out* or *expended,* as money. 2 K. 12 : 13. (7.) *to escape, to be delivered,* construed with an accus. Ecc. 7 : 18. So 1 Sam. 14 : 41, *to escape,* in the drawing of lots, (antith. נִלְכַּד *to be taken.*)

Hiph. הוֹצִיא. 1. *to bring, lead,* or *draw forth* or *out,* persons or things. Gen. 24 : 53. Ex. 4 : 6, 7. Also *to cause to spring up,* spoken of the earth, Gen. 1 : 12, 24. Especially (1.) הוֹצִיא דִבָּה *to spread an evil report.* Num. 14 : 37. comp. Deut. 22 : 14, 19. (in both cases construed with עַל.) and Neh. 6 : 19. (2.) causat. of Kal no. (6.) *to lay* or *charge an expense on* any one, construed with עַל, 2 K. 15 : 20.

Hoph. *to be brought out.* Ezek. 25:22. 38:8. 47:8.

Deriv. מוֹצָא, מוֹצָאָה, תּוֹצָאוֹת, צֶאֱצָאִים, צֵאָה, צוֹאָה.

יְצָא Chald. Only in Shaph. שֵׁיצִיא and שֵׁיצִי, in the Targums, *to bring* a matter *to an issue, to finish* it. Hence שֵׁיצִיא Ezra 6:15. *finished.*

יָצַב i. q. נָצַב *to place.* In Kal not used.

Hithpa. הִתְיַצֵּב.

1. *to place* or *present one's self.* Ex. 2:4. 1 Sam. 17:16 וַיִּתְיַצֵּב אַרְבָּעִים יוֹם *and he presented himself (for combat) forty days.* Job 33:5. Construed with עַל, *to rise up against* any one, Ps. 2:2. elsewhere הִתְיַצֵּב עַל יְהוָה *to present one's self before Jehovah,* waiting for his commands, Job 1:6. 2:1 Zech. 6:5.

2. with לִפְנֵי and בִּפְנֵי, *to stand before* any one; either as a conqueror, Deut. 9:2. 7:24. 11:25. Josh. 1:5. or as innocent in a judicial sense, Job 41:2. [10.] Ps. 5:6. with עִם, 2 Chr. 20:6.

3. with לְ, *to stand by, to assist.* Ps. 94:16.

יְצַב Chald. *to be certain, true.*

Pa. *to tell the truth.* Dan. 7:19. Comp. verse 16.

יָצַג in Kal not used.

Hiph. הִצִּיג 1. *to cause to stand, to establish.* Am. 5:15 הַצִּיגוּ בַשַּׁעַר מִשְׁפָּט *establish righteousness in the gate.*

2. *to leave behind.* Gen. 33:15.

3. *to place, set;* e. g. persons, Gen. 43:9. things, 30:38.

4. *to lay, spread, sternere.* Judg. 6:37. Sometimes we find הִצִּיק in the same signification, Josh. 7:23. 2 Sam. 15:24.

Hoph. fut. יֻצַּג, *to be left behind.* Ex. 10:24. Comp. the verb kindred in meaning הִנִּיחַ.

יִצְהָר m. *oil.* Deut. 7:13. Zech. 4:14 בְּנֵי הַיִּצְהָר *the anointed.* (Root צהר literally *to shine;* comp. זָהַב no. 2.)

יִצְחָק (*he laughs;* comp. Gen. 17:17, 19.) proper name of the son of Abraham and Sarah. Gen. XXI—XXVIII. More rarely written יִשְׂחָק (from שָׂחַק *to laugh,*) Ps. 105:9. Jer. 33:26. Am. 7:9. In the last passage it is parallel and synonymous with Israel. Sept. Ἰσαάκ.

יָצִיא m. *proceeding,* a passive participle with an active signification. 2 Chr. 32:21.

יַצִּיב m. Chald. adj.

1. *true, certain.* Dan. 2:45. 3:24. —מִן יַצִּיב *certainly, truly,* 2:8.

2. *valid, established.* Dan. 6:12.

יָצִיעַ see the following article.

יָצַע *to spread for a bed, to lay under, sternere,* Part. יָצוּעַ (1.) *a bed, couch.* Ps. 63:7. Job 17:13. Also *a marriage bed,* Gen. 49:4. (2.) *a story, floor.* Vulg. *tabulatum.* 1 K. 6:5, 6, 10. (in the Keri יָצִיעַ). Ezek. 41:6 ff. The word denotes especially the three stories of side chambers (צְלָעוֹת,) which surrounded the temple of Solomon. Comp. Hirt's Tempel Salomo's, p. 24, 25.

Hiph. הִצִּיעַ *to spread out, to make for a bed.* Ps. 139:8 וְאַצִּיעָה שְּׁאוֹל *and if I make hades my bed.* Is. 58:5.

Hoph. Is. 14:11 תַּחְתֶּיךָ יֻצַּע רִמָּה *under thee shall worms lie.* Est. 4:13. comp. Is. 58:5.

Deriv. מַצָּע.

I. יָצַק, fut. יִצֹק, (once יָצַק 1 K. 22:35 intrans. *it poured itself out,*) imper. צַק 2 K. 4:41. and יְצֹק Ezek. 24:3. infin. צֶקֶת.

1. *to pour forth* or *out,* as liquids. Gen. 28:18. 35:14.—Intrans. *to be poured out,* Job 38:38 *when the dust is poured out into a solid mass;* i. e. when the dust cleaves together on account of the rain.

2. *to cast* metallic vessels or instruments. Ex. 25:12. 26:37. 36:36.—יָצוּק *molten, cast,* 1 K. 7:24, 30. and so *hard, firm,* as metal, Job 41:15, 16. [41:23, 26.]

Hoph. הוּצַק. 1. *to be poured out.* Lev. 21:10. Ps. 45:3.

2. *to be molten* or *cast,* spoken of metal. 1 K. 7:23, 33. Job 37:18. Metaphorically מֻצָּק *firm, fearless,* Job 11:15.

Deriv. out of course מוּצָק, מוּצָקָה.

II. יָצַק found only in Hiph. i. q. הִצִּיג *to place, spread.* Josh. 7:23. 2 Sam. 15:24.

יְצֻקָה verbal from יָצַק no. I. *a pouring out* or *casting.* 1 K. 7:24.

I. יָצַר, fut. יִצֶּר, יִיצֶר, also יִצֹּר Is. 44:12. Jer. 1:5 Keri.

1. *to form, make, create, fingere.* Is. 44:10, 12. Gen. 2:7, 8, 19. Ps. 94:9 יֹצֵר עַיִן *he who formed the eye.* Ps. 33:15. 99:5. Hence *to make* generally, Ps. 74:17. Is. 44:21 יְצַרְתִּיךָ עֶבֶד לִי *I have made thee my servant;* comp. 49:5.—Part. יֹצֵר *a potter,* Ps. 94:9, 20.—כְּלִי יוֹצֵר *an earthen vessel,* Ps. 2:9.

2. metaphorically *to imagine, devise.* 2 K. 19:25. Jer. 18:11. Ps. 94:20.

Niph. pass. Is. 43:10.

Pu. יֻצַּר *to be appointed, destined.* Ps. 139:16.

Hoph. i. q. Niph. Is. 54:17.

II. יָצַר i. q. צוּר, but used intrans. *to be straitened.* Found only in the fut. יֵצֶר, plur. יֵצְרוּ, Prov. 4:12. Is. 49:19. Job 18:7. Elsewhere used impersonally יֵצֶר לוֹ *he was straitened,* (in the preterite צַר לוֹ from צָרַר;) signifying (1.) *he was in trouble, it went ill with him.* Judg. 2:15. 10:9. Job 20:22. (2.) *he was distressed.* Gen. 32:8. Also in the feminine form used as a neuter, 1 Sam. 30:6. (3.) *he took it ill.* 2 Sam. 13:2.

יֵצֶר m. with suff. יִצְרוֹ, verbal from יָצַר no. I. dec. VI. g.

1. *something formed by an artificer, a form, frame.* Is. 29:16. Hab. 2:18. Ps. 103:14 כִּי הוּא יָדַע יִצְרֵנוּ *for he knows our frame,* i. e. how and whereof we are formed.

2. metaphorically *an imagination, thought,* or *device,* (of the heart.) Gen. 8:21. 6:6. Deut. 31:21. Is. 26:3 יֵצֶר סָמוּךְ *whose thoughts are firm.*

יְצֻרִים masc. plur. Job 17:7. *forms* or *form* (of the body). Vulg. *members.*

יָצַת found only in the fut. יִצַּת.

1. *to set on fire,* construed with בְּ. Is. 9:17.

2. pass. *to be burned,* as in Niph. Is. 33:12. Jer. 40:2. 51:58. (The form יִצַּתּוּ has a Dagesh forte euphonic, like יֵחַתּוּ Job 21:13.)

Niph. pret. נִצַּת.

1. *to be burned,* or *laid waste by fire.* Jer. 2:15. 9:9, 11.

2. *to be kindled,* spoken of anger; construed with בְּ *against* any one, 2 K. 22:13, 17.

Hiph. הוֹצִית only 2 Sam. 14:30 Keth. elsewhere הִצִּית *to set on fire.* These phrases are used indiscriminately, הִצִּית אֵשׁ בְּ Jer. 17:27. 21:14. or with עַל, Jer. 11:16. and הִצִּית דָּבָר בָּאֵשׁ Josh. 8:19. Jer. 32:29. or without בָּאֵשׁ, Jer. 51:50.

יֶקֶב m. dec. VI. a. 1. *the wine-fat, ὑπολήνιον, lacus,* into which the wine flowed from the press. Joel 2:24. 4:13. [3:13.] Prov. 3:10. It was usually dug into the ground or hewed into the rock, Is. 5:2.

2. *the press itself.* Job 24:11.

יְקַבְצְאֵל (*God will collect*) Neh. 11:25. i. q. קַבְצְאֵל Josh. 15:21. 2 Sam. 23:20. proper name of a city in the south part of the tribe of Judah.

יָקַד, fut. יֵקַד Is. 10:16. and יֵקַד Deut. 32:22. *to kindle, to burn.*

Hoph. הוּקַד *to burn, to be kindled.* Lev. 6:2, 5, 6. [6:9, 12, 13.] Used metaphorically of anger, Jer. 15:14. 17:4.

Deriv. out of course מוֹקֵד, יְקֹד.

יְקַד Chald. *idem.* Part. fem. יָקִדְתָּא and יָקִידְתָּא *burning.* Dan. 3:6, 11, 23, 26.

יְקֵדָה f. Chald. verbal from יְקַד, *a burning.* Dan. 7:11.

יִקְּהָה f. (with Dagesh forte euphonic.) *obedience.* Gen. 49:10. Prov. 30:17. (Root Arab. وقه *to obey.*)

יְקוֹד m. verbal from יָקַד *a burning.* Is. 10:16.

יְקוּם m. verbal from קוּם, *whatever exists or is, a substance.* Gen. 7:4, 23, Deut. 11:6.

יָקוֹשׁ Hos. 9:8. and יָקוּשׁ Ps. 91:3. Prov. 6:5. Jer. 5:26. m. *a fowler.* Root. יָקֹשׁ. The form יָקוּשׁ is properly an active participial form, the other is a passive form with an active signification.

יָקְטָן proper name of a son of Heber and descendant of Shem, Gen. 10:25, 26. from whom many Arabian tribes were derived, Gen. 10:26—30. By the Arabian writers he is called قحطان *Kachtan*. See Bocharti Phaleg. III. cap. 15.

יַקִּיר m. verbal adj. from יָקַר, *dear, beloved.* Jer. 31:20.

יַקִּיר adj. Chald. 1. *hard.* Dan. 2:11.

2. *mighty, honoured, noble.* Ezra 4:10.

יָקַע only in the fut. יֵקַע, i. q. נָקַע.

1. *to be wrenched, dislocated,* or *put out of joint, luxari,* spoken of members of the body. Gen. 32:26.

2. metaphorically *to be alienated* or *removed from* any one, construed with מִן and מֵעַל. Jer. 6:8. Ezek. 23:17, 18.

Hiph. הוֹקִיעַ *to suspend* or *nail up on a stake, ἀνασκολοπίζειν,* as a punishment to criminals, perhaps literally *to dislocate the limbs.* Num. 25:4. 2 Sam. 21: 6, 9, 12.

יָקַץ only in the fut. יִיקַץ, יִקַץ, once יִיקֶץ Gen. 9:24. *to awake.* Gen. 28:16. 41:4, 7. For the preterite, הֵקִיץ Hiph. of קוּץ is used.

יָקַר, fut. יֵיקַר, also יֵקַר Ps. 72:14. and יֵקַר Ps. 49:9.

1. *to be heavy, difficult.* Metaphorically *to be incomprehensible* Ps. 139: 17. Comp. Dan. 2:11.

2. *to be dear, costly, precious.* Ps. 49:9. 1 Sam. 26:21 אֲשֶׁר יָקְרָה נַפְשִׁי בְּעֵינֶיךָ *because my life was dear to thee,* i. e. because thou sparedst it. 2 K. 1:13, 14. Ps. 72:14. Zech. 11:13 *the price* אֲשֶׁר יָקַרְתִּי מֵעֲלֵיהֶם *at which I was valued by them.*

3. *to be honoured, respected.* 1 Sam. 18:30.

Hiph. הוֹקִיר *to make rare.* (See the adj. no. 4.) Is. 13:12. Prov. 25:17.

Deriv. out of course יְקָר.

יָקָר fem. יְקָרָה, verbal adj. from יָקַר.

1. *heavy.* See the verb.

2. *dear, costly, precious.*—אֶבֶן יְקָרָה used collectively *costly stones,* i. e. either precious stones, 1 K. 10:2, 10, 11. or valuable stones for building, 2 Chr. 3: 7. So אֲבָנִים יְקָרוֹת 1 K. 5:31. 7:9ff.—Ps. 45:10 *kings' daughters* בְּיִקְּרוֹתֶיךָ *were among thy beloved;* (the Dagesh is euphonic.) Ps. 36:8 מַה־יָּקָר חַסְדְּךָ אֱלֹהִים *how precious is thy grace, O God.* 116:5. comp. 72:14.

3. *magnificent, majestic.* Job 31:26.

4. *rare.* 1 Sam. 3:1.

5. Prov. 17:27 יְקַר רוּחַ Keri perhaps *quiet of spirit,* after the Arab. وقر *to be quiet.* In the Kethib קַר רוּחַ.

יְקָר m. (with Kamets impure,) verbal from יָקַר, dec. I.

1. *worth, costliness.* Prov. 20:15. Used as a concrete, כָּל־יְקָר *every precious thing,* Job 28:10. Jer. 20:5.

2. *honour, respect.* Ps. 49:13, 21. Est. 1:20.

3. *magnificence, splendour.* Est. 1:4. Ps. 37:20 יְקַר כָּרִים *the splendour of the fields.*

יְקָר m. Chald. 1. *costly things.* Dan. 2:6. comp. Is. 3:17. 10:3 Targ.

2. *honour, majesty.* Dan. 2:37. 4:27, 33. [4:30, 36.]

יָקֹשׁ 1 pers. יָקֹשְׁתִּי, i. q. נָקַשׁ and קוּשׁ, *to lay snares.* Ps. 141:9. Jer. 50:24. For the fut. we find יְקֹשׁוּן from קוּשׁ, Is. 29:21. Part. יוֹקֵשׁ *a fowler,* Ps. 124:7.

Niph. נוֹקַשׁ *to be ensnared, taken,* Is. 8:15. *to ensnare one's self,* Prov. 6:2. Ps. 9:17. Metaphorically *to be seduced,* Deut. 7:25.

Pu. part. יוּקָשִׁים for מְיֻקָּשִׁים *ensnared.* Ecc. 9:12.

Deriv. מוֹקֵשׁ, יָקוֹשׁ.

יָקְתְאֵל 1. proper name of a city in the tribe of Judah. Josh. 15:38.

2. the name, which king Amaziah gave to *Selah,* an Arabian city which he took. 2 K. 14:7. As an appellative, perhaps *præmium Dei,* from وقت, *constituit;* Ethiop. conj. IV. *constituit præmium.*

יָרֵא, fut. יִירָא, imper. יְרָא, infin. יְרֹא Josh. 22:25. and with לְ, לֵרֹא for לִירֹא 1 Sam. 18:29. elsewhere uniformly fem. יִרְאָה.

1. *to fear, to be afraid.*—אַל תִּירָא *fear not,* Gen. 15:1. 21:17. Construed with an accus. of the person *feared,* Num. 14:9. 21:34. with מִן, Deut. 1:29. and מִפְּנֵי Josh. 11:6. On the contrary with לְ of the person or thing *for* which one fears, Josh. 9:24. Prov. 31:21. Construed with לְ and מִן before an infinitive, *to be afraid to* do any thing, Gen. 19:30. 46:3.

2. *to honour, fear, reverence, revereri;* e. g. one's parents, Lev. 19:3. the general, Josh. 4:14. the sanctuary, Lev. 19:30. an oath, 1 Sam. 14:26. Hence יָרֵא אֶת אֱלֹהִים *to fear God,* whether in a more natural, Ex. 14:31. 1 Sam. 12:18. or in a more spiritual sense, Ex. 1:17. Prov. 3:7 *fear God, and depart from evil.* Job 1:9. In this latter sense it is equivalent to *being virtuous, pious.* Sometimes without אֱלֹהִים, Jer. 44:10.

Niph. נוֹרָא *to be feared.* Ps. 130:4. Part. נוֹרָא (1.) *fearful, terrible.* Deut. 1:19. 8:15. Joel 2:11. 3:4. [2:31.] (2.) *worthy of reverence, holy.* Gen. 28:17. (3.) *wonderful, great, noble.* Ps. 66:3, 5. Ex. 15:12. Plur. נוֹרָאוֹת *wonderful deeds,* as of men, Ps. 45:5. but particularly of God, Deut. 10:21. 2 Sam. 7:23. Used also as an adv. *in a wonderful manner,* Ps. 139:14. (comp. נִפְלָאוֹת.)

Pi. יֵרֵא *to terrify, to make afraid.* 2 Sam. 14:15.

Deriv. out of course מוֹרָא.

יָרֵא m. const. יְרֵא, verbal adj. from יָרֵא dec. V. e.

1. *fearing.* Joined with personal pronouns it forms a periphrasis for the finite verb, as יָרֵא אָנֹכִי *I fear,* Gen. 32:12. אֲנַחְנוּ יְרֵאִים *we fear,* I Sam. 23:3. אֵינֶנּוּ יָרֵא *he fears not,* Ecc. 8:13. It is construed in a similar manner with the verb, as יָרֵא אֶת יְהוָֹה *fearing Jehovah,* 2 K. 4:1.

2. more as an adj. *fearful.* Deut. 20:8. יְרֵא אֱלֹהִים *fearing God,* Gen. 22:12. Job 1:1, 8. 2:3.

יִרְאָה f. dec. X. 1. strictly an infin. from יָרֵא, as Neh. 1:11 לְיִרְאָה אֶת־שְׁמֶךָ *to fear thy name.* 2 Sam. 3:11 מִיִּרְאָתוֹ אֹתוֹ *because he feared him.*

2. as a subst. *fear.* Ps. 55:6. Jon. 1:10 וַיִּירְאוּ הָאֲנָשִׁים יִרְאָה גְדוֹלָה *and the men feared exceedingly.* With suff. יִרְאָתְךָ *the fear of thee,* Deut. 2:25. and in an active signification, Job 4:6.

3. *holy fear, reverence.* Ps. 2:11. 5:8. יִרְאַת יְהוָֹה *the fear of Jehovah, virtue, religion, piety.* Prov. 1:7 יִרְאַת יְהוָֹה רֵאשִׁית דָּעַת *the fear of Jehovah is the beginning of wisdom.* Job 28:28. Also *religion* objectively considered, *truths of religion,* Ps. 19:10. Also without יְהוָֹה, Job 4:5. 15:4.

4. *dreadfulness.* Ezek. 1:18.

יָרֵב i. q. יָרִיב *an adversary.* מֶלֶךְ יָרֵב Hos. 5:13. 10:9. *the hostile king.* According to others: *the revenger,* for אֲשֶׁר יָרִיב לוֹ *one who contends,* Vulg. *ultor.* Chald. *idem.* Others: *the great* or *mighty king,* (comp. Syr. ܪܰܒ *to be great, mighty,*) as a title of the Assyrian kings; comp. 2 K. 18:19.

יְרֻבַּעַל m. (for יָרֹב בַּעַל *Baal contends,* see Judg. 6:32.) the name, which Gideon bears from Judg. 6:32. onward; for which we also find יְרֻבֶּשֶׁת (*the idol contends*) 2 Sam. 11:21, an interpretation of the other name. Sept. Ἰεροβάαλ. Comp. אִישׁ־בֹּשֶׁת and אֶשְׁבַּעַל.

יָרָבְעָם m. (read Yarobeam, for יָרֹב עָם *the people are many*).

1. *Jeroboam,* the son of Nebat, first king of the ten tribes, and author of the worship of the golden calves. 1 K. 12:14.

2. son of Joash, likewise king of Israel. 2 K. 14:24—29.

יָרַד, fut. יֵרֵד, and יֵרֵד, וַיֵּרֶד, more rarely וַיֵּרַד imper. רֵד, רְדָה, infin. absol. יָרֹד (Gen. 43:20.) once רְדָה Gen. 48:52. infin. const. רֶדֶת, with suff. רִדְתִּי.

1. *to go down, to descend.* Frequently

to go from a higher to a lower country; hence used constantly of a journey into Egypt, Gen. 12:10. 26:2ff. into Philistia and the country on the sea, 1 Sam. 13:20. 23:4, 8, 11. towards the south, 1 Sam. 25:1. 26:2. 30:15. or from a city, (considered as placed on an eminence,) Ruth 3:3, 6. 1 Sam. 9:27. The place *to* which one goes stands with לְ, אֶל, ה ָ—, or in the accus. Ps. 55:16 יֵרְדוּ שְׁאוֹל חַיִּים *let them descend alive into hades.* Job 7:9. 17:16. 33:24. Hence Part. יֹרְדֵי־בוֹר *they who go down into the pit,* Prov. 1:12.

2. spoken of inanimate objects; as of a road, *to lead down,* Prov. 7:27. of a boundary, *to extend down* or *southwardly,* Num. 34:11, 12. Josh. 18:13 ff. of the day, *to decline,* Judg. 19. 11. of streams, *to flow down,* Deut. 9:21. By a common idiom of the Hebrew language, it is also spoken of the object *from* which any thing flows down, as Lam. 3:48 פַּלְגֵי מַיִם תֵּרַד עֵינִי *mine eye flows down in streams of water.* 1:16. Jer. 9:17. 13:17. 14:17. Ps. 119:136. Comp. Is. 15:3 יֹרֵד בַּבֶּכִי *he flows down in tears.*

3. *to fall;* spoken of a wall, Deut. 28:52. of a wood which is felled, Is. 32:19. Zech. 11:2. of a besieged city, Deut. 20:20. Metaphorically *to fall,* in wealth, in outward circumstances, Deut. 28:43.

Hiph. הוֹרִיד 1. *to make to go down, to bring down,* either persons or things. Gen. 37:25. 43:10, 21. *to let down,* (by a cord), Josh. 2:15, 18. *to let* or *take down,* Gen. 24:18, 46. 44:11. Num. 1:51. 4:5. *to cast down,* Hos. 7:12. *to bring down* a citadel, Prov. 21:22. *to conquer* a people, Prov. 21:22.

Hoph. הוּרַד pass. of Hiph. Gen. 39:1. Is. 14:11ff.

יַרְדֵּן a proper name, *Jordan,* the largest river of Palestine, commonly with the article, in Greek Ἰορδάνης. Root ירד *to flow down,* comp. Syr. ܝܘܪܕܢܐ *a sea.*—אֶרֶץ יַרְדֵּן *the country on the Jordan,* Ps. 42:7. By the Arabians it is now called *El Sharai, (the ford.)*

I. יָרָה, infin. יְרֹה, יָרוֹה, and יְרוֹא 2 Chr. 26:15. imper. יְרֵה, fut. יִירֶה.

1. *to throw, cast.* Ex. 15:4. as a lot, Josh. 18:6. an arrow, 1 Sam. 20:36, 37. Ps. 11:2. 64:5. Num. 21. 30. Part. יֹרֶה *an archer,* 1 Chr. 10:3.

2. *to found, fundamenta jacere,* Job 38:6. *to raise* (a monument), Gen. 31:51. (So Syr. ܫܕܐ; *to throw* and *to found.*)

3. *to sprinkle, to wet.* Hos. 6:3. (So many other words, e. g. זָרַק *to throw* and *to sprinkle.*) Part. יוֹרֶה *the early rain,* (see art. יוֹרֶה).

Niph. *to be shot through with arrows.* Fut. יִיָּרֶה Ex. 19:13.

Hiph. הוֹרָה 1. as in Kal, *to throw, cast,* Job 30:19. Especially *to shoot an arrow,* 1 Sam. 20:20, 36. Fut. apoc. וַיּוֹר 2 K. 13:17. Part. מוֹרֶה *an archer,* 1 Sam. 31:3. It is found with the Aramean orthography, 2 Sam. 11:24 וַיֹּרְאוּ הַמּוֹרְאִים *and the archers shot;* comp. 2 Chr. 26:15.

2. *to sprinkle, to wet.* Part. מוֹרֶה i. q. יוֹרֶה *the early rain,* Joel 2:23. Ps. 84:7.

II. יָרָה found only in Hiph. הוֹרָה.

1. *to shew, direct.* Gen. 46:28. Prov. 6:13 מֹרֶה בְּאֶצְבְּעֹתָיו *making signs with his fingers.* Construed with two accus. Ex. 15:25.

2. *to instruct, teach.* Ex. 35:34. Mic. 3:11. Construed with an accus. of the person, Job 6:24. 8:10. 12:7, 8. with an accus. of the thing, Is. 9:14. Hab. 2:18. Hence with two accus. Ps. 27:11. 86:11. 119:33. with בְּ of the thing, Job 27:11. Ps. 25:8, 12. 32:8. more rarely with אֶל, 2 Chr. 6:27, or מִן, Is. 2:3. Mic. 4:2. With a dative of the person and an accus. of the thing, Deut. 33:10. Hos. 10:12.

Note. These two significations nos. I. and II. are probably connected; see Gesenius' Auszug, Vorrede, p. VII.

יְרוּאֵל proper name of a desert, mentioned only 2 Chr. 20:16. Literally *dwelling of God;* see יְרוּשָׁלַיִם.

יָרוֹק m. verbal from יָרַק, (q. v.) *something green*. Job 39 : 8.

יְרוּשָׁלֵם and יְרוּשָׁלַיִם, a proper name, *Jerusalem*, the chief city of Palestine, situated on the borders of the tribes Judah and Benjamin. The latter form יְרוּשָׁלַיִם predominates in the later writings of the Hebrews, and is derived from the other form which should be pointed יְרוּשָׁלֵם, (comp. the Chald.) So out of שֹׁמְרוֹן, שָׁמְרַיִן, was formed שָׁמְרַיִן; out of עֶפְרוֹן, עֶפְרַיִן. The Masoretes, being familiar only with the latter form, have given an erroneous punctuation to the ancient. On the Jewish medals both modes of spelling occur. The signification of this proper name is *people* or *dwelling of peace;* namely, יְרוּ i. q. Arab. وري=מְתִים *people*, but perhaps in Heb. *a dwelling*, (hence יְרוּאֵל *dwelling of God;* comp. Arab. اهل *people*, literally *a tent, dwelling*,) and שָׁלֵם *peace*. The abbreviation שָׁלֵם (q. v.) may be the more ancient appellation, and on that account retained in poetry. In Greek Ἱερουσαλήμ and Ἱεροσόλυμα.

יְרוּשְׁלֶם and יְרוּשְׁלֵם Chald. *idem*. Dan. 5 : 2. 6 : 11. Ezra 4 : 8.

יָרֵחַ m. prim. dec. V. a. *the moon*. Gen. 37 : 9. Deut. 4 : 19. Ps. 72 : 5 לִפְנֵי יָרֵחַ *before the moon was*.

יֶרַח m. denom. from יָרֵחַ, dec. VI. d.

1. *a month, a Hebrew lunar month*, 1 K. 6 : 37, 38. 8 : 2.

2. Gen. 10 : 26. a country of Arabia. See Bocharti Phaleg, lib. 3. cap. 19. p. 124. J. D. Michaëlis Spicileg. Geogr. Hebr. exteræ, T. II. p. 160.

יְרַח Chald. *a month*. Ezra 6 : 15.

יְרֵחוֹ Num. 22 : 1. also יְרִיחוֹ Josh. 2 : 1, 2, 3. and יְרִיחֹה 1 K. 16 : 34. *Jericho*, a celebrated city of Palestine, not far from Jordan and the Dead Sea, in the tribe of Benjamin, and the most fruitful part of all Palestine.

יָרַט prob. *to be corrupt, perverse*. (Arab. ورط *to throw down, to ruin*.) Num. 22 : 32. The Samaritan text has, by way of gloss, הרע.

יָרִיב m. verbal from רִיב, dec. III. a. *an opponent, adversary*. Ps. 35 : 1. Jer. 18 : 19. Is. 49 : 24.

יְרִיעָה f. dec. X. *a covering, curtain*, Especially (1.) *the covering of a tent*. Is. 54 : 2. Jer. 4 : 20. 49 : 29. Spoken of the curtains of the tabernacle of the congregation, Ex. 26 : 1 ff. 36 : 8 ff. (2.) *carpet, tapestry*, Cant. 1 : 5.

יָרֵךְ const. יֶרֶךְ, with suff. יְרֵכִי, dec. V. c.

1. *thigh, hip, loins*. Gen. 24 : 2. Ex. 1 : 4 יֹצְאֵי יֶרֶךְ יַעֲקֹב *they who came out of the loins of Jacob*, i. e. those descended from him. Gen. 46 : 26. Jud. 8 : 30.

2. *side*, e. g. of the tent, Ex. 40 : 22, 24. of the altar, Lev. 1 : 11. 2 K. 16 : 14. (In the feminine form יַרְכָה or יְרֵכָה this is the predominant meaning; comp. the Greek μηρὸς and the Heb. צֵלָע.

3. that part of a candlestick where the main shaft (קָנֶה) receives the feet. Ex. 25 : 31. 37 : 17.

Dual יְרֵכַיִם Ex. 28 : 42 מִמָּתְנַיִם וְעַד יְרֵכַיִם *from the loins even unto the thighs*. The word denotes here, as elsewhere, *the lower part of the hip*, or *upper part of the thigh;* but מָתְנַיִם denotes *the upper part of the hip*, including the small of the back, ὀσφύς, *coxa*. Cant. 7 : 2.

יַרְכָה or יְרֵכָה fem. of יָרֵךְ, used only of inanimate objects, *a side*, as of a country. Gen. 49 : 13.

Dual יַרְכָתַיִם, const. יַרְכְּתֵי.

1. *the side*, (losing its dual signification, like מַיִם.) Ps. 48 : 3 יַרְכְּתֵי צָפוֹן *the north*. Especially *the hinder*, i. e. the western, *side;* e. g. of the tabernacle of the congregation, Ex. 26 : 23, 27. (so 36 : 27, 28, 32.) of the temple, 1 K. 6 : 16. Ezek. 46 : 23.

2. *the hindmost, innermost, deepest part* generally, *recessus*. 1 Sam. 24 : 4 יַרְכְּתֵי הַמְּעָרָה *the back part of the cave*. Is. 14 : 15 and Ezek. 32 : 23 יַרְכְּתֵי בוֹר *the deepest parts of the pit*. Am. 6 : 10 and Ps. 128 : 3 יַרְכְּתֵי הַבַּיִת *the innermost part*

of the house. Jon. 1:5. Jud. 19:1, 18 יַרְכְּתֵי הַר אֶפְרַיִם prob. *the innermost regions of mount Ephraim*, as in 2 K. 19:23.

3. *the remotest countries.*—יַרְכְּתֵי צָפוֹן *the remotest countries of the north*, Is. 14:13. יַרְכְּתֵי אָרֶץ *the remotest countries of the earth*, Jer. 6:22. 25:32. (Comp. כַּנְפוֹת הָאָרֶץ.)

יַרְכָה f. Chald. *thigh.* Dan. 2:32.

יַרְמוּת proper name of a city in the plain of the tribe of Judah, anciently the seat of a Canaanitish king. Josh. 10:3. 12:11. 15:35. Neh. 11:29.

יִרְמְיָה and יִרְמְיָהוּ (for יְרִמֶה יָהּ literally *Jehovah throws*, e.g. the lightning,) proper name of a celebrated prophet, son of Hilkiah. Jer. 1:1. 27:1. Dan. 9:2. Sept. Ἱερεμίας.

I. יָרַע i.q. רוּעַ. Found only in the fut. יֵרַע, the preterite Kal רַע being supplied from רוּעַ (which wants the fut.) and the Hiph. הֵרַע from the root רָעַע.

1. *to be evil, wicked.*—The following constructions are worthy of notice; (1.) יֵרַע לִי *it shall go ill with me.* Ps. 106:32. (2.) וַיֵּרַע בְּעֵינַי *it appeared ill to me, it displeased me.* Gen. 21:11. 38:10. 48:17. 1 Sam. 8:6. Construed with לְ, Neh. 13:8. and with the intensitive addition רָעָה גְדוֹלָה, Neh. 2:10. Jon. 4:1. In a different construction 1 Chr. 21:7 וַיֵּרַע בְּעֵינֵי הָאֱלֹהִים עַל הַדָּבָר הַזֶּה *and this thing displeased God.* (3.) *to be envious*, spoken of the eye. Deut. 28:54.

2. *to be sad.* (Opposite of יָטַב, טוֹב *to be joyful.*) Spoken of the countenance, Neh. 2:3. of the heart, 1 Sam. 1:8. Deut. 15:10 לֹא יֵרַע לְבָבְךָ בְּתִתְּךָ לוֹ *let it not grieve thy heart to give to him.* In verse 9, the same is expressed of the eye.

3. *to be pernicious, hurtful*, construed with לְ. 2 Sam. 20:6.

II. יָרַע i.q. Arab. ورع and يرع *to be fearful, distressed.* Is. 15:4 נַפְשׁוֹ יָרְעָה לוֹ *his heart is distressed.* This verb is distinguished from no. I. by being used in the preterite.

יָרַק *to spit.* In the preterite Num. 12:14. Deut. 25:9. In the infin. absol. Num. 12:14. The future is formed from רָקַק.

יֶרֶק m. dec. IV. a. *greenness.* 2 K. 19:26. Especially *an herb, vegetable*, as גַּן הַיָּרָק *a garden of vegetables*, Deut. 11:10. 1 K. 21:2. אֲרֻחַת יָרָק *a portion* or *dish of herbs*, Prov. 15:17. (Syr. ܝܘܪܩܢܐ, ܝܪܩܐ *an herb.*)

יָרָק m. *greenness, verdure, foliage.* Ex. 10:15.—כָּל־יֶרֶק עֵשֶׂב *every green herb*, Gen. 1:30. 9:3.

יֵרָקוֹן m. 1. *paleness of countenance*, perhaps literally *the greenish yellow* or *whitish death colour*, which the Greeks call χλωρός. Comp. ὠχρός. Jer. 30:6.

2. *jaundice, blasting* or *withering of plants.* Deut. 28:22. 1 K. 8:37. Am. 4:9. (Arab. يرقان *idem.*)

יְרַקְרַק m. 1. *greenish, yellowish*, χλωρίζων, spoken of clothes infected with the leprosy. Lev. 13:49. 14:37.

2. *yellowness, yellow colour of gold.* Ps. 68:14.

יָרַשׁ and יָרֵשׁ, fut. יִירַשׁ, imp. רֵשׁ and רַשׁ, infin. רֶשֶׁת, with suff. רִשְׁתּוֹ.

1. *to take into possession*, construed with an accus. of the thing. Deut. 1:8, 21. 2:24 הָחֵל רָשׁ *begin to take into possession.*

2. *to possess.* Lev. 25:46.—יָרַשׁ אֶרֶץ *to possess the land (quietly)*, i.e. (in the mind of a Hebrew) *to be blessed, to be happy*, Ps. 25:13. 37:9, 11, 22, 29. comp. Mat. 5:5.

3. *to inherit.* Gen. 21:10.—Part. יוֹרֵשׁ *an heir*, Jer. 49:1.—Construed with an accus. of the thing, Num. 27:11. 36:8. with an accus. of the person, *to inherit from* any one, *to be* his *heir*, Gen. 15:3, 4.

4. *to drive from a possession, to dispossess, disinherit.* Deut. 2:12 וּבְנֵי עֵשָׂו יִירָשׁוּם וַיַּשְׁמִידוּם מִפְּנֵיהֶם *and the children of Esau dispossessed them, and destroyed them from before them.* verses 21, 22. 9:1. 11:23. 12:2, 29. 18:14. 19:1. 31:3. Prov. 30:23 *and a handmaid that dispossesses her mistress*, i.e. that

takes her place. (This signification is derived from no. 3. *to succeed, as it were, to the possessions of another.*)

Niph. *to be disinherited, to become poor,* pass. of Kal no. 4. Gen. 45:11. Prov. 20:13. Kindred with רוּשׁ *to be poor.*

Pi. יֵרַשׁ 1. *to take into possession,* i. q. Kal no. 1. Deut. 28:42.

2. *to deprive of a possession, to make poor,* i. q. Kal no. 4. Judg. 14:15.

Hiph. הוֹרִישׁ 1. *to give for a possession, to make to possess, to bequeath;* construed with two accus. Judg. 11:24. 2 Chr. 20:11. Job 13:26 וְתוֹרִישֵׁנִי עֲוֹנוֹת נְעוּרָי *and (that) thou makest me to possess the sins of my youth,* i. e. thou imputest them to me. Construed with לְ, Ezra 9:12.

2. *to take into possession,* i. q. Kal no. 1. e. g. a country, Num. 14:24. a city, Josh. 8:7. 17:12. a mountain, Judg. 1:19.

3. *to drive from a possession,* and simply *to drive out.* Ex. 34:24. Num. 32:21. 33:52. Deut. 4:38. Also *to cast out* inanimate objects, Job 20:15 *God shall cast them out of his belly.* Hence

4. *to make* any one *poor.* (See Niph.) 1 Sam. 2:7.

5. *to destroy.* (The verbs הֵסֵם, פָּרַח also embrace the two ideas *to drive out* and *to destroy.*) Num. 14:12.

Deriv. out of course מוֹרָשׁ, and perhaps רֶשֶׁת.

יְרֵשָׁה f. (Num. 24:18.) and **יְרֻשָּׁה** f. dec. X. verbals from יָרַשׁ, *a possession.* Deut. 2:5, 9, 19. Josh. 12:6, 7.

יָשַׂם i. q. שׂוּם, but used intransitively, *to be set, placed;* (comp. יָצַר and צוּר.) Fut. וַיִּישֶׂם Gen. 50:26. 24:33. Judg. 12:3 (in the two last passages only in Kethib.)

יִשְׂרָאֵל (*a wrestler with God,* from שָׂרָה *to wrestle* and אֵל; see Gen. 32:29. and Hos. 12:4.) *Israel,* a later name of Jacob, employed more frequently as the name of the people, while Jacob generally denotes the patriarch himself. Hence בְּנֵי יִשְׂרָאֵל and יִשְׂרָאֵל m. (1.) *Israelites* generally.—אֶרֶץ יִשְׂרָאֵל *land of Israel, Palestine,* 1 Sam. 13:19. 2 K. 6:23. Ezek. 27:17. also simply יִשְׂרָאֵל as fem. Is. 19:24. (2.) after the division of the kingdom under Rehoboam, *the kingdom of the ten tribes,* in opposition *to the kingdom of Judah.* (3.) after the exile, especially in the time of the Maccabees, *the Jewish nation,* (1 Mac. 3:35. 4:11, 30:31. and on the Jewish medals;) hence in the Chronicles, *Israel* is used for *the kingdom of Judah,* 2 Chr. 12:1. 15:17. 19:8. 21:2, 4. 23:2. 24:25. The Gentile noun is יִשְׂרְאֵלִי *an Israelite,* 2 Sam. 17:25. and fem. יִשְׂרְאֵלִית *an Israelitess,* Lev. 24:10.

יִשָּׂשכָר a proper name, *Issachar,* the fifth son of Jacob; also the tribe named from him, the boundaries of which are given Josh. 19:17—23. Its etymological signification is given Gen. 30:18. Simonis (Anal. Lect. Masoreth. p. 5.) makes the probable conjecture, that the consonants of the Kethib should be pointed יֶשׁ־שָׂכָר, and that a constant Keri is to be understood for the present vowel-points, namely, יִשָּׂכָר.

יֵשׁ (Aram. ܐܝܬ אִיתַי; Arab. أَيْسَ, لَيْسَ) with Makkeph following יֶשׁ־, with suff. יֶשְׁךָ, יֶשְׁכֶם, יֶשְׁנוֹ.

1. *there is, there are;* (comp. the negation אַיִן i. q. לֹא יֵשׁ). Most frequently placed before the noun, as Gen. 28:16. rarely after it, as 1 Sam. 21:5 כִּי־אִם לֶחֶם קֹדֶשׁ יֵשׁ *but there is holy bread.* Is. 43:8. Joined with a participle it forms a periphrasis for the finite verb, Judg. 6:36 אִם יֶשְׁךָ מוֹשִׁיעַ *if thou savest.* Gen. 24:42, 49. When joined with plural nouns, *there are, there were,* 2 K. 2:16. Ezra 10:44.—יֵשׁ וָיֵשׁ *it is certainly so,* 2 K. 10:15.—יֶשׁ־לִי *I have,* (i. q. הָיָה לִי,) Gen. 43:7. Hence כָּל־אֲשֶׁר יֶשׁ־לוֹ *every thing which he had,* Gen. 39:5.—Prov. 8:21 לְהַנְחִיל אֹהֲבַי יֵשׁ *est (mihi,) quod dem diligentibus me;* comp. 2 Chr. 25:9.

2. especially, *there exists, there is extant.* Ruth 3:12. Jer. 5:1. Ecc. 1:10. יֵשׁ דָּבָר שֶׁיֹּאמַר *there exist things of which*

one may say. 2 : 21. 7 : 15. 8 : 14. Prov. 13 : 7 יֵשׁ מִתְעַשֵּׁר *there is that appeareth rich.* 11 : 24. 18 : 24.—יֵשׁ־אֲשֶׁר *fuerunt qui,* for *quidam;* and when repeated, *there are some, there are others,* Neh. 5 : 2, 3, 4. (Comp. the Syr. ܐܺܝܬ Mat. 13 : 8.)

יָשַׁב fut. יֵשֵׁב, infin. absol. יָשׁוֹב (1 Sam. 20 : 5.) const. שֶׁבֶת, with suff. שִׁבְתִּי, imper. שֵׁב, שְׁבָה.

1. *to seat one's self, to sit;* sometimes construed with a pleonastic dative, Gen. 21 : 16 וַתֵּשֶׁב לָהּ *she seated herself.* The place of sitting is preceded by בְּ, עַל, or is put in the accus. Ps. 9 : 12 יֹשֵׁב צִיּוֹן *sitting or enthroned on Zion.* 80 : 2 יֹשֵׁב הַכְּרֻבִים *sitting on the cherubim.* 99 : 1. Is. 37 : 16. The more special constructions are (1.) *to sit as judge* or *regent.* Ps. 9 : 8. 55 : 20. (2.) *to sit in ambush, to lie in wait.* Ps. 10 : 8. 17 : 12. Job 38 : 40. Hence construed with לְ, *insidiari,* Jer. 3 : 2. (3.) construed with עִם, *to have intercourse with* any one. Ps. 26 : 4, 5. comp. 1 : 1. and הָלַךְ עִם, בּוֹא עִם. (4.) Ps. 122 : 5 כִּי שָׁמָּה יָשְׁבוּ כִסְאוֹת לְמִשְׁפָּט *for there the thrones are set for judgment.* יָשְׁבוּ is here used of inanimate objects, as the verb *to stand* in English.

2. *to continue.* Gen. 24 : 55. 29 : 19. Construed with an accus. 25 : 27 יֹשֵׁב אֹהָלִים *continuing in tents,* i. e. at home. Hos. 3 : 3 תֵּשְׁבִי לִי *continue to me,* i. e. devote thyself to me alone. Also of inanimate objects, Gen. 49 : 24.

3. *to dwell.* Gen. 18 : 6. Construed with an accus. *to inhabit,* Gen. 4 : 20. Ps. 22 : 4 יוֹשֵׁב תְּהִלּוֹת יִשְׂרָאֵל *dwelling amidst the praises of Israel.* 107 : 10.

4. pass. *to be inhabited,* or *habitable,* spoken of a city or country. Is. 13 : 20. Jer. 17 : 6, 25. Ezek. 26 : 20. (Comp. ναίω, ναιετάω in Homer).

Niph. נוֹשַׁב *to be inhabited.* Ex. 16 : 35.

Hiph. הוֹשִׁיב 1. *to cause to sit,* or *dwell, to set.* Ps. 68 : 7. 113 : 9. 1 Sam. 2 : 8.

2. causat. of Kal no. 4. *to make to be inhabited.* Ezek. 36 : 33. Is. 54 : 3.

3. *to let dwell with one's self,* (as a wife,) *to marry.* Ezra 10 : 2, 10, 14, 17, 18. Neh. 13 : 23, 27. (In Ethiop. ושב conj. IV. *idem;* in Span. *casarse.*)

יֵשׁוּעַ contraction of יְהוֹשֻׁעַ, and used chiefly after the Babylonish captivity in later Hebrew.

1. *Joshua,* the successor of Moses. Neh. 8 : 17.

2. a high-priest after the captivity. Ezra 2 : 2. 3 : 2. Neh. 7 : 2. In Greek Ἰησοῦς.

יְשׁוּעָה f. verbal from יָשַׁע, dec. X.

1. *help, deliverance, salvation.*—יְשׁוּעַת יְהוָֹה *help obtained from God.* Ex. 14 : 13. As a concrete, Is. 26 : 18.

2. *victory.* (See הוֹשִׁיעַ no. I. a.) 1 Sam. 14 : 45, 47. 2 Chr. 20 : 17. Hab. 3 : 8.

3. *prosperity, happiness.* Job 30 : 15.

יֶשַׁח m. dec. VI found only Mic. 6 : 14. *empty stomach, emptiness of the belly.* (In Arab. by transpos. وحش conj. IV. *to be famished with hunger.*)

יָשַׁט found only in Hiph. הוֹשִׁיט *to stretch out.* Est. 4 : 11. 5 : 2. 8 : 4. (In Syr. and Chald. *idem.*)

יְשִׁימוֹן m. verbal from יָשַׁם, *a waste, desert.* Ps. 68 : 8. 78 : 40. 106 : 14.

יְשִׁימוֹת plur. fem. verbal from יָשַׁם, *destruction.* Ps. 55 : 16 Kethib. Comp. the proper name בֵּית־הַיְשִׁימוֹת (*house of the desert*) Num. 33 : 49. Josh. 12 : 3. 13 : 20. Ezek. 25 : 9. a place not far from the Dead Sea.

יָשִׁישׁ m. dec. III. a. *an old* or *aged man.* Job 12 : 12. 15 : 10. 29 : 8. 32 : 6. Also יָשֵׁשׁ (q. v.)

יָשַׁם i. q. שָׁמֵם *to be desolate,* only in the fut. תֵּשַׁם Gen. 47 : 19. Ezek. 12 : 19. 19 : 7. plur. תִּישַׁמְנָה Ezek. 6 : 6. Deriv. יְשִׁימוֹן, יְשִׁימוֹת.

יִשְׁמָעֵאל (*God hears*) a proper name, *Ishmael,* the son of Abraham by Hagar, and progenitor of many Arabian tribes. See Gen. 25 : 12—18. Hence יִשְׁמְעֵאלִים *Ishmaelites, Arabians,* Gen. 37 : 25. 39 : 1. Judg. 8 : 24. (comp. verse 22. Ps. 83 : 7.)

I. יָשֵׁן *to be old.* Found only in Niph. נוֹשַׁן strictly *to be made old;* (1.) *to remain long,* (in a land). Deut. 4:25. (2.) *to be deeply rooted, to become inveterate,* spoken of the leprosy. Lev. 13:11. (3.) *to grow old,* spoken of grain. Lev. 26:10 יָשָׁן נוֹשָׁן *grain of the preceding year that has grown old.*

Deriv. יָשָׁן.

II. יָשֵׁן, fut. יִישַׁן, infin. יְשׁוֹן *to sleep, to fall asleep.* Gen. 2:21. 41:5. Applied to the sleep of death, Job 3:13. Ps. 13:4 פֶּן אִישַׁן הַמָּוֶת *lest I sleep the sleep of death.*

Pi. *to cause to sleep.* Judg. 16:19.

Deriv. שֵׁנָה, יָשֵׁן, שְׁנָת.

יָשָׁן, fem. יְשָׁנָה, verbal adj. from יָשַׁן, dec. IV. a. *old,* in opposition to *new* or *fresh;* spoken only of things, e.g. of grain, Lev. 25:22. Cant. 7:14. of a gate. Neh. 3:6. 12:39. of a pool, Is. 22:11.

יָשֵׁן fem. יְשֵׁנָה, plur. const. יְשֵׁנֵי, verbal adj. from יָשֵׁן, dec. V. f. *sleeping.* Joined with pronouns and substantives it forms a periphrásis for the verb, 1 K. 3:20 אֲמָתְךָ יְשֵׁנָה *thine handmaid was asleep.* Cant. 5:2. 1 Sam. 26:7, 12.

יָשַׁע in Kal not used. In Arab. وسع *to be wide, enlarged;* an idea, which in the Shemitish languages often indicates *deliverance* or *happiness.*

Hiph. הוֹשִׁיעַ 1. *to help, succour;* construed with an accus. Ex. 2:17. Ps. 3:8. 6:5. with a dat. Josh. 10:6. Ps. 72:4. 86:16. 116:6. When spoken of Jehovah, whose power is efficient, *to give victory,* (comp. יְשׁוּעָה,) Deut. 20:4. Josh. 22:22. 2 Sam. 8:6, 14— הוֹשִׁיעָה לִּי יָדִי *mine own hand hath given me the victory,* that is, without the aid of another, Judg. 7:2. Job 40:14. Ps. 98:1. A similar phrase is formed with זְרוֹעַ, Ps. 44:4. Is. 59:16. 63:5. sometimes with the idea of rashness, 1 Sam. 25:26, 33. comp. verse 31.

2. *to deliver, set free;* construed with מִן, Ps. 7:2. 34:7. 44:8. or with מִיַּד, Judg. 2:16, 18. 3:31.

Niph. 1. *to be aided, assisted, to obtain victory.* Deut. 33:29. Part. נוֹשָׁע *victorious,* Zech. 9:9. Ps. 33:16.

2. *to be freed, delivered.* Num. 10:9. Ps. 33:16.

יֵשַׁע and יֶשַׁע, with suff. יִשְׁעִי, יִשְׁעֲךָ Ps. 85:8. verbal from יָשַׁע, dec. VI.

1. *help, salvation, deliverance.* Ps. 13:6. 50:23. Construed with an accus. like its verb, Hab. 3:13 לְיֵשַׁע אֶת מְשִׁיחֶךָ *for the help of thine anointed.*

2. *prosperity, happiness.* Job 5:4, 11. Ps. 132:17. Is. 61:10.

יְשַׁעְיָהוּ (*salvation of Jehovah*) *Isaiah,* a proper name. The most celebrated person of this name is the prophet, Is. 1:1. 2 K. 19:20. Sept. Ἡσαΐας. Vulg. *Isaias.*

יָשְׁפֵה Ex. 28:20. 39:13. and יָשְׁפֶה Ezek. 28:13. *jasper,* a precious stone of different colours.

יָשַׁר, fut. יִישַׁר, (once יִשַּׁרְנָה 1 Sam. 6:12.)

1. *to be straight, even.* 1 Sam. 6:12 וַיִּשַּׁרְנָה הַפָּרוֹת בַּדֶּרֶךְ literally *and the kine were strait on the way,* i. e. they went directly on. (For the grammatical form, see Gesenius' Lehrgeb. § 81. 2.)

2. metaphorically *to be right;* found only in the phrase יָשַׁר בְּעֵינֵי *to be right in the eyes of* any one, *to please* him, Num. 23:27. Judg. 14:3, 7. 1 Sam. 18:20, 26. 2 Sam. 17:4. 19:6. 1 K. 9:12.

3. perhaps *to be happy.* (Arab. يسر *idem.* Comp. טוֹב no. 4.) Hab. 2:4 הִנֵּה עֻפְּלָה לֹא יָשְׁרָה נַפְשׁוֹ בּוֹ *behold, whose soul is incredulous, it shall not be happy for it.* Others: *behold, froward, not modest is his soul,* literally *tumidus, non planus est animus in eo.*

Pi. 1. *to make straight* or *even;* e.g. a path, Is. 40:3. Also *to make straight another's paths,* for *to give him prosperity,* Is. 45:13. Prov. 3:6. *to make straight one's own paths,* for *to walk in a straight path,* Prov. 9:15.

2. *to lead, direct;* e.g. a water course, 2 Chr. 32:30. the thunder, Job 37:3.

3. *to esteem right*, or *to observe strictly*. Ps. 119 : 128.

Pu. part. זָהָב מְיֻשָּׁר *gold beaten out, thin gold*. 1 K. 6 : 35.

Hiph. fut. יַיְשִׁר i. q. Pi. Ps. 5 : 9 Keri. (In the Kethib הושר.) Intrans. Prov. 4 : 25.

Deriv. out of course מִישׁוֹר, מֵישָׁרִים.

יָשָׁר, fem. יְשָׁרָה, verbal from יָשַׁר, dec. IV. a.

1. *straight*, *rectus*. Ezek. 1 : 7, 23. Used especially of the way, Jer. 31 : 9. Job 33 : 27 יָשָׁר הֶעֱוֵיתִי *the straight I have made crooked*.

2. *right*, especially when construed with בְּעֵינֵי. Judg. 17 : 6 הַיָּשָׁר בְּעֵינָיו *what seemed to him right*. Deut. 12 : 25, 28 הַיָּשָׁר בְּעֵינֵי יְהוָה *what is pleasing to Jehovah*. Construed with לִפְנֵי, Prov. 14 : 12. 16 : 25.

3. *righteous, upright, virtuous*. Job 1 : 1, 8. Ps. 11 : 7. So יִשְׁרֵי־לֵב Ps. 7 : 11 and יִשְׁרֵי־דֶרֶךְ 37 : 14. Especially do the Jews bear this name, (comp. צַדִּיק,) Dan. 11 : 17.—סֵפֶר הַיָּשָׁר *the book of the righteous*, a collection of Hebrew national songs now lost, Josh. 10 : 3. 2 Sam. 1 : 18. As an abstract noun, *righteousness*, Ps. 37 : 37.

4. *true, faithful*; spoken of God. Deut. 32 : 4. Ps. 119 : 137.

5. *happy, prosperous*. Ezra 8 : 21.

יֹשֶׁר m. verbal from יָשַׁר, dec. VI. p.

1. *straightness*. Prov. 2 : 13. 4 : 11.

2. *right, duty, obligation*. Job 6 : 25. 33 : 23. Prov. 11 : 24. 14 : 2. 17 : 26.

3. *righteousness, uprightness*; construed for the most part with לֵב or לֵבָב. Deut. 9 : 5. Ps. 25 : 21. 119 : 7. Job 33 : 3.

יִשְׁרָה or **יְשָׁרָה** f. const. יִשְׁרַת, verbal from יָשַׁר, *idem*. 1 K. 3 : 6.

יְשֻׁרוּן m. *Jeshurun*, a poetical name for *Israel*, found only Deut. 32 : 15. 33 : 5, 26. Is. 44 : 2. It signifies most probably *the upright, the virtuous*, as if from יָשַׁר, after the form זְבוּלוּן, but at the same time with an allusion to the name יִשְׂרָאֵל. וּן appears to be the termination of diminutives, here used *by way of endearment*. Others derive it as a dimin. directly from יִשְׂרָאֵל; in the Veneto-Greek version Ἰσραηλίσκος.

יָשֵׁשׁ m. i. q. יָשִׁישׁ, *old*. 2 Chr. 36 : 17.

יַת Chald. i. q. Heb. אֵת, a sign of the accusative case. Dan. 3 : 12.

יְתִב Chald. i. q. Heb. יָשַׁב.

1. *to seat one's self, to sit*. Dan. 7 : 9. 10 : 26.

2. *to dwell*. Ezra 4 : 17.

Aph. הוֹתֵב *to cause to dwell, to set*. Ezra 4 : 10.

יָתֵד f. const. יְתַד, plur. יְתֵדוֹת, dec. V. a.

1. *a peg* or *pin*, to be driven into the wall. Ezek. 15 : 3. but especially *a tent-pin*, Ex. 27 : 19. 35 : 18. 38 : 31. Judg. 4 : 21, 22. The driving of such a pin is with the Hebrews indicative of a firm and permanent situation, Is. 22 : 23. Hence

2. metaphorically *a firm, secure dwelling place*. Ezra 9 : 8. In verse 9, the same idea is denoted by גָּדֵר. (Comp. the verbs נָטַע, נָתַשׁ.)

3. also metaphorically *a superior, chief, princeps civitatis*. Zech. 10 : 4. Comp. פִּנָּה.

4. *a spade, shovel*. Deut. 23 : 13.—Judg. 16 : 14 יְתַד הָאֶרֶג *spatha textoris*.

יָתוֹם m. dec. III. a. *an orphan*. Ex. 22 : 22, 24. Deut. 10 : 18. 14 : 29. Also simply *fatherless*, Job 24 : 9. (Arab. يتم *to become an orphan*.)

יְתוּר m. verbal from תּוּר no. 1. (after the form יְקוּם,) *what one spies* or *finds out*. Job 39 : 8.

יַתִּיר Chald. 1. adj. *very great, eminent, extraordinary*. Dan. 2 : 31. 5 : 12, 14.

2. adv. יַתִּירָה *very, exceeding*. Dan. 3 : 22. 7 : 7, 10.

יַתִּיר proper name of a city of the priests in the hill-country of the tribe of Judah. Josh. 15 : 48. 21 : 14. 1 Sam. 30 : 27. 1 Chr. 6 : 42.

יָתַם. For the fut. אֵיתָם Ps. 19 : 14. see the verb תָּמַם.

יָתַר *to remain, to be left*. In Kal not used, except in the part. יוֹתֵר *the rest*,

1 Sam. 15:15. (For several other significations of this form, see the articles יוֹתֵר and יוֹתֶרֶת.)

Hiph. הוֹתִיר 1. *to let remain, to leave.* Ex. 10:15. 12:10. Ps. 79:11 הוֹתֵר בְּנֵי תְמוּתָה *preserve* (liter. *superstites fac*) *the sons of death*, i. e. those doomed to die.

2. *to make to abound*, construed with an accus. of the person and בְּ of the thing. Deut. 28:11. 30:9.

3. intrans. *to have the preference.* Gen. 49:4 אַל־תּוֹתַר *thou shalt not have the preference*, i. e. the birth-right.

Niph. נוֹתַר 1. *to be left.* Ex. 10:15. Part. נוֹתָר, fem. נוֹתֶרֶת, *the rest*, Gen. 30:36. Ex. 28:10. 29:34.

2. *to stay behind.* Gen. 32:25.

3. *to acquire the superiority* or *victory.* (In Syr. Ethpa. *præstans, excellens fuit.*) Dan. 10:13 וַאֲנִי נוֹתַרְתִּי שָׁם אֵצֶל מַלְכֵי פָרָס *and I there acquired the superiority with the kings of Persia.*

Deriv. out of course יוֹתֵר, יוֹתֶרֶת, מוֹתָר, מֵיתָר.

I. יֶתֶר m. with suff. יִתְרוֹ, verbal from יָתַר, dec. VI. h.

1. *the rest, the remainder.*—יֶתֶר הָעָם *the rest of the people*, Judg. 7:6.—Joel 1:4 יֶתֶר הָאַרְבֶּה *what was left by the locusts.*

2. *abundance, superfluity.*—עַל יֶתֶר *in abundance*, Ps. 31:24. יִתְרָם *their abundance*, Job 4:21. 22:20.

3. *excellence, dignity.* שְׂפַת יֶתֶר *excellent speech*, Prov. 17:7. Used as a concrete, Gen. 49:3 יֶתֶר שְׂאֵת וְיֶתֶר עָז *the first in dignity, the first in strength.*

4. adv. *eminently, very much.* Is. 56:12. Dan. 8:9. otherwise יֶתֶר.

5. *besides.* Num. 31:32. See יוֹתֵר no. 4.

II. יֶתֶר m. dec. VI. h. *a cord*, Judg. 16:7 ff. *string of a bow*, Ps. 11:2. *bridle*, (parall. רֶסֶן,) Job 30:11 Kethib יִתְרוֹ פִתַּח *he lets his bridle loose*, i. e. acts without restraint. According to the Keri, *he* (*God*) *loosens my nerves*, i. e. disarms me, not accordant with the parallel clause. Comp. מֵיתָר.

יִתְרָה fem. of יֶתֶר, dec. X. *remainder, abundance.* Is. 15:7. Jer. 48:36.

יִתְרוֹ proper name of the father-in-law of Moses, also called יֶתֶר and חֹבָב Ex. 3:1. 4:18.

יִתְרוֹן m. verbal from יָתַר.

1. *advantage, profit.* Ecc. 1:3. 2:11. 3:9. 5:8, 15. 10:10.

2. *excellence.* Ecc. 2:13.

כ

The letter *Caph* (Heb. כַּף *the hollow hand,*) is the eleventh in the alphabet, and as a numerical sign denotes 20.

It is a palatal of an intermediate character, and therefore commuted sometimes with the smoother palatal ג, (see p. 97.) and sometimes with the rougher ק, (see p. 97. no. 2.) Comp. further דָּכָה and דָּקַק *to be beaten in pieces;* מָכַךְ and מָקַק no. 2. *to sink, to fall;* רָכַךְ and רָקַק *to be thin, tender.*

Sometimes, though more rarely, it is interchanged with the gutturals ח and ע; e. g. חֹלֶד Arab. خلد and كلد *a mole;* חָרִיץ Arab. كريض *cheese;* כְּבָר and חָבוֹר *the river Chaboras;* כְּפִיר Arab. غفر and غفر *a young lion;* כָּתַר and עָטַר *to surround, to crown.*

כְּ a prefix prep. and conj. (also written כְּמוֹ and כְּדֵי in the same sense; see דַּי.)

1. *as.* Gen. 3:4. Dan. 10:18 כְּמַרְאֵה אָדָם *something in a human form.*—כְּ....כְּ *as .... so,* Lev. 7:7. 24:16. Gen. 44:18 כָּמוֹךָ כְּפַרְעֹה *as thou, so Pharaoh,* i. e. thou art as Pharaoh. Sometimes the copulative וְ intervenes, Dan. 11:29. Josh. 14:11. Ezek. 18:4.

2. *according to, after, secundum.* 2 K. 1:17 כִּדְבַר־יְהוָה *according to the word of Jehovah.* 1 Sam. 13:14 אִישׁ כִּלְבָבוֹ *a man after his own heart.* Ps. 7:18 כְּצִדְקוֹ *according to his righteousness.*

3. *about, nearly, almost,* (before words of number, measure, or time.) Ruth 1:4 כְּעֶשֶׂר שָׁנִים *about ten years.* 1 K. 22.6. Ruth 2:17 כְּאֵיפָה *about an ephah.* Gen. 39:11 כְּהַיּוֹם הַזֶּה *about this time.* Dan. 9:21 כְּעֵת מִנְחַת־עֶרֶב *about the*

time of the evening offering. Ex. 9:18 כָּעֵת מָחָר *about the time of to-morrow*, i. e. to-morrow. כַּיּוֹם *now*, Gen. 25:31.— כִּמְעַט *about a little*, i. e. little is wanting, almost; see מְעַט.

4. before an infin. *when, as.* Gen. 39:18 כַּהֲרִימִי קוֹלִי *when I lifted up my voice.* Deut. 16:6 כְּבוֹא הַשֶּׁמֶשׁ *when the sun is gone down.* 24:13. More rarely before a participle, Gen. 38:29 וַיְהִי כְּמֵשִׁיב יָדוֹ *and when he drew back his hand.* 40:10. So before a verbal noun, Is. 23:5 כַּאֲשֶׁר שֵׁמַע צֹר *when they hear concerning Tyre*, i. e. at the report concerning Tyre.

5. כְּ is sometimes redundant and may be omitted in translating. In these cases it is called by grammarians *Caph veritatis.* Neh. 7:2 הוּא כְּאִישׁ אֱמֶת *he was a faithful man;* liter. *as a faithful man is wont to be.* Job 24:14 בַּלַּיְלָה יְהִי כַגַּנָּב *by night he is a thief*, i. e. he acts as a thief. Hos. 4:4. 5:10. Is. 1:7. 13:6.

Note. With suffixes only כָּהֶם, כָּכֶם, *as ye, as they.* The other suffixes are annexed to the form כְּמוֹ, כָּמוֹנִי, q. v.

I. **כָּאַב**, fut. יִכְאַב, *to have pain;* either in body, Gen. 34:25. or in mind, Ps. 69:30. Prov. 14:13. Job 14:22.

Hiph. *to occasion pain, to make sad.* Job 5:18. Ezek. 28:24. Construed with an accus. of the person, Ezek. 13:22.

Deriv. out of course מַכְאֹב.

II. **כָּאַב** prob. i. q. Syr. ܟܒܐ *nocuit;* or Arab. كَبَّ *perdidit, destruxit;* (comp. מאס no. II. i. q. מסס.) Hence Hiph. *to destroy.* 2 K. 3:19.

כְּאֵב m. verbal from כָּאַב no. I. dec. I. (with Tseri impure,) *pain, grief.* Job 2:13. 16:6. Is. 17:21. 65:14.

כָּאָה *to be sad, desponding.* In Kal not used. (Syr. ܟܐܐ *to chide*, hence *to grieve.* Kindred with כָּהָה.)

Hiph. *to make sad*, as the heart. Ezek. 13:22.

Niph. *to be grieved, humbled.* Dan. 11:30. Ps. 109:16.

כָּאֶה m. verbal adj. from כָּאָה, *desponding, unhappy.* Plur. כָּאִים Ps. 10:10 Keri. But the reading of the Kethib is preferable. See חֵלְכָה.

כָּבֵד and **כָּבַד**, fut. יִכְבַּד.

1. *to be heavy.* Job 6:3. Hence spoken of sin, *to be grievous, very great*, Gen. 18:20.

2. *to lie* or *fall heavily on* any one, *to be chargeable*, or *troublesome to* him; construed with עַל. Is. 24:20. Neh. 5:18. 2 Sam. 13:25 וְלֹא נִכְבַּד עָלֶיךָ *that we be not chargeable unto thee;* comp. 14:26.—כָּבְדָה יַד־יְהוָה עַל *the hand of God lies heavily on* any one, i. e. God brings upon him troubles, afflictions. 1 Sam. 5:11. Ps. 32:4. Construed with אֶל, 1 Sam. 5:6.

3. *to be dull*, of hearing or of vision. Gen. 48:10. Is. 59:1.

4. *to be hard, obdurate;* spoken of the heart. Ex. 9:7.

5. *to be honoured, respected, mighty, gravem esse.* Job 14:21. Ezek. 27:25. Is. 66:25.

6. *to be* or *become violent, vehement, gravem esse.* Judg. 20:34. 1 Sam. 31:3.

Pi. כִּבֵּד 1. causat. of Kal no. 4. *to harden.* 1 Sam. 6:6.

2. causat. of Kal no. 5. *to honour.* Judg. 13:17. 2 Sam. 10:3. In reference to the Deity, Is. 29:13. also with לְ, Ps. 86:9. Dan. 11:38. Is. 43:23 וּזְבָחֶיךָ לֹא כִבַּדְתָּנִי *thou hast not honoured me with thy sacrifices.*

Hiph. 1. *to make heavy*, or *grievous.* 1 K. 12:10. Is. 47:6.

2. *to oppress* a people, construed with עַל. Neh. 5:15.

3. *to make hard, heavy*, or *obdurate;* e. g. the ears, Is. 6:10. Zech. 7:11. the heart, Ex. 9:34.

4. *to make to be honoured* or *distinguished.* Is. 8:23. [9:1.] Intrans. *to acquire honour*, 2 Chr. 25:19.

Niph. 1. *to be rich* or *abundant in* any thing. Part. Prov. 8:24 מַעְיָנוֹת נִכְבַּדֵּי מָיִם *fountains abounding in water.*

2. pass. of Pi. no. 2. *to be honoured.* Gen. 34:19.—נִכְבַּדֵּי־אֶרֶץ *the most ho-*

nourable of the earth, Is. 23:8,9. (The Dagesh in ר is euphonic.) Plur. fem. נִכְבָּדוֹת *glorious things*, Ps. 87:3.

3. reflex. *to shew one's self great* or *glorious, to glorify one's self.* Hag. 1:8. With בְּ *in* any one, Ex. 14:4,17,18. Lev. 10:3. Ezek. 39:13.

Hithpa. 1. *to multiply one's self, to be numerous.* Nah. 3:15.

2. *to honour one's self, to be proud.* Prov. 12:9.

Deriv. out of course כָּבוֹד.

כָּבֵד, const. כְּבַד Ex. 4:10. and כֶּבֶד Is. 1:4. verbal from כָּבֵד, dec. V. d.

1. as an adj. *heavy*, Prov. 27:3. *burdensome*, spoken of an employment, Ex. 18:18. Num. 11:14. *laden*, (with iniquity), Is. 1:4. *severe, sore*, spoken of a famine, Gen. 12:10. 41:31.

2. *slow*, (of speech). Ex. 4:10. hence *unintelligible*, Ezek. 3:5.

3. *great, numerous.*—חַיִל כָּבֵד *a numerous host*, 1 K. 10:2. So in Germ. *eine schwere Menge.*

4. *rich, abounding.* Gen. 13:2.

5. as a subst. *the liver.* (Arab. كَبِد,) perhaps literally *the most precious;* comp. כָּבוֹד no. 4. Ex. 29:13,22. Lev. 3:4,10. Lam. 2:11 נִשְׁפַּךְ לָאָרֶץ כְּבֵדִי *my liver is poured out upon the earth*, as indicative of violent grief.

כָּבֹד verbal adj. from כָּבֵד, found only in the fem. כְּבוּדָּה *glorious, magnificent*, Ezek. 23:41. Ps. 45:14. Also collectively, *costly articles*, Judg. 18:21.

כֹּבֶד m. verbal from כָּבֵד.

1. *weight, heaviness.* Prov. 27:3.

2. *vehemence, heat, rage*, (of battle.) Is. 21:15. comp. 1 Sam. 31:3.

3. *multitude.* Nah. 3:3.

כְּבֵדוּת f. denom. from כָּבֵד, *difficulty.* Ex. 14:25.

כָּבָה *to go out, to be extinguished;* spoken of the fire, Lev. 6:5,6. [6:12, 13.] of the light, 1 Sam. 3:3. Spoken metaphorically of the anger of God, 2 K. 22:17. also in another figure, Is. 43:17 *they are extinct, they go out like tow.*

Pi. *to extinguish, put out.* Is. 1:31. 42:3. Jer. 4:4. 21:12. 2 Sam. 21:17 וְלֹא תְכַבֶּה אֶת־נֵר יִשְׂרָאֵל *that thou extinguish not the light of Israel.*

כָּבוֹד m. (fem. only Gen. 49:6.) verbal from כָּבֵד, dec. III. a. literally *weight, gravitas;* hence

1. *honour, praise.* Ps. 19:2. 79:9. 96:8.—כְּבוֹד יִשְׂרָאֵל *the honourable of Israel*, comp. Mic. 1:15. Is. 5:13. 8:7. 17:3,4.

2. *majesty, glory.*—מֶלֶךְ הַכָּבוֹד *the glorious* or *majestic king*, Ps. 24:7,8,9.—כִּסֵּא הַכָּבוֹד *the glorious throne*, 1 Sam. 2:8.—כְּבוֹד לְבָנוֹן *the glory* or *ornament of Lebanon*, Is. 35:2. 60:13. comp. 10:18.—Especially כְּבוֹד יְהוָה (Sept. δόξα Κυρίου,) *the glory of Jehovah*, i. e. the shining splendour which surrounds the Deity, when he appears to men, called by the Rabbins *the Shechinah*, Ex. 24:16. 40:34. 1 K. 8:10,11. 2 Chr. 7:1. Is. 6:3,4. Ezek. 1:28. 3:12,23. 8:4. 10:4,18. 11:22. comp. in N.T. Luke 2:9. It is represented as a bright fire, Ex. 24:17. 33:18. from which lightnings proceed, Lev. 9:23. Num. 16:35. Ps. 18:13. and which is usually covered with smoke, 1 K. 8:10,11.

3. *abundance, riches.* Ps. 49:17. Is. 10:3. 66:12.

4. poetically for *the heart, soul;* prob. liter. i. q. כָּבֵד *the liver.* Gen. 49:6 בִּקְהָלָם אַל־תֵּחַד כְּבֹדִי *with their assembly let not my heart be united.* Ps. 16:9. 57:9. 108:2.

כְּבוּדָּה see **כָּבֹד**.

כָּבוּל proper name of a district of Galilee, containing 20 cities, which Solomon gave to king Hiram. 1 K. 9:13. The following notice of Josephus (Antiq. VIII. 5. 3.) applies here, although its correctness may be doubted, as the word is not found in the Shemitish languages. "Μεθερμηνευόμενον γὰρ τὸ Χαβαλὼν, κατὰ Φοινίκων γλῶτταν οὐκ ἀρέσκων σημαίνει."

כַּבִּיר m. verbal adj. from כָּבַר, dec. I.
1. *great, mighty.* Job 34:17, 24. 36:5.—מַיִם כַּבִּירִים *mighty waters,* Is. 17:12. 28:2. כַּבִּיר יָמִים *grandævus,* Job 15:10. (So in Arab.)

2. *many, much.* Job 31:25. Is. 16:14.

כְּבִיר m. *something twisted* or *platted, a quilt.* 1 Sam. 19:13, 16. Comp. the kindred words מִכְבָּר *a lattice-work;* מַכְבֵּר *a net, covering;* כְּבָרָה *a sieve;* and מִכְמָר, מִכְמוֹר *a net.*

כֶּבֶל m. dec. VI. a. *a fetter.* Ps. 105:18. 149:8. (Arab. and Syr. *idem.*) Root כבל, in Syr. Chald. Arab. *to bind, to fetter.*

כָּבַס *to wash, cleanse,* namely, clothes, in Greek πλύνειν; (comp. רָחַץ *to wash* the body, in Greek λούειν.) In Kal only part. כּוֹבֵס Is. 7:3. 36:2. *a washer, fuller,* πλύντης, κναφεύς, *fullo.* The fuller in this operation made use of lie, and trod the clothes with his feet in a trough.

Pi. 1. i. q. Kal. Gen. 49:11. Ex. 19:10. Part. מְכַבֵּס i. q. כֹּבֵס, Mal. 3:2.

2. metaphorically *to purify* the heart. Ps. 51:4, 9. Jer. 4:14. the metaphor sometimes being continued, Jer. 2:22. Mal. 3:2.

Pu. pass. Lev. 13:58. 15:17.

Hothpa. pass. הֻכַּבֵּס Lev. 13:55, 56.

כָּבַר in Kal not used, *to be great* or *numerous;* comp. כַּבִּיר.

Hiph. *to make many, to multiply.* Job 35:16. Part. מַכְבִּיר *abundance,* Job 36:31. (comp. מִשְׁחוֹת.)

I. כְּבָר adv. 1. *already, formerly, long ago.* Ecc. 1:10. 3:15. 4:2. 9:6.

2. *now.* Ecc. 9:7. (Syr. ܟܒܪ *formerly, now.*)

II. כְּבָר *Ghaboras,* the proper name of a river in Mesopotamia, otherwise called חָבוֹר, (q. v.) Ezek. 1:3. 3:15, 23. 10:15, 22. Syr. ܟܒܪ, ܟܒܘܪ.

כְּבָרָה f. *a sieve.* Am. 9:9. See כְּבִיר.

כִּבְרָה f. dec. X. a long measure, the exact extent of which is not known. Gen. 35:16. 48:7. 2 K. 5:19. In the Chaldaic version פְּרַס־אַרְעָא *aratio terræ,* (from פְּרַב *aravit,*) and then i. q. *jugerum;* from which perhaps the Hebrew word is formed by transposition. The Sept. adds in Gen. 48:7, ἱππόδρομος, a common measure among the Arabians, thought to equal about a French mile.

כֶּבֶשׂ m. dec. VI. a. and h. *a lamb of one year and upwards, agnus mediæ ætatis;* hence the frequent addition, בֶּן־שְׁנָתוֹ *a year old,* Num. 7:15, 21, 23, 39, 45, 51, 57, 63, 69, 75. and in the plur. בְּנֵי שָׁנָה, *idem,* 7:17, 23, 29, 35, 41. (Arab. كَبْش *idem.*)

כִּבְשָׂה 2 Sam. 12:3. and כַּבְשָׂה Lev. 14:10. Num. 6:14. fem. of כֶּבֶשׂ, dec. XII. *an ewe-lamb about a year old.* We sometimes, though more rarely, find כֶּשֶׂב and כִּשְׂבָּה, by transposition.

כָּבַשׁ fut. יִכְבּוֹשׁ.

1. *to tread under foot.* Metaphorically Zech. 9:15 וְכָבְשׁוּ אַבְנֵי־קֶלַע *they shall tread the sling-stones under foot,* i. e. they shall not be injured by them. (Comp. Job 41:20, 21. [41:28, 29.] Mic. 7:19 יִכְבּוֹשׁ עֲוֹנֹתֵינוּ *he will suppress our iniquities.*

2. *to subdue, subject, subjugate.* Gen. 1:28. Jer. 34:16. with the addition לַעֲבָדִים, 2 Chr. 28:10. Jer. 34:10. Neh. 5:5.

3. Est. 7:8. prob. *vim inferre fœminæ, subigere fœminam.* (So in Arab. كَبَس, and كَبْس *coitus.*)

Pi. *to subdue,* i. q. Kal no. 2. 2 Sam. 8:11.

Niph. 1. pass. of Kal no. 2. Num. 32:22, 29. Josh. 18:1.

2. pass. of Kal no. 3. Neh. 5:5 at the close.

כֶּבֶשׁ m. *a footstool.* 2 Chr. 9:18. Syr. ܟܘܒܫܐ *idem.*

כִּבְשָׁן m. *a furnace, a smelting oven,* different from תַּנּוּר a kind of baker's oven. Gen. 19:28. Ex. 9:8, 10. 19:18. (Arab. قبس *to kindle.*)

כַּד f. plur. כַּדִּים, dec. VIII. h. *a pail* or *bucket*, κάδος, *cadus*, for carrying water, Gen. 24:14 ff. Ecc. 12:6. 1 K. 18:34. also for keeping meal, 1 K. 17: 12, 14, 16. It was carried on the shoulder. 1 K. 18:24. (Arab. كدّ *to draw from a well.*)

כְּדַב, fem. כִּדְבָה, Chald. adj. i. q. Heb. כָּזָב *lying, false.* Dan. 2:9.

כְּדֵי see דַּי.

כְּדִי see דִּי.

כַּדְכֹּד m. Ezek. 27:16. Is. 54:12. name of a precious stone, most probably of a red colour; comp. Arab. كذكذة *rubedo maxima*, and Heb. כִּידוֹד *sparks.* (In Chald. כַּדְכְּדָנָא, כַּדְכּוֹדִין Ex. 39:11. *idem.*)

כֹּה adv. prim. 1. *thus.* Gen. 32:5. Ex. 3:15.—כֹּה אָמַר יְהוָה *thus saith Jehovah*, Jer. 2:2. 7:20. 9:16, 22.—כֹּה...וְכֹה *in this manner....in that manner*, 1 K. 22:20.

2. *here*, (more rarely.) Gen. 31:37. When doubled, *here....there*, Num. 11: 31.—עַד־כֹּה *hither*, or rather *thither*, Gen. 22:5. Ex. 2:12 כֹּה וָכֹה *hither and thither.*

3. in reference to time, *now.*—עַד־כֹּה *to the present time, hitherto*, Ex. 7:16. Josh. 17:14. 1 K. 18:45 עַד־כֹּה וְעַד־כֹּה *so and so long*, i. e. in the mean time.

כָּה Chald. i. q. Heb. כֹּה no. 3. Once Dan. 7:18 עַד־כָּה *hitherto.* Comp. the Heb. אֵיכָה.

כָּהָה 1. *to be extinguished, to go out, to be dull, dim;* spoken of a light. See the adj. Is. 42:3.

2. *to be weak, dull, dim;* as the eyes from old age, Deut. 34:7. Zech. 11: 17. Gen. 27:1. or from sorrow, Job 17:7.

3. *to despond, to intermit.* Is. 42:4.

Pi. כִּהָה and כֵּהָה for the most part intrans.

1. *to become paler, to disappear;* spoken of the spots of the leprosy. Lev. 13:6, 21, 26, 28, 56.

2. in a moral sense, *to be low spirited, desponding, to faint.* Ezek. 21:12. comp. Is. 61:3.

3. trans. *to dispirit, chide, rebuke, increpare.* 1 Sam. 3:13 וְלֹא כִהָה בָּם *and he rebuked* or *restrained them not.* Comp גָּעַר.

כֵּהֶה found only in the fem. כֵּהָה, verbal adj. from כָּהָה dec. X.

1. *going out, expiring*, spoken of a lamp. Is. 42:3.

2. *weak*, spoken of the eyes. 1 Sam. 3:2 וְעֵינָיו הֵחֵלּוּ כֵהוֹת *and his eyes began (to wax) dim.* Comp. a similar construction Gen. 9:20.

3. *diminishing, disappearing.* Lev. 13:39.

4. *desponding.* רוּחַ כֵּהָה *a desponding heart*, Is. 61:3.

כֵּהָה f. verbal from כָּהָה, *an extinguishing, healing*, or *alleviating.* Nah. 3:19. Comp. גֵּהָה.

כְּהַל Chald. *to be able*, construed with לְ and an infin. Dan. 2:26. 4:15. [4:18.] 5:8, 15.

כֹּהֵן m. dec. VII. b. *a priest;* very frequently.—כֹּהֵן הָרֹאשׁ 2 Chr. 19:11. 24: 11. 26:20. and הַכֹּהֵן הַגָּדוֹל Lev. 21:10. Num. 35:25, 28. Josh. 20:6. *the high-priest;* also הַכֹּהֵן הַמָּשִׁיחַ Lev. 4:3, 5. *the anointed priest.* The Chaldaic version sometimes renders it *princeps*, as in Gen. 41:45. Ps. 110:4. So it is generally supposed to mean 2 Sam. 8:18, where the sons of David are called כֹּהֲנִים, instead of which we find in the parallel passage 1 Chr. 18:17 וּבְנֵי דָוִיד הָרִאשֹׁנִים לְיַד הַמֶּלֶךְ *and the sons of David were the first on the side of the king;* comp. 1 K. 4:5. 2 K. 10:11. But this meaning of the word is not at all proved by a reference to these parallel passages; for the sons of David 2 Sam. 8:18, were probably *priests* or *ecclesiastical counsellors*, though they were not *Levitical* priests. The writer of Chronicles, however, chose not to give the name כֹּהֵן to any but Levitical priests. See De Wette's Beyträge zur Einleit. ins

A. T. Bändchen I. p. 81, 82. also Gesenius' Geschichte der hebräischen Sprache und Schrift. p. 41. Hence the verb

כִּהֵן Piel, denom. from כֹּהֵן.

1. *to serve as priest, to administer the priest's office.* Ex. 31:10. usually construed with לְ, Ex. 28:41. 40:13, 15. Hos. 4:6.

2. *to become a priest.* Deut. 10:6.

3. Is. 61:10 כֶּחָתָן יְכַהֵן פְּאֵר prob. *as the bridegroom adorns in priestly style his turban,* i. e. puts on a turban of priestly magnificence. Others: *makes rich his turban,* comp. Syr. ܟܗܢ Pe. and Ethpa. *to be* or *become rich, opulent, happy;* ܟܘܗܢܐ *glory, magnificence.*

כָּהֵן emph. כָּהֲנָא, plur. כָּהֲנִין, Chald. *a priest.* Ezra 7:12, 16, 21.

כְּהֻנָּה f. denom. from כֹּהֵן, dec. X. *the priesthood, the office of a priest.* Ex. 29:9. 40:15. Num. 16:10. 25:13.

כַּו plur. כַּוִּין, Chald. *a window.* Dan. 6:11. (In Syr. and Arab. *idem.*)

כּוּב found only Ezek. 30:5. a southern country mentioned in connexion with Egypt and Ethiopia. We may compare it with *Cobe,* a harbour of Ethiopia; or with *Cobium,* a place in Mareotis. Another reading נוּב *Nubia* is supported by the Arabic version, and suits the context.

כּוֹבַע m. plur. כּוֹבָעִים, dec. II. c. *a helmet,* usually of metal among the Hebrews. 1 Sam. 17:5. Ezek. 27:10. 38:5. Elsewhere written קוֹבַע.

כָּוָה found only in Niph. *to be burned.* Prov. 6:28. Is. 43:2.

Deriv. מִכְוָה, כִּי, כְּוִיָּה.

כֹּחַ (Dan. 11:6.) more commonly כֹּחַ, dec. I. a.

1. *power, strength.* Ezra 10:13 *but the people are many, and the weather is rainy,* וְאֵין כֹּחַ לַעֲמוֹד בַּחוּץ *and we are not able to stand without.* (Comp. עָצַר כֹּחַ under עָצַר.) Job 26:2 לְלֹא כֹחַ *to the weak.* —Used also of God, Num. 14:17. Job 23:6. 30:18.

2. *ability, aptness, fitness.* Dan. 1:4.

3. *ability, means, goods, facultates.* Job 6:22. 36:19. Prov. 5:10. comp. Ezra 2:69.

4. *the strength of the earth,* poetically for *its fruits, produce.* Gen. 4:12. Job 31:39.

כְּוִיָּה f. verbal from כָּוָה, *a mark burnt in, a burnt spot.* Ex. 21:25.

כּוֹכָב m. prim. dec. II. b. *a star.* Gen. 37:9. Ps. 8:5. (Arab. and Syr. *idem.*)

כּוּל *to measure,* (as in Syr. Chald. and Arab.) in Kal only Is. 40:12.

Pilp. כִּלְכֵּל 1. *to hold in itself, to comprehend, contain.* 1 K. 8:27. 2 Chr. 6:18.

2. *to support* or *sustain, to provide with the means of living.* Gen. 45:11. 50:21. 1 K. 4:7. 17:4. Construed with two accus. Gen. 47:12. 1 K. 18:4, 13.

3. *to hold out, to endure.* Mal. 3:2. Prov. 18:14. Jer. 20:9.

4. *to hold up, to defend, sustain.* Ps. 112:5 *he defends his conduct before the court.* Ps. 55:23 וְהוּא יְכַלְכְּלֶךָ *and he will sustain thee.*

Pass. כָּלְכַּל *to be nourished* or *supported.* 1 K. 20:27.

Hiph. הֵכִיל 1. i. q. Pilp. no. 1. 1 K. 7:26, 38. Ezek. 23:32 מִרְבָּה לְהָכִיל *containing much.*

2. i. q. Pilp. no. 3. Jer. 6:11. 10:10. Joel 2:11.

Note. The significations given above are mostly embraced in the Lat. *tenere* and its compounds, as also in the English word *to hold* followed by various prepositions.

כּוּמָז m. Ex. 35:22. Num. 31:50. a golden ornament worn by the Israelites in the desert, perhaps a *bracelet* or *necklace* of gold balls, such as are found native in Arabia; comp. Arab. كمز *conglobavit,* and Diod. Sic. III. 45.

כּוּן in Kal not used; literally *to*

stand up. Hence כֵּן. In Arab. كان *to be;* comp. Lat. *existere* (*to be.*)

Pilel כּוֹנֵן 1. *to raise up, erect;* e. g. a throne, Ps. 9:8. 2 Sam. 7:13. particularly *to raise up* what is falling, *to establish, confirm*, Ps. 7:10. 40:3. 68:10.

2. *to found;* e. g. a city, Ps. 107:36. the earth, Ps. 24:2. 119:90. the heavens, Prov. 3:19.

3. *to direct;* e.g. an arrow to the mark, Ps. 7:13. 11:2. the heart, (see Hiph. no. 4.) and so, לֵב being understood, *to direct one's heart, to attend, purpose*, Job 8:8. Is. 51:13.

4. *to prepare, form, make.* Deut. 32:6. Ps. 8:4.

Pulal כּוֹנַן 1. *to be prepared.* Ezek. 28:13.

2. *to be established.* Ps. 37:23.

Hithpalel הִתְכּוֹנֵן (Prov. 24:3.) elsewhere הִכּוֹנֵן.

1. *to be founded, established.* Prov. 24:3. Num. 21:27.

2. *to make one's self ready, to prepare.* Ps. 59:5.

Hiph. הֵכִין i. q. Pilel.

1. *to raise up, erect, place;* e. g. a seat, Job 29:7. Ps. 103:19. *to establish*, Ps. 89:5. 2 Sam. 7:12. *to strengthen*, Ps. 10:17.

2. *to appoint*, to an office. 2 Sam. 5:12. Josh. 4:4.

3. *to found.* 1 K. 6:19. Ps. 65:7.

4. *to direct;* e. g. an arrow, Ps. 7:14. the countenance, Ezek. 4:3. the way, 2 Chr. 27:6. Especially הֵכִין לֵב לְ *to direct one's heart* or *attend to* any thing, 2 Chr. 12:14. 30:19. and elliptically without לֵב, 1 Sam. 23:22. Judg. 12:6. 1 Chr. 28:2. Also הֵכִין לֵב אֶל יְהֹוָה *to direct the heart to Jehovah*, 1 Sam. 7:3. and without לֵב, Job 11:13.

5. *to prepare*, in the broadest sense; e. g. food, Gen. 43:15. ~~16~~.

Hoph. pass. of Hiph. nos. 1, 2, 5.

Niph. pass. of Pilel and Hiph. but used more metaphorically.

1. *to be placed upright, to stand.* Ps. 93:2.—נְכוֹן הַיּוֹם literally *erectum diei, mid-day*, when the sun is directly overhead, σταθερὸν ἦμαρ, Prov. 4:18. Especially *to stand firm, to abide*, Ps. 101:7 *he that speaketh lies shall not stand before mine eyes.* Job 21:8. Metaphorically (1.) *to be becoming, right, suitable.* Ex. 8:22. [26.] Job 42:7, 8. Ps. 5:10. (2.) *to be upright.* Ps. 78:37 לִבָּם לֹא נָכוֹן עִמּוֹ *their heart was not upright with him;* (comp. שָׁלֵם) (3.) *to be firm, right.*—רוּחַ נָכוֹן *a right spirit*, Ps. 51:12. Gen. 41:32 נָכוֹן הַדָּבָר מֵעִם הָאֱלֹהִים *the thing was established by God.* (4.) *to be confident, fearless*, construed with לֵב. Ps. 57:8. 108:2. 112:7. (5.) *to be certain.* —אֶל נָכוֹן *with certainty*, 1 Sam. 26:4. 23:23.

2. *to be prepared, ready.* Prov. 19:29. Neh. 8:11. Job 15:23. Imper. הִכּוֹן *hold thyself ready*, Ezek. 38:7. Am. 4:12.

Deriv. כֵּן, כַּוָּן, כִּיּוֹן, מָכוֹן, מְכוֹנָה, תְּכוּנָה.

כּוּן 1 Chr. 18:8. a Phenician city, which in the parallel passage 2 Sam. 8:9, is called בֵּרֹתַי *Berytus.*

כַּוָּן m. dec. I. *a small cake* or *wafer*, offered to the Gods, *libum*, πόπανον. Jer. 7:18. 44:19. Sept. χαυῶνες, χαβῶνες. Root כּוּן, in Pi. כַּוֵּן (Chald. כַּוֵּן) *to prepare.* Others derive it incorrectly from כָּוָה.

I. כּוֹס f. plur. כֹּסוֹת (Jer. 35:5.) dec. I. *a cup.* (In Syr. and Arab. *idem.*) Gen. 40:11, 13, 21. Ps. 116:13 כּוֹס יְשׁוּעוֹת אֶשָּׂא *I will take the cup of deliverance*, i. e. I will consecrate to Jehovah a cup of gratitude for deliverance.—Jehovah is often represented as holding a cup in his hand, from which he lets the nations drink and become intoxicated, so as to fall and perish, Is. 51:17, 22. Jer. 25:15. 49:12. 51:7. Lam. 4:21. Hab. 2:16. Ezek. 23:31, 32, 33. So in the Arabian poets. Ps. 16:5 יְהֹוָה מְנָת־חֶלְקִי וְכוֹסִי *Jehovah is my portion and my cup*, i. e. my inheritance, possession; comp. Deut. 4:19.

II. כּוֹס Lev. 11:17. Deut. 14:16. Ps. 102:7. according to the ancient versions, *an owl.* According to Bochart (Hieroz. P. II. p. 267.) *the pelican*, from כּוֹס *a cup*, which he refers to the bag under the throat; comp. in Lat. *truo* from *trua*.

כּוּר m. dec. I. *an oven, smelting furnace*. Ezek. 22:18, 20, 22. Prov. 17:3. 27:21. Metaphorically Is. 48:10 *I have tried thee in the furnace of affliction*. Deut. 4:20 *and he has brought you out of the iron furnace, from Egypt*. 1 K. 8:51. (Arab. and Syr. *idem*; perhaps from كار *to be round*.)

כּוּר־עָשָׁן (*smoking furnace*) proper name of a city in the tribe of Simeon. 1 Sam. 30:30. Also simply עָשָׁן Josh. 15:42. 19:7. 1 Chr. 4:32. 6:44.

כּוֹר i. q. כֹּר q. v.

כּוּשׁ f. *Ethiopia*, in the widest sense, including the southern part of Arabia, the original seat of all the Ethiopians. The Arabian Cush appears principally intended in Gen. 10:7, 8. Num. 12:1. 2 Chr. 14:8. 21:16. Hab. 3:7. But the African in Jer. 13:23. Is. 18:1. Zeph. 3:10. In other passages the place intended is less certain, as Job 28:19. Am. 9:7. Jer. 38:7, 10, 12. 39:16.—In Gen. 2:13, Ethiopia is probably meant, but in the sense of a widely-extended southern country. See the art. גִּיחוֹן. It is to no purpose to seek here for another כּוּשׁ, as Michaëlis has done in the name كاش in Chowarasmia. See Bocharti Phaleg, Lib. IV. cap. 2. but especially Michaëlis Spicileg. Geogr. Hebræorum exteræ, P. I. p. 143 ff. The gentile noun is כּוּשִׁי, fem. כּוּשִׁית, plur. כּוּשִׁיִּים, *an Ethiopian*, Jer. 38:7, 10, 12. Num. 12:1.

כּוּשָׁן f. Hab. 3:7. i. q. כּוּשׁ.

כּוֹשָׁרָה f. dec. X. *prosperity, affluence, abundance*. Ps. 68:7. Root כָּשֵׁר no. 2.

כּוּת 2 K. 17:30. and כּוּתָה verse 24. the original residence of a people, who, after the carrying away of the ten tribes, were transplanted by the king of Assyria into their place, and, by mixing with the inhabitants that remained behind, formed the race of the Samaritans, who in Chaldaic and Talmud. are hence called כּוּתִים. The situation of Cuthah is uncertain. Josephus (Antiq. IX. 14. § 2.) places it in Persia. Another opinion makes it a country near Sidon, since the Samaritans have professed to be of Sidonian origin; (Josephi Antiq. XI. 8. § 6. XII. 5. § 5.) See Michaëlis Spicileg. Geogr. Hebræorum exteræ. P. I. p. 104 ff.

כֹּתֶרֶת see כּוֹתֶרֶת.

כָּזַב in Kal only in the part. כֹּזֵב Ps. 116:11. More frequently in Pi. כִּזֵּב *to lie*. Job 6:28. 34:6. Construed with לְ *to lie to* any one, *to deceive* him, Ps. 78:36. 89:36 אִם לְדָוִד אֲכַזֵּב *shall I lie to David?* i. e. shall I break my divine promise? (comp. Num. 23:19.) Ezek. 13:19. with בְּ in the same sense, 2 K. 4:16. Used metaphorically of water which dries up and deceives the hope of the traveller, Is. 58:11. Comp. אַכְזָב.

Hiph. *to make* or *prove* any one *a liar*. Job 24:25.

Niph. pass. of Hiph. *to be proved false*. Job 41:1. [41:9.]

כָּזָב m. verbal from כָּזַב, dec. IV. a.

1. *a lie, deception*. Ps. 4:3. 5:7. Prov. 6:19.

2. *something false*, e. g. an idol. Ps. 40:5. Am. 2:5.

כֹּזֵבָא 1 Chr. 4:22. prob. i. q. כְּזִיב.

כְּזִיב Gen. 38:5. i. q. אַכְזִיב a place in the tribe of Judah, Josh. 15:44.

כֹּחַ *strength*, see כּוֹחַ.

כָּחַד in Kal not used; perhaps *to be concealed, invisible*.

Pi. כִּחֵד 1. *to conceal*. Job 27:11. Ps. 40:11. Construed with מִן of the person *from* whom, Josh. 7:19. 1 Sam. 3:17, 18. Jer. 38:14, 25.

2. *to deny*. Is. 3:9. Job 6:10. (In Ethiop. כחד *to renounce*, e. g. Christ, Satan.)

Hiph. הִכְחִיד 1. *to hide*. Job 20:12.

2. *to destroy*, e. g. a people. Ex. 23:23. Zech. 11:8. (In both significations the idea is that of the Greek ἀφανίζειν.)

Niph. 1. pass. of Pi. no. 1. 2 Sam. 18:13. Ps. 69:6. 139:15. Hos. 5:3.

2. pass. of Hiph. no. 2. Job 4:7. 15:28. 22:20. With the addition *from the earth*, Ex. 9:15.

כָּחַל, Arab. كَحَلَ *to paint the eyes with alcohol*, i. e. with stibium or black oxid of antimony. Ezek. 23:40. This eye paint of the Hebrew women, (also called פּוּךְ, in Greek στίμμι,) is a fine mineral powder, with which, when moistened, the women paint the inside of the eyelids, leaving a narrow black rim around the edge. Comp. Hartmann's Hebräerin am Putzische, Th. ii. p. 149ff. Th. iii. p. 198ff. Böttiger's Sabina, p. 22. 48.

כָּחַשׁ literally *to lie*, (see Piel;) but in Kal used only metaphorically, (like כָּזַב q. v.) *to waste away, deficere*. Ps. 109:24 בְּשָׂרִי כָּחַשׁ מִשָּׁמֶן *my flesh wastes away from fatness*, i. e. from being fat, it becomes lean. Comp. כַּחַשׁ.

Pi. כִּחֵשׁ 1. *to lie*. Lev. 19:11. Hos. 4:2. 1 K. 13:18 כִּחֵשׁ לוֹ *he lied to him*.

2. *to deny*. Gen. 18:15. Josh. 7:11. Construed with בְּ of the person and thing, Lev. 5:21, 22. Job 8:18. Hence כִּחֵשׁ בַּיהוָֹה *to deny Jehovah*, Is. 59:13. Jer. 5:12. with לְ, Job 31:28. Also without יְהוָֹה in the same sense, Prov. 30:9 פֶּן אֶשְׂבַּע וְכִחַשְׁתִּי *lest I be full and deny God.*

3. *to dissemble, flatter*, used of conquered enemies who feign submission. Ps. 18:45. 66:3. 81:16.

4. *to deceive* (one's expectation), hence *to waste away, to fail*. Hos. 9:2. Hab. 3:17. Comp. the Lat. *spem mentita seges, fundus mendax*.

Niph. Deut. 33:29. and Hithpa. 2 Sam. 22:45. i. q. Kal no. 3. *to flatter* or *submit to* a conqueror.

כַּחַשׁ m. verbal from כָּחַשׁ, dec. VI. c.

1. *a lie, deception, hypocrisy*. Nah. 3:1. Hos. 12:1. [11:12.]

2. *leanness*. Job 16:8. See the verb in Kal.

כֶּחָשׁ m. (for כַּחָשׁ,) verbal from כָּחַשׁ, dec. I. *lying, a liar*. Is. 30:9.

I. **כִּי** m. (for כְּוִי,) subst. *a mark burnt in, a brand, stigma*. Is. 3:24. (Root כָּוָה *to be burned*, whence the Arab. كَيّ *a mark burnt in.*)

II. **כִּי** a primitive particle, probably in its primary acceptation a relative pronoun, i. q. אֲשֶׁר, Gen. 4:25. Deut. 14:29. Ps. 90:4. (These passages, however, are all capable of a different interpretation.) Hence (like the Greek ὅτι, and Latin *quod*,) used as a conj.

1. *that, quod*. Gen. 1:4.—וַיְהִי כִּי *it came to pass that*, Job 1:5.—*That, so that, ut, ita ut*, construed with a future used as a subjunctive, Deut. 14:24. Judg. 9:28.—הֲכִי literally *is it so that*, (French *est—ce que*,) hence as an interrogative particle, i. q. Lat. *an?* Job 6:22. 2 Sam. 9:1. Also *is it not so that*, (French *n'est—ce pas que*,) hence i. q. Lat. *nonne? vere*, 2 Sam. 23:19.

2. *for, because*. Gen. 3:14, 17. Deut. 23:8. Gen. 41:49. Comp. יַעַן כִּי, עַל כִּי *because*.

3. *if*. Ex. 3:21. Lev. 21:9. 1 Sam. 24:20.

4. *when, quum*. Hos. 11:1.

5. *yet, although*. Ps. 116:10. Ex. 5:11. also גַּם־כִּי and כִּי גַם (Ecc. 4:14.)

6. i. q. כִּי אִם *but*. Gen. 45:8. Ex. 16:8. 1 K. 21:15.

7. *yea rather, immo*. Ps. 44:23. 49:11. 130:4.

8. It is often used at the beginning of a proposition, where it may be omitted in translating, like the Germ. *ja!* Zech. 3:8. 2 Sam. 19:23. So before the direct address, like the Greek ὅτι, Ruth 1:10. Josh. 2:24. 1 Sam. 10:19. and after oaths, 1 Sam. 26:16. 14:44. 25:34. 2 Chr. 18:13.

9. at the beginning of the apodosis or turn of the sentence, *so, then*. Gen. 22:17. 31:42. Num. 22:33. Job 8:6. 37:20.

כִּי אִם 1. i. q. אִם *if*, the force of כִּי being lost. 1 Sam. 20:9. Ex. 22:22.

2. *that.* Gen. 47:18.

3. *unless,* (comp. אִם no. 5.) Gen. 32:27. Lev. 22:6. Hence in swearing i. q. אִם לֹא, 2 K. 5:20. 2 Sam. 15: 21. Jer. 51:14, Judg. 15:7.

4. after a negation, *except, other than.* Gen. 28:17. Est. 2:15.

5, *but.* Gen. 32:29. 40:14. 1 Sam. 8:19. Ps. 1:2.

כִּיד m. dec. I. *destruction, misfortune.* Job 21:20. (Arab. كيد literally *insidiæ,* and hence *destruction.*)

כִּידוֹד m. dec. I. found only Job 41: 11. [41:19.] *sparks.* Arab. كيد כִּיד *a striking of fire.*)

כִּידוֹן m. 1. *a dart, javelin,* probably different from חֲנִית *a spear.* Job 41:21. [41:29.] 1 Sam. 17:6, 45. Josh. 8: 18, 26. The etymology is unknown. Some connect it with כִּיד *destruction,* (like חֶרֶב from חָרַב;) but it is more probably i. q. קתין Arab. قتين *a spear, lance.*

2. proper name of a country, 1 Chr. 13:9 גֹּרֶן כִּידֹן, in the parallel passage 2 Sam. 6:6 גֹּרֶן נָכוֹן.

כִּידוֹר m. found only Job 15:24. prob. *the tumult of war.* Vulg. *prœlium.* Syr. Arab. *bellum.* (Root כדר, in Arab. *turbari.*)

כִּיּוּן found only Am. 5:26 כִּיּוּן צַלְמֵיכֶם *the frame* or *carriage of your idols.* Vulg. *imaginem idolorum vestrorum.* Root כון particularly the Piel כּוֹנֵן, כִּוֵּן *to put up, prepare, form;* (see כּוּן.) Others, following the Syriac version and some Jewish commentators, make כִּיּוּן i. q. Arab. كيوان *the star Saturn;* namely, *Saturn, your idol,* the plur. צַלְמֵיכֶם being used poetically. But this does not accord so well with the parallel clause.

כִּיּוֹר and כִּיֹּר m. dec. I.

1. *a basin,* particularly for washing. Ex. 30:18, 28. 31:9. 35:16. 39:39. 1 K. 7:38.—כִּיּוֹר אֵשׁ *a pan of fire.* Zech. 12:6.

2. *a round stage* or *scaffold,* on which king Solomon stood, when he consecrated the temple. 2 Chr. 6:13.

Plur. כִּיּוֹרִים 2 Chr. 4:6. and כִּיֹּרוֹת 1 K. 7:38, 40, 43. (Root prob. כור=Arab. كار *to be round.*)

כֵּילַי Is. 32:5. and כֵּלַי verse 7. *a deceiver, a fraudulent man.* Vulg. *fraudulentus.* Prob. for נְכִילַי, from נָכַל. ־ַי is the termination of adjectives in Chaldaic, as ־ִי in Hebrew.

כֵּילַפּוֹת plur. fem. Ps. 74:6. *hammers* or *hatchets,* for striking. (Chald. קוּלְפָא *a cudgel, club.*)

כִּימָה f. *the Pleiades, the Seven Stars.* Am. 5:8. Job 9:9. 38:31. Literally *a heap, collection,* from the root כום=Arab. كام conj. II. *to heap up;* كومة *a heap.* The Asiatic poets often speak of the band of the Pleiades; hence we may explain Job 38:31 הַתְקַשֵּׁר מַעֲדַנּוֹת כִּימָה *canst thou fasten the bands of the Pleiades?*

כִּיס m. *a bag, purse.* (In Syr. and Arab. *idem.*) (1.) for gold. Prov. 1:14. Is. 46:6. (2.) for the weights of the merchant, such as is used at the present day in the east. Deut. 25:13. Mic. 6: 11. Hence אַבְנֵי כִיס *the weights of the bag,* Prov. 16:11.

כִּירַיִם dual, found only Lev. 11:35. Sept. χυτρόποδες, i. e. prob. *the bricks* or *stones, on which the Nomades place the pot over the fire,* a kind of hearth, *ollæ sustentaculum.*

כִּישׁוֹר found only Prov. 31:19. according to the Jewish commentators, *the distaff.*

כָּכָה adv. i. q. כֹּה or כָּה *thus.* Ex. 12: 11. 29:35. Num. 8:26. Comp. אֵיכָכָה *how?*

כִּכָּר f. dec. II. b. literally *a circle,* prob. for כִּרְכָּר, from the root כור in Arab. *to be round.* Hence

1. *circuit, surrounding country.* Neh. 12:28—כִּכַּר הַיַּרְדֵּן *the country on the Jordan,* Gen. 13:10, 11. 1 K. 7:47. in

other places simply הַכִּכָּר, Gen. 13 : 12. 19 : 17.

2. with לֶחֶם, *a round cake* or *loaf,* (the usual form of bread in ancient times,) *placenta.* Ex. 29 : 23. 1 Sam. 2 : 36. Prov. 6 : 26. Plur. m. כִּכְּרוֹת לֶחֶם Judg. 8 : 5. 1 Sam. 10 : 3.

3. as a weight, *a talent,* Syr. ܟܟܪܐ. It appears from Ex. 38 : 25, 26, to have contained 3000 shekels of the sanctuary. Zech. 5 : 7. כִּכַּר זָהָב *a talent of gold,* 1 K. 9 : 14. 10 : 10, 14. Dual כִּכָּרַיִם *two talents,* and used before a genitive, as כִּכְּרַיִם כֶּסֶף 2 K. 5 : 23. Plur. כִּכָּרִים f. 1 Chr. 22 : 14. 29 : 7. Ezra 8 : 26.

כִּכַּר, plur. כַּכְּרִין, Chald. *idem.* Ezra 7 : 22.

כֹּל, כּוֹל (Jer. 33 : 8 Kethib,) before Makkeph כָּל־, m. verbal from כָּלַל, dec. VIII. d. a subst. *all, the whole, totality.* But generally it is more convenient to render it in English as an adj.

1. *all.* Thus כָּל־הָאָדָם *all men,* literally *the whole of men;* כָּל־הַחַיָּה *all animals.* —With suff. כֻּלָּנוּ *all of us,* כֻּלְּכֶם *all of you,* כֻּלָּם *all of them.*

2. *every one, omnis.*—כָּל־הָאָדָם *every man.* בְּכָל־שָׁנָה *every year,* Est. 9 : 21. הַכֹּל כַּאֲשֶׁר לַכֹּל *every one is as the other,* i. e. all are alike, Ecc. 9 : 2.

3. *the whole.* כָּל־הַיּוֹם *the whole day,* Is. 28 : 24. כָּל־עַמִּי *my whole people,* Gen. 41 : 40. כָּל־הָאַיִל *the whole ram,* Ex. 29 : 18. With suff. כֻּלֵּךְ, כֻּלְּךָ *the whole of thee, thou wholly,* Is. 22 : 1. Mic. 2 : 12. מִצְרַיִם כֻּלָּהּ *the whole of Egypt,* Ezek. 29 : 2.

4. *some one, some thing.* כֹּל דָּבָר *any thing,* Ruth 4 : 7. לֹא כֹל *nothing,* Num. 11 : 6.

5. *of all kinds* or *sorts.* Lev. 19 : 23 כָּל־עֵץ *trees of all kinds.* Neh. 13 : 16. 1 Chr. 29 : 2.

6. in connexion with certain particles, as כָּל־עוֹד *so long as,* Job 27 : 3. כָּל־עֻמַּת שֶׁ *just as, exactly as,* Ecc. 5 : 15.

Note. In the three first significations כֹּל is followed by the article. In significations nos. 5, 6. the article is omitted.

כֹּל Chald. *idem.* With Makkeph כָּל־, more frequently with א parag. כֹּלָּא, as in Dan. 2 : 40. 4 : 9, 18, 25. [4 : 12, 21, 28.]

כָּלָא nearly synonimous with עָצַר.

1. *to hold back, to restrain, to retain.* Num. 11 : 28. Ecc. 8 : 8. Ps. 40 : 10. Construed with מִן of the action, 1 Sam. 25 : 33. Ps. 119 : 101. With מִן of the person, *to withhold from* any one, Gen. 23 : 6. Ps. 40 : 12. Comp. Hag. 1 : 10.

2. *to shut up, to confine.* Jer. 32 : 2, 3. Ps. 88 : 9. Intrans. *to shut itself up,* Hag. 1 : 10.

Niph. 1. *to be restrained,* hence *to cease.* Gen. 8 : 2. Ex. 36 : 6.

Note. This verb often borrows its form from כָּלָה. Hence כְּלִתַנִי 1 Sam. 25 : 33. כָּלוּ 1 Sam. 6 : 10. יִכְלֶה Gen. 23 : 6. and כָּלִאתִי Ps. 119 : 101. On the contrary כַּלֵּא infin. Pi. has the signification of כַּלֵּה or כַּלּוֹת.

Deriv. out of course כְּלוּא, כְּלִיא, מִכְלָה, מִכְלָאוֹת.

כֶּלֶא m. with suff. כִּלְאוֹ verbal from כָּלָא. dec. VI. h. *a prison.* Jer. 52 : 33. 2 K. 25 : 29. More commonly בֵּית כֶּלֶא, בֵּית הַכֶּלֶא 2 K. 17 : 4. 22 : 27. Plur. בָּתֵּי כְלָאִים Is. 42 : 22.

כִּלְאַיִם dual, *of two kinds.* (Arab. كلا *two,* in Ethiop. *of two kinds.*) Lev. 19 : 19. Deut. 22 : 9.

כֶּלֶב m. dec. VI. a.

1. *a dog.* This animal in the east often runs wild without an owner, and becomes fierce and dangerous. Ps. 22 : 17, 21. As an unclean animal it is used by the Hebrews as a word of reproach, 2 K. 8 : 13. especially *a dead dog.* 1 Sam. 24 : 15. 2 Sam. 9 : 8. 16 : 9. or *a dog's head,* 2 Sam. 3 : 8.

2. *puer mollis, scortum virile,* (comp. κύνες Rev. 22 : 15.) Deut. 23 : 18. elsewhere קָדֵשׁ.

כָּלֵב *Caleb,* the proper name of a contemporary of Joshua. Num. 13 : 7. 14 : 6 ff. Josh. 15 : 14.

כָּלָה 1. *to be completed, finished.* Ex. 39 : 32. 1 K. 6 : 38.

2. *to be over, past.* Gen. 41:53. Is. 24:13 אִם כָּלָה בָצִיר *when the vintage is over.* 32:10. Is. 10:25 וְכָלָה זַעַם *and the anger (of God) shall be over.* 16:4.

3. *to be prepared* or *ready for* any one, spoken particularly of something evil. Prov. 22:8 וְשֵׁבֶט עֶבְרָתוֹ יִכְלֶה *and the rod of correction for him is prepared.* Construed with מֵעִם, מֵאֵת of the person *by* whom, Est. 7:7. 1 Sam. 20:7, 9. 25:17.

4. *to be consumed, to be all gone.* Gen. 21:15. 1 K. 17:16.

5. *to waste away, vanish, disappear;* spoken of a cloud, Job 7:9. of smoke, Ps. 37:20. of time, Job 7:6. Ps. 31:11. Lam. 2:11 *mine eyes waste away from weeping.* In Hebrew we often find the phrases כָּלְתָה נַפְשִׁי Ps. 84:3. כָּלְתָה רוּחִי Ps. 143:7. and כָּלוּ עֵינַי Ps. 69:4. *my soul, my spirit, my eyes faint* or *languish for* any thing, i. e. I languish. These phrases are also used of disappointed hope, Job 11:20. 17:5. Jer. 14:6. Lam. 4:17. Comp. the similar construction with חוּס.

6. *to be destroyed, to perish,* spoken of men. Jer. 16:4. Ezek. 5:13. Ps. 39:11.

7. *to be fulfilled,* spoken of a prophecy. Ezra 1:1. Dan. 12:7.

Note. The fut. תִּכְלָה after the analogy of verbs לא, occurs once 1 K. 17:14.

Pi. כִּלָּה 1. *to complete, finish.* Gen. 2:2. 6:16. Construed with לְ and an infin. *to finish* or *cease to* do any thing, Gen. 24:15 הוּא טֶרֶם כִּלָּה לְדַבֵּר *he had not yet finished speaking.* 43:1. Num. 7:1. Deut. 31:24. with מִן, Ex. 34:33. Lev. 16:20. This signification may often be expressed in English by means of adverbs, as *to speak through, to eat up.*

2. *to prepare.* Prov. 16:30 כִּלָּה רָעָה *he prepares,* i. e. devises, *mischief.* See Kal no. 3.

3. *to consume, let pass away,* as time. Ps. 78:33 *he lets their days pass away like breath.* 90:9. Is. 49:4 לְתֹהוּ וְהֶבֶל כֹּחִי כִלֵּיתִי *for nought and in vain have I spent my strength.*—כִּלָּה עֵינֵי פ׳ *to cause the eyes of any one to fail,* i. e. to cause any one to languish, Job 31:16. 1 Sam. 2:33. Lev. 26:16.

4. *to consume, destroy;* as men, nations, through hunger, Gen. 41:30. Jer. 14:12. also generally, 2 Sam. 21:5.—עַד כַּלֵּה 2 K. 13:17, 19. and עַד־לְכַלֵּה 2 Chr. 31:1. *even to destruction.*—עַד־כַּלּוֹתָם *until they are destroyed,* 1 Sam. 15:18.

5. *to fulfil,* (a prophecy.)

Pu. כֻּלָּה and כֻּלּוּ *to be finished, ended.* Gen. 2:1. Ps. 72:20.

Deriv. out of course כְּלִי, כִּלָּיוֹן, תַּכְלִית, מִכְלוֹת, תִּכְלָה.

Note. Some forms of כָּלָה borrow their signification from כָּלָא q. v.

כָּלֶה, fem. כָּלָה, verbal from כָּלָה, dec. X. *languishing, failing,* spoken of the eye; see the verb, Kal no. 5, and Pi. no. 3. Deut. 28:32.

כָּלָה f. verbal from כָּלָה, dec. XI. a.

1. *destruction.*—עָשָׂה כָלָה *to cause* or *make utter destruction,* Jer. 4:27. 5:10. Neh. 9:31. Nah. 1:8, 9. This phrase is construed with בְּ, Jer. 30:11. and with אֵת of the person destroyed, Jer. 5:18. 46:28. Ezek. 11:13. 20:17.

2. as an adv. *entirely, wholly, altogether.* Gen. 18:21. Ex. 11:1. So לְכָלָה 2 Chr. 12:12.

כַּלָּה f. dec. X. 1. *a bride.* Cant. 4:8ff. Jer. 2:32. (Root כלל, Syr. Pa. ܟܠܠ *to crown, to put on a marriage garland.*)

2. *a daughter-in-law.* Gen. 38:11, 24. Comp. the different significations of חָתָן.

כְּלוּא m. verbal from כָּלָא, *a prison,* i. q. כֶּלֶא. Found only in the Keri of Jer. 37:4. 52:31. In the Kethib is כְּלִיא.

כְּלוּב m. *a basket;* (1.) for fruit, Am. 8:1, 2. (2.) for a bird-cage, Jer. 5:27. (Syr. *idem.* In Greek κλωβός, κλουβός, κλοβὸς *a cage,* the word being derived from the east.)

כְּלוּלוֹת fem. plur. denom. from כַּלָּה.

bridal state, condition of a bride. Jer. 2 : 2.

I. **כֶּלַח** m. *soundness, strength, activity,* i. q. Syr. ܟܠܚ Job 5 : 26 תָּבוֹא בְכֶלַח אֱלֵי־קָבֶר *thou shalt come to the grave in full strength,* i. e. as an active old man. 30 : 2 עָלֵימוֹ אָבַד כָּלַח *whose activity is lost.* Others derive the signification *old age* from chap. 5 : 26. and apply it to 30 : 2. thus, *in whom old age languishes,* not suited to the connexion.

II. **כֶּלַח** found only Gen. 10 : 11. a city mentioned in connexion with several Assyrian cities, perhaps i. q. חֲלַח q. v. (comp. כְּבָר and חָבוֹר.) See Michaëlis Supplem. p. 767.

כְּלִי m. in pause כֶּלִי, with suff. כֶּלְיְךָ, plur. כֵּלִים, const. כְּלֵי, irreg. (from כָּלָה *to be completed, ready.*)

1. *a vessel, utensil.* Gen. 31 : 37. 45 : 20. Ps. 2 : 9.—כְּלֵי כֶסֶף, כְּלֵי זָהָב *vessels of gold, of silver,* Ex. 3 : 22. 11 : 2.—כְּלֵי־, בֵית יְהוָה Jer. 27 : 18. and כְּלֵי יְהוָה Is. 52 : 11. *the vessels of the temple.*—כְּלֵי גוֹלָה *furniture for travelling,* Ezek. 12 : 7.

2. *a cloth, garment.* כְּלִי גֶבֶר *a man's garment,* Deut. 22 : 5.

3. *an instrument, tool.*—כְּלֵי־שִׁיר *musical instruments,* 2 Chr. 34 : 12. Am. 6 : 5. also without שִׁיר in the same sense, Ps. 71 : 22. Metaphorically כְּלֵי זַעַם יְהוָה *instruments of the divine anger,* Is. 13 : 5. Jer. 50 : 25.

4. *a vessel, boat.* Is. 18 : 2.

5. *a weapon.* Gen. 27 : 3. Often joined with מִלְחָמָה, Judg. 18 : 11, 16. כְּלֵי־מָוֶת *deadly weapons,* Ps. 7 : 14. נֹשֵׂא כֵלִים *armour-bearer,* 1 Sam. 14 : 1, 6, 7 ff. 31 : 4, 5, 6.

כֵּלַי see **כִּילַי**.

כְּלִיא m. verbal from כָּלָא, *a prison.* Found only in the Kethib of Jer. 37 : 4. 52 : 31.

כִּלָּיוֹן m. const. כִּלְיוֹן, verbal from כָּלָה, dec. III. d.

1. *a languishing* (of the eyes). Deut. 28 : 65. See כָּלָה no. 5.

2. *destruction.* Is. 10 : 22.

כְּלָיוֹת plur. fem. const. כִּלְיוֹת, dec. XI. c.

1. *the reins, kidneys,* Ex. 29 : 13, 22. Job 16 : 13.—חֵלֶב כִּלְיוֹת אֵילִים *the kidney fat of rams,* Is. 34 : 6. comp. Deut. 32 : 14.

2. by a metonymy, *the inward parts,* like לֵב, with which it is frequently connected. Jer. 11 : 20 בֹּחֵן כְּלָיוֹת וָלֵב *trying the reins and the heart.* 17 : 10. 20 : 12. Ps. 7 : 10. כָּלוּ כִלְיֹתַי *my reins languish,* i. e. I languish, I fail from languishing, Job 19 : 27. (comp. כָּלָה no. 5.)—Ps. 16 : 7 יִסְּרוּנִי כִלְיוֹתָי *my reins,* i. e. my inward parts, *admonish me.* 73 : 21. Prov. 23 : 16. (In Chald. and Arab. *idem.* Kindred with כְּלָאִים.)

כָּלִיל m. verbal from כָּלַל, dec. III. a.

1. as an adj. *perfect, complete.* Ezek. 28 : 12 כְּלִיל יֹפִי *perfect in beauty.* 27 : 3. Lam. 2 : 15. Ezek. 16 : 14.

2. as a subst. *the whole.* Judg. 20 : 40 כְּלִיל הָעִיר *the whole of the city.* Ex. 28 : 31 כְּלִיל תְּכֵלֶת *all of bluish purple.* 39 : 22. Num. 4 : 6.

3. as an adv. *wholly, utterly.* Is. 2 : 18. Lev. 6 : 15. [22.]

4. i. q. עוֹלָה *a whole burnt-offering, holocaustum.* Deut. 33 : 10. Ps. 51 : 21.

כָּלַל *to complete, make perfect.* Found only Ezek. 27 : 4, 11. Deriv. כֹּל, כָּלִיל, מִכְלָל, מִכְלוֹל, מַכְלֻלִים.

כְּלַל Chald. *idem.* Hence Shaph. שַׁכְלֵל Ezra 5 : 11. 6 : 14. Pass. אִשְׁתַּכְלַל Ezra 4 : 13, 16. In the Kethib of Ezra 4 : 12. we find אשכללו, with the omission of ת.

כָּלַם in Kal not used. In Arab. *to wound.*

Hiph. הִכְלִים and הֶכְלִים (1 Sam. 25 : 7.)

1. *to put to shame, to make ashamed.* Job 11 : 3. Prov. 25 : 8. Ps. 44 : 10. Hence *to bring shame* or *disgrace* on any one, Prov. 28 : 7.

2. *to reproach.* 1 Sam. 20 : 34.

3. *to hurt, injure.* 1 Sam. 25 : 7. Judg. 18 : 7.

Hoph. 1. *to be made ashamed, to be frustrated in one's hope.* Jer. 14 : 3. Comp. Niph.

2. *to be hurt, injured.* 1 Sam. 25 : 15.

Niph. 1. *to be ashamed, to feel ashamed,* synonymous with בּוֹשׁ. Num. 12 : 14. Construed with מִן of the thing *of* which one is ashamed, Ezek. 16 : 27, 54.

2. *to be brought to shame, to be disgraced.* Jer. 31 : 19. Ps. 35 : 4.

3. *to be insulted.* 1 Chr. 19 : 5.

כִּלְמַד name of a place or country, probably in Arabia. Once Ezek. 27 : 23.

כְּלִמָּה f. verbal from כָּלַם, dec. X. *shame, reproach.* Ps. 69 : 8. Jer. 51 : 51. Ezek. 16 : 54.

כַּלְנֵה Gen. 10 : 10. כַּלְנֵה Am. 6 : 2. and כַּלְנוֹ Is. 10 : 9. proper name of an Assyrian city; according to the Targums, Eusebius, Jerome and others, *Ctesiphon,* a great city on the eastern bank of the Tigris, over against Seleucia. See Bocharti Phaleg, Lib. IV. cap. 18. Michaëlis Spicileg. Geogr. Hebræor. exter. T. 1. p. 228.

כָּמַהּ *to long* or *languish after* any thing, i. q. כָּלָה no. 5. Ps. 63 : 2. (Arab. كمه *to be dim of sight, to be weak.*)

כַּמָּה see מָה.

כְּמוֹ, כָּמוֹ i. q. כְּ. 1. *as.* Before substantives it is used only in poetry; but before most of the suffixes it is the usual form for כְּ; as כָּמוֹנִי, כָּמוֹךָ, כָּמוֹהוּ, כָּמוֹהָ, כָּמוֹנוּ; in the other persons more frequently כָּכֶם, כָּהֵם, rarely כְּמוֹכֶם, כְּמוֹהֶם.

2. *when.* Gen. 19 : 15.

כְּמוֹשׁ m. 1 K. 11 : 7. 2 K. 23 : 13. Jer. 48 : 7. the national god of the Moabites and Ammonites, (Judg. 11 : 24.) which under Solomon was also worshipped at Jerusalem. Hence עַם כְּמוֹשׁ *the people of Chemosh,* i. e. Moab, Num. 21 : 29. Sept. Χαμώς. Vulg. *Chamos.* The pagan Arabians are said by tradition to have worshipped him under the form of a black stone.

כַּמֹּן m. *cumin,* Arab. كمون, Greek κύμινον, *cuminum.* Is. 28 : 25, 27. The *cuminum* of the ancients is the *cuminum sativum* of Linnæus.

כָּמַס found only Deut. 32 : 34. *to hide, conceal;* without doubt synonymous with כָּנַס, which is substituted for it in the Samar. text. See מִכְמָס.

כָּמַר found only in Niph. נִכְמַר.

1. *to be burned, to burn.* Lam. 5 : 10 *our skin burns, as an oven, from the heat of hunger.* (Talmud. כמר *calefactio.*)

2. metaphorically *to be kindled, excited;* spoken of affection, construed with עַל, 1 K. 3 : 26. with אֶל, Gen. 43 : 29. spoken of compassion, Hos. 11 : 8. (Perhaps we may likewise compare חמר, Arab. خمر *to rise by fermenting,* in Talmud. *to burn.*)

Deriv. כִּמְרִיר.

כְּמָרִים masc. plur. *idolatrous priests.* 2 K. 23 : 5. Hos. 10 : 5. Zeph. 1 : 4. (Syr. ܟܘܡܪܐ *a priest* generally; the idolatrous priests of Palestine being, as might be expected, derived from Syria.)

כִּמְרִיר m. prob. *a deadly heat, sultriness, hot breath,* from כָּמַר, of the same form with שַׁפְרִיר, (except that it has Hirik under the first syllable.) Job 3 : 5 יְבַעֲתֻהוּ כִּמְרִירֵי יוֹם *the heats of the day terrify him;* comp. particularly Lam. 5 : 10. (see Bellermann Metrik der Hebräer. p. 178.) Others: *the blackness* or *the sadness of the day,* from the Syr. ܟܡܪ *to be sad.* Others, following the ancient versions, make כ the Caph veritatis, and מְרִירֵי *bitterness, misfortune.*

I. כֵּן 1. strictly a participle from כּוּן, dec. I. a. *rectus,* hence metaphorically, *upright, honest, sincere.* Gen. 42 : 11, 19, 31. Is. 16 : 6 לֹא־כֵן *insincerity, falsehood, non rectum.* As an adv. *right, rightly, recte,* Num. 27 : 7. 36 : 5. 2 K. 7 : 9. Ecc. 8 : 10.

2. *the same.* Ps. 127 : 2. 1 Sam. 23 : 17. and then as an adv. (1.) *thus, so.* Gen. 29 : 26. Josh. 2 : 21. 2 Sam. 5 : 5. (2.) *then, therefore.* Ps. 48 : 6. see לָכֵן. (3.) before the latter clause of a sentence nearly pleonastic, *so, then.* 1 Sam. 9 : 13. (4.) when כְּ or כַּאֲשֶׁר precedes, *as....so.* Ex. 1 : 12. Hos. 4 : 7. Also כְּ being un-

derstood, Hos. 11:2. Judg. 5:15 (*as*) *Issachar, so Barak.*

In composition we find (1.) אַחֲרֵי, אַחַר כֵּן *after* (*it was so*) *that, after that.* (2.) בְּכֵן *then, on this account*, as in Chaldaic. Ecc. 8:10. Est. 4:16. (3.) לָכֵן *therefore, on this account*, Judg. 10:13. 1 Sam. 3:14. *yet*, (Arab. لكن,) Hos. 2:11. [2:9.] Jer. 16:14. 30:16. Ezek. 39:25. (4.) עַל־כֵּן *therefore, on this account.* Gen. 20:6. Also for עַל־כֵּן אֲשֶׁר *because that, propterea quod*, Gen. 38:26. Ps. 42:7. 45:3. Num. 11:31. 14:43. (5.) עַד־כֵּן *till now, as yet.* Neh. 2:16.

II. **כֵּן**, with suff. כַּנִּי, כַּנּוֹ, verbal from כָּנַן i. q. כּוּן, dec. VII. c.

1. *a place.* Gen. 40:13. 41:13. Dan. 11:20, 21, 38 עַל כַּנּוֹ *in his stead, loco ejus.* So in verse 7, where כַּנּוֹ stands for עַל כַּנּוֹ. (Sept. Vulg. *a set* or *slip;* but in that case what is the force of the suffix?)

2. *a frame, stand, basis.* Is. 33:23 כֵּן־תָּרְנָם *the support of their mast*, in Greek *μεσόδμη*, i. e. the cross timber in a ship on which the mast is raised. Spoken also of the wash-stand in the court, Ex. 30:18, 28. 31:9. 35:16. 38:28. Lev. 8:11. 1 K. 7:31 מַעֲשֵׂה־כֵן *after the manner of a base* or *pedestal.*

III. **כֵּן** Is. 51:6. prob. the sing. of כִּנִּים, (q. v.) Others render it כְּמוֹ־כֵן *just so, in like manner.*

כִּנִּים masc. plur. Ex. 8:17, 18. Ps. 105:31. Sept. *σκνῖφες*; Vulg. *sciniphes;* a species of very small sharp stinging gnats, found in the swampy tracts of Egypt, (*Culex reptans*, Linn. or *culex molestus*, Forsk.) Comp. Philo (De Vita Mosis Liber, P. II. p. 97. ed. Mangey.) Odmann verm. Samml. aus der Naturkunde, H. I. cap. 6. The Jewish commentators and Josephus (Antiq. II. 14. § 3.) with less probability make these insects *lice.* Hence in the Talmud כִּנָּה *a louse.* So Bochart (Hieroz. T. II. p. 572 ff.)

Note כֵּן in Is. 51:6, is probably the singular of this noun.

כָּנָה in Kal not used. In Arab. conj. I. II. IV. V. and in Chald. *to call by an honourable surname* or *title, blandè loqui.*

Pi. 1. *idem.* Is. 44:5 וּבְשֵׁם יִשְׂרָאֵל יְכַנֶּה *he shall call upon the name of Israel*, i. e. address him in a friendly manner. 45:4 בִּשְׁמֶךָ אֲכַנְּךָ *I have called thee by thy name*, i. e. have called upon thee in a friendly or flattering manner.

2. *to flatter* generally. Job 32:21, 22.

כַּנֵּה found only Ezek. 27:23. proper name of a city, prob. a contraction of כַּלְנֵה *Ctesiphon*, (q. v.) One MS. of De Rossi reads כַּלְנֵה. (Comp. קַח for לְקַח.)

כַּנָּה Ps. 80:16. see **כָּנַן**.

כְּנָוֹת plur. masc. *fellow-labourers, colleagues.* It has the feminine termination, like אַחְוָה. Ezra 4:7. (Syr. ܟܢܬܐ, plur. ܟܢܘܬܐ, *σύνδουλος.* The singular, which no longer occurs, was prob. כְּנָת, like מְנָת, plur. מְנָאוֹת, מְנָיוֹת.)

כְּנָת Chald. *idem.* With suff. כְּנָוָתֵהּ Ezra 5:6. כְּנָוָתְהוֹן Ezra 4:9, 17, 23. 5:3. 6:6, 13.

כִּנּוֹר m. plur. ־ִים and ־וֹת, in Greek *κινύρα*, a stringed instrument of the Hebrews and Greeks, celebrated for its having expressed the pious feelings of David. Gen. 4:21. Ps. 33:2. 43:4. 49:5. 71:22. 1 Sam. 16:16, 23. Josephus (Antiq. x. 12. § 3.) describes it as having ten strings, and played upon by a plectrum; but this does not accord with 1 Sam. 16:23. 18:10. 19:9. where David is said to have played upon it with his hand. (Arab. كِنَّارَةٌ *a harp, sound.*)

כִּנָּם i. q. כִּנִּים *gnats.* Ex. 8:13, 14. (The termination ־ָם, unless it should be read ־ִם, has probably a collective signification.)

כְּנֵמָא adv. Chald. *thus, in this manner.* Ezra 4:8. 5:4, 9, 11. 6:13. Prob. i. q. כֵּן with the termination מא, ما, which also in Arabic is annexed to many particles without affecting their signification.

כָּנַן i. q. Arab. كَنَّ *to cover, protect,* (comp. גָּנַן, جَنَّ.) Imper. כַּנָּה Ps. 80:16. Others make it a subst. *a set* or *slip,* (comp. כֵּן Dan. 11:7.) but with less evidence.

כָּנַס 1. *to collect, heap up;* e.g. stones, Ecc. 3:5. *treasures,* Ecc. 2:8, 26. *water,* Ps. 33:7.

2. *to assemble, bring together,* as men. Est. 4:16. 1 Chr. 22:2.

Pi. *to assemble, bring together,* as men. Ezek. 22:21. 39:28. Ps. 147:2.

Hithpa. *to hide* or *cover one's self.* Is. 28:20 וְהַמַּסֵּכָה צָרָה כְּהִתְכַּנֵּס *and the covering is too narrow to hide one's self therein.* (Aram. כְּנַס *to collect;* Arab كنز *to collect, heap up,* also *to conceal;* else كنس.)

כָּנַע in Kal not used.

Hiph. הִכְנִיעַ *to humble, bow down.* Job 40:12. Ps. 107:12. Is. 25:5. Especially *to subdue* or *conquer* an enemy, 2 Sam. 8:1. 1 Chr. 17:10. 18:1. Ps. 81:15.

Niph. נִכְנַע 1. *to be humbled, to be subdued.* Judg. 3:30. 8:28. 11:33. 1 Sam. 7:13.

2. *to humble one's self before* any one, especially before God or before a divine ambassador, construed with לִפְנֵי, מִפְּנֵי and מִלְּפָנַי. 1 K. 21:29 *hast thou seen how Ahab has humbled himself before me?* 2 K. 22:19. 2 Chr. 12:7. 30:11. 33:23. 36:12. (Chald. Ithp. *idem.* Arab. كنع conj. I. IV. *to be humble.*)

כִּנְעָה f. dec. XI. c. found only in Jer. 10:17. according to the Sept. ὑπόστασις, *goods, substance.* Usually rendered incorrectly *wares,* as if from כְּנַעֲנִי *a merchant.* From the Arab. كنع *concupivit* it would denote, *valuables;* (comp. חֶמְדָּה.)

כְּנַעַן m. a proper name.

1. *Canaan,* the son of Ham, and progenitor of the Canaanites. Gen. 9:18 ff. 10:6.

2. *the country* or *people of Canaan,* including what was afterwards called Palestine and Phenicia; but in a more restricted sense, (1.) *the country west of Jordan,* in opposition to *Gilead.* Num. 33:51. Josh. 22:9. (2.) *Phenicia* alone. Is. 23:11. (3.) *Philistia.* Zeph. 2:5.—שְׂפַת כְּנַעַן *the language of Canaan,* i. e. the Hebrew, which the Hebrews adopted from the Canaanites.—That *Canaan* was the domestic name of the same people which the Greeks called *Phenicians,* is evident from the Phenician medals, on which we find the word כנען. The ancient Carthaginians also gave themselves this name. See Gesenius' Geschichte der. Hebr. Sprache und Schrift, p. 16, 227.

3. i. q. אִישׁ כְּנַעַן *a Canaanite.* Hos. 12:8. and this for *a merchant* generally, Is. 23:8 כִּנְעָנֶיהָ *her merchants.* Comp. Ezek. 17:4.

כְּנַעֲנִי, fem. כְּנַעֲנִית plur. כְּנַעֲנִים, a gentile noun from כְּנַעַן.

1. *a Canaanite.* Judg. 1:1 ff. For the different tribes included under this name, see Gen. 10:15—19. Sometimes it has a more special signification, as in Gen. 13:7. 15:20. Num. 13:30. Josh. 11:3.

2. as the Canaanites were many of them devoted to traffic, *a merchant, a dealer.* Job 40:30. [41:6.] Prov. 31:24. So כַּשְׂדִּי *a Chaldean* for *an astrologer.*

כָּנַף in Syr. Chald. and Talmud. *to collect, gather together;* hence prob. in Hebrew, (like אָסַף, קָבַץ,) *to take away.* Is. 30:20 לֹא יִכָּנֵף עוֹד מוֹרֶיךָ *no longer shall thy teachers be taken from thee.*

כָּנָף f. dec. IV. f.

1. *a wing.*—בַּעַל כָּנָף Prov. 1:16. and בַּעַל כְּנָפַיִם Ecc. 10:20. *winged, a bird.*—כָּל־כָּנָף *every fowl,* Gen. 7:14. Often used metaphorically, as כַּנְפֵי רוּחַ *the wings of the wind,* Ps. 18:21. 104:3. כַּנְפֵי שַׁחַר *the wings of the morn,* 139:9. In the Psalms often in phrases like the following, Ps. 17:8 בְּצֵל כְּנָפֶיךָ תַּסְתִּירֵנִי *hide me under the shadow of thy wings.* 36:8. 57:2.

2. *the corner* or *skirt* of a garment,

πτέρυξ, πτερύγιον. 1 Sam. 24 : 5, 11. Num. 15 : 38. Zech. 8 : 13 כְּנַף אִישׁ יְהוּדִי *the skirt of a Jew*. Also of a bed-covering, Deut. 23 : 1 וְלֹא יְגַלֶּה כְּנַף אָבִיו *and he shall not remove the bed-covering of his father*, i. e. he shall not defile his father's bed. 27 : 20. comp. Ezek. 16 : 8. Ruth 3 : 9 *spread thy covering over thine handmaid*, i. e. *in tori societatem me recipias;* (comp. Theocr. Idyll. XVIII. 19. and ἐπισκιάζειν Luke 1 : 35.)

3. *the wing of an army, ala exercitus*, (comp. אֲגַפִּים.) Is. 8 : 8.

4. *end, corner, boundary*. Is. 24 : 16 כְּנַף הָאָרֶץ *the end of the earth*. Especially in the plur. Job 37 : 3. 38 : 13 כַּנְפוֹת הָאָרֶץ *the ends of the earth;* and Is. 11 : 12. Ezek. 7 : 2 אַרְבַּעַת כַּנְפוֹת הָאָרֶץ *the four ends of the earth*. The earth appears to have been considered as four-cornered like a mantle.

5. *a battlement* or *pinnacle* of the temple. Dan. 9 : 27. Comp. πτερύγιον τοῦ ἱεροῦ, Matt. 4 : 5.

Dual כְּנָפַיִם f. const. כַּנְפֵי, occurring in the significations nos. 1. 2. 3. and often applied to more than two, as שֵׁשׁ כְּנָפַיִם *six wings*, Is. 6 : 2. אַרְבַּע כְּנָפַיִם *four wings*, Ezek. 1 : 6. 10 : 21.

Plur. כַּנְפוֹת m. occurring in the signification no. 2. Deut. 22 : 12. and besides in signif. no. 4.

כִּנֶּרֶת Deut. 3 : 17. כִּנְּרוֹת 1 K. 15 : 20. and כִּנֲרוֹת Josh. 11 : 2. a city in the tribe of Naphtali, on the Sea of Galilee, which was hence called יָם כִּנֶּרֶת Num. 34 : 11. (The later name was גִּנֵּסַר, Γεννησαρέτ.)

כְּנַשׁ Chald. *to collect*, i. q. Heb. כָּנַס. Infin. Dan. 3 : 2.

Ithpa. *to assemble, to meet*. Dan. 3 : 3, 27.

כֵּס m. Ex. 17 : 16. most prob. a corrupt reading for נֵס *a banner, standard*. Comp. ver. 15. The common reading is usually explained as if i. q. כִּסֵּא *a throne*, which is the reading of the Samar. text.

כֶּסֶא Prov. 7 : 20. and כֶּסֶה Ps. 81 : 4. *the time of full moon*. (Syr. ܟܣܐ *the 14th day of the month, the full moon*, as it were *the ides;* also *the festival celebrated at that time*.)

כִּסֵּא m. prim. (twice כִּסֵּה Job 26 : 9. 1 K. 10 : 19.) with suff. כִּסְאֲךָ, plur. כִּסְאוֹת dec. VII.

1. *a seat*. 2 K. 4 : 10. Particularly *a raised seat, cathedra;* e. g. of the high-priest, 1 Sam. 1 : 9. 4 : 13. of a judge, namely, *a judgment seat*, Ps. 122 : 5. Neh. 3 : 7.

2. *a throne*.—כִּסֵּא הַמַּמְלָכָה 2 Sam. 7 : 13. or הַמַּלְכוּת 1 Chr. 22 : 10. *a royal throne*. (Arab. كُرْسِيّ, Aram. ܟܘܪܣܝܐ כָּרְסֵא *idem;* whence it appears that the Dagesh forte in ס is an assimilated ר.)

כַּשְׂדָּי Chald. *a Chaldean*, i. q. כַּשְׂדִּי. Ezra 5 : 12.

כָּסָה in Kal found only in the participles כֹּסֶה Prov. 12 : 16, 23. and כְּסוּי Ps. 32 : 1. elsewhere only in

Pi. כִּסָּה 1. *to cover*. The person or thing *covered* is usually put in the accus. Ex. 10 : 5. Num. 9 : 15. 22 : 5. but is sometimes preceded by עַל, (see the kindred verbs of covering סָכַךְ, כָּפַר,) Num. 16 : 33 וַתְּכַס עֲלֵיהֶם הָאָרֶץ *and the earth covered them*. Job 21 : 26 וְרִמָּה תְּכַסֶּה עֲלֵיהֶם *and worms cover them*. 2 Chr. 5 : 8. by לְ, Is. 11 : 9.—When followed by a double complement, *to cover* a person or thing with any thing, it is construed (1.) with an accus. of the person and בְּ of the thing. Lev. 17 : 13 וְכִסָּהוּ בֶּעָפָר *and he covered it with earth*. Num. 4 : 5, 8, 11. (2.) with a double accus. of the person and thing. Ezek. 18 : 7, 16. 16 : 10. (3.) with עַל of the person and בְּ of the thing. Ps. 44 : 20. (4.) with עַל of the person and an accus. of the thing, Ezek. 24 : 7. comp. Job 36 : 32.

2. *to cover* or *clothe one's self*. Gen. 38 : 14. Deut. 22 : 12. Jon. 3 : 6 וַיְכַס שַׂק *and he covered himself with a mourning garment*. (In Arab. كَسَا *to put on*, construed with an accus.)

3. *to conceal, to keep secret*, as in Chaldaic. Prov. 10 : 18. 12 : 16, 23. Job

31:33. In a somewhat different sense, Job 23:17 וּמִפָּנַי כִּסָּה אֹפֶל and (since) he did (not) conceal from me misfortune, i.e. did not deliver me from it.

4. *to cover* or *pardon* (sin), construed with עַל. Prov. 10:12. Neh. 3:37. [4:5.] Ps. 32:1 כְּסוּי חֲטָאָה *whose sin is forgiven.* (Comp. כִּפֶּר.)

5. construed with אֶל, *to discover one's self to* any one, (comp. סֵתֶר and הִסְתִּיר;) or *to commit one's self secretly*, Ps. 143:9.

Pu. כֻּסָּה and כֻּסָּה pass. *to be covered;* construed with בְּ, 1 Chr. 21:16. Ecc. 6:4. with an accus. Ps. 80:11. Prov. 24:31.

Niph. pass. Jer. 51:42.

Hithpa. *to clothe one's self*, construed with בְּ, 1 K. 11:29. with an accus. Jon. 3:8.

Deriv. מִכְסֶה, מְכַסֶּה, כֶּסֶה, כְּסוּת, כָּסוּי.

כֶּסֶה i. q. **כֶּסֶא** q. v.

כְּסוּחָה Is. 5:25. see **סוּחָה**.

כָּסוּי m. verbal from כָּסָה, dec. III. c. *a covering.* Num. 4:6, 14.

כְּסוּת verbal from כָּסָה, dec. I.

1. *a covering.* Job 24:7. 26:6.—כְּסוּת עֵינַיִם *a covering for the eyes, a veil*, Gen. 20:16.

2. *a garment.* Deut. 22:12.

כָּסַח *to cut off* (a plant). Is. 33:12. Ps. 80:17. (In Syr. and Chald. *to prune* the vine.)

כְּסִיל m. verbal from כָּסַל, dec. I.

1. *a fool.* Prov. 1:32. 10:1, 18. 13:19, 20. 14:8, 24, 33. 15:2, 7. elsewhere only in Ecc. and in some of the Psalms.

2. Job 9:9. 38:31. Am. 5:8. a constellation in the heavens; according to the ancient versions, *Orion*, which in Aram. and Arab. is called *the giant.* According to an eastern tradition this was Nimrod, the founder of Babylon, afterwards translated to the skies. Michaëlis and others suppose, that this story may have been known to the ancient Hebrews, and that כְּסִיל *the foolish* or *impious one* is a name given to the deified Nimrod. Plur. כְּסִילִים Is. 13:10. *the giants* (of heaven), meaning probably several constellations similar to Orion.—The Rabbins interpret it *Sirius*, which is called in Arabic سُهَيْل *stultulus.*

כְּסִילוּת f. denom. from כָּסַל, *folly.* Prov. 9:13.

כָּסַל *to be foolish.* Jer. 10:8. More usually written סָכַל, q. v.

I. **כֶּסֶל** (Job 15:27.) plur. כְּסָלִים, *the internal muscles of the loins*, in the region of the kidneys, covered with fat, ψόαι, ψοῖαι, ψύαι, *lumbi.* Lev. 3:4, 10, 15. 4:9. 7:4. Job 15:27 וַיַּעַשׂ פִּימָה עֲלֵי כָסֶל *and (since) he put fat on the loins.* —*The inward parts* generally, Ps. 38:8. Comp. Bocharti Hieroz. T. I. p. 506 ff.

II. **כֶּסֶל** m. verbal from כָּסַל, dec. VI. h.

1. *folly.* Ecc. 7:25.

2. *hope, confidence.* (The origin of this signification is unknown.) Ps. 78:7. Prov. 3:26.

כִּסְלָה fem. of כֶּסֶל no. II.

1. *folly.* Ps. 85:9.

2. *hope.* Job 4:6.

כִּסְלֵו m. Zech. 7:1. Neh. 1:1. in Greek Χασελεῦ 1 Mac. 1:54. the ninth month of the Hebrews, answering to part of November and part of December.

כַּסְלֻחִים masc. plur. Gen. 10:14. 1 Chr. 1:12. a people, spoken of as a colony of the Egyptians; according to Bochart (Phaleg. IV. 31.) *the Colchians*, whom the Greek writers constantly represent as of Egyptian origin. The similarity of the two names, however, is quite remote.

כָּסַם *to shear.* Once Ezek. 44:20.

כֻּסֶּמֶת f. Ex. 9:32. Is. 28:25. Plur. כֻּסְּמִים Ezek. 4:9. *spelt, triticum, spelta* Linn. the ζέα of the Greeks, the *far* and *adoreum* of the Romans, a species of grain resembling wheat with *shorn* ears.

כָּסַס *to reckon, count.* Once Ex.

12:4. So the Sept. Chald. Syr. Deriv. כֶּסֶם.

כָּסַף, fut. יִכְסֹף. 1. *to be greedy* or *long for* any thing, construed with לְ. Ps. 17:12.

2. *to have compassion, bene cupere.* Job 14:15.

Niph. 1. i. q. Kal no 1. *to long for.* Gen. 31:30. Ps. 84:3.

2. as in Chaldaic. *to blush, to be ashamed.* Zeph. 2:1. הַגּוֹי לֹא נִכְסָף *O people, without shame.*

כֶּסֶף m. dec. VI. a.

1. *silver.* Gen. 23:15 אַרְבַּע מֵאֹת שֶׁקֶל־כֶּסֶף 400 *shekels of silver.* The word שֶׁקֶל is more frequently omitted; as אֶלֶף כֶּסֶף 1000 (*shekels of*) *silver,* Gen. 20:16. עֶשְׂרִים כֶּסֶף 20 (*shekels of*) *silver,* 37:28.

2. i. q. *money* generally, (like ἀργύριον, *argent.*) Gen. 23:13. Deut. 23:20. Plur. *pieces of money,* Gen. 42:25, 35.

כְּסַף Chald. *idem.* emph. כַּסְפָּא Dan. 2:35. 5:2, 4, 23.

כָּסִפְיָא found only Ezra 8:17. name of a country, perhaps *Caspia,* the country on the Caspian sea.

כֶּסֶת f. plur. כְּסָתוֹת, verbal from כָּסָה, dec. VI. h. *a cushion, pillow.* Ezek. 13:18, 20. Sept. προσκεφάλαια. Vulg. *pulvilli.* According to the Rabbins *pulvinar longius, a bolster.*—The feminine termination ת is, in the formation of the plural, treated as if radical; comp. דֶּלֶת, plur. דְּלָתוֹת.

כְּעַן adv. Chald. *now.* Dan. 2:23. עַד כְּעַן *till now,* Ezra 5:16.

כְּעֶנֶת and כְּעֶת see עֵת.

כָּעַס, fut. יִכְעַס.

1. *to be grieved, out of humour, displeased.* Ecc. 5:16. 7:9. Neh. 3:33. [4:1.]

2. *to be angry.* Ezek. 16:42. construed with אֶל of the person, 2 Chr. 16:10.

Pi. כִּעֵס Deut. 32:21. 1 Sam. 1:6. i. q. Hiph.

Hiph. הִכְעִיס 1. *to cause ill-humour, to vex, grieve, trouble.* 1 Sam. 1:7. Neh. 3:37. [4:5.] Ezek. 32:9.

2. *to make angry, to provoke to anger;* spoken particularly of men who offend Jehovah by their sins, especially by idolatry. Deut. 31:29. 32:16. 1 K. 14:9, 15. 16:2, 7, 13 ff. Also without an accus. 1 K. 21:22 אֶל הַכַּעַס אֲשֶׁר הִכְעַסְתָּ *on account of the anger to which thou hast provoked (me).* 2 K. 21:6.

כַּעַס m. verbal from כָּעַס, dec. VI. c.

1. *grief, vexation, sorrow.* Ecc. 1:18. 2:23. Prov. 17:25. 21:19 אֵשֶׁת מְדוֹנִים וָכָעַס *a contentious and peevish* or *vexatious woman.* Deut. 32:27 כַּעַס אוֹיֵב *vexation from an enemy.*

2. *anger.* Deut. 32:19. Ezek. 20:28. Plur. כְּעָסִים *provocations to anger,* 2 K. 23:26.

כַּעַשׂ m. dec. VI. c. *idem.* Only Job 5:2. 6:2. 10:17. 17:7.

כַּף f. with suff. כַּפִּי, dec. VIII. h. (Arab. كَفّ,) verbal from כָּפַף, literally *something crooked* or *hollowed out.*

1. *the hollow hand, the palm;* and so *the hand itself.*—In animals *the paw,* Lev. 11:27.—מִכַּף פ׳ *out of the hand of any one,* (like מִיַּד,) particularly after verbs of delivering, 1 Sam. 4:3. 2 Sam. 14:16.—Judg. 12:3 וָאָשִׂימָה נַפְשִׁי בְכַפִּי *I took my life in my hand,* i. e. I put it at hazard, or I exposed myself to great danger, 1 Sam. 19:5. 28:21. Job 13:14. comp. Ps. 119:109.—To express the plural the dual כַּפַּיִם is constantly used, except in the phrase כַּפּוֹת הַיָּדַיִם, which in 1 Sam. 5:4. 2 K. 9:35. denotes *hands cut off,* and in Dan. 10:10, *the palms of the hands.* The plural form in other places denotes *handles,* as of a bar, Cant. 5:5. (Comp. יָדוֹת.)

2. joined with רֶגֶל, *the sole of the foot.* Deut. 28:65 מָנוֹחַ לְכַף רַגְלֶךָ *rest for the sole of thy foot,* i. e. a peaceful residence; comp. Gen. 8:9.—Plur. כַּפּוֹת Josh. 3:13. 4:18. Is. 60:14. With פְּעָמִים instead of רֶגֶל, 2 K. 19:24.

3. *a pan, dish;* found only in the plur. כַּפּוֹת. Ex. 25:29. Num. 7:84, 86.

כַּף־הַקֶּלַע *the hollow* or *cavity of a sling,* 1 Sam. 25:29. כַּף־הַיָּרֵךְ *the socket of the hip-bone, acetabulum femoris,* Gen. 32: 26, 33.

4. כַּפּוֹת תְּמָרִים Lev. 23:40. *palm branches,* from their *crooked form.* See כִּפָּה, and comp. the Lat. *palma,* which denotes both *the hand* and *a palm branch.*

כֵּף m. dec. I. *a rock.* Plur. כֵּפִים Jer. 4:29. Job 30:6. (In Syr. and Chald. the usual word to express this idea; hence in the N. T. Κηφᾶς i. q. Πέτρος.)

כָּפָה *to bend, incline,* hence *to tame.* Chald. כְּפָא *inclinavit, subegit, coercuit,* perhaps *to turn away.* Prov. 21:14 מַתָּן בַּסֵּתֶר יִכְפֶּה אָף *a secret present tameth anger.* Others compare כָּבָה *to extinguish,* or the Arab. كفي *to turn away.*

כִּפָּה f. dec. X. *a palm branch.* (Comp. כַּפּוֹת.) Is. 9:13. 19:15 כִּפָּה וְאַגְמוֹן *palm branch and rush,* a proverbial expression for highest and lowest.—*A branch* generally, Job 15:32.

כְּפוֹר m. dec. I. 1. *a cup, bowl.* 1 Chr. 28:17. Ezra 1:10. 8:27. Perhaps *a covered cup,* from כָּפַר *to cover.*

2. *hoar frost.* Ex. 16:14. Ps. 147: 16. Job 38:29. According to Simonis so called from its *covering* the ground.

כָּפִיס found only Hab. 2:11. *a cross-beam, rafter.* Root כפס i. q. Syr. ܟܦܣ *connexuit.* Sept. κάνθαρος, i. q. *cantherius* in Vitruv. IV. 2. Jerome: *lignum, quod ad continendos parietes in medio structuræ ponitur,* vulgo ἱμάντωσις, (comp. Ecclus. 22:16.)

כְּפִיר m. dec. I. 1. *a young lion,* namely, such an one as already goes abroad for prey, different from גּוּר. (Ezek. 19:2, 3.) Ps. 17:12. 104:21. Judg. 14:5. Metaphorically (1.) *dangerous enemies.* Ps. 34:11. 35:17. 58:7. comp. Jer. 2:15. Ezek. 32:2. (2.) *young heroes* or *defenders of a state.* Ezek. 38:13. comp. Nah. 2:14. (Arab. غفر and غُفْر *the young of several animals,* also *a young lion.* Comp. עֹפֶר.)

כְּפִירָה proper name of a city of the Hivites, which was allotted to the tribe of Benjamin. Josh. 9:17. 18:26. Ezra 2:25. Neh. 7:29. (As an appellative, i. q. כָּפָר *a village.*)

כָּפַל *to double.* Ex. 26:9. Part. כָּפוּל *doubled,* 28:16. 39:9. (In Aram. with פ, ܥܦܠ *to be doubled;* כְּפַל *to double.*)

Niph. pass. Ezek. 21:19. [14.]

כֶּפֶל m. verbal from כָּפַל, dec. VI. h. *a doubling.* כֶּפֶל רִסְנוֹ *his double jaws,* Job 41:5. [41:13.] Dual כִּפְלַיִם *double, twice as much,* Job 11:6. Is. 40:2.

כָּפַן *to long for, to desire.* (In Aram. *to be hungry.*) Once Ezek. 17:7 *this vine stretched out its roots with desire after him.*

כָּפָן m. verbal from כָּפַן, *hunger.* Job 5:22. 30:3.

כָּפַף *to bend, to bow down.* Is. 58:5. Intrans. *to bow one's self down,* Ps. 57: 7. Part. כְּפוּפִים *the bowed down,* Ps. 145: 14. 146:8.

Niph. *to bow down* or *humble one's self before* any one, construed with לְ. Mic. 6:6. (In Aram. *idem.*)

כָּפַר *to cover, overlay.* Gen. 6:14. Deriv. כַּפֹּרֶת *a cover.* (Arab. كفر *to cover;* conj. II. *to expiate;* comp. غفر 1. *to cover;* 2. *to forgive.*)

Pi. כִּפֶּר, fut. יְכַפֵּר.

1. *to pardon, forgive,* (literally *to cover* an offence, comp. כִּסָּה;) construed with an accus. of the offence, Ps. 65: 4. 78:38. with עַל, Jer. 18:23. Ps. 79: 9. or with לְ, Deut. 21:8. Sometimes with a double לְ of the person and thing, Ezek. 16:63. (The construction with עַל comes from the signification of *covering;* comp. כִּסָּה.)

2. causat. *to effect* or *procure forgiveness;* and that (1.) in respect to the offence, *to expiate, to make an atonement;* construed with עַל, Lev. 4:35. with בְּעַד (*for,*) Ex. 32:30. with מִן, Num. 6:11 (2.) in respect to the offender, *to make an atonement, to purify;* usually con-

strued with עַל. Ex. 30:15. Lev. 4:20. with בְּעַד (*for*,) Lev. 16:6, 11, 24. Ezek. 45:17. with בְּ, Lev. 17:11. Spoken also of the *purification* of sacred things, construed with עַל, Lev. 16:18. with an accus. Lev. 16:33.—An example of the full construction is found Lev. 5:18 וְכִפֶּר עָלָיו הַכֹּהֵן עַל שִׁגְגָתוֹ *and the priest shall purify him from his offence.* (3.) in respect to the person offended, *to appease, to pacify.* Gen. 32:21. Prov. 16:14. Also *to expiate* a threatening calamity, i. e. to avert it by a sin-offering, Is. 47:11.—The offering *whereby* any offence is expiated, or any person is purified, is preceded by בְּ, 2 Sam. 21:3. Num. 5:8.

Pu. 1. *to be blotted out, obliterari;* because a writing was *covered* by drawing the style over it. Is. 28:18 וְכֻפַּר בְּרִיתְכֶם *abolebitur fœdus vestrum.* (In Aram. ܟܦܪ, כְּפַר *abstersit, diluit, abolevit.*)

2. *to be expiated*, spoken of an offence. Is. 6:7. 22:14. 27:9.

3. *to be purified*, spoken of an offender. Ex. 29:33. Num. 35:33.

Hithpa. fut. יִתְכַּפֵּר 1 Sam. 3:14. and Nithpa. נִכַּפֵּר Deut. 21:8. *to be expiated,* spoken of an offence.

Deriv. out of course כְּפוֹר.

כָּפָר m. dec. IV. a. *a village.* Cant. 7:12. 1 Chr. 27:25. Neh. 6:2.

I. **כֹּפֶר** m. *idem.* 1 Sam. 6:18.

II. **כֹּפֶר** m. verbal from כִּפֶּר, dec. VI. p.

1. *pitch.* Gen. 6:14. (In Aram. and Arab. *idem.*) So called from its use for *smearing* or *covering.* (Comp. כָּפַר in Kal and Pu.)

2. *a ransom.* Ex. 21:30. 30:12 כֹּפֶר נַפְשׁוֹ *a ransom for his soul.* Is. 43:3 כָּפְרְךָ *thy ransom.*

III. **כֹּפֶר** m. dec. VI. p. in Greek κύπρος, *the alhenna* of the Arabians, (*Lawsonia inermis*, Linn.) a plant resembling privet, with clustering, whitish, and fragrant flowers. Cant. 1:14 אֶשְׁכֹּל הַכֹּפֶר *a cluster of alhenna.* Plur. כְּפָרִים Cant. 4:13, Comp. O. Celsii Hierobot. T. I. p. 222. Odmann's verm. Sammlungen aus der Naturkunde, Heft. 1. cap. 7.

כִּפֻּרִים plur. masc. verbal from כִּפֶּר, *atonement, expiation.* Ex. 29:36. 30:10, 16.—יוֹם הַכִּפֻּרִים *the day of atonement,* Lev. 23:27. 25:9.

כַּפֹּרֶת f. verbal from כִּפֶּר, *the cover* or *lid of the ark of the covenant.* Ex. 25:17 ff. 30:6. 31:7. בֵּית הַכַּפֹּרֶת *the place of the ark of the covenant,* i. e. the most holy place, 1 Chr. 28:11. Sept. incorrectly ἱλαστήριον, from the signif. of the root *to expiate;* Vulg. *propitiatorium;* Luth. *Gnadenstuhl;* C. V. *mercy-seat.*

כָּפַשׁ prob. i. q. כָּבַשׁ = Arab. كَبَسَ *to cover, to cover over,* e. g. with earth; conj. IV. *idem.* Lam. 3:16 הִכְפִּישַׁנִי בָּאֵפֶר *he hath covered me with ashes.*

כְּפַת Chald. *to bind, fetter.* Pret. Peil, Dan. 3:21. Pa. *idem.* 3:20, 23, 24.

I. **כַּפְתֹּר** m. plur. כַּפְתֹּרִים, dec. I.

1. an ornament on the golden candlestick; *a knob* or *protuberance.* Ex. 25:31, 33, 34 ff. 37:17 ff. Sept. σφαιρωτῆρες. Vulg. *sphærulæ.* Josephus, (Antiq. III. 6. § 7. *pomegranate.* (Comp. in Syr. ܟܘܦܪܐ *balaustium (malogranati;)* ܟܦܪ *folliculos aut globulos emisit;* and ܟܘܦܪܐ *capsula lini*).

2. *the knob* or *the capital of a pillar,* perhaps in the form of a pomegranate or its flower. Am. 9:1. Zeph. 2:14.

II. **כַּפְתּוֹר** Jer. 47:4. Am. 9:7. and plur. כַּפְתֹּרִים Gen. 10:14. Deut. 2:23. name of a country and people, whence the Philistines are said to have originated. The Caphtorim, according to the passages above referred to, came originally from Egypt, and settled in Caphtor, whence again a colony went to the southern parts of Canaan, and called themselves פְּלִשְׁתִּים. (For the explanation of Gen. 10:14, see Vater in loc.) Most of the ancient versions have rendered the word *Cappadocia;* but the appellation אִי Jer. 47:4, shews that it was an island or at least a maritime country. More probably *Cyprus*, though the evidence from ancient writers in its favour is small, (see, however, Theodoret on Jer. 47 : 4. and Is. 9 : 12.) or *Crete*, in support of which we may refer to the name כְּרֵתִי *a Philistine*, (q. v.) J. D. Michaëlis Spicileg. Geogr. Hebr. exter. T. I. p. 292—308. Supplem. p. 1338.

I. כַּר, m. plur. כָּרִים, dec. II. d.

1. *a pasture*. Is. 30 : 23. Ps. 65 : 14. לָבְשׁוּ כָרִים הַצֹּאן *the pastures are clothed with flocks*.

2. *a pasture lamb, a fat lamb*; often mentioned with rams and he-goats, Deut. 32 : 14. Is. 34 : 6. Ezek. 39 : 18. which passages shew that the meaning *a ram*, which is adopted by some, is not correct. That it means a *fat* lamb is evident from the context of the same passages, and also from Am. 6 : 4. 1 Sam. 15 : 9. 2 K. 3 : 4. Ps. 37 : 20. Jer. 51 : 40. Vulg. *agnus*; Syr. *saginatus*; Chald. פַּטִּים *pinguis*.—Is. 16 : 1 שִׁלְחוּ כַר מֹשֵׁל אֶרֶץ *send ye the (tribute) lambs to the prince of the land*. (Neither of these two significations is found in the kindred dialects. Among the Ionians, however the words κὰρ, κάρα, καρὸς, κάρνος denote *a sheep, a pasture*. See Bocharti Hieroz. T. I. p. 429.)

3. כָּרִים Ezek. 4 : 2. 21 : 27. [22.] *battering rams, arietes*. (The Arab. كبس signifies 1. *aries*; 2. *aries ferreus, machina bellica*.) It may also be derived from כָּרָה *to bore through*, (Ps. 40 : 7.) *to penetrate*; as if from a singular כָּרֶה.

II. כַּר, in the phrase כַּר הַגָּמָל Gen. 31 : 34. *a camel's saddle, a camel's tent*, a small tent, which is fastened on the back of a camel, and in which the women usually sit. (Arab. كور and قر.) See Jahn's Bibl. Archäol. Th. 1. B. 1. p. 287. Hartmann's Hebräerin, Th. 2. p. 397.

כֹּר m. dec. I. a measure for both liquid and dry things. 1 K. 5 : 2, 25. [4 : 22. 5 : 11.] Ezek. 45 : 14. i. q. חֹמֶר, consequently containing 10 ephahs or 10 baths. (In Aram. כּוֹר, ܟܘܪܐ i. q. Heb. חֹמֶר.) In Hellenistic Greek the name κόρος has been retained.

כְּרָא Chald. *to be grieved*. Ithpe. Dan. 7 : 15 אֶתְכְּרִיַּת רוּחִי *doluit animus meus*.

כִּרְבֵּל a quadriliteral, *to gird, to put on, to clothe*, i. q. Aram. כְּבַל, with epenthetic ר. Pass. מְכֻרְבָּל *clothed*, 1 Chr. 15 : 27. Hence

כַּרְבְּלָא f. Chald. *a mantle, cloak*. Dan. 3 : 21.

I. כָּרָה *to dig*, (as in Chald. and Arab.) e. g. a well, Gen. 26 : 25. a pit, Ps. 7 : 16. 57 : 7. Hence metaphorically of plotting, laying snares, Prov. 16 : 27 אִישׁ בְּלִיַּעַל כֹּרֶה רָעָה *the wicked man plotteth evil*.—Ps. 40 : 7 אָזְנַיִם כָּרִיתָ לִּי *thou hast bored* or *opened the ears for me*, i. e. (thus) hast thou revealed to me. Comp. גָּלָה. Deriv. מִכְרֶה.

II. כָּרָה *to buy*. Deut. 2 : 6. Hos. 3 : 2. (In Arab. كرا conj. I. III. IV. *to rent, to hire*.)

III. כָּרָה *to give a feast, to prepare a banquet*. 2 K. 6 : 23. Job 40 : 30 [41 : 6] יִכְרוּ עָלָיו חַבָּרִים interrogatively, *shall the companions feast over him?* that is, after his capture. The interpretation, however, which admits of the most philological proof, is the following, *they hire magicians against him*; compare كرا على *to hire against* any one, (see no. II.) and see חָבַר.

כֵּרָה f. 1. *a feast, banquet*. 2 K. 6 : 23. See כָּרָה no. III.

2. Zeph. 2 : 6 נְוֹת כְּרֹת רֹעִים of difficult interpretation, usually rendered *pens which the shepherds have dug*, as if from כָּרָה no. I. or else *pastures*, as if i. q. כָּרִים.

כְּרוּב, plur. כְּרוּבִים, dec. I. *the cherub*, a poetical being, in the writings of the ancient Hebrews, whose form was compounded of that of a man, an ox, a lion, and an eagle, the well known symbols of might and power, Ezek. 1:10. comp. Rev. 4:6, 7. They first appear as the keepers of Paradise, after man was driven out, Gen. 3:24. then usually as the supporters of the throne of Jehovah, or rather as the bearers of his moving throne, hence Ps. 18:11. 2 Sam. 22:11 וַיִּרְכַּב עַל כְּרוּב וַיָּעֹף *he rode on the cherubim and did fly.* Ps. 8:2 יֹשֵׁב הַכְּרֻבִים *thou who sittest or art enthroned on the cherubim.* 1 Sam. 4:4. 2 Sam. 6:2. In conformity with this idea, two cherubim were made upon the cover of the ark of the covenant in the holy of holies, and between the wings of these cherubim the Deity was considered as enthroned, Ex. 25:18ff. 1 K. 6:23. In as much as they are frequently mentioned in connexion with thunder and lightning, they have been compared with the *equi tonantes* of Jupiter, but the similitude in such comparisons must not be pressed too far. (The most probable among the many derivations of this word which have been proposed, is that from the Syr. ܟܪܘܒ *potens, magnus, fortis.*)

כָּרוֹז m. Chald. *a herald.* Emph. כָּרוֹזָא, Dan. 3:4. (Syr. ܟܪܘܙܐ.) From

כְּרַז *to cry out publicly, to make proclamation.* Aph. *idem.* Dan. 5:29.

כָּרִי found only 2 K. 11:4, 19 הַכָּרִי וְהָרָצִים, a designation of the *body-guard* under the later kings, corresponding to the כְּרֵתִי וּפְלֵתִי under king David; comp. 2 Sam. 20:23, where הַכְּרִי וְהַפְּלֵתִי stands in the Kethib, and הַכְּרֵתִי in the Keri. The latter appears to be the more easy reading, but of the same import with the former. For כָּרִי may be derived from כָּרָה no. I. *to bore through,* and denote *a headsman, executioner,* i. q. כְּרֵתִי. Others interpret the word *Carians,* i. e. Carian soldiers in the service of the Israelitish kings. Others, after the Syriac version, *runners,* as if from Arab. كَرَا *velox fuit* jumentum, *vehementer cucurrit;* (see כִּרְכָּרוֹת.)

כְּרִית proper name of a brook by which Elijah dwelt. Only 1 K. 17:3, 5.

כְּרִיתוּת and כְּרִיתֻת f. verbal from כָּרַת, dec. I. *a divorce.*—סֵפֶר כְּרִיתֻת Deut. 24:1, 3. Is. 50:1. סֵפֶר כְּרִיתֻתֶיהָ Jer. 3:8. *a bill of divorce.*

כַּרְכֹּב m. with suff. כַּרְכֻּבּוֹ, dec. VIII. e. Ex. 27:5. 38:4. *an enclosure, border, ledge,* about the middle of the altar, and above the brazen grate, perhaps to catch things falling from the altar. (In Syr. and Chald. ܟܪܟ *to surround, enclose, intrench.* The quadriliteral is formed by combining this root with כרב i. q. Arab. كرب *arctius constrinxit,* or the ב is joined on without any special signification.)

כַּרְכֹּם m. *curcuma, yellow root, Indian saffron.* Cant. 4:14. Sept. κρόκος. (Chald. כּוּרְכְּמָא, כּוּרְכָּם *saffron;* כַּרְכֵּם *to colour with saffron.* Arab. كُرْكُم *idem.*)

כַּרְכְּמִישׁ Is. 10:9. Jer. 46:2. 2 Chr. 35:20. a city on the Euphrates; most probably *Circesium, Cercusium,* Arab. قَرْقِيسِيَة, a celebrated and strong city, situated on the east side of the Euphrates, at the mouth of the Chaboras. See J. D. Michaëlis Supplem. p. 1352.

כִּרְכָּרוֹת f. according to the Jewish commentators, *camels, dromedaries.* Is. 66:20. Root כרכר *saltavit* 2 Sam. 6:14. comp. in Arab. كِرَة *camelus strenuus,* كَرَي *vehementer cucurrit, saltavit,* spoken particularly of camels. See Bocharti Hieroz. T. I. p. 90.

כֶּרֶם m. (fem. Is. 27:2, 3.) prim. dec. VI. a. *a vineyard.* Ex. 22:4. Deut. 20:6. 28:30.—כֶּרֶם זַיִת *an olive-yard,* Judg. 15:5.—Job 24:18 לֹא יִפְנֶה דֶּרֶךְ כְּרָמִים *they turn themselves not to the vineyards,* i. e. to cultivated regions where men dwell. (Arab. كَرْم *idem,* كَرْم *a pleasant, fruitful land* generally.) Hence

כֹּרֵם m. denom. from כֶּרֶם, dec. VII. a. *a vine dresser.* Joel 1:11. Is. 61:5.

כַּרְמִיל m. in later Hebrew, i. q. תּוֹלַעַת שָׁנִי, (q. v.) *the crimson colour*, (taken from the kermes or turtle-insect, coccus ilicis, Linn.) also *crimson cloth.* 2 Chr. 2:6, 13. 3:14. Most probably of Persian origin, namely, from كرمال a red colour taken from insects, compounded of كرم *a worm*, and آل *shining red;* comp. *vermeil* from *vermiculus.*

I. **כַּרְמֶל** m. with suff. כַּרְמִלּוֹ, dec. VIII. g.

1. *a fruitful field, a finely cultivated country*, a quadriliteral etymologically connected with כֶּרֶם, often in opposition to מִדְבָּר. Is. 10:18. 16:10. 29:17. 32:15, 16. Jer. 2:7. 2 K. 19:23 יַעַר כַּרְמִלּוֹ *the forest of his fruitful field*, i. e. his forest which terminates in a fruitful field.

2. Lev. 23:14. 2 K. 4:42. more fully גֶּרֶשׂ כַּרְמֶל Lev. 2:14. according to the ancient versions, *pounded* or *bruised kernels* or *ears*. The derivation of this sense, or its connexion with the preceding, is not certain. The Jewish lexicographers render it *green ears*, which does not suit the passages.

3. proper name of a fruitful promontory on the Mediterranean Sea, on the southern boundary of the tribe of Asher. Josh. 19:26. 1 K. 18:19ff. Is. 33:9. Relandi Palæstina, p. 327. Cant. 7:6 רֹאשֵׁךְ עָלַיִךְ כַּכַּרְמֶל *thy head (is) as Carmel*, i. e. as thickly covered with hair, as Carmel with foliage. (Hair and foliage are often compared together by poets.) Others make כַּרְמֶל here i. q. כַּרְמִיל *crimson*, but without reason.

4. a city on the west of the Dead Sea, situated on a height, Josh. 15:55. 1 Sam. 25:5. now called *El Kirmel*, a lime-stone mountain. See Relandi Palæstina, p. 695. Seetzen in Zach's monatl. Correspondenz, B. 17. p. 134.

Note. The gentile noun is כַּרְמְלִי 1 Sam. 30:5. 2 Sam. 23:35. fem. ־ית 1 Sam. 27:3. *a Carmelite, a Carmelitess.*

כָּרְסֵא Chald. *a seat, throne*, i. q. Heb. כִּסֵּא. Dan. 5:20. With suff. כָּרְסְיֵהּ 7:9. Plur. כָּרְסָוָן 7:9.

כִּרְסֵם found only Ps. 80:14. *to lay waste, to root up;* spoken of a boar. (Arab. كرسم *to eat up, to gnaw in pieces;* Chald. כְּרַסַם *to eat off.* It is derived from the simple כָּסַם, either by inserting ר, or by combining it with the kindred כרם, in Syr. *præscidit.*)

כָּרַע *to bend* or *let one's self down*, usually with the addition עַל בִּרְכַּיִם *on the knees.* Judg. 7:5, 6. 1 K. 8:54. 2 K. 1:13. Ezra 9:5. Also כָּרְעוּ בִּרְכַּיִם *the knees bend* or *bow*, Is. 45:23. Job 4:4. This verb is used (1.) to express reverence to a prince or to the Deity, and then frequently joined with הִשְׁתַּחֲוָה. Ps. 95:6. Construed with לְ of the person, Is. 45:23 כִּי לִי תִּכְרַע כָּל־בֶּרֶךְ *for to me every knee shall bow.* Also with לִפְנֵי, Ps. 22:30. 72:9. It sometimes denotes entire prostration, 2 Chr. 7:3 וַיִּכְרְעוּ אַפַּיִם אַרְצָה *and they bowed down with their faces to the ground.* (2.) to express a sinking down on the knees from weakness, previous to falling. Job 4:4 בִּרְכַּיִם כֹּרְעוֹת *the sinking knees.* Ps. 20:9 כָּרְעוּ וְנָפָלוּ *they sink and fall.* 2 K. 9:24 *he sunk down in his chariot.* Judg. 5:27. Also for repose, Gen. 49:9 כָּרַע רָבַץ *he bends and lies down.* (3.) to express the posture of a woman in travail. 1 Sam. 4:19. comp. Job 39:4, where the same is spoken of the wild goats. (In Ethiopia the women bring forth in a kneeling posture.) (4.) כָּרַע עַל אִשָּׁה *to bend down on a woman, comprimere fœminam.* Job 31:10. Comp. *incurvare*, Martial. XI. 44. *inclinare*, Juvenal. IX. 26. X. 224.

Hiph. 1. *to cast down* (an enemy). Ps. 17:13. 18:40. 78:31.

2. *to bend down*, (with sorrow). Judg. 11:35.

כְּרָעַיִם dual fem. *the legs*, Lev. 1:13. Am. 3:12. *the legs* of a locust, with which he leaps, Lev. 11:21.

כַּרְפַּס *fine white linen* or *cotton cloth.* Est. 1:6. (In Arab. and Pers. كرفس and كرباس; whence κάρπασος, *carbasus*, a species of fine flax which the classics speak of as brought from India and the east. Celsii Hierobot. T. II. p. 157. The word is said to exist also in the Sanscrit language.)

כָּרַר found only in Pilp. כִּרְכֵּר *to dance,* 2 Sam. 6:14, 16. i. q. רִקֵּד in the parallel passage 1 Chr. 15:29. See under כִּרְכָּרוֹת.

כָּרֵשׂ found only Jer. 51:34. *the belly.* (In Aram. ܟܪܣ , ܟܪܣܐ , כַּרְסָא i. q. בֶּטֶן.)

כּוֹרֶשׁ a proper name, *Cyrus,* king of Persia. Ezra 1:1, 7, 8. Is. 44:28. 45:1. 2 Chr. 36:22, 23. Dan. 1:21. 6:29. 10:1. The Greeks uniformly interpret it *the sun,* and correctly; comp. the Pers. خور (*khor*) and خورشيد (*khorshid*) *the sun.* The Hebrew form is either a contraction of *khorshid,* or else *khor* with a servile ש annexed, as perhaps in דָּרְיָוֶשׁ *Darius.*

כָּרַת, fut. יִכְרֹת.

1. *to cut, to cut off;* e. g. a part of a garment, 1 Sam. 24:5, 12. a branch of a tree, Num. 13:23, 24. the prepuce, Ex. 4:25. Hence כָּרוּת Lev. 22:24. and כְּרוּת שָׁפְכָה Deut. 23:2. *abscissus quoad veretrum.*

2. *to chop off, to hew down;* e. g. the head, 1 Sam. 5:4. wood in a forest, Deut. 19:5.—כֹּרְתֵי הָעֵצִים *hewers of wood,* 2 Chr. 2:10. Applied to the cutting down of images, Ex. 34:13. Judg. 6:25, 26, 30.

3. *to root out, to destroy,* (as men.) Jer. 11:19. See Niph. and Hiph.

4. כָּרַת בְּרִית *to make an agreement,* or *covenant, to strike a league,* like ὅρκια τέμνειν, *icere fœdus,* a phraseology derived from the custom of slaughtering and *dividing asunder* the victims, on occasion of making a covenant, (comp. Gen. 15:10. Jer. 34:18, 19. So σπονδὴ *a libation,* also *a covenant,* whence *spondere, sponsio.*) It is usually construed with עִם and אֵת (אֶת,) *with* any one, Gen. 15:18. Ex. 24:8. but in cases where on one side a condition is made or assented to, it is construed with לְ, Josh. 9:6 וְעַתָּה כִּרְתוּ־לָנוּ בְרִית *now make a covenant with us,* i. e. give us peace, lay upon us the conditions of peace. Verse 7 ff. 1 Sam. 11:1, 2. Ex. 23:32. 34:12, 15. Deut. 7:2. Job 31:1 בְּרִית כָּרַתִּי לְעֵינָי *I had made a covenant with my eyes,* i. e. I had imposed a law upon them; comp. 2 Sam. 5:3. 1 Chr. 11:3. Hence spoken of Jehovah's making a covenant with men, 2 Chr. 21:7. Is. 55:3. 61:8. Jer. 32:40. Ezra 10:3 וְעַתָּה נִכְרָת־בְּרִית לֵאלֹהֵינוּ לְהוֹצִיא כָל־נָשִׁים *and now let us vow to our God to put away all our wives.* In all these constructions בְּרִית is sometimes omitted; as 1 Sam. 20:16. 22:8. 2 Chr. 7:18. Is. 57:8 וַתִּכְרָת־לָךְ מֵהֶם *et fœdere conjunxisti tibi (quosdam) ex iis.* Vulg. *fœdus pepigisti cum eis.* Instead of בְּרִית we find אֲמָנָה *a covenant,* Neh. 10:1. and דָּבָר, Hag. 2:5. (comp. Ps. 105:9.)

Niph. 1. pass. of Kal no. 2. Job 14:7. Is. 55:13.

2. *to be separated, to separate itself.* Josh. 3:13 מֵי הַיַּרְדֵּן יִכָּרֵתוּן *then the waters of Jordan separated themselves.* 4:7.

3. *to be banished.* Zech. 14:2. Comp. כְּרִיתוּת *a divorce.*

4. *to be consumed.* Num. 11:33 *the flesh was yet between their teeth,* טֶרֶם יִכָּרֵת *(and) not yet consumed.*

5. *to be rooted out, to be destroyed.* Gen. 9:11. Ps. 37:9. Prov. 2:22. 10:31.—So in the formula of the Mosaic law נִכְרְתָה הַנֶּפֶשׁ הַהִוא מֵעַמֶּיהָ *that soul shall be destroyed from its people,* Gen. 17:14. Lev. 7:20, 21. or מִיִּשְׂרָאֵל *from Israel,* Ex. 12:15. Num. 19:13. מִתּוֹךְ הַקָּהָל *from the midst of the congregation,* Num. 19:20. מֵעֲדַת יִשְׂרָאֵל *from the congregation of Israel,* Ex. 12:19. also simply נִכְרְתָה *it shall be destroyed,* Lev. 17:14. 20:17. This formula denotes capital punishment generally, without defining the mode; see Ex. 31:14. comp. 35:2. and Num. 15:32.

6. *to perish* generally, i. q. אָבַד; e. g. as a land, *perire (fame),* Gen. 41:36. as a hope, *to be frustrated,* Prov. 24:14 וְתִקְוָתְךָ לֹא תִכָּרֵת *and thy hope shall not be frustrated;* (comp. אָבַד Job 8:13.) 1 K.

2:4 לֹא יִכָּרֵת לְךָ אִישׁ מֵעַל כִּסֵּא יִשְׂרָאֵל *there shall not perish* or *fail to thee a man on the throne of Israel.* 8:25. 9:5. Is. 48:19. Jer. 33:17, 18. 35:19. — Josh. 9:23 לֹא יִכָּרֵת מִכֶּם עֶבֶד *there shall not fail among you a servant,* i. e. ye shall be bondmen for ever.

Hiph. 1. i. q. Kal no. 3. *to root out, to destroy;* as individual persons, Lev. 17:10. nations, Josh. 23:4. Zeph. 3:6. Ezek. 25:7. instruments of idolatry, Lev. 26:30.

2. *to separate, withdraw.* 1 Sam. 20:15 וְלֹא תַכְרִית אֶת חַסְדְּךָ מֵעִם בֵּיתִי עַד עוֹלָם *and thou shalt not withdraw thy kindness from my house for ever.*

Hoph. הָכְרַת pass. Joel 1:9.

כְּרֻתוֹת fem. plur. verbal from כָּרַת, *hewn timber.* 1 K. 6:36. 7:12.

I. כְּרֵתִי found only in the phrase הַכְּרֵתִי וְהַפְּלֵתִי 2 Sam. 8:18. 15:18. 20:7, 23. *headsmen and runners,* that is, the body guard of David. The word כְּרֵתִי is here prob. i. q. טַבָּח *a headsman, an executioner,* (from כָּרַת no. 2.) i. e. a member of the body guard, it being well known that capital punishments in the east are executed by the body guard, or by their chief. (See טַבָּחִים.) Comp. 1 K. 2:25, 34, 46. with Dan. 2:14. Some interpret the word *Philistine,* (after no. II.) but this meaning is improbable, (1.) because David would hardly have employed this hated nation in so important a service; and (2.) because the analogy of the word פְּלֵתִי requires that it should be an appellative.

II. כְּרֵתִי m. a gentile noun, i. q. פְּלִשְׁתִּי, *a Philistine,* or perhaps an inhabitant of only the southern and maritime parts of Philistia. 1 Sam. 30:14. Ezek. 25:16. Zeph. 2:5. — The Sept. and the Syriac version render it *a Cretan;* and this has led, not without reason, to the supposition that the Cherethites were descendants of the Cretans, and that כַּפְתּוֹר *Caphtor* is Crete itself. According to an account in Stephanus Byzantinus, (under the art. Gaza,) the Cretans under Minos undertook an expedition to Gaza, where there exists a temple of Jupiter Cretensis, called Marnas. This may be a historical vestige of the emigration of the Philistines from Caphtor or Crete. Others derive the name from כָּרַת *to banish* Zech. 14:2. hence i. q. ἀλλόφυλοι.

כֶּשֶׂב m. and כִּשְׂבָּה f. by transposition, i. q. כֶּבֶשׂ *a lamb.* Gen. 30:32, 33, 35. Lev. 3:7. 5:6.

כֶּשֶׂד proper name of the son of Nahor and nephew of Abraham. Gen. 22:22. It is not improbable, that he is here referred to as the progenitor or founder of the nation of the כַּשְׂדִּים *Chaldeans.*

כַּשְׂדִּים plur. a gentile noun.

1. *the Chaldeans,* i. e. the inhabitants of Babylon and Babylonia, being often parallel with יֹשְׁבֵי בָבֶל. Is. 43:14. 48:14, 20. Jer. 21:9. 32:4, 24, 25, 28, 29. Ezek. 23:14, 23. Hab. 1:6—11.—אֶרֶץ כַּשְׂדִּים *Chaldea,* Jer. 24:5. 25:12. Ezek. 12:13. Is. 23:13. also simply כַּשְׂדִּים f. Jer. 50:10. 51:24, 35. כַּשְׂדִּימָה *to Chaldea,* Ezek. 16:29. 23:16. In its widest sense it included Mesopotamia, hence אֶרֶץ כַּשְׂדִּים Ezek. 1:3, spoken of the country on the Chaboras, and כַּשְׂדִּימָה 11:24. So אוּר כַּשְׂדִּים Gen. 11:28. *Ur of the Chaldees,* i. e. Ur in Mesopotamia. In their irruptions into Palestine, they came from the north, (Jer. 1:14. 4:6. 6:1.) by Hemath and Riblah, the usual route from Babylon, Ezek. 26:7. Jer. 39:5. 52:9.—In opposition to the hypothesis of Michaëlis and Schlözer that the Chaldeans were a northern people of perhaps Sclavonic origin, and different from the Shemitish Babylonians, see Adelung's Mithridat, Th. 1. p. 314 ff. Rosenmüller on Hab. 1:6. and Gesenius' greater Lexicon, p. 489.

2. as Chaldea was the country where astrology eminently flourished, *an astrologer, a Magian,* as the word *Chaldæus* is used in the classic writers. Dan. 2:2, 4.

כַּשְׂדַּי, plur. כַּשְׂדָּאֵי, Chald.

1. *a Chaldean.* Dan. 3:8.

2. *an astrologer.* Dan. 2:10. 4:4. [4:7.]

כָּשִׂיתָ found only Deut. 32:15. i. q. כָּסָה, but, like the Arab. كسا (which otherwise corresponds to כָּסָה) conj. VIII. specially *to be covered with fat.* So the Hebrew commentators; and 3 MSS. read כסית. Comp. Job 15:27.

כַּשִּׁיל m. *an axe, hatchet,* from כָּשַׁל, in Piel *to fell.* Ps. 74:6. (In Chald. *idem,* Jer. 46:22 Targ.)

כָּשַׁל, fut. יִכְשׁוֹל once Prov. 4:16 Kethib, (elsewhere the fut. of Niphil is used.)

1. *to shake, totter, to be weak, feeble.* Ps. 109:24 בִּרְכַּי כָּשְׁלוּ מִצּוֹם *my knees totter from fasting;* comp. Is. 35:3. Neh. 4:4. [10.] כּוֹשֵׁל *feeble, tottering,* Is. 5:27.

2. *to stumble, to trip in walking.* Ps. 27:2 הֵמָּה כָּשְׁלוּ וְנָפָלוּ *they stumble and fall.* Is. 31:3. 59:14. Jer. 50:32. Construed with בְּ *on* any thing, Lev. 26:37. Nah. 3:3. *To fall, sink,* generally, Is. 3:8. Hos. 4:5.

Niph. נִכְשַׁל, fut. יִכָּשֵׁל (this tense is wanting in Kal,) i. q. Kal.

1. *to totter.* 1 Sam. 2:4 נִכְשָׁלִים *the tottering.*

2. *to stumble, to fall.* Prov. 4:12. Jer. 31:9. Figuratively *to be rendered unhappy,* Ezek. 33:12.

Pi. Ezek. 36:14 Kethib, and Hiph.

1. *to cause to totter, to make feeble.* Lam. 1:14.

2. *to cause to stumble* or *fall.* 2 Chr. 25:8. 28:23. Jer. 18:19. In a moral sense, *to cause to err, to seduce,* Mal. 2:8.

Deriv. out of course כִּשָּׁל, מִכְשׁוֹל, מַכְשֵׁלָה.

כִּשָּׁלוֹן m. verbal from כָּשַׁל, *a fall.* Prov. 16:18.

כָּשַׁף in Kal not used. In Syr. Ethpa. *to pray, to make a prayer, to perform divine worship;* as in Acts 4:32. 13:1. (for the Greek λειτουργεῖν.) Phil. 1:4 (for δέησιν ποιεῖν.) This, like many other sacred words of the Syrians, see כְּמָרִים, קָסַם, סָגַד, בַּעַל,) is restricted by the Hebrews to idolatrous services. Hence

Pi. כִּשֵּׁף *to practise magic,* (liter. *to pronounce* or *mutter over magic spells.*) 2 Chr. 33:6. Part. מְכַשֵּׁף *a magician,* Ex. 7:11. Deut. 18:10. Dan. 2:2. Mal. 3:5. Fem. מְכַשֵּׁפָה *a sorceress,* Ex. 22:18. Sept. φαρμακός, and the verb φαρμακεύεσθαι; Vulg. *maleficus, maleficis artibus inservire.*

כֶּשֶׁף m. verbal from כִּשֵּׁף, dec. VI. *magic.* Nah. 3:4.

כַּשָּׁף m. verbal from כִּשֵּׁף, dec. I. *a magician.* Jer. 27:9.

כָּשֵׁר, fut. יִכְשַׁר. 1. *to be right, proper, suitable.* Est. 8:5 וְכָשֵׁר הַדָּבָר לִפְנֵי הַמֶּלֶךְ *and the thing shall seem right before the king.* (So in Chald.)

2. *to be happy, to prosper.* (In Syr. *idem.*) Ecc. 11:6.

Hiph. *to give success.* Ecc. 10:10.

כִּשְׁרוֹן m. verbal from כָּשֵׁר.

1. *success, prosperity, happy course.* Ecc. 2:21. 4:4. See כּוֹשָׁרָה.

2. *gain, advantage.* Ecc. 5.10. (Syr. ܟܘܫܪܐ in both senses.)

כָּתַב, fut. יִכְתֹּב.

1. *to write;* construed with עַל *on* any thing, Deut. 6:9. 11:20. with אֶל, Jer. 36:2. Ezek. 2:10. with בְּ, Neh. 7:5. 8:14. 13:1. with an accus. Is. 44:5 יִכְתֹּב יָדוֹ לַיהוָה *he writes on his hand, I am Jehovah's;* comp. Ex. 32:15. Ezek. 2:10. and Rev. 13:16. (But Gesenius in his Iesaia, Leip. 1821. renders Is. 44:5 thus: *he writes with his hand, I am Jehovah's.*)—כָּתַב סֵפֶר אֶל פ׳ *to write a letter to any one,* 2 Sam. 11:14. with עַל, 2 Chr. 30:1.—כָּתַב עַל *to prescribe to* any one, 2 K. 22:13. Ps. 40:8. also with אֶל, Est. 9:23. and with לְ, Prov. 22:20. Hos. 8:12.—Ezra 4:7 כָּתוּב אֲרָמִית *written in the Aramean character,* as distinguished from the language.

2. *to describe, write down.* Num. 33:2. Judg. 8:14. Josh. 18:4, 6, 8. Ps. 87:6 יְהוָה יִסְפֹּר בִּכְתוֹב עַמִּים *Jehovah reckons,*

in writing down the people. Is. 4:3 כָּל־הַכָּתוּב לַחַיִּים *every one that is written among the living;* comp. Jer. 22:30. Ps. 69:29.

3. *to write, ordain, resolve.* Is. 65:6. Job 13:26.

Niph. pass. Est. 1:19. 2:28.

Pi. i. q. Kal. Once Is. 10:1.

Deriv. out of course מִכְתָּב.

כְּתָב m. (with Kamets impure,) verbal from כָּתַב, dec. I. found only in later Hebrew.

1. *a writing.* Est. 3:14. 8:8. כְּתָב־הַדָּת *the writing of the edict,* Est. 4:8.—2 Chr. 2:10 וַיֹּאמֶר בִּכְתָב *and he answered in writing.*

2. *a book.* Dan. 10:21. Especially *a catalogue,* Ezek. 13:9. Ezra 2:62. Neh. 7:64.

כְּתָב m. Chald.

1. *a writing.* Dan. 5:8, 15, 16, 24.

2. *a precept, prescription.* Ezra 6:18. 7:22 דִּי לָא כְתָב *without prescription,* i. e. without limitation, as much as was necessary.

כְּתַב Chald. *to write.* Dan. 5:5. 6:26. 7:1.

כְּתֹבֶת f. verbal from כָּתַב, *a writing, marking.* Lev. 19:28. See קַעֲקַע.

כִּתִּים and כִּתִּיִּים plur. *the Chittim,* the name of a western people, Gen. 10:4. Dan. 11:30. Ezek. 27:6. which in a wider sense may have been sometimes used for *western people* or *the west* generally, (synonymous with אִיִּים,) as the Roman poets used *India, Syria* for *the east* generally. Num. 24:24. Is. 23:12. Jer. 2:10.—What particular part of the west was primarily and strictly designated by this word has been disputed. According to the Vulg. *Italy;* according to Josephus, (Antiq. I. 7. 1.) *Cyprus;* according to others, *Macedonia* or *the north of Greece.* For the latter Χεττιιμ is evidently taken 1 Mac. 1:1. and Κιτιαιοι 8:5. and perhaps the word is so used in Dan. 11:30. Comp. Bocharti Phaleg. p. 137. J. D. Michaëlis Spicileg. T. 1. p. 103 ff. Supplem. p. 1377 ff. also Gesenius on Is. 23:1, where he advocates the opinion of Josephus.

כָּתִית m. verbal from כָּתַת, *beaten oil.* Ex. 27:20. 29:40. Lev. 24:2. which, as R. Salomo affirms, was obtained not from the press, but by bruising the olives with a pestle in a mortar, by which means only the purest and best oil was extracted.

כֹּתֶל m. dec. VI. p. *a wall.* Cant. 2:9.

כְּתַל Chald. *idem.* Dan. 5:5. Plur. כֻּתְלַיָּא, (like גְּבַר, גֻּבְרַיָּא,) Ezra 5:8.

כָּתַם in Kal not used; *to be soiled, stained, spotted.* (Syr. Pa. ܟܬܡ *to soil;* Ethpa. *to be dirty, black, spotted.*)

Niph. Jer. 2:22.

כֶּתֶם m. *gold,* i. q. זָהָב, but used only in poetry. Job 28:16, 19. 31:24. Prov. 25:12. Ps. 45:10. Dan. 10:5. Cant. 5:11. Michaëlis (Supplem. p. 1381.) supposes, that כָּתַם denoted particularly *to have dark yellow spots,* in support of which he refers to the Arab. اكتتم *cum quid valde flavum est;* hence he explains כֶּתֶם *yellow (gold).* Others derive it from the Arab. كتم *to conceal,* as if, *aliquid absconditum, pretiosum.* Perhaps, however, like the other names of metals, it is a primitive.

כְּתֹנֶת f. and כֻּתֹּנֶת f. dec. XIII. c. *an under garment, close coat,* χιτων, *tunica.* Gen. 37:3 ff. Ex. 28:4, 39. This garment, which was used also by women, (2 Sam. 13:18. Cant. 5:3.) was worn next to the skin, had sleeves, and usually reached down to the knees. For the women it was longer. (Arab. كتن *linen, linen cloth;* Chald. כִּתָּן, כִּתָּנָא, כִּיתָּן, Syr. ܟܬܢ *idem;* comp. Arab. قطن, قطن *cotton, cotton cloth.* Out of this substance the garment was made, and hence acquired its name. From the east the Greeks obtained their word χιτων.) Plur. כֻּתֳּנוֹת Ex. 28:40. 29:8.

40:14. const. כָּתְנוֹת Gen. 3:21. Ex. 39:27.

כָּתֵף f. const. כֶּתֶף, dec. V. c.

1. *the shoulder.* (A double member, and of fem. gen. different from שְׁכֶם masc. q. v.) Is. 49:22. Neh. 9:29 וַיִּתְּנוּ כָתֵף סוֹרֶרֶת *and they shewed a rebellious shoulder* i. e. they shewed themselves rebellious; comp. Zech. 7:11.

2. applied to things without life, *a side;* e. g. of a building, 1 K. 6:8. 7:39. of the sea, Num. 34:11. of a city or country, (in a geographical sense,) Josh. 15:8, 10, 11. 18:12 ff. Is. 11:14 כָתֵף פְּלִשְׁתִּים *the side* or *country of the Philistines.* Better under no. 1. see Gesen. on Is. 11:14.

Plur. כְּתֵפוֹת f. const. כִּתְפוֹת, with suff. כְּתֵפָיו.

1. *sides.*—כִּתְפוֹת הַשַּׁעַר *latera portæ, the space by the side of the door,* Ezek. 41:2, 26.

2. *the shoulder-pieces* (of the high-priest's ephod). Ex. 28:7, 12. 39:4, 7, 18, 20.

3. *the shoulder of the axle-tree.* 1 K. 7:30, 34.

I. כָּתַר in Kal not used.

Pi. *to surround,* especially in a hostile manner. Judg. 20:43. Ps. 22:13.

Hiph. *idem.* Hab. 1:4. Also in a good sense, with בְּ, Ps. 142:8. Intrans. *to be surrounded* or *crowned,* (see כֶּתֶר,) Prov. 14:18 עֲרוּמִים יַכְתִּרוּ דָעַת *the prudent are crowned with knowledge.*

II. כָּתַר Pi. *to wait,* construed with לְ. Job 36:2. (as in Aram.)

כֶּתֶר m. verbal from כָּתַר no. I. *a crown* or *diadem* of the Persian king, Est. 6:8. or of the queen, Est. 1:11. 2:17. By the Greeks it was called κίταρις, κίδαρις, Curt. III. 3.

כֹּתֶרֶת f. plur. כֹּתָרוֹת, verbal from כָּתַר, dec. XIII. k. *the chapiter of a pillar.* 1 K. 7:16 ff. 2 Chr. 4:12.

כָּתַשׁ *to pound* or *bruise,* (in a mortar.) Prov. 27:22. In Aram. more frequent. Deriv. מַכְתֵּשׁ.

כָּתַת, fut. יִכֹּת. 1. *to hammer, beat, forge.* Joel 4:10. [3:10.] כָּתוּת *contusus (testiculos,)* a kind of castration, Lev. 22:24.

2. *to break in pieces,* e. g. a vessel. Is. 30:14. Figuratively *to scatter* an enemy, Ps. 89:24. (i. q. פָּרַץ.)

Pi. כִּתֵּת i. q. Kal no. 1. Is. 2:4. no. 2. 2 K. 18:4. 2 Chr. 34:7.

Pu. *to be destroyed.* 2 Chr. 15:6 *nation was destroyed of nation, and city of city,* descriptive of a state of anarchy.

Hiph. fut. וַיַּכּוּם, *to scatter* or *beat down* (an enemy). Num. 14:45. Deut. 1:44.

Hoph. fut. יֻכַּת *to be broken down, destroyed;* spoken of images, Mic. 1:7. of persons, Job 4:20. Jer. 46:5.

Deriv. מַכְתֵּה, כָּתִית.

ל

לָמֶד *Lamed* is the twelfth letter of the alphabet, and as a numerical sign denotes 30. The name signifies perhaps i. q. מַלְמֵד *an ox-goad,* and has reference to its form.

This letter is commuted, as in Greek, with the other semi-vowels, (1.) With נ, as לָחַץ and נָחַץ *to press;* נִדְנָה Chald. לִדְנָא, לָדֵן *a sheath;* לִשְׁכָּה and נִשְׁכָּה *a cell, chamber;* פְּסַנְתֵּר, ψαλτήρ, ψαλτήριον; comp. the Doric ἦνθον, βέντιον, for ἦλθον, βέλτιον. (2.) With ר, especially in Aramean, and in the comparison of Hebrew with Aramean, as אֲלוּ for אֲרוּ *behold;* אַלְמְנוֹת Is. 13:22. i. q. אַרְמְנוֹת *palaces;* חֲלָצַיִם *loins,* Chald. חֲרַץ; מַזָּלוֹת and מַזָּרוֹת *the zodiac;* שַׁרְשְׁרוֹת *chains,* Chald. and Arab. שַׁלְשְׁלָה, سلسلة, Ethiop. and modern Arab. שנשל; comp. κρίβανος and κλίβανος *an oven;* λείριον and *lilium.* Hence there is a paronomasia in the words לָכִישׁ and רֶכֶשׁ Mich. 1:13. (3.) Rarely with מ, as גֻּלְגֹּלֶת Arab. جمجمة *a scull.*

לְ a prefix preposition, i. q. אֶל, of

which it is probably a contraction; (in poetry also לְמוֹ, q. v.)

1. most frequently a sign of the dative case. But more rarely

2. it serves to form a periphrasis for the genitive, as 1 Sam. 14:16 הַצֹּפִים לְשָׁאוּל *the watchmen of Saul*, liter. *which belonged to Saul.* (Comp. אֲשֶׁר לְ p. 60.) Used thus in marking dates, Ezek. 1:2 בַּחֲמִשָּׁה לַחֹדֶשׁ *on the fifth* (*day*) *of the month.* 40:1. Dan. 2:1. in naming authors, (called *Lamed auctoris*, and found also in Arabic,) Hab. 3:1 תְּפִלָּה לַחֲבַקּוּק *the prayer of Habakkuk;* מִזְמוֹר לְדָוִד *the psalm of David.* before the material, Lev. 13:48. Ezra 1:11. Ps. 12:7.

3. It is found in the later writings likewise before the nominative and accusative; (1.) before the nomin. 1 Chr. 3:2 הַשְּׁלִשִׁי לְאַבְשָׁלוֹם *the third* (*was*) *Absalom;* in the parallel passage 2 Sam. 3:3, simply הַשְּׁלִשִׁי אַבְשָׁלוֹם. 1 Chr. 7:1. 24:20, 21. 2 Chr. 7:21. Ecc. 9:4. When thus used, it may sometimes be rendered *as*, Ex. 21:2 יֵצֵא לַחָפְשִׁי *to go out as free.* Gen. 9:4 דִּמְכֶם לְנַפְשֹׁתֵיכֶם *your blood, as your lives.* (2.) before the accus. Lam. 4:5 הָאֹכְלִים לְמַעֲדַנִּים *who fed on dainties.* Job 5:2. Ps. 135:11. (Many verbs, which are construed with an accus. and אֵת in the more ancient writings, are joined with לְ in the more modern.)

4. *unto.*—לְשָׂבְעָה *even to satiety*, Ezek. 39:19.

5. *concerning, de.* Is. 5:1. Hence דִּבֶּר, אָמַר *to speak, to say concerning* any thing, Gen. 20:13. Ps. 22:31.

6. *from, by.*—לְ.... וְעַד *from .... to*, Neh. 3:15. Especially after a passive verb, to express the efficient cause, (answering to the Greek dative,) בָּרוּךְ אַתָּה לַיהוָה *blessed art thou by* or *of Jehovah*, 1 Sam. 15:13. Gen. 14:19. comp. הָרָה לְ *to become pregnant by* any one.

7. *in, at, on*, in specifications of time and place. לָעֶרֶב *at evening*, Gen. 49:27. לַבְּקָרִים *every morning*, Ps. 73:14. לְעֵת עֶרֶב *at evening*, Gen. 8:11. לְיַד *at the side.* לְפֶתַח אָהֳלוֹ *at the door of his tent*, Num. 11:10. לְשִׁבְעַת הַיָּמִים *in seven days.* Gen. 7:10. Also before numbers, לְמֵאָה וְעֶשְׂרִים *an hundred and twenty*, 2 Chr. 5:12.

8. *as it respects, in reference to.* Gen. 17:20. 1 K. 10:23 לְעֹשֶׁר וּלְחָכְמָה *in riches and wisdom.* Job 32:4 לְיָמִים *in years.*

9. *for.* Gen. 24:4. 47:24.—נִלְחַם לְ *to fight for* any one.

10. *on account of.* Lev. 19:28.—לָכֵן *therefore.*

11. *after, according to.* Num. 4:29 *after their families.* Gen. 1:11 לְמִינוֹ *after his kind.*

12. *before.* לְעֵינֵי *before the eyes of* any one, Gen. 23:11.—Gen. 45:1 לְכֹל הַנִּצָּבִים עָלָיו *before all that stood by him.*

13. *in, into.* לִרְקָמוֹת *in garments of party-coloured needlework*, Ps. 45:15. Lam. 5:15 *our dance is turned into mourning.* Joel 3:4. [2:31.]

14. *with.* Gen. 46:26. Ps. 56:10. 118:6.

15. i. q. כְּ *as if, tanquam.* Job 39:16 *she treats her young ones* לְלֹא לָהּ *as if they were not hers.*

16. before other prepositions, it is sometimes pleonastic; as לְמִן i. q. מִן.

17. as a conj. *that*, before the future, (as in Chald. and Arab.) 1 K. 6:19.

18. before an infin. it forms a kind of gerund, and may be variously rendered; as *to*, Gen. 24:25. *till that*, Is. 7:15. *so that*, Is. 10:2. *when*, Ex. 14:27. *that*, 1 K. 16:7. *while, as*, Gen. 2:3. especially לֵאמֹר *while he spake.* (The opposite of these different phrases is constantly expressed by לְבִלְתִּי.) This infin. with לְ serves also for a periphrasis of the future; and likewise to express an obligation, ability, or necessity. See Gesenius Lehrgeb. §. 211.

With suff. לִי; לְךָ (לְכָה Gen. 27:37.) in pause לָךְ; לוֹ, לָהּ; לָנוּ; לָכֶם, fem. לָכֵנָה; לָהֶם, לָהֶן. These datives, strictly datives of personal advantage, are used pleonastically after many verbs, especially in the imper. and fut. as e. g. בְּרַח לְךָ *flee thou*, Gen. 27:43. דְּמֵה לְךָ *be thou like*, Cant. 2:17. 8:14. יֵחָבֶל לוֹ *he shall perish*, Prov. 13:13. לֶךְ לְךָ *get thee away*, Gen. 12:1. 22:2. תֵּדְעִי לָךְ *thou knowest*, Cant.

1:8. This idiom prevails more in the later writers, whose style approaches the Aramean.

לֹא more rarely לוֹא, (35 times, as the Masora states,) a primitive adv. of negation.

1. *not.*

2. *no.* Gen. 19:2.

3. *nothing.* Job 6:21. comp. Dan. 4:32. [4:35.]

4. *without.* i. q. בְּלֹא. 1 Chr. 2:30 *and Seled died* לֹא בָנִים *without children.* Ps. 59:4. 2 Sam. 23:4. לֹא דֶרֶךְ *without way,* Job 12:24.

5. the interrogative הֲ being understood, i. q. הֲלֹא *nonne?* Jon. 4:11. Job 14:16. Lam. 3:36. (In Talmud. frequently.) So הֲלֹא Ex. 8:22. 1 Sam. 20:9.

6. *lest, that not.* Ex. 28:32.

7. In combination with adjectives it gives them a negative signification; as לֹא עָז *without strength,* Prov. 30:25. לֹא חָסִיד *merciless,* Ps. 43:1. Also joined with substantives, לֹא אִישׁ *without inhabitant,* Job 38:26 לֹא דָבָר *nothing.* לֹא כֹל *no one;* Gen. 3:1 לֹא תֹאכְלוּ מִכֹּל עֵץ הַגָּן *ye shall eat of no tree of the garden.* Josh. 11:11. 1 Sam. 14:24. In a somewhat different construction, לֹא־אֵל *that which is not God, an idol,* Deut. 32:21. comp. לֹא עֵץ *that which is not wood, a man,* Is. 10:15.

Combined with prepositions, (1.) בְּלֹא *without.* Ezek. 22:29. also לֹא בְּ, as לֹא בִמְחִיר *without price,* Is. 45:13. (Syr. ܒܠܥܕ, *sine.*) (2.) הֲלֹא *nonne?* Gen. 4:7. Often used affirmatively, as if i. q. *ecce!* Deut. 11:30. 1 Sam. 20:37 הֲלֹא הַחֵצִי מִמְּךָ וָהָלְאָה *behold, the arrow is beyond thee.* 2 Sam. 15:25. Ruth 2:8. In the books of Kings we often meet with הֲלֹא, where the writer of Chronicles has substituted הִנֵּה, 2 K. 15:36. 20:20. 21:17. comp. 2 Chr. 27:7. 32:32. 33:18. 35:27. See Gesenius Gesch. der Hebr. Sprache, p. 39. In Samar. הלא is the common word for הִנֵּה. So in Rabbinic. (3.) לְלֹא *without.* 2 Chr. 15:3.

Note. The word לֹא stands in some places for לוֹ *to him,* (15 times, as the Masora states,) e. g. Ex. 21:8. Lev. 11:21. 1 Sam. 2:3. 2 Sam. 16:18. Probably merely an incorrect orthography.

לָא Chald. 1. *not.*

2. *nothing.* Dan. 4:32. [4:35.]

לָאַב an obsol. root. See תַּלְאוּבָה.

לֹא דְבָר (*without pasture*) a place in Gilead, 2 Sam. 17:27. which in chap. 9:4, 5, is called לוֹ דְבָר.

לָאָה kindred with לָהָה, in Kal (Gen. 19:11. Job 4:2, 5.) and Niph.

1. *to exert,* or *fatigue one's self,* especially *to labour to no purpose.* Construed with an infin. with and without לְ, Gen. 19:11. Jer. 9:5. 20:9.

2. *to be wearied, exhausted.* Prov. 26:15. Job 4:5. Spoken of things without life, Ps. 68:10 נַחֲלָתְךָ וְנִלְאָה *thine inheritance, when it was exhausted.*

3. *to be tired* or *wearied of* any thing. Is. 1:14. 16:12. Jer. 6:11. 15:6.

4. *to loathe* or *abhor* generally, *ægre ferre.* Job 4:2. In a stronger sense, Ex. 7:18.

Hiph. הֶלְאָה 1. *to make weary, to exhaust.* Job 16:7. Ezek. 24:12.

2. *to weary* the patience of any one. Is. 7:13. Mic. 6:3.

Deriv. תְּלָאָה.

לָאַט i. q. לוּט *to cover.* 2 Sam. 19:5. Comp. p. 2.—לָאט Job 15:11. see under אַט.

לְאַט adv. *gently,* see אַט.

לָאט i. q. לָט; hence בַּלָּאט *secretly, privately,* Judg. 4:21. otherwise בַּלָּט 1 Sam. 18:22. 24:5.

לָאַךְ an obsol. root. In Arab. and Ethiop. *to send.*

Deriv. מַלְאָךְ, מְלָאכָה, מַלְאָכוּת.

לְאֹם m. with suff. לְאֻמִּי, plur. לְאֻמִּים, dec. VIII. d.

1. *a people, nation.* Gen. 25:23. 27:29. Ps. 2:1. 7:8. 9:9.

2. proper name of an Arabian tribe. Gen. 25:3. The name has been compared with 'Αλλουμαιωται in Ptolemy.

לֵב m. prim. before Makkeph (when a tone-syllable follows) לֶב־, with suff. לִבִּי, dec. VIII. i. and

לֵבָב m. const. לְבַב, plur. לְבָבוֹת ,לְבָבִים dec. IV. b.

1. *the heart.*—בְּלֵב וָלֵב *with a double* or *deceitful heart*, Ps. 12:3. comp. 1 Chr. 12:33 בְּלֹא לֵב וָלֵב *with undivided heart.* 1 Sam. 13:14 אִישׁ כִּלְבָבוֹ *a man after his heart;* comp. 2:35. Jer. 3:15.—The Hebrews regard the heart rather as the seat of intellect than of feeling, Neh. 7:5 *God put it into my mind.* 1 K. 10:24 *the wisdom which God had put into his mind;* (comp. φρὴν, *cor, cordatus.*) Hence (1.) *mind, purpose, intention.*—הָיָה עִם לְבָבִי *I had in mind,* 1 K. 8:17, 18. 1 Chr. 22:7. 28:2. 2 Chr. 1:11. 29:10. (2.) *understanding, knowledge, insight.* Job 12:3 גַּם לִי לֵבָב כְּמוֹכֶם *I also have understanding as well as you.* 34:10 אַנְשֵׁי לֵבָב *men of understanding.*—חֲסַר־לֵב *one without understanding, a fool,* Prov. 7:7. 9:4. See the denom. נִלְבַּב. (3.) *courage, spirit.*—רַךְ הַלֵּבָב *faint hearted,* Deut. 20:8. Gen. 42:28 וַיֵּצֵא לִבָּם *and their courage failed them.* 1 Sam. 17:32. 2 Sam. 7:27. 17:10. (Syr. ܠܒܝܒܳܐ *spirited, confident.*) (4.) with suffixes it forms a periphrasis of the personal pronouns. Ex. 9:14. (Comp. *cor,* in Ennius apud Gellium, VII. 2.)—In some phrases the Hebrews use *heart* for *stomach,* (comp. the Greek καρδιαλγία, *a cramp in the stomach;*) as סְעַד לֵב *to support* or *strengthen the stomach.* So the Lithuanians express heart, soul, and stomach, by one word.

2. *middle, midst;* e.g. of the sea, Ex. 15:8.—of heaven, Deut. 4:11. 2 Sam. 18:14 בְּלֵב הָאֵלָה *on the turpentine-tree.*

לֵב Chald. *idem.* Dan. 7:28.

לוּבִים see לְבִים.

לְבִי see לְבָאוֹת, לְבָאִים.

I. לָבַב denom. from לֵב.

Niph. *to become wise, to acquire understanding.* Job 11:12. (Syr. ܠܰܒܶܒ *cordatum fecit, animum addidit;* Ethpa. *cordatus, confortatus est.*) Others, without sufficient ground, *corde privari;* for there is no example of the privative signification of Piel being transferred to Niph.

Pi. לִבֵּב *to steal the heart, to wound the heart,* spoken of one beloved. Cant. 4:9.

II. לָבַב denom. from לְבִיבָה, *to make cakes.* 2 Sam. 13:6, 8.

לֵבָב m. *heart;* see לֵב.

לְבַב m. Chald. *idem.* With suff. לִבְבָךְ ,לִבְבֵהּ, Dan. 2:30. 5:22.

לְבַד *alone;* see בַּד.

לִבָּה fem. of לֵב, dec. X. *the heart.* Ezek. 16:30. Plur. לִבּוֹת Ps. 7:10. Prov. 15:11.

לַבָּה a contraction of לֶהָבָה, *a flame.* Ex. 3:2. Comp. יַקְטִיל for יְהַקְטִיל.

לְבֹנָה see לְבוֹנָה.

לְבוּשׁ ,לְבֻשׁ m. verbal from לָבֵשׁ, dec. I.

1. *a garment,* usually in poetry. Job 24:7, 10. 31:19. 38:14. Est. 6:9, 10, 11.

2. *a spouse, consort.* (After a common figure in Arabic; as in Cor. Sur. II. 183 "women are your *garment* and you are theirs.") As fem. Mal. 2:16.

לָבַט, Arab. لَبَطَ *to throw to the ground.* Niph. *to fall, to perish.* Prov. 10:8, 10. Hos. 4:14.

לָבִי dec. VI. plur. masc. לְבָאִים *lions,* Ps. 57:5. plur. fem. לְבָאוֹת *lionesses,* Nah. 2:13.

לָבִיא *a lion,* perhaps *a lioness;* comp. Gen. 49:9. Num. 24:9. Job 4:11. Used only in poetry. Arab. لَبْوَةٌ, لَبِيَةٌ, لَبَاةٌ *a lioness;* but all these forms have the feminine termination.) Comp. Bocharti Hieroz. I. p. 719.

לְבִיָּא f. (for לְבִיָּה,) Ezek. 19 : 2. *a lioness.*

לְבִיבוֹת fem. plur. a kind of cake or pudding, which was cooked in a pan, and was so soft as to be poured out. 2 Sam. 13 : 6—8, 10. See לִבֵּב. Sept. κολλυρίδες. Vulg. *sorbitiunculæ.* (Arab. لُبَاب *wheaten flour,* لُبَاب *a crumb of bread.*)

לָבַן 1. *to be white.* In Kal not used. See לָבָן, לְבָנָה.

2. denom. from לְבֵנָה, *to make bricks.* Gen. 11 : 3. Ex. 5 : 7, 14. (Arab. لَبَنَ *idem.*)

Hiph. 1. trans. *to make white,* metaphorically *to purify, cleanse.* Dan. 11 : 35.

2. intrans. *to be white.* Ps. 51 : 9. Is. 1 : 18. Joel 1 : 7.

Hithpa. *to purify* or *cleanse one's self.* Dan. 12 : 10.

לָבָן, fem. לְבָנָה, verbal adj. from לָבַן, dec. IV. a. and XI. c. *white.* Ex. 16 : 31. Lev. 13 : 3 ff.

לָבֵן, const. לְבֶן, verbal adj. from לָבַן, *white.* Gen. 49 : 12.

לְבָנָה fem. of לָבָן, *alba* scil. *luna, the moon,* used only in poetry. Cant. 6 : 10. Is. 24 : 23. 30 : 26. Comp. in Arab. قَمَر *the moon,* from قَمِرَ *to be white.*)

לְבֵנָה f. plur. ־ִים, verbal from לָבַן, dec. XI. b. *a brick,* made of clay dried in the sun and then burnt. Gen. 11 : 3. Ezek. 4 : 1. *White* clay, like chalk, was used for this purpose, (Vitruv. II. 3.) hence the name. (Arab. لَبِن.) Comp. מַלְבֵּן.

לִבְנֶה m. Gen. 30 : 37. Hos. 4 : 13. according to the Sept. and the Arabic version in Gen. *styrax, the storax-tree.* (Arab. لُبْنَى *idem.*)—But the Sept. in Hosea, and the Vulg. in Gen. render it λεύκη, *populus (alba,) the white poplar.* See Celsii Hierobot. P. I. p. 292. comp. J. D. Michaëlis Supplem. p. 1404.

לִבְנָה f. verbal from לָבַן, dec. X.

1. *whiteness,* hence *clearness, transparency.* Ex. 24 : 10.

2. proper name of a city of refuge in the plain of the tribe of Judah, anciently the residence of a king. Josh. 10 : 29. 12 : 15. 15 : 42. 21 : 13. 2 K. 8 : 22. 19 : 8, 23, 31.

3. also of a station of the Israelites in the desert. Num. 33 : 20.

לְבֹנָה and לְבוֹנָה f. verbal from לָבַן, dec. X.

1. *incense,* in Greek λίβανος. Lev. 2 : 1, 15. The *white* incense was most esteemed, see Plin. N. H. XII. 14. hence its name. It is mentioned as a production of Arabia, (Is. 60 : 6. Jer. 6 : 20.) and also of Palestine, (Cant. 4 : 6, 14.) unless in the latter passages it denotes *balsamic plants* in general.

2. name of a city near Shiloh. Once Judg. 21 : 19.

לִבְנַת see שִׁיחוֹר לִבְנָת.

לְבָנוֹן *Lebanon,* proper name of a great range of mountains between Syria and Palestine, consisting of two principal chains, *the proper Lebanon* or *Libanus,* and *Antilibanus,* between which lay *the valley of Bukka,* (בִּקְעַת הַלְּבָנוֹן Josh. 11 : 17. 12 : 7.) See שִׂרְיוֹן, שְׂנִיר, חֶרְמוֹן. It derives its name (*white mountain*) from the constant snow, (Jer. 18 : 14.) with which the eastern chain is covered; hence in Chald. and Arab. טוּר תַּלְגָּא and جبال الثلج *snow mountain.* Comp. *Alpes,* evidently connected with ἄλφος, *albus, white.* It stands with and without the article, like the names of mountains generally. See Relandi Palæstina, p. 311. Odmann's verm. Sammlungen aus der Naturkunde, Heft II. no. 9.

לָבַשׁ and לָבֵשׁ, fut. יִלְבַּשׁ.

1. *to put on;* construed with an ac-

cus. of the garment, Lev. 6:3, 4. 16:23, 24, 32. with בְּ, Est. 6:8. (Comp. Arab. لبس med. Kesr. construed with an accus. of the garment, or with ب.)

Part. Paul לָבוּשׁ construed with an accus. or genitive; e. g. לָבוּשׁ בַּדִּים Ezek. 9:2. לְבוּשׁ הַבַּדִּים verse 11 ff. Comp. חָגוּר.

2. metaphorically in very many connexions. Ps. 104:1 הוֹד וְהָדָר לָבָשְׁתָּ *thou puttest on glory and majesty.* Job 7:5 לָבַשׁ בְּשָׂרִי רִמָּה *my body has put on worms,* i. e. is covered with worms. Ps. 65:14 לָבְשׁוּ כָרִים הַצֹּאן *the pastures are covered with sheep.* So *to put on shame,* frequently is, *to be covered with shame,* Job 8:22. Ps. 35:26. 109:29. *to put on righteousness,* Job 29:14. *to put on terror,* Ezek. 26:16. *to put on salvation,* 2 Chr. 6:41. etc. Comp. the Homeric phrases δῦσιν ἀλκήν, Il. XIII. 742. ἐνδῦναι ἀλκήν, XX. 381. ἐπιέννυσθαι ἀλκήν Od. IX. 214.—Job 29:14 צֶדֶק לָבַשְׁתִּי וַיִּלְבָּשֵׁנִי *I put on righteousness, and it put me on,* i. e. it filled me. So the Spirit of God is said *to put on,* i. e. to fill any one, Judg. 6:34. 1 Chr. 12:18. 2 Chr. 24:20. comp. Luke 24:49.

Pu. part. מְלֻבָּשִׁים Ezra 3:10. and מְלֻבָּשִׁים בְּגָדִים 1 K. 22:10. 2 Chr. 18:9. *clothed,* scil. in royal or priestly garments.

Hiph. 1. *to clothe* any one; construed with an accus. 2 Chr. 28:15. Usually with a double accus. of the person and thing, Gen. 41:42. Ex. 28:41. In a different construction, Gen. 27:16 *the skins* הִלְבִּישָׁה עַל יָדָיו *she put over his hands.* Metaphorically *to clothe* one with salvation, Ps. 132:16. Is. 61:10.

2. i. q. Kal, *to put on.* Jer. 4:30.

לְבַשׁ, fut. יִלְבַּשׁ, Chald. *idem,* construed with an accus. Dan. 5:7, 16.

Aph. הַלְבִּישׁ (with the Hebrew form) Dan. 5:29.

לְבֻשׁ see לְבוּשׁ.

לֹג m. a small measure for liquids, according to the Rabbins containing 6 egg shells or a 12th part of a hin. Lev. 14:10, 12, 15, 21, 24. (Arab. لج *idem;* Syr. ܠܓܐ *a basin, dish.*)

לֹד *Lydda,* (now *Loddo,*) proper name of a large village in the tribe of Benjamin, in later times the seat of a Rabbinical school. Neh. 7:37. 11:35. 1 Chr. 8:12. Ezra 2:33. See Relandi Palæstina, p. 877.

לָה Chald. *nothing,* i. q. לָא. Dan. 4:32 [35] Keth.

לַהַב m. dec. VI. c. **לֶהָבָה** and **לֶהָבֶת** f. dec. XI.

1. *a flame.* Joel 2:5. Job 41:13. [21.] Plur. לֶהָבוֹת Ps. 105:32. const. לַהֲבוֹת 29:7.

2. *the flaming* or *glittering part* of a spear or sword, i. e. the point or blade. 1 Sam. 17:7. Nah. 3:3. Job 39:23. Also without חֶרֶב, Judg. 3:22.

לְהָבִים masc. plur. Gen. 10:13. probably i. q. לוּבִים *Libyans;* comp. the analogies on p. 163.

לַהַג found only Ecc. 12:12. (where the corresponding phrase in the parallel clause is *to make books.* (According to Kimchi, *to learn* or *to read.* In Arab. لهج *to be eager* or *bent upon* any thing. Hence Aben Ezra: *ardent study.* Sept. μελέτη. Vulg. *meditatio.* Luth. *Predigen.*

לָהָה i. q. לָאָה *to be wearied, exhausted.* (Comp. פָּאָה and כָּהָה.) Gen. 47:13 וַתֵּלַהּ אֶרֶץ מִצְרַיִם—מִפְּנֵי הָרָעָב *and the land of Egypt was exhausted by the famine.* (In Chald. לְהָה is the common word for the Heb. לָאָה.)

לָהַהּ in Kal not used. Hithpal. Prov. 26:18 כְּמִתְלַהְלֵהַּ prob. *an insane* or *mad man* Sept. πειρώμενοι, *tentati* (scil. *a diabolo.*) Veneto-Gr. ἐξιστάς. (Syr. ܐܬܠܗܠܗ *obstupuit, horruit;* but the ideas *stupuit* and *amens fuit* are often embraced in the same verb.)

לָהַט *to burn, to flame.* (So in Syr. and Chald.). Ps. 104:4. 57:5 לֹהֲטִים *(men) flaming* or *breathing flames.*

Pi. לִהֵט 1. *to burn, consume;* spoken of a flame. Joel 1:19. 2:3. Ps. 83:15. 106:18.

2. *to cause to burn, to kindle.* Job 41:13.

לַהַט m. verbal from לָהַט.

1. *a flame.*

2. *the flaming part* or *blade* (of a sword). Gen. 3:24. See לַהַב.

לְהָטִים dec. VI. c. *magic arts, enchantments,* i. q. לָטִים. Ex. 7:11. See the analogies on p. 163.

לָהַם, Arab. لَهِمَ *to swallow eagerly;* whence لُهَمٌ *a glutton.*

Part. Hithpa. מִתְלַהֲמִים *what is eagerly swallowed, dainty bits.* Prov. 18:8. 26:22.

לָהֵן *on this account, therefore.* Ruth 1:13.

לָהֵן Chald. 1. *idem.* Dan. 2:6, 9. 4:24. [27.] Also כָּל־קֳבֵל דִּי *on this account, because.*

2. *besides, nisi,* compounded of לָא *not,* and הֵן *if.* Dan. 2:11. 3:28. 6:8.

3. *but.* Ezra 5:12.

לַהֲקָה f. dec. X. found only 1 Sam. 19:20. prob. *the congregation, company,* i. q. קְהִלָּה by a transposition. So the Sept. Syr. Arab. Chald.

לוֹ for לֹא *not.* 1 Sam. 2:16. 20:2. Job 6:21.

לוֹ דְבָר see **לֹא דְבָר**.

לוּ Arab. لَوْ, a primitive particle.

1. *if.* Judg. 8:19. Ezek. 14:15.

2. *O that! O si! utinam.* Construed with a fut. Gen. 17:18. Job 6:2. with an imper. Gen. 23:13. (comp. אִם.) with a part. Ps. 81:14. Joined with the preterite, it gives it the force of a pluperfect, Num. 14:2 לוּ מַתְנוּ *O that we had died!* 20:3 לוּ גָוַעְנוּ *idem.* Sometimes it is barely concessive, Gen. 30:34 לוּ יְהִי כִדְבָרֶךָ *it may be as thou sayest.*

3. *O that not!* Gen. 50:15. Sept. μή ποτε. Vulg. *ne forte.*

לוּא i. q. לוּ. 1 Sam. 14:30. Is. 63:19.

לוּבִים masc. plur. 2 Chr. 12:3. 16:8. Nah. 3:9. and לֻבִים Dan. 11:43. *the Libyans,* always joined with the Egyptians and Ethiopians. See לְהָבִים.

לוּד a proper name.

1. Gen. 10:22. a people of Shemitish origin, according to Josephus *the Lydians.*

2. Ezek. 27:10. 30:5. Is. 66:19. and לוּדִים Gen. 10:13. Jer. 46:9. a people of Africa or Egypt. See J. D. Michaëlis Spicileg. T. 1. p. 256—260. 2. p. 114, 115.

לָוָה 1. *to adhere to* any one, *to accompany* him. Ecc. 8:15 וְהוּא יִלְוֶנּוּ בַעֲמָלוֹ *and this accompanies him,* i. e. continues to him, *in his labour.* Hence

2. *to borrow of* any one, as it were, *to be dependent on* him, *nexum esse.* Deut. 28:12. Ps. 37:21.

Niph. i. q. Kal no. 1. *to be joined to* any one; construed with עַל, Num. 18:2, 4. Dan. 11:31. with אֶל, Ex. 29:34. Is. 56:3. Jer. 50:5. Zech. 2:15. with עִם, Ps. 83:9.

Hiph. causat. of Kal no. 2. *to lend, mutuum dare.* Is. 24:2 כַּמַּלְוֶה כַּלֹּוֶה *as the lender, so the borrower.* Prov. 22:7. Ps. 112:5. Construed with an accus. of the person, Deut. 28:12, 44. Prov. 19:17. with two accusatives, Ex. 22:24.

לוּז 1. *to bend, to bend away.* (Arab. لَاذَ *to bend, incline.*)

2. *to depart.* Prov. 3:21.

Niph. *to be bent, to be perverted.* Part. נָלוֹז *a perverse* or *corrupt man, a sinner,* Prov. 3:32. (For this change of signification, comp. עָוָה and עִקֵּשׁ.) Neut. נָלוֹז *what is perverse* or *sinful,* Is. 30:12. More full Prov. 14:2 נְלוֹז דְּרָכָיו *whose ways are perverted;* and 2:15 נְלוֹזִים בְּמַעְגְּלוֹתָם *idem.*

Hiph. fut. יַלִּיזוּ, (with Chaldaic form, like יַשִּׁיקוּ from נָשַׁק,) i. q. Kal, *to depart.* Prov. 4:21.

Deriv. לְזוּת.

לוּז m. 1. *the almond-tree.* Gen. 30:37. (In Arab. and Syr. *idem.*)

2. proper name of a city, which was afterwards called בֵּית־אֵל. (See p. 75.) Josh. 18:3. Prob. different from the place mentioned Judg. 1:26.

לוּחַ m. dec. I. *a tablet.* (In Syr. and Arab. *idem.*) (1.) of stone, to engrave upon. לֻחֹת הַבְּרִית Deut. 9:9. and לֻחֹת הָעֵדֻת Ex. 31:18. *tablets of the law.* (2.) of wood. 1 K. 7:36. Cant. 8:9 לוּחַ אָרֶז *boards of cedar.* Dual לֻחֹתַיִם *the boarding of ships,* Ezek. 27:5. (3.) in a metaphorical sense, Prov. 3:3 *write it on the tablet of thine heart;* comp. Jer. 17:1.

לוּחִית name of a Moabitish city. Is. 15:5. Jer. 48:5.

לוּט *to cover, to wrap up.* Part. pass. 1 Sam. 21:10. Fut. 1 K. 19:13. (See the kindred word לָאַט, and the deriv. לָט.)

לוֹט m. verbal from לוּט.

1. *a covering, veil.* Is. 25:7 הַלּוֹט עַל־כָּל־הָעַמִּים *the veil over all nations,* i. e. prob. a mourning veil over their faces.

2. proper name of the nephew of Abraham. Gen. 13:1 ff. 19:1 ff. By an incestuous intercourse with his own daughters, he was the progenitor of the Ammonites and Moabites, who are therefore called *the children of Lot,* Deut. 2:9. Ps. 83:9.

לֵוִי m. 1. *Levi,* proper name of a son of Jacob by Leah. Gen. 29:34.

2. a patronymic noun for לֵוִיִּי *a Levite.* Plur. לְוִיִּם *Levites,* Josh. 21:1 ff. the tribe of priests among the Hebrews.

לֵוָי m. plur. לֵוָיֵא, Chald. *Levites.* Ezra 6:16.

לִוְיָה f. dec. X, *a crown, garland.* Prov. 1:9. 4:9. Root לָוָה, in Arab. also *to weave, twist.* Hence

לִוְיָתָן m. (from לִוְיָה and the adjective termination ָן;) liter. *the twisted animal;* hence *any great sea monster,* Ps. 74:14. 104:26. particularly *a great serpent,* Is. 27:1. *a crocodile,* Job 40:25 ff. [41:1 ff.] Comp. Bocharti Hieroz. P. II. Lib. v. cap. 16—18.

לוּל, plur. לוּלִים, *winding stairs.* 1 K. 6:8. (In Chald. *idem.*) Comp. לֻלָאוֹת.

לוּלֵא Gen. 43:10. Judg. 14:18. 2 Sam. 2:27. and לוּלֵי Gen. 31:42. Deut. 32:27. *unless,* (compounded of לוּ *if* and לֹא i. q. לֹא, לֵא *not.*)

I. לוּן and לִין.

1. *to pass the night, to remain through the night.* Gen. 19:2. Spoken also of inanimate objects, Ex. 23:18. Lev. 19:13.

2. *to lodge, dwell;* for the most part metaphorically. Ps. 25:13 *his soul dwells in prosperity.* Job 17:2. 29:19. 41:14. [41:22] Also *to turn in,* in order to lodge. Ps. 30:6.

3. *to abide, continue, remain.* Ps. 49:13 וְאָדָם בִּיקָר בַּל־יָלִין *but (such) a man abideth not in prosperity.* Job 19:4.

Hiph. *to cause to abide.* Jer. 4:14.

Hithpal. i. q. Kal. Ps. 91:1. Job 39:28.

Deriv. מָלוֹן, מְלוּנָה.

II. לוּן in Kal not used.

Niph. *to murmur against* any one, construed with עַל. Fut. יִלֹּנוּ Ex. 15:24. Num. 14:2. 17:6.

Hiph. *idem.* Num. 14:29. Fut. יַלִּין Ex. 17:3. also תַּלִּינוּ Ex. 16:7. Part. מַלִּינִים. Ex. 16:8. Num. 14:27. instead of מְלִינִים, יָלִינוּ. In Rabbinic, this punctuation is more frequent. Comp. לְזוּת Prov. 4:21.

Deriv. תְּלוּנָה.

לוּעַ *to swallow, to swallow down.* Obad. 16. (Deriv. לֹעַ *the throat.* Syr. ܠܥܐ *to lick.* Comp. לָעַע.)

לוּץ 1. prob. *to speak in an unintelligible (foreign) language,* i. q. לָעַז. Comp. Hiph.

2. *to mock, scoff, scorn,* (strictly *to stammer* like any one, comp. לָעַג.) Part. לֵץ *a scoffer, scorner,* Prov. 22:10. 24:9. particularly *one who ridicules things sacred,* (comp. זֵד.) Ps. 1:1. Prov. 9:7,

8. 13; 1. 14:6. 15:12. 19:25. Is. 29:20. So the preterite 9:12.

Hiph. 1. *to interpret* an unknown language. (Comp. Kal no. 1.) Hence Part. מֵלִיץ *an interpreter*, Gen. 42:23. *a mediator, messenger* generally, 2 Chr. 32:31. Is. 43:27. Job 33:23 מַלְאָךְ מֵלִיץ *a mediating angel*, i. e. prob. one's protecting angel in heaven.

2. i. q. Kal no. 2. *to mock, deride.* Construed with an accus. Ps. 119:51. Prov. 14:9. with a dat. Prov. 3:34.

Hithpal. הִתְלוֹצֵץ *to shew one's self arrogant* or *wicked.* Is. 28:22.

Deriv. מְלִיצָה, לָצוֹן.

לוּשׁ *to knead.* Gen. 18:6. 1 Sam. 28:24.

לְוָת Chald. strictly *connexion;* hence as a prep. *with.* Ezra 4:12 מִן לְוָתָךְ *from with thee, de chez toi*, i. q. מֵעִמָּךְ. (Syr. *idem.*)

לְזוּת f. *perverseness, frowardness.* Prov. 4:24. Root לָזָה i. q. לוּז.

לַח, plur. לַחִים, dec. VIII. 1. adj. *moist, green, fresh, recens;* spoken of wood, Gen. 30:3. of grapes, Num. 6:3. Also *new, not used*, spoken of cords, Judg. 16:7, 8. (Root לחח, comp. in Ethiop. ለሐለ *to moisten;* Rabbin. לֵיחָה, לַחְלוּחִית, לֵיחוּת *humor, vigor.*)

לֵחַ m. verbal from the same root, dec. I. *freshness, activity, vigour.* Deut. 34:7.

לְחוּם or **לָחוּם** m. with suff. also לְחוּמִי, (like חָרוּל, plur. חֲרֻלִּים.)

1. *food.* Job 20:23 יַמְטֵר עָלֵימוֹ בִּלְחוּמוֹ *he causes it to rain upon them for their food*, as if i. q. לְלַחְמוֹ.

2. *flesh, body.* Zeph. 1:17. (Arab. لَحْم, plur. لُحُوم, *flesh.*)

לְחִי f. in pause לֶחִי, with suff. לֶחְיִי, dual לְחָיַיִם, const. לְחָיֵי, dec. VI.

1. *a jaw-bone.* Judg. 15:15—17. Job 40:26. Ps. 3:8.

2. *a cheek.*—To be smitten on the cheek is a sign of humiliation and disgrace, Mic. 4:14. 1 K. 22:24. Lam. 3:30.

3. proper name of a country on the borders of Philistia. Judg. 15:9, 14, 19. more full רָמַת לְחִי verse 17. The etymology of the name is given Judg. 15:17.

לָחַךְ *to lick.* (In Syr. and Arab. *idem.* Kindred with לָקַק.) In Kal only Num. 22:4.

Pi. לִחֵךְ 1. *to lick.*—לִחֵךְ עָפָר *to lick the dust*, i. e. to throw one's self in the dust, Ps. 72:9. Mic. 7:17. Is. 49:23.

2. *to lick up, to eat off, carpere.* Num. 22:4.

לָחַם, fut. יִלְחַם.

1. *to eat, consume.* Prov. 4:17. Construed with בְּ, Prov. 9:5. Ps. 141:4. Deut. 32:24 לְחֻמֵי רֶשֶׁף *consumed by disease.*

2. *to war, fight.* (Comp. אָכַל no. 2. and such passages as Num. 14:9 כִּי לַחְמֵנוּ הֵם *for they are our food*, i. e. we will eat them as food; and the Homeric phrase, πολέμοιο μέγα στόμα, Il. xxii. 8.) Construed with אֵת, Ps. 35:1. with לְ, 56:2, 3.

Niph. נִלְחַם, infin. pleon. נִלְחוֹם, i. q. Kal no. 2. *to fight, contend.* 1 Sam. 17:10 נִלָּחֲמָה יָחַד *let us fight together.* The person *against* whom one fights, is put in the accus. Josh. 10:25. or is preceded by בְּ Ex. 1:10. by עִם, 2 K. 13:12. 14:15. by אֶל, Jer. 1:19. 15:20. by עַל, Neh. 4:8.—The person *for* whom, is preceded by לְ, Ex. 14:14, 25. Deut. 1:30. or by עַל, Judg. 9:17.—*To fight against* a city, *to besiege it*, is construed with בְּ, Judg. 9:45. and with עַל, Jer. 34:22. 37:8.

Deriv. out of course לְחוּם, מִלְחָמָה.

לָחֶם m. a verbal from the Piel of לָחַם, *war, a besieging.* Judg. 5:8 לָחֶם שְׁעָרִים *a besieging of the gates*, i. e. they besieged the gates.

לֶחֶם com. gen. verbal from לָחַם, dec. VI. a.

1. *food.*—לֶחֶם אֱלֹהִים *the food of God*, i. e. the offerings. Lev. 21:8, 17. Jer. 11:19 עֵץ בְּלַחְמוֹ *the tree with its food,*

i. e. fruit. לֶחֶם הַפֶּחָה *the food of the governor*, i. e. the allowance for his table, Neh. 5:18. comp. verse 15.

2. *bread.* (Arab. لَحْم specially *flesh.*)—לֶחֶם הַפָּנִים *the shew-bread*, Ex. 25:30. If numerals immediately precede, then כִּכְּרוֹת is to be supplied, 1 Sam. 10:4 שְׁתֵּי־לֶחֶם *two (loaves) of bread;* comp. verse 3. אָכַל לֶחֶם *to eat bread*, i. e. to take a meal, see אָכַל no. I. (1.) Perhaps particularly *wheat*, Is. 28:28.

לְחֶם Chald. *food, a meal, feast.* Dan. 5:1.

לְחֵנָה f. Chald. *a concubine.* Dan. 5:2, 3, 23.

לָחַץ, fut. יִלְחַץ, *to press, squeeze.* Num. 22:25. 2 K. 6:32. Particularly *to oppress* a weaker or tributary people, Ex. 23:9. Judg. 1:34.

Niph. *to press one's self.* Num. 22:25.

לַחַץ m. verbal from לָחַץ dec. VI. c.

1. *oppression* of a people. Ex. 3:9.

2. *affliction, distress* generally. Job 36:15. 1 K. 22:27 לֶחֶם לַחַץ וּמַיִם לַחַץ *bread and water of affliction*, i. e. such as are enjoyed in times of affliction.

לָחַשׁ in Kal not used.

Pi. 1. strictly *to whisper, mussitare*, (see Hithpa.) In Syr. and Talmud. *idem.*

2. *to conjure*, from the *muttering over* of magic spells. Ps. 58:6.

Hithpa. *to whisper.* 2 Sam. 12:19. Ps. 41:8.

לַחַשׁ m. verbal from לָחַשׁ, dec. VI. c.

1. *a whispering, sighing* or *calling for help.* Is. 26:16.

2. *magic, conjuration.* Is. 3:3. Particularly *the charming of serpents*, Jer. 8:17. Ecc. 10:11.

3. *a charm, amulet.* Plur. לְחָשִׁים Is. 3:20. (Comp. in Arab. رَقَى *to practise magic*, and *to fortify one's self by amulets against magic.*) These amulets were female ornaments, prob. engraved precious stones or the like, which the orientals make use of for amulets. Schröder and others: *small serpents*, worn for ornaments; but without equal etymological support.

לָט verbal adj. from לוּט, dec. I. *concealed, private.* Hence בַּלָּט as an adv. *secretly, softly*, Ruth 3:7. 1 Sam. 18:22. 24:5. Plur. לָטִים *secret arts, magic arts*, Ex. 7:22. 8:3, 14. See לְהָטִים 7:11.

לֹט m. Gen. 37:25. 43:11. commonly interpreted *ladanum*, in Greek λῆδον, λήδανον, in Lat. *ledum, ladanum*, a fragrant gum, which distils on the leaves of the cistus ladanifera, or Creticus. The ancient versions interpret variously. Sept. Vulg. στακτή. Syr. Chald. *pistachio-nuts.* Arab. *chesnuts.* See Celsii Hierob. T. I. p. 280—288. Comp. J.D. Michaëlis Supplem. p.1424.

לְטָאָה f. probably a species of lizard. Once Lev. 11:30. Sept. χαλαβώτης. Vulg. *stellio.* Root either לְטָא Chald. i. q. לוּט *to conceal;* or the Arab. لَطَأَ and لَطِئَ *adhæsit terræ.*

לָטַשׁ, fut. יִלְטֹשׁ.

1. *to hammer, to forge.* Gen. 4:22.

2. *to sharpen* by hammering; e. g. a ploughshare, 1 Sam. 13:20. a sword, Ps. 7:13. Hence *to sharpen* generally. Metaph. Job 16:9 יִלְטוֹשׁ עֵינָיו לִי *he sharpens his eyes upon me*, i. e. he casts upon me cutting or penetrating looks.

Pu. pass. Ps. 52:4.

לֹיָה for לִוְיָה, and this a contraction of לִוְיָה = לִוְיָה *a crown, garland.* Plur. *garlands, festoons*, in architecture, 1 K. 7:29, 30, 36.

לַיִל Is. 16:3. const. לֵיל Ex. 12:42. Is. 15:1. 30:29. more commonly לַיְלָה (with He paragogic,) plur. לֵילוֹת, m. *night.* Also *by night*, Gen. 14:15. Ex. 13:22. So לֵילוֹת Ps. 16:7.—יוֹמָם וָלַיְלָה *by day and by night*, Ex. 13:21.—הַלַּיְלָה *this night*, Gen. 19:5, 34. Metaphorically *misfortune, adversity*, Job 35:10. Mic. 3:6. Comp. חֹשֶׁךְ.

Note. In Aramean the final ־ָה is treated as if radical, and in the emphatic state is changed into Yod. Hence

לֵילְיָא m. Chald. *idem.* Dan. 2:19. 5:30. 7:2, 7, 13.

לִילִית f. Is. 34:14. strictly *nocturna*, (from לַיִל, with the adjective termination ־ִי, ־ִית,) *a nocturnal spectre*, an imaginary creature of Jewish superstition. According to the Rabbins, a spectre, in the form of a beautifully adorned woman, which lays wait by night for children, and kills them; like to the Lamiæ, Striges, (Ovid. Fast. VI. 123.) and Ἐμπούσαι of the Romans and Greeks. See Bocharti Hieroz. T. II. p. 831. and Buxtorfii Lex. Chald. et Talmud. p. 1140.

לִין see **לוּן** no. I.

לַיִשׁ m. 1. *a lion*. Job 4:11. Prov. 30: 30. (Arab. لَيْثٌ, Chald. לֵיתָא *idem.*)

2. name of a place on the northern boundary of Palestine, otherwise called דָּן. Judg. 18:7, 29. With ־ָה local, Is. 10:30, where others understand a different place near Jerusalem; comp. Ἐλασα 1 Mac. 9:5. Vulg. *Laisa.*

לָכַד fut. יִלְכֹּד.

1. *to take, catch;* e. g. in a net, Am. 3:5. Ps. 35:8. in a pit, Jer. 18:22. Metaphorically Job 5:13 *he taketh the wise in their own craftiness.* Prov. 5:22.

2. *to take prisoner*, in war. Num. 21:32. Also *to take away* things, 1 Chr. 18:4. Judg. 7:24 וְלִכְדוּ לָהֶם אֶת הַמַּיִם *intercipite illis aquam.*

3. *to take* or *break into* (a city). Josh. 8:12.

4. *to take out, to choose out;* spoken of Jehovah who selects any one by the lot. Comp. אָחַז no. 7. Josh. 7:14 הַשֵּׁבֶט אֲשֶׁר יִלְכְּדֶנּוּ יְהוָה *the tribe which Jehovah shall choose*, i. e. determine by lot. Verse 17.

Niph. pass. of Kal no. 1. Ps. 9:16. no. 2. Jer. 51:56. no. 3. 1 K. 16:18. no. 4. 1 Sam. 10:20, 21.

Hithpa. *to hold* or *hang together.* Job 41:9 [41:17] יִתְלַכְּדוּ *they* (the scales of the crocodile) *hold together.* 38:30 פְּנֵי תְהוֹם יִתְלַכָּדוּ *the surfaces of the deep hold together*, that is, through the frost. Comp. אָחַז no. 4.

Deriv. out of course מַלְכֹּדֶת.

לֶכֶד m. verbal from לָכַד, *a being taken.* Prov. 3:26.

לְכָה 1. strictly the imper. of הָלַךְ, *go thou.* Num. 10:29.

2. as an interj. of exhortation, *up, come on.* Gen. 31:44. The verbal signification is entirely lost, for it is addressed to women as well as men, Gen. 19:32.

לָכִישׁ proper name of a city in the plain of the tribe of Judah, anciently the residence of a Canaanitish king. Josh. 10:3. 12:11. 15:39. Neh. 11: 30. Jer. 34:7. Mic. 1:13. Called by Josephus Λαχεῖς (Ant. VIII. 3.) and Λαχεῖσα (Ant. IX. 10.)

לָכֵן see **כֵּן**.

לֻלָאוֹת, const. לֻלְאֹת, fem. plur. *loops*, for the taches or hooks (קְרָסִים,) by which the curtains of the tabernacle of the congregation were fastened together. Ex. 26:4 ff. 36:11 ff. Root לוּל prob. *to wind*, hence לוּלִים *winding-stairs.* The form is like that of תְּאֹדִים, and the singular was perhaps לוּלִי.

לָמַד, fut. יִלְמַד.

1. *to accustom one's self* to any thing, construed with אֶל, Jer. 10:2.

2. *to learn*, (comp. אָלַף;) construed (1.) with an infin. with and without לְ, Is. 1:17. Deut. 14:23. 17:19. 18:9. (2.) with an accus. Deut. 5:1. Is. 26: 10. Part. pass. 1 Chr. 5:18 לְמוּדֵי מִלְחָמָה *skilful in war.* (The participle has here the signification of Pual.)

Pi. לִמֵּד *to teach.* 2 Chr. 17:7. Construed (1.) with an accus. of the person, Ps. 71:17. Cant. 8:2. (2.) with a double accus. of the person and of the thing, Deut. 4:1. Ps. 25:4. Jer. 2:33. Ecc. 12:9. (3.) more rarely with an accus. of the person and a dative of the thing, Ps. 18:35. 144:1. Also with an accus. and infin. Ps. 143:10. (4.) with a dative of the person, Job 21:22.

Pu. 1. *to be accustomed, inured.* Hos. 10:11.

2. *to be taught, to be skilful.* Cant. 3:8. See מְלַמֵּד ,תַּלְמִיד ,לִמּוּד.

לָמָּה and לָמָה, see מָה.

לְמוֹ poetically for לְ. Job 27:14. 29:21. So כְּמוֹ for כְּ, בְּמוֹ for בְּ.

לִמּוּד and לִמֻּד verbal adj. from the Piel of לָמַד, dec. I.

1. *accustomed, practised.* Jer. 2:24. 13:23. Is. 50:4 לְשׁוֹן לִמּוּדִים *the tongue of the practised*, i. e. the practised tongue.

2. *a scholar, disciple, follower.*—לִמּוּדֵי יְהוָה *the disciples of Jehovah*, i. e. those to whom Jehovah communicates his revelations, Is. 8:16. 54:13.

לְמַעַן *on account of, because.* See מַעַן.

לֹעַ m. verbal from לוּעַ, dec. I. *throat, swallow.* Once Prov. 23:2. (Chald. לוֹעָא *idem.*)

לָעַב found only in Hiph. *to mock, deride*, construed with בְּ. 2 Chr. 36:16. (Chald. אִתְלַעַב, Arab. conj. I. II. IV. *idem.*)

לָעַג 1. *to speak unintelligibly*, especially *to speak in a foreign language.* (Syr. ܠܥܓ *to stammer.* Comp. לָעַז *to speak in a foreign tongue*, and لجلج *to stammer.* By transposition עִלֵּג, علج *speaking in a foreign tongue.*) See Niph.

2. *to laugh at, deride, mock;* (liter. *to imitate the stammering of another.*) Prov. 1:26. Construed with a dative of the person, Prov. 17:5. Ps. 2:4 יְהוָה יִלְעַג לָמוֹ *Jehovah will laugh at them.* 59:9. Job 22:19. With a pleonastic dative of personal advantage, Ps. 80:7.

Niph. *to speak in a foreign or barbarous tongue.* Is. 33:19.

Hiph. *to deride, mock.* Job 21:3. Construed with לְ, also with בְּ, 2 Chr. 30:10. and with עַל, Neh. 2:19.

לַעַג m. verbal from לָעַג, dec. VI. c.

1. *scorn, derision*, Ps. 79:4. Ezek. 23:32. 36:4. *cause of derision*, Hos. 7:16.

2. *a wicked, blasphemous speech.* (Comp. לוּץ.) Job 34:7.

לָעֵג verbal adj. from לָעַג, dec. V. b.

1. *speaking in a foreign* or *barbarous tongue.* Is. 28:11.

2. *a scorner.* Ps. 35:16 לַעֲגֵי מָעוֹג literally *cake-scorners, table-wits, parasites*, ψωμοκόλακες, κνισσοκόλακες. See מָעוֹג.

לָעָה Arab. لغا and لغي *to speak any thing rashly* or *inconsiderately*, Job 6:3 עַל־כֵּן דְּבָרַי לָעוּ *therefore my words were rash* or *inconsiderate.* Comp. לָעַע.

לָעַז *to speak unintelligibly* or *in a foreign language.* Ps. 114:1. (Syr. ܠܥܙ *barbare*, pecul. *Ægyptiace locutus est.*)

לָעַט *to eat*, particularly *with greediness* or *daintiness.* Found only in Hiph. Gen. 25:30 הַלְעִיטֵנִי נָא *let me eat, I pray thee.*

לַעֲנָה f. *wormwood.* Jer. 9:14. 23:15. Lam. 3:15, 19. Prov. 5:4. Like bitter herbs generally, (see מָרַר and its derivatives, also πικρος in the N. T.) the Hebrews probably used it to denote *poison;* comp. Deut. 29:17. Rev. 8:10, 11.

לַפִּיד m. dec. I. (Syr. ܠܰܡܦܺܝܕܳܐ.)

1. *a torch.* Judg. 7:16. Job 12:5 לַפִּיד בּוּז *lampas despecta, abjecta*, i. e. something entirely worthless or useless.

2. *a flame.* Gen. 15:17. Dan. 10:6 *his eyes were as flames of fire.*

לָפַת, Arab. لفت, *to bend, bow*, Judg. 16:29.

Niph. 1. *to bend one's self.* Ruth 3:8.

2. *to turn* (on one's way). Job 6:18.

לָצוֹן, m. verbal from לוּץ, *scorn, derision, contempt of every thing great and good.* Prov. 1:22. Hence אַנְשֵׁי לָצוֹן i. q. לֵצִים, Is. 28:14. Prov. 29:8.

לָצַץ i. q. לִיץ *to mock, scorn.* Part. לֹצְצִים Hos. 7:5.

לָקַח, fut. יִקַּח, imper. קַח, more rarely לְקַח, infin. absol. לָקוֹחַ, const. קַחַת.

1. *to take.*—Often pleonastically, as Gen. 12:5 *and Abram took Sarai,—and they went out into the land of Canaan.* Deut. 4:20. 15:17. Jer. 23:31 הַלֹּקְחִים לְשׁוֹנָם וַיִּנְאֲמוּ נְאֻם *that take* or *use their tongues and speak oracles.* So 2 Sam. 18:18. Sometimes לוֹ *sibi* is annexed pleonastically, Lev. 15:14, 29. Job 2:8.—לָקַח אִשָּׁה *to take a wife,* Gen. 4:19. 6:2. 1 Sam. 25:43. Also spoken of the father, לָקַח אִשָּׁה לִבְנוֹ *he took a wife for his son,* Ex. 21:10. also elliptically, Ex. 34:16 וְלָקַחְתָּ מִבְּנֹתָיו לְבָנֶיךָ *and thou shalt* (*not*) *take of his daughters* (*wives*) *for thy sons.* Comp. נָשָׂא.

2. *to seize* or *lay hold of.* Ezek. 8:3. Ps. 18:17.

3. *to take away,* spoken e. g. of an enemy. Gen. 4:12. 27:35 וַיִּקַּח בִּרְכָתֶךָ *he has taken away thy blessing.* Ps. 31:14 לָקַחַת נַפְשִׁי *to take away my life.* Jer. 15:15 אַל תִּקָּחֵנִי *take me not away.*—In a somewhat different sense, Gen. 5:24 לָקַח אֹתוֹ אֱלֹהִים *God took him away.* 2 K. 2:3, 5. (Comp. Od. δ', 561.)

4. *to take, capture, occupare,* the cities or possessions of an enemy. Num. 21:25. Spoken metaphorically of captivating persons or things, Prov. 6:25. 11:30.

5. *to receive, obtain, acquire.* Num. 23:20.

6. *to admit, take up, receive;* e. g. counsel, Prov. 2:1. prayer, Ps. 6:10. Also *to take* a person *under one's protection,* Ps. 49:16. 73:24.

8. *to fetch, to cause to be brought.* Gen. 20:2 וַיִּקַּח אֶת־שָׂרָה *he caused Sarah to be brought.* 27:13 לֵךְ קַח לִי *go and fetch to me.* Verse 45. 42:16.

9. *to lead, bring.* Gen. 48:9. Job 32:20. Prov. 24:11. Gen. 18:5, 7, 8. Particularly *to bring* for an offering, Gen. 15:10. Ex. 25:2. 35:5.

Niph. נִלְקַח 1. pass. of Kal no. 3. 1 Sam. 4:11 ff. 2 K. 2:9.

2. pass. of Kal no. 6. Est. 2:8, 16. But the passive significations are more frequently denoted by the

Pret. Pu. לֻקַּח and fut. Hoph. יֻקַּח.

1. *to be taken.* Gen. 3:23.

2. *to be taken away.* Judg. 17:2.

3. *to be brought.* Gen. 12:15. 18:4.

Hithpa. Part. אֵשׁ מִתְלַקַּחַת Ex. 9:24. Ezek. 1:4. *a continuous fire,* i. e. a mass of fire. See the synon. הִתְהַלֵּךְ.

Deriv. out of course מִקָּח, מַלְקוֹחַ, מַלְקָחַיִם.

לֶקַח m. verbal from לָקַח, dec. VI. i.

1. *doctrine.* Prov. 4:2. Deut. 32:2. (In Syr. ܩܒܠ *to receive* for *to learn.* In Hebrew, comp. לָקַח Prov. 2:1.)

2. *speech* generally. Job 11:4.

3. *knowledge.* Prov. 1:5. 9:9. Is. 29:24.

4. *fair speech, flattery,* by which one captivates another. Prov. 7:21. Comp. the verb no. 4.

לָקַט in Kal and Pi. *to collect, gather,* especially from the ground, as ears, Ruth 2:3, 7, 15. manna, Ex. 16:4, 18. stones, Gen. 31:46. flowers, Cant. 6:2. Also in Gen. 47:14.

Pu. Is. 27:12. and Hithpa. Judg. 11:3. *to assemble, come together,* as men. (Arab. and Aram. *idem.*)

Deriv. out of course יַלְקוּט.

לֶקֶט m. verbal from לָקַט, *the gleaning* of fields and vineyards. Lev. 19:9. 23:22.

לָקַק, fut. יָלֹק, formed by an onomatopœia, *to lick,* spoken only of dogs. 1 K. 21:19. 22:38. Also *to lap,* as a dog when drinking, Judg. 7:5.

Pi. *idem.* Judg. 7:6, 7.

לָקַשׁ in Syr. Pa. *to be late,* spoken of fruit. Hence מַלְקוֹשׁ *the latter rain.* In Hebrew *to glean, to gather the last fruits.* Job 24:6. (In some MSS. יִלְקֹשׁוּ, a correct gloss.)

לֶקֶשׁ m. verbal from לָקַשׁ, *later grass, aftermath.* Am. 7:1.

לָשָׁד m. dec. VIII. h.

1. *sap, life-blood, vital power, vigour.* Ps. 32:4 נֶהְפַּךְ לְשַׁדִּי *my moisture is*

changed, i.e. dried up. (Arab. لسد *suxit*, whence *succus*.)

2. Num. 11:8 לְשַׁד הַשָּׁמֶן *an oil cake.* Sept. ἐγκρὶς ἐξ ἐλαίου. Vulg. *panis oleatus.*

לָשׁוֹן com. gen. (more frequently fem.) dec. III. a.

1. *a tongue.* Ps. 10:7.—בַּעַל הַלָּשׁוֹן *a conjurer, exorcist,* Ecc. 10:11. Especially *a wicked, slanderous tongue,* Ps. 140:12 אִישׁ לָשׁוֹן *a man of an evil tongue, a slanderer.* Job 5:21. Jer. 18:18. Prov. 10:31 לְשׁוֹן תַּהְפֻּכוֹת *the perverted* or *false tongue.* 17:20. (In Chald. this is called *lingua tertia;* comp. Sir. 28:15. Used by a metonymy for (1.) *speech, prayer.* Job 15:5 לְשׁוֹן עֲרוּמִים *crafty speech,* Prov. 16:1. (2.) *language.* Dan. 1:4. Gen. 10:5 אִישׁ לִלְשֹׁנוֹ *each after his language.* 20:31. Hence (3.) *a people,* speaking one language. Is. 66:18 כָּל־הַגּוֹיִם וְהַלְּשֹׁנוֹת *all nations and languages.* (See the Chald. לִשָּׁן.)

2. applied also to things without life, as (1.) לְשׁוֹן זָהָב *a bar of gold,* Josh. 7:21, 24. Vulg. *regula aurea.* (2.) לְשׁוֹן אֵשׁ *a flame of fire,* Is. 5:24. comp. Acts 2:3. (3.) לְשׁוֹן הַיָּם *a tongue of the sea,* i.e. a bay or gulf, Josh. 15:5. 18:19. Is. 11:15. and simply לָשׁוֹן Josh. 15:2. So we say *a tongue of land.* (So also in the Arabian geographers.)

לִשְׁכָּה f. dec. XII. b. *a chamber, cell,* particularly in the temple. 1 Chr. 9:26. Ezek. 40:17, 45. 42:1 ff. Neh. 10:38 ff. Also *a dining-room,* 1 Sam. 9:22. *an office* or *chamber for business* in the royal palace, Jer. 36:12. Synonymous with נִשְׁכָּה. The etymology is unknown.

לֶשֶׁם m. 1. a precious stone, mentioned only Ex. 28:19. 39:12. Sept. λιγύριον, Vulg. *ligurius, an opal.*

2. Josh. 19:47. a city, otherwise called לַיִשׁ and דָּן.

לָשַׁן Po. denom. from לָשׁוֹן, *to slander.* Ps. 101:5 Kethib מְלוֹשְׁנִי, in the Keri מְלָשְׁנִי, *a calumniator, slanderer.* (Arab. لسن *to calumniate.*)

Hiph. *idem.* Prov. 30:10.

לִשָּׁן Chald. *a tongue.* Always in the phrase עַמְמַיָּא אֻמַּיָּא וְלִשָּׁנַיָּא *peoples, nations, and tongues,* i. e. nations of different languages, Dan. 3:4, 7, 31. 5:19. 6:26. 7:15.

לֶשַׁע a proper name found only Gen. 10:19. according to Jerome, (in Quæst.) *Callirhoe,* a place on the east of the Dead Sea.

לֶתֶךְ m. found only Hos. 3:2. name of a certain measure; according to the Jewish interpreters and the Vulg. *corus dimidius, a half-homer;* which is rendered probable by its connexion with חֹמֶר.

מ

Mem is the 13th letter of the Hebrew alphabet, and as a numerical sign denotes 40. The signification of the name is doubtful. The Greek name μῦ leads to the conjecture that מֵם was not the original designation.

This letter is commuted (1.) most frequently with the other labials, especially ב and ף. See ב. (2.) Also with ן; e.g. אִם Syr. ܐܶܢ *if;* בֹּהֶן Arab. بهم *the thumb;* בָּטְנִים *pistachio-nuts,* comp. Syr. ܒܛܡܬܐ *pistazia terebinthus,* Linn. דָּשֵׁן Arab. دسم *to be fat;* הֶרְצַנִּים, comp. the Samar. and Arab. חצרם *unripe grapes;* שָׂטַם and שָׂטַן *to be hostile.* (3.) rarely with ל. See the letter ל.

מַ־ i. q. מָה. See **מָה** Note.

מִ־ *out of, from.* See the full form **מִן**.

מָא Chald. i. q. מָה *what, something.* מָא דִּי *that which,* Ezra 6:8.

מַאֲבוּס m. verbal from אָבַס no. 1. dec. I. *a barn, granary.* Jer. 50:26. Sept. ἀποθήκη.

מְאֹד 1. subst. dec. I. *strength, force, vehementia.* Deut. 6:5 בְּכָל־מְאֹדֶךָ *with all thy strength.* 2 K. 23:25. (Root אוּד or

אִיר = Arab. آدَ (med. Ye) *to be firm, strong;* أَيْد *strength, force.*)

2. usually an adv. *exceedingly, very, especially, vehementer.*—Also doubled, Gen. 7:19. Num. 14:7. Ps. 46:2 עֶזְרָה בְצָרוֹת נִמְצָא מְאֹד *a help in trouble has he been especially found*; i. e. a powerful help has he been found; comp. 31:12. 1 Sam. 20:19 תֵּרֵד מְאֹד *descende vehementer* for *descende festinus.* Vulg.

The combinations with prepositions point to the original meaning of the noun; as (1.) בִּמְאֹד מְאֹד *exceedingly, vehementissime,* liter. *cum vehementia, vehementia,* Gen. 17:2, 6, 20. Ezek. 9:9. (2.) עַד־לִמְאֹד *idem.* 2 Chr. 16:14. (3.) עַד־מְאֹד *idem.* Gen. 27:33. 1 K. 1:4. Dan. 8:8. The latter expression is sometimes equivalent to עַד עוֹלָם *for ever,* Ps. 119:43. Is. 64:8. (So invertedly לָנֶצַח *in æternum* sometimes denotes *vehementer, prorsus.*)

מֵאָה f. const. מְאַת, dec. XI. b.

1. *a hundred.*—The Hebrews say indiscriminately מְאָה שָׁנָה Gen. 17.17. and מְאַת שָׁנָה Gen. 25:7. *a hundred years.* Both forms also signify *a hundred times,* Prov. 17:10. Ecc. 8:12. Dual מָאתַיִם (with Syriac punctuation for מְאָתַיִם) *two hundred,* Gen. 11:23. Plur. מֵאוֹת *hundreds,* also simply *a hundred,* 2 Chr. 25:9 Kethib. Also מאיות (read מֵאָיוֹת) in the Kethib of 2 K. 11:4, 9, 10, 15. Comp. the Arab. مائة.

2. prob. *interest, usury, the rate per cent.* Neh. 5:11. Vulg. *centesima.* It is uncertain whether the rate per cent was reckoned by the month or by the year.

3. proper name of a tower in Jerusalem. Neh. 3:1. 12:39.

מְאָה Chald. *idem.* Dual מָאתַיִן Ezra 6:17.

מַאֲוַיִּים masc. plur. verbal from אָוָה, dec. VIII. *desires.* Ps. 140:9.

מאום the Aramean orthography for מוּם *a spot, blemish.* Dan. 1:4. Job 31:7. The א stands in otio.

מְאוּמָה *something.* Always preceded by the negative אֵין, *nothing.* 1 K. 18:43. Ecc. 5:13. Jer. 39:10.

מָאוֹר m. plur. ־ִים and וֹת, verbal from אוֹר, dec. III. a.

1. *light.* Ps. 90:8. Spoken of the sun and moon, Gen. 1:14, 16. Ps. 74:16 מְנֹרַת הַמָּאוֹר *the candlestick,* in the tabernacle, Num. 4:9, 16.

2. *a candlestick.* Ex. 25:6.

3. מְאוֹר עֵינַיִם *the shining of the eyes,* i. e. a serene or friendly countenance. Prov. 15:30.

מְאוּרָה f. dec. X. *a hole, cavern.* Is. 11:8. (It is i. q. מְעָרָה *a cavern,* by a commutation of א and ע.)

מֹאזְנַיִם dual, dec. I. *a balance, scales.* liter. *two scales.* (It stands for מוֹזְנַיִם from וזן. = Arab. وزن *to weigh.*) Lev. 19:36. Job 31:6.

מֹאזְנַיִן Chald. *idem.* Dan. 5:27.

מַאֲכָל m. verbal from אָכַל, dec. II. b. *food.* Gen. 2:9. עֵץ מַאֲכָל *a fruit-tree,* Lev. 19:23. צֹאן מַאֲכָל, *sheep intended for food,* Ps. 44:12.

מַאֲכֹלֶת m. verbal from אָכַל, *idem.* Is. 9:4 מַאֲכֹלֶת אֵשׁ *food for fire, fuel.* Verse 18.

מַאֲכֶלֶת f. plur. מַאֲכָלוֹת, verbal from אָכַל, dec. XIII. 1. *an instrument for eating, a knife.* Gen. 22:6, 10. Judg. 19:29. Prov. 30:14.

מַאֲמַצִּים masc. plur. verbal from אָמֵץ, dec. VIII. *forces,* joined with כֹּחַ Job 36:19. comp. אַמִּיץ כֹּחַ Job 9:4. Is. 40:26.

מַאֲמָר m. verbal from אָמַר, dec. II. b. *a word, command;* found only in later Hebrew, Est. 1:15. 2:20. 9:32.

מֵאמַר Chald. *idem.* Dan. 4:14. [4:17.]

מָאן Chald. *a vessel,* i. q. Heb. כְּלִי Dan. 5:2, 3, 23.

מָאֵן in Kal not used. (Syr. ܡܐܠ impers. *tædet me.*)

Pi. מֵאֵן *to refuse, decline.* 1 Sam. 28:

23. Construed with an infin. with and without לְ, Ex. 7:14. Num. 22:14. Ps. 77:3.

מָאֵן verbal adj. from מָאֵן, *refusing*. Joined with the personal pronouns it forms a periphrasis of the finite verb, Ex. 7:27 אִם מָאֵן אַתָּה *if thou refusest*. 9:2. 10:4.

מֵאֵן m. plur. מֵאֲנִים, verbal from the Piel of מָאֵן, *idem*. Jer. 13:10.

I. מָאַס, fut. יִמְאַס.

1. *to reject*. (Opposite of בָּחַר *to choose*.) Is. 7:15, 16. 41:9. Job 34:33. It is construed with an accus. and with בְּ, and is spoken most frequently (1.) of God, who rejects his people, Jer. 6:30. 7:29. 14:19. or (2.) of men, who reject God and his commandments, 1 Sam. 15:23. 2 K. 17:15.

2. *to despise, not to regard*. Prov. 15:32. Job 19:18. Infin. מָאוֹס Lam. 3:45, as a subst. *contempt*.

Niph. pass. Ps. 15:4. Is. 54:6.

II. מָאַס i. q. the kindred מָסַס *to melt away, to disappear*. (So in Chald. מְאַךְ i. q. מָכַךְ, and מְאַס i. q. מסס.)

Niph. Ps. 58:8 יִמָּאֲסוּ כְמוֹ־מַיִם *let them melt away as water*. Job 7:5 עוֹרִי רָגַע וַיִּמָּאֵס *my skin heals and breaks out again*, i. e. sanie diffluit.

מַאֲפֶה m. verbal from אָפָה, dec. IX. a. *something baked*. Lev. 2:4.

מַאֲפֵל m. verbal from obsol. אָפַל, *darkness*. Josh. 24:7.

מַאְפֵּלְיָה f. verbal from obsol. אָפַל, *darkness*, hence *lateness, unseasonableness, backwardness*. (Comp. אָפִיל.) Jer. 2:31 אֶרֶץ מַאְפֵּלְיָה *a backward land*. Vulg. *terra serotina*. Comp. verse 6. (For the form of this noun, comp. לַיְלָה Chald. לֵילְיָא q. v.)

מָאַר in Kal not used.

Hiph. הַמְאִיר perhaps i. q. הִמְרִיר, (comp. מָאַס no. II.) *to make bitter*, particularly *to cause severe pain*. Ezek. 28:24 סִלּוֹן מַמְאִיר *a painful*, i. e. a pricking, *thorn*. —צָרַעַת מַמְאֶרֶת *a painful* or *malignant leprosy*, Lev. 13:51, 52. 14:44. Others derive the word from the Arab. مأر *recruduit vulnus*.

מַאֲרָב m. verbal from אָרַב, dec. II. b.

1. *a lurking-place, place of ambush*. Josh. 8:9. Ps. 10:8.

2. *a party in ambush*. 2 Chr. 13:13.

מְאֵרָה f. verbal from אָרַר, dec. X. *a curse*. Prov. 3:33. 28:27. Mal. 2:2.

מֵאֵת compounded of מִן or מֵ־ and אֵת. See מִן.

מִבְדָּלוֹת fem. plur. verbal from בָּדַל, *separate places*. Josh. 16:9.

מָבוֹא m. (perhaps fem. 2 K. 16:18.) plur. ־ִים and וֹת, verbal from בּוֹא, dec. III. a. *an entrance*. Judg. 1:24, 25 מְבוֹא הָעִיר *the entrance of the city*. Prov. 8:3 מְבוֹא פְתָחִים *at the entrance of the gates*, (like פֶּתַח שְׁעָרִים *before the gates*.) —מְבוֹא הַשֶּׁמֶשׁ *the setting of the sun, the west*, Deut. 11:30. Ps. 50:1. *to the west*, Josh. 1:4.—Ezek. 27:3 מְבוֹאֹת יָם *the entrances of the sea*.

מְבוּכָה f. verbal from בּוּךְ, dec. X. *consternation, perplexity*. Is. 22:5. Mic. 7:4.

מַבּוּל m. verbal from יָבַל no. 2. *a flood, deluge, inundation*; spoken of Noah's flood, Gen. 6:17. 7:6, 7, 10, 17. 9:11, 28. 10:1, 32. of the waters above, on which God is enthroned, Ps. 29:10.

מְבוּסָה f. verbal from בּוּס, *a treading down* or *under foot*, e. g. of a conquered country. Is. 18:2, 7. 22:5.

מַבּוּעַ m. plur. ־ִים, verbal from נָבַע, dec. I. *a spring, fountain*. Is. 35:7. 49:10. Ecc. 12:6.

מְבוּקָה f. *emptiness, desolation*. Once Nah. 2:11. Root בּוּק=בָּקַק *to be empty*.

מְבוּשִׁים plur. masc. verbal from בּוֹשׁ, dec. III. c. *the secret parts, pudenda*. Deut. 25:11.

מִבְחָר m. verbal from בָּחַר, dec. II. b. *the choicest, best*. Is. 22:7 מִבְחַר עֲמָקַיִךְ

thy choicest valleys. 37:24 מִבְחַר בְּרוֹשָׁיו *thy choicest firs.* Jer. 22:7.

מִבְחוֹר m. verbal from בָּחַר, *idem.* 2 K. 3:19. 19:23.

מַבָּט m. verbal from נָבַט, dec. I. *the object to which one looks with hope* or *expectation.* Is. 20:5, 6.

מֶבָּט m. verbal from נָבַט, dec. I. *hope, expectation.* Zech. 9:5.

מִבְטָא m. verbal from בָּטָא, dec. I. *something rashly said.* Joined with שְׂפָתַיִם, Num. 30:7, 9.

מִבְטָח m. with suff. מִבְטַחִי, plur. מִבְטַחִים, verbal from בָּטַח, dec. II. a. and VIII. 1.

1. *confidence,* Prov. 22:19. Hence *object of confidence,* Ps. 40:15. 65:6. 71:5.

2. *safety, security.* Job 18:14. Is. 32:18.

מַבְלִיגִית f. verbal from בָּלַג, dec. I. *serenity, satisfaction, consolation.* Jer. 8:18.

מִבְנֶה m. verbal from בָּנָה, dec. IX. a. *a building.* Once Ezek. 40:2.

מִבְצָר m. plur. ־ִים, (once וֹת Dan. 11:15.) verbal from בָּצַר, dec. II. b. *a fortified place, a fortress.* Is. 17:3. עִיר, עָרֵי מִבְצָר *a fenced city, fenced cities,* Num. 32:17, 36. Josh. 10:20. 19:35. Perhaps applied to fortified temples, Dan. 11:39.

מִבְרָח m. verbal from בָּרַח, dec. II. c. liter. *flight;* hence, the abstract being used for the concrete, *a fugitive.* Ezek. 17:21.

מְבַשְּׁלוֹת plur. fem. strictly Piel part. of בָּשַׁל, *places for boiling, fire-places.* Ezek. 46:23.

מָג m. *a Magian, a Persian* or *Median priest.* (Pers. مغ *a Magian, a worshipper of fire;* which is said to be strictly i. q. *méh* or *megh,* denoting *great, excellent.*) Jer. 39:8 רַב־מָג *the chief Magian,* who, as Justin and Curtius state, was wont to accompany the king in his wars.

מְגֹאָל, see גָּאַל under the word גָּאַל no. I.

מִגְבָּלוֹת plur. fem. Ex. 28:14. liter. *borderings, edges;* see גַּבְלוּת.

מִגְבָּעָה f. dec. X. *the cap* or *turban of the common priests,* different from מִצְנֶפֶת *the turban of the high-priest.* Ex. 28:40. 29:9. 39:28. Comp. Josephi Antiq. III. 7. § 7. [otherwise cap. 8, § 2.] (In Syr. ܡܘܟܒܐ *a hat, cap;* Ethiop. ቆብዕ *a turban;* compare the letter ג, p. 98.)

מֶגֶד m. dec. VI. a. *costly* or *precious gifts,* (particularly of nature.) Deut. 33:13 מֶגֶד שָׁמַיִם *the precious gifts of heaven.* Verses 14, 15, 16. Spoken particularly of fruits, Cant. 4:13 פְּרִי מְגָדִים *precious fruits.* So verse 16. 7:14 כָּל־מְגָדִים *all kinds of precious fruits.* Vulg. constantly *poma.* (Syr. ܡܓܕܐ *fructus aridus.*) The deriv. מִגְדָּנוֹת presents the same idea, but in a different relation.

מְגִדּוֹ Judg. 1:27. 1 K. 4:12. 9:15. 2 K. 9:27. and מְגִדּוֹן Zech. 12:11. name of a fenced city belonging to the tribe of Manasseh, but within the limits of the tribe of Issachar, anciently the seat of a Canaanitish king. Sept. Μαγιδδώ; Vulg. *Mageddo*.—עֵמֶק מְגִדּוֹ *the plain* or *valley about Megiddo,* 2 Chr. 35:22. מֵי מְגִדּוֹ *the waters of Megiddo,* i. e. prob. the brook Kishon; comp. verse 21. 4:13.

מִגְדּוֹל and מִגְדֹּל a city in Egypt, not far from the Red Sea. Ex. 14:2. Num. 33:7. Jer. 44:1. 46:14. Ezek. 29:10. 30:6.

מִגְדָּל, plur. ־ִים and וֹת, verbal from גָּדַל, dec. II. b.

1. *a tower.* Gen. 11:4, 5. Particularly *a tower for defence,* Judg. 8:9. 9:46 ff. 2 Chr. 14:6. *a watch-tower,* in a vineyard, Is. 5:2. or by a herd, Gen. 35:21. Mic. 4:8.

2. *a high scaffold, a stage* or *pulpit.* Neh. 8:4. comp. 9:4.

3. *an espalier.* Cant. 5:13. (Parall. עֲרוּגָה.)

מִגְדָּנוֹת plur. fem. denom. from מֶגֶד, *costly* or *precious things*. Gen. 24:53. 32:23. Ezra 1:6. This signification is evident from 2 Chr. 21:3.

מָגוֹג Gen. 10:2. Ezek. 38:2. 39:6. proper name of a northern people, obscurely known to the Hebrews, which the Arabian and other eastern writers speak of under the names *Yagug* and *Magug*. They place this people in the unknown north-eastern parts of Asia, and have many fabulous traditions concerning them. The king of this people is גּוֹג, q. v. See Cor. Sur. XVIII. 94—99. XXI. 96. Assemani Biblioth. Orient. T. III. P. II. 16. 17. 20. Klaproth's Asiat. Magazin, Th. I. p. 138. D'Herbelot's Orient. Bibliotheque, Art. *Jagiouge* and *Magiouge*.

מָגוֹר m. verbal from גּוּר no. I. dec. III. c.

1. *a dwelling*. Ps. 55:16.

2. plur. מְגוּרִים *a sojourning, a residence among strangers, a pilgrimage*. Gen. 17:8 אֶרֶץ מְגֻרֶיךָ *the land wherein thou sojournest*. 28:4. Often used figuratively of one's residence on earth, Gen. 47:9. Ps. 119:54.

מָגוֹר m. plur. מְגוּרִים (Lam. 2:22.) verbal from גּוּר no. II. dec. III. f. *fear, terror*. Ps. 31:14. Jer. 6:25. 29:3, 10.

מְגוֹרָה f. verbal from גּוּר no. II. dec. X. *idem*. Prov. 10:24.

I. מְגוּרָה f. verbal from גּוּר no. I. 2. *a storehouse*. Hag. 2:19.

II. מְגוּרָה fem. of מָגוֹר, dec. X. *fear*. Ps. 34:5. comp. Prov. 10:24.

מַגְזֵרָה f. verbal from גָּזַר no. 2. dec. XI. b. *an axe* for felling wood. 2 Sam. 12:31.

מַגָּל m. *a sickle*. Jer. 50:16. Joel 4:13. [3:13.] (Arab. مِنْجَل, Syr. ܡܰܓܠܳܐ *idem*. But the root is uncertain.)

מְגִלָּה f. verbal from גָּלַל, dec. X. *a roll, book, volumen*. Jer. 36:14 ff. Ezek. 2:9. Ps. 40:8 מְגִלַּת־סֵפֶר *the roll of the book*, i. e. the book of the law.

מְגִלָּה f. Chald. *idem*. Ezra 6:2.

מְגַמָּה f. dec. X. found only Hab. 1:9 מְגַמַּת פְּנֵיהֶם *desiderium vultus ipsorum*. (The word is used to denote *desiderium, anhelitus*, by Kimchi on Ps. 27:8. Comp. גמם Arab. جَمَّ *appetebat, prope fuit, instititque res.*) The following word קָדִימָה may be rendered *forwards*.

מִגֵּן found only in Pi. מִגֵּן *to give, deliver*. Prov. 4:9. Gen. 14:20.

מָגֵן m. (with Kamets impure,) with suff. מָגִנִּי, plur. מָגִנִּים, const. מָגִנֵּי; strictly part. Hiph. of גָּנַן *to protect*, dec. VIII. i. *a shield*. Judg. 5:8. It appears from 1 K. 10:16, 17. 2 Chr. 9:16. that מָגֵן denotes a smaller kind of shield than צִנָּה; of course i. q. ἀσπὶς, *clypeus, a light shield* or *buckler*.—אִישׁ מָגֵן *an armed man*, i. e. a robber, Prov. 6:11. 24:34. Used metaphorically (1.) of God, Gen. 15:1. Ps. 3:4. 18:3, 31. 144:2. Ps. 7:11 מָגִנִּי עַל אֱלֹהִים *my shield* or *defence is with God;* comp. 89:19. (2.) מָגִנֵּי־אֶרֶץ *the shields of the land*, i. e. its princes or protectors, Ps. 47:10. Hos. 4:18.

מְגִנָּה f. dec. X. found only Lam. 3:65 מְגִנַּת־לֵב either *a covered* or *obdurate heart*, (from גָּנַן;) or else *madness of heart*, (from the Arab. جُنَّ pass. *to rave, to be mad*. Comp. the parallel sentiment Deut. 28:28).

מִגְעֶרֶת f. verbal from גָּעַר, *the rebuke* or *curse* (of God). Deut. 28:20.

מַגֵּפָה f. (with Tseri impure,) verbal from נָגַף, dec. X.

1. *an overthrow, discomfiture*. 1 Sam. 4:17.

2. *a plague*, (sent by God.) Ex. 9:14. Spoken of a pestilential disease, Num. 14:37. 17:13. [16:48.] of the plague on the Philistines, 1 Sam. 6:4.

מָגַר Syr. ܡܓܰܪ *to fall*. Part. pass. (as if pass. of Piel; comp. בֵּרוּךְ.) Ezek.

21:17 מְגוּרֵי אֶל חֶרֶב *thrown* or *given up to the sword.* Others: *destroyed by the sword.*

Pi. מִגֵּר *to throw down.* Ps. 89:45.

מְגַר Chald. *idem.* Pa. מַגֵּר *to throw down, destroy.* Ezra 6:12.

מְגֵרָה f. (with Tseri impure,) verbal from גָּרַר, dec. X. *a saw.* 2 Sam. 12:31. 1 K. 7:9.

מִגְרוֹן proper name of a city in the tribe of Benjamin. Only 1 Sam. 14:2. Is. 10:28.

מִגְרָעוֹת plur. fem. (verbal from גָּרַע *to lessen, shorten, narrow;*) *narrowings, narrowed rests, rebatements.* 1 K. 6:6.

מֶגְרָפָה f. (verbal from גָּרַף *to carry away,*) in Syriac and Arabic *a wooden shovel.* So Joel 1:17 *the grain disappears under the shovels.* But it does not appear how this is a consequence of drought. The rendering of the Jewish commentators is better suited to the context, namely, *clods,* (as if from גָּרַף in the signification *to shovel away.*)

מִגְרָשׁ m. dec. II. b. Plur. ־ִים, and once ־וֹת Ezek. 27:28.

1. the Aramean infin. of גָּרַשׁ no. 3. Ezek. 36:3.

2. *a pasture,* Germ. *Trift,* (from גָּרַשׁ *to drive, to drive out,*) or *a vacant, empty place,* (comp. the Syr. ܡܓܪܫܐ *nudus, vacuus.*) It is applied (1.) to the vacant space about the temple, Ezek. 45:2. about Jerusalem, Ezek. 48:17. about Tyre, 27:28. (2.) particularly to the suburbs of the Levitical cities for pasturing cattle, Num. 35:2 ff. Josh. 21:11 ff. 1 Chr. 6:40 ff. [6:55 ff.]—1 Chr. 13:2 עָרֵי מִגְרְשֵׁיהֶם *the cities with suburbs,* i. e. Levitical cities.

מַד, with suff. מִדּוֹ and מַדִּי, plur. מַדִּים and מִדִּין (Judg. 5:10.) verbal from מָדַד, dec. VIII. f. and h.

1. *measure.* Job 11:9. Jer. 13:25 מְנָת מִדַּיִךְ *the portion of thy measures,* i. e. the portion measured out to thee.

2. *a garment.* Ps. 109:18. Lev. 6:3. [6:10.]

מַדְבַּח Chald. *an altar.* Ezra 7:17. Root דְּבַח *to offer.*

מִדְבָּר m. verbal from דָּבַר, dec. II. b.

1. *speech.* Cant. 4:3. See דָּבַר no. 2.

2. *a wilderness, an uncultivated and comparatively barren country,* into which cattle are *driven* to feed, Germ. *Trift.* (In Syr. *idem.* See דָּבַר no. 1. *to drive.*) Ps. 65:13. יִרְעֲפוּ נְאוֹת מִדְבָּר *the pastures of the wilderness drop* (*fatness*). Jer. 9:9. 23:10.

3. *an actual waste, a sandy desert.* Is. 32:15. 35:1. 50:2.—מִדְבַּר שְׁמָמָה *a desolate wilderness,* Joel 2:3. 4:19. [3:19.] Joined with the article, הַמִּדְבָּר *the desert,* i. e. the desert of Arabia, Gen. 14:6. 16:7. Ex. 3:1. 13:18. Deut. 11:24. Different portions of this desert occur likewise under special names; see the proper names סִין, סִינַי, פָּארָן, שׁוּר, etc.—מִדְבַּר יְהוּדָה *the plain* or *desert of Judah,* Josh. 15:61. Judg. 1:16. Ps. 63:1.

מָדַד, pret. מָדְדוּ, also מַדּוֹתִי, infin. מֹד, fut. יָמֹד.

1. i. q. Arab. مدّ *to stretch out, to extend.* See Hithpa. and the deriv. מִדָּה.

2. *to measure,* literally *to stretch out* the measuring line. Ezek. 40:5 ff. 41:1 ff. Applied likewise to measures of capacity, Ruth 3:15. Metaphorically Is. 65:7 *I will measure their former conduct into their bosom,* i. e. I will recompense it.

Niph. pass. Jer. 31:37. 33:22.

Pi. מִדֵּד i. q. Kal. 2 Sam. 8:2.

Po. מוֹדֵד *idem.* Hab. 3:6 *he measured the earth* (with a glance). Others, following the Sept. and Chaldaic version, *he made the earth to quake,* as if from מוּר in Arab. (med. Ye) *to be moved.*

Hithpo. הִתְמוֹדֵד *to stretch one's self.* 1 K. 17:21.

Deriv. מִדָּה, מַד, מֵמַד.

מְדַד m. Job 7:4. prob. *an escaping, fleeing away,* from נָדַד, (comp. the fut. יִדַּד Gen. 31:40.) The whole passage may be rendered thus: *when I lie down, I say, when shall I arise,* וּמִדַּד עָרֶב *and (when) shall the night be gone?*

מִדָּה f. verbal from מָדַד, dec. X.

1. *extension, great extent.*—אִישׁ מִדָּה *a man of great stature,* 1 Chr. 11:23.—אַנְשֵׁי מִדָּה *men of stature,* Is. 45:24.—בֵּית מִדּוֹת *a spacious house,* Jer. 22:14.

2. *a measure, length measured out,* Ex. 26:2, 8. — קָו מִדָּה *a measuring line,* Zech. 2:5. Metaphorically Ps. 39:5.

3. i. q. מַד no. 2. *a garment.* Plur. מִדּוֹת Ps. 133:2.

4. as in Chald. *tribute.* Neh. 5:4.

מִדָּה m. Chald. *tribute, pars cuivis demensa.* Ezra 4:20. 6:8. By a resolution of the Dagesh forte into Nun, it is sometimes written מִנְדָּה, Ezra 4:13. 7:24.

מַדְהֵבָה f. found only Is. 14:4. according to the Jewish commentators, *exactress of gold,* (spoken of Babylon,) as if a denom. from דְּהַב=זָהָב *gold,* and formed in the part. Hiph. fem. Others: *extortion,* as if from the Arab. ذهب conj. I. IV. *abduxit, abstulit.*—Another reading is found in an edition of the Hebrew Bible published at Thessalonica in 1600, namely, מַרְהֵבָה *oppression,* from רָהַב, which is also parallel with נִגַּשׂ Is. 3:5. This last reading is preferred by Michaëlis, Gesenius, and others.

מַדְו m. plur. with suff. מַדְוֵיהֶם, dec. VI. a. *a garment.* 2 Sam. 10:4. 1 Chr. 19:4. Root מָדַד=מָדָה.

מַדְוֶה m. verbal from דָּוָה, dec. IX. a. *sickness, disease.* Deut. 7:15. 28:60.

מַדּוּחִים masc. plur. verbal from נָדַח, *seductions.* Lam. 2:14.

I. מָדוֹן m. plur. מְדָנִים, verbal from דִּין.

1. *strife, contention, dissension.* Prov. 15:18. 16:28. 17:14.

2. *object of contention,* Germ. *Zankapfel.* Ps. 80:7.

II. מָדוֹן m. verbal from מָדַד=מָדָה, *extension, extent.* 2 Sam. 21:20 Keri אִישׁ מָדוֹן *vir longus,* i. q. אִישׁ מִדָּה 1 Chr. 20:6. The Kethib is to be read מִדִּין in the same sense.

מַדּוּעַ *wherefore? on what account?* for the most part interrogatively, Josh. 17:14. 2 Sam. 19:42. but sometimes without an interrogation, Ex. 3:3.—Job 21:4 אִם־מַדּוּעַ לֹא־תִקְצַר רוּחִי *wherefore should I not be angry.* אִם only strengthens the interrogation, or is pleonastic. (Perhaps compounded of מַה־יָּדוּעַ *quâ mente? on what account?*)

מְדוֹר Chald. verbal from דּוּר, *a dwelling-place, residence.* Dan. 4:22, 29. [4:25, 32.] 5:21.

מְדוּרָה f. denom. from דּוּר no. 3. dec. X. *a pile of wood,* literally *the place of a pile of wood;* comp. מַעֲצָן. Ezek. 24:9. Is. 30:33.

מְדוּשָׁה f. verbal from דּוּשׁ, dec. X. *a threshing;* hence, as a concrete, *what threshes* or *is threshed.* Is. 21:10. See under גֹּרֶן no. 2.

מִדְחֶה m. verbal from דָּחָה, *ruin, destruction.* Prov. 26:28.

מַדְחֵפוֹת plur. fem. verbal from דָּחַף, *concitatio.* Ps. 140:12 לְמַדְחֵפֹת *concitatè, in haste, speedily, urgently.*

מָדַי *Media.* Gen. 10:2. Dan. 5:28. Est. 1:3. (Syr. ܡܕܝ *idem.*) The gentile noun is מָדַי *a Mede,* Dan. 11:1.

מַדַּי a contraction of מַה־דַּי *what is enough.* 2 Chr. 30:3.

מִדֵּי see דַּי.

מִדְיָן m. found only in the plur. מִדְיָנִים, verbal from דִּין, *strife, contention.* Prov. 18:18. 19:13. and more frequently in the Keri for מְדָנִים. See מָדוֹן.

מִדְיָן f. *Midian,* proper name of an Arabian tribe, near Mount Sina, (Ex. 3:1. 18:5.) and on the east side of Canaan, near the Moabites, Amorites, and Amalekites, (Judg. 6:7.—8:28.) In some passages the names *Midianite* and *Ishmaelite* appear to be almost synonymous, as Gen. 37:28. Judg. 7:12; comp. 8:22, 24.

מְדִינָה f. verbal from דִּין, dec. X. liter. *a jurisdiction;* hence

1. *a province,* e. g. *a district of the Persian empire.* Est. 1:1, 22. 3:12, 14. —בְּנֵי הַמְּדִינָה Ezra 2:1. Neh. 7:6. *the children of the province,* i. e. the Israelites who returned from the provinces of Persia.

2. *a land, country.* Dan. 11:24 וּבְמִשְׁמַנֵּי מְדִינָה יָבוֹא *and into the fertile land,* i. e. Palestine, *he shall enter.* Lam. 1:1. Ezek. 19:8. Ecc. 2:8. (comp. Ezra 4:13.) Ecc. 5:7. See the following article.

מְדִינָה f. Chald. 1. *a province.* Dan. 3:2, 3.

2. *a land, country.* Dan. 2:48, 49. 3:1, 12, 30. Ezra 5:8.

מְדֹכָה f. verbal from דּוּךְ, *a mortar.* Num. 11:8.

מַדְמֵן proper name of a city in the territory of Moab. Jer. 48:2. As an appellative i. q. מַדְמֵנָה.

מַדְמֵנָה f. 1. denom. from דֹּמֶן, *a dung-hill, dung-heap.* Is. 25:10.

2. proper name of a city in the tribe of Benjamin. Is. 10:31.

מְדָנִים i. q. מְדוֹנִים and מִדְיָנִים, verbal from דִּין, *strife, contention, discord.* Prov. 6:14, 19. 10:12.

מַדָּע and **מַדַּע** m. verbal from יָדַע, dec. II. only in later Hebrew. (Chald. מַנְדַּע; Syr. ܡܕܥܐ, ܡܕܥ, ܡܕܥܐ.)

1. *knowledge.* 2 Chr. 1:11, 12. 2 Chr. 1:10. Dan. 1:4, 17.

2. *thought.* Ecc. 10:20. Sept. συνείδησις.

מֹדָע see **מוֹדַע.**

מַדְקָרוֹת plur. fem. verbal from דָּקַר, dec. XI. *piercings.* Prov. 12:18.

מַדְרֵגָה f. dec. X. *a cliff, precipice.* Cant. 2:14. Ezek. 38:20. Root דָּרַג, in Arab. and Chald. *gradatim ascendit.*

מִדְרָךְ m. verbal from דָּרַךְ, dec. II. b. *a place to tread upon, a footing.* Deut. 2:5.

מִדְרָשׁ m. (verbal from דָּרַשׁ *to examine,*) dec. II. b. *an exposition, interpretation.* (In Rabbinic frequent.) 2 Chr. 24:27 מִדְרַשׁ סֵפֶר הַמְּלָכִים *the exposition of the book of kings.* 13:22. Others incorrectly, *book* generally, after the Arab. مدرس *liber.*

מָה, מַה־, מֶה, and **מַה,** (see the Note.)

1. *what?* spoken of things, as מִי of persons. Judg. 11:12 מַה־לִּי וָלָךְ *what have we, I and thou, to do with each other?* comp. 2 Sam. 16:10. 19:23. Without a copula, Jer. 2:18 מַה־לָּךְ לְדֶרֶךְ מִצְרַיִם *what hast thou to do with the way of Egypt?* Hos. 14:9.

2. without an interrogation, *what, whatever, something, any thing.* Prov. 9:13 בַּל־יָדְעָה מָּה *she careth for nothing.* 2 Sam. 18:23 וִיהִי מָה אָרוּצָה־נָּא *whatever it may be,* i. e. howsoever, *let me, I pray thee, run.* Job 13:13, 14. Joined with שֶׁ, *that, which, what,* Ecc. 1:9. 3:15, 22. 6:10. (Aram. ܡܕܡ, *idem.*)

3. before substantives, *what, of what sort, qualis.* Josh. 22:16 מָה־הַמַּעַל הַזֶּה *what a transgression is this!* 1 Sam. 28:14. 1 K. 9:13.

4. *how?* Gen. 44:16 מַה־נִּצְטַדָּק *how shall we justify ourselves?* Ex. 10:26. Gen. 28:17 מַה־נּוֹרָא *how dreadful!*

5. *wherefore?* (So the Lat. *quid?* for *cur?*) Judg. 8:1. Ps. 42:12.

6. *not,* (as in Chald. and Arab.) The negation arises from the reproachful inquiry. Cant. 8:4 מַה־תָּעִירוּ וּמַה־תְּעֹרְרוּ אֶת־הָאַהֲבָה *O wake not, disturb not the lovely one;* liter. *why wake ye, why disturb ye the lovely one?* Comp. 2:7. 3:5. where אִם is used to express the negation. The transition to this sense is found in such passages as Job 16:6. 31:1, 20, 24. where the ancient versions for the most part have expressed the negation. See particularly לָמָּה.

The most frequent combinations of this word with prepositions are the following:

1. בַּמֶּה *whereby?* Judg. 16:5. *why?* 2 Chr. 7:21.

2. כַּמָּה (1.) *how many?* Gen. 47 : 8. 1 K. 22 : 16 עַד־כַּמָּה פְעָמִים *how many times?* Without an interrogation, *so many*, Zech. 7 : 3 זֶה כַּמָּה שָׁנִים *these so many years*. (2.) *how long?* Ps. 35 : 17. Job 7 : 19. (3.) *what, how great*. Zech. 2 : 6. [2 : 2.] (4.) *how often*. Ps. 78 : 40. (Syr. ܟܡܐ *idem*.)

3. לָמָּה (*Milêl*) and לָמָה (*Milra*,) the latter form usually before gutturals and the word יְהוָה. (1.) *wherefore?* Gen. 4 : 6. 12 : 18. Ps. 2 : 1. Without an interrogation, Dan. 10 : 20. With more intensity לָמָּה זֶּה *wherefore then?* See זֶה. (2.) *lest, that not*. Dan. 1 : 10.—שַׁלָּמָה *idem*, Cant. 1 : 7. (Aram. לְמָה, ܠܡܢܐ, ܠܡܘܢܐ *idem*.)

4. לְמָה *since, because*. 1 Chr. 15 : 13 לְמַבָּרִאשׁוֹנָה *since at the beginning*. (Comp. 2 Chr. 30 : 3.)

5. עַד־מָה *how long?* Ps. 74 : 9. 79 : 5. Num. 24 : 22.

6. עַל־מָה *wherefore?* Num. 22 : 32. Jer. 9 : 11.

Note. This word is pointed (1.) with Pathah before the letters ה, ח, ע, or before Makkeph and Dagesh euphonic. (2.) with Segol before ה, ח, and ע, with Kamets. (3.) with Kamets before א and ר with and without Makkeph. (4.) Sometimes it is united both in pronunciation and orthography with the following word, as מַזֶּה *what is this?* Ex. 4 : 2. מַלָּכֶם *what have you?* Is. 3 : 15. Mal. 1 : 13.

מָה Chald. *what*, as in Heb. with and without an interrogation.—מָה דִי *that which*, Dan. 2 : 28. Combined with prepositions, (1.) כְּמָה *how, how very*. Dan. 3 : 33. (2.) לְמָה Ezra 4 : 22. and דִּי לְמָה 7 : 23. *lest, that not*.

מָהַהּ found only in Hithpalp. הִתְמַהְמַהּ *to linger, tarry, delay*. Gen. 19 : 16. 43 : 10. 2 Sam. 15 : 28.

מְהוּמָה f. verbal from הוּם, dec. X.

1. *tumult, commotion*. 2 Chr. 15 : 5; (antith. שָׁלוֹם *peace*.) Prov. 15 : 16.

2. *consternation, confusion*. Deut. 7 : 23. 1 Sam. 5 : 9, 11 מְהוּמַת מָוֶת *a deadly consternation*.

מָהִיר m. verbal adj. from מָהַר, dec. III. a. *quick*; hence, *ready, apt, skilful*, at any art or business. Prov. 22 : 29. Is. 16 : 5. Ps. 45 : 2. (Syr. ܡܗܝܪܐ *idem*; Arab. مهر *to be experienced, to be skilful*.)

מָהַל i. q. מוּל *to circumcise*. (In Chald. more frequent. Compare the analogies, p. 147.) Hence, by a figure common with the Arabians, *to adulterate* or *dilute* wine, Is. 1 : 22.

מַהֲלָךְ m. verbal from הָלַךְ, dec. II. b.

1. *a way, journey*. Neh. 2 : 6. Jon. 3 : 3, 4.

2. *a walk, passage, ambulacrum*. Ezek. 42 : 4.—But מַהְלְכִים Zech. 3 : 7. denotes *companions*, and is the plur. part. Hiph. from הָלַךְ *to go, to accompany*.

מַהֲלָל m. verbal from הָלַל, dec. II. b. *praise, commendation*. Prov. 27 : 21 *what the crucible is to gold,—that let a man be to the mouth that praiseth him*, i. e. let him examine the praise carefully.

מַהֲלֻמּוֹת plur. fem. verbal from הָלַם, *strokes, blows*. Prov. 18 : 6. 19 : 29.

מַהֲמֹרוֹת plur. fem. found only Ps. 140 : 11. according to the Hebrew commentators, *pits*. (So in Talmud. But the etymology is unknown.)

מַהְפֵּכָה f. verbal from הָפַךְ, dec. X. *overthrow, destruction*. Deut. 29 : 22. In some places it is used as an infin. (like יִרְאָה,) Is. 13 : 19 כְּמַהְפֵּכַת אֱלֹהִים אֶת סְדֹם *as when God destroyed Sodom*. Jer. 50 : 40. Amos 4 : 11.

מַהְפֶּכֶת f. verbal from הָפַךְ, *a wooden frame, in which the feet, perhaps also the hands and head of prisoners were confined, shackles, stocks, pillory, nervus, cippus*. Jer. 20 : 2, 3. 29 : 26. 2 Chr. 16 : 10 בֵּית הַמַּהְפֶּכֶת *a house of stocks, a prison*.

I. **מָהַר** *to hasten, to be in haste*, in Kal only Ps. 16 : 4.

Pi. מִהֵר 1. *to hasten, to make haste*; construed with a finite verb with and without the copula, e. g. 1 Sam. 17 : 48. Gen. 19 : 22 מַהֵר הִמָּלֵט *hasten (and) deliver thyself.* With an infin. with and without לְ, e. g. Ex. 2 : 18. 10 : 16. This verb may be often expressed in English by the adverbs, *hastily, quickly, suddenly, soon,* Gen. 27 : 20 מַה־זֶּה מִהַרְתָּ לִמְצֹא *how then hast thou found it so quickly?* Ex. 2 : 18. The infin. מַהֵר is likewise used as an adv. *in haste, quickly,* Judg. 2 : 17, 23. Ps. 79 : 8.

2. trans. *to hasten, to do in haste, to urge on.* Is. 5 : 19. Gen. 18 : 6 מַהֲרִי שְׁלֹשׁ סְאִים קֶמַח *bring quickly three seahs of flour.* 1 K. 22 : 9.

Niph. נִמְהַר *to be too much hurried, to be over hasty, rash, inconsiderate.* Job 5 : 13 עֲצַת נִפְתָּלִים נִמְהָרָה *the counsel of the crafty is over hasty,* i. e. is carried headlong. Hence part. נִמְהָר *inconsiderate,* Is. 32 : 4. *timid, fearful,* 35 : 4. *impetuous, violent,* Hab. 1 : 6.

II. מָהַר *to buy, purchase,* namely, a wife, by a dowry or present to the father. Ex. 22 : 15. See מֹהַר. (Comp. אָרַשׂ.)

מָהֵר verbal adj. from מָהַר, *hastening,* Zeph. 1 : 14.

מֹהַר m. verbal from מָהַר, no. II. *a portion* or *dowry,* paid by the bridegroom for his bride. Gen. 34 : 12. Ex. 22 : 16. 1 Sam. 18 : 25. (Syr. and Arab. *idem.*)

מְהֵרָה f. verbal from מָהַר, *haste, celerity, quickness.* Ps. 147 : 15. Hence בִּמְהֵרָה Ecc. 4 : 12. and מְהֵרָה as an adv. *hastily, quickly,* Num. 17 : 11. [16 : 46.]

מַהֲתַלּוֹת plur. fem. verbal from הָתַל, *deceits.* Is. 30 : 10.

מוֹ an enclitic syllable, annexed to the prefixes בְּ, כְּ, לְ, to make them independent words, as לְמוֹ, כְּמוֹ, בְּמוֹ, the signification not being affected thereby. These lengthened forms are exclusively poetical.

מוֹאָב *Moab,* in later times *Moabitis,* a people and country on the east side of the Dead Sea, extending to the brook Arnon. (As the name of a people, of the masc. gen. Jer. 48 : 11, 13. as the name of a country, fem. Jer. 48 : 4.)—עַרְבוֹת מוֹאָב *the plains of Moab,* mentioned Deut. 34 : 1, 8. Num. 22 : 1. in which the Israelites encamped for a long time, were beyond the Arnon, over against Jericho, and are also called אֶרֶץ מוֹאָב Deut. 28 : 69. [29 : 1.] 32 : 49. but did not pertain to the proper territory of Moab, which the Israelites are expressly said not to have entered, Judg. 11 : 18. 2 Chr. 20 : 10.—In Gen. 19 : 30—38. the name is derived from מֵאָב *ex patre.* The gentile noun is מוֹאָבִי, fem. מוֹאָבִיָּה or מוֹאָבִית, Ruth 4 : 5. 2 Chr. 24 : 26.

מוּאל the Aramean orthography for מוּל *over against.* Neh. 12 : 38. Comp. מאום.

מוֹבָא m. dec. II. b. i. q. מָבוֹא *entrance.* Ezek. 43 : 11. and 2 Sam. 3 : 25 Keri. In both passages, this form appears to have been adopted on account of its similarity with מוֹצָא, with which it is connected.

מוּג *to flow, dissolve, melt.* Metaphorically *to melt, faint, despond,* (from fear.) Comp. מָסַס. Ezek. 21 : 20. [15.] Ps. 46 : 7. Amos 9 : 5. Transitively Is. 67 : 6 תְּמוּגֵנוּ *thou causest us to despond.*

Niph. 1. *to melt away* or *disappear,* spoken of people, 1 Sam. 14 : 16.

2. *to despond* (from fear.) Ex. 15 : 15. Josh. 2 : 9, 24. Ps. 75 : 4.

Po. מוֹגֵג *to let dissolve, to soften, to melt.* Ps. 65 : 11 בִּרְבִיבִים תְּמֹגְגֶנָּה *thou softenest it (the thirsty earth) with showers.* Metaphorically Job 30 : 22 תְּמֹגְגֵנִי תֻּשִׁיָּה liter. *thou meltest away my prosperity.*

Hithpo. 1. *to flow, overflow.* Am. 9 : 13.

2. *to melt* or *despond,* (from fear.) Nah. 1 : 5. Ps. 107 : 26.

מוּד see מָדַד Po.

מֹדַע, מוֹדַע m. Prov. 7 : 4. and מוֹדַע Ruth 2 : 1 Keri; verbal from יָדַע, *familiarity, acquaintance;* and as a concrete, *a friend, an acquaintance.*

מוֹדַעַת fem. of מוֹדָע, dec. XIII. m. *idem*, used as a concrete. Ruth 3 : 2.

מוֹט, fut. יָמוּט, in Kal and Niph. *to move, quake, tremble;* spoken of the mountains, Ps. 46 : 3. 60 : 4. of a country or kingdom, Ps. 46 : 7. 60 : 4. of persons, Prov. 10 : 30. 12 : 3. Ps. 10 : 6. In the same sense we find מָטָה רֶגֶל פ׳ *the foot of any one slides,* Deut. 32 : 35. Ps. 38 : 17. comp. Lev. 25 : 35 *if thy brother become poor* וּמָטָה יָדוֹ עִמָּךְ *and his hand tremble with thee,* i. e. if he loses his substance.

Hiph. *declinare fecit, to cause to fall, to let come down.* Ps. 55 : 4. 140 : 11 Kethib.

Hithpo. i. q. Kal and Niph. Is. 24 : 19.

מוֹט m. verbal from מוּט, dec. I.

1. *a moving, shaking, trembling.* Ps. 66 : 9. 121 : 3.

2. *a bar, pole, vectis,* for moving things. Num. 13 : 23.

3. *a frame* or *carriage*, consisting of several bars or poles. Num. 4 : 10, 12.

4. *a yoke.* Nah. 1 : 12. See מוֹטָה.

מוֹטָה fem. of מוֹט, dec. X.

1. *a bar, pole, vectis.* 1 Chr. 15 : 15. See מוֹט no. 2.

2. מֹטוֹת עֹל *vectes jugi,* Lev. 26 : 13. Ezek. 34 : 27. a piece of wood bent round the neck of the ox, so that its two ends might be fastened into the wooden yoke.

3. *the yoke* itself. Is. 58 : 6, 9. Jer. 27 : 2. 28 : 10, 12. Ezek. 30 : 18.

מוּךְ i. q. מָכַךְ *to be reduced in circumstances, to become poor.* Lev. 25 : 25, 35, 39, 47.

מוּל *to circumcise* (the foreskin). Gen. 21 : 4. Ex. 12 : 44. Metaphorically Deut. 10 : 16 וּמַלְתֶּם אֵת עָרְלַת־לְבַבְכֶם *and circumcise the foreskin of your hearts,* i.e. remove the impurity of your hearts. 30 : 6.

Niph. pass. Gen. 17 : 10, 13. Metaphorically Jer. 4 : 4 הִמֹּלוּ לַיהוָה *circumcise yourselves for Jehovah,* i. e. purify your hearts before him.

Hiph. *to destroy* (a people). Ps. 118 : 10, 11, 12.

Hithpal. הִתְמוֹלֵל *to be cut off, blunted,* spoken of arrows. Ps. 58 : 8 חִצָּו כְּמוֹ יִתְמֹלָלוּ *his arrows are as it were blunted.*

מוּל Deut. 1 : 1. elsewhere מוּל, a preposition.

1. *before, coram.* Ex. 18 : 19 מוּל הָאֱלֹהִים *before God.*

2. *over against,* e. g. a city. Deut. 3 : 29. 4 : 46. 11 : 30. Josh. 19 : 46.—1 K. 7 : 5 מוּל מֶחֱזָה אֶל־מֶחֱזָה *window over against window.*

It occurs equally often in combination, as (1.) אֶל מוּל *over against, towards.* Ex. 34 : 3. Josh. 8 : 33. 9 : 1. (2.) אֶל מוּל פְּנֵי *before, in fronte.* Ex. 26 : 9 אֶל מוּל פְּנֵי הָאֹהֶל *in front of the tent.* 28 : 25 אֶל מוּל פָּנָיו *to the front.* 28 : 37. 34 : 3. (3.) מִמּוּל (a.) *à coram,* i. q. מֵעִם. 2 Sam. 5 : 22. Mic. 2 : 8 מִמּוּל שַׂלְמָה *from over the under garment.* (b.) i. q. מוּל *over against.* 1 K. 7 : 38. Num. 22 : 5.

מוֹלָדָה proper name of a city in the southern part of the tribe of Judah, which was transferred to the tribe of Simeon. Josh. 15 : 26. 19 : 2. 1 Chr. 4 : 28. Neh. 11 : 26.

מוֹלֶדֶת f. verbal from יָלַד, dec. XIII. a.

1. *birth, origin, descent.* Est. 2 : 10, 20. Plur. מוֹלְדוֹת *natales, origines,* Ezek. 16 : 3, 4.—אֶרֶץ מוֹלֶדֶת *the country of one's birth, native land,* Gen. 11 : 28. 24 : 7.

2. i. q. אֶרֶץ מוֹלֶדֶת. Gen. 12 : 1. 24 : 4.

3. *kindred, fellow-countrymen* generally. Est. 8 : 6.

4. *children, posterity, descendants, proles.* Gen. 48 : 6. Lev. 18 : 9, 11.

מוּלָה f. verbal from מוּל dec. X. *circumcision.* Ex. 4 : 26.

מוּם m. dec. I. *a stain, blemish.* (In Syr. *idem.*)

1. *a bodily injury, blemish, defect.* Lev. 21 : 17 ff. 22 : 20, 21, 25. It belongs to beauty to be *without blemish,* 2 Sam. 14 : 25. Cant. 4 : 7.

2. *a stain, blemish,* in a moral sense. Deut. 32 : 5. Job 11 : 15. 31 : 7.

מוּסַב m. verbal from סָבַב *circuit* (of a house). Ezek. 41:7.

מוֹסָד verbal from יָסַד, dec. II. b. found only in the plur. מוֹסָדוֹת Jer. 51:26. const. מוֹסְדֵי, מוֹסְדוֹת, *foundations*, e. g. of a building, Jer. 51:26. of the earth, Prov. 8:29. of the heavens, 2 Sam. 22:8. Hence, because they remain after the destruction of the building, *ruins*, Is. 58:12.

מוּסָד m. verbal from יָסַד, dec. II. b. *idem*. Is. 28:16.

מוּסָדָה f. verbal from יָסַד, dec. XI. a.

1. *idem*. Ezek. 41:8 Keri. In the Kethib מיסדות.

2. *an institution* or *appointment* (of God). Comp. the root יָסַד Kal and Pi. no. 2. Is. 30:32 מַטֵּה מוּסָדָה *the rod of correction appointed of God*.

מוּסַךְ m. verbal from סָכַךְ, dec. II. b. *a covered walk*. 2 K. 16:18 Keri. In the Kethib מֵיסַךְ.

מוֹסֵר for מַאְסֵר verbal from אָסַר found only in the plur. ־ִים and ־וֹת, m. *bonds*, *fetters*, *vincula*. Ps. 2:3. 107:14. 116:16. As a proper name מוֹסֵר and ־וֹת a station of the Israelites in the desert.

מוּסָר m. verbal from יָסַר, dec. II. b.

1. *warning*, *correction*, as of God to men, of parents to children. Ps. 50:17. Jer. 2:30. Prov. 1:8. 4:1. 5:12. 8:33. Hence also, *a warning* or *instructive example*, Ezek. 5:15. comp. the verb 23:48.

2. *instruction*, *knowledge*, *wisdom*, parallel with חָכְמָה, דַּעַת. Prov. 1:2. 4:13. 23:23. 6:23.

3. *chastisement*, *punishment*. Job 5:17 מוּסַר שַׁדַּי *the chastisement of the Almighty*. Prov. 22:15 שֵׁבֶט מוּסָר *the rod of chastisement*. 23:15 אַל תִּמְנַע מִנַּעַר מוּסָר *withhold not chastisement from a child*. Job 12:18 מוּסַר מְלָכִים פִּתֵּחַ *he loosens the chastisement*, i. e. the violence, *of kings*.

I. **מוֹעֵד** m. verbal from יָעַד, dec. VII. a.

1. *an appointed* or *definite time*. Gen. 17:21 לַמּוֹעֵד הַזֶּה בַּשָּׁנָה הָאַחֶרֶת *about this time in the coming year*. Jer. 8:7 *the stork* יָדְעָה מוֹעֲדֶיהָ *knows her times of passage*. Gen. 1:14 וְהָיוּ לְאֹתֹת וּלְמוֹעֲדִים *they shall be for signs and for times*, i. e. signs of times. Hab. 2:3 עוֹד חָזוֹן לַמּוֹעֵד *the vision refers to a somewhat remote time*. Dan. 8:19. 11:27, 35. Especially (1.) *a year*, in the indefinite language of prophecy. Dan. 12:7. comp. 7:25. (2.) *a festival*.—מוֹעֲדֵי יְהוָֹה *festivals of Jehovah*, Lev. 23:2, 4, 37, 44. —יוֹם מוֹעֵד *idem*, Hos. 9:5. 12:10. Hence, *a festival sacrifice*, *victim*, 2 Chr. 30:22. (comp. חַג no. 2.)

2. *a meeting*, (comp. מוֹעֵד no. 2.) Job 30:23. Is. 33:20. Num. 16:2 קְרִאֵי מוֹעֵד *those invited to the meeting*; otherwise קְרִיאֵי הָעֵדָה.—Is. 14:13 הַר־מוֹעֵד *the mount of meeting* (of the gods,) *the mount of the gods*, prob. with reference to some fabulous mountain in the remotest north. (So Caucasus is called *the abode of the gods*, Spanhem. ad Callim. Hymn. in Del. v. 70.)—אֹהֶל מוֹעֵד *the tent of meeting*, *the tabernacle of the congregation* so called. According to Ex. 25:22. Num. 17:19. [17:4.] it was the tent where God *met with* Moses, hence *a tabernacle of conference*, *place of an oracle*; but perhaps also *the tent for meetings of the people on festival occasions*. Comp. no. 3. The Germ. *Stiftshütte* is a translation of the Greek σκήνη μαρτυρίου, or the Lat. *tabernaculum testimonii*, as if מוֹעֵד were derived from עוּד *testari*; comp. מִשְׁכַּן עֵדוּת *the tent of the law*. Num. 9:15.

3. *appointed place of meeting*. Josh. 8:40.—מוֹעֵד אֵל *place of meeting with God*, i. e. the temple, Lam. 2:6. Ps. 74:4. So in the plur. Ps. 74:8. of the halls of the temple, or as a pluralis excellentiæ, or, (if the psalm pertains to the time of the Maccabees,) of the Jewish synagogues.

4. *a concerted sign*, *signal*. Judg. 20:38.

II. **מוֹעֵד** verbal from מָעַד, dec. VII. a. *a slipping*, liter. *that which slips*; (comp. אֵיד *destruction*.) Job 12:5.

מוֹעָד m. verbal from יָעַד, dec. II. b. prob. *a collection, congregation, host.* Is. 14 : 31 אֵין בּוֹדֵד בְּמוֹעָדָיו *no one is by himself in their hosts,* i. e. they advance in close order; comp. 5 : 27.

מוֹעָדָה f. plur. מוֹעָדוֹת, verbal from יָעַד, *a festival.* 2 Chr. 8 : 13.

מוּעָדָה f. verbal from יָעַד, liter. *a place fixed upon for safety, a place of refuge, asylum.* Josh. 20 : 9 עָרֵי הַמּוּעָדָה *free cities, cities of refuge, urbes asyli.* (Syr. ܡܥܕܘܐ *refuge, harbour;* ܒܝܬ ܡܥܕܘܐ *an asylum.*)

מוֹעֶדֶת see מָעַד.

מוּעָף m. verbal from the Hoph. of עוּף no. II. *darkness.* Is. 8 : 23. [9 : 1.]

מוֹעֵצָה f. i. q. עֵצָה, verbal from יָעַץ, dec. XI. b. found only in the plur. מוֹעֵצוֹת *counsels, plans, purposes, devices.* Ps. 5 : 11. 81 : 13. Prov. 1 : 31 מִמֹּעֲצֹתֵיהֶם יִשְׂבָּעוּ *they shall be filled with their own devices,* i. e. with the consequences of them.

מוּעָקָה f. verbal from the Hoph. of עוּק, *an oppressive burden.* Ps. 66 : 11.

מוֹפֵת m. (perhaps for מֹאפֵת; comp. the Arab. أَفْتٌ *a wonder.*) dec. VII.

1. *a wonder, a wonderful occurrence, portentum, prodigium;* e. g. in heaven, Joel 3 : 3. [2 : 30.] Hence *a miracle* wrought by God or his messengers, Ex. 4 : 21. 7 : 3, 9. 11 : 9. Deut. 4 : 34. 6 : 22. Ps. 105 : 27. Particularly *a sign, token, pledge, omen,* given by a prophet for the accomplishment of something future; comp. אוֹת no. (4.) 1 K. 13 : 3 —5. Deut. 13 : 2, 3.

2. *a symbol, emblem, a type of a future event,* contained in some action, Lat. *portentum.* See אוֹת no. (5.) Is. 8 : 18 *behold I and the children which Jehovah has given me,* לְאֹתוֹת וּלְמוֹפְתִים *are emblems and symbols,* i. e. on account of our significant names we are symbols of future events. 20 : 3. Zech. 3 : 8 אַנְשֵׁי מוֹפֵת *typical* or *symbolical men.* So in N. T. τύπος, Rom. 5 : 14. Sometimes the prophet performs an action, and asserts that it is ominous or emblematic of something future, Ezek. 12 : 6, 11. 24 : 24, 27.

מוּץ (kindred with מָצָה and מָצַץ,) *to oppress.* Part. מֵץ *an oppressor,* Is. 16 : 4. Deriv. מִיץ.

מוֹץ see **מֹץ** *chaff.*

מוֹצָא m. verbal from יָצָא, dec. I.

1. *a going out, coming forth, rising.* Num. 33 : 2. Also *the rising* of the sun, Ps. 19 : 7.

2. *place of rising.*—מוֹצָא מַיִם *a place where water rises, a spring,* Is. 41 : 18. מוֹצָא הַשֶּׁמֶשׁ *the place where the sun rises, the east,* Ps. 75 : 7. 65 : 9 מוֹצָאֵי בֹקֶר וָעֶרֶב תַּרְנִין *thou makest the goings forth of the morning and of the evening to rejoice.* (The word מוֹצָא is here applied to the evening by the figure called zeugma.) Hence *a door, gate, passage out,* Ezek. 42 : 11.

3. *that which comes out.*—מוֹצָא שְׂפָתַיִם *that which comes out of the lips,* Num. 30 : 13. Deut. 23 : 24.

4. *origin, descent, race.* 1 K. 10 : 28.

מוֹצָאָה fem. of מוֹצָא, dec. X.

1. *origin, descent.* Mic. 5 : 1.

2. plur. מוֹצָאוֹת *a privy, sink, loca in quæ effertur stercus;* see צֵאָה, צוֹאָה. 2 K. 10 : 27 Keri.

מוּצָק m. verbal from יָצַק, *the pouring out* or *casting* of metals. 1 K. 7 : 37.

2. *something cast* or *solid.* Job 37 : 10.

מוּצָק m. verbal from the Hoph. of צוּק, *straitness, oppression.* Job 36 : 16.

מוּצָקָה f. verbal from יָצַק, dec. X. *a tunnel, funnel, infundibulum.* Zech. 4 : 2.

מוּק found only in Hiph. הֵמִיק *to imitate, to mock, deride.* Ps. 73 : 8. (Aram. Pa. מַיֵּק, ܡܰܝܶܩ *idem.*)

מוֹקֵד m. verbal from יָקַד, dec. VII. b.

1. *heat, burning.* Is. 33 : 14.

2. *materials for burning, brush, dry wood.* Ps. 102 : 4.

מוֹקְדָה f. verbal from יָקַד, *the place*

on the altar where the victim was burnt, perhaps *the pile of wood.* Lev. 6:2. [6:9.]

מוֹקֵשׁ m. verbal from יָקַשׁ, dec. VII. b.

1. *a snare, a springe;* e. g. for animals, birds, Job 40:24. Am. 3:5 (פַּח appears here to denote *snares lying on the ground.*) מוֹקְשֵׁי־מָוֶת *snares of death,* Ps. 18:6.

2. metaphorically *an object by which any one is seduced and caused to fall.* Ex. 10:7 עַד־מָתַי יִהְיֶה זֶה לָנוּ לְמוֹקֵשׁ *how long shall he be to us for a snare?* i. e. bring us into misfortune? 23:33. 34:12. Deut. 7:16. Josh. 23:13. Plur. ־ִים, once ־וֹת Ps. 141:9.

מוֹר see מֹר.

מוּר in Kal not used.

Hiph. הֵמִיר 1. *to change, exchange.* Lev. 27:33. Construed with בְּ of the thing *for* which the exchange is made, Ps. 106:20. Jer. 2:11. Hos. 4:7.

2. used absolutely, *to undergo change, to suffer alteration.* Ps. 15:4 *he swears* וְלֹא יָמִר *and changes not,* i. e. breaks not his oath. 46:3 לֹא נִירָא בְּהָמִיר אָרֶץ *we will not fear, though the earth change:* (comp. 102:27.)—In Jer. 2:11, we find הֵימִיר for הֵמִיר.

Niph. נָמַר, (as if from מָרַר,) *to be altered.* Jer. 48:11.

Deriv. תְּמוּרָה.

מוֹרָא m. verbal from יָרֵא, dec. II. b.

1. *fear.* Gen. 9:2 מוֹרַאֲכֶם *the fear of you.* Deut. 11:25. Mal. 1:6.

2. *the object of fear* or *reverence.* Is. 8:12, 13. Ps. 76:12.

3. *something astonishing* or *wonderful,* Deut. 26:8. 34:12. Jer. 32:21. Plur. מוֹרָאִים Deut. 4:34.

מוֹרַג m. Is. 41:15. Plur. מוֹרִגִּים 2 Sam. 24:22. and מוֹרִיגִים (after the Chaldaic form) 1 Chr. 21:23. prim. dec. VIII. f. *a threshing sledge* or *dray, trahea, a plank armed with iron* or *sharp stones,* which was drawn by oxen, like a sledge, over the grain, to cut the straw in pieces, after which it was winnowed. In Span. *trillo.* (Arab. نورج by a commutation of מ and נ.)

מוֹרָד m. verbal from יָרַד, dec. II. b.

1. *a descent, declivity.* Josh. 7:5. 10:11.

2. 1 K. 7:29 מַעֲשֵׂה מוֹרָד *work hanging down, festoons.*

I. מוֹרֶה m. verbal from יָרָה no. I.

1. *an archer.* See יָרָה no. I. Hiph. no. 1.

2. *the early rain.* See יָרָה no. I. Hiph. no. 2.

II. מוֹרֶה m. verbal from יָרָה no. II. 2. *a teacher.* Is. 9:14. Hence i. q. חָכָם *wise,* spoken of God, Job 36:22. Others adopt the rendering of the Sept. δυνάστης, comp. the Aram. מָרֵא ܡܪܐ *a lord;* but would not this be written in Hebrew מָרֵא? Others make it i. q. מוֹרָא no. 2. *the object of fear, the dreadful one.* (Comp. Ps. 9:21.)

As a proper name אֵלוֹן מוֹרֶה Gen. 12:6. and אֵלוֹנֵי מוֹרֶה Deut. 11:30. *the turpentine-trees of Moreh,* in the neighbourhood of Shechem; and גִּבְעַת הַמּוֹרֶה *the hill of Moreh,* in the valley of Jezreel, Judg. 7:1.

I. מוֹרָה m. *a razor.* Judg. 13:5. 16:7. 1 Sam. 1:11. (Root prob. מָרָה Arab. مرى *ubera strinxit, plagis perstrinxit,* whence *novacula stringens.* According to others, i. q. מוֹרָא *timor,* the razor being so called from the danger in using it.)

II. מוֹרָה Ps. 9:21 Kethib, i. q. מוֹרָא *fear, terror,* which is the reading of the Keri.

מוֹרָט see מָרַט.

מוֹרִיָּה see מֹרִיָּה.

מוֹרָשׁ m. const. מוֹרַשׁ, verbal from יָרַשׁ, (with Kamets impure,) *a possession.* Obad. 17. Is. 14:23. Job 17:11 מוֹרָשֵׁי לְבָבִי *the possessions,* i. e. the fondest hopes, *of my heart.*

מוֹרָשָׁה f. verbal from יָרַשׁ *idem.* Ex. 6:8. Deut. 33:4.

מוֹרֶשֶׁת גַּת Mic. 1:14. a place in the neighbourhood of Eleutheropolis, the birth-place of the prophet Micah, The gentile noun is מֹרַשְׁתִּי, Mic. 1:1. Jer. 26:18.

I. **מוּשׁ** 1. *to depart.* Num. 14:44. Josh. 1:8.

2. causat. *to put away, to remove.* Zech. 3:9.

Hiph. 1. as in Kal no 1. *to depart, cease.* Ex. 13:22. Jer. 17:8 וְלֹא יָמִישׁ מֵעֲשׂוֹת פֶּרִי *and it shall not cease from yielding fruit.*

2. causat. as in Kal no. 2. *to remove, withdraw.* Mic. 2:3, 4.

3. *to let escape.* Nah. 3:1.

II. **מוּשׁ** i. q. מָשַׁשׁ *to feel, touch.* Gen. 27:21.

מוֹשָׁב m. verbal from יָשַׁב, dec. II. b.

1. *a seat, stool,* 1 Sam. 20:18, 25.

2. *a company* or *circle of persons sitting together, consessus.* Ps. 1:1. 107:32.

3. *a habitation.* Gen. 27:39.—בֵּית־מוֹשָׁב *a dwelling-house,* Lev. 25:29. Hence (1.) *the time of dwelling.* Ex. 12:40. (2.) as a concrete, *people dwelling together.* 2 Sam. 9:12 כֹּל־מוֹשַׁב בֵּית צִיבָא *all that dwell in the house of Ziba.*

4. *the situation* (of a city). 2 K. 2:19.

מוֹשְׁכוֹת fem. plur. dec. VII. a. *bands, fetters.* Job 38:31. (Arab. مسكة *compes,* from مسك *to hold, to hold fast.*)

מוֹשָׁעוֹת plur. fem. verbal from יָשַׁע, *deliverance, salvation.* Ps. 68:21.

מוּת, pret. מֵת, מַתִּי.

1. *to die.* 1 Sam. 25:37 וַיָּמָת לִבּוֹ בְּקִרְבּוֹ *then died his heart within him.* Comp. חָיָה. Gen. 45:27. Judg. 15:19. Part. מֵת *a dead man, a corpse,* also, as an epicene, for *the corpse of a woman,* Gen. 23:4. (So in German, *ein Kranker, ein Todter.*)—Spoken of inanimate nature, Job 14:8. hence Gen. 47:19 *wherefore should we die, we and our land?* Comp. הָרַג Ps. 78:47. and Bocharti Hieroz. P. I. p. 1.

2. *to perish, be destroyed,* spoken of a state, Am. 2:2. *to become wretched* or *unfortunate,* Prov. 15:10. Hos. 13:1. See מָוֶת.

Pil. מוֹתֵת and Hiph. הֵמִית *to kill, slay.* (More frequently in Hiph.) 1 Sam. 14:13. 2 Sam. 1:16. Judg. 16:30. Part. מְמִתִים *the destroyers,* prob. *the angels of death,* Job 33:22.

Hoph. הוּמַת *to be killed.* Deut. 21:22. 1 Sam. 19:11.

Deriv. out of course תְּמוּתָה, מָוֶת.

מָוֶת m. with ה paragogic הַמָּוְתָה Ps. 116:15. const. מוֹת, plur. מוֹתִים Ezek. 28:10. verbal from מוּת, dec. VI. e.

1. *death.*—כְּלֵי מָוֶת *deadly weapons,* Ps. 7:14. יָשֵׁן מָוֶת *to sleep the sleep of death,* Ps. 13:4. בֶּן־מָוֶת and אִישׁ מָוֶת *one condemned to die,* 1 K. 2:26. 2 Sam. 19:28. Sometimes death is personified, as in Ps. 49:15.

2. *the region of the dead, the subterranean world, hades.* Job 28:22. שַׁעֲרֵי־מָוֶת *the gates of hades,* Ps. 9:14. חַדְרֵי־מָוֶת *the chambers of hades.* Prov. 7:27.

3. *adversity, ruin, destruction,* in opposition to חַיִּים *prosperity, happiness.* Prov. 11:19. 12:28.

4. *pestilence.* Jer. 15:2. 18:21. 43:11. Job 27:15. Comp. θάνατος, Rev. 6:8. 18:8. Chald. מוֹתָא *pestilence,* and the Heb. דֶּבֶר.

מוֹת Chald. *idem.* Ezra 7:26.

מוֹתָר m. verbal from יָתַר, dec. II. b.

1. *pre-eminence.* Ecc. 3:19.

2. *abundance.* Prov. 14:23. 21:5.

מִזְבֵּחַ m. const. מִזְבַּח, plur. מִזְבְּחוֹת, verbal from זָבַח, dec. VII. d. *an altar.*—הַמִּזְבֵּחָה *upon the altar,* Lev. 1:9, 13, 15. 2 Chr. 29:22.—מִזְבַּח הָעֹלָה *the altar of burnt-offering,* Ex. 30:28. also called מִזְבַּח הַנְּחֹשֶׁת *the brazen altar,* in front of the temple or tabernacle, in the open air, Ex. 39:39.—מִזְבַּח הַקְּטֹרֶת *the altar of incense,* also called *the golden* *altar*, in the sanctuary, Ex. 30 : 27. 1 K. 7 : 48.

מֶזֶג m. *mixed wine, spiced wine.* Cant. 7 : 3. (Root מזג, in Arab. and Aram. *to mix.*) Comp. מָסַךְ.

מָזֶה m. adj. dec. IX. b. found only Deut. 32 : 24 מְזֵי רָעָב *exhausted* or *consumed by hunger.* Comp. the kindred roots מָצָה, מָצַץ, Arab. מזז *to suck.*

מָזֶו m. plur. מְזָוִים, dec. VI. a. i. q. זָוִית *a corner.* Once Ps. 144 : 13.

מְזוּזָה f. dec. X. *a door-post.* Ex. 12 : 7. 21 : 6. Deut. 6 : 9. Root perhaps זוז *to move*, because the door-post is that on which the door *turns* or *is moved.*

מָזוֹן m. verbal from זוּן, *food.* Gen. 45 : 23.

מָזוֹן Chald. *idem.* Dan. 4 : 9. [4 : 12.]

I. מָזוֹר m. verbal from זוּר no. I. dec. III. a. literally *the bandage of a wound*, hence *the wound itself.* Hos. 5 : 13. Metaphorically Jer. 30 : 13.

II. מָזוֹר m. *a snare, insidiæ.* Obad. 7. So Sept. Vulg. Chald. Syr. Root זוּר no. II. see in Arab. زار *to lie, to deceive.* According to others, liter. *a net*, from מזר in Aram. *to stretch out.*

מֵזַח Ps. 109 : 19. Is. 23 : 10. and מְזִיחַ m. Job 12 : 21. *a girdle.* The etymology is unknown.

מַזָּלוֹת fem. plur. 2 K. 23 : 5. *the constellations of the zodiac.* (In Chald. and Rabbin. *idem*, also *a lucky star.* In Arab. مَنْزِل *a house, dwelling.* The Arabians call the zodiac *the circle of palaces*, i. e. the twelve palaces in which the sun dwells.) See מַזָּרוֹת.

מַזְלֵג m. *a flesh-hook, a flesh-fork.* 1 Sam. 2 : 13, 14. The etymology is uncertain.

מִזְלָגָה f. found only in the plur. מִזְלָגוֹת dec. XI. b. *idem.* Ex. 27 : 3. 38 : 3.

מְזִמָּה f. verbal from זָמַם, dec. X.

1. *a thought.* Ps. 10 : 4. Particularly *a plan, purpose, device*, Job 42 : 2. Most frequently in a bad sense, Ps. 10 : 2. 21 : 12. 37 : 7. Jer. 23 : 20.

2. as a quality of mind, *wisdom, discretion.* Prov. 1 : 4. 3 : 21. 5 : 2. 8 : 12. Also in a bad sense, *craft, maliciousness*, Prov. 12 : 2 אִישׁ מְזִמּוֹת *a crafty man.* 14 : 17.—בַּעַל מְזִמּוֹת *idem*, 24 : 8.

3. *wickedness.* Job 21 : 27. Ps. 139 : 20.

מִזְמוֹר m. verbal from זָמַר no. II, dec. I. *a song.* Only in the superscriptions of the Psalms, e. g. Ps. III. IV. V. VI. VIII. IX. etc.

מְזַמְּרוֹת plur. fem. verbal from זָמַר no. I. *knives* or rather *snuffers*, as appurtenances of the candlestick. 1 K. 7 : 50. 2 K. 12 : 14. Jer. 52 : 18.

מַזְמֵרָה f. verbal from זָמַר no. I. dec. XI. b. *a pruning-knife.* Is. 2 : 4. 18 : 5. Joel 4 : 10. [3 : 10.]

מִזְעָר adv. *a little, in small quantity* or *number.* Is. 10 : 25. 29 : 17. 24 : 6. (Root זְעֵר Chald. *to be small* or *few*; comp. in Heb. צָעִיר.)

מְזָרִים plur. Job 37 : 9. in opposition to חֶדֶר *the south*, hence prob. *the north*, or some northern star. Vulg. *Arcturus*, Sept. ἀκρωτήρια (perhaps ἀρκτῷα, ἀρκτοῦρος.) Chald. *fenestræ τῶν Mesarim.* According to Kimchi: (*venti*) *dispergentes*, i. e. north winds. According to others, i. q. מַזָּרוֹת 38 : 32.

מַזָּרוֹת plur. fem. Job 38 : 32. prob. i. q. מַזָּלוֹת (see the letter ל) *the constellations of the zodiac.* Sept. μαζουρώθ. Chald. מַזָּלַיָּא. Vulg. *lucifer.* Others: *northern crown*; (comp. נֵזֶר.)

מִזְרֶה m. verbal from זָרָה, *a winnowing fan* or *shovel.* Is. 30 : 24. Jer. 15 : 7.

מִזְרָח m. verbal from זָרַח, dec. II. b. *the sun-rising, the east.* Ps. 103 : 12. *Towards the east* is expressed by מִזְרָח Neh. 12 : 37. by מִזְרַח הַשֶּׁמֶשׁ, Deut. 4 : 47. by מִזְרָחָה, Ex. 27 : 13. and by מִזְרְחָה שָׁמֶשׁ, Deut. 4 : 41.—מִזְרַח יְרִיחוֹ *on the east of Jericho*, Josh. 4 : 19.

מִזְרָע m. verbal from זָרַע, *a sown field, standing corn*. Is. 19 : 7.

מִזְרָק m. plur. ־ִים and ־וֹת, verbal from זָרַק, dec. II. b. liter. *a vessel used for sprinkling;* hence *a large dish,* Num. 7 : 13, 19 ff. *a basin,* Ex. 38 : 3. Num. 4 : 14. *a drinking vessel,* Am. 6 : 6.

מֵחַ m. adj. (Root מחח in Arab. conj. IV. *to be full of marrow,* spoken of bones; *to be fat,* spoken of sheep.) dec. I.

1. *fat,* particularly *a fat sheep.* Ps. 66 : 15.

2. *rich, opulent,* like דָּשֵׁן. Is. 5 : 17.

מֹחַ m. verbal from the same root, *marrow.* Job 21 : 24. (Arab. and Aram. *idem.*)

מָחָא i. q. Aram. מְחָא *to smite together, to clap.* Ps. 98 : 8 נְהָרוֹת יִמְחֲאוּ־כָף *let the streams clap their hands,* i. e. rejoice. Is. 55 : 12.

Pi. *idem,* with יָד. Ezek. 25 : 6.

מְחָא Chald. *to smite.* Dan. 2 : 34, 35. Part. מָחֵא Dan. 5 : 19, better מַחֵא part. Aph. of חֲיָא *to keep alive.*

Pa. מַחֵא *idem.—To smite on the hand,* for *to restrain, hinder,* Dan. 4 : 32. [4 : 35.] (So in Talmud. and Arab.)

Ithpe. *to be fastened* or *nailed.* Ezra 6 : 11.

מַחֲבֵא m. verbal from חָבָא, *a hiding-place, a lurking-place.* Is. 32 : 2.

מַחֲבֹאִים masc. plur. verbal from חָבָא dec. I. *idem.* 1 Sam. 23 : 23.

מַחְבֶּרֶת f. verbal from חָבַר no. I. dec. XIII. a. *the place of joining, the juncture;* e. g. of the parts of the curtain, Ex. 26 : 4, 5. of the front and hinder parts of the ephod, Ex. 28 : 27. 39 : 20.

מְחַבְּרוֹת fem. plur. verbal from חָבַר.

1. *beams,* so called from their *binding* the parts of the house together. 2 Chr. 34 : 11.

2. *iron hooks.* 1 Chr. 22 : 3.

מַחֲבַת f. (a contraction of מַחֲבֶנֶת, as מִשְׁרַת of מִשְׁרְתָה;) *a frying* or *baking pan.* Lev. 2 : 5. Ezek. 4 : 3. See חֲבִתִּים.

מַחֲגֹרֶת f. verbal from חָגַר, *a girdle.* Is. 3 : 24.

I. מָחָה 1. *to wipe off, to wash out,* Num. 5 : 23. E. g. *to wipe away* tears, Is. 25 : 8. *to wipe* the mouth, Prov. 30 : 20. *to blot out* or *erase* from a book, Ex. 32 : 32, 33. *to blot out* sin, i. e. to pardon it, Ps. 51 : 3, 11. Is. 43 : 25. 44 : 22.

2. *to destroy,* (a people, a state.) The origin of this signification is seen 2 K. 21 : 13 *I will wipe,* i. e. destroy, *Jerusalem, as one wipeth a dish; he wipeth it and turneth it upside down.* Gen. 6 : 7. 7 : 4. *To destroy* the name or remembrance of any one, Ex. 17 : 14. Deut. 9 : 14.

Niph. fut. apoc. יִמַּח for יִמָּחֶה, pass. of Kal, especially of no. 2. *to be destroyed.* Ezek. 6 : 6. Judg. 21 : 17. Spoken of שֵׁם *the name* or *memory* of any one, Deut. 25 : 6.

Hiph. i. q. Kal. fut. apoc. תֶּמַח Neh. 13 : 14. Jer. 18 : 23.—Prov. 31 : 3 וּדְרָכֶיךָ לַמְחוֹת מְלָכִין usually rendered: *and* (*give not*) *thy ways to destroy kings,* as a caution against a fondness for war. Better: *to the destroyers of kings,* i. e. to harlots; as if מחות were the fem. plur. of an adj. מָחֶה. Others derive the same signification from a change in the vowel-points, לְמֹחוֹת מְלָכִין.

II. מָחָה i. q. מָחָא *to strike,* (as a geographical line,) *to reach to, pertinere ad;* construed with עַל. Deut. 34 : 11. Deriv. מְחִי.

מְחוּגָה f. verbal from חוּג, *a compass, an instrument for drawing circles.* Is. 44 : 13.

מָחוֹז m. dec. III. a. *the sea-coast.* Once Ps. 107 : 30. (In Chald. *idem,* also *a country.* Arab. حَوْزٌ *border, side, country.* The ancient versions render it, *haven.*)

מָחוֹל m. verbal from חוּל, dec. III. a. *a circular dance, a dance.* Ps. 30 : 12. 149 : 3. 150 : 4. See the verb, Kal no. 3. and Pilel no. 1.

מְחוֹלָה or מְחֹלָה f. verbal from חוּל, dec. X. *idem.* Cant. 7:1. [6:13.] Plur. Ex. 15:20.

מַחֲזֶה m. verbal from חָזָה, dec. IX. a. *a sight, vision.* Gen. 15:1. Num. 24:4, 16.

מֶחֱזָה f. verbal from חָזָה, *a window.* 1 K. 7:4, 5.

מְחִי m. verbal from מָחָה no. II. dec. VI. *a smiting.* Ezek. 26:9 מְחִי קָבָלּוֹ Chald. *percussio tormentorum suorum,* which rendering makes קְבָל or קָבָל the name for *an engine used in sieges.* Others make the whole phrase, (*percussio rei oppositæ,*) to denote *a battering-ram.*

מִחְיָה f. verbal from חָיָה, dec. X.

1. *the preservation of life.* Gen. 45:5. 2 Chr. 14:12. Ezra 9:8, 9.

2. *means of living, support.* Judg. 6:4.

3. prob. *a sign, mark, indication.* Lev. 13:10 מִחְיַת חַי בָּשָׂר *an indication of raw flesh.* Verse 24 וְהָיְתָה מִחְיַת־הַמִּכְוָה *and there shall be a mark of burning.*

מְחִיר m. dec. I. (prob. kindred with מָכַר *to sell,* and מָחַר *to buy.*

1. *price.* Prov. 17:16. 27:26. בִּמְחִיר *for a price, for money,* 2 Sam. 24:24. לֹא בִמְחִיר *without price,* i. q. חִנָּם, Is. 45:13. 55:1.

2. *a reward.* Mic. 3:11. Deut. 23:28.

מַחֲלֶה m. verbal from חָלָה no. I. dec. IX. a. *sickness, disease.* Prov. 18:14. 2 Chron. 21:15.

מַחֲלָה f. verbal from חָלָה no. I. *idem.* Ex. 15:26.

מְחֹלָה f. see מְחוֹלָה.

מְחֹלָתִי m. a gentile noun, *a Meholathite, an inhabitant of* אָבֵל־מְחוֹלָה *Abelmeholah,* q. v. 1 Sam. 18:19. 2 Sam. 21:8.

מְחִלָּה f. verbal from חָלַל, dec. X. *a hole, cave.* Is. 2:19.

מַחֲלֻיִים masc. plur. verbal from חָלָה, *sicknesses.* 2 Chr. 24:25.

מַחֲלָף m. dec. II. b. *a knife, a knife for slaying victims.* Ezra 1:9. Syr. ܡܚܠܦܐ, Rabbin. חִלּוּף *idem.*)

מַחְלְפוֹת plur. fem. dec. II. b. Judg. 16:13, 19. *braided locks* or *tufts of hair.* (The sense of *braiding* is allied to that of *changing,* which is found in the Piel and Hiphil of the root חָלַף.)

מַחֲלָצוֹת plur. fem. *costly garments.* Is. 3:22. Zech. 3:4. Root חָלַץ i. q. Arab. خلع חלע (by a commutation of ץ and ע, see ע) *to clothe in a costly manner;* hence, خِلْعَة *a costly garment, a kaftan.* See N. G. Schröder De Vestitu Mulierum Heb. p. 206—225.

מַחֲלֹקֶת f. with suff. מַחֲלֻקְתּוֹ, plur. מַחְלְקוֹת, verbal from חָלַק, dec. XIII. f.

1. *smoothness,* hence *a slipping away, an escaping.* So in the proper name סֶלַע הַמַּחְלְקוֹת *Sela-hammahlekoth,* 1 Sam. 23:28.

2. *a division, class;* spoken particularly of the division of the Levites and priests into 24 courses, (ἐφημέριαι, κλῆροι.) 1 Chr. 27:1 ff. 2 Chr. 8:14. 31:2. 35:4.

מָחֲלַת Ps. 53:1. 88:1. prob. i. q. Ethiop. *mahhlet,* κιθάρα. Others: *a pipe,* i. q. נְחִילָה.

מַחְמָאוֹת plur. fem. found only Ps. 55:22 חָלְקוּ מַחְמָאוֹת פִּיו, according to this punctuation, *smooth are the milky words of his mouth,* as if מַחְמָאָה were a denom. from חֶמְאָה. But it would better suit the parallelism, to read with Kimchi and others מֵחֶמְאוֹת, *his mouth is smoother than cream* or *butter.*

מַחְמָד m. plur. מַחְמַדִּים, verbal from חָמַד, dec. VIII. a.

1. *desire, object of desire.* מַחְמַד עֵינֶיךָ *what thine eyes desire.* 1 K. 20:6.

2. *pleasantness, agreeableness, loveliness.* Cant. 5:16. Hos. 9:16 מַחֲמַדֵּי בִטְנָם *the beloved of their womb,* i. e. their most beloved offspring.

3. *costliness, precious things.* Is. 64: 10. Joel 4:5. [3:5.] 2 Chr. 36:19.

מַחֲמַדִּים m. verbal from חָמַד, *precious things.* Lam. 1:7, 10.

מַחְמָל m. dec. II. b. Ezek. 24:21 מַחְמַל נַפְשְׁכֶם *that which your soul desires* or *loves.* The root חָמַל *to pity,* may here have the kindred sense of *love, affection,* and be synonymous with חָמַד. Some MSS. read מחמד. But חמל is in Arab. i. q. נָשָׂא, and joined with אֶל signifies *desiderio ferri ad aliquam rem;* whence it would be exactly synonymous with מַשָּׂא נֶפֶשׁ in verse 25.

מַחְמֶצֶת f. verbal from חָמֵץ, *any thing leavened.* Ex. 12:19, 20.

מַחֲנֶה m. (fem. Gen. 32:9.) verbal from חָנָה, dec. IX. a.

1. *an encampment,* either of an army, or of a Nomadic tribe, *castra.* Gen. 32:8. 33:8. Ex. 16:13.

2. *a host, army.* Ex. 14:24. Judg. 4:16. *a multitude* or *company of men* generally, Gen. 50:9. *an army* or *swarm* (of locusts), Joel 2:11.

Dual מַחֲנָיִם Cant. 7:1. [6:13.]

Plur. מַחֲנִים Num. 13:19. and מַחֲנוֹת.—מַחֲנוֹת יְהוָה *the courts in which the priests of Jehovah lodged,* 2 Chr. 31:2.

מַחֲנֵה־דָן (*the camp of Dan*) a place near Kirjath-jearim in the tribe of Judah. Judg. 18:12.

מַחֲנַיִם (*two hosts* of angels; see Gen. 32:2.) proper name of a city beyond Jordan, in the tribe of Gad, near the tribe of Manasseh, assigned to the Levites. Josh. 13:26, 30. 21:36. 2 Sam. 2:8, 12, 29. 17:24, 27. 1 K. 2:8. 4:14.

מַחֲנָק m. verbal from חָנַק, *strangling,* also *death* generally, parallel with מָוֶת. Job 7:15.

מַחְסֶה m. with suff. מַחְסִי, verbal from חָסָה, dec. IX. a. *refuge, a place of refuge.* Is. 25:4. Ps. 104:18. Spoken of Jehovah, Ps. 62:9. 46:2. 61:4. Joel 4:16. [3:16.] Ps. 71:7.

מַחְסוֹם m. verbal from חָסַם, *a basket* or *muzzle for the mouth.* Ps. 39:2.

מַחְסוֹר m. (plur. Prov. 24:34.) verbal from חָסֵר, dec. I. *want.*—כָּל־מַחְסוֹרְךָ *every want of thine.* Judg. 19:20. Used absolutely, *poverty, indigence,* Prov. 28:27. Prov. 21:17 אִישׁ מַחְסוֹר *a man of poverty,* i. e. a poor man.

מָחַץ 1. *to shake* or *agitate;* e. g. the foot in blood. Ps. 68:24.

2. *to break* or *smite in pieces,* e. g. the head of any one, Ps. 68:22. 110:6. the loins, Deut. 33:11. Metaphorically Job 36:12 *by his wisdom he smiteth the haughtiness* (*of the sea*).

מַחַץ m. *the place smitten, stroke.* Is. 30:26.

מַחְצֵב m. verbal from חָצַב, *a hewing,*—אַבְנֵי מַחְצֵב *hewn stones,* 2 K. 12:13. 22:6.

מֶחֱצָה f. verbal from חָצָה, dec. IX. a. *the half.* Num. 31:36, 43.

מַחֲצִית f. verbal from חָצָה, dec. I.

1. *the half.* Ex. 30:13.

2. *the middle.* Neh. 8:3.

מָחַק *to smite.* Judg. 5:26. In Arab. مَحَقَ *to destroy.*

מֶחְקָר m. verbal from חָקַר, dec. II. b. *what is searched into, the inmost part,* i. q. חֵקֶר, no. 2. Ps. 95:4.

מָחָר subst. and adv.

1. *to-morrow, on the morrow.*—לְמָחָר *idem,* Num. 11:18.—כָּעֵת מָחָר *to-morrow about this time,* 1 K. 19:2. or more fully, מָחָר כָּעֵת הַזֹּאת, Josh. 11:6.—כָּעֵת מָחָר הַשְּׁלִשִׁית *about this time to-morrow* (*or*) *the day after to-morrow,* 1 Sam. 20:12.

2. *in future, in time to come.* Ex. 13:14. Josh. 4:6, 21. בְּיוֹם מָחָר *idem,* Gen. 30:33. Comp. מָחֳרָת.

מַחֲרָאָה f. *a sink, privy.* 2 K. 10:27 Kethib. See חֲרָאִים.

מַחֲרֵשָׁה and מַחֲרֶשֶׁת f. 1 Sam. 13:20. the names of two different cutting instruments, one of which is prob. *a ploughshare,* (from חָרַשׁ no. 3.) but the other, some *cutting* tool, (from חָרַשׁ no. I.)

The plur. מַחְתְּשׁוֹת verse 21. appears to embrace both the above mentioned instruments, at least it stands in the place of both.

מָחֳרָת f. const. מָחֳרַת, *the morrow, the following day;* comp. מָחָר. Joined with יוֹם Num. 11:32. but elsewhere without it.—לְמָחֳרָת *on the morrow,* Jon. 4:7. מִמָּחֳרָת *idem,* Gen. 19:34. Ex. 9:6.—With a genitive following, like the French *lendemain,* Lev. 23:11. 15:16 מִמָּחֳרַת הַשַּׁבָּת *on the day after the sabbath.* Num. 33:3. 1 Sam. 20:27. — מָחֳרָתָם 1 Sam. 30:17. perhaps with an adverbial termination, like יוֹמָם.

מַחְשֹׂף m. verbal from חָשַׂף, *a place stripped* or *made bare, a streak.* Gen. 30:37.

מַחֲשָׁבָה and מַחֲשֶׁבֶת f. plur. מַחֲשָׁבוֹת, const. מַחְשְׁבוֹת, verbal fro... חָשַׁב.

1. *view, design.* 2 Sa... 14:14.

2. *project, plan, device.* Job 5:12. Prov. 12:5. Particularly *an evil device,* with and without the addition of רַע, Est. 8:3, 5. 9:25. Ezek. 38:10.

3. *cunning* or *mechanical work.* Ex. 31:4. 35:33, 35.

מַחְשָׁךְ m. verbal from חָשַׁךְ, dec. VIII. a. *darkness.* Is. 29:15. Ps. 88:19 מְיֻדָּעַי מַחְשָׁךְ *mine acquaintance are (in) darkness,* i. e. invisible to me. Plur. מַחֲשַׁכִּים *dark places,* Ps. 88:7. 74:20 מַחֲשַׁכֵּי־אֶרֶץ *the lurking-places of the country.* Particularly *hades,* Ps. 143:3.

מַחְתָּה f. verbal from חָתָה, dec. X.

1. *a coal-pan, a fire-pan.* Ex. 27:3. 38:3. Perhaps in the form of a fire-shovel, comp. Num. 16:6 ff.

2. prob. *small tongs* or *snuffers.* Ex. 25:38. 37:23.

מְחִתָּה f. verbal from חָתַת, dec. X. liter. *a breaking in pieces;* hence

1. *destruction,* Prov. 10:14. 13:3. 18:7. Jer. 17:17. *something destroyed, ruins,* Ps. 89:40.

2. *discouragement, consternation.* Prov. 10:15. See the root, signif. no. 2.

3. *terror.* Prov. 10:29. 21:15. Is. 54:14. (See חָתַת Niph. Pi. Hiph.)

מַחְתֶּרֶת f. verbal from חָתַר, *a breaking through* or *in,* as of a thief. Ex. 22:1. Jer. 2:34.

מְטָה, מְטָא Chald. 1. *to come, arrive.* Dan. 7:22.

2. *to come to* any person or place. Dan. 6:24, 25. 7:13.

3. *to reach.* Dan. 4:8, 17, 19. [4:11, 20, 22.]

4. *to come upon* or *befal* any one, construed with עַל. Dan. 4:21, 25. [4:24, 28.]

Note this verb is etymologically connected with the Heb. מָצָא, but differs from it in signification.

מַטְאֲטֵא m. *a besom, broom;* see טֵאטֵא.

מַטְבֵּחַ m. from טָבַח, *a slaughter, overthrow.* Is. 14:21.

מַטֶּה m. (fem. Mic. 6:9.) Plur. ־וֹת, once ־ִים Hab. 3:15. verbal from נָטָה *to stretch out,* in Niph. *to extend itself;* comp. נְטִישָׁה from נָטַשׁ; dec. IX. a.

1. *a bough, branch.* Ezek. 19:11 ff.

2. *a staff, stick, rod.* Ex. 4:2.—שָׁבַר מַטֵּה־לֶחֶם *to break the staff of bread,* i. e. to cause a famine, since bread is said by the Hebrews to support the heart, (comp. סָעַד,) Lev. 26:26. Ps. 105:16. Ezek. 4:16. 5:16. 14:12.—Particularly *a rod of correction,* Is. 9:3 מַטֵּה שִׁכְמוֹ *the rod for his back.* 10:5, 24. Nah. 1:13. Ezek. 7:10. Hence *punishment,* Mic. 6:9.

3. *a tribe* of the Israelites, (comp. שֵׁבֶט;) e. g. מַטֵּה לֵוִי *the tribe of Levi,* Num. 1:49. also מַטֵּה בְּנֵי מְנַשֶּׁה *the tribe of the children of Manasseh,* Josh. 13:29.—רָאשֵׁי הַמַּטּוֹת *the heads of the tribes,* 1 K. 8:1.

4. perhaps *an arrow, javelin,* (like Lat. *hasta.*) Hab. 3:9, 14.

5. *an inclining* or *sinking downwards, a low* or *deep place.* Hence, with He local, מַטָּה an adv. *down, downwards, beneath,* Deut. 28:43. Prov. 15:24. With prepositions, (1.) לְמַטָּה (a.) *downwards.* Ecc. 3:21. (b.) *beneath, below.* 2 K. 19:30. (c.) *under, below.* 1 Chr.

27:23. *from twenty years old and under.* (d.) *less than.* Ezra 9:13 *below our misdeeds,* i.e. less than they deserve. (2.) מִלְמַטָּה *beneath.* Ex. 26:24. 27:5.

מִטָּה f. verbal from נָטָה, as in Greek κλίνη from κλίνω; dec. X.

1. *a bed.* Gen. 47:31.

2. *a cushion,* to sit upon at meals, Est. 1:6. Ezek. 23:41. *a couch, sofa,* generally, Am. 3:12. 6:4.

3. *a portable bed, litter, sedan.* Cant. 3:7.

4. *a bier.* 2 Sam. 3:31.

מֻטָּה, מֻטֶּה, plur. וֹת—, verbal from the Hophal of נָטָה.

1. *a stretching out.* Is. 8:8.

2. *a bending* or *perversion of justice.* Ezek. 9:9.

מַטְוֶה m. verbal from טָוָה, *something spun.* Ex. 35:25.

מְטִיל m. *a forged* or *wrought bar of iron.* Once Job 40:18. Root מטל Arab. *to work, to forge,* particularly iron.

מַטְמוֹן, plur. מַטְמֹנִים, verbal from טָמַן, dec. I. a. and c.

1. *a place where any thing is buried.* Particularly *a subterranean granary,* Jer. 41:8.

2. *a subterranean treasure,* Prov. 2:4. Job 3:21. *a treasure* generally, Gen. 43:23.

מַטָּע m. verbal from נָטַע dec. I. and II. *a planting.* Ezek. 17:7. 34:29.

מַטְעַמִּים masc. plur. Gen. 27:4 ff. and **מַטְעַמּוֹת** fem. plur. Prov. 23:3, 6. verbals from טָעַם, *dainties, savoury meats.*

מִטְפַּחַת f. verbal from טָפַח, dec. XIII. m. Ruth 3:15. Plur. מִטְפָּחוֹת Is. 3:22. *a wide garment for women.*

מָטַר *to rain.* In Kal not used.

Hiph. הִמְטִיר *to cause to rain.* Gen. 7:4. Applied also to the sending of hail, Ex. 9:23. lightning, Ps. 11:6. manna, Ex. 16:4. Ps. 78:24. (In Syr. Chald. and Arab. *idem.*)

Niph. *to be rained upon.* Am. 4:7.

מָטָר m. plur. const. מִטְרוֹת, verbal from מָטַר, dec. IV. a. *rain.* Ex. 9:33. Job 37:6.

מַטָּרָה f. verbal from נָטַר.

1. *a prison.* Neh. 3:25. 12:39.

2. *aim, mark, object, scopus,* (from נטר Arab. *to see,* like σκόπος from σκέπτομαι.) 1 Sam. 20:20. Job 16:12. Also with the Aramean orthography מַטָּרָא, Lam. 3:12.

מִי an interrogative pronoun.

1. *who?*—As a genitive, בַּת־מִי *whose daughter?* Gen. 24:23.—Judg. 21:8 מִי אֶחָד מִשִּׁבְטֵי יִשְׂרָאֵל *what one among the tribes of Israel?* comp. 2 Sam. 3:23. Rarely in reference to things, like מָה, Gen. 33:8. Judg. 9:28 וּמִי שְׁכֶם כִּי נַעַבְדֶנּוּ *and what is Shechem that we should serve him?* 13:17.—Also without an interrogation, e. g. Gen. 43:22. hence *whoever,* Judg. 7:3 מִי יָרֵא וְחָרֵד *whoever is fearful and afraid.* Is. 54:15. With אֲשֶׁר following, Ex. 32:33. 2 Sam. 20:11.

2. *how?* (like *qui?* for *quomodo?*) Am. 7:2, 5. Ruth. 3:16. Is. 51:19.

מֵידְבָא proper name of a city in the tribe of Reuben, situated in a plain of the same name. Num. 21:30. Josh. 13:9, 16. 1 Chr. 19:7. According to Is. 15:2, it belonged afterwards to Moab. Otherwise written Μηδαβᾶ, 1 Mac. 9:36. and Μιδάβη, Μηδάβα, Josephi Antiq. XIII. 1. 17. 23. XIV. 2.

מֵיטָב m. verbal from יָטַב, dec. II. b. *the best of any thing.* 1 Sam. 15:9, 15 מֵיטַב הַצֹּאן *the best sheep.* Ex. 22:5 מֵיטַב שָׂדֵהוּ וּמֵיטַב כַּרְמוֹ *the best of his own field, and the best of his own vineyard.* Gen. 47:6 בְּמֵיטַב הָאָרֶץ *in the best part of the land.* Verse 11.

מִיכָאֵל (*who is as God*) *Michael,* proper name of one of the seven archangels before the throne of God. He was the particular patron of the Jewish people. Dan. 10:13, 21. 12:1.

מִיכָה *Micah,* proper name of a

prophet. It is a contraction of מִיכָיְהוּ (*who is as Jehovah.*) Mic. 1:1.

מִיכַל 1. masc. 2 Sam. 17:20 מִיכַל הַמַּיִם *a small brook.* Root מכל, in Arab. *to have little water*, spoken of a well.

2. fem. *Michal*, proper name of a daughter of Saul, and wife of David. 1 Sam. 14:49. 19:11 ff. 2 Sam. 6:16 ff.

מַיִם masc. plur. prim. irreg. const. מֵי, also מֵימֵי, with suff. מֵימֶיךָ.

1. *water* or *waters.* (The singular in Arabic is ماءٌ מא *water.*)—מַיִם חַיִּים *living water*, i. e. fresh, Gen. 26:19. מַיִם קְדֹשִׁים *holy water*, Num. 5:17. Sometimes construed with a verb *preceding* in the singular; with a verb *following*, only in Num. 19:13, 20.—With He local הַמַּיְמָה *to the water.*—Water in which one sinks or is overwhelmed is used to represent adversity, Ps. 18:17. 32:6. 69:2, 3, 16. Job 27:20.

2. i. q. זֶרַע *seed.* Is. 48:1. (Arab. ماءٌ *semen.*) Better *waters* or *fountain*; see Gesenius on Is. 48:1.

מִין m. dec. I. *sort, kind, species.* Gen. 1:11 פְּרִי לְמִינוֹ *fruit after its kind.* Verses 12, 24. Lev. 11:15.

מֵינֶקֶת *a nurse*, see the Hiph. of יָנַק.

מֵיסַךְ 2 K. 16:18 Kethib, i. q. מוּסַךְ, q. v.

מֵיפַעַת Josh. 21:37. Jer. 48:21. and מֵפַעַת Josh. 13:18. a Levitical city in the tribe of Reuben beyond Jordan, subsequently belonging to the Moabites. In the Kethib of Jer. 48:21. it is written מוֹפַעַת.

מִיץ m. dec. I. *a pressing, wringing, churning.* Prov. 30:33. See מוּץ.

מִישׁוֹר m. verbal from יָשַׁר.

1. *a level country, a plain.* Is. 40:4. 42:16. Ps. 143:10. This name is applied particularly to the plain in the tribe of Reuben, near the city מֵידְבָא; hence joined with the article, Deut. 3:10. 4:43. Josh. 13:9, 16, 17, 21. 20:8. Jer. 48:21.

2. *right, righteousness.* Ps. 45:7. As an adv. *righteously.* Ps. 67:5.

מֵישָׁרִים plur. masc. verbal from יָשַׁר, dec. I.

1. *straightness.* Is. 26:7. Hence with בְּ and לְ, as an adv. *aright, smoothly, rectà*, Prov. 23:31. Cant. 7:10.

2. *uprightness, sincerity;* and as an adv. *sincerely*, Cant. 1:4.

3. *righteousness*, as of a judge. Ps. 99:4. בְּמֵישָׁרִים Ps. 9:9. and מֵישָׁרִים Ps. 58:2. *with righteousness, righteously. Right, justice*, generally, Prov. 1:3. 8:6. Ps. 17:2.

4. *unity, peace.*—עָשָׂה מֵישָׁרִים *to make peace*, Dan. 11:6. comp. verse 17. and Mal. 2:6.

מֵיתָר m. found only in the plur. i. q. יֶתֶר no. II. dec. II. b.

1. *string of a bow.* Ps. 21:13.

2. *a tent cord.* Num. 3:37. 4:32. Jer. 10:20.

מַכְאוֹב and מַכְאֹב m. plur. ־ים and ־וֹת, verbal from כָּאַב, dec. I.

1. *pain.* Job 33:19.

2. metaphorically, *sorrow, grief.* Ex. 3:7. Lam. 1:12, 18.

מַכְבִּיר *abundance*, see כָּבַר.

מִכְבָּר m. dec. II. b. *a grate, a lattice-work.* Ex. 27:4. 38:4, 5, 30. See כָּבִיר.

מַכְבֵּר m. 2 K. 8:15. *something woven, a mattress*, here perhaps κωνωπεῖον, *a fly net.* See כָּבִיר.

מַכָּה f. plur. ־ים and ־וֹת, verbal from נָכָה, dec. X.

1. *a smiting.* Deut. 25:3. 2 Chr. 2:9 חִטִּים מַכּוֹת usually rendered as if i. q. חִטֵּי מַכּוֹת *wheat beaten* or *threshed out*, perhaps a corruption of מַכֹּלֶת, as it is called in 1 K. 5:25. [5:11.] Used particularly of the plagues sent by God, Lev. 26:21. Deut. 28:59, 61. 29:21.

2. *an overthrow, slaughter;* in battle, Josh. 10:10, 20. Judg. 11:33. 15:8. or more immediately from God, 1 Sam. 6:19.

3. *a wound.* 1 K. 22:35. Is. 1:6.

מִכְוָה f. verbal from כָּוָה, dec. X. a. *a place* or *spot burnt*. Lev. 13 : 24, 25, 28.

מָכוֹן m. verbal from כון *to stand*, dec. III. a.

1. *a place*. Ezra 2 : 68. Particularly *a dwelling-place* (of Jehovah). Ex. 15 : 17. 1 K. 8 : 23, 39, 43. Ps. 33 : 14.

2. *foundation*. Ps. 89 : 15. 97 : 2. 104 : 5.

מְכוֹנָה and מְכֹנָה f. verbal from כּוּן, dec. X.

1. *a place*. Ezra 3 : 3.

2. *a stand* or *base*, 1 K. 7 : 27—36.

3. proper name of a city in the tribe of Judah. Neh. 11 : 28.

מְכוּנָה f. verbal from כּוּן, dec. X. *a place* or *foundation*. Zech. 5 : 11.

מְכוּרָה f. Ezek. 16 : 3. and מְכוֹרָה 21 : 35. 29 : 14. dec. X. *birth*, *origin*. The etymology is obscure. The Hebrew commentators explain it by מְגוּרָה *a dwelling*. Others derive it from כּוּר i. q. כָּרָה *to dig*, hence *effossiones* for *origines*, by a metaphor taken from mining; comp. Is. 51 : 1.

מָכִיר m. (*sold*) proper name of a son of Manasseh, father of Gilead. Gen. 50 : 25. Hence used poetically for *Manasseh*, Judg. 5 : 13.—The gentile noun is מָכִירִי.

מָכַךְ (kindred with מוּךְ,) *to sink*, *to be overthrown*. Ps. 106 : 43.

Niph. fut. יִמַּךְ, *to sink* or *settle down*, spoken of a building. Ecc. 10 : 18.

Hoph. plur. הֻמְּכוּ for הֻמַּכּוּ *they sink away*. Job 24 : 24.

מִכְלָה m. verbal from כָּלָא *to shut up*, *confine*, which often commutes its א for ה; dec. II. a. *a pen*, *fold*, for sheep. Hab. 3 : 17. Plur. מִכְלְאוֹת Ps. 50 : 9. 78 : 70.

מִכְלוֹל m. verbal from כָּלַל, *perfection*, *perfect beauty*. Ezek. 23 : 12. 38 : 4 לְבֻשֵׁי מִכְלוֹל *perfectly* or *gorgeously apparelled*, *vestiti perfectè*.

מִכְלוֹת plur. fem. verbal from כָּלָה, found only 2 Chr. 4 : 21 מִכְלוֹת זָהָב *perfectiones auri*, i. e. *perfect* or *pure gold*. Comp. כָּלָה adv. *entirely*.

מִכְלָל m. verbal from כָּלַל, dec. II. b. *perfection*. Ps. 50 : 2.

מַכְלֻלִים masc. plur. verbal from כָּלַל, liter. *ornaments*, hence *costly garments*. Ezek. 27 : 24. comp. particularly מִכְלוֹל.

מַכֹּלֶת f. *food*. Once 1 K. 5 : 25. [5 : 11.] a contraction of מַאֲכֹלֶת, or else of the Syriac form מַאְכֹּלֶת, from the root אָכַל.

מִכְמַנִּים masc. plur. dec. VIII. h. *treasures*. Once Dan. 11 : 43. Root כמן, in Syr. and Chald. *to conceal*, *to be concealed*.

מִכְמָס Ezra 2 : 27. מִכְמָשׂ 1 Sam. 13 : 2, 5. מִכְמָשׂ Neh. 11 : 31. (as an appellative, *concealed*, *a treasure*, see כמס,) name of a place in the tribe of Benjamin, according to 1 Sam. 13 : 5. on the east of Beth-aven. In 1 Mac. 9 : 73, it is called Μαχμάς, in Josephus Μαχμά. Antiq. VI. 6. XIII. 2.

מִכְמָר m. Is. 51 : 20. and מַכְמֹר Ps. 141 : 10. *a net*, *snare*. It is i. q. כְּבִיר, מִכְבָּר, מַכְבֵּר (q. v.) by a commutation of מ and ב.

מִכְמֶרֶת f. Hab. 1 : 15, 16. and מִכְמֹרֶת Is. 19 : 8. *a net*, *drag*.

מִכְמָשׂ see מִכְמָס.

מִכְנָס verbal from כָּנַס, found only in the dual or plur. const. מִכְנְסֵי *breeches* (of the priests). Ex. 28 : 42. 39 : 28. Lev. 6 : 3. 16 : 4. Ezek. 44 : 18. Vulg. *feminalia*. According to Josephus (Antiq. III. 8.) they reached only to the middle of the thigh.

מֶכֶס m. (perhaps from כָּסַס, like מֶקֶר from קָרַר,) dec. VI. h. *a tribute*. Num. 31 : 28, 37—41. (Aram. and Arab. ܡܟܣܐ, مَكْس *census*, *vectigal*.) Hence

מִכְסָה f. denom. from מֶכֶס, dec. X.

1. *number*. Ex. 12 : 4.

2. *amount*, *price*. Lev. 27 : 23.

מִכְסֶה m. verbal from כָּסָה, dec. IX.

a. *a covering*, of a tent, Ex. 26:14. 36:19. of a ship, Gen. 8:13.

מְכַסֶּה liter. part. Pi. from כָּסָה, dec. IX. a.

1. *a covering, stragula.* Is. 14:11. 23:18. Also of a ship, Ezek. 27:7.

2. *the fat caul over the inwards, omentum.* Lev. 9:19. Expressed more fully הַחֵלֶב הַמְכַסֶּה אֶת־הַקֶּרֶב Ex. 29:13, 22.

מַכְפֵּלָה f. (*a doubling*) a country near Hebron, where Sarah was buried. Gen. 23:9, 17, 19. 25:9. 49:30. 50:13.

מָכַר, fut. יִמְכֹּר, *to sell.* Gen. 37:27, 28. Construed with בְּ of the price, Ps. 44:13.—*To sell one's daughter*, i. e. to give her in marriage, the father on such occasions receiving a price or portion (מֹהַר) from the bridegroom, Gen. 31:15. Ex. 21:7.—*To sell a people*, i. e. to deliver them to their enemies, spoken of Jehovah, Deut. 32:30. Judg. 2:14 וַיִּמְכְּרֵם בְּיַד אוֹיְבֵיהֶם *and he sold them into the hand of their enemies.* 3:8. 4:2, 9.

Niph. נִמְכַּר 1. *to be sold.* Lev. 25:34. Metaphorically Is. 50:1.

2. *to sell one's self* (for a slave). Lev. 25:39, 42, 47.

Hithpa. 1. *to be sold.* Deut. 28:68.

2. *to sell one's self*, in the phrase הִתְמַכֵּר לַעֲשׂוֹת הָרָע *to sell one's self*, i. e. to give one's self up, *to do iniquity*, 1 K. 21:20, 25. 2 K. 17:17.

Derivatives out of course מִמְכָּר, מִמְכֶּרֶת.

מֶכֶר m. with suff. מִכְרִי, verbal from מָכַר, dec. VI. h.

1. *something presented for sale, merchandise, venum, venale.* Neh. 13:16.

2. *price* or *worth* of any thing. Num. 20:19.

3. prob. *property, substance.* Deut. 18:8.

מַכָּר m. verbal from נָכַר, dec. I. *an acquaintance, friend.* 2 K. 12:6, 8.

מִכְרֶה m. verbal from כָּרָה, dec. IX. a. *a pit, mine.* Zeph. 2:9.

מְכֵרָה f. found only Gen. 49:5. prob. *a sword, weapon.* Hence כְּלֵי חָמָס מְכֵרֹתֵיהֶם *instruments of cruelty (are) their swords.* Jerome: *arma eorum.* The root in that case is supposed to be כּוּר i. q. Arab. كار conj. II. *prostravit;* comp. כָּרָה *to dig, to bore through.* Others make it synonymous with מְגוּרָה (in Ezek.) *a dwelling.* Hence *weapons of violence (are in) their dwellings.* Others explain it *plans, purposes*, from the Ethiop. מכר *consilium cepit;* or *craft, deceit*, from the Arabic verb which signifies *to deceive.*

מִכְשׁוֹל m. verbal from כָּשַׁל, dec. I.

1. *a stumbling block* or *stone.* Lev. 19:14. Is. 8:14 צוּר מִכְשׁוֹל *a stone of stumbling.* 57:14. Metaphorically Ezek. 3:20 וְנָתַתִּי מִכְשׁוֹל לְפָנָיו הוּא יָמוּת *then I will throw a stumbling block before him, and he shall die.* Is. 6:21. Metaphorically, (1.) *a cause of falling* or *of misfortune.* Ezek. 18:30. 44:12. Ps. 119:165. (2.) *a seducement* or *cause of sin.* (Comp. the verb, Mal. 2:8.) Ezek. 7:19. 14:3 מִכְשׁוֹל עֲוֹנָם *their seducement to sin*, i. e. their idols. (3.) *offence of heart, scruple of conscience.* 1 Sam. 25:31.

מַכְשֵׁלָה f. verbal from כָּשַׁל, dec. X.

1. *ruin* (of a state). Is. 3:6.

2. *a cause of stumbling, a seducement to sin.* In the plur. spoken of idols, Zeph. 1:3.

מִכְתָּב m. verbal from כָּתַב, dec. I.

1. *a writing.* Ex. 32:16. Deut. 10:4.

2. *a letter.* 2 Chr. 21:12.

3. *a song.* Is. 38:9, where it occurs as a title. Comp. מִכְתָּם.

מְכִתָּה f. verbal from כָּתַת, dec. X. *a breaking in pieces.* Is. 30:14.

מִכְתָּם m. in the superscriptions of Psalms XVI. LVI. LVII. LVIII. LIX. LX. most prob. i. q. מִכְתָּב Is. 38:9. (by a commutation of ם and ב, see p. 63.) *a writing*, by way of eminence *a song.* Others derive it from כֶּתֶם *gold*, hence *a golden piece, carmen aureum*, a commendatory title; but כֶּתֶם is barely a poetical name for gold, and there appears no special reason in these psalms for this designation.

מִכְתָּשׁ m. verbal from כָּתַשׁ.

1. *a mortar*. Prov. 27:22.

2. Judg. 15:19 prob. *the cavity for the teeth*, in Greek ὀλμίσκος, Lat. *mortariolum*. See Bocharti Hieroz. T. I. p. 202.

3. Zeph. 1:11, probably the name of a place in or near Jerusalem.

מָלֵא, fut. יִמְלָא. intrans. *to be* or *become full*. Josh. 3:15. Construed with an accus. of the thing which fills, Gen. 6:13 מָלְאָה הָאָרֶץ חָמָס *the earth is full of wickedness*. Judg. 16:27 וְהַבַּיִת מָלֵא הָאֲנָשִׁים וְהַנָּשִׁים *and the house was full of men and women*. Job 32:18 כִּי מָלֵתִי מִלִּים *for I am full of words*. 2 K. 6:17. Ps. 10:7. 26:10. 33:5. 48:11. 65:10. 104:24. Is. 11:9. 14:21. 27:6. Jer. 23:10. 46:12. 51:5. Ezek. 9:9. with לְ, Hab. 2:14. with מִן perhaps Is. 2:5. Used also (1.) of time, *to be fulfilled* or *completed*. Gen. 25:24 וַיִּמְלְאוּ יָמֶיהָ לָלֶדֶת *and her time was fulfilled that she should be delivered*. 29:21 כִּי מָלְאוּ יָמָי *for my time is completed*. 50:3 כִּי כֵּן יִמְלְאוּ יְמֵי הַחֲנֻטִים *for so long does the time of embalming last*; (comp. Est. 2:12.) Lev. 8:33. 12:4, 6. Lam. 4:18. Jer. 25:34. (2.) of a desire, *to be fulfilled* or *satisfied*. Ex. 15:9 תִּמְלָאֵמוֹ נַפְשִׁי *my desire respecting them shall be satisfied*, liter. *my soul shall be full of them*. The suffix ־ֵמוֹ is the accus. of the thing filling, which the verb requires after it.

2. trans. *to fill, to make full*. (In Arabic it is written in the preceding signification with med. E; in this with med. A.) (1.) Construed with an accus. of the place filled, Gen. 1:22 מִלְאוּ אֶת־הַמַּיִם בַּיַּמִּים *fill the waters in the seas*. Verse 28. 9:1. Ex. 40:34 וּכְבוֹד יְהוָה מָלֵא אֶת־הַמִּשְׁכָּן *and the glory of Jehovah filled the dwelling*. Verse 35. 1 K. 8:10, 11. Ezek. 10:3. Ex. 32:29. So Est. 7:5 *where is he*, אֲשֶׁר מְלָאוֹ לִבּוֹ לַעֲשׂוֹת כֵּן *whom his heart has filled*, i. e. who has dared, *to do thus*. Comp. Ecc. 8:11. (2.) Spoken of the person filling, as in Piel, and construed with a double accus. of the place filled and of the thing which fills, Ezek. 8:17 כִּי מָלְאוּ אֶת־הָאָרֶץ חָמָס *for they fill the land with wickedness*. 30:11 וּמָלְאוּ אֶת־הָאָרֶץ חָלָל *and they fill the land with the slain*. 28:16. Jer. 16:18 וְתוֹעֲבוֹתֵיהֶם מָלְאוּ אֶת־נַחֲלָתִי *and they fill mine inheritance with their abominations*. Rarely with מִן before the thing filling, Ex. 16:32 מְלֹא הָעֹמֶר מִמֶּנּוּ *fill an omer with it*. Comp. Lev. 9:17.

Note. In Ezek. 28:16, מָלוּ stands for מָלְאוּ. In Job 32:18, מָלֵתִי for מָלֵאתִי. The infin. is מְלֹאת and מְלֹאות.

Niph. 1. *to be filled, to be full*; construed with an accus. of the thing, as in Kal. Gen. 6:11 וַתִּמָּלֵא הָאָרֶץ חָמָס *and the earth was full of wickedness*. Ex. 1:7 וַתִּמָּלֵא הָאָרֶץ אֹתָם *and the land was full of them*. 1 K. 7:14 וַיִּמָּלֵא אֶת־הַחָכְמָה וְאֶת־הַתְּבוּנָה *and he was filled with skill and understanding*. 2 K. 3:17. Construed with מִן, Ezek. 32:6. It has the signification of Kal no. 1. (1.) Ex. 7:25. of Kal no. 1. (2.) Ecc. 6:7.

2. *to come to an end, to perish*. Job 15:32 בְּלֹא יוֹמוֹ תִּמָּלֵא *before his time he* (scil. נַפְשׁוֹ *his soul*) *perishes*; i. q. מָלְאוּ יָמָיו *his days are completed*.

Note. Niphal is perfectly synonymous with Kal no. 1. but the preterite of Kal and the future of Niphal are in more common use.

Pi. מִלֵּא, rarely מִלָּא (Jer. 51:34.) infin. מַלֵּא and מַלֹּאות, fut. יְמַלֵּא, once יְמַלֶּה (Job 8:21.)

1. *to fill*. Spoken of a person filling, and construed with a double accus. of the thing filling and the place filled, like Kal no. 2. (2.) Ex. 28:3. 35:35 מִלֵּא אֹתָם חָכְמַת לֵב *he filled them with a wise heart*. Job 3:15 הַמְמַלְאִים בָּתֵּיהֶם כָּסֶף *who filled their houses with silver*. 22:18. Ps. 107:9. 129:7. Is. 33:5. Jer. 41:9. 1 K. 18:35. More rarely with מִן of the thing filling, Ps. 127:5 *happy is the man* אֲשֶׁר מִלֵּא אֶת־אַשְׁפָּתוֹ מֵהֶם *who fills his quiver with them*. Jer. 51:34. Lev. 9:17. The following metaphorical sig-

nifications and phrases are worthy of notice;

2. *to fulfil, complete,* or *pass* a certain time. Gen. 29 : 27 מַלֵּא שְׁבֻעַ זֹאת *fulfil her week.* Verse 28. Job 39 : 2 תִּסְפֹּר יְרָחִים תְּמַלֶּאנָה *canst thou number the months which they fulfil,* i. e. go with young. Also causat. *to cause to pass* or *be completed,* Dan. 9 : 2 לְמַלֹּאות לְחָרְבוֹת יְרוּשָׁלַםִ שִׁבְעִים שָׁנָה *to make seventy years to pass over the desolations of Jerusalem.* Comp. 2 Chr. 36 : 21.

3. *to satisfy* desire, hunger, or the like. Job 38 : 39. Prov. 6 : 30.

4. *to fulfil* a petition, Ps. 20 : 6. a promise, 1 K. 8 : 15 *who spake with his mouth to David my father, and with his hand hath fulfilled it.* Verse 24. Jer. 44 : 25. a prophecy, 1 K. 2 : 27 לְמַלֵּא אֶת־דְּבַר יְהוָה *to fulfil the word of Jehovah.*

5. *to make complete in number.* Ex. 23 : 26 *I will complete the number of thy days,* i. e. I will cause thee to reach the full term of life. Comp. Is. 65 : 20. —1 Sam. 18 : 27 *and David brought their foreskins,* וַיְמַלְאוּם לַמֶּלֶךְ *and they gave them in full number to the king.* —1 K. 1 : 14 *and I will come after thee* וּמִלֵּאתִי אֶת־דְּבָרָיִךְ *and make thy words complete,* i. e. add what is wanting, supplebo verba tua.

6. מִלֵּא אֶת־יַד־פְּלֹנִי *to fill the hand of any one,* i. e. to transmit to him the office of priest. Ex. 28 : 41. 29 : 9. Lev. 21 : 10. Num. 3 : 3. Judg. 17 : 5.

7. מִלֵּא אֶת־יָדוֹ לַיהוָה *to fill one's hand for Jehovah,* i. e. to give to him liberally. 1 Chr. 29 : 5. 2 Chr. 29 : 31. Comp. Ex. 32 : 29.—2 Chr. 13 : 9 *every one who cometh to present a bullock and seven rams, becomes a priest.*

8. מִלֵּא אֲבָנִים *to set* or *enchase precious stones.* Ex. 28 : 17. 31 : 5. 35 : 33. Pual, Cant. 5 : 14.

9. מִלֵּא יָדוֹ בַקֶּשֶׁת *to fill one's hand with the bow,* i. e. to take the bow into his hand. 2 K. 9 : 24. This phrase differs from מִלֵּא הַקֶּשֶׁת i. q. דָּרַךְ הַקֶּשֶׁת *to bend the bow,* Zech. 9 : 13. So in the Syriac version, ܡܠܘ ܩܫܬܐ Ps. 11 : 2. for the Heb. דָּרַךְ; and in Arab. ملا conj. IV. *valide traxit* arcum.

10. When connected with another verb, it serves sometimes for a periphrasis of the adverb *fully.* Jer. 4 : 5 קִרְאוּ מַלְאוּ *clamate plenâ voce.* Sept. κεκράξατε μέγα. Syr. *clamate altâ voce.* Vulg. *clamate fortiter.* Comp. 12 : 6. The same use of the word is found in Arabic; as املا النظر الي *intense intuitus est* aliquem. Comp. Frähn on Nah. 1 : 10. Here belongs the elliptical construction מִלֵּא אַחֲרֵי יְהוָה for מִלֵּא לָלֶכֶת אַחֲרֵי יְהוָה *to follow Jehovah fully, to yield him perfect obedience,* Num. 14 : 24. 32 : 11, 12. Deut. 1 : 36. Josh. 14 : 8, 9, 14. 1 K. 11 : 6. J. D. Michaëlis incorrectly resolves the phrase thus: *implet quæ sunt post Jehovam,* i. e. vestigia Jehovæ premit. Vulg. simply *sequi Deum.* Sept. for the most part συνακολουθεῖν. Chald. אַשְׁלִים בָּתַר דַּחְלְתָא דַיְיָ *implere post timorem Dei.*

Pu. see Piel no. 8.

Hithpa. *to assemble* or *come together in full number,* construed with עַל, *against* any one. Job 16 : 10. Arabic ملا conj. VI. *concordârunt et unanimes fuerunt* aliquâ in re, construed with على. Comp. מְלֹא; and the Arab. ملا *turba, cœtus.*

מְלָא Chald. *to fill.* Dan. 2 : 35.

Ithpe. *to be filled.* Dan. 3 : 19.

מָלֵא, fem. מְלֵאָה, verbal adj. from מָלֵא, dec. V. e. and X.

1. intrans. *full.*—כֶּסֶף מָלֵא *full price,* Gen. 23 : 9. Generally construed with an accus. Deut. 6 : 11 בָּתִּים מְלֵאִים כָּל־טוּב *houses full of every good thing.* 34 : 9. More rarely with a genitive, Jer. 6 : 11 מְלֵא יָמִים *stricken in years, plenus dierum.* Is. 1 : 21. As a neuter adjective it stands (1.) for the subst. *fulness.* Ps. 73 : 10 מֵי מָלֵא *waters of fulness,* i. e. full streams. (2) for the adv. *plene;* and hence *plenâ voce,* Jer. 12 : 6. *pleno numero,* Nah. 1 : 10.

2. trans. *filling.* Is. 6 : 1. Jer. 23 : 24.

מְלֹא, מְלוֹא, once **מְלוֹ** (Ezek. 41:8.) m. verbal from מָלֵא, dec. I.

1. *that wherewith any space is filled.* (Generally to be expressed in English by the word or syllable *full.*)—מְלֹא חָפְנֵיכֶם *your hands full,* Ex. 9:8. Judg. 6:38 מְלוֹא הַסֵּפֶל מָיִם *a bason-full of water.* Applied also to measures of length, Ezek. 41:8 מְלוֹ הַקָּנֶה *the length of the measuring rod.* 1 Sam. 28:20 *and he fell* מְלֹא קוֹמָתוֹ *his whole length.*

2. *a multitude.* Gen. 48:19 מְלֹא הַגּוֹיִם *a multitude of nations.* Is. 31:4.

מְלֵאָה f. verbal from מָלֵא, dec. X. *fulness, abundance, plenty,* (of grain and wine,) presented as tithes or first fruits. Used particularly of grain, Ex. 22:28. Deut. 22:9. of wine, Num. 18:27.

מִלֻּאָה f. verbal from מָלֵא, dec. X. *a setting* or *enchasing* of precious stones. Ex. 28:17, 20. 39:13. See the root, Piel no. 8.

מִלֻּאִים masc. plur. verbal from מָלֵא, dec. I.

1. *a consecration* or *initiation into the priest's office.* Lev. 8:33. Ex. 29:22, 26, 27, 31. See the root, Piel no. 6.

2. *a consecration-offering,* (comp. e.g. חַטָּאת *a sin,* and *a sin-offering.*) Lev. 7:37. 8:28, 31.

3. i.q. מִלֻּאָה *a setting* of precious stones. Ex. 25:7. 35:9.

מַלְאָךְ m. verbal from obsol. לָאַךְ, dec. II. b.

1. *a messenger.* Job 1:14. 1 Sam. 11:3.

2. particularly *a messenger of God;* and (1.) *an angel,* usually expressed by מַלְאַךְ יְהוָה. Gen. 16:7. 21:17. 22:11, 15. Comp. De Wette Bibl. Dogmatik des A. and N. T. p. 64. 143. (2.) *a prophet,* or *a priest.* Hag. 1:13. Mal. 2:7. 3:1. Ecc. 5:5. (3.) spoken of the Israelitish people. Is. 42:19.

מְלָאכָה (a Syriasm for מַלְאָכָה) f. const. מְלֶאכֶת, with suff. מְלַאכְתְּךָ, plur. const. מַלְאֲכוֹת, verbal from obsol. לָאַךְ, dec. XI. h.

1. *business.* (The root לָאַךְ *to send* has here the kindred signification *to order, to execute.*) Gen. 39:11. Ex. 20:9, 10.

2. *work, labour,* of an artificer, mechanic.—מְלֶאכֶת עוֹר *any thing made of skin,* Lev. 13:48.—מְלֶאכֶת בֵּית יְהוָה *work on the house of Jehovah,* 1 Chr. 23:4. Ezra 3:8.—עֹשֵׂי הַמְּלָאכָה *the labourers,* 2 K. 12:12. אֲשֶׁר עַל הַמְּלָאכָה *the overseers of the work,* 1 K. 5:30. [5:16.] But עֹשֵׂה הַמְּלָאכָה in Neh. 2:16. denotes *one concerned in public business,* and in Est. 3:9. 9:3. perhaps particularly *an overseer of the royal treasury.* Vulg. *arcarius.* Comp. 1 Chr. 29:6.

3. *goods, substance, res alicujus.* Ex. 22:7, 10. Particularly *cattle,* Gen. 33:14. 1 Sam. 15:9. comp. מִקְנֶה.)

מַלְאָכִי m. (*angelical*) *Malachi,* proper name of a prophet. Mal. 1:1. Sept. in the superscription Μαλαχίας, in the text ἄγγελος. Vulg. *Malachias.*

מַלְאֲכוּת f. const. מַלְאֲכוּת, denom. from מַלְאָךְ, dec. III. a. *a message.* Hag. 1:13.

מִלֵּאת f. Cant. 5:12. *fulness, perfect beauty.*

מַלְבּוּשׁ m. verbal from לָבַשׁ, dec. I. *a garment,* i.q. לְבוּשׁ. 2 K. 10:22.

מַלְבֵּן m. (denom. from לְבֵנָה *a brick,*) *a brick-kiln.* Jer. 43:9. Nah. 3:14.

מִלָּה f. plur. ־ִים and ־ִין, verbal from מָלַל, dec. X.

1. *a word, speech,* (synonymous with דָּבָר,) in Aramean the common word, but in Hebrew used only in poetry. Prov. 23:9. Ps. 19:5. 139:4. 2 Sam. 23:2. Also *a proverb, by-word,* Job 30:9 וָאֱהִי לָהֶם לְמִלָּה *and I am to them for a by-word.*

2. *a thing,* like דָּבָר. Job 32:11.

מִלָּה f. Chald. emphat. מִלְּתָא, plur. מִלִּין.

1. *a word, speech.* Dan. 4:28, 30. [4:31, 33.] 5:15.

2. *a thing.* Dan. 2:8, 15, 17.

מְלוֹ, מְלוֹא, see **מְלֹא.**

מְלֻאִים see מִלּוּאִים.

מִלּוֹא m. name of the fortress at Jerusalem, or of some part of the fortifications. 2 Sam. 5 : 9. 1 K. 9 : 15, 24. 11 : 27. 1 Chron. 11 : 8. 2 Chr. 32 : 5. See Hamelsveld Bibl. Geographie, Th. 2. p. 35 ff. Prob. the same with בֵּית מִלּוֹא 2 K. 12 : 21. But *Millo* Judg. 9 : 6, 20. is prob. different.

מַלּוּחַ m. in Greek ἅλιμος, *atriplex halimus*, Linn. a plant resembling lettuce, the green leaves of which, either raw or boiled, furnished food for poor people. Job 30 : 4.

מְלוּכָה f. verbal from מָלַךְ, *a kingdom*. —עִיר הַמְּלוּכָה *the royal city*, 2 Sam. 12 : 26. זֶרַע הַמְּלוּכָה *the royal line*, Jer. 41 : 1. Dan. 1 : 3. עָשָׂה מְלוּכָה *to exercise dominion, to rule*, 1 K. 21 : 7.

מָלוֹן m. verbal from לוּן, dec. III. a. *a lodging-place, an inn*. Gen. 42 : 27. 43 : 21. Ex. 4 : 24.

מְלוּנָה fem. of מָלוֹן.

1. *a shed* or *lodge*, for the watchman in a garden. Is. 1 : 8.

2. particularly *a hanging bed*, such as travellers, or the keepers of gardens and vineyards, in hot climates, suspend from high trees, for safety by night from wild beasts. Is. 24 : 20. See Niebuhr's Description de l'Arabie.

I. מָלַח (in Arab. with ح) *to salt*. Lev. 2 : 13.

Pu. pass. Ex. 30 : 35.

Hoph. הָמְלַח, infin. absol. הָמְלֵחַ, *to be washed with salt water*, spoken of a new-born child. Ezek. 16 : 4.

II. מָלַח (in Arab. with خ) *to depart quickly, to pass away*. Only in Niph. *dispelli*. Is. 51 : 6 כִּי־שָׁמַיִם כֶּעָשָׁן נִמְלָחוּ *for the heavens pass away like smoke*.

I. מֶלַח m. dec. VI. *salt*.—יָם הַמֶּלַח *the salt sea*, see יָם.—גֵּיא מֶלַח *the valley of salt*, see גַּי.—בְּרִית מֶלַח Num. 18 : 19. 2 Chr. 13 : 5. (comp. Lev. 2 : 13.) *a covenant of salt, fœdus salitum*, i. e. a solemn covenant, because salt is sacred, and the contracting parties in a covenant partake of it.—נְצִיב מֶלַח *a pillar of salt*, Gen. 19 : 26.

II. מֶלַח or מָלָח found only in the plur. מְלָחִים *torn garments, rags, panni*. Jer. 38 : 11, 12. Root ملخ in Arab. and Ethiop. *to pull, to tear*.

מְלַח Chald. denom. from מְלַח, *to eat salt*. Ezra 4 : 14.

מְלַח Chald. *salt*. Ezra 4 : 14.

מַלָּח m. (with Kamets impure,) denom. from מֶלַח i. q. ἅλς *the salt sea*, dec. I. *a mariner*. Ezek. 27 : 9, 26, 29. Jon. 1 : 5.

מְלֵחָה f. verbal from מָלַח, *salted*, of course *unfruitful land*. Job 39 : 6. Ps. 107 : 34. Joined with אֶרֶץ, Jer. 17 : 6. Comp. Virg. Æn. II. 238. *Salsa tellus —Frugibus infelix*.

מִלְחָמָה f. once מִלְחֶמֶת (1 Sam. 13 : 22.) with suff. מִלְחַמְתִּי, plur. מִלְחָמוֹת, verbal from לָחַם, dec. XI. f.

1. *war*.—עָשָׂה מִלְחָמָה *to carry on war*, construed with אֵת (אֶת) and with עִם, *with* any one. Gen. 14 : 2. Deut. 20 : 12, 20.—הָיְתָה מִלְחָמָה בְּ *there was war with* any one, 2 Sam. 21 : 15, 20. אִישׁ מִלְחָמָה *a man of war, a warrior*, Num. 31 : 27. also, *an enemy in war*, 1 Chr. 18 : 10.

2. *battle, slaughter*. Ex. 13 : 17. Job 39 : 25.

3. by a metonymy, *a weapon*, i. q. כְּלֵי מִלְחָמָה. Ps. 76 : 4. comp. Hos. 1 : 7.

מָלַט in Kal not used. Liter. *to be smooth, slippery;* hence *to slip away, to escape*.

Pi. מִלֵּט and מִלַּט 1. *to let escape* (from danger), *to deliver*. Job 6 : 23. 29 : 12. מִלֵּט נַפְשׁוֹ *to save one's life*, 1 Sam. 19 : 11. 2 Sam. 19 : 6.

2. *ova parere*. Is. 34 : 15. See Hiph. no. 2.

Hiph. 1. *to deliver*. Once Is. 31 : 5.

2. *to bear, bring forth*. Is. 66 : 7.

Niph. 1. *to be delivered*. Ps. 22 : 6.

More frequently reflex. *to deliver one's self, to escape.* Gen. 19:19. 1 Sam. 30:17.

2. *to hasten, to go quickly,* (without the idea of flight.) 1 Sam. 20:29 אִמָּלְטָה נָּא *let me, I pray thee, go quickly.*

Hithpa. i.q. Niph. Job 19:20 וָאֶתְמַלְּטָה בְּעוֹר שִׁנָּי (*scarcely*) *am I escaped with the skin of my teeth,* a proverbial phrase for *there is scarcely a sound spot in my body.*—Job 41:11 [41:19] *sparks of fire fly out.*

מֶלֶט m. *mortar, cement.* Jer. 43:9. This word is found in some occidental languages, as in Greek *μάλθα, soft wax, pitch,* to spread over the bottoms of vessels; in Ital. malta, *mud, clay.* Root מְלַט Syr. ܡܠܛ *to spread over.*

מְלִילָה f. dec. X. *an ear of corn.* Once Deut. 23:26. Prob. from מלל=מול, נָמַל. Job 24:24. *to cut off* ears of corn.

מְלִיצָה f. verbal from לִיץ.

1. liter. *an interpretation,* hence *what needs an interpretation, an enigma, riddle, dark saying.* Prov. 1:6.

2. *a satire.* Hab. 2:6.

מָלַךְ, fut. יִמְלֹךְ. 1. *to be king, to reign;* construed with בְּ or עַל. Josh. 13:12, 21. Judg. 4:2. 1 Sam. 12:14.

2. *to become king.* 2 Sam. 15:10.

Hiph. *to cause to be king;* construed with an accus. 1 Sam. 15:35. 1 K. 1:43. with a dative, 1 Chr. 29:22.

Hoph. הָמְלַךְ *to be made king.* Dan. 9:1.

Niph. *to consult, to take counsel.* Neh. 5:7. In Syr. the predominant meaning. Compare the Latin *consulere* and *consul.*

Deriv. out of course מַמְלָכוּת, מַמְלָכָה, מְלוּכָה.

מֶלֶךְ m. with suff. מַלְכִּי, plur. מְלָכִים, once מְלָכִין (Prov. 31:3.) and once with Aleph as a mater lectionis מַלְאָכִים (2 Sam. 11:1.) verbal from מָלַךְ, dec. VI. a. *a king.*—מֶלֶךְ מְלָכִים *the king of kings,* a title of the king of Babylon, Ezek. 26:7. Spoken frequently of Jehovah, Ps. 5:3. 44:5. 48:3. 68:25. Is. 8:21. also of false gods, Am. 5:26. comp. Zeph. 1:5. Comp. *βασιλεὺς,* Hom. Il. γ. 351. π. 233.

מֶלֶךְ m. Chald. emph. מַלְכָּא, מַלְכָּה, plur. מַלְכִין, also מְלָכִים Ezra 4:13. *a king,* as in Heb.—מֶלֶךְ מַלְכַיָּא *the king of kings,* Dan. 2:36, 37. Ezra 7:12. a title of the Persian and other Asiatic monarchs; in Pers. *Shahinshah.* See Brissonius De regio Persarum Principatu, § 3.—In Dan. 7:17, מַלְכִין stands for *kingdoms.*

מְלַךְ m. Chald. with suff. מִלְכִּי, *advice, counsel.* Dan. 4:24. [4:27.]

מֹלֶךְ always joined with the article הַמֹּלֶךְ, (*the king,*) *Molech,* proper name of an idol of the Ammonites, to which also the Hebrews sometimes offered human sacrifices in the valley of Hinnom. Lev. 18:21. 20:2 ff. 1 K. 11:7. 2 K. 23:10. Aqu. Symm. Theod. Vulg. Μολὸχ, *Moloch.* His brazen image, the Rabbins say, resembled an ox as to the head, and a man as to the other parts. It was hollow within, and made hot beneath; and the children to be sacrificed were placed in its arms. A similar description is given of an image at Carthage, by the name of Saturn; see Carpzov Apparat. Antiqu. Sac. Cod. p. 87. 404.

מַלְכֹּדֶת f. verbal from לָכַד, dec. XIII. f. *a net, snare,* for taking animals. Job 18:10.

מַלְכָּה fem. of מֶלֶךְ, dec. XII. a. *a queen.* Est. 1:9 ff. 7:1 ff. Plur. מְלָכוֹת *queens, sultanas of princely blood,* different from פִּלַגְשִׁים, Cant. 6:8, 9.

מַלְכָּה Chald. *idem.* Dan. 5:12.

מַלְכוּ f. Chald. const. מַלְכוּת, emph. מַלְכוּתָא.

1. *reign, rule, dominion.* Dan. 4:28. [4:31.] Ezra 4:24. 6:15.

2. *a kingdom.* Dan. 2:39, 41, 44. Plur. מַלְכְוָתָא Dan. 2:44. 7:23.

מַלְכוּת f. denom. from מֶלֶךְ.

1. *royalty, royal dignity,* or *authority, reign,* used almost exclusively in the

later writers, and equivalent to מַמְלָכָה in the more ancient. 1 Chr. 12:23 מַלְכוּת שָׁאוּל *the royal authority of Saul.* Dan. 1:1. *in the third year* לְמַלְכוּת יְהוֹיָקִים *of the reign of Jehoiakim.* 2:1. 8:1. 1 Chr. 26:31. —בֵּית הַמַּלְכוּת *the royal palace,* (otherwise called בֵּית־הַמֶּלֶךְ,) Est. 1:9. 2:16. 5:1 וַתִּלְבַּשׁ אֶסְתֵּר מַלְכוּת *and Esther put on the royal garments.*

2. *a kingdom.*—מַלְכוּת יְהוּדָה *the kingdom of Judah,* 2 Chr. 11:17. מַלְכוּת כַּשְׂדִּים *the kingdom of the Chaldeans,* Dan. 9:1. Plur. מַלְכֻיוֹת Dan. 8:22.

מַלְכִּי־צֶדֶק m. (*king of righteousness*) *Melchisedek,* proper name of a king of Salem, and priest of Jehovah. Gen. 14:18. Ps. 110:4.

מַלְכָּם i. q. מִלְכֹּם and מֹלֶךְ, an idol of the Ammonites and Moabites. Jer. 49:1, 3. Zeph. 1:5. (In Am. 1:15, the word is an appellative, and does not belong here.) As the proper name of a person, 1 Chr. 8:9.

מִלְכֹּם *Milcom* i. q. *Molech,* an idol of the Ammonites. 1 K. 11:5, 33. 2 K. 23:13.

מְלֶכֶת f. found only Jer. 7:18. 44:17, 18, 19, 25 מְלֶכֶת הַשָּׁמַיִם, an object of idolatrous worship to the Israelitish women. According to the Sept. in Jer. XLIV. and the Vulg. in all the passages, i. q. מַלְכַּת הַשָּׁמַיִם *the queen of heaven,* perhaps *Astarte, the moon.* Another explanation is followed by many MSS. which read in full מלאכת, from which the punctuation of the common reading appears to be derived, namely, *worship of heaven,* i. e. the abstract being put for the concrete, the god or goddess of heaven. Chald. *stella cœli.* Syr. *cultus cœli.*

מָלַל as in Aram. *to speak.* In Kal only Prov. 6:13.

Pi. *idem.* Job 8:2. Ps. 106:2 מִי יְמַלֵּל גְּבוּרוֹת יְהוָה *who can speak the mighty deeds of Jehovah?*

Deriv. מִלָּה.—For the forms יִמַּל and יְמוֹלֵל, see נָמַל and מוּל.

מַלֵּל Chald. found only in Pa. מַלֵּל *to speak.* Dan. 7:8, 11, 20, 25.

מַלְמַד m. dec. II. b. Judg. 3:31 מַלְמַד הַבָּקָר *an ox-goad,* for driving oxen. Root لمد i. q. لدم *to strike, smite.*

מָלַץ *to be smooth.* Comp. the kindred root מָלַט. Used only metaphorically, *to be pleasant,* Ps. 119:103.

מֶלְצַר, with the article הַמֶּלְצַר, Dan. 1:11, 16. *a steward,* οἰκονόμος, in the Babylonian court. It is usually considered a proper name; but the prefixing of the article, and its etymological meaning, (comp. Pers. مالسر *præfectus palatii seu thesauri,*) are in favour of its being an appellative.

מָלַק *to break,* but without separating entirely. Lev. 1:15. 5:8. Others: *to pinch off.* Sept. ἀποκνίζω.

מַלְקוֹחַ m. verbal from לָקַח, dec. I.

1. *prey, booty, spoil;* but strictly only of living animals. Hence Num. 31:13 אֶת־הַשְּׁבִי וְאֶת־הַמַּלְקוֹחַ וְאֶת־הַשָּׁלָל *captivos et prædam et exuvias.* In verses 11, 27, 32, it includes *the captives* (שְׁבִי.) Is. 49:24, 25.

2. מַלְקוֹחַיִם *the jaws, fauces.* Ps. 22:16.

מַלְקוֹשׁ m. verbal from לָקַשׁ, *the latter rain,* which in Palestine falls in the months of March and April, before the harvest. Deut. 11:14. Jer. 3:3. 5:24. Comp. יוֹרֶה and מוֹרֶה *the early rain.*

מֶלְקָחַיִם masc. dual, verbal from לָקַח.

1. *pincers, tongs.* Is. 6:6.

2. *snuffers.* 1 K. 7:49. 2 Chr. 4:21.

מַלְקָחַיִם masc. dual, dec. I. i. q. מֶלְקָחַיִם no. 2. Ex. 25:38. 37:23.

מֶלְתָּחָה f. *a chamber in which clothes are kept, a wardrobe.* 2 K. 10:22. (In Ethiop. ለብሐ *vestis byssina.*)

מַלְתָּעוֹת plur. fem. dec. X. *eyeteeth, dentes canini.* Ps. 58:7. See מְתַלְּעוֹת.

מַמְּגֻרָה f. (with Dagesh euphonic,) dec. X. Joel 1:17. *a storehouse, gra-*

nary, corn-loft. Derived either from מָגַר Arab. *vendidit,* or directly from the subst. מְגוּרָה *a storehouse,* by prefixing מ; like דּוּר, מְדוּרָה *a pile of wood;* מְרַאֲשׁוֹת, מַרְגְּלוֹת, etc.

מְמַדִּים masc. plur. dec. VIII. verbal from מָדַד, *the measures* or *measuring rods.* Job 38:5.

מָמוֹת found only in the plur. מְמוֹתִים, verbal from מוּת, dec. III. a.

1. *deaths, mortes.* Jer. 16:4. Ezek. 28:8.

2. 2 K. 11:2 Kethib, as a concrete, *the killed.* In the Keri מוּמָתִים.

מַמְזֵר m. found only Deut. 23:3. Zech. 9:6. according to the Rabbins and the ancient versions in Deut. *a bastard.* The etymology is doubtful. Perhaps we may compare מזר Syr. ܡܙܪ in Aph. *to despise,* in Arab. by transposition, מרז *idem.*

מִמְכָּר m. verbal from מָכַר, dec. II. b.

1. *a sale.* Lev. 25:27, 29, 50.

2. *something sold.* Lev. 25:25 מִמְכַּר אָחִיו *that which his brother hath sold.* Verses 28, 33. Ezek. 7:13.

3. *something for sale, venale.* Lev. 25:14. Neh. 13:20.

מִמְכֶּרֶת fem. of מִמְכָּר, *a sale* or *selling.* Lev. 25:42.

מַמְלָכָה f. const. מַמְלֶכֶת, with suff. מַמְלַכְתִּי, plur. מַמְלָכוֹת, verbal from מָלַךְ, dec. XI. f.

1. *a kingdom.*

2. *royal authority* or *dominion, reign.* 1 K. 11:11. 14:8.—עִיר הַמַּמְלָכָה *the royal city,* Josh. 10:2. 1 Sam. 27:5.—בֵּית הַמַּמְלָכָה *the royal residence,* Am. 7:13.

מַמְלָכוּת f. const. מַמְלְכוּת, verbal from מָלַךְ, dec. III. c. *idem.* Josh. 13:12 ff.

מִמְסָךְ m. verbal from מָסַךְ, *mixed wine, spiced wine.* Prov. 23:30. Is. 65:11.

מֶמֶר m. *bitterness, affliction, grief.* Prov. 17:25. Root מָרַר; comp. תֶּקֶם from קוּם, חֶגֶל from גָּלַל, מֶסֶס.

מַמְרֵא Gen. 23:17, 19. 35:27. *Mamre,* and אֵלֹנֵי מַמְרֵא 13:18. 18:1. *the turpentine trees of Mamre,* a country not far from Hebron, so called from מַמְרֵא an Amorite, and confederate with Abraham. 14:13, 24.

מַמְרֹרִים masc. plur. (with Dagesh euphonic,) verbal from מָרַר, *bitterness, bitter lot.* Job 9:18.

מִמְשַׁח m. *extension, measure.* Ezek. 28:14 כְּרוּב מִמְשַׁח Vulg. *Cherub extentus,* i. e. Cherub alis extentis. Comp. Ex. 25:20. Root משׁח in Aram. *to stretch out, extend.*

מִמְשָׁל m. verbal from מָשַׁל no. I. dec. II. b.

1. *dominion.* Dan. 11:3, 5.

2. plur. מִמְשָׁלִים 1 Chr. 26:6. as a concrete, *rulers, princes.*

מֶמְשָׁלָה f. verbal from מָשַׁל no. I. *dominion.* Mic. 4:8.

מֶמְשֶׁלֶת f. plur. מֶמְשָׁלוֹת, מַמְשְׁלוֹת, verbal from מָשַׁל no. I. dec. XIII. a.

1. *rule, dominion.* Gen. 1:16. Ps. 136:8, 9.

2. *a kingdom, a dominion.* 2 K. 20:13.

3. as a concrete, *leaders, princes, chiefs, the general staff.* 2 Chr. 32:9. See מִמְשָׁל no. 2.

מִמְשָׁק m. dec. II. b. found only Zeph. 2:9 מִמְשַׁק חָרוּל *a place where nettles grow, possessio urticæ.* Root מָשַׁק, prob. *to possess;* see מֶשֶׁק.

מַמְתַּקִּים masc. plur. from מָתַק, dec. VIII. *sweetness.* Cant. 5:16.

מָן m. with suff. מַנְךָ (in some MSS. without Dagesh) Neh. 9:20. dec. VIII. *the Arabian manna,* a sweet gum, which, in Arabia and other parts of the east, especially in the months of July and August, before sunrise, and more frequently after a heavy mist, oozes out of the leaves of several trees, particularly of the hedysarum alhagi, Linn. and is gathered by the inhabitants in small transparent kernels. Ex. 16:31 ff. Num. 11:6. Comp. Niebuhr's Description de l'Arabie. J. E. Faber Historia

Mannæ in Faber and Reiske Opusc. med. Arab. p. 121. (According to Ex. 16:14, 31, it derives its name from מָן *what?* which word, however, occurs only in Chaldaic.)

מַן, before Makkeph מַן־, Chald.

1. *who? what?* Ezra 5:3, 9. Dan. 3:15. Without an interrogation, Ezra 5:4.

2. מַן־דִּי *whosoever, quicunque.* Dan. 3:6, 11. 4:14. [4:17.]

מֵן m. plur. מִנִּים, *a string.* Ps. 150:4. Syr. ܡܢܝܢ. Here perhaps also Ps. 45:9 מִנִּי (as an uncommon plural form for מִנִּים, although the existence of such a form is not fully demonstrated.)

מִן and מִ־, before gutturals מֵ, more rarely מִ, with suff. מִמֶּנִּי, (in poetry מִנִּי, מֶנִּי;) מִמְּךָ, מִמֵּךְ; מִמֶּנּוּ, (in poetry מִנְּהוּ, מֶנְהוּ;) מִמֶּנּוּ; מִכֶּם; מֵהֶם; a prefix preposition.

1. *from.* (Most probably originally a noun from מנן in Arab. *to divide, allot,* (comp. מנה,) and signifying *a part;* whence perhaps in Ps. 68:24 לְשׁוֹן כְּלָבֶיךָ מֵאֹיְבִים מִנֵּהוּ liter. *the tongue of thy dogs, from the enemies is its portion.* Hence מִמֶּנִּי liter. *à parte meâ,* i. e. à me.)—מִבֶּטֶן *from the womb, from one's birth,* Judg. 16:17. מִמְּךָ וָהֵנָּה *on this side of thee,* 1 Sam. 20:21. מִמְּךָ וָהָלְאָה *on that side of thee,* verse 22.—מִן....עַד, מִן....וְעַד *from ....to, as well....as also,* after a negation, *neither....nor,* Gen. 14:23 אִם מִחוּט וְעַד שְׂרוֹךְ נַעַל *neither a thread nor a shoe-latchet,* 31:24. Ex. 22:3. Deut. 29:10.—Before מִן, we must often supply the word *some,* Lev. 5:9 מִדָּם *some of the blood.* Ex. 17:5 מִזִּקְנֵי יִשְׂרָאֵל *some of the elders of Israel.* Dan. 11:5.

2. *of, out of.* Ps. 45:14 מִמִּשְׁבְּצוֹת זָהָב *of cloth wrought with gold.*

3. *at, in, on, by,* in specifications of time and place.—מִצַּד *by the side of,* Deut. 31:26. מִקֵּץ *at the end of,* Deut. 15:1. מִשְּׁנַת־הַיֹּבֵל *in the year of jubilee,* Lev. 27:17. מִשְּׁלֹשׁ חֳדָשִׁים *after three months,* Gen. 38:24. מִמַּעַל *above,* Deut. 5:8. מִתַּחַת *beneath,* 1 K. 8:23. More frequently followed by לְ; as מִמַּעַל לְ *above,* Dan. 12:6. מִחוּץ לְ־ *without,* Lev. 9:11.

4. *on account of, concerning, de.* Lev. 6:11 [6:18] מֵאִשֵּׁי יְהוָה *concerning the offerings of Jehovah.* Deut. 7:7 מֵרֻבְּכֶם *on account of your multitude.*

5. *towards, to, versus.* מִקֶּדֶם *towards the east,* Gen. 13:11. comp. Judg. 7:1. מֵרָחוֹק *to a distance,* Prov. 7:19. Is. 22:3. 23:6.

6. *against.*—חָטָא מִן *to sin against,* עָמַד מִן *to stand against,* Dan. 11:8. Deut. 33:7.

7. *before, in presence of.*—יָרֵא מִן *to fear before* any one. Often synonymous with לִפְנֵי, Nah. 1:5 הָרִים רָעֲשׁוּ מִמֶּנּוּ *mountains tremble before him.* Num. 32:22 נְקִיִּם מֵיְהוָה וּמִיִּשְׂרָאֵל *innocent before Jehovah and before Israel.* Gen. 3:14 *be accursed in presence of all cattle and all the beasts of the field.* 4:11 *be accursed before the earth,* i. e. let the world regard thee as accursed.

8. *more than, præ.* Judg. 2:19 הִשְׁחִיתוּ מֵאֲבוֹתָם *they sinned more than their fathers.* Jer. 5:3. Hence it is used in comparisons, to express the comparative degree, as טוֹב מִזָּהָב *better than gold.* Sometimes the tertium comparationis is omitted, as Job 11:17 מִצָּהֳרַיִם יָקוּם חֶלֶד *more (clear) than the noon-day rises thy life.* Ps. 62:10.

9. *by, through,* expressing the efficient cause. Job 7:14. Cant. 3:10. Ecc. 12:11.

10. *without.* Job 11:15 מִמּוּם *without spot.* 21:9 מִפָּחַד *without fear.*

11. before an infin. (1.) *because.* מֵאַהֲבַת יְהוָה אֶתְכֶם *because Jehovah loved you,* Deut. 7:8. (2.) *since that.* 2 Chr. 31:10. (3.) usually *so that....not.* Gen. 27:1 *his eyes were dim* מֵרְאֹת *so that he could not see.* Ex. 14:5 מֵעָבְדֵנוּ *that they should not serve us.* 1 Sam. 8:7. Is. 24:10. The infin. הֱיוֹת is sometimes to be supplied, as 1 Sam. 15:23 *he has rejected thee* מִמֶּלֶךְ *from being king,* i. e. that thou be no longer king. 1 K. 15:13. Jer. 2:25. 48:2 נַכְרִיתֶנָּה מִגּוֹי *let us cut it off from being a nation.*

12. before a future, as a conj. *that*

not, lest. Deut. 33:11 מִן יְקוּמוּן Sept. μὴ ἀναστήσονται. Vulg. *non consurgant.*

The following combinations are worthy of notice; (1.) מֵאַחַר and מֵאַחֲרֵי *from behind.* 2 Sam. 7:8 מֵאַחַר הַצֹּאן *from behind,* i. e. from following, *the sheep.* (2.) מֵאֵצֶל *from the side of* any one, *from* any one. 1 Sam. 17:30. 1 K. 3:20. (3.) מֵאֵת i. q. מֵעִם *from the side of,* also simply *from.* Job 2:10. Ex. 27:21 *let this be an eternal statute* מֵאֵת בְּנֵי יִשְׂרָאֵל *on the part of the children of Israel.* (4.) מִבֵּין *from between, out of;* see בֵּין. (5.) מִבַּעַד *idem;* see בַּעַד. (6.) מִנֶּגֶד *from over against.* (7.) מֵעַל *from above, from upon;* see עַל. (8.) מֵעִם *from with;* see עִם. So in Chald. מִן־קֳדָם, מִן־לְוָת.

Note. The force of מִן is sometimes, though more rarely, entirely lost; as מֵאַחֲרֵי *after;* מֵאֵצֶל *with;* מֵעַל *beside,* Jer. 36:21. As synonymous with מִן we find לְמִן, לְמִנִּי, Judg. 19:30. Ex. 9:18.

מִן Chald. *idem.*—מִן־דִּי *because, since,* Dan. 3:22.—מִן־יַצִּיב, מִן־קְשֹׁט *certainly, truly,* Dan. 2:8, 47. With suff. מִנִּי, מִנָּה, מִנֵּהּ, מִנְּהוֹן.

מְנָא Chald. see **מְנָה**

מְנָאוֹת, see **מְנָת**.

מַנְגִּינָה f. verbal from נָגַן, dec. X. *a satire,* i. q. נְגִינָה. Lam. 3:63.

מִנְדָּה f. Chald. i. q. מִדָּה (by a resolution of the Dagesh forte into Nun), *tribute, custom.* Ezra 4:13. 7:24. Root מדד.

מַנְדַּע m. Chald. i. q. Heb. מַדָּע (by a resolution of the Dagesh forte into Nun.) Root יְדַע *to know,* fut. יִנְדַּע.

1. *knowledge, intelligence.* Dan. 2:21. 5:12.

2. *understanding, mental faculties.* Dan. 4:31, 33. [4:34, 36.]

מָנָה 1. *to number, to count;* e. g. a people. 1 Chr. 21:1, 17. 27:24.

2. *to levy, muster,* an army. 1 K. 20:25.

3. *to appoint.* Is. 65:12.

Niph. 1. *to be numbered, counted.* Gen. 13:16. Ecc. 1:15.

2. *to be reckoned, accounted.* Is. 53:12.

Pi. 1. *to appoint, assign;* construed with לְ. Dan. 1:5. Job 7:3. Ps. 61:8 מַן יִנְצְרֻהוּ *appoint* or *grant that they may preserve him.*

2. *to appoint, destine, order;* spoken of God. Jon. 2:1. 4:6, 7, 8.

3. *to set* or *appoint over* any thing. Dan. 1:11.

Pu. pass. 1 Chr. 9:29.

מְנָה or **מְנָא** Chald. *to count, number.* Dan. 5:26. Part. pass. מְנֵא *numbered,* verses 25, 26.

Pa. מַנִּי *to appoint* to an office. Dan. 2:24, 49. 3:12. Ezra 7:25.

מָנֶה m. dec. IX. b. (Arab. مَنٌّ, Syr. ܡܢܝܐ;) *a maneh,* a Hebrew weight, which according to 1 K. 10:17. comp. 2 Chr. 9:16. contained 100 shekels. Another statement is found in Ezek. 45:12 *twenty shekels, five and twenty shekels, fifteen shekels, shall be your maneh.* We may supply between these numbers either *and* or *or.* In the first case we have one maneh of 60 shekels; in the latter 3 different manehs of 20, 25, and 15 shekels.

מָנָה verbal from מָנָה, dec. X. and XI. a.

1. *a part, portion.* Ex. 29:26. Lev. 7:33. Particularly of food. 1 Sam. 1:4.—שָׁלַח מָנוֹת *to send portions,* from a banquet, Neh. 8:10, 12.

2. i. q. חֵלֶק *lot, destiny.* Jer. 13:25.

מֹנֶה found only in the plur. מֹנִים *times,* Lat. *vices.* Gen. 31:7, 41. Liter. *parts,* (from מָנָה *to number;*) comp. יָד no. 7.

מִנְהָג m. verbal from נָהַג, dec. II. b. *a driving* of a chariot. 2 K. 9:20.

מִנְהָרָה f. dec. X. *a hole, cavern.* Judg. 6:2. Root נהר in Arab. *to dig.*

מָנוֹד m. verbal from נוּד, dec. III. a. Ps. 44:15 מְנוֹד רֹאשׁ *a shaking of the head,* i. e. an object at which the head is shaken.

מָנוֹחַ m. plur. מְנוֹחִים Ps. 116:7. verbal from נוּחַ, dec. III. f.

1. *a resting-place.* Gen. 8:9. Deut. 28:65.

2. *rest.* Lam. 1:3. Also *rest* or *provision* for a woman by marriage, Ruth 3:1.

מְנוּחָה fem. of מָנוֹחַ, dec. X.

1. *a resting-place.* Num. 10:33. Mic. 2:10.

2. *rest, state of quietness.* Ruth 1:9. (comp. 3:1.) Jer. 45:3. — מֵי מְנוּחוֹת *still waters,* Ps. 23:2. Particularly *the quiet possession of Canaan,* Ps. 95:11. Deut. 12:9.

מָנוֹן m. according to the Jewish commentators, *a child, soboles,* (see נין and נִין.) Prov. 29:21 *if any one delicately bringeth up his servant from a child,* וְאַחֲרִיתוֹ יִהְיֶה מָנוֹן *then shall he afterwards become his son.* Luth. *so will er darnach ein Junker seyn.* Others: *ingratitude,* from מנן in Arab. *benefacta exprobravit.*

מָנוֹס, with suff. מְנוּסִי, verbal from נוּס, dec. III. f.

1. *a flight.* Jer. 46:5.

2. *a refuge.* Ps. 142:5. Job 11:20.

מְנוּסָה fem. of מָנוֹס, dec. X. *a flight.* Lev. 26:36. Is. 52:12.

מָנוֹר m. dec. III. a. *jugum.* (Syr. and Arab. נִיר *jugum aratorium* et *textorium.*)—מְנוֹר אֹרְגִים *a weaver's beam,* 1 Sam. 17:7. 2 Sam. 21:19.

מְנוֹרָה f. verbal from נוּר, dec. X. *a candlestick,* particularly *the great candlestick* or *chandelier* in the tabernacle of the congregation. Ex. 25:31 ff. 30:27. 31:8. 37:17. 39:37.

מִנְּזָרִים masc. plur. (with Dagesh euphonic,) dec. I. Nah. 3:17. *chiefs, princes, optimates,* i. q. נָזִיר Gen. 49:26. Deut. 33:16.

מִנְחָה f. verbal from מנח in Arab. *to give,* dec. XII. b.

1. *a present, gift.* Gen. 32:14.

2. particularly *a present* or *offering* to the deity. Gen. 4:3, 4, 5. In the Mosaic ritual *a meat* or *a drink offering,* such as was brought with the animal sacrifice, Lev. 2:1, 4. 5:6. 6:7 ff. 7:9. Hence זֶבַח וּמִנְחָה *sacrifice and offering,* Ps. 40:7.

3. *a tribute, custom,* to a ruling nation. 2 Sam. 8:2, 6. 1 K. 5:1. [4:21.] 2 K. 17:4. Ps. 72:10.

מִנְחָה Chald. *idem.* Dan. 2:46. Ezra 7:17.

מְנִי Is. 65:11. name of an idol, perhaps *the god of destiny,* from מָנָה, (like גַּד.) Comp. مناة *Manah,* one of the three daughters of God in the mythology of the Arabians before the time of Mohammed.

מִנִּי Jer. 51:27. (perhaps Ps. 45:9.) name of a country, according to the Syriac and Chaldaic versions, *Armenia;* but most prob. only a province of that country, as it is mentioned in connexion with אֲרָרָט (q.v.) Bochart (Phaleg, lib. I. cap. 3. p. 19, 20.) compares Μινυὰς, a district of Armenia. Josephi Antiq. I. 3. 6.

מִנִּי i. q. מִן, a poetic form with paragogic Yod. Judg. 5:14. Is. 46:3. Also written מִנֵּי Is. 30:11.

מְנָיוֹת, see מְנָת.

מִנְיָן m. Chald. *number.* Ezra 6:17. Root מְנָא.

מִנִּית a place in the territory of the Ammonites. Judg. 11:33. Wheat was brought from this place to the market of Tyre, Ezek. 27:17.

מִנְלֶה dec. IX. a. prob. *a possession, prosperous condition.* With suff. מִנְלָם Job 15:29. Root נָלָה Is. 33:1. *to finish, make an end,* i. q. Arab. نَالَ (med Ye,) whence نَال, نَيْل *power, substance, possession.*

מָנַע *to hold back, stop, check.* Ezek. 31:15 וָאֶמְנַע נַהֲרוֹתֶיהָ *and I will check its streams.* Construed (1.) with מִן, *to restrain* or *preserve* from any thing. 1 Sam. 25:26, 34 אֲשֶׁר מְנָעֲנִי מֵהָרַע אֹתָךְ *who has restrained me from doing evil to thee.* Jer. 2:25 מִנְעִי רַגְלֵךְ מִיָּחֵף *preserve thy foot from being unshod,* i. e. run not so fast as to lose thy shoes. 31:16. (2.) with an accus. of the thing and מִן of the person, *to withhold from* any one, *to deny* or *refuse* him. Gen. 30:2 אֲשֶׁר מָנַע מִמֵּךְ פְּרִי בָטֶן *who hath withheld from thee the fruit of the womb.* 2 Sam. 13:13. 1 K. 20:7. Job 22:7. More rarely with לְ of the person, Ps. 84:12. or with an accus. of the person and מִן of the thing, Num. 24:11. Ecc. 2:10.

Niph. *to be kept back, stopped.* Jer. 3:3.

2. reflex. *to hold one's self back, to forbear.* Num. 22:16.

3. *to be withheld* or *denied,* construed with מִן. Job 38:15.

מַנְעוּל m. verbal from נָעַל, dec. I. *a bar.* Cant. 5:5. Neh. 3:3.

מִנְעָל m. verbal from נָעַל, dec. II. b. *idem.* Deut. 33:25.

מַנְעַמִּים masc. plur. dec. VIII. *dainties, delicacies.* Ps. 141:4. Root נָעַם, in Arab. spoken also of rich food.

מְנַעַנְעִים masc. plur. 2 Sam. 6:5. name of a musical instrument, according to the Vulg. *sistra;* liter. part. Pi. from נוּעַ *to be shaken, agitated.*

מְנַקִּית found only in the plur. מְנַקִּיּוֹת, *dishes for receiving the blood of victims.* Ex. 25:29. 37:16. Num. 4:7. (Syr. *idem,* from the root ܢܩܐ in Pa. *to pour out, libare.*)

מֵנֶקֶת f. *a nurse.* See the Hiph. of יָנַק.

מְנַשֶּׁה m. (*causing to forget,* see Gen. 42:51.) *Manasseh,* the son of Joseph, who, being adopted by his grandfather, inherited equally with the sons of Jacob. Gen. 48:1ff. The territory of this tribe lay one half on the east, and one half on the west of Jordan, Josh. 17:8ff. The patronymic noun is מְנַשִּׁי, Num. 4:43.

מְנָת f. for מְנָאת, (from מָנָה,) irreg. plur. מְנָאוֹת Neh. 12:44. and מְנָיוֹת 12:47. 13:10. (with Kamets impure,) *a part, portion.* Ps. 63:11 מְנָת שֻׁעָלִים יִהְיוּ *a portion* or *prey for foxes shall they be, pars vulpium erunt.* Ps. 11:6 מְנָת כּוֹסָם *this shall be the portion of their cup.* 16:5. Particularly *a portion of food,* see the passages in Nehemiah.

מָס m. Job 6:14. *unhappy, afflicted, cast down.* Root מָסַס.

מַס m. dec. VIII. f. *tribute, soccage,* more fully מַס עֹבֵד, 1 K. 9:21. 2 Chr. 8:8.—הָיָה לָמַס Deut. 20:11. Judg. 1:30, 33:35. Is. 31:8. and הָיָה לְמַס עֹבֵד Gen. 49:15. Josh. 16:10. *to become tributary, to be obliged to serve.*—נָתַן לָמַס Josh. 17:13. שׂוּם לָמַס Judg. 1:28. and שׂוּם מַס עַל Est. 10:1. *to impose a tribute on* any one, *to make* him *tributary.*—אֲשֶׁר עַל הַמַּס *an overseer over the tribute,* an important officer in the court of Israel, 2 Sam. 20:24. 1 K. 4:6. 12:18.—שָׂרֵי מִסִּים *collectors of tribute, taskmasters,* Ex. 1:11. The etymology is uncertain.

מֵסַב m. verbal from סָבַב, dec. VIII. f.

1. subst. *a circle of persons sitting together, a divan, consessus.* Cant. 1:12. comp. the root סָבַב 1 Sam. 16:11.

2. as an adv. *round about.* 1 K. 6:29.

3. plur. const. as a prep. *round about.* 2 K. 23:5 מְסִבֵּי יְרוּשָׁלַיִם *round about Jerusalem.* מְסִבּוֹת *idem,* Job 37:12.

מַסְגֵּר m. verbal from סָגַר, strictly part. Hiph.

1. *a smith.* 2 K. 24:14, 16. Jer. 24:1. 29:2.

2. *a place of confinement, a prison,* liter. *that which encloses.* Ps. 142:8. Is. 24:22.

מִסְגֶּרֶת f. plur. מִסְגְּרוֹת, verbal from סָגַר, dec. XII. a.

1. *a prison.* Ps. 18:46. Mic. 7:17.

2. *a border, ridge.* Ex. 25:25ff. 37:14.

3. 1 K. 7:28, 29, 31, 32, 35, 36. 2 K. 16:7. *ornaments* or *decorations* of the brazen bases or stands for the molten sea. It appears from verses 28, 29, 31. that they were four-cornered plates on

the four sides of each stand. Comp. Syr. ܣܒܢܐ.

מֻסָּד m. *foundation* of a building. 1 K. 7:9. Root יָסַד *to found,* whose Yod assimilates itself in many forms of the verb.

מִסְדְּרוֹן m. *a colonnade, porch, porticus,* denom. from שְׂדֵרָה ,סָדַר *a row.* Once Judg. 3:23.

מָסָה i. q. מָסַס *to dissolve.* (In Chald. מְסָא, Syr. ܡܣܐ *to dissolve, rot, decay.*)

Hiph. 1. *to cause to dissolve* or *run down.* Ps. 6:7 בְּדִמְעָתִי עַרְשִׂי אַמְסֶה *I make my bed to run down with tears.* 147:18. Fut. apoc. וַיַּמֵּס 39:12.

2. metaphorically with לֵב, *to cause the heart to melt, to throw into consternation.* Plur. הִמְסִיו for הִמְסוּ Josh. 14:8.

מִסָּה, const. מִסַּת, dec. X. *enough, sufficient.* (Syr. ܡܣܬܐ, Chald. כְּמִסַּת.) Deut. 16:10 מִסַּת נִדְבַת־יָדְךָ *as much as thy hand can give.*

מַסָּה f. verbal from נָסָה, dec. X. *a temptation.*

1. spoken of the miracles of Jehovah, by which he tried the people of Israel. Deut. 4:34. 7:19. 29:2.

2. *a tempting of Jehovah,* i. e. a murmuring against him. Ps. 95:8. Hence the name of a place in the desert מַסָּה, Ex. 17:7. Deut. 6:16. 9:22. 33:8.

3. *a suffering* or *trial* from God, i. q. πειρασμός in N. T. Job 9:23.

מַסְוֶה m. *a covering, veil.* Ex. 34:33, 34, 35. Root סָוָה not used. Arab. سوية *a covering* for a camel.

מְסוּכָה f. i. q. מְשׂוּכָה *a thorn hedge, a quick hedge.* Mic. 7:4. Root שׂוּךְ *to hedge, to hedge about.*

מַסָּח m. verbal from נָסַח, *a keeping off.* 2 K. 11:6.

מִסְחָר m. dec. II. b. *traffic, commerce.* 1 K. 10:15. Root סָחַר *to traffic.*

מָסַךְ *to mix,* i. q. מָזַג, μίσγω, *misceo.* Ps. 102:15. Is. 19:14 יְהוָה מָסַךְ בְּקִרְבָּהּ רוּחַ עִוְעִים *Jehovah has poured out in the midst of them a spirit of giddiness,* i. e. has brought consternation among them. Used especially of the mixing of wine with spices to make it more intoxicating, Prov. 9:2, 5. Is. 5:22.

Deriv. מִמְסָךְ ,מֶסֶךְ.

מֶסֶךְ m. verbal from מָסַךְ, *mixed wine, spiced wine.* Ps. 75:9.

מָסָךְ m. const. מְסַךְ, verbal from סָכַךְ, dec. IV. a. *a covering.* 2 Sam. 17:19. particularly *the curtain* before the door of the tabernacle of the congregation, Ex. 26:36 ff. 39:38. 40:5. and before the gate of the court. 35:17. 39:40. More fully פָּרֹכֶת הַמָּסָךְ *the veil of the covering,* 35:12. 39:34. 40:21.—Is. 22:8 וַיְגַל אֵת־מָסַךְ יְהוּדָה *and he removed the covering of Judah,* i. e. he exposed them to every reproach.

מְסֻכָּה f. verbal from סָכַךְ, dec. X. *a covering.* Ezek. 28:13.

I. **מַסֵּכָה** f. verbal from נָסַךְ no. I. dec. X.

1. *a casting* or *pouring out* of metal. —עֵגֶל מַסֵּכָה *a molten calf,* Ex. 32:4, 8. אֱלֹהֵי מַסֵּכָה *molten gods,* Ex. 34:17.

2. particularly *a molten image.* Deut. 9:12. Judg. 17:3, 4.

3. *a covenant, a making of peace,* σπονδή. Is. 30:1.

II. **מַסֵּכָה** f. verbal from נָסַךְ no. II. *a covering.* Is. 25:7.

מִסְכֵּן m. *poor, unfortunate.* Ecc. 4:13. 9:15, 16. It is a quadriliteral and the מ is radical. (Found in all the cognate dialects. Likewise in several western languages; as in Ital. *meschino, meschinello;* in Portug. *mesquinho,* subst. *mesquinhez;* in French *mesquin,* subst. *mesquinerie, poverty, indigence,* for the most part in the sense of reproach.)

מִסְכֵּנוּת f. denom. from מִסְכֵּן, *poverty, want.* Deut. 8:9. See סָכַן.

מִסְכְּנוֹת plur. fem. *stores, magazines,* by transposition for מִכְנָסוֹת, from

מַס to heap up, comp. נָמַס. Ex. 1:11. 1 K. 9:19. 2 Chr. 8:4.

מַסֶּכֶת f. threads of yarn, a web; perhaps more particularly the warp or woof. Judg. 16:13, 14. Root נָסַךְ, in the signification here of the Arab. נשג نسج to weave.

מְסִלָּה f. verbal from סלל, dec. X.

1. a way, highway. Judg. 20:31, 32. 1 Sam. 6:12. Is. 40:3. Metaphorically a manner of life, Prov. 16:17.

2. a flight of steps, a stair-case, i. q. סֻלָּם. 2 Chr. 9:11.

מַסְלוּל m. verbal from סָלַל, a way, path. Is. 35:8.

מַסְמְרִים masc. plur. Is. 41:7. מַסְמְרִים 1 Chr. 22:3. and מַסְמְרוֹת 2 Chr. 3:9. Jer. 10:4. nails, pegs. (Chald. סַמֵּר to nail, to fasten with nails; Arab. مسمار a nail.)

מָסַס to dissolve, melt, faint. In Kal only Is. 10:18. Kindred with מָסָה.

Niph. נָמַס, in pause נָמָס, fut. יִמַּס, infin. הִמֵּס.

1. to melt, flow asunder or down. Ex. 16:21. Ps. 68:3. Is. 34:3. Judg. 15:14 and his bands melted, i. e. loosed, from off his hands.—Spoken of scabby or mangy cattle, 1 Sam. 15:9. of a sick person, Is. 10:18.

2. used figuratively with לֵב, to faint or fail, (from fear or alarm.) Deut. 20:8. Josh. 2:11. 5:1. The figure is sometimes continued, as Josh. 7:5 the heart of the people melted וַיְהִי לְמָיִם and became as water. More rarely to faint or waste away, (from sorrow or pain,) Ps. 22:15. Comp. Ovid. Ex Ponto, I. 2. 57. Also without לֵב in both these acceptations, 2 Sam. 17:10 and also the valiant man הִמֵּס יִמָּס shall utterly faint or despond. Spoken of inanimate nature, Ps. 97:5. Mic. 1:4.—Ps. 112:10 he melts away, (for grief.)

Hiph. to cause to faint, to discourage. Deut. 1:28.

Deriv. מַס, תֶּמֶס.

Note. Several forms of the root מָאַס borrow their signification from מָסַס. See מָאַס no. II.

מַסָּע m. a dart. Job 41:18. [41:26.] (Arab. منزع sagitta, telum.)

מַסַּע m. verbal from נָסַע, dec. II. c.

1. a removing, breaking up, marching, departing, (of a Nomadic people,) strictly the Aram. infin. Deut. 10:11 לְמַסַּע לִפְנֵי הָעָם to march before the people. Num. 10:2 לְמַסַּע אֶת־הַמַּחֲנוֹת for marching with the camps. Hence as a subst. a journey, march, Ex. 40:38. Deut. 10:6.

2. a station, encampment. Ex. 17:1 לְמַסְעֵיהֶם after their encampments. Num. 10:6, 12.

3. a quarry. 1 K. 6:7 אֶבֶן שְׁלֵמָה מַסָּע unhewn stone from the quarry. Sept. λίθοις ἀκροτόμοις ἀργοῖς.

מִסְעָד m. verbal from סָעַד, a support, balustrade. 1 K. 10:12.

מִסְפֵּד m. const. מִסְפַּד, with suff. מִסְפְּדִי, verbal from סָפַד, dec. VII. d. a lamentation. Gen. 50:10. Amos 5:16, 17.

מִסְפּוֹא m. fodder, provender, for cattle. Gen. 24:25, 32. 42:47. 43:24. Root in Chald. סְפָא Pe. and Aph. cibavit.

מִסְפַּחַת f. i. q. סַפַּחַת the scab. Lev. 13:6, 7, 8.

מִסְפָּחוֹת pl. fem. dec. XI. a. cushions or coverings, to sleep upon. Ezek. 13:18, 21. Symm. ὑπαυχένια. Vulg. cervicalia. Root סָפַח to pour out, perhaps to spread under. In Ethiop. ספח lectum expandit, stravit.

מִסְפָּר m. verbal from סָפַר, dec. II. b.

1. number. As an accus. used adverbially, in or by number, after the number, Ex. 16:16 מִסְפַּר נַפְשֹׁתֵיכֶם after the number of your persons. Job 1:5. 2 Sam. 21:20 עֶשְׂרִים וְאַרְבַּע מִסְפָּר twenty four in number.—אֵין מִסְפָּר Gen. 41:49. לְאֵין מִסְפָּר 1 Chr. 22:4. and עַד־אֵין מִסְפָּר Job 5:9. 9:10. without number, innumerable. The opposite of these phrases is מִסְפָּר numerable, i. e. a few; e. g. מְתֵי

אַנְשֵׁי מִסְפָּר, *few people*, Gen. 34:30. Deut. 4:27. also preceded by a noun in the absolute state, יָמִים מִסְפָּר *a few days*, Num. 9:20.

2. *a relation, narration.* (Comp. the verb in Pi.) Judg. 7:15.

מָסַר in Kal only Num. 31:16 לִמְסָר מַעַל בַּיהוָה *to attempt rebellion against Jehovah.* So it may be rendered, in conformity with the Syr. ܡܣܰܪ *opus aggressus* seu *ausus est.* But the text is perhaps corrupted, and should be written לִמְעֹל מַעַל as in the parallel passages Num. 5:6. 2 Chr. 36:14. Ezek. 14:12.

Niph. *to be numbered, reviewed,* (so the Sept. comp. מסר in Samar. *visitavit;*) or *to be selected out* or *given up,* (comp. the Talmud. מסר *tradidit.*) Num. 31:5.

מָסֹרֶת f. a contraction of מַאֲסֹרֶת, verbal from אָסַר, dec. XIII. *a bond, fetter.* Ezek. 20:37.

מֹסָר dec. II. b. i. q. מוּסָר *warning, instruction.* Job 33:16. Root יָסַר *to admonish, instruct.*

מִסְתּוֹר m. verbal from סָתַר, dec. I. *a place of concealment, a covert, a refuge.* Is. 4:6.

מִסְתָּר m. verbal from סָתַר, dec. II. b. *a place of concealment, a lurking-place, a place for lying in wait.* Ps. 10:9. 17:12. Lam. 3:10.

מַעְבָּד m. dec. II. b. *an action, deed, work.* Job 34:24. Also in Chaldaic, Dan. 4:34. Root עֲבַד Chald. *to do, to make.*

מַעֲבֶה m. verbal from עָבָה, dec. IX. a. *thickness.* 1 K. 7:46 בְּמַעֲבֵה הָאֲדָמָה *in thick earth.*

מַעֲבָר m. verbal from עָבַר, dec. II. b.

1. *a ford, a shallow part of a river.* Gen. 32:23.

2. *a narrow pass.* 1 Sam. 13:23.

3. *place of passing.* Is. 30:32 כֹּל מַעֲבַר מַטֵּה מוּסָדָה *every place where the destined scourge passes.*

מַעְבָּרָה f. plur. מַעְבָּרוֹת, verbal from עָבַר, dec. X.

1. *a ford* or *passage of a river.*— מַעְבְּרוֹת הַיַּרְדֵּן *the fords of Jordan,* Judg. 3:28. 12:5, 6.

2. *a narrow pass.* Is. 10:29. 1 Sam. 14:4.

מַעְגָּל m. plur. ־ִים and ־וֹת, verbal from עָגַל *to roll,* or denom. from עֲגָלָה *a waggon;* dec. II. b.

1. *a track of a carriage.* Ps. 65:12.

2. *a path* generally. Ps. 140:6. Often metaphorically, *a manner of life,* (like נְתִיבָה, דֶּרֶךְ.) Ps. 23:3.

מַעְגָּלָה f. (denom. from עֲגָלָה *a waggon,*) *a bulwark* or *fortification formed by the carriages of an army.* 1 Sam. 17:20. 26:5, 7.

מָעַד *to totter, slide, slip.* Ps. 18:37. Job 12:5 מוֹעֲדֵי רָגֶל *those whose feet slip.* Prov. 25:19 רֶגֶל מוּעָדֶת *a tottering foot.* The ancient grammarians regarded it as an uncommon form of the participle Kal, for מוֹעֶדֶת. It may be the participle Pual for מְמוּעֶדֶת; or perhaps it should be read מוֹעֶדֶת.

Hiph. *to cause to shake.* Ps. 69:24.

I. **מַעֲדַנִּים**, also מַעֲדַנִּים and מַעֲדַנּוֹת, found only in the plur. verbals from עָדַן.

1. *delight, joy.* Prov. 29:17. As an adv. *with delight, cheerfully,* 1 Sam. 15:32.

2. *delicate food, dainties.* Gen. 49:20. Lam. 4:5.

II. **מַעֲדַנּוֹת** masc. plur. *bands,* by transposition for מַעֲנַדּוֹת, from עָנַד *to bind, tie.* Job 38:31 מַעֲדַנּוֹת כִּימָה *the bands of the Pleiades;* see כִּימָה.

מַעְדֵּר m. verbal from עָדַר, *a mattock, weeding-hook, hoe, sarculum.* Is. 7:25.

מָעָה f. dec. XI. a. *a small stone, a gravel stone.* Is. 48:19 כִּמְעֹתָיו according to the ancient versions, *ut lapilli ejus.* (In Chald. and Talmud. מָעָא *obolus, nummulus,* a kindred idea.)

מֵעֶה m. dec. IX. b. found only in the plur. מֵעִים. (The singular is found in Arabic.)

1. *bowels.*—יָצָא מִמְּעֵי פ׳ *prodire e visceribus alicujus, to be descended from*

any one, Gen. 15:4. (comp. 25:23.) 2 Sam. 7:12. 16:11.

2. *the inward parts* generally, and particularly *the womb*. Gen. 25:23. Ruth 1:11 הַעוֹד־לִי בָנִים בְּמֵעַי *shall I yet bear children?*—מִמְּעֵי אִמִּי *from my mother's womb*, Is. 49:1. Ps. 71:6.

3. in a metaphorical sense, *the inward parts, the heart*. Job 30:27 מֵעַי רֻתְּחוּ *my heart boiled*. Lam. 1:10. Is. 16:11. Ps. 40:9 תּוֹרָתְךָ בְּתוֹךְ מֵעָי *thy law is in my heart*.

4. *the belly, body*. Cant. 5:14. Comp. the Chald.

מְעִין masc. plur. Chald. i. q. Heb. מֵעִים no. 4. Dan. 2:32.

מָעוֹג m. i. q. עֻגָה *a cake*. 1 K. 17:12. comp. verse 13. — Ps. 35:16 לַעֲגֵי מָעוֹג liter. *sanniones placentæ, mockers at feasts*, i. e. parasites who support themselves by their wit. In Talmud. לְשׁוֹן עוּגָה *sermo placentæ, the talk of a parasite*. See לַעַג no. 2.

מָעוֹז m. more rarely מָעֹז, (with Kamets impure,) with suff. מָעוּזִּי, מָעֻזִּי, plur. מָעֻזִּים, verbal from עָזַז *to be strong, fast;* dec. VIII. d. *a fortress, fortification*. Judg. 6:26. Dan. 11:7, 10. עָרֵי מָעוֹז, Is. 17:9. Metaphorically *a defence*. Ps. 60:9 מָעוֹז רֹאשִׁי *the defence of my head*, i.e. my helmet. Is. 23:4 מָעוֹז הַיָּם *the fortress of the sea*, i. e. Sidon; comp. ver. 14. Ezek. 30:15. Spoken of Jehovah, Ps. 31:5. 37:39. 43:2 אֱלֹהֵי מָעֻזִּים *the god of fortresses*, Dan. 11:38. a Syrian deity forced upon the Jews by Antiochus Epiphanes.—מָעוּזְנֶיהָ for מָעוּזֶּיהָ with Nun epenthetic, which is unusual in the noun suffixes, Is. 23:11.

מָעוֹן m. plur. מְעוֹנִים 1 Chr. 4:41. verbal from עוּן, dec. III. a. and f.

1. *a dwelling*, (1.) of God. Ps. 68:6. Deut. 26:15. (2.) of wild beasts. Nah. 2:12. Jer. 9:10. 10:22. 51:37. —In 1 Sam. 2:29, 31. as an accus. used adverbially, *to the dwelling*, like בַּיִת *to the house*.

2. *a place of refuge*. Ps. 90:1.

3. proper name of a city in the tribe f Judah, not far from Carmel. Josh. 15:55. 1 Sam. 25:2. Hence מִדְבַּר־מָעוֹן *the wilderness of Maon*, 1 Sam. 23:24, 25.

4. name of a people mentioned in connexion with the Amalekites, Sidonians, Philistines, etc. Judg. 10:12. Plur. מְעוּנִים 1 Chr. 4:41 Keri. 2 Chr. 26:7. In the last passage they are joined with the Arabians. The Sept. has rendered it 1 Chr. 4:41. Μιναῖοι, i. e. an Arabian people on the Red Sea, whose chief city is Κάρνα.

מְעוֹנָה and **מְעֹנָה** fem. of מָעוֹן, dec. X. *a dwelling*. Jer. 21:13. Particularly (1.) of God. Ps. 76:3. (2.) of wild beasts. Ps. 104:22. Am. 8:4.

מְעוֹן, see **בֵּית מְעוֹן, בַּעַל מְעוֹן, בֵּית בַּעַל מְעוֹן**.

מָעוּף m. verbal from עוּף no. II. dec. III. c. *darkness*. Is. 8:22.

מָעוֹר m. dec. III. a. plur. מְעוֹרִים *pudenda*. Hab. 2:15. Root עוּר Arab. عَارَ i. q. عري עָרָה *to be bare, naked*.

מָעֹז see **מָעוֹז**.

מָעַט *to be little, small, few in number*. Lev. 25:16 לְפִי מְעֹט הַשָּׁנִים *according as the years are few*. Ex. 12:4. Neh. 9:32. Also *to become few*, Ps. 107:39.

Pi. מִעֵט intrans. as in Kal. Ecc. 12:3.

Hiph. הִמְעִיט 1. *to make small* or *few, to diminish*. Lev. 25:16. Num. 26:54. 33:54. (See no. 2.) Jer. 20:24 פֶּן תַּמְעִטֵנִי *lest thou make me (the people) few in number*. Ezek. 29:15.—The action to which this verb relates must often be supplied from the context, as Num. 11:32 הַמַּמְעִיט אָסַף עֲשָׂרָה חֳמָרִים *he who gathered little, gathered ten homers*. Ex. 16:17, 18. 2 K. 4:3 *borrow for thee empty vessels* אַל תַּמְעִיטִי, scil. לִשְׁאֹל, *and not a few*.

2. *to give little* or *less*. Num. 35:8. Ex. 30:15 וְהַדַּל לֹא יַמְעִיט *and the poor man shall not give less*.

מְעַט, less frequently מְעָט, dec. VIII. h.

1. as an adj. *a little, a few, paucus*. Num. 26:54 לַמְעַט *to the few*. Plur. מְעַטִּים *few*, Ps. 109:8. Ecc. 5:1.

2. more frequently as an adv. *a little*,

parum. מְעַט מַיִם *a little water,* Gen. 18:4. 24:17, 43. מְעַט אֹכֶל *a little food,* 43:2. More rarely after the noun, as מְתֵי מְעָט *few people,* Deut. 26:5. עֵזֶר מְעָט *little help,* Dan. 11:34.—Also of time, *a short time,* Ruth 2:7. Ps. 37:10. of space, 2 Sam. 16:1.—מְעַט מְעַט *by little and little, gradually, peu à peu,* Ex. 23:30. Deut. 7:22.—הַמְעַט מִכֶּם *is it too little for you?* Num. 16:9.—Ezek. 16:20 הַמְעַט מִתַּזְנֻתָיִךְ *was there too little of thy idolatry?*

In combination with a prefix, כִּמְעַט (1.) i. q. מְעַט *little, few,* 1 Chr. 16:19. Ps. 105:12. *a little,* 2 Sam. 19:37.—כִּמְעַט רֶגַע *a little moment,* Is. 26:20. Ezra 9:8. (2.) *almost,* liter. *within a little, little was wanting.* Gen. 26:10. Ps. 73:2. 119:87. (3.) *soon, shortly.* Ps. 81:15. 94:17. (4.) *scarcely.* Cant. 3:4. (5.) *suddenly.* Ps. 2:12. Job 32:22. (6.) *as nothing,* i. e. nothing worth. Prov. 10:20.

מָעֹט, fem. מְעֻטָּה, dec. VIII. d. found only Ezek. 21:20. *smooth,* and spoken of a sword, *glittering, sharp,* synonymous with מרט. (In Arab. معط *glaber fuit.*)

מַעֲטֶה m. verbal from עָטָה, dec. IX. a. *a garment, covering.* Is. 61:3.

מַעֲטָפוֹת f. plur. verbal from עָטַף no. I. *mantles.* Is. 3:22.

מְעִי m. *a heap of rubbish, ruins,* i. q. עִי. Is. 17:1.

מְעִיל m. dec. I. *an upper garment,* which appears from 2 Sam. 13:8. and the description of the high-priest's dress, to have been not a mantle, but a second and larger tunic without sleeves. (Comp. Hartmann's Hebräerin, Th. 3. p. 312.) It was worn by women, 2 Sam. 13:8. by magistrates, Job 1:20. 2:12. especially by kings, 1 Sam. 15:27. 18:4. 24:5, 12. and priests, 1 Sam. 28:14. The high-priest wore it under the ephod. Hence מְעִיל הָאֵפוֹד Ex. 28:31. 39:22. (The etymology is doubtful. If the מ is servile, then we may collate the word with עיל Arab. غيل *ampla vestis,* from غال *tenuis, subtilis fuit.* But if מָעַל is the root, its significations probably were 1. *to cover;* 2. *to act under cover, to deceive.* Comp. בָּגַד *to deceive,* בֶּגֶד *a garment;* دجل *to cover, deceive.*)

מֵעִים *bowels,* see מֵעֶה.

מַעְיָן m. with suff. מַעְיָנוֹ, plur. מַעְיָנִים, const. מַעְיְנֵי; and מַעְיָנוֹת, const. מַעְיְנוֹת; i. q. עַיִן *a spring, fountain.* Gen. 7:11. 8:2. Ps. 84:7 *and they pass through a valley of weeping,* מַעְיָן יְשִׁיתוּהוּ *they make it a well.* Ps. 87:7 כָּל־מַעְיָנַי בָּךְ *all my springs or fountains are in thee (Zion,)* i. e. all my joys or daily delights. Others: *all my views are directed to thee;* comp. עַיִן.

מָעַךְ *to press, squeeze, crush.* Lev. 22:24 מָעוּךְ *with broken testicles, castrated.* 1 Sam. 26:7 וַחֲנִיתוֹ מְעוּכָה בָאָרֶץ *his spear was pressed into the ground.*

Pu. *to be pressed,* in an immodest manner, spoken of the breasts of females. Ezek. 23:3.

מַעֲכָה 2 Sam. 10:6, 8. 1 Chr. 19:6, 7. and מַעֲכָת Josh. 13:13. a people and country, east of Jordan, at the foot of Antilibanus. More fully אֲרַם מַעֲכָה, 1 Chr. 19:6. The gentile noun is מַעֲכָתִי Deut. 3:14. Josh. 12:5. 13:11. 2 K. 25:23. Comp. אָבֵל בֵּית מַעֲכָה.

מָעַל, fut. יִמְעַל and יִמְעֹל.

1. *to sin, transgress, deal faithlessly.* Prov. 16:10. 2 Chr. 26:18. 29:6, 19. Neh. 1:8.

2. joined with בַּיהוָה, *to sin against Jehovah,* especially *to apostatize from him.* Deut. 32:51. Most frequently in the phrase מָעַל מַעַל בַּיהוָה *to transgress against Jehovah,* 1 Chr. 5:25. 10:13. 2 Chr. 12:2.

3. joined with בְּ of the thing, *to offend in* any thing. Josh. 7:1. 22:20. 1 Chr. 2:7.

I. מַעַל m. verbal from מָעַל, *a sin, transgression,* always in the phrase מָעַל מַעַל בְּ. See the verb.

II. מַעַל m. a contraction of מַעְלָה

from עָלָה, liter. *what is above;* hence as an adv. *above.* Found only in the compositions,

1. מִמַּעַל *from above.* Is. 45:8. Also simply *above.* Deut. 5:8.—מִמַּעַל לְ *above, upon,* Gen. 22:9 מִמַּעַל לָעֵצִים *upon the wood.* Dan. 12:6 מִמַּעַל לְמֵימֵי הַיְאֹר *upon the waters of the river.* Also i. q. עַל *by, about,* Is. 6:2.

2. with ה local, מַעְלָה (1.) *upwards.*—מַעְלָה מַעְלָה *higher and higher,* Deut. 28:43. (2.) *above.* 1 Sam. 9:2. especially of time, Num. 1:20. (3.) *forward, afterwards.* 1 Sam. 16:13.

מֹעַל m. Neh. 8:6. *a lifting up,* a contraction of מַעֲלָה from עָלָה.

מֶעָל Chald. plur. מֶעָלִין, *setting* of the sun. Dan. 6:15. Root עֲלַל *to go in.*

מַעֲלֶה m. verbal from עָלָה, dec. IX. a.

1. *a rising, place of rising.* Neh. 12:37.

2. *a raised place, suggestus.* Neh. 9:4.

3. *a hill, ascent.*—מַעֲלֵה הָעִיר *the ascent to the city,* 1 Sam. 9:11. 2 Sam. 15:30.

4. מַעֲלֵה עַקְרַבִּים (*hill of scorpions*) Num. 34:4. Josh. 15:3. a place on the southern boundary of Palestine.

מַעֲלָה f. verbal from עָלָה, dec. X.

1. *an ascending* or *going up.* Ezra 7:9. Metaphorically מַעֲלוֹת רוּחֲכֶם *that which rises in your hearts,* Ezek. 11:5. comp. עָלָה אֶל לֵב.

2. *height, a high degree.* 1 Chr. 17:17.

3. *a step, stair.* Ex. 20:23. 1 K. 10:19.

4. *a degree,* on a sun-dial. 2 K. 20:9, 10, 11. Is. 38:8.

5. *a loft, story,* i. q. עֲלִיָּה. Am. 9:6.

6. שִׁיר הַמַּעֲלוֹת the superscription of Ps. cxx. and of those that follow to the cxxxiv. liter. *a song of degrees,* prob. a designation having reference to a certain versification common to these fifteen Psalms. So the Syrians call a certain class of poems ܡܣܩܬܐ ܕܙܡܪ̈ܐ *scalæ odarum.* A conjecture concerning the origin of these designations may be found in the A. L. Z. 1813. no. 205. Others: *trochaic songs,* but it is not probable that metre existed in Hebrew poetry. Others: *pilgrim songs, carmina ascensionum,* sung by those who went up to Jerusalem to worship, (comp. עָלָה Ps. 122:4.) but this explanation is suited to only a few of them, e. g. to Ps. cxxii.

מַעֲלִיל i. q. מַעֲלָל Zech. 1:4 Kethib.

מַעֲלָל m. verbal from עָלַל, dec. II. b. *a deed, work, action.* Found only in the plur. מַעֲלָלִים (1.) *great deeds, miracles, facinora Dei.* Ps. 77:12. 78:7. (2.) *actions* (of men). Zech. 1:6.—הֵיטִיב ,הֵרַע מַעֲלָלִים *to make one's actions good* or *bad,* i. e. to act well or ill, Jer. 35:15.

מַעֲמָד m. verbal from עָמַד, dec. II. b. *an establishment.* 1 K. 10:5.

מָעֳמָד m. Ps. 69:3. *a place for standing, a bottom.* So Sept. Chald. Others make it the part. Hoph.

מַעֲמָסָה f. *a burden.* Zech. 12:3. Root עָמַס *to load.*

מַעֲמַקִּים masc. plur. dec. VIII. *depths.* Is. 51:10. Ps. 69:3. Root עָמַק *to be deep.*

מַעַן a contraction of מַעֲנֶה, from ענה Arab. عنى *to have in view, to purpose;* liter. a subst. *object, purpose.* Only in the combination לְמַעַן.

1. before verbs, *that, so that;* construed with a fut. Gen. 27:25. Ex. 4:5. with an infin. Am. 2:7. Ezek. 21:20.

2. before substantives, (1.) *on account of.* 1 K. 8:41. With suff. לְמַעֲנִי, לְמַעַנְךָ. (2.) *according to, secundum,* i. q. כְּ. לְמַעַן שִׁמְךָ *according to thy name,* Ps. 109:21. 25:11. 31:4. לְמַעַן חַסְדֶּךָ *according to thy grace,* i. q. כְּחַסְדְּךָ, Ps. 6:5. 44:27.

3. *on this account,* (for לְמַעַן זֹאת 1 K. 11:39.) Ps. 30:13. 51:6. Hos. 8:4.

4. לְמַעַן אֲשֶׁר *that, ut,* Josh. 3:4. *that, quod,* Gen. 18:19. *on this account,* Lev. 17:5.

מַעֲנֶה m. verbal from עָנָה, dec. IX. a.

1. *an answer.* Prov. 15:1, 23.

2. *a hearing.* Prov. 16:1.

3. *a refutation, confutation.* Job 32: 3, 5.

4. *end, object.* Prov. 16:4. (comp. Arab. عني *to have in view.*)

מַעֲנָה f. dec. X. *a furrow.* Ps. 129: 3 Keth. 1 Sam. 14:14. Usually derived from עָנָה *subegit.*

מַעֲנִית f. *idem.* Ps. 129:3 Keri.

מְעֹנָה f. *a dwelling;* see מְעוֹנָה

מַעֲצֵבָה f. verbal from עָצַב, *sorrow.* Is. 50:11.

מַעֲצָד m. *an axe, hatchet.* Is. 44:12. Jer. 10:3. (Arab. معضد *idem;* root عضد *to hew.* In Talmud. *idem.*)

מַעְצוֹר m. verbal from עָצַר, *restraint, hindrance.* 1 Sam. 14:6.

מַעְצָר m. verbal from עָצַר, *restraint.* Prov. 25:28.

מַעֲקֶה m. *a battlement* or *balustrade,* round the flat roof of an oriental house. Deut. 22:8. Root עקה Arab. عقا *retinuit, detinuit.*

מַעֲקַשִּׁים masc. plur. verbal from עָקַשׁ, *crooked paths.* Is. 42:16.

מַעַר m. a contraction of מַעֲרֶה from עָרָה.

1. *nakedness,* i. q. עֶרְוָה. Nah. 3:5.

2. *vacant space.* 1 K. 7:36 כְּמַעַר אִישׁ *according to the space of each one.*

1. מַעֲרָב m. verbal from עָרַב no. I. 2. dec. II. b.

1. *traffic, commerce, exchange.* Ezek. 27:9, 27 עֹרְבֵי מַעֲרָבֵךְ *those who carry on thy traffic.*

2. *merchandise.* Ezek. 27:13, 17, 19, 27 at the beginning, 33, 34.

II. מַעֲרָב m. verbal from עָרַב no. III. dec. II. b. *the place of sunset, the west.* Ps. 75:7. 103:12. 107:3. Is. 43:5.

מַעֲרָבָה f. verbal from עָרַב no. III. *idem.* Is. 45:6.

מַעֲרֶה m. *an open plain without wood.* Judg. 20:33. (Arab. عروة *vacant ground about a city.*)

מַעֲרוֹת fem. plur. 1 Sam. 17:23 Keth. perhaps a corruption of מַעַרְכוֹת the reading of the Keri. If the Kethib gives any meaning in Hebrew, we may collate it with the Arab. عروة *caterva hominum.*

מְעָרָה f. const. מְעָרַת, plur. מְעָרוֹת, dec. X.

1. *a hole, cave, cavern.* Gen. 19:30. 1 Sam. 24:4, 8. Root עור Arab. غار *to be deep, to be excavated;* غار *a hole, cavern.*

2. Josh. 13:4. according to some a proper name of a place. Vulg. *Maara.*

מַעֲרִיץ m. dec. I. *fear, reverence,* or *the object of fear* or *reverence.* Is. 8:13. Root עָרַץ *to fear.*

מַעֲרָךְ m. verbal from עָרַךְ, dec. II. b. *arrangement, purpose.* Prov. 16:1 מַעַרְכֵי לֵב *the purposes of the heart.*

מַעֲרָכָה f. verbal from עָרַךְ, dec. XI. a.

1. *an arranging, a setting in order.* נֵרוֹת הַמַּעֲרָכָה *the lamps* (of the sacred candlestick) *set in order,* Ex. 39:37. Applied to the arranging of wood on an altar, Judg. 6:26. comp. the verb Gen. 22:9.

2. *order of battle, battle-array.* 1 Sam. 4:16. 17:22, 48.

מַעֲרֶכֶת f. verbal from עָרַךְ, dec. XIII. b.

1. *order of battle,* also *an army in battle-array.* 1 Sam 17:8.

2. *a row,* e. g. of the shew-bread. Lev. 24:6. Hence לֶחֶם הַמַּעֲרֶכֶת *the shew-bread,* for the more ancient name לֶחֶם הַפָּנִים, Neh. 10:34. Also without לֶחֶם, 2 Chr. 2:3. So in the same sense מַעֲרֶכֶת לֶחֶם 2 Chr. 13:11.—שֻׁלְחַן הַמַּעֲרֶכֶת *the table with the shew-bread,* 2 Chr. 29:18.

מַעֲרֻמִּים masc. plur. dec. VIII. *the naked.* 2 Chr. 28:15. Root ערם in Arab. *to make naked.*

מַעֲרָצָה f. *sudden violence, terror.* Is. 10:33. Root עָרַץ *to fear;* comp. עָרִיץ.

מַעֲשֶׂה m. verbal from עָשָׂה, dec. IX. a.

1. *a deed, action, concern, business.*

Gen. 44:15. 47:3. Spoken frequently of the mighty deeds of Jehovah, Ps. 86:6. Judg. 2:10. Also *facinus*, as 1 Sam. 20:19 בְּיוֹם הַמַּעֲשֶׂה *die facinoris*, namely, when Saul attempted to kill David.

2. *a work, labour, something done or wrought.* מַעֲשֵׂה יְדֵי יְהוָה *a work of Jehovah*, Ps. 8:4, 7. 19:2 מַעֲשֵׂה יְדֵי אָדָם *a work of men's hands*, often a designation for *idols*, Deut. 4:28. Ps. 115:4. 135:15. Applied to ingenious mechanical labour, מַעֲשֵׂה חֹשֵׁב *damask-work*, Ex. 26:1, 31. מַעֲשֵׂה רֶשֶׁת *lattice-work*, 27:4. Also *a poetical work*, ποίημα, Ps. 45:2.

3. *property, res*, like מְלָאכָה; particularly *the produce of the field*, Ex. 23:16. *cattle*, 1 Sam. 25:2.

מַעֲשֵׂר m. const. מַעְשַׂר, with suff. מַעְשְׂרוֹ, plur. מַעַשְׂרוֹת, denom. from עָשָׂר, עֶשֶׂר, dec. VII. d. *the tenth part, tithes*. Gen. 14:20. Deut. 14:23, 28. 26:12. שְׁנַת הַמַּעֲשֵׂר *the year of tithes*, i. e. every third year, in which the people made a feast of the tithes in their own houses. Deut. 26:12. Comp. De Wette jüd. Archäologie, p. 247. Jahn's Bibl. Archæol. p. 492.

מַעֲשַׁקּוֹת fem. plur. *oppressions*. Prov. 28:16. Root עָשַׁק *to oppress*.

מֹף *Memphis*, proper name of an Egyptian city. Hos. 9:6. Otherwise called נֹף, Is. 19:13. Jer. 2:16. By the Arabian geographers this city is called منف, מנף, by the modern Copts ΜΕΝΦ, ΜΕΝΟΥΦ and ΝΟΥΦ, from which we may explain both the Hebrew forms, and also the Greek name Μέμφις. Plutarch (De Iside et Osiride, p. 359. or p. 639 ed. Stephan.) interprets the name ὅρμον ἀγαθῶν (from Copt. meh *full* and nouphi *good*;) or τάφον Ὀσίριδος (from Copt. mhau *a grave*, and onphi εὐεργέτης, as Osiris is called.) See Jablonskii Opusc. ed. te Water. T. I. p. 137, 150, 179. T. II. p. 131.

מִפְגָּע m. *an attack*, or *an object of attack*. Job 7:20. Root פָּגַע.

מַפֻּחַ m. verbal from נָפַח, *bellows*. Jer. 6:29.

מַפָּח m. verbal from נָפַח, dec. II. b. Job 11:20 מַפַּח נֶפֶשׁ *the breathing out* or *expiring of the soul;* comp. the phrase נָפַח נֶפֶשׁ Jer. 15:9. Job 31:39.

מֵפִיץ m. *a hammer, a battle-hammer, a maul*. Prov. 25:18. Strictly part. Hiph. from פּוּץ *to smite in pieces*.

מַפָּל m. verbal from נָפַל, dec. II. b. strictly *that which hangs down*, or *falls off*. Job 41:51 [41:23] מַפְּלֵי בְשָׂרוֹ *the fleshy dewlaps*. Am. 8:6 מַפַּל בַּר *the refuse of the wheat*.

מִפְלָאָה f. verbal from פָּלָא, dec. XI. a. *a wonderful work, a miracle*. Job 37:16.

מִפְלַגָּה f. verbal from פָּלַג, dec. X. *a class, division*. 2 Chr. 35:12.

מַפֵּלָה f. Is. 17:1. and **מַפֵּלָה** f. 23:13. 25:2. verbals from נָפַל, *buildings fallen down, ruins*.

מִפְלָט m. verbal from פָּלַט, *an escaping, flying away*. Ps. 55:9.

מִפְלֶצֶת f. dec. XIII. a. *an image, idol*. 1 K. 15:13. Root פָּלַץ *to terrify;* comp. Syr. ܡܦܠܨܬܐ *idolum*, from ܦܠܨ *to fear*.

מִפְלָשׂ m. dec. II. b. *a waving, balancing*, spoken of clouds. Job 37:16. Root פָּלַשׂ=פָּלַס in Pi. *to weigh*.

מַפֶּלֶת f. verbal from נָפַל, dec. XIII. a.

1. *fall, ruin*. Prov. 29:16. Spoken of the destruction of a kingdom, Ezek. 26:15, 18. 27:27. 31:16.

2. *something fallen, a fallen trunk*. Ezek. 31:13.

3. *a dead body, a corpse*, like *cadaver* from *cadere*, πτῶμα from πίπτω. Judg. 14:8.

מִפְעָל m. dec. II. b. Prov. 8:22. and **מִפְעָלָה** f. dec. XI. a. Ps. 46:9. 66:5. verbals from פָּעַל, *a work* of God.

מֵפַעַת, see **מֵיפַעַת**.

מַפֵּץ m. *a hammer.* Jer. 51:20. strictly part. Hiph. from נָפַץ *to smite in pieces.*

מַפָּץ m. verbal from נָפַץ, dec. II. b. *a smiting in pieces.* Ezek. 9:2.

מִפְקָד m. verbal from פָּקַד, dec. II. b.

1. *a numbering* or *census* of a people. 2 Sam. 24:9.

2. *a command.* 2 Chr. 31:13.

3. *an appointed place.* Ezek. 43:21.

4. שַׁעַר הַמִּפְקָד name of one of the gates of Jerusalem. Neh. 3:31.

מִפְרָץ m. dec. II. b. *a haven, harbour.* Judg. 5:17. (Arab. فُرْضَةٌ *a haven, place of anchoring.*)

מַפְרֶקֶת f. dec. XIII. a. *the neck.* 1 Sam. 4:18. (Chald. פִּרְקָא, פְּרַק *idem.*)

מִפְרָשׂ m. verbal from פָּרַשׂ, dec. II. b.

1. *a stretching out, a spreading.* Job 36:29.

2. *a flag, banner.* Ezek. 27:7.

מִפְשָׂעָה f. verbal from פָּשַׂע, *the thigh, the hip, organon gressûs.* 1 Chr. 19:4.

מַפְתֵּחַ m. verbal from פָּתַח, *a key.* Judg. 3:25. Is. 22:22.

מִפְתָּח m. verbal from פָּתַח, dec. II. b. *an opening.* Prov. 8:6.

מִפְתָּן m. dec. II. b. *a sill, threshold.* 1 Sam. 5:4,5. Ezek. 9:3,4. 10:4,18. The etymology is obscure.

מֹץ, once in full מוֹץ (Zeph. 2:2.) *chaff.* Is. 41:15. Usually in phrases such as Ps. 35:5 יִהְיוּ כְּמֹץ לִפְנֵי רוּחַ *let them be as chaff before the wind.* 1:4. Job 21:18. Is. 17:13.

מָצָא, fut. יִמְצָא, imper. מְצָא, infin. מְצֹא.

1. *to find.* Gen. 2:20. 1 Sam. 10:7 *do what thine hand shall find,* i. e. what shall come to thine hand. 25:8. Ecc. 9:10. Spoken more rarely of the understanding, *to find out, discover, comprehend,* Ecc. 3:11. 7:27. 8:17. comp. Judg. 14:18, where it is used of the *solving* of a riddle.

2. *to get, obtain, acquire,* (as in Lat. *invenire cognomen, laudem;*) e. g. wisdom, Prov. 3:13. favour (see חֵן;) a vision from Jehovah, Lam. 2:9. fenced cities by conquest, 2 Sam. 20:6. a harvest, Gen. 26:12.—2 Sam. 18:22 אֵין בְּשׂוֹרָה מֹצֵאת *there is no tidings of any importance.* Also *to meet with* affliction, Ps. 116:3 צָרָה וְיָגוֹן אֶמְצָא *I found* or *met with affliction and sorrow.* Prov. 6:33. Hos. 12:9. (Comp. no. 3, where the same idea is somewhat differently expressed.)—*My hand acquires any thing,* for *I acquire it,* or *attain to it,* Lev. 12:8. 25:28.

3. *to befall* or *happen to* any one, construed with an accus. Gen. 44:34. Ex. 18:8 כָּל־הַתְּלָאָה אֲשֶׁר מְצָאָתַם בַּדֶּרֶךְ *all the trouble which had befallen them in the way.* Num. 20:14. 32:23.—יָדִי מָצְאָה פ׳ *my hand comes upon any one* (in punishment), 1 Sam. 23:17. with לְ, Is. 10:10. Ps. 21:9. (In Aram. מְטָא, ܡܛܐ *idem.* See no. 2.)

4. construed with a dative, *to suffice* or *be sufficient.* Num. 11:22. Judg. 21:14. (Comp. the German *hinlangen, hinreichen;* the Greek ἱκνούμενος, ἱκανός, *sufficient,* from ἱκνέομαι.)

5. more rarely *to seek.* 1 Sam. 20:21 לֵךְ מְצָא אֶת־הַחִצִּים *go, seek the arrows.* Verse 36. Comp. Job 33:10.

Niph. נִמְצָא 1. *to be found.*

2. *to be found* or *be* in any place. Gen. 47:14 כָּל־הַכֶּסֶף הַנִּמְצָא בְאֶרֶץ מִצְרַיִם *all the money which was found in the land of Egypt.* 1 Chr. 4:41. 2 Chr. 34:32. Hence used absolutely, *to exist, to be present,* Gen. 19:15 שְׁתֵּי בְנֹתֶיךָ הַנִּמְצָאֹת *thy two daughters which are present,* in opposition to those which were absent. Comp. verse 14. Ezra 8:25.

3. spoken of God, *to let himself be found (of men),* i. e. to hear or answer them, (comp. דָּרַשׁ.) 1 Chr. 28:9 אִם תִּדְרְשֶׁנּוּ יִמָּצֵא לָךְ *if thou wilt seek him, he will be found of thee,* i. e. he will hear thee. 2 Chr. 15:2,4,15. Jer. 29:13.

4. *to be acquired* or *possessed* by any one, construed with לְ, (comp. Kal no. 2.) Deut. 21:17 כֹּל אֲשֶׁר־יִמָּצֵא לוֹ *all which shall be possessed by him.* Josh. 17:16.

Jer. 15:16 נִמְצְאוּ דְבָרֶיךָ *thy words were gotten (by me).*

Hiph. הִמְצִיא *to cause to find* or *to participate.* Job 34:11. 37:13.

2. *to cause to come, to deliver up.* 2 Sam. 3:8 לֹא הִמְצִיתִךָ בְּיַד דָּוִד *I have not delivered thee up into the hand of David.* Zech. 11:6.

5. *to present,* construed with אֶל. Lev. 9:12, 13, 18.

מַצָּב m. const. מַצַּב, verbal from נָצַב, dec. II. b.

1. *the place where any thing stands.* Josh. 4:3, 9. Metaphorically *state, condition,* Is. 22:19.

2. *a military post, a garrison.* 1 Sam. 13:23. 14:1, 4. 2 Sam. 23:14.

מֻצָּב m. strictly part. Hoph. from נָצַב, *a post, garrison.* Is. 29:3.

מַצָּבָה fem. of מַצָּב, *idem.* 1 Sam. 14:12.

מַצֵּבָה f. const. מַצֶּבֶת, verbal from נָצַב, dec. XI. b. *something raised up, a pillar, monument, cippus.* Gen. 28:18, 22. Ex. 24:4. Particularly *the statue* or *image of a god,* e. g. מַצֶּבֶת הַבַּעַל *the image of Baal,* 2 K. 3:2. 10:26. 18:4. 23:14. Mic. 5:13.

מַצֶּבֶת f. verbal from נָצַב, dec. XIII a.

1. i. q. מַצֵּבָה *a pillar.* Gen. 35:14, 20.

2. *a monument.* 2 Sam. 18:18.

3. *a stock, trunk, root,* (from נָצַב in the signif. *to plant.*) Is. 6:13.

מְצָד, plur. מְצָדוֹת, (with Kamets impure,) dec. I. *a fortress, strong hold, castle on a mountain,* 1 Chr. 11:7 וַיֵּשֶׁב דָּוִיד בַּמְצָד *and David dwelt in the fortress,* i. e. in Zion. Jer. 48:41. 51:30. Probably used frequently of places strong by nature, as high mountains or rocks, (Arab. مصاد *the top of a mountain,*) 1 Sam. 23:14, 19, 29. 1 Chr. 12:8, 16. Comp. Judg. 6:2. Ezek. 33:27. See מָצוֹד, מְצוּדָה.

מָצָה 1. *to squeeze* or *wring out* moisture. Judg. 6:38. (Chald. and Syr. *idem.*)

2. *to swallow down, to drink with eagerness.* Is. 51:17 *the cup of intoxication thou hast drunken and swallowed down,* i. e. thou hast emptied it to the dregs. Ps. 75:9. Ezek. 23:34. (Syr. *idem.* See the Heb. מוּץ, מָצַץ; and comp. מָזָה.)

Niph. 1. pass. of Kal no. 1. *to be wrung out,* spoken of blood. Lev. 1:15. 5:9.

2. pass. of Kal no. 2. Ps. 73:10.

מַצָּה f. dec. X. *something unleavened.* (The etymology is obscure. Usually derived from מָצָה=מָצַץ *to press out* or *to press together;* hence *pressed together, close, heavy,* in opposition to *what is leavened* or *light.*)—חַלַּת מַצָּה *an unleavened cake,* Lev. 8:26. Plur. חַלּוֹת מַצּוֹת *unleavened cakes,* Num. 6:15, also simply מַצּוֹת in the same sense, Ex. 12:15, 18.—חַג הַמַּצּוֹת *the feast of unleavened bread, the passover,* Ex. 23:15. 34:18.

מַצָּה f. verbal from נָצָה, *strife, contention.* Prov. 13:10. 17:19.

מִצְהָלָה f. verbal from צָהַל, dec. XI. a. *a neighing, snorting.* Jer. 8:16. 13:27.

I. **מָצוֹד** m. dec. III. a. Ecc. 9:14. **מְצוֹדָה** dec. X. Is. 29:7. Ezek. 19:9. and most frequently **מְצוּדָה** dec. X. i. q. מְצָד *the height* or *top of a mountain.* Job 39:28. 1 Sam. 22:4. Hence *a castle on a mountain, a fortress,* Ecc. 9:14. 2 Sam. 5:7. Used metaphorically of God, Ps. 18:3. 31:4. 71:3. 91:2.

II. **מָצוֹד** m. verbal from צוּד, dec. III. a. and f.

1. *a catching, hunting.* Prov. 12:12.

2. *a net.* Ecc. 7:27.

I. **מְצוֹדָה** and **מְצוּדָה**, see **מָצוֹד** no. I.

II. **מְצוֹדָה** Ecc. 9:12. and **מְצוּדָה** dec. X. verbals from צוּד.

1. *a prey, booty.* Ezek. 13:21.

2. *a net.* Ecc. 9:12. Ezek. 12:13.

מִצְוָה f. verbal from צָוָה, dec. X. *a command.* 2 K. 18:36. Spoken of the commands of God, Deut. 6:1, 25. 7: 11. Lev. 4:13 אַחַת מִכָּל־מִצְוֹת יְהוָה אֲשֶׁר לֹא תֵעָשֶׂינָה *one of the commands of Jehovah, which should not be done,* i. e. one of his prohibitions.—מְנָת הַלְוִיִּם *what was ordered to be given to the Levites,* Neh. 13:5. comp. מִשְׁפָּט.

מְצוֹלָה Ex. 15:5. Neh. 9:11. and מְצוּלָה f. dec. X. i. q. צוּלָה *the depth,* particularly of the sea, Jon. 2:4. Mic. 7:19. of a river, Zech. 10:11. of mud, Ps. 69:3. See צוּלָה.

מָצוֹק m. verbal from צוּק, *oppression, affliction, straitness.* Ps. 119:143. Jer. 19:9.

מָצוּק m. dec. III. a.

1. *a steep mountain* or *hill.* 1 Sam. 14:5. (Talmud. צוק *mons altus et præceps.* Arab. طاق الجبل *mons altus, rupes montium eminentes.*)

2. *foundation* (of the earth). 1 Sam. 2:8. The earth appears to have been regarded as resting on mountains.

מְצוּקָה f. verbal from צוּק, dec. X. *straitness, affliction, trouble.* Job 15: 24. Plur. Ps. 25:17.

I. מָצוֹר m. with suff. מְצוֹרֵךְ (Ezek. 4:8.) verbal from צוּר, dec. III. a. and f.

1. *straitness, affliction.* Deut. 28: 53 ff.

2. *a siege.* Ezek. 4:7. בּוֹא בַמָּצוֹר *to be besieged,* spoken of a city, 2 K. 24:10. 25:2.

3. *a wall* or *bulwark* against a city besieged. Deut. 20:20. Ezek. 4:2. Mic. 4:14.

4. *a fortification, fortress.* 2 Chr. 32:10. Hab 2:1. More frequently עִיר מָצוֹר *a fortress, a fenced city,* Ps. 31:22.

II. מָצוֹר i. q. מִצְרַיִם *Eygpt,* the proper name of a country. (The Hebrews may have conceived of this name as derived from no. I. since the ancients often speak of the natural strength of Egypt. Diod. I. 18. Comp. Bocharti Phaleg, IV. 24.) יְאֹרֵי מָצוֹר *the streams of Egypt,* Is. 19:6. 37:25. 2 K. 19:24.

מְצוּרָה f. verbal from צוּר, dec. X.

1. *a wall* or *bulwark* against a city besieged. Is. 29:3.

2. *a fortress, citadel.* 2 Chr. 11:11. More frequently עָרֵי מְצוּרָה *fenced cities,* 2 Chr. 14:5 עָרֵי מְצוּרוֹת *idem,* 2 Chr. 11: 10.

מַצּוּת f. verbal from נָצָה, dec. I. i. q. מַצָּה *strife, contention.* Is. 41:12.

מֵצַח com. gen. (Ezek. 3:8. Is. 48: 4.) with suff. מִצְחוֹ, dec. VI. i. *the forehead, brow, front.* 1 Sam. 17:49.—מֵצַח אִשָּׁה זוֹנָה *the (shameless) front of an harlot,* Jer. 3:3.—Ezek. 3:7 חִזְקֵי מֵצַח *of a bold forehead.* Verses 8, 9. Is. 48: 4 מִצְחֲךָ נְחוּשָׁה *thy forehead is of brass.*

מִצְחָה f. dec. X. *greaves.* 1 Sam. 17:6. See מֵצַח. (The Hebrews employed the same word to express *forehead, shin-bone, greaves,* on account of their resemblance to each other in their external surface.)

מְצִלָּה f. plur. מְצִלּוֹת, verbal from צָלַל no. I. dec. X. *a small metallic plate,* such as was suspended from horses or camels in the east for the sake of ornament. Zech. 14:20. See מְצִלְתַּיִם.

מְצֻלָּה f. verbal from צָלַל no. II. *a shady place.* Zech. 1:8.

מְצִלְתַּיִם dual, verbal from צָלַל no. I. *a cymbal,* a musical instrument consisting of two plates which were struck together, *cymbala.* 1 Chr. 13:8. Ezra 3:10. Neh. 12:27. See צֶלְצְלִים.

מִצְנֶפֶת f. (verbal from צָנַף *to wind, to wrap round;*) *the turban* of the high-priest, Ex. 28:4, 30. of the king, Ezek. 21:31. The Bible says nothing of the difference between this and the turban of the common priest. For the suppositions of the Rabbins, see Braun, De Vestitu Sacerd. Heb. p. 625 ff.

מַצָּע m. verbal from יָצַע, *a bed.* Is. 28:20.

מִצְעָד m. verbal from צָעַד, dec. II. b. *a step, going, course.* Ps. 37:23. Prov. 20:24.—בְּמִצְעָדָיו *at his steps,* i. e. in his train, Dan. 11:43. comp. בְּרַגְלָיו Judg. 4:10.

מִצְעִירָה f. *very small, subparvus, parvulus*, compounded of מִן and צְעִירָה, (comp. מִנּאֹל.) Dan. 8:9.

מִצְעָר m. verbal from צָעַר, dec. II. b.

1. *something small* or *insignificant*. Gen. 19:20. Job 8:7. לְמִצְעָר *for a short time*, Is. 63:18.

2. *a small number*.—מִצְעַר אֲנָשִׁים *a small number of men*, 2 Chr. 24:24.

3. Ps. 42:7. prob. the proper name of a peak of Mt. Libanus, not far from Hermon. Others: *a small mountain*.

מִצְפֶּה m. verbal from צָפָה, dec. IX. a.

1. *a high place affording an extensive prospect, a watch-tower*. Is. 21:8. 2 Chr. 20:24.

2. proper name (1.) of a city in the plain of the tribe of Judah. Josh. 15: 38. (2.) of a city in Moab. 1 Sam. 22: 3. (3.) of a valley in the region of Mount Libanus. Josh. 11:8. comp. 11: 3. (4.) of a city in the tribe of Gad, otherwise called מִצְפָּה. Judg. 11:29. See מִצְפָּה no. 1. (5.) of a city in the tribe of Benjamin, otherwise called מִצְפָּה. Josh. 18:26. See מִצְפָּה no. 2.

מִצְפָּה (*a high place, watch-tower.*)

1. proper name of a place in Gilead, beyond Jordan. Judg. 10:17. 11:11, 34. In Judg. 11:29, called מִצְפֵּה־גִלְעָד.

2. also of a place in the tribe of Benjamin, where assemblies of the people were often held, (once called מִצְפֶּה Josh. 18:26.) Judg. 10:1. 21:1. 1 Sam. 7: 5. 10:17. King Asa strengthened it for a frontier fortification against the kingdom of Israel, 1 K. 15:22. 2 Chr. 16:6. Afterwards the governor Gedaliah had his residence here, Jer. 40: 6. comp. Neh. 3:7, 19.

מַצְפֻּנִים masc. plur. verbal from צָפַן, dec. I. *hidden places*. Obad. 6.

מָצַץ *to suck, to sip with pleasure*. Is. 66:11. See מָצָה no. 2. (Arab. and Chald. *idem*.)

מֵצַר m. verbal from צָרַר, (like מֵסַב from סָבַב,) dec. VIII. k. *a strait, affliction, distress*. Ps. 118:5. Plur. מְצָרִים, const. מְצָרֵי, Lam. 1:3. Ps. 116:3.

מִצְרַיִם fem. dual, *Egypt*, the name of a country. Construed with a verb in the singular, Hos. 9:6. Josephus makes the name to be of Coptic origin. (Antiq. I. 6. 2.) But nothing resembling it is found in the present remains of the Coptic language, in which this country bears the name of χημι, see חָם. In Arab. and Chald. مصر, מְצַר, as an appellative, signifies *limes*. The Arabians preserve the word in the singular (مصر.) The dual, which is used in Hebrew and Syriac, may have respect to the division of the country by the Nile, or to Upper and Lower Egypt. The gentile noun is מִצְרִי, plur. מִצְרִים, *an Egyptian;* fem. מִצְרִית *an Egyptian woman*.

מַצְרֵף m. verbal from צָרַף, *a crucible*. Prov. 17:3. 27:21.

מַק m. (verbal from מָקַק, comp. Ps. 38:6.) *rottenness, corruption*. Is. 3:24 וְהָיָה תַחַת בֹּשֶׂם מַק *and instead of a sweet smell shall be rottenness*, i. e. a bad smell. 5:24 *their root shall be as rottenness*, i. e. as rotten wood.

מַקָּבָה f. (verbal from נָקַב, see Hab. 3:15.) dec. X. *a hammer*. 1 K. 6:7. Is. 44:12. Jer. 10:4.

מַקֶּבֶת f. verbal from נָקַב.

1. i. q. מַקָּבָה *a hammer*. Judg. 4:21.

2. *a hollow* or *cleft of a rock*. Is. 51:1.

מַקֵּדָה proper name of a city in the plain of the tribe of Judah, formerly the seat of a Canaanitish king. Josh. 10:10. 12:16. 15:41.

מִקְדָּשׁ m. verbal from קָדַשׁ, dec. II. b.

1. *a holy place, a sanctuary*, spoken of the tabernacle of the congregation and of the temple. Ex. 25:8. Lev. 12: 4. 21:12. Num. 10:21. 18:1. Plur. מִקְדָּשִׁים *sanctuaries*, spoken of the temple, Jer. 51:51. and of high places (בָּמוֹת), Am. 7:9.—מִקְדַּשׁ מֶלֶךְ *a place consecrated to the king*, Am. 7:13.

2. *something consecrated* or *to be consecrated*. Num. 18 : 29. Metaphorically מִקְדְּשֵׁי אֵל prob. *the holy purposes of God*, Ps. 73 : 17.

3. *an asylum, place of refuge*. Is. 8 : 14. Ezek. 11 : 16.

מַקְהֵלִים plur. masc. Ps. 26 : 12. and **מַקְהֵלוֹת** plur. fem. Ps. 68 : 27. verbals from קָהַל, *places of meeting*. The latter occurs also as the proper name of a station of the Israelites in the desert, Num. 33 : 25.

מִקְוֵא see **מִקְוֶה** no II.

I. **מִקְוֶה** m. verbal from קָוָה no. I. dec. IX. a.

1. *hope, confidence*. 1 Chr. 29 : 15. Ezra 10 : 2. Also *an object of hope* or *confidence*, Jer. 14 : 8. 17 : 13. 50 : 7.

II. **מִקְוֶה** m. verbal from קָוָה no. II. dec. IX. a.

1. *a collection* or *company of men*. Under this signification we may place the difficult passage 1 K. 10 : 28 וּמִקְוֵה סֹחֲרֵי הַמֶּלֶךְ *and the caravans of the merchants of the king* יִקְחוּ מִקְוֵה בִּמְחִיר. According to the common punctuation מִקְוֵה, the latter part of this verse hardly gives any meaning, for מִקְוֵה must be rendered *yarn*, (comp. Arab. قوي *torsit funem;* and Heb. קַו, תִּקְוָה.) But it is not probable that the historian has used the word here in two different acceptations, and in the following verse horses are still the subject of discourse. It is better, therefore, to point the word מִקֹּוֵא *from Coa*, as in the Vulgate, probably referring to *Co*, an island in the Nile. The Masoretic punctuators could very easily make this mistake. Or the second מקוה ought perhaps to be rejected from the text. It is wanting in Cod. 172 Kennic. but is found in all the versions. The writer of Chronicles has adopted the Chaldaic form מִקְוֵא, 2 Chr. 1 : 16.

2 מִקְוֵה הַמַּיִם *a collection of waters*. Gen. 1 : 10. Ex. 7 : 19. Lev. 11 : 36.

מִקְוָה f. verbal from קָוָה, *a place of collecting, a reservoir*. Is. 22 : 11.

מָקוֹם com. gen. plur. מְקוֹמוֹת, (verbal from קוּם in the signif. *to stand*,) dec. III. a.

1. *a place*. Gen. 1 : 9. 24 : 23, 25. 28 : 11, 17. Job 16 : 18 אַל יְהִי מָקוֹם לְזַעֲקָתִי *let there be no place* (of concealment) *for my cry*, i. e. let it rise incessantly before God. Before the relative pronoun, the const. state is always used, as מְקוֹם אֲשֶׁר *the place where*, Lev. 4 : 33. 14 : 13. Jer. 22 : 12. So also when the relative is omitted, as in Ps. 104 : 8. Job 18 : 21.—מְקוֹם is sometimes used pleonastically, as מְקוֹם אֲשֶׁר *loco, quo* for *ubi*, Est. 4 : 3. 8 : 17. Ecc. 11 : 3. Ezek. 6 : 13. So in Syr. ܐܬܪ ܕ.)

2. particularly *a dwelling-place*. Gen. 30 : 25. Ex. 3 : 8. Num. 24 : 25.

3. *a place, city, village*. מְקוֹם שְׁכֶם *the village of Shechem*, Gen. 12 : 6. 18 : 24.

4. *instead of, loco*. Is. 33 : 21.

מָקוֹר m. verbal from קוּר, dec. III. a. *a well, fountain*. מְקוֹר חַיִּים *the fountain of happiness*, Ps. 36 : 10. מְקוֹר דָּמִים *the fountain of blood;* an euphemistic expression for *muliebria pudenda*, Lev. 12 : 7. 20 : 18. also 20 : 18. without דָּמִים in the same sense.—Ps. 68 : 27 מִמְּקוֹר יִשְׂרָאֵל *ye of the fountain of Israel*, i. e. ye descendants of Israel. Comp. מַיִם no. 2.

מִקָּח m. verbal from לָקַח, dec. II. b. *a taking, receiving*. 2 Chr. 19 : 7.

מַקָּחוֹת plur. fem. *wares, articles for sale, venalia*. Neh. 10 : 32. The root לָקַח *to take*, has the signif. *to buy*, Neh. 10 : 31. comp. in Talmud מקח *emtio*.

מִקְטָר m. verbal from קָטַר, dec. II. b. *a burning* of incense. Ex. 30 : 1.

מִקְטֶרֶת f. verbal from קָטַר, dec. XIII. a. *a censer*. 2 Chr. 26 : 19. Ezek. 8 : 11.

מַקֵּל, const. מַקַּל and מַקֵּל, plur. מַקְלוֹת prim. dec. VII. a. and h. *a staff*. Gen. 30 : 37 ff.—מַקֵּל יָד *a hand staff*, a kind of weapon, Ezek. 39 : 9. (Chald. מקל יד *spiculum*, Castell.)

מִקְלָט m. dec. II. b. *an asylum, a place of protection,* for the manslayer from the avenger of blood. עָרֵי מִקְלָט *cities of refuge,* Num. 35 : 6—15. Josh. 20 : 2. Root Chald. קְלַט *to receive,* particularly a fugitive.)

מִקְלַעַת f. verbal from קָלַע no. 2. dec. XIII. m. *a sculpture, carved work, graving.* 1 K. 6 : 18. Plur. מִקְלָעוֹת, const. מִקְלְעוֹת, 1 K. 6 : 29, 32. 7 : 31.

מִקְנֶה m. verbal from קָנָה, dec. IX. a.

1. *something bought.* Gen. 49 : 32.

2. *a possession,* but used only of cattle, which among Nomadic tribes is the principal and almost the only property. (For a similar reason, *oxen* in Holstein are called *goods.* Comp. Greek κτῆνος, *cattle,* liter. i. q. κτῆμα, *a possession.*—אַנְשֵׁי מִקְנֶה *people who raise cattle,* Gen. 46 : 32, 34. אֶרֶץ מִקְנֶה *pasturage land,* Num. 32 : 1, 4. — This word denotes both oxen and sheep, but does not include horses or asses. See e. g. Gen. 26 : 14. and particularly 47 : 17.

מִקְנָה fem. of מִקְנֶה, dec. X.

1. *a buying, purchasing.*—סֵפֶר הַמִּקְנָה *a bill of purchase,* Jer. 32 : 11 ff.

2. *something bought.* מִקְנַת כֶּסֶף *a slave bought with money,* Gen. 17 : 12, 13, 23.

3. *price of purchase.* Lev. 25 : 16, 51.

4. *a possession.* Gen. 23 : 18.

מִקְסָם m. verbal from קָסַם, dec. II. b. *a divining, divination.* Ezek. 12 : 24. 13 : 7.

מִקְצוֹעַ m. plur. ־ִים and ־וֹת, dec I. *a corner.* Neh. 3 : 19, 20, 24, 25. Ex. 26 : 24. 36 : 29. Root קָצַע prob. *to cut off.*

מַקְצוּעָה f. dec. X. prob. *a plane* or some similar instrument. Is. 44 : 13. Targ. אִזְמֵל *a knife* generally, also *a plane iron.* Root קָצַע *to scrape off.*

מִקְצָת f. *a part.* Dan. 1 : 2. Neh. 7 : 70. Comp. the Chald. קְצָת. Root קְצָה in Chald. *to divide.*

מָקַק in Kal not used.

Niph. נָמַק 1. *to flow* or *run down.* Ps. 38 : 6 נָמַקּוּ חַבּוּרֹתָי *my sores run down,* i. e. suppurate.

2. *to consume* or *waste away, tabescere;* spoken of the eyes and tongue, Zech. 14 : 12. of persons, Lev. 26 : 39. Ezek. 24 : 23. 33 : 10. Is. 34 : 4 נָמַקּוּ כָּל־צְבָא הַשָּׁמַיִם *all the host of heaven shall waste away.*

Hiph. הֵמַק causat. of Niph. Zech. 14 : 12.

Deriv. מַק.

מִקְרָא m. verbal from קָרָא, dec. I.

1. *a calling together,* liter. the Aramean infin. of קָרָא. Num. 10 : 2. לְמִקְרָא הָעֵדָה *to call together the assembly.*

2. *an assembly called together, an assembly.* מִקְרָא קֹדֶשׁ *a sacred assembly,* such as was called together on the sabbath, and on the first and seventh days of the great festivals, Lev. 23 : 2 ff. Num. 28 : 18, 25. Without קֹדֶשׁ, Is. 1 : 13.

3. *something read, a writing.* Neh. 8 : 8.

מִקְרֶה m. verbal from קָרָה, dec. IX. a.

1. *an accident, chance.* 1 Sam. 6 : 9. 20 : 26. Ruth 2 : 3.

2. *fate, destiny.* Ecc. 2 : 14 מִקְרֶה אֶחָד יִקְרֶה אֶת־כֻּלָּם *one destiny happeneth to them all.* Verse 15. 3 : 19. 9 : 2, 3.

מְקָרֶה m. *the beams of a house.* Ecc. 10 : 18. See קָרָה *to lay the beams of a house.*

מְקֵרָה f. verbal from קָרַר, *a cooling, coolness.* Judg. 3 : 20, 24.

מִקְשֶׁה m. strictly *turned work,* from קָשָׁה i. q. Arab. قشا among other significations *opere tornatili elaboravit lignum.* Comp. מִקְשָׁה.) Hence Is. 3 : 4. מַעֲשֵׂה מִקְשֶׁה *twisted* or *plaited hair.*

I. מִקְשָׁה fem. of מִקְשֶׁה, *turned* or *rounded work.* Ex. 25 : 18 מִקְשָׁה תַּעֲשֶׂה אֹתָם *opere tornatili facias eos* (*cherubos.*) It appears from comparing 1 K. 6 : 23. with verse 28, that the cherubim were made of olive wood and covered with gold; hence this word is incorrectly rendered *massive* or *beaten,* as if from קָשָׁה *to be hard, solid.* Used also of the golden candlestick, Ex. 25 : 31, 36. 37 : 17, 22. Num. 8 : 4. of the silver trumpets, Num. 10 : 2. of a pillar, Jer. 10 : 5.

II. מִקְשָׁה m. (for מִקְשָׁא,) denom. from קִשֻּׁא, Is. 1:8. *a cucumber* or *melon garden.*

I. מַר m. *a drop.* Is. 40:15. Root in Arab. مَرَّ *to flow.*

II. מַר, fem. מָרָה, verbal adj. from מָרַר, *to be bitter,* dec. VIII. k.

1. *bitter.* Is. 5:20. Prov. 27:7. Spoken of water, *briny,* Ex. 15:23. Used abstractly, *bitterness.* 1 Sam. 15:32.

2. *afflictive, acerbus,* Prov. 5:4. Am. 8:10. *destructive, pernicious,* Jer. 2:19. 2 Sam. 2:26. Ps. 64:4. Used substantively, מֵי הַמָּרִים Num. 5:18, 19, 24.

3. *troubled, afflicted,* construed for the most part with נֶפֶשׁ. 1 Sam. 30:6. Job 21:25.—מַר נֶפֶשׁ used as an adj. 1 Sam. 1:10. 22:2. also as a subst. *sorrow,* Job 7:41. 10:1.

4. *bitter, lamentable.* צְעָקָה גְדוֹלָה וּמָרָה *a loud and bitter cry,* Gen. 27:34. Est. 4:1. Ezek. 27:31 מִסְפֵּד מַר *a bitter lamentation.* As an adv. מַר Is. 33:7. and מָרָה Ezek. 27:30. *bitterly.*

5. *violent, cruel, acerbus, acer.* (Comp. Arab. مرير *validus, fortis.*) Hab. 1:6. —מָרֵי נֶפֶשׁ *idem,* Judg. 18:25. 2 Sam. 17:8. This association of ideas is seen in Judg. 14:14, where עַז *strong* is placed in opposition to מָתוֹק *sweet.*

מֹר and מוֹר, before Makkeph מָר־ (Ex. 30:23.) m. dec. I. *myrrh,* a white balsam, which distils from a small thorny tree in Arabia like the acacia. The ancients, however, differ in their account of it. Ps. 45:9. Prov. 7:17. Cant. 3:6. 4:14. 5:6, 13. (Arab. *idem.* Root مر *to drop, distil.*) See Celsii Hierobot. T. I. p. 520 ff.

מָרָא prob. i. q. Arab. مري *to urge* a horse *on rapidly with a whip.*

Hiph. intrans. in reference to the ostrich's clapping its wings in running. Job 39:18 כָּעֵת בַּמָּרוֹם תַּמְרִיא *when she* (*the ostrich*) *moves herself forward,* namely, by clapping her wings. The ancient versions render it, *to lift one's self.*

Note. מֹרְאָה Zeph. 3:1, stands for מֹרָה *rebellis;* see מָרָה.

מָרֵא Chald. *a lord.* Dan. 2:47. 4:16, 21. 5:23. (In Syr. and Arab. *idem.*)

מְרֹאדַךְ בַּלְאֲדָן proper name of a Babylonish king. Is. 39:1. Also written בּ׳ בְּרֹאדַךְ q. v. He lived in the time of Hezekiah. See מְרֹדָךְ.

מַרְאֶה m. verbal from רָאָה, dec. IX. a.

1. *a looking, seeing.* Lev. 13:12. לְכָל־מַרְאֵה עֵינֵי הַכֹּהֵן *wheresoever the priest looketh.* Deut. 28:34 מַרְאֵה עֵינֶיךָ *what thine eyes see.* Verse 67. Is. 11:3. Ezek. 23:16.

2. *sight, vision.* Ex. 3:3. Ezek. 8:4. 11:24. 43:3. Dan. 8:16.

3. *appearance, form.* Ex. 24:17. Ezek. 1:16, 28. Frequently after a noun in regimen, as יְפַת מַרְאֶה Gen. 12:11. טוֹבַת מַרְאֶה 24:16. 26:7. *of a beautiful form;* also נֶחְמָד לְמַרְאֶה *desirable in appearance,* Gen. 2:9.—In the prophetic style, it is used, like דְּמוּת (see no. 3.) to express the indistinct forms which appear in vision, Dan. 10:18 וַיִּגַּע־בִּי כְּמַרְאֵה אָדָם *and there touched me something, like a human form.* Ezek. 8:2. Connected with דְּמוּת, 1:27. Plur. מַרְאִים in the same connexion as the singular, Dan. 1:13, 15. Ezek. 1:5, 13. 10:22. Cant. 2:14.

מַרְאָה fem. of מַרְאֶה, dec. X.

1. *a sight, vision,* i. q. חָזוֹן. Dan. 10:7, 8, 16. מַרְאֹת הַלַּיְלָה *nightly visions,* Gen. 46:2. מַרְאוֹת אֱלֹהִים *visions sent from God,* Ezek. 8:3. 40:2.

2. *a mirror.* Ex. 38:8. (Arab. مِرْآة *idem.*) Comp. רְאִי.

מֻרְאָה f. dec. X. *the crop of a bird.* Lev. 1:16. (Arab. مَرِيء *idem,* from مرأ *to digest well,* and spoken of food, *to be digestible.*)

מָרֵאשָׁה Josh. 15:44. and מָרֵשָׁה 2 Chr. 11:8. 14:8, 9. Mic. 1:15. in Greek Μαρισά 2 Mac. 12:35. proper name of a fenced city in the plain of the tribe of Judah. See Josephi Antiq. VIII. 3, 6. XII. 12. XIV. 2, 8, 10, 27. Bella Jud. I. 6.)

מְרַאֲשׁוֹת plur. fem. denom. from רֹאשׁ, dec. X. *place of* or *about the head*, (comp. מַרְגְּלוֹת *the place of the feet.*) The accusative is used adverbially, *at the head*, i. e. near or under the head, 1 Sam. 19:13 מְרַאֲשֹׁתָיו *at his head.* Verse 16. 26:7, 11, 16. 1 K. 19:6. Gen. 28:11, 18. With a double plural termination, (like בָּמוֹתֵי,) 1 Sam. 26:12 מֵרַאֲשֹׁתֵי שָׁאוּל *from the head of Saul*, for מִמְּרַאֲשֹׁתֵי ש׳.

מַרְאֲשׁוֹת plur. fem. denom. from רֹאשׁ, *idem.* Jer. 13:18.

מַרְבַדִּים plur. fem. verbal from רָבַד, dec. VIII. *coverings, mattresses.* Prov. 7:16. 31:22.

מַרְבָּה f. verbal from רָבָה, *greatness, largeness;* as a concrete, *large, ample.* Ezek. 23:32.

מַרְבֶּה m. verbal from רָבָה, dec. IX. a. *greatness, increase.* Is. 9:6.

מַרְבִּית f. verbal from רָבָה, dec. I.

1. *greatness, multitude.* 2 Chr. 9:6. 30:18.

2. *the greatest part.* 1 Chr. 12:29.

3. *increase of a family, offspring, soboles.* 1 Sam. 2:33.

4. *usury, interest*, liter. *increase of the capital.* Lev. 25:37. (Comp. Greek τόκος *usury*, from τίκτω *to bear;* and Lat. *fœnus*, from *feo, to bear*, whence *fœtus, fœcundus, fœnum.* See Gellius XVI. 13. In Arab. comp. ربا conj. IV. *to lend on usury;* رِبًا *usury;* Syr. ܪܒܐ *idem.*)

מַרְבֵּץ m. verbal from רָבַץ *a place to lie down in, a couching place.* Zeph. 2:15.

מַרְבָּץ dec. II. b. i. q. מַרְבֵּץ. Ezek. 25:5.

מַרְבֵּק m. *a place of fattening, a stall.* Am. 6:4. עֵגֶל מַרְבֵּק, *a calf of the stall*, i. e. a fatted calf, 1 Sam. 28:24. Jer. 46:21. Mal. 3:20. [4:2.] Root רָבַק in Chald. *to fatten.*

מַרְגּוֹעַ m. verbal from רָגַע, *rest, a resting place.* Jer. 6:16.

מַרְגְּלוֹת plur. fem. denom. from רֶגֶל, dec. X. *place of* or *about the feet.* Ruth 3:5 ff. Dan. 10:6. (Comp. מְרַאֲשׁוֹת.) Used adverbially in the accus. *at the feet*, Ruth 3:8.

מַרְגֵּמָה f. *a heap of stones.* (Root רָגַם *to throw stones;* Arab. رجم *to heap up stones.*) Thus Prov. 26:8 כִּצְרוֹר אֶבֶן בְּמַרְגֵּמָה *as a bag of precious stones in a heap of stones.* Luth. *als ob man Edelsteine auf den Rabenstein würfe.* The Sept. renders the word *a sling*, (in like manner from רָגַם *to throw stones*,) hence the whole passage, *as if one binds a precious stone on a sling.* The expression is proverbial like Matt. 7:6.

מַרְגֵּעָה f. verbal from רָגַע, *rest, quiet dwelling.* Is. 28:12.

מָרַד, fut. יִמְרֹד, *to revolt* or *rebel*, as subjects or tributaries from their masters. Gen. 14:4. Construed with בְּ, 2 K. 18:7, 20. 24:1, 20. more rarely with עַל, Neh. 2:19. 2 Chr. 13:6.—מָרַד בַּיהוָֹה *to decline from* or *rebel against Jehovah*, (by the practice of idolatry,) Josh. 22:16 ff. Ezek. 2:3. Dan. 9:9.—מֹרְדֵי־אוֹר *those who rebel against the light*, i. e. hate it or declare war against it, Job 24:13.

מְרַד Chald. *to rebel*, as in Heb. Ezra 4:19.

מֶרֶד m. verbal from מָרַד, *rebellion.* Josh. 22:22.

מָרָד Chald. adj. *rebellious.* Fem. מָרָדָא, emph. מָרָדְתָּא, Ezra 4:12, 15.

מַרְדּוּת f. verbal from מָרַד, *rebellion, refractoriness.* 1 Sam. 20:30. (In Arab. *idem.*)

מְרֹדַךְ m. proper name of an idol of the Babylonians. Jer. 50:2. Like אֵל and בַּעַל, it is often compounded with other words to form proper names of persons. Comp. מְרֹאדַךְ בַּלְאֲדָן, אֱוִיל מְרֹדַךְ, *Mesessimordacus*, *Sisimardocus*, etc. Assyrian and Babylonian names.

מָרְדֳּכַי proper name of a Jew living in Persia, who was the foster father of Esther, and afterwards vizier or prime-minister in the court of Ahasuerus. Est. II.—X. Sept. Μαρδοχαῖος. Like Esther, it is probably of Persian origin; comp. مردك (*mardach*) *homunculus.*

מֻרְדָּף m. Is. 14:6. strictly part. Hoph. from רָדַף, but here used substantively, *persecution.*

I. מָרָה *to be refractory, perverse, rebellious.* Deut. 21:18, 20. Ps. 78:8. Construed (1.) with an accus. of the person or thing against which any one is refractory, Jer. 4:17. Ps. 105:28. Most frequently מָרָה אֶת־פִּי יְהוָֹה *to rebel against the command of Jehovah*, Num. 20:24. 27:14. 1 Sam. 12:15. (2.) with בְּ, Ps. 5:11. Hos. 14:1.

Hiph. הִמְרָה, fut. apoc. וַתֶּמֶר (Ezek. 5:6.)

1. *to contend with* any one. (In Arab. conj. III. *idem.*) Job 17:2 בְּהַמְּרוֹתָם תָּלַן עֵינִי *my eye dwells on their contention* (against me), i.e. I must constantly behold their contention against me. (The Dagesh in מ is euphonic.)

2. *to be rebellious.* Ps. 106:7. It is construed (1.) with an accus. Ps. 78:17, 40, 56. Hence הִמְרָה אֶת־פִּי יְהוָֹה *to rebel against the commandment of the Lord*, Deut. 1:26, 45. Josh. 1:18. Also in the same sense with עֵינַיִם, Is. 3:8. (2.) with בְּ, Ps. 106:43. Ezek. 20:8. (3.) with עִם, Deut. 9:7, 24.

Deriv. מְרִי.

II. מָרָה i.q. מָרַר *to be bitter.* 2 K. 14:26 עֳנִי מֹרֶה *the bitter affliction.* So all the ancient versions. If pointed מָרָה, the gender would be incorrect. Comp. מְרִי Job 23:2. So invertedly a form from מָרַר Ex. 23:21. derives its signification from מָרָה.

מְרָה f. dual מְרָתַיִם (strictly *double rebellion*) a prophetical name of Babylon. Jer. 50:21.

מָרָה (*bitterness*) Ex. 15:23. Num. 33:8. proper name of a place in the desert of Arabia, so called from the bitterness of its waters. Comp. Pococke Beschreibung des Morgenlandes, Th. I. p. 234. of the German translation.

מָרָּה (read *morra*) f. verbal from מָרַר, dec. X. *grief, sorrow.* Prov. 14:10.

מֹרָה f. verbal from מָרַר, dec. X. *idem.* Gen. 26:35 מֹרַת רוּחַ *bitterness of heart.*

מָרוּד m. verbal from רוּד, dec. III.c. *persecution.* Lam. 3:19. Plur. מְרוּדִים Lam. 1:7. Used as a concrete Is. 58:7 מְרוּדִים *persecuted.* So all the ancient versions.

מֵרוֹז proper name of a city in the northern part of Palestine. Once Judg. 5:23. Jerome, (in his Onomast.) Est autem nunc vicus, Merrus nomine, in duodecimo milliario urbis Sebaste, juxta Dothaim.

מְרוֹחַ m. Lev. 21:21 מְרוֹחַ אָשֶׁךְ *with broken testicles.* Root מָרַח; in Arab. also among other significations, *to rub* or *bruise in pieces;* comp. مرخ *arbor, quæ confricta ignem reddit.*

מָרוֹם m. verbal from רוּם, dec. III.a.

1. *a height, high place.* Hab. 2:9. Ps. 7:8. הַר מְרוֹם יִשְׂרָאֵל *the high mountain of Israel*, Ezek. 17:23. 20:40. 34:14. Spoken often of heaven, Ps. 18:17. Jer. 25:30. Also, *on high*, Is. 37:23 וַתִּשָּׂא מָרוֹם עֵינֶיךָ *and thou hast lifted up thine eyes on high.* 40:26. As a concrete *the highest*, Ps. 92:9. and collectively, *the high ones*, i.e. the princes, Is. 24:4.

2. *pride;* as an adv. *proudly, arrogantly.* Ps. 56:3.

3. *something remote* or *far off*, (comp. רוּם Is. 30:18.) Ps. 10:5 מָרוֹם מִשְׁפָּטֶיךָ מִנֶּגְדּוֹ *thy judgments are far from him.*

מֵרוֹם (*height*) a proper name. מֵי מֵרוֹם *waters of Merom*, Josh. 11:5, 7. a lake, called in Greek *Samochonitis*, extending to the Jordan, 60 stadia long, and 30 broad.

מֵרוֹץ m. verbal from רוּץ, *race, course.* Ecc. 9:11.

I. מְרוּצָה fem. of מֵרוֹץ, dec. X. *idem.* 2 Sam. 18:27. Jer. 23:10.

II. מְרוּצָה f. verbal from רוּץ, *oppression.* Jer. 22:17. It borrows its signification from רָצַץ.

מְרוּקִים masc. plur. dec. I. *a purifying, cleansing.* Est. 2:12. Root מָרַק.

מָרוֹת (*bitterness*) proper name of a city in Judah. Once Mic. 1:12.

מַרְזֵחַ *an outcry, lamentation.* Jer. 16:5. See the following article.

מִרְזַח m. *an outcry, rejoicing.* Am. 6:7. Comp. Arab. رزح *a raising of the voice* from joy or sorrow; مرزيح *an outcry.*)

מָרַח i. q. Arab. مرخ *to rub in, to overspread,* e. g. the body with oil; conj. IV. *to soften.* It is used in Hebrew of the application of a soft substance to a wound, (comp. Is. 1:6,) Is. 38:21 *let them take dried figs,* וְיִמְרְחוּ עַל הַשְּׁחִין *and lay them on the sore,* or *and rub them on the sore.* Sept. καὶ τρίψον καὶ κατάπλασαι. Deriv. מָרוֹחַ.

מֶרְחָב m. verbal from רָחַב, dec. II. b. *a broad place.* Hab. 1:6. Often used figuratively Ps. 18:20 וַיּוֹצִיאֵנִי לַמֶּרְחָב *he brought me forth into a broad place,* i. e. he gave me freedom, happiness. (Comp. the opposite phrase צַר *straitness.*) Ps. 31:9. 118:5. In a bad sense Hos. 4:16 כְּכֶבֶשׂ בַּמֶּרְחָב *as a sheep going astray.*

מֶרְחָק m. verbal from רָחַק, dec. VIII. a. *remoteness, a remote place.* Is. 10:3. 17:13. אֶרֶץ מֶרְחָק *a distant land,* Is. 13:5. Plur. מֶרְחַקִּים Zech. 10:9. אֶרֶץ מֶרְחַקִּים Jer. 8:19. מֶרְחַקֵּי־אָרֶץ Is. 8:9. *distant lands.*

מַרְחֵק m. verbal from רָחַק, dec. VIII. a. *idem.* Plur. מַרְחַקִּים Is. 33:17.

מַרְחֶשֶׁת f. verbal from רָחַשׁ, *a vessel for boiling* or *frying.* Lev. 2:7. 7:9.

מָרַט kindred with מָלַט q. v.

1. *to make smooth* or *to sharpen* a sword. Ezek. 21:14, 33.

2. *to make smooth* the head of any one, *to pluck off the hair.* Ezra 9:3. Neh. 13:25 וָאֶמְרְטֵם *I plucked off their hair.* Is. 50:6 וּלְחָיַי לְמֹרְטִים *and my cheeks to them that plucked off the hair.* Ezek. 29:18 כָּל־כָּתֵף מְרוּטָה *every shoulder is bald,* from constantly bearing burdens.

Niph. *to become bald.* Lev. 13:40, 41.

Pu. 1. *to be smooth* or *polished.* 1 K. 7:45.

2. *to be sharpened,* spoken of the sword. Part. fem. מוֹרָטָה for מְמֹרָטָה, Ezek. 21:15, 16.

3 עַם מוֹרָט Is. 18:2, 7. most probably *populus acer,* i. e. celer, vehemens. Comp. חַד no. 2. Hab. 1:8.

מְרַט Chald. *to pluck.* See Heb. מָרַט no. 2. Dan. 7:4.

I. מְרִי m. in pause מֶרִי, with suff. מִרְיְךָ, מִרְיָם, verbal from מָרָה no. I. dec. VI. l. *obstinacy, rebellion.* Prov. 17:11. Ezek. 2:5 כִּי בֵּית מְרִי הֵמָּה *for they are an obstinate house,* i. e. generation. בְּנֵי מֶרִי *the obstinate* or *refractory,* Num. 17:25. Hence used elliptically for אִישׁ, אַנְשֵׁי מְרִי, Ezek. 2:7 כִּי מְרִי הֵמָּה *for they are rebellious.* Verse 8. 44:6.

II. מְרִי probably verbal from מָרָה no. II. *bitterness.* Job 23:2.

מְרִיא m. *fat, well-fed;* particularly as a subst. *a fatted calf,* μοσχὸς σιτιυτός. It is generally connected with שׁוֹר and בָּקָר, 2 Sam. 6:13. 1 K. 1:9, 19, 25. As an epithet, Ezek. 39:18 פָּרִים מְרִיאֵי בָשָׁן *bullocks fed in Bashan.* Comp. further Is. 1:11. 11:6. Am. 5:22. Root מָרָא i. q. Arab. مرأ *to digest well,* hence *to flourish, become fat.* Chald. Pa. *to fatten.* (Comp. בָּרִיא, בָּרָה.)

מְרִיבָה f. verbal from רִיב, dec. X.

1. *strife, contention.* Gen. 13:8. Ex. 17:7. Num. 27:14.

2. מֵי מְרִיבָה (*waters of contention*) name of a spring in the desert of Sin, where the people contended against Jehovah. Num. 20:13, 24. Deut. 33:8. Ps. 81:8. 106:32. Also in the same sense מֵי מְרִיבוֹת קָדֵשׁ Ezek. 47:19.

מֹרִיָּה and **מוֹרִיָּה** f. proper name of a hill in Jerusalem, on which Solomon built the temple. 2 Chr. 3:1. Gen. 22:2 אֶרֶץ הַמֹּרִיָּה *the country of Moriah.* It was separated from Mount Zion by a valley, afterwards connected by a bridge. See Josephi Antiq. xv. 14. Bella Judaica, iv. 14. vi. 6. ix. 13. In the two passages above named there is an allusion to the derivation of the word from רָאָה *to see.* The Samar. text Gen. 22:2. has מוראה.

מִרְיָם f. (liter. *their rebellion*) *Miriam,* the sister of Moses, a musician and prophetess. Ex. 15:20. Num. 12:1. Mic. 6:4. In Greek Μαριάμ, Μαρία.

מְרִירוּת f. verbal from מָרַר, *sorrow, trouble.* Ezek. 21:11.

מְרִירִים see **כִּמְרִיר**.

מְרִירִי m. verbal adj. from מָרַר, *bitter, poisonous.* Deut. 32:24. Comp. מְרֹרָה.

מֹרֶךְ m. liter. *softness,* hence metaphorically *fear.* Lev. 26:36. Sept. δειλία. (In Rabbin. נמרך *mollescere,* Syr. ܡܪܟ *attenuavit.* For the figure, comp. רַךְ לֵבָב.)

מֶרְכָּב m. verbal from רָכַב, dec. II. b.

1. *a chariot, waggon.* 1 K. 5:6. [4:26.]

2. *the seat of a chariot.* Cant. 3:10. Lev. 15:9.

מֶרְכָּבָה fem. of מֶרְכָּב, *a chariot, waggon.* 2 Sam. 15:1. 1 K. 7:33. Const. מִרְכֶּבֶת Gen. 41:43. With suff. מֶרְכַּבְתּוֹ Gen. 46:29. 1 Sam. 8:11. Plur. מַרְכָּבוֹת, const. מַרְכְּבוֹת, Joel 2:5. Ex. 15:4. Is. 2:7.

מַרְכֹּלֶת f. verbal from רָכַל, dec. XIII. f. *a market, place of traffic.* Ezek. 27:24.

מִרְמָה f. (verbal from רָמָה in Piel *to deceive,*) dec. X. *deception.* Gen. 27:35. 34:13.—אַבְנֵי מִרְמָה *false weights,* Mic. 6:11.—מֹאזְנֵי מִרְמָה *a false balance,* Prov. 11:1.—Metaphorically *goods unjustly acquired,* Jer. 5:27.—Plur. מִרְמוֹת Ps. 10:7. 35:20.

מִרְמָס m. verbal from רָמַס, *what is trodden under foot.* Is. 5:5. 7:25. 10:6. Ezek. 34:19.

מֵרֵעַ m. (with two Tseris impure,) dec. I. i. q. רֵעַ *a friend, companion.* With suff. מֵרֵעֵהוּ, plur. מֵרֵעִים, Gen. 26:26. Judg. 14:20. 15:6. Most probably the part. Hiph. from רעע, with the signification of רָעָה no. 2. The first Tseri is impure, like the Kamets in מָגֵן, מָסָךְ, מָעֹז.

מִרְעֶה m. verbal from רָעָה, dec. IX. a. *fodder* or *pasture* for cattle. Gen. 47:4. Joel 1:18. Job 39:8.

מַרְעִית f. verbal from רָעָה, dec. I.

1. *a feeding, pasturing;* used of shepherds. צֹאן מַרְעִיתִי *the sheep which I feed,* Jer. 23:1. Ps. 74:1.

2. *the herd* itself. Jer. 10:21.

I. **מַרְפֵּא** m. and **מַרְפֵּה** (Jer. 8:15.) verbal from רָפָא *to heal.*

1. *healing, cure.* 2 Chr. 21:18 אֵין מַרְפֵּא *so that there was no cure.* 36:16. Jer. 14:19.

2. *health, vigour.* Prov. 4:22. 16:24. 12:18. 13:17.

3. *deliverance* (from adversity). Prov. 6:15. 29:1. Mal. 3:20.

4. *a remedy, cure.* Jer. 33:6.

II. **מַרְפֵּא** verbal from רָפָה=רָפָא, dec. I. *quietness, calmness, gentleness.* Prov. 14:30 לֵב מַרְפֵּא *a quiet, gentle spirit.* 15:4 מַרְפֵּא לָשׁוֹן *gentleness of tongue,* i. e. mild language. Ecc. 10:4 *gentleness pacifies great offences.*

מִרְפָּשׂ m. verbal from רָפַשׂ, dec. II. a. *fouled* or *troubled water.* Ezek. 34:19.

מָרַץ in Kal not used. According to Kimchi, *to be vehement, strong, powerful,* a meaning which suits all the passages where the word occurs.

Niph. Job 6:25 מַה־נִּמְרְצוּ אִמְרֵי־יֹשֶׁר *how powerful are the words of truth!* 1 K. 2:8 קְלָלָה נִמְרֶצֶת *a grievous curse.* Mic. 2:10 חֶבֶל נִמְרָץ *a sore destruction, corruptio vehementissima.*

Hiph. *to make violent, to excite.* Job 16:3 מַה־יַּמְרִיצְךָ *what excites* or *emboldens thee?*

Note. As it is uncertain whether the Rabbins in giving this interpretation have followed their knowledge of the usus loquendi, or have been guided, as they frequently were, by conjecture, a different explanation has been adopted by others with considerable plausibility, In Job 6:25, it is supposed equivalent, to מָלַץ *to be sweet,* (as it is read in 1 MS.) and in the other places to signify, *ægrum esse, to be sick;* comp. the Arab. مرض *to be sick.*

מַרְצֵעַ m. verbal from רָצַע, *an awl.* Ex. 21:6. Deut. 15:17.

מַרְצֶפֶת f. verbal from רָצַף, *a pavement.* 2 K. 16:17.

מָרַק *to cleanse, polish, furbish,* as metals. 2 Chr. 4:16 נְחֹשֶׁת מָרוּק *polished brass.* Jer. 46:4 מִרְקוּ הָרְמָחִים *furbish the spears.*

Pu. מֹרַק pass. Lev. 6:21. [6:28.] (In Arab. and Syr. *idem.*)

Deriv. תַּמְרוּקִים, מְרוּקִים.

מָרָק m. dec. IV. a. *broth, soup.* Judg. 6:19, 20. Also Is. 65:4 Keri. (Arab. *idem.*)

מֶרְקָח m. verbal from רָקַח, dec. II. b. *an aromatic herb.* Cant. 5:13.

מֶרְקָחָה f. verbal from רָקַח, *ointment.* Ezek. 24:10. perhaps *a pot of ointment,* Job 41:23. [41:31.]

מִרְקַחַת f. verbal from רָקַח.

1. *an anointing.* Ex. 30:25. 2 Chr. 16:14.

2. *ointment,* 1 Chr. 9:30.

מָרַר 1. *to be bitter.* (So in all the dialects.) In Kal impers. מַר לִי *amarum est mihi, I am troubled, grieved,* Lam. 1:4. Construed with מִן *about* any one, Ruth 1:13.

2. *to be grieved.* 1 Sam. 30:6.

Niph. fut. יִמַּר (for יִמָּר.) *to become bitter.* Is. 24:9. The preterite נָמַר Jer. 48:11. comes from מוּר.

Pi. fut. יְמָרֵר. 1. *to make bitter, to imbitter.* Ex. 1:14. Is. 22:4 אֲמָרֵר בַּבֶּכִי *I will weep bitterly.*

2. *to irritate, provoke, irritare, lacessere;* comp. Hithpa. Gen. 49:23.

Hiph. הֵמַר, infin. הָמֵר.

1. *to imbitter.* Job 27:2.

2. construed with לְ, *to afflict.* Ruth 1:20 הֵמַר לִי שַׁדַּי *the Almighty hath afflicted me.* Comp. הֵרַע לְ verse 21.

3. בְּכִי being omitted, *to weep bitterly.* Zech. 12:10.

Note. In Ex. 23:21, תַּמֵּר for תָּמֵר derives its signification from מָרָה.

Hithpa. *to be provoked, irritated.* Dan. 8:7. (Syr. ܐܬܡܪܡܪ *to provoke, excite to anger.*)

Deriv. out of course מַר, מָרָה, מְרִירִי, תַּמְרוּרִים, מַמְּרֹרִים, מֶמֶר, מְרִירוּת.

מְרֵרָה f. verbal from מָרַר, dec. X. *gall.* Job 16:13.

מְרֹרִים masc. plur. verbal from מָרַר, dec. III. a. *bitter herbs.* Ex. 12:8. Num. 9:11. Sept. πικρίδες. Vulg. *lactucæ agrestes.* For the herbs so named by the Jews, see Carpzov Apparat. ad Antiquit. Sac. Cod. p. 402 ff. In Lam. 3:15. it corresponds to לַעֲנָה *wormwood* in the parallel clause.

מְרֹרָה f. verbal from מָרַר, dec. X.

1. plur. מְרֹרֹת *bitternesses.* Deut. 32:32 אַשְׁכְּלֹת מְרֹרֹת *bitter grapes.* Metaphorically Job 13:26 כִּי תִכְתֹּב עָלַי מְרֹרוֹת *for thou writest,* i. e. decreest, *against me bitter things.*

2. *gall.* Job 20:25.

3. *poison.* Job 20:14 מְרוֹרַת פְּתָנִים *the poison of adders.* Perhaps strictly *the gall of adders,* which, according to Pliny, (N. H. XI. 37.) is the seat of their poison. But *bitterness* and *poison* are otherwise kindred ideas in Hebrew. (See מְרִירִי *poisonous;* Syr. ܡܪܪܬܐ and Zabian מורא *poison.*)

מָרְאֲשָׁה see **מְרַאֲשָׁה.**

מִרְשַׁעַת f. verbal from רָשַׁע, *wickedness.* Used as a concrete *wicked,* (comp. Lat. *scelus* for *scelesta.*) 2 Chr. 24:7.

מַשָּׂא m. verbal from נָשָׂא *to bear,* dec. I.

1. *a bearing,* construed like an infin. Num. 4:24 לַעֲבֹד וּלְמַשָּׂא *to labour and to bear.* 2 Chr. 20:25 לְאֵין מַשָּׂא *so that it was not to be borne;* comp. 35:3. More as a substantive, Num. 4:19, 27, 31, 32, 47.

2. *a burden.* 2 K. 5:17. Jer. 17:21 ff. Num. 11:11. הָיָה לְמַשָּׂא *to become a burden,* 2 Sam. 15:33. 19:36. with עַל, Job 7:20.

3. מַשָּׂא נֶפֶשׁ *that to which the heart cleaves.* Ezek. 24:25. Comp. נָשָׂא no. 1. (3.)

4. *a proverb, saying,* (from נָשָׂא *efferre.*) Prov. 30:1. 31:1 מַשָּׂא אֲשֶׁר יִסְּרַתּוּ אִמּוֹ *the sayings which his mother taught him.* Particularly *an oracle* from God, 2 K. 9:25. or from a prophet, Is. 13:1 מַשָּׂא בָּבֶל *an oracle concerning Babel.* 15:1. 17:1. 19:1.

5. *a present, gift,* like מִנְחָה, (comp. נשא in Pi.) 2 Chr. 17:11.

6. perhaps *a song,* see נָשָׂא no. 1. (5.) 1 Chr. 15:27 שַׂר הַמַּשָּׂא *the chorister.* Sept. ἄρχων τῶν ᾠδῶν. So also Kimchi. Others: *the overseer over the burden* or *bearing* (of the ark).

מַשֹּׂא (read *masso*) m. 2 Chr. 19:7 מַשֹּׂא פָנִים *partiality.* See נָשָׂא no. 3. (1.)

מַשָּׂאָה fem. of מַשָּׂא, *a burning, conflagration.* Is. 30:27. See מַשְׂאֵת no. 3.

מַשְׂאֵת const. מַשְׂאַת, plur. מַשְׂאֹת.

1. *a lifting up.* Ps. 141:2.

2. *a burden.* Zeph. 3:18.

3. *a mounting up,* particularly of smoke in a conflagration. Judg. 20:38 מַשְׂאַת הֶעָשָׁן *the smoke rising up.* Ver. 40. Comp. מַשָּׂאָה.

4. *a banner,* i. q. נֵס, perhaps strictly, *a signal by a lighted fire, a lantern,* as if from signif. no. 3. Jer. 6:1.

5. *a tax, duty.* 2 Chr. 24:6, 9. Ezek. 20:40.

6. *a proverb.* Lam. 2:14.

7. *a present,* comp. נָשָׂא in Pi. Est. 2:18. Jer. 40:5. Particularly *the mess* or *portion which the host sets before his guest* (γέρας,) or *sends to him.* Gen. 43:34. 2 Sam. 11:8.

Note. מַשְּׂאוֹת Ezek. 17:9. is the Aram. infin. from נְשָׂא, like מַשָּׂא. Comp. מַלְאוֹת infin. Pi. for מַלֵּא.

מַשּׁאוֹת plur. fem. Ps. 74:3 according to some editions. See מַשּׁוּאוֹת.

מִשְׂגָּב m. with suff. מִשְׂגַּבִּי, verbal from שָׂגַב, dec. VIII. a.

1. *a height.* Is. 25:12.

2. *a hill, rock,* as a place of security; hence *a refuge.* Ps. 9:10. 18:3. 46:8, 12.

מְשׂוּכָה f. verbal from שׂוּךְ, dec. X. *a thorn-hedge.* Is. 5:5. Prov. 15:19. Also מְסוּכָה Mic. 7:4.

מַשּׂוֹר m. *a saw.* Is. 10:15. Root נָשַׂר = Chald. נְסַר *to saw.*

מְשׂוּרָה f. a measure for liquids. Lev. 19:35. Ezek. 4:11, 16. Root מָשַׂר Arab. مشر conj. II. *to divide.*

מָשׂוֹשׂ m. verbal from שׂוּשׂ, dec. III. a. *joy,* also *the object of joy.* Ps. 48:3. Is. 8:6. 24:11.

מִשְׂחָק m. verbal from שָׂחַק, *laughter,* also *the object of laughter* or *scorn.* Hab. 1:10.

מַשְׂטֵמָה f. 1. *a snare, pit,* i. q. פַּח. Hos. 9:8. Root שׂטם, Syr. ܣܛܡ *vinxit, compedivit.* Hence

2. *destruction, ruin.* Hos. 9:7. Others: *hatred, persecution,* from שָׂטַם.

מַשְׂכִּיל *a song.* See שָׂכַל.

מַשְׂכִּית f. 1. *an image, figure, picture.* (Comp. שְׂכִיָּה, שָׂכָה.) Ezek. 8:12 חַדְרֵי מַשְׂכִּית *chambers of imagery,* i. e. chambers whose walls were painted with idolatrous figures. Comp. verses 10, 11. — אֶבֶן מַשְׂכִּית Lev. 26:1. and מַשְׂכִּיּוֹת Num. 33:52. *stones with idolatrous figures.* Prov. 25:11 תַּפּוּחֵי זָהָב בְּמַשְׂכִּיּוֹת כָּסֶף *golden apples with silver figures.* Others: *in silver dishes* or *baskets,* from שָׂכָה=שָׂכַךְ.

2. *an image, idea, thought.* Ps. 73: 7. Prov. 18:11.

מַשְׂכֹּרֶת f. verbal from שָׂכַר, dec. XIII. f. *a reward.* Gen. 29:15. 31: 7, 41.

מַשְׂמְרוֹת fem. plur. *nails.* Ecc. 12: 11. See מַסְמְרִים.

מִשְׂפָּח m. *a shedding of blood.* Is. 5:7. Root שָׂפַח or סָפַח *to pour*, in Arabic particularly *to shed* blood.

מִשְׂרָה f. *dominion, government.* Is. 9:5, 6. Root שָׂרָה=שָׂרַר and שׂוּר *to rule.*

מִשְׂרְפוֹת plur. fem. verbal from שָׂרַף, dec. II. b.

1. *a burning;* e. g. of lime. Is. 33: 12. (comp. Gen. 11:3.)

2. *a burning;* e. g. of corpses. Jer. 34:5. (comp. 2 Chr. 16:14.)

3. מִשְׂרְפוֹת מַיִם (*flowings of water*, from the Chald. שְׂרַף Ithpe. *stillavit,*) proper name of a city or country near Sidon. Josh. 11:8. 13:6.

מַשְׂרֵת m. *a pan.* 2 Sam. 13:9. (Chald. מַסְרֵיתָא, מַסְרִיתָא, מַסְרֵת *idem.*)

מַשׁ Gen. 10:23. *Mount Masius*, a part of the Gordiean chain, north of Nesibis, called by the Arabians *Judi.*

מַשָּׁא m. verbal from נָשָׁא.

1. *usury.* נָשָׁא מַשָּׁא *to exact usury.* Neh. 5:7.

2. *a debt, obligation.* Neh. 10:32.

מֵשָׁא found only Gen. 10:30. a boundary of Joktanite Arabia, which is very difficult to be defined. If the eastern boundary is intended, we may best compare the *Mesene* of the ancients, *Maishan* and *Moshan*, two cities in the country of the modern Bassora. Whence the Syrians give the name *Maishan* to the whole country on the Tigris and Euphrates below Seleucia. Comp. סְפָר.

מַשְׁאָב m. verbal from שָׁאַב, dec. VIII. a. *a water trough,* (for cattle,) *canalis.* Judg. 5:11.

מַשָּׁאָה f. verbal from נָשָׁא, *a debt, obligation, debitum.* Deut. 24:10. Prov. 22:26. i. q. מַשָּׁא no. 2.

מַשָּׁאוֹן m. *fraud, deception.* Prov. 26:26. Root נָשָׁא *to deceive.*

מַשָּׁאוֹת Ps. 74:3. see מַשּׁוּאוֹת.

מִשְׁאָל proper name of a Levitical city in the tribe of Asher. Josh. 19:26. 21:30. In 1 Chr. 6:59. [74.] it is written מָשָׁל a contraction of מִשְׁאָל.

מִשְׁאָלָה f. verbal from שָׁאַל, dec. XI. a. *a petition, request.* Ps. 20:6. 37:4.

מִשְׁאֶרֶת *a kneading trough,* or rather *a wooden dish to contain the dough,* such as is now in use in the east. Ex. 7:28 (joined with תַּנּוּר.) 12:34. Deut. 28:5, 17. The derivation is doubtful. If written with שׂ instead of שׁ, it might come from שְׂאֹר *sour dough, leaven.*

מִשְׁבְּצוֹת plur. fem. verbal from שָׁבַץ.

1. *cloth embroidered* or *interwoven with gold threads,* joined with זָהָב. Ps. 45:14. See שָׁבַץ no. 1.

2. *ouches* or *cavities* in which precious stones are set. Ex. 28:11, 13, 14, 25. 39:13, 16. See the root signif. no. 2.

מַשְׁבֵּר m. *the entrance of the womb, matrix.* Is. 37:3. 2 K. 19:3. Strictly part. Hiph. from שָׁבַר, q. v.

מִשְׁבָּר m. dec. II. b.

1. i. q. מַשְׁבֵּר, *womb, matrix.* Hos. 13: 13.

2. Plur. *waves, breakers, billows.* Ps. 42:8. 88:8. Jon. 2:4.—מִשְׁבְּרֵי־יָם *the billows of the sea,* Ps. 93:4.

מִשְׁבַּתִּים plur. masc. dec. VIII. *destruction, ruin.* Lam. 1:7. comp. שָׁבַת Hiph. no. 3.

מִשְׁגֶּה m. verbal from שָׁגָה, *an error, oversight.* Gen. 43:12.

מָשָׁה *to draw, to draw out.* Ex. 2:10.

Hiph. *idem.* 2 Sam. 22:17. Ps. 18: 17. Syr. ܡܫܐ *idem.*

מֹשֶׁה m. *Moses,* the great leader and lawgiver of the Israelites. Sept. Μωϋσῆς. In Ex. 2:10, there is given a Hebrew derivation of this word (namely, *drawing out,* as if a part. from מָשָׁה), but the education of Moses among the Egyptians would lead us to regard it as of Egyptian origin. So Josephus interprets it, (Antiq. II. 9. § 6.) *drawn out of the water*, from μω *water*, and υσης *saved*; (comp. μω *water* and *oushe to save*; see Jablonski, ed. te Water, T. I. p. 152—157.) which is favoured by the Greek manner of writing the name. According to this, the name was slightly altered by the Hebrews to give it a significancy in their own language.

מַשֶּׁה m. verbal from נָשָׁה, dec. IX. a. *a debt.* Deut. 15:2.

מְשׁוֹאָה f. 1. *desolation.* Zeph. 1:15.

2. *a desolate place.* Job 30:3. 38:27. See שׁוֹאָה.

מַשּׁוּאוֹת plur. fem. 1. Ps. 73:18. *treacherous, deceitful places*, from נָשָׁה *to deceive.*

2. Ps. 74:3 מַשֻּׁאוֹת נֶצַח *eternal ruins.* Without Dagesh it might come from שָׁאָה. But with Dagesh it must either be derived from נָשָׁא in the signification of שָׁאָה; or it must be read, as in some editions, מַשָּׂאוֹת with *Sin*, from נָשָׂא *to destroy*, (Job 32:22. Gen. 18:24. 27:21.)

מְשׁוּבָה f. verbal from שׁוּב, dec. I.

1. *apostacy, rebellion, falling away.* Prov. 1:32. מְשׁוּבַת פְּתָיִם *the falling away of fools* (from wisdom). Particularly *rebellion* against Jehovah, Jer. 8:5. Hos. 11:5 מְשׁוּבָתִי *rebellion against me.* Plur. מְשׁוּבוֹת Jer. 2:19.

2. as a concrete, מְשֻׁבָה יִשְׂרָאֵל *rebellious Israel*, Jer. 3:6, 8, 11, 12.

מְשׁוּגָה f. dec. I. *an error.* Job 19:4. Root שָׁגָה=שׁוּג and שָׁגַג.

מָשׁוֹט m. verbal from שׁוּט, *an oar.* Ezek. 27:29.

מִשּׁוֹט m. dec. I. i. q. מָשׁוֹט, *an oar.* Ezek. 27:6. Root שָׁטַט i. q. שׁוּט *to row.*

מָשַׁח, fut. יִמְשַׁח, infin. also מָשְׁחָה (Ex. 28:29.)

1. *to rub over with oil, to anoint.* Ex. 29:2. מָשַׁח מָגֵן *to rub over a shield with oil*, to make the leather more supple and impenetrable to water, Is. 21:5. 2 Sam. 1:21. Once *to rub over* with paint, Jer. 22:14.

2. *to anoint, to consecrate by unction*; e. g. a priest, Ex. 28:41. a prophet, 1 K. 19:16. a king, 1 Sam. 10:1. 2 Sam. 2:7. 1 K. 1:34. Also elliptically 2 Sam. 19:11 *Absalom whom we anointed* (*king*) *over us.* Hence also *to consecrate* generally, Is. 61:1. That wherewith one anoints or is anointed is put in the accus. Ps. 45:8. Am. 6:5. or is construed with בְּ, Ps. 89:21.

מְשַׁח Chald. *oil.* Ezra 6:9. 7:22.

I. **מִשְׁחָה** f. verbal from מָשַׁח, dec. XII. b. *an anointing.*—שֶׁמֶן הַמִּשְׁחָה *the anointing oil*, Ex. 25:6. 29:7, 21. שֶׁמֶן מִשְׁחַת קֹדֶשׁ *the holy anointing oil*, Ex. 30:25, 31.

II. **מִשְׁחָה** f. dec. XII. b. *a part, portion, portio, demensio.* Lev. 7:35. Root משח, Syr. ܡܫܚ, Arab. مسح *mensus est.* See מִמְשַׁח, and מָשְׁחָה.

I. **מָשְׁחָה** f. an infin. from מָשַׁח *to anoint.* See above.

II. **מָשְׁחָה** f. *a part, portion.* Num. 18:8. See מִשְׁחָה no. II.

מַשְׁחִית strictly the part. Hiph. from שָׁחַת, dec. I.

1. *destruction, desolation*, strictly *that which destroys, desolates.* Ex. 12:13. Ezek. 5:16. 21:36 חָרָשֵׁי מַשְׁחִית *artifices perniciei.* 25:15.

2. *a trap, snare*, which takes and destroys. Jer. 5:26.

3. הַר הַמַּשְׁחִית 2 K. 23:13. *the mount of corruption*, a name given to Mount Olivet from the numerous idols which were worshipped there. So the kingdom of Babylon is called by this name, Jer. 51:25.

מִשְׁחָר m. i. q. שַׁחַר, *the dawn.* Ps. 110:3.

מַשְׁחֵת m. i. q. מַשְׁחִית, *destruction.* Ezek. 9:1.

מִשְׁחַת m. verbal from שָׁחַת, *destruction, something destroyed.* Is. 52:14.

מַשְׁחִית m. verbal from שָׁחַת, *corruption, something corrupted.* Lev. 22 : 25.

מִשְׁטוֹחַ m. Ezek. 47 : 10. and **מִשְׁטַח** Ezek. 26 : 5, 14. verbal from שָׁטַח, *the place where any thing is spread* or *stretched out.*

מִשְׁטָר m. dec. II. b. *dominion.* Job 38 : 33 אִם תָּשִׂים מִשְׁטָרוֹ בָאָרֶץ *canst thou fix its dominion over the earth?* See שׁטר.

מֶשִׁי m. Ezek. 16 : 10, 13. according to the Jewish commentators, *silk.* By its derivation from מָשָׁה *to draw*, it may denote *ravellings of silk*, according to the notice of Pliny (H. N. XI. cap. 22.) that silk came from eastern Asia, in cloth half silk, and was unravelled in Greece, and again rewoven into cloth of entire silk.

מָשִׁיחַ m. verbal from מָשַׁח, dec. III. a.

1. strictly pass. part. *anointed.* 2 Sam. 1 : 21. הַכֹּהֵן הַמָּשִׁיחַ *the anointed priest*, i. e. the high-priest, Lev. 4 : 3, 5, 16.

2. as a subst. *an anointed one, a prince.* Dan. 9 : 25, 26. More frequently מְשִׁיחַ יְהוָה *the anointed of Jehovah, the king*, 1 Sam. 24 : 7, 11.

3. spoken also of priests, patriarchs. Ps. 105 : 15.

מָשַׁךְ, fut. יִמְשֹׁךְ,

1. *to seize, take.* (Arab. *idem.*) Ex. 12 : 21 מִשְׁכוּ וּקְחוּ לָכֶם צֹאן *take for yourselves sheep.*

2. *to hold, to hold fast;* construed with בְּ. Judg. 5 : 14.

3. *to draw.* Judg. 4 : 7. Cant. 1 : 4. Gen. 37 : 28. Particularly (1.) מְשֹׁךְ הַיּוֹבֵל Ex. 19 : 13. and מָשַׁךְ בְּקֶרֶן הַיּוֹבֵל Josh. 6 : 5. *to blow the jubilee horn.* It does not necessarily follow from this word that the blast of this instrument consisted in a protracted sound, as in the trumpet. Comp. Arab. جلب *to draw;* in conj. I. II. also i. q. הֵרִיעַ *to cry aloud, to blow with a trumpet.* (2.) מָשַׁךְ הַקֶּשֶׁת *to bend* or *stretch the bow.* 1 K. 22 : 34. Is. 66 : 19. (3.) מֶשֶׁךְ הַזָּרַע *to draw out seed*, i. e. sow it along the furrows. Am. 9 : 13. comp. Ps. 126 : 6. (4.) Hos. 7 : 5 מָשַׁךְ יָדוֹ אֶת־לֹצְצִים *he stretches out his hand with scorners*, i. e. he becomes their companion.

4. *to take* or *snatch away.* Ps. 28 : 3. Ezek. 32 : 20. Job 24 : 22.

5. *to draw out, extend, prolong.* Neh. 9 : 30. Ps. 36 : 11 מְשֹׁךְ חַסְדְּךָ לְיֹדְעֶיךָ *prolong thy grace to thy worshippers.* 85 : 6. 109 : 12. Jer. 31 : 3 מְשַׁכְתִּיךְ חָסֶד *I have prolonged favour to thee.* (So in Syr. ܢܓܕ *to draw*, whence ܢܘܓܪܐ *long duration.*) Hence

6. *to make durable, to strengthen.* Ecc. 2 : 3 לִמְשׁוֹךְ בַּיַּיִן אֶת־בְּשָׂרִי *to strengthen my body with wine.* (Syr. ܥܫܢ *induruit.*) Comp. Pu.

7. *to spread out.* Judg. 4 : 6 מָשַׁכְתָּ בְּהַר תָּבוֹר *thou shalt spread thyself out on Mount Tabor.* 20 : 37 וַיִּמְשֹׁךְ הָאֹרֵב *and the ambush spread themselves out.* See the Targum on these two places.

Niph. *to be put off, prolonged.* Is. 13 : 22. Ezek. 12 : 25, 28.

Pu. 1. *to be drawn out, delayed.* Prov. 13 : 12.

2. pass. of Kal no. 6. *to be strong, courageous, mighty.* Is. 18 : 2, 7 גּוֹי מְמֻשָּׁךְ, comp. Arab. مسيكة *vir fortis, validus, strenuus.* Others, with the Sept. *stretched out, longus.*

מֶשֶׁךְ m. 1. *possession.* Job 28 : 18. From מָשַׁךְ *to hold* or *possess.*

2. Ps. 126 : 6 מֶשֶׁךְ הַזָּרַע *the drawing out of seed*, i. e. the scattering of it along; (comp. Am. 9 : 13.)

3. *Moschians*, the proper name of a nation inhabiting the Moschian mountains between Iberia, Armenia, and Colchis. Ps. 120 : 5. In other places always in connexion with תּוּבַל, תֻּבַל *the Tibarenes*, Gen. 10 : 2. Ezek. 27 : 13. 32 : 26. 38 : 2, 3. 39 : 1. These two neighbouring nations are also joined together by Herod. (III. 94. VII. 78.) The Samaritan MSS. have מושך and משך, Sept. Μοσὸχ, Vulg. *Mosoch*, meaning probably as above.

מִשְׁכָּבוֹת see **מוֹשְׁכוֹת**. Comp. the root, signif. no. 2.

מִשְׁכָּב m. verbal from שָׁכַב, dec. II. b.

1. *a lying down.* 2 Sam. 4:5 מִשְׁכַּב הַצָּהֳרָיִם *a lying down* or *taking rest at noon.* Ps. 41:4.

2. *a lying together, coition.* Lev. 18:22 *and with men shalt thou not lie* מִשְׁכְּבֵי־אִשָּׁה *as with a woman.* 20:13. Num. 31:17 מִשְׁכַּב זָכָר *the lying with a man.* Verses 18, 35.

3. *a couch, bed.* Gen. 49:4. 2 Sam. 17:28.

4. *a coffin.* 2 Chr. 16:14.

מִשְׁכַּב m. Chald. *a bed,* i. q. Heb. מִשְׁכָּב no. 3. Dan. 2:28, 29.

מִשְׁכָּן m. verbal from שָׁכַן, plur. ־ים and ־ות.

1. *a dwelling.* Ps. 26:8. מִשְׁכְּנוֹת יְהוָה *the dwellings of Jehovah,* i. e. the temple, a poetical use of the plural, Ps. 84:2. 132:5. Used also of our last dwelling, *the grave,* Is. 22:16.

2. particularly *a tent.* Cant. 1:8. Very frequently used *of the tabernacle of the congregation* in the wilderness, Ex. 25:9. 26:1 ff. 40:9 ff. More full מִשְׁכַּן הָעֵדוּת *the tabernacle of the law,* Ex. 38:21. Num. 1:50, 53. 10:11. From Ex. 26:7. it appears to have denoted particularly the frame and boarding, in opposition to אֹהֶל *the covering.* Hence מִשְׁכַּן אֹהֶל מוֹעֵד Ex. 39:32. 40:2, 6, 29.

I. **מָשַׁל**, fut. יִמְשֹׁל, *to rule, to be master.* Prov. 6:7. Construed with בְּ, Gen. 3:16. 4:7. Is. 3:4. more rarely with עַל, Prov. 28:15. Sometimes it signifies *to be placed over* any thing, Gen. 24:2. Construed with לְ and an infin. *to have power to do* any thing, Ex. 21:8.

Hiph. הִמְשִׁיל *to cause to rule, to appoint ruler.* Ps. 8:7. Dan. 11:39. Infin. used substantively, *dominion,* Job 25:2.

Deriv. out of course מִמְשָׁל, מֶמְשָׁלָה.

II. **מָשַׁל** in Kal, a denom. from מָשָׁל.

1. *to utter a metaphor* or *comparison.* Ezek. 24:3.

2. *to utter a proverb.* Ezek. 12:23. 17:2. 18:2, 3.

3. *to sing satires.* Joel 2:17.

Niph. *to be* or *become similar, to be like;* construed with אֶל, Is. 14:10. with עִם, Ps. 28:1. 143:7. with כְּ, Ps. 49:13, 21.

Pi. i. q. Kal, *to speak in parables.* Ezek. 21:5. [20:49.]

Hiph. *to compare.* Is. 46:5.

Hithpa. as in Niph. *to be like, similar;* construed with כְּ. Job 30:19. (Arab. مثل *to be like.* Syr. and Chald. ܡܬܠ, מְתַל *idem.*)

I. **מֹשֶׁל** m. verbal from מָשַׁל no. I. dec. VI. p. *dominion.* Zech. 9:10.

II. **מֹשֶׁל** verbal from מָשַׁל no. II. dec. VI. p. *something like* or *similar.* Job 41:25.

מָשָׁל m. prim. dec. IV. a.

1. *a comparison, similitude, parable.* Ezek. 17:2. 24:3.

2. *a sentiment, maxim,* expressed for the most part by the orientalists in a pithy comparison. (Comp. e. g. Prov. 26:1, 2, 3, 6, 7, 8, 9, 11, 14, 17.) Prov. 1:1, 6. 10:1. 25:1. 26:7, 9. Ecc. 12:9. Job 13:12. 1 K. 4:32. [5:12].) And because such maxims often become proverbial (1 Sam. 24:13.) hence

3. *a proverb,* παροίμια; e. g. 1 Sam. 10:12. Ezek. 18:2, 3. 12:22, 23. Comp. παραβολὴ Luke 4:13.

4. *figurative discourse* generally; hence *a song, poem.* Num. 23:7, 18. Job 27:1. 29:1. Ps. 49:5. 78:2. Particularly *a satiric song,* or *a song of triumph,* over the destruction of one's enemies. Is. 14:4. Mic. 2:4. Hab. 2:6. הָיָה לְמָשָׁל וְלִשְׁנִינָה *to be* or *become a satire and reproach,* Deut. 28:37. 1 K. 9:7. (Arab. مَثَل *a comparison, fable, proverb;* in the plur. *verses.*)

מְשֹׁל an infin. used as a noun, i. q. מָשָׁל no. 4. Job 17:6.

מִשְׁלָח m. verbal from שָׁלַח, dec. II. b.

1. *a place sent to.* Is. 7:25 מִשְׁלַח שׁוֹר *a place whither oxen are driven.*

2. joined with יָד and יָדַיִם, *that to which one puts his hand, business.*

Deut. 15:10. 23:21. 28:8, 20. 12:7, 18.

מִשְׁלוֹחַ, מִשְׁלַח m. verbal from שָׁלַח.

1. *a sending*. Est. 9:19, 22.

2. joined with יָד, *that on which one lays his hand, booty*. Is. 11:14.

מִשְׁלַחַת fem. of the preceding.

1. *a sending*. Ps. 78:49.

2. *a dismission*, from service or captivity. Ecc. 8:8. Comp. the verb in Pi. no. 2.

מְשֻׁלָּשׁ m. *three, a triad, trias*. Gen. 38:24. See שָׁלֹשׁ *three*.

מְשַׁמָּה f. verbal from שָׁמַם, dec. X.

1. *a desolation*. Ezek. 6:14. 33:28. Plur. Is. 15:6.

2. *an astonishment*. Ezek. 5:15.

מִשְׁמָן m. verbal from שָׁמֵן, dec. VIII. a. *fatness*. Is. 17:4 מִשְׁמַן בְּשָׂרוֹ *his fat body*. Plur. מִשְׁמַנִּים, (1.) *the fat, fertile parts of a country*. Gen. 27:28, 39. Dan. 11:24. (2.) as a concrete, *the fat*, i. e. the fleshy, muscular, stout, (spoken of warriors.) Ps. 78:31. Is. 10:16.

מַשְׁמַנִּים masc. plur. *fat* or *dainty bits*. Neh. 8:10.

מִשְׁמָע m. verbal from שָׁמַע, dec. II. b. *a hearing, what is heard*. Is. 11:3.

מִשְׁמַעַת fem. of the preceding.

1. *the more private audience of monarchs*, to which only the higher officers were admitted. 1 Sam. 22:14 וְסָר אֶל מִשְׁמַעְתֶּךָ *and having access to thy private audience*. 2 Sam. 23:23. 1 Chr. 11:25.

2. *obedience*. As a concrete, *obedient, subject*, Is. 11:14.

מִשְׁמָר m. verbal from שָׁמַר, dec. II. b.

1. *a post, a place where one keeps watch*. Neh. 7:3. Jer. 51:12. Hence *the persons watching, a watch*, Neh. 4:3, 16. [4:9, 22.] Job 7:12.

2. *custody, confinement, a prison*. Gen. 40:3 ff. 42:17.

3. *that which one keeps* or *preserves*. Prov. 4:23 מִכָּל־מִשְׁמָר *before all things which thou keepest*.

4. *what is observed, a custom, usage*. Neh. 13:14.

5. as a concrete, *observantia* for *quem observant, imperator*. Ezek. 38:7.

מִשְׁמֶרֶת, plur. מִשְׁמָרוֹת, fem. of the preceding, dec. XIII. a.

1. *a watch* or *watching*. 2 K. 11:5, 6.

2. *the place where one keeps watch*. Is. 21:8. Hab. 2:1. also *persons keeping watch*, Neh. 7:3. 12:9. 13:30.

3. *a keeping* or *preserving*. Ex. 12:6. 16:32, 33, 34. As a concrete, *what is kept* or *preserved*, 1 Sam. 22:23.

4. *what is observed, a law, command, usage*. Gen. 26:5. Lev. 18:30. 22:9.

5. *the care* or *management of a business*. Num. 4:27, 31 זֹאת מִשְׁמֶרֶת מַשָּׂאָם *this is the management of their burden*, i. e. this is what they have to bear. Num. 3:31. Hence שָׁמַר מִשְׁמֶרֶת הַמִּשְׁכָּן Num. 1:53. or הַקֹּדֶשׁ 3:28. or יְהוָה Lev. 8:35. *to do service in the tent of the congregation*, more rarely, simply *to keep watch*.

6. *the adherence to* any one, *sequi partes alicujus*. 1 Chr. 12:29 מַרְבִּיתָם שֹׁמְרִים מִשְׁמֶרֶת בֵּית שָׁאוּל Vulg. *magna pars eorum adhuc sequebatur domum Saul*.

מִשְׁנֶה m. verbal from שָׁנָה, dec. IX. a.

1. *the second place*, in succession or rank; usually put after a noun in regimen. כֹּהֵן הַמִּשְׁנֶה *the second priest, the next to the high-priest*, (כֹּהֵן הָרֹאשׁ.) 2 K. 25:18. Jer. 52:24. Plur. כֹּהֲנֵי הַמִּשְׁנֶה *sacerdotes secundarii*, 2 K. 23:4. מִרְכֶּבֶת הַמִּשְׁנֶה *the second chariot*, Gen. 41:43. אָחִיהוּ מִשְׁנֵהוּ *his second brother*, 2 Chr. 31:12. הָעִיר מִשְׁנֶה *the second part of the city*, Neh. 11:9. also simply מִשְׁנֶה 2 K. 22:14. Zeph. 1:10.

2. as a concrete, *the second*. מִשְׁנֵה הַמֶּלֶךְ *the second after the king*, 2 Chr. 28:7. comp. 1 Sam. 23:17. Est. 10:3. Tob. 1:22. particularly *the second brother*, 1 Chr. 5:12. 1 Sam. 8:2.—Plur. אֲחֵיהֶם הַמִּשְׁנִים *their other brothers after the eldest*, 1 Chr. 15:18 כְּפוֹרֵי כֶסֶף מִשְׁנִים *silver cups of a second quality*, Ezra 1:10.—1 Sam. 15:9 הַמִּשְׁנִים (*cattle*) *of less value*, in opposition to מֵיטָב. Perhaps *autumn lambs, secundo partu editi*.

3. *a doubling, double.* Ex. 16:22. Is. 61:7.

4. *a duplicate, copy.* Deut. 17:18. Josh. 8:32.

מְשִׁסָּה f. verbal from שָׁסַס, dec. X. *plunder, booty, prey.*—הָיָה לִמְשִׁסָּה *to become a prey*, 2 K. 21:14. נָתַן לִמְשִׁסָּה *to give for a prey*, Is. 42:24.

מִשְׁעוֹל m. *a narrow path, hollow way.* Num. 22:24 מִשְׁעוֹל הַכְּרָמִים *a path between the vineyards.* Comp. שֹׁעַל *the hollow hand.*

מִשְׁעִי only Ezek. 16:4 לְמִשְׁעִי, according to Jarchi: *ad nitorem.* It stands then for מִשְׁעָה, (like הָחֳלִי for הָחֳלָה,) from שָׁעָה=שָׁעַע. According to others, from משׁע Arab. مشع conj. II. *to wash off, to cleanse,* conj. V. *to wash one's self;* comp. Syr. ܡܫܥܐ *splendidus;* hence לְמִשְׁעִי *for purifying,* the infin. with Yod paragogic.

מַשְׁעֵן m. verbal from שָׁעַן, dec. II. b. *a stay, staff, support.* Is. 3:1. Metaphorically Ps. 18:19.

מַשְׁעֵן m. verbal from שָׁעַן, *idem.* Is. 3:1 מַשְׁעֵן וּמַשְׁעֵנָה *every stay* or *support.* The combining of the masculine and feminine forms expresses universality.

מִשְׁעֶנֶת fem. of the preceding, *a staff.* Judg. 6:21. 2 K. 4:31. 18:21.

מִשְׁפָּחָה f. const. מִשְׁפַּחַת, with suff. מִשְׁפַּחְתִּי, Plur. מִשְׁפָּחוֹת, const. מִשְׁפְּחוֹת, dec. XI. g. Root שׁפח in Ethiop. *to spread out,* in Arab. سفح *idem.*

1. *a kind, species,* of animals. Gen. 8:19. of inanimate things, Jer. 15:3.

2. *a tribe.* Gen. 10:18, 20, 31, 32. 12:3. Used of a whole people, Ezek. 20:32. Jer. 8:3. 25:9. Mic. 2:3.

3. *a subdivision of a tribe, a family,* among the Israelites. Ex. 6:14ff. Num. 1:2 לְמִשְׁפְּחֹתָם לְבֵית אֲבֹתָם *after their families, after the house of their fathers;* comp. verse 20 ff. 26:5 ff. Deut. 29:17. Josh. 7:14ff. 21:5ff. 1 Sam. 20:29 זֶבַח מִשְׁפָּחָה לָנוּ *we have a family sacrifice.* More rarely and inaccurately, i. q. שֵׁבֶט, e. g. Josh. 7:17 מִשְׁפַּחַת יְהוּדָה i. q. in the preceding verse שֵׁבֶט יְהוּדָה.

מִשְׁפָּט m. verbal from שָׁפַט, dec. II. b.

1. *judgment, the act of judging.* Lev. 19:15. Ezek. 21:32 [21:27] עַד בֹּא אֲשֶׁר לוֹ הַמִּשְׁפָּט *until he come who shall exercise judgment.*—בּוֹא בְמִשְׁפָּט עִם *to go* or *enter into judgment with* any one, Job 9:32. 22:4. Ps. 143:2. comp. Job 14:3. Ecc. 11:9. בַּעַל מִשְׁפָּטִי *one that contends in judgment with me,* i. e. my adversary, Is. 50:8. Particularly *a sentencing to punishment,* Is. 53:8.

2. *a judgment, judicial decision.* 1 K. 3:28. 20:40. Ps. 17:2. Plur. מִשְׁפְּטֵי יְהוָה *the decisions* or *counsels of Jehovah,* Ps. 19:10. 119:75, 137. Particularly *a sentence of punishment,* דִּבֶּר מִשְׁפָּטִים אֶת־פ׳ *to pronounce sentence against any one,* Jer. 1:16. 4:12. 39:5. 52:9. 2 K. 25:6. See the same phrase under no. 4.

3. *guilt, liability to punishment.* מִשְׁפַּט דָּמִים *blood-guiltiness,* Ezek. 7:23. Jer. 51:9. Deut. 21:22 חֵטְא מִשְׁפַּט־מָוֶת *a sin which incurs death;* comp. 19:6.

4. *a cause, a suit at law.* Num. 27:5. Job 13:18. 23:4 עָשָׂה מִשְׁפַּט פְּלוֹנִי *to conduct,* or *manage the cause of any one, to be his advocate,* Deut. 10:18. Ps. 9:5. (Comp. רִיב and דִּין.) דִּבֶּר מִשְׁפָּטִים אֶת *to plead* or *contend with* any one, Jer. 12:1.

5. *a right, privilege;* e. g. מִשְׁפַּט הַגְּאֻלָּה *the right of redemption,* Jer. 32:7. מִשְׁפַּט הַמֶּלֶךְ *the right* or *prerogative of the king,* 1 Sam. 8:9, 11. Particularly *what belongs to any one by law,* Deut. 18:3 מִשְׁפַּט הַכֹּהֲנִים *what belongs to the priests,* i. e. their due, 1 Sam. 2:13.

6. *right, righteousness, justice,* i. q. צֶדֶק. Deut. 32:4 כָּל־דְּרָכָיו מִשְׁפָּט *all his ways are righteousness,* i. e. righteous. מִשְׁפָּט וּצְדָקָה *justice and righteousness.* Jer. 22:15. 23:5. מֹאזְנֵי מִשְׁפָּט *just balances,* Prov. 16:11. בְּלֹא מִשְׁפָּט *with unrighteousness,* Jer. 22:13.

7. *a law,* i. q. חֹק. Ex. 21:1. 24:3. particularly *a divine law,* Lev. 18:4, 5, 26. 19:37. 20:22.

8. *a custom, usage.* 1 K. 18:28. 2 K. 11:14. 17:33, 34, 40. Hence

9. *a mode, manner*. Ex. 26:30. 2 K. 1:7 מֶה מִשְׁפַּט הָאִישׁ *what was the manner of the man?* Judg. 13:12 מַה־יִּהְיֶה מִשְׁפַּט הַנַּעַר וּמַעֲשֵׂהוּ *what shall the manner and conduct of the child be?*

מִשְׁפְּתַיִם dual, Gen. 49:14. Judg. 5:16. i. q. שְׁפַתַּיִם Ps. 68:14. probably *folds for cattle,* particularly the open summer stalls, in which cattle, in warmer climates, pass the whole summer; from שׁפת *to place,* like *stabula,* (comp. Virg. Georg. III. 228. and the note of Voss thereon,) from *stare.* Usually rendered *water-troughs* for cattle; but the root سفت signifies not *to drink* generally, but *to drink without being satisfied* or *refreshed,* so as only to increase thirst. The reason of the dual form does not appear.

מֶשֶׁק m. found only Gen. 15:2. best explained by Simonis, *a possession,* i. q. מֶשֶׁךְ, by a commutation of כ and ק, (see כ.) Hence בֶּן־מֶשֶׁק *a son of possession,* i. e. a possessor, and the whole clause thus, *the possessor of my house will be Eliezer that Damascene.* Another deriv. from the same root is מִמְשָׁק. —Onkelos, Pseudojon. Vulg. *filius procurationis, dispensator.*

מַשָּׁק m. verbal from שָׁקַק (with a Chaldaic form.) dec. II. b. *a running about.* Is. 33:4.

מַשְׁקֶה m. verbal from שָׁקָה, dec. IX. a.

1. as a Hiph. part. *a cupbearer.*

2. *drink.* Lev. 11:34. 1 K. 10:21 כְּלֵי מַשְׁקֵה *drinking vessels.*

3. *a well watered country.* Gen. 13:10. Ezek. 45:15.

מִשְׁקוֹל m. verbal from שָׁקַל, *weight.* Ezek. 4:10.

מַשְׁקוֹף m. *the lintel, the timber over the door posts.* Ex. 12:7, 22, 23. Comp. שְׁקֻפִים, שָׁקַף.

מִשְׁקָל m. verbal from שָׁקַל, *weight.* Lev. 19:35. 1 Chr. 22:3 אֵין מִשְׁקָל *so as not to be weighed.* Verse 14.

מִשְׁקֶלֶת fem. of the preceding, Is. 28:17. and מִשְׁקֹלֶת 2 K. 21:13. *a perpendicle, plummet.*

מִשְׁקָע m. verbal from שָׁקַע, dec. II. b. *a pool, pond,* where water subsides. Ezek. 34:18.

מִשְׁרָה f. verbal from שׁרה *to dissolve,* dec. X. *a solution, liquor.* Num. 6:3 מִשְׁרַת־עֲנָבִים *drink formed by dissolving* or *macerating grapes.*

מַשְׁרוֹקִיתָא verbal from שׁרק, Chald. *a pipe, reed, flute.* Dan. 3:5, 7, 10, 25.

מָשַׁשׁ i. q. מוּשׁ no. II. *to touch, feel.* Gen. 27:12. comp. מוּשׁ verse 21.

Pi. 1. *idem.* Gen. 31:34, 37.

2. *to grope in darkness.* Deut. 28:29. Job 5:14. Construed with an accus. Job 12:15.

Hiph. *idem.* Ex. 10:21.

מִשְׁתֶּה m. verbal from שָׁתָה, dec. IX. a.

1. *a drinking.* Est. 5:4. 7:2. בֵּית מִשְׁתֵּה הַיַּיִן *a chamber for drinking wine,* Est. 7:8.

2. *drink.* Dan. 1:10. Ezra 3:7.

3. *a banquet, συμπόσιον.* Est. 1:3. 2:18. 8:17.

מִשְׁתֵּה, emph. מִשְׁתְּיָא, Chald. *idem.* Dan. 5:10.

מֵת m. (active part. from מות *to die,*) *a dead person, a corpse,* see מוּת. Plur. מֵתִים *dead idols,* in opposition to Jehovah the living God, Ps. 106:28. Is. 8:19.

מְתִים and defect. מְתִם m. dec. VII. i. found only in the plur. *men,* (not *people* generally.) Deut. 2:34 מְתִם וְהַנָּשִׁים וְהַטָּף *men and women and children.* 3:6. Job 11:3. Is. 3:25. מְתֵי מִסְפָּר *few people,* Gen. 34:30. Ps. 26:4. Job 11:11. (Sing. מת met, in Ethiop. *vir,* pecul. *maritus.* It occurs besides in proper names, in the form מְתוּ, like אָב, const. אֲבִי, Chald. אֲבוּ, e. g. מְתוּשֶׁלַח.)

מַתְבֵּן m. i. q. תֶּבֶן, *straw.* Is. 25:10.

מֶתֶג m. with suff. מִתְגִּי, dec. VI. h. *a bridle.* Ps. 32:9. Prov. 26:3.

מָתוֹק adj. fem. מְתוּקָה, plur. מְתוּקִים,

verbal from מָתַק, dec. III. f. *sweet.* Judg. 14:14, 18. Ecc. 5:11. Ps. 19:11. Used abstractly *sweetness*, Ezek. 3:4 לְמָתוֹק *for sweetness.*

מָתַח *to stretch out.* Is. 40:22. (In Syr. and Chald. *idem.*) Deriv. אַמְתַּחַת *a sack.*

מָתַי prim. *when?* (In Arab. *idem.*) For the most part interrogatively, Gen. 30:30. Prov. 6:9. more rarely without an interrogation, Prov. 23:35 מָתַי אָקִיץ *when I wake.*—לְמָתַי Ex. 8:5. and עַד מָתַי *how long?* 1 Sam. 16:1. Prov. 6:9. אַחֲרֵי מָתַי *after how long a time?* Jer. 13:27.

מַתְכֹּנֶת f. verbal from תָּכַן, dec. XIII. f.

1. *measure*, Ezek. 45:11. *daily task, tale*, Ex. 5:8. comp. תֹּכֶן verse 18. Ex. 30:32 בְּמַתְכֻּנְתּוֹ *after its measure*, i. e. proportion of the ingredients. 2 Chr. 24:13 *and they set the house of God* עַל מַתְכֻּנְתּוֹ *after its (former) measure.*

מַתְּלָאָה Mal. 1:13. a contraction of מַה־תְּלָאָה *what a weariness.* See the note to the art. מָה.

מְתַלְּעוֹת plur. fem. Job 29:17. Prov. 30:14. Joel 1:6. and by transposition מַלְתָּעוֹת Ps. 58:7. *the front cutting teeth*, or *the projecting eye teeth, dentes canini*, which in wild animals are very dangerous. Root לָתַע Arab. لتع *to bite*, or תָּלַע Arab. تلع *to project, be prominent.* The former derivation is for cutting teeth, the latter for eye teeth.

מְתֹם m. verbal from תָּמַם, *something sound* or *uninjured.* Ps. 38:4, 8. Is. 1:6. In Judg. 20:48, it is a corrupt reading for מְתִם *men*, which is found in several MSS.

מַתָּן m. verbal from נָתַן, dec. I. *a gift, present.* Gen. 34:12. אִישׁ מַתָּן *one who gives gifts*, Prov. 19:6.

מַתָּנָה fem. of the preceding, dec. XI. a.

1. *a gift, present.* Gen. 25:6. Particularly *a bribe*, Ecc. 7:7. *an offering*, Ex. 28:38.

2. proper name of a place between the desert and the territory of Moab. Num. 21:18, 19.

מַתְּנָא Chald. i. q. Heb. מַתָּנָה *a present.* Dan. 2:6, 48. 5:17.

מָתְנַיִם dual masc. *the loins, the upper part of the hip*, including the small of the back, ὀσφύς; on which the girdle is worn, 2 K. 4:29. 9:1. Gen. 37:34. or a burden is borne, Ps. 66:11. the seat of pain in parturition, Is. 21:3. Nah. 2:11. For its distinction from יָרֵךְ see that article. (Arab. and Syr. *idem.* Root מָתַן, متن *to be firm*, whence אֲמִתַּי.)

מָתַק, fut. יִמְתַּק, *to be* or *become sweet.* Ex. 15:25. Job 21:33 מָתְקוּ לוֹ רִגְבֵי־נָחַל *the clods of the valley rest sweetly upon him, est ei terra levis.* 24:20 מְתָקוֹ רִמָּה for מְתָקָה לוֹ רִמָּה *the worm is sweet to him.* Others take מָתַק in the Syriac signification, *to suck;* hence *the worm feeds upon him.*

Hiph. 1. *to sweeten.* Ps. 55:15 אֲשֶׁר יַחְדָּו נַמְתִּיק סוֹד *we took sweet counsel together.*

2. intrans. *to be sweet.* Job 20:12.

Deriv. out of course מַמְתַּקִּים.

מֶתֶק m. verbal from מָתַק, *sweetness.* Prov. 27:9. Metaphorically *pleasure*, 16:21.

מֹתֶק m. verbal from מָתַק, *idem.* Judg. 9:11.

מִתְקָה proper name of a station of the Israelites in the desert of Arabia. Once Num. 33:28.

מַתָּת f. a contraction of מַתֶּנֶת fem. of מַתָּן, *a gift, present.* Prov. 25:14. Ecc. 3:13. Ezek. 46:5, 11.

נ (ן)

Nun, the 14th letter of the alphabet, and as a numerical sign denoting 50. The name נוּן denotes in Syr. Chald. and Arab. *a fish.* This does not suit the common square character, and the final character was probably of later origin.

In the Phenician alphabets it is more crooked, but the character in the original alphabet was perhaps still more conformed to its name.

The commutation of this letter with Lamed and Mem, has already been noticed under those letters. It is also interchanged (1.) with ר, yet very rarely, e. g. נָגַהּ Chald. דְּנַח *to rise*, as the sun; שְׁנַיִם Aram. תְּרֵין *two*. (2.) with י as the first radical; e. g. יָאָה and נָאָה *to be fair, becoming*; יָצַב and נָצַב *to place*; יָקֹשׁ and נָקַשׁ *to lay snares*. Comp. Gesen. Lehrgebäude, p. 453.

I. נָא a primitive particle, expressive of respectful entreaty or exhortation, *I pray you*, Lat. *quæso*, Germ. *doch*. It is joined (1.) with the imper. in a request or admonition. Gen. 12:13 אִמְרִי־נָא *say, I pray thee.* 24:2 שִׂים־נָא *put, I pray thee.* 24:45. Judg. 12:6 אֱמָר־נָא *say, I pray thee*, or *say now*. Also in negative sentences, with אַל and the future, Gen. 18:3 אַל־נָא תַעֲבֹר *pass not away, I pray thee.* Verse 32 אַל־נָא יִחַר לַאדֹנָי *let not the Lord, I pray thee, be angry.* (2.) with the future, to express the optative. Ps. 124:1 יֹאמַר־נָא יִשְׂרָאֵל *may Israel now say.* 129:1. Cant. 7:9. Particularly with the first person, in requesting permission, Ex. 3:3. 4:18 אֵלְכָה נָּא *I will go, if thou permittest*, or *let me go, I pray thee.* 1 K. 1:12 אִיעָצֵךְ נָא עֵצָה *let me give thee counsel.* Cant. 3:2. Is. 5:1. Num. 20:17 נַעְבְּרָה־נָּא *let us pass through, we pray thee.* Comp. Gen. 44:18. 18:4. (3.) with אִם, *if indeed*, εἴ ποτε, ἐάν, *si quidem*. Gen. 18:3 אִם־נָא מָצָאתִי *if indeed I have found.* 24:42. 30:27. 33:9. (4.) with אַל, *nay* or *no, I pray thee.* Gen. 33:10 אַל־נָא *nay, I pray thee.* 19:18. (5.) הִנֵּה־נָא *behold now.* Gen. 12:11. 16:2. (6.) אוֹי־נָא *alas now.* Lam. 5:16. Jer. 4:31. 45:3.

Note. The frequent use of this particle appears to indicate courtesy and respect; see Gen. 18:3. 19:7, 8, 18, 19.

II. נָא adj. *raw, half-boiled*, spoken of flesh. Ex. 12:9. Root נִיא Arab. نَاءَ for نِيءَ *to be raw, half-boiled.*

נֹא a proper name, Ezek. 30:14, 15, 16. Jer. 46:25. in full נֹא אָמוֹן Nah. 3:8. *Thebes*, the ancient capital of Upper Egypt. Sept. in Ezek. Διόσπολις, in Nah. μερὶς Ἀμμών. The latter appears to be an etymological explanation of the word after the Coptic. In that language NOH signifies *a cord, measuring line*, hence *a portion measured out*, and נֹא אָמוֹן *portio, possessio Amonis*, i. e. the seat of the god Amon, or the place where he was principally worshipped. See Jablonskii Opuscula, ed. te Water T. I. p. 163—168.

נֹאד m. plur. נֹאדוֹת, (once נֹאוד Judg. 4:19 Keth.) dec. I. *a leather bag* or *bottle*. Judg. 4:19 נֹאד הֶחָלָב *a bottle of milk.* 1 Sam. 16:20. Josh. 9:4, 13. Wine bottles were hung up in the smoke, Ps. 119:83.

נָאָה *to be fair, beautiful*; kindred with יָאָה. The doubling of the last radical, (comp. הִשְׁתַּחֲוָה from שָׁחָה,) gives rise to a quadriliteral נַאֲוָה and by contraction נָאוָה, plur. נָאווּ, *to be beautiful.* Cant. 1:10. 2:14. 4:3. Is. 52:7.

נָאוֶה, fem. נָאוָה, verbal adj. from נָאָה, dec. IX. a. and X.

1. *fair, beautiful.* Cant. 1:5. 6:4.

2. *fit, becoming, suitable.* Ps. 33:1 לַיְשָׁרִים נָאוָה תְהִלָּה *praise becometh the upright*, i. e. it becometh them to praise God. 93:5 לְבֵיתְךָ נַאֲוָה קֹדֶשׁ *holiness becometh thine house.* 147:1. Prov. 17:7. 19:10. 26:1.

נָאָה found only in the plural const. נְאוֹת, i. q. נָוָה, נְוֶה.

1. *a dwelling, habitation.* Ps. 74:20. 83:13. Lam. 2:2.

6. *a grassy place, green, pasture.* נְאוֹת מִדְבָּר *the pastures of the desert*, Ps. 65:13. Jer. 9:10. 23:9. נְאוֹת דֶּשֶׁא *green pastures*, Ps. 23:2.

נָאַם *to utter, to utter an oracle.* As a finite verb found only in Jer. 23:31. (In a single MS. Zech. 4:2.) Part. pass. נְאֻם *an oracle*, in the phrase נְאֻם יְהוָה *an oracle of Jehovah*, i.e. (thus) saith Jehovah, occurring frequently in the prophets, who repeat the oracles, as it were, from the mouth of Jehovah. Applied more rarely to the prophets themselves, Num. 24:3 נְאֻם בִּלְעָם *the oracle of Balaam.* Verse 15. Also to poets, 2 Sam. 23:1. Prov. 30:1.—Ps. 36:1 נְאֻם פֶּשַׁע *an oracle* or *song concerning wickedness.* See De Wette in loc. Others: *an oracle of wickedness.*

נָאַף, fut. יִנְאַף, and Pi. נִאֵף, part. מְנָאֵף, *to commit adultery*, spoken both of the man and woman. Ex. 20:14. Lev. 20:10. Construed with an accus. Prov. 6:32 נֹאֵף אִשָּׁה *he who committeth adultery with a woman.* Lev. 20:10. Jer. 29:23. Like the kindred word זָנָה it is often applied figuratively to the unfaithfulness of the Israelites towards Jehovah, to their apostacy and idolatry. Jer. 3:8 אֲשֶׁר נִאֲפָה מְשֻׁבָה יִשְׂרָאֵל *because rebellious Israel committed adultery.* 5:7. 9:1. 23:14. Construed in like manner with an accus. Jer. 3:9 וַתִּנְאַף אֶת־הָאֶבֶן וְאֶת־הָעֵץ *she committed adultery with stones and stocks.* Ezek. 23:37.

נִאֻפִים masc. plur. verbal from נָאַף, dec. I. *adultery.* Jer. 13:27. Ezek. 23:43.

נַאֲפוּפִים masc. plur. verbal from נָאַף, dec. I. *idem.* Hos. 2:4 [2:2] וְתָסֵר—נַאֲפוּפֶיהָ מִבֵּין שָׁדֶיהָ *let her put away adultery from her (open) breasts*, that is, as in the parallel clause, *let her put away fornication from her countenance.* The coquettish look and exposed breasts are here the signs of fornication and adultery.

נָאַץ, fut. יִנְאַץ, *to despise, to reject with contempt*, often *to mock, insult;* e. g. a people, Jer. 33:24. doctrine, instruction, Prov. 1:30. 5:12. 15:5. the counsel of God, 107:11. Spoken of God, who rejects men, Deut. 32:19. Lam. 2:6. Also absolutely Jer. 14:21 *cast not off for thy name's sake.* (Comp. the kindred verbs נָזָה and מָאַס).

Pi. נִאֵץ, fut. יְנָאֵץ.

1. i. q. Kal, *to despise, contemn.* Is. 60:14. Particularly God, Ps. 10:3, 13. 74:18. Is. 1:4.

2. causat. *to give occasion to despise* or *blaspheme.* 2 Sam. 12:14.

Hiph. fut. יָנֵאץ, intrans. *to be despised.* Ecc. 12:5. The form is Syriac for יָנֹאץ.

Hithpo. *to be despised, blasphemed.* Is. 52:5 מִנֹּאָץ for מִתְנֹאֵץ.

נְאָצָה f. verbal from נָאַץ, *reproach, blasphemy.* Is. 37:3.

נֶאָצָה f. plur. נֶאָצוֹת, Neh. 9:18, 26. and נֶאָצוֹתֶיךָ Ezek. 35:12. verbal from נָאַץ, *idem.*

נָאַק i. q. אָנַק *to groan, lament.* Ezek. 30:24. Job 24:12.

נְאָקָה f. const. נַאֲקַת, verbal from נָאַק, dec. XI. d. *a groaning, lamentation.* Ex. 2:24. 6:5.

נָאַר found only in Pi. נֵאֵר *to abhor, reject.* Lam. 2:7. Ps. 89:40. (Arab. نار med. Vav, *abhorruit ab* aliqua re, *refugit.*)

נֹב proper name of a sacerdotal city in the tribe of Benjamin, not far from Jerusalem. 1 Sam. 22:11, 19. Neh. 11:32. Is. 10:32.—נֹבֶה (נֹבָה?) *to Nob,* 1 Sam. 21:2. 22:9.

נָבָא in Kal not used. In Arab. *to bring forth*, particularly words; hence *to shew, announce.* Deriv. נָבִיא, נְבוּאָה.

Ni. נִבָּא 1. *to deliver an oracle from God, to speak as God's ambassador*, whatever the object may be. Jer. 23:21. Joel 3:1. Num. 11:25, 27. Of importance is Am. 3:8 *the lion roareth, who will not be afraid? the Lord Jehovah speaks,* מִי לֹא יִנָּבֵא *who will not be his messenger?* Since such oracles generally refer to the future, hence

2. *to prophesy, to predict future events in the name of God.* 1 K. 22:8, 10, 12, 13. Construed with לְ, Jer. 20:6. with אֶל, Jer. 26:11. with עַל, Jer. 25:13.

3. *to sing songs* or *hymns*, (the singer being inspired of God.) 1 Sam. 10:11. 19:19, 20. 1 Chr. 25:2, 3. 1 K. 18:29. Once נִבֵּית for נִבֵּאתָ Jer. 26:9.

Hithpa. הִתְנַבֵּא, sometimes הִתְנַבָּא (Ezek. 37:10. Jer. 23:13.) infin. הִתְנַבּוֹת 1 Sam. 10:13 (like verbs ל״ה.)

1. i. q. Niph. 1 Sam. 10:5, 6. 19:21, 23, 24.

2. *to act like a madman*, μαίνεσθαι. 1 Sam. 18:10. Inspiration and madness were both attended with singular motions of the body and even with violent convulsions and contortions. Hence the Greek *μάντις the enraptured soothsayer*, from *μαίνομαι to rave, to be mad;* and the Lat. *fatuus* (from *fari*) *a soothsayer, a fool; furor, madness* and *inspiration.* For this reason we find in Jer. 29:26, מְשֻׁגָּע וּמִתְנַבֵּא connected; and in 2 K. 9:11, Elisha's disciple is called in reproach מְשֻׁגָּע *a fool.*

נְבָא Chald. Ethpa. הִתְנַבִּי *to prophesy.* Ezra 5:1.

נְבָה see נב.

נְבוֹ 1. proper name of a mountain beyond Jordan, over against Jericho. Deut. 32:48. 34:1.

2. of a city in the tribe of Reuben, near Mount Nebo. Num. 32:3, 38. Is. 15:2.

3. of a city in the tribe of Judah. Ezra 2:29. 10:43. By way of distinction called נְבוֹ אַחֵר Neh. 7:33.

4. of an idol of the Chaldeans. Is. 46:1. The planet Mercury has this name among the Zabians. It is found also in the composition of several Chaldean names of persons. See, besides *Nebuchadnezzar*, other names not found in the Bible, as *Nabonassar, Nabopolasser, Nabonebus*, etc.

נְבוּאָה f. verbal from נָבָא, dec. X. *a prophecy.* Neh. 6:12. 2 Chr. 15:8. Hence *a writing of a prophet*, 2 Chr. 9:29.

נְבוּאָה Chald. *idem.* Ezra 6:14.

נְבוּכַדְנֶאצַּר and נְבוּכַדְרֶאצַּר (the latter in some passages of Jeremiah,) *Nebuchadnezzar*, king of Babylon, who destroyed Jerusalem, and led the Jews into captivity. Sept. Ναβουχοδονόσορ. Arab. *Bochtonassar.* It occurs frequently in Jeremiah, Daniel, and the books of Kings. Like other Assyrian and Babylonish names, this word is best explained from the Persian; (see Gesenius' Gesch. der Hebr. Sprache and Schrift, p. 63.) hence according to Lorsbach, i. q. *Nebu-godan-sar* i. e. Nebo (see נְבוֹ) deorum princeps.

נְבִזְבָּה f. Chald. *a present, gift.* Dan. 2:6. 5:17. comp. Jer. 40:5. Deut. 33:24. Targ. Jonath. Root probably בְּזַבְּ *erogare, expendere*, whence נְבִזְבָּה and, by a not uncommon syncope of ו, נְבִזְבָּה. It is commonly, but erroneously, regarded as the Greek νόμισμα *a coin*, (by a commutation of מ and ב,) for neither *coin* nor *money* suits the context. According to others, i. q. Pers. *nowasish, blanda tractatio.*

נָבַח *to bark.* Once Is. 56:10. (In Arab. *idem.*)

נֹבַח proper name of a city in Gilead. Once Judg. 8:11.

נִבְחַז an idol of the Avites. 2 K. 17:31. The Hebrew interpreters render it *latrator*, (as if from נָבַח,) and say that this idol had the form of a dog. Traces of the ancient worship of an idol in the form of this animal have been discovered in Syria in modern times. Comp. Ikenii Dissert. de Nibchas, in his Dissert. 1749. p. 143 ff.

נָבַט in Kal not used.

Pi. נִבַּט, once Is. 5:30. and

Hiph. הִבִּיט.

1. *to look, to direct the eye, to behold, regarder*, (different from רָאָה.) Job 35:5 הַבֵּט שָׁמַיִם וּרְאֵה *look to heaven and see.* Ps. 142:5. It is construed (1.) with אַחֲרֵי, *to look after* any one, Ex. 33:8. and אַחֲרָיו *to look behind one's self*, 1 Sam. 24:9. Gen. 19:17 אַל תַּבִּיט אַחֲרֶיךָ *look not behind thee.* Verse 26 וַתַּבֵּט אִשְׁתּוֹ מֵאַחֲרָיו *and his (Lot's) wife looked back from after him.* She ought to have followed after her husband, but instead of it, shewed a disposition to return, hence it is correctly rendered as to the sense, but not literally, in the Vulg. *respiciens*

uxor ejus post se. (2.) with אֶל, *to look upon* or *unto, to behold.* Ex. 3 : 6. Num. 21 : 9. Particularly with hope. Is. 51 : 1, 2. Ps. 34 : 6. Also *to look on, respect, regard,* 1 Sam. 16 : 7. Is. 66 : 2. Ps. 119 : 6. comp. verse 15, where it is construed with an accus. Also construed with לְ, instead of אֶל, Ps. 74 : 20. 104 : 32. or with עַל, Hab. 2 : 15. (3.) with an accus. *to regard;* spoken particularly of God, *to regard with favour.* Am. 5 : 22. Ps. 84 : 10. Lam. 4 : 16. Also used absolutely in the same sense, Ps. 13 : 4. Is. 64 : 8.

2. *to see, perceive with the eye,* i. q. רָאָה. Num. 12 : 8. 1 Sam. 2 : 32. Is. 38 : 11. Ps. 10 : 14.

3. construed with בְּ, *to see with satisfaction.* Ps. 92 : 12. Comp. רָאָה בְ, חָזָה בְ.

4. trans. *to let* or *cause to see.* Hab. 1 : 3. Deriv. מַבָּט, מֶבָּט.

נָבִיא m. verbal from נָבָא, dec. III. a.

1. *interpres Dei, one employed by God to make known his will to men.* Judg. 6 : 8. 2 Sam. 7 : 2. This signification is illustrated by Ex. 7 : 1 נְתַתִּיךָ אֱלֹהִים לְפַרְעֹה וְאַהֲרֹן אָחִיךָ יִהְיֶה נְבִיאֶךָ *thou shalt, in reference to Pharaoh,* i. e. in conversation with him, *be the God,* i. e. the sovereign director, *and Aaron, thy brother, shall be thine interpreter;* comp. 4 : 16 וְהוּא יִהְיֶה לְּךָ לְפֶה *and he shall be thy mouth,* also Jer. 15 : 19. Deut. 18 : 18. (In Greek προφήτης, ὑποφήτης, strictly *an interpreter of the divine oracles.*) Hence

2. *a friend* or *confidant of God;* spoken e. g. of Abraham, Gen. 20 : 7. of the patriarchs generally, Ps. 105 : 15. of Moses, Deut. 34 : 10.

3. *a prophet, one inspired of God to instruct the people and foretel future events.* Deut. 13 : 2. 1 Sam. 9 : 9. 1 K. 22 : 7 הַאֵין פֹּה נָבִיא לַיהוָה עוֹד *is there not here a prophet of Jehovah further?* 2 K. 3 : 11. 2 Chr. 28 : 9. This name is also used in reference to false gods, as נְבִיאֵי הַבַּעַל *prophets of Baal,* 1 K. 18 : 19, 40. 2 K. 10 : 19. נְבִיאֵי הָאֲשֵׁרָה *prophets of Astarte,* 1 K. 18 : 19.—Those to be educated as prophets whether younger or older (2 K. 4 : 1.) were called בְּנֵי הַנְּבִיאִים *sons of the prophets,* i. e. their disciples, 1 K. 20 : 35. 2 K. 2 : 3, 5, 7, 15. 4 : 1, 38. 5 : 22. 6 : 1. 9 : 1. Comp. *filii magorum,* i. e. disciples of the Magians, among the Persians.

4. *a minstrel, poet,* considered as one inspired of God. See נְבִיאָה no. 3.

נְבִיא Chald. *idem.* Ezra 5 : 1, 2. 6 : 14.

נְבִיאָה fem. of נָבִיא.

1. *a prophetess, a woman that foretels future events.* 2 K. 22 : 14. 2 Chr. 34 : 22. Neh. 6 : 14. Judg. 4 : 4.

2. *the wife of a prophet.* Is. 8 : 3.

3. *a poetess, a female musician.* Ex. 15 : 20. See נָבִיא no. 4.

נְבָיוֹת *Nabatheans,* the proper name of an Arabian tribe, according to Gen. 25 : 13. 28 : 9. of the race of Ishmael. Is. 60 : 7. (Arab. نَبَط and نَبِيط.) Comp. Diod. Sic. II. 48. Reland's Palæstina, p. 90 ff.

נֶבֶךְ found only in the plur. Job 38 : 16 נִבְכֵי־יָם usually *the heights of the sea,* comp. Arab. نَبْك *collis acuto vertice,* from نبك conj. VIII. *eminuit, altus fuit.* A better sense is given by the Sept. πηγὴ θαλάσσης, comp. Arab. نبع and Chald. נְבַג *to spring up.*

נָבֵל, fut. יִבֹּל. 1. *to wither, to fall off;* spoken of leaves and flowers. Ps. 1 : 3. 37 : 2. Is. 1 : 30. Hence in comparisons, as Is. 34 : 4 *all their host* (*the host of heaven*) *shall fall down, as the leaves of the vine fall.* Ps. 37 ; 2.

2. *to sink down, to be exhausted.* Ex. 18 : 18. Is. 24 : 4. Job 14 : 18 הַר־נוֹפֵל יִבּוֹל *a mountain falling continues to lie.* (Kindred with נָפַל and בָּלָה.) Deriv. נְבֵלָה *a corpse.*

3. *to act foolishly, wickedly.* Prov. 30 : 32. See the noun נָבָל. (The ideas of remissness and foolishness are in like manner connected in several Arabic words.)

Pi. נִבֵּל 1. *to lightly esteem, to reject.* Deut. 32 : 15. Mic. 7 : 6.

2. *to disgrace, dishonour.* Nah. 3:6. Jer. 14:21 אַל־תְּנַבֵּל כִּסֵּא כְבוֹדֶךָ *dishonour not the throne of thy glory.* (Comp. נְבָלָה.)

נָבָל m. verbal from נָבֵל, dec. IV. a.

1. *foolish, a fool.* Prov. 17:7, 21. Jer. 17:11. Hence, by a common association of ideas in the Shemitish dialects,

2. *a wicked, ungodly man.* (Comp. חָכָם, אֱוִיל.) 1 Sam. 25:25. 2 Sam. 3:33. Job 2:10. This meaning is illustrated by Ps. 14:1. 53:2 אָמַר נָבָל בְּלִבּוֹ אֵין אֱלֹהִים *the fool saith in his heart, there is no God.* (So in Arabic the synonymous word كافر denotes *an atheist, unbelieving, wicked.*)

נֵבֶל and נֶבֶל m. plur. נְבָלִים, const. נִבְלֵי, dec. VI. g. and h.

1. *a vessel, bottle;* particularly *an earthen wine-bottle.* Is. 30:14 נֵבֶל יוֹצְרִים *an earthen vessel.* Lam. 4:2 נִבְלֵי חֶרֶשׂ *earthen vessels;* comp. Jer. 13:12. 48:12. Metaphorically Job 38:37 נִבְלֵי שָׁמַיִם *the bottles of heaven.*

2. the name of a musical instrument, a kind of harp or lyre, in Greek νάβλα (נַבְלָא) in Lat. *nablium,* e. g. Ovid. A. A. III. 327. Josephus (Antiq. Jud. VII. 10.) represents it as having 12 strings, which were played on by the hand. Jerome gives it the form of an inverted Delta (∇.) The wine jugs (נְבָלִים *cadi*) of the ancients were usually in the form of a sugar loaf, and the resemblance to this may have given name to the musical instrument. נֵבֶל עָשׂוֹר Ps. 33:2. 144:9. perhaps *a harp of ten strings.* Ps. 57:9. 81:3. 92:4. 108:3. Is. 5:12. Am. 5:23. 6:5. Instead of this we meet also with כְּלִי־נֶבֶל Ps. 71:22. and plur. כְּלֵי־נְבָלִים 1 Chr. 16:5. Is. 22:24.

נְבָלָה f. verbal from נָבֵל.

1. *folly, foolishness.* Job 42:8 לְבִלְתִּי עֲשׂוֹת עִמָּכֶם נְבָלָה *that I may not deal with you after your folly,* for כְּנִבְלַתְכֶם. Is. 32:6.

2. *wickedness.* 1 Sam. 25:25. Is. 9:16.

3. *a wicked deed.* Judg. 19:23, 24. 2 Sam. 13:12. The full phrase used of a person guilty of a gross crime, especially of lewdness, is עָשָׂה, עָשְׂתָה נְבָלָה בְּיִשְׂרָאֵל *he, she has committed a scandalous crime in Israel,* Deut. 22:21. Judg. 20:10. Jer. 29:23. comp. עָשׂוּ זִמָּה וּנְבָלָה בְּיִשְׂרָאֵל Judg. 20:6. So Gen. 34:7, before Israel existed as a people.

נְבֵלָה f. const. נִבְלַת, with suff. נִבְלָתִי (Is. 26:19.) and נִבְלָתוֹ, נִבְלָתְךָ, *a corpse* (of a man), Is. 26:19. *a carcase* (of an animal), Lev. 5:2. 7:24. Used by way of reproach of idols, Jer. 16:18. Comp. פֶּגֶר Lev. 26:30. (Root נָבַל no. 2. comp. מַפֶּלֶת from נָפַל.)

נַבְלוּת f. verbal from נָבֵל, dec. I. *private parts, pudenda.* Hos. 2:12. [2:10.] See נָבֵל Pi. no. 2. and Chald. נְבוּל *fœditas, obscœnitas.*

נָבַע *to spring, to flow.* Prov. 18:4 נַחַל נֹבֵעַ *a flowing brook.* (Chald. Syr. and Arab. *idem.*)

Hiph. הִבִּיעַ. 1. liter. *to let flow out.* Prov. 1:23 אַבִּיעָה לָכֶם רוּחִי *I will pour out my spirit upon you.* Especially *to pour forth* words, Prov. 15:2, 28 פִּי רְשָׁעִים יַבִּיעַ רָעוֹת *the mouth of the wicked poureth out evil things.* Hence it is used without any further addition in an evil sense, Ps. 59:8. 94:4.

2. *to announce.* (Comp. e. g. נָטַף.) Ps. 19:3. 78:2. 145:7. (Syr. ܢܒܥ Aph. *vulgavit.*)

נֶבְרַשְׁתָּא f. Chald. *a candlestick.* Dan. 5:5. (Arab. and Syr. *idem.*)

נֶגֶב m. *the south.* (Root נגב in Syr. and Chald. *to be dry.*) גְּבוּל־נֶגֶב *the southern boundary,* Josh. 15:4. פְּאַת־נֶגֶב *on the south side,* Num. 35:5. נֶגֶב כִּנְרוֹת *on the south of lake Cinneroth,* Josh. 11:2. Hence אֶרֶץ נֶגֶב Josh. 15:19. and simply נֶגֶב Ps. 126:4. *a south land.* Particularly (1.) *the southern part of Palestine,* whether joined with אֶרֶץ, Gen. 20:1. 24:62. or without it, Gen. 13:3. Deut. 34:3. Josh. 10:40. (2.) *Egypt.* So at least Dan. 11:5 ff מֶלֶךְ הַנֶּגֶב *the king of the south*, in prophetic language, for *the king of Egypt*.

With ה־ parag. נֶגְבָּה *to the south*, Ex. 40:24. Josh. 17:9, 10 נֶגְבָּה לְאֶפְרַיִם *to the south of Ephraim*, or as in 18:3 נֶגְבָּה מִן הָהָר *to the south of the mount*. Also בַּנֶּגְבָּה Josh. 15:21. and לַנֶּגְבָּה 1 Chr. 26: 17. where the ה has no significancy.

נָגַד in Kal not used. Probably literally *to be before, in conspectu esse, to be evident*. Arab. *clara et manifesta fuit* res.

Hiph. הִגִּיד 1. *to declare, shew, make known*; usually construed with a dative of the person, Gen. 3:11. 9:22. 29: 12. 37:5. rarely with an accus. Ezek. 43:10. Job 26:4. Also without cases, Job 42:3.

2. *to announce, publish*. Ps. 111:6. Particularly *to publish with commendation, to praise*, Ps. 9:12. 71:17. 92:3. comp. 75:10 וַאֲנִי אַגִּיד לְעֹלָם *but I will praise for ever*.

3. *to betray*. Job 17:5 לְחֵלֶק יַגִּיד רֵעִים (*who*) *betrays his friends for a prey*, i. e. to the plunderer.

3. *to solve* a riddle. Judg. 14:19. Comp. Chald. אַחֲוָיָה.

Hoph. הֻגַּד, fut. יֻגַּד, infin. pleonast. הֻגֵּד, pass. of Hiph. Josh. 9. 24. Ruth 2:11. Is. 7:2.

נְגַד Chald. *to flow*. Dan. 7:10.

נֶגֶד strictly a subst. dec. VI. k. *what is before* or *in front*. מִנֶּגֶד *a facie*, Judg. 9:17 *he cast his life* מִנֶּגֶד *from himself*, i. e. away. Hence as an adv. (1.) *over against*. 2 K. 2:7, 15. 3:22. Deut. 28:66 *and thy life shall hang over against thee*, i. e. thou shalt be in constant danger of thy life. (2.) *against*. 2 Sam. 18:13.

לְנֶגֶד and נֶגֶד as a prep. (1.) *before, coram, in conspectu*. Job 4:16 נֶגֶד עֵינָי *before my eyes*. Ex. 34:10 נֶגֶד כָּל־עַמְּךָ *before thy whole people*.—נֶגֶד הַשָּׁמֶשׁ *coram sole*, i. e. as long as the sun exists; comp. Deut. 21:22, 23. (2.) *over against*. Ex. 19: 2. Josh. 3:16. (3.) *against, contra*. 1 K. 21:10. Ecc. 4:12. (4.) *near, in the neighbourhood of*. 1 Chr. 8:32. Neh. 3:10.

With other prepositions, (1.) מִנֶּגֶד *from before*. Is. 1:16 מִנֶּגֶד עֵינָי *from before mine eyes*. Jon. 2:5. Prov. 14:7 לֵךְ מִנֶּגֶד לְאִישׁ כְּסִיל *to go away from the foolish man*. (2.) כְּנֶגֶד only Gen. 2:18, 20 כְּנֶגְדּוֹ *over against him, suited to him*. Sept. verse 18 κατ' αὐτόν; verse 20 ὅμοιος αὐτῷ.

נָגַהּ *to shine, to give light, to beam*. Job 22:28. 18:5. (In Syr. *idem*.)

Hiph. 1. *to cause to shine*. Is. 13:10.

2. *to enlighten*. Ps. 18:29. 2 Sam. 22:29.

נֹגַהּ f. verbal from נָגַהּ, dec. VI. a. *brightness, shining*; particularly of the fire, Is. 4:5. of the sun, 2 Sam. 23:4. of the moon, Is. 60:19. of the sword, Hab. 3:11. of the shechinah or majestic presence of Jehovah (כְּבוֹד יְהוָה,) Ezek. 10:4. Hab. 3:4. Ps. 18:13. — Prov. 4:18, probably referring to the rising sun.

נֹגַהּ, emph. נָגְהָא, Chald. *brightness, shining*, of the dawn. Dan. 6:20.

נְגֹהָה *brightness*. Plur. Is. 59:9.

נָגַח, fut. יִגַּח, *to push*, spoken of horned animals. Ex. 21:28.

Pi. *idem*. Ezek. 34:21. Dan. 8:4. Figuratively of a conqueror overthrowing nations before him, Deut. 33:17. 1 K. 22:11. Ps. 44:6.

Hithpa. liter. *to push one's self*, hence *to carry on war against* any one. Dan. 11:40. (In Chald. *idem*.)

נַגָּח m. verbal from נָגַח, *apt* or *wont to push*. Ex. 21:29, 36.

נָגִיד m. dec. III. a.

1. *a prince*. (Root נָגַד Arab. نَجُدَ *to be high-spirited, courageous*, whence نَجِيد *high-spirited, noble, a prince*.) 1 Sam. 9:16. 10:1. Plur. *chiefs, nobles*, generally, Job 29:10. Used abstractly, *nobilia, honesta*, Prov. 8:6.

2. *an overseer* generally; e. g. over the temple, 1 Chr. 9:11. 2 Chr. 31:13. over the palace, 2 Chr. 28:7. over an

army, *a captain*, 1 Chr. 13:1. 2 Chr. 32:21.

נְגִינָה f. verbal from נָגַן, dec. X.

1. *a stringed instrument* of music. So in the titles of Psalms IV. VI. LIV. LV. LXVII. LXXVI.

2. *music on a stringed instrument.* Lam. 5:14. Is. 38:20.

3. *a song for a stringed instrument.* Ps. 77:7. Particularly *a satiric song,* Lam. 3:14. Job 30:9.

נָגַן in Kal found only in the part. נֹגְנִים Ps. 68:26. otherwise Pi. נִגֵּן *to play on a stringed instrument.* 1 Sam. 16:16, 17, 18, 23. 2 K. 3:15. Ps. 33:3 הֵיטִיבוּ נַגֵּן *touch skilfully the strings.* Is. 23:16. (In Chald. *idem.*) Deriv. מְנַגִּינָה.

נָגַע, fut. יִגַּע, infin. נְגֹעַ, with suff. נָגְעוֹ, also גַּעַת.

1. *to touch,* usually construed with בְּ Gen. 3:3. Lev. 5:3. 6:11. [6:18.] more rarely with עַל, Is. 6:7. Dan. 10:16. with אֶל, Num. 4:15. Hag. 2:12. But in this sense it is applied to denote (1.) *to injure.* Gen. 26:11 הַנֹּגֵעַ בָּאִישׁ הַזֶּה וּבְאִשְׁתּוֹ *whosoever toucheth this man or his wife.* Verse 29. Josh. 9:19. (2.) *to lie with* a woman. Prov. 6:29. Construed with אֶל, Gen. 20:6. (3.) joined with לֵב, *to touch* or *affect the heart.* 1 Sam. 10:26. (4.) *to injure* a plant, spoken of a pernicious wind. Ezek. 17:10.

2. *to reach unto* any thing; construed with בְּ, Hos. 4:2. with עַד, Mic. 1:9. Is. 16:8. Jer. 4:10. with אֶל, Jer. 51:9. with עַל, Judg. 20:34, 41. Comp. Job 4:5. 5:19.

3. *to come to* a person or thing, construed with בְּ, 2 Sam. 5:8. with אֶל, Jon. 3:6. Dan. 9:21. Used absolutely *to come, arrive,* Ezra 3:1. Neh. 7:73. Comp. הִגִּיעַ.

4. *to smite.* Gen. 32:26, 33. Spoken particularly of Jehovah, and construed with בְּ, 1 Sam. 6:9. Job 19:21. Part. נָגוּעַ *smitten, punished of God,* Ps. 73:14. Is. 53:4.

Niph. *to be beaten,* spoken of an army; or rather *to make as if one were beaten.* Josh. 8:15. This last turn of the signification is more common in Hithpael.

Pi. *to smite,* i. q. Kal no. 4. used particularly in reference to divine judgments, (comp. נָגַף, נֶגַע.) Gen. 12:17. 2 K. 15:5.

Pu. pass. Ps. 73:5.

Hiph. 1. i. q. Kal no. 1. *to touch;* construed with לְ, Ex. 4:25. with אֶל, Ex. 12:22. with עַל, Is. 6:7.

2. i. q. Kal no. 2. *to reach unto* any thing; construed with לְ, Gen. 28:12. with עַד, Is. 8:8.—*To befal, happen,* as an event, Ecc. 8:14. Est. 9:26 (with אֶל.)—*My hand attains to any thing,* i. e. I obtain or possess it, Lev. 5:7. Comp. מָצָא no. 2.

3. i. q. Kal no. 3. *to come to;* construed with עַד, Ps. 107:18. with אֶל, 1 Sam. 14:9. Also *to come to* any thing, i. e. to attain it, Est. 4:14 הִגַּעַתְּ לַמַּלְכוּת *thou hast attained to royal dignity.* Used absolutely, *to come;* spoken of persons, Est. 6:14. especially of time, Ezek. 7:12. Ecc. 12:1.

4. causat. of Kal no. 1. *to cause to touch,* particularly in the phrase הִגִּיעַ לָאָרֶץ עַד עָפָר, *to cause to touch the earth, the dust,* i. e. to throw to the ground, Is. 25:12. 26:5. Lam. 2:2.—In like manner Is. 5:8 *woe to them who cause house to touch on house,* i. e. who acquire many houses.

נֶגַע m. with suff. נִגְעוֹ, plur. נְגָעִים, const. נִגְעֵי, verbal from נָגַע, dec. VI. i.

1. *a stroke, blow, wound,* also collect. *blows.* Prov. 6:33. Deut. 17:8. 21:5. Used most frequently of God's *strokes* or *the plagues* which he sends on men, Gen. 12:17. Ex. 11:1.

2. נֶגַע צָרַעַת Lev. 13:3, 9, 20, 25. and without צָרַעַת verses 22, 29. *the plague of leprosy,* also *this plague* in garments, 13, 14. and in walls, 14:39 ff. Hence

3. *one infected with the leprosy* or *so suspected.* Lev. 13:4, 13, 17, 31 נֶגַע הַנֶּתֶק *one infected with the scall,* for which we find barely נֶתֶק, verse 33.—In verse 50, it denotes *a garment infected with the leprosy.*

נָגַף, fut. יִגֹּף. 1. *to smite.* Spoken particularly of Jehovah, who ordains human calamities or plagues, 2 Chr. 21:18. Ex. 7:27. [8:2.] or causes death, 1 Sam. 25:38. Ps. 89:24.— Sometimes this language is used when Jehovah suffers his people to be beaten before their enemies, 1 Sam. 4:3 *wherefore hath Jehovah smitten us this day before the Philistines?* Judg. 20:35. 2 Chr. 13:15. 21:14. Comp. Niph.

2. *to push, thrust;* spoken of a man, Ex. 21:22. of horned cattle, 21:35.

3. *to stumble, to knock against* any thing. Prov. 3:23. Ps. 91:12.

Niph. נִגַּף *to be smitten,* spoken of an army. Judg. 20:36. 1 Sam. 4:10. Usually construed with לִפְנֵי 1 Sam. 4:2 *Israel was smitten before the Philistines.* Lev. 26:17.

Hithpa. *to stumble,* spoken of the feet. Jer. 13:16. Comp. Kal no. 3.

Deriv. out of course מַגֵּפָה.

נֶגֶף m. verbal from נָגַף.

1. *a plague* or *destructive calamity sent by God.* Ex. 12:13, 30:12.

2. *stumbling, offence.* Is. 8:14.

נָגַר in Kal not used. Prob. *to flow.* (In Aram. נְגַר *to draw* and *to flow.*)

Niph. 1. *to be poured out, to flow away.* 2 Sam. 14:14. Job 20:28.

2. *to be stretched out.* Ps. 77:3.

Hiph. הִגִּיר. 1. *to pour out.* Ps. 75:9.

2. *to throw down,* as stones from a mountain. Mic. 1:6.

3. *to throw to, give up, yield,* in the phrase הִגִּיר פ׳ עַל יְדֵי חֶרֶב *to give up any one to the power of the sword,* Ezek. 35:5. Jer. 18:21. Ps. 63:11. Incorrectly rendered *fundere per manus gladii.*

Hoph. *to be poured out* or *thrown down,* spoken of water. Mic. 1:4.

נָגַשׂ, fut. יִגֹּשׂ, once יִנְגּוֹשׂ (Is. 58:3.)

1. *to urge, press, drive on to labour.* Is. 58:3. Hence נוֹגֵשׂ *task-master, bailiff,* Ex. 3:7. Is. 9:3. Job 3:18. Also *a driver* of cattle, Job 39:7.

2. *to press* a debtor, Deut. 15:2, 3. *to exact* tribute, construed with two accus. 2 K. 23:35. Hence נוֹגֵשׂ Dan. 11:20. *an exactor of tribute.*

3. *to oppress* a subject people, also *to rule over* generally. Part. נוֹגֵשׂ *a ruler,* Is. 3:12. 14:2. 60:17. Zech. 10:4. (So in Ethiop. whence the king of Ethiopia is called *Negush.*)

Niph. נִגַּשׂ 1. *to be hard pressed* (by an enemy). 1 Sam. 13:6.

2. *to be oppressed, injured.* Is. 53:7.

3. *to be wearied out,* spoken of an army. 1 Sam. 14:24.

נָגַשׁ, not used in the pret. Kal, but instead of it the pret. Niph. נִגַּשׁ, fut. Kal יִגַּשׁ, imper. גַּשׁ, גְּשָׁה, also גֶּשׁ (Gen. 19:9.) infin. גֶּשֶׁת, *to draw near, to approach.* Gen. 19:9 גֶּשׁ־הָלְאָה *approach nearer.* Construed most frequently with אֶל of the object, Gen. 27:22. with לְ, Judg. 20:23. with עַד, Gen. 33:3. with עַל, Ezek. 44:13. with an accus. Num. 4:19 בְּגִשְׁתָּם אֶת־קֹדֶשׁ הַקֳּדָשִׁים *when they approach the most holy place.* 1 Sam. 9:18. with בְּ, Is. 65:5. Am. 9:13. Job 41:8 [41:16] אֶחָד בְּאֶחָד יִגַּשׁוּ *one (of the scales) joins to another.* Particularly (1.) *to approach* a woman, *to have conjugal intercourse with* her. Ex. 19:15. (2.) *to draw near to* Jehovah, *to turn to* him. Is. 29:13.

Hiph. הִגִּישׁ. 1. *to lead* or *bring near,* as persons. Gen. 48:10, 13.

2. *to bring near,* as things. Gen. 27:25. 2 Sam. 13:11. 17:29. Particularly offerings, Am. 5:25.

3. *to cause to penetrate.* Job 40:19.

4. more rarely, i. q. Kal, *to draw near.* Am. 9:10. Is. 41:22. 45:21.

Hoph. הֻגַּשׁ pass. of Hiph. no. 1. 2 Sam. 3:34. of no. 2. Mal. 1:11.

Hithpa. *to draw near.* Is. 45:20.

נֵד m. *a heap* (of fruit). Is. 17:11. Elsewhere used figuratively of *a heap* or *pile* of waters, Ps. 33:7 כֹּנֵס כַּנֵּד מֵי הַיָּם *he gathereth together the waters of the sea as an heap.* So Josh. 3:13, 16 *then the waters which came down from above stood* נֵד אֶחָד *as an heap.* In the same connexion, Ex. 15:8. Ps. 78:13. The same idea is expressed Ex. 14:22, by חוֹמָה *a wall.* Comp. Virg. Georg. iv. 361.

נָדָא found only 2 K. 17 : 21 Keth. an Aramean form for נָדָה, hence in Hiph. *to drive away, to remove.* The Keri וַיַּדַּח is a correct explanatory gloss.

נָדַב *to drive on, to excite to* any thing. (Arab. *vocavit, invitavit ad aliquid.*) Only in the phrase Ex. 25 : 2. כָּל־אִישׁ אֲשֶׁר יִדְּבֶנּוּ לִבּוֹ *every one whom his heart urges on,* i. e. who acts voluntarily. 35 : 21, 29.

Hithpa. 1. *to excite one's self, to shew one's self willing, to act voluntarily.* Neh. 11 : 2. Particularly in reference to military service, Judg. 5 : 2, 9. Comp. Ps. 110 : 3.

2. *to give freely, willingly, to bring a voluntary gift.* 1 Chr. 29 : 9, 14, 17. Ezra 1 : 6. 2 : 68. 3 : 5.

3. *to serve voluntarily,* construed with לְ. 2 Chr. 17 : 16.

Deriv. out of course נָדִיב.

נְדַב Chald. Ithpa. i. q. Heb.

1. *to be willing* or *disposed for* any thing, construed with לְ. Ezra 7 : 13.

2. *to give voluntarily.* Ezra 7 : 15, 16. הִתְנַדָּבוּת *what is given freely,* an Aramean infin. ibid.

נְדָבָה f. verbal from נָדַב, dec. XI. c.

1. *voluntariness, freewill.* Hence בִּנְדָבָה *voluntarily, freely,* Num. 15 : 3. Ps. 54 : 8. and without בְּ, Deut. 23 : 24. Hos. 14 : 5. Ps. 110 : 3 עַמְּךָ נְדָבֹת *thy people is willing,* the abstract being used for the concrete.

2. *a voluntary gift, a freewill offering,* in opposition to נֶדֶר *the performance of a vow.* Ex. 35 : 29. Lev. 22 : 23 נְדָבָה תַּעֲשֶׂה אֹתוֹ *as a freewill offering thou mayest offer it.* Also *a present* for the temple, Ezra 1 : 4. comp. verse 7.

3. *copiousness, plenty, largitas.* Ps. 68 : 10 גֶּשֶׁם נְדָבוֹת *a copious rain, pluvia larga.*

Note. The ideas *to give freely, to be liberal, to give abundantly,* are closely connected, and often in Arabic occur under the same root. Comp. Lat. *largus* and *largiri.*

נִדְבָּךְ m. Chald. *a wall* or *structure.* Ezra 6 : 4. (In Chald. and Talmud. *idem.*)

נָדַד (kindred with נוּד,) pret. נָדְדוּ, infin. נְדֹד, fut. יִדֹּד and יִדַּד.

1. trans. *to move,* e. g. the wing. Is. 10 : 14.

2. *to wander about;* spoken of a bird, Prov. 27 : 8. Is. 16 : 2. of men, Job 15 : 23. Part. נֹדֵד *a wandering fugitive,* Is. 16 : 3. 21 : 14. Jer. 49 : 5.

3. most frequently, *to flee.* Ps. 31 : 15. 55 : 8. 68 : 13. Spoken of a bird, *to fly away,* Jer. 4 : 25. 9 : 9.

Poal נֹדַד *to flee away.* Nah. 3 : 17.

Hiph. הֵנֵד *to frighten, chase away.* Job 18 : 18.

Hoph. הֻנַד *to be thrust away,* 2 Sam. 23 : 6. and with another form, fut. יֻדַּד, *to be frightened away, to flee.* Job 20 : 8.

Hithpo. *to flee.* Ps. 64 : 9.

נְדַד Chald. *to flee.* Dan. 6 : 19.

נְדֻדִים masc. plur. verbal from נָדַד, *the tossings* of a wakeful person on his bed. Job 7 : 4.

נָדָה in Kal not used, i. q. נוּד and נָדַד *to flee, depart.* (Syr. *idem.*)

Pi. נִדָּה 1. *to remove,* construed with לְ. Am. 6 : 3.

2. *to cast out, exclude.* Is. 66 : 5. (In Rabbin. נִדּוּי *a casting out of the synagogue.*)

נִדָּה f. dec. X. *impurity, uncleanness, something unclean, hateful, abominable,* in a physical and moral sense. (Syr. ܢܕܝ *nauseavit.*) Particularly (1.) *uncleanness of a woman arising from her monthly courses,* Lev. 12 : 2. 15 : 19, 20. Hence *the monthly courses,* Lev. 15 : 24, 25, 33. (2.) מֵי־הַנִּדָּה Num. 19 : 9, 13, 20, 21. *the waters of impurity,* i. e. the water with which any thing unclean is purified, water of purification. Comp. Zech. 13 : 1 לְחַטָּאת וּלְנִדָּה *for sin and uncleanness,* i. e. as an expiation and purification. (3.) *something unclean, abominable,* spoken of idolatry. 2 Chr. 29 : 5. Ezra 9 : 11. Lam. 1 : 17.

4. *an abominable deed*, spoken of incest. Lev. 20 : 21.

נֵדֶה m. *a liberal gift, present*, as the price of prostitution. Ezek. 16 : 33. Root נָדָה Arab. ندا *uvidus*, 2. *liberalis fuit*. Comp. נֵדֶן.

נָדַח, fut. יִדַּח. 1. *to push, thrust, expel.* 2 Sam. 14 : 14. See Hiph.

2. *immittere* (securim.) Deut. 20 : 19. See the kindred verbs דָּחָה, נָדָה, דָּחַח.

Hiph. הִדִּיחַ 1. *to throw down, to cast out.* Ps. 62 : 5. Ps. 5 : 11.

2. *to cast out, eject, expel.* 2 Chr. 13 : 9. Deut. 30 : 1. Jer. 8 : 3. Spoken of the scattering of a flock, Jer. 23 : 2. 50 : 17.

3. *to urge on, seduce.* Deut. 13 : 13. Prov. 7 : 21. Construed with מִן, *to turn* or *seduce away from* any one, Deut. 13 : 5, 10.

4. *to bring* a calamity on any one, construed with עַל. 2 Sam. 15 : 14.

Niph. נִדַּח 1. pass. of Hiph. no. 2. *to be driven out*, Jer. 40 : 12. Part. נִדָּח *one driven out, a fugitive*, Is. 16 : 3, 4. 27 : 13. Also used collectively Deut. 30 : 4. Neh. 1 : 9. So the fem. נִדָּחָה Mic. 4 : 6. Zeph. 3 : 19. With suff. נִדָּחוֹ *one whom he hath banished*, 2 Sam. 14 : 13. —Metaph. Job 6 : 13 וְתֻשִׁיָּה נִדְּחָה מִמֶּנִּי *hope is driven away from me.*—Spoken of cattle, *to wander about, to go astray*, Deut. 22 : 1. Ezek. 34 : 4, 16.

2. pass. of Hiph. no. 3. *to be seduced* or *led astray*. Deut. 4 : 19. 30 : 17.

3. *immitti, impelli*, (see Kal no. 2.) Deut. 19 : 5 *he who goes into a wood with his neighbour to hew wood*, וְנִדְּחָה יָדוֹ בַגַּרְזֶן לִכְרֹת הָעֵץ *and his hand fetches a stroke with the axe to cut down the tree;* liter. *impellitur* or *impellit se manus ejus cum securi.*

Pu. *to be pushed* or *driven.* Is. 8 : 22 וַאֲפֵלָה מְנֻדָּח *pushed into darkness.* Comp. Jer. 23 : 12.

Hoph. part. מֻדָּח *chased, driven.* Is. 13 : 14.

Deriv. מַדּוּחִים.

נָדִיב m. verbal from נָדַב, dec. III. a.

1. *voluntary, giving voluntarily.* Generally in the phrase נְדִיב לֵב Ex. 35 : 5, 22. 2 Chr. 29 : 31. (See נָדַב Kal and Hithpa.) Ps. 51 : 14 רוּחַ נְדִיבָה *a willing heart.*

2. *liberal.* Prov. 19 : 6.

3. *noble, noble minded*, from the connexion of nobleness with liberality. Is. 32 : 5, 8. Prov. 17 : 7, 26.

4. subst. *one noble in rank, a prince.* Job 34 : 18. Ps. 107 : 40. 113 : 8. Also in the bad sense, *a tyrant*, Job 21 : 28. Is. 13 : 2.

נְדִיבָה f. denom. from נָדִיב, *nobility*, also *prosperity* generally. Job 30 : 15.

I. **נָדָן** m. dec. IV. a. *a sheath.* 1 Chr. 21 : 27. See נְדָנָה.

II. **נֵדֶן** i. q. נֵדֶה m. dec. IV. a. *a liberal gift, present*, as the price of prostitution. Ezek. 16 : 33. Root נָדָה, the final Nun being afformative. Cod. 409 of De Rossi reads נִדְנַיִךְ instead of נְדָנַיִךְ.

נִדְנֶה m. Chald. *a sheath.* (So in Chald. נְדָן and נִדְנָה, also לְדָן ,לִדְנָא, see the letter ל. The ה־ is paragogic as in אַרְיֵה.) By a particular metaphor this word is used to denote *the body*, as *the sheath* or *covering* of the soul. Dan. 7 : 15 *my spirit was grieved* בְּגוֹ נִדְנֶה *in the body.* The same metaphor is used in Plin. N. H. VII. 52 seu 53. *donec cremato eo inimici remeanti animæ velut vaginam ademerint.* So the Nazareans call the body *a garment.* See Niebuhr's Reisebeschreibung, Th. 2. p. 439ff.

נָדַף, fut יִנְדֹּף (Ps. 68 : 3.) and יִדֹּף.

1. *to drive out, dispellere*, e. g. stubble, smoke. Ps. 1 : 4. 68 : 3.

2. *to drive out, put to flight, overcome.* Job 32 : 13.

Niph. נִדָּף pass. of no. 1. Is. 41 : 2. Ps. 68 : 3. עָלֶה נִדָּף *a leaf blown about by the wind*, Lev. 26 : 36. Job 13 : 25. Infin. const. הִנְדֹּף Ps. 68 : 3.

נָדַר, fut. יִדֹּר ,יִדַּר ,וַיִּדֹּר (1 Sam. 1 : 11. *to vow, to make a vow*, for the performance of any thing. Construed with a dative of the person, Gen. 31 : 13. Deut. 23 : 24. Frequently נָדַר נֶדֶר *vovere votum*, Judg. 11 : 39. 2 Sam. 15 : 8. Different from אָסַר *to make a vow of abstinence.*

נֶדֶר and **נֵדֶר** m. with suff. נִדְרִי, plur. נְדָרִים, const. נִדְרֵי, verbal from נָדַר, dec. VI. g.

1. *a vow.* נָדַר נְדָרִים *vovere vota,* see above. שִׁלֵּם נְדָרִים Ps. 22:26. and עָשָׂה נְדָרִים Judg. 11:39, *to pay* or *perform vows.*

2. *an offering promised by vow.* Lev. 7:16. in opposition to נְדָבָה *a free-will offering.*

נֹהַּ m. found only in Ezek. 7:11. according to the Jewish commentators, *a lamentation,* for נְהִי, (after the form קֹדֶשׁ,) from נָהָה, But not suitably to the context. Better from נוּהַּ Arab. نَاهَ *eminuit;* hence *greatness, excellence, beauty.* Sept. cod. Alex. ὡραϊσμός.

I. **נָהַג**, fut. יִנְהַג. 1. *to guide, lead;* e.g. a flock. Gen. 31:18. Ex. 3:1. Construed with בְּ, Is. 11:6. comp. Ps. 80:2 נֹהֵג כַּצֹּאן יוֹסֵף *who leadest Joseph, like sheep.*—Cant. 8:2.

2. *to drive* a beast of burden. 2 K. 4:24 נְהַג וָלֵךְ *drive forward* (*the ass*). 9:20 כִּי בְשִׁגָּעוֹן יִנְהָג *for he driveth* (*the horse*) *on furiously.* Hence נָהַג עֲגָלָה *to drive a chariot* or *waggon,* 2 Sam. 6:3. construed with בְּ, 1 Chr. 13:7.

3. *to lead away,* e.g. prisoners. 1 Sam. 30:2. Is. 20:4.

4. as in Chald. *to be accustomed to* any thing. Ecc. 2:3 וְלִבִּי נֹהֵג בַּחָכְמָה *and my heart being accustomed to wisdom,* i.e. cleaving to wisdom. Others, intrans. *my heart walking in wisdom.* Others compare לָהַג, see the letter ל.

Pi. נִהַג, fut. יְנַהֵג. 1. i.q. Kal no 1. *to lead,* Deut. 4:27. 28:37. *to bring,* Ex. 10:13 *and Jehovah brought an east wind on the land.* Ps. 78:26.

2. trans. of Kal no. 2. Ex. 14:25 וַיְנַהֲגֵהוּ בִּכְבֵדֻת *and caused them to drive them heavily.*

3. *to take away,* i. q. Kal no. 3. Gen. 31:26.

II. **נָהַג** i. q. נָהַק, נָהָה, *to sigh, pant, gasp.* In Arab. and Syr. *idem.* Only in Pi. Nah. 2:8.

נָהָה *to lament.* Ezek. 32:18. Mic. 2:4 נָהָה נְהִי נִהְיָה *they lament with a doleful lamentation.* Deriv. נְהִי, נִי.

Niph. *to assemble,* as in Chald. 1 Sam. 7:2 *the whole house of Israel assembled after Jehovah,* i.e. they united to follow Jehovah. The phrase is analogous with הָלַךְ אַחֲרֵי יְהוָֹה, מִלֵּא. An etymological connexion with the signification of Kal is possible; comp. זָעַק *to cry;* Niph. *convocari, congregari.*

נְהוֹר Chald. *light.* Dan. 2:22 Keri, as is common in Chald. The Kethib has נְהִירָא as in Syriac. See נְהַר no. 2.

נְהִי m. in pause נֶהִי, verbal from נָהָה, *a lamentation.* Jer. 9:17. Am. 5:16 יוֹדְעֵי נֶהִי *those who are skilled in lamentation.*

נִהְיָה fem. of נְהִי, 1. *a lamentation.* Mic. 2:4.

2. fem. of an adj. נִהְיִ, *forbidden.* Prov. 13:19 תַּאֲוָה נִהְיָה תֶּעֱרַב לְנָפֶשׁ *forbidden desire is sweet to the soul.* Root نَهَى in Arab. *to forbid, hinder.* The formation of the fem. נִהְיָה from the masc. נִהְיִ, is entirely analogous to the forms נְהִי m. and נְהִיָה f. *a lamentation,* and to the declension of the form נְהִי generally. The ancient versions have all missed the meaning.

נָהִיר see **נְהוֹר**.

נַהִירוּ Chald. verbal from נְהַר no. II. *illumination, wisdom.* Dan. 5:11, 14. Syr. *idem.*

נָהַל in Kal not used.

Pi. נִהַל, fut. יְנַהֵל.

1. *to lead, guide.* Ex. 15:13. 2 Chr. 28:15 וַיְנַהֲלוּם בַּחֲמֹרִים *and they led them upon asses.* Ps. 23:2 עַל מֵי מְנֻחוֹת יְנַהֲלֵנִי *he leads me by still waters.* 31:4. Is. 49:10. 51:18. It includes here the idea of *care* and *protection.* Hence

2. *to protect.* 2 Chr. 32:22. (Comp. 1 Chr. 22:18.)

3. *to provide for.* Gen. 47:17.

Hithpa. *to march, proceed.* Gen. 33:14.

נַהֲלֹל m. dec. I.

1. prob. *pastures,* from נָהַל *to drive* (cattle); comp. מִדְבָּר. Is. 7:19.

2. proper name of a city in the tribe of Zebulun. Judg. 1:30. Also written נַהֲלָל Josh. 19:15.

נָהַם, fut. יִנְהֹם, (synon. with שָׁאַג.)

1. *to roar*, as a lion. Prov. 28:15. Is. 5:29.

2. *to rage, foam*, as the sea. Is. 5:30.

3. *to sigh, groan*. Ezek. 24:23. Prov. 5:11. Arab. and Syr. *idem*. Kindred with הָמָה q. v.

נַהַם m. verbal from נָהַם, *the roaring* of a lion. Prov. 19:12. 20:2.

נְהָמָה f. const. נַהֲמַת, verbal from נָהַם, dec. XI. d.

1. *the raging* of the sea. Is. 5:30.

2. *a groaning*. Ps. 38:9.

נָהַק, fut. יִנְהַק, *to cry as an ass, to bray*. Job 6:5. Also in a different connexion, 30:7. (In Chald. and Arab. *idem*.)

I. **נָהַר** *to run, flow, confluere*. (In Arab. *idem*.) Whence נָהָר. Used only metaphorically of nations, Is. 2:2 וְנָהֲרוּ אֵלָיו כָּל־הַגּוֹיִם *and all nations shall flow unto it*. Jer. 31:12. 51:44. Construed with עַל, Mic. 4:1.

II. **נָהַר** as in Aramean, *to shine, to be clear, bright;* hence figuratively *to rejoice, to have a bright countenance*. (Comp. אוֹר no. 2.) Ps. 34:6. Is. 60:5. Deriv. נְהָרָה, נְהוֹר, נְהִירוּ. It is kindred with נוּר *to shine*. See the letter ה.

נָהָר m. verbal from נָהַר no. I. dec. IV. a. *a stream, river*. נְהַר פְּרָת *the river Euphrates*, Gen. 15:18. This river is also called by way of eminence נָהָר and הַנָּהָר, Gen. 31:21. Ex. 23:31. Ps. 72:8. hence עֵבֶר הַנָּהָר *the country beyond the Euphrates*, Is. 7:20. also *on this side of the Euphrates*, Ezra 8:36. See עֵבֶר.—It is likewise used of *the currents* or *streams* of the sea, Jon. 2:3 וְנָהָר יְסֹבְבֵנִי *and the sea surrounded me*.

Dual נַהֲרַיִם (as if from a sing. נַהַר,) *the two rivers*, used of the Tigris and Euphrates, only in the phrase אֲרַם נַהֲרַיִם *Syria of the two rivers*, i. e. Mesopotamia, Gen. 24:10. Deut. 23:5.

Plur. נְהָרִים, more frequently נְהָרוֹת, const. נַהֲרוֹת.

נְהַר m. Chald. *a stream*. Dan. 7:10. עֲבַר נַהֲרָה *the country on this side of the river (Euphrates)*, Ezra 4:10, 16, 17, 20.

נְהָרָה f. verbal from נָהַר no. II. *light, the light of the sun*. Job 3:4.

נוּא or **נִיא** in Kal not used; except in Num. 32:7 Keth. *to remove, forsake*. (Arab. נוא *idem*.)

Hiph. הֵנִיא.

1. *to hold back, forbid, make of no effect*. Ps. 33:10. Num. 30:6 אִם הֵנִיא אָבִיהָ אֹתָהּ *but if her father forbid her*. Verses 9, 12.

2. *to cause to turn away from* any one, construed with מִן. Num. 32:7, 9.

3. intrans. *to refuse*. Ps. 141:8. The full reading יָנִיא is found in 36 MSS.

Deriv. תְּנוּאָה.

נוּב 1. *to sprout, shoot, germinate*. Ps. 92:15.

2. *to grow, increase*, spoken of riches. Ps. 62:11. Comp. מַרְבִּית.

3. *to utter, bring forth*, spoken of the mouth. Prov. 10:31.

Pil. נוֹבֵב *to make to sprout, to cause to flourish*. Zech. 9:17.

Deriv. תְּנוּבָה, נִיב.

נוֹב or **נוּב** Is. 57:19 Keth. i. q. נִיב q. v.

I. **נוּד** (comp. the kindred נָדַד.)

1. *to shake*, as a reed. 1 K. 14:15. (In Arab. *idem*.)

2. *to wander about*, as a fugitive. Jer. 4:1. Gen. 4:12, 14 נָע וָנָד *a fugitive and a vagabond*. Ps. 56:9.

3. *to flee*. Ps. 11:1. Jer. 49:30.

Hiph. הֵנִיד.

1. *to move, shake;* hence with בְּרֹאשׁ *to shake the head*, Jer. 18:16.

2. *to cause to wander about, to frighten* or *chase away*. 2 K. 21:8. Ps. 36:12.

Hithpa. הִתְנוֹדֵד.

1. *to shake, to reel to and fro*. Is. 24:20.

2. *to shake the head*. Jer. 48:27.

Deriv. מָנוֹד.

II. **נוּד** construed with a dative, *to*

pity, lament any one. According to some, liter. *to shake the head,* as a sign of mourning, (comp. Job 16:4, 5.) and then to be referred to no. 1. It is used (1.) in reference to a person living, *to pity, comfort,* and construed with לְ. Job 2:11. 42:11. Is. 51:19. Jer. 16:5. (2.) in reference to a dead person, *to lament, bewail.* Jer. 22:10.

Hithpa. *to mourn, lament.* Jer. 31:18.

נוּד Chald. *to flee.* Dan. 4:11.

נוֹד m. *flight, banishment.* (Ps. 56:9.) Hence the proper name of a country into which Cain removed after his banishment, Gen. 4:16.

I. נָוָה *to dwell;* (see נָוֶה, נָוָה.) Hab. 2:5 גֶּבֶר יָהִיר וְלֹא יִנְוֶה *the arrogant man, he dwells not* (*quietly*), i.e. he keeps not still, but makes war on others.

II. נָוָה *to be beautiful,* i. q. נָאָה, נָאוָה.

Hiph. *to exalt, to praise.* Ex. 15:2. Sept. δοξάσω αὐτόν. Vulg. *glorificabo eum.*

נָוֶה const. נְוֵה, with suff. נָוְךָ, נָוֵהוּ, נְוֵהֶם, plur. נְאוֹת q. v. verbal from נָוָה no. 1.

1. *a dwelling, habitation.* Prov. 3:33. 21:20. Is. 35:7 נְוֵה תַנִּים *a habitation of dragons.*

2. *a pasture* for flocks. Hos. 9:13. Is. 65:10. Jer. 23:3.

I. נָוָה fem. of נָוֶה, dec. XI. a.

1. *a dwelling.* Job 8:6.

2. *a pasture.* Zeph. 2:6.

3. adj. fem. from נָוֶה *an inhabitant.* Ps. 68:13 נְוַת בַּיִת *a domestic woman, domi habitans.*

II. נָוָה a contraction of נָאוָה *pulchra.* Jer. 6:2.

נוּחַ, fut. יָנוּחַ.

1. *to rest,* spoken of Noah's ark, Gen. 8:4. *to encamp,* spoken of an army, Is. 7:2, 19. 2 Sam. 21:10. *to descend on* any one, spoken of the spirit of God, Num. 11:25, 26. comp. Is. 11:2.

2. *to rest, to have repose.* Ex. 20:11. 23:12. Deut. 5:14. Also *to have rest from trials, persecutions,* construed with מִן, Job 3:26. Est. 9:22. Impers. Job 3:12 אָז יָנוּחַ לִי *then should I have rested.* Is. 23:12. Neh. 9:28. — 2 K. 2:15 *the spirit of Elijah rests upon Elisha.* Is. 25:10. Particularly (1.) *to abide, continue.* Ecc. 7:9 *anger resteth in the bosom of a fool.* Prov. 14:33. Ps. 125:3 *the sceptre of the wicked shall not rest on the lot of the righteous;* comp. Is. 20:32. (2.) *to be still, silent.* 1 Sam. 25:9. (In Syr. and Chald. *idem.* In Arab. comp. ناخ *in genua procubuit camela.*)

Hiph. הֵנִיחַ 1. *to let* or *set down.* Ezek. 37:1. 40:2. Ex. 17:11.

2. *to make* or *cause to rest.* Ezek. 44:30. Is. 30:32. Usually construed with the dative, *to give rest,* Is. 28:12. 14:3. Most frequently applied to Jehovah, who gives his people their desired rest by the promised possession of Canaan and the subjugation of the neighbouring nations, Ex. 33:14 הֲנִחֹתִי לָךְ *I will give thee rest.* Josh. 1:13, 15. Deut. 3:20. 12:10. וְהֵנִיחַ לָכֶם מִכָּל־אֹיְבֵיכֶם מִסָּבִיב *and he will give you rest from all your enemies round about.* 25:19. Josh. 21:44. (Comp. in N. T. καταπαύω, κατάπαυσις.)

3. הֵנִיחַ חֵמָתוֹ *to cool* or *abate one's anger.* Ezek. 5:13. 16:42. 21:22. [21:17.] 24:13. Zech. 6:8.

Hoph. הוּנַח *there is rest given,* construed with a dat. Lam. 5:5.

Deriv. out of course מְנוּחָה, הֲנָחָה, מָנוֹחַ, נַחַת.

נוֹחַ verbal from נוּחַ, *rest.* Est. 9:16, 17, 18. With suff. נוֹחֶךָ 2 Chr. 6:41.

נוּט i. q. מוּט *to shake, to tremble, to be moved.* Once Ps. 79:1. Sept. σαλευθήτω ἡ γῆ. Vulg. *moveatur terra.*

נְוָלוּ f. Chald. Ezra 6:11. and נְוָלִי Dan. 2:5. *a dunghill.* Root נְוַל i. q. נְבַל *to dirty, soil.* Hence Dan. 2:5 *and your houses shall be made a dunghill,* i. e. levelled with the earth.

נוּם *to sleep, to slumber,* i. q. יָשֵׁן. Particularly from indolence, sluggishness. Nah. 3:18. Is. 56:10. Ps. 121:3. Is. 5:27. (In Syr. and Arab. more frequent.) Deriv. out of course תְּנוּמָה.

נוּמָה f. verbal from נוּם, *sleep, sluggishness.* Prov. 23:21.

נוּן in Niph. (according to the Keri,) or in Hiph. (according to the Kethib,) *sobolescere.* Ps. 72:17 לִפְנֵי שֶׁמֶשׁ יִנּוֹן שְׁמוֹ *as long as the sun exists, shall his name flourish.* Deriv. נִין *soboles*, also probably מָנוֹן. Comp. further the Syr. and Chald. נוּן *a fish*, so called from its rapid propagation.

נוּס *to flee before* any person or thing; construed with מִן, Is. 24:18. with לִפְנֵי, Deut. 28:25. Josh. 7:4. with מִפְּנֵי, 2 Sam. 23:11. Lev. 26:36 וְנָסוּ מְנֻסַת חֶרֶב *they shall flee, as before the sword.* Spoken of inanimate objects, e. g. of waves, Ps. 104:7. of a shadow, Cant. 2:17. 4:6. Once נָס לוֹ *il s'enfuit,* Is. 31:8. comp. לְ p. 290.

Pil. נוֹסֵס *to chase, drive.* Is. 59:19 *a compressed stream,* רוּחַ יְהוָה נֹסְסָה בוֹ *which the wind of Jehovah has driven up.*

Hiph. הֵנִיס 1. *to put to flight.* Deut. 32:30.

2. *to save by flight, to remove secretly.* Ex. 9:20. Judg. 6:11.

Hithpal. הִתְנוֹסֵס *to flee.* Ps. 60:6.

Deriv. מָנוֹס, מְנוּסָה.

נוּעַ 1. *to move, to be moved,* spoken of the lips. 1 Sam. 1:13.

2. particularly *to shake, tremble.* Is. 6:4. 7:2. 19:1. Ex. 20:15.

3. *to stagger, to be giddy.* Is. 24:19. 29:9 *they are giddy, but not from strong drink.* Ps. 107:27.

4. *to move with a waving motion.* Job 28:4. דַּלּוּ מֵאֱנוֹשׁ נָעוּ *they (the miners) descend, they move away from men.* Judg. 9:9 לָנוּעַ עַל הָעֵצִים *to move over the trees,* i. e. to rule over them. 11:13.

5. *to wander.* Am. 4:8. 8:12. Lam. 4:14, 15. Jer. 14:10. Comp. the kindred verbs נָדַד and נוּד.

Niph. pass. of Hiph. *to be shaken,* spoken of a fruit-tree, Nah. 3:12. *to be shaken,* as in a sieve, *to be sifted,* Am. 9:9.

Hiph. 1. *to shake;* e. g. corn in a sieve, Am. 9:9. the head, in derision, (according to others, *to nod* with the head,) Ps. 22:8. 109:25. Lam. 2:15. 2 K. 19:21. In a somewhat different construction, Job 16:4 אָנִיעָה עֲלֵיכֶם בְּמוֹ רֹאשִׁי *I could shake my head at you,* i. e. make a mock of you by gestures; comp. Jer. 18:16. Also *to shake* the hand, in derision, Zeph. 2:15.

2. *to move, disturb.* 2 K. 23:18.

3. *to cause to rove* or *wander, to drive about,* πλάζω. Num. 32:13. Ps. 59:12. 2 Sam. 15:20.

4. *to cause to stand,* though in a feeble manner. Dan. 10:10 *and behold, an hand touched me* וַתְּנִיעֵנִי עַל־בִּרְכַּי וְכַפּוֹת יָדָי *and helped me to stand on my tottering knees and hands.*

Deriv. מְנַעַנְעִים.

נוּף 1. *to swing, wave, move to and fro,* (as the hands, etc.) See Hiph. Hence

2. *to sprinkle,* which is done by *waving* the hand. Prov. 7:17.

Hiph. הֵנִיף 1. *to move to and fro, to wave, shake;* particularly (1.) *to sift, winnow.* Is. 30:28. (2.) *to wave,* e. g. the hand, for a sign. Is. 13:2. More frequently construed with עַל, *to shake* the hand *against* any one, Is. 11:15. 19:16. Zech. 2:13. [2:9.] Also with עַל, *to lay* the hand *on* any thing, Job 31:21. or with אֶל, 2 K. 5:11. (3.) *to move, lift up, brandish,* (a stick, or an instrument.) Is. 10:15 אִם יִתְגַּדֵּל הַמַּשּׂוֹר עַל מְנִיפוֹ *shall the saw boast itself against him who draws it?* כְּהָנִיף שֵׁבֶט אֶת־מְרִימָיו *as if the staff shook them that lifted it up?* *To move* or *put in* a sickle, Deut. 23:25. Construed with עַל, Ex. 20:25. Josh. 8:31. (4.) very frequently in the language of the ritual law, *to move this way and that way* (perhaps also *up and down*) an offering before Jehovah, a peculiar rite, which was observed in particular offerings, especially in the thank-offerings, partly before and partly after the slaughter of the victim. Comp. the use of the word *porricere,* as applied to Roman sacrifices; and *the elevation* of the host in the Roman Catholic service. Lev. 7:30. 8:27, 29. 9:21. 10:15. 14:12, 24. 23:11, 12, 20. Num.

5:25. 6:20. In the offering of living animals and in the consecration of the Levites, a *leading about* is perhaps intended, as is expressed in the version of Saadias,) Ex. 35:22. Num. 8:11—21. Comp. Carpzov. Apparat. ad Antiquit. Sacri Cod. p. 709 ff. Bauer's gottesdienstl. Alterthümer, Th. I. p. 137.

2. *to scatter in small particles, to sprinkle.* Ps. 68:10 *thou sendest a plentiful rain, O God.*

Hoph. הוּנַף pass. of no. 1. (4.) Ex. 29:27.

Pil. נוֹפֵף i. q. Hiph. no. 1. *to shake* the hand against any thing. Is. 10:32.

Deriv. out of course נֹפֶת, תְּנוּפָה.

נוֹף m. verbal from נוּף, *height, elevation.* Ps. 48:3 יְפֵה־נוֹף הַר־צִיּוֹן *mount Zion raises itself beautifully, pulcher elatione (est) mons Zion.* Arab. نَوْفٌ *idem.* Root נוּף and נִיף in Arab. *imminuit* rei, *eminuit* supra rem. See also נָפָה. Entirely a distinct word from נֹף *Memphis.*

I. **נוּץ** *to flee, to wander about in flight.* Lam. 4:15. In Arab. *fugit, effugit, aufugit*; also *motus, agitatus fuit,* like the kindred verbs נוּד and נוּעַ.

II. **נוּץ** *to flourish.* (In Arab. نَاضَ med. Vav. *to glitter, to shine,* a sense often interchanged with that of *flourishing;* comp. the art. צִיץ.)

Hiph. הֵנֵץ *idem.* Cant. 6:11. 7:13. (In the Targums אָנֵיץ *idem.*)

Note. The verbals נֵץ, נִצָּה, נִצָּן are derived from the kindred form נָצַץ q. v.

נוֹצָה f. *the feather of the wing, a feather grown, penna.* Ezek. 17:3, 7. Job 39:13. Root נָצָה q. v.—For נֹצָה Lev. 1:16, see below.

נוּק *to suck,* i. q. יָנַק. Hence, according to the present punctuation, וַתְּנִיקֵהוּ *and she suckled him,* Ex. 2:9. But if pointed וַתֵּינִקֵהוּ it might be formed from יָנַק.

נוּר m. Chald. *fire.* Dan. 3:6, 11, 15, 17. 7:9. Root נוּר, نَارٌ *to shine,* comp. the kindred form נָהַר no. II. The derivatives in Hebrew from the same root are נִיר, נֵר, מְנוֹרָה.

נוּשׁ Syr. ܢܘܫ i. q. the more common אָנַשׁ *to be sick.* Used metaphorically of the soul. Ps. 69:21.

נָזָה, fut. apoc. יַז and יֵז.

1. i. q. Arab. نَزَا *to spring, to leap,* e. g. for joy. See Hiph.

2. *to spout, spatter, to be sprinkled;* spoken of liquids. Lev. 6:20. [27.] 2 K. 9:33. Is. 63:3.

Hiph. הִזָּה, fut. apoc. יַז.

1. *to cause to leap,* for joy or admiration. So perhaps Is. 52:15 כֵּן יַזֶּה גּוֹיִם רַבִּים עָלָיו *so shall he cause many nations to wonder at him.* Sept. οὕτω θαυμάσονται ἔθνη πολλὰ ἐπ' αὐτῷ.

2. trans. *to sprinkle.* Ex. 29:21. Lev. 4:6, 17. 5:9. 14:7.

נָזִיד m. dec. III. a. *pottage.* Gen. 25:29, 34. Root נָזַד i. q. זִיד no. II. According to others, the part. Niph. for נָזוֹד.

נָזִיר m. verbal from נָזַר, dec. III. a.

1. *separated from others, distinguished,* hence *a prince.* Gen. 49:26. (Perhaps a denom. from נֵזֶר.)

2. *one consecrated, a Nazarite,* a particular kind of ascetic among the Hebrews bound to God by certain vows. Num. 6:13 ff. Am. 2:11, 12. Lam. 4:7. More full נְזִיר אֱלֹהִים *one consecrated to God,* Judg. 13:5, 7. 16:17. As it was one usage of the Nazarites not to cut their hair, hence

3. metaphorically, *the vine not pruned,* which was so left, by divine command, in the Sabbatical year and the year of Jubilee. Lev. 25:5, 11. Comp. in Lat. *herba virgo,* in Talmud. בתולת שקמה *the sycomore in its unpruned state, virginitas sycomori.*

נָזַל, fut. יִזַּל. 1. *to run, to flow.* Num. 24:7. Ps. 147:18. Part. plur. נוֹזְלִים *the flowing,* a poetical epithet for *waters,* Ex. 15:8. Is. 44:3. Used metaphorically of speech, Deut. 32:2 *my speech drops as the dew.* Also of fragrant odours, Cant. 4:16.

2. *to run,* spoken of the place from

which any thing runs; (comp. הָלַךְ no. 5.) Jer. 9:17 וְעַפְעַפֵּינוּ יִזְּלוּ מָיִם *and our eyelashes run down with water.* Is. 45:8. Job 36:28.

3. *to dissolve, melt.* Judg. 5:5 הָרִים נָזְלוּ מִפְּנֵי יְהוָה *the mountains melt* or *dissolve before Jehovah.* Sept. *are shaken* or *tremble,* as if it were pointed נָזֹלּוּ, as it is Is. 64:1, 3. in a connexion exactly similar. The Masoretes appear here to have been inconsistent with themselves; unless we admit that נָזְלוּ may stand grammatically for נָזֹלּוּ. This is probably the case, see art. זָלַל, and Gesen. Lehrgeb. p. 372.

Hiph. הִזִּיל *to cause to flow.* Is. 48:21.—The same form occurs also under זָלַל no. I.

נֶזֶם m. with suff. נִזְמִי, plur. נְזָמִים, const. נִזְמֵי, dec. VI. h. *a nose* or *ear-ring.* In the former sense expressly, Gen. 24:47. Is. 3:21. Prov. 11:22. in the latter, Gen. 35:4. In other passages uncertain, Judg. 8:24, 25. Job 42:11. Comp. Jahn's Bibl. Archäologie, Th. I. § 153. and A. Th. Hartmann's Hebräerin, Th. II. p. 166. Th. III. p. 205 ff.

נְזַק Chald. *to suffer injury.* Part. נָזִק Dan. 6:3.

Aph. הַנְזֵק *to injure, endamage.* Ezra 4:13, 15, 22.

נֵזֶק m. *injury, damage.* Est. 7:4.

נָזַר in Kal not used.

Niph. 1. *to separate one's self.* Joined with מֵאַחֲרֵי יְהוָה *to fall off from the worship of Jehovah,* Ezek. 14:7.

2. *to abstain* or *refrain from* any thing, construed with מִן. Lev. 22:2. Used absolutely, Zech. 7:3. (Syr. Ethpe. *idem.*)

3. construed with לְ, *to consecrate one's self* to any thing. Hos. 9:20. It here becomes synonymous with the kindred נָדַר *to vow,* and the Arab. نذر *to vow, to consecrate.*

Hiph. הִזִּיר 1. *to cause to avoid.* Lev. 15:31 וְהִזַּרְתֶּם אֶת־בְּנֵי יִשְׂרָאֵל מִטֻּמְאָתָם *and cause that the children of Israel separate themselves from their uncleanness.* The old versions: *warn,* after the Arab. نذر conj. IV. *to warn.*

2. *to consecrate,* construed with לְ. Num. 6:12.

3. intrans. i. q. Niph. no. 2. *to abstain,* construed with מִן. Num. 6:3.

4. *to consecrate* or *devote one's self,* joined with לַיהוָה *to Jehovah.* Num. 6:2, 5, 6.

Deriv. out of course נָזִיר.

נֵזֶר m. verbal from נָזַר, dec. VI. g.

1. *a diadem,* literally *insigne, a mark of separation* or *distinction.* Particularly of the king, 2 Sam. 1:10. 2 K. 11:22. of the high-priest, Ex. 29:6. Comp. נָזִיר.

2. *a consecration.* Lev. 21:12. Particularly *the consecration* of a Nazarite, (נָזִיר,) Num. 6:4, 5, 9 רֹאשׁ נִזְרוֹ *the head of his consecration,* i. e. his consecrated head. Verse 12.

3. by a metonymy, *the consecrated head* of the Nazarite. Num. 6:19. Then without this reference, *an unshaven head of hair,* Jer. 7:29. (Comp. נָזִיר no. 3.)

נָחָה in Kal pret. and imper. and in Hiph. fut. and infin. *to lead, guide.* Ex. 32:34. Num. 23:7. Most frequently of God who *leads* men, Ps. 5:9. 27:11. 31:4.—Job 12:23 שֹׁטֵחַ לַגּוֹיִם וַיַּנְחֵם *he enlarges the nations and leads them (back again),* namely, to their narrower bounds. *To remove,* as troops and chariots, 1 K. 10:26.

נִחוּמִים masc. plur. verbal from נָחַם, dec. I.

1. *consolation.* Is. 57:18. Zech. 1:13. (Several MSS. and editions have נִחֻמִּים with Dagesh forte.)

2. *compassion.* Hos. 11:8.

נָחוּשׁ m. denom. adj. from נְחֹשֶׁת *made of brass, brazen.* Job 6:12.

נְחוּשָׁה strictly fem. of the preceding, used abstractly *æneum,* hence i. q. נְחֹשֶׁת *æs, brass.* Lev. 26:19. Job 41:19. Is. 45:2 דַּלְתוֹת נְחוּשָׁה *brazen gates.* Job 40:18 אֲפִיקֵי נְחוּשָׁה *brazen pipes.* 28:2 אֶבֶן יָצוּק נְחוּשָׁה *and ore they melt into brass.*

נְחִילָה f. Ps. 5:1. name of a musical instrument, perhaps *a flute*, for נְחִלָה from חָלַל *to bore through*, comp. (וְחָקָה,) whence חָלִיל *a pipe*. The root נָחַל may have taken its signification from חלל.

נְחִירִים masc. plur. *nostrils*. Job 41:12. Syr. in sing. *the nose*. Root נָחַר.

נָחַל 1. *to inherit, to acquire an inheritance*. Judg. 11:2. comp. Num. 18:20.

2. *to acquire a possession, to possess;* e. g. reputation, goods. Prov. 3:35. 11:29. 28:10. Frequently used of the acquisition and possession of the land of Canaan by the Israelites, Ex. 23:30. 32:13. Num. 18:20. In other places it is said of Jehovah, *he takes Israel for a possession*, i. e. he takes it to himself as his own property, Ex. 34:9. Zech. 2:12.

3. as in Piel, *to divide for a possession*, construed with לְ. Num. 34:17 אֲשֶׁר יִנְחֲלוּ לָכֶם אֶת־הָאָרֶץ *who shall divide to you the land*. Verse 18. Josh. 19:49. Perhaps also Ex. 34:9 וּנְחַלְתָּנוּ *put us in possession*.

Pi. נִחֵל *to divide for a possession*. Josh. 13:32. Construed with a double accus. of the person and thing, Josh. 14:1. Num. 34:29. With לְ of the person, Josh. 19:51.

Hiph. הִנְחִיל 1. *to cause to inherit;* and that (1.) *to leave behind as an inheritance*, construed with a dative, 1 Chr. 28:8. (2.) *to divide out as an inheritance*, construed with two accus. Deut. 21:16.

2. *to give into possession*. Is. 49:8. Very commonly with two accus. of the person and thing, Prov. 8:21. 13:22. Zech. 8:12. Particularly *to divide out the land of Canaan*, Deut. 1:38. 3:28. 12:10. 19:3. 31:7. Jer. 3:18. 12:14. Also without an accus. of the thing, Deut. 32:8 בְּהַנְחֵל עֶלְיוֹן גּוֹיִם *when the Most High assigned to the nations (their dwellings)*.

Hoph. *to acquire for a possession*. Job 7:3 כֵּן הָנְחַלְתִּי לִי יַרְחֵי־שָׁוְא *so shall I acquire to myself months of vanity*.

Hithpa. 1. i. q. Kal no. 2. *to acquire for a possession, to possess*, construed with an accus. Num. 32:18. Is. 14:2.

2. trans. i. q. Kal no. 3. Piel, and Hiph. Lev. 25:46 וְהִתְנַחַלְתֶּם אֹתָם לִבְנֵיכֶם אַחֲרֵיכֶם *and ye shall leave them for an inheritance to your children after you*. So all the ancient versions. This signification may also be applied to Num. 33:54. 34:13. Ezek. 47:13. although such a transitive signification is not often found in Hithpael.

נַחַל 1. *a valley with a brook*, i. q. Arab. وَادٍ. Gen. 26:19.—נַחַל אֶשְׁכֹּל *the valley of Eshcol*, Num. 13:23.

2. *a brook, stream*. Gen. 32:24. Ps. 74:15. Is. 30:33 נַחַל גָּפְרִית בֹּעֵרָה *a stream of burning sulphur*. Particularly *a torrent*, raised high by showers, but dried up in summer, Job 6:15 *my brethren are faithless, like a brook*, which, drying up suddenly, disappoints the hopes of the traveller who visits it. (Comp. אַכְזָב.)—נַחַל מִצְרַיִם *the brook of Egypt*, a frequent description of the southern boundary of Palestine, Num. 34:5. Josh. 15:4, 47. 1 K. 8:65. 2 K. 24:7. Is. 27:12. Among the ancient translators, Saadias, Abusaid and Sept. (Is. 27:12.) give the only suitable explanation, namely, *El-Arish*, otherwise Ῥινοκορούρα, the boundary between Syria and Egypt, in a sandy soil, where there is a summer brook. This is to be distinguished from נְהַר מִצְרַיִם *the river of Egypt*, i. e. the Nile, Gen. 15:18. Comp. Faber zu (Harmer's) Beobachtungen über den Orient, Th. 2. p. 209.

3. probably *the perpendicular descent* or *shaft of a mine*. Job 28:4 פָּרַץ נַחַל *they lay open a shaft*.

נַחְלָה (*Milêl*) i. q. נַחַל *a brook*. Ps. 124:4, where it is construed as a masc. of course the ־ָה is paragogic.

נַחֲלָה f. verbal from נָחַל, dec. XII. e.

1. *an inheritance*. Prov. 19:14 נַחֲלַת אָבוֹת *an inheritance from the fathers*.

2. *a property, possession*. Num. 18:21. Deut. 4:21. Josh. 13:23 נַחֲלַת

בְּנֵי רְאוּבֵן *the possession of the sons of Reuben.* Num. 26:62.—נַחֲלַת יְהוָֹה *the possession of Jehovah,* i. e. the Israelites whom Jehovah had taken to himself, Deut. 4:20. 9:26, 29. Ps. 28:9. This phrase is taken in a different sense, Ps. 127:3 נַחֲלַת יְהוָֹה *a possession of Jehovah,* i. e. a gift from him.—יֵשׁ לִי חֵלֶק וְנַחֲלָה בְּ *I have a portion and possession in* any thing, see חֵלֶק no. 2.

3. *the lot* or *destiny* of any one, i. q. חֵלֶק no. 4. Job 20:29. 27:13. 31:2.

נַחֲלִיאֵל (*valley of God*) proper name of a station of the Israelites in the desert. Once Num. 21:19.

נַחֲלָת f. i. q. נַחֲלָה with the uncommon feminine termination ־ָת. Ps. 16:6.

נָחַם in Kal not used.

Niph. 1. *to suffer pain, to be grieved,* about any person or thing; hence (1.) *to have pity, compassion, sympathy.* Jer. 15:6 נִלְאֵיתִי הִנָּחֵם *I am weary of compassion.* It is construed with עַל, Ps. 90:13. with אֶל, Judg. 21:6. with לְ, verse 15. with מִן, Judg. 2:18. (2.) *to feel regret, to repent.* (Comp. Germ. *reuen* with Eng. *to rue.*) Ex. 13:17. Gen. 6:6, 7. Construed most frequently with עַל, Ex. 32:12, 14. Jer. 8:6. 18:8, 10. with אֶל, 2 Sam. 24:16. Jer. 26:3.

2. pass. or reflex. of Pi. *to console* or *comfort one's self.* Gen. 38:12. Construed with עַל, *about* any thing, 2 Sam. 13:39. and with אַחֲרֵי *for the loss of* any one, Gen. 24:67.

3. *to take revenge, to avenge one's self,* from the *consolation* and satisfaction which the vindictive orientalist feels therein, construed with מִן. Is. 1:24. (Comp. Ezek. 5:13. 31:16. 32:31.) See Hithpa.

Pi. נִחַם *to shew sympathy, to comfort, console.* Construed with an accus. of the person, Gen. 50:21. Job 2:11. The thing *about* which consolation is given, is preceded by מִן, Gen. 5:29. by עַל, Is. 22:4. 1 Chr. 19:2. Sometimes it conveys the idea of mercy or relief, as when spoken of God, Is. 12:1. 49:13. 51:3, 12. 52:9.

Pu. pass. Is. 54:11.

Hithpa. הִתְנַחֵם, once הִנֶּחָם (Ezek. 5:13.) i. q. Niph. but of more rare occurrence.

1. *to be grieved;* and so (1.) *to have compassion,* construed with עַל. Deut. 32:36. Ps. 135:14. (2.) *to repent.* Num. 23:19.

2. *to console one's self.* Gen. 27:25. Ps. 119:52.

3. *to take revenge.* Gen. 27:42 הִנֵּה עֵשָׂו אָחִיךָ מִתְנַחֵם לְךָ לְהָרְגֶךָ *behold Esau, thy brother, will take revenge on thee, by killing thee.*

Deriv. out of course נִחוּמִים, תַּנְחוּמִים.

נֹחַם m. verbal from נָחַם, *repentance.* Hos. 13:14.

נֶחָמָה f. (with Kamets impure) verbal from נָחַם, dec. X. *comfort, consolation.* Job 6:10. Ps. 119:50.

נַחְנוּ i. q. אֲנַחְנוּ *we.* Only Gen. 42:11. Ex. 16:7, 8. Num. 32:32. 2 Sam. 17:12. Lam. 3:42. (Arab. نَحْنُ.)

נָחַץ i. q. לָחַץ *to press, urge, urgere.* (Comp. under the letter ל.) Part. pass. liter. *pressed,* for *pressing, urgent,* 1 Sam. 21:9.

נַחַר m. dec. VI. c. Job 39:20. and

נַחֲרָה f. dec. X. Jer. 8:16. *the snorting* of a horse. Root in Syr. and Arab. *to snort, snore.* Deriv. נְחִירַיִם.

נָחַשׁ found only in Pi. נִחֵשׁ.

1. strictly a denominative from נָחָשׁ, *to augur from the appearance of serpents,* a mode of divination, common among the ancients, to which they gave the name of ὀφιομαντεία. See Bocharti Hieroz. T. I. p. 21. Lev. 19:26. Deut. 18:10. 2 K. 17:17. 21:6.

2. *to perceive, discover, find out,* generally, like οἰωνίζομαι and *auguror,* without farther respect to the etymology. Gen. 30:27 נִחַשְׁתִּי וַיְבָרְכֵנִי יְהוָה בִּגְלָלֶךָ *I perceive that Jehovah has blessed me on your account.* 44:15 *knew ye not* כִּי נַחֵשׁ יְנַחֵשׁ אִישׁ אֲשֶׁר כָּמֹנִי *that a man like me would certainly find* (*it*) *out.* Verse 5 וְהוּא נַחֵשׁ יְנַחֵשׁ בּוֹ *and he could certainly*

find it out. Others: (*the cup*) *by which he augurs*, with reference to a divination by cups, κυλικομαντεία. Comp. Burder's Oriental Customs, p. 41. edit. Philad.

3. 1 K. 20:33 וְהָאֲנָשִׁים יְנַחֲשׁוּ Vulg. *et acceperunt viri pro omine*, i. e. they took the words of Ahab (in verse 32) as a good omen. Others less plausibly after no. 2. *and when the men perceived* (*what his meaning was*), *they hastened*, etc.

נַחַשׁ m. verbal from נָחַשׁ, dec. VI. c.

1. *divination, magic.* Num. 23:23.

2. *omen, augurium, quod aliquis captat.* Num. 24:1. comp. 23:3, 15.

נָחָשׁ m. prim. dec. IV. a.

1. *a serpent.* Gen. 3:1 ff. Ex. 4:3. 7:15.

2. *the serpent* or *dragon*, a constellation between the greater and lesser bear. Job 26:13.

3. proper name of a city otherwise unknown. 1 Chr. 4:12.

נְחָשׁ m. Chald. *brass.* Dan. 2:32, 45. 4:20. Syr. ܢܚܫܐ. See the following article.

נְחֹשֶׁת com. gen. (masc. Ezek. 1:7. Dan. 10:6. fem. 1 Chr. 18:8.) with suff. נְחֻשְׁתְּךָ, dec. XIV. e. and f.

1. *brass.* Gen. 4:22. Ex. 26:11, 37.

2. *money, æs.* Ezek. 16:36 יַעַן הִשָּׁפֵךְ נְחֻשְׁתֵּךְ Vulg. *quia effusum est æs tuum.*

3. *a brazen fetter.* Lam. 3:7. Particularly in the dual נְחֻשְׁתַּיִם Judg. 16:21. 2 Sam. 3:34, *fetters* for *both* hands or feet.

נְחֻשְׁתָּן m. a denom. from נְחֹשֶׁת and the adj. termination ָן, *brazen, æneus*, spoken particularly of the brazen serpent, to which the Israelites burnt incense till the time of Hezekiah. 2 K. 18:4.

נָחַת, fut. יִנְחַת and יֵחַת, *to descend, to come down*, in Aram. the prevalent word for the Heb. יָרַד. Jer. 21:13 מִי יֵחַת עָלֵינוּ *who shall come down to us?* (here in a hostile sense.) Ps. 38:3 וַתִּנְחַת עָלַי יָדֶךָ *and thy* (*punitive*) *hand has come down upon me*; (comp. the deriv. נַחַת Is. 30:30.) Plur. יֵחַתּוּ Job 21:13. *they descend*, for יֵחֲתוּ, with Dagesh euphonic, comp. נְחִתִּים 2 K. 6:9. and נִקְבָּרִים for נִקְבָּרִים, יְחַלּוּ Job 29:21. for יָחֵלּוּ. Metaphorically Prov. 17:10 תֵּחַת גְּעָרָה בְמֵבִין *a reproof descends into a wise man*, i. e. it makes an impression upon him; (comp. 18:8. 26:22.) תֵּחַת has the tone on the penult, according to grammarians on account of the moveable Sheva following, and need not on that account to be formed from חָתַת, which would not suit the passage.

Niph. נִחַת i. q. Kal. Ps. 38:3 כִּי חִצֶּיךָ נִחֲתוּ בִי *for thine arrows have come down upon me*, i. e. have hit me.

Pi. נִחֵת *to press down, to stretch*, (a bow,) Ps. 18:35. *to press down, to level*, (the furrows, by copious rains,) Ps. 65:11.

Hiph. *to bring down.* Imper. הַנְחַת Joel 4:11. [3:11.]

נְחַת Chald. *to descend.* Part. נָחִת Dan. 4:10, 20.

Aph. fut. יַחֵת, imper. אַחֵת, part. מְהַחֵת.

1. *to bring* or *carry down.* Ezra 5:15.

2. *to deposit, to lay up.* Ezra 6:1, 5.

Hoph. הָנְחַת *to be deposed* or *thrown down.* Dan. 5:20.

I. נַחַת m. verbal from נָחַת.

1. *a descent, a coming down.* Is. 30:30 נַחַת זְרוֹעוֹ *the descent*, i. e. the blow, *of his arm*; comp. Ps. 38:3.

2. *a setting down, what is set down*; comp. נְחַת in Aph. Job 36:16 נַחַת שֻׁלְחָנְךָ *that which is set on thy table.*

II. נַחַת f. verbal from נוּחַ, *rest, quietness.* Is. 30:15. Ecc. 4:6 מְלֹא כַף נָחַת *a hand full* (*with*) *quietness.* 6:5.

נָחֵת verbal adjective from נָחַת, *descending.* Found only in the plural with Dagesh euphonic נְחִתִּים 2 K. 6:9.

נָטָה, fut. יִטֶּה, apoc. יֵט, וַיֵּט, וַיֵּט.

1. *to stretch out*, e. g. the hand. Spoken of Jehovah, *to stretch out* the hand over any thing, as a sign of its destruction. Jer. 51:25. Ezek. 6:14. 14:9, 13. Is. 5:25 עוֹד יָדוֹ נְטוּיָה *his hand is*

still stretched out.—נָטָה קַו עַל *to stretch out* or *apply the measuring line to* any thing, Job 38:5. Is. 44:13. Lam. 2:8. —Ps. 102:12 צֵל נָטוּי *a shadow stretched out and gradually disappearing;* comp. 109:23.

2. *to spread out,* e. g. a tent. Gen. 12:8. 26:25. Is. 40:22 הַנּוֹטֶה כַדֹּק שָׁמַיִם *who spreadeth out the heavens as a garment.*—נָטָה רָעָה עַל *tendere insidias* alicui, a metaphor taken from the spreading of nets, Ps. 21:12.—1 Chron. 21:10 שָׁלוֹשׁ אֲנִי נֹטֶה עָלֶיךָ *three things I spread before* or *offer thee.* In the parallel passage 2 Sam. 24:12, we find נוֹטֵל.—Intrans. *to spread itself out,* Job 15:29.

3. *to incline.* Gen. 49:15. Ps. 119:112. 62:4 קִיר נָטוּי *a wall inclined* or *about to fall.*—Intrans. *to incline itself;* spoken of the day, Judg. 19:8. of the shadow on the sun-dial, 2 K. 20:10.—Ps. 73:2 כִּמְעַט נָטָיוּ רַגְלָי *his feet had almost slipped.*

4. *to turn, lead.* Is. 66:12. Gen. 39:21. More frequently intrans. *to turn one's self,* Num. 20:17. 22:23. 26:33. construed with אֶל *to* any one, Gen. 38:16. with מִן and מֵעִם *from* any person or thing, Job 31:7. 1 K. 11:9. with אַחֲרֵי *to turn to the side* or *party of* any one, Ex. 23:2. Judg. 9:3. 1 K. 2:28. also *to be devoted to* any thing, 1 Sam. 8:3.

5. *to go away, depart.* 1 Sam. 14:7 נְטֵה לָךְ *go away.*

Niph. pass. of no. 1. *to be stretched out,* spoken of the measuring line, Zech. 1:16. *to stretch itself out, to extend,* as a valley, Num. 24:6. as a shadow, Jer. 6:4.

Hiph. הִטָּה, fut. יַטֶּה, apoc. יֵט, יַט, וַיֵּט, imper. apoc. הַט.

1. *to stretch out,* i. q. Kal no. 1. but of more rare occurrence. E. g. the hand, Is. 31:3. Jer. 6:12. 15:6. — Intrans. *to stretch itself out,* Am. 2:8.

2. *to spread out,* i. q. Kal no. 2. Is. 54:2. 2 Sam. 21:10, (with לְ.) Spoken of a tent, 2 Sam. 16:22.

3. *to incline, bend down.* Gen. 24:14. Particularly (1.) the ear, Jer. 7:24, 26. 11:8. Construed with לְ, Ps. 17:6. (2.) the heart, 2 Sam. 19:15. Construed with אֶל of the person, 1 K. 8:58. Prov. 2:2 הַטֶּה לִבְּךָ לַתְּבוּנָה *incline thine heart to understanding.* 1 K. 11:2 *they will incline your heart after their gods.* Hence in a bad sense, *to seduce,* Prov. 7:21. Is. 44:20. (3.) הִטָּה חֶסֶד עַל פ׳ *to shew favour to any one,* Ezra 7:28. 9:9. comp. in Kal Gen. 39:21.

4. trans. of Kal no. 4. (1.) *to turn away.* Jer. 5:25. Num. 22:23. (2.) *to lead astray.* Job 24:4. comp. Am. 2:7. (3.) *to lead aside.* 2 Sam. 3:27. (4.) *to put away.* Ps. 27:9. Intrans. *to depart,* Job 23:11. Is. 30:11. Ps. 125:5.

5. *to bend, pervert;* particularly in the phrase הִטָּה מִשְׁפָּט, 1 Sam. 8:3. and with a genitive following, Ex. 23:6. Deut. 27:19. Lam. 3:35. *to wrest* or *pervert the right of* any one in judgment. Without addition, Ex. 23:2 לִנְטֹת אַחֲרֵי רַבִּים לְהַטֹּת *to follow the multitude to wrest (judgment).* Also with an accusative of the person, *to turn* any one *aside* (in judgment), Prov. 18:5. Is. 10:2. 29:21. Am. 5:12.

Hoph. part. מֻטֶּה Is. 8:8. Ezek. 9:9. used as a subst. see the art. מֻטֶּה.

Deriv. מַטֶּה, מִטָּה.

נְטִיעִים masc. plur. verbal from נָטַע *plants.* Ps. 144:12.

נְטִיפוֹת fem. plur. (verbal from נָטַף *to drop,*) *ear-pendants,* particularly of pearls, so called from their form; liter. *drops.* Judg. 8:26. Is. 3:19. (Arab. نُطْفَة *idem.* Comp. σταλάγμιον *a pendant,* from σταλάζω *to drop.*)

נְטִישׁוֹת fem. plur. *branches.* Is. 18:5. Jer. 5:10. 48:32. Root נָטַשׁ in Niph. *to spread out.*

נָטַל, fut. יִטּוֹל. 1. *to take up.* Is. 40:15 כַּדַּק יִטּוֹל *as the dust which (one)* or *(the wind) takes up.*

2. *to lay upon* or *before* any one. 2 Sam. 24:11 שָׁלוֹשׁ אָנֹכִי נוֹטֵל עָלֶיךָ *three things I offer thee.* (In the parallel passage 1 Chr. 21:10, נוֹטֶה.) In Jer. 21:8, the same sense is expressed by נָתַן לִפְנֵי.

Lam. 3:28 כִּי נָטַל עָלָיו *because (God) has laid it upon him.* Part. pass. *laden,* Zeph. 1:11.

Pi. *to bear.* Is. 63:9.

נְטַל Chald. *to lift up.* Dan. 4:31. [4:34.] Pret. pass. Dan. 7:4.

נֵטֶל m. verbal from נָטַל, *heaviness, weight.* Prov. 27:3.

נָטַע, fut. יִטַּע, infin. נְטוֹעַ and טַעַת.

1. *to plant,* also *to set with plants.* Ezek. 36:36. Construed with two accus. Is. 5:2.

2. metaphorically *to plant, settle, establish,* (a people.) Am. 9:15. Jer. 24:6 *I will plant them and not pluck them up.* 32:41. 42:10. 45:4. Ps. 44:3. 80:9. Ex. 15:17. 2 Sam. 7:10. Comp. the oppos. נָתַשׁ, likewise מַטָּע, and יָתֵד Ezra 9:8.

3. *to drive in* (a nail). Ecc. 12:11. Also *to set up* (an image), Deut. 16:21.

4. *to pitch* or *erect* a tent, *tentorium figere,* from the *driving in* of the tent-pins. Dan. 11:45. Hence applied to the tent of heaven, Is. 51:16.

Deriv. מַטָּע, נְטִיעִים.

נֶטַע m. with suff. נִטְעֵךְ, plur. נְטָעִים, const. נִטְעֵי, verbal from נָטַע, dec. VI. i.

1. *a plant.* Job 14:9.

2. *a planting.* Is. 17:11.

3. *a place planted, a plantation.* Is. 17:10. 1 Chr. 4:23.

נְטַע m. verbal from נָטַע, dec. IV. a. *a plant.* Found only in the const. state נְטַע, Is. 5:7.

נָטַף, fut. יִטֹּף, *to drop, to fall in drops.* (Also in Aram. and Arab. In Ethiop. נטב.) Job 29:22. Usually spoken of the object whence any thing drops, (comp. הָלַךְ no. 5.) Joel 4:18 [3:18] יִטְּפוּ הֶהָרִים עָסִיס *the mountains drop down new wine.* Cant. 5:5, 13. Judg. 5:4. Also in the same way metaphorically of the lips, Cant. 4:11 נֹפֶת תִּטֹּפְנָה שִׂפְתוֹתַיִךְ *thy lips drop down* or *distil honey.* Prov. 5:3.

Hiph. 1. *to let* or *cause to drop.* Am. 9:13.

2. metaphorically *to let flow out,* as words, *to speak, prophesy.* Mic. 2:6, 11. Ezek. 21:2, 7. Am. 7:16. Comp. נָבָא.

Deriv. out of course נְטִיפוֹת.

נָטָף m. verbal from נָטַף, dec. IV. a.

1. *a drop.* Job 36:27.

2. a fragrant gum which *distils* from some plant. Ex. 30:34 Sept. στάκτη. According to the Jewish commentators, *opobalsamum;* according to others, *storax.*

נְטֹפָה proper name of a city not far from Bethlehem in Judea. Ezra 2:22. Neh. 7:26. The gentile noun is נְטוֹפָתִי 2 Sam. 23:28, 29. 2 K. 25:23.

נָטַר, fut. יִטּוֹר, once יִנְטוֹר (Jer. 3:5.) kindred with נָצַר.

1. *to watch, guard.* Cant. 1:6. 8:11, 12. (In Aram. and Arab. *idem.*)

2. *to keep, retain,* namely אַף *anger,* which must always be supplied. Ps. 103:9 לֹא לְעוֹלָם יִטּוֹר *he will not retain (anger) for ever.* Jer. 3:5, 12. Construed with לְ of the person, Nah. 1:2. with אֵת, Lev. 19:18. Comp. שָׁמַר Jer. 3:5. Job 10:14.

Deriv. מַטָּרָה.

נְטַר Chald. *to lay up,* with בְּלִבָּא *in the heart.* Dan. 7:28. comp. Luke 2:19.

נָטַשׁ, fut. יִטֹּשׁ, *to leave, forsake,* (kindred as to sense with עָזַב, הֵנִיחַ, and שָׁמַט.) Particularly

1. *to forsake, reject,* i. q. עָזַב; e. g. spoken of Jehovah, in reference to his people, Judg. 6:13. 1 Sam. 12:22. 1 K. 8:57. 2 K 21:14. Is. 1:6. of the people, in reference to Jehovah, Deut. 32:15.

2. *to leave under the care* or *protection of* any one, construed with עַל. 1 Sam. 17:20, 22, 28.

3. *to let go, to give up as lost.* 1 Sam. 10:2.

4. *to let lie without using,* e. g. the land in the Sabbatical year. Ex. 23:11.

5. *to let go, to remit,* (a debt.) Neh. 10:32.

6. *to leave off,* e. g. contention. Prov. 17:14.

7. *to suffer, allow, permit;* construed with an accus. of the person and לְ of the action. Gen. 31:28.

8. *to throw down, cast away.* Ezek. 29:5 וּנְטַשְׁתִּיךָ הַמִּדְבָּרָה *and I will cast thee into the desert.* 32:4.

9. *to spread out, to scatter,* comp. שָׁטַשׁ. 1 Sam. 13:16 נְטֻשִׁים *scattered.* Intrans. *to extend itself,* 1 Sam. 4:2 וַתִּטֹּשׁ הַמִּלְחָמָה *and the battle extended itself.* Comp. Niph. no. 3.

10. *to draw out* (a sword); liter. *to set it free.* Is. 21:15. Comp. Syr. שְׁמַט *to draw out* the sword.

Niph. 1. *to be loosed, relaxari,* spoken of cords. Is. 33:23.

2. *to be thrown down.* Am. 5:2. Comp. Kal no. 8.

3. *to spread itself out;* spoken of a vine, Is. 16:8. of a host, Judg. 15:9. 2 Sam. 5:18, 22. Comp. Kal no. 9.

Pu. *to be forsaken.* Is. 32:14.

נִי a contraction of נְהִי *a lamentation.* Ezek. 27:32 בְּנִיהֶם *in lamento eorum.* So the Masora. But eleven MSS. several ancient editions, the Sept. Arab. Theod. and Syr. read בְּנֵיהֶם.

נִיב m. verbal from נוּב, dec. I.

1. *fruit, proventus.* Mal. 1:12.

2. נִיב שְׂפָתַיִם Is. 57:19. *proventus labiorum, the fruit of the lips,* i. e. prob. offerings presented by the lips, praises, thanksgivings; comp. καρπὸς χειλέων, Heb. 13:15. Hence *I create the fruit of the lips,* i. e. give occasion for thanksgivings. In the Kethib נוב, comp. Chald. נוֹב *fructus.*

נִיד m. verbal from נוּד, found only Job 16:5 נִיד שְׂפָתַי *the motion of my lips,* i. e. my words, or the consolation of my lips. In שְׂפָתַיִם lies in either case the idea of *idle* talk.

נִידָה f. Lam. 1:8. prob. i. q. נִדָּה *an abomination,* verse 17. See several analogies under the art. נָקִים. Others: *a fugitive,* as if from נוּד.

נָיוֹת, in the Kethib נְוִית, (*dwellings,*) proper name of a place in or near Ramah, where David resided when he fled to Samuel. 1 Sam. 19:18, 19, 22, 23. 20:1. Targ. *domus doctrinæ,* intending *the buildings of the prophetical school* at Ramah.

נִיחוֹחַ m. *sweetness, pleasantness,* found only in the phrase רֵיחַ נִיחוֹחַ *a pleasant smell.* Applied exclusively to offerings, Gen. 8:21 וַיָּרַח יְהוָה אֶת־רֵיחַ הַנִּיחֹחַ *and Jehovah smelled a pleasant odour.* Lev. 2:12. Very frequently after the precepts of the ritual law רֵיחַ נִיחוֹחַ לַיהוָה *a pleasant odour to Jehovah,* Lev. 1:9, 13, 17. Num. 15:7 ff. Root נוּחַ or נִיחַ, whence in Talmud. נִיחָא *gratum, acceptum.*

נִיחֹחַ Chald. *a sweet odour, a pleasant smell,* (without רֵיחַ.) Plur. *sweet odours,* Dan. 2:46. Ezra 6:10. (The significations in Hebrew and Chaldaic stand here in the inverted order; comp. the root בָּשַׂם in Hebrew *to be fragrant,* in Chald. *to be acceptable,* where they stand in the natural order. Comp. also the opposite בְּאַשׁ.)

נִין m. verbal from נוּן, dec. I. *offspring, posterity, proles, soboles.* Only in the phrase נִין וָנֶכֶד, Gen. 21:23. Job 18:19. Is. 14:22.

נִינְוֵה *Nineveh,* the capital of the kingdom of Assyria. Gen. 10:11, 12. Jon. 1:2. 3:3. By the Greeks and Romans called *Ninus,* in Ammian also *Nineve.* For its situation, see Bochart's Phaleg, lib. IV. cap. 20. Mannert's Geographie der Griechen and Römer, B. V. p. 440 ff.

נִיס Jer. 48:44 Keth. i. q. נָס *fleeing,* liter. pass. *fled.*

נִיסָן m. *Nisan,* the first month of the Hebrews, (in the older writings חֹדֶשׁ הָאָבִיב.) Neh. 2:1. Est. 3:7. (In Aram. and Arab. *idem.*)

נִיצוֹץ m. *a spark.* Once Is. 1:31. (Root נָצַץ *to sparkle, shine,* whence נִיצוּץ in Talmud. *a spark,* i. q. נִץ and נִצְנָא in Chald.)

נִיר i. q. נֵר m. verbal from נוּר, dec. I. *a light, lamp.* 2 Sam. 22:29.

I. נִיר m. verbal from נוּר, dec. I. i. q. נֵר *a light, lamp;* used metaphorically for *posterity.* 1 K. 11:36 לְמַעַן הֱיוֹת־נִיר לְדָוִיד עַבְדִּי כָּל־הַיָּמִים *so that David my servant may have a light alway,* i. e. so that his posterity may continue; comp. 15:4. 2 K. 8:19. 2 Chr. 21:7.

II. נִיר m. *land first broken up for tillage, fallow ground, novale.* Prov. 13:23. Jer. 4:3. Hos. 10:12. Root נִיר.

נִיר *to dig up, to cultivate.* Jer. 4:3. Hos. 10:12.

נָכָא i. q. נָכָה *to smite.* Hence according to some the Niph. Job 30:8 נִכְּאוּ מִן־הָאָרֶץ *they are driven out from the land.* Perhaps better as Niph. from כָּאָה (with Dagesh euphonic) *increpantur e terra,* i. e. increpando pelluntur e terra.

נָכֵא verbal adj. from נָכָא, dec. V. e. *smitten, broken down, contrite.* Fem. רוּחַ נְכֵאָה *a broken spirit,* Prov. 15:13. 17:22. 18:14. Comp. Is. 66:2 נְכֵה רוּחַ *contrite in spirit.*

נְכָאִים masc. plur. verbal from נָכָא, *beaten down, in ruins.* Is. 16:7.

נְכֹאת f. Gen. 37:25. 43:11. *spicery,* Sept. θυμίαμα. Saad. *siliqua.* Aqu. στύραξ. (In Arab. نكاث i. q. نكعة *gummi, gummi tragacanthæ.*)

I. נֶכֶד m. dec. VI. *offspring, proles.* Only in the phrase נִין וָנֶכֶד; see נִין. The derivation is uncertain.

II. נֶכֶד Job 31:3 in several MSS. and editions for the usual נֵכֶר. It corresponds to the Arab. نكد *vita misera.*

נָכָה in Kal not used.

Hiph. הִכָּה, imper. הַכֵּה and הַךְ, fut. יַכֶּה, וַיַּכֶּה and וַיַּךְ.

1. *to smite.*—הִכָּה כַף *to clap the hands,* in joy, 2 K. 11:12. also in disapprobation, Ezek. 22:13, (comp. תָּקַע.) — 1 Sam. 24:6 וַיַּךְ לֵב־דָּוִד אֹתוֹ *and David's heart smote him;* comp. 2 Sam. 24:10. Spoken particularly (1.) of Jehovah or his messengers, *to smite* with a sickness or plague, (comp. נֶגַע, נָגַף.) Gen. 19:11. *and the men* הִכּוּ בַּסַּנְוֵרִים *they (the angels) smote with blindness.* Num. 14:12. *I will smite them with pestilence.* 1 Sam. 5:6. Ex. 7:25 *after Jehovah had smitten the river,* i. e. changed it into blood; comp. verse 20. Zech. 10:11. (2.) *to smite* (in battle). Gen. 14:15. Deut. 4:46. (3.) *to take* (a besieged city). 1 Chr. 20:1. 2 K. 3:19.

2. *to beat in pieces, to smite down,* spoken e. g. of hail. Ex. 9:25.—Ps. 3:8 *for thou smitest all my enemies on the jawbone,* a metaphor taken from wild beasts. Am. 3:15.

3. *to slay, kill.* Gen. 4:15. Ex. 2:12. Sometimes the accus. נֶפֶשׁ *quoad vitam* is added, Gen. 37:21 לֹא נַכֶּנּוּ נָפֶשׁ *let us not kill him.* Deut. 19:6, 11. Lev. 24:18. Construed with בְּ, 2 Sam. 23:10 וַיַּךְ בַּפְּלִשְׁתִּים *he caused an overthrow among the Philistines,* liter. *he slew (men) among the Philistines.* 2 Sam. 24:17. Ezek. 9:7. 2 Chr. 28:5, 17. See particularly 1 Sam. 6:19. In a different construction 1 Sam. 18:7 הִכָּה שָׁאוּל בַּאֲלָפָיו *Saul has slain his thousands.* 21:12. 29:5.—הִכָּה לְפִי חָרֶב *to smite with the edge of the sword,* see חֶרֶב. Also *to kill* or *tear in pieces,* spoken of a beast of prey, 1 K. 20:36. Jer. 5:6.

4. *to thrust, to thrust through, ferire.* 1 Sam. 18:11 אַכֶּה בְדָוִד וּבַקִּיר *I will thrust through David and through the wall.* 19:10. 26:8. 2 Sam. 2:23. *To push with horns,* Dan. 8:7.

5. *to smite, ferire,* with an arrow or sling stone. 1 Sam. 17:49. 1 K. 22:34. 2 K. 9:24.

6. *to smite,* in other connexions. Spoken of the sun, Jon. 4:7, 8. Ps. 121:6. *the sun shall not smite thee by day, nor the moon by night;* where it is applied to the moon by a kind of zeugma, although some travellers speak of an injurious influence of the moonlight; (comp. Hoph. Ps. 102:5. Hos. 9:16.)

7. joined with שָׁרָשִׁים, *to take root.* Hos. 14:6.

Hoph. הֻכָּה, once הוּכָּה (Ps. 102:5.) pass. particularly of Hiph. nos. 1. 3. also of no. 6.

Niph. pass. 2 Sam. 11:15.

Pu. pass. Ex. 9:31, 32.

נָכֶה verbal adj. from נָכָה, dec. IX. b. *smitten, wounded.*—נְכֵה רַגְלַיִם *injured in the feet, lame,* 2 Sam. 4:4. 9:3.—נְכֵה רוּחַ *contrite* or *broken in spirit,* Is. 66:2. Comp. נְכָא.

נֵכֶה verbal from נָכָה, found only in the plur. נֵכִים Ps. 35:15. *wounding* (with the tongue), i. e. reviling, slandering. Comp. Jer. 18:18.

נְכוֹ and **נְכֹה** *Necho,* king of Egypt. 2 K. 23:29, 33. 2 Chr. 35:20. 36:4. Jer. 46:2. Sept. Νεχαω. In Herod. II. 158, 159. 4:42 Νεκώς, Νεκώ.

נָכוֹן proper name of a threshing floor. 2 Sam. 6:6. In the parallel passage of Chronicles, כִּידוֹן.

נָכֹחַ adj. dec. III. a. *right, upright, straight.* Prov. 8:9. Is. 57:2 הֹלֵךְ נְכֹחוֹ *he who walketh in his (Jehovah's) uprightness,* i. e. practises what is righteous before God. (Comp. 33:15.) Fem. נְכֹחָה *right, righteousness,* Am. 3:10. Is. 59:24. Plur. נְכֹחוֹת *idem,* Is. 26:10. 30:10.

נֹכַח liter. a subst. *what is straight and forward.* Hence לְנֹכַח adv. *straight forward,* Prov. 4:25. Further נֹכַח (as if in the accus.) a preposition (1.) *against, over against.* Ex. 26:35. 40:24. אֶל נֹכַח *directly against,* Num. 19:4. עַד נֹכַח *ad contra,* Judg. 19:10. 20:43. (2.) *before.*—נֹכַח יְהוָה *before Jehovah,* i. e. pleasing to him, Judg. 18:6. נֹכַח פְּנֵי יְהוָה *before the face of Jehovah,* Lam. 2:19. hence *manifest to him,* Jer. 17:16. comp. Prov. 5:21. שׂוּם נֹכַח פְּנֵי *to place* any thing *before one's face,* i. e. to regard it with favour, Ezek. 14:7. and verse 3, with נָתַן.—לְנֹכַח *before,* Gen. 30:38. *for,* Gen. 25:21.

נֶכַח, with suff. נִכְחוֹ, dec. VI. i. *over against.* Ex. 14:2. Ezek. 46:9.

נָכַל *to act deceitfully.* Mal. 1:14. (So in Syr. Chald. and Samar.)

Pi. *to practise deceit against* any one, construed with לְ. Num. 25:18.

Hithpa. *idem;* construed with אֶת, Gen. 37:18. with בְּ, Ps. 105:25.

Deriv. כִּילַי.

נֵכֶל m. plur. נְכָלִים, const. נִכְלֵי, verbal from נָכַל, dec. VI. g. *craft, cunning, deceit.* Num. 25:18.

נֶכֶס m. plur. נְכָסִים, dec. VI. *riches, treasures,* an Aramean word adopted into the later Hebrew. 2 Chr. 1:11, 12. Ecc. 5:18. 6:2. Josh. 22:8.

נְכַס Chald. plur. נִכְסִין, *idem.* Ezra 6:8. 7:26 עֲנָשׁ נִכְסִין *a mulct, fine, confiscation of goods.* Comp. after two different transpositions כָּנַס and מַטְמוֹן.

נָכַר in Kal not used.

Niph. נִכַּר 1. *to be known,* pass. of Hiph. Lam. 4:8.

2. pass. or reflex. of Pi. no. 3. *to let one's self be unknown, to dissemble,* like Hithpa. no. 2. Prov. 26:24.

Pi. נִכֵּר 1. *to regard.* Job 34:19.

2. *to understand, find out.* Job 21:29.

3. *to mistake.* (On the privative signification, see the note.) Deut. 32:27.

4. *to despise, reject.* (Arab. conj. I. and IV. *contempsit, repudiavit, improbavit.*) Jer. 19:4 *and they have despised this place,* or, after the Sept. and Vulg. *they have estranged this place (to me),* namely, by devoting it to strange gods. 1 Sam. 23:7 נִכַּר אֹתוֹ אֱלֹהִים בְּיָדִי *God has rejected him* (and given him) *into my hand.*

Hiph. הִכִּיר 1. *to regard.* Gen. 31:32. Neh. 6:12.—הִכִּיר פָּנִים *to have respect of persons, to be partial,* spoken of judges, i. q. נָשָׂא פָּנִים Deut. 1:17. 16:19. Prov. 24:23. 28:21. comp. Is. 3:9.

2. *to perceive, discern.* Gen. 27:23. 37:33. 38:25, 26.

3. *to acknowledge.* Deut. 21:17. Is. 61:9.

4. *to know,* Lat. *noscere,* only in poetry. Job 24:13, 17, 34:25. Is. 63:16.

5. *to know,* Lat. *scire,* i. q. יָדַע, only in the later books. Neh. 13:24 אֵינָם מַכִּירִים לְדַבֵּר יְהוּדִית *they know not how to*

speak Jewish.—הִכִּיר לְ i. q. הֵדַע בֵּין *to discriminate between,* Ezra 3 : 13.

6. *to be concerned,* or *to care for* any one. Ps. 142 : 5. Ruth 2 : 10, 19.

Hithpa. 1. *to be known, distinguished,* pass. of Hiph. no. 2. Prov. 20 : 11.

2. pass. of Pi. no 3. *to dissemble.* Gen. 42 : 7. 1 K. 14 : 5, 6.

Deriv. נָכְרִי, נֵכָר, מַכָּר, הַכָּרָה.

Note. The privative signification *not to know,* (in Pi. no. 3. Niph. no. 2. Hithpa. no. 2. and in the deriv. נָכְרִי, נֵכָר,) is in Arab. its only signification, where it often occurs. Thus نكر *not to know, to deny, to despise, reject;* intrans. *to be unfortunate,* (see נֹכֶר, נֵכָר;) conj. II. *to disguise,* also *to disguise one's self, to dissemble.* It is, however, by no means uncommon, that the same root in different dialects, or in the different conjugations of the same dialect, should express directly opposite ideas. Comp. אָבָה in Heb. *to be willing;* in Arab. *to be unwilling.* حَبَّ *to love;* construed with ب *not to love;* خبا *to be extinguished,* and *to be kindled.* חָטָא *to sin,* חִטֵּא *to expiate sin.* قسط fut. A. and O, *to be righteous, equitable, to give just measure;* (comp. the Heb. קֹשֶׁט,) and fut. I, *to be unjust, to take advantage of, to deceive,* which in Ethiop. is the common and only meaning. שֵׁרֵשׁ *to root up;* שֹׁרֵשׁ and הִשְׁרִישׁ *to take root.* Perhaps בֵּרֵךְ *to bless* and *to curse.* Comp. in German the inseparable prepositions *ent* and *ver,* which in composition sometimes express a negation or antithesis, and sometimes not. Denominatives in Hebrew, like those compounds in German, have often the privative signification, as e. g. דִּשֵּׁן, זִנֵּב, לִבֵּב, עֵרָה.

נֵכָר, const. נֵכַר (Deut. 31 : 16.) verbal from נָכַר, dec. VI. i.

1. *foreignness, a strange place.* Always after a noun in regimen, בֶּן־נֵכָר *a stranger,* Gen. 17 : 12, 27. Ex. 12 : 43. Sometimes in the sense of *an enemy,* Ps. 18 : 45, 46.—אֱלֹהֵי נֵכָר *strange gods,* Gen. 35 : 2.

2. *any thing strange* or *foreign,* particularly with reference to idolatry. Neh. 13 : 30. 2 Chr. 14 : 2.

נֶכֶר m. Job 31 : 3. and **נֹכֶר** Obad. 12. *misfortune, destruction.* (Arab. نُكْر *idem.* See the note under the verb.)

נָכְרִי, fem. נָכְרִיָּה, plur. נָכְרִים, denom. adj. (from נֵכָר=נֹכֶר *foreignness,* and the adjective termination ־ִי,) *strange, a stranger.* Ex. 2 : 22. Jer. 2 : 21.—נָכְרִיָּה *a strange woman,* in opposition to one's wife, *an adulteress,* i. q. זָרָה, Prov. 5 : 20. 6 : 24. 7 : 5. 23 : 27. (In Samar. comp. נוכראה *alienigena* and *meretrix,* Castelli Heptagl. p. 2310.)

נְכֹת Is. 39 : 2. 2 K. 20 : 13. בֵּית נְכֹתֹה prob. *his treasure-house,* as it is rendered by the Syr. Chald. and Arab. although no philological support can be found for it. Aqu. Symm. Vulg. *house of spicery,* (comp. נְכֹאת,) but הַבְּשָׂמִים follows afterwards.

נָלָה prob. i. q. Arab. ניל نال *to complete,* (whence מִנְלָה q. v.) Hence Hiph. Is. 33 : 1 כַּנְּלֹתְךָ probably for כְּהַנְלֹתְךָ (as it is read in one MS.) *when thou hast completed,* i. e. ceased. The Dagesh forte is euphonic. Cappellus conjectures that the true reading is כַּכְלֹתְךָ, but it appears that all the versions read it with נ.

נְמִבְזָה found only 1 Sam. 15 : 9. *mean, of little worth.* Sept. ἠτιμωμένον. Vulg. *vile.* Evidently i. q. נִבְזָה; but the form is without analogy. Perhaps it may have arisen from two different readings נִבְזָה and מִבְזָה.

נָמַל i. q. מוּל *to circumcise.* Pret. נְמַלְתֶּם Gen. 17 : 11. To this root is usually referred the Niph. נִמּוֹל Gen. 17 : 26, 27. Part. נִמּוֹלִים 34 : 22. But these latter are properly Chaldaic forms from מוּל, (for נִמַּל, comp. לִין for לִין), as the Niph. of נָמַל would be נִמַּל.

נְמָלָה f. Prov. 6 : 6. Plur. נְמָלִים 30 : 25. *an ant, pismire.* Arab. نَمْلَة *idem.*

נָמֵר m. dec. V. a. *a leopard.* Is. 11:6. Jer. 5:6. Hab. 1:8. Syr. and Arab. *idem.* Stw. נמר *to be spotted.*

נְמַר Chald. *idem.* Dan. 7:6.

נִמְרֹד *Nimrod,* the proper name of a son of Cush and founder of the kingdom of Babylon. Gen. 10:8, 10:—אֶרֶץ נִמְרֹד *the land of Nimrod,* i.e. Babylonia, Mic. 5:5.

נֵס with suff. נִסִּי, verbal from נסס no. II. dec. VIII. b. (Syr. ܢܶܣܳܐ *signum, meta, scopus.*)

1. *a high pole.* Num. 21:8, 9.

2. *the flag* of a ship. Ezek. 27:7. Is. 33:23.

3. *a flag, banner,* raised on high mountains, sometimes to assemble the people for war, and sometimes after a flight. Is. 5:26. 11:12. 12:3. 18:3. 62:10, Jer. 4:6, 21. Ps. 60:6.

4. metaphorically *a warning.* Num. 26:10.

נְסִבָּה f. strictly part. fem. Niph. from סָבַב, *a turn* or *change of things, an event.* 2 Chr. 10:15.

נָסַג i. q. סוג *to make way, depart.* In Kal only in the infin. absol. נָסוֹג Is. 59:13. and fut. יִסַּג Mic. 2:6.

Hiph. הִסִּיג 1. *to take back* or *away.* Mic. 6:14 תַּסֵּג *thou shalt take away* (*thy goods*).

2. *to remove* (boundaries). Deut. 19:14. 27:17. Hos. 5:10. and written with שׂ, יַשִּׂיגוּ Job 24:2.

Hoph. הֻסַּג *to be turned back, to be perverted.* Is. 59:14.

נָסָה in Kal not used.

Pi. נִסָּה *to try, tempt, put to the test;* used (1.) absolutely, 1 Sam. 17:39 כִּי לֹא נִסִּיתִי *for I have not tried* (*them*). Judg. 6:39. or with an infin. Deut. 4:34. 28:56. Job 4:2 הֲנִסָּה דָבָר אֵלֶיךָ *shall a man try a word with thee?*

2. with an accus. of the person. 1 K. 10:1 *she came* לְנַסֹּתוֹ בְּחִידוֹת *to try him with riddles.* Dan. 1:12, 14. Particularly (1.) spoken of God, who *tries* men by afflictions. Gen. 22:1. Ex. 16:4. Judg. 2:22. (2.) and of men, who *tempt* God by unbelief or despondency. Ex. 17:2, 7. Deut. 6:16. Ps. 78:18, 41, 56. Is. 7:12. *I will not ask* (*it*) *and will not tempt Jehovah.*

Deriv. מַסָּה.

נָסַח, fut. יִסַּח. 1. *to pluck* or *tear away;* from one's dwelling, Ps. 52:7. from one's country, Prov. 2:22. (comp. נָתַשׁ.)

2. *to tear down* (a house). Prov. 15:25.

Niph. *to be torn away,* or *driven out,* from a country. Deut. 28:63.

נְסַח Chald. i. q. Heb. Ithpe. Ezra 6:11.

נָסִיךְ m. verbal from נָסַךְ, dec. III. a.

1. *a drink-offering.* Deut. 32:38.

2. *a molten image,* i. q. מַסֵּכָה. Dan. 11:8.

3. *one anointed, a prince.* Josh. 13:21. Ps. 83:12. Ezek. 32:30. Mic. 5:4.

I. נָסַךְ *to pour, to pour out.* Is. 29:10. Particularly (1.) in honour of a deity, *to make a libation,* σπένδω, *libare.* Ex. 30:9. Hos. 9:4. Hence Is. 30:1 נָסַךְ מַסֵּכָה *to pour out libations,* σπένδεσθαι σπονδὴν, i. e. to make a covenant; (comp. in Lat. *spondere,* derived immediately from the Greek σπονδὴ, σπένδω. (2.) *to melt, cast, found.* Is. 40:19. 44:10. (3.) *to anoint* (a king). Ps. 2:6. (Comp. the kindred verb סוּךְ.)

Niph. *to be anointed.* Prov. 8:23.

Pi. i. q. Kal no. 1. *to make a libation* of any thing. 1 Chr. 11:18.

Hiph. *to pour out* a drink-offering, *to make a libation* of anything. Gen. 35:14. Num. 28:7. Jer. 7:18. Ps. 16:4.

Hoph. pass. Ex. 25:29. 37:16.

Deriv. נֶסֶךְ, נָסִיךְ, מַסֵּכָה.

II. נָסַךְ i. q. the kindred סָכַךְ *to cover.* Is. 25:7 מַסֵּכָה הַנְּסוּכָה *the covering which is covered.* Comp. מַסֵּכָה no. 3.

נְסַךְ *to pour out,* as a libation. Especially in Pa. Dan. 2:46, where it is applied also to meat-offerings by a kind of zeugma.

נֶסֶךְ and נֵסֶךְ m. with suff. נִסְכִּי, plur. נְסָכִים, const. נִסְכֵּי, verbal from נָסַךְ, dec. VI. g.

1. *a drink-offering.* Gen. 35:14. Jer. 7:18. מִנְחָה וָנֶסֶךְ *a meat and drink offering.* Joel 1:9.

2. *a molten image,* i. q. מַסֵּכָה. Is. 41:29. 48:5.

נְסַךְ, emph. נִסְכָּא, Chald. *a drink offering.* Ezra 7:17.

נִסְמָן found only Is. 28:25. according to the Sept. Aqu. Theod. Vulg. *millet,* though without confirmation from the kindred dialects. Others make it an epithet of שְׂעֹרָה, *fat barley,* (as if from سمن *to be fat,*) but the gender does not suit, and *to be fat* in Hebrew is written with שׁ.

I. נָסַס *to waste away, to be sick.* (Syr. ܢܣ Ethpa. *idem;* ܢܣܝܣܐ *sick.*) Is. 10:18 כִּמְסֹס נֹסֵס *as a sick man wastes away.* מסס and נסס are almost synonymous, and are brought together for the sake of the paranomasia.

II. נָסַס prob. *to lift up,* (whence נֵס;) comp. the Arab. نص *to lift up.*

Hithpo. Zech. 9:16 אַבְנֵי נֵזֶר מִתְנוֹסְסוֹת עַל־אַדְמָתוֹ *consecrated stones lift themselves up in his land.* So perhaps Ps. 60:6, where, however, לְהִתְנוֹסֵס can be derived from נוס.

נָסַע 1. strictly i. q. Arab. نزع נזע *to tear out; to pluck up,* e. g. the door-posts. Judg. 16:3, 14. Particularly *to pluck up* the tent-pins, in order to remove, Is. 33:20. Hence

2. *to break up, to remove,* spoken of a nomadic horde. Gen. 35:16. 37:17. Num. 10:18. 33:3 ff. Also of an army, Ex. 14:10. 2 K. 19:8. of a tent, Num. 1:51. of the ark of the covenant, 10:35. and metaphorically of a strong wind, Num. 11:31.

3. *to march, journey,* spoken of nomadic people, Gen. 12:9. 33:17. of the ark of the covenant, Num. 10:33.

Niph. 1. *to be broken up* or *removed,* spoken of a tent. Is. 38:12.

2. *to be torn away.* Job 4:21.

Hiph. הִסִּיעַ 1. *to tear up,* as a tree, Job 19:10. as a vine, Ps. 80:9. *to dig out,* as stones, Ecc. 10:9. 1 K. 5:31. [5:17.]

2. causat. of no. 2. *to let* or *cause to remove.* Ex. 15:22. Ps. 78:26.

3. causat. of no. 3. *to lead, guide.* Ps. 78:52.

4. *to bear away, remove,* as things. 2 K. 4:4.

Deriv. מַסָּע.

נְסַק in Aramean the common word for the Hebrew עָלָה, *to ascend, mount up.* Once Ps. 139:8.

נְסַק Chald. *idem.* Aph. הַסִּיק, infin. הַנְסָקָה, *to take up.* Dan. 3:22. 6:24.

Hoph. (with the Hebrew form,) pass. of Aph. הֻסַּק 6:24.

נִסְרֹךְ an idol of the Ninevites. 2 K. 19:37.

נָסַת. For the forms יְסִיתְ, מְסִית, which appear to pertain here, see the art. סות.

נְעוּרִים masc. plur. denom. from נַעַר, dec. I.

1. *childhood, boyhood.* Gen. 46:34.

2. *youth, the state* or *condition of a young man.* Ps. 71:5, 17.—אֵשֶׁת נְעוּרֶיךָ *the wife of thy youth.* Prov. 5:18.—בְּנֵי הַנְּעוּרִים *the children of youth,* Ps. 127:4. Used figuratively of *the infancy* of a nation, Jer. 2:2. 3:4. Ezek. 16:22, 60.

נְעוּרוֹת fem. plur. denom. from נַעַר, *idem.* Jer. 32:30.

נָעִים m. adj. *pleasant, lovely, agreeable.* Ps. 133:1. Spoken e. g. of a song, Ps. 147:1. of the harp, Ps. 81:3. of one beloved, Cant. 1:16. Plur. נְעִימִים *pleasant places,* Ps. 16:6. also *prosperity, pleasure,* Job 36:11. נְעִימוֹת *pleasant places,* Ps. 16:11.

נָעַל 1. *to bolt, bar.* 2 Sam. 13:17, 18. Judg. 3:23, 24. Deriv. מִנְעָל, מַנְעוּל.

2. *to shoe, to furnish with shoes;* construed with two accus. Ezek. 16:10 וָאֶנְעֲלֵךְ תָּחַשׁ *I have shod thee with badgers' skins.* (The putting on and cord-

ing of sandals has some similarity with barring or bolting.)

Hiph. *to shoe.* 2 Chr. 28:15.

נַעַל f. verbal from נָעַל, dec. VI. c. *a shoe, sandal.* Gen. 14:23. Ps. 60:10 *upon Edom cast I my shoe,* i. e. it is the place where I throw my cast-off shoes. (Parall. *Moab is my wash-bason.*) 108:10. שְׂרוֹךְ הַנַּעַל *a shoe-latchet,* Gen. 14:23. and נַעֲלַיִם *a pair of shoes,* (Am. 2:6. 8:6.) figuratively for *something small* or *trifling.*

Dual נַעֲלַיִם Am. 2:6. 8:6. and plur. נְעָלִים, once נְעָלוֹת Josh. 9:5.

נָעֵם, fut. יִנְעַם, *to be pleasant, lovely;* spoken of a country, Gen. 49:15. of one beloved, Cant. 7:6. of a friend, 2 Sam. 1:26. Impers. Prov. 24:25 לַמּוֹכִיחִים יִנְעָם *to those that punish it shall be well.* Comp. טוֹב, יִיטַב לִי *it goes well with me.* Deriv. מַנְעַמִּים.

נֹעַם m. verbal from נָעֵם. 1. *pleasantness.* Prov. 3:17. — אִמְרֵי נֹעַם *pleasant,* i. e. enticing, *words,* Prov. 15:26. 16:24.

2. *beauty, majesty, glory.* Ps. 27:4. נֹעַם יְהוָה *the glory of the Lord.* Comp. טוּב יְהוָה verse 13. Ex. 33:19.

3. *grace, mercy.* Ps. 90:17. (Comp. *χάρις, gratia,* and the Germ. *Huld* from *hold.*)

נַעֲמָן m. verbal from נָעֵם, dec. II. b. *pleasantness.* Is. 17:10 נִטְעֵי נַעֲמָנִים *pleasant plantations.*

נַעֲמָתִי a gentile noun, Job 2:11. 11:1. This refers not to נַעֲמָה a city in the tribe of Judah, (Josh. 15:41.) but to some other place of the same name.

נַעֲצוּץ m. dec. I. a kind of thorn-bush, prob. the species called in Arab. نعض, which denotes, according to Celsius (Hierob. ii. 191.) a wild thorny species of the lotus. Plur. נַעֲצוּצִים *thorn-bushes* generally, Is. 7:19. Root Chald. נְעַץ *fixit, infixit.*

I. **נָעַר** 1. *to shake out.* Neh. 5:13. Is. 33:15.

2. *to shake off.* Is. 33:9 נֹעֵר בָּשָׁן וְכַרְמֶל *Bashan and Carmel shake off (their leaves).*

Niph. 1. *to shake off from one's self,* as bonds. Judg. 16:20.

2. pass. of Pi. *to be driven out.* Job 38:13. Ps. 109:23.

Pi. *to drive in,* construed with בְּ. Ex. 14:27 וַיְנַעֵר יְהוָה אֶת מִצְרַיִם בְּתוֹךְ הַיָּם *and Jehovah drove the Egyptians into the midst of the sea.* Ps. 136:15. Comp. Neh. 5:13. (Arab. نفض *to shake,* conj. VIII. *to be driven.*)

Hithpa. *to shake one's self free from* any thing, construed with מִן. Is. 52:2.

Deriv. נַעַר no. II. נְעֹרֶת.

II. **נָעַר** *to roar,* (spoken of young lions, as in Syriac.) Jer. 51:38. It may perhaps be derived from no. I. from the terror or *shaking* of the lion's roar.

I. **נַעַר** m. dec. VI. c. prim.

1. *a child,* even *a suckling.* Ex. 2:6. Judg. 13:5, 7. 1 Sam. 1:24 וְהַנַּעַר נָעַר *and the boy was yet small.*

2. *a young man,* spoken e. g. of Joseph, Gen. 37:2. of Solomon, when he was already king, 1 K. 3:7. 1 Sam. 30:17 אַרְבַּע מֵאוֹת אִישׁ־נַעַר *four hundred young men.*

3. *a servant,* like *παῖς, puer.* 2 K. 5:20. 8:4. Also military servants, 1 K. 20:15 נַעֲרֵי שָׂרֵי הַמְּדִינוֹת *the people of the princes of the provinces.* Verses 17, 19. 2 K. 19:6.

Note. In the Pentateuch, by a peculiar idiom, it is used for both *puer* and *puella,* hence instead of נַעֲרָה. Gen. 24:14, 28, 55. 34:3, 12. Deut 22:15 ff. But the Keri in all these places has נַעֲרָה. (comp. הוא.) Out of the Pentateuch, it is thus used only in Ruth 2:21 עִם הַנְּעָרִים Sept. *μετὰ τῶν κορασίων;* comp. verses 8, 22, 23.

Deriv. נֹעַר, נְעוּרִים.

II. **נַעַר** m. verbal from נָעַר no. I. *the wandering, straying,* spoken of cattle. Zech. 11:16.

נֹעַר m. denom. from נַעַר *youth, the state* or *condition of a young man,* i. q.

נְעוּרִים. Job 33:25. 36:14. Prov. 29:20. For Job 36:14. Ps. 88:16. some have adopted the sense *expulsion*, (as if from נָעַר,) but this signification is in neither passage necessary.

נַעֲרָה fem. of נַעַר, dec. XII. e.

1. *a young female, a maiden.* Judg. 19:3 ff. Est. 2:9, 13. Sometimes applied to a young married woman, Ruth 2:6. Comp. בְּתוּלָה.

2. *a hand-maid, maid-servant.* Prov. 9:3. 31:15.

3. proper name of a city on the borders of the tribe of Ephraim, Josh. 16:7. which in 1 Chr. 7:28, is called נַעֲרָן.

נְעֹרֶת f. verbal from נָעַר no. 1. *tow, the coarse part of flax*, so called because *beaten* or *shaken out.* Judg. 16:9. Is. 1:31.

נֹף *Memphis*, a proper name, see מֹף

I. **נָפָה** f. verbal from נוּף, dec. X. *a sieve, winnowing-fan.* Is. 30:28.

II. **נָפָה** f. dec. X. *exaltation.* Only in the proper name נָפַת־דּוֹר (*height of Dor*,) see דּוֹר.

נָפַח i. q. פּוּחַ. 1. *to breathe, blow.* Gen. 2:7.

2. *to blow* or *breathe on*, construed with בְּ. Ezek. 37:9.—נָפַח בָּאֵשׁ, and without בְּ, *to blow* or *kindle the fire*, Ezek. 22:20, 21. Is. 54:16.—דּוּד נָפוּחַ *a boiling* or *hot caldron*, Job 41:12. [41:20.] Jer. 1:13.

3. *to blow away*, construed with בְּ. Hag. 1:9.

4. with נֶפֶשׁ, *to breathe out life.* Jer. 15:9.

Pu. *to be kindled*, spoken of the fire. Job 20:26.

Hiph. 1. with נֶפֶשׁ, *to let* or *cause to expire*, (but in a hyperbolical sense.) Job 31:39.

2. metaphorically *to blow away*, for *to lightly esteem, to despise.* Mal. 1:13.

Deriv. מַפָּח, מַפֻּחַ, תַּפּוּחַ.

נֹפַח found only Num. 21:30. a city beyond Jordan, in the territory of Moab, according to some the same with נֹבַח, 32:42. Judg. 8:11.

נְפִילִים plur. masc. *giants.* Gen. 6:4. Num. 13:33. (In Chald. נְפִלָא, נְפִלִין spoken of Orion and other giant forms in the heavens.) Root, according to the Jewish commentators, נָפַל; hence נָפִיל in an active sense, *irruens, grassans.* Perhaps better derived from the Arab. נבל نبيلة نبيل *magnus, corpore magno.*

נֹפֶךְ m. the name of a precious stone which cannot be defined with certainty. Ex. 28:18. 39:11. Ezek. 27:16. 28:13.

נָפַל 1. *to fall;* e. g. spoken of a house, city, Judg. 7:13. Ezek. 13:12. also in war, 2 Sam. 1:4. often with the addition בַּחֶרֶב, Ps. 78:64.—נָפַל לְמִשְׁכָּב *to fall sick, tomber malade*, Ex. 21:18.—Part. נֹפֵל (with a preterite signification,) *that which has fallen* or *lies along*, Judg. 3:25. 1 Sam. 5:3. 31:8. Deut. 21:1. *lying asleep, sleeping*, Num. 24:4. It is also used in the following phrases, (1.) *to descend*, as a divine revelation. Is. 9:7. Comp. in Chald. Dan. 4:28. (2.) with עַל, *to fall on* any one, spoken of sleep or terror. Gen. 15:12. Ex. 15:16. Josh. 2:9. Est. 8:17. (3.) *to fall away* (and pass over) *to* any one, i. q. Greek διαπίπτειν, also πίπτειν. Construed with עַל, 1 Chr. 12:19, 20. Jer. 21:9. Is. 54:15. with אֶל, Jer. 37:13. without cases, 1 Sam. 29:3. (4.) *to fall, to be cast*, as a lot. Ezek. 24:6. Jon. 1:7. (5.) *to fall to* any one, in a division, construed with לְ. Num. 34:2. Judg. 18:1. Comp. Ps. 16:6. (6.) *to fall before* or *in comparison with* any one, i. e. to yield or be inferior to him; construed with מִן, Job 12:3. 13:2. with לִפְנֵי, Est. 6:13. Comp. Neh. 6:16. (7.) *excidere consilio*, construed with מִן. Ps. 5:11. Comp. Ovid. Met. II. 328. *magnis tamen excidit ausis.* (8.) *to be vain, fruitless, irritum cadere.* Num. 6:12. Spoken particularly of empty promises, Josh. 21:45. 23:14. More full נָפַל אַרְצָה *to fall to the ground*, 2 K. 10:10. Comp. in Greek πίπτειν ἔραζε, εἰς γῆν. (9.) *to fall* or *turn out*, like *accidere* from *cadere.* Ruth 3:1'

אֵיךְ יִפֹּל הַדָּבָר *how the matter turns out.* Comp. in Chald. Ezra 7:20. (10.) *to fall, sink, be despondent,* spoken of the countenance. Gen. 4:5, 6. Oppos. נָשָׂא פָנִים *to keep a joyful countenance.* See Hiph. no. 8. (11.) *to fall into ruin,* spoken of houses, Am. 9:11. *to become lean,* spoken of the body, Num. 5:22, 27.

2. In other places it expresses more of a voluntary action, to be rendered in English sometimes by *to fall* and sometimes by other verbs; (comp. the Syr. ܢܦܠ in N. T. for *βάλλεσθαι,* and for *πίπτειν.*) Thus (1.) *to fall on* the neck of any one, i. e. to embrace him. Gen. 33:4. 45:14. 46:29. (2.) *to fall down, to prostrate one's self.* 2 Sam. 1:2. Job 1:20. Gen. 17:3. (3.) *to fall* or *rush on* a sword. 1 Sam. 31:4, 5. 1 Chr. 10:4. (4.) *to fall upon, to attack,* spoken of an enemy. Job 1:15. Construed with בְּ, *to surprise,* Josh. 11:7. (5.) *to leap down, alight.* Gen. 24:64. 2 K. 5:21. (6.) *to encamp,* spoken of a host. Judg. 7:12. *to dwell,* spoken of a people, Gen. 25:18. Comp. 16:12. (7.) נָפְלָה תְחִנָּתִי לְפָנָי *my prayer is laid down before* any one, i. e. I pray to him in a humble manner, Jer. 36:7. also *to be accepted,* 37:20, 42.

Hiph. הִפִּיל causat. of Kal in most of its significations; hence

1. *to let fall.* Num. 35:23. Gen. 2:21. (comp. Prov. 19:15.)

2. *to throw down, to throw to the ground.* Deut. 25:2. Dan. 11:12.

3. *to fell,* as trees. 2 K. 3:19, 25. 6:5.

4. *to cast,* as the lot. Ps. 22:19. Prov. 1:14. Also without גּוֹרָל 1 Sam. 14:42 הַפִּילוּ בֵּינִי וּבֵין יוֹנָתָן בְּנִי *cast (lots) between me and Jonathan my son.* So perhaps Job 6:27.

5. *to let fall to* any one, *to distribute to* him, construed with לְ. Josh. 13:6. 23:4. Ezek. 45:1. 47:22.

6. *to leave,* or *cause to be unfulfilled,* causat. of no. 1. (8.) 1 Sam. 3:19. Est. 6:10.

7. הִפִּיל תְּחִנָּה לִפְנֵי *to present a prayer before* any one. Jer. 38:26. 42:9. Dan. 9:18, 20. Comp. Kal no 1. (7.)

8. הִפִּיל פָּנִים *to let the countenance fall, to look gloomy.* Comp. Kal no. 2. (10.) Jer. 3:12. Job 29:24.

9. *to bring forth.* Comp. *cadere* in the Latin poets, e. g. Stat. Theb. I. 60. Val. Flacc. I. 355. and Il. XIX. 110. Is. 26:19 וָאָרֶץ רְפָאִים תַּפִּיל *and the earth shall cast forth its dead;* Schultens: *abortiet,* comp. נֵפֶל *an untimely birth.*

10. intrans. *to leave off, to cease from* any thing. Judg. 2:19 לֹא הִפִּילוּ מִמַּעַלְלֵיהֶם *they ceased not from their doings.*

Hithpa. 1. *to throw one's self down.* Deut. 9:18, 25. Ezra 10:1.

2. with עַל, *to fall on* any one. Gen. 43:18.

Deriv. נֵפֶל, מַפָּל, מַפֵּלָה, מַפֶּלֶת.

נְפַל Chald. fut. יִפֵּל. i. q. Heb.

1. *to fall.* Dan. 7:20. 4:28 קָל מִן שְׁמַיָּא נְפַל *there fell a voice from heaven.* Comp. in Heb. Is. 9:7.

2. *to fall down, to prostrate one's self.* Dan. 2:46. 3:6, 7, 10, 11.

3. *to be cast.* Dan. 3:23.

4. *to fall out, to happen, accidere.* Ezra 7:20.

נֵפֶל m. verbal from נָפַל, dec. VI. h. *an untimely birth, an abortion, abortus.* Job 3:16. Ps. 58:9. Ecc. 6:3. (So in Arab. سِقْط *abortus,* from سقط *to fall.* Also comp. the verb in Hiph. no. 9.)

נִפְלַל found only Ezek. 28:23. a quadriliteral, or conj. Pilel, i. q. נָפַל which stands in the parallel passages (30:4. 32:20.)

נָפַץ i. q. synon. פּוּץ, (whence a part of its tenses and conjugations are supplied.)

1. *to dash* or *break in pieces;* e. g. a vessel. Judg. 7:19. Jer. 22:28.

2. *to scatter, disperse;* e. g. an army, a people. Is. 11:12.

3. reflex. *to spread abroad, to scatter.* 1 Sam. 13:11. Is. 33:3. Gen. 9:19 מֵאֵלֶּה נָפְצָה כָל־הָאָרֶץ *from them the whole earth,* i. e. the people of the whole earth, *spread themselves abroad.* (Comp. 10:5).

Pi. 1. i. q. Kal no. 1. *to break* or *dash in pieces;* e. g. an earthen vessel, Ps. 2:9. children against a rock, Ps. 137:9.

2. *to disperse* or *scatter* a people. Jer. 13:14. 51:20, 23. Infin. נַפֵּץ as a subst. *the dispersed of the Jews, διασπορά,* Dan. 12:17.

Deriv. מַפֵּץ, מַפָּץ.

נֶפֶץ m. *a violent shower, a flood.* Is. 30:30. Root נפץ in Aram. *to pour out;* comp. e. g. זרק *to scatter,* and *to sprinkle, pour out.*

נְפַק Chald. *to go forth, proceed.* Dan. 2:14. 3:26. 5:5. Spoken of an edict. Dan. 2:13 וְדָתָא נֶפְקַת, comp. Luke 2:1 ἐξῆλθε δόγμα. Imper. plur. פֻּקוּ Dan 3:26.

Aph. הַנְפֵּק, הַנְפִּיק *to bring out.* Dan. 5: 2, 3. Ezra 5:14. 6:8.

נִפְקָא f. emph. נִפְקְתָא, Chald. *expense, cost, what is paid out* or *expended.* Ezra 6:4, 8. Root נפק in Aph. *to pay out, to expend.* Comp. יָצָא no. 6.

נָפַשׁ found only in Niph. *to take breath, to refresh one's self,* after fatigue. Ex. 23:12. 31:17. 2 Sam. 16:14.

נֶפֶשׁ com. gen. but more frequently fem. with suff. נַפְשִׁי, plur. נְפָשׁוֹת, once נְפָשִׁים (Ezek. 13:20.) verbal from נָפַשׁ, dec. VI. a.

1. *breath.* Job 41:13. [41:21.]—נֶפֶשׁ חַיָּה *a living breath,* Gen. 1:30.

2. *life, the vital principle in animal bodies, anima,* which was supposed to reside in the *breath;* (comp. רוּחַ, and in Lat. *animus* from ἄνεμος.) Gen. 35:18 וַיְהִי בְּצֵאת נַפְשָׁהּ *and when her breath* or *life departed from her.* 1 K. 17:21 תָּשָׁב־נָא נֶפֶשׁ־הַיֶּלֶד הַזֶּה עַל־קִרְבּוֹ *let the life of this child, I pray thee, return again within him.* Ex. 21:23 נֶפֶשׁ תַּחַת נָפֶשׁ *life for life.* Ps. 56:7 קִוּוּ נַפְשִׁי *they wait for my life,* i. e. they hope to take away my life. The following phrases deserve notice; (1.) אֶל נַפְשׁוֹ *for one's life, to save one's life.* 1 K. 19:3. 2 K. 7:7. (2.) בְּנֶפֶשׁ *at the hazard of life.* 2 Sam. 23: 17. 18:13 Keri. 1 K. 2:23 בְנַפְשׁוֹ דִּבֶּר אֲדֹנִיָּהוּ אֶת־הַדָּבָר הַזֶּה *at the hazard of his life has Adonijah said this thing.* Lam. 5: 9. Comp. בְּרָאשֵׁינוּ 1 Chr. 12:19. (3.) בְּנֶפֶשׁ also *for the life (taken away,)* i. e. for the death of any one. Jon. 1:14. 2 Sam. 14:7. (4.) הִכָּה נֶפֶשׁ *to smite dead, cædere quoad vitam;* see נָכָה.

3. *a living being, that which has life.* Josh. 10:28 כָּל־הַנֶּפֶשׁ *every living thing.* Verses 30, 32, 35, 37. More full נֶפֶשׁ חַיָּה. Gen. 1:20, 24. 2:7. Particularly spoken of men, Ezek. 22:25 נֶפֶשׁ אָכָלוּ *they devour men.* Prov. 11:25 נֶפֶשׁ בְּרָכָה *a beneficent man, a liberal soul.*—It is used especially (1.) in the Mosaic laws to denote *any one, any person.* Lev. 4:2. נֶפֶשׁ כִּי תֶחֱטָא *if a person sin.* 5:1, 2, 4, 15, 17. 6:2. (2.) in enumerations, e. g. שִׁבְעִים נֶפֶשׁ *seventy souls* or *persons,* Ex. 1:5. In opposition to animals, Num. 31:46. comp. Gen. 14:21. (3.) particularly of slaves. Gen. 12:5 הַנֶּפֶשׁ אֲשֶׁר־עָשׂוּ בְחָרָן *the souls which they had acquired in Haran.* Ezek. 27:13. Comp. Rev. 18:13. 1 Mac. 10:33. (4.) נֶפֶשׁ מֵת (the latter is in the genitive), *a dead body, a corpse.* Num. 6:6 עַל־נֶפֶשׁ מֵת לֹא יָבֹא *he shall come at no dead body.* Lev. 21: 11. Then without מֵת, as טָמֵא לָנֶפֶשׁ Num. 5:2. and טְמֵא נֶפֶשׁ Lev. 22:4. *one rendered unclean by a dead body.*

4. *the soul, spirit,* as the seat of the volitions and affections. Hence frequently connected with לֵב, or construed like the same. Deut. 26:16 בְּכָל־לְבָבְךָ וּבְכָל־נַפְשְׁךָ *with all thy heart and with all thy soul.* Cant. 1:7 שֶׁאָהֲבָה נַפְשִׁי *thou, whom my soul loveth.* 1 Sam. 1:15 *and I poured out my soul before Jehovah.* Ex. 23:9 יְדַעְתֶּם אֶת נֶפֶשׁ הַגֵּר *ye know the feelings of a stranger,* and so Prov. 12: 10. Particularly (1.) with suffixes, it forms a periphrasis of the personal pronouns; as נַפְשִׁי *I,* Ps. 3:3. 7:3. 11:1. 35:3, 7. נַפְשֵׁךְ *thou,* Is. 51:23. Also *I myself,* Job 9:21. (2.) by a peculiar idiom, the Hebrew says, *my soul hungers,* (Prov. 27:7.) *thirsts,* (Prov. 25: 25.) *fasts,* (Ps. 69:15.) *is cold,* (Job 24:7 according to the Sept.)

5. *desire.* Gen. 23:8. 2 K. 9:15. Also *the object of desire,* Prov. 13:4.

Particularly (1.) *the desire of eating, hunger*. Prov. 6:30.—נֶפֶשׁ בַּעַל *a hungry man*, Prov. 23:2. Is. 56:11. By a metonymy, *that which satisfies hunger*, Is. 58:10. (2.) *desire of revenge, murder*. Ex. 15:9. Ps. 27:12. 41:3.

6. *scent, fragrancy, odour*, derived from signif. no. 1. Is. 3:20 בָּתֵּי נֶפֶשׁ *smelling bottles*.

נֶפֶת f. prob. i. q. נוֹף and נָפָה *an elevation, height*. Once Josh. 17:11 שְׁלֹשֶׁת הַנָּפֶת. Chald. *tres regiones*.

נֹפֶת f. verbal from נוּף no. II. *honey as dropped from the comb*, hence more full נֹפֶת צוּפִים *destillatio favorum*, Ps. 19:11.—Cant. 4:11. Prov. 5:3. 24:13 נֹפֶת מָתוֹק עַל חִכֶּךָ *honey is a sweet thing to thy palate;* where it is not necessary to consider נֹפֶת as masc.

נַפְתּוּלִים plur. masc. *wrestlings*. Once Gen. 30:8. Root פָּתַל Niph. *to wrestle, contend.*

נַפְתֻּחִים plur. masc. Gen. 10:13. 1 Chr. 1:11. an Egyptian people, concerning whom nothing is known with certainty. The word has been collated with Νέφθυς, according to Plutarch (de Iside, p. 96. ed. Squire,) the remotest bounds of the country, washed by the sea; (comp. Copt. *nephthos, terminalis;* which would place this people to the east of Pelusium on the sea of Sirbonis. See Michaëlis Spicileg. Geogr. Hebr. Exteræ, T. I. p. 269. Jablonskii Opusc. ed. te Water, T. I. p. 161.

נַפְתָּלִי *Naphtali*, the son of Jacob by Bilhah, and progenitor of the tribe which bears his name. For the etymology, see Gen. 30:8. The possessions of this tribe are marked out. Josh. 19:32—39. In Greek Νεφθαλείμ.

נֵץ m. verbal from נָצַץ (q. v.) dec. VIII. b.

1. *a blossom, flower*, i. q. נִצָּה and נִצָּן. Gen. 40:10.

2. *a hawk*. Lev. 11:16. Deut. 14:15. Job 39:26. Sept. ἱέραξ. Vulg. *accipiter*. Samar. נצצה. Comp. Bocharti Hieroz. T. II. p. 226.

נָצָא *to fly, to fly away*. Jer. 48:9. נָצֹא תֵּצֵא *avolando exibit*. The words נָצֹא, תֵּצֵא and נָצֹא make here a paronomasia. For the signification, see נָצַץ no. 3.

נָצַב *to place*, i. q. the kindred יָצַב. From נָצַב are formed the conjugations Niphal and Hiphil, from יָצַב the conjugation Hithpael.

Niph. נִצַּב 1. *to be set* or *placed over* any thing, construed with עַל. 1 Sam. 22:9. Ruth 2:5, 6. Hence part. נִצָּב *an overseer, officer*, 1 K. 4:5. 5:7. [4:27.]

2. *to place* or *present one's self*. Ex. 34:2. וְנִצַּבְתָּ לִי שָׁם *and thou shalt present thyself to me there*.

3. *to stand*. Gen. 37:7. Ex. 15:8. Ps. 45:10. Particularly *to stand firm*, Ps. 39:6. Zech. 11:16 הַנִּצָּבָה לֹא יְכַלְכֵּל *the firm*, i. e. the sound, *he will not nourish*. Sept. τὸ ὁλόκληρον.

Hiph. הִצִּיב 1. *to make* or *cause to stand*. Ps. 78:13.

2. *to place, set;* e. g. a trap. Jer. 5:26. a pillar, Gen. 35:20, an altar, 33:20. a monument, 1 Sam. 15:12. comp. Jer. 31:21. a heap of stones, 2 Sam. 18:17.

3. *to straighten, point, sharpen*. 1 Sam. 13:21. לְהַצִּיב הַדָּרְבָן *to sharpen the goads*.

4. *to fix, establish*, e. g. boundaries. Ps. 74:17. Deut. 32:8.

Hoph. הֻצַּב and הָצַב.

1. *to be placed*. Gen. 28:12.

2. *to be planted*, the common signification in Aram. Judg. 9:6.

3. prob. *to be fixed, to be determined*. Nah. 2:8 וְהֻצַּב גֻּלְּתָה הֹעֲלָתָה *and it is determined; it (Nineveh) shall be carried away captive*. (Comp. Chald. יְצִיב *firm, established;* and Arab. نصب conj. I. med. Kesr. conj. VIII. *præparatum fuit*.) Others: *they place themselves*, (in martial array.) Perhaps the word pertained originally to the preceding verse, and had other vowel-points.

Deriv. out of course נְצִיב, מַצָּב, מַצֵּבָה, מַצֶּבֶת.

נִצְבָה Chald. emph. נִצְבְּתָא, *firmness*.

strength, of iron. Dan. 2:41. Theod. ἀπὸ τῆς ῥίζης τῆς σιδηρᾶς. Vulg. *de plantario ferri*, as if from the Syr. נְצַב *to plant;* but *root* is prob. used here for *natural state, temperament, condition*, like the Arab. أَصْل.

נִצָּב m. (strictly part. Niph. from נָצַב,) *the haft* or *handle* of a dagger, liter. *something inserted.* Judg. 3:22. Comp. the verb Josh. 6:26. 1 K. 16:34. (Arab. نِصَاب *the handle* of a sword, knife, etc.)

I. **נָצָה** in Kal not used. In Syr. and Chald. נְצָא the usual word for the Heb. רִיב *to contend.* In Arab. strictly *to strike.*

Hiph. הִצָּה *to contend, strive.* Num. 26:9 בְּהַצֹּתָם עַל יְהוָה *when they contended against Jehovah.* Also *to carry on war,* Ps. 60:2 בְּהַצּוֹתוֹ אֶת־אֲרַם נַהֲרַיִם *when he carried on war with Mesopotamia.*

Niph. נִצָּה *to contend with one another.* Ex. 2:13. 21:22. Deut. 25:11 כִּי יִנָּצוּ אֲנָשִׁים יַחְדָּו *when men contend together.* Lev. 24:10. 2 Sam. 14:6. Deriv. מַצָּה, מַצּוּת.

II. **נָצָה** *to be laid waste.* Jer. 4:7 עָרַיִךְ תִּצֶּינָה *thy cities shall be laid waste.* Sept. αἱ πόλεις καθαιρεθήσονται.

Niph. *idem.* Is. 37:26 גַּלִּים נִצִּים *waste heaps of stones.* 2 K. 19:25. (In Arab. نقا *to draw out* or *off*, e. g. a garment, a sword; *to make bare;* hence perhaps to *strip* the ground, *to lay waste;* comp. עָרָה. Or it may be collated with the Samar. נצץ *to be set on fire, to be burnt up.*)

נִצָּה f. verbal from נָצַץ no. 2. dec. X. *a blossom, flower.* Job 15:33. Is. 18:5.

נוֹצָה f. dec. X. Lev. 1:16. *the dirt* or *filth* in the crop of a bird. Prob. strictly Part. Niph. from יָצָא, for נוֹצָא, *quod excernitur, excrementum;* comp. צֵאָה and צוֹאָה.

נָצַח in Kal not used. In Arab. *to be pure, upright, faithful;* In Syr. (1.) *to be shining;* (2.) *to conquer.*

Pi. נִצַּח 1. *to be placed over* any thing, *to have the oversight* of it, construed with עַל and לְ. 1 Chr. 23:4. Ezra 3:8, 9. Part. מְנַצֵּחַ *an overseer,* 2 Chr. 2:1, 17. 34:12.

2. used in reference to music, prob. *to preside over the singing, to lead in the singing.* 1 Chr. 15:21 *and Mattithiah* and others *played on harps, on the octave,* לְנַצֵּחַ *as precentors.* (Comp. verse 19 לְהַשְׁמִיעַ *to sing loud,* with verse 21 עַל עֲלָמוֹת *with a female voice;* q. v.) Here belongs the expression לַמְנַצֵּחַ in the superscriptions of 53 psalms, and in Hab. 3:19. *a precentor, chorister.* So Rashi, Aben Ezra, Kimchi, and most of the moderns. Others make it the Syr. Infin. Pa. (comp. in Chald. Dan. 5:12.) *to lead in singing.* Targ. *ad laudandum.* The former interpretation is favoured by the frequent phrase לַמְנַצֵּחַ עַל יְדוּתוּן *to the overseer over the Jeduthunites,* which is analogous with the construction under no. 1.

Niph. found only Jer. 8:5 מְשֻׁבָה נִצַּחַת *an entire declension.* See נֵצַח no. 5.

נְצַח Chald. Ithpe. *to conquer, surpass.* Dan. 6:4. (In Syr. *idem.*)

I. **נֵצַח** and **נֶצַח**, with suff. נִצְחִי, dec. VI. i.

1. *permanency, perpetuity, eternity.* (Kindred with the primary signification of the verb *to be faithful.*) Ps. 74:3 מַשֻּׁאוֹת נֶצַח *perpetual desolations.*—עַד נֵצַח *to eternity,* Ps. 49:20. Job 34:36.—נֶצַח, לָנֶצַח as an adv. *forever,* Is. 13:20. 34:10 לְנֵצַח נְצָחִים *idem.*

2. *hope, confidence.* Lam. 3:18 אָבַד נִצְחִי *my hope is perished.* Perhaps also 1 Sam. 15:29 נֵצַח יִשְׂרָאֵל *the confidence of Israel.*

3. *truth, uprightness.* Hab. 1:4 לֹא יֵצֵא לָנֶצַח מִשְׁפָּט *judgment does not proceed according to truth.* (Comp. Is. 42:3.) Perhaps Prov. 21:28.

4. *glory, praise.* 1 Chr. 29:11. Perhaps also 1 Sam. 15:29 נֵצַח יִשְׂרָאֵל *gloria Israelis,* spoken of Jehovah.

5. *perfection, completeness;* hence נֶצַח and לָנֶצַח *entirely,* Ps. 13:2 עַד אָנָה יְהוָה

הִשְׁכָּחֵנִי נֶצַח *how long, O Lord, wilt thou entirely forget me?* Luth. *Herr, wie lange willst du mein sogar vergessen?* Ps. 79:5. Job 23:7.

II. **נֵצַח** m. dec. VI. i. *the juice which spatters from the pressed grapes.* Is. 63:3, 6. Root نضح and نضخ *to spatter, sprinkle,* i. q. Heb. הִזָּה.

נְצִיב m. verbal from נָצַב, dec. I.

1. *something raised up, a pillar,* i. q. מַצֵּבָה, (comp. in Arab. נצב, נציבה *idem.*) Gen. 19:26 נְצִיב מֶלַח *a pillar of salt.*

2. *a military post* or *station.* 1 Sam. 10:5. 13:3, 4.

3. *a garrison.* 2 Sam. 8:6, 14.

4. *an overseer,* i. q. נִצָּב. 1 K. 4:7, 19.

נָצַל in Kal not used; prob. *to draw* or *tear away.*

Pi. 1. *to take, to take away.* 2 Chr. 20:25.

2. *to rob* any one, construed with an accus. of the person. Ex. 3:22. 12:36.

3. *to tear away from danger, to save.* Ezek. 14:14. See Hiph.

Hiph. הִצִּיל 1. i. q. Pi. *to take away,* construed with מִן. Gen. 31:9, 16. Ps. 119:43. 2 Sam. 20:6 וְהִצִּיל עֵינֵנוּ *and escape from our eyes.*

2. *to deliver, free.* For the most part construed with מִן, Ps. 18:49. 34:5, 18. Mic. 5:5. with מִיַּד *out of the hand* or *power of* any one, Gen. 32:12. 37:21, 22. Ex. 3:8. 18:10. also with מִכַּף, Is. 38:6.—הִצִּיל נַפְשׁוֹ *to save one's life* or *soul.* Ezek. 3:19, 21. אֵין מַצִּיל *there is no helper,* Ps. 7:3. 50:22. Is. 5:29. Construed with a dative of the person, only Jon. 4:6.

Hoph. הֻצַּל *to be drawn out.* Am. 4:11. Zech. 3:2.

Niph. 1. pass. of Hiph. no. 2. *to be delivered* or *saved.* Is. 20:6. Jer. 7:10.

2. reflex. *to deliver one's self.* Prov. 6:3, 5. Construed with אֶל, Deut. 23:16 אֲשֶׁר יִנָּצֵל אֵלֶיךָ *who shall have escaped to thee.*

Hithpa. *to take away from one's self, to put off.* Ex. 33:6 וַיִּתְנַצְּלוּ בְנֵי־יִשְׂרָאֵל אֶת־עֶדְיָם *then the children of Israel put off their ornaments.* For this meaning of the conjugation Hithpael, comp. the art. פָּרַק, פָּשַׁט.

Deriv. הַצָּלָה.

נְצַל Chald. Aph. הַצֵּל i. q. Heb. הִצִּיל no. 2. Dan. 3:29. 6:15, 28.

נִצָּן m. dec. II. b. *a flower.* Cant. 2:12. Root נָצַץ.

נָצַע see **יָצַע**.

נָצַץ 1. strictly *to shine, sparkle.* Once Ezek. 1:7. Deriv. נִיצוֹץ.

2. *to blossom,* (as in Chald.) whence the deriv. נֵץ no. 1. נִצָּה, נִצָּן; comp. הֵנֵץ *to blossom.* (Words of *shining* are often made to signify *verdure* and *blossoming;* see זִיו, and comp. Simonis Arcanum Formarum, p. 352.) With *blossoming* or *sprouting,* the Shemite also connects *the plumage* of birds; hence

3. *to fly;* (comp. פרח in Chald. *to sprout,* in Syr. *to fly.*) Deriv. נֵץ *a hawk.* Comp. the kindred forms נָצָא *to fly,* and נוצה *a wing.*

נָצַק see **יָצַק**.

נָצַר, fut. יִצֹּר, more rarely יִנְצֹר, i. q. נָטַר.

1. *to watch, keep guard;* e. g. a vineyard. Job 27:18.—מִגְדַּל נֹצְרִים *a watch-tower,* 2 K. 17:9. Often spoken of Jehovah, *to guard, protect, defend,* Deut. 32:10. Ps. 31:24. Construed with מִן of the thing, Ps. 32:7 מִצַּר תִּצְּרֵנִי *thou shalt preserve me from trouble.* 12:8. 64:2. 140:2. Also taken in a bad sense, Job 7:20 נֹצֵר הָאָדָם *O thou that watchest for men.*—Is. 49:6 נְצִירֵי יִשְׂרָאֵל *the preserved of Israel.* Is. 1:8 כְּעִיר נְצוּרָה *as a delivered city.* Only once with עַל, Ps. 141:3 נִצְּרָה עַל־דַּל שְׂפָתָי *watch over the door of my lips,* i. e. over my mouth. (The Dagesh is euphonic.)

2. *to keep, observe;* e. g. a covenant, Deut. 33:9. Ps. 25:10. the precepts of God, Ps. 105:45. Ex. 34:7 נֹצֵר חֶסֶד לָאֲלָפִים *keeping mercy to the thousandth generation.*

3. *to keep, hide, conceal.* Is. 48:6 נְצֻרוֹת וְלֹא יְדַעְתָּם *hidden things which thou didst not know.* 65:4 וּבַנְּצוּרִים יָלִינוּ *they*

lodge in concealed places. Hence נְצֻרַת־לֵב *subtle of heart,* Prov. 7:10.

4. *to watch* or *observe* (a city), i. e. prob. *to shut* it *in, to besiege* it. 2 Sam. 11:16 בִּשְׁמוֹר יוֹאָב אֶל הָעִיר *when Joab besieged the city.* So Jer. 4:16 נֹצְרִים *besiegers.* Also, according to some, Is. 1:8 עִיר נְצוּרָה *a besieged city.*

נֵצֶר m. *a twig, branch, shoot.* Is. 11:1. 14:19. 60:21. Dan. 11:7. (Root نضر *to be green.*)

נְקֵא Chald. *pure.* Dan. 7:9. Root נְקָא i. q. Heb. נָקָה. q. v.

נָקַב, fut. יִקֹּב and יִנְקֹב.

1. *to bore.* 2 K. 12:10. Construed with an accus. *to bore through, pierce,* Job 40:24, 26. [41:2.] 2 K. 18:21. Hag. 1:6. צְרוֹר נָקוּב *a bag with holes.* Hab. 3:14 נָקַבְתָּ רֹאשׁ פְּרָזָו *thou didst pierce the head of their leaders.* (In Chald. Syr. and Arab. *idem,* very common.) Deriv. מַקֶּבֶת, מַקָּבָה, נְקֵבָה.

2. *to cut, divide, separate, distinguere,* and hence *distincte dicere, to specify, to name.* (Comp. פָּרַשׁ in Heb. and Aram. *to pierce, divide, distinguish.*) Gen. 30:28 נָקְבָה שְׂכָרְךָ עָלַי *name to me thy wages.* Is. 62:2. Part. pass. נְקֻבִים *the called by name, the famous,* Am. 6:1. (comp. 1 Chr. 12:31.) In Arab. نقيب *dux, tribunus, princeps.*

3. i. q. קָבַב *to curse, execrate, blaspheme.* (So in Arab. سب *to cut* or *bore through,* metaphorically *to revile, curse.*) Lev. 24:11, 16. Num. 23:8, 25. Job 3:8. 5:3. Prov 11:26. (The ambiguity of the word נָקַב has caused the passage Lev. 24:11. to be misunderstood, and to be interpreted of a simple utterance of the name of God, see יְהוָה.)

Niph. pass. of no. 2. Num. 1:17 *these men* אֲשֶׁר נִקְּבוּ בְּשֵׁמוֹת *who are specified by name.* 1 Chr. 12:31. 16:41. 2 Chr. 28:15. 31:19. (Comp. the Arab. לקב لقب *to name,* by a commutation of ל and נ.)

נֶקֶב m. dec. VI. Ezek. 28:13. prob. *a casket, pala gemmarum* (according to Jerome,) literally *an excavation, incisio,* from נָקַב. Comp. חֹק. Others: *pipes;* from נָקַב *to bore through,* like חָלִיל from חָלַל, which does not suit the context.

נְקֵבָה f. verbal from נָקַב, *a female,* in opposition to זָכָר *a male;* the appropriate designation of sex in men and animals.—זָכָר וּנְקֵבָה *a male and a female, a man and a woman,* Gen. 1:27. Lev. 3:1, 6. 4:28, 32. 5:6. 12:5.

נָקֹד m. plur. נְקֻדִּים, dec. VIII. d. *speckled, spotted,* spoken of sheep and goats. Gen. 30:32 ff. 31:8 ff. (Also in Chald.)

נֹקֵד m. *a herdsman, an owner of cattle.* Am. 1:1. Applied to the king of Moab, 2 K. 3:4. Strictly a denom. from נָקַד Arab. نَقَد and نَقَد a species of sheep and goats with short feet, and of an ugly form; whence נֹקֵד, (like פָּרָשׁ from פָּרַשׁ, בָּקָר from בָּקַר,) Arab. نَقَّاد *one who keeps such cattle.* But in Hebrew the signification was probably more general, *a herdsman.* See Bocharti Hieroz. T. I. p. 441.

נְקֻדָּה f. dec. X. *a point, dot,* on a gold or pearl chain. Cant. 1:11. See נָקֹד.

נִקֻּדִים masc. plur. 1. *crumbs of bread, frusta;* (comp. נָקֹד *a point, dot.*) Josh. 9:5, 12.

2. a kind of pastry, *small cakes.* 1 K. 14:3. Sept. κολλυρία. Vulg. *crustulam.*

נָקָה *to be pure, innocent.* In Kal only Jer. 49:12 נָקֹה a pleonastic infin. used with the Niph.

Niph. נִקָּה 1. *to be pure,* metaphorically *to be innocent;* construed with מִן of the crime, Ps. 19:14. Num. 5:31. of the person, Judg. 15:3 נִקֵּיתִי מִפְּלִשְׁתִּים *I shall not be guilty to the Philistines.*

2. *to be free from punishment, to go unpunished,* without the idea of innocence. Ex. 21:19, 28. Num. 5:19. Prov. 6:29 לֹא יִנָּקֶה כָּל־הַנֹּגֵעַ בָּהּ *whosoever*

toucheth her shall not go unpunished. 11:21.

3. *to be free*, from an oath, from an obligation. Gen. 24:8, 41.

4. *to be emptied out, to be stripped, laid waste*, spoken of a city. (So in Arab. conj. X.) Is. 3:26 נִקָּתָה לָאָרֶץ תֵּשֵׁב *desolate she shall sit upon the ground.* Also spoken of persons, *to be destroyed* or *rooted out*, Zech. 5:3.

Pi. נִקָּה 1. *to pronounce innocent, to acquit.* Job 9:28. Construed with מִן, Ps. 19:13. Job 10:14.

2. *to let go unpunished, to remit, forgive.* Ex. 20:7. 1 K. 2:9. Joel 4:21 [3:21] וְנִקֵּיתִי דָמָם לֹא נִקֵּיתִי *and I will remit their blood-guiltiness, which I have not remitted.* Comp. Ex. 34:7 *who forgives iniquity, transgression, and sin,* וְנַקֵּה לֹא יְנַקֶּה *but will not always forgive*, etc. Num. 14:18. also Jer. 30:11. 46:28. Nah. 1:3.

נָקִי, plur. נְקִיִּים, verbal adj. from נָקָה, dec. VIII. m.

1. *pure, innocent.* Ex. 23:7. Job 4:7. 9:25.—דָּם נָקִי *innocent blood*, Deut. 19:10, 13. 2 Sam. 3:28 נָקִי אָנֹכִי מִדְּמֵי אַבְנֵר *I am innocent of the blood of Abner.*

2. *free, clear;* from responsibility or obligation, construed with מִן. Gen. 24:41. Num. 32:22. from military service, Deut. 24:5. 1 K. 15:22.

נָקִיא (with א in otio) i. q. נָקִי. Joel 4:19. [3:19.] Jon. 1:14 Keth.

נִקָּיוֹן m. verbal from נָקָה, dec. III. d. *purity, cleanness.* Am. 4:6 נִקְיוֹן שִׁנַּיִם *cleanness of teeth*, i. e. hunger. נִקְיוֹן כַּפַּי *the cleanness of my hands*, i. e. my innocency, Gen. 20:5. Hence *moral purity, innocence*, Ps. 26:6. 73:13.

נָקִיק or **נְקִיק** found only in the const. state, Jer. 13:4 נְקִיק הַסָּלַע *a cleft of the rock;* and in the plur. נְקִיקֵי הַסְּלָעִים Is. 7:19. Jer. 16:16. The root נקק is found in none of the Shemitish dialects.

נָקֹט i. q. קוּט and קוּץ *to loathe* or *be weary of* any thing, construed with בְּ. Job 10:1. The future and other forms are made from קוּט.

נָקַם, infin. נְקֹם, fut. יִקֹּם, *to avenge, revenge, to take revenge.* Lev. 19:18. Construed (1.) with an accus. of the person or thing *for* which the revenge is taken, Deut. 32:43. 1 Sam. 24:23. Also in the following construction, Lev. 26:25 חֶרֶב נֹקֶמֶת נְקַם בְּרִית *the sword which avenges the covenant;* comp. Jer. 51:36. (2.) with מִן of the person or thing *on* which revenge is taken, 1 Sam. 24:13. with מֵאֵת, Num. 31:2. with מִיַּד, 2 K. 9:7. with לְ, Nah. 1:2. Ezek. 25:12. with an accus. Josh. 10:13.—Some examples of the full construction are 1 Sam. 24:13 נְקָמַנִי יְהוָה מִמֶּךָּ *Jehovah avenge me of thee.* Num. 31:2. Once with עַל, Ps. 99:8.

Niph. 1. *to revenge one's self.* Ezek. 25:15. The person *on* whom revenge is taken, is construed with בְּ, Judg. 15:7. 1 Sam. 18:25. with מִן, Is. 1:24. Judg. 16:28 אִנָּקְמָה נְקַם־אַחַת מִשְּׁתֵי עֵינַי מִפְּלִשְׁתִּים *I will take one revenge of the Philistines on account of my two eyes.*

2. *to suffer revenge, to be punished.* Ex. 21:20. Comp. Hoph. no. 2.

Pi. i. q. Kal. 2 K. 9:7. Jer. 51:36.

Hoph. fut. יֻקַּם.

1. *to be revenged.* Gen. 4:24.

2. *to suffer revenge, to be punished.* Gen. 4:15. Ex. 21:22. See Niph. no. 2.

Hithpa. 1. *to revenge one's self*, as in Niph. Jer. 5:9, 29. 9:8.

Part. מִתְנַקֵּם *revengeful, vindictive.* Ps. 8:3. 44:17.

נָקָם m. dec. IV. a. and **נְקָמָה** f. with suff. נִקְמָתִי, plur. נְקָמוֹת, dec. XI. c.

1. *revenge.* Deut. 32:35. *To take revenge* is expressed by הֵשִׁיב, Deut. 32:41, 43. by לָקַח, Is. 47:3. Jer. 20:10. by עָשָׂה, Ps. 149:7. Ezek. 25:17. and construed with לְ, מִן, or בְּ of the person. Also עָשָׂה בִנְקָמָה *to execute vengeance.* Ezek. 25:15. נָתַן נִקְמָתוֹ בְּ *to execute one's vengeance on* any one, Ezek. 25:14. Num. 31:3. נָתַן נְקָמוֹת לְ *to avenge* any one, *to give* him *satisfaction*, Ps. 18:48. comp. Judg. 11:36. The genitive following often expresses the thing *for* which revenge is taken, Jer. 50:28

נִקְמַת הֵיכָלוֹ *the vengeance for his temple,* comp. 51:36.

2. *desire of revenge.* Lam. 3:60.

נָקַע i. q. יָקַע *to move one's self away,* metaphorically *to be alienated.* Ezek. 23:18, 22, 28. Of this form occurs only the preterite, of יָקַע the future.

I. **נָקַף** *to make a circle, to go round, revolve;* spoken of time. Is. 29:1 חַגִּים יִנְקֹפוּ *let the festivals go round.*

Hiph. הִקִּיף 1. *to go round* a place. Hence הַקֵּף and הַקֵּיף Josh. 6:3, 11. *circumeundo,* used adverbially for *circum, round about.*

2. *to surround, compass.* Construed with an acccus. 1 K. 7:24. Ps. 22:17. with עַל, 2 K. 6:14. Ps. 17:9. 88:18. with an accus. of the thing and עַל of the person, *to surround with* any thing, Job 19:6 וּמְצוּדוֹ עָלַי הִקִּיף *and he has surrounded me with his net.* Lam. 3:4.

3. *to go round, to elapse,* spoken of time. Job 1:5 כִּי הִקִּיפוּ יְמֵי הַמִּשְׁתֶּה *when the days of feasting had ended.*

4. used elliptically. Lev. 19:27 לֹא תַקִּפוּ פְּאַת רֹאשְׁכֶם *ye shall not round the corners of your heads.* Symm. οὐ περιζυγώσετε κύκλῳ τὴν πρόσοψιν, in reference to some religious custom, like that of the Arabians, who cut off the hair all round the head, but left it standing on the crown; see Herod. III. 8. IV. 175.

II. **נָקַף** *to smite, to hew,* kindred with נָכָה. In Chald. and Arab. *idem.* In Kal not used.

Pi. נִקֵּף 1. *to cut down,* e. g. a thicket. Is. 10:34.

2. Job 19:26. prob. *to destroy* (the body).

נֹקֶף m. verbal from נָקַף no. II. *the beating* of an olive-tree. Is. 17:6. 24:13. (Chald. נִיקְפָא *an olive-tree.*)

נִקְפָּה f. verbal from נָקַף no. I. *a cord.* Is. 3:24.

נָקַר, fut. יִקֹּר, and Pi. נִקֵּר *to bore, pierce, bore out, dig out.* (In Arab. and Aram. *idem.*) Used particularly of the *digging out* of the eyes, Num. 16:14. Judg. 16:21. of the *picking out* of the same by birds, Prov. 30:17.

Niph. *to be pierced.* Job 30:17 לַיְלָה עֲצָמַי נִקַּר *by night my bones are pierced* (with pain).

Pu. *to be dug out.* Is. 51:1. Here metaphorically *to be descended.*

נְקָרָה or **נִקְרָה**, found only in the phrase נִקְרַת הַצּוּר Ex. 33:22. *the cleft* or *cavity of a rock.* Plur. נְקִרוֹת הַצֻּרִים Is. 2:21.

נָקַשׁ i. q. יָקַשׁ and קוּשׁ *to lay snares, to ensnare.* Intrans. Ps. 9:17 בְּפֹעַל כַּפָּיו נוֹקֵשׁ רָשָׁע *the wicked is ensnared by the work of his own hands.* Or נוֹקֵשׁ may be the part. Niph. i. q. נוֹקָשׁ, (after the form נָקֵל i. q. נָקַל.)

Niph. *to be ensnared, seduced.* Deut. 12:30.

Pi. *to lay snares.* Ps. 38:18. 109:11 יְנַקֵּשׁ נוֹשֶׁה לְכָל־אֲשֶׁר־לוֹ *the creditor takes every thing which is his,* liter. *laqueos injiciat omni,* cet.

Hithpa. *to lay snares, to lie in wait,* construed with בְּ. 1 Sam. 28:9.

נְקַשׁ Chald. *to smite, strike.* Dan. 5:6 *and his knees smote one against another.* In Syr. *idem.*

נֵר m. plur. נֵרוֹת, verbal from נוּר, dec. VII. e. Zeph. 1:12. *a light, lamp.* Spoken of the lamps in the great candlestick, Ex. 29:37. 35:14. Often used metaphorically (1.) *the light of Israel* for *a great man in Israel.* 2 Sam. 21:17. (2.) *prosperity;* comp. אוֹר no. 3. the figure, however, being continued. Prov. 13:9 נֵר רְשָׁעִים יִדְעָךְ *the light of the wicked is extinguished.* 20:20. 31:18. Ps. 18:29. Job 29:3.

נִר Prov. 21:4. *idem.*

נֵרְגַל 2 K. 17:30. an idol of the Cuthites. Hence the proper name נֵרְגַל שַׂרְאֶצֶר Jer. 39:3, 13. and *Neriglissar,* The best explanation is from the Aram. נִירִיג *the planet Mars.*

נִרְגָּן m. *a slanderer, tale-bearer.* Prov. 16:28. 18:8. 26:20, 22. The final Nun is afformative, the initial Nun radical; comp. the Arab. نَيْرَجٌ *a tale-bearer, sycophant*; نَيْرَجَةٌ *sycophancy.*

נֵרְדְּ m. with suff. נִרְדִּי, plur. נְרָדִים, *nard*, a fragrant shrub, *andropogon nardus*, Linn. Cant. 1:12. 4:13, 14. See Celsii Hierobot. T. II. p. 1 ff.

נָשָׂא, fut. יִשָּׂא, infin. שְׂאֵת, with a prefix לָשֵׂאת, rarely נְשֹׂא (Is. 1:14.) infin. absol. נָשׂוֹא.

1. *to lift* or *raise up.* Gen. 7:17. 29:1. Is. 5:26. Its principal uses are the following (1.) *to lift up* the eyes, frequently in the phrase, *he lifted up his eyes and saw*, Gen. 13:10, 14. 18:2. 31:10. 33:1, 5. 43:29. Construed with אֶל, *to look*, e.g. on an object of affection. Gen. 39:7. on idols, with reverence, Ezek. 18:6, 12, 15. 23:27. comp. Deut. 4:19. on Jehovah, Ps. 123:1. Comp. below under no. 3.—(2.) *to lift up* the hand, construed with בְּ *against* any one. 2 Sam. 20:21. Very frequently as the gesture of one taking an oath, and hence the same as *to swear*, Ex. 6:8. Construed with לְ, Ps. 106:26. Ezek. 20:6 ff. Neh. 9:15. Comp. Gen. 14:22. and Virg. Æn. xii. 196. More rarely *to lift up* the hand, as a supplicant. Ps. 28:2. 63:5. (3.) נָשָׂא נֶפֶשׁ אֶל *to raise one's heart* to any thing, i.e. to long for or desire it. Deut. 24:15. Hos. 4:8. Prov. 19:18. Particularly with אֶל יְהוָה, Ps. 25:1. 86:4. 143:8. (4.) נָשָׂא רֹאשׁוֹ *to lift up the head* of any one, *to exalt* him, *caput extollere in civitate.* Judg. 8:28. Ps. 83:3. Different from the phrase נָשָׂא רֹאשׁ פ׳ מִבֵּית כֶּלֶא *to lift up the head of any one from the prison, to let him come out*, 2 K. 25:27. and without the addition מ׳ כ׳, Gen. 40:13, 20. Another meaning of the phrase may be found under no. 3. (2.)—(5.) נָשָׂא קוֹל *to lift up the voice*; spoken of a person weeping, Gen. 27:38. of one calling aloud, Judg. 9:7. of one rejoicing. Is. 24:14.—נָשָׂא מָשָׁל *to lift* or *take up a song*, Num. 23:7 ff. Job 27:1. Is. 14:4. So with זִמְרָה, Ps. 81:3. Hence (6.) *to utter, speak, efferre, proferre* aliquid, e.g. the name of God, Ex. 20:7. a false report, Ex. 23:1. a reproach, Ps. 15:2. (Comp. מַשָּׂא no. 4.) (7.) without addition, *to lift up* (the voice), *to begin.* Num. 14:1 וַתִּשָּׂא כָּל־הָעֵדָה וַיִּבְכּוּ *and the whole congregation began and wept.* Is. 3:7. Job 21:12 יִשְׂאוּ בְּתֹף וְכִנּוֹר *they begin with the timbrel and harp.* Is. 42:2, 11. See מַשָּׂא no. 6. (8.) *one's heart raises him to any thing*, i.e. it makes him willing or excites him to it. Comp. נָדַב. Ex. 35:21 כָּל־אִישׁ אֲשֶׁר־נְשָׂאוֹ לִבּוֹ *every one whose heart excited him.* Verse 26. 36:2. In a different sense 2 K. 14:10 נְשָׂאֲךָ לִבֶּךָ *thine heart has lifted thee up*, i.e. thou hast become arrogant. (9.) with עַל, *to put* or *set on* any thing. Gen. 31:17. Lev. 22:9. (10.) intrans. *to raise one's self, to rise.* Ps. 89:10. Nah. 1:5. *To be placed* in the balance, i.e. to be weighed, Job 6:2.

2. *to bear*, e.g. fruit, as a tree. Ezek. 17:8. Particularly (1.) *to bear away.* 1 Sam. 17:34. comp. Hos. 5:14. Judg. 16:31. (2.) *to suffer, endure, bear.* Is. 1:14. Mic. 7:9. Construed with בְּ, Job 7:13. (3.) נָשָׂא עָוֹן *to bear the guilt* of any person or thing, Is. 53:12. Num. 14:33. Construed with בְּ, Ezek. 18:19, 20. נָשָׂא עֲוֹנוֹ, חֶטְאוֹ, *to bear one's sin, to suffer for it*, Lev. 5:1, 17. Num. 5:31. 9:13. 14:34. Ezek. 23:35 שְׂאִי זִמָּתֵךְ וְאֶת תַּזְנוּתַיִךְ *bear thou thy lewdness and thy whoredoms.*—Without farther addition, *to suffer, to be punished*, Job 34:31. (4.) *to bring*; spoken of a wind, Ex. 10:13. of a ship, 1 K. 10:11.

3. *to take.* Gen. 27:3. 45:19.—נָשָׂא אִשָּׁה *to take a wife*, in later Hebrew for לָקַח אִשָּׁה, 2 Chr. 11:21. 13:21. Ezra 10:44. Then elliptically Ezra 9:2 *for they have taken of their daughters* (*wives*) *for themselves and for their sons.* Verse 12. Neh. 13:25. 2 Chr. 24:3.—Particularly (1.) *to accept*; with פָּנִים *to accept the person of* any one, *to be gracious to* him. Gen. 32:21. Mal. 1:8, 9.—Hence (a.) in a good sense, *to ac-*

cept the person of any one, *to do any thing from respect* or *regard to* him. Gen. 19:21. Job 42:8. Lam. 4:16. Prov. 6:35 לֹא־יִשָּׂא פְּנֵי כָל־כֹּפֶר *he regards no ransom.* Part. נְשׂוּא פָנִים *esteemed, honoured, honourable,* 2 K. 5:1. Is. 9:14. (b.) in a bad sense, *to be partial,* spoken of a judge. Lev. 19:15. Deut. 10:17. Mal. 2:9 נֹשְׂאִים פָּנִים בַּתּוֹרָה *being partial in the law;* comp. הִכִּיר פָּנִים, in N. T. πρόσωπον λαμβάνειν. (2.) *to take away.* Dan. 1:16. Gen. 40:19 *within three days* יִשָּׂא פַרְעֹה אֶת־רֹאשְׁךָ מֵעָלֶיךָ *Pharaoh shall take thine head from off thee.* (In this passage there is a play on the meaning of the phrase נָשָׂא רֹאשׁ, verses 13, 30. See above under no. 1. (4.)—Also *to carry away by force* or *violence,* Job 27:21. 32:22. Particularly נָשָׂא עָוֹן פ׳ *to take away the guilt of any one,* Lev. 10:17. Hence *to forgive* (sins), Ps. 32:5. 85:3. Gen. 50:17. Construed with a dative of the person, Gen. 18:24, 26. Hos. 1:6. Is. 2:9. Part. pass. נְשׂוּא עָוֹן *whose sin is forgiven,* Is. 33:24. and נְשׂוּי פֶּשַׁע *idem,* Ps. 32:1. (3.) *to take* the number of any thing. For the most part with רֹאשׁ *the sum,* Ex. 30:12. Num. 1:2, 49. or with מִסְפָּר *the number,* Num. 3:40. (4.) *to receive, to bear.* Ps. 24:5. Ecc. 5:18.

Niph. נִשָּׂא 1. *to rise, to be raised up, to be elevated.* Ezek. 1:19—21. Ps. 94:2. Is. 40:4. 52:13. Part. נִשָּׂא *lifted up, exalted,* synon. with רָם, Is. 2:2.

2. *to be borne,* Ex. 25:28. Is. 49:22. *to be carried away,* 2 K. 20:17.

Pi. נִשֵּׂא and נַשֵּׂא.

1. *to lift up, exalt.* 2 Sam. 5:12. With נֶפֶשׁ, *to long for, to desire,* Jer. 22:27. 44:14.

2. *to assist, help, sublevare.* Est. 9:3. Ps. 28:9. Especially by presents, 1 K. 9:11. Hence

3. *to make presents,* construed with לְ. 2 Sam. 19:43.

4. *to take away.* Am. 4:2.

Hiph. הִשִּׂיא 1. causat. of Kal no. 2. (3.) *to let* any one *bear* iniquity. Lev. 22:16.

2. with אֶל, *to set* or *apply to* any thing, e. g. a cord. 2 Sam. 17:13.

Hithpa. הִתְנַשֵּׂא and הִנַּשֵּׂא *to lift one's self up, to rise,* Num. 23:24. 16:3. 24:7. 1 K. 1:5. *to act proudly,* Prov. 30:32.

Deriv. נָשִׂיא, מְשׂוּאָה, מַשְּׂאֵת, נְשֻׂאָה, מַשָּׂא, מַשָּׂאָה, שְׂאֵת, שִׂיא, מַשְׂאֵת.

נְשָׂא Chald. 1. *to take.* Ezra 5:15.

2. *to take* or *carry away,* spoken of the wind. Dan. 2:35.

Ithpa. *to lift one's self against* any one, construed with עַל. Ezra 4:19.

נִשֵּׂאת f. strictly Part. Niph. *a gift;* (comp. נָשָׂא Pi.) 2 Sam. 19:43.

I. **נָשַׂג** in Kal not used.

Hiph. הִשִּׂיג 1. *to reach unto, to overtake.* Gen. 31:25. 2 Sam. 15:14. Gen. 47:9. Lev. 26:5.

2. *to fall upon* or *befal* any one, spoken of a blessing or curse, Deut. 28:2, 15, 45. of iniquity, Ps. 40:13. of anger, Ps. 69:25.

3. *to acquire, obtain.* Is. 35:10. 51:11. *My hand can acquire* any thing, a frequent phrase for *I am able to get* it, Lev. 14:31 ff. 25:26. Ezek. 46:7. Construed with לְ, Lev. 5:11. Used absolutely for *to become rich,* Lev. 25:47.

4. causat. *to bring,* e. g. one's hand to his mouth. 1 Sam. 14:26. (Comp. the kindred מָצָא.)

II. **נָשַׂג** Hiph. הִשִּׂיג i. q. הִסִּיג *to remove* (boundaries). Job 24:2.

נְשׂוּאָה f. verbal from נָשָׂא, dec. X. *what is carried, a load, burden.* Is. 46:1.

נָשִׂיא m. strictly part. pass. from נָשָׂא, liter. *elatus,* but used to designate

1. *a prince.* 1 K. 11:34. Spoken of the king, Ezek. 12:10. 45:7 ff. 46:2 ff. particularly of the princes of the tribes of Israel, Num. 7:11 ff. or of the Ismaelites, Gen. 17:20. Among the Israelites, these were also called נְשִׂיאֵי הָעֵדָה *the princes of the congregation,* Num. 4:34. נְשִׂיאֵי הָאָבוֹת, 1 K. 8:1. 2 Chr. 5:2 instead of נְשִׂיאֵי בָּתֵּי הָאָבוֹת. Also used

of the family chiefs, Num. 3:24, 30, 35. Hence Eleazer was called נְשִׂיא נְשִׂיאֵי הַלֵּוִי the chief of the chiefs of Levi, Num. 3:32. comp. also 1 Chr. 7:41.

2. plur. נְשִׂיאִים vapours, which form clouds. Jer. 10:13. 51:16. Hence clouds, Ps. 135:7. Prov. 25:14. (Arab. نَشَأ and نَشْء nubes elata seu primum concrescens.)

נָשַׂק in Kal not used.

Hiph. הִשִּׂיק to kindle. Is. 44:15. Ezek. 39:9.

Niph. to be kindled. Ps. 78:21. (In Chald. אַסִּיק idem.)

נָשׁ found only in the plur. נָשִׁים f. women, employed as the plural of אִשָּׁה, but derived by abbreviation from אֲנָשִׁים. (Arab. نِسَاء, نِسْوَة women.)

I. **נָשָׁא** in Kal not used; perhaps to err, wander, (kindred with נָשָׁה to forget.) Hence in Syr. ܢܫܝܐ an error.

Hiph. הִשִּׁיא to lead astray; hence

1. to deceive; construed with a dative, 2 K. 18:29. with an accus. e.g. in the parallel passage, 2 Chr. 32:15. 2 K. 19:10. Jer. 37:9 אַל תַּשִּׁאוּ נַפְשֹׁתֵיכֶם deceive not yourselves. Ps. 55:16. Keri יַשִּׁי מָוֶת עָלֵימוֹ let death deceive (and break in suddenly) upon them.

2. to seduce. Gen. 3:13. Jer. 49:16.

Niph. to be deceived. Is. 19:13.

II. **נָשָׁא** i.q. נָשָׁה no. II. to lend on usury, construed with בְּ. Neh. 5:7. Hence נֹשֵׁא בוֹ Is. 24:2. and נֹשֶׁא 1 Sam. 22:2. a creditor.

Hiph. to press, spoken of a creditor, construed with בְּ. Ps. 89:23.

Deriv. מַשָּׁא, מַשָּׁאָה.

נָשַׁב i.q. נָשַׁם and נָשַׁף to blow, spoken of the wind. Is. 40:7.

Hiph. 1. to let blow. Ps. 147:18.

2. to drive away by blowing. Gen. 15:11.

I. **נָשָׁה** 1. to forget. Lam. 3:17.

2. to forsake, neglect. Jer. 23:39.

Niph. i.q. Kal, (strictly pass. of Hiph.) Is. 44:21.

Pi. to cause to forget, construed with two accus. Gen. 41:51.

Hiph. הִשָּׁה i.q. Pi. Job 39:17. 11:6 כִּי יַשֶּׁה לְךָ אֱלוֹהַּ מֵעֲוֺנֶךָ that God causes thee to forget of thine iniquity, i.e. that he remits part of it.

II. **נָשָׁה** i.q. נָשָׁא no. II.

1. to loan to any one, mutuum dare, construed with בְּ of the person. Deut. 24:11. Neh. 5:10. Jer. 15:10.—נֹשֶׁה a creditor, 2 K. 4:1. Ps. 129:11.

2. to receive as usury, construed with בְּ of the person. Neh. 5:11 the per cent אֲשֶׁר אַתֶּם נֹשִׁים בָּהֶם which ye have taken from them. Part. נֹשֶׁה an usurer, Ex. 22:24.

3. to borrow, mutuum accipere, construed with an accus. by which it is distinguished from no. 1. Jer. 15:10 לֹא נָשִׁיתִי וְלֹא נָשׁוּ בִי I have borrowed nothing of them, and they have loaned me nothing. Is. 24:2 כַּנֹּשֶׁה כַּאֲשֶׁר נֹשֵׁא בוֹ as the debtor, so the creditor.

Hiph. i.q. Kal no. 1. construed with בְּ, to lend or loan to any one. Deut. 15:2. 24:10.

נְשִׁי m. dec. VI. 1. a debt, debitum. 2 K. 4:7. Root נָשָׁה no. II.

נְשִׁיָּה f. forgetfulness. Ps. 88:13. Root נָשָׁה no. I.

נָשֶׁה m. Gen. 32:33. i.q. Arab. نَسًا nervus seu tendo, qui per femur et crus ad talos fertur, prob. nervus ischiaticus.

נְשִׁיקָה f. verbal from נָשַׁק, dec. X. a kiss. Cant. 1:2. Prov. 27:6.

נָשַׁךְ, fut. יִשֹּׁךְ (Ecc. 10:11.) and יִשַּׁךְ (Prov. 23:32.)

1. to bite; spoken of serpents, Gen. 49:17. Num. 21:6 ff. of men, Mic. 3:5.

2. metaphorically to oppress, vex. Hab. 2:7.

3. to take as usury. Deut. 23:20. See Hiph.

Pi. i.q. Kal no. 1. Num. 21:6. Jer. 8:17.

Hiph. הִשִּׁיךְ to lend on usury, construed with a dative of the person. Deut. 23:21. Hence

נֶשֶׁךְ m. verbal from נָשַׁךְ, dec. VI. in-

terest, usury. Ps. 15:5. Ezek. 18:8, 13. שׂוּם נֶשֶׁךְ עַל *to lay usury on* any one, Ex. 22:24. (Comp. in Aram. נְשַׁךְ, نكت *to bite,* whence נִכְסָא *usury;* in Arab. قرض *to gnaw,* conj. III. *to take usury.* So in Lucan, I. 171. *usura vorax.*)

נִשְׁכָּה dec. XII. b. i. q. לִשְׁכָּה *a small chamber* or *cell* in the temple. Neh. 3:30. 12:44. 13:7.

נָשַׁל, fut. יִשַּׁל (intrans.)

1. *to put off,* e. g. the shoe. Ex. 3:5. Josh. 5:15.

2. *to cast out* a nation from a country. Deut. 7:1, 22.

3. *to slip off.* Deut. 19:5 וְנָשַׁל הַבַּרְזֶל מִן הָעֵץ *and the iron shall slip off from the handle.*

4. intrans. *to fall off,* as berries from an olive-tree. Fut. יִשַּׁל Deut. 28:40.

נָשַׁם, fut. אֶשֹּׁם Is. 42:14. *to breathe,* hence *to puff, to be angry.* (But the fut. אֶשֹּׁם may come from שָׁמַם.) Hence

נְשָׁמָה f. verbal from נָשַׁם, dec. XI. c.

1. *breath;* particularly (1.) *the angry breath* or *anger* of God. Is. 30:33. Ps. 18:16. (2.) his *life-giving* or *inspiring breath.* Job 32:5. 33:4. 26:4.

2. *breath, the vital principle in the human body;* (comp. נֶפֶשׁ no. 2.) Gen. 2:7. Job 27:3.

3. *a living being,* i. q. נֶפֶשׁ no. 3. Deut. 20:16. Josh. 10:40.

4. *the soul.* Prov. 20:27.

נִשְׁמָא Chald. *the breath of life, life.* Dan. 5:23.

נָשַׁף *to breathe, blow.* Ex. 15:10. Is. 40:24. Comp. by transposition נָפַשׁ.

נֶשֶׁף m. with suff. נִשְׁפִּי, dec. VI. h.

1. *twilight.* 2 K. 7:5, 7. Jer. 13:16. (1.) *morning, twilight, dawn.* 1 Sam. 30:17. Job 7:4. (2.) *evening twilight.* Job 24:15. Prov. 7:9. (If derived from נָשַׁף, it would denote strictly *the cool of the day,* i. q. רוּחַ הַיּוֹם Gen. 3:8. hence *the evening.*)

2. also perhaps *darkness,* as כּוֹכְבֵי נִשְׁפּוֹ Job 3:9, and *night,* Is. 21:4. Comp. נשׁף.

נָשַׁק, fut. יִשַּׁק and יִשַּׁק (1 K. 19:20.) strictly *to join, arrange.* See Hiph. (Arab. نسق *to arrange.*) Hence

1. *to put in order, to arm,* (whence נֶשֶׁק.) 2 Chr. 17:17 נֹשְׁקֵי קֶשֶׁת *armed with the bow.* Ps. 78:9.

2. *to kiss, os adjungere ori,* construed with a dative, Gen. 27:26. 2 Sam. 15:5. with a suff. Cant. 1:2. with אֶת, 1 Sam. 20:41. Ps. 85:11 צֶדֶק וְשָׁלוֹם נָשָׁקוּ *righteousness and peace kiss each other.* (Parall. *meet together.*) Also *to kiss* the hand, as a mode of adoration, Job 31:27. comp. 1 K. 19:18. Hos. 13:2. *to kiss,* as an act of homage, Ps. 2:12. The meaning is uncertain Gen. 41:40, where it is said of Joseph, עַל פִּיךָ יִשַּׁק כָּל־עַמִּי perhaps *all my people shall kiss thy mouth,* i. e. they shall do thee homage; if so, this mark of homage consisted in kissing the mouth, (as, according to some Rabbins, was the custom among the Indians and Ethiopians.) Or, *at thy command shall all my people arm themselves.* Others: *my people shall run,* as if from שָׁקַק.)

Pi. i. q. Kal no. 2. *to kiss.* Gen. 31:28, 55. Ps. 2:12.

Hiph. *to touch,* construed with אֶל. Ezek. 3:13. Comp. 1:9. where the same idea is expressed by חָבַר.

Deriv. out of course מַשָּׁק.

נֵשֶׁק and נֶשֶׁק m. verbal from נָשַׁק.

1. *armour.* 1 K. 10:25. Ezek. 39:9, 10. Ps. 140:8 בְּיוֹם נָשֶׁק *in the day of armour,* i. e. of battle.

2. *an armory, arsenal.* Neh. 3:19. Perhaps the same building which in 1 K. 7:2, is called בֵּית יַעַר הַלְּבָנוֹן *the house of the forest of Lebanon* wherein Solomon laid up much splendid armour, see 1 K. 10:17. Comp. Is. 22:8.

נֶשֶׁר m. dec. VI. h. *an eagle.* (Arab. نسر, Syr. ܢܫܪܐ *idem.*) Deut. 32:11. Ezek. 17:3, 10. In common life, this word among the Hebrews included also *the vulture.* So in Job 39:27. Prov. 30:17. (comp. Mat. 24:28.) where it is said to eat carrion, and in Mic. 1:16.

where it is said to have a bald head, (*vultur barbatus*, Linn.) Comp. Ps. 103:5. So the Greeks, Romans, and Arabians; see Bocharti Hieroz. P. II. p. 312ff.—Ps. 103:5 *so that thy youth renews itself like the eagle*, for the eagle often changes his feathers, as the snake does his skin.

נְשַׁר, plur. נִשְׁרִין, Chald. *idem*. Dan. 4:30. 7:4.

נָשַׁת *to dry up, to become dry*, spoken of water. Hence Is. 41:17 לְשׁוֹנָם בַּצָּמָא נָשָׁתָּה *their tongue becomes dry with thirst*. Jer. 51:30 *their strength is dried up*.

Niph. *to become dry*, spoken of water, Is. 19:5. We find in the same signification נִתַּשׁ Jer. 18:14.

נִשְׁתְּוָן m. in Heb. and Chald. a *letter*. Ezra 4:7, 18, 23. 5:5. 7:11. Prob. from the Pers. نبشتن nobishten, also novishen, nevisten *to write*, by a transposition of the dental ת.

נָתַח found only in Pi. נִתַּח *to cut in pieces*, particularly an animal body. Ex. 29:17. Lev. 1:6, 12. 8:20.

נֵתַח, plur. נְתָחִים, verbal from נָתַח, dec. VI. i. *a piece cut off*, particularly of flesh. Lev. 1:8ff. Ezek. 24:4.

נָתִיב m. dec. III. a. and נְתִיבָה f. dec. X. plur. נְתִיבִים.

1. strictly an adj. *beaten, trodden*, (from נתב in Arab. *to raise*, then *to beat* or *tread* a path; comp. סָלַל.)—דֶּרֶךְ נְתִיבָה *a beaten path*, Prov. 12:28. and without דֶּרֶךְ, *idem*, Judg. 5:6. (Oppos. *a by-path*.) Hence

2. *a way, path* generally, only in poetry. Job 18:10. 28:7. 41:24. נְתִיבוֹת בֵּיתוֹ *the paths to his dwelling*, Job 38:20.

נְתִינִים masc. plur. *the devoted, consecrated*, (comp. particularly Num. 8:19.) hence *servants of the temple* or *of the sanctuary*, who performed the inferior services in the same. Ezra 8:17, 20. Neh. 3:31. 7:46, 60, 73. 11:3, 21. In Chald. Ezra 7:24.

נָתַךְ found only in the fut. יִתַּךְ, (kindred with נָתַן,) *to be poured out, to flow*. Job 3:24. Metaphorically spoken of anger, 2 Chr. 12:7. 34:25. Jer. 42:18. 44:6. of a curse, Dan. 9:11. of punishment, verse 27.

Niph. i. q. Kal, but found only in the pret.

1. i. q. Kal, *to be poured out*, spoken of water, rain, Ex. 9:33. of anger, 2 Chr. 34:21. Jer. 7:20.

2. *to melt, dissolve*. (See the Aram. Ezek. 22:21. 24:11.

Hiph. הִתִּיךְ, once infin. הַנְתִּיךְ (Ezek. 22:20.)

1. *to pour out;* e. g. milk, Job 10:10. money, 2 K. 22:9.

2. *to melt*. Ezek. 22:20.

Hoph. pass. *to be melted*. Ezek. 22:22.

Deriv. הִתּוּךְ.

נָתַן fut. יִתֵּן, וַיִּתֵּן, imper. תֵּן, תְּנָה, infin. absol. נָתוֹן, const. תֵּת (for תֶּנֶת,) with suff. תִּתִּי, rarely נְתֹן.

1. *to give;* construed with a dative of the person, rarely with a suffix instead of the dative, Josh. 15:19 נְתַתָּנִי *thou hast given to me*. Impers. Prov. 13:10 רַק בְּזָדוֹן יִתֵּן מַצָּה *only from arrogance arises* (Germ. *es gibt*,) *contention*.—מִי יִתֵּן *who will give?* expressive of a wish, for *O that some one would give*, Judg. 9:29. Ps. 55:7. Hence merely as a periphrasis for the Lat. *utinam, O that*, Ex. 16:3 מִי יִתֵּן מוּתֵנוּ *O that we had died*. Deut. 28:67 מִי יִתֵּן עֶרֶב *O that it were evening*.

2. *to lay, set, place*. Gen. 1:17. 9:13. E. g. *to lay* snares, Ps. 119:110. *to place* bulwarks, Ezek. 26:8.—נָתַן בְּרִית *to establish a covenant*, Gen. 9:12 נָתַן לִפְנֵי *to lay before* any one, 1 K. 9:7. נָתַן לִבּוֹ לְ *to give one's heart to* any thing, i. e. to determine to do it, Ecc. 1:13, 17. 8:16. or to give attention to it, Ecc. 7:21. 8:9. Particularly נָתַן עַל *to place* or *appoint over* any thing, Gen. 41:41, 43. Deut. 17:15.

3. *to make, to do*, i. q. שׂוּם, עָשָׂה.—נָתַן מוֹפֵת *to work a miracle*, Ex. 7:9. Particularly *to make into* any thing, construed with two accus. Gen. 17:4. Ex.

7:1. with לְ before the predicate, Gen. 17:20. 48:4. Jer. 1:5. more rarely with בְּ, Is. 41:2.

4. *to permit, allow, grant,* (derived immediately from signif. no. 1.) construed with an accus. of the person and an infin. of the action, (with and without לְ.) Gen. 20:6 עַל־כֵּן לֹא נְתַתִּיךָ לִנְגֹּעַ אֵלֶיהָ *therefore have I not permitted thee to touch her.* 31:7. Ex. 3:19. Judg. 1:34. 15:1. 1 Sam. 18:2. Job 9:18. Only once with a dative of the person, 2 Chr. 20:10.

5. *to give forth, yield, edere;* e. g. a smell, Cant. 1:12. particularly with קוֹל *the voice,* (see קוֹל.)—Job 1:22 וְלֹא נָתַן תִּפְלָה לֵאלֹהִים *and he uttered nothing rash against God.* Comp. נָתַן תֹּף *to strike the timbrel,* Ps. 81:3.

6. *to hold, regard;* construed with בְּ. 1 K. 10:27 וַיִּתֵּן אֶת־הַכֶּסֶף כָּאֲבָנִים *and he regarded silver as stones.* Gen. 42:30. with לִפְנֵי, 1 Sam. 1:16.

Niph. pass. of Kal, *to be given, placed, made,* etc.

Hoph. only in the fut. יֻתַּן, *idem.*

Note. In the preterite, the final Nun assimilates itself to the afformative, hence נָתַתִּי, נָתַתָּ. Once occurs תַּתָּה 2 Sam. 22:41. for נָתַתָּה, like רַד Judg. 19:11. for יָרַד.

Deriv. מַתַּת, מַתָּנָה, מַתָּן, נְתִינִים.

נְתַן Chald. found only in the fut. יִנְתֵּן and infin. מִנְתַּן, *to give,* as in Heb. Ezra 4:13. 7:20. The deficient tenses are supplied from יְהַב. Deriv. מַתְּנָא.

נָתַס *to tear up, proscindere* terram, kindred with נָתַץ and נָתַשׁ. Job 30:13 נָתְסוּ נְתִיבָתִי *they tear up* or *destroy my path.* (4 MSS. read נָתְצוּ, which gives the same sense.)

נָתַע an Aramean form for נָתַץ *to strike out* (the teeth). See the letter ע.

Niph. pass. Job 4:10.

נָתַץ, fut. יִתֹּץ. 1. *to tear down, to destroy;* e. g. houses, statues, altars. Lev. 24:45. Judg. 6:30ff. 8:17.

2. *to destroy,* e. g. persons. Job 19:10. Ps. 52:7.

3. *to break* or *strike out,* e. g. teeth. Ps. 58:7. Comp. נָתַע.

Pi. i. q. Kal no 1. 2 Chr. 31:1. 33:3.

Niph. Pu. and Hoph. pass. of Kal no. 1. Jer. 4:26. Judg. 6:28. *To fall down,* spoken of rocks, Nah. 1:6.

נָתַק 1. *to pluck* or *tear off.* Jer. 22:24.

2. *to draw off,* (from a place,) in war. Judg. 20:32. See Niph. and Hiph.

3. Part. pass. נָתוּק *castratus, avulsis testiculis.* Lev. 22:24.

Pi. *to tear up* or *asunder,* e. g. roots, Ezek. 17:9. fetters, Ps. 2:3. 107:14. a yoke, Is. 58:6.—Ezek. 23:34 *thou shalt tear thine own breasts thereon,* i.e. on the sherds.

Hiph. 1. *to draw off,* i. q. Kal no. 2. Josh. 8:6.

2. *to separate.* Jer. 12:3.

Niph. *to be broken,* e. g. spoken of a cord or string. Is. 5:27. Jer. 10:20. Metaphorically Job 17:11.

2. *to be torn away,* from a dwelling. Job 18:14.—Josh. 4:18. *and when the soles of the feet of the priests were lifted up* (and placed) *on the dry ground.*

3. *to be plucked away, withdrawn.* Jer. 6:29. Josh. 8:16.

Hoph. הָנְתַּק i. q. Niph. no. 3. Judg. 20:31.

נֶתֶק m. 1. *the scall, the leprosy of the head and beard.* Lev. 13:30ff.

2. *one infected with the scall.* Lev. 13:33. See נֶגַע no. 3. Root Arab. نتق *to pull out the hair;* intrans. *to lose the hair.*

נָתַר, fut. יִתַּר, *to spring, leap;* hence *to quake* or *tremble,* as the heart, Job 37:1.

Pi. *idem,* spoken of the locust. Lev. 11:21.

Hiph. 1. *to cause to quake.* Hab. 3:6.

2. as in Chald. *to strip* or *break off,* (a yoke.) Is. 58:6. Hence הַתִּיר אֲסוּרִים *to set prisoners free,* Ps. 105:20. 146:7. Job 6:9 יַתֵּר יָדוֹ וִיבַצְּעֵנִי *O that he would loose his hand,* (which is now, as it were, tied,) *and destroy me.* In 2 Sam.

22 : 33, this verb makes no sense. Probably the reading is corrupted.

נְתַר Chald. *to fall off*, spoken of leaves or fruit. Aph. *to shake* or *strip off*, e. g. leaves. Dan. 4 : 11.

נֶתֶר m. the νίτρον or λίτρον of the Greeks, *the mineral alkali*, (comp. בֹּרִית *the vegetable alkali.*) Prov. 25 : 20. It is mixed with oil and used for soap in the east to the present day. So Jer. 2 : 22. See Beckmann's Beyträge zur Geschichte der Erfindungen, Th. 4. p. 15 ff. J. D. Michaëlis De Nitro, § 10.

נָתַשׁ, fut. יִתּשׁ.

1. *to root out*, strictly plants, (see Hoph. Ezek. 19 : 12.) hence *to destroy*, e. g. a city, Ps. 9 : 7. idols, Mic. 5 : 13.

2. metaphorically *to drive out* of a country. Comp. the oppos. נָטַע. Deut. 29 : 27. 1 K. 14 : 15. Jer. 24 : 6 וּנְטַעְתִּים וְלֹא אֶתּוֹשׁ *and I will plant them, and not root them out.*

Niph. 1. pass. of Kal no. 2. Jer. 18 : 14. 31 : 9. Am. 9 : 15. Spoken of the destruction of a kingdom, Dan. 11 : 4.

2. i. q. נָשַׁת (Is. 19 : 5.) *to dry up*, spoken of water. Jer. 18 : 14.

Hoph. pass. Ezek. 19 : 12.

ס

Samech, the 15th letter of the alphabet, and as a numerical sign denoting 60. The name סָמֶךְ is perhaps i. q. Syr. ܣܡܟܐ *consessus, triclinium*, and has reference to the circular form of the common square character. In pronunciation, it probably differed nothing from שׂ.

The Arabians have no Samech, but use Sin س in its stead. The Syrians have only the Samech. The Hebrews, speaking a dialect in many respects intermediate, have both of these letters. In most cases the orthography is fixed, and a word is spelt either uniformly with שׂ or uniformly with ס; e. g. שָׂדֶה, שׂוּם, and סוּר, סָבַב; comp. e. g. סָכַל *to be foolish*, and שָׂכַל *to be wise;* רָמַס *to tread down*, and רָמַשׂ *to be stirring*. In some words, however, שׂ and ס are used promiscuously; e. g. כַּעַס and כַּעַשׂ *vexation;* סכך and שׂכך *to be interwoven;* מְסוּכָה and מְשׂוּכָה *a thorn-hedge*. In Chaldaic ס is often used, where שׂ is retained in Hebrew; e. g. שְׂאֹר Chald. סְאוֹר *leaven;* שָׂבַר Chald. סְבַר *to wait for;* etc. In Syr. ܣ is used for both of these letters.

In the collation of Heb. with Arab. for the Heb. ס and שׂ, we often find in Arabic שׁ ش, but not in the majority of cases, as has been sometimes falsely asserted.

This commutation is more rare in Hebrew and Aramean; e. g. סִרְיוֹן and שִׁרְיוֹן *a coat of mail;* אֶשְׁכֹּל Aram. סִתְּלָא *a cluster of grapes;* כָּנַס and כָּנַשׁ *to collect;* שָׁמַר Chald. סְמַר Ithpa. *to guard;* שָׁפַךְ and סָפַח *to pour out*, etc. In Judg. 12 : 6, it is mentioned as a peculiarity of the Ephraimites that they pronounced ס instead of שׁ. This letter is also found interchanged with ז and צ, see under these letters.

סְאָה, plur. סְאִים, f. *measure.* (See Is. 27 : 8. below.) Particularly a definite measure for grain; containing according to the Rabbins the third part of an ephah, according to Jerome on Mat. 13 : 33. a modius and a half. Gen. 18 : 6. 1 Sam. 25 : 18. Dual סָאתַיִם *2 seahs*, 2 K. 7 : 1, 16. a Syriac contraction, like סָאתַיִם for סְאָתַיִם.—Is. 27 : 8 בְּסַאסְּאָה is prob. a contraction of בְּסְאָה סְאָה, (with Dagesh forte conjunctivum, after the analogy of מַלָּכֶם for מַה־לָּכֶם,) hence liter. *measure by measure, peu à peu*, i. e. moderately; (comp. לְמִשְׁפָּט Jer. 30 : 11. 46 : 28.) So Aqu. Symm. Theodot. Syr. Chald.—From the form סָאתָא, the Greek σάτον (in the Sept. N. T. and Josephus) is derived.

סְאוֹן m. *a shoe*, or rather *greave* of the warrior, *ocrea, caliga.* (Chald. סֵין, Syr. ܣܐܘܢܐ.) Is. 9 : 4 כָּל־סְאוֹן סֹאֵן *every greave of the armed with greaves*, i. e. of the warrior. Root סָאַן.

סָאַן *calceavit.* Only in the part. סֹאֵן. See the preceding article.

סַאסְּאָה Is. 27:8. See סְאָה.

סָבָא *to drink to excess.* Is. 56:12. Part. סֹבֵא *a drunkard,* Deut. 21:20. Part. pass. סָבוּא *drunken, potus,* Nah. 1:10.

סָבָא Ezek. 23:42 Keth. i. q. סוֹבְאִים in the Keri.

סֹבֶא m. verbal from סָבָא, dec. VI. p.

1. *wine,* only in poetry. Is. 1:22. Nah. 1:10.

2. *a banquet.* Hos. 4:18.

סְבָא proper name of a people derived from Cush (Gen. 10:7.) and their territory. According to Josephus, (Antiq. Jud. II. 10. 2.) probably *Meroë,* a province of Ethiopia, surrounded by the branches of the Nile. Is. 43:3. Ps. 72:10. (where סְבָא is spoken of as a rich people.) The gentile noun in the plur. is סְבָאִים Is. 45:14. where they are represented as of a great stature; comp. Herod. 3:20 concerning the Ethiopians. See Michaëlis Spicileg. Geogr. Hebræor. Ext. T. I. p. 177 ff. and his Supplem. p. 1707.

סָבַב, pret. סַבּוּ and סַבּוֹתִי, infin. סְבֹב and סֹב, fut. יָסֹב, also יִסֹּב, plur. יָסֹבּוּ.

1. *to turn.* 1 Sam. 15:27. Construed with לְ, 1 K. 2:15. with אֶל, Num. 36:7. with עַל, Hab. 2:16. *to* any one. Also construed with מִן, מֵעַל, Gen. 42. 24. *from* any one. Sometimes *to be added* or *joined,* 1 Sam. 22:17, 18. 2 Sam. 18:15, 30. When spoken of inanimate things, *to be brought,* 1 Sam. 5:8. See Hiph. no. 1. (2.)

2. *to turn about, to turn back.* 2 K. 9:18, 19. Cant. 2:17. Hence adverbially, like שׁוּב, Ps. 71:21 וְתִסֹּב תְּנַחֲמֵנִי *thou wilt comfort me again.*

3. *to go about* in a place, as it were, *to be constantly turning one's self.* Cant. 3:3. 5:7. 2 Chr. 17:9. 23:2. Construed with an accus. *to go through,* Is. 23:16. 1 Sam. 7:16.

4. *to go round* a place, construed with an accus. Deut. 2:3. Josh. 6:3, 4, 7. sometimes for the purpose of avoiding it, Num. 21:4. Judg. 11:18.

5. *to surround, encompass.* Ps. 18:6. 22:17. Also in a hostile manner, Ecc. 9:14. and then construed with אֶל, 2 K. 8:21. and with עַל, Job 16:13. Judg. 20:5. As an adv. Gen. 37:7 וְהִנֵּה תְסֻבֶּינָה אֲלֻמֹּתֵיכֶם וַתִּשְׁתַּחֲוֶיןָ *and behold your sheaves did obeisance round about.* Particularly

6. *to surround* or *sit at* a table. 1 Sam. 16:11. לֹא נָסֹב *we will not sit down.* Comp. מֵסַב.

7. *to be changed,* pass. of Pi. Hiph. no. 4. construed with בְּ. Zech. 14:10.

8. *to be the occasion of* any thing. (Arab. سبب *to occasion;* Talmud. סִבָּה *cause, occasion.*) 1 Sam. 22:22 אָנֹכִי סַבֹּתִי בְּכָל נֶפֶשׁ *I have been the occasion to every soul* (*lost*), i. e. I have caused their death.

Niph. נָסַב, fut. יִסַּב, יִסֹּבּוּ.

1. i. q. Kal no. 1. *to turn.* Ezek. 1:9. Spoken of boundaries, Num. 34:4, 5. Josh. 15:3. Jer. 6:12 נָסַבּוּ בָתֵּיהֶם לַאֲחֵרִים *their houses shall turn to others.* Comp. in Kal Num. 36:7.

2. *to surround,* i. q. Kal no. 5. Judg. 19:22. Construed with עַל, *to surround in a hostile manner,* Gen. 19:4. Josh. 7:9.

Pi. סִבֵּב *to change, alter.* Once 2 Sam. 14:20.

Po. סוֹבֵב 1. i. q. Kal no. 3. *to go about.* Cant. 3:2. Construed with an accus. *to go through,* Ps. 59:7, 15.

2. *to go round, compass,* (a place,) construed with an accus. Ps. 26:6. with עַל, Ps. 55:11.

3. *to surround, enclose.* Jon. 2:4, 6. Ps. 7:8. Construed with two accus. Ps. 32:7, 10. Particularly *to surround* in order to protect, Deut. 32:10. (comp. Hom. Il. I. 37.) Jer. 31:22 נְקֵבָה תְּסוֹבֵב גָּבֶר *the woman protects the man.*

Hiph. הֵסֵב, fut. יָסֵב.

1. causat. of Kal no. 1. *to cause to turn about.* Ex. 13:18. Hence (1.) *to turn about.* 1 K. 8:14. 2 K. 20:2. 2 Sam. 3:12 לְהָסֵב אֵלֶיךָ אֶת־כָּל־יִשְׂרָאֵל *to turn*

about all Israel to thee. 1 Chr. 10:14. 1 K. 18:37 הֲסִבֹּתָ אֶת־לִבָּם אֲחֹרַנִּית *thou hast turned their heart back again.* (2.) *to bring about.* 1 Sam. 5:8 וַיַּסֵּבּוּ אֶת־אֲרוֹן אֱלֹהֵי יִשְׂרָאֵל *and they brought about (thither) the ark of the God of Israel.* Verses 9, 10. 1 Chr. 13:3. 2 Sam. 20:12.

2. i. q. Kal no. 4. *to go round* a place. Josh. 6:11.

3. *to surround*, i. q. Kal no. 5. Ps. 140:10. Causat. *to cause to surround, to carry round*, as a wall, 2 Chr. 14:6.

4. *to change, alter;* comp. Kal no. 7. 2 K. 23:34 וַיַּסֵּב אֶת־שְׁמוֹ יְהוֹיָקִים *and he changed his name into Jehoiakim.* 24:17. (Comp. Hoph. Num. 32:38.)

Hoph. הוּסַב, fut. יוּסַב.

1. *to turn*, spoken of the valves of a door, Ezek. 41:24. *to roll*, spoken of the threshing waggon, Is. 28:27.

2. *to be surrounded.* Ex. 28:11. 39:6, 13.

3. *to be changed.* See Hiph. no. 4.

Deriv. מֵסַב, מוּסָב, סָבִיב, נְסִבָּה, סִבָּה.

סִבָּה f. verbal from סָבַב, *a turn of events.* 1 K. 12:15. i. q. נְסִבָּה in the parallel passage, 2 Chr. 10:15.

סָבִיב m. verbal from סָבַב, dec. III. a. as a subst. *circuit.* 1 Chr. 11:8. Hence מִסָּבִיב Num. 16:27. and סָבִיב as an adv. *round about*, Gen. 23:17. Ex. 16:13. Also doubled סָבִיב סָבִיב Ezek. 40:5ff. סָבִיב לְ as a prep. *round about* any thing, as סָבִיב לַמִּשְׁכָּן *round about the tent*, Ex. 40:33. Num. 1:53.

Plur. m. סְבִיבִים 1. *persons round about, neighbours.* Jer. 48:17, 39.

2. *country round about, les environs.* Jer. 33:3 בִּסְבִיבֵי יְרוּשָׁלַםִ *in the environs of Jerusalem.* Ps. 76:12. 89:8. 97:2.

3. as an adv. *round about.* Ps. 50:3 סְבִיבָיו נִשְׂעֲרָה מְאֹד *it is very tempestuous round about him.* Jer. 46:14.

Plur. fem. סְבִיבוֹת.

1. *country round about.* Jer. 17:26. Num. 22:4. Dan. 9:16.

2. in the const. state used as a prep. *round about.* Num. 11:24 סְבִיבוֹת הָאֹהֶל *round about the tent.* Ezek. 6:5. Ps. 79:3. With suff. סְבִיבוֹתַי *round about me*, etc.

סָבַךְ *to interweave, fold together*, as branches. Part. pass. Nah. 1:10.

Pu. Job 8:17. (Arab. شبك *idem.*)

סְבָךְ m. (with Kamets impure) verbal from סָבַךְ, *branches interwoven, a thicket.* Gen. 22:13. Ps. 74:5.

סֹבֶךְ, with suff. סֻבְּכוֹ (with Dagesh forte euphonic), verbal from סָבַךְ, dec. VI. o. Jer. 4:7. *idem.* Plur. סִבְכֵי הַיַּעַר *thickets of the wood*, (from a sing. form סְבַךְ,) Is. 9:17. 10:34. The same word is written with שׂ שׂוֹבֶךְ and שׂוֹבְכָה.

סַבְּכָא f. Chald. Dan. 3:5. and שַׂבְּכָא verses 7, 10, 15. *sambuca*, in Greek σαμβύκη, a three-cornered stringed instrument, similar to the harp. (Comp. נֵבֶל.) Comp. Vitruv. vi. 1. x. 22. The Chaldaic word appears to be borrowed from the Greek, like סוּמְפֹּנְיָה.

סָבַל, fut. יִסְבֹּל, *to bear*, particularly a heavy load. Is. 46:4, 7. Gen. 49:15. Metaphorically *to bear* the guilt of any one, Is. 53:11. Lam. 5:7. (In Chald. and Syr. *idem.*)

Pu. part. *loaded*, hence *fruitful, prolific*, spoken of cattle, Ps. 144:14.

Hithpa. הִסְתַּבֵּל *to be burdensome.* Ecc. 12:5.

סְבַל Chald. i. q. Heb. סָבַל, also *to lift up*, (comp. נָשָׂא,) *to erect.*

Poal pass. *to be erected.* Ezra 6:3.

סַבָּל m. verbal from סָבַל, *a porter.* 2 Chr. 2:1, 17. 34:13.—1 K. 5:29 [5:15] נֹשֵׂא סַבָּל where the two words are in apposition, or else the latter must be pointed סֵבֶל.

סֵבֶל m. verbal from סָבַל, *a burden.* 1 K. 11:28. Ps. 81:7.

סֹבֶל with suff. סֻבֳּלוֹ (with Dagesh forte euphonic, like סֻבְּכוֹ,) *a burden.* Is. 10:27. 14:27. עֹל סֻבֳּלוֹ *the yoke which he bears*, Is. 9:3.

סְבָלָה or **סִבְלָה** f. found only in the plur. const. סִבְלוֹת *burdens, oppressive service*, Ex. 1:11. 2:11. 5:4, 5. 6:6, 7.

סִבֹּלֶת the Ephraimitish pronunciation for שִׁבֹּלֶת *an ear of corn.* Judg. 12 : 6.

סְבַר in Syr. *to believe,* in Chald. *to hope.* Somewhat differently Dan. 7 : 25 יִסְבַּר לְהַשְׁנָיָה *he thinketh to change,* like the Heb. חָשַׁב לְ. Comp. Gen. 37 : 8 Targ.

סִבְרַיִם found only Ezek. 47 : 16. a city of Syria, between Damascus and Hemath.

סַבְתָּה Gen. 10 : 7. (21 MSS. read סַבְתָּא,) and סַבְתָּא 1 Chr. 1 : 9. a people or country of the Cushites. Most probably *Sabatha* or *Sabota,* a considerable city in Arabia Felix, according to Pliny VI. 28. § 32. the principal city of the Atramites, a tribe of Sabeans, on the Red Sea, Comp. XII. 14. § 32 *thus collectum Sabota camelis convehitur.* Michaëlis (Supplem. p. 1712) proposes also for comparison سبتة the Arabic name for *Ceuta,* (in Moses Chorenensis *Septa,*) on the gulf of Cadiz.

סַבְתְּכָה and סַבְתְּכָא in the same passages, but far more uncertain. Targ. זנגאי, דנגאי prob. meaning *Zingis,* a city in the extremity of Ethiopia.

סג, plur. סִיגִים, see סִיגִים.

סָגַד, fut. יִסְגֹּד, *to fall down, to worship;* construed with לְ, (Is. 44 : 15, 17, 19. 46 : 6.) used only in reference to idols.

סְגִד, fut. יִסְגֻּד, Chald. i. q. Heb. סָגַד, construed with לְ. Dan. 2 : 46. 3 : 5 ff. (Syr. ܣܓܕ. Arab. سجد *idem,* whence مسجد *a mosque.*

סְגֻלָּה f. dec. X. *a possession, property, treasure.* 1 Chr. 29 : 3. Ecc. 2 : 8. סְגֻלַּת יְהֹוָה used frequently of Israel, Ex. 19 : 5. Deut. 7 : 6. 14 : 2. 26 : 18. (Chald. סְגוּלָה *idem.* Root סְגַל, סִיגֵל *to acquire.*)

סֶגֶן or סָגָן, found only in the plur. סְגָנִים.

1. strictly *a deputy, lieutenant,* under the prince, often joined with פֶּחָה. Jer. 51 : 23, 28, 57. Ezek. 23 : 6, 12, 23. comp. Is. 41 : 25. See the Chald.

2. *a prefect, overseer, officer* generally, spoken of the officers at Jerusalem under Ezra and Nehemiah. Ezra 9 : 2. Neh. 2 : 16. 4 : 8, 13. [4 : 14, 19.] 5 : 7. 7 : 5. 12 : 40. Prob. originally derived from the Pers. شحنه שחנה *vicarius, prætor, præfectus,* by a commutation of ח and ג.

סְגַן m. Chald. *a deputy, overseer, governor,* of a province. Dan. 3 : 2, 27. 6 : 8.—Dan. 2 : 48 רַב סִגְנִין *the chief overseer,* of the Magians.

סְגוֹר m. verbal from סָגַר.

1. *an enclosure.* Hos. 13 : 8 סְגוֹר לִבָּם *the enclosure of their heart,* i. e. their breast.

2. Job 28 : 15. i. q. זָהָב סָגוּר, see סָגַר.

3. Ps. 35 : 3. perhaps *a lance, spear,* comp. Arab. شجار *hasta lignea;* or *a battle-axe,* comp. Greek σάγαρις, (Herod. VII. 64.) and Armen. *sacr.* The connexion of the passage, and the parallelism of the preceding verse, add great confirmation to this interpretation. The passage, however, is capable of the usual explanation, (סְגֹר as imper. of סָגַר,) *draw out the spear, and stop (the way) against my persecutors.*

סָגַר, fut. יִסְגֹּר, (kindred with סָכַר,) *to shut* or *close up.* Used without an accus. of the object, Gen. 7 : 16. Is. 22 : 22. with an accus. and the prepositions בְּעַד and עַל, Gen. 19 : 6, 10. 1 K. 11 : 27. Job 3 : 10. 1 Sam. 1 : 6 כִּי סָגַר יְהֹוָה בְּעַד רַחְמָהּ *because Jehovah had shut up her womb.* (See בְּעַד no. 4.) Job 12 : 14 יִסְגֹּר עַל אִישׁ *he shuts up a man.* Intrans. Josh. 6 : 1 וִירִיחוֹ סֹגֶרֶת וּמְסֻגֶּרֶת מִפְּנֵי בְּנֵי יִשְׂרָאֵל *and Jericho was straitly shut up before the children of Israel.* Or, the first participle may refer to the shutting-to of the gates, and the second to the fastening of the same by bars. Chald. *et Jericho erat clausa foribus ferreis et roborata vectibus æneis.*

Part. pass. סָגוּר *laid up, costly.*—זָהָב סָגוּר *costly* or *fine gold,* in opposition to common gold, 1 K. 6 : 20, 21. 7 : 49, 50. 10 : 21. 2 Chr. 4 : 20, 21. 9 : 20.

Niph. pass. of Kal, *to be shut*, spoken of doors and gates, Is. 45 : 1. *to be shut in*, spoken of persons, Num. 12 : 14, 15. 1 Sam. 23 : 7. Reflex. *to shut one's self in*, Ezek. 3 : 24.

Pi. סִגֵּר i. q. Hiph. nos. 2. 3.

1. *to deliver*. 1 Sam. 17 : 46. 24 : 19. 26 : 8. Hence

2. *to give up*. 2 Sam. 18 : 28.

Pu. *to be shut up*. Is. 24 : 10. Jer. 13 : 19.

Hiph. 1. *to shut up*, e. g. a house, Lev. 14 : 38. *to shut in*, a person, Lev. 13 : 4, 5, 11.

2. *to deliver*, (as usually explained, strictly *concludendum tradidit*, but perhaps antiphrastically for *reclusit, resignavit*. Comp. נָכַר.) Construed with אֶל, Deut. 23 : 16. Obad. 14. and בְּיַד, 1 Sam. 23 : 16. Ps. 31 : 9. Lam. 2 : 7.

3. *to give* or *deliver up*. Deut. 32 : 30. Am. 6 : 8. Construed with לְ, Ps. 78 : 48.

Deriv. מִסְגֶּרֶת, מַסְגֵּר, סוּגַר, סְגוֹר.

סְגַר Chald. *idem*. Dan. 6 : 23.

סַגְרִיר m. *rain*. Prov. 27 : 15. (In Syr. and Chald. *idem*. Samar. אסגר *pluvia*. Root شجر *aquam effudit*.)

סַד m. *stocks, nervus*, i. q. מַהְפֶּכֶת, a wood, into which the feet of prisoners were inserted. Job 13 : 27. 33 : 11. (Syr. ܣܕܐ, Chald. סַדָּא *idem*. Root سدّ *occlusit, obstruxit*.)

סְדֹם *Sodom*, the proper name of the southernmost (Gen. 19 : 15.) of the four cities in the vale of Siddim which were sunk in the Dead Sea. Sept. Σόδομα. Vulg. *Sodoma*.

סָדִין m. dec. III. a. *a linen undergarment*, a kind of shirt or shift worn next the skin. Judg. 14 : 12, 13. Is. 3 : 23. Prov. 31 : 24. (Syr. ܣܘܕܢܐ in N. T. for σουδάριον Luke 19 : 20. for λέντιον John 13 : 4. Root סְדַן, in Arab. سدن i. q. سدل *laxavit, dimisit* vestem suam, (see the letter ל,) whence سدن *a covering*, سدانة *sindones*. Sept. usually σινδών, the etymological connexion of which with the Hebrew word is uncertain.

סֵדֶר m. *order*. Job 10 : 22. (Syr. ܣܕܪܐ *idem*. Chald. סְדַר i. q. Hebr. עָרַךְ *to arrange, set in order*.) Comp. שְׂדֵרָה.

סַהַר m. *a rounding*. Found only Cant. 7 : 3 אַגַּן הַסַּהַר *a round goblet*. (Syr. ܣܗܪܐ *the moon*; comp. שַׂהֲרֹן. The root סהר appears to be synonymous with סָחַר, (comp. the letter ה,) and to have signified, *to surround*; whence סְהַר Talmud. *maceria, sepes*. See סֹהַר.)

סֹהַר m. *a castle, fortress, tower*. (Root סָהַר=סָחַר *to surround, close in, munivit*, comp. סֹחֵרָה *a shield*, Syr. ܣܘܚܪܐ *munimentum, arx, palatium*.) Hence בֵּית הַסֹּהַר *a house of confinement, a prison*, Gen. 39 : 20—23. 40 : 3, 5. The Samar. text reads סוהר, for explanation.

סוֹא proper name of an Egyptian king, contemporary with Hosea king of Israel. 2 K. 17 : 4. The name signifies according to Jablonski, *a chief, prince*, or *prince of the dwelling*, (*shooneh*.) Perhaps the same person with *Sevechus* in Manetho, or *Sabaco* in Herod. II. 137.

I. **סוּג** or **סוֹג** (once שׂוּג 2 Sam. 1 : 22.) i. q. נָסַג *to depart*, particularly from God, Ps. 80 : 19. 53 : 4. Prov. 14 : 14 סוּג לֵב *whose heart is rebellious*, i. e. wicked, perverse; comp. Ps. 44 : 19.

Niph. נָסוֹג, fut. יִסּוֹג, *to decline, fall away*, usually with the addition אָחוֹר. Is. 50 : 5. Ps. 35 : 4 יִסֹּגוּ אָחוֹר וְיַחְפְּרוּ *let them turn back and be brought to confusion*. 40 : 15. 70 : 3. 129 : 5. Is. 42 : 17. Jer. 46 : 5. Particularly as in Kal, *to decline from Jehovah*; with מֵאַחֲרֵי יְהוָה Zeph. 1 : 6. without addition, Ps. 44 : 19. 78 : 57.

Deriv. סִיג.

II. **סוּג** *to hedge round, to encompass*. (Syr. ܣܝܓ, Chald. סְיַג, in Hebrew elsewhere סוֹךְ.) Cant. 7:3 סוּגָה בַּשּׁוֹשַׁנִּים *encompassed with lilies.*

סוּג found only Ezek. 22:18 Keth. i. q. סִיג *a dross.*

סוּגַר m. *a prison, cage,* for lions. Ezek. 19:9. Sept. κημός. Vulg. *cavea.*

סוֹד m. dec. I. 1. *a circle* or *company of persons sitting together.* It is a contraction of יְסוֹד Arab. وِسَاد *an eastern sofa, divan,* from יָסַד in the signification of وسد *sternere lectulum.* Comp. יָסַד in Niph.) Jer. 6:11 סוֹד בַּחוּרִים *the circle of young men.* 15:17 סוֹד מְשַׂחֲקִים *the circle of scorners.* Ezek. 13:9. Ps. 64:3. 111:1. Particularly *a body of counsellors,* Ps. 89:8. Job 15:8. Jer. 23:18.

2. *a common consultation of many persons together.* Prov. 15:21 בְּאֵין סוֹד *without consultation.* Oppos. בְּרֹב יוֹעֲצִים. Ps. 83:4.

3. *confidential talk* or *intercourse.* Ps. 55:15. Job 19:19 מְתֵי סוֹדִי *my confidential friends.*—סוֹד יְהוָה *close intercourse with Jehovah, confidence in him,* Ps. 25:14. Prov. 3:32. Job 29:4.

4. *a secret;* hence גָּלָה, גִּלָּה סוֹד, *to reveal a secret,* Prov. 11:13. 20:19. 25:9. Amos 3:7.

סוּחָה f. prob. i. q. סְחִי *sweepings, dirt, filth.* Is. 5:25 כַּסּוּחָה, Sept. ὡς κοπρία. Vulg. *quasi stercus.* Chald. כְּסַחִיתָא. Others make the כ radical, and compare it with the Arab. كسح כסח *to sweep out.* But the adverb of comparison כְּ is naturally expected here.

סוּךְ i. q. נָסַךְ no. 3. *to anoint,* applied to the anointing of the body after washing, and not to the anointing of a king or the like; hence different from מָשַׁח. 2 Chr. 28:15. Ezek. 16:9. Reflex. *to anoint one's self,* Ruth 3:3. Dan. 10:2. 2 Sam. 12:20. The matter *with* which one is anointed is put in the accus. (comp. מָשַׁח Am. 6:6.) Deut. 28:40 וְשֶׁמֶן לֹא תָסוּךְ *but with oil thou shalt not anoint thyself.* Mic. 6:15. 2 Sam. 14:2. Deriv. אָסוּךְ. The part. מֵסִיךְ derives its signification from סָכַךְ, and is equivalent to מֵסֵךְ.

סוּמְפֹּנְיָה f. Chald. Dan. 3:5, 10, 15. for which in verse 10 Keth. we find סִיפֹנְיָא, the Greek word συμφωνία, *a bagpipe.* (Comp. Serv. on Æn. xi. 27.) In the latter form the Mem is thrown out, as in the Syr. ܨܦܘܢܝܐ. The Hebrew interpreters render it by שַׂבָּ. The Hebrew Tractatus Shilte Haggibborim (Ugolini Thes. Vol. XXXII.) describes the *samponja* as a bag pipe, consisting of two pipes thrust through a leathern bag, of a mournful sound. The shalm is at the present day called in Italy *samponja,* in Asia Minor *sambonja.*

סְוֵנֵה *Syene,* the southernmost city in Egypt, through which the tropic of Cancer passes, by the Copts called *Sovan,* Arab. أُسْوَان *Asvan.* Ezek. 29:10. 30:6. In both passages it stands in the accus. *to Syene,* but the final ה־ is not on that account to be taken as the ה local. (comp. נֹבָה.) See Jablonskii Opusc. ed. te Water, T. I. p. 328. Michaëlis Spicileg. T. II. p. 40.

סוּס m. dec. I.

1. *a horse.* Gen. 47:17. Is. 2:7.

2. *a swallow.* Is. 38:14. Jer. 8:7. but in the latter place the Keri has סִיס. So the Sept. Theod. Jerome; but the Hebrew commentators render it *the crane.* See Bocharti Hieroz. T. II. p. 60.

סוּסָה f. Cant. 1:9. *a mare.*

סוֹף m. *an end,* the Aramean word for the more ancient and usual Hebrew word קֵץ. Ecc. 3:11. 7:2. 12:13. 2 Chr. 20:16. Joel 2:20. Root סוּף.

סוֹף, emph. סוֹפָא, Chald. *idem.* Dan. 4:8, 19. 6:27. 7:28.

סוּף *to cease, to come to an end.* Is. 66:17. Est. 9:28. (In Syr. and Chald. *idem.*)

Hiph. *to cause to cease, to put an end to* any thing. Zeph. 1:2, 3. Jer. 8:13

אָסֹף אֲסִיפֵם *I will surely consume them.* For the infin. pleon. the kindred form אָסֹף is here employed; comp. אָסַף no. 4. (Comp. Is. 28:28.)

סוּף Chald. *idem*, applied to *the fulfilment* of a prophecy. Dan. 4:30. (Comp. the kindred verb כָּלָה no. 7.)

Aph. *to put an end to* any thing. Dan. 2:44.

סוּף m. *a reed;* particularly (1.) *the sea-grass, φῦκος, fucus.* Jon. 2:6. Hence יַם־סוּף *the sea of reeds*, i. e. the Red Sea, Ps. 106:7, 9, 22. 136:13. In Egypt this sea-grass is called *sari;* hence the sea is called *the sea of Sari.* See Michaëlis Supplem. ad Lex. Heb. p. 1726. Jablonskii Opusc. ed. te Water, T. I. p. 266. Bocharti Opp. T. II. p. 1191. (2.) a reed found in the Nile, also called by the Egyptians *sari.* Ex. 2:3, 5. Is. 19:6. Plin. H. N. XIII. 23. §45. (3.) proper name of a place. Once Deut. 1:1.

סוּפָה f. verbal from סוּף, dec. X. *a violent wind, hurricane, whirlwind.* Job 21:18. 27:20. 37:9. Prov. 10:25. Is. 17:13. With ה paragogic סוּפָתָה Hos. 8:7.

סוּר, fut. יָסוּר, with ו convers. וַיָּסַר.

1. *to turn away, to depart;* construed with מִן, Ex. 32:8. Judg. 16:17. Gen. 49:10. with מֵעִם, 1 Sam. 18:12. with מֵעַל Num. 12:10. 14:9, 1 Sam. 28:15. with מֵאַחֲרֵי, 1 Sam. 12:20. 2 K. 10:29. 18:6. 2 Chr. 25:27. with בְּ, Hos. 7:14. with an accus. 2 Chr. 8:15. Prov. 11:22 סָרַת טָעַם *without discretion*, liter. *recedens mente.* Used absolutely to signify (1.) *to depart* (from the ways of God), *to decline, degenerate.* Ps. 14:3. Jer. 5:23. Deut. 11:16. Dan. 9:11. (2.) in a passive sense, *to be removed.* 1 K. 15:14 הַבָּמוֹת לֹא סָרוּ *and the high places were not removed.* 22:44. 2 K. 12:4. 14:4. 15:4. comp. Job 15:30 יָסוּר בְּרוּחַ פִּיו *he is taken away by the breath of his mouth.*

2. *to be gone, to pass away.* 1 Sam. 15:32 *the bitterness of death is past.* Hos. 4:18.—Job 15:30 לֹא יָסוּר מִנִּי חֹשֶׁךְ *he shall not escape from darkness*, i. e. from calamity.

3. *to turn in* or *lodge with* any one, construed with אֶל. Judg. 4:18. 18:3, 15. Gen. 19:2, 3.

4. *to approach to* any thing. Ex. 3:3 אָסֻרָה־נָּא וְאֶרְאֶה *I will approach and see.* Verse 4. Ruth 4:1. 1 K. 20:39. Construed with עַל, 22:32. Also *to have access*, 1 Sam. 22:14 וְסָר אֶל מִשְׁמַעְתֶּךָ *and having access (like him) to thy private audience.*

Hiph. הֵסִיר, fut. יָסִיר, with ו convers. וַיָּסַר (as in Kal).

1. *to turn away.* Deut. 7:4. Hence (1.) *to take off,* e. g. a ring from the finger, Gen. 41:42. the head of any one, i. e. to cause him to be executed, 1 Sam. 17:46. 2 Sam. 5:6. 16:9. (2.) *to put off* one's clothes. Gen. 38:14. (3.) *to take away, remove;* e. g. the altars of the idols, 2 K. 18:4. the necromancers, 1 Sam. 28:3. the curse, Josh. 7:13.

2. *to let* any thing *be brought*, construed with אֵלָיו *to one's self.* 2 Sam. 6:10.

Hoph. הוּסַר pass. Lev. 4:31. Dan. 11:31.

Pil. סוֹרֵר i. q. Hiph. *to cause to deviate, to turn aside.* Once Lam. 3:11.

סוּר 1. part. pass. *driven out, exiled.* Is. 49:21 גֹּלָה וְסוּרָה *a captive and exile.* Also in an active sense, Jer. 17:13 Keri סוּרַי *those who have departed from me.*

2. prob. *the wild shoots* or *branches of the vine,* liter. *what degenerates.* Comp. סִיג *dross,* from סוּג.) Jer. 2:21 סוּרֵי הַגֶּפֶן נָכְרִיָּה *wild shoots of a strange vine.*

3. name of a gate of the temple. Once 2 K. 11:6. In the parallel passage 2 Chr. 23:5, it is called שַׁעַר הַיְסוֹד *the gate of the foundation.*

סוּת or **סִית** in Kal not used.

Hiph. הֵסִית, also הִסִּית (Jer. 38:22.) fut. יָסִית, also יַסִּית part. מֵסִית, (comp. לִין from לוּן.)

1. *to take* or *drive away;* construed with מִן, *to take* or *drive away from* any

place, Job 36:18 פֶּן יְסִיתְךָ בְסָפֶק *lest he take thee away with his stroke.* 2 Chr. 18:31. Job 36:16.

2. *to urge, induce, persuade.* Josh. 15:18. Judg. 1:14. 2 Chr. 18:2. Particularly *to entice to evil, to seduce,* Deut. 13:7. 1 K. 21:25. Job 36:18.

3. *to excite* or *stir up against* any one, construed with בְּ of the person. 1 Sam. 26:19. Job 2:3. Jer. 43:3.

סוּת m. dec. I. *a garment.* Once Gen. 49:11. Parall. לְבֻשׁ. Sept. περιβολή. Vulg. *pallium.* Prob. i. q. כְּסוּת by an aphæresis of כְּ, like פְּלֵי for נְבָלֵי, בַּל for יְגַל, etc. although no other example is known, in which initial Caph is dropped. The Samaritan text has the full reading כסות.

סָחַב. *to draw* or *drag away,* e. g. a dead body. 2 Sam. 17:13. Jer. 15:3 (*I will send*) אֶת־הַכְּלָבִים לִסְחֹב *dogs to drag them away.* 22:19. 49:20. (Arab. سحب *to draw,* e. g. a garment on the ground.)

סְחָבָה f. found only in the plur. Jer. 38:11, 12. *torn garments.* (Root סָחַב *to drag,* prob. also *to tear, rend.*)

סָחָה *to wipe* or *sweep off.* Only in Pi. Ezek. 26:4. (Arab. سَحَا *idem.* Syr. ܣܚܘܪܐ *a brush, broom.* Chald. סְחָה *to wash.*) Hence

סְחִי m. verbal from סָחָה, *sweepings, filth, dirt,* metaphorically *something of little worth.* Lam. 3:45. (Chald. סְחִיתָא *dirt, mud.*)

סָחִישׁ 2 K. 19:29. (in the parallel passage Is. 37:30, שָׁחִיס,) *that which grows up of itself the third year after sowing.* Comp. סָפִיחַ. Sept. in the Book of Kings αὐτόματα. Aqu. and Theod. in Isaiah αὐτοφυῆ. For an illustration of the thing, see Strabo, xr. p. 767 (aliter 502).

סָחַף 1. *to throw down,* as in Syr. See Niph.

2. *to inundate,* spoken of a rain. Prov. 28:3. (So in Arab.)

Niph. *prosterni.* Jer. 46:15.

סָחַר *to go* or *move about,* (in Chald. i. q. סָבַב.) Jer. 14:18. *To pass through* or *traverse* a land, construed with an accus. Gen. 34:10, 21. particularly for the sake of traffic, Gen. 42:34 וְאֶת הָאָרֶץ תִּסְחָרוּ *and ye may traverse* or *traffic in the land.* Hence part. סֹחֵר *a travelling merchant* or *trader, a pedlar,* Gen. 23:16. 37:28. סֹחֲרֵי הַמֶּלֶךְ *the merchants of the king,* i. e. the agents which he employed to make purchases, 1 K. 10:28. 2 Chr. 1:16. Spoken of navigators, Prov. 31:14. Is. 23:2. In a still more general sense Is. 47:15 סֹחֲרַיִךְ *those with whom thou hast had intercourse.*—Fem. סֹחֶרֶת *a female trader,* Ezek. 27:12, 16, 18.

Pilp. סְחַרְחַר *to flutter, palpitate,* spoken of the heart. Ps. 38:11.

Deriv. out of course מִסְחָר.

סְחַר m. verbal from סָחַר, dec. IV. a.

1. *a place of trade, mart, emporium.* Is. 23:3.

2. *something acquired by trading, merchandise.* Is. 45:14 סְחַר כּוּשׁ *the merchandise of Ethiopia;* comp. Prov. 3:14.

סַחַר m. verbal from סָחַר, dec. VI. c.

1. *something acquired by trading, merchandise.* Is. 23:18.

2. *an acquisition* generally. Prov. 3:14 כִּי טוֹב סַחְרָהּ מִסְּחַר כָּסֶף *for the acquisition of it is better than that of silver,* i. e. it is better to acquire it, than to acquire silver. 31:18.

סְחֹרָה f. verbal from סָחַר, dec. X. *traffic, trade;* and used as a concrete, *a trader.* Ezek. 27:15 סְחֹרַת יָדֵךְ i. q. סֹחֲרֵי יָדֵךְ verse 21. *thy traders.*

סֹחֵרָה f. *a shield.* Once Ps. 91:4. The root סָחַר i. q. סָבַב *to surround,* has here the idea of *protection;* comp. ܣܘܚܪܐ *a tower, citadel,* and סֹחֵר. Hence not exactly *a round shield,* as Jahn supposes, (Archæol. II. 2. p. 404.)

סֹחֶרֶת f. Est. 1:6. a substance employed with several species of marble for making a pavement. Sept. πάρινος

3 H

λίθος. Better perhaps *tortoise-shell*, (comp. סֹחֵרָה,) according to Hartmann (Hebräerin, Th. 3. p. 353.) Others: *black marble*, comp. Syr. סחורתא *lapis niger tinctorius*.

סֵטִים masc. plur. i. q. שֵׂטִים *sins, transgressions*. Ps. 101:3. Root סוּט i. q. שָׂטָה *to deviate, to sin*.

סִיג m. verbal from סוּג, Ezek. 22:18 Keri, and plur. סִגִים, *dross, recrement, scoria, the baser metal which is separated from the purer in smelting*. (See בְּדִיל.) Ezek. 22:18, 19. Is. 1:22, 25. Prov. 25:4 הָגוֹ סִיגִים מִכָּסֶף *separate the dross from the silver*. 26:23 כֶּסֶף סִיגִים *silver-dross*, i. e. unrefined silver. It is once written in the singular סוּג Ezek. 22:18 Keth. and in the plural many manuscripts and editions have סִגִים, Is. 1:22, 25. Ezek. 22:18, 19. (For this commutation of the forms, see e.g. קִים.)

סִיוָן m. Esth. 8:9, the third month of the Hebrew year, which corresponds to part of May and part of June. Root perhaps Chald. סְוָה *to rejoice;* hence *pleasure-month*.

סִיחוֹן m. proper name of a king of the Amorites in Heshbon. Numb. 21:21, 23. Ps. 135:11.

סִין (liter. *mire;* comp. the Aram. סִין ܣܝܢܐ,) Ezek. 30:15, 16. the proper name of a strong city in Egypt, according to Jerome *Pelusium* (perhaps from the Greek πηλὸς,) in Arab. طينة (*the miry*,) on the eastern boundary of Egypt, and defended by the swamps which lie round it. Hence מִדְבַּר־סִין Ex. 16:1. 17:1. Numb. 33:12. *the desert of Sin*, a part of Arabia Deserta, towards Egypt, between Elim and Mount Sinai.

סִינִי a gentile noun.

1. a people in the country of Lebanon. Gen. 10:17. 1 Chr. 1:15. Strabo (XVI. p. 78C. aliter 1096.) speaks of a city there called *Sinna*, in Jerome (Quæst. Hebr. in Genesin) *Sine*, according to Breidenbach's Travels, (published in 1486,) p. 47. a village *Sya*. See Michaëlis Spicileg. Geogr. Exter. T. II. p. 27.

2. אֶרֶץ סִינִים Is. 49:12. a land very distant from Palestine. From the context, it appears to be situated to the south or east. Sept. ἐκ γῆς Περσῶν. As a southern country, it has been compared with סִין *Pelusium*, and סְוֵנֵה *Syene*, but these are merely cities, and not sufficiently remote. It were better to understand it of an eastern country, perhaps *China*, Arab. صين, Syr. ܨܝܢܝ, with צ. It is by no means improbable that together with מָגוֹג *Scythia* and הֹדּוּ *India*, the Hebrews may have heard at least of the name of *China*, as a very distant country.

סִינַי, usually הַר סִינַי *Mount Sinai*, a well-known mountain in Arabia Deserta, consisting of two peaks, of which the lower and western is properly called חֹרֵב, (though now known by the name of *Sinai*,) the higher and eastern peak is the proper סִינַי (now *Mount Catharine*.) The Arabians call it *Jebel Musa* (*the mount of Moses*.) Ex. 19:11, 23. 24:16. 34:2, 4. See Bellermann's Handb. der Bibl. Literatur, Th. III. p. 229. Hence מִדְבַּר סִינַי *the desert about Sinai*, Ex. 19:1, 2. Lev. 7:38. Num. 1:1, 19. 9:1.

סִיס *a swallow*. Jer. 8:7 Keri. In the Kethib סוּס q. v.

סִיסְרָא m. (*order of battle*, comp. the Syr. ܣܝܣܪܐ,) *Sisera*, a general under Jabin, king of Canaan. Judg. 4:2ff. Ps. 83:10.

סִיפֹנְיָה Dan. 3:10. In the Keri סוּמְפֹּנְיָה q. v.

I. **סִיר** (perhaps from סוּר Hiph. *removit*.)

1. with the plur. סִירִים, *a thorn*. Is. 34:13. Hos. 2:8. Ecc. 7:6 (first occurr.) Nah. 1:10 כִּי עַד סִירִים סְבֻכִים *for as thorns*, i. e. as a thorn-hedge, *they are folded together*, a description of great

wickedness, (comp. Mic. 7:4. Ezek. 2:6.)

2. *a fish-hook, angle*; from its similarity to *a thorn*. (Comp. חוח *a thorn* and *a hook*.) Plur. ות, Am. 4:2.

II. סִיר com. gen. (Jer. 1:13. Ezek. 24:6.)

1. *a pot, kettle, caldron*. (Root סור prob. Arab. سار *to boil with anger*.) Ezek. 11:3, 7. סִיר הַבָּשָׂר *a flesh-pot*, Ex. 16:3. Ecc. 7:6 כְּקוֹל הַסִּירִים תַּחַת הַסִּיר *as the crackling of thorns under the pot*; (comp. Ps. 58:10.) Plur. סִירוֹת Ex. 38:3. 1 K. 7:45.

2. *a basin*. Ps. 60:10 סִיר רַחְצִי *my wash-basin*.

סָךְ m. *a multitude of people*. Once Ps. 42:5. (comp. Talmud. and Chald. סַךְ *summa, collectio, complexus*.)

סֹךְ m. with suff. סֻכּוֹ, once סֻכּוֹ, verbal from סָכַךְ no. II. dec. VIII. d.

1. *a booth, tent, dwelling*. Ps. 27:5. 76:3.

2. *a thicket*, as the covert of the lion. Ps. 10:9. Jer. 25:38.

סֻכָּה fem. of סֹךְ, dec. X.

1. *a booth, tent, tabernacle*, made of boughs and bushes. Jon. 4:5. Is. 4:6. חַג הַסֻּכּוֹת *the feast of tabernacles*, Lev. 23:34. Deut. 16:13.—Am. 9:11. by way of contempt for *a small house*.

2. *a hedge, enclosure*, for cattle. Gen. 33:17.

3. *a shelter, shed, dwelling*, generally. Ps. 31:21. Job 36:29. *the noise of his* (*God's*) *dwelling*. Ps. 18:12.

4. *a thicket*, as the dwelling of the lion. Job 38:40.

סֻכּוֹת (*booths*) 1. proper name of a city in the tribe of Gad. Josh. 13:27. Judg. 8:5. 1 K. 7:46. For the derivation of the name, see Gen. 33:17. עֵמֶק סֻכּוֹת Ps. 60:8. 108:8. prob. *ager Succoth, the field of Succoth*.

2. also of the first encampment of the Israelites in their march out of Egypt. Ex. 12:37. 13:20. Num. 33:5. Pliny (H. N. vi. 29.) mentions there a place called *Sucha*.

3. סֻכּוֹת בְּנוֹת 2 K. 17:30. (*booths of the daughters*) an object of idolatrous worship among the Babylonians. According to the most common opinion, they were *small tents* or *booths*, in which the Babylonish maidens devoted themselves to the service of Milytta; see Herod. i. 199. Strabo xvi. p. 1081 or 743.

סִכּוּת f. dec. I. i. q. סֹךְ or סֻכָּה, Am. 5:26. *a booth* or *tabernacle*, which the Israelites are said to have carried about in the wilderness with them in honour of an idol (מֹלֶךְ,) perhaps an imitation on a small scale of the tabernacle of the congregation. Diodorus Siculus (xx. 25.) mentions a similar σκηνὴ ἱερὰ in the camp of the Carthaginians.

סֻכִּיִּים an African people, mentioned 2 Chr. 12:3, along with Lybians and Ethiopians. Sept. and Vulg. *Troglodytæ*.

I. סָכַךְ (once שָׂכַךְ Ex. 33:22.)

1. *to cover, spread over*. Ex. 40:3. for the most part construed with עַל, (comp. the synon. כָּסָה,) 1 K. 8:7. וַיָּסֹכּוּ הַכְּרֻבִים עַל־הָאָרוֹן *and the cherubim covered the ark*, liter. *they covered over the ark*. Ex. 25:20. 37:9. comp. Ezek. 28:14, 16. Construed with two accus. Job 40:22 יְסֻכֻּהוּ צֶאֱלִים צִלְלוֹ *the shady trees cover him with their shadow*.

2. *to hide* or *conceal one's self*. Lam. 3:44 סַכֹּתָה בֶעָנָן *thou concealest thyself in a cloud*. Verse 43.

3. *to protect*, construed with לְ. Ps. 140:8. Part. סוֹכֵךְ *something which protects* or *defends, a moveable roof employed by assailants, vinea*, Nah. 2:6.

Hiph. הֵסֵךְ i. q. Kal, *to cover, protect*, construed with עַל, Ps. 5:12. with לְ, Ps. 91:4. הֵסֵךְ רַגְלָיו 1 Sam. 24:4. Judg. 3:24. *to cover one's feet*, according to Josephus (Antiq. vi. 14.) and the Talmudists an euphemism for *to obey a call of nature*. Less applicable is the explanation of the Syriac and Arabic versions in Sam. and of Josephus (Antiq. v. 4. § 2.) *to take rest, to sleep*. See, however, J. D. Michaelis

Supplem. p. 1743. Glassii Philol. Sacra, ed. Dathe, p. 891.

Hoph. *to be covered.* Ex. 25:29. 37:16.

Pilp. סִכְסֵךְ most prob. *to arm.* (Comp. Arab. شَكَّ *totum se operuit armis;* شِكَّةٌ *arma, panoplia;* and سَكَّ *to fasten gates with iron.*) Is. 9:10 וְאֶת אֹיְבָיו יְסַכְסֵךְ *and he will arm his enemies.* 19:2 וְסִכְסַכְתִּי מִצְרַיִם בְּמִצְרַיִם *I will arm the Egyptians against the Egyptians.* Others: *to mingle* or *join together*, (comp. סָכַךְ no. II.)

Deriv. מוּסָךְ, מָסָךְ.

II. סָכַךְ i. q. שָׂכַךְ and שׂוּךְ *to weave.* Ps. 139:13 תְּסֻכֵּנִי בְּבֶטֶן אִמִּי *thou hast woven* or *formed me in my mother's womb.* Comp. Job 10:11. Others: *to cover, protect;* as in no. I.

Hiph. הֵסֵךְ *to hedge,* construed with בְּעַד, *to hedge round.* Job 3:23. 38:8.

Deriv. סֹךְ, סֻכָּה, סֻכּוֹת.

סָכַל in Kal not used. Syr. *to be foolish.* Comp. by transposition כָּסַל.

Pi. *to make* any one *appear foolish, to frustrate.* 2 Sam. 15:31. Is. 44:25. Comp. הוֹלֵל.

Hiph. liter. *to make foolish;* joined with עָשׂוֹ, *to act foolishly,* Gen. 31:28. also without this addition, 1 Sam. 26:21. (In Aram. Aph. *idem.*)

Niph. 1. *to act foolishly.* 1 Sam. 13:13. 2 Chr. 16:9.

2. *to sin.* 2 Sam. 24:10. 1 Chr. 21:8. Comp. כְּסִיל, נָבָל, and other synonymes. The root שָׂכַל is not to be confounded with this root.

סָכָל m. verbal from סָכַל, dec. IV. a. *foolish, a fool.* Jer. 4:22. 5:21. Ecc. 2:19. 7:17.

סֶכֶל m. verbal from סָכַל, *folly,* and as a concrete, *fools.* Ecc. 10:6.

סִכְלוּת f. verbal from סָכַל, *folly,* an Aramean word. Ecc. 2:3,12,13. 7:25. 10:1,13. Once שִׂכְלוּת 1:17 (Syr. *idem*).

I. סָכַן, fut. יִסְכֹּן. 1. *to be useful, profitable;* construed with לְ or עַל. Job 22:2. 35:3. Without cases, Job 15:3.

2. intrans. *to receive profit, to be profited, proficere.* Job 34:9.

3. *to take care of, to nurse, to manage,* derived from signif. no. 1. Part. סֹכֵן οἰκόνομος, *a steward, one set over the royal palace,* Is. 22:15. Fem. סֹכֶנֶת *a nurse* (of the king), 1 K. 1:2, 4.

Hiph. הִסְכִּין 1. *to be wont, to be accustomed.* Num. 22:30.

2. *to be* or *become acquainted with* any thing. Ps. 139:3 כָּל־דְּרָכַי הִסְכַּנְתָּה *thou art acquainted with all my ways.* Parall. *to know.* Job 22:21 הַסְכֶּן־נָא עִמּוֹ *acquaint thyself with him.*

II. סָכַן as in Chald. *to be in danger.*

Niph. *idem.* Ecc. 10:9.

III. סָכַן Pu. מְסֻכָּן Is. 40:20 (if the punctuation is correct,) i. q. מִסְכֵּן *poor;* hence הַמְסֻכָּן תְּרוּמָה *he who is too poor for an oblation.*

I. סָכַר i. q. סָגַר *to shut up.* (Syr. and Arab. *idem.*) In Kal not used.

Niph. *to be shut up, to be stopped.* Gen. 8:2. Ps. 63:12.

Pi. i. q. סִגֵּר and הִסְגִּיר *to deliver up.* Is. 19:4.

II. סָכַר i. q. שָׂכַר *to hire, to bribe.* Ezra 4:5.

סָכַת in Kal not used.

Hiph. *to be silent.* Once Deut. 27:9. (Arab. سَكَتَ conj. I. IV. *idem.* Samar. *to attend.*) Sept. σιώπα. Vulg. *attende.*

סַל m. plur. סַלִּים, dec. VIII. h. *a basket.* Gen. 40:17. Ex. 29:3, 31. Comp. סַלְסִלּוֹת.

סִלָּא (i. q. מְסִלָּה *a way*) the proper name of a place not far from Jerusalem. 2 K. 12:21.

סָלָא prob. strictly i. q. סָלַל *to raise up,* hence *to hang the balance, to weigh.* Comp. נָשָׂא Job 6:2. and in Lat. *pendeo, to hang,* with *pendo, to hang the balance, to weigh.* Only in Pual, Lam. 4:2 הַמְסֻלָּאִים בַּפָּז *to be weighed,* i. e. to be compared, *with fine gold.* See סָלָה no. I.

סָלַד prob. i. q. Chald. סְלַד *to burn, to be consumed.* Found only in Pi. Job 6:10 וַאֲסַלְּדָה בְחִילָה *although I be consumed with pain.* Sept. ἡλλόμην, Vulg. *saliebam;* (comp. صلد *to leap, spring.*) Others: *to harden one's self;* (comp. Arab. صلد *dura fuit* terra.)

I. סָלָה i. q. סָלָא *to weigh.*

Pu. Job 28:16 לֹא תְסֻלֶּה בְּכֶתֶם אוֹפִיר *it shall not be weighed,* i. e. valued, *with gold of Ophir.*

II. סָלָה as in Aramean, *to reject, despise.* Ps. 119:118.

Pi. *idem.* Lam. 1:15.

סֶלָה (*Milêl*) a musical term, very frequent in the Psalms, besides which it is found in Hab. 3:3, 9, 13. It usually occurs at the end of a period or strophe; but sometimes at the end only of a clause, as in Ps. 55:20. 57:4. Hab. 3:3, 9. In the explanation of this difficult word, it is undoubtedly safest to follow the usus loquendi of the Hebrew dialect. Derived from the Hebrew סָלָה, (whence סֶלֶה, after the form בֶּכֶה, הֶגֶה, and with ה ָ parag. סֶלָה,) it would signify *an elevation* of the voice, (as was long ago observed by Kimchi, Lib. Rad. Venet. 5340. p. 327.) and so perhaps be a sign for changing the key or for repeating the tune some notes higher. See Forkel's Gesch. der Musik, Th. 1. p. 144. and Herder's Geist der Hebr. Poësie, Th. 2. p. 376.) So the Sept. διάψαλμα, i. e. μέλους διαλλαγή, (see Schleusner's Nov. Thes. V. T.) Another explanation, *pause,* as if from the Syr. ܫܠܐ *quievit,* is uncertain, because this Syriac word corresponds to the Heb. שָׁלָה q. v. although the letters ס and שׂ are sometimes interchanged, (see the letter ס.)

Others regard it, not as a proper word, but as an abbreviation containing the initial or most important letters in several words; such abbreviations, furnished with vowels, being very common among the modern Jews and Arabians. The deciphering of the word on this principle must be very arbitrary. The two following have been proposed, סֹב לְמַעְלָה הַשָּׁר *redi sursum, cantor,* (*da capo;*) סִימָן לְשַׁנּוֹת הַקּוֹל *signum mutandæ vocis.* The use of abbreviations among the ancient Hebrews has, however, never yet been proved. Comp. Michaëlis Supplem. p. 1760. See Rosenmülleri Comment. in Psalm. T. I. p. LIX. Noldii Concord. Particul. Heb. p. 940. ed. Tymp. Eichhorn's Bibl. der Bibl. Literatur, Th. 5. p. 542ff.

סִלּוֹן m. *a thorn, brier.* Ezek. 28:24. Sept. σκόλοψ. (Chald. סִלּוֹנָא, סִילְוָא, Arab. سُلّاء *thorns of the date-palm.*)

סַלּוֹן m. dec. I. Ezek. 2:6. i. q. the preceding article, but taken figuratively. Comp. עַקְרַבִּים. Others: *despisers, scorners,* as if from סָלָה=סָלַל no. II.

סָלַח fut. יִסְלַח, *to forgive,* construed with a dative. Ex. 34:9. 1 K. 8:31, 34, 36, 39.

Niph. *to be forgiven,* spoken of sin. Lev. 4:20, 26, 31. 5:10, 13.

Deriv. out of course סְלִיחָה.

סַלָּח m. verbal from סָלַח, *forgiving, ready to forgive.* Ps. 86:5.

סְלִיחָה f. verbal from סָלַח, dec. X. *forgiveness.* Ps. 130:4. Plur. Neh. 9:17.

סַלְכָה proper name of a city on the borders of the kingdom of Bashan. Deut. 3:10. Josh. 12:5. 13:11. 1 Chr. 5:11.

סָלַל 1. *to raise* or *lift up.* See Pilp. Comp. סָלָה, סָלָא.

2. *to raise, throw,* or *cast up.* Jer. 50:26 סָלּוּהָ כְמוֹ־עֲרֵמִים *cast her up as heaps.* Particularly

3. *to raise* or *build* a way *by throwing up dirt, aggerare, aggesto aggere planare.* (Comp. רוּם Is. 49:11.) Is. 57:14. 62:10. Prov. 15:19. Jer. 18:15. Job 19:12 וַיָּסֹלּוּ עָלַי דַּרְכָּם *they raised for themselves a way to me.* 30:12. Without דֶּרֶךְ, Ps. 68:5 סֹלּוּ *build ye* (*the way.*)

Pilp. *to raise up, exalt.* Prov. 4:8 סַלְסְלֶהָ *exalt her (wisdom).*

Hithpo. הִסְתּוֹלֵל, denom. from סֹלְלָה, *to make one's self a wall, to oppose one's self,* construed with בְּ. Ex. 9:17 עוֹדְךָ מִסְתּוֹלֵל בְּעַמִּי *thou yet opposest thyself to my people.*

Deriv. מַסְלוּל, סֻלָּם, מְסִלָּה, סֹלְלָה.

סֹלְלָה f. verbal from סָלַל, dec. X. *a mound, trench, rampart.* Jer. 33:4. Particularly one thrown round a besieged city by the enemy, 2 K. 19:32. Ezek. 4:2. 2 Sam. 20:15. Comp. דָּיֵק.

סֻלָּם m. *a ladder, flight of stairs* or *steps.* Gen. 28:12. (Arab. *idem.*) Root סָלַל, with the termination ־ָם i. q. ־ָן.

סַלְסִלּוֹת fem. plur. *baskets.* i. q. סַלִּים. Is. 6:9. Sept. *κάρταλλα.* Vulg. *cartalla.*

סֶלַע m. dec. VI. d.

1. *a rock.* Often metaphorically, Ps. 18:3. יְהוָה סַלְעִי *Jehovah is my rock.* 31:4. 42:10.

2. proper name of the ancient capital of Edom, afterwards called *Petra,* whence *Arabia Petræa* has its name. 2 K. 14:7. Is. 16:1. Relandi Palæstinâ, p. 926—951.

3. also of a place in the northern part of Arabia. Judg. 1:36.

סָלְעָם m. a four-footed, winged, edible species of locust. Once Lev. 11:22. Root Chald. סַלְעַם *to consume,* i. q. בָּלַע.

סָלַף found only in Pi.

1. *to pervert.* Ex. 23:8 וִיסַלֵּף דִּבְרֵי צַדִּיקִים *and it (the bribe) perverts the cause of the righteous.* Deut. 16:19.

2. *to turn up, destroy,* (a way;) comp. הָפַךְ. Prov. 19:3 אִוֶּלֶת אָדָם תְּסַלֵּף דַּרְכּוֹ *the folly of a man turns up his way,* i. e. makes it uneven.

3. *to overthrow, evertere.* Job 12:19. Prov. 21:12. 13:6. 22:12.

סֶלֶף m. verbal from סָלַף, *rudeness* of speech. Prov. 15:4. Oppos. מַרְפֵּא לָשׁוֹן *mild language.*

2. *perverseness, falsehood.* Prov. 11:3. Oppos. תֻּמָּה.

סְלִק Chald. *to mount up.* Dan. 7:3, 8, 20. Pret. pass. *idem,* Dan. 2:29. Ezra 4:12. In Syr. and Samar. *idem.*

סֹלֶת com. gen. (masc. Ex. 29:40. fem. Lev. 2:5. and often, probably because the ת was erroneously regarded as a feminine termination,) dec. VI. p. *meal.* Ezek. 16:13, 19. 1 Chr. 9:29. Gen. 18:6.—סֹלֶת חִטִּים *wheat meal,* Ex. 29:2. (Arab. سُلْت *barley, peeled barley,* ἄλφιτα, from سلت *to make bare, to peel off.* In Chald. סוּלְתָּא *idem,* whence the verb סַלֵּת *to sift meal.*)

סַם found only in the plur. סַמִּים *sweet spices.* Ex. 30:34. קְטֹרֶת הַסַּמִּים *incense of sweet spices,* Ex. 30:7. 40:27. Root סמם Arab. شَمّ *to smell.*

סְמָדַר m. prim. *a vine-blossom.* Cant. 7:12. 2:13, 15. (In Chald. and Syr. *idem.*)

סָמַךְ, fut. יִסְמֹךְ. 1. *to lay* or *rest on* any thing; as in the phrase סָמַךְ יָד עַל *to lay the hand on* any thing, Ex. 29:10, 15, 19. Lev. 1:4. 3:2. 8:14.—Am. 5:19 וְסָמַךְ יָדוֹ עַל הַקִּיר *and he rested his hand upon the wall,* spoken of one that had fled to his own house and supported himself by the wall of his dwelling.

2. intrans. *to lie on* any one. Ps. 88:8 עָלַי סָמְכָה חֲמָתֶךָ *thine anger lies hard on me.*

3. *to uphold, support.* Ps. 37:17, 24. 54:6. Ezek. 30:6 סֹמְכֵי מִצְרַיִם *those that uphold Egypt, the allies of Egypt.* Construed with לְ, Ps. 145:14. Part. pass. סָמוּךְ, *supported,* i. e. firm, unshaken, Ps. 112:8. Is. 26:3.

4. *to support* or *sustain* any one *with* any thing, construed with two accus. Gen. 27:37 דָּגָן וְתִירוֹשׁ סְמַכְתִּיו *with corn and wine have I sustained him.* Ps. 51:14.

5. *to draw near.* Ezek. 24:2. (This signification is derived from no. 1. *to rest on* any thing, hence in Rabbinic *to be joined to it, to be near;* סָמוּךְ *near.*)

Niph. *to be supported,* Judg. 16:29.

to support one's self, Ps. 71 : 6. Is. 48 : 2. Metaphorically 2 Chr. 32 : 8.

Pi. *to refresh*. Cant. 2 : 5. (Comp. סָעַד.)

סֶמֶל and **סֵמֶל** m. *an image, statue.* Ezek. 8 : 3, 5. Deut. 4 : 16. 2 Chr. 33 : 7 פֶּסֶל הַסֶּמֶל, where פֶּסֶל denotes *signum sculptum*, and סֶמֶל *imago*. The etymology is uncertain.

סָמַן see נִסְמָן.

סָמַר *to shudder, shiver*. Ps. 119 : 120.

Pi. *idem;* also *to stand on end*, spoken of the hair. Job 4 : 15.

סָמָר m. Jer. 51 : 27. prob. *with rough or bristly hair*, ὀρθόθριξ, an epithet of the insect יֶלֶק.

סְנָאָה proper name of a city in Judah. Ezra 2 : 53. Neh. 7 : 38. With the article, Neh. 3 : 3. The root סנא in Aram. is i. q. Heb. שָׂנֵא *to hate*.

סַנְבַלַּט *Sanballat*, proper name of a Persian governor in Moab. Neh. 2 : 10. 4 : 1. 6 : 1, 2, 12, 14. 13 : 28.

סְנֶה m. prim. *a bush, a thorn-bush*. Ex. 3 : 2ff. Deut. 33 : 16. (Syr. ܣܢܝܐ *idem*. Arab. سنا and سنا particularly *the senna bush*.)

סֶנֶה proper name of a rocky cliff over against Gibeah. 1 Sam. 14 : 4. (As an appellative, perhaps *a height, hill*, from سنا *to raise up*.)

סַנְוֵרִים masc. plur. *blindness*. Gen. 19 : 11. 2 K. 6 : 18. Root Chald. quadriliteral סַנְוֵר *to blind, dazzle.*

סַנְחֵרִיב *Sennacherib*, king of Assyria, about the year 720 before Christ, (2 K. 18 : 13. 19 : 16—36.) in Herod. (II. 141.) Σαναχάριβος. He was murdered by his two sons in the temple of Nisroch.

סַנְסִנִּים masc. pl. Cant. 7 : 9. *branches or leaves of the palm-tree*. Prob. kindred with סַלְסִלּוֹת *baskets*, and זַלְזַלִּים *tendrils*.

סְנַפִּיר m. *a fin*. Lev. 11 : 9. Deut. 14 : 9.

סָס m. *a moth*, an insect that eats clothes. Is. 51 : 8. (Syr. ܣܣܐ, Arab. سُوس *a moth, a corn-worm, a louse*, or the like. In Greek σής.)

סָעַד, fut. יִסְעַד. 1. *to stay, sustain, hold up*. Ps. 18 : 36. Prov. 20 : 28. Is. 9 : 6. Hence *to aid, assist, support*, Ps. 20 : 3. 41 : 4. 94 : 18.

2. סָעַד לֵב *to stay the heart*, i. e. to refresh the stomach, by taking food. (See לֵב no. 1.) Gen. 18 : 5 סַעֲדוּ לִבְּכֶם *refresh yourselves by food*. Ps. 104 : 15. Judg. 19 : 8. Intrans. 1 K. 13 : 7 סְעָדָה *refresh thyself*. Comp. רִפֵּדָה.)

Deriv. מִסְעָד.

סְעַד Chald. *to help, aid, assist*, construed with לְ. Ezra 5 : 2.

סָעָה found only Ps. 55 : 9 רוּחַ סֹעָה *a sweeping tempest*. Arab. سعى *to run, to rush*, spoken also of a violent storm.

סְעִיף m. dec. I.

1. *a fissure, cleft*. סְעִיף הַסֶּלַע *a cleft of the rock*, Judg. 15 : 8, 11. Plur. סְעִפֵי הַסְּלָעִים *the clefts of the rocks*, Is. 2 : 21. 57 : 5.

2. *a branch*. Is. 17 : 6. 27 : 10. See סְעַפָּה. (These two significations are found united in the Arab. שׁעבה شُعْبَة from شعب *to divide*, by a commutation of ב and פ.) Hence

סָעַף in Pi. a denom. from סְעִיף no. 2. *to cut off branches*. Is. 10 : 33.

סְעִפִּים masc. plur. *divided opinions, sects, parties*. (Root סָעַף = شعب *to divide.*) 1 K 18 : 21 *how long halt ye* עַל שְׁתֵּי הַסְּעִפִּים *between two opinions?* i. e. between the service of Baal and the service of Jehovah.

סֵעֲפִים masc. plur. Ps. 119 : 113. perhaps *the hesitating* or *sceptical in religion*. Luther: *the light-minded*. Others: *the foolish* or *mad*, i. e. the wicked; comp. Arab. شغاف *madness, violent passion*.

סְעַפּוֹת plur. fem. *branches*. Ezek. 31 : 6, 8. Comp. סְעִיף and סַרְעַפָּה.

סָעַר 1. *to move with violence, to rage;* spoken of the sea, Jon. 1:11, 13. of enemies, Hab. 3:15.

2. *to be tossed about,* by affliction. Is. 54:11. comp. Pi.

Niph. *to be moved* or *disquieted,* by fear. 2 K. 6:11.

Pi. סֵעֵר *to disperse* or *scatter* a people. Zech. 7:14.

Poal, *to be blown away,* spoken of stubble. Hos. 13:3. Comp. שָׂעַר.

סַעַר m. verbal from סָעַר, dec. VI. c. *a storm, tempest.* Jon. 1:4, 12. Jer. 23:19. 25:32.

סְעָרָה f. verbal from סָעַר, dec. XI. d. *idem.* Is. 29:6. also רוּחַ סְעָרָה Ps. 107:25. Ezek. 1:3. and רוּחַ סְעָרוֹת Ezek. 13:11, 13. (See שָׂעַר and שְׂעָרָה.)

סַף m. with suff. סִפִּי, plur. סִפִּים, dec. VIII. f.

1. *the threshold.* Judg. 19:27. 2 K. 12:10. (In Chald. and Samar. *idem.*) See the denom. הִסְתּוֹפֵף.

2. *a basin.* Ex. 12:22. Zech. 12:2. Plur. ־ִים, Jer. 52:19. and ־וֹת, 1 K. 7:50.

סָפַד, fut. יִסְפֹּד, *to mourn, lament, bewail;* particularly for one dead. Zech. 12:12. The person *lamented* is preceded by לְ, 1 K. 14:13. Gen. 23:2. by עַל, 2 Sam. 11:26. once by לִפְנֵי, 2 Sam. 3:31.—Is. 32:12, according to the usual reading *ubera plangunt,* but the true reading is prob. שָׂדִים; so that this passage furnishes no support to the sense *planctus,* as a gesture of grief. On the contrary this word denotes rather *a mournful noise,* comp. Mic. 1:8. Jer. 22:18. 34:5.

Deriv. מִסְפֵּד.

I. **סָפָה** 1. perhaps i. q. אָסַף *to snatch up.* See Niph. no. 1.

2. *to take off* the beard, Is. 7:20. *to take away* life, Ps. 40:15. *to destroy,* Gen. 18:21, 24.

3. intrans. *to be taken away, to perish.* Am. 3:12. Jer. 12:4. Ps. 73:19.

Niph. 1. *to be snatched up, to be seized.* Is. 13:15.

2. *to perish.* Gen. 19:15. Particularly in battle, 1 Sam. 12:25. 26:10. 27:1.

Hiph. *to bring together, to heap up.* Deut. 32:23. Sept. συνάξω. Others place this under no. II. *addam.*

II. **סָפָה** i. q. יָסַף, found only in the infin. סְפוֹת (a mode which is wanting to the verb יָסַף in Kal,) *to add.* Is. 30:1. Particularly *to add to* any thing, *to increase it.* (See יָסַף no. 2.) Num. 32:14. The imper. סְפוּ Is. 29:1. Jer. 7:21. may be formed with equal ease from יָסַף.

סִפּוּן m. verbal from סָפַן, *a covering* of the temple. 1 K. 6:15.

סְפוֹרָה f. verbal from סָפַר, dec. X. *a number.* Ps. 71:15.

I. **סָפַח** in Kal not used. Prob. i. q. סָפָה and אָסַף *to add.*

Niph. *to be joined, to cleave, adhere;* construed with עַל. Is. 14:1.

Pu. *to be gathered.* Job 30:7.

Hithpa. i. q. Niph. construed with בְּ. 1 Sam. 26:19.

II. **סָפַח** i. q. שָׁפַךְ Arab. سفح.

1. *to pour out.* See Piel.

2. *to anoint.* (Comp. נָסַךְ, Syr. ܢܣܟ *to pour out;* Aph. *to anoint and induct a bishop.*) 1 Sam. 2:36 סְפָחֵנִי נָא אֶל אַחַת הַכְּהֻנּוֹת *appoint me, I pray thee, in some priesthood.*

Pi. *to pour out.* Hab. 2:15.

סַפַּחַת f. *the scab.* Lev. 13:2, 6. 14:56. also מִסְפַּחַת 13:7, 8. Strictly *a bald place on the head occasioned by the scab* or *itch;* comp. שִׂפַּח.

סָפִיחַ m. verbal from סָפַח no. II. liter *effusum;* hence

1. *the grain which springs up of itself the second year after a field has been sown.* Lev. 25:5, 11. 2 K. 19:29. Is. 37:30. Comp. סָחִישׁ.

2. *an overflowing.* Job 14:19.

סְפִינָה f. *a ship.* Once Jon. 1:5. (Syr. and Arab. *idem.*) Root סָפַן *to cover with boards.*

סַפִּיר m. plur. ־ִים, dec. I. *a sapphire.* Ex. 28:18. 39:11. Job 28:6, 16. Ezek. 1:26. (Syr. ܣܦܝܠܐ, Chald. סַפִּירָא.)

סֵפֶל m. *a dish, bowl.* Only Judg. 5:25. 6:38. (In Chald. and Talmud. *idem.* See Bocharti Hieroz. I. p. 549.)

סָפַן, fut. יִסְפֹּן. 1. *to cover, contignare,* construed with two accus. 1 K. 6:9. 7:3.

2. *to cover with boards, to wainscot.* 1 K. 7:7. Jer. 22:14. Hag. 1:4.

3. *to conceal, lay up,* like the kindred forms שָׂפַן and צָפַן. Deut. 33:21 כִּי שָׁם חֶלְקַת מְחֹקֵק סָפוּן *for there is the portion of the leader laid up.*

Deriv. out of course סְפִינָה, סִפֻּן.

סָפַף found only in Hithpo. הִסְתּוֹפֵף, denom. from סַף, *to stand on the threshold, to be a doorkeeper.* Ps. 84:11.

I. סָפַק, fut. יִסְפֹּק.

1. *to smite.* Particularly (1.) ס׳ עַל יָרֵךְ *to smite one's self on the thigh,* as a gesture of displeasure and grief. Jer. 31:19. Construed with אֶל, Ezek. 21:17. [21:12.] comp. Il. XII. 162. XV. 397. Od. XIII. 198. (2.) סָפַק אֶת־כַּפַּיִם *to smite the hands together;* as a gesture of displeasure. Num. 24:10. Construed with עַל, as a gesture of contempt, (comp. Lat. *explodere aliquem,*) Lam. 2:15. Job 27:23, (where 31 MSS. read it with שׂ.) Without כַּפַּיִם, *idem,* Job 34:37. In some passages it is written with שׂ.

2. *to chastise,* spoken of God. Job 34:26.

II. סָפַק Syr. ܣܦܩ, *to vomit.* Once Jer. 48:26.

סֵפֶק dec. VI. g. *abundance, sufficientia.* Job 20:22. Root שָׂפַק.

סָפַר, fut. יִסְפֹּר. 1. *to count, number.* Gen. 15:5. Lev. 15:13, 28.

2. *to write.* (From signif. no. 1. comes *to enumerate, relate, tell;* (see Pi. nos. 2. 3.) whence *to write,* comp. 2 Chr. 2:10 וַיֹּאמֶר בִּכְתָב *and he answered in writing;* comp. קָרָא *to call* and *to read.* It is not necessary then to derive this verb from the Arab. شَفَرَ *scalpsit,* or to make סֹפֵר a denom. from סֵפֶר *a book.*) Found only in the part. סֹפֵר *a writer,* Ps. 45:2. Ezek. 9:2, 3. Particularly (1.) *a secretary of state,* an important officer of the crown, who gave out commissions in the name of the king. 2 Sam. 8:17. 20:25. 2 K. 12:11. 19:2. 22:3 ff. (2.) in the later writings, *one skilled in the scriptures, one learned in the law,* γραμματεύς. 1 Chr. 27:32. Ezra 7:6. Ezra bears this name, Neh. 8:1 ff. 12:26, 36. Ezra 7:11. (3.) in a military sense, *an inspector-general,* who had the charge of reviewing and recruiting the army. Jer. 37:15. 52:25. 2 K. 25:19. comp. 2 Chr. 26:11. Is. 33:18.—In Judg. 5:14, it appears to have a more extended signification and to denote *a general, a military leader.*

Niph. *to be numbered, counted.* Gen. 16:10. 32:13.

Pi. 1. *to number, count,* i. q. Kal. Job 38:37. Ps. 40:6.

2. *to relate, tell.* Gen. 24:66. 40:9. Particularly *to announce with commendation, to praise,* Ps. 19:2. 78:4.—Job 28:27 *then did he (God) see it (wisdom,) and made it known* (in his works).

3. used absolutely, *to speak, to talk, sermones facere.* Ps. 64:6. 73:15. Hence 69:27 אֶל מַכְאוֹב חֲלָלֶיךָ יְסַפֵּרוּ *concerning the pain of thy wounded they speak,* (with pleasure.)

Pu. סֻפַּר pass. of no. 2. *to be related, told.* Ps. 22:31. Job 37:20.

Deriv. out of course מִסְפָּר, סְפֹרָה.

סְפַר m. Chald. 1. *a writer, scribe.* Ezra 4:8, 9, 17, 23. here *the royal scribe* which attended the governor.

2. *one learned in the scriptures.* Ezra 7:12, 21.

סֵפֶר m. with suff. סִפְרִי, plur. סְפָרִים, const. סִפְרֵי, verbal from סָפַר, dec. VI. g.

1. *writing, scriptura.* Is. 29:11, 12 יֹדֵעַ הַסֵּפֶר *one who understands writing.* Dan. 1:4 סֵפֶר וּלְשׁוֹן כַּשְׂדִּים *the writing and language of the Chaldeans.* Verse 17.

2. *a writing, something written;* spoken of a bill of sale, Jer. 32:11 ff. of a written accusation, Job 31:35. of a bill of divorce, Deut. 24:1, 3. Of course

3. *a book.* Ex. 17:14.—סֵפֶר הַתּוֹרָה *the book of the law,* Josh. 1:8. 8:34. also called מְגִלַּת־סֵפֶר *the volume of the book.* Ps. 40:8.—סֵפֶר חַיִּים *the book of life,* in which the living are written down before God, Ps. 69:29. comp. Dan. 12: 1. Rev. 20:12, 15.—סְפָרִים Dan. 9:2, *the (holy) scriptures,* τὰ γράμματα, which were perhaps already united into a volume before the writing of the book of Daniel.—עֲשׂוֹת סְפָרִים Ecc. 12:12, *to make books,* used by way of contempt.

4. *a letter, an epistle.* 2 Sam. 11:14.

סְפַר Chald. plur. סִפְרִין, *a book.* Ezra 4:15. Dan. 7:10.

סְפָר m. verbal from סָפַר.

1. *a numbering.* 2 Chr. 2:16.

2. Gen. 10:30. (with ה local סְפָרָה) a boundary of Joktanitish Arabia, probably on the south. (See מֵשָׁא.) The names of places which present themselves for comparison are (1.) *Saphar* of Pliny (VI. 23.) ظفار, מפאר of Abulfeda, a city in the middle of Yemen. (2.) *Dofar,* in the mountainous district, and near the northern boundary of Yemen. Neither of these places corresponds perfectly.

סְפָרַד found only Obad. 20. name of a country where some of the Israelitish captives lived. Vulg. *Bosphorus.* The Syr. Chald. and modern Hebrew commentators, *Spain.* Both of these explanations are undoubtedly false, but nothing more certain can be substituted in their place. Some have conjectured *Sipphara,* but the Hebrew for this is probably סְפַרְוַיִם.

סִפְרָה fem. of סֵפֶר *a book.* Ps. 56:9.

סְפַרְוַיִם 2 K. 17:24. 18:34. 19: 13. Is. 36:19. 37:13. a city under the government of the Assyrians, whence colonists were sent into the country of Samaria. Prob. Σιπφάρα, in Mesopotamia, on the Euphrates. The gentile noun is סְפָרְוִים 2 K. 17:31. and also סְפָרִים again in the same verse in Kethib.

סָקַל *to stone,* construed with an accus. of the person. Ex. 19:13. 21: 28. Frequently with the addition בָּאֲבָנִים, Deut. 13:11. 17:5. 22:24. Comp. the synonymous verb רָגַם.

Niph. pass. Ex. 19:13. 21:28 ff.

Pi. 1. as in Kal, *to stone, to overwhelm with stones.* 2 Sam. 16:6, 13.

2. *to free from stones,* with a privative signification like גִּנֵּב, סִקֵּל. Is. 5:2. Joined with מֵאֶבֶן, 62:10.

Pu. pass. *to be stoned.* 1 K. 21:14, 15.

סַר, fem. סָרָה, dec. VIII. k. *discontented, displeased, sullen.* 1 K. 20:43. 21:4, 5. (Root סרר Arab. شرّ *to be evil,* here, as in German, signifying *to look evil* or *displeased.*)

סָרָב m. (with Kamets impure) dec. I. *refractory, rebellious.* Ezek. 2:6. (In Syr. and Chald. *idem.*) On account of its connexion with סַלּוֹנִים and עַקְרַבִּים, some Jewish commentators have rendered it *thorns* or *nettles,* (comp. סָרַף *to burn,*) a very suitable interpretation, if it were only better supported.

סַרְבָּל m. Chald. *wide Persian hosen* or *breeches.* Dan. 3:21, 27. (In Syr. Arab. and Chald. *idem;* but in Aram. used also for *a wide garment* of any kind. Pers. شلوار by transposition. This article of dress has passed with its name into the western languages, as in Greek σαράβαρα, σαράβαλλα, σαράπαρα; in Lat. *sarabara, saraballa;* in Span. *ceroulas;* in Hungarian and Sclavonic *shalwary,* in Polish *sharmvari.*)

סַרְגוֹן proper name of a king of Assyria. Once Is. 20:1. He was probably the predecessor of Sennacherib, as his general Tartan was also general under Sennacherib. Others suppose *Sargon* to have been another name of *Sennacherib.* (For its appellative signification, comp. Pers. سرجونة *prince of the sun.*)

סָרָה f. verbal from סוּר.

1. *a deviation from the law, a sin.* Deut. 19:16.

2. particularly *declension* or *apostacy* from Jehovah. Deut. 13:6. Jer. 28:16. 29:32. Is. 1:5. 31:6. 59:13.

3. *cessation, intermission.* Is. 14:6.

סָרַח 1. *to pour out, to stretch out.* Am. 6:4, 7. Intrans. Ezek. 17:6 גֶּפֶן סֹרַחַת *vitis late fusa.*

2. *to be superfluous, to hang over, redundare.* Ex. 26:12. Part. pass. סָרוּחַ *redundans,* verse 13. Ezek. 23:15 סְרוּחֵי טְבוּלִים *with long turbans hanging down, redundantes mitris.*

Niph. *to be poured* or *shaken out.* Metaphorically Jer. 49:7 נִסְרְחָה חָכְמָתָם *is their wisdom poured out?*

סֶרַח m. verbal from סָרַח, *a superfluity, something hanging over.* Ex. 26:12.

סִרְיוֹן i. q. שִׁרְיוֹן, dec. I. *a coat of mail, a brigandine.* Jer. 46:4. 51:3.

סָרִיס m. const. סְרִיס, plur. סָרִיסִים, const. סָרִיסֵי and סְרִיסֵי, Syr. ܣܪܝܣܐ.

1. *an eunuch.* Is. 56:3, 4. (Root Arab. سرس *impotens esse ad venerem.*) Eunuchs were employed particularly as keepers of the harem, (Est. 2:3, 14, 15. 4:5.) but also in other capacities, Est. 1:10, 12, 15.—רַב הַסָּרִיסִים Dan. 1:3. or שַׂר הַסָּרִיסִים verse 7 ff. *the prince of the eunuchs,* who had the charge of the noble youths. Hence

2. *a courtier, chamberlain* generally, only that we are unable to decide in particular cases whether the original idea is retained or lost. 1 Sam. 8:15. 1 K. 22:9. 2 K. 9:32. 20:18. 24:12, 15. 25:19 (where a סָרִיס is placed over the men of war.) Jer. 34:19. 41:16. Especially Gen. 37:36. 39:1. where the סָרִיס is married.

סָרַךְ, plur. סָרְכִין, Chald. *an overseer, prefect.* Dan. 6:3 ff. (In the Targums for שׁוֹטֵר.) It is here employed of the three ministers which were placed over the governors of the 120 provinces of the Persian empire.

סֶרֶן dec. VI. a. found only in the plur. סְרָנִים, const. סַרְנֵי.

1. *an axle-tree.* 1 K. 7:30. In ancient times axle-trees, especially in waggons, were fastened to the wheels and turned round with them.

2. *princes,* used exclusively of the five princes or lords of the Philistines, in their five principal cities. Josh. 13:3. Judg. 3:3. 16:5 ff. 1 Sam. 6:4 ff. 5:8 ff. 29:6. Comp. Arab. قُطْب *axis, polus;* (2.) *dominus, princeps,* (quasi *cardo populi*).

סַרְעַפָּה f. dec. X. *a branch, bough,* i. q. סְעִפָּה. Ezek. 31:5. (Syr. ܣܪܥܦ. *to sprout, shoot.* For the insertion of ר, see the letter ר.)

סָרַף an Aramean orthography for שָׂרַף *to burn.* Part. Pi. מְסָרֵף *the burner* (of human corpses), *the kindler of the funeral pile,* Am. 6:10. Comp. particularly שְׂרֵפָה. 23 MSS. of Kennicot and several others of De Rossi read מְשָׂרֵף.

סִרְפָּד m. Is. 55:13. name of a plant, which cannot be determined with certainty. Sept. Theod. Aqu. κόνυζα. Vulg. *urtica.*

סָרַר *to be refractory, rebellious, perverse;* spoken of animals, Hos. 4:16. of a son, Deut. 21:18, 20. Ps. 78:8. Jer. 5:23. Neh. 9:29 וַיִּתְּנוּ כָתֵף סוֹרֶרֶת *they shewed a rebellious shoulder,* i. e. they conducted themselves perversely. Zech. 7:11. Jer. 6:28 סָרֵי סוֹרְרִים *falling off to the rebellious.* Often used of a people which rebels against God, Is. 30:1. 65:2. Ps. 68:19. Is. 1:23. Hos. 9:15.

סְתָו, in Keri סְתָיו, m. *winter.* Cant. 2:11. (In Aram. and Arab. *idem.*)

סָתַם 1. *to stop up,* e. g. wells of water. 2 K. 3:19, 25. 2 Chron. 32:3, 4.

2. *to close up, to keep secret.* Dan. 8:26. 12:4, 9. Part. pass. סָתוּם *something concealed; a secret.* Ezek. 28:3.

Niph. *to be closed,* spoken of breaches in a wall. Neh. 4:1. [4:7.]

Pi. i. q. Kal no. 1. Gen. 26:15, 18. See שָׁתַם.

סָתַר *to hide* or *conceal one's self.* In Kal only Prov. 22:3 Kethib. The Keri is וְנִסְתָּר, as in 27:12.

Niph. 1. *to be concealed.* Job 3:23. Construed with מִן, Ps. 38:10. Is. 40:27. Gen. 31:49 *when we shall be concealed*, i. e. separated, *from each other.* Hos. 13:14 *repentance is hidden from mine eyes*, i. e. I experience it not. Also with מִפְּנֵי, Deut. 7:20. with מִלִּפְנֵי, Jer. 16:17. with מִנֶּגֶד, Am. 9:3. Part. נִסְתָּרוֹת *secret things*, Deut. 29:28. *secret sins, sins committed ignorantly*, Ps. 19:13.

2. *to hide one's self.* 1 Sam. 20:5, 19. Construed with מִן, Ps. 55:13. and with מִפְּנֵי, Gen. 4:14.

Pi. *to hide, conceal.* Is. 16:3.

Pu. *to be concealed, secret.* Prov. 27:5.

Hiph. הִסְתִּיר 1. *to cover, to hide;* followed by פָּנִים *the face.* Ex. 3:6. Either from shame, Is. 53:3. or so as not to see, Ps. 10:11. 51:11 הַסְתֵּר פָּנֶיךָ מֵחֲטָאָי *hide thy face from my sins*, i. e. overlook them. Spoken particularly of Jehovah, as a mark of displeasure or anger, Ps. 30:8. 104:29. Construed with מִן of the person, Ps. 22:25. 27:9. 88:15. Used elliptically Is. 57:17 אַכֵּהוּ הַסְתֵּר וְאֶקְצֹף *I smote them (the people,) I hid (my face) and was angry.*

2. *to hide, to keep secret* or *concealed;* construed with מִן *from* any one, 1 Sam. 20:2. with מִפְּנֵי, 2 K. 11:2. Job 3:10. וַיַּסְתֵּר עָמָל מֵעֵינָי *nor hid sorrow from mine eyes*, i. e. did not deliver me from it.

3. *to protect, defend.* Ps. 31:21. 27:5. 64:3.

Hithpa. הִסְתַּתֵּר *to hide one's self.* 1 Sam. 23:19. 26:1. Is. 29:14.

Deriv. out of course מִסְתָּר, מִסְתּוֹר.

סְתַר Chald. found only in Pa.

1. *to conceal.* Part. pass. *secret things*, Dan. 2:22.

2. *to destroy.* Ezra 5:12. (In Syr. Pe. and in the Targums, *idem.* This signification is connected with the preceding. Both signify *to remove out of sight.* See כָּחַד and הִכְחִיד.)

סֵתֶר, with suff. סִתְרִי, verbal from סָתַר, dec. VI. g.

1. *a covering.* Job 22:14. 24:15. Ps. 81:8 בְּסֵתֶר רַעַם *in the covering of thunder*, i. e. the thunder clouds. Ps. 18:12.

2. *secrecy, a secret place* or *thing.* Judg. 3:19 דְּבַר־סֵתֶר *something secret.* 1 Sam. 25:20 סֵתֶר הָהָר *a secret place of the mountain.*—לֶחֶם סְתָרִים *bread in secret*, Prov. 9:17. — בַּסֵּתֶר *in secret, secretly*, 1 Sam. 19:2. 2 Sam. 12:12.

3. *a shelter, protection.* Ps. 32:7. 91:1. 119:114.

סִתְרָה fem. of סֵתֶר no. 3. *a shelter, protection.* Deut. 32:38.

ע

Ain, the 16th letter of the alphabet, and as a numerical sign denoting 70. The name עַיִן signifies *an eye*, and has reference to the round form of this letter in the Phenician alphabet.

The Arabians have two letters corresponding to the Hebrew and Aramean *Ain*, ع and غ, the former a soft guttural, the latter a *g* or *gh*, pronounced from the throat with a rattling sound peculiar to the orientalists. These two sounds probably existed in the Hebrew as a living language, though perhaps less definitely marked than in Arabic. Hence some Hebrew words spelt with ע, (as is the case also with ח,) have two different significations, according as the corresponding word in Arabic is written with ع or غ; e. g. עָטָה Arab. عَطَي *to seize*, and עָטָה Arab. غَطَا *to cover;* comp. the articles צֶבַע and אֶצְבַּע, עָשָׂה, עָשָׁה. The Sept. expresses it sometimes by a spiritus lenis or asper, and sometimes by γ; e. g. עֲמָלֵק, Ἀμαλήκ; עִבְרִי, Ἑβραῖος; עַזָּה, Γάζα; עֲמֹרָה, Γόμοῤῥα.

Ain is interchanged (1.) with א, (see p. 1.) (2.) rarely with ג, כ and (only in Chald.) with ק; e. g. נְבַע i. q. נְבַע, נָבַע *to spring, to stream;* אַרְעָא and אַרְקָא *the earth;* שְׁמַע and שְׁמַק *to hear;* (3.) with צ, more frequently than with the last mentioned, especially in the collation of Aramean words, in which ע often stands for the Hebrew צ; e. g. אַרְעָא, אֶרֶץ *the earth;* עֲמַר, צֶמֶר *wool;* עוק, צוק *to press.* In Greek, comp. ὀλίγος and ὀλίζος; φύγω, φεύγω, and φυζάω, φύζημι. The cause of this remarkable change lies perhaps in the pronunciation of צ like גס *ghs*, from which the flat pronunciation of the Arameans left out the sound of ס and retained only that of ע.

עָב m. an architectural term, prob. *a threshold*, forming the entrance to a colonnade or temple. 1 K. 7 : 6. Ezek. 41:25. Plur. עֻבִּים *idem*, verse 26.

עָב com. gen. (masc. Is. 19 : 1. Ecc. 11:31. fem. 1 K. 18 : 44.) const. עַב, plur. עָבִים, עָבֵי, and עָבוֹת.

1. *darkness.* (Root עוב or עיב q. v.) Ex. 19 : 9 בְּעַב הֶעָנָן *in the darkness of a cloud.* Ps. 18 : 12.

2. *a cloud* itself. Job 36 : 29. 37 : 11, 16.

3. *a thicket of a wood.* Plur. עָבִים Jer. 4 : 29.

עָבַד, fut. יַעֲבֹד. 1. *to labour.* Ex. 20 : 9 שֵׁשֶׁת יָמִים תַּעֲבֹד *six days shalt thou labour.* Deut. 5 : 13. Ecc. 5 : 11. (From this signif. is derived the Chald. עֲבַד i. q. עָשָׂה *to make, do;* and the derivatives עֲבַד, מַעֲבָד.)

2. *to labour upon, to cultivate*, construed with an accus. of the thing. E. g. the ground, Gen. 2 : 5. 3 : 23. 4 : 2. *a vineyard*, Deut. 28 : 39.—Is. 19 : 9 עֹבְדֵי פִשְׁתִּים *those who cultivate flax.* Ezek. 48 : 18 עֹבְדֵי הָעִיר *those who labour on the city*, i. e. in building the walls. Elliptically Deut. 15 : 19 *thou shalt not labour (the ground) with the firstling of thy bullock.*

3. *to labour for another, to serve.* Construed with an accus. of the person, Gen. 27 : 40. 29 : 15. 30 : 26. with לְ, 1 Sam. 4 : 9. 2 Sam. 16 : 19. with עִם, Gen. 29 : 25, 30. Lev. 25 : 40. Also with לִפְנֵי, *to serve before* any one, 2 Sam. 16 : 19. Spoken likewise of a whole nation, *to serve* or *be tributary to* another nation, Gen. 14 : 4. 15 : 14. With two accus. Gen. 30 : 29 יָדַעְתָּ אֵת אֲשֶׁר עֲבַדְתִּיךָ *thou knowest what service I have rendered thee.*

4. construed with בְּ, *to impose labour* or *service* on any one. Lev. 25 : 39 לֹא תַעֲבֹד בּוֹ עֲבֹדַת עָבֶד *thou shalt not lay on him the service of a bond-servant.* Verse 46. Ex. 1 : 14. Jer. 22 : 13. 25 : 14. 30 : 8. Hence we may explain Gen. 15 : 13 וַעֲבָדוּם וְעִנּוּ אֹתָם *they (the Egyptians) shall impose on them (the Israelites) and shall afflict them.* The suffix pronoun ם may be resolved into בָּם, (comp. Job 6 : 4. 31 : 18. Ps. 42 : 5.)

5. *to serve, worship*, (Jehovah or idols.) Construed with an accus. Ex. 3 : 12. 9 : 1, 13. rarely with לְ, Jer. 44 : 3. Judg. 2 : 13. — Job 36 : 11 אִם יִשְׁמְעוּ וְיַעֲבֹדוּ *if they obey and serve (God).*

6. *to offer, to present*, (to God.) Is. 19 : 21. Construed with two accus. Ex. 10 : 26. Comp. the Greek ἔρδω, ῥέζω, the Latin *facio*, and עָשָׂה Ex. 10 : 15.

Niph. 1. *to be laboured.* Deut. 21 : 4.

2. *to be cultivated.* Ezek. 36 : 9, 34.

3. *to be served, honoured.* Ecc. 5 : 8.

Pu. 1. *to be laboured.* Deut. 21 : 3. Comp. 15 : 19.

2. pass. of Kal no. 4. עֻבַּד בְּ *labour is imposed on* any one, Is. 14 : 3.

Hiph. 1. causat. of Kal no. 1. *to cause to work, to keep at work.* Ex. 1 : 13. 6 : 5.

2. causat. of Kal no. 3. Ezek. 29 : 18. Hence *to make tributary*, Jer. 17 : 4.

3. causat. of no. 5. 2 Chr. 34 : 33.

4. *to weary out* or *fatigue by hard labour, to weary out* in any way. Is. 43 : 23, 24 אַךְ הֶעֱבַדְתַּנִי בְּחַטֹּאותֶיךָ *but thou hast wearied me by thy sins.* Parall. הוֹגִיעַ.

Hiph. i. q. Kal, *to serve.* תָעָבְדֵם *thou shalt serve them*, Ex. 20 : 5. 23 : 24. Deut. 5 : 9. and נָעָבְדֵם *we will serve them*, Deut. 13 : 3. Others consider this as an uncommon form of the fut. Kal.

עֲבַד Chald. *to make, do*, i. q. Heb.

עֲבִידָה. Dan. 3:1, 15.—עֲבַד קְרָב *to make war,* Dan. 7:21. Construed with בְּ, Dan. 4:32. [4:35.] and עִם, Ezra 6:8. *to treat* or *deal with* any one.

Ithpe. *to be made, to take place, to happen.* Ezra 4:19. 5:8. 7:26. Dan. 3:29.

Deriv. עֲבַד, עֲבִידָא.

עֶבֶד m. verbal from עָבַד, dec. VI. a. *a servant.*—Gen. 9:25 עֶבֶד עֲבָדִים *a servant of servants,* i. e. a most abject servant. Particularly (1.) *a servant* (of the king), *a courtier, a military officer.* 1 Sam. 16:17. 18:22. 22:6. 28:7. (2.) *a servant* (of God), an honourable title of pious and holy men, as of Moses, Deut. 34:5. Josh. 1:1, 13, 15. of Joshua, Josh. 24:29. Judg. 2:8. of the prophets, Jer. 7:25. 26:5. 29:19 44:4. of Job, Job 1:8. 2:3. 42:8. of David, Ps. 18:1. 36:1. 89:4, 21. more rarely of pious men generally, Ps. 113:1. 134:1. 34:23. 69:37. This phrase is used in a different sense Jer. 23:9. 27:6. where it is applied to the king of Babylon, as an instrument in the hand of God. (3.) The phrase *thy servant* is employed by inferiors in conversing with their superiors to express the *first* person, as *my lord* (see אָדוֹן) to express the *third* person. Dan. 10:17 *how can the servant of this my lord speak with this my lord?* i. e. how can I speak with thee? *Thy servant,* therefore, sometimes alternates with the first person; e. g. Gen. 44:32 *for thy servant became surety for the lad to my father.* This epithet is sometimes applied to one's absent kindred; e.g. Gen. 44:27. *thy servant, my father, spake to us.* 30:31. 32:20. (4.) once applied to inanimate things by a zeugma. Gen. 47:19.

עֲבַד Chald. *idem.*—עֲבַד אֱלָהָא *a servant* or *worshipper of God,* Dan. 3:26. 6:21. Ezra 5:11.

עֲבָד m. (with Kamets impure) verbal from עָבַד, dec. I. *a work, deed.* Once Ecc. 9:1.

עֲבֹדָה f. verbal from עָבַד, dec. X. 1. *labour.* Ex. 1:14. Lev. 25:39 עֲבֹדַת עָבֶד *the labour of a bond-servant.* 23:7 כָּל־מְלֶאכֶת עֲבֹדָה *every business connected with labour.*

2. *a work, business.* Num. 4:47 לַעֲבֹד עֲבֹדַת עֲבֹדָה וַעֲבֹדַת מַשָּׂא *to perform the business of the service and the business of the burden.* (In 1 Chr. 9:19, the same is expressed by מְלֶאכֶת הָעֲבֹדָה.) Is. 28:21. 32:17 וַעֲבֹדַת הַצְּדָקָה הַשְׁקֵט *and the work,* i. e. effect, *of righteousness shall be peace.* (Chald. עֲבִידָא, שֹׁלְתָא i. q. מַעֲשֶׂה *a work,* also *a reward;* comp. the latter passages.)

3. *tillage, cultivation of land, agriculture.* 1 Chr. 27:26. Neh. 10:38.

4. *service.* Gen. 30:26. Neh. 3:5. 1 Chr. 26:30 עֲבֹדַת הַמֶּלֶךְ *the service of the king.* Ps. 104:14 עֵשֶׂב לַעֲבֹדַת הָאָדָם *herb for the service,* i. e. use, *of man.* Used particularly of service in the tabernacle or temple, e.g. עֲבֹדָה בְּאֹהֶל מוֹעֵד Num. 4:23, 35. or עֲבֹדַת אֹהֶל מוֹעֵד Ex. 30:17. עֲבֹדַת בֵּית יְהוָה 1 Chr. 9:13. also without addition, 1 Chr. 28:14. Ex. 35:24. Spoken also of a single religious usage, Ex. 12:25, 26. 13:5.—עָבַד עֲבֹדָה *to do service,* Gen. 30:26.

5. *implements, utensils, appertenances.* Num. 3:26, 31, 36.

עֲבֻדָּה f. verbal from עָבַד, *a body of servants* or *domestics, familia.* Gen. 26:14. Job 1:3. 34:25.

עַבְדּוֹן proper name of a Levitical city in the tribe of Asher. Josh. 21:30. 1 Chr. 6:59. Without doubt this is the true reading Josh 19:28, instead of עֶבְרֹן. It is so read in 20 MSS. of Kennicott and De Rossi.

עַבְדוּת f. denom. from עֶבֶד, dec. I. *servitude, the state of a servant.* Ezra 9:8, 9.

עֹבַדְיָהוּ and **עֹבַדְיָה** m. (*servant of Jehovah*) the proper name of several persons, among whom the prophet of this name (Obad. 1.) is the most famous.

עָבָה *to be thick, fat.* Deut. 32:15. 1 K. 12:10. (Syr. ܥܒܳܐ *to be thick, close.*) Deriv. עָבִי, עֳבִי, מַעֲבֶה.

עֲבוֹט m. dec. I. *a pledge*. Deut. 24: 10, 11, 12. Root עָבַט.

עֲבוּר liter. a subst. *transition*. Found only in composition בַּעֲבוּר (1.) a prep. signifying (a.) *on account of*. 1 Sam. 12:22. With suff. בַּעֲבוּרִי, בַּעֲבוּרְךָ *on my account, on thy account*, 1 Sam. 23:10. Gen. 3:17. (b.) *for, in exchange for*. Am. 2:6. (2.) a conj. signifying (a.) *so that;* construed with a fut. Gen. 27:4. Ex. 9:14. with an infin. 2 Sam. 10:3. more full בַּעֲבוּר אֲשֶׁר, Gen. 27:10. also לְבַעֲבוּר with an infin. 2 Sam. 14:20. 17: 15. (b.) *because*, construed with a prep. Mic. 2:10. (c.) *so long as, while*. 2 Sam. 12:21.

עֲבוּר m. dec. III. a. *grain*. Josh. 5: 11, 12. (Syr. ܥܒܘܪܐ, Chald. עִבּוּר *idem*.)

עָבַט, fut. יַעֲבֹט. 1. prob. *to change, exchange*. See Pi. (Comp. עָבַת *to weave*.)

2. *to give a pledge, to borrow by giving a pledge, mutuum accipere*. Deut. 24:10 לַעֲבֹט עֲבֹטוֹ *that he may give his pledge*. 15:6 וְאַתָּה לֹא תַעֲבֹט *and thou shalt not borrow by giving pledges*.

Pi. *to change, alter*. Joel 2:7 *they shall not alter their course*, i. e. they shall go straight on.

Hiph. *to loan* or *lend, mutuum dare*. Construed with an accus. Deut. 15:6. with two accus. verse 8.

Deriv. עֲבוֹט, עַבְטִיט.

עַבְטִיט m. verbal from עָבַט, *debt, guilt, criminality*. Hab. 2:6.

עֳבִי m. verbal from עָבָה, *thickness*. Job 15:26. 2 Chr. 4:17 בַּעֲבִי הָאֲדָמָה *in thick*, i. e. adhesive, *earth*. Vulg. *in terra argillosa*.

עֳבִי m. with suff. עָבְיוֹ, verbal from עָבָה, dec. VI. q. *thickness*. 1 K. 7:26. Jer. 52:21.

עֲבִידָה f. Chald.

1. *work, labour*. Ezra 4:24. 5:8. 6:7, 18.

2. *business*, especially *public business*. Dan. 2:49. 3:12. Comp. מְלָאכָה Neh. 2:16.

עָבַר, fut. יַעֲבֹר.

1. *to pass, to go* or *pass on*. Ps. 42: 5. Am. 5:5 וּבְאֵר שֶׁבַע לֹא תַעֲבֹרוּ *to Beersheba ye shall not pass*.—עָבַר וְשָׁב *to pass and return*, Ezek. 35:7. Zech. 7:14. 9:8. Ex. 32:27. עָבַר וְיָצָא *to go in and out*, Mic. 2:13. Also (1.) with לִפְנֵי, *to go before*. Gen. 33:3. Ex. 17:5. (2.) with אַחֲרֵי, *to go after*. 2 Sam. 20: 13. (3.) עָבַר בִּבְרִית *to enter into a covenant*. Deut. 29:11. (comp. בּוֹא בְאָלָה Neh. 10:30.)

2. *to go* or *pass through* a place, construed with an accus. Judg. 11:29. usually with בְּ, Gen. 12:6. 30:32. Is. 8:21. with בֵּין, *to pass through* or *between*, Gen. 15:17. Lam. 3:44 *thou concealedst thyself in a cloud*, מֵעֲבוֹר תְּפִלָּה *so that our prayer should not pass through*.

3. *to pass by;* used absolutely, Gen. 37:28. construed with עַל, 1 K. 9:8. 2 K. 4:9. Jer. 18:17. with מֵעַל, Gen. 18:3. with עַל פְּנֵי, Ex. 34:6. with לִפְנֵי, 2 K. 4:31. with מִן, Is. 40:27 *my cause passes by God, præterit Deum*, i. e. is unnoticed by him. Ps. 81:7 כַּפָּיו מִדּוּד תַּעֲבֹרְנָה *his hands pass by the labourers' basket*, i. e. are freed from bearing it. Also with בְּ, Ps. 103:16. with an accus. 32:32. 2 Sam. 18:23. Job 21:29 עֹבְרֵי דֶרֶךְ *those who pass by the way*. Metaphorically (1.) *to pass by, elapse*, spoken of time. Cant. 2:11. Jer. 8:20. (2.) עָבַר עַל פֶּשַׁע *to pass by sin*, i. e. to forgive it. Mic. 7:18. Then with a dative of the person, Am. 7:8. 8:2. (3.) כֶּסֶף עֹבֵר *current money*. 2 K. 12:5. More full עֹבֵר לַסֹּחֵר *current with the merchant*, Gen. 23:16.

4. *to pass over*, e. g. a river; construed with an accus. Gen. 31:21. with בְּ, Josh. 3:11. 2 Sam. 15:23. Jer. 2: 10 עִבְרוּ אִיֵּי כִתִּיִּים *pass over to the isles of Chittim*. Metaphorically *to transgress* the law, Jer. 34:18. 2 K. 18:12. Dan. 9:11.

5. *to overflow*, spoken of water. Is. 8:8. 54:9. Nah. 1:8. Metaphorically of a devastating army, Dan. 11:10, 40. and in other phrases borrowed from water, Ps. 124:4 נַחְלָה עָבַר עַל נַפְשֵׁנוּ *the*

stream had overwhelmed our life, i. e. our head. 38:5. Jer. 23:9 *as a man* עֲבָרוֹ יַיִן *whom wine has overwhelmed*, i. e. overcome. Comp. בָּלַע.

6. *to pass away, to go on*. Gen. 18:5. 2 Sam. 18:9. Hence *to disappear, perish*, Ps. 37:36. Job 34:20. Is. 29:5. Est. 9:28. עָבַר בַּשֶּׁלַח *to perish by the sword*, Job 33:18.

7. construed with עַל, *to come on* any one, (comp. בּוֹא with an accus.) Num. 5:14 וְעָבַר עָלָיו רוּחַ קִנְאָה *and (if) the spirit of jealousy come upon him*. Spoken of evil, Nah. 3:19. Job 13:13 וְיַעֲבֹר עָלַי מָה *let come upon me what will*. Passively, *to be laid on* any one, Deut. 24:5.

8. i. q. Arab. عَبَرَ *to drop, to ooze out*. מֹר עֹבֵר *myrrha lachrymans*, i. e. myrrh which flows out of itself, the purest myrrh. Cant. 5:5, 13.

9. causat. as in Hiph. Ezek. 48:14 Keth.

Niph. *transiri*, spoken of a river. Ezek. 47:5.

Pi. 1. *to bar, repagulavit*. 1 K. 6:21. (Chald. עַבַּר *idem*; עַבְרָא *a bar*.)

2. *to conceive, to become pregnant*, liter. *transire fecit* seu *recepit semen virile*. Job 21:10 שׁוֹרוֹ עִבַּר *his cow becomes pregnant*. (In Chald. Kal, Pael and Ethpa. *idem*; comp. the synon. עֲדָה, Pa. and Aph. *concepit*.)

Hiph. הֶעֱבִיר causat. of Kal no. 1. (i. q. הֵבִיא.)

1. *to bring, present, consecrate*. Ex. 13:12. Ezek. 23:37. Particularly הֶעֱבִיר לַמֹּלֶךְ *to consecrate to Moloch*, Lev. 18:21. Jer. 32:35. Ezek. 16:21. more full ה׳ ל׳ בָּאֵשׁ *to consecrate to Moloch in the fire*, 2 K. 23:10. Ezek. 20:31. the usual phrase to express the burning of children in the valley of Hinnom in honour of Moloch; (comp. Jer. 7:31. 19:5. Ps. 106:37.)—In 2 Chr. 28:3, we find expressly וַיַּבְעֵר *he burnt*, for וַיַּעֲבֵר in 2 K. 16:3. (Some have understood this of a bare passing through the fire or of a lustration; comp. Carpzov. Apparat. ad Antiq. Sac. Cod. p. 487. but erroneously.)

2. *to cause to pass, to conduct*; construed with two accus. 2 Sam. 19:16. Num. 32:5. and with בְּ, Ps. 78:13. 136:14.—הֶעֱבִיר קוֹל בְּ *to let one's voice go through* a place, *to cause to be publicly proclaimed*, Ex. 36:6. Ezra 1:1. 10:7. Comp. הֶעֱבִיר שׁוֹפָר *to cause the trumpet to sound*, Lev. 25:9.

3. *to cause to pass by*. 1 Sam. 16:9, 10. 1 Sam. 20:36 *he shot an arrow* לְהַעֲבִרוֹ *to pass by him*, i. e. beyond him. Metaphorically הֶעֱבִיר חַטָּאָה *to let sin pass by* i. e. to forgive it, 2 Sam. 12:13. 24:10. Job 7:21.

4. causat. of Kal no. 4. *to carry over* (a river), Gen. 32:23. *to remove, transferre*, Gen. 47:21 וְאֶת־הָעָם הֶעֱבִיר אֹתוֹ לֶעָרִים *and the people he removed into (other) cities*.

5. causat. of Kal no. 4. metaphorically, *to cause to trangress*. 1 Sam. 2:24.

6. *to carry away*, 2 Chr. 35:23. *to take away, remove*; e. g. *to put off* a garment, Jon. 3:6. *to take off* a ring, Est. 8:2. *to remove*, idols, false prophets, 2 Chr. 15:8. Zech. 13:2. Also *to turn away*, Est. 8:3.

Hithpa. 1. *to be arrogant, haughty*. Prov. 14:16. (Comp. עֶבְרָה no. 2.)

2. *to become angry, to be wroth*. (Comp. עֶבְרָה no. 3.) Ps. 78:21, 59. Construed with בְּ, Ps. 78:62. with עִם, Ps. 89:39. with עַל, Prov. 26:17. with an accus. Prov. 20:2 מִתְעַבְּרוֹ *he who becomes wroth with him (the king.)* The suffix pronoun may also be resolved into בּוֹ.

(Comp. Arab. جَارَ *to go beyond, to be angry, to be arrogant*.)

Deriv. out of course מַעֲבָר, עֲבוּר, עֶבְרָה.

עֵבֶר m. with suff. עֶבְרוֹ, dec. VI. j.

1. *what is on the other side*.—עֵבֶר הַיַּרְדֵּן τὸ πέραν τοῦ Ἰορδάνου, *the part of Palestine beyond Jordan*, Gen. 50:10, 11. Deut. 1:1. Is. 8:23. [9:1.]—עֵבֶר הַנָּהָר *the country beyond the Euphrates*, Josh. 24:2, 3. Once in the plur. עֶבְרֵי נָהָר Is. 7:20.—אֶל־עֵבֶר הַיָּם *beyond the sea*, Deut. 30:13.—מֵעֵבֶר Num. 21:13. and מֵעֵבֶר לְ *on the other side*, Num. 22:1.

2. sometimes *that which is on this side*, as if used by one living on the other side. 1 K. 4 : 24.

3. *side, quarter* generally. 1 Sam. 14 : 40 לְעֵבֶר אֶחָד repeated, *on one side, on the other side*. Ex. 28 : 26. Plur. Jer. 49 : 32 מִכָּל־עֲבָרָיו *on all sides*. Ex. 32 : 15.

4. אֶל עֵבֶר (1.) *over against*, i. q. אֶל־מוּל. Josh. 22 : 11. (2.) עַל עֵבֶר פְּנֵי *in front, before*. Ex. 25 : 37. Ezek. 1 : 9 אִישׁ אֶל עֵבֶר פָּנָיו *each before him*.

5 *Eber* or *Heber*, proper name of the progenitor of the Hebrews. Gen. 10 : 24, 25. 11 : 14, 15. Hence בְּנֵי עֵבֶר Gen. 10 : 21. and in poetry עֵבֶר Num. 24 : 24. for *Hebrews*. Most of the names in those tables seem to stand for nations rather than for individuals. Comp. Gesenius' Gesch. der Hebr. Sprache und Schrift, p. 11.

עֲבַר Chald. *idem*. עֲבַר נַהֲרָא *the other side of the Euphrates*, Ezra 4 : 10 ff.

עֲבָרָה f. verbal from עָבַר.

1. *a ferry-boat*. 2 Sam. 19 : 19.

2. 2 Sam. 15 : 28 Keth. עֲבָרוֹת i. q. Keri עַרְבוֹת *plains*.

עֶבְרָה f. verbal from עָבַר, dec. XII. c.

1. *excess*. Prov. 21 : 24 עֶבְרַת זָדוֹן *excessive wickedness*. Job 40 : 11 עֶבְרוֹת אַפֶּךָ *thy excessive wrath*.

2. *arrogance, pride*. (See עָבַר Hithpa.) Jer. 48 : 30. Is. 16 : 6. Ps. 7 : 7.

3. *wrath, anger*. Is. 14 : 6. Particularly *the wrath of God exhibited in punishment*, Is. 9 : 18. 10 : 6.—יוֹם עֶבְרָה *the day of divine indignation*, Prov. 11 : 4. Zeph. 1 : 15, 18. Comp. Prov. 11 : 23.

עִבְרִי, plur. עִבְרִים and עִבְרִיִּים, fem. עִבְרִיָּה, plur. עִבְרִיּוֹת, a gentile noun, *a Hebrew* or *Hebrewess*. The sacred writers regard this word as a patronymic from עֵבֶר, (q. v.) otherwise it might be considered as originally an appellative from עֵבֶר *the country on the other side*, hence *those who live on the other side* or *come from thence*, (a name which might very properly be given by the Canaanites to the migrating horde under Abraham, Gen. 14 : 13.) or, according to others, by transposition i. q. עֲרָבִים *inhabitants of the desert, nomades*. It was the proper name of the people, by which they were known to foreigners, (as to Pausanias, Tacitus, Josephus;) and thus distinguished from בְּנֵי יִשְׂרָאֵל the common domestic name. Comp. a similar distinction between the words *Canaanite* and *Phenician, Dutch* and *German*. Hence it is used in the Bible principally by way of antithesis to other nations, Gen. 40 : 15. 43 : 32. Ex. 1 : 15, 19. 2 : 7, 11, 13. 3 : 18. 5 : 3. 7 : 16. 9 : 1, 13. 21 : 2. Deut. 15, 12. (Jer. 34 : 9, 14.) 1 Sam. 13 : 3, 7. 14 : 11, 21. 29 : 3. Jon. 1 : 9. or when a foreigner is introduced speaking, e. g. an Egyptian, Gen. 39 : 14, 17. 41 : 12. Ex. 1 : 16. 2 : 6. or a Philistine, 1 Sam. 4 : 6, 9. 13 : 19. 14 : 11. 29 : 3.—1 Sam. 13 : 3, 7. makes perhaps the only exception. Comp. Gesenius' Gesch. der Hebr. Sprache, p. 9—12.

עֲבָרִים Jer. 22 : 20. in full הַר־הָעֲבָרִים Num. 27 : 12. Deut. 32 : 49. and עִיֵּי הָעֲבָרִים Num. 33 : 47, 48. proper name of certain mountains beyond Jordan, over against Jericho, of which Mount Nebo (see נְבוֹ) appears to have made a part.

עַבְרֹנָה proper name of a station of the Israelites, not far from Ezion-gaber, on the coast of the Red Sea. Num. 33 : 34.

עָבַשׁ found only Joel 1 : 17. according to the Hebrew commentators i. q. עָשַׁשׁ *to rot, to become rotten* or *mouldy*, as seed under the ground from heat. Comp. in Greek πύθομαι, Hesiod. Scut. Herc. 153.

עָבַת *to be twisted* or *woven*, as appears from the derivatives.

Pi. *to perplex, pervert*. Mic. 7 : 3.

עָבֹת, fem. עֲבֻתָּה, verbal adj. from עָבַת, dec. VIII. d. *thick, bushy, covered with foliage*, spoken of trees. Ezek. 20 : 28. Lev. 23 : 40. Ezek. 6 : 13. (In Syr. with Teth ܛܒܝܬܐ.)

עֲבֹת, plur. עֲבֹתִים and עֲבֹתוֹת, verbal from עָבַת, dec. I. *something twisted* or *woven;* hence

1. *a line, cord*. Judg. 15 : 13, 14.

Plur. *cords, bands, vincula,* Ps. 2:3. Ezek. 3:25. 4:8.

2. *wreathen work.* Ex. 28:24. מַעֲשֵׂה עֲבֹת *idem,* Ex. 28:14. 39:17.

3. *a thick branch.* Ezek. 19:11. 31:3, 10, 14.

עָגַב, fut. יַעְגַּב, *to love,* especially in a bad sense, construed with an accus. and עַל. Ezek. 23:5 ff. עֹגְבִים *lovers,* Jer. 4:30.

עֲגָבִים masc. plur. verbal from עָגַב.

1. *loveliness, pleasantness.* Ezek. 33:32 שִׁיר עֲגָבִים *a lovely song.*

2. *what is pleasing to God.* (Arab. عجب *gratia, beneplacitum Dei.*) Ezek. 33:31 כִּי עֲגָבִים בְּפִיהֶם הֵמָּה עֹשִׂים *for with the mouth they do what is pleasing to God;* antith. *but their heart goeth after unrighteous gain.*

עֲגָבָה or **עַגְבָה** f. verbal from עָגַב, *lust, lewdness.* Ezek. 23:11.

עֻגָה and **עֻגָּה** f. dec. X. *a small cake baked under the ashes,* in Greek ἐγκρυφίας, a common food to this day among the orientals, especially when travelling. Gen. 18:6. Num. 11:8. 1 K. 17:13. עֻגַת רְצָפִים *a cake baked on hot stones,* 1 K. 19:6. Root עוג, comp. מָעוֹג.

עָגוּר m. name of a bird of passage, Jer. 8:7. which, together with the swallow, is said to pip or chirp, Is. 38:14. According to Bochart (Hieroz. II. 68.) *the crane,* but without sufficient ground.

עָגִיל m. dec. III. a. *a ring,* particularly *an ear-ring.* Ezek. 16:12. Num. 31:50. See the following article.

עָגֹל, fem. עֲגֻלָּה, dec. VIII. d. adj. *round, rounded.* 1 K. 7:23 ff. Root עגל in Syr. Pa. *to roll.*

עֵגֶל m. with suff. עֶגְלִי, plur. const. עֶגְלֵי, dec. VI. j. and **עֶגְלָה** f. dec. X.

1. *a calf* male and female, *vitulus* and *vitula.* Lev. 9:3. Mic. 6:6. עֵגֶל מַסֵּכָה *a molten calf,* Ex. 32:4.

2. *a bullock, a heifer,* as in Lat. *vitulus, vitula,* in old Germ. *Kalbe.* Hos. 10:11 עֶגְלָה מְלֻמָּדָה *a heifer that is broken,* comp. Jer. 31:18. 50:11. Judg. 14:18 לוּלֵא חֲרַשְׁתֶּם בְּעֶגְלָתִי *if ye had not ploughed with my heifer.* Spoken of a three-year old heifer, Gen 15:9. Metaphorically עֶגְלֵי עַמִּים *the bullocks of the nations,* i. e. their leaders, princes, Ps. 68:31.

3. עֶגְלַת שְׁלִשִׁיָּה Is. 15:5. Jer. 48:34. name of an unknown place.

עֲגָלָה f. with suff. עֶגְלָתוֹ dec. XI. e. *a cart, waggon.* Gen. 45:19 ff. 1 Sam. 6:7 ff. Spoken of the threshing waggon, Is. 28:27, 28. of the chariot of war, Ps. 46:10. Root עגל *to roll.*

עָגַם *to be sad, sorrowful,* construed with נֶפֶשׁ. Job 30:25. See אָגַם no. 3.

עָגַן found only in Niph. *to stay, detineri,* as in Chald. Ruth 1:13 הֲלָהֵן תֵּעָגֵנָה *would you on that account stay or forbear?* for תֵּעָגַנָּה; comp. Is. 60:4. Sept. κατισχεθήσεσθε.

עַד m. 1. as a subst. *eternity,* i. q. עוֹלָם. Liter. perhaps *time, duration,* as if from the root עָדָה *to go, to pass away,* spoken of time, comp. עָבַר.—לָעַד *for ever,* Ps. 9:19. 19:10. In the same sense also לְעוֹלָם וָעֶד, Ps. 9:6. עוֹלָם וָעֶד, Ps. 10:16. 21:5. 45:7.—עֲדֵי־עַד *to eternity,* Ps. 83:18. עַד־עוֹלְמֵי־עַד *to eternal ages,* Is. 45:17. אֲבִי־עַד *eternal father,* Is. 9:5. הַרְרֵי־עַד Hab. 3:6. and הוֹרֵי־עַד Gen. 49:26. *eternal mountains.*

2. also as a subst. *booty, prey.* (From עדה no. I. 2. *to fall upon, to rob.* Chald. עֲדָא, עֲדִי, עֲדָאָא *idem.*) Gen. 49:27. Zeph. 3:8. Is. 33:23.

3. as a prep. plur. עֲדֵי, with suff. עָדַי, *unto, until,* spoken of time and space; (derived from signif. no. 1. *time.*) עַד־אָנָה *how long?* Hab. 1:2. *when?* Job 18:2 עַד־מְאֹד *to the greatest, vehementissime.* עַד.... עַד *as well.... as,* Num. 8:4 מִן...עַד *from.... to,* Ex. 28:42. Sometimes (1.) simply *to,* e. g. שׁוּב עַד *to return to,* Lam. 3:40. הָלַךְ עַד *to go to,* 1 Sam. 9:9. Ps. 65:3. (2.) *even, so much as.* עַד אֶחָד *so much as one,* Judg. 4:16. 2 Sam. 17:22. (3.) *even to,* i. e. as, like as. Nah. 1:10 עַד־סִירִים *like thorns.* 1 Chr. 4:27. (4.) הִתְבּוֹנֵן עַד *to hearken or attend*

to any one; (elsewhere with עַל.) Num. 23:18. Job 32:12.

4. also as a prep. *during, while,* Judg. 3:26 עַד־הִתְמַהְמְהָם *while they delayed.* 2 K. 9:22 עַד־זְנוּנֵי אִיזֶבֶל *during the fornications of Jezebel,* i. e. while they continue. Ezra. 10:14 עַד־לַדָּבָר הַזֶּה *during this matter.* Doubled 1 K. 18:45 עַד־כֹּה וְעַד כֹּה *in the mean while.*

5. as a conj. עַד אֲשֶׁר and simply עַד *until,* construed with a pret. Josh. 2:22. with a fut. Num. 11:20. So עַד אִם Gen. 24:19. עַד כִּי Gen. 26:13.

6. also as a conj. *during, while;* construed with a part. Job 1:18. with a fut. 8:23. So עַד שֶׁ *so long as, quamdiu,* Cant. 1:12. and perhaps עַד־כִּי, Gen. 49:10.

עַד Chald. a prep. and conj. as in Heb.

I. **עֵד** m. strictly a part. from עוד, dec. I.

1. *a witness.* Prov. 19:5, 9. Is. 8:2. Also spoken of inanimate objects, Gen. 31:44, 48. Is. 19:20.

2. *witness, testimony.*—עָנָה עֵד בְּ *to give testimony against* any one, Ex. 20:13. Deut. 5:17. 31:21.

3. *a commander.* Is. 55:4.

II. **עֵד**, plur. עִדִּים, dec. VIII. b. liter. *time,* (comp. עִדָּן;) hence *the time of the monthly discharge in females.* (Arab. عِدَّةٌ *tempus menstruum.*) Is. 64:5 בֶּגֶד עִדִּים *vestis menstruis polluta.*

עֹד see **עוֹד** *yet.*

עָדַד found only in Po. עוֹדֵד *to lift up, to support.* Ps. 146:9. 147:6.

Hithpo. *to be raised up.* Ps. 20:9.

I. **עָדָה** Arab, عدا for عدو.

1. *to go* or *pass by,* synonymous with עָבַר Job 28:8. Deriv. עַד no. 1. עֲדִי no. I.

2. *to fall upon in a hostile manner;* (whence Arab. عَدُوٌّ *an enemy.*) Comp. עָבַר, חָלַף, חָלַךְ. Deriv. עַד *booty.*

Hiph. *to remove, put off,* e. g. a garment. Prov. 25:20. comp. הֶעֱבִיר Jon. 3:6.

II. **עָדָה** Arab. عدى *to adorn* or *attire one's self with* any thing, construed with an accus. like לָבַשׁ. (In Chald. *idem.*) Job 40:10 עֲדֵה־נָא גָאוֹן *adorn thyself with majesty.*—עָדָה עֲדִי *to put on ornaments,* Ezek. 23:40. Jer. 4:30. Hos. 2:15. [2:13.] Jer. 31:4 תַּעְדִּי תֻפַּיִךְ *thou shalt adorn thyself with thy tabrets,* the small tabrets being a kind of ornament to the dancing women.

Hiph. *to adorn* any one *with* any thing, construed with two accus. Ezek. 16:11.

Deriv. עֲדִי no. II.

עֲדָה, עֲדָא, fut. יֶעְדֵּא, יֶעְדֵּה, Chald. i. q. Heb. no. I.

1. *to go* or *come on* any one, construed with בְּ. Dan. 3:27.

2. *to go away, depart,* construed with מִן. Dan. 4:28. [4:31.]

3. *to pass away, to be abolished;* spoken of a kingdom, Dan. 7:14. of a law, Dan. 6:9, 13. [6:8, 12.]

Aph. causat. of Pe. no. 2. *to take away,* Dan. 5:20. 7:26. *to depose* (kings), 2:21.

I. **עֵדָה** f. const. עֲדַת, verbal from יָעַד, dec. XI. b. *a collection.* Particularly

1. *the Israelitish people,* which is called עֲדַת יִשְׂרָאֵל *the congregation of Israel,* Ex. 12:3. עֲדַת בְּנֵי יִשְׂרָאֵל *the congregation of the children of Israel,* 16:1, 2, 9. but usually הָעֵדָה *the congregation,* Lev. 4:15. It is also called עֲדַת יְהוָה *the congregation of Jehovah,* Num. 27:17.

2. in a bad sense, *a gang, faction.* Ps. 22:17. עֲדַת קֹרַח *the faction of Korah,* Num. 16:5.

3. *those pertaining to one's household, familia.* Job 16:7. 15:34.

4. *a swarm* (of bees). Judg. 14:8.

II. **עֵדָה** f. plural עֵדוֹת, verbal from עוד, dec. X.

1. *a female witness.* Gen. 31:52.

2. *testimony.* Gen. 21:30.

3. *an institution, ordinance, precept,* (of God.) Ps. 119:22, 24, 59, 79, 138, 146, 168.

עֵדוּת f. verbal from עוד.

1. *an ordinance, precept,* (of God,) i. q. עֵדָה no. 3. Very frequent in the plural form עֵדוֹת (edwot) with an Aramean inflexion, (like מַלְכוּ, plur. מַלְכָן.) Ps. 119:14, 36, 99. Neh. 9:34.

2. *the law,* i. q. תּוֹרָה; by way of eminence, *the tablets of the law.* Ex. 25:21. 16:34. אֲרוֹן הָעֵדוּת *the ark of the law.* Ex. 25:22. אֹהֶל הָעֵדוּת *the tent of the law,* Num. 9:15. 17:23. 18:2.

3. Ps. 60:1. and 80:1. name of a musical instrument, i. q. Arab. عُود *lyra;* or *a song adapted to such an instrument;* or else perhaps *a law, a writing,* and thence *a song,* (like מִכְתָּב, מִכְתָּם.)

I. עֲדִי m. with suff. עֶדְיֵךְ, verbal from עָדָה no. I. dec. VI. prob. *old age.* Ps. 103:5. Chald. *senectus.* Antith. נְעוּרִים. Comp. עַד *eternity.*

II. עֲדִי, in pause עֶדִי, with suff. עֶדְיוֹ, verbal from עָדָה no. II. dec. VI.

1. *an ornament.* Ex. 33:4, 6. Jer. 4:30. עֲדִי עֲדָיִים *a most beautiful ornament,* Ezek. 16:7.

2. *the ornament* or *harness of a horse.* Ps. 32:9.

I. עָדִין, fem. עֲדִינָה, as an adj. *luxurious, given to pleasure.* Is. 47:8.

II. עֲדִין dec. III. a. perhaps *a striking, percussio* hastæ. (Comp. Arab. عدن conj. II. *malleo mucronato percussit.*) Hence 2 Sam. 23:8 Keth. עֲדִינוֹ הָעֶצְנִי according to Simonis *percussio hastæ ejus,* comp. the parallel passage 1 Chr. 11:11 עוֹרֵר אֶת חֲנִיתוֹ, *lifting up his spear,* which is taken from 2 Sam. 23:18.

עֲדֻלָּם proper name of a city in the plain of the tribe of Judah, once the residence of a Canaanitish king. Rehoboam caused it to be fortified. Josh. 12:15. 15:35. Mic. 1:15. Neh. 11:30. Sept. Ὀδολλάμ. In its neighbourhood was *the cave of Adullam,* 1 Sam. 22:1. 2 Sam. 23:13. The gentile noun is עֲדֻלָּמִי Gen. 38:1, 12.

עָדַן found only in Hithpa. *to enjoy* or *delight one's self.* Neh. 9:25. (Arab. غَدَنٌ *pleasure, luxury.*) Deriv. עֵדֶן, מַעֲדַנִּים, עֶדְנָה.

עֵדֶן and עֵדֶן m. verbal from עָדַן, dec. VI. j and k.

1. *pleasure, loveliness.* Plur. Ps. 36:9. 2 Sam. 1:24 עִם עֲדָנִים *in a lovely manner.*

2. proper name (1.) of the country in which the garden of our first parents was placed. Gen. 2:8. 4:16. Hence גַּן עֵדֶן *the garden of Eden,* 2:15. 3:23, 24. (2.) of a pleasant valley near Damascus. Am. 1:5. (3.) of a country of Mesopotamia or Assyria; under the power of the Assyrians, 2 K. 19:12. Is. 37:12. and in Ezek. 27:23, joined with אַשּׁוּר. Perhaps *Maedon* مَعْدن in Diarbekir, towards the Tigris.

עֲדֶן, עֲדֶנָה a contraction of עַד־הֵנָּה *till now, hitherto, yet.* Ecc. 4:2, 3.

עֶדְנָה f. verbal from עָדַן, *pleasure.* Gen. 18:12.

עִדָּן m. Chald. 1. *time.* Dan. 2:8 ff. 3:5, 15. 7:12. (Syr. ܥܶܕܳܢ; Arab. عَدَان *idem.* Kindred with עַד *a long time, eternity;* and with עַד no. II.)

2. *a year.* Dan. 4:13, 20, 22, 29. [4:16, 23, 25, 32.] Dan. 7:25 עַד עִדָּן וְעִדָּנִין וּפְלַג עִדָּן *for a year, years (two years,) and half a year,* i. e. three years and a half. Comp. Josephi Jud. Bell. I. 1. See מוֹעֵד no. I. (1.) and יָמִים no. 4.

עָדַף *to be over; to remain;* spoken e. g. of food, Gen. 16:23. of money, Lev. 25:27. of persons, Num. 3:46, 48, 49. *to hang over,* spoken of tapestry, Ex. 26:12, 13.

Hiph. *to have over.* Ex. 16:18.

I. עָדַר in Kal not used. Arab. غدر *to forsake in a faithless manner;* conj. III. *to forsake.*

Niph. נֶעְדַּר 1. *to be left behind, to remain.* 2 Sam. 17:22.

2. *to be lacking, wanting, missing.* 1 Sam. 30:19. Is. 40:26. 59:15.

Pi. עִדֵּר *to lack, want.* 1 K. 5:7. [4:27.]

II. עָדַר 1. *to arrange, put in order.* 1 Chron. 12:38 עֹדְרֵי מַעֲרָכָה בְּלֵבָב שָׁלֵם *arranging the order of battle,* i. e. in battle-array, *with an upright heart.* Sept. παρατασσόμενοι παράταξιν. Elliptically verse 33 לַעֲדֹר בְּלֹא לֵב וָלֵב *in battle-array with one heart.* Deriv. עֵדֶר.

2. as in Chald. *to clean, to weed.* Is. 5:6. 7:25. (Syr. ܡܥܕܪܐ *a plough-share.*) Deriv. מַעְדֵּר *a weeding-hook, mattock.*

עֵדֶר m. with suff. עֶדְרוֹ, verbal from עָדַר, dec. VI. j. *a herd* or *flock.* Gen. 29:2, 3, 8. עֵדֶר יְהוָה *the flock of Jehovah,* i. e. the Israelitish people, Jer. 13:17.

עֲדָשִׁים masc. plur. *lentiles.* Gen. 25:34. 2 Sam. 17:28. (Arab. عدس *idem.*)

עַוָּא 2 K. 17:24. see עִוָּה.

עוּב Lam. 2:1. see עִיב.

עוֹבָל Gen. 10:28. a city or country of Arabia, in the Samaritan text and in 1 Chr. 1:22, עֵיבָל. The latter name occurs also as a tribe or country of Idumea, Gen. 36:23. (Comp. Vater in locos.) These names may be collated with Γοβαλίτις in Josephus, (II. 1. III. 1.) a country of Arabia, inhabited by Edomites and Amalekites, and *Gebalene,* the country about Petra. They may also have some connexion with the Arab. جبل *a mountain.*

עוּג *to bake* (a cake). Ezek. 4:12. Deriv. מָעוֹג, עֻגָה.

עוּגָב m, Gen. 4:21. Job 21:12. 30:31. and עֻגָב Ps. 150:4, (where several MSS. and editions read עֻגָּב;) the name of a musical instrument, prob. *the shalm, bagpipe.* So the Hebrew translators, Targums, and Jerome uniformly. It is used likewise in the Chaldee paraphrase Dan. 3:5, 10, 15. for סוּמְפֹּנְיָה q. v.

עוֹד, more rarely עֹד, originally an infin. absol. from עוּד *to turn back, to repeat;* hence *redeundo, iterando.* Used only as an adv.

1. *again, a second time.* Gen. 4:25. Judg. 13:8.

2. *repeatedly, continually.* Gen. 46:29 וַיֵּבְךְּ עַל צַוָּארָיו עוֹד *and he wept on his neck continually.* Ruth 1:14. Ps. 84:5. Jer. 2:9.

3. *further, moreover.* Ecc. 3:16. With a negative, *no longer,* Joel 2:19. Deut. 31:2.

4. most frequently *yet,* and with a negative, *no more.* Gen. 7:4. 8:10. 29:7. כָּל־עוֹד *so long as, all the while that,* Job 27:3. With suff. עוֹדֶנִּי *I (am) yet;* עוֹדְךָ *thou (art) yet;* עוֹדֶנּוּ, עוֹדֶנָּה, עוֹדָם, עוֹדֵינוּ. Joined with a participle, עוֹדָם מְדַבְּרִים *they were yet speaking,* Est. 6:14. Also in composition

5. בְּעוֹד (1.) *while yet.* Comp. בְּעֶצֶם. Jer. 15:9 בְּעֹד יוֹמָם *while it is yet day.* 2 Sam. 12:22. Ps. 104:33 בְּעוֹדִי *while yet I live, so long as I live,* 146:2. (2.) *within.* Gen. 40:13 בְּעוֹד שְׁלֹשֶׁת יָמִים *within three days.* Gen. 40:13.

2. מֵעוֹד *since.*—מֵעוֹדִי *since I existed,* Gen. 48:15. Num. 22:30 מֵעוֹדְךָ עַד־הַיּוֹם הַזֶּה *since I was thine to this day.*

עוּד Arab. عاد. 1. *to turn, to turn about.* Hence

2. *to repeat.* (Comp. שׁוּב.) Hence the infin. absol. עוֹד adv. *again, yet,* (q. v.)

3. *to say repeatedly, to testify.* In Kal only Lam. 2:13 Keth. See Hiph.

Pi. עִוֵּד *to surround.* Ps. 119:61.

Hiph. הֵעִיד 1. strictly *to say repeatedly, to affirm, assert;* hence

2. *to testify, to give evidence.* Amos 3:13. The person testified *against* is expressed by the suffix pronoun, 1 K. 21:20.

2. *to call* or *take to witness against* any one, construed with בְּ. Deut. 4:26. 30:19. 31:28. Is. 8:2. *To affirm solemnly, to protest, obtestari,* construed with בְּ of the person, Gen. 43:3 הָעֵד הֵעִד בָּנוּ הָאִישׁ לֵאמֹר *the man protested against us, saying.* Deut. 8:19. 32:46. 1 K. 2:42. Zech. 3:6.

4. *to admonish,* frequently spoken of Jehovah, construed with בְּ of the person, Ps. 50:7. 81:9. 2 K. 17:13. With an accus. and עַל, Lam. 2:13. Jer. 6:10. Particularly *to chide, rebuke, upbraid,* (comp. יִסַּר,) Neh. 13:15, 21.

5. *to command, ordain, prescribe.* (See עֵדָה no. 3. and עֵדוּת.) 2 K. 17:15 אֶת־עֵדְוֹתָיו אֲשֶׁר הֵעִיד בָּם *his precepts, which he gave them.* Neh. 9:34. 1 Sam. 8:9.

6. *to praise,* (comp. μαρτυρέω Luke 4:22.) Job 29:11.

Hoph. הוּעַד *to be shewn, testified.* Ex. 21:29.

Deriv. עֵד, עֵדָה, עֵדוּת, תְּעוּדָה.

עָוָה 1. *to be crooked, to be perverted.* In Kal not used. See Niph. Pi. Hiph.

3. *to deal perversely, to sin,* (comp. e.g. חָבַל no. I.) Dan. 9:5. Construed with עַל of the person, Est. 1:16.

Niph. 1. *to be bowed down.* Ps. 38:7. Especially from pain, (like the pangs of a woman in child-birth,) Is. 21:3 נַעֲוֵיתִי מִשְּׁמֹעַ *I am bent down so as not to hear.*

2. *to be perverted.* Prov. 12:8 נַעֲוֵה־לֵב *of a perverse heart.* Fem. נַעֲוָה as a subst. *perverseness,* 1 Sam. 20:30 בֶּן־נַעֲוַת הַמַּרְדּוּת *thou son of obstinate perverseness,* i. e. thou obstinate and perverse son.

Pi. *to turn up.* Lam. 3:9 נְתִיבֹתַי עִוָּה *he turned up my paths.* Is. 24:1.

Hiph. 1. *to pervert;* e. g. justice, Job 33:27. one's way or conduct, i. e. to act perversely, Jer. 3:21. Hence without דֶּרֶךְ,

2. *to act perversely* or *wickedly.* 2 Sam. 7:14. 19:20. 24:17.

Deriv. עִוְעִים, עָוֹן, עַוָּה.

עַוָּה 2 K. 18:34. 19:13. Is. 37:13. and עַוָּא 2 K. 17:24. proper name of a city from which colonies were sent to Samaria. The inhabitants are called עַוִּים 2 K. 17:31. Some compare a Phenician city *Avatha.* (See Relandi Palæstina, pp. 232, 233.) Others עַוִּים, see below.

עַוָּה f. *destruction.* Ezek. 21:32. [21:27.] See the root עָוָה in Piel.

עוֹז *strength,* see עֹז.

עוּז Arab. عاذ *to flee.* In Kal not used.

Hiph. 1. *to cause to flee, to bring into a place of safety.* Ex. 9:19.

2. intrans. *to flee.* Is. 10:31. Jer. 4:6. 6:1.

עַוִּי, plur. עַוִּים, a gentile noun, *Avites,* the original inhabitants of Philistia before the Philistines came from Caphtor. Deut. 2:23. Josh. 13:3.

עֲוָיָא or עֲוָיָא f. plur. עֲוָיָן, Chald. *perverseness, sin.* Dan. 4:24. [4:27.] Root עָוָה.

I. עֲוִיל m. *unrighteous, ungodly.* Job 16:11. Root עוּל.

II. עֲוִיל *a child,* i. q. עוּל. Job 21:11. perhaps also 19:18. See עוּל.

עֲוִית name of a city in the territory of Edom. Once Gen. 36:35.

עוּל or עִיל *to give milk, to suckle,* spoken of animals. 1 Sam. 6:7, 10. Gen. 33:13. Part. עָלוֹת *(ewes) giving milk, (ewes) that have young,* Ps. 78:71. Is. 40:11. (Arab. غال med. Je *to be pregnant and at the same time to give suck.*)

עוּל m. dec. I. *a child.* Is. 49:15. 65:20. See the verb עוּל and the noun עוֹלֵל. (In modern Arabic عايل *puer.* In Syr. ܥܘܠܐ *idem.*)

עָוַל, Pi. עִוֵּל *to act unrighteously* or *wickedly.* Ps. 71:4. Is. 26:10. (In Syr. *idem.*) Hence

עַוָּל m. verbal from עָוַל, *wicked, unrighteous.* Job 18:21. 27:7. 29:17.

עָוֶל, with suff. עַוְלוֹ, and עָוֶל m. verbal from עָוַל, dec. VI. a. *iniquity, injustice,* e. g. in judgment, Lev. 19:15. in traffic, Ezek. 28:18.—עָשָׂה עָוֶל *to practise iniquity,* Ezek. 3:20.

עַוְלָה f. verbal from עָוַל, dec. XII. f. *idem.* Job 6:29, 30. 11:14. 13:7.—בְּנֵי עַוְלָה *the unrighteous, the wicked,* 2 Sam. 3:34. and without בֵּן, *an unrighteous man,* Job 24:20. Ps. 107:42. With ה paragogic עַוְלָתָה Ps. 92:16. also contracted עֹלָתָה Job 5:16. Plur. עוֹלֹת Ps. 58:3. 64:7. (See also עַלְוָה.)

עוֹלָה *a burnt-offering.* See עֹלָה.

עוֹלָל, plur. עוֹלָלִים, and **עֹלָל**, plur. עֹלָלִים, m. *a child* male or female; frequently joined with יוֹנֵק *a suckling*, Jer. 44:7. Lam. 2:11. but strictly *a child more advanced*, which plays in the street, (Jer. 6:11. 9:20.) asks for bread, (Lam. 4:4.) goes into captivity, (Lam. 1:5.) but which is still borne upon the arm, (2:20.) Applied to children in the womb, Job 3:16. The same signification belongs to מְעוֹלֵל Is. 3:12. עֲוִיל, עוּל, comp. also תַּעֲלוּלִים. (The etymology is uncertain. It cannot be derived from עוּל *to suckle;* since it does not properly include *a suckling*. Better, according to Schultens, liter. *a weaned child*, from עלל, in Arab. *to soothe for the loss of any thing*, particularly a child for the loss of its mother's breast; or from the Heb. עָלַל in the sense *to be active, busy*, for the signification *to play, sport*, is not demonstrable.)

עוֹלֵלוֹת *a gleaning*. See **עֹלֵלוֹת**.

עוֹלָם m. rarely עֹלָם, dec. II. b.

1. *eternity*. Sometimes to be understood in a loose sense for *a long period*, e.g. Deut. 15:17 *so shall he be thy servant for ever*, i.e. all his life long. 1 Sam. 27:12. Ps. 21:5 *thou gavest him long life* עוֹלָם וָעֶד *for ever and ever*. 1 K. 1:31 יְחִי אֲדֹנִי הַמֶּלֶךְ לְעֹלָם *let my lord the king live for ever*. Neh. 2:3. In other places it is to be taken strictly, e.g. חָיָה לְעֹלָם *to live for ever, to be immortal*, (like God,) Gen. 3:22. Deut. 32:40. It refers (1.) to time to come, e.g. בְּרִית עוֹלָם *an eternal covenant*, Gen. 9:16. לְעֹלָם *for ever, always*, Gen. 6:3. 13:15. 1 Sam. 13:13. (2.) to time past, יְמוֹת עוֹלָם *the days of old, former times*, Deut. 32:7. מֵעוֹלָם *in ancient days, in former times*, Gen. 6:4.—Ezek. 26:20 עַם עוֹלָם *the people of former times*, i.e. the manes of the dead. Plur. עוֹלָמִים *eternity*, and as an adv. *eternally*, Ps. 61:5. 77:6. 145:13. Is. 26:4.

2. In Chald. and Talmud. *the world*, like the Greek *αἰών*. Hence prob. *worldly-mindedness, love of the world*, like *κόσμος* in N. T. Ecc. 3:11.

עִוְעִים masc. plur. *perverseness*. Is. 19:14, for עֲוָיִם, from עָוָה. Vulg. *vertigo, giddiness*, which likewise makes very good sense.

עוּן *to dwell*, not used. Hence מָעוֹן and

עוֹנָה f. verbal from obsol. עוּן, dec. X. *cohabitation, duty of marriage*. Once Ex. 21:10. (Talmud. *idem.*) — Hos. 10:10 Keri, according to the usual punctuation, עוֹנֹת in the Targums *furrows*, (comp. מַעֲנָה;) but it is better to point the word עֲוֹנֹת *sins*.

עֹן in Kethib for עַיִן q.v.

עָוֹן m. rarely עָווֹן, plur. עֲוֹנִים and עֲוֹנוֹת, dec. III. a. liter. *perverseness*, from עָוָה. Hence

1. *sin, guilt, iniquity*. Gen. 4:13. 15:16. Job 31:11 עָוֹן פְּלִילִים *a crime to be punished by the judges;* comp. verse 28. 19:29 עֲוֹנוֹת חֶרֶב *a crime to be punished by the sword*. Ezek. 21:30 [21:25] עֲוֹן קֵץ *a crime which leads to destruction*. Verse 34. 35:5. comp. Gen. 15:16 *the iniquity of the Amorites is not yet full*.

2. more rarely, *punishment for sin, suffering, affliction*. 2 Sam. 16:12. Is. 5:18.

I. **עוּף** *to fly;* spoken of birds, Is. 31:5. Prov. 26:2. of the arrow, Ps. 91:5. Metaphorically *to fly away*, spoken of a dream, Job 20:8. of human life, Ps. 90:10. of an army, Is. 60:8. comp. 11:14.

Pil. עוֹפֵף 1. *to fly*, as in Kal. Gen. 1:20. Is. 6:2.

2. *to brandish* (a sword). Ezek. 32:10.

Hiph. *to let fly*. Prov. 23:5 Keri.

Hithpalel, *to fly away, to disappear*. Hos. 9:11.

II. **עוּף** 1. *to be darkened, to be in darkness*. Once Job 11:17 תָּעֻפָה כַּבֹּקֶר תִּהְיֶה *(now) thou art in darkness*, i.e. in adversity, *(then) shalt thou be as the morning*. (Syr. ܥܛܦ *to wrap up*.) Deriv. עֵיפָה, מוּעָף, מָעוּף.

2. *to be wrapt in darkness, to be faint*,

weary. Fut. וַיָּעַף (to distinguish it from וַיָּעָף *he flew*,) 1 Sam. 14:28. Judg. 4:21. Comp. עָפַף. (Syr. ܥܛܦ *to be weary, faint;* Ethpa. *to faint*, or *swoon away*. Comp. עָיֵף *faint, weary;* and the kindred verb יָעַף *to be weary*.)

עוֹף m. collect. *birds, fowls*. Gen. 1:21, 30. In Chald. *idem*. Dan. 2:38. 7:6.

עוּץ *to advise, to take counsel*, i. q. יָעַץ. Found only in the imper. עֻצוּ, Judg. 19:30. Is. 8:10.

עוּץ f. *Uz*, the proper name of a people and country, according to the Sept. Αὐσῖτις, Αὐσῖται, a people and country in the northern part of Arabia Deserta, between Palestine on the east and Mesopotamia on the west. The Bible appears to ascribe to this people a diversity of origin, namely, immediately from Aram, Gen. 10:23. from Nahor an Aramean. 22:21. from Seir, whose posterity dwelt in Idumea, 36:28. Such differences are likewise found in reference to other nations mentioned in the book of Genesis. (Comp. Vater's Commentar. üb. d. Pentateuch, Th. I. p. 152.) The other passages where this word occurs are Job 1:1. comp. verse 3, where Job is called בֶּן־קֶדֶם *an inhabitant of the east*, (see קֶדֶם.) Jer. 25:20, where the kings of Uz are mentioned between those of Egypt and Philistia; and Lam. 4:21, where the territory of Edom extends to Uz. There is no necessity, according to this view, for supposing different places of this name. Comp. particularly Rosenmülleri Comment. in Job. Prolegom. § 5. For other views, see Bocharti Phaleg. II. 8. Eichhorn's Einleit. in das A. T. § 639.

עוּק or **עִיק** *to bow* or *be pressed down;* in Hiph. *to bow* or *press down*. Both conjugations are found Am. 2:13. (In Aram. עוּק, ܥܘܩ i. q. Heb. צוּק *to be pressed*.) Deriv. עָקָה, מוּעָקָה.

עוֹר m. dec. I.

1. *the human skin*. Ex. 34:30, 35. Job 7:5.

2. *the hide or skin of an animal*. Gen. 3:21. Plur. עוֹרוֹת *skins*, Gen. 27:16.

3. *leather*, מְלֶאכֶת עוֹר *something made of leather*, Lev. 13:48.

עוּר 1. *to awake from sleep;* hence *to rouse* or *get up*. In Kal found only in the imper. עוּרָה, fem. עוּרִי, *awake! up!* Ps. 44:24 עוּרָה לָמָּה תִישַׁן אֲדֹנָי *awake, why sleepest thou, O Lord!* Ps. 7:7. Is. 51:9.

2. *to be awake, to watch*. Cant. 5:2. Mal. 2:13 עֵר וְעֹנֶה *the watching and answering*, prob. a proverbial phrase for *every living being*, (like עָצוּר וְעָזוּב,) the origin of which, however, has not been satisfactorily explained. Jerome: *magister et discipulus*.

3. causat. *to stir up*. Job 41:2 [41:10] Keri. In the Kethib יְעִיר the fut. of Hiph.

Niph. נֵעוֹר, fut. יֵעוֹר, pass. of Pi. and Hiph.

1. *to be waked* or *roused from sleep*. Job 14:12. Zech. 4:1.

2. *to be stirred* or *raised up, to rise up;* spoken of a wind, Jer. 25:32. of a people, Jer. 6:22. Joel 4:12. [3:12.] of Jehovah, Zech. 2:17. [2:13.]

Pil. עוֹרֵר 1. *to awaken* from sleep. Cant. 2:7. 3:5. 8:4.

2. *to stir up, excite*, e. g. contention, Prov. 10:12. *to call forth*, e. g. strength, Ps. 80:3.—Job 3:8 עֲתִידִים עֹרֵר לִוְיָתָן *skilful to stir up the leviathan*.

3. *to lift up, brandish*, e. g. a spear, 2 Sam. 23:18. a scourge, Is. 10:26.

4. *to raise up, to build*. Is. 23:13 עֹרְרוּ אַרְמְנוֹתֶיהָ *they* (*the Chaldeans*) *builded her palaces*. Parall. הֵקִימוּ. (Comp. the Greek ἐγείρειν ναὸν, τρόπαιον.)

Hiph. i. q. Pi.

1. *to awaken from sleep*. Zech. 4:1. Cant. 2:7. 3:5. 8:4.

2. *to stir up*, e. g. the leviathan, Job 41:2 [41:10] Keth.—Deut. 32:11 כְּנֶשֶׁר יָעִיר קִנּוֹ *as the eagle stirreth up her nest*, i. e. her nestlings. Jerome: *provocat ad volandum*. Frequently used of Jehovah, *to raise up* any one, Is. 45:13. Jer. 50:9. *to stir up* the spirit of

any one, i. e. to urge him on, 1 Chr. 5: 26. 2 Chr. 21:16.

3. intrans. *to awake.* Ps. 35:23. Construed with עַל *for* any one, Job 8:6.

Hithpal. 1. *to awake, to rise up.* Is. 51:17. 64:6. Construed with עַל *against* any one, Job 17:8.

2. *to rejoice, be elated.* Job 31:29.

עוּר Chald. *chaff.* Once Dan. 2:35. (Arab. and Syr. *idem.*)

עָוַר *to be blind;* comp. the Arab. عور *to be blind of one eye.* Hence Pi. עִוֵּר *to blind, to deprive of sight.* 2 K. 25:7. Jer. 39:7. Metaphorically Ex. 23:8. Deut. 16:19. Syr. ܥܘܪ *idem.*

עִוֵּר m. verbal adj. from עָוַר, dec. VII. h. *blind.* Ex. 4:11. Lev. 19:14. Metaphorically Is. 42:7. Ps. 146:8.

עִוָּרוֹן m. verbal from עָוַר, *blindness.* Deut. 28:28. Zech. 12:4.

עַוֶּרֶת f. verbal from עָוַר, *idem.* Lev. 22:22.

עוּשׁ *to assemble* or *gather together.* Once Joel 4:11.

עוּת found only Is. 50:4. Vulg. *sustentare.* Aqu. ὑποστηρίσαι. Comp. the Arab. غاث *succurrit, sustentavit.* Others, following the Septuagint, *tempestive loqui,* as if a denom. from עֵת.

עָוַת found only in Pi. עִוֵּת *to bend, make crooked, pervert.* Ecc. 7:13. E.g. judgment, Job 8:3. 34:12. comp. Amos 8:5. also in reference to the person, Lam. 3:36 *to subvert a man in his cause.* Job 19:6. Ps. 119:78. עִוֵּת דֶּרֶךְ *to pervert the way of* any one, *to lead astray,* Ps. 146:9.

Pu. part. *crooked.* Ecc. 1:15.

Hithpa. *to bend one's self, to bow down.* Ecc. 12:3.

עַוָּתָה f. (with Kamets impure) strictly the Aramean infin. from עָוַת, *wrong, oppression.* Lam. 3:59.

עַז, fem. עַזָּה, plur. עַזִּים, verbal from עָזַז, dec. VIII. h.

1. as an adj. *strong, mighty;* spoken of a nation, Num. 13:28. of the wind, Ex. 14:21. of the waves, Neh. 9:11. Is. 43:16. of anger, Gen. 49:7. Prov. 21:14.

2. *strong, well-fortified, munitus.* Num. 21:24.

3. *hard, cruel.* מֶלֶךְ עַז *a cruel king,* Is. 19:4.—עַז־פָּנִים *of a fierce* or *cruel countenance,* Deut. 28:50. Dan. 8:23.

4. as a subst. *strength.* Gen. 49:3.

עֵז f. plur. עִזִּים dec. VIII. b. (Arab. عنز idem.)

1. *a goat.*—גְּדִי עִזִּים *a kid,* Gen. 27:9. —שֵׂה עִזִּים *an animal of the goat kind,* Deut. 14:4.

2. Plur. עִזִּים *goats' hair.* Ex. 26:7. 36:14. 1 Sam. 19:13.

עֹז, rarely עוֹז (Prov. 31:17, 25.) before Makkeph עָז־, with suff. עֻזִּי, also עָזִּי, עֻזְּךָ, עֻזּוֹ, verbal from עָזַז, dec. VIII. d. and e.

1. *strength, might, power,* of God or man.—As an adv. *with strength, powerfully,* Judg. 5:21.

2. *strength, security.* מִגְדַּל עֹז *a strong tower,* Judg. 9:51. Ps. 30:8 הֶעֱמַדְתָּה לְהַרְרִי עֹז *thou hast made my mountain to stand strong.* Hence metaphorically *a refuge, protection,* Ps. 28:8 יְהֹוָה עֹז לָמוֹ *Jehovah is their refuge.* 46:2. 62:8.

3. i. q. כָּבוֹד (with which it is often connected,) *glory, majesty.* Hab. 3:4. Ps. 96:6 עֹז וְתִפְאֶרֶת *glory and majesty.* Ps. 132:8 אֲרוֹן עֻזֶּךָ *the ark* (*the seat*) *of thy majesty,* spoken of the ark of the covenant, otherwise called אֲרוֹן כְּבוֹד יְהֹוָה. 2 Chr. 6:41. Hence עֹז Ps. 78:61. for *the ark of the covenant;* comp. 1 Sam. 4:21, 22.

4. *praise.* Ps. 8:3. 29:1. 68:35. 99:4. Ex. 15:2. 2 Chr. 30:21 כְּלֵי־עֹז *instrumenta laudis, in laudatione Dei adhibita.*

5. עֹז פָּנִים Ecc. 8:1. *an arrogant* or *wicked look.*

עֲזָאזֵל m. found only Lev. 16:8, 10, 26. a difficult word, which has been variously explained. It denotes (1.) the place in the wilderness whither the second goat was sent. Thus ver. 10 לַעֲזָאזֵל, וְשִׁלַּח אֶת־הַשָּׂעִיר לַעֲזָאזֵל הַמִּדְבָּרָה and ver. 26 לַעֲזָאזֵל. Accordingly some Jewish commentators (see Bocharti Hieroz. I. p. 650.) have rendered it, *a rough desert mountain.* The form of the word is considered then as an Arabic pluralis fractus عزازل from عزل *to separate*, particularly *from human society;* hence *solitudes, deserts,* i. q. אֶרֶץ גְּזֵרָה in verse 22.—Or (2.) the name of an evil demon, supposed to reside in the wilderness, to which this goat was devoted and sent away. This would accord well with verse 8, where there is an antithesis between לַיהוָה and לַעֲזָאזֵל. The later Jews, as well as the early Christians and Mohammedans, speak of an evil angel of this name. See Spencer de Leg. Hebr. ritualibus, Lib. III. Diss. VIII. Reland de Relig. Mohammed. p. 189. But as the Pentateuch gives no proper names of angels and is entirely silent concerning evil angels, it is possible that *Asasel* is the name of an idol, and that this rite on the day of expiation was in imitation of some idolatrous ceremony. The names of idols are not unfrequently transferred to evil angels, comp. *Adrammelech.* Or (3.) less plausibly, according to the Sept. Symm. Theod. Vulg. the name of the goat itself, (Sept. ἀποπομπαῖος, Vulg. *emissarius*, Symm. ἀπερχόμενος and ἀπολελυμένος;) and to be rendered *the goat sent off.* In this case it is derived from עֵז *a goat* and אָזַל *to go away;* but עֵז denotes *a she-goat*, not *a he-goat;* and the rendering of לְ by *as* is considerably harsh.

עָזַב, fut. יַעֲזֹב.

1. *to leave* or *forsake* a place, person, or thing; e. g. Jehovah, Is. 1:4. Deut. 31:16. Jer. 5:19. a law or covenant, Prov. 28:4.

2. *to leave behind, to leave* in any way, Gen. 39:12, 13. 50:8. 39:6 וַיַּעֲזֹב כָּל־אֲשֶׁר לוֹ בְּיַד יוֹסֵף *and he left all that he had in the hand of Joseph.* Mal. 3:19. Construed with לְ, אֶל, and עַל, *to leave* or *commit to* any one, Ps. 49:11 וְעָזְבוּ לַאֲחֵרִים חֵילָם *and they leave their goods to others.* Job 39:11. Intrans. Ps. 10:14 עָלֶיךָ יַעֲזֹב חֵלְכָה *the unfortunate commits himself to thee.*

3. *to leave off, cease,* construed with לְ and an infin. Hos. 4:10. comp. Prov. 28:13.

4. *to give up, to dismiss.* Gen. 24:27 אֲשֶׁר לֹא עָזַב חַסְדּוֹ מֵעִם *who has not dismissed his favour from* etc. Ruth 2:20. Ps. 37:8 עֲזֹב חֵמָה *dismiss anger.*

5. *to set free,* the opposite of *to shut up.* Hence עָצוּר וְעָזוּב *the shut up and the set free,* i. e. the bond and the free, a proverbial expression for *all even to the lowest,* Deut. 32:36. 1 K. 14:10. 21:21. 2 K. 9:8. 14:26. Others: *the married* (comp. Arab. أَعْصَرُ *paterfamilias,*) *and the single* (comp. Arab. الْعَزَبُ *cœlebs.*) Others: *the laid up and the neglected,* i. e. the costly and the worthless, every thing whatever; but the phrase refers to persons wherever it occurs.

Niph. *to be forsaken.* Neh. 13:11. Is. 7:16.

Pu. *idem.* Is. 32:14.

עִזָּבוֹן m. dec. III. d. found only in the plur. עִזְבוֹנִים, probably a technical word of merchants, nearly synonymous with מַעֲרָב *trade, commerce,* (from עָזַב *to give up, transfer,* hence *to sell.*) Hence

1. *a market-place, bazaar, a fair.* Ezek. 27:19 *Dan and Javan* מְאוּזָּל בְּעִזְבוֹנַיִךְ נָתָנוּ *brought cloth to thy fairs.* Verse 16. So in verses 12, 14, 22, where the prefix בְּ is omitted before this word, but inserted before the wares.

2. *merchandize,* joined with הוֹן. Ezek. 27:27, 33. Comp. סַחַר.

עַזָּה *Gaza,* the proper name of a considerable city on the southern boundary of Palestine, one of the five principal cities of the Philistines. Sept. Γαζά. It was assigned to the tribe of Judah, (Josh. 15:47.) by whom it was actually taken, (Judg. 1:18.) but afterwards lost again. 1 Sam. 6:17. See Relandi Palæstina, p. 788—800. Bellermann's

Handbuch der Bibl. Literatur, Th. III. p. 24. The gentile noun is עַזָּתִי Judg. 16:2.

עֲזוּבָה *f.* verbal from עָזַב, *a forsaking* or *leaving desolate, derelictio.* Is. 6:12. comp. the verb Is. 17:2. Jer. 4:29.

עִזּוּז m. verbal from עָזַז, *strong.* Ps. 24:8. As a collective, *the strong, the mighty,* Is. 43:17.

עֱזוּז m. verbal from עָזַז, dec. I. *strength;* of war, Is. 42:25. of God, Ps. 78:4. 145:6.

עָזַז, fut. יָעֹז, infin. עֲזוֹז. 1. *to be* or *shew one's self strong, mighty.* Ps. 89:14. 68:29 עוּזָּה אֱלֹהִים *shew thyself mighty, O God.* 52:9. Judg. 3:10 וַתָּעָז יָדוֹ עַל כּוּשַׁן רִשְׁעָתַיִם *and his hand was strong against Chushan-rishathaim,* i.e. he conquered him. 6:2. Dan. 11:12 וְלֹא יָעוֹז *and he shall not be strong,* i. e. prevail. Ps. 9:20. Prov. 8:28 בַּעֲזוֹז עִינוֹת תְּהוֹם *when the fountains of the deep were strong;* i. e. raged with violence; comp. מַיִם עַזִּים Neh. 9:11. Is. 43:16. (Syr. ܥܙ Ethpa. *infremuit, efferbuit.*)

2. causat. *to make strong* or *mighty.* Ecc. 7:19 הַחָכְמָה תָּעֹז לֶחָכָם וגו׳ *wisdom makes a wise man stronger than ten* etc. Arab. عَزَّ fut. O. *to make strong.* Others: *protects him more than ten* etc. Comp. then עֹז no. 2. and מָעוֹז.

Hiph. הֵעֵז, joined with פָּנִים, *to put on a fierce* or *impudent countenance.* Prov. 7:13. Construed with בְּ, 21:29. Comp. עַז no. 3. עֹז no. 5.

Deriv. עַז, עֹז, עֵז, עָזוּז, עֱזוּז, מָעוֹז.

עֻזִּיָּה and **עֻזִּיָּהוּ** (*strength of Jehovah*) *Uzziah,* the proper name of a king of Judah. 2 K. 15:13, 30, 32, 34. Is. 1:1. 6:1. 7:1. Hos. 1:1. Am. 1:1. In the second book of Kings, (chap. 14:21. 15:1, 6, 8, 23, 27.) it is likewritten עֲזַרְיָה and עֲזַרְיָהוּ, without any mention of a change in his name. The latter forms, therefore, may have arisen from an error of the ancient transcribers. Such corruptions are nowhere more frequent than in proper names.

עָזְנִיָּה f. Lev. 11:13. Deut. 14:12. according to the Sept. and Jerome, *the ospray,* or *sea-eagle.* (Arab. عُزَن in the lexicons, *nomen avis, aut aquila, aut aquilæ similis.*)

עָזַק found only in Pi. עִזֵּק *to dig about.* Is. 5:2. (Arab. عزق *idem.*) Also *to dig in, to engrave;* hence

עִזְקָא f. Chald. *a seal-ring.* Dan. 6:18. (Syr. ܥܙܩܬܐ *idem.*)

עֲזֵקָה proper name of a city in the tribe of Judah. Josh. 10:10. 15:35. 1 Sam. 17:1. Neh. 11:30. Jer. 34:2. Relandi Palæstina, p. 603.

עָזַר, fut. יַעְזֹר, plur. יַעְזְרוּ, *to help, aid, assist,* most commonly construed with an accus. of the person; e. g. עָזְרֵנִי *help me,* Ps. 109:26. etc. More rarely and in the later writings with לְ, 2 Sam. 8:5. 21:17. 1 Chr. 18:5. 22:17. 2 Chr. 19:2. 26:13. 28:16, Job 26:2. with עִם, 1 Chr. 12:21. with אַחֲרֵי, 1 K. 1:7 וַיַּעְזְרוּ אַחֲרֵי אֲדֹנִיָּה *and they helped the party of Adonijah.*

Niph. *to obtain help, to be helped, juvari.* 2 Chr. 26:15. 1 Chr. 5:20 וַיֵּעָזְרוּ עֲלֵיהֶם *and they were helped against them,* i. e. God gave them the victory over them. Dan. 11:34. So the Arabians say: *adjutus est (a Deo),* for *vicit.*

Hiph. part. with the Aramean form מְעַזְּרִים 2 Chr. 28:23. *helping,* as in Kal.

עֵזֶר m. with suff. עֶזְרִי, verbal from עָזַר, dec. VI. j. *help.* Often as a concrete, *a helper,* Ps. 70:6. 115:9. even a female, Gen. 2:18, 20.

עֶזְרָא *Ezra,* the proper name of a well-known priest and scribe, who was very active in promoting the return of the Jews. Neh. 7:1. 12:1.

עֶזְרָה f. Ps. 22:20. Is. 10:3. and **עֶזְרָת** (like זִמְרָת) Ps. 60:13. 108:13. with He paragogic עֶזְרָתָה Ps. 44:27. verbal from עָזַר, dec. XII. c. *help.*

עֲזָרָה f. 1. a later Aramean word for the more ancient חָצֵר *a court* (before the temple). 2 Chr. 4:9. 6:13. (In the Targums frequently.) The derivation is not clear, prob. as if from עזר in Arab. *cohibuit, prohibuit*, kindred with עָצַר *to shut in.*

2. *a settle* or *terrace* (of the altar), prob. because in the court of the temple. Ezek. 43:14, 17, 20.

עֶזְרָתִי see עֲזָרָה.

עֵט m. (prob. a verbal from the Arab. غطل med. Vav. *to dig in.*)

1. *an iron style* or *pen for writing.* Job 19:24. Jer. 17:1.

2. perhaps also *a reed for writing, calamus.* Jer. 8:8. comp. the use of the penknife, (Jer. 36:23.)

עֵטָא Chald. verbal from יְעַט i. q. Heb. עֵצָה *counsel, understanding, wisdom.* Dan. 2:14 הֲתִיב עֵטָא וּטְעֵם לְאַרְיוֹךְ *he replied to Arioch wisdom and understanding*, i. e. he made to him a wise and rational address; comp. Prov. 26:16.

I. עָטָה (in Arab. with ع) *to seize, to lay hold of.* Is. 22:17. Construed with אֶל, *to seize unjustly* or *improperly*, 1 Sam. 15:19. and 14:32, (where the Keri ויעט is the correct reading.) For the form מְעֻטָּה Ezek. 21:20, see under מָרַט.

II. עָטָה (in Arab. with غ.)

1. *to cover*, construed with עַל, liter. *to cover over* any thing. (Comp. כָּסָה and other verbs of covering.) Lev. 13:45. Ezek. 24:17, 22. Mic. 3:7.

2. *to cover* or *clothe one's self, to put on* a garment, construed with an accus. Ps. 104:2 עֹטֶה אוֹר כַּשַּׂלְמָה *he puts on light, as a garment.* 109:19, 29. 71:13. Jer. 43:12 וְעָטָה אֶת־אֶרֶץ מִצְרַיִם כַּאֲשֶׁר יַעְטֶה וגו׳ *and he shall put on the land of Egypt, as a shepherd puts on his garment*, a bolder figure than the more common expression הָפַךְ *to overturn* or *destroy* a country. Part. fem. עֹטְיָה Cant. 1:7. *a covered female*, i. e. either a mourner, or a harlot, which were distinguished by their dress. See Gen. 38:14.

Hiph. הֶעֱטָה *to cover*, construed with two accus. Ps. 84:7 גַּם־בְּרָכוֹת יַעְטֶה מוֹרֶה *also the early rain covers it with blessings.* Also with עַל before the object *covered*, Ps. 89:46.

Deriv. מַעֲטֶה.

עֲטִין m. dec. I. prob. i. q. Chald. עִטְנָא *a side*, (by a commutation of ט and נ, see page 303.) Job 21:24 עֲטִינָיו מָלְאוּ חָלָב *his sides are full of milk*, i. e. full with milk, or well nourished. Better to read חֵלֶב, *full of fat.* Sept. ἔγκατα. Vulg. *viscera.* Syr. *latera ejus.*

עֲטִישָׁה m. dec. X. *a sneezing.* Job 41:10. [41:18.] Arab. عطس *to sneeze*; Chald הִתְעַטֵּשׁ *idem.*)

עֲטַלֵּף m. dec. VII. f. *a bat.* Lev. 11:19. Is. 2:20. Perhaps compounded of غطل *caliginosa fuit* nox and עָף *volans.* The ע is often lost in composition.

עָטַף, fut. יַעֲטֹף.

1. *to cover, to clothe*, i. q. עָטָה, for which it frequently stands in Chaldaic. (Arab. عطف conj. IV. *to put on.* Syr. ܥܛܦ *to be clothed.*) Ps. 73:6.

2. *to be covered, concealed*, construed with an accus. Ps. 65:14 עֲמָקִים יַעַטְפוּ בָר *the valleys are covered with corn.* Without cases, Job 23:9 יַעְטֹף יָמִין *he is concealed in the south.* Deriv. מַעֲטָפוֹת *garments.*

3. *to be covered in night*; hence *to faint, languish, waste away.* (Comp. עוּף no. II. 2.) Ps. 102:1. 61:3 בַּעֲטֹף לִבִּי *when my heart languishes.* Is. 57:16. Part. pass. עָטוּף *wasted*, Lam. 2:19. Also *weak, feeble* in any way, spoken of cattle, Gen. 30:42.

Niph. i. q. Kal no. 3. Lam. 2:11.

Hiph. *idem.* Gen. 30:42.

Hithpa. *to faint, languish.* Ps. 142:4 בְּהִתְעַטֵּף עָלַי רוּחִי *when my spirit faints within me.* 143:4. 77:4. Joined with נֶפֶשׁ, Jon. 2:7. Ps. 107:5.

עָטַר *to surround*; either in a hostile manner, construed with אֶל, 1 Sam. 23:26, or for protection, with two accus. Ps. 5:13.

Pi. עִטֵּר *to crown.* Construed with two accus. Ps. 8:6. 65:12. 103:4. with a dative of the person, Cant. 3:11.

Hiph. Is. 23:8 צֹר הַמַּעֲטִירָה *Tyre, the crowning*, i. e. the distributor of crowns.

עֲטָרָה f. const. עֲטֶרֶת, plur. עֲטָרוֹת, verbal from עָטַר, dec. XI. d. *a crown, diadem.* 2 Sam. 12:30. Often figuratively, e. g. Job 19:9 *he hath taken the crown from my head.* Prov. 12:4 *a virtuous woman is a crown to her husband.* 14:24. 16:31. 17:6.

עֲטָרוֹת (*crowns*) a proper name.

1. a city in the tribe of Gad. Num. 32:3, 34.

2. another in the tribe of Ephraim, Josh. 16:7. which is also called עַטְרוֹת אַדָּר (*the crowns of Addar*) Josh. 16:5. 18:13.

3. עַטְרוֹת בֵּית יוֹאָב (*the crowns of the house of Joab*) a city in the tribe of Judah. Once 1 Chr. 2:54.

4. עַטְרוֹת שׁוֹפָן a city in the tribe of Gad. Once Num. 32:35.

עִי m. (a contraction of עֱוִי, from עָוָה *to overturn, destroy,*) plur. עִיִּים, dec. VIII.

1. *a heap, ruin.* Mic. 1:6. Jer. 26:17. Mic. 3:12. Ps. 79:1. Comp. מְעִי.

2. עִיִּים Num. 33:45. and more in full עִיֵּי הָעֲבָרִים verse 44. 21:11. (*hills of Mount Abarim,*) a part of Mount Abarim.

3. עִיִּים a city in the tribe of Judah. Josh. 15:29.

עַי proper name of a Canaanitish city, the residence of a king, west of Bethel, and on the northern boundary of the tribe of Benjamin. Gen. 12:8. 13:3. Josh. 7:2 ff. 8:1 ff. Ezra 2:28. Sept. Ἀγγαί. Vulg. *Hai.* Instead of this name we find עַיָּא Neh. 11:31. and עַיָּת Is. 10:28.

עִיב or עוּב found only in the fut. יָעִיב Lam. 2:1. according to the Sept. Vulg. and the Hebrew commentators, *to darken, obscure;* (comp. עוּף no. II.) Hence עָב *darkness, a cloud.* Or according to the Arab. عاب med. Je *to disgrace;* comp. the Syr. ܥܝܒ *idem.*

עֵיבָל a proper name.

1. a various reading for עוֹבָל q. v.

2. the northern peak of Mount Ephraim, (גְּרִזִים is the southern,) a naked unfruitful rock. Deut. 11:29. Josh. 8:30. Sept. Γαιβάλ. Vulg. *Hebal.*

עִיּוֹן (*ruins*) the proper name of a fortified city in the tribe of Naphtali. 1 K. 15:20. 2 Chr. 16:4.

עֵיוֹת f. 1 Chr. 1:46 Keth. for עֲוִית q. v.

עִיט Arab. غاط for غيظ *to become wroth, to fall into a passion.* 1 Sam. 25:14 וַיָּעַט בָּהֶם *and he became wroth with them.* (Syr. ܐܬܚܡܛ *to be displeased, angry;* ܚܡܛܐ *displeasure, anger.*) Hence

עַיִט m. verbal from עִיט, dec. VI. f.

1. *a ravenous beast.* Jer. 12:9. Particularly

2. as a collective, *birds of prey.* Gen. 15:11. Is. 18:6. 46:11. Ezek. 39:4.

עֵיטָם the proper name of a city in the tribe of Judah, 1 Chr. 4:3, 32. 2 Chr. 11:6. and of a rock named therefrom, Judg. 15:8, 11.

עֵילוֹם m. i. q. עוֹלָם *eternity.* 2 Chr. 33:7.

עֵילָם the proper name of a country, strictly *Elymais* in the south of Media, but used generally in a wider sense for *Media* itself. So e. g. Dan. 8:2, where it includes the city Shushan. Gen. 10:22. 14:1. Is. 11:11. 22:6. Jer. 25:25. 49:34 ff. Ezek. 32:24. In most of these passages Elam is represented as a contentious people, causing disturbance to the neighbouring nations. Strabo says as much concerning the inhabitants of Elymais. See Bocharti Geogr. Sacra, II. 2. Michaëlis Spicileg. II. 68.

עָיָם (with Kamets impure) *ardour, violence.* Once Is. 11:15 בַּעְיָם רוּחוֹ *by his violent wind.* Sept. ἐν πνεύματι βιαίῳ.

עַיִן com. gen. (more frequently fem.) dual עֵינַיִם (which stands also for the plural Zech. 3:9.) prim. dec. VI. f.

1. *an eye.*—רָאָה לְעַיִן *to see with the eye,* Ezek. 12:12. The following phrases are worthy of notice, (1.) לְעֵינֵי פ׳ *before the eyes of any one.* Gen. 23:11, 18. Ex. 4:30. (2.) בְּעֵינֵי פ׳ *in the eyes,* i. e. in the judgment or opinion, *of any one.* It often conveys the idea of *seeming* or *appearing.* Gen. 19:14 וַיְהִי כִמְצַחֵק בְּעֵינֵי חֲתָנָיו *but he appeared to his sons-in-law to jest.* 29:20. 2 Sam. 10:3. Hence טוֹב, רַע בְּעֵינַי *what appears to me good, evil.* See the articles טוֹב, יָטַב, יָשַׁר, רָעַע, etc. (3.) מֵעֵינֵי פ׳ *behind the back* or *without the knowledge of any one.* Num. 15:24. (4.) בֵּין עֵינַיִם *between the eyes, on the forehead.* Ex. 13:9, 16. Deut. 6:8. 11:18. Spoken also of the fore-part of the head, Deut. 14:1. (5.) שִׂים עַיִן עַל *to fix the eye on* any one, usually *to regard* him *with favour,* (like שִׂים פָּנִים עַל *to regard with anger.*) E. g. Gen. 44:22 אָשִׂימָה עֵינִי עָלָיו *I will be gracious to him.* Jer. 39:12, 40:4. Job 24:23. Ezra 5:5. Construed with אֶל, Ps. 33:18. 34:16. with בְּ, Deut. 11:12. (comp. further Zech. 12:4. 1 K. 8:29, 52.)—But in Am. 9:8, in a bad sense, it is used of the angry countenance of Jehovah, (otherwise פָּנִים.) So in verse 4, with the addition לְרָעָה; on the contrary Jer. 24:6, in a good sense, with לְטוֹבָה. In the N. T. comp. 1 Pet. 3:12.—Since many of the passions, such as envy, pride, pity, desire, are expressed by the eye, so in the biblical style they are often ascribed to this organ, though strictly applicable only to the person. (Comp. the articles חוּס, כָּלָה no. 5. רַע, רוּע.) Further עֵינַיִם רָמוֹת *proud eyes,* i. e. pride, arrogance, Prov. 6:17. Ps. 18:28. comp. רוּם עֵינַיִם *pride, arrogance.*

2. *a bead* or *bubble,* in wine. Prov. 23:31.

3. perhaps *a look.* Cant. 4:9 לִבַּבְתִּנִי בְּאַחַד מֵעֵינַיִךְ *thou hast stolen my heart by one of thy looks.* Others: *with one (look) from thine eyes.*

4. *face, countenance,* like פָּנִים. Ps. 6:8.—עַיִן בְּעַיִן *face to face,* Num. 14:14. Is. 52:8. Some other passages, usually placed under this signification, belong elsewhere; e. g. 1 Sam. 16:12 יְפֵה עֵינַיִם *with beautiful eyes;* so Gen. 29:17. See יָפֶה. Hence

5. *the surface.* Ex. 10:5 עֵין הָאָרֶץ *the surface of the land.* Verse 15. Num. 22:5, 11.

6. *appearance, form.* Num. 11:7. Lev. 13:5, 55. Ezek. 1:4 ff. 10:9. Dan. 10:6.

7. with a plur. עֲיָנוֹת, const. עֵינוֹת, *a spring, fountain;* (comp. מַעְיָן.) Gen. 16:7. 24:29, 30, 42. The eye is *a fountain* of tears, which may have led to this signification of the word. The plur. fem. or neuter is used to express things without life, see Gesenius' Lehrgeb. § 125. 3.

8. In the preceding signification, it stands before many geographical names; the most remarkable of which are (1.) עֵין גֶּדִי (*fountain of the kid*) a city in the tribe of Judah, not far from the southern point of the Dead Sea, fruitful in palms. In Pliny, (Hist. Nat. v. 17.) *Engadda.* Josh. 15:62. 1 Sam. 24:1. Ezek. 47:10. Cant. 1:14. Its more ancient name was חַצְצוֹן תָּמָר q. v. (2.) עֵין דֹּאר Ps. 83:11. and עֵין דּוֹר Josh. 17:11. 1 Sam. 28:7. a city in the tribe of Manasseh. (3.) עֵין מִשְׁפָּט (*fountain of judgment*) found only Gen. 14:7. i. q. מֵי מְרִיבָה (*waters of contention*) name of a fountain in the desert of Sin, otherwise called קָדֵשׁ. The name is there used by a prolepsis, for it originated at a later period, see Num. 10:1—13. (4.) עֵין עֶגְלַיִם (*fountain of two calves*) a place on the northern point of the Dead Sea. Once Ezek. 47:10. (5.) עֵין רֹגֵל (*fountain of the spy,* or, according to the Targum, *of the fuller,* for he treads his clothes with his feet, comp. רָגַל,) a fountain on the south-east of Jerusalem, on the borders of the tribes of Judah and Benjamin. Josh. 15:7. 18:16. 2 Sam. 17:17. 1 K. 1:9. According to Josephus, (Antiq. VII. 11.) it was situated in the king's pleasure-garden.

9. without addition עַיִן (1.) the name of a Levitical city in the tribe of Simeon. Josh. 15:32. 19:7. 21:16. 1 Chr. 4:32.—Out of עַיִן וְרִמּוֹן Josh. 15:32, is

formed עֵין רִמּוֹן Neh. 11:28. (2.) also of a place in the north-east of Palestine. Num. 34:11.

עָיִן m. denom. from עַיִן, (after the form בֹּשֶׁר, פֹּרֶם,) *looking askance, envious.* 1 Sam. 18:9 Keri. In the Kethib עוֹן. (Arab. عاين *idem.*)

עֵינַיִם Gen. 38:14, 21. and **עֵינָם** Josh. 15:34, (with the ancient dual form, comp. Gesen. Gesch. der Hebr. Sprache und Schrift, p. 49, 51.) a place in the tribe of Judah.

עָיֵף *to be wearied, exhausted.* Jer. 4:31. Hence

עָיֵף, fem. עֲיֵפָה, verbal adj. from עוּף, dec. III. a. *wearied, exhausted, languishing;* from fatigue, hunger, and particularly thirst. Gen. 25:29, 30. Job 22:7. Ps. 63:2. נֶפֶשׁ עֲיֵפָה *the weary soul,* Jer. 31:25. Prov. 25:25. אֶרֶץ עֲיֵפָה *a thirsty land,* Ps. 143:6. Is. 32:2. Comp. עוּף no. II. 2. and יָעֵף.

עֵיפָה f. verbal from עוּף no. II. 1.

1. *darkness.* Amos 4:13. With He paragogic עֵיפָתָה, Job 10:22.

2. name of a Midianitish country and people. Gen. 25:4. Is. 60:6. 1 Chr. 1:33.

עַיִר m. with suff. עִירֹה (Gen. 49:11.) plur. עֲיָרִים, *a young ass, an ass colt.* Zech. 9:9. Job 11:12 עַיִר פֶּרֶא *the wild ass's colt.* It is applied also to the animal when grown, so as to be rode upon, Judg. 10:4. 12:14. and to bear burdens, Is. 30:6. Comp. also Gen. 32:16.

I. **עִיר** f. plur. once עֲיָרִים, (Judg. 10:4.) usually עָרִים (from an obsol. sing. עָר q. v.) *a city.* (Some erroneously suppose the primary signification to have been *a cavern,* like the Arab. غار, and Heb. מְעָרָה, referring to Gen. 4:17. Ps. 31:22.)—עִיר אֱלֹהִים *the city of God,* Ps. 46:5. 87:3. Is. 60:14. and עִיר הַקֹּדֶשׁ *the holy city,* Neh. 11:1. Is. 52:1. Dan. 9:24. for *Jerusalem.*—עִיר הַמַּיִם *the city of waters,* a part of the city Rabbah, 2 Sam. 12:27.—Ecc. 10:15 *the labour of the foolish wearieth him, he knows not how* לָלֶכֶת אֶל עִיר *to go to the city,* perhaps a proverbial phrase for *to find his way,* as if spoken of a wanderer.

2. Several proper names of cities are compounded of this word; (1.) עִיר הַמֶּלַח (*the city of salt*) in the desert of the tribe of Judah, near the Salt Sea. Josh. 15:62. (2.) עִיר הַתְּמָרִים (*the city of palms*) *Jericho,* so called from the multitude of palms growing there. (See Plin. Hist. Nat. v. 14. Tacit. Hist. v. 6. Josephi Bell. Jud. I. 6. 18. IV. 8.) Deut. 34:3. Judg. 1:16. 2 Chr. 28:15.

II. **עִיר** perhaps *anger, hostile attack.* (Comp. the Arab. غار med. Vav *to attack, assault.*) Jer. 15:8 הִפַּלְתִּי עָלֶיהָ פִּתְאֹם עִיר וּבֶהָלוֹת. Sept. ἐπέῤῥιψα ἐπ' αὐτὴν ἐξαίφνης τρόμον καὶ σπουδήν. Hos. 11:9 לֹא אָבוֹא בְּעִיר *I come not with anger.* The former signification, *city,* may, however, be applied to both of these passages; thus in Jer. *I will let come suddenly upon it cities and terror;* and in Hos. according to Lowth, *non sum urbicola,* i. e. homo.—In Ps. 73:20, בָּעִיר stands prob. for בְּהָעִיר *in awaking,* and pertains not here.

עִיר m. Chald. *a watcher,* a name of angels in the later Jewish demonology, being so called because, according to the doctrine of the Persians, they *watch over* the souls of men. Dan. 4:10, 14, 20. (In the Syriac liturgies it is applied to archangels, e. g. to Gabriel. Afterwards it came to be applied rather to evil angels, like ἐγρήγοροι in the book of Enoch and in the fathers.)

עֵירֹם, **עֵרֹם**, plur. עֵירֻמִּים, dec. VIII. d. i. q. עָרוֹם.

1. adj. *naked.* Gen. 3:7, 10, 11.

2. subst. *nakedness.* Ezek. 16:7 וְאַתְּ עֵרֹם וְעֶרְיָה *yet thou wast nakedness and bareness,* i. e. naked and bare, the abstract being used for the concrete; comp. קֹדֶשׁ, שָׁלוֹם. Verses 22, 39. 23:29.

עַיִשׁ *the constellation of the bear.* See עָשׁ.

עַיָּת a proper name, see עַי.

עַכָּבִישׁ m. *a spider*. Job 8:14. Is. 59:5. Arab. عنكبوت, Chald. עַכּוּבִיתָא *idem*. This quadriliteral appears to be compounded of עכש Arab. عكش *to weave*, (spoken of the spider,) and עכב *to be light, nimble*.

עַכְבָּר m. prim. dec. II. b.

1. *a mouse*, particularly a *field-mouse*. 1 Sam. 6:4, 5, 11, 18.

2. probably also other edible animals of the glis genus. Lev. 11:29. Is. 66:17. So in Arab. this word signifies i. q. يربوع *the jerboa, mus jaculus*, Linn. which is used for food. See Bocharti Hieroz. T. I. p. 1017.

עַכּוֹ *Acco*, the proper name of a city and haven in the tribe of Asher. Judg. 1:31. In Greek Ἄκη, more frequently *Ptolemais*, in the time of the crusades *Acca*, now *Acre*. See Relandi Palæstina, p. 534—542.

עָכוֹר (*troubling*, comp. Josh. 7:26.) name of a valley not far from Jericho. Josh. 15:7. Is. 65:10. Hos. 2:17.

עָכָן m. proper name of an Israelite, who, by taking of the accursed thing (חֵרֶם,) caused an overthrow among his people. Josh. 7:1. 22:20. In the parallel passage 1 Chr. 2:7, he is called עָכָר which name suits the etymology Josh. 7:26. The reading in Joshua, however, is not to be changed. The derivation only is less accurate; (comp. Gesen. Geschichte der Hebr. Sprache und Schrift, p. 43.)

עֶכֶס m. dec. VI. k. *a fetter for the foot*. (Arab. عكس *idem*.) Prov. 7:22. usually rendered *he* (*the inexperienced young man*) *goeth after her* (*the wicked woman*) *suddenly, as the ox goeth to the slaughter*, וּכְעֶכֶס אֶל־מוּסַר אֱוִיל *and as in fetters to the correction of the fool*, i. e. to his own correction. The Sept. and Chald. render עֶכֶס *a dog*, a meaning well suited to the connexion, but not confirmed by philological evidence. Plur. עֲכָסִים Is. 3:18. *bracelets* or *rings for the ankles*, a female ornament, which occasioned a clinking in walking. Hence

עִכֵּס Pi. denom. from עֶכֶס, *to adorn one's self with ankle-rings*, or, what is better, *to make a tinkling with them*, *to excite attention*. Is. 3:16.

עָכַר 1. strictly *to stir up*, e. g. water; *to make* it *turbid*. (So in Arab. med. Kesr.) Hence metaphorically

2. *to trouble* any one. Judg. 11:35. Usually by bringing or occasioning evil, Gen. 34:30. Josh. 6:18. 7:25. 1 Sam. 14:29 עָכַר אָבִי אֶת הָאָרֶץ *my father troubleth the land*. 1 K. 18:17, 18. Prov. 11:17 עֹכֵר שְׁאֵרוֹ אַכְזָרִי *the cruel man troubleth his own flesh*, i. e. renders himself unhappy. Verse 29 עֹכֵר בֵּיתוֹ יִנְחַל רוּחַ *he who troubleth his own house shall inherit the wind*.

Niph. 1. *to be excited*, spoken of grief. Ps. 39:3.

2. *to be brought into adversity*, *to be destroyed*. Prov. 15:6.

עַכְשׁוּב m. a quadriliteral, *an adder*. Ps. 140:4. The root עכש signifies in Arabic, *to bend together*, conj. V. *to coil up*. The ב appears to be annexed, as in many quadriliterals. See כַּרְבֵּל.

עַל (for עָלָה) verbal from עָלָה, strictly a subst. *whatever is high* or *uppermost*. Hos. 7:16 יָשׁוּבוּ לֹא עָל *they return not to the Most High*, or else *to things above*, πρὸς τὰ ἄνω. 11:7 אֶל עַל יִקְרָאֻהוּ *they call them* (*the people*) *to the Most High*. Hence as an adv. (1.) *above*. מֵעָל *from above*, Gen. 27:39. 49:25. and simply *above*, Ps. 50:4.

2. *high*. 2 Sam. 23:1 הֻקַם עָל (*who*) *is exalted high*. Hence in the const. state

עַל (Heb. and Chald.) plur. const. עֲלֵי (used only in poetry,) with suff. עָלַי, עָלֶיךָ, עָלָיו, עָלֵינוּ, עֲלֵיכֶם, עֲלֵיהֶם, poetically עָלֵימוֹ; (Chald. עֲלוֹהִי, עֲלַיְנָא, עֲלֵיהוֹם;) a preposition.

1. *upon*.—Used particularly (1.) after verbs of covering; see כָּסָה, etc. (2.) to express a duty or obligation, which lies on any one. 2 Sam. 18:11 עָלַי לָתֵת *I*

should have given. 1 K. 4:7. Ezra 10: 4. Neh. 13:13. (3.) to express a weight or load which lies on any one. Is. 1:14. Comp. כָּבֵד.

2. *over, above, concerning.* Gen. 41: 33. Ps. 29:3. Is. 1:1.—דִּבֶּר עַל *to speak concerning* any thing, צִוָּה עַל *to give command concerning* any thing, Gen. 18:19. Comp. Joel 1:3. 1 K. 22:8. Also *more than,* Gen. 48:22 עַל אַחֶיךָ *more than thy brethren.* Job 22:24. 23: 2. Used of time, *beyond,* Lev. 15:25 עַל נִדָּתָהּ *beyond the time of her purification.*

3. i. q. אֶל *to.* 2 Sam. 15:4 עָלַי יָבוֹא *he shall come to me.* Gen. 38:12. 2 Sam. 15:20.—דִּבֶּר עַל לֵב *to speak to the heart* or *satisfaction of* any one. נָפַל עַל פ׳ *to fall to any one.*—Also to express the dative in later Hebrew, Job 33:23 אִם יֵשׁ עָלָיו *if there is given to him.* Est. 3:9 אִם עַל הַמֶּלֶךְ טוֹב *if it is good* or *pleasing to the king.*

4. *near, by, at.* עַל עַיִן *by a fountain,* Gen. 16:7. 24:30 עַל הַגְּמַלִּים עַל הָעָיִן *by the camels at the well.* Ps. 7:11 מָגִנִּי עַל אֱלֹהִים *my shield is with God,* i. e. he holds my shield.

5. *against.* Is. 1:25. Mic. 4:11 קוּם עַל *to rise up against.* חָנָה עַל עִיר *to encamp against* or *besiege a city.* חָשַׁב עַל *to devise plans against* any one.

6. *before, ante.* Ex. 27:21 *the curtain which is before the law.* (Derived from signif. no. 2.) הִשְׁתַּחֲוָה עַל *to bow down before* any one, Lev. 26:1. עַל פְּנֵי *before the face of* any one. (Derived from signif. no. 4.)

7. *in.* Hos. 11:8 נֶהְפַּךְ עָלַי לִבִּי *my heart is turned within me.* Ps. 42:5, 6, 7, 12. 43:5. 142:4.

8. *for.* Est. 7:7. כִּפֶּר עַל *to atone for.* הִלָּחֵם עַל *to contend for,* Judg. 9:17. הִתְפַּלֵּל, עַל *to pray for.*

9. *on account of, because of.* Ps. 44: 23. Ruth 1:19. Frequently before an infin. e. g. עַל אָמְרֵךְ *on account of thy saying,* i. e. because thou sayest, Jer. 2:35. עַל כֵּן *therefore, on this account,* (see כֵּן.) עַל דְּבַר *on account of.* עַל אֲשֶׁר as a conj. *because,* Deut. 29:24. 2 Sam. 3: 30. Est. 8:7. also simply עַל in the same sense, Gen. 31:20.

10. *after, according to, secundum.* Ps. 110:4.

11. *although.* Job 16:17 עַל לֹא חָמָס בְּכַפַּי *although there is no injustice in my hands.* 34:6. Is. 53:9. Joined with an infin. Job 10:7 עַל־דַּעְתְּךָ *although thou knowest.*

12. *from, by;* e. g. in the phrase *to live from* or *by* any thing. Gen. 27:40. Deut. 8:3. Is. 38:16.

13. *with, together with.* Ex. 35:22 אֲנָשִׁים עַל הַנָּשִׁים *the men together with the women.* Gen. 32:12.

14. *besides, without,* (from signif. no. 2. *more than.*) Gen. 31:50. Ps. 16:2 טוֹבָתִי בַּל עָלֶיךָ *there is no happiness for me without thee.*

15. Other compositions, מֵעַל (1.) *from above* or *on.* Ex. 40:36. 2 Sam. 12: 30. Ex. 3:5. (2.) the force of מִן being lost, simply i. q. עַל. Est. 3:1 מֵעַל הַשָּׂרִים *above the princes.* Jer. 36:21 מֵעַל הַמֶּלֶךְ *by the king.* Ps. 108:5. (3.) מֵעַל לְ *above* or *over* any thing. (Antith. מִתַּחַת לְ.) Gen. 1:7. Neh. 12:31. Jon. 4:6.

עֹל m. more rarely **עוֹל**, with suff. עֻלּוֹ, dec. VIII. d. *a yoke,* a crooked piece of wood fastened to the pole of the carriage and laid upon the necks of the team, by which they draw. Num. 19: 2. Deut. 21:3. For the most part figuratively, *bondage, servitude.* 1 Sam. 6: 7. 1 K. 12:11. Is. 9:3.

עֵלָּא Chald. *above, over,* followed by מִן. Dan. 6:3.

עִלֵּג m. adj. dec. VII. a. *stuttering, stammering.* Is. 32:4. Comp. by transposition לָעַג. (Arab. علج *speaking a foreign tongue.*)

עָלָה, fut. יַעֲלֶה.

1. *to go up, ascend, mount.* It is used absolutely, or construed with עַל, Is. 14: 14. with אֶל, Ex. 24:13, 15, 18. 34:4. with לְ Is. 22:1. with בְּ, Ps. 24:3. Cant. 7:9. also with an accus. of the place *ascended,* Gen. 49:4 כִּי עָלִיתָ מִשְׁכְּבֵי אָבִיךָ *for thou ascendedst the bed of thy father.*

Prov. 21 : 22. Often simply, *to go from a lower country to one situated higher,* (comp. יָרַד;) e. g. uniformly of a journey from Egypt to Palestine, Gen. 13 : 1. 44 : 24. Ex. 1 : 10. of the return from exile, Ezra 2 : 1. Neh. 7 : 6. Hos. 1 : 11. of frequenting the gate or seat of judgment, (as a place of distinction or elevation,) Num. 16 : 12. Deut. 17 : 8. 25 : 7. Judg. 4 : 5. Ruth 4 : 1.

2. Used of things without life; e. g. of a way, *to lead*, Judg. 20 : 31. of a country, *to stretch* or *extend itself*, Josh. 16 : 1. 18 : 12. of a lot, *to come up*, (out of the shaken urn,) Lev. 16 : 9, 10. Josh. 18 : 11. of a city, *to ascend in flames*, Judg. 20 : 40. Jer. 48 : 15. of plants, *to shoot* or *grow up*, Gen. 40 : 10. 41 : 22. Deut. 29 : 22. Comp. Gen. 49 : 9. Part. עוֹלֶה Job 36 : 33 prob. *what shoots up, a plant.* Sometimes (1.) to be rendered passively, e. g. *to be used* or *employed*, spoken of a razor, Judg. 16 : 17. *to be put on*, spoken of a garment, Lev. 19 : 19. of a bandage, Jer. 8 : 22 עָלְתָה אֲרֻכָה *a bandage is put on*; see אֲרוּכָה. (2.) by a common Hebraism, (see Gesenius' Lehrgeb. § 218. 4.) spoken of the thing which is ascended. Prov. 24 : 31 וְהִנֵּה עָלָה כֻלּוֹ קִמְּשֹׂנִים *behold, the whole of it (the field) grows up with thorns*, i. e. only thorns grow up therein. Is. 34 : 13. 5 : 6. Am. 8 : 8 and 9 : 5 עָלְתָה כַיְאֹר כֻּלָּהּ *the whole land ascends as by the Nile*, i. e. it is overflown as by the Nile. (Comp. Jer. 46 : 7, 8.)

3. metaphorically *to rise, increase, advance*; e. g. spoken of a battle, 1 K. 22 : 35. of one increasing in wealth, Deut. 28 : 43. Construed with עַל, *to excel*, Prov. 31 : 29.—עָלָה אֶל לֵב *to come into mind*, Jer. 3 : 16. 7 : 31. 19 : 5. 32 : 35. Is. 65 : 17.

4. pass. of Hiph. no. 3. *tolli, auferri.* Job 36 : 20.

5. pass. of Hiph. no. 4. *to be inserted* or *entered*. 1 Chr. 27 : 24.

Niph. pass. of Hiph.

1. *to be brought up.* Ezra 1 : 11.

2. *to be driven away*, Jer. 37 : 11. *to be led away*, Num. 16 : 24, 27. 2 Sam. 2 : 27.

3. *to be exalted*, spoken of God. Ps. 47 : 10. 97 : 9.

Hiph. 1. *to lead* or *bring up*, (persons or things.) Gen. 37 : 28. 1 Sam. 8 : 8. 2 Sam. 2 : 3.—הֶעֱלָה הַנֵּרוֹת *to put up the lamps*, Ex. 25 : 37. Usually construed with an accus. once with a dative, Ezek. 26 : 3.

2. *to present* an offering on the altar. Is. 57 : 6. especially הֶעֱלָה עֹלוֹת *to present burnt-offerings*, Lev. 14 : 20. Job 1 : 5.

3. *to take away, tollere, auferre.* Ps. 102 : 25.

4. *to enrol, in tabulas referre.* 1 K. 9 : 21.

Hoph. הֹעֲלָה (for הָעֳלָה) *to be brought up*, Nah. 2 : 8. *to be presented*, spoken of an offering, Judg. 6 : 28. *to be entered, inserted, recorded*, pass. of Hiph. no. 4. 2 Chr. 20 : 34.

Hithpa. *to exalt one's self, to glory.* Jer. 51 : 3.

Deriv. עָל, עַל, עֹלֶה, עִלִּי, עֶלְיוֹן, מַעַל, תְּעָלָה, מַעֲלָה.

עָלֶה m. const. עֲלֵה, dec. IX. b. *a leaf.* Gen. 3 : 7. 8 : 11.

עִלָּה Chald. *a cause, occasion, pretext.* Dan. 6 : 5, 6. (In Aram. and Arab. *idem.* Root עלל Arab. *to give cause or occasion*; conj. VI. VIII. *to use a pretext.* Comp. Heb. עָלַל.)

I. **עֹלָה**, more rarely **עוֹלָה** f. verbal from עָלָה, dec. X.

1. strictly *quicquid ascendit in altare*, i. e. altari imponitur; but used by way of eminence for *a burnt-offering*, (see הֶעֱלָה no. 2.) which was entirely consumed, ὁλόκαυστον. Gen. 22 : 3, 6. Lev. 1 : 4 ff.

2. *a step.* Ezek. 40 : 26.

II. **עֹלָה** f. i. q. עַוְלָה *unrighteousness, iniquity.* With He paragogic עֹלָתָה, Job 5 : 16.

עֲלָה, עֲלָתָא Chald. *a burnt-offering.* Plur. עֲלָוָן Ezra 6 : 9.

עַלְוָה f. Hos. 10 : 9. i. q. עַוְלָה (as it is read in several MSS.) *iniquity.*

עֲלוּמִים masc. plur. denom. from עֶלֶם and עַלְמָה, *youth*, *the state* or *condition of a young man* or *woman*. Ps. 89:46. Is. 54:4. Job 33:25. 20:11 עַצְמוֹתָיו מָלְאוּ עֲלוּמָיו *his bones are full of youth.*

עֲלוּקָה f. found only Prov. 30:15. according to the Sept. Vulg. Gr. Venet. *the horse-leech*, (Arab. عَلَقَةٌ, Syr. ܥܠܘܩܐ,) whose insatiable thirst for blood might very well serve for a proverb. The Arab. علوق signifies *calamitas, gravis casus, fatum, quod homini impendit;* whence Bochart (Hieroz. II. 801.) makes it a personification of fate as a hideous monster. Others: *desire*, (personified, comp. Arab. علق *propensum esse in aliquem, amare.*) Others, by conjecture, *the locust.*

עָלַז i. q. עָלַס and עָלַץ *to be glad, to exult, rejoice.* 2 Sam. 1:20. Ps. 68:5. Construed with בְּ *concerning* any thing, 149:5. Hab. 3:18. Spoken also of the inanimate creation, Ps. 96:12. Sometimes in the sense of arrogant exultation, Ps. 94:3. Is. 23:12. comp. 5:14. See עַלִּיז.

עָלֵז m. verbal adj. from עָלַז, *rejoicing.* Is. 5:14.

עֲלָטָה f. *thick darkness.* Gen. 15:17. Ezek. 12:6, 7, 12. (Arab. غلط *to be thick, dense;* and by transposition غَطَلَ *to be very dark.*)

עֵלִי *Eli*, the proper name of a well-known high-priest. 1 Sam. 1:3ff. Sept. Ἡλί, Vulg. *Heli.*

עֱלִי m. *a pestle.* Prov. 27:22. Root עָלָה, but perhaps in the signification of علا in Arab. conj. II. *to strike repeatedly.*

עִלִּי found only in the fem. עִלִּית *the upper.* Josh. 15:19. Judg. 1:15.

עִלָּי Chald. *the upper, the highest.*— אֱלָהָא עִלָּאָה *the most high God*, Dan. 3:26, 32. 5:18, 21. and עִלָּאָה *the Most High*, 4:14, 21. [4:17, 24.] 7:25. In the Kethib uniformly עליא, after the Syriac form ܥܠܝܐ.

עֲלִיָּה f. dec. X.

1. *a loft, an upper chamber, a covered place on the flat roof of an oriental house.* Judg. 3:23, 25. 1 K. 17:19, 23. 2 K. 4:10. Used metaphorically of the chambers of heaven, Ps. 104:3, 13.

2. *a step, ascent.* 2 Chr. 9:4.

עֶלְיוֹן, fem. עֶלְיוֹנָה, verbal adj. from עָלָה, dec. I. and X.

1. *upper, higher*, the opposite of תַּחְתּוֹן. Gen. 40:17. 2 K. 18:17. Ezek. 42:5.

2. *the Most High*, i. e. God. אֵל עֶלְיוֹן, Gen. 14:18. יְהוָה עֶלְיוֹן, Ps. 7:18. אֱלֹהִים עֶלְיוֹן, Ps. 57:3. and simply עֶלְיוֹן, Ps. 9:3. 21:8.

עֶלְיוֹן m. Chald. plur. majest. עֶלְיוֹנִין *the Most High*, Dan. 7:22, 25.

עַלִּיז m. verbal from עָלַז, dec. I. *rejoicing, joyful.* Is. 24:8. Sometimes in a bad sense, *rejoicing from pride* or *arrogance*, Is. 22:2. Zeph. 2:15. Hence Zeph. 3:11 עַלִּיזֵי גַּאֲוָתֵךְ *thy proud rejoicers.* Is. 13:3.

עֲלִיל Ps. 12:7. usually *a crucible.* More correctly *a work-shop*, from עָלַל *to work, to labour.*

עֲלִילָה f. verbal from עָלַל, dec. X. *an action, deed, work, facinus*, i. q. מַעֲלָל; found in the sing. only Ps. 14:1. 66:5. elsewhere in the plural.

1. *deeds, mighty works*, (of God.) Is. 12:4. Ps. 9:12. 77:13.

2. *actions* (of men). Zeph. 3:7. הִשְׁחִיתוּ כֹּל עֲלִילוֹתָם *they pervert all their actions*, i. e. they act perversely, wickedly, Ps. 14:1. 141:4. Ezek. 14:22. In all these passages there is a reference to *evil* actions, which is expressed more definitely Deut. 22:14, 17.

עֲלִילִיָּה f. i. q. עֲלִילָה no. 1. *a work* (of God). Jer. 32:19.

עֲלִיצוּת f. verbal from עָלַץ, dec. I. *joy, rejoicing.* Hab. 3:14.

עִלִּית f. Chald. *an upper chamber*, i. q. Heb. עֲלִיָּה. Dan. 6:11.

I. עָלַל *to do* or *perform* any thing, whether good or evil. Derivatives עֲלִילָה and מַעֲלָל *an action, deed.*

Poel, עוֹלֵל, construed with לְ, *to conduct towards* any one, used only in a bad sense, like עֲלִילָה. Lam. 1:22. 2:20 לְמִי עוֹלַלְתָּ כֹּה *to whom thou hast done thus (evil).* 3:51 עֵינִי עוֹלְלָה לְנַפְשִׁי *mine eye causes pain to my soul,* i. e pains me from much weeping. Job 16:15 עֹלַלְתִּי בֶעָפָר קַרְנִי *I have defiled* (comp. also Hithpa.) *my horn,* i. e. my head, *with dust.* (Others, after the Aramean, *indidi in cinerem caput meum.* But in an Arameism of this kind, we should have expected the Aramean form, the conj. Aphel only being used in that dialect.)

Poal, pass. Lam. 1:12. *as my sorrow* אֲשֶׁר עוֹלַל לִי *which has been brought upon me.*

Hithpa. הִתְעַלֵּל.

1. *to perform* a mighty deed, spoken of God, construed with בְּ *on* or *to* any one. Ex. 10:2. 1 Sam. 6:6.

2. *to treat* any one *ill,* construed with בְּ. 1 Sam. 31:4. 1 Chr. 10:4. Jer. 38:19. Num. 22:29. Also *to do violence* to a woman, Judg. 19:25. The ancient translators have rendered it in most passages, *to deride,* (Sept. ἐμπαίζω; Vulg. *illudo*); which does not agree with the analogy of the verb and its derivatives, and is inconsistent with its use in some passages, e. g. Ex. 10:2. Judg. 19:25.

Hithpo. *to execute, perform,* (an action.) Ps. 141:4.

Deriv. עֹלָה, עוֹלֵל, עֲלִילָה, מַעֲלָל, תַּעֲלוּל.

II. עָלַל found only in Po. עוֹלֵל *to make a gleaning, to glean.* Lev. 19:10. Construed with an accus. Deut. 34:21. Metaphorically Jer. 6:9. (In Arab. علل conj. II. *to drink repeatedly, to pluck, to smite.*) Deriv. עֹלֵלוֹת.

III. עָלַל whence part. Po. מְעוֹלֵל *a child,* i. q. עוֹלֵל. Is. 3:12. See עוֹלֵל.

עֲלַל Chald. 1. *to go in, to enter.* In Syr. *idem.* Pret. עַל Dan. 2:16. Fem. עַלַּת, in Kethib עָלַלַת, 5:10. Part. עָלִּין, in Kethib עָלְלִין, Dan. 4:4. [4:7.] 5:8.

2. *to go down, to set,* spoken of the sun. Dan. 6:15. Comp. the Heb. בּוֹא.

Aph. *to bring in,* construed for the most part with לְ. Pret. הַנְעֵל (with epenthetic נ, instead of Dagesh forte, in ע,) Dan. 2:25. 6:19. Imper. הַעֵל, 2:24. Infin. הַעָלָה, 5:7. and הַנְעָלָה, 4:3. [4:6.]

Hoph. הֻעַל pass. Dan. 5:13, 15.

עֹלֵלוֹת, const. עֹלְלוֹת, fem. sing. (like חָכְמוֹת, comp. Judg. 8:2. Is. 17:6.) *a gleaning.* Jer. 49:9. Obad. 1:5. Is. 17:6. Root עָלַל no. II.

עָלַם *to cover, conceal.* In Kal found only in the part. pass. עֲלֻמִים *concealed* or *secret (sins),* Ps. 90:8.

Niph. נֶעְלַם *to be concealed, hidden.* Nah. 3:11. The person *from* whom any thing is concealed is preceded by מִן, Lev. 5:2 or by מֵעֵינֵי, Lev. 4:13. Num. 5:13. Part. נַעֲלָמִים *disguised men, dissemblers,* Ps. 26:4.

Hiph. הֶעְלִים.

1. *to conceal from* any one, construed with מִן. 2 K. 4:27.

2. הֶעְלִים עֵינַיִם מִן *to hide the eyes from* any one; as a refusal of assistance, Is. 1:15. comp. Prov. 28:27. as a neglecting to punish, Lev. 20:4. 1 Sam. 12:3, (construed with בְּ,) or as an expression of contempt, Ezek. 22:26.—הֶעְלִים אֹזֶן *to cover the ear, to refuse to hear,* Lam. 3:56.

3. *to obscure.* Job 42:3.

4. perhaps intrans. *to conceal one's self,* like other verbs of covering, e. g. עָטָה, כָּסָה. Ps. 10:1. Or עֵינַיִם is to be supplied as in no. 2.

Hithpa. *to conceal one's self.* Job 6:16. Construed with מִן, *to conceal one's self* or *withdraw from* any thing, Deut. 22:1, 3, 4. Ps. 55:2 אַל תִּתְעַלַּם מִתְּחִנָּתִי *withdraw not from my supplication.* Is. 58:7.

Deriv. תַּעֲלֻמָה.

עָלַם m. emph. עָלְמָא, Chald. i. q. Heb.

עָלַם *eternity, a long duration;* either future, Dan. 3:33. 4:31. [4:34.] 7:27. or past, Ezra 4:15. Hence Dan. 2:20 מִן עָלְמָא וְעַד עָלְמָא *from eternity to eternity.*

עֶלֶם m. *a lad, a young man.* 1 Sam. 17:56. 20:22. and

עַלְמָה fem. of עֶלֶם, dec. XII. a. *a young woman, mulier nubilis.* Gen. 24:43. Ex. 2:8. Ps. 68:26. Cant. 1:3. 6:8. Prov. 30:19. Is. 7:14. (Syr. ܥܠܡ Pa. and Ethpa. *to grow up, to become marriageable.* Arab. غَلِمَ *coeundi cupidus fuit.*) Deriv. עֲלוּמִים.

עַלְמוֹן 1. the proper name of a place in the tribe of Benjamin. Josh. 21:18. which in the parallel passage 1 Chr. 6:45, [6:60,] is called עָלֶמֶת.

2. עַלְמֹן דִּבְלָתָיְמָה Num. 33:46. a station of the Israelites.

עֲלָמוֹת plur. fem. a kind of tune or harmony in music. 1 Chr. 15:20. Ps. 46:1. perhaps *the female voice* or *manner,* which the chorister imitated. Comp. Forkel's Gesch. der Musik, Th. I. p.142. In the former passage it appears to stand more in reference to high and low; see מוּת.

עַלְמוּת Ps. 9:1. perhaps i. q. the preceding article, in which case עַל is to supplied; (unless the true reading be עֲלָמוֹת.) In Ps. 48:15, the context requires that it should be read as two words עַל־מָוֶת *even unto death.* In both passages the MSS. and editions vary, some writing it in one, others in two words. This, however, has but little weight, for anciently words closely connected in sense were often written as one. (See Gesenius' Gesch. der Hebr. Sprache und Schrift, p. 171.)

עֵלְמִי Chald. plur. עֵלְמָיֵא, *an Elamite,* from עֵילָם q. v. Ezra 4:9.

עַלְמוֹן see **עָלֶמֶת**

עָלַס i. q. עָלַז and עָלַץ *to exult, rejoice.* Job 20:18.

Niph. Job 39:13 כְּנַף רְנָנִים נֶעֱלָסָה *the wing of the ostrich moves nimbly* or *joyfully.* Comp. Il. II. 462, ἀγαλλόμεναι πτερύγεσσι.

Hithpa. *to rejoice, take pleasure,* (in love.) Prov. 7:18.

עָלַע found only in Piel, *to swallow down, to drink.* Job 39:30. (Kindred with לוּעַ.)

עֲלַע Chald. i. q. Heb. צֵלָע *a rib,* hence *a great tooth* or *tusk.* Dan. 7:5.

עָלַף in Kal not used.

1. *to cover.*

2. *to be wrapt in night,* hence *to be feeble, to faint.* (Comp. עָטַף, עָיֵף.)

Pu. 1. *to be covered.* Cant. 5:14.

2. *to swoon away, to faint.* Is. 51:20.

Hithpa. 1. *to cover* or *disguise one's self.* Gen. 38:14.

2. *to faint,* from heat, Jon. 4:8. from thirst. Am. 8:13.

עֻלְפֶּה m. verbal from Pual of עָלַף, (with ה paragogic,) *fainting, sorrowful.* Ezek. 31:15.

עָלַץ, fut. יַעֲלֹץ i. q. עָלַז and עָלַס *to exult, rejoice, be glad.* Prov. 11:10. 28:12.—עָלַץ בַּיהוָה *to rejoice in Jehovah,* Ps. 5:12. 9:3. 1 Sam. 2:1. Construed with לְ, *to exult* or *rejoice over* any one's calamity, *insultare* alicui, Ps. 25:2. Used metaphorically of inanimate nature, 1 Chr. 16:32.

עַם and **עָם** com. gen. (the former word being used with the conjunctive accents, the latter with the disjunctive accents and with the article as הָעָם,) with suff. עַמִּי, dec. VIII. h. *a people.* —בְּנֵי עַמִּי *the sons of my people,* i. e. my fellow-countrymen, Gen. 23:11.—בַּת עַמִּי *the daughter of my people,* i. e. my people or country, (see בַּת no. 3.) Applied to animals, Prov. 30:25, 26. Ps. 74:14.

Plur. עַמִּים (rarely in the Chaldaic form עֲמָמִים, const. עַמְמֵי, Neh. 9:22, 24. Judg. 5:14.) *peoples, nations,* particularly *the tribes of Israel.* Gen. 49:10. Deut. 32:8. 33:3, 19. But הָעַמִּים and עַמֵּי הָאָרֶץ on the contrary denote *other nations besides the Jews, gentiles.* Sometimes the plural stands for the singular, as Lev. 19:16 *thou shalt not go about as a tale-bearer* בְּעַמֶּיךָ *among thy people.* 21:1. Hos. 10:14. נֶאֱסַף אֶל עַמָּיו *to be gathered to his people,* i. e. to die. נִכְרַת מֵעַמָּיו *to be cut off from his people;* see כָּרַת Niph. no. 5.

עַם Chald. *idem.* Plur. עַמְמִין, emph. עַמְמַיָּא, Dan. 3:4, 7, 31. 5:19. 6:26. 7:14.

עִם, with suff. עִמִּי, עִמְּךָ, עִמּוֹ, עִמָּנוּ, עִמָּכֶם, עִמָּם and עִמָּהֶם, liter. *connexion, union,* (from Arab. عَمَّ *to be in common;* comp. עַם *a people,* עֻמָּה,) but used only as a preposition.

1. *with.* Gen. 27:44. Ex. 22:29. 1 Sam. 17:42 אַדְמֹנִי עִם יְפֵה־מַרְאֶה *red-haired and therewith beautiful of countenance.*—עִם זֶה *with all this, notwithstanding this,* Neh. 5:18.—Ps. 72:5 עִם שָׁמֶשׁ *so long as the sun shall endure.* Comp. Dan. 3:33. [4:3.] and Ovid. Amor. I. 15. 16. *cum sole et luna.*—Also, like the Latin *penes, in the power of* the body or mind, as Job 15:9 תָּבִין וְלֹא עִמָּנוּ הוּא *dost thou know (any thing), which was not with us,* i. e. which we knew not; (comp. 14:5.) Ps. 50:11. Job 23:14. 10:13.—עִם לְבָבִי like *apud animum meum,* Ecc. 1:16. Josh. 14:7.—It forms a periphrasis for the genitive case, Job 23:10 דֶּרֶךְ עִמָּדִי *my walk.*

2. *before;* e. g. עִם אֵל *before God,* Job 9:2. 27:13.

3. *against;* e. g. נִלְחַם עִם *to fight against* any one, 2 K. 13:12. 14:15. Comp. Ps. 94:16. 55:19.

4. *like as, pariter ac.* Ecc. 2:16 הֶחָכָם עִם הַכְּסִיל *the wise man as well as the fool.* Job 9:26. 21:8. Ps. 73:5. Ecc. 7:11. מֵעִם *from with, in respect to,* Gen. 44:32. Job 28:4. 1 Sam. 16:14 *the spirit of Jehovah departed* מֵעִם שָׁאוּל *from Saul.* More rarely i. q. עִם, 2 Sam. 3:28. Job 34:33 מֵעִמְּךָ *according to thy mind;* (comp. no. 2.)

עִם Chald. *with;* also *in,* e. g. עִם לֵילְיָא *in the night,* Dan. 7:2. עִם דָּר וְדָר *so long as the generations of men last,* Dan. 3:33. 4:31. [4:34.]

I. **עָמַד**, fut. יַעֲמֹד.

1. *to stand, stay.* 1 Sam. 20:38 *make speed, haste,* אַל תַּעֲמֹד *stay not.* (1.) Construed with לִפְנֵי, *to stand before* any one, particularly as a servant before his master; hence *to serve,* e. g. a king or general, Gen. 41:46. Deut. 1:38. Jehovah, 1 K. 17:1. 18:15. Also without לִפְנֵי, Dan. 1:4.—In Lev. 18:23, עָמַד לִפְנֵי is used in reference to copulation. (2.) construed with עַל, *to stand by, to assist.* Dan. 12:1. Est. 8:11. 9:16. (Comp. קוּם לְ.) Also *to rely upon* any thing, Ezek. 33:26. (3.) *to stand still;* spoken of the sea, Jon. 1:15. of the sun, Josh. 10:13. construed with מִן, *to cease from* any thing, Gen. 29:35.

2. *to stand firm, to abide.* Ps. 33:11. 102:27. Est. 3:4 עָמַד בַּמִּלְחָמָה *to stand in battle,* Ezek. 13:5. Particularly with לִפְנֵי, *to stand before* any one, *to withstand* or *resist* him, Ps. 76:8. 130:3. 147:7. Nah. 1:16. more rarely with בִּפְנֵי, Josh. 21:44. 23:9. with נֶגֶד, Ecc. 4:12. with מִן, Dan. 11:8. Without cases, Dan. 11:15, 25. Hence

3. *to continue, abide, stay,* spoken of persons and things. Ex. 9:28. Lev. 13:5. Dan. 10:17. Construed with בְּ, *to continue* or *abide in* any thing, Is. 47:12. Ecc. 8:3. 2 K. 23:4. Also with an accus. Ezek. 17:14 *to keep the covenant* לְעָמְדָהּ *(and) to abide therein.*—Also *to continue to live,* Ex. 21:21.

4. *to stand up, to arise,* (from signif. no. 1.) i. q. קוּם, found only in later Hebrew. Dan. 12:1, 13. Spoken particularly of a new prince, Dan. 8:23. 11:2, 3, 20. Ecc. 4:15. of a war, 1 Chr. 20:4. Construed with עַל, *to rise up against* any one, Dan. 8:25. 11:14. 1 Chr. 21:1. comp. Lev. 19:16.

5. pass. of Hiph. *to be set, placed, appointed.* Ezra 10:14 יַעַמְדוּ־נָא שָׂרֵינוּ *let our rulers be appointed,* i. e. let us appoint our rulers. Dan. 11:31.

Hiph. הֶעֱמִיד 1. causat. of Kal no. 1. *to make to stand, to place,* Ps. 31:9.

Lev. 14:11. *to fix* or *settle* one's countenance on any one, 2 K. 8:11.

2. *to cause to endure, to preserve.* 1 K. 15:4. 2 Chr. 9:8. Prov. 29:4. Also *to establish, confirm*, i. q. קִיֵּם, 2 Chr. 35:2. Dan. 11:14. *to confirm* or *fulfil the vision.*

3. *to place* or *appoint* to an office. 1 K. 12:32. 1 Chr. 15:16.

4. *to raise up, to erect*, e. g. statues. 2 Chr. 33:19. a house, Ezra 2:68. 9:9. *To stir up, to excite*, Neh. 6:7. Dan. 11:11, 13.

5. *to ordain, establish.* 2 Chr. 30:5. Construed with לְ *for* any one, 33:8.

6. intrans. *to continue.* 2 Chr. 18:34.

Hoph. *to be placed* or *presented.* Lev. 16:10.

Deriv. out of course מַעֲמָד, עַמּוּד.

II. עָמַד found only in Hiph. Ezek. 29:7 וְהַעֲמַדְתָּ לָהֶם כָּל־מָתְנָיִם by transposition for הַמְעַדְתָּ וגו׳ *and thou causedst their loins to shake.* Comp. Ps. 69:24. It is difficult to determine whether there is an actual transposition in this place, or an error of the transcribers.

עִמָּד i. q. עִם, a preposition, but found only with the suff. ־ִי, עִמָּדִי.

1. *with;* freq.

2. *in, within.* Job 6:3 *the arrows of the Almighty* עִמָּדִי *(stick) in me.* Sept. ἐν σώματί μου.

עֹמֶד m. verbal from עָמַד, dec. VI. o.

1. *a place.* Dan. 8:17, 18.

2. *a pulpit, stage.* 2 Chr. 34:31.

עֶמְדָּה f. verbal from עָמַד, dec. X. *an abiding place, a dwelling.* Mic. 1:11.

עֻמָּה f. liter. a subst. *union, connexion.* (Root עמם in Arab. *to be in common.* Comp. עִם.) Found only in the const. state עֻמַּת, also לְעֻמַּת, with suff. לְעֻמָּתִי, once לְעֻמּוֹת (Ezek. 45:7.) a preposition.

1. *near by.* Ex. 25:27. 28:27.

2. *against.* 2 Sam. 16:13. Ezek. 3:8.

3. *over against.* 1 Chr. 26:16.

4. *as, like as*, i. q. עִם no. 4. 1 Chr. 24:31. 26:12. Ecc. 7:14. Comp. 5:15 כָּל־עֻמַּת *exactly as.* (Comp. כָּל־אֲשֶׁר Job 27:3.)

5. מִלְּעֻמַּת *near by.* 1 K. 7:20.

עַמּוּד m. verbal from עָמַד, dec. I.

1. *a pillar.* Judg. 16:25, 26. 1 K. 7:2ff. עַמּוּד הֶעָנָן *the pillar of cloud*, Ex. 33:9, 10. and עַמּוּד הָאֵשׁ *the pillar of fire*, Ex. 13:22. Spoken of the pillars of heaven, Job 26:11. of the earth, Job 9:6.

2. *a stage, pulpit.* 2 K. 11:14. 23:3.

עַמּוֹן m. (liter. *from* or *of the people*, as if from עַם *a people* and the termination וֹן, like קַדְמוֹן from קֶדֶם, רִאשׁוֹן from רֹאשׁ, hence it is explained by בֶּן־עַמִּי Gen. 19:38.) *Ammon*, a proper name. 1 Sam. 11:11. More frequently בְּנֵי עַמּוֹן *the Ammonites*, a people which dwelt north-east of the Moabites from the Arnon to the Jabbok. Num. 21:24. Deut. 2:37. 3:16. See Relandi Palæstina, p. 103. —The gentile noun is עַמּוֹנִי, fem. עַמּוֹנִית, 1 K. 11:1. Neh. 13:23.

עָמוֹס *Amos*, proper name of a well-known prophet. Amos 1:1. 7:8ff. 8:2.

עַמִּיק Chald. adj. *deep, unsearchable.* Dan. 2:22.

עָמִיר m. *a sheaf*, i. q. עֹמֶר. Amos 2:13. Mic. 4:12. Zech. 12:6.

עָמִית m. dec. III. a. *a friend, neighbour, fellow-man*, synonymous with רֵעַ. Lev. 5:20. 18:20. 19:15.—Zech. 13:7 גֶּבֶר עֲמִיתִי *my neighbour*, spoken by Jehovah of the Jewish nation. Root prob. עמם=עָמָה *to bind together*, (whence עַם and עִמָּה.) The form then is feminine, and is to be compared with such examples as קְנֵה, פֶּחָה, etc.

עָמַל, fut. יַעֲמֹל, *to labour*, particularly *to weariness.* Prov. 16:26. Ps. 127:1. Construed with בְּ, *to labour on* any thing, Jon. 4:10. Ecc. 2:21.—Ecc. 1:3 בְּכָל־עֲמָלוֹ שֶׁיַּעֲמֹל *in all his labour, with which he wearieth himself.* In Arab. عمل *to labour* or *make* in any way.)

עָמָל m. verbal from עָמַל, dec. IV. c.

1. *wearisome labour, toil,* Ecc. 1:3. 2:11.

2. *the fruit of labour.* Ps. 105:44. Ecc. 2:19.

3. *trouble, adversity,* like *labor,* κάματος, πόνος. Gen. 41:51. Deut. 26:7. Job 3:10. 16:2 מְנַחֲמֵי עָמָל *troublesome comforters.*

4. *iniquity, injustice,* i. q. אָוֶן. Num. 23:21. Is. 10:1.

עָמֵל m. verbal adj. from עָמַל, dec. V. b.

1. *wearying one's self.* Joined with suffix pronouns, it forms a periphrasis of the finite verb. Ecc. 2:22. 4:8. 9:9.

2. as a subst. *a workman, faber.* Judg. 5:26.

3. *afflicted, unhappy.* Job 3:20.

4. in the abstract, *affliction, unhappiness.* Job 20:22.

עֲמָלֵק and **עֲמָלֵקִים** m. *Amalek, the Amalekites,* a people between Palestine and Arabia, on the south-west of Edom; comp. Gen. 14:7. Ex. 17:13. Num. 13:29.—In Gen. 36:12, 16. Amalek is said to be a grandson of Esau, and the prince of an Arabian tribe; yet, according to Gen. 14:7, this tribe had an earlier origin. The traditions of the Arabians favour the latter idea. See Relandi Palæstina, p. 78—82. J. D. Michaëlis Spicileg. Geogr. Hebræorum Exter. T. I. p. 170—177. Also his Supplem. p. 1927. Vater's Comment. über den Pentateuch, Th. I. p. 140.

עָמַם 1. *to obscure;* metaphorically *to excel.* Ezek. 31:8.

2. *to be obscure, unknown.* Ezek. 28:3 כָּל־סָתוּם לֹא עֲמָמוּךָ *no secret thing is unknown to thee.* (In Aram. and Arab. with غ *idem.*)

Hoph. הוּעַם *to be obscured, tarnished.* Lam. 4:1.

עֲמָמִים and Chald. עַמְמִין, *nations, peoples.* See עַם.

עִמָּנוּאֵל (*God with us*) the symbolical and prophetical name of a child, whose birth was to indicate the liberation of the Jewish state. Is. 7:15.

עָמַס (once עָמַשׂ Neh. 4:11.) fut. יַעֲמֹס.

1. *to lift up, to carry.* Zech. 12:3. Is. 46:3.

2. *to load, lade,* a beast of burden. Gen. 44:13 וַיַּעֲמֹס אִישׁ עַל חֲמֹרוֹ *and each one laded his ass.* Neh. 13:15. Ps. 68:20.

Hiph. הֶעֱמִיס, construed with עַל, *to load* or *burden* any one. 1 K. 12:11. 2 Chr. 10:11.

Deriv. מַעֲמָסָה.

עָמַק *to be deep.* Metaphorically *to be unsearchable.* Ps. 92:6. (In Arab. and Aram. *idem.*)

Hiph. 1. *to make deep.* Is. 30:33. Often adverbially, Is. 7:11 הַעְמֵק שְׁאָלָה *make deep, ask,* i. e. ask for something out of the deep. Jer. 49:8, 30 הֶעְמִיקוּ לָשֶׁבֶת *make deep your dwellings,* i. e. dwell deep in the earth. Hos. 9:9.

2. *to keep deep, to conceal.* Is. 29:15.

Deriv. out of course מַעֲמַקִּים.

עָמֹק, fem. עֲמֻקָּה, verbal adj. from עָמַק, dec. VIII. d.

1. *deep.* Lev. 13:3 ff.

2. metaphorically *unsearchable.* Ps. 64:7. Ecc. 7:24.

עָמֵק or **עֵמֶק** verbal from עָמַק, dec. IV. e. *idem.* Found only in the plur. const. עִמְקֵי שָׂפָה *of unintelligible speech,* Is. 33:19. Ezek. 3:5, 6.

עֵמֶק, with suff. עִמְקִי, dec. VI. g.

1. *a valley,* liter. *a low plain,* as a cultivated place, (Job 39:10. Ps. 65:14. Cant. 2:1.) as a place for combat, (Job 39:21.) It is evidently distinguished from the kindred words, בִּקְעָה, נַחַל, גַּיְא; whence the same place has only one of these epithets applied to it. The name עֵמֶק is applied to the valleys, e. g. of אַיָּלוֹן, יְהוֹשָׁפָט, יִזְרְעֶאל, etc. Comp. עֵמֶק הַמֶּלֶךְ *the king's dale,* not far from the Dead Sea, Gen. 14:17. 2 Sam. 18:18.

2. *an inhabitant of the valley,* i. q. אִישׁ הָעֵמֶק. 1 Chr. 12:15.

עֹמֶק m. verbal from עָמַק, *depth.* Prov. 25:3.

עָמַר in Kal not used.

Pi. עִמֵּר *to bind sheaves.* Ps. 129:7. Deriv. עֹמֶר, עָמִיר.

Hithpa. construed with בְּ, *to make slaves* or *treat as such;* (comp. עָבַד בְּ.) Deut. 21:4. 24:7. The primary signification appears to be *colligavit, coërcuit;* hence *subjecit* (as in Samar.)

עֹמֶר, plur. עֳמָרִים, dec. VI. m.

1. *a sheaf,* i. q. עָמִיר. Lev. 23:10 ff. Job 24:10.

2. *an omer,* a measure which according to Ex. 16:36, contains the tenth part of an ephah. 16:22, 32, 33.

עֲמַר Chald. *wool,* i. q. Heb. צֶמֶר. Dan. 7:9.

עֲמֹרָה *Gomorrah,* the proper name of one of the four cities in the vale of Siddim, which were sunk in the Dead Sea. Gen. 10:19. 13:10. Sept. Γομόῤῥα, Vulg. *Gomorrha.*

עָמְרִי proper name of a king of Israel. 1 K. 16:16 ff. 2 K. 8:26. Mic. 6:16. Sept. Ἀμβρί.

עָמַשׂ i. q. עָמַס *to bear.* Neh. 4:11. [4:17.]

עֵנָב m. dec. IV. b. *a grape.* Deut. 32:14. Plur. עֲנָבִים, const. עִנְּבֵי (with Dagesh forte euphonic,) Lev. 25:5. Deut. 32:32.

עָנַג in Kal not used. (In Arab. *to be beautiful and coquettish, to make amorous gestures;* spoken of females.)

Pu. *to be delicate.* Jer. 6:2.

Hithpa. 1. i. q. Pu. Deut. 28:56. comp. Is. 55:2.

2. construed with עַל, *to rejoice in* any thing; e. g. in God, Job 22:26. 27:10. in peace, Ps. 37:11. Construed with מִן, *idem,* Is. 66:11.

3. *to make one's self merry about* any thing, construed with עַל. Is. 57:4.

Deriv. תַּעֲנוּג.

עָנֹג, fem. עֲנֻגָּה, verbal adj. from עָנַג, dec. VIII. d. *delicate, luxurious.* Deut. 28:26, 54. Is. 47:1.

עֹנֶג m. verbal from עָנַג, *pleasure, enjoyment, luxury.* Is. 13:22. 58:13.

עָנַד *to bind on.* Found only Job 31:36. Prov. 6:21. Comp. מַעֲדַנּוֹת.

I. **עָנָה** (a proper verb ל״ה.)

1. *to answer.* It is construed (1.) with an accus. of the person, Job 1:7. Gen. 23:14. Cant. 5:6. So in Greek ἀμείβομαι τινά. (2.) with an accus. of the thing which any one answers, Prov. 18:23. Job 40:2. So Job 33:13 כָּל־דְּבָרָיו לֹא יַעֲנֶה *he answereth not about any of his matters,* i. e. gives no account of them. Hence (3.) with a double accus. of the person and thing, 1 Sam. 20:10. Mic. 6:5. Jer. 23:27.

2. *to hear,* liter. *to answer* a prayer, used particularly of God. 1 Sam. 9:17. 14:39. Ps. 3:5. 4:2. Ps. 22:22 מִקַּרְנֵי רֵמִים עֲנִיתָנִי *hear (and deliver) me from the horns of the gazelle.* Construed with an accus. of the thing, *to impart, grant* any thing, Ecc. 10:19 הַכֶּסֶף יַעֲנֶה אֶת־הַכֹּל *money imparts every thing.* Comp. Hos. 2:22, 23. With two accus. *to grant* any one any thing, Ps. 65:6.

3. *to begin to speak,* particularly in later Hebrew. Job 3:2 וַיַּעַן אִיּוֹב וַיֹּאמַר *then began Job and said.* Cant. 2:10. Is. 14:10. Zech. 1:10. 3:4. 4:11, 12. Construed with an accus. of the person, *to address* any one, Zech. 1:11.

4. עָנָה בְ *to give testimony, to testify,* namely, by *answering* the inquiries of the judge; sometimes *for* a person, Gen. 30:33. 1 Sam. 12:3. but for the most part *against* him, 2 Sam. 1:16. Num. 35:30. Deut. 19:18. Job 16:8 כַּחֲשִׁי בְּפָנַי יַעֲנֶה *my leanness testifies to my face.*—More full עָנָה עֵד בְּ *to bear witness against* any one, Ex. 20:16. comp. Deut. 31:21. The thing *testified* is put in the accus. Deut. 19:16.

5. *to pass a sentence, responsum dare;* spoken of the judge. Ex. 23:2. Spoken of Jehovah, *to announce,* as an oracle, Gen. 41:16. comp. Deut. 20:11. 1 Sam. 9:17 וַיהוָה עָנָהוּ *then Jehovah announced to him.*

6. *to cry, shout,* for the onset or for victory, Ex. 32:18. Jer. 51:14. as the jackal, Is. 13:22.

7. *to sing.* Ex. 15:21. Construed with לְ, *to praise* or *celebrate by singing,* 1 Sam. 21:10. 29:5. Ps. 147:7.

Niph. 1. *to be answered.* Job 11:2.

2. *to be heard.* Job 19:7. Prov. 21:13.

3. as if pass. of Hiph. i. q. Kal, *to answer*, construed with לְ. Ezek. 14:4, 7.

Pi. i. q. Kal no. 7. *to sing.* Ex. 32:18. Ps. 88:1. Is. 27:2.

II. עָנָה (for ענו, a proper verb ל״ו, comp. the derivatives עָנִי, עֲנָוָה.)

1. *to bestow labour* or *toil on* any thing, *to busy one's self* therewith, construed with בְּ. Ecc. 1:14. 3:10. Syr. ܥܢܐ, Arab. عني with ب *idem.*)

2. *to suffer, to be bowed down* or *oppressed.* Ps. 116:10. 119:67. Zech. 10:2. Is. 31:4 וּמֵהֲמוֹנָם לֹא יַעֲנֶה *and is not bowed down before their multitude,* i. e. does not lose his labour. 25:5 זְמִיר עָרִיצִים יַעֲנֶה *the triumphal song of the tyrant is bowed down* or *brought low.* (Arab. عنا *to be bowed down, to be humble.*)

Niph. 1. *to be* or *become afflicted.* Ps. 119:107.

2. reflex. *to bow down* or *humble one's self,* construed with מִפְּנֵי. Ex. 10:3. The infin. לֵעָנוֹת stands here for לְהֵעָנוֹת.

Pi. 1. *to oppress, afflict, humble.* Gen. 16:6. 15:13. 31:50. Ex. 22:22. Ps. 102:24 עִנָּה בַדֶּרֶךְ כֹּחִי *he (the enemy) has humbled my strength in the way.* 88:8 כָל־מִשְׁבָּרֶיךָ עִנִּיתָ *with all thy waves thou hast afflicted me.*

2. joined with אִשָּׁה, *comprimere feminam, to deflour* or *ravish a woman.* Gen. 34:2. Deut. 22:24, 29. Judg. 19:24. 20:5.

3. joined with נֶפֶשׁ, *to afflict the soul,* i. e. to fast. Lev. 16:31. 23:27, 32. Num. 29:7.

Pu. *to be oppressed, humbled.* Ps. 119:71. Is. 53:4, Infin. עֻנּוֹתוֹ *his misery, his affliction,* Ps. 132:1.

Hiph. i. q. Pi. no. 1. 1 K. 8:35. 2 Chr. 6:26 כִּי תַעֲנֵם *when thou hast afflicted them.* Ecc. 5:19 כִּי הָאֱלֹהִים מַעֲנֶה בְּשִׂמְחַת לִבּוֹ *for God humbleth him in the joy of his heart.* Others: *if God hears him through the joy of his heart,* i. e. imparts to him the joy of his heart.

Hithpa. 1. *to humble one's self.* Gen. 16:9. Particularly before God, Dan. 10:12.

2. *to be afflicted,* as in Kal. 1 K. 2:26.

עֲנָה, עֲנָא Chald. 1. *to answer.* Dan. 2:7, 10. 3:14, 16. 5:8. 6:14.

2. more frequently *to begin to speak,* as in Heb. no. 3. Dan. 2:20. 3:9, 19, 24, 26, 28. 4:16, 27. [4:19, 30.] Construed with לְ of the person, Dan. 2:47.

עָנָו, plur. עֲנָוִים, const. עַנְוֵי, verbal from עָנָה no. II. 2. dec. IV. c.

1. *afflicted, oppressed, poor, unhappy.* Ps. 9:13. 10:12, 17.—עַנְוֵי־אֶרֶץ *the poor of the earth,* Is. 11:4. Ps. 76:10. Prov. 3:34. For the most part involving the idea of *humility,* or *virtuous suffering,* comp. particularly Ps. 25:9. 37:11. 69:33.

2. *meek.* Num. 12:3.

עֲנָוָה strictly the fem. of עָנָו, dec. XI. d. used substantively.

1. *humility.* Prov. 15:33. 18:12. 22:4. Zeph. 2:3.

2. *mildness, goodness,* spoken of God. Ps. 18:36.

עַנְוָה f. i. q. עֲנָוָה no. 2. Ps. 45:5.

עֲנוֹק see עֲנָק.

עֱנוּת f. Ps. 22:25 עֱנוּת עָנִי *the affliction of the afflicted.* Others, after the Sept. Vulg. Chald. *the cry of the afflicted,* (parall. שַׁוְעוֹ,) but עָנָה is used neither in Hebrew (see no. I. 6.) nor in the other dialects to express *lamentation.*

עָנִי, fem. עֲנִיָּה, plur. עֲנִיִּים, const. עֲנִיֵּי, verbal adj. from עָנָה no. II. dec. VIII. m.

1. *poor, helpless;* often in reference to the national distresses of the Israelites. (Comp. De Wette in den Studien, Th. 3. p. 209.) Ex. 22:24. Deut. 24:12. Ps. 10:2, 9. 14:6. 18:28.

2. *humble, lowly.* Zech. 9:9. For the plur. עֲנִיִּים the Kethib often has עֲנָוִים, e. g. Ps. 9:19. Is. 32:7.

עֳנִי, in pause עֹנִי, with suff. עָנְיִי, verbal

from עָנָה no. II. dec. VI. q. *affliction, oppression, suffering, misery.* Gen. 16:11. 31:42. 41:52. בְּנֵי עֹנִי *the children of affliction*, i. e. the afflicted, Prov. 31:5. לֶחֶם עֹנִי *the bread of affliction*, Deut. 16:3.

עִנְיָן m. dec. II. b. 1. *a business, employment.* Ecc. 2:26. 1:13 עִנְיַן רָע *a troublesome business.*

2. *a matter, thing,* (as in Chald.) Ecc. 4:8 עִנְיַן רָע *an evil thing.* 5:13 בְּעִנְיַן רָע *by an evil matter*, i. e. by an evil occurrence. 2:23 כַּעַס עִנְיָנוֹ *grief is his portion.* 8:16. (Comp. עָנָה no. II. 1.)

עֲנָמִים found only Gen. 10:13. a people of Egyptian origin, otherwise unknown.

עֲנַמֶּלֶךְ proper name of an idol of the inhabitants of Sippharа. Once 2 K. 17:31. It appears to be compounded of ענם=صنم *an image, statue,* and מֶלֶךְ *a king.* The former part of this composition is found also in the proper name Ἐνεμεσσαρ, (Tob. 1:2, 13, 15, 16.) i. e. ענמאסר, (comp. שלמנאסר.)

עָנָן m. const. עֲנַן, dec. IV. c. *a cloud.* Gen. 9:14. Ex. 13:21, 22. 14:19. Hence the denom. עָנַן.

עֲנָן Chald. *idem.* Plur. const. עֲנָנֵי, Dan. 7:13.

עָנַן, in Pi. עִנֵּן, denom. from עָנָן, *to gather clouds.* Gen. 9:14. Hence many likewise derive

עוֹנֵן Po. fut. יְעוֹנֵן, part. מְעוֹנֵן, *to augur from the appearances of the clouds*, a species of divination. Lev. 19:26. Deut. 18:10, 14. 2 K. 21:6. But we have no proof that this mode of divination was known in ancient times. Better to render it, like the Talmudists (Surenhusii Mishna, T. IV. p. 224.) and several ancient versions, *to fascinate, enchant, bewitch,* by the eye, (Ital. *indocchiatura,*) and to derive it from עַיִן. Comp. the Arab. عان *oculo maligno petivit,* also עָיַן and עוּן.

עֲנָנָה f. *a cloud.* Job 3:5.

עָנָף *a bough, branch.* Ezek. 17:8, 23. With suff. עַנְפְּכֶם Ezek. 36:8, (as if from עֶנֶף.)

עֲנַף Chald. *idem.* Dan. 4:9, 11. [4:12, 14.]

עָנֵף m. *full of branches.* Ezek. 19:10.

עָנַק liter. *to surround like a necklace* (עֲנָק.) Ps. 73:6 עֲנָקַתְמוֹ גַאֲוָה *pride surroundeth him like a necklace.* The *collum resupinum* is, in poetic language, an indication of pride.

Hiph. הֶעֱנִיק *to give to* any one. Deut. 15:14 הַעֲנֵיק תַּעֲנִיק לוֹ מִצֹּאנְךָ *thou shalt surely give to him from thy flock.* (Arab. عنق, with علي, *facilem se alicui præbuit,* Samar. ענק *subvenit* alicui, *adjuvit* eum.) Others: liter. *thou shalt load upon him, collo imponas.*

I. **עֲנָק** m. *a necklace, an ornament for the neck.* Cant. 4:9. Plur. ־ִים and ־וֹת, Prov. 1:9. Judg. 8:26.

II. **עֲנָק**, once עֲנוֹק (Josh. 21:11.) found only in the phrases בְּנֵי עֲנָק, בְּנֵי הָעֲנָק, Num. 13:33. יְלִידֵי הָעֲנָק, Num. 13:22, 28. *sons of Anak;* and עֲנָקִים *the Anakites,* Deut. 1:28. 2:10, 11, 21. an ancient race of giants, which before the irruption of the Israelites into Palestine dwelt in the neighbourhood of Hebron and in some other places, (Josh. 11:21.) but were destroyed, excepting a small remnant in the Philistine cities, Gaza, Gath, and Ashdod. (The word appears to have been originally an appellative, comp. عنق *homines, principes.*)

עָנַשׁ, fut. יַעֲנֹשׁ, 1. *to amerce* or *impose a fine on* any one, construed with two accus. Deut. 22:19. Also *to exact* from a conquered enemy, 2 Chr. 36:3. Sometimes this fine or contribution is in natural productions, Am. 2:8.

2. *to punish* in any way, construed with לְ. Prov. 17:26.

3. *to suffer, to be punished.* Prov. 21:11.

Niph. 1. *to be amerced* or *fined.* Ex. 21:22.

2. *to suffer* or *be punished* in any way. Prov. 22:3. 27:12.

עֹנֶשׁ m. verbal from עָנַשׁ.
1. *a fine, contribution.* 2 K. 23 : 33.
2. *a punishment.* Prov. 19 : 19.

עֲנָשׁ m. Chald. *a mulct, fine.* Ezra 7 : 26.

עֱנָת, whence כְּעֶנֶת, Chald. see עֵת.

עֲנָתוֹת proper name of a Levitical city in the tribe of Benjamin, the birthplace of Jeremiah. Josh. 21 : 18. Is. 10 : 30. Jer. 1 : 1. The gentile noun is עַנְּתֹתִי 2 Sam. 23 : 27.

עָסִיס m. dec. III. a. *new wine.* Joel 1 : 5. 4 : 18. [3 : 18.] Amos 9 : 13. Root עָסַס.

עָסַס *to tread down.* Mal. 3 : 21. [4 : 3.]

עער Is. 15 : 5 יְעֹעֵרוּ, to judge from the context, i. q. יְעוֹרְרוּ, or יְעָרְעָרוּ *they stir up* (a cry). Vulg. *clamorem levabunt.* The form appears to be a corruption of one of the two given above.

עֵפָה see אֵיפָה.

עֳפִי m. plur. עֳפָאִים, dec. VI. q. *a bough, branch, foliage.* Ps. 104 : 12. See the following article.

עֳפִי Chald. *a bough, branch,* as in Heb. Dan. 4 : 9, 11, 18. [4 : 12, 14, 21.] (Syr. ܥܽܘܦܳܐ *a bough, top of a tree;* ܥܽܘܦܳܐ *foliage.*)

עָפַל prob. *tumuit,* (comp. אָפַל.) Hence *to be arrogant, contumacious, rash,* (against God.) Comp. זִיד.

Pu. *idem.* Hab. 2 : 4.

Hiph. 14 : 44 וַיַּעְפִּלוּ לַעֲלוֹת וגו׳ *they were rash and went up;* comp. Deut. 1 : 43 וַתָּזִדוּ וַתַּעֲלוּ הָהָרָה.

עֹפֶל m. *a hill.* Is. 32 : 14. Mic. 4 : 8. With the article, (*the hill,*) proper name of an eminence on the eastern part of Mount Zion, which was surrounded and fortified with a wall. 2 K. 5 : 24. 2 Chr. 27 : 3. 33 : 14. Neh. 3 : 27. 11 : 21. comp. Josephi Bell. Jud. VI. 6.

עפלים (to be pronounced עֳפָלִים or עֲפָלִים) in the Kethib of Deut. 28 : 27. 1 Sam. 5 : 6 ff. *tumours on the fundament, hemorrhoids.* (Arab. عفل in men *a tumour on the fundament;* in women *a swelling on the pudenda.*) The Keri in all these passages has טְחֹרִים q. v.

עַפְעַף and עַפְעַפַּיִם dual, found only in the const. state עַפְעַפֵּי, *eye-lashes.* Job 16 : 16. Ps. 132 : 4. עַפְעַפֵּי שָׁחַר *the eye-lashes of the morning dawn,* i. e. the beams emitted from the rising sun, Job 3 : 9. 41 : 10. [41 : 18.] (The Arabian and Greek poets have the same figure.)

עָפָר m. dec. IV. c. *dust, earth.* Gen. 2 : 7. 26 : 15. Lev. 14 : 42, 45. Hab. 1 : 10. Plur. const. עַפְרוֹת Prov. 8 : 26. Job 28 : 6.—Used only rarely of the fine floating dust (otherwise called אָבָק,) as Ps. 18 : 43.—שָׁכַב עַל עָפָר *to lie in the dust* or *grave,* Job 20 : 11. 21 : 26. So with לֶעָפָר, Job 7 : 21.—יָרַד עָפָר *to descend to the grave,* Ps. 22 : 30. 30 : 10.—שׁוּב אֶל עָפָר *to return to the dust,* Gen. 3 : 19. Ps. 104 : 29.—עָפָר וָאֵפֶר *dust and ashes,* a figurative expression for humility, frailty, Gen. 18 : 27. Ps. 103. 14.—אָכַל עָפָר *to eat the dust,* spoken of the serpent, Gen. 3 : 14. comp. Is. 65 : 16. Hence

עִפֵּר Pi. denom. from עָפָר, *to cover with earth.* 2 Sam. 16 : 13.

עֹפֶר m. prim. dec. VI. m. *the young of the stag, roe,* or *gazelle.* Cant. 2 : 9, 17. 4 : 5. 7 : 4. 8 : 14. Arab. غُفْر and غَفْر *a young wild goat.*)

עָפְרָה 1. proper name of a place in the tribe of Benjamin. Josh. 18 : 23. 1 Sam. 13 : 17. In Mic. 1 : 10, בֵּית לְעַפְרָה.

2. also of a place in the tribe of Manasseh. Judg. 6 : 11. 8 : 27. 9 : 5.

עֶפְרוֹן 1. proper name of a city on the borders of the tribe of Benjamin. 2 Chr. 13 : 19. The Keri has עֶפְרַיִן.

2. also of a mountain on the borders of the tribes Judah and Benjamin. Josh. 15 : 9.

עֹפֶרֶת f. *lead.* Ex. 15 : 10. אֶבֶן הָעֹפֶרֶת *a weight of lead,* Zech. 5 : 8.

עֵץ m. plur. עֵצִים, const. עֲצֵי, dec. VII. f.
1. *a tree;* freq.

2. *wood.* Also *a post, gibbet, gallows, patibulum,* Gen. 40 : 19. Deut. 21 : 22. Josh. 10 : 26. The plur. עֵצִים denotes *logs* or *pieces of wood,* whether *billets* for burning, Lev. 1 : 7. 4 : 12. or *timber* for building and the like.—עֲצֵי שִׁטִּים *acacia wood,* Ex. 25 : 10 ff.

עָצַב 1. *to labour, make, form;* (see Pi. no. 1.) Deriv. עָצָב and עֹצֶב *an image, idol;* עֶצֶב *vas fictile.* Particularly *to perform hard* or *fatiguing labour,* (comp. עִצָּבוֹן.) Hence

2. *to suffer pain,* (see עֶצֶב, עֹצֶב, עַצֶּבֶת, עִצָּבוֹן *pain.*) Comp. Niph. no. 1.

3. *to be pained* or *distressed in mind, dolere,* or trans. *to occasion pain* or *distress, to grieve, to afflict.* 1 K. 1 : 6. 1 Chr. 4 : 10. Is. 54 : 6. Comp. Niph. no. 2. Pi. and Hiph.

Niph. 1. *to hurt one's self with* any thing, construed with בְּ. Ecc. 10 : 9.

2. *to grieve* or *vex one's self.* Gen. 45 : 5. 1 Sam. 20 : 3. Construed with אֶל, (1 Sam. 20 : 34.) and with עַל, (2 Sam. 19 : 3.) of the thing *about* which one is vexed.

Pi. 1. *to make, form.* (Comp. Kal no. 1.) Job 10 : 8.

2. *to grieve, vex.* (Comp. Kal no. 3.) Is. 63 : 10. Ps. 56 : 6.

Hiph. i. q. Pi. no. 2. *to vex, to excite to anger,* e. g. the Deity. Ps. 78 : 40.

2. perhaps *to serve, worship,* (comp. עָבַד *to labour* and *to serve.*) Jer. 44 : 19 לְהַעֲצִבָהּ *to worship her* (*the queen of heaven.*) Vulg. *ad colendum eam.* Others: *to form an image of her.* (Comp. Kal no. 1.)

Hithpa. 1. *to grieve* or *trouble one's self.* Gen. 6 : 6.

2. *to be angry.* Gen. 34 : 7. See Hiph. no. 1.

Deriv. out of course מַעֲצֵבָה.

עֲצַב Chald. found only in the part. עֲצִיב *troubled, afflicted.* Dan. 6 : 21.

עָצָב found only in the plur. עֲצַבִּים, const. עֲצַבֵּי, verbal from עָצַב, *idols, images.* 1 Sam. 31 : 9. 2 Sam. 5 : 21. Hos. 4 : 17. (See the root no. 1.)

עָצֵב m. verbal from עָצַב, plur. with suff. עַצְּבֵיכֶם (with Dagesh forte euphonic,) *a labourer, servant.* Is. 58 : 3.

עֶצֶב and **עֶצֶב** m. verbal from עָצַב, dec. VI. a.

1. *fatiguing labour, toil.* Prov. 10 : 22. Plur. עֲצָבִים *hard earnings, labores,* Prov. 5 : 10. לֶחֶם הָעֲצָבִים *bread acquired by hard labour,* Ps. 127 : 2.

2. *pain,* (of a woman in childbirth.) Gen. 3 : 16.

3. *sorrow, affliction, bitterness.* Prov. 15 : 1 דְּבַר עֶצֶב *a bitter* or *angry word.* See the verb in Hiph.

4. *an earthen vessel, vas fictile.* Jer. 22 : 28. (See Kal no. 1.)

עֹצֶב m. verbal from עָצַב, dec. VI. p.

1. *an image,* like עָצָב. Is. 48 : 5. Ps. 139 : 24 דֶּרֶךְ עֹצֶב *idolatry.*

2. *pain.* 1 Chr. 4 : 9. Is. 14 : 3.

עִצָּבוֹן m. const. עִצְּבוֹן, verbal from עָצַב, dec. III. d.

1. *labour, toil.* Gen. 3 : 17. 5 : 29.

2. *pain.* Gen. 3 : 16 עִצְּבוֹנֵךְ וְהֵרֹנֵךְ *thy pain and thy conception,* i. e. the pain of thy conception.

עַצֶּבֶת f. const. עַצֶּבֶת (as if from עַצָּבָה,) plur. const. עַצְּבוֹת, verbal from עָצַב, dec. XIII. k.

1. *pain, suffering.* Job 9 : 28. Ps. 16 : 4.

2. *affliction, sorrow.* Ps. 147 : 3 מְחַבֵּשׁ לְעַצְּבוֹתָם *he bindeth up their wounds,* i. e. the wounds of their soul. Prov. 10 : 10. Joined with לֵב, 15 : 13.

עָצָה *to shut* or *close* (the eyes). Once Prov. 16 : 30. (Ethiop. ዐፀወ *clausit portam.* Arab. conj. VII. *connivit oculis.*)

עָצֶה m. *the chine, spine, back-bone.* Lev. 3 : 9. According to others, i. q. Arab. عصعص *os coccygis.* See Bocharti Hieroz. I. p. 497.

I. **עֵצָה** fem. of עֵץ, used collectively, *wood,* i. q. עֵצִים. Jer. 6 : 6.

II. **עֵצָה** f. const. עֲצַת, verbal from יָעַץ, dec. XI. b.

1. *counsel* given or received. 2 Sam. 16:20. Ps. 119:24 אַנְשֵׁי עֲצָתִי *my counsellors.*

2. *purpose, design, plan,* Is. 19:3. אִישׁ עֲצָתִי *the man whom I have selected for my purpose,* Is. 46:11. עָשָׂה עֵצָה *to form a design* or *purpose,* Is. 30:1.

3. *wisdom, reflection, consilium,* as a quality of mind. Is. 11:2. Prov. 8:14. Jer. 32:19 גְּדֹל הָעֵצָה *magnus consilio.* 1 Chr. 12:19 בְּעֵצָה *with reflection.* Plur. עֵצוֹת, once with suff. עֲצָתָיִךְ Is. 47:13. Elsewhere usually מוֹעֵצוֹת.

עָצוּם m. verbal from עָצַם, dec. III. c.

1. *strong, mighty.* Num. 14:12 גּוֹי גָּדוֹל וְעָצוּם *a great and strong people.* Deut. 4:38.

2. *numerous.* Joel 1:6. Ps. 35:18.

3. Plur. עֲצוּמִים *the strong ones,* prob. a poetical epithet, (like אַבִּיר, לְבָנָה,) for *strong members, teeth, claws.* Hence Ps. 10:10 וְנָפַל בַּעֲצוּמָיו חֵלְכָּאִים *the unhappy fall into his claws.* Others: *his strong ones,* i.e. his young lions.

עֶצְיוֹן גֶּבֶר (*the spine of a man*) proper name of a haven in Idumea, on the Elanitic gulf, whence Solomon sent ships to Ophir, in later times called *Berenice.* Num. 33:35. Deut. 2:8. 1 K. 9:26. 22:49.

עָצַל found only in Niph. *to be slothful.* Judg. 18:19.

עָצֵל m. verbal from עָצַל, *slothful, sluggish, lazy.* Prov. 6:6, 9. 13:4. 15:19.

עַצְלָה f. Prov. 19:15. and עַצְלוּת 31:27. verbals from עָצַל, *sloth, idleness.* Dual עֲצַלְתַּיִם *double,* i.e. great, *idleness.* Ecc. 10:18.

I. **עָצַם** and **עָצֵם** (Ps. 38:20.)

1. *to be strong, mighty.* Gen. 26:16. More frequently inchoatively, *to become mighty,* Ex. 1:7, 20. Dan. 8:8, 24. 11:23.

2. *to be numerous.* Ps. 38:20. 40:6, 13. (See עָצוּם.) These two ideas are embraced likewise in the kindred verbs רָבַב and רָבָה. (Arab. عظم *idem.*)

Pi. עִצֵּם (denom. from עֶצֶם *a bone,*) *exossare, to gnaw flesh from a bone.* Jer. 50:17. Comp. גָּרַם.

Hiph. *to make strong.* Ps. 105:24.

II. **עָצַם** Is. 33:15. and in Pi. עִצֵּם, followed by עֵינַיִם, *to shut* or *close the eyes.* 29:10. (Arab. لعصم *to bind up.*)

עֶצֶם f. verbal from עָצַם, dec. VI. a.

1. *a bone.* Gen. 2:23 עֶצֶם מֵעֲצָמַי *bone of my bones.* Plur. עֲצָמִים and more frequently עֲצָמוֹת, the latter form being used generally, (but not exclusively,) of the bones of a dead person, in reference to burial, etc. (Comp. רוּחַ, נְשָׁמָה.) Ex. 13:19. Josh. 24:32. 2 Sam. 21:12—14. 2 K. 23:14, 18, 20.

2. *body, form, appearance.* Lam. 4:7.

3. *the same, very, itself,* in reference to things; e. g. בְּעֶצֶם הַיּוֹם הַזֶּה *on this same day.* Gen. 7:13. 17:23, 26. Ex. 24:10 כְּעֶצֶם הַשָּׁמַיִם *as the heaven itself.* Job 21:23 בְּעֶצֶם תֻּמּוֹ *in the midst of prosperity.* (In a similar way the Arabians use عين *an eye.*)

4. proper name of a city in the tribe of Simeon. Josh. 15:29. 19:3. 1 Chr. 4:29.

עֹצֶם m. verbal from עָצַם, dec. VI. p.

1. *strength.* Deut. 8:17. Job 30:21.

2. *body, frame,* i. q. עֶצֶם no. 2. Ps. 139:15.

עָצְמָה f. verbal from עָצַם, dec. X.

1. *strength.* Is. 40:29.

2. *multitude.* Is. 47:9. Nah. 3:9.

עַצְמוֹן proper name of a city on the southern boundary of Palestine. Num. 34:4, 5. Josh. 15:4.

עֲצֻמוֹת f. verbal from עָצַם, *strong reasons, arguments.* Is. 41:21. (In Talmud. עֲצָמוֹת *argumenta valida, rationes;* Arab. עצמה *defensio, tutamen.*)

עֶצֶן found only 2 Sam. 23:8. prob. *a spear.* Comp. Arab. عصن *a bough, branch.* See under the art. עֵדֶן.

עָצַר, fut. יַעֲצֹר and יַעְצֹר.

1. *to stop, hold back, detain.* 1 K. 18:44. Judg. 13:16. Construed with

בְּ, Job 12:15 יַעְצֹר בַּמַּיִם *he holdeth back the waters.* 4:2. 29:9.

2. *to shut up,* e.g. heaven, that it may not rain, Deut. 11:17. 2 Chr. 7:13. a woman that she may not bear, Gen. 16:2. 20:18 (where בְּעַד pertains to the construction, see בַּעַד no. 4.) Hence also *to imprison,* 2 K. 17:4. Jer. 33:1. 36:5. 39:15.—1 Chr. 12:1 עָצוּר מִפְּנֵי שָׁאוּל *shut up* or *kept close because of Saul.*

3. *to rule, coërcere imperio.* 1 Sam. 9:17. See עֶצֶר.

4. עָצַר כֹּחַ (only in later Hebrew,) *to retain strength.* Dan. 10:8, 16. 11:6. 2 Chr. 13:20. Construed with לְ, *to have power* or *be able to* do any thing, 1 Chr. 29:14. 2 Chr. 2:5. 22:9. Also without כֹּחַ, 2 Chr. 20:37. 14:10.

Niph. 1. *to be stopped.* Num. 17:13, 15. [16:48, 50.] 2 Sam. 24:21, 25. Ps. 106:30.

2. *to be shut up,* spoken of heaven. 1 K. 8:35. 2 Chr. 6:26.

עֹצֶר m. verbal from עָצַר, dec. VI.

1. *the shutting up.* Prov. 30:16 עֹצֶר רָחַם *the shutting up of the womb,* i.e. the barren womb.

2. *oppression.* Ps. 107:39. Is. 53:8.

עֶצֶר m. verbal from עָצַר, *government, restraint.* Judg. 18:7. See the verb no. 3.

עֲצָרָה f. and more frequently עֲצֶרֶת, dec. XI. d.

1. *an assembly.* Jer. 9:1.

2. particularly *a festival meeting of the people,* πανήγυρις. Joel 1:14. 2 K. 10:20. Am. 5:21. Is. 1:13.

3. by way of eminence, *the festival meeting of the people on the seventh day of the passover,* or *on the eighth of the feast of tabernacles,* synonymous with מִקְרָא קֹדֶשׁ. Lev. 23:36. Comp. Num. 29:35. Deut. 16:8. 2 Chr. 7:9. Neh. 8:18. (Comp. in Arab. جمعة *a meeting, a day of meeting, Friday* the festival of the Mohammedans.)

עָקַב, fut. יַעְקֹב, (denom. from עָקֵב *the heel,*) *to hold* any one *by the heel.* Hos. 12:4 בַּבֶּטֶן עָקַב אֶת־אָחִיו *in the womb he took his brother by the heel.* Comp. אָחַז בַּעָקֵב. Particularly *to trip up the heel of* any one, *supplantare;* hence *to act deceitfully,* Gen. 27:36. Jer. 9:3.

Pi. *to stop* or *hold back* any thing, *retardare.* Job 37:4.

עָקֵב m. const. עֲקֵב, plur. const. עִקְבֵי (in some editions עִקְּבֵי with Dagesh forte euphonic.)

1. *the heel.* Gen. 3:15. Ps. 56:7. Job 18:9. Jer. 13:22. Cant. 1:8.

2. *the hoof* (of a horse). Gen. 49:17. Judg. 5:22.

3. with a plur. עֲקֵבוֹת fem. (or neut.) *a footstep, trace.* Ps. 77:20. 89:52. (Comp. Cant. 1:8.)

4. metaphorically *the hinder part of an army,* Josh. 8:13. Gen. 49:19.

5. as a verbal adj. from עָקַב, *a lier in wait, insidiator.* Ps. 49:6.

עָקֹב m. 1. subst. *an eminence, a hill.* (Arab. عقب and عقبة *clivus, clivositas montis.*) Is. 40:4.

2. adj. *deceitful.* Jer. 17:9.

3. adj. (denom. from עָקֵב *the heel, a footstep,*) Hos. 6:8 עֲקֻבָּה מִדָּם *with footsteps of blood.*

עֵקֶב m. 1. *the end, the extremity* of any thing. (Arab. عقب.) Hence adv. *to the end, for ever,* Ps. 119:33, 112.

2. *a reward, recompence.* Ps. 19:12. Prov. 22:4. liter. *the consequences of an action,* comp. λοισθήϊα *a reward,* from λοῖσθος *the last.* Hence עַל עֵקֶב Ps. 40:16. 70:4. and עֵקֶב Is. 5:23. as an adv. *on account of, for the sake of,* liter. *as a reward of, in præmium.* Further as a conj. *because that,* Num. 14:24. Deut. 7:12. more in full, עֵקֶב אֲשֶׁר Gen. 26:5. and עֵקֶב כִּי Am. 4:12.

עָקְבָה f. verbal from עָקַב, *fraud, deceit.* 2 K. 10:19.

עָקַד, fut. יַעֲקֹד, Arab. عقد, *to bind.* Gen. 22:9. Hence

עָקֹד, plur. עֲקֻדִּים, verbal adj. from עָקַד, dec. VIII. d. *striped, covered with rings* or *bands.* Gen. 30:35 ff. 31:8 ff.

עֲקָה f. dec. X. *oppression*. Ps. 55: 4. Root עוק *to oppress*.

עָקַל *to wind, twist*.

Pu. part. *perverted, perverse*. Hab. 1:4. (Syr. ܥܩܠ *perversus*, Arab. عقل *to bind together*.)

עֲקַלְקַל verbal adj. from עָקַל, dec. VIII. a. *crooked*. Judg. 5:6 אֳרָחוֹת עֲקַלְקַלּוֹת *by-ways*. So Ps. 125:5 עֲקַלְקַלּוֹת without addition, *idem*.

עֲקַלָּתוֹן m. verbal from עָקַל, *crooked*, spoken of the serpent. Is. 27:1.

עָקַר *to root out, to pluck up*, (any thing planted.) Ecc. 3:2. (In Syr. and Chald. *idem*.)

Niph. *to be destroyed*, spoken of a city. Zeph. 2:4.

Pi. *to hough* or *hamstring, to disable by cutting the sinews of the ham*; e. g. a horse, Josh. 11:6, 9. 2 Sam. 8:4. 1 Chr. 18:4. an ox, Gen. 49:6. (Arab. عقر *idem*.)

עֲקַר Chald. *to pluck up*. Ithpe. pass. Dan. 7:8.

עֵקֶר m. *a stem, trunk, truncus*, metaphorically *a stock, family*. Lev. 25: 47. (Chald. עִקַּר.)

עָקָר, fem. עֲקָרָה and עֲקֶרֶת, *barren, unfruitful*, spoken of a man or woman. Gen. 11:30. 25:21. 29:31. Deut. 7: 14. (Syr. and Arab. *idem*.)

עִקַּר m. Chald. *a stock, stump*. Dan. 4:12, 20. [4:15, 23.]

עַקְרָב m. plur. עַקְרַבִּים, dec. VIII. a.

1. *a scorpion*. Ezek. 2:6. (Arab. *idem*.) See also מַעֲלֵה עַקְרַבִּים.

2. *a whip* or *scourge armed with knots and thorns*. 1 K. 12:11, 14. 2 Chr. 10:11, 14. So in Lat. *scorpio*, i. q. virga nodosa et aculeata.

עֶקְרוֹן proper name of one of the five cities of the Philistines, by whom it was constantly possessed although it was assigned at first to the tribe of Judah, (Josh. 15:45.) and afterwards to the tribe of Dan, (Josh. 19:43.) Josh. 13: 3. 15:11. 19:43. Judg. 1:18. 1 Sam. 5:10. 2 K. 1:2. Sept. 'Ακκαρὼν, 'Ακκαρών. The gentile noun is עֶקְרוֹנִי Josh. 13:3. 1 Sam. 5:10.

עָקַשׁ *to distort, pervert*. Job 9:20 וַיַּעְקְשֵׁנִי *he perverts me*, i. e. perverts my cause.

Pi. *idem*. Mic. 3:9.—*To pervert* one's ways, i. e. to act perversely or falsely, Is. 59:8. Prov. 19:9.

Niph. נֶעְקַשׁ דְּרָכִים *he whose ways are perverse*. Prov. 28:18.

Deriv. מַעֲקַשִּׁים.

עִקֵּשׁ m. verbal adj. from עָקַשׁ, dec. VII. a. *perverse, froward*.—לֵבָב עִקֵּשׁ *a perverse heart*, Ps. 101:4. and עִקֶּשׁ־לֵב *perverse of heart*, Prov. 11:20. 17:20. עִקֵּשׁ שְׂפָתָיו *perverse in his lips*, i. e. of a false speech, Prov. 19:1. Without addition, *false*, Deut. 32:5. Ps. 18:27. Prov. 8:8. Hence

עִקְּשׁוּת f. denom. from עִקֵּשׁ dec. I. joined with פֶּה, *perverseness of mouth, deceitful speech*. Prov. 4:24. 6:12. comp. 19:1.

I. עָר m. an obsolete form, i. q. עִיר *a city*; whence the plural עָרִים. In the sing. עָר Num. 21:15. Deut. 2:9. and in full עָר־מוֹאָב (*the city of Moab*) Num. 21:28. Is. 15:1. the proper name of the metropolis of Moab, on the southern bank of Arnon, otherwise called רַבָּה (*the great*,) in Greek *Areopolis*, now *Mab, Mob, Arrabat*. See Relandi Palæstina p. 577.

II. עָר m. dec. I. *an enemy*, i. q. צַר. (See the letter ע, p. 471.) 1 Sam. 28: 16. Plur. Ps. 9:7. 139:20. In Chald. *idem*, Dan. 4:16. [4:19.]

I. עָרַב 1. *to mix*. In Kal not used. See Hithpa. (In Chald. and Syr. more common.) Deriv. עֵרֶב *the woof, weft*.

2. *to exchange, barter*. Ezek. 27:9, 27. Deriv. מַעֲרָב.

3. *to stand in the place of* any one, construed with an accus. of the person; and that (1.) *to be surety for* any one by pledging his own life. Gen. 43:9. 44:32. Is. 38:14 עָרְבֵנִי *be thou surety*

for me, i. e. take me under thy protection. Ps. 119:122. Job 17:3. עָרְבֵנִי עִמָּךְ *put me in a surety with thee.* (2.) *to be surety for* any one, by paying the debts which he has contracted. Prov. 11:15. 20:16. 27:13. Also with לְ, Prov. 6:1. and with לִפְנֵי, 17:18. Deriv. תַּעֲרֻבָה, עֲרֻבָּה.

4. *to pledge, to give as a pledge*, construed with an accus. of the thing. Neh. 5:3 בָּתֵּינוּ אֲנַחְנוּ עֹרְבִים *our houses we are obliged to pledge* or *mortgage*. עָרַב אֶת לִבּוֹ *to pledge one's heart*, i. e. to venture or dare, Jer. 31:21. (Or עָרַב is causat. of no. II. *alacrem fecit.*)

Hithpa. 1. *to interfere, intermeddle*, construed with בְּ. Prov. 14:10.

2. *to be familiar* or *have intercourse with* any one; construed with בְּ, Ps. 106:35. Ezra 9:2. with לְ, Prov. 20:19. with עִם, 24:21. with אֵת, Is. 36:8. 2 K. 18:23. (In the two last passages it signifies *to enter into a negociation.*)

II. עָרֵב, fut. יֶעֱרַב, *to be sweet, pleasant*, construed with לְ of the person; spoken e. g. of sleep, Prov. 3:24. of offerings, presents, Jer. 6:20. Construed with עַל, Ps. 104:34. Ezek. 16:37 אֲשֶׁר עָרַבְתְּ עֲלֵיהֶם *whom thou hast pleased.* (In Arab. comp. عَرِبَ *alacer, lubens fuit.*)

III. עָרַב (In Arab. with غ.)

1. *to remove, pass away, disappear.* Is. 24:11 עָרְבָה כָּל־שִׂמְחָה *all joy disappears.*

2. *to set*, spoken of the sun; hence *to grow dark, to become evening.* Judg. 19:9.

Hiph. *to do at evening.* Infin. הַעֲרֵב *at evening*, strictly *vespere faciendo*, like הַשְׁכֵּם *mane faciendo*, for *mane.* 1 Sam. 17:16. See מַעֲרָב, עֶרֶב.

עֲרַב Chald. *to mix.*

Pa. *idem.* Dan. 2:43.

Ithpa. pass. ibid.

עָרֵב m. verbal from עָרֵב no. II. *sweet, pleasant, acceptable.* Prov. 20:17. Cant. 2:14.

עָרֹב m. the fourth of the Egyptian plagues, the name of a biting insect, (comp. the Arab. عرب *to eat*,) perhaps *blatta orientalis* seu *Ægyptia*, Linn. (Oedmann's verm. Sammlungen, H. II. p. 150.) one of the most troublesome plagues in all parts of the world, and epecially in Egypt. Sept. κυνόμυια, *the dog-fly.* Aqu. παμμυῖα. Jerome: *omne genus muscarum*, (prob. deriving it from עָרַב *to mix.*) But that עָרֹב is not a general term, but the name of a definite species of animal, is evident from Ex. 8:29, 31.

עֲרָב f. 2 Chr. 9:14. and עֲרַב Is. 21:13. Ezek. 27:21. *Arabia.* The gentile noun is עַרְבִי *an Arabian*, also עַרָבִי Neh. 2:19. plur. עַרְבִים 2 Chr. 21:16. 22:1. and עַרְבִיאִים 2 Chr. 17:11. Is. 13:20. Jer. 2:3.

עֵרֶב m. with the article הָעֵרֶב, verbal from עָרַב no. I. 1.

1. as a collective, *strangers, those who do not belong to a people but have mingled with them;* spoken, e. g. of the strangers who had joined the Israelites, Ex. 12:38. Neh. 13:3. hence of allied nations, Jer. 25:20. 50:37. Ezek. 30:5. 1 K. 10:15 מַלְכֵי הָעֶרֶב *kings of the Israelitish allies* or *tributaries;* comp. Jer. 25:24. Chald. *reges auxiliorum.*

2. *the woof* or *weft.* Lev. 13:48—59.

I. עֶרֶב com. gen. (fem. 1 Sam. 20:5.) verbal from עָרַב no. III. dec. VI. a. *the evening.*—בָּעֶרֶב *at evening*, also לְעֵת עֶרֶב Gen. 8:11. 24:11. עֶרֶב (as an accus. used adverbially) Ex. 16:6. and לָעֶרֶב (in poetry) Ps. 59:7, 15. 90:6. Gen. 49:27. Plur. עַרְבוֹת, once Jer. 5:6.

Dual עַרְבַּיִם, found only in the phrase בֵּין הָעַרְבַּיִם *between the two evenings*, Ex. 16:12. 30:8. the time when, according to Ex. 12:6. Lev. 23:5. Num. 9:3. the paschal lamb was slain, and according to Ex. 29:39, 41. Num. 28:4. the daily evening offering was presented; which was (1.) according to the Karaites and Samaritans, prob. *the time between sunset and dark*, (comp. Deut. 16:6.) (2.) according to the Pharisees (see Joseph Bell. Jud. VI. 9. § 3.) and the

Rabbinists, *from the time when the sun begins to decline* (called by the Arabians *the small evening*, in Greek δειλη πρωΐα,) *until actual sunset*, (called by the Arabians *the proper evening*, in Greek δειλη ὀψία.) See Bocharti Hieroz. T. I. p. 559.

II. עֲרָב or עָרָב m. found only in the plur. עֲרָבִים, const. עַרְבֵי, *a willow, willow-tree*, (Arab. with غ.) Is. 44:4. Job 40:22. In Ps. 137:2, we are to understand *the oriental mourning willow, salix Babylonica*, Linn.) Is. 15:7 נַחַל הָעֲרָבִים (*the brook of willows*) proper name of a brook, probably on the southern boundary of Moab.

עֹרֵב m. plur. עֹרְבִים, prim. dec. VII. a.

1. *the raven*. Gen. 8:7. Is. 34:11. Ps. 147:9. (Arab. غُرَابٌ *idem*.) Sometimes used in a wider sense, including several kindred species of birds, (as e. g. in Arabic, *the crow*.)

2. proper name of a Midianitish prince. Judg. 7:25. 8:3. Ps. 83:12. From him a certain rock was named, Judg. 7:25. Is. 10:26. Lev. 11:15. Deut. 14:14.

עֲרָבָה f. dec. XI. d.

1. *a plain*. Ezek. 47:8.

2. particularly *a waste, desert*. Is. 33:9. Jer. 50:12. 51:43.

3. When joined with the article, הָעֲרָבָה by way of eminence (1.) *the country between the Dead Sea and the Elanitic gulf*. Deut. 1:1. 2:8. Josh. 12:1. whence the Dead Sea is likewise called יָם הָעֲרָבָה *the Sea of the plain*, Deut. 4:49. Josh. 3:16. (2.) *the plain of the tribe of Judah*. 2 Sam. 4:7. 2 K. 25:4. נַחַל הָעֲרָבָה *the brook of the plain*, i. e. the Kidron, Am. 6:14. comp. 2 K. 14:25.

4. a city in the tribe of Benjamin, otherwise called בֵּית הָעֲרָבָה. Josh. 18:18.

Note. The root ערב borrows its signification perhaps from עבר in Ethiop. *sterilis, aridus fuit*, by a transposition of the letters.

עֲרֻבָּה f. verbal from עָרַב no. I. dec. X.

1. *bail, surety*. Prov. 17:18. (See עָרַב no. I. 3.)

2. *a pledge*. (See עָרַב no. I. 4.) 1 Sam. 17:18 וְאֶת־עֲרֻבָּתָם תִּקָּח *and receive their pledge*.

עֵרָבוֹן m. verbal from עָרַב, *a pledge*. Gen. 38:17, 18, 20. (See עָרַב no. I. 4.) This word appears to have passed, probably as a commercial term, out of the Hebrew or Phenician into the western languages, as in Greek ἀῤῥαβών, in Latin *arrhabo, earnest* or *purchase money*.

עַרְבָתִי a gentile noun from עֲרָבָה no. 4. q. v. 2 Sam. 23:31.

עָרַג, fut. יַעֲרֹג.

1. *to mount up*, i. q. Arab. عرج. See עֲרוּגָה.

2. construed with עַל and אֶל, *to look up with longing, to long for* any thing. (Arab. conj. II. *institit, intentus fuit* rei.) Ps. 42:2. Joel 1:20. The Jewish commentators make it denote *the cry of the deer*, but this does not suit the passage in Joel. Comp. further עֲרוּגָה. See Bocharti Hieroz. P. I. p. 883.

עֲרָד proper name of a Canaanitish royal city, in the south of Palestine, according to Judg. 1:16, in the desert of Judah. Num. 21:1. 33:40. Josh. 12:14.

עֲרָד m. Chald. i. q. עָרוֹד *the wild ass, onager*. Dan. 5:21.

עָרָה *to be naked*. In Kal not used.

Pi. עֵרָה, fut. with Vav convers. וַתְּעַר.

1. *to make bare*. Is. 3:17. 22:6. Zeph. 2:14 אַרְזָה עֵרָה *the cedar wainscotting they make bare*, i. e. they tear off.

2. *to make bare* (the foundation), i. e. to destroy. Ps. 137:7. Infin. עָרוֹת Hab. 3:13. (Comp. גָּלָה, גִּלָּה Ezek. 13:14. Mic. 1:6.)

3. *to empty* or *pour out*. Gen. 24:20. 2 Chr. 24:11. Ps. 141:8 אַל תְּעַר נַפְשִׁי *pour not out my life*, i. e. deliver it not up. Comp. Hiph. Is. 53:12.

Hiph. 1. *to make bare*. Lev. 20:18, 19.

2. *to pour out*. Is. 53:12 הֶעֱרָה לַמָּוֶת נַפְשׁוֹ

he poured out his life unto death, i. e. he gave it up.

Niph. *to be poured out,* pass. of Pi. and Hiph. Is. 32:15.

Hithpa. 1. *to make one's self bare.* Lam. 4:21.

2. *to pour* or *spread one's self out.* Ps. 37:35.

Deriv. out of course מַעַר, עָרִי, עֶרְוָה, מַעֲרָה, תַּעַר, comp. also מְעֹרִים.

עָרָה, plur. עָרוֹת Is. 19:7. verbal from עָרָה, dec. X. *an open place, a place naked of wood,* (see מַעַר, מַעֲרָה,) here applied to the pastures on the banks of the Nile.

עֲרוּגָה f. Cant. 5:13. 6:2. Ezek. 17:7, 10. according to the ancient translators, *a bed* in a garden, perhaps *a raised bed,* (from עָרַג.) More conformably to the etymology, *an espalier,* comp. Arab. مَعْرَج *a ladder.*

עָרוֹד m. found only Job 39:5. the more Aramean name for פֶּרֶא, *the wild ass, onager.*

עֶרְוָה f. verbal from עָרָה, dec. X.

1. *nakedness.* Hos. 2:11. [2:9.] Metaphorically עֶרְוַת הָאָרֶץ *the nakedness of a country, the part in which it is most exposed,* Gen. 42:9, 12.

2. *the private parts, pudenda.* Gen. 9:22, 23. עֶרְוַת אָבִיו *the nakedness of his father,* i. e. of his father's wife, Lev. 20:11. comp. 18:8, 16. 1 Sam. 20:30 לְבֹשֶׁת עֶרְוַת אִמֶּךָ *to the shame of thy mother's nakedness,* a reproachful expression.

3. *offensiveness, shamefulness.* Deut. 23:15 עֶרְוַת דָּבָר *any thing offensive* or *indecent,* (in reference to filth.) So Deut. 24:1, (in reference to some defect found in a woman.)

עַרְוָה Chald. *injury, dishonour,* (of the king.) Ezra 4:14.

עָרוֹם, plur. עֲרוּמִּים, fem. עֲרֻמָּה, adj. dec. VIII. d. *naked.* Job 1:21. It also signifies (1.) *poorly clad.* Job 22:6. 24:7, 10. (2.) *stripped of one's upper garment, having on only an under garment* (כְּתֹנֶת.) 1 Sam. 19:24. Is. 20:2. Comp. John 21:7. (Root עָרַם Arab. عَرِمَ *to make bare,* med. Kesr. *to be shameless.*) Deriv. מַעֲרֻמִּים.

עָרוּם m. verbal from עָרַם, dec. III. c.

1. *wise, prudent.* Prov. 12:16, 23. 13:16.

2. *cunning, crafty.* Gen. 3:1. Job 5:12. 15:5.

עָרוֹם see עֵירֹם.

עֲרוֹעֵר and **עֲרֹעֵר**. 1. prob. i. q. עַרְעָר (Jer. 17:6. Ps. 102:18.) strictly *naked,* hence *needy, driven out.* Jer. 48:6. Sept. Vulg. Chald. *myrica, the tamarisk.* Others, after the Arab. عَرْعَر *the juniper bush.* Others, after the Arab. غُرْغُر *the Guinea fowl.*

2. proper name of a city of the Gadites, on the river Arnon. Num. 32:34. Deut. 2:36. 3:12. Josh. 12:2. 13:25. also written עַרְעוֹר Judg. 11:26.—Is. 17:2 עָרֵי עֲרֹעֵר *the cities about Aroer,* perhaps *the cities beyond Jordan* generally.

3. name of a place in the tribe of Judah. 1 Sam. 30:28.

עָרוּץ or as in other MSS. עָרוּץ *something terrible* or *awful.* (Root עָרַץ no. 1.) Job 30:6 בַּעֲרוּץ נְחָלִים *in the awful valleys.*

עֶרְיָה f. i. q. עֶרְוָה verbal from עָרָה, *nakedness.* Ezek. 16:7 וְאַתְּ עֵרֹם וְעֶרְיָה *thou wast nakedness and bareness,* i. e. naked and bare.—In Hab. 3:9, it is a pleonastic accus. after תֵּעוֹר.

עֲרִיסָה dec. X. found only in the plur. Num. 15:20, 21. Neh. 10:38. Ezek. 44:30. *dough,* or *pastry.* Sept. and Vulg. in Num. φύραμα, *pulmentum;* in Neh. and Ezek. σῖτος, *cibus.* (In Rabbin. עֲרָסָן *far hordei vetusti.*)

עֲרִיפִים masc. plur. prob. *clouds, heaven,* from עָרַף *to drop.* Is. 5:30. Syr. and Vulg. *darkness.* Perhaps kindred with עֲרָפֶל.

עָרִיץ m. (for עָרִּיץ with Dagesh forte, hence the Kamets is impure,) dec. I.

1. *strong, mighty,* spoken of Jehovah. Jer. 20:11.

2. in a bad sense, *violent, tyrannical;* and as a subst. *a tyrant, oppressor.* Ps.

37:35. Job 15:20. 27:13. Is. 13:11.—Ezek. 28:7 עָרִיצֵי־גוֹיִם *the most violent nations*. 30:11. 31:12. 32:12. comp. Is. 25:3. Root prob. עָרַץ no. II. according to others, no. I. hence liter. *terrible*.

עֲרִירִי, plur. עֲרִירִים, adj. dec. I. *solitary, forsaken, childless*. Gen. 15:3. Lev. 20:20, 21. Jer. 22:30. Root עָרַר no. 2.

עָרַךְ, fut. יַעֲרֹךְ. 1. *to set right, to arrange, prepare;* e.g. the wood upon the altar, Gen. 22:9. Lev. 1:7. the shew-bread, 24:8. (comp. מַעֲרֶכֶת no. 2.) the table for a feast, Prov. 9:2. armour for battle, Jer. 46:3. Particularly (1.) עָרַךְ מִלְחָמָה *to arrange the battle*, i.e. to put one's self in battle-array, Judg. 20: 20, 22. Construed with אֵת and לִקְרַאת *against* any one, 1 Sam. 17:2. Gen. 14:8. Part. עֹרְכֵי מִלְחָמָה 1 Chr. 12:33, 35. and עֲרוּךְ מִלְחָמָה Joel 2:5. also simply עָרוּךְ Jer. 6:23. 50:42. *put in battle-array*. (2.) עָרַךְ מִלִּים *to prepare* or *utter words*, construed with אֶל *against* any one. Job 32:14. Without מִלִּים, *idem*, Job 37:19 לֹא נַעֲרֹךְ מִפְּנֵי חֹשֶׁךְ *we spake nothing by reason of darkness* or *ignorance*. Ps. 5:4 בֹּקֶר אֶעֱרָךְ־לְךָ *in the morning I direct* (my words) *to thee;* or intrans. *I direct myself to thee*. (3.) עָרַךְ מִשְׁפָּט *to order* or *exhibit one's cause*. Job 13:18. 23:4. comp. Ps. 50:21.

2. intrans. *to put* or *set one's self* (in battle-array). Judg. 20:30, 33. 1 Sam. 4:2. 17:21. construed with עַל, לְ, לִקְרַאת *against* any one, 2 Sam. 10:9, 10, 17. Jer. 50:9, 14.—Job 6:4 יַעַרְכוּנִי for יַעַרְכוּ עָלַי *they set themselves in array against me*. 33:5.

3. construed with לְ, *to compare, liken*, Is. 40:18 מַה־דְּמוּת תַּעַרְכוּ לוֹ *what likeness will ye compare to him?* and Ps. 89:7. 40:6 אֵין עֲרֹךְ אֵלֶיךָ *nothing is to be compared with thee*. Job 28:17, 19, (in both passages the suffix ־ֶנָּה stands for the dative.)

4. as in Hiph. *to value, esteem, regard*. Job 36:19 הֲיַעֲרֹךְ שׁוּעֲךָ *will he regard thy riches?* or as if pass. of Hiph. *will thy riches be regarded* (*by him*)?

Hiph. *to value, appraise*. Lev. 27: 8 ff. 2 K. 23:35.

עֵרֶךְ m. with suff. עֶרְכִּי, verbal from עָרַךְ, dec. VI. j.

1. *whatever is arranged* or *put in order, a row;* spoken of the shew-bread, Ex. 40:23.—Judg. 17:10 עֵרֶךְ בְּגָדִים *a suit of clothing*.

2. *armour*. Job 41:4. [41:12.]

3. *valuation, estimation*. Lev. 27:2 בְּעֶרְכְּךָ נְפָשֹׁת *so that thou hast souls to value*. 5:15 בְּעֶרְכְּךָ *according to thy valuation* or *estimation*. Ps. 55:14 אַתָּה אֱנוֹשׁ כְּעֶרְכִּי *thou a man whom I equal to myself*. Hence

4. *price of valuation*, Lev. 27:4, 7, 13, 15. *worth* generally, Job 28:13.

עָרַל 1. *to be uncircumcised*. See עָרֵל.

2. denom. from עָרְלָה, *to regard as uncircumcised*, i.e. as unclean, *to reject*. Lev. 19:23.

Niph. *to shew one's foreskin, præputiatum sisti, cerni*. Hab. 2:16. Here in reference to a drunken man's shamefully exposing his nakedness.

עָרֵל m. const. עֲרַל (Ezek. 44:9.) and עֲרַל (Ex. 6:12.) adj. dec. V. d. *uncircumcised*. Gen. 17:14. Ex. 12:48. Often a name of reproach for those who were not Israelites, e.g. for a Philistine, 1 Sam. 17:26, 36. 14:6. 31:4. Metaphorically עֲרַל שְׂפָתַיִם *of uncircumcised lips, not eloquent*, (as it were *tongue-tied*,) Ex. 6:12, 30. Lev. 26:41 לְבָבָם הֶעָרֵל *their uncircumcised heart*. Comp. Ezek. 44:9. Jer. 6:10 עֲרֵלָה אָזְנָם *their ear is uncircumcised*, i.e. not open.

עָרְלָה f. plur. עֲרָלוֹת, dec. XI. d.

1. *the prepuce, foreskin*. 1 Sam. 18: 25. 2 Sam. 3:14. בְּשַׂר הָעָרְלָה *membrum præputiatum*, Gen. 17:11—24. Lev. 12:3. Metaphorically עָרְלַת־לֵב *the foreskin of the heart, impurity of heart*, Deut. 10:16. Jer. 4:4.

2. applied to the fruit of the three first years, because they were regarded by the law as unclean. Lev. 19:23.

I. עָרַם *to be crafty, prudent.* (Syr. Ethpe. *idem;* ܥܪܝܡܐ, עֲרִימָא *crafty, malicious.*) In Kal only 1 Sam. 23 : 22.

Hiph. 1. *to be crafty,* as in Kal, 1 Sam. 23 : 22.

2. *to be wise, prudent.* Prov. 15 : 5. 19 : 25.

3. *to make crafty.* Ps. 83 : 4 יַעֲרִימוּ סוֹד *they devise crafty counsels.*

Deriv. עָרוּם, עֹרֶם, עָרְמָה.

II. עָרַם found only in Niph. *to be heaped up.* Ex. 15 : 8. (Syr. and Arab. *idem.*) Deriv. עֲרֵמָה.

עָרֹם *naked,* see עָרוֹם.

עֹרֶם m. verbal from עָרַם, dec VI. m. *cunning, craftiness.* Job 5 : 13.

עָרְמָה f. verbal from עָרַם.

1. *craft, deceit.* Ex. 21 : 14.

2. *wisdom, prudence.* Prov. 1 : 4. 8 : 5.

עֲרֵמָה f. (with Tseri impure,) plur. וֹת, once ־ִים (Jer. 50 : 26.) dec. X. *a heap;* e. g. of rubbish, Neh. 3 : 34. [4 : 2.] of grain, Cant. 7 : 3. of sheaves, Ruth 3 : 7. Root עָרַם no. II.

עַרְמוֹן m. dec. I. *the plane-tree, the oriental maple, platanus orientalis,* Linn. Gen. 30 : 37. Ezek. 31 : 8. See Celsii Hierobot. T. I. p. 513.

עַרְעוֹר Judg. 11 : 26. see עֲרוֹעֵר no. 2.

עַרְעָר adj. liter. *naked;* hence *poor, forsaken.* Root עָרַר q. v. Ps. 102 : 18. Jer. 17 : 6. Comp. עֲרוֹעֵר no. 1.

עַרְעֵר and עַרְעֵרִי see עֲרוֹעֵר.

I. עָרַף i. q. רָעַף *to drop.* Deut. 32 : 2. 33 : 28.

II. עָרַף denom. from עֹרֶף.

1. *to break the neck of* an animal, *to decollate.* Ex. 13 : 13. 34 : 20. Deut. 21 : 4, 6. Is. 66 : 3.

2. metaphorically *to throw down,* (an altar.) Hos. 10 : 2.

עֹרֶף m. dec. VI. m. prim. *the neck.* Lev. 5 : 8. The following phrases are worthy of notice; (1.) נָתַן עֹרֶף *to turn the back, to turn away.* 2 Chr. 29 : 6. (2.) פָּנָה עֹרֶף אֶל *to turn the back to* a person. Jer. 2 : 27. 32 : 33. (3.) פָּנָה עֹרֶף Josh. 7 : 12. and הָפַךְ עֹרֶף 7 : 8. *to flee, terga vertere.* Hence (4.) Ex. 23 : 27 נָתַתִּי אֶת־כָּל־אֹיְבֶיךָ אֵלֶיךָ עֹרֶף *I have made all thine enemies turn their backs to thee,* i. e. have put them all to flight. Ps. 18 : 41. (5.) קְשֵׁה עֹרֶף *stiff-necked,* see קָשֶׁה.

עֲרָפֶל m. a quadriliteral, *thick mist, darkness.* Deut. 4 : 11. Ps. 18 : 10. (Syr. *idem.*)

I. עָרַץ, fut. יַעֲרֹץ.

1. *to fear, to be afraid.* Deut. 1 : 29. Construed with מִפְּנֵי of the person, Deut. 7 : 21. 20 : 3. 31 : 6. also with an accus. Job 31 : 34.

2. trans. *to terrify, to make afraid.* Job 13 : 25. Ps. 10 : 18. Is. 2 : 19, 21.

Note. The primary signification appears to have been *to quake,* as in the Arab. عرص.

Niph. part. נַעֲרָץ *fearful, to be feared* or *reverenced,* parallel with נוֹרָא. Ps. 89 : 8.

Hiph. intrans. *to tremble, to be afraid.* Is. 8 : 12. Construed with an accus. 29 : 23.

Deriv. עָרוּץ, מַעֲרָצָה, מַעֲרִיץ, and prob. עָרִיץ.

II. עָרַץ (Arab. with ض) *to resist, withstand.* Is. 47 : 12 אוּלַי תַּעֲרוֹצִי *if so be thou mayest resist.* According to the old translators, *to become strong, to gain strength.* Comp. עָרִיץ.

עָרַק *to flee.* (In Syr. and Arab. *idem.*) Job 30 : 3 הָעֹרְקִים צִיָּה *they flee into the wilderness.* Part. plur. עֹרְקִים *veins, arteries, nerves.* (So in Talmud. and the Arab. عُرُوق; comp. עַרְקָא *a band, strap,* and גִּיד.) Job 30 : 17 וְעֹרְקַי לֹא יִשְׁכָּבוּן *my nerves rest not.*—The root ערק signifies also in Arab. and Syr. Pa. *to gnaw.* Hence Vulg. in verse 3, *they gnaw the dry ground;* and in verse 17, *my gnawers,* i. e. pains, *rest not.*

עַרְקִי a gentile noun, *an Arkite, an inhabitant of the city Arce* (in Greek Ἄρκη, also *Cæsarea Libani,*) in Syria, some miles north of Tripolis. Magnificent ruins of this place are said to be remaining to this day. Gen. 10:17.

ערר i. q. עָרָה. 1. *to be naked.* In Kal found only in the imper. עֹרָה *make thyself bare,* Is. 32:11.

2. *to be solitary, forsaken.* Deriv. עֲרִירִי, עַרְעָר, עֲרוֹעֵר.

Pilp. עַרְעֵר and Hithpalp. הִתְעַרְעֵר Jer. 51:58. *to be made bare, to be destroyed to the foundation.* Comp. עָרָה Ps. 137:7. Hab. 3:13.

ערשׂ f. (Cant. 1:16.) plur. עֲרָשׂוֹת, dec. VI. a. *a bed, couch.* Deut. 3:11. Ps. 6:7. (Syr. and Chald. *idem.*)

עֵשֶׂב m. with suff. עֶשְׂבָּם, plur. const. עִשְּׂבוֹת (with Dagesh forte euphonic) (Prov. 27:25.) dec. VI. g. and j. *an herb,* and collect. *herbs,* particularly for fodder, or for the table. Gen. 1:11, 12. 2:5. 3:18. Ex. 10:12, 15. (Arab. عُشْبٌ *idem.*)

עֲשַׂב, emph. עִשְׂבָּא, Chald. *idem.* Dan. 2:30. 4:21, 22, 29. [4:24, 25, 32.]

I. **עָשָׂה**, fut. יַעֲשֶׂה, apoc. יַעַשׂ.

1. *to make, do, act.* Gen. 1:7. 6:22. Prov. 13:16. Sometimes redundant, as Gen. 31:26. (1.) The thing *into* which any thing is made or converted is preceded by לְ, Gen. 12:2. Ex. 32:10. or the verb has two accus. (see נָתַן no. 3. and שׂוּם,) Am. 4:13. Ex. 30:24 וְעָשִׂיתָ אֹתוֹ שֶׁמֶן מִשְׁחַת קֹדֶשׁ *thou shalt make it into a holy ointment.* Hos. 2:10. 8:4. Hence we may say, that the material of which a thing is made is put in the accus. (comp. בָּנָה, יָצַר, and Gesen. Lehrgeb. § 219. 2.) Ex. 38:3 כָּל־כֵּלָיו עָשָׂה נְחֹשֶׁת *all the vessels thereof he made of brass.* 25:39. 36:14. 37:24. 30:25. More rarely as in Ex. 27:3 לְכָל־כֵּלָיו תַּעֲשֶׂה נְחֹשֶׁת *for all the vessels thereof thou shalt take brass.* Verse 19.—(2.) construed with לְ of the person, *to do to* any one; sometimes in a good sense, e. g. Ex. 13:8. Deut. 11:5. sometimes in a bad sense, e. g. Ex. 14:11. Gen. 27:55. Also *to do an injury, to injure,* Gen. 22:12. 19:8. More rarely with an accus. Jer. 33:9. Is. 42:16. comp. Ezek. 23:25.—Also *to have business,* 1 K. 20:40. and construed with עִם, *to have business with* a person, Ruth 2:19.—עָשָׂה מִלְחָמָה *to carry on war,* Gen. 14:2. עָשָׂה חֶסֶד *to exercise love* or *kindness,* construed with עִם and אֶת *towards* a person, Gen. 24:12. 40:14.

2. *to labour in* any thing, *to be busied* therein, construed with בְּ. Ex. 5:9. Neh. 4:15. In a somewhat different sense, Ex. 31:4 לַעֲשׂוֹת בַּזָּהָב וּבַכֶּסֶף *to labour in gold and silver.* Verse 5. 2 Chr. 2:13.

3. *to execute* or *accomplish* any thing, spoken particularly of Jehovah. Ps. 37:5. 22:32. 52:11. Dan. 8:24 וְהִצְלִיחַ וְעָשָׂה *he shall prosper and shall execute it.* Dan. 11:7, 17, 28, 30, 32.

4. *to prepare, to get ready;* e. g. *to dress* food, Gen. 18:7, 8. Judg. 13:15. *to trim* the beard, (comp. the French phrase *faire la barbe,*) 2 Sam. 19:25. *to pare* the nails, Deut. 21:12.

5. *to make, acquire,* e. g. riches, Gen. 31:1. Deut. 8:17, 18. slaves, Gen. 12:5.

6. *to pass* or *spend* time. Ecc. 6:12. comp. in Greek ποιεῖν χρόνον, Acts 15:33.

7. *to keep one's self, to abide,* as in Lat. *agere.* Ruth 2:19 אָנָה עָשִׂית *where hast thou abode?* Job 23:9.—עָשָׂה טוֹב *to prosper,* εὖ πράττειν, Ecc. 3:12.

8. *to produce,* e. g. *to bear* fruit, Gen. 1:11, 12. Is. 5:2, 10. *to put forth* branches, Job 14:9. Ezek. 17:8. *to yield* meal, (spoken of the stock,) Hos. 8:7. *to put* fat on the loins, Job 15:27. *to give* milk, Is. 7:22.

9. *to offer, present,* as in Greek ῥέζειν, ἔρδειν, construed with לְ. Ex. 10:25. 29:36, 38, 39, 41. 1 K. 18:23.

10. *to appoint,* (to an office.) 1 K. 12:31. 1 Sam. 12:6. Comp. Jer. 37:15.

11. *to celebrate* or *keep,* (the sabbath, the passover.) Ex. 12:48. Num. 9:10, 14.

Niph. נַעֲשָׂה, fem. נַעֲשְׂתָה, *to be made.* Lev. 7:24. Ps. 107:37. Frequently *to be done,* Num. 15:34. Gen. 20:9. Comp. 29:26. 34:7.

Pu. *to be made.* Ps. 139:15.

Deriv. מַעֲשֶׂה.

II. עָשָׂה in Kal Ezek. 23:21. and in Piel, verses 3, 8. *to press, squeeze,* (the breast.) (Chald. עַשִּׂי *idem.*)

עֵשָׂו (according to Gen. 25:25, *covered with hair,* comp. the Arab. عثا *to be hairy,*) *Esau,* the son of Isaac and elder brother of Jacob. His posterity, *the Idumeans,* are for the most part called אֱדוֹם q. v. but sometimes, especially in poetry, עֵשָׂו. Deut. 2:4 ff. Obad. 6, 18. Jer. 49:8, 10.—הַר עֵשָׂו Obad. 8, 9, 19.

עָשׂוֹר m. 1. *ten,* i. q. עֶשֶׂר and עֲשָׂרָה. Once Gen. 24:55.

2. *the tenth;* in the phrase בֶּעָשׂוֹר לַחֹדֶשׁ *on the tenth of the month,* Ex. 12:3. Lev. 16:29.

3. נֵבֶל עָשׂוֹר Ps. 33:2. 144:9. and עָשׂוֹר Ps. 92:4. *a harp of ten strings.*

עֲשִׂירִי m. *the tenth.* Fem. עֲשִׂירִיָּה and עֲשִׂירִית *a tenth part,* Ex. 16:36. Lev. 5:11. Is. 6:13.

עָשַׂק found only in Hithpa. *to strive, contend.* Gen. 26:20. (In Chald. and Talmud. *idem.*)

עֶשֶׂר f. and עֲשָׂרָה, עֲשֶׂרֶת m. *ten.* Plur. עֲשָׂרוֹת m. *tens,* Ex. 18:21. Deut. 1:15.

עָשָׂר m. and עֶשְׂרֵה f. *idem,* but used only in composition with the units to express the numbers from 11 to 19, (like *decim* for *decem,* and *teen* for *ten.*) Hence in the masc. אַחַד עָשָׂר *eleven,* אַרְבָּעָה עָשָׂר *fourteen,* also *the eleventh, the fourteenth.* In the fem. אַחַת עֶשְׂרֵה *eleven,* שֵׁשׁ עֶשְׂרֵה *sixteen;* also *the eleventh,* etc.

Plur. עֶשְׂרִים com. gen.

1. *twenty,* joined with the sing. and plur. Gen. 31:38. Lev. 27:5.

2. *the twentieth.* Num. 10:11.

עֲשַׂר f. and עַשְׂרָא m. Chald. *ten.* Dan. 7:7, 20, 24.

Plur. עֶשְׂרִין *twenty.* Dan. 6:2.

עָשַׂר, fut. יַעְשֹׂר, denom. from עֶשֶׂר, *to impose tithes, to take the tenth part of* any thing, construed with an accus. 1 Sam. 8:15, 17.

Pi. *to pay tithes, to pay a tenth part.* Gen. 28:22. Neh. 10:38. Deut. 14:22.

Hiph. i. q. Pi. *to pay* or *give tithes.* Deut. 26:12. Neh. 10:39.

Deriv. מַעֲשֵׂר.

עֲשָׂרָה see עֶשֶׂר.

עֶשְׂרֵה see עָשָׂר.

עִשָּׂרוֹן m. plur. עֶשְׂרֹנִים, dec. III. e. *the tenth part,* a measure of grain or flour. Lev. 14:10. 23:13, 17. According to the Sept. Num. 15:4, *the tenth part of an ephah,* equivalent, therefore, to *an omer.*

I. עָשׁ m. *a moth.* Job 4:19. 13:28. 27:18. Root עשש Arab. عث *to gnaw* (wool).

II. עָשׁ *the constellation of the bear, ursa major.* Job 9:9. comp. Niebuhr's Beschreib. von Arabien, p. 114. עַיִשׁ f. Job 38:32. prob. *idem.* Her sons (בָּנֶיהָ) are the three stars in the tail of the bear. So in Arab. Comp. Bocharti Hieroz. II. p. 114. Michaëlis Supplem. p. 1907. Lach in Eichhorn's allgem. Bibliothek der Bibl. Litteratur, Th. VII. p. 397. The etymology is obscure.

עָשׁוֹק m. verbal from עָשַׁק, *an oppressor.* Jer. 22:3. i. q. עֹשֵׁק 21:12.

עֲשׁוּקִים masc. plur. verbal from עָשַׁק, *oppressions, violent acts.* Ecc. 4:1. Am. 3:9.

עָשׁוֹת m. adj. *forged, laboured, wrought.* Once Ezek. 27:19. Root עָשָׁה.

עָשִׁיר m. verbal from עָשַׁר, dec. III. a. *rich.* Prov. 10:15. 14:20. 18:11.—In Is. 53:9, the parallel clause has רְשָׁעִים *the wicked,* from the natural association of *poverty* with *humility,* and *riches* with *pride;* which occurs so frequently in the Hebrew writers. Comp. Job 27:19, with verse 13.

עָשַׁן, fut. יֶעְשַׁן, *to smoke.* Ex. 19:18. Used metaphorically of the divine anger, Deut. 29:19. Ps. 74:1. 80:5.

עָשֵׁן m. verbal adj. from עָשַׁן, dec. V. b. *smoking.* Ex. 20:18. Is. 7:4.

עָשָׁן m. const. עֲשַׁן (as if from עֶשֶׁן,) verbal from עָשַׁן, dec. IV. h. *smoke, vapour*. Gen. 15:17. Job 41:12. [41:20.] Ps. 18:9 עָלָה עָשָׁן בְּאַפּוֹ *a smoke went up out of his nostrils*, an image of divine anger. Is. 65:5.

עָשַׁק, fut. יַעֲשֹׁק. 1. *to press* or *extort from* any one.—עָשַׁק עֹשֶׁק *to practise extortion* or *oppression*, Ezek. 18:18.

2. *to cheat* or *defraud* a person, construed with an accus. of the person and thing. Mal. 3:5 עֹשְׁקֵי שְׂכַר שָׂכִיר *who defraud the labourer of his reward.* Lev. 19:13. Deut. 24:14. Mic. 2:2 עָשְׁקוּ גֶבֶר וּבֵיתוֹ *they defraud a man and (take away) his house.*

3. *to oppress* in any way, *to exercise violence* or *injustice;* e. g. on the poor or helpless, Prov. 14:31. Ecc. 4:1. on a people, spoken of a conqueror, Is. 52:4. Jer. 50:33. on a man, spoken of God, Job 10:3.

4. Prov. 28:17 אָדָם עָשֻׁק בְּדַם נָפֶשׁ *a man oppressed with* or *guilty of bloodshed.*

5. spoken of a river, *to be proud, arrogant, to overflow its banks.* Job 40:23.

Pu. מְעֻשָּׁקָה *oppressed.* Is. 23:12.

עֹשֶׁק m. verbal from עָשַׁק.

1. *oppression, extortion.* Ecc. 5:7. Ezek. 22:7, 12.

2. *whatever is obtained by oppression* or *extortion,* Lev. 5:23. [6:4.] Ps. 62:11. *unrighteous gain* of any kind, Ecc. 7:7.

עָשְׁקָה f. verbal from עָשַׁק, *oppression, straitness.* Is. 38:14 עָשְׁקָה־לִּי *I am straitened.* (The Metheg here does not prove that we are to read *âsheka*, with Kamets long, any more than in שָׁמְרֵנִי, בָּתֵּיהֶם.)

עָשַׁר, fut. יַעֲשֹׁר, *to be* or *become rich.* Job 15:29. Hos. 12:9. (Aram. עֲתַר *idem.*)

Hiph. 1. *to enrich, to make rich.* Gen. 14:23. Ps. 65:10 רַבַּת תַּעְשְׁרֶנָּה *thou enrichest it (the earth) abundantly.*

2. intrans. *to become rich.* Ps. 49:17. Prov. 10:4. Construed with an accus. of the thing, Dan. 11:2.

Hithpa. *to represent one's self as rich.* Prov. 13:7.

עֹשֶׁר m. verbal from עָשַׁר, dec. VI. m. *riches.* 1 Sam. 17:25.

עָשֵׁשׁ *to be consumed, to waste away;* spoken of the eye, Ps. 6:8. of the spirit and bones, 31:10, 11. (comp. כָּלָה.)

עָשַׁת 1. *to labour, fabricari.* See the deriv. עַשְׁתּוֹת, עֶשֶׁת.

2. *to be made smooth* or *polished, to be bright, to shine.* Metaphorically Jer. 5:28.

Hithpa. *to think* or *be mindful of* any one, construed with לְ. Jon. 1:6. See the Chald. Deriv. עֶשְׁתֹּנוֹת, עַשְׁתּוֹת.

עֲשִׁת, עֲשַׁת Chald. *to think, purpose,* like the Lat. *machinari.* Dan. 6:4. This signification is derived from that of עָשַׁת no. 1. comp. e. g. חָשַׁב *to think, purpose,* with חֹשֵׁב *an artificer.*

עֶשֶׁת m. verbal from עָשַׁת, *artificial work.* Cant. 5:14.

עַשְׁתּוּת f. verbal from עָשַׁת, *a thought.* Job 12:5 לְעַשְׁתּוּת שַׁאֲנָן *in the thought of him that is at ease,* i. q. בְּעֵינֵי. Some read עַשְׁתּוֹת in the plural.

עַשְׁתֵּי m. found only in combination with the numeral *ten,* as עַשְׁתֵּי עָשָׂר m. and עַשְׁתֵּי עֶשְׂרֵה f. *eleven, the eleventh.* Deut. 1:3. Jer. 39:2. Ex. 26:1. According to Simonis, liter. *cogitationes ultra decem,* i. e. *ten* (counted on the fingers,) and *one* (in thought.)

עֶשְׁתֹּנוֹת fem. plur. verbal from עָשַׁת, *thoughts, purposes.* Ps. 146:4.

עַשְׁתֹּרֶת f. Ἀστάρτη, *Astarte,* a Phenician goddess, whose worship was introduced also among the Israelites (1 K. 11:5, 33. 2 K. 23:13.) and the Philistines (1 Sam. 31:10.) Probably synonymous with אֲשֵׁרָה q. v. The Greeks compare her, after their manner, sometimes with *Juno,* sometimes with *Diana,* but most frequently with *Venus;* to which last her lascivious worship appears to correspond, (Lev. 19:29. Deut. 23:18. 2 K. 23:7.) She is usually joined with בַּעַל, thus denoting the male and female powers of nature. (Is not this perhaps connected with the appellative עַשְׁתְּרוֹת *proles*, or *agni*, as the Roman goddess *Ops* with *ovis*, οἶς?) Comp. Creuzer's Symbolik, Th. 2. p. 55, 60. De Wette's Hebr. jüd. Archäologie, p. 281.

Plur. הָעַשְׁתָּרוֹת Judg. 2:13. 10:6. 1 Sam. 7:3, 4. 12:10. 31:10. a kind of pluralis excellentiæ, and synonymous in signification with the singular, comp. 1 Sam. 31:10. or like תְּרָפִים, spoken of *the statues or images of Astarte.*

I. **עַשְׁתְּרוֹת** plur. fem. עַשְׁתְּרוֹת צֹאן *the increase of the flocks*, Deut. 7:13. 28:4, 18, 51. Sept. τὰ ποίμνια τῶν προβάτων. Vulg. *greges avium.* The etymology is unknown.

II. **עַשְׁתָּרוֹת** Deut. 1:4. Josh. 13:12. also עַשְׁתְּרֹת קַרְנַיִם Gen. 14:5. a city of Og, king of Bashan. The latter word קַרְנַיִם some refer to two summits between which the city was situated, others to the image of Astarte, which is said to have had the head of a bull. The gentile noun is עַשְׁתְּרָתִי 1 Chr. 11:44.

עֵת com. gen. (Cant. 2:12, Jer. 51:33.) before Makkeph עֶת־, with suff. עִתּוֹ, plur. עִתִּים and עִתּוֹת, prim. dec. VIII. b. *time.*—As an adv. *a long time*, Hos. 13:13. לֹא עֵת *before the time*, Job 22:16.—Est. 1:13 יֹדְעֵי הָעִתִּים and 1 Chr. 12:32 יוֹדְעֵי בִינָה לָעִתִּים *those who know the times*, i. e. astrologers.—כְּעֵת חַיָּה, see חַי adj. no. 4.—Particularly (1.) *a time of prosperity.* Ps. 81:16. (2.) *a time of adversity.* Is. 13:22. 27:7. Comp. יוֹם no. 1. parag. 2.

Plur. עִתִּים and עִתּוֹת (1.) *destinies.* Ps. 31:16, 1 Chr. 29:30. Job 24:1. (2.) *times*, Lat. *vices.* Neh. 9:28 עִתִּים רַבּוֹת *many times.*

Deriv. עַתָּה, עִתִּי.

עֵת Chald. With a preposition כְּעֶת Ezra 4:17. and with epenthetic נ, as a solution of the Dagesh forte omitted, וּכְעֶנֶת *and so on.* Ezra 4:10, 11. 7:12. Root prob. عيس to repeat often and to weariness; hence literally *secundum id quod sæpius dictum est.*

עָתַד In Arab. *to be ready, prepared.* In Kal not used.

Pi. *to prepare, make ready.* Prov. 24:27.

Hithpa. *to be prepared, ready, destined.* Job 15:28.

Deriv. עָתִיד.

עַתָּה adv. (from עֵת *time*,) liter. *at the time.* Hence

1. *now, at this moment.*—מֵעַתָּה *from this moment.* עַד־עַתָּה *until now.*

2. *soon, shortly, presently*, liter. *after some time.* Job 7:21. 8:6. etc. Is. 43:19. Mic. 7:10. In the Kethib it is sometimes written without ה, (עַתְּ,) Ps. 74:6. Ezek. 23:43.

עַתּוּד m. dec. 1. *a he-goat.* Gen. 31:10, 12. As the leader of the herd, Is. 1:11. Jer. 51:40. Metaphorically *a leader of the people, a prince*, Is. 14:9. Zech. 10:2.

עָתוּד i. q. עָתִיד. Is. 10:13 Keri. Est. 8:13 Keth.

עִתִּי adj. (from עֵת *time*,) *present*, or *fit*, *opportunus.* Lev. 16:21.

עָתִיד m. verbal adj. from עָתַד, dec. III. a.

1. *ready.* (In Syr. and Arab. *idem.*) Est. 3:14. 8:13 Keri. Job 15:24.

2. *skilful.* Job 3:8.

Plur. עֲתִידוֹת (1.) *whatever is impending, things destined.* Deut. 32:35. (2.) *goods, riches, substance, what one has acquired for himself*, τὰ ὑπάρχοντα. Is. 10:13 Keth.

עֲתִיד Chald. *ready.* Dan. 3:15.

עָתִיק m. adj. *beautiful, shining.* Is. 23:18. (Arab. عتق *to be beautiful, to shine.*) See עָתֵק.

עַתִּיק adj. dec. I.

1. *weaned.* Is. 28:9. (See עָתַק no. 1.)

2. *old.* 1 Chr. 4:22. (See עָתַק no. 2.)

עַתִּיק Chald. *old.* Dan. 7:9, 13, 22.

עָתַם found only in Niph. Is. 9:18 נֶעְתַּם אֶרֶץ usually rendered *the land is* *darkened*, from collating the Arab. عتم *to be dark.* But the Sept. Chald. more in accordance with the parallel member, *terra combusta est.*

עָתַק, fut. יֶעְתַּק. 1. *to be removed,* or *transferred* from a place. Job 14:18. 18:4. See עָתִיק no. 1.

2. *ætate provehi, to grow old.* Ps. 6: 8. Job 21:7. Deriv. עַתִּיק no. 2.

Hiph. 1. causat. of Kal no. 1. *to remove, dimovere, transferre.* Job 9:5.

2. particularly *to remove* one's tent, *to break up,* spoken of a nomade. Gen. 12:8. 26:22.

3. *to transcribe, copy, compile.* Prov. 25:1. Sept. ἐξεγράψαντο. Vulg. *transtulerunt.* (In Talmud. *to transcribe, translate.*)

4. *to take away.* Job 32:15 הֶעְתִּיקוּ מֵהֶם מִלִּים *they took away from them speech,* i. e. they could say nothing.

Note. Other significations of this root, see in the derivatives עָתָק, עָתִיק, עָתֵק.

עָתָק m. adj. *bold, wicked.*—דִּבֶּר עָתָק *to speak wickedly,* Ps. 31:19. 75:6. 94:4. 1 Sam. 2:3. (In Arab. عتق in a good sense, *openness, frankness, freedom.*)

עָתֵק m. adj. *beautiful, shining.* See עָתִיק. Prov. 8:18 הוֹן עָתֵק *shining riches.* Vulg. *opes superbæ.*

I. **עָתַר**, fut. יֶעְתַּר, *to pray, supplicate, entreat,* (God,) construed with לְ and אֶל. Gen. 25:21. Ex. 8:26. [8:30.] 10: 18. Job 33:26.

Niph. *to be entreated by* any one, *to hear* him, construed with a dative. Gen. 25:21 וַיֵּעָתֶר לוֹ יְהוָה *and Jehovah heard him.* 2 Sam. 21:14. Is. 19:22. The infin. נַעְתּוֹר 1 Chr. 5:20. is used for the finite verb.

Hiph. i. q. Kal. Ex. 8:25. [8:29.] 10:17. Construed with לְ and בְּעַד *to pray for* any one, Ex. 8:5, 24. [8:9, 28.]

II. **עָתַר** as in Chaldaic, *to be rich,* kindred with עָשַׁר. In Kal not used.

Niph. *idem.* Prov. 27:6 *abundant are the kisses of an enemy.*

Hiph. Ezek. 35:13 וְהַעְתַּרְתֶּם עָלַי דִּבְרֵיכֶם *ye have multiplied (proud) speeches against me.*

I. **עָתָר** m. verbal from עָתַר no. I. dec. IV. c. *a suppliant.* Zeph. 3:10.

II. **עָתָר** Ezek. 8:11. prob. i. q. Aram. עֲטַר, عطر (see the letter ע,) *scent, vapour.* Hence עֲתַר עֲנַן הַקְּטֹרֶת *the scent of the cloud of incense.* So the Sept. Vulg. Chald. Syr. Others: *the multitude of the clouds* etc. Comp. עָתַר no. II.

עֲתֶרֶת f. verbal from עָתַר no. II. *riches, abundance.* Jer. 33:6.

פ

Pe, the 17th letter of the alphabet, and as a numerical sign denoting 80. The name פֵּא is prob. i. q. פֶּה *a mouth,* hence in Greek πῖ (פִּי.)

In Hebrew this letter was sometimes pronounced like *p;* and not always like *ph,* as in Arabic. Though Jerome and others deny this, yet it is rendered certain by some Shemitish words, which passed at an early date into the Greek language, and are written with π; as פִּלֶּגֶשׁ πάλλαξ, יָשְׁפֵה ἴασπις, כַּרְפַּס κάρπασος, comp. פָּרַס πέρσαι, etc.

The commutation of פ with other letters is comparatively rare. For its interchange with ב and מ, see the examples given under ב.

פֹּא i. q. פֹּה *here.* Job 38:11.

פָּאָה found only in the fut. Hiph. Deut. 32:26 אַפְאֵיהֶם. Sept. διασπερῶ αὐτούς. (Arab. فأى *fidit, diffidit.*) According to others, a denom. from פֵּאָה *a corner,* hence *to drive into corners.*

פֵּאָה f. const. פְּאַת, dec. XI. b.

1. *a corner;* e. g. of a field, Lev. 19: 9. of a bed, Am. 3:12.

2. פְּאַת זָקָן *the corner* or *extremity of*

the beard, i. e. prob. mustaches, (like the Syr. ܦܐܬܐ.) Lev. 19:27. 21:5.—קְצוּצֵי פֵאָה all whose mustaches are cut or *shorn*, a name of reproach for some Arabian tribes, Jer. 9:25. 25:23. 49:32. (The Jewish commentators understand *the beard on the cheeks and upper lip.*)

3. *a side, region, country;* e. g. פְּאַת־יָם *the west side*, Josh. 18:14. פְּאַת צָפוֹן *the north side*, Ex. 26:20.—Jer. 48:45 פְּאַת מוֹאָב *the side* or *country of Moab.* Dual const. פַּאֲתֵי מוֹאָב *the sides of Moab.* The dual here has reference to the *two* sides of the country, comp. יַרְכָתַיִם, יָדַיִם.

פָּאַר in Kal not used.

Pi. פֵּאֵר 1. *to adorn, beautify, glorify;* e. g. the sanctuary, Is. 60:7, 13. the people of God, Is. 55:5. the poor by helping them, Ps. 149:4. (comp. the Latin phrase *ornare beneficiis.*)

2. denom. from פֹּארָה, *to search the branches, to glean.* Deut. 24:20.

Hithpa. 1. *to be adorned, beautified, glorified;* spoken of Jehovah, Is. 60:21. 61:3. particularly of his glorifying himself in the people, construed with בְּ, Is. 44:23. 49:3.—Ex. 8:5 [8:9] הִתְפָּאֵר עָלַי usually rendered *be thou glorified above me*, i. e. thou shalt have honour before me. The ancient translators, more agreeably to the context, *command* or *appoint to me*, (באר=פאר.)

2. *to boast one's self, to glory;* construed with עַל *against* any one. Judg. 7:2. Is. 10:15.

Deriv. out of course תִּפְאֶרֶת.

פְּאֵר m. verbal from פֵּאֵר, dec. VI. t. *a head-dress, turban.* Ezek. 24:17, 23. 26:10. worn by the priests, Ex. 39:28. by the bridegroom, Is. 61:10. Ezek. 24:17. by women, Is. 3:20.

פארה f. (for פֹּארָה by a Syriasm,) Ezek. 17:6. 31:5ff. and פֻּארָה f. (for פֹּארָה by a Syriasm,) Is. 10:33. verbals from פֵּאֵר, dec. X. *a branch* or *bough with leaves*, liter. *the ornament of the trees*, like the Lat. *comá arborum.* Deriv. פֵּאֵר no. 2. Plur. פֹּארֹתָיו, for פֹּארוֹתָיו, Ezek. 31:8.

פָּארוּר m. (for פָּארוּר,) verbal from פֵּאֵר, *beauty, shining countenance,* (i. q. זִיו.) Joel 2:6 כָּל־פָּנִים קִבְּצוּ פָארוּר *all faces gather in,* i. e. lose, *their brightness.* Nah. 2:11. (Comp. Joel 2:10. 4:15.) For a different explanation, see Gesen. on Is. 13:8.

פָּארָן proper name of a desert between Midian and Egypt, which bears this name at the present day. Gen. 21:21. Num. 10:12. 1 K. 11:18. Hence הַר־פָּארָן Hab. 3:3. and הָרֵי פָארָן Deut. 33:2. *the mountains of Paran.*—אֵיל פָּארָן *the turpentine-tree of Paran,* Gen. 14:6.

פַּג, plur. פַּגִּים, dec. VIII. h. *small unripe figs*, growing over winter, *grossi, grossuli.* Cant. 2:13. Sept. ὄλυνθοι. Root פגג in Arab. conj. VII. *to be unripe.*

פִּגּוּל m. adj. dec. X. *impure, abominable, an abomination*, spoken of food, i. q. שֶׁקֶץ. Lev. 7:18. 19:7. Used as a subst. בְּשַׂר פִּגּוּל *unclean flesh*, Ezek. 4:14.

פָּגַע 1. *to meet, meet with, light upon;* construed with an accus. Ex. 23:4. 1 Sam. 10:5. with בְּ, Gen. 28:11. 32:2.

2. *to fall on* any one, construed with בְּ. 1 Sam. 22:17, 18. particularly for to injure, Ruth 2:22. or to kill, hence *to kill, slay*, Judg. 8:21. 15:12. 2 Sam. 1:15. Also with an accus. of the person and בְּ of the thing, Ex. 5:3 פֶּן יִפְגָּעֵנוּ בַּדֶּבֶר *lest he slay us with the pestilence.*

3. *to reach to, border on, be contiguous, pertinere ad* aliquid, spoken of a territory; construed with בְּ, Josh. 16:7. 17:10. with אֶל, 19:11.

4. *to address with a supplication, to urge, supplicate, entreat,* construed with בְּ of the person. Ruth 1:16. Jer. 7:16. 27:18. With לְ of the person *for* whom, Gen. 23:8.

5. as in Syriac, *to visit,* hence *to regard with favour,* like פָּקַד. Is. 47:3 וְלֹא אֶפְגַּע אָדָם *and I will spare no man.* 64:4.

Hiph. 1. *to cause to fall, to let fall.* Is. 53:6 הִפְגִּיעַ בּוֹ אֵת עֲוֺן כֻּלָּנוּ *he causes to fall on him the iniquity of us all.* According to this we should render Jer.

15:11 *I will in the time of adversity let the enemy come upon thee.* But this does not accord with the preceding clause. Hence perhaps (comp. Ex. 5: 3.) *I will through thee meet the enemy in an hour of adversity*, i. e. I will announce to him through thee adversity.

2. i. q. Kal no. 2. *to fall on, to seize, attack.* Part. מַפְגִּיעַ *an enemy*, Job 36:32.

3. i. q. Kal no. 4. *to supplicate, entreat*, construed with בְּ. Jer. 36:25. Also with לְ of the person *for* whom, Is. 53:12. 59:16.

Deriv. מִפְגָּע.

פֶּגַע m. verbal from פָּגַע, *an occurrence, incident.* 1 K. 5:18. Ecc. 9:11. See Hiph. no. 1.

פָּגַר *to be weary, faint.* Found only in Pi. 1 Sam. 30:10, 21. (In Talmud. *to be idle.* In Syr. [Syriac] by a commutation of ב and פ, *attenuatus est*; [Arabic] *weak, faint.*) Hence

פֶּגֶר m. plur. const. פִּגְרֵי, verbal from פָּגַר, dec. VI. h. *a corpse* or *carcase.* Gen. 15:11. Metaphorically פִּגְרֵי גִלּוּלֵיכֶם *the ruins of your idols*, Lev. 26:29. Once with the addition מֵת *dead*, Is. 37:36.

פָּגַשׁ fut. יִפְגֹּשׁ. 1. *to meet* a person, construed with an accus. Gen. 32:18. 33:8. Ex. 4:27. Is. 34:14.

2. *to fall on, attach*, i. q. פָּגַע no. 2. Ex. 4:24. Hos. 13:8.

Niph. *to meet together.* Ps. 85:11. Prov. 22:2.

Pi. *to meet.* Job 5:14.

פָּדָה, synonymous with גָּאַל.

1. *to redeem, ransom.* Ex. 13:13. Construed with בְּ of the price, e. g. Ex. 34:20 פֶּטֶר חֲמוֹר תִּפְדֶּה בְשֶׂה *the firstling of an ass thou shalt redeem with a sheep.*

2. *to set free, let go*, spoken of the priest. Num. 18:15, 16, 17.

3. *to deliver* from slavery. Deut. 7: 8. 13:6. Jer. 15:21. 31:11.

4. *to deliver* in any way. Job 5:20. 1 K. 1:29. 2 Sam. 4:9. Ps. 71:23.

Niph. pass. of Kal no. 1. Lev. 19:20. of Kal no. 3. Is. 1:27.

Hiph. הֶפְדָּה causat. of Kal no. 1. Ex. 21:8.

Hoph. only in the infin. pleon. הָפְדֵּה, Lev. 19:20.

Deriv. פִּדְיוֹן, פְּדוּיִם, פְּדוּת, פִּדְיוֹם, פְּדוּיִם.

פְּדוּיִים masc. plur. verbal from פָּדָה, dec. I. *ransom, price of deliverance.* Num. 3:46 ff. Also as a part. pass. *the delivered.*

פְּדוּת f. verbal from פָּדָה, *deliverance, redemption.* Ps. 111:9. 130:7. Is. 50:2.

פִּדְיוֹם m. Num. 3:49. and פִּדְיוֹן Ex. 21:30. Ps. 49:10. verbals from פָּדָה, *a ransom.*

פַּדָּן m. dec. II. b. *a plain, a field.* Found only in the phrase פַּדַּן אֲרָם *the plain of Syria*, i. e. Mesopotamia. Gen. 31:18. 28:2 ff. Once simply פַּדָּן *idem.* In Hos. 12:13, we find instead of it שְׂדֵה אֲרָם.

פָּדַע according to the usual reading, i. q. פָּדָה *to deliver.* Once Job 33:24 פְּדָעֵהוּ *deliver him.* Some MSS. however, read פְּרָעֵהוּ, which gives good sense and might easily be corrupted.

פֶּדֶר m. with suff. פִּדְרוֹ, dec. VI. h. *fat, grease.* Lev. 1:8, 12. 8:20.

פֶּה m. (strictly for פֶּאֶה, like שֶׂה,) const. פִּי, with suff. פִּי *my mouth*; פִּיךָ; פִּיו, פִּיהוּ; פִּיהֶם, poet. פִּימוֹ; prim.

1. *the mouth.*—פֶּה אֶל פֶּה *mouth to mouth, orally*, Num. 12:8.—פֶּה אֶחָד *with one accord*, Josh. 9:2.—Ex. 4:16 *and he shall be thy mouth*, i. e. thy spokesman. Gen. 25:28 בְּפִיו *to his mouth*, i. e. taste. Metaphorically עַל פִּי *according to the word* or *oracle*, Num. 3:16, 39, 51. *by the testimony*, Deut. 17:6. *by the command*, Gen. 45:21.

2. *an aperture, opening*; e. g. of a sack, Gen. 42:27. of a well, Gen. 29: 2.—פִּי רֹאשׁוֹ *the opening of the head*, i. e. the head (of a garment), Gen. 28:32.

3. *an edge.* So in the phrase הִכָּה לְפִי חֶרֶב *to smite with the edge of the sword.* Plur. פִּים *edges* (of cutting instruments), 1 Sam. 13:21.—פֵּיוֹת and פִּיפִיּוֹת *idem*, Judg. 3:16. Prov. 5:4. See פִּיפִיּוֹת.

4. *an edge, border*; (perhaps liter.

lip,) e. g. spoken of the collar of a coat, Ps. 133 : 2. Job 30 : 18. of the shore of the sea, Prov. 8 : 29.—פֶּה לָפֶה 2 K. 10 : 21. 21 : 16. and מִפֶּה אֶל פֶּה Ezra 9 : 11. *from one side to the other.*

5. *a part.* Deut. 21 : 17 פִּי שְׁנַיִם *two parts, a double portion.* 2 K. 2 : 9 פִּי שְׁנַיִם *two (third) parts.* Zech. 13 : 8. See יָד no. 7.

6. In combination it forms a periphrasis for prepositions or conjunctions; as (1.) כְּפִי (a.) *according to, in proportion to, secundum.* Lev. 25 : 52. Num. 6 : 21. (b.) *like, as.* Job 33 : 6 אֲנִי כְפִיךָ לָאֵל *I am like thee before God.* (c.) *so that.* Zech. 2 : 4. [1 : 21.] (d.) כְּפִי אֲשֶׁר *because.* Mal. 2 : 9. (2.) לְפִי (a.) *according to, secundum.* Ex. 12 : 4. Gen. 47 : 12 לְפִי הַטָּף *according to the number of the family.* (b.) simply i. q. לְ. Hos. 10 : 12. Before an infin. *when*, Num. 9 : 17. Jer. 29 : 10. (3.) עַל פִּי *according to, secundum.* Lev. 27 : 8, 18. Hence עַל פִּי הַדְּבָרִים *according to the thing itself, as the truth is.*

פֹּה and פוֹ adv. prim. See פֹּא, אֵיפֹה.

1. *here;* freq.

2. *hither.* 1 Sam. 16 : 11. Ezra 4 : 2.

3. מִפֹּה *hence.* Ezek. 40 : 21, 26, 34, 37.

פוּג 1. *to be cold, to lose one's animal warmth.* Gen. 45 : 26 וַיָּפָג לִבּוֹ *but his heart continued cold.*

2. *to relax, to be wearied, to be inactive,* an idea connected with that of *coldness.* Ps. 77 : 3. Metaphorically Hab. 1 : 4 *the law is inactive, friget lex.*

Niph. *to be weak, feeble.* Ps. 38 : 9.

פוּגָה f. verbal from פוּג, dec. X. *rest, relaxation.* Lam. 2 : 18. See הֲפוּגָה.

פוּחַ i. q. נָפַח *to blow.* Cant. 2 : 17 עַד שֶׁיָּפוּחַ הַיּוֹם *until the day blows,* i. e. grows cool, from the springing up of the evening breeze. 4 : 6. Comp. רוּחַ.

Hiph. 1. *to blow through* or *upon.* Cant. 4 : 16.

2. *to kindle* (a fire), construed with בְּ. Ezek. 21 : 36. Metaphorically *to put in commotion,* construed with an accus. Prov. 29 : 8 *they put a city in commotion.*

3. metaphorically *to breathe out, utter, efflare;* in a bad sense, as יָפִיחַ כְּזָבִים *efflare mendacia.* Prov. 6 : 19. 14 : 5. 19 : 5, 9. in a good sense, Prov. 12 : 17.

4. *to snort,* hence *to hasten.* Hab. 2 : 3. Comp. שׁוֹאֵף Ecc. 1 : 6.

5. *to snuff at angrily, to puff at,* construed with בְּ and לְ. Ps. 10 : 5. 12 : 6 יָפִיחַ לוֹ אֲשֶׁר *whom man snuffs at,* i. e. the oppressed.

פוּט proper name of an African people, according to Josephus (Antiq. I. 7.) *the inhabitants of Mauritania,* where there is a river called *Phut.* Comp. Plin. H. N. v. 1. According to the Sept. and Vulg. *Libyans.* Gen. 10 : 6. Jer. 46 : 9. Ezek. 27 : 10. 38 : 5. Nah. 3 : 9.

פּוֹטִי פֶרַע an Egyptian proper name, *Poti-pherah,* the father-in-law of Joseph. Gen. 41 : 45. 46 : 20. Jablonski makes it i. q. Copt. ΠΗΟΝΤ-ΦΡΗ *sacerdos solis.*

פּוֹטִיפַר an Egyptian proper name, *Potiphar,* the captain of Pharaoh's body-guard. Gen. 39 : 1. It has been explained by the Copt. ΠΙΩΤ-ΦΡΡΟ *father,* i. e. prime minister *of Pharaoh.* Comp. אָב no. 6.

פּוּךְ m. 1. *an ornament, decoration.* 1 Chr. 29 : 2 אַבְנֵי פוּךְ וְרִקְמָה *stones for ornament and of various colours.* Sept. λίθοι πολυτελεῖς καὶ ποικίλοι.

2. particularly *eye paint, stibium,* (see the article כָּחַל.)—שׂוּם עֵינַיִם בַּפּוּךְ *to paint the eyes with stibium,* 2 K. 9 : 30. Comp. Jer. 4 : 30.—Is. 54 : 11 *I will lay thy stones in stibium,* i. e. I will use it for lime or cement.—This word occurs also in the proper name קֶרֶן הַפּוּךְ (*a box of paint.*)

פּוֹל m. *a bean.* 2 Sam. 17 : 28. Ezek. 4 : 9.

פּוּל proper name 1. of a people remote from Palestine. Is. 66 : 19. Vulg. *Africa.* According to Bochart (Phaleg, IV. 26.) *Philæ* or *Elephantina,* an island of the Nile, in Upper Egypt.

2. of an Assyrian king. 2 K. 15 : 19.

פּוּם and פֻּם m. emph. פּוּמָא, Chald. i. q. Heb. פֶּה.

1. *a mouth.* Dan. 7:5.

2. *an aperture, opening.* Dan. 6:18.

פּוּן found only Ps. 88:16 אָפוּנָה Sept. ἐξηπορήθην. Vulg. *conturbatus sum.* Comp. perhaps the Arab. אפן *consilii inops fuit,* like אָרַשׁ and רוּשׁ.

פּוּנֹן proper name of a city in Idumea, between Petra and Zoar, celebrated for its mines. Num. 33:42, 43. See Relandi Palæstina, p. 952.

פּוּץ found only in the fut. and imper. i. q. נָפַץ q. v.

1. *to smite* or *dash in pieces.* See Pilel, Pilpel, Hithpa.

2. *to scatter,* but only in a reflexive sense, *to scatter one's self, to go astray;* spoken of a flock, Ezek. 34:5. Zech. 13:7. of a people, Gen. 11:4. 1 Sam. 11:11. 14:34.

3. *to overflow.* Zech. 1:17. Prov. 5:16.

Niph. *to be* or *become scattered;* spoken of a flock, Ezek. 34:6. of nations, Gen. 10:18. Ezek. 11:17.

Pilel פּוֹצֵץ *to break in pieces* a rock, spoken of the hammer. Jer. 23:29.

Pilpel פִּצְפֵּץ *to dash in pieces,* as a man against a rock. Job 16:12.

Hiph. 1. trans. *to scatter;* e. g. one's enemies, by lightning, arrows, Ps. 18:15. 144:6. seed, Is. 28:25. nations, Deut. 4:27. 28:64. 30:3. Is. 24:1. Part. מֵפִיץ *a scatterer, devastator,* Nah. 2:2.

2. *to chase, drive, exagitare.* Job 18:11. Ezek. 34:21.

3. intrans. *to be scattered, to rush out;* spoken of the east wind, Job 38:24. of the people, Ex. 5:12. 1 Sam. 13:8.

Hithpulal, *to be broken in pieces,* spoken of the mountains. Hab. 3:6.

Note. The form הֲפִיצוֹתִיכֶם *I will scatter you,* Jer. 25:34. belongs to the uncommon conjugation Tiphel. See Gesen. Lehrgeb. § 73:4. The Vulg. Aqu. Symm. and several editions read תְּפוֹצוֹתֵיכֶם *dispersiones vestræ,* which is not so well suited to the context.

Deriv. out of course מֵפִיץ *a hammer.*

פּוּץ m. verbal from פּוּץ, dec. I. *dispersion.* Zeph. 3:10 בַּת פּוּצַי *the daughter of my dispersion,* i. e. those dispersed by me.

I. **פּוּק** *to stumble.* Is. 28:7.

Hiph. *idem.* Jer. 10:4.

Deriv. פִּיק, פּוּקָה.

II. **פּוּק** *to go out,* i. q. Chald. נְפַק.

Hiph. 1. *to give out, afford, supply, suppeditare.* Ps. 144:13. Is. 58:10.

2. *to cause a person to give, to get* or *acquire* from him. Prov. 3:13. 12:2. 8:35. 18:22.

3. *to let* or *cause to be accomplished.* Ps. 140:9 אַל תָּפֵק *let not be accomplished.*

פּוּקָה f. verbal from פּוּק no. I. *a stumbling-stone, an offence,* i. q. מִכְשׁוֹל. 1 Sam. 25:31.

פּוּר and **פָּרַר** *to break, rive, shatter.* In Kal found only in the infin. פּוֹר, Is. 24:19.

Pilel פּוֹרֵר *to divide* (the sea). Ps. 74:13.

Hithpal. *to be broken, shattered.* Is. 24:19.

Pilpel פַּרְפֵּר *to break in pieces.* Job 16:12.

Hiph. הֵפִיר (Ps. 33:10. Ezek. 17:19.) and הֵפֵר, in pause הֵפַר.

1. *to break;* but only metaphorically *to break or violate,* e. g. a covenant, Is. 33:8. Ezek. 17:16. Lev. 26:44. the law, Ps. 119:126.

2. *to frustrate, defeat, bring to nought,* (a purpose.) 2 Sam. 15:34. Ps. 33:10. comp. Job 5:13. Prov. 15:22. Is. 44:25.

3. *to annul, to make void* or *of none effect;* e. g. a vow, Num. 30:9, 13. the fear of God, Job 15:4. righteousness, Job 40:8. Construed with מִן, *to turn away from* a person, Ps. 89:34. So with עִם (for מֵעִם), Ps. 85:5. Intrans. *to come to nought, to fail,* Ecc. 12:5.

Hoph. *to be frustrated, to be brought to nought.* Is. 8:10. Jer. 33:21.

Deriv. פּוּרָה.

פּוּר m. dec. I. *a lot,* a Persian word which is explained Est. 3:7, by גּוֹרָל.

(Comp. Pers. بر, بارہ *a part.*) Hence Plur. יְמֵי הַפּוּרִים Est. 9:31. and simply פּוּרִים 9:29, 32. *the feast of Purim*, which was celebrated by the Jews on the 14th and 15th of the month Adar, in commemoration of the destruction which was meditated for them by Haman.

פּוּרָה f. *a wine-press.* Is. 63:3. Hag. 2:16. Root פּוּר *to break* or *bruise.*

I. **פּוּשׁ** and **פִּישׁ**, Arab. فاش med. Je *to move proudly;* hence spoken of a horseman, *to leap proudly*, Hab. 1:8 of calves, *to leap wantonly, to frisk, lascivire*, Mal. 3:20 [4:2] פִּשְׁתֶּם (from פִּשׁ.) Sept. σκιρτήσετε. Jer. 50:11.

II. **פּוּשׁ** Niph. *to be scattered, spread abroad.* Nah. 3:18. So in Chald. See פּשׁ.

פָּז m. verbal from פָּזַז no. I. *pure gold.* Ps. 21:4. Lam. 4:2. Is. 13:12. It is distinguished from common gold, Ps. 19:11. 119:127. Prov. 8:19. and in Ecc. 5:11, it is used as an epithet of כֶּתֶם.

I. **פָּזַז** In Kal not used. Prob. i. q. Arab. فض מצץ *to purify* metals.

Hoph. part. זָהָב מוּפָז 1 K. 10:18. for which we find in 2 Chr. 9:17 זָהָב טָהוֹר *pure gold.*

Deriv. פָּז.

II. **פָּזַז** *to be active, strong.*

Niph. Gen. 49:24 וַיָּפֹזּוּ זְרֹעֵי יָדָיו *the power of his hands continues strong.* (Syr. ܦܙܙ *hard, heavy.*)

Pi. 2 Sam. 6:16 מְפַזֵּז וּמְכַרְכֵּר *leaping nimbly and dancing.* In the parallel passage. 1 Chr. 15:29 מְרַקֵּד וּמְשַׂחֵק *dancing and sporting.*

פָּזַר *to scatter*, i. q. בָּזַר, פָּזַר. In Kal found only in the part. pass. Jer. 50:17.

Pi. 1. as in Kal, *to scatter*, e. g. a people, Ps. 89:11. the bones of any one, Ps. 53:6.—Jer. 3:13 וַתְּפַזְּרִי אֶת־דְּרָכַיִךְ *thou hast roved.*

2. *to disperse, to give bountifully.* Ps. 112:9. Prov. 11:24.

Niph. pass. Ps. 141:7.

Pu. pass. Est. 3:8.

פַּח m. plur. פַּחִים, const. פַּחֵי, (like אַחִים, with Dagesh forte implied,) verbal from פָּחַח, dec. VIII. l.

1. *a net, snare, gin.* Job 18:19. particularly of the fowler, Ecc. 9:12. Prov. 7:23.—*To lay snares* is expressed in Hebrew by נָתַן פַּח, Ps. 119. 110. טָמַן פַּח, 140:6. יָקֹשׁ פַּח, 141:9.

2. metaphorically, *an object which causes to fall* or *brings into misfortune;* comp. מוֹקֵשׁ no. 2. Josh. 23:13. Ps. 69:23. Is. 8:15. Hence *ruin, destruction*, Is. 24:17. Jer. 48:43. See פַּחַת.

3. Ps. 11:6 פַּחִים prob. *crooked lightning.* Comp. in Arab. *cords* or *chains*, used in this signification; also in Greek μάστιξ *lightning*, Hom. Il. XIII. 812.)

4. פַּחִים *thin plates.* Ex. 39:3. Num. 17:3.

פָּחַד, fut. יִפְחַד. 1. *to tremble, to be afraid.* Deut. 28:66. Is. 12:2. Construed with מִן, Ps. 27:1. and with מִפְּנֵי, Is. 19:16. of the person *feared.* Also with אֶל of the thing *for* which one fears, Is. 19:17.—פָּחַד פַּחַד *timere timorem*, Job 3:25.—פָּחַד אֶל רֵעֵהוּ *to communicate one's fear to his neighbour*, Jer. 36:16. comp. Gen. 42:28. Also used of a trembling for joy, Is. 60:5. Jer. 33:9.

2. *to hasten, trepidare.* Hos. 3:5. Comp. חָרַד, נֶחְפַּז, נִבְהַל.

Pi. 1. intrans. *to quake, tremble.* Is. 51:13.

2. *to be cautious, circumspect.* Prov. 28:14. Antith. הִקְשָׁה לֵב.

Hiph. *to cause to shake.* Job 4:14.

I. **פַּחַד** m. with suff. פַּחְדִּי, verbal from פָּחַד, dec. VI. c.

1. *fear, terror.* Ex. 15:16. Job 13:11. פַּחַד הַיְּהוּדִים *the fear of the Jews*, i.e. which the Jews caused, Est. 8:17. 9:3.—פַּחַד יְהוָֹה *the fear* or *terror which Jehovah inspires*, Is. 2:10, 19. 2 Chr. 14:13.

2. joined with אֱלֹהִים, *the fear of God, piety.* Ps. 36:2.

3. *the object of fear* or *reverence.* Gen. 31:42 פַּחַד יִצְחָק *the fear of Isaac,*

i. e. Jehovah. Verse 53. Plur. פְּחָדִים Job 15:21.

II. פַּחַד, Arab. فَخِذ, dec. VI. c. *a hip, thigh, femur.* Job 40:17.

פַּחְדָּה f. verbal from פָּחַד, dec. XII. a. *fear, terror.* Jer. 2:19.

פֶּחָה m. irreg. const. פַּחַת, with suff. פֶּחָתְךָ but also פֶּחָם Neh. 5:14 (from an obsol. masc. form,) plur. פַּחוֹת const. פַּחֲוֹת, *a satrap, governor, deputy, viceroy,* (of a province,) an officer under the ancient Chaldean and Persian monarchs. Est. 3:12. 8:9. 9:3. Spoken of the governor of Judea under the Persians, Hag. 1:1, 14. 2:2, 21. Neh. 5:14, 18.—In 1 K. 10:15. 20:24. it is perhaps used by anticipation.

פֶּחָה, const. פַּחַת, plur. פַּחֲוָתָא, Chald. i. q. Heb. Ezra 5:3, 14. 6:7. Dan. 3:2, 3, 27. 6:8.

פָּחַז 1. i. q. Arab. فخر *to be proud, vain-glorious.* Hence part. פֹּחֲזִים spoken of false prophets, Zeph. 3:4.

2. *to be arrogant, rash.* Judg. 9:4. (Syr. ܦܚܙ *to be arrogant, licentious, wanton.* Chald. *to boil up, to boil over.* That the primary signification of the word has reference to water, is evident from the following article.)

פַּחַז m. liter. *a boiling* or *flowing over,* spoken of water; hence *arrogance, wantonness.* Gen. 49:4 פַּחַז כַּמַּיִם for פָּחַזְתָּ כַּמַּיִם *thou boilest over, like water,* indicative of arrogance and wantonness. Symm. ὑπερέζεσας. Vulg. *effusus es.*

פַּחֲזוּת f. verbal from פָּחַז, dec. I. *vain-glory, boasting.* Jer. 23:32.

פָּחַח prob. *to spread out,* hence *to make thin.* Hence פַּח *a net,* and *a thin plate.* (Syr. Ethpa. *attenuatus est.*)

Hiph. הָפֵחַ denom. from פַּח, *to spread a net, to ensnare.* Is. 42:22. So Sept. Vulg. Syr. and the Hebrew interpreters.

פֶּחָם m. 1. liter. *a black coal.* (Root פחם Chald. and Arab. *to be coal-black.*) Prov. 26:21.

2. also *a burning coal.* Is. 44:12. 54:16.

פֶּחָר m. Chald. *a potter.* Dan. 2:41. (Syr. and Arab. *idem.*)

פַּחַת m. plur. פְּחָתִים, dec. VI. c. *a pit.* 2 Sam. 17:9. As representing destruction, it is joined, by way of paronomasia, with פַּחַד and פַּח, Is. 24:17. Jer. 48:43 פַּחַד וָפַחַת וָפָח עָלֶיךָ *terror and the pit and the snare shall be upon thee.* Lam. 3:27 פַּחַד וָפַחַת *fear and a pit.* Root פחת in Syr. *to dig, to dig out.* Hence also

פְּחֶתֶת f. *a hole,* (in a garment infected with the leprosy.) Lev. 13:55.

פִּטְדָה f. the name of a precious stone, Ezek. 28:17. Ezek. 28:13. principally obtained from Ethiopia, Job 28:19. by the ancient translators rendered *a topaz,* i. e. the chrysolite of the moderns.

פַּטִּישׁ m. *a hammer.* Is. 41:7. Jer. 23:29. Metaphorically Jer. 50:23 *the hammer,* i. e. the desolator, *of the whole earth.* Root فطس *to pound out* iron.

פַּטִּישׁ m. Chald. Dan. 3:21 Keth. In the Keri פַּטְּשׁ i. q. Syr. ܦܛܫܐ *an under garment.* Hence the Jewish Targumist פתגניכם, as should be read instead of פתגניכם.

פָּטַר 1. *to cleave, burst open,* spoken e. g. of flowers. 1 K. 6:18, 29, 32, 35.

2. trans. *to let break open, to let loose,* e. g. water. Prov. 17:14. Hence

3. metaphorically *to let loose, set free, dismiss.* (In Chald. the prevalent meaning.) 2 Chr. 23:8. 1 Chr. 9:33 Keri פְּטוּרִים *free from service.* In the Keth. פְּטִירִים.

3. intrans. *to go* or *slip away, to withdraw,* with a fut. יִפְטֹר. 1 Sam. 19:10.

Hiph. הִפְטִיר בְּשָׂפָה *to cleave the lips,* i. e. to open the mouth wide, as an expression of contempt. Ps. 22:8. (comp. 35:21. Job 16:11.)

פֶּטֶר m. verbal from פָּטַר, dec. VI. *what first breaks through.* Hence פֶּטֶר רֶחֶם *what first breaks out of the womb, a firstling*, Ex. 13:2. 34:19. Also without רֶחֶם in the same sense, Ex. 13:12, 13. 34:20.

פִּטְרָה f. verbal from פָּטַר, dec. X. *idem*. Num. 8:16.

פִּי see פֶּה *a mouth*.

פִּי־בֶסֶת found only Ezek. 30:17. proper name of a city in Egypt, according to the Sept. and Jerome, *Bubastos* on the eastern mouth of the Nile.

פִּיד m. dec. I. *calamity, destruction*. Job 30:24. 31:29. (12:5.?) Prov. 24:22. (Arab. فَادَ med. Vav and Je *to die*; conj. IV. *to destroy*.)

פֵּיָה fem. of פֶּה, i. q. פֶּה no. 3. *the edge of a sword*. Judg. 3:16.

פִּי־הַחִירוֹת (*opening of caverns*) proper name of a place on the Red Sea. Ex. 14:2, 9. Num. 33:7. Also without פִּי, verse 8.

פִּיחַ m. *dust, ashes*, verbal from פּוּחַ Hiph. *to blow away*. Ex. 9:8, 10.

פִּילֶגֶשׁ *a concubine*, see פִּלֶגֶשׁ.

פִּימָה f. *fat, fatness*. Job 15:27. Arab. فَيِمَ *to be fat*.

פִּיפִיּוֹת fem. plur. *double edge, two edges*. Ps. 149:6. Is. 41:15. Comp. פֶּה no. 3.

פִּיק m. *a tottering*. Nah. 2:11. Root פּוּק.

פִּישׁוֹן proper name of a river, which according to Gen. 2:11, issued from Eden and flowed round Havilah; comp. Ecclus. 24:25. Josephus (Antiq. Jud. I. 3.) makes it *the Ganges*; comp. חֲוִילָה. Others, (after Reland,) *the Phasis*. Comp. J. D. Michaëlis Supplem. p. 2008.

פַּךְ m. *a vial, flask, bottle*. 1 Sam. 10:1. 2 K. 9:1, 3. Root פָּכָה.

פָּכָה in Pi. *to run* or *flow out*. Once Ezek. 47:2. See פַּךְ.

פָּלָא in Kal not used.

1. *to separate*, like פָּלָה. See Pi. Hiph. no. 1. (Chald. Pa. *to select, remove.*)

2. *to distinguish, to make great* or *extraordinary*. See Niph. Hiph. no. 2.

Niph. *to be great* or *extraordinary, insignem, ingentem esse*. 2 Sam. 1:26. Dan. 11:36 יְדַבֵּר נִפְלָאוֹת *he will speak great things*, i. e. seditious blasphemies, (comp. Dan. 7:11. Apoc. 13:5.)

2. *to be difficult to do* or *conceive of, arduum esse*, construed with בְּעֵינֵי. 2 Sam. 13:2. Zech. 8:6. Construed with מִן, *to be too difficult* or *too hard for* any one, Gen. 18:14. Deut. 17:8. 30:11. Hence

3. *to be wonderful*. Ps. 118:23. 139:14. Part. plur. fem. נִפְלָאוֹת *wonderful deeds, marvellous works*, (of Jehovah;) sometimes in reference to the works of creation, Ps. 9:2. 26:7. 40:6. and sometimes to the miracles wrought for the Israelites, Ex. 34:10. Josh. 3:5. As a subst. it may have an adjective agreeing with it, as Ps. 136:4. The plur. is also used as an adv. *wonderfully, marvellously*, Job 37:5. Dan. 8:24.

Pi. *to consecrate, dedicate*, (liter. *to separate*;) particularly a vow, either in making it, Lev. 27:2. or in performing it, Lev. 22:21. Num. 15:3, 8.

Hiph. הִפְלִיא and הִפְלָא (the latter Deut. 28:59. Is. 28:29. as if from פָּלָה.)

1. i. q. Pi. *to consecrate, to set apart*. Num. 6:2.

2. *to make great* or *extraordinary*. Deut. 28:59. Ps. 31:22. Infin. הַפְלֵא as an adv. 2 Chr. 2:8.

3. *to make wonderful*. Is. 28:29. Construed with עִם, *to deal wonderfully with* a person, 29:14.—לְהַפְלִיא as an adv. *wonderfully*, Joel 2:26.

Hithpa. *to shew one's self great* or *powerful towards* a person, construed with בְּ. Job 10:16.

פֶּלֶא m. with suff. פִּלְאֲךָ, verbal from פָּלָא, dec. VI. h.

1. *something great* or *wonderful, a wonder, miracle*. Ex. 15:11. Ps. 77:12, 15. Plur. פְּלָאִים as an adv. *wonderfully*, Lam. 1:9.—פְּלָאוֹת *wonderful events*, Dan. 12:6.

מֻצְהָב *shining like gold.* Ezra 8:27. Kindred with זָהָב *gold.*

צָהֹב m. *gold-coloured, yellow,* spoken of the hair. Lev. 13:30 ff.

I. **צָהַל** 1. *to neigh,* spoken of the horse. Jer. 5:8.

2. metaphorically *to rejoice,* spoken of men. Is. 12:6. 24:14.

Pi. Is. 10:30 צַהֲלִי קוֹלֵךְ *let thy voice resound,* i. e. cry aloud, from alarm, terror. (Comp. רָנַן.)

Deriv. מִצְהָלָה.

II. **צָהַל** i. q. צָהַר or זָהַר *to shine.* Comp. the letter ל, p. 290. Found only in Hiph. causat. Ps. 104:15.

צָהַר found only in Hiph. denom. from יִצְהָר, *to make or press oil.* Job 24:11.

צֹהַר m. dec. VI. n. *light.* (Comp. זֹהַר and טֹהַר.) Gen. 6:16 צֹהַר תַּעֲשֶׂה לַתֵּבָה *light,* i. e. a window, *shalt thou make for the ship.* Comp. 8:6. (Others make it *the deck,* comp. the Arab. ظَهْر *the back, surface.*)

Dual צָהֳרַיִם *noon, mid-day,* liter. *double light.* Gen. 43:16, 25. Deut. 28:29. Used as an emblem of prosperity, Job 11:17. Ps. 47:6.

צַו or **צָו**, prob. *a precept,* (from צָוָה, like קַו, קָו, from قوي, קָוָה.) Hos. 5:11. *for he follows willingly after the commandment* (of men). According to this we should render Is. 28:10, 13 צַו לָצָו צַו לָצָו *precept upon precept, precept upon precept.* Others: *filth on filth,* (as if i. q. צוֹאָה, צֹאָה;) comp. verse 8.; but this does not agree so well with verse 13. Others make it the inarticulate sound of the drunken man, comp. verse 11.

צוֹא m. dec. I. *dirty,* spoken of garments. Zech. 3:3, 4. (Syr. ܨܐܐ *to be dirty, odious.*)

צוֹאָה f. dec. X. *dirt, filth.* Is. 28:8 קִיא צֹאָה *vomitus fœdus.* Metaphorically *sin, guilt,* Is. 4:4. Prov. 30:12. Used as an euphemistic expression for *human dung* in the Keri of Is. 36:12. 2 K. 18:27.

צַוָּאר m. and **צַוָּר** (Neh. 3:5.) const. צַוַּאר, dec. II. b.

1. *the neck,* Germ. *Hals.*—בְּצַוָּאר *with a stretched out* or *proud neck,* Job 15:26. Ps. 75:6.

2. *the neck,* Germ. *Nakken.* Lam. 5:5. Hence used in reference to a yoke or burden, Hos. 10:11. Lam. 1:14.

Plur. צַוָּארִים, const. צַוְּארֵי, used of an individual, Gen. 27:16. 33:4. 45:14. —צַוָּארוֹת *colla,* Mic. 2:3.

צוֹבָא, צוֹבָה proper name of a city in Mesopotamia, otherwise called *Nesibin, Nisibis, Antiochia Mygdoniæ,* 1 Sam. 14:47. 2 Sam. 8:3. 23:36. 2 Chr. 8:3. Its territory is denominated אֲרַם צוֹבָה Ps. 60:2. 2 Sam. 10:6, 8. It was the residence of a king, who in the time of David carried on several considerable wars with Israel.

צוּד (comp. צָדָה,) *to lie in wait,* construed with an accus. (1.) *to hunt, take,* (wild beasts.) Gen. 27:3, 5, 33. Job 38:39. (2.) *to lay snares,* e. g. for birds. Lev. 17:13. Lam. 3:52. Mic. 7:2. (3.) צוּד נֶפֶשׁ *to seek the life,* of a person. Prov. 6:26. (4.) in the other dialects also *to fish;* see צִידוֹן.

Pil. i. q. Kal no. (3.) Ezek. 13:18, 20.

Hithpa. הִצְטַיֵּד, see under צַיִד.

Deriv. מְצוּדָה, מָצוֹד, צַיָּד, צַיִד.

צָוָה found only in Pi. צִוָּה.

1. *to command* any one; construed with an accus. of the person, (like the Lat. *jubere aliquem,*) Gen. 26:11. more rarely with עַל, Gen. 2:16. 28:6. Est. 2:10, 20. with אֶל, Gen. 50:16. with לְ, Ex. 1:22. The command usually follows directly after לֵאמֹר, or indirectly in an infin. e. g. Gen. 3:11. The thing *commanded* is put also in the accus. hence a double accus. of the person and thing, Gen. 6:22. Ex. 25:22.

2. *to commission, depute, send,* (a person,) without mentioning the thing enjoined. Jer. 14:14. 23:32. Construed with עַל of the person *sent to,* Est. 4:5.

2. as a concrete, *wonderful, extraordinary.* Is. 9:5.

פִּלְאִי Judg. 13:18 Keth. *wonderful.* In the Keri פֶּלִי. The feminine of the first form is found in the Kethib of Ps. 139:6 פלאיה, read פְּלִאיָה, for which the Keri reads פְּלִיאָה from a singular פֶּלִא.

פָּלַג *to divide.* In Kal not used.

Niph. *to be divided.* Gen. 10:25. 1 Chr. 1:19 בְּיָמָיו נִפְלְגָה הָאָרֶץ *in his days the earth was divided.*

Pi. *to divide.* Ps. 55:10 פַּלַּג לְשׁוֹנָם *divide their tongues,* i. e. make them disunited in their counsels. Job 38:25 מִי־פִלַּג לַשֶּׁטֶף תְּעָלָה *who divideth a passage for the showers?*

פְּלַג Chald. *idem.* Part. pass. Dan. 2:41.

פֶּלֶג m. dec. VI. a. *a brook.* Ps. 65:10. Plur. פַּלְגֵי מַיִם *water brooks,* Ps. 1:3. 119:136.

פְּלַג Chald. *half.* Dan. 7:25.

פְּלַגּוֹת plur. fem. *brooks.* Judg. 5:15, 16. Job 20:17.

פְּלֻגָּה f. verbal from פָּלַג, dec. X. *a division* or *class* of the priests, otherwise called מַחֲלֹקֶת. 2 Chr. 35:5. In Chald. *idem,* Ezra 6:18.

פִּלֶגֶשׁ and פִּילֶגֶשׁ, plur. פִּילַגְשִׁים, of the common or epicene gender.

1. *a concubine.* Gen. 35:22. In full אִשָּׁה פִילֶגֶשׁ Judg. 19:1. 2 Sam. 15:16. 20:3.

2. *a paramour.* Ezek. 23:20 וַתַּעְגְּבָה עַל פִּלַגְשֵׁיהֶם *and she doted upon their paramours;* comp. verse 5. (In Chald. פַּלְקְתָּא, פִּילַקְתָּא *idem.* The Greek words πάλλαξ, παλλακίς, and the Latin *pellex,* are probably derived from the Hebrew.)

פְּלָדָה f. dec. XII. a. *iron, steel.* (Syr. and Arab. *idem.*) Plur. Nah. 2:4.

פָּלָה i. q. פָּלָא. 1. *to separate.*

2. *to distinguish.*

Niph. pass. of no. 1. Ex. 33:16. of no. 2. Ps. 139:14.

Hiph. 1. *to separate.* Ex. 8:18. [8:22.] Construed with בֵּין, *to make a distinction between,* Ex. 9:4. 11:7.

2. *to distinguish,* Ps. 4:4. *to make great,* Ps. 17:7.

פָּלַח *to cleave, cut, furrow.* Ps. 141:7. (In Arab. *to cut, furrow, cultivate the ground.*)

Pi. 1. *to divide, cleave,* spoken of an arrow. Prov. 7:23. Job 16:13 יְפַלַּח כִּלְיוֹתַי *he cleaveth my reins asunder.*

2. *to cut up,* e. g. fruit. 2 K. 4:39.

3. *to let break forth, to bring forth,* e. g. young. Job 39:3. Comp. פָּטַר.

פְּלַח Chald. *to serve,* (God or idols,) construed with an accus. and with לְ. Dan. 3:12ff. 7:14, 24. (In the Targums, *to labour, to serve.*)

פֶּלַח m. verbal from פָּלַח.

1. *a piece* or *slice cut off.* Cant. 4:3. 1 Sam. 30:12 פֶּלַח דְּבֵלָה *a slice of a cake of dried figs.*

2. *a mill-stone,* so named from its cut or flat surface which it turns to the other stone. The upper is called פֶּלַח רֶכֶב *the loose mill-stone* or *the runner,* Judg. 9:53. 2 Sam. 11:21. also simply רֶכֶב; the lower is called פֶּלַח תַּחְתִּית, Job 41:16. [41:24.]

פָּלְחָן m. Chald. *worship, service of God.* Ezra 7:19.

פָּלַט synonymous with מָלַט, comp. the letter ב.

1. *to be smooth, slippery.*

2. *to escape.* Ezek. 7:16. (Syr. and Arab. *idem.*)

Pi. 1. *to let escape* (from danger), *to deliver.* Ps. 18:3. 40:18. Construed with מִן, Ps. 18:49. 17:13. with מִיַּד, 71:4.

2. intrans. *to escape, to be delivered.* Job 23:7.

3. *to bear, bring forth.* Job 21:10. Comp. מָלַט no. 2. In this signification we find the part. only of פִּלֵּט, the pret. only of מִלֵּט, the fut. imper. and infin. of both.

Hiph. *to deliver,* Mic. 6:14. *to bear away* (the prey), Is. 5:29.

Deriv. out of course מִפְלָט, פְּלֵיטָה, פָּלִיט.

פֶּלֶט m. verbal from פָּלַט, *deliverance.* Ps. 32:7 *thou shalt compass me about with songs of deliverance.*

פִּלְאִי *wonderful,* see פֶּלֶא.

פִּלְיָא *wonderful,* see פֶּלֶא.

פָּלִיט and **פָּלֵיט** m. verbal from פָּלַט, dec. III. a. *one escaped, a fugitive.* Gen. 14:13. Josh. 8:22. In the plur. פְּלִיטִים, פְּלֵטִים, Is. 66:19. Jer. 44:14. Const. and with suff. פְּלִיטֵי, פְּלִיטָיו, Jer 44:28. Ezek. 6:8.

פְּלֵיטָה and **פְּלֵטָה** f. verbal from פָּלַט, dec. X.

1. *deliverance.* Joel 3:5. [2:32.] Obad. 17.

2. *that which escapes or is delivered.* Ex. 10:5. Particularly as a collective, *a part saved, a remnant of men escaped,* (from an overthrow,) 2 Sam. 15:14. 2 K. 19:30, 31. Ezra. 9:8.

פָּלִיל m. verbal from פָּלַל, dec. III. a. found only in the plur. פְּלִילִים *judges.* Ex. 21:22. Job 31:11 עָוֹן פְּלִילִים *a transgression to go before the judges.*

פְּלִילָה f. verbal from פָּלַל, *justice, equity, righteousness,* i. q. צֶדֶק and מִשְׁפָּט. Is. 16:3.

פְּלִילִי m. denom. adj. from פָּלִיל, *pertaining to a judge, judicialis.* Job 31:28. (Comp. verse 11.) Fem. פְּלִילִיָּה *judiciale,* used substantively for *judicium, judgment,* Is. 28:7.

פֶּלֶךְ m. with suff. פִּלְכּוֹ, dec. VI. h.

1. *a district, circle, circuit, small province.* Neh. 3:9 ff. E. g. פֶּלֶךְ יְרוּשָׁלַיִם *the district of Jerusalem,* verse 9. (In Chald. פִּלְכָּא, Arab. فَلْكَةٌ *idem.*)

2. *a spindle.* Prov. 31:19. (Arab. فَلْكَةٌ *idem,* in Talmud. פלך, פלכה, פלכה; also פִּלֵּךְ *to spin.*)

3. *a staff, crutch.* 2 Sam. 3:29. Sept. σκυτάλη.

פָּלַל in Kal not used. Probably its primary signification was *to cut, separate,* hence *to decide.* Kindred with פָּלָא and פָּלָה *to separate;* in Chald. פְּלַל conj. Aph. *to decide.*

Pi. פִּלֵּל 1. *to judge.* 1 Sam. 2:25. Construed with לְ, *to adjudge to* a person, *adjudicare,* Ezek. 16:52.

2. *to think, believe.* Gen. 48:11.

Deriv. פְּלִילִי, פְּלִילָה, פָּלִיל.

Hithpa. *to pray.* (1.) The deity *to* which a person prays is preceded by לְ, or אֶל. Gen. 20:17. Num. 11:2. (2.) The person *for* whom one prays is preceded by בְּעַד, Deut. 9:20. 1 Sam. 7:5. by עַל, Job 42:8. by לְ, 1 Sam. 2:25. (3.) The thing *about* which one prays is preceded by אֶל, 1 Sam. 1:27. Deriv. תְּפִלָּה *prayer.*

פַּלְמֹנִי see the following article.

פְּלֹנִי m. i. q. Greek ὁ καὶ ὁ δεῖνα, *some one, a certain one,* always followed by אַלְמֹנִי. 1 Sam. 21:2 אֶל מְקוֹם פְּלֹנִי אַלְמוֹנִי *to such and such a place.* 2 K. 6:8. As if in the vocative case, Ruth 4:2 שְׁבָה־פֹּה פְּלֹנִי אַלְמֹנִי *sit down here, such an one,* ὦ οὗτος, *O bone.* (Arab. فلان, Syr. ܦܠܢ *idem.*) From combining the two words arose in common language the quadriliteral פַּלְמוֹנִי Dan. 8:13.

פָּלַס in Kal not used.

Pi. 1. *to make straight, smooth, even, to beat* (a path). Ps. 78:50 *he beat a path for his anger,* i. e. he gave it free course. Prov. 4:26 *make straight the path of thy feet,* i. e. go in a straight path.

2. *to weigh out.* Metaphorically Ps. 58:3.

3. *to weigh, observe, ponder.* Prov. 5:21.

Deriv. מִפְלָשׂ, and

פֶּלֶס m. verbal from פָּלַס, *scales, a balance;* properly *steelyards,* like the Arab. تَفْلِيس Prov. 16:11. Is. 40:12.

פָּלַץ found only in Hithpa. *to be shaken, to quake, tremble.* Job 9:6. Deriv. out of course מִפְלָצֶת, פַּלָּצוּת.

פַּלָּצוּת f. verbal from פָּלַץ, *a quaking, fear, trembling.* Job 21:6. Ps. 55:6.

פָּלַשׁ found only in Hithpa. *to cover* or *sprinkle one's self;* e.g. בָּאֵפֶר *with ashes,* Jer. 6:26. Ezek. 27:30. עָפָר *with dust,* Mic. 1:10. Also without addition, in the same sense, Jer. 25:34.

פְּלֶשֶׁת f. *Philistia,* the proper name of a country in the south-western part of Palestine. Gen. 10:14. Ex. 15:14. Is. 14:28. In Josephus Παλαιστίνη (Antiq. Jud. I. 7. II. 6. VI. 1. VIII. 2. IX. 13.) which he uses likewise for *all Canaan,* e.g. Antiq. Jud. VIII. 4. comp. Relandi Palaestina, p. 38 ff. 73 ff. The gentile noun is פְּלִשְׁתִּי, plur. פְּלִשְׁתִּים, also פְּלִשְׁתִּיִּים (Am. 9:8.) *a Philistine,* Is. 2:6.

פְּלֵתִי m. *royal messengers, state courtiers,* who, with the כְּרֵתִי *headsmen,* formed the body-guard of the Hebrew kings. 2 Sam. 8:18. 15:18. etc. Root Arab. فلت i. q. פָּלַט *to escape, to flee away;* فَلَتْ *swift, swift-footed.*

פֶּן (always with Makkeph following.)

1. conj. construed with the fut. (1.) *that not, lest, ne, ne forte.* Gen. 19:19. Lev. 10:7. Ps. 2:12. (2.) *that not, quod non.* Judg. 15:12.

2. conj. construed with the pret. *that not, lest.* 2 Sam. 20:6. 2 K. 2:16.

3. adv. *not.* Prov. 5:6.

פַּנַּג found only Ezek. 27:17. prob. a kind of pastry. (In Rabbin. לחם פנג *opus dulciarium.*) Perhaps kindred with פָּנַק *deliciari.* So in Chald. קְלוֹיָא i. e. κολία, a kind of sweetened pastry.

פָּנָה, fut. apoc. יִפֶן, also אֵפֶן, תֵּפֶן.

1. *to turn, to turn away.* Deut. 30:17. Particularly (1.) for the purpose of departing. Ex. 7:23. 10:6. 32:15. Hence (2.) *to go to* a place. 1 K. 17:3. Construed with a pleonastic dative לְךָ, Deut. 1:40. 2:3. Josh. 22:4.—1 Sam. 14:47 בְּכֹל אֲשֶׁר יִפְנֶה *whithersoever he went* or *turned himself.* (3.) *to go* or *pass away.* Metaphorically Ps. 90:9 *all our days pass away.* Jer. 6:4. פָּנָה הַיּוֹם *the day declines* or *passes away.* (4.) *to turn one's self* to a person, construed with אֶל; e. g. to God, Is. 45:22. to idols, Lev. 19:4. Deut. 29:17. Also once with בְּ, Job 6:28. (5.) *to approach, draw near.*—לִפְנוֹת הַבֹּקֶר *at the approach of morning, towards morning,* Ex. 14:27. Judg. 19:26. לִפְנוֹת עֶרֶב *towards evening,* Deut. 23:12.

2. particularly *to turn one's eyes, to look.* Ex. 2:12. Is. 8:21. Construed with אֶל, *to look towards* a place, Ex. 16:10. Spoken of God or a king, *to look graciously, to regard with favour,* Ps. 25:16. 2 Sam. 9:8. Spoken of inanimate objects, *to be turned towards* a place, *spectare* aliquam regionem, Ezek. 8:3. 11:1. 44:1.

3. trans. as in Hiph. *to turn, incline;* only in the phrase פָּנָה עֹרֶף. See עֹרֶף.

Pi. פִּנָּה 1. *to destroy.* Zeph. 3:15.

2. *to clear, empty;* e. g. a house, Gen. 24:31. Lev. 14:36. a way, Is. 40:3. 57:14.

Hiph. הִפְנָה, fut. apoc. יֵפֶן.

1. trans. *to turn, incline,* e. g. the back. Jer. 48:39. 1 Sam. 10:9.

2. intrans. *to turn one's self, terga vertere.* Jer. 46:5, 21. 49:24. Construed with אֶל, Jer. 47:3.

Hoph. 1. *to be turned, to look,* (to a place.) Ezek. 9:2.

2. *to turn one's self,* i. q. Hiph. no. 2. Jer. 49:8.

פִּנָּה f. plur. וֹת, once ־ים (Zech. 14:10.) dec. X.

1. *a corner.* Prov. 7:8.—רֹאשׁ פִּנָּה Ps. 118:22. and אֶבֶן פִּנָּה Job 38:6. *the corner stone.*

2. *a battlement in a wall, pinna.* 2 Chr. 26:15. Zeph. 1:16.

3. figuratively *the head* or *leader of a people,* (comp. Ps. 118:22. Is. 28:16.) Is. 19:13. Zech. 10:4. 1 Sam. 14:38. Judg. 20:2. For similar metaphorical expressions, see under פִּנַּת יָתֵד.

פְּנוּאֵל Gen. 32:32. Judg. 8:8. and פְּנִיאֵל Gen. 32:31. (*the face of God,* פְּנוּ and פְּנִי being probably the obsolete singular of פָּנִים, comp. מְתוּ, plur. מְתִים.)

proper name of a place beyond Jordan. For the origin of the name, see Gen. xxxii.

פָּנִים masc. plur. const. פְּנֵי.

1. *a face, countenance.*—Also to express the plur. *faces*, Ezek. 1:6 אַרְבָּעָה פָנִים *four faces.*—פָּנִים אֶל פָּנִים *face to face*, Gen. 32:31. also פָּנִים בְּפָנִים, Deut. 5:4.—לֶחֶם הַפָּנִים *the shew-bread*, and שֻׁלְחַן הַפָּנִים *the table of shew-bread*, Num. 4:7. The following phrases are worthy of notice; (1.) שׂוּם פָּנִים לְ *to direct one's face to* a thing, *to have* it *before him, to purpose.* Jer. 42:15, 17. 44:12. 2 K. 12:18. Dan. 11:17. So with נָתַן, 2 Chr. 20:3. Dan. 9:3. Also without a verb, 2 Chr. 32:2 וּפָנָיו לַמִּלְחָמָה *and (that) his purpose was to fight.* (Comp. הֵכִין פָּנִים אֶל Ezek. 4:3. and Luke 9:53.) (2.) שׂוּם פָּנִים אֶל *to direct one's face* or *look to* a place. Ezek. 6:2. So with עַל, 1 K. 2:15. (3.) שׂוּם פָּנִים בְּ *to direct one's anger against* a person. Lev. 20:5. Sometimes with the addition לְרָעָה וְלֹא לְטוֹבָה, Jer. 21:10. comp. לְרָעָה Jer. 44:11. (Comp. שׂוּם עַיִן עַל under the word עַיִן no. 1. (5.)—Hence (4.) נָתַן פָּנִים בְּ *to set* or *execute one's anger against* a person. Lev. 20:3, 6. 26:17. Ezek. 14:8. 15:17. Hence without a verb, Ps. 34:17 פְּנֵי יְהוָה בְּעֹשֵׂי רָע *the face*, i. e. the anger, *of Jehovah is against evil-doers.* Antith. verse 16.

2. *appearance, looks.* 1 Sam. 1:18 *and her (sorrowful) looks continued no longer.* So Job 9:27. Metaphorically *a state, condition*, Prov. 27:23.

3. *surface, facies, superficies;* e. g. of the earth, Gen. 2:6. Is. 14:21. of the water, Job 38:30. See אֶל פְּנֵי, עַל פְּנֵי.

4. *the front* or *forepart.* In an army, *the front* or *van*, (in Greek πρόσωπον,) Joel 2:20. Hence as an adv. פָּנִים *before*, (antith. אָחוֹר,) Ezek. 2:10.—לְפָנִים *forwards*, Jer. 7:24. and spoken of time, *in ancient times, formerly*, Deut. 2:10, 12. Josh. 11:10. 14:15.—מִלְּפָנִים *from ancient times*, Is. 41:26.

5. i. q. פֶּה *a mouth*, and hence *the edge*, spoken of iron. Ecc. 10:10.

6. *a person, personal presence*, πρόσωπον. Spoken of Jehovah, Ex. 33:14 פָּנַי יֵלֵכוּ *my presence shall go with you*, i. e. I myself, or I in person will go with you. 2 Sam. 17:11. Lam. 4:16 *the presence of Jehovah scatters them.* Ps. 21:10. (So in the phrases הִכִּיר פָּנִים, נָשָׂא.) Hence it serves for a periphrasis of the pronoun, Prov. 7:13. Ps. 80:17. particularly in a reflexive sense, Ezek. 6:9.

In the significations which follow, it is combined with prepositions, and often loses its primary meaning.

7. לִפְנֵי, with suff. לְפָנַי, לְפָנֶיךָ, etc. liter. *before the face of* a person; hence (1.) *before*, (in space.) לִפְנֵי יְהוָה *before Jehovah*, i. e. before the tent of the congregation, Lev. 9:5. Ex. 34:34. metaphorically *pleasing to Jehovah*, Ps. 19:15. Hence (2.) *east of.* Josh. 8:14. Gen. 23:17. Comp. קֶדֶם. (3.) *before*, (in time.) Am. 1:1. Before an infin. *before that*, Gen. 13:10. (4.) *against.* 1 Chr. 14:8. (5.) i. q. בְּיַד *in* or *into the power of* any one. Josh. 10:12. 1 K. 8:46. Comp. Gen. 24:51 *behold, Rebekah is before thee*, i. e. is committed to thee. 34:10. 2 Chr. 14:6. Ezek. 23:24. Is. 8:4. (6.) *for;* e. g. נָתַן לִפְנֵי *to count for, to regard as*, 1 Sam 1:16. (7.) i. q. בְּעֵינֵי *in the judgment* or *opinion of* any one. Gen. 10:9. Prov. 14:12. Gen. 6:13. בָּא לְפָנַי *is come before me*, i. e. is resolved upon by me.—לִפְנָי 1 K. 6:17, is regarded as an adj. from לִפְנֵי, with the Aramean termination of adjectives, *anterius.*

8. מִפְּנֵי liter. *from the face of* a person, *a facie;* hence (1.) *from, away from.* Num. 20:6. 1 Sam. 25:10. (2.) *before*, (in space.) Ex. 14:19. (3.) *on account of.* Deut. 28:20. Is. 10:27. 17:9. 57:1. Jer. 9:6.—מִפְּנֵי אֲשֶׁר conj. *because*, Ex. 19:18. (4.) *towards, versus.* Jer. 1:13.

9. מִלִּפְנֵי (1.) *away from.* Ex. 35:20. Lev. 9:24. Num. 17:11. (2.) *before, on account of;* e. g. *to fear before* a person, 1 Sam. 18:12. *to cry on account of*, 1 Sam. 8:18.

10. עַל פְּנֵי *on the surface of;* hence

(1.) *upon, over*. Gen. 1:2. 11:8. Lev. 16:14. (2.) *in, near*; e.g. Gen. 1:20 עַל־פְּנֵי הָרָקִיעַ *in the firmament*. Gen. 23:3. (3.) *before*, (in time and space,) 2 Chr. 3:17. Gen. 11:28. Also *in preference to*, Deut. 21:16. (4.) *east of*. Gen. 25:18. Josh. 15:8. (5.) *toward, versus*. Gen. 18:16. (6.) *with, together with*. Ex. 20:3. Num. 3:4.

11. אֶל־פְּנֵי (1.) *before*, i. q. לִפְנֵי. Lev. 9:5. (2.) *on the surface of*; e.g. אֶל־פְּנֵי הַשָּׂדֶה *into the field*, Lev. 14:53. (3.) אֶל־פָּנָיו Deut. 7:10. prob. *at the moment, on the spot*. Vulg. *statim*. Antith. לֹא יְאַחֵר.

12. אֵת־פְּנֵי *before*. Gen. 19:13. Hence מֵאֵת פְּנֵי *from before*, Gen. 27:30. Ps. 42:3. אֵרָאֶה פְּנֵי אֱלֹהִים for א׳ אֶת־פְּנֵי אֱלֹהִים *I shall appear before God*; comp. Ex. 34:24. Deut. 16:16.

פְּנִים (1 K. 6:29.) and פְּנִימָה adv. *within, inwardly*. (The etymology is obscure.) 1 K. 6:18. 2 K. 7:11. Ps. 45:14. *the king's daughter is all glorious* פְּנִימָה *within*, i.e. in the palace, redundant like ἐν μεγάροισι in Hom. Also *in*, Lat. *introrsum*, 2 Chr. 29:18. —לִפְנִימָה *inwardly*, 1 K. 6:30. *introrsum*, Ezek. 41:3.—לִפְנִימָה לְ *within, inward*, Ezek. 40:16. מִפְּנִימָה *from within*, 1 K. 6:19, 21. 2 Chr. 3:4.

פְּנִימִי fem. ־ִית, denom. adj. from פְּנִים, *inner*. Antith. חִיצוֹן. 1 K. 6:27. 7:3, 12.

פְּנִינִים masc. plur. Prov. 3:15 Keri. 8:11. 20:15. 31:10. Job 28:18. (In Prov. 3:15 Keth. פְּנִיִּים) a costly substance, prob. *corals*; comp. Lam. 4:7. and see the article אָדֹם. Others: *red gems*, (*sardii, pyropi*,) but the constant use of the plural contradicts this idea. Neither does the name occur among precious stones, Ex. 39:10 ff. According to Bochart (Hieroz. II. Lib. v. cap. 6. 7.) *pearls*, which leads him to render אָדַם (Lam. 4:7.) *to be white, shining*, but without sufficient evidence.

פָּנַק Pi. *to bring up delicately, to spoil by tenderness*. Once Prov. 29:21. (In Aram. and Arab. *idem*.)

פַּס dec. VIII. h. found only in the phrase כְּתֹנֶת פַּסִּים Gen. 37:3, 23. 2 Sam. 13:18, 19. according to Josephus (Antiq. Jud. VII. 8. § 1.) an under garment, with sleeves, which hung down to the heels and was worn by persons of rank over the common tunic; hence the addition קְטַלִּים in 2 Sam. 13:18. The Sept. in Gen. χιτὼν ποικίλος. The Syr. a *flounced garment*. Jonath. *paragoda*, a kind of *tunica prætexta*. Symm. in Gen. Sept. in Sam. χειριδωτός. Several derivations are possible. The most plausible is that from the Chaldee, *tunica talaris et manicata, a tunic reaching down to the hands and feet*. Comp. Hartmann's Hebräerin, Th. 3. p. 280. Concerning this double tunic, See Schroeder, De Vestibus Mulierum, p. 237.

פַּס m. Chald. joined with יְדָא, *the palm of the hand*. Dan. 5:5, 24. Syr. ܦܣܐ *the palm* of the hand or *sole* of the foot, according as *hand* or *foot* is to be supplied.

פָּסַג Pi. פַּסֵּג in Chald. *to divide, distribute*. Ps. 48:14 פַּסְּגוּ אַרְמְנוֹתֶיהָ *divide her palaces*, i.e. walk about them, or consider them separately. Perhaps the word signified in Hebrew, *to distinguish, attend to, consider*, (like בִּין.) This would suit the context better.

פִּסְגָּה proper name of a mountain peak, in the territory of Moab, the southern limit of the kingdom of Sihon. Num. 21:20. 23:14. Deut. 3:27. 34:1. Josh. 12:3. (Chald. פִּסְגָּא, *a piece, part*.)

פִּסָּה f. dec. X. prob. *an abundance*, found only Ps. 72:16 יְהִי פִסַּת בַּר בָּאָרֶץ *let there be an abundance of corn in the land*. Root prob. פסס=فَسَّ *diffudit*; comp. Chald. פְּשָׂה *to spread itself out, to be fruitful*, and the Heb. פָּשָׂה.

I. פָּסַח liter. *to pass over*. Hence תִּפְסַח (*passage*) *Thapsacus*, proper name of a city, situated at a celebrated passage over the river Euphrates. Particularly *to pass by and spare, to spare*, construed with עַל, Ex. 12:13, 23, 27. Is. 31:5. (Comp. עָבַר עַל.)

II. פָּסַח *to limp, halt, be lame.* (Arab. فسخ *to be dislocated.*) 1 K. 18:21 *how long halt ye between two opinions;* i. e. how long waver ye between two opinions? The Arabians likewise say *claudicare* (in religione).

Pi. *idem.* 1 K. 18:26, (where it is spoken in derision of the fruitless dance of the priests of Baal.)

Niph. *to become lame.* 2 Sam. 4:4.

פֶּסַח m. verbal from פָּסַח no. I. dec. VI. d.

1. *the paschal lamb,* offered according to Ex. 12:27. in commemoration of the *sparing* of the Israelitish first-born in Egypt. Ex. 12:21.—אָכַל הַפֶּסַח *to eat the paschal lamb,* 2 Chr. 30:18. Plur. פְּסָחִים 2 Chr. 30:17.

2. *the feast of the passover.* Num. 9:4 ff. Josh. 5:11. This strictly denoted only the paschal meal on the evening of the 14th of Nisan; the 15th and the succeeding days were called *the feast of unleavened bread.* Lev. 23:5. The Greek word *πάσχα, pascha,* is derived from the Aramean form פַּסְחָא.

פִּסֵּחַ m. verbal from פָּסַח no. II. dec. VII. a. Lev. 21:18. 2 Sam. 9:13.

פָּסִיל or פְּסִיל, verbal from פָּסַל, found only in the plur. פְּסִלִים.

1. *images, idols.* Deut. 7:25. Jer. 8:19. 51:52.

2. perhaps *quarries,* like the Syr. ܦܣܝܠܐ. Judg. 3:19, 26.

פָּסַל, fut. יִפְסֹל, *to cut* or *hew out,* of stone. Ex. 34:1, 4. Deut. 10:3. also Hab. 2:18. (Syr. *idem.*)

פֶּסֶל m. with suff. פִּסְלִי, verbal from פָּסַל, dec. VI. h. *a graven image, an idol.* Ex. 20:4. Judg. 17:3, 4. In the plural always פְּסִילִים. See פָּסִיל.

פְּסַנְתֵּרִין Chald. Dan. 3:7. and פְּסַנְטֵרִין Dan. 3:5, 10, 15. the Greek *ψαλτὴς,* *a psaltery,* a stringed instrument like the harp, by a commutation of ל and נ. See ל.

פָּסַס *to cease, fail, disappear,* kindred with אָפֵס. Once Ps. 12:2. Comp. the letter א.

פָּעָה *to cry,* as a woman in child-birth. Once Is. 42:14. (Syr. and Chald. *to cry, bleat,* spoken of a flock.)

פָּעִי see פָּעוּ.

פְּעוֹר m. name of a mountain in the territory of Moab. Num. 23:28. Hence בַּעַל פְּעוֹר Num. 25:3, 5. and simply פְּעוֹר Num. 23:18. 31:16. Josh. 22:17. a Moabitish idol, in honour of which the young women of Moab prostituted themselves. Comp. also בֵּית פְּעוֹר.

פָּעַל, fut. יִפְעַל, i. q. עָשָׂה, but used only in poetry.

1. *to make, do, prepare.* Ex. 15:17. Deut. 32:27. Ps. 7:14.

2. used particularly in reference to moral actions; as פֹּעֵל צֶדֶק *doing righteousness,* Ps. 15:2. פֹּעֲלֵי אָוֶן *evil-doers,* Ps. 5:6. Construed with לְ, *to do* or *shew* a person, either good, Job 22:17. Ps. 31:20. or evil, Job 7:20. The latter is also expressed by בְּ, Job 35:6.

Deriv. out of course מִפְעָל.

פֹּעַל, with suff. פָּעֳלוֹ, פָּעָלְךָ (poolcha,) more rarely פָּעֳלוֹ (Is. 1:31. Jer. 22:13.) plur. פְּעָלִים, verbal from פָּעַל, dec. VI. n. i. q. מַעֲשֶׂה, but seldom used except in poetry.

1. *an action, deed,* (of God.) Ps. 64:10. Spoken particularly of God's judgments on the wicked, Is. 5:12. Hab. 3:2. (comp. מַעֲשֶׂה Is. 5:19. 10:12.)—רַב פְּעָלִים *great in mighty acts,* 2 Sam. 23:20.

2. *a work, a thing made.* Is. 1:31.—פֹּעַל יָדַי *the work of my hands,* i. e. men, Is. 45:11.

3. *an action,* in a moral sense. Ps. 28:4. Prov. 24:12, 29. Sometimes by way of eminence, *an evil action,* Job 36:9. (comp. עֲלִילָה.)

4. *a reward of labour,* comp. פְּעֻלָּה. Job 7:2. Jer. 22:13.

5. *an acquisition.* Prov. 21:6.

פְּעֻלָּה f. verbal from פָּעַל. dec. X.

1. *a work, action.* Prov. 11:18.

2. *a reward, wages.* Lev. 19:13. Ps. 109:20.

פָּעַם 1. *to strike, smite.* Deriv. פַּעַם *an anvil,* פַּעֲמוֹן *a bell.*

2. *to drive* or *urge on,* spoken of the spirit of God. Judg. 13:25.

Niph. *to be pushed* or *driven about, to be disquieted,* Gen. 41:8. Dan. 2:3. Ps. 77:5 נִפְעַמְתִּי *I am disquieted.*

Hithpa. i. q. Niph. Dan. 2:1.

פַּעַם, plur. פְּעָמִים, fem. (also masc. in signif. no. 3. Judg. 16:28.) verbal from פָּעַם, dec. VI. c.

1. *a foot.* Ps. 17:5. 57:7. Plur. פַּעֲמוֹת *feet* (of the ark of the covenant), Ex. 25:12.

2. *a footstep.* Ps. 119:133. 140:5. Metaphorically Judg. 5:28 *the steps of his chariots.*

3. *a time* or *repetition* of a thing, *vicis una,* liter. *a step* or *blow.*—פַּעַם אַחַת *once,* Josh. 6:3, 11, 14. *at once,* Is. 66:8. Dual פַּעֲמַיִם *twice,* Gen. 27:36. שָׁלֹשׁ פְּעָמִים *three times,* כַּמֶּה פְעָמִים *how many times?* 1 K. 22:16. פַּעַם וּשְׁתַּיִם *once and again, semel et iterum,* Neh. 13:20. הַפַּעַם *this time,* Ex. 9:27. 10:17. *now,* Gen. 29:35. 46:30. כְּפַעַם בְּפַעַם *this time as the other, as at other times,* Num. 24:1. Judg. 16:20. 1 Sam. 20:25. פַּעַם ... פַּעַם *sometimes ... sometimes,* Prov. 7:12.

4. *an anvil,* see the root signif. no. 1. Is. 41:7.

פַּעֲמוֹן m. verbal from פָּעַם *to strike,* dec. I. *a bell.* Ex. 28:33. 39:25, 26.

פָּעַר joined with פֶּה and פֶּה (Job 16:10.) *to open wide the mouth,* as an expression of longing desire, Job 29:23. Ps. 119:131. or of ravenous voracity, e. g. spoken of wild beasts, Job 16:10. of hades, Is. 5:14. (Syr. and Arab. *idem.*)

פָּצָה, fut. יִפְצֶה. 1. *to open* (the mouth). Ezek. 2:8. Is. 10:14. Spoken e. g. of wild animals, Ps. 22:14. of the earth, Gen. 4:11. of men, as an expression of derision, construed with עַל, Lam. 2:16. 3:46. or to utter foolish or rash speeches, Job 35:16. Judg. 11:35, 36. Ps. 66:13, 14.

2. *to tear away, save, deliver.* Ps. 144:7, 10, 11. (So in Syr. Chald. and Arab. فصى conj. II. IV.)

פָּצַח 1. *to break in pieces,* like the Arab. فضخ. See Pi.

2. *to break out* into rejoicing, in the phrase פָּצַח רִנָּה. Is. 14:7. 44:23. 49:13. Also, as in Ps. 98:4. פִּצְחוּ רַנְּנוּ *break out, rejoice,* i. e. break out into rejoicing. Is. 52:9.

Pi. *to break in pieces,* (bones.) Mic. 3:3.

פְּצִירָה f. *bluntness, obtuseness, dullness,* (in cutting instruments.) (Arab. فطار *a blunt notched sword.*) 1 Sam. 13:21.

פָּצַל found only in Pi. *to pill.* Gen. 30:37, 38. (Comp. بصل *to pill;* whence בָּצָל *an onion.*)

פְּצָלוֹת fem. plur. verbal from פָּצַל, *places pilled.* Gen. 30:37

פָּצַם found only in Pi. *to break, cleave,* (the earth.) Ps. 60:4. (Arab. *idem.*)

פָּצַע *to wound, mutilate.* Cant. 5:7. Deut. 23:2 פְּצוּעַ דַּכָּה *mutilated by bruising,* i. e. an eunuch made by bruising the testicles. (In Arab. *to press, mash.*)

פֶּצַע m. with suff. פִּצְעִי, verbal from פָּצַע, dec. VI. i. *a wound, bruise, contusion.* Ex. 21:25. Is. 1:6.

פָּצַר or **פָּצַר**, fut. יִפְצַר. joined with בְּ of the person, *to press* or *urge* any one; with entreaties, Gen. 19:3. 33:11. with violence, Gen. 19:9. It is synonymous with פָּרַץ בְּ q. v.

Hiph. *to be wilful, obstinate,* (perhaps liter. *to let one's self be urged, to be deaf to the representations of others.*) 1 Sam. 15:23 הַפְצַר (the infin. used substantively), *stubbornness, wilfulness,* parallel with מְרִי. According to Schultens (Opp. min. p. 168.) the primary signification is *obtundere;* hence *obtundere precibus*, and Hiph. *obtundere animum, obtusum esse, pertinaciter agere.*

פָּקַד fut. יִפְקֹד. *to look on* or *after* a thing. 2 K. 9:34. Particularly with a concern for it, *prospicere* alicui rei, Jer. 23:2. Spoken frequently of Jehovah, Ex. 3:16. 4:31. 1 Sam. 2:21. Ps. 106:4.

2. *to visit.* Construed with בְּ, *to visit with* a present, (comp. בְּ no. 2.) Judg. 15:1. 1 Sam. 17:18 אֶת אַחֶיךָ תִּפְקֹד לְשָׁלוֹם *thou shalt visit thy brethren to inquire for their health.* (Comp. שָׁאַל לְשָׁלוֹם לְ)

3. *to examine, prove.* Ps. 17:3.

4. *to visit, punish, animadvertere in* aliquem. Job 31:14. 35:15. Is. 26:14. The crime punished is put in the accus. 1 Sam. 15:2. Ps. 89:33. The person punished is generally preceded by עַל, Jer. 9:24. 44:13. also by אֶל, Jer. 46:25. and sometimes put in the accus. Ps. 59:6. This verb is most frequently construed with an accus. of the crime, and with עַל of the person, as Ex. 20:5 פֹּקֵד עֲוֹן אָבוֹת עַל בָּנִים *visiting the iniquity of the fathers upon the children.* 32:34. 34:7. Num. 14:18. Is. 13:11. Once with בְּ of the person, Jer. 9:8.

5. *to number, review, muster,* (a people, an army.) Num. 1:44 ff. 3:39 ff. 1 K. 20:15. Part. pass. פְּקוּדִים *the numbered* or *enrolled, qui in censum veniebant,* Num. 1:21 ff. 2:4 ff. Ex. 30:14. See Hothpa. and deriv. מִפְקָד.

6. *to miss in reviewing.* 1 Sam. 20:6. 25:15. Is. 34:16. See Niph.

7. causat. *to give the oversight, to place* a person *over* any thing; construed with עַל, Num. 4:27. 27:16. with אֵת (אֶת *penes,*) Gen. 40:4. and without cases, Num. 3:10. Deut. 20:9. Metaphorically Jer. 15:3. Part. pass. פְּקֻדִים *overseers, officers,* Num. 31:48. 2 K. 11:15. (Comp. Niph. Hiph. and פָּקִיד.)

8. after the Chaldaic, *to give commission, to commission, to command,* construed with עַל of the person. 2 Chr. 36:23. Ezra 1:2. Job 36:23 מִי פָקַד עָלָיו דַּרְכּוֹ *who hath prescribed to him his way?* 34:13 *who has committed to him the earth?* i. e. set him over it. Deriv. פִּקּוּד *a command.*

9. *to deposit, lay up.* 2 K. 5:24. See פִּקָּדוֹן *a deposit.*

Niph. 1. pass. of Kal no. 4. Is. 24:22.

2. pass. of no. 6. Num. 31:49.

3. pass. of no. 7. *præfici.* Neh. 7:1.

Pi. *to muster,* i. q. Kal no. 5. Once Is. 13:4.

Pu. 1. *to be numbered.* Ex. 38:21.

2. *to be missed.* Is. 38:10 *I am deprived of the rest of my years, desideror reliquos annos meos.*

Hiph. 1. i. q. Kal no. 7. *to appoint.* 2 K. 25:23. Construed with עַל *over* any thing, Gen. 39:5. 41:34. with לְ, 1 K. 11:28. Metaphorically Lev. 26:16.

2. i. q. Kal no. 9. *to lay down.* Jer. 36:20. Is. 10:28. Hence *to commit to* a person; construed with עַל יְדֵי, 2 Chr. 12:10. with בְּיַד, Ps. 31:6. with אֵת (אֶת) *penes,* (like *deponere apud* aliquem,) Jer. 40:7. 41:10.

Hoph. הָפְקַד, part. מֻפְקָדִים.

1. *to be punished.* Jer. 6:6. pass. of Kal no. 4.

2. *to be appointed* or *set over* a thing. 2 Chr. 34:10, 12.

3. *to be deposited with* a person, construed with אֵת (אֶת.) Lev. 5:23. [6:4.]

Hithpa. *to be numbered, reviewed.* Judg. 20:15, 17. 21:9.

Hothpa. plur. הָתְפָּקְדוּ, *idem.* Num. 1:47. 2:33. 26:62. 1 K. 20:27.

פְּקֻדָּה f. verbal from פָּקַד, dec. X.

1. *care, providence.* Job 10:12.

2. *punishment.* Is. 10:3. Plur. Ezek. 9:1.

3. *a counting, reckoning.* 1 Chr. 23:11.

4. *an office, business, service,* i. q. מִשְׁמֶרֶת, מִשְׁמָר. Num. 4:16. Ps. 109:8.

5. as a concrete, *an officer,* and collect. *officers.* 2 Chr. 24:11. Is. 60:17. Parall. נֹגְשִׂים. Comp. Num. 3:32.

6. *a watch;* also *persons keeping watch.* Comp. מִשְׁמֶרֶת, מִשְׁמָר. 2 K. 11:18.

2 Chr. 23:18. Hence בֵּית הַפְּקֻדּוֹת *a house of custody, a prison*, Jer. 52:11.

7. *substance, goods;* derived from signif. no. 4. (Comp. מְלָאכָה, מַעֲשֶׂה, פֹּעַל.) Is. 15:4.

פִּקָּדוֹן m. verbal from פָּקַד, *what is laid up, a deposit*. Gen. 41:36. Lev. 5:21, 23.

פְּקִדֻת f. denom. from פָּקִיד *an office, employment*. Jer. 37:13.

פְּקוֹד m. verbal from פָּקַד.

1. *punishment*, as an allegorical name of Babylon. Jer. 50:21.

2. *oversight*, and as a concrete, i.q. פָּקִיד. Ezek. 23:23.

פִּקּוּדִים masc. plur. verbal from פָּקַד, *commands, precepts*. Ps. 103:18. 111:7.

פָּקִיד m. verbal from פָּקַד, dec. III. a. *an overseer, officer*. Gen. 41:34. Neh. 11:9, 22. Used of a military officer, 2 K. 25:19.

פָּקַח *to open;* (1.) with עֵינַיִם, *to open the eyes*. 2 K. 4:35. Job 27:19. Construed with עַל, *to open one's eyes* on a person, i.e. to be gracious to him, Zech. 12:4. Comp. under עַיִן no. 1. (5.) In a somewhat different sense, Job 14:3.—*To open the eyes of* a person, spoken of God; i.e. (a.) to give sight to a blind man, 2 K. 6:17. Ps. 146:8. Is. 42:7. or (b.) to let a person see what is usually concealed from mortal eyes, Gen. 21:19. (2.) with אָזְנַיִם, *to open the ears*. Is. 42:20.

Niph. *to be opened*, spoken of the eyes of the blind. Is. 35:5. Metaphorically as in Kal no. (1.) (b.) Gen. 3:5, 7.

פִּקֵּחַ m. verbal adj. from פָּקַח, dec. VII. a. *seeing, not blind*. Ex. 4:11. Metaphorically Ex. 23:8.

פֶּקַח m. (*an opening, deliverance,*) *Pekah*, the proper name of a king of Israel, contemporary with Isaiah. 2 K. 15:25 ff. Is. 7:1. 2 Chr. 28:6.

פְּקַחְיָה (*deliverance of Jehovah*) proper name of a king of Israel, the predecessor of the preceding. 2 K. 15:22 ff.

פְּקַח־קוֹחַ m. verbal from פָּקַח, *deliverance from prison*. Is. 61:1. Comp. פָּתַח Is. 14:17. It should be written as one word, comp. Is. 2:20. Jer. 46:20.

פְּקָעִים masc. plur. *wild cucumbers*, as an artificial ornament in architecture. 1 K. 6:18. 7:24.

פַּקֻּעֹת fem. plur. 2 K. 4:39. *wild cucumbers, cucumeres asinini*, oblong, and of a bitter taste, by the Hebrews esteemed poisonous. They break open under the gentlest pressure, and shoot out their seed; hence the root פקע in Syr. and Arab. *to crash, to burst*.

פַּר and פָּר m. (the latter form in pause and with the article, as הַפָּר, לַפָּר) plur. פָּרִים, dec. II. a. and c. *a bull, bullock, juvencus*. Hence the frequent addition פַּר בֶּן־בָּקָר, Ex. 29:1.—Ps. 69:32 שׁוֹר פָּר *a beef which is a bullock*. Comp. Judg. 6:25 פַּר הַשּׁוֹר *a bullock*. It is once used in Judg. 6:25, of a seven years' old bullock. See פָּרָה.

פֶּרֶא, once פֶּרֶה (Jer. 2:24.) of the common or epicene gender, (masc. Ps. 104:11. fem. Jer. 2:24.) dec. VI. a. *the wild ass, onager*, now chiefly found in Tartary under the name of *kulan*. Gen. 16:12. Ps. 104:11. Job 6:5. 11:12. 24:5. 39:5. It is synonymous with עָרוֹד. Arab. *idem;* in Chald. פְּרָא *to run*.

פָּרָא i.q. פָּרָה *to bear fruit*.

Hiph. הִפְרִיא intrans. *to be fruitful*. Once Hos. 13:15. Others make it a denom. from פֶּרֶא.

פֹּארֹת fem. plur. *boughs, branches, twigs*. See פֹּארָה.

פַּרְבָּר m. 1 Chr. 26:18. and פַּרְוָר dec. II. b. 2 K. 23:11. *a suburb*. (In Chald. *idem*.)

פָּרַד *to separate*. In Kal only Ezek. 1:11.

Niph. 1. *to separate one's self, to part*. 2 Sam. 1:23. Construed with מִן *from* a person, Judg. 4:11. with מֵעַל, Gen. 13:9 ff.

2. *to be divided* or *dispersed*. Neh. 4:13. [4:19.] Gen. 10:5, 32. (Comp. Gen. 25:23. and נָפַץ Gen. 9:19.)

3. Part. נִפְרָד *a singular person*. Prov. 18:1.

Pi. intrans. *to separate one's self, to go aside*. Hos. 4:14.

Pu. *to be scattered, dispersed*. Est. 3:8.

Hiph. 1. *to separate;* construed with an accus. Gen. 30:40. with בֵּין, (liter. *to make a separation between*,) Ruth 1:17. 2 K. 2:11.

2. *to scatter, disperse*. Deut. 32:8.

Hithpa. 1. *to be separated*. Job 41:9. [41:17.] Ps. 22:15.

2. *to be scattered*. Job 4:11.

פֶּרֶד m. with suff. פִּרְדּוֹ, dec. VI. h. *a mule*. 2 Sam. 18:9. 1 K. 1:33.

פְּרֻדוֹת fem. plur. *grains, seed*. Joel 1:17. (Syr. ܦܪܕܐ *granum*.)

פַּרְדֵּס m. Cant. 4:13. Ecc. 2:5. Neh. 2:8. *a garden of trees, a park for animals*, a word derived from the Persian, in which it denotes *the royal park*. Hence the Greek παράδεισος.

פָּרָה *to be fruitful, to bear fruit;* spoken (1.) of plants, Ps. 128:3. Is. 32:12 שֹׁרֶשׁ פֹּרֶה רֹאשׁ *a root bearing poison*. Is. 11:1. בֵּן פֹּרָת *a fruitful branch*, Gen. 49:22. (see בֵּן no. 8.) Metaphorically Is. 45:8. (2.) of animals and men, Ex. 1:7. 23:30.—פְּרוּ וּרְבוּ *be fruitful and multiply*, Gen. 1:22.

Hiph. fut. apoc. וַיֶּפֶר, *to make fruitful*. Gen. 17:6, 20. 41:52. 48:4.

Deriv. פְּרִי.

פָּרָה fem. of פַּר, dec. X. *a young cow, a heifer*. Num. 19:2 ff. Gen. 41:2 ff. Spoken of a milch or breeding cow, 1 Sam. 6:7 ff. Job 21:10; of one that bears the yoke, Hos. 4:16. Metaphorically פָּרוֹת הַבָּשָׁן *the cows of Bashan*, i. e. the wanton women of Samaria.

פָּרָה see **פֶּרֶא**.

פַּרְוַיִם 2 Chr. 3:6. name of a country which furnished gold. Bochart conjectures it without ground to be the same with אוֹפִיר.

פַּרְוָר see **פַּרְבָּר**.

פָּרוּר m. *a pot, kettle*. Num. 11:8. Judg. 6:19. In Arab. فار *to boil*.

פֵּרוֹת found only Is. 2:20 לַחְפֹּר־פֵּרוֹת, for which, however, we ought probably to read לַחֲפַרְפֵּרוֹת, according to Jerome, *moles*. Those who make two words of it collate the Arab. فار *a mouse*.

פָּרָז m. dec. IV. a. *a leader*. Hab. 3:14. In Arab. فرز *to separate, decide, appoint;* hence liter. i. q. שֹׁפֵט.

פְּרָזוֹן *idem*. Judg. 5:7. With suff. פִּרְזוֹנוֹ verse 11.

פְּרָזוֹת plur. fem. liter. *plains, flat open country*, in opposition to *walled cities in hilly country*. Ezek. 38:11. Est. 9:19 עָרֵי הַפְּרָזוֹת *the cities of the open country*, in opposition to the capital, verse 18. Zech. 2:8 [2:4] *absque muro habitabitur Jerusalem*. Hence

פְּרָזִי m. denom. from פְּרָזוֹת, *an inhabitant of the flat country*. Est. 9:19. Deut. 3:5. 1 Sam. 6:18.

פְּרִזִּי a gentile noun, *a Perizzite*, one of the Canaanitish tribes driven out by the Israelites, which according to Josh. 11:3. 17:15, 16. dwelt on the mountains. Gen. 13:7. 15:20. Ex. 3:8, 17. In Greek Φερεζαῖος. Lat. *Pherezæus*.

פַּרְזֶל m. Chald. i. q. Heb. בַּרְזֶל *iron*. Dan. 2:33 ff.

פָּרַח 1. *to sprout, blossom*. Num. 17:20, 23. [17:5, 8.] Cant. 6:11. Often used figuratively (1.) of a prosperous person or people, Ps. 92:8. Is. 27:6. (2.) Hos. 10:4 *therefore punishment shall spring up as a poison*.

2. *to break out*, spoken of sores or of the leprosy. Lev. 13:12 ff. 14:43. Ex. 9:9, 10.

3. prob. *to fly*, as in Chald. So in the difficult passage Ezek. 13:20. (For the connexion of the ideas *to blossom* and *to fly*, see נָצָה.)

Hiph. 1. *to make to flourish.* Ezek. 17:24.

2. as in Kal, *to flourish.* Ps. 92:14. Job 14:9.

פֶּרַח m. with suff. פִּרְחוֹ, verbal from פָּרַח, dec. VI. i. *a blossom.* Num. 17:23. As an artificial ornament, Ex. 25:33.

פִּרְחַח m. verbal from פָּרַח, *a brood,* used by way of reproach. Job 30:12.

פָּרַט found only Am. 6:5. prob. *to sing,* according to the Vulg.

פֶּרֶט m. *what is left behind* or *omitted,* in the vintage. Lev. 19:10. (Arab. فرط conj. II. IV. *to leave behind, to forget.*)

פְּרִי m. with suff. פִּרְיוֹ, פִּרְיְךָ, in pause פֶּרִי, verbal from פָּרָה, dec. VI. l.

1. *fruit,* either of trees or of the ground.—עֵץ פְּרִי *a fruit-tree.*—אֶרֶץ פְּרִי *a fruitful land,* Ps. 107:34. — Is. 4:2 פְּרִי הָאָרֶץ i. q. צֶמַח יְהוָה in the parallel clause, and referring to the Messiah.

2. פְּרִי בֶטֶן *the fruit of the body.* Gen. 30:2. Deut. 7:13. 28:4. So without בֶּטֶן, Lam. 2:20. Hence it denotes *posterity,* Ps. 21:11.

3. metaphorically *the consequences* (of an action). Often with the figure continued, Is. 3:10 *for they shall eat the fruit of their actions.* Prov. 1:31. Hos. 10:13. Jer. 17:10. Ps. 104:13 *through the fruit of thy works,* i. e. through thy power, *the earth is satisfied.* Prov. 31:16 פְּרִי כַפַּיִם *an acquisition of the hands.* Is. 10:12 פְּרִי גֹדֶל לְבַב *the fruit of arrogance,* i. e. what arises from arrogance.

פָּרִיץ m. const. פְּרִיץ (Is. 35:9.) plur. פָּרִיצִים, const. פָּרִיצֵי, *violent, ravenous.* Is. 35:9 פְּרִיץ חַיּוֹת *a ravenous beast.* Ps. 17:4 אָרְחוֹת פָּרִיץ *the ways of the violent.* Root פָּרַץ no. 4. and 7.

פֶּרֶךְ m. *rigour, tyranny, oppression.* Ex. 1:13, 14. (In Syr. and Arab. *to crush;* in Chald. also *to break in pieces.*)

פָּרֹכֶת f. *the curtain between the holy and the holy of holies,* in the tent of the congregation. Ex. 26:31 ff. Lev. 16:2 ff. Comp. perhaps the Arab. فرق *to separate.*

פָּרַם, fut. יִפְרֹם, *to tear* or *rend* (garments). Lev. 10:6. 13:45. 21:10.

פָּרַס *to break, divide.*—פָּרַס לֶחֶם לְ *to break one's bread* to a person, Is. 58:7. and without לֶחֶם, Jer. 16:7. Comp. פָּרַשׂ no. II.

Hiph. (denom. from פַּרְסָה *a split hoof, a cloven foot,*) *to have a split hoof, to part the hoof,* for the most part joined with פַּרְסָה. Lev. 11:3, 6, 7, 26. Deut. 14:7. Ps. 69:32.—In Lev. 11:4, it is said of the camel וּפַרְסָה אֵינֶנּוּ מַפְרִיס which we are necessitated to render, *but he divideth not the hoof entirely.*

פָּרַס *Persia, the Persians,* a proper name. 2 Chr. 36:20, 22. Ezra 4:5 ff. 6:14. Dan. 5:28. 6:12, 28.

פְּרַס Chald. *to divide.* Dan. 5:25—28. Part. pass. פְּרִיס verse 28.

פֶּרֶס found only Lev. 11:13. a species of eagle, which Bochart (Hieroz. II. p. 185.) supposes to be *the sea-eagle, ospray, ossifraga.*

פַּרְסָה f. plur. וֹת and once ־ים (Zech. 11:16.) verbal from פָּרַס, dec. XII. a.

1. *the hoof* (of a horse). Is. 5:28. Jer. 47:3.

2. *a split hoof, cloven foot.* Ex. 10:26. Zech. 11:16.

פַּרְסִי *a Persian.* Neh. 12:22.

פָּרְסִי Chald. emph. פָּרְסָיָא, *idem.* Dan. 6:29.

I. **פָּרַע** *to lead, command,* (in war.) Arab. فرع *summum tenuit.* Judg. 5:2 בִּפְרֹעַ פְּרָעוֹת בְּיִשְׂרָאֵל *that the leaders led* (*courageously*) *in Israel.* Deriv. פְּרָעוֹת.

II. **פָּרַע** 1. *to make bare,* e. g. the head. Num. 5:18. Particularly by shearing, Lev. 10:6. 21:10. Part. פָּרוּעַ *made bare, uncovered,* Lev. 13:45.

2. *to set at liberty, to make lawless,* e. g. a people. Ex. 32:25.

3. *to forsake, reject,* (a way, counsel.) Prov. 1:25. 4:15. 8:33. 13:18. 15:32.

4. *to remit punishment.* Ezek. 24:14.

Niph. pass. of Kal no. 2. Prov. 29:18.

Hiph. 1. causat. of Kal no. 2. *to cause to be lawless* or *unbridled.* 2 Chr. 28:19.

2. *to let rest* (from labour), construed with מִן. Ex. 5:4. (In Arab. فرغ conj. I. IV. *to be free from labour.*)

פֶּרַע m. *a lock* or *bush of hair.* Num. 6:5. Ezek. 44:20. Root פרע no. II.

פַּרְעֹה, in Greek Φαραώ, *Pharaoh,* the name of nearly all the kings of Egypt, which are mentioned in the Old Testament, strictly a mere title of royalty. Gen. XL. XLI. XLVII. Ex. I.—X. etc. The usual expression is, *Pharaoh king of Egypt,* without the mention of his particular name; e. g. 1 K. 3:1. 2 K. 17:7. 18:21. But sometimes this is added, e. g. *Nechoh,* 2 K. 23:29. *Hophra,* Jer. 44:30. The appellative signification of the word, according to Josephus, (Antiq. Jud. VIII. 6. 2.) and the Coptic, (see Jablonskii Opusc. ed. te Water, T. I. p. 374.) is *king.* The Hebrew might associate it with פְּרָעוֹת *principes.* See the following article.

פְּרָעוֹת masc. plur. verbal from פרע no. I. dec. XII. a. *nobles, princes.* Deut. 32:42. Judg. 5:2. It has the feminine termination, like אָבוֹת *fathers.*

פַּרְעֹשׁ m. *a flea.* 1 Sam. 24:15.

פִּרְעָתוֹן proper name of a city in the tribe of Ephraim. Judg. 12:15. In Greek Φαραθωνί. 1 Macc. 9:50. The gentile noun is פִּרְעָתֹנִי Judg. 12:13, 15.

פַּרְפַּר proper name of a small river, which rises in Lebanon, and unites with the Amana not far from Damascus, now *Fege* or *Alfaige.* 2 K. 5:12.

פָּרַץ, fut. יִפְרֹץ. 1. *to tear* or *break forth.* Gen. 38:29. Particularly *to break down* (a wall), Ecc. 3:3. 10:8. Neh. 1:3, 5. Construed with בְּ, 2 K. 14:13.—עִיר פְּרוּצָה *a city with walls torn down,* Prov. 25:28.

2. *to scatter,* (an army, the enemy.) 2 Sam. 5:20. Ps. 60:3.—1 Chr. 13:2 *let us scatter and send,* i. e. let us send every where.

3. intrans. *to spread itself* or *increase,* spoken of a people. Gen. 28:14. Ex. 1:12. Hos. 4:10 וְלֹא יִפְרֹצוּ *and they spread* or *increase not.* Spoken of one's substance and flocks, Job 1:10. Gen. 30:30. Also of the person, in reference to his substance, Gen. 30:43.

4. *to break in.* Mic. 2:13. Job 28:4 פָּרַץ נַחַל *they break* or *lead in a shaft,* in reference to mining. Job 16:14 יִפְרְצֵנִי *he breaks in upon me.* Construed with בְּ, *to break in* or *cause an overthrow among* a people, Ex. 19:22, 24. 2 Sam. 6:8. 1 Chr. 15:13. Also spoken of the overthrow itself, Ps. 106:29.

5. *to urge with entreaties,* construed with בְּ. 1 Sam. 28:23. 2 Sam. 13:25, 27.

6. *to overflow, to abound in* a thing, (derived from signif. no. 3.) construed with an accus. (like verbs of *plenty* generally.) Prov. 3:10.

7. *to act with violence,* (from signif. no. 4.) Hos. 4:2. See פָּרִיץ.

Niph. pass. of no. 3. 1 Sam. 3:1 אֵין נִפְרָץ *not spread abroad, rare.*

Pu. pass. of Kal no. 1. Neh. 1:3.

Hithpa. *to break away.* 1 Sam. 25:10.

פֶּרֶץ m. plur. ־ִים (Am. 4:3.) and ־וֹת (Ezek. 13:5.) verbal from פָּרַץ, dec. VI. h.

1. *a gap, breach,* in a wall. 1 K. 11:27. Am. 4:3. Job 30:14 *they come (upon me) as through a wide breach.* Vulg. *quasi rupto muro.*—עָמַד בַּפֶּרֶץ *to stand in the breach,* a figure taken from sieges, Ezek. 22:30. (comp. 13:5.) Ps. 106:23.

2. *a breaking out* (of water). 2 Sam. 5:20.

3. *a breaking in, an attack.* Job 16:14.

4. *an overthrow.* Judg. 21:15. Ps. 144:14. Hence פֶּרֶץ עֻזָּה (*overthrow of Uzzah*) the name of a place, 2 Sam. 6:8. 1 Chr. 13:11.

פָּרַק 1. *to break off,* construed with מֵעַל. Gen. 27:40. Ex. 32:2.

2. *to tear in pieces,* spoken of a wild animal. Ps. 7:3.

3. *to snatch away, to deliver*, i. q. הִצִּיל. Ps. 136:24. Lam. 5:8.

Pi. 1. *to rend* or *tear in pieces.* 1 K. 19:11.

2. *to tear off.* Zech. 11:16 פַּרְסֵיהֶן יְפָרֵק *he tears off their claws*, i. e. lets them alone.

Hithpa. 1. *to be broken in pieces.* Ezek. 19:12.

2. *to break off from one's self, sibi avellere,* Ex. 32:3, 24.

פְּרַק Chald. *to redeem, expiate.* Dan. 4:24. [4:27.]

פָּרָק, const. פְּרַק, Is. 65:4 Keth. i. q. Keri מְרַק *broth*, by a commutation of פ and מ. See the letter ב.

פֶּרֶק m. verbal from פָּרַק.

1. *violence, robbery.* Nah. 3:1.

2. *a cross-way.* Obad. 14.

פָּרַר see the kindred פּוּר.

I. פָּרַשׂ, fut. יִפְרֹשׂ, *to spread* or *stretch out*, e. g. a garment, Num. 4:6, 8. the hands, construed with אֶל, Ex. 9:29, 33. with עַל, Lam. 1:10. with לְ, Ps. 44:21. In a different sense Prov. 31:20 *she stretched out her hand to the needy*, i. e. she gives to them liberally. Metaphorically Prov. 13:16 *the fool spreadeth out folly, præ se fert stultitiam.*

Niph. *to be spread abroad* or *scattered.* Ezek. 17:21. See Pi. no. 2.

Pi. פֵּרֵשׂ 1. as in Kal, *to spread out* (the hands). Ps. 143:6. Is. 1:15. 65:2. Construed with בְּ, Lam. 1:17.

2. *to scatter.* Ps. 68:15. Zech. 2:10. Comp. Niph.

Deriv. מִפְרָשׂ.

II. פָּרַשׂ i. q. פָּרַס *to break, divide in pieces.* Mic. 3:3. Lam. 4:4.

פָּרַשׁ 1. liter. *to separate, distinguish.* (So in Chald. and Syr. whence פָּרוּשׁ, ܦܪܝܫܐ *a Pharisee.*)

2. *to decide, determine, explain.* (Comp. נָקַב no. 2.) Lev. 24:12.

Niph. *to be scattered.* Ezek. 34:12. Several MSS. and ancient editions read this word with *Sin*, which is to be preferred.

Pu. pass. *to be determined, explained, made clear.* Num. 15:34. Neh. 8:8 מְפֹרָשׁ *exactly* or *literally.* Comp. Ezra 4:18. and Gesenius' Gesch. der Hebr. Sprache, p. 45.

Hiph. *to wound, sting.* Prov. 23:32.

פְּרַשׁ Chald. *idem.* Part. pass. Pa. Ezra 4:18 מְפָרַשׁ *exactly* or *literally.* Syr. *fideliter.*

פָּרָשׁ m. (with the first Kamets impure,) once פָּרָשׁ (Ezek. 26:10.) plur. פָּרָשִׁים, dec. I.

1. *a horseman.* Gen. 50:9. Ex. 14:9, 17. (Arab. فَارِس.)

2. *a horse*, which is rode, (like *eques* for *equus*, cui quis inequitatur. See Bocharti Hieroz. T. I. p. 35. ed. Lips.) Is. 28:28. Hab. 1:8. Hence Is. 21:7, 9. 2 Sam. 1:6. בַּעֲלֵי הַפָּרָשִׁים *horsemen.*

פֶּרֶשׁ m. with suff. פִּרְשׁוֹ, dec. VI. h. *filth, dung.* Lev. 4:11. 8:17. Ex. 29:14. Mal. 2:3.

פָּרָשָׁה f. (with two Kamets pure) verbal from פָּרַשׁ, dec. X. *declaration, specification.* Est. 4:7. 10:2.

פַּרְשֶׁגֶן m. Heb. and Chald. *a copy.* Ezra 4:11, 23. 5:6. 7:11. (Also in the Targums.) Instead of it we find פַּתְשֶׁגֶן Est. 3:14. 4:8.

פַּרְשְׁדֹן or פַּרְשְׁדוֹנָה found only Judg. 3:22. according to the Chaldaic version, *dung*, (i. q. פֶּרֶשׁ,) hence וַיֵּצֵא הַפַּרְשְׁדֹנָה *that the dung came out from him.* On the contrary the Sept. Vatic. καὶ ἐξῆλθεν ('Αὼδ) τὴν προστάδα. So Kimchi. Could we refer וַיֵּצֵא to the sword, (comp. Zech. 13:7.) then it might be rendered, *and it (the sword) went through his bones.* Comp. Arab. فرشد *to spread out the feet.*

פַּרְשֵׁז a quadriliteral, i. q. פָּרַשׂ *to spread.* Once Job 26:9. The ז arises from the combination of פָּרַשׂ with פרז Arab. فرز *to separate, spread out;* comp. פְּרָזוֹן *a plain.*

פְּרָת *Euphrates,* a proper name, Gen. 2:14. 15:18. Deut. 1:7. This river, not Ephrata, is without doubt intended Jer. 13:4—7.

פֹּרָת f. Gen. 49:22. see פָּרָה.

פַּרְתְּמִים masc. plur. *princes, nobles;* among the Persians, Est. 1:3. 6:9. among the Jews, Dan. 1:3. A Persian word, comp. in Pehlvi, *pardom* (*the first,*) and in Parsee, *pardomim* (*the nobles.*) Kleuker's Zend-Avesta, Th. 2. p. 82. Th. 3. p. 162.

פָּשָׂה *to spread,* spoken of the leprosy. Lev. 13:5 ff. (Arab. فشا, Aram. פְּשָׂא *idem.*)

פָּשַׂע *to go,* construed with בְּ *against* a thing. Is. 27:4. (Aram. פְּסַע *idem.*) Deriv. out of course מִפְשָׂעָה.

פֶּשַׂע m. verbal from פָּשַׂע, *a step,* 1 Sam. 20:3.

פָּשַׂק *to spread asunder, to open widely,* e. g. the lips. Prov. 13:3.

Pi. *to spread asunder, to open widely,* e. g. the feet. Ezek. 16:25.

פַּשׁ m. *a multitude.* Job 35:15. See פַּשׁ no. II. As to the form it is derived from פּוּשׁ.

פָּשַׁח found only in Pi. *to tear in pieces, to lacerate.* Lam. 3:11. (So in Aram.)

פַּשְׁחוּר proper name of a priest and chief overseer of the temple in the time of Jeremiah. Jer. 20:3. 38:1. In the former passage there is an allusion to the signification of the name, prob. *prosperity round about;* (this quadriliteral being compounded of פּוּשׁ in Arab. *to be wide, spacious,* and סְחוֹר *round about.*) Antith. מָגוֹר מִסָּבִיב.

פָּשַׁט, fut. יִפְשֹׁט.

1. *to put off,* construed with an accus. of the garment, (like לָבַשׁ *to put on.*) Lev. 6:4. 16:23. Is. 32:11 פְּשֹׁטָה *put off* (thy garments).

2. *to pillage, plunder, fall on,* (in order to plunder,) e. g. a city, country; construed with בְּ, 2 Chr. 25:13. 28:18. with an accus. 1 Sam. 30:14. with אֶל, 1 Sam. 27:8. with עַל, Judg. 9:33.

3. *to spread one's self out,* spoken of a hostile army. 1 Chr. 14:9, 12. Trop. Nah. 3:16.

Pi. *to strip* or *plunder,* (the slain.) 1 Sam. 31:8. 2 Sam. 23:10. 1 Chr. 10:8.

Hiph. 1. *to cause to put off, to strip* a person. Construed (1.) with a double accus. of the person and thing. Num. 20:26, 28. Gen. 37:23. (2.) with an accus. of the thing *stripped off.* 1 Sam. 31:9. Job 22:6. And that with מֵעַל of the person, Job 19:9. Mic. 3:3. with מִמּוּל, Mic. 2:8. (3.) with an accus. of the person. Hos. 2:3. [2:5.]

2. *to flay* cattle. (Comp. Mic. 3:3. above.) Lev. 1:6. 2 Chr. 29:34. 35:11.

Hithpa. *to strip one's self, sibi exuere* aliquid. 1 Sam. 18:4.

פָּשַׁע 1. *to fall away, revolt, rebel;* construed with בְּ *from* or *against* any one, 2 K. 1:1. 3:5, 7. with מִתַּחַת, 2 K. 8:20, 22.

2. particularly *to rebel against* God, *to apostatize from* him, *to sin against* him. 1 K. 8:50. Is. 1:2. Jer. 2:29. Construed with עַל Hos. 8:1. Hence

3. *to sin, to transgress.* Prov. 28:21. Part. פֹּשְׁעִים *sinners, transgressors,* Is. 1:28. 46:8.

Niph. Prov. 18:19 אָח נִפְשָׁע *a brother offended.*

פֶּשַׁע m. with suff. פִּשְׁעִי, verbal from פָּשַׁע, dec. VI. i.

1. *revolt, sedition.* Prov. 28:2.

2. *sin, transgression, crime.* Gen. 31:36. 50:17. Job 33:9. 34:6, 37. Ps. 32:1. Perhaps stronger than חַטָּאת, comp. Job 34:37.

3. *punishment for sin.* Dan. 9:24.

4. *a sin-offering.* Mic. 6:7.

פְּשַׁר Chald. *to interpret, explain,* (dreams.) Infin. Dan. 5:16.

Pa. *idem.* Dan. 5:12.

פְּשַׁר m. emph. פִּשְׁרָא, Chald. *an explanation, interpretation.* Dan. 2:4 ff. 4:4 ff.

פֵּשֶׁר m. i. q. Chald. פְּשַׁר. Ecc. 8:1.

פִּשְׁתָּה Hos. 2:7, 11. plur. פִּשְׁתִּים.

1. *flax, linen.* Lev. 13:47. Jer. 13:1.

2. פִּשְׁתֵּי הָעֵץ *cotton.* Josh. 2:6. This is frequently cultivated at the present day in Palestine. Others make it i. q. עֲצֵי פִשְׁתִּים *the wood*, i. e. the stalks, *of flax.*

פִּשְׁתָּה f. 1. i. q. פִּשְׁתָּה. Ex. 9:31.

2. *a light, lamp*, from its *linen* or *cotton* wick. Is. 42:3. 43:17.

פַּת f. with suff. פִּתִּי, plur. פִּתִּים, verbal from פָּתַת, dec. VIII. f. *a piece, crumb, morsel*, (of bread.) Gen. 18:5. Judg. 19:5. Also without לֶחֶם, Job 31:17. Ps. 147:17.

פֹּת m. with suff. פָּתְהֵן.

1. *pudendum muliebre.* Is. 3:17. (Arab. فوت *interstitium.*)

2. plur. פֹּתוֹת *the hinge of a door*, or rather *the hole in which the hinge moves, cardo femina.* 1 K. 7:50.

פְּתָאִים plur. of פֶּתִי q. v.

פִּתְאֹם adv. (from פֶּתַע, with an adverbial termination ם, as in שִׁלְשֹׁם, and by a commutation of א and ע, see page 1.) *in a moment, suddenly.* Josh. 10:9. Job 22:10. Also בְּפִתְאֹם 2 Chr. 29:36. In combination with פֶּתַע, בְּפֶתַע פִּתְאֹם Num. 6:9. לְפֶתַע פִּתְאֹם Is. 29:5. and פִּתְאֹם לְפֶתַע Is. 30:13. Used as a substantive in the genitive, Prov. 3:25 פַּחַד פִּתְאֹם *sudden terror.*

פַּתְבַּג Heb. and Chald. Dan. 1:5, 8, 13, 15. 11:26. *costly food, delicacies*, from the royal table. Syr. ܦܛܒܓܐ *dainties, pastry-work.* Perhaps liter. *food of the gods*, from the Pers. بت (bot) *an idol*, (comp. Chald. פַּתְכַר *idolum*,) and باد also باج (bag) *food.*

פִּתְגָם Chald. emph. פִּתְגָמָא.

1. *a word.* Dan. 3:16.

2. *an order, edict.* Ezra 4:17.

3. *a letter, epistle*, λόγος. Ezra 5:7.

4. *a matter, thing.* Ezra 6:11. Dan. 4:14.

Note. This word has the same meaning in Syriac; but it is probably of Persian origin; comp. the Pers. *peigham* (*a word*,) in Pehlvi *pedam.*

פִּתְגָם in later Hebrew, *an edict, sentence.* Est. 1:20. Ecc. 8:11.

פָּתָה 1. *to be open, wide.* Prov. 20:19. פֹּתֶה שְׂפָתָיו *the babbler*, whose mouth is always *open.* See Hiph.

2. *to be open-hearted, susceptible of impressions;* hence *to be easily enticed* or *seduced.* (Arab. *to be young, open-hearted, ingenuous.*) Deut. 11:16 פֶּן־יִפְתֶּה לְבַבְכֶם *lest your heart be enticed.* Job 31:27. Part. פֹּתֶה *simple, easily seduced*, i. q. פֶּתִי Job 5:2. Fem. Hos. 7:11.

Niph. *to be persuaded*, in a good sense, Jer. 20:7. *to be enticed to* a thing, construed with עַל, Job 31:9.

Pi. 1. *to persuade.* Jer. 20:7. Particularly to something injurious, 1 K. 22:20 ff. to reveal a secret, Judg. 14:15. 16:5. 2 Sam. 3:25.

2. *to entice, seduce.* Ex. 22:15. Prov. 1:10. 16:29.

3. *to dissemble* in any way. Ps. 78:36. Prov. 24:28 וַהֲפִתִּיתָ בִּשְׂפָתֶיךָ *wouldest thou dissemble with lips?* i. e. thou shouldest not etc.

Pu. *to be persuaded*, Prov. 25:15. *to be enticed, allured*, Ezek. 14:9. Jer. 20:10.

Hiph. *to make wide, to enlarge.* Fut. apoc. יַפְתְּ, Gen. 9:27.

פִּתּוּחַ m. verbal from פִּתַּח Pi. no. 5. dec. I. *a graving, graven work.* 2 Chr. 2:13. Zech. 3:9. More frequently in the plur. פִּתּוּחִים Ex. 28:11, 21, 36. 39:6.

פְּתוֹר proper name of a place in Mesopotamia, on the Euphrates, the residence of Balaam. Num. 22:5. 23:7. Deut. 23:5.

פְּתוֹת i. q. פַּת *a piece.* Ezek. 13:19. Root פָּתַת.

פָּתַח 1. *to open;* e. g. the mouth, Ps. 39:10. the hand, i. e. *to be liberal*, construed with לְ of the person, Deut. 15:8, 11. the ear, i. e. *to instruct.* Is.

50:5. (comp. 48:8.)—Am. 8:5 נִפְתְּחָה בָּר *that we may open* (and sell) *the grain.*

2. *to draw* (the sword). Ps. 37:14. Ezek. 21:33.

3. *to open, disclose, utter, ore proferre.* Ps. 49:5 *I will utter my song on the harp.* Comp. פֶּתַח.

4. *to let loose, dismiss, set free,* (a prisoner.) Is. 14:17.

Niph. 1. *to be opened* or *open.* Ezek. 1:1.

2. *to be loosed.* Is. 5:27.

3. *to be let loose, to be set at liberty.* Job 12:14. Comp. Jer. 1:14.

Pi. 1. *to open,* as in Kal. Job 41:6. [41:14.]

2. *to loosen, to unbind;* e. g. fetters, Job 30:11. 38:31. 39:5. Ps. 116:16. a girdle, Ps. 30:12. Is. 20:2. Part. מְפַתֵּחַ *one who loosens his girdle,* i. e. returns from the battle, 1 K. 20:11. Construed also with an accus. of the person *unfettered,* Jer. 40:4. or *ungirded,* Is. 45:1.

3. intrans. *to open itself.* Cant. 7:13. Is. 48:8.

4. *to plough, furrow, terram aperire.* Is. 28:24.

5. *to engrave, sculpere;* e. g. on wood, 1 K. 7:36. on precious stones, Ex. 28:36. *To hew* or *cut* stones in any way, Zech. 3:9. (See פִּתּוּחִים.)

Pu. pass. of Pi. no. 5. Ex. 39:6.

Hithpa. *to loose from one's self.* Is. 52:2.

פְּתַח Chald. *to open.* Dan. 6:11. 7:10.

פֶּתַח m. with suff. פִּתְחִי, plur. פְּתָחִים, const. פִּתְחֵי, dec. VI. i.

1. *a door.*—בְּפֶתַח and as an accus. פֶּתַח *before* or *at the door,* Gen. 18:1, 10. 19:11. Job 31:34. So הַפֶּתְחָה Gen. 19:6.

2. *a gate.* Is. 3:26.—פֶּתַח שַׁעַר *at the entrance of the gate,* Josh. 20:4. Judg. 9:35. comp. Prov. 1:21. Metaphorically פִּתְחֵי פִיךָ *the doors of thy mouth,* Prov. 8:34.

פֵּתַח m. verbal from פָּתַח, *the opening* or *insight imparted by any thing.* Ps. 119:130. (In Syr. Aph. *to enlighten, to give insight.* In Arab. conj. X. *to explain.*)

פִּתְחוֹן m. const. פִּתְחוֹן, verbal from פָּתַח, dec. III. d. *an opening,* joined with פֶּה. Ezek. 16:63. 29:21.

פֶּתִי m. in pause פֶּתִי, plur. פְּתָיִים and פְּתָאִים, verbal from פָּתָה, dec. VI. l.

1. *simple, inexperienced,* liter. *open to every impression, easily seduced.* (See פָּתָה.) Prov. 7:7. 22:3. 27:12. Used particularly of credulity, Prov. 14:15. of innocency, Ps. 116:6.

2. as an abstract, *simplicity, folly.* Prov. 1:22.

פְּתַי m. Chald. with suff. פְּתָיֵהּ, *width, breadth.* Dan. 3:1. Ezra 6:3.

פְּתַיּוּת f. verbal from פָּתָה, *simplicity;* as a concrete, *simple.* Prov. 9:13.

פְּתִיגִיל found only Is. 3:24. *a girdle for females,* according to Symm. and Jerome, *a stomacher, strophium.* The composition of this word is doubtful. Perhaps from פְּתִי *wideness,* or פְּתַג in Chald. *linen,* and גִּיל, comp. גִּלָּא *pallium, stola.*

פְּתִיחוֹת fem. plur. *drawn swords.* Ps. 55:22. See פָּתַח no. 2.

פָּתִיל m. verbal from פָּתַל, dec. III. a. *a thread, string, cord.* Num. 19:15. Judg. 16:9. Used of the cord by which the Orientalist suspends his sealring, (see חוֹתָם,) Gen. 38:18, 25.

פָּתַל in Kal not used. (Arab. *to twist, to spin.*)

Niph. 1. *to wrestle, to struggle.* Gen. 30:8. Deriv. נַפְתּוּלִים.

2. *to be perverted, false, deceitful.* Prov. 8:8. Job 5:13.

Hithpa. *to shew one's self false.* Ps. 18:27. In the parallel passage 2 Sam. 22:27. is תִּתַּפָּל. which appears to be a corruption of תִּתְפַּתָּל,

Deriv. out of course פָּתִיל.

פְּתַלְתֹּל verbal from פָּתַל, *crooked, perverse, false.* Deut. 32:5.

פִּתֹם proper name of an Egyptian city, mentioned only Ex. 1:11. In Herod. II. 158. called Πάτουμος, by the Arabians in later times *Fijum, Fajum,* which is also applied to the province.

פֶּתֶן m. plur. פְּתָנִים, dec. VI. a. *an adder,* a species of poisonous serpent. Is. 11:8. Ps. 58:5. 91:13. (Arab. بتن according to Forskål *coluber bätän.*)

פֶּתַע m. *a moment.* Hence as an adv.

1. *in a moment, suddenly.* Prov. 6:15. 29:1. Comp. פִּתְאֹם.

2. *unintentionally, undesignedly.* Num. 35:22.

פָּתַר, fut. יִפְתֹּר, *to interpret, explain,* (dreams.) Gen. 40:8 ff. Chald. פְּשַׁר.

פִּתְרוֹן m. verbal from פָּתַר, dec. X. *an interpretation.* Gen. 40:5, 8, 12.

פַּתְרוֹס proper name of a country in Egypt. Is. 11:11. Jer. 44:1, 15. Ezek. 29:14. 30:14. Sept. Παθούρης, i. e. in Coptic, *the south land,* perhaps for *Thebais,* or *Upper Egypt.* Here was anciently a district called *Nomos Phaturites.* Plin. H. N. v. 9. The inhabitants of this country are called פַּתְרֻסִים, Gen. 10:14. See Jablonskii Opusc. ed. te Water, T. I. p. 198. and J. D. Michaëlis Spicileg. Geogr. Hebræorum exter. T. I. p. 271—274.

פַּתְשֶׁגֶן *a copy,* see פַּרְשֶׁגֶן.

פָּתַת *to break.* Lev. 2:6. Deriv. פַּת, פְּתוֹת.

צ

Tsade, the 18th letter of the alphabet, and as a numerical sign denoting 90.

To the Hebrew Tsade correspond two letters in Arabic, namely, ص *Tsad* or *Zad,* in which the sound of *s* prevails, and ض *Dad,* in which the sound of *d* is more distinctly heard; besides the Arabic ظ *Da,* which in pronunciation does not differ from the latter. This difference of pronunciation probably existed likewise in Hebrew, although it was not regarded in writing; hence the same root in Hebrew has different significations, according as the corresponding letter in Arabic is ص or ض or ظ.

This letter is interchanged (1.) with ט, particularly in Aramean. In Heb. comp. נָצַר and נָטַר *to watch, guard;* טָהֵר *to be pure* and צָהַר *to be clear;* טָבַע *to press in, to sink,* and צָבַע *to dip in, to colour.* (2.) by making the sound of *s* more audible, with שׂ, ס and ז, e. g. עָלַץ and עָלַס *to rejoice;* נָתַץ and נָתַס *to tear down;* שָׂחַק and צָחַק *to deride.* Comp. ז, p. 164. (3.) with ע, see above p. 429.

צֵאָה f. (with Tseri impure) dec. X. *dung, filth, excrement.* Ezek. 4:12. Deut. 23:14. Prob. for יְצָאָה, from יָצָא *efferri,* comp. מוֹצָא, צוֹא, צוֹאָה.

צֶאֱלִים m. Job 40:21, 22. *shady bushes,* prob. an Aramean form for צְלָלִים. So מָכַךְ Aram. מְאַךְ, מָסַס Aram. מְאַס, comp. also in Heb. מָאַס no. II. It is thus rendered by the Vulg. Syr. Kimchi and Aben Ezra.

צֹאן f. (as an epicene noun applied also in the feminine gender to male animals, Gen. 31:10. though it is sometimes construed as masc.) a collective noun denoting *small cattle,* i. e. sheep and goats, (the μῆλα of Homer,) particularly *sheep.* Gen. 27:9. Lev. 1:10. 22:21. The corresponding nomen unitatis, or noun expressing an individual, is שֶׂה, hence Ex. 21:37 [22:1.] *if a man steal a head of small cattle* (שֶׂה,) *then he shall restore four head of small cattle* (אַרְבַּע הַצֹּאן.) Ezek. 45:15. Sometimes goats are separately mentioned, and then צאן denotes *sheep,* 1 Sam. 25:2. (So in Arab.)

צַאֲנָן a proper name, Mic. 1:11. prob. i. q. צְנָן Josh. 15:37. a city in the tribe of Judah. As an appellative it would signify *the place of flocks.*

צֶאֱצָאִים masc. plur. const. צֶאֱצָאֵי, verbal from יָצָא, dec. I.

1. *productions* (of the earth). Is. 34:1. 42:5. Job 31:8.

2. metaphorically *children, offspring.* Is. 22:24. 65:23. 61:9. Job 5:25. 21:8. 27:14. More in full צֶאֱצָאֵי מֵעֶיךָ *the offspring of thy bowels,* Is. 48:19.

צָב m. dec. VIII. a.

1. a kind of chariot or litter. Plur. צַבִּים Is. 66:20. Sept. λαμπήνη. Num. 7:3 עֶגְלֹת־צָב. Sept. ἁμάξαι λαμπηνικαί. Vulg. *plaustra tecta,* comp. the Arab. ضَبَّ conj. II. *to cover.*

2. a species of lizard, (Arab. ضَبٌّ.) Lev. 11:29. Bocharti Hieroz. I. p. 1044—1063.

צָבָא 1. *to go forth* or *march out to war, to carry on war.* Num. 31:42. Is. 31:4. Construed with עַל *against* a person, Num. 31:7. Is. 29:7, 8. (Arab. صبا *idem.*)

2. *to go forth to the service of the temple,* a kind of militia sacra. Num. 4:23. 8:24. 1 Sam. 2:22.

Hiph. liter. *to lead out to war.* 2 K. 25:19. Jer. 52:25.

צָבָא m. plur. צְבָאוֹת, verbal from צָבָא, dec. IV. g.

1. *a host,* particularly *a military host, an army.*—שַׂר הַצָּבָא *the general of the host,* Gen. 21:22.—אַנְשֵׁי הַצָּבָא *the soldiers, warriors,* Num. 31:53.—יָצָא בַצָּבָא Deut. 24:5. לַצָּבָא Num. 31:27, 28. usually יָצָא צָבָא Num. 1:3ff. *to go to the host, to go forth to war.* Spoken also of the body of Levites who go forth to the service of the temple, Num. 4:23, 35, 39, 43.

2. צְבָא הַשָּׁמַיִם *the host of heaven,* denoting (1.) *the host of angels,* which surround the throne of Jehovah. 1 K. 22:19. 2 Chr. 18:18. Ps. 103:21. 148:2. Hence Josh. 5:14, 15 שַׂר צְבָא יְהוָה *the prince of God's host.* Comp. Luke 2:13. (2.) *the stars.* Jer. 33:22. Is. 40:26. for the most part as an object of idolatrous worship, Deut. 4:19. 17:3. 2 K. 17:16. 21:3, 5. Sometimes only the sun and moon (Deut. 17:3. Jer. 8:2.) and sometimes the stars also (Deut. 4:19. Dan. 8:10.) are separately mentioned. It appears then that this expression embraced every thing in heaven, both angels and heavenly bodies. Comp. Job 38:7. Dan. 4:32. Hence (3.) צְבָא הַמָּרוֹם *the powers on high,* Is. 24:21. in opposition to *the kings of the earth.* Comp. Is. 34:4. 45:12. Ps. 33:6.—In one passage Gen. 2:1, צָבָא is applied to the earth, *whatever is on the earth,* (i. q. מְלֹא,) by a zeugma, which is resolved Neh. 9:6. Hence אֱלֹהֵי צְבָאוֹת, and more frequently יְהוָה אֱלֹהֵי צְבָאוֹת, also barely יְהוָה צְבָאוֹת, and אֱלֹהִים צְבָאוֹת, (e. g. Ps. 80:8, 15.) *God of the heavenly hosts,* synonymous with אֱלֹהֵי הַשָּׁמַיִם *God of heaven,* in the later books. (See שָׁמַיִם, שְׁמַיָּא.) According to others, it denoted originally *the God of war,* (comp. Ps. 24:10. with ver. 8. 1 Sam. 17:45.) and was afterwards made to denote *the God of the powers of heaven.* This epithet of God does not occur in Genesis nor in the book of Judges.

3. *warfare, hard service, affliction.* Job 7:1. 10:17. 14:14. Is. 40:2. Dan. 10:1 וֶאֱמֶת הַדָּבָר וְצָבָא גָדוֹל *and the oracle is true and* (relates to) *great affliction.*

צְבָאִים and **צְבָאוֹת**, see צְבִי *a gazelle.*

צְבָא Chald. fut. יִצְבֵּא, *to will, to choose.* Dan. 4:14, 22, 29. [4:17, 25, 32.] 5:19:21. (Syr. and Arab. *idem.*) Deriv. צְבוּ.

צְבֹאִים Hos. 11:8. צְבֹיִם and צְבֹיִּים Gen. 10:19. 14:2. Deut. 29:22. proper name of a city in the vale of Siddim, which was sunk with Sodom and Gomorrah in the Dead Sea.

I. **צָבָה** i. q. צָבָא *to go forth to war, to carry on war.* Is. 29:7 צֹבֶיהָ *they who carry on war against her,* i. q. צֹבְאִים עָלֶיהָ.

II. **צָבָה** *to swell,* spoken of the belly. Num. 5:27.

Hiph. causat. *to make to swell.* Num. 5:22. Hence

צָבֶה, fem. צָבָה, verbal adj. from צָבָה, *swelling.* Num. 5:21.

צְבוּ Chald. 1. liter. *will, purpose,* (from צְבָא *to will.*) Hence

2. *a matter, business, concern,* Syr. ܨܒܘ. Dan. 6:18. Comp. חֵפֶץ no. 4.

צָבוּעַ m. found only Jer. 12:9. *a hyena,* (Arab. ضبع.) Sept. ὑαίνη. Or else, *a wild beast* generally. (Comp. Talmud. צבועים *beasts of prey,* like the Arab. سباع *feræ rapaces.* See Bocharti Hieroz. P. I. p. 829.)

צְבִי m. in pause צֶבִי, dec. VI. l.

1. *honour, majesty, glory.* Is. 4:2. 24:16. 28:1, 4, 5.—צְבִי מַמְלָכוֹת *the glory of kingdoms,* i. e. Babylon, Is. 13:19. —אֶרֶץ הַצְּבִי *the glorious land,* i. e. the land of Israel, Dan. 11:16, 41. Also simply צְבִי in the same sense, Dan. 8:9. So in the Rabbinical writings, comp. Ezek. 20:6, 15. Jer. 3:19.—Dan. 11: 45 הַר צְבִי קֹדֶשׁ *the glorious holy mount,* i. e. the mount of the temple.

2. *a gazelle.* (Arab. ظبي, Aram. טַבְיָא.) 1 K. 5:3. [4:23.] Is. 13:14. Prov. 6:5. See Bocharti Hieroz. T. I. p. 924 ff. 895 ff. and Rosenmüller's notes thereon, T. II. p. 304 of the Leipsic edit. Plur. צְבָיִם, צְבָאִים 2 Sam. 2:18. צְבָאִים 1 Chr. 12:9. and צְבָאוֹת Cant. 2:7. 3:5.

צְבִיָּה fem. of צְבִי, *the female gazelle.* Cant. 4:5. 7:4.

צְבִיִּים see **צְבֹאִים**.

צָבַט, fut. יִצְבֹּט, *to reach* or *hold out.* Once Ruth 2:14.

צְבַע Chald. *to wet, moisten.* Pa. Dan. 4:22. [4:25.]

Ithpa. אִצְטַבַּע pass. Dan. 4:12, 20, 30. [4:15, 23, 33.] Otherwise *to immerse, colour,* as in Syr. and Arab. Hence

צֶבַע m. dec. VI. i. *what is coloured, a party-coloured garment.* Judg. 5:30. —שְׁלַל צְבָעִים ibid.

צְבֹעִים (*hyenas*) proper name of a valley and of a city in the tribe of Benjamin. 1 Sam. 13:18. Neh. 11:34.

צָבַר, fut. יִצְבֹּר, *to heap up;* e. g. grain. Gen. 41:35. treasures, Job 27: 16. Chald. צְבַר and Arab. *idem.*)

צִבֻּרִים masc. plur. verbal from צָבַר, *heaps.* 2 K. 10:8.

צֶבֶת or **צֶבֶת**, plur. צְבָתִים, *a sheaf, bundle.* Once Ruth 2:16. (Chald צְבַת *to bind.*)

צַד m. with suff. צִדִּי, plur. ־ִים, dec. VIII. f.

1. *a side.*—עַל צַד *at the side,* Is. 60:4. —מִצַּד *by the side,* Deut. 31:26. Josh. 12:9. By way of eminence, it is used of the *left* side, Ps. 91:7. (Antith. יָמִין.) 1 Sam. 20:25. With He paragogic, צִדָּה *to the side,* 1 Sam. 20:20.

2. *an adversary, opponent.* Judg. 2:3. Arab. صد and ضد *to turn away;* conj. III. *to oppose.*

צַד Chald. *a side.*—מִצַּד *on the part of,* Dan. 6:5.—לְצַד *against,* Dan. 7:25.

צְדָא Chald. *a purpose, intention.* Dan. 3:14 הַצְדָא *was it an intention?* Comp. Heb. צְדִיָּה, צָדָה.

צְדָד or **צְדָדָה** a place on the northern boundary of Palestine. Only Num. 34:8. Ezek. 47:15.

צָדָה *to seek after* a person, construed with an accus. Ex. 21:13. Joined with נֶפֶשׁ, *to seek after the life of* a person, 1 Sam. 24:12. Kindred with צוּד *to hunt* or *lie in wait for* wild beasts. Deriv. צְדִיָּה, צְדָא.

Niph. as in Aram. *to be laid waste.* Zeph. 3:6.

צֵדָה see **צֵידָה**.

צְדִיָּה f. verbal from צָדָה, *a purpose, intention, design.* Num. 35:20, 22.

צַדִּיק m. verbal adj. from צָדַק, dec. I.

1. *he that has a righteous cause.* Ex. 9:27. 23:8. Hence *innocent,* Gen. 18: 23 ff. 20:4.

2. *just, righteous,* (spoken of God, of a king, judge.) Ps. 7:10. 119:4.

3. *blameless, virtuous, pious.* Gen. 6:9. 7:1. Prov. 10:3 ff.

4. *true, faithful.* Neh. 9:8. Is. 41:26.

5. perhaps *victorious, a conqueror.* Is. 49:24. Comp. צְדָקָה no. 7.

צָדַק, fut. יִצְדַּק, prob. liter. *to be straight,* i. q. יָשַׁר. (Comp. צֶדֶק Ps. 23:3.) In Syr. ܙܕܩ *to be right, suitable.* In Arab. صدق *to be upright, true.*

1. *to have a just* or *righteous cause,* (in a contention at law.) Gen. 38:26 צָדְקָה מִמֶּנִּי *her cause is more just than mine.* Job 9:15, 20. 10:15. 13:18. 34:5. Also *to be right,* (in an assertion,) Job 33:12. 11:2.

2. *to be just, righteous;* spoken of Jehovah, Ps. 51:6. of the law, Ps. 19:10.

3. *to be innocent, blameless.* Job 15:14. 22:3. 35:7.—צָדַק עִם אֵל *to appear innocent before God,* Job 9:2. 25:4.—צָדַק מֵאֱלוֹהַ *idem,* Job 4:17.

4. *to be justified, to justify one's self,* as if the pass. of Pi. and Hiph. Is. 43:9, 26. 45:25. Ezek. 16:52.

Niph. *to be justified.* Dan. 8:14 נִצְדַּק קֹדֶשׁ *the sanctuary shall be justified,* i. e. its honour shall be maintained, it shall be safe. See צֶדֶק and צְדָקָה no. 6.

Pi. 1. *to justify.* Ezek. 16:51, 52. Jer. 3:11 צִדְּקָה נַפְשָׁהּ *she justifies herself,* i. e. appears just.

2. *to esteem* or *pronounce just.* Job 33:32. Joined with נַפְשׁוֹ, *to pronounce one's self just,* Job 32:2.

Hiph. 1. *to pronounce innocent, to acquit, absolve,* (spoken of a judge.) Ex. 23:7. Deut. 25:1. Is. 5:23. Construed with לְ, Is. 53:11.

2. *to make righteous, to lead to righteousness.* Dan. 12:4.

Hithpa. הִצְטַדֵּק *to justify* or *defend one's self.* Gen. 44:16.

Note. The antithesis is constantly made by רָשַׁע.

צֶדֶק m. with suff. צִדְקִי, verbal from צָדַק, dec. VI. h.

1. *straightness.* Ps. 23:3 מַעְגְּלֵי־צֶדֶק *straight paths.*

2. *what is right, right.* Job 36:3. Ps. 15:2.—Lev. 19:36 מֹאזְנֵי צֶדֶק *just balances.*—זִבְחֵי צֶדֶק *suitable sacrifices* or *sacrifices according to law,* Deut. 33:19.

3. *righteousness,* (of a judge, of Jehovah.) Ps. 35:24, 28.—צֶדֶק וּמִשְׁפָּט *righteousness and justice,* Ps. 89:15. 97:2.

4. *innocency, blamelessness,* Ps. 37:6. Job 8:6. *a just* or *righteous cause,* Ps. 17:1. Job 6:29.

5. *truth.* Ps. 52:5. Is. 45:19.

6. *deliverance, salvation, prosperity,* as the consequence of righteousness, (according to the usual ideas of retribution,) i. q. יֶשַׁע, יְשׁוּעָה. Is. 45:8. 51:5. 62:1. Jer. 33:16. Dan. 9:24. Ps. 132:9. comp. verse 16.

צְדָקָה f. verbal from צָדַק, dec. XI. c.

1. *what is right* or *fit.* Joel 2:23 הַמּוֹרֶה לִצְדָקָה *the early rain as it is wanted.* Also *a right* or *interest* in a thing, Neh. 2:20.

2. *righteousness, justice,* (of a judge, of God.)—מִשְׁפָּט וּצְדָקָה *righteousness and justice,* 2 Sam. 8:15. Jer. 9:23.

3. *blamelessness, innocency,* Job 27:6. Prov. 12:28. 15:9. *a just* or *righteous cause,* Gen. 30:33. Ps. 18:21. Dan. 9:7.

4. *merit, desert of good.* Gen. 15:6 *and he counted it to him as a merit.* Deut. 6:25.

5. *favour, beneficence.* Ps. 24:5. Prov. 10:2. Mic. 6:5. (Comp. the Chald.)

6. *salvation, deliverance, prosperity,* i. q. יֶשַׁע, יְשׁוּעָה. Is. 45:8. 48:18. 51:6, 8. Hence

7. *victory.* Judg. 5:11.

צִדְקָה Chald. *beneficence, alms.* Dan. 4:24. [4:27.]

צִדְקִיָּהוּ (*righteousness of Jehovah*) Sept. Σεδεκίας, Vulg. *Sedecias,* proper name of a king of Judah, which was given to him by king Nebuchadnezzar, instead of his former name מַתַּנְיָה. 2 K. 24:17. 1 Chr. 3:15. Jer. 1:3.

צָהַב *to shine like gold.* Part. Hoph.

מֻצְהָב *shining like gold.* Ezra 8 : 27. Kindred with זָהָב *gold.*

צָהֹב m. *gold-coloured, yellow,* spoken of the hair. Lev. 13 : 30 ff.

I. **צָהַל** 1. *to neigh,* spoken of the horse. Jer. 5 : 8.

2. metaphorically *to rejoice,* spoken of men. Is. 12 : 6. 24 : 14.

Pi. Is. 10 : 30 צַהֲלִי קוֹלֵךְ *let thy voice resound,* i. e. cry aloud, from alarm, terror. (Comp. רָנַן.)

Deriv. מִצְהָלָה.

II. **צָהַל** i. q. צָהַר or זָהַר *to shine.* Comp. the letter ל, p. 290. Found only in Hiph. causat. Ps. 104 : 15.

צָהַר found only in Hiph. denom. from יִצְהָר, *to make* or *press oil.* Job 24 : 11.

צֹהַר m. dec. VI. n. *light.* (Comp. זָהַר and טֹהַר.) Gen. 6 : 16 צֹהַר תַּעֲשֶׂה לַתֵּבָה *light,* i. e. a window, *shalt thou make for the ship.* Comp. 8 : 6. (Others make it *the deck,* comp. the Arab. ظَهْر *the back, surface.*)

Dual צָהֳרַיִם *noon, mid-day,* liter. *double light.* Gen. 43 : 16, 25. Deut. 28 : 29. Used as an emblem of prosperity, Job 11 : 17. Ps. 47 : 6.

צַו or **צָו**, prob. *a precept,* (from צִוָּה, like קַו, קָו, from قوي ,קָוָה.) Hos. 5 : 11. *for he follows willingly after the commandment* (of men). According to this we should render Is. 28 : 10, 13 צַו לָצָו צַו לָצָו *precept upon precept, precept upon precept.* Others: *filth on filth,* (as if i. q. צֹאָה ,צוֹא;) comp. verse 8. ; but this does not agree so well with verse 13. Others make it the inarticulate sound of the drunken man, comp. verse 11.

צוֹא m. dec. I. *dirty,* spoken of garments. Zech. 3 : 3, 4. (Syr. ܙܘܐ *to be dirty, odious.*)

צוֹאָה f. dec. X. *dirt, filth.* Is. 28 : 8 קִיא צֹאָה *vomitus fœdus.* Metaphorically *sin, guilt,* Is. 4 : 4. Prov. 30 : 12. Used as an euphemistic expression for *human dung* in the Keri of Is. 36 : 12. 2 K. 18 : 27.

צַוָּאר m. and **צַוָּר** (Neh. 3 : 5.) const. צַוַּאר, dec. II. b.

1. *the neck,* Germ. *Hals.*—בְּצַוָּאר *with a stretched out* or *proud neck,* Job 15 : 26. Ps. 75 : 6.

2. *the neck,* Germ. *Nakken.* Lam. 5 : 5. Hence used in reference to a yoke or burden, Hos. 10 : 11. Lam. 1 : 14.

Plur. צַוָּארִים, const. צַוְּארֵי, used of an individual, Gen. 27 : 16. 33 : 4. 45 : 14. —צַוָּארוֹת *colla,* Mic. 2 : 3.

צוֹבָא ,צוֹבָה proper name of a city in Mesopotamia, otherwise called *Nesibin, Nisibis, Antiochia Mygdoniæ,* 1 Sam. 14 : 47. 2 Sam. 8 : 3. 23 : 36. 2 Chr. 8 : 3. Its territory is denominated אֲרַם צוֹבָה Ps. 60 : 2. 2 Sam. 10 : 6, 8. It was the residence of a king, who in the time of David carried on several considerable wars with Israel.

צוּד (comp. צָדָה,) *to lie in wait,* construed with an accus. (1.) *to hunt, take,* (wild beasts.) Gen. 27 : 3, 5, 33. Job 38 : 39. (2.) *to lay snares,* e. g. for birds. Lev. 17 : 13. Lam. 3 : 52. Mic. 7 : 2. (3.) צוּד נֶפֶשׁ *to seek the life,* of a person. Prov. 6 : 26. (4.) in the other dialects also *to fish* ; see צִידוֹן.

Pil. i. q. Kal no. (3.) Ezek. 13 : 18, 20.

Hithpa. הִצְטַיֵּד, see under צַיִד.

Deriv. צַיִד ,צֵיד ,צַיָּד ,מָצוֹד ,מְצוּדָה.

צָוָה found only in Pi. צִוָּה.

1. *to command* any one; construed with an accus. of the person, (like the Lat. *jubere aliquem,*) Gen. 26 : 11. more rarely with עַל, Gen. 2 : 16. 28 : 6. Est. 2 : 10, 20. with אֶל, Gen. 50 : 16. with ל, Ex. 1 : 22. The command usually follows directly after לֵאמֹר, or indirectly in an infin. e. g. Gen. 3 : 11. The thing *commanded* is put also in the accus. hence a double accus. of the person and thing, Gen. 6 : 22. Ex. 25 : 22.

2. *to commission, depute, send,* (a person,) without mentioning the thing enjoined. Jer. 14 : 14. 23 : 32. Construed with על of the person *sent to,* Est. 4 : 5.

Ezra 8:17. 1 Chr. 22:12. or *on whose account* the charge is given, Gen. 12:20. 2 Sam. 14:8. In the latter case also with אֶל, Ex. 6:13. with לְ, Ps. 91:11. Used in reference to inanimate objects, Am. 9:4. Ps. 42:9.

3. construed with an accus. of the person and עַל of the thing, *to appoint* a person *over* any thing. Neh. 7:2. 5:14. 1 Sam. 13:14. 25:30.

4. *to appoint, ordain, esse jubere.* Ps. 68:29 צִוָּה אֱלֹהֶיךָ עֻזֶּךָ *thy God hath appointed thy prosperity.* Ps. 111:9. Is. 45:12.

5. צַוֵּה לְבֵיתוֹ or אֶל בֵּיתוֹ *to put one's house in order, to give one's last charge to his family.* 2 Sam. 17:23. 2 K. 20:1. Is. 38:1. (In Rabbin. צַוָּאָה *a testament.*)

Deriv. צַו, מִצְוָה.

צָוַח *to shout,* for joy. Is. 42:11.

צְוָחָה f. verbal from צָוַח, dec. XI. c. *a cry,* either of joy or sorrow. Is. 24:11. Jer. 14:2.

צוּלָה f. *the depth* or *bottom of the sea.* Is. 44:27. More frequently called מְצוּלָה, מְצֻלָה. Kindred with the root צָלַל no. II.

צוּם *to fast.* (In Arab. and Aram. *idem.*) Judg. 20:26. Zech. 7:5 הֲצוֹם צַמְתֻּנִי *did ye fast to me?*

צוֹם m. verbal from צוּם, dec. I. *fasting, a fast.* 2 Sam. 12:6. Plur. צוֹמוֹת Est. 9:31.

צוֹעַר see **צֹעַר**.

צוּף *to overflow.* Lam. 3:54.

Hiph. 1. *to cause to overflow.* Deut. 11:4.

2. *to make to swim.* 2 K. 6:6.

Deriv. out of course צָפָה.

צוּף m. verbal from צוּף, dec. X. *honey distilling of itself, pure honey.* Prov. 16:24. Plur. צוּפִים Ps. 19:11.

I. **צוּק** found only in the fut. יָצוּק, i. q. יָצַק *to pour out.* Job 28:2. 29:6.

II. **צוּק** *to be straitened, pressed.* In Kal found only Is. 26:16 צָקוּן לַחַשׁ probably *they press out sighs.*

Hiph. הֵצִיק 1. *to straiten, afflict, oppress,* construed with a dative and accus. Deut. 28:53 ff. Jer. 19:9. E. g. a city, Is. 29:7. Part. מֵצִיק *an oppressor,* Is. 51:13.

2. *to urge* or *press,* (with words,) construed with לְ. Judg. 16:16.

Deriv. out of course מוּצָק, מָצוֹק, מְצוּקָה.

צוֹק m. verbal from צוּק no. II. *oppression, affliction, trouble.* Dan. 9:25.

צוּקָה f. verbal from צוּק no. II. *oppression, compression, affliction, trouble.* Prov. 1:27. Is. 8:22 מְעוּף צוּקָה *darkness of compression,* i. e. thick darkness. 30:6.

צוּץ see **צִיץ**.

צוֹר, צֹר *Tyre,* the proper name of a celebrated commercial city in Phenicia. 2 Sam. 5:11. 1 K. 5:15. 7:13. Ps. 45:13. Ezek. 26:2. The Greek name Τύρος is probably derived from an Aramean pronunciation טוּר, טָרָא, like מֹר (מָרָא) μύῤῥα.

I. **צוּר**, fut. יָצוּר, apoc. וַיָּצַר.

1. *to press, straiten,* hence *to besiege,* (a city;) construed with עַל, Dan. 1:1. with אֶל, Deut. 20:19. with an accus. 1 Chr. 20:1. Causat. *to cause to straiten* or *besiege,* Is. 29:3. Deriv. מָצוֹר, מְצוּרָה, צַר, צָרָה.

2. *to press, persecute,* i. q. צָרַר no. II. Deut. 2:9. Ex. 23:22. Part. צָרִים Est. 8:11.

3. trans. *to make hostile, to instigate.* Judg. 9:31.

II. **צוּר** i. q. צָרַר *to bind together.* Pret. צַרְתָּ Deut. 14:25. Fut. וַיָּצֻרוּ 2 K. 12:11. וַיָּצַר 2 K. 5:23.

III. **צוּר** i. q. יָצַר *to form, make.* So the fut. וַיָּצַר Ex. 32:4. 1 K. 7:15. and אֱצוּרְךָ Jer. 1:5 Keth. (In Arab. and Aram. *idem.*) Deriv. צוּר no. III. צוּרָה.

I. **צוּר** m. dec. I.

1. *a rock.* Job 18:4. 24:8. Metaphorically צוּר יִשְׂרָאֵל *the rock of Israel,* i. e. God, Is. 30:29. Deut. 32:37 *the rock in which they trusted.* Ps. 18:3, 32, 47. Plur. צוּרוֹת Job 28:10.

2. *a stone.* Is. 8:14.

II. **צוּר** m. *sharpness, edge,* (from

צר i. q. Arab. صار *dissecuit, divisit.*) Ps. 89:44 צר חֶרֶב *the edge of the sword.* Josh. 5:2, 3 חַרְבוֹת צֻרִים *sharp knives.* Comp. צֹר Ex. 4:25.

III. צוּר m. dec. I. *form.* Ps. 49:15 Keri. See the following article.

צוּרָה f. dec. X. *form.* Ezek. 43:11. See the verb צור no. III.

צַוָּר i. q. צַוָּאר *the neck,* q. v.

צַוְּרֹנִים masc. plur. *the neck.* Cant. 4:9. The וֹן here may be a terminatio diminutiva et charitativa. Others: *an ornament for the neck, a necklace.*

צוּת Hiph. *to kindle, set on fire,* i. q. הִצִּית. Is. 27:4.

צַח m. verbal adj. from צָחַח, dec. VIII. l.

1. *white and shining.* Cant. 5:10.

2. *shined upon by the sun, hot, bright, clear.* Is. 18:4 חֹם צַח *a clear heat.* Jer. 4:11 רוּחַ צַח *a hot wind.* Arab. (with ض) and Syr. *idem.*

3. metaphorically *clear,* spoken of words. Is. 32:4.

צִחֶה adj. dec. IX. a. *dry, parched.* Is. 5:13. Root צְחָא in Aram. *to thirst.*

צָחַח 1. *to be white and shining.* Lam. 4:7.

2. *apricum esse,* see צַח.

Deriv. צַח, צָחִיחַ, צְחִיחָה, צְחִיחִי, צַחְצָחוֹת.

צָחִיחַ m. verbal from צָחַח, dec. I. *shined upon and burnt by the sun, parched.* Ezek. 24:7, 8. 26:4, 14.

צְחִיחָה f. verbal from צָחַח, *a dry land, a parched country.* Ps. 68:7.

צְחִיחִי, plur. ־ִים Neh. 4:7 [4:13] Keth. verbal from צָחַח, *idem.*

צַחְצָחוֹת fem. plur. verbal from צָחַח, *parched countries.* Is. 58:11.

צַחֲנָה f. dec. X. *an ill savour, a stink.* Joel 2:20. Syr. ܨܚܢܬܐ *a bad stench.*

צָחַק *to laugh.* Gen. 18:12 ff. Construed with לְ *about* any one, Gen. 21:6. Comp. שָׂחַק.

Pi. 1. *to jest, joke, sport.* Gen. 19:14. Construed with אֶת *with* a person, Gen. 26:8.

2. *to mock, insult.* Gen. 21:9. Construed with בְּ of the person, Gen. 39:14, 17.

3. *to play, to dance with music.* Judg. 16:25.

צְחֹק m. verbal from צָחַק, *laughter.* Gen. 21:6.

צַחַר m. *a dazzling whiteness, candor.* Ezek. 27:18. (Arab. conj. XI. *idem.*)

צָחֹר adj. dec. III. a. *white,* spoken of the she-ass. Judg. 5:10. Vulg. *nitens.* Syr. *albus.* (In Arabic, however, صُحُور spoken of the ass, denotes *party-coloured, spotted with white and red;* which meaning can be applied to the Hebrew.)

צִי m. *a ship.* Is. 33:21. Plur. צִים Num. 24:24. and צִיִּים Dan. 11:30.

צִיִּי (denom. from צִי, צִיָּה *a waste, desert,*) found only in the plur. צִיִּים *inhabitants of the desert;* used (1.) of men, Ps. 72:9. 74:14. (2.) of animals, Is. 13:21. 23:13. 34:14. Jer. 50:39. According to Bochart (Hieroz. T. II. p. 209. of the Leips. edit.) *wild cats,* like the Arab. ضَيْوَن *cats.* Otherwise comp. صُوَّة (צִוָּה) *a collection of wild animals,* particularly *of lions.*

צַיִד m. verbal from צוּד, dec. VI. f.

1. *a hunting.* Gen. 10:9.

2. *game, venison,* Gen. 25:28. *prey, booty,* Job 38:41.

3. *food.* Neh. 13:15. Ps. 132:15. Particularly *food for a journey, viaticum,* Josh. 9:5, 14. See צֵידָה.

Hithpa. הִצְטַיֵּד denom. from צַיִד, *to furnish one's self with provision for a journey.* Josh. 9:13.

צֵידָה or צֵדָה fem of צַיִד.

1. *food.* Ps. 78:25.

2. *food for a journey, viaticum.* Gen. 42:25. 45:21. (Arab. زَادَ *idem.*)

צַיָּד m. verbal from צוּד, dec. I. *a hunter.* Jer. 16:16.

צִידוֹן f. (*a fishing*) *Sidon*, the proper name of a celebrated commercial city in Phenicia, now called *Said*. Gen. 10: 15, 19. 49:13. The gentile noun is צִידֹנִי *a Sidonian*.

צִיָּה f. dec. X. *dryness, aridity*. Job 24:19. Hence אֶרֶץ צִיָּה *a dry land, a desert*, Ps. 63:2. 107:35. Without אֶרֶץ, in the same sense, Ps. 78:17. Root Arab. צוה صوي *to dry up*.

צָיוֹן m. *a dry land*. Is. 25:5. 32:2. Comp. צִיָּה.

צִיּוֹן f. *Zion*, the proper name of a part of Jerusalem, consisting of the more elevated southernmost mountain and the upper part of the city. In the poets and prophets it is often used for Jerusalem itself. See Relandi Palæstina, p. 846.

צִיּוּן m. dec. I. *a sign, memorial, a stone set up*. 2 K. 23:17. Sometimes as a way-mark, Jer. 31:21. and sometimes as a sepulchral monument, Ezek. 39:15. Root prob. צוה Syr. ܨܘܐ *to place*.

צִין and צִן *Zin*, the proper name of a desert in the south of Palestine, towards Idumea. Num. 13:21. 20:1. 34:3, 4. Josh. 15:1, 3. See Relandi Palæstina, p. 113.

צִינֹק m. *a prison*. Jer. 29:26. Root צנק in Samar. *to shut up*.

צִיץ, fut. יָצִיץ, pret. צָץ. (In Arab. צאץ.)

1. *to shine*. Ps. 132:18. Comp. the kindred root נָצַץ.

2. *to put forth flowers, to blossom*. Num. 17:23. [17:8.] Ps. 103:15. Often metaphorically *to flourish*, Ps. 92:8.

Hiph. *to peep, to look secretly*. Cant. 2:9.

צִיץ m. verbal from צוּץ, dec. X.

1. *something shining*, particularly the gold plate which the high-priest wore on his forehead. Ex. 28:36—38. Comp. Ps. 132:18.

2. *a flower*. Job 14:2. Plur. צִצִּים, (comp. קִשּׁוֹת, קְמִים,) 1 K. 6:18.

3. *a wing*. Jer. 48:9. For this change of signification, see נָצָה.

צִיצָה f. verbal from צִיץ dec. X. *a flower*. Is. 28:4.

צִיצִת f. 1. *a forelock*. Ezek. 8:3. (This signification is kindred with צִיץ no. 3. *a wing*. Comp. נָצָה strictly *to pluck, strike*.)

2. *a fringe, tassel*, such as the Israelites wore on the corners of their upper garments and esteemed sacred. Num. 15:38, 39.

צִקְלַג, צִיקְלַג, צִקְלָג, צִיקְלָג proper name of a city in the tribe of Simeon, but at times under the dominion of the Philistines. Josh 15:31. 19:5. 1 Sam. 30:1. 2 Sam. 1:1.

I. צִיר m. verbal from צור no. III. dec. I.

1. *an idol*. Is. 45:16.

2. *form*. Ps. 49:15 Keth.

II. צִיר m. dec. I. *a messenger*. Prov. 13:17. 25:13. Is. 18:2. Arab. صار med. Je *to go, arrive*. Hence a verb in

Hithpa. הִצְטַיֵּר *to set out on one's way*. Josh. 9:4. But the various reading with ד, as in verse 12, is to be preferred to the common reading.

III. צִיר m. dec. I. *something winding or twisting itself*. (Arab. ضور conj. V. *to writhe from pain*.) Hence

1. *a hinge of a door*. Prov. 26:14.

2. Plur. i. q. חֲבָלִים *throes* or *pangs* (of a woman in childbirth). Is. 13:8. 21: 3. 1 Sam. 4:19. Metaphorically *strong terrors*, which are often compared with the pains of childbirth, Dan. 10:16.

צֵל m. with suff. צִלִּי, verbal from צָלַל no. III. dec. VIII. b. *a shadow*. It is used (1.) to indicate *frailty*. Job 8:9. Ps. 102:12. (2.) to express *protection, shelter*, the figure sometimes being continued and sometimes not. Ps. 17:8. 36:8. Is. 16:3 *make thy shadow at mid-day as in the night*, i. e. afford a secure refuge from the burning heat. Is. 25:4 *thou (Jehovah) art a shadow from the heat.* As plurals, see צְלָלִים and צִלְלֵים.

צְלָא Chald. found only in Pa. *to pray.* Dan. 6:11. Ezra 6:10.

צָלָה *to roast.* 1 Sam. 2:15. Jer. 44:16. (Arab. *idem.*) Deriv. צָלִי.

צְלוּל, in Keri צְלִיל, found only Judg. 7:13 צְלִיל לֶחֶם שְׂעֹרִים usually rendered *a baked barley-cake*, from צָלָה=צָלַל. Better with the Sept. Chald. *placenta panis hordacei*, perhaps after the Chald. צִלְצוּל *cingulum.*

צָלִי m. verbal from צָלָה, dec. III. a. *roasted.* Ex. 12:8, 9.

I. **צָלַח** (Arab. with ص.)

1. *to be fit, useful*, construed with לְ. Jer. 13:7, 10.

2. *to succeed, prosper, flourish;* spoken of an undertaking, Is. 53:10. 54:17. of a plant, Ezek. 17:9, 10.

3. *to succeed* (in an undertaking,) spoken of a person. Ps. 45:5. Jer. 22:30.

Hiph. 1. trans. *to make prosperous, to bless;* (1.) an undertaking, spoken of God. Gen. 24:21, 56. 39:3, 23. (2.) a person, construed with an accus. 2 Chr. 26:5. with לְ, Neh. 1:11. 2:20.

2. *to accomplish*, or *execute happily* or *prosperously.* 2 Chr. 7:11. Dan. 8:25. Particularly with דְּרָכָיו, דַּרְכּוֹ, *to prosper in one's ways, to succeed.* Deut. 28:29. Ps. 37:7 מַצְלִיחַ דַּרְכּוֹ *he that prospers in his ways, the prosperous man.*

3. intrans. as in Kal no. 2. *to prosper*, spoken of an undertaking. Judg. 18:5.

4. as in Kal no. 3. *to prosper* (in an undertaking), spoken of a person. 1 K. 22:12, 15. 1 Chr. 22:13. 29:23. 2 Chr. 18:14. Prov. 28:13. Jer. 2:37.

II. **צָלַח** i. q. עָבַר.

1. *to pass over.* 2 Sam. 19:18.

2. *to fall upon*, construed with an accus. Amos 5:6. with עַל, spoken of the spirit of God which comes upon a person, Judg. 14:19. 15:14. 1 Sam. 10:10. 11:6. With אֶל, 1 Sam. 16:13. 18:10.

צְלַח Chald. i. q. Heb. צָלַח no. I. Aph. הַצְלַח (with the Heb. form.)

1. trans. *to bless, prosper, promote,* (a person.) Dan. 3:30.

2. *to execute prosperously.* Ezra 6:14.

3. intrans. *to succeed, prosper.* Ezra 5:8.

4. *to prosper, to be promoted.* Dan. 6:29.

צַלַּחַת f. *a dish, bowl.* Prov. 19:24. 26:15. Plur. צְלָחוֹת (as if from צְלָחָה,) 2 Chr. 35:13.

צְלֹחִית f. *idem.* 2 K. 2:20.

צְלִיל see **צְלוּל**.

I. **צָלַל** (Arab. with ص) *to tingle,* spoken of the ears. 1 Sam. 3:11. 2 K. 21:13. Also metaphorically *to quiver,* spoken of the lips, Hab. 3:16. Deriv. צִלְצַל, מְצִלְתַּיִם, צֶלְצְלִים.

II. **צָלַל** (Arab. with ض) *to sink.* Ex. 15:10. Deriv. צוּלָה, מְצוֹלָה.

III. **צָלַל** (Arab. with ظ) *to be shaded, to be dark.* Neh. 13:19.

Hiph. part. מֵצַל *shadowing.* Ezek. 31:3.

Deriv. out of course צֵל, מְצִלָּה.

צֵלֶל, with suff. צִלְלוֹ, plur. צְלָלִים, verbal from צָלַל no. III. dec. VI. g. *a shadow.* Cant. 2:17. Jer. 6:4.

צֶלֶם m. with suff. צַלְמוֹ, dec. VI. a. *a form, image, likeness,* Gen. 1:27. 5:3. 9:6. *a shadowy image, a shadow,* Ps. 39:7. *an idol,* 2 K. 11:18. Amos 5:26. Metaphorically *an imagination, fancy,* Ps. 73:20.

צֶלֶם, צְלֵם m. Chald. emph. צַלְמָא, *an image, idol.* Dan. 2:31 ff. 3:1 ff.

צַלְמוֹן proper name of a mountain in Samaria, not far from Sichem. Judg. 9:48. It is represented by the poet Ps. 68:15, as covered with snow.

צַלְמֹנָה a station of the Israelites in the desert. Once Num. 33 : 41.

צַלְמָוֶת f. liter. *death-shade, shadow of death,* (from צֵל *a shadow,* and מָוֶת *death,*) hence poetically *thick darkness.* Job 3 : 5. 10 : 21. 28 : 3. 34 : 22. 38 : 17 שַׁעֲרֵי צַלְמָוֶת *the gates of darkness.* Is. 9 : 1. [9 : 2.]

צָלַע *to halt, limp,* liter. *to incline to one side,* (צֵלָע.) Gen. 32 : 32. Part. fem. הַצֹּלֵעָה used collectively, *those that halt,* spoken of the flocks, but in a metaphorical sense, Mic. 4 : 6, 7. Zeph. 3 : 19.

צֶלַע m. verbal from צָלַע, dec. VI. d. *a halting, falling.* Ps. 35 : 15. 38 : 18.

צֵלָע f. const. צֵלַע and צֶלַע, with suff. צַלְעִי, dec. IV. i.

1. *a rib.* Gen. 2 : 21, 22.

2. *a side.* Job 18 : 12. 20 : 10 שֹׁמְרֵי צַלְעִי *those who guard my side,* i. e. my most intimate friends. Spoken also of inanimate objects, as of the tent, Ex. 26 : 26, 27. Plur. צְלָעִים m. *the sides* or *leaves of a folding door,* 1 K. 6 : 34. Elsewhere uniformly צְלָעוֹת, const. צַלְעוֹת, *sides,* of the altar, Ex. 38 : 7. of the ark of the covenant, Ex. 25 : 14.

3. *a side-chamber* (of the temple). 1 K. 6 : 3. Ezek. 41 : 6 ff. Also collectively, like יָצִיעַ, *a whole story of side-chambers,* 1 K. 6 : 8. or even *the three stories,* Ezek. 41 : 5, 9, 11.—בֵּית צְלָעוֹת Ezek. 41 : 9, is the space for these side-chambers between the two walls of the temple. Comp. Josephi Antiq. Jud. III. 3. § 2.

4. Plur. צְלָעוֹת *boards,* (as it were *ribs.*) 1 K. 6 : 15, 16.

5. proper name of a city in the tribe of Benjamin, where Saul was buried. Josh. 18 : 28. 2 Sam. 21 : 14.

צְלָצַל m. Deut. 28 : 42. prob. a species of locust, so called from the *shrill noise* which it makes. See צָלַל no. 1.

צִלְצַל dec. II. a.

1. *a fishing instrument, a hook.* Job 40 : 31. [41 : 7.]

2. *a rattling, rustling.* Is. 18 : 1 אֶרֶץ צִלְצַל כְּנָפָיִם *the land of rustling wings.* See Gesen. in loc. Others : *the land of shadowing wings,* i. e. under whose wings the Israelites find protection. By which Egypt is then intended. Others : γῆ ἀμφίσκιος, *terra utrinque umbrosa,* having reference to the situation of Ethiopia, which lies between the tropics, so that the shadow is one half of the year on the north side, and the other half on the south.

צֶלְצְלִים masc. plur. const. צִלְצְלֵי, *a cymbal,* Lat. *cymbala,* similar to what is now used in field music. 2 Sam. 6 : 5. Root צָלַל no. I. Besides the larger cymbals, there were also smaller ones or *castanets,* consisting of metallic plates of the size of a button, which the dancing women wore on their fingers and smote together. Both these kinds are probably referred to by the phrases צִלְצְלֵי שָׁמַע and צִלְצְלֵי תְרוּעָה, Ps. 150 : 5. See Jahn's Bibl. Archaeol. § 96.

צָם, plur. צַמִּים Job 5 : 5. prob. i. q. צְמֵאִים *the thirsty.* Targ. *prædones,* comp. Arab. צמים صَمِيم *vir magnus, durus, validus.*

צָמֵא, fut. יִצְמָא, *to thirst.* Ex. 17 : 3. Metaphorically *to thirst* or *long after* a person or thing, construed with לְ, Ps. 42 : 3. 63 : 2.

צָמֵא m. verbal adj. from צָמֵא dec. V. e. *thirsty.* Is. 21 : 14.

צָמָא m. verbal from צָמֵא dec. IV. g. *thirst.* Ezek. 19 : 13. Jer. 48 : 18.

צִמְאָה f. verbal from צָמֵא, *thirst.* Once Jer. 2 : 25.

צִמָּאוֹן m. verbal from צָמֵא, *a dry* or *thirsty land.* Deut. 8 : 15. Is. 35 : 7.

צָמַד in Kal not used. In Syr. and Arab. (with ض) *to bind, fasten.*

Niph. found only in the phrase נִצְמַד לְבַעַל־פְּעוֹר *to join* or *consecrate one's self to Baal-peor.* Num. 25 : 3, 5. Ps. 106 : 28.

Pu. *to be fastened.* 2 Sam. 20 : 8.

Hiph. joined with מִרְמָה, *to frame deceit, nectere fraudem.* Ps. 50 : 19.

Deriv. צָמִיד, and

צֶמֶד m. with suff. צִמְדּוֹ, dec. VI. h.

1. *a pair, couple, yoke;* e.g. of oxen, 1 Sam. 11:7. of asses, Judg. 19:10.—2 K. 9:25 רֹכְבִים צְמָדִים *riding by pairs.*

2. a measure of land, equal to what a person might plough in one day, *an acre,* Lat. *jugum, jugerum.* 1 Sam. 14: 14. Is. 5:10.

צִמָּה f. i. q. צָמָא *thirst.* Is. 5:13.

צַמָּה f. dec. X. *a veil.* Cant. 4:1. 6:7. Is. 47:2. Root צמם Chald. *to cover.*

צִמּוּק m. dec. I. *dried grapes* or *raisins,* or rather *cakes made of them,* in Ital. *simmuki.* 1 Sam. 25:18. 2 Sam. 16:1. Root צָמַק.

צָמַח *to sprout* or *spring up;* spoken of plants, Gen. 2:5. 41:6. of hair, Lev. 13:37.—Ecc. 2:6 יַעַר צוֹמֵחַ עֵצִים *the forest which springs up with trees.* Metaphorically *to spring up, to arise,* spoken of new occurrences, Is. 42:9. 43:19. 58:8.

Pi. i. q. Kal. Ezek. 16:7. Judg. 16: 22.

Hiph. *to let spring up, to cause to grow.* Gen. 2:9. Construed with two accus. Ps. 147:8. Metaphorically *to arise,* spoken of deliverance or salvation, Is. 45:8. 61:11.

צֶמַח m. with suff. צִמְחוֹ, verbal from צָמַח, dec. VI. i. *a sprout, shoot.* Gen. 19:25. Metaph. צֶמַח יְהוָה *the sprout* or *branch of Jehovah,* i. e. the Messiah, the expected restorer of the Jewish state, Is. 4:2. Jer. 23:5. 33:15. Zech. 3:8. 6:12.

צָמִיד m. verbal from צָמַד, dec. III. a.

1. *a bracelet.* Gen. 24:22, 30.

2. *a lid* or *cover* for a vessel. Num. 19:15.

צַמִּים masc. sing. (after the form צַדִּיק,) *a snare.* Job 18:9. Root צמם Arab. طمّ *to weave,* or ضمّ *to bind.*

צְמִיתֻת f. liter. *destruction,* from צָמַת, hence לִצְמִיתֻת *for ever, absolutely, entirely,* i. q. כָּלָה. Lev. 25:23, 30.

צָמַק *to be dry,* spoken of the breasts. Hos. 9:14. Deriv. צִמּוּק.

צֶמֶר m. with suff. צַמְרִי dec. VI. h. *wool.* Lev. 13:47. Deut. 22:11. Is. 1: 18. Hence

צַמֶּרֶת f. *the foliage of trees,* as if *lana seu coma arborum.* Ezek. 17:3, 22. 31:3, 10, 14. For similar transfers of words from the animal to the vegetable kingdom, see under the articles זַלְזַל, פֶּרַח, נֵצֶר, צִיץ, יוֹנֶקֶת; also comp. ἀἰς ἄωτος, *the flower,* i. e. the skin, *of the sheep,* (Hom. Od. I. 443.)

צְמָרִי proper name of a Syrian people, mentioned only Gen. 10:18. Some have very justly compared the name with that of the city *Simyra,* the ruins of which Shaw describes under the name of *Sumra.*

צְמָרַיִם proper name of a city in the tribe of Benjamin. Josh. 18:22. 2 Chr. 13:4.

צָמַת *to root out, to cut off.* Lam. 3:53.

Niph. *to be destroyed, to perish.* Job 6:17. 23:17.

Pi. i. q. Kal. Ps. 119:139.

Hiph. i. q. Kal. Ps. 54:7. 69:5. 101:5.

Pilel צִמְּתֻתְנִי i. q. Kal. Ps. 88:17.

Note. In the other dialects, this root signifies *to be silent.*

צֵן m. *a thorn.* Plur. צִנִּים Prov. 22: 5. Spoken of a thorn-hedge, Job 5:5. where perhaps we may comp. צִנְצֶנֶת *a basket of grain.*

צִן see צִין.

צֹנֶא com. gen. Num. 32:24. and צֹנֶה Ps. 8:8. i. q. צֹאן *small cattle,* particularly *sheep.* (Arab. ضَنَأ conj. IV. *to have much cattle.*)

I. **צִנָּה** f. i. q. צֵן *a thorn,* hence *a hook, fish-hook,* like חֹחַ, סִיר. Plur. צִנּוֹת Am. 4:2.

II. **צִנָּה** dec. X. *a shield.* Ps. 35:2.

91 : 4. Ezek. 23 : 24. and that of the larger size, (comp. 1 K. 10 : 16, 17.) *scutum*, θυρεός, which covered the whole body of the soldier. Root צָנַן prob. i. q. صان *custodivit, protexit*.

III. צִנָּה dec. X. *coolness*. Prov. 25 : 13. Root צְנַן Chald. *to be cool*. Others: *a vessel*, comp. צִנְצֶנֶת.

צָנוֹף or צָנוּף dec. III. a. i. q. צָנִיף *a turban*. Is. 62 : 3 Keth.

צִנּוֹר m. dec. I. *a water-course, a water-fall*. 2 Sam. 5 : 8. Ps. 42 : 8. (In Chald. *idem*.)

צָנַח 1. *to alight*. Josh. 15 : 18.

2. prob. causat. *to make to descend* or *sink*, i. q. הוֹרִיד. Judg. 4 : 21 *she smote the nail through his temples*, וַתִּצְנַח בָּאָרֶץ *and made it sink into the ground*. So the Sept. Vulg. Chald.

צְנִינִים masc. plur. *thorns*. Num. 33 : 55. Josh. 23 : 13. See צֵן.

צָנִיף m. dec. III. a. *a turban, head-band*; for men, Job 29 : 14. for women, Is. 3 : 23. for the high-priest, Zech. 3 : 5. Root צָנַף *to wind round*. See מִצְנֶפֶת.

צָנַם found only in the part. pass. צָנוּם *thin, dry, withered*, spoken of ears. Gen. 41 : 23. (In Talmud. *idem*, in Samar. *hard*. Syr. ܨܘܢܥܐ *a rock*.)

צַנָּן see צַאֲנָן.

צָנַע *to be low, humble, modest*. Part. pass. (with an active signification,) Prov. 11 : 2. In Chald. *idem*.

Hiph. *to act humbly*. Mic. 6 : 8.

צָנַף fut. יִצְנֹף, *to wrap up* or *roll round*, (with a turban.) Lev. 16 : 4.— Is. 22 : 18 צָנוֹף יִצְנָפְךָ צְנֵפָה *he shall roll thee up as a ball*. Deriv. out of course מִצְנֶפֶת, צָנִיף.

צְנֵפָה f. verbal from צָנַף, *a ball*. Is. 22 : 18. See the preceding article.

צִנְצֶנֶת f. *a pot* or *basket*, to keep things in. Ex. 16 : 33. Root צנן prob. i. q. Arab. صان *to keep, lay up*.

צַנְתָּרוֹת fem. plur. dec. XI. a. *tubes, pipes*, through which the oil ran from the oil-vessel (גֻּלָּה) into the lamps. Zech. 4 : 12. According to Simonis, a quadriliteral compounded of צִנּוֹר *a pipe* and נָתַר *to flow*.

צָעַד *to go, proceed, move*. Prov. 7 : 8. Jer. 10 : 5. Particularly *to move solemnly*, 2 Sam. 6 : 13. hence spoken of Jehovah, Judg. 5 : 4. Ps. 68 : 8. Construed with an accus. *to march through* (a country), Hab. 3 : 12.—Gen. 49 : 22 בָּנוֹת צָעֲדָה עֲלֵי שׁוּר *the daughters* (*of the tree*), i. e. the branches, *reach over the wall*. By a change of the vowel-points, בְּנוֹת צְעָדָה i. q. Arab. بنات صعدة *filiæ ascensionis*, i. e. feræ, onagri.

Hiph. *to lead, bring*. Job 18 : 14.

Deriv. out of course מִצְעָד.

צַעַד m. verbal from צָעַד, dec. VI. c. *a step*. 2 Sam. 6 : 13. Ps. 18 : 37.

צְעָדָה f. verbal from צָעַד, dec. X.

1. *a step, marching*, (of God.) 2 Sam. 5 : 24.

2. *a short chain for the feet*, extending from one foot to the other, worn by the eastern women to give them a short fashionable gait. (Arab. مصعاد *idem*.) Comp. אֶצְעָדָה.

צָעָה 1. *to bend, incline, tilt*, (Arab. صغى,) e. g. a vessel, for the purpose of drawing off the liquor. Jer. 48 : 12.

2. *to be bent down* by fetters. Is. 51 : 14.

3. *to lay down*, in reference to copulation. Jer. 2 : 20.

4. *to go with neck bent back, to walk proudly*. Is. 63 : 1. (Others: *to be proud*, comp. the Arab. طغى *erravit, aberravit, superbus fuit*, i. q. Heb. שָׂטָה.)

Pi. i. q. Kal no. 1. Jer. 48 : 12.

צָעוֹר i. q. צָעִיר in the Kethib of Jer. 14 : 3. 48 : 4.

צָעִיף m. dec. III. a. *a veil, covering*. Gen. 24 : 65. 38 : 14. (Root Arab. ضعف conj. II. III. IV. *to double*; hence perhaps *the double veil*, of which one part hung down in front before the eyes, and the other part was thrown back over them.

צָעִיר m. dec. III. a.

1. as an adj. *small.* Particularly (1.) *minor natu.* Gen. 19:31. With the addition יָמִים Job 30:1. (2.) *low, of little influence,* Judg. 6:15. *despised.* Ps. 119:141.

2. proper name of a place. Once 2 K. 8:21.

צְעִירָה f. denom. from צָעִיר, dec. X. *minority, youth.* Gen. 43:33.

צָעַן *to wander, to remove,* spoken of the nomades. (Arab. ظعن.) Perhaps liter. *to lade beasts for a journey.* Comp. טָעַן no. I. Is. 33:20.

צֹעַן *Zoan,* proper name of an ancient city in Lower Egypt, according to the Sept. and Targums, *Tanis,* on the eastern mouth of the Nile. Num. 13:22. Is. 19:11, 13. 30:4. Ezek. 30:14.

צַעֲצֻעִים masc. plur. *the work of a sculptor, statuary.* 2 Chr. 3:10. Root prob. צוע Arab. صاغ *finxit, conflavit, artem aurifabri exercuit.* The last idea, however, does not apply, see 1 K. 6:23.

צָעַק i. q. זָעַק *to cry,* particularly for help. Deut. 22:24, 27. Construed with אֶל of the person, Gen. 41:55. Judg. 4:3. with לְ, 2 Chr. 13:14. Also with an accus. of the thing *about* which a person cries, Job 19:7.

Pi. i. q. Kal. Once 2 K. 2:12.

Hiph. *to call together,* like הִזְעִיק. 1 Sam. 10:17.

Niph. pass. of Hiph. *to be called* or *to come together.* Judg. 7:23, 24. 10:17.

צְעָקָה f. verbal from צָעַק, dec. XI. d. *a cry,* particularly for assistance. Ex. 3:9. Job 34:28. Jer. 48:5. Gen. 19:13 צַעֲקָתָם *the cry concerning them.*

צָעַר *to be small.* (Comp. זָעִיר, מִזְעָר.) Metaphorically *to be brought low, to be debased,* Jer. 30:19. Job 14:21. (antith. כָּבֵד.) Zech. 13:7. Deriv. מִצְעָר, צְעִירָה, צָעִיר.

צֹעַר and צוֹעַר (*smallness,* comp. Gen. 19:20.) proper name of a city on the southern extremity of the Dead Sea. Gen. 13:10. 19:22, 30. Is. 15:5. Jer. 48:34. Its more ancient name was בֶּלַע.

צָפַד *to adhere, to stick fast.* Lam. 4:8. (Arab. صفد *to bind.*)

I. צָפָה 1. *to look about,* particularly down from a height.—Spoken metaphorically of inanimate objects, Cant. 7:5. —Part. צוֹפֶה *a watchman,* (in a tower or steeple,) 1 Sam. 14:16. 2 Sam. 13:34. 18:24. Metaphorically *a prophet,* who should, like a watchman, warn the people, Jer. 6:17. Ezek. 3:17. comp. Hab. 2:1—Hos. 9:8 צֹפֶה אֶפְרַיִם *Ephraim looks out* (after oracles).

2. *to observe narrowly,* construed with an accus. Prov. 15:3. 31:27. with בְּ, Ps. 66:7. with בֵּין, Gen. 31:49.

3. *to lie in wait,* construed with לְ. Ps. 37:32. Job 15:22.

Pi. 1. i. q. Kal no. 1. 1 Sam. 4:13. Part. מְצַפֶּה *a watchman,* Is. 21:6. Applied metaphorically to prophets, Mic. 7:4. The thing *looked out for* is preceded by אֶל, Lam. 4:17. by בְּ, Mic. 7:7. Ps. 5:4.

Deriv. מִצְפֶּה, מִצְפָּה, צְפִיָּה.

II. צָפָה found only in Pi. צִפָּה *to overlay,* (with gold, silver,) construed with two accus. Ex. 25:24. 1 K. 6:20 ff.

Pu. pass. Ex. 26:32. Prov. 26:23. Deriv. צִפּוּי.

III. צָפָה perhaps i. q. Arab. ضفا *abundavit.* Is. 21:5 צָפֹה הַצָּפִית *every thing is in abundance, redundat redundantia.* Better: *they keep a watch,* according to no. I. See Gesen. in loc. Others, from the Arab. صفا *clarum, defæcatum fuit* vinum, *they refine the wine.*

צָפָה f. verbal from צוּף, dec. X. *a swimming.* Ezek. 32:6.

צִפּוּי m. verbal from צָפָה no. II. *a metallic overlaying* or *covering.* Num. 17:3, 4. Is. 30:22.

צָפוֹן m. (fem. in signif. no. 2.) dec. III. a.

1. *the north.* (Perhaps liter. *the concealed, dark place,* like πρὸς ζόφον in Homer.) Num. 34 : 7.—מִצְּפוֹן לְ *on the north of,* Josh. 8 : 11, 13.—With ה ָ parag. צָפוֹנָה *northward,* Gen. 13 : 14. also with prepositions אֶל הַצָּפוֹנָה Ezek. 8 : 14. לַצָּפוֹנָה 1 Chr. 26 : 17. *towards the north.* מִצָּפוֹנָה Josh. 15 : 10. and מִצָּפוֹנָה לְ Judg. 21 : 19. *on the north side.*

2. *the north wind.* Cant. 4 : 16.

3. *the northern hemisphere,* poetically for *the whole heaven.* Job 26 : 7.

צְפוֹנִי m. denom. adj. from צָפוֹן, *coming from the north,* spoken of the locusts. Joel 2 : 20.

צְפוּעַ Ezek. 4 : 15 Keth. i. q. צָפִיעַ.

צִפּוֹר, plur. צִפֳּרִים, com. gen.

1. *a sparrow.* Ps. 84 : 4. Prov. 26 : 2. Root צפר in Arab. *to chirp.*

2. *any small bird,* particularly *a singing bird.* Ps. 11 : 1. 104 : 17. 124 : 7. Job 40 : 29. Prov. 6 : 5. 7 : 23.

3. *a bird* generally. Deut. 4 : 17. 14 : 11. Lev. 14 : 4. Gen. 7 : 14 כָּל הָעוֹף לְמִינֵהוּ כֹּל צִפּוֹר כָּל כָּנָף *every fowl after his kind, every bird of every sort.* Comp. Ezek. 17 : 23. 39 : 4, 17. Ps. 148 : 10.

צַפַּחַת f. *a cruise* or *cup* ; e. g. for water, 1 Sam. 26 : 11 ff. for oil, 1 K. 17 : 12. Chald. צְפִיחָה *idem.* Arab. by transposition צחפה *a dish, vessel.*

צְפִיָּה f. verbal from צָפָה, no. I. dec. X. *a watching,* i. q. מִצְפֶּה. Lam. 4 : 17.

צַפִּיחִת f. *a cake, wafer.* Ex. 16 : 31. Root נפח=מסח *to spread out.* Comp. in Greek πλακοῦς, *a cake.*

צְפִין Ps. 17 : 14 Keth. i. q. צָפוּן, see צָפַן no. 2.

I. **צָפִיעַ** m. dec. III. a. *dung,* (of cattle.) Ezek. 4 : 15 Keri. (Arab. ضفع *idem.*)

II. **צְפִיעוֹת** plur. Is. 22 : 24. of very difficult explanation ; according to the Targum and Kimchi, synonymous with the preceding word צֶאֱצָאִים *offspring, issue.* But no confirmation of this sense has yet been found in the kindred dialects. Others : *diadems.* See J. D. Michaëlis Supplem. p. 2132.

צָפִיר m. dec. III. a. *a he-goat.* Dan. 8 : 5, 21. Ezra 6 : 17.

I. **צְפִירָה** f. dec. X. *a crown, diadem.* Is. 28 : 5. Root צפר Arab. ضفر *to weave a garland.*

II. **צְפִירָה** Ezek. 7 : 7, 10. Root Arab. صفر *to be waste, empty, to die.*

צָפִית f. verbal from צָפָה. Is. 21 : 5. See under צָפָה no. III.

צָפַן, fut. יִצְפֹּן. 1. *to conceal.* Ex. 2 : 2. Part. pass. צָפוּן *concealed, inaccessible, sacred,* Ezek. 7 : 22. Particularly in order to give protection, Ps. 27 : 5. 83 : 4 צְפוּנֶי יְהוָה *those under Jehovah's protection, his clients.*

2. *to preserve, lay up.* Part. צְפוּנִים *goods, treasures,* Ps. 17 : 14. Construed with לְ, *to lay up for* a person, Ps. 31 : 20.—צָפַן בְּלֵב *to lay up in one's heart,* Job 10 : 13.—צָפַן אִתּוֹ *to lay up with one's self,* Prov. 2 : 1. 7 : 1.

3. *to keep* a person *from* any thing, construed with מִן. Job 17 : 4.

4. *to hold back, to stop.* Prov. 27 : 16.

5. *to hide one's self ;* particularly *to lie in wait,* construed with לְ of the person. Prov. 1 : 11, 18. Ps. 10 : 8. Without an object following, Ps. 56 : 7.

Niph. 1. *to be concealed from* or *unknown to* a person, construed with מִן. Job 24 : 1. Jer. 16 : 17.

2. *to be finished, determined, appointed,* construed with לְ. Job 15 : 20.

Hiph. i. q. Kal no. 1. *to conceal.* Ex. 2 : 3. Job 14 : 13.

Deriv. מַצְפּוּנִים, צָפוֹן.

צְפַנְיָה (*Jehovah conceals*) *Zephaniah,* proper name of a well-known prophet. Zeph. 1 : 1. Sept. Σοφονίας. Vulg. *Sophonias.*

צָפְנַת פַּעְנֵחַ an Egyptian name, which Pharaoh gave to Joseph. Gen. 41 : 45. The reading of the Sept.

Ψοθομφανηχ and Ψονθομφανήχ comes nearer to the proper Egyptian pronunciation; comp. the Copt. *Psot-em-phanech* (i. e. *salus seculi.*) Jerome: *servator mundi.* The original orthography of the word is perhaps corrupted in the Hebrew, (comp. מֹשֶׁה, אַבְרֵךְ,) in which language it is explained by *revelator occulti*, (Targ. Syr. Kimchi;) but we can hardly conceive that the word should be of Hebrew origin. See Jablonskii Opusc. ed. te Water, T. I. p. 207—216.

צֶפַע m. Is. 14:29. and צִפְעֹנִי Is. 11: 8. 59:5. Prov. 23:32. Plur. צִפְעֹנִים Jer. 8:17. prob. *the horned serpent.* Aqu. βασίλισκος. Vulg. *regulus.* (According to Michaëlis, derived from the Arab. צופעה *cidaris*, hence *apicatus, coronatus;* according to Bochart from صفع *to breathe poison*, inasmuch as the ancients ascribed this property to the basilisk.)

צָפַף found only in Pilp. צִפְצֵף *to pip, chirp*, as a bird, τρίζειν, στρουθίζειν. Is. 10:14. 38:14. Then used metaphorically of *the gentle whispering*, (*vox exigua*, Virg. Æn. VI. 492.) which the ancients ascribed to departed spirits, or rather of the voice of the necromancers who sought to imitate the manes. Is. 8:19.

צַפְצָפָה f. according to the Hebrew interpreters, *a willow-tree, salix.* Ezek. 17:5, where בְּ must be supplied. (In Arab. *idem.*) Others: *a plain;* hence *in a plain*, by supplying בְּ. (So in Arab.)

צָפַר (Arab. with ض) *to run, to go away.* Judg. 7:3.

צְפַר m. Chald. plur. צִפְּרִין, *a bird, fowl.* Dan. 4:9, 11, 18, 30. [4:12, 14, 21, 33.]

צְפַרְדֵּעַ m. dec. VII. a. *a frog.* Ex. 7:27, 28. 8:1 ff. Used as a collective noun and then of the fem. gen. *frogs*, Ex. 8:2. [8:6.]

צִפֹּרֶן m. dec. VI. b.

1. *a nail* (of the finger). Deut. 21: 12. Hence

2. *the (diamond) point of a style*, liter. *its nail.* Jer. 17:1. Comp. Plin. N. H. XXXVII. cap. 4. (Chald. טְפַר *idem.*)

צֶפֶת f. *the capital* or *chapiter* (of a pillar). 2 Chr. 3:15. Root Syr. ܨܦܐ *to adorn.*

צִצִּים see **צִיץ**.

צִקְלַג see **צִיקְלַג**.

צִקְלוֹן m. found only 2 K. 4:42. *a bag, pouch.* Perhaps from the Arab. صقل צקל *a side*, hence *a side-bag.*

צַר, with disjunctive accents and with the article צָר, with suff. צָרִי, plur. צָרִים, const. צָרֵי, dec. VIII. k.

I. *an adversary, enemy, persecutor*, i. e. אֹיֵב, but found only in the later books; e. g. Est. 7:4, 6. Neh. 4:11. 9:27. Root צרר no. II. Comp. צָר, צָרִים.

II. *affliction, distress*, from צרר no. III. Ps. 4:2. 44:11. 78:42—צַר לִי for בִּהְיוֹת צַר לִי *when I was afflicted*, Ps. 18:7. 66:14. 106:44.—102:3 בְּיוֹם צַר לִי *in the day when I was afflicted.* The fem. is צָרָה.

III. *a stone*, i. q. צֹר, צוּר. Is. 5:28.

צֹר m. 1. *a rock*, i. q. צוּר no. 1. Ezek. 3:9.

2. *a knife.* Ex. 4:25. Comp. צוּר no. 3.

3. *Tyre.* i. q. צוֹר q. v.

צָרַב in Niph. *to be burned.* Ezek. 21:3. [20:47.] Kindred with צָרַף, צָרָה. In Chald. צְרָבָה *adustio.*

I. **צָרֶבֶת** f. verbal adj. from צָרַב, *burning, scorching.* Prov. 16:27.

II. **צָרֶבֶת** Lev. 13:23, 28. according to the Sept. Vulg. Chald. *a mark*, from Arab. ضرب *to impress, smite.*

צְרֵדָה proper name of a city in the tribe of Manasseh, not far from Scythopolis. 1 K. 11:26. 2 Chr. 4:17. In its stead we find צְרֵרָה Judg. 7:22, (where, however, the true reading is with ד;) and it is evidently the same place with צָרְתָן Josh. 3:16. 1 K. 4:12. 7:46.

צָרָה (with Kamets impure) fem. of צַר.

1. *a female adversary*, particularly *a rival.* 1 Sam. 1:6.

II. *distress, trouble.* Is. 8:22. With He parag. Ps. 120:1 בַּצָּרָתָה לִּי *when I was in distress;* comp. Jon. 2:3.

צָרוֹר see צָרַר.

צָרַח, Arab. صرخ, *to cry aloud.* Zeph. 1:14.

Hiph. *to shout for battle,* Is. 42:13.

צֹרִי *a Tyrian,* a gentile noun from צֹר *Tyre.* 1 K. 7:14. Ezra 3:7.

צְרִי m. Gen. 37:25. and צֳרִי Gen. 43:11. Jer. 8:22. 46:11. 51:8. in pause צֹרִי Ezek. 27:17. *the juice of the balsam bush, opobalsamum,* a production of Gilead, used for the healing of external wounds. Root צרה Arab. ضري *to flow, distil.* Comp. Bocharti Hieroz. T. I. p. 628. Celsii Hierobot. II. 180—185. and for a different view, J. D. Michaëlis Supplem. p. 2142. Warnekros in the Repertorium für morgenländ. Litteratur, Th. XV. p. 227. and Jahn's Bibl. Archaeol. § 74.

צְרִיחַ m. dec. III. a. *a high building, a palace, tower.* Judg. 9:46, 49. Spoken of old watchtowers, 1 Sam. 13:6. (Arab. صرح *a tower.*)

צֹרֶךְ m. dec. VI. p. *need, necessity.* 2 Chr. 2:15. (In Chald. and Rabbin. more common.)

צָרַע see under צָרַעַת.

צִרְעָה f. Ex. 23:28. Deut. 7:20. Josh. 24:12. according to the ancient versions and the Hebrew interpreters, *hornets.* Comp. Bocharti Hieroz. II. p. 534. Perhaps *plagues, public calamities, plagæ Dei,* (from صرع *to cast down.*)

צָרְעָה proper name of a city in the plain of the tribe of Judah, but afterwards assigned to the tribe of Dan. Josh. 15:32. 19:41. Judg. 13:2. The gentile noun is צָרְעִי 1 Chr. 2:54. and צָרְעָתִי verse 53. 4:2.

צָרַעַת f. dec. XIII. m. *the leprosy;* either in men, Lev. 13:2 ff. or in houses and garments, Lev. 13:47—59. 14:33—37. In men strictly *the white leprosy,* comp. Ex. 4:6. Num. 12:10. Hence the denom. צָרוּעַ Lev. 13:44. 22:4. and מְצֹרָע 2 K. 5:1, 27. 15:5. *leprous, infected with the leprosy.*

צָרַף, fut. יִצְרֹף. 1. *to melt, fuse,* particularly the precious metals—Hence צֹרֵף *a founder* or *workman* in gold and silver, Judg. 17:4. Prov. 25:4.

2. particularly *to refine* gold, silver, etc. by the fire, *to separate* the dross. Ps. 12:7. Is. 1:25.

3. metaphorically *to refine, purify.* Dan. 11:35. Part. pass. צָרוּף *purified, pure,* Ps. 18:31. 119:140.

4. *to try, examine, prove.* Ps. 17:3. 26:2. 105:19.

Niph. pass. Dan. 12:10.

Pi. i. q. Kal no. 1. Part. מְצָרֵף Mal. 3:2, 3.

צָרְפַת (now *Sarfend,*) a contraction of צְרֶפֶנֶת, hence with He parag. צָרְפָתָה, *Sarepta,* proper name of a Phenician city between Tyre and Sidon. 1 K. 17:9, 10. Obad. 20.

I. צָרַר (Arab. with ص.)

1. *to bind up* or *together,* (in a cloth or bundle.) Ex. 12:34. Job 26:8. Prov. 30:4. 1 Sam. 25:29 *bound up in the bundle of the living,* i. e. written in the book of the living. Hos. 13:12 *the iniquity of Ephraim is bound up,* i. e. taken away, comp. Job 14:17.

2. *to embrace* or *hold fast.* Hos. 4:19.

3. *to shut up.* 2 Sam. 20:3.

Note. Of this verb there occur in Kal the pret. צָרַר, part. pass. צָרוּר, imper. צוֹר Is. 8:16. to which some add צְרוֹר Prov. 26:8, as an infin. Some other tenses and persons borrow their form from צוּר. See צוּר no. II.

Deriv. צְרוֹר.

II. צָרַר (Arab. with ض.)

1. *to be hostile to, to persecute.* Num. 33:55. Is. 11:13. Construed with a dative, Num. 25:18. Hence part. צֹרֵר i. q. צַר *a persecutor, an enemy,* Ps. 6:8. 7:5. 23:5.

2. *to be jealous, to be a rival.* Lev. 18:18.

Deriv. צָרָה, צַר.

III. צָרַר i. q. צוּר no. I. but used intrans. *to be narrow* or *straitened.* Pret. צַר, fem. צָרָה Is. 49:20. Construed impersonally צַר לִי (1) *I am in a strait, I am in trouble.* Ps. 31:10. 69:18. Judg. 11:7. 1 Sam. 28:15. 2 Sam. 24:14. (2.) *I am much grieved,* construed with עַל. 2 Sam. 1:26.—In a similar construction occurs also the fut. וַיֵּצֶר לוֹ, see יָצַר no. II.

Hiph. הֵצַר, infin. הָצֵר.

1. trans. *to oppress, distress, afflict;* construed with a dative. Deut. 28:52. Jer. 10:18. Neh. 9:27. Fut. יָצֵר 1 K. 8:37.

2. intrans. as in Kal, *to be distressed,* construed with a dative. 2 Chr. 28:22. 33:12. Part. אִשָּׁה מְצֵרָה *a woman in childbirth,* Jer. 48:41. 49:22.

Deriv. מֵצַר.

צְרֹר and צְרוֹר m. verbal from צָרַר no. I. dec. I.

1. *a bundle, pack.* 1 Sam. 25:29. Particularly *a purse* or *bag* for money, Gen. 42:35. Prov. 7:20. For Prov. 26:8, see מַרְגֵּמָה.

2. i. q. צוֹר, *a stone, a small stone,* 2 Sam. 17:13. *a grain, kernel,* Amos 9:9.

צְרֵרָה and צָרְתָן, see צְרֵדָה.

ק

Koph, the 19th letter of the alphabet, and as a numerical sign denoting 100.

The name קוֹף is i.q. Arab. قُفٌّ *foramen acus* vel *securis.*

For its few commutations with the other palatals, see the letters כ, ג.

קִיא m. verbal from קוֹא, dec. I. *a vomit, matter thrown from the stomach,* Prov. 26:11.

קָאַת f. with the article הַקָּאַת, const. קְאַת, a water-fowl, (Lev. 11:18. Deut. 14:17.) which also inhabits waste places, (Is. 34:11. Zeph. 2:14. Ps. 102:7.) according to the ancient versions, *the pelican.* Root prob. קוֹא *to vomit,* from *the vomiting up* of muscles and other indigestible things, which is done by the pelican and other water birds.

קַב m. 2 K. 6:25. *a cab,* a measure according to the Rabbins containing the sixth part of a seah, (סְאָה.)

קָבַב *to execrate, curse.* i. q. נָקַב no. 3. q. v. From this form come only the pret. infin. and imper. Num. 23:8 ff. 24:1. Imper. with suff. קָבְנוֹ Num. 23:13, with Nun epenthetic.

קֵבָה f. *the stomach* or *maw of animals that chew the cud, echinus.* Deut. 18:3. (Arab. قِبَةٌ *idem.*)

קֻבָּה found only Num. 25:8. prob. i.q. Arab. قَبٌّ, قَبْبٌ *the part between the ribs and the rump.* Sept. μήτρα. Vulg. *genitalia.* Perhaps also קֳבָה stands for נְקֻבָה i. q. Chald. נְקוּבָה *the fundament,* from נָקַב *to pierce.*

קֻבָּה f. *a sleeping chamber.* Once Num. 25:8. (Arab. قُبَّةٌ *idem.* Hence the Span. *alcova,* Engl. *alcove.*)

קִבּוּץ m. dec. I. *a company, multitude.* Is. 57:13. Root קָבַץ.

קְבוּרָה f. verbal from קָבַר, dec. X. *a grave, sepulchre.* Gen. 35:20.

קָבַל in Kal not used.

Pi. קִבֵּל 1. *to take, receive,* synonymous with לָקַח; but used only in later Hebrew. 2 Chr. 29:16, 22. Ezra 8:30.

2. *to accept.* Job 2:10. Esth. 4:4. 9:23, 27. Applied to the receiving of instruction, Prov. 19:20.

3. *to take up.* 1 Chr. 12:18.

Hiph. *to stand over against one another.* Ex. 26:5. 36:12.

קְבַל found only in Pa. *to receive.* Dan. 2:6. 6:1. 7:18.

קֳבֵל and קֳבֵל Chald. strictly i. q. נֶגֶד *what is before* or *in front.* Hence לָקֳבֵל, with suff. לָקֳבְלָךְ, as a preposition,

1. *before.* Dan. 2:31. 3:3. 5:1.

2. *over against.* Dan. 5:5.

3. *on account of, because of.* Dan. 5:10. Ezra 4:16.

4. in combination with other particles, (1.) לָקֳבֵל דִּי as a conj. *because that.* Ezra 6:13. (2.) כָּל־קֳבֵל־דִּי *idem,* Dan. 6:5, 23. *wherefore,* Dan. 2:10. *as,* Dan. 2:40. 6:11. (3.) כָּל־קֳבֵל־דְּנָה *for this cause.* Dan. 2:12, 24.

קָבָל, in other editions קֹבֶל, (read *kŏbāl,*) i. q. קֹבֶל, a prep. *before.* 2 K. 15:10 קָבָל עָם *before the people.* The form resembles that of the Chald. קֳדָם.

קֹבֶל m. whence קָבְלוֹ Ezek. 26:9. in other editions קַבָּלוֹ *kabollo* (like קָטְנִי from קֹטֶן.) See מְחִי.

קָבַע 1. *to defraud, rob.* Mal. 3:8, 9.

2. *to spoil,* construed with two accus. Prov. 22:23.

קֻבַּעַת f. a kind of cup. Is. 51:17, 22. (Arab. قبعة *the calix of a flower;* comp. כּוֹבַע and קוֹבַע.)

קָבַץ, fut. יִקְבֹּץ, *to gather together,* (persons or things.) Gen. 41:48. 1 K. 20:1.

Niph. *to gather one's selves together, to assemble.* Is. 34:15. 43:9.

Pi. 1. as in Kal, *to assemble, gather together.* Deut. 30:3, 4. Jer. 31:10. Is. 11:12, 13, 14.

2. i. q. אָסַף no. 4. *to draw in, withdraw, lose.* Joel 2:6. Nah. 2:11. See פָּארוּר.

Pu. pass. of Pi. no. 1. Ezek. 38:8.

Hithpa. reflex. Josh. 9:2. Judg. 9:47.

קַבְצְאֵל see יְקַבְצְאֵל.

קְבֻצָה f. verbal from קָבַץ, dec. X. *a collecting, gathering.* Ezek. 22:20.

קָבַר, fut. יִקְבֹּר, *to bury.* Gen. 23:4, 19. 25:9.

Niph. pass. Ruth 1:17. Judg. 8:32.

Pi. i. q. Kal. 1 K. 11:15.

Pu. pass. Gen. 25:10.

קֶבֶר m. with suff. קִבְרִי, plur. קְבָרִים, const. קִבְרֵי, and קְבָרוֹת, const. קִבְרוֹת, m. verbal from קָבַר, dec. VI. h. *a grave, sepulchre.* Ps. 5:10. Gen. 23:9, 20.

קִבְרוֹת־הַתַּאֲוָה (*graves of lusting*) name of a place in the desert, the occasion of which is given Num. 11:34. Comp. Num. 33:16. Deut. 9:22.

קָדַד found only in the fut. יִקֹּד, plur. יִקְּדוּ, (with a Chaldaic form,) *to incline, bend, bow.* 1 Sam. 24:9. 28:14. It is usually followed by הִשְׁתַּחֲוָה, Gen. 24:26. Ex. 12:27. 34:8. Num. 22:31. 1 K. 1:16.

קִדָּה f. Ex. 30:24. Ezek. 27:19. according to the Syr. Chald. Vulg. *the Arabian cassia,* i. q. קְצִיעָה. Root. قدّ *to split.*

קְדוּמִים masc. plur. found only Judg. 5:21 נַחַל קְדוּמִים perhaps *the brook of ancient days,* i. e. celebrated from ancient days. Sept. Vatic. χειμάῤῥους ἀρχαίων. Chald. *rivus, in quo facta sunt Israeli signa et fortia facta ab antiquis.* Or, *brook of slaughters,* comp. קֶדֶם no. 3. and the Arab. قدم *to be bold, courageous.*

קָדוֹשׁ and קָדֹשׁ verbal adj. from קָדַשׁ, dec. III. a. *holy;* spoken of Jehovah, Ps. 99:3. of the people, Lev. 11:44. of sacred places, Lev. 6:9. [6:17.]—קָדוֹשׁ *the holy one,* i. e. by way of eminence, Jehovah, Job 6:10. Is. 40:25. Hab. 3:3. Also קְדוֹשׁ יִשְׂרָאֵל *the holy one of Israel* i. e. Jehovah, Ps. 71:22. and in Isaiah, frequently.

Plur. קְדוֹשִׁים *the holy ones,* by which is denoted (1.) *angels,* particularly in later Hebrew, (see קַדִּישׁ.) Dan. 8:13. Job 5:1. 15:15. Zech. 14:5. Ps. 89:6, 8. perhaps Deut. 33:3. Hence (2.) *the pious.* Ps. 16:3. 34:10. (3.) *the Jews,* (see again קַדִּישׁ.) Dan. 8:24. (4.) as a pluralis excellentiæ, *Jehovah.* Hos. 12:1. Josh. 24:19. Prov. 9:10. 30:3.

קָדַח (in Arab. *to strike fire.*)

1. *to kindle, to cause to burn.* Jer. 17:4. Is. 50:11. 64:1.

2. *to kindle itself.* Deut. 32:22. Jer. 15:14.

קַדַּחַת f. verbal from קָדַח, *a hot fever,* Lev. 26:16. Deut. 28:22.

קָדִים m. verbal from קָדַם.

1. liter. *what is before* or *in front.* Hab. 1:9 קָדִימָה *forwards.*

2. *the east,* i. q. קֶדֶם. Ezek. 47:18. 48:1.

3. *the east wind,* in full רוּחַ קָדִים. This in the east is an extremely tempestuous wind, Job 27:21. Is. 27:8. Jer. 18:17. also felt at sea, Ps. 48:8. Ezek. 27:26. and by its scorching heat blasting the grain and plants, Gen. 41:6, 23. Jon. 4:8. Metaphorically like רוּחַ, *something vain, vanity,* Hos. 12:2.

קַדִּישׁ Chald. adj. *holy;* e. g. אֱלָהִין קַדִּישִׁין *the holy gods,* Dan. 4:5, 6. [4:8, 9.] 5:11. Used particularly (1.) of angels, Dan. 4:10. [4:13.] See קְדוֹשִׁים no. (1.) (2.) of the Jews, Dan. 7:21. in full קַדִּישֵׁי עֶלְיוֹנִין *the saints of the Most High,* Dan. 7:18, 22, 25. comp. 1 Esd. 8:70 ἅγιοι τοῦ ὑψίστου.

קָדַם found only in Pi. קִדֵּם.

1. *to precede, go before.* Ps. 68:26. Construed with an accus. of the person, Ps. 89:15.

2. *to be beforehand, to anticipate,* construed with an accus. Ps. 17:13. 119:148. Hence with an infin. it forms a periphrasis of the adverb *before,* Jon. 4:2 קִדַּמְתִּי לִבְרֹחַ *I fled before,* i. e. recently.

3. *to fall upon.* Ps. 18:6, 19.

4. *to do early, to rise up early,* i. q. הִשְׁכִּים. Ps. 119:147.

5. *to meet,* construed with an accus. of the person; particularly with help, Ps. 59:11. 79:8. Job 3:12. Also spoken of an adverse event, Job 30:27. Is. 37:33 לֹא יְקַדְּמֶנָּה מָגֵן *no shield shall meet it* (*the city,*) i. e. shall be turned to it. Construed with בְּ of the thing, *to bring,* (comp. בְּ no. 2.) Deut. 23:5. Micah 6:6. Neh. 13:2. So without בְּ, Ps. 21:4.

Hiph. 1. i. q. Pi. no. 3. *to fall on a person,* (spoken of a calamity,) construed with בְּעַד. Am. 9:10.

2. *to be first in doing a service,* construed with an accus. Job 41:3. [41:11.]

Deriv. out of course קָדִים, קְדוּמִים.

קֶדֶם m. verbal from קָדַם, dec. VI. a.

1. strictly *what is before* or *in front.* As an adv. *before,* Ps. 139:5. Hence

2. *the east, the east country.* (comp. אָחוֹר.) Job 23:8.—מִקֶּדֶם *towards the east,* Gen. 2:8. 12:8.—מִקֶּדֶם לְ *to the east of,* Gen. 3:24.—בְּנֵי קֶדֶם *the sons of the east,* i. e. the Bedouin Arabs in the deserts east of Palestine, Job 1:3. Is. 11:14. Jer. 49:28. Ezek. 25:4. 1 K. 5:10. [4:30.] Judg. 6:3 ff. Here belong also מַלְכֵי קֶדֶם Is. 19:11. אֶרֶץ קֶדֶם Gen. 25:6. and אֶרֶץ בְּנֵי קֶדֶם Gen. 29:1. —The following passage is more doubtful, Is. 2:6 מָלְאוּ מִקֶּדֶם *they are full of the east,* i. e. prob. of the magic arts of the Syrians and Chaldeans. Comp. 9:11.

3. spoken of time, *former times,* used in poetry for עוֹלָם. Ps. 44:2. Is. 23:7. —מִקֶּדֶם *from former times,* Ps. 74:12. 77:6, 12. As an adv. (1.) *aforetime,* Jer. 30:20. Lam. 5:21. (2.) *a long time,* Ps. 55:20. (The usual expresion in prose is לְפָנִים, מִלְּפָנִים.) Also as a prep. *before,* Prov. 8:22. Plur. *primordia,* Prov. 8:23.

קֵדֶם *idem;* hence קֵדְמָה *towards the east,* Gen. 25:6. Ex. 27:13.

קֳדָם, קֳדָם Chald. prep. *before,* in space; more rarely in time, e. g. Dan. 7:7. With suff. in the plur. as קָדָמַי, קֳדָמוֹהִי.—מִן קֳדָם i. q. Heb. מִלִּפְנֵי, מִפְּנֵי *a coram,* e. g. Dan. 2:15. for the most part simply i. q. מִן, Dan. 2:6. 6:27. or קֳדָם, Dan. 5:24.

קִדְמָה dec. X. i. q. קֶדֶם nos. 1. 2. used only in the const. state, as a preposition, *before,* i. e. to the east of. Gen. 2:14. 4:16. 1 Sam. 13:5. Ezek. 39:11.

קַדְמָה f. verbal from קָדַם, dec. X. *origin,* Is. 23:7. *former state,* Ezek. 16:55. Used in the const. state, as a prep. and with the omission of אֲשֶׁר, as a conj. *before that,* Ps. 129:6.

קַדְמָה Chald. *idem.*—מִן־קַדְמַת as a prep. *before,* hence מִן קֳדָם דְּנָה Dan. 6:11. מִקַּדְמַת דְּנָה Ezra 5:11. *before, aforetime.*

קַדְמוֹן, fem. ־ָה, denom. adj. from קֶדֶם, *eastern.* Ezek. 47:8.

קַדְמֹנִי m. ־ִית f. denom. adj. from קֶדֶם.

1. *front, fore.* Ezek. 10:19. 11:1.

2. *eastern.*—הַיָּם הַקַּדְמֹנִי *the eastern sea,* i. e. the Dead Sea, in opposition to *the western* or *Mediterranean,* Ezek. 47:18. Joel 2:20.

3. *ancient, belonging to former times.* Ezek. 38:17. Plur. קַדְמֹנִים *the ancients* or *forefathers,* Job 18. 20. 1 Sam. 24:14 מְשַׁל הַקַּדְמֹנִי *a proverb of the ancients,* (where the singular is used collectively.) Plur. fem. קַדְמֹנִיּוֹת *things of old,* Is. 43:18.

4. proper name of a Canaanitish people. Gen. 15:19.

קַדְמַי Chald. *the first.* Plur. Dan. 7:24. Fem. emph. קַדְמָיְתָא Dan. 7:4. plur. קַדְמָיָתָא Dan. 7:8.

קָדְקֹד m. with suff. קָדְקֳדוֹ, dec. VII. j. *the crown, head.* Gen. 49:26. Deut. 33:16. More in full קָדְקֹד שֵׂעָר *the hairy crown* or *scalp,* Ps. 68:22.

קָדַר 1. *to be black, to be dark-coloured,* spoken e. g. of the skin burnt by the sun, Job 30:28. *to grow black,* spoken of the day, of the sun and moon, Jer. 4:28. Joel 2:10. 4:15. [3:15.] Mic. 3:6.

2. *to be dirty, muddy, turbid,* spoken of a river. Job 6:16. Hence *to go in dirty garments, to be in mourning.* Part. קֹדֵר *a mourner,* Ps. 35:14. 38:7. 42:10.

Hiph. 1. *to make dark.* Ezek. 32:7, 8.

2. *to cause to mourn.* Ezek. 31:15.

Hithpa. *to blacken one's self, to become black.* 1 K. 18:45.

קֵדָר m. a proper name.

1. the son of Ishmael. Gen. 25:13.

2. a tribe of Arabian nomades descended from Kedar. Cant. 1:5. Is. 42:11. 60:7. Jer. 49:28. Ezek. 27:21. also called בְּנֵי קֵדָר Is. 21:17. In Pliny (H. N. v. 11.) *Cedrei.*

קִדְרוֹן (*the turbid,* comp. Job 6:16.) a brook and valley of the same name between Jerusalem and Mount Olivet. The brook empties itself into the Dead Sea. 2 Sam. 15:23. 1 K. 2:37. 15:13. 2 K. 23:4. Jer. 31:40.

קַדְרוּת f. verbal from קָדַר, *blackness, darkness.* Is. 50:3.

קְדֹרַנִּית adv. *mournfully, in sadness,* from קָדַר. Mal. 3:14.

קָדַשׁ and קָדֵשׁ (Num. 17:2.) fut. יִקְדַּשׁ.

1. *to be sacred* or *holy,* Ex. 29:37. 30:29. *to become sacred* or *holy,* Ex. 29:21.—Is. 65:5 קְדַשְׁתִּיךָ *I am holier than thou,* for קָדַשְׁתִּי מִמְּךָ. The primary meaning was probably *to be clean,* comp. Lev. 11:43, 44. Deut. 23:14. 2 Sam. 11:4.

2. *to be consecrated, to fall to the sanctuary.* Deut. 22:9.

Niph. 1. *to be sanctified.* Ex. 29:43. Is. 5:16.

2. *to be regarded* or *treated as holy, to be hallowed.* Lev. 10:3. 22:32.

3. *to shew one's self holy* or *glorious in* a person, construed with בְּ; either by benefits, Ezek. 20:41. 28:25. or by judgments, Ezek. 28:22. Num. 20:13.

Pi. קִדֵּשׁ 1. *to make holy, to consecrate, dedicate, sanctify;* e. g. a person for the priest's office, Ex. 28:41. an altar, Ex. 29:36. a people, Ex. 19:10, 14. Josh. 7:13. comp. Job 1:5. a finished building, Neh. 3:1. Particularly *to consecrate* as an offering to God, *Deo consecrare,* Ex. 13:2. Comp. Hiph.

2. *to regard as holy,* e. g. a priest, Lev. 21:8. the sabbath, Ex. 20:8. God, Deut. 32:51.

3. *to pronounce holy,* (spoken of Jehovah,) e. g. the sabbath, Gen. 2:3. the people, Lev. 20:8. 21:8.

4. *to appoint, institute, proclaim,* (something holy;) e. g. a fast, Joel 1:14. 2:15, (parall. קָרָא.) a festival assembly, 2 K. 10:20.—קַדֵּשׁ מִלְחָמָה *to sanc-*

tify a war, i. e. to prepare one's self for it, (which was connected with religious solemnities, comp. Ps.110:3. 1Sam.7:9, 10.) Joel 4:9.[3:9.] Jer.6:4. Mic.3:5.

5. *to separate as holy*. Ex. 19:23.

Pu. 1. pass. of Pi. no. 1. Ezek. 48:11.

2. pass. of Pi. no. 4. Is. 13:3 לִמְקֻדָּשָׁי *my consecrated ones, those whom I have consecrated for war*.

Hiph. 1. i. q. Pi. no. 1. *Deo consecrare*. Lev. 27:14 ff. Judg. 17:3. 2 Sam. 8:11.

2. i. q. Pi. no. 2. *to sanctify, to regard as holy*. Is. 8:13. 29:23. Num. 20:12.

3. i. q. Pi. no. 3. *to pronounce holy*. Jer. 1:5. 1 K. 9:3.

4. *to set apart, appoint*. Jer. 12:3. Zeph. 1:7.

Hithpa. 1. *to sanctify* or *purify one's self*, (by washings, lustrations.) Ex. 19:22. 2 Chr. 5:11. 29:15. Comp. Kal no. 1.

2. *to shew one's self holy* or *glorious*. Ezek. 38:23.

3. *to be kept* or *celebrated*, spoken of a festival. Is. 30:29.

Deriv. out of course מִקְדָּשׁ, קָדוֹשׁ, קֹדֶשׁ.

קָדֵשׁ m. verbal from קָדַשׁ, dec. V. a.

1. *a male prostitute, a sodomite, puer mollis*, liter. *one consecrated*. Deut. 23:18. 1 K. 14:24. 15:12. Fem. קְדֵשָׁה *a female prostitute, a harlot*, Gen. 38:21, 22. Deut. 23:18. In the religious worship of the Arameans, which prevailed also at times among the Hebrews, both maidens and boys prostituted themselves in honour of their idols. Comp. Num. 25:1—15. Herod. i. 150. and the passages already quoted.

2. קָדֵשׁ and קָדֵשׁ בַּרְנֵעַ Num. 34:4. Deut. 1:2, 19. 2:14. proper name of a place in the desert, which lay south of Palestine, between Idumea and Egypt. Gen. 14:7. Num. 13:3. 27:14. 33:36, 37. See Relandi Palæstina, p. 114.

קֶדֶשׁ 1. a city in the south of the tribe of Judah. Josh. 15:23.

2. a city in the tribe of Naphtali. Josh. 12:22. 19:37. 21:32. Judg. 4:6. 1 Chr. 6:61. Also written קֶדֶשׁ Judg. 4:9.

3. a city in the tribe of Issachar. 1 Chr. 6:57. Also called קִשְׁיוֹן. Josh. 19:20. 21:28.

קֹדֶשׁ m. once קוֹדֶשׁ (Dan. 11:30.) with suff. קָדְשִׁי, plur. קֳדָשִׁים, also קָדָשִׁים, (read *kŏdashim*,) verbal from קָדַשׁ, dec. VI. m.

1. *holiness*. Ps. 89:36. Usually employed as a genitive after another noun for a periphrasis of the adjective *holy*; as שֵׁם קָדְשִׁי *my holy name*, Lev. 20:3 רוּחַ קָדְשְׁךָ *thy holy spirit*, Ps. 51:13.

2. *a holy place, a sanctuary*, spoken of the tabernacle of the congregation and of the temple. Ex. 28:43. 29:30. 35:19. 39:1. And particularly i. q. הֵיכָל *the holy place before the oracle*, 1 K. 8:8.

3. *what is holy* or *sacred*, the abstract being used for the concrete. Lev. 12:4. 21:6 וְהָיוּ קֹדֶשׁ *and they* (*the priests*) *shall be holy*. Jer. 2:3.

4. *something consecrated, a sacred gift*. Particularly in the plur. הַקֳּדָשִׁים Lev. 21:22. 22:2, 3, 15.

5. קֹדֶשׁ קָדָשִׁים (1.) *what is very holy*, spoken e. g. of the altar and sacred utensils, Ex. 29:37. of the sacred gifts, etc. Plur. קָדְשֵׁי קֳדָשִׁים *idem*, Lev. 21:22. Ezek. 42:13. (2.) *the holy of holies* in the temple, otherwise called דְּבִיר. Ex. 26:33, 34. More in full בֵּית קֹדֶשׁ הַקֳּדָשִׁים 2 Chr. 3:8, 10. Sometimes simply הַקֹּדֶשׁ, Ezek. 41:23.

קָהָה *to be blunted*, spoken of teeth. Jer. 31:29, 30. Ezek. 18:2.

Pi. קֵהָה *idem*, intrans. spoken of iron. Ecc. 10:10. Comp. כָּהָה.

קָהַל in Kal not used.

Hiph. *to assemble, call together*, (a people.) Num. 8:9. 10:7. 20:8.

Niph. *to assemble, come together*. Num. 16:3.

Deriv. out of course מַקְהֵלִים, מַקְהֵלוֹת.

קָהָל m. verbal from קָהַל, dec. IV. a. *an assembly, congregation*; particularly of the Israelitish people. This people is called הַקָּהָל Lev. 4:13. קְהַל יִשְׂרָאֵל Deut. 31:30. קְהַל יְהוָה Num. 16:3. 20:4.—קְהַל גּוֹיִם Gen. 35:11. and קְהַל עַמִּים Gen. 28:3. 48:4. *a multitude of nations.*

קְהִלָּה f. verbal from קָהַל, dec. X. *a congregation.* Deut. 33:4. Neh. 5:7.

קֹהֶלֶת *Koheleth,* the proper name by which Solomon is distinguished in the Book of Ecclesiastes. It is usually construed as masc. and without the article, Ecc. 1:1, 2, 12. 12:9, 10. once with the article, 12:8. (like many proper names which have an appellative signification, see Gesenius' Lehrgeb. § 167. 1.) and once construed as feminine, 7:27. from a reference to the feminine termination. This feminine form occurs in several proper names of men, e.g. סֹפֶרֶת Ezra 2:55. פֹּכֶרֶת 2:57. also in some masculine appellatives, e. g. פֶּחָה, כְּנָת, q. v. and in Arabic much more frequently.

The greatest difficulty attends the explanation of this proper name, which evidently has some significancy. The two following have been proposed from the Hebrew language, (1.) *the assembler,* or rather *preacher before an assembly,* Lat. *concionator.* Sept. ἐκκλησιαστής. Vulg. *Ecclesiastes.* Luth. *Prediger.* (2.) *the collector,* (namely, of maxims, proverbs, etc.) Symm. παροιμιαστής. But קָהַל signifies only *to assemble* people, not *to collect* things.—In Arabic, the root قهل signifies *exaruit* cutis, pecul. *ex multa spirituali exercitatione;* conj. V. *lente incessit, debili et infirmo statu fuit;* comp. كهل *to be old.* Hence קֹהֶלֶת would signify *an old man who has reflected much and had great experience.* It is in Arabic too, that this feminine form most frequently occurs. See Bocharti Hieroz. T. I. p. 88. Jahn's Einleit. in das A. T. Th. 2. p. 828. Carpzov. Introductio in V. T. T. II. p. 200. Dindorf, Quomodo nomen Kohelet Salomoni tribuatur? Leip. 1791. 4.

קַו and **קָו** m. with suff. קַוָּם, dec. VIII. a.

1. *a cord, line.* 1 K. 7:23. Particularly *a measuring cord* or *line,* Ezek. 47:3. 2 K. 21:13 *I will stretch over Jerusalem the measuring line of Samaria,* i. e. I will destroy it like Samaria, comp. Is. 34:11. The same phrase is also used in reference to rebuilding, Zech. 1:16. With the former use of it is connected Is. 18:2 גּוֹי קַו־קָו *a people of measuring lines;* i. e. whose business is to lay waste. Others: *a people of strength,* comp. Arab. قُوَّة *a line,* and *strength.* Metaphorically perhaps *a rule, precept,* like the Germ. *Richtschnur,* Is. 28:10. Comp. צַו.

2. *a musical chord,* hence *a sound.* Ps. 19:5.

קוא *to vomit.* Metaphorically Lev. 18:28.

Hiph. *idem.* Prov. 23:8. Metaphorically Lev. 18:28.

Deriv. קֵא, קִיא.

קוֹבַע m. i. q. כּוֹבַע *a helmet.* 1 Sam. 17:38. Ezek. 23:24.

קָוָה in Kal found only in the part. קֹוֶה, and Pi. קִוָּה, *to wait* or *look for, to wait on;* construed with an accus. Job 30:26. with אֶל, Ps. 27:14. 37:34. with לְ, Jer. 8:15. 14:19. Particularly (1.) קַוֵּה יְהוָה and לַיהוָה *to wait on Jehovah,* i. e. to confide in him. Ps. 25:5. 39:8. 40:2. (2.) *to lie in wait for* a person. Ps. 119:95. 56:7.

Niph. *to gather themselves together;* spoken of nations, Jer. 3:17. of waters, Gen. 1:9. The ideas *to wait* and *to assemble* are not very remote from each other; the signification of Niphal, therefore, is not to be separated from that of Kal.

Deriv. out of course מִקְוֶה, מִקְוָה, תִּקְוָה.

קָוֶה 1 K. 7:23 Keth. i. q. קַו.

קוֹחַ Is. 61:1. See פְּקַחְקוֹחַ.

I. **קוּט** i. q. קוּץ *to loathe, abhor, be grieved with,* construed with בְּ of the thing. Fut. אָקוּט Ps. 95:10. For the pret. we find נָקֹטָה Job 10:1.

Niph. *idem.* Ezek. 20:43. 36:31.

For the third person we find נָקֹטּוּ, (as if from קָטַט,) Ezek. 6:9.

Hithpal. הִתְקוֹטֵט *to be grieved.* Ps. 119:158. 139:21.

II. קוּט or קוֹט i. q. Arab. قطّ *to be cut off.* Job 8:14 אֲשֶׁר יָקוֹט כִּסְלוֹ *cujus spes præciditur.*

קוֹל m. plur. קוֹלוֹת and קֹלוֹת, dec. I.

1. *a voice.* (Root קול Arab. قال *to speak.*)—In the accusative קוֹלִי *with* (all) *my voice,* i. e. with a loud voice, Ps. 142:2. קוֹל גָּדוֹל *with a loud voice,* Ezek. 11:13. Ezra 10:12. קוֹל אֶחָד *with one voice,* i. e. with one consent, Ex. 24:3.—קוֹל יְהוָה *the voice of Jehovah,* i. e. the thunder, Ps. 29:3 ff.—נָתַן קוֹל *to lift up one's voice,* Gen. 45:2. Ps. 104:12. spoken of Jehovah, *to thunder,* Ps. 77:18. construed with לְ, *to call to,* Prov. 2:3.— נָתַן קוֹל בְּ *to proclaim in* a country, 2 Chr. 24:9.—נָתַן בְּקוֹל i. q. נָתַן קוֹל, Jer. 12:8. applied to the roaring of thunder, Ps. 46:7. 68:34.

2. *a report, rumour.* Gen. 45:16. Jer. 3:9.

3. *a sound, noise,* of inanimate things. 2 Sam. 15:10. Ezek. 1:24.

קוּם, fut. יָקוּם, apoc. וַיָּקָם, pret. once after the Arabic form קָאם (Hos. 10:14.)

1. *to stand* or *get up, to rise, arise.* Often used pleonastically, as Gen. 22:3 וַיָּקָם וַיֵּלֶךְ *and he rose up and went.* Job 1:20. With a redundant dative of the pronoun, קוּמִי לָךְ *rise up,* Cant. 2:10. The person *against* whom one rises up is preceded by עַל, Ps. 3:2. 54:5. 86:14. Is. 31:2. by אֶל, Gen. 4:8. by בְּ, Ps. 27:12. Job 16:8, (here *to stand up against* one, as a witness, comp. עָנָה בְּ.) In the participle the same object is expressed by suffixes, as קָמַי *they that rise up against me,* Ps. 18:40. קָמָיו Deut. 33:11.

2. *to stand,* in different relations; (1.) *to last, endure.* Job 15:29. Amos 7:2, 5. 1 Sam. 24:21. 13:14. (2.) *to continue,* construed with לְ *to* a person, Lev. 25:30. with עַל *in* a thing, Is. 32:8. (3.) *to prosper,* construed with לְ. Job 22:28. Is. 8:10. 14:24. Prov. 19:21. (4.) *to come to pass, to be fulfilled,* spoken of a prediction, i. q. בּוֹא no. 2. (2.) Jer. 44:28, 29. Antith. נָפַל no. 1. (8.)—(5.) *to be legal, valid;* spoken e. g. of testimony, Deut. 19:15. of a vow, Num. 30:5 ff. (6.) *to stand by, assist,* construed with לְ. Ps. 94:16. (7.) *to stand before, resist,* construed with לִפְנֵי. Josh. 7:13. (8.) קָמוּ עֵינָיו *the eyes were fixed* or *set.* 1 K. 14:4. comp. 1 Sam. 4:15. (9.) pass. of Pi. *to be made sure, to be confirmed.* Gen. 23:17, 20.

Pi. קִיַּם (used chiefly in the later books,) causat. of Kal no. 2. in many relations; (1.) *to confirm, establish, ratify.* Ruth 4:7. Esth. 9:29, 31 at the beginning. (2.) *to impose a duty, to lay under an obligation,* construed with עַל, (comp. in Chald. קַיֵּם עַל *to bind by an oath.*) Est. 9:21, 31 in the middle. (3.) קִיֵּם עֲלֵיהֶם *to take on one's self.* Est. 9:27, 31 at the end. (4.) *to perform, keep,* (an oath.) Ps. 119:106. (5.) *to bring to pass.* Ezek. 13:6. (6.) *to preserve alive.* Ps. 119:28. (In the Targums more common.)

Pil. קוֹמֵם 1. causat. of Kal no. 1. *to raise up,* (ruins, old foundations.) Is. 44:26. 58:12. 61:4.

2. intrans. *to rise up.* Mic. 2:8.

Hiph. הֵקִים 1. *to raise up* persons or things; e. g. a judge, Judg. 2:18. a prophet, Jer. 29:15. a tent, Ex. 26:30. a statue, Deut. 16:22.—הֵקִים שֵׁם לְ Deut. 25:7. Ruth 4:5, 10. and הֵקִים זֶרַע לְ Gen. 38:8. *to raise up a name* or *posterity* to a person, i. e. to continue his race according to the levirate law.

2. *to make to stand;* hence *to appoint,* e. g. a king. Deut. 28:36.

3. *to make to stand still, to check, quiet.* Ps. 107:29.

4. causat. of Kal no. 2. (4.) *to accomplish, fulfil;* an oath, Gen. 26:3. a promise, 1 Sam. 1:23.

5. causat. of Kal no. 2. (5.) *to make valid, to establish.* Num. 30:14, 15.

Hoph. הוּקַם pass. of Hiph. no. 1. Ex.

40:17. of no. 2. 2 Sam. 23:1. of no. 4. Jer. 35:14.

Hithpal. הִתְקוֹמֵם *to rise up*. Ps. 17:7. Construed with לְ *against* a person, Job 20:27. also simply with a suffix, מִתְקוֹמְמַי *my enemy*, Job 27:7. Ps. 59:2.

Deriv. out of course קִים, מָקוֹם, יְקוּם, קָם, תְּקוּמָה, תְּקוֹמֵם, קָמָה, קוֹמָה.

קוּם Chald. 1. *to rise up*. Dan. 3:24.

2. *to stand*. Dan. 3:3. 7:17.

Pa. קַיֵּם e. g. קַיָּם קְיָם *to issue* or *establish a decree*, Dan. 6:8.

Aph. הֲקִים, once אֲקִים (Dan. 3:1.) plur. הֲקִימוּ, part. מְהָקֵים, fut. יְקִים and יְהָקֵים.

1. *to raise* or *set up*, e. g. a statue. Dan. 3:1 ff.

2. *to appoint*, e. g. a prince or governor. Dan. 6:2.

Hoph. הֳקִים (after the Hebrew form) *to stand*. Dan. 7:4.

Deriv. קְיָם, קַיָּם.

קוֹמָה f. verbal from קוּם, dec. X. *height*. Gen. 6:15. Is. 37:24 *the height of his cedars*, i. e. his high cedars. Spoken of persons, *tallness*, *stature*, 1 Sam. 16:7. 28:20 מְלֹא קוֹמָתוֹ *his whole length*. Ezek. 13:18 כָּל־קוֹמָה *every stature*, i. e. people of every size.

קוֹמְמִיּוּת adv. *upright*. Lev. 26:13. Root קוּם.

קוּן found only in Pil. קוֹנֵן *to set up a lamentation*, *to lament*. 2 Sam. 1:17. Construed with עַל and אֶל *over* a person or thing, 2 Sam. 3:33. Ezek. 27:32. Deriv. קִינָה.

קוּס see קָסַם.

קוֹעַ Ezek. 23:23. prob. i. q. the preceding word שׁוֹעַ, with which it forms a paronomasia, according to the Hebrew interpreters, Vulg. and others, *a prince*, *nobleman*. Perhaps liter. *admissarius*, (comp. the Arab. قاع conj. I. VIII.) and then figuratively *princeps*, (like עַתּוּד.) Or שׁוֹעַ וְקוֹעַ may form an antithesis, *high and low*, the latter being kindred with the Arab. وكع, whose derivatives signify *to be low*, *base*, *ignoble*.

קוֹף m. dec. I. *an ape*. 1 K. 10:22. Hence the Greek words κῆπος, κῆβος, κεῖβος, which denote several species of monkies.

I. קוּץ i. q. קוּט.

1. *to loathe*, *abhor*; construed with בְּ of the person. Lev. 20:23. Num. 21:5.

2. *to be afraid*, construed with מִפְּנֵי. Ex. 1:12. Num. 22:3. Is. 7:16.

Hiph. הֵקִיץ *to throw into fear* or *consternation*, *to besiege*, (a city.) Is. 7:6. In Arab. it has the same signification.

II. קוּץ found only in Hiph. הֵקִיץ intrans. *to awake*, i. q. יָקַץ. Ps. 3:6. 73:20. Imper. הָקִיצָה, i. q. עוּרָה, *awake*, Ps. 35:23. Applied to *the awaking* from the sleep of death, Job 14:12. Dan. 12:2.

III. קוּץ or קִיץ Is. 18:6. prob. denom. from קַיִץ, hence *to summer*, *to pass the summer*. (Arab. قاظ med. Je *idem*.) See חָרַף no. III.

קוֹץ m. dec. I. *a thorn*. Gen. 3:18. Is. 32:13.

קְוֻצּוֹת fem. plur. dec. X. *locks*. Cant. 5:2, 11. Syr. ܩܘܨܬܐ *idem*. Arab. קצה قُصَّة *antiæ*, *capillus frontis*.

קוּר *to dig*, particularly for water. Is. 37:25. Deriv. מָקוֹר.

Hiph. *to let spring up*, e. g. water. Jer. 6:7.

Pilp. קַרְקַר *to destroy*, as in Chaldaic. Is. 22:5 מְקַרְקַר קִר *they destroy* or *pull down the wall*. (Talmud. קרקורא דקיר *destructio parietis*.—It appears to be a denominative, with a privative signification, from קִיר *a wall*.) Num. 24:17 וְקַרְקַר כָּל־בְּנֵי־שֵׁת *and it shall destroy all the children of arrogance*. Sept. προνομεύσει. Vulg. *vastabit*.

קוּרִים masc. plur. dec. I. *thin threads*, *a web*. Is. 59:5, 6. (Arab. قور *funiculus*.)

קוֹרָה f. dec. X. *a beam*, so called perhaps because beams *meet* and *cross* each other. (See קָרָה Pi.) 2 K. 6:2, 5.

Cant. 1:12. By a synecdoche, *a house*, (like the Greek *μέλαθρον*,) Gen. 19:8.

קוֹשׁ i. q. יָקֹשׁ *to lay snares*. Found only in the fut. Is. 29:21 יְקֹשׁוּן, or as in other MSS. יְקֹשׁוּן.

קַט adv. *only*, i. q. Arab. قَطُّ. Ezek. 16:47.

קֶטֶב m. and קֹטֶב, with suff. קָטָבְךָ (read *kotobcha*) Hos. 13:14. dec. VI.

1. *destruction, devastation;* usually derived from קטב in Chald. and Arab. *secuit*. Is. 28:2 שַׂעַר קָטֶב *a destructive* or *devastating storm*.

2. particularly *pestilence, contagion*. Deut. 32:24. Ps. 91:6. Hos. 13:14.

קְטוֹרָה f. verbal from קָטַר, *incense*. Deut. 33:10.

קָטַט Ezek. 6:9. comp. קוּט.

קָטַל, fut. יִקְטֹל, *to kill, slay*. Only Ps. 139:19. Job 13:15. 24:14.

קְטַל Chald. *idem*. Part. act. קָטֵל Dan. 5:19. Pret. pass. קְטִיל Dan. 5:30. 7:11.

Pa. קַטֵּל *idem*, in reference to the death of many. Dan. 2:14. 3:32. (In Syr. Pe. *interfecit* unum; Pa. *interfecit* plures.)

Ithpe. pass. Dan. 2:13.

Ithpa. pass. Dan. 2:13.

קֶטֶל m. verbal from קָטַל, *slaughter*. Obad. 9.

קָטֹן, fut. יִקְטַן, *to be small, little*. 2 Sam. 7:19. Gen. 32:11.

Hiph. *to make small*. Am. 8:5.

קָטָן, fem. קְטַנָּה, plur. קְטַנִּים, dec. VIII. a. and קָטֹן, verbal adj. from קָטֹן.

1. *small;* freq.

2. *young*. Gen. 9:24. 27:15.

3. *small, unimportant;* spoken of persons, Is. 36:9. of things, Ex. 18:22, 26.

4. as a subst. *the little finger*. With suff. קָטָנִּי (*katŏni*) 1 K. 12:10.

קָטַף, fut. יִקְטֹף, *to pluck off* or *up*. Deut. 23:26. Job 30:4.

Niph. *to be cut off*. Job 8:12.

קָטַר in Kal not used. In Arab. قطر *to emit fragrance*.

Pi. קִטֵּר *to burn incense in honour of a god*, construed with לְ. Jer. 7:9. 11:13. Always as an idolatrous act. Part. fem. מְקַטְּרוֹת *altars of incense*, 2 Chr. 30:14.

Pu. מְקֻטֶּרֶת *incense*. Cant. 3:6.

Hiph. i. q. Pi. 1 K. 3:3. 11:8. For the most part construed with an accus. of the incense or victim, Ex. 29:18. Lev. 1:9, 17. 2:2, 16.

Hoph. הָקְטַר pass. Lev. 6:15. [6:22.] Part. מֻקְטָר *incense*, Mal. 1:11.

Deriv. מִקְטֶרֶת, מִקְטָר, קִיטוֹר, קְטֹרֶת, קְטוֹרָה, מְקַטְּרָה.

קְטַר found only in the plur. קִטְרִין Chald. *knots;* particularly (1.) *joints*. Dan. 5:6. (2.) metaphorically *difficult problems*. Dan. 5:12, 16. Root קְטַר=קָשַׁר *to bind*.

קָטֹר found only Ezek. 46:22 חֲצֵרוֹת קְטֻרוֹת prob. *uncovered courts*. Comp. Syr. ܒܰܝܬܳܐ ܩܛܺܝܪܳܐ *domus sine tecto*.

קְטֹרֶת f. with suff. קְטָרְתִּי, verbal from קָטַר, dec. XIII. e.

1. *incense*. Ex. 30:1 ff. Lev. 4:7. 10:1. Is. 1:13.

2. *an offering*. Ps. 66:15 קְטֹרֶת אֵילִים *an offering of rams*.

קִיא m. dec. I. *a vomit*. Jer. 48:26. Is. 19:14. 28:8. Root קוֹא *to vomit*.

קָיָה i. q. קוֹא *to vomit*. Imper. קְיוּ Jer. 25:27.

קַיִט Chald. i. q. Heb. קַיִץ *summer*. Dan. 2:35.

קִיטוֹר m. verbal from קָטַר.

1. *smoke*. Gen. 19:28. Ps. 119:83.

2. *vapour*. Ps. 148:8.

קִים dec. I. i. q. קָם *an adversary, enemy*. Job 22:20. Sept. ὑπόστασις, as if they read קִימָם.

קְיָם m. Chald. *an order, edict*, Dan. 6:8.

קַיָּם Chald. *established, sure*. Dan. 4:23. [4:26.]

קִימָה f. verbal from קוּם, dec. X. *a rising up*. Lam. 3:63.

קִמּוֹשׁ see קִימוֹשׁ.

קַיִן m. dec. VI. f.

1. *a spear.* 2 Sam. 21:16. Root قان med. Je *to forge.*

2. *Cain,* the son of Adam. Gen. 4:1. According to this passage, from קָנָה, see קָנָה no 4.

3. the name of a people, *the Kenites.* Num. 24:22. Judg. 4:11. See קֵינִי.

קִינָה f. plur. ־ִים and ־וֹת, verbal from קִין, dec. X. *a lamentation.* Jer. 7:29. 9:9, 19. 19:1. Josh. 15:22.

קֵינִי Gen. 15:19. Judg. 4:11, 17. קֵנִי 1 Sam. 27:10. קִינִי 1 Chr. 2:55. *the Kenites,* a Canaanitish people, which according to 1 Sam. 15:6. (comp. Num. 24:20, 21.) dwelt among the Amalekites. According to Judg. 1:16. 4:11. they appear to have been descended from Hobab the brother-in-law of Moses.

קַיִץ dec. VI. f.

1. *summer, the warm season of the year,* in opposition to חֹרֶף. Gen. 8:22. Ps. 74:17.

2. *fruit, dried fruit,* perhaps by way of eminence, *figs.* Jer. 40:10, 12. Am. 8:1, 2. 2 Sam. 16:1. Comp. Faber zu Harmer's Beobachtungen, Th. I. p. 387 ff.

קִיצוֹן, fem. קִיצוֹנָה, *last, uttermost.* Ex. 26:4, 10. 36:11, 17. It has its form from קַיִץ, but its signification from the kindred forms קֵץ, קָצָה.

קִיקָיוֹן m. Jon. 4:6—10. according to Jerome, Syr. *the palma Christi,* (Lat. *ricinus,* Arab. *Elcheroa,* Egypt. κίκι, κοῦκι,) a biennial plant, which shoots up to the height of a small tree, but like all plants of a rapid growth withers immediately from the slightest injury. According to the Sept. *the gourd.* See Bocharti Hieroz. T. II. p. 293, 623. Celsii Hierob. P. II. p. 273—282. Faber zu Harmer's Beobacht. Th. I. p. 140—151. Rosenmüller in Jon. 4:6.

קִיקָלוֹן m. found only Hab. 2:16. prob. compounded of קִי קָלוֹן (whence 9 MSS. write it in two words,) *shameful vomit.* The word קִי is i. q. קִיא.

קִיר once קִר (Is. 22:5.) plur. קִירוֹת, com. gen.

1. *a wall.* 1 K. 6:5. Spoken of *the wall* or *side* of an altar, Lev. 1:15. 5:9. of the heart, Jer. 4:19. of the city, Num. 35:4. Josh. 2:15. Is. 25:4 זֶרֶם קִיר *stormy weather which breaks down walls.*

2. prob. i. q. קִרְיָה *a city,* hence as a proper name, (1.) קִיר מוֹאָב Is. 15:1. (*the city of Moab,*) in later times called *Karach,* Χαράκμωβα. It is generally thought to be the same with (2.) קִיר חֶרֶשׂ Is. 16:11. Jer. 48:31, 36. and קִיר חֲרֶשֶׂת Is. 16:7. 1 K. 3:25. a city in Moab.

3. name of a people and country under the dominion of the Assyrians, Is. 22:6. to which the conquered inhabitants of Damascus were carried away, 2 K. 16:9. Amos 1:5. and whence the Arameans had emigrated, Am. 9:7. Most prob. a country on the river Cyrus where the name *Kur, Kura,* is preserved to this day.

קִישׁוֹן proper name of a brook, which rises on mount Tabor, and empties itself into the bay of Acco. Judg. 4:7. 5:21. 1 K. 18:40. Ps. 83:10.

קִיתָרֹס Chald. the Greek κίθαρις, *a harp.* In the Kethib of Dan. 3:5, 7, 10.

קַל, fem. קַלָּה, plur. קַלִּים, verbal adj. from קָלַל, dec. VIII. h. *light, swift.* 2 Sam. 2:18. Am. 2:14, 15.—As a subst. *a swift animal,* Is. 30:16.—As an adv. *swiftly,* Joel 4:4. [3:4.]

קָל m. Chald. i. q. Heb. קוֹל *a voice.* Dan. 3:5.

קֹל see קוֹל.

I. קָלָה, Arab. قلى, *to roast in the fire.* Part. pass. קָלוּי Lev. 2:14. Josh. 5:11. Comp. קָלִי. Also *to burn* men, as a mode of execution, Jer. 29:22.

Niph. part. *a burnt place, a burn, inflammation.* Ps. 38:8.

II. קָלָה i. q. קָלַל.

Niph. *to be lightly esteemed, despised, disgraced.* Deut. 25:3. Is. 3:5. 16:14. Prov. 12:9.

Hiph. *to lightly esteem.* Deut. 27:16.

Deriv. קָלוֹן.

קָלוֹן m. verbal from קָלָה, no. II. dec. III. a.

1. *contempt,* Prov. 13:18. *reviling,* Prov. 22:10.

2. *shame, disgrace.* Prov. 3:35. 6:33.

3. *pudenda muliebria.* Nah. 3:5. Jer. 13:26.

4. *a shameful deed.* Prov. 18:3.

קָלִי m. and קָלִיא (with א in otio) 1 Sam. 17:17. verbal from קָלָה, *roasted grain* or *pulse.* Lev. 23:14. 2 Sam. 17:28.

קַלַּחַת f. *a pot, kettle.* 1 Sam. 2:14. Mic. 3:3. The etymology is uncertain.

קָלַט found only in the part. pass. קָלוּט Levit. 22:23. *unusually small, dwarfish.* Arab. قلطي *idem.*

קָלַל 1. *to be light.* See Hiph. Hence

2. *to be small, to be lessened* or *abated.* Gen. 8:11. כִּי קַלּוּ הַמַּיִם מֵעַל הָאָרֶץ *that the waters were abated from off the earth.* Verse 8.

3. *to be small, mean, vile.* Job 40:4. Nah. 1:14. Comp. קָלָה no. II.

4. *to be swift.* 2 Sam. 1:23. Hab. 1:8. Job 7:6. 9:25.

Niph. נָקַל and נָקַל, fut. יִקַּלּוּ (Is. 30:16.) and יֵקַל (for יִקַּל, like יֵבַד.)

1. *to be easy, light, facilem esse,* construed with a dative of the person. Prov. 14:6.—The form נָקַל with לְ is used impersonally, *it is a light thing,* 2 K. 20:10.

2. *to be small,* construed with בְּעֵינֵי. 1 Sam. 18:23. Used impers. נָקַל מִן *it is too small* or *not enough that,* Is. 49:6. Ezek. 8:17. Part. נָקַל, fem. נְקַלָּה, *small;* e.g. עַל נְקַלָּה *slightly,* Jer. 6:14. 8:11.

3. *to be lightly esteemed, to be despised.* 2 Sam. 6:22. Gen. 16:4, 5.

4. *to be swift.* Is. 30:16.

Pi. קִלֵּל *to curse, to blaspheme;* construed with an accus. Gen. 8:21. Lev. 19:14. once with בְּ, Is. 8:21. 1 Sam. 3:13 *because he knew* כִּי מְקַלְלִים לָהֶם בָּנָיו *that his sons were bringing a curse on themselves.*

Pilp. קִלְקֵל 1. *to move, shake.* Ezek. 21:26. [21:21.] Arab. قلقل.

2. *to smooth, polish;* hence *to sharpen.* Ecc. 10:10. Comp. the adj. קָלָל *smooth.*

Hiph. הֵקַל, infin. הָקֵל, fut. יָקֵל.

1. *to make light,* construed with מִן and מֵעַל. 1 K. 12:10. 1 Sam. 6:5. Without an object following, Ex. 18:22 הָקֵל מֵעָלֶיךָ *make* (it) *lighter for thyself.* Jon. 1:5.—1 K. 12:4 הָקֵל מֵעֲבֹדַת אָבִיךָ הַקָּשָׁה *make thou the grievous service of thy father lighter.* Verse 9.

2. *to despise, contemn.* 2 Sam. 19:44. Ezek. 22:7. Is. 8:23.

Hithpalp. *to move one's self, to tremble.* Jer. 4:24.

קָלָל m. verbal adj. from קָלַל, Dan. 10:6. Ezek. 1:7. spoken of brass, prob. *smooth, polished.* The idea is not remote from that of *lightness.* Comp. in Chald. גְּלָל *politura.* Vulg. *æs candens.*

קְלָלָה f. const. קִלְלַת, verbal from קָלַל, dec. XI. c.

1. *a reviling.* 2 Sam. 16:12.

2. *a curse.* Gen. 27:12. Used as a concrete, *one accursed,* Deut. 21:23.

קָלַס in Kal not used.

Pi. *to mock, scorn, deride.* Ezek. 16:31 *as a* (common) *harlot* לְקַלֵּס אֶתְנָן *that scorneth the* (offered) *hire,* to obtain the more.

Hithpa. *idem,* construed with בְּ. 2 K. 2:23. Ezek. 22:5. Hab. 1:10. Hence

קֶלֶס m. verbal from קָלַס, *scorn, derision.* Ps. 44:14. Jer. 20:8.

קַלָּסָה f. verbal from קָלַס, *idem.* Ezek. 22:4.

קָלַע 1. *to throw* or *sling.* Judg. 20:16. Metaphorically Jer. 10:18.

2. *to cut in, to engrave.* 1 K. 6:29,

32, 35. prob. from קָלַע, i. q. Lat. *funda*, *any cavity like that of a sling, engraved work* in wood or stone. Deriv. מִקְלַעַת.

Pi. i. q. Kal. 1 Sam. 17:49. 25:29.

קֶלַע m. verbal from קָלַע, dec. VI. d.

1. *a sling.* 1 Sam. 17:40.

2. *a curtain, hanging.* Ex. 27:9 ff. 35:17. Num. 3:26. (In Chald. *idem.* Arab. *a sail.*)

3. 1 K. 6:34. most probably a corrupted reading for צְלָעִים, as in the former part of the verse, *valves* or *leaves of a door,* and here in cod. 150 of Kennicott.

קַלָּע m. verbal from קָלַע, dec. I. *a slinger.* 2 K. 3:25.

קְלֹקֵל m. verbal from קָלַל, *mean, vile,* spoken of food. Num. 21:5. The form is like that of חֲצֹצְר.

קִלְּשׁוֹן m. *a pointed* or *pronged instrument.* (In Chald. *idem.* Ecc. 12:11 Targ.) 1 Sam. 13:21 שְׁלֹשׁ קִלְּשׁוֹן *a three-pronged instrument, a pitch-fork,* or the like.

קָמָה f. verbal from קוּם, dec. X. *standing corn, a crop yet standing.* Judg. 15:5. Ex. 22:5. Plur. Judg. 15:5.

קִמּוֹשׁ m. Is. 34:13. קִימוֹשׁ Hos. 9:6. and plur. קִמְּשֹׂנִים Prov. 24:31. *a prickly plant, a nettle, thistle.* Celsii Hierobot. T. II. p. 206.

קֶמַח m. dec. VI. *meal.* Gen. 18:6. Num. 5:15. (Arab. *wheat, grain.*)

קָמַט 1. *to fetter, to bind hands and feet.* Job 16:8.

2. *to cast into fetters, to drag away.* (In Chald. *idem.*)

Pu. pass. of no. 2. Job 22:16.

קָמַל *to become sickly and die,* spoken of plants. Is. 19:6. 33:9. (In Syr. used of men. In Arab. of plants destroyed by insects.)

קָמַץ *to take,* particularly *with a full hand.* Lev. 2:2. 5:12. Num. 5:26.

קֹמֶץ m. with suff. קֻמְצוֹ, verbal from קָמַץ, dec. VI. o.

1. *a handful.* Lev. 2:2. 5:12. 6:8.

2. *a sheaf, a bundle of ears which one takes in his hand, manipulus.* Gen. 41:47 לִקְמָצִים *in full bundles,* i. e. in abundance.

קִמְּשׁוֹן see קִמּוֹשׁ.

קֵן m. const. קַן, with suff. קִנּוֹ, verbal from קָנַן perhaps i. q. Arab. قان *to make, form.*

1. *a bird's nest.* Deut. 22:6. Is. 10:14. Hence *the nestlings, the young birds in the nest,* Deut. 32:11. Is. 16:2.

2. metaphorically *a dwelling,* (the figure, however, being preserved.) Num. 24:21. Job 29:18.

3. Plur. קִנִּים *cells, small dwellings.* Gen. 6:14.

קָנָא in Kal not used.

Pi. קִנֵּא 1. *to be zealous for* a person or thing, *to defend the rights of a person with zeal,* construed with לְ of the person. Num. 25:11, 13. 2 Sam. 21:2. 1 K. 19:10.

2. *to be jealous;* e. g. of one's wife, construed with an accus. Num. 5:14. of a rival, construed with בְּ Gen. 30:1.

3. *to be envious of* a person; construed with בְּ, Gen. 37:11. with an accus. Gen. 26:14. with לְ, Ps. 106:16.

4. *to emulate.* Prov. 3:31.

5. *to be indignant about* a thing, construed with בְּ. Prov. 23:17. 24:1.

6. trans. *to excite* a person *to jealousy by* any thing, construed with an accus. and בְּ. Deut. 32:21. 1 K. 14:22.

Hiph. i. q. Pi. no. 6. Deut. 32:16, 21. Ps. 78:58.

Deriv. out of course קַנּוֹא.

קְנָא Chald. *to buy, purchase.* Ezra 7:17. i. q. Heb. קָנָה.

קַנָּא m. verbal from קָנָא, *jealous, one who permits not his rights to be injured,* spoken of Jehovah. Ex. 20:5. 34:14. Deut. 4:24.

קִנְאָה f. verbal from קָנָא, dec. XII. b.

1. *zeal, ardour.* 2 K. 10:16. Is. 9:6 קִנְאַת יְהוָה צְבָאוֹת *the zeal of Jehovah of hosts* (for his people.)—קִנְאַת־עָם *zeal for the people,* Is. 26:11. Also *ardent* or *zealous love* generally, Cant. 8:6.

2. *jealousy.* Is. 11:13. Particularly

in reference to love, Prov. 6:34. 27:4.—Ezek. 8:3 סֵמֶל הַקִּנְאָה הַמַּקְנֶה *the image of jealousy which excites* (God) *to jealousy.*

3. *envy.* Ecc. 4:4. 9:6.

4. *anger, indignation.* Deut. 29:19. Ps. 79:5.

5. *impatience.* Job 5:2.

קָנָה, fut. יִקְנֶה, apoc. יִקֶן.

1. *to get, gain, acquire.* Prov. 4:7. 15:32. 16:16. 19:8.

2. *to buy.* Gen. 25:10. 47:22.

3. particularly *to redeem, ransom;* e. g. from captivity. Is. 11:11. Neh. 5:8.

4. *to obtain for a possession, to obtain.* Gen. 4:1.

5. *to own, possess.* Is. 1:3.

6. *to prepare, form, make.* (In Syr. *idem.* In Arab. קין قان med. Je *formavit, concinnavit.*) Ps. 139:13. Gen. 14:19, 22. Deut. 32:6. Prov. 8:22.

Hiph. Zech. 13:5. prob. i.q. Kal, *to buy, purchase.*—The form מַקְנֶה Ezek. 8:3. stands for מַקְנִיא, see קָנָא.

Deriv. מִקְנֶה, מִקְנָה, קִנְיָן.

קָנֶה m. dec. IX. b.

1. *a cane, reed, rush.* Is. 42:3. 36:6. Ps. 68:31 חַיַּת קָנֶה *the wild beast of the reeds,* i. e. the crocodile, as a symbol of Egypt.

2. *sweet cane, sweet calamus,* (*acorus calamus,* Linn.) Is. 43:24. in full קְנֵה בֹשֶׂם Ex. 30:23. and קָנֶה הַטּוֹב Jer. 6:20.

3. *a stalk of corn.* Gen. 41:5, 22.

4. *a measuring reed* or *rod;* in full קְנֵה הַמִּדָּה. Ezek. 40:3, 5. Hence

5. *a measure of six cubits.* Ezek. 41:8.

6. *the beam of a balance, a balance.* Is. 46:6.

7. *the upper bone of the arm, the os humeri.* Job 31:22.

8. *a branch of a candlestick.* Ex. 25:31 ff. Plur. קָנִים Ex. 25:32. and קָנוֹת Ex. 25:36. 37:22.

קַנּוֹא m. verbal from קָנָא, *jealous,* spoken of God, i. q. קַנָּא. Josh. 24:19. Nah. 1:2.

קְנַז proper name of a descendant of Esau, from whom an Arabian country is named. Gen. 36:11, 15, 42.

קְנִזִּי a Canaanitish people, whose place of residence cannot be definitely ascertained. Gen. 15:19. Num. 32:12.

קֵינִי see **קֵנִי**.

קִנְיָן m. verbal from קָנָה, dec. II. b.

1. *that which one gets* or *acquires.* Prov. 4:7. Lev. 22:11.

2. *a possession, substance, property.* Gen. 34:23.

3. perhaps *a creature,* (comp. קָנָה no. 6.) Ps. 104:24. Sept. κτίσις.

קִנָּמוֹן, const. קִנְּמָן (Ex. 30:23.) dec. III. h. *cinnamon.* Prov. 7:17. Cant. 4:14.—Herodotus (III. 111.) mentions expressly that the Greeks obtained their κίνναμον or κιννάμωμον from the Phenicians; of course from a people speaking a Shemitish dialect. The derivation of the word from קנם Arab. قنم *to smell strong,* is doubtful; since the use of this word is confined to the rancid smell of oil.

קִנֵּן denom. from קֵן, *to nest, to make a nest.* Ps. 104:17. Is. 34:15. 48:28.

Pu. *idem.* Jer. 22:23.

קִנְצֵי Job 18:2. see **קֵץ**.

קְנָת (*a possession*) a city in the country of Gilead. Num. 32:42. 1 Chr. 2:23. See Relandi Palaestina, p. 681.

קָסַם, fut. יִקְסֹם, *to divine;* spoken of false prophets, as a forbidden and unlawful practice, Deut. 18:10, 14. 2 K. 17:17. Mic. 3:6, 7, 11. or at least accompanied with some reproach, as in the case of Balaam, Josh. 13:22. of the prophets of the Philistines, 1 Sam. 6:2. of the necromancer, 28:8.—The deriv. קֶסֶם in signif. no. 3. is taken in a good sense.—The word in Syriac is more common; comp. the remark made under the articles קְסָמִים, כִּשֵּׁף, נִחֵשׁ. Deriv. out of course מִקְסָם.

קֶסֶם m. verbal from קָסַם, dec. VI.

1. *divination*. Ezek. 13:6, 23. 21:26. 1 Sam. 15:23.

2. *the wages of divination*. Num. 22:7. (Comp. פְּעֻלָּה.)

3. prob. in a good sense, *an oracle*. Prov. 16:10.

קָסַס found only in Po. קוֹסֵס i. q. קוֹצֵץ *to cut off*. Ezek. 17:9.

קֶסֶת f. *a vessel, cup*. (Aram. קַסְטָא *idem*, for the most part as a measure for liquids, *a sextary*. Ethiop. קסח *hydria*.) Hence קֶסֶת הַסֹּפֵר *a writer's vessel, an inkhorn*, Ezek. 9:2, 3, 11.

קְעִילָה proper name of a city in the tribe of Judah. Josh. 15:44. 1 Sam. 23:1. 1 Chr. 4:19. See Relandi Palæstina, p. 698.

קַעֲקַע m. *a mark cut* or *burnt into the skin*. Lev. 19:28. (In Talmud. קעקע and קיעקע *scalpsit, inussit*.)

קְעָרָה f. const. קַעֲרַת, plur. קְעָרוֹת, const. קַעֲרוֹת, but with suff. קְעָרֹתָיו, *a dish, charger*. Num. 7:13 ff. (Arab. قعران *a deep dish*, from قعر *to be deep*.)

קָפָא 1. *to coagulate, curdle*, spoken of milk, (see Hiph.) *to be congealed*, spoken of the floods, Ex. 15:8.

2. *to draw in one's self, to sit with one's feet under him*. Zeph. 1:12. comp. Jer. 48:11.

Hiph. causat. of no. 1. *to make to curdle*. Job 10:10. (In Talmud. *idem*. In Syr. and Arab. under the kindred form קפה.)

קִפָּאוֹן m. verbal from קָפָא, *ice, frost*. Zech. 14:6.

קָפַד as in Chald. *to cut off*. Found only in Pi. Is. 38:12 קִפַּדְתִּי כָאֹרֵג חַיַּי Vulg. *præcisa est, velut a texente, vita mea*. Hence

קִפֹּד or **קִפּוֹד**, with He paragogic קְפָדָה, verbal from קָפַד, *destruction*, Ezek. 7:25.

קִפֹּד m. *the hedge-hog*. Is. 14:23. 34:11. Zeph. 2:14. (Arab. קנפד, Syr. ܩܘܦܕܐ *idem*. Root ܩܦܕ *horruit*, Ethpe. *contractus est*.)

קִפּוֹז m. Is. 34:15. according to the ancient translators i. q. קִפֹּד, which is the reading of 6 MSS. But the animal here is represented as oviparous and brooding over its young, which will not apply to the hedgehog. Better, therefore, according to Bochart (Hieroz. T. II. p. 408.) *the arrow snake, serpens jaculus*, Arab. قفّازة from قفز in Chald. and Arab. *to spring, to seize with a spring*.

קָפַץ, fut. יִקְפֹּץ. *to contract, close, shut*; e. g. the mouth, Job 5:16. Ps. 107:42. the hand, Deut. 15:7. Metaphorically *to shut up* or *restrain* compassion, Ps. 77:10. The phrase *to shut up the hand from a person*, signifies *to be niggardly towards him*. Kindred with קָמַץ.

Niph. *to be gathered*, hence i. q. נֶאֱסַף *to die*. Job 24:24.

Pi. *to spring, leap*. Cant. 2:8. (Chald. *idem*.)

קֵץ m. with suff. קִצִּי, verbal from קָצַץ, dec. VIII. b. *an end*, either of space or time. Job 28:3. 6:11.—אֵין קֵץ *without end*, Ecc. 12:12.—מִקֵּץ *after*, e. g. מִקֵּץ אַרְבָּעִים יוֹם *after forty days*, Gen. 8:6. 16:3. 41:1. in the later writers also לְקֵץ, 2 Chr. 18:2. Dan. 11:6, 13.—Particularly (1.) *the end* or *destruction* of a people. Gen. 6:13. Ezek. 7:2. עֲוֹן קֵץ. *a crime which brings destruction*, Ezek. 21:30, 34. 35:5. (2.) *the end* or *fulfilment* of a prophecy. Hab. 2:3. (3.) עֵת קֵץ Dan. 8:17. or מוֹעֵד קֵץ verse 19. *the time of the end*, also קֵץ הַיָּמִים Dan. 12:13. *the end of days*, according to the theological views of the later Jews, the time immediately preceding the advent of the Messiah's kingdom, and represented as full of calamity and trouble.

Plur. const. קִנְצֵי for קִצֵּי (by a resolution of the Dagesh forte after the Chaldaic manner,) Job 18:2 עַד־אָנָה תְּשִׂימוּן קִנְצֵי לְמִלִּין *when will ye make an end of words?*

Deriv. קִיצוֹן.

קָצַב, fut. יִקְצֹב. Comp. חָצַב, חָסַם.

1. *to cut off*, e. g. a piece of wood. 2 K. 6 : 6.

2. *to shear* (sheep.) Cant. 4 : 2.

קֶצֶב m. verbal from קָצַב, dec. VI. h.

1. *form*, liter. *cut*, French *taille*. 1 K. 6 : 25. 7 : 37.

2. קִצְבֵי הָרִים Jon. 2 : 7. prob. *the ends*, i. e. the foundations, *of the mountains*, (in the depths of the sea.) Vulg. *extrema montium*.

קָצָה *to hew* or *cut off*, like קָצַץ. Metaphorically *to destroy* (nations,) Hab. 2 : 10.

Pi. *idem*. Prov. 26 : 6 מְקַצֶּה רַגְלַיִם *one that has his feet cut off*. 2 K. 10 : 32 *Jehovah began* לְקַצּוֹת בְּיִשְׂרָאֵל *to cut off in Israel*, i. e. to take off one part after another.

Hiph. *to scrape*, i. q. קָצַע. Lev. 14 : 41, 43.

Deriv. out of course מִקְצָה, קָצֶה, קֵצֶו, קְצָת.

קָצֶה m. const. קְצֵה, plur. const. קְצֵי, verbal from קָצָה, dec. IX. b.

1. i. q. קֵץ *the end, the uttermost part*; e. g. of the earth, Is. 5 : 26. of heaven, Is. 13 : 5. Ps. 19 : 7.—מִקְצֵה שְׁלֹשֶׁת יָמִים *after three days*, Josh. 3 : 2. 9 : 16.—מִקָּצֶה *from* (every) *end* or *quarter*, Gen. 19 : 4. Jer. 51 : 31. Hence

2. *the whole, the sum*. Gen. 47 : 2 מִקְצֵה אֶחָיו *from the whole number of his brethren*. Ezek. 33 : 2. Comp. Num. 22 : 41. Is. 56 : 11. Comp. the fem. קָצָה no. 2.

קֵצֶה m. verbal from קָצָה, *an end*. Is. 2 : 7. Nah. 2 : 10.

קָצָה f. plur. const. קְצוֹת, verbal from קָצָה, dec. XI. a. i. q. קָצֶה.

1. *an end, extremity*. Ex. 25 : 19. Job 26 : 14 קְצוֹת דְּרָכָיו *the extreme parts of his works*.

2. *the sum, crowd, mass*. 1 K. 12 : 31. 13 : 33.

קֶצֶו m. verbal from קָצָה, dec. VI a. *an end*. Found only in the plur. const. קַצְוֵי אֶרֶץ *the ends of the earth*, Ps. 48 : 11. 65 : 6.

קֶצַח m. found only Is. 28 : 25, 27. *black cumin, nigella melanthium*, according to the Sept. Vulg. and the Rabbins. See Celsii Hierobot. P. II. p. 70.

קָצִין m. dec. III. a.

1. *a judge, magistrate, ruler*. Is. 1 : 10. 3 : 6, 7. Mic. 3 : 9. 1. Root קָצָה, in Arab. with ض, *to determine, judge*, (kindred with قصي *to cut, to cut off*;) whence قاضي *a judge, cadi*. The ן, therefore, is servile.

2. *a leader in war, a general, a captain*. Josh. 10 : 24. Judg. 11 : 6, 11. Is. 22 : 3. Dan. 11 : 18. Comp. שֹׁפֵט.

3. *a prince, chief*. Prov. 6 : 7. 25 : 15.

קְצִיעוֹת plur. fem. *the Arabian cassia*, a bark resembling cinnamon, prob. *laurus cassia*, Linn. Ps. 45 : 9. See Celsii Hierobot. T. II. p. 360.

קָצִיר m. verbal from קָצַר, dec. III. a.

1. *harvest*. Gen. 8 : 22. Hence (1.) *the grain gathered in*. Lev. 19 : 9. 23 : 22. (2.) collect. *the reapers*. Is. 17 : 5.

2. *a bough, branch*. Ps. 80 : 12. Job 14 : 9.

קָצַע in Kal not used. Prob. *to cut off*, i. q. קָצָה. In Arab. قطع *idem*.

Hiph. *to scrape*, i. q. קָצָה Hiph. Lev. 14 : 41.

Hoph. part. מְהֻקְצָעוֹת i. q. מִקְצֹעִים *corners*. Ezek. 46 : 22. Liter. *what is cut off, the place of cutting off*.

Deriv. מַקְצֻעָה, מִקְצֹעִים.

קָצַף, fut. יִקְצֹף, *to be wroth* or *angry*; construed with עַל, Gen. 40 : 2. 41 : 10. Ex. 16 : 20. with אֶל, Josh. 22 : 18.

Hiph. *to provoke to anger*, e. g. Jehovah. Deut. 9 : 7, 8, 22.

Hithpa. i. q. Kal. Is. 8 : 21.

קְצַף Chald. *idem*. Dan. 2 : 12.

קֶצֶף m. with suff. קִצְפִּי, verbal from קָצַף, dec. VI. h. and k.

1. *wrath, anger*, particularly of Jehovah. Josh. 9 : 20. 22 : 20. Zech. 1 : 2. 2 Chr. 19 : 10.

2. *a chip, splinter.* Hos. 10 : 7. Sept. φρύγανον. (Arab. قصف *debile, flaccum fuit* lignum.) Hence also

קְצָפָה f. verbal from קָצַף, *a fragment, a broken piece.* Joel 1 : 7. Sept. συγκλασμός.

קָצַץ *to cut off;* e. g. the hand, Deut. 25 : 12. the mustaches, Jer. 9 : 25. 25 : 23. (In Arab. *to cut* the nails and hair.)

Pi. קִצֵּץ and קִצֵּץ.

1. *to cut off;* a cord, Ps. 129 : 4. the hand, the thumb, Judg. 1 : 6. 2 Sam. 4 : 12. (the point of) a spear, Ps. 46. 10.

2. *to cut* (into wires). Ex. 39 : 3.

3. *to strip.* 2 K. 18 : 16. 24 : 13.

Pu. pass. Judg. 1 : 7.

קְצַץ Chald. Pa. *to cut off.* Dan. 4 : 11. [4 : 14.]

קָצַר 1. with a fut. יִקְצֹר, *to cut down,* particularly grain; hence *to mow, reap.* Jer. 12 : 13. Lev. 19 : 9. 25 : 5. Part. קֹצֵר *a reaper,* Ruth 2 : 3 ff. Metaphorically Job 4 : 8 *they that sow wickedness shall reap it.* Prov. 22 : 8.

2. קָצַר (as it appears from the adj.) with a fut. יִקְצַר, intrans. *to be short.* Is. 28 : 20. Particularly (1.) קָצְרָה יָדִי *my hand is* (too) *short,* i. e. I am (too) weak. Num. 11 : 23. Construed with מִן and an infin. Is. 50 : 2. (2.) קָצְרָה רוּחִי, נַפְשִׁי, *I am impatient, grieved, vexed.* Num. 21 : 4, 5. Judg. 16 : 16. Construed with בְּ *about* a thing, Judg. 10 : 16.

Pi. *to shorten.* Ps. 102 : 24.

Hiph. 1. *idem.* Ps. 89 : 46.

2. *to reap.* Job 24 : 6 Keth.

Deriv. out of course קָצִיר.

קָצֵר m. verbal from קָצַר, dec. V. a. *short.* Ezek. 42 : 5. Particularly (1.) קְצַר יָד *weak, feeble,* Is. 37 : 27. (2.) קְצַר רוּחַ Prov. 14 : 29. and קְצַר אַפַּיִם Prov. 14 : 17. *impatient, irascible, passionate.* (3.) קְצַר יָמִים *short lived.* Job 14 : 1.

קֹצֶר m. verbal from קָצַר, dec. VI. found only in the phrase קֹצֶר רוּחַ *impatience.* Ex. 6 : 9.

קְצָת f. (for קְצָאת after the form מְנָת,) verbal from קָצָה, *an end,* i. q. קָצֶה. Dan. 1 : 5, 15 מִקְצָת יָמִים עֲשָׂרָה *at the end of ten days.* In verse 18, occurs לְמִקְצָת. Plur. קְצוֹת *the ends,* Ex. 38 : 5. particularly *the ends* (of the earth), Ps. 65 : 9.

קְצָת f. const. קְצָת, Chald.

1. *a part.* Dan. 2 : 42.

2. *an end.* Dan. 4 : 31. [4 : 34.]

קַר, plur. קָרִים, verbal adj. from obsol. קָרַר, dec. VIII. k.

1. *cold, cool.* Prov. 25 : 25. Jer. 18 : 14

2. *quiet.* Prov. 17 : 27 Keth קַר רוּחַ *of a quiet spirit.* See יָקָר no. 5.

קֹר see **קִיר**.

קֹר m. verbal from obsol. קָרַר, *cold.* Gen. 8 : 22.

I. **קָרָא** *to call.* The subordinate significations and constructions are the following; (1.) *to call* a person or thing; construed with a dative of the object, Lev. 9 : 1. Hos. 11 : 1 with אֶל, Gen. 3 : 9. 49 : 1 with an accus. Gen. 27 : 1. Prov. 18 : 6 *his mouth calleth for strokes.* Ruth 4 : 11 קְרָא שֵׁם בְּבֵית לָחֶם, *call,* i. e. acquire, *fame in Bethlehem.* (2.) *to call out to* any one, construed with אֶל. Is. 6 : 3. Ex. 3 : 4. (3.) *to call to* or *on* any one, particularly for help; construed with אֶל, Ps. 4 : 4. 30 : 9. with an accus. Hos. 7 : 11. particularly in reference to Jehovah, Ps. 14 : 4. 18 : 7. (4.) *to call together,* e. g. an assembly. Joel 1 : 14. Hence (5.) *to invite, bid.* 1 Sam. 9 : 13, 22.—קָרָא לְשָׁלוֹם לְ— *to invite to peace, to offer peace,* Deut. 20 : 10. Judg. 21 : 13. (6.) *to announce, proclaim.* Joel 4 : 9. [3 : 9.] Jer. 2 : 2. 3 : 12. 7 : 2.—קָרָא דְרוֹר לְ— *to proclaim liberty to* a person, Is. 61 : 1. Jer. 34 : 8, 15, 17, Used absolutely, *to preach,* Jon. 1 : 2. (7.) *to celebrate, praise,* (like אָמַר with an accus.) Prov. 20 : 6 אִישׁ חַסְדּוֹ יִקְרָא *each celebrates his own goodness.* (8.) *to call, choose, appoint,* i. q. בָּחַר. Is. 42 : 6. 48 : 12. 49 : 1. 51 : 2. Somewhat stronger is the nearly synonymous phrase קָרָא בְשֵׁם פ׳ *to call* or *choose by name,* Is. 43 : 1. 45 : 3, 4. Comp. Ex. 31 : 2. (9.) *to call on, to invoke,* construed with בְּ. Is. 59 : 4. Particularly

קָרָא בְּשֵׁם יְהוָה *to invoke* or *praise the name of Jehovah*, Gen. 4:26. 12:8. Ex. 33:19. Ps. 79:6. 105:1. Is. 64:6. So in reference to idols, 1 K. 18:26. Also used in the same signification without בְּ, e.g. Lam. 3:55. Ps. 99:6. Deut. 32:3. comp. Ruth 4:14. More rarely in reference to men, Ps. 49:12. In a somewhat different sense, Is. 44:5 זֶה יִקְרָא בְשֵׁם יַעֲקֹב *this one praises the name of Jacob*, i.e. cleaves to him.

2. *to name*; construed with an accus. of the name and a dative of the person or thing, Gen. 1:5 וַיִּקְרָא אֱלֹהִים לָאוֹר יוֹם *and God named the light day*. Verses 8, 10. 31:47. rarely with a double accus. Is. 60:18. Num. 32:41. The following construction is very frequent, Gen. 4:25 וַתִּקְרָא אֶת־שְׁמוֹ שֵׁת *and she named his name Seth*. 4:26. 5:2, 3, 29. 11:9.—קָרָא שֵׁם לְ *to give a name to* a person, Ruth 4:17. Gen. 26:18. Ps. 147:3.

3. *to read*. Ex. 24:7. Deut. 17:19.

Niph. 1. *to be called*. Jer. 44:26. Est. 3:12. 6:1. 8:9.

2. *to be named*. Properly construed with a dative of the person, Gen. 2:23. 1 Sam. 9:9. Is. 1:26. 32:5. 62:4, 12. Then also with a double nominative, Zech. 8:3. Is. 48:2. 54:5. 56:7. and with שֵׁם, e.g. Gen. 17:5 לֹא יִקָּרֵא עוֹד אֶת־שִׁמְךָ אַבְרָם *thy name shall no more be called Abram*. 35:10. Deut. 25:10. Dan. 10:1. Construed with בְּ, *to be named after* any one, Gen. 21:12. with בְּשֵׁם, *to name one's self after* a person, i.e. to confess or cleave to him, Is. 43:7. 48:1.—נִקְרָא שְׁמִי עַל *my name is given to* a thing, i.e. it is named after me, 2 Sam. 12:28. Is. 4:1. hence *it pertains* or *is consecrated to me*; e.g. in reference to Jehovah, spoken of the Israelitish people, Deut. 28:10. Is. 63:19. of the temple, 1 K. 8:43. of Jerusalem, Dan. 9:18, 19.

Pu. קֹרָא 1. *to be called*. Ezek. 10:13. Is. 48:12. (2.) *to be named*. Is. 65:1. For the most part construed with a dative, Is. 48:8. 58:12. 61:3. 62:2.

Deriv. out of course קֹרֵא, קְרִיאָה, מִקְרָא.

II. קָרָא i. q. קָרָה *to meet* or *befal* a person, spoken of an event, destiny, construed with an accus. Gen. 49:1. 42:4, 38. Lev. 10:19. Infin. strictly קְרֹאת (like יְשֹׁאת,) hence לִקְרַאת and by a Syriasm לִקְרַאת, with suff. לִקְרָאתִי, לִקְרַאתְכֶם, used as a prep. (1.) *to meet, obviam*. Gen. 46:29. Ex. 4:27. 18:7. Josh. 11:20 לְחַזֵּק אֶת־לִבָּם לִקְרַאת הַמִּלְחָמָה *to harden their heart to meet the war*. (2.) *over against*. Gen. 15:10. 1 Sam. 4:2.

Niph. 1. *to meet*, spoken of persons, construed with עַל, Ex. 5:3. with לִפְנֵי, 2 Sam. 18:9. *to fall in the way of* a person, spoken of things, Deut. 22:6.

2. without cases, *to happen, to be by chance*. 2 Sam. 1:6. 20:1.

Hiph. *to cause to happen*, e.g. a misfortune. Jer. 32:23.

קְרָא Chald. fut. יִקְרֵא, יִקְרָה.

1. *to call*. Dan. 3:4. 4:11. [4:14.] 5:7.

2. *to read*. Dan. 5:8, 16, 17.

קֹרֵא m. *a partridge*, liter. *the caller* or *crier*, from קָרָא. 1 Sam. 26:20. Jer. 17:11. In the latter passage there is an allusion to a fabulous story of the ancients, (see Bocharti Hieroz. T. II. p. 84, 85.) that the partridge steals the eggs of other birds, and broods over them. According to Faber (zu Harmer's Beobachtungen, Th. I. p. 305.) *the partridge of Damascus, tetrao orientalis*.

קָרַב and קָרֵב, fut יִקְרַב, infin. קְרֹב, also קִרְבָה. *to approach, to draw near*, spoken of persons and things. Josh. 10: 24. Construed with אֶל of the person or thing, Gen. 37:18. Ex. 14:20. more rarely with לְ, Job 33:22. with בְּ, Ps. 91:10. with לִפְנֵי, particularly in reference to Jehovah, Ex. 16:9. Lev. 16:1. The more special constructions are (1.) spoken of Jehovah, *to draw near with help*. Ps. 69:19. Lam. 3:57. (2.) קָרַב אֶל אִשָּׁה *to draw near a woman*, i.e. to lie with her, Gen. 20:4. Is. 8:3. (3.) *to draw near, to advance*, in a hostile manner. Deut. 20:2. Construed with עַל, Ps. 27:2. Comp. קְרָב.

(4.) joined with an infin. of another verb, *to be near* to a thing. Gen. 47:29. 1 K. 2:1.

Niph. *to come near*, as in Kal. Ex. 22:7. Josh. 7:14.

Pi. קֵרֵב 1. *to bring near*, Is. 41:21. 46:13. *to grant access*, Ps. 65:5. In a hostile sense, *to let advance*, Job 31:37. Hos. 7:6, (in the latter passage perhaps intrans. as in Kal.)

2. *to bring* or *join together*. Ezek. 37:17.

3. *to be near*, as in Kal, construed with לְ and an infin. Ezek. 36:8.

Hiph. 1. *to let draw near*. Ezek. 22:4. Also *to cause to come near*, Num. 8:9, 10. *to give access*, Jer. 30:21.

2. *to bring*; a gift, Judg. 3:18. 5:25. an offering, Num. 9:13. (See קָרְבָּן.)

3. *to bring or join together*. Is. 5:8.

4. intrans. *to draw near, to approach*. Ex. 14:10.

5. joined with an infin. of another verb, *to be near to* doing a thing. Gen. 12:11. Is. 26:17.

Deriv. out of course קָרוֹב.

קָרֵב m. verbal adj. from קָרַב, dec. V. a. *approaching, drawing near*. Deut. 20:3. 1 K. 4:27. [5:7.].

קְרֵב Chald. plur. קְרִבוּ, *to draw* or *come near*. Dan. 3:26. 6:13.

Pa. *to bring, offer*. Ezra 7:17.

Aph. 1. *to bring near*, Dan. 7:13.

2. *to bring, to offer*. Ezra 6:10, 17.

קְרָב m. (with Kamets impure) verbal from קָרַב, dec. I. *war, battle, contest*, see קָרַב no. (3.) In Hebrew used almost exclusively in poetry. Ps. 55:19, 22. Job 38:23.

קְרָב Chald. *idem*. Dan. 7:21.

קֶרֶב m. with suff. קִרְבִּי, dec. VI. h.

1. *the middle* or *inner part*. Hence בְּקֶרֶב as a prep. *in the midst, within*; also simply *in, among*, (like בְּתוֹךְ,) e. g. בְּקֶרֶב הָאָרֶץ *in the earth*, Ex. 8:18. [8:22.] בְּקֶרֶב הַכְּנַעֲנִי *among the Canaanites*, Judg. 1:32.

2. particularly *the inner part of the body*. (1.) *the bowels, inwards*. Gen. 41:21. Ex. 29:13, 22. (2.) *the heart*, as the seat of thought and affection. Ps. 5:10. 64:7.

קִרְבָה f. const. קִרְבַת, verbal from קָרַב, dec. XI. c. *a drawing near*. Ps. 73:28. Is. 58:2.

קָרְבָּן m. const. קָרְבַּן, plur. with suff. קָרְבְּנֵיהֶם Lev. 7:38, (more correctly in other MSS. קָרְבָּנֵיהֶם,) Arab. قُرْبَان, *an offering, oblation* of any kind. Lev. 2:1, 4, 12, 13. 7:13. 9:7, 15. See הִקְרִיב no. 2.

קֻרְבָּן m. verbal from קָרַב dec. II. b. *a presenting* or *offering*. Neh. 10:35. 13:31.

קַרְדֹּם m. dec. VIII. d. *an axe*. With suff. קַרְדֻּמּוֹ 1 Sam. 13:20. Plur. קַרְדֻּמִּים 1 Sam. 13:21. also וֹת Ps. 74:5. (Arab. كَرْزَم כרזם *idem*. It appears to be kindred with פָּרַס q. v.)

קָרָה f. verbal from obsol. קָרַר, dec. X. *cold*. Prov. 25:20.

קָרָה, fut. יִקְרֶה, apoc. יִקֶר, *to meet* any one, construed with an accus. spoken of persons, Deut. 25:18. and of fate, destiny, Ecc. 2:14. 9:11. Gen. 44:29. of punishment, 1 Sam. 28:10. Ruth 2:3 וַיִּקֶר מִקְרֶהָ חֶלְקַת הַשָּׂדֶה לְבֹעַז liter. *and her lot fell on a piece of land which belonged to Boaz*. Construed with לְ, only Dan. 10:14. Without cases, Is. 41:22.

Niph. 1. as in Kal, *to meet*, (spoken only of persons;) construed with עַל, Ex. 3:18. (comp. 5:3.) with אֶל, Num. 23:4, 16. with לִקְרַאת verse 3.

2. *to be by chance*. 2 Sam. 1:6.

Pi. קֵרָה *to frame* or *lay beams for* a house or gate, *contignare*, liter. *to make the beams meet together*. (Comp. קוֹרָה *a beam*.) 2 Chr. 34:11. Neh. 2:8. 3:3, 6. Also *to construct, build* generally, Ps. 104:3.

Hiph. 1. *to cause to meet*, construed with לִפְנֵי. Gen. 27:20. 24:12 הַקְרֵה־נָא לְפָנַי הַיּוֹם *cause it* (*the object of my journey*) *to meet me this day*.

2. *to make a suitable selection, obvium facere.* Num. 35:11.

Note. This verb is written nearly as often with א; see קָרָא no. II.

Deriv. מִקְרֶה, מִקְרָה, קָרֶה, קְרִי, קוֹרָה.

קָרוֹב m. verbal adj. from קָרַב, dec. III. a.

1. *near*, in space or time. Gen. 45:10. Deut. 22:2. With suff. קְרֹבוֹ for קָרוֹב לוֹ Ps. 148:14.—Ps. 75:2. קָרוֹב שְׁמֶךָ *thy name is near*, i. e. thy praise is in our mouths. (Perhaps also *known*, as in Arab.) Plur. קְרוֹבַי *my nearest friends*, Job 19:14.

2. *kindred, allied*, construed with לְ and אֶל. Ruth 2:20. Num. 27:11.

3. *short, of short continuance.* (Arab. قريب *idem.*) Job 17:12. מִקָּרוֹב *for a short time*, Job 20:5. *shortly, soon*, Ezek. 7:8.

קָרַח 1. intrans. *to be bald, smooth.*

2. *to make smooth*, hence *to shave, to make a bald place.* Lev. 21:5. Mic. 1:16.

Niph. impers. *a baldness is made*, construed with לְ *in honour of* a person. Jer. 16:6.

Hiph. i. q. Kal. Ezek. 27:31.

Hoph. pass. מֻקְרָח *shorn, made bald.* Ezek. 29:18.

קֶרַח m. verbal from קָרַח.

1. *ice*, so called from its *smoothness.* Job 6:16. 37:10. 38:29.

2. *crystal*, like the Greek κρύσταλλος, from its resemblance to *ice*, Ezek. 1:22.

3. *cold.* Gen. 31:40. Jer. 36:30.

קֹרַח m. verbal from קָרַח, dec. VI. n.

1. i. q. קֶרַח no. 1. *ice*, or rather *hail.* Ps. 147:17.

2. proper name (1.) of a son of Esau. Gen. 36:5, 14. (2.) of a son of Eliphaz, also of an Idumean district. Gen. 36:16. (3.) of a Levite who conspired against Moses. Ex. 6:21. Num. 16:1 ff. Hence *the children of Korah*, a Levitical family of singers, the authors of several Psalms, e. g. XLII. XLIV. LXXXIV. LXXXV.

קֵרֵחַ m. verbal from קָרַח, *one who has a bald spot on the hind part of his head, bald-pated*, different from גִּבֵּחַ. Lev. 13:40. 2 K. 2:23. (In Syr. ܩܪܚ *having a smooth forehead.*)

קָרְחָה, once קָרְחָא, f. verbal from קָרַח, dec. X. *a bald spot on the back part of the head*, different from גַּבַּחַת. Lev. 21:5. Spoken of as a sign of mourning, Jer. 48:37. Ezek. 7:18. Used also for *a bald spot on the fore part of the head*, (otherwise called גַּבַּחַת,) Deut. 14:1.

קָרַחַת f. verbal from קָרַח, dec. XIII. m.

1. i. q. קָרְחָה. Lev. 13:42, 43.

2. metaphorically *a bareness of hair on the back side of cloth.* Lev. 13:55.

קְרִי m. in pause קֶרִי, verbal from קָרָה, *contrariness, opposition;* found only in the phrase הָלַךְ קְרִי עִם *to act in opposition* or *walk contrary to* a person, Lev. 26:21, 23. with בְּקֶרִי, verses 24, 27, 40, 41. So in verse 28 וְהָלַכְתִּי עִמָּכֶם בַּחֲמַת קֶרִי *I will in anger walk contrary to you.*

קָרִיא m. verbal from קָרָא no. I. dec. III. a. *called, invited, deputed.* Num. 16:2. and 1:16 Keth.

קְרִיאָה f. verbal from קָרָא, *a preaching, proclamation.* Jon. 3:2.

קִרְיָה f. dec. X. *a city*, i. q. עִיר, but almost solely in poetry. Is. 1:21, 26. 22:2. 25:2. 26:5. 32:13. (In Aram. and Arab. *idem;* in the latter rather *a small city, a village.* It is either primitive, and then kindred with קִיר no. 2. עִיר; or, what is better, a verbal from קָרָה *to build, contignare.*)

The following proper names of cities are compounded of it; (1.) קִרְיַת אַרְבַּע Gen. 23:2. Josh. 15:54. 20:7. the ancient name of Hebron. In this name אַרְבַּע is not the numeral *four*, but *Arba* the proper name of a man; (see אַרְבַּע.) With the article קִרְיַת הָאַרְבַּע (*the city of Arba;*)—(2.) קִרְיַת חֻצוֹת (*city of streets*) in the territory of Moab. Once Num. 22:39. (3.) קִרְיַת יְעָרִים (*city of forests*) in the tribe of Judah, on the western boundary of the tribe of Benjamin. Josh. 9:17. 18:15. Judg. 18:

12. 1 Sam. 6 : 21. With the article קִרְיַת הַיְּעָרִים (*the city of forests,*) and by corruption קִרְיַת עָרִים Ezra 2 : 25. Only a different name is קִרְיַת־בַּעַל Josh. 15 : 60. 18 : 14. (4.) קִרְיַת־סַנָּה Josh. 15 : 49. (*city of the law,*) and קִרְיַת סֵפֶר (*city of writing,*) a city in the tribe of Judah, otherwise called דְּבִיר. Josh. 15 : 15, 16. Judg. 1 : 11, 12. (5.) קִרְיָתַיִם (*double city*) proper name (a.) of a city in the tribe of Reuben. Num. 32 : 37. Josh. 13 : 19. It was afterwards possessed by the Moabites, Jer. 48 : 1, 3. Ezek. 25 : 9. (b.) of a city in the tribe of Naphtali. 1 Chr. 6 : 61. also called קַרְתָּן, (an ancient dual form from קֶרֶת) Josh. 21 : 32.

קָרַם *to cover*, construed with עַל, like other verbs of covering. Ezek. 37 : 6 קָרַמְתִּי עֲלֵיכֶם עוֹר *I will cover you with skin.* Intrans. with a fut. יִקְרַם, verse 8.

קֶרֶן f. prim. dec. VI. a.

1. *a horn.*—Hence (1.) *a vessel of horn*, or *a horn used as a vessel.* 1 Sam. 16 : 1, 13. 1 K. 1 : 39. (2.) *a horn*, as a musical instrument. Josh. 6 : 5. (3.) *a horn*, as a symbol of *strength*, the figure, which is taken from a bull, being retained more or less. Jer. 48 : 25 *the horn of Moab is broken*, i. e. his power is weakened. Comp. Lam. 2 : 3. Ps. 75 : 11. Ps. 132 : 17 *then will I cause a horn to bud to David*, i. e. exalt his power. Comp. Ezek. 29 : 21. Am. 6 : 13 לָקַחְנוּ לָנוּ קַרְנָיִם *we have gained strength.* (Comp. Hor. Od. III. 21. 18, *et addis cornua pauperi.* Ovid. A. A. I. 139.) Ps. 18 : 3 קֶרֶן יִשְׁעִי *the horn of my salvation*, i. e. my powerful deliverer or helper. (Others: *the top of my salvation*, after signif. no. 2. *a peak.*) (4.) used in several phrases, where we employ the word *head.* Job 16 : 15 *I have defiled my horn*, i. e. my head, *with dust.*—*To exalt the horn* or *head* of any one, i. e. to give dignity and power, Ps. 89 : 18. 92 : 11. —*To exalt one's horn* or *head*, i. e. to be arrogant, Ps. 75 : 5, 6.—*My horn exalts itself*, i. e. I acquire new strength, Ps. 89 : 25. 112 : 9.—In this first signification, instead of the plural we find the dual קַרְנַיִם and קְרָנַיִם Dan. 8 : 3, 6, 20. (as if from קֶרֶן ;) rarely the plur. קְרָנוֹת Zech. 2 : 1, 4. [1 : 18, 21.] Ps. 75 : 11. But קַרְנוֹת is used Ezek. 27 : 15, for *horns of ivory*, from a false popular opinion of the ancients that ivory consisted of *the horns* of an animal, (Plin. H. N. XVIII. § 1.)

2. *the top* or *summit of a mountain*, (like the syllable *horn* in the Swiss words *Schreckhorn, Buchhorn.*) Is. 5 : 1. (So in Arab.)

3. קַרְנוֹת הַמִּזְבֵּחַ *horns of the altar*, i. e. projecting points, which were fixed on the four corners of the altar, prob. in the form of horns. Lev. 4 : 7, 18, 25, 30, 34. 8 : 15. 9 : 9. 16 : 18. It cannot denote merely the corners, see Ex. 27 : 2.

4. *a beam, ray.* In the dual used for *flashes of lightning*, Hab. 3 : 4. The Arabian poets also compare the beams of the sun with his horns; hence the poetical expression, *gazelle* for *sun;* (see אַיֶּלֶת.) Hence

קָרַן *to emit rays, to shine*, spoken of the countenance of Moses. Ex. 34 : 29, 30, 35. But Aqu. and Vulg. render it, *to be horned.* Hence Christian painters have represented Moses as horned.

Hiph. *to have horns.* Ps. 69 : 32.

קֶרֶן, emph. קַרְנָא, Chald. *a horn*, Dan. 3 : 5 ff. 7 : 8. Dual קַרְנַיִן used also for the plural, Dan. 7 : 8, 20, 24.

קָרַס found only Is. 46 : 1. perhaps *to be bowed down*, like the parall. כָּרַע, comp. קָרַס. (According to the versions, *to be broken in pieces*, for which we may compare קָרַשׁ, in Arab. *amputavit*, or by transposition שָׁבַר *to break in pieces.*) Hence

קֶרֶס m. verbal from קָרַס, dec. VI. a. *a hook* or *pin*, connected with a loop. Ex. 26 : 6, 11, 33. 35 : 11. 39 : 33.

קַרְסֻלִּים plur. or קַרְסֻלַּיִם dual, prob. *ankles.* Ps. 18 : 37. 2 Sam. 22 : 37. Vulg. *tali.* (Likewise in the Targum Ezek. 47 : 3, for *ankles*, and in Judg. 1 : 6, for *great toes.*)

קָרַע 1. *to rend, to tear in pieces;*

particularly clothes, as a sign of mourning, Gen. 37:29, 34. 44:13. heaven, spoken of God, Is. 63:19. [64:1.]

2. *to tear open.*—קָרַע עֵינַיִם בַּפּוּךְ Jer. 4:30. *to tear open the eyes with stibium*, with a reference to the mode of procedure in the painting of the eyes, (see כָּחַל;) a strong expression used perhaps designedly.

3. *to tear off* or *away.* Lev. 13:56. 1 Sam. 15:28 *Jehovah has torn away the kingdom of Israel from thee.* 28:17. 1 K. 11:11:

4. *to cut in pieces,* (with a knife.) Jer. 36:23.

5. *to cut out.* Jer. 22:14.

6. *to revile, verbis proscindere,* Ps. 35:15. (Arab. قرع conj. II. *increpuit, corripuit.* Comp. נָקַב nos. 1, 2, 3.)

Niph. pass. spoken e. g. of the altar. 1 K. 13:3, 5.

קְרָעִים masc. plur. verbal from קָרַע, *pieces of a garment, rags.* 1 K. 11:30, 31. Prov. 23:21.

קָרַץ (in Arab. with ص,) *to bite, to nip.* Particularly (1.) joined with שְׂפָתַיִם, *to bite one's lips,* as a mark of maliciousness. Prov. 16:30. (2.) joined with עַיִן Prov. 10:10. Ps. 35:19. and בְּעֵינָיו Prov. 6:13. *to wink with the eyes,* as a mark of falsehood.

Pu. Job 33:6 מֵחֹמֶר קֹרַצְתִּי גַם אָנִי liter. *from the clay was I also nipped* or *broken off.* The figure is taken from the potter, who nips off a piece of clay from the mass.

קֶרֶץ m. *destruction.* Jer. 46:20. (Root Arab. قرض *consumsit, exterminavit.*)

קְרַץ m. Chald. *a piece,* from the Heb. קָרַץ. Found only in the phrase אֲכַל קַרְצֵי דִי *to eat the pieces of* a person, a metaphorical expression for *to slander* or *inform against* him. Dan. 3:8. 6:25. (In Syr. *idem.* In Arab. *to eat the flesh of* a person, for *to slander;* also simply اكل conj. IV. *to calumniate;* أكلة *calumny.*)

קַרְקַע m. a quadriliteral, *the ground, bottom;* as (1.) *the floor* or *pavement* of the tabernacle or temple. Num. 5:17. 1 K. 6:15, 16, 30. (2.) *the bottom* of the sea. Am. 9:3. (In Chald. *idem.* In Arab. قرق *solum planum et æquabile.*)

קָרַר *to be cold, cool.* In Hebrew not in use. Deriv. קַר, קֹר, קָרָה, מְקֵרָה.

קֶרֶשׁ m. dec. VI. h. *a board* or *plank.* Ex. 26:15 ff. 36:20 ff. Ezek. 27:6. The etymology is uncertain; perhaps from Arab. قرش *amputavit.*

קֶרֶת f. i. q. קִרְיָה *a city.* Job 29:7. Prov. 8:3. 9:3. Chald. קִרְיָא *idem.* This form of the word is still retained in *Cirta, Tigranocerta,* etc. names of cities.

קַרְתָּן proper name of a city in the tribe of Naphtali, otherwise called קִרְיָתַיִם. Josh. 21:32. ־ָן is an ancient termination of the dual, and the two names are synonymous.

קְשָׂה and קַשְׂוָה found only in the plur. קְשָׂוֹת Ex. 25:29. 37:16. const. קְשׂוֹת Num. 4:7. *bowls, dishes.* (Chald. קַסְוָה, plur. קַסְוָת *idem.*)

קְשִׂיטָה f. Gen. 33:19. Josh. 24:32. Job 42:11. prob. a coin of unknown value, or a certain weight made use of in reckoning, (comp. Arab. قسط *a balance,* also a certain measure; قسط conj. V. *to divide equally;*) perhaps also a vessel used in barter, (comp. Syr. ܩܣܛܐ i. q. Heb. קֶסֶת *a vessel.*) Faber zu Harmer's Beob. üb. den Orient, Th. II. p. 15—19. The ancient versions for the most part render it *a lamb.* According to Rabbi Akiba (Bocharti Hieroz. T. I. 3. c. 43.) a certain coin bore this name in Africa, in comparatively modern times.

קַשְׂקֶשֶׂת f. plur. קַשְׂקַשִּׂים (1 Sam. 17:5.) and קַשְׂקְשׂוֹת (Ezek. 29:4.) *a scale.* Lev. 11:9 ff.—שִׁרְיוֹן קַשְׂקַשִּׂים *a coat of mail of scales,* 1 Sam. 17:5.

קַשׁ m. verbal from קָשַׁשׁ, *straw, halm,* Ex. 15:7. *stubble,* Is. 5:24. 47:14.

Particularly *flying stubble, chaff*, Job 13:25.

קִשֻּׁאִים masc. plur. Num. 11:5. a species of cucumbers or melons, *pumkins*, with an oblong, green, sweet-tasted fruit; Arab. قثّا, now called in Egypt, *chate*, hence *cucumis chate*, Linn. Deriv. מִקְשָׁה no. II. *a melon-garden.*

קָשַׁב *to give attention, to be attentive, to hearken.* In Kal only Is. 32:3.

Hiph. joined with אֹזֶן, *to incline one's ear attentively, to hearken.* Ps. 10:17. Prov. 2:2. Hence without אֹזֶן, intrans. as in Kal; construed with בְּ, Ps. 66:19. with לְ, Ps. 5:3. Is. 48:18. with אֶל, Ps. 142:7. Neh. 9:34. with עַל, Prov. 17:4. 29:12. with an accus. Job 13:6.

קֶשֶׁב m. verbal from קָשַׁב, *attention.* Is. 21:7.

קַשָּׁב m. verbal adj. from קָשַׁב, dec. I. *attentive.* Ps. 130:2.

קַשֻּׁב, fem. קַשֻּׁבָה verbal adj. from קָשַׁב, *attentive.* Neh. 1:6, 11.

קָשָׁה 1. *to be hard*, spoken e.g. of words. 2 Sam. 19:44. Also *to be cruel, terrible*, spoken of anger, Gen. 49:7.

2. *to be heavy, difficult, hard.* 1 Sam. 5:7. Deut. 15:18. Spoken of a cause in law, Deut. 1:17.

Niph. part. נִקְשֶׁה *burdened, oppressed, troubled.* Is. 8:21.

Pi. *to make hard* or *heavy.* Gen. 35:16 וַתְּקַשׁ בְּלִדְתָּהּ *she had hard labour.* In verse 17, the same is expressed by the Hiph.

Hiph. הִקְשָׁה, fut. apoc. וַיַּקֶשׁ.

1. *to harden*, e.g. (1.) the heart, *to render obdurate.* Ex. 7:3. Deut. 2:30. Ps. 95:8. Prov. 28:14. (2.) one's neck, i.e. *to be stiff-necked.* Deut. 10:16. 2 K. 17:14. Without עֹרֶף, Job 9:4.

2. *to make heavy* or *grievous.* 1 K. 12:4. 2 K. 2:10 הִקְשִׁיתָ לִשְׁאוֹל *thou hast asked a hard thing.* Ex. 13:15 כִּי הִקְשָׁה פַרְעֹה לְשַׁלְּחֵנוּ *when Pharaoh made difficulties about letting us go.*

קָשֶׁה, fem. קָשָׁה, verbal adj. from קָשָׁה, dec. IX. b. and XI. a.

1. *hard*; spoken e.g. of words, Gen. 42:7, 30. of servitude, Ex. 1:14. 6:9. 1 K. 12:4.—Job 30:25 קְשֵׁה־יוֹם *one whose day is hard*, i.e. an unfortunate man. Particularly (1.) joined with עֹרֶף, *stiff-necked.* Ex. 32:9. 34:9. (2.) joined with פָּנִים, *of a bold front, impudent, shameless.* Ezek. 2:4. (3.) joined with לֵב, *of a hard, inflexible heart.* Ezek. 3:7. So without addition, Is. 48:4.

2. *heavy, difficult.* Judg. 4:24. Ex. 18:26.

3. *firm.* Cant. 8:6.

4. *violent*; spoken of the wind, Is. 27:8. of a battle, 2 Sam. 2:17.

5. *powerful, mighty, gravis auctoritate.* 2 Sam. 3:39.

Deriv. קְשִׁי, מַקְשָׁה, מִקְשָׁה no. I.

קְשׁוֹט Chald. *truth.* (See the Heb. קֹשֶׁט.) Dan. 4:34. [4:37.]—מִן קְשֹׁט *in truth, certainly*, Dan. 2:47.

קָשַׁח Arab. قسح i.q. קָשָׁה *to be hard.* In Kal not used.

Hiph. 1. *to harden* (the heart.) Is. 63:17.

2. *to treat harshly*, Job 39:16.

קֹשֶׁט m. Ps. 60:6. and קֹשְׁטְ Prov. 22:21. *truth.* (Aram. קוּשְׁטָא, ܩܘܫܛܐ *idem.* In Arab. قسط *to be right, equitable.*)

קְשִׁי m. verbal from קָשָׁה, *hardness, obduracy, stubbornness.* Deut. 9:27.

קָשַׁר, fut. יִקְשֹׁר. 1. *to bind, fetter.* Gen. 38:28. Metaphorically Gen. 44:30. Prov. 22:15.

2. *to enter into a conspiracy, to conspire*, construed with עַל *against* a person. 1 K. 15:27. 16:9, 16. 2 K. 10:9. In full קָשַׁר קֶשֶׁר.

3. part. pass. *bound, close*, hence *strong.* Gen. 30:42. For this transition of meaning, see חָזַק no. 3.

Niph. 1. pass. of Kal no. 1. Metaphorically 1 Sam. 18:1.

2. *to be joined together, to be closed*, spoken of a wall. Neh. 3:38. [4:6.]

Pi. i.q. Kal no. 1. Job 38:31.

Pu. part. מְקֻשָּׁרוֹת *the strong* (*sheep*), Gen. 30:41. see Kal no. 3.

Hithpa. i. q. Kal no. 2. 2 K. 9:14. 2 Chr. 24:25, 26.

קֶשֶׁר m. with suff. קִשְׁרוֹ, verbal from קָשַׁר, dec. VI. h. *a conspiracy*. See קָשַׁר no. 2. 2 K. 11:14.—קָשַׁר קֶשֶׁר *to form a conspiracy*, 2 K. 12:21. 14:19. 15:30. This name is also given to the combination of Israel and Syria against Judah, Is. 8:12, because it was opposed to the people of God, and was an unnatural alliance.

קִשֻּׁרִים masc. plur. verbal from קָשַׁר, *a girdle*, an ornament worn by women. Is. 3:20. Jer. 2:32.

קָשַׁשׁ in Kal only Zeph. 2:1. see Hithpa.

Po. קוֹשֵׁשׁ *to search after, to collect;* e. g. straw, Ex. 5:7, 12. wood, Num. 15:32.

Hithpo. Zeph. 2:1 הִתְקוֹשְׁשׁוּ וָקוֹשּׁוּ *collect yourselves*, i. e. go into yourselves, examine yourselves. The ancient versions: *assemble yourselves together*.

Deriv. קַשׁ.

קֶשֶׁת, plur. קְשָׁתוֹת, const. קַשְּׁתוֹת, com. gen. (masc. 1 Sam. 2:22. fem. Ps. 18:35.)

1. *a bow*, to shoot with.—דָּרַךְ קֶשֶׁת *to stretch the bow*, see דָּרַךְ.—בֶּן־קֶשֶׁת *the son of the bow*, i. e. the arrow, Job 41:20. [41:28.]—*to break the bow of* any one, i. e. to destroy his power, Hos. 1:5. Jer. 49:35. comp. Ps. 76:4.

2. as a collect. *archers*. Is. 21:17. 22:3.

2. *a rain-bow*. Gen. 9:13 ff. Ezek. 1:28.

3. 2 Sam. 1:18. *the song of the bow*, the title of the elegy on Saul and Jonathan, from the incidental naming of the bow in verse 22. The titles of the chapters of the Koran, as well as of most other oriental works, appear to us equally unsuitable.—Hence the denom.

קַשָּׁת m. denom. from קֶשֶׁת, *an archer*. Gen. 21:20.

קַתְרוֹס Chald. the constant Keri for the Kethib קִיתָרֹס *a harp*. It is the more usual form in the Targums, but on that account less to be approved.

ר

Resh, the 20th letter of the alphabet, and as a numerical sign denoting 200. The name רֵישׁ=רֹאשׁ denotes *a head*, and has reference to the shape of the letter in the Phenician alphabet (𐤓,) whence by inversion the Greek Ῥῶ (Ρ.) For the interchange of this letter with ל and נ, see those letters. Here observe (1.) that ר sometimes assimilates itself to the following letter; e. g. אֲשֶׁר, whence שֶׁ with Dagesh following, (for the omission of the א, see p. 2.) דַּרְמֶשֶׂק, usually דַּמֶּשֶׂק *Damascus;* יַבֹּק Arab. يرموك name of a river; כָּרְסֵא Heb. כִּסֵּא *a throne*. (2.) that between the first and second radicals a ר is sometimes inserted, and then a quadriliteral is formed; as e. g. פַּרְזֶל i. q. כָּבַל *to bind, fetter;* סַרְעַפָּה and סְעִיף *a branch;* שַׂרְעַפִּים and שְׂעִפִּים *thoughts*.

רָאָה, fut. יִרְאֶה, apoc. יֵרֶא, with Vav convers. וַיַּרְא, וַיֵּרֶא, infin. absol. רָאֹה, רָאוֹ, const. רְאוֹת.

1. *to see, look;* very freq. Usually construed with an accus. once with לְ, Ps. 64:6. with עַל, *to look upon* a thing, Ex. 5:21. with בֵּין, *to see the difference between*, Mal. 3:18.—So in the phrase *to see the face of a king*, i. e. to be his confidant, 2 K. 25:19. Est. 1:14.—Ecc. 12:3 הָרֹאוֹת בָּאֲרֻבּוֹת *which look through the windows*.

2. construed with בְּ, *to look upon or view with interest* or *sympathy;* (1.) with satisfaction, *to rejoice in* a thing. Job 3:9. 20:17. Particularly in the destruction of one's enemies, Ps. 22:18. 37:34. 54:9. 112:8 עַד אֲשֶׁר יִרְאֶה בְצָרָיו *until he rejoices in his enemies*, i. e. in their destruction, Obad. 12. (2.) with

grief. Gen. 21:16 אַל־אֶרְאֶה בְּמוֹת הַיָּלֶד *let me not see the death of the child.* 44:34. Est. 8:6. (Comp. בְּ no. 17.)

3. *to look on, to view.* Lev. 13:3, 5, 17. Prov. 23:31. Cant. 1:6: Construed with בְּ, Gen. 34:1. Cant. 6:11. Ecc. 11:4 רֹאֶה בֶעָבִים *he who vieweth the clouds.* Particularly spoken of God, *to look on,* in order to relieve, Ex. 4:31 וְכִי רָאָה אֶת־עָנְיָם *and that he looked on their affliction.* Ps. 9:14. 25:18. 31:8. Construed with בְּ, Gen. 29:32. 1 Sam. 1:11.

4. *to look* or *see to* a thing, *to take care for* it, construed with an accus. (like יָדַע.) Gen. 39:23. Ps. 37:37. Prov. 23:33. 1 K. 12:16 רְאֵה בֵיתְךָ דָּוִד *see to thine house,* i. e. take care for thine house, *O David.* Is. 26:10.

5. *to see, know, discern.* Jer. 20:12. Ecc. 1:16.

6. *to visit.* 2 Sam. 13:5. 2 K. 8:29. 2 Chr. 22:6.

7. *to choose, select.* Gen. 22:8. 41:33. Deut. 12:13. Part. pass. רָאוּי *select, chosen,* Est. 2:9.

8. *to see* or *experience;* e. g. good, Ps. 34:13. Ecc. 3:13. 6:6. construed with בְּ, Jer. 29:32. evil, Lam. 3:1. Prov. 27:12. *To enjoy* life, Ecc. 9:9. *to suffer* death, Ps. 89:49. *to have a part in* the grave, Ps. 16:10. 49:10. Construed with בְּ, Obad. 13.

Niph. 1. *to be seen.* 1 K. 6:18.

2. *to shew one's self, to appear;* construed with אֶל. Lev. 13:19. 1 K. 18:1.—נִרְאָה אֶת־פְּנֵי יְהוָֹה *to appear before Jehovah,* i. e. to visit his sanctuary, Ex. 34:23, 24. Deut. 31:11. 1 Sam. 1:22. comp. Ex. 23:17. Ps. 42:3. Spoken particularly of Jehovah, Gen. 12:7. 17:1. 18:1. More rarely with לְ, Jer. 31:3.

Pu. *to be seen.* Once Job 33:21.

Hiph. הֶרְאָה and הִרְאָה, fut. apoc. וַיַּרְא (like Kal) 2 K. 11:4.

1. *to cause to see, to shew,* construed with two accus. 2 K. 8:13. Nah. 3:5. Amos 7:1.

2. metaphorically like Kal no. 8. *to cause to experience* good or evil. Ps. 60:5. 71:20. Ecc. 2:24. Construed with בְּ of the thing, Ps. 50:23. 91:16.

Hoph. *to be shewn,* liter. *to be made to see.* Ex. 25:40 אֲשֶׁר אַתָּה מָרְאֶה בָּהָר *which thou hast been shewn in the mount.* 26:30. Deut. 4:35. Lev. 13:49 הָרְאָה אֶת הַכֹּהֵן *it shall be shewn to the priest.*

Hithpa. הִתְרָאָה *to look on one another.* Gen. 42:1. Also in a hostile sense, *to see one another in battle, to try each other's strength,* 2 K. 14:8, 11. Comp. the old German proverb, *sich die Köpfe,* oder *das Weisse im Auge besehn.*

Deriv. out of course רְאוּת, רְאִי, רֳאִי, מַרְאֶה, מַרְאָה, Chald. רֵו.

רָאָה found only Deut. 14:13. prob. a corrupted reading for דָּאָה, as in the parallel passage Lev. 11:14. See דָּאָה.

רֹאֶה m. a participial noun from רָאָה, dec. IX. a.

1. *a seer, prophet,* according to 1 Sam. 9:9, the more ancient name for נָבִיא. It is used by way of eminence of Samuel, 1 Sam. 9:9 ff. 1 Chr. 9:22. 26:28. 29:29. of another prophet, 2 Chr. 16:7, 10.

2. i. q. רְאִי, *a vision.* Is. 28:7.

רְאוּבֵן *Reuben,* the proper name of the eldest son of Jacob, (who, however, lost his birthright,) and progenitor of the tribe which was named from him. The most natural etymology would be, *see, a son!* But a different derivation is given Gen. 29:32.

רְאוּת f. verbal from רָאָה, *a seeing.* Ecc. 5:10 Keri.

רְאִי f. verbal from רָאָה, *a mirror.* Job 37:18. See מַרְאָה no. 2. Arab. رئي, *idem.*

רֳאִי, in pause רֹאִי, verbal from רָאָה.

1. *a sight, vision.* Gen. 16:13. See the art. בְּאֵר לַחַי רֹאִי.

2. i. q. מַרְאֶה *an appearance, form.* 1 Sam. 16:12. Job 33:21 *his flesh consumes away* מֵרֹאִי *out of view.*

3. *a spectacle, gazing stock,* παράδειγμα. Nah. 3:6.

רְאֵם see רְאֵים.

רִאשׁוֹן see רִאשׁוֹן.

רָאַם Zech. 14:10. i. q. רוּם *to be high.* See under the letter א, p. 1, 2.

רְאֵם m. Num. 23:22. Deut. 33: 17. רְאֵים Ps. 92:11. רֵים Job 39:9, 10. Plur. רְאֵמִים Ps. 29:6. also רֵמִים Ps. 22: 22. *the wild buffalo.* (Arab. رِئم a species of gazelle, which sense some apply to the Hebrew; but the signification of the Arabic here is only cognate, and not identical. The Greek βούβαλος, βούβαλις, is also used of the gazelle, and the Arabians call stags and antelopes wild oxen. See Schultens in Job 39:9, 10. De Wette's Commentar in Ps. 22: 22. comp. Bocharti Hieroz. T. I. p. 948 ff.) Sept. Vulg. *monoceros, unicornis, rhinoceros;* against which see Bochart.

רָאמוֹת strictly part. act. plur. for רָמוֹת (Prov. 24:7.) and then

1. *heights;* used only as a proper name (1.) of a city in Gilead, otherwise called רָמֹת, רָמַת מִצְפֶּה. Deut. 4:43. Josh. 20:8. 1 Chr. 6:65. (2.) of a city in the tribe of Issachar. 1 Chr. 6:58. perhaps i. q. רֶמֶת Josh. 19:21. and יַרְמוּת Josh. 21:29.

2. a costly substance, according to the Hebrew interpreters, *red corals.* Job 28:18. Ezek. 27:16.

רָאשׁ *poor.* See רוּשׁ.

רֵאשׁ m. a different orthography for רֵישׁ *poverty.* Prov. 30:8.

רֵאשׁ Chald. i. q. Heb. ראשׁ.

1. *a head.* Dan. 2:38.—חֶזְוֵי רֵאשִׁי *the visions of my head* or *fancy,* or better simply *my visions,* making רֵאשִׁי merely a periphrasis of the personal pronoun. Dan. 4:2, 7, 10. [4:5, 10, 13.] 7:15.

2. *the sum, amount.* Dan. 7:1.

Plur. רָאשִׁין Dan. 7:6. also after the Hebrew form רָאשֵׁין Ezra 5:10. *heads, chiefs.*

I. ראשׁ m. (for רְאשׁ or רֹאשׁ by a Syriasm,) plur. רָאשִׁים (for רְאָשִׁים,) once ראשׁיו (Is. 15:2.) prim. irreg.

1. *a head.*—נָתַן בְּרֹאשׁ פ׳ *to let come on the head of any one,* Ezek. 9:10. 11: 21. 16:43. 17:19. 22:31.—בְּרָאשֵׁינוּ *with the danger of our heads,* 1 Chr. 12:19. comp. בְּנַפְשׁוֹ under נֶפֶשׁ no. 2. (2.)

2. *the first* or *highest* in its kind. Hence (1.) *a head, chief, leader.* 1 Sam. 15:17.—ראשׁ בֵּית אָבוֹת and simply ר׳ אָבוֹת *the head of a family,* Ex. 6:14, 25. Num. 7:2. 32:28. 36:1. (2.) *a chief city, metropolis.* Josh. 11:10. Is. 7:8. (3.) *the highest place, first rank.*—כֹּהֵן הָרֹאשׁ *the high-priest,* 2 Chr. 19:11. instead of which we find in 2 Chr. 24:6, simply הָרֹאשׁ, after no. (1.)—Job 29: 25 אֵשֵׁב ראשׁ *I sat in the highest place.* Amos 6:7 בְּרֹאשׁ גֹּלִים *at the head of the captives.* (4.) *the top* or *highest part,* as of a mountain, Gen. 8:5. 2 K. 1:9. of a tower, Gen. 11:4. of a pillar, 1 K. 7: 19. of an ear of corn, Job 24:24.—ראשׁ פִּנָּה *the head stone of the corner,* (not *the foundation stone,*) Ps. 118:22. Metaphorically ראשׁ שִׂמְחָה *the highest joy,* Ps. 137:6. רָאשֵׁי בְשָׂמִים *the most costly spices,* Cant. 4:14. Ezek. 27:22.

3. *the first;* e. g. ראשׁ הֳחָדָשִׁים *the first month,* Ex. 12:2. hence *the beginning,* as מֵרֹאשׁ *from the beginning,* Is. 40:21. 41:26. 48:16. אַרְבָּעָה רָאשִׁים *four beginnings of streams,* Gen. 2:10. (So the Lat. *caput,* Caes. de Bello Gall. VIII. 41. § 4. Pomp. Mela, II. 4.) ראשׁ דֶּרֶךְ *the beginning of the way, a cross-way,* Ezek. 16:25 ר׳ חוצות *the beginning* or *head of the streets,* Lam. 2:19.

4. *the sum, the whole number.* Lev. 5: 24 [6:5] בְּרֹאשׁוֹ *according to the sum.* Ps. 119:160 ראשׁ דְּבָרְךָ *the sum of thy words.* Hence נָשָׂא ראשׁ *to take the sum, to number, measure.* See נָשָׂא no. 3. (3.) Hence

5. *a company, multitude, host;* particularly of warriors. Judg. 7:16, 20. 9:34, 37, 43. 1 Sam. 11:11.

Deriv. רִאשׁוֹן, רֵאשִׁית, מְרַאֲשׁוֹת.

II. **ראשׁ** and **רוֹשׁ** (Deut. 32:32.)

1. a poisonous plant, Deut. 29:17: which grows in the fields, Hos. 10:4. bears fruit in clusters, Deut. 32:32. (unless this verse falls under signif. no. 2.) and is bitter, Ps. 69:22. Lam. 3: 5. Hence its frequent connexion with

לַעֲנָה *wormwood*, Deut. 29:17. Lam. 3:19.—מֵי רֹאשׁ *poisonous water* or *bitter water*, Jer. 8:14. 9:14. 23:15. Its specific meaning cannot be determined. Perhaps *night-shade;* or according to Michaëlis, *darnel, lolium temulentum;* or according to Oedmann, *the poisonous coloquintida;* or according to Celsius (Hierob. II. 46 ff.) *the cicuta.*

2. *poison* of any kind. Deut. 32:33.

III. רֹאשׁ Ezek. 38:2, 3. 39:1. proper name of a Scythian people, mentioned in connexion with Meshech and Tubal, in the northern parts of Asia Minor. The Byzantine writers speak of a rude and savage people about the northern Taurus, called Ῥῶς, (*Russians?*) See J. D. Michaëlis Supplem. p. 2225.

רֵאשָׁה f. plur. רָאשׁוֹת, dec. X. *a beginning*, i. q. רֹאשׁ no. 3. The form of the word resembles the Syr. ܪܫܐ. Ezek. 36:11.

רֹאשָׁה f. i. q. רֹאשׁ no. 2. in the phrase הָאֶבֶן הָרֹאשָׁה *the chief corner stone*, Zech. 4:7.

רִאשׁוֹן (by a Syriasm for רִאשׁוֹן, as in the Kethib of Josh. 21:10. Job 15:7. and in the Samar. Pentateuch constantly,) a denom. adj. from רֹאשׁ, (with an epenthetic Yod, like קִיצוֹן from קֵץ,) fem. רִאשֹׁנָה, *the first*, in time, order, or dignity. Plur. רִאשֹׁנִים *the forefathers*, Deut. 19:14.—יָמִים רִאשֹׁנִים *the first days*, Deut. 10:10.—הָרִאשֹׁנוֹת *the former things, the former events*, Is. 41:22.—Fem. רִאשֹׁנָה as an adv. *first, foremost*, Gen. 33:2. 38:28. *before*, Dan. 11:29. more commonly בָּרִאשֹׁנָה *first*, Num. 10:13, 14. *at the first*, Gen. 13:4. Is. 1:26. לָרִאשֹׁנָה *at the first*, Judg. 18:29. (See רִישׁוֹן.)

רִאשֹׁנִי, fem. ־ִית, *idem*, Jer. 25:1.

רַאֲשׁוֹת see מְרַאֲשׁוֹת.

רֵאשִׁית f. once רֵשִׁית (Deut. 11:12.) denom. from רֹאשׁ = Chald. רֵאשׁ *caput, princeps*, (with the termination ־ִית, see Gesen. Lehrgeb. § 122. 2.) dec. I. liter. *principium.*

1. *a beginning*. Gen. 1:1. 10:10. Jer. 28:1.

2. *a former state.* Job 42:12.

3. *the first in its kind, a firstling, first-fruits.* Gen. 49:3 רֵאשִׁית אוֹנִי *the first-fruits of my strength.*—רֵאשִׁית דַּרְכּוֹ *the first-fruits of his creation*, Prov. 8:22. comp. Job 40:19. Spoken particularly of the first-fruits which were brought into the temple, Lev. 2:12. 23:10. Deut. 18:4. 26:10. Hence רֵאשִׁית גּוֹיִם *the first*, i. e. the most eminent *of the nations*, Num. 24:21. Am. 6:1.

I. רַב, in pause רָב, fem. רַבָּה, plur. רַבִּים, verbal adj. from רָבַב, dec. VIII. h.

1. *much, many, numerous;* as מִקְנֶה רַב *much cattle*, Num. 32:1. עֲבֻדָּה רַבָּה *a numerous train of servants*, Gen. 26:14. רַבַּת בָּנִים *having many children*, 1 Sam. 2:5.—Ex. 19:21 וְנָפַל מִמֶּנּוּ רָב, *and many of them fall.* Plur. יָמִים רַבִּים, *many days, a long time*, Gen. 21:34. As an adv. *much, exceedingly, sufficient, enough*, Ps. 123:3. Gen. 33:9. Also joined with substantives, Ps. 18:15 בְּרָקִים רָב *lightnings in abundance.* (Comp. מְעַט.)—רַב עַתָּה *it is now enough, it suffices*, 2 Sam. 24:16. 1 K. 19:4. Also in the same sense רַב לָךְ Deut. 3:26. רַב לָכֶם Ezek. 45:9. Num. 16:3. Construed with an infin. Deut. 1:6 רַב לָכֶם שֶׁבֶת *ye have dwelt long enough.* 2:3. with מִן, Ezek. 44:6 רַב לָכֶם מִכָּל תּוֹעֲבוֹתֵיכֶם *desist from all your abominations.* 1 K. 12:28. Ex. 9:28. Fem. רַבָּה in like manner as an adv. *much, sufficient*, Ps. 62:3. more frequently in the const. state רַבַּת, Ps. 65:10. 120:6. 123:4.

2. *great, mighty.* Ps. 31:20 מָה רַב טוּבְךָ *how great is thy goodness!* 145:7. Is. 63:1 רַב לְהוֹשִׁיעַ *mighty to save.* Plur. רַבִּים *the great, the mighty*, Job 35:10. As a subst. *greatness*, Ps. 145:7. Is. 63:7.

3. *older, major natu.* Gen. 25:23. Plur. רַבִּים *the aged*, Job 32:9.

4. as a subst. *a chief, captain, leader, prince*, i. q. שַׂר, particularly in later Hebrew; e. g. רַב טַבָּחִים *the captain of the body guard*, 2 K. 25:8. רַב סָרִיסִים *a captain of the eunuchs*, Dan. 1:3. Est. 1:8.

II. רַב m. dec. VIII. h. Job 16:13. according to the versions, *an arrow*, or *an archer*. See רָבַב no. II.

רַב Chald. 1. *great*. Dan. 2:10, 31, 35, 45.

2. subst. *a chief, head, captain*. Dan. 5:11. 2:48.

Plur. רַבְרְבִן (from an obsol. sing. רברב,) Dan. 3:33. [4:3.] 2:48. 7:3, 7, 17.—מַלִּל רַבְרְבָן *to speak great things*, i. e. to make arrogant or blasphemous speeches, Dan. 7:8, 20. Comp. Rev. 13:5. and in Heb. נִפְלָא.

רָב see רִיב.

רֹב (strictly an infin. from רָבַב,) in the later books also written in full רוֹב (Job 35:9. Est. 10:3.) before Makkeph רָב־, with suff. רֻבָּם, verbal from רָבַב no. I. dec. VIII. d.

1. *multitude, number*. Lev. 25:16. Is. 1:11. לָרֹב *abundantly, very much*, Gen. 30:30. 48:16. Deut. 1:10. Plur. Hos. 8:12 Keri.

2. *greatness*. רָב־כֹּחַ *greatness of strength*, Ps. 33:16. 51:3.

I. רָבַב *to be* or *become many* or *numerous*. Gen. 6:1. Ps. 3:2. 69:5. 104:24. Is. 59:12. Found only in the pret. and in the infin. רֹב; the other tenses are formed from רָבָה.

Pu. denom. from רְבָבָה, *to be increased to myriads*. Ps. 144:13.

Deriv. רַב, רַבָּה, רֹב, רְבָבָה, רִבּוֹא, רְבִיבִים.

II. רָבַב or רָבַב *to shoot arrows*. (Perhaps kindred with רָמָה, by a commutation of מ and ב, see ב.) Hence the pret. רֹבּוּ *they shoot arrows*, Gen. 49:23. Some likewise place here Ps. 18:15 בְּרָקִים רָב *he shoots out lightning*. See the deriv. רַב no. II.

Note. These two roots nos. I. and II. were made distinct by Kimchi.

רְבָבָה f. verbal from רָבַב, dec. XI. c. *a myriad, ten thousand*. Judg. 20:10. Plur. רְבָבוֹת *myriads*, for the most part used as an indefinitely large number, Ps. 3:7. 91:7. Deut. 33:17.

רָבַד, *to cover, to overspread*. Prov. 7:16. Deriv. מַרְבַדִּים,

רָבָה, fut. apoc. יִרֶב and יֶרֶב.

1. *to be* or *become many* or *numerous, to increase*. Gen. 1:22, 28. 9:1, 7. Ex. 1:20.

2. *to be great*, Gen. 43:34. Job 33:12. *to become great, to grow*, Deut. 30:16. Gen. 21:20 וַיְהִי רֹבֶה קַשָּׁת *and he became, as he grew up, an archer*. Vulg. *factusque est juvenis sagittarius*.

Pi. רִבָּה 1. *to make numerous, to increase*. Judg. 9:29. Ps. 44:13 לֹא רִבִּיתָ בִּמְחִירֵיהֶם *thou hast not increased* (thy wealth) *by their price*, i. e. thou hast sold them for nothing.

2. *to nourish, to bring up*. Ezek. 19:2. Lam. 2:22.

Hiph. הִרְבָּה, fut. יַרְבֶּה, apoc. יֶרֶב, imper. apoc. הֶרֶב, infin. absol. הַרְבֵּה and הַרְבָּה (the latter used as an adv.) infin. const. הַרְבּוֹת.

1. *to make numerous, to increase*. Gen. 3:16. Prov. 22:16 הַרְבּוֹת לוֹ *to increase for himself* (riches,) i. e. to enrich himself. Comp. Ps. 44:13. Construed with לְ, Hos. 10:1.

2. *to make great, enlarge*. 1 Chr. 4:10. Job 34:37 *and he maketh great his words against God*, i. e. he uttereth arrogant speeches, (see רַב in Chald.)

3. *to have much* or *many*. 1 Chr. 7:4. 4:27. 8:40. 23:11. Lev. 11:42.

4. *to give much*. Ex. 30:15. Antith. הַמְעִיט.

5. joined with an infin. with and without לְ, it forms a periphrasis for the adv. *much*. 1 Sam. 1:12 הִרְבְּתָה לְהִתְפַּלֵּל *she prayed much*. Ex. 36:5. Ps. 78:38. Am. 4:4. Also when followed by a finite verb, as 1 Sam. 2:3.—Infin. absol. הַרְבֵּה used as an adv. *much*, (liter. *making much*,) Ecc. 5:11. 2 Sam. 1:4. rarely הַרְבּוֹת Prov. 25:27.—הַרְבֵּה מְאֹד *very much*, Neh. 2:2. 3:33. [4:1.] Also with substantives, 2 Sam. 8:8 נְחֹשֶׁת הַרְבֵּה מְאֹד *very much brass*. 12:2. 1 K. 5:9. [4:29.] Gen. 15:1 שְׂכָרְךָ הַרְבֵּה מְאֹד *thy reward shall be very much*, i. e. very great. Also joined with the plural, 1 K. 10:11.—לְהַרְבֵּה *in abundance*, Neh. 5:

18. הַרְבּוֹת also used as a subst. *multitude*, Am. 4:9.

Deriv. out of course הַרְבּוּת, מַרְבִּית, אַרְבֶּה, תַּרְבִּית.

רְבָה Chald. *to be* or *become great*. Dan. 4:8, 19. [4:11, 22.]

Pa. *to make great, to exalt*. Dan. 2:48.

רַבָּה liter. *a chief city*, comp. the Syr. ܪܰܒܬܳܐ. Hence the proper name (1) of the metropolis of the Ammonites; called in full רַבַּת בְּנֵי עַמּוֹן, Deut. 3:11. also simply רַבָּה, 2 Sam. 11:1. 12:27 (2.) of the metropolis of the Moabites, otherwise called עָר and עָר־מוֹאָב, Josh. 13:25.

רִבּוֹ and **רִבּוֹא** f. (for רִבּוֹת, by casting off ת, Syr. ܪܶܒܘܳ,) *ten thousand, a myriad*, i. q. רְבָבָה, but found only in the later writers. Ezra 2:64. 1 Chr. 29:7. Plur. רִבּאוֹת Dan. 11:12.

רִבּוֹ Chald. *idem*. Plur. רִבְּוָן, (Syr. ܪܶܒܘܳܢ,) in Keri רִבְבָן, *myriads*. Dan. 7:10.

רְבוּ Chald. emph. רְבוּתָא, *greatness*. Dan. 4:19, 33. [4:22, 36.] 5:18.

רִבּוֹת f. i. q. רִבּוֹ *ten thousand, a myriad*. Neh. 7:71. Dual רִבּוֹתַיִם *two myriads*, Ps. 68:18.

רְבִיבִים masc. plur. verbal from רָבַב, *showers of rain*, so called from the *multitude* of drops. Deut. 32:2. Arab. رَبَبٌ, *aqua copiosa*.

רָבִיד m. dec. III. a. Ezek. 16:11. Gen. 41:42. *a chain, necklace*. Root רָבַד here prob. i. q. רבט ربط, *ligavit, revinxit*.

רְבִיעִי, fem. ־ִית, (denom. adj. from רֶבַע, אַרְבַּע *four*,) *the fourth*.—בְּנֵי רְבִיעִים *the children of the fourth*, i. e. of the fourth generation, 2 K. 10:30. 15:12. Fem. רְבִיעִית also *a fourth part*, Ex. 29:40.

רְבִיעַי, fem. רְבִיעָאָה, Chald. *idem*. Dan. 2:40. 7:23.

רָבַךְ *to intermix, to mingle with a liquid*. Found only in the part. Hoph. Lev. 6:14. [6:21.] 7:12. 1 Chr. 23:29.

רִבְלָה proper name of a city on the northern boundary of Palestine, in the province of חֲמָת. Num. 34:11. 2 K. 23:33, 25:6. Jer. 39:5. 52:10. The Babylonians, in their irruptions into Palestine, were wont to pass by Riblah and Hamath.

I. **רָבַע** 1. i. q. רָבַץ *to lie*, by a Chaldaic commutation of ע and צ. See רֶבַע no. I.

2. *to copulate* or *lie with*, construed with an accus. Lev. 18:23. 20:16.

Hiph. *to let copulate* or *gender*. Lev. 19:19.

II. **רָבַע** in some forms a denom. from אַרְבַּע *four*; as the part. pass. רָבוּעַ *four-cornered, four-square*, Ex. 27:1. 28:16. part. Pu. מְרֻבָּע *idem*, 1 K. 7:31.

I. **רֶבַע** m. with suff. רִבְעִי, verbal from רָבַע no. I. dec. VI. i. *a lying down*. Ps. 139:3.

II. **רֶבַע** (denom. from אַרְבַּע *four*,) dec. VI. i.

1. *a fourth part*. Ex. 29:40.

2. *a side, quarter*, so called from their number. Ezek. 1:8, 17. 43:17.

II. **רֹבַע** m. denom. from אַרְבַּע, *a fourth part*. 2 K. 6:25. Arab. رُبْعٌ *idem*.

II. **רֹבַע** m. *a multitude of people*. Num. 23:10. (Arab. رَبْعٌ *cœtus, caterva hominum*.) Others: *concubitus*, (see רָבַע no. I. 2.) hence *soboles*.

רִבֵּעִים masc. plur. denom. from אַרְבַּע, *posterity in the fourth generation*. Ex. 20:5. 34:7.

רָבַץ, fut. יִרְבַּץ, Arab. رَبَضَ.

1. strictly *to lie for repose on the breast with the fore-feet stretched out*; spoken of quadrupeds, as the lion, dog, etc. Gen. 29:2. 49:9, 14. Is. 11:6. Also in an inchoative sense, Num. 22:27.

2. used metaphorically of men in a peaceful state, Job 11:19. 17:2. of

waters, Gen. 49 : 25. of a curse, Deut. 29 : 19.

Hiph. 1. *to cause to lie down* or *rest*, e. g. a flock. Cant. 1 : 7. Ezek. 34 : 15. Is. 13 : 20.

2. *to lay* (stones in cement). Is. 54 : 11. Deriv. out of course מַרְבֵּץ, מַרְבֵּץ.

רֶבֶץ m. verbal from רָבַץ, dec. VI. g.

1. *a place of lying down*, (for animals.) Is. 65 : 10.

2. *a place of resting*, (for men.) Prov. 24 : 15.

רִבְקָה *Rebekah*, the wife of Isaac. Gen. 22 : 23. 24 : 15 ff. (Root רבק *to feed, to fatten.*)

רַבְרַב see **רַב** Chald.

רַבְרְבָן m. Chald. *a noble*. Dan. 5 : 1.

רֶגֶב or **רֶגֶב** m. dec. VI. g. *a lump* or *clod of earth*. Job 38 : 38. 21 : 33 *the clods of the valley lie softly upon him, est ei terra levis.*

רָגַז, fut. יִרְגַּז. 1. *to quake, tremble*. Ps. 4 : 5. Is. 32 : 10, 11. Construed with מִפְּנֵי *before* any thing, Deut. 2 : 25. Is. 64 : 2. Spoken also of inanimate nature, Joel 2 : 10. Is. 5 : 25. Ps. 18 : 8. of a quaking for joy, Jer. 33 : 9.—Mic. 7 : 17 יִרְגְּזוּ מִמִּסְגְּרֹתֵיהֶם *they tremble out of their prisons*, i. e. they flee trembling out of their prisons.

2. *to be thrown into commotion*, Is. 14 : 9. *to be disquieted*, 2 Sam. 7 : 10.

3. *to be moved;* with grief, 2 Sam. 19 : 1. [18 : 33.] with anger, hence *to be angry*, Prov. 29 : 9. Is. 28 : 21.

4. *to rage*, construed with לְ. Ezek. 16 : 43. See Hithpa.

Hiph. 1. *to make to tremble, to shake.* Is. 14 : 16. 23 : 11. E. g. inanimate nature, Is. 13 : 13. Job 9 : 6.

2. *to disquiet*. 1 Sam. 28 : 15. Construed with לְ, Jer. 50 : 34.

3. *to provoke, to excite to anger*. Job 12 : 6. See Kal no 3.

Hithpa. *to rage against* a person, construed with אֶל. Is. 37 : 28, 29.

רְגַז Chald. *to be angry.*

Aph. *to excite to anger*. Ezra 5 : 12.

רְגַז Chald. *anger*. Dan. 3 : 13.

רַגָּז m. verbal from רָגַז, *trembling*. Deut. 28 : 65.

רֹגֶז m. verbal from רָגַז, dec. VI. p.

1. *disquiet, trouble*. Job 3 : 26. 14 : 1. Is. 14 : 3.

2. *a raging*. Job 3 : 17. Spoken of a horse, Job 39 : 24. of thunder, Job 37 : 2.

3. *anger*. Hab. 3 : 2.

רָגְזָה f. verbal from רָגַז, *a quaking, trembling*. Ezek. 12 : 18.

רָגַל denom. from רֶגֶל, *to run about*, and that as a tale-bearer and as a spy. Hence in Kal *to calumniate*, Ps. 15 : 3.

Pi. 1. i. q. Kal, *to calumniate*, construed with בְּ. Once 2 Sam. 19 : 28.

2. *to spy out*, construed with an accus. Josh. 14 : 7. Judg. 18 : 2, 14, 17. 2 Sam. 10 : 3. Part. מְרַגֵּל *a spy*, Gen. 42 : 9 ff. Josh. 6 : 22. Comp. רָכַל.

רֶגֶל com. gen. (more frequently fem.) with suff. רַגְלִי, prim. dec. VI. a.

1. *the foot*. Is. 1 : 6. 3 : 16.—בְּרֶגֶל פ׳ *at the foot* or *in the track of any one*, i. e. behind or after him, Ex. 11 : 8. Judg. 4 : 10. 5 : 15. 8 : 5. 1 Sam. 15 : 17. 25 : 27. More rarely לְרֶגֶל Gen. 30 : 30. and לְרַגְלָיו Hab. 3 : 5. (Antith. לְפָנָיו.) 1 Sam. 25 : 42. Job 13 : 11.—הִשְׁקָה בְרֶגֶל Deut. 11 : 10. *to water with the foot*, i. e. by the help of a machine which was trodden by the feet, and which is used in Egypt at the present day for the watering of gardens. See Philo de Confusione Linguar. T. III. p. 330. and Niebuhr's Reisebeschreibung, Th. I. p. 149.

2. metaphorically *a step, pace*. Gen. 33 : 14 לְרֶגֶל הַמְּלָאכָה *according to the pace of the cattle*, i. e. according as they can go.

Dual רַגְלַיִם, also used in a plural sense Lev. 11 : 23, 42.

Plur. רְגָלִים *times*, Lat. *vices*, (like פְּעָמִים liter. *steps*.) Ex. 23 : 14. Num. 22 : 28, 32, 33.

Deriv. רַגְלִי, תִּרְגַּל, רָגַל.

רְגַל and **רֶגֶל** Chald. *a foot.* Dual רַגְלַיִן, emph. רַגְלַיָּא, Dan. 2:41, 7:7.

רַגְלִי m. denom. from רֶגֶל, *a footman;* but only in a military sense, *a foot soldier.* Ex. 12:37. Num. 11:21. Plur. ־ִים, Jer. 12:5.

רָגַם *to stone,* i. q. סָקַל; construed (1.) with an accus. of the person, Lev. 24:14. for the most part with the addition of בָּאֶבֶן Lev. 20:2, 27. בָּאֲבָנִים Num. 14:10. or אֶבֶן Lev. 24:23. (2.) with בְּ of the person, Lev. 24:16. and the addition of אֶבֶן, 1 K. 12:18. Liter. *to throw stones at* a person. (3.) with עַל of the person, Ezek. 23:47 רָגְמוּ עֲלֵיהֶם אֶבֶן *they shall throw stones at them.* In Arab. *idem.* The kindred רכם signifies *to heap up* in any way. Hence in Hebrew

רִגְמָה f. verbal from רָגַם, dec. X. *a crowd, press, band.* Ps. 68:28.

רָגַן in Kal Is. 29:24. and in Niph. Deut. 1:27. Ps. 106:25. *to murmur, rebel, to be refractory,* construed with בְּ *against* a person.

רָגַע 1. *to rest.* Job 7:5 עוֹרִי רָגַע וַיִּמָּאֵס *my skin rests,* i. e. closes up, is sound, *and breaks out anew.* See Hiph. no. 1. (In Ethiop. רגע *to contract, curdle;* comp. קְפָא. Hence the Syriac version: *cutis contracta est.*)

2. *to stir up;* occurring three times in the phrase רֹגַע הַיָּם וַיֶּהֱמוּ גַלָּיו *he stirreth up the sea, and its waves roar,* Is. 51:15. Sept. *ταράσσων.* Vulg. *conturbo.* Chald. *increpans.*) Jer. 31:35. Job 26:12. (This signification appears to be the opposite of no. 1. comp. נָעַר.)

Niph. *to rest,* spoken of the sword. Jer. 47:6.

Hiph. 1. *to have rest, to dwell quietly.* Deut. 28:65. Is. 34:14. Comp. the derivatives רָגַע, מַרְגֵּעָה, מַרְגּוֹעַ.

2. trans. *to cause to rest, to give rest.* Jer. 31:2. 50:34.

3. as in Arabic, *to restore.* (Arab. رجع *to turn back;* conj. VIII. *to bring back, to restore.*) Is. 51:4 מִשְׁפָּטִי לְאוֹר עַמִּים אַרְגִּיעַ *my law will I restore for a light to the nations.*

4. denom. from רֶגַע, *to pass a moment, to do in a moment.* Jer. 49:19 כִּי אַרְגִּיעָה אֲרִיצֶנּוּ *for I will in a moment make him run away.* 50:44. Prov. 12:19 עַד־אַרְגִּיעָה *till I can pass a moment,* i. e. for a moment.

רָגֵעַ m. verbal from רָגַע, dec. V. a. *living quietly.* Ps. 35:20. See the verb. in Hiph. no. 1.

רֶגַע m. verbal from רָגַע, dec. VI. *a moment.* (Perhaps liter. *a moving, stirring,* from רָגַע no. 2. like *momentum* for *movimentum.*) Ex. 33:5. Is. 54:7. Then as an adv. רֶגַע Job 34:20. בְּרֶגַע Job 21:13. and כְּרֶגַע Ps. 73:19. Lam. 4:6. *in a moment, suddenly.*—כִּמְעַט רֶגַע *idem,* Is. 26:20. Ezra 9:8.—לִרְגָעִים (1.) *every moment, repeatedly.* Job 7:18. Is. 27:3. (2.) *suddenly.* Ezek. 26:16.

רָגַשׁ *to rage, tumultuate,* spoken of nations. Ps. 2:1. (In the Targums used for the Heb. הָמָה.)

רְגַשׁ i. q. Heb. Aph. *idem,* also *to run together in a tumult.* Dan. 6:7, 12, 16.

רֶגֶשׁ m. Ps. 55:15. and רִגְשָׁה f. dec. X. Ps. 64:3. verbals from רָגַשׁ, *a bustling multitude, a multitude* generally.

רָדַד *to spread out, to stretch on the ground, to subject, sternere,* e. g. nations. Ps. 144:2. Is. 45:1, (where the infin. רַד is used for רֹד.) Comp. the kindred verb רָדָה.

Hiph. *to spread out,* hence *to overlay with metal spread out.* 1 K. 6:32. Deriv. רְדִיד.

I. **רָדָה**, fut. apoc. יֵרְדְּ.

1. *to tread* (with the feet), e. g. the wine-press. Joel 4:13. [3:13.] Construed with בְּ *upon* a person, Ps. 49:15. with an accus. Is. 14:6.

2. *to subjugate, rule;* construed with בְּ, Gen. 1:28. Lev. 26:17. with an accus. Ezek. 34:4. Ps. 68:28. also without cases, Num. 24:19. 1 K. 4:24.—Lam. 1:13 *from above he sendeth*

fire into my bones, and it (the fire) ruleth therein.

Pi. whence the fut. apoc. יַרְדְּ Judg. 5:13 (twice) *he maketh to rule;* but it is highly probable that the true punctuation in both cases is יֵרֶד *descendit.*

Hiph. *to cause to rule.* Is. 41:2.

II. רָדָה *to take, to take away,* in reference to the gathering of honey. Judg. 14:9. Sept. ἐξεῖλε. Vulg. *sumpsit.* Chald. נְסַח *avulsit.* According to the Rabbins, *divellere id quod cohæret,* e.g. one loaf of bread from another.

רָדִיד m. verbal from רָדַד, dec. III. a. *a large thin upper garment,* worn by women and thrown over their other clothes when they went out. Is. 3:23. Cant. 5:7. (In Chald. and Syr. *idem.*)

רָדַם found only in the Niph. נִרְדַּם.

1. *to lie in a deep sleep.* Prov. 10:5. Jon. 1:5, 6.

2. *to sink down stupified* or *senseless.* Dan. 8:18. 10:9. Ps. 76:7. Comp. Judg. 4:21.

Deriv. תַּרְדֵּמָה.

רֹדָנִים 1 Chr. 1:7. see דֹּדָנִים.

רָדַף, fut. יִרְדֹּף. 1. *to run* or *follow after;* construed with an accus. Ps. 23:6. with אַחֲרֵי, Judg. 3:28 רִדְפוּ אַחֲרַי *follow after me.* Metaphorically *to follow after* righteousness, Prov. 21:21. peace, Ps. 34:15. the wind, Hos. 12:2.

2. *to pursue, persecute;* without cases, Gen. 14:14. with an accus. verse 15. with אַחֲרֵי, Gen. 35:5. Ex. 14:4. with לְ, Job 19:28. with אֶל, Judg. 7:25.

3. *to chase, to put to flight.* Lev. 26:36.

Niph. pass. of Kal. Lam. 5:5.—Part. נִרְדָּף Ecc. 3:15. prob. *that which is past,* liter. *that which has escaped.*

Pi. i. q. Kal, but only in poetry.

Pi. *to run after* a person or thing. Prov. 12:11. 28:19. E. g. righteousness, Prov. 15:9.—Prov. 19:7 *he runs after words,* i. e. relies upon them.

2. *to pursue, persecute.* Nah. 1:8. Prov. 13:21.

Pu. pass. Is. 17:13.

Hiph. i. q. Kal, *to persecute.* Judg. 20:43.

Deriv. מֻרְדָּף.

רָהַב 1. *to urge, press upon, attack.* Prov. 6:3 רְהַב רֵעֶיךָ *urge thy friend.* Is. 3:5 יִרְהֲבוּ הַנַּעַר בַּזָּקֵן *the young man crowds* or *presses the old man.* Parall. נִגַּשׂ *to press.* (In Aram. *to rage.*)

2. perhaps *to fear,* (like the Arab. intrans. رَهِبَ.) So Is. 60:5, according to several MSS. where it stands with פָּחַד. The usual reading is רָחַב.

Hiph. 1. *to disconcert* or *embarrass.* Cant. 6:5.

2. *to strengthen.* Ps. 138:3.

רַהַב m. verbal from רָהַב, dec. VI. c.

1. *rage, insolence, pride.* Job 9:13 עֹזְרֵי רַהַב *the proud helpers.* Spoken of the sea, Job 26:12.

2. a poetical name of Egypt. Is. 30:7. 51:9. Ps. 87:4. 89:11. In the first passage there is an allusion to the significancy of the name in Hebrew. But this furnishes no proof of its Hebrew origin; although no plausible Egyptian derivation has yet been suggested. See Jablonskii Opusc. ed. te Water, T. I. p. 228.

רָהָב m. verbal from רָהַב, dec. IV. a. *proud, haughty.* Ps. 40:5.

רֹהַב m. verbal from רָהַב, dec. VI. p. *pride;* and by a metonymy, *the object of pride.* Ps. 90:10

רָהָה *to be afraid,* i. q. the parallel פָּחַד, found only Is. 44:8. So in the ancient versions, except the Sept.

רַהַט m. dec. VI. c. 1. *a watering-trough* for cattle. Gen. 30:38, 41, Ex. 2:16.

2. plur. *turns, windings,* hence prob. *braided locks.* Cant. 7:6. Root Aram. רְהַט *to run,* i. q. Heb. רוּץ, (see the letter ה.)

רָהִיטִים masc. plur. *a ceiled* or *arched covering.* Cant. 1:17 Keri. Vulg. *laquearia.* This signification is derived from רַהַט no. 1. comp. φάτνωμα from φάτνη *a crib.*

רֵו Chald. *form, appearance.* Dan. 3:25. Root Heb. רָאָה *to see.*

רוב see רִיב.

רוד *to wander, rove.* (In Arab. *to run about, to search round.*) Jer. 2:31. Hos. 12:1 [11:12] יְהוּדָה עֹד רָד עִם אֵל *Judah wanders still from God;* עִם being used here for מֵעִם; comp. שָׁלֵם, תָּמִים, עִם אֵל.

Hiph. 1. *to wander about,* spoken of an afflicted person or mourner. Ps. 55:3. Synonymous with הִים.

2. *to desire, seek, to strive to accomplish.* (Arab. *idem.*) Gen. 27:40 כַּאֲשֶׁר תָּרִיד *when thou shalt seek to effect it.*

Deriv. מְרוּדִים.

רָוָה 1. *to be abundantly supplied with drink, to drink to satiety,* like שָׂבַע *to eat to satiety.* (In Aram. yet stronger, *to become drunk.*) It is construed, like all verbs of *fullness,* with an accus. or with מִן of that *with* which a person is satisfied, Jer. 46:10.

2. *to enjoy* or *to take pleasure in* any thing. Ps. 36:9. Prov. 7:18 נִרְוֶה דֹדִים *we will take our fill of love.*

Pi. 1. intrans. as in Kal, *to be satisfied with drink.* Is. 34:5, 7.

2. trans. *to water, wet, moisten,* e. g. fields. Ps. 65:11. Construed with two accus. Is. 16:9 אֲרַיָּוֶךְ דִּמְעָתִי *I will water thee with my tears.* (The form אֲרַיָּוֶךְ is transposed for אֲרַוָּיֵךְ.)

3. *to satisfy, refresh,* construed with two accus. Jer. 31:14. Prov. 5:19.

Hiph. 1. *to satiate with drink.* Jer. 31:25. Lam. 3:15. Also *to water* a field, Is. 55:10.

2. *to satisfy* with fat, (as in Ps. 36:9. Jer. 31:14.) Is. 43:24.

רָוֶה m. verbal adj. from רָוָה, dec. IX. b. *satisfied with drink, drunken.* Deut. 29:18. Hence *well watered,* spoken of a garden, Is. 58:11.

רְוָיָה f. verbal from רָוָה, *abundance of drink, plenty of water.* Ps. 66:12. Ps. 23:5 כּוֹסִי רְוָיָה *my cup is abundance,* i. e. always full.

רוח Hiph. הֵרִיחַ *to smell.* See רֵיחַ.

רוּחַ com. gen. (comp. 1 K. 19:11.) dec. I.

1. *wind, air in motion.* Gen. 8:1. Job 1:19.—אַרְבַּע רוּחוֹת *the four winds,* hence also *the four quarters of heaven,* Ezek. 37:9. 42:20. 1 Chr. 9:24.—כַּנְפֵי רוּחַ *the wings of the wind,* Ps. 18:11.—רוּחַ יְהוָֹה *a wind of God,* Is. 40:7. 59:15. (Also Gen. 1:2. according to some, but erroneously.) 2 K. 2:16. 1 K. 18:12. Ezek. 3:14. 11:24.—רוּחַ הַיּוֹם Gen. 3:8. *the windy* or *cool part of the day,* i. e. the evening, since in the east a refreshing breeze is wont to arise some hours before sunset. Comp. Cant. 2:17. 4:6.

2. *a breathing* or *exhalation, a breath.* Job 7:7.—רוּחַ פֶּה *a breath of the mouth* (of Jehovah), i. e. his creative power, Ps. 33:6—Hence indicative of *frailty, vanity,* Job 15:2 דַּעַת רוּחַ *vain knowledge.* 16:3. לָרוּחַ *in vain,* Ecc. 5:15.—Also *the vital and animal breath* in men and animals, Job 17:1. 19:17.—רוּחַ חַיִּים *the breath of life,* Gen. 6:17. 7:15, 22.

3. *a snuffing* (of the nose). Job 4:9. Hence *anger,* Judg. 8:3. Is. 25:4. Zech. 6:8.

4. *the anima* or *animal soul, the vital principle of animals which was placed by the ancients in the breath, the spirit, life,* i. q. נֶפֶשׁ. 1 Sam. 30:12. Judg. 15:19. 1 K. 10:5 וְלֹא הָיָה בָהּ עוֹד רוּחַ *then there was no more life in her,* i. e. she was beside herself. Ecc. 3:21. 8:8. 12:7. Ezek. 37:8. Inasmuch as this spirit was considered as coming immediately from God, (Ecc. 12:7.) it is called רוּחַ אֱלוֹהַּ, Job 27:3. comp. Num. 16:22. Metaphorically *a* (miraculous) *principle of life,* in things otherwise inanimate, Ezek. 10:17. Zech. 5:9.

5. *the animus* or *rational soul, the mind, intellect, spirit.* Gen. 41:8 וַתִּפָּעֶם רוּחוֹ *and his mind was disquieted.*—רוּחַ נְכֵאָה *a dejected mind,* Prov. 17:22. 18:14.—Hence קְשַׁת־רוּחַ *sorrowful of spirit;* גְּבַהּ רוּחַ *proud of spirit,* etc. Metaphorically *a disposition, inclination;* e. g. to jealousy, Num. 5:14. to fornication, Hos. 4:12. to justice, Is. 28:6.

to discord, Judg. 9:23. generally, Ezek. 1:12. Also *courage*, Josh. 2:11. 5:1.

6. רוּחַ אֱלֹהִים or רוּחַ יְהוָה *the spirit of God* or *Jehovah*, more rarely, by way of eminence, רוּחַ, הָרוּחַ, *the spirit*, (Num. 27:18. Hos. 9:7.) or רוּחַ קָדְשׁוֹ *his (God's) holy spirit*, (Ps. 51:13. Is. 63:10, 11.) By this name is denoted the life-giving breath or power of God in men and animals, Job 27:3. 33:4. Ps. 104:30. Gen. 6:3. which operates also through inanimate nature, Job 26:13. which moved over the chaotic mass at the creation, Gen. 1:3. and produces whatever is noble and good in man, by making him wise, Job 32:8. by leading him to virtue, Ps. 51:13. and by guiding him generally, Hag. 2:5. Ps. 143:10. Neh. 9:20. But it is especially applied to extraordinary powers and gifts; e.g. of the artificer, Ex. 31:3. 35:31. of the warrior, Judg. 3:10. 6:34. 11:29. 13:25. of the ruler, Is. 11:1 ff. of the prophet, Num. 24:2. 1 Sam. 10:6, 10. 19:20, 23. of the interpreter of dreams, Gen. 41:38. Hence אִישׁ הָרוּחַ *a prophet*, Hos. 9:7. and הָרוּחַ 1 K. 22:21. 2 Chr. 18:20. *the spirit of the prophets* or *the power which inspires them*, (personified.) This spirit David acquires at his anointing, 1 Sam. 16:13. It departs from Saul, 1 Sam. 16:14. That of Elijah rests on Elisha, 2 K. 2:15. A part of the spirit of Moses is transferred to the 70 elders, Num. 11:17. It is promised to all men in the golden age, Joel 3:1. [2:28.] Is. 44:3. 59:21.—In this sense of *divine power*, it is sometimes opposed to בָּשָׂר *flesh* or *human power*, as Is. 31:3 סוּסֵיהֶם בָּשָׂר וְלֹא רוּחַ *their horses are flesh and not spirit*, i. e. something earthly, and not any thing divine. Zech. 4:6.

7. In such passages as Job 6:4. Is. 30:1. Ps. 139:7. it may be regarded, like נֶפֶשׁ, as a mere periphrasis of the personal pronoun.

רוּחַ Chald. 1. *wind*. Dan. 7:2.

2. *a spirit*. Dan. 4:5. [4:8.]

רָוַח *to be* or *become wide*. Used impers. יִרְוַח לִי *I find room, I am relieved*, Job 32:20. 1 Sam. 16:23. Antith. צַר לִי.

Pu. מְרֻוָּח *wide, spacious*. Jer. 22:14.

רֶוַח m. verbal from רָוַח.

1. *width, space*. Gen. 32:17.

2. *relief, enlargement*. Est. 4:14.

רְוָחָה f. verbal from רָוַח, dec. X. *relief*. Ex. 8:11. [8:15.] Lam. 3:56.

רוּם, fut. יָרוּם, apoc. יָרֹם, with Vav convers. וַיָּרָם.

1. *to be lifted up, exalted, elevated*. Gen. 7:17. Job 22:12.—רָם לֵב *the heart is lifted up* (with pride), Deut. 8:14. 17:20. So רָמוּ עֵינַיִם *the eyes are lifted up* (with pride), Prov. 30:13. Construed with עַל *to be exalted* (in triumph) *over* a person, Ps. 13:3. Also *to grow up*, once Ex. 16:20 וַיָּרֻם תּוֹלָעִים *and there grew up worms*. (By this unusual punctuation, instead of וַיָּרָם, the authors of the vowel-points meant perhaps to derive the word from רמם, a denom. from רִמָּה *a worm*.) Also *to be raised* or *built*, spoken of a way, (comp. סָלַל.) Is. 49:11. *to be exalted* or *praised*, spoken of God, Ps. 18:47. 46:11.—Mic. 5:9 *thy hand is exalted over thine enemies*. Hence *to be mighty, victorious, to prevail*, Ps. 140:9. Num. 24:7. particularly with יָד, Deut. 32:27.

2. *to be remote* or *distinct from* doing a thing, construed with an infin. Is. 30:18. Comp. מָרוֹם no. 3.

Part. רָם, fem. רָמָה. 1. *high, exalted, lifted up*.—יָד רָמָה *with a high hand*, i. e. publicly, triumphantly, proudly, Ex. 14:8. Num. 33:3. also *presumptuously, wickedly*, Num. 15:30. In a different sense Is. 26:11 רָמָה יָדְךָ *thy hand was lifted up*, (to inflict punishment.) Plur. רָמִים *the heights of heaven*, Ps. 78:69.

2. *great of stature, longus*. Deut. 1:28. 2:10, 21.

3. *mighty*. Deut. 1:28. Spoken of יָד *the hand*, Deut. 32:27.

4. *loud*, spoken of the voice, (like *altus*.) Deut. 27:14.

5. *proud*. Job 21:22. עֵינַיִם רָמוֹת *proud eyes*, Ps. 18:28.

6. *difficult to be comprehended, ar-*

duus intellectu. Prov. 24:7, where it is written חָאמוֹת after the Arabic form. Comp. שָׂגַב.

Niph. see under רָמַם.

Pilel רוֹמֵם 1. *to raise, to lift up.* 1 Sam. 2:7.—Particularly (1.) *to exalt* one that is low or oppressed. Ps. 37:34. (2.) *to place in safety, to make secure.* Ps. 27:5. 18:49. (3.) *to exalt, let conquer.* Job 17:4.

2. *to raise up* (a building). Ezra 9:9.

3. *to exalt, praise.* Ps. 30:2. 34:4.

4. *to cause to grow.* Ezek. 31:4.

5. *to bring up, nourish, educate.* Is. 1:2. 23:4.

Pulal רוֹמַם pass. *to be exalted.* Ps. 75:11. Part. *exalted,* Neh. 9:5.

Hiph. 1. *to lift up;* e.g. the head, Ps. 3:4. the hand, Ps. 89:43. the head or horn of a person, i.e. to increase his strength, (see קֶרֶן,) Ps. 75:5, 6. 148:14.

2. *to raise up,* e.g. a banner, a monument. Gen. 31. 45. Is. 62:10.

3. *to lift up;* e.g. the hand, construed with בְּ *against* a person, 1 K. 11:27. or as the gesture of swearing, Gen. 14:22. the voice, Gen. 39:18. 2 K. 19:22. construed with בְּ, 1 Chr. 15:16. 2 Chr. 5:13 כְּהָרִים קוֹל בַּחֲצֹצְרוֹת *when they lifted up their voice with trumpets.* Elliptically 1 Chr. 25:5 לְהָרִים קֶרֶן *ad clangendum tuba.* הֵרִים קוֹל לְ *to call to* a person, Is. 13:2. Of *the raising* or *levying* a tribute, Num. 31:28.

4. *to bring* (tribute or gifts to the temple and to the priests, תְּרוּמָה.) Num. 15:19, 20. 31:52. Also gifts or largesses to the people, Lat. viscerationes, 2 Chr. 30:24. 35:7—9.

5. *to bring* as an offering on the altar. Lev. 2:9. 4:8.

6. *to take away,* like *tollere.* Ezek. 21:31. Is. 57:15.

Hoph. pass. of no. 4. Ex. 29:27. of no. 6. Dan. 8:11.

Hithpal. *to exalt one's self proudly.* Dan. 11:36. Here belongs likewise אֵרוֹמָם Is. 33:10, for אֶתְרוֹמָם by an assimilation of the ת.

Deriv. out of course מָרוֹם, רָמוּת, רָמָה, תְּרוּמָה, תְּרוּמִיָּה.

רוּם Chald. *idem.* Peil רִם *to be lifted up.* Dan. 5:20.

Pal. רוֹמֵם *to exalt, praise.* Dan. 4:34. [4:37.]

Aph. *to lift up.* Dan. 5:19.

Ithpal. *to lift one's self up.* Dan. 5:23.

רוּם m. verbal from רוּם, *height.* Prov. 25:3. Joined with עֵינַיִם Prov. 21:4. Is. 10:12. and with לֵב Jer. 48:29. also without addition Is. 2:11, 17. *pride, arrogance.*

רוּם Chald. *idem.* Dan. 3:1.

רוֹם Hab. 3:10. and רוֹמָה Mic. 2:3. verbals from רוּם, but used as an adv. *proudly, on high.*

רוּמָה name of a place, perhaps the same which is otherwise called אֲרוּמָה. 2 K. 23:36.

רוֹמָם m. verbal from רוּם, dec. II. b. *exaltation, praise.* Ps. 66:17. Plur. fem. רוֹמְמוֹת Ps. 149:6.

רוֹמֵמוּת f. verbal from רוּם, dec. III. b. *a lifting up.* Is. 33:3. Strictly Syr. infin. Palel.

רוּן, Arab. ران med. Je *to conquer, to get the upper-hand;* in Kal not used. The fut. יָרֹן pertains to רָנַן.

Hithpal. pass. Ps. 78:65 כְּגִבּוֹר מִתְרוֹנֵן מִיָּיִן *as a mighty man overcome by wine.* The same phrase occurs in Arabic. In Heb. comp. Niph. הָלַם, עָבַר no. 5.

I. **רוּעַ** found only in the pret. רַע, and the infin. רֹעַ, i. q. יָרַע (whence the fut.)

1. *to be evil, wicked.*—(1.) רַע בְּעֵינֵי פ׳ *it is disagreeable to* a person, *it displeases* him. Num. 11:10. (2.) רָעָה עֵינוֹ בְּ *to be envious* or *unkind to* a person. Deut. 15:9.

2. *to be sad,* joined with פָּנִים. Ecc. 7:3.

3. *to be pernicious,* construed with לְ. 2 Sam. 19:8.

Niph. fut. יֵרוֹעַ.

1. *to degenerate, to become worse.* (Antith. *to become wise.*) Prov. 13:20.

2. *to experience ill, to suffer injury.* Prov. 11:15. (רַע here is a noun added

merely to give intensity, like חָרָה with אַף.)

Hiph. הֵרַע and הֵרֵעַ (formed from רָעַע.)

1. *to make evil*, e. g. one's doings. Gen. 44:5 הֲרֵעֹתֶם אֲשֶׁר עֲשִׂיתֶם liter. *ye have made evil what ye have done*, i. e. ye have done evil in so doing. Jer. 38:9. Hence with לַעֲשׂוֹת 1 K. 14:9. and with מַעַלְלִים Mic. 3:4. *to act ill*. Hence

2. without addition, *to act wickedly, to sin*. Is. 1:16. Jer. 7:26. Part. מֵרַע מֵרֵעַ, *an evil-doer*, Is. 1:4. Ps. 37:9.

3. *to do* or *treat ill;* construed with a dative of the person, Ex. 5:23. Num. 11:11. with an accus. Num. 16:15. with עַל, 1 K. 17:20. with בְּ, 1 Chr. 16:22. with עִם, Gen. 31:7. Comp. the opposite term הֵיטִיב.

Hithpal הִתְרוֹעֵעַ i. q. Niph. no. 2. *to experience ill, to suffer injury*. Prov. 18:24 אִישׁ רֵעִים לְהִתְרוֹעֵעַ *a man of many acquaintances shall suffer injury thereby.*

Deriv. רָעָה, רֹעַ, רַע.

II. רוּעַ or רִיעַ in Kal not used.

Hiph. הֵרִיעַ 1. *to cry aloud*. Job 30:5. Particularly (1.) *to rejoice, exult*. Judg. 15:14. 1 Sam. 10:24. Construed with a dative, Ps. 47:2. (2.) *to lament*. Mic. 4:9. Is. 15:4. (3.) *to shout for battle*. Josh. 6:16. 1 Sam. 17:20.

2. *to blow* (with a trumpet). Num. 10:9 וַהֲרֵעֹתֶם בַּחֲצֹצְרוֹת *then shall ye blow with the trumpets*. Joel 2:1.—In Num. 10:7, it is distinguished from תָּקַע, and made synonymous with תָּקַע תְּרוּעָה *to sound an alarm*, Num. 10:5, 6.

Pul. רוֹעַע *to be celebrated with rejoicing*, Is. 16:10.

Hithpal. *to rejoice*. Ps. 60:10. 65:14.

Deriv. תְּרוּעָה.

רוּף see רָפַף.

רוּץ 1. *to run*. Prov. 18:10 בּוֹ יָרוּץ *he runneth to it* (for protection). Metaphorically Ps. 119:32 *I will run*, i. e. pursue with ardour, *the way of thy commandments*. Hab. 2:2 *so that the reader may run*, i. e. read fluently. Spoken of things without life, Ps. 147:15.

2. *to rush upon, to assail;* construed with אֶל and עַל, Job 15:26. 16:14. with an accus. Ps. 18:30.

Part. plur. רָצִים and רָצִין [2 K. 11:13.) *runners, state-couriers*, among the Persians, who published the royal edicts in the provinces. Est. 3:13, 15. 8:14. Among the Hebrews, they made a part of the royal body-guard under Saul, 1 Sam. 22:17. and the later kings, 2 K. 10:25. 11:6 ff. and correspond probably to the פְּלֵתִי under David. Comp. further 1 K. 1:5. 14:27. 2 Sam. 15:1.

Pilel רוֹצֵץ i. q. Kal. Nah. 2:5.

Hiph. *to cause to run, to put to flight*. Jer. 49:19. 50:44. hence *to fetch in haste, to bring* or *carry quickly*, Gen. 41:14. 1 Sam. 17:17. Ps. 68:32 כּוּשׁ תָּרִיץ יָדָיו לֵאלֹהִים *Ethiopia bears quickly her hands to God*, prob. with presents.

Deriv. מֵרוֹץ, מְרוּצָה.

Note. Several forms of רוץ; e. g. יָרֻץ, Niph. נָרוֹץ, deriv. מְרוּצָה, have their signification from רָצַץ q. v.

רוּק see רִיק.

רוּר *to run* or *ooze with, to emit*, e. g. spittle, semen. Lev. 15:3. Deriv. רִיר.

רוֹשׁ *poison*, see רֹאשׁ.

רוּשׁ *to be poor* or *in want*. Ps. 34:11. Part. רָשׁ sometimes רָאשׁ, (Prov. 10:4. 13:23.) *poor, needy*, Prov. 14:20. 18:23.

Hithpal. *to appear poor*. Prov. 13:7.

Deriv. רֵישׁ, רִישׁ.

Note. The passages Jer. 5:17. Mal. 1:4. pertain to רָשַׁשׁ.

רוּת *Ruth*, proper name of an ancestor of the house of David, the heroine of the small book which bears her name. Ruth 1:4.

רָז m. Chald. *a secret*. Dan. 2:18, 19. 4:6. [4:9.] (Syr. ܐܪܙ also ܪܰܙ *to keep secret;* ܐܪܙܐ *a secret.*)

רָזָה 1. *to be* or *to make lean*. (In Arab. رذي *to be wearied, enervated.*)

2. *to cause to waste away, to destroy*, (see רָזֶה.) Zeph. 2:11.

Niph. *to become lean.* Is. 17 : 4.
Deriv. out of course רָזוֹן, רָזִי.

רָזֶה m. verbal from רָזָה, dec. IX. b. *lean*, spoken of a country. Num. 13 : 20.

I. **רָזוֹן** m. verbal from רָזָה.

1. *leanness, consumption.* Is. 10 : 16. Hence *destructive disease* generally. Ps. 106 : 15.

2. *diminution, smallness, scantiness,* Mic. 6 : 10 אֵיפַת־רָזוֹן *the scant ephah.*

II. **רָזוֹן** i. q. רֹזֵן, (after the form עָשׁוֹק i. q. עֹשֵׁק,) *a prince.* Prov. 14 : 28.

רָזִי m. verbal from רָזָה no. 2. *destruction, wo.* Is. 24 : 16 רָזִי לִי i. q. the following phrase אוֹי לִי *wo unto me!*

רָזַם by a transposition of the letters, (which in the dentals is common,) i. q. Arab. and Aram, رمز, רְמַז, *to wink with the eyes*, here as an expression of arrogance. Job 15 : 12. Some MSS. read ירמזון.

רָזַן Arab. رزن, *to be respected* or *honoured, to conduct with gravity* or *dignity.* Found only in the part. רֹזֵן liter. *the respected* or *dignified*, used as a poetical epithet for *a prince* or *king*, Judg. 5 : 3. Ps. 2 : 2. Prov. 8 : 15. 31 : 4. Is. 40 : 23. See רָזוֹן no. II.

רָחַב *to be wide, broad, large;* e. g. spoken of the heart, *to be enlarged* (with joy), Is. 60 : 5. of the mouth, *to be opened wide*, 1 Sam. 2 : 1.

Niph. part. *wide, large.* Is. 30 : 23.

Hiph. 1. *to enlarge.* Is. 57 : 8. Ex. 34 : 24 *I will enlarge thy borders.* (1.) Construed with לְ of the person, *to make room* or *procure access for* any one. Prov. 18 : 16. Also *to deliver* (from affliction), Ps. 4 : 2. (2.) joined with פֶּה, *to open the mouth wide.* Ps. 81 : 11. Construed with עַל *against* any one, in derision, Ps. 35 : 21. Is. 57 : 4. (3.) joined with נֶפֶשׁ, *to enlarge one's desire*, i. e. to open wide one's jaws. Is. 5 : 14. Hab. 2 : 5. (4.) joined with לֵב, *to open the heart* (to knowledge). Ps. 119 : 32. comp. רְחַב לֵב.

2. intrans. Ps. 25 : 17, according to the usual reading. Better by conjecture הַרְחִיבוּ.

Deriv. out of course מֶרְחָב.

רָחָב m. verbal adj. from רָחַב, dec. IV. a. and XI. d. *wide, broad, large;* spoken e. g. of a country. Ex. 3 : 8.—רְחַב יָדַיִם *wide on both sides*, a stronger expression, Ps. 104 : 25. Gen. 34 : 21.—רְחַב לֵב Ps. 101 : 5. and רְחַב נֶפֶשׁ Prov. 28 : 25. *puffed up, proud, arrogant.* The former is also used substantively for *arrogance*, Prov. 21 : 4.

רַחַב m. verbal from רָחַב, dec. VI. c. *a broad place.* Job 36 : 16.

רֹחַב m. verbal from רָחַב, dec. VI. m.

1. *breadth.* Gen. 6 : 15. Ezek. 40 : 6 ff.

2. joined with לֵב, *largeness of understanding, comprehensive understanding.* 1 K. 5 : 9. [4 : 29.]

רְחֹב and **רְחוֹב** f. (Dan. 9 : 25.) plur. רְחֹבוֹת (as masc. Zech. 8 : 5.) verbal from רָחַב, dec. I.

1. *a street*, so called from its being *broad*, (like the Greek πλατεῖα, *platea.*) Gen. 19 : 2. Judg. 19 : 20.

2. *the open space before the gate of an oriental city*, where courts were held, and bargains made, *the oriental forum.* 2 Chron. 32 : 6. comp. Neh. 8 : 1, 3, 16. Ezra 10 : 9 רְחוֹב בֵּית הָאֱלֹהִים *the open space before the house of God.*

3. proper name of a city in the tribe of Asher, in the valleys below Mount Libanus. Num. 13 : 21. Josh. 19 : 28. 21 : 31. also called בֵּית רְחוֹב Judg. 18 : 28.

4. also of a Syrian district or people, 2 Sam. 10 : 8. likewise called *Beth-rehob* verse 6. comp. 1 Chr. 19 : 6.

רְחֹבוֹת (*streets* or *room*, see Gen. 26 : 22.)

1. proper name of a well. Gen. 26 : 22.

2. רְחֹבֹת עִיר (*streets of the city*) an Assyrian city. Once Gen. 10 : 11. It occurs nowhere else, and the ancient versions do not agree. See J. D. Michaëlis Spicileg. T. I. p. 240—244. Perhaps the same with

3. רְחֹבוֹת הַנָּהָר Gen. 36 : 37. with which

some have collated رحبة, *Rachbah*, a city on the Euphrates between Cercusium and Ana.

רְחַבְעָם *enlargement of the people*, as if Ἐυρυδήμος,) *Rehoboam*, the son of Solomon and first king of the two tribes of Benjamin and Judah. 1 K. 11 : 43.

רַחוּם m. verbal adj. from רָחַם, *merciful, compassionate*, spoken only of God, and for the most part joined with חַנּוּן. Deut. 4 : 31. Ps. 86 : 15.

רָחוֹק m. verbal adj. from רָחַק, dec. III. a.

1. *remote, distant*, in space, more rarely in time. 2 Sam. 7 : 19. 1 K. 8 : 41. Used abstractly or as a neuter, *remoteness, distance*, Josh. 3 : 4. מֵרָחוֹק *at a distance, far off*, Ps. 10 : 1. מֵרָחוֹק Gen. 22 : 4. and לְמֵרָחוֹק Job 39 : 29. *from afar, far off*.

2. *dear, costly*, as to price. Prov. 31 : 10. (The same metaphor is found in Arabic.)

רְחִיטֵים Cant. 1 : 17 Keth. prob. a corrupted reading for רָהִיטִים, which is found in the Keri.

רֵחַיִם dual, *a hand-mill* of the Orientalists, consisting of two stones of which the upper one turns round on the lower, (see פֶּלַח and רֶכֶב.) Ex. 11 : 5. Num. 11 : 8. Is. 47 : 2. (Arab. رحي, dual رحوان, *a mill*.)

רַחִיק Chald. *far, distant, remote*. Ezra 6 : 6.

רָחֵל f. dec. V. a.

1. *an ewe*. Gen. 31 : 38. 32 : 14. Then *a sheep* generally, Is. 53 : 7. Cant. 6 : 6.

2. *Rachel*, proper name of a wife of Jacob. Gen. 29 : 6.

רָחַם or **רָחֵם** *to love*. Ps. 18 : 2. (In Syr. and Arab. *idem*.)

Pi. רִחַם *to have compassion, to pity*, construed with an accus. Ex. 33 : 19. Deut. 13 : 18. 30 : 3. Is. 9 : 16. 14 : 1. with עַל, Ps. 103 : 13. It is used only of the affection of parents for children, Ps. 103 : 13. Is. 49 : 15. and that of God to men.

Pu. רֻחַם *to find mercy*. Prov. 28 : 13. Hos. 14 : 4. comp. 1 : 6.

רֶחֶם, more rarely רַחַם m. once fem. (Jer. 20 : 17.) dec. VI. a.

1. *the womb*. Job 31 : 15.—מֵרֶחֶם *from the womb*, Ps. 22 : 11. For the phrase *to close the womb*, i. e. to make unfruitful, see עָצַר, סָגַר. For the phrase *to open the womb*, i. e. to make fruitful, see פָּתַח.

2. *a maiden, female*, from their distinguishing member. (Comp. in Engl. *woman*, for *womb-man*.) Judg. 5 : 30.

רָחָם m. Lev. 11 : 18. and **רָחָמָה** Deut. 14 : 17. *the carrion-kite, vultur percnopterus*, Linn. Arab. رخم and رخمة. See Bocharti Hieroz. T. II. p. 297—322. Root רחם *pium esse*; from which this bird is named, (like חֲסִידָה *the stork*,) see Bochart, p. 318, 319.

רַחֲמָה i. q. רַחַם no. 2. *a maiden*. Dual רַחֲמָתַיִם Judg. 5 : 30.

רַחֲמִים masc. plur. dec. I.

1. *the chief intestines*, as the heart, liver, etc. *viscera*, τὰ σπλάγχνα. Prov. 12 : 10. Hence, because the heart is the seat of love, compassion, etc.

2. *tender love* or *affection*, particularly towards relatives, *pietas*. Gen. 43 : 30. Am. 1 : 11. 1 K. 3 : 26. So in N. T. τὰ σπλάγχνα 2 Cor. 6 : 12. 7 : 15.

3. *favour, grace*, i. q. חֵן, חֶסֶד. Gen. 43 : 14. In reference to the unfortunate, *mercy, compassion*, Is. 47 : 6. Used particularly of God, *grace, goodness, mercy*, Ps. 25 : 6. 40 : 12.—נָתַן רַחֲמִים לְ Deut. 13 : 17. and שׂוּם רַחֲמִים לְ Is. 47 : 6. *to shew mercy to* a person,—נָתַן פ׳ לְרַחֲמִים לִפְנֵי *to give one person favour with* another, 1 K. 8 : 50. Ps. 106 : 46.

רַחֲמִין Chald. *idem*. Dan. 2 : 18.

רַחֲמָנִי m. verbal adj. from רִחַם, dec. VIII. m. *merciful, compassionate*. Lam. 4 : 10.

רָחַף *to shake, totter*, as the bones from terror. Jer. 23 : 9.

Pi. *to hover, flutter*, as an eagle over her young, Deut. 32:11. *to brood*, as the life-giving power of God over the mighty deep at the creation, Gen. 1:2. (In Syr. *to brood.*)

רָחַץ, fut. יִרְחַץ, infin. רָחְצָה.

1. *to wash, cleanse;* used only in reference to the body, Gen. 18:4. 43:31. or other flesh, Ex. 29:17. Different from כָּבַס, which applies to garments.

2. *to wash one's self, to bathe.* Ex. 2:5. Ruth 3:3.

Pu. רֻחַץ *to be washed.* Prov. 30:12.

Hithpa. i. q. Kal no. 2. Job 9:30.

רַחַץ m. verbal from רָחַץ, dec. VI. c. *a washing.* Ps. 60:10.

רַחְצָה f. verbal from רָחַץ, *a bathing* or *washing place.* Cant. 4:2. 6:6.

רְחַץ Chald. Ithpe. construed with עַל, *to trust in* a person or thing. Dan. 3:28.

רָחַק, fut. יִרְחַק, infin. רָחְקָה, *to be removed, distant.* Ps. 103:12. Construed with מִן and מֵעַל, Jer. 2:5. Ezek. 8:6. 11:15. 44:10. (In Syr. and Chald. *idem.*) Particularly (1.) spoken of God, *to be far off*, in reference to giving aid. Ps. 22:12, 20. 35:22. (2.) *to keep one's self, to abstain, avoid.* Ex. 23:7. Ecc. 3:5.

Pi. רִחַק *to put far away.* Is. 6:12. 29:13.

Hiph. 1. trans. as in Pi.

2. intrans. *to be* or *go far off.* Gen. 44:4. Josh. 8:4. Infin. הַרְחֵק as an adv. *at a distance, far off*, Gen. 21:16.

Deriv. out of course רָחוֹק, מֶרְחָק.

רָחֵק m. verbal adj. from רָחַק, dec. V. a. *removing one's self.* Ps. 73:27 רְחֵקֶיךָ *they that remove far from thee.*

רָחַשׁ *to swell* or *boil up.* Ps. 45:2 רָחַשׁ לִבִּי דָּבָר טוֹב *my heart boils up with a good matter.* (Syr. *idem.*) Deriv. מַרְחֶשֶׁת.

רַחַת f. Is. 30:24. prob. *a winnowing shovel* or *fan*, from רוּחַ, like *ventilabrum* from *ventus*, after the form מַחַת.

רָטַב, fut. יִרְטַב, *to be wet* or *soaked through*, as by the rain. Job 24:8. Particularly *to be moist, juicy*, like fresh plants; hence

רָטֹב m. verbal from רָטַב, *moist, juicy, in fresh verdure.* Job 8:16.

רָטָה found only Job 16:11 וְעַל־יְדֵי רְשָׁעִים יִרְטֵנִי Vulg. *et manibus impiorum me tradidit;* comp. either the Arab. رطا *to throw*, e. g. an arrow, (Sept. ἔῤῥιψε,) or رتا (by a commutation of ט and ת,) *constrinxit*, comp. הִסְגִּיר in the parallel member.

רֶטֶט m. *fear, terror.* Jer. 49:24. (Chald. רְטַט *to tremble, to be afraid.*)

רֻטֲפַשׁ a quadriliteral pass. Job 33:25. *to revive, to become fresh again.* (In Arab. by transposition طرفش *idem.* It is supposed to be compounded of רָטַב *to be juicy* and טָפַשׁ *to be thick, fat.*)

רָטַשׁ found only in Pi.

1. *to dash in pieces*, as little children on the rocks, (otherwise נִפֵּץ Ps. 137:9.) 2 K. 8:12.

3. *to strike to the ground* generally. Is. 13:18. (So in Chald.)

Pu. pass. of no. 1. Is. 13:16. Hos. 10:14. 14:1. Nah. 3:10.

רִי m. Job 37:11. according to some, i. q. Arab. رِيّ for רְוִי *a watering*, from the root רָוָה. See however בְּרִי.

רִיב, pret. רָב, רַבֹּתָ, also רִיבוֹתָ, infin. absol. רֹב (Judg. 11:25. Job 40:2.)

1. *to contend* or *strive* with any one, in words or deeds. Is. 57:16. Ps. 103:9. Construed with עִם, Gen. 26:20. with אֵת (*with,*) Judg. 8:1. with אֶל, Job 33:13, with בְּ, Gen. 31:36. with an accus. Job 10:2. Is. 27:8. The person *for* whom one contends is preceded by לְ, Judg. 6:31. Job 13:8. the thing *about* which, by עַל, Gen. 26:21.

2. *to manage the cause of* any one, *to plead for* or *defend*, construed with an accus. Is. 1:17. 51:22. More in full רִיב אֵת רִיב פ׳, 1 Sam. 24:16. 25:39 *blessed be Jehovah* אֲשֶׁר רָב אֶת־רִיב חֶרְפָּתִי מִיַּד נָבָל *who hath taken vengeance on Nabal for my affront;* (it is construed here

with מִיַּד, on account of the accessory idea *to take revenge.*) Ps. 43:1 רִיבָה רִיבִי מִגּוֹי לֹא חָסִיד *plead my cause,* (and deliver me,) *from an unmerciful people.*

Hiph. i.q. Kal. 1 Sam. 2:10. Hos. 4:4.

Deriv. out of course יָרִיב, מְדִינָה

רִיב rarely רִב m. plur. ־ִים and ־וֹת verbal from רִיב, dec. I.

1. *a strife, contention.* Gen. 13:7. Deut. 25:1. אִישׁ רִיבִי *my adversary,* Job 31:35. comp. Is. 41:11.

2. *a cause, matter of contention.* Ex. 23:2. אִישׁ רִיב *one who has a cause,* Judg. 12:2. See the verb signif. no. 2.

רִיחַ in Kal not used.

Hiph. הֵרִיחַ. 1. *to smell.* (It is kindred with רוּחַ *wind, breath;* inasmuch as fragrant substances *breathe out* an odour.) Gen. 8:21. 27:27.

2. construed with בְּ, *to take delight in smelling, to smell with pleasure,* (comp. רָאָה, חָזָה בְּ.) Ex. 30:38. Lev. 26:31. Hence

3. metaphorically *to take delight in* a thing, in any way. Am. 5:21. Is. 11: 3 וַהֲרִיחוֹ בְּיִרְאַת יְהוָה *and in the fear of Jehovah is his delight.* For the connexion of the ideas of *fragrancy* and *acceptableness,* see under the articles נִיחֹחַ, בֶּשֶׂם.

רֵיחַ m. verbal from רִיחַ, dec. I. *exhalation, scent, smell.* Cant. 2:13. 7: 14. Gen. 27:27. Metaphorically Job 14:9. comp. Judg. 16:9. Very frequently in the phrase רֵיחַ נִיחֹחַ, see נִיחֹחַ.

רֵיחַ Chald. *idem.* Dan. 3:27.

רֵים see **רְאֵם** *a buffalo.*

רֵיעַ see **רוּעַ** no. II.

רֵיעַ the full orthography for רֵעַ *a neighbour, friend.* Job 6:27.

רִיפוֹת *bruised corn.* 2 Sam. 17:19. Prov. 27:22. The etymology is obscure, if וֹת is the fem. plur. termination. If the ת is radical, then comp. the Arab. رفت, *to bruise in pieces.*

רִיפַת Gen. 10:3. proper name of an unknown people, of the race of the Cimmerians. It has been collated with *the Riphean mountains.*

רִיק *to be empty.* In Kal not used.

Hiph. 1. *to empty,* Gen. 42:35. Jer. 48:12. *to leave empty,* i. e. unsatisfied, Is. 32:6.

2. *to pour out.* Ecc. 11:3. Zech. 4: 12. Ps. 18:43.

3. *to draw* or *make bare* (the sword). Ex. 15:9. Lev. 26:33 וַהֲרִיקֹתִי אַחֲרֵיכֶם חָרֶב *I will draw out the sword after you.* Ps. 35:3. Ezek. 5:2, 12. 12:14. Here belongs the common reading of Gen. 14:14 וַיָּרֶק *and he caused to draw* (the sword), i. e. he armed them. Perhaps the reading of the Samar. text וַיָּדֶק *he reviewed them,* from דוּק in Aram. *to number, review,* is to be preferred. So Sept. Vulg.

Hoph. pass. of no. 1. Jer. 48:11.

רִיק m. verbal adj. from רִיק, *empty.* Jer. 51:34. Used abstractly or as a neuter, *an empty* or *vain thing, vanity,* Ps. 2:1. 4:3. As an adv. רִיק Ps. 73: 13. לָרִיק Lev. 26:16. בְּדֵי רִיק Jer. 51:58. *in vain, to no purpose.*

רֵיק and **רֵק** verbal adj. from רִיק, dec. I.

1. *empty.* Gen. 37:24. Is. 29:8 רֵקָה נַפְשׁוֹ *his hunger is unsatisfied.* Comp. 32:6.

2. *vain, futile.* Deut. 32:47.

3. *poor, stripped of every thing.* Neh. 5:13.

4. *good for nothing, base, wicked.* Judg. 9:4. 11:3. 2 Sam. 6:20.

רֵיקָם an adv. from רִיק, denoting (1.) *with empty hands.* Gen. 31:42. (2.) *in vain, without success.* 2 Sam. 1:22. (3.) *without cause, frustra.* Ps. 25:3. 7:5.

רִיר m. verbal from רוּר, dec. I. *spittle.* 1 Sam. 21:14.—רִיר חַלָּמוּת, see חַלָּמוּת.

רִישׁ m. Prov. 13:18. רֵישׁ 28:19. and רָאשׁ 6:11. 30:8. verbal from רוּשׁ, dec. I. *poverty.*

רִישׁוֹן the Syriac orthography for רִאשׁוֹן *former, first.* Job 8:8.

רַךְ, fem. רַכָּה, verbal adj. from רָכַךְ, dec. VIII. h.

1. *tender;* spoken e.g. of children,

Gen. 33:13. of a calf for the table, Gen. 18:7.

2. *tender, delicate, delicately brought up.* Deut. 28:54, 56.

3. *soft, flattering.* Prov. 15:1.—רַכּוֹת *soft words,* Job 40:27. [41:3.]

4. *weak.* 2 Sam. 3:39. עֵינַיִם רַכּוֹת *weak eyes,* Gen. 29:17. Sept. ἀσθενεῖς. Vulg. *lippi.* The Orientalist regarded this as a great defect in regard to beauty, (comp. the opposite יְפֵה־עֵינַיִם 1 Sam. 17:42. *having beautiful eyes,* spoken in commendation of David.)

5. רַךְ לֵבָב *fearful, timid.* Deut. 20:8. 2 Chr. 13:7.

רָכַב, fut. יִרְכַּב i. q. Lat. *vehi.*

1. *to ride,* on the back of an animal; construed with עַל, Gen. 24:61. Num. 22:30. with בְּ, Neh. 2:12. with an accus. 2 K. 9:18, 19.

2. *to ride,* in a vehicle. Jer. 17:25. 22:4. Spoken particularly of Jehovah's *riding* on the wings of the cherub, Ps. 18:11. upon the clouds, Is. 19:1. upon the heavens, Deut. 33:26. Ps. 68:34.

Hiph. 1. *to cause to ride,* on the back of an animal. Est. 6:9. 1 K. 1:33. Ps. 66:12.

2. *to cause to ride,* in a vehicle; construed with an accus. of the person, Gen. 41:43. 2 Chr. 35:24. or of the draught-animal, Hos. 10:11. Here belongs the phrase הִרְכִּיב עַל בָּמוֹתֵי־אָרֶץ, see בָּמָה plur.

2. *to set* a thing *in a cart* or *waggon.* 2 Sam. 6:3. 2 K. 23:30.

4. simply *to place* or *set,* e.g. the hand. 2 K. 13:16.

Deriv. out of course מֶרְכָּב, מֶרְכָּבָה, רְכוּב.

רֶכֶב m. (f. Nah. 2:5.) verbal from רָכַב, dec. VI. h.

1. *cavalry.* Is. 21:7.

2. *a chariot* or *waggon.* Judg. 5:28. Usually as a collective noun, *chariots, a train of chariots,* Gen. 50:9. (The plur. is found only in Cant. 1:9.) Particularly *war-chariots,* Ex. 14:9.—רֶכֶב בַּרְזֶל *iron chariots, currus falcati,* Josh. 17:18.—עָרֵי הָרֶכֶב *chariot cities,* where the war-chariots were kept, 2 Chr. 1:14. 8:6. 9:25.—This word is often so used, that what is said of it refers strictly to the horses or to the men in the chariot; as e.g. 2 Sam. 8:4 *and David houghed all the chariots,* i.e. the horses pertaining to them. 10:18 *and David killed of the Syrians seven hundred chariots,* i.e. the men and horses belonging to them. 2 K. 7:14 שְׁנֵי רֶכֶב סוּסִים *two span of horses.*

3. *the upper mill-stone, the runner.* Deut. 24:6. 2 Sam. 11:21.

רֵכָב a proper name, *Rechab,* the progenitor of the Rechabites, a wandering tribe of Kenites, whom Jonadab the son of Rechab bound by a solemn vow, not to practise agriculture, nor to drink wine, but to live for ever a strict nomadic life. 2 K. 10:15, 23. Jer. 35:1 ff. 1 Chr. 2:55. Comp. a similar law of the Nabatheans, in Diod. Sic. XIX. 92.

רַכָּב m. verbal from רָכַב, dec. I.

1. *a horseman.* 2 K. 9:17.

2. *a charioteer, driver of a war-chariot.* 1 K. 22:34.

רְכוּב m. verbal from רָכַב, dec. I. *a chariot.* Ps. 104:3.

רְכוּשׁ more rarely רְכֻשׁ m. verbal from רָכַשׁ, dec. I. *substance, goods, possessions.* Gen. 14:16.—רְכוּשׁ הַמֶּלֶךְ *the private substance* or *property of the king,* 2 Chr. 35:7.—שָׂרֵי הָרְכוּשׁ *the overseers of the* (royal) *substance,* 1 Chr. 27:31. 28:1.

רָכִיל m. verbal from רָכַל, *calumny, slander,* (see רָכַל no. 2.) Hence אַנְשֵׁי רָכִיל *slanderers, tale-bearers,* Ezek. 22:9.—הָלַךְ רָכִיל *to go about as a tale-bearer,* Lev. 19:16. Prov. 11:13. 20:19.

רָכַךְ 1. *to be tender, soft,* or *to be softened;* spoken of the heart. 2 K. 22:19.

2. *to be soft, effeminate.* Deut. 28:56.

3. *to be soft, supple, smooth;* spoken of fat, and metaphorically of words. Ps. 55:22.

Niph. fut. יֵרַךְ spoken of the heart, *to be fearful* or *afraid.* Deut. 20:3. Is. 7:4. Jer. 51:46. See רַךְ no. 5.

Pu. *to be mollified* or *softened,* spoken of a wound. Is. 1:6.

Hiph. *to terrify, make afraid,* e. g. the heart. Job 23:16.

רָכַל *to go about, to go up and down,* i. q. רָגַל. Particularly (1.) as a trader, i. q. סָחַר hence *to trade, traffic.* Part. רֹכֵל *a trader, merchant,* Ezek. 27:13, 15, 17 ff. רֹכֶלֶת *a female merchant.* Ezek. 27:3, 20, 23. Deriv. מַרְכֹּלֶת, רְכֻלָּה *a market.* (2.) as a tale-bearer, whence רָכִיל.

רְכֻלָּה f. verbal from רָכַל, dec. X. *trade, traffic.* Ezek. 28:5, 16, 18.

רָכַס *to bind on.* Ezek. 28:28. 39:21.

רֹכֶס m. verbal from רָכַס, dec. VI. o. *a conspiracy, plot,* (like קֶשֶׁר,) or else *cords, snares.* Ps. 31:21.

רְכָסִים masc. plur. *rough* or *steep places.* Is. 40:4. Arab. ركس, *præcipitem dedit.*

רָכַשׁ *to get, acquire.* Gen. 12:5. 31:18. Deriv. רְכוּשׁ.

רֶכֶשׁ m. *a swift horse,* as it appears, a peculiar and noble breed. Mic. 1:13. 1 K. 5:8, [4:28,] (where it is coupled with סוּסִים) Arab. ركض רכץ *to gallop;* (for the interchange of צ and שׁ, see under the letter שׁ. Syr. ܪܰܟܫܳܐ *a horse,* particularly *a stallion.* See Bocharti Hieroz. T. I. p. 95.

רָם *high,* see **רוּם**.

רֵם *a buffalo,* see **רְאֵם**.

רָמָה 1. *to throw.* Only Ex. 15:1, 21.

2. *to shoot* (with a bow). Jer. 4:29. Ps. 78:9.

Pi. רִמָּה *to deceive, beguile,* (primarily *to cause to fall, to trip up;* comp. the Lat. *fallo* with the Greek σφάλλω and perhaps the Engl. *to fall*) Prov. 26:19. Gen. 29:25. Construed with לְ 1 Chr. 12:17 לְרַמּוֹתַנִי לְצָרַי *to deceive* (and betray) *me to mine enemies,* an instance of the constructio prægnans.

Deriv. תַּרְמִית, תָּרְמָה, מִרְמָה, רְמִיָּה.

רָמָה f. (with Kamets impure) verbal from רוּם *to be high,* dec. X.

1. *a height, high place.* 1 Sam. 22:6. Particularly for the worship of idols, Ezek. 16:24, 25, 39. Comp. בָּמָה.

2. proper name of several cities; (1.) of a city in the tribe of Benjamin, (Judg. 19:23. Is. 10:29.) situated north of Jerusalem. Josh. 18:25. Judg. 4:5. Jer. 31:15. Hos. 5:8. 1 K. 15:17. (2.) of a city in Mount Ephraim, the birth-place and residence of Samuel. 1 Sam. 1:19. 2:11. 7:17. 15:34. 16:13. More in full רָמָתַיִם צוֹפִים 1 Sam. 1:1. —1 Mac. 11:34. Ῥαμαθέμ. (3.) of a city in the tribe of Naphtali. Josh. 19:36. Perhaps the same as Josh. 19:29. (4.) רָמַת הַמִּצְפֶּה (*height of the watch-tower*) Josh. 13:26. a city in Gilead, otherwise called רָאמוֹת, רָמוֹת q. v. (5.) רָמַת לְחִי (*height of the jaw-bone*) Judg. 15:17. a place named by Samson.—The gentile noun is רָמָתִי 1 Chr. 27:27.

רְמָא, רְמָה Chald.

1. *to throw, cast.* Dan. 3:21, 24. 6:17.

2. *to set, place,* e. g. a throne. Dan. 7:9. Comp. Rev. 4:2 θρόνος ἔκειτο and יָרָה *to erect, raise up,* Gen. 31:51.

3. *to lay* or *impose,* (a tribute.) Ezra 7:24.

Ithpe. pass. *to be cast.* Dan. 3:6, 15.

רִמָּה f. *a worm.* Job 25:6. Particularly *worms* arising from putridity, Ex. 16:25. Job 7:5. 21:26. (Arab. רמם *to rot;* رمّة *rottenness,* also a *worm arising from rottenness.*)

רִמּוֹן m. dec. I.

1. *a pomegranate.* Cant. 4:3. As an artificial ornament, Ex. 28:33, 34. e. g. on the chapiter of a pillar, 2 K. 25:17.

2. *a pomegranate-tree.* Joel 1:12.

3. a proper name (1.) of a city in the tribe of Simeon, on the southern boundary of Palestine. Josh. 15:32. 19:7. Zech. 14:10. (2.) of a rock not far from Gibeah. Judg. 20:45, 47. It was hither that Saul and his men went, 1 Sam. 14:2. (3.) רִמּוֹן הַמְּתֹאָר (*a round pomegranate*) a city in the tribe of Zebulun, Josh. 19:13. comp. רִמּוֹנוֹ 1 Chr.

6:62. [6:77.] (4.) רִמֹּן פֶּרֶץ (*split pomegranate*) a station of the Israelites. Num. 33:19.

רָמוֹת (*heights.*)

1. proper name of a city in Gilead, otherwise called רָאמוֹת. Josh. 21:38. 1 K. 4:13.

2. רָמוֹת נֶגֶב (*heights towards the south*) a city in the tribe of Simeon, otherwise called רָאמַת־נֶגֶב. 1 Sam. 30:37.

רָמוּת f. Ezek. 32:5. according to the present punctuation, from רוּם *to be high*, hence *high heaps* (of corpses). Better to be pointed רִמּוֹתֶךָ (though this plural does not occur elsewhere,) *with thy worms.*

רֹמַח m. plur. רְמָחִים, dec. VI. n. *a spear, javelin,* (as a part of heavy armour.) Num. 25:7. Judg. 5:8. Jer. 46:4. (In Aram. and Arab. *idem.*)

רַמִּי, plur. הָרַמִּים 2 Chr. 22:5. i. q. הָאֲרַמִּים *the Syrians.* Comp. 2 K. 8:28. For the omission of אֲ in the beginning of words, see p. 1.

רְמִיָּה f. verbal from רָמָה.

1. *deceit.* Job 13:7.—לְשׁוֹן רְמִיָּה *a deceitful tongue,* Ps. 120:2, 3.—קֶשֶׁת רְמִיָּה *a deceitful bow,* i. e. one that misses the mark, Ps. 78:57. Hos. 7:16.

2. *slackness, remissness, remissio.* (Comp. Arab. رمى conj. VII. *laxum, remissum fuit* negotium, kindred with רָפָה.) Prov. 12:24. כַּף רְמִיָּה *a slack hand,* Prov. 10:4. As an adv. *remissly.* Jer. 48:10.

רַמָּךְ f. dec. I. *a mare.* Once Est. 8:10. (Arab. رَمَكَة *idem.*)

רָמַם i. q. רוּם *to be high, exalted.* Pret. רֹמּוּ Job 22:12. and רוֹמּוּ 24:24. (In both passages several MSS. and editions omit the Dagesh, and the forms would then be derived from רוּם.) Part. fem. רוֹמֵמָה *high, exalted, alta,* Ps. 118:16.

Niph. imper. plur. הֵרֹמּוּ Num. 17:10. and fut. יֵרֹמּוּ Ezek. 10:15, 17, 19. *to be lifted up, to rise.* (The authorities for omitting the Dagesh are here much less.)

רָמַס, fut. יִרְמֹס, *to tread with the feet,* as clay by the potter. Is. 41:25. Particularly *to tread down, to trample on,* 2 K. 7:17, 20. Dan. 8:7, 10. Is. 63:3. 16:4 רֹמֵס *the oppressor, conculcator,* 1:12 רְמֹס חֲצֵרָי *to tread my courts,* here with the accessory idea of *profanation;* comp. Rev. 11:2. 1 Mac. 3:45. (Comp. the kindred verb רָפַס.)

Niph. pass. Is. 28:3.

רָמַשׂ, fut. יִרְמֹשׂ. 1. *to move,* spoken of living creatures. Gen. 1:30. 7:8, 21 (at the beginning.) 8:19. Construed with an accus. *to move* or *be alive with* any thing, (comp. הָלַךְ no. 5.) Gen. 9:2 אֲשֶׁר תִּרְמֹשׂ הָאֲדָמָה *with which the earth moves,* i. e. which moves upon the earth. Lev. 20:25.

2. particularly *to creep,* as worms. Gen. 7:14. 8:17.

רֶמֶשׂ m. 1. verbal from רָמַשׂ.

1. *that which moves* (on the earth), *four-footed beasts* in opposition to *fowls.* Gen. 7:14. Ps. 148:10. Spoken of *fishes,* Ps. 104:25.

2. *worms.* Gen. 1:24, 25, 26.

רֹן (strictly infin. from רָנַן,) dec. VIII. e. *a shout of joy, a rejoicing.* Ps. 32:7 רָנֵּי פַלֵּט *shouts for deliverance.*

רָנָה i. q. רָנַן *to rattle,* as arrows in a quiver, or else *to whiz,* as arrows shot from the bow. Job 39:23. See Bocharti Hieroz. T. I. p. 134. In the latter case אַשְׁפָּה *quiver* must stand for *arrows.*

רִנָּה f. verbal from רָנַן, dec. X.

1. *a cry,* e. g. of a herald, for assistance. Ps. 17:1. 61:2. 1 K. 22:36.

2. *a rejoicing, shout of joy.* Ps. 30:6. 42:5.

רָנַן, fut. יָרֹן, (once יָרוּן as if from רוּן Prov. 29:6.)

1. *to cry aloud.* Prov. 1:20. 8:3. Particularly for help, Lam. 2:19.

2. *to raise a shout of joy, to rejoice, exult.* Lev. 9:24. Job 38:7. Spoken of inanimate nature, Is. 44:23. 49:13.

Pi. רִנֵּן i. q. Kal no. 2. *to shout, rejoice.* Ps. 98:4. 132:16. Construed with an accus. of the person or thing, *to praise* or *celebrate with joy,* Ps. 51:

16. 59:17. with בְּ, Ps. 33:1. 89:13. with אֶל, Ps. 84:3. with לְ, 95:1.

Pu. pass. Is. 16:10.

Hiph. הִרְנִין 1. *to rejoice.* Deut. 32: 43. with לְ, Ps. 81:2.

2. trans. *to make to rejoice.* Ps. 65: 9. Job 29:13.

Deriv. out of course רֹן, רִנָּה.

רְנָנָה f. verbal from רָנַן, dec. XI. c. *a rejoicing.* Job 3:7. 20:5. Plur. וֹת Ps. 63:6.

רְנָנִים plur. fem. prob. a poetic word for *ostriches*, otherwise called בְּנוֹת יַעֲנָה Job 39:13. Vulg. *struthio.* The name is derived from *the buzzing* of the wings, (comp. רָנָה Job 39:23.) or from *the cry* of the female ostrich, (comp. the article יַעֲנָה;) hence the female ostrich is called by the Arabians, زمار *song.* See Bocharti Hieroz. II. p. 248.

רִסָּה a station of the Israelites in the desert. Num. 33:21, 22.

I. רְסִיסִים masc. plur. verbal from רָסַס, dec. I. *drops.* Cant. 5:2.

II. רְסִיסִים *ruins.* Amos 6:11. Root Chald. רְסַס i. q. רָצַץ *to dash in pieces.*

רֶסֶן m. dec. VI. h.

1. *a bridle.* Ps. 32:9. Job 30:11. Is. 30:28. According to the latter passage it was drawn *over* the jaw-bone like a halter, but served, however, to guide the animal.

2. *the inner part of the jaw, the corner of the mouth.* Job 41:5 [41:13] כֶּפֶל רִסְנוֹ *his double jaws.* Comp. the Greek χαλινοὶ *the corners of the mouth,* where the bridle is put, and the Germ. *Gebiss.*

3. proper name of an Assyrian city. Once Gen. 10:12.

רָסַס *to wet, moisten.* Ezek. 46:14. (Chald. רְסַס *idem.*) Deriv. רְסִיסִים no. I.

רַע f. with the distinctive accents רָע, fem. רָעָה, plur. רָעִים, verbal adj. from רָעַע in the sense of רוּעַ, dec. VIII. k.

1. *bad, of a bad quality.* Lev. 27:10. Deut. 17:1. Particularly *morally bad, evil, wicked,* spoken of men, purposes, actions, Gen. 6:5. 8:21. 1 Sam. 25:3. —לֵב רָע *an evil heart,* Jer. 3:17. 7:24. —רַע בְּעֵינֵי פ' *evil in the eyes of a person, displeasing to him,* Gen. 38:7. frequently in the phrase הָרַע בְּעֵינֵי יְהוָה *what displeased Jehovah,* 1 K. 11:6. 14:22. more rarely with עַל, Ecc. 2:17. with לִפְנֵי, Neh. 2:1. Hence רַע and fem. רָעָה as a subst. *evil,* Job 1:1. Ps. 97:10. and often put as a genitive after another noun, e. g. עֲצַת רָע *a wicked counsel,* Ezek. 11:2. אַנְשֵׁי רָע *wicked men,* Prov. 28:5.

2. *ugly, ill-favoured,* particularly with מַרְאֶה. Gen. 41:3.

3. *evil, unfortunate, calamitous.* Jer. 7:6 לְרַע לָכֶם *so that it may go ill with you,* i. e. to your hurt, for לִהְיוֹת רַע לָכֶם; (comp. טוֹב no. 1. 25:7.—עָשָׂה רָעָה עִם *to do ill to* any one, Gen. 26:29. 31:29. Hence as a subst. רַע and רָעָה *evil, adversity, trouble,* Gen. 19:19. 44:4. 50:15.

4. *evil, pernicious, dangerous.*—חַיָּה רָעָה *an evil beast,* Gen. 37:33 דָּבָר רָע *any evil* or *pernicious thing,* 2 K. 4:41.

5. רַע עַיִן *having an evil eye, envious.* Prov. 23:6. 28:22.

6. *sad;* spoken of the heart, Prov. 25:20. of the countenance, Gen. 40:7. Neh. 2:2.

I. רֵעַ verbal from רוּעַ no II. dec. I. *a cry, shout.* Ex. 32:17. Mic. 4:9.

II. רֵעַ m. a contraction of רֵעֶה verbal from רָעָה no. II. dec. I.

1. *a companion, acquaintance, friend.* Job 2:11. 19:21. Prov. 25:17. Not so strong a term as אֹהֵב *a loving* or *close friend,* comp. Prov. 18:24. Often followed by לְ instead of a genitive, Job 30:29 רֵעַ לִבְנוֹת יַעֲנָה *a companion of ostriches,* i. e. like to ostriches. Prov. 19:6.

2. *one beloved, a lover, spouse, husband.* Cant. 5:16. Jer. 3:1, 20. Hos. 3:1. Comp. רַעְיָה.

3. *another person, a neighbour, fellow-being.* Ex. 20:17 ff. 22:25. Hence אִישׁ and רֵעַ *the one, the other;* e. g. Judg. 6:29 וַיֹּאמְרוּ אִישׁ אֶל רֵעֵהוּ *and they said one to another.* Gen. 11:3. 1 Sam. 10:11. 20:41. Used likewise of inanimate

things, Gen. 15:10. Comp. אָח no. 7. More rarely in the same sense without אִישׁ, e. g. Is. 34:14 שָׂעִיר עַל רֵעֵהוּ יִקְרָא *one satyr calls to another.*

4. *a thought, will, purpose,* (i. q. Chald. רְעוּת ,רַעְיוֹן.) Ps. 139:2, 17. prob. also Job 32:22. Root רְעָה Chald. *to will*, and رَعَى; Ethpa. *to think.*

רֹעַ m. rarely רוֹעַ, verbal from רָעַע in the sense of רוּעַ.

1. *badness, bad quality.* Jer. 24:2, 3, 8. Especially in a moral sense, *wickedness, evil,* Jer. 4:4. 21:12. 23:2. 26:3.

2. *ugliness.* Gen. 41:19.

3. *sadness.*—רֹעַ לֵב *sadness of heart,* Neh. 2:2. רֹעַ פָּנִים *a sad countenance,* Ecc. 7:3.

רָעֵב, fut. יִרְעַב, *to be hungry, to hunger,* Ps. 34:11. 50:12. *to suffer from famine, to be famished,* Gen. 41:55. Construed with לְ, *to hunger* after any thing, Jer. 42:14.

Hiph. *to cause to hunger.* Deut. 8:3. Prov. 10:3.

רָעֵב, fem. רְעֵבָה, verbal from רָעֵב, dec. V. a. *hungry,* 2 Sam. 17:29. Job 5:8. Is. 8:22. *consumed* or *weakened by hunger,* Job 18:12.

רָעָב m. verbal from רָעֵב, dec. IV. a.

1. *hunger.* Lam. 5:10.

2. *a famine.* Gen. 12:10. 41:30 ff. Am. 8:11.

רַעֲבוֹן m. verbal from רָעֵב, dec. III. *idem.* Ps. 37:19. Gen. 42:19 שֶׁבֶר רַעֲבוֹן בָּתֵּיכֶם *grain for the hunger,* i. e. for the wants, *of your families.*

רָעַד *to quake, tremble.* Ps. 104:32. (Arab. *idem.*)

Hiph. intrans. *idem.* Dan. 10:11. Ezra 10:9.

רַעַד m. Ex. 15:15. and **רְעָדָה** f. Ps. 2:11. 48:7. verbals from רָעַד, *a quaking, trembling.*

I. **רָעָה**, Arab. رَعَى, fut. apoc. יֵרַע.

1. *to feed* (a flock), *pascere.* Gen. 30:36. Construed with an accus. more rarely with בְּ, 1 Sam. 16:11. 17:34. Without a case following, *to wander about as a nomade,* Num. 14:33. Part. רֹעֶה *a shepherd,* fem. רֹעָה *a shepherdess,* Gen. 29:9.—Metaphorically *to feed* a people, i. e. to lead or guide them, spoken (1.) of a prince, e. g. 2 Sam. 5:2. 7:7. Jer. 23:2 ff. Construed with בְּ, Ps. 78:71. In Is. 44:28, Cyrus is called *the shepherd of Jehovah.* Comp. the Homeric phrase ποιμένες λαῶν (2.) of God, e. g. Ps. 23:1 *Jehovah is my shepherd, I shall not want.* 28:9. 80:2. (3.) Prov. 10:21 שִׂפְתֵי צַדִּיק יִרְעוּ רַבִּים *the lips of the righteous guide many.* Part. רֹעֶה *a guide, teacher, wise man,* Ecc. 12:11.

2. *to feed, graze, pasci,* spoken of cattle. Is. 5:17. 11:7. The pasture *fed upon* is put in the accus. Jer. 50:19. Ezek. 34:14, 18, 19. Mic. 7:14. Metaphorically *to eat up, to consume,* Mic. 5:5 *they shall consume the land of Assyria with the sword.* Job 20:26 יֵרַע שָׂרִיד בְּאָהֳלוֹ *it (the fire) shall consume him that is left in his tabernacle.* Jer. 22:22. 2:16 יִרְעוּךְ קָדְקֹד *they shall consume the crown of thy head.* Job 24:21 רֹעֶה עֲקָרָה *who oppresseth the barren.* (Chald. *confringens.*) In the two last examples the meaning approaches near to that of רָעַע *to break in pieces.*

3. *to support, nourish,* spoken of food. Hos. 9:2 *the threshing-floor and wine-press shall not nourish them.*

Hiph. i. q. Kal. Once Ps. 78:72.

Deriv. מַרְעִית ,מִרְעֶה ,רְעִי.

II. **רָעָה** *to take delight* or *pleasure in* a person or thing. (Chald. רְעָה *idem,* i. q. Heb. רָצָה. In Arab. comp. رضى.) Construed (1.) with an accus. of the person, *to take pleasure in* or *to associate with* any one. Prov. 13:20. 28:7. 29:3. Deriv. רֵעֶה ,רֵעַ no. II. 1—3. מֵרֵעַ *a male friend;* רְעוּת ,רַעְיָה *a female friend.* (2.) with an accus. of the thing, *to take pleasure in* or *pursue after* any thing. Prov. 15:14 *the mouth of fools* יִרְעֶה אִוֶּלֶת *takes pleasure in folly, sectatur stultitiam.* Ps. 37:3 רְעֵה אֱמוּנָה *sectare veritatem.*

—רְעָה רוּחַ *to pursue after the wind, inania sectari*, Hos. 12:2. comp. Is. 44:20. also רְעוּת, and רַעְיוֹן רוּחַ.

Pi. רֵעָה *to choose*, or *to treat as one's friend*. Judg. 14:20.

Hithpa. construed with אֶת, *to have intercourse* or *make friendship with* any one. Prov. 22:24.

רָעָה f. verbal from רָעַע in the sense of רוּעַ, dec. X. *evil, adversity, destruction;* see רַע nos. 1. 3.

רֵעֶה m. verbal from רָעָה no. II. *a companion, acquaintance, friend*, i. q. the more frequent רֵעַ. 2 Sam. 15:37. 16:16. 1 K. 4:5.

רֵעָה fem. of רֵעֶה, dec. X. *a female companion*. Plur. רֵעוֹת Ps. 45:15. Judg. 11:38.

רֹעָה strictly an infin. fem. from רָעַע, *a breaking*. Prov. 25:19.

רְעוּת, fem. of רְעוּ i. q. רֵעָה, רֵעַ, (after the form כַּלָּה=כְּלִי, מַת=מְתוּ *a man*.)

1. *a female friend* or *companion*. Est. 1:19. Ex. 11:2. Joined with אִשָּׁה, *the one, the other*, Is. 34:15, 16. Jer. 9:19.

2. *a desiring, striving after* a thing. רְעוּת רוּחַ *a striving for the wind, a vain endeavour*, Ecc. 1:14. 2:11, 17, 26. 4:4, 6. 6:9. comp. רָעָה רוּחַ Hos. 12:2, under the article רָעָה no. II. (2.) and the Chald. רְעוּת.

רְעוּת Chald. *will, pleasure*. Ezra 5:17. 7:18.

רְעִי m. verbal from רָעָה no. 1. *a pasture*. 1 K. 5:3 [4:23] בְּקַר רְעִי *pastured oxen*.

רֹעִי m. denom. from רֹעֶה, with the adjective termination ִי, *pertaining to a shepherd*. Is. 38:12. Also *a shepherd* himself, Zech. 11:17.

רַעְיָה f. verbal from רָעָה no. I. dec. X. *a female friend* or *lover*, like the Lat. *amica*. Cant. 1:9, 15. 2:2, 10, 13. 4:7. Comp. רֵעַ no. 2. Plur. רַעְיֹתַי Judg. 11:37 Keth. *my companions*, or it may be pointed רְעוּתַי (as if from רְעוּת).

רַעְיוֹן m. i. q. רְעוּת no. 2. *a desire, endeavour, exertion*. Ecc. 2:22 רַעְיוֹן לִבּוֹ *the desire of his heart*.—רַעְיוֹן רוּחַ i. q. רְעוּת רוּחַ *a vain endeavour*, Ecc. 1:17. 4:16.

רַעְיוֹן m. Chald. *a thought*. Dan. 4:16. [4:19] רַעְיֹנֹהִי יְבַהֲלֻנֵּהּ *his thoughts terrified him*, i. e. he was terrified. 5:6, 10. 7:28. Spoken of nightly visions, Dan. 2:29, 30. Root רְעָה *to think*.

רָעַל *to tremble, to shake*. Found only in Hoph. *to be shaken, to tremble*. Nah. 2:4. (Syr. Pe. *to tremble;* Aph. *to shake*.) Deriv. תַּרְעֵלָה, and

רַעַל m. verbal from רָעַל, dec. VI. c.

1. *giddiness, intoxication*. Zech. 12:2.

2. Plur. רְעָלוֹת Is. 3:19. *veils*, Arab. رِعْل, prob. from their *tremulous* motion, when worn.

רָעַם 1. *to be agitated, to tremble*. Ezek. 27:35.

2. *to roar, to rage*, spoken of the sea. Ps. 96:11. 98:7. 1 Chr. 16:32.

3. *to thunder*. (In Syr. *idem*.) Only in Hiph. and in the noun רַעַם.

4. *to be angry*. In like manner only in Hiph. (Syr. Ethpe. *idem*. Arab. رغم conj. III. V. *to be angry*.)

Hiph. 1. *to cause it to thunder, to thunder*, spoken of Jehovah. Ps. 29:3. Job 40:9. 1 Sam. 2:10.

2. *to provoke to anger, to cause to fret*. 1 Sam. 1:6.

רַעַם m. verbal from רָעַם, dec. VI. c.

1. *a raging, tumult*. Job 39:25.

2. *thunder*. Ps. 77:19. 81:8. Metaphorically Job 26:14 רַעַם גְּבוּרֹתוֹ מִי יִתְבּוֹנָן *the thunder of his power who can understand?*

רַעְמָה f. verbal from רָעַם.

1. *a trembling, shivering;* hence *the trembling mane* of a horse, Job 39:19 הֲתַלְבִּישׁ צַוָּארוֹ רַעְמָה *canst thou clothe his neck with its trembling mane?* According to the Chaldaic version, *majesty*, from רַעַם=רוּם.

2. Gen. 10:7. Ezek. 27:22. proper name of a city or country belonging to a tribe of Cushites. Sept. in Gen. Ῥέγμα,

a city on the Persian gulf mentioned by Ptolemy and Steph. Byzant. See Bocharti Phaleg, IV. cap. 5. J.D. Michaëlis Spicileg. T. I. p. 193.

רַעְמְסֵס Gen. 47:11. and רַעְמְסֵס Ex. 1:11. 12:37. Num. 33:3, 5. proper name of a city and country (Gen. 47:11.) in Lower Egypt. Of importance in this place is a passage of the Sept. Gen. 46:28, where for the Heb. אַרְצָה גֹּשֶׁן stands καθ' Ἡρώων πόλιν, εἰς γῆν Ῥαμεσσῆ. According to this the city of Raamses is *Heroopolis*, and the country a part of the land of Goshen. See Jablonski De Terra Gosen, in his Opusc. ed. te Water, T. II. p. 136. and in opposition to him J.D. Michaëlis Supplem. p. 2256.

רָעַן found only in Pil. רַעֲנַן *to be green, to be covered with leaves.* Job 15:32. Cant. 1:16. In both passages, however, it may be regarded as an adjective. Some traces of the simple root רען are found in Syriac. Hence

רַעֲנָן m. verbal from רַעֲנַן, dec. II. a.

1. *green;* spoken of trees in full growth, Deut. 12:2. 2 K. 16:4. of a leaf, Jer. 17:8. The verdant tree is employed as an emblem of *prosperity,* Ps. 37:35. 52:10. 92:15.

2. *fresh,* spoken of oil. Ps. 92:11.

רַעֲנַן Chald. *to be flourishing,* spoken of a person. Dan. 4:1. [4:4.]

רָעַע, fut. יָרֹעַ, infin. רֹעָה (Is. 24:19. Prov. 25:19.)

1. *to break* or *dash in pieces.* (In Aram. *idem.*) Jer. 15:12. Ps. 2:9. Job 34:24.

2. intrans. *to be broken in pieces.* Jer. 11:16.

3. intrans. *to be terrified.* Is. 8:9. Comp. חָתַת no. 2.) Others derive it in this passage from רוּעַ. See Gesen. in loc.

Hiph. הֵרַע has its signification from רוּעַ *to be evil,* q. v.

Hithpo. הִתְרֹעֲעָה *to be violently shaken* or *thrown down.* Is. 24:19. Perhaps *to be ruined, to perish,* Prov. 18:24. but this can also be derived from רוּעַ no. I. This same form occurs likewise under רוּעַ no. II.

רְעַע Chald. *to break in pieces.* Pa. *idem.* Dan. 2:40.

רָעַף, fut. יִרְעַף, *to drop, distil.* Prov. 3:20. Ps. 65:12, 13. (In Arab. *idem.*)

Hiph. *to let drop,* spoken of heaven; of course i. q. Kal. Is. 45:8.

רָעַץ i. q. רָעַע and רָצַץ *to break* or *dash in pieces.* Ex. 15:6. Metaphorically *to oppress, vex,* (a people,) Judg. 10:8.

רָעַשׁ 1. *to wave, shake,* spoken e. g. of fruit. Ps. 72:16.

2. *to be shaken, to quake, tremble.* Ezek. 38:20. 26:15. Spoken of inanimate nature, e. g. of the earth, Judg. 5:4. Is. 13:13 *the earth shall quake from its place;* (comp. Job 9:6.) of the heavens, Joel 2:10. 4:16. [3:16.] of the mountains, Jer. 4:24. Nah. 1:5.

Niph. i. q. Kal. Once Jer. 50:46.

Hiph. 1. *to shake, put in motion.* Hag. 2:6, 7.

2. *to make to tremble.* Ps. 60:4. Is. 14:16.

3. *to cause to leap* or *spring,* e. g. a horse. Job 39:20 הֲתַרְעִישֶׁנּוּ כָּאַרְבֶּה *causest thou him to leap as the locust?* Comp. נָתַר *to leap,* spoken of locusts; Hiph. *to cause to quake;* also נָקַף.

רַעַשׁ m. verbal from רָעַשׁ, dec. IV. c.

1. *a shaking;* e. g. of a spear. Job 41:21. [41:29.] Particularly *an earthquake,* 1 K. 19:11. Am. 1:1. Zech. 15:5.

2 *tumult, noise;* e. g. of a chariot, Nah. 3:2. of battle, Is. 9:4. Jer. 10:22. of a snorting horse, Job 39:24.

3. *a trembling.* Ezek. 12:18.

רָפָא 1. liter. *to mend, repair.* Found only in Niph. and Pi. no. 1.

2. *to cure, to heal.* (Comp. ἀκεῖσθαι, *sarcire, sanare.*) It is construed with an accus. and dative, as well of the wound or sickness as of the person; e. g. with an accus. Ps. 60:4. with a dative, Num. 12:13. 2 K. 20:5. Part. רֹפֵא *a physician,* Gen. 50:2. 2 Chr. 16:12. Used impersonally, Is. 6:10 וְרָפָא לוֹ *and lest he should be healed, et ne curatio fiat illi.*

3. metaphorically *to restore;* e.g. a land, people. 2 Chr. 7:14. comp. verse 13. Hos. 7:1. 11:3. Ps. 30:3. This figure and its opposite are found Deut. 32:39 *I wound and I heal.* Jer. 17:14. 30:17. Since this restoration to former prosperity was connected with the forgiveness of past sins on the part of Jehovah; hence

4. *to forgive, pardon.* 2 Chr. 30:20. Jer. 3:22. Hos. 14:5. Comp. Ps. 41:5. 103:3.

5. *to comfort.* Job 13:4 רֹפְאֵי אֱלִל *comforters of no value.* For the transition to this signification, see such passages as Ps. 147:3. Jer. 6:14. 8:11.

Niph. 1. pass. of no. 1. Jer. 19:11.

2. *to be healed.* Lev. 13:37. Construed with a dative, Is. 53:5. נִרְפָּא לָנוּ *we are healed.* Spoken of water, *to be made drinkable,* 2 K. 2:22. Ezek. 47:8, 9.

Pi. *to repair* (a broken altar), 1 K. 18:30.

2. *to heal,* Ezek. 34:4. *to make wholesome* or *potable,* e.g. unwholesome water. 2 K. 2:21.

3. trans. *to cause to be healed.* Ex. 21:19. רַפֹּא יְרַפֵּא *he shall cause him to be thoroughly healed.*

Hithpa. *to let himself be healed.* 2 K. 8:22.

Deriv. מַרְפֵּא, רְפֻאוֹת, רִפְאוּת.

Note. The root רָפָא often borrows its form from רָפָה, (comp. קָרָא i. q. קָרָה,) sometimes in respect to the consonants, and sometimes barely as to the vowels, which then follow the analogy of verbs ל״ה. Here pertain the imper. רְפָה Ps. 60:4. fut. תִּרְפֶּינָה Job 5:18. Niph. נִרְפְּתָה Jer. 51:9. infin. הֵרָפֵה 19:11. fut. יֵרָפוּ 2 K. 2:22. Pi. רִפֵּא Jer. 6:14.

רָפָא i. q. רָפֶה *weak, without strength.* Hence only the plur. רְפָאִים *the weak ones,* i.e. the shades, the inhabitants of hades, whom the ancient Hebrews conceived of as without strength and without sensation, (εἴδωλα καμόντων.) Ps. 88:11. Prov. 2:18. 9:18. 21:16. Is. 14:9. 26:14, 19. Hence Is. 14:10 גַּם אַתָּה חֻלֵּיתָ כָמוֹנוּ *hast thou also become weak* or *feeble as we?*

רִפְאוּת f. verbal from רָפָא, *a healing, recovery.* Prov. 3:8.

רְפֻאוֹת plur. fem. verbal from רָפָא, *medicine.* Jer. 30:13. 46:11. Ezek. 30:21.

רָפָאִי found only in the plur. רְפָאִים a gentile noun, *the Rephaim* or *sons of Raphah,* (יְלִדֵי הָרָפָה 2 Sam. 21:16, 18.) a Canaanitish race of giants, that lived beyond the Jordan, Gen. 14:5. 15:20. Josh. 17:15. from whom Og the giant king of Bashan was descended, Deut. 3:11. In a broader sense it appears to have included all the giant tribes of Canaan, (see אֵימִים, זַמְזֻמִּים, עֲנָקִים.) Deut. 2:11, 20. In subsequent times *the sons of Raphah* appear to have been men of extraordinary strength among the Philistines, see 2 Sam. 21:16, 18.

רָפַד, fut. יִרְפַּד, *to spread out, sternere,* kindred with רָבַד. Job 41:22. [41:30.]

Pi. 1. *to spread* a bed or couch, *sternere* lectum. Job 17:14.

2. *to support,* hence *to refresh* one wearied. Cant. 2:5. Comp. סָעַד no. 2.

Deriv. רְפִידָה.

רָפָה, fut. apoc. יִרֶף.

1. *to be slack, to hang down.* Used particularly of the hands, 2 Chr. 15:7 אַל יִרְפּוּ יְדֵיכֶם *let not your hands be slack.* Hence this phrase denotes *to be dispirited, to despond,* 2 Sam. 4:1 וַיִּרְפּוּ יָדָיו *then his hands became slack.* i.e. he was dispirited. Is. 13:7. Jer. 6:24. 50:43. Ezek. 7:17. 21:12. Zeph. 3:16. Also without יָדַיִם, Jer. 49:24 רָפְתָה דַמֶּשֶׂק *Damascus is dispirited.*

2. construed with מִן, *to desist from* a person or thing. Ex. 4:26. Judg. 8:3. Neh. 6:9.

3. *to sink;* spoken of the day, Judg. 19:9. of burning stubble, Is. 5:24.

Niph. *to be remiss, idle, lazy.* Ex. 5:8, 17.

Pi. 1. *to slacken* or *loosen,* e.g. a girdle. Job 12:21. Particularly joined with יָדַיִם, *to slacken the hands of* a person, i. e. to dishearten or discourage him, (comp. Kal no. 1.) Jer. 38:4. Ezra 4:4.

2. *to let down.* Ezek. 1:24, 25.

Hiph. הִרְפָּה, imper. and fut. apoc. הֶרֶף and יֶרֶף.

1. intrans. *to let go* or *alone, to desist from* a person or thing; construed with מִן, Judg. 11:37. Deut. 9:14. with לְ, 2 K. 4:27. 1 Sam. 11:3. Also with an accus. *to let lie, to leave, forsake,* Neh. 6:3. Ps. 138:8. Deut. 4:31. 31:6, 8. Josh. 1:5, (where it is synonymous with עָזַב.) Joined with an infin. Prov. 4:13. Without cases, Ps. 46:11. 1 Sam. 15:16.

2. *to dismiss, let go,* construed with an accus. Cant. 3:4. Job 7:19. 27:6.

3. causat. of no. 1. *to cause to cease, to withdraw.* 2 Sam. 24:16 הֶרֶף יָדֶךָ *withdraw thine hand,* i. e. cease from destroying. Construed with מִן, Josh. 10:6.

Hithpa. 1. *to behave one's self slackly, remissly, idly.* Josh. 18:3. Prov. 18:9.

2. *to let one's courage fail, to be dispirited.* Prov. 24:10.

Note. רָפָה borrows the form of רָפָא only once, (part. Pi. מְרַפֵּא Jer. 38:4.) but the forms of רָפָה have frequently the signification of רָפָא. See the note under רָפָה.

רָפֶה m. verbal from רָפָה, dec. IX. b.

1. *slack, remiss,* particularly with יָדַיִם 2 Sam. 17:2.—יָדַיִם רָפוֹת *slack hands,* as indicating *dejection, despondency,* Job 4:3. Is. 35:3.

2. *weak, feeble.* Num. 13:18.

רְפִידָה f. dec. X. *the support,* prob. *the frame* (of a portable couch). Cant. 3:10. Root רָפַד Pi. no. 2.

רְפִידִים (*stays*) a station of the Israelites in their march through the wilderness. Ex. 17:1. 19:2.

רִפְיוֹן m. *slackness, remissness;* joined with יָדַיִם, *despondency, fear.* See רָפָה no. 1.

רָפַס and **רָפַשׂ**, (both forms being used promiscuously,) fut. יִרְפֹּשׂ (Ezek. 34:18.) 32:2. *to tread with the feet,* particularly *to make waters turbid.* Kindred with רָמַס.

Niph. Prov. 25:26 מַעְיָן נִרְפָּשׂ *a troubled* or *turbid fountain.*

Hithpa. הִתְרַפֵּס liter. *to let one's self be trodden on,* hence *to submit one's self.* Prov. 6:3. Ps. 68:31 מִתְרַפֵּס בְּרַצֵּי כָסֶף *who submits himself with bars of silver,* i. e. brings bars of silver.

Deriv. מִרְפָּשׂ.

רְפַס Chald. *to tread in pieces.* Dan. 7:7.

רַפְסֹדוֹת fem. plur. *floats, rafts.* 2 Chr. 2:15. a later word, as it appears, for the more ancient דֹּבְרוֹת 1 K. 5:23. [5:9.] Perhaps compounded of רְפָא *sarcire* and אַסְדָא Talmud. *a float.*

רָפַף *to shake, tremble.* Found only in Po. Job 26:11. (Arab. رفّ Chald. רפרף *to tremble.*)

רָפַק found only in Hithpa. *to lean, to support one's self.* Cant. 8:5. (Arab. رفق conj. VIII. *idem.*)

רָפַשׂ see **רָפַס**.

רֶפֶשׁ m. *mire,* i. q. the following word טִיט Once Is. 57:20. (In Talmud. *idem.*)

רְפָתִים masc. plur. Hab. 3:17. according to the Rabbins, *stalls.* Sept. Vulg. Arab. *cribs.* (In Arab. رُفْتٌ *straw,* perhaps *a bed of straw.*)

רַץ m. verbal from רָצַץ, dec. VI. h. *a piece, a bar,* (of silver.) Ps. 68:31.

רָץ m. *a runner.* See **רוּץ**.

רָצָא i. q. רוּץ *to run.* Once Ezek. 1:14.

רָצַד in Pi. only Ps. 68:17. *to look askance, to be envious.* (Arab. رصد *to observe narrowly,* particularly for to lay wait.)

רָצָה (Arab. with ض.)

1. *to be well pleased with* or *to take delight in* a person or thing; construed with an accus. Ps. 102:15. Job 14:6. Is. 42:1. Jer. 14:10. with בְּ, Ps. 49:14. 147:10. 149:4. Particularly *to*

accept graciously a person with a present, Gen. 33:10. Mal. 1:8. or with offerings and prayers, spoken of the Deity, Job 33:26. Ezek. 20:40. Ps. 51:18. Also *to be on good terms* or *in friendship with* a person, construed with עִם, Ps. 50:18. Job 34:9. (Comp. רָעָה no. II. with which this verb here agrees in signification.) Construed with an infin. *to be pleased to do* a thing, Ps. 40:14. Used absolutely, *to be gracious*, Ps. 77:8. Am. 5:22.

2. i.q. Hiph. *to pay off, discharge*, Lev. 26:34, 41. 2 Chr. 36:21.

Niph. 1. *to be well pleasing, to be graciously received*, used only in reference to offerings, (see Kal no. 1.) Lat. *litare*. Lev. 19:7. 22:23, 27. 7:18. 22:25. 1:4. (In the two last passages there is a pleonastic dative of the pronoun לוֹ, לָכֶם.) It is synonymous with הָיָה לְרָצוֹן Lev. 22:20.

2. prob. *to be paid off* or *discharged*, pass. of Hiph. Is. 40:2. See Hiph.

Pi. *to seek the favour of* a person. Job 20:10 *his sons must seek the favour of the poor;* or else *must satisfy* or *propitiate them;* (Arab. رضى conj. II.) here by the restoration of plundered goods.

Hiph. *to satisfy* (a creditor), hence *to pay off*, (like הִרְצָה in Talmud). Lev. 26:34 *then shall the land rest and pay its sabbaths*. In the beginning of the verse and in 2 Chr. 36:21, Kal is used in the same connexion. Comp. Lev. 26:41, 43. and in Niph. Is. 40:2. Others: *and the land shall be satisfied with its sabbaths*, and so in the other passages; but an ironical expression here appears out of place.

Hiph. *to make one's self pleasing*, construed with אֶל. 1 Sam. 29:4.

Deriv. רָצוֹן.

רָצוֹן m. verbal from רָצָה, dec. III. a.

1. *acceptance, delight, satisfaction*. Prov. 14:35.—לְרָצוֹן Is. 56:7. Jer. 6:20. and עַל רָצוֹן Is. 60:7. *for acceptance* (with God), i. e. well-pleasing to him. Ex. 28:38 לְרָצוֹן לָהֶם לִפְנֵי יְהוָה *for acceptance for them with Jehovah;* i. e. to make them acceptable to Jehovah; comp. Lev. 22:20, 21. 19:5 לִרְצֹנְכֶם *so that you may be accepted, rite, ita ut litet*. 22:19, 29. 23:11.

2. *what is acceptable, an object of delight*. Prov. 11:1, 20. 12:22. 15:8. 16:13. Particularly *what is acceptable to God*, Prov. 10:32. Mal. 2:13.

3. *grace, favour, good-will;* e. g. of a king, Prov. 16:15. 19:12. particularly of God, Ps. 5:13. 30:7. Is. 49:8 בְּעֵת רָצוֹן *in a time of favour*. Hence *expressions of favour, benefits*. Ps. 145:16. Deut. 33:23.

4. *will, pleasure*, (i. q. Chald. רְעוּת.) Ps. 40:9. 103:21. 2 Chr. 15:15 בְּכָל־רְצוֹנָם *with their whole will*, i. e. with all their heart.—עֲשׂוֹת כִּרְצוֹנוֹ *to do as one pleases*, Est. 1:8. particularly as a description of absolute power, Dan. 8:4. 11:3, 16. construed with בְּ, *to treat* a person *as one pleases*, Neh. 9:24, 37. Est. 9:5.

5. *self-will, wantonness*. Gen. 49:6.

רָצַח 1. *to dash in pieces*. See Pi. no. 1. and the deriv. רֶצַח.

2. *to slay, kill*. Num. 35:6 ff.—רָצַח נֶפֶשׁ *to smite dead*, Deut. 22:20. comp. הִכָּה no. 3.

Niph. pass. of Kal no. 2. Judg. 20:4.

Pi. 1. *to dash in pieces, destroy*. Ps. 62:4.

2. i. q. Kal no. 2. Is. 1:21.

רֶצַח m. verbal from רָצַח, *a wounding, slaying, slaughter*. Ps. 42:11 *for a wounding in my bones*, i. e. to my bitterest anguish. Ezek. 21:27.

רָצַע *to pierce, bore through*. Ex. 21:6. (Arab. conj. IV. *idem*.) Deriv. מַרְצֵעַ.

רָצַף *to arrange with art*, particularly stones for a pavement. Applied also to the inlaying of wood-work, Cant. 3:10. Deriv. out of course מַרְצֶפֶת.

רֶצֶף m. verbal from רָצַף, dec. VI. h.

1. *a hot stone*, which the orientalists made use of to roast meat upon, or to

throw into milk or broth in order to heat it. 1 K. 19:6 עֻגַת רְצָפִים *a cake baked on hot stones.* According to the Rabbins, *coals.*

2. proper name of a city subject to the Assyrians. Is. 37:12. Perhaps Ῥησαφα of Ptolemy, in Palmyrene, Arab. رُصَافَة.

רִצְפָּה com. gen. verbal from רָצַף, dec. X.

1. i. q. רֶצֶף *a hot stone.* Is. 6:6. Vulg. *calculus.* According to the Sept. and the Rabbins, *a coal.*

2. *a pavement, pavimentum.* Est. 1:6. 2 Chr. 7:3. Ezek. 40:17, 18.

רָצַץ (Arab. with ض,) kindred with רָצַע.

1. *to smite* or *dash in pieces, to bruise.* Is. 42:3 קָנֶה רָצוּץ *a bruised reed.* 36:6. 2 K. 18:21.

2. metaphorically *to oppress, treat with violence;* often connected with עָשַׁק. 1 Sam. 12:3, 4. Am. 4:1. Is. 58:6. Deut. 28:33.

Note. The fut. יָרוּץ Is. 42:4. תָּרֻץ Ecc. 12:6. (as if from רוּץ,) is used intransitively, *to be bruised* or *broken.*

Niph. נָרוֹץ, (as if from רוּץ,) pass. of Kal no. 1. Ecc. 12:6. Ezek. 29:7.

Pi. רִצֵּץ *to dash in pieces.* Ps. 74:14.

2. i. q. Kal no. 2. Job 20:19. 2 Chr. 16:10.

Po. רוֹצֵץ i. q. Kal and Pi. no. 2. Judg. 10:8. This form Nah. 2:5, pertains to רוּץ *to run.*

Hiph. fut. תָּרֶץ, (as if from רוּץ,) Judg. 9:53. *to dash in pieces.*

Hithpo. *to struggle.* Gen. 25:22.

Deriv. מְרוּצָה, רַץ.

רַק verbal from רָקַק no. I. dec. VIII. h.

1. as an adj. *thin.* Gen. 41:19, 20, 27.

2. as an adv. (1.) *only.* Gen. 6:5. Is. 4:1. After a negation, *except,* Josh. 11:22. (2.) at the beginning of a sentence, *indeed, certainly, surely.* Gen. 20:11. Num. 5:6. Ps. 32:6 רַק לְשֵׁטֶף מַיִם רַבִּים וגו׳ *surely, as to the floods of great waters,* etc.

רֵק *empty,* see **רֵיק**.

רֹק m. with suff. רֻקִּי, verbal from רָקַק no. II. dec. VIII. d. *spittle.* Job 7:19. 30:10. Is. 50:6.

רָקַב, fut. יִרְקַב, *to be worm-eaten, to rot,* spoken of wood. Is. 40:20. Metaphorically Prov. 10:7. comp. the Rabbinic phrase, *ascendit putredo in nomen alicujus.* Hence

רָקָב m. verbal from רָקַב, dec. IV. a.

1. *a being eaten by worms, rottenness.* Job 13:28. Hos. 5:12.

2. *rottenness* or *an internal wasting* (of the bones). Prov. 12:4. 14:30. Metaphorically Hab. 3:16.

רִקָּבוֹן m. i. q. רָקָב no. 1. verbal from רָקַב, *rottenness.* Job 41:19. [41:27.]

רָקַד *to skip, dance.* Ecc. 3:4. Spoken of inanimate nature, Ps. 114:4, 6.

Pi. *to leap, to dance.* 1 Chr. 15:29. Is. 13:21. Job 21:11. Applied also to *the jolting up and down* of a swift chariot on a rough road, Nah. 3:2. Joel 2:5.

Hiph. *to cause to skip.* Ps. 29:6. Comp. רָעַשׁ and נָתַר.

רַקָּה f. verbal from רָקַק no. I. dec. X.

1. liter. *thinness,* hence *the temples, tempora.* Judg. 4:21, 22. 5:26.

2. poetically *cheeks.* Cant. 4:3. 6:7. Comp. *tempora,* Prop. II. 24:3.

רָקַח *to spice, season;* particularly oil in the preparing of ointments. Ex. 30:33. Part. רֹקֵחַ *a maker of ointments, an apothecary,* 30:35. Ecc. 10:1.

Pu. pass. 2 Chr. 16:14.

Hiph. *to spice* or *season* (flesh). Ezek. 24:10.

Deriv. out of course מִרְקַחַת, מֶרְקָחָה, מִרְקַחַת.

רֶקַח m. verbal from רָקַח, *a spicing* or *seasoning.* יֵין הָרֶקַח *spiced wine,* Cant. 8:2.

רֹקַח m. verbal from רָקַח, dec. VI.

that which is seasoned, an ointment, a confection. Ex. 30 : 25.

רַקָּח m. verbal from רָקַח, dec. I. *a confectionary, apothecary, pigmentarius.* 1 Sam. 8 : 13. Neh. 3 : 8.

רִקֻּחִים masc. plur. verbal from רָקַח, dec. I. *ointments, perfumes.* Is. 57 : 9.

רָקִיעַ m. verbal from רָקַע, dec. III. a. in full רְקִיעַ הַשָּׁמַיִם (Gen. 1 : 14, 15, 17.) *the expanse,* i. e. the arch or vault, *of heaven,* which the ancients supposed to rest like a hollow hemisphere on the earth. The Hebrews appear to have regarded it as transparent like a crystal or sapphire, (Ezek. 1 : 22. Dan. 12 : 3. Ex. 24 : 10. Apoc. 4 : 6.) of course as something different from the brazen or iron heaven of the Homeric poetry. Over this arch they placed the waters, Gen. 1 : 7. 7 : 11. Ps. 104 : 3. 148 : 4. Sept. *στερέωμα.* Vulg. *firmamentum.* Luth. *Veste.*

רָקִיק m. verbal from רָקַק no. I. dec. III. a. *a thin cake, a wafer.* Ex. 29 : 2, 23. Lev. 8 : 26.

רָקַם 1. *to variegate, to make party-coloured.* (In Arab. *to mark with points;* conj. II. *to draw lines.*)

2. particularly *to work cloth with various colours.* Part. רֹקֵם *one that works cloth with various colours,* Ex. 26 : 36. 27 : 16. 28 : 39. 38 : 18. different from חֹשֵׁב *a worker in damask,* q. v. Others: *an embroiderer.* (Span. *recamare,* Ital. *ricamare, to embroider.*) As opposed to this explanation, see Ps. 139 : 15. comp. Job 10 : 11. and Hartmann's Hebräerin, Th. 3. p. 138 ff.

Pu. Ps. 139 : 15 *when I was curiously wrought in the lowest parts of the earth.*

רִקְמָה f. verbal from רָקַם, dec. XII. b.

1. *a variegation of colour,* spoken of the eagle, Ezek. 17 : 3. of many coloured stones, 1 Chr. 29 : 2. comp. פּוּךְ.

2. *a party-coloured cloth* or *garment.* Ezek. 16 : 13, 16. 27 : 16. Plur. Ps. 45 : 15. Dual רִקְמָתַיִם *two party-coloured garments,* or joined with צֶבַע, *stuff worked on both sides,* Judg. 5 : 30.

רָקַע 1. *to stamp* (with the feet), to express indignation, Ezek. 6 : 11. to express joy, Ezek. 25 : 6.

2. *to stamp* or *beat out.* See Piel. Hence

3. *to spread out,* but only solid bodies, as e. g. the earth, Ps. 136 : 6. Is. 42 : 5, (here in reference also to plants by a zeugma.) 44 : 24. (In Syr. *to found, establish.*)

4. *to tread down.* 2 Sam. 22 : 43.

Pi. *to beat* or *hammer out,* e. g. metallic plates, Ex. 39 : 3. Num. 17 : 4. [16 : 39.] *to overlay,* (with metallic plates,) Is. 40 : 19.

Pu. part. *beat* or *spread into plates.* Jer. 10 : 9.

Hiph. i. q. Kal no. 3. *to spread out,* e. g. the heavens. Job 37 : 18.

Deriv. רָקִיעַ, and

רִקֻּעִים masc. plur. verbal from רָקַע, dec. I. *metallic plates.* Num. 17 : 3. [16 : 38.]

I. רָקַק, Arab. رَقَّ, *to be thin,* a root not in use. Deriv. רַק, רַקָּה, רָקִיק.

II. רָקַק i. q. יָרַק *to spit on.* Found only in the fut. Lev. 15 : 8. Deriv. רֹק.

רָשׁ *poor,* see רוּשׁ.

רִשְׁיוֹן m. dec. I. *a grant, permission.* Ezra. 3 : 7. (Chald. רְשָׁא *to have permission, to be able;* רְשׁוּת *permission.*)

רֵשִׁית *a beginning,* see רֵאשִׁית.

רָשַׁם *to note, write down.* Dan. 10 : 21. (Arab. رشم *idem.*)

רְשַׁם Chald. *idem.* Fut. יִרְשֻׁם Dan. 6 : 9. Peil. רְשִׁים pass. Dan. 5 : 24, 25.

רָשַׁע (the opposite of צָדַק.)

1. *to be guilty, to be liable to punishment.* Job 9 : 29. 10 : 7, 15.

2. *to be wicked, to act wickedly.* 1 K. 8 : 47. Dan. 9 : 15. Construed with מִן *against* a person, Ps. 18 : 22.

Hiph. 1. *to pronounce guilty, to condemn,* spoken particularly of a judge. Ex. 22 : 8. Deut. 25 : 1. Job 32 : 3. Is. 50 : 9.

2. intrans. *to be wicked, to act wickedly.* 2 Chr. 20:35, (with לַעֲשׂוֹת.) 22:3. Job 34:12. Dan. 12:10. 11:32 מַרְשִׁיעֵי בְרִית *who do wickedly against the covenant.*

3. prob. *to conquer, be victorious.* (The Hebrews, regarding every victory and every overthrow as a kind of divine judgment, very naturally associated *a righteous cause* with *victory*, and *an unrighteous cause* with *defeat;* e.g. זָכָה *to be innocent*, in Syr. *to conquer;* צֶדֶק *righteousness* and *deliverance;* comp. יְשׁוּעָה *deliverance* and *victory.* So here *to represent as unrighteous, to conquer.*) 1 Sam. 14:47 *and whithersoever he turned himself,* יַרְשִׁיעַ *he conquered* or *was victorious.* Sept. ἐσώζετο. Vulg. *superabat.* Others make the primary signification of רָשַׁע *to be restless, to disturb the peace;* here, therefore, *to spread disturbance, terror.*

רָשָׁע (the opposite of צַדִּיק,) verbal adj. from רָשַׁע, dec. IV. a.

1. *one that has an unrighteous cause,* (in law.) Ex. 23:7. Deut. 25:1.

2. *guilty, punishable.* Gen. 18:23, 25.—רָשָׁע לָמוּת *guilty of death,* Num. 35:31.

3. *wicked, ungodly,* and as a subst. *a wicked* or *ungodly person.* Ps. 1:1, 4. Often spoken of the heathen, as foes of the Israelites, in opposition to עֲנָוִים *the virtuous* (Israelitish) *sufferers,* Ps. 10:2. comp. 84:11. 125:3. Comp. οἱ ἄνομοι, used for *the heathen,* 1 Macc. 2:44. 3:5. Acts 2:23.

רֶשַׁע m. with suff. רִשְׁעִי, verbal from רָשַׁע, dec. VI. i.

1. *unrighteousness, injustice,* the opposite of צֶדֶק.—אֹצְרוֹת רֶשַׁע *treasures of wickedness,* i.e. wealth unjustly acquired, Mic. 6:10. מֹאזְנֵי רֶשַׁע *a false balance,* Mic. 6:11.

2. *wickedness.* Ps. 5:5. 45:8. Plur. Job 34:26 תַּחַת רְשָׁעִים *on account of wickedness.*

רִשְׁעָה f. verbal from רָשַׁע, dec. X.

1. *guilt.* Deut. 25:2.

2. *wickedness.* Is. 9:17. Mal. 3:15.

רֶשֶׁף m. dec. VI. h.

1. *a flame, strong heat.* (So in Chald. Ps. 78:48 Targ.) Cant. 8:6.

2. *the flame of Jehovah* or *the lightning.* Probably Ps. 78:48. Hence Ps. 76:4 רִשְׁפֵי קָשֶׁת *the lightnings of the bow,* a poetical expression for *the arrows.* So prob. also בְּנֵי רֶשֶׁף Job 5:7, *arrows;* (or else *sons of the flame,* i.e. sparks.)

3. *a burning pestilence,* (comp. חֵמָה *heat* and *poison.*) Deut. 32:24 לְחֻמֵי רֶשֶׁף *devoured of the burning pestilence.* Hab. 3:5, (parall. דֶּבֶר *pestilence;*) or it may be placed under no. 2. *lightning.*

Note. On account of Job 5:7, where the ancient translators have rendered the word *bird, bird of prey,* (comp. Arab. رشف, conj. VIII. *in altum elatus, sublatus est;*) many critics have made this the primary signification, and have endeavoured to apply it to the other passages; in opposition to whom, see G. Th. Steger Comment. de Vocabulo רֶשֶׁף. Kiliæ, 1808. and Gesenius' larger Lexicon, p. 1077.

רָשַׁשׁ *to break in pieces, to destroy.* In Kal not used.

Po. *idem.* Jer. 5:17.

Pu. pass. Mal. 1:4.

רֶשֶׁת f. with suff. רִשְׁתִּי, (perhaps strictly an infin. from יָרַשׁ *to take into possession,* hence *to take, catch,*) dec. VI. h.

1. *a net.* Ps. 57:7. 9:16. 31:5. Lam. 1:13.—פָּרַשׂ רֶשֶׁת עַל *to spread* or *throw a net over* any thing, Ezek. 12:13. 17:20. 32:3.

2. *net-work, lattice-work.* Ex. 27:4.

רַתּוֹק m. Ezek. 7:23. and **רַתּוּקָה** dec. X. 1 K. 6:21 Keth. *a chain.* Root רָתַק.

רָתַח *to boil.*

Pi. *to cause to boil.* Ezek. 24:5.

Pu. *to be agitated,* spoken of the bowels. Job 30:27.

Hiph. i.q. Pi. Job 41:23. [41:31.] (In Syr. and Chald. *idem.*)

רֶתַח m. verbal from רָתַח, dec. VI. i. *a boiling.* Ezek. 24:5.

רָתַם *to bind*, hence *to yoke* or *harness*. Mic. 1:13. (Comp. אָסַר no. 4.) In Arab. *to bind a thread about the finger*. Hence

רֹתֶם m. (fem. in the Kethib of 1 K. 19:4.) plur. רְתָמִים, dec. VI. 1 K. 19:4, 5. Job 30:4. Ps. 120:4. according to the Jewish interpreters and Jerome, *the juniper-tree*; more correctly i. q. Arab. رَتَم *broom*, (*spartium junceum*, Linn.) which grows common in the desert parts of Arabia, has yellowish flowers and a bitter root, and can serve, therefore, only for a very poor nourishment, (see Job 30:4.) Probably so called from its use *in binding*. See Celsii Hierobot. T. I. Œdmann's verm. Sammlungen aus der Naturkunde. H. II. cap. 8.

רָתַק *to bind, to chain*. In Arab. *to bind, shut up, close*.

Niph. prob. in a privative sense, *to be unbound, to be loosed*, Ecc. 12:6 Keri. The Kethib reads יִרְחַק *it is removed*.

Pu. *to be bound, fettered*. Nah. 3:10.

Deriv. רַתּוֹק and

רַתֻּקוֹת fem. plur. verbal from רָתַק, *chains*. Is. 40:19.

רְתֵת m. Hos. 13:1 i. q. רֶטֶט *terror*. (Aram. رَتّ, רְתַת *to terrify*; רְתִיתָא *terror*.)

שׂ

The relation of *Sin* to *Samech* has been already explained under that letter. In this lexicon *Sin* is everywhere regarded as a distinct letter from *Shin*, and placed before it; a circumstance, which must be borne in mind in the looking out of words. In adopting this arrangement, the example of the Arabic lexicographers has been followed.

שְׂאֹר m. *leaven*. Ex. 12:15, 19. (Chald. סְאוֹר *idem*. In Arab. سَارَ med. Vav *to rise, ferment*, spoken of wine, of anger.)

שְׂאֵת m. (strictly an infin. from נָשָׂא,) with suff. שְׂאֵתִי.

1. *a raising* (of the countenance), hence *joy*. Gen. 4:7. It is in this case regarded as the opposite of נָפְלוּ פָנִים in verse 6. Others: *acceptance, forgiveness*, after נָשָׂא no. 3. (1.) (a.)

2. *a rising, swelling*, on the skin. Lev. 13:2, 10, 19.

3. *exaltation, dignity*. Gen. 49:3. Job 13:11.

4. *a judicial sentence*, (comp. מַשָּׂא no. 4. and נָשָׂא no 1. (6.) *to pronounce*.) Hab. 1:7. Others: *arrogance*.

שְׂבָךְ m. dec. II. c. i. q. שְׂבָכָה. 1 K. 7:17. Root סָבַךְ *to weave*.

שְׂבָכָה fem. of שְׂבָךְ, dec. X.

1. *a net*. Job 18:8.

2. *a lattice, lattice-work*. 2 K. 1:2. 1 K. 7:18, 20, 41. With such lattice-work the chapiters of the pillars were overspread.

שַׂבְּכָא *the sambuca*, see סַבְּכָא.

שְׂבָם Num. 32:3. and שִׂבְמָה verse 38. Josh. 13:19. Is. 16:8, 9. proper name of a city in the tribe of Reuben, abounding in vines.

שָׂבַע and שָׂבֵעַ.

1. *to be satisfied, satiated, filled*; strictly with food, (comp. רָוָה *to be satisfied with drink*,) but sometimes also in reference to drink, Am. 4:8. and spoken of the earth or trees, Prov. 30:16. Ps. 104:16. The thing *with* which a person is satisfied is put in the accus. e. g. שָׂבַע לֶחֶם *to be satisfied with bread*, Ex. 16:12. Job 27:14. Ecc. 5:9. or is preceded by מִן, Prov. 14:14. 18:20. by בְּ, Ps. 66:5. or is expressed by לְ before an infin. Ecc. 1:8. Metaphorically *to be satisfied* or *filled* with reproach, Lam. 3:30. Hab. 2:11. with contempt, Ps. 123:3. with adversity, Ps. 88:4. Sometimes in reference to affluence and its occasioning pride, Prov. 30:9 *lest I be full and deny God*. Hos. 13:6.

2. *to be tired, weary, disgusted,* (with any thing.) Is. 1:11. Job 7:4. Prov. 25:17.—שְׂבַע יָמִים *to be full of days,* 1 Chr. 23:1. 2 Chr. 24:15.

Pi. *to satisfy.* Ezek. 7:19. Construed with a double accus. of the person and thing, Ps. 90:14.

Hiph. *to satisfy.* Ps. 107:9. Construed with a double accus. of the person and thing, Ps. 81:17. 132:15. with מִן of the thing, Ezek. 32:4. with בְּ, Ps. 103:5. Once with לְ of the person, Ps. 145:16. Trop. Ps. 91:16.

שָׂבֵעַ m. verbal adj. from שָׂבַע, dec. V. a.

1. *full, satisfied.* Prov. 27:7. 1 Sam. 2:5.

2. *full, tired, weary* (of any thing).—שְׂבַע יָמִים *full of days,* Gen. 35:29. Job 42:17. also simply שָׂבֵעַ in the same sense, Gen. 25:8.

3. *rich* or *abounding in* any thing. שְׂבַע רָצוֹן *rich in* (God's) *grace.* Deut. 33:23. Job 14:1. 10:15.

שָׂבָע m. verbal from שָׂבַע, *satiety,* hence *abundance, plenty.* Prov. 3:10. Gen. 41:29 ff.

שֹׂבַע m. verbal from שָׂבַע, dec. VI. p.

1. *satiety.* לָשֹׂבַע *to satiety, to the full,* Ex. 16:3.

2. *fulness.* Ps. 16:11.

שִׂבְעָה f. Ezek. 16:49. and **שָׂבְעָה** f. Ruth 2:18. verbals from שָׂבַע, dec. X. *fullness, satiety.*—לְשָׂבְעָה *to satiety, to the full,* Is. 23:18. Ezek. 39:19.

שָׂבַר *to observe, view,* construed with בְּ. Neh. 2:13, 15. (In Chald. סְבַר i. q. Heb. בִּין.)

Pi. 1. *to wait.* Ruth 1:13.

2. *to hope.* Est. 9:1. Construed with אֶל and לְ of the person, Ps. 104:27. 119:166. (So in Aram. in Pe. and Pa.)

3. perhaps *to praise, to announce with praise.* Is. 38:18. i. q. ܫܰܒܰܚ in Syr. The second signification, however, applies very well.

שֵׂבֶר or **שֶׂבֶר** m. found only with suff. שִׂבְרִי, verbal from שָׂבַר, dec. VI. g. *hope.* Ps. 119:116. 146:5.

שָׂגָא i. q. Aram. סְגָא *to become great, to grow.* See שָׂגָה. Found only in Hiph. *to make great, to exalt.* Job 12:23. 36:24.

שְׂגָא Chald. *idem.* Ezra 4:22.—שְׁלָמְכוֹן יִשְׂגֵּא *may your peace be great,* a form of salutation, Dan. 6:26.

שָׂגַב i. q. רוּם, but (excepting Deut. 2:36.) used only in poetry.

1. *to rise, mount.* Job 5:11.

2. *to be high,* (See Niph.) Hence spoken of a city, *to be fast, strong, invincible,* Deut. 2:36.

Niph. 1. *to be high.* Prov. 18:11.

2. *to be exalted,* spoken of God. Ps. 148:13. Is. 2:11.

3. *to be high, incomprehensible, inconceivable.* Ps. 139:6.

4. *to be protected, to be safe.* Prov. 18:10. (Comp. מִשְׂגָּב.)

Pi. *to raise up,* but only in a figurative sense, (like Niph. no. 4.) *to protect, defend.* Ps. 20:2. 69:30. 91:14. Construed with מִן, *to defend from* any one, Ps. 59:2. 107:41.

Pu. pass. *to be protected, to be safe.* Prov. 29:25.

Hiph. intrans. *to be exalted.* Job 36:22.

שָׂגַג i. q. שָׂגָא and שָׂגָה. Found only in Pil. שִׂגְשֵׂג *to cause to grow.* Is. 17:11.

שָׂגָה *to become great, to grow,* i. q. שָׂגָא. Job 8:7, 11. Ps. 92:13.

Hiph. *to make great, to increase.* Ps. 73:12.

שַׂגִּיא m. verbal from שָׂגָא, *great.* Job 36:26. 37:23.

שַׂגִּיא Chald. 1. *great.* Dan. 2:31.

2. *much, many.* Dan. 2:48. 4:9.

3. as an adv. *very, valde.* Dan. 2:12. 5:9.

שָׂדַד found only in Pi. *to harrow.* Is. 28:24. Job 39:10. Hos. 10:11.

שָׂדֶה m. plur. שָׂדוֹת, const. always שְׂדֵה, dec. IX. b.

1. *a field, a piece of cultivated ground.* Gen. 23:17. 47:20, 24. In

opposition to a garden or vineyard, Ex. 22:4. Num. 20:17.

2. *a field* generally; e g. חַיַּת הַשָּׂדֶה *the wild beasts of the field*, Is. 43:20. אִישׁ שָׂדֶה *a man living in the field, a hunter*, Gen. 25:27.

3. *a country, territory*, like the Lat. *ager*. Gen. 14:7 שְׂדֵה הָעֲמָלֵקִי *the territory of the Amalekites*. Gen. 32:3. Ruth 1:6.

4. שְׂדֵה־אֲרָם i. q. פַּדַּן־אֲרָם *the plain of Syria*, i. e. Mesopotamia. Hos. 12:13.

שָׂדַי poetically for שָׂדֶה *a field*. Ps. 8:8. 50:11. 80:14, etc. That it is the singular, and not the ancient plural form with ַי for ִים, is shewn by Ps. 96:12. In Arabic the termination ـَي is the usual one for the Heb. ֶה.

שִׂדִּים in full עֵמֶק הַשִּׂדִּים *the vale of Siddim*, which afterwards became the Dead Sea. Gen. 14:3, 8, 18.

שְׂדֵרָה f. dec. X. i. q. סֵדֶר *an order, row;* of soldiers, 2 K. 11:8, 15. of chambers, 1 K. 6:9.

שֶׂה com. gen. (for שֶׂיֶה, like פֶּה for פֶּאֶה,) const. שֵׂה, with suff. שֵׂיוֹ and שֵׂיהוּ (from שָׂיָה), prim. irreg. *one of the smaller cattle, a sheep* or *goat*, the nomen unitatis corresponding to צֹאן *small cattle*, q. v. Gen. 22:7, 8. 30. 32. Ex. 12:3 ff. Sometimes defined more accurately, Deut. 14:4 שֵׂה כְשָׂבִים וְשֵׂה עִזִּים *a sheep and a goat*. The same relation exists between the words שׁוֹר *one of the larger cattle*, and בָּקָר *large cattle* collectively.

שָׂהֵד m. (with Kamets impure, like the Aramean participle,) dec. VII. a. *a witness*. Once Job 16:19. (In Chald. and Syr. with ס, *idem*.) Hence

שָׂהֲדוּתָא f. Syr. and Chald. *testimony*. Gen. 31:47.

שַׂהֲרֹנִים masc. plur. small ornaments in the form of a half moon, worn on the neck by men and women, also by camels. Judg. 8:21, 26. Is. 3:18. Sept. μηνίσκοι. Vulg. *lunulæ*. In Aram. סַהֲרָא *the moon*, (see סַהַר.) ון is the termination of diminutives, as in אִישׁוֹן.

שׂוּב *to have gray hairs*, see שִׂיב.

שׂוֹבֶךְ dec. VI. i. q. סְבַךְ *thick branches, a thicket*. 2 Sam. 18:9. See סְבַךְ.

שׂוּג i. q. סוּג *to turn back*. Only in Niph. 2 Sam. 1:22, where several MSS. and editions read it with ס.

שׂוּד *to white-wash, to plaster*, see שִׂיד.

שׂוּחַ found only Gen. 24:63. i. q. שִׂיחַ here *to meditate*, (Vulg. *ad meditandum*,) or else *to walk, wander, obambulare*, i. q. Arab. ساح med. Je. Comp. the subst. שִׂיחַ no. 3.

שׂוּט or שִׂיט i. q. שָׂטָה *to incline to any thing*. Ps. 40:5. Deriv. שֵׂטִים, סֵטִים.

שׂוּךְ *to hedge in, to hedge round*. (See the kindred forms סוּג and סָכַךְ, no. II.) Job 1:10 שַׂכְתָּ בַעֲדוֹ *thou hedgest him round about*, i. e. thou protectest him. The same phrase also denotes *to hedge in, to give no way of escape*, (comp. גָּדַר,) Job 3:23. 38:8. Hos. 2:8. [2:6.]

Pil. שׂוֹכֵךְ *to twist, weave*. Job 10:11 בַּעֲצָמוֹת וְגִידִים תְּשֹׂכְכֵנִי *out of bones and muscles hast thou woven me;* comp. Ps. 139:13.

Deriv. out of course מְסוּכָה and מְשׂוּכָה; comp. שׂוֹכֵךְ no. II.

שׂוֹךְ m. dec. I. Judg. 9:49. and שׂוֹכָה f. dec. X. Judg. 9:48. verbals from שׂוּךְ, *a bough, branch*. (Chald. סוֹךְ and שׂוֹךְ, Syr. ܣܘܟܐ *idem*.)

שׂוֹכֹה proper name of a city in the plain of the tribe of Judah. Josh. 15:35. From this place Antigonus Sochæus obtained his surname.

שׂוּם and שִׂים, fut. יָשִׂים, apoc. יָשֵׂם, וַיָּשֶׂם, once יָשׂוּם (Ex. 4:11.) imper. שִׂים, infin. absol. שׂוֹם, const. שׂוּם, rarely שִׂים (Job 20:4.)

1. *to set, place, put*, in any manner. The following are the phrases most worthy of notice; (1.) *to arrange* (an army). Job 1:17. Josh. 8:2, 13. also

intrans. (or by an ellipsis of the accus. מִלְחָמָה *aciem,*) *to set themselves in battle-array,* 1 K. 20 : 12. Ezek. 23 : 24. (comp. in Hiph. Ezek. 21 : 21. [21 : 16.]) 1 Sam. 15 : 2 אֲשֶׁר שָׂם לוֹ בַּדֶּרֶךְ *when he arrayed himself against him in the way.* The verbs עָרַךְ (see no. 2.) and שִׁית are used in a similar elliptical manner. (2.) *to ordain, establish.* Gen. 47 : 26. Ex. 21 : 13. (3) *to appoint.* Hos. 2 : 2. [1 : 11.] Construed with two accus. 1 Sam. 8 : 1. or with לְ of the predicate, Gen. 45 : 9. Ex. 2 : 14. Construed with עַל of the thing, *to place* or *appoint over* any thing, Ex. 1 : 11. 5 : 14. (4.) *to lay upon* a person; construed with עַל of the person, Ex. 5 : 8. 22 : 24. with בְּ, Deut. 7 : 15. Also *to impute* or *charge to* a person, construed with לְ, Deut. 22 : 14, 17. with בְּ, 1 Sam. 22 : 15. Job 4 : 18. with עַל, Judg. 9 : 24. (5.) *to put on* (a garment). Ruth 3 : 3. (6.) *to place* (a surety). Job 17 : 3. (7.) שׂוּם שֵׁם לְ *to give a name to* a person. Dan. 1 : 7. comp. Judg. 8 : 31. Neh. 9 : 7. Comp. in Chald. Dan. 5 : 12. (8.) שׂוּם שְׁמוֹ *to put one's name* in a place, i. e. to fix his dwelling there, spoken of Jehovah. Deut. 12 : 5, 21. 14 : 24 לָשׂוּם שְׁמוֹ שָׁם *to let his name dwell there.* 1 K. 9 : 3. 11 : 36. 2 K. 21 : 4. Synonymous with שַׁכֵּן שְׁמוֹ Deut. 12 : 11. 26 : 2. (9.) שׂוּם בָּנִים *to beget children.* Ezra 10 : 44. (10.) שׂוּם בְּאָזְנֵי פ׳ *to instruct a person about* any thing. Ex. 17 : 14. (11.) שׂוּם לֵב *to attend, consider, animum advertere.* Is. 41 : 22. Hag. 2 : 15, 18. Without לֵב, *idem,* Is. 41 : 20. Job 34 : 23. Judg. 19 : 30. See a similar ellipsis under הֵכִין no 4. The thing *attended to* is preceded by עַל, Job 1 : 8. by אֶל, Ex. 9 : 21. by לְ, Deut. 32 : 46. Ezek. 40 : 4. by בְּ, Job 23 : 6. (12.) שׂוּם עַל לֵב *to lay to heart.* Is. 57 : 1, 11. Also with אֶל, 2 Sam. 13 : 33. with בְּ, 1 Sam. 21 : 13. In the same sense שׂוּם לֵב לְ 1 Sam. 9 : 20. Elliptically Ps. 50 : 23 שָׂם דֶּרֶךְ scil. עַל לִבּוֹ *who lay his way to heart.* (13.) שׂוּם עַל לֵב also *to purpose, resolve.* Dan. 1 : 8. Mal. 2 : 2. (14.) שׂוּם פָּנִים *to direct one's face,* see under פָּנִים no. 1. (1.) to (3.)—(15.) שׂוּם עַיִן עַל *to direct one's eye to* any one, see עַיִן no. 1. (5.)—(16.) used absolutely, *to heap up.* Job 36 : 13 *the wicked* יָשִׂימוּ אַף *heap up* (God's) *wrath.*

2. *to make,* i. q. נָתַן no. 3. Gen. 4 : 15. 6 : 16.—שׂוּם אֹתוֹת *to perform miracles,* Ex. 10 : 2. Ps. 78 : 43. Particularly *to make into* any thing, (like τίθημι in Homer,) construed with two accus. Ps. 39 : 9. Josh. 8 : 28. with לְ of the predicate, Gen. 21 : 13, 18. or with כְּ, *to make as,* Gen. 32 : 13. 1 K. 19 : 2. The construction is peculiar in Is. 25 : 2 שַׂמְתָּ מֵעִיר לַגַּל *I will make the city an heap.*

3. *to give;* e. g. honour, Josh. 7 : 19. Is. 42 : 12. peace, Num. 6 : 26. *To give* or *shew* favour, Is. 47 : 6. Synonymous with נָתַן.

Hiph. i. q. Kal, found only in the imper. הָשִׂימִי Ezek. 21 : 21. [21 : 16.] and the part מְשִׂים Job 4 : 20.

Hoph. only Gen. 24 : 33 Keri. (See יָשַׂם.)

Deriv. תְּשׂוּמֶת.

שׂוּם Chald. *to set, put, place.* Particularly (1.) *to appoint.* Ezra 5 : 14. (2.) *to issue* (an edict). Dan. 3 : 10, 29. 4 : 3. [4 : 6.] Ezra 4 : 19 ff. (3.) שׂוּם טְעֵם עַל *to regard.* Dan. 3 : 15. (4.) שׂוּם בָּל לְ *to be concerned for* a person. Dan. 6 : 13. (5.) שׂוּם שֻׁם דִּי פ׳ *to name* a person. Dan. 5 : 12.

I. שׂוּר i. q. סוּר *to turn away, to depart.* Hos. 9 : 12.

II. שׂוּר i. q. שָׂרַר *to exercise dominion, to rule.* Fut. וַיָּשַׂר Judg. 9 : 22.

Hiph. הֵשִׂיר *to appoint princes.* Hos. 8 : 4. Comp. also מִשְׂרָה.

III. שׂוּר i. q. שָׂרָה *to contend, struggle.* Hos. 12 : 5. Fut. וַיָּשַׂר.

IV. שׂוּר *to saw,* i. q. Chald. נְסַר. Fut. וַיָּשַׂר 1 Chr. 20 : 3. See מַשּׂוֹר.

שׂוֹרָה f. Is. 28 : 25. see שׂוֹרָה.

שׂוֹרֵק see שֹׂרֵק.

שׂוּשׂ and שִׂישׂ, fut. יָשִׂישׂ, once יָשׂוּשׂ (Is. 35 : 1.) imper. שִׂישׂ, infin. absol. שׂוֹשׂ,

const. שׂוּשׂ, *to rejoice*. Job 3:22. Construed with עַל, Deut. 28:63. 30:9. with בְּ, Is. 65:19. Ps. 119:14.—שׂוּשׂ בַּיהוָה *to rejoice in Jehovah*, Ps. 40:17. 70:5. Construed with an accus. Is. 35:1 יְשֻׂשׂוּם *they shall rejoice for them*, i. e. for the divine judgments mentioned in the preceding chapter.

Deriv. מָשׂוֹשׂ, שָׂשׂוֹן.

שֵׂחַ m. dec. I. *a thought*. Amos 4:13. Root. שִׂיחַ *to meditate*.

שָׂחָה *to swim*. Is. 25:11.

Hiph. *to make to swim*, a hyperbolical expression for *to moisten*. Ps. 6:7.

שָׂחוּ f. (Milel, a segolated form for שְׂחִי,) *a swimming*. Ezek. 47:5.

שְׂחוֹק see שְׂחֹק.

שָׂחַט *to press, to press out*. Gen. 40:11. (In Chald. סְחַט *idem*.)

שָׂחַק i. q. צָחַק, but more frequent.

1. *to laugh, smile*. Ecc. 3:4. Construed with אֶל, *to smile on* a person, Job 29:24. with לְ, *to laugh at, to deride*, particularly what is weak and cannot hurt us. Job 5:22. 39:7, 18, 22. 41:21. Ps. 2:4. with עַל, in the same sense, Ps. 52:8. Job 30:1.

2. i. q. Pi. no. 3. Judg. 16:27.

Pi. שִׂחֵק, fut. יְשַׂחֵק.

1. *to mock, deride*. Jer. 15:17.

2. *to play, sport*, spoken e.g. of children, Zech. 8:5. of animals in the sea, Ps. 104:26. comp. Job 40:20, 29. [41:5.]—2 Sam. 2:14 *let the young men arise*, וִישַׂחֲקוּ לְפָנֵינוּ *and play*, i.e. contend, *before us*.

3. *to dance*, with vocal and instrumental music, the constant accompaniment of dancing in the east. Judg. 16:25. 1 Sam. 18:7. 2 Sam. 6:5, 21. 1 Chr. 13:8. 15:29. Hence Jer. 30:19 קוֹל מְשַׂחֲקִים *the voice of dancers*. 31:4 בִּמְחוֹל מְשַׂחֲקִים *in the dance of the dancers*. Prov. 8:30, 31.

Hiph. *to deride*, construed with עַל. 2 Chr. 30:10.

Deriv. מִשְׂחָק and

שְׂחֹק and **שְׂחוֹק** m. verbal from שָׂחַק.

1. *a laughing*. Job 8:21.

2. *an object of laughter* or *derision*. Job 12:4. Jer. 20:7.

3. *sport*. Prov. 10:23.

שֵׂט, plur. שֵׂטִים *transgressions*, Hos. 5:2. i.q. סֵטִים Ps. 101:3. Root שׂוּט.

שָׂטָה, fut. apoc. יֵשְׂטְ.

1. *to deviate* from a way. (In Aram. סְטָא *idem*.) Prov. 4:15.

2. *to be unfaithful*, spoken of a married woman. Num. 5:12. Sometimes with the addition תַּחַת הָאִישׁ Num. 5:19, 20, 29. for מִתַּחַת; comp. Ezek. 23:5. with Hos. 4:12.

שָׂטַם, fut יִשְׂטֹם, i. q. שָׂטַן, (comp. the letter ם, p.303.) *to hate, persecute*. Gen. 27:41. 50:15. Job 16:9. 30:21.

שָׂטַן *to be hostile, to oppose, persecute*. (Aram. with ס, Arab. with ش *idem*.) Ps. 38:21. 109:4. 71:13. 109:20, 29.

שָׂטָן verbal from שָׂטַן.

1. *an adversary, opponent*. (Arab. شَيْطَان *idem*.) E. g. in war, 1 K. 4:18. [5:4.] 11:14, 23, 25. 1 Sam. 29:4. before a court, Ps. 109:6. (comp. Zech. 3:1, 2.) and generally *one that obstructs another's way*, 2 Sam. 19:23. Num. 22:22 *the angel of Jehovah placed himself in the way* לְשָׂטָן לוֹ *to resist him*, verse 32.

2. with the article הַשָּׂטָן *the adversary*, by way of eminence, *Satan*, an evil angel, according to the later theological views of the Jews, who excites men to evil, (1 Chr. 12:1. comp. 2 Sam. 24:1.) and accuses and calumniates them before God, Zech. 3:1, 2. Job 1:7. 2:2 ff. Comp. Rev. 12:10 ὁ κατήγωρ τῶν ἀδελφῶν ἡμῶν, ὁ κατηγορῶν αὐτῶν ἐνώπιον τοῦ Θεοῦ ἡμῶν ἡμέρας καὶ νυκτός. The article (which fails only 1 Chr. 12:1.) shews that the appellative is used here κατ' ἐξοχήν, and makes it almost a proper name. So הַבַּעַל *the god Baal*, הַמִּדְבָּר, הַכִּכָּר, הָהָר. It is in violation of the principles of grammar, criticism, and hermeneutics, that some read in Job

שָׂטָן and render it περιοδεύτης, *a traveller*, as if from שׁוּט.

שִׂטְנָה f. verbal from שָׂטַן.

1. *an accusation.* Ezra 4:6.

2. proper name of a well, so called from *a contention* of Isaac with the Philistines. Gen. 26:21.

שִׂיא m. dec. X. *height, greatness, excellency.* Job 20:6. Synonymous with שׂוֹא, שְׂאֵת. Root נָשָׂא.

שִׂיאֹן another name of Mount Hermon. Deut. 4:48.

שִׂיב *to have gray hairs.* 1 Sam. 12:2. (In Syr. and Arab. with ش *idem.*) Part. שָׂב Job 15:10. Hence

שֵׂיב m. dec. I. (1 K. 14:4.) and

שֵׂיבָה f. dec. X. verbals from שִׂיב.

1. *the gray hairs* (of an old man). Gen. 42:38. 44:29, 31.—אִישׁ שֵׂיבָה *a man of gray hairs,* Deut. 32:25.

2. *old age.* Gen. 15:15. 25:8. By a metonymy, *a person in advanced years,* Ruth 4:15.

שִׂיג m. *a departure, journey.* 1 K. 18:27. Comp. Arab. שׂוּגן *abitio et adventus,* from ساج *lentiore gradu incessit;* or Chald. סְגָה *incessit* i.q. הָלַךְ, hence סִגְיָא *incessus.*

שִׂיד *to cover with lime, to plaster.* (Arab. with ش *idem.*) Deut. 27:2, 4.

שִׂיד m. *lime, plaster, white-wash,* to spread over walls. Deut. 27:2, 4. Is. 33:12. This sense suits also Am. 2:1. comp. Is. 33:12.

שִׂיחַ 1. *to meditate,* particularly on religious subjects. Ps. 77:47. Construed with בְּ *about* a thing, Ps. 119:15, 23, 27, 48, 78, 148. Ps. 77:13.

2. *to speak to* or *address* a person, construed with לְ, Job 12:8. with an accus. Prov. 6:22 תְשִׂיחֶךָ *it shall talk with thee.* Construed with בְּ, *to speak about* a person, Ps. 69:13.

3. *to sing,* comp. the Lat. *meditari carmen.* Judg. 5:10. Ps. 145:5. Construed with בְּ, Ps. 105:2. Comp. שׂוּחַ.

4. *to sigh, lament.* Ps. 55:18. Job 7:11.

Note. These various significations are all united in the synonymous word הָגָה q. v.

Pil. שׂוֹחֵחַ *to meditate.* Ps. 143:5. Is. 53:8. where others apply the significations of Kal no. 2. and no. 4.

Deriv. שֵׂחַ and

I. **שִׂיחַ** m. verbal from שִׂיחַ, dec. I.

1. *a speech, discourse.* 2 K. 9:11.

2. *a lamentation, complaint.* Job 7:13. 9:27. 21:4. 23:2. Ps. 142:3. 1 Sam. 1:16.

3. 1 K. 18:27 שִׂיחַ לוֹ *he is in deep thought,* or *he has business.* So the Hebrew interpreters, (comp. דָּבָר *verbum, res*). Others: *he has a journey,* comp. שׂוּחַ.

II. **שִׂיחַ** m. plur. שִׂיחִים, dec. I. *a plant, shrub, bush.* Gen. 2:5. 21:15. Job 30:4, 7. (Aram. ܫܝܚܐ *tamariscus*).

שִׂיחָה fem. of שִׂיחַ no. I. *a thought, subject of pious meditation.* Ps. 119:97, 99. Job 15:4 שִׂיחָה לִפְנֵי אֵל *pious meditation on God,* (parall. *fear of God;*) or *prayer to God,* comp. שִׂיחַ no. I. 2.

שִׂים *to put, place,* see **שׂוּם**.

שֵׂךְ m. plur. שִׂכִּים, verbal from שָׂכַךְ no. II. dec. VIII. b. *a thorn.* Num. 33:55. (Arab. شَوْكٌ *a thorn*).

שֹׂךְ verbal from שָׂכַךְ no. II. dec. VIII. d. *a hedge.* Lam. 2:6.

שֻׂכָּה f. verbal from שָׂכַךְ no. II. dec. X. *a sharp instrument, a dart,* liter. *a thorn, goad.* Job 40:31. [41:7.] (Arab. شَوْكَة *a goad, a pointed instrument.*)

שֶׂכְוִי m. i.q. מַשְׂכִּית *thought, understanding, heart,* (from Chald. סְכָא *to regard, consider.*) Job 38:36. Comp. טֻחוֹת p. 223. Others: *a meteor, an appearance in the air,* see p. 223.

שְׂכִיָּה f. dec. X. *a sight, picture.* Is. 2:16. כָּל־שְׂכִיּוֹת הַחֶמְדָּה *all pleasant sights.* It appears to be a general expression embracing all the preceding particulars in verses 13—16. Targ. *costly palaces.*

שַׂכִּין m. *a knife.* Prov. 23:2. (In Chald. and Arab. *idem.*)

שָׂכִיר m. verbal from שָׂכַר, dec. III. a. *a hireling, a day-labourer.* Ex. 22:14. Lev. 19:13. Is. 16:14 *in three years* כִּשְׁנֵי שָׂכִיר *as the years of an hireling,* i. e. exactly at this time, as the labourer is exact about the time for which he is hired.

שְׂכִירָה f. verbal from שָׂכַר, *a hiring.* Is. 7:20 תַּעַר הַשְּׂכִירָה *a hired razor, novacula conductionis.*

I. **שָׂכַךְ** i. q. סָכַךְ no. I. *to cover.* Ex. 33:22.

II. **שָׂכַךְ** i. q. סָכַךְ no. II. and שׂוּךְ *to weave, to hedge.* Deriv. שׂוֹךְ, שֹׂךְ, שׂוֹכָה.

שָׂכַל *to act wisely, prudently.* Once 1 Sam. 18:30. (In Arab. شكل *to interweave,* intrans. *to be interwoven, intricate;* hence שֶׂכֶל *cunning.*)

Pi. *to interweave, to cross.* (See Kal according to its Arabic signification.) Gen. 48:14 שִׂכֵּל אֶת־יָדָיו according to the ancient versions, *he laid his hand crosswise.* According to the Hebrew usage, it would be *he laid his hand wisely,* i. e. carefully, or wittingly.

Hiph. 1. *to look at.* Gen. 3:6 וְנֶחְמָד הָעֵץ לְהַשְׂכִּיל *and the tree was desirable to look at.* Vulg. *aspectu delectabile.* (In Chald. אִסְתַּכַּל *idem.* Arab. شَكْل *form, appearance.*)

2. *to consider, to attend to;* construed with an accus. Deut. 32:29. Ps. 64:10. with עַל, Prov. 16:20. with אֶל, Neh. 8:13. Ps. 41:2 מַשְׂכִּיל אֶל דָּל *he that considereth* or *regardeth the poor.* Also with בְּ, Dan. 9:13.

3. *to have understanding, to be* or *become wise* or *intelligent.* Ps. 2:10. 94:8. Construed with בְּ, Dan. 1:4. comp. verse 17. Also *to conduct wisely,* Jer. 20:11. 23:5. Part. מַשְׂכִּיל *wise, intelligent,* Prov. 10:5. hence *religious, pious,* Ps. 14:2. Dan. 11:33, 35. 12:3, 10. (Comp. חָכָם, חָכְמָה.) Infin. הַשְׂכֵּל Jer. 3:15. and הַשְׂכֵּל Prov. 1:3. 21:16. as a subst. *wisdom, understanding.*

4. i. q. הִצְלִיחַ *to prosper* (in an undertaking). Josh. 1:7, 8. 2 K. 18:7. Is. 52:13. Jer. 10:21. Prov. 17:8.—Also the two latter significations causatively; hence

5. *to make wise, to instruct.* Ps. 32:8. Construed with two accus. Dan. 9:22. with לְ of the person, Prov. 21:11.

6. *to cause to prosper.* 1 K. 2:3.

Part. מַשְׂכִּיל used substantively *a song, poem,* Ps. 47:8. and in the superscriptions of 13 Psalms, (viz. XXXII. XLII. LII. LIII. LIV. etc.) Probably derived from the Arabic signification of the root, (see Kal,) *to be interwoven, intricate,* in the derivatives also *figuratum esse,* (comp. חִידָה;) and the participial form acquires here an abstract signification, like מַכְבִּיר *fulness,* מַשְׁחִית *destruction.* According to strict Hebrew usage, it would denote *knowledge,* hence *poetry,* (comp. Arab. شِعْر *knowledge, poetry,*) the poets in antiquity being wise men and preservers of knowledge.

שְׂכַל Chald. Ithpa. *to consider,* construed with בְּ. Dan. 7:8.

שֶׂכֶל and **שֵׂכֶל** m. with suff. שִׂכְלוֹ, verbal from שָׂכַל, dec. VI. g.

1. *understanding, intelligence.* 1 Chr. 22:12. 26:14.—שֵׂכֶל טוֹב *good understanding,* Prov. 13:15. Ps. 111:10. 2 Chr. 30:22.—שׂוּם שֶׂכֶל *to give the understanding* or *sense* of any thing, Neh. 8:8.

2. *craft, cunning.* Dan. 8:25.

3. *prosperity.* Prov. 3:4.

שִׂכְלוּת f. i. q. סִכְלוּת *folly.* Ecc. 1:17. Several MSS. and editions read it with ס.

שָׂכְלְתָנוּ f. Chald. *understanding.* Dan. 5:11, 12.

שָׂכַר, fut. יִשְׂכֹּר, *to hire.* Gen. 30:16. E. g. soldiers, 2 Sam. 10:6. Particularly *to bribe*, Neh. 6:12, 13. 13:2. 2 K. 7:6.

Niph. *to let one's self for hire.* 1 Sam. 2:5.

Hithpa. *idem.* Hagg. 1:6.

Deriv. out of course מַשְׂכֹּרֶת, שְׂכִירָה, שָׂכִיר.

שֶׂכֶר m. verbal from שָׂכַר, dec. IV. a.

1. *hire.* Ex. 22:15 אִם שָׂכִיר הוּא בָּא בִּשְׂכָרוֹ *if he (the owner) was a hireling, and brought it for hire.*

2. *wages, reward,* (of a labourer.) Gen. 30:28, 32. Deut. 15:18. Also *a reward* generally, Gen. 15:1.

שֶׂכֶר m. verbal from שָׂכַר, dec. VI. *a reward.* Prov. 11:18.—Is. 19:10 after the usual reading עֹשֵׂי שֶׂכֶר *they that earn wages.* It would be more accordant with the parallel clause to read שֵׁכָר q. v.

שְׂלָו m. plur. שַׂלְוִים, dec. VI. γ. *a quail.* Ex. 16:13. Num. 11:31, 32. Ps. 105:40 Keth. where the Keri reads שְׂלָיו. (Arab. سلوى *idem,* from سلي *to be fat,* whence *the quail* goes in Arabic by other names denoting *fatness.*) On the multitude of quails in Arabia, see Diod. Sic. I. p. 38 ed. Rhodom. Sept. ὀρτυγομήτρα. Vulg. *coturnix.* See Bocharti Hieroz. II. p. 92. Faber zu Harmer's Beobachtungen üb. d. Orient, Th. 2. p. 441. Niebuhr's Beschr. v. Arabien, p. 176.

שַׂלְמָה by transposition for שִׂמְלָה *a garment.* Ex. 22:8. Mic. 2:8.

שְׂמֹאל or **שְׂמאוֹל** m. dec. I.

1. *the left side.*—עַל שְׂמֹאל *to the left,* Gen. 24:49.—מִשְּׂמֹאל *on the left,* 1 K. 7:49. 2 Chr. 4:8. and with a genitive or dative following, Gen. 48:13.—שְׂמֹאל and הַשְּׂמֹאל (used adverbially in the accus.) *towards the left,* Gen. 13:9. Deut. 5:32. Hence. יַד־שְׂמֹאל *the left hand,* liter. *the hand of the left side,* Judg. 3:21. Ezek. 39:3.

2. without יָד, *the left hand.* Gen. 48:14. Cant. 2:6. 8:3.

3. *the north.* Job 23:9. Gen. 14:15 מִשְּׂמֹאל לְדַמָּשֶׂק *on the north of Damascus.* (In Arab. שאם شام *the country on the left,* i. e. Syria, in opposition to ימן يمن *the country on the right,* i. e. Yemen or Arabia. Comp יָמִין.) Hence the denom. verb in

Hiph. הִשְׂמְאִיל, הַשְׂמְאִיל (1 Chr. 12:2.) and הַשְׂמִיל (2 Sam. 14:19.)

1. *to turn one's self to the left.* Gen. 13:9. Is. 30:21.

2. *to be left-handed, to use the left hand.* 1 Chr. 12:2.

שְׂמָאלִי and **שְׂמָלִי**, fem. ־ִית, denom. adj. from שְׂמֹאל, *left, situated on the left, sinister.* 1 K. 7:21. 2 K. 11:11.

שָׂמַח and **שָׂמֵחַ**, fut. יִשְׂמַח, *to be joyful, to rejoice;* construed with בְּ of the thing, 1 Sam. 2:1. Ps. 122:1. with עַל, Is. 9:16. [9:17.] 39:2. Jon. 4:6. with מִן, Prov. 5:18, (where, however, several MSS. read בְּ.)—שָׂמַח בַּיהוָֹה *to rejoice in Jehovah,* Ps. 9:3. 32:11. 97:12. 104:34. Construed with לְ it expresses a malicious joy, or a rejoicing in the calamities of others, (like רָאָה בְּ.) Ps. 35:19, 24. 38:17. Is. 14:8. Mic. 7:8. (comp. however Amos 6:13.) שָׂמַח לִפְנֵי יְהוָֹה *to rejoice before Jehovah,* in reference to the sacrificial feasts in the temple, Lev. 23:40. Deut. 12:7, 12, 18. 14:26. Is. 9:2. [9:3.]

Pi. שִׂמַּח *to gladden, to make joyful, to make to rejoice.* Deut. 24:5. Prov. 27:11. When the joy arises from the misfortunes of others, construed with לְ, Ps. 30:2. with עַל, Lam. 2:17. with מִן, 2 Chr. 20:27.

Hiph. i. q. Pi. Ps. 89:43.

שָׂמֵחַ m. verbal adj. from שָׂמַח, dec. V. a. and f. *joyful, rejoicing.* Deut. 16:15. etc. Plur. const. once שְׂמֵחַי Ps. 35:26. elsewhere שְׂמֵחֵי.

שִׂמְחָה f. verbal from שָׂמַח, dec. XII. b.

1. *joy, rejoicing.*—שָׂמַח שִׂמְחָה גְדוֹלָה *to rejoice greatly,* 1 K. 1:40. Jon. 4:6.

2. *festivity, mirth.* Prov. 21:17 אֹהֵב שִׂמְחָה *he that loves festivity.*—עָשָׂה שִׂמְחָה *to make feasts,* Neh. 8:12. 12:27. 2 Chr. 30:23.

3. *a loud shout, a joyful acclama-*

tion. Neh. 12 : 43. Gen. 31 : 27. 2 Chr. 23 : 18. 29 : 30.

שְׂמִיכָה f. *a mattress, covering*. Judg. 4 : 18. Root סָמַךְ (with ס, as some MSS. read it here;) Comp. Syr. ܡܣܡܟܐ *a couch, sofa*.

שְׂמַל, see under **שְׂמֹאל**.

שְׂמָלִי *sinister*, see **שְׂמָאלִי**

שִׂמְלָה f. dec. XII. b. *a garment*, for men and women, (Deut. 22 : 5.) particularly *the broad robe* of the orientalist, Gen. 9 : 23. 1 Sam. 21 : 10. which served him also for his bed-covering, Deut. 22 : 17.

שְׂמָמִית (for which several MSS. read שְׂמָמִת), a poisonous species of lizard. Prov. 30 : 28. Sept. καλαβώτης. Vulg. *stellio*. (In Arab. سام שאם a poisonous lizard with spots like the leprosy, from سام and سم *to poison*.) See Bocharti Hieroz. T. II. p. 1084.

שָׂנֵא, fut. יִשְׂנָא, infin. שְׂנֹאת.

1. *to hate*, construed with an accus. and with לְ. Deut. 4 : 42. 19 : 4. Part. שׂוֹנֵא *a hater, an enemy*, Ps. 35 : 19. 38 : 20.

2. when used in opposition to אָהַב, merely comparatively, *to love less, to slight*, (אָהַב signifying *to love more, to prefer*.) Deut. 21 : 15 ff. comp. Matt. 6 : 24. Luke 14 : 26.

Niph. pass. Prov. 14 : 17.

Pi. found only in the part. מְשַׂנֵּא *an enemy*, Ps. 55 : 13. 68 : 2.

שְׂנֵא Chald. *to hate*, Part. שָׂנֵא *an enemy*, Dan. 4 : 16. [4 : 19.]

שִׂנְאָה f. dec. X. 1. strictly infin. of שָׂנֵא. Deut. 1 : 27.

2. *hatred*. שָׂנֵא שִׂנְאָה גְדוֹלָה *to hate exceedingly*, 2 Sam. 13 : 15. comp. Ps. 139 : 22. Ps. 25 : 19.

שְׂנִיר according to Deut. 3 : 9. name of a ridge of mountains among the Amorites, usually called Hermon. (See חֶרְמוֹן.) In other passages (1 Chr. 5 : 23. Cant. 4 : 8.) it is used in a more restricted sense and distinguished from Hermon; comp. Ezek. 27 : 5. The name is still preserved among the Arabians, and its appellative signification, (comp. سنور *lorica*,) is the same as that of שִׁרְיוֹן, which, according to Deut. 3 : 9. is the name of the same mountain among the Sidonians.

שְׂעִפִּים masc. plur. dec. I. i. q. שְׂעִפִּים *thoughts*, (concerning the insertion of ר, see under the article ר, p. 536.) Job 20 : 2. 4 : 13 *in thoughts of nightly visions*, i. e. in dreams; comp. Dan. 2 : 29, 30.

שָׂעִיר m. dec. III. a.

1. *hairy, rough*. Gen. 27 : 11, 23.

2. *a buck, he-goat*. Lev. 4 : 24. 16 : 9. as an object of idolatrous worship, (like the practice of the Egyptians,) Lev. 17 : 7. 2 Chr. 11 : 15. Fem. שְׂעִירָה.

3. Is. 13 : 21. 34 : 14. שְׂעִירִים inhabitants of impassable deserts, which dance and call to each other, perhaps, according to the popular belief, *wild men in the form of he-goats*, like the Grecian satyrs. The Arabians had such fabulous monsters in abundance; (see Bocharti Hieroz. II. 844.) They speak also of the voices of nightly spectres in the woods; comp. the Heb. לִילִית. Sept. δαιμόνια.

4. plur. שְׂעִירִים *showers*. Deut. 32 : 2. Comp. שָׂעַר *to shudder*.

שֵׂעִיר proper name of a mountainous country on the south of Palestine and the Dead Sea. Esau is said to have dwelt here, (Gen. 32 : 3. 33 : 14, 16.) and Josephus (Antiq. I. 19.) derives *Seir* from עֵשָׂו *the hairy*, (see the art. עֵשָׂו. According to other notices, it was originally inhabited by Horites, (Gen. 14 : 6. Deut. 2 : 12.) among whom occurs a leader or head of a tribe named שֵׂעִיר (Gen. 36 : 20—30.) These Horites were driven out by the descendants of Esau, who in after times dwelt in this region, Deut. 2 : 4 ff. 2 Chr. 20 : 10. As an appellative שֵׂעִיר denotes *hairy*, hence perhaps *woody*, which would be a very suitable name for this country. Comp. שְׂעִירָה no. 2.

שְׂעִירָה 1. fem. of שָׂעִיר, dec. X. *a she-goat.* Lev. 4 : 23. 5 : 6.

2. name of an unknown place, perhaps a wood or mountain, to which Ehud fled. Judg. 3 : 26.

שָׂעַר i. q. Greek φρίσσω, φρίττω.

1. *to shudder, shiver,* from fear, alarm. Ezek. 27 : 35. Jer. 2 : 12. Construed with עַל *for* a thing, Ezek. 32 : 10. Construed with an accus. *to fear, reverence,* φρίσσω τινά, Deut. 32 : 17.

2. i. q. סָעַר *to rage, roar, assail with violence.* Ps. 58 : 10 יִשְׂעָרֶנּוּ *it (the storm) assails him with violence.*

2. *to stand on end,* spoken of hair, *to be rough, bristly, horrere.* Deriv. שְׂעֹרָה, שַׂעֲרָה, שֵׂעָר, שָׂעִיר, שְׂעִיר. (Arab. شعر *to be hairy.*)

Niph. *to rage, be tempestuous.* Ps. 50 : 3.

Pi. *to carry away in a storm.* Job 27 : 21.

Hithpa. *to storm, to rage like a storm.* Dan. 11 : 40. comp. סָעַר Hab. 3 : 14.

שַׂעַר m. verbal from שָׂעַר, dec. VI. c.

1. *a shuddering, horror.* Job 18 : 20. Ezek. 27 : 35.

2. i. q. סַעַר *a storm, tempest.* Is. 28 : 2.

3. *hair,* as if the const. state of שֵׂעָר. Is. 7 : 20.

שֵׂעָר m. const. שְׂעַר, with suff. שְׂעָרוֹ, verbal from שָׂעַר, dec. IV. b. *hair.* Lev. 13 : 3 ff. for the most part collectively, (as in Arab.)—אִישׁ בַּעַל שֵׂעָר *a hairy* or *rough man.* 2 K. 1 : 8. comp. Gen. 25 : 25. See שַׂעֲרָה.

שְׂעַר Chald. *idem.* Dan. 3 : 27. 7 : 9.

שְׂעָרָה f. i. q. סְעָרָה *a tempest.* Job 9 : 17. Nah. 1 : 3.

שַׂעֲרָה f. verbal from שָׂעַר, dec. XII. e. *a hair,* i. q. שֵׂעָר. (Arab. *a single hair.*) Judg. 20 : 16 אֶל הַשַּׂעֲרָה *at a hair.* Used collectively, Job 4 : 15. 1 Sam. 14 : 45. Plur. Ps. 40 : 13. 69 : 5.

שְׂעֹרָה f. (masc. Is. 28 : 25.?) verbal from שָׂעַר, dec. X. *barley,* so called from *the roughness* of its ears. (Comp. כֻּסֶּמֶת *spelt,* from כָּסַם.) In the singular spoken of the plant as it grows, Job 31 : 40. Joel 1 : 11.

Plur. שְׂעֹרִים spoken of the grain, see חֹמֶר שְׂעֹרִים.—חִטָּה *a homer of barley,* Lev. 27 : 16. אֵיפָה שְׂעֹרִים *an ephah of barley,* Ruth 2 : 17. קְצִיר שְׂעֹרִים *barley harvest,* Ruth 1 : 22. This last example furnishes no exception to the usual distinction between the singular and the plural.

שָׂפָה, f. dual שְׂפָתַיִם, const. שִׂפְתֵי with suff. שְׂפָתָיו, plur. only in the const. state שִׂפְתוֹת, as if from שֶׂפֶת. prim. irreg.

1. *a lip.*—אִישׁ שְׂפָתַיִם *a man of lips, a babbler,* Job 11 : 2. דְּבַר שְׂפָתַיִם *babbling, idle talk,* 2 K. 18 : 20. Prov. 13 : 23. comp. Prov. 10 : 8. Lev. 5 : 4. Ps. 106 : 33. Trop. (1.) *speech, words;* e. g. שִׂפְתֵי־שָׁקֶר *lying lips,* i. e. false words, Prov. 10 : 18. Ps. 120 : 2. שְׂפָתַיִם דֹּלְקִים *burning lips,* i. e. warm professions of friendship, Prov. 26 : 23. — Ps. 81 : 6 שְׂפַת לֹא יָדַעְתִּי אֶשְׁמָע *the speech of one that I knew not I heard.* Ezek. 36 : 3. (2.) *a language, dialect.* Gen. 11 : 1 ff. Is. 19 : 18. 33 : 19 עִמְקֵי שָׂפָה *of an unintelligible language, barbarians.*

2. *a border,* e. g. of a vessel, 1 K. 7 : 26. of a garment, Ex. 28 : 32. of a river, the sea, Gen. 22 : 17: 41 : 3. of a country, Judg. 7 : 22.

שָׂפַח, found only in Pi. שִׂפַּח Is. 3 : 17. *to make bald,* (the head,) particularly *to cause the hair to fall off by sickness.* Comp. סַפַּחַת.

שָׂפָם m. dec. IV. a. *the beard,* perhaps *the whole chin;* comp. זָקָן. 2 Sam. 19 : 25 לֹא עָשָׂה שְׂפָמוֹ *he had not trimmed his beard.* עָטָה אֶת, עַל הַשָּׂפָם *to cover the beard* or *chin,* as an expression of sorrow, Lev. 13 : 45. Ezek. 24 : 17, 22. Mic. 3 : 7.

שָׂפַן *to cover, hide, conceal,* i. q. סָפַן and צָפַן. Deut. 33 : 19 שְׂפֻנֵי טְמוּנֵי *the* *most hidden treasures.* Vulg. *thesauri absconditi.*

I. שָׂפַק i. q. סָפַק *to clap* (the hands). Job 27:23 according to several MSS.

Hiph. Is. 2:6 בְּיַלְדֵי נָכְרִים יַשְׂפִּיקוּ *plaudunt filiis peregrinorum,* or *dextras jungunt peregrinis;* comp. in Arab. سفق *to shake hands,* as in a covenant or bargain.

II. שָׂפַק Syr. ܣܦܩ *to suffice.* 1 K. 20:10. See סָפַק.

שֶׂפֶק m. *the stroke* or *chastisement* (of God). Job. 36:18. See סָפַק Job 34:26.

שַׂק m. with suff. שַׂקּוֹ, plur. שַׂקִּים, dec. VIII. h.

1. *coarse,* particularly *hair cloth.* (In Ethiop. *a hairy garment* of the pilgrims and eastern monks, *a coarse tent-covering, coarse linen* generally.) So the Greek σάκος, σάκκος, *cilicium;* and *saccus* in Jerome, *a garment for pilgrims.* (Comp. Rev. 6:12.) Is. 3:23 מַחֲגֹרֶת שָׂק *a hairy girdle.*

2. *a bag made of coarse* or *hair cloth.* Gen. 42:25, 27, 35. Lev. 11:32.

3. *a mourning garment made of coarse* or *hair cloth.* Gen. 37:34. 2 Sam. 3:31. Est. 4:1. Joel 1:8. Jon. 3:6. As the dress of a prophet, Is. 20:2.

שָׂקַד found only Lam. 1:14. in Niph. according to the Hebrew interpreters, *to be fastened* or *bound.* Chald. *aggravatum est.* The Sept. Vulg. read נִשְׁקַד.

שָׂקַר found only in Pi. Is. 3:16 מְשַׂקְּרוֹת עֵינַיִם *ogling* or *winking with their eyes.* (Chald. סְקַר *to look on,* סַקְרָנִית *circumspectatrix.*) Sept. ἐν νεύμασιν ὀφθαλμῶν. Others: *fucantes oculos,* (comp. Chald. סְקַר *to paint,*) but not so well suited to the context.

שַׂר m. plur. שָׂרִים, fem. שָׂרָה q. v. verbal from שָׂרַר, dec. VIII. k.

1. *a captain, commander, chief;* e. g. of the body-guard, Gen. 37:36. of the cup-bearers, 40:9.—שַׂר הַצָּבָא *the commander of the host,* 21:22.—שָׂרֵי מִקְנֶה *the overseers of the herds,* Gen. 47:6. —שַׂר הָעִיר *the commander of the city, præfectus urbis,* 1 K. 22:26.

2. *a chief, prince, courtier.* Gen. 12:15.

3. according to the theological views of the later Jews, *an archangel,* one of the seven principal angels which surround the throne of God and act as patrons of particular nations in the heavenly court, οἱ ἑπτὰ ἄγγελοι, οἳ ἐνώπιον τοῦ Θεοῦ ἑστήκασι (Rev. 8:2.) Dan. 10:13, 20.

שָׂרַג *to interweave.* (Chald. and Syr. סְרַג *idem,* at least in the derivatives.) Comp. שָׂרַךְ.

Pu. *to be interwoven.* Job 40:17.

Hithpa. *to be interwoven, to be fastened.* Lam. 1:14.

Deriv. שָׂרִיגִים.

שָׂרַד *to escape, flee,* (after a general overthrow.) Josh. 10:20. (Arab. and Syr. *idem.*) Deriv. שָׂרִיד.

שְׂרָד m. found only in the phrase בִּגְדֵי־שְׂרָד Ex. 31:10. 35:19. 39:1, 41. according to most of the ancient versions, *clothes of service* or *office.* Sept. Ex. 39:1 στολαὶ λειτουργικαί. Comp. the phrase subjoined to the three last passages לְשָׁרֵת בַּקֹּדֶשׁ *to serve in the sanctuary.* They were distinct, however, from *the holy garments,* (בִּגְדֵי הַקֹּדֶשׁ) Perhaps better: *party-coloured garments,* comp. the Samar. סרדה *a party-coloured garment.*

שֶׂרֶד m. Is. 44:13. according to Kimchi, *red earth.* According to the Arab. سِرَاد *an awl,* here perhaps a pointed instrument with which the workman marked out the form of the image on the rough block.

I. שָׂרָה *to contend, struggle* with a person; construed with עִם, Gen. 32:28. with אֶת, Hos. 12:4. (Arab. شرا conj. III. *idem.*) The fut. is formed from שׂוּר no. III.

II. שָׂרָה i. q. שָׂרַר and שׂוּר no. II. *to rule.* Deriv. מִשְׂרָה. Here belongs, according to the common interpretation, the part. fem. שׂוֹרָה Is. 28:25 חִטָּה שׂוֹרָה *triticum principale*, i.e. egregium, bonum. Better perhaps: *fat wheat;* comp. the Arab. شار *to be fat*. Others make it a substantive denoting a particular species of grain. Others make it an error of the transcribers, arising from the following word שְׂעֹרָה, since the ancient versions omit it.

שָׂרָה, fem. of שַׂר, dec. X.

1. *a princess*. Judg. 5:29. Est. 1:18. Is. 49:23. Also spoken of concubines of the first rank and noble birth, (מְלָכוֹת Cant. 6:8.) 1 K. 11:3.

2. *Sarah*, a proper name, see שָׂרַי.

שְׂרוֹךְ m. *a shoe-latchet*, a string which fastened the sandal to the foot. Gen. 14:23. Is. 5:27. Root שָׂרַךְ *to weave*.

שְׂרוּקִים masc. plur. dec. X. *noble shoots* or *tendrils of the vine*. Is. 16:8. See שׂרק.

שָׂרַט *to make an incision* (in the body). Lev. 21:5.

Niph. *to tear* or *hurt one's self* (by lifting.) Zech. 12:3.

שֶׂרֶט m. Lev. 19:28. and **שָׂרֶטֶת** f. 21:5. verbals from שָׂרַט, *an incision* (in the body).

שָׂרַי *Sarai*, the proper name of the wife of Abraham. On occasion of the promise to her of a numerous posterity, this name was changed into שָׂרָה (Gen. 17:15.) without doubt in the sense of *princess*. Various explanations of the former name have been attempted, but to very little purpose, see Gesenius' larger Lexicon, p. 1309. The point of the passage in Genesis is undoubtedly this, that a more suitable and significant name was substituted for one which was less appropriate or had no meaning at all.

שָׂרִיגִים masc. plur. (with Kamets impure,) dec. I. *vine-branches*. Gen. 40:10, 12. Joel 1:7. Root שָׂרַג *to interweave*.

שָׂרִיד m. verbal from שָׂרַד, dec. III. a. *one surviving* or *escaping* (after a general overthrow), i.q. פָּלִיט. Num. 21:35. 24:19. Deut. 3:3. Josh. 8:22. Used collectively, Is. 1:9. Judg. 5:13. Spoken of things, *that which is left*, Job 20:21.

שָׂרִיק *combed*, verbal adj. from שָׂרַק q. v.

שָׂרַךְ i. q. שָׂרַג *to interweave, make intricate*.

Pi. Jer. 2:23 *a swift camel* מְשָׂרֶכֶת דְּרָכֶיהָ *that makes her ways intricate*, i.e. that runs wild with the desire of copulation. (In Arab. شرك *to run wild from sexual desire*, spoken of animals.)

Deriv. שְׂרוֹךְ.

שָׂרַע *to stretch out, to stretch forth*. Part. pass. שָׂרוּעַ *having a member preternaturally large*, Lev. 21:18. 22:23.

Hithpa. *to stretch one's self out*. Is. 28:20.

שַׂרְעַפִּים masc. plur. dec. X. *thoughts*. Ps. 94:19. 139:23. Comp. שְׂעִפִּים; and on the insertion of ר, see under that letter.

שָׂרַף, fut. יִשְׂרֹף. 1. *to burn*, e.g. cities, houses, altars. Is. 1:7. Lev. 4:21. 8:17. 9:11. Josh. 11:9. and often with the addition of בָּאֵשׁ *in the fire*. Used also in reference to the burning and other funeral rites of a dead body, Jer. 34:5.

2. *to burn* (bricks). Gen. 11:3.

Niph. pass. *to be burned*. Lev. 4:12.

Pu. pass. *to be burned*. Lev. 10:16.

Deriv. מִשְׂרָפָה, שְׂרֵפָה.

I. **שָׂרָף** m. dec. IV. a. a species of poisonous serpent. Num. 21:8. Deut. 8:5. With the addition of נָחָשׁ, Num. 21:6.—שָׂרָף מְעוֹפֵף *a flying serpent, draco volans*, Is. 14:29. 30:6.—It is usually collated with the Greek πρηστήρ, καύσων, a species of serpent so named from its *burning* breath; but the ideas *heat* and *poison* are connected in several other words. Comp. חֵמָה, נָשַׁךְ. See Bocharti Hieroz. T. III. p. 221. ed. Lips.

II. **שָׂרָף** found only in the plur.

שְׂרָפִים Is. 6:2, 6. a kind of angel or archangel, with 6 wings, and a voice with which they praise God. According to Kimchi, מַלְאֲכֵי־אֵשׁ *fiery angels*, perhaps with reference to the shining fiery appearance of such celestial beings, (Ezek. 1:13. 2 K. 2:11. 6:17. Matt. 28:3.) But שָׂרַף signifies *to burn*, not *to shine;* and the splendour referred to (כָּבוֹד) is common to all the divine messengers. The more probable derivation, therefore, is from the Arab. شرف *to be noble, excellent*, (whence, شريف *a prince, a noble;*) hence liter. *nobles* or *princes*, comp. שַׂר no. 3.

שְׂרֵפָה f. (with Tseri impure,) verbal from שָׂרַף, dec. X.

1. *a burning, conflagration.* Gen. 11:3. Lev. 10:6. הַר שְׂרֵפָה *a burnt, desolate mountain*, Jer. 51:25. Particularly *the solemn burning of a corpse*, 2 Chr. 16:14. 21:19.

2. *matter to be burnt, fuel for the fire.* Is. 9:4. 64:10.

שָׂרַק *to comb, hatchel*, e.g. flax. (Syr. and Chald. *idem.*) Hence Is. 19:9. פִּשְׁתִּים שְׂרִיקוֹת *combed flax.*

שֹׂרֵק m. Is. 5:2. Jer. 2:21. שֹׂרֵקָה f. Gen. 49:11.

1. a choice species of vine, the grapes of which, as the Jewish commentators say, have very small and scarcely perceptible stones, and which at this day is called *serki* in Morocco. Pers. *kishmis.* See Niebuhr's Reisebeschr. Th. II. p. 169. Beschr. von Arabien, p. 147. Root prob. Syr. ܣܪܩ *to empty out;* hence ܣܪܝܩܐ *empty.* See שׂוֹרֵק.

2. name of a valley between Ascalon and Gaza, prob. so called from its producing this vine. Judg. 16:4.

שָׂרֹק m. plur. שְׂרֻקִּים, dec. VII. d. *reddish, fox-coloured*, spoken of horses, Zech. 1:8. (In Arab. by transposition اشقر *a reddish horse, having also a red mane and tail.*)

שָׂרַר *to have dominion, to bear rule.* Part. שֹׂרֵר Est. 1:22. Fut. יָשֹׂר Is. 32:1. Prov. 8:16. Synonymous with שׂוּר no. II.

Hithpa. *to make one's self a ruler*, construed with עַל. Num. 16:13.

Deriv. שַׂר, שָׂרָה.

שָׂשׂוֹן m. const. שְׂשׂוֹן, verbal from שׂוּשׂ, (with the signification of שׂוּשׂ,) dec. III. a. *joy, gladness*, usually joined with שִׂמְחָה. Is. 22:13. 35:10. 51:3, 11.— שֶׁמֶן שָׂשׂוֹן *oil of joy*, wherewith guests were anointed, Ps. 45:8. Is. 61:3.

שָׂתַם i. q. סָתַם *to stop* or *shut up.* Lam. 3:8 שָׂתַם תְּפִלָּתִי *he stoppeth up my prayer*, that it may not reach him; comp. verse 44.

שָׂתַר *to cleave, split.*

Niph. *to be split, to break out*, (spoken of the עֳפָלִים.) 1 Sam. 5:9. Comp. סָתַר

ש

Shin, usually reckoned together with *Sin* as the 21st letter of the alphabet, and as a numerical sign denoting 300.

The name שִׁין i. q. שֵׁן *a tooth*, is derived from the *pronged* form of the letter in all the ancient Shemitish alphabets.

There are three letters in Arabic which correspond to the Hebrew Shin more or less; (1.) most frequently س, e.g. שָׁלוֹם Arab. سلام *peace.* (2.) more rarely ش, e.g. שֶׁמֶשׁ Arab. شمس *the sun.* In both of these cases the Shin is retained in Aram. (3.) ث, e.g. שְׁמֹנָה Arab. ثمان *eight;* שֶׁלֶג Arab. ثلج *snow.* In this case the Aramean dialects have ת, ܬܡܢܐ, תְּמָנֵי *eight;* תְּלַג

ثلج *snow.* Sometimes, but more rarely, ت is found in Arabic, e.g. שָׁבַר Arab. تبر *to break in pieces.* In the Hebrew itself, comp. שָׁרַשׁ and תָּרַה χαρέδριον, בְּרוֹשׁ and בְּרוֹת *a fir-tree.* (4.) There are some examples in which the same Hebrew word with שׁ has two corresponding Arabic words; (a.) שֶׁלַח *a dart,* in Arabic written with س and ش. (b.) שָׁקַל *to weigh,* in Arab. with ش and ث. (c.) גֶּשֶׁם Arab. جسم, جثمان, جسمان *body.*—On the contrary מָשַׁל *to rule,* (prob. in Arabic with *Sin,*) is a different root from מָשַׁל Arab. مثل Syr. מְתַל *to be like.*—From nos. 2, 3. flow (5.) the examples where שׁ is interchanged with ז and ץ; e.g. שׁוּל Arab. ذيل *a trail;* רֶכֶשׁ Arab. ركض *a noble horse;* חֹמֶשׁ Rabbin. חוּמְצָא *inguen.* Perhaps also there is some cognation between רֶשֶׁף *heat* and רִצְפָּה *a coal;* רָשַׁשׁ and רָצַץ *to break in pieces.*

.שֶׁ, more rarely .שַׁ (Judg. 5 : 7. Cant. 1 : 7. Job 19 : 29.) and שְׁ (Ecc. 2 : 22. 3 : 18.) i. q. אֲשֶׁר (of which it is a contraction, by omitting א at the beginning, see p. 1. and assimilating the ר to the following letter, see p. 536.) but found only in later Hebrew, and in the poetic style, e.g. Judg. 5 : 7.

1. a relative pronoun, *who, which, what.* Ecc. 1 : 11. Cant. 1 : 7. 3 : 1, 2, 3. —כְּשֶׁ i. q. כַּאֲשֶׁר *as,* (liter. *secundum id quod,*) Ecc. 5 : 14.

2. merely a sign of relation, nota relationis; e.g. שֶׁשָּׁם *whither,* Ecc. 1 : 7. Ps. 122 : 4.

3. with לְ following, it makes a periphrasis of the sign of the genitive case. Cant. 3 : 7 מִטָּתוֹ שֶׁלִּשְׁלֹמֹה *the sedan of Solomon,* liter. *his sedan, which* (belonged) *to Solomon,* or *Solomon's his sedan.* 1 : 6 כַּרְמִי שֶׁלִּי *my vineyard.* (Comp. אֲשֶׁר no. 3.) This pleonastic use of the suffix belongs to the Aramean style.

4. as a conj. (1.) *that, ut, quod.* Job 19 : 29. Ecc. 1 : 17. 2 : 24.—כִּמְעַט שֶׁ *scarcely that,* Cant. 3 : 4. עַד שֶׁ *until that,* Judg. 5 : 7. שַׁלָּמָה *lest, that not,* Cant. 1 : 7. See p. 311. (2.) *because.* Cant. 1 : 6. (3.) *for.* Cant. 5 : 2.

שָׁאַב, fut. יִשְׁאַב, *to draw, haurio.* Gen. 24 : 11, 13 ff. Josh. 9 : 21, 23, 27. Is. 12 : 2. (In Chald. *idem.*) Deriv. מַשְׁאַבִּים.

שָׁאַג fut. יִשְׁאַג.

1. *to roar;* spoken strictly of the lion, Judg. 14 : 5. Ps. 104 : 21. Job 37 : 4. comp. Am. 1 : 2. Joel 4 : 16. [3 : 16.] of savage enemies, Ps. 74 : 4.

2. *to groan,* spoken of a person in extreme pain. Ps. 38 : 9.

שְׁאָגָה f. const. שַׁאֲגַת, verbal from שָׁאַג dec. XI. d.

1. *the roaring* (of a lion). Is. 5 : 29.

2. *a groan, groaning,* (of one in distress.) Job 3 : 24. Ps. 22 : 2. 32 : 3.

שָׁאָה and **שׁוֹא** (the former only is used as a verb, and that rarely, but both are important on account of their derivatives.)

1. *to make a noise, tumult,* spoken of water, of a crowd of people and the like, (see שָׁאוֹן, שֵׁאת;) *to shout,* (see שָׁאוֹן;) *to crash,* (see תְּשֻׁאוֹת;) hence spoken of a storm, (see שׁוֹאָה *a storm, tempest.*)

2. *to be destroyed with noise* or *crashing.* Is. 6 : 11 at the beginning.

3. *to be laid waste.* Deriv. שׁוֹאָה, מְשׁוֹאָה, שְׁאִיָּה *desolation,* more rarely שָׁאוֹן.

Niph. 1. *to make a noise* or *tumult,* spoken of waters. Is. 17 : 12, 13.

2. *to be laid waste,* spoken of a country. Is. 6 : 11 at the end.

Hiph. *to lay waste.* Infin לְהַשְׁאוֹת Is. 37 : 26. לְהַשּׁוֹת (without א) 2 K. 19 : 25 Keth.

Hithpa. הִשְׁתָּאָה *to gaze* or *wonder at,* construed with לְ. Gen. 24 : 21. (The ideas *astonishment* and *desolation* are united also in the word שָׁמַם q. v.) Sept. καταμανθάνω. Vulg. *contemplor.*

שֹׁאָה see **שׁוֹאָה**.

שַׁאֲוָה Prov. 1 : 27 Keth. i. q. שׁוֹאָה.

שְׁאוֹל, **שְׁאֹל** com. gen. (Is. 14 : 9.

Jer. 5:14. Job 26:6.) *the lower world, the region of ghosts, the orcus* or *hades* of the Hebrews; in which thick darkness reigns, (Job 10:21, 22.) and where all men after death live as ghosts (רְפָאִים q. v.) without thought or sensation. To it are attributed valleys (Prov. 9: 18.) and gates (Is. 38:10.) The wicked descend into it by the openings in the earth. (Num. 16:30 ff.) The etymology is uncertain. Usually collated with the Arab. شال med. Je *to go downwards, to sink;* but the examples, (in Scheidius ad Cant. Hiskiæ, p. 21 ff.) prove merely the signification *to settle,* spoken of a sediment; which lies too remote.

שָׁאוֹן m. verbal from שָׁאָה, dec. III. a.

1. *noise, tumult;* of waters, Ps. 65: 8. of a calling or shouting, Jer. 25:31. Ps. 74:23. Particularly *the bustle* or *tumult* of a multitude of people, Is. 5: 14. 13:4. 24:8. of war, Am. 2:2. Hos. 10:14.—Jer. 48:45 בְּנֵי שָׁאוֹן *tumultuous warriors.*

2. *destruction.* Ps. 40:3 בּוֹר שָׁאוֹן *pit of destruction.* Jer. 46:18.

שְׁאָט m. (with Kamets impure,) verbal from שׁוּט, dec. I. *contempt.* With suff. שָׁאטְךָ Ezek. 25:6.—בִּשְׁאָט בְּנֶפֶשׁ *with contempt of soul,* (for every thing about them,) i. e. with arrogance, *cum fastu,* 36:5. comp. 25:15.

שְׁאִיָּה f. verbal from שָׁאָה, *a crash.* Is. 24:12.

שָׁאַל and **שָׁאֵל**, fut. יִשְׁאַל.

1. *to ask, demand, require, seek;* construed with an accus. of the thing. Job 31:30 לִשְׁאֹל בְּאָלָה נַפְשׁוֹ *to demand with a curse his (the enemy's) life,* i. e. his death. So Jon. 4:8 וַיִּשְׁאַל אֶת־נַפְשׁוֹ לָמוּת *and he asked death for himself.* 1 K. 19:4. The person *of* whom any thing is asked, is preceded by מִן, Ps. 2:8. by מֵאֵת, 1 Sam. 8:10. or put in an accus. (like αἰτεῖν τινά, τί.) Hence with two accus. Ps. 137:3. Deut. 14:26.

2. *to ask, beg, request,* construed with an accus. of the thing, and מִן, מֵעִם, מֵאֵת of the person. Ps. 21:5. Deut. 18:16.

3. *to inquire of, to interrogate,* construed with an accus. of the person. Gen. 24:47. Job 40:7. and with לְ, Job 8:8.—Josh. 9:14 but *they inquired not of the mouth of Jehovah.* In this expression the neglect of a duty is implied, comp. Is. 30:2. Gen. 24:57.—The thing *for* which one inquires is preceded by לְ, Judg. 13:18. Gen. 32:29. by עַל, Neh. 1:2. or put in an accus. Hag. 2:11. Is. 45:11.

4. particularly *to inquire of* or *consult,* as an oracle, and then construed with בְּ; hence שָׁאַל בַּיהוָה *to inquire of Jehovah,* Judg. 1:1. 18:5. 20:18. construed with לְ *for* a person, 1 Sam. 22:10, 13, 15. Num. 27:21.—שָׁאַל בַּתְּרָפִים *to inquire of* or *consult the teraphim,* Ezek. 21:26.

5. שָׁאַל לְשָׁלוֹם לְ *to inquire after the health of* any one, particularly as a salutation. Gen. 43:27. 1 Sam. 10:4. 17:22. 30:21. Ex. 18:7. also שָׁאַל לְשָׁלוֹם פ' 2 Sam. 11:7.

6. *to borrow, to ask as a loan,* (derived from signif. nos. 1. 2.) Ex. 3:22. 11:2. 12:35. Part. שָׁאוּל *borrowed,* 1 Sam. 1:28. 2 K. 6:5. See Hiph.

7. *to beg, to ask alms.* Prov. 20:4. Comp. Pi.

Niph. *to ask for one's self,* (like the Greek αἰτοῦμαι, *mihi peto,* different from αἰτέω.) 1 Sam. 20:6, 28. Neh. 13:6.

Pi. שִׁאֵל 1. *to ask, inquire.* 2 Sam. 20:18.

2. i. q. Kal no. 7. *to beg.* Ps. 109:10.

Hiph. *to lend.* Ex. 12:36. 1 Sam. 1:28. Comp. Kal no. 6.

Deriv. out of course מִשְׁאָלָה.

שְׁאֵל Chald. 1. *to ask, beg, request.* Construed with two accus. Ezra 7:21.

2. *to ask, inquire;* construed with לְ of the person, Ezra 5:9. and an accus. of the thing, verse 10.

שְׁאֵלָה f. with suff. שְׁאֵלָתִי, also שֶׁאֱלָתָם (Ps. 106:15.) and by contraction שֵׁלָתֵךְ (1 Sam. 1:17.) verbal from שָׁאַל, dec. X. and XI.

1. *a petition, request.*—שָׁאַל שְׁאֵלָה *to make a request,* Judg. 8:24. 1 K. 2:16. נָתַן שְׁאֵלָה *to grant a request,* Est. 5:6, 8.—בָּאָה שְׁאֵלָה *a request is granted,* Job 6:8.

2. *what is lent, a loan.* 1 Sam. 2:20. Comp. the verb no. 6.

שְׁאֵלָא Chald. emph. שְׁאֵלְתָא, *a wish, request;* hence also *an affair, matter, concern.* (Comp. חֵפֶץ no. 4.) Dan. 4:14. [4:17] מֵאמַר קַדִּישִׁין שְׁאֵלְתָא *and the matter is the command of the holy ones.*

שָׁאַן in Kal not used. In Pil. (as a quadriliteral,) שַׁאֲנַן *to be at rest, to live quietly.* Jer. 30:10. 48:11. Job 3:18. Hence

שַׁאֲנָן, plur. שַׁאֲנַנִּים, verbal adj. from שָׁאַן, dec. VIII. a.

1. *quiet.* Is. 33:20. Particularly *living in peace, security, prosperity,* Job 12:5. comp. שַׁלְאֲנָן 21:23. Inasmuch as prosperity and security often lead to carelessness and forgetfulness of God; hence

2. *careless, proud, arrogant,* (*secundis rebus ferox,* Sallust. Jug. 94.) Ps. 123:4. Am. 6:1. Is. 32:9, 11, 18. (Comp. שָׁלֵו, שַׁלְוָה, part. בֹּטֵחַ and עָלֵז; also Schulten's Animadv. in Job 26:5.)

3. as a subst. *pride, arrogance.* Is. 37:29. 2 K. 19:28.

שָׁאַס see **שָׁסַס**.

שָׁאַף 1. *to breathe with open mouth, to snuff up,* e. g. the air, construed with an accus. Jer. 2:24. 14:6. hence *to gape, aspire, long after,* Job 7:2. 36:20. *to strive for,* Job 5:5. Construed with עַל Am. 2:7 *they long after the dust of the earth on the head of the poor;* i. e. they long to bring the *poor* into that condition.

2. *to snort, snuff;* hence (1.) *to hasten after* a thing. Ecc. 1:5. Comp. הֵפִיחַ Hab. 2:3. (2.) *to snort at, assail with violence,* spoken of wild animals and metaphorically of savage enemies. Ps. 56:2, 3. 57:4. Am. 8:4. Ezek. 36:3. Spoken of Jehovah, Is. 42:14.

שָׁאַר *to remain.* 1 Sam. 16:11.

Niph. pass. of Hiph.

1. *to remain, to be left.* Gen. 7:23. 42:38. Is. 11:11.

2. *to continue, to be kept back.* Ex. 8:5, 7. [8:9, 11.] Num. 11:26. Job 21:34 וּתְשׁוּבֹתֵיכֶם נִשְׁאַר מָעַל *your answers continue false.*

Hiph. 1. *to let remain, to leave.* Ex. 10:12.

2. *to leave behind.* Joel 2:14.

3. intrans. *to be left, to remain.* Num. 21:35. Deut. 3:3.

שְׁאָר m. (with Kamets impure,) verbal from שָׁאַר, *the rest, remnant, remainder.* Is. 10:20, 21, 22. 11:11.

שְׁאָר m. Chald. const. שְׁאָר, *idem.* Ezra 4:7, 9, 10, 17. 7:18.

שְׁאָר יָשׁוּב (*a remnant shall return*) the symbolical proper name of a son of the prophet Isaiah. Is. 7:3. comp. 10:21.

שְׁאֵר m. dec. I.

1. *flesh,* i. q. בָּשָׂר, but almost exclusively in poetry. Ps. 73:26. 78:20, 27. Jer. 51:35 חֲמָסִי וּשְׁאֵרִי עַל בָּבֶל *my violence and my flesh come upon Babylon,* i. e. the violence done to me, and my flesh, which it has consumed, come upon it; (comp. אֵל no. 1. (2.) and no. 2.)

2. *one related by blood.* Lev. 21:2. 18:12, 13, 17. Num. 27:11. In Lev. 18:6, and 25:49. more in full שְׁאֵר בְּשָׂרוֹ. Comp. בָּשָׂר no. 4.

שַׁאֲרָה fem. of שְׁאֵר, *blood relationship,* hence as a concrete, *kindred by blood.* Lev. 18:17.

שְׁאֵרִית f. by contraction שֵׁרִית (1 Chr. 12:38.) verbal from שָׁאַר, dec. I. *a remnant of people,* particularly after a general overthrow. Jer. 11:23. 44:14. Mic. 7:18. Zeph. 2:7. Comp. שָׂרִיד, פְּלֵיטָה.—Ps. 76:11 שְׁאֵרִית חֵמֹת *the remainder of his wrath,* i. e. that which is not exerted, his whole wrath.

שְׁאֵת f. (for שְׁאֵה fem. of שֵׁא verbal from שָׁאָה, like רֵעַ, רֵעָה from רָעָה,) *destruction.* Lam. 3:47. By contraction שֵׁת Num. 24:17. see שֵׁת below.

שְׁבָא *Sheba, Sabeans,* (as the name of a country, fem. as the name of a people, masc.) a people and country in Arabia Felix; celebrated for affording incense, spicery, gold, and precious stones, 1 K. 10:1 ff. Is. 60:6. Jer. 6:20. Ezek. 27:22. Ps. 72:15. also for carrying on commerce, Ezek. 27:22. Ps. 72:10. Joel 4:8. [3:8.] Job 6:19. In Job 1:15, it is used for *the* (plundering) *Arabs* generally, and is feminine, although *the people* are intended; the name of the country being used for the name of the people.—There appears to be a threefold derivation of this people in Genesis; namely, (1.) from a grandson of Cush, Gen. 10:7. (2.) from a son of Joktan, Gen. 10:28. (So also in the traditions of the Arabians.) (3.) from a grandson of Abraham by Keturah, Gen. 25:3.—In the first and last accounts the name is connected with Dedan; (see דְּדָן, שְׁבָא.)

שְׁבָבִים masc. plur. *small pieces.* Hos. 8:6. (Chald. שְׁבַב *to break in pieces;* שִׁבְבָא *a piece.*)

שָׁבָה, fut. apoc. יִשְׁבְּ, *to take prisoner, to carry away captive.* Gen. 34:29. 1 K. 8:48. Gen. 31:26 שְׁבֻיוֹת חֶרֶב *taken prisoner with the sword in hand;* comp. 2 K. 6:22. Also *to carry away* cattle, 1 Chr. 5:21. or other substance, 2 Chr. 21:17.

Niph. pass. of Kal. Gen. 14:14, Ex. 22:9.

Deriv. שְׁבוּת, שְׁבִי, שִׁבְיָה, שְׁבִית.

שְׁבוֹ m. name of a precious stone. Ex. 28:19. 39:12. Sept. ἀχάτης. Vulg. *achates.*

שְׁבוּל or שְׁבוֹל Jer. 18:15 Keth. for שְׁבִיל q. v.

שָׁבוּעַ f. also שָׁבֻעַ (Gen. 29:27, 28.) dual. שְׁבֻעַיִם (Lev. 12:5.) plur. שָׁבֻעִים m. שָׁבֻעוֹת, const. שְׁבֻעוֹת, liter. *the number seven,* ἑβδομάς; hence

1. *seven days, a week,* ἑβδομάς, *septimana.* Gen. 29:27, 28. Dan. 10:2 שְׁלֹשָׁה שָׁבֻעִים יָמִים *three weeks long.* (See p. 244.) חַג שָׁבֻעוֹת *the feast of* (seven) *weeks* or *of Pentecost,* from the time which intervened between the Passover and this feast, Deut. 16:9. In full Tob. 2:1 ἁγία ἑπτὰ ἑβδομάδων. On the contrary Ezek. 45:21 חַג שְׁבֻעוֹת יָמִים *the festival of seven days,* is spoken of the feast of the Passover which lasted seven days.

2. *seven years, a week of years,* Dan. 9:24 ff.

שְׁבוּעָה and שְׁבֻעָה f. verbal from שָׁבַע, dec. X. *an oath.* Gen. 26:3. 24:8.—שְׁבֻעַת יְהוָֹה *an oath by Jehovah,* Ex. 22:10. Ecc. 8:2. Particularly (1.) *an oath in covenanting.* 2 Sam. 21:7.—בַּעֲלֵי שְׁבוּעָה לְ *bound to* a person *by an oath,* ἔνορκοι, Neh. 6:18. (2.) *an oath of imprecation, a curse;* in full שְׁבֻעַת הָאָלָה Num. 5:21. hence לְאָלָה וְלִשְׁבֻעָה *for a curse,* ibid. Comp. Dan. 9:11. Is. 65:15.

שְׁבוּת and שְׁבִית f. (the two forms being frequently interchanged in the Keri and Kethib,) verbal from שָׁבָה, dec. I. *captivity,* and as a concrete, *captives.* Num. 21:29.—שׁוּב שְׁבוּת *to bring back the captives,* (of a people,) Deut. 30:3. Jer. 29:24. 30:3. Ezek. 29:14. 39:25. Amos 9:14. Zeph. 3:20. Ps. 14:7. 53:7. 126:1, 4. hence used metaphorically of the restoration of prosperity, or the bringing back to a former state, Job 42:10 וַיהוָה שָׁב אֶת־שְׁבוּת אִיּוֹב *and Jehovah restored again the prosperity of Job.* Ezek. 16:53. Comp. verse 55. Hos. 6:11, (if these words are to be joined to the beginning of the following chapter.)

I. שָׁבַח (Arab. with ح) found only in Pi. שִׁבַּח.

1. *to praise, commend.* Ecc. 8:15. Particularly *to praise* God, Ps. 63:4. 117:1. 147:12.

2. *to pronounce happy.* Ecc. 4:2. Comp. the Chald.

Hithpa. *to praise one's self, to glory,* construed with בְּ of the thing. Ps. 106:47. 1 Chr. 16:35.

II. שָׁבַח (Arab. with ح) *to submit.*

Pi. *to check, still, quiet;* e. g. the waves, Ps. 89:10. anger, Prov. 29:11.

Hiph. i. q. Pi. *to still* (the waves). Ps. 65 : 8.

שְׁבַח Chald. found only in Pa. שַׁבַּח *to commend, praise.* See the Heb. no. I. Dan. 2 : 23. 4 : 31, 34. [4 : 34, 37.]

שֵׁבֶט and **שֵׁבֶט**, com. gen. with suff. שִׁבְטִי, plur. שְׁבָטִים, const. שִׁבְטֵי, dec. VI. g.

1. *a stick, staff, rod,* Lev. 27 : 32. Ps. 2 : 9. Particularly for chastisement, (Prov. 10 : 13. 13 : 24. 22 : 8.) hence *a rod of correction,* Job 9 : 34. 21 : 9. 37 : 13. Is. 10 : 5. 11 : 4 שֵׁבֶט פִּיו *the rod* or *scourge of his mouth,* metaphorically for a command to chastise.

2. *the staff of a ruler, a sceptre.* Gen. 49 : 10. Num. 24 : 17.

3. *a measuring staff* or *rod*; also *a portion of land assigned by measure, a lot, inheritance.* Ps. 74 : 2 שֵׁבֶט נַחֲלָתֶךָ *the possession assigned to thee.* Jer. 10 : 16. 51 : 19.

4. *a spear, javelin.* 2 Sam. 18 : 14. Comp. מַטֶּה no. 4.

5. *a tribe, tribus,* spoken of the tribes of Israel. (See מַטֶּה no. 3.) Ex. 28 : 21. Judg. 20 : 2. also i. q. מִשְׁפָּחָה *a family, a subdivision of a tribe,* Num. 4 : 18. Judg. 20 : 12. 1 Sam. 9 ; 21.

שְׁבַט Chald. *a tribe,* i. q. Heb. שֵׁבֶט no. 5. Ezra 6 : 17.

שְׁבָט m. the eleventh month of the Jewish ecclesiastical year, corresponding to part of January and part of February in our calendar. (So in Syr. and Arab.) Zech. 1 : 7.

שְׁבִי m. in pause שֶׁבִי, with suff. שִׁבְיוֹ, שִׁבְיֵךְ, verbal from שָׁבָה, dec. VI. l.

1. as an adj. *captive, a prisoner,* (after the form פְּתִי.) Ex. 12 : 29. Fem. שִׁבְיָה Is. 52 : 2.

2. as a subst. *captivity,* and as a concrete *captives, prisoners.* שָׁבָה שְׁבִי *to carry away prisoners,* Num. 21 : 1. Ps. 68 : 19. and בַּשְּׁבִי, הָלַךְ שְׁבִי, *to go into captivity,* Jer. 22 : 22. 30 : 16. Lam. 1 : 5. Used in reference to animals, Amos 4 : 10.

שָׁבִיב m. dec. III. a. *a flame.* Job 18 : 5. See the following article.

שְׁבִיב Chald. *idem.* Dan. 3 : 22. Plur. 7 : 9. (Arab. شبّ *to kindle,* and intrans. *to burn.*)

שִׁבְיָה fem. of שְׁבִי no. 2. *captivity, captives.* 2 Chr. 28 : 5. Neh. 4 : 4.

שְׁבִיל m. dec. I. *a way, path.* Ps. 77 : 20. Jer. 18 : 15, where in the Kethib we find שבול. Root שָׁבַל no. 1.

שְׁבִיסִים masc. plur. Is. 3 : 18. *caps of net-work, cauls;* comp. the Lat. *reticulum,* Varr. de Ling. Lat. IV. 19. (So in Talmud.) Root שָׁבַס prob. i. q. שָׁבַץ *to weave, make into a net.* According to others, *small suns,* like the Arab. شُبَيْسَة (a denom. from شمس, *the sun,*) a kind of spangle worn on the hair. Comp. in the same connexion שַׂהֲרֹנִים *small moons.*

שְׁבִיעִי, fem. ־ִית, an ordinal adj. (from שֶׁבַע *seven,*) *the seventh.* Gen. 2 : 2. Ex. 21 : 2.

שְׁבִית f. i. q. שְׁבוּת q. v. *captivity.* Num. 21 : 29.

שָׁבַל, Arab. سبل, a root not in use.

1. *to go.* Hence שְׁבִיל.

2. *to mount up, to grow.* (Arab. conj. IV. *to form ears.*) See שֹׁבֶל, שִׁבֹּלֶת no. 2.

3. *to flow, stream, overflow.* Comp. שֹׁבֶל, שִׁבֹּלֶת, שַׁבְּלוּל. For these transitions of meaning, see הָלַךְ, יָרַד, עָלָה, עָבַר.

שִׁבֹּל m. *a branch,* from שָׁבַל no. 2. (Comp. עָלֶה *a leaf,* from עָלָה.) Zech. 4 : 12 שִׁבֲּלֵי הַזֵּיתִים *olive branches.* The Dagesh forte is euphonic, as in סֻבְּכוֹ (from סְבַךְ) Jer. 4 : 7. and the Hateph-pattah as in סֻבֳּלוֹ Is. 9 : 3. 10 : 27. (The reading שִׁבְלֵי is contrary to the authority of the Masora.)

שֹׁבֶל m. *the trail or train of a garment.* Is. 47 : 2. (Arab. سَبَلَة *idem.* Root שָׁבַל no. 3.)

שַׁבְּלוּל m. according to the Hebrew interpreters and the Talmud, *a snail.*

Ps. 58:9 כְּמוֹ שַׁבְּלוּל תֶּמֶס יַהֲלֹךְ *as the snail which melts away as it walks,* i. e. which gradually wastes away by the moisture which it imparts in crawling. Root שָׁבַל no. 3. *to flow, dissolve,* (like λείμαξ, *limax,* from λείβω, *to flow,* λείβομαι, *to dissolve.*) In Chald. חִילְּזָא *idem,* with ח; comp. שִׁבֹּלֶת *an ear,* Chald. שׁוּבְּלָא.

שִׁבֹּלֶת f. plur. שִׁבֳּלִים.

1. *an ear of corn,* (from שָׁבַל no.2.) Job 24:24. Gen. 41:5 ff. Is. 17:5. (Arab. سُنْبُلَة by a resolution of the Dagesh forte into Nun.)

2. *a stream,* (see שָׁבַל no. 3.) Ps. 69: 3, 16. Is. 27:12.

שֶׁבְנָא and **שֶׁבְנָה** (prob. *a fresh, blooming young man;* comp. the Arab. شَابٌّ,) *Shebna,* the proper name of a prefect of the palace under Hezekiah, who was deprived of his office and succeded by Eliakim, (Is. 22:15.) but he afterwards appears with Eliakim as a private secretary of the king, (Is. 36:3. 2 K. 18:18. 26:37. 19:2.) This ought not to surprise us, considering the capriciousness of eastern monarchs in bestowing their favours.

שָׁבַע *to swear,* in Kal found only in the part. pass. Ezek. 21:28 שְׁבֻעֵי שְׁבֻעוֹת *jurantes juramenta.* (Prob. a denom. from שֶׁבַע *seven,* liter. *to affirm over seven victims,* or *with some other reference to seven, the sacred number.*) More commonly in

Niph. נִשְׁבַּע *to swear;* construed (1.) with בְּ of the person or thing *by* which a person swears, Gen. 21:23. 22:16.—*To swear by a god* was considered as an acknowledgement of him; thus of Jehovah, Deut. 6:13. 10:20. of idols, Amos 8:14.—*To swear by an unfortunate man,* means that the person who breaks his word shall become like him, Ps. 102:9. comp. Is. 65:15. (2.) with לְ of the person *to* whom one swears, Gen. 24:7. 21:23. Also with a dative of the person and an accus. of the thing *promised* by an oath, Gen. 50:24. Ex. 13:5. 33:1.—נִשְׁבַּע לֵאלֹהִים *to swear* (fidelity) *to God, nomen dare Deo,* 2 Chr. 15:14. comp. Is. 19:18. Zeph. 1:5, (where the prefix לְ interchanges with בְּ.)

Hiph. 1. *to make to swear, to bind by an oath.* Num. 5:19. Gen. 50:5. Hence

2. *to adjure, conjure, obtestari, to beseech solemnly, to beg earnestly.* Cant. 2:7. 3:5. 5:9. 1 K. 22:16.

Deriv. שְׁבוּעָה.

שֶׁבַע f. const. שְׁבַע, and **שִׁבְעָה**, const. שִׁבְעַת.

1. *seven,* placed either before or after the noun. When placed before, it is used either in the const. state, (Gen. 8:10.) or in the state absolute, (Num. 23:1.) It is put more rarely after the noun, as שְׁנַת־שֶׁבַע *the seventh year,* 2 K. 12:2.—The Hebrews employed *seven* (1.) as a round or indefinite number, to express a small number, (as we use *ten.*) Gen. 41.2 ff. 1 Sam. 2:5. Is. 4:1. Ruth 4:15. Prov. 26:25. So especially in poetic fictions, as Job 1:2, 3. 2:13. (2.) as a sacred number, like many other nations. Thus seven offerings in making a covenant, Gen. 21:28. seven lamps in the golden candlestick, Ex. 37:23. the blood was sprinkled seven times, Lev. 4:6, 17. etc. (See Fr. Gedicke verm. Schriften, p. 32—60.)—שִׁבְעָה עָשָׂר m. and שְׁבַע עֶשְׂרֵה f. *seventeen.*

2. *seven times,* usually as an indefinite or round number. Ps. 119:164. Prov. 24:16.

Dual שִׁבְעָתַיִם *seven fold or seven times.* Gen. 4:15, 24. Ps. 12:7. 2 Sam. 21: 9 Keth.

Plur. שִׁבְעִים *seventy,* for the most part as a round number. Gen. 50:3. So *seven and seventy,* Gen. 4:24.

Deriv. שָׁבַע.

שִׁבְעָה Gen. 26:33. proper name of a well so called, according to this passage, from an oath. It was perhaps originally pronounced with other vowels שְׁבֻעָה which signifies *an oath.* (Comp.

Gesenius' Gesch. der Hebr. Sprache und Schrift, p. 186.)

שִׁבְעָנָה m. i. q. שִׁבְעָה, *seven.* Once Job 42:13.

שָׁבַץ in Kal not used. In Syr. *to mingle, to weave;* in Arab. conj. V. *to be interwoven, intricate.* In Hebrew used only in Piel and Pual.

Pi. 1. Ex. 28:39. *to work with checker-work on white cloth,* so that the checks or cells resembled the settings of precious stones, (see signif. no. 2.) So in Greek σφενδόνη (1.) *the bezel of a ring;* (2.) a certain figure woven on cloth. According to Salmasius, *opus ocellatum;* better, *opus tessellatum, reticulatum.* Deriv. מִשְׁבְּצוֹת no. 1. תַּשְׁבֵּץ; comp. שְׁבִיסִים.

2. *to set* (precious stones). Pu. pass. Ex. 28:20. Deriv. מִשְׁבְּצוֹת no. 2.

שָׁבָץ m. found only 2 Sam. 1:9. according to the Targums, *perplexity, terror;* (comp. the verb שָׁבַץ.) But as the article shews the word to have a more specific meaning, better according to the Rabbins, *a cramp,* or according to others, *a giddiness.*

שְׁבַק Chald. *to leave.* Dan. 4:12, 20, 23. [4:15, 23, 26.] (Syr. *idem.*)

Ithpe. *to be left.* Dan. 2:44.

שָׁבַר, fut. יִשְׁבֹּר.

1. trans. *to break in pieces.* Jer. 2:20. 19:10. Several phrases in which this verb occurs may be found under the articles זְרוֹעַ, מַטֶּה, קֶשֶׁת. Hos. 2:20 וְקֶשֶׁת וְחֶרֶב וּמִלְחָמָה אֶשְׁבּוֹר מִן הָאָרֶץ *I will break in pieces the bow, the sword, and the weapons of war,* (and remove them) *out of the land.* Applied to the destruction of ships by the wind, Ezek. 27:26.

2. *to tear in pieces,* spoken of wild animals. 1 K. 13:26, 28. And generally of injuries to the body. Part. שָׁבוּר *broken, maimed,* Lev. 22:22. See Niph. no. 2. Metaphorically *to break* or *wound* the heart, Ps. 69:21. 147:3.

3. *to assuage* or *quench* thirst, *frangere sitim.* Ps. 104:11.

4. *to destroy.* Dan. 11:26. Ezek. 30:21. See Niph. no. 3. and שֶׁבֶר.

5. *to cut off, measure off, appoint.* Job 38:10 וָאֶשְׁבֹּר עָלָיו חֻקִּי *when I appointed my bounds about it* (*the sea*). Comp. גָּזַר.

6. denom. from שֶׁבֶר no. 6. (1.) *to buy* (grain); joined with שֶׁבֶר, Gen. 47:14. with בַּר, 42:3. also without addition, 42:5. Is. 55:1. (2.) *to sell* (grain). Gen. 41:56.

Niph. pass. 1. *to be broken in pieces, frangi.* Is. 14:29. Spoken of ships, *to be dashed in pieces, to founder,* Ezek. 27:34. Jon. 1:4.

2. *to be torn in pieces.* Ps. 124:7. Spoken of cattle, *to be hurt, injured,* Ex. 22:9, 13. Ezek. 34:4, 15. Zech. 11:16 הַנִּשְׁבָּרֶת *the hurt, injured.* Metaphorically with לֵב, *to be of a contrite heart,* Ps. 34:19. Is. 61:1. Ps. 51:19. Perhaps trans. as in Kal, Ezek. 6:9.

3. *to be broken in pieces, to be overthrown,* spoken of an army, Dan. 11:22. 2 Chr. 14:12. *to be destroyed, to perish,* spoken of a state, of a city, of individuals, Is. 8:15. 24:10. 28:13. Jer. 48:4. Dan. 8:25. 11:4. Ezek. 30:8.

Pi. שִׁבֵּר i. q. Kal no. 1. *to break* or *smite in pieces;* e. g. the teeth, Ps. 3:8. images, altars, 2 K. 18:4. 23:14. ships, Ps. 48:8.

Hiph. 1. *to let break through,* in reference to the birth of a first child, (comp. מַשְׁבֵּר.) Is. 66:9 הַאֲנִי אַשְׁבִּיר וְלֹא אוֹלִיד *should I cause to break through,* i. e. to open the womb, *and not cause to bring forth?* Comp. Hos. 13:13. Is. 37:3.

2. denom. from שֶׁבֶר, *to sell* (grain). Gen. 42:6. Am. 8:5, 6.

Hoph. pass. *to be wounded, hurt,* spoken of the heart, i. q. Niph. no. 2. Jer. 8:21.

Deriv. מַשְׁבֵּר, מִשְׁבָּר, שִׁבָּרוֹן, שֶׁבֶר.

שֶׁבֶר and **שֵׁבֶר**, with suff. שִׁבְרִי, verbal from שָׁבַר dec VI. g. and h.

1. *a breaking.* Is. 30:14.

2. *a wound, injury, breach.* Lev. 21:19. 24:20. Metaphorically *a*

breach or *wound* (of a state), Ps. 60 : 4. —שֶׁבֶר רוּחַ *a broken heart, sorrow*, Is. 65 : 14.

3. *ruin, destruction*; of a state, Lam. 2 : 11. 3 : 47. of individual persons, Prov. 16 : 18. Is. 1 : 28.

4. *a solution, explanation*, (of a dream.) Judg. 7 : 15.

5. plur. שְׁבָרִים *terror*. Job 41 : 17. [41 : 25.] This metaphorical signification is found in many verbs of *breaking*, e. g. חָתַת.

6. *grain*, perhaps so called from its being *broken* in the mill. Gen. 42 : 1 ff. Ex. 8 : 5. etc. Comp. שָׁבַר no 6.

שִׁבָּרוֹן m. verbal from שָׁבַר, dec. III. d.

1. *a breaking*. Ezek. 21 : 6 שִׁבְרוֹן מָתְנַיִם *a breaking of the loins*, as an image of extreme pain.

2. *destruction*. Jer. 17 : 18.

שָׁבַת, fut. יִשְׁבֹּת and יִשְׁבַּת (Lev. 26 : 34.)

1. *to cease to do* any thing, construed with מִן and an infin. Job 32 : 1. Jer. 31 : 36. Hos. 7 : 4. Hence

2. used absolutely, *to rest from labour, to keep holyday*, Ex. 23 : 12, 34 : 21. Spoken of a country, *to lie uncultivated*, Lev. 26 : 34, 35. comp. 25 : 2. Construed with מִן *to rest from* a labour, Gen. 2 : 2, 3. Ex. 31 : 17. Comp. Is. 33 : 8 שָׁבַת עֹבֵר אֹרַח *the wayfaring man resteth*, i. e. travels no more. 14 : 4. Lam. 5 : 14 *the elders rest from the gate*, i. e. they visit it no more.

3. *to cease to be, to have an end*. Gen. 8 : 22. Is. 24 : 8. Lam. 5 : 15.

Niph. i. q. Kal no. 3. strictly pass. of Hiph. *to cease to be, to have an end*. Is. 17 : 3. Ezek. 6 : 6. 30 : 18. 33 : 28.

Hiph. 1. *to make to cease from* doing any thing; construed with מִן and an infin. Ezek. 34 : 10. with לְבִלְתִּי and an infin. Josh. 22 : 25.

2. *to let rest* or *cease*, (as a person from labour,) construed with מִן. Ex. 5 : 5. (as a work,) 2 Chr. 16 : 5. Neh. 4 : 11.

3. *to still, quiet*. Ps. 8 : 3.

4. *to make to cease, to put an end to*, e. g. a war, Ps. 46 : 10. contention, Prov. 18 : 18. rejoicing, Is. 16 : 10. also Jeremiah 48 : 35. Amos 8 : 4. Ruth 4 : 14 אֲשֶׁר לֹא הִשְׁבִּית לָךְ גֹּאֵל *who has not left thee without a kinsman*. Lev. 2 : 13.

5. *to put away, to remove*, construed with מִן, i. q. הֵסִיר. Ex. 12 : 15. Lev. 26 : 6. Ezek. 34 : 25. 23 : 27, 48. 30 : 13. Is. 30 : 11. Jer. 7 : 34. Ps. 119 : 119.

I. **שֶׁבֶת** m. with suff. שִׁבְתּוֹ, verbal from שָׁבַת, dec. VI. h.

1. *a ceasing*. Prov. 20 : 3. comp. 18 : 18. 22 : 10.

2 *an interruption, loss of time*. Ex. 21 : 19.

II. **שֶׁבֶת** f. the infin. of יָשַׁב *to dwell*, q. v.

שַׁבָּת com. gen. (masc. Lev. 25 : 4. fem. Ex. 31 : 14.) const. שַׁבַּת, with suff. שַׁבַּתּוֹ, plur. שַׁבָּתוֹת, const. שַׁבְּתוֹת, verbal from שָׁבַת, *a day of rest, a sabbath*, the seventh day of the week among the Jews. Ex. 16 : 25 שַׁבָּת הַיּוֹם לַיהוָֹה *to day is a day of rest to Jehovah*.—שַׁבַּת שַׁבָּת *every sabbath*, 1 Chr. 9 : 32.—שַׁבַּת שָׁנִים *the sabbatical year*, every seventh year which was a year of release, Lev. 25 : 4, 8. (In Lev. 23 : 15, some adopt the signification, *a week*, as in Syr. and Greek Mat. 28 : 1. but this is not necessary.)

שַׁבָּתוֹן m. verbal from שָׁבַת, *idem*, but with a more intense signification. Ex. 16 : 23. Lev. 23 : 24. For the most part in the phrase שַׁבַּת שַׁבָּתוֹן Ex. 31 : 15. 35 : 2. Lev. 16 : 31. *a great festival*.

שָׁגַג i. q. שָׁגָה.

1. *to wander, to go astray*. Hence

2. *to err, transgress*, (from mistake or ignorance.) Ps. 119 : 67. Num. 15 : 28. שָׁגַג שְׁגָגָה *to be guilty of a transgressing*, Lev. 5 : 18. According to this we may render Gen. 6 : 3 בְּשַׁגַּם הוּא בָשָׂר *on account of their transgressing, they are flesh*, i. e. collect. on account of their transgressions; (as if an infin. after the form שַׁךְ Jer. 5 : 26.) But all the ancient versions render it, *because he is flesh*, as if it were compounded of בְּ, שֶׁ = אֲשֶׁר and גַּם = גַּם *also*. This is more accordant with the context, but

has the following difficulties; (1.) the use of the prefix שֶׁ in Genesis, and that in prose. To this, however, it may be answered in part, that the solemn speeches of Jehovah, even in the prosaic portions of the Old Testament, abound with poetic forms. See Gen. 1:24 חַיְתוֹ, comp. verse 25 חַיַּת. In like manner verse 10 יַמִּים. (2.) that בְּשַׁגָּם stands for בְּ although it has a *lesser* distinctive accent. But similar exceptions in regard to the lesser distinctives sometime occur. (3.) that גַּם is apparently superfluous. But it may perhaps be rendered, *because he is also flesh*, (and not barely spirit.) The sentence, however, would still appear to drag.

שְׁגָגָה f. verbal from שָׁגַג, dec. XI. c. *an error, mistake.* Ecc. 5:5. חָטָא בִשְׁגָגָה *to sin through inadvertence* or *ignorance*, Lev. 4:2, 27. Num. 15:27.

שָׁגָה (comp. שָׁגַג.)

1. *to wander about.* Ezek. 34:6. Construed with מִן, *to wander from* the way, and metaphorically from the commands of God, Prov. 19:27.

2. *to transgress, to do wrong.* Lev. 4:13. 1 Sam. 26:21, with the accessory idea of inadvertence or ignorance.

3. *to be giddy, to be intoxicated;* from wine, Is. 28:7. Prov. 20:1. from love, Prov. 5:20 *wherefore art thou intoxicated, my son, with (the love of) a strange woman?* Verse 14.

Hiph. 1. *to lead astray.* Deut. 27:18.

2. metaphorically *to let wander*, construed with מִן, Ps. 119:10. *to seduce, entice*, Job 12:16.

Deriv. מִשְׁגֶּה, comp. also מְשׂוּגָה, שְׁגִיאָה.

שָׁגַח found only in Hiph. *to look, see, view;* e. g. from a window, Cant. 2:9. Construed with אֶל, Is. 14:16. Also with מִן, Ps. 33:14. (In Chald. *providere*, הַשְׁגָּחָה *providentia.*)

שְׁגִיאָה f. dec. X. *a transgression from ignorance* or *inadvertence.* Ps. 19:13. Root שָׁגָא i. q. שָׁגָה.

שִׁגָּיוֹן m. Ps. 7:1. and in the plur. שִׁגְיֹנוֹת Hab. 3:1. *a song, an ode*, (comp. Syr. [Syriac] *cantilena, cantio*, from [Syriac] Pa. *cecinit;*) or (after the Arab. שגי *to be sad, distressed,*) *a lamentation*, to be rendered then in Habakkuk, *after the manner of a lamentation.*

שָׁגַל *to lie with* (a woman). Deut. 28:30.

Niph. pass. Is. 13:16. Zech. 14:2.

Pu. Jer. 3:2.

Note. The Masoretes regarded this word as low and obscene, and have, therefore, substituted שׁכב for it in the Keri.

שֵׁגָל f. *a wife, spouse*, e. g. of the Persian king. Neh. 2:6. Prob. also Ps. 45:10.

שֵׁגַל f. Chald. *idem*, spoken of the wives of the king of Babylon. Dan. 5:2, 3, 23. different from לְחֵנָן *concubines.*

שָׁגַע in Kal not used. In Arab. *to be bold*, also *to rave, be mad.*

Pu. part. מְשֻׁגָּע.

1. *mad, raving.* 1 Sam. 21:16. Deut. 28:34.

2. *an enthusiast, fanatic;* spoken of false prophets, Jer. 29:26. Hos. 9:7. also reproachfully of true prophets, 2 K. 9:11.

Hithpa. *to rave, to make one's self a mad man.* 1 Sam. 21:15, 16.

Deriv. שִׁגָּעוֹן.

שִׁגָּעוֹן m. verbal from שָׁגַע, *madness.* Deut. 28:28. 2 K. 9:20.

שֶׁגֶר m. Ex. 13:12. const. שְׁגַר Deut. 7:13. 28:4. *an offspring, young, fœtus.* (Root Syr. and Chald. *misit, emisit.*)

שַׁד Lam. 4:3. dual שָׁדַיִם, const. שְׁדֵי m. (Hos. 9:14. Cant. 4:5.) *breasts;* spoken of men, Cant. 4:5. 8:1. of animals, Gen. 49:25. (In Aram. תַּד.) See שֹׁד.

שֵׁד found only in the plur. שֵׁדִים m. *idols*, liter. *lords*, like בְּעָלִים. Deut. 32:

17. Ps. 106:37. Root שׁוּד Arab. سَادَ med. Je *to rule;* whence سَيِّدٌ *a lord.* Syr. ܫܺܐܕܳܐ *an evil demon.* Sept. δαιμόνια. Vulg. *dæmonia.* The names of idols are often used by the later Jews for demons.

I. שַׁד m. i. q. שֹׁד, prim. *a mother's breast.* Job 24:9. Is. 60:16.

II. שֹׁד, once שׁוֹד (Job 5:21.) verbal from שָׁדַד.

1. *violence, oppression;* either actively, Prov. 21:7. 24:2. or passively, Ps. 12:6 שֹׁד עֲנִיִּים *the oppression of the poor.* Also *goods obtained by violence,* Am. 3:10.

2. *desolation, destruction;* often joined with שֶׁבֶר. Is. 51:19. 59:7. Jer. 48:3.—Hab. 2:17 שֹׁד בְּהֵמוֹת *desolation by wild beasts.*

שָׁדַד 1. *to oppress, destroy.* Ps. 17:9. Prov. 11:3. Part. שֹׁדְדֵי לַיְלָה *nightly robbers,* Obad. 5. Part. pass. שָׁדוּד *slain, dead,* Judg. 5:27. (In Arab. 1. *to fall on;* 2. *to strengthen;* conj. II. *to harden;* conj. III. *to be more violent than another, to overcome.*)

2. *to desolate, lay waste;* a country or city, Ps. 137:8. Jer. 25:36. a people, Jer. 47:4, 7. 49:28. Ps. 91:6. Jer. 5:6.

Note. The inflection of this verb is in part regular, and in part contracted; e. g. pret. שָׁדְדוּ, with suff. שַׁדּוּנִי, fut. יָשׁוּד Ps. 91:6, (as if from שׁוּד,) with suff. יְשָׁדְדֵם Jer. 5:6. and יְשָׁדֵּם Prov. 11:3.

Niph. *to be laid waste.* Mic. 2:4.

Pi. i. q. Kal no. 1. Prov. 19:26. 24:15.

Pu. שֻׁדַּד and שֻׁדַּד (Nah. 3:7.) *to be laid waste,* pass. of Kal no. 2. Is. 15:1. 23:1. Jer. 4:13. 48:1.

Po. *to destroy.* Hos. 10:2.

Hoph. הוּשַׁד pass. Is. 35:1. Hos. 10:14.

שִׁדָּה fem. of שַׁד, dec. X. liter. *a lady, princess,* whence *a wife, concubine.* (Comp. سَيِّدَةٌ *domina, conjux.* Instead of ־ָה stands Hirik defective with Dagesh forte following; comp. שְׁלִשִׁים and שְׁלֹשִׁים, קִמּוֹשׁ and קִמְּשׁוֹנִים.) Ecc. 2:8 שִׁדָּה וְשִׁדּוֹת *a wife and wives,* i. e. concubines of every description. Compare the context, which requires that the harem should be mentioned among the delights of an eastern king, and the preceding word תַּעֲנֻגוֹת *luxuriousness,* (comp. Cant. 7:7.) Aben Ezra derives this same signification, but less suitably, from שַׁד *the female breast,* whence *a female,* like רַחַם Judg. 5:30.

שַׁדַּי m. *the Almighty,* an epithet of Jehovah, sometimes in the phrase אֵל שַׁדַּי, Gen. 17:1. 28:3. Ex. 6:3. and sometimes standing by itself, Job 5:17, and frequently in this book. Ruth 1:20, 21. The form is the pluralis excellentiæ from a sing. שַׁד *mighty,* (comp. Arab. شَدِيدٌ *mighty, violent,* under the root שָׁדַד.) ־ַי is the ancient plural termination, as in אֲדֹנָי. Sept. generally παντοκράτωρ. Vulg. in the Pentateuch *Omnipotens.*

שַׁדּוּן Job 19:29. not a proper word, but compounded of the prefix שֶׁ=אֲשֶׁר. and דִּין *judgment,* hence *that there is a judgment.* So in the Keri, שַׁדִּין.

I. שְׁדֵמָה f. Is. 37:27. *blighted grain,* i. q. שְׁדֵפָה in the parallel passage 2 K. 19:26. by a commutation of מ and ף. See under the letter ב.

II. שְׁדֵמָה, plur. שְׁדֵמוֹת, const. שַׁדְמוֹת, dec. XI. d. *a field.* Jer. 31:40. 2 K. 23:4. Deut. 32:32. In the two remaining passages (Is. 16:8. Hab. 3:17.) it is construed with a verb in the singular. It is found in none of the kindred dialects, but the signification given above is sufficiently evident from the connection and from the ancient versions.

שָׁדַף *to burn, blacken, blast, blight,* spoken of the injurious effects of the east wind on the grain. Gen. 41:23, 27. (Arab. with ס *to be dark, to be black;* Chald. שְׁדַף *to burn.*) Hence

שִׁדָּפָה f. verbal from שָׁדַף, *blighted grain.* 2 K. 19:26.

שִׁדָּפוֹן m. verbal from שָׁדַף, *a blasting* (of corn or grain). 1 K. 8:37. Amos 4:9. Deut. 28:22. According to Gen. 41:6 ff. it is sometimes an effect of the east wind.

שְׁדַר Chald. Ithpa. *to exert one's self,* construed with לְ. Dan. 6:15. Elsewhere in Chald. and Rabbin. שְׁדַל; see the letter לְ, p. 290.

שֹׁהַם m. name of a precious stone. Gen. 2:12. Ex. 28:9, 20. 35:9, 27. Job 28:16. Ezek. 28:13. Most of the ancient versions make it *the sardonyx.* Others: *the flesh-coloured onyx with whitish lines;* (comp. the Arab. مسهم *a striped garment.*)

שׁו Job 15:31 Keth. i. q. שָׁוְא.

שׁוֹא i. q. the root שָׁאָה q. v.

שׁוֹא m. dec. I. *ruin, destruction.* Ps. 35:17. Root שׁוֹא = שָׁאָה. See the fem. שׁוֹאָה.

שָׁוְא m. (read *shav*) a segolated form, like מָוֶת, but without the furtive Segol, like קֹשְׁטְ. Root שׁוּא, (whence שָׁוְא, like מָוֶת from מוּת,) Arab. (with ل) *to be bad, wicked.*

1. *what is vain, vanity.* Job 15:31. —הַבְלֵי שָׁוְא *vain idols,* Ps. 31:7. Hence

2. *what is useless, to no purpose* or *in vain.* Mal. 3:14 שָׁוְא עֲבֹד אֱלֹהִים *it is in vain to serve God.* Hence לַשָּׁוְא *in vain, to no purpose,* Jer. 2:30. 4:30. 6:29.

3. *what is false* or *deceitful, a lie, falsehood.* Ps. 12:3. 41:7. Job 31:5. שֵׁמַע שָׁוְא *a false report,* Ex. 23:1. עֵד שָׁוְא *a false witness,* Deut. 5:17.—Ex. 20:7 לֹא תִשָּׂא אֶת־שֵׁם יְהוָה לַשָּׁוְא *thou shalt not utter the name of Jehovah on a falsehood,* i. e. thou shalt not swear falsely; comp. Ps. 24:4.

4. *wickedness,* (comp. אָוֶן.) מְתֵי שָׁוְא *the wicked,* Job 11:11.—Is. 5:18 חַבְלֵי הַשָּׁוְא *cords of wickedness.*

5. *trouble, affliction, destruction.* Job 7:3. Is. 30:28 נָפַת שָׁוְא *the sieve* or *winnowing-fan of destruction.*

שׁוֹאָה f. verbal from שׁוֹא = שָׁאָה q. v. dec. X.

1. *a storm, tempest.* Prov. 1:27 *when your fear cometh as a tempest.* (In the Kethib שַׁאֲוָה.) Ezek. 38:9.

2. *sudden destruction, ruin.* Ps. 63:10 לְשׁוֹאָה יְבַקְשׁוּ נַפְשִׁי *they seek after my life to destroy it.* Is. 10:3. 47:11. Ps. 35:8.

3. *desolation.* Usually connected, by way of paronomasia, with the synonymous word מְשׁוֹאָה. Zeph. 1:15. Hence *desolated countries, ruins,* Job 30:3, 14. 38:27.

שׁוּב, infin. absol. שׁוֹב, fut. יָשׁוּב, apoc. יָשֹׁב.

1. *to turn, turn back, to return.*—עֹבֵר וָשָׁב *he that goeth and he that returneth,* Ezek. 35:7. Zech. 7:14. 9:8. (Comp. בָּא וְיֹצֵא.) The following constructions are worthy of notice, (1.) with לְ and אֶל, *to turn* or *return to* a person or thing, e. g. to Jehovah, 1 K. 8:33. Ps. 22:28. So with עַל, 2 Chr. 30:9. with עַד, Is. 19:22. Joel 2:12. Amos 4:6 ff. with בְּ, Hos. 12:7. Without addition, *to return, be converted,* Jer. 3:12, 14, 22. 2 Chr. 6:24. Is. 1:27 שָׁבֶיהָ *her (Zion's) converted citizens.* (2.) with מִן, *to cease, desist;* e.g. from a purpose, Jer. 4:28. from good, Ezek. 18:24. from evil, Ezek. 3:19. 14:6. Job 36:10. from anger, Ex. 32:12. Also in phrases as *my anger ceases* or *is turned away from* a person, Gen. 27:45. 2 Chr. 12:12. and without addition, שָׁב אַפִּי *my anger ceases,* Gen. 27:44. Is. 5:25. 12:1. Prov. 25:10 *and thy shame cease not.* (3.) with מֵאַחֲרֵי, *to turn back from* a person whom one has followed, Ruth 1:16. or persecuted, 2 Sam. 2:26, 30. hence *to turn away, to apostatize;* e.g. from Jehovah, Josh. 22:16, 23, 29. 1 Sam. 15:11. (without addition, Josh. 23:12.) (4.) *to come back to the possession of* a thing, construed with אֶל. Ezek. 7:13. Is. 23:17. Lev. 25:10.

2. spoken of things without life, *to go* or *come back*, particularly in the following phrases; (1.) *to be turned into* any thing *again;* e. g. Is. 29:17. comp. Gen. 3:19. Ecc. 3:20. (2.) *to be given back* (to its former owner), construed with לְ. Lev. 27:24. Deut. 28:31. 1 Sam. 7:14. 1 K. 12:26. (3.) *to be recalled, to continue unfulfilled,* spoken of a command, a prophecy, (the opposite of בּוֹא *to be fulfilled.*) Is. 45:23. 55:11. Ezek. 7:13. (4.) *to be recovered, to be restored;* spoken of cities, Ezek. 35:9 Keri. 1 Sam. 7:14. comp. Ezek. 16:55. of a diseased member, 1 K. 13:6. 2 K. 5:10, 14. Ex. 4:7.

3. joined with another verb, it forms a periphrasis of the adverbs *again, anew.* It is then connected with a finite verb with and without a copula; e. g. Gen. 30:31 אָשׁוּבָה אֶרְעֶה *I will feed again.* 26:18. Josh. 5:2. 2 K. 1:13 וַיָּשָׁב וַיִּשְׁלַח *and he sent again.* 20:5. Is. 6:13. With an infin. Job 7:7.

4. causat. as in Hiph. (1.) *to lead or bring back.* Num. 10:36. Ps. 85:5. Particularly in the phrase שׁוּב שְׁבוּת *to bring back captives,* see שְׁבוּת. (2.) *to restore.* Nah. 2:3. The Kethib frequently has יָשׁוּב in a causative sense, where the Keri has יָשִׁיב.

Pil. שׁוֹבֵב 1. *to lead or bring back.* Jer. 50:19.

2. *to convert.* Is. 49:5. See Kal no. 1. (1.)

3. *to make rebellious, to pervert.* Is. 47:10. See Kal no. 1. (3.)

4. *to restore.* Is. 58:12. Prob. Ps. 60:3.

5. שׁוֹבֵב נֶפֶשׁ *to animate* or *invigorate the soul.* Ps. 23:3. Comp. הֵשִׁיב נֶפֶשׁ.

Pul. שׁוֹבַב pass. whence the part. מְשׁוֹבֶבֶת *brought back,* i. e. escaped, delivered, Ezek. 38:8.

Hiph. הֵשִׁיב, fut. יָשִׁיב, apoc. יָשֵׁב, וַיָּשֶׁב, *to cause to turn back;* hence

1. *to bring* or *lead back,* e. g. prisoners. Jer. 32:44. 33:11. 49:6, 39. Hence *to drive back, to keep off, to hinder,* Job 9:12. 11:10. 23:13. Is. 14:27. 43:13. Particularly (1.) joined with פָּנִים, *to turn away the face of* a person, i. e. to refuse or deny his request. 1 K. 2:16, 17, 20. 2 Chr. 6:42. (2.) with נֶפֶשׁ, *to bring back the life of* a person, i. e. to relieve or refresh him. Ruth 4:15. Lam. 1:11, 16, 19. Metaphorically Ps. 19:8. (By weariness life is as it were exhausted, by refreshment it is restored again, comp. 1 Sam. 30:12. Judg. 15:19.) (3.) with אַף, חֵמָה, *to still* or *assuage anger.* Job 9:13. Ps. 78:38. 106:23. Construed with מִן *from* a person, Prov. 24:18.—הֵשִׁיב חֲמַת יְהוָה מִן *to turn away the wrath of Jehovah from* a person, Num. 25:11. Ezra 10:14.

2. *to give back, to restore,* construed with a dative of the person. Ex. 22:25. Deut. 22:2. Particularly *to make good, replace;* e. g. what is stolen, Lev. 5:23. [6:4.] a trespass, Num. 5:7. Hence (1.) *to compensate, recompense;* construed with a dative, Ps. 18:21. 116:12. with עַל, Ps. 94:23. and without a mention of the person, Prov. 17:13. with an accus. and dative, Gen. 50:15. (2.) הֵשִׁיב דָּבָר *to return word, to answer,* construed with an accus. of the person, (like עָנָה.) 1 K. 12:6, 9, 16. Also *to bring word* or *answer,* Num. 22:8. 13:27. 2 Sam. 24:13. The former is also expressed with אֲמָרִים, Prov. 22:21. with מִלִּין, Job 35:4. without addition, 2 Chr. 10:16. Job 35:5.

3. *to bring again, to bring repeatedly;* as a tribute, 2 K. 3:4. 17:3. 2 Chr. 27:5. Ps. 72:10. an offering, Num. 18:9. So in Lat. *sacra referre,* Virg. Georg. I. 339. Æn. V. 598. 603.

4. *to recal, revoke,* e. g. a blessing, Num. 23:20. an edict, Est. 8:5, 8 אֵין לְהָשִׁיב *it is irrevocable.* Am. 1:3 ff *for many transgressions of Damascus I will not revoke it,* scil. what I have decreed. (Comp. verses 4, 5. and Num. 23:20.)

5. *to restore.* Is. 1:26. Dan. 9:25.

6. simply *to turn, direct, apply.* Hence (1.) הֵשִׁיב אֶל לֵב *to lay to heart, to*

consider. Deut. 4:39. 30:1. With עַל, Is. 46:8. Hence *to repent*, 1 K. 8:47. (2.) with פָּנִים, *to turn away one's face*, Ezek. 14:6. and without פָּנִים, 18:30, 32. Construed with לְ, *to turn one's face to* a place, Dan. 11:18, 19.

Hoph. הוּשַׁב *to be brought, led, given back.* Gen. 42:28. 43:12. Num. 5:8. etc.

Deriv. out of course תְּשׁוּבָה, מְשׁוּבָה, שִׁיבָה.

שׁוֹבָב m. verbal adj. from שׁוּב, dec. II. b. *rebellious, backsliding.* Jer. 3:14, 22. Is. 57:17.

שׁוֹבֵב, fem. שׁוֹבֵבָה, verbal adj. from שׁוּב, *rebellious, backsliding.* Jer. 31:22. 49:4.

שׁוֹד *desolation*, see **שֹׁד**.

שׁוּד, whence the fut. יָשׁוּד, see **שָׁדַד**.

I. **שָׁוָה** 1. *to be even.* See Pi.

2. *to be equal*, e. g. in value, construed with בְּ. Prov. 3:15. 8:11. Est. 7:4. כִּי אֵין הַצָּר שֹׁוֶה בְּנֵזֶק הַמֶּלֶךְ *although the enemy could not equal*, i. e. make good, *the damage of the king.* Used passively, שָׁוָה לִי *it was recompensed to me, æquitum est mihi*, Job 33:27.

3. *to be like*, construed with לְ. Prov. 26:4. Is. 40:25.

4. *to be sufficient, to satisfy.* Est. 5:13 כָּל־זֶה אֵינֶנּוּ שֹׁוֶה לִי *all this satisfies me not.*

5. *suitable, serviceable, useful.* Est. 3:8 לַמֶּלֶךְ אֵין שֹׁוֶה *it is not useful to the king.*

Pi. 1. *to make plain* or *even.* Is. 28:25. Joined with נֶפֶשׁ, *to quiet one's spirit, to compose one's mind, animum componere*, Ps. 131:2. So prob. elliptically Is. 38:13 שִׁוִּיתִי עַד בֹּקֶר *I quieted myself*, i.e. I waited, *till morning.* Vulg. and Jerome, *sperabam usque ad mane.* The word כָּאֲרִי must then (contrary to the accents) be joined to the following clause. Others, after signif. no. 2. *ponebam* (me) *usque ad mane sicut leonem* (rugientem,) *I was like till morning to a* (roaring) *lion.* Targ. *rugiebam, ut leo.* Or, *assimilabam* (me).

2. *to place, put, ponere.* (In the Targums more frequent. So שַׁוִּי *to place and to compare.*) Ps. 16:8. 21:6. 89:20 שִׁוִּיתִי עֵזֶר עַל גִּבּוֹר *I have given help to the mighty.* 119:30. שַׁוֵּה פְרִי *to prepare fruit*, Hos. 10:1. Construed with כְּ, *to make as* or *like*, Ps. 18:34.

Hiph. *to compare, liken.* Lam. 2:13.

II. **שָׁוָה**, in Chald. Ithpa. *to fear.* In Hebrew not used in Kal. Hence perhaps

Pi. Job 30:22 Keth. תְּמֹגְגֵנִי תְּשַׁוֶּה *thou makest me despond, thou terrifiest me.* (In the Keri תּוּשִׁיָּה.) The Syriac version likewise has two verbs here.

Nithpa. (a conjugation, uncommon in pure Hebrew, but frequent in Rabbinic, see Gesenius' Lehrgeb. §. 71. 4. Anm.) Prov. 27:15 *a continual dropping in a very rainy day* וְאֵשֶׁת מִדְיָנִים נִשְׁתָּוָה *and a contentious woman one must be afraid of.* Others after no. I. *are like to each other.* Vulg. *comparantur.* Greek Venet. ἰσοῦται. But so direct and apparently weak a mode of expressing the comparison is uncommon in the Proverbs. Others change the vowel-pointing, and read נִשְׁתָּוָה *which raves* or *storms;* comp. סְתָו *winter*, and the Greek χειμασθῆναι ἀπειλαῖς, κεχειμάνται φρένες. Targ. *uxor litigiosa, quæ rixatur.*

שְׁוָה or **שְׁוָא** Chald. i. q. Heb. שָׁוָה no. I. *to be equal, like, suitable.* Pa. Dan. 5:21 Keri וְלִבְבֵהּ עִם חֵיוְתָא שַׁוִּי *and his heart they made like to the beasts*, i. e. his heart was made like to the beasts. The Kethib reads שְׁוִי part. pass. of Kal, which is better suited to the passage.

Ithpa. *to be made into* any thing. Dan. 3:29.

שָׁוֵה Gen. 14:17. proper name of a valley, which is also called *the king's dale.* The latter name occurs likewise 2 Sam. 18:18. but there is nothing to determine its locality. If it be the same with שָׁוֵה קִרְיָתַיִם Gen. 14:5. it was probably in the neighbourhood of Kiriathaim; but there are two cities of this name, see p. 534.

שׁוּחַ (kindred with שָׁחָה and שָׁחַח.)

1. *to sink down.* Prov. 2:18 שָׁחָה אֶל־מָוֶת בֵּיתָהּ *her house sinks down to hades;* or (since בַּיִת is elsewhere uniformly masc.) *she sinks down to hades with her house,* liter. *quoad domum suam.* Deriv. שׁוּחָה, שִׁיחָה and שַׁחַת *a pit.*

2. *to be bowed down.* Ps. 44:26 שָׁחָה לֶעָפָר נַפְשֵׁנוּ *our soul is bowed down to the dust.* Lam. 3:20 Keri תָּשׁוֹחַ עָלַי נַפְשִׁי *my soul is bowed down within me.* Comp. Ps. 42:7.

שׁוּחַ proper name of a son of Abraham by Keturah. Gen. 25:2. Hence the patronymic and gentile noun שׁוּחִי *a Shuhite,* Job 2:11. 8:1. 25:1. the name of a tribe in Arabia Deserta, called Σαυχῖται, Σακχαῖοι by Ptolemy, (xv. 5.)

שׁוּחָה f. verbal from שׁוּחַ, *a pit, abyss.* Jer. 2:6. 18:20. Prov. 22:14.

I. שׁוּט 1. *to row.* Part. שָׁטִים *rowers,* Ezek. 27:8, 26. (Arab. ساط *to whip,* whence שׁוֹט *a whip, scourge.*) Deriv. מָשׁוֹט, שַׁיִט.

2. *to run to and fro, to seek.* Num. 11:8.—שׁוּט בָּאָרֶץ *to rove* or *wander through the earth* or *a country,* Job 1:7. 2:2. particularly for the purpose of reviewing, 2 Sam. 24:2, 8. (These two significations may be connected; comp. the German verbs *peitschen, rudern.*)

Pil. שׁוֹטֵט i. q. Kal no. 2. Jer. 5:1. Am. 8:12. Zech. 4:10 *the eyes of Jehovah* מְשׁוֹטְטִים בְּכָל־הָאָרֶץ *which run to and fro through the whole earth.* 2 Chr. 16:9. Metaphorically *to run over* or *examine* (a writing), Dan. 12:4.

Hithpa. i. q. Pi. Jer. 49:3.

II. שׁוּט Aram. ܫܳܛ i. q. שָׁאַט *to despise, contemn.* Part. שָׁאטִים Ezek. 16:57. 28:24, 26. See שָׁאַט.

שׁוֹט m. verbal from שׁוּט, dec. I. *a whip, scourge.* Prov. 26:3. 1 K. 12:11. שׁוֹט לָשׁוֹן *the scourge of the* (slanderous) *tongue,* Job 5:21. Particularly *the scourge* of God with which he punishes men, Is. 10:26. Job 9:23. Is. 28:15, 18 שׁוֹט שׁוֹטֵף *the overflowing scourge,* an incongruous figure, for *a grievous calamity.* (The Arabians have similar expressions; see the Coran, Sur. 88:12. 89:33.)

שׁוּל m. dec. I.

1. *a hem.* Ex. 28:33, 34.

2. *the train* or *trail* (of a garment). Is. 6:1. גִּלָּה שׁוּלַיִם *to turn up the trail* (of one's garment), indicative of the greatest dishonour, Jer. 13:22, 26. Nah. 3:5. Root שׁוּל Arab. سَالَ *to be broad, slack, to hang down.*

שׁוֹלָל m. verbal from שָׁלַל.

1. *stripped, naked.* Mic. 1:8. Or perhaps more specifically *bare-footed,* (so the Sept. Syr.) Comp. נָשַׁל *to put off* (the shoe).

2. *captive, prisoner.* Job 12:17, 19.

שׁוּלַמִּית *Shulammith,* proper name of the maiden, whose praises are sung in a part, according to others, through the whole of Canticles. Cant. 7:1. It may be a gentile noun, *a Shulamite* or *Shunamite,* from שׁוּנֵם also called *Sulem;* or the fem. of שְׁלֹמֹה, after the Arabic form سُلَيْمَان *Suleiman.*

שׁוּם m. dec. I. *garlick.* Num. 11:5. Comp. Celsii Hierobot. T. II. p. 53.

שׁוּנֵם proper name of a city in the tribe of Issachar. Josh. 19:18. 1 Sam. 28:4. 2 K. 4:8. According to Eusebius, (under the word σουνὴμ,) there was a place *Sulem* (by a commutation of *l* and *n,*) five Roman miles south of mount Tabor. The gentile noun is שׁוּנַמִּי, fem. ־ִית, 1 K. 1:3. 2:17. 2 K. 4:12.

שָׁוַע or שׁוּעַ found only in Pi. שִׁוַּע *to cry,* particularly for help, construed with אֶל. Ps. 30:3. 88:14. 72:12. Hence

I. שׁוּעַ m. Is. 22:5. and שֶׁוַע Job 30:28. verbals from שִׁוַּע, *a cry for help.*

II. שׁוֹעַ, also שׁוּעַ (Job 36:19.) dec. I.

1. *rich, opulent,* Job 34:19. Ezek. 23:23. *riches,* Job 36:19.

2. *noble, liberal, magnanimous.* Is. 32:5. The root שׁוּעַ borrows its signification here from יָשַׁע Arab. وسع *to be broad*, also *to be rich, mighty;* conj. VIII. X. *to be noble-minded, liberal.*

שֶׁוַע m. dec. VI. d. Ps. 5:3. and שַׁוְעָה f. dec. X. verbals from שָׁוַע, *a cry for help, a supplication.* Ps. 18:7. 39:13. 102:2.

שׁוּעָל m. dec. I. *a fox.* Cant. 2:15. Lam. 5:18. Ezek. 13:4. Ps. 63:11. Neh. 3:35. (Arab. ثُعَالَة more frequently ثعلب, with ب annexed; comp. the proper name שַׁעַלְבִּים, which is also written שַׁעַלְבִים.) Under this name is included also in common life *the jackal,* (Pers. شغل *shagal;*) comp. Niebuhr's Beschreib. von Arabien, p. 166. and this meaning has been applied to Judg. 15:4. and Ps. 63:11. since the jackal is common in Palestine and feeds on carrion. But both of these circumstances are also true of the fox, and the jackal has another name in Hebrew (אִי.) See Bocharti Hieroz. T. II. p. 190 ff. of the Leips. edit. Faber zu Harmer's Beobachtungen, Th. 2. p. 270. Faber's Archäologie, Th. 1. p. 140.

שׁוֹעֵר m. (denom. from שַׁעַר *a gate,*) dec. VII. b. *a porter.* 2 K. 7:10, 11. 2 Chr. 31:14.

שׁוּף 1. *to break* or *smite in pieces.* (So in Chald. Ps. 94:5. Deut. 9:21 Targ. for the Heb. כָּתַת; and more frequently the kindred verbs שְׁפָא, שְׁפַף, for the Heb. דָּכָה, דָּכָא etc.) Job 9:17 אֲשֶׁר בִּשְׂעָרָה יְשׁוּפֵנִי *who breaks me in pieces with a tempest.* Sept. ἐκτρίψῃ. Vulg. *conteret.*

2. i. q. Lat. *ferio,* Greek πλήττω, *to smite, strike;* also spoken of the serpent, *to bite.* Gen. 3:15 הוּא יְשׁוּפְךָ רֹאשׁ וְאַתָּה תְּשׁוּפֶנּוּ עָקֵב *he (the seed of the woman) shall smite thee on the head, and thou shalt bite him on the heel.* In Hebrew both these ideas are expressed by the same word נָכָה; and in Arabic by ضرب. Syr. ܢܫܘܦ *conteret,* ܬܫܘܦܝܗ *feries.* Jerome, *conteret — insidiaberis.* See Eichhorn's Urgesch. herausgegeben von Gabler, Th. II. B. 1. p. 189 ff. B. 2. p. 281 ff.

3. perhaps also *to press.* Ps. 139:11 חֹשֶׁךְ יְשׁוּפֵנִי *tenebræ prement,* i. e. occultabunt *me;* comp. *noctepremi,* Æn. VI. 828. *silentio premere, nubibus pressus.* Or, *darkness is dark about me.* In this case שׁוּף is supposed to derive its meaning from נֶשֶׁף *twilight, darkness.* Sept. καλύψει. Symm. ἐπισκεπάσει. Others compare the Arab. شاف *vidit,* conj. V. *ex alto prospexit;* hence *the darkness sees me.*

שׁוֹפָר m. plur. שׁוֹפָרוֹת, dec. II. b. *a horn, trumpet, lituus,* different from חֲצֹצְרָה. Ex. 19:16. Lev. 25:9. Jerome on Hos. 5:8, buccina pastoralis est et cornu recurvo efficitur, unde et proprie Hebraice *sophar,* Græce κερατίνη, appellatur. Sept. σάλπιγξ, κερατίνη. The proper verb to express *the blowing* of this instrument is תָּקַע, q. v. That it was made of horn, or at least in the shape of a horn, is evident from its being interchanged with קֶרֶן, e. g. Josh. 6:5. comp. verses 4, 6, 8, 13. Job 39:25 בְּדֵי שׁוֹפָר. (Arab. سبور *idem.*)

שׁוֹק m. dec. I. *a leg, thigh.* Cant. 5:15. Ps. 147:10 לֹא בְשׁוֹקֵי הָאִישׁ יִרְצֶה *he takes no pleasure in the legs of a man,* i. e. in infantry, in opposition to cavalry. Judg. 15:8 וַיַּךְ אוֹתָם שׁוֹק עַל יָרֵךְ *and he smote them hip and thigh,* a proverbial expression, for *he smote them all.* (עַל here signifies *with, together with;* see עַל no. 13.) Spoken also of animals, Ex. 29:22, 27. 1 Sam. 9:24.—Dual שׁוֹקַיִם Prov. 26:7.—Kindred with שׁוּק and שָׁקַק *to run.*

שׁוּק in Kal not used. Prob. *to run,* like שָׁקַק, comp. שׁוֹק *a thigh,* and שׁוּק *a street.*

Hiph. *to run over, to overflow.* Joel 2:24 הֵשִׁיקוּ הַיְקָבִים תִּירוֹשׁ *the fats shall overflow with wine.* 4:13. [3:13.] It governs an accus. like verbs of plenty.

Pil. שׁוֹקֵק causat. of Hiph. *to cause to*

overflow, to water abundantly. Ps. 65:10.

שׁוֹק m. verbal from שׁוּק, dec. VI. *a. a street.* Prov. 7:8. Ecc. 12:4, 5. Plur. שְׁוָקִים, (like דְּוָדִים from דּוֹד,) Cant. 3:2.

שׁוֹר m. plur. שְׁוָרִים (Hos. 12:12.) dec. VI. *z. an ox, an animal of the ox kind,* without respect to age or sex. Is. 1:3. Used particularly in general notices of different animals, Ex. 22:1. [21:37.] Lev. 22:23, 28. 27:26. Num. 18:17. Deut. 14:4. For the collective noun, the Hebrews used בָּקָר q.v. to which שׁוֹר has the same relation, as שֶׂה to צֹאן. In Gen. 32:6, it is, however, used collectively like the other nomina unitatis עֶבֶד, שִׁפְחָה, חֲמוֹר, for *servants, maidens, asses,* (but the collective noun צֹאן is subjoined, probably because שֶׂה appeared unappropriate.) In many passages the connection shews that *a calf,* (Lev. 22:27.) or *a cow,* (Job 21:10.) is intended; but the word itself is generic. It is an epicene noun and of the masculine gender even when spoken of female animals, Job 21:10 שׁוֹרוֹ עִבַּר *his cow becomes pregnant.* (In Arab. ثور *an ox;* in Aram. תּוֹרָא also *a calf.*)

I. **שׁוּר**, fut. יָשׁוּר, *to see, behold, view.* Job 7:8. 24:15. Construed with an accus. Num. 23:9. Job 35:5. Particularly (1.) *to look down.* Cant. 4:8. (2.) *to look graciously.* Hos. 14:9. (3.) *to lay wait.* Jer. 5:26. Hos. 13:7. (4.) *to regard.* Job 33:14. 35:13.

II. **שׁוּר** *to go, to travel, journey.* (Arab. سار, שׁיר *idem;* comp. in Chald. שְׁיָרָא *a caravan.* Also in Palmyr. comp. Tychsen's Element. Syr. p. 74.) Ezek. 27:25 אֳנִיּוֹת תַּרְשִׁישׁ שָׁרוֹתַיִךְ מַעֲרָבֵךְ *the ships of Tarshish are thy caravans for thy traffic,* i. e. they go out in caravans or squadrons to carry on thy commerce. Construed with בְּ, *to go with* a thing, i. e. to carry it, (comp. בְּ no. 2.) Is. 57:9. Deriv. תְּשׁוּרָה *a present.*

III. **שׁוּר** i. q. שִׁיר *to sing,* q. v.

I. **שׁוּר** m. dec. I. i. q. שׁוֹרֵר *an enemy.* Ps. 92:12.

II. **שׁוּר** dec. I.

1. i. q. Arab. سور *a wall.* Gen. 49:22. Ps. 18:30. Plur. שׁוּרוֹת Job 24:11 בֵּין שׁוּרֹתָם *between their walls,* i. e. in their houses.

2. proper name of a city on the borders of Egypt towards Palestine, (Gen. 16:7. 20:1. 25:18. 1 Sam. 15:7. 27:8.) according to Josephus (Antiq. Jud. vi. 7. § 3. comp. 1 Sam. 15:7.) *Pelusium.* The desert from Palestine to Shur is called Ex. 15:22 מִדְבַּר שׁוּר, Num. 33:8 מִדְבַּר אֵתָם, now *Jofar.*

שׁוּר Chald. *a wall.* Ezra 4:13, 16.

שׁוּשַׁן m. 1 K. 7:19. in pause שׁוֹשָׁן 7:22, 26. more frequently שׁוֹשַׁנָּה f. plur. שׁוֹשַׁנִּים, dec. VIII. h. and X.

1. *a lily,* various species of which are native in the east and grow in the fields. Cant. 2:1, 2, 16. 4:5. 6:2. 7:3. Hos. 14:6. The Greek authors also were acquainted with the name σοῦσον for *lily,* e. g. Dioscor. iii. 116. Athen. xii. 1. —מַעֲשֵׂה שׁוֹשָׁן *lily-work,* (an ornament on the pillars of the temple,) perhaps *work in the form of the lotus,* for the lotus is like the lily and was common in Egypt as a decoration for pillars, and the Hebrew architecture generally has a Phenico-Egyptian character, 1 K. 7:19, 22, 66. (Arab. and Syr. *idem.*) Comp. Celsii Hierob. I. p. 383 ff.

2. שׁוּשַׁן עֵדוּת Ps. 60:1. and שׁשַׁנִּים Ps. 45:1. 69:1. 80:1. name of a musical instrument. If so called from its resemblance to *a lily,* then we may suppose it to have been *a cymbal.*

3. as a proper name, Dan. 8:2. Neh. 1:1. Est. 1:2, 5. *Shushan* or *Susa,* on the river Choaspes, the metropolis of Susiana and winter residence of the Persian kings. (The summer residence was אַחְמְתָא.) In its place is now a city called *Suster* or *Tuster.*

שׁוּשַׁנְכָיֵא a gentile noun, Chald. *the*

inhabitants of Susa. See the preceding article, no. 3. Ezra 4:9.

שׁוּת *to set, place,* see שִׁית.

שֵׁיזִב Chald. found only in the uncommon conj. שֵׁיזִב, שֵׁיזֵב *to free, deliver.* Fut. יְשֵׁיזִב, infin. שֵׁיזָבָה, Dan. 3:15, 17, 28. 6:17, 28. In the Targums more common.

שָׁזַף *to see, look on, behold.* Job 20:9. 28:7. (So all the ancient versions. In Rabbin. שזף *idem.*) Cant. 1:6 שֶׁשְּׁזָפַתְנִי הַשָּׁמֶשׁ *for the sun has looked,* i. e. shined, *on me.*

שָׁזַר Arab. شزر *to turn from right to left* or *inwards, to twist.* Found only in the Hoph. part. שֵׁשׁ מָשְׁזָר *fine twined linen,* Ex. 26:1, 31, 36. 27:9, 18. 28:6, 8, 15 ff.

שַׁח m. verbal from שָׁחַח, *bowed down, cast down.* Job 22:29 שַׁח עֵינַיִם *the cast down.*

שָׁחַד *to give a present,* particularly for freeing a person from punishment. Job 6:22. Construed with an accus. of the person, *to load with presents,* Ezek. 16:33. Hence

שֹׁחַד m. verbal from שָׁחַד, *a gift, present.* 1 K. 15:19. Particularly to purchase deliverance from punishment, 2 K. 16:8. Prov. 6:35. (comp. Job 6:22.) or to bribe any one, e.g. a judge, Ex. 23:8. Deut. 10:17. Is. 5:23.—לָקַח שֹׁחַד *to receive a bribe,* Ps. 15:5. 26:10. 1 Sam. 8:3. Prov. 17:8 אֶבֶן חֵן הַשֹּׁחַד בְּעֵינֵי בְעָלָיו *a precious stone is a gift to its master,* i. e. to him that receives it; (comp. בַּעַל no. 1.)

שָׁחָה (comp. שׁוּחַ and שָׁחַח.)

1. *to bow down.* Is. 51:23. In Chald. more frequent.

2. *to sink down.* Comp. the deriv. שְׁחוּת, שְׁחִית.

Hiph. הִשְׁחָה *to cause to bow down.* Prov. 12:25.

Hithpal. הִשְׁתַּחֲוָה (with a doubling of the third radical, like נַאֲוָה, נָאוָה, for נָאָה,) fut. apoc. יִשְׁתַּחוּ, in pause יִשְׁתָּחוּ (Milêl,) infin. (after the Chaldaic form) הִשְׁתַּחֲוָיָה (2 K. 5:18.)

1. *to bow down, to prostrate one's self,* as a testimony of respect and reverence, προσκυνεῖν; often with the addition of אַפַּיִם אַרְצָה *with the face to the earth.* Gen. 19:1. 42:6. 48:12. The person *before* whom one prostrates himself is preceded by לְ, Gen. 23:7. 37:7, 9, 10. more rarely by לִפְנֵי, 23:12. This token of respect was shewn sometimes to equals, Gen. 23:7. 37:7, 9, 10. 33:3, 6. sometimes to superiors, e. g. to kings and princes, 2 Sam. 9:8. and especially to the Deity; hence

2. *to prostrate one's self* (before God), *to worship, adore.* Gen. 22:5. 1 Sam. 1:3. Sometimes without a prostration, as upon one's bed, Gen. 47:31. 1 K. 1:47.—This prostration was also a sign of homage or allegiance; hence

3. *to do homage.* Ps. 45:12 *he is thy lord,* הִשְׁתַּחֲוִי לוֹ *do homage to him.*

Note. מִשְׁתַּחֲוִיתֶם Ezek. 8:16, is probably a corrupted reading for מִשְׁתַּחֲוִים.

שִׁחוֹר see שִׁיחוֹר.

שְׁחוּת f. verbal from שָׁחָה no. 2. dec. I. *a pit.* Prov. 28:10. Comp. שׁוּחַ.

שָׁחַח i. q. שׁוּחַ and שָׁחָה.

1. *to stoop, bow down, couch,* as animals lurking for prey. Job 38:40.

2. *to be brought low, to be bowed down,* Ps. 107:39. Job 9:13. Is. 2:11, 17. *to bend* or *bow one's self,* Is. 60:14 וְהָלְכוּ אֵלַיִךְ שְׁחוֹחַ *and they shall come bending unto thee.* Prov. 14:19.

3. *to be bowed down* (with sorrow). Ps. 35:14. 38:7. Lam. 3:20 Keri.

4. *to sink.* Hab. 3:6 *the eternal hills do sink.* Ps. 10:10.

Note. The forms which occur are שַׁחוֹתִי, שַׁחוּ and שֹׁחוּ, fut. יָשֹׁחַ.

Niph. 1. *to be bowed down.* Is. 2:9. 5:15.

2. *to be depressed, made low,* spoken of the voice and of singers. Ecc. 12:4. Is. 29:4 וּמֵעָפָר תִּשַּׁח אִמְרָתֵךְ *out of the dust shall thy depressed speech come.*

Hiph. *to bring* or *throw down.* Is. 25:12. 26:5.

Hithpo. *to be cast down*, spoken of the soul. Ps. 42 : 7, 12. 43 : 5.

Deriv. שַׁח.

שָׁחַט 1. *to kill, slay*, (animals.) Gen. 37 : 31. Particularly for sacrifice, Lev. 1 : 5, 11. Hos. 5 : 2 שַׁחֲטָה שֵׂטִים הֶעְמִיקוּ *in slaying* (of sacrifices) *they sin greatly*. In reference to the sacrifice of human beings, Gen. 22 : 10. Is. 57 : 5.

2. *to kill, murder*, (men.) 2 K. 25 : 7. Jer. 39 : 6. חֵץ שׁוֹחֵט Jer. 9 : 7 Keth. *a deadly arrow*. In the Keri שָׁחוּט probably in the same sense.

3. זָהָב שָׁחוּט 1 K. 10 : 16, 17. 2 Chr. 9 : 15, 16. prob. *gold mixed with alloy*. (In Arabic, this verb, like the Heb. מָהַל, is applied to the *adulteration* of wine.) Sept. *beaten gold*; comp. by transposition, שָׁטַח *to spread out*.

שְׁחִין m. dec. I. *a bile, sore, ulcer*. Ex. 9 : 9, 11. Lev. 13 : 18—20.—שְׁחִין מִצְרַיִם *the botch of Egypt*, prob. *the elephantiasis*, which is endemic in Egypt. It affects particularly the feet, which immediately swell up, lose their flexibility, and become stiff like the feet of elephants, whence the name of the disease. Deut. 28 : 27, 35.—It is used of the sores of the leprosy, or of the elephantiasis, Job 2 : 7. Comp. Schilling de Lepra, p. 184. Plin. XXVI. § 5. (Root Arab. سخن *to be hot, inflamed*; Syr. ܫܚܢ *to suppurate*.)

שָׁחִיס m. Is. 37 : 30. *that which grows up of itself the third year after sowing*, i. q. סָחִישׁ in the parallel passage, q. v. Some MSS. read here שָׁחִישׁ, others שחיש.

שְׂחִיף m. *thinness*. Ezek. 41 : 16 שְׂחִיף עֵץ *thin wood*. See שָׁחַף.

שְׁחִית f. plur. שְׁחִיתוֹת, dec. 1. *a pit*. Ps. 107 : 20. Lam. 4 : 20. Root שׁוּחַ no. 2. *to sink*.

שַׁחַל m. *a lion*, used only in poetry. Job 4 : 10. 10 : 16. 28 : 8. Ps. 91 : 13. Prov. 26 : 13. Hos. 5 : 14. 13 : 7. According to Bochart (Hieroz. I. 717.) strictly *the blackish lion of Syria*, (Plin. H. N. VIII. 17.) comp. שָׁחֹר *black*, (by a commutation of ל and ר.) Better as a poetical epithet, *the roarer*, comp. Arab. سَحَالٌ *vox in pectore reciprocata*, spec. *rugitus*.

שְׁחֵלֶת f. Ex. 30 : 34. according to most of the versions, Jewish commentators and Talmudists, ὄνυξ, *unguis odoratus, onycha, blatta Byzantina* of the shops. It consists of the shells of several kinds of muscles, which, when burnt, yield a smell like to castoreum. See Dioscorid. II. 10. and the passages from the Arabic writers quoted by Bochart, (Hieroz. T. II. p. 803 ff.) Root שָׁחַל prob. i. q. Arab. سحل *to shell or flake off*, (comp. שִׁיחְלָא *a date-shell*,) hence שְׁחֵלָה *a muscle-shell*. If it were not for the authority of the ancient versions, the collation of the word with the Syr. ܫܚܠ *to distil, exude*, would lead to the idea of a resinous fragrant substance of the vegetable kingdom, perhaps *bdellium*; and this Bochart prefers, since Dioscorides and Pliny have compared the pieces of this gum, on account of their smoothness, with *nails* (*unguibus*).

שָׁחַף Arab. سحف *to be lean, to waste away*. Hence

שַׁחַף m. Lev. 11 : 16. name of a bird, according to the Sept. and Vulg. *larus*, *the sea-gull*, a very *lank* bird. But the birds mentioned in connexion with it are not sea-fowls. Hence others: *the horned owl, the night-owl*, the *leanest* of all birds, although it is a great eater.

שַׁחֶפֶת f. verbal from obsol. שָׁחַף, *a consumption, tabes*. Lev. 26 : 16. Deut. 28 : 22.

שַׁחַץ m. *majesty, pride*. (Arab. شَخْصٌ, Talmud. שַׁחַץ *idem*.) Found only Job 28 : 8. 41 : 26 [41 : 34] בְּנֵי שַׁחַץ Vulg. *filii superbiæ*, *the haughty ones*, spoken of great beasts of prey, e. g. lions, etc. The Targum has *lions* in chap. 28 : 8. but the meaning is evidently more general in chap. 41:26. Comp. Bocharti Hieroz. I. p. 718.

שָׁחַק 1. *to pound* or *bruise in pieces*. Ex. 30:36. Metaphorically Ps. 18:43.

2. *to wear away.* Job 14:19 אֲבָנִים שָׁחֲקוּ מַיִם *the waters wear away the stones.* (In Arab. *to wear out*, e. g. a garment.)

שַׁחַק m. dec. VI. c.

1. *dust.* Is. 40:15.

2. *a cloud,* (comp. سحق *nubes tenuis.*) Found only in the plur. Job 36:28. Ps. 78:23. Prov. 3:20, (which passages ascribe to them rain.) Ps. 77:18, (which ascribes to them thunder.) In Job 38:37, their number is spoken of.

3. Plur. i. q. שָׁמַיִם and רָקִיעַ, *the heavens, the sky.* Job 37:18 *canst thou, like him, spread out the sky which is strong like a molten mirror?* Prov. 8:28. Job 37:21. It often stands in parallelism with שָׁמַיִם and as the residence of Jehovah, Deut. 33:26. Job 35:5. Ps. 68:35. So in the singular, Ps. 89:7, 38. (In Samar. שחקיה stands for שָׁמַיִם Gen. 7:19.)

I. **שָׁחַר** *to be black,* (In Aram. *idem.*) Job 30:30 עוֹרִי שָׁחַר מֵעָלַי *my skin is black* (and comes off) *from me.*

Deriv. שָׁחֹר, שְׁחַרְחֹר.

II. **שָׁחַר** *to seek.* In Kal only Prov. 11:27.

Pi. שִׁחֵר *to seek;* construed with an accus. Job 7:21. Prov 7:15. 8:17. with לְ, Job 24:5.—Prov. 13:24 אֹהֲבוֹ שִׁחֲרוֹ מוּסָר *he that loveth him* (*his son*) *seeketh,* i. e. prepareth, *for him correction.* The suffix here supplies the place of a dative. The phrase *to seek God* denotes (1.) *to turn one's self to him.* Hos. 5:15. Ps. 78:34. Construed with אֶל, Job 8:5. (2.) *to long after him.* Ps. 63:2. Is. 26:9. (This verb is usually derived from the noun שַׁחַר *the dawn,* and made to signify primarily *to do early, to hasten,* then *to seek after* any thing. Arab. سحر conj. IV. *to do early.* Comp. הִשְׁכִּים.)

שַׁחַר m. *the morning light, dawn.* (Arab. سَحَرٌ *idem.*) Gen. 19:15. Josh. 6:15.—כַּנְפֵי שָׁחַר *the wings of the dawn,* Ps. 139:9.—בֶּן־שַׁחַר *the morning star,* Is. 14:12.—Hos. 6:3 כְּשַׁחַר נָכוֹן מֹצָאוֹ *his rising,* i. e. the appearance of Jehovah, *is sure as the morning.* Comp. 10:15 בַּשַּׁחַר נִדְמֹה נִדְמָה *in the morning,* i. e. early, *he perisheth.* As an adv. *early, in the morning,* Ps. 57:9. 108:2. Metaphorically (1.) *a rising, appearance, breaking out,* (of misfortune.) Is. 47:11. (2.) *prosperity.* Is. 8:20 *to the law, to the testimony; if they do not speak according to this word,* i. e. thus, אֲשֶׁר אֵין לוֹ שָׁחַר (then know) *that no dawn will rise,* i. e. no prosperity will smile, *upon it* (*the people*). The words *then know* are to be supplied, as in chap. 7:9. or we may supply *say to them* and retain the usual sense of אֲשֶׁר. Whether אֲשֶׁר can have the force of כִּי signif. no. 8. or 9. is doubtful. Others make שַׁחַר here i. q. Arab. سحر *magic, deception;* hence *if they speak not according to this oracle, in which is no deception,* etc. But this parenthetic clause encumbers the sense.

שָׁחֹר m. verbal adj. from שָׁחַר, dec. III. a. *black;* spoken e. g. of the hair, Lev. 13:31, 37. of horses, Zech. 6:2, 6. of the skin tanned by the sun, Cant. 1:5.

שְׁחוֹר m. verbal from שָׁחַר, *blackness.* Lam. 4:8.

שִׁיחוֹר see **שִׁחוֹר**.

שַׁחֲרוּת f. *youth.* Ecc. 11:10.

שְׁחַרְחֹר, fem. שְׁחַרְחֹרֶת, *black,* spoken of the countenance. Cant. 1:6.

שָׁחַת in Kal not used.

Pi. שִׁחֵת 1. trans. *to destroy;* e. g. a vineyard, Jer. 12:10. a people, Num. 32:15. Is. 14:20. *to lay waste* a city or country, Josh. 22:33. Gen. 19:13. 2 Sam. 24:16. *to break down* walls, Ezek. 26:4. *to destroy* an individual person, 2 Sam. 1:14. — Amos 1:11

וְשִׁחֵת רַחֲמָיו *he destroyed* or *cast off his compassion*. Ezek. 28:17 שִׁחַתָּ חָכְמָתְךָ עַל יִפְעָתֶךָ *thou destroyest thy wisdom for the sake of thy beauty;* i. e. thou forgettest the one for the other.

2. intrans. *to behave wickedly, to sin.* Ex. 32:7. Deut. 9:12. 32:5.

Hiph. 1. *to corrupt, destroy, lay waste;* also *to kill, slay.* 2 Chr. 24:23. מַלְאָךְ מַשְׁחִית *the destroying angel,* 2 Sam. 24:16. also simply הַמַּשְׁחִית *the destroyer,* Ex. 12:23.—אַל תַּשְׁחֵת in the superscriptions of Psalms LVII. LVIII. LIX. LXXV. prob. the beginning of some song, like which these Psalms were to be sung.

2. הִשְׁחִית דַּרְכּוֹ Gen. 6:12. or עֲלִילוֹת Zeph. 3:7. *to corrupt one's way,* or *one's actions,* i. e. to act wickedly. Deut. 4:16. 31:29. Judg. 2:19. Is. 1:4. Comp. הֵרַע.

Note. In the phrases אִישׁ מַשְׁחִית Prov. 28:24. and בַּעַל מַשְׁחִית Prov. 18:9. the word מַשְׁחִית is probably a noun, *vir perniciei;* (see p. 361.) In the former passage, it is taken in an active sense, *a destroyer, murderer;* in the latter, in a reflexive sense, *a waster, spendthrift.*

Hoph. הָשְׁחַת pass. Prov. 25:26. Mal. 1:14.

Niph. 1. *to be marred* or *spoiled.* Jer. 13:7.

2. *to be laid waste* or *desolated.* Ex. 8:20. [8:24.]

3. *to be corrupt,* in a moral sense. Gen. 6:11, 12.

Deriv. out of course מַשְׁחִית, מִשְׁחָת, מָשְׁחָת, מַשְׁחֵת.

שְׁחַת Chald. *to destroy, corrupt.* Found only in the part. pass. Dan. 2:9 מִלָּה כִדְבָה וּשְׁחִיתָה *false and corrupt words.* Taken in the abstract sense, as a noun of the neuter gender, *wickedness, crime,* Dan. 6:5.

I. **שַׁחַת** m. verbal from שָׁחַת, *corruption, putrefaction, putredo.* Job 17:14.

II. **שַׁחַת** f. verbal from שׁוּחַ, (like נַחַת from נוּחַ,) dec. VI. c.

1. *a pit,* Ps. 94:13. Prov. 26:27. Ezek. 19:4, 8. *a miry pit, a ditch,* Job 9:31.

2. *the grave.* Ps. 30:10. Job 33:18.

שִׁטָּה f. (for שִׁנְטָה, Arab. سنط,) *the acacia, spina Ægyptia* of the ancients, (*mimosa Nilotica,* Linn.) a great tree, with thick branches, which grows in Egypt and Arabia. Its bark is covered with stiff black thorns, and it bears pods like lupines. From its sap the gum Arabic is obtained. The wood, when old, is nearly as black and as hard as ebony. Is. 41:19. Celsii Hierobot. T. I. p. 499. Jablonskii Opuscula ed. te Water, T. I. p. 260.

Plur. שִׁטִּים 1. *acacia wood.* Ex. 25:5. 10, 13. 26:26. 27:1, 6.

2. proper name of a valley, in the territory of Moab, on the borders of Palestine, the last station of the Israelites. Num. 25:1. Josh. 2:1. 3:1. Mic. 6:5. In full נַחַל הַשִּׁטִּים Joel 4:18. [3:18.]

שָׁטַח *to spread out, enlarge.* Job 12:23 שֹׁטֵחַ לַגּוֹיִם *he enlargeth the nations.* Particularly *to spread out* or *scatter* (on the ground); e. g. bones, Jer. 8:2. quails, Num. 11:32. peeled grain, 2 Sam. 17:19.

Pi. *to stretch out* (the hands). Ps. 88:10.

שֹׁטֵט m. verbal from Pil. of שׁוּט, *a whip, scourge,* i. q. שׁוֹט. Josh. 23:13.

שָׁטַף, fut. יִשְׁטֹף. 1. *to gush* or *stream out, to flow in abundance.* Ps. 78:20. —גֶּשֶׁם שֹׁטֵף *a gushing rain,* Ezek. 13:13. 38:22. Spoken metaphorically of an army, *to overflow, overrun,* Dan. 11:10, 26, 40.—Is. 10:22 שׁוֹטֵף צְדָקָה *it overflows with righteousness* or *judgment;* (צְדָקָה being here i. q. מִשְׁפָּט.)

2. *to overflow, overwhelm, inundate.* Is. 30:28. 66:12. Construed with an accus. Ps. 69:3 שִׁבֹּלֶת שְׁטָפָתְנִי *the stream overwhelms me.* Verse 16. 124:4. Jer. 47:2. Is. 43:2. Cant. 8:6.

3. *to sweep* or *wash away.* Is. 28:17. Job 14:19 *floods wash away the dust of the earth.* Ezek. 16:9. Construed

with an accus. *to wash, rinse*, Lev. 15:11. 1 K. 22:38.

4. metaphorically *to rush*, spoken of a horse. Jer. 8:6. Comp. no. 1.

Niph. 1. *to be overrun* (by an army). Dan. 11:22.

2. *to be washed* or *rinsed*. Lev. 15:12.

Pu. i.q. Niph. no. 2. Lev. 6:21.

שֶׁטֶף and **שֵׁטֶף** m. verbal from שָׁטַף.

1. *an overflowing of waters*. Job 38:25. Spoken metaphorically of an effusion of anger, Prov. 27:4, of the devastation of an army, Dan. 11:22 זְרֹעוֹת הַשֶּׁטֶף *the overwhelming forces*.

2. *a flood, inundation*. Ps. 32:6. Nah. 1:8. Dan. 9:26 קִצּוֹ בַשֶּׁטֶף *his end is with a flood*, i. e. sudden; comp. בַּשַּׁחַר Hos. 10:15.

שָׁטַר Arab. سَطَرَ *to oversee, direct, manage*, (construed with على.) In Hebrew found only in the part. שֹׁטֵר *an overseer, officer*. It is applied (1.) to the officers of the Israelites in Egypt, and in their march through the wilderness. Ex. 5:6—19, (where they have the oversight of the people at work.) Num. 11:16, (where the 70 elders have this name.) Deut. 20:9. 29:9. 31:28. Josh. 1:10. 3:2, (where they make regulations in the camp.) 8:33. 23:2. 24:1.—(2.) to officers in the cities of Israel. Deut. 16:18. 1 Chr. 23:4. 26:29. 2 Chr. 19:11. 34:13. (3.) to higher officers; e. g. 2 Chr. 26:11, (where the newly-raised army is placed under two leaders, a סֹפֵר and a שֹׁטֵר.) Prov. 6:7, (where it is joined with מֹשֵׁל and קָצִין.)—Targ. סָרֵךְ, סַרְכָן *an overseer*. Vulg. *magistri, duces, exactores*. Sept. and Syr. on the contrary, in most places, γραμματεύς, *scriba*, (comp. Arab. سطر *to write*;) whence some modern critics have supposed them to be *writers of genealogical tables*, which, however, does not suit the context of the passages.

שְׁטַר Chald. Dan. 7:5. prob. a false reading for סְטַר *a side*, which is found in several MSS. and editions, and is expressed by the ancient versions. (In the Targums סְטַר, which is also read in 11 MSS. Syr. ܣܛܪܐ, Arab. سَطْر *idem*.)

שַׁי m. *a present*, found only in the phrase הוֹבִיל שַׁי *to bring presents*. Ps. 68:30. 76:12. Is. 18:7. Not found in the kindred dialects in this signification.

I. **שִׁיבָה** f. verbal from שׁוּב dec. X. *a returning*; as a concrete, *those that return*. Ps. 126:1.

II. **שִׁיבָה** f. (for יְשִׁיבָה) verbal from יָשַׁב, dec. X. *a dwelling, residence*. 2 Sam. 19:33.

שָׁיָה. To this root belongs, according to the most correct grammatical analogy, the usual reading תֶּשִׁי, Deut. 32:18. Sept. ἐγκατέλιπες. Vulg, *dereliquisti*. (Comp. יְהִי from הָיָה.) This root may be i. q. שָׁוָה, (comp. הָיָה and הָוָה,) in the signification of the Arab. سوي conj. IV. *to set aside, to leave*. But it is more probable, that the true root is נָשָׁה *to forget, forsake*, (comp. Job 28:4.) A slight change only in the reading would then be necessary, namely תַּשִּׁי, (like תֶּמְחִי Jer. 18:23, for תֶּמְחֶה.) This derivation is favoured by the reading of the Samaritan text תשא, תשה; and appears to have been adopted by most of the ancient versions.

שִׁיזֵב *to free, deliver*, see **שׁוּב**.

שִׁיחָה verbal from שׁוּחַ, dec. X. *a pit*, i. q. שׁוּחָה. Ps. 119:85. 57:7 Keth.

שִׁחֹר, שִׁחוֹר, שִׁיחוֹר m. *Sihor*, the proper name of a river, *the Nile*. So necessarily Is. 23:3 זֶרַע שִׁחֹר קְצִיר יְאוֹר *the seed of Sihor, the harvest of the Nile*. (Vulg. *Nili*.) Jer. 2:18 *what hast thou to do in the way to Egypt, to drink the waters of Sihor? or what hast thou to do in the way to Assyria, to drink the waters of the river (Euphrates)?* If a Hebrew etymology is to be adopted here, as is probable from the following article, then this word may be derived from שָׁחַר *to be black*; hence liter. *the black, turbid river*, whence the Greek name Μίλας, and the Lat. *Melo,* see Serv. ad Virg. Georg. IV. 291. In two passages (Josh. 13:3. 1 Chr. 13:5.) it is used to express the southern boundary of Palestine, like נַחַל מִצְרַיִם *the brook of Egypt,* i. e. Ῥινοκόρουρα, (see p. 383.) and it has therefore been supposed by some to denote this same stream. But this sense is not necessary, for the Nile may very well be regarded as the boundary of Palestine, (comp. Gen. 15:18.)

שִׁיחוֹר לִבְנָת Josh. 19:26. name of a river on the borders of the tribe of Asher, according to Michaëlis, *fluvius vitri, the glass river,* i. e. the river Belus, out of the sands of which glass was first made. (See לִבְנָה no. 1.)

שַׁיִט m. verbal from שׁוּט.

1. i. q. שׁוֹט *a whip, scourge.* Is. 28:15 Keth.

2. *an oar,* i. q. מָשׁוֹט. Is. 33:21.

שִׁילֹה found only Gen. 49:10 עַד כִּי יָבֹא שִׁילֹה. The full reading שִׁילֹה is found in most Jewish MSS. and in nearly all the editions; the defective reading שִׁלֹה in only 25 Jewish MSS. of Kennicott and 13 of De Rossi, but in all the Samaritan MSS. and the ancient versions appear to have so read it. A few MSS. only have שִׁילוֹ and שִׁלוֹ.

All these various readings may be explained, if we regard it as one word, whether a proper name or an appellative. The following are the most plausible explanations; (1.) as a proper name, i. q. *Shiloh,* in the following article. According to this, the clause might be rendered, *till they come to Shiloh,* i. e. to the land of Canaan; or *so long as they go to Shiloh,* (comp. עַד שֶׁ. *quamdiu* Cant. 1:12.) i. e. for ever. (This form actually has the meaning *to Shiloh,* Judg. 21:20. 1 Sam. 4:4.) (2.) as an appellative, *pacificus, the bringer of peace, the prince of peace,* (comp. Is. 9:6.) from שָׁלָה, after the form קִיטוֹר, כִּידוֹר. It may then be compared with the name of Solomon, (i. e. *the peaceable,* 1 Chr. 22:9.) and to him the Samaritans expressly refer this prophecy, (Repert. f. Bibl. und morgenl. Literatur, Th. 16. p. 168.) Among the moderns it is also referred to Solomon by Alexius ab Aquilino, (de Pent. Sam. p. 100.) Rosenmüller (de Vers. Pent. Pers. ad h.l.) Others compare שִׁלְיָה *the afterbirth,* hence *offspring;* rendering the whole clause, *so long as the latest posterity.*—Entirely different the ancient versions. They regard it as compounded of .שֶׁ i. q. אֲשֶׁר and לֹה i. q. לוֹ *to him,* and suppose it pointed שֶׁלֹּה or שֶׁלּוֹ. Hence the meaning, *till he comes to whom it (the sceptre or the dominion) belongs.* Comp. Ezek. 21:32 עַד־בֹּא אֲשֶׁר לוֹ הַמִּשְׁפָּט *till he comes to whom the right belongs,* (Sept. ᾧ καθήκει,) i. e. the Messiah. Perhaps Ezekiel had reference to this passage in Genesis, and gives its true interpretation. Aqu. Symm. and Sept. (according to the majority of MSS.) ᾧ ἀπόκειται. Syr. Saad. *is, cujus est.* Onkelos: *Messias, cujus est regnum.* Targ. Jerus. Sept. (according to the usual reading) τὰ ἀποκείμενα αὐτῷ, *what is reserved for him.*

שִׁילוֹ (Judg. 21:21. Jer. 7:12.) שִׁלוֹ (Judg. 21:19. 1 Sam. 1:24. 3:21.) most frequently שִׁלֹה (Josh. 18:1, 8. Judg. 18:31. 1 Sam. 1:3, 9. 1 K. 2:27.) proper name of a city in the tribe of Ephraim, where the people assembled (Josh. 18:1.) to set up the tabernacle of the congregation, which continued there till the time of Eli. 1 Sam. 4:3. It was situated north of Bethel on a high mountain. The full form was שִׁילוֹן, hence the gentile noun שִׁילֹנִי 1 K. 11:29. 12:15. Neh. 11:5. *a Shilonite, an inhabitant of Shiloh.*

שֵׁילָל Mic. 1:8 Keth. i. q. שׁוֹלָל q. v.

שִׁילֹנִי see שִׁילוֹ.

שַׁיִן m. plur. שֵׁינִים, dec. I. *urine.* Is. 36:12.

שֵׁיצִא Chald. *to finish.* See יְצָא.

שִׁיר, rarely שׁוּר (1 Sam. 18:6 Keth.)

to sing. Prov, 25:20 שָׁר בַּשִּׁירִים *one that singeth songs*. Job 33:27 יָשֹׁר עַל אֲנָשִׁים *he singeth among men*, (comp. Prov. 25:20.) It is construed (1.) with an accus. of the words sung, Ps. 7:1. or of the thing celebrated, Ps. 21:14. 59:17. 89:2. (2.) with לְ, *to praise* or *celebrate* a person, Ps. 13:6. 27:6. 33:3. also *to sing to* or *before* a person, Is. 5:1.

Pil. שׁוֹרֵר *idem*. Zeph. 2:14. Job 36:24 אֲשֶׁר שֹׁרְרוּ אֲנָשִׁים *which men praise*. Part. מְשׁוֹרֵר *a singer*, 1 Chr. 9:33. 15:16. Neh. 12:28 ff. 13:5.

Hoph. pass. Is. 26:1.

שִׁיר m. verbal from שִׁיר, dec. I.

1. *a song*. Judg. 5:12. Ps. 30:1. In the superscriptions of Psalms XLVIII. LXVI. LXXXIII. CVIII. we find שִׁיר מִזְמוֹר connected; in others מִזְמוֹר שִׁיר Ps. LXV. LXVII. LXVIII. LXXXVII. prob. merely pleonastic.—Particularly *a song of joy*, Am. 8:3, 10.—Cant. 1:1 שִׁיר הַשִּׁירִים *the song of songs*, i. e. the most beautiful song, (as the title of the book;) comp. עֲדִי עֲדָיִים *the most beautiful ornament*, Ezek. 16:7. עֶבֶד עֲבָדִים *the most abject servant;* שְׁמֵי שָׁמַיִם *the highest heaven*, 1 K. 8:27. This superscription, (perhaps not from the author himself,) contains a commendation of the book, like that of Psalm XLV. שִׁיר יְדִידֹת *a lovely song*. Others correctly, *a song of the many songs*, comp. 1 K. 5:12. [4:32.] or *a song composed of several songs*.

2. *a choir of singers*. 2 Chr. 29:28.

3. *instrumental music*. כְּלֵי שִׁיר *instruments of music*, 1 Chr. 16:42. 2 Chr. 7:66. 34:12. Am. 6:5.—Neh. 12:28. בְּשִׁיר מְצִלְתַּיִם *music of cymbals*.

שִׁירָה fem. of שִׁיר dec. X. *a song*. Deut. 31:19 ff. Ps. 18:1. Is. 5:1.

שַׁיִשׁ, Syr. ܫܝܫܐ, *white marble, alabaster*. 1 Chr. 29:2. Comp. שֵׁשׁ no. 1.

שִׁישַׁק m. proper name of a king of Egypt, in the time of Jeroboam. 1 K. 11:40. 14:25. 2 Chr. 12:5. The Greek writers appear to make no mention of him.

שִׁית, fut. יָשִׁית, apoc. יָשֶׁת, וַיָּשֶׁת, infin. absol. שֹׁת (Is. 22:7.) synonymous with שׂוּם in nearly all its significations.

1. *to lay, put, set, place;* e. g. שִׁית מֹקְשִׁים *to lay snares*, Ps. 140:6.—Jer. 3:19 אֵיךְ אֲשִׁיתֵךְ בַּבָּנִים *how shall I place thee among the children?* It is construed with an accus. rarely with לְ, Ps. 73:18. The more special constructions are (1.) *to arrange* (an army), and then with the omission of an accus. מַחֲנֶה or מִלְחָמָה, *to set one's self in array*, like שׂוּם no. 1. (1.) Ps. 3:7 אֲשֶׁר שָׁתוּ עָלָי *who have set themselves against me*. Is. 22:7. (2.) *to constitute, appoint*. 1 K. 11:34. Construed with עַל *over* a thing, Gen. 41:33. (3.) construed with עַל of the person, *to lay on* any one. Ps. 9:21 *lay fear upon them*. Particularly something to be done, Ex. 21:22. Also *to charge, impute, make responsible*, Num. 12:11. See שׂוּם no. 1. (4.)—(4.) with עִם, *to set* or *compare with* any thing, Job 30:1. Comp. עָרַךְ no. 3. (5.) שִׁית לֵב, *to pay attention, to regard, animum advertere*. 1 Sam. 4:20. Ps. 62:11. Construed with לְ, *to lay to heart*, Ex. 7:23. 2 Sam. 13:20. Prov. 22:17. Jer. 31:21. Construed with אֶל, *to regard*, Job 7:17. (6.) שִׁית יָד עִם *to have intercourse* or *to associate with* a person. Ex. 23:1. comp. מָשַׁךְ יָד אֶת־לֹצְ' Hos. 7:5. (7.) שִׁית פָּנִים *to set one's face* towards a place, Num. 24:1. With עֵינַיִם *to direct one's eyes* to a place, Ps. 17:11. (8.) *to put on* (ornaments). Ex. 33:4.—Intrans. *to be put*, Job 38:11 פֹּא יָשִׁית בִּגְאוֹן גַּלֶּיךָ *here let* (a limit) *be put to the pride of thy waves*, i. e. to thy proud waves. 10:20 שִׁית מִמֶּנִּי *let me alone*.

2. *to make, work, do;* e. g. שִׁית אֹתוֹת *to work miracles*, Ex. 10:1. Particularly *to make into* or *like* any thing, construed with two accus. Is. 5:6. Jer. 22:6. Ps. 21:7. also with לְ of the predicate, Jer. 2:15. Construed with כְּ, *to make as* or *like*, Is. 16:3. Hos. 2:5. [2:3.] Ps. 83:14.

3. *to give;* e.g. Gen. 4:25. Intrans. *to be given, prepared*, Hos. 6:11 *also*

for thee, O Judah, is an harvest prepared.

Hoph. pass. Ex. 21 : 30.

Deriv. שִׁית, שְׁתָה.

שַׁיִת m. with suff. שִׁיתוֹ, dec. VI. *a thorn.* Is. 5 : 6. 7 : 23—25. 10 : 17.

שִׁית m. verbal from שִׁית, dec. I. *dress, attire.* Prov. 7 : 10. Ps. 73 : 6. Comp. the verb no. 1. (8.)

שַׁךְ see שָׂכָה.

I. שָׁכַב, infin. and imper. שְׁכַב, fut. יִשְׁכַּב.

1. *to lay one's self down,* particularly for sleep, (Gen. 19 : 4. 28 : 11. 1 Sam. 3 : 5, 6, 9.) or in death, hence וַיִּשְׁכַּב עִם אֲבֹתָיו *and he slept with his fathers,* the usual expression for the death of a king, 1 K. 2 : 10. 11 : 43. 14 : 20, 31. 15 : 8, 24. 16 : 6, 28.

2. *to lie.* Construed with an accus. of the place, hence שֹׁכְבֵי קֶבֶר *those that lie in the grave,* Ps. 88 : 6. שֹׁכֶבֶת חֵיקֶךָ *she that lieth in thy bosom,* Mic. 7 : 5. Also used absolutely, *to lie quietly,* Lev. 26 : 6. *to rest,* Ecc. 2 : 23.

3. with עִם and אֵת *to lie with* a person, an euphemism. More frequently used of the man, Gen. 26 : 10. 30 : 15, 16. 39 : 7, 12. 34 : 2. Ex. 22 : 18. Deut. 22 : 23 ff. 2 Sam. 12 : 11. but also of the woman, Gen. 19 : 32. The particle אֵת must here be rendered *with,* like עִם, and not as the sign of the accusative, although with suffixes it is written אוֹת, e. g. Lev. 15 : 18, 24. (see אֵת no. III.) The construction with the accus. is indeed uniformly found in the Keri, where שָׁגַל stands in the text; namely, in Kal Deut. 28 : 30. in Niph. Is. 13 : 16. Zech. 14 : 2. in Pu. Jer. 3 : 2. but the Masoretes have given here the construction of the verb שָׁגַל to the less offensive verb שָׁכַב.

Hiph. *to cause to lie, to cast down,* 2 Sam. 8 : 2. *to lay down,* 1 K. 17 : 19. *to cause to rest,* Hos. 2 : 20. [2 : 18.]

Hoph. הָשְׁכַּב, part. מֻשְׁכָּב, *to be laid,* 2 K. 4 : 32. *to lie,* Ezek. 32 : 19, 32.

Deriv. out of course מִשְׁכָּב.

II. שָׁכַב perhaps after the Arabic usage, i. q. سكب *to pour out.*

Hiph. Job 38 : 37 וְנִבְלֵי שָׁמַיִם מִי יַשְׁכִּיב *and the bottles of heaven, who pours them out?* Others, after no. I. *who arranges the vessels of heaven,* i. e. the clouds. The former explanation is favoured by verse 38.

שְׁכָבָה f. verbal from שָׁכַב no. I. dec. XI. c.

1. *a lying.* שִׁכְבַת הַטַּל Ex. 16 : 13, 14. *a lying of dew,* i. e. dew lying.

2. *copulation, coition.* שִׁכְבַת־זֶרַע *coition with emission of seed,* also *emission of seed,* Lev. 15 : 16, 17, 32. 22 : 4. hence שָׁכַב אֶת־אִשָּׁה שִׁכְבַת־זֶרַע *to have conjugal intercourse with a woman,* Lev. 15 : 18. 19 : 20. Num. 5 : 13.

שְׁכֹבֶת f. verbal from שָׁכַב no. I. dec. XIII. e. i. q. שְׁכָבָה no. 2. hence נָתַן אֶת־שְׁכָבְתּוֹ בְּאִשָּׁה *to have conjugal intercourse with a woman,* Lev. 18 : 23. 20 : 15. Num. 5 : 20. also נָתַן אֶת־שְׁכָבְתּוֹ לְזֶרַע אֶל Lev. 18 : 20.

שָׁכָה *to wander, rove;* comp. the Ethiop. ሰከየ *erravit.* Here belongs the part. Hiph. Jer. 5 : 8 *like well-fed horses* מַשְׁכִּים הָיוּ *they wander about* with desire; (comp. Jer. 2 : 23. Prov. 7 : 11. and שָׁגָה no. 3.) But may not מַשְׁכִּים stand adverbially in the sing. for מַשְׁכִּימִים, in this sense, *in the morning they are like well-fed horses,* (comp. Is. 5 : 11.)?

שְׁכוֹל m. verbal from שָׁכֹל.

1. *the loss of children.* Is. 47 : 8, 9.

2. *a forsaking, abandoning.* Ps. 35 : 12.

שַׁכּוּל m. verbal from שָׁכֹל, dec. I. *robbed of children* or *young,* spoken e. g. of a she-bear. 2 Sam. 17 : 8. Hos. 13 : 8. Also *without young,* Cant. 4 : 2. 6 : 6.

שִׁכּוֹר, שִׁכֹּר m. verbal from שָׁכַר, dec. I. *drunken, intoxicated,* 1 Sam. 25 : 36. 1 K. 16 : 9. 20 : 16. Fem. שִׁכֹּרָה 1 Sam. 1 : 13.

שָׁכַח and שָׁכֵחַ (Is. 49 : 14. Prov. 2 : 17.) fut. יִשְׁכַּח, *to forget,* construed with an accus. Gen. 40:23. Ps. 9:13. Construed with מִן and an infin. Ps. 102:5. Also *to leave from forgetfulness*, Deut. 24:19.

Niph. *to be forgotten.* Gen. 41:30. Ps. 31:13. Job 28:4 נִשְׁכָּחִים מִנִּי רָגֶל *forgotten*, i. e. untried, *by* (human) *feet.* Deut. 31:21 לֹא תִשָּׁכַח מִפִּי זַרְעוֹ *it* (*the song*) *shall not be forgotten out of the mouths of their seed.*

Pi. Lam. 2:6. and Hiph. Jer. 23:27. *to cause to forget.*

Hithpa. i. q. Niph. Ecc. 8:10.

שָׁכֵחַ m. verbal from שָׁכַח, dec. V. f. *forgetting, forgetful.* Is. 65:11. Plur. const. שִׁכְחֵי Ps. 9:18.

שְׁכַח Chald. *to find.*

Ithpe. הִשְׁתְּכַח *to be found.* Dan. 2:35. Ezra 6:2.

Aph. הַשְׁכַּח 1. *to find.* Dan. 2:25. 6:6, 12.

2. *to obtain, acquire.* Ezra 7:16. Comp. מָצָא no. 2.

שָׁכַךְ, infin. שֹׁךְ.

1. *to settle, subside;* spoken of water, Gen. 8:1. of anger, Est. 2:1. 7:10.

2. *to bow down, to stoop,* spoken of a fowler. Jer. 5:26 כְּשַׁךְ יְקוּשִׁים *as fowlers stoop* or *bow down.*

Hiph. *to still* (an uproar). Num. 17:20. [17:5.]

שָׁכֹל, fut. יִשְׁכַּל, *to lose children, to become childless,* construed with an accus. Gen. 27:45 לָמָה אֶשְׁכַּל גַּם שְׁנֵיכֶם *wherefore should I lose you both?* 43:14 וַאֲנִי כַּאֲשֶׁר שָׁכֹלְתִּי שָׁכָלְתִּי *and if I be childless, let me be childless.* 1 Sam. 15:33. Part. pass. שְׁכֻלָה *childless,* Is. 49:21.

Pi. שִׁכֵּל 1. *to make childless.* Gen. 42:36. 1 Sam. 15:33. Spoken particularly (1.) of wild beasts which devour children. Lev. 26:22 *I will send on you wild beasts of the field, which shall make you childless.* Ezek. 5:17. 14:15. comp. Hos. 9:12. (2.) of the loss of young men in battle. Deut. 32:25 מִחוּץ תְּשַׁכֶּל־חֶרֶב *without,* i. e. in the field, *the sword makes childless.* Lam. 1:20. Jer. 15:7. Ezek. 36:13—15.

2. *to miscarry, to cast one's young, abortare.* Gen. 31:38. Ex. 23:26. Spoken metaphorically of the vine, *to be unfruitful,* Mal. 3:11.

3. trans. *to occasion abortions.* 2 K. 2:19. Part. מְשַׁכֶּלֶת *an abortion,* verse 21.

Hiph. 1. i. q. Pi. no. 1. (2.) *to destroy young men in war.* Jer. 50:9.

2. *to miscarry.* Hos. 9.14. See Pi. no. 2.

שִׁכֻּלִים masc. plur. verbal from שָׁכֹל, dec. I. *a childless state* or *condition.* Is. 49:20.

שַׁכֻּלוֹת fem. plur. verbal from שָׁכֹל, *deprived, bereaved.* Jer. 18:21.

שַׁכְלֵל see **כָּלַל**.

שָׁכַם found only in Hiph. הִשְׁכִּים.

1. *to rise up early;* both with and without the addition בַּבֹּקֶר, Gen. 19:2, 27. 20:8. 28:18. 31:55. Construed with לְ, *to rise up early after* any thing, Cant. 7:13. Joined with another verb, it forms a periphrasis of the adverb *early,* Hos. 6:5 טַל מַשְׁכִּים הֹלֵךְ *the dew which passeth away early.* 13:3. Hence infin. absol. הַשְׁכֵּם as an adv. *early,* Prov. 27:14.

2. *to urge with ardour* or *earnestness.* Jer. 7:13 אֲדַבֵּר אֲלֵיכֶם הַשְׁכֵּם וְדַבֵּר *I have spoken unto you most urgently.* 11:7 כִּי הָעֵד הַעִדֹתִי הַשְׁכֵּם וְהָעֵד *I have protested most earnestly.* 7:25. 25:3. 26:5. 32:33. 35:14, 15. 44:4. 2 Chr. 36:15. Zeph. 3:7 הִשְׁכִּימוּ הִשְׁחִיתוּ עֲלִילוֹתָם *they were most eager to do wickedly.*

Note. In Jer. 25:3, we find אַשְׁכִּים an infin. after the Chaldaic form for הַשְׁכֵּם.—For מַשְׁכִּים Jer. 5:8, see under שָׁכָה.

שְׁכֶם m. in pause שֶׁכֶם (Ps. 21:13.) with suff. שִׁכְמוֹ, dec. VI. a.

1. *the shoulder, the upper part of the back.* It is constantly regarded as a single member of the masc. gen. and thus distinguished from כָּתֵף, (see Job 31:22.) It is used (1.) as the part on which a burden is borne; e. g.

Gen. 9 : 23. Hence Is. 9 : 5 *the government shall be on his shoulder*, i. e. it shall be given him. 22 : 22 *I will lay upon his shoulder the key of the house of David;* (עַל שְׁכֶם is here i. q. עַל יַד.) Comp. further Zeph. 3 : 9 *to serve God* שְׁכֶם אֶחָד *with one shoulder*, i. e. with one accord. (2.) in the phrase *to turn the neck* or *back*. 1 Sam. 10 : 9 כְּהַפְנֹתוֹ שִׁכְמוֹ לָלֶכֶת *when he had turned his back to go.* (Comp. פָּנָה עֹרֶף Josh. 7 : 12. Jer. 48 : 39.) Hence we may explain Ps. 21 : 13 כִּי תְּשִׁיתֵמוֹ שֶׁכֶם *for thou shalt make them turn their back, facies ut terga dent;* (comp. נָתַן עֹרֶף Ps. 18 : 41.) Sept. ὅτι θήσεις αὐτοὺς νῶτον. Vulg. *quoniam pones eos dorsum.* (3.) Is. 9 : 3 מַטֵּה שִׁכְמוֹ *the rod for their back.*

2. *a part, portion.* Gen. 48 : 22. So the connexion requires and the ancient versions have rendered it.

3. proper name of a city on Mount Ephraim, pertaining to the Levites, and a city of refuge for the manslayer. Josh. 20 : 7. 21 : 20, 21. Sept. Συχὲμ, (comp. Acts 7 : 16.) Vulg. *Sichem.* In the times of the Romans there was a city here called *Flavia Neapolis*, hence the present name among the Arabians *Naplos* or *Naplus*. With He paragogic שְׁכֶמָה *to Shechem*, Hos. 6 : 9. See Relandi Palæstina, p. 1004—1010. Bachiene Beschreibung von Palästina, Th. 2. § 536 ff.

שִׁכְמָה f. i. q. שְׁכֶם no. 1. Job 31 : 22 כְּתֵפִי מִשִּׁכְמָה תִפּוֹל *let my shoulder fall from my neck.* According to the printed edition of the Masora, the ה here is marked with a Raphe, which denotes the absence of a Mappik, it is, therefore, not a suffix, but the word is a new form of the feminine gender. According to some MSS. (see J. H. Michaëlis and Jahn on the passage,) the ה has a Mappik, and the word comes from שְׁכֶם, (*from its neck.*) In that case this word should be entirely omitted as a distinct article.

שָׁכַן, שָׁכֵן, fut. יִשְׁכֹּן.

1. *to let itself down, to rest,* spoken e. g. of the pillar of fire and the cloud. Num. 9 : 17, 22. 10 : 12. Ex. 24 : 16. Hence

2. *to encamp,* Num. 24 : 2. *to lie quietly, to rest,* spoken e. g. of lions, Deut. 33 : 20. of men, Judg. 5 : 17. Prov. 7 : 11 בְּבֵיתָהּ לֹא יִשְׁכְּנוּ רַגְלֶיהָ *her feet rest not in her house.*

3. *to dwell.* Gen. 9 : 27. 2 Sam. 7 : 10 וְשָׁכַן תַּחְתָּיו *and they (the people) shall dwell in their place.* שֹׁכְנִי סְנֶה *the dweller in the thorn-bush,* Deut. 33 : 16. Part. pass. שָׁכוּן used actively, like the French *logé*, Judg. 8 : 11.—Construed with an accus. *to inhabit,* Ps. 68 : 7.—שָׁכַן אֶרֶץ *to inhabit the land, to be in peaceable possession of the land,* Prov. 2 : 21. 10 : 30. Ps. 37 : 29. and without אֶרֶץ in the same sense, Ps. 102 : 29.—Construed with a pleonastic dative, Ps. 120 : 6 שָׁכְנָה לָּהּ *habitabit sibi.*—Spoken of a tent, *to be pitched, set up,* Josh. 22 : 19.

4. pass. *to be inhabited,* like יָשַׁב no. 4. Jer. 50 : 39. 33 : 16. 46 : 26. Is. 13 : 20.

5. metaphorically *to possess* or *be familiar with* a thing. Prov. 8 : 12 אֲנִי חָכְמָה שָׁכַנְתִּי עָרְמָה *I wisdom possess prudence.* (In Arab. سكن *to dwell, to be accustomed, to be familiar.*)

Pi. *to cause to dwell.* Jer. 7 : 7. Num. 14 : 30. Frequently used of Jehovah, *to let* his name *dwell* in a place, i. e. to make his residence there, Deut. 12 : 11. 14 : 23. 16 : 6, 11. 26 : 2. Comp. שׁוּם שְׁמוֹ under the art. שׂוּם no. 1. (8.) Prob. elliptically Ps. 78 : 61 *the tent in which he let* (his name) *dwell among men.* Hence the Jewish term שְׁכִינָה *the Shechinah, the presence of God.*

Hiph. *to cause to dwell.* Gen. 3 : 24. Job 11 : 14. Joined with אֹהֶל, *to pitch a tent,* Josh. 18 : 1. (comp. in Kal Josh. 22 : 19.)—Ps. 7 : 6 כְּבוֹדִי לֶעָפָר יַשְׁכֵּן *in the dust let him make me to dwell,* i. e. let him prostrate me in the dust.

Deriv. out of course מִשְׁכָּן.

שְׁכַן Chald. *idem.* Dan. 4 : 18. [4 : 21.]

Pa. שַׁכֵּן *to let dwell.* Ezra 6:12. Comp. Heb. Pi.

שָׁכֵן a participial noun from שָׁכַן, dec. V. a.

1. *an inhabitant.* Is. 33:24. Hos. 10:5.

2. *a neighbour.* Prov. 27:10. Spoken also of neighbouring states, cities, Jer. 50:40. 49:18. Ps. 44:14. 79:12.

שֶׁכֶן m. with suff. שִׁכְנוֹ, verbal from שָׁכַן, dec. VI. h. *a dwelling.* Once Deut. 12:5.

שָׁכַר, fut. יִשְׁכַּר.

1. *to drink to the full,* (i. q. רָוָה.) Hag. 1:6. Particularly *to drink to hilarity,* Cant. 5:1. Gen. 43:34.

2. *to be intoxicated.* Gen. 9:21. Construed with an accus. of the drink, Is. 49:26. Applied sometimes to a hardened state of mind, the effect of a divine judgment, which leads men on to their own destruction, Is. 29:9. 51:21. Lam. 4:21. Nah. 3:11. Comp. תַּרְעֵלָה, טוּשׂ.

Pi. *to make drunken, to inebriate.* 2 Sam. 11:13. Particularly spoken of Jehovah, *to make* a nation *drunken,* i.e. to cause it to hasten to its own destruction. Jer. 51:7. Is. 63:6.

Hiph. *idem.* Jer. 51:57. Deut. 32:42.

Hithpa. *to act like a drunken person.* 1 Sam. 1:14.

Deriv. out of course שִׁכּוֹר.

שֵׁכָר m. verbal from שָׁכַר, *strong* or *intoxicating drink, temetum,* a general expression for wine and other strong drinks, prepared from grain, fruit, honey, dates, etc. See Hieron. Opp. ed. Martian. T. IV. p. 364. (In Arab. سكر by way of eminence, *date-wine.*) Hence in Num. 28:7, it denotes *wine;* but occurs usually in the phrase יַיִן וְשֵׁכָר *wine and* (other) *strong drink,* Lev. 10:9. Num. 6:3. Judg. 13:4, 7. and in the poets in parallelism with יַיִן, Is. 5:11. 24:9. 28:7. 29:9. 56:12. Prov. 20:1. 31:6. Mic. 2:1.—In Is. 5:22, it appears to denote a kind of spiced wine, (comp. מֶסֶךְ, רֹקַח.)

שִׁכָּרוֹן m. verbal from שָׁכַר, *drunkenness.* Ezek. 23:33. 39:19.

שַׁל m. *an error, fault.* 2 Sam. 6:7. Root שָׁלָה no. II.

שֶׁל a particle used in later Hebrew and in Rabbinic, compounded of .שֶׁ i. q. אֲשֶׁר and לְ. (See .שֶׁ no. 2.) In Rabbinic it is often employed as a sign of the genitive case, (comp. p. 60.) but in Biblical Hebrew, we find only בְּשֶׁל *on account of,* (comp. בַּאֲשֶׁר Gen. 39:9, 23.) Jon. 1:7 בְּשֶׁלְּמִי *on whose account,* comp. verse 8 בַּאֲשֶׁר לְמִי. Verse 12 בְּשֶׁלִּי *on my account.* (In Aram. בְּדִיל *on account of,* compounded of בְּ, דִּי and לְ.) בְּשֶׁל אֲשֶׁר *although, quantumvis,* liter. *in* (omni) *eo, quod,* Ecc. 8:17. It corresponds to the Aram. בְּדִיל דִּי, which, however, usually signifies *because.* Is not perhaps the true reading בְּכָל אֲשֶׁר?

שַׁלְאֲנָן m. adj. *at ease, quiet.* Job 21:23. A quinqueliteral formed by the union of the two synonymes שָׁלָה and שַׁאֲנָן; or else simply from the latter by inserting ל; like זַלְעָפָה *heat,* comp. זעף in Syr. Ethp. *to be burned.*

שָׁלַב in Kal not used. In Arab. ثلب *crenatim fregit.* It appears from this and from the noun שְׁלַבִּים, that it must have expressed the idea of *parallel uniformity.*

Pu. part. Ex. 26:17 *one board shall have two tenons,* מְשֻׁלָּבֹת אִשָּׁה אֶל אֲחֹתָהּ *parallel to each other.* Sept. ἀντιπίπτοντας ἕτερον τῷ ἑτέρῳ. Hence

שְׁלַבִּים masc. plur. *ledges, corner ledges.* 1 K. 7:28, 29. (In Chald. שְׁלַב *the step of a ladder.*) It appears here to denote *the ledges* or *ridges,* which covered the junctures of the sides of the bases, and were made so broad as to contain graven work.

שֶׁלֶג m. Arab. ثلج, Aram. תַּלְגָּא, *snow.* Job 24:19. Ps. 147:16. Is. 1:18. Hence the verb denom. in

Hiph. הִשְׁלִיג *to be covered with snow.* Ps. 68:15 *when the Almighty scattered kings in it* (*the country*,) תַּשְׁלֵג בְּצַלְמוֹן *it was covered with snow* (from the bodies of the slain,) *like Salmon;* comp. Virg. Æn. v. 865. xii. 36, *campi ossibus albent.* A recent overthrow is also referred to in these passages. בְּ is used by way of comparison, like כְּ. (See בְּ no.16.) Others: *when the Almighty scattered kings therein, there was rest in the shade;* comp. ثلج *to be cooled*, metaphorically *to be peaceful, joyful*, conj. IV. *to make joyful;* and צַלְמוֹן according to Theodotion, *a shade.*

I. שָׁלָה and שָׁלָו *to be quiet*, particularly *to enjoy a peaceful prosperity.* Job 3:26. 12:6. Ps. 122:6. Pret. שָׁלַוְתִּי Job 3:26. fut. יִשְׁלָיוּ. Deriv. שָׁלֵו, שַׁלְוָה, שְׁלִי, שָׁלֵו.

II. שָׁלָה as in Chaldaic, *to err, fail, transgress.*

Niph. *idem.* 2 Chr. 29:11.

Hiph. *to lead astray, to deceive.* 2 K. 4:28.

Deriv. שַׁל.

III. שָׁלָה i. q. שָׁלַל *to draw out* or *off*, (comp. נָשַׁל.) Found only in the fut. apoc. יֵשֶׁל, (for יִשְׁלֶה,) Job 27:8 כִּי יֵשֶׁל אֱלוֹהַּ נַפְשׁוֹ *when God draws out his soul*, scil. from the body, which was regarded as a sheath or receptacle for the soul, (comp. נִדְנֶה.) Chald. *quando Deus animum ejus excusserit.* Perhaps more pertinently, (according to Schnurrer,) ישל is taken for יִשְׁאַל *he requires*, like the Arab. يسل for يسال, from سال; but in that case the word must be pointed differently.

שְׁלָה Chald. *to be at rest.* Dan. 4:1. [4:4.]

שָׁלָה Chald. *an error, something amiss.* Dan. 3:29. Keth. i. q. שָׁלוּ, שָׁלוּת.

שֵׁלָה 1 Sam. 1:17. See שְׁאֵלָה.

שִׁלֹה name of a city, see שִׁילוֹ.

שַׁלְהֶבֶת f. *a flame.* Job 15:30. Ezek. 21:3. [20:47.] (Root Chald. and Syr. שַׁלְהֵב *to burn*, a quadriliteral, or conj. Shaphel of the verb לְהַב.) Cant. 8:6 שַׁלְהֶבֶת־יָהּ *a flame of Jehovah*, i. e. a most vehement flame. Acccording to the recension of Ben Asher, and most MSS. it is written as one word, the Mappik also is frequently wanting, and ה is written with Sheva. But this has no effect on the meaning of the word.

שִׁלוֹ name of a city, see שִׁילוֹ.

שָׁלֵו m. שְׁלֵוָה f. plur. const. שַׁלְוֵי, verbal from שָׁלָה no. I. dec. V.

1. *quiet, peaceable.* 1 Chr. 4:40. Particularly *living in peace*, Job 16:12. Ps. 73:12. As a subst. *rest, quietness*, Job 20:20.

2. in a bad sense, *careless, wicked, forgetful of God;* comp. שַׁאֲנָן no. 2. Ezek. 23:42.—Also written שָׁלֵיו q. v.

שֶׁלֶו m. verbal from שָׁלָה no. I. dec. VI. a. *quietness, rest, uninterrupted prosperity.* Ps. 30:7.

שַׁלְוָה f. verbal from שָׁלָה no. I. dec. XII. a.

1. i. q. שֶׁלֶו, *quietness, peace, prosperity.* Prov. 17:1. Ps. 122:7. Ezek. 16:49. Plur. בְּשַׁלְוֹתַיִךְ *in the time of thy prosperity*, Jer. 22:21. בְּשַׁלְוָה *in the midst of peace*, Dan. 8:25. 11:21. (comp. Job 15:21.) with the accessory idea of *suddenness*, as in Chald. and Syr. בִּשְׁלָיָה, מִן שְׁלִיָה, ܡܢ ܫܠܝ. Comp. Dan. 11:24.

2. in a bad sense, *carelessness, a criminal security, forgetfulness of God.* Prov. 1:32. See שָׁלֵו.

שְׁלֵוָה f. Chald. *rest, tranquillity.* Dan. 4:24. [4:27.]

שִׁלּוּחִים masc. plur. verbal from שִׁלַּח, dec. I.

1. *a dismission, sending off.* Ex. 18:2. hence *a bill of divorce*, Mic. 1:14.

2. *the disposing of a daughter in marriage*, also *a gift given on such an occasion.* 1 K. 9:16. Comp. שִׁלַּח Jud. 12:9.

שָׁלוֹם m. verbal from שָׁלַם, dec. III. a.

1. as an adj. *prosperous, in health*,

well, integer. Gen. 47:27 הֲשָׁלוֹם אֲבִיכֶם *is your father well?* 1 Sam. 25:6. 2 Sam. 17:3. 20:9. Job 5:24. Ps. 38:4 אֵין שָׁלוֹם בַּעֲצָמַי *there is nothing sound in my bones.*

2. *in full number, the whole.* Jer. 13:19.

3. *safe, secure, enjoying peace.* Job 21:9. Plur. *those enjoying peace,* Ps. 69:23.

4. *friendly, peaceably disposed.* Ps. 55:21.

5. as a subst. *health, integritas.* The following phrases are worthy of notice; (1.) הֲשָׁלוֹם לוֹ *is he well?* the usual form of inquiry concerning the health of an absent person, Gen. 29:6. 2 K. 4:26. The answer is שָׁלוֹם, Gen. 29:6. Without ה, interrogatively, 2 Sam. 18:29. also affirmatively, Gen. 43:28. comp. Deut. 29:18 שָׁלוֹם יִהְיֶה־לִּי *I shall prosper.* Hence (2.) שָׁאַל לְשָׁלוֹם לְ *to inquire after the health* or *welfare of* any one, (see under שָׁאַל no. 5.) Comp. further 2 Sam. 11:7 וַיִּשְׁאַל דָּוִד לִשְׁלוֹם הַמִּלְחָמָה *and David inquired how the war prospered.* Somewhat similar Gen. 37:14 רְאֵה אֶת־שְׁלוֹם אַחֶיךָ *see whether it be well with thy brethren.* With יָדַע, Est. 2:11. with פָּקַד, 1 Sam. 17:18. Elliptically 2 K. 10:13 *we have come down* (to look) *after the welfare of the sons of the king,* i. e. to visit them. (3.) שָׁלוֹם לְךָ, לָכֶם, Judg. 6:23. 19:20. Dan. 10:19. Gen. 43:23. *peace be to thee* or *to you,* the language of consolation and encouragement, hence thrice with the addition אַל תִּירָא, אַל תִּירְאוּ. Comp. 1 Sam. 20:21 כִּי שָׁלוֹם לְךָ *for there is peace to thee,* and not evil. Verse 7. Used also to express satisfaction, 2 K. 4:23 וַתֹּאמֶר שָׁלוֹם *and she said, peace,* i. e. let it be so. (In Hebrew it is never used as a salutation.) (4.) שָׁלוֹם as an exclamation, *hail!* 2 Sam. 18:28. 1 Chr. 12:18 שָׁלוֹם שָׁלוֹם לְךָ *hail, hail to thee.*

6. *prosperity, a prosperous event.* הֲשָׁלוֹם *is it any thing prosperous?* 1 K. 2:13. 2 K. 5:21. 9:11. 17:22.

7. *peace.* קָרָא לְשָׁלוֹם לְ *to offer peace to* any one, Deut. 20:10. Judg. 21:13. עָנָה שָׁלוֹם אֶת *to answer peaceably, to accept of peace,* Deut. 20:11. עָשָׂה שָׁלוֹם לְ *to give peace to* any one, Josh. 9:15. אִישׁ שָׁלוֹם *a man of peace,* i. e. a lover of peace, Ps. 37:37.—דִּבְרֵי שָׁלוֹם (with) *words of peace,* Deut. 2:26.

8. *friendship, good understanding,* אִישׁ שְׁלוֹמִי *my friend,* Ps. 41:10. Jer. 20:10. 38:22. Obad. 7. דֹּבְרֵי שָׁלוֹם *that speak friendly,* Ps. 28:3. comp. Est. 9:30.

שִׁלּוּם *recompense,* see שִׁלֵּם.

שָׁלוֹשׁ *three,* see שָׁלֹשׁ.

שָׁלוּת or **שָׁלוּ** f. Chald. *an error, fault.* Dan. 6:5. Ezra 4:22. Root שְׁלָה no. II.

שָׁלַח fut. יִשְׁלַח, infin. שְׁלֹחַ, שְׁלֹחַ, once שְׁלֹחַ (Is. 58:9.)

1. *to send* a person or thing. The person or thing *sent* is put in the accus. also once preceded by לְ, 2 Chr. 17:7. The person *sent to* is preceded by אֶל, very rarely and only in imitation of the Chaldaic, by עַל, Neh. 6:3. Jer. 29:31. Often used absolutely without a direct complement, Gen. 31:4. 41:8, 14. the person sometimes being preceded by בְּיַד, e. g. 1 K. 2:25 וַיִּשְׁלַח הַמֶּלֶךְ בְּיַד בְּנָיָהוּ *and the king sent by the hand of Benaiah,* i. e. he sent Benaiah. Ex. 4:13 שְׁלַח־נָא בְּיַד־תִּשְׁלָח *send by whom thou wilt send.* With a pleonastic dative שְׁלַח לְךָ, Num. 13:2.

2. *to send* (a commission, charge). Prov. 26:6 שֹׁלֵחַ דְּבָרִים בְּיַד כְּסִיל *he that sends orders by the hand of a fool.* Gen. 38:25 שָׁלְחָה אֶל חָמִיהָ לֵאמֹר *she sent to her father-in-law, saying.* 1 K. 20:5. 2 K. 5:8. Without לֵאמֹר 1 Sam. 20:21. 1 K. 5:23 [5:9] עַד־הַמָּקוֹם אֲשֶׁר תִּשְׁלַח אֵלַי *to the place which thou shalt appoint me.* 20:9. 12:11. Jer. 42:5, 21. 43:1.

3. *to commission,* construed with two accus. 2 Sam. 11:22 *and he shewed David* אֵת כָּל־אֲשֶׁר שְׁלָחוֹ יוֹאָב *all wherewith Joab had intrusted him.* 1 K. 14:6. Is. 55:11.

4. *to stretch out, to put forth;* e. g.

the finger in scorn, Is. 58:9. a rod, Ps. 110:2. 1 Sam. 14:27. a sickle, Joel 4:13. [3:13.] comp. Rev. 14:15, 18. (like the Lat. *falcem immittere segeti*, or perhaps *to put to, to apply*.) Particularly *to stretch out* the hand, Gen. 3: 22. 8:9. 19:10. 48:14. Job 1:11. This latter phrase is often used pleonastically, like *he rose up*, etc.—שָׁלַח יָד בְּ *to lay the hand on* a person or thing, Job 28:9. and this denoting (1.) *to injure* or *do violence to* a person. Gen. 37:22. 1 Sam. 26:9. Est. 8:7. also with אֶל in the same sense, Gen. 22:12. Ex. 24:11. (2.) *to take unjustly, to plunder*, (a thing.) Ex. 22:7. Ps. 125: 3. Dan. 11:42.—שָׁלַח יָד עַל *to put forth the hand after* any thing, 1 K. 13:4. 1 Chr. 13:10. construed with מִן, *to draw back the hand from*, Cant. 5:4. —In each of these cases יָד may be omitted; as Ps. 18:17 יִשְׁלַח מִמָּרוֹם *he stretched out* (his hand) *from above*. 2 Sam. 6:6. Obad. 13. Part. pass. שָׁלוּחַ *stretched out, slim, slender*, Gen. 49: 21. (Comp. Pi. no. 11.) Comp. שְׁלֻחוֹת *shoots*.

5. *to set free, to let loose*, i. q. Pi. no. 3. Ps. 50:19 *thou lettest loose thy mouth to evil*.

Niph. pass. Infin. נִשְׁלוֹחַ used for the finite verb, Est. 3:13.

Pi. שִׁלַּח 1. *to send*, i. q. Kal no. 1. but used more rarely. Gen. 19:13. 28:6. Construed with עַל *to* any one, 2 Chr. 32:31. Often in reference to plagues, pestilence, wild beasts, which Jehovah sends on his people; construed with בְּ, Deut. 32:24. 7:20. 2 K. 17:25. Ps. 78:45. with אֶל, Ezek. 14:19. with עַל, 5:17.

2. *to let go, to dismiss*. Ex. 8:28. [8:32.] 9:7, 28. Jud. 7:8. שִׁלַּח בָּנוֹת הַחוּצָה *locare filias*, Judg. 12:9.

3. *to set free* or *loose*. Gen. 32:27. Lev. 14:7. Particularly prisoners. Zech. 9:11. 1 K. 20:42. 1 Sam. 20:22 *go*, כִּי שִׁלַּחֲךָ יְהוָה *for Jehovah sets you free*.—שִׁלַּח חָפְשִׁי *to set free*, see under חָפְשִׁי.—שִׁלַּח מָדוֹן *to let loose strife, to occasion strife*, Prov. 6:14, 19. 16:28.

4. *to accompany one departing, to send forward*, προπέμπειν. Gen. 18:16. 31:27.

5. *to chase* or *drive away*. Gen. 3: 23. 1 K. 9:7. Is. 50:1. *repudiare* (feminam,) Deut. 21:14. 22:19, 29. Jer. 3:8. Comp. שִׁלּוּחִים.

6. *to let hang down*; e. g. the hair, Ezek. 44:20. *to let down* (by a cord), Jer. 38:6, 11. *to give* or *yield up*, construed with בְּ and בְּיַד, Job 8:4 וַיְשַׁלְּחֵם בְּיַד פִּשְׁעָם *then gave he them up to their transgression*. Ps. 81:13.

7. *to throw off, to rid* or *divest one's self of* a thing. Job 30:11 *they throw off the bridle before me*, i. e. they rid themselves of all restraint before me. 39:3 *they rid themselves of their pains*, i. e. of their young.

8. *to throw*, e. g. arrows at a mark, 1 Sam. 20:20. fire into a city, Am. 1: 4 ff. Hos. 8:14.

9. *to push away, propellere*. Job 30: 12.

10. שִׁלַּח בָּאֵשׁ *to set on fire, mettre à feu*. Ps. 74:7. Judg. 1:8. 20:48. 2 K. 8:12.

11. joined with יָד, *to stretch out* the hand. Prov. 31:19, 20. (Comp. Kal no. 4.) Spoken of a tree, *to spread out* its branches, Jer. 17:8. Ezek. 17:6, 7. 31:5. Ps. 80:12. Metaphorically *to spread out* (a people), Ps. 44:3.

Pu. 1. *to be sent*; freq.

2. *to be put away*. Is. 50:1.

3. *to be driven out*. Is. 16:2.

4. *to be forsaken*. Is. 27:10.

5. *to be let loose, set free*. Prov. 29: 15 נַעַר מְשֻׁלָּח *a child left to himself*.

Hiph. i. q. Pi. no. 1. *to send*, e. g. misfortune, plagues, etc. construed with בְּ. Lev. 26:22. Am. 8:11.

Deriv. out of course מִשְׁלַח, מִשְׁלוֹחַ, מִשְׁלַחַת.

שְׁלַח, fut. יִשְׁלַח, Chald.

1. *to send, to send away*. Dan. 3:2. Construed with עַל of the person *sent to*, Ezra 4:11, 18. 5:7, 17.

2. joined with יָד, *to stretch out the hand*. Dan. 5:24. Construed with לְ, *aggredi* aliquid, Ezra 6:12.

שֶׁלַח m. with suff. שִׁלְחוֹ, verbal from שָׁלַח, dec. VI. i.

1. *a sprout, shoot.* Cant. 4:13.

2. *a pointed weapon, a spear, dart, sword.* (Arab. سِلَاح *a dart, weapon;* مُسَلَّح *armed.*) 2 Chr. 32:5. 23:10. Joel 2:8.—עָבַר בַּשֶּׁלַח *to perish by the sword,* hence *to perish in any way,* Job 33:18. 36:12.

3. proper name of a son of Arphaxad. Gen. 10:24. 11:12. The other names of persons with which this is joined represent at the same time nations or tribes. But there is no evidence that the same is the case with the name Selah.

4. name of a conduit and pool, near Mount Zion, prob. the same with שִׁלֹחַ. Neh. 3:15. Vulg. *Siloe.*

שִׁלֹחַ *Siloah,* a spring and conduit on the south-west of Jerusalem. Is. 8:6. otherwise called גִּחוֹן, see גִּחוֹן no. 1. In the Sept. and Josephus, Σιλωάμ; so in the N. T. John 9:7. Vulg. *Siloe.* See Relandi Palæstina, p. 858.

שְׁלֻחוֹת fem. plur. verbal from שָׁלַח, *shoots, branches, tendrils.* Is. 16:8. See the verb in Kal no. 4.

שֻׁלְחָן m. plur. שֻׁלְחָנוֹת, dec. II. b. *a table.* Ex. 25:23 ff. עָרַךְ שֻׁלְחָן *to spread* or *set a table,* (for a meal,) Ps. 23:5. Prov. 9:2.—שֻׁלְחַן הַפָּנִים *the table of shew-bread,* Num. 4:7. also called שֻׁלְחַן הַמַּעֲרֶכֶת 1 Chr. 28:16. 2 Chr. 29:18. which appears to have been the later name, see the art. מַעֲרֶכֶת.—אֹכְלֵי שֻׁלְחָנְךָ *those that eat at thy table,* 2 Sam. 19:29. 1 K. 2:7. for אֹכְלִים עַל שֻׁלְחָנְךָ, comp. 2 Sam. 9:11.

שָׁלַט fut. יִשְׁלֹט, a word belonging to the later Hebrew.

1. *to rule over* any thing; construed with בְּ. Ecc. 8:9. with עַל, Neh. 5:15.

2. *to be master of* any thing. Ecc. 2:19. Est. 9:1.

Hiph. 1. *to let rule.* Ps. 119:133.

2. *to give power* or *permission, potestatem alicujus rei dare.* Ecc. 5:18. 6:2. Comp. מָשַׁל Ex. 21:8.

שְׁלֵט, fut. יִשְׁלַט, Chald.

1. *to rule over* any thing, construed with בְּ. Dan. 2:39. 5:7, 16.

2. *to have power over* any thing. Dan. 3:27.

3. construed with בְּ, *to fall on, attack.* Dan. 6:25.

Aph. *to appoint ruler.* Dan. 2:38, 48.

שֶׁלֶט found only in the plur. שְׁלָטִים, const. שִׁלְטֵי, dec. VI. h. *a shield.* 2 Sam. 8:7 שִׁלְטֵי הַזָּהָב *the golden shields.* 2 K. 11:10 *the spears and the shields of king David.* In the parallel passage 2 Chr. 23:9, מָגִנִּים is likewise added. According to Cant. 4:4. Ezek. 27:11, the שְׁלָטִים were hung up on the walls for ornament; and in the former passage מָגֵן is so used, that שֶׁלֶט which follows appears to be a repetition of the same sense. Jer. 51:11 *sharpen the arrows,* מִלְאוּ הַשְּׁלָטִים *fill the shields,* i. e. present yourselves with them, or fill your hands with them; (comp. Zech. 9:13, with 2 K. 9:24.) The signification given above is adopted by most critics since Kimchi, suits the context of all the passages, and is the best supported by the kindred dialects. The Syriac and Chaldaic versions have often retained the same word, and from them we can learn with most certainty its true signification. Now in two passages (1 Chr. 18:7. 2 Chr. 23:9.) the Chaldaic version renders it *scuta,* and in the Targum of Jer. 13:23, we find שִׁלְטֵי רִקְמָתֵהּ *scuta varietatis ejus,* spoken of the variegated spots of the leopard. Others: *quivers,* on account of Jer. 51:11.

שִׁלְטוֹן m. verbal from שָׁלַט, *mighty, powerful.* Ecc. 8:4, 8.

שִׁלְטוֹן Chald. *an officer, ruler.* Dan. 3:2, 3.

שָׁלְטָן, const. שָׁלְטָן, Chald. *might, power, dominion.* Dan. 3:33. [4:3.] 4:19. [4:22.] 7:6, 14. 6:27 בְּכָל־שָׁלְטָן מַלְכוּתִי *in the whole dominion of my kingdom.* Plur. *dominions, kingdoms,*

Dan. 7:27. Arab. سلطان *dominion*, and as a concrete, *a lord*.

שַׁלֶּטֶת f. *shameless, impudent*, spoken of a whore. Ezek. 16:30. Arab. سليطة *mulier clamosa et impudica*. Vulg. *procax*.

שְׁלִי m. in pause שֶׁלִי, verbal from שָׁלָה no. I. *rest, quiet, stillness*. 2 Sam. 3:27 בַּשֶּׁלִי *quietly, secretly*.

שִׁלְיָה f. verbal from שָׁלָה no. III. dec. X. *the after-birth*. Deut. 28:57. (In the Arabic medical writers سلى. In Talmud. סִלְיָתָא, also שִׁלְיָא.)

שָׁלֵיו and **שְׁלֵיו** (Jer. 49:31.) m. i. q. שָׁלֵו, verbal adj. from שָׁלָה no. I. *quiet, at ease*. Job 21:23.

שַׁלִּיט m. verbal from שָׁלַט, dec. I.

1. adj. *having power over* any thing, construed with בְּ. Ecc. 8:8.

2. subst. *a mighty* or *powerful man, a ruler*. Ecc. 7:19. 10:5. Gen. 42:6.

שַׁלִּיט Chald. 1. adj. *mighty, powerful, having power*. Dan. 2:10. 4:23. [4:26.] Construed with בְּ *over* any thing, Dan. 4:14, 22, 29. [4:17, 25, 32.] 5:21.

2. construed with לְ, *permitted to* be done. Ezra 7:24.

3. subst. *a powerful man, a ruler, officer*. Dan. 2:15. 5:29. Ezra 4:20.

שָׁלִישׁ and **שָׁלִשׁ** m. (with Kamets impure,) dec. I.

1. a hollow measure of unknown dimensions. Is. 40:12. Usually rendered *triens, triental*. Hence Ps. 80:6 וַתַּשְׁקֵמוֹ בִּדְמָעוֹת שָׁלִישׁ *thou givest them tears to drink by measure*, for בְּשָׁלִישׁ. Sept. ἐν μέτρῳ, *in mensura*.

2. Plur. a musical instrument, mentioned in connection with tabrets, perhaps *a triangle*, as in modern Turkish music. 1 Sam. 18:6.

3. a distinguished kind of warriors or combatants, perhaps strictly *the riders in the war-chariots*, ἀναβάται, παραβάται. Ex. 14:7 *he took all the chariots of Egypt* וְשָׁלִשִׁם עַל כֻּלּוֹ *and warriors in each of them*. 15:4. Sept. in chap. 14:7, τριστάται, and in chap. 15:4, ἀναβάται τριστάται. (Τριστάτης has this meaning, according to Origen, because there were three in each chariot, of whom the first fought, the second protected him with a shield, and the third guided the horses.) In 1 K. 9:22, שָׁלִשִׁים and שָׂרֵי־רִכְבּוֹ are joined together; comp. 2 K. 9:25. In other passages they appear to make a part of the body-guard of the Israelitish kings, 1 K. 9:22. 2 K. 10:25. 1 Chr. 11:11. 12:18, (where their leader is called רֹאשׁ הַשָּׁלִשִׁים, in the parallel passage 2 Sam. 23:8 רֹאשׁ הַשָּׁלִשִׁי without the final Mem.) These may indeed be the same, only having a different employment in time of peace.—שָׁלִישׁ in the singular is often prob. i. q. רֹאשׁ הַשָּׁלִשִׁים, and occurs as a high officer attending on the king, 2 K. 9:25. 15:25. 7:2, 17, 19. The etymology in Hebrew is perhaps analogous to that of the Greek word τριστάτης. It has also been collated with the Latin *tribunus*, but the origin of this word is entirely different. Other derivations and explanations, e. g. *one of the thirty*, (comp. 2 Sam. 23:23. 1 Chr. 11:25.) or *officers of the third rank*, are not suited to the first passages where the word evidently stands in connection with the war-chariots.—Prov. 22:20 שָׁלִשִׁים Keri prob. *principalia*, i. e. *nobilia*, comp. 8:6.

שְׁלִישִׁי m. שְׁלִישִׁיָּה, שְׁלִישִׁית f. plur. שְׁלִשִׁים, (ordinal adj. from שָׁלֹשׁ, שְׁלוֹשׁ *three*,) *the third*. The fem. signifies also (1.) *the third part*, scil. חֶלְקָה. Num. 15:6, 7. 2 Sam. 18:2. (2.) *the third time*. Ezek. 21:19. [21:14.] (3.) *the third day, the day after to-morrow*. 1 Sam. 20:12 כָּעֵת מָחָר הַשְּׁלִשִׁית *about this time to-morrow or the day after*. (4.) in Is. 15:5. Jer. 48:34, it forms a part of a proper name; see עֶגְלָה.

שָׁלַךְ in Kal not used.

Hiph. 1. *to throw, cast*. Gen. 37:22.

Num. 35:20, 22. E. g. to the ground, Ezek. 28:17.—הִשְׁלִיךְ עַל יְהוָה *to cast upon Jehovah*, i. e. to commit to him, Ps. 55:23. הִשְׁלִיךְ אַחֲרָיו Ps. 50:17. and אַחֲרֵי גֵוּוֹ 1 K. 14:9. Neh. 9:26. Is. 38:17. Ezek. 23:35. *to cast behind one's back*, i. e. to despise, contemn.—Job 29:17 מִשִּׁנָּיו אַשְׁלִיךְ טָרֶף *I cast the spoil out of his teeth.*

2. *to cast away.* 2 K. 7:15. Ezek. 20:8. הִשְׁלִיךְ נַפְשׁוֹ מִנֶּגֶד *to expose one's life*, Judg. 9:17.

3. *to expel, banish*, out of a country. Deut. 29:27. Amos 4:3, (where, however, 1 MS. reads it in Hoph. which is prob. correct.) Spoken of Jehovah, הִשְׁלִיךְ מֵעַל פָּנָיו *to drive from his presence, to reject*, 2 K. 13:23. 17:20. Jer. 7:15.

4. *to cast down, destroy*, e. g. a house, Jer. 9:18. Job 18:7 וְתַשְׁלִיכֵהוּ עֲצָתוֹ *and his own counsel shall cast him down.*

Hoph. הָשְׁלַךְ and הֻשְׁלַךְ pass. of no. 1. Ezek. 19:12. Ps. 22:11 עָלֶיךָ הָשְׁלַכְתִּי מֵרָחֶם *upon thee have I cast myself from the womb*, i. e. in thee have I trusted. Also of no. 2. Is. 14:19. of no. 4. Dan. 8:11.

שָׁלָךְ m. verbal from שָׁלַךְ, Lev. 11:17. Deut. 14:17. prob. *the plungeon, cormorant*, καταῤῥάκτης of the ancients, *pelecanus Bassanus*, Linn. It derives its name from this circumstance, that it keeps watch on the high cliffs, and when it sees a fish in the water, it *shoots down* like an arrow into the water, and seizes its prey. Sept. καταῤῥάκτης. Vulg. *mergulus*. Syr. and Chald. *trahens pisces*. Comp. Bocharti Hieroz. P. II. Lib. II. cap. 21. Oedmann's verm. Sammlungen aus der Naturkunde, H. III. p. 68.

שַׁלֶּכֶת f. verbal from שָׁלַךְ.

1. *the falling* (of a tree). Is. 6:13.

2. name of a gate of the temple. 1 Chr. 26:16.

שָׁלַל 1. i. q. Arab. سَلَّ *to draw out or off.* Ruth 2:16. Comp. נָשַׁל and שָׁלָה no. III.

2. *to plunder, spoil.* Construed with an accus. of the thing, Ezek. 26:12. of the person, Ezek. 39:10. Zech. 2:12. [2:8.]—שָׁלַל שָׁלָל *to make booty*, Is. 10:6. Ezek. 29:19. It is inflected sometimes regularly, and sometimes defectively. The forms which occur are שָׁלַל, שָׁלְלוּ, שׁוֹלְלַי; infin. שְׁלֹל and שֹׁל, fut. יָשֹׁל.

Hithpo. אִשְׁתּוֹלֵל (with the Aramean form,) for הִשְׁתּוֹלֵל *to be spoiled, to become a prey.* Ps. 76:6. Is. 59:15.

שָׁלָל m. verbal from שָׁלַל, dec. IV. a.

1. *a prey, spoil, booty*, liter. *spolium, exuviæ.*—חִלֵּק שָׁלָל *to divide the spoil*, Gen. 49:27. Ps. 68:13.—Jer. 21:9 וְהָיְתָה לּוֹ נַפְשׁוֹ לְשָׁלָל *he shall have his life as a booty*, i. e. it shall be preserved to him. Jer. 38:2. 39:18.

2. *booty, gain, profit.* Prov. 31:11.

שָׁלֵם, fut. יִשְׁלַם.

1. *to be completed* or *finished*; spoken e. g. of a building, 1 K. 7:51. Neh. 6:15. of a space of time, Is. 60:20.

2. *to live in peace* or *affluence, to prosper, integrum esse.* Job 9:4 *who hath hardened himself against him* וַיִּשְׁלָם *and prospered?* 22:21 הַסְכֶּן־נָא עִמּוֹ וּשְׁלָם *acquaint now thyself with him and prosper.*

3. *to have peace, friendship.* Part. שׁוֹלְמִי *my friend, one at peace with me*, i. q. אִישׁ שְׁלוֹמִי, Ps. 7:5. Part. pass. שְׁלוּמִים *peaceable*, 2 Sam. 20:19. See Pu. no. 3.

Pi. שִׁלֵּם 1. *to complete* or *finish*, (a building.) 1 K. 9:25.

2. *to preserve, to keep uninjured.* Job 8:6.

3. *to restore, make good*; e. g. what has been stolen, Ex. 21:37. a debt, Ps. 37:21. 2 K. 4:7. Hence in general *to pay* or *perform*; e. g. a vow, Ps. 50:14. Is. 19:21. an offering, Hos. 14:3.

4. *to recompense, requite, reward*; construed with an accus. of the thing, Jer. 16:18. 32:18. with a dative of the person, 2 K. 9:26. with the accus. and dative together, שִׁלֵּם גְּמוּלוֹ לְ *to recompense one's actions upon him*, see גְּמוּל no. 1. The person is sometimes, though more rarely, put in the accus. e. g. Ps. 31:24. Prov. 13:21 וְאֶת־צַדִּיקִים יְשַׁלֶּם טוֹב *but prosperity rewards the righteous.* Ps. 35:12. The thing is also preceded by בְּ, Jer.

50:29. Ps. 62:13. (Synonymous with הֵשִׁיב.)

5. *to grant, impart in any way,* (from signif. no. 3.) e. g. consolations, Is. 57:18. but it may perhaps be rendered, *to impart again.*

Pu. 1. pass. of Pi. no. 3. *to be paid, discharged,* spoken of a vow. Ps. 65:2.

2. *to be recompensed.* Jer. 18:20. Spoken of a person, *to obtain recompense.* (comp. שִׁלֵּם with an accus. of the person.) Prov. 11:31 הֵן צַדִּיק בָּאָרֶץ יְשֻׁלָּם *behold, the righteous shall be recompensed in the earth.* 13:13.

3. *to be devoted to God.* Part. מְשֻׁלָּם *devoted to God,* Is. 42:19. Parall. עֶבֶד יְהוָה. Comp. Kal. no. 3. particularly Hiph. no. 3.

Hiph. 1. *to complete, execute, perform.* Job 23:14. Is. 44:26, 38.

2. *to make an end of* a thing. Is. 38:12, 13.

3. *to make* or *have peace with* a person; construed with אֶת, Josh. 10:1, 4. with עִם, Deut. 20:12. 1 K. 22:45. Particularly *to make peace by submitting one's self,* construed with אֶל, Josh. 11:19. (Comp. the Arab. سلم conj. IV. *to devote or submit one's self,* particularly to God, hence اسلام (*Islam*) *submission to God, religion;* مسلم (*Moslem*) *one devoted to God, a believer;* comp. שָׁלֵם עִם יְיָ *devoted to God,* and Pu. no. 3.)

4. causat. *to make a friend* of any one. Prov. 16:7.

Hoph. *to be at peace with* any one, construed with לְ. Job 5:23.

Deriv. out of course שָׁלוֹם, שִׁלּוּם.

שְׁלַם Chald. *to complete.* Part. Pe. שְׁלִים *completed,* Ezra 5:16.

Aph. *to restore, give back.* Ezra 7:19.

שְׁלָם m. Chald. i. q. Heb. שָׁלוֹם *prosperity, peace,* Ezra 5:7. Dan. 3:31. 6:26.

שָׁלֵם, fem. שְׁלֵמָה, verbal adj. from שָׁלַם, dec. V. a

1. *completed, finished.* 2 Chr. 8:16.

2. *complete, full;* e. g. אֶבֶן שְׁלֵמָה *a full weight,* Deut. 25:15. spoken of iniquity, Gen. 15:16. גָּלוּת שְׁלֵמָה *the prisoners in full number,* Am. 1:6, 9. (comp. Jer. 13:19.)

3. *uninjured, safe, integer.* Gen. 33:18. Spoken of a host, Nah. 1:12. אֲבָנִים שְׁלֵמוֹת *unhewn stones,* Deut. 27:6. 1 K. 6:7.

4. *at peace, friendly.* (See the verb in Pu. Hiph. Hoph.) Gen. 34:21 שְׁלֵמִים הֵם אִתָּנוּ *they are at peace with us.*

5. *devoted,* particularly to God. 1 Chr. 28:9. 2 Chr. 15:17. 16:9. 2 K. 20:3. Sometimes with the addition עִם יְהוָה, 1 K. 8:61. 11:4. 15:3, 14. Comp. the verb in Hiph. no. 3.

6. a proper name, i. q. יְרוּשָׁלַםִ *Jerusalem,* (comp. p. 256.) Gen. 14:18. Ps. 76:3. Josephus (Antiq. Jud. I. 10.) τὴν μέντοι Σόλυμα ὕστερον ἐκάλεσαν Ἱεροσόλυμα. See Relandi Palaestina, p. 976. (In Arab. شَلَم، شَلْم and شَلَّم *Jerusalem.* Its appellative signification here is *health, peace,* i. q. שָׁלוֹם.)

שֶׁלֶם m. verbal from שָׁלַם, dec. VI. a. *a thank-offering, victima.* Am. 5:22. More frequently in the plural זֶבַח שְׁלָמִים Lev. 3:1 ff. (where the rites accompanying this offering are described.) 7:11 ff. Num. 7:17 ff. also simply שְׁלָמִים Lev. 9:4. The same offering, which in Lev. 7:12, is called זֶבַח הַתּוֹדָה *a sacrifice of praise,* is called in verses 13, 15 זֶבַח תּוֹדַת שְׁלָמָיו *his sacrifice of praise and thanksgiving.*—Sometimes, though rarely, this word denotes offerings, on mournful occasions, its original import being disregarded, Judg. 20:26. 21:4.

שִׁלֵּם m. verbal from שִׁלֵּם, *recompense.* Deut. 32:35.

שִׁלֻּם and **שִׁלּוּם** m. verbal from שִׁלֵּם, dec. I. *idem.* Hos. 9:7. Mic. 7:3. Plur. Is. 34:8.

שִׁלֻּמָה fem. of שִׁלֵּם, dec. X. *recompense, punishment.* Ps. 91. 8.

שַׁלֻּם m. proper name of a king of Israel. 2 K. 15:8—16.

שְׁלֹמֹה a proper name, *Solomon*, the son of David, king of Israel. Sept. Σαλωμών, in Josephus and the N. T. Σολομών. Its appellative import, which is alluded to 1 Chr. 22:9. is *peaceable*, (comp. the Saxon name *Frederick*, i.e. peaceable;) from שָׁלוֹם and the termination ה or ו, equivalent to ן, (comp. שִׁילֹה, שִׁילוֹן,) which is added to abstract nouns to give them the force of concretes. See Gesenius' Lehrgeb. § 122. 1. p. 513.

שַׁלְמַן Hos. 10:14. more at length שַׁלְמַנְאֶסֶר 2 K. 17:3. 18:9. proper name of a king of Assyria between Tiglath-pileser and Sennacherib. Sept. Σαλαμανασσάρ. Vulg. *Salmanassar.* (The syllable אסר undoubtedly signifies *prince*, and is found in several Assyrian names, e.g. תִּגְלַת־פִּלְאֶסֶר, on which account it is sometimes omitted. For שלמן no suitable explanation has yet been found in Persian.)

שַׁלְמֹנִים masc. plur. verbal from שִׁלֵּם, *recompenses;* hence *rewards, bribes.* Is. 1:23.

שָׁלַף, fut. יִשְׁלֹף, *to draw out* or *off;* e.g. a shoe, Ruth 4:7, 8. grass, Ps. 129:6. an arrow from the body which it has penetrated, Job 20:25. and most frequently a sword, Num. 22:23, 31. Josh. 5:13. אֶלֶף שֹׁלֵף חֶרֶב *a thousand men with drawn swords*, i.e. armed men, Judg. 8:10. 20:2, 15, 17, 46. 2 Sam. 24:9. (In Chald. more frequent.)

שֶׁלֶף a proper name. Gen. 10:26. 1 Chr. 1:20. a people of Arabia Felix, prob. the Σαλαπηνοί of Ptolemy, (Lib. vi. p. 154.) but nothing farther is known of them.

שָׁלֹשׁ and **שָׁלוֹשׁ**, const. שְׁלֹשׁ, before Makkeph שְׁלָשׁ־ (Ex. 21:11.) f. and שְׁלֹשָׁה, const. שְׁלֹשֶׁת, m. dec. III. a. and XIII. e.

1. *three.* שָׁלֹשׁ שָׁנִים *three years;* rarely after the noun, e.g. עָרִים שָׁלֹשׁ *three cities*, Josh. 21:32. בִּשְׁנַת שָׁלֹשׁ *in the third year*, 2 K. 18:1. שְׁלֹשׁ עֶשְׂרֵה *thirteen.* (With suff. שְׁלָשְׁתְּכֶם *ye three*, Num. 12:4. שְׁלָשְׁתָּם *they three*, Num. 12:4.

2. *three times.* Job 33:29.

Plur. שְׁלֹשִׁים com. gen. *thirty.* Used as an ordinal, 1 K. 16:23.

Deriv. out of course שָׁלִשׁ, שְׁלִישִׁי, מְשֻׁלָּשׁ.

שָׁלִישׁ see **שָׁלִישׁ**.

שִׁלֵּשׁ Pi. denom. from שָׁלֹשׁ.

1. *to divide into three parts.* Deut. 19:3.

2. *to repeat the third time.* 1 K. 18:34.

3. *to do on the third day.* 1 Sam. 20:19 וְשִׁלַּשְׁתָּ תֵּרֵד *and on the third day thou shalt come down.*

Pu. 1. *to be triple, three-fold.* Ecc. 4:12. Ezek. 42:6.

2. *to be three years old.* Gen. 15:9.

שִׁלֵּשִׁים masc. plur. denom. from שָׁלֹשׁ, *posterity of the third generation, grand-children.* Ex. 20:5. 37:7. בְּנֵי שִׁלֵּשִׁים *great grand-children*, Gen. 50:23. (Comp. רִבֵּעַ.)

שָׁלִשָׁה name of a district or country in Palestine. Once 1 Sam. 9:4. In it was probably situated the city בַּעַל־שָׁלִשָׁה 2 K. 4:42. This latter is called by Eusebius *Beth-Shalisha*, and is placed by him 15 Roman miles north of Diospolis.

שִׁלְשֹׁם adv. (from שָׁלֹשׁ, שלש and the adverbial termination ־ֹם) *three days ago, the day before yesterday*, always joined with תְּמוֹל, e.g. תמול שלשם *yesterday and the day before*, i.e. heretofore, Ex. 5:8. כִּתְמוֹל שִׁלְשֹׁם *as yesterday and the day before*, i.e. as heretofore, Gen. 31:3. 2 K. 13:5. מִתְּמוֹל שִׁלְשֹׁם *in time past, beforetime*, Deut. 19:6. Josh. 20:5. גַּם תְּמוֹל גַּם שִׁלְשֹׁם *both yesterday and the day before*, i.e. in time past, 2 Sam. 5:2.

שָׁם adv. 1. *there.* מִשָּׁם *thence.* אֲשֶׁר־שָׁם *where*, for the most part separated by intervening words, Gen. 13:3. 2 Sam. 15:21. also connected, 2 Chr. 6:11. שָׁם שָׁם *here, there*, Is. 28:10.

2. i. q. שָׁמָּה *thither.* 1 Sam. 2:14. 2 K. 19:32. Joined with אֲשֶׁר, *whither*, 1 K. 18:10. Jer. 19:14.

3. spoken of time, *then*, (like the Greek ἐκεῖ and the Lat. *ibi.*) Ps. 14:5.

132:17. Judg. 5:11. מִשָּׁם *from that time*, Hos. 2:17. [2:15.]

4. with ה paragogic שָׁמָּה (*Milêl*, hence read *shamma;*) (1.) *thither*. Gen. 19:20. (2.) more rarely i. q. שָׁם *there*. Is. 34:15. Jer. 18:2. (3.) with אֲשֶׁר, *whither;* more rarely *where*, e. g. 2 K. 23:8.

שֵׁם m. const. שֵׁם, sometimes before Makkeph שֶׁם־, with suff. שְׁמִי, שִׁמְךָ, שִׁמְכֶם, plur. שֵׁמוֹת, const. שְׁמוֹת, dec. VII. e.

1. *a name.*—בְּשֵׁם פ׳ *in the name of any one*, Ex. 5:23. Est. 3:12. בְּשֵׁם יְהוָה *in the name of Jehovah*, Jer. 11:21. 26:9. קָרָא בְשֵׁם, see under the article קָרָא. Particularly, *a celebrated name, celebrity, renown*, אַנְשֵׁי שֵׁם *men of renown*, Num. 16.2. 1 Chr. 5:24. Gen. 6:4. Antith. Job 30:8 בְּנֵי בְלִי שֵׁם *the children of the ignoble*, i. e. the ignoble. עָשָׂה לוֹ שֵׁם Gen. 11:4. Jer. 32:20. and שׂוּם לוֹ שֵׁם 2 Sam. 7:23. *to make for one's self a name.*—Zeph. 3:19 שַׂמְתִּים לִתְהִלָּה וּלְשֵׁם *I will make them for a praise and a name.* Verse 20. Deut. 26:19. Gen. 9:27 בְּאָהֳלֵי שֵׁם *in tents of renown.* Sometimes specifically, *a good name*, Ecc. 7:1. Prov. 22:1.

2. *a rumour, report.* שֵׁם רָע *an ill report*, Deut. 22:14, 19. Neh. 6:13 הָיָה לָהֶם לְשֵׁם רָע *it should be to them* (the occasion) *for an ill report* (concerning me).

3. שֵׁם יְהוָה *the name of Jehovah*, particularly in the following significations and connexions; (1.) *the praise* or *glory of Jehovah*, e. g. Is. 48:9 לְמַעַן שְׁמִי *for my name's sake, for my praise* or *glory.* Ps. 79:9. 106:8. Ezek. 20:44. 1 K. 8:41. (In other passages this phrase signifies, *according to his name*, i. e. according to what his name Jehovah signifies; see מַעַן no. 2.) Ps. 138:2 עַל־כָּל־שִׁמְךָ *above all thy name*, i. e. above all that has been said in praise of thee. Hence (2.) *Jehovah*, considered as the object of prayer, worship, or praise; e. g. קָרָא בְשֵׁם יְהוָה *to call on the name of Jehovah;* comp. the phrases under signif. no. 1. אֹהֲבֵי שְׁמֶךָ *they that love thy name*, Ps. 5:12. יֹדְעֵי שְׁמֶךָ *they that know thy name*, Ps. 9:11. יִרְאֵי שְׁמֶךָ *they that fear thy name*, Ps. 61:6. 91:14. 99:3. (3.) *the presence of Jehovah*, (comp. פָּנִים,) or *Jehovah*, considered as every where present; e. g. Ex. 23:21 כִּי שְׁמִי בְּקִרְבּוֹ *for my name is in him* (*the angel*). 1 K. 8:29 יִהְיֶה שְׁמִי שָׁם *there* (*in the temple*) *shall my name dwell.* 2 K. 23:27. 1 K. 3:2 *no house was yet built for the name of Jehovah.* 5:17, 19. [5:3, 5.] 8:17, 20. שׂוּם, שַׁכֵּן שְׁמוֹ *to place his name*, or *cause it to dwell* any where; see under שׂוּם and שָׁכַן. Also considered as present and mighty to help, Ps. 54:3 *O God!* בְּשִׁמְךָ הוֹשִׁיעֵנִי *by thy name*, i. e. by thy powerful presence, *save me.* 44:6. 124:8. 89:25. 20:2. Is. 30:27. Hence

4. שֵׁם and הַשֵּׁם Levit. 24:11, 16. Deut. 28:58. used, by way of eminence, for *Jehovah.* (The Samaritans read שֵׁם=שִׁימָא for יְהוָה, as the Jews read אֲדֹנָי.)

5. *a monument*, which preserves the name or memory of a person. 2 Sam. 8:13. Is. 55:13.

6. *Shem*, the second son of Noah. Gen. 5:32. According to the genealogical table in Gen. x. the nations of south-western Asia, as the Persians, Assyrians, Syrians, Hebrews, and a part of the Arabians, were descended from him. See on this subject Gesenius' Gesch. der Hebr. Sprache and Schrift, p. 5, 6.

שֻׁם m. Chald. *a name.* Dan. 4:5. [4:8.] Ezra 5:1. With suff. שְׁמֵהּ (from שֻׁם) Dan. 2:20, 26. 4:5. [4:8.] 5:12. Ezra 5:14 וִיהִיבוּ לְשֵׁשְׁבַּצַּר שְׁמֵהּ *and they were given to Sheshbazzar, as his name was*, liter. *they were given to him whose name was Sheshbazzar.* Plur. שְׁמָהָן Ezra 5:4, 10.

שָׁמַד in Kal not used.

Hiph. הִשְׁמִיד 1. *to destroy*, e. g. cities, altars. Lev. 26:30. Num. 33:52.

2. more frequently *to destroy*, e. g. men, nations. Deut. 1:27. 2:12, 21, 22, 23. Est. 3:6. Infin. הַשְׁמֵד used as a subst. *destruction*, Is. 14:23. Infin.

with suff. הִשְׁמִידָם, הַשְׁמִידְךָ, Deut. 7:24. 28:48. Josh. 11:14.

Niph. pass. 1. *to be laid waste;* spoken of a plain, Jer. 48:8. of high places, Hos. 10:8.

2. *to be destroyed.* Gen. 34:30. Ps. 37:38.

שְׁמַד Chald. Aph. *to destroy.* Dan. 7:26.

שַׁמָּה f. verbal from שָׁמַם, dec. X.

1. *a desolation.* Is. 5:9. Jer. 2:15. Ps. 73:19 אֵיךְ הָיוּ לְשַׁמָּה *how have they become a desolation!*

2. *astonishment, amazement.* Jer. 8:21. Particularly *an object of astonishment,* Deut. 28:37. Jer. 19:8 לְשַׁמָּה וְלִשְׁרֵקָה *for an astonishment and a derision.* 25:9, 18. 51:37.

שְׁמָהָן Chald. plur. *names,* see שֵׁם.

שְׁמוּאֵל m. a proper name, *Samuel,* son of Elkanah, a judge and high-priest in Israel, who first gave to the people a king. According to 1 Sam. 1:20, the name is a contraction of שְׁמוּעַ אֵל (*heard of God,*) by the omission of ע. As it is now written, it may be compounded of שְׁמוּ i. q. שֵׁם *a name,* (like מְתוּ=מַת, רֵעַ=רֵעוּ *a man;*) hence liter. *the name of God.* Comp. Gesenius' Gesch. der Hebr. Sprache, p. 49.

שְׁמוּעָה and **שְׁמֻעָה** f. verbal from שָׁמַע, dec. X.

1. *news, tidings.* 1 Sam. 4:19. Either of good, (Prov. 15:30. 25:25.) or of evil, (Jer. 49:23. Ps. 112:7.) e. g. of the approach of a formidable enemy, Jer. 10:22. Particularly *a message* from God, Is. 53:1. Jer. 49:14. hence

2. *instruction, doctrine.* Is. 28:9.

3. *a rumour, report.* 2 Chr. 9:6.

שָׁמַט synonymous with נָטַשׁ.

1. *to remit* (a debt). Deut. 15:2.

2. *to cause to rest, to let lie uncultivated,* as the ground. Ex. 23:11.

3. construed with מִן *to cease from* any thing. Jer. 17:4.

4. *to cause to fall, to throw down.* 2 K. 9:33.

5. *to break loose, to set one's self free.* 2 Sam. 6:6 כִּי שָׁמְטוּ הַבָּקָר *for the oxen would set themselves free.* (Comp. the synon. נָטַשׁ no. 10. *to draw out,* in Niph. *to be loosed.*)

Niph. *to be scattered,* liter. *to be loosed.* Ps. 141:6. Comp. the synon. נָטַשׁ no. 9. Others: *to be dismissed.* Others: *to be thrown down;* comp. Kal. no. 4.

Hiph. i. q. Kal no. 1. *to release, remit.* Deut. 15:3.

שְׁמִטָּה f. verbal from שָׁמַט, *a remission, release.* Deut. 15:1, 2. שְׁנַת־הַשְּׁמִטָּה *the year of release,* Deut. 15:9. 31:10. This was every seventh year, when debts were cancelled and agriculture intermitted.

שָׁמַיִם masc. plur. const. שְׁמֵי, *the heaven* or *heavens.* (The singular is found in the Arab. سَمَآءٌ from سما *to be high.* The corresponding form of the singular may in Hebrew have been שָׁמַי, whence the plur. שָׁמַיִם, like גַּי, plur. גַּיִם. Comp. מַיִם.) With ה parag. הַשָּׁמַיְמָה *to* or *towards heaven,* Gen. 15:5. 28:12.—אֱלֹהֵי הַשָּׁמַיִם *the God of heaven,* a frequent phrase in the later books, (See the Chald.) 2 Chr. 36:23. Ezra 1:2. Neh. 1:4, 5. 2:4, 20. Ps. 136:26. Jon. 1:9. in connection with יְהוָה, Gen. 24:3, 7. שָׁמַיִם וּשְׁמֵי הַשָּׁמַיִם *the heaven and the heaven of heavens,* a rhetorical expression for *the highest* or *most holy heavens,* Deut. 10:14. 1 K. 8:27. 2 Chr. 2:5. הַשָּׁמַיִם וְהָאָרֶץ *the heaven and the earth,* i. e. the universe, Gen. 1:1. 2:1. 14:19, 22. The Hebrews conceived of heaven as a solid arch, (see רָקִיעַ;) as resting on pillars, (Job 26:11.) as having foundations, (2 Sam. 22:8.) and a gate, (Gen. 28:17.) and as sending down rain from its open doors or sluices, (Ps. 78:23. 2 K. 7:2, 19.)

שְׁמַיִן emph. שְׁמַיָּא, Chald. *idem.* Sometimes used where we might expect the word *God,* Dan. 4:23. [4:26.] אֱלָהּ שְׁמַיָּא *the God of heaven,* Dan. 2:18, 37.

Ezra 5:11, 12. 6:9, 10. Comp. Tob. 10:12. Rev. 11:13.

שְׁמִינִי, fem. ־ִית, (denom. from שְׁמֹנֶה *eight,*) *the eighth.* Ex. 22:29. The fem. שְׁמִינִית *octava* is used in reference to music, and denotes a particular tone, (not a musical instrument as is commonly supposed,) Ps. 6:1. 12:1. From 1 Chr. 15:21, it appears to have been the lowest of the three parts or voices; according to Forkel, *the fundamental base,* sung by men.

שָׁמִיר m. dec. III. a.

1. *a thorn, a thorn-bush,* (In Arab. سمر.) Is. 5:6. 7:23, 24, 25. 9:17. 10:17. 27:4. 32:13.

2. *a diamond.* (In Arab. سامور.) Jer. 17:1. Ezek. 3:9. Zech. 7:12. (The root سمر signifies *to pierce, to nail;* whence the Hebrew מַסְמֵר *a nail;* and prob. also שָׁמִיר in both significations, the diamond being used to engrave with.)

3. proper name of a city in the tribe of Judah. Josh. 15:48.

4. also of another in Mount Ephraim. Judg. 10:1, 2.

שָׁמֵם, imper. שֹׁם, fut. יֵשַׁם, plur. יֵשַׁמּוּ, i. q. יָשַׁם and אָשַׁם no. II.

1. *to be laid waste, made desolate.* Ezek. 33:28. 35:12, 15. Part. שׁוֹמֵם *desolate,* Lam. 1:4. 3:11. spoken of persons, *faint, desponding,* Lam. 1:13, 16. Plur. fem. שׁוֹמֵמוֹת *waste places, desolations, vastata,* Is. 61:4 שֹׁמְמוֹת רִאשֹׁנִים *the desolations of former generations.* Dan. 9:18, 26 נֶחֱרֶצֶת שֹׁמֵמוֹת *the decreed desolations.*

2. more rarely trans. *to lay waste.* Ezek. 36:3 יַעַן בְּיַעַן שַׁמּוֹת וְשָׁאֹף אֶתְכֶם *because they have laid you waste and destroyed you;* (שַׁמּוֹת is strictly a verbal noun, but used here as an infin.) Part. שֹׁמֵם *a desolater, ravager,* Dan. 9:27 פֶּשַׁע הַשֹּׁמֵם *the wickedness of the desolater,* Dan. 8:13, and שִׁקּוּץ שֹׁמֵם *the abomination of the desolater,* Dan. 12:11. prob. the idolatrous altar which Antiochus Epiphanes caused to be built on the altar of burnt-offerings at Jerusalem. Comp. 1 Macc. 1:54. 6:7. In the plur. *the abominations of the desolater,* Dan. 9:27. perhaps idols.

3. *to be solitary, single,* spoken of a woman. 2 Sam. 13:20. Is. 54:1. (The ideas *desolate* and *single* are kindred and found united in the synonymous word גַּלְמוּד. Comp. the figure Is. 62:4.)

4. *to be amazed, astonished.* 1 K. 9:8. Jer. 18:16. Construed with עַל of the thing, Is. 52:14. Jer. 2:12.

Niph. נָשַׁם 1. *to be laid waste, made desolate,* i. q. Kal. Jer. 12:11. Spoken of persons, *to faint, languish,* Lam. 4:5. Spoken of a way, *to be solitary, deserted,* Lev. 26:22. Is. 33:8. Comp. Kal no. 3.

2. i. q. Kal no. 4. *to be amazed, astonished.* Jer. 4:9. Construed with עַל of the thing, Job 18:20.

Po. part. מְשׁוֹמֵם.

1. *a desolater, ravager.* Dan. 9:27. 11:31. See Kal no. 1.

2. *solitary,* spoken of a mourner. Ezra 9:3, 4. Else *astonished,* comp. Hiph. no. 2.

Hiph. הֵשַׁם, fut. יַשִּׁים, infin. הַשְׁמֵם, part. מַשְׁמִים.

1. i. q. Kal no. 2. *to lay waste.* Lev. 26:31, 32. Ezek. 30:12, 14.

2. *to be amazed, astonished, confounded.* Ezek. 3:16. Construed with עַל of the thing, Mic. 6:13.

3. trans. *to amaze, astonish.* Ezek. 32:10.

Hoph. הָשַּׁם (hosham,) plur. הָשַׁמּוּ, (for הָשְׁמַם, which is read in some MSS. and editions.)

1. *to be waste, desolate.* Lev. 26:34, 35, 43.

2. *to be amazed, astonished.* Job 21:5.

Hithpo. הִשְׁתּוֹמֵם, fut. once תִּשּׁוֹמֵם Ecc. 7:16.

1. *to destroy one's self.* Ecc. 7:16.

2. *to be astonished, amazed, confounded.* Is. 59:16. 63:5. Dan. 8:27. Ps. 143:4.

Deriv. out of course מְשַׁמָּה, מְשׁוֹמָה.

שְׁמַם Chald. Ithpo. אֶשְׁתּוֹמֵם *to be astonished, amazed.* Dan. 4:16. [4:19.]

שָׁמֵם m. verbal adj. from שָׁמֵם, dec. V. a. *desolate, waste.* Dan. 9:17.

שְׁמָמָה f. verbal from שָׁמֵם, dec. XI. c.

1. *desolation, a waste.* Is. 1:7.—מִדְבַּר שְׁמָמָה *a desolate wilderness,* Jer. 12:10.—שְׁמָמָה וּמְשַׁמָּה *wasting and desolation,* i. e. an entire desolation, Ezek. 33:28, 29. 35:3.

2. *amazement, astonishment.* Ezek. 7:27.

שִׁמֲמָה f. (for שְׁמָמָה,) verbal from שָׁמֵם, dec. X. *idem.* Ezek. 35:7, 9.

שִׁמָּמוֹן m. verbal from שָׁמֵם, *amazement, astonishment.* Ezek. 4:16. 12:19.

שָׁמַן or **שָׁמֵן**, fut. יִשְׁמַן, *to be* or *become fat.* Deut. 32:15. Jer. 5:28.

Hiph. 1. *to make fat, to cover with fat;* e. g. the heart, i. e. to render it obdurate or insensible, Is. 6:10. (comp. Ps. 119:70.)

2. *to become fat.* Neh. 9:25.

שָׁמֵן verbal adj. from שָׁמַן, dec. V. a. *fat;* (1.) spoken of persons, *stout, robust,* Judg. 3:29. Comp. מִשְׁמַנִּים no. 2. (2.) of a country, Num. 13:20. of bread, Gen. 49:20.

שֶׁמֶן m. (fem. Cant. 1:3.) with suff. שַׁמְנִי, plur. שְׁמָנִים, verbal from שָׁמַן, dec. VI. a.

1. *fat, fatness.* Ps. 109:24.—מִשְׁתֵּה שְׁמָנִים *a fat* or *sumptuous feast,* Is. 25:6.—בֶּן־שֶׁמֶן, see בֵּן no. 5.

2. *oil.* Gen. 28:18. עֵץ שֶׁמֶן *a wild olive-tree, oleaster,* different from זַיִת *the common olive-tree,* Neh. 8:15. 1 K. 6:23.

3. *spiced oil, ointment,* Ps. 133:2. Prov. 21:17. Applied as a remedy, Is. 1:6.

מִשְׁמַנִּים masc. plur. verbal from שָׁמַן, dec. VIII. h. *fat, fatness,* (of the earth.) Gen. 27:28, 39 מִשְׁמַנֵּי אֶרֶץ for מִשְׁמַנֵּי, (parall. מִטַּל;) in verse 28, *of the fatness of the earth;* in verse 39, *without fatness of earth.*

שְׁמֹנֶה f. and **שְׁמֹנָה**, const. **שְׁמֹנַת**, m. *eight.* Plur. שְׁמֹנִים com. gen. *eighty.* Deriv. שְׁמִינִי.

שָׁמַע and **שָׁמֵעַ** 1. *to hear;* construed with an accus. rarely with בְּ, Job 26:14. The latter particularly with the accessory idea of hearing *with pleasure* or *satisfaction,* Ps. 92:12. The person or thing *heard* is put in the accus. Gen. 23:8, 11, 15. or is preceded by לְ, Job 31:35. by אֶל, 2 Sam. 12:16. by בְּקוֹל, Gen. 30:6. Deut. 1:45. by לְקוֹל, Gen. 3:17. The phrase *to hear* a person or thing denotes (1.) *to listen, to be attentive.* Gen. 23:8. Job 31:35. (2.) *to hearken, obey.* Gen. 39:10. Neh. 13:27. Ex. 24:7 *all which Jehovah hath spoken* נַעֲשֶׂה וְנִשְׁמָע *we will do and obey.* (3.) *to hear, answer,* spoken of God. Ps. 10:17. 28:2. 54:4.

2. *to understand.* Gen. 11:7. 42:23. Part. שֹׁמֵעַ prob. *intelligent, understanding,* i. q. מֵבִין 1 K. 3:9. Prov. 21:28.

Niph. 1. *to be heard,* construed with לְ *by* a person. Neh. 6:1, 7.

2. *to shew one's self obedient* or *submissive.* Ps. 18:45.

Pi. *to cause to hear, to summon,* construed with an accus. of the person. 1 Sam. 15:4. 23:8.

Hiph. 1. *to cause to hear* or *be heard.* Jer. 48:4. Construed with a double accus. of the person and thing, 2 K. 7:6. Ps. 143:8. also with אֶל of the person, Ezek. 36:15. Also הִשְׁמִיעַ בְּקוֹל Ezek. 27:30. Ps. 26:7. like נָתַן בְּקוֹל.

2. *to announce;* construed with an accus. of the thing, Is. 45:21. with an accus. of the person, Is. 44:8. 48:5. with two accus. 48:6.

3. *to call together* or *upon by proclamation.* 1 K. 15:22. Jer. 50:29. 51:27.

4. in reference to music, intrans. *to sing,* Neh. 12:42. *to play,* 1 Chr. 15:28. 16:5. Particularly *to sound on a high note,* 1 Chr. 15:19. Comp. נִצַּח. (Arab. مُسْمِعَةٌ *a songstress;* سَمَاعٌ *music.*)

Deriv. out of course כִּשְׁמֻעָה ,כְּשֵׁמַע ,שְׁמוּעָה.

שְׁמַע Chald. *to hear*, construed with עַל *concerning* a person. Dan. 5 : 14, 16.

Ithpe. *to shew one's self obedient* or *submissive*. Dan. 7 : 27.

שֶׁמַע m. with suff. שִׁמְעִי, verbal from שָׁמַע, dec. VI. i.

1. *a hearing*. Job 42 : 5.

2. *a message, intelligence, news*, i. q. שְׁמוּעָה. Hos. 7 : 12 כְּשֵׁמַע לַעֲדָתָם *as the news went to their assembly*.

3. *a report, rumour;* e. g. שֵׁמַע רָע *an evil report*. Ex. 23 : 1. Ps. 18 : 45 לְשֵׁמַע אֹזֶן *at the bare report* (of me). The genitive subjoined expresses the person to whom the report relates; e. g. שֵׁמַע שְׁלֹמֹה *the fame of Solomon*, 1 K. 10 : 1. In English it may sometimes be omitted in translating, e. g. Gen. 29 : 13 כִּשְׁמֹעַ לָבָן אֶת־שֵׁמַע יַעֲקֹב *when Laban heard concerning Jacob*. Is. 66 : 19.

4. in reference to music, *a high sound* or *note*, (see הִשְׁמִיעַ no. 4.) Ps. 150 : 5 בְּצִלְצְלֵי שָׁמַע *cymbals of a high sound*.

שֹׁמַע m. verbal from שָׁמַע, dec. VI. p. *report, fame*. Josh. 6 : 27. 9 : 9.

שְׁמֻעָה see **שְׁמוּעָה**.

שִׁמְעוֹן (*a hearing*) *Simeon*, proper name of a son of Jacob by Leah, and progenitor of the tribe which is named from him. Gen. 29 : 33. The territory assigned to this tribe is described Josh. 19 : 1—9. In Greek Συμεών.

שֶׁמֶץ m. *a short gentle sound, a whispering*. (Arab. شمص *celeriter loqui*.) Job 4 : 12. 26 : 14. In Talmud. שֶׁמֶץ signifies *a little*, which suits the passages and is the rendering of the Targum and Syriac version. But the former interpretation is to be preferred, because the following article שִׁמְצָה may be explained from the same Arabic root. Both may likewise be explained by a collation with שֵׁמַע, see the following article.

שִׁמְצָה f. once Ex. 32 : 25 לְשִׁמְצָה בְּקָמֵיהֶם *so as to be overthrown by their enemies;* comp. the Arabic root شمص *to drive away, thrust, smite*, pass. *to hasten*. According to the ancient versions and Jewish commentators, *an ill report, disgrace*, comp. שֵׁמַע (by a commutation of צ and ע;) whence שֶׁמֶץ likewise may be explained.

שָׁמַר, fut. יִשְׁמֹר.

1. *to keep, watch, guard;* construed with an accus. rarely with אֶל, 1 Sam. 26 : 15. with עַל, verse 16. Prov. 6 : 22. with בְּ, 2 Sam. 18 : 12. Construed with מִן, *to guard* or *preserve from* any thing, Ps. 121 : 7. 140 : 5. Part. שֹׁמֵר *a watchman, guard*, Cant. 3 : 3. spoken of a shepherd, 1 Sam. 17 : 20.

2. *to keep, preserve, lay up*. Ex. 22 : 6. Particularly *to keep in memory*, Gen. 37 : 11. Ps. 130 : 3. Job 10 : 14 וּשְׁמַרְתָּנִי *thou keepest* (it) *in memory concerning me*. Particularly *to keep* or *retain* (anger), Amos 1 : 11 עֶבְרָתוֹ שְׁמָרָה נֶצַח *he kept his anger for ever;* (שְׁמָרָה pointed in this way and with the accent on the penult, is of the masc. gen. and the ה is paragogic.) Hence by an ellipsis of עֶבְרָה or אַף, (like נָטַר no. 2.) Jer. 3 : 5 אִם יִשְׁמֹר לָנֶצַח *will he retain* (his anger) *for ever?*

3. *to watch, mark, observe*. 1 Sam. 1 : 12. Ps. 17 : 4 *I observed the ways of the violent*, scil. for the purpose of avoiding them. In a different sense, Prov. 2 : 20. Construed with עַל, Job 14 : 16. with אֶל, Ps. 59 : 10. Sometimes in a bad sense, *to lie in wait for*, Job 13 : 27. 33 : 11. Ps. 56 : 7.

4. *to observe, keep;* e. g. a covenant, Gen. 17 : 9, 10. the commands of God, 1 K. 11 : 10. the sabbath, Is. 56 : 2, 6. a promise, 1 K. 3 : 6. 8 : 24. Construed with לְ before an infin. *to take heed to* do any thing, Num. 23 : 12. 2 K. 10 : 31.

5. *to worship, reverence;* e. g. Ps. 31 : 7. Hos. 4 : 10. Comp. Virg. Georg. IV. 212, *observant regem non sic Ægyptus*, etc.

6. *to watch, besiege*, (a city.) 2 Sam. 11 : 16. Comp. נָצַר no. 4.

7. as in Niph. *to beware of*, construed with מִן. Josh. 6 : 18.

Niph. 1. *to be guarded, preserved.* Ps. 37:28.

2. reflex. *to take heed, to beware.* Most frequently in the imper. הִשָּׁמֶר לְךָ פֶּן *take heed lest,* Gen. 24:6. 31:24, 29. more rarely without לְךָ, 1 Sam. 19:2. comp. Is. 7:4. In other passages it is construed with מִן before a noun or an infin. and it then denotes (1.) *to be cautious* or *careful before* any one. Ex. 23:21. (2.) *to abstain, hold back from* any thing. Deut. 23:10. also with a simple infin. Ex. 19:12.—הִשָּׁמֵר בְּנַפְשׁוֹ *to take heed for one's life,* Jer. 17:21. also לְנַפְשׁוֹ Deut. 4:15. More rarely construed with בְּ of the thing *guarded against,* 2 Sam. 20:10.

Pi. i. q. Kal no. 5. Jon. 2:9.

Hithpa. 1. *to be observed,* pass. of Kal no. 4. Mic. 6:16.

2. *to take heed, beware,* construed with מִן. Ps. 18:24.

Deriv. out of course אַשְׁמֻרָה, אַשְׁמֹרֶת, מִשְׁמָרָה, מִשְׁמָר.

שֶׁמֶר m. verbal from שָׁמַר, dec. VI. h. found only in the plur. שְׁמָרִים.

1. *lees* or *dregs of wine,* so called from their *preserving* the strength and colour of the wine which was left to stand upon them. קָפָא עַל שְׁמָרָיו and שָׁקַט, Jer. 48:11. Zeph. 1:12. *to rest upon one's lees,* i. e. to continue quietly in one's former condition, a proverbial expression taken from wine.

2. *wine kept on the lees.* Is. 25:6 שְׁמָרִים מְזֻקָּקִים *wine on the lees well refined.*

שְׁמֻרָה f. verbal from שָׁמַר, dec. X. *an eyelid,* quasi *custodia oculi.* Ps. 77:5.

שָׁמְרָה f. verbal from שָׁמַר, *a watch.* Ps. 141:3.

שִׁמֻּרִים m. verbal from שָׁמַר, *the observance* (of a festival), *a festival.* Ex. 12:43. Comp. שְׁמֻר הַשָּׁנָה.

שֹׁמְרוֹן f. *Samaria,* a proper name; (1.) the metropolis of the kingdom of Israel and the royal residence, situated on a mountain of the same name. 1 K. 16:24. Am. 4:1. 6:1. In later times named by Herod Σεβάστη, (Josephi Antiq. Jud. xv. 7. § 7.) Now a small village called *Sebaste,* also *Shemrun, Shemrin.* (2.) name of a country.—עָרֵי שֹׁמְרוֹן *the cities of Samaria,* 2 K. 17:26. 23:19. הָרֵי שֹׁמְרוֹן *the mountains of Samaria,* Jer. 31:5. So the calf at Bethel is called, Hos. 8:5, 6, *the calf of Samaria. The cities of Samaria* are spoken of under Jeroboam by a prolepsis, 1 K. 13:32. The gentile noun is שֹׁמְרֹנִי 2 K. 17:29.

שָׁמְרַיִן Chald. Ezra. 4:10, 17. i. q. Heb. שֹׁמְרוֹן *Samaria,* as the name of a city.

שְׁמַשׁ Chald. Pa. שַׁמֵּשׁ *to serve, wait upon.* Dan. 7:10.

שֶׁמֶשׁ com. gen. (Ps. 104:19. Gen. 15:19.) with suff. שִׁמְשׁוֹ, prim. dec. VI. h.

1. *the sun.*—תַּחַת הַשָּׁמֶשׁ *under the sun,* i. e. on the earth, a frequent expression in Ecclesiastes, as chap. 1:3, 9, 14. 2:11.—לִפְנֵי שֶׁמֶשׁ *in the sun-shine.* Job 8:16. The *rising* of the sun is expressed by the verbs יָצָא, זָרַח, and its *setting* by בּוֹא. As an image of *light* and *prosperity,* Ps. 84:12.

2. Plur. שִׁמְשׁוֹת Is. 54:12. *battlements, pinnacles, turrets,* (on a wall.) Liter. *beams of the sun;* otherwise called by the Hebrews *horns,* (comp. קֶרֶן no. 4. and קָרַן,) hence *artificial horns, teeth.* Sept. ἐπάλξεις.

שִׁמְשׁוֹן *Samson,* the proper name of an Israelitish judge, the Hercules of the Hebrews. Judg. 13:24 ff. Sept. Σαμψών, which Josephus (Antiq. Jud. v. 10.) interprets ἰσχυρός; but his explanations have little philological weight, (see Gesenius' Gesch. der Hebr. Sprache, p. 81, 82.) and שִׁמְשׁוֹן is rather a dimin. from שֶׁמֶשׁ *the sun,* like שַׁהֲרֹן from שַׂהַר *the moon.*

שֵׁן com. gen. before Makkeph שֶׁן, with suff. שִׁנּוֹ, prim. dec. VIII. b.

1. *a tooth.* Ex. 21:24, 27.

2. particularly *an elephant's tooth, ivory.* 1 K. 10:18. Cant. 5:14. בָּתֵּי שֵׁן *ivory palaces,* i. e. palaces inlaid with

ivory, Am. 3 : 15. Ps. 45 : 9. Comp. קֵן no. 1.

3. *the tooth of a rock, a sharp cliff.* 1 Sam. 14 : 4. Job 39 : 28. Comp. Syr. ܫܢܢܐ *cliffs.*

4. proper name of a place, perhaps of a rock. 1 Sam. 7 : 12.

Dual שִׁנַּיִם *teeth,* (the dual number referring to the two rows.) Gen. 49 : 12. Am. 4 : 6. Used also for the plural, 1 Sam. 2 : 13, (the plural itself not occurring.)

שָׁנָא (after the Chaldaic form) i. q. שָׁנָה *to be changed.* Lam. 4 : 1.

Pu. *idem.* Ecc. 8 : 1. See שָׁנָה.

שְׁנָא, fut. יִשְׁנֵא, Chald.

1. *to be changed* or *altered.* Dan. 6 : 18. 3 : 27. Particularly *to be changed for the worse, in pejus mutari;* and spoken of the countenance, *to lose its brightness,* Dan. 5 : 6.

2. *to be different, diverse.* Dan. 7 : 3, 19, 23, 24.

Pa. 1. *to change, alter, transform.* Dan. 4 : 13 [4 : 16] *his heart they shall change,* i. e. it shall be changed.

2. *to violate, transgress,* (a royal command.) Dan. 3 : 28. (In Syr. more common.)

3. part. pass. *different, diverse.* Dan. 7 : 7.

Ithpa. *to change itself, to be altered.* Dan. 2 : 9. Spoken of the countenance, Dan. 3 : 19. 7 : 28.

Aph. 1. *to change, alter;* e. g. times and seasons, Dan. 2 : 21. a royal command, Dan. 6 : 9, 16.

2. *to transgress.* Ezra 6 : 11, 12.

שִׁנְאָן m. verbal from שָׁנָא, *a repetition.* Ps. 68 : 18 אַלְפֵי שִׁנְאָן *thousands of repetition,* i. e. repeated or many thousands.

שֵׁנָא f. i. q. שֵׁנָה *sleep.* Ps. 127 : 2. Root יָשֵׁן *to sleep.*

שְׁנָא f. Chald. *idem.* Dan. 6 : 19. Root. יְשֵׁן *to sleep.*

שָׁנָה, fut. יִשְׁנֶה, (comp. the Chald. שְׁנָא.)

1. *to alter, to change* or *be changed.* Mal. 3 : 6. Lam. 4 : 1, (where it is written with א.)

2. *to be different, diverse;* construed with מִן. Est. 1 : 7. 3 : 8.

3. *to be of a different opinion.* Part. plur. שׁוֹנִים *schismatics,* Prov. 24 : 21.

4. *to repeat, to do a second time,* (comp. שְׁנַיִם *two.*) Neh. 13 : 21 אִם תִּשְׁנוּ *if ye do* (so) *again.* 1 Sam. 26 : 8. 2 Sam. 20 : 10. Prov. 17 : 9 שֹׁנֶה בְדָבָר *he who repeateth a matter* (which has been forgotten,) i. e. he that stirs it up anew. 1 K. 18 : 34.

Niph. *to be repeated.* Gen. 41 : 32.

Pi. שִׁנָּה (once שִׁנֵּא 2 K. 25 : 29.)

1. *to change, alter;* e. g. one's promise, Ps. 89 : 35. one's way, Jer. 2 : 36. right, i. e. to pervert it, Prov. 31 : 5.

2. *to change* (garments). Jer. 52 : 33. 2 K. 25 : 29.

3. *to change* or *disfigure* (the countenance). Job 14 : 20.

4. *to remove, change the place of* a thing. Est. 2 : 9.

5. שִׁנָּה אֶת־טַעְמוֹ *to dissemble one's understanding,* i. e. to act like a madman. Ps. 34 : 1. 1 Sam. 21 : 14. (In Syr. ܫܢܐ without addition, *to be mad.*)

Pu. *to be changed, disfigured.* Ecc. 8 : 1, (where it is written with א.)

Hithpa. *to disguise one's self.* 1 K. 14 : 2.

Deriv. מִשְׁנֶה.

שָׁנָה f. plur. שָׁנִים, poetically שָׁנוֹת, dec. XI. a. *a year,* (perhaps liter. *a repetition* or *return* of the same seasons or natural appearances, see שָׁנָה no. 4. and comp. *annus,* i. q. annulus, *a ring, circle;* Greek ἐνιαυτὸς, ἔτος, λυκάβας.) שָׁנָה שָׁנָה Deut. 14 : 22. שָׁנָה בְשָׁנָה 15 : 20. מִדֵּי שָׁנָה בְּשָׁנָה 1 Sam. 7 : 16. *from year to year.*—שְׁנַת שְׁתַּיִם שָׁלוֹשׁ *the year two, three,* i. e. the second, third year; freq. Sometimes שָׁנָה is repeated; e. g. בִּשְׁנַת שֵׁשׁ מֵאוֹת שָׁנָה *in the six hundredth year,* Gen. 7 : 11. Plur. שָׁנִים *some years,* 2 Chr. 18 : 2.

Dual שְׁנָתַיִם *two years;* often joined with יָמִים, *two years long,* (see יָמִים no. 2.) Gen. 41 : 1. Jer. 28 : 3, 11. 2 Sam. 13 : 23.

שְׁנָה f. Chald. *a year*. Plur. שְׁנִין Dan. 6:1.

שֵׁנָה f. (for יְשֵׁנָה) *sleep, a dream*. Ps. 90:5. Root יָשֵׁן *to sleep*.

שֶׁנְהַבִּים masc. plur. 1 K. 10:22. 2 Chr. 9:21. *elephant's teeth, ivory*. The plural number refers to the multitude of separate teeth, comp. שִׁנַּיִם,הָבְנִים. Sept. ὀδόντες ἐλεφάντινοι. Chald. שֵׁן דְּפִיל *dens elephanti*. שֵׁן evidently denotes *a tooth*, (see above no. 2.) but the signification of the latter part הַבִּים is unknown; and the form of the word may be so corrupted as to disguise its original meaning entirely.

שָׁנִי m. *the crimson dye*, also *cloth* or *thread coloured therewith, the coccus* of the ancients. It stands sometimes alone, as Gen. 38:28, 30. Jer. 4:30. sometimes in the phrase תּוֹלַעַת שָׁנִי Ex. 25:4. or שְׁנִי תוֹלַעַת Lev. 14:4. Plur. שָׁנִים Is. 1:18. Prov. 31:21. This colour is derived from the turtle insect, (in Arab. قرمز *kermez*, in Heb. תּוֹלַעַת, *coccus ilicis*, Linn.) which is found on the leaves of the holly. The eggs of this insect yield the dye. The root is שָׁנָה in Arab. سني *splenduit*, since scarlet garments were admired for their brightness; hence in Aram. זְהוֹרִי,זְהוֹר, ܙܘܗܪܐ *coccus*, from זהר *to shine*. Others explain it *double-dyed*, (from שָׁנָה no. 4. *to repeat*,) δίβαφον, which, however, is applicable to the Tyrian purple only, and not to the crimson dye. See Braun de Vestitu Sacerdotum, p. 237 ff. Bocharti Hieroz. T. III. p. 527 ff. ed. Rosenmüller.

שֵׁנִי, fem. שֵׁנִית, *second*. The fem. is also used adverbially, *a second time*, Gen. 22:15. 41:5. Plur. שֵׁנִים *second*, Gen. 6:16. Num. 2:16.

שְׁנַיִם masc. dual, *two*. (Etymologically connected with שָׁנָה *to repeat*.) שְׁנַיִם שְׁנַיִם *two and two*, Gen. 7:9, 15. The const. state שְׁנֵי is used before the subst. With suff. שְׁנֵיהֶם *duo illi*, Gen. 2:25.

Fem. שְׁתַּיִם for שְׁנְתַּיִם, as it would be written, if regularly formed, (comp. the Arab. اثنتان.) The syllable נְ is thrown out by a syncope, and the Dagesh in ת appears to be a Dagesh lene. Const. שְׁתֵּי.—שְׁתַּיִם also signifies *a second time*, e.g. פַּעַם וּשְׁתַּיִם *semel et iterum*, Neh. 13:20. בִּשְׁתַּיִם *idem*, Job 33:14.

The contracted forms שְׁנֵים and שְׁתֵּים are used only in connection with *ten*, to express the number *twelve*; as שְׁנֵים עָשָׂר *twelve*, m. שְׁתֵּים עֶשְׂרֵה *twelve*, f. This punctuation is the usual one in Syriac for the dual.

שְׁנִינָה *mockery, scorn, derision*, liter. *a sharp pungent speech*. הָיָה לִשְׁנִינָה *to be a derision*, Deut. 28:37. 1 K. 9:7. Root שָׁנַן, comp. particularly Ps. 64:4. 140:4.

שָׁנַן *to sharpen*; e.g. the sword, Deut. 32:41. the tongue, Ps. 64:4. 140:4. i.e. to speak in a sharp insulting manner. Part. pass. שָׁנוּן *sharp*, Ps. 45:5. Is. 5:28.

Pi. *to inculcate*. Deut. 6:7.

Hithpo. *to be penetrated* or *pierced* (with pain). Ps. 73:21.

Deriv. שְׁנִינָה.

שָׁנַס found only in Pi. שִׁנֵּס *to gird up*. Once 1 K. 18:46. So all the ancient versions and the context requires it.

שִׁנְעָר a proper name, *Shinar*, the territory of Babylon. Gen. 10:10. 11:2. 14:1. Jer. 11:11. Dan. 1:2. Zech. 5:11. The boundaries of this country are defined in Gen. 10:10. and depend on the interpretation given to the names of cities mentioned in that verse. If אֶרֶךְ signifies *Edessa*, then Shinar must have extended so far as to embrace Mesopotamia; but this is doubtful, and the occurrence of *Singara* as the name of a river, a chain of mountains, and a city, in the north of Mesopotamia, is not a sufficient confirmation. See Bocharti Phaleg. I. 5. Vater's Anm. zu Gen. 10:10. J.D. Michaëlis Spicileg. T.I. p. 231.

שְׁנַת f. i. q. שֵׁנָה *sleep*. Ps. 132:4. Root יָשֵׁן *to sleep*.

שָׁסָה *to spoil, to plunder*, construed with an accus. of the thing. Hos. 13:15. Used absolutely, Ps. 44:11. Part. שֹׁסִים *spoilers*, Judg. 2:14. 1 Sam. 23:1. Synon. שָׁסַס.

Po. שׁוֹשֵׂה for שׁוֹסֵה (as it stands in several MSS.) *idem*. Is. 10:13.

שָׁסַס, fut. יָשֹׁס, *idem*, construed with an accus. 1 Sam. 17:53. Judg. 2:14. Part. שֹׁאסַי, by a Syriasm for שֹׁסַיִךְ, Jer. 30:16 Kethib, after the form رَأْسٌ, from رَسٌّ.

Niph. pass. *to be plundered* or *spoiled*. Is. 13:16. Zech. 14:2.

Deriv. מְשִׁסָּה.

שָׁסַע *to make an incision, to cleave, split;* hence שֹׁסַע שֶׁסַע פַּרְסָה *to divide the hoof, to have a cloven foot*, Lev. 11:3, 7, 26. Comp. הִפְרִיס.

Pi. 1. *to break, rend*. Lev. 1:17.

2. *to tear in pieces*, e. g. a lion. Judg. 14:6.

3. metaphorically *to chide, rebuke, verbis dilacerare*, i. q. גָּעַר. 1 Sam. 24:8. Sept. ἔπεισε. Chald. *quietos reddidit*.

שֶׁסַע m. *a cleft*, see שָׁסַע in Kal.

שִׁסֵּף found only in Pi. *to hew in pieces*. 1 Sam. 15:33. Sept. ἔσφαξε. Vulg. *in frusta concidit*. Only in Hebrew.

I. **שָׁעָה** *to look, see*. It is construed (1.) with אֶל, *to regard graciously*. Gen. 4:4, 5. (2.) *to look with confidence to* any thing; construed with בְּ, Ex. 5:9. with עַל, Is. 17:7. 31:1. with אֶל, 17:8. (3.) *to look away from* any thing, construed with מִן and מֵעַל. Job 14:6 שְׁעֵה מֵעָלָיו וְיֶחְדָּל *look away from him that he may rest*. 7:19. Is. 22:4. (4.) *to look about* (for help). 2 Sam. 22:42.

Hiph. imper. הָשַׁע (as if from שָׁעַע) *look away*. Ps. 39:14. Or we may read הָשַׁע, by apocope for הַשְׁעֵה.

Hithpa. fut. apoc. יִשְׁתָּע, *to look around* (for help), *to be dismayed*, i. q. Kal no. (4.) Is. 41:10, 23.

II. **שָׁעָה** *to spread over, to close*, i. q. שָׁעַע. Is. 32:3 *the eyes of the seeing shall not be closed*.

שָׁעָה f. Chald. Dan. 4:16. emph. שַׁעְתָּא, שָׁעֲתָה, *a short time, a moment*, elsewhere also *an hour*. Hence בַּהּ שַׁעֲתָא *in the same moment*, i. e. immediately, Dan. 3:6, 15. 4:30. [4:33.] 5:5. Dan. 4:16 [4:19] כְּשָׁעָה חֲדָא *for a short time*. (In Arab. سَاعَةٌ *idem*. In Dutch the word *Stondt* has both significations.)

שַׁעֲטָה f. dec. X. *a stamping* (of horses' hoofs). Jer. 47:3. (Arab. with شَطّ *idem*.

שַׁעַטְנֵז Lev. 19:19. Deut. 22:11. *cloth made of different threads*. Sept. κίβδηλον, *adulterated*. The etymology is obscure. Some have supposed it to be derived from the Coptic; perhaps *shontnes*, i. e. *byssus complicatus seu fimbriatus* (comp. שֵׁשׁ, in Egypt. *shont*.) For derivations out of the Shemitish dialects, see Bocharti Hieroz. T. I. p. 486, 487.

שֹׁעַל m. with suff. שָׁעֳלוֹ, plur. שְׁעָלִים, const. שַׁעֲלֵי, *the hollow hand*, Is. 40:12. *a handful*, 1 K. 20:10. Ezek. 13:19. (Syr. ܫܘܥܠܐ *idem*. In Hebrew, comp. מִשְׁעוֹל *a hollow way*.)

שַׁעֲלִים m. name of a country. 1 Sam. 9:4. According to most interpreters, i. q. the following article.

שַׁעַלְבִים Judg. 1:35. 1 K. 4:9. and **שַׁעַלַבִּין** Josh. 19:42. proper name of a city in the tribe of Dan. See Relandi Palæstina, p. 988. (As an appellative *foxes*, comp. the Arab. ثَعْلَبٌ *a fox*, i. q. שׁוּעָל.) The gentile noun is שַׁעַלְבֹנִי 2 Sam. 23:32. 1 Chr. 11:33.

שָׁעַן found only in Niph.

1. *to lean, rest;* construed with עַל *upon* a thing. 2 Sam. 1:6.—נִשְׁעַן עַל יַד פ׳ *to lean on the hand of any one*, as oriental monarchs on the hand of their

officers, 2 K. 5:18. 7:2, 17. Construed with עַל, also *to lean against* a thing, Judg. 16:26.

2. metaphorically *to rely upon, to trust in;* construed with עַל, Is. 10:20. 31:1. with אֶל, Prov. 3:5. with בְּ, Is. 50:10. without cases, Job 24:23.

3. *to lie down, to rest.* Gen. 18:4.

4. in a geographical sense, *to border* or *bound* on a country. Num. 21:15.

Deriv. מַשְׁעֵן, מַשְׁעֵנָה, מִשְׁעָן.

שָׁעַע in Aram. *to make smooth, rub, spread over;* also *to caress, flatter.* (Comp. חָלָק, חִלָּה פָנִים.) In Heb. in Kal, *to be overspread, to be closed,* Is. 29:9. see below Hithpalp. no. 2.

Hiph. imper. הָשַׁע, *to overspread, close* (the eyes). Is. 6:10. (In Aram. שַׁע *idem.*)

Pilp. שִׁעֲשַׁע 1. *to rejoice, delight.* Ps. 94:19.

2. *to delight one's self, to play.* Is. 11:8. Construed with an accus. of the thing, Ps. 119:70. These significations are derived from the Aramean signification of Kal.

Palp. שֳׁעֲשַׁע *to be flattered, caressed.* Is. 66:12.

Hithpalp. הִשְׁתַּעֲשַׁע

1. *to delight in* and thing, construed with בְּ. Ps. 119:16, 47.

2. pass. of Hiph. *to be dazzled* or *blinded.* Is. 29:9 הִשְׁתַּעַשְׁעוּ וָשֹׁעוּ *be ye dazzled and blinded,* i. e. be ye astonished, as in the first clause of the verse.

Deriv. שַׁעֲשֻׁעִים.

שָׁעַר *to think, estimate.* Once Prov. 23:7. (Chald. שְׁעַר *to measure.* Arab. سعر *to fix a price.*) Hence

I. **שַׁעַר** m. verbal from שָׁעַר, dec. VI. c. *a measure.* Once Gen. 26:12 מֵאָה שְׁעָרִים *an hundred measures,* i. e. an hundred fold.

II. **שַׁעַר** com. gen. prim. dec. VI. c.

1. *a gate, porta.* (Arab. ثغر *idem.* Syr. and Chald. by transposition תְּרַע.) In the gate the orientals have their market, (see רְחוֹב,) and their courts of judgment, (Prov. 22:22. Amos 5:10, 12, 15.) Thither the people assemble to pass away time, Gen. 19:1. hence Ps. 69:13 *they that sit in the gate,* i. e. the idle. Ruth 3:11 כָּל־שַׁעַר עַמִּי *the whole assembly of my people.* שַׁעֲרֵי אֶרֶץ *the gates* or *entrances of the land,* Jer. 15:7. Nah. 3:13 בִּשְׁעָרֶיךָ *within thy gates,* i. e. in thy cities, Deut. 12:12. 14:27. hence Deut. 16:5 בְּאַחַד שְׁעָרֶיךָ *in one of thy cities.* 17:2. Comp. further 1 K. 8:37. 2 Chr. 6:28. The gates of Jerusalem, which are all to be sought for in the ancient or original wall, are as follows, passing from the west to the south and east; (1.) שַׁעַר הָעַיִן *the fountain-gate,* Neh. 2:14. 3:15. 12:37. prob. so called from the fountain of Siloah. (2.) שַׁעַר הָאַשְׁפֹּת Neh. 2:13. 3:14. 12:31. and by contraction שׁ׳ הַשֹּׁפֹת 3:13. *the dung-gate.* (3.) שַׁעַר הַגַּיְא *the valley-gate.* Neh. 2:13, 15. 3:13. (4.) שַׁעַר הַפִּנָּה Is. 31:38. and שַׁעַר הַפֹּנִים Zech. 14:10. *the corner-gate.* (5.) שׁ׳ אֶפְרַיִם *the gate of Ephraim,* Neh. 8:16. supposed to be the same with *the gate of Benjamin,* Jer. 37:13. 38:7. Zech. 14:10. (6.) שַׁעַר הַיְשָׁנָה *the old gate,* Neh. 3:6. 12:39. prob. the same with שַׁעַר הָרִאשׁוֹן *the first gate,* Zech. 14:10. (7.) *the fish-gate.* Neh. 3:3. 12:39. (8.) *the sheep-gate.* Neh. 3:1. 12:39. (9.) שׁ׳ הַמִּפְקָד *the review-gate.* Neh. 3:31. Vulg. *porta judicialis.* (10.) *the horse-gate.* Neh. 3:28. Jer. 31:40. (11.) *the water-gate.* Neh. 3:26. 12:37. (12.) שׁ׳ הַחַרְסִית, see that article. (13.) שׁ׳ הַמַּטָּרָה *the prison-gate,* Neh. 12:39. according to some the same with no. (9.) —Comp. Bachiene Beschreibung von Palästina, Th. II. § 94—107. Faber's Archäologie der Hebräer, Th. I. p. 336. Other gates were not gates of the city, but of the temple; comp. the articles סוּר, שַׁלֶּכֶת, יְסוֹד.

2. particularly *the great gate* of a royal citadel or palace, (Est. 2:19, 21.) hence *a royal citadel* or *palace, a seraglio, the porte.* Est. 4:2, 6.

Deriv. שׁוֹעֵר *a porter, watchman at a gate.*

שֹׁעָר or **שׁוֹעָר**, plur. שֹׁעָרִים, dec. II. b. *vile, mean, detestable,* spoken of figs. Jer. 29:17. See the following articles.

שַׁעֲרוּרָה *something terrible, horrible.* Jer. 5:30. 23:14.

שַׁעֲרוּרִי adj. *terrible, horrible.* Jer. 18:13.

Note. The three preceding articles are connected with שָׂעַר *to shudder,* written with Sin.

שַׁעֲרַיִם *(two gates)* name of a city in the tribe of Judah. Josh. 15:36. 1 Sam. 17:52. 1 Chr. 4:31.

שַׁעֲשֻׁעִים masc. plur. dec. I. *pleasure, delight,* also *an object of pleasure* or *delight, deliciæ.* Prov. 8:30. Ps. 119:24. Jer. 31:20 יֶלֶד שַׁעֲשֻׁעִים *a child in whom one delights.* Root שָׁעַע, Pilp. שִׁעֲשַׁע.

שָׁפָה in Kal not used. Prob. as in Aramean, *to rub off* or *in pieces;* Pa. *to make smooth* or *bald.*

Niph. pass. Is. 13:2 הַר נִשְׁפֶּה *a naked* or *bald mountain.* Sept. ὄρος πεδινόν.

Pu. Job 33:21 שֻׁפּוּ עַצְמוֹתָיו *his bones are naked* or *stripped of flesh;* or perhaps *atteruntur.*

Deriv. שְׁפִי.

שָׁפָה or **שְׁפָה** found only in the plur. 2 Sam. 17:29 שְׁפוֹת בָּקָר according to the Targum, Syr. and the Jewish interpreters, *cheese of kine;* (comp. the Talmud. שׁפה *to filter.*) According to the Arabic version, *cow-milk,* (comp. شفي the name for *sweet milk* among the Brebers.)

שְׁפוֹט m. verbal from שָׁפַט, dec. I. c. *punishment.* 2 Chr. 20:9. Comp. the root no. 3. Plur. שְׁפוּטִים *punishments,* i. q. שְׁפָטִים, Ezek. 23:10.

שִׁפְחָה f. plur. שְׁפָחוֹת, dec. XII. b. *a maid-servant, a hand-maid.* Gen. 16:1. 29:24. Comp. 1 Sam. 25:41 הִנֵּה אֲמָתְךָ לְשִׁפְחָה *behold, thy hand-maid is your servant.*

שָׁפַט fut. יִשְׁפֹּט 1. *to judge,* construed with an accus. Ex. 18:22, 26. Deut. 16:18. Ezek. 16:38 וּשְׁפַטְתִּיךְ מִשְׁפְּטֵי נֹאֲפוֹת *I will judge thee as adulteresses are judged.* When joined with בֵּין .... וּבֵין, or בֵּין .... לְ, *to judge* or *decide between, to act as umpire,* Gen. 16:5. 31:53. Is. 2:4. Part. שֹׁפֵט *a judge.* Deut. 16:18.

2. *to do justice to* any one, spoken of a judge; or *to plead for* any one, spoken of an advocate. Comp. דִּין no. 2. and רִיב no. 2. Ps. 10:18. 26:1. Is. 1:17 שִׁפְטוּ יָתוֹם *do justice to the fatherless.* 11:4. More in full שָׁפַט מִשְׁפַּט פ׳ Jer. 5:28. Lam. 3:59.—Construed with מִן, *do justice to* a person (and deliver him) *from* any one, 1 Sam. 24:16. Comp. 2 Sam. 18:19, 31. Ps. 43:1.

3. *to condemn, punish,* κατακρίνω. 1 Sam. 3:13. Obad. 21. Ps. 109:31. Comp. שְׁפוֹט.

4. *to command, rule;* since *judging* and *ruling* are connected in the east, and sitting in judgment is one of the principal employments of an oriental monarch, (1 Sam. 8:20. 2 Chr. 1:10.) Part. שֹׁפֵט *a ruler,* Am. 2:3. Ps. 2:10. and so, whenever it is used of the Judges, who between the days of Joshua and David rose up as saviours of their country, to deliver them from foreign bondage, Judg. 2:16, 18. Ruth 1:1. 2 K. 23:22. Yet it appears concerning some of them that they acted in fact as judges, (Judg. 4:5.) Comp. קָצִין. The name *suffetes* among the Carthaginians is of the same origin.

Niph. 1. *to be judged.* Ps. 37:33.

2. *to contend with* a person. Prov. 29:9. Is. 43:26. Construed usually with אֵת (אֶת and אֵת *with,*) Ezek. 17:20. 20:35, 36. also with עִם, Joel 4:2. [3:2.] with לְ, Jer. 25:31, (more in the sense of no. 3.) The thing contended *about* is preceded by עַל, Jer. 2:35. or put in the accus. 1 Sam. 12:7. Ezek. 17:20.

3. *to execute punishment, to punish,* particularly when spoken of Jehovah. So in several of the passages referred

to above; also Ezek. 38:22 *I will punish him with pestilence and with blood.* Is. 66:16. comp. 2 Chr. 22:8.

Po. only in the part. מְשֹׁפְטִי *my judge*, Job 9:15.

Deriv. out of course שְׁפוֹט, מִשְׁפָּט.

שְׁפַט Chald. part. שָׁפֵט *a judge*. Ezra 7:25.

שֶׁפֶט found only in the plur. שְׁפָטִים m. verbal from שָׁפַט, dec. VI. *judgments, punishments.* עָשָׂה שְׁפָטִים בְּ *to execute judgments on* any one, Ex. 12:12. Num. 33:4. See מִשְׁפָּט no. 2.

שְׁפִי m. plur. שְׁפָיִים, dec. VI. 1. *a hill*, particularly *one that is open* or *not covered with wood.* Jer. 4:11. 12:12 שְׁפָיִים בַּמִּדְבָּר *hills in the desert.* Is. 41:18, (parall. בְּקָעוֹת.) 49:9. Jer. 3:2, 21. 7:29. 14:6. Num. 23:3 וַיֵּלֶךְ שֶׁפִי *and he went up a hill.* (In Syr. ܫܦܝܐ *planities.*)

שְׁפִיפֹן m. Gen. 49:17. a species of serpent; according to Jerome, *the horned serpent* or *cerastes*, so called from its two antennæ, which it sticks in the sand, and stretches out after its prey. (Arab. سُفّ a spotted serpent like the cerastes, *hæmorrhous.*) See Bocharti Hieroz. II. p. 416 ff.

שַׁפִּיר Chald. adj. *pleasant, fair.* Dan. 4:9, 18. [4:12, 21.]

שָׁפִיר m. name of an unknown place, Mic. 1:11.

שָׁפַךְ, fut. יִשְׁפֹּךְ.

1. *to pour, to pour out.* Is. 57:6.— שָׁפַךְ דָּם *to shed blood*, Gen. 9:6. 37:22. Trop. שָׁפַךְ נַפְשׁוֹ *to pour out one's soul*, scil. in tears and lamentations, Ps. 42:5. with לִפְנֵי יְהוָֹה subjoined, *to lament before Jehovah*, 1 Sam. 1:15. Ps. 62:9. —ש׳ חֲמָתוֹ עַל *to pour out one's anger on* a person, Ezek. 22:22. 14:19.

2. *to throw up*, e.g. a wall. 2 K. 19:32. See סֹלְלָה.

Niph. *to be poured out.* 1 K. 13:5. Ps. 22:15 *I am poured out like water.*

Pu. *idem.* Ps. 73:2 שֻׁפְּכוּ אֲשֻׁרָי *my steps are poured out*, i.e. they slip.

Hithpa. *to be poured out.* Lam. 4:1. Spoken of the soul, (1.) *to pour itself out* (in lamentations). Job 30:16. (2.) *to be breathed out, to expire.* Lam. 2:12.

שֶׁפֶךְ m. verbal from שָׁפַךְ, dec. VI. *a place of pouring out.* Lev. 4:12.

שָׁפְכָה f. verbal from שָׁפַךְ, *the privy member, the penis.* Deut. 23:2.

שָׁפֵל, fut. יִשְׁפַּל, infin. שְׁפַל, (like שָׁכֵב.)

1. *to be made low, to sink*, e.g. spoken of a mountain, Is. 40:4. *to be overthrown*, spoken of a city, Is. 32:19.

2. *to be suppressed, depressed*, spoken of a voice or sound. Ecc. 12:4.

3. metaphorically *to be humbled.* Is. 2:9, 11, 12, 17. 5:15. 10:33. Infin. שְׁפַל רוּחַ *to be of a humble spirit*, Prov. 16:19. Comp. שָׁפָל.

Hiph. 1. *to make low, to bring down.* (Antith. הֵרִים.) Ps. 18:28. 75:8.

2. *to bring to the ground, to throw down.* Is. 25:12.

3. In connection with other verbs, it may be rendered adverbially; e.g. Jer. 13:18 הַשְׁפִּילוּ שֵׁבוּ *sit down low.* Ps. 113:6.

4. intrans. *to be brought low, to be cast down.* Job 22:29.

שְׁפַל Chald. found only in Aph.

1. *to bring down.* Dan. 5:19.

2. *to oppress, subdue, deprimere.* Dan. 7:24.

3. joined with לְבַב, *to humble one's heart.* Dan. 5:22.

שָׁפָל verbal adj. from שָׁפֵל, dec. IV. a.

1. *low, deep, sunk down;* spoken of a tree, Ezek. 17:24. of the leprosy, Lev. 13:20, 21.

2. *low, mean, contemptible.* Job 5:11. 2 Sam. 6:22.

3. שְׁפַל רוּחַ *humble, lowly in spirit.* Prov. 29:23. Is. 57:15. Also without רוּחַ in the same sense, ibid.

שְׁפַל Chald. *low.* Dan. 4:14. [4:17.]

שֵׁפֶל m. verbal from שָׁפֵל, dec. VI. g. *lowness, a low place* or *condition.* Ecc. 10:6. Ps. 136:23.

שִׁפְלָה f. verbal from שָׁפֵל, *lowness, a low place.* Is. 32:19.

שְׁפֵלָה f. verbal from שָׁפֵל, dec. X. *a low country,* with the article הַשְּׁפֵלָה *the low country* or *the plain,* i. e. the south-western portion of Palestine, between the mountains and the Mediterranean Sea. Josh. 11:16. Jer. 32:44. 33:13.

שִׁפְלוּת f. verbal from שָׁפֵל, joined with יָדַיִם, *a slacking* or *letting down of the hands, idleness, remissness.* Ecc. 10:18. Comp. רָפָה nos. 1. 2.

שְׁפָם proper name of a place in the eastern part of the tribe of Judah. Num. 34:10, 11. Prob. i. q. שִׁפְמוֹת 1 Sam. 30:28. The gentile noun is שִׁפְמִי 1 Chr. 27:27.

שָׁפָן m. a quadruped, which is joined with the hare and chews the cud, Lev. 11:5. Deut. 14:7. inhabits the mountains and rocks, Ps. 104:18. and is a gregarious and cunning animal, Prov. 30:26. These notices agree best with the different species of *the jerboa,* (Arab. يربوع, Greek χοιρογρύλλιος, *mus jaculus,* Linn.) which has two long hind feet, and springs with the agility of the locust. It lives in the sand and shews great skill in constructing its habitation. Root perhaps شفن *ingenio pollens, astutus.* The Rabbins render it, *the rabbit.* See Bocharti Hieroz. T. I. p. 1001 ff. Oedmann's verm. Sammlungen, H. 4. p. 48.

שֶׁפַע m. Deut. 33:19. and **שִׁפְעָה** f. dec. X.

1. *a multitude;* e. g. of horses or camels, Is. 60:6. Ezek. 26:10. of waters, Job 22:11. 38:34. Particularly *a multitude of people,* 2 K. 9:17.

2. *abundance, superfluity,* spoken e. g. of the rich gifts of the sea. Deut. 33:19. (Syr. ܣܦܥ *to overflow.*)

שָׁפַר *to be fair, shining,* (comp. שְׁפַרְפַּר,) *pleasant, acceptable;* construed with עַל. Ps. 16:6. comp. Dan. 4:24. [4:27.]

Pi. *to adorn, garnish.* Job 26:13 בְּרוּחוֹ שָׁמַיִם שִׁפְרָה *by his* (creating) *spirit he adorns the heavens* (with stars, etc.). The gender of שִׁפְרָה agrees with רוּחַ, instead of אֱלֹהִים.

שְׁפַר, fut. יִשְׁפַּר, Chald. *to be fair, pleasant, acceptable;* construed with עַל, Dan. 4:24. [4:27.] with קֳדָם, Dan. 3:32. [4:2.] 6:2. (In Syr. *idem.*)

שֶׁפֶר m. verbal from שָׁפַר.

1. *fairness, pleasantness.* Gen. 49:21.

2. name of a mountain in Arabia Deserta. Num. 33:23, 24.

שַׁפְרִיר m. Jer. 43:10 Keri (in the Keth. שַׁפְרוּר,) *a covering, stratum,* here *a covering of the throne.* Arab سفرة *a covering for the floor of a tent.* Others, from שָׁפַר, *an elegant covering.*

שְׁפַרְפָּרָא m. Chald. *the dawn of the morning.* Dan. 6:20. (Arab. سفر *eluxit, emicuit* aurora.)

שָׁפַת fut. יִשְׁפֹּת, i. q. שׂוּם.

1. *to set, put, place.* 2 K. 4:38. Ezek. 24:3. Ps. 22:16 לַעֲפַר מָוֶת תִּשְׁפְּתֵנִי *in the dust of death shalt thou put me.*

2. *to give.* Is. 26:12.

שְׁפַתַּיִם masc. dual.

1. Ps. 68:14. *folds for cattle,* i. q. מִשְׁפְּתַיִם q. v.

2. Ezek. 40:43. prob. *stalls,* in the courts of the temple, where the sacrificial victims were fastened.

שֶׁצֶף m. found only Is. 54:8 בְּשֶׁצֶף קֶצֶף perhaps *an effusion of anger,* i. q. שֶׁטֶף, which occurs Prov. 27:4, in the same connection. Or, *violence of anger,* comp. Arab. شظف *to be hard, violent.*

שָׁקַד fut. יִשְׁקֹד 1. *to be sleepless.* Ps. 102:8. Hence *to watch, to be wakeful,* Ezra 8:29. Ps. 127:1.

2. *to watch over* a thing, *invigilare alicui rei.* Jer. 1:12. Is. 29:20 שֹׁקְדֵי אָוֶן *invigilantes iniquitati.* Jer. 44:27. Comp. 31:28.

3. *to lie in wait,* spoken of the leopard. Jer. 5:6.

Pu. part. (denom. from שָׁקֵד,) *having the form of almond flowers.* Ex. 25: 33, 34.

שָׁקֵד m. verbal from שָׁקַד dec. V. a.

1. *an almond-tree.* Ecc. 12:5.

2. *an almond.* Gen. 43:11. Num. 17:23. [17:8.]

Note. This tree is probably so called from the earliness of its flowers and fruit; (comp. שָׁקַד *to watch,* hence *to hasten;*) to which etymology there is an allusion Jer. 1:11. See Celsii Hierobot. T. I. p. 297.

שָׁקָה *to drink.* In Kal not used.

Hiph. *to make to drink, to water;* e. g. cattle, Gen. 24:46. a country, Gen. 2:6. Part. מַשְׁקֶה *a cup-bearer,* Gen. 40:1. הַמַּשְׁקִים אֶת־פַּרְעֹה *the cup-bearers of Pharaoh,* Gen. 41:9. Construed with two accus. of the person and thing, Gen. 19:32. Judg. 4:19. Job 22:7.

Niph. Amos 8:8 Keth. See שָׁקַע.

Pu. *to be watered, moistened.* Job 21:24 *the marrow of his bones is moistened.* i. e. is fresh. Comp. Prov. 3:8. 15:30. 17:22.

Deriv. מַשְׁקֶה, שֹׁקֶת, שִׁקּוּי, שִׁקּוּי.

שִׁקֻּי m. verbal from שָׁקָה, dec. I. *drink.* Ps. 102:10.

שִׁקּוּי, plur. שִׁקּוּיִים, verbal from שָׁקָה, dec. I. *idem.* Hos. 2:7. [2:5.] Trop. Prov. 3:8 *moisture to thy bones.* Comp. the verb in Pual.

שִׁקּוּץ m. verbal from שָׁקַץ, dec. I. *an abomination,* particularly in a religious sense; spoken of unclean things, (perhaps garments,) Nah. 3:6. unclean food, Zech. 9:7. and most frequently of idols, 1 K. 11:5. 2 K. 23: 13. Dan. 9:27 שִׁקּוּץ מְשֹׁמֵם *the abomination,* i. e. the idol, *of the desolater.* 11:31. 12:11. 2 K. 23:24.

שָׁקַט, fut. יִשְׁקֹט, *to rest, to have repose.* Is. 62:1. Jer. 47:6, 7. Spoken particularly of a country or city, *to have rest* or *peace, to be free from war,* Judg. 3:11. 5:31. 8:28. Jer. 30:10. 46:27. hence with the addition מִמִּלְחָמָה Josh. 11:23. 14:15. Also *to keep quiet,* Judg. 18:7, 27. Is. 18:4. *to be still* (from fear), Ps. 76:9. Spoken of God, *to be inactive,* so as not to grant assistance, i. q. חָרַשׁ, Ps. 83:2.

Hiph. 1. *to give rest.* Job 34:29. Construed with לְ, Ps. 94:13.

2. *to still, appease,* e. g. strife. Prov. 15:18.

3. intrans. *to keep still, to be quiet.* Is. 7:4. 57:20. Hence infin. הַשְׁקֵט as a subst. *rest,* Is. 30:15. 32:17.

4. *to make still and sultry.* Job 37:17.

שֶׁקֶט m. verbal from שָׁקַט, *rest, peace.* 1 Chr. 22:9.

שָׁקַל, fut. יִשְׁקֹל, *to weigh.* 2 Sam. 14:26. 2 Sam. 18:12 *although I should weigh in my hand,* i. e. have weighed or paid to me. Trop. Job 6:2. 31:6. Particularly *to weigh out, to pay,* construed with לְ, Gen, 23:16. with עַל יְדֵי, Est. 3:9. with עַל, 4:7.

Niph. *to be weighed* or *paid out.* Ezra 8:33. Job 6:2.

שֶׁקֶל m. verbal from שָׁקַל, dec. VI. h.

1. a weight of the Hebrews, supposed equal to 240 grains of Troy weight. 1 Sam. 17:5. 2 Sam. 14:26. Particularly for weighing uncoined gold or silver, Gen. 23:15, 16. In this sense, the word שֶׁקֶל is frequently omitted; see כֶּסֶף, זָהָב. *The shekel of the sanctuary* (Ex. 30:15.) appears to have been different from *the king's shekel,* (2 Sam. 14:26.) but the difference between the two is not known.

2. *price,* i. q. כֶּסֶף. Amos 8:5.

שִׁקְמִים m. 1 K. 10:27. Is. 9:9. Amos 7:14. and שִׁקְמוֹת f. found only in the plur. (the sing. שקמה occurs in the Mishnah.) Ps. 78.47. *a sycamore-tree,* in Greek *συκόμορος, συκάμινος, ficus sycomorus vera,* Forsk. the leaves of which resemble mulberry-leaves, and the fruit figs. The fruit grows out of the trunk and larger branches. To ripen the fruit it is necessary, when the season approaches, to ascend the tree, and scrape or rub each berry about the middle. (Comp. בּוֹלֵס.) It furnishes after all only a poor nourishment, see Am. 7:14. Comp. Warnekros Hist. Natur. Sycomori, in the Repertor. für morgenländ. Literatur, Th. XI. no. 7. Th. XII. no. 3. Celsii Hierob. T. I. p. 310.

שָׁקַע 1. *to sink, to sink down*, spoken of a country, Jer. 51:64. *to be overflown*, Amos 9:5 שָׁקְעָה כִּיאֹר מִצְרָיִם *as by the stream of Egypt it is overflown.*

2. *to burn down*, spoken of a fire. Num. 11:2.

Niph. Amos 8:8 Keri, as in Kal Am. 9:5. In the Kethib נִשְׁקָה, the ע is omitted by a syncope, as in בַּל for בַּעַל.

Hiph. 1. *to let sink*, e. g. waters. Ezek. 32:14.

2. *to let down, to sink, demergere.* Job 40:25. [41:1.] בְּחֶבֶל תַּשְׁקִיעַ לְשֹׁנוֹ *canst thou let down a cord and draw up his tongue therewith?*

שְׁקַעֲרוּרֹת plur. fem. found only Lev. 14:37. *cavities, hollow places.* Sept. κοιλάδας. Vulg. *valliculæ.* This quadriliteral is either compounded of שָׁקַע *to sink* and قعر *to be deep*, (whence קְעָרָה *a dish,*) or is formed from the latter root by prefixing Shin, like שַׁלְהֶבֶת, לָהַב.

שָׁקַף in Kal not used; prob. *to overlay*, particularly timber; hence *to roof* or *cover* a house. (Arab. سقف *contignare.*) Deriv. שֶׁקֶף, שְׁקֻפִים, מַשְׁקוֹף.

Niph. and Hiph. *to bend forward*, in order to see; hence *to look for* a thing, and spoken of things, *to project, stick out, imminere;* e. g. הִשְׁקִיף מִשָּׁמַיִם *to look down from heaven*, Ps. 14:2. 53:3. 85:12. בְּעַד הַחַלּוֹן *through a window*, Gen. 26:8. Judg. 5:28. 2 Sam. 6:16. Spoken of a mountain, *to overlook a country*, Num. 21:20. 23:28. Jer. 6:1 כִּי רָעָה נִשְׁקְפָה מִצָּפוֹן *for evil threatens from the north.* (Arab. سقف *to be long and hanging down.*)

שֶׁקֶף m. 1 K. 7:5 *all the doors and posts* רְבֻעִים שָׁקֶף *were square, covered*, prob. in opposition to *arched.* Root שָׁקַף.

שְׁקֻפִים masc. plur. verbal from שָׁקַף, *timber overlaid.* 1 K. 7:4. Hence 1 K. 6:4 חַלּוֹנֵי שְׁקֻפִים אֲטֻמִים *windows of closed timber*, i. q. חַלֹּנִים אֲטֻמוֹת; see under the article אָטַם.

שָׁקַץ *to be abominable, loathsome.* In Kal not used.

Pi. שִׁקֵּץ 1. *to loathe, abominate.* Ps. 22:25. Particularly what is ceremonially unclean, Lev. 11:11. Deut. 7:26.

2. *to make unclean, to pollute.* Lev. 11:43. 20:25.

Deriv. שֶׁקֶץ, שִׁקּוּץ.

שֶׁקֶץ m. verbal from שָׁקַץ, *an abomination*, particularly *what is ceremonially unclean.* Lev. 11:10 שֶׁקֶץ הֵם לָכֶם *let them be an abomination unto you.* Verses 12, 13, 20, 23, 41, 42. Is. 66:17.

שִׁקֻּץ see שִׁקּוּץ.

I. **שָׁקַק**, fut. יָשֹׁק, (kindred with שׁוּק,) *to run about, to run to and fro.* Is. 33:4. Joel 2:9, (where it is spoken of locusts).

Hithpalp. הִשְׁתַּקְשֵׁק Nah. 2:5. *idem.*

Deriv. מַשָּׁק.

II. **שָׁקַק** *to be desirous, eager;* spoken e.g. of a thirsty person, Is. 29:8. Ps. 107:9. of a greedy bear, Prov. 28.15. (Arab. شاق conj. I. and VIII. *to desire;* whence in Hebrew the verbal noun תְּשׁוּקָה *desire.*)

שָׁקַר, fut. יִשְׁקֹר *to lie, to deceive*, construed with a dative of the person. Gen. 21:23.

Pi. *idem.* 1 Sam. 15:29. Construed (1.) with ל of the person, *to deceive*, Lev. 19:11. (2.) with בְּ of the thing, as שׁ׳ בִּבְרִית, בֶּאֱמוּנָה *to violate a covenant, faithfulness*, Ps. 44:18. 89:34. also without addition, Is. 63:8.

שֶׁקֶר m. verbal from שָׁקַר, dec. VI. h.

1. *a lie, falsehood, deception.*—דִּבְרֵי שֶׁקֶר *false words*, Ex. 5:9. עֵד שֶׁקֶר *a false witness.* Deut. 19:18. נִשְׁבַּע לַשֶּׁקֶר *to swear falsely*, Lev. 5:24. [6:5.] 19:12. נִבָּא בַשֶּׁקֶר *to prophesy falsely*, Jer. 5:31. 20:6. 29:9. Ps. 33:17 שֶׁקֶר הַסּוּס לִתְשׁוּעָה *a horse is a vain thing for safety.*—לַשֶּׁקֶר 1 Sam. 25:21. Jer. 3:23. and שֶׁקֶר Ps. 38:20. 69:5. 119:78, 86. as an

adv. *in vain, to no purpose, without cause.* Plur. שְׁקָרִים *lies,* Ps. 101:7.

2. i. q. אִישׁ שֶׁקֶר *a liar,* Prov. 17:4. as הֵלֶךְ 2 Sam. 12:4, for אִישׁ הֵלֶךְ.

שֹׁקֶת f. Gen. 24:20. plur. const. שִׁקֲתוֹת (as if from שִׁקָה) Gen. 30:38. *watering-troughs,* for cattle to drink out of. Root שָׁקָה *to drink.*

שַׁר or **שָׁרָה** found only in the plur. שָׁרוֹת Jer. 5:10. *walls,* i. q. שׁוּרוֹת. So the Sept. Vulg. Chald. and the context requires it.

שֹׁר m. with suff. שָׁרֵּךְ, dec. VII. e. i. q. שֹׁרֶר.

1. prob. *a nerve, sinew, muscle.* (Comp. שָׁרִיר and the Chald. שְׁרִיר *firm.*) Collect. Prov. 3:8 רִפְאוּת תְּהִי לְשָׁרֶּךָ *healing shall it be to thy sinews* or *muscles,* as the seat of strength. Parall. *to thy bones.*

2. *the navel,* strictly *the navel-string.* (Arab. سُرّ *idem.*) Ezek. 16:4. Comp. שָׁרִיר Job 40:16.

שְׁרָא and **שְׁרֵא** Chald.

1. *to loosen, solve, explain.* Dan. 5:16. Part. שְׁרַיִן *loose,* 3:25. Used particularly of the loosing or untying of a beast of burden, in order to rest; hence

2. *to turn in, to lodge, dwell.* Dan. 2:22. So the Greek καταλύω, *to unloose,* whence κατάλυμα, *a lodging.*

Pa. 1. *to loosen, solve, explain.* Dan. 5:12.

2. *to begin.* Ezra 5:2. (Comp. הֵחֵל *to begin,* from חָלַל *to loosen.*)

Ithpa. pass. of no. 1. Dan. 5:6 קִטְרֵי חַרְצֵהּ מִשְׁתָּרַיִן *the joints of his loins were loosed,* i. e. he could not keep himself upright.

שַׁרְאֶצֶר proper name of a son of Sennacherib, king of Assyria, who murdered his father. Is. 37:38. 2 K. 19:37.

שָׁרָב m. 1. *the heat* (of the sun). Is. 49:10. (Chald. שְׁרָב *idem.* Arab. سَرَاب *an undulous motion of the sand in the deserts of Arabia, occasioned by the rays of the sun.* See the Koran, sur. 24:39.)

2. *the parched ground* or *glimmering waste.* Is. 35:7.

שַׁרְבִיט m. i. q. שֵׁבֶט *a sceptre,* with ר inserted after the Chaldaic manner, (see the letter ר, p. 536.) found only in the later Hebrew. Est. 4:11. 5:2. 8:4.

שָׁרָה i. q. Aram. שְׁרָא *to loosen.*

Pi. שֵׁרָה *idem.* Jer. 15:11 Keri שֵׁרִיתִךָ לְטוֹב *I will loosen thee for good,* i. e. I will deliver you. The word לְטוֹב is added here probably because שֵׁרָה was also used in a bad sense, for *to let loose, to forsake.* In the Kethib שֵׁרוֹתִךָ q. v.

Deriv. מִשְׁרָה, שֵׁרוּת.

שֵׁרָה f. plur. שֵׁרוֹת, Is. 3:19. *chains, bracelets.* (Chald. שֵׁיר. Comp. שַׁרְשְׁרָה, שַׁרְשָׁה. Root Arab. سار *to string together,* hence *to build.*)

שָׁרוֹן *Sharon,* proper name of a level district in Palestine, extending from Joppa to Cæsarea, abounding in fruitful fields and rich pastures. Josh. 12:18. Cant. 2:1. Is. 33:9. 35:2. 65:10. 1 Chr. 27:29. See Relandi Palæstina, p. 188, 370. Some have adopted another Sharon beyond Jordan, from 1 Chr. 5:16. but this is not necessary. See Reland, ubi supra. The gentile noun is שָׁרוֹנִי 1 Chr. 27:29.

שְׁרוּקוֹת Jer. 18:16 Keth. see **שְׁרִיקוֹת**.

שֵׁרוּת f. *a beginning,* found only Jer. 15:11 Keth. Root Chald. שְׁרָא *to begin,* whence שֵׁרוּ *a beginning.*

שִׁרְיָה f. Job 41:18. [41:26.] **שִׁרְיָן** 1 K. 22:34. Is. 59:17. most frequently **שִׁרְיוֹן** m. dec. I.

1. *a coat of mail, habergeon.* 1 Sam. 17:5, 38. Plur. ־ִים Neh. 4:10. and ־וֹת 2 Chr. 26:14. Syr. ܫܪܝܢܐ *idem.* (Root perhaps Arab. شَرِيَ *micuit, coruscavit* fulgur.) Also written סִרְיוֹן q.v.

2. שִׂרְיֹן the name of mount שְׂנִיר among the Sidonians. Deut. 3 : 9. See שְׂנִיר.

שְׁרִיקוֹת fem. plur. verbal from שָׁרַק, dec. X.

1. *a hissing, derision.* Jer. 18 : 16 Keri. In the Kethib שְׁרוּקֹת.

2. *a fifing, piping.* Judg. 5 : 16. שְׁרִקוֹת עֲדָרִים *the piping by the herds,* (made by the herdsmen.) Sept. συρισμούς.

שָׁרִיר *hard, firm, solid,* Chald. שְׁרִיר *idem;*) found only in the plur. שְׁרִירֵי בִטְנוֹ Job 40 : 16. *the firm parts,* or perhaps particularly *the muscles of the belly;* (comp. שֹׁר and שֹׁרֶר *a muscle, navel-string.* Hence the abstract noun

שְׁרִירוּת f. denom. from the preceding, *hardness, firmness;* metaphorically *obduracy, stubbornness,* always joined with לֵב and לֵב הָרָע. Deut. 29 : 18. Ps. 81 : 13. Jer. 3 : 17. 7 : 24. 9 : 13. 11 : 8. (Aram. ܫܪܝܪܘܬܐ *firmness* in a good sense, *truth.*)

שֵׁרִית see שְׁאֵרִית.

שְׁרֵמוֹת fem. plur. Jer. 31 : 40 Keth. prob. only a false reading for שְׁדֵמוֹת *fields,* as is read in the Keri, in 6 MSS. and several editions. Comp. as a parallel passage 2 K. 23 : 4.

שָׁרַץ, fut. יִשְׁרֹץ. 1. *to multiply* or *propagate itself abundantly,* spoken of men and animals. (Ethiop. *propullulavit.*) Gen. 8 : 17. 9 : 7. Ex. 1 : 7.

2. *to creep, crawl, swarm,* spoken of worms and smaller fishes. Gen. 7 : 21 כָּל־הַשֶּׁרֶץ הַשֹּׁרֵץ עַל הָאָרֶץ *every worm which creepeth upon the earth.* Lev. 11 : 29, 41, 42, 43.

3. *to swarm* or *abound with* any thing, spoken of a place, construed with an accus. (Comp. הָלַךְ no. 5. and similar verbs.) Gen. 1 : 20 יִשְׁרְצוּ הַמַּיִם שֶׁרֶץ *let the waters swarm with creeping things.* Verse 21. Ex. 7 : 28. Ps. 105 : 30.

שֶׁרֶץ m. verbal from שָׁרַץ, dec. VI.

1. *a worm, reptile.* Gen. 7 : 21. Lev. 5 : 2. 11 : 29. שֶׁרֶץ הָעוֹף *a winged reptile,* with a special reference to the bat, Lev. 11 : 20, 21, 23. Deut. 14 : 19.

2. *smaller fishes.* Gen. 1 : 20.—שֶׁרֶץ הַמַּיִם Lev. 11 : 10.

שָׁרַק, fut. יִשְׁרֹק.

1. *to hiss.* Construed with לְ, *to hiss to* any one, *to lure by hissing;* e. g. flies, Is. 7 : 18. nations, Is. 5 : 26. Zech. 10 : 8.

2. *to hiss* (from scorn). 1 K. 9 : 8. Lam. 2 : 15, 16. Construed with עַל *at* a person or thing, Jer. 19 : 8. 49 : 17. Job 27 : 23 וְיִשְׁרֹק עָלָיו מִמְּקֹמוֹ *they shall hiss him away from his place.*

3. *to pipe,* συρίζειν; found only in the deriv. מַשְׁרוֹקִיתָא, שְׁרִיקוֹת.

שְׁרֵקָה f. verbal from שָׁרַק, *a hissing, derision, scorn.*—הָיָה לִשְׁרֵקָה *to be for a derision,* Jer. 19 : 8. 25 : 9. 29 : 18.

שָׁרַר *to be evil-minded, hostile.* (Arab. شَرَّ *idem.*) Found only in the part. שׁוֹרֵר *an enemy,* Ps. 27 : 11. 54 : 7. 56 : 33. 59 : 11. Synonymous with שׁוּר no. I.

שֹׁרֶר dec. VI. p. i. q. שֹׁר *the navel.* Cant. 7 : 3.

שֹׁרֶשׁ m. plur. שָׁרָשִׁים (read shŏrashim, like קָדָשִׁים kŏdashim,) dec. VI. m.

1. *a root.* Is. 5 : 24. Job 30 : 4.

2. *what springs up from the root, a shoot, branch.* Is. 53 : 2. 11 : 10 שֹׁרֶשׁ יִשַׁי *the shoot of Jesse,* i. e. the expected king of the race of David, the Messiah; comp. ῥίζα Δαβίδ, Rev. 5 : 5. Used collectively, Is. 14 : 30. Prov. 12 : 3, 12.

3. *the lowest part of a thing;* e. g. *the foot* (of a mountain), Job 28 : 9. *the bottom* (of the sea), Job 36 : 30. *the sole* (of the foot), Job 13 : 27. So *planta pedis.*

4. *a plantation, settlement, colony,* (of a people.) Judg. 5 : 14. Comp. the figure of *planting a people,* under the articles נָטַע and שָׁתַל.

5. שֹׁרֶשׁ דָּבָר *the ground of contention* or *complaint, radix causæ.* Job 19 : 28.

שֵׁרֵשׁ Pi. denom. from שֹׁרֶשׁ, (with a privative signification,) *to root up* or *out.* Ps. 52 : 7. Job 31 : 12.

Pu. שֹׁרַשׁ *to be rooted out.* Job 31 : 8.

Poel, שֹׁרֵשׁ *to take root.* Is. 40 : 24.

Poal, *idem*. Jer. 12:2.

Hiph. i. q. Po. *to take root;* joined with שָׁרָשִׁים, Ps. 80:10. without this addition, Job 5:3. Is. 27:6. In the two last passages, it is taken figuratively for *to prosper*.

שְׁרֹשׁ Chald. *a root*. Dan. 4:12. [4:15.]

שַׁרְשָׁה, plur. const. שַׁרְשׁוֹת *chains*. Ex. 28:22. Comp. שַׁרְשְׁרָה.

שְׁרֹשׁוּ (shroshu,) in the Keri שְׁרֹשִׁי, Chald. fem. *a rooting out*, and metaphorically *a banishment*. Ezra 7:26. comp. 10:8. Comp. שֹׁרֶשׁ no 4.

שַׁרְשְׁרָה f. *a chain*. Ex. 28:14. 39:15. The form is a reduplication of שַׁרְה *a chain*. (Arab. سلسلة, Chald. שַׁלְשְׁלָה, שַׁלְשֶׁלֶת. By contraction שַׁרְשָׁה q. v.)

שָׁרַת found only in Pi. שֵׁרֵת *to serve, wait upon;* construed for the most part with an accus. Gen. 39:4. 40:4. Num. 3:6. 1 K. 1:15. with לְ, Num. 4:9.—שֵׁרֵת אֶת־יְהוָה *to serve* or *minister unto Jehovah*, spoken of the priests, in reference to the ceremonial worship, Num. 18:2. 1 Sam. 2:11. 3:1. also without this addition, Num. 3:31. 4:12. שֵׁרֵת בְּשֵׁם יְהוָה Deut. 18:5, 7. *to minister on the name of Jehovah*, after the analogy of קָרָא ,בֵּרֵךְ בְּשֵׁם יְהוָה, the idea of divine worship suggesting immediately that of invocation and prayer.

שָׁשָׁה see **שָׁסָה**.

I. **שֵׁשׁ** m. 1. *white marble*. Est. 1:6. Cant. 5:15. elsewhere שַׁיִשׁ.

2. *byssus, fine white Egyptian cotton*, also *cloth made of it*. Gen. 41:42. Ex. 26:1. 27:9, 18. 28:39. Prov. 31:22. The later name is בּוּץ q. v. Under each of them *linen* is sometimes included, the orientalists usually expressing *cotton* and *linen* by the same word; (comp. פִּשְׁתֵּי־הָעֵץ *cotton*, كتّان *linen*, قطن *cotton*, comp. Ezek. 44:17. with Lev. 16:4.) The word appears to be of Hebrew, or at least of Shemitish origin, from a root שׁוּשׁ *to be white*, whence שֵׁשׁ, שַׁיִשׁ, Syr. ܫܘܫܐ *white marble;* שׁוֹשַׁן *a lily;* (of course like בּוּץ from the Arab. باض *to be white;*) it is called, however, in Egypt. *shensh*, and perhaps the Hebrews adopted the Egyptian name, though with some reference to its significancy in Heb. Comp. בְּהֵמוֹת ,יָם ,מֹשֶׁה. Celsii Hierobot. T. II. p. 259. Hartmann's Hebräerin, Th. 3. p. 34—36. Faber zu Harmer's Beobachtungen üb. den Orient, Th. 2. p. 380 ff. (Faber, however, makes a distinction between שֵׁשׁ and בּוּץ.)

II. **שֵׁשׁ** and **שִׁשָּׁה**, const. שֵׁשֶׁת, m. *six*, a contraction of שִׁדְשׁ, (like עֵת, by contraction לֵד, *to bring forth*,) Arab. سدس. Plur. שִׁשִּׁים com. gen. *sixty*. Deriv. שִׁשָּׁה, שִׁשִּׁי.

שָׁשָׁא found only in Pi. שִׁשֵּׁא *to lead astray, to seduce*. Ezek. 39:2. In Ethiop. ሰሰወ conj. V. *obire*, hence trans. *deducere, seducere*. Sept. κατοδηγήσω σε, aliter κατάξω σε. Chald. *errare te faciam*, Vulg. *seducam*.

שֵׁשְׁבַּצַּר a proper name, prob. the Persian name which Zerubbabel bore in the Persian court. Ezra 1:8. 5:14.

שִׁשָּׁה Pi. (denom. from שֵׁשׁ *six*,) *to divide into six parts, to pay a sixth part*. Ezek. 45:13.

שֶׁשִׁי Ezek. 16:13 Kethib for שֵׁשׁ. The form appears to be chosen for the sake of a paronomasia with מֶשִׁי, and is not grammatically correct, at least it is against the true origin of שֵׁשׁ from שַׁיִשׁ. The same, however, is true of the denom. שִׁשָּׁה.

שִׁשִּׁי, fem. ־ִית, (ordinal adj. from שֵׁשׁ *six*,) *sixth*. The fem. also denotes *the sixth part*, Ezek. 4:11. 45:13.

שֵׁשַׁךְ Jer. 25:26. 51:41. *Sheshach*, another name for *Babylon*. This is evident from the connexion, but the derivation of the word is obscure. The Hebrew interpreters and Jerome suppose it formed from בבל, after a Cabbalistic mode of writing, called *Atbash*, which consists in substituting ת for א, ש for ב, etc. But supposing this mode of writing to be sufficiently ancient, no reason appears why this secret name should be used in connexion with the real name, as in Jer. 51 : 41. Others make it i. q. שׁכתך, χαλκόπυλος, from سلّك *to fasten a gate with iron*. Others, *the arrogant*, from שׁשׁא in Syr. *rest*, hence perhaps *arrogance*, (comp. שַׁאֲנָן,) and ך formative as in Chald. Others make it the name of a Babylonian goddess.

שָׁשַׁר, in pause שָׁשָׁר, a red colour, perhaps *red earth, ruddel*, Jer. 22 : 14. Ezek. 23 : 14. Sept. μίλτος, used in Homer to denote *rubrica, ruddle*, the most celebrated kind of which was brought from Sinope, hence Vulg. *sinopis*, (comp. Plin. xxxv. 5 seu 13.) which includes likewise the *terra lemnia*. Chald. and Syr. *idem*. The Hebrew interpreters understand by it *vermilion*. (Arab. أشزر *red, of a brick colour*. Perhaps the word should be pointed שֶׁשֶׁר.)

שָׁת, found only in the plur. שָׁתוֹת m. verbal from שִׁית, *foundations, pillars*. Ps. 11 : 3 *the foundations are thrown down*. Aqu. τὰ θεμέλια. Is. 19 : 10 וְהָיוּ שָׁתֹתֶיהָ מְדֻכָּאִים according to the present vowel-pointing, *and all her pillars*, i. e. all the nobles of Egypt, *shall be afflicted*. But this furnishes no parallelism to, *all that earn wages are sad*. This is obtained by pointing the word שֹׁתְתֶיהָ, as if from שָׁתָה i. q. שָׁתָה *to weave*; thus *her weavers are afflicted*. Or, if the other clause be pointed שֵׁכָר שֹׁשֵׁי (after the Sept. Syr.) *they that prepare intoxicating drink*, and שתות be taken in the signification of שָׁתָה *to drink*. Comp. then Joel 1 : 5. The punctuators were evidently guided by the parallel passage Ps. 11 : 3. and their authority on that account is of less weight.

I. שֵׁת m. plur. שֵׁתוֹת.

1. *the posteriors, buttocks*. Is. 20 : 4. 2 Sam. 10 : 4. (Arab. إست, Syr. إقما *nates*.) Root שִׁית *to set*, hence *the seat*, comp. Germ. *Gesass;* the form, however, is borrowed from שתות.

2. *Seth*, the proper name of the third son of Adam. Gen. 4 : 25, 26. 5 : 3, 6. In the first passage the name is derived from שִׁית *to set, to give*.

II. שֵׁת f. a contraction of שְׁאֵת (Lam. 3 : 47.) hence *noise, tumult of war*, Num. 24 : 17, Root שָׁאָה. In the parallel passage Jer. 48 : 45, we find in its stead שָׁאוֹן.

שֵׁת and שֵׁת Chald. *six*, i. q. שֵׁשׁ. Dan. 3 : 1. Ezra 6 : 15. Plur. שִׁתִּין *sixty*, Dan. 3 : 1.

שָׁתָה, fut. יִשְׁתֶּה, apoc. יֵשְׁתְּ.

1. *to drink*. In Syr. Chald. and Ethiop. *idem*.) Construed with בְּ, *to drink from* a vessel, (comp. the French phrase, *boire dans une tasse*,) Am. 6 : 6. Figuratively Job 15 : 16 שֹׁתֶה כַמַּיִם עַוְלָה *he that drinketh iniquity like water*, i. e. practiseth it eagerly. Also passively, Prov. 26 : 6 *the lame man must drink*, i. e. suffer, *injury*.—Job 21 : 20 *he shall drink of the wrath of the Almighty;* comp. כּוֹס.

2. *to sit at table, to banquet*. Est. 7 : 1. See מִשְׁתֶּה.

Niph. pass. Once Lev. 11 : 34.

Note. The Hiphil of this verb is not in use, but is supplied by the synonymous verb הִשְׁקָה, which on the other hand wants the conjugations Kal and Niphal.

Deriv. מִשְׁתֶּה, שְׁתִי, שְׁתִיָּה.

שְׁתָה and שְׁתָא Chald. *idem*. Dan. 5 : 1, 2, 23. Pret. with א prosthetic אִשְׁתִּיו *they drank*, Dan. 5 : 3, 4. (So in Syr.) Construed with בְּ, *to drink out of* a vessel, like the French *boire dans une tasse*, Dan. 5 : 3. Deriv. מִשְׁתְּיָא.

שָׁתוֹת see שָׁת.

שְׁתִי m. verbal from שָׁתָה.

1. *a drinking, banqueting*. Ecc. 10 : 17.

2. *the warp* (in a web). Lev. 13:48 ff. (Syr. ܐܫܬܝ *to weave*, Arab. أَسْتَى *to fix the web, to stretch the warp.*) Comp. עֵרֶב *the woof.* Others understand by שְׁתִי and עֵרֶב different kinds of cloth, which is better suited to verses 52, 57.

שְׁתִיָּה f. verbal from שָׁתָה, *a drinking.* Est. 1:8.

שְׁתַּיִם f. *two*, see **שְׁנַיִם**

שָׁתַל, fut. יִשְׁתֹּל, *to plant*, more rarely and in poetry. Ps. 1:3. 92:14. Ezek. 17:8. 19:10, 13. Hos. 9:13. Hence

שָׁתִל m. verbal from שָׁתַל, dec. I. *a twig, branch, plant.* 128:3.

שָׁתַם prob. *to open.* In Chald. *to bore through.* (Comp. חָלַל *to bore through*, in Hiph. *to open, begin*; כָּרָה *to bore* for *to open* Ps. 40:7, used in the same connection as שָׁתַם.) Found only Num. 24: 3, 15 שְׁתֻם הָעָיִן *having his eyes opened*, i. q. גְּלוּי עֵינָיִם verse 4. For the force of this phrase, which denotes a divine revelation, see particularly Gen. 3:5. Ps. 40:7.

שָׁתַן found only in the part. Hiph. מַשְׁתִּין *a pisser.* (In Talmud. we find likewise the fut. and infin.) Used only in the phrase מַשְׁתִּין בְּקִיר *a pisser against the wall*, i. e. a man, a low expression used by way of contempt. 1 K. 16:11 *he slew all the house of Baasha, he left him not one that pisseth against the wall, neither of his kinsfolks nor of his friends.* 1 Sam. 25:22, 34. 1 K. 14:10. 21:21. 2 K. 9:8. (The same expression is found also in Syriac, see Assemani Biblioth. Orient. T. II. p. 260.) Others understand *a dog*, (but the expression would apply only to the male;) comp. the curse of Aurelian in Vopiscus: *canem in hoc oppido non relinquam.* But the mention of kinsfolks and friends afterwards, as in 1 K. 16:11. is against this explanation; neither is it suited to 1 K. 14:10. 21:21. 2 K. 9:8, where עָצוּר וְעָזוּב follows.

שָׁתַק, fut. יִשְׁתֹּק, *to be still, to rest;* spoken e. g. of the waves, Jon. 1:11, 12. Ps. 107:30. of contention, Prov. 26:20.

שְׁתַר בּוֹזְנַי (in Pers. *a shining star*;) proper name of a Persian governor. Ezra 5:3. 6:6.

שָׁתַת i. q. שִׁית *to set, place.* Hence the pret. שַׁתּוּ Ps. 49:15 כַּצֹּאן לִשְׁאוֹל שַׁתּוּ *like sheep one removes them to hades.* (Comp. Ps. 88:7.) 73:9.

ת

Tav, the last letter of the alphabet, and as a numerical sign denoting 400. For the significancy of the name and the original form of the letter, see the article תָּו. Its sound was like that of the Greek ϑ, or of the English *th* in *thin*; but perhaps not equally strong in all words. The Arabians distinguish in writing between the simple *t* ت (*Te*,) and the *th* ث (*The*,) which last is sometimes pronounced nearly as שׂ. See שׂ no. (3.) On the whole this letter is seldom commuted with others, and generally corresponds to ت in Arabic. For its interchange with ט, see p. 220. It is very rarely that it corresponds to the Arab. ث, as תָּקַף Arab. ثَقُفَ *to be strong.*

תָּא m. dec. I. *a chamber.* 1 K. 14:28. Ezek. 40:7 ff. (In Chald. תָּוָא, תָּוָן, Syr. ܬܘܢܐ, ܬܘܘܢܐ.) Plur. תָּאִים, once תָּאוֹת Ezek. 40:12. Root תָּוָה = ثوي *to dwell.*

I. **תָּאַב** *to desire, long for*, construed with לְ. Ps. 119:40, 174. In Chald. more frequent. Deriv. תַּאֲבָה.

II. **תָּאַב** found only in the part. Pi. מְתָאֵב i. q. מְתָעֵב *abhorring*, Am. 6:8. This commutation of ע and א is frequent in Aramean, see p. 1.

תַּאֲבָה f. verbal from תָּאַב no. I. *a desire, longing.* Ps. 119:20.

תָּאָה found only in Pi. fut. תְּתָאוּ Num. 34:7, 8. Sept. καταμετρήσετε. Syr. *determinabitis.* The root תָּאָה has here probably the signification of תָּוָה *to mark out, to describe;* comp. נָאוָה, נָאָה, and נָוָה no. II. *to be fair;* נָוֶה, נָוָה *a dwelling, pasture,* plur. const. נְאוֹת. That the form התאויתם verse 10, ought to be differently pointed and to be placed under this root, has been already observed under the article אָוָה no. II. p. 15.

תְּאוֹ Deut. 14:5. and **תּוֹא** Is. 51:20. a species of gazelle or wild-goat. Sept. Vulg. in Deut. Aqu. Symm. Theod. Vulg. in Is. ὄρυξ. The Targums: *bos sylvestris,* a kindred idea, (comp. רְאֵם.) See Bocharti Hieroz. T. I. p. 973.

תַּאֲוָה f. verbal from אָוָה no. I. dec. X.

1. *a wish, desire,* Ps. 10:17. Prov. 11:23. *the thing desired,* Ps. 21:3. Prov. 10:24.

2. in a bad sense, *lust, lusting, concupiscence,* also *the thing lusted after.* Num. 11:4 הִתְאַוּוּ תַּאֲוָה *they fell a lusting.* Ps. 78:29, 30.—קִבְרוֹת הַתַּאֲוָה *the graves of lusting,* Num. 11:34, 35.—מַאֲכַל תַּאֲוָה *dainty meat,* Job 33:20.

3. *something desirable, pleasant* or *lovely.* (Comp. מַחְמָד, חֶמְדָּה.) Gen. 3:6. 49:26. Prov. 19:22 תַּאֲוַת אָדָם חַסְדּוֹ *the loveliness* or *ornament of a man is his kindness.*

תְּאוֹם, תְּאֹם m. verbal from תָּאַם, dec. I. *a twin.* Gen. 38:27. Cant. 4:5. Plur. contracted תּוֹמִם Gen. 25:24. const. תָּאֳמֵי Cant. 7:4.

תַּאֲלָה f. verbal from אָלָה, dec. X. *a curse.* Lam. 3:65.

תָּאַם *to be doubled.* Ex. 26:24. 36:29. (In Syr. and Arab. *to be a twin.*)

Hiph. *to bear twins.* Cant. 4:2. 6:6.

Deriv. תְּאוֹם, תּוֹם.

תַּאֲנָה f. dec. X. *sexual desire* or *heat* in animals, most probably from אָנָה no. II. *to meet,* liter. *occursus venereus, concubitus.* Comp. עֵת no. (2.) Jer. 2:24 תַּאֲוָתָהּ מִי יְשִׁיבֶנָּה *the urgency of her desire, who can restrain it?* Others derive it from the Arab. أَنَى *to be ripe* or *ready,* hence *ripeness* (for love), an euphemism for *wantonness, sexual desire;* but an euphemism would hardly be expected in this place.

תְּאֵנָה f. plur. תְּאֵנִים. dec. X.

1. *a fig-tree.* Judg. 9:10. Prov. 27:18. The phrase *to sit under one's vine and under one's fig-tree,* is descriptive of a state of peace and prosperity, 1 K. 5:5. [4:25.] Zech. 3:10. Mic. 4:4.—In Gen. 3:7, we are not to think of the common fig-tree, but of *the pisang, paradise* or *Adam's fig-tree,* the leaves of which are large and strong like parchment, and serve for packing goods, for table-cloths, mats, etc. See Celsii Hierob. T. II. p. 389.

2. *a fig.* 2 K. 20:7.

תֹּאֲנָה f. (for תַּאֲנָה,) *an occasion.* Judg. 14:4. Comp. אָנָה no. II. particularly in Hithpa.

תַּאֲנִיָּה f. verbal from אָנָה no. I. *mourning, sadness, sorrow.* Is. 29:2. Lam. 2:5.

תְּאֻנִים masc. plur. *labour, toil, trouble.* Ezek. 24:12 תְּאֻנִים הֶלְאָת *it (the pot) wearieth me* (with) *hard labour.* Vulg. *multo labore sudatum est.* Root אין Arab. אין *lassus, defatigatus fuit;* comp. אָוֶן no. 3. *trouble, affliction.*

תָּאַר *to be drawn, marked out,* spoken of a boundary. Josh. 15:9, 11. 18:14, 17.

Pi. *to mark out, describe.* Is. 44:13.

תֹּאַר m. with suff. תָּאֳרוֹ, תָּאֳרָם, verbal from תָּאַר, dec. VI. n.

1. *form, visage.* 1 Sam. 28:14. Lam. 4:8. יְפֵה תֹאַר, יְפַת תֹּאַר *beautiful of form,* spoken for the most part of persons, Gen. 29:17. 39:6. also of animals, Gen. 41:18, 19.

2. *a beautiful form, beauty.* Is. 53:2. 1 Sam. 16:18 אִישׁ תֹּאַר *vir formæ,* i. e. formosus.

תְּאַשּׁוּר m. Is. 41:19. 60:13. name

of a tree which the ancient versions render variously, *cedar, fir, poplar,* etc. Most probably a species of cedar, called in the east *sherbin*. Chald. *box-tree;* see the article אַשּׁוּר no. 2.

תֵּבָה f. dec. X. strictly *a box, chest,* (Chald. תֵּיבוּתָא *idem;* Arab. تَابُوتٌ *a chest, coffin;*) hence *a vessel, boat, ship,* e. g. that of Noah, Gen. 6:14 ff. that wherein Moses was exposed when an infant, Ex. 2:5. Sept. κιβωτός. Vulg. *arca*. C.V. *an ark*.

תְּבוּאָה f. verbal from בּוֹא, dec. X.

1. *produce, increase,* e. g. of a country, Josh. 8:12. of the threshing-floor, Num. 18:30. of the wine-press, ibid. of the vineyard, Deut. 22:15.

2. *gain, profit;* e. g. תְּבוּאַת רָשָׁע *the gain of the wicked,* Prov. 10:16. 15:6. תְּבוּאַת חָכְמָה *the profit of wisdom,* Prov. 3:14. 8:19.

3. metaphorically *the fruit* or *consequences* of any thing; e. g. תְּבוּאַת שְׂפָתָיו *the consequences of his words,* Prov. 18:20. Comp. פְּרִי no. 3.

תְּבוּן m. verbal from בִּין, dec. III. c. *wisdom, understanding.* Hos. 13:2.

תְּבוּנָה f. verbal from בִּין, dec. X.

1. *wisdom, understanding.* Deut. 32:28. Often in the plural, Ps. 49:4.

2. plur. *arguments, proofs.* Job 32:11.

תְּבוּסָה f. verbal from בּוּס dec. X. *a treading down, ruin, destruction.* 2 Chr. 22:7.

תָּבוֹר 1. the proper name of a mountain in Galilee, on the borders of the tribes Zebulun and Naphtali. Josh. 19:22. Judg. 4:6. 8:18. Ps. 89:13. Jer. 46:18. Hos. 5:1. In Josephus Ἰταβύριον, Ἀταβύριον. Relandi Palæstina, p. 331—336.

2. also of a grove of turpentine trees in the tribe of Benjamin. 1 Sam. 10:3.

תֵּבֵל f. (with two Tseris impure,) used in poetry for אֶרֶץ.

1. *the earth, the globe, the world.* 1 Sam. 2:8. Ps. 18:16. 93:1. 96:10. Twice with אֶרֶץ subjoined, Prov. 8:31 תֵּבֵל אַרְצוֹ *the circuit of his earth.* Job 37:12. comp. Ps. 90:2 אֶרֶץ וְתֵבֵל. Particularly *the inhabited earth,* Is. 14:17. (comp. אֶרֶץ Zech. 14:10.) hence metaphorically *the inhabitants of the earth,* Ps. 9:9. 24:1. 33:8. 96:13. 98:9.

2. *a land, country;* in reference to the kingdom of Babylon, Is. 13:11. to that of Israel, Is. 24:4. Comp. the Latin phrase *orbis Romanus.* (Syr. ܬܐܒܝܠ, ܬܒܠ *idem.*) Root perhaps יָבַל *to bring forth,* (comp. יְבוּל,) hence liter. *the fruitful,* i. e. the earth.

תֶּבֶל m. *shameful pollution,* particularly in respect to sins of lewdness. Lev. 18:23 after the prohibition of sodomy, תֶּבֶל הוּא *it would be a shameful pollution,* i. e. a wicked scandalous deed. 20:12. Synonymous with נְבָלָה no. 3. Root בָּלַל *to mix, mingle,* (after the analogy of חָמָס from מָסַס,) with the accessory idea of *pollution, profanation.* So in Chald. בַּלְבֵּל e. g. Gen. 49:4 Targ. comp. in Arab. بل *to be impious, to commit adultery.*

תֻּבַל see תּוּבַל.

תַּבְלִית f. dec. I. *destruction, annihilation.* Is. 10:25. Root בָּלָה *to consume.* Some MSS. and editions read תַּכְלִיתָם, a word probably more familiar and intelligible to the copyist, and chosen on that account. See תַּכְלִית.

תְּבַלֻּל m. found only Lev. 21:20 תְּבַלֻּל בְּעֵינוֹ *having a white spot* (λεύκωμα) *on his eye.* Vulg. *albuginem habens in oculo.* Comp. Tob. 2:9. 3:17. 6:8. where the Hebrew translator uses this word for the Greek λεύκωμα. Root בָּלַל *to stain, pollute,* comp. תֶּבֶל. The Targums render it *a snail,* meaning here *blear-eyedness;* comparing it with the Chald. חִלְזוֹנָא *a snail.* But this in Hebrew would be שַׁבְּלוּל.

תֶּבֶן m. *straw,* which by threshing

with the pointed threshing waggon (מוֹרַג) was broken into small pieces, like our *chopped straw.* Job 21:18. It was used as fodder for cattle, Gen. 24:25. Is. 11:7. 65:25. and in the preparation of clay for bricks, Gen. 5:7 ff. Deriv. מַתְבֵּן.

תַּבְנִית f. verbal from בָּנָה.

1. *a style* or *mode of building.* Ps. 144:12.

2. *a model, pattern,* after which any thing is built. Ex. 25:9, 40. 2 K. 16:10.

3. *an image, likeness.* Deut. 4:16—18. Ezek. 8:10. Hence Ezek. 8:3. וַיִּשְׁלַח תַּבְנִית יָד *he stretched out as it were a hand,* liter. *the image of a hand.* 10:8. Comp. דְּמוּת no. 3.

תַּבְעֵרָה (*a burning*) proper name of a place in the desert. Num. 11:3. Deut. 9:22.

תֵּבֵץ proper name of a place not far from Sichem. Judg. 9:50. 2 Sam. 11:21.

תִּגְלַת פִּלְאֶסֶר *Tiglath-pileser,* proper name of a king of Assyria, contemporary with Ahaz king of Judah. 2 K. 15:29. 16:10. This name is also written תִּגְלַת פְּלֶסֶר 2 K. 16:7. תִּלְּגַת פִּלְנְאֶסֶר 1 Chr. 5:6. 2 Chr. 28:20. and תִּלְּגַת פִּלְנֶסֶר 1 Chr. 5:26. The latter part of this compound name occurs likewise with a slight change in the royal name *Nabopolassar,* and signifies prob. *magnus princeps,* (Pers. پلاسر, according to Lorsbach's Archiv für morgenl. Litt. Th. 2. p. 247.) The former part may be the Pers. تكل *juvenis imberbis.*

תַּגְמוּל m. verbal from גָּמַל, dec. I. *a benefit,* i. q. גְּמוּל. Ps. 116:12.

תִּגְרָה f. verbal from גָּרָה, dec. X. *strife, contention.* Once Ps. 39:11 מִתִּגְרַת יָדְךָ אֲנִי כָלִיתִי *by the contention.* i. e. blows, punishment, *of thy hand I am consumed.* (In Chald. *idem.*)

תֹּגַרְמָה Gen. 10:3. and **תּוֹגַרְמָה** 1 Chr. 1:6. Ezek. 27:14. 38:6. name of a northern country, from which horses and mules were brought to Tyre. (See Ezek. 27:14.) Sept. by transposition Θοργαμα, Θεργαμα, Θυργυμα, Θυργαβα; and some Hebrew MSS. תרגמה. This leads us to *Armenia,* as the most probable explanation of the word, since the Armenians derive themselves from *Torgom* a descendant of Gomer, and call themselves *the house of Torgom.* Armenia is also represented by the Greeks as rich in horses. Comp. J. D. Michaëlis Spicileg. Geogr. T. I. p. 67—78.

תִּדְהָר m. name of a tree, perhaps *the plane-tree;* found only Is. 41:19. 60:13. The ancient translators fluctuate between *the beech, pine, cypress, larch,* etc. Comp. Celsii Hierobot. T. II. p. 271.

תְּדִירָא f. Chald. *a going round in a circle, continuance,* i. q. תָּמִיד. Adv. בִּתְדִירָא *constantly, continually,* Dan. 6:17, 21. (Root דּוּר *to move in a circle,* whence דּוֹר *a generation, periodus.*)

תַּדְמֹר 1 K. 9:18. Keri, and 2 Chr. 8:4. a city built by Solomon, on a fruitful spot surrounded by barren deserts, between Damascus and the Euphrates. In the Kethib of 1 K. 9:18 תָּמָר (*a palm-tree,*) and hence without doubt is derived the well-known Grecian name *Palmyra.* Among the Arabians the ruins of this city still bear the name of *Tadmor.*

תֹּהוּ (for תֹּהֶו a segolated form like קֹדֶשׁ, hence the word is penacuted.) Root in Chald. תְּהָא *to be confounded, to be desolate,* (comp. שָׁמֵם;) whence תְּהִי, תְּהָיָא, *waste.* Arab. تيه *empty.* Syr. ܬܘܗ *idem,* a contraction of תֹּהוּ.

1. as a subst. *emptiness, desolateness,* Gen. 1:2. Job 26:7. *a desert,* Deut. 32:10. Job 6:18. 12:24. Is. 24:10 קִרְיַת תֹּהוּ *the desolate city.* 34:11 קַו תֹהוּ וְאַבְנֵי בֹהוּ *the line of wasting and the plummet of desolation.*

2. metaphorically *emptiness, vanity,* and as a concrete, *something vain* or *of no value,* synonymous with הֶבֶל. Is. 41:29. 44:9. 49:4. 59:4. 1 Sam.

12:21. Hence parallel with אַיִן *nothing*, Is. 40:17, 23.

3. as an adv. *in vain*, like הֶבֶל. Is. 45:19.

תְּהוֹם com. gen. plur. תְּהוֹמוֹת, dec. I. Root prob. הוּם i. q. הָמָה *to rage* or *be tumultuous*, as the sea.

1. *a flood, deep water*, used poetically for מַיִם *waters*. Deut. 8:7. Ps. 42:8 תְּהוֹם אֶל תְּהוֹם קֹרֵא *flood calleth after*, i. e. followeth after, *flood*. Ps. 78:15. Ezek. 31:4. תְּהוֹם רַבָּה *the great waters*, spoken of the sea, Gen. 7:11. So Ps. 36:7. Amos 7:4. Job 28:14. 38:16, 30. Plur. Ex. 15:3, 8. Ps. 33:7.

2. *the abyss*, spoken of the abysses of the earth. Ps. 71:20. (Syr. ܬܗܘܡܐ *a flood* and *an abyss*.)

תְּהִלָּה f. verbal from הָלַל, dec. X.

1. *praise, glory*. Ps. 22:26. 48:11. 51:17. Hence (1.) *an object of praise, something praised*. Deut. 26:19. לִתְהִלָּה לְשֵׁם וּלְתִפְאָרֶת *to be a praise, a name, and an honour*. Jer. 13:11. 33:9. Zeph. 3:19, 20. (2.) *an object of boasting, ground of praise, boast, praise*. Jer. 17:14 אַתָּה תְהִלָּתִי *thou (Jehovah) art my boast*. 48:2. Deut. 10:21. Plur. תְּהִלּוֹת *laudes*, Ps. 78:4. Is. 60:6.

2. *a song of praise*. Ps. 22:4. 66:2. 145:1. The Jews call the whole collection of Psalms תְּהִלִּים *songs of praise*, a name which applies strictly to only a part of them. The plur. in ־ִים occurs nowhere else.

תָּהֳלָה f. found only Job 4:18. *a fault, error, defect*. Sept. σκολιόν τι. Vulg. *pravum quid*. Syr. *stupor*. Chald. *iniquitas*. If the ת be radical, then this word may be collated with the Arab. تهل. But the ת may be servile, and the word derived from the root יהל Arab. وهل, *to err, to fail*, whence وهل *an error*. Hence a verbal noun תּוֹהֳלָה, תּוֹהֵלָה, for which may be substituted תָּהֳלָה, as inversely הוֹעֲלָה for הֶעֱלָה Judg. 6:28. וַיַּעְמֵד for וָאֶעְמֵד Num. 23:7.

תַּהֲלוּכָה f. verbal from הָלַךְ, dec. X. *a procession, company, guard*. Neh. 12:31.

תַּהְפּוּכָה f. verbal from הָפַךְ, found only in the plur.

1. *perverseness, folly*. Deut. 32:20.

2. *falsehood, deceit*. Prov. 2:12, 14. 6:14. לְשׁוֹן תַּהְפֻּכוֹת *the false tongue*.

תָּו m. (for תָּוֶה,) verbal from תָּוָה no. I.

1. *a mark, sign*. Ezek. 9:4. (Arab. تَوِيٌّ *a mark in the form of a cross*, which was branded on the flanks or neck of horses and camels; hence prob. the name of the letter ת, which in the ancient Phenician alphabet and on Jewish coins has the form of a cross (†), and from which the Greeks and Romans have borrowed the form of their T.)

2. *the signature* or *subscription* (of a complaint), or *the complaint* itself. Job 31:35. The term probably refers not to the use of alphabetical characters, but simply to the signature of a writing by drawing a cross or the like; (see no. I.) Parall. סֵפֶר.

תּוֹא *a gazelle*, see **תְּאוֹ**.

תּוּב, fut. יְתוּב, Chald. i. q. Heb. שׁוּב *to return*. Dan. 4:31, 33. [4:34. 36.]

Aph. הֲתִיב (with a Hebrew form) *to cause to return, to restore, to give* or *send back*. Ezra 5:5. 6:5.—הֲתִיב פִּתְגָם i. q. Heb. הֵשִׁיב דָּבָר *to return answer, to answer*, construed with an accus. of the person, Ezra 5:11. Dan. 3:16. Also without פִּתְגָם *idem*, Dan. 2:14.

תּוּבַל Ezek. 27:13. 38:2, 3. Is. 66:19. and תֻּבַל Gen. 10:2. Ezek. 32:26. 39:1. *the Tibarenes*, a people of Pontus in Asia Minor, west of מֶשֶׁךְ *the Moschians*, in connection with whom they are generally mentioned. See מֶשֶׁךְ no. 3.

תּוּבַל קַיִן *Tubal-cain*, the proper name of a son of Lamech, the inventor of smithery. Gen. 4:22. To this the appellative meaning of the word has reference, for *Tubal* signifies in Persian *the dross* or *slacks of brass and iron;* and קַיִן in Arab. and Pers. *a smith.* Is this account then of Persian origin?

תּוּגָה f. verbal from יָגָה, dec. X. *grief, sorrow.* Prov. 14:13. 17:21. Ps. 119:28.

תּוֹגַרְמָה see תֹּגַרְמָה.

תּוֹדָה f. (verbal from יָדָה no. II. Hiph. *to confess, praise;*) dec. X.

1. *a confession, acknowledgment.* Josh. 7:19. Ezra 10:11.

2. *praise, thanks, thanksgiving.* Ps. 26:7. 42:5. זָבַח תּוֹדָה *to offer thanksgiving,* (not *to bring thank-offerings,*) Ps. 50:14, 23. 107:22. 116:17. זֶבַח הַתּוֹדָה *a thank-offering,* Lev. 22:29. So in the same sense זֶבַח תּוֹדַת שְׁלָמִים Lev. 7:13, 15. comp. verse 12.

3. i. q. זֶבַח תּוֹדָה *a thank-offering.* Ps. 56:13.

4. *a choir of singers.* Neh. 12:31, 38, 40.

תְּוַהּ Chald. *to be astonished, terrified, to tremble from fear.* Dan. 3:24.

I. תָּוָה in Kal not used.

Pi. *to make a mark* or *sign.* 1 Sam. 21:14 וַיְתָו עַל דַּלְתוֹת הַשַּׁעַר *and he scrabbled on the doors of the gate.*

Hiph. *to make a mark* or *sign,* joined with תָּו. Ezek. 9:4.

II. תָּוָה *to repent, grieve.* (In Syr. *idem.*)

Hiph. causat. *to cause to repent* or *to be grieved.* Ps. 78:41.

תּוֹחֶלֶת f. verbal from יָחַל, dec. XIII. a. *a hope, expectation.* Ps. 39:8. Prov. 10:28.

תָּוֶךְ m. const. תּוֹךְ, with suff. תּוֹכִי, dec. VI. e. *the middle, the midst.* Sometimes as a genitive after another noun, Judg. 16:29 עַמּוּדֵי הַתָּוֶךְ *the middle pillars.*—בְּתוֹךְ *in the midst;* denoting (1.) *among, inter.* Gen. 35:2. Lev. 20:14. (2.) *in the midst of,* or simply *in.* 1 Sam. 9:14. 18:10 בְּתוֹךְ הַבַּיִת *in the house.* (3.) *through the midst.* עָבַר בְּתוֹךְ *to go through the midst,* Ezek. 9:4. Ex. 14:29.—מִתּוֹךְ liter. *from the midst;* hence simply *out of,* Jer. 51:6. *from,* Ex. 33:11.—אֶל תּוֹךְ *into the midst of,* Num. 17:12. [16:47.] 19:6. Comp. the synon. קֶרֶב. Deriv. תִּיכוֹן.

תֹּךְ i. q. תֹּךְ *oppression,* q. v.

תּוֹכֵחָה f. verbal from יָכַח, dec. X. *chastisement, punishment,* i. q. תּוֹכַחַת no. 4. Ps. 149:7. Hos. 5:9.

תּוֹכַחַת f. with suff. תּוֹכַחְתִּי, plur. תּוֹכָחוֹת, verbal from יָכַח, dec. XIII. m.

1. *a proving, proof, demonstration.* Job 13:6. Plur. *arguments, proofs,* Job 23:4. *contradictions,* Ps. 38:15. Prov. 29:1 אִישׁ תּוֹכָחוֹת *a man of contradictions,* i.e. a refractory man.

2. *warning, admonition.* Prov. 1:23, 25, 30. 3:11. 5:12. Plur. תּוֹכְחוֹת מוּסָר *instructive reproofs,* Prov. 6:23.

3. *censure, reproach, reproof.* Prov. 27:5. 29:15. Particularly *a complaint* or *censure* (of God,) Hab. 2:1.

4. *chastisement, punishment.* Ps. 73:14. Plur. Ps. 39:12. Ezek. 5:15 תּוֹכְחוֹת חֵמָה *angry chastisements* 25:17.

תּוֹלְדֹת fem. plur. verbal from יָלַד, dec. X.

1. *families, generations.* Num. 1:20 ff. לְתוֹלְדֹתָם *according to their generations,* Gen. 10:32. 25:13. Ex. 6:16. Hence סֵפֶר תּוֹלְדֹת *a family register,* Gen. 5:1. This family register often began thus אֵלֶּה תּוֹלְדֹת וגו׳ *these are the generations and so forth,* Gen. 10:1. 11:10. 25:12, 19. 36:1, 9. Ruth 4:18.—As the most ancient history among the orientals consisted in a great measure of genealogical accounts, hence

2. *a family history* of any kind. Gen. 6:9 אֵלֶּה תּוֹלְדֹת נֹחַ *this is the history of Noah.* 37:2. and

3. *a history,* in a still wider sense. Gen. 2:4 *this is the history of the heavens and the earth.* Comp. יָלַד and the Syr. ܬܘܠܕܬܐ *a family, genealogy, history* generally. See Castelli Lex. Syr. ed. Mich. p. 937.

תּוֹלָלִים masc. plur. found only

Ps. 137:3 תּוֹלָלֵינוּ according to the Targums, *prædatores nostri*, as if it stood for שׁוֹלָלֵינוּ by a commutation of שׁ and ת. But שׁוֹלָל has a passive signification, *to be plundered* or *spoiled*. The comparison is more close with the Syr. תלל Ethpa. *to rave, rage,* hence תּוֹלָלֵינוּ *they that raged against us.* Gr. anon. οἱ καταλαζονευόμενοι ἡμᾶς. Still better after the Arab. تَلَّ *to cast down,* conj. IV. *to fetter, carry away in chains;* hence *our tyrants, despots.*

תּוֹלָע m. **תּוֹלֵעָה, תּוֹלַעַת** f. Plur. תּוֹלָעִים.

1. *a worm of any kind;* spoken e.g. of those which arise from putridity, Ex. 16:20. Is. 14:11. 66:24. of the worm which destroys the palma Christi, Jon. 4:7. of insects which gnaw the grape-vine, Deut. 28:39. As an image of weakness and vileness, Ps. 22:7. Job 25:6.

2. particularly תּוֹלַעַת שָׁנִי *the kermez, the turtle insect,* also *the colour prepared from it;* see שָׁנִי. More rarely תּוֹלָע stands alone for *the crimson dye, crimson garments,* Lam. 4:5. Is. 1:18.

תּוּם. From this root are derived some forms, which have the signification of תָּמַם.

תּוֹמִים *twins,* see **תְּאֹמִים.**

תּוֹמָן Gen. 36:15 Keth. for תֵּימָן, but prob. a corrupted reading.

תּוֹעֵבָה f. const. תּוֹעֲבַת, verbal from תָּעַב, dec. XI. b.

1. *an abomination.* Prov. 21:27. 28:9. תּוֹעֲבַת יְהוָה *an abomination to Jehovah,* Prov. 3:32. 11:1, 20. Spoken particularly of what is unclean or forbidden by ceremonial laws, Gen. 43:32 *for this* (*the eating with Hebrews*) *is an abomination to the Egyptians.* 46:34. Deut. 14:3. Hence also of idols and other things pertaining to idolatry, 2 K. 23:13. See שִׁקּוּץ, שֶׁקֶץ.

2. *an abominable deed* or *practice,* particularly in reference to idolatry. 1 K. 14:24. 2 K. 16:3. 21:2. Ezra 9:1. Ezek. 16:2.

תּוֹעָה f. verbal from תָּעָה.

1. *apostacy* (from God). Is. 32:6.

2. *hurt, injury.* Neh. 4:2. [4:8.]

תּוֹעָפוֹת plur. fem. verbal from יָעַף, dec. XI. a.

1. *swift course, swiftness.* Num. 23:22. 24:8 תּוֹעֲפֹת רְאֵם לוֹ *he has the swiftness of the buffalo.*

2. *weariness, wearisome labour;* see יָעֵף no. 2. Hence prob. *earnings, possession, substance, treasure;* comp. יְגִיעַ no. 3. Ps. 95:4 תּוֹעֲפוֹת הָרִים *the treasures of the mountains.* Job 22:25 כֶּסֶף תּוֹעָפוֹת *silver of treasures,* i.e. treasures of silver. According to some interpreters, in all these passages, *heights,* by a transposition of the letters, from the root יפע Arab. يفع *ascendit, altus fuit,* hence Num. 23:22 *an upright course.* Ps. 95:4 *heights of the mountains.* Job 22:25 *silver of heaps,* i.e. heaps of silver. But the signification given above is equally well suited to the passages, and is better supported by Hebrew usage.

תּוֹצָאוֹת f. plur. verbal from יָצָא *to go out,* dec. XI. a.

1. *a place of going out, a gate.* Ezek. 48:30.

2. *a place of rising, a spring.* Prov. 4:23 תּוֹצְאוֹת חַיִּים *the well-springs of life,* i.e. of happiness.

3. *a going forth, extremity, limit,* (of a boundary.) Num. 34:4, 5, 8, 9. Josh. 15:4.

4. metaphorically *deliverance.* Ps. 68:21 לַמָּוֶת תּוֹצָאוֹת *deliverance in regard to death,* i.e. from death. Comp. יָצָא Ecc. 7:18.

I. **תּוֹר** m. dec. I. *a turtle-dove, turtur,* so called from the noise which it makes. Gen. 15:9. Lev. 12:6. Used as a word of endearment to one beloved, Cant. 2:12. Ps. 74:19 תּוֹרֶךָ *thy turtle-dove,* i.e. thy persecuted affrighted people, with the accessory idea of affection.

II. **תּוֹר** m. dec. I.

1. *a row, order, turn.* Est. 2:12, 15.

2. *a row* or *string of pearls* or *metallic beads,* which hung down over the face. Cant. 1:10. 11.

III. **תּוֹר** 1 Chr. 17:17. *a manner,* i. q. תּוֹרָה no. 3. which stands in the parallel passage 2 Sam. 7:19. If the reading is correct, then the word may be derived from no. II. *a row,* or be a contraction of תּוֹרָה=תֹּרָה.

תּוֹר Chald. *an ox,* i. q. Heb. שׁוֹר. Plur. תּוֹרִין *oxen.* Dan. 4:22, 29, 30. [4:25, 32, 33.] 5:21. Ezra 6:9, 17.

תּוּר 1. *to go about,* particularly as a spy; hence *to spy out,* e. g. a land, construed with an accus. Num. 13:17, 18, 22. 14:6 ff. Also *to search out, discover,* Deut. 1:33. Num. 10:33. Ezek. 20:6. Trop. *to search out, explore,* Ecc. 7:25. used absolutely, Ecc. 2:3. also construed with עַל, Ecc. 1:13.

2. *to go about,* as a merchant. 1 K. 10:15. Comp. רָכַל and סָחַר.

3. construed with אַחֲרֵי, *to follow.* Trop. Num. 15:39.

Hiph. 1. i. q. Kal no. 1. *to spy out.* Judg. 1:23.

2. *to direct* a person or *shew* him *the right way.* Prov. 12:26 יָתֵר מֵרֵעֵהוּ צַדִּיק *the righteous man shews his neighbour the right way;* parall. *the way of the wicked leads them astray.* (Chald. תַּיָּר *a guide.*)

Deriv. יָתוּר.

תּוֹרָה f. verbal from יָרָה, (in Hiph. *to teach,*) dec. X.

1. *instruction, doctrine, precept, admonition.* Job 22:22. E. g. from parents, Prov. 1:8. 3:1. 4:2. 7:2. from God, i. e. a revelation, an oracle, Is. 1:10. 8:16, 20. 42:4, 21.

2. *a law* (of Moses). Lev. 6:9, 14. 25. 7:1, 7. Also collectively *laws,* Lev. 13:9. 16:4.—סֵפֶר הַתּוֹרָה *the book of the law,* Josh. 1:8. 8:34. 2 K. 22:8, 11. Neh. 8:3. 13:3.

3. *a mode, manner,* i. q. חֹק, מִשְׁפָּט. 2 Sam. 7:19.

4. *a rule, direction,* (for building a house.) Ezek. 43:12.

תּוֹשָׁב m. (verbal from יָשַׁב *to dwell,*) dec. I. *a sojourner, a stranger dwelling in another country without the rights of citizenship, inquilinus.* Lev. 22:10. 25:47. Ps. 39:13. Plur. const. 1 K. 17:1.

תּוּשִׁיָּה f. used only in poetry.

1. *wisdom, understanding.* (Used as synonymous with חָכְמָה, עֵצָה, דַּעַ.) Job 11:6. כִּפְלַיִם לְתוּשִׁיָּה *twice as much wisdom.* 12:16 עֹז וְתוּשִׁיָּה *might and wisdom.* 26:3. Prov. 3:21. 8:14. 18:1. Is. 28:29. הִפְלִא עֵצָה הִגְדִּיל תּוּשִׁיָּה *whose counsel is wonderful and whose wisdom is great.* Perhaps Mic. 6:9. Hence also i. q. עֵצָה *purpose, plan,* Job 5:12 לֹא תַעֲשֶׂינָה יְדֵיהֶם תּוּשִׁיָּה *their hands execute not their purpose.* Vulg. *quod cœperant.*

2. *help, deliverance, salvation.* Job 6:13 תּוּשִׁיָּה נִדְּחָה מִמֶּנִּי *has deliverance fled from me?* Parall. עֶזְרָה. Prov. 2:7. According to some also Mic. 6:9. Job 30:22 Keri. (The most natural root is יָשָׁה Arab. وسى *to support, help,* which fully illustrates this last signification; but the sense of *wisdom* is not found in any of the roots with which this word has been collated. The ideas, however, of *wisdom* or *virtue* and *salvation* or *prosperity,* are connected. Comp. צֶדֶק and צְדָקָה no. 6.)

תּוֹתָח m. *a club, cudgel.* Job 41:21. [41:29.] Sept. σφῦρα. Vulg. *malleus.* Root יָתַח Arab. وتخ *fuste percussit.*

תָּזַז found only in Hiph. הֵתַז *to cut off.* Is. 18:5. Sept. ἀποκόψει, aliter κατακόψει. (Found likewise in Talmudic.) The Hebrew interpreters explain it by כָּרַת.

תַּזְנוּת f. verbal from זָנָה, dec. I. *whoredom, fornication;* metaphorically *idolatry.* Ezek. 16:25, 26, 29. 23:8. Plur. תַּזְנוּתִים Ezek. 16:15, 20, 22. 23:7 ff.

תַּחְבֻּלוֹת and תַּחְבּוּלוֹת fem. plur. dec. X.

1. *a leading, guidance, direction.* Job 37:12. Particularly *the guidance* or *management* of a state, Prov. 11:14. (Most prob. a denom. from חֹבֵל *a pilot, gubernator.*)

2. *the art of leading* or *governing.* Hence *a wise plan* or *counsel,* Prov. 1:5. 20:18. 24:6. Also in a bad sense, Prov. 12:5.

תְּחוֹת Chald. prep. *under,* i. q. Heb. תַּחַת. Dan. 7:27. It is strictly a noun, and with suffixes is always put in the plur. e. g. תְּחוֹתוֹהִי *under it,* Dan. 4:9, 18. [4:12, 21.]

תְּחִלָּה f. verbal from חָלַל (in Hiph. *to begin,*) dec. X. *the beginning.* Hos. 1:2. Prov. 9:10. בַּתְּחִלָּה *at the beginning, before, at the first,* Gen. 13:3. 41:21. 43:18, 20. Is. 1:26.

תַּחֲלוּאִים masc. plur. (verbal from חָלָה=חָלָא *to be sick,*) dec. I. *sicknesses, diseases.* Deut. 29:21. Ps. 103:3. Jer. 16:4 מְמוֹתֵי תַחֲלֻאִים יָמֻתוּ *deaths of sicknesses,* i. e. grievous deaths, *they shall die.* 14:18 תַּחֲלוּאֵי־רָעָב as a concrete, *the famished by hunger.*

תַּחְמָס m. (verbal from חָמַס *to be violent, rapacious,*) Lev. 11:16. Deut. 14:15. name of an unclean bird. According to Bochart, (Hieroz. P. II. p. 232.) *the male ostrich,* which in Arabic is called ظليم *impius, iniquus,* (comp. Job 39:17 ff. Lam. 4:3.) from ظلم, which corresponds exactly to the Heb. חָמַס. The preceding בַּת יַעֲנָה must then be taken here in a narrower sense for *the female ostrich.* Sept. and Vulg. *night owl;* Jonath. *the swallow.* Other Jewish interpreters make it a generic name for any *bird of prey,* from חָמַס *to be violent.*

תְּחִנָּה f. (verbal from חָנַן *to pity,*) dec. X.

1. *favour, pity, compassion.* Josh. 11:20. Ezra 9:8.

2. *a prayer, supplication,* (see the verb חָנַן Hithpa. *to supplicate.*) Ps. 6:10. 55:2. 119:170.

תַּחֲנוּנִים masc. plur. dec. I. *prayers, supplications,* i. q. תְּחִנּוֹת. Ps. 28:2, 7. 31:23. 116:1. Root חָנַן Hithpa. *to supplicate.*

תַּחֲנוּנוֹת fem. plur. verbal from חָנַן, dec. X. *supplications.* Ps. 86:6.

תַּחֲנוֹת f. verbal from חָנָה, *a place of encamping, a camp.* 2 K. 6:8.

תְּחַפְנְחֵס Ezek. 30:18. and תַּחְפַּנְחֵס Jer. 43:7, 8, 9. 44:1. 46:14. also 2:16 Keri, where the Kethib reads תְּחַפְנֵס.

1. the proper name of a city in Egypt. Sept. Τάφνη, Τάφναι, undoubtedly meaning *Daphne,* not far from Pelusium, a frontier fortress of the Egyptians towards Syria. Jablonski (Opusc. P. I. p. 343.) supposes the Egyptian name of the city to have been *Taphe-eneh,* i. e. caput seculi seu terræ, having reference to the situation of the city on the very borders of Egypt.

2. תַּחְפְּנֵיס the proper name of an Egyptian queen. 1 K. 11:19, 20.

תַּחְרָא m. *a linen coat of mail* or *habergeon,* θώραξ, *lorica,* a closely woven linen garment furnished with a coat of mail in the upper part about the neck. Ex. 28:32. 39:23. Root חָרָא, Syr. Ethp. *to fight, contend;* Aph. *to prepare for contest;* kindred with the Heb. חָרָה *to burn, to be hot.*

תַּחֲרָה *to emulate, vie, contend.* Strictly an uncommon conjugation, (after the form תִּרְגַּל, תַּרְגֵּם,) from חָרָה Hithpa. *to become angry,* from jealousy or envy, (comp. in Syr. Ethpe. *to contend.*) Jer. 12:5 אֵיךְ תְּתַחֲרֶה אֶת־הַסּוּסִים *how canst thou contend with horses?* 22:15 כִּי אַתָּה מְתַחֲרֶה בָאֶרֶז *because thou viest* (with others) *in cedar houses.*

תַּחַשׁ m. found only in the connexion עוֹר תַּחַשׁ *tahash skin* or *leather,* Num. 4:6 ff. Plur. עֹרֹת תְּחָשִׁים *tahash skins,* Ex. 25:5. 26:14. 35:23. 39:

34. and in the same sense simply תַּחַשׁ Num. 4:25. Ezek. 16:10. It has been thought to be the name of an animal, or of a colour, (like שָׁנִי, תְּכֵלֶת,) or of a preparation of leather, (like *morocco.*) The first appears to be favoured by the construction of the word, particularly by the use of the plural, and by Ex. 39:34, where תְּחָשִׁים is used as a genitive; (שָׁנִי and תְּכֵלֶת are construed somewhat differently.) But to determine what animal is intended is difficult. Several Hebrew interpreters and the Talmudists explain it by *the weasel, marten;* others, from the similarity of the names, by the Germ. *Dachs, the badger;* but the Arab. תחש تخس and نخس denotes *the dolphin,* under which the ancients may have included *the seal.* (See Faber's Archäologie der Hebräer, p. 115. Beckmann ad Antigonum Carystium, cap. 60.) *Seal skins* would certainly give a very good sense. All the ancient versions make it a colour; e. g. Sept. ὑακίνθινα; Aqu. Symm. ἰάνθινα; Chald. and Syr. *crimson;* Arab. *pelles nigræ* or *cæruleæ;* and Bochart coincides with them, (Hieroz. T. I. p. 989.) A. Th. Hartmann (Th. 3. p. 230.) thinks it to denote a preparation of leather, namely, *red morocco.*—It occurs as the proper name of a person Gen. 22:24, which slightly favours the first interpretation.

תַּחַת m. 1. *what is under* or *below.* Hence מִתַּחַת Ex. 20:4. Josh. 2:11. and תַּחַת as an accus. used adverbially, *below, beneath.* In the const. state used as a prep. (1.) *under.* Often in composition as (a.) מִתַּחַת *from under.* Ex. 6:6. (b.) מִתַּחַת לְ *beneath, under, below.* Gen. 1:7 מִתַּחַת לָרָקִיעַ *beneath the firmament.* Ex. 30:4. also in a geographical sense, Gen. 35:8. 1 Sam. 7:11. without לְ, Ezek. 42:9. Job 26:5. (c.) תַּחַת לְ i. q. תַּחַת *under.* Cant. 2:6. (d.) אֶל תַּחַת *under;* with the accessory idea of direction to a place, Zech. 3:10. sometimes without this accessory idea, 1 Sam. 21:5.—Some verbs of *pressing down,* or of *motion downwards* generally, appear to be construed with תַּחַת, (as verbs of *shutting* or *closing* with בְּעַד,) in which cases it may be omitted in translating, Amos 2:13 אָנֹכִי מֵעִיק תַּחְתֵּיכֶם *I will press you down.* Job 36:20. 40:12.—With suffixes, it is usually put in the plural, e, g. תַּחְתָּיו, תַּחְתַּי; yet the following forms occur in the singular, תַּחְתֵּנִי. תַּחְתָּם, תַּחְתֶּנָּה, (2.) *between, inter.* Is. 10:4.

2. *what is under a person, a place, spot.* Zech. 6:12 מִתַּחְתָּיו יִצְמָח *from his place he shall shoot up.* Comp. Ex. 10:23. Hence (1.) as an accus. used adverbially, *on* or *in the place* or *spot.* Ex. 16:29 שְׁבוּ אִישׁ תַּחְתָּיו *continue each in his place.* 1 Sam. 14:9. Judg. 7:21. 2 Sam. 2:23. 7:10. 1 Chr. 17:9. Job 36:16 רַחַב לֹא מוּצָק תַּחְתֶּיהָ *to a broad place, where is no straitness.* (2.) *in the place of, instead of, loco.* Lev. 16:32. Est. 2:17. Ps. 45:17 תַּחַת אֲבֹתֶיךָ יִהְיוּ בָנֶיךָ *instead of thy fathers shall be thy sons.* (3.) *for, in exchange for, in compensation for.* Gen. 30:15. 1 K. 21:2. 1 Sam. 2:20. תַּחַת מָה *wherefore?* Jer. 5:19. Hence תַּחַת אֲשֶׁר as a conj. (a.) *instead that.* Deut. 28:62. (b.) *because that.* Deut. 21:14. 2 K. 22:17. תַּחַת כִּי *idem,* Deut. 4:37. Also simply תַּחַת *because,* before an infin. Is. 60:15 תַּחַת הֱיוֹתֵךְ עֲזוּבָה *because thou wast forsaken.* Job 34:26 תַּחַת רְשָׁעִים for תַּחַת הֱיוֹתָם ר׳ *because they are wicked.*

3. proper name of a station of the Israelites in the wilderness. Once Num. 33:26.

תְּחוֹת Chald. *idem.* Dan. 4:11 [4:14] מִן־תְּחוֹתוֹהִי *from under it.*

תַּחְתִּי m. ־יָּה and ־ית f. denom. from תַּחַת *low, inferior.* Ps. 86:13. Job 41:16. Gen. 6:16. תַּחְתִּיּוֹת אֶרֶץ *the lower* or *lowest parts of the earth, inferiora, infima terræ,* i. e. hades, Is. 44:23. Ps. 139:15. In the same sense אֶרֶץ תַּחְתִּיּוֹת liter. *terra inferiorum,* Ezek. 26:20. 32:18, 24. comp. בּוֹר תַּחְתִּיּוֹת *the lowest pit,* Ps. 88:7. Lam. 3:55.

תַּחְתּוֹן, fem. תַּחְתּוֹנָה, *idem.* Josh. 18:13. 1 K 6:6.

תִּיכוֹן, m. תִּיכֹנָה f. denom. adj. from תָּוֶךְ, *middle, in the middle.* Ex. 26:28. Ezek. 42:6.

תֵּימָא Is. 21:14. Jer. 25:23. and **תֵּמָא** Job 6:19. proper name of a country and people in the northern part of Arabia Deserta, on the borders of the Syrian desert, so called from *Thema*, a son of Ishmael, (Gen. 25:15.)

תֵּימָן m. strictly *what lies to the right*, (comp. יָמִין ,יָמַן;) hence

1. *the south.* (Comp. the note under אָחוֹר no. 2.) Job 9:9. תֵּימָנָה *towards the south*, Ex. 26:18, 35. 27:9.

2. poetically for *the south wind.* Ps. 78:26. Cant. 4:16. Here of the fem. gen. scil. רוּחַ. Comp. צָפוֹן.

3. a city, district and people in the east of Idumea, named after תֵּימָן a grandson of Esau. Gen. 36:11, 15. Jer. 49:7, 20. Ezek. 25:13. Hab. 3:3. Obad. 9. (as the name of a people, masc. Obad. 9.) The Temanites were celebrated for their wisdom and their proverbs, (Jer. 49:7. Obad. 8. Bar. 3:22, 23.) hence the choice of Eliphaz the Temanite, as one of the speakers in the book of Job, chap. 2:11. 22:1. The patronymic תֵּימָנִי occurs further in Gen. 36:34.

תִּימָרָה f. dec. XI. a. found only in the phrase תִּימְרוֹת עָשָׁן *pillars of smoke,* Cant. 3:6. Joel 3:3. [2:30.] (In Talmud. תִּמֵּר *to mount up straight like a pillar*, spoken of smoke; תִּמְרָא *a pillar of smoke; columna* solis vel lunæ orientis. Arab. تَامُور *a tower.* Kindred with תֹּמֶר ,תָּמָר *a palm-tree.*)

תִּירוֹשׁ and **תִּירשׁ** m. dec. I. *new wine, must.* Gen. 27:28 אֶרֶץ דָּגָן וְתִירוֹשׁ *a land of corn and wine,* Deut. 33:28. 2 K. 18:32. Is. 36:17. Root יָרַשׁ *to seize* (the head), hence in Syr. ܬܺܝܪܳܘܫ *new wine.* liter. *intoxicating drink.*

תִּירָס m. Gen. 10:2. name of a northern tribe of the race of Japheth. The similarity of the names suggests to us *Thrace;* and this explanation has been adopted by Josephus, Jerome, Jonathan, and the Jerusalem Targum. See Bocharti Phaleg, Lib. III. cap. 2. p. 151 ff.

תַּיִשׁ m. plur. תְּיָשִׁים, dec. VI. *a buck, he-goat.* Prov. 30:31. Gen. 30:35. 32:15. (Arab. تَيْس *a he-goat, roe-buck.*)

תֹּךְ m. *oppression, violence.* Ps. 10:7. 55:12. Written in full תּוֹךְ 72:14. Root תָּכַךְ q.v.

תָּכָה found only in Pu. according to the Jewish interpreters, *to be joined, connected;* perhaps better *to rest, to be encamped,* after the Arab. تكأ conj. VIII. Hence Deut. 33:3 וְהֵם תֻּכּוּ לְרַגְלֶךָ *and they are encamped at thy feet,* scil. the Israelites at the foot of Mount Sinai. Others read תָּכוּ *they abide,* (from תוך Syr. *to continue, abide,*) hence the whole clause, *and they* (*the saints*) *abide by thy host.*

I. **תְּכוּנָה** f. verbal from כּוּן, dec. X. *a place, seat.* Job 23:3.

II. **תְּכוּנָה** f. verbal from תָּכַן, dec. X.

1. *arrangement, structure,* Ezek. 43:11. i. q. תָּכְנִית verse 10.

2. *costliness, costly apparatus.* Nah. 2:10. Comp. תָּכְנִית no. 2.

תֻּכִּיִּים masc. plur. 1 K. 10:22. also תּוּכִּיִּים 2 Chr. 9:21. according to the Targ. Syr. Arab. Jerome and the Jewish interpreters, *peacocks;* according to the conjecture of others, *pheasants,* which are common in Arabia Felix, where Ophir appears to be situated. It is in favour of the first interpretation, that the peacock on the Malabar coast is called *Togei.* The word appears to be a foreign one, and is found in none of the kindred dialects. The Greeks have the name ταὼς or ταῶς in common with the Persians and Arabians, who call *the peacock* طاوس, hence the Chald.

מים. See Bocharti Hieroz. T. II. p. 135 ff.

תָּכַךְ an obsolete root, *to oppress, rob,* i. q. עָשַׁק, גָּזַל. (Chald. *damno affecit, multavit.* Syr. ܬܟܟ i. q. Heb. גָּזַל.) Hence תֹּךְ, תְּכָכִים.

תְּכָכִים masc. plur. verbal from obsol. תָּכַךְ, *oppressions,* particularly of the poor. Prov. 29 : 13 אִישׁ תְּכָכִים *the oppressor* (of the poor), *the hard-hearted rich man.* Sept. δανειστής. Vulg. *creditor.* In the parallel passage, Prov. 22 : 2, we find simply עָשִׁיר *the rich man,* but with the accessory idea of *oppression.*

תִּכְלָה f. verbal from כָּלָה, *completeness, perfection.* Ps. 119 : 96. Others: *hope* or *confidence,* or *the object thereof,* from תְּכַל Syr. ܬܟܠ *to hope, trust.*

תַּכְלִית f. verbal from כָּלָה, dec. I.

1. *completion, perfection.* Job 11 : 7. Ps. 139 : 22 תַּכְלִית שִׂנְאָה *the perfection of hatred,* i. e. extreme hatred.

2. *an end.* Neh. 3 : 21. Job 26 : 10. עַד תַּכְלִית אוֹר עִם חֹשֶׁךְ *to where light ends in darkness.* 27 : 3 לְכָל־תַּכְלִית הוּא חוֹקֵר *into every end,* i. e. into all depths, *he searches.*

תְּכֵלֶת f. *bluish purple,* also *cloth* or *thread coloured therewith.* Ex. 26 : 4, 31. Num. 4 : 6 ff. Ezek. 23 : 6. 27 : 7, 24. Sept. generally ὑάκινθος, ὑακίνθινος, i. e. *bluish purple, violet coloured.* So Jerome, Vulg. This colour was procured from the juice of the חִלָּזוֹן, a purple shell-fish in the Mediterranean Sea, *conchylium* of the ancients, *helix ianthina,* Linn. This word is almost constantly joined with אַרְגָּמָן, *reddish purple.* See Bocharti Hieroz. T. II. 720—742. T. III. 655—686. of the Leips. edit. Braun de Vestitu Sacerdot. p. 187—200. A. Th. Hartmann's Hebräerin, Th. 3. p. 128 ff. Luther: *yellow silk,* after Aben Ezra and R. Salomo, who ascribe to the חִלָּזוֹן *a yellow colour.*

תָּכַן *to weigh,* metaphorically *to prove, try, examine accurately.* Prov. 16 : 2 תֹּכֵן רוּחוֹת יְהוָה *Jehovah trieth the spirits.* 21 : 2. 24. 12.

Niph. liter. *to be weighed out;* hence *to be levelled,* spoken of a way, and metaphorically *to be right,* spoken of an action, (like יָשַׁר.) Ezek. 18 : 25, 29 לֹא יִתָּכֵן דֶּרֶךְ אֲדֹנָי *the way of the Lord is not right.* 33 : 17, 20. 1 Sam. 2 : 3. Comp. תָּכַן.

Pi. תִּכֵּן 1. *to weigh out, to level,* e. g. horizontal objects. Job 28 : 25.

2. *to measure* or *mete out.* Is. 40 : 12 *who meted out heaven with the span?* Parall. שָׁקַל, מָדַד.

3. *to fix, establish.* Ps. 75 : 4.

4. *to lead, direct.* Is. 40 : 13 מִי תִכֵּן אֶת־רוּחַ יְהוָה *who directed the spirit of the Lord?* Parall. *who was his counsellor and taught him?*

Pu. part. *weighed out,* spoken of money. 2 K. 12 : 12.

Deriv. out of course תְּכוּנָה no. II. מַתְכֹּנֶת.

תֹּכֶן m. verbal from תָּכַן.

1. *a task, portion of labour measured out, pensum.* Ex. 5 : 18.

2. *a measure.* Ezek. 45 : 11.

תָּכְנִית f. verbal from תָּכַן.

1. *a measure, pattern, structure.* Ezek. 43 : 10.

2. *an ornament, beauty.* Ezek. 28 : 12 *one perfecting beauty,* i. e. perfect in beauty.

תַּכְרִיךְ m. Est. 8 : 15. *a mantle, a wide garment,* here *stola Medica talaris* of the king. (In Chald. *idem.*) Root כרך in Syr. and Chald. *to wrap about, to cover.*

תֵּל m. with suff. תִּלִּי, verbal from תָּלַל, dec. VIII. b. *a hill.* Josh. 11 : 13. Particularly *a heap of stones* or *rubbish,* Deut. 13 : 17. Josh. 8 : 28. Jer. 49 : 2. It occurs in composition with the following names of places; (1.) תֵּל אָבִיב (*heap of ears of corn*) Ezek. 3 : 15. a place in Mesopotamia, perhaps *Thelabba* on d'Anville's Map, l' Euphrate et le Tigre, between 36° and 37½ of longitude, and 53° and 54° of latitude. (2.) תֵּל חַרְשָׁא (*hill of the wood,* see חֹרֶשׁ,) a place in Babylonia. Ezra 2 : 59. Nehem. 7 : 61.

(3.) תֵּל מֶלַח (*a hill of salt*) likewise a place in Babylonia. Ezra 2:59. Neh. 7:61. (Names of places beginning with *Tel* are common in Assyria, Mesopotamia, and Syria.)

תָּלָא i.q. תָּלָה *to hang, to be suspended*, found only in the part. pass. Deut. 28:66 *thy life shall be suspended before thee*, i.e. it shall be in constant danger. Hos. 11:7 עַמִּי תְּלוּאִים לִמְשׁוּבָתִי *my people are inclined to apostacy.* So in Greek ἐξαρτάομαι τινὸς πράγματος, *to be addicted to any thing.*

תְּלָאָה f. verbal from לָאָה, (according to its form, from לוּא, comp. תְּעָלָה from עָלָה,) *labour, trouble, distress.* Ex. 18:8. Num. 20:14. Neh. 9:32.

תַּלְאוּבָה f. *dryness, drought.* Once Hos. 13:5 אֶרֶץ תַּלְאֻבוֹת *a dry land.* Root לָאַב Arab. لاب and لهب *to burn, to be dry.*

תְּלַאשָּׂר 2 K. 19:12. and **תְּלַשָּׂר** Is. 37:12. proper name of a city in Syria or Mesopotamia. It occurs besides only in the Jerusalem Targum Gen. 14:1, 9, for the Heb. אֶלָּסָר, and in the same Targum and Jonathan Gen. 10:12, for the Heb. רֶסֶן. But these passages do not help us to determine its locality. If differently pointed, we might explain the first syllable תֵּל by *hill*, which occurs in the names of several Syrian and Mesopotamian cities; (comp. תֵּל.) The latter part might then be collated with *Sharra*, in the desert of Gezira, half a mile from the Euphrates.

תִּלְבֹּשֶׁת f. verbal from לָבַשׁ, *a garment, clothing.* Is. 59:17.

תְּלַג Chald. *snow*, i.q. Heb. שֶׁלֶג. Dan. 7:9.

תִּלְגַּת פִּלְסֶר see תִּגְלַת פ׳.

תָּלָה *to hang, to suspend.* (In Chald. and Syr. *idem.*) 2 Sam. 18:10. Job 26:7. תָּלָה עַל הָעֵץ *to hang on a stake, to crucify*, a mode of executing criminals among the Israelites, Deut. 21:22. Persians, Est. 7:10. 5:14. and Egyptians, Gen. 40:19.

Niph. pass. Lam. 5:12.

Pi. i.q. Kal. Ezek. 27:10, 11.

Deriv. תְּלִי.

תְּלוּנָה f. verbal from לוּן no. II. dec. X. found only in the plur. *murmurings.* Ex. 16:7 ff. Num. 14:27.

תְּלִי m. verbal from תָּלָה, dec. VI. l. *a quiver.* Once Gen. 27:3. So all the ancient versions except Onk. and Syr. which render it *a sword.* The root תָּלָה *to hang up*, and the context favour the former signification.

תְּלִיתַי Chald. (denom. adj. from תְּלָת *three*,) *third.* Dan. 2:39.

תָּלַל *to raise* or *heap up.* Part. pass. תָּלוּל *high, exalted, aggestus*, Ezek. 17:22. Deriv. תֵּל *a hill, a heap.*—For the form הֵתַל, see under הָתַל.

תֶּלֶם m. dec. VI. a. *a furrow* (for seed). Job 21:38. 39:10. Ps. 65:11. In Arab. *idem.*

תַּלְמִיד m. verbal from לָמַד, *a disciple, scholar.* 1 Chr. 25:8. (In Syr. and Arab. *idem.*)

תָּלַע found only in the Pu. part. מְתֻלָּע, denom. from תּוֹלָע, *clothed in crimson.* Nah. 2:4.—For מַתְלְעוֹת, see under מ.

תַּלְפִּיּוֹת plur. fem. *an armoury, a place where weapons were hung up*, as on the turrets and walls of eastern cities. Cant. 4:4. comp. Ezek. 27:10, 11. Prob, compounded of תֵּל (from תָּלָה *to hang up*,) and פִּיּוֹת *ora*, i.e. acies, comp. פֶּה no. 3.

תְּלַאשָּׂר see תְּלַשָּׂר.

תְּלָת, fem. תְּלָתָא, Chald. *three*, i.q. Heb. שָׁלשׁ. יוֹם תְּלָתָא *the third day*, Ezra 6:15. Plur. תְּלָתִין, *thirty*, Dan. 6:8, 13.

תַּלְתְּ, emph. תַּלְתָּא. *idem.* Dan. 5:16, 29.

תַּלְתִּי m. *third.* Dan. 5:7. The form is in imitation of the Hebrew. Elsewhere written תְּלִיתַי.

תַּלְתַּלִּים masc. plur. *hanging down, flowing,* spoken of the hair. Cant. 5: 11. (In Arab. تَلْتَل *agitavit, commovit, concussit.*)

תָּם, fem. תַּמָּה, verbal adj. from תָּמַם dec. VIII. a. *integer*, but used only in a moral sense, *innocent, blameless, upright, righteous,* i. q. יָשָׁר Job 1:1. 8:20. 9:20, 21, 22. Gen. 25:26 וְיַעֲקֹב אִישׁ תָּם יֹשֵׁב אֹהָלִים *and Jacob was a virtuous man, keeping at home,* in opposition to the ruder character of his brother. Used abstractly in the neuter gender, *innocency, uprightness,* Ps. 37:37. Fem. תַּמָּתִי *my innocent one,* a word of endearment to one beloved, Cant. 5:2. 6:9.

תַּם only with ה paragogic תַּמָּה, Chald. *there,* i. q. שָׁם. Ezra 5:17. 6:6, 12.

תָּמִים masc. plur. a contraction of תְּאוֹמִים *doubled, double.* Ex. 26:24. 36:29. (See תָּאַם.)

תֹּם m. (once תּוֹם Prov. 10:9.) before Makkeph תָּם, with suff. תֻּמִּי, verbal from תָּמַם, dec. VIII. d.

1. *fulness, completion.* Is. 47:9 בְּתֻמָּם *in their fulness.* Hence

2. i. q. שָׁלוֹם *safety, security, prosperity.* Job 21:23 בְּעֶצֶם תֻּמּוֹ *in the midst of his prosperity.* Ps. 41:13.

3. in a moral sense, *innocency, integrity, uprightness.* תָּם־לֵבָב *integrity of heart,* Gen. 20:5, 6. הָלַךְ בְּתֹם Prov. 10:9 and בְּתֻמִּי Ps. 26:1. *to walk uprightly.* —1 K. 22:34 *he stretched the bow* לְתֻמּוֹ *in his innocency,* i. e. without aiming at any one. 2 Sam. 15:11 הֹלְכִים לְתֻמָּם *going in their innocency,* i. e. without being privy to the plans of Absalom.

4. plur. תֻּמִּים *truth,* (Sept. ἀλήθεια,) joined with אוּרִים *light,* i. e. revelation, (Sept. δήλωσις,) prob. oracular images in the breast-plate of the high-priest. See אוּרִים.

תֵּמָא see **תֵּימָא**.

תֻּמָּה fem. of תֹּם, dec. X. *innocency, uprightness, integrity.* Job 2:3, 9. 27:5. 31:6.

תָּמַהּ *to wonder, to be astonished;* construed with אֶל *at* any thing. Ecc. 5:7. Is. 13:8 אִישׁ אֶל רֵעֵהוּ יִתְמָהוּ *they look astonished one at another;* comp. Gen. 34:22. Often with the accessory idea of *fear,* Ps. 48:6. Job 26:11. Jer. 4:9.

Hithpa. *idem.* Hab. 1:5.

Deriv. תִּמָּהוֹן.

תְּמַהּ m. Chald. *a wonder, miracle,* τέρας. Dan. 3:32, 33. 6:28.

תִּמָּהוֹן m. verbal from תָּמַהּ dec. III. d. *astonishment, fear, terror.* Deut. 28:28, (where it is joined with לֵבָב.) Zech. 12:4.

תַּמּוּז m. a deity of the Syrians, which was likewise worshipped by mourning women among the Hebrews. Ezek. 8:14. It is the proper Syriac name for the *Adonis* of the Greeks, (i. q. אָדוֹן *lord.*) See Creuzer's Symbolik des Alterthums, Th. 2. p. 86 ff.—Moses Maimonides (More Nebochim, III. c. 29. ed. Buxtorf,) explains it, after a story of the Sabians, for an idolatrous priest who was murdered by his king, because he recommended the worship of the stars and the constellations. At his death, it is said, all the idols of the whole earth came together in one night into a Babylonian temple to mourn for him. See Carpzov Apparat. ad Antiquit. Sac. Cod. p. 492.

תְּמוֹל m. adv. *yesterday.* Very frequently connected with שִׁלְשֹׁם *the day before yesterday,* for *formerly.* See שִׁלְשֹׁם. Job 8:9 תְמוֹל אֲנַחְנוּ *we are of yesterday, hesterni sumus,* as if it were an adjective. Synonymous with אֶתְמוֹל.

תְּמוּנָה f. dec. X. Root מִין prob. i. q. Arab. مان med. Je *to lie, deceive.*

1. *an image, figure, likeness;* often joined with פֶּסֶל. Ex. 20:4. Deut. 4:16, 23, 25.—Job 4:16 תְּמוּנָה לְנֶגֶד עֵינָי *an image* (an airy form) *moved before mine eyes.*

2. *sight, appearance, form,* (of God.) Num. 12:2. Ps. 17:15.

תְּמוּרָה f. (verbal from מוּר Hiph. *to exchange,*) dec. X.

1. *a changing, exchange.* Ruth 4:7. Job 28:17 וּתְמוּרָתָהּ כְּלִי פָז *and the exchange of it (of wisdom) shall (not) be for a jewel of fine gold.* Hence *the thing exchanged,* Lev. 27:10, 33.

2. *recompence, restitution, compensatio.* Job 15:31 כִּי שָׁוְא תִּהְיֶה תְמוּרָתוֹ *for vanity shall be his recompence.* 20:18 כְּחֵיל תְּמוּרָתוֹ וְלֹא יַעֲלֹס *as substance to be restored, he shall not rejoice therein.*

תְּמוּתָה f. verbal from מוּת, *death.* Found only in the phrase בְּנֵי־תְמוּתָה *a son of death,* i.e. one condemned to die, Ps. 79:11. 102:21.

תָּמִיד m. 1. subst. *constant continuance.* Used only as a genitive after other nouns, (comp. e.g. קֹדֶשׁ no. 1.) for a periphrasis of the adjective *constant, continual;* as אַנְשֵׁי תָמִיד *men hired constantly,* Ezek. 39:14. עֹלַת הַתָּמִיד *the continual,* i.e. the daily, or morning and evening, *burnt-offering,* Num. 28:6, 10, 15, 23, 24. לֶחֶם הַתָּמִיד *the continual bread,* i.e. the shew-bread, Num. 4:7.

2. i.q. עֹלַת הַתָּמִיד *the daily offering.* Dan. 8:11, 12, 13. 11:31.

3. as an adv. *constantly, always, for ever.* Ps. 16:8. 25:15. 34:2. The root מוּד is prob. kindred with נוּד, נָגַד, and signifies i.q. מוּט *to move along, to proceed, continue,* hence *continuance;* comp. עַד from עָדָה, דּוּר, and the Chald. תְּדִירָא from דּוּר.

תָּמִים, fem. תְּמִימָה, verbal adj. from תָּמַם, dec. III. a.

1. *complete, whole.* Lev. 3:9. 25:30. Josh. 10:13.

2. *without blemish, sound, uninjured, integer,* spoken of sacrificial victims. Ex. 12:5. Lev. 1:3. Spoken of persons, *sound, whole,* Prov. 1:12.

3. *perfect.* תְּמִים דֵּעִים *perfect in knowledge,* Job 36:4. 37:16. Ps. 19:8.

4. most frequently in a moral sense, *blameless, innocent, upright.* Gen. 6:9. 17:1. תְּמִימֵי־דָרֶךְ *they that are of a blameless walk,* Ps. 119:1. תָּמִים עִם אֵל *blameless towards God,* i.e. entirely devoted to him, Deut. 18:13. Ps. 18:24. (In 2 Sam. 22:24, with לְ.) Comp. שָׁלֵם nos. 4, 5.

5. subst. *innocency, uprightness, sincerity,* as if the neuter of the adj. Josh. 24:14. Judg. 9:16, 19. Hence הָלַךְ בְּתָמִים Ps. 84:12. and הֹלֵךְ תָּמִים Ps. 15:2. *to walk uprightly.* 1 Sam. 14:41 הָבָה תָמִים *give truth.*

תָּמַךְ, fut. יִתְמֹךְ.

1. *to lay hold of;* construed with an accus. Gen. 48:17. with בְּ, Prov. 28:17. 5:5.

2. *to hold, to hold fast,* construed with an accus. Am. 1:5, 8. Metaphorically Prov. 4:4.

3. *to obtain, acquire,* e.g. honour. Prov. 11:16. 29:23.

4. *to keep up, to support,* construed with בְּ. Ex. 17:12 *they supported his hands.* Spoken of God, *to support, uphold,* construed with בְּ, Ps. 41:13. 63:9. with an accus. Ps. 16:5.

5. recipr. as if in Niph. *to hold together, to follow each other.* Job 36:17 דִּין וּמִשְׁפָּט יִתְמֹכוּ *crime and punishment follow each other.* Comp. אָחַז and לָכַד Hithpa.

Niph. pass. *to be holden.* Prov. 5:22.

תָּמַם, fut. יִתֹּם, rarely יִתּוֹם Ezek. 47:12. יֵתַם Ezek. 24:11. אֵיתָם Ps. 19:14. plur. in pause יִתָּמּוּ Ps. 102:28.

1. *to be finished, completed.* 1 K. 6:22. 7:22.—עַד תֻּמָּם *till they were finished,* Deut. 31:24, 30.

2. trans. *to complete, finish,* i.q. כָּלָה no. 1. Ps. 64:7 תַּמְנוּ *we have completed it.* Hence with לְ before an infin. *to finish an action,* Josh 5:8. 3:17. 4:1, 11.

3. *to be ended, to be past, to cease,* spoken particularly of time. Gen. 47:18. Ps. 102:28 שְׁנוֹתֶיךָ לֹא יִתָּמּוּ *thy years cease not.* Ezek. 47:12 וְלֹא יִתֹּם פִּרְיוֹ *and the fruit thereof shall not cease.* Deut. 34:8.

4. *to be complete* or *in full number.* 1 Sam. 16:11 הֲתַמּוּ הַנְּעָרִים *are thy children all here?* Num. 17:13. Gen. 47:18 אִם תַּם הַכֶּסֶף אֶל אֲדֹנִי *if our money is all spent* (and given) *to my lord.* Jer. 27:8.

5. *to be consumed*, i. q. כָּלָה no. 4. Jer. 36 : 23. 37 : 21. Gen. 47 : 15.

6. *to be destroyed, to perish*, i. q. כָּלָה no. 6. Num. 32 : 13 עַד תֹּם כָּל־הַדּוֹר *till the whole generation was destroyed*. Josh. 5 : 6. Jer. 27 : 8. עַד תֻּמּוֹ 1 K. 14 : 10. and עַד תֻּמָּם Deut. 2 : 15. Josh. 8 : 24. *to his* or *their entire destruction*. (Elsewhere עַד־כַּלֵּה, see כָּלָה no. 4.)

7. *to be innocent, blameless, to appear innocent*. Ps. 19 : 14. Comp. Hiph. no. 6.

Niph. fut. plur. יִתַּמּוּ, *to be destroyed, annihilated*, i. q. Kal no. 6. Num. 14 : 35. Ps. 104 : 35. Jer. 14 : 15.

Note. The fut. יִתֹּם has also been considered as a fut. Niph. (comp. יְרוֹמוּ, יֵרוֹמוּ,) but this form has the significations only of Kal nos. 1, 2, 3, 4.—יִתַּמּוּ on the contrary is rather passive like no. 6. *to be destroyed*. There is another plural form יִתְּמוּ (Deut. 34 : 8. Ps. 102 : 28,) which is evidently Kal. See Kal no. 3.

Hiph. הֵתֵם (once infin. הֲתִימְךָ, as if from תּוּם,) fut. יָתֵם.

1. intrans. *to be complete* or *in full number*. Dan. 8. 23 כְּהָתֵם הַפֹּשְׁעִים *when their sins shall be full*, liter. *when they shall be full sinners*. 9 : 24 Keri. Ezek. 24 : 10 הָתֵם הַבָּשָׂר *that the flesh may be ready*.

2. trans. *to complete, execute, finish*. 2 Sam. 20 : 18.

3. *to end, leave off, cease*. Is. 33 : 1 כַּהֲתִימְךָ שׁוֹדֵד *when thou hast ceased to spoil*.

4. *to cause to cease*; construed with מִן, *to remove*, Ezek. 22 : 15.

5. *to count up*, i. q. שִׁלֵּם. 2 K. 22 : 4.

6. in a moral sense, *to keep blameless* or *upright*. Job 22 : 3 כִּי תַתֵּם דְּרָכֶיךָ *if thou keepest thy way blameless*.

Hithpa. הִתַּמֵּם *to treat with uprightness*, construed with עִם. Ps. 18 : 26.

Deriv. תֹּם, תָּם, תָּמִים, מְתֹם.

תֵּמָן see **תֵּימָן**.

תִּמְנָה proper name of a city in the tribe of Judah. Josh. 15 : 10, 57. 2 Chr. 28 : 18. In Greek Θάμνα.

תִּמְנָע f. proper name of the concubine of Eliphaz, the son of Esau. Gen. 36 : 12, 22. 1 Chr. 1 : 39. She gave name to one of the Edomitish tribes, Gen. 36 : 40. 1 Chr. 1 : 51.

תִּמְנָתָה f. proper name of a city in the territory of the Philistines, Judg. 14 : 1. which was assigned to the tribe of Dan, Josh. 19 : 43. In Greek Θαμναθὰ, 1 Macc. 9 : 50. Hence the gentile noun תִּמְנִי Judg. 15 : 6.

תִּמְנַת חֶרֶס Judg. 2 : 9. for which we find תִּמְנַת־סֶרַח Josh. 19 : 50. 24 : 30. a city in Mount Ephraim. See Relandi Palæstina, p. 1043.

תֶּמֶס m. verbal from מָסַס, *a dissolving, melting, wasting away*. Ps. 58 : 9. Comp. under the art. שַׁבְּלוּל.

תָּמָר m. dec. IV. a. 1. *a palm-tree, a date-palm, phœnix dactylifera*. Joel 1 : 12.—עִיר הַתְּמָרִים *the city of palms*, see under the art. עִיר.

2. proper name of a place on the southern boundary of Palestine. Ezek. 47 : 19. 48 : 28.

תֹּמֶר m. *a palm-tree*, or perhaps *a pillar*. Comp. מִקְשָׁה. Jer. 10 : 5.

תִּמֹּרָה f. plur. תִּמֹּרִים Ezek. 41 : 18. and תִּמֹּרוֹת, dec. X. *a palm-branch*, an ornament in architecture, comp. תָּמָר. 1 K. 6 : 29, 32, 35. Ezek. 41 : 18, 19.

תַּמְרוּק m. plur. תַּמְרוּקִים, verbal from מָרַק, dec. I.

1. *a purification, cleansing*. Est. 2 : 12. The maidens received into the harem of the Persian king underwent a course of purification and anointing with perfumes for twelve months; hence

2. *precious ointments for purification*. Est. 2 : 3, 9.

3. metaphorically *means of purification* or *amendment*. Prov. 20 : 30 Keri.

I. **תַּמְרוּרִים** masc. plur. verbal from מָרַר, *bitternesses*. בְּכִי תַמְרוּרִים *bitter weeping*, Jer. 31 : 15. 6 : 26. Hence as an adv. *bitterly*, Hos. 12 : 15.

II. **תַּמְרוּרִים** masc. plur. *erect pillars*, probably for way-marks. Jer. 31 : 21.

Comp. תִּימָרָה and the Arab. تامور ,تامورة *a tower.*

תַּמְרִיק i. q. תַּמְרוּק Prov. 20:30 Keth.

תַּן or **תָּן** m. found only in the plur. תַּנִּים and תַּנִּין, *a jackal, a wild dog,* otherwise called אִי. A mournful noise is attributed to it, (Job 30:29. Mic. 1:8.) it inhabits desolate places, (Is. 13:22. 43:20. 34:13.) hence מְקוֹם תַּנִּים Ps. 44:20. and מְעוֹן תַּנִּים Jer. 9:10. 10:22. 49:33. *the dwelling of jackals,* i. e. the desert. In Jer. 14:6, they are said to snuff up the air; and in Lam. 4:3, to suckle their young. (In Arab. تينان *a wolf,* a kindred species of animal. Comp. the articles פֶּרֶא ,אִיִּם.) According to Bochart (Hieroz. II. p. 429.) the תַּנִּים are the same with the תַּנִּינִים *great serpents, sea monsters,* like לִוְיָתָן; but with this several of the notices given above do not agree; e. g. Lam. 4:3, where the whale race cannot be intended, for fierce ravenous animals are certainly spoken of in that verse.

תָּנָה i. q. נָתַן *to give, to distribute presents,* in order to hire aid. Hos. 8:10 גַּם כִּי יִתְנוּ בַגּוֹיִם *although they give gifts among the nations.* Others read יִתְּנוּ from נָתַן.

Pi. *to praise, to celebrate;* construed with an accus. Judg. 5:11. with לְ, 11:40. (In Chald. תַּנֵּי i. q. סַפֵּר *to relate.* Arab. ثنى conj. IV. *laude celebravit.*)

Hiph. i. q. Kal. Hos. 8:9 אֶפְרַיִם הִתְנוּ אֲהָבִים *Ephraim hires foreign alliances.*

Deriv. אֶתְנָה ,אֶתְנָן.

תַּנָּה found only in the plur. תַּנּוֹת f. Mal. 1:3. according to the Sept. Syr. *dwellings,* comp. Arab. ثناة *a dwelling.* According to others, i. q. תַּנִּים *jackals.*

תְּנוּאָה f. verbal from נוא, dec. X.

1. *a forsaking, withdrawing.* Num. 14:34 וִידַעְתֶּם אֶת־תְּנוּאָתִי *ye shall know what it is for me to forsake you.*

2. *hostility.* Job 33:10 הֵן תְּנוּאוֹת עָלַי יִמְצָא *behold, he seeketh hostility against me.* (Root נוא Arab. *to rise up as an enemy against* a person.)

תְּנוּבָה f. verbal from נוּב, dec. X. *fruit, produce, increase, proventus.* Deut. 32:13. Judg. 9:11. Lam. 4:9.

תְּנוּךְ m. joined with אֹזֶן, *the tip of the ear.* Ex. 29:20. Lev. 8:23, 24. 14:14. Root תְּנַךְ in Syr. Ethpe. *desiit, defecit.*

תְּנוּמָה f. verbal from נוּם, dec. X. *sleep, slumber.* Job 33:15. Particularly from laziness or inactivity, Prov. 6:10. 24:33. Ps. 132:4.

תְּנוּפָה f. verbal from נוּף, dec. X.

1. *a moving this way and that way, a shaking, waving;* e.g. of the hand, Is. 19:16, (as a gesture of threatening.) 30:32 מִלְחֲמוֹת תְּנוּפָה *tumultuous wars, bella agitationis.*

2. *a waving* or *moving this way and that way before Jehovah,* a ceremony in the consecration of offerings; hence *what is consecrated in this manner;* e.g. חֲזֵה תְּנוּפָה *the wave-breast,* Ex. 29:27. Lev. 7:34. זְהַב הַתְּנוּפָה *the consecrated gold,* Ex. 38:24.

תַּנּוּר m. *a baking oven.* Ex. 7:28. [8:3.] Lev. 2:4. 7:9. 11:35. In the east it often consists only of a large conical pot, which is first heated and then cakes are baked on its sides. Jahn's Bibl. Archäol. Th. I. B. 1. p. 213. and B. 2. p. 182. Beckmann's Beyträge zur Geschichte der Erfindungen, Th. 11. p. 419. In a similiar way the κλίβανος of the Greeks appears to have been formed. See Schneider sub voce. (Prob. compounded of אַתּוּן Chald. *an oven* and נוּרָא *fire.*)

תַּנְחוּמִים masc. plur. verbal from נָחַם, dec. I.

1. *consolations, comfort.* Is. 66:11. Jer. 16:7.

2. *pity, compassion.* Ps. 94:19.

תַּנְחוּמוֹת f. plur. verbal from נָחַם, dec. X. *consolations.* Job 15:11. 21:2.

תַּנִּים masc. sing. Ezek. 29:3. *a great serpent, a sea monster,* i. q. תַּנִּין, which is the reading of several MSS.

תַּנִּין m. plur. תַּנִּינִים, dec. I.

1. *a great fish, a sea monster.* Gen. 1:21. Job 7:12. Is. 27:1.

2. *a serpent,* Ex. 7:9 ff. Deut. 32:33. Ps. 91:13. *a dragon,* Jer. 51:34. also *a crocodile,* comp. Ezek. 29:3. Comp. the article תַּן.

תִּנְיָן Chald. *second.* Dan. 7:5. It is derived from שְׁנָה Chald. תנה *to double.* (The Chaldaic word for *two* is תְּרֵין q. v.)

תִּנְיָנוּת adv. *a second time, again.* Dan. 2:7.

תִּנְשֶׁמֶת f. 1. Lev. 11:30. an unclean quadruped, mentioned in connection with several species of lizards, according to Bochart (Hieroz. T. I. p. 1083.) *the chameleon,* from נָשַׁם *to breathe,* it being supposed by the ancients to live solely on the air which it inhales. Sept. Vulg. *a mole.* Saad. *lacerta Gecko.*

2. Lev. 11:18. Deut. 14:16. an unclean water-fowl. Sept. πορφυρίων, *the sea-gull.* Vulg. *the swan.* Syr. a species of heron. Perhaps *the pelican,* from נָשַׁם, with reference to the *inflation* or *expansion* of its pouch.

תָּעַב in Kal not used. Comp. תָּאַב no. II.

Pi. תִּעֵב 1. *to loathe, abominate, abhor.* Deut. 7:26. Job 9:31. 19:19. Ps. 5:7.

2. *to make to be abhorred, to pollute.* Ezek. 16:25. Is. 49:7 מְתָעֵב־גּוֹי *he that pollutes* or *is supposed to pollute the people,* i. e. the abhorred of the people.

Hiph. *to make abominable* or *shameful.* Ps. 14:1 הִתְעִיבוּ עֲלִילָה *they make their actions abominable,* i. e. they act abominably. Hence without עֲלִילָה in the same sense, 1 K. 21:26. Ezek. 16:52. Comp. הִשְׁחִית, הֵרַע.

Niph. pass. *to be an aversion, abhorrence.* 1 Chr. 21:6. Job 15:16. Is. 14:19.

Deriv. תּוֹעֵבָה.

תָּעָה. fut. יִתְעֶה, apoc. יֵתַע.

1. *to wander about.* Gen. 21:14. 37:15. Ex. 23:4. Construed with an accus. *to wander through* a place, Is. 16:8.—21:4 תָּעָה לְבָבִי *my heart is giddy* or *disquieted.* 28:7 תָּעוּ מִן הַשֵּׁכָר *they are giddy from intoxicating drink.*

2. construed with מִן, *to wander from,* e. g. the commands of God. Ps. 119:110. comp. Prov. 21:16. With מֵעַל יְהֹוָה *from the worship of God,* Ezek. 44:10, 15. with מֵאַחֲרֵי יְהֹוָה Ezek. 14:11. Hence used absolutely, *to go astray,* (from the path of virtue and religion,) Ps. 58:4. Ezek. 48:11. תֹּעֵי לֵבָב Ps. 95:10. and תֹּעֵי רוּחַ *the erring in heart, the foolish,* Is. 29:24. (Chald. טְעָה by a commutation of ת and ט, *to practise idolatry;* in Syr. *to cherish heretical opinions.*)

3. *to be unfortunate, to be wretched;* comp. אָבַד. Prov. 14:22.

Niph. 1. *to stagger, to be giddy.* Is. 19:14.

2. *to err, to go astray,* in a moral sense. Job 15:31.

Hiph. fut. apoc. יַתַע.

1. *to cause to wander,* Job 12:24. Ps. 107:40. *to cause to stagger,* Job 12:25.

2. *to lead astray,* e. g. a flock. Jer. 50:6. Metaphorically *to seduce,* e. g. a people, Is. 3:12. 9:15. particularly to idolatry, 2 K. 21:9. Construed with מִן, *to seduce from* the right way, Is. 63:17.

3. prob. intrans. Jer. 42:20 Keri הִתְעֵיתֶם בְּנַפְשׁוֹתֵיכֶם *ye err at the expense of your lives.* It appears also to be intrans. Prov. 10:17.

Deriv. תּוֹעָה.

תְּעוּדָה f. verbal from עוּד.

1. *a precept* or *doctrine from God, an oracle,* synonymous with תּוֹרָה no. 1. Is. 8:16, 20. See עוּד Hiph. nos. 4, 5.

2. *a law, custom, usage.* Ruth 4:7. Comp. חֹק no. 4.

תְּעָלָה f. const. תְּעָלַת, verbal from עָלָה, (like תְּלָאָה, from לָאָה, perhaps strictly from עָלָה=עוּל;) dec. X.

1. *a channel, trench.* I K. 18:32. Job 38:25 מִי פִלַּג לַשֶּׁטֶף תְּעָלָה *who divided to the shower its channel?* i. e. who led it through the air to all countries? Hence *a conduit, a water-course,* Is. 7:3. 36:2. Ezek. 31:4.

2. *a plaster* or *bandage* for a wound. Jer. 30:13. 46:11. Comp. תְּעָלָה אֲרֻכָה

to lay on a plaster or *bandage*, Jer. 30:17. 33:6.

תַּעֲלוּלִים masc. plur. dec. I.

1. *an evil destiny*, which befals a person. Is. 66:4. See עָלַל no. I. Po.

2. Is. 3:4. i. q. עוֹלָל, עוֹלֵל *a child, a babe*. The abstract form is used for the concrete, like the Germ. *Kinderey-en* for *Kinder*.

תַּעֲלֻמָה f. verbal from עָלַם, dec. X. *what is hid* or *concealed*. Job 28:11. Plur. *secrets*, Job 11:6. Ps. 44:22.

תַּעֲנוּג, plur. ־ִים and וֹת, from עָנַג, dec. I.

1. *pleasure, luxuriousness*. Mic. 2:9. Prov. 19:10.

2. *delight, desire*. Mic. 1:16 בְּנֵי תַּעֲנוּגָיִךְ *the children of thy delight*, i. e. who are thy delight. In reference to sexual desire, Cant. 7:7. Ecc. 2:8.

תַּעֲנִית f. dec. I. *self-mortification, fasting*. Ezra 9:5. See עָנָה no. 3.

תַּעְנָךְ Josh. 21:25. 1 Chr. 7:29. and

תַּעֲנָךְ Josh. 12:21. Judg. 1:27. a city in the tribe of Manasseh, on this side of the Jordan.

תָּעַע in Kal not used.

Pilp. תִּעְתַּע *to mock, deride*. Gen. 27:12. So most of the ancient versions. The signification *to deceive* would suit the context better, and is also well adapted to the derivative תַּעְתֻּעִים. This meaning may be derived from the former, (comp. הֵתֵל *to deride* and *to deceive*;) or may be borrowed from the root תָּעָה *to err*.

Hithpalp. *to mock, deride*. 2 Chr. 36:16.

Deriv. תַּעְתֻּעִים.

תַּעֲצֻמוֹת fem. plur. *strength*. Ps. 68:36. Root עָצַם.

תַּעַר m. with suff. תַּעְרִי, dec. VI. c.

1. *a sharp knife, a razor*. Num. 6:5. 8:7. Is. 7:20.—תַּעַר הַסֹּפֵר *the writer's knife*, prob. used to sharpen the point of his calamus, Jer. 36:23.

2. *the sheath* (of a sword). 1 Sam. 17:51. Ezek. 21:8, 10, 35. Jer. 47:6.—Root prob. עָרָה *to be bare*, Pi. *to make bare, to empty out*, perhaps synonymous with הֵרִיק *to empty out* and *to draw* (a sword from its sheath). Or perhaps *nudans cutem*.—תַּעַר stands for תְּעָרָה a verbal from the conj. Piel. (See Gesenius' Lehrgeb. § 121. p. 508.)

תַּעֲרֻבָה f. verbal from עָרַב no. I. 3. dec. X. *suretiship*. 2 K. 14:14 בְּנֵי תַּעֲרֻבוֹת *hostages*.

תַּעְתֻּעִים masc. plur. Jer. 10:15. 51:18. Spoken of idols, מַעֲשֵׂה תַּעְתֻּעִים Jerome: *opus risu dignum*. Better, *a work of deceit*, see the root תָּעַע.

תֹּף m. plur. תֻּפִּים, dec. VIII. d.

1. *the tabret* or *kettle-drum* of the orientals, consisting of a broad hoop, with a skin stretched over it, and round metallic plates on the border. It was played upon particularly by dancing women. Ex. 15:20. Judg. 11:34. Jer. 31:4. (comp. Ps. 68:26.) Comp. Niebuhr's Reise, Th. 1. p. 181.

2. Ezek. 28:13. *a casket, tympanum gemmæ*. Comp. נֶקֶב.

תִּפְאָרָה f. more frequently תִּפְאֶרֶת, with suff. תִּפְאַרְתּוֹ, verbal from פָּאַר, dec. XIII. a.

1. *ornament, splendour, beauty*. Ex. 28:2, 40. Is. 3:18. 52:1 בִּגְדֵי תִפְאַרְתֵּךְ *thy beautiful garments*. Ezek. 16:17. Prov. 28:12 בַּעֲלֹץ צַדִּיקִים רַבָּה תִפְאָרֶת *when the righteous rejoice, there is much splendour*, i. e. the garments of joy are put on.

2. *glory, praise, honour*. Judg. 4:9. שֵׁם תִּפְאֶרֶת *a glorious name*, Is. 63:14. Is. 10:12. 13:19 תִּפְאֶרֶת גְּאוֹן כַּשְׂדִּים *the glory of the pride of the Chaldeans*, i. e. the city Babylon. Hence

3. spoken of the mercy-seat, as the seat of the glory of Jehovah. Ps. 78:61. Comp. עֹז no. 3.

תַּפּוּחַ m. (verbal from נָפַח *to breathe*, also *to emit fragrance*, comp. Cant. 7:9.) dec. I.

1. *an apple*. Cant. 7:9. Prov. 25:11. (Arab. تُفَّاحٌ *idem*, but including also *citrons, peaches, apricots*.)

2 *an apple-tree.* Cant. 2 : 3. 8 : 5.

3. proper name of a city in the tribe of Judah. Josh. 12 : 17. 15 : 34.

4. also of a city on the bounds of the tribes Ephraim and Manasseh. Josh. 16 : 8.

תְּפוֹצָה f. verbal from פּוּץ, dec. X. *a scattering, dispersion.* Jer. 25 : 34. But the reading is doubtful, see the note under פּוּץ.

תֻּפִינִים masc. plur. dec. I. only Lev. 6 : 14. [6 : 21.] prob. *small pieces, crumbs.* It is then derived from פָּתַן i. q. אפן Arab. أفن *diminuit,* perhaps *comminuit.* Sept. in several MSS. ἐρικτά, *bruised.* The following words מִנְחַת פִּתִּים (as) *a meat-offering in pieces,* appear to be explanatory. Others derive it from אָפָה *to bake.* So the Sept. in the common text ἑλικτά.

I. תָּפֵל m. *what is unseasoned* or *unsavoury.* Job 6 : 6. Metaphorically *what is insipid, foolish, absurd,* Lam. 2 : 14. See תִּפְלָה. (Arab. تفل *to be unseasoned;* in Chald. *to be unsalted.*)

II. תָּפֵל m. *lime, white-wash,* to spread over walls. Ezek. 13 : 10 ff. 22 : 28. (Arab. طفل, Chald. טְפֵל *idem,* by a commutation of ט and ת.)

תֹּפֶל name of a place in the desert. Once Deut. 1 : 1.

תִּפְלָה f. i. q. תָּפֵל no. I. *what is insipid, absurd, foolish.* Job 1 : 22. 24 : 12. Jer. 23 : 13.

תְּפִלָּה f. (verbal from פָּלַל Hithpo. *to pray,*) dec. X. *a prayer.* Ps. 4 : 2, 6, 10. Ps. 109 : 4 וַאֲנִי תְפִלָּה for וַאֲנִי אִישׁ תְּפִלָּה *and I prayed* (for them). 109 : 7. נָשָׂא תְפִלָּה Is. 37 : 4. and הִתְפַּלֵּל תְּפִלָּה Neh. 1 : 6. *orare preces.* It is used in the superscriptions of Psalms XVII. LXXXVI. XC. CII. CXLII. and in Ps. 72 : 20, the Psalms I.—LXXII. are included under the general name of תְּפִלּוֹת דָּוִד *the prayers of David.* Since many of these compositions are not properly prayers, it is evident that the word must have been used in a broader sense; and that it denotes

2. *an ode, song of praise.* So Hab. 3 : 1. Also the verb הִתְפַּלֵּל is used 1 Sam. 2 : 1, more in the sense of *praising* God, than of *praying* to him.

תִּפְלֶצֶת f. (verbal from פָּלַץ Hithpa.) dec. XIII. a. *fear, terror.* Jer. 49 : 16 תִּפְלַצְתְּךָ *the fear of thee.*

תִּפְסַח *Thapsacus,* the proper name of a considerable city on the western bank of the Euphrates, which formed the limit of the kingdom of Solomon to the north-east. It had its name from פָּסַח *transiit,* since at this place there was a celebrated passage of the Euphrates. 1 K. 5 : 4. [4 : 24.] Perhaps also 2 K. 15 : 16, which some suppose to be a different place situated nearer Samaria.

תָּפַף *to smite, strike,* e. g. the tabret. Ps. 68 : 26.

Po. *to beat* (on the heart or breast). Nah. 2 : 8.

Deriv. תֹּף.

תָּפַר *to sew together.* Gen. 3 : 7. Ecc. 3 : 7. Job 16 : 15.

Pi. *idem.* Ezek. 13 : 18.

תָּפַשׂ, fut. יִתְפֹּשׂ. 1. *to lay hold of;* construed with an accus. Gen. 39 : 12. 1 K. 18 : 40. with בְּ, Deut. 9 : 17. Is. 3 : 6.

2. *to take prisoner,* 2 K. 7 : 12. *to take* or *capture* (a city), Josh. 8 : 8. Deut. 20 : 19. hence *to have possession of, to hold, tenere,* Jer. 40 : 10.

3. *to hold, handle, guide, manage;* e. g. the sickle, Jer. 50 : 16. the bow, Amos 2 : 15. Jerem. 46 : 9. the oar, Ezek. 27 : 29. the harp, Gen. 4 : 21. the law, Jer. 2 : 8.

4. תָּפַשׂ שֵׁם אֱלֹהִים Prov. 30 : 9. *to take in vain the name of God,* i. e. to deny or abjure him; comp. כִּחֵשׁ in the first member.

5. *to set, enchase.* Part. pass. תָּפוּשׂ זָהָב *inlaid* or *overlaid with gold,* Hab. 2 : 19. Comp. אָחַז 1 K. 6 : 10.

Niph. pass. of Kal no. 2. *to be taken.* Ezek. 19 : 4, 8. Jer. 50 : 46. Ps. 10 : 2.

Pi. i. q. Kal no. 1. *to touch.* Prov. 30:28.

תֹּפֶת f. 1. *what causes loathing or vomiting, an abhorrence.* (Root Chald. תּוּף *to spit out.*) Job 17:6 וְתֹפֶת לְפָנִים אֶהְיֶה liter. *I was an abhorrence before them.*

2. a place in or near the valley of Hinnom, celebrated as the seat of idolatry, particularly of the worship of Moloch. 2 K. 23:10. Jer. 7:31, 32. 19:6, 13, 14. With He paragogic תָּפְתֶּה, Is. 30:33.

תִּפְתָּיֵא plur. Chald. name of certain officers or magistrates among the Chaldeans, prob. *lawyers* or *judges.* Dan. 3:2, 3. (In Arab. conj. IV. افتى *to pass sentence, to give counsel;* hence مفتي *a mufti,* liter. *a wise counsellor.* Others: *provincial officers,* from פְּתִי, פְּתָאָה, *the plain, the country.* Sept. οἱ ἐπ' ἐξουσιῶν. Vulg. *præfecti.*

תִּקְוָה f. dec. X. 1. i. q. קַו *a cord, line.* Josh. 2:18, 21. The root קָוָה appears to have had the signification of *twisting,* whence that of *strength* was derived, (as in חול, חֵיל.)

2. *an expectation, hope,* from קָוָה. Ruth 1:12. Job 5:16. 7:6. Zech. 9:12 אֲסִירֵי הַתִּקְוָה *prisoners of hope.* Also *the object of hope* or *expectation,* Job 6:8.

תְּקוּמָה f. *a withstanding, resisting.* Lev. 26:37. Root קוּם no. 2.

תְּקוֹמֵם m. dec. VII. b. i. q. מִתְקוֹמֵם *one that rises up, an enemy.* Ps. 139:21.

תְּקוֹעַ proper name of a village, south-east of Jerusalem, near which the great desert commenced, (hence מִדְבַּר תְּקוֹעַ 2 Chr. 20:20, comp. 1 Macc. 9:33.) the birth-place of the prophet Amos. 2 Sam. 14:2. 1 Chr. 2:24. Jer. 6:1. Amos 1:1. In Greek Θεκωὲ 1 Macc. 9:33. Relandi Palæstina, p. 1028.

תְּקוּפָה f. (verbal from קוּף i. q. נָקַף no. I.) dec. X. *a going round, a circuit;* e. g. of the sun. Ps. 19:7. — לִתְקוּפַת הַשָּׁנָה *at the end of the year,* 2 Chr. 24:23. comp. Ex. 34:22, where the לְ is wanting. — לִתְקֻפוֹת הַיָּמִים *at the end of the time* (of pregnancy). 1 Sam. 1:20.

תַּקִּיף m. adj. verbal from תָּקַף, *strong, mighty.* Ecc. 6:10.

תַּקִּיף m. Chald. verbal from תְּקֵף.
1. *hard, strong.* Dan. 2:40, 42.
2. *mighty.* Dan. 3:33. [4:3.]

תְּקַל Chald. *to weigh,* i. q. Heb. שָׁקַל. Part. pass. תְּקִל for תְּקִיל *weighed,* Dan. 5:25. Pret. Peil. *to be weighed,* 5:27.

תָּקַן *to be* or *become straight.* A later Aramean word. Ecc. 1:15. Comp. the kindred verb תָּכַן in Pi.

Pi. 1. *to make straight.* Ecc. 7:13.

2. joined with מְשָׁלִים, *aptare, adornare parabolas.* Ecc. 12:9.

תְּקַן Chald. *idem.* Hoph. (with the Hebrew inflection,) *to be restored, re-established.* Dan. 4:33. [4:36.]

תָּקַע 1. *to strike, smite, clap;* particularly with כַּף *the hand,* and that (1.) as a sign of joy. Ps. 47:2. (2.) as a sign of malicious joy and scorn, construed with עַל *over* a person. Nah. 3:19. (3.) as a sign of becoming surety. Prov. 17:18. 22:26. With לְ following of the person *for* whom, Prov. 6:1. Also without כַּף in the same sense, Prov. 11:15.

2. *to smite* or *drive in,* e. g. a nail. Judg. 4:21. Is. 22:23, 25. Hence *to fasten by nailing,* 1 Sam. 31:10. 1 Chr. 10:10. Judg. 16:14. Hence also תָּקַע אֹהֶל *to pitch* or *strike a tent,* scil. by driving in the tent-pins, Gen. 31:25. Jer. 6:3.

3. *to thrust in,* e. g. a spear, sword, Judg. 3:21. 2 Sam. 18:14. Hence *to cast* or *throw,* e. g. into the sea, Ex. 10:19.

4. *to blow with a trumpet;* construed with בְּ of the instrument, Num. 10:3, 4, 8. without בְּ, Ps. 81:4. Jer. 4:5. 6:1. 51:27. In Num. 10:6, 7, תָּקַע שׁוֹפָר *to blow the trumpet,* (as a signal for calling the people together,) is distinguished from הֵרִיעַ and תָּקַע תְּרוּעָה *to sound an alarm,* (as a signal for moving.)

Niph. pass. of Kal no. 2. Job 17:3

מִי הוּא לְיָדִי יִתָּקֵעַ *who is it that will strike hands with me?* i. e. will become surety for me? Pass. of no. 4. Is. 27:13. Amos 3:6.

תֵּקַע m. Ps. 150:3. and תָּקוֹעַ m. Ezek. 7:14. verbals from תָּקַע, *a blowing with the trumpet.*

תָּקַף *to prevail over* or *oppress* a person, construed with an accus. Job 14:20. 15:24. Ecc. 4:12. (Arab. تقف *idem.* Comp. the Chald.) Deriv. out of course תֹּקֶף.

תְּקֵף Chald. *to be* or *become great* or *strong.* Dan. 4:8, 19. [4:11, 22.] 5:20 רוּחֵהּ תִּקְפַת *his mind became arrogant.*

Pa. *to confirm, establish.* Dan. 6:8.

תֹּקֶף verbal from תָּקַף, dec. VI. p. *power, authority.* Est. 9:29. 10:2. Dan. 11:17.

תְּקֹף m. Chald. emph. תָּקְפָּא, *idem.* Dan. 4:27. [4:30.]

תֹּר *a turtle-dove,* see **תּוֹר** no. I.

תַּרְבּוּת f. verbal from רָבָה, dec. I. *offspring, brood, soboles,* probably used by way of contempt. Num. 32:14.

תַּרְבִּית f. verbal from רָבָה, *interest, usury,* i. q. מַרְבִּית q. v. Lev. 25:36. Prov. 28:8. Ezek. 18:8 ff. In some passages it is joined with נֶשֶׁךְ. If the two words differ in meaning then תַּרְבִּית is the interest *exclusive* of the principal.

תִּרְגַּל a quadriliteral, *to teach to go, to guide the steps of* a person. Hos. 11:3. It is a denom. from רֶגֶל, with prosthetic ת, as in Aram. תַּלְמֵד *to teach,* from לָמַד *to learn.*

תַּרְגֵּם Chald. a quadriliteral, *to expound, explain, interpret.* Part. pass. מְתֻרְגָּם *interpreted,* Ezra 4:7.

תַּרְדֵּמָה f. (with Tseri impure,) verbal from רָדַם, dec. X.

1. *deep sleep.* Gen. 2:21. 15:12. 1 Sam. 26:12.

2. *sluggishness, inactivity.* Is. 29:10. Prov. 19:15.

תִּרְהָקָה *Tirhakah,* the proper name of a king of Ethiopia. Is. 37:9. 2 K. 19:9. In Strabo, (B. xv. p. 472 ed. Casaub.) he is called Τεάρκων; in Manetho, who makes him the third king of Ethiopia, Ταρακός.

תֶּרַח (*delay*) name of a station of the Israelites in the desert. Num. 33:27.

תְּרוּמָה f. verbal from רוּם, dec. X.

1. *a present, gift.* Prov. 29:4 אִישׁ תְּרוּמוֹת *one that receives bribes.*

2. particularly *a gift to the priests* or *the temple, an offering;* spoken e. g. of contributions to the tabernacle of the congregation, Ex. 25:2, 3. 30:13, 14. of the contributions to the priests, Lev. 7:32. 22:12. Hence שְׂדֵי תְרוּמֹת *fields of first-fruits,* i. e. where the first-fruits grow, 2 Sam. 1:21. Synonymous with תְּרוּמַת־יָד Deut. 12:11, 17. and תְּרוּמַת־יְהוָה Ex. 30:14, 15. See הֵרִים no. 4.

3. particularly *the heave-offering,* (with reference to a certain rite of moving it up and down, comp. תְּנוּפָה *the wave-offering.*) Ex. 29:27 שׁוֹק הַתְּרוּמָה *the heave-shoulder.* Lev. 7:34. etc. Comp. הֵרִים no. 5.

תְּרוּמִיָּה i. q. תְּרוּמָה no. 2. strictly *what pertains to an offering.* Ezek. 48:12.

תְּרוּעָה f. verbal from רוּעַ no. II. dec. X.

1. *a cry of jubilee.* Job 8:21. 33:26. הֵרִיעַ תְּרוּעָה *to raise a cry of jubilee,* 1 Sam. 4:5. Ezra 3:11, 13.

2. *a shout for battle.* Amos 1:14. Jer. 4:19. 49:2 הֵרִיעַ תְּרוּעָה *to raise a shout for battle,* Josh. 6:5, 20.

3. *the sound of a trumpet.* Lev. 25:9 יוֹם תְּרוּעָה *the day of sounding the trumpet,* namely, the first day of the seventh month, new year's day, Lev. 23:24. Num. 29:1—6. זִבְחֵי תְרוּעָה *an offering with the sounding of a trumpet,* Ps. 27:6. comp. Num. 10:10. Ps. 89:16.

תְּרוּפָה f. *a healing* or *refreshment.* Ezek. 47:12. Sept. ὑγίεια, whence in Rev. 22:2, θεραπεία. Vulg. *medicina.* The root רוּף prob. borrows its signification from רָפָא *to heal,* whence מַרְפֵּא *a healing, cure.*

תִּרְזָה f. Is. 44:14. name of a tree;

according to some, *the holly*, from תרז Arab. ترز *to be strong, hard.* See Celsii Hierobot. T. II. p. 270.

תְּרֵין Chald. const. תְּרֵי, *two.* Fem. תַּרְתֵּין Dan. 6 : 1. Ezra 4 : 24. Derived from the Heb. שְׁנַיִם by a commutation of נ and ר, see נ.

תַּרְמָה *a lie, deceit.* Judg. 9 : 31. Root רָמָה Pi. *to deceive.*

תַּרְמִית f. *deception.* Jer. 8 : 5. 23 : 26. But in Jer. 14 : 14 Keth. we find תַּרְמוּת. Root רָמָה Pi. *to deceive.*

תֹּרֶן m. 1. *the mast of a ship.* Is. 33 : 23. Ezek. 27 : 5.

2. i. q. נֵס prob. *a flag, banner,* raised on mountains for a signal. Is. 30 : 17. (Perhaps to be collated with the Rabbin. תורניתא *pinus.*)

תְּרַע m. Chald. 1. *a door, opening,* i. q. Heb. שַׁעַר, whence it is formed by transposition. Dan. 3 : 26.

2. *the porte,* i. e. the palace of eastern kings, so called from the great gate which leads to the seraglio and the other public buildings. Dan. 2 : 49 *and Daniel was placed over the royal palace,* i. e. he was made prefect of the palace. Comp. שַׁעַר no. 2. (Syr. and Arab. *idem.*)

תָּרָע Chald. (with Kamets impure,) *a porter, watchman at a gate.* Ezra 7 : 24. It is a denom. like שֹׁעֵר from שַׁעַר.

תַּרְעֵלָה f. verbal from רָעַל, *giddiness, intoxication;* hence יֵין תַּרְעֵלָה *intoxicating wine,* Ps. 60 : 5. and כּוֹס הַתַּרְעֵלָה *the cup of intoxication,* Is. 51 : 17, 22. See this figure further under כּוֹס.

תְּרָפִים masc. plur. a kind of penates or household gods, (Gen. 31 : 19, 34. 1 Sam. 19 : 13, 16.) which the superstitious used for domestic oracles, (Ezek. 21 : 26. Zech. 10 : 2.) From 1 Sam. 19 : 13, 16, it appears that they were as large as life, and had a human form. The plural here קָדָשִׁים appears to be the pluralis excellentiæ, and to refer to a single image; but in Gen. 31 : 34, it is construed with the plural. The other passages are Judg. 17 : 5. 18 : 14 ff. 2 K. 23 : 24. Hos. 3 : 4. With their use as oracles agrees the etymology of the word from תרף in Syr. *percontari, inquirere.*

תִּרְצָה *pleasantness*) proper name of a city in the kingdom of Israel, which was the residence of the kings from Jeroboam to Omri. Josh. 12 : 24. 1 K. 14 : 17. 15 : 21. 2 K. 15 : 14. Its situation is represented as pleasant, Cant. 6 : 4.

תַּרְשִׁישׁ *Tartessus,* the proper name of a city and country in Spain, the most celebrated emporium in the west to which the Phenicians and Hebrews traded. That it was situated in the west is evident from Gen. 10 : 4, where it is joined with Elishah, Kittim, and Dodanim; comp. Ps. 72 : 10, where it is connected with אִיִּים *the islands of the west.* According to Ezek. 38 : 13, it was an important place of trade; according to Jer. 10 : 9, it exported silver, and according to Ezek. 27 : 12, 25, silver, iron, tin, and lead to the Tyrian market. They embarked for this place from Joppa, Jon. 1 : 3. 4 : 2. In Is. 23 : 1, 6, 10, it is evidently represented as an important Phenician colony. It is named among other distant states, Is. 66 : 19. That these notices agree with *Tartessus,* has been shewn by Bochart, (Geogr. Sacra, Lib. III. cap. 7. p. 165 ff.) J. D. Michaëlis, (Spicileg. Geogr. Hebr. exteræ, P. I. p. 82—103.) and Bredow, (Histor. Untersuchungen, St. 2. p. 260—303.) The Greek name Ταρτησσος is derived from a harder Aramean pronunciation of the word תַּרְשִׁישׁ; but another orthography with σ was also known to the Greeks, for in Polybius and Stephanus Byzantinus occurs Ταρσηϊον, as synonymous with Ταρτησσος.—אֳנִיּוֹת תַּרְשִׁישׁ *Tarshish ships,* is employed Is. 23 : 1, 4. 60 : 9. to denote *large merchant ships bound on long voyages,* (perhaps distinguished by their construction from the common Phenician ships,) even though they were sent to other countries instead of Tarshish; (comp. the Eng. phrase *an*

Indiaman.) Ps. 48:8. Is. 2:16. So it is used of the ships which went to Ophir, 1 K. 22:49. 1 K. 10:22. (comp. 9:28.) In the interval between the composition of the Books of Kings and that of Chronicles, this name seems to have been transferred to denote any distant country; hence the Tarshish ships which went to Ophir, (see 1 K. 22:49. etc.) are said expressly by the writer of Chronicles to have gone to Tarshish. See 2 Chr. 9:21. 20:36, 37. and comp. Bredow, p. 293—295. and Gesenius' Gesch. der Hebr. Sprache und Schrift, p. 42. There is no necessity then for the definite adoption of a second Tarshish, (perhaps in India or Ethiopia;) and the ancient versions are evidently incorrect, which render תַּרְשִׁישׁ *the sea*, and אֳ׳ תַּרְשִׁישׁ *ships of the sea.*

2. a precious stone which probably derived its name from Tartessus, (like אוֹפִיר for *Ophiritic gold.*) Ex. 28:20. 39:13. Ezek. 1:16. 10:9. 28:13. Cant. 5:14. Dan. 10:6. The Sept. and Josephus make it *the chrysolite*, which is *the topaz* of the moderns; and this explanation is adopted by Braun, (de Vestitu Sacerdot. II. 7.) Others: *amber*, which, however, does not suit Ex. 28:20. 39:13.

תִּרְשָׁתָא (always with the article,) a title given to Nehemiah, Ezra 2:63. Neh. 7:65, 70, (where it stands alone;) and more clearly Neh. 8:9. 10:2 נְחֶמְיָה הוּא הַתִּרְשָׁתָא. This word occurs only in that part of Nehemiah, which is supposed to be inserted by another hand; viz. from chap. 7:6, to 10:10. Probably a title belonging to him as governor (פֶּחָה;) comp. perhaps the Pers. تُرش, تَرش *dark, rigid, austere*, hence *a rigid governor*, or the like.

תַּרְתָּן m. *Tartan*, the proper name of an Assyrian general, under the kings Sargon, (Is. 20:1.) and Sennacherib, (2 K. 18:17.)

תַּרְתָּק proper name of an idol of the Avites, (שֵׁמִּים.) 2 K. 17:31.

תְּשׂוּמֶת f. verbal from שׂוּם, found only Lev. 5:21 תְּשׂוּמֶת יָד *something put into the hand, a deposit* or *trust.* The distinction between this word and פִּקָּדוֹן is not known.

תְּשֻׁאוֹת fem. plur. (verbal from שָׁאָה=שׁוֹא.)

1. *noise, clamour.* Job 39:7. Particularly *the bustle* or *tumult of a multitude*, Is. 22:2. Synon. שָׁאוֹן.

2. *a crashing noise.* Job 36:29.

תִּשְׁבִּי m. a gentile noun, *a Tishbite*, spoken of Elijah. 1 K. 17:1. 21:17. It is derived from תִּשְׁבֶּה or תִּשְׁבָּה, in Greek Θισβή Tob. 1:2. a city in the tribe of Naphtali. See Relandi Palaestina, p. 1035.

תַּשְׁבֵּץ m. verbal from שָׁבַץ, *cloth worked in checkers* or *cells.* (See the verb.) Hence כְּתֹנֶת תַּשְׁבֵּץ *a coat of checkered cloth*, Ex. 28:4.

תְּשׁוּעָה f. verbal from שׁוּעַ i. q. יָשַׁע, dec. X.

1. *help, deliverance, salvation.* Ps. 37:39. 40:11. 71:15.

2. *victory.* 2 Sam. 19:3. 2 K. 5:1. Comp. יְשׁוּעָה.

תְּשׁוּקָה f. verbal from שׁוּק i. q. שָׁקַק no. II. dec. X. *desire, longing.* Gen. 3:16. 4:7. Cant. 7:11.

תְּשׁוּרָה f. *a gift, present.* 1 Sam. 9:7. It is also used in the Jewish translation of Dan. 2:6. 5:17. for the Chald. נְבִזְבָּה *a gift.* Root שׁוּר no. II. *to go, to travel*; construed with בְּ, *to bring, present*; comp. Is. 57:9.

תְּשִׁיעִי, fem. ־ִיָּה, *ninth*, denom. from תֵּשַׁע. Num. 7:60.

תֵּשַׁע, const. תְּשַׁע, f. and **תִּשְׁעָה**, const. תִּשְׁעַת, m. *nine.* Also *ninth*, in the numbering of days, e. g. בְּתִשְׁעָה לַחֹדֶשׁ *on the ninth of the month*, Lev. 23:32. Plur. תִּשְׁעִים com. gen. *ninety.*

LONDON: PRINTED BY R. WATTS, ORIENTAL TYPE-FOUNDER, CROWN COURT, TEMPLE BAR.

Princeton University Library
32101 073303529

Lightning Source UK Ltd.
Milton Keynes UK
UKHW031250111120
373211UK00003B/172